Presented

ON THIS

DAY OF

THE YEAR

BY

Here's HOPE Holy Bible

KING JAMES VERSION

Holman Bible Publishers
Nashville, Tennessee

ISBN: 1-5581-9856-3

2 3 4 5 6 7 8 03 02 01 00

Printed in the United States

R

Books of the Bible

Old Testament

New Testament

THE
OLD TESTAMENT

THE FIRST BOOK OF MOSES
COMMONLY CALLED

GENESIS

1 IN the beginning God created the heaven
and the earth.
2 And the earth was without form, and void;
and darkness *was* upon the face of the deep.
And the Spirit of God moved upon the face of
the waters.
3 ¶ And God said, Let there be light: and
there was light.
4 And God saw the light, that *it was* good:
and God divided the light from the darkness.
5 And God called the light Day, and the darkness he called Night. And the evening and the
morning were the first day.
6 ¶ And God said, Let there be a firmament
in the midst of the waters, and let it divide the
waters from the waters.
7 And God made the firmament, and divided
the waters which *were* under the firmament
from the waters which *were* above the firmament: and it was so.
8 And God called the firmament Heaven.
And the evening and the morning were the second day.
9 ¶ And God said, Let the waters under the
heaven be gathered together unto one place,
and let the dry *land* appear: and it was so.
10 And God called the dry *land* Earth; and
the gathering together of the waters called he
Seas: and God saw that *it was* good.
11 And God said, Let the earth bring forth
grass, the herb yielding seed, *and* the fruit tree
yielding fruit after his kind, whose seed *is* in
itself, upon the earth: and it was so.
12 And the earth brought forth grass, *and*
herb yielding seed after his kind, and the tree
yielding fruit, whose seed *was* in itself, after his
kind: and God saw that *it was* good.
13 And the evening and the morning were
the third day.
14 ¶ And God said, Let there be lights in the
firmament of the heaven to divide the day from
the night; and let them be for signs, and for seasons, and for days, and years:
15 And let them be for lights in the firmament of the heaven to give light upon the earth:
and it was so.
16 And God made two great lights; the
greater light to rule the day, and the lesser light
to rule the night: *he made* the stars also.
17 And God set them in the firmament of the
heaven to give light upon the earth,
18 And to rule over the day and over the
night, and to divide the light from the darkness:
and God saw that *it was* good.
19 And the evening and the morning were
the fourth day.
20 And God said, Let the waters bring forth
abundantly the moving creature that hath life,
and fowl *that* may fly above the earth in the
open firmament of heaven.
21 And God created great whales, and every
living creature that moveth, which the waters
brought forth abundantly, after their kind, and
every winged fowl after his kind: and God saw
that *it was* good.
22 And God blessed them, saying, Be fruitful,
and multiply, and fill the waters in the seas, and
let fowl multiply in the earth.
23 And the evening and the morning were
the fifth day.
24 ¶ And God said, Let the earth bring forth
the living creature after his kind, cattle, and
creeping thing, and beast of the earth after his
kind: and it was so.
25 And God made the beast of the earth after
his kind, and cattle after their kind, and every
thing that creepeth upon the earth after his
kind: and God saw that *it was* good.
26 ¶ And God said, Let us make man in our
image, after our likeness: and let them have dominion over the fish of the sea, and over the
fowl of the air, and over the cattle, and over all
the earth, and over every creeping thing that
creepeth upon the earth.
27 So God created man in his *own* image, in
the image of God created he him; male and female created he them.
28 And God blessed them, and God said unto
them, Be fruitful, and multiply, and replenish
the earth, and subdue it: and have dominion
over the fish of the sea, and over the fowl of the
air, and over every living thing that moveth
upon the earth.
29 ¶ And God said, Behold, I have given you
every herb bearing seed, which *is* upon the face
of all the earth, and every tree, in the which *is*
the fruit of a tree yielding seed; to you it shall
be for meat.
30 And to every beast of the earth, and to
every fowl of the air, and to every thing that
creepeth upon the earth, wherein *there is* life, *I
have given* every green herb for meat: and it
was so.
31 And God saw every thing that he had
made, and, behold, *it was* very good. And the
evening and the morning were the sixth day.

2 THUS the heavens and the earth were finished, and all the host of them.
2 And on the seventh day God ended his
work which he had made; and he rested on the
seventh day from all his work which he had
made.
3 And God blessed the seventh day, and
sanctified it: because that in it he had rested
from all his work which God created and made.
4 ¶ These *are* the generations of the heavens
and of the earth when they were created, in the
day that the LORD God made the earth and the
heavens,
5 And every plant of the field before it was in
the earth, and every herb of the field before it
grew: for the LORD God had not caused it to
rain upon the earth, and *there was* not a man to
till the ground.
6 But there went up a mist from the earth,
and watered the whole face of the ground.
7 And the LORD God formed man *of* the dust
of the ground, and breathed into his nostrils the
breath of life; and man became a living soul.
8 ¶ And the LORD God planted a garden eastward in E'den; and there he put the man whom
he had formed.
9 And out of the ground made the LORD God
to grow every tree that is pleasant to the sight,
and good for food; the tree of life also in the
midst of the garden, and the tree of knowledge
of good and evil.
10 And a river went out of E'den to water the
garden; and from thence it was parted, and became into four heads.
11 The name of the first *is* Pi'son: that *is* it

which compasseth the whole land of Hav'i-lah, where *there is* gold;

12 And the gold of that land *is* good: there *is* bdellium and the onyx stone.

13 And the name of the second river *is* Gi'-hon: the same *is* it that compasseth the whole land of E-thi-o'pi-a.

14 And the name of the third river *is* Hid'de-kel: that *is* it which goeth toward the east of As-syr'i-a. And the fourth river *is* Eu-phra'tes.

15 And the LORD God took the man, and put him into the garden of E'den to dress it and to keep it.

16 And the LORD God commanded the man, saying, Of every tree of the garden thou mayest freely eat:

17 But of the tree of the knowledge of good and evil, thou shalt not eat of it: for in the day that thou eatest thereof thou shalt surely die.

18 ¶ And the LORD God said, *It is* not good that the man should be alone; I will make him an help meet for him.

19 And out of the ground the LORD God formed every beast of the field, and every fowl of the air; and brought *them* unto Ad'am to see what he would call them: and whatsoever Ad'-am called every living creature, that *was* the name thereof.

20 And Ad'am gave names to all cattle, and to the fowl of the air, and to every beast of the field; but for Ad'am there was not found an help meet for him.

21 And the LORD God caused a deep sleep to fall upon Ad'am, and he slept: and he took one of his ribs, and closed up the flesh instead thereof;

22 And the rib, which the LORD God had taken from man, made he a woman, and brought her unto the man.

23 And Ad'am said, This *is* now bone of my bones, and flesh of my flesh: she shall be called Woman, because she was taken out of Man.

24 Therefore shall a man leave his father and his mother, and shall cleave unto his wife: and they shall be one flesh.

25 And they were both naked, the man and his wife, and were not ashamed.

3 NOW the serpent was more subtil than any beast of the field which the LORD God had made. And he said unto the woman, Yea, hath God said, Ye shall not eat of every tree of the garden?

2 And the woman said unto the serpent, We may eat of the fruit of the trees of the garden:

3 But of the fruit of the tree which *is* in the midst of the garden, God hath said, Ye shall not eat of it, neither shall ye touch it, lest ye die.

4 And the serpent said unto the woman, Ye shall not surely die:

5 For God doth know that in the day ye eat thereof, then your eyes shall be opened, and ye shall be as gods, knowing good and evil.

6 And when the woman saw that the tree *was* good for food, and that it *was* pleasant to the eyes, and a tree to be desired to make *one* wise, she took of the fruit thereof, and did eat, and gave also unto her husband with her; and he did eat.

7 And the eyes of them both were opened, and they knew that they *were* naked; and they sewed fig leaves together, and made themselves aprons.

8 And they heard the voice of the LORD God walking in the garden in the cool of the day: and Ad'am and his wife hid themselves from the presence of the LORD God amongst the trees of the garden.

9 And the LORD God called unto Ad'am, and said unto him, Where *art* thou?

10 And he said, I heard thy voice in the garden, and I was afraid, because I *was* naked; and I hid myself.

11 And he said, Who told thee that thou *wast* naked? Hast thou eaten of the tree, whereof I commanded thee that thou shouldest not eat?

12 And the man said, The woman whom thou gavest *to be* with me, she gave me of the tree, and I did eat.

13 And the LORD God said unto the woman, What *is* this *that* thou hast done? And the woman said, The serpent beguiled me, and I did eat.

14 And the LORD God said unto the serpent, Because thou hast done this, thou *art* cursed above all cattle, and above every beast of the field; upon thy belly shalt thou go, and dust shalt thou eat all the days of thy life:

15 And I will put enmity between thee and the woman, and between thy seed and her seed; it shall bruise thy head, and thou shalt bruise his heel.

16 Unto the woman he said, I will greatly multiply thy sorrow and thy conception; in sorrow thou shalt bring forth children; and thy desire *shall be* to thy husband, and he shall rule over thee.

17 And unto Ad'am he said, Because thou hast hearkened unto the voice of thy wife, and hast eaten of the tree, of which I commanded thee, saying, Thou shalt not eat of it: cursed *is* the ground for thy sake; in sorrow shalt thou eat *of* it all the days of thy life;

18 Thorns also and thistles shall it bring forth to thee; and thou shalt eat the herb of the field;

19 In the sweat of thy face shalt thou eat bread, till thou return unto the ground; for out of it wast thou taken: for dust thou *art*, and unto dust shalt thou return.

20 And Ad'am called his wife's name Eve; because she was the mother of all living.

21 Unto Ad'am also and to his wife did the LORD God make coats of skins, and clothed them.

22 ¶ And the LORD God said, Behold, the man is become as one of us, to know good and evil: and now, lest he put forth his hand, and take also of the tree of life, and eat, and live for ever:

23 Therefore the LORD God sent him forth from the garden of E'den, to till the ground from whence he was taken.

24 So he drove out the man; and he placed at the east of the garden of E'den Cher'u-bims, and a flaming sword which turned every way, to keep the way of the tree of life.

4 AND Ad'am knew Eve his wife; and she conceived, and bare Cain, and said, I have gotten a man from the LORD.

2 And she again bare his brother A'bel. And A'bel was a keeper of sheep, but Cain was a tiller of the ground.

3 And in the process of time it came to pass, that Cain brought of the fruit of the ground an offering unto the LORD.

4 And A'bel, he also brought of the firstlings of his flock and of the fat thereof. And the LORD had respect unto A'bel and to his offering:

5 But unto Cain and to his offering he had not respect. And Cain was very wroth, and his countenance fell.

6 And the LORD said unto Cain, Why art thou
wroth? and why is thy countenance fallen?
7 If thou doest well, shalt thou not be accepted? and if thou doest not well, sin lieth at
the door. And unto thee *shall be* his desire, and
thou shalt rule over him.
8 And Cain talked with A'bel his brother: and
it came to pass, when they were in the field,
that Cain rose up against A'bel his brother, and
slew him.
9 ¶ And the LORD said unto Cain, Where *is*
A'bel thy brother? And he said, I know not: *Am*
I my brother's keeper?
10 And he said, What hast thou done? the
voice of thy brother's blood crieth unto me
from the ground.
11 And now *art* thou cursed from the earth,
which hath opened her mouth to receive thy
brother's blood from thy hand;
12 When thou tillest the ground, it shall not
henceforth yield unto thee her strength; a fugitive and a vagabond shalt thou be in the earth.
13 And Cain said unto the LORD, My punishment *is* greater than I can bear.
14 Behold, thou hast driven out this day from
the face of the earth; and from thy face shall I
be hid; and I shall be a fugitive and a vagabond
in the earth; and it shall come to pass, *that* every one that findeth me shall slay me.
15 And the LORD said unto him, Therefore
whosoever slayeth Cain, vengeance shall be
taken on him sevenfold. And the LORD set a
mark upon Cain, lest any finding him should kill
him.
16 ¶ And Cain went out from the presence of
the LORD, and dwelt in the land of Nod, on the
east of E'den.
17 And Cain knew his wife; and she conceived, and bare E'noch: and he builded a city,
and called the name of the city, after the name
of his son, E'noch.
18 And unto E'noch was born I'rad: and I'rad
begat Me-hu'ja-el: and Me-hu'ja-el begat Me-
thusa-el: and Me-thusa-el begat La'mech.
19 ¶ And La'mech took unto him two wives:
the name of the one *was* A'dah, and the name of
the other Zil'lah.
20 And A'dah bare Ja'bal: he was the father
of such as dwell in tents, and *of such as have*
cattle.
21 And his brother's name *was* Ju'bal: he
was the father of all such as handle the harp
and organ.
22 And Zil'lah, she also bare Tu'bal–cain, an
instructer of every artificer in brass and iron:
and the sister of Tu'bal–cain *was* Na'a-mah.
23 And La'mech said unto his wives, A'dah
and Zil'lah, Hear my voice; ye wives of La'-
mech, hearken unto my speech: for I have slain
a man to my wounding, and a young man to my
hurt.
24 If Cain shall be avenged sevenfold, truly
La'mech seventy and sevenfold.
25 ¶ And Ad'am knew his wife again; and
she bare a son, and called his name Seth: For
God, *said she,* hath appointed me another seed
instead of A'bel, whom Cain slew.
26 And to Seth, to him also there was born a
son; and he called his name E'nos: then began
men to call upon the name of the LORD.

5 THIS *is* the book of the generations of Ad'-
am. In the day that God created man, in
the likeness of God made he him;
2 Male and female created he them; and
blessed them, and called their name Ad'am, in
the day when they were created.
3 ¶ And Ad'am lived an hundred and thirty
years, and begat a *son* in his own likeness, after
his image; and called his name Seth:
4 And the days of Ad'am after he had begotten Seth were eight hundred years: and he begat sons and daughters:
5 And all the days that Ad'am lived were
nine hundred and thirty years: and he died.
6 And Seth lived an hundred and five years,
and begat E'nos:
7 And Seth lived after he begat E'nos eight
hundred and seven years, and begat sons and
daughters:
8 And all the days of Seth were nine hundred
and twelve years: and he died.
9 ¶ And E'nos lived ninety years, and begat
Ca-i'nan:
10 And E'nos lived after he begat Ca-i'nan
eight hundred and fifteen years, and begat sons
and daughters:
11 And all the days of E'nos were nine hundred and five years: and he died.
12 ¶ And Ca-i'nan lived seventy years, and
begat Ma-ha'la-le-el:
13 And Ca-i'nan lived after he begat Ma-ha'-
la-le-el eight hundred and forty years, and begat
sons and daughters:
14 And all the days of Ca-i'nan were nine
hundred and ten years: and he died.
15 ¶ And Ma-ha'la-le-el lived sixty and five
years and begat Ja'red:
16 And Ma-ha'la-le-el lived after he begat
Ja'red eight hundred and thirty years, and begat
sons and daughters:
17 And all the days of Ma-ha'la-le-el were
eight hundred ninety and five years: and he
died.
18 ¶ And Ja'red lived an hundred sixty and
two years, and he begat E'noch:
19 And Ja'red lived after he begat E'noch
eight hundred years, and begat sons and daughters:
20 And all the days of Ja'red were nine hundred sixty and two years: and he died.
21 ¶ And E'noch lived sixty and five years,
and begat Me-thu'se-lah:
22 And E'noch walked with God after he begat Me-thu'se-lah three hundred years, and begat sons and daughters:
23 And all the days of E'noch were three
hundred sixty and five years:
24 And E'noch walked with God: and he *was*
not; for God took him.
25 And Me-thu'se-lah lived an hundred
eighty and seven years, and begat La'mech.
26 And Me-thu'se-lah lived after he begat
La'mech seven hundred eighty and two years,
and begat sons and daughters:
27 And all the days of Me-thu'se-lah were
nine hundred sixty and nine years: and he died.
28 ¶ And La'mech lived an hundred eighty
and two years, and begat a son:
29 And he called his name No'ah, saying,
This *same* shall comfort us concerning our
work and toil of our hands, because of the
ground which the LORD hath cursed.
30 And La'mech lived after he begat No'ah
five hundred ninety and five years, and begat
sons and daughters:
31 And all the days of La'mech were seven
hundred seventy and seven years: and he died.
32 And No'ah was five hundred years old:
and No'ah begat Shem, Ham, and Ja'pheth.

6 AND it came to pass, when men began to
multiply on the face of the earth, and
daughters were born unto them,

2 That the sons of God saw the daughters of
men that they *were* fair; and they took them
wives of all which they chose.
3 And the LORD said, My spirit shall not always strive with man, for that he also *is* flesh:
yet his days shall be an hundred and twenty
years.
4 There were giants in the earth in those
days; and also after that, when the sons of God
came in unto the daughters of men, and they
bare *children* to them, the same *became* mighty
men which *were* of old, men of renown.
5 ¶ And GOD saw that the wickedness of
man *was* great in the earth, and *that* every
imagination of the thoughts of his heart *was*
only evil continually.
6 And it repented the LORD that he had made
man on the earth, and it grieved him at his
heart.
7 And the LORD said, I will destroy man
whom I have created from the face of the earth;
both man, and beast, and the creeping thing,
and the fowls of the air; for it repenteth me that
I have made them.
8 But No'ah found grace in the eyes of the
LORD.
9 ¶ These *are* the generations of No'ah: No'-
ah was a just man *and* perfect in his generations, *and* No'ah walked with God.
10 And No'ah begat three sons, Shem, Ham,
and Ja'pheth.
11 The earth also was corrupt before God,
and the earth was filled with violence.
12 And God looked upon the earth, and, behold, it was corrupt; for all flesh had corrupted
his way upon the earth.
13 And God said unto No'ah, The end of all
flesh is come before me; for the earth is filled
with violence through them; and, behold, I will
destroy them with the earth.
14 ¶ Make thee an ark of gopher wood;
rooms shalt thou make in the ark, and shalt
pitch it within and without with pitch.
15 And this *is the fashion* which thou shalt
make it *of:* The length of the ark *shall be* three
hundred cubits, the breadth of it fifty cubits,
and the height of it thirty cubits.
16 A window shalt thou make to the ark, and
in a cubit shalt thou finish it above; and the
door of the ark shalt thou set in the side thereof;
with lower, second, and third *stories* shalt thou
make it.
17 And, behold, I, even I, do bring a flood of
waters upon the earth, to destroy all flesh,
wherein *is* the breath of life, from under
heaven; *and* every thing that *is* in the earth
shall die.
18 But with thee will I establish my covenant; and thou shalt come into the ark, thou,
and thy sons, and thy wife, and thy sons' wives
with thee.
19 And of every living thing of all flesh, two
of every *sort* shalt thou bring into the ark, to
keep *them* alive with thee; they shall be male
and female.
20 Of fowls after their kind, and of cattle after their kind, of every creeping thing of the
earth after his kind, two of every *sort* shall
come unto thee, to keep *them* alive.
21 And take thou unto thee of all food that is
eaten, and thou shalt gather *it* to thee; and it
shall be for food for thee, and for them.
22 Thus did No'ah; according to all that God
commanded him, so did he.

7 AND the LORD said unto No'ah, Come thou
and all thy house into the ark; for thee
have I seen righteous before me in this generation.
2 Of every clean beast thou shalt take to thee
by sevens, the male and his female: and of
beasts that *are* not clean by two, the male and
his female.
3 Of fowls also of the air by sevens, the male
and the female; to keep seed alive upon the face
of all the earth.
4 For yet seven days, and I will cause it to
rain upon the earth forty days and forty nights;
and every living substance that I have made
will I destroy from off the face of the earth.
5 And No'ah did according unto all that the
LORD commanded him.
6 And No'ah *was* six hundred years old when
the flood of waters was upon the earth.
7 ¶ And No'ah went in, and his sons, and his
wife, and his sons' wives with him, into the ark,
because of the waters of the flood.
8 Of clean beasts, and of beasts that *are* not
clean, and of fowls, and of every thing that
creepeth upon the earth,
9 There went in two and two unto No'ah into
the ark, the male and the female, as God had
commanded No'ah.
10 And it came to pass after seven days, that
the waters of the flood were upon the earth.
11 ¶ In the six hundredth year of No'ah's
life, in the second month, the seventeenth day
of the month, the same day were all the fountains of the great deep broken up, and the windows of heaven were opened.
12 And the rain was upon the earth forty
days and forty nights.
13 In the selfsame day entered No'ah, and
Shem, and Ham, and Ja'pheth, the sons of No'-
ah, and No'ah's wife, and the three wives of his
sons with them, into the ark;
14 They, and every beast after his kind, and
all the cattle after their kind, and every creeping thing that creepeth upon the earth after his
kind, and every fowl after his kind, every bird
of every sort.
15 And they went in unto No'ah into the ark,
two and two of all flesh, wherein *is* the breath
of life.
16 And they that went in, went in male and
female of all flesh, as God had commanded him:
and the LORD shut him in.
17 And the flood was forty days upon the
earth; and the waters increased, and bare up the
ark, and it was lift up above the earth.
18 And the waters prevailed, and were increased greatly upon the earth; and the ark
went upon the face of the waters.
19 And the waters prevailed exceedingly
upon the earth; and all the high hills, that *were*
under the whole heaven, were covered.
20 Fifteen cubits upward did the waters prevail; and the mountains were covered.
21 And all flesh died that moved upon the
earth, both of fowl, and of cattle, and of beast,
and of every creeping thing that creepeth upon
the earth, and every man:
22 All in whose nostrils *was* the breath of
life, of all that *was* in the dry *land,* died.
23 And every living substance was destroyed
which was upon the face of the ground, both
man, and cattle, and the creeping things, and
the fowl of the heaven; and they were destroyed
from the earth: and No'ah only remained *alive,*
and they that *were* with him in the ark.
24 And the waters prevailed upon the earth
an hundred and fifty days.

8

AND God remembered No'ah, and every
living thing, and all the cattle that *was*
with him in the ark: and God made a wind to
pass over the earth, and the waters asswaged;
2 The fountains also of the deep and the windows of heaven were stopped, and the rain
from heaven was restrained;
3 And the waters returned from off the earth
continually: and after the end of the hundred
and fifty days the waters were abated.
4 And the ark rested in the seventh month,
on the seventeenth day of the month, upon the
mountains of Ar'a-rat.
5 And the waters decreased continually until
the tenth month: in the tenth *month*, on the first
day of the month, were the tops of the mountains seen.
6 ¶ And it came to pass at the end of forty
days, that No'ah opened the window of the ark
which he had made:
7 And he sent forth a raven, which went
forth to and fro, until the waters were dried up
from off the earth.
8 Also he sent forth a dove from him, to see
if the waters were abated from off the face of
the ground;
9 But the dove found no rest for the sole of
her foot, and she returned unto him into the
ark, for the waters *were* on the face of the
whole earth: then he put forth his hand, and
took her, and pulled her in unto him into the
ark.
10 And he stayed yet other seven days; and
again he sent forth the dove out of the ark;
11 And the dove came in to him in the evening; and, lo, in her mouth *was* an olive leaf
pluckt off: so No'ah knew that the waters were
abated from off the earth.
12 And he stayed yet other seven days; and
sent forth the dove; which returned not again
unto him any more.
13 ¶ And it came to pass in the six hundredth and first year, in the first *month*, the first
day of the month, the waters were dried up
from off the earth: and No'ah removed the covering of the ark, and looked, and, behold, the
face of the ground was dry.
14 And in the second month, on the seven
and twentieth day of the month, was the earth
dried.
15 ¶ And God spake unto No'ah, saying,
16 Go forth of the ark, thou, and thy wife,
and thy sons, and thy sons' wives with thee.
17 Bring forth with thee every living thing
that *is* with thee, of all flesh, *both* of fowl, and
of cattle, and of every creeping thing that
creepeth upon the earth: that they may breed
abundantly in the earth, and be fruitful, and
multiply upon the earth.
18 And No'ah went forth, and his sons, and
his wife, and his sons' wives with him:
19 Every beast, every creeping thing, and every fowl, *and* whatsoever creepeth upon the
earth, after their kinds, went forth out of the
ark.
20 ¶ And No'ah builded an altar unto the
LORD; and took of every clean beast, and of every clean fowl, and offered burnt offerings on
the altar.
21 And the LORD smelled a sweet savour; and
the LORD said in his heart, I will not again curse
the ground any more for man's sake; for the
imagination of man's heart *is* evil from his
youth; neither will I again smite any more every
thing living, as I have done.
22 While the earth remaineth, seedtime and
harvest, and cold and heat, and summer and
winter, and day and night shall not cease.

9

AND God blessed No'ah and his sons, and
said unto them, Be fruitful, and multiply,
and replenish the earth.
2 And the fear of you and the dread of you
shall be upon every beast of the earth, and upon
every fowl of the air, upon all that moveth *upon*
the earth, and upon all the fishes of the sea; into
your hand are they delivered.
3 Every moving thing that liveth shall be
meat for you; even as the green herb have I giv-
en you all things.
4 But flesh with the life thereof, *which is* the
blood thereof, shall ye not eat.
5 And surely your blood of your lives will I
require; at the hand of every beast will I require
it, and at the hand of man; at the hand of every
man's brother will I require the life of man.
6 Whoso sheddeth man's blood, by man shall
his blood be shed: for in the image of God made
he man.
7 And you, be ye fruitful, and multiply; bring
forth abundantly in the earth, and multiply
therein.
8 ¶ And God spake unto No'ah, and to his
sons with him, saying,
9 And I, behold, I establish my covenant with
you, and with your seed after you;
10 And with every living creature that *is* with
you, of the fowl, of the cattle, and of every
beast of the earth with you; from all that go out
of the ark, to every beast of the earth.
11 And I will establish my covenant with
you; neither shall all flesh be cut off any more
by the waters of a flood; neither shall there any
more be a flood to destroy the earth.
12 And God said, This *is* the token of the covenant which I make between me and you and
every living creature that *is* with you, for perpetual generations:
13 I do set my bow in the cloud, and it shall
be for a token of a covenant between me and
the earth.
14 And it shall come to pass, when I bring a
cloud over the earth, that the bow shall be seen
in the cloud:
15 And I will remember my covenant, which
is between me and you and every living creature of all flesh; and the waters shall no more
become a flood to destroy all flesh.
16 And the bow shall be in the cloud; and I
will look upon it, that I may remember the everlasting covenant between God and every living
creature of all flesh that *is* upon the earth.
17 And God said unto No'ah, This *is* the token of the covenant, which I have established
between me and all flesh that *is* upon the earth.
18 ¶ And the sons of No'ah, that went forth
of the ark, were Shem, and Ham, and Ja'pheth:
and Ham *is* the father of Ca'naan.
19 These *are* the three sons of No'ah: and of
them was the whole earth overspread.
20 And No'ah began *to be* an husbandman,
and he planted a vineyard:
21 And he drank of the wine, and was
drunken; and he was uncovered within his tent.
22 And Ham, the father of Ca'naan, saw the
nakedness of his father, and told his two brethren without.
23 And Shem and Ja'pheth took a garment,
and laid *it* upon both their shoulders, and went
backward, and covered the nakedness of their
father; and their faces *were* backward, and they
saw not their father's nakedness.
24 And No'ah awoke from his wine, and

knew what his younger son had done unto him.
25 And he said, Cursed *be* Ca'naan; a servant
of servants shall he be unto his brethren.
26 And he said, Blessed *be* the LORD God of
Shem; and Ca'naan shall be his servant.
27 God shall enlarge Ja'pheth, and he shall
dwell in the tents of Shem; and Ca'naan shall be
his servant.
28 ¶ And No'ah lived after the flood three
hundred and fifty years.
29 And all the days of No'ah were nine hundred and fifty years: and he died.

10 NOW these *are* the generations of the
sons of No'ah, Shem, Ham, and Ja'-
pheth: and unto them were sons born after the
flood.
2 The sons of Ja'pheth; Go'mer, and Ma'gog,
and Mad'a-i, and Ja'van, and Tu'bal, and Me'-
shech, and Ti'ras.
3 And the sons of Go'mer; Ash'ke-naz, and
Ri'phath, and To-gar'mah.
4 And the sons of Ja'van; E-li'shah, and Tar'-
shish, Kit'tim, and Dod'a-nim.
5 By these were the isles of the Gen-tiles divided in their lands; every one after his tongue,
after their families, in their nations.
6 ¶ And the sons of Ham; Cush, and Miz'ra-
im, and Phut, and Ca'naan.
7 And the sons of Cush; Se'ba, and Hav'i-lah,
and Sab'tah, and Ra'a-mah, and Sab'te-chah:
and the sons of Ra'a-mah; She'ba, and De'dan.
8 And Cush begat Nim'rod: he began to be a
mighty one in the earth.
9 He was a mighty hunter before the LORD:
wherefore it is said, Even as Nim'rod the
mighty hunter before the LORD.
10 And the beginning of his kingdom was
Ba'bel, and E'rech, and Ac'cad, and Cal'neh, in
the land of Shi'nar.
11 Out of that land went forth As'shur, and
builded Nin'e-veh, and the city Re-ho'both, and
Ca'lah,
12 And Re'sen between Nin'e-veh and Ca'-
lah: the same *is* a great city.
13 And Miz'ra-im begat Lu'dim, and An'a-
mim, and Le'ha-bim, and Naph'tu-him,
14 And Path-ru'sim, and Cas'lu-him, (out of
whom came Phi-lis'tim,) and Caph'to-rim.
15 ¶ And Ca'naan begat Si'don his first born,
and Heth,
16 And the Jeb'u-site, and the Am'or-ite, and
the Gir'ga-site,
17 And the Hi'vite, and the Ark'ite, and the
Sin'ite,
18 And the Ar'vad-ite, and the Zem'a-rite,
and the Ha'math-ite: and afterward were the
families of the Ca'naan-ites spread abroad.
19 And the border of the Ca'naan-ites was
from Si'don, as thou comest to Ge'rar, unto Ga'-
za; as thou goest, unto Sod'om, and Go-mor'-
rah, and Ad'-mah, and Ze-bo'im, even unto La'-
sha.
20 These *are* the sons of Ham, after their
families, after their tongues, in their countries,
and in their nations.
21 ¶ Unto Shem also, the father of all the
children of E'ber, the brother of Ja'pheth the elder, even to him were *children* born.
22 The children of Shem; E'lam, and As'shur,
and Arphax'ad, and Lud, and A'ram.
23 And the children of A'ram; Uz, and Hul,
and Ge'ther, and Mash.
24 And Arphax'ad begat Sa'lah; and Sa'lah
begat E'ber.
25 And unto E'ber were born two sons: the
name of one *was* Pe'leg; for in his days was the
earth divided; and his brother's name *was* Jok'-
tan.
26 And Jok'tan begat Al-mo'dad, and She'-
leph, and Ha'zar-ma'veth, and Je'rah,
27 And Ha-do'ram, and U'zal, and Dik'lah,
28 And O'bal, and A-bim'a-el, and She'ba,
29 And O'phir, and Hav'i-lah, and Jo'bab: all
these *were* the sons of Jok'tan.
30 And their dwelling was from Me'sha, as
thou goest unto Se'phar a mount of the east.
31 These *are* the sons of Shem, after their
families, after their tongues, in their lands, after
their nations.
32 These *are* the families of the sons of No'-
ah, after their generations, in their nations: and
by these were the nations divided in the earth
after the flood.

11 AND the whole earth was of one language, and of one speech.
2 And it came to pass, as they journeyed
from the east, that they found a plain in the
land of Shi'nar; and they dwelt there.
3 And they said one to another, Go to, let us
make brick, and burn them thoroughly. And
they had brick for stone, and slime had they for
morter.
4 And they said, Go to, let us build us a city
and a tower, whose top *may reach* unto heaven;
and let us make us a name, lest we be scattered
abroad upon the face of the whole earth.
5 And the LORD came down to see the city
and the tower, which the children of men
builded.
6 And the LORD said, Behold, the people *is*
one, and they have all one language; and this
they begin to do: and now nothing will be restrained from them, which they have imagined
to do.
7 Go to, let us go down, and there confound
their language, that they may not understand
one another's speech.
8 So the LORD scattered them abroad from
thence upon the face of all the earth: and they
left off to build the city.
9 Therefore is the name of it called Ba'bel;
because the LORD did there confound the language of all the earth: and from thence did the
LORD scatter them abroad upon the face of all
the earth.
10 ¶ These *are* the generations of Shem:
Shem *was* an hundred years old, and begat
Arphax'ad two years after the flood:
11 And Shem lived after he begat Arphax'ad
five hundred years, and begat sons and daughters.
12 And Arphax'ad lived five and thirty years,
and begat Sa'lah:
13 And Arphax'ad lived after he begat Sa'lah
four hundred and three years, and begat sons
and daughters.
14 And Sa'lah lived thirty years, and begat
E'ber:
15 And Sa'lah lived after he begat E'ber four
hundred and three years, and begat sons and
daughters.
16 And E'ber lived four and thirty years, and
begat Pe'leg:
17 And E'ber lived after he begat Pe'leg four
hundred and thirty years, and begat sons and
daughters.
18 And Pe'leg lived thirty years, and begat
Re'u:
19 And Pe'leg lived after he begat Re'u two
hundred and nine years, and begat sons and
daughters.

20 And Re'u lived two and thirty years, and begat Se'rug:

21 And Re'u lived after he begat Se'rug two hundred and seven years, and begat sons and daughters.

22 And Se'rug lived thirty years, and begat Na'hor:

23 And Se'rug lived after he begat Na'hor two hundred years, and begat sons and daughters.

24 And Na'hor lived nine and twenty years, and begat Te'rah:

25 And Na'hor lived after he begat Te'rah an hundred and nineteen years, and begat sons and daughters.

26 And Te'rah lived seventy years, and begat A'bram, Na'hor, and Ha'ran.

27 ¶ Now these *are* the generations of Te'rah: Te'rah begat A'bram, Na'hor, and Ha'ran; and Ha'ran begat Lot.

28 And Ha'ran died before his father Te'rah in the land of his nativity, in Ur of the Chal'dees.

29 And A'bram and Na'hor took them wives: the name of A'bram's wife *was* Sa'rai; and the name of Na'hor's wife, Mil'cah, the daughter of Ha'ran, the father of Mil'cah, and the father of Is'cah.

30 But Sa'rai was barren; she *had* no child.

31 And Te'rah took A'bram his son, and Lot the son of Ha'ran his son's son, and Sa'rai his daughter in law, his son A'bram's wife; and they went forth with them from Ur of the Chal'dees, to go into the land of Ca'naan; and they came unto Ha'ran, and dwelt there.

32 And the days of Te'rah were two hundred and five years: and Te'rah died in Ha'ran.

12 NOW the LORD had said unto A'bram, Get thee out of thy country, and from thy kindred, and from thy father's house, unto a land that I will shew thee:

2 And I will make of thee a great nation, and I will bless thee, and make thy name great; and thou shalt be a blessing:

3 And I will bless them that bless thee, and curse him that curseth thee: and in thee shall all families of the earth be blessed.

4 So A'bram departed, as the LORD had spoken unto him; and Lot went with him: and A'bram *was* seventy and five years old when he departed out of Ha'ran.

5 And A'bram took Sa'rai his wife, and Lot his brother's son, and all their substance that they had gathered, and the souls that they had gotten in Ha'ran; and they went forth to go into the land of Ca'naan; and into the land of Ca'naan they came.

6 ¶ And A'bram passed through the land unto the place of Si'chem, unto the plain of Mo'reh. And the Ca'naan-ite *was* then in the land.

7 And the LORD appeared unto A'bram, and said, Unto thy seed will I give this land: and there builded he an altar unto the LORD, who appeared unto him.

8 And he removed from thence unto a mountain on the east of Beth'-el, and pitched his tent, *having* Beth'-el on the west, and Ha'i on the east: and there he builded an altar unto the LORD, and called upon the name of the LORD.

9 And A'bram journeyed, going on still toward the south.

10 ¶ And there was a famine in the land: and A'bram went down into E'gypt to sojourn there; for the famine *was* grievous in the land.

11 And it came to pass, when he was come near to enter into E'gypt, that he said unto Sa'rai his wife, Behold now, I know that thou *art* a fair woman to look upon:

12 Therefore it shall come to pass, when the E-gyptians shall see thee, that they shall say, This *is* his wife: and they will kill me, but they will save thee alive.

13 Say, I pray thee, thou *art* my sister: that it may be well with me for thy sake; and my soul shall live because of thee.

14 ¶ And it came to pass, that, when A'bram was come into E'gypt, the E-gyptians beheld the woman that she *was* very fair.

15 The princes also of Pha'raoh saw her, and commended her before Pha'raoh: and the woman was taken into Pha'raoh's house.

16 And he entreated A'bram well for her sake: and he had sheep, and oxen, and he asses, and menservants, and maidservants, and she asses, and camels.

17 And the LORD plagued Pha'raoh and his house with great plagues because of Sa'rai A'bram's wife.

18 And Pha'raoh called A'bram, and said, What *is* this *that* thou hast done unto me? why didst thou not tell me that she *was* thy wife?

19 Why saidst thou, She *is* my sister? so I might have taken her to me to wife: now therefore behold thy wife, take *her*, and go thy way.

20 And Pha'raoh commanded *his* men concerning him: and they sent him away, and his wife, and all that he had.

13 AND A'bram went up out of E'gypt, he, and his wife, and all that he had, and Lot with him, into the south.

2 And A'bram *was* very rich in cattle, in silver, and in gold.

3 And he went on his journeys from the south even to Beth'-el, unto the place where his tent had been at the beginning, between Beth'-el and Ha'i;

4 Unto the place of the altar, which he had made there at the first: and there A'bram called on the name of the LORD.

5 ¶ And Lot also, which went with A'bram, had flocks, and herds, and tents.

6 And the land was not able to bear them, that they might dwell together: for their substance was great, so that they could not dwell together.

7 And there was a strife between the herdmen of A'bram's cattle and the herdmen of Lot's cattle: and the Ca'naan-ite and the Per'izzite dwelled then in the land.

8 And A'bram said unto Lot, Let there be no strife, I pray thee, between me and thee, and between my herdmen and thy herdmen; for we *be* brethren.

9 *Is* not the whole land before thee? separate thyself, I pray thee, from me: if *thou wilt take* the left hand, then I will go to the right; or if *thou depart* to the right hand, then I will go to the left.

10 And Lot lifted up his eyes, and beheld all the plain of Jor'dan, that it *was* well watered every where, before the LORD destroyed Sod'om and Go-mor'rah, *even* as the garden of the LORD, like the land of E'gypt, as thou comest unto Zo'ar.

11 Then Lot chose him all the plain of Jor'dan; and Lot journeyed east: and they separated themselves the one from the other.

12 A'bram dwelled in the land of Ca'naan, and Lot dwelled in the cities of the plain, and pitched *his* tent toward Sod'om.

13 But the men of Sod'om *were* wicked and sinners before the LORD exceedingly.

14 ¶ And the LORD said unto A'bram, after that Lot was separated from him, Lift up now thine eyes, and look from the place where thou art northward, and southward, and eastward, and westward:

15 For all the land which thou seest, to thee will I give it, and to thy seed for ever.

16 And I will make thy seed as the dust of the earth: so that if a man can number the dust of the earth, *then* shall thy seed also be numbered.

17 Arise, walk through the land in the length of it and in the breadth of it; for I will give it unto thee.

18 Then A'bram removed *his* tent, and came and dwelt in the plain of Mam're, which *is* in He'bron, and built there an altar unto the LORD.

14

AND it came to pass in the days of Am'ra-phel king of Shi'nar, A'ri-och king of El'la-sar, Ched-or-la'o-mer king of E'lam, and Ti'dal king of nations;

2 *That these* made war with Be'ra king of Sod'om, and with Bir'sha king of Go-mor'rah, Shi'nab king of Ad'-mah, and Shem'e-ber king of Ze-boi'im, and the king of Be'la, which is Zo'-ar.

3 All these were joined together in the vale of Sid'dim, which is the salt sea.

4 Twelve years they served Ched-or-la'o-mer, and in the thirteenth year they rebelled.

5 And in the fourteenth year came Ched-or-la'o-mer, and the kings that *were* with him, and smote the Reph'a-ims in Ash'te-roth Kar-na'im, and the Zu'zims in Ham, and the E'mims in Sha'veh Kir-i-a-tha'im,

6 And the Ho'rites in the mount Se'ir, unto El–pa'ran, which *is* by the wilderness.

7 And they returned, and came to En–mish'-pat, which *is* Ka'desh, and smote all the country of the Am'a-lek-ites, and also the Am'or-ites, that dwelt in Haz'e-zon–ta'mar.

8 And there went out the king of Sod'om, and the king of Go-mor'rah, and the king of Ad'-mah, and the king of Ze-boi'im, and the king of Be'la (the same *is* Zo'ar;) and they joined battle with them in the vale of Sid'dim;

9 With Ched-or-la'o-mer the king of E'lam, and with Ti'dal king of nations, and Am'ra-phel king of Shi'nar, and A'ri-och king of El'la-sar; four kings with five.

10 And the vale of Sid'dim *was full of* slimepits; and the kings of Sod'om and Go-mor'rah fled, and fell there; and they that remained fled to the mountain.

11 And they took all the goods of Sod'om and Go-mor'rah, and all their victuals, and went their way.

12 And they took Lot, A'bram's brother's son, who dwelt in Sod'om, and his goods, and departed.

13 ¶ And there came one that had escaped, and told A'bram the He'brew; for he dwelt in the plain of Mam're the Am'or-ite, brother of Esh'col, and brother of A'ner: and these *were* confederate with A'bram.

14 And when A'bram heard that his brother was taken captive, he armed his trained *servants*, born in his own house, three hundred and eighteen, and pursued *them* unto Dan.

15 And he divided himself against them, he and his servants, by night, and smote them, and pursued them into Ho'bah, which *is* on the left hand of Da-mas'cus.

16 And he brought back all the goods, and also brought again his brother Lot, and his goods, and the women also, and the people.

17 ¶ And the king of Sod'om went out to meet him after his return from the slaughter of Ched-or-la'o-mer, and of the kings that *were* with him, at the valley of Sha'veh, which *is* the king's dale.

18 And Mel-chiz'e-dek king of Sa'lem brought forth bread and wine: and he *was* the priest of the most high God.

19 And he blessed him, and said, Blessed *be* A'bram of the most high God, possessor of heaven and earth:

20 And blessed be the most high God, which hath delivered thine enemies into thy hand. And he gave him tithes of all.

21 And the king of Sod'om said unto A'bram, Give me the persons, and take the goods to thyself.

22 And A'bram said to the king of Sod'om, I have lift up mine hand unto the LORD, the most high God, the possessor of heaven and earth,

23 That I will not *take* from a thread even to a shoelatchet, and that I will not take any thing that *is* thine, lest thou shouldest say, I have made A'bram rich:

24 Save only that which the young men have eaten, and the portion of the men which went with me, A'ner, Esh'col, and Mam're; let them take their portion.

15

AFTER these things the word of the LORD came unto A'bram in a vision, saying, Fear not, A'bram: I *am* thy shield, *and* thy exceeding great reward.

2 And A'bram said, Lord GOD, what wilt thou give me, seeing I go childless, and the steward of my house *is* this E-li-e'zer of Da-mas'cus?

3 And A'bram said, Behold, to me thou hast given no seed: and, lo, one born in my house is mine heir.

4 And, behold, the word of the LORD *came* unto him, saying, This shall not be thine heir; but he that shall come forth out of thine own bowels shall be thine heir.

5 And he brought him forth abroad, and said, Look now toward heaven, and tell the stars, if thou be able to number them: and he said unto him, So shall thy seed be.

6 And he believed in the LORD; and he counted it to him for righteousness.

7 And he said unto him, I *am* the LORD that brought thee out of Ur of the Chal'dees, to give thee this land to inherit it.

8 And he said, Lord GOD, whereby shall I know that I shall inherit it?

9 And he said unto him, Take me an heifer of three years old, and a she goat of three years old, and a ram of three years old, and a turtledove, and a young pigeon.

10 And he took unto him all these, and divided them in the midst, and laid each piece one against another: but the birds divided he not.

11 And when the fowls came down upon the carcases, A'bram drove them away.

12 And when the sun was going down, a deep sleep fell upon A'bram; and, lo, an horror of great darkness fell upon him.

13 And he said unto A'bram, Know of a surety that thy seed shall be a stranger in a land *that is* not theirs, and shall serve them; and they shall afflict them four hundred years;

14 And also that nation, whom they shall serve, will I judge: and afterward shall they come out with great substance.

15 And thou shalt go to thy fathers in peace; thou shalt be buried in a good old age.

16 But in the fourth generation they shall

come hither again: for the iniquity of the Am'or-ites *is* not yet full.

17 And it came to pass, that, when the sun went down, and it was dark, behold a smoking furnace, and a burning lamp that passed between those pieces.

18 In the same day the LORD made a covenant with A'bram, saying, Unto thy seed have I given this land, from the river of E'gypt unto the great river, the river Eu-phra'tes:

19 The Ken'ites, and the Ken'iz-zites, and the Kad'mon-ites,

20 And the Hit'tites, and the Per'iz-zites, and the Reph'a-ims,

21 And the Am'or-ites, and the Ca'naan-ites, and the Gir'ga-shites, and the Jeb'u-sites.

16 NOW Sa'rai A'bram's wife bare him no children: and she had an handmaid, an E-gyp'tian, whose name *was* Ha'gar.

2 And Sa'rai said unto A'bram, Behold now, the LORD hath restrained me from bearing: I pray thee, go in unto my maid; it may be that I may obtain children by her. And A'bram hearkened to the voice of Sa'rai.

3 And Sa'rai A'bram's wife took Ha'gar her maid the E-gyp'tian, after A'bram had dwelt ten years in the land of Ca'naan, and gave her to her husband A'bram to be his wife.

4 ¶ And he went in unto Ha'gar, and she conceived: and when she saw that she had conceived, her mistress was despised in her eyes.

5 And Sa'rai said unto A'bram, My wrong *be* upon thee: I have given my maid into thy bosom; and when she saw that she had conceived, I was despised in her eyes: the LORD judge between me and thee.

6 But A'bram said unto Sa'rai, Behold, thy maid *is* in thy hand; do to her as it pleaseth thee. And when Sa'rai dealt hardly with her, she fled from her face.

7 ¶ And the angel of the LORD found her by a fountain of water in the wilderness, by the fountain in the way to Shur.

8 And he said, Ha'gar, Sa'rai's maid, whence camest thou? and whither wilt thou go? And she said, I flee from the face of my mistress Sa'rai.

9 And the angel of the LORD said unto her, Return to thy mistress, and submit thyself under her hands.

10 And the angel of the LORD said unto her, I will multiply thy seed exceedingly, that it shall not be numbered for multitude.

11 And the angel of the LORD said unto her, Behold, thou *art* with child, and shalt bear a son, and shalt call his name Ish'ma-el; because the LORD hath heard thy affliction.

12 And he will be a wild man; his hand *will be* against every man, and every man's hand against him; and he shall dwell in the presence of all his brethren.

13 And she called the name of the LORD that spake unto her, Thou God seest me: for she said, Have I also here looked after him that seeth me?

14 Wherefore the well was called Be'er-la-hai'-roi; behold, *it is* between Ka'desh and Be'red.

15 ¶ And Ha'gar bare A'bram a son: and A'bram called his son's name, which Ha'gar bare, Ish'ma-el.

16 And A'bram *was* fourscore and six years old, when Ha'gar bare Ish'ma-el to A'bram.

17 AND when A'bram was ninety years old and nine, the LORD appeared to A'bram, and said unto him, I *am* the Almighty God; walk before me, and be thou perfect.

2 And I will make my covenant between me and thee, and will multiply thee exceedingly.

3 And A'bram fell on his face: and God talked with him, saying,

4 As for me, behold, my covenant *is* with thee, and thou shalt be a father of many nations.

5 Neither shall thy name any more be called A'bram, but thy name shall be A'bra-ham; for a father of many nations have I made thee.

6 And I will make thee exceeding fruitful, and I will make nations of thee, and kings shall come out of thee.

7 And I will establish my covenant between me and thee and thy seed after thee in their generations for an everlasting covenant, to be a God unto thee, and to thy seed after thee.

8 And I will give unto thee, and to thy seed after thee, the land wherein thou art a stranger, all the land of Ca'naan, for an everlasting possession; and I will be their God.

9 ¶ And God said unto A'bra-ham, Thou shalt keep my covenant therefore, thou, and thy seed after thee in their generations.

10 This *is* my covenant, which ye shall keep, between me and you and thy seed after thee; Every man child among you shall be circumcised.

11 And ye shall circumcise the flesh of your foreskin; and it shall be a token of the covenant betwixt me and you.

12 And he that is eight days old shall be circumcised among you, every man child in your generations, he that is born in the house, or bought with money of any stranger, which *is* not of thy seed.

13 He that is born in thy house, and he that is bought with thy money, must needs be circumcised: and my covenant shall be in your flesh for an everlasting covenant.

14 And the uncircumcised man child whose flesh of his foreskin is not circumcised, that soul shall be cut off from his people; he hath broken my covenant.

15 ¶ And God said unto A'bra-ham, As for Sa'rai thy wife, thou shalt not call her name Sa'rai, but Sa'rah *shall* her name *be*.

16 And I will bless her, and give thee a son also of her: yea, I will bless her, and she shall be *a mother* of nations; kings of people shall be of her.

17 Then A'bra-ham fell upon his face, and laughed, and said in his heart, Shall a *child* be born unto him that is an hundred years old? and shall Sa'rah, that is ninety years old, bear?

18 And A'bra-ham said unto God, O that Ish'ma-el might live before thee!

19 And God said, Sa'rah thy wife shall bear thee a son indeed; and thou shalt call his name I'saac: and I will establish my covenant with him for an everlasting covenant, *and* with his seed after him.

20 And as for Ish'ma-el, I have heard thee: Behold, I have blessed him, and will make him fruitful, and will multiply him exceedingly; twelve princes shall he beget, and I will make him a great nation.

21 But my covenant will I establish with I'saac, which Sa'rah shall bear unto thee at this set time in the next year.

22 And he left off talking with him, and God went up from A'bra-ham.

23 ¶ And A'bra-ham took Ish'ma-el his son, and all that were born in his house, and all that were bought with his money, every male among

the men of A'bra-ham's house; and circumcised the flesh of their foreskin in the selfsame day, as God had said unto him.

24 And A'bra-ham *was* ninety years old and nine, when he was circumcised in the flesh of his foreskin.

25 And Ish'ma-el his son *was* thirteen years old, when he was circumcised in the flesh of his foreskin.

26 In the selfsame day was A'bra-ham circumcised, and Ish'ma-el his son.

27 And all the men of his house, born in the house, and bought with money of the stranger, were circumcised with him.

18 AND the LORD appeared unto him in the plains of Mam're: and he sat in the tent door in the heat of the day;

2 And he lift up his eyes and looked, and, lo, three men stood by him: and when he saw *them*, he ran to meet them from the tent door, and bowed himself toward the ground,

3 And said, My Lord, if now I have found favour in thy sight, pass not away, I pray thee, from thy servant:

4 Let a little water, I pray you, be fetched, and wash your feet, and rest yourselves under the tree:

5 And I will fetch a morsel of bread, and comfort ye your hearts; after that ye shall pass on: for therefore are ye come to your servant. And they said, So do, as thou hast said.

6 And A'bra-ham hastened into the tent unto Sa'rah, and said, Make ready quickly three measures of fine meal, knead *it*, and make cakes upon the hearth.

7 And A'bra-ham ran unto the herd, and fetcht a calf tender and good, and gave *it* unto a young man; and he hasted to dress it.

8 And he took butter, and milk, and the calf which he had dressed, and set *it* before them; and he stood by them under the tree, and they did eat.

9 ¶ And they said unto him, Where *is* Sa'rah thy wife? And he said, Behold, in the tent.

10 And he said, I will certainly return unto thee according to the time of life; and, lo, Sa'rah thy wife shall have a son. And Sa'rah heard *it* in the tent door, which *was* behind him.

11 Now A'bra-ham and Sa'rah *were* old *and* well stricken in age; *and* it ceased to be with Sa'rah after the manner of women.

12 Therefore Sa'rah laughed within herself, saying, After I am waxed old shall I have pleasure, my lord being old also?

13 And the LORD said unto A'bra-ham, Wherefore did Sa'rah laugh, saying, Shall I of a surety bear a child, which am old?

14 Is any thing too hard for theLORD? At the time appointed I will return unto thee, according to the time of life, and Sa'rah shall have a son.

15 Then Sarah denied, saying, I laughed not; for she was afraid. And he said, Nay; but thou didst laugh.

16 ¶ And the men rose up from thence, and looked toward Sod'om: and A'bra-ham went with them to bring them on the way.

17 And the LORD said, Shall I hide from A'bra-ham that thing which I do;

18 Seeing that A'bra-ham shall surely become a great and mighty nation, and all the nations of the earth shall be blessed in him?

19 For I know him, that he will command his children and his household after him, and they shall keep the way of the LORD, to do justice and judgment; that the LORD may bring upon A'bra-ham that which he hath spoken of him.

20 And the LORD said, Because the cry of Sod'om and Go-mor'rah is great, and because their sin is very grievous;

21 I will go down now, and see whether they have done altogether according to the cry of it, which is come unto me; and if not, I will know.

22 And the men turned their faces from thence, and went toward Sod'om: but A'braham stood yet before the LORD.

23 ¶ And A'bra-ham drew near, and said, Wilt thou also destroy the righteous with the wicked?

24 Peradventure there be fifty righteous within the city: wilt thou also destroy and not spare the place for the fifty righteous that *are* therein?

25 That be far from thee to do after this manner, to slay the righteous with the wicked: and that the righteous should be as the wicked, that be far from thee: Shall not the Judge of all the earth do right?

26 And the LORD said, If I find in Sod'om fifty righteous within the city, then I will spare all the place for their sakes.

27 And A'bra-ham answered and said, Behold now, I have taken upon me to speak unto the Lord, which *am but* dust and ashes:

28 Peradventure there shall lack five of the fifty righteous: wilt thou destroy all the city for *lack of* five? And he said, If I find there forty and five, I will not destroy *it*.

29 And he spake unto him yet again, and said, Peradventure there shall be forty found there. And he said, I will not do *it* for forty's sake.

30 And he said *unto him*, Oh let not the Lord be angry, and I will speak: Peradventure there shall thirty be found there. And he said, I will not do *it*, if I find thirty there.

31 And he said, Behold now, I have taken upon me to speak unto the Lord: Peradventure there shall be twenty found there. And he said, I will not destroy *it* for twenty's sake.

32 And he said, Oh let not the Lord be angry, and I will speak yet but this once: Peradventure ten shall be found there. And he said, I will not destroy *it* for ten's sake.

33 And the LORD went his way, as soon as he had left communing with A'bra-ham: and A'bra-ham returned unto his place.

19 AND there came two angels to Sod'om at even; and Lot sat in the gate of Sod'om: and Lot seeing *them* rose up to meet them; and he bowed himself with his face toward the ground;

2 And he said, Behold now, my lords, turn in, I pray you, into your servant's house, and tarry all night, and wash your feet, and ye shall rise up early, and go on your ways. And they said, Nay; but we will abide in the street all night.

3 And he pressed upon them greatly; and they turned in unto him, and entered into his house; and he made them a feast, and did bake unleavened bread, and they did eat.

4 ¶ But before they lay down, the men of the city, *even* the men of Sod'om, compassed the house round, both old and young, all the people from every quarter:

5 And they called unto Lot, and said unto him, Where *are* the men which came in to thee this night? bring them out unto us, that we may know them.

6 And Lot went out at the door unto them, and shut the door after him,

7 And said, I pray you, brethren, do not so wickedly.

8 Behold now, I have two daughters which have not known man; let me, I pray you, bring them out unto you, and do ye to them as *is* good in your eyes: only unto these men do nothing; for therefore came they under the shadow of my roof.

9 And they said, Stand back. And they said *again*, This one *fellow* came in to sojourn, and he will needs be a judge: now will we deal worse with thee, than with them. And they pressed sore upon the man, *even* Lot, and came near to break the door.

10 But the men put forth their hand, and pulled Lot into the house to them, and shut to the door.

11 And they smote the men that *were* at the door of the house with blindness, both small and great: so that they wearied themselves to find the door.

12 ¶ And the men said unto Lot, Hast thou here any besides? son in law, and thy sons, and thy daughters, and whatsoever thou hast in the city, bring *them* out of this place:

13 For we will destroy this place, because the cry of them is waxen great before the face of the LORD; and the LORD hath sent us to destroy it.

14 And Lot went out, and spake unto his sons in law, which married his daughters, and said, Up, get you out of this place; for the LORD will destroy this city. But he seemed as one that mocked unto his sons in law.

15 ¶ And when the morning arose, then the angels hastened Lot, saying, Arise, take thy wife, and thy two daughters, which are here; lest thou be consumed in the iniquity of the city.

16 And while he lingered, the men laid hold upon his hand, and upon the hand of his wife, and upon the hand of his two daughters; the LORD being merciful unto him: and they brought him forth, and set him without the city.

17 ¶ And it came to pass, when they had brought them forth abroad, that he said, Escape for thy life; look not behind thee, neither stay thou in all the plain; escape to the mountain, lest thou be consumed.

18 And Lot said unto them, Oh, not so, my Lord:

19 Behold now, thy servant hath found grace in thy sight, and thou hast magnified thy mercy, which thou has shewed unto me in saving my life; and I cannot escape to the mountain, lest some evil take me, and I die:

20 Behold now, this city *is* near to flee unto, and it *is* a little one: Oh, let me escape thither, (*is* it now a little one?) and my soul shall live.

21 And he said unto him, See, I have accepted thee concerning this thing also, that I will not overthrow this city, for the which thou hast spoken.

22 Haste thee, escape thither; for I cannot do any thing till thou be come thither. Therefore the name of the city was called Zo'ar.

23 ¶ The sun was risen upon the earth when Lot entered into Zo'ar.

24 Then the LORD rained upon Sod'om and upon Go-mor'rah brimstone and fire from the LORD out of heaven;

25 And he overthrew those cities, and all the plain, and all the inhabitants of the cities, and that which grew upon the ground.

26 ¶ But his wife looked back from behind him, and she became a pillar of salt.

27 ¶ And A'bra-ham gat up early in the morning to the place where he stood before the LORD:

28 And he looked toward Sod'om and Gomor'rah, and toward all the land of the plain, and beheld, and, lo, the smoke of the country went up as the smoke of a furnace.

29 ¶ And it came to pass, when God destroyed the cities of the plain, that God remembered A'bra-ham, and sent Lot out of the midst of the overthrow, when he overthrew the cities in the which Lot dwelt.

30 ¶ And Lot went up out of Zo'ar, and dwelt in the mountain, and his two daughters with him; for he feared to dwell in Zo'ar: and he dwelt in a cave, he and his two daughters.

31 And the firstborn said unto the younger, Our father *is* old, and *there is* not a man in the earth to come in unto us after the manner of all the earth:

32 Come, let us make our father drink wine, and we will lie with him, that we may preserve seed of our father.

33 And they made their father drink wine that night: and the firstborn went in, and lay with her father; and he perceived not when she lay down, nor when she arose.

34 And it came to pass on the morrow, that the firstborn said unto the younger, Behold, I lay yesternight with my father: let us make him drink wine this night also; and go thou in, *and* lie with him, that we may preserve seed of our father.

35 And they made their father drink wine that night also: and the younger arose, and lay with him; and he perceived not when she lay down, nor when she arose.

36 Thus were both the daughters of Lot with child by their father.

37 And the firstborn bare a son, and called his name Mo'ab: the same *is* the father of the Mo'ab-ites unto this day.

38 And the younger, she also bare a son, and called his name Ben–am'mi: the same *is* the father of the children of Am'mon unto this day.

20 AND A'bra-ham journeyed from thence toward the south country, and dwelled between Ka'desh and Shur, and sojourned in Ge'rar.

2 And A'bra-ham said of Sa'rah his wife, She *is* my sister: and A-bim'e-lech king of Ge'rar sent, and took Sa'rah.

3 But God came to A-bim'e-lech in a dream by night, and said to him, Behold, thou *art but* a dead man, for the woman which thou hast taken; for she *is* a man's wife.

4 But A-bim'e-lech had not come near her: and he said, Lord, wilt thou slay also a righteous nation?

5 Said he not unto me, She *is* my sister? and she, even she herself said, He *is* my brother: in the integrity of my heart and innocency of my hands have I done this.

6 And God said unto him in a dream, Yea, I know that thou didst this in the integrity of thy heart; for I also withheld thee from sinning against me: therefore suffered I thee not to touch her.

7 Now therefore restore the man *his* wife; for he *is* a prophet, and he shall pray for thee, and thou shalt live: and if thou restore *her* not, know thou that thou shalt surely die, thou, and all that *are* thine.

8 Therefore A-bim'e-lech rose early in the morning, and called all his servants, and told all these things in their ears: and the men were sore afraid.

9 Then A-bim'e-lech called A'bra-ham, and said unto him, What hast thou done unto us? and what have I offended thee, that thou hast brought on me and on my kingdom a great sin? thou hast done deeds unto me that ought not to be done.

10 And A-bim'e-lech said unto A'bra-ham, What sawest thou, that thou hast done this thing?

11 And A'bra-ham said, Because I thought, Surely the fear of God *is* not in this place; and they will slay me for my wife's sake.

12 And yet indeed *she is* my sister; she *is* the daughter of my father, but not the daughter of my mother; and she became my wife.

13 And it came to pass, when God caused me to wander from my father's house, that I said unto her, This *is* thy kindness which thou shalt shew unto me; at every place whither we shall come, say of me, He *is* my brother.

14 And A-bim'e-lech took sheep, and oxen, and menservants, and womenservants, and gave *them* unto A'bra-ham, and restored him Sa'rah his wife.

15 And A-bim'e-lech said, Behold, my land *is* before thee: dwell where it pleaseth thee.

16 And unto Sa'rah he said, Behold, I have given thy brother a thousand *pieces* of silver: behold, he *is* to thee a covering of the eyes, unto all that *are* with thee, and with all *other*: thus she was reproved.

17 ¶ So A'bra-ham prayed unto God: and God healed A-bim'e-lech, and his wife, and his maidservants; and they bare *children*.

18 For the LORD had fast closed up all the wombs of the house of A-bim'e-lech, because of Sa'rah A'bra-ham's wife.

21 AND the LORD visited Sa'rah as he had said, and the LORD did unto Sa'rah as he had spoken.

2 For Sa'rah conceived, and bare A'bra-ham a son in his old age, at the set time of which God had spoken to him.

3 And A'bra-ham called the name of his son that was born unto him, whom Sa'rah bare to him, I'saac.

4 And A'bra-ham circumcised his son I'saac being eight days old, as God had commanded him.

5 And A'bra-ham was an hundred years old, when his son I'saac was born unto him.

6 ¶ And Sa'rah said, God hath made me to laugh, *so that* all that hear will laugh with me.

7 And she said, Who would have said unto A'bra-ham, that Sa'rah should have given children suck? for I have born *him* a son in his old age.

8 And the child grew, and was weaned: and A'bra-ham made a great feast the *same* day that I'saac was weaned.

9 ¶ And Sa'rah saw the son of Ha'gar the E-gyp'tian, which she had born unto A'bra-ham, mocking.

10 Wherefore she said unto A'bra-ham, Cast out this bondwoman and her son: for the son of this bondwoman shall not be heir with my son, *even* with I'saac.

11 And the thing was very grievous in A'bra-ham's sight because of his son.

12 ¶ And God said unto A'bra-ham, Let it not be grievous in thy sight because of the lad, and because of thy bondwoman; in all that Sa'rah hath said unto thee, hearken unto her voice; for in I'saac shall thy seed be called.

13 And also of the son of the bondwoman will I make a nation, because he *is* thy seed.

14 And A'bra-ham rose up early in the morning, and took bread, and a bottle of water, and gave *it* unto Ha'gar, putting *it* on her shoulder, and the child, and sent her away: and she departed, and wandered in the wilderness of Be'er-she'ba.

15 And the water was spent in the bottle, and she cast the child under one of the shrubs.

16 And she went, and sat her down over against *him* a good way off, as it were a bowshot: for she said, Let me not see the death of the child. And she sat over against *him*, and lift up her voice, and wept.

17 And God heard the voice of the lad; and the angel of God called to Ha'gar out of heaven, and said unto her, What aileth thee, Ha'gar? fear not; for God hath heard the voice of the lad where he *is*.

18 Arise, lift up the lad, and hold him in thine hand; for I will make him a great nation.

19 And God opened her eyes, and she saw a well of water; and she went, and filled the bottle with water, and gave the lad drink.

20 And God was with the lad; and he grew, and dwelt in the wilderness, and became an archer.

21 And he dwelt in the wilderness of Pa'ran: and his mother took him a wife out of the land of E'gypt.

22 ¶ And it came to pass at that time, that A-bim'e-lech and Phi'chol the chief captain of his host spake unto A'bra-ham, saying, God *is* with thee in all that thou doest:

23 Now therefore swear unto me here by God that thou wilt not deal falsely with me, nor with my son, nor with my son's son: *but* according to the kindness that I have done unto thee, thou shalt do unto me, and to the land wherein thou hast sojourned.

24 And A'bra-ham said, I will swear.

25 And A'bra-ham reproved A-bim'e-lech because of a well of water, which A-bim'e-lech's servants had violently taken away.

26 And A-bim'e-lech said, I wot not who hath done this thing: neither didst thou tell me, neither yet heard I *of it*, but to day.

27 And A'bra-ham took sheep and oxen, and gave them unto A-bim'e-lech; and both of them made a covenant.

28 And A'bra-ham set seven ewe lambs of the flock by themselves.

29 And A-bim'e-lech said unto A'bra-ham, What *mean* these seven ewe lambs which thou hast set by themselves?

30 And he said, For *these* seven ewe lambs shalt thou take of my hand, that they may be a witness unto me, that I have digged this well.

31 Wherefore he called that place Be'er-she'ba; because there they sware both of them.

32 Thus they made a covenant at Be'er-she'ba: then A-bim'e-lech rose up, and Phi'chol the chief captain of his host, and they returned into the land of the Phi-lis'tines.

33 ¶ And A'bra-ham planted a grove in Be'er-she'ba, and called there on the name of the LORD, the everlasting God.

34 And A'bra-ham sojourned in the Phi-lis'tines' land many days.

22 AND it came to pass after these things, that God did tempt A'bra-ham, and said unto him, A'bra-ham: and he said, Behold, *here* I *am*.

2 And he said, Take now thy son, thine only *son* I'saac, whom thou lovest, and get thee into the land of Mo-ri'ah; and offer him there for a

burnt offering upon one of the mountains which
I will tell thee of.
3 ¶ And A'bra-ham rose up early in the
morning, and saddled his ass, and took two of
his young men with him, and I'saac his son, and
clave the wood for the burnt offering, and rose
up, and went unto the place of which God had
told him.
4 Then on the third day A'bra-ham lifted up
his eyes, and saw the place afar off.
5 And A'bra-ham said unto his young men,
Abide ye here with the ass; and I and the lad
will go yonder and worship, and come again to
you.
6 And A'bra-ham took the wood of the burnt
offering, and laid *it* upon I'saac his son; and he
took the fire in his hand, and a knife; and they
went both of them together.
7 And I'saac spake unto A'bra-ham his father, and said, My father: and he said, Here *am*
I, my son. And he said, Behold the fire and the
wood: but where *is* the lamb for a burnt offering?
8 And A'bra-ham said, My son, God will provide himself a lamb for a burnt offering: so they
went both of them together.
9 And they came to the place which God had
told him of; and A'bra-ham built an altar there,
and laid the wood in order, and bound I'saac his
son, and laid him on the altar upon the wood.
10 And A'bra-ham stretched forth his hand,
and took the knife to slay his son.
11 And the angel of the LORD called unto him
out of heaven, and said, A'bra-ham, A'bra-ham:
and he said, Here *am* I.
12 And he said, Lay not thine hand upon the
lad, neither do thou any thing unto him: for now
I know that thou fearest God, seeing thou hast
not withheld thy son, thine only *son* from me.
13 And Abraham lifted up his eyes, and
looked, and behold behind *him* a ram caught in
a thicket by his horns: and A'bra-ham went and
took the ram, and offered him up for a burnt
offering in the stead of his son.
14 And A'bra-ham called the name of that
place Je-ho'vah–ji'reh: as it is said *to* this day,
In the mount of the LORD it shall be seen.
15 ¶ And the angel of the LORD called unto
A'bra-ham out of heaven the second time,
16 And said, By myself have I sworn, saith
the LORD, for because thou hast done this thing,
and hast not withheld thy son, thine only *son:*
17 That in blessing I will bless thee, and in
multiplying I will multiply thy seed as the stars
of the heaven, and as the sand which *is* upon
the sea shore; and thy seed shall possess the
gate of his enemies;
18 And in thy seed shall all the nations of the
earth be blessed; because thou hast obeyed my
voice.
19 So A'bra-ham returned unto his young
men, and they rose up and went together to Be'-
er–she'ba; and A'bra-ham dwelt at Be'er–she'-
ba.
20 ¶ And it came to pass after these things,
that it was told A'bra-ham, saying, Behold, Mil'-
cah, she hath also born children unto thy
brother Na'hor;
21 Huz his firstborn, and Buz his brother,
and Ke-mu'el the father of A'ram,
22 And Che'sed, and Ha'zo, and Pil'dash, and
Jid'laph, and Beth-u'el.
23 And Beth-u'el begat Re-bek'ah: these
eight Mil'cah did bear to Na'hor, A'bra-ham's
brother.
24 And his concubine, whose name *was*
Reu'mah, she bare also Te'bah, and Ga'ham,
and Tha'hash, and Ma'a-chah.

23 AND Sa'rah was an hundred and seven
and twenty years old: *these were* the
years of the life of Sa'rah.
2 And Sa'rah died in Kir'jath–ar'ba; the same
is He'bron in the land of Ca'naan: and A'bra-
ham came to mourn for Sa'rah, and to weep for
her.
3 ¶ And A'bra-ham stood up from before his
dead, and spake unto the sons of Heth, saying,
4 I *am* a stranger and a sojourner with you:
give me a possession of a buryingplace with
you, that I may bury my dead out of my sight.
5 And the children of Heth answered A'bra-
ham, saying unto him,
6 Hear us, my lord: thou *art* a mighty prince
among us: in the choice of our sepulchres bury
thy dead; none of us shall withhold from thee
his sepulchre, but that thou mayest bury thy
dead.
7 And A'bra-ham stood up, and bowed himself to the people of the land, *even* to the children of Heth.
8 And he communed with them, saying, If it
be your mind that I should bury my dead out of
my sight; hear me, and intreat for me to E'-
phron the son of Zo'har,
9 That he may give me the cave of Mach-pe'-
lah, which he hath, which *is* in the end of his
field; for as much money as it is worth he shall
give it me for a possession of a buryingplace
amongst you.
10 And E'phron dwelt among the children of
Heth: and E'phron the Hit'tite answered A'bra-
ham in the audience of the children of Heth,
even of all that went in at the gate of his city,
saying,
11 Nay, my lord, hear me: the field give I
thee, and the cave that *is* therein, I give it thee;
in the presence of the sons of my people give I it
thee: bury thy dead.
12 And A'bra-ham bowed down himself before the people of the land.
13 And he spake unto E'phron in the audience of the people of the land, saying, But if
thou *wilt give it,* I pray thee, hear me: I will give
thee money for the field; take *it* of me, and I will
bury my dead there.
14 And E'phron answered A'bra-ham, saying
unto him,
15 My lord, hearken unto me: the land *is*
worth four hundred shekels of silver; what *is*
that betwixt me and thee? bury therefore thy
dead.
16 And A'bra-ham hearkened unto E'phron;
and A'bra-ham weighed to E'phron the silver,
which he had named in the audience of the sons
of Heth, four hundred shekels of silver, current
money with the merchant.
17 ¶ And the field of E'phron, which *was* in
Mach-pe'lah, which *was* before Mam're, the
field, and the cave which *was* therein, and all
the trees that *were* in the field, that *were* in all
the borders round about, were made sure
18 Unto A'bra-ham for a possession in the
presence of the children of Heth, before all that
went in at the gate of his city.
19 And after this, A'bra-ham buried Sa'rah
his wife in the cave of the field of Mach-pe'lah
before Mam're: the same *is* He'bron in the land
of Ca'naan.
20 And the field, and the cave that *is* therein,
were made sure unto A'bra-ham for a possession of a buryingplace by the sons of Heth.

24 AND A'bra-ham was old, *and* well stricken in age: and the LORD had blessed A'bra-ham in all things.

2 And A'bra-ham said unto his eldest servant of his house, that ruled over all that he had, Put, I pray thee, thy hand under my thigh:

3 And I will make thee swear by the LORD, the God of heaven, and the God of the earth, that thou shalt not take a wife unto my son of the daughters of the Ca'naan-ites, among whom I dwell:

4 But thou shalt go unto my country, and to my kindred, and take a wife unto my son I'saac.

5 And the servant said unto him, Peradventure the woman will not be willing to follow me unto this land: must I needs bring thy son again unto the land from whence thou camest?

6 And A'bra-ham said unto him, Beware thou that thou bring not my son thither again.

7 ¶ The LORD God of heaven, which took me from my father's house, and from the land of my kindred, and which spake unto me, and that sware unto me, saying, Unto thy seed will I give this land; he shall send his angel before thee, and thou shalt take a wife unto my son from thence.

8 And if the woman will not be willing to follow thee, then thou shalt be clear from this my oath: only bring not my son thither again.

9 And the servant put his hand under the thigh of A'bra-ham his master, and sware to him concerning that matter.

10 ¶ And the servant took ten camels of the camels of his master, and departed; for all the goods of his master *were* in his hand: and he arose, and went to Mes-o-po-ta'mi-a, unto the city of Na'hor.

11 And he made his camels to kneel down without the city by a well of water at the time of the evening, *even* the time that women go out to draw *water*.

12 And he said, O LORD God of my master A'bra-ham, I pray thee, send me good speed this day, and shew kindness unto my master A'-bra-ham.

13 Behold, I stand *here* by the well of water; and the daughters of the men of the city come out to draw water:

14 And let it come to pass, that the damsel to whom I shall say, Let down thy pitcher, I pray thee, that I may drink; and she shall say, Drink, and I will give thy camels drink also: *let the same be* she *that* thou hast appointed for thy servant I'saac; and thereby shall I know that thou hast shewed kindness unto my master.

15 ¶ And it came to pass, before he had done speaking, that, behold, Re-bek'ah came out, who was born to Beth-u'el, son of Mil'cah, the wife of Na'hor, A'bra-ham's brother, with her pitcher upon her shoulder.

16 And the damsel *was* very fair to look upon, a virgin, neither had any man known her: and she went down to the well, and filled her pitcher, and came up.

17 And the servant ran to meet her, and said, Let me, I pray thee, drink a little water of thy pitcher.

18 And she said, Drink, my lord: and she hasted, and let down her pitcher upon her hand, and gave him drink.

19 And when she had done giving him drink, she said, I will draw *water* for thy camels also, until they have done drinking.

20 And she hasted, and emptied her pitcher into the trough, and ran again unto the well to draw *water*, and drew for all his camels.

21 And the man wondering at her held his peace, to wit whether the LORD had made his journey prosperous or not.

22 And it came to pass, as the camels had done drinking, that the man took a golden earring of half a shekel weight, and two bracelets for her hands of ten *shekels* weight of gold;

23 And said, Whose daughter *art* thou? tell me, I pray thee: is there room *in* thy father's house for us to lodge in?

24 And she said unto him, I *am* the daughter of Beth-u'el the son of Mil'cah, which she bare unto Na'hor.

25 She said moreover unto him, We have both straw and provender enough, and room to lodge in.

26 And the man bowed down his head, and worshipped the LORD.

27 And he said, Blessed *be* the LORD God of my master A'bra-ham, who hath not left destitute my master of his mercy and his truth: I *being* in the way, the LORD led me to the house of my master's brethren.

28 And the damsel ran, and told *them of* her mother's house these things.

29 ¶ And Re-bek'ah had a brother, and his name *was* La'ban: and La'ban ran out unto the man, unto the well.

30 And it came to pass, when he saw the earring and bracelets upon his sister's hands, and when he heard the words of Re-bek'ah his sister, saying, Thus spake the man unto me; that he came unto the man; and, behold, he stood by the camels at the well.

31 And he said, Come in, thou blessed of the LORD; wherefore standest thou without? for I have prepared the house, and room for the camels.

32 ¶ And the man came into the house: and he ungirded his camels, and gave straw and provender for the camels, and water to wash his feet, and the men's feet that *were* with him.

33 And there was set *meat* before him to eat: but he said, I will not eat, until I have told mine errand. And he said, Speak on.

34 And he said, I *am* A'bra-ham's servant.

35 And the LORD hath blessed my master greatly; and he is become great: and he hath given him flocks, and herds, and silver, and gold, and menservants, and maidservants, and camels, and asses.

36 And Sa'rah my master's wife bare a son to my master when she was old: and unto him hath he given all that he hath.

37 And my master made me swear, saying, Thou shalt not take a wife to my son of the daughters of the Ca'naan-ites, in whose land I dwell:

38 But thou shalt go unto my father's house, and to my kindred, and take a wife unto my son.

39 And I said unto my master, Peradventure the woman will not follow me.

40 And he said unto me, The LORD, before whom I walk, will send his angel with thee, and prosper thy way; and thou shalt take a wife for my son of my kindred, and of my father's house:

41 Then shalt thou be clear from *this* my oath, when thou comest to my kindred; and if they give not thee *one*, thou shalt be clear from my oath.

42 And I came this day unto the well, and said, O LORD God of my master A'bra-ham, if now thou do prosper my way which I go:

43 Behold, I stand by the well of water; and it shall come to pass, that when the virgin cometh forth to draw *water*, and I say to her, Give me, I

pray thee, a little water of thy pitcher to drink;
44 And she say to me, Both drink thou, and I
will also draw for thy camels: *let* the same *be*
the woman whom the LORD hath appointed out
for my master's son.
45 And before I had done speaking in mine
heart, behold, Re-bek'ah came forth with her
pitcher on her shoulder; and she went down
unto the well, and drew *water:* and I said unto
her, Let me drink, I pray thee.
46 And she made haste, and let down her
pitcher from her *shoulder,* and said, Drink, and
I will give thy camels drink also: so I drank, and
she made the camels drink also.
47 And I asked her, and said, Whose daughter *art* thou? And she said, The daughter of
Beth-u'el, Na'hor's son, whom Mil'cah bare
unto him: and I put the earring upon her face,
and the bracelets upon her hands.
48 And I bowed down my head, and worshipped the LORD, and blessed the LORD God of
my master A'bra-ham, which had led me in the
right way to take my master's brother's daughter unto his son.
49 And now if ye will deal kindly and truly
with my master, tell me: and if not, tell me; that
I may turn to the right hand, or to the left.
50 Then La'ban and Beth-u'el answered and
said, The thing proceedeth from the LORD: we
cannot speak unto thee bad or good.
51 Behold, Re-bek'ah *is* before thee, take *her,*
and go, and let her be thy master's son's wife,
as the LORD hath spoken.
52 And it came to pass, that, when A'bra-
ham's servant heard their words, he worshipped the LORD, *bowing himself* to the earth.
53 And the servant brought forth jewels of
silver, and jewels of gold, and raiment, and
gave *them* to Re-bek'ah: he gave also to her
brother and to her mother precious things.
54 And they did eat and drink, he and the
men that *were* with him, and tarried all night;
and they rose up in the morning, and he said,
Send me away unto my master.
55 And her brother and her mother said, Let
the damsel abide with us a *few* days, at the least
ten; after that she shall go.
56 And he said unto them, Hinder me not,
seeing the LORD hath prospered my way; send
me away that I may go to my master.
57 And they said, We will call the damsel,
and enquire at her mouth.
58 And they called Re-bek'ah, and said unto
her, Wilt thou go with this man? And she said, I
will go.
59 And they sent away Re-bek'ah their sister,
and her nurse, and A'bra-ham's servant, and his
men.
60 And they blessed Re-bek'ah, and said
unto her, Thou *art* our sister, be thou *the
mother* of thousands of millions, and let thy
seed possess the gate of those which hate them.
61 ¶ And Re-bek'ah arose, and her damsels,
and they rode upon the camels, and followed
the man: and the servant took Re-bek'ah, and
went his way.
62 And I'saac came from the way of the well
La-hai'roi; for he dwelt in the south country.
63 And I'saac went out to meditate in the
field at the eventide: and he lifted up his eyes,
and saw, and, behold, the camels *were* coming.
64 And Re-bek'ah lifted up her eyes, and
when she saw I'saac, she lighted off the camel.
65 For she *had* said unto the servant, What
man *is* this that walketh in the field to meet us?
And the servant *had* said, It *is* my master:
therefore she took a veil, and covered herself.
66 And the servant told I'saac all things that
he had done.
67 And I'saac brought her into his mother
Sa'rah's tent, and took Re-bek'ah, and she became his wife; and he loved her: and I'saac was
comforted after his mother's *death.*

25 THEN again A'bra-ham took a wife, and
her name *was* Ke-tu'rah.
2 And she bare him Zim'ran, and Jok'shan,
and Me'dan, and Mid'i-an, and Ish'bak, and
Shu'ah.
3 And Jok'shan begat She'ba, and De'dan.
And the sons of De'dan were As-shu'rim, and
Le-tu'shim, and Le-um'mim.
4 And the sons of Mid'i-an; E'phah, and E'-
pher, and Ha'noch, and A-bi'dah, and El'da-ah.
All these *were* the children of Ke-tu'rah.
5 ¶ And A'bra-ham gave all that he had unto
I'saac.
6 But unto the sons of the concubines, which
A'bra-ham had, A'bra-ham gave gifts, and sent
them away from I'saac his son, while he yet
lived, eastward, unto the east country.
7 And these *are* the days of the years of A'-
bra-ham's life which he lived, an hundred threescore and fifteen years.
8 Then A'bra-ham gave up the ghost, and
died in a good old age, an old man, and full of
years; and was gathered to his people.
9 And his sons I'saac and Ish'ma-el buried
him in the cave of Mach-pe'lah, in the field of
E'phron the son of Zo'har the Hit'tite, which *is*
before Mam're;
10 The field which A'bra-ham purchased of
the sons of Heth: there was A'bra-ham buried,
and Sa'rah his wife.
11 ¶ And it came to pass after the death of
A'bra-ham, that God blessed his son I'saac; and
I'saac dwelt by the well La-hai'roi.
12 ¶ Now these *are* the generations of Ish'-
ma-el, A'bra-ham's son, whom Ha'gar the E-
gyp'tian, Sa'rah's handmaid, bare unto A'bra-
ham:
13 And these *are* the names of the sons of
Ish'ma-el, by their names, according to their
generations: the firstborn of Ish'ma-el, Ne-ba'-
joth; and Ke'dar, and Ad'be-el, and Mib'sam,
14 And Mish'ma, and Du'mah, and Mas'sa,
15 Ha'dar, and Te'ma, Je'tur, Na'phish, and
Ked'e-mah:
16 These *are* the sons of Ish'ma-el, and these
are their names, by their towns, and by their
castles; twelve princes according to their nations.
17 And these *are* the years of the life of Ish'-
ma-el, an hundred and thirty and seven years:
and he gave up the ghost and died; and was
gathered unto his people.
18 And they dwelt from Hav'i-lah unto Shur,
that *is* before E'gypt, as thou goest toward As-
syr'i-a: *and* he died in the presence of all his
brethren.
19 ¶ And these *are* the generations of I'saac,
A'bra-ham's son: A'bra-ham begat I'saac:
20 And I'saac was forty years old when he
took Re-bek'ah to wife, the daughter of Beth-
u'el the Syr'i-an of Pa'dan–a'ram, the sister to
La'ban the Syr'i-an.
21 And I'saac intreated the LORD for his wife,
because she *was* barren: and the LORD was intreated of him, and Re-bek'ah his wife conceived.
22 And the children struggled together
within her; and she said, If *it be* so, why *am* I
thus? And she went to enquire of the LORD.
23 And the LORD said unto her, Two nations

are in thy womb, and two manner of people
shall be separated from thy bowels: and *the one*
people shall be stronger than *the other* people;
and the elder shall serve the younger.
24 ¶ And when her days to be delivered
were fulfilled, behold, *there were* twins in her
womb.
25 And the first came out red, all over like an
hairy garment; and they called his name E'sau.
26 And after that came his brother out, and
his hand took hold on E'sau's heel; and his
name was called Ja'cob: and I'saac *was* threescore years old when she bare them.
27 And the boys grew: and E'sau was a cunning hunter, a man of the field; and Ja'cob *was* a
plain man, dwelling in tents.
28 And I'saac loved E'sau, because he did eat
of *his* venison: but Re-bek'ah loved Ja'cob.
29 ¶ And Ja'cob sod pottage: and E'sau
came from the field, and he *was* faint:
30 And E'sau said to Ja'cob, Feed me, I pray
thee, with that same red *pottage;* for I *am* faint:
therefore was his name called E'dom.
31 And Ja'cob said, Sell me this day thy
birthright.
32 And E'sau said, Behold, I *am* at the point
to die: and what profit shall this birthright do to
me?
33 And Ja'cob said, Swear to me this day;
and he sware unto him: and he sold his birthright unto Ja'cob.
34 Then Ja'cob gave E'sau bread and pottage
of lentiles; and he did eat and drink, and rose
up, and went his way: thus E'sau despised *his*
birthright.

26 AND there was a famine in the land, beside the first famine that was in the days
of A'bra-ham. And I'saac went unto A-bim'e-
lech king of the Phi-lis'tines unto Ge'rar.
2 And the LORD appeared unto him, and said,
Go not down into E'gypt; dwell in the land
which I shall tell thee of:
3 Sojourn in this land, and I will be with thee,
and will bless thee; for unto thee, and unto thy
seed, I will give all these countries, and I will
perform the oath which I sware unto A'bra-ham
thy father;
4 And I will make thy seed to multiply as the
stars of heaven, and will give unto thy seed all
these countries; and in thy seed shall all the nations of the earth be blessed;
5 Because that A'bra-ham obeyed my voice,
and kept my charge, my commandments, my
statutes, and my laws.
6 ¶ And I'saac dwelt in Ge'rar:
7 And the men of the place asked *him* of his
wife; and he said, She *is* my sister: for he feared
to say, *She is* my wife; lest, *said he,* the men of
the place should kill me for Re-bek'ah; because
she *was* fair to look upon.
8 And it came to pass, when he had been
there a long time, that A-bim'e-lech king of the
Phi-lis'tines looked out at a window, and saw,
and, behold, I'saac *was* sporting with Re-bek'ah
his wife.
9 And A-bim'e-lech called I'saac, and said,
Behold, of a surety she *is* thy wife: and how
saidst thou, She *is* my sister? And I'saac said
unto him, Because I said, Lest I die for her.
10 And A-bim'e-lech said, What *is* this thou
hast done unto us? one of the people might
lightly have lien with thy wife, and thou shouldest have brought guiltiness upon us.
11 And A-bim'e-lech charged all *his* people,
saying, He that toucheth this man or his wife
shall surely be put to death.
12 Then I'saac sowed in that land, and received in the same year an hundredfold: and the
LORD blessed him.
13 And the man waxed great, and went forward, and grew until he became very great:
14 For he had possession of flocks, and possession of herds, and great store of servants:
and the Phi-lis'tines envied him.
15 For all the wells which his father's servants had digged in the days of A'bra-ham his
father, the Phi-lis'tines had stopped them, and
filled them with earth.
16 And A-bim'e-lech said unto I'saac, Go
from us; for thou art much mightier than we.
17 ¶ And I'saac departed thence, and
pitched his tent in the valley of Ge'rar, and
dwelt there.
18 And I'saac digged again the wells of water, which they had digged in the days of A'bra-
ham his father; for the Phi-lis'tines had stopped
them after the death of A'bra-ham: and he
called their names after the names by which his
father had called them.
19 And Isaac's servants digged in the valley,
and found there a well of springing water.
20 And the herdmen of Ge'rar did strive with
Isaac's herdmen, saying, The water *is* ours: and
he called the name of the well E'sek; because
they strove with him.
21 And they digged another well, and strove
for that also: and he called the name of it Sit'-
nah.
22 And he removed from thence, and digged
another well; and for that they strove not: and
he called the name of it Re-ho'both; and he said,
For now the LORD hath made room for us, and
we shall be fruitful in the land.
23 And he went up from thence to Be'er-
she'ba.
24 And the LORD appeared unto him the
same night, and said, I *am* the God of A'bra-
ham thy father: fear not, for I *am* with thee, and
will bless thee, and multiply thy seed for my
servant A'bra-ham's sake.
25 And he builded an altar there, and called
upon the name of the LORD, and pitched his tent
there: and there Isaac's servants digged a well.
26 ¶ Then A-bim'e-lech went to him from
Ge'rar, and A-huz'zath one of his friends, and
Phi'chol the chief captain of his army.
27 And I'saac said unto them, Wherefore
come ye to me, seeing ye hate me, and have
sent me away from you?
28 And they said, We saw certainly that the
LORD was with thee: and we said, Let there be
now an oath betwixt us, *even* betwixt us and
thee, and let us make a covenant with thee;
29 That thou wilt do us no hurt, as we have
not touched thee, and as we have done unto
thee nothing but good, and have sent thee away
in peace: thou *art* now the blessed of the LORD.
30 And he made them a feast, and they did
eat and drink.
31 And they rose up betimes in the morning,
and sware one to another: and I'saac sent them
away, and they departed from him in peace.
32 And it came to pass the same day, that
Isaac's servants came, and told him concerning
the well which they had digged, and said unto
him, We have found water.
33 And he called it She'bah: therefore the
name of the city *is* Be'er-she'ba unto this day.
34 ¶ And E'sau was forty years old when he
took to wife Ju'dith the daughter of Be-e'ri the
Hit'tite, and Bash'e-math the daughter of E'lon
the Hit'tite:

35 Which were a grief of mind unto I'saac and to Re-bek'ah.

27

AND it came to pass, that when I'saac was old, and his eyes were dim, so that he could not see, he called E'sau his eldest son, and said unto him, My son: and he said unto him, Behold, *here am* I.

2 And he said, Behold now, I am old, I know not the day of my death:

3 Now therefore take, I pray thee, thy weapons, thy quiver and thy bow, and go out to the field, and take me *some* venison;

4 And make me savoury meat, such as I love, and bring *it* to me, that I may eat; that my soul may bless thee before I die.

5 And Re-bek'ah heard when I'saac spake to E'sau his son. And E'sau went to the field to hunt *for* venison, *and* to bring *it*.

6 ¶ And Re-bek'ah spake unto Ja'cob her son, saying, Behold, I heard thy father speak unto E'sau thy brother, saying,

7 Bring me venison, and make me savoury meat, that I may eat, and bless thee before the LORD before my death.

8 Now therefore, my son, obey my voice according to that which I command thee.

9 Go now to the flock, and fetch me from thence two good kids of the goats; and I will make them savoury meat for thy father, such as he loveth:

10 And thou shalt bring *it* to thy father, that he may eat, and that he may bless thee before his death.

11 And Ja'cob said to Re-bek'ah his mother, Behold, E'sau my brother *is* a hairy man, and I *am* a smooth man:

12 My father peradventure will feel me, and I shall seem to him as a deceiver; and I shall bring a curse upon me, and not a blessing.

13 And his mother said unto him, Upon me *be* thy curse, my son: only obey my voice, and go fetch me *them*.

14 And he went, and fetched, and brought *them* to his mother: and his mother made savoury meat, such as his father loved.

15 And Re-bek'ah took goodly raiment of her eldest son E'sau, which *were* with her in the house, and put them upon Ja'cob her younger son:

16 And she put the skins of the kids of the goats upon his hands, and upon the smooth of his neck:

17 And she gave the savoury meat and the bread, which she had prepared, into the hand of her son Ja'cob.

18 ¶ And he came unto his father, and said, My father: and he said, Here *am* I; who *art* thou, my son?

19 And Ja'cob said unto his father, I *am* E'sau thy firstborn; I have done according as thou badest me: arise, I pray thee, sit and eat of my venison, that thy soul may bless me.

20 And I'saac said unto his son, How *is it* that thou hast found *it* so quickly, my son? And he said, Because the LORD thy God brought *it* to me.

21 And I'saac said unto Ja'cob, Come near, I pray thee, that I may feel thee, my son, whether thou *be* my very son E'sau or not.

22 And Ja'cob went near unto I'saac his father; and he felt him, and said, The voice *is* Ja'cob's voice, but the hands *are* the hands of E'sau.

23 And he discerned him not, because his hands were hairy, as his brother E'sau's hands: so he blessed him.

24 And he said, *Art* thou my very son E'sau? And he said, I *am*.

25 And he said, Bring *it* near to me, and I will eat of my son's venison, that my soul may bless thee. And he brought *it* near to him, and he did eat: and he brought him wine, and he drank.

26 And his father I'saac said unto him, Come near now, and kiss me, my son.

27 And he came near, and kissed him: and he smelled the smell of his raiment, and blessed him, and said, See, the smell of my son *is* as the smell of a field which the LORD hath blessed:

28 Therefore God give thee of the dew of heaven, and the fatness of the earth, and plenty of corn and wine:

29 Let people serve thee, and nations bow down to thee: be lord over thy brethren, and let thy mother's sons bow down to thee: cursed *be* every one that curseth thee, and blessed *be* he that blesseth thee.

30 ¶ And it came to pass, as soon as I'saac had made an end of blessing Ja'cob, and Ja'cob was yet scarce gone out from the presence of I'saac his father, that E'sau his brother came in from his hunting.

31 And he also had made savoury meat, and brought it unto his father, and said unto his father, Let my father arise, and eat of his son's venison, that thy soul may bless me.

32 And I'saac his father said unto him, Who *art* thou? And he said, I *am* thy son, thy firstborn E'sau.

33 And I'saac trembled very exceedingly, and said, Who? where *is* he that hath taken venison, and brought *it* me, and I have eaten of all before thou camest, and have blessed him? yea, *and* he shall be blessed.

34 And when E'sau heard the words of his father, he cried with a great and exceeding bitter cry, and said unto his father, Bless me, *even* me also, O my father.

35 And he said, Thy brother came with subtilty, and hath taken away thy blessing.

36 And he said, Is not he rightly named Ja'cob? for he hath supplanted me these two times: he took away my birthright; and, behold, now he hath taken away my blessing. And he said, Hast thou not reserved a blessing for me?

37 And I'saac answered and said unto E'sau, Behold, I have made him thy lord, and all his brethren have I given to him for servants; and with corn and wine have I sustained him: and what shall I do now unto thee, my son?

38 And E'sau said unto his father, Hast thou but one blessing, my father? bless me, *even* me also, O my father. And E'sau lifted up his voice, and wept.

39 And I'saac his father answered and said unto him, Behold, thy dwelling shall be the fatness of the earth, and of the dew of heaven from above;

40 And by thy sword shalt thou live, and shalt serve thy brother; and it shall come to pass when thou shalt have the dominion, that thou shalt break his yoke from off thy neck.

41 ¶ And E'sau hated Ja'cob because of the blessing wherewith his father blessed him: and E'sau said in his heart, The days of mourning for my father are at hand; then will I slay my brother Ja'cob.

42 And these words of E'sau her elder son were told to Re-bek'ah: and she sent and called Ja'cob her younger son, and said unto him, Behold, thy brother E'sau, as touching thee, doth comfort himself, *purposing* to kill thee.

43 Now therefore, my son, obey my voice;

and arise, flee thou to La'ban my brother to Ha'ran;

44 And tarry with him a few days, until thy brother's fury turn away;

45 Until thy brother's anger turn away from thee, and he forget *that* which thou hast done to him: then I will send, and fetch thee from thence: why should I be deprived also of you both in one day?

46 And Re-bek'ah said to I'saac, I am weary of my life because of the daughters of Heth: if Ja'cob take a wife of the daughters of Heth, such as these *which are* of the daughters of the land, what good shall my life do me?

28 AND I'saac called Ja'cob, and blessed him, and charged him, and said unto him, Thou shalt not take a wife of the daughters of Ca'naan.

2 Arise, go to Pa'dan–a'ram, to the house of Beth-u'el thy mother's father; and take thee a wife from thence of the daughters of La'ban thy mother's brother.

3 And God Almighty bless thee, and make thee fruitful, and multiply thee, that thou mayest be a multitude of people;

4 And give thee the blessing of A'bra-ham, to thee, and to thy seed with thee; that thou mayest inherit the land wherein thou art a stranger, which God gave unto A'bra-ham.

5 And I'saac sent away Ja'cob: and he went to Pa'dan–a'ram unto La'ban, son of Beth-u'el the Syr'i-an, the brother of Re-bek'ah, Ja'cob's and E'sau's mother.

6 ¶ When E'sau saw that I'saac had blessed Ja'cob, and sent him away to Pa'dan–a'ram, to take him a wife from thence; and that as he blessed him he gave him a charge, saying, Thou shalt not take a wife of the daughters of Ca'naan;

7 And that Ja'cob obeyed his father and his mother, and was gone to Pa'dan–a'ram;

8 And E'sau seeing that the daughters of Ca'naan pleased not I'saac his father;

9 Then went E'sau unto Ish'ma-el, and took unto the wives which he had Ma'ha-lath the daughter of Ish'ma-el A'bra-ham's son, the sister of Ne-ba'joth, to be his wife.

10 ¶ And Ja'cob went out from Be'er–she'ba, and went toward Ha'ran.

11 And he lighted upon a certain place, and tarried there all night, because the sun was set; and he took of the stones of that place, and put *them for* his pillows, and lay down in that place to sleep.

12 And he dreamed, and behold a ladder set up on the earth, and the top of it reached to heaven: and behold the angels of God ascending and descending on it.

13 And, behold, the LORD stood above it, and said, I *am* the LORD God of A'bra-ham thy father, and the God of I'saac: the land whereon thou liest, to thee will I give it, and to thy seed;

14 And thy seed shall be as the dust of the earth, and thou shalt spread abroad to the west, and to the east, and to the north, and to the south: and in thee and in thy seed shall all the families of the earth be blessed.

15 And, behold, I *am* with thee, and will keep thee in all *places* whither thou goest, and will bring thee again into this land; for I will not leave thee, until I have done *that* which I have spoken to thee of.

16 ¶ And Ja'cob awaked out of his sleep, and he said, Surely the LORD is in this place; and I knew *it* not.

17 And he was afraid, and said, How dreadful *is* this place! this *is* none other but the house of God, and this *is* the gate of heaven.

18 And Ja'cob rose up early in the morning, and took the stone that he had put *for* his pillows, and set up *for* a pillar, and poured oil upon the top of it.

19 And he called the name of that place Beth'–el: but the name of that city *was called* Luz at the first.

20 And Ja'cob vowed a vow, saying, If God will be with me, and will keep me in this way that I go, and will give me bread to eat, and raiment to put on,

21 So that I come again to my father's house in peace; then shall the LORD be my God:

22 And this stone, which I have set *for* a pillar, shall be God's house: and of all that thou shalt give me I will surely give the tenth unto thee.

29 THEN Ja'cob went on his journey, and came into the land of the people of the east.

2 And he looked, and behold a well in the field, and, lo, there *were* three flocks of sheep lying by it; for out of that well they watered the flocks: and a great stone *was* upon the well's mouth.

3 And thither were all the flocks gathered: and they rolled the stone from the well's mouth, and watered the sheep, and put the stone again upon the well's mouth in his place.

4 And Ja'cob said unto them, My brethren, whence *be* ye? And they said, Of Ha'ran *are* we.

5 And he said unto them, Know ye La'ban the son of Na'hor? And they said, We know *him*.

6 And he said unto them, *Is* he well? And they said, *He is* well: and, behold, Ra'chel his daughter cometh with the sheep.

7 And he said, Lo, *it is* yet high day, neither *is it* time that the cattle should be gathered together: water ye the sheep, and go *and* feed *them*.

8 And they said, We cannot, until all the flocks be gathered together, and *till* they roll the stone from the well's mouth; then we water the sheep.

9 ¶ And while he yet spake with them, Ra'chel came with her father's sheep: for she kept them.

10 And it came to pass, when Ja'cob saw Ra'chel the daughter of La'ban his mother's brother, and the sheep of La'ban his mother's brother, that Ja'cob went near, and rolled the stone from the well's mouth, and watered the flock of La'ban his mother's brother.

11 And Ja'cob kissed Ra'chel, and lifted up his voice, and wept.

12 And Ja'cob told Ra'chel that he *was* her father's brother, and that he *was* Re-bek'ah's son: and she ran and told her father.

13 And it came to pass, when La'ban heard the tidings of Ja'cob his sister's son, that he ran to meet him, and embraced him, and kissed him, and brought him to his house. And he told La'ban all these things.

14 And La'ban said to him, Surely thou *art* my bone and my flesh. And he abode with him the space of a month.

15 ¶ And La'ban said unto Ja'cob, Because thou *art* my brother, shoudest thou therefore serve me for nought? tell me, what *shall* thy wages *be?*

16 And La'ban had two daughters: the name of the elder *was* Le'ah, and the name of the younger *was* Ra'chel.

17 Le'ah *was* tender eyed; but Ra'chel was
beautiful and well favoured.
18 And Ja'cob loved Ra'chel; and said, I will
serve thee seven years for Ra'chel thy younger
daughter.
19 And La'ban said, *It is* better that I give her
to thee, than that I should give her to another
man: abide with me.
20 And Ja'cob served seven years for Ra'-
chel; and they seemed unto him *but* a few days,
for the love he had to her.
21 ¶ And Ja'cob said unto La'ban, Give *me*
my wife, for my days are fulfilled, that I may go
in unto her.
22 And La'ban gathered together all the men
of the place, and made a feast.
23 And it came to pass in the evening that he
took Le'ah his daughter, and brought her to
him; and he went in unto her.
24 And La'ban gave unto his daughter Le'ah
Zil-pah his maid *for* an handmaid.
25 And it came to pass, that in the morning,
behold, it *was* Leah: and he said to La'ban,
What *is* this thou hast done unto me? did not I
serve with thee for Ra'chel? wherefore then
hast thou beguiled me?
26 And La'ban said, It must not be so done in
our country, to give the younger before the
firstborn.
27 Fulfil her week, and we will give thee this
also for the service which thou shalt serve with
me yet seven other years.
28 And Ja'cob did so, and fulfilled her week:
and he gave him Ra'chel his daughter to wife
also.
29 And La'ban gave to Ra'chel his daughter
Bil'hah his handmaid to be her maid.
30 And he went in also unto Ra'chel, and he
loved also Ra'chel more than Le'ah, and served
with him yet seven other years.
31 ¶ And when the LORD saw that Le'ah *was*
hated, he opened her womb: but Ra'chel *was*
barren.
32 And Le'ah conceived, and bare a son, and
she called his name Reu'ben: for she said,
Surely the LORD hath looked upon my affliction;
now therefore my husband will love me.
33 And she conceived again, and bare a son;
and said, Because the LORD hath heard that I
was hated, he hath therefore given me this *son*
also: and she called his name Sim'e-on.
34 And she conceived again, and bare a son;
and said, Now this time will my husband be
joined unto me, because I have born him three
sons: therefore was his name called Le'vi.
35 And she conceived again, and bare a son:
and she said, Now will I praise the LORD: therefore she called his name Ju'dah; and left bearing.

30 AND when Ra'chel saw that she bare
Ja'cob no children, Ra'chel envied her
sister; and said unto Ja'cob, Give me children,
or else I die.
2 And Ja'cob's anger was kindled against
Ra'chel: and he said, *Am* I in God's stead, who
hath withheld from thee the fruit of the womb?
3 And she said, Behold my maid Bil'hah, go
in unto her; and she shall bear upon my knees,
that I may also have children by her.
4 And she gave him Bil'hah her handmaid to
wife: and Ja'cob went in unto her.
5 And Bil'hah conceived, and bare Ja'cob a
son.
6 And Ra'chel said, God hath judged me, and
hath also heard my voice, and hath given me a
son: therefore called she his name Dan.
7 And Bil'hah Ra'chel's maid conceived
again, and bare Ja'cob a second son.
8 And Ra'chel said, With great wrestlings
have I wrestled with my sister, and I have prevailed: and she called his name Naph'ta-li.
9 When Le'ah saw that she had left bearing,
she took Zil-pah her maid, and gave her Ja'cob
to wife.
10 And Zil-pah Le'ah's maid bare Ja'cob a
son.
11 And Le'ah said, A troop cometh: and she
called his name Gad.
12 And Zil-pah Le'ah's maid bare Ja'cob a
second son.
13 And Le'ah said, Happy am I, for the
daughters will call me blessed: and she called
his name Ash'er.
14 ¶ And Reu'ben went in the days of wheat
harvest, and found mandrakes in the field, and
brought them unto his mother Le'ah. Then Ra'-
chel said to Le'ah, Give me, I pray thee, of thy
son's mandrakes.
15 And she said unto her, *Is it* a small matter
that thou hast taken my husband? and wouldest
thou take away my son's mandrakes also? And
Ra'chel said, Therefore he shall lie with thee to
night for thy son's mandrakes.
16 And Ja'cob came out of the field in the
evening, and Le'ah went out to meet him, and
said, Thou must come in unto me; for surely I
have hired thee with my son's mandrakes. And
he lay with her that night.
17 And God hearkened unto Le'ah, and she
conceived, and bare Ja'cob the fifth son.
18 And Le'ah said, God hath given me my
hire, because I have given my maiden to my
husband: and she called his name Is'sa-char.
19 And Le'ah conceived again, and bare Ja'-
cob the sixth son.
20 And Le'ah said, God hath endued me *with*
a good dowry; now will my husband dwell with
me, because I have born him six sons: and she
called his name Zeb'u-lun.
21 And afterwards she bare a daughter, and
called her name Di'nah.
22 ¶ And God remembered Ra'chel, and God
hearkened to her, and opened her womb.
23 And she conceived, and bare a son; and
said, God hath taken away my reproach:
24 And she called his name Jo'seph; and said,
The LORD shall add to me another son.
25 ¶ And it came to pass, when Ra'chel had
born Jo'seph, that Ja'cob said unto La'ban,
Send me away, that I may go unto mine own
place, and to my country.
26 Give *me* my wives and my children, for
whom I have served thee, and let me go: for
thou knowest my service which I have done
thee.
27 And La'ban said unto him, I pray thee, if I
have found favour in thine eyes, *tarry: for* I
have learned by experience that the LORD hath
blessed me for thy sake.
28 And he said, Appoint me thy wages, and I
will give *it*.
29 And he said unto him, Thou knowest how
I have served thee, and how thy cattle was with
me.
30 For *it was* little which thou hadst before I
came, and it is *now* increased unto a multitude;
and the LORD hath blessed thee since my coming: and now when shall I provide for mine own
house also?
31 And he said, What shall I give thee? And
Ja'cob said, Thou shalt not give me any thing: if
thou wilt do this thing for me, I will again feed
and keep thy flock.

32 I will pass through all thy flock to day, removing from thence all the speckled and spotted cattle, and all the brown cattle among the sheep, and the spotted and speckled among the goats: and *of such* shall be my hire.

33 So shall my righteousness answer for me in time to come, when it shall come for my hire before thy face: every one that *is* not speckled and spotted among the goats, and brown among the sheep, that shall be counted stolen with me.

34 And La′ban said, Behold, I would it might be according to thy word.

35 And he removed that day the he goats that were ringstraked and spotted, and all the she goats that were speckled and spotted, *and* every one that had *some* white in it, and all the brown among the sheep, and gave *them* into the hand of his sons.

36 And he set three days' journey betwixt himself and Ja′cob: and Ja′cob fed the rest of La′ban's flocks.

37 ¶ And Ja′cob took him rods of green poplar, and of the hazel and chesnut tree; and pilled white strakes in them, and made the white appear which *was* in the rods.

38 And he set the rods which he had pilled before the flocks in the gutters in the watering troughs when the flocks came to drink, that they should conceive when they came to drink.

39 And the flocks conceived before the rods, and brought forth cattle ringstraked, speckled, and spotted.

40 And Ja′cob did separate the lambs, and set the faces of the flocks toward the ringstraked, and all the brown in the flock of La′ban; and he put his own flocks by themselves, and put them not unto La′ban's cattle.

41 And it came to pass, whensoever the stronger cattle did conceive, that Ja′cob laid the rods before the eyes of the cattle in the gutters, that they might conceive among the rods.

42 But when the cattle were feeble, he put *them* not in: so the feebler were La′ban's, and the stronger Ja′cob's.

43 And the man increased exceedingly, and had much cattle, and maidservants, and menservants, and camels, and asses.

31 AND he heard the words of La′ban's sons, saying, Ja′cob hath taken away all that *was* our father's; and of *that* which *was* our father's hath he gotten all this glory.

2 And Ja′cob beheld the countenance of La′ban, and, behold, it *was* not toward him as before.

3 And the LORD said unto Ja′cob, Return unto the land of thy fathers, and to thy kindred; and I will be with thee.

4 And Ja′cob sent and called Ra′chel and Le′ah to the field unto his flock,

5 And said unto them, I see your father's countenance, that it *is* not toward me as before; but the God of my father hath been with me.

6 And ye know that with all my power I have served your father.

7 And your father hath deceived me, and changed my wages ten times; but God suffered him not to hurt me.

8 If he said thus, The speckled shall be thy wages; then all the cattle bare speckled: and if he said thus, The ringstraked shall be thy hire; then bare all the cattle ringstraked.

9 Thus God hath taken away the cattle of your father, and given *them* to me.

10 And it came to pass at the time that the cattle conceived, that I lifted up mine eyes, and saw in a dream, and, behold, the rams which leaped upon the cattle *were* ringstraked, speckled, and grisled.

11 And the angel of God spake unto me in a dream, *saying,* Ja′cob: And I said, Here *am* I.

12 And he said, Lift up now thine eyes, and see, all the rams which leap upon the cattle *are* ringstraked, speckled, and grisled: for I have seen all that La′ban doeth unto thee.

13 I *am* the God of Beth′-el, where thou anointedst the pillar, *and* where thou vowedst a vow unto me: now arise, get thee out from this land, and return unto the land of thy kindred.

14 And Ra′chel and Le′ah answered and said unto him, *Is there* yet any portion or inheritance for us in our father's house?

15 Are we not counted of him strangers? for he hath sold us, and hath quite devoured also our money.

16 For all the riches which God hath taken from our father, that *is* ours, and our children's: now then, whatsoever God hath said unto thee, do.

17 ¶ Then Ja′cob rose up, and set his sons and his wives upon camels;

18 And he carried away all his cattle, and all his goods which he had gotten, the cattle of his getting, which he had gotten in Pa′dan–a′ram, for to go to I′saac his father in the land of Ca′naan.

19 And La′ban went to shear his sheep: and Ra′chel had stolen the images that *were* her father's.

20 And Ja′cob stole away unawares to La′ban the Syr′i-an, in that he told him not that he fled.

21 So he fled with all that he had; and he rose up, and passed over the river, and set his face *toward* the mount Gil′e-ad.

22 And it was told La′ban on the third day that Ja′cob was fled.

23 And he took his brethren with him, and pursued after him seven days' journey; and they overtook him in the mount Gil′e-ad.

24 And God came to La′ban the Syr′i-an in a dream by night, and said unto him, Take heed that thou speak not to Ja′cob either good or bad.

25 ¶ Then La′ban overtook Ja′cob. Now Ja′cob had pitched his tent in the mount: and La′ban with his brethren pitched in the mount of Gil′e-ad.

26 And La′ban said to Ja′cob, What hast thou done, that thou hast stolen away unawares to me, and carried away my daughters, as captives *taken* with the sword?

27 Wherefore didst thou flee away secretly, and steal away from me; and didst not tell me, that I might have sent thee away with mirth, and with songs, with tabret, and with harp?

28 And hast not suffered me to kiss my sons and my daughters? thou hast now done foolishly in *so* doing.

29 It is in the power of my hand to do you hurt: but the God of your father spake unto me yesternight, saying, Take thou heed that thou speak not to Ja′cob either good or bad.

30 And now, *though* thou wouldest needs be gone, because thou sore longedst after thy father's house, *yet* wherefore hast thou stolen my gods?

31 And Ja′cob answered and said to La′ban, Because I was afraid: for I said, Peradventure thou wouldest take by force thy daughters from me.

32 With whomsoever thou findest thy gods, let him not live: before our brethren discern

thou what *is* thine with me, and take *it* to thee.
For Ja'cob knew not that Ra'chel had stolen
them.
33 And La'ban went into Ja'cob's tent, and
into Le'ah's tent, and into the two maidservants' tents; but he found *them* not. Then went
he out of Le'ah's tent, and entered into Ra'chel's
tent.
34 Now Ra'chel had taken the images, and
put them in the camel's furniture, and sat upon
them. And La'ban searched all the tent, but
found *them* not.
35 And she said to her father, Let it not displease my lord that I cannot rise up before thee;
for the custom of women *is* upon me. And he
searched, but found not the images.
36 ¶ And Ja'cob was wroth, and chode with
La'ban: and Ja'cob answered and said to La'-
ban, What *is* my trespass? what *is* my sin, that
thou hast so hotly pursued after me?
37 Whereas thou hast searched all my stuff,
what hast thou found of all thy household stuff?
set *it* here before my brethren and thy brethren,
that they may judge betwixt us both.
38 This twenty years *have* I *been* with thee;
thy ewes and thy she goats have not cast their
young, and the rams of thy flock have I not eat-
en.
39 That which was torn *of beasts* I brought
not unto thee; I bare the loss of it; of my hand
didst thou require it, *whether* stolen by day, or
stolen by night.
40 *Thus* I was; in the day the drought consumed me, and the frost by night; and my sleep
departed from mine eyes.
41 Thus have I been twenty years in thy
house; I served thee fourteen years for thy two
daughters, and six years for thy cattle: and thou
hast changed my wages ten times.
42 Except the God of my father, the God of
A'bra-ham, and the fear of I'saac, had been with
me, surely thou hadst sent me away now empty. God hath seen mine affliction and the labour
of my hands, and rebuked *thee* yesternight.
43 ¶ And La'ban answered and said unto Ja'-
cob, *These* daughters *are* my daughters, and
these children *are* my children, and *these* cattle
are my cattle, and all that thou seest *is* mine:
and what can I do this day unto these my
daughters, or unto their children which they
have born?
44 Now therefore come thou, let us make a
covenant, I and thou; and let it be for a witness
between me and thee.
45 And Ja'cob took a stone, and set it up *for*
a pillar.
46 And Ja'cob said unto his brethren, Gather
stones; and they took stones, and made an
heap: and they did eat there upon the heap.
47 And La'ban called it Je'gar-sa-ha-du'tha:
but Ja'cob called it Gal'e-ed.
48 And La'ban said, This heap *is* a witness
between me and thee this day. Therefore was
the name of it called Gal'e-ed;
49 And Miz'pah; for he said, The LORD watch
between me and thee, when we are absent one
from another.
50 If thou shalt afflict my daughters, or if
thou shalt take *other* wives beside my daughters, no man *is* with us; see, God *is* witness betwixt me and thee.
51 And La'ban said to Ja'cob, Behold this
heap, and behold *this* pillar, which I have cast
betwixt me and thee;
52 This heap *be* witness, and *this* pillar *be*
witness, that I will not pass over this heap to
thee, and that thou shalt not pass over this heap
and this pillar unto me, for harm.
53 The God of A'bra-ham, and the God of
Na'hor, the God of their father, judge betwixt
us. And Ja'cob sware by the fear of his father
I'saac.
54 Then Ja'cob offered sacrifice upon the
mount, and called his brethren to eat bread: and
they did eat bread, and tarried all night in the
mount.
55 And early in the morning La'ban rose up,
and kissed his sons and his daughters, and
blessed them: and La'ban departed, and returned unto his place.

32 AND Ja'cob went on his way, and the
angels of God met him.
2 And when Ja'cob saw them, he said, This *is*
God's host: and he called the name of that place
Ma-ha-na'im.
3 And Ja'cob sent messengers before him to
E'sau his brother unto the land of Se'ir, the
country of E'dom.
4 And he commanded them, saying, Thus
shall ye speak unto my lord E'sau; Thy servant
Ja'cob saith thus, I have sojourned with La'ban,
and stayed there until now:
5 And I have oxen, and asses, flocks, and
menservants, and womenservants: and I have
sent to tell my lord, that I may find grace in thy
sight.
6 ¶ And the messengers returned to Ja'cob,
saying, We came to thy brother E'sau, and also
he cometh to meet thee, and four hundred men
with him.
7 Then Ja'cob was greatly afraid and distressed: and he divided the people that *was*
with him, and the flocks, and herds, and the
camels, into two bands;
8 And said, If E'sau come to the one company, and smite it, then the other company
which is left shall escape.
9 ¶ And Ja'cob said, O God of my father A'-
bra-ham, and God of my father I'saac, the LORD
which saidst unto me, Return unto thy country,
and to thy kindred, and I will deal well with
thee:
10 I am not worthy of the least of all the mercies, and of all the truth, which thou hast
shewed unto thy servant; for with my staff I
passed over this Jor'dan; and now I am become
two bands.
11 Deliver me, I pray thee, from the hand of
my brother, from the hand of E'sau: for I fear
him, lest he will come and smite me, *and* the
mother with the children.
12 And thou saidst, I will surely do thee
good, and make thy seed as the sand of the sea,
which cannot be numbered for multitude.
13 ¶ And he lodged there that same night;
and took of that which came to his hand a present for E'sau his brother;
14 Two hundred she goats, and twenty he
goats, two hundred ewes, and twenty rams,
15 Thirty milch camels with their colts, forty
kine, and ten bulls, twenty she asses, and ten
foals.
16 And he delivered *them* into the hand of
his servants, every drove by themselves; and
said unto his servants, Pass over before me, and
put a space betwixt drove and drove.
17 And he commanded the foremost, saying,
When E'sau my brother meeteth thee, and asketh thee, saying, Whose *art* thou? and whither
goest thou? and whose *are* these before thee?
18 Then thou shalt say, *They be* thy servant

Ja'cob's; it *is* a present sent unto my lord E'sau:
and, behold, also he *is* behind us.
19 And so commanded he the second, and
the third, and all that followed the droves, saying, On this manner shall ye speak unto E'sau,
when ye find him.
20 And say ye moreover, Behold, thy servant
Ja'cob *is* behind us. For he said, I will appease
him with the present that goeth before me, and
afterward I will see his face; peradventure he
will accept of me.
21 So went the present over before him: and
himself lodged that night in the company.
22 And he rose up that night, and took his
two wives, and his two womenservants, and his
eleven sons, and passed over the ford Jab'bok.
23 And he took them, and sent them over the
brook, and sent over that he had.
24 ¶ And Ja'cob was left alone; and there
wrestled a man with him until the breaking of
the day.
25 And when he saw that he prevailed not
against him, he touched the hollow of his thigh;
and the hollow of Ja'cob's thigh was out of
joint, as he wrestled with him.
26 And he said, Let me go, for the day breaketh. And he said, I will not let thee go, except
thou bless me.
27 And he said unto him, What *is* thy name?
And he said, Ja'cob.
28 And he said, Thy name shall be called no
more Ja'cob, but Is'ra-el: for as a prince hast
thou power with God and with men, and hast
prevailed.
29 And Ja'cob asked *him,* and said, Tell *me,* I
pray thee, thy name. And he said, Wherefore *is*
it *that* thou dost ask after my name? And he
blessed him there.
30 And Ja'cob called the name of the place
Pe-ni'el: for I have seen God face to face, and
my life is preserved.
31 And as he passed over Pe-nu'el the sun
rose upon him, and he halted upon his thigh.
32 Therefore the children of Is'ra-el eat not
of the sinew which shrank, which *is* upon the
hollow of the thigh, unto this day: because he
touched the hollow of Ja'cob's thigh in the
sinew that shrank.

33 AND Ja'cob lifted up his eyes, and
looked, and, behold, E'sau came, and
with him four hundred men. And he divided the
children unto Le'ah, and unto Ra'chel, and unto
the two handmaids.
2 And he put the handmaids and their children foremost, and Le'ah and her children after,
and Ra'chel and Jo'seph hindermost.
3 And he passed over before them, and
bowed himself to the ground seven times, until
he came near to his brother.
4 And E'sau ran to meet him, and embraced
him, and fell on his neck, and kissed him: and
they wept.
5 And he lifted up his eyes, and saw the
women and the children; and said, Who *are*
those with thee? And he said, The children
which God hath graciously given thy servant.
6 Then the handmaidens came near, they and
their children, and they bowed themselves.
7 And Le'ah also with her children came
near, and bowed themselves: and after came
Jo'seph near and Ra'chel, and they bowed
themselves.
8 And he said, What *meanest* thou by all this
drove which I met? And he said, *These are* to
find grace in the sight of my lord.
9 And E'sau said, I have enough, my brother;
keep that thou hast unto thyself.
10 And Ja'cob said, Nay, I pray thee, if now I
have found grace in thy sight, then receive my
present at my hand: for therefore I have seen
thy face, as though I had seen the face of God,
and thou wast pleased with me.
11 Take, I pray thee, my blessing that is
brought to thee; because God hath dealt graciously with me, and because I have enough.
And he urged him, and he took *it.*
12 And he said, Let us take our journey, and
let us go, and I will go before thee.
13 And he said unto him, My lord knoweth
that the children *are* tender, and the flocks and
herds with young *are* with me: and if men
should overdrive them one day, all the flock will
die.
14 Let my lord, I pray thee, pass over before
his servant: and I will lead on softly, according
as the cattle that goeth before me and the children be able to endure, until I come unto my
lord unto Se'ir.
15 And E'sau said, Let me now leave with
thee *some* of the folk that *are* with me. And he
said, What needeth it? let me find grace in the
sight of my lord.
16 ¶ So E'sau returned that day on his way
unto Se'ir.
17 And Ja'cob journeyed to Suc'coth, and
built him an house, and made booths for his cattle: therefore the name of the place is called
Suc'coth.
18 ¶ And Ja'cob came to Sha'lem, a city of
Shechem, which *is* in the land of Ca'naan, when
he came from Pa'dan–a'ram; and pitched his
tent before the city.
19 And he bought a parcel of a field, where
he had spread his tent, at the hand of the children of Ha'mor, She'chem's father, for an hundred pieces of money.
20 And he erected there an altar, and called
it El–e-lo'he–Is'ra-el.

34 AND Di'nah the daughter of Le'ah,
which she bare unto Ja'cob, went out to
see the daughters of the land.
2 And when Shechem the son of Ha'mor the
Hi'vite, prince of the country, saw her, he took
her, and lay with her, and defiled her.
3 And his soul clave unto Di'nah the daughter of Ja'cob, and he loved the damsel, and
spake kindly unto the damsel.
4 And Shechem spake unto his father Ha'-
mor, saying, Get me this damsel to wife.
5 And Ja'cob heard that he had defiled Di'-
nah his daughter: now his sons were with his
cattle in the field: and Ja'cob held his peace until they were come.
6 ¶ And Ha'mor the father of Shechem went
out unto Ja'cob to commune with him.
7 And the sons of Ja'cob came out of the field
when they heard *it:* and the men were grieved,
and they were very wroth, because he had
wrought folly in Is'ra-el in lying with Ja'cob's
daughter; which thing ought not to be done.
8 And Ha'mor communed with them, saying,
The soul of my son Shechem longeth for your
daughter: I pray you give her to him to wife.
9 And make ye marriages with us, *and* give
your daughters unto us, and take our daughters
unto you.
10 And ye shall dwell with us: and the land
shall be before you; dwell and trade ye therein,
and get you possessions therein.
11 And Shechem said unto her father and
unto her brethren, Let me find grace in your

eyes, and what ye shall say unto me I will give.
12 Ask me never so much dowry and gift,
and I will give according as ye shall say unto
me: but give me the damsel to wife.
13 And the sons of Ja'cob answered Shechem and Ha'mor his father deceitfully, and
said, because he had defiled Di'nah their sister:
14 And they said unto them, We cannot do
this thing, to give our sister to one that is uncircumcised; for that *were* a reproach unto us:
15 But in this will we consent unto you: If ye
will be as we *be*, that every male of you be circumcised;
16 Then will we give our daughters unto you,
and we will take your daughters to us, and we
will dwell with you, and we will become one
people.
17 But if ye will not hearken unto us, to be
circumcised; then will we take our daughter,
and we will be gone.
18 And their words pleased Ha'mor, and
Shechem Ha'mor's son.
19 And the young man deferred not to do the
thing, because he had delight in Ja'cob's daughter: and he *was* more honourable than all the
house of his father.
20 ¶ And Ha'mor and Shechem his son came
unto the gate of their city, and communed with
the men of their city, saying,
21 These men *are* peaceable with us; therefore let them dwell in the land, and trade
therein; for the land, behold *it is* large enough
for them; let us take their daughters to us for
wives, and let us give them our daughters.
22 Only herein will the men consent unto us
for to dwell with us, to be one people, if every
male among us be circumcised, as they *are* circumcised.
23 *Shall* not the cattle and their substance
and every beast of theirs *be* ours? only let us
consent unto them, and they will dwell with us.
24 And unto Ha'mor and unto Shechem his
son hearkened all that went out of the gate of
his city; and every male was circumcised, all
that went out of the gate of his city.
25 ¶ And it came to pass on the third day,
when they were sore, that two of the sons of
Ja'cob, Sim'e-on and Le'vi, Di'nah's brethren,
took each man his sword, and came upon the
city boldly, and slew all the males.
26 And they slew Ha'mor and Shechem his
son with the edge of the sword, and took Di'nah
out of She'chem's house, and went out.
27 The sons of Ja'cob came upon the slain,
and spoiled the city, because they had defiled
their sister.
28 They took their sheep, and their oxen, and
their asses, and that which *was* in the city, and
that which *was* in the field,
29 And all their wealth, and all their little
ones, and their wives took they captive, and
spoiled even all that *was* in the house.
30 And Ja'cob said to Sim'e-on and Le'vi, Ye
have troubled me to make me to stink among
the inhabitants of the land, among the Ca'naan-
ites and the Per'iz-zites: and I *being* few in number, they shall gather themselves together
against me, and slay me; and I shall be destroyed, I and my house.
31 And they said, Should he deal with our
sister as with an harlot?

35 AND God said unto Ja'cob, Arise, go up
to Beth'-el, and dwell there: and make
there an altar unto God, that appeared unto
thee when thou fleddest from the face of E'sau
thy brother.
2 Then Ja'cob said unto his household, and to
all that *were* with him, Put away the strange
gods that *are* among you, and be clean, and
change your garments:
3 And let us arise, and go up to Beth'-el; and
I will make there an altar unto God, who answered me in the day of my distress, and was
with me in the way which I went.
4 And they gave unto Ja'cob all the strange
gods which *were* in their hand, and *all their* earrings which *were* in their ears; and Ja'cob hid
them under the oak which *was* by Shechem.
5 And they journeyed: and the terror of God
was upon the cities that *were* round about
them, and they did not pursue after the sons of
Ja'cob.
6 ¶ So Ja'cob came to Luz, which *is* in the
land of Ca'naan, that *is*, Bethel, he and all the
people that *were* with him.
7 And he built there an altar, and called the
place El-bethel: because there God appeared
unto him, when he fled from the face of his
brother.
8 But Deb'o-rah Re-bek'ah's nurse died, and
she was buried beneath Beth'-el under an oak:
and the name of it was called Al'lon-bach'uth.
9 ¶ And God appeared unto Ja'cob again,
when he came out of Pa'dan-a'ram, and blessed
him.
10 And God said unto him, Thy name *is* Ja'-
cob: thy name shall not be called any more Ja'-
cob, but Is'ra-el shall be thy name: and he called
his name Is'ra-el.
11 And God said unto him, I *am* God Almighty: be fruitful and multiply; a nation and a
company of nations shall be of thee, and kings
shall come out of thy loins;
12 And the land which I gave A'bra-ham and
I'saac, to thee I will give it, and to thy seed after
thee will I give the land.
13 And God went up from him in the place
where he talked with him.
14 And Ja'cob set up a pillar in the place
where he talked with him, *even* a pillar of stone:
and he poured a drink offering thereon, and he
poured oil thereon.
15 And Ja'cob called the name of the place
where God spake with him, Beth'-el.
16 ¶ And they journeyed from Beth'-el; and
there was but a little way to come to Eph'rath:
and Ra'chel travailed, and she had hard labour.
17 And it came to pass, when she was in hard
labour, that the midwife said unto her, Fear not;
thou shalt have this son also.
18 And it came to pass, as her soul was in
departing, (for she died) that she called his
name Ben-o'ni: but his father called him Ben'ja-
min.
19 And Ra'chel died, and was buried in the
way to Eph'rath, which *is* Beth'-le-hem.
20 And Ja'cob set a pillar upon her grave:
that *is* the pillar of Ra'chel's grave unto this
day.
21 ¶ And Is'ra-el journeyed, and spread his
tent beyond the tower of E'dar.
22 And it came to pass, when Is'ra-el dwelt in
that land, that Reu'ben went and lay with Bil'-
hah his father's concubine: and Is'ra-el heard *it*.
Now the sons of Ja'cob were twelve:
23 The sons of Le'ah; Reu'ben, Ja'cob's firstborn, and Sim'e-on, and Le'vi, and Ju'dah, and
Is'sa-char, and Zeb'u-lun:
24 The sons of Ra'chel; Jo'seph, and Ben'ja-
min:
25 And the sons of Bil'hah, Ra'chel's handmaid; Dan, and Naph'ta-li:
26 And the sons of Zil-pah, Le'ah's hand-

maid; Gad, and Ash'er: these *are* the sons of
Ja'cob, which were born to him in Pa'dan–a'-
ram.
27 ¶ And Ja'cob came unto I'saac his father
unto Mam're, unto the city of Ar'bah, which *is*
He'bron, where A'bra-ham and I'saac sojourned.
28 And the days of I'saac were a hundred
and fourscore years.
29 And I'saac gave up the ghost, and died,
and was gathered unto his people, *being* old and
full of days: and his sons E'sau and Ja'cob buried him.

36 NOW these *are* the generations of E'-
sau, who *is* E'dom.
2 E'sau took his wives of the daughters of
Ca'naan; A'dah the daughter of E'lon the Hit'-
tite, and A-ho-lib'a-mah the daughter of A'nah
the daughter of Zib'e-on the Hi'vite;
3 And Bash'e-math Ish'ma-el's daughter, sister of Ne-ba'joth.
4 And A'dah bare to E'sau El'i-phaz; and
Bash'e-math bare Reu'el;
5 And A-ho-lib'a-mah bare Je'ush, and Ja-a'-
lam, and Ko'rah: these *are* the sons of E'sau,
which were born unto him in the land of Ca'-
naan.
6 And E'sau took his wives, and his sons, and
his daughters, and all the persons of his house,
and his cattle, and all his beasts, and all his substance, which he had got in the land of Ca'naan;
and went into the country from the face of his
brother Ja'cob.
7 For their riches were more than that they
might dwell together; and the land wherein they
were strangers could not bear them because of
their cattle.
8 Thus dwelt E'sau in mount Se'ir: E'sau *is*
E'dom.
9 ¶ And these *are* the generations of E'sau
the father of the E'dom-ites in mount Se'ir:
10 These *are* the names of E'sau's sons; El'i-
phaz the son of A'dah the wife of E'sau, Reu'el
the son of Bash'e-math the wife of E'sau.
11 And the sons of El'i-phaz were Te'man,
O'mar, Ze'pho, and Ga'tam, and Ke'naz.
12 And Tim'na was concubine to El'i-phaz E'-
sau's son; and she bare to El'i-phaz Am'a-lek:
these *were* the sons of A'dah E'sau's wife.
13 And these *are* the sons of Reu'el; Na'hath,
and Ze'rah, Sham'mah, and Miz'zah: these were
the sons of Bash'e-math E'sau's wife.
14 ¶ And these were the sons ofA-ho-lib'a-
mah, the daughter of A'nah the daughter of
Zib'e-on, E'sau's wife: and she bare to E'sau Je'-
ush, and Ja-a'lam, and Ko'rah.
15 ¶ These *were* dukes of the sons of E'sau:
the sons of El'i-phaz the firstborn *son* of E'sau;
duke Te'man, duke O'mar, duke Ze'pho, duke
Ke'naz,
16 Duke Ko'rah, duke Ga'tam, *and* duke
Am'a-lek: these *are* the dukes *that came* of El'i-
phaz in the land of E'dom; these *were* the sons
of A'dah.
17 ¶ And these *are* the sons of Reu'el E'sau's
son; duke Na'hath, duke Ze'rah, duke Sham'-
mah, duke Miz'zah: these *are* the dukes *that
came* of Reu'el in the land of E'dom; these *are*
the sons of Bash'e-math E'sau's wife.
18 ¶ And these *are* the sons of A-ho-lib'a-
mah E'sau's wife; duke Je'ush, duke Ja-a'lam,
duke Ko'rah: these *were* the dukes *that came* of
A-ho-lib'a-mah the daughter of A'nah, E'sau's
wife.
19 These *are* the sons of E'sau, who *is* E'dom,
and these *are* their dukes.
20 ¶ These *are* the sons of Se'ir the Ho'rite,
who inhabited the land; Lo'tan, and Sho'bal,
and Zib'e-on, and A'nah,
21 And Di'shon, and E'zer, and Di'shan:
these *are* the dukes of the Ho'rites, the children
of Se'ir in the land of E'dom.
22 And the children of Lo'tan were Ho'ri and
He'mam; and Lo'tan's sister *was* Tim'na.
23 And the children of Sho'bal *were* these;
Al'van, and Man'a-hath, and E'bal, She'pho, and
O'nam.
24 And these *are* the children of Zib'e-on;
both A'jah, and A'nah: this *was that* A'nah that
found the mules in the wilderness, as he fed the
asses of Zib'e-on his father.
25 And the children of A'nah *were* these; Di'-
shon, and A-ho-lib'a-mah the daughter of A'-
nah.
26 And these *are* the children of Di'shon;
Hemdan, and Esh'ban, and Ith'ran, and Che'ran.
27 The children of E'zer *are* these; Bil'han,
and Za'a-van, and A'kan.
28 The children of Di'shan *are* these; Uz, and
A'ran.
29 These *are* the dukes *that came* of the Ho'-
rites; duke Lo'tan, duke Sho'bal, duke Zib'e-on,
duke A'nah,
30 Duke Di'shon, duke E'zer, duke Di'shan:
these *are* the dukes *that came* of Ho'ri, among
their dukes in the land of Se'ir.
31 ¶ And these *are* the kings that reigned in
the land of E'dom, before there reigned any
king over the children of Is'ra-el.
32 And Be'la the son of Be'or reigned in E'-
dom: and the name of his city *was* Din'ha-bah.
33 And Be'la died, and Jo'bab the son of Ze'-
rah of Boz'rah reigned in his stead.
34 And Jo'bab died, and Hu'sham of the land
of Tem'a-ni reigned in his stead.
35 And Hu'sham died, and Ha'dad the son of
Be'dad, who smote Mid'i-an in the field of Mo'-
ab, reigned in his stead: and the name of his city
was A'vith.
36 And Ha'dad died, and Sam'lah of Mas're-
kah reigned in his stead.
37 And Sam'lah died, and Saul of Re-ho'both
by the river reigned in his stead.
38 And Saul died, and Ba'al–ha'nan the son
of Ach'bor reigned in his stead.
39 And Ba'al–ha'nan the son of Ach'bor died,
and Ha'dar reigned in his stead: and the name
of his city *was* Pa'u; and his wife's name *was*
Me-het'a-bel, the daughter of Ma'tred, the
daughter of Mez'a-hab.
40 And these *are* the names of the dukes *that
came* of E'sau, according to their families, after
their places, by their names; duke Tim'nah,
duke Al'vah, duke Je'theth,
41 Duke A-ho-lib'a-mah, duke E'lah, duke
Pi'non,
42 Duke Ke'naz, duke Te'man, duke Mib'zar,
43 Duke Mag'di-el, duke I'ram: these *be* the
dukes of E'dom, according to their habitations
in the land of their possession: he *is* E'sau the
father of the E'dom-ites.

37 AND Ja'cob dwelt in the land wherein
his father was a stranger, in the land of
Ca'naan.
2 These *are* the generations of Ja'cob. Jo'-
seph, *being* seventeen years old, was feeding
the flock with his brethren; and the lad *was*
with the sons of Bil'hah, and with the sons of
Zil-pah, his father's wives: and Jo'seph brought
unto his father their evil report.
3 Now Is'ra-el loved Jo'seph more than all his

children, because he *was* the son of his old age: and he made him a coat of *many* colours.

4 And when his brethren saw that their father loved him more than all his brethren, they hated him, and could not speak peaceably unto him.

5 ¶ And Jo'seph dreamed a dream, and he told *it* his brethren: and they hated him yet the more.

6 And he said unto them, Hear, I pray you, this dream which I have dreamed:

7 For, behold, we *were* binding sheaves in the field, and, lo, my sheaf arose, and also stood upright; and, behold, your sheaves stood round about, and made obeisance to my sheaf.

8 And his brethren said to him, Shalt thou indeed reign over us? or shalt thou indeed have dominion over us? And they hated him yet the more for his dreams, and for his words.

9 ¶ And he dreamed yet another dream, and told it his brethren, and said, Behold, I have dreamed a dream more; and, behold, the sun and the moon and the eleven stars made obeisance to me.

10 And he told *it* to his father, and to his brethren: and his father rebuked him, and said unto him, What *is* this dream that thou hast dreamed? Shall I and thy mother and thy brethren indeed come to bow down ourselves to thee to the earth?

11 And his brethren envied him: but his father observed the saying.

12 ¶ And his brethren went to feed their father's flock in Shechem.

13 And Is'ra-el said unto Jo'seph, Do not thy brethren feed *the flock* in Shechem? come, and I will send thee unto them. And he said to him, Here *am I*.

14 And he said to him, Go, I pray thee, see whether it be well with thy brethren, and well with the flocks; and bring me word again. So he sent him out of the vale of He'bron, and he came to Shechem.

15 ¶ And a certain man found him, and, behold, *he was* wandering in the field: and the man asked him, saying, What seekest thou?

16 And he said, I seek my brethren: tell me, I pray thee, where they feed *their flocks*.

17 And the man said, They are departed hence; for I heard them say, Let us go to Do'than. And Jo'seph went after his brethren, and found them in Do'than.

18 And when they saw him afar off, even before he came near unto them, they conspired against him to slay him.

19 And they said one to another, Behold, this dreamer cometh.

20 Come now therefore, and let us slay him, and cast him into some pit, and we will say, Some evil beast hath devoured him: and we shall see what will become of his dreams.

21 And Reu'ben heard *it*, and he delivered him out of their hands; and said, Let us not kill him.

22 And Reu'ben said unto them, Shed no blood, *but* cast him into this pit that *is* in the wilderness, and lay no hand upon him; that he might rid him out of their hands, to deliver him to his father again.

23 ¶ And it came to pass, when Jo'seph was come unto his brethren, that they stript Jo'seph out of his coat, *his* coat of *many* colours that *was* on him;

24 And they took him, and cast him into a pit: and the pit *was* empty, *there was* no water in it.

25 And they sat down to eat bread: and they lifted up their eyes and looked, and, behold, a company of Ish'me-el-ites came from Gil'e-ad with their camels bearing spicery and balm and myrrh, going to carry *it* down to E'gypt.

26 And Ju'dah said unto his brethren, What profit *is it* if we slay our brother, and conceal his blood?

27 Come, and let us sell him to the Ish'me-el-ites and let not our hand be upon him; for he *is* our brother *and* our flesh. And his brethren were content.

28 Then there passed by Mid'i-an-ites merchantmen; and they drew and lifted up Jo'seph out of the pit, and sold Jo'seph to the Ish'me-el-ites for twenty *pieces* of silver: and they brought Jo'seph into E'gypt.

29 ¶ And Reu'ben returned unto the pit; and, behold, Jo'seph *was* not in the pit; and he rent his clothes.

30 And he returned unto his brethren, and said, The child *is* not; and I, whither shall I go?

31 And they took Jo'seph's coat, and killed a kid of the goats, and dipped the coat in the blood;

32 And they sent the coat of *many* colours, and they brought *it* to their father; and said, This have we found: know now whether it *be* thy son's coat or no.

33 And he knew it, and said, *It is* my son's coat; an evil beast hath devoured him; Jo'seph is without doubt rent in pieces.

34 And Ja'cob rent his clothes, and put sackcloth upon his loins, and mourned for his son many days.

35 And all his sons and all his daughters rose up to comfort him; but he refused to be comforted; and he said, For I will go down into the grave unto my son mourning. Thus his father wept for him.

36 And the Mid'i-an-ites sold him into E'gypt unto Pot'i-phar, an officer of Pha'raoh's, *and* captain of the guard.

38 AND it came to pass at that time, that Ju'dah went down from his brethren, and turned in to a certain A-dul'lam-ite, whose name *was* Hi'rah.

2 And Ju'dah saw there a daughter of a certain Ca'naan-ite, whose name *was* Shu'ah; and he took her, and went in unto her.

3 And she conceived, and bare a son; and he called his name Er.

4 And she conceived again, and bare a son; and she called his name O'nan.

5 And she yet again conceived, and bare a son; and called his name She'lah: and he was at Che'zib, when she bare him.

6 And Ju'dah took a wife for Er his firstborn, whose name *was* Ta'mar.

7 And Er, Ju'dah's firstborn, was wicked in the sight of the LORD; and the LORD slew him.

8 And Ju'dah said unto O'nan, Go in unto thy brother's wife, and marry her, and raise up seed to thy brother.

9 And O'nan knew that the seed should not be his; and it came to pass, when he went in unto his brother's wife, that he spilled *it* on the ground, lest that he should give seed to his brother.

10 And the thing which he did displeased the LORD: wherefore he slew him also.

11 Then said Ju'dah to Ta'mar his daughter in law, Remain a widow at thy father's house, till She'lah my son be grown: for he said, Lest peradventure he die also, as his brethren *did*. And Ta'mar went and dwelt in her father's house.

12 ¶ And in process of time the daughter of Shu'ah Ju'dah's wife died; and Ju'dah was comforted, and went up unto his sheepshearers to Tim'nath, he and his friend Hi'rah the A-dul'-lam-ite.

13 And it was told Ta'mar, saying, Behold thy father in law goeth up to Tim'nath to shear his sheep.

14 And she put her widow's garments off from her, and covered her with a veil, and wrapped herself, and sat in an open place, which *is* by the way to Tim'nath; for she saw that She'lah was grown, and she was not given unto him to wife.

15 When Ju'dah saw her, he thought her *to be* an harlot; because she had covered her face.

16 And he turned unto her by the way, and said, Go to, I pray thee, let me come in unto thee; (for he knew not that she *was* his daughter in law.) And she said, What wilt thou give me, that thou mayest come in unto me?

17 And he said, I will send *thee* a kid from the flock. And she said, Wilt thou give *me* a pledge, till thou send *it?*

18 And he said, What pledge shall I give thee? And she said, Thy signet, and thy bracelets, and thy staff that *is* in thine hand. And he gave *it* her, and came in unto her, and she conceived by him.

19 And she arose, and went away, and laid by her veil from her, and put on the garments of her widowhood.

20 And Ju'dah sent the kid by the hand of his friend the A-dul'lam-ite, to receive *his* pledge from the woman's hand: but he found her not.

21 Then he asked the men of that place, saying, Where *is* the harlot, that *was* openly by the way side? And they said, There was no harlot in this *place.*

22 And he returned to Ju'dah, and said, I cannot find her; and also the men of the place said, *that* there was no harlot in this *place.*

23 And Ju'dah said, Let her take *it* to her, lest we be shamed: behold, I sent this kid, and thou hast not found her.

24 ¶ And it came to pass about three months after, that it was told Ju'dah, saying, Ta'mar thy daughter in law hath played the harlot; and also, behold, she *is* with child by whoredom. And Ju'dah said, Bring her forth, and let her be burnt.

25 When she *was* brought forth, she sent to her father in law, saying, By the man, whose these *are, am* I with child: and she said, Discern, I pray thee, whose *are* these, the signet, and bracelets, and staff.

26 And Ju'dah acknowledged *them,* and said, She hath been more righteous than I; because that I gave her not to She'lah my son. And he knew her again no more.

27 ¶ And it came to pass in the time of her travail, that, behold, twins *were* in her womb.

28 And it came to pass, when she travailed, that *the one* put out *his* hand: and the midwife took and bound upon his hand a scarlet thread, saying, This came out first.

29 And it came to pass, as he drew back his hand, that, behold, his brother came out: and she said, How hast thou broken forth? *this* breach *be* upon thee: therefore his name was called Pharez.

30 And afterward came out his brother, that had the scarlet thread upon his hand: and his name was called Za'rah.

39

AND Jo'seph was brought down to E'gypt; and Pot'i-phar, an officer of Pha'raoh, captain of the guard, an E-gyp'tian, bought him of the hands of the Ish'me-el-ites, which had brought him down thither.

2 And the LORD was with Jo'seph, and he was a prosperous man; and he was in the house of his master the E-gyp'tian.

3 And his master saw that the LORD *was* with him, and that the LORD made all that he did to prosper in his hand.

4 And Jo'seph found grace in his sight, and he served him: and he made him overseer over his house, and all *that* he had he put into his hand.

5 And it came to pass from the time *that* he had made him overseer in his house, and over all that he had, that the LORD blessed the E-gyp'tian's house for Jo'seph's sake; and the blessing of the LORD was upon all that he had in the house, and in the field.

6 And he left all that he had in Jo'seph's hand; and he knew not ought he had, save the bread which he did eat. And Jo'seph was *a* goodly *person,* and well favoured.

7 ¶ And it came to pass after these things, that his master's wife cast her eyes upon Jo'seph; and she said, Lie with me.

8 But he refused, and said unto his master's wife, Behold, my master wotteth not what *is* with me in the house, and he hath committed all that he hath to my hand;

9 *There is* none greater in this house than I; neither hath he kept back any thing from me but thee, because thou *art* his wife: how then can I do this great wickedness, and sin against God?

10 And it came to pass, as she spake to Jo'seph day by day, that he hearkened not unto her, to lie by her, *or* to be with her.

11 And it came to pass about this time, that *Joseph* went into the house to do his business; and *there was* none of the men of the house there within.

12 And she caught him by his garment, saying, Lie with me: and he left his garment in her hand, and fled, and got him out.

13 And it came to pass, when she saw that he had left his garment in her hand, and was fled forth,

14 That she called unto the men of her house, and spake unto them, saying, See, he hath brought in an He'brew unto us to mock us; he came in unto me to lie with me, and I cried with a loud voice:

15 And it came to pass, when he heard that I lifted up my voice and cried, that he left his garment with me, and fled, and got him out.

16 And she laid up his garment by her, until his lord came home.

17 And she spake unto him according to these words, saying, The He'brew servant, which thou hast brought unto us, came in unto me to mock me:

18 And it came to pass, as I lifted up my voice and cried, that he left his garment with me, and fled out.

19 And it came to pass, when his master heard the words of his wife, which she spake unto him, saying, After this manner did thy servant to me; that his wrath was kindled.

20 And Jo'seph's master took him, and put him into the prison, a place where the king's prisoners *were* bound: and he was there in the prison.

21 ¶ But the LORD was with Jo'seph, and shewed him mercy, and gave him favour in the sight of the keeper of the prison.

22 And the keeper of the prison committed

to Jo'seph's hand all the prisoners that *were* in the prison; and whatsoever they did there, he was the doer *of it*.

23 The keeper of the prison looked not to any thing *that was* under his hand; because the LORD was with him, and *that* which he did, the LORD made *it* to prosper.

40 AND it came to pass after these things, *that* the butler of the king of E'gypt and *his* baker had offended their lord the king of E'gypt.

2 And Pha'raoh was wroth against two *of* his officers, against the chief of the butlers, and against the chief of the bakers.

3 And he put them in ward in the house of the captain of the guard, into the prison, the place where Jo'seph *was* bound.

4 And the captain of the guard charged Jo'seph with them, and he served them: and they continued a season in ward.

5 ¶ And they dreamed a dream both of them, each man his dream in one night, each man according to the interpretation of his dream, the butler and the baker of the king of E'gypt, which *were* bound in the prison.

6 And Jo'seph came in unto them in the morning, and looked upon them, and, behold, they *were* sad.

7 And he asked Pha'raoh's officers that *were* with him in the ward of his lord's house, saying, Wherefore look ye *so* sadly to day?

8 And they said unto him, We have dreamed a dream, and *there is* no interpreter of it. And Jo'seph said unto them, *Do* not interpretations *belong* to God? tell me *them*, I pray you.

9 And the chief butler told his dream to Jo'seph, and said to him, In my dream, behold, a vine *was* before me;

10 And in the vine *were* three branches: and it *was* as though it budded, *and* her blossoms shot forth; and the clusters thereof brought forth ripe grapes:

11 And Pha'raoh's cup *was* in my hand: and I took the grapes, and pressed them into Pha'raoh's cup, and I gave the cup into Pha'raoh's hand.

12 And Jo'seph said unto him, This *is* the interpretation of it: The three branches *are* three days:

13 Yet within three days shall Pha'raoh lift up thine head, and restore thee unto thy place: and thou shalt deliver Pha'raoh's cup into his hand, after the former manner when thou wast his butler.

14 But think on me when it shall be well with thee, and shew kindness, I pray thee, unto me, and make mention of me unto Pha'raoh, and bring me out of this house:

15 For indeed I was stolen away out of the land of the He'brews: and here also have I done nothing that they should put me into the dungeon.

16 When the chief baker saw that the interpretation was good, he said unto Jo'seph, I also *was* in my dream, and, behold, *I had* three white baskets on my head:

17 And in the uppermost basket *there was* of all manner of bakemeats for Pha'raoh; and the birds did eat them out of the basket upon my head.

18 And Jo'seph answered and said, This *is* the interpretation thereof: The three baskets *are* three days:

19 Yet within three days shall Pha'raoh lift up thy head from off thee, and shall hang thee on a tree; and the birds shall eat thy flesh from off thee.

20 ¶ And it came to pass the third day, *which was* Pha'raoh's birthday, that he made a feast unto all his servants: and he lifted up the head of the chief butler and of the chief baker among his servants.

21 And he restored the chief butler unto his butlership again; and he gave the cup into Pha'raoh's hand:

22 But he hanged the chief baker: as Jo'seph had interpreted to them.

23 Yet did not the chief butler remember Jo'seph, but forgat him.

41 AND it came to pass at the end of two full years, that Pha'raoh dreamed: and, behold, he stood by the river.

2 And, behold, there came up out of the river seven well favoured kine and fatfleshed; and they fed in a meadow.

3 And, behold, seven other kine came up after them out of the river, ill favoured and leanfleshed; and stood by the *other* kine upon the brink of the river.

4 And the ill favoured and leanfleshed kine did eat up the seven well favoured and fat kine. So Pha'raoh awoke.

5 And he slept and dreamed the second time: and, behold, seven ears of corn came up upon one stalk, rank and good.

6 And, behold, seven thin ears and blasted with the east wind sprung up after them.

7 And the seven thin ears devoured the seven rank and full ears. And Pha'raoh awoke, and, behold, *it was* a dream.

8 And it came to pass in the morning that his spirit was troubled; and he sent and called for all the magicians of E'gypt, and all the wise men thereof: and Pha'raoh told them his dream; but *there was* none that could interpret them unto Pha'raoh.

9 ¶ Then spake the chief butler unto Pha'raoh, saying, I do remember my faults this day:

10 Pha'raoh was wroth with his servants, and put me in ward in the captain of the guard's house, *both* me and the chief baker:

11 And we dreamed a dream in one night, I and he; we dreamed each man according to the interpretation of his dream.

12 And *there was* there with us a young man, an He'brew, servant to the captain of the guard; and we told him, and he interpreted to us our dreams; to each man according to his dream he did interpret.

13 And it came to pass, as he interpreted to us, so it was; me he restored unto mine office, and him he hanged.

14 ¶ Then Pha'raoh sent and called Jo'seph, and they brought him hastily out of the dungeon: and he shaved *himself*, and changed his raiment, and came in unto Pha'raoh.

15 And Pha'raoh said unto Jo'seph, I have dreamed a dream, and *there is* none that can interpret it: and I have heard say of thee, *that* thou canst understand a dream to interpret it.

16 And Jo'seph answered Pha'raoh, saying, *It is* not in me: God shall give Pha'raoh an answer of peace.

17 And Pha'raoh said unto Jo'seph, In my dream, behold, I stood upon the bank of the river:

18 And, behold, there came up out of the river seven kine, fatfleshed and well favoured; and they fed in a meadow:

19 And, behold, seven other kine came up after them, poor and very ill favoured and lean-

fleshed, such as I never saw in all the land of
E'gypt for badness:
20 And the lean and the ill favoured kine did
eat up the first seven fat kine:
21 And when they had eaten them up, it
could not be known that they had eaten them;
but they *were* still ill favoured, as at the beginning. So I awoke.
22 And I saw in my dream, and, behold,
seven ears came up in one stalk, full and good:
23 And, behold, seven ears, withered, thin,
and blasted with the east wind, sprung up after
them:
24 And the thin ears devoured the seven
good ears: and I told *this* unto the magicians;
but *there was* none that could declare *it* to me.
25 ¶ And Jo'seph said unto Pha'raoh, The
dream of Pha'raoh *is* one: God hath shewed
Pha'raoh what he *is* about to do.
26 The seven good kine *are* seven years; and
the seven good ears *are* seven years: the dream
is one.
27 And the seven thin and ill favoured kine
that came up after them *are* seven years; and
the seven empty ears blasted with the east wind
shall be seven years of famine.
28 This *is* the thing which I have spoken unto
Pha'raoh: What God *is* about to do he sheweth
unto Pha'raoh.
29 Behold, there come seven years of great
plenty throughout all the land of E'gypt:
30 And there shall arise after them seven
years of famine; and all the plenty shall be forgotten in the land of E'gypt; and the famine
shall consume the land;
31 And the plenty shall not be known in the
land by reason of that famine following; for it
shall be very grievous.
32 And for that the dream was doubled unto
Pha'raoh twice; *it is* because the thing *is* established by God, and God will shortly bring it to
pass.
33 Now therefore let Pha'raoh look out a
man discreet and wise, and set him over the
land of E'gypt.
34 Let Pha'raoh do *this*, and let him appoint
officers over the land, and take up the fifth part
of the land of E'gypt in the seven plenteous
years.
35 And let them gather all the food of those
good years that come, and lay up corn under
the hand of Pha'raoh, and let them keep food in
the cities.
36 And that food shall be for store to the land
against the seven years of famine, which shall
be in the land of E'gypt; that the land perish not
through the famine.
37 ¶ And the thing was good in the eyes of
Pha'raoh, and in the eyes of all his servants.
38 And Pha'raoh said unto his servants, Can
we find *such a one* as this *is*, a man in whom the
Spirit of God *is*?
39 And Pha'raoh said unto Jo'seph, Forasmuch as God hath shewed thee all this, *there is*
none so discreet and wise as thou *art*:
40 Thou shalt be over my house, and according unto thy word shall all my people be ruled:
only in the throne will I be greater than thou.
41 And Pha'raoh said unto Jo'seph, See, I
have set thee over all the land of E'gypt.
42 And Pha'raoh took off his ring from his
hand, and put it upon Jo'seph's hand, and arrayed him in vestures of fine linen, and put a
gold chain about his neck;
43 And he made him to ride in the second
chariot which he had; and they cried before
him, Bow the knee: and he made him *ruler* over
all the land of E'gypt.
44 And Pha'raoh said unto Jo'seph, I *am*
Pha'raoh, and without thee shall no man lift up
his hand or foot in all the land of E'gypt.
45 And Pha'raoh called Jo'seph's name
Zaph'nath-pa-a-ne'ah; and he gave him to wife
As'e-nath the daughter of Po-tiphe-rah priest of
On. And Jo'seph went out over *all* the land of
E'gypt.
46 ¶ And Jo'seph *was* thirty years old when
he stood before Pha'raoh king of E'gypt. And
Jo'seph went out from the presence of Pha'-
raoh, and went throughout all the land of E'-
gypt.
47 And in the seven plenteous years the
earth brought forth by handfuls.
48 And he gathered up all the food of the
seven years, which were in the land of E'gypt,
and laid up the food in the cities: the food of the
field, which *was* round about every city, laid he
up in the same.
49 And Jo'seph gathered corn as the sand of
the sea, very much, until he left numbering; for
it was without number.
50 And unto Jo'seph were born two sons before the years of famine came, which As'e-nath
the daughter of Po-tiphe-rah priest of On bare
unto him.
51 And Jo'seph called the name of the firstborn Ma-nas'seh: For God, *said he*, hath made
me forget all my toil, and all my father's house.
52 And the name of the second called E'phra-
im: For God hath caused me to be fruitful in the
land of my affliction.
53 ¶ And the seven years of plenteousness,
that was in the land of E'gypt, were ended.
54 And the seven years of dearth began to
come, according as Jo'seph had said: and the
dearth was in all lands; but in all the land of
E'gypt there was bread.
55 And when all the land of E'gypt was famished, the people cried to Pha'raoh for bread:
and Pha'raoh said unto all the E-gyptians; Go
unto Jo'seph; what he saith to you, do.
56 And the famine was over all the face of
the earth: And Jo'seph opened all the storehouses, and sold unto the E-gyptians; and the
famine waxed sore in the land of E'gypt.
57 And all countries came into E'gypt to Jo'-
seph for to buy *corn*; because that the famine
was *so* sore in all lands.

42 NOW when Ja'cob saw that there was
corn in E'gypt, Ja'cob said unto his sons,
Why do ye look one upon another?
2 And he said, Behold, I have heard that
there is corn in E'gypt: get you down thither,
and buy for us from thence; that we may live,
and not die.
3 ¶ And Jo'seph's ten brethren went down to
buy corn in E'gypt.
4 But Ben'ja-min, Jo'seph's brother, Ja'cob
sent not with his brethren; for he said, Lest peradventure mischief befall him.
5 And the sons of Is'ra-el came to buy *corn*
among those that came: for the famine was in
the land of Ca'naan.
6 And Jo'seph *was* the governor over the
land, *and* he *it was* that sold to all the people of
the land: and Jo'seph's brethren came, and
bowed down themselves before him *with* their
faces to the earth.
7 And Jo'seph saw his brethren, and he knew
them, but made himself strange unto them, and
spake roughly unto them; and he said unto

them, Whence come ye? And they said, From the land of Ca′naan to buy food.

8 And Jo′seph knew his brethren, but they knew not him.

9 And Jo′seph remembered the dreams which he dreamed of them, and said unto them, Ye *are* spies; to see the nakedness of the land ye are come.

10 And they said unto him, Nay, my lord, but to buy food are thy servants come.

11 We *are* all one man's sons; we *are* true *men,* thy servants are no spies.

12 And he said unto them, Nay, but to see the nakedness of the land ye are come.

13 And they said, Thy servants *are* twelve brethren, the sons of one man in the land of Ca′naan; and, behold, the youngest *is* this day with our father, and one *is* not.

14 And Jo′seph said unto them, That *is it* that I spake unto you, saying, Ye *are* spies:

15 Hereby ye shall be proved: By the life of Pha′raoh ye shall not go forth hence, except your youngest brother come hither.

16 Send one of you, and let him fetch your brother, and ye shall be kept in prison, that your words may be proved, whether *there be any* truth in you: or else by the life of Pha′raoh surely ye *are* spies.

17 And he put them all together into ward three days.

18 And Jo′seph said unto them the third day, This do, and live; *for* I fear God:

19 If ye *be* true *men,* let one of your brethren be bound in the house of your prison: go ye, carry corn for the famine of your houses:

20 But bring your youngest brother unto me; so shall your words be verified, and ye shall not die. And they did so.

21 ¶ And they said one to another, We *are* verily guilty concerning our brother, in that we saw the anguish of his soul, when he besought us, and we would not hear; therefore is this distress come upon us.

22 And Reu′ben answered them, saying, Spake I not unto you, saying, Do not sin against the child; and ye would not hear? therefore, behold, also his blood is required.

23 And they knew not that Jo′seph understood *them;* for he spake unto them by an interpreter.

24 And he turned himself about from them, and wept; and returned to them again, and communed with them, and took from them Sim′e-on, and bound him before their eyes.

25 ¶ Then Jo′seph commanded to fill their sacks with corn, and to restore every man's money into his sack, and to give them provision for the way: and thus did he unto them.

26 And they laded their asses with the corn, and departed thence.

27 And as one of them opened his sack to give his ass provender in the inn, he espied his money; for, behold, it *was* in his sack's mouth.

28 And he said unto his brethren, My money is restored; and, lo, *it is* even in my sack: and their heart failed *them,* and they were afraid, saying one to another, What *is* this *that* God hath done unto us?

29 ¶ And they came unto Ja′cob their father unto the land of Ca′naan, and told him all that befell unto them; saying,

30 The man, *who is* the lord of the land, spake roughly to us, and took us for spies of the country.

31 And we said unto him, We *are* true *men;* we are no spies:

32 We *be* twelve brethren, sons of our father; one *is* not, and the youngest *is* this day with our father in the land of Ca′naan.

33 And the man, the lord of the country, said unto us, Hereby shall I know that ye *are* true *men;* leave one of your brethren *here* with me, and take *food for* the famine of your households, and be gone:

34 And bring your youngest brother unto me: then shall I know that ye *are* no spies, but *that* ye *are* true *men: so* will I deliver you your brother, and ye shall traffick in the land.

35 ¶ And it came to pass as they emptied their sacks, that, behold, every man's bundle of money *was* in his sack: and when *both* they and their father saw the bundles of money, they were afraid.

36 And Ja′cob their father said unto them, Me have ye bereaved *of my children:* Jo′seph *is* not, and Sim′e-on *is* not, and ye will take Ben′-ja-min *away:* all these things are against me.

37 And Reu′ben spake unto his father, saying, Slay my two sons, if I bring him not to thee: deliver him into my hand, and I will bring him to thee again.

38 And he said, My son shall not go down with you; for his brother is dead, and he is left alone: if mischief befall him by the way in the which ye go, then shall ye bring down my gray hairs with sorrow to the grave.

43 AND the famine *was* sore in the land.

2 And it came to pass, when they had eaten up the corn which they had brought out of E′gypt, their father said unto them, Go again, buy us a little food.

3 And Ju′dah spake unto him, saying, The man did solemnly protest unto us, saying, Ye shall not see my face, except your brother *be* with you.

4 If thou wilt send our brother with us, we will go down and buy thee food:

5 But if thou wilt not send *him,* we will not go down: for the man said unto us, Ye shall not see my face, except your brother *be* with you.

6 And Is′ra-el said, Wherefore dealt ye *so* ill with me, *as* to tell the man whether ye had yet a brother?

7 And they said, The man asked us straitly of our state, and of our kindred, saying, *Is* your father yet alive? have ye *another* brother? and we told him according to the tenor of these words: could we certainly know that he would say, Bring your brother down?

8 And Ju′dah said unto Is′ra-el his father, Send the lad with me, and we will arise and go; that we may live, and not die, both we, and thou, *and* also our little ones.

9 I will be surety for him; of my hand shalt thou require him: if I bring him not unto thee, and set him before thee, then let me bear the blame for ever:

10 For except we had lingered, surely now we had returned this second time.

11 And their father Is′ra-el said unto them, If *it must be* so now, do this; take of the best fruits in the land in your vessels, and carry down the man a present, a little balm, and a little honey, spices, and myrrh, nuts, and almonds:

12 And take double money in your hand; and the money that was brought again in the mouth of your sacks, carry *it* again in your hand; peradventure it *was* an oversight:

13 Take also your brother, and arise, go again unto the man:

14 And God Almighty give you mercy before the man, that he may send away your other

brother, and Ben'ja-min. If I be bereaved *of my*
children, I am bereaved.
15 ¶ And the men took that present, and
they took double money in their hand, and Ben'-
ja-min; and rose up, and went down to E'gypt,
and stood before Jo'seph.
16 And when Jo'seph saw Ben'ja-min with
them, he said to the ruler of his house, Bring
these men home, and slay, and make ready; for
these men shall dine with me at noon.
17 And the man did as Jo'seph bade; and the
man brought the men into Jo'seph's house.
18 And the men were afraid, because they
were brought into Jo'seph's house; and they
said, Because of the money that was returned in
our sacks at the first time are we brought in;
that he may seek occasion against us, and fall
upon us, and take us for bondmen, and our
asses.
19 And they came near to the steward of Jo'-
seph's house, and they communed with him at
the door of the house,
20 And said, O sir, we came indeed down at
the first time to buy food:
21 And it came to pass, when we came to the
inn, that we opened our sacks, and, behold, *ev-*
ery man's money *was* in the mouth of his sack,
our money in full weight: and we have brought
it again in our hand.
22 And other money have we brought down
in our hands to buy food: we cannot tell who
put our money in our sacks.
23 And he said, Peace *be* to you, fear not:
your God, and the God of your father, hath giv-
en you treasure in your sacks: I had your money. And he brought Sim'e-on out unto them.
24 And the man brought the men into Jo'-
seph's house, and gave *them* water, and they
washed their feet; and he gave their asses provender.
25 And they made ready the present against
Jo'seph came at noon: for they heard that they
should eat bread there.
26 ¶ And when Jo'seph came home, they
brought him the present which *was* in their
hand into the house, and bowed themselves to
him to the earth.
27 And he asked them of *their* welfare, and
said, *Is* your father well, the old man of whom
ye spake? *Is* he yet alive?
28 And they answered, Thy servant our father *is* in good health, he *is* yet alive. And they
bowed down their heads, and made obeisance.
29 And he lifted up his eyes, and saw his
brother Ben'ja-min, his mother's son, and said,
Is this your younger brother, of whom ye spake
unto me? And he said, God be gracious unto
thee, my son.
30 And Jo'seph made haste; for his bowels
did yearn upon his brother: and he sought
where to weep; and he entered into *his* chamber, and wept there.
31 And he washed his face, and went out,
and refrained himself, and said, Set on bread.
32 And they set on for him by himself, and
for them by themselves, and for the E-gyptians,
which did eat with him, by themselves: because
the E-gyptians might not eat bread with the
He'brews; for that *is* an abomination unto the
E-gyptians.
33 And they sat before him, the firstborn according to his birthright, and the youngest according to his youth: and the men marvelled
one at another.
34 And he took *and sent* messes unto them
from before him: but Ben'ja-min's mess was
five times so much as any of theirs. And they
drank, and were merry with him.

44 AND he commanded the steward of his
house, saying, Fill the men's sacks *with*
food, as much as they can carry, and put every
man's money in his sack's mouth.
2 And put my cup, the silver cup, in the
sack's mouth of the youngest, and his corn
money. And he did according to the word that
Jo'seph had spoken.
3 As soon as the morning was light, the men
were sent away, they and their asses.
4 *And* when they were gone out of the city,
and not *yet* far off, Jo'seph said unto his steward, Up, follow after the men; and when thou
dost overtake them, say unto them, Wherefore
have ye rewarded evil for good?
5 *Is* not this *it* in which my lord drinketh, and
whereby indeed he divineth? ye have done evil
in so doing.
6 ¶ And he overtook them, and he spake
unto them these same words.
7 And they said unto him, Wherefore saith
my lord these words? God forbid that thy servants should do according to this thing:
8 Behold, the money, which we found in our
sacks' mouths, we brought again unto thee out
of the land of Ca'naan: how then should we
steal out of thy lord's house silver or gold?
9 With whomsoever of thy servants it be
found, both let him die, and we also will be my
lord's bondmen.
10 And he said, Now also *let* it *be* according
unto your words: he with whom it is found shall
be my servant; and ye shall be blameless.
11 Then they speedily took down every man
his sack to the ground, and opened every man
his sack.
12 And he searched, *and* began at the eldest,
and left at the youngest: and the cup was found
in Ben'ja-min's sack.
13 Then they rent their clothes, and laded every man his ass, and returned to the city.
14 ¶ And Ju'dah and his brethren came to
Jo'seph's house; for he *was* yet there: and they
fell before him on the ground.
15 And Jo'seph said unto them, What deed *is*
this that ye have done? wot ye not that such a
man as I can certainly divine?
16 And Ju'dah said, What shall we say unto
my lord? what shall we speak? or how shall we
clear ourselves? God hath found out the iniquity
of thy servants: behold, we *are* my lord's servants, both we, and *he* also with whom the cup
is found.
17 And he said, God forbid that I should do
so: *but* the man in whose hand the cup is found,
he shall be my servant; and as for you, get you
up in peace unto your father.
18 ¶ Then Ju'dah came near unto him, and
said, Oh my lord, let thy servant, I pray thee,
speak a word in my lord's ears, and let not thine
anger burn against thy servant: for thou *art*
even as Pha'raoh.
19 My lord asked his servants, saying, Have
ye a father, or a brother?
20 And we said unto my lord, We have a father, an old man, and a child of his old age, a
little one; and his brother is dead, and he alone
is left of his mother, and his father loveth him.
21 And thou saidst unto thy servants, Bring
him down unto me, that I may set mine eyes
upon him.
22 And we said unto my lord, The lad cannot
leave his father: for *if* he should leave his father, *his father* would die.

23 And thou saidst unto thy servants, Except your youngest brother come down with you, ye shall see my face no more.

24 And it came to pass when we came up unto thy servant my father, we told him the words of my lord.

25 And our father said, Go again, *and* buy us a little food.

26 And we said, We cannot go down: if our youngest brother be with us, then will we go down: for we may not see the man's face, except our youngest brother *be* with us.

27 And thy servant my father said unto us, Ye know that my wife bare me two *sons:*

28 And the one went out from me, and I said, Surely he is torn in pieces; and I saw him not since:

29 And if ye take this also from me, and mischief befall him, ye shall bring down my gray hairs with sorrow to the grave.

30 Now therefore when I come to thy servant my father, and the lad *be* not with us; seeing that his life is bound up in the lad's life;

31 It shall come to pass, when he seeth that the lad *is* not *with us,* that he will die: and thy servants shall bring down the gray hairs of thy servant our father with sorrow to the grave.

32 For thy servant became surety for the lad unto my father, saying, If I bring him not unto thee, then I shall bear the blame to my father for ever.

33 Now therefore, I pray thee, let thy servant abide instead of the lad a bondman to my lord; and let the lad go up with his brethren.

34 For how shall I go up to my father, and the lad *be* not with me? lest peradventure I see the evil that shall come on my father.

45 THEN Jo′seph could not refrain himself before all them that stood by him; and he cried, Cause every man to go out from me. And there stood no man with him, while Jo′seph made himself known unto his brethren.

2 And he wept aloud: and the E-gyptians and the house of Pha′raoh heard.

3 And Jo′seph said unto his brethren, I *am* Jo′seph; doth my father yet live? And his brethren could not answer him; for they were troubled at his presence.

4 And Jo′seph said unto his brethren, Come near to me, I pray you. And they came near. And he said, I *am* Jo′seph your brother, whom ye sold into E′gypt.

5 Now therefore be not grieved, nor angry with yourselves, that ye sold me hither: for God did send me before you to preserve life.

6 For these two years *hath* the famine *been* in the land: and yet *there are* five years, in the which *there shall* neither *be* earing nor harvest.

7 And God sent me before you to preserve you a posterity in the earth, and to save your lives by a great deliverance.

8 So now *it was* not you *that* sent me hither, but God: and he hath made me a father to Pha′raoh, and lord of all his house, and a ruler throughout all the land of E′gypt.

9 Haste ye, and go up to my father, and say unto him, Thus saith thy son Jo′seph, God hath made me lord of all E′gypt: come down unto me, tarry not:

10 And thou shalt dwell in the land of Go′shen, and thou shalt be near unto me, thou, and thy children, and thy children's children, and thy flocks, and thy herds, and all that thou hast:

11 And there will I nourish thee; for yet *there are* five years of famine; lest thou, and thy household, and all that thou hast, come to poverty.

12 And, behold, your eyes see, and the eyes of my brother Ben′ja-min, that *it is* my mouth that speaketh unto you.

13 And ye shall tell my father of all my glory in E′gypt, and of all that ye have seen; and ye shall haste and bring down my father hither.

14 And he fell upon his brother Ben′ja-min's neck, and wept; and Ben′ja-min wept upon his neck.

15 Moreover he kissed all his brethren, and wept upon them: and after that his brethren talked with him.

16 ¶ And the fame thereof was heard in Pha′raoh's house, saying, Jo′seph's brethren are come: and it pleased Pha′raoh well, and his servants.

17 And Pha′raoh said unto Jo′seph, Say unto thy brethren, This do ye; lade your beasts, and go, get you unto the land of Ca′naan;

18 And take your father and your households, and come unto me: and I will give you the good of the land of E′gypt, and ye shall eat the fat of the land.

19 Now thou art commanded, this do ye; take you wagons out of the land of E′gypt for your little ones, and for your wives, and bring your father, and come.

20 Also regard not your stuff; for the good of all the land of E′gypt *is* yours.

21 And the children of Is′ra-el did so: and Jo′seph gave them wagons, according to the commandment of Pha′raoh, and gave them provision for the way.

22 To all of them he gave each man changes of raiment; but to Ben′ja-min he gave three hundred *pieces* of silver, and five changes of raiment.

23 And to his father he sent after this *manner;* ten asses laden with the good things of E′gypt, and ten she asses laden with corn and bread and meat for his father by the way.

24 So he sent his brethren away, and they departed: and he said unto them, See that ye fall not out by the way.

25 ¶ And they went up out of E′gypt, and came into the land of Ca′naan unto Ja′cob their father,

26 And told him, saying, Jo′seph *is* yet alive, and he *is* governor over all the land of E′gypt. And Ja′cob's heart fainted, for he believed them not.

27 And they told him all the words of Jo′seph, which he had said unto them: and when he saw the wagons which Jo′seph had sent to carry him, the spirit of Ja′cob their father revived:

28 And Is′ra-el said, *It is* enough; Jo′seph my son *is* yet alive: I will go and see him before I die.

46 AND Is′ra-el took his journey with all that he had, and came to Be′er–she′ba, and offered sacrifices unto the God of his father I′saac.

2 And God spake unto Is′ra-el in the visions of the night, and said, Ja′cob, Ja′cob. And he said, Here *am* I.

3 And he said I *am* God, the God of thy father: fear not to go down into E′gypt; for I will there make of thee a great nation:

4 I will go down with thee into E′gypt; and I will also surely bring thee up *again:* and Jo′seph shall put his hand upon thine eyes.

5 And Ja′cob rose up from Be′er–she′ba: and the sons of Is′ra-el carried Ja′cob their father,

and their little ones, and their wives, in the wagons which Pha'raoh had sent to carry him.

6 And they took their cattle, and their goods, which they had gotten in the land of Ca'naan, and came into E'gypt, Ja'cob, and all his seed with him:

7 His sons, and his sons' sons with him, his daughters, and his sons' daughters, and all his seed brought he with him into E'gypt.

8 ¶ And these *are* the names of the children of Is'ra-el, which came into E'gypt, Ja'cob and his sons: Reu'ben, Ja'cob's firstborn.

9 And the sons of Reu'ben; Ha'noch, and Phal'lu, and Hez'ron, and Car'mi.

10 ¶ And the sons of Sim'e-on; Je-mu'el, and Ja'min, and O'had, and Ja'chin, and Zo'har, and Sha'ul the son of a Ca'naan-it-ish woman.

11 ¶ And the sons of Le'vi; Ger'shon, Ko'-hath, and Me-ra'ri.

12 ¶ And the sons of Ju'dah; Er, and O'nan, and She'lah, and Pha'rez, and Za'rah: but Er and O'nan died in the land of Ca'naan. And the sons of Pha'rez were Hez'ron and Ha'mul.

13 ¶ And the sons of Is'sa-char; To'la, and Phu'vah, and Job, and Shim'ron.

14 ¶ And the sons of Zeb'u-lun; Se'red, and E'lon, and Jah'le-el.

15 These *be* the sons of Le'ah, which she bare unto Ja'cob in Pa'dan–a'ram, with his daughter Di'nah: all the souls of his sons and his daughters *were* thirty and three.

16 ¶ And the sons of Gad; Ziph'i-on, and Hag'gi, Shu'ni, and Ez'bon, E'ri, and Ar'o-di, and A-re'li.

17 ¶ And the sons of Ash'er; Jim'nah, and Ishu-ah, and Is'u-i, and Be-ri'ah, and Se'rah their sister: and the sons of Be-ri'ah; He'ber, and Mal'chi-el.

18 These *are* the sons of Zil-pah, whom La'-ban gave to Le'ah his daughter, and these she bare unto Ja'cob, *even* sixteen souls.

19 The sons of Ra'chel Ja'cob's wife; Jo'seph, and Ben'ja-min.

20 ¶ And unto Jo'seph in the land of E'gypt were born Ma-nas'seh and E'phra-im, which As'e-nath the daughter of Po-tiphe-rah priest of On bare unto him.

21 ¶ And the sons of Ben'ja-min *were* Be'lah, and Be'cher, and Ash'bel, Ge'ra, and Na'a-man, E'hi, and Rosh, Mup'pim, and Hup'pim, and Ard.

22 These *are* the sons of Ra'chel, which were born to Ja'cob: all the souls *were* fourteen.

23 ¶ And the sons of Dan; Hu'shim.

24 ¶ And the sons of Naph'ta-li; Jah'ze-el, and Gu'ni, and Je'zer, and Shil'lem.

25 These *are* the sons of Bil'hah, which La'-ban gave unto Ra'chel his daughter, and she bare these unto Ja'cob: all the souls *were* seven.

26 All the souls that came with Ja'cob into E'gypt, which came out of his loins, besides Ja'-cob's sons' wives, all the souls *were* threescore and six;

27 And the sons of Jo'seph, which were born him in E'gypt, *were* two souls: all the souls of the house of Ja'cob, which came into E'gypt, *were* threescore and ten.

28 ¶ And he sent Ju'dah before him unto Jo'-seph, to direct his face unto Go'shen; and they came into the land of Go'shen.

29 And Jo'seph made ready his chariot, and went up to meet Is'ra-el his father, to Go'shen, and presented himself unto him; and he fell on his neck, and wept on his neck a good while.

30 And Is'ra-el said unto Jo'seph, Now let me die, since I have seen thy face, because thou *art* yet alive.

31 And Jo'seph said unto his brethren, and unto his father's house, I will go up, and shew Pha'raoh, and say unto him, My brethren, and my father's house, which *were* in the land of Ca'naan, are come unto me;

32 And the men *are* shepherds, for their trade hath been to feed cattle; and they have brought their flocks, and their herds, and all that they have.

33 And it shall come to pass, when Pha'raoh shall call you, and shall say, What *is* your occupation?

34 That ye shall say, Thy servants' trade hath been about cattle from our youth even until now, both we, *and* also our fathers: that ye may dwell in the land of Go'shen; for every shepherd *is* an abomination unto the E-gyptians.

47 THEN Jo'seph came and told Pha'raoh, and said, My father and my brethren, and their flocks, and their herds, and all that they have, are come out of the land of Ca'naan; and, behold, they *are* in the land of Go'shen.

2 And he took some of his brethren, *even* five men, and presented them unto Pha'raoh.

3 And Pha'raoh said unto his brethren, What *is* your occupation? And they said unto Pha'-raoh, Thy servants *are* shepherds, both we, *and* also our fathers.

4 They said moreover unto Pha'raoh, For to sojourn in the land are we come; for thy servants have no pasture for their flocks; for the famine *is* sore in the land of Ca'naan: now therefore, we pray thee, let thy servants dwell in the land of Go'shen.

5 And Pha'raoh spake unto Jo'seph, saying, Thy father and thy brethren are come unto thee:

6 The land of E'gypt *is* before thee; in the best of the land make thy father and brethren to dwell; in the land of Go'shen let them dwell: and if thou knowest *any* men of activity among them, then make them rulers over my cattle.

7 And Jo'seph brought in Ja'cob his father, and set him before Pha'raoh: and Ja'cob blessed Pha'raoh.

8 And Pha'raoh said unto Ja'cob, How old *art* thou?

9 And Ja'cob said unto Pha'raoh, The days of the years of my pilgrimage *are* an hundred and thirty years: few and evil have the days of the years of my life been, and have not attained unto the days of the years of the life of my fathers in the days of their pilgrimage.

10 And Ja'cob blessed Pha'raoh, and went out from before Pha'raoh.

11 ¶ And Jo'seph placed his father and his brethren, and gave them a possession in the land of E'gypt, in the best of the land, in the land of Ra-me'ses, as Pha'raoh had commanded.

12 And Jo'seph nourished his father, and his brethren, and all his father's household, with bread, according to *their* families.

13 ¶ And *there was* no bread in all the land; for the famine *was* very sore, so that the land of E'gypt and *all* the land of Ca'naan fainted by reason of the famine.

14 And Jo'seph gathered up all the money that was found in the land of E'gypt, and in the land of Ca'naan, for the corn which they bought: and Jo'seph brought the money into Pha'raoh's house.

15 And when money failed in the land of E'-gypt, and in the land of Ca'naan, all the E-gyptians came unto Jo'seph, and said, Give us

bread: for why should we die in thy presence? for the money faileth.

16 And Jo'seph said, Give your cattle; and I will give you for your cattle, if money fail.

17 And they brought their cattle unto Jo'seph: and Jo'seph gave them bread *in exchange* for horses, and for the flocks, and for the cattle of the herds, and for the asses: and he fed them with bread for all their cattle for that year.

18 When that year was ended, they came unto him the second year, and said unto him, We will not hide *it* from my lord, how that our money is spent; my lord also hath our herds of cattle; there is not ought left in the sight of my lord, but our bodies, and our lands:

19 Wherefore shall we die before thine eyes, both we and our land? buy us and our land for bread, and we and our land will be servants unto Pha'raoh: and give *us* seed, that we may live, and not die, that the land be not desolate.

20 And Jo'seph bought all the land of E'gypt for Pha'raoh; for the E-gyptians sold every man his field, because the famine prevailed over them: so the land became Pha'raoh's.

21 And as for the people, he removed them to cities from *one* end of the borders of E'gypt even to the *other* end thereof.

22 Only the land of the priests bought he not; for the priests had a portion *assigned them* of Pha'raoh, and did eat their portion which Pha'raoh gave them: wherefore they sold not their lands.

23 Then Jo'seph said unto the people, Behold, I have bought you this day and your land for Pha'raoh: lo, *here is* seed for you, and ye shall sow the land.

24 And it shall come to pass in the increase, that ye shall give the fifth *part* unto Pha'raoh, and four parts shall be your own, for seed of the field, and for your food, and for them of your households, and for food for your little ones.

25 And they said, Thou hast saved our lives: let us find grace in the sight of my lord, and we will be Pha'raoh's servants.

26 And Jo'seph made it a law over the land of E'gypt unto this day, *that* Pha'raoh should have the fifth *part;* except the land of the priests only, *which* became not Pha'raoh's.

27 ¶ And Is'ra-el dwelt in the land of E'gypt, in the country of Go'shen; and they had possessions therein, and grew, and multiplied exceedingly.

28 And Ja'cob lived in the land of E'gypt seventeen years: so the whole age of Ja'cob was an hundred forty and seven years.

29 And the time drew nigh that Is'ra-el must die: and he called his son Jo'seph, and said unto him, If now I have found grace in thy sight, put, I pray thee, thy hand under my thigh, and deal kindly and truly with me; bury me not, I pray thee, in E'gypt:

30 But I will lie with my fathers, and thou shalt carry me out of E'gypt, and bury me in their buryingplace. And he said, I will do as thou hast said.

31 And he said, Swear unto me. And he sware unto him. And Is'ra-el bowed himself upon the bed's head.

48

AND it came to pass after these things, that *one* told Jo'seph, Behold, thy father *is* sick: and he took with him his two sons, Ma-nas'seh and E'phra-im.

2 And *one* told Ja'cob, and said, Behold, thy son Jo'seph cometh unto thee: and Is'ra-el strengthened himself, and sat upon the bed.

3 And Ja'cob said unto Jo'seph, God Almighty appeared unto me at Luz in the land of Ca'naan, and blessed me,

4 And said unto me, Behold, I will make thee fruitful, and multiply thee, and I will make of thee a multitude of people; and will give this land to thy seed after thee *for* an everlasting possession.

5 ¶ And now thy two sons, E'phra-im and Ma-nas'seh, which were born unto thee in the land of E'gypt before I came unto thee into E'gypt, *are* mine; as Reu'ben and Sim'e-on, they shall be mine.

6 And thy issue, which thou begettest after them, shall be thine, *and* shall be called after the name of their brethren in their inheritance.

7 And as for me, when I came from Pa'dan, Ra'chel died by me in the land of Ca'naan in the way, when yet *there was* but a little way to come unto Eph'rath: and I buried her there in the way of Eph'rath; the same *is* Beth'-le-hem.

8 And Is'ra-el beheld Jo'seph's sons, and said, Who *are* these?

9 And Jo'seph said unto his father, They *are* my sons, whom God hath given me in this *place.* And he said, Bring them, I pray thee, unto me, and I will bless them.

10 Now the eyes of Is'ra-el were dim for age, *so that* he could not see. And he brought them near unto him; and he kissed them, and embraced them.

11 And Is'ra-el said unto Jo'seph, I had not thought to see thy face: and, lo, God hath shewed me also thy seed.

12 And Jo'seph brought them out from between his knees, and he bowed himself with his face to the earth.

13 And Jo'seph took them both, E'phra-im in his right hand toward Is'ra-el's left hand, and Ma-nas'seh in his left hand toward Is'ra-el's right hand, and brought *them* near unto him.

14 And Is'ra-el stretched out his right hand, and laid *it* upon E'phra-im's head, who *was* the younger, and his left hand upon Ma-nas'seh's head, guiding his hands wittingly; for Ma-nas'seh *was* the firstborn.

15 ¶ And he blessed Jo'seph, and said, God, before whom my fathers A'bra-ham and I'saac did walk, the God which fed me all my life long unto this day,

16 The Angel which redeemed me from all evil, bless the lads; and let my name be named on them, and the name of my fathers A'bra-ham and I'saac; and let them grow into a multitude in the midst of the earth.

17 And when Jo'seph saw that his father laid his right hand upon the head of E'phra-im, it displeased him: and he held up his father's hand, to remove it from E'phra-im's head unto Ma-nas'seh's head.

18 And Jo'seph said unto his father, Not so, my father: for this *is* the firstborn; put thy right hand upon his head.

19 And his father refused, and said, I know *it,* my son, I know *it:* he also shall become a people, and he also shall be great: but truly his younger brother shall be greater than he, and his seed shall become a multitude of nations.

20 And he blessed them that day, saying In thee shall Is'ra-el bless, saying, God make thee as E'phra-im and as Ma-nas'seh: and he set E'phra-im before Ma-nas'seh.

21 And Is'ra-el said unto Jo'seph, Behold, I die: but God shall be with you, and bring you again unto the land of your fathers.

22 Moreover I have given to thee one portion above thy brethren, which I took out of the

hand of the Am'or-ite with my sword and with
my bow.

49 AND Ja'cob called unto his sons, and
said, Gather yourselves together, that I
may tell you *that* which shall befall you in the
last days.
2 Gather yourselves together, and hear, ye
sons of Ja'cob; and hearken unto Is'ra-el your
father.
3 ¶ Reu'ben, thou *art* my firstborn, my
might, and the beginning of my strength, the
excellency of dignity, and the excellency of
power:
4 Unstable as water, thou shalt not excel; because thou wentest up to thy father's bed; then
defiledst thou *it*: he went up to my couch.
5 ¶ Sim'e-on and Le'vi *are* brethren; instruments of cruelty *are in* their habitations.
6 O my soul, come not thou into their secret;
unto their assembly, mine honour, be not thou
united: for in their anger they slew a man, and
in their selfwill they digged down a wall.
7 Cursed *be* their anger, for *it was* fierce; and
their wrath, for it was cruel: I will divide them
in Ja'cob, and scatter them in Is'ra-el.
8 ¶ Ju'dah, thou *art he* whom thy brethren
shall praise: thy hand *shall be* in the neck of
thine enemies; thy father's children shall bow
down before thee.
9 Ju'dah *is* a lion's whelp: from the prey, my
son, thou art gone up: he stooped down, he
couched as a lion, and as an old lion; who shall
rouse him up?
10 The sceptre shall not depart from Ju'dah,
nor a lawgiver from between his feet, until Shi'-
loh come; and unto him *shall* the gathering of
the people *be*.
11 Binding his foal unto the vine, and his
ass's colt unto the choice vine; he washed his
garments in wine, and his clothes in the blood
of grapes:
12 His eyes *shall be* red with wine, and his
teeth white with milk.
13 ¶ Zeb'u-lun shall dwell at the haven of the
sea; and he *shall be* for an haven of ships; and
his border *shall be* unto Zi'don.
14 ¶ Is'sa-char *is* a strong ass couching
down between two burdens:
15 And he saw that rest *was* good, and the
land that *it was* pleasant; and bowed his shoulder to bear, and became a servant unto tribute.
16 ¶ Dan shall judge his people, as one of the
tribes of Is'ra-el.
17 Dan shall be a serpent by the way, an adder in the path, that biteth the horse heels, so
that his rider shall fall backward.
18 I have waited for thy salvation, O LORD.
19 ¶ Gad, a troop shall overcome him: but he
shall overcome at the last.
20 ¶ Out of Ash'er his bread *shall be* fat, and
he shall yield royal dainties.
21 ¶ Naph'ta-li *is* a hind let loose: he giveth
goodly words.
22 ¶ Jo'seph *is* a fruitful bough, *even* a fruitful bough by a well; *whose* branches run over
the wall:
23 The archers have sorely grieved him, and
shot *at him*, and hated him:
24 But his bow abode in strength, and the
arms of his hands were made strong by the
hands of the mighty *God* of Ja'cob; (from
thence *is* the shepherd, the stone of Is'ra-el:)
25 *Even* by the God of thy father, who shall
help thee; and by the Almighty, who shall bless
thee with blessings of heaven above, blessings
of the deep that lieth under, blessings of the
breasts, and of the womb:
26 The blessings of thy father have prevailed
above the blessings of my progenitors unto the
utmost bound of the everlasting hills: they shall
be on the head of Jo'seph, and on the crown of
the head of him that was separate from his
brethren.
27 ¶ Ben'ja-min shall ravin *as* a wolf: in the
morning he shall devour the prey, and at night
he shall divide the spoil.
28 ¶ All these *are* the twelve tribes of Is'ra-
el: and this *is it* that their father spake unto
them, and blessed them; every one according to
his blessing he blessed them.
29 And he charged them, and said unto them,
I am to be gathered unto my people: bury me
with my fathers in the cave that *is* in the field of
E'phron the Hit'tite,
30 In the cave that *is* in the field of Mach-
pe'lah, which *is* before Mam're, in the land of
Ca'naan, which A'bra-ham bought with the field
of E'phron the Hit'tite for a possession of a
buryingplace.
31 There they buried A'bra-ham and Sa'rah
his wife; there they buried I'saac and Re-bek'ah
his wife; and there I buried Le'ah.
32 The purchase of the field and of the cave
that *is* therein *was* from the children of Heth.
33 And when Ja'cob had made an end of
commanding his sons, he gathered up his feet
into the bed, and yielded up the ghost, and was
gathered unto his people.

50 AND Jo'seph fell upon his father's face,
and wept upon him, and kissed him.
2 And Jo'seph commanded his servants the
physicians to embalm his father: and the physicians embalmed Is'ra-el.
3 And forty days were fulfilled for him; for so
are fulfilled the days of those which are embalmed: and the E-gyptians mourned for him
threescore and ten days.
4 And when the days of his mourning were
past, Jo'seph spake unto the house of Pha'raoh,
saying, If now I have found grace in your eyes,
speak, I pray you, in the ears of Pha'raoh, saying,
5 My father made me swear, saying, Lo, I
die: in my grave which I have digged for me in
the land of Ca'naan, there shalt thou bury me.
Now therefore let me go up, I pray thee, and
bury my father, and I will come again.
6 And Pha'raoh said, Go up, and bury thy father, according as he made thee swear.
7 ¶ And Jo'seph went up to bury his father:
and with him went up all the servants of Pha'-
raoh, the elders of his house, and all the elders
of the land of E'gypt,
8 And all the house of Jo'seph, and his brethren, and his father's house: only their little ones,
and their flocks, and their herds, they left in the
land of Go'shen.
9 And there went up with him both chariots
and horsemen: and it was a very great company.
10 And they came to the threshingfloor of A'-
tad, which *is* beyond Jor'dan, and there they
mourned with a great and very sore lamentation: and he made a mourning for his father
seven days.
11 And when the inhabitants of the land, the
Ca'naan-ites, saw the mourning in the floor of
A'tad, they said, This *is* a grievous mourning to
the E-gyptians: wherefore the name of it was

called A'bel-miz'ra-im, which *is* beyond Jor'-dan.

12 And his sons did unto him according as he commanded them:

13 For his sons carried him into the land of Ca'naan, and buried him in the cave of the field of Mach-pe'lah, which A'bra-ham bought with the field for a possession of a buryingplace of E'phron the Hit'tite, before Mam're.

14 ¶ And Jo'seph returned into E'gypt, he, and his brethren, and all that went up with him to bury his father, after he had buried his father.

15 ¶ And when Jo'seph's brethren saw that their father was dead, they said, Jo'seph will peradventure hate us, and will certainly requite us all the evil which we did unto him.

16 And they sent a messenger unto Jo'seph, saying, Thy father did command before he died, saying,

17 So shall ye say unto Jo'seph, Forgive, I pray thee now, the trespass of thy brethren, and their sin; for they did unto thee evil: and now, we pray thee, forgive the trespass of the servants of the God of thy father. And Jo'seph wept when they spake unto him.

18 And his brethren also went and fell down before his face; and they said, Behold, we *be* thy servants.

19 And Jo'seph said unto them, Fear not: for *am* I in the place of God?

20 But as for you, ye thought evil against me; *but* God meant it unto good, to bring to pass, as *it is* this day, to save much people alive.

21 Now therefore fear ye not: I will nourish you, and your little ones. And he comforted them, and spake kindly unto them.

22 ¶ And Jo'seph dwelt in E'gypt, he, and his father's house: and Jo'seph lived an hundred and ten years.

23 And Jo'seph saw E'phra-im's children of the third *generation:* the children also of Ma'-chir the son of Ma-nas'seh were brought up upon Jo'seph's knees.

24 And Jo'seph said unto his brethren, I die: and God will surely visit you, and bring you out of this land unto the land which he sware to A'bra-ham, to I'saac, and to Ja'cob.

25 And Jo'seph took an oath of the children of Is'ra-el, saying, God will surely visit you, and ye shall carry up my bones from hence.

26 So Jo'seph died, *being* an hundred and ten years old: and they embalmed him, and he was put in a coffin in E'gypt.

THE SECOND BOOK OF MOSES

COMMONLY CALLED

EXODUS

1 NOW these *are* the names of the children of Is'ra-el, which came into E'gypt; every man and his household came with Ja'cob.

2 Reu'ben, Sim'e-on, Le'vi, and Ju'dah,

3 Is'sa-char, Zeb'u-lun, and Ben'ja-min,

4 Dan, and Naph'ta-li, Gad, and Ash'er.

5 And all the souls that came out of the loins of Ja'cob were seventy souls: for Jo'seph was in E'gypt *already.*

6 And Jo'seph died, and all his brethren, and all that generation.

7 ¶ And the children of Is'ra-el were fruitful, and increased abundantly, and multiplied, and waxed exceeding mighty; and the land was filled with them.

8 Now there arose up a new king over E'-gypt, which knew not Jo'seph.

9 And he said unto his people, Behold, the people of the children of Is'ra-el *are* more and mightier than we:

10 Come on, let us deal wisely with them; lest they multiply, and it come to pass, that, when there falleth out any war, they join also unto our enemies, and fight against us, and *so* get them up out of the land.

11 Therefore they did set over them taskmasters to afflict them with their burdens. And they built for Pha'raoh treasure cities, Pi'thom and Ra-am'ses.

12 But the more they afflicted them, the more they multiplied and grew. And they were grieved because of the children of Is'ra-el.

13 And the E-gyptians made the children of Is'ra-el to serve with rigour:

14 And they made their lives bitter with hard bondage, in morter, and in brick, and in all manner of service in the field: all their service, wherein they made them serve, *was* with rigour.

15 ¶ And the king of E'gypt spake to the He'-brew midwives, of which the name of the one *was* Shiphrah, and the name of the other Pu'ah:

16 And he said, When ye do the office of a midwife to the He'brew women, and see *them* upon the stools; if it *be* a son, then ye shall kill him: but if it *be* a daughter, then she shall live.

17 But the midwives feared God, and did not as the king of E'gypt commanded them, but saved the men children alive.

18 And the king of E'gypt called for the midwives, and said unto them, Why have ye done this thing, and have saved the men children alive?

19 And the midwives said unto Pha'raoh, Because the He'brew women *are* not as the E-gyp'tian women; for they *are* lively, and are delivered ere the midwives come in unto them.

20 Therefore God dealt well with the midwives: and the people multiplied, and waxed very mighty.

21 And it came to pass, because the midwives feared God, that he made them houses.

22 And Pha'raoh charged all his people, saying, Every son that is born ye shall cast into the river, and every daughter ye shall save alive.

2 AND there went a man of the house of Le'-vi, and took *to wife* a daughter of Le'vi.

2 And the woman conceived, and bare a son: and when she saw him that he *was a* goodly *child,* she hid him three months.

3 And when she could not longer hide him, she took for him an ark of bulrushes, and daubed it with slime and with pitch, and put the child therein; and she laid *it* in the flags by the river's brink.

4 And his sister stood afar off, to wit what would be done to him.

5 ¶ And the daughter of Pha'raoh came down to wash *herself* at the river; and her maidens walked along by the river's side; and when she saw the ark among the flags, she sent her maid to fetch it.

6 And when she had opened *it,* she saw the child: and, behold, the babe wept. And she had compassion on him, and said, This *is one* of the He′brews' children.

7 Then said his sister to Pha′raoh's daughter, Shall I go and call to thee a nurse of the He′brew women, that she may nurse the child for thee?

8 And Pha′raoh's daughter said to her, Go. And the maid went and called the child's mother.

9 And Pha′raoh's daughter said unto her, Take this child away, and nurse it for me, and I will give *thee* thy wages. And the woman took the child, and nursed it.

10 And the child grew, and she brought him unto Pha′raoh's daughter, and he became her son. And she called his name Moses: and she said, Because I drew him out of the water.

11 ¶ And it came to pass in those days, when Mo′ses was grown, that he went out unto his brethren, and looked on their burdens: and he spied an E-gyp′tian smiting an He′brew, one of his brethren.

12 And he looked this way and that way, and when he saw that *there was* no man, he slew the E-gyp′tian, and hid him in the sand.

13 And when he went out the second day, behold, two men of the He′brews strove together: and he said to him that did the wrong, Wherefore smitest thou thy fellow?

14 And he said, Who made thee a prince and a judge over us? intendest thou to kill me, as thou killedst the E-gyp′tian? And Mo′ses feared, and said, Surely this thing is known.

15 Now when Pha′raoh heard this thing, he sought to slay Mo′ses. But Mo′ses fled from the face of Pha′raoh, and dwelt in the land of Mid′i-an: and he sat down by a well.

16 Now the priest of Mid′i-an had seven daughters: and they came and drew *water,* and filled the troughs to water their father's flock.

17 And the shepherds came and drove them away: but Mo′ses stood up and helped them, and watered their flock.

18 And when they came to Reu′el their father, he said, How *is it that* ye are come so soon to day?

19 And they said, An E-gyp′tian delivered us out of the hand of the shepherds, and also drew *water* enough for us, and watered the flock.

20 And he said unto his daughters, And where *is* he? why *is* it *that* ye have left the man? call him, that he may eat bread.

21 And Mo′ses was content to dwell with the man: and he gave Mo′ses Zip-po′rah his daughter.

22 And she bare *him* a son, and he called his name Ger′shom: for he said, I have been a stranger in a strange land.

23 ¶ And it came to pass in process of time, that the king of E′gypt died: and the children of Is′ra-el sighed by reason of the bondage, and they cried, and their cry came up unto God by reason of the bondage.

24 And God heard their groaning, and God remembered his covenant with A′bra-ham, with I′saac, and with Ja′cob.

25 And God looked upon the children of Is′ra-el, and God had respect unto *them.*

3 NOW Mo′ses kept the flock of Je′thro his father in law, the priest of Mid′i-an: and he led the flock to the backside of the desert, and came to the mountain of God, *even* to Ho′reb.

2 And the angel of the LORD appeared unto him in a flame of fire out of the midst of a bush: and he looked, and, behold, the bush burned with fire, and the bush *was* not consumed.

3 And Mo′ses said, I will now turn aside, and see this great sight, why the bush is not burnt.

4 And when the LORD saw that he turned aside to see, God called unto him out of the midst of the bush, and said, Mo′ses, Mo′ses. And he said, Here *am* I.

5 And he said, Draw not nigh hither: put off thy shoes from off thy feet, for the place whereon thou standest *is* holy ground.

6 Moreover he said, I *am* the God of thy father, the God of A′bra-ham, the God of I′saac, and the God of Ja′cob. And Mo′ses hid his face; for he was afraid to look upon God.

7 ¶ And the LORD said, I have surely seen the affliction of my people which *are* in E′gypt, and have heard their cry by reason of their taskmasters; for I know their sorrows;

8 And I am come down to deliver them out of the hand of the E-gyptians, and to bring them up out of that land unto a good land and a large, unto a land flowing with milk and honey; unto the place of the Ca′naan-ites, and the Hit′tites, and the Am′or-ites, and the Per′iz-zites, and the Hi′vites, and the Jeb′u-sites.

9 Now therefore, behold, the cry of the children of Is′ra-el is come unto me: and I have also seen the oppression wherewith the E-gyptians oppress them.

10 Come now therefore, and I will send thee unto Pha′raoh, that thou mayest bring forth my people the children of Is′ra-el out of E′gypt.

11 ¶ And Mo′ses said unto God, Who *am* I, that I should go unto Pha′raoh, and that I should bring forth the children of Is′ra-el out of E′gypt?

12 And he said, Certainly I will be with thee; and this *shall be* a token unto thee, that I have sent thee: When thou hast brought forth the people out of E′gypt, ye shall serve God upon this mountain.

13 And Mo′ses said unto God, Behold, *when* I come unto the children of Is′ra-el, and shall say unto them, The God of your fathers hath sent me unto you; and they shall say to me, What *is* his name? what shall I say unto them?

14 And God said unto Mo′ses, I AM THAT I AM: and he said, Thus shalt thou say unto the children of Is′ra-el, I AM hath sent me unto you.

15 And God said moreover unto Mo′ses, Thus shalt thou say unto the children of Is′ra-el, The LORD God of your fathers, the God of A′bra-ham, the God of I′saac, and the God of Ja′cob, hath sent me unto you: this *is* my name for ever, and this *is* my memorial unto all generations.

16 Go, and gather the elders of Is′ra-el together, and say unto them, The LORD God of your fathers, the God of A′bra-ham, of I′saac, and of Ja′cob, appeared unto me, saying, I have surely visited you, and *seen* that which is done to you in E′gypt:

17 And I have said, I will bring you up out of the affliction of E′gypt unto the land of the Ca′naan-ites, and the Hit′tites, and the Am′or-ites, and the Per′iz-zites, and the Hi′vites, and the Jeb′u-sites, unto a land flowing with milk and honey.

18 And they shall hearken to thy voice: and thou shalt come, thou and the elders of Is′ra-el, unto the king of E′gypt, and ye shall say unto him, The LORD God of the He′brews hath met with us: and now let us go, we beseech thee, three days' journey into the wilderness, that we may sacrifice to the LORD our God.

19 ¶ And I am sure that the king of E′gypt

will not let you go, no, not by a mighty hand.

20 And I will stretch out my hand, and smite E'gypt with all my wonders which I will do in the midst thereof: and after that he will let you go.

21 And I will give this people favour in the sight of the E-gyptians: and it shall come to pass, that, when ye go, ye shall not go empty:

22 But every woman shall borrow of her neighbour, and of her that sojourneth in her house, jewels of silver, and jewels of gold, and raiment: and ye shall put *them* upon your sons, and upon your daughters; and ye shall spoil the E-gyptians.

4 AND Mo'ses answered and said, But, behold, they will not believe me, nor hearken unto my voice: for they will say, The LORD hath not appeared unto thee.

2 And the LORD said unto him, What *is* that in thine hand? And he said, A rod.

3 And he said, Cast it on the ground. And he cast it on the ground, and it became a serpent; and Mo'ses fled from before it.

4 And the LORD said unto Mo'ses, Put forth thine hand, and take it by the tail. And he put forth his hand, and caught it, and it became a rod in his hand:

5 That they may believe that the LORD God of their fathers, the God of A'bra-ham, the God of I'saac, and the God of Ja'cob, hath appeared unto thee.

6 ¶ And the LORD said furthermore unto him, Put now thine hand into thy bosom. And he put his hand into his bosom: and when he took it out, behold, his hand *was* leprous as snow.

7 And he said, Put thine hand into thy bosom again. And he put his hand into his bosom again; and plucked it out of his bosom, and, behold, it was turned again as his *other* flesh.

8 And it shall come to pass, if they will not believe thee, neither hearken to the voice of the first sign, that they will believe the voice of the latter sign.

9 And it shall come to pass, if they will not believe also these two signs, neither hearken unto thy voice, that thou shalt take of the water of the river, and pour *it* upon the dry *land:* and the water which thou takest out of the river shall become blood upon the dry *land.*

10 ¶ And Mo'ses said unto the LORD, O my Lord, I *am* not eloquent, neither heretofore, nor since thou hast spoken unto thy servant: but I *am* slow of speech, and of a slow tongue.

11 And the LORD said unto him, Who hath made man's mouth? or who maketh the dumb, or deaf, or the seeing, or the blind? have not I the LORD?

12 Now therefore go, and I will be with thy mouth, and teach thee what thou shalt say.

13 And he said, O my Lord, send, I pray thee, by the hand *of him whom* thou wilt send.

14 And the anger of the LORD was kindled against Mo'ses, and he said, *Is* not Aar'on the Le'vite thy brother? I know that he can speak well. And also, behold, he cometh forth to meet thee: and when he seeth thee, he will be glad in his heart.

15 And thou shalt speak unto him, and put words in his mouth: and I will be with thy mouth, and with his mouth, and will teach you what ye shall do.

16 And he shall be thy spokesman unto the people: and he shall be, *even* he shall be to thee instead of a mouth, and thou shalt be to him instead of God.

17 And thou shalt take this rod in thine hand, wherewith thou shalt do signs.

18 ¶ And Mo'ses went and returned to Je'thro his father in law, and said unto him, Let me go, I pray thee, and return unto my brethren which *are* in E'gypt, and see whether they be yet alive. And Je'thro said to Mo'ses, Go in peace.

19 And the LORD said unto Mo'ses in Mid'i-an, Go, return into E'gypt: for all the men are dead which sought thy life.

20 And Mo'ses took his wife and his sons, and set them upon an ass, and he returned to the land of E'gypt: and Mo'ses took the rod of God in his hand.

21 And the LORD said unto Mo'ses, When thou goest to return into E'gypt, see that thou do all those wonders before Pha'raoh, which I have put in thine hand: but I will harden his heart, that he shall not let the people go.

22 And thou shalt say unto Pha'raoh, Thus saith the LORD, Is'ra-el *is* my son, *even* my firstborn:

23 And I say unto thee, Let my son go, that he may serve me: and if thou refuse to let him go, behold, I will slay thy son, *even* thy firstborn.

24 ¶ And it came to pass by the way in the inn, that the LORD met him, and sought to kill him.

25 Then Zip-po'rah took a sharp stone, and cut off the foreskin of her son, and cast *it* at his feet, and said, Surely a bloody husband *art* thou to me.

26 So he let him go: then she said, A bloody husband *thou art*, because of the circumcision.

27 ¶ And the LORD said to Aar'on, Go into the wilderness to meet Mo'ses. And he went, and met him in the mount of God, and kissed him.

28 And Mo'ses told Aar'on all the words of the LORD who had sent him, and all the signs which he had commanded him.

29 ¶ And Mo'ses and Aar'on went and gathered together all the elders of the children of Is'ra-el:

30 And Aar'on spake all the words which the LORD had spoken unto Mo'ses, and did the signs in the sight of the people.

31 And the people believed: and when they heard that the LORD had visited the children of Is'ra-el, and that he had looked upon their affliction, then they bowed their heads and worshipped.

5 AND afterward Mo'ses and Aar'on went in, and told Pha'raoh, Thus saith the LORD God of Is'ra-el, Let my people go, that they may hold a feast unto me in the wilderness.

2 And Pha'raoh said, Who *is* the LORD, that I should obey his voice to let Is'ra-el go? I know not the LORD, neither will I let Is'ra-el go.

3 And they said, The God of the He'brews hath met with us: let us go, we pray thee, three days' journey into the desert, and sacrifice unto the LORD our God; lest he fall upon us with pestilence, or with the sword.

4 And the king of E'gypt said unto them, Wherefore do ye, Mo'ses and Aar'on, let the people from their works? get you unto your burdens.

5 And Pha'raoh said, Behold, the people of the land now *are* many, and ye make them rest from their burdens.

6 And Pha'raoh commanded the same day the taskmasters of the people, and their officers, saying,

7 Ye shall no more give the people straw to make brick, as heretofore: let them go and gather straw for themselves.

8 And the tale of the bricks, which they did make heretofore, ye shall lay upon them; ye shall not diminish *ought* thereof: for they *be* idle; therefore they cry, saying, Let us go *and* sacrifice to our God.

9 Let there more work be laid upon the men, that they may labour therein; and let them not regard vain words.

10 ¶ And the taskmasters of the people went out, and their officers, and they spake to the people, saying, Thus saith Pha'raoh, I will not give you straw.

11 Go ye, get you straw where ye can find it: yet not ought of your work shall be diminished.

12 So the people were scattered abroad throughout all the land of E'gypt to gather stubble instead of straw.

13 And the taskmasters hasted *them,* saying, Fulfil your works, *your* daily tasks, as when there was straw.

14 And the officers of the children of Is'ra-el, which Pha'raoh's taskmasters had set over them, were beaten, *and* demanded, Wherefore have ye not fulfilled your task in making brick both yesterday and to day, as heretofore?

15 ¶ Then the officers of the children of Is'ra-el came and cried unto Pha'raoh, saying, Wherefore dealest thou thus with thy servants?

16 There is no straw given unto thy servants, and they say to us, Make brick: and, behold, thy servants *are* beaten; but the fault *is* in thine own people.

17 But he said, Ye *are* idle, *ye are* idle: therefore ye say, Let us go *and* do sacrifice to the LORD.

18 Go therefore now, *and* work; for there shall no straw be given you, yet shall ye deliver the tale of bricks.

19 And the officers of the children of Is'ra-el did see *that* they *were* in evil *case,* after it was said, Ye shall not minish *ought* from your bricks of your daily task.

20 ¶ And they met Mo'ses and Aar'on, who stood in the way, as they came forth from Pha'raoh:

21 And they said unto them, The LORD look upon you, and judge; because ye have made our savour to be abhorred in the eyes of Pha'raoh, and in the eyes of his servants, to put a sword in their hand to slay us.

22 And Mo'ses returned unto the LORD, and said, Lord, wherefore hast thou *so* evil entreated this people? why *is* it *that* thou hast sent me?

23 For since I came to Pha'raoh to speak in thy name, he hath done evil to this people; neither hast thou delivered thy people at all.

6

THEN the LORD said unto Mo'ses, Now shalt thou see what I will do to Pha'raoh: for with a strong hand shall he let them go, and with a strong hand shall he drive them out of his land.

2 And God spake unto Mo'ses, and said unto him, I *am* the LORD:

3 And I appeared unto A'bra-ham, unto I'saac, and unto Ja'cob, by *the name of* God Almighty, but by my name JE-HO'VAH was I not known to them.

4 And I have also established my covenant with them, to give them the land of Ca'naan, the land of their pilgrimage, wherein they were strangers.

5 And I have also heard the groaning of the children of Is'ra-el, whom the E-gyptians keep in bondage; and I have remembered my covenant.

6 Wherefore say unto the children of Is'ra-el, I *am* the LORD, and I will bring you out from under the burdens of the E-gyptians, and I will rid you out of their bondage, and I will redeem you with a stretched out arm, and with great judgments:

7 And I will take you to me for a people, and I will be to you a God: and ye shall know that I *am* the LORD your God, which bringeth you out from under the burdens of the E-gyptians.

8 And I will bring you in unto the land, concerning the which I did swear to give it to A'bra-ham, to I'saac, and to Ja'cob; and I will give it you for an heritage: I *am* the LORD.

9 ¶ And Mo'ses spake so unto the children of Is'ra-el: but they hearkened not unto Mo'ses for anguish of spirit, and for cruel bondage.

10 And the LORD spake unto Mo'ses, saying,

11 Go in, speak unto Pha'raoh king of E'gypt, that he let the children of Is'ra-el go out of his land.

12 And Mo'ses spake before the LORD, saying, Behold, the children of Is'ra-el have not hearkened unto me; how then shall Pha'raoh hear me, who *am* of uncircumcised lips?

13 And the LORD spake unto Mo'ses and unto Aar'on, and gave them a charge unto the children of Is'ra-el, and unto Pha'raoh king of E'gypt, to bring the children of Is'ra-el out of the land of E'gypt.

14 ¶ These *be* the heads of their fathers' houses: The sons of Reu'ben the firstborn of Is'ra-el; Ha'noch, and Pal'lu, Hez'ron, and Car'mi: these *be* the families of Reu'ben.

15 And the sons of Sim'e-on; Je-mu'el, and Ja'min, and O'had, and Ja'chin, and Zo'har, and Sha'ul the son of a Ca'naan-it-ish woman: these *are* the families of Sim'e-on.

16 ¶ And these *are* the names of the sons of Le'vi according to their generations; Ger'shon, and Ko'hath, and Me-ra'ri: and the years of the life of Le'vi *were* an hundred thirty and seven years.

17 The sons of Ger'shon; Lib'ni, and Shi'mi, according to their families.

18 And the sons of Ko'hath; Am'ram, and Iz'har, and He'bron, and Uz'zi-el: and the years of the life of Ko'hath *were* an hundred thirty and three years.

19 And the sons of Me-ra'ri; Ma'ha-li and Mu'shi: these *are* the families of Le'vi according to their generations.

20 And Am'ram took him Joch'e-bed his father's sister to wife; and she bare him Aar'on and Mo'ses: and the years of the life of Am'ram *were* an hundred and thirty and seven years.

21 ¶ And the sons of Iz'har; Ko'rah, and Ne-pheg, and Zich'ri.

22 And the sons of Uz'zi-el; Mish'a-el, and El'za-phan, and Zith'ri.

23 And Aar'on took him E-lish'e-ba, daughter of Am-min'a-dab, sister of Na-ash'on, to wife; and she bare him Na'dab, and A-bi'hu, E-le-a'zar, and Ith'a-mar.

24 And the sons of Ko'rah; As'sir, and El'ka-nah, and A-bi'a-saph: these *are* the families of the Kor'hites.

25 And E-le-a'zar Aar'on's son took him *one* of the daughters of Pu'ti-el to wife; and she bare him Phin'e-has: these *are* the heads of the fathers of the Le'vites according to their families.

26 These *are* that Aar'on and Mo'ses, to whom the LORD said, Bring out the children of

Is'ra-el from the land of E'gypt according to their armies.

27 These *are* they which spake to Pha'raoh king of E'gypt, to bring out the children of Is'ra-el from E'gypt: these *are* that Mo'ses and Aar'-on.

28 ¶ And it came to pass on the day *when* the LORD spake unto Mo'ses in the land of E'-gypt,

29 That the LORD spake unto Mo'ses, saying, I *am* the LORD: speak thou unto Pha'raoh king of E'gypt all that I say unto thee.

30 And Mo'ses said before the LORD, Behold, I *am* of uncircumcised lips, and how shall Pha'-raoh hearken unto me?

7 AND the LORD said unto Mo'ses, See, I have made thee a god to Pha'raoh: and Aar'on thy brother shall be thy prophet.

2 Thou shalt speak all that I command thee: and Aar'on thy brother shall speak unto Pha'-raoh, that he send the children of Is'ra-el out of his land.

3 And I will harden Pha'raoh's heart, and multiply my signs and my wonders in the land of E'gypt.

4 But Pha'raoh shall not hearken unto you, that I may lay my hand upon E'gypt, and bring forth mine armies, *and* my people the children of Is'ra-el, out of the land of E'gypt by great judgments.

5 And the E-gyptians shall know that I *am* the LORD, when I stretch forth mine hand upon E'gypt, and bring out the children of Is'ra-el from among them.

6 And Mo'ses and Aar'on did as the LORD commanded them, so did they.

7 And Mo'ses *was* fourscore years old, and Aar'on fourscore and three years old, when they spake unto Pha'raoh.

8 ¶ And the LORD spake unto Mo'ses and unto Aar'on, saying,

9 When Pha'raoh shall speak unto you, saying, Shew a miracle for you: then thou shalt say unto Aar'on, Take thy rod, and cast *it* before Pha'raoh, *and* it shall become a serpent.

10 ¶ And Mo'ses and Aar'on went in unto Pha'raoh, and they did so as the LORD had commanded: and Aar'on cast down his rod before Pha'raoh, and before his servants, and it became a serpent.

11 Then Pha'raoh also called the wise men and the sorcerers: now the magicians of E'gypt, they also did in like manner with their enchantments.

12 For they cast down every man his rod, and they became serpents: but Aar'on's rod swallowed up their rods.

13 And he hardened Pha'raoh's heart, that he hearkened not unto them; as the LORD had said.

14 ¶ And the LORD said unto Mo'ses, Pha'-raoh's heart *is* hardened, he refuseth to let the people go.

15 Get thee unto Pha'raoh in the morning; lo, he goeth out unto the water; and thou shalt stand by the river's brink against he come; and the rod which was turned to a serpent shalt thou take in thine hand.

16 And thou shalt say unto him, The LORD God of the He'brews hath sent me unto thee, saying, Let my people go, that they may serve me in the wilderness: and, behold, hitherto thou wouldest not hear.

17 Thus saith the LORD, In this thou shalt know that I *am* the LORD: behold, I will smite with the rod that *is* in mine hand upon the waters which *are* in the river, and they shall be turned to blood.

18 And the fish that *is* in the river shall die, and the river shall stink; and the E-gyptians shall loathe to drink of the water of the river.

19 ¶ And the LORD spake unto Mo'ses, Say unto Aar'on, Take thy rod, and stretch out thine hand upon the waters of E'gypt, upon their streams, upon their rivers, and upon their ponds, and upon all their pools of water, that they may become blood; and *that* there may be blood throughout all the land of E'gypt, both in *vessels of* wood, and in *vessels of* stone.

20 And Mo'ses and Aar'on did so, as the LORD commanded; and he lifted up the rod, and smote the waters that *were* in the river, in the sight of Pha'raoh, and in the sight of his servants; and all the waters that *were* in the river were turned to blood.

21 And the fish that *was* in the river died; and the river stank, and the E-gyptians could not drink of the water of the river; and there was blood throughout all the land of E'gypt.

22 And the magicians of E'gypt did so with their enchantments: and Pha'raoh's heart was hardened, neither did he hearken unto them; as the LORD had said.

23 And Pha'raoh turned and went into his house, neither did he set his heart to this also.

24 And all the E-gyptians digged round about the river for water to drink; for they could not drink of the water of the river.

25 And seven days were fulfilled, after that the LORD had smitten the river.

8 AND the LORD spake unto Mo'ses, Go unto Pha'raoh, and say unto him, Thus saith the LORD, Let my people go, that they may serve me.

2 And if thou refuse to let *them* go, behold, I will smite all thy borders with frogs:

3 And the river shall bring forth frogs abundantly, which shall go up and come into thine house, and into thy bedchamber, and upon thy bed, and into the house of thy servants, and upon thy people, and into thine ovens, and into thy kneadingtroughs:

4 And the frogs shall come up both on thee, and upon thy people, and upon all thy servants.

5 ¶ And the LORD spake unto Mo'ses, Say unto Aar'on, Stretch forth thine hand with thy rod over the streams, over the rivers, and over the ponds, and cause frogs to come up upon the land of E'gypt.

6 And Aar'on stretched out his hand over the waters of E'gypt; and the frogs came up, and covered the land of E'gypt.

7 And the magicians did so with their enchantments, and brought up frogs upon the land of E'gypt.

8 ¶ Then Pha'raoh called for Mo'ses and Aar'on, and said, Intreat the LORD, that he may take away the frogs from me, and from my people; and I will let the people go, that they may do sacrifice unto the LORD.

9 And Mo'ses said unto Pha'raoh, Glory over me: when shall I intreat for thee, and for thy servants, and for thy people, to destroy the frogs from thee and thy houses, *that* they may remain in the river only?

10 And he said, To morrow. And he said, *Be it* according to thy word: that thou mayest know that *there is* none like unto the LORD our God.

11 And the frogs shall depart from thee, and from thy houses, and from thy servants, and

from thy people; they shall remain in the river only.

12 And Mo′ses and Aar′on went out from Pha′raoh: and Mo′ses cried unto the LORD because of the frogs which he had brought against Pha′raoh.

13 And the LORD did according to the word of Mo′ses; and the frogs died out of the houses, out of the villages, and out of the fields.

14 And they gathered them together upon heaps: and the land stank.

15 But when Pha′raoh saw that there was respite, he hardened his heart, and hearkened not unto them; as the LORD had said.

16 ¶ And the LORD said unto Mo′ses, Say unto Aar′on, Stretch out thy rod, and smite the dust of the land, that it may become lice throughout all the land of E′gypt.

17 And they did so; for Aar′on stretched out his hand with his rod, and smote the dust of the earth, and it became lice in man, and in beast; all the dust of the land became lice throughout all the land of E′gypt.

18 And the magicians did so with their enchantments to bring forth lice, but they could not: so there were lice upon man, and upon beast.

19 Then the magicians said unto Pha′raoh, This *is* the finger of God: and Pha′raoh's heart was hardened, and he hearkened not unto them; as the LORD had said.

20 ¶ And the LORD said unto Mo′ses, Rise up early in the morning, and stand before Pha′raoh; lo, he cometh forth to the water; and say unto him, Thus saith the LORD, Let my people go, that they may serve me.

21 Else, if thou wilt not let my people go, behold, I will send swarms *of flies* upon thee, and upon thy servants, and upon thy people, and into thy houses: and the houses of the E-gyptians shall be full of swarms *of flies*, and also the ground whereon they *are*.

22 And I will sever in that day the land of Go′shen, in which my people dwell, that no swarms *of flies* shall be there; to the end thou mayest know that I *am* the LORD in the midst of the earth.

23 And I will put a division between my people and thy people: to morrow shall this sign be.

24 And the LORD did so; and there came a grievous swarm *of flies* into the house of Pha′raoh, and *into* his servants' houses, and into all the land of E′gypt: the land was corrupted by reason of the swarm *of flies*.

25 ¶ And Pha′raoh called for Mo′ses and for Aar′on, and said, Go ye, sacrifice to your God in the land.

26 And Mo′ses said, It is not meet so to do; for we shall sacrifice the abomination of the E-gyptians to the LORD our God: lo, shall we sacrifice the abomination of the E-gyptians before their eyes, and will they not stone us?

27 We will go three days' journey into the wilderness, and sacrifice to the LORD our God, as he shall command us.

28 And Pha′raoh said, I will let you go, that ye may sacrifice to the LORD your God in the wilderness; only ye shall not go very far away: intreat for me.

29 And Mo′ses said, Behold, I go out from thee, and I will intreat the LORD that the swarms *of flies* may depart from Pha′raoh, from his servants, and from his people, to morrow: but let not Pha′raoh deal deceitfully any more in not letting the people go to sacrifice to the LORD.

30 And Mo′ses went out from Pha′raoh, and intreated the LORD.

31 And the LORD did according to the word of Mo′ses; and he removed the swarms *of flies* from Pha′raoh, from his servants, and from his people; there remained not one.

32 And Pha′raoh hardened his heart at this time also, neither would he let the people go.

9 THEN the LORD said unto Mo′ses, Go in unto Pha′raoh, and tell him, Thus saith the LORD God of the He′brews, Let my people go, that they may serve me.

2 For if thou refuse to let *them* go, and wilt hold them still,

3 Behold, the hand of the LORD is upon thy cattle which *is* in the field, upon the horses, upon the asses, upon the camels, upon the oxen, and upon the sheep: *there shall be* a very grievous murrain.

4 And the LORD shall sever between the cattle of Is′ra-el and the cattle of E′gypt: and there shall nothing die of all *that is* the children's of Is′ra-el.

5 And the LORD appointed a set time, saying, To morrow the LORD shall do this thing in the land.

6 And the LORD did that thing on the morrow, and all the cattle of E′gypt died: but of the cattle of the children of Is′ra-el died not one.

7 And Pha′raoh sent, and, behold, there was not one of the cattle of the Is′ra-el-ites dead. And the heart of Pha′raoh was hardened, and he did not let the people go.

8 ¶ And the LORD said unto Mo′ses and unto Aar′on, Take to you handfuls of ashes of the furnace, and let Mo′ses sprinkle it toward the heaven in the sight of Pha′raoh.

9 And it shall become small dust in all the land of E′gypt, and shall be a boil breaking forth *with* blains upon man, and upon beast, throughout all the land of E′gypt.

10 And they took ashes of the furnace, and stood before Pha′raoh; and Mo′ses sprinkled it up toward heaven; and it became a boil breaking forth *with* blains upon man, and upon beast.

11 And the magicians could not stand before Mo′ses because of the boils; for the boil was upon the magicians, and upon all the E-gyptians.

12 And the LORD hardened the heart of Pha′raoh, and he hearkened not unto them; as the LORD had spoken unto Mo′ses.

13 ¶ And the LORD said unto Mo′ses, Rise up early in the morning, and stand before Pha′raoh, and say unto him, Thus saith the LORD God of the He′brews, Let my people go, that they may serve me.

14 For I will at this time send all my plagues upon thine heart, and upon thy servants, and upon thy people; that thou mayest know that *there is* none like me in all the earth.

15 For now I will stretch out my hand, that I may smite thee and thy people with pestilence; and thou shalt be cut off from the earth.

16 And in very deed for this *cause* have I raised thee up, for to shew *in* thee my power; and that my name may be declared throughout all the earth.

17 As yet exaltest thou thyself against my people, that thou wilt not let them go?

18 Behold, to morrow about this time I will cause it to rain a very grievous hail, such as hath not been in E′gypt since the foundation thereof even until now.

19 Send therefore now, *and* gather thy cattle, and all that thou hast in the field; *for upon* ev-

ery man and beast which shall be found in the
field, and shall not be brought home, the hail
shall come down upon them, and they shall die.
20 He that feared the word of the LORD
among the servants of Pha'raoh made his servants and his cattle flee into the houses:
21 And he that regarded not the word of the
LORD left his servants and his cattle in the field.
22 ¶ And the LORD said unto Mo'ses, Stretch
forth thine hand toward heaven, that there may
be hail in all the land of E'gypt, upon man, and
upon beast, and upon every herb of the field,
throughout the land of E'gypt.
23 And Mo'ses stretched forth his rod toward
heaven: and the LORD sent thunder and hail,
and the fire ran along upon the ground; and the
LORD rained hail upon the land of E'gypt.
24 So there was hail, and fire mingled with
the hail, very grievous, such as there was none
like it in all the land of E'gypt since it became a
nation.
25 And the hail smote throughout all the land
of E'gypt all that *was* in the field, both man and
beast; and the hail smote every herb of the field,
and brake every tree of the field.
26 Only in the land of Go'shen, where the
children of Is'ra-el *were*, was there no hail.
27 ¶ And Pha'raoh sent, and called for Mo'-
ses and Aar'on, and said unto them, I have
sinned this time: the LORD *is* righteous, and I
and my people *are* wicked.
28 Intreat the LORD (for *it is* enough) that
there be no *more* mighty thunderings and hail;
and I will let you go, and ye shall stay no longer.
29 And Mo'ses said unto him, As soon as I
am gone out of the city, I will spread abroad my
hands unto the LORD; *and* the thunder shall
cease, neither shall there be any more hail; that
thou mayest know how that the earth *is* the
LORD'S.
30 But as for thee and thy servants, I know
that ye will not yet fear the LORD God.
31 And the flax and the barley was smitten:
for the barley *was* in the ear, and the flax *was*
bolled.
32 But the wheat and the rie were not smitten: for they *were* not grown up.
33 And Mo'ses went out of the city from
Pha'raoh, and spread abroad his hands unto the
LORD: and the thunders and hail ceased, and the
rain was not poured upon the earth.
34 And when Pha'raoh saw that the rain and
the hail and the thunders were ceased, he
sinned yet more, and hardened his heart, he and
his servants.
35 And the heart of Pha'raoh was hardened,
neither would he let the children of Is'ra-el go;
as the LORD had spoken by Mo'ses.

10 AND the LORD said unto Mo'ses, Go in
unto Pha'raoh: for I have hardened his
heart, and the heart of his servants, that I might
shew these my signs before him:
2 And that thou mayest tell in the ears of thy
son, and of thy son's son, what things I have
wrought in E'gypt, and my signs which I have
done among them; that ye may know how that I
am the LORD.
3 And Mo'ses and Aar'on came in unto Pha'-
raoh, and said unto him, Thus saith the LORD
God of the He'brews, How long wilt thou refuse
to humble thyself before me? let my people go,
that they may serve me.
4 Else, if thou refuse to let my people go, behold, to morrow will I bring the locusts into thy
coast:
5 And they shall cover the face of the earth,
that one cannot be able to see the earth: and
they shall eat the residue of that which is escaped, which remaineth unto you from the hail,
and shall eat every tree which groweth for you
out of the field:
6 And they shall fill thy houses, and the
houses of all thy servants, and the houses of all
the E-gyptians; which neither thy fathers, nor
thy fathers' fathers have seen, since the day
that they were upon the earth unto this day.
And he turned himself, and went out from Pha'-
raoh.
7 And Pha'raoh's servants said unto him,
How long shall this man be a snare unto us? let
the men go, that they may serve the LORD their
God: knowest thou not yet that E'gypt is destroyed?
8 And Mo'ses and Aar'on were brought again
unto Pha'raoh: and he said unto them, Go, serve
the LORD your God: *but* who *are* they that shall
go?
9 And Mo'ses said, We will go with our
young and with our old, with our sons and with
our daughters, with our flocks and with our
herds will we go; for we *must hold* a feast unto
the LORD.
10 And he said unto them, Let the LORD be so
with you, as I will let you go, and your little
ones: look *to it;* for evil *is* before you.
11 Not so: go now ye *that are* men, and serve
the LORD; for that ye did desire. And they were
driven out from Pha'raoh's presence.
12 ¶ And the LORD said unto Mo'ses, Stretch
out thine hand over the land of E'gypt for the
locusts, that they may come up upon the land of
E'gypt, and eat every herb of the land, *even* all
that the hail hath left.
13 And Mo'ses stretched forth his rod over
the land of E'gypt, and the LORD brought an
east wind upon the land all that day, and all
that night; *and* when it was morning, the east
wind brought the locusts.
14 And the locusts went up over all the land
of E'gypt, and rested in all the coasts of E'gypt:
very grievous *were they;* before them there
were no such locusts as they, neither after them
shall be such.
15 For they covered the face of the whole
earth, so that the land was darkened; and they
did eat every herb of the land, and all the fruit
of the trees which the hail had left: and there
remained not any green thing in the trees, or in
the herbs of the field, through all the land of
E'gypt.
16 ¶ Then Pha'raoh called for Mo'ses and
Aar'on in haste; and he said, I have sinned
against the LORD your God, and against you.
17 Now therefore forgive, I pray thee, my sin
only this once, and intreat the LORD your God,
that he may take away from me this death only.
18 And he went out from Pha'raoh, and intreated the LORD.
19 And the LORD turned a mighty strong
west wind, which took away the locusts, and
cast them into the Red sea; there remained not
one locust in all the coasts of E'gypt.
20 But the LORD hardened Pha'raoh's heart,
so that he would not let the children of Is'ra-el
go.
21 ¶ And the LORD said unto Mo'ses, Stretch
out thine hand toward heaven, that there may
be darkness over the land of E'gypt, even darkness *which* may be felt.
22 And Mo'ses stretched forth his hand
toward heaven; and there was a thick darkness
in all the land of E'gypt three days:
23 They saw not one another, neither rose

any from his place for three days: but all the children of Is'ra-el had light in their dwellings.

24 ¶ And Pha'raoh called unto Mo'ses, and said, Go ye, serve the LORD; only let your flocks and your herds be stayed: let your little ones also go with you.

25 And Mo'ses said, Thou must give us also sacrifices and burnt offerings, that we may sacrifice unto the LORD our God.

26 Our cattle also shall go with us; there shall not an hoof be left behind; for thereof must we take to serve the LORD our God; and we know not with what we must serve the LORD, until we come thither.

27 ¶ But the LORD hardened Pha'raoh's heart, and he would not let them go.

28 And Pha'raoh said unto him, Get thee from me, take heed to thyself, see my face no more; for in *that* day thou seest my face thou shalt die.

29 And Mo'ses said, Thou hast spoken well, I will see thy face again no more.

11 AND the LORD said unto Mo'ses, Yet will I bring one plague *more* upon Pha'raoh, and upon E'gypt; afterwards he will let you go hence: when he shall let *you* go, he shall surely thrust you out hence altogether.

2 Speak now in the ears of the people, and let every man borrow of his neighbour, and every woman of her neighbour, jewels of silver, and jewels of gold.

3 And the LORD gave the people favour in the sight of the E-gyptians. Moreover the man Mo'ses *was* very great in the land of E'gypt, in the sight of Pha'raoh's servants, and in the sight of the people.

4 And Mo'ses said, Thus saith the LORD, About midnight will I go out into the midst of E'gypt:

5 And all the firstborn in the land of E'gypt shall die, from the firstborn of Pha'raoh that sitteth upon his throne, even unto the firstborn of the maidservant that *is* behind the mill; and all the firstborn of beasts.

6 And there shall be a great cry throughout all the land of E'gypt, such as there was none like it, nor shall be like it any more.

7 But against any of the children of Is'ra-el shall not a dog move his tongue, against man or beast: that ye may know how that the LORD doth put a difference between the E-gyptians and Is'ra-el.

8 And all these thy servants shall come down unto me, and bow down themselves unto me, saying, Get thee out, and all the people that follow thee: and after that I will go out. And he went out from Pha'raoh in a great anger.

9 And the LORD said unto Mo'ses, Pha'raoh shall not hearken unto you; that my wonders may be multiplied in the land of E'gypt.

10 And Mo'ses and Aar'on did all these wonders before Pha'raoh: and the LORD hardened Pha'raoh's heart, so that he would not let the children of Is'ra-el go out of his land.

12 AND the LORD spake unto Mo'ses and Aar'on in the land of E'gypt, saying,

2 This month *shall be* unto you the beginning of months: it *shall be* the first month of the year to you.

3 ¶ Speak ye unto all the congregation of Is'ra-el, saying, In the tenth *day* of this month they shall take to them every man a lamb, according to the house of *their* fathers, a lamb for an house:

4 And if the household be too little for the lamb, let him and his neighbour next unto his house take *it* according to the number of the souls; every man according to his eating shall make your count for the lamb.

5 Your lamb shall be without blemish, a male of the first year: ye shall take *it* out from the sheep, or from the goats:

6 And ye shall keep it up until the fourteenth day of the same month: and the whole assembly of the congregation of Is'ra-el shall kill it in the evening.

7 And they shall take of the blood, and strike *it* on the two side posts and on the upper door post of the houses, wherein they shall eat it.

8 And they shall eat the flesh in that night, roast with fire, and unleavened bread; *and* with bitter *herbs* they shall eat it.

9 Eat not of it raw, nor sodden at all with water, but roast *with* fire; his head with his legs, and with the purtenance thereof.

10 And ye shall let nothing remain until the morning; and that which remaineth of it until the morning ye shall burn with fire.

11 ¶ And thus shall ye eat it; *with* your loins girded, your shoes on your feet, and your staff in your hand; and ye shall eat it in haste: it *is* the LORD's passover.

12 For I will pass through the land of E'gypt this night, and will smite all the firstborn in the land of E'gypt, both man and beast; and against all the gods of E'gypt I will execute judgment: I *am* the LORD.

13 And the blood shall be to you for a token upon the houses where ye *are*: and when I see the blood, I will pass over you, and the plague shall not be upon you to destroy *you*, when I smite the land of E'gypt.

14 And this day shall be unto you for a memorial; and ye shall keep it a feast to the LORD throughout your generations; ye shall keep it a feast by an ordinance for ever.

15 Seven days shall ye eat unleavened bread; even the first day ye shall put away leaven out of your houses: for whosoever eateth leavened bread from the first day until the seventh day, that soul shall be cut off from Is'ra-el.

16 And in the first day *there shall be* an holy convocation, and in the seventh day there shall be an holy convocation to you; no manner of work shall be done in them, save *that* which every man must eat, that only may be done of you.

17 And ye shall observe *the feast of* unleavened bread; for in this selfsame day have I brought your armies out of the land of E'gypt: therefore shall ye observe this day in your generations by an ordinance for ever.

18 ¶ In the first *month*, on the fourteenth day of the month at even, ye shall eat unleavened bread, until the one and twentieth day of the month at even.

19 Seven days shall there be no leaven found in your houses: for whosoever eateth that which is leavened, even that soul shall be cut off from the congregation of Is'ra-el, whether he be a stranger or born in the land.

20 Ye shall eat nothing leavened; in all your habitations shall ye eat unleavened bread.

21 ¶ Then Mo'ses called for all the elders of Is'ra-el, and said unto them, Draw out and take you a lamb according to your families, and kill the passover.

22 And ye shall take a bunch of hyssop, and dip *it* in the blood that *is* in the bason, and strike the lintel and the two side posts with the blood that *is* in the bason; and none of you shall

go out at the door of his house until the morning.

23 For the LORD will pass through to smite the E-gyptians; and when he seeth the blood upon the lintel, and on the two side posts, the LORD will pass over the door, and will not suffer the destroyer to come in unto your houses to smite *you.*

24 And ye shall observe this thing for an ordinance to thee and to thy sons for ever.

25 And it shall come to pass, when ye be come to the land which the LORD will give you, according as he hath promised, that ye shall keep this service.

26 And it shall come to pass, when your children shall say unto you, What mean ye by this service?

27 That ye shall say, It *is* the sacrifice of the LORD's passover, who passed over the houses of the children of Is'ra-el in E'gypt, when he smote the E-gyptians, and delivered our houses. And the people bowed the head and worshipped.

28 And the children of Is'ra-el went away, and did as the LORD had commanded Mo'ses and Aar'on, so did they.

29 ¶ And it came to pass, that at midnight the LORD smote all the firstborn in the land of E'gypt, from the firstborn of Pha'raoh that sat on his throne unto the firstborn of the captive that *was* in the dungeon; and all the firstborn of cattle.

30 And Pha'raoh rose up in the night, he, and all his servants, and all the E-gyptians; and there was a great cry in E'gypt; for *there was* not a house where *there was* not one dead.

31 ¶ And he called for Mo'ses and Aar'on by night, and said, Rise up, *and* get you forth from among my people, both ye and the children of Is'ra-el; and go, serve the LORD, as ye have said.

32 Also take your flocks and your herds, as ye have said, and be gone; and bless me also.

33 And the E-gyptians were urgent upon the people, that they might send them out of the land in haste; for they said, We *be* all dead *men.*

34 And the people took their dough before it was leavened, their kneadingtroughs being bound up in their clothes upon their shoulders.

35 And the children of Is'ra-el did according to the word of Mo'ses; and they borrowed of the E-gyptians jewels of silver, and jewels of gold, and raiment:

36 And the LORD gave the people favour in the sight of the E-gyptians, so that they lent unto them *such things as they required.* And they spoiled the E-gyptians.

37 ¶ And the children of Is'ra-el journeyed from Ra-me'ses to Suc'coth, about six hundred thousand on foot *that were* men, beside children.

38 And a mixed multitude went up also with them; and flocks, and herds, *even* very much cattle.

39 And they baked unleavened cakes of the dough which they brought forth out of E'gypt, for it was not leavened; because they were thrust out of E'gypt, and could not tarry, neither had they prepared for themselves any victual.

40 ¶ Now the sojourning of the children of Is'ra-el, who dwelt in E'gypt, *was* four hundred and thirty years.

41 And it came to pass at the end of the four hundred and thirty years, even the selfsame day it came to pass, that all the hosts of the LORD went out from the land of E'gypt.

42 It *is* a night to be much observed unto the LORD for bringing them out from the land of E'gypt: this *is* that night of the LORD to be observed of all the children of Is'ra-el in their generations.

43 ¶ And the LORD said unto Mo'ses and Aar'on, This *is* the ordinance of the passover: There shall no stranger eat thereof:

44 But every man's servant that is bought for money, when thou hast circumcised him, then shall he eat thereof.

45 A foreigner and an hired servant shall not eat thereof.

46 In one house shall it be eaten; thou shalt not carry forth ought of the flesh abroad out of the house; neither shall ye break a bone thereof.

47 All the congregation of Is'ra-el shall keep it.

48 And when a stranger shall sojourn with thee, and will keep the passover to the LORD, let all his males be circumcised, and then let him come near and keep it; and he shall be as one that is born in the land: for no uncircumcised person shall eat thereof.

49 One law shall be to him that is homeborn, and unto the stranger that sojourneth among you.

50 Thus did all the children of Is'ra-el; as the LORD commanded Mo'ses and Aar'on, so did they.

51 And it came to pass the selfsame day, *that* the LORD did bring the children of Is'ra-el out of the land of E'gypt by their armies.

13 AND the LORD spake unto Mo'ses, saying,

2 Sanctify unto me all the firstborn, whatsoever openeth the womb among the children of Is'ra-el, *both* of man and of beast: it *is* mine.

3 ¶ And Mo'ses said unto the people, Remember this day, in which ye came out from E'gypt, out of the house of bondage; for by strength of hand the LORD brought you out from this *place:* there shall no leavened bread be eaten.

4 This day came ye out in the month A'bib.

5 ¶ And it shall be when the LORD shall bring thee into the land of the Ca'naan-ites, and the Hit'tites, and the Am'or-ites, and the Hi'vites, and the Jeb'u-sites, which he sware unto thy fathers to give thee, a land flowing with milk and honey, that thou shalt keep this service in this month.

6 Seven days thou shalt eat unleavened bread, and in the seventh day *shall be* a feast to the LORD.

7 Unleavened bread shall be eaten seven days; and there shall no leavened bread be seen with thee, neither shall there be leaven seen with thee in all thy quarters.

8 ¶ And thou shalt shew thy son in that day, saying, *This is done* because of that *which* the LORD did unto me when I came forth out of E'gypt.

9 And it shall be for a sign unto thee upon thine hand, and for a memorial between thine eyes, that the LORD's law may be in thy mouth: for with a strong hand hath the LORD brought thee out of E'gypt.

10 Thou shalt therefore keep this ordinance in his season from year to year.

11 ¶ And it shall be when the LORD shall bring thee into the land of the Ca'naan-ites, as he sware unto thee and to thy fathers, and shall give it thee,

12 That thou shalt set apart unto the LORD all that openeth the matrix, and every firstling that cometh of a beast which thou hast; the males *shall be* the LORD's.

13 And every firstling of an ass thou shalt re-

deem with a lamb; and if thou wilt not redeem
it, then thou shalt break his neck: and all the
firstborn of man among thy children shalt thou
redeem.
14 ¶ And it shall be when thy son asketh
thee in time to come, saying, What *is* this? that
thou shalt say unto him, By strength of hand
the LORD brought us out from E'gypt, from the
house of bondage:
15 And it came to pass, when Pha'raoh
would hardly let us go, that the LORD slew all
the firstborn in the land of E'gypt, both the firstborn of man, and the firstborn of beast: therefore I sacrifice to the LORD all that openeth the
matrix, being males; but all the firstborn of my
children I redeem.
16 And it shall be for a token upon thine
hand, and for frontlets between thine eyes: for
by strength of hand the LORD brought us forth
out of E'gypt.
17 ¶ And it came to pass, when Pha'raoh had
let the people go, that God led them not *through*
the way of the land of the Phi-lis'tines, although
that *was* near; for God said, Lest peradventure
the people repent when they see war, and they
return to E'gypt:
18 But God led the people about, *through* the
way of the wilderness of the Red sea: and the
children of Is'ra-el went up harnessed out of the
land of E'gypt.
19 And Mo'ses took the bones of Jo'seph
with him: for he had straitly sworn the children
of Is'ra-el, saying, God will surely visit you; and
ye shall carry up my bones away hence with
you.
20 ¶ And they took their journey from Suc'-
coth, and encamped in E'tham, in the edge of
the wilderness.
21 And the LORD went before them by day in
a pillar of a cloud, to lead them the way; and by
night in a pillar of fire, to give them light; to go
by day and night:
22 He took not away the pillar of the cloud
by day, nor the pillar of fire by night, *from* before the people.

14 AND the LORD spake unto Mo'ses, saying,
2 Speak unto the children of Is'ra-el, that
they turn and encamp before Pi-ha-hi'roth, between Mig'dol and the sea, over against Ba'al-
ze'phon: before it shall ye encamp by the sea.
3 For Pha'raoh will say of the children of Is'-
ra-el, They *are* entangled in the land, the wilderness hath shut them in.
4 And I will harden Pha'raoh's heart, that he
shall follow after them; and I will be honoured
upon Pha'raoh, and upon all his host; that the E-
gyptians may know that I *am* the LORD. And
they did so.
5 ¶ And it was told the king of E'gypt that
the people fled: and the heart of Pha'raoh and of
his servants was turned against the people, and
they said, Why have we done this, that we have
let Is'ra-el go from serving us?
6 And he made ready his chariot, and took
his people with him:
7 And he took six hundred chosen chariots,
and all the chariots of E'gypt, and captains over
every one of them.
8 And the LORD hardened the heart of Pha'-
raoh king of E'gypt, and he pursued after the
children of Is'ra-el: and the children of Is'ra-el
went out with an high hand.
9 But the E-gyptians pursued after them, all
the horses *and* chariots of Pha'raoh, and his
horsemen, and his army, and overtook them en-
camping by the sea, beside Pi-ha-hi'roth, before
Ba'al-ze'phon.
10 ¶ And when Pha'raoh drew nigh, the children of Is'ra-el lifted up their eyes, and, behold,
the E-gyptians marched after them; and they
were sore afraid: and the children of Is'ra-el
cried out unto the LORD.
11 And they said unto Mo'ses, Because *there*
were no graves in E'gypt, hast thou taken us
away to die in the wilderness? wherefore hast
thou dealt thus with us, to carry us forth out of
E'gypt?
12 *Is* not this the word that we did tell thee in
E'gypt, saying, Let us alone, that we may serve
the E-gyptians? For *it had been* better for us to
serve the E-gyptians, than that we should die in
the wilderness.
13 ¶ And Mo'ses said unto the people, Fear
ye not, stand still, and see the salvation of the
LORD, which he will shew to you to day: for the
E-gyptians whom ye have seen to day, ye shall
see them again no more for ever.
14 The LORD shall fight for you, and ye shall
hold your peace.
15 ¶ And the LORD said unto Mo'ses, Wherefore criest thou unto me? speak unto the children of Is'ra-el, that they go forward:
16 But lift thou up thy rod, and stretch out
thine hand over the sea, and divide it: and the
children of Is'ra-el shall go on dry *ground*
through the midst of the sea.
17 And I, behold, I will harden the hearts of
the E-gyptians, and they shall follow them: and
I will get me honour upon Pha'raoh, and upon
all his host, upon his chariots, and upon his
horsemen.
18 And the E-gyptians shall know that I *am*
the LORD, when I have gotten me honour upon
Pha'raoh, upon his chariots, and upon his horsemen.
19 ¶ And the angel of God, which went before the camp of Is'ra-el, removed and went behind them; and the pillar of the cloud went from
before their face, and stood behind them:
20 And it came between the camp of the E-
gyptians and the camp of Is'ra-el; and it was a
cloud and darkness *to them*, but it gave light by
night *to these:* so that the one came not near the
other all the night.
21 And Mo'ses stretched out his hand over
the sea; and the LORD caused the sea to go *back*
by a strong east wind all that night, and made
the sea dry *land*, and the waters were divided.
22 And the children of Is'ra-el went into the
midst of the sea upon the dry *ground:* and the
waters *were* a wall unto them on their right
hand, and on their left.
23 ¶ And the E-gyptians pursued, and went
in after them to the midst of the sea, *even* all
Pha'raoh's horses, his chariots, and his horsemen.
24 And it came to pass, that in the morning
watch the LORD looked unto the host of the E-
gyptians through the pillar of fire and of the
cloud, and troubled the host of the E-gyptians,
25 And took off their chariot wheels, that
they drave them heavily: so that the E-gyptians
said, Let us flee from the face of Is'ra-el; for the
LORD fighteth for them against the E-gyptians.
26 ¶ And the LORD said unto Mo'ses, Stretch
out thine hand over the sea, that the waters
may come again upon the E-gyptians, upon
their chariots, and upon their horsemen.
27 And Mo'ses stretched forth his hand over
the sea, and the sea returned to his strength
when the morning appeared; and the E-gyptians

fled against it; and the LORD overthrew the E-
gyptians in the midst of the sea.
28 And the waters returned, and covered the
chariots, and the horsemen, *and* all the host of
Pha'raoh that came into the sea after them;
there remained not so much as one of them.
29 But the children of Is'ra-el walked upon
dry *land* in the midst of the sea; and the waters
were a wall unto them on their right hand, and
on their left.
30 Thus the LORD saved Is'ra-el that day out
of the hand of the E-gyptians; and Is'ra-el saw
the E-gyptians dead upon the sea shore.
31 And Is'ra-el saw that great work which
the LORD did upon the E-gyptians: and the people feared the LORD, and believed the LORD, and
his servant Mo'ses.

15 THEN sang Mo'ses and the children of
Is'ra-el this song unto the LORD, and
spake, saying, I will sing unto the LORD, for he
hath triumphed gloriously: the horse and his
rider hath he thrown into the sea.
2 The LORD *is* my strength and song, and he
is become my salvation: he *is* my God, and I
will prepare him an habitation; my father's
God, and I will exalt him.
3 The LORD *is* a man of war: the LORD *is* his
name.
4 Pha'raoh's chariots and his host hath he
cast into the sea: his chosen captains also are
drowned in the Red sea.
5 The depths have covered them: they sank
into the bottom as a stone.
6 Thy right hand, O LORD, is become glorious
in power: thy right hand, O LORD, hath dashed
in pieces the enemy.
7 And in the greatness of thine excellency
thou hast overthrown them that rose up against
thee: thou sentest forth thy wrath, *which* consumed them as stubble.
8 And with the blast of thy nostrils the waters were gathered together, the floods stood
upright as an heap, *and* the depths were con-
gealed in the heart of the sea.
9 The enemy said, I will pursue, I will overtake, I will divide the spoil; my lust shall be satisfied upon them; I will draw my sword, my
hand shall destroy them.
10 Thou didst blow with thy wind, the sea
covered them: they sank as lead in the mighty
waters.
11 Who *is* like unto thee, O LORD, among the
gods? who *is* like thee, glorious in holiness,
fearful *in* praises, doing wonders?
12 Thou stretchedst out thy right hand, the
earth swallowed them.
13 Thou in thy mercy hast led forth the people *which* thou hast redeemed: thou hast guided
them in thy strength unto thy holy habitation.
14 The people shall hear, *and* be afraid: sorrow shall take hold on the inhabitants of Pal-es-
ti'na.
15 Then the dukes of E'dom shall be amazed;
the mighty men of Mo'ab, trembling shall take
hold upon them; all the inhabitants of Ca'naan
shall melt away.
16 Fear and dread shall fall upon them; by
the greatness of thine arm they shall be *as* still
as a stone; till thy people pass over, O LORD, till
the people pass over, *which* thou hast purchased.
17 Thou shalt bring them in, and plant them
in the mountain of thine inheritance, *in* the
place, O LORD, *which* thou hast made for thee to
dwell in, *in* the Sanctuary, O LORD, *which* thy
hands have established.
18 The LORD shall reign for ever and ever.
19 For the horse of Pha'raoh went in with his
chariots and with his horsemen into the sea,
and the LORD brought again the waters of the
sea upon them; but the children of Is'ra-el went
on dry *land* in the midst of the sea.
20 ¶ And Mir'i-am the prophetess, the sister
of Aar'on, took a timbrel in her hand; and all the
women went out after her with timbrels and
with dances.
21 And Mir'i-am answered them, Sing ye to
the LORD, for he hath triumphed gloriously; the
horse and his rider hath he thrown into the sea.
22 So Mo'ses brought Is'ra-el from the Red
sea, and they went out into the wilderness of
Shur; and they went three days in the wilderness, and found no water.
23 ¶ And when they came to Ma'rah, they
could not drink of the waters of Ma'rah, for
they *were* bitter: therefore the name of it was
called Ma'rah.
24 And the people murmured against Mo'ses,
saying, What shall we drink?
25 And he cried unto the LORD; and the LORD
shewed him a tree, *which* when he had cast into
the waters, the waters were made sweet: there
he made for them a statute and an ordinance,
and there he proved them,
26 And said, If thou wilt diligently hearken to
the voice of the LORD thy God, and wilt do that
which is right in his sight, and wilt give ear to
his commandments, and keep all his statutes, I
will put none of these diseases upon thee, which
I have brought upon the E-gyptians: for I *am*
the LORD that healeth thee.
27 ¶ And they came to E'lim, where *were*
twelve wells of water, and threescore and ten
palm trees: and they encamped there by the waters.

16 AND they took their journey from E'-
lim, and all the congregation of the children of Is'ra-el came unto the wilderness of Sin,
which *is* between E'lim and Si'nai, on the fifteenth day of the second month after their departing out of the land of E'gypt.
2 And the whole congregation of the children
of Is'ra-el murmured against Mo'ses and Aar'on
in the wilderness:
3 And the children of Is'ra-el said unto them,
Would to God we had died by the hand of the
LORD in the land of E'gypt, when we sat by the
flesh pots, *and* when we did eat bread to the
full; for ye have brought us forth into this wilderness, to kill this whole assembly with hunger.
4 ¶ Then said the LORD unto Mo'ses, Behold,
I will rain bread from heaven for you; and the
people shall go out and gather a certain rate
every day, that I may prove them, whether they
will walk in my law, or no.
5 And it shall come to pass, that on the sixth
day they shall prepare *that* which they bring in;
and it shall be twice as much as they gather
daily.
6 And Mo'ses and Aar'on said unto all the
children of Is'ra-el, At even, then ye shall know
that the LORD hath brought you out from the
land of E'gypt:
7 And in the morning, then ye shall see the
glory of the LORD; for that he heareth your murmurings against the LORD: and what *are* we,
that ye murmur against us?
8 And Mo'ses said, *This shall be*, when the
LORD shall give you in the evening flesh to eat,
and in the morning bread to the full; for that the
LORD heareth your murmurings which ye mur-

mur against him: and what *are* we? your murmurings *are* not against us, but against the
LORD.
9 ¶ And Mo'ses spake unto Aar'on, Say unto
all the congregation of the children of Is'ra-el,
Come near before the LORD: for he hath heard
your murmurings.
10 And it came to pass, as Aar'on spake unto
the whole congregation of the children of Is'ra-
el, that they looked toward the wilderness, and,
behold, the glory of the LORD appeared in the
cloud.
11 ¶ And the LORD spake unto Mo'ses, saying,
12 I have heard the murmurings of the children of Is'ra-el: speak unto them, saying, At
even ye shall eat flesh, and in the morning ye
shall be filled with bread; and ye shall know
that I *am* the LORD your God.
13 And it came to pass, that at even the
quails came up, and covered the camp: and in
the morning the dew lay round about the host.
14 And when the dew that lay was gone up,
behold, upon the face of the wilderness *there*
lay a small round thing, *as* small as the hoar
frost on the ground.
15 And when the children of Is'ra-el saw *it*,
they said one to another, It *is* manna: for they
wist not what it *was*. And Mo'ses said unto
them, This *is* the bread which the LORD hath
given you to eat.
16 ¶ This *is* the thing which the LORD hath
commanded, Gather of it every man according
to his eating, an omer for every man, *according*
to the number of your persons; take ye every
man for *them* which *are* in his tents.
17 And the children of Is'ra-el did so, and
gathered, some more, some less.
18 And when they did mete *it* with an omer,
he that gathered much had nothing over, and he
that gathered little had no lack; they gathered
every man according to his eating.
19 And Mo'ses said, Let no man leave of it till
the morning.
20 Notwithstanding they hearkened not unto
Mo'ses; but some of them left of it until the
morning, and it bred worms, and stank: and
Mo'ses was wroth with them.
21 And they gathered it every morning, every man according to his eating: and when the
sun waxed hot, it melted.
22 ¶ And it came to pass, *that* on the sixth
day they gathered twice as much bread, two
omers for one *man:* and all the rulers of the
congregation came and told Mo'ses.
23 And he said unto them, This *is that* which
the LORD hath said, To morrow *is* the rest of the
holy sabbath unto the LORD: bake *that* which ye
will bake *to day*, and seethe that ye will seethe;
and that which remaineth over lay up for you to
be kept until the morning.
24 And they laid it up till the morning, as
Mo'ses bade: and it did not stink, neither was
there any worm therein.
25 And Mo'ses said, Eat that to day; for to
day *is* a sabbath unto the LORD: to day ye shall
not find it in the field.
26 Six days ye shall gather it; but on the seventh day, *which is* the sabbath, in it there shall
be none.
27 ¶ And it came to pass, *that* there went out
some of the people on the seventh day for to
gather, and they found none.
28 And the LORD said unto Mo'ses, How long
refuse ye to keep my commandments and my
laws?
29 See, for that the LORD hath given you the
sabbath, therefore he giveth you on the sixth
day the bread of two days; abide ye every man
in his place, let no man go out of his place on
the seventh day.
30 So the people rested on the seventh day.
31 And the house of Is'ra-el called the name
thereof Manna: and it *was* like coriander seed
white; and the taste of it *was* like wafers *made*
with honey.
32 ¶ And Mo'ses said, This *is* the thing
which the LORD commandeth, Fill an omer of it
to be kept for your generations; that they may
see the bread wherewith I have fed you in the
wilderness, when I brought you forth from the
land of E'gypt.
33 And Mo'ses said unto Aar'on, Take a pot
and put an omer full of manna therein, and lay
it up before the LORD, to be kept for your generations.
34 As the LORD commanded Mo'ses, so Aar'-
on laid it up before the Testimony, to be kept.
35 And the children of Is'ra-el did eat manna
forty years, until they came to a land inhabited;
they did eat manna, until they came unto the
borders of the land of Ca'naan.
36 Now an omer *is* the tenth *part* of an e-
phah.

17 AND all the congregation of the children of Is'ra-el journeyed from the wilderness of Sin, after their journeys, according
to the commandment of the LORD, and pitched
in Reph'i-dim: and *there was* no water for the
people to drink.
2 Wherefore the people did chide with Mo'-
ses, and said, Give us water that we may drink.
And Mo'ses said unto them, Why chide ye with
me? wherefore do ye tempt the LORD?
3 And the people thirsted there for water;
and the people murmured against Mo'ses, and
said, Wherefore *is* this *that* thou hast brought
us up out of E'gypt, to kill us and our children
and our cattle with thirst?
4 And Mo'ses cried unto the LORD, saying,
What shall I do unto this people? they be almost
ready to stone me.
5 And the LORD said unto Mo'ses, Go on before the people, and take with thee of the elders
of Is'ra-el; and thy rod, wherewith thou smotest
the river, take in thine hand, and go.
6 Behold, I will stand before thee there upon
the rock in Ho'reb; and thou shalt smite the
rock, and there shall come water out of it, that
the people may drink. And Mo'ses did so in the
sight of the elders of Is'ra-el.
7 And he called the name of the place Mas'-
sah, and Mer'i-bah, because of the chiding of
the children of Is'ra-el, and because they
tempted the LORD, saying, Is the LORD among
us, or not?
8 ¶ Then came Am'a-lek, and fought with
Is'ra-el in Reph'i-dim.
9 And Mo'ses said unto Josh'u-a, Choose us
out men, and go out, fight with Am'a-lek: to
morrow I will stand on the top of the hill with
the rod of God in mine hand.
10 So Josh'u-a did as Mo'ses had said to him,
and fought with Am'a-lek: and Mo'ses, Aar'on,
and Hur went up to the top of the hill.
11 And it came to pass, when Mo'ses held up
his hand, that Is'ra-el prevailed: and when he let
down his hand, Am'a-lek prevailed.
12 But Mo'ses' hands *were* heavy; and they
took a stone, and put *it* under him, ahd he sat
thereon; and Aar'on and Hur stayed up his
hands, the one on the one side, and the other on

the other side; and his hands were steady until the going down of the sun.

13 And Josh'u-a discomfited Am'a-lek and his people with the edge of the sword.

14 And the LORD said unto Mo'ses, Write this *for* a memorial in a book, and rehearse *it* in the ears of Josh'u-a: for I will utterly put out the remembrance of Am'a-lek from under heaven.

15 And Mo'ses built an altar, and called the name of it Je-ho'vah–nis'si:

16 For he said, Because the LORD hath sworn *that* the LORD *will have* war with Am'a-lek from generation to generation.

18 WHEN Je'thro, the priest of Mid'i-an, Mo'ses' father in law, heard of all that God had done for Mo'ses, and for Is'ra-el his people, *and* that the LORD had brought Is'ra-el out of E'gypt;

2 Then Je'thro, Mo'ses' father in law, took Zip-po'rah, Mo'ses' wife, after he had sent her back,

3 And her two sons; of which the name of the one *was* Ger'shom; for he said, I have been an alien in a strange land:

4 And the name of the other *was* E-li-e'zer; for the God of my father, *said he, was* mine help, and delivered me from the sword of Pha'-raoh:

5 And Je'thro, Mo'ses' father in law, came with his sons and his wife unto Mo'ses into the wilderness, where he encamped at the mount of God:

6 And he said unto Mo'ses, I thy father in law Je'thro am come unto thee, and thy wife, and her two sons with her.

7 ¶ And Mo'ses went out to meet his father in law, and did obeisance, and kissed him; and they asked each other of *their* welfare; and they came into the tent.

8 And Mo'ses told his father in law all that the LORD had done unto Pha'raoh and to the E-gyptians for Is'ra-el's sake, *and* all the travail that had come upon them by the way, and *how* the LORD delivered them.

9 And Je'thro rejoiced for all the goodness which the LORD had done to Is'ra-el, whom he had delivered out of the hand of the E-gyptians.

10 And Je'thro said, Blessed *be* the LORD, who hath delivered you out of the hand of the E-gyptians, and out of the hand of Pha'raoh, who hath delivered the people from under the hand of the E-gyptians.

11 Now I know that the LORD *is* greater than all gods: for in the thing wherein they dealt proudly *he was* above them.

12 And Je'thro, Mo'ses' father in law, took a burnt offering and sacrifices for God: and Aar'-on came, and all the elders of Is'ra-el, to eat bread with Mo'ses' father in law before God.

13 ¶ And it came to pass on the morrow, that Mo'ses sat to judge the people: and the people stood by Mo'ses from the morning unto the evening.

14 And when Mo'ses' father in law saw all that he did to the people, he said, What *is* this thing that thou doest to the people? why sittest thou thyself alone, and all the people stand by thee from morning unto even?

15 And Mo'ses said unto his father in law, Because the people come unto me to enquire of God:

16 When they have a matter, they come unto me; and I judge between one and another, and I do make *them* know the statutes of God, and his laws.

17 And Mo'ses' father in law said unto him, The thing that thou doest *is* not good.

18 Thou wilt surely wear away, both thou, and this people that *is* with thee: for this thing *is* too heavy for thee; thou art not able to perform it thyself alone.

19 Hearken now unto my voice, I will give thee counsel, and God shall be with thee: be thou for the people to God-ward, that thou mayest bring the causes unto God:

20 And thou shalt teach them ordinances and laws, and shalt shew them the way wherein they must walk, and the work that they must do.

21 Moreover thou shalt provide out of all the people able men, such as fear God, men of truth, hating covetousness; and place *such* over them, *to be* rulers of thousands, *and* rulers of hundreds, rulers of fifties, and rulers of tens.

22 And let them judge the people at all seasons: and it shall be, *that* every great matter they shall bring unto thee, but every small matter they shall judge: so shall it be easier for thyself, and they shall bear *the burden* with thee.

23 If thou shalt do this thing, and God command thee *so*, then thou shalt be able to endure, and all this people shall also go to their place in peace.

24 So Mo'ses hearkened to the voice of his father in law, and did all that he had said.

25 And Mo'ses chose able men out of all Is'-ra-el, and made them heads over the people, rulers of thousands, rulers of hundreds, rulers of fifties, and rulers of tens.

26 And they judged the people at all seasons: the hard causes they brought unto Mo'ses, but every small matter they judged themselves.

27 ¶ And Mo'ses let his father in law depart; and he went his way into his own land.

19 IN the third month, when the children of Is'ra-el were gone forth out of the land of E'gypt, the same day came they *into* the wilderness of Si'nai.

2 For they were departed from Reph'i-dim, and were come *to* the desert of Si'nai, and had pitched in the wilderness; and there Is'ra-el camped before the mount.

3 And Mo'ses went up unto God, and the LORD called unto him out of the mountain, saying, Thus shalt thou say to the house of Ja'cob, and tell the children of Is'ra-el;

4 Ye have seen what I did unto the E-gyptians, and *how* I bare you on eagles' wings, and brought you unto myself.

5 Now therefore, if ye will obey my voice indeed, and keep my covenant, then ye shall be a peculiar treasure unto me above all people: for all the earth *is* mine:

6 And ye shall be unto me a kingdom of priests, and an holy nation. These *are* the words which thou shalt speak unto the children of Is'-ra-el.

7 ¶ And Mo'ses came and called for the elders of the people, and laid before their faces all these words which the LORD commanded him.

8 And all the people answered together, and said, All that the LORD hath spoken we will do. And Mo'ses returned the words of the people unto the LORD.

9 And the LORD said unto Mo'ses, Lo, I come unto thee in a thick cloud, that the people may hear when I speak with thee, and believe thee for ever. And Mo'ses told the words of the people unto the LORD.

10 ¶ And the LORD said unto Mo'ses, Go

unto the people, and sanctify them to day and
to morrow, and let them wash their clothes,
11 And be ready against the third day: for
the third day the LORD will come down in the
sight of all the people upon mount Si'nai.
12 And thou shalt set bounds unto the people
round about, saying, Take heed to yourselves,
that ye go *not* up into the mount, or touch the
border of it: whosoever toucheth the mount
shall be surely put to death:
13 There shall not an hand touch it, but he
shall surely be stoned, or shot through; whether
it be beast or man, it shall not live: when the
trumpet soundeth long, they shall come up to
the mount.
14 ¶ And Mo'ses went down from the mount
unto the people, and sanctified the people; and
they washed their clothes.
15 And he said unto the people, Be ready
against the third day: come not at *your* wives.
16 ¶ And it came to pass on the third day in
the morning, that there were thunders and
lightnings, and a thick cloud upon the mount,
and the voice of the trumpet exceeding loud; so
that all the people that *was* in the camp trembled.
17 And Mo'ses brought forth the people out
of the camp to meet with God; and they stood
at the nether part of the mount.
18 And mount Si'nai was altogether on a
smoke, because the LORD descended upon it in
fire: and the smoke thereof ascended as the
smoke of a furnace, and the whole mount
quaked greatly.
19 And when the voice of the trumpet
sounded long, and waxed louder and louder,
Mo'ses spake, and God answered him by a
voice.
20 And the LORD came down upon mount Si'-
nai, on the top of the mount: and the LORD
called Mo'ses *up* to the top of the mount; and
Mo'ses went up.
21 And the LORD said unto Mo'ses, Go down,
charge the people, lest they break through unto
the LORD to gaze, and many of them perish.
22 And let the priests also, which come near
to the LORD, sanctify themselves, lest the LORD
break forth upon them.
23 And Mo'ses said unto the LORD, The people cannot come up to mount Si'nai: for thou
chargedst us, saying, Set bounds about the
mount, and sanctify it.
24 And the LORD said unto him, Away, get
thee down, and thou shalt come up, thou, and
Aar'on with thee: but let not the priests and the
people break through to come up unto the
LORD, lest he break forth upon them.
25 So Mo'ses went down unto the people,
and spake unto them.

20

AND God spake all these words, saying,
2 I *am* the LORD thy God, which have
brought thee out of the land of E'gypt, out of
the house of bondage.
3 Thou shalt have no other gods before me.
4 Thou shalt not make unto thee any graven
image, or any likeness *of any thing* that *is* in
heaven above, or that *is* in the earth beneath, or
that *is* in the water under earth:
5 Thou shalt not bow down thyself to them,
nor serve them: for I the LORD thy God *am* a
jealous God, visiting the iniquity of the fathers
upon the children unto the third and fourth *generation* of them that hate me;
6 And shewing mercy unto thousands of
them that love me, and keep my commandments.
7 Thou shalt not take the name of the LORD
thy God in vain; for the LORD will not hold him
guiltless that taketh his name in vain.
8 Remember the sabbath day, to keep it holy.
9 Six days shalt thou labour, and do all thy
work:
10 But the seventh day *is* the sabbath of the
LORD thy God: *in it* thou shalt not do any work,
thou, nor thy son, nor thy daughter, thy manservant, nor thy maidservant, nor thy cattle, nor
thy stranger that *is* within thy gates:
11 For *in* six days the LORD made heaven and
earth, the sea, and all that in them *is*, and rested
the seventh day: wherefore the LORD blessed
the sabbath day, and hallowed it.
12 ¶ Honour thy father and thy mother: that
thy days may be long upon the land which the
LORD thy God giveth thee.
13 Thou shalt not kill.
14 Thou shalt not commit adultery.
15 Thou shalt not steal.
16 Thou shalt not bear false witness against
thy neighbour.
17 Thou shalt not covet thy neighbour's
house, thou shalt not covet thy neighbour's
wife, nor his manservant, nor his maidservant,
nor his ox, nor his ass, nor any thing that *is* thy
neighbour's.
18 ¶ And all the people saw the thunderings,
and the lightnings, and the noise of the trumpet,
and the mountain smoking: and when the people saw *it*, they removed, and stood afar off.
19 And they said unto Mo'ses, Speak thou
with us, and we will hear: but let not God speak
with us, lest we die.
20 And Mo'ses said unto the people, Fear
not: for God is come to prove you, and that his
fear may be before your faces, that ye sin not.
21 And the people stood afar off, and Mo'ses
drew near unto the thick darkness where God
was.
22 ¶ And the LORD said unto Mo'ses, Thus
thou shalt say unto the children of Is'ra-el, Ye
have seen that I have talked with you from
heaven.
23 Ye shall not make with me gods of silver,
neither shall ye make unto you gods of gold.
24 ¶ An altar of earth thou shalt make unto
me, and shalt sacrifice thereon thy burnt offerings, and thy peace offerings, thy sheep, and
thine oxen: in all places where I record my
name I will come unto thee, and I will bless
thee.
25 And if thou wilt make me an altar of
stone, thou shalt not build it of hewn stone: for
if thou lift up thy tool upon it, thou hast polluted it.
26 Neither shalt thou go up by steps unto
mine altar, that thy nakedness be not discovered thereon.

21

NOW these *are* the judgments which
thou shalt set before them.
2 If thou buy an He'brew servant, six years
he shall serve: and in the seventh he shall go out
free for nothing.
3 If he came in by himself, he shall go out by
himself: if he were married, then his wife shall
go out with him.
4 If his master have given him a wife, and
she have born him sons or daughters; the wife
and her children shall be her master's, and he
shall go out by himself.
5 And if the servant shall plainly say, I love
my master, my wife, and my children; I will not
go out free:
6 Then his master shall bring him unto the

judges; he shall also bring him to the door, or
unto the door post; and his master shall bore his
ear through with an aul; and he shall serve him
for ever.
7 ¶ And if a man sell his daughter to be a
maidservant, she shall not go out as the menservants do.
8 If she please not her master, who hath betrothed her to himself, then shall he let her be
redeemed: to sell her unto a strange nation he
shall have no power, seeing he hath dealt deceitfully with her.
9 And if he have betrothed her unto his son,
he shall deal with her after the manner of
daughters.
10 If he take him another *wife:* her food, her
raiment, and her duty of marriage, shall he not
diminish.
11 And if he do not these three unto her, then
shall she go out free without money.
12 ¶ He that smiteth a man, so that he die,
shall be surely put to death.
13 And if a man lie not in wait, but God deliver *him* into his hand; then I will appoint thee
a place whither he shall flee.
14 But if a man come presumptuously upon
his neighbour, to slay him with guile; thou shalt
take him from mine altar, that he may die.
15 ¶ And he that smiteth his father, or his
mother, shall be surely put to death.
16 ¶ And he that stealeth a man, and selleth
him, or if he be found in his hand, he shall
surely be put to death.
17 ¶ And he that curseth his father, or his
mother, shall surely be put to death.
18 ¶ And if men strive together, and one
smite another with a stone, or with *his* fist, and
he die not, but keepeth *his* bed:
19 If he rise again, and walk abroad upon his
staff, then shall he that smote *him* be quit: only
he shall pay *for* the loss of his time, and shall
cause *him* to be thoroughly healed.
20 ¶ And if a man smite his servant, or his
maid, with a rod, and he die under his hand; he
shall be surely punished.
21 Notwithstanding, if he continue a day or
two, he shall not be punished: for he *is* his money.
22 ¶ If men strive, and hurt a woman with
child, so that her fruit depart *from her,* and yet
no mischief follow: he shall be surely punished,
according as the woman's husband will lay
upon him; and he shall pay as the judges *deter-
mine.*
23 And if *any* mischief follow, then thou
shalt give life for life,
24 Eye for eye, tooth for tooth, hand for
hand, foot for foot,
25 Burning for burning, wound for wound,
stripe for stripe.
26 ¶ And if a man smite the eye of his servant, or the eye of his maid, that it perish; he
shall let him go free for his eye's sake.
27 And if he smite out his manservant's
tooth, or his maidservant's tooth; he shall let
him go free for his tooth's sake.
28 ¶ If an ox gore a man or a woman, that
they die: then the ox shall be surely stoned, and
his flesh shall not be eaten; but the owner of the
ox *shall be* quit.
29 But if the ox were wont to push with his
horn in time past, and it hath been testified to
his owner, and he hath not kept him in, but that
he hath killed a man or a woman; the ox shall
be stoned, and his owner also shall be put to
death.
30 If there be laid on him a sum of money,
then he shall give for the ransom of his life
whatsoever is laid upon him.
31 Whether he have gored a son, or have
gored a daughter, according to this judgment
shall it be done unto him.
32 If the ox shall push a manservant or a
maidservant; he shall give unto their master
thirty shekels of silver, and the ox shall be
stoned.
33 ¶ And if a man shall open a pit, or if a
man shall dig a pit, and not cover it, and an ox
or an ass fall therein;
34 The owner of the pit shall make *it* good,
and give money unto the owner of them; and
the dead *beast* shall be his.
35 ¶ And if one man's ox hurt another's, that
he die; then they shall sell the live ox, and divide the money of it; and the dead *ox* also they
shall divide.
36 Or if it be known that the ox hath used to
push in time past, and his owner hath not kept
him in; he shall surely pay ox for ox; and the
dead shall be his own.

22 IF a man shall steal an ox, or a sheep,
and kill it, or sell it; he shall restore five
oxen for an ox, and four sheep for a sheep.
2 ¶ If a thief be found breaking up, and be
smitten that he die, *there shall* no blood *be shed*
for him.
3 If the sun be risen upon him, *there shall be*
blood *shed* for him; *for* he should make full restitution; if he have nothing, then he shall be sold
for his theft.
4 If the theft be certainly found in his hand
alive, whether it be ox, or ass, or sheep; he shall
restore double.
5 ¶ If a man shall cause a field or vineyard to
be eaten, and shall put in his beast, and shall
feed in another man's field; of the best of his
own field, and of the best of his own vineyard,
shall he make restitution.
6 ¶ If fire break out, and catch in thorns, so
that the stacks of corn, or the standing corn, or
the field, be consumed *therewith;* he that kindled the fire shall surely make restitution.
7 ¶ If a man shall deliver unto his neighbour
money or stuff to keep, and it be stolen out of
the man's house; if the thief be found, let him
pay double.
8 If the thief be not found, then the master of
the house shall be brought unto the judges, *to
see* whether he have put his hand unto his
neighbour's goods.
9 For all manner of trespass, *whether it be*
for ox, for ass, for sheep, for raiment, *or* for any
manner of lost thing, which *another* challeng-
eth to be his, the cause of both parties shall
come before the judges; *and* whom the judges
shall condemn, he shall pay double unto his
neighbour.
10 If a man deliver unto his neighbour an ass,
or an ox, or a sheep, or any beast, to keep; and
it die, or be hurt, or driven away, no man seeing
it:
11 *Then* shall an oath of the LORD be between
them both, that he hath not put his hand unto
his neighbour's goods; and the owner of it shall
accept *thereof,* and he shall not make *it* good.
12 And if it be stolen from him, he shall
make restitution unto the owner thereof.
13 If it be torn in pieces, *then* let him bring it
for witness, *and* he shall not make good that
which was torn.
14 ¶ And if a man borrow *ought* of his neighbour, and it be hurt, or die, the owner thereof
being not with it, he shall surely make *it* good.

15 *But* if the owner thereof *be* with it, he
shall not make *it* good: if it *be* an hired *thing*, it
came for his hire.
16 ¶ And if a man entice a maid that is not
betrothed, and lie with her, he shall surely en-
dow her to be his wife.
17 If her father utterly refuse to give her unto
him, he shall pay money according to the dowry
of virgins.
18 ¶ Thou shalt not suffer a witch to live.
19 ¶ Whosoever lieth with a beast shall
surely be put to death.
20 ¶ He that sacrificeth unto *any* god, save
unto the LORD only, he shall be utterly destroyed.
21 ¶ Thou shalt neither vex a stranger, nor
oppress him: for ye were strangers in the land
of E'gypt.
22 ¶ Ye shall not afflict any widow, or fatherless child.
23 If thou afflict them in any wise, and they
cry at all unto me, I will surely hear their cry;
24 And my wrath shall wax hot, and I will
kill you with the sword; and your wives shall be
widows, and your children fatherless.
25 ¶ If thou lend money to *any of* my people
that is poor by thee, thou shalt not be to him as
an usurer, neither shalt thou lay upon him
usury.
26 If thou at all take thy neighbour's raiment
to pledge, thou shalt deliver it unto him by that
the sun goeth down:
27 For that *is* his covering only, it *is* his raiment for his skin: wherein shall he sleep? and it
shall come to pass, when he crieth unto me,
that I will hear; for I *am* gracious.
28 ¶ Thou shalt not revile the gods, nor curse
the ruler of thy people.
29 ¶ Thou shalt not delay *to offer* the first of
thy ripe fruits, and of thy liquors: the first born
of thy sons shalt thou give unto me.
30 Likewise shalt thou do with thine oxen,
and with thy sheep: seven days it shall be with
his dam; on the eighth day thou shalt give it me.
31 ¶ And ye shall be holy men unto me: neither shall ye eat *any* flesh *that is* torn of beasts
in the field; ye shall cast it to the dogs.

23 THOU shalt not raise a false report: put
not thine hand with the wicked to be an
unrighteous witness.
2 ¶ Thou shalt not follow a multitude to *do*
evil; neither shalt thou speak in a cause to decline after many to wrest *judgment:*
3 ¶ Neither shalt thou countenance a poor
man in his cause.
4 ¶ If thou meet thine enemy's ox or his ass
going astray, thou shalt surely bring it back to
him again.
5 If thou see the ass of him that hateth thee
lying under his burden, and wouldest forbear to
help him, thou shalt surely help with him.
6 Thou shalt not wrest the judgment of thy
poor in his cause.
7 Keep thee far from a false matter; and the
innocent and righteous slay thou not: for I will
not justify the wicked.
8 ¶ And thou shalt take no gift: for the gift
blindeth the wise, and perverteth the words of
the righteous.
9 ¶ Also thou shalt not oppress a stranger:
for ye know the heart of a stranger, seeing ye
were strangers in the land of E'gypt.
10 And six years thou shalt sow thy land, and
shalt gather in the fruits thereof:
11 But the seventh *year* thou shalt let it rest
and lie still; that the poor of thy people may eat:
and what they leave the beasts of the field shall
eat. In like manner thou shalt deal with thy
vineyard, *and* with thy oliveyard.
12 Six days thou shalt do thy work, and on
the seventh day thou shalt rest: that thine ox
and thine ass may rest, and the son of thy handmaid, and the stranger, may be refreshed.
13 And in all *things* that I have said unto you
be circumspect: and make no mention of the
name of other gods, neither let it be heard out
of thy mouth.
14 ¶ Three times thou shalt keep a feast unto
me in the year.
15 Thou shalt keep the feast of unleavened
bread: (thou shalt eat unleavened bread seven
days, as I commanded thee, in the time appointed of the month A'bib; for in it thou camest out from E'gypt: and none shall appear before me empty:)
16 And the feast of harvest, the firstfruits of
thy labours, which thou hast sown in the field:
and the feast of ingathering, *which is* in the end
of the year, when thou hast gathered in thy labours out of the field.
17 Three times in the year all thy males shall
appear before the Lord GOD.
18 Thou shalt not offer the blood of my sacrifice with leavened bread; neither shall the fat of
my sacrifice remain until the morning.
19 The first of the firstfruits of thy land thou
shalt bring into the house of the LORD thy God.
Thou shalt not seethe a kid in his mother's milk.
20 ¶ Behold, I send an Angel before thee, to
keep thee in the way, and to bring thee into the
place which I have prepared.
21 Beware of him, and obey his voice, provoke him not; for he will not pardon your transgressions: for my name *is* in him.
22 But if thou shalt indeed obey his voice,
and do all that I speak; then I will be an enemy
unto thine enemies, and an adversary unto
thine adversaries.
23 For mine Angel shall go before thee, and
bring thee in unto the Am'or-ites, and the Hit'-
tites, and the Per'iz-zites, and the Ca'naan-ites,
and Hi'vites, and the Jeb'u-sites: and I will cut
them off.
24 Thou shalt not bow down to their gods,
nor serve them, nor do after their works: but
thou shalt utterly overthrow them, and quite
break down their images.
25 And ye shall serve the LORD your God,
and he shall bless thy bread, and thy water; and
I will take sickness away from the midst of
thee.
26 ¶ There shall nothing cast their young,
nor be barren, in thy land: the number of thy
days I will fulfil.
27 I will send my fear before thee, and will
destroy all the people to whom thou shalt come,
and I will make all thine enemies turn their
backs unto thee.
28 And I will send hornets before thee, which
shall drive out the Hi'vite, the Ca'naan-ite, and
the Hit'tite, from before thee.
29 I will not drive them out from before thee
in one year; lest the land become desolate, and
the beast of the field multiply against thee.
30 By little and little I will drive them out
from before thee, until thou be increased, and
inherit the land.
31 And I will set thy bounds from the Red
sea even unto the sea of the Phi-lis'tines, and
from the desert unto the river: for I will deliver
the inhabitants of the land into your hand; and
thou shalt drive them out before thee.

32 Thou shalt make no covenant with them, nor with their gods.

33 They shall not dwell in thy land, lest they make thee sin against me: for if thou serve their gods, it will surely be a snare unto thee.

24 AND he said unto Mo'ses, Come up unto the LORD, thou, and Aar'on, Na'dab, and A-bi'hu, and seventy of the elders of Is'ra-el; and worship ye afar off.

2 And Mo'ses alone shall come near the LORD: but they shall not come nigh; neither shall the people go up with him.

3 ¶ And Mo'ses came and told the people all the words of the LORD, and all the judgments: and all the people answered with one voice, and said, All the words which the LORD hath said will we do.

4 And Mo'ses wrote all the words of the LORD, and rose up early in the morning, and builded an altar under the hill, and twelve pillars, according to the twelve tribes of Is'ra-el.

5 And he sent young men of the children of Is'ra-el, which offered burnt offerings, and sacrificed peace offerings of oxen unto the LORD.

6 And Mo'ses took half of the blood, and put *it* in basons; and half of the blood he sprinkled on the altar.

7 And he took the book of the covenant, and read in the audience of the people: and they said, All that the LORD hath said will we do, and be obedient.

8 And Mo'ses took the blood, and sprinkled *it* on the people, and said, Behold the blood of the covenant, which the LORD hath made with you concerning all these words.

9 ¶ Then went up Mo'ses, and Aar'on, Na'dab, and A-bi'hu, and seventy of the elders of Is'ra-el:

10 And they saw the God of Is'ra-el: and *there was* under his feet as it were a paved work of a sapphire stone, and as it were the body of heaven in *his* clearness.

11 And upon the nobles of the children of Is'ra-el he laid not his hand: also they saw God, and did eat and drink.

12 ¶ And the LORD said unto Mo'ses, Come up to me into the mount, and be there: and I will give thee tables of stone, and a law, and commandments which I have written; that thou mayest teach them.

13 And Mo'ses rose up, and his minister Josh'u-a: and Mo'ses went up into the mount of God.

14 And he said unto the elders, Tarry ye here for us, until we come again unto you: and, behold, Aar'on and Hur *are* with you: if any man have any matters to do, let him come unto them.

15 And Mo'ses went up into the mount, and a cloud covered the mount.

16 And the glory of the LORD abode upon mount Si'nai, and the cloud covered it six days: and the seventh day he called unto Mo'ses out of the midst of the cloud.

17 And the sight of the glory of the LORD *was* like devouring fire on the top of the mount in the eyes of the children of Is'ra-el.

18 And Mo'ses went into the midst of the cloud, and gat him up into the mount: and Mo'ses was in the mount forty days and forty nights.

25 AND the LORD spake unto Mo'ses, saying,

2 Speak unto the children of Is'ra-el, that they bring me an offering: of every man that giveth it willingly with his heart ye shall take my offering.

3 And this *is* the offering which ye shall take of them; gold, and silver, and brass,

4 And blue, and purple, and scarlet, and fine linen, and goats' *hair,*

5 And rams' skins dyed red, and badgers' skins, and shittim wood,

6 Oil for the light, spices for anointing oil, and for sweet incense,

7 Onyx stones, and stones to be set in the ephod, and in the breastplate.

8 And let them make me a sanctuary; that I may dwell among them.

9 According to all that I shew thee, *after* the pattern of the tabernacle, and the pattern of all the instruments thereof, even so shall ye make *it.*

10 ¶ And they shall make an ark *of* shittim wood: two cubits and a half *shall be* the length thereof, and a cubit and a half the breadth thereof, and a cubit and a half the height thereof.

11 And thou shalt overlay it with pure gold, within and without shalt thou overlay it, and shalt make upon it a crown of gold round about.

12 And thou shalt cast four rings of gold for it, and put *them* in the four corners thereof; and two rings *shall be* in the one side of it, and two rings in the other side of it.

13 And thou shalt make staves *of* shittim wood, and overlay them with gold.

14 And thou shalt put the staves into the rings by the sides of the ark, that the ark may be borne with them.

15 The staves shall be in the rings of the ark: they shall not be taken from it.

16 And thou shalt put into the ark the testimony which I shall give thee.

17 And thou shalt make a mercy seat *of* pure gold: two cubits and a half *shall be* the length thereof, and a cubit and a half the breadth thereof.

18 And thou shalt make two cherubims *of* gold, *of* beaten work shalt thou make them, in the two ends of the mercy seat.

19 And make one cherub on the one end, and the other cherub on the other end: *even* of the mercy seat shall ye make the cherubims on the two ends thereof.

20 And the cherubims shall stretch forth *their* wings on high, covering the mercy seat with their wings, and their faces *shall look* one to another; toward the mercy seat shall the faces of the cherubims be.

21 And thou shalt put the mercy seat above upon the ark; and in the ark thou shalt put the testimony that I shall give thee.

22 And there I will meet with thee, and I will commune with thee from above the mercy seat, from between the two cherubims which *are* upon the ark of the testimony, of all *things* which I will give thee in commandment unto the children of Is'ra-el.

23 ¶ Thou shalt also make a table *of* shittim wood: two cubits *shall be* the length thereof, and a cubit the breadth thereof, and a cubit and a half the height thereof.

24 And thou shalt overlay it with pure gold, and make thereto a crown of gold round about.

25 And thou shalt make unto it a border of an hand breadth round about, and thou shalt make a golden crown to the border thereof round about.

26 And thou shalt make for it four rings of gold, and put the rings in the four corners that *are* on the four feet thereof.

27 Over against the border shall the rings be
for places of the staves to bear the table.
28 And thou shalt make the staves *of* shittim
wood, and overlay them with gold, that the table may be borne with them.
29 And thou shalt make the dishes thereof,
and spoons thereof, and covers thereof, and
bowls thereof, to cover withal: *of* pure gold
shalt thou make them.
30 And thou shalt set upon the table shewbread before me alway.
31 ¶ And thou shalt make a candlestick *of*
pure gold: *of* beaten work shall the candlestick
be made: his shaft, and his branches, his bowls,
his knops, and his flowers, shall be of the same.
32 And six branches shall come out of the
sides of it; three branches of the candlestick out
of the one side, and three branches of the candlestick out of the other side:
33 Three bowls made like unto almonds,
with a knop and a flower in one branch; and
three bowls made like almonds in the other
branch, *with* a knop and a flower: so in the six
branches that come out of the candlestick.
34 And in the candlestick *shall be* four bowls
made like unto almonds, *with* their knops and
their flowers.
35 And *there shall be* a knop under two
branches of the same, and a knop under two
branches of the same, and a knop under two
branches of the same, according to the six
branches that proceed out of the candlestick.
36 Their knops and their branches shall be of
the same: all it *shall be* one beaten work *of* pure
gold.
37 And thou shalt make the seven lamps
thereof: and they shall light the lamps thereof,
that they may give light over against it.
38 And the tongs thereof, and the snuffdishes
thereof, *shall be of* pure gold.
39 *Of* a talent of pure gold shall he make it,
with all these vessels.
40 And look that thou make *them* after their
pattern, which was shewed thee in the mount.

26 MOREOVER thou shalt make the tabernacle *with* ten curtains *of* fine twined
linen, and blue, and purple, and scarlet: *with*
cherubims of cunning work shalt thou make
them.
2 The length of one curtain *shall be* eight and
twenty cubits, and the breadth of one curtain
four cubits: and every one of the curtains shall
have one measure.
3 The five curtains shall be coupled together
one to another; and *other* five curtains *shall be*
coupled one to another.
4 And thou shalt make loops of blue upon the
edge of the one curtain from the selvedge in the
coupling; and likewise shalt thou make in the
uttermost edge of *another* curtain, in the coupling of the second.
5 Fifty loops shalt thou make in the one curtain, and fifty loops shalt thou make in the edge
of the curtain that *is* in the coupling of the second; that the loops may take hold one of another.
6 And thou shalt make fifty taches of gold,
and couple the curtains together with the
taches: and it shall be one tabernacle.
7 ¶ And thou shalt make curtains *of* goats'
hair to be a covering upon the tabernacle:
eleven curtains shalt thou make.
8 The length of one curtain *shall be* thirty cubits, and the breadth of one curtain four cubits:
and the eleven curtains *shall be all* of one measure.
9 And thou shalt couple five curtains by
themselves, and six curtains by themselves, and
shalt double the sixth curtain in the forefront of
the tabernacle.
10 And thou shalt make fifty loops on the
edge of the one curtain *that is* outmost in the
coupling, and fifty loops in the edge of the curtain which coupleth the second.
11 And thou shalt make fifty taches of brass,
and put the taches into the loops, and couple
the tent together, that it may be one.
12 And the remnant that remaineth of the
curtains of the tent, the half curtain that remaineth, shall hang over the backside of the
tabernacle.
13 And a cubit on the one side, and a cubit on
the other side of that which remaineth in the
length of the curtains of the tent, it shall hang
over the sides of the tabernacle on this side and
on that side, to cover it.
14 And thou shalt make a covering for the
tent *of* rams' skins dyed red, and a covering
above *of* badgers' skins.
15 ¶ And thou shalt make boards for the tabernacle *of* shittim wood standing up.
16 Ten cubits *shall be* the length of a board,
and a cubit and a half *shall be* the breadth of
one board.
17 Two tenons *shall there be* in one board,
set in order one against another: thus shalt thou
make for all the boards of the tabernacle.
18 And thou shalt make the boards for the
tabernacle, twenty boards on the south side
southward.
19 And thou shalt make forty sockets of silver under the twenty boards; two sockets under
one board for his two tenons, and two sockets
under another board for his two tenons.
20 And for the second side of the tabernacle
on the north side *there shall be* twenty boards:
21 And their forty sockets *of* silver; two
sockets under one board, and two sockets under another board.
22 And for the sides of the tabernacle westward thou shalt make six boards.
23 And two boards shalt thou make for the
corners of the tabernacle in the two sides.
24 And they shall be coupled together beneath, and they shall be coupled together above
the head of it unto one ring: thus shall it be for
them both; they shall be for the two corners.
25 And they shall be eight boards, and their
sockets *of* silver, sixteen sockets; two sockets
under one board, and two sockets under another board.
26 ¶ And thou shalt make bars *of* shittim
wood; five for the boards of the one side of the
tabernacle,
27 And five bars for the boards of the other
side of the tabernacle, and five bars for the
boards of the side of the tabernacle, for the two
sides westward.
28 And the middle bar in the midst of the
boards shall reach from end to end.
29 And thou shalt overlay the boards with
gold, and make their rings *of* gold *for* places for
the bars: and thou shalt overlay the bars with
gold.
30 And thou shalt rear up the tabernacle according to the fashion thereof which was
shewed thee in the mount.
31 ¶ And thou shalt make a veil *of* blue, and
purple, and scarlet, and fine twined linen of
cunning work: with cherubims shall it be made:
32 And thou shalt hang it upon four pillars of
shittim *wood* overlaid with gold: their hooks
shall be of gold, upon the four sockets of silver.

33 ¶ And thou shalt hang up the veil under the taches, that thou mayest bring in thither within the veil the ark of the testimony: and the veil shall divide unto you between the holy *place* and the most holy.

34 And thou shalt put the mercy seat upon the ark of the testimony in the most holy *place*.

35 And thou shalt set the table without the veil, and the candlestick over against the table on the side of the tabernacle toward the south: and thou shalt put the table on the north side.

36 And thou shalt make an hanging for the door of the tent, *of* blue, and purple, and scarlet, and fine twined linen, wrought with needle work.

37 And thou shalt make for the hanging five pillars *of* shittim *wood*, and overlay them with gold, *and* their hooks *shall be of* gold: and thou shalt cast five sockets of brass for them.

27 AND thou shalt make an altar *of* shittim wood, five cubits long, and five cubits broad; the altar shall be foursquare: and the height thereof *shall be* three cubits.

2 And thou shalt make the horns of it upon the four corners thereof: his horns shall be of the same: and thou shalt overlay it with brass.

3 And thou shalt make his pans to receive his ashes, and his shovels, and his basons, and his fleshhooks, and his firepans: all the vessels thereof thou shalt make *of* brass.

4 And thou shalt make for it a grate of network *of* brass; and upon the net shalt thou make four brasen rings in the four corners thereof.

5 And thou shalt put it under the compass of the altar beneath, that the net may be even to the midst of the altar.

6 And thou shalt make staves for the altar, staves *of* shittim wood, and overlay them with brass.

7 And the staves shall be put into the rings, and the staves shall be upon the two sides of the altar, to bear it.

8 Hollow with boards shalt thou make it: as it was shewed thee in the mount, so shall they make *it*.

9 ¶ And thou shalt make the court of the tabernacle: for the south side southward *there shall be* hangings for the court *of* fine twined linen of an hundred cubits long for one side:

10 And the twenty pillars thereof and their twenty sockets *shall be of* brass; the hooks of the pillars and their fillets *shall be of* silver.

11 And likewise for the north side in length *there shall be* hangings of an hundred *cubits* long, and his twenty pillars and their twenty sockets *of* brass; the hooks of the pillars and their fillets *of* silver.

12 ¶ And *for* the breadth of the court on the west side *shall be* hangings of fifty cubits: their pillars ten, and their sockets ten.

13 And the breadth of the court on the east side eastward *shall be* fifty cubits.

14 The hangings of one side *of the gate shall be* fifteen cubits: their pillars three, and their sockets three.

15 And on the other side *shall be* hangings fifteen *cubits*: their pillars three, and their sockets three.

16 ¶ And for the gate of the court *shall be* an hanging of twenty cubits, *of* blue, and purple, and scarlet, and fine twined linen, wrought with needlework: *and* their pillars *shall be* four, and their sockets four.

17 All the pillars round about the court *shall be* filleted with silver; their hooks *shall be of* silver, and the sockets *of* brass.

18 ¶ The length of the court *shall be* an hundred cubits, and the breadth fifty every where, and the height five cubits *of* fine twined linen, and their sockets *of* brass.

19 All the vessels of the tabernacle in all the service thereof, and all the pins thereof, and all the pins of the court, *shall be of* brass.

20 ¶ And thou shalt command the children of Is'ra-el, that they bring thee pure oil olive beaten for the light, to cause the lamp to burn always.

21 In the tabernacle of the congregation without the veil, which *is* before the testimony, Aar'on and his sons shall order it from evening to morning before the LORD: *it shall be* a statute for ever unto their generations on the behalf of the children of Is'ra-el.

28 AND take thou unto thee Aar'on thy brother, and his sons with him, from among the children of Is'ra-el, that he may minister unto me in the priest's office, *even* Aar'on, Na'dab and A-bi'hu, E-le-a'zar and Ith'a-mar, Aar'on's sons.

2 And thou shalt make holy garments for Aar'on thy brother for glory and for beauty.

3 And thou shalt speak unto all *that are* wise hearted, whom I have filled with the spirit of wisdom, that they may make Aar'on's garments to consecrate him, that he may minister unto me in the priest's office.

4 And these *are* the garments which they shall make; a breastplate, and an ephod, and a robe, and a broidered coat, a mitre, and a girdle: and they shall make holy garments for Aar'on thy brother, and his sons, that he may minister unto me in the priest's office.

5 And they shall take gold, and blue, and purple, and scarlet, and fine linen.

6 ¶ And they shall make the ephod *of* gold, *of* blue, and *of* purple, *of* scarlet, and fine twined linen, with cunning work.

7 It shall have the two shoulderpieces thereof jointed at the two edges thereof; and *so* it shall be joined together.

8 And the curious girdle of the ephod, which *is* upon it, shall be of the same, according to the work thereof; *even of* gold, *of* blue, and purple, and scarlet, and fine twined linen.

9 And thou shalt take two onyx stones, and grave on them the names of the children of Is'ra-el:

10 Six of their names on one stone, and *the other* six names of the rest on the other stone, according to their birth.

11 With the work of an engraver in stone, *like* the engravings of a signet, shalt thou engrave the two stones with the names of the children of Is'ra-el: thou shalt make them to be set in ouches of gold.

12 And thou shalt put the two stones upon the shoulders of the ephod *for* stones of memorial unto the children of Is'ra-el: and Aar'on shall bear their names before the LORD upon his two shoulders for a memorial.

13 ¶ And thou shalt make ouches *of* gold;

14 And two chains *of* pure gold at the ends; *of* wreathen work shalt thou make them, and fasten the wreathen chains to the ouches.

15 ¶ And thou shalt make the breastplate of judgment with cunning work; after the work of the ephod thou shalt make it; *of* gold, *of* blue, and *of* purple, and *of* scarlet, and *of* fine twined linen, shalt thou make it.

16 Foursquare it shall be *being* doubled; a

span *shall be* the length thereof, and a span *shall be* the breadth thereof

17 And thou shalt set in it settings of stones, *even* four rows of stones: *the first* row *shall be* a sardius, a topaz, and a carbuncle: *this shall be* the first row.

18 And the second row *shall be* an emerald, a sapphire, and a diamond.

19 And the third row a ligure, an agate, and an amethyst.

20 And the fourth row a beryl, and an onyx, and a jasper: they shall be set in gold in their inclosings.

21 And the stones shall be with the names of the children of Is'ra-el, twelve, according to their names, *like* the engravings of a signet; every one with his name shall they be according to the twelve tribes.

22 ¶ And thou shalt make upon the breastplate chains at the ends *of* wreathen work *of* pure gold.

23 And thou shalt make upon the breastplate two rings of gold, and shalt put the two rings on the two ends of the breastplate.

24 And thou shalt put the two wreathen *chains* of gold in the two rings *which are* on the ends of the breastplate.

25 And *the other* two ends of the two wreathen *chains* thou shalt fasten in the two ouches, and put *them* on the shoulderpieces of the ephod before it.

26 ¶ And thou shalt make two rings of gold, and thou shalt put them upon the two ends of the breastplate in the border thereof, which *is* in the side of the ephod inward.

27 And two *other* rings of gold thou shalt make, and shalt put them on the two sides of the ephod underneath, toward the forepart thereof, over against the *other* coupling thereof, above the curious girdle of the ephod.

28 And they shall bind the breastplate by the rings thereof unto the rings of the ephod with a lace of blue, that *it* may be above the curious girdle of the ephod, and that the breastplate be not loosed from the ephod.

29 And Aar'on shall bear the names of the children of Is'ra-el in the breastplate of judgment upon his heart, when he goeth in unto the holy *place,* for a memorial before the LORD continually.

30 ¶ And thou shalt put in the breastplate of judgment the U'rim and the Thum'mim; and they shall be upon Aar'on's heart, when he goeth in before the LORD: and Aar'on shall bear the judgment of the children of Is'ra-el upon his heart before the LORD continually.

31 ¶ And thou shalt make the robe of the ephod all *of* blue.

32 And there shall be an hole in the top of it, in the midst thereof: it shall have a binding of woven work round about the hole of it, as it were the hole of an habergeon, that it be not rent.

33 ¶ And *beneath* upon the hem of it thou shalt make pomegranates *of* blue, and *of* purple, and *of* scarlet, round about the hem thereof; and bells of gold between them round about:

34 A golden bell and a pomegranate, a golden bell and a pomegranate, upon the hem of the robe round about.

35 And it shall be upon Aar'on to minister: and his sound shall be heard when he goeth in unto the holy *place* before the LORD, and when he cometh out, that he die not.

36 ¶ And thou shalt make a plate *of* pure gold, and grave upon it, *like* the engravings of a signet, HOLINESS TO THE LORD.

37 And thou shalt put it on a blue lace, that it may be upon the mitre; upon the forefront of the mitre it shall be.

38 And it shall be upon Aar'on's forehead, that Aar'on may bear the iniquity of the holy things, which the children of Is'ra-el shall hallow in all their holy gifts; and it shall be always upon his forehead, that they may be accepted before the LORD.

39 ¶ And thou shalt embroider the coat of fine linen, and thou shalt make the mitre *of* fine linen, and thou shalt make the girdle *of* needlework.

40 ¶ And for Aar'on's sons thou shalt make coats, and thou shalt make for them girdles, and bonnets shalt thou make for them, for glory and for beauty.

41 And thou shalt put them upon Aar'on thy brother, and his sons with him; and shalt anoint them, and consecrate them, and sanctify them, that they may minister unto me in the priest's office.

42 And thou shalt make them linen breeches to cover their nakedness; from the loins even unto the thighs they shall reach:

43 And they shall be upon Aar'on, and upon his sons, when they come in unto the tabernacle of the congregation, or when they come near unto the altar to minister in the holy *place;* that they bear not iniquity, and die: *it shall be* a statute for ever unto him and his seed after him.

29 AND this *is* the thing that thou shalt do unto them to hallow them, to minister unto me in the priest's office: Take one young bullock, and two rams without blemish,

2 And unleavened bread, and cakes unleavened tempered with oil, and wafers unleavened anointed with oil: *of* wheaten flour shalt thou make them.

3 And thou shalt put them into one basket, and bring them in the basket, with the bullock and the two rams.

4 And Aar'on and his sons thou shalt bring unto the door of the tabernacle of the congregation, and shalt wash them with water.

5 And thou shalt take the garments, and put upon Aar'on the coat, and the robe of the ephod, and the ephod, and the breastplate, and gird him with the curious girdle of the ephod:

6 And thou shalt put the mitre upon his head, and put the holy crown upon the mitre.

7 Then shalt thou take the anointing oil, and pour *it* upon his head, and anoint him.

8 And thou shalt bring his sons, and put coats upon them.

9 And thou shalt gird them with girdles, Aar'on and his sons, and put the bonnets on them: and the priest's office shall be theirs for a perpetual statute: and thou shalt consecrate Aar'on and his sons.

10 And thou shalt cause a bullock to be brought before the tabernacle of the congregation: and Aar'on and his sons shall put their hands upon the head of the bullock.

11 And thou shalt kill the bullock before the LORD, *by* the door of the tabernacle of the congregation.

12 And thou shalt take of the blood of the bullock, and put *it* upon the horns of the altar with thy finger, and pour all the blood beside the bottom of the altar.

13 And thou shalt take all the fat that covereth the inwards, and the caul *that is* above the

liver, and the two kidneys, and the fat that *is*
upon them, and burn *them* upon the altar.
14 But the flesh of the bullock, and his skin,
and his dung, shalt thou burn with fire without
the camp: it *is* a sin offering.
15 ¶ Thou shalt also take one ram; and Aar'-
on and his sons shall put their hands upon the
head of the ram.
16 And thou shalt slay the ram, and thou
shalt take his blood, and sprinkle *it* round about
upon the altar.
17 And thou shalt cut the ram in pieces, and
wash the inwards of him, and his legs, and put
them unto his pieces, and unto his head.
18 And thou shalt burn the whole ram upon
the altar: it *is* a burnt offering unto the LORD: it
is a sweet savour, an offering made by fire unto
the LORD.
19 ¶ And thou shalt take the other ram; and
Aar'on and his sons shall put their hands upon
the head of the ram.
20 Then shalt thou kill the ram, and take of
his blood, and put *it* upon the tip of the right ear
of Aar'on, and upon the tip of the right ear of
his sons, and upon the thumb of their right
hand, and upon the great toe of their right foot,
and sprinkle the blood upon the altar round
about.
21 And thou shalt take of the blood that *is*
upon the altar, and of the anointing oil, and
sprinkle *it* upon Aar'on, and upon his garments,
and upon his sons, and upon the garments of his
sons with him: and he shall be hallowed, and his
garments, and his sons, and his sons' garments
with him.
22 Also thou shalt take of the ram the fat and
the rump, and the fat that covereth the inwards,
and the caul *above* the liver, and the two kidneys, and the fat that *is* upon them, and the
right shoulder; for it *is* a ram of consecration:
23 And one loaf of bread, and one cake of
oiled bread, and one wafer out of the basket of
the unleavened bread that *is* before the LORD:
24 And thou shalt put all in the hands of
Aar'on, and in the hands of his sons; and shalt
wave them *for* a wave offering before the LORD.
25 And thou shalt receive them of their
hands, and burn *them* upon the altar for a burnt
offering, for a sweet savour before the LORD: it
is an offering made by fire unto the LORD.
26 And thou shalt take the breast of the ram
of Aar'on's consecration, and wave it *for* a
wave offering before the LORD: and it shall be
thy part.
27 And thou shalt sanctify the breast of the
wave offering, and the shoulder of the heave offering, which is waved, and which is heaved up,
of the ram of the consecration, *even* of *that*
which *is* for Aar'on, and of *that* which is for his
sons:
28 And it shall be Aar'on's and his sons' by a
statute for ever from the children of Is'ra-el: for
it *is* an heave offering: and it shall be an heave
offering from the children of Is'ra-el of the sacrifice of their peace offerings, *even* their heave
offering unto the LORD.
29 ¶ And the holy garments of Aar'on shall
be his sons' after him, to be anointed therein,
and to be consecrated in them.
30 *And* that son that is priest in his stead
shall put them on seven days, when he cometh
into the tabernacle of the congregation to minister in the holy *place*.
31 ¶ And thou shalt take the ram of the consecration, and seethe his flesh in the holy place.
32 And Aar'on and his sons shall eat the flesh
of the ram, and the bread that *is* in the basket,
by the door of the tabernacle of the congregation.
33 And they shall eat those things wherewith
the atonement was made, to consecrate *and* to
sanctify them: but a stranger shall not eat
thereof, because they *are* holy.
34 And if ought of the flesh of the consecrations, or of the bread, remain unto the morning,
then thou shalt burn the remainder with fire: it
shall not be eaten, because it *is* holy.
35 And thus shalt thou do unto Aar'on, and
to his sons, according to all *things* which I have
commanded thee: seven days shalt thou consecrate them.
36 And thou shalt offer every day a bullock
for a sin offering for atonement: and thou shalt
cleanse the altar, when thou hast made an
atonement for it, and thou shalt anoint it, to
sanctify it.
37 Seven days thou shalt make an atonement
for the altar, and sanctify it; and it shall be an
altar most holy: whatsoever toucheth the altar
shall be holy.
38 ¶ Now this *is that* which thou shalt offer
upon the altar; two lambs of the first year day
by day continually.
39 The one lamb thou shalt offer in the morning; and the other lamb thou shalt offer at even:
40 And with the one lamb a tenth deal of
flour mingled with the fourth part of an hin of
beaten oil; and the fourth part of an hin of wine
for a drink offering.
41 And the other lamb thou shalt offer at
even, and shalt do thereto according to the
meat offering of the morning, and according to
the drink offering thereof, for a sweet savour,
and offering made by fire unto the LORD.
42 *This shall be* a continual burnt offering
throughout your generations *at* the door of the
tabernacle of the congregation before the LORD:
where I will meet you, to speak there unto thee.
43 And there I will meet with the children of
Is'ra-el, and *the tabernacle* shall be sanctified
by my glory.
44 And I will sanctify the tabernacle of the
congregation, and the altar: I will sanctify also
both Aar'on and his sons, to minister to me in
the priest's office.
45 ¶ And I will dwell among the children of
Is'ra-el, and will be their God.
46 And they shall know that I *am* the LORD
their God, that brought them forth out of the
land of E'gypt, that I may dwell among them: I
am the LORD their God.

30 AND thou shalt make an altar to burn
incense upon: *of* shittim wood shalt
thou make it.
2 A cubit *shall be* the length thereof, and a
cubit the breadth thereof; foursquare shall it be:
and two cubits *shall be* the height thereof: the
horns thereof *shall be* of the same.
3 And thou shalt overlay it with pure gold,
the top thereof, and the sides thereof round
about, and the horns thereof; and thou shalt
make unto it a crown of gold round about.
4 And two golden rings shalt thou make to it
under the crown of it, by the two corners
thereof, upon the two sides of it shalt thou
make *it;* and they shall be for places for the
staves to bear it withal.
5 And thou shalt make the staves *of* shittim
wood, and overlay them with gold.
6 And thou shalt put it before the veil that *is*
by the ark of the testimony, before the mercy
seat that *is* over the testimony, where I will
meet with thee.

7 And Aar′on shall burn thereon sweet incense every morning: when he dresseth the
lamps, he shall burn incense upon it.
8 And when Aar′on lighteth the lamps at
even, he shall burn incense upon it, a perpetual
incense before the LORD throughout your generations.
9 Ye shall offer no strange incense thereon,
nor burnt sacrifice, nor meat offering; neither
shall ye pour drink offering thereon.
10 And Aar′on shall make an atonement
upon the horns of it once in a year with the
blood of the sin offering of atonements: once in
the year shall he make atonement upon it
throughout your generations: it *is* most holy
unto the LORD.
11 ¶ And the LORD spake unto Mo′ses, saying,
12 When thou takest the sum of the children
of Is′ra-el after their number, then shall they
give every man a ransom for his soul unto the
LORD, when thou numberest them; that there be
no plague among them, when *thou* numberest
them.
13 This they shall give, every one that passeth among them that are numbered, half a
shekel after the shekel of the sanctuary: (a
shekel *is* twenty gerahs:) and half shekel *shall
be* the offering of the LORD.
14 Every one that passeth among them that
are numbered, from twenty years old and
above, shall give an offering unto the LORD.
15 The rich shall not give more, and the poor
shall not give less than half a shekel, when *they*
give an offering unto the LORD, to make an
atonement for your souls.
16 And thou shalt take the atonement money
of the children of Is′ra-el, and shalt appoint it
for the service of the tabernacle of the congregation; that it may be a memorial unto the children of Is′ra-el before the LORD, to make an
atonement for your souls.
17 ¶ And the LORD spake unto Mo′ses, saying,
18 Thou shalt also make a laver *of* brass, and
his foot *also of* brass, to wash *withal:* and thou
shalt put it between the tabernacle of the congregation and the altar, and thou shalt put water therein.
19 For Aar′on and his sons shall wash their
hands and their feet thereat:
20 When they go into the tabernacle of the
congregation, they shall wash with water, that
they die not; or when they come near to the
altar to minister, to burn offering made by fire
unto the LORD:
21 So they shall wash their hands and their
feet, that they die not: and it shall be a statute
for ever to them, *even* to him and to his seed
throughout their generations.
22 ¶ Moreover the LORD spake unto Mo′ses,
saying,
23 Take thou also unto thee principal spices,
of pure myrrh five hundred *shekels,* and of
sweet cinnamon half so much, *even* two hundred and fifty *shekels,* and of sweet calamus
two hundred and fifty *shekels,*
24 And of cassia five hundred *shekels,* after
the shekel of the sanctuary, and of oil olive an
hin:
25 And thou shalt make it an oil of holy ointment, an ointment compound after the art of
the apothecary: it shall be an holy anointing oil.
26 And thou shalt anoint the tabernacle of
the congregation therewith, and the ark of the
testimony,
27 And the table and all his vessels, and the
candlestick and his vessels, and the altar of incense,
28 And the altar of burnt offering with all his
vessels, and the laver and his foot.
29 And thou shalt sanctify them, that they
may be most holy: whatsoever toucheth them
shall be holy.
30 And thou shalt anoint Aar′on and his
sons, and consecrate them, that *they* may minister unto me in the priest's office.
31 And thou shalt speak unto the children of
Is′ra-el, saying, This shall be an holy anointing
oil unto me throughout your generations.
32 Upon man's flesh shall it not be poured,
neither shall ye make *any other* like it, after the
composition of it: it *is* holy, *and* it shall be holy
unto you.
33 Whosoever compoundeth *any* like it, or
whosoever putteth *any* of it upon a stranger,
shall even be cut off from his people.
34 ¶ And the LORD said unto Mo′ses, Take
unto thee sweet spices, stacte, and onycha, and
galbanum; *these* sweet spices with pure frankincense: of each shall there be a like *weight:*
35 And thou shalt make it a perfume, a con-
fection after the art of the apothecary, tempered together, pure *and* holy:
36 And thou shalt beat *some* of it very small,
and put of it before the testimony in the tabernacle of the congregation, where I will meet
with thee: it shall be unto you most holy.
37 And *as for* the perfume which thou shalt
make, ye shall not make to yourselves according to the composition thereof: it shall be unto
thee holy for the LORD.
38 Whosoever shall make like unto that, to
smell thereto, shall even be cut off from his people.

31 AND the LORD spake unto Mo′ses, saying,
2 See, I have called by name Be-zal′e-el the
son of U′ri, the son of Hur, of the tribe of Ju′-
dah:
3 And I have filled him with the spirit of God,
in wisdom, and in understanding, and in knowledge, and in all manner of workmanship,
4 To devise cunning works, to work in gold,
and in silver, and in brass,
5 And in cutting of stones, to set *them,* and in
carving of timber, to work in all manner of
workmanship.
6 And I, behold, I have given with him A-ho′-
li-ab, the son of A-his′a-mach, of the tribe of
Dan: and in the hearts of all that are wise
hearted I have put wisdom, that they may make
all that I have commanded thee;
7 The tabernacle of the congregation, and the
ark of the testimony, and the mercy seat that *is*
thereupon, and all the furniture of the tabernacle,
8 And the table and his furniture, and the
pure candlestick with all his furniture, and the
altar of incense,
9 And the altar of burnt offering with all his
furniture, and the laver and his foot,
10 And the cloths of service, and the holy
garments for Aar′on the priest, and the garments of his sons, to minister in the priest's office,
11 And the anointing oil, and sweet incense
for the holy *place:* according to all that I have
commanded thee shall they do.
12 ¶ And the LORD spake unto Mo′ses, saying,
13 Speak thou also unto the children of Is′ra-
el, saying, Verily my sabbaths ye shall keep: for

it *is* a sign between me and you throughout
your generations; that *ye* may know that I *am*
the LORD that doth sanctify you.
14 Ye shall keep the sabbath therefore; for it
is holy unto you: every one that defileth it shall
surely be put to death: for whosoever doeth *any*
work therein, that soul shall be cut off from
among his people.
15 Six days may work be done; but in the
seventh *is* the sabbath of rest, holy to the LORD:
whosoever doeth *any* work in the sabbath day,
he shall surely be put to death.
16 Wherefore the children of Is'ra-el shall
keep the sabbath, to observe the sabbath
throughout their generations, *for* a perpetual
covenant.
17 It *is* a sign between me and the children of
Is'ra-el for ever: for *in* six days the LORD made
heaven and earth, and on the seventh day he
rested, and was refreshed.
18 ¶ And he gave unto Mo'ses, when he had
made an end of communing with him upon
mount Si'nai, two tables of testimony, tables of
stone, written with the finger of God.

32 AND when the people saw that Mo'ses
delayed to come down out of the mount,
the people gathered themselves together unto
Aar'on, and said unto him, Up, make us gods,
which shall go before us; for *as for* this Mo'ses,
the man that brought us up out of the land of
E'gypt, we wot not what is become of him.
2 And Aar'on said unto them, Break off the
golden earrings, which *are* in the ears of your
wives, of your sons, and of your daughters, and
bring *them* unto me.
3 And all the poeple brake off the golden earrings which *were* in their ears, and brought
them unto Aar'on.
4 And he received *them* at their hand, and
fashioned it with a graving tool, after he had
made it a molten calf: and they said, These *be*
thy gods, O Is'ra-el, which brought thee up out
of the land of E'gypt.
5 And when Aar'on saw *it,* he built an altar
before it; and Aar'on made proclamation, and
said, To morrow *is* a feast to the LORD.
6 And they rose up early on the morrow, and
offered burnt offerings, and brought peace offerings; and the people sat down to eat and to
drink, and rose up to play.
7 ¶ And the LORD said unto Mo'ses, Go, get
thee down; for thy people, which thou broughtest out of the land of E'gypt, have corrupted
themselves:
8 They have turned aside quickly out of the
way which I commanded them: they have made
them a molten calf, and have worshipped it, and
have sacrificed thereunto, and said, These *be*
thy gods, O Is'ra-el, which have brought thee up
out of the land of E'gypt.
9 And the LORD said unto Mo'ses, I have seen
this people, and, behold, it *is* a stiffnecked people:
10 Now therefore let me alone, that my
wrath may wax hot against them, and that I
may consume them: and I will make of thee a
great nation.
11 And Mo'ses besought the LORD his God,
and said, LORD, why doth thy wrath wax hot
against thy people, which thou hast brought
forth out of the land of E'gypt with great power,
and with a mighty hand?
12 Wherefore should the E-gyptians speak,
and say, For mischief did he bring them out, to
slay them in the mountains, and to consume
them from the face of the earth? Turn from thy
fierce wrath, and repent of this evil against thy
people.
13 Remember A'bra-ham, I'saac, and Is'ra-el,
thy servants, to whom thou swarest by thine
own self, and saidst unto them, I will multiply
your seed as the stars of heaven, and all this
land that I have spoken of will I give unto your
seed, and they shall inherit *it* for ever.
14 And the LORD repented of the evil which
he thought to do unto his people.
15 ¶ And Mo'ses turned, and went down
from the mount, and the two tables of the testimony *were* in his hand: the tables *were* written
on both their sides; on the one side and on the
other *were* they written.
16 And the tables *were* the work of God, and
the writing *was* the writing of God, graven upon
the tables.
17 And when Josh'u-a heard the noise of the
people as they shouted, he said unto Mo'ses,
There is a noise of war in the camp.
18 And he said, *It is* not the voice of *them*
that shout for mastery, neither *is it* the voice of
them that cry for being overcome: *but* the noise
of *them that* sing do I hear.
19 ¶ And it came to pass, as soon as he came
nigh unto the camp, that he saw the calf, and
the dancing: and Mo'ses' anger waxed hot, and
he cast the tables out of his hands, and brake
them beneath the mount.
20 And he took the calf which they had
made, and burnt *it* in the fire, and ground *it* to
powder, and strawed *it* upon the water, and
made the children of Is'ra-el drink *of it.*
21 And Mo'ses said unto Aar'on, What did
this people unto thee, that thou hast brought so
great a sin upon them?
22 And Aar'on said, Let not the anger of my
lord wax hot: thou knowest the people, that
they *are set* on mischief.
23 For they said unto me, Make us gods,
which shall go before us: for *as for* this Mo'ses,
the man that brought us up out of the land of
E'gypt, we wot not what is become of him.
24 And I said unto them, Whosoever hath
any gold, let them break *it* off. So they gave *it*
me: then I cast it into the fire, and there came
out this calf.
25 ¶ And when Mo'ses saw that the people
were naked; (for Aar'on had made them naked
unto *their* shame among their enemies:)
26 Then Mo'ses stood in the gate of the
camp, and said, Who *is* on the LORD's side? *let*
him come unto me. And all the sons of Le'vi
gathered themselves together unto him.
27 And he said unto them, Thus saith the
LORD God of Is'ra-el, Put every man his sword
by his side, *and* go in and out from gate to gate
throughout the camp, and slay every man his
brother, and every man his companion, and every man his neighbour.
28 And the children of Le'vi did according to
the word of Mo'ses: and there fell of the people
that day about three thousand men.
29 For Mo'ses had said, Consecrate yourselves to day to the LORD, even every man upon
his son, and upon his brother; that he may bestow upon you a blessing this day.
30 ¶ And it came to pass on the morrow,
that Mo'ses said unto the people, Ye have
sinned a great sin: and now I will go up unto the
LORD; peradventure I shall make an atonement
for your sin.
31 And Mo'ses returned unto the LORD, and
said, Oh, this people have sinned a great sin,
and have made them gods of gold.
32 Yet now, if thou wilt forgive their sin—;

and if not, blot me, I pray thee, out of thy book which thou hast written.

33 And the LORD said unto Mo′ses, Whosoever hath sinned against me, him will I blot out of my book.

34 Therefore now go, lead the people unto *the place* of which I have spoken unto thee: behold, mine Angel shall go before thee: nevertheless in the day when I visit I will visit their sin upon them.

35 And the LORD plagued the people, because they made the calf, which Aar′on made.

33

AND the LORD said unto Mo′ses, Depart, *and* go up hence, thou and the people which thou hast brought up out of the land of E′gypt, unto the land which I sware unto A′bra-ham, to I′saac, and to Ja′cob, saying, Unto thy seed will I give it:

2 And I will send an angel before thee; and I will drive out the Ca′naan-ite, the Am′or-ite, and the Hit′tite, and the Per′iz-zite, the Hi′vite, and the Jeb′u-site:

3 Unto a land flowing with milk and honey: for I will not go up in the midst of thee; for thou *art* a stiffnecked people: lest I consume thee in the way.

4 ¶ And when the people heard these evil tidings, they mourned: and no man did put on him his ornaments.

5 For the LORD had said unto Mo′ses, Say unto the children of Is′ra-el, Ye *are* a stiffnecked people: I will come up into the midst of thee in a moment, and consume thee: therefore now put off thy ornaments from thee, that I may know what to do unto thee.

6 And the children of Is′ra-el stripped themselves of their ornaments by the mount Ho′reb.

7 And Mo′ses took the tabernacle, and pitched it without the camp, afar off from the camp, and called it the Tabernacle of the congregation. And it came to pass, *that* every one which sought the LORD went out unto the tabernacle of the congregation, which *was* without the camp.

8 And it came to pass, when Mo′ses went out unto the tabernacle, *that* all the people rose up, and stood every man *at* his tent door, and looked after Mo′ses, until he was gone into the tabernacle.

9 And it came to pass, as Mo′ses entered into the tabernacle, the cloudy pillar descended, and stood *at* the door of the tabernacle, and *the LORD* talked with Mo′ses.

10 And all the people saw the cloudy pillar stand *at* the tabernacle door: and all the people rose up and worshipped, every man *in* his tent door.

11 And the LORD spake unto Mo′ses face to face, as a man speaketh unto his friend. And he turned again into the camp: but his servant Josh′u-a, the son of Nun, a young man, departed not out of the tabernacle.

12 ¶ And Mo′ses said unto the LORD, See, thou sayest unto me, Bring up this people: and thou hast not let me know whom thou wilt send with me. Yet thou hast said, I know thee by name, and thou hast also found grace in my sight.

13 Now therefore, I pray thee, if I have found grace in thy sight, shew me now thy way, that I may know thee, that I may find grace in thy sight: and consider that this nation *is* thy people.

14 And he said, My presence shall go *with thee,* and I will give thee rest.

15 And he said unto him, If thy presence go not *with me,* carry us not up hence.

16 For wherein shall it be known here that I and thy people have found grace in thy sight? *is it* not in that thou goest with us? so shall we be separated, I and thy people, from all the people that *are* upon the face of the earth.

17 And the LORD said unto Mo′ses, I will do this thing also that thou hast spoken: for thou hast found grace in my sight, and I know thee by name.

18 And he said, I beseech thee, shew me thy glory.

19 And he said, I will make all my goodness pass before thee, and I will proclaim the name of the LORD before thee; and will be gracious to whom I will be gracious, and will shew mercy on whom I will shew mercy.

20 And he said, Thou canst not see my face: for there shall no man see me, and live.

21 And the LORD said, Behold, *there is* a place by me, and thou shalt stand upon a rock:

22 And it shall come to pass, while my glory passeth by, that I will put thee in a clift of the rock, and will cover thee with my hand while I pass by:

23 And I will take away mine hand, and thou shalt see my back parts: but my face shall not be seen.

34

AND the LORD said unto Mo′ses, Hew thee two tables of stone like unto the first: and I will write upon *these* tables the words that were in the first tables, which thou brakest.

2 And be ready in the morning, and come up in the morning unto mount Si′nai, and present thyself there to me in the top of the mount

3 And no man shall come up with thee, neither let any man be seen throughout all the mount; neither let the flocks nor herds feed before that mount.

4 ¶ And he hewed two tables of stone like unto the first; and Mo′ses rose up early in the morning, and went up unto mount Si′nai, as the LORD had commanded him, and took in his hand the two tables of stone.

5 And the LORD descended in the cloud, and stood with him there, and proclaimed the name of the LORD.

6 And the LORD passed by before him, and proclaimed, The LORD, The LORD God, merciful and gracious, longsuffering, and abundant in goodness and truth,

7 Keeping mercy for thousands, forgiving iniquity and transgression and sin, and that will by no means clear *the guilty;* visiting the iniquity of the fathers upon the children, and upon the children's children, unto the third and to the fourth *generation.*

8 And Mo′ses made haste, and bowed his head toward the earth, and worshipped.

9 And he said, If now I have found grace in thy sight, O Lord, let my Lord, I pray thee, go among us; for it *is* a stiffnecked people; and pardon our iniquity and our sin, and take us for thine inheritance.

10 ¶ And he said, Behold, I make a covenant: before all thy people I will do marvels, such as have not been done in all the earth, nor in any nation: and all the people among which thou *art* shall see the work of the LORD: for it *is* a terrible thing that I will do with thee.

11 Observe thou that which I command thee this day: behold, I drive out before thee the Am′or-ite, and the Ca′naan-ite, and the Hit′tite,

and the Per′iz-zite, and the Hi′vite, and the Jeb′-
u-site.
12 Take heed to thyself, lest thou make a
covenant with the inhabitants of the land
whither thou goest, lest it be for a snare in the
midst of thee:
13 But ye shall destroy their altars, break
their images, and cut down their groves:
14 For thou shalt worship no other god: for
the LORD, whose name *is* Jealous, *is* a jealous
God:
15 Lest thou make a covenant with the inhabitants of the land, and they go a whoring
after their gods, and do sacrifice unto their
gods, and *one* call thee, and thou eat of his sacrifice;
16 And thou take of their daughters unto thy
sons, and their daughters go a whoring after
their gods, and make thy sons go a whoring after their gods.
17 Thou shalt make thee no molten gods.
18 ¶ The feast of unleavened bread shalt
thou keep. Seven days thou shalt eat unleavened bread, as I commanded thee, in the time of
the month A′bib: for in the month A′bib thou
camest out from E′gypt.
19 All that openeth the matrix *is* mine; and
every firstling among thy cattle, *whether* ox or
sheep, *that is male*.
20 But the firstling of an ass thou shalt redeem with a lamb: and if thou redeem *him* not,
then shalt thou break his neck. All the firstborn
of thy sons thou shalt redeem. And none shall
appear before me empty.
21 ¶ Six days thou shalt work, but on the
seventh day thou shalt rest: in earing time and
in harvest thou shalt rest.
22 ¶ And thou shalt observe the feast of
weeks, of the firstfruits of wheat harvest, and
the feast of ingathering at the year's end.
23 ¶ Thrice in the year shall all your men-
children appear before the Lord GOD, the God
of Is′ra-el.
24 For I will cast out the nations before thee,
and enlarge thy borders: neither shall any man
desire thy land, when thou shalt go up to appear
before the LORD thy God thrice in the year.
25 Thou shalt not offer the blood of my sacrifice with leaven; neither shall the sacrifice of
the feast of the passover be left unto the morning.
26 The first of the firstfruits of thy land thou
shalt bring unto the house of the LORD thy God.
Thou shalt not seethe a kid in his mother's milk.
27 And the LORD said unto Mo′ses, Write
thou these words: for after the tenor of these
words I have made a covenant with thee and
with Is′ra-el.
28 And he was there with the LORD forty
days and forty nights; he did neither eat bread,
nor drink water. And he wrote upon the tables
the words of the covenant, the ten commandments.
29 ¶ And it came to pass, when Mo′ses came
down from mount Si′nai with the two tables of
testimony in Mo′ses' hand, when he came down
from the mount that Mo′ses wist not that the
skin of his face shone while he talked with him.
30 And when Aar′on and all the children of
Is′ra-el saw Mo′ses, behold, the skin of his face
shone; and they were afraid to come nigh him.
31 And Mo′ses called unto them; and Aar′on
and all the rulers of the congregation returned
unto him: and Mo′ses talked with them.
32 And afterward all the children of Is′ra-el
came nigh: and he gave them in commandment
all that the LORD had spoken with him in mount
Si′nai.
33 And *till* Mo′ses had done speaking with
them, he put a veil on his face.
34 But when Mo′ses went in before the LORD
to speak with him, he took the veil off, until he
came out. And he came out, and spake unto the
children of Is′ra-el *that* which he was commanded.
35 And the children of Is′ra-el saw the face of
Mo′ses, that the skin of Mo′ses' face shone: and
Mo′ses put the veil upon his face again, until he
went in to speak with him.

35 AND Mo′ses gathered all the congregation of the children of Is′ra-el together,
and said unto them, These *are* the words which
the LORD hath commanded, that *ye* should do
them.
2 Six days shall work be done, but on the
seventh day there shall be to you an holy day, a
sabbath of rest to the LORD: whosoever doeth
work therein shall be put to death.
3 Ye shall kindle no fire throughout your
habitations upon the sabbath day.
4 ¶ And Mo′ses spake unto all the congregation of the children of Is′ra-el, saying, This *is* the
thing which the LORD commanded, saying,
5 Take ye from among you an offering unto
the LORD: whosoever *is* of a willing heart, let
him bring it, an offering of the LORD; gold, and
silver, and brass,
6 And blue, and purple, and scarlet, and fine
linen, and goats' *hair*,
7 And rams' skins dyed red, and badgers'
skins, and shittim wood,
8 And oil for the light, and spices for anointing oil, and for the sweet incense,
9 And onyx stones, and stones to be set for
the ephod, and for the breastplate.
10 And every wise hearted among you shall
come, and make all that the LORD hath commanded;
11 The tabernacle, his tent, and his covering,
his taches, and his boards, his bars, his pillars,
and his sockets,
12 The ark, and the staves thereof, *with* the
mercy seat, and the veil of the covering,
13 The table, and his staves, and all his vessels, and the shewbread,
14 The candlestick also for the light, and his
furniture, and his lamps, with the oil for the
light,
15 And the incense altar, and his staves, and
the anointing oil, and the sweet incense, and the
hanging for the door at the entering in of the
tabernacle,
16 The altar of burnt offering, with his brasen grate, his staves, and all his vessels, the laver and his foot,
17 The hangings of the court, his pillars, and
their sockets, and the hanging for the door of
the court,
18 The pins of the tabernacle, and the pins of
the court, and their cords,
19 The cloths of service, to do service in the
holy *place*, the holy garments for Aar′on the
priest, and the garments of his sons, to minister
in the priest's office.
20 ¶ And all the congregation of the children
of Is′ra-el departed from the presence of Mo′-
ses.
21 And they came, every one whose heart
stirred him up, and every one whom his spirit
made willing, *and* they brought the LORD's offering to the work of the tabernacle of the con-

gregation, and for all his service, and for the holy garments.

22 And they came, both men and women, as many as were willing hearted, *and* brought bracelets, and earrings, and rings, and tablets, all jewels of gold: and every man that offered *offered* an offering of gold unto the LORD.

23 And every man, with whom was found blue, and purple, and scarlet, and fine linen, and goats' *hair,* and red skins of rams, and badgers' skins, brought *them.*

24 Every one that did offer an offering of silver and brass brought the LORD's offering: and every man, with whom was found shittim wood for any work of the service, brought *it.*

25 And all the women that were wise hearted did spin with their hands, and brought that which they had spun, *both* of blue, and of purple, *and* of scarlet, and of fine linen.

26 And all the women whose heart stirred them up in wisdom spun goats' *hair.*

27 And the rulers brought onyx stones, and stones to be set, for the ephod, and for the breastplate;

28 And spice, and oil for the light, and for the anointing oil, and for the sweet incense.

29 The children of Is'ra-el brought a willing offering unto the LORD, every man and woman, whose heart made them willing to bring for all manner of work, which the LORD had commanded to be made by the hand of Mo'ses.

30 ¶ And Mo'ses said unto the children of Is'ra-el, See, the LORD hath called by name Be-zal'e-el the son of U'ri, the son of Hur, of the tribe of Ju'dah;

31 And he hath filled him with the spirit of God, in wisdom, in understanding, and in knowledge, and in all manner of workmanship;

32 And to devise curious works, to work in gold, and in silver, and in brass,

33 And in the cutting of stones, to set *them,* and in carving of wood, to make any manner of cunning work.

34 And he hath put in his heart that he may teach, *both* he, and A-ho'li-ab, the son of A-his'-a-mach, of the tribe of Dan.

35 Them hath he filled with wisdom of heart, to work all manner of work, of the engraver, and of the cunning workman, and of the embroiderer, in blue, and in purple, in scarlet, and in fine linen, and of the weaver, *even* of them that do any work, and of those that devise cunning work.

36 THEN wrought Be-zal'e-el and A-ho'li-ab, and every wise hearted man, in whom the LORD put wisdom and understanding to know how to work all manner of work for the service of the sanctuary, according to all that the LORD had commanded.

2 And Mo'ses called Be-zal'e-el and A-ho'li-ab, and every wise hearted man, in whose heart the LORD had put wisdom, *even* every one whose heart stirred him up to come unto the work to do it:

3 And they received of Mo'ses all the offering, which the children of Is'ra-el had brought for the work of the service of the sanctuary, to make it *withal.* And they brought yet unto him free offerings every morning.

4 And all the wise men, that wrought all the work of the sanctuary, came every man from his work which they make;

5 ¶ And they spake unto Mo'ses, saying, The people bring much more than enough for the service of the work, which the LORD commanded to make.

6 And Mo'ses gave commandment, and they caused it to be proclaimed throughout the camp, saying, Let neither man nor woman make any more work for the offering of the sanctuary. So the people were restrained from bringing.

7 For the stuff they had was sufficient for all the work to make it, and too much.

8 ¶ And every wise hearted man among them that wrought the work of the tabernacle made ten curtains *of* fine twined linen, and blue, and purple, and scarlet: *with* cherubims of cunning work made he them.

9 The length of one curtain *was* twenty and eight cubits, and the breadth of one curtain four cubits: the curtains *were* all of one size.

10 And he coupled the five curtains one unto another: and *the other* five curtains he coupled one unto another.

11 And he made loops of blue on the edge of one curtain from the selvedge in the coupling: likewise he made in the uttermost side of *another* curtain, in the coupling of the second.

12 Fifty loops made he in one curtain, and fifty loops made he in the edge of the curtain which *was* in the coupling of the second: the loops held one *curtain* to another.

13 And he made fifty taches of gold, and coupled the curtains one unto another with the taches: so it became one tabernacle.

14 ¶ And he made curtains *of* goats' *hair* for the tent over the tabernacle: eleven curtains he made them.

15 The length of one curtain *was* thirty cubits, and four cubits *was* the breadth of one curtain: the eleven curtains *were* of one size.

16 And he coupled five curtains by themselves, and six curtains by themselves.

17 And he made fifty loops upon the uttermost edge of the curtain in the coupling, and fifty loops made he upon the edge of the curtain which coupleth the second.

18 And he made fifty taches *of* brass to couple the tent together, that it might be one.

19 And he made a covering for the tent *of* rams' skins dyed red, and a covering *of* badgers' skins above *that.*

20 ¶ And he made boards for the tabernacle *of* shittim wood, standing up.

21 The length of a board *was* ten cubits, and the breadth of a board one cubit and a half.

22 One board had two tenons, equally distant one from another: thus did he make for all the boards of the tabernacle.

23 And he made boards for the tabernacle; twenty boards for the south side southward:

24 And forty sockets of silver he made under the twenty boards; two sockets under one board for his two tenons, and two sockets under another board for his two tenons.

25 And for the other side of the tabernacle, *which is* toward the north corner, he made twenty boards,

26 And their forty sockets of silver; two sockets under one board, and two sockets under another board.

27 And for the sides of the tabernacle westward he made six boards.

28 And two boards made he for the corners of the tabernacle in the two sides.

29 And they were coupled beneath, and coupled together at the head thereof, to one ring: thus he did to both of them in both corners.

30 And there were eight boards; and their sockets *were* sixteen sockets of silver, under every board two sockets.

31 ¶ And he made bars of shittim wood; five

for the boards of the one side of the tabernacle,
32 And five bars for the boards of the other
side of the tabernacle, and five bars for the
boards of the tabernacle for the sides westward.
33 And he made the middle bar to shoot
through the boards from the one end to the other.
34 And he overlaid the boards with gold, and
made their rings *of* gold *to be* places for the
bars, and overlaid the bars with gold.
35 ¶ And he made a veil *of* blue, and purple,
and scarlet, and fine twined linen: *with* cherubims made he it of cunning work.
36 And he made thereunto four pillars *of*
shittim *wood*, and overlaid them with gold:
their hooks *were of* gold; and he cast for them
four sockets of silver.
37 ¶ And he made an hanging for the tabernacle door *of* blue, and purple, and scarlet, and
fine twined linen, of needlework;
38 And the five pillars of it with their hooks:
and he overlaid their chapiters and their fillets
with gold: but their five sockets *were of* brass.

37 AND Be-zal'e-el made the ark *of* shittim
wood: two cubits and a half *was* the
length of it, and a cubit and a half the breadth
of it, and a cubit and a half the height of it:
2 And he overlaid it with pure gold within
and without, and made a crown of gold to it
round about.
3 And he cast for it four rings of gold, *to be*
set by the four corners of it; even two rings
upon the one side of it, and two rings upon the
other side of it.
4 And he made staves *of* shittim wood, and
overlaid them with gold.
5 And he put the staves into the rings by the
sides of the ark, to bear the ark.
6 ¶ And he made the mercy seat *of* pure
gold: two cubits and a half *was* the length
thereof, and one cubit and a half the breadth
thereof.
7 And he made two cherubims *of* gold,
beaten out of one piece made he them, on the
two ends of the mercy seat;
8 One cherub on the end on this side, and another cherub on the *other* end on that side: out
of the mercy seat made he the cherubims on the
two ends thereof.
9 And cherubims spread out *their* wings on
high, *and* covered with their wings over the
mercy seat, with their faces one to another;
even to the mercy seatward were the faces of
the cherubims.
10 ¶ And he made the table *of* shittim wood:
two cubits *was* the length thereof, and a cubit
the breadth thereof, and a cubit and a half the
height thereof:
11 And he overlaid it with pure gold, and
made thereunto a crown of gold round about.
12 Also he made thereunto a border of an
handbreadth round about; and made a crown of
gold for the border thereof round about.
13 And he cast for it four rings of gold, and
put the rings upon the four corners that *were* in
the four feet thereof.
14 Over against the border were the rings,
the places for the staves to bear the table.
15 And he made the staves *of* shittim wood,
and overlaid them with gold to bear the table.
16 And he made the vessels which *were* upon
the table, his dishes, and his spoons, and his
bowls, and his covers to cover withal, *of* pure
gold.
17 ¶ And he made the candlestick *of* pure
gold: *of* beaten work made he the candlestick;
his shaft, and his branch, his bowls, his knops,
and his flowers, were of the same:
18 And six branches going out of the sides
thereof; three branches of the candlestick out of
the one side thereof, and three branches of the
candlestick out of the other side thereof:
19 Three bowls made after the fashion of almonds in one branch, a knop and a flower; and
three bowls made like almonds in another
branch, a knop and a flower: so throughout the
six branches going out of the candlestick.
20 And in the candlestick *were* four bowls
made like almonds, his knops, and his flowers:
21 And a knop under two branches of the
same, and a knop under two branches of the
same, and a knop under two branches of the
same, according to the six branches going out
of it.
22 Their knops and their branches were of
the same: all of it *was* one beaten work *of* pure
gold.
23 And he made his seven lamps, and his
snuffers, and his snuffdishes, *of* pure gold.
24 *Of* a talent of pure gold made he it, and
all the vessels thereof.
25 ¶ And he made the incense altar *of* shittim wood: the length of it *was* a cubit, and the
breadth of it a cubit; *it was* foursquare; and two
cubits *was* the height of it; the horns thereof
were of the same.
26 And he overlaid it with pure gold, *both*
the top of it, and the sides thereof round about,
and the horns of it: also he made unto it a
crown of gold round about.
27 And he made two rings of gold for it under the crown thereof, by the two corners of it,
upon the two sides thereof, to be places for the
staves to bear it withal.
28 And he made the staves *of* shittim wood,
and overlaid them with gold.
29 ¶ And he made the holy anointing oil, and
the pure incense of sweet spices, according to
the work of the apothecary.

38 AND he made the altar of burnt offering
of shittim wood: five cubits *was* the
length thereof, and five cubits the breadth
thereof; *it was* foursquare; and three cubits the
height thereof.
2 And he made the horns thereof on the four
corners of it; the horns thereof were of the
same: and he overlaid it with brass.
3 And he made all the vessels of the altar, the
pots, and the shovels, and the basons, *and* the
fleshhooks, and the firepans: all the vessels
thereof made he *of* brass.
4 And he made for the altar a brasen grate of
network under the compass thereof beneath
unto the midst of it.
5 And he cast four rings for the four ends of
the grate of brass, *to be* places for the staves.
6 And he made the staves *of* shittim wood,
and overlaid them with brass.
7 And he put the staves into the rings on the
sides of the altar, to bear it withal; he made the
altar hollow with boards.
8 ¶ And he made the laver *of* brass, and the
foot of it *of* brass, of the lookingglasses of *the*
women assembling, which assembled *at* the
door of the tabernacle of the congregation.
9 ¶ And he made the court: on the south side
southward the hangings of the court *were of*
fine twined linen, an hundred cubits:
10 Their pillars *were* twenty, and their brasen sockets twenty; the hooks of the pillars and
their fillets *were of* silver.

11 And for the north side *the hangings were* an hundred cubits, their pillars *were* twenty, and their sockets of brass twenty; the hooks of the pillars and their fillets *of* silver.

12 And for the west side *were* hangings of fifty cubits, their pillars ten, and their sockets ten; the hooks of the pillars and their fillets *of* silver.

13 And for the east side eastward fifty cubits.

14 The hangings of the one side *of the gate were* fifteen cubits; their pillars three, and their sockets three.

15 And for the other side of the court gate, on this hand and that hand, *were* hangings of fifteen cubits; their pillars three, and their sockets three.

16 All the hangings of the court round about *were* of fine twined linen.

17 And the sockets for the pillars *were of* brass; the hooks of the pillars and their fillets *of* silver; and the overlaying of their chapiters *of* silver; and all the pillars of the court *were* filleted with silver.

18 And the hanging for the gate of the court *was* needlework, *of* blue, and purple, and scarlet, and fine twined linen: and twenty cubits *was* the length, and the height in the breadth *was* five cubits, answerable to the hangings of the court.

19 And their pillars *were* four, and their sockets *of* brass four; their hooks *of* silver, and the overlaying of their chapiters and their fillets *of* silver.

20 And all the pins of the tabernacle, and of the court round about, *were of* brass.

21 ¶ This is the sum of the tabernacle, *even* of the tabernacle of testimony, as it was counted, according to the commandment of Mo'ses, *for* the service of the Le'vites, by the hand of Ith'a-mar, son to Aar'on the priest.

22 And Be-zal'e-el the son of U'ri, the son of Hur, of the tribe of Ju'dah, made all that the LORD commanded Mo'ses.

23 And with him *was* A-ho'li-ab, son of A-his'a-mach, of the tribe of Dan, an engraver, and a cunning workman, and an embroiderer in blue, and in purple, and in scarlet, and fine linen.

24 All the gold that was occupied for the work in all the work of the holy *place*, even the gold of the offering, was twenty and nine talents, and seven hundred and thirty shekels, after the shekel of the sanctuary.

25 And the silver of them that were numbered of the congregation *was* an hundred talents, and a thousand seven hundred and threescore and fifteen shekels, after the shekel of the sanctuary:

26 A bekah for every man, *that is*, half a shekel, after the shekel of the sanctuary, for every one that went to be numbered, from twenty years old and upward, for six hundred thousand and three thousand and five hundred and fifty *men*.

27 And of the hundred talents of silver were cast the sockets of the sanctuary, and the sockets of the veil; an hundred sockets of the hundred talents, a talent for a socket.

28 And of the thousand seven hundred seventy and five *shekels* he made hooks for the pillars, and overlaid their chapiters, and filleted them.

29 And the brass of the offering *was* seventy talents, and two thousand and four hundred shekels.

30 And therewith he made the sockets to the door of the tabernacle of the congregation, and the brasen altar, and brasen grate for it, and all the vessels of the altar,

31 And the sockets of the court round about, and the sockets of the court gate, and all the pins of the tabernacle, and all the pins of the court round about.

39 AND of the blue, and purple, and scarlet, they made cloths of service, to do service in the holy *place*, and made the holy garments for Aar'on; as the LORD commanded Mo'ses.

2 And he made the ephod *of* gold, blue, and purple, and scarlet, and fine twined linen.

3 And they did beat the gold into thin plates, and cut *it into* wires, to work *it* in the blue, and in the purple, and in the scarlet, and in the fine linen, *with* cunning work.

4 They made shoulderpieces for it, to couple *it* together: by the two edges was it coupled together.

5 And the curious girdle of his ephod, that *was* upon it, *was* of the same, according to the work thereof; *of* gold, blue, and purple, and scarlet, and fine twined linen; as the LORD commanded Mo'ses.

6 ¶ And they wrought onyx stones inclosed in ouches of gold, graven, as signets are graven, with the names of the children of Is'ra-el.

7 And he put them on the shoulders of the ephod, *that they should be* stones for a memorial to the children of Is'ra-el; as the LORD commanded Mo'ses.

8 ¶ And he made the breastplate *of* cunning work, like the work of the ephod; *of* gold, blue, and purple, and scarlet, and fine twined linen.

9 It was foursquare; they made the breastplate double: a span *was* the length thereof, and a span the breadth thereof, *being* doubled.

10 And they set in it four rows of stones: *the first* row *was* a sardius, a topaz, and a carbuncle: this *was* the first row.

11 And the second row, an emerald, a sapphire, and a diamond.

12 And the third row, a ligure, an agate, and an amethyst.

13 And the fourth row, a beryl, an onyx, and a jasper: *they were* inclosed in ouches of gold in their inclosings.

14 And the stones *were* according to the names of the children of Is'ra-el, twelve, according to their names, *like* the engravings of a signet, every one with his name, according to the twelve tribes.

15 And they made upon the breastplate chains at the ends, *of* wreathen work *of* pure gold.

16 And they made two ouches *of* gold, and two gold rings; and put the two rings in the two ends of the breastplate.

17 And they put the two wreathen chains of gold in the two rings on the ends of the breastplate.

18 And the two ends of the two wreathen chains they fastened in the two ouches, and put them on the shoulderpieces of the ephod, before it.

19 And they made two rings of gold, and put *them* on the two ends of the breastplate, upon the border of it, which *was* on the side of the ephod inward.

20 And they made two *other* golden rings, and put them on the two sides of the ephod underneath, toward the forepart of it, over against the *other* coupling thereof, above the curious girdle of the ephod.

21 And they did bind the breastplate by his

rings unto the rings of the ephod with a lace of blue, that it might be above the curious girdle of the ephod, and that the breastplate might not be loosed from the ephod; as the LORD commanded Mo'ses.

22 ¶ And he made the robe of the ephod *of* woven work, all *of* blue.

23 And *there was* an hole in the midst of the robe, as the hole of an habergeon, *with* a band round about the hole, that it should not rend.

24 And they made upon the hems of the robe pomegranates *of* blue, and purple, and scarlet, *and* twined *linen*.

25 And they made bells *of* pure gold, and put the bells between the pomegranates upon the hem of the robe, round about between the pomegranates;

26 A bell and a pomegranate, a bell and a pomegranate, round about the hem of the robe to minister *in;* as the LORD commanded Mo'ses.

27 ¶ And they made coats *of* fine linen *of* woven work for Aar'on, and for his sons,

28 And a mitre *of* fine linen, and goodly bonnets *of* fine linen, and linen breeches *of* fine twined linen,

29 And a girdle *of* fine twined linen, and blue, and purple, and scarlet, *of* needlework; as the LORD commanded Mo'ses.

30 ¶ And they made the plate of the holy crown *of* pure gold, and wrote upon it a writing, *like to* the engravings of a signet, HOLINESS TO THE LORD.

31 And they tied unto it a lace of blue, to fasten *it* on high upon the mitre; as the LORD commanded Mo'ses.

32 ¶ Thus was all the work of the tabernacle of the tent of the congregation finished: and the children of Is'ra-el did according to all that the LORD commanded Mo'ses, so did they.

33 ¶ And they brought the tabernacle unto Mo'ses, the tent, and all his furniture, his taches, his boards, his bars, and his pillars, and his sockets,

34 And the covering of rams' skins dyed red, and the covering of badgers' skins, and the veil of the covering,

35 The ark of the testimony, and the staves thereof, and the mercy seat,

36 The table, *and* all the vessels thereof, and the shewbread,

37 The pure candlestick, *with* the lamps thereof, *even with* the lamps to be set in order, and all the vessels thereof, and the oil for light,

38 And the golden altar, and the anointing oil, and the sweet incense, and the hanging for the tabernacle door,

39 The brasen altar, and his grate of brass, his staves, and all his vessels, the laver and his foot,

40 The hangings of the court, his pillars, and his sockets, and the hanging for the court gate, his cords, and his pins, and all the vessels of the service of the tabernacle, for the tent of the congregation,

41 The cloths of service to do service in the holy *place,* and the holy garments for Aar'on the priest, and his sons' garments, to minister in the priest's office.

42 According to all that the LORD commanded Mo'ses, so the children of Is'ra-el made all the work.

43 And Mo'ses did look upon all the work, and, behold, they had done it as the LORD had commanded, even so had they done it: and Mo'ses blessed them.

40 AND the LORD spake unto Mo'ses, saying,

2 On the first day of the first month shalt thou set up the tabernacle of the tent of the congregation.

3 And thou shalt put therein the ark of the testimony, and cover the ark with the veil.

4 And thou shalt bring in the table, and set in order the things that are to be set in order upon it; and thou shalt bring in the candlestick, and light the lamps thereof.

5 And thou shalt set the altar of gold for the incense before the ark of the testimony, and put the hanging of the door to the tabernacle.

6 And thou shalt set the altar of the burnt offering before the door of the tabernacle of the tent of the congregation.

7 And thou shalt set the laver between the tent of the congregation and the altar, and shalt put water therein.

8 And thou shalt set up the court round about, and hang up the hanging at the court gate.

9 And thou shalt take the anointing oil, and anoint the tabernacle, and all that *is* therein, and shalt hallow it, and all the vessels thereof: and it shall be holy.

10 And thou shalt anoint the altar of the burnt offering, and all his vessels, and sanctify the altar: and it shall be an altar most holy.

11 And thou shalt anoint the laver and his foot, and sanctify it.

12 And thou shalt bring Aar'on and his sons unto the door of the tabernacle of the congregation, and wash them with water.

13 And thou shalt put upon Aar'on the holy garments, and anoint him, and sanctify him; that he may minister unto me in the priest's office.

14 And thou shalt bring his sons, and clothe them with coats:

15 And thou shalt anoint them, as thou didst anoint their father, that they may minister unto me in the priest's office: for their anointing shall surely be an everlasting priesthood throughout their generations.

16 Thus did Mo'ses: according to all that the LORD commanded him, so did he.

17 ¶ And it came to pass in the first month in the second year, on the first *day* of the month, *that* the tabernacle was reared up.

18 And Mo'ses reared up the tabernacle, and fastened his sockets, and set up the boards thereof, and put in the bars thereof, and reared up his pillars.

19 And he spread abroad the tent over the tabernacle, and put the covering of the tent above upon it; as the LORD commanded Mo'ses.

20 ¶ And he took and put the testimony into the ark, and set the staves on the ark, and put the mercy seat above upon the ark:

21 And he brought the ark into the tabernacle, and set up the veil of the covering, and covered the ark of the testimony; as the LORD commanded Mo'ses.

22 ¶ And he put the table in the tent of the congregation, upon the side of the tabernacle northward, without the veil.

23 And he set the bread in order upon it before the LORD; as the LORD had commanded Mo'ses.

24 ¶ And he put the candlestick in the tent of the congregation, over against the table, on the side of the tabernacle southward.

25 And he lighted the lamps before the LORD; as the LORD commanded Mo'ses.

26 ¶ And he put the golden altar in the tent
of the congregation before the veil:
27 And he burnt sweet incense thereon; as
the LORD commanded Mo'ses.
28 ¶ And he set up the hanging *at* the door
of the tabernacle.
29 And he put the altar of burnt offering *by*
the door of the tabernacle of the tent of the congregation, and offered upon it the burnt offering
and the meat offering; as the LORD commanded
Mo'ses.
30 ¶ And he set the laver between the tent of
the congregation and the altar, and put water
there, to wash *withal*.
31 And Mo'ses and Aar'on and his sons
washed their hands and their feet thereat:
32 When they went into the tent of the congregation, and when they came near unto the
altar, they washed; as the LORD commanded
Mo'ses.
33 And he reared up the court round about
the tabernacle and the altar, and set up the
hanging of the court gate. So Mo'ses finished
the work.
34 ¶ Then a cloud covered the tent of the
congregation, and the glory of the LORD filled
the tabernacle.
35 And Mo'ses was not able to enter into the
tent of the congregation, because the cloud
abode thereon, and the glory of the LORD filled
the tabernacle.
36 And when the cloud was taken up from
over the tabernacle, the children of Is'ra-el went
onward in all their journeys:
37 But if the cloud were not taken up, then
they journeyed not till the day that it was taken
up.
38 For the cloud of the LORD *was* upon the
tabernacle by day, and fire was on it by night, in
the sight of all the house of Is'ra-el, throughout
all their journeys.

THE THIRD BOOK OF MOSES

COMMONLY CALLED

LEVITICUS

1 AND the LORD called unto Mo'ses, and
spake unto him out of the tabernacle of the
congregation, saying,
2 Speak unto the children of Is'ra-el, and say
unto them, If any man of you bring an offering
unto the LORD, ye shall bring your offering of
the cattle, *even* of the herd, and of the flock.
3 If his offering *be* a burnt sacrifice of the
herd, let him offer a male without blemish: he
shall offer it of his own voluntary will at the
door of the tabernacle of the congregation before the LORD.
4 And he shall put his hand upon the head of
the burnt offering; and it shall be accepted for
him to make atonement for him.
5 And he shall kill the bullock before the
LORD: and the priests, Aar'on's sons, shall bring
the blood, and sprinkle the blood round about
upon the altar that *is by* the door of the tabernacle of the congregation.
6 And he shall flay the burnt offering, and cut
it into his pieces.
7 And the sons of Aar'on the priest shall put
fire upon the altar, and lay the wood in order
upon the fire:
8 And the priests, Aar'on's sons, shall lay the
parts, the head, and the fat, in order upon the
wood that *is* on the fire which *is* upon the altar:
9 But his inwards and his legs shall he wash
in water: and the priest shall burn all on the
altar, *to be* a burnt sacrifice, an offering made
by fire, of a sweet savour unto the LORD.
10 ¶ And if his offering *be* of the flocks,
namely, of the sheep, or of the goats, for a burnt
sacrifice; he shall bring it a male without blemish.
11 And he shall kill it on the side of the altar
northward before the LORD: and the priests,
Aar'on's sons, shall sprinkle his blood round
about upon the altar.
12 And he shall cut it into his pieces, with his
head and his fat: and the priest shall lay them in
order on the wood that *is* on the fire which *is*
upon the altar:
13 But he shall wash the inwards and the
legs with water: and the priest shall bring *it* all,
and burn *it* upon the altar: it *is* a burnt sacrifice,
an offering made by fire, of a sweet savour unto
the LORD.
14 ¶ And if the burnt sacrifice for his offering to the LORD *be* of fowls, then he shall bring
his offering of turtledoves, or of young pigeons.
15 And the priest shall bring it unto the altar,
and wring off his head, and burn *it* on the altar;
and the blood thereof shall be wrung out at the
side of the altar:
16 And he shall pluck away his crop with his
feathers, and cast it beside the altar on the east
part, by the place of the ashes:
17 And he shall cleave it with the wings
thereof, *but* shall not divide *it* asunder: and the
priest shall burn it upon the altar, upon the
wood that *is* upon the fire: it *is* a burnt sacrifice,
an offering made by fire, of a sweet savour unto
the LORD.

2 AND when any will offer a meat offering
unto the LORD, his offering shall be *of* fine
flour; and he shall pour oil upon it, and put
frankincense thereon:
2 And he shall bring it to Aar'on's sons the
priests: and he shall take thereout his handful
of the flour thereof, and of the oil thereof, with
all the frankincense thereof; and the priest shall
burn the memorial of it upon the altar, *to be* an
offering made by fire, of a sweet savour unto
the LORD:
3 And the remnant of the meat offering *shall*
be Aar'on's and his sons': *it is* a thing most holy
of the offerings of the LORD made by fire.
4 ¶ And if thou bring an oblation of a meat
offering baken in the oven, *it shall be* unleavened cakes of fine flour mingled with oil, or unleavened wafers anointed with oil.
5 ¶ And if thy oblation *be* a meat offering
baken in a pan, it shall be *of* fine flour unleavened, mingled with oil.
6 Thou shalt part it in pieces, and pour oil
thereon: it *is* a meat offering.
7 ¶ And if thy oblation *be* a meat offering
baken in the fryingpan, it shall be made *of* fine
flour with oil.
8 And thou shalt bring the meat offering that
is made of these things unto the LORD: and

when it is presented unto the priest, he shall bring it unto the altar.

9 And the priest shall take from the meat offering a memorial thereof, and shall burn *it* upon the altar: *it is* an offering made by fire, of a sweet savour unto the LORD.

10 And that which is left of the meat offering *shall be* Aar'on's and his sons': *it is* a thing most holy of the offerings of the LORD made by fire.

11 No meat offering, which ye shall bring unto the LORD, shall be made with leaven: for ye shall burn no leaven, nor any honey, in any offering of the LORD made by fire.

12 ¶ As for the oblation of the firstfruits, ye shall offer them unto the LORD: but they shall not be burnt on the altar for a sweet savour.

13 And every oblation of thy meat offering shalt thou season with salt; neither shalt thou suffer the salt of the covenant of thy God to be lacking from thy meat offering: with all thine offerings thou shalt offer salt.

14 And if thou offer a meat offering of thy firstfruits unto the LORD, thou shalt offer for the meat offering of thy firstfruits green ears of corn dried by the fire, *even* corn beaten out of full ears.

15 And thou shalt put oil upon it, and lay frankincense thereon: it *is* a meat offering.

16 And the priest shall burn the memorial of it, *part* of the beaten corn thereof, and *part* of the oil thereof, with all the frankincense thereof: *it is* an offering made by fire unto the LORD.

3 AND if his oblation *be* a sacrifice of peace offering, if he offer *it* of the herd; whether *it be* a male or female, he shall offer it without blemish before the LORD.

2 And he shall lay his hand upon the head of his offering, and kill it *at* the door of the tabernacle of the congregation: and Aar'on's sons the priests shall sprinkle the blood upon the altar round about.

3 And he shall offer of the sacrifice of the peace offering an offering made by fire unto the LORD; the fat that covereth the inwards, and all the fat that *is* upon the inwards,

4 And the two kidneys, and the fat that *is* on them, which *is* by the flanks, and the caul above the liver, with the kidneys, it shall he take away.

5 And Aar'on's sons shall burn it on the altar upon the burnt sacrifice, which *is* upon the wood that *is* on the fire: *it is* an offering made by fire, of a sweet savour unto the LORD.

6 ¶ And if his offering for a sacrifice of peace offering unto the LORD *be* of the flock; male or female, he shall offer it without blemish.

7 If he offer a lamb for his offering, then shall he offer it before the LORD.

8 And he shall lay his hand upon the head of his offering, and kill it before the tabernacle of the congregation: and Aar'on's sons shall sprinkle the blood thereof round about upon the altar.

9 And he shall offer of the sacrifice of the peace offering an offering made by fire unto the LORD; the fat thereof, *and* the whole rump, it shall he take off hard by the backbone; and the fat that covereth the inwards, and all the fat that *is* upon the inwards,

10 And the two kidneys, and the fat that *is* upon them, which *is* by the flanks, and the caul above the liver, with the kidneys, it shall he take away.

11 And the priest shall burn it upon the altar: *it is* the food of the offering made by fire unto the LORD.

12 ¶ And if his offering *be* a goat, then he shall offer it before the LORD.

13 And he shall lay his hand upon the head of it, and kill it before the tabernacle of the congregation: and the sons of Aar'on shall sprinkle the blood thereof upon the altar round about.

14 And he shall offer thereof his offering, *even* an offering made by fire unto the LORD; the fat that covereth the inwards, and all the fat that *is* upon the inwards,

15 And the two kidneys, and the fat that *is* upon them, which *is* by the flanks, and the caul above the liver, with the kidneys, it shall he take away.

16 And the priest shall burn them upon the altar: *it is* the food of the offering made by fire for a sweet savour: all the fat *is* the LORD's.

17 *It shall be* a perpetual statute for your generations throughout all your dwellings, that ye eat neither fat nor blood.

4 AND the LORD spake unto Mo'ses, saying,

2 Speak unto the children of Is'ra-el, saying, If a soul shall sin through ignorance against any of the commandments of the LORD *concerning things* which ought not to be done, and shall do against any of them:

3 If the priest that is anointed do sin according to the sin of the people; then let him bring for his sin, which he hath sinned, a young bullock without blemish unto the LORD for a sin offering.

4 And he shall bring the bullock unto the door of the tabernacle of the congregation before the LORD; and shall lay his hand upon the bullock's head, and kill the bullock before the LORD.

5 And the priest that is anointed shall take of the bullock's blood, and bring it to the tabernacle of the congregation:

6 And the priest shall dip his finger in the blood, and sprinkle of the blood seven times before the LORD, before the veil of the sanctuary.

7 And the priest shall put *some* of the blood upon the horns of the altar of sweet incense before the LORD, which *is* in the tabernacle of the congregation; and shall pour all the blood of the bullock at the bottom of the altar of the burnt offering, which *is at* the door of the tabernacle of the congregation.

8 And he shall take off from it all the fat of the bullock for the sin offering; the fat that covereth the inwards, and all the fat that *is* upon the inwards,

9 And the two kidneys, and the fat that *is* upon them, which *is* by the flanks, and the caul above the liver, with the kidneys, it shall he take away,

10 As it was taken off from the bullock of the sacrifice of peace offerings: and the priest shall burn them upon the altar of the burnt offering.

11 And the skin of the bullock, and all his flesh, with his head, and with his legs, and his inwards, and his dung,

12 Even the whole bullock shall he carry forth without the camp unto a clean place, where the ashes are poured out, and burn him on the wood with fire: where the ashes are poured out shall he be burnt.

13 ¶ And if the whole congregation of Is'ra-el sin through ignorance, and the thing be hid from the eyes of the assembly, and they have done *somewhat against* any of the commandments of the LORD *concerning things* which should not be done, and are guilty;

14 When the sin, which they have sinned against it, is known, then the congregation shall offer a young bullock for the sin, and bring him before the tabernacle of the congregation.

15 And the elders of the congregation shall lay their hands upon the head of the bullock before the LORD: and the bullock shall be killed before the LORD.

16 And the priest that is anointed shall bring of the bullock's blood to the tabernacle of the congregation:

17 And the priest shall dip his finger *in some* of the blood, and sprinkle *it* seven times before the LORD, *even* before the veil.

18 And he shall put *some* of the blood upon the horns of the altar which *is* before the LORD, that *is* in the tabernacle of the congregation, and shall pour out all the blood at the bottom of the altar of the burnt offering, which *is at* the door of the tabernacle of the congregation.

19 And he shall take all his fat from him, and burn *it* upon the altar.

20 And he shall do with the bullock as he did with the bullock for a sin offering, so shall he do with this: and the priest shall make an atonement for them, and it shall be forgiven them.

21 And he shall carry forth the bullock without the camp, and burn him as he burned the first bullock: it *is* a sin offering for the congregation.

22 ¶ When a ruler hath sinned, and done *somewhat* through ignorance *against* any of the commandments of the LORD his God *concerning things* which should not be done, and is guilty;

23 Or if his sin, wherein he hath sinned, come to his knowledge; he shall bring his offering, a kid of the goats, a male without blemish:

24 And he shall lay his hand upon the head of the goat, and kill it in the place where they kill the burnt offering before the LORD: it *is* a sin offering.

25 And the priest shall take of the blood of the sin offering with his finger, and put *it* upon the horns of the altar of burnt offering, and shall pour out his blood at the bottom of the altar of burnt offering.

26 And he shall burn all his fat upon the altar, as the fat of the sacrifice of peace offerings: and the priest shall make an atonement for him as concerning his sin, and it shall be forgiven him.

27 ¶ And if any one of the common people sin through ignorance, while he doeth *somewhat against* any of the commandments of the LORD *concerning things* which ought not to be done, and be guilty;

28 Or if his sin, which he hath sinned, come to his knowledge: then he shall bring his offering, a kid of the goats, a female without blemish, for his sin which he hath sinned.

29 And he shall lay his hand upon the head of the sin offering, and slay the sin offering in the place of the burnt offering.

30 And the priest shall take of the blood thereof with his finger, and put *it* upon the horns of the altar of burnt offering, and shall pour out all the blood thereof at the bottom of the altar.

31 And he shall take away all the fat thereof, as the fat is taken away from off the sacrifice of peace offerings; and the priest shall burn *it* upon the altar for a sweet savour unto the LORD; and the priest shall make an atonement for him, and it shall be forgiven him.

32 And if he bring a lamb for a sin offering, he shall bring it a female without blemish.

33 And he shall lay his hand upon the head of the sin offering, and slay it for a sin offering in the place where they kill the burnt offering.

34 And the priest shall take of the blood of the sin offering with his finger, and put *it* upon the horns of the altar of burnt offering, and shall pour out all the blood thereof at the bottom of the altar:

35 And he shall take away all the fat thereof, as the fat of the lamb is taken away from the sacrifice of the peace offerings; and the priest shall burn them upon the altar, according to the offerings made by fire unto the LORD: and the priest shall make an atonement for his sin that he hath committed, and it shall be forgiven him.

5 AND if a soul sin, and hear the voice of swearing, and *is* a witness, whether he hath seen or known *of it;* if he do not utter *it,* then he shall bear his iniquity.

2 Or if a soul touch any unclean thing, whether *it be* a carcase of an unclean beast, or a carcase of unclean cattle, or the carcase of unclean creeping things, and *if* it be hidden from him; he also shall be unclean, and guilty.

3 Or if he touch the uncleanness of man, whatsoever uncleanness *it be* that a man shall be defiled withal, and it be hid from him; when he knoweth *of it,* then he shall be guilty.

4 Or if a soul swear, pronouncing with *his* lips to do evil, or to do good, whatsoever *it be* that a man shall pronounce with an oath, and it be hid from him; when he knoweth *of it,* then he shall be guilty in one of these.

5 And it shall be, when he shall be guilty in one of these *things,* that he shall confess that he hath sinned in that *thing:*

6 And he shall bring his trespass offering unto the LORD for his sin which he hath sinned, a female from the flock, a lamb or a kid of the goats, for a sin offering; and the priest shall make an atonement for him concerning his sin.

7 And if he be not able to bring a lamb, then he shall bring for his trespass, which he hath committed, two turtledoves, or two young pigeons, unto the LORD; one for a sin offering, and the other for a burnt offering.

8 And he shall bring them unto the priest, who shall offer *that* which *is* for the sin offering first, and wring off his head from his neck, but shall not divide *it* asunder:

9 And he shall sprinkle of the blood of the sin offering upon the side of the altar; and the rest of the blood shall be wrung out at the bottom of the altar: it *is* a sin offering.

10 And he shall offer the second *for* a burnt offering, according to the manner: and the priest shall make an atonement for him for his sin which he hath sinned, and it shall be forgiven him.

11 ¶ But if he be not able to bring two turtledoves, or two young pigeons, then he that sinned shall bring for his offering the tenth part of an ephah of fine flour for a sin offering; he shall put no oil upon it, neither shall he put *any* frankincense thereon: for it *is* a sin offering.

12 Then shall he bring it to the priest, and the priest shall take his handful of it, *even* a memorial thereof, and burn *it* on the altar, according to the offerings made by fire unto the LORD: it *is* a sin offering.

13 And the priest shall make an atonement for him as touching his sin that he hath sinned in one of these, and it shall be forgiven him: and *the remnant* shall be the priest's, as a meat offering.

14 ¶ And the LORD spake unto Mo'ses, saying,

15 If a soul commit a trespass, and sin through ignorance, in the holy things of the LORD; then he shall bring for his trespass unto the LORD a ram without blemish out of the flocks, with thy estimation by shekels of silver, after the shekel of the sanctuary, for a trespass offering:

16 And he shall make amends for the harm that he hath done in the holy thing, and shall add the fifth part thereto, and give it unto the priest: and the priest shall make an atonement for him with the ram of the trespass offering, and it shall be forgiven him.

17 ¶ And if a soul sin, and commit any of these things which are forbidden to be done by the commandments of the LORD; though he wist *it* not, yet is he guilty, and shall bear his iniquity.

18 And he shall bring a ram without blemish out of the flock, with thy estimation, for a trespass offering, unto the priest: and the priest shall make an atonement for him concerning his ignorance wherein he erred and wist *it* not, and it shall be forgiven him.

19 It *is* a trespass offering: he hath certainly trespassed against the LORD.

6 AND the LORD spake unto Mo'ses, saying,
2 If a soul sin, and commit a trespass against the LORD, and lie unto his neighbour in that which was delivered him to keep, or in fellowship, or in a thing taken away by violence, or hath deceived his neighbour;

3 Or have found that which was lost, and lieth concerning it, and sweareth falsely; in any of all these that a man doeth, sinning therein:

4 Then it shall be, because he hath sinned, and is guilty, that he shall restore that which he took violently away, or the thing which he hath deceitfully gotten, or that which was delivered him to keep, or the lost thing which he found,

5 Or all that about which he hath sworn falsely; he shall even restore it in the principal, and shall add the fifth part more thereto, *and* give it unto him to whom it appertaineth, in the day of his trespass offering.

6 And he shall bring his trespass offering unto the LORD, a ram without blemish out of the flock, with thy estimation, for a trespass offering, unto the priest:

7 And the priest shall make an atonement for him before the LORD: and it shall be forgiven him for any thing of all that he hath done in trespassing therein.

8 ¶ And the LORD spake unto Mo'ses, saying,

9 Command Aar'on and his sons, saying, This *is* the law of the burnt offering: It *is* the burnt offering, because of the burning upon the altar all night unto the morning, and the fire of the altar shall be burning in it.

10 And the priest shall put on his linen garment, and his linen breeches shall he put upon his flesh, and take up the ashes which the fire hath consumed with the burnt offering on the altar, and he shall put them beside the altar.

11 And he shall put off his garments, and put on other garments, and carry forth the ashes without the camp unto a clean place.

12 And the fire upon the altar shall be burning in it; it shall not be put out: and the priest shall burn wood on it every morning, and lay the burnt offering in order upon it; and he shall burn thereon the fat of the peace offerings.

13 The fire shall ever be burning upon the altar; it shall never go out.

14 ¶ And this *is* the law of the meat offering: the sons of Aar'on shall offer it before the LORD, before the altar.

15 And he shall take of it his handful, of the flour of the meat offering, and of the oil thereof, and all the frankincense which *is* upon the meat offering, and shall burn *it* upon the altar *for* a sweet savour, *even* the memorial of it, unto the LORD.

16 And the remainder thereof shall Aar'on and his sons eat: with unleavened bread shall it be eaten in the holy place; in the court of the tabernacle of the congregation they shall eat it.

17 It shall not be baken with leaven. I have given it *unto them for* their portion of my offerings made by fire; it *is* most holy, as *is* the sin offering, and as the trespass offering.

18 All the males among the children of Aar'on shall eat of it. *It shall be* a statute for ever in your generations concerning the offerings of the LORD made by fire: every one that toucheth them shall be holy.

19 ¶ And the LORD spake unto Mo'ses, saying,

20 This *is* the offering of Aar'on and of his sons, which they shall offer unto the LORD in the day when he is anointed; the tenth part of an ephah of fine flour for a meat offering perpetual, half of it in the morning, and half thereof at night.

21 In a pan it shall be made with oil; *and when it is* baken, thou shalt bring it in: *and* the baken pieces of the meat offering shalt thou offer *for* a sweet savour unto the LORD.

22 And the priest of his sons that is anointed in his stead shall offer it: *it is* a statute for ever unto the LORD; it shall be wholly burnt.

23 For every meat offering for the priest shall be wholly burnt: it shall not be eaten.

24 ¶ And the LORD spake unto Mo'ses, saying,

25 Speak unto Aar'on and to his sons, saying, This *is* the law of the sin offering: In the place where the burnt offering is killed shall the sin offering be killed before the LORD: it *is* most holy.

26 The priest that offereth it for sin shall eat it: in the holy place shall it be eaten, in the court of the tabernacle of the congregation.

27 Whatsoever shall touch the flesh thereof shall be holy: and when there is sprinkled of the blood thereof upon any garment, thou shalt wash that whereon it was sprinkled in the holy place.

28 But the earthen vessel wherein it is sodden shall be broken: and if it be sodden in a brasen pot, it shall be both scoured, and rinsed in water.

29 All the males among the priests shall eat thereof: it *is* most holy.

30 And no sin offering, whereof *any* of the blood is brought into the tabernacle of the congregation to reconcile *withal* in the holy *place*, shall be eaten: it shall be burnt in the fire.

7 LIKEWISE this *is* the law of the trespass offering: it *is* most holy.

2 In the place where they kill the burnt offering shall they kill the trespass offering: and the blood thereof shall he sprinkle round about upon the altar.

3 And he shall offer of it all the fat thereof; the rump, and the fat that covereth the inwards,

4 And the two kidneys, and the fat that *is* on them, which *is* by the flanks, and the caul *that is* above the liver, with the kidneys, it shall he take away:

5 And the priest shall burn them upon the altar *for* an offering made by fire unto the LORD: it *is* a trespass offering.

6 Every male among the priests shall eat thereof: it shall be eaten in the holy place: it *is* most holy.

7 As the sin offering *is,* so *is* the trespass offering: *there is* one law for them: the priest that maketh atonement therewith shall have *it.*

8 And the priest that offereth any man's burnt offering, *even* the priest shall have to himself the skin of the burnt offering which he hath offered.

9 And all the meat offering that is baken in the oven, and all that is dressed in the fryingpan, and in the pan, shall be the priest's that offereth it.

10 And every meat offering, mingled with oil, and dry, shall all the sons of Aar'on have, one *as much* as another.

11 And this *is* the law of the sacrifice of peace offerings, which he shall offer unto the LORD.

12 If he offer it for a thanksgiving, then he shall offer with the sacrifice of thanksgiving unleavened cakes mingled with oil, and unleavened wafers anointed with oil, and cakes mingled with oil, of fine flour, fried.

13 Besides the cakes, he shall offer *for* his offering leavened bread with the sacrifice of thanksgiving of his peace offerings.

14 And of it he shall offer one out of the whole oblation *for* an heave offering unto the LORD, *and* it shall be the priest's that sprinkleth the blood of the peace offerings.

15 And the flesh of the sacrifice of his peace offerings for thanksgiving shall be eaten the same day that it is offered; he shall not leave any of it until the morning.

16 But if the sacrifice of his offering *be* a vow, or a voluntary offering, it shall be eaten the same day that he offereth his sacrifice: and on the morrow also the remainder of it shall be eaten:

17 But the remainder of the flesh of the sacrifice on the third day shall be burnt with fire.

18 And if *any* of the flesh of the sacrifice of his peace offerings be eaten at all on the third day, it shall not be accepted, neither shall it be imputed unto him that offereth it: it shall be an abomination, and the soul that eateth of it shall bear his iniquity.

19 And the flesh that toucheth any unclean *thing* shall not be eaten; it shall be burnt with fire: and as for the flesh, all that be clean shall eat thereof.

20 But the soul that eateth *of* the flesh of the sacrifice of peace offerings, that *pertain* unto the LORD, having his uncleanness upon him, even that soul shall be cut off from his people.

21 Moreover the soul that shall touch any unclean *thing, as* the uncleanness of man, or *any* unclean beast, or any abominable unclean *thing,* and eat of the flesh of the sacrifice of peace offerings, which *pertain* unto the LORD, even that soul shall be cut off from his people.

22 ¶ And the LORD spake unto Mo'ses, saying,

23 Speak unto the children of Is'ra-el, saying, Ye shall eat no manner of fat, of ox, or of sheep, or of goat.

24 And the fat of the beast that dieth of itself, and the fat of that which is torn with beasts, may be used in any other use: but ye shall in no wise eat of it.

25 For whosoever eateth the fat of the beast, of which men offer an offering made by fire unto the LORD, even the soul that eateth *it* shall be cut off from his people.

26 Moreover ye shall eat no manner of blood, *whether it be* of fowl or of beast, in any of your dwellings.

27 Whatsoever soul *it be* that eateth any manner of blood, even that soul shall be cut off from his people.

28 ¶ And the LORD spake unto Mo'ses, saying,

29 Speak unto the children of Is'ra-el, saying, He that offereth the sacrifice of his peace offerings unto the LORD shall bring his oblation unto the LORD of the sacrifice of his peace offerings.

30 His own hands shall bring the offerings of the LORD made by fire, the fat with the breast, it shall he bring, that the breast may be waved *for* a wave offering before the LORD.

31 And the priest shall burn the fat upon the altar: but the breast shall be Aar'on's and his sons'.

32 And the right shoulder shall ye give unto the priest *for* an heave offering of the sacrifices of your peace offerings.

33 He among the sons of Aar'on, that offereth the blood of the peace offerings, and the fat, shall have the right shoulder for *his* part.

34 For the wave breast and the heave shoulder have I taken of the children of Is'ra-el from off the sacrifices of their peace offerings, and have given them unto Aar'on the priest and unto his sons by a statute for ever from among the children of Is'ra-el.

35 ¶ This *is the portion* of the anointing of Aar'on, and of the anointing of his sons, out of the offerings of the LORD made by fire, in the day *when* he presented them to minister unto the LORD in the priest's office;

36 Which the LORD commanded to be given them of the children of Is'ra-el, in the day that he anointed them, *by* a statute for ever throughout their generations.

37 This *is* the law of the burnt offering, of the meat offering, and of the sin offering, and of the trespass offering, and of the consecrations, and of the sacrifice of the peace offerings;

38 Which the LORD commanded Mo'ses in mount Si'nai, in the day that he commanded the children of Is'ra-el to offer their oblations unto the LORD, in the wilderness of Si'nai.

8 AND the LORD spake unto Mo'ses, saying,

2 Take Aar'on and his sons with him, and the garments, and the anointing oil, and a bullock for the sin offering, and two rams, and a basket of unleavened bread;

3 And gather thou all the congregation together unto the door of the tabernacle of the congregation.

4 And Mo'ses did as the LORD commanded him; and the assembly was gathered together unto the door of the tabernacle of the congregation.

5 And Mo'ses said unto the congregation, This *is* the thing which the LORD commanded to be done.

6 And Mo'ses brought Aar'on and his sons, and washed them with water.

7 And he put upon him the coat, and girded him with the girdle, and clothed him with the robe, and put the ephod upon him, and he girded him with the curious girdle of the ephod, and bound *it* unto him therewith.

8 And he put the breastplate upon him: also he put in the breastplate the U'rim and the Thum'mim.

9 And he put the mitre upon his head; also

upon the mitre, *even* upon his forefront, did he put the golden plate, the holy crown; as the LORD commanded Mo'ses.

10 And Mo'ses took the anointing oil, and anointed the tabernacle and all that *was* therein, and sanctified them.

11 And he sprinkled thereof upon the altar seven times, and anointed the altar and all his vessels, both the laver and his foot, to sanctify them.

12 And he poured of the anointing oil upon Aar'on's head, and anointed him, to sanctify him.

13 And Mo'ses brought Aar'on's sons, and put coats upon them, and girded them with girdles, and put bonnets upon them; as the LORD commanded Mo'ses.

14 And he brought the bullock for the sin offering: and Aar'on and his sons laid their hands upon the head of the bullock for the sin offering.

15 And he slew *it;* and Mo'ses took the blood, and put *it* upon the horns of the altar round about with his finger, and purified the altar, and poured the blood at the bottom of the altar, and sanctified it, to make reconciliation upon it.

16 And he took all the fat that *was* upon the inwards, and the caul *above* the liver, and the two kidneys, and their fat, and Mo'ses burned *it* upon the altar.

17 But the bullock, and his hide, his flesh, and his dung, he burnt with fire without the camp; as the LORD commanded Mo'ses.

18 ¶ And he brought the ram for the burnt offering: and Aar'on and his sons laid their hands upon the head of the ram.

19 And he killed *it;* and Mo'ses sprinkled the blood upon the altar round about.

20 And he cut the ram into pieces; and Mo'ses burnt the head, and the pieces, and the fat.

21 And he washed the inwards and the legs in water; and Mo'ses burnt the whole ram upon the altar: it *was* a burnt sacrifice for a sweet savour, *and* an offering made by fire unto the LORD; as the LORD commanded Mo'ses.

22 ¶ And he brought the other ram, the ram of consecration: and Aar'on and his sons laid their hands upon the head of the ram.

23 And he slew *it;* and Mo'ses took of the blood of it, and put *it* upon the tip of Aar'on's right ear, and upon the thumb of his right hand, and upon the great toe of his right foot.

24 And he brought Aar'on's sons, and Mo'ses put of the blood upon the tip of their right ear, and upon the thumbs of their right hands, and upon the great toes of their right feet: and Mo'ses sprinkled the blood upon the altar round about.

25 And he took the fat, and the rump, and all the fat that *was* upon the inwards, and the caul *above* the liver, and the two kidneys, and their fat, and the right shoulder:

26 And out of the basket of unleavened bread, that *was* before the LORD, he took one unleavened cake, and a cake of oiled bread, and one wafer, and put *them* on the fat, and upon the right shoulder:

27 And he put all upon Aar'on's hands, and upon his sons' hands, and waved them *for* a wave offering before the LORD.

28 And Mo'ses took them from off their hands, and burnt *them* on the altar upon the burnt offering: they *were* consecrations for a sweet savour: it *is* an offering made by fire unto the LORD.

29 And Mo'ses took the breast, and waved it *for* a wave offering before the LORD: *for* of the ram of consecration it was Mo'ses' part; as the LORD commanded Mo'ses.

30 And Mo'ses took of the anointing oil, and of the blood which *was* upon the altar, and sprinkled *it* upon Aar'on, *and* upon his garments, and upon his sons, and upon his sons' garments with him; and sanctified Aar'on, *and* his garments, and his sons, and his sons' garments with him.

31 ¶ And Mo'ses said unto Aar'on and to his sons, Boil the flesh *at* the door of the tabernacle of the congregation: and there eat it with the bread that *is* in the basket of consecrations, as I commanded, saying, Aar'on and his sons shall eat it.

32 And that which remaineth of the flesh and of the bread shall ye burn with fire.

33 And ye shall not go out of the door of the tabernacle of the congregation *in* seven days, until the days of your consecration be at an end: for seven days shall he consecrate you.

34 As he hath done this day, *so* the LORD hath commanded to do, to make an atonement for you.

35 Therefore shall ye abide *at* the door of the tabernacle of the congregation day and night seven days, and keep the charge of the LORD, that ye die not: for so I am commanded.

36 So Aar'on and his sons did all things which the LORD commanded by the hand of Mo'ses.

9 AND it came to pass on the eighth day, *that* Mo'ses called Aar'on and his sons, and the elders of Is'ra-el;

2 And he said unto Aar'on, Take thee a young calf for a sin offering, and a ram for a burnt offering, without blemish, and offer *them* before the LORD.

3 And unto the children of Is'ra-el thou shalt speak, saying, Take ye a kid of the goats for a sin offering; and a calf and a lamb, *both* of the first year, without blemish, for a burnt offering;

4 Also a bullock and a ram for peace offerings, to sacrifice before the LORD; and a meat offering mingled with oil: for to day the LORD will appear unto you.

5 ¶ And they brought *that* which Mo'ses commanded before the tabernacle of the congregation: and all the congregation drew near and stood before the LORD.

6 And Mo'ses said, This *is* the thing which the LORD commanded that ye should do: and the glory of the LORD shall appear unto you.

7 And Mo'ses said unto Aar'on, Go unto the altar, and offer thy sin offering, and thy burnt offering, and make an atonement for thyself, and for the people: and offer the offering of the people, and make an atonement for them; as the LORD commanded.

8 ¶ Aar'on therefore went unto the altar, and slew the calf of the sin offering, which *was* for himself.

9 And the sons of Aar'on brought the blood unto him: and he dipped his finger in the blood, and put *it* upon the horns of the altar, and poured out the blood at the bottom of the altar:

10 But the fat, and the kidneys, and the caul above the liver of the sin offering, he burnt upon the altar; as the LORD commanded Mo'ses.

11 And the flesh and the hide he burnt with fire without the camp.

12 And he slew the burnt offering; and Aar'on's sons presented unto him the blood, which he sprinkled round about upon the altar.

13 And they presented the burnt offering

unto him, with the pieces thereof, and the head:
and he burnt *them* upon the altar.
14 And he did wash the inwards and the legs,
and burnt *them* upon the burnt offering on the
altar.
15 ¶ And he brought the people's offering,
and took the goat, which *was* the sin offering
for the people, and slew it, and offered it for sin,
as the first.
16 And he brought the burnt offering, and offered it according to the manner.
17 And he brought the meat offering, and
took an handful thereof, and burnt *it* upon the
altar, beside the burnt sacrifice of the morning.
18 He slew also the bullock and the ram *for* a
sacrifice of peace offerings, which *was* for the
people: and Aar'on's sons presented unto him
the blood, which he sprinkled upon the altar
round about,
19 And the fat of the bullock and of the ram,
the rump, and that which covereth *the inwards*,
and the kidneys, and the caul *above* the liver:
20 And they put the fat upon the breasts, and
he burnt the fat upon the altar:
21 And the breasts and the right shoulder
Aar'on waved *for* a wave offering before the
LORD; as Mo'ses commanded.
22 And Aar'on lifted up his hand toward the
people, and blessed them, and came down from
offering of the sin offering, and the burnt offering, and peace offerings.
23 And Mo'ses and Aar'on went into the tabernacle of the congregation, and came out, and
blessed the people: and the glory of the LORD
appeared unto all the people.
24 And there came a fire out from before the
LORD, and consumed upon the altar the burnt
offering and the fat: *which* when all the people
saw, they shouted, and fell on their faces.

10 AND Na'dab and A-bi'hu, the sons of
Aar'on, took either of them his censer,
and put fire therein, and put incense thereon,
and offered strange fire before the LORD, which
he commanded them not.
2 And there went out fire from the LORD, and
devoured them, and they died before the LORD.
3 Then Mo'ses said unto Aar'on, This *is it*
that the LORD spake, saying, I will be sanctified
in them that come nigh me, and before all the
people I will be glorified. And Aar'on held his
peace.
4 And Mo'ses called Mish'a-el and El'za-
phan, the sons of Uz'zi-el the uncle of Aar'on,
and said unto them, Come near, carry your
brethren from before the sanctuary out of the
camp.
5 So they went near, and carried them in
their coats out of the camp; as Mo'ses had said.
6 And Mo'ses said unto Aar'on, and unto E-
le-a'zar and unto Ith'a-mar, his sons, Uncover
not your heads, neither rend your clothes; lest
ye die, and lest wrath come upon all the people:
but let your brethren, the whole house of Is'ra-
el, bewail the burning which the LORD hath kindled.
7 And ye shall not go out from the door of
the tabernacle of the congregation, lest ye die:
for the annointing oil of the LORD *is* upon you.
And they did according to the word of Mo'ses.
8 ¶ And the LORD spake unto Aar'on, saying,
9 Do not drink wine nor strong drink, thou,
nor thy sons with thee, when ye go into the tabernacle of the congregation, lest ye die: *it shall*
be a statute for ever throughout your generations:
10 And that ye may put difference between
holy and unholy, and between unclean and
clean;
11 And that ye may teach the children of Is'-
ra-el all the statutes which the LORD hath spoken unto them by the hand of Mo'ses.
12 ¶ And Mo'ses spake unto Aar'on, and
unto E-le-a'zar and unto Ith'a-mar, his sons that
were left, Take the meat offering that remaineth
of the offerings of the LORD made by fire, and
eat it without leaven beside the altar: for it *is*
most holy:
13 And ye shall eat it in the holy place, because it *is* thy due, and thy sons' due, of the
sacrifices of the LORD made by fire: for so I am
commanded.
14 And the wave breast and heave shoulder
shall ye eat in a clean place; thou, and thy sons,
and thy daughters with thee: for *they be* thy
due, and thy sons' due, *which* are given out of
the sacrifices of peace offerings of the children
of Is'ra-el.
15 The heave shoulder and the wave breast
shall they bring with the offerings made by fire
of the fat, to wave *it for* a wave offering before
the LORD; and it shall be thine, and thy sons'
with thee, by a statute for ever; as the LORD
hath commanded.
16 ¶ And Mo'ses diligently sought the goat
of the sin offering, and, behold, it was burnt:
and he was angry with E-le-a'zar and Ith'a-mar,
the sons of Aar'on *which were* left *alive*, saying,
17 Wherefore have ye not eaten the sin offering in the holy place, seeing it *is* most holy, and
God hath given it you to bear the iniquity of the
congregation, to make atonement for them before the LORD?
18 Behold, the blood of it was not brought in
within the holy *place*: ye should indeed have
eaten it in the holy *place*, as I commanded.
19 And Aar'on said unto Mo'ses, Behold, this
day have they offered their sin offering and
their burnt offering before the LORD; and such
things have befallen me: and *if* I had eaten the
sin offering to day, should it have been accepted in the sight of the LORD?
20 And when Mo'ses heard *that*, he was content.

11 AND the LORD spake unto Mo'ses and
to Aar'on, saying unto them,
2 Speak unto the children of Is'ra-el, saying,
These *are* the beasts which ye shall eat among
all the beasts that *are* on the earth.
3 Whatsoever parteth the hoof, and is clovenfooted, *and* cheweth the cud, among the
beasts, that shall ye eat.
4 Nevertheless these shall ye not eat of them
that chew the cud, or of them that divide the
hoof: *as* the camel, because he cheweth the cud,
but divideth not the hoof; he *is* unclean unto
you.
5 And the coney, because he cheweth the
cud, but divideth not the hoof; he *is* unclean
unto you.
6 And the hare, because he cheweth the cud,
but divideth not the hoof; he *is* unclean unto
you.
7 And the swine, though he divide the hoof,
and be clovenfooted, yet he cheweth not the
cud; he *is* unclean to you.
8 Of their flesh shall ye not eat, and their carcase shall ye not touch; they *are* unclean to you.
9 ¶ These shall ye eat of all that *are* in the
waters: whatsoever hath fins and scales in the
waters, in the seas, and in the rivers, them shall
ye eat.
10 And all that have not fins and scales in the

seas, and in the rivers, of all that move in the
waters, and of any living thing which *is* in the
waters, they *shall be* an abomination unto you:
11 They shall be even an abomination unto
you; ye shall not eat of their flesh, but ye shall
have their carcases in abomination.
12 Whatsoever hath no fins nor scales in the
waters, that *shall be* an abomination unto you.
13 ¶ And these *are they which* ye shall have
in abomination among the fowls; they shall not
be eaten, they *are* an abomination: the eagle,
and the ossifrage, and the ospray,
14 And the vulture, and the kite after his
kind;
15 Every raven after his kind;
16 And the owl, and the night hawk, and the
cuckow, and the hawk after his kind,
17 And the little owl, and the cormorant, and
the great owl,
18 And the swan, and the pelican, and the
gier eagle,
19 And the stork, the heron after her kind,
and the lapwing, and the bat.
20 All fowls that creep, going upon *all* four,
shall be an abomination unto you.
21 Yet these may ye eat of every flying
creeping thing that goeth upon *all* four, which
have legs above their feet, to leap withal upon
the earth;
22 *Even* these of them ye may eat; the locust
after his kind, and the bald locust after his kind,
and the beetle after his kind, and the grasshopper after his kind.
23 But all *other* flying creeping things, which
have four feet, *shall be* an abomination unto
you.
24 And for these ye shall be unclean: whosoever toucheth the carcase of them shall be unclean until the even.
25 And whosoever beareth *ought* of the carcase of them shall wash his clothes, and be unclean until the even.
26 *The carcases* of every beast which divideth the hoof, and *is* not clovenfooted, nor cheweth the cud, *are* unclean unto you: every one
that toucheth them shall be unclean.
27 And whatsoever goeth upon his paws,
among all manner of beasts that go on *all* four,
those *are* unclean unto you: whoso toucheth
their carcase shall be unclean until the even.
28 And he that beareth the carcase of them
shall wash his clothes, and be unclean until the
even: they *are* unclean unto you.
29 ¶ These also *shall be* unclean unto you
among the creeping things that creep upon the
earth; the weasel, and the mouse, and the tor-
toise after his kind,
30 And the ferret, and the chameleon, and
the lizard, and the snail, and the mole.
31 These *are* unclean to you among all that
creep: whosoever doth touch them, when they
be dead, shall be unclean until the even.
32 And upon whatsoever *any* of them, when
they are dead, doth fall, it shall be unclean;
whether *it be* any vessel of wood, or raiment, or
skin, or sack, whatsoever vessel *it be,* wherein
any work is done, it must be put into water, and
it shall be unclean until the even; so it shall be
cleansed.
33 And every earthen vessel, whereinto *any*
of them falleth, whatsoever *is* in it shall be unclean; and ye shall break it.
34 Of all meat which may be eaten, *that* on
which *such* water cometh shall be unclean: and
all drink that may be drunk in every *such* vessel
shall be unclean.
35 And every *thing* whereupon *any part* of
their carcase falleth shall be unclean; *whether it
be* oven, or ranges for pots, they shall be broken
down: *for* they *are* unclean, and shall be unclean unto you.
36 Nevertheless a fountain or pit, *wherein
there is* plenty of water, shall be clean: but that
which toucheth their carcase shall be unclean.
37 And if *any part* of their carcase fall upon
any sowing seed which is to be sown, it *shall be*
clean.
38 But if *any* water be put upon the seed, and
any part of their carcase fall thereon, it *shall be*
unclean unto you.
39 And if any beast, of which ye may eat, die;
he that toucheth the carcase thereof shall be
unclean until the even.
40 And he that eateth of the carcase of it
shall wash his clothes, and be unclean until the
even: he also that beareth the carcase of it shall
wash his clothes, and be unclean until the even.
41 And every creeping thing that creepeth
upon the earth *shall be* an abomination; it shall
not be eaten.
42 Whatsoever goeth upon the belly, and
whatsoever goeth upon *all* four, or whatsoever
hath more feet among all creeping things that
creep upon the earth, them ye shall not eat; for
they *are* an abomination.
43 Ye shall not make yourselves abominable
with any creeping thing that creepeth, neither
shall ye make yourselves unclean with them,
that ye should be defiled thereby.
44 For I *am* the LORD your God: ye shall
therefore sanctify yourselves, and ye shall be
holy; for I *am* holy: neither shall ye defile yourselves with any manner of creeping thing that
creepeth upon the earth.
45 For I *am* the LORD that bringeth you up
out of the land of E'gypt, to be your God: ye
shall therefore be holy, for I *am* holy.
46 This *is* the law of the beasts, and of the
fowl, and of every living creature that moveth
in the waters, and of every creature that creepeth upon the earth:
47 To make a difference between the unclean
and the clean, and between the beast that may
be eaten and the beast that may not be eaten.

12 AND the LORD spake unto Mo'ses, saying,
2 Speak unto the children of Is'ra-el, saying,
If a woman have conceived seed, and born a
man child: then she shall be unclean seven
days; according to the days of the separation
for her infirmity shall she be unclean.
3 And in the eighth day the flesh of his foreskin shall be circumcised.
4 And she shall then continue in the blood of
her purifying three and thirty days; she shall
touch no hallowed thing, nor come into the
sanctuary, until the days of her purifying be fulfilled.
5 But if she bear a maid child, then she shall
be unclean two weeks, as in her separation: and
she shall continue in the blood of her purifying
three-score and six days.
6 And when the days of her purifying are fulfilled, for a son, or for a daughter, she shall
bring a lamb of the first year for a burnt offering, and a young pigeon, or a turtledove, for a
sin offering, unto the door of the tabernacle of
the congregation, unto the priest:
7 Who shall offer it before the LORD, and
make an atonement for her; and she shall be
cleansed from the issue of her blood. This *is* the
law for her that hath born a male or a female.
8 And if she be not able to bring a lamb, then

she shall bring two turtles, or two young pigeons; the one for the burnt offering, and the other for a sin offering: and the priest shall make an atonement for her, and she shall be clean.

13 AND the LORD spake unto Mo′ses and Aar′on, saying,

2 When a man shall have in the skin of his flesh a rising, a scab, or bright spot, and it be in the skin of his flesh *like* the plague of leprosy; then he shall be brought unto Aar′on the priest, or unto one of his sons the priests:

3 And the priest shall look on the plague in the skin of the flesh: and *when* the hair in the plague is turned white, and the plague in sight *be* deeper than the skin of his flesh, it *is* a plague of leprosy: and the priest shall look on him, and pronounce him unclean.

4 If the bright spot *be* white in the skin of his flesh, and in sight *be* not deeper than the skin, and the hair thereof be not turned white; then the priest shall shut up *him that hath* the plague seven days:

5 And the priest shall look on him the seventh day: and, behold, *if* the plague in his sight be at a stay, *and* the plague spread not in the skin; then the priest shall shut him up seven days more:

6 And the priest shall look on him again the seventh day: and, behold, *if* the plague *be* somewhat dark, *and* the plague spread not in the skin, the priest shall pronounce him clean: it *is but* a scab: and he shall wash his clothes, and be clean.

7 But if the scab spread much abroad in the skin, after that he hath been seen of the priest for his cleansing, he shall be seen of the priest again:

8 And *if* the priest see that, behold, the scab spreadeth in the skin, then the priest shall pronounce him unclean: it *is* a leprosy.

9 ¶ When the plague of leprosy is in a man, then he shall be brought unto the priest;

10 And the priest shall see *him:* and, behold, *if* the rising *be* white in the skin, and it have turned the hair white, and *there be* quick raw flesh in the rising;

11 It *is* an old leprosy in the skin of his flesh, and the priest shall pronounce him unclean, and shall not shut him up: for he *is* unclean.

12 And if a leprosy break out abroad in the skin, and the leprosy cover all the skin of *him that hath* the plague from his head even to his foot, wheresoever the priest looketh;

13 Then the priest shall consider: and, behold, *if* the leprosy have covered all his flesh, he shall pronounce *him* clean *that hath* the plague: it is all turned white: he *is* clean.

14 But when raw flesh appeareth in him, he shall be unclean.

15 And the priest shall see the raw flesh, and pronounce him to be unclean: *for* the raw flesh *is* unclean: it *is* a leprosy.

16 Or if the raw flesh turn again, and be changed unto white, he shall come unto the priest;

17 And the priest shall see him: and, behold, *if* the plague be turned into white; then the priest shall pronounce *him* clean *that hath* the plague: he *is* clean.

18 ¶ The flesh also, in which, *even* in the skin thereof, was a boil, and is healed,

19 And in the place of the boil there be a white rising, or a bright spot, white, and somewhat reddish, and it be shewed to the priest;

20 And if, when the priest seeth it, behold, it *be* in sight lower than the skin, and the hair thereof be turned white; the priest shall pronounce him unclean: it *is* a plague of leprosy broken out of the boil.

21 But if the priest look on it, and, behold, *there be* no white hairs therein, and *if* it *be* not lower than the skin, but *be* somewhat dark; then the priest shall shut him up seven days:

22 And if it spread much abroad in the skin, then the priest shall pronounce him unclean: it *is* a plague.

23 But if the bright spot stay in his place, *and* spread not, it *is* a burning boil; and the priest shall pronounce him clean.

24 ¶ Or if there be *any* flesh, in the skin whereof *there is* a hot burning, and the quick *flesh* that burneth have a white bright spot, somewhat reddish, or white;

25 Then the priest shall look upon it: and, behold, *if* the hair in the bright spot be turned white, and it *be in* sight deeper than the skin; it *is* a leprosy broken out of the burning: wherefore the priest shall pronounce him unclean: it *is* the plague of leprosy.

26 But if the priest look on it, and, behold, *there be* no white hair in the bright spot, and it *be* no lower than the *other* skin, but *be* somewhat dark; then the priest shall shut him up seven days:

27 And the priest shall look upon him the seventh day: *and* if it be spread much abroad in the skin, then the priest shall pronounce him unclean: it *is* the plague of leprosy.

28 And if the bright spot stay in his place, *and* spread not in the skin, but it *be* somewhat dark; it *is* a rising of the burning, and the priest shall pronounce him clean: for it *is* an inflammation of the burning.

29 ¶ If a man or woman have a plague upon the head or the beard;

30 Then the priest shall see the plague: and, behold, if it *be* in sight deeper than the skin; *and there be* in it a yellow thin hair; then the priest shall pronounce him unclean: it *is* a dry scall, *even* a leprosy upon the head or beard.

31 And if the priest look on the plague of the scall, and, behold, it *be* not in sight deeper than the skin, and *that there is* no black hair in it; then the priest shall shut up *him that hath* the plague of the scall seven days:

32 And in the seventh day the priest shall look on the plague: and, behold, *if* the scall spread not, and there be in it no yellow hair, and the scall *be* not in sight deeper than the skin;

33 He shall be shaven, but the scall shall he not shave; and the priest shall shut up *him that hath* the scall seven days more:

34 And in the seventh day the priest shall look on the scall: and, behold, *if* the scall be not spread in the skin, nor *be* in sight deeper than the skin; then the priest shall pronounce him clean: and he shall wash his clothes, and be clean.

35 But if the scall spread much in the skin after his cleansing;

36 Then the priest shall look on him: and, behold, if the scall be spread in the skin, the priest shall not seek for yellow hair; he *is* unclean.

37 But if the scall be in his sight at a stay, and *that* there is black hair grown up therein; the scall is healed, he *is* clean: and the priest shall pronounce him clean.

38 ¶ If a man also or a woman have in the skin of their flesh bright spots, *even* white bright spots;

39 Then the priest shall look: and, behold, *if*

the bright spots in the skin of their flesh *be* darkish white; it *is* a freckled spot *that* groweth in the skin; he *is* clean.

40 And the man whose hair is fallen off his head, he *is* bald; *yet is* he clean.

41 And he that hath his hair fallen off from the part of his head toward his face, he *is* forehead bald: *yet is* he clean.

42 And if there be in the bald head, or bald forehead, a white reddish sore; it *is* a leprosy sprung up in his bald head, or his bald forehead.

43 Then the priest shall look upon it: and, behold, *if* the rising of the sore *be* white reddish in his bald head, or in his bald forehead, as the leprosy appeareth in the skin of the flesh;

44 He is a leprous man, he *is* unclean: the priest shall pronounce him utterly unclean; his plague *is* in his head.

45 And the leper in whom the plague *is*, his clothes shall be rent, and his head bare, and he shall put a covering upon his upper lip, and shall cry, Unclean, unclean.

46 All the days wherein the plague *shall be* in him he shall be defiled; he *is* unclean: he shall dwell alone; without the camp *shall* his habitation *be*.

47 ¶ The garment also that the plague of leprosy is in, *whether it be* a woollen garment, or a linen garment;

48 Whether *it be* in the warp, or woof, of linen, or of woollen; whether in a skin, or in any thing made of skin;

49 And if the plague be greenish or reddish in the garment, or in the skin, either in the warp, or in the woof, or in any thing of skin; it *is* a plague of leprosy, and shall be shewed unto the priest:

50 And the priest shall look upon the plague, and shut up *it that hath* the plague seven days:

51 And he shall look on the plague on the seventh day: if the plague be spread in the garment, either in the warp, or in the woof, or in a skin, *or* in any work that is made of skin; the plague *is* a fretting leprosy; it *is* unclean.

52 He shall therefore burn that garment, whether warp or woof, in woollen or in linen, or any thing of skin, wherein the plague is: for it *is* a fretting leprosy; it shall be burnt in the fire.

53 And if the priest shall look, and, behold, the plague be not spread in the garment, either in the warp, or in the woof, or in any thing of skin;

54 Then the priest shall command that they wash *the thing* wherein the plague *is*, and he shall shut it up seven days more:

55 And the priest shall look on the plague, after that it is washed: and, behold, *if* the plague have not changed his colour, and the plague be not spread; it *is* unclean; thou shalt burn it in the fire; it *is* fret inward, *whether* it *be* bare within or without.

56 And if the priest look, and, behold, the plague *be* somewhat dark after the washing of it; then he shall rend it out of the garment, or out of the skin, or out of the warp, or out of the woof:

57 And if it appear still in the garment, either in the warp, or in the woof, or in any thing of skin; it *is* a spreading *plague*: thou shalt burn that wherein the plague *is* with fire.

58 And the garment, either warp, or woof, or whatsoever thing of skin *it be*, which thou shalt wash, if the plague be departed from them, then it shall be washed the second time, and shall be clean.

59 This *is* the law of the plague of leprosy in a garment of woollen or linen, either in the warp, or woof, or any thing of skins, to pronounce it clean, or to pronounce it unclean.

14 AND the LORD spake unto Mo'ses, saying,

2 This shall be the law of the leper in the day of his cleansing: He shall be brought unto the priest:

3 And the priest shall go forth out of the camp; and the priest shall look, and, behold, *if* the plague of leprosy be healed in the leper;

4 Then shall the priest command to take for him that is to be cleansed two birds alive *and* clean, and cedar wood, and scarlet, and hyssop:

5 And the priest shall command that one of the birds be killed in an earthen vessel over running water:

6 As for the living bird, he shall take it, and the cedar wood, and the scarlet, and the hyssop, and shall dip them and the living bird in the blood of the bird *that was* killed over the running water:

7 And he shall sprinkle upon him that is to be cleansed from the leprosy seven times, and shall pronounce him clean, and shall let the living bird loose into the open field.

8 And he that is to be cleansed shall wash his clothes, and shave off all his hair, and wash himself in water, that he may be clean: and after that he shall come into the camp, and shall tarry abroad out of his tent seven days.

9 But it shall be on the seventh day, that he shall shave all his hair off his head and his beard and his eyebrows, even all his hair he shall shave off: and he shall wash his clothes, also he shall wash his flesh in water, and he shall be clean.

10 And on the eighth day he shall take two he lambs without blemish, and one ewe lamb of the first year without blemish, and three tenth deals of fine flour *for* a meat offering, mingled with oil, and one log of oil.

11 And the priest that maketh *him* clean shall present the man that is to be made clean, and those things, before the LORD, *at* the door of the tabernacle of the congregation:

12 And the priest shall take one he lamb, and offer him for a trespass offering, and the log of oil, and wave them *for* a wave offering before the LORD:

13 And he shall slay the lamb in the place where he shall kill the sin offering and the burnt offering, in the holy place: for as the sin offering *is* the priest's, *so is* the trespass offering: it *is* most holy:

14 And the priest shall take *some* of the blood of the trespass offering, and the priest shall put *it* upon the tip of the right ear of him that is to be cleansed, and upon the thumb of his right hand, and upon the great toe of his right foot:

15 And the priest shall take *some* of the log of oil, and pour *it* into the palm of his own left hand:

16 And the priest shall dip his right finger in the oil that *is* in his left hand, and shall sprinkle of the oil with his finger seven times before the LORD:

17 And of the rest of the oil that *is* in his hand shall the priest put upon the tip of the right ear of him that is to be cleansed, and upon the thumb of his right hand, and upon the great toe of his right foot, upon the blood of the trespass offering:

18 And the remnant of the oil that *is* in the priest's hand he shall pour upon the head of him

that is to be cleansed: and the priest shall make
an atonement for him before the LORD.
19 And the priest shall offer the sin offering,
and make an atonement for him that is to be
cleansed from his uncleanness; and afterward
he shall kill the burnt offering:
20 And the priest shall offer the burnt offering and the meat offering upon the altar: and
the priest shall make an atonement for him, and
he shall be clean.
21 And if he *be* poor, and cannot get so
much; then he shall take one lamb *for* a trespass offering to be waved, to make an atonement for him, and one tenth deal of fine flour
mingled with oil for a meat offering, and a log
of oil;
22 And two turtledoves, or two young pigeons, such as he is able to get; and the one
shall be a sin offering, and the other a burnt
offering.
23 And he shall bring them on the eighth day
for his cleansing unto the priest, unto the door
of the tabernacle of the congregation, before
the LORD.
24 And the priest shall take the lamb of the
trespass offering, and the log of oil, and the
priest shall wave them *for* a wave offering before the LORD:
25 And he shall kill the lamb of the trespass
offering, and the priest shall take *some* of the
blood of the trespass offering, and put *it* upon
the tip of the right ear of him that is to be
cleansed, and upon the thumb of his right hand,
and upon the great toe of his right foot:
26 And the priest shall pour of the oil into the
palm of his own left hand:
27 And the priest shall sprinkle with his right
finger *some* of the oil that *is* in his left hand
seven times before the LORD:
28 And the priest shall put of the oil that *is* in
his hand upon the tip of the right ear of him that
is to be cleansed, and upon the thumb of his
right hand, and upon the great toe of his right
foot, upon the place of the blood of the trespass
offering:
29 And the rest of the oil that *is* in the
priest's hand he shall put upon the head of him
that is to be cleansed, to make an atonement for
him before the LORD.
30 And he shall offer the one of the turtledoves, or of the young pigeons, such as he can
get;
31 *Even* such as he is able to get, the one *for*
a sin offering, and the other *for* a burnt offering,
with the meat offering: and the priest shall
make an atonement for him that is to be
cleansed before the LORD.
32 This *is* the law *of him* in whom *is* the
plague of leprosy, whose hand is not able to get
that which pertaineth to his cleansing.
33 ¶ And the LORD spake unto Mo'ses and
unto Aar'on, saying,
34 When ye be come into the land of Ca'-
naan, which I give to you for a possession, and I
put the plague of leprosy in a house of the land
of your possession;
35 And he that owneth the house shall come
and tell the priest, saying, It seemeth to me
there is as it were a plague in the house:
36 Then the priest shall command that they
empty the house, before the priest go *into it* to
see the plague, that all that *is* in the house be
not made unclean: and afterward the priest
shall go in to see the house:
37 And he shall look on the plague, and, behold, *if* the plague *be* in the walls of the house
with hollow strakes, greenish or reddish, which
in sight *are* lower than the wall;
38 Then the priest shall go out of the house
to the door of the house, and shut up the house
seven days:
39 And the priest shall come again the seventh day, and shall look: and, behold, *if* the
plague be spread in the walls of the house;
40 Then the priest shall command that they
take away the stones in which the plague *is*,
and they shall cast them into an unclean place
without the city:
41 And he shall cause the house to be
scraped within round about, and they shall pour
out the dust that they scrape off without the
city into an unclean place:
42 And they shall take other stones, and put
them in the place of those stones; and he shall
take other morter, and shall plaister the house.
43 And if the plague come again, and break
out in the house, after that he hath taken away
the stones, and after he hath scraped the house,
and after it is plaistered;
44 Then the priest shall come and look, and,
behold, *if* the plague be spread in the house, it *is*
a fretting leprosy in the house: it *is* unclean.
45 And he shall break down the house, the
stones of it, and the timber therof, and all the
morter of the house; and he shall carry *them*
forth out of the city into an unclean place.
46 Moreover he that goeth into the house all
the while that it is shut up shall be unclean until
the even.
47 And he that lieth in the house shall wash
his clothes; and he that eateth in the house shall
wash his clothes.
48 And if the priest shall come in, and look
upon it, and, behold, the plague hath not spread
in the house, after the house was plaistered:
then the priest shall pronounce the house clean,
because the plague is healed.
49 And he shall take to cleanse the house
two birds, and cedar wood, and scarlet, and
hyssop:
50 And he shall kill the one of the birds in an
earthen vessel over running water:
51 And he shall take the cedar wood, and the
hyssop, and the scarlet, and the living bird, and
dip them in the blood of the slain bird, and in
the running water, and sprinkle the house seven
times:
52 And he shall cleanse the house with the
blood of the bird, and with the running water,
and with the living bird, and with the cedar
wood, and with the hyssop, and with the scarlet:
53 But he shall let go the living bird out of
the city into the open fields, and make an atonement for the house: and it shall be clean.
54 This *is* the law for all manner of plague of
leprosy, and scall,
55 And for the leprosy of a garment, and of a
house,
56 And for a rising, and for a scab, and for a
bright spot:
57 To teach when *it is* unclean, and when *it is*
clean: this *is* the law of leprosy.

15 AND the LORD spake unto Mo'ses and
to Aar'on, saying,
2 Speak unto the children of Is'ra-el, and say
unto them, When any man hath a running issue
out of his flesh, *because of* his issue he *is* unclean.
3 And this shall be his uncleanness in his issue: whether his flesh run with his issue, or his

flesh be stopped from his issue, it *is* his uncleanness.
4 Every bed, whereon he lieth that hath the
issue, is unclean: and every thing, whereon he
sitteth, shall be unclean.
5 And whosoever toucheth his bed shall
wash his clothes, and bathe *himself* in water,
and be unclean until the even.
6 And he that sitteth on *any* thing whereon
he sat that hath the issue shall wash his clothes,
and bathe *himself* in water, and be unclean until the even.
7 And he that toucheth the flesh of him that
hath the issue shall wash his clothes, and bathe
himself in water, and be unclean until the even.
8 And if he that hath the issue spit upon him
that is clean; then he shall wash his clothes, and
bathe *himself* in water, and be unclean until the
even.
9 And what saddle soever he rideth upon
that hath the issue shall be unclean.
10 And whosoever toucheth any thing that
was under him shall be unclean until the even:
and he that beareth *any of* those things shall
wash his clothes, and bathe *himself* in water,
and be unclean until the even.
11 And whomsoever he toucheth that hath
the issue, and hath not rinsed his hands in water, he shall wash his clothes, and bathe *himself*
in water, and be unclean until the even.
12 And the vessel of earth, that he toucheth
which hath the issue, shall be broken: and every
vessel of wood shall be rinsed in water.
13 And when he that hath an issue is
cleansed of his issue; then he shall number to
himself seven days for his cleansing, and wash
his clothes, and bathe his flesh in running water, and shall be clean.
14 And on the eighth day he shall take to him
two turtledoves, or two young pigeons, and
come before the LORD unto the door of the tabernacle of the congregation, and give them unto
the priest:
15 And the priest shall offer them, the one
for a sin offering, and the other *for* a burnt offering; and the priest shall make an atonement
for him before the LORD for his issue.
16 And if any man's seed of copulation go
out from him, then he shall wash all his flesh in
water, and be unclean until the even.
17 And every garment, and every skin,
whereon is the seed of copulation, shall be
washed with water, and be unclean until the
even.
18 The woman also with whom man shall lie
with seed of copulation, they shall *both* bathe
themselves in water, and be unclean until the
even.
19 ¶ And if a woman have an issue, *and* her
issue in her flesh be blood, she shall be put
apart seven days: and whosoever toucheth her
shall be unclean until the even.
20 And every thing that she lieth upon in her
separation shall be unclean: every thing also
that she sitteth upon shall be unclean.
21 And whosoever toucheth her bed shall
wash his clothes, and bathe *himself* in water,
and be unclean until the even.
22 And whosoever toucheth any thing that
she sat upon shall wash his clothes, and bathe
himself in water, and be unclean until the even.
23 And if it *be* on *her* bed, or on any thing
whereon she sitteth, when he toucheth it, he
shall be unclean until the even.
24 And if any man lie with her at all, and her
flowers be upon him, he shall be unclean seven
days; and all the bed whereon he lieth shall be
unclean.
25 And if a woman have an issue of her blood
many days out of the time of her separation, or
if it run beyond the time of her separation; all
the days of the issue of her uncleanness shall be
as the days of her separation: she *shall be* unclean.
26 Every bed whereon she lieth all the days
of her issue shall be unto her as the bed of her
separation: and whatsoever she sitteth upon
shall be unclean, as the uncleanness of her
separation.
27 And whosoever toucheth those things
shall be unclean, and shall wash his clothes, and
bathe *himself* in water, and be unclean until the
even.
28 But if she be cleansed of her issue, then
she shall number to herself seven days, and after that she shall be clean.
29 And on the eighth day she shall take unto
her two turtles, or two young pigeons, and
bring them unto the priest, to the door of the
tabernacle of the congregation.
30 And the priest shall offer the one *for* a sin
offering, and the other *for* a burnt offering; and
the priest shall make an atonement for her before the LORD for the issue of her uncleanness.
31 Thus shall ye separate the children of Is'-
ra-el from their uncleanness; that they die not
in their uncleanness, when they defile my tabernacle that *is* among them.
32 This *is* the law of him that hath an issue,
and *of him* whose seed goeth from him, and is
defiled therewith;
33 And of her that is sick of her flowers, and
of him that hath an issue, of the man, and of the
woman, and of him that lieth with her that is
unclean.

16 AND the LORD spake unto Mo'ses after
the death of the two sons of Aar'on,
when they offered before the LORD, and died;
2 And the LORD said unto Mo'ses, Speak unto
Aar'on thy brother, that he come not at all
times into the holy *place* within the veil before
the mercy seat, which *is* upon the ark; that he
die not: for I will appear in the cloud upon the
mercy seat.
3 Thus shall Aar'on come into the holy *place:*
with a young bullock for a sin offering, and a
ram for a burnt offering.
4 He shall put on the holy linen coat, and he
shall have the linen breeches upon his flesh, and
shall be girded with a linen girdle, and with the
linen mitre shall he be attired: these *are* holy
garments; therefore shall he wash his flesh in
water, and *so* put them on.
5 And he shall take of the congregation of
the children of Is'ra-el two kids of the goats for
a sin offering, and one ram for a burnt offering.
6 And Aar'on shall offer his bullock of the sin
offering, which *is* for himself, and make an
atonement for himself, and for his house.
7 And he shall take the two goats, and present them before the LORD *at* the door of the
tabernacle of the congregation.
8 And Aar'on shall cast lots upon the two
goats; one lot for the LORD, and the other lot for
the scapegoat.
9 And Aar'on shall bring the goat upon
which the LORD's lot fell, and offer him *for* a sin
offering.
10 But the goat, on which the lot fell to be the
scapegoat, shall be presented alive before the
LORD, to make an atonement with him, *and* to
let him go for a scapegoat into the wilderness.

11 And Aar'on shall bring the bullock of the
sin offering, which *is* for himself, and shall
make an atonement for himself, and for his
house, and shall kill the bullock of the sin offering which *is* for himself:
12 And he shall take a censer full of burning
coals of fire from off the altar before the LORD,
and his hands full of sweet incense beaten
small, and bring *it* within the veil:
13 And he shall put the incense upon the fire
before the LORD, that the cloud of the incense
may cover the mercy seat that *is* upon the testimony, that he die not:
14 And he shall take of the blood of the bullock, and sprinkle *it* with his finger upon the
mercy seat eastward; and before the mercy seat
shall he sprinkle of the blood with his finger
seven times.
15 ¶ Then shall he kill the goat of the sin offering, that *is* for the people, and bring his blood
within the veil, and do with that blood as he did
with the blood of the bullock, and sprinkle it
upon the mercy seat, and before the mercy seat:
16 And he shall make an atonement for the
holy *place*, because of the uncleanness of the
children of Is'ra-el, and because of their transgressions in all their sins: and so shall he do for
the tabernacle of the congregation, that remaineth among them in the midst of their uncleanness.
17 And there shall be no man in the tabernacle of the congregation when he goeth in to
make an atonement in the holy *place*, until he
come out, and have made an atonement for
himself, and for his household, and for all the
congregation of Is'ra-el.
18 And he shall go out unto the altar that *is*
before the LORD, and make an atonement for it;
and shall take of the blood of the bullock, and of
the blood of the goat, and put *it* upon the horns
of the altar round about.
19 And he shall sprinkle of the blood upon it
with his finger seven times, and cleanse it, and
hallow it from the uncleanness of the children
of Is'ra-el.
20 ¶ And when he hath made an end of reconciling the holy *place*, and the tabernacle of
the congregation, and the altar, he shall bring
the live goat:
21 And Aar'on shall lay both his hands upon
the head of the live goat, and confess over him
all the iniquities of the children of Is'ra-el, and
all their transgressions in all their sins, putting
them upon the head of the goat, and shall send
him away by the hand of a fit man into the wilderness:
22 And the goat shall bear upon him all their
iniquities unto a land not inhabited: and he shall
let go the goat in the wilderness.
23 And Aar'on shall come into the tabernacle
of the congregation, and shall put off the linen
garments, which he put on when he went into
the holy *place*, and shall leave them there:
24 And he shall wash his flesh with water in
the holy place, and put on his garments, and
come forth, and offer his burnt offering, and the
burnt offering of the people, and make an
atonement for himself, and for the people.
25 And the fat of the sin offering shall he
burn upon the altar.
26 And he that let go the goat for the scapegoat shall wash his clothes, and bathe his flesh
in water, and afterward come into the camp.
27 And the bullock *for* the sin offering, and
the goat *for* the sin offering, whose blood was
brought in to make atonement in the holy *place*,
shall *one* carry forth without the camp; and
they shall burn in the fire their skins, and their
flesh, and their dung.
28 And he that burneth them shall wash his
clothes, and bathe his flesh in water, and afterward he shall come into the camp.
29 ¶ And *this* shall be a statute for ever unto
you: *that* in the seventh month, on the tenth
day of the month, ye shall afflict your souls, and
do no work at all, *whether it be* one of your own
country, or a stranger that sojourneth among
you:
30 For on that day shall *the priest* make an
atonement for you, to cleanse you, *that* ye may
be clean from all your sins before the LORD.
31 It *shall be* a sabbath of rest unto you, and
ye shall afflict your souls, by a statute for ever.
32 And the priest, whom he shall anoint, and
whom he shall consecrate to minister in the
priest's office in his father's stead, shall make
the atonement, and shall put on the linen
clothes, *even* the holy garments:
33 And he shall make an atonement for the
holy sanctuary, and he shall make an atonement for the tabernacle of the congregation,
and for the altar, and he shall make an atonement for the priests, and for all the people of
the congregation.
34 And this shall be an everlasting statute
unto you, to make an atonement for the children of Is'ra-el for all their sins once a year.
And he did as the LORD commanded Mo'ses.

17

AND the LORD spake unto Mo'ses, saying,
2 Speak unto Aar'on, and unto his sons, and
unto all the children of Is'ra-el, and say unto
them; This *is* the thing which the LORD hath
commanded, saying,
3 What man soever *there be* of the house of
Is'ra-el, that killeth an ox, or lamb, or goat, in
the camp, or that killeth *it* out of the camp,
4 And bringeth it not unto the door of the
tabernacle of the congregation, to offer an offering unto the LORD before the tabernacle of the
LORD; blood shall be imputed unto that man; he
hath shed blood; and that man shall be cut off
from among his people:
5 To the end that the children of Is'ra-el may
bring their sacrifices, which they offer in the
open field, even that they may bring them unto
the LORD, unto the door of the tabernacle of the
congregation, unto the priest, and offer them
for peace offerings unto the LORD.
6 And the priest shall sprinkle the blood
upon the altar of the LORD *at* the door of the
tabernacle of the congregation, and burn the fat
for a sweet savour unto the LORD.
7 And they shall no more offer their sacrifices unto devils, after whom they have gone a
whoring. This shall be a statute for ever unto
them throughout their generations.
8 ¶ And thou shalt say unto them, Whatsoever man *there be* of the house of Is'ra-el, or of
the strangers which sojourn among you, that
offereth a burnt offering or sacrifice,
9 And bringeth it not unto the door of the
tabernacle of the congregation, to offer it unto
the LORD; even that man shall be cut off from
among his people.
10 ¶ And whatsoever man *there be* of the
house of Is'ra-el, or of the strangers that sojourn among you, that eateth any manner of
blood; I will even set my face against that soul
that eateth blood, and will cut him off from
among his people.
11 For the life of the flesh *is* in the blood: and
I have given it to you upon the altar to make an

atonement for your souls for it *is* the blood *that* maketh an atonement for the soul.

12 Therefore I said unto the children of Is'ra-el, No soul of you shall eat blood, neither shall any stranger that sojourneth among you eat blood.

13 And whatsoever man *there be* of the children of Is'ra-el, or of the strangers that sojourn among you, which hunteth and catcheth any beast or fowl that may be eaten; he shall even pour out the blood thereof, and cover it with dust.

14 For *it is* the life of all flesh; the blood of it *is* for the life thereof: therefore I said unto the children of Is'ra-el, Ye shall eat the blood of no manner of flesh: for the life of all flesh *is* the blood thereof: whosoever eateth it shall be cut off.

15 And every soul that eateth that which died *of itself*, or that which was torn *with beasts, whether it be* one of your own country, or a stranger, he shall both wash his clothes, and bathe *himself* in water, and be unclean until the even: then shall he be clean.

16 But if he wash *them* not, nor bathe his flesh; then he shall bear his iniquity.

18

AND the LORD spake unto Mo'ses, saying,

2 Speak unto the children of Is'ra-el, and say unto them, I am the LORD your God.

3 After the doings of the land of E'gypt, wherein ye dwelt, shall ye not do: and after the doings of the land of Ca'naan, whither I bring you, shall ye not do: neither shall ye walk in their ordinances.

4 Ye shall do my judgments, and keep mine ordinances, to walk therein: I *am* the LORD your God.

5 Ye shall therefore keep my statutes, and my judgments: which if a man do, he shall live in them: I *am* the LORD.

6 ¶ None of you shall approach to any that is near of kin to him, to uncover *their* nakedness: I *am* the LORD.

7 The nakedness of thy father, or the nakedness of thy mother, shalt thou not uncover: she *is* thy mother; thou shalt not uncover her nakedness.

8 The nakedness of thy father's wife shalt thou not uncover: it *is* thy father's nakedness.

9 The nakedness of thy sister, the daughter of thy father, or daughter of thy mother, *whether she be* born at home, or born abroad, *even* their nakedness thou shalt not uncover.

10 The nakedness of thy son's daughter, or of thy daughter's daughter, *even* their nakedness thou shalt not uncover: for theirs *is* thine own nakedness.

11 The nakedness of thy father's wife's daughter, begotten of thy father, she *is* thy sister, thou shalt not uncover her nakedness.

12 Thou shalt not uncover the nakedness of thy father's sister: she *is* thy father's near kinswoman.

13 Thou shalt not uncover the nakedness of thy mother's sister: for she *is* thy mother's near kinswoman.

14 Thou shalt not uncover the nakedness of thy father's brother, thou shalt not approach to his wife: she *is* thine aunt.

15 Thou shalt not uncover the nakedness of thy daughter in law: she *is* thy son's wife; thou shalt not uncover her nakedness.

16 Thou shalt not uncover the nakedness of thy brother's wife: it *is* thy brother's nakedness.

17 Thou shalt not uncover the nakedness of a woman and her daughter, neither shalt thou take her son's daughter, or her daughter's daughter, to uncover her nakedness; *for* they *are* her near kinswomen: it *is* wickedness.

18 Neither shalt thou take a wife to her sister, to vex *her*, to uncover her nakedness, beside the other in her life *time*.

19 Also thou shalt not approach unto a woman to uncover her nakedness, as long as she is put apart for her uncleanness.

20 Moreover thou shalt not lie carnally with thy neighbour's wife, to defile thyself with her.

21 And thou shalt not let any of thy seed pass through *the fire* to Mo'lech, neither shalt thou profane the name of thy God: I *am* the LORD.

22 Thou shalt not lie with mankind, as with womankind: it *is* abomination.

23 Neither shalt thou lie with any beast to defile thyself therewith: neither shall any woman stand before a beast to lie down thereto: it *is* confusion.

24 Defile not ye yourselves in any of these things: for in all these the nations are defiled which I cast out before you:

25 And the land is defiled: therefore I do visit the iniquity thereof upon it, and the land itself vomiteth out her inhabitants.

26 Ye shall therefore keep my statutes and my judgments, and shall not commit *any* of these abominations; *neither* any of your own nation, nor any stranger that sojourneth among you:

27 (For all these abominations have the men of the land done, which *were* before you, and the land is defiled;)

28 That the land spue not you out also, when ye defile it, as it spued out the nations that *were* before you.

29 For whosoever shall commit any of these abominations, even the souls that commit *them* shall be cut off from among their people.

30 Therefore shall ye keep mine ordinance, that *ye* commit not *any one* of these abominable customs, which were committed before you, and that ye defile not yourselves therein: I *am* the LORD your God.

19

AND the LORD spake unto Mo'ses, saying,

2 Speak unto all the congregation of the children of Is'ra-el, and say unto them, Ye shall be holy: for I the LORD your God *am* holy.

3 ¶ Ye shall fear every man his mother, and his father, and keep my sabbaths: I *am* the LORD your God.

4 ¶ Turn ye not unto idols, nor make to yourselves molten gods: I *am* the LORD your God.

5 ¶ And if ye offer a sacrifice of peace offerings unto the LORD, ye shall offer it at your own will.

6 It shall be eaten the same day ye offer it, and on the morrow: and if ought remain until the third day, it shall be burnt in the fire.

7 And if it be eaten at all on the third day, it *is* abominable; it shall not be accepted.

8 Therefore *every one* that eateth it shall bear his iniquity, because he hath profaned the hallowed thing of the LORD: and that soul shall be cut off from among his people.

9 ¶ And when ye reap the harvest of your land, thou shalt not wholly reap the corners of thy field, neither shalt thou gather the gleanings of thy harvest.

10 And thou shalt not glean thy vineyard, neither shalt thou gather *every* grape of thy vineyard; thou shalt leave them for the poor and stranger: I *am* the LORD your God.

11 ¶ Ye shall not steal, neither deal falsely,
neither lie one to another.
12 ¶ And ye shall not swear by my name
falsely, neither shalt thou profane the name of
thy God: I *am* the LORD.
13 ¶ Thou shalt not defraud thy neighbour,
neither rob *him:* the wages of him that is hired
shall not abide with thee all night until the
morning.
14 ¶ Thou shalt not curse the deaf, nor put a
stumblingblock before the blind, but shalt fear
thy God: I *am* the LORD.
15 ¶ Ye shall do no unrighteousness in judgment: thou shalt not respect the person of the
poor, nor honour the person of the mighty: *but*
in righteousness shalt thou judge thy neighbour.
16 ¶ Thou shalt not go up and down *as* a
talebearer among thy people: neither shalt thou
stand against the blood of thy neighbour: I *am*
the LORD.
17 ¶ Thou shalt not hate thy brother in thine
heart: thou shalt in any wise rebuke thy neighbour, and not suffer sin upon him.
18 ¶ Thou shalt not avenge, nor bear any
grudge against the children of thy people, but
thou shalt love thy neighbour as thyself: I *am*
the LORD.
19 ¶ Ye shall keep my statutes. Thou shalt
not let thy cattle gender with a diverse kind:
thou shalt not sow thy field with mingled seed:
neither shall a garment mingled of linen and
woollen come upon thee.
20 ¶ And whosoever lieth carnally with a
woman, that *is* a bondmaid, betrothed to an
husband, and not at all redeemed, nor freedom
given her; she shall be scourged; they shall not
be put to death, because she was not free.
21 And he shall bring his trespass offering
unto the LORD, unto the door of the tabernacle
of the congregation, *even* a ram for a trespass
offering.
22 And the priest shall make an atonement
for him with the ram of the trespass offering
before the LORD for his sin which he hath done:
and the sin which he hath done shall be forgiven him.
23 ¶ And when ye shall come into the land,
and shall have planted all manner of trees for
food, then ye shall count the fruit thereof as uncircumcised: three years shall it be as uncircumcised unto you: it shall not be eaten of.
24 But in the fourth year all the fruit thereof
shall be holy to praise the LORD *withal.*
25 And in the fifth year shall ye eat of the
fruit thereof, that it may yield unto you the increase thereof: I *am* the LORD your God.
26 ¶ Ye shall not eat *any thing* with the
blood: neither shall ye use enchantment, nor
observe times.
27 Ye shall not round the corners of your
heads, neither shalt thou mar the corners of thy
beard.
28 Ye shall not make any cuttings in your
flesh for the dead, nor print any marks upon
you: I *am* the LORD.
29 ¶ Do not prostitute thy daughter, to cause
her to be a whore; lest the land fall to whoredom, and the land become full of wickedness.
30 ¶ Ye shall keep my sabbaths, and reverence my sanctuary: I *am* the LORD.
31 ¶ Regard not them that have familiar
spirits, neither seek after wizards, to be defiled
by them: I *am* the LORD your God.
32 ¶ Thou shalt rise up before the hoary
head, and honour the face of the old man, and
fear thy God: I *am* the LORD.
33 ¶ And if a stranger sojourn with thee in
your land, ye shall not vex him.
34 *But* the stranger that dwelleth with you
shall be unto you as one born among you, and
thou shalt love him as thyself; for ye were
strangers in the land of E'gypt: I *am* the LORD
your God.
35 ¶ Ye shall do no unrighteousness in judgment, in meteyard, in weight, or in measure.
36 Just balances, just weights, a just ephah,
and a just hin, shall ye have: I *am* the LORD your
God, which brought you out of the land of E'-
gypt.
37 Therefore shall ye observe all my statutes,
and all my judgments, and do them: I *am* the
LORD.

20

AND the LORD spake unto Mo'ses, saying,
2 Again, thou shalt say to the children of Is'-
ra-el, Whosoever *he be* of the children of Is'ra-
el, or of the strangers that sojourn in Is'ra-el,
that giveth *any* of his seed unto Mo'lech; he
shall surely be put to death: the people of the
land shall stone him with stones.
3 And I will set my face against that man,
and will cut him off from among his people; because he hath given of his seed unto Mo'lech, to
defile my sanctuary, and to profane my holy
name.
4 And if the people of the land do any ways
hide their eyes from the man, when he giveth of
his seed unto Mo'lech, and kill him not:
5 Then I will set my face against that man,
and against his family, and will cut him off, and
all that go a whoring after him, to commit
whoredom with Mo'lech, from among their people.
6 ¶ And the soul that turneth after such as
have familiar spirits, and after wizards, to go a
whoring after them, I will even set my face
against that soul, and will cut him off from
among his people.
7 ¶ Sanctify yourselves therefore, and be ye
holy: for I *am* the LORD your God.
8 And ye shall keep my statutes, and do
them: I *am* the LORD which sanctify you.
9 ¶ For every one that curseth his father or
his mother shall be surely put to death: he hath
cursed his father or his mother; his blood *shall
be* upon him.
10 ¶ And the man that committeth adultery
with *another* man's wife, *even he* that committeth adultery with his neighbour's wife, the a-
dulterer and the adulteress shall surely be put
to death.
11 And the man that lieth with his father's
wife hath uncovered his father's nakedness:
both of them shall surely be put to death; their
blood *shall be* upon them.
12 And if a man lie with his daughter in law,
both of them shall surely be put to death: they
have wrought confusion; their blood *shall be*
upon them.
13 If a man also lie with mankind, as he lieth
with a woman, both of them have committed an
abomination: they shall surely be put to death;
their blood *shall be* upon them.
14 And if a man take a wife and her mother,
it *is* wickedness: they shall be burnt with fire,
both he and they; that there be no wickedness
among you.
15 And if a man lie with a beast, he shall
surely be put to death: and ye shall slay the
beast.
16 And if a woman approach unto any beast,
and lie down thereto, thou shalt kill the woman,

and the beast: they shall surely be put to death; their blood *shall be* upon them.

17 And if a man shall take his sister, his father's daughter, or his mother's daughter, and see her nakedness, and she see his nakedness; it *is* a wicked thing; and they shall be cut off in the sight of their people: he hath uncovered his sister's nakedness; he shall bear his iniquity.

18 And if a man shall lie with a woman having her sickness, and shall uncover her nakedness; he hath discovered her fountain, and she hath uncovered the fountain of her blood: and both of them shall be cut off from among their people.

19 And thou shalt not uncover the nakedness of thy mother's sister, nor of thy father's sister: for he uncovereth his near kin: they shall bear their iniquity.

20 And if a man shall lie with his uncle's wife, he hath uncovered his uncle's nakedness: they shall bear their sin; they shall die childless.

21 And if a man shall take his brother's wife, it *is* an unclean thing: he hath uncovered his brother's nakedness; they shall be childless.

22 ¶ Ye shall therefore keep all my statutes, and all my judgments, and do them: that the land, whither I bring you to dwell therein, spue you not out.

23 And ye shall not walk in the manners of the nation, which I cast out before you: for they committed all these things, and therefore I abhorred them.

24 But I have said unto you, Ye shall inherit their land, and I will give it unto you to possess it, a land that floweth with milk and honey: I *am* the LORD your God, which have separated you from *other* people.

25 Ye shall therefore put difference between clean beasts and unclean, and between unclean fowls and clean: and ye shall not make your souls abominable by beast, or by fowl, or by any manner of living thing that creepeth on the ground, which I have separated from you as unclean.

26 And ye shall be holy unto me: for I the LORD *am* holy, and have severed you from *other* people, that ye should be mine.

27 ¶ A man also or woman that hath a familiar spirit, or that is a wizard, shall surely be put to death: they shall stone them with stones: their blood *shall be* upon them.

21 AND the LORD said unto Mo'ses, Speak unto the priests the sons of Aar'on, and say unto them, There shall none be defiled for the dead among his people:

2 But for his kin, that is near unto him, *that is*, for his mother, and for his father, and for his son, and for his daughter, and for his brother,

3 And for his sister a virgin, that is nigh unto him, which hath had no husband; for her may he be defiled.

4 *But* he shall not defile himself, *being* a chief man among his people, to profane himself.

5 They shall not make baldness upon their head, neither shall they shave off the corner of their beard, nor make any cuttings in their flesh.

6 They shall be holy unto their God, and not profane the name of their God: for the offerings of the LORD made by fire, *and* the bread of their God, they do offer: therefore they shall be holy.

7 They shall not take a wife *that is* a whore, or profane; neither shall they take a woman put away from her husband: for he *is* holy unto his God.

8 Thou shalt sanctify him therefore; for he offereth the bread of thy God: he shall be holy unto thee: for I the LORD, which sanctify you, *am* holy.

9 ¶ And the daughter of any priest, if she profane herself by playing the whore, she profaneth her father: she shall be burnt with fire.

10 And *he that is* the high priest among his brethren, upon whose head the anointing oil was poured, and that is consecrated to put on the garments, shall not uncover his head, nor rend his clothes;

11 Neither shall he go in to any dead body, nor defile himself for his father, or for his mother;

12 Neither shall he go out of the sanctuary, nor profane the sanctuary of his God; for the crown of the anointing oil of his God *is* upon him: I *am* the LORD.

13 And he shall take a wife in her virginity.

14 A widow, or a divorced woman, or profane, *or* an harlot, these shall he not take: but he shall take a virgin of his own people to wife.

15 Neither shall he profane his seed among his people: for I the LORD do sanctify him.

16 ¶ And the LORD spake unto Mo'ses, saying,

17 Speak unto Aar'on, saying, Whosoever *he be* of thy seed in their generations that hath *any* blemish, let him not approach to offer the bread of his God.

18 For whatsoever man *he be* that hath a blemish, he shall not approach: a blind man, or a lame, or he that hath a flat nose, or any thing superfluous,

19 Or a man that is brokenfooted, or brokenhanded,

20 Or crookbackt, or a dwarf, or that hath a blemish in his eye, or be scurvy, or scabbed, or hath his stones broken;

21 No man that hath a blemish of the seed of Aar'on the priest shall come nigh to offer the offerings of the LORD made by fire: he hath a blemish; he shall not come nigh to offer the bread of his God.

22 He shall eat the bread of his God, *both* of the most holy, and of the holy.

23 Only he shall not go in unto the veil, nor come nigh unto the altar, because he hath a blemish; that he profane not my sanctuaries: for I the LORD do sanctify them.

24 And Mo'ses told *it* unto Aar'on, and to his sons, and unto all the children of Is'ra-el.

22 AND the LORD spake unto Mo'ses, saying,

2 Speak unto Aar'on and to his sons, that they separate themselves from the holy things of the children of Is'ra-el, and that they profane not my holy name *in those things* which they hallow unto me: I *am* the LORD.

3 Say unto them, Whosoever *he be* of all your seed among your generations, that goeth unto the holy things, which the children of Is'ra-el hallow unto the LORD, having his uncleanness upon him, that soul shall be cut off from my presence: I *am* the LORD.

4 What man soever of the seed of Aar'on *is* a leper, or hath a running issue; he shall not eat of the holy things, until he be clean. And whoso toucheth any thing *that is* unclean *by* the dead, or a man whose seed goeth from him;

5 Or whosoever toucheth any creeping thing, whereby he may be made unclean, or a man of whom he may take uncleanness, whatsoever uncleanness he hath;

6 The soul which hath touched any such shall be unclean until even, and shall not eat of the

holy things, unless he wash his flesh with water.
7 And when the sun is down, he shall be
clean, and shall afterward eat of the holy
things; because it *is* his food.
8 That which dieth of itself, or is torn *with*
beasts, he shall not eat to defile himself therewith: I *am* the LORD.
9 They shall therefore keep mine ordinance,
lest they bear sin for it, and die therefore, if
they profane it: I the LORD do sanctify them.
10 There shall no stranger eat *of* the holy
thing: a sojourner of the priest, or an hired servant, shall not eat *of* the holy thing.
11 But if the priest buy *any* soul with his
money, he shall eat of it, and he that is born in
his house: they shall eat of his meat.
12 If the priest's daughter also be *married*
unto a stranger, she may not eat of an offering
of the holy things.
13 But if the priest's daughter be a widow, or
divorced, and have no child, and is returned
unto her father's house, as in her youth, she
shall eat of her father's meat: but there shall no
stranger eat thereof.
14 ¶ And if a man eat *of* the holy thing unwittingly, then he shall put the fifth *part* thereof
unto it, and shall give *it* unto the priest with the
holy thing.
15 And they shall not profane the holy things
of the children of Is′ra-el, which they offer unto
the LORD;
16 Or suffer them to bear the iniquity of trespass, when they eat their holy things: for I the
LORD do sanctify them.
17 ¶ And the LORD spake unto Mo′ses, saying,
18 Speak unto Aar′on, and to his sons, and
unto all the children of Is′ra-el, and say unto
them, Whatsoever *he be* of the house of Is′ra-el,
or of the strangers in Is′ra-el, that will offer his
oblation for all his vows, and for all his freewill
offerings, which they will offer unto the LORD
for a burnt offering;
19 *Ye shall offer* at your own will a male
without blemish, of the beeves, of the sheep, or
of the goats.
20 *But* whatsoever hath a blemish, *that* shall
ye not offer: for it shall not be acceptable for
you.
21 And whosoever offereth a sacrifice of
peace offerings unto the LORD to accomplish *his*
vow, or a freewill offering in beeves or sheep, it
shall be perfect to be accepted; there shall be no
blemish therein.
22 Blind, or broken, or maimed, or having a
wen, or scurvy, or scabbed, ye shall not offer
these unto the LORD, nor make an offering by
fire of them upon the altar unto the LORD.
23 Either a bullock or a lamb that hath any
thing superfluous or lacking in his parts, that
mayest thou offer *for* a freewill offering; but for
a vow it shall not be accepted.
24 Ye shall not offer unto the LORD that
which is bruised, or crushed, or broken, or cut;
neither shall ye make *any offering thereof* in
your land.
25 Neither from a stranger's hand shall ye offer the bread of your God of any of these; because their corruption *is* in them, *and* blemishes *be* in them: they shall not be accepted for
you.
26 ¶ And the LORD spake unto Mo′ses, saying,
27 When a bullock, or a sheep, or a goat, is
brought forth, then it shall be seven days under
the dam; and from the eighth day and thenceforth it shall be accepted for an offering made
by fire unto the LORD.
28 And *whether it be* cow or ewe, ye shall not
kill it and her young both in one day.
29 And when ye will offer a sacrifice of
thanksgiving unto the LORD, offer *it* at your
own will.
30 On the same day it shall be eaten up; ye
shall leave none of it until the morrow: I *am* the
LORD.
31 Therefore shall ye keep my commandments, and do them: I *am* the LORD.
32 Neither shall ye profane my holy name;
but I will be hallowed among the children of
Is′ra-el: I *am* the LORD which hallow you,
33 That brought you out of the land of E′-
gypt, to be your God: I *am* the LORD.

23 AND the LORD spake unto Mo′ses, saying,
2 Speak unto the children of Is′ra-el, and say
unto them, *Concerning* the feasts of the LORD,
which ye shall proclaim *to be* holy convocations, *even* these *are* my feasts.
3 Six days shall work be done: but the seventh day *is* the sabbath of rest, an holy convocation; ye shall do no work *therein:* it *is* the sabbath of the LORD in all your dwellings.
4 ¶ These *are* the feasts of the LORD, *even*
holy convocations, which ye shall proclaim in
their seasons.
5 In the fourteenth *day* of the first month at
even *is* the LORD's passover.
6 And on the fifteenth day of the same month
is the feast of unleavened bread unto the LORD:
seven days ye must eat unleavened bread.
7 In the first day ye shall have an holy convocation: ye shall do no servile work therein.
8 But ye shall offer an offering made by fire
unto the LORD seven days: in the seventh day *is*
an holy convocation: ye shall do no servile work
therein.
9 ¶ And the LORD spake unto Mo′ses, saying,
10 Speak unto the children of Is′ra-el, and
say unto them, When ye be come into the land
which I give unto you, and shall reap the harvest thereof, then ye shall bring a sheaf of the
firstfruits of your harvest unto the priest:
11 And he shall wave the sheaf before the
LORD, to be accepted for you: on the morrow
after the sabbath the priest shall wave it.
12 And ye shall offer that day when ye wave
the sheaf an he lamb without blemish of the
first year for a burnt offering unto the LORD.
13 And the meat offering thereof *shall be* two
tenth deals of fine flour mingled with oil, an offering made by fire unto the LORD *for* a sweet
savour: and the drink offering thereof *shall be*
of wine, the fourth *part* of an hin.
14 And ye shall eat neither bread, nor
parched corn, nor green ears, until the selfsame
day that ye have brought an offering unto your
God: *it shall be* a statute for ever throughout
your generations in all your dwellings.
15 ¶ And ye shall count unto you from the
morrow after the sabbath, from the day that ye
brought the sheaf of the wave offering; seven
sabbaths shall be complete:
16 Even unto the morrow after the seventh
sabbath shall ye number fifty days; and ye shall
offer a new meat offering unto the LORD.
17 Ye shall bring out of your habitations two
wave loaves of two tenth deals: they shall be of
fine flour; they shall be baken with leaven; *they*
are the firstfruits unto the LORD.
18 And ye shall offer with the bread seven
lambs without blemish of the first year, and one

young bullock, and two rams: they shall be *for* a
burnt offering unto the LORD, with their meat
offering, and their drink offerings, *even* an offering made by fire, of sweet savour unto the
LORD.
19 Then ye shall sacrifice one kid of the goats
for a sin offering, and two lambs of the first
year for a sacrifice of peace offerings.
20 And the priest shall wave them with the
bread of the firstfruits *for* a wave offering before the LORD, with the two lambs: they shall be
holy to the LORD for the priest.
21 And ye shall proclaim on the selfsame
day, *that* it may be an holy convocation unto
you: ye shall do no servile work *therein: it shall*
be a statute for ever in all your dwellings
throughout your generations.
22 ¶ And when ye reap the harvest of your
land, thou shalt not make clean riddance of the
corners of thy field when thou reapest, neither
shalt thou gather any gleaning of thy harvest:
thou shalt leave them unto the poor, and to the
stranger: I *am* the LORD your God.
23 ¶ And the LORD spake unto Mo'ses, saying,
24 Speak unto the children of Is'ra-el, saying,
In the seventh month, in the first *day* of the
month, shall ye have a sabbath, a memorial of
blowing of trumpets, an holy convocation.
25 Ye shall do no servile work *therein:* but ye
shall offer an offering made by fire unto the
LORD.
26 ¶ And the LORD spake unto Mo'ses, saying,
27 Also on the tenth *day* of this seventh
month *there shall be* a day of atonement: it
shall be an holy convocation unto you; and ye
shall afflict your souls, and offer an offering
made by fire unto the LORD.
28 And ye shall do no work in that same day:
for it *is* a day of atonement, to make an atonement for you before the LORD your God.
29 For whatsoever soul *it be* that shall not be
afflicted in that same day, he shall be cut off
from among his people.
30 And whatsoever soul *it be* that doeth any
work in that same day, the same soul will I destroy from among his people.
31 Ye shall do no manner of work: *it shall be*
a statute for ever throughout your generations
in all your dwellings.
32 It *shall be* unto you a sabbath of rest, and
ye shall afflict your souls: in the ninth *day* of the
month at even, from even unto even, shall ye
celebrate your sabbath.
33 ¶ And the LORD spake unto Mo'ses, saying,
34 Speak unto the children of Is'ra-el, saying,
The fifteenth day of this seventh month *shall be*
the feast of tabernacles *for* seven days unto the
LORD.
35 On the first day *shall be* an holy convocation: ye shall do no servile work *therein.*
36 Seven days ye shall offer an offering made
by fire unto the LORD: on the eighth day shall be
an holy convocation unto you; and ye shall offer
an offering made by fire unto the LORD: it *is* a
solemn assembly; *and* ye shall do no servile
work *therein.*
37 These *are* the feasts of the LORD, which ye
shall proclaim *to be* holy convocations, to offer
an offering made by fire unto the LORD, a burnt
offering, and a meat offering, a sacrifice, and
drink offerings, every thing upon his day:
38 Beside the sabbaths of the LORD, and beside your gifts, and beside all your vows, and
beside all your freewill offerings, which ye give
unto the LORD.
39 Also in the fifteenth day of the seventh
month, when ye have gathered in the fruit of
the land, ye shall keep a feast unto the LORD
seven days: on the first day *shall be* a sabbath,
and on the eighth day *shall be* a sabbath.
40 And ye shall take you on the first day the
boughs of goodly trees, branches of palm trees,
and the boughs of thick trees, and willows of
the brook; and ye shall rejoice before the LORD
your God seven days.
41 And ye shall keep it a feast unto the LORD
seven days in the year. *It shall be* a statute for
ever in your generations: ye shall celebrate it in
the seventh month.
42 Ye shall dwell in booths seven days; all
that are Is'ra-el-ites born shall dwell in booths:
43 That your generations may know that I
made the children of Is'ra-el to dwell in booths,
when I brought them out of the land of E'gypt: I
am the LORD your God.
44 And Mo'ses declared unto the children of
Is'ra-el the feasts of the LORD.

24 AND the LORD spake unto Mo'ses, saying,
2 Command the children of Is'ra-el, that they
bring unto thee pure oil olive beaten for the
light, to cause the lamps to burn continually.
3 Without the veil of the testimony, in the
tabernacle of the congregation, shall Aar'on order it from the evening unto the morning before
the LORD continually: *it shall be* a statute for
ever in your generations.
4 He shall order the lamps upon the pure
candlestick before the LORD continually.
5 ¶ And thou shalt take fine flour, and bake
twelve cakes thereof: two tenth deals shall be in
one cake.
6 And thou shalt set them in two rows, six on
a row, upon the pure table before the LORD.
7 And thou shalt put pure frankincense upon
each row, that it may be on the bread for a memorial, *even* an offering made by fire unto the
LORD.
8 Every sabbath he shall set it in order before
the LORD continually, *being taken* from the children of Is'ra-el by an everlasting covenant.
9 And it shall be Aar'on's and his sons'; and
they shall eat it in the holy place: for it *is* most
holy unto him of the offerings of the LORD made
by fire by a perpetual statute.
10 ¶ And the son of an Is'ra-el-it-ish woman,
whose father *was* an E-gyp'tian, went out
among the children of Is'ra-el: and this son of
the Is'ra-el-it-ish *woman* and a man of Is'ra-el
strove together in the camp;
11 And the Is'ra-el-it-ish woman's son blasphemed the name *of the LORD,* and cursed. And
they brought him unto Mo'ses: (and his mother's name *was* Shel'o-mith, the daughter of
Dib'ri, of the tribe of Dan:)
12 And they put him in ward, that the mind
of the LORD might be shewed them.
13 And the LORD spake unto Mo'ses, saying,
14 Bring forth him that hath cursed without
the camp; and let all that heard *him* lay their
hands upon his head, and let all the congregation stone him.
15 And thou shalt speak unto the children of
Is'ra-el, saying, Whosoever curseth his God
shall bear his sin.
16 And he that blasphemeth the name of the
LORD, he shall surely be put to death, *and* all the
congregation shall certainly stone him: as well
the stranger, as he that is born in the land, when

he blasphemeth the name *of the* LORD, shall be put to death.

17 ¶ And he that killeth any man shall surely be put to death.

18 And he that killeth a beast shall make it good; beast for beast.

19 And if a man cause a blemish in his neighbour; as he hath done, so shall it be done to him;

20 Breach for breach, eye for eye, tooth for tooth: as he hath caused a blemish in a man, so shall it be done to him *again*.

21 And he that killeth a beast, he shall restore it: and he that killeth a man, he shall be put to death.

22 Ye shall have one manner of law, as well for the stranger, as for one of your own country: for I *am* the LORD your God.

23 ¶ And Mo′ses spake to the children of Is′ra-el, that they should bring forth him that had cursed out of the camp, and stone him with stones. And the children of Is′ra-el did as the LORD commanded Mo′ses.

25 AND the LORD spake unto Mo′ses in mount Si′nai, saying,

2 Speak unto the children of Is′ra-el, and say unto them, When ye come into the land which I give you, then shall the land keep a sabbath unto the LORD.

3 Six years thou shalt sow thy field, and six years thou shalt prune thy vineyard, and gather in the fruit thereof;

4 But in the seventh year shall be a sabbath of rest unto the land, a sabbath for the LORD: thou shalt neither sow thy field, nor prune thy vineyard.

5 That which groweth of its own accord of thy harvest thou shalt not reap, neither gather the grapes of thy vine undressed: *for* it is a year of rest unto the land.

6 And the sabbath of the land shall be meat for you; for thee, and for thy servant, and for thy maid, and for thy hired servant, and for thy stranger that sojourneth with thee,

7 And for thy cattle, and for the beast that *are* in thy land, shall all the increase thereof be meat.

8 ¶ And thou shalt number seven sabbaths of years unto thee, seven times seven years; and the space of the seven sabbaths of years shall be unto thee forty and nine years.

9 Then shalt thou cause the trumpet of the jubile to sound on the tenth *day* of the seventh month, in the day of atonement shall ye make the trumpet sound throughout all your land.

10 And ye shall hallow the fiftieth year, and proclaim liberty throughout *all* the land unto all the inhabitants thereof: it shall be a jubile unto you; and ye shall return every man unto his possession, and ye shall return every man unto his family.

11 A jubile shall that fiftieth year be unto you: ye shall not sow, neither reap that which groweth of itself in it, nor gather *the grapes* in it of thy vine undressed.

12 For it *is* the jubile; it shall be holy unto you: ye shall eat the increase thereof out of the field.

13 In the year of this jubile ye shall return every man unto his possession.

14 And if thou sell ought unto thy neighbour, or buyest *ought* of thy neighbour's hand, ye shall not oppress one another:

15 According to the number of years after the jubile thou shalt buy of thy neighbour, *and* according unto the number of years of the fruits he shall sell unto thee:

16 According to the multitude of years thou shalt increase the price thereof, and according to the fewness of years thou shalt diminish the price of it: for *according* to the number *of the years* of the fruits doth he sell unto thee.

17 Ye shall not therefore oppress one another; but thou shalt fear thy God: for I *am* the LORD your God.

18 ¶ Wherefore ye shall do my statutes, and keep my judgments, and do them; and ye shall dwell in the land in safety.

19 And the land shall yield her fruit, and ye shall eat your fill, and dwell therein in safety.

20 And if ye shall say, What shall we eat the seventh year? behold, we shall not sow, nor gather in our increase:

21 Then I will command my blessing upon you in the sixth year, and it shall bring forth fruit for three years.

22 And ye shall sow the eighth year, and eat *yet* of old fruit until the ninth year; until her fruits come in ye shall eat *of* the old *store*.

23 ¶ The land shall not be sold for ever: for the land *is* mine; for ye *are* strangers and sojourners with me.

24 And in all the land of your possession ye shall grant a redemption for the land.

25 ¶ If thy brother be waxen poor, and hath sold away *some* of his possession, and if any of his kin come to redeem it, then shall he redeem that which his brother sold.

26 And if the man have none to redeem it, and himself be able to redeem it;

27 Then let him count the years of the sale thereof, and restore the overplus unto the man to whom he sold it; that he may return unto his possession.

28 But if he be not able to restore *it* to him, then that which is sold shall remain in the hand of him that hath bought it until the year of jubile: and in the jubile it shall go out, and he shall return unto his possession.

29 And if a man sell a dwelling house in a walled city, then he may redeem it within a whole year after it is sold; *within* a full year may he redeem it.

30 And if it be not redeemed within the space of a full year, then the house that *is* in the walled city shall be established for ever to him that bought it throughout his generations: it shall not go out in the jubile.

31 But the houses of the villages which have no wall round about them shall be counted as the fields of the country: they may be redeemed, and they shall go out in the jubile.

32 Notwithstanding the cities of the Le′vites, *and* the houses of the cities of their possession, may the Le′vites redeem at any time.

33 And if a man purchase of the Le′vites, then the house that was sold, and the city of his possession, shall go out in *the year of* jubile: for the houses of the cities of the Le′vites *are* their possession among the children of Is′ra-el.

34 But the field of the suburbs of their cities may not be sold; for it *is* their perpetual possession.

35 ¶ And if thy brother be waxen poor, and fallen in decay with thee; then thou shalt relieve him: *yea, though he be* a stranger, or a sojourner; that he may live with thee.

36 Take thou no usury of him, or increase: but fear thy God; that thy brother may live with thee.

37 Thou shalt not give him thy money upon usury, nor lend him thy victuals for increase.

38 I *am* the LORD your God, which brought

you forth out of the land of E'gypt, to give you
the land of Ca'naan, *and* to be your God.
39 ¶ And if thy brother *that dwelleth* by thee
be waxen poor, and be sold unto thee; thou
shalt not compel him to serve as a bondservant:
40 *But* as an hired servant, *and* as a sojourner, he shall be with thee, *and* shall serve
thee unto the year of jubile:
41 And *then* shall he depart from thee, *both*
he and his children with him, and shall return
unto his own family, and unto the possession of
his fathers shall he return.
42 For they *are* my servants, which I brought
forth out of the land of E'gypt: they shall not be
sold as bondmen.
43 Thou shalt not rule over him with rigour;
but shalt fear thy God.
44 Both thy bondmen, and thy bondmaids,
which thou shalt have, *shall be* of the heathen
that are round about you; of them shall ye buy
bondmen and bondmaids.
45 Moreover of the children of the strangers
that do sojourn among you, of them shall ye
buy, and of their families that *are* with you,
which they begat in your land: and they shall be
your possession.
46 And ye shall take them as an inheritance
for your children after you, to inherit *them for* a
possession; they shall be your bondmen for
ever: but over your brethren the children of Is'-
ra-el ye shall not rule one over another with rigour.
47 ¶ And if a sojourner or stranger wax rich
by thee, and thy brother *that dwelleth* by him
wax poor, and sell himself unto the stranger *or*
sojourner by thee, or to the stock of the stranger's family:
48 After that he is sold he may be redeemed
again; one of his brethren may redeem him:
49 Either his uncle, or his uncle's son, may
redeem him, or *any* that is nigh of kin unto him
of his family may redeem him; or if he be able,
he may redeem himself.
50 And he shall reckon with him that bought
him from the year that he was sold to him unto
the year of jubile: and the price of his sale shall
be according unto the number of years, according to the time of an hired servant shall it be
with him.
51 If *there be* yet many years *behind*, according unto them he shall give again the price of
his redemption out of the money that he was
bought for.
52 And if there remain but few years unto
the year of jubile, then he shall count with him,
and according unto his years shall he give him
again the price of his redemption.
53 *And* as a yearly hired servant shall he be
with him: *and the other* shall not rule with rigour over him in thy sight.
54 And if he be not redeemed in these *years*,
then he shall go out in the year of jubile, *both*
he, and his children with him.
55 For unto me the children of Is'ra-el *are*
servants; they *are* my servants whom I brought
forth out of the land of E'gypt: I *am* the LORD
your God.

26 YE shall make you no idols nor graven
image, neither rear you up a standing
image, neither shall ye set up *any* image of
stone in your land, to bow down unto it: for I
am the LORD your God.
2 ¶ Ye shall keep my sabbaths, and reverence my sanctuary: I *am* the LORD.
3 ¶ If ye walk in my statutes, and keep my
commandments, and do them;
4 Then I will give you rain in due season, and
the land shall yield her increase, and the trees
of the field shall yield their fruit.
5 And your threshing shall reach unto the
vintage, and the vintage shall reach unto the
sowing time: and ye shall eat your bread to the
full, and dwell in your land safely.
6 And I will give peace in the land, and ye
shall lie down, and none shall make *you* afraid:
and I will rid evil beasts out of the land, neither
shall the sword go through your land.
7 And ye shall chase your enemies, and they
shall fall before you by the sword.
8 And five of you shall chase an hundred, and
an hundred of you shall put ten thousand to
flight: and your enemies shall fall before you by
the sword.
9 For I will have respect unto you, and make
you fruitful, and multiply you, and establish my
covenant with you.
10 And ye shall eat old store, and bring forth
the old because of the new.
11 And I will set my tabernacle among you:
and my soul shall not abhor you.
12 And I will walk among you, and will be
your God, and ye shall be my people.
13 I *am* the LORD your God, which brought
you forth out of the land of E'gypt, that ye
should not be their bondmen; and I have broken
the bands of your yoke, and made you go upright.
14 ¶ But if ye will not hearken unto me, and
will not do all these commandments;
15 And if ye shall despise my statutes, or if
your soul abhor my judgments, so that ye will
not do all my commandments, *but* that ye break
my covenant:
16 I also will do this unto you; I will even
appoint over you terror, consumption, and the
burning ague, that shall consume the eyes, and
cause sorrow of heart: and ye shall sow your
seed in vain, for your enemies shall eat it.
17 And I will set my face against you, and ye
shall be slain before your enemies: they that
hate you shall reign over you; and ye shall flee
when none pursueth you.
18 And if ye will not yet for all this hearken
unto me, then I will punish you seven times
more for your sins.
19 And I will break the pride of your power;
and I will make your heaven as iron, and your
earth as brass:
20 And your strength shall be spent in vain:
for your land shall not yield her increase, neither shall the trees of the land yield their fruits.
21 ¶ And if ye walk contrary unto me, and
will not hearken unto me; I will bring seven
times more plagues upon you according to your
sins.
22 I will also send wild beasts among you,
which shall rob you of your children, and destroy your cattle, and make you few in number;
and your *high* ways shall be desolate.
23 And if ye will not be reformed by me by
these things, but will walk contrary unto me;
24 Then will I also walk contrary unto you,
and will punish you yet seven times for your
sins.
25 And I will bring a sword upon you, that
shall avenge the quarrel of *my* covenant: and
when ye are gathered together within your
cities, I will send the pestilence among you; and
ye shall be delivered into the hand of the enemy.
26 *And* when I have broken the staff of your
bread, ten women shall bake your bread in one
oven, and they shall deliver *you* your bread

again by weight: and ye shall eat, and not be satisfied.

27 And if ye will not for all this hearken unto me, but walk contrary unto me;

28 Then I will walk contrary unto you also in fury; and I, even I, will chastise you seven times for your sins.

29 And ye shall eat the flesh of your sons, and the flesh of your daughters shall ye eat.

30 And I will destroy your high places, and cut down your images, and cast your carcases upon the carcases of your idols, and my soul shall abhor you.

31 And I will make your cities waste, and bring your sanctuaries unto desolation, and I will not smell the savour of your sweet odours.

32 And I will bring the land into desolation: and your enemies which dwell therein shall be astonished at it.

33 And I will scatter you among the heathen, and will draw out a sword after you: and your land shall be desolate, and your cities waste.

34 Then shall the land enjoy her sabbaths, as long as it lieth desolate, and ye *be* in your enemies' land; *even* then shall the land rest, and enjoy her sabbaths.

35 As long as it lieth desolate it shall rest; because it did not rest in your sabbaths, when ye dwelt upon it.

36 And upon them that are left *alive* of you I will send a faintness into their hearts in the lands of their enemies; and the sound of a shaken leaf shall chase them; and they shall flee, as fleeing from a sword; and they shall fall when none pursueth.

37 And they shall fall one upon another, as it were before a sword, when none pursueth: and ye shall have no power to stand before your enemies.

38 And ye shall perish among the heathen, and the land of your enemies shall eat you up.

39 And they that are left of you shall pine away in their iniquity in your enemies' lands; and also in the iniquities of their fathers shall they pine away with them.

40 If they shall confess their iniquity, and the iniquity of their fathers, with their trespass which they trespassed against me, and that also they have walked contrary unto me;

41 And *that* I also have walked contrary unto them, and have brought them into the land of their enemies; if then their uncircumcised hearts be humbled, and they then accept of the punishment of their iniquity:

42 Then will I remember my covenant with Ja'cob, and also my covenant with I'saac, and also my covenant with A'bra-ham will I remember; and I will remember the land.

43 The land also shall be left of them, and shall enjoy her sabbaths, while she lieth desolate without them: and they shall accept of the punishment of their iniquity: because, even because they despised my judgments, and because their soul abhorred my statutes.

44 And yet for all that, when they be in the land of their enemies, I will not cast them away, neither will I abhor them, to destroy them utterly, and to break my covenant with them: for I *am* the LORD their God.

45 But I will for their sakes remember the covenant of their ancestors, whom I brought forth out of the land of E'gypt in the sight of the heathen, that I might be their God: I *am* the LORD.

46 These *are* the statutes and judgments and laws, which the LORD made between him and the children of Is'ra-el in mount Si'nai by the hand of Mo'ses.

27 AND the LORD spake unto Mo'ses, saying,

2 Speak unto the children of Is'ra-el, and say unto them, When a man shall make a singular vow, the persons *shall be* for the LORD by thy estimation.

3 And thy estimation shall be of the male from twenty years old even unto sixty years old, even thy estimation shall be fifty shekels of silver, after the shekel of the sanctuary.

4 And if it *be* a female, then thy estimation shall be thirty shekels.

5 And if *it be* from five years old even unto twenty years old, then thy estimation shall be of the male twenty shekels, and for the female ten shekels.

6 And if *it be* from a month old even unto five years old, then thy estimation shall be of the male five shekels of silver, and for the female thy estimation *shall be* three shekels of silver.

7 And if *it be* from sixty years old and above; if *it be* a male, then thy estimation shall be fifteen shekels, and for the female ten shekels.

8 But if he be poorer than thy estimation, then he shall present himself before the priest, and the priest shall value him; according to his ability that vowed shall the priest value him.

9 And if *it be* a beast, whereof men bring an offering unto the LORD, all that *any man* giveth of such unto the LORD shall be holy.

10 He shall not alter it, nor change it, a good for a bad, or a bad for a good: and if he shall at all change beast for beast, then it and the exchange thereof shall be holy.

11 And if *it be* any unclean beast, of which they do not offer a sacrifice unto the LORD, then he shall present the beast before the priest:

12 And the priest shall value it, whether it be good or bad: as thou valuest it, *who art* the priest, so shall it be.

13 But if he will at all redeem it, then he shall add a fifth *part* thereof unto thy estimation.

14 ¶ And when a man shall sanctify his house *to be* holy unto the LORD, then the priest shall estimate it, whether it be good or bad: as the priest shall estimate it, so shall it stand.

15 And if he that sanctified it will redeem his house, then he shall add the fifth *part* of the money of thy estimation unto it, and it shall be his.

16 And if a man shall sanctify unto the LORD *some part* of a field of his possession, then thy estimation shall be according to the seed thereof: an homer of barley seed *shall be valued* at fifty shekels of silver.

17 If he sanctify his field from the year of jubile, according to thy estimation it shall stand.

18 But if he sanctify his field after the jubile, then the priest shall reckon unto him the money according to the years that remain, even unto the year of the jubile, and it shall be abated from thy estimation.

19 And if he that sanctified the field will in any wise redeem it, then he shall add the fifth *part* of the money of thy estimation unto it, and it shall be assured to him.

20 And if he will not redeem the field, or if he have sold the field to another man, it shall not be redeemed any more.

21 But the field, when it goeth out in the jubile, shall be holy unto the LORD, as a field devoted; the possession thereof shall be the priest's.

22 And if *a man* sanctify unto the LORD a

field which he hath bought, which *is* not of the fields of his possession;
23 Then the priest shall reckon unto him the worth of thy estimation, *even* unto the year of the jubile: and he shall give thine estimation in that day, *as* a holy thing unto the LORD.
24 In the year of the jubile the field shall return unto him of whom it was bought, *even* to him to whom the possession of the land *did belong*.
25 And all thy estimations shall be according to the shekel of the sanctuary: twenty gerahs shall be the shekel.
26 ¶ Only the firstling of the beasts, which should be the LORD's firstling, no man shall sanctify it; whether *it be* ox, or sheep: it *is* the LORD's.
27 And if *it be* of an unclean beast, then he shall redeem *it* according to thine estimation, and shall add a fifth *part* of it thereto: or if it be not redeemed, then it shall be sold according to thy estimation.
28 Notwithstanding no devoted thing, that a man shall devote unto the LORD of all that he hath, *both* of man and beast, and of the field of his possession, shall be sold or redeemed: every devoted thing *is* most holy unto the LORD.
29 None devoted, which shall be devoted of men, shall be redeemed; *but* shall surely be put to death.
30 And all the tithe of the land, *whether* of the seed of the land, *or* of the fruit of the tree, *is* the LORD's: *it is* holy unto the LORD.
31 And if a man will at all redeem *ought* of his tithes, he shall add thereto the fifth *part* thereof.
32 And concerning the tithe of the herd, or of the flock, *even* of whatsoever passeth under the rod, the tenth shall be holy unto the LORD.
33 He shall not search whether it be good or bad, neither shall he change it: and if he change it at all, then both it and the change thereof shall be holy; it shall not be redeemed.
34 These *are* the commandments, which the LORD commanded Mo'ses for the children of Is'ra-el in mount Si'nai.

THE FOURTH BOOK OF MOSES
COMMONLY CALLED

NUMBERS

1 AND the LORD spake unto Mo'ses in the wilderness of Si'nai, in the tabernacle of the congregation, on the first *day* of the second month, in the second year after they were come out of the land of E'gypt, saying,
2 Take ye the sum of all the congregation of the children of Is'ra-el, after their families, by the house of their fathers, with the number of *their* names, every male by their polls;
3 From twenty years old and upward, all that are able to go forth to war in Is'ra-el: thou and Aar'on shall number them by their armies.
4 And with you there shall be a man of every tribe; every one head of the house of his fathers.
5 ¶ And these *are* the names of the men that shall stand with you: of *the tribe* of Reu'ben; E-li'zur the son of Shed'e-ur.
6 Of Sim'e-on; She-lu'mi-el the son of Zu-ri-shad'da-i.
7 Of Ju'dah; Nah'shon the son of Am-min'a-dab.
8 Of Is'sa-char; Ne-than'e-el the son of Zu'ar.
9 Of Zeb'u-lun; E-li'ab the son of He'lon.
10 Of the children of Jo'seph: of E'phra-im; E-lish'a-ma the son of Am-mi'hud: of Ma-nas'-seh; Ga-ma'li-el the son of Pe-dah'zur.
11 Of Ben'ja-min; Ab'i-dan the son of Gid-e-o'ni.
12 Of Dan; A-hi-e'zer the son of Am-mi-shad'da-i.
13 Of Ash'er; Pa'gi-el the son of Oc'ran.
14 Of Gad; E-li'a-saph the son of Deu'el.
15 Of Naph'ta-li; A-hi'ra the son of E'nan.
16 These *were* the renowned of the congregation, princes of the tribes of their fathers, heads of thousands in Is'ra-el.
17 ¶ And Mo'ses and Aar'on took these men which are expressed by *their* names:
18 And they assembled all the congregation together on the first *day* of the second month, and they declared their pedigrees after their families, by the house of their fathers, according to the number of the names, from twenty years old and upward, by their polls.
19 As the LORD commanded Mo'ses, so he numbered them in the wilderness of Si'nai.
20 And the children of Reu'ben, Is'ra-el's eldest son, by their generations, after their families, by the house of their fathers, according to the number of the names, by their polls, every male from twenty years old and upward, all that were able to go forth to war;
21 Those that were numbered of them, *even* of the tribe of Reu'ben, *were* forty and six thousand and five hundred.
22 ¶ Of the children of Sim'e-on, by their generations, after their families, by the house of their fathers, those that were numbered of them, according to the number of the names, by their polls, every male from twenty years old and upward, all that were able to go forth to war;
23 Those that were numbered of them, *even* of the tribe of Sim'e-on, *were* fifty and nine thousand and three hundred.
24 ¶ Of the children of Gad, by their generations, after their families, by the house of their fathers, according to the number of the names, from twenty years old and upward, all that were able to go forth to war;
25 Those that were numbered of them, *even* of the tribe of Gad, *were* forty and five thousand six hundred and fifty.
26 ¶ Of the children of Ju'dah, by their generations, after their families, by the house of their fathers, according to the number of the names, from twenty years old and upward, all that were able to go forth to war;
27 Those that were numbered of them, *even* of the tribe of Ju'dah, *were* threescore and fourteen thousand and six hundred.
28 ¶ Of the children of Is'sa-char, by their generations, after their families, by the house of their fathers, according to the number of the names, from twenty years old and upward, all that were able to go forth to war;
29 Those that were numbered of them, *even* of the tribe of Is'sa-char, *were* fifty and four thousand and four hundred.

30 ¶ Of the children of Zeb′u-lun, by their generations, after their families, by the house of their fathers, according to the number of the names, from twenty years old and upward, all that were able to go forth to war;

31 Those that were numbered of them, *even* of the tribe of Zeb′u-lun, *were* fifty and seven thousand and four hundred.

32 ¶ Of the children of Jo′seph, *namely,* of the children of E′phra-im, by their generations, after their families, by the house of their fathers, according to the number of the names, from twenty years old and upward, all that were able to go forth to war;

33 Those that were numbered of them, *even* of the tribe of E′phra-im, *were* forty thousand and five hundred.

34 ¶ Of the children of Ma-nas′seh, by their generations, after their families, by the house of their fathers, according to the number of the names, from twenty years old and upward, all that were able to go forth to war;

35 Those that were numbered of them, *even* of the tribe of Ma-nas′seh, *were* thirty and two thousand and two hundred.

36 ¶ Of the children of Ben′ja-min, by their generations, after their families, by the house of their fathers, according to the number of the names, from twenty years old and upward, all that were able to go forth to war;

37 Those that were numbered of them, *even* of the tribe of Ben′ja-min, *were* thirty and five thousand and four hundred.

38 ¶ Of the children of Dan, by their generations, after their families, by the house of their fathers, according to the number of the names, from twenty years old and upward, all that were able to go forth to war;

39 Those that were numbered of them, *even* of the tribe of Dan, *were* threescore and two thousand and seven hundred.

40 ¶ Of the children of Ash′er, by their generations, after their families, by the house of their fathers, according to the number of the names, from twenty years old and upward, all that were able to go forth to war;

41 Those that were numbered of them, *even* of the tribe of Ash′er, *were* forty and one thousand and five hundred.

42 ¶ Of the children of Naph′ta-li, throughout their generations, after their families, by the house of their fathers, according to the number of the names, from twenty years old and upward, all that were able to go forth to war;

43 Those that were numbered of them, *even* of the tribe of Naph′ta-li, *were* fifty and three thousand and four hundred.

44 These *are* those that were numbered, which Mo′ses and Aar′on numbered, and the princes of Is′ra-el, *being* twelve men: each one was for the house of his fathers.

45 So were all those that were numbered of the children of Is′ra-el, by the house of their fathers, from twenty years old and upward, all that were able to go forth to war in Is′ra-el;

46 Even all they that were numbered were six hundred thousand and three thousand and five hundred and fifty.

47 ¶ But the Le′vites after the tribe of their fathers were not numbered among them.

48 For the LORD had spoken unto Mo′ses, saying,

49 Only thou shalt not number the tribe of Le′vi, neither take the sum of them among the children of Is′ra-el:

50 But thou shalt appoint the Le′vites over the tabernacle of testimony, and over all the vessels thereof, and over all things that *belong* to it: they shall bear the tabernacle, and all the vessels thereof; and they shall minister unto it, and shall encamp round about the tabernacle.

51 And when the tabernacle setteth forward, the Le′vites shall take it down: and when the tabernacle is to be pitched, the Le′vites shall set it up: and the stranger that cometh nigh shall be put to death.

52 And the children of Is′ra-el shall pitch their tents, every man by his own camp, and every man by his own standard, throughout their hosts.

53 But the Le′vites shall pitch round about the tabernacle of testimony, that there be no wrath upon the congregation of the children of Is′ra-el: and the Le′vites shall keep the charge of the tabernacle of testimony.

54 And the children of Is′ra-el did according to all that the LORD commanded Mo′ses, so did they.

2 AND the LORD spake unto Mo′ses and unto Aar′on, saying,

2 Every man of the children of Is′ra-el shall pitch by his own standard, with the ensign of their father's house: far off about the tabernacle of the congregation shall they pitch.

3 And on the east side toward the rising of the sun shall they of the standard of the camp of Ju′dah pitch throughout their armies: and Nah′shon the son of Am-min′a-dab *shall be* captain of the children of Ju′dah.

4 And his host, and those that were numbered of them, *were* threescore and fourteen thousand and six hundred.

5 And those that do pitch next unto him *shall be* the tribe of Is′sa-char: and Ne-than′e-el the son of Zu′ar *shall be* captain of the children of Is′sa-char.

6 And his host, and those that were numbered thereof, *were* fifty and four thousand and four hundred.

7 *Then* the tribe of Zeb′u-lun: and E-li′ab the son of He′lon *shall be* captain of the children of Zeb′u-lun.

8 And his host, and those that were numbered thereof, *were* fifty and seven thousand and four hundred.

9 All that were numbered in the camp of Ju′dah *were* an hundred thousand and fourscore thousand and six thousand and four hundred, throughout their armies. These shall first set forth.

10 ¶ On the south side *shall be* the standard of the camp of Reu′ben according to their armies: and the captain of the children of Reu′ben *shall be* E-li′zur the son of Shed′e-ur.

11 And his host, and those that were numbered thereof, *were* forty and six thousand and five hundred.

12 And those which pitch by him *shall be* the tribe of Sim′e-on: and the captain of the children of Sim′e-on *shall be* She-lu′mi-el the son of Zu-ri-shad′da-i.

13 And his host, and those that were numbered of them, *were* fifty and nine thousand and three hundred.

14 Then the tribe of Gad: and the captain of the sons of Gad *shall be* E-li′a-saph the son of Reu′el.

15 And his host, and those that were numbered of them, *were* forty and five thousand and six hundred and fifty.

16 All that were numbered in the camp of Reu′ben *were* an hundred thousand and fifty and one thousand and four hundred and fifty,

throughout their armies. And they shall set
forth in the second rank.
17 ¶ Then the tabernacle of the congregation
shall set forward with the camp of the Le'vites
in the midst of the camp: as they encamp, so
shall they set forward, every man in his place
by their standards.
18 ¶ On the west side *shall be* the standard
of the camp of E'phra-im according to their
armies: and the captain of the sons of E'phra-im
shall be E-lish'a-ma the son of Am-mi'hud.
19 And his host, and those that were numbered of them, *were* forty thousand and five
hundred.
20 And by him *shall be* the tribe of Ma-nas'-
seh: and the captain of the children of Ma-nas'-
seh *shall be* Ga-ma'li-el the son of Pe-dah'zur.
21 And his host, and those that were numbered of them, *were* thirty and two thousand
and two hundred.
22 Then the tribe of Ben'ja-min: and the captain of the sons of Ben'ja-min *shall be* Ab'i-dan
the son of Gid-e-o'ni.
23 And his host, and those that were numbered of them, *were* thirty and five thousand
and four hundred.
24 All that were numbered of the camp of
E'phra-im *were* an hundred thousand and eight
thousand and an hundred, throughout their
armies. And they shall go forward in the third
rank.
25 ¶ The standard of the camp of Dan *shall
be* on the north side by their armies: and the
captain of the children of Dan *shall be* A-hi-e'-
zer the son of Am-mi-shad'da-i.
26 And his host, and those that were numbered of them, *were* threescore and two thousand and seven hundred.
27 And those that encamp by him *shall be*
the tribe of Ash'er: and the captain of the children of Ash'er *shall be* Pa'gi-el the son of Oc'-
ran.
28 And his host, and those that were numbered of them, *were* forty and one thousand and
five hundred.
29 ¶ Then the tribe of Naph'ta-li: and the
captain of the children of Naph'ta-li *shall be* A-
hi'ra the son of E'nan.
30 And his host, and those that were numbered of them, *were* fifty and three thousand
and four hundred.
31 All they that were numbered in the camp
of Dan *were* an hundred thousand and fifty and
seven thousand and six hundred. They shall go
hindmost with their standards.
32 ¶ These *are* those which were numbered
of the children of Is'ra-el by the house of their
fathers: all those that were numbered of the
camps throughout their hosts *were* six hundred
thousand and three thousand and five hundred
and fifty.
33 But the Le'vites were not numbered
among the children of Is'ra-el; as the LORD commanded Mo'ses.
34 And the children of Is'ra-el did according
to all that the LORD commanded Mo'ses: so they
pitched by their standards, and so they set forward, every one after their families, according
to the house of their fathers.

3 THESE also *are* the generations of Aar'on
and Mo'ses in the day *that* the LORD spake
with Mo'ses in mount Si'nai.
2 And these *are* the names of the sons of
Aar'on; Na'dab the firstborn, and A-bi'hu, E-le-
a'zar, and Ith'a-mar.
3 These *are* the names of the sons of Aar'on,
the priests which were anointed, whom he consecrated to minister in the priest's office.
4 And Na'dab and A-bi'hu died before the
LORD, when they offered strange fire before the
LORD, in the wilderness of Si'nai, and they had
no children: and E-le-a'zar and Ith'a-mar ministered in the priest's office in the sight of Aar'on
their father.
5 ¶ And the LORD spake unto Mo'ses, saying,
6 Bring the tribe of Le'vi near, and present
them before Aar'on the priest, that they may
minister unto him.
7 And they shall keep his charge, and the
charge of the whole congregation before the
tabernacle of the congregation, to do the service of the tabernacle.
8 And they shall keep all the instruments of
the tabernacle of the congregation, and the
charge of the children of Is'ra-el, to do the service of the tabernacle.
9 And thou shalt give the Le'vites unto Aar'-
on and to his sons: they *are* wholly given unto
him out of the children of Is'ra-el.
10 And thou shalt appoint Aar'on and his
sons, and they shall wait on their priest's office:
and the stranger that cometh nigh shall be put
to death.
11 And the LORD spake unto Mo'ses, saying,
12 And I, behold, I have taken the Le'vites
from among the children of Is'ra-el instead of
all the firstborn that openeth the matrix among
the children of Is'ra-el: therefore the Le'vites
shall be mine;
13 Because all the firstborn *are* mine; *for* on
the day that I smote all the firstborn in the land
of E'gypt I hallowed unto me all the firstborn in
Is'ra-el, both man and beast: mine shall they be:
I *am* the LORD.
14 ¶ And the LORD spake unto Mo'ses in the
wilderness of Si'nai, saying,
15 Number the children of Le'vi after the
house of their fathers, by their families: every
male from a month old and upward shalt thou
number them.
16 And Mo'ses numbered them according to
the word of the LORD, as he was commanded.
17 And these were the sons of Le'vi by their
names; Ger'shon, and Ko'hath, and Me-ra'ri.
18 And these *are* the names of the sons of
Ger'shon by their families; Lib'ni, and Shim'e-i.
19 And the sons of Ko'hath by their families;
Am'ram, and Iz'e-har, He'bron, and Uz'zi-el.
20 And the sons of Me-ra'ri by their families;
Mah'li, and Mu'shi. These *are* the families of the
Le'vites according to the house of their fathers.
21 Of Ger'shon *was* the family of the Lib'-
nites, and the family of the Shim'ites: these *are*
the families of the Ger'shon-ites.
22 Those that were numbered of them, according to the number of all the males, from a
month old and upward, *even* those that were
numbered of them *were* seven thousand and
five hundred.
23 The families of the Ger'shon-ites shall
pitch behind the tabernacle westward.
24 And the chief of the house of the father of
the Ger'shon-ites *shall be* E-li'a-saph the son of
La'el.
25 And the charge of the sons of Ger'shon in
the tabernacle of the congregation *shall be* the
tabernacle, and the tent, the covering thereof,
and the hanging for the door of the tabernacle
of the congregation,
26 And the hangings of the court, and the
curtain for the door of the court, which *is* by the
tabernacle, and by the altar round about, and
the cords of it for all the service thereof.

27 ¶ And of Ko'hath *was* the family of the Am'ram-ites, and the family of the Iz'e-har-ites, and the family of the He'bron-ites, and the family of the Uz'zi-el-ites: these *are* the families of the Ko'hath-ites.

28 In the number of all the males, from a month old and upward, *were* eight thousand and six hundred, keeping the charge of the sanctuary.

29 The families of the sons of Ko'hath shall pitch on the side of the tabernacle southward.

30 And the chief of the house of the father of the families of the Ko'hath-ites *shall be* E-liz'a-phan the son of Uz'zi-el.

31 And their charge *shall be* the ark, and the table, and the candlestick, and the altars, and the vessels of the sanctuary wherewith they minister, and the hanging, and all the service thereof.

32 And E-le-a'zar the son of Aar'on the priest *shall be* chief over the chief of the Le'vites, *and have* the oversight of them that keep the charge of the sanctuary.

33 ¶ Of Me-ra'ri *was* the family of the Mah'-lites, and the family of the Mu'shites: these *are* the families of Me-ra'ri.

34 And those that were numbered of them, according to the number of all the males, from a month old and upward, *were* six thousand and two hundred.

35 And the chief of the house of the father of the families of Me-ra'ri *was* Zu'ri-el the son of Ab-i-ha'il: *these* shall pitch on the side of the tabernacle northward.

36 And *under* the custody and charge of the sons of Me-ra'ri *shall be* the boards of the tabernacle, and the bars thereof, and the pillars thereof, and the sockets thereof, and all the vessels thereof, and all that serveth thereto,

37 And the pillars of the court round about, and their sockets, and their pins, and their cords.

38 ¶ But those that encamp before the tabernacle toward the east, *even* before the tabernacle of the congregation eastward, *shall be* Mo'-ses, and Aar'on and his sons, keeping the charge of the sanctuary for the charge of the children of Is'ra-el; and the stranger that cometh nigh shall be put to death.

39 All that were numbered of the Le'vites, which Mo'ses and Aar'on numbered at the commandment of the LORD, throughout their families, all the males from a month old and upward, *were* twenty and two thousand.

40 ¶ And the LORD said unto Mo'ses, Number all the firstborn of the males of the children of Is'ra-el from a month old and upward, and take the number of their names.

41 And thou shalt take the Le'vites for me (I *am* the LORD) instead of all the firstborn among the children of Is'ra-el; and the cattle of the Le'-vites instead of all the firstlings among the cattle of the children of Is'ra-el.

42 And Mo'ses numbered, as the LORD commanded him, all the firstborn among the children of Is'ra-el.

43 And all the firstborn males by the number of names, from a month old and upward, of those that were numbered of them, were twenty and two thousand two hundred and threescore and thirteen.

44 ¶ And the LORD spake unto Mo'ses, saying,

45 Take the Le'vites instead of all the firstborn among the children of Is'ra-el, and the cattle of the Le'vites instead of their cattle; and the Le'vites shall be mine: I *am* the LORD.

46 And for those that are to be redeemed of the two hundred and threescore and thirteen of the firstborn of the children of Is'ra-el, which are more than the Le'vites;

47 Thou shalt even take five shekels apiece by the poll, after the shekel of the sanctuary shalt thou take *them:* (the shekel *is* twenty gerahs:)

48 And thou shalt give the money, wherewith the odd number of them is to be redeemed, unto Aar'on and to his sons.

49 And Mo'ses took the redemption money of them that were over and above them that were redeemed by the Le'vites:

50 Of the firstborn of the children of Is'ra-el took he the money; a thousand three hundred and threescore and five *shekels,* after the shekel of the sanctuary:

51 And Mo'ses gave the money of them that were redeemed unto Aar'on and to his sons, according to the word of the LORD, as the LORD commanded Mo'ses.

4 AND the LORD spake unto Mo'ses and unto Aar'on, saying,

2 Take the sum of the sons of Ko'hath from among the sons of Le'vi, after their families, by the house of their fathers,

3 From thirty years old and upward even until fifty years old, all that enter into the host, to do the work in the tabernacle of the congregation.

4 This *shall be* the service of the sons of Ko'-hath in the tabernacle of the congregation, *about* the most holy things:

5 ¶ And when the camp setteth forward, Aar'on shall come, and his sons, and they shall take down the covering veil, and cover the ark of testimony with it:

6 And shall put thereon the covering of badgers' skins, and shall spread over *it* a cloth wholly of blue, and shall put in the staves thereof.

7 And upon the table of shewbread they shall spread a cloth of blue, and put thereon the dishes, and the spoons, and the bowls, and covers to cover withal: and the continual bread shall be thereon:

8 And they shall spread upon them a cloth of scarlet, and cover the same with a covering of badgers' skins, and shall put in the staves thereof.

9 And they shall take a cloth of blue, and cover the candlestick of the light, and his lamps, and his tongs, and his snuffdishes, and all the oil vessels thereof, wherewith they minister unto it:

10 And they shall put it and all the vessels thereof within a covering of badgers' skins, and shall put *it* upon a bar.

11 And upon the golden altar they shall spread a cloth of blue, and cover it with a covering of badgers' skins, and shall put to the staves thereof:

12 And they shall take all the instruments of ministry, wherewith they minister in the sanctuary, and put *them* in a cloth of blue, and cover them with a covering of badgers' skins, and shall put *them* on a bar:

13 And they shall take away the ashes from the altar, and spread a purple cloth thereon:

14 And they shall put upon it all the vessels thereof, wherewith they minister about it, *even* the censers, the fleshhooks, and the shovels, and the basons, all the vessels of the altar; and they shall spread upon it a covering of badgers' skins, and put to the staves of it.

15 And when Aar'on and his sons have made
an end of covering the sanctuary, and all the
vessels of the sanctuary, as the camp is to set
forward; after that, the sons of Ko'hath shall
come to bear *it:* but they shall not touch *any*
holy thing, lest they die. These *things are* the
burden of the sons of Ko'hath in the tabernacle
of the congregation.
16 ¶ And to the office of E-le-a'zar the son of
Aar'on the priest *pertaineth* the oil for the light,
and the sweet incense, and the daily meat offering, and the anointing oil, *and* the oversight of
all the tabernacle, and of all that therein *is,* in
the sanctuary, and in the vessels thereof.
17 ¶ And the LORD spake unto Mo'ses and
unto Aar'on, saying,
18 Cut ye not off the tribe of the families of
the Ko'hath-ites from among the Le'vites:
19 But thus do unto them, that they may live,
and not die, when they approach unto the most
holy things: Aar'on and his sons shall go in, and
appoint them every one to his service and to his
burden:
20 But they shall not go in to see when the
holy things are covered, lest they die.
21 ¶ And the LORD spake unto Mo'ses, saying,
22 Take also the sum of the sons of Ger'shon,
throughout the houses of their fathers, by their
families;
23 From thirty years old and upward until fifty years old shalt thou number them; all that
enter in to perform the service, to do the work
in the tabernacle of the congregation.
24 This *is* the service of the families of the
Ger'shon-ites, to serve, and for burdens:
25 And they shall bear the curtains of the
tabernacle, and the tabernacle of the congregation, his covering, and the covering of the badgers' skins that *is* above upon it, and the hanging for the door of the tabernacle of the
congregation,
26 And the hangings of the court, and the
hanging for the door of the gate of the court,
which *is* by the tabernacle and by the altar
round about, and their cords, and all the instruments of their service, and all that is made for
them: so shall they serve.
27 At the appointment of Aar'on and his sons
shall be all the service of the sons of the Ger'-
shon-ites, in all their burdens, and in all their
service: and ye shall appoint unto them in
charge all their burdens.
28 This *is* the service of the families of the
sons of Ger'shon in the tabernacle of the congregation: and their charge *shall be* under the
hand of Ith'a-mar the son of Aar'on the priest.
29 ¶ As for the sons of Me-ra'ri, thou shalt
number them after their families, by the house
of their fathers;
30 From thirty years old and upward even
unto fifty years old shalt thou number them, every one that entereth into the service, to do the
work of the tabernacle of the congregation.
31 And this *is* the charge of their burden, according to all their service in the tabernacle of
the congregation; the boards of the tabernacle,
and the bars thereof, and the pillars thereof,
and sockets thereof,
32 And the pillars of the court round about,
and their sockets, and their pins, and their
cords, with all their instruments, and with all
their service: and by name ye shall reckon the
instruments of the charge of their burden.
33 This *is* the service of the families of the
sons of Me-ra'ri, according to all their service,
in the tabernacle of the congregation, under the
hand of Ith'a-mar the son of Aar'on the priest.
34 ¶ And Mo'ses and Aar'on and the chief of
the congregation numbered the sons of the Ko'-
hath-ites after their families, and after the
house of their fathers,
35 From thirty years old and upward even
unto fifty years old, every one that entereth into
the service, for the work in the tabernacle of the
congregation:
36 And those that were numbered of them by
their families were two thousand seven hundred and fifty
37 These *were* they that were numbered of
the families of the Ko'hath-ites, all that might
do service in the tabernacle of the congregation, which Mo'ses and Aar'on did number according to the commandment of the LORD by
the hand of Mo'ses.
38 And those that were numbered of the sons
of Ger'shon, throughout their families, and by
the house of their fathers,
39 From thirty years old and upward even
unto fifty years old, every one that entereth into
the service, for the work in the tabernacle of the
congregation,
40 Even those that were numbered of them,
throughout their families, by the house of their
fathers, were two thousand and six hundred
and thirty.
41 These *are* they that were numbered of the
families of the sons of Ger'shon, of all that
might do service in the tabernacle of the congregation, whom Mo'ses and Aar'on did number according to the commandment of the
LORD.
42 ¶ And those that were numbered of the
families of the sons of Me-ra'ri, throughout
their families, by the house of their fathers,
43 From thirty years old and upward even
unto fifty years old, every one that entereth into
the service, for the work in the tabernacle of the
congregation,
44 Even those that were numbered of them
after their families, were three thousand and
two hundred.
45 These *be* those that were numbered of the
families of the sons of Me-ra'ri, whom Mo'ses
and Aar'on numbered according to the word of
the LORD by the hand of Mo'ses.
46 All those that were numbered of the Le'-
vites, whom Mo'ses and Aar'on and the chief of
Is'ra-el numbered, after their families, and after
the house of their fathers,
47 From thirty years old and upward even
unto fifty years old, every one that came to do
the service of the ministry, and the service of
the burden in the tabernacle of the congregation,
48 Even those that were numbered of them,
were eight thousand and five hundred and fourscore.
49 According to the commandment of the
LORD they were numbered by the hand of Mo'-
ses, every one according to his service, and according to his burden: thus were they numbered of him, as the LORD commanded Mo'ses.

5 AND the LORD spake unto Mo'ses, saying,
2 Command the children of Is'ra-el, that
they put out of the camp every leper, and every
one that hath an issue, and whosoever is defiled
by the dead:
3 Both male and female shall ye put out,
without the camp shall ye put them; that they
defile not their camps, in the midst whereof I
dwell.
4 And the children of Is'ra-el did so, and put

them out without the camp: as the LORD spake unto Mo'ses, so did the children of Is'ra-el.

5 ¶ And the LORD spake unto Mo'ses, saying,

6 Speak unto the children of Is'ra-el, When a man or woman shall commit any sin that men commit, to do a trespass against the LORD, and that person be guilty;

7 Then they shall confess their sin which they have done: and he shall recompense his trespass with the principal thereof, and add unto it the fifth *part* thereof, and give *it* unto *him* against whom he hath trespassed.

8 But if the man have no kinsman to recompense the trespass unto, let the trespass be recompensed unto the LORD, *even* to the priest; beside the ram of the atonement, whereby an atonement shall be made for him.

9 And every offering of all the holy things of the children of Is'ra-el, which they bring unto the priest, shall be his.

10 And every man's hallowed things shall be his: whatsoever any man giveth the priest, it shall be his.

11 ¶ And the LORD spake unto Mo'ses, saying,

12 Speak unto the children of Is'ra-el, and say unto them, If any man's wife go aside, and commit a trespass against him,

13 And a man lie with her carnally, and it be hid from the eyes of her husband, and be kept close, and she be defiled, and *there be* no witness against her, neither she be taken *with the manner;*

14 And the spirit of jealousy come upon him, and he be jealous of his wife, and she be defiled: or if the spirit of jealousy come upon him, and he be jealous of his wife, and she be not defiled:

15 Then shall the man bring his wife unto the priest, and he shall bring her offering for her, the tenth *part* of an ephah of barley meal; he shall pour no oil upon it, nor put frankincense thereon; for it *is* an offering of jealousy, an offering of memorial, bringing iniquity to remembrance.

16 And the priest shall bring her near, and set her before the LORD:

17 And the priest shall take holy water in an earthen vessel; and of the dust that is in the floor of the tabernacle the priest shall take, and put *it* into the water:

18 And the priest shall set the woman before the LORD, and uncover the woman's head, and put the offering of memorial in her hands, which *is* the jealousy offering: and the priest shall have in his hand the bitter water that causeth the curse:

19 And the priest shall charge her by an oath, and say unto the woman, If no man have lain with thee, and if thou hast not gone aside to uncleanness *with another* instead of thy husband, be thou free from this bitter water that causeth the curse:

20 But if thou hast gone aside *to another* instead of thy husband, and if thou be defiled, and some man have lain with thee beside thine husband:

21 Then the priest shall charge the woman with an oath of cursing, and the priest shall say unto the woman, The LORD make thee a curse and an oath among thy people, when the LORD doth make thy thigh to rot, and thy belly to swell;

22 And this water that causeth the curse shall go into thy bowels, to make *thy* belly to swell, and *thy* thigh to rot: And the woman shall say, Amen, amen.

23 And the priest shall write these curses in a book, and he shall blot *them* out with the bitter water:

24 And he shall cause the woman to drink the bitter water that causeth the curse: and the water that causeth the curse shall enter into her, *and become* bitter.

25 Then the priest shall take the jealousy offering out of the woman's hand, and shall wave the offering before the LORD, and offer it upon the altar:

26 And the priest shall take an handful of the offering, *even* the memorial thereof, and burn *it* upon the altar, and afterward shall cause the woman to drink the water.

27 And when he hath made her to drink the water, then it shall come to pass, *that,* if she be defiled, and have done trespass against her husband, that the water that causeth the curse shall enter into her, *and become* bitter, and her belly shall swell, and her thigh shall rot: and the woman shall be a curse among her people.

28 And if the woman be not defiled, but be clean; then she shall be free, and shall conceive seed.

29 This *is* the law of jealousies, when a wife goeth aside *to another* instead of her husband, and is defiled;

30 Or when the spirit of jealousy cometh upon him, and he be jealous over his wife, and shall set the woman before the LORD, and the priest shall execute upon her all this law.

31 Then shall the man be guiltless from iniquity, and this woman shall bear her iniquity.

6 AND the LORD spake unto Mo'ses, saying,

2 Speak unto the children of Is'ra-el, and say unto them, When either man or woman shall separate *themselves* to vow a vow of a Naz'a-rite, to separate *themselves* unto the LORD:

3 He shall separate *himself* from wine and strong drink, and shall drink no vinegar of wine, or vinegar of strong drink, neither shall he drink any liquor of grapes, nor eat moist grapes, or dried.

4 All the days of his separation shall he eat nothing that is made of the vine tree, from the kernels even to the husk.

5 All the days of the vow of his separation there shall no razor come upon his head: until the days be fulfilled, in the which he separateth *himself* unto the LORD, he shall be holy, *and* shall let the locks of the hair of his head grow.

6 All the days that he separateth *himself* unto the LORD he shall come at no dead body.

7 He shall not make himself unclean for his father, or for his mother, for his brother, or for his sister, when they die: because the consecration of his God *is* upon his head.

8 All the days of his separation he *is* holy unto the LORD.

9 And if any man die very suddenly by him, and he hath defiled the head of his consecration; then he shall shave his head in the day of his cleansing, on the seventh day shall he shave it.

10 And on the eighth day he shall bring two turtles, or two young pigeons, to the priest, to the door of the tabernacle of the congregation:

11 And the priest shall offer the one for a sin offering, and the other for a burnt offering, and make an atonement for him, for that he sinned by the dead, and shall hallow his head that same day.

12 And he shall consecrate unto the LORD the days of his separation, and shall bring a lamb of the first year for a trespass offering: but the

days that were before shall be lost, because his separation was defiled.

13 ¶ And this *is* the law of the Naz'a-rite, when the days of his separation are fulfilled: he shall be brought unto the door of the tabernacle of the congregation:

14 And he shall offer his offering unto the LORD, one he lamb of the first year without blemish for a burnt offering, and one ewe lamb of the first year without blemish for a sin offering, and one ram without blemish for peace offerings,

15 And a basket of unleavened bread, cakes of fine flour mingled with oil, and wafers of unleavened bread anointed with oil, and their meat offering, and their drink offerings.

16 And the priest shall bring *them* before the LORD, and shall offer his sin offering, and his burnt offering:

17 And he shall offer the ram *for* a sacrifice of peace offerings unto the LORD, with the basket of unleavened bread: the priest shall offer also his meat offering, and his drink offering.

18 And the Naz'a-rite shall shave the head of his separation *at* the door of the tabernacle of the congregation, and shall take the hair of the head of his separation, and put *it* in the fire which *is* under the sacrifice of the peace offerings.

19 And the priest shall take the sodden shoulder of the ram, and one unleavened cake out of the basket, and one unleavened wafer, and shall put *them* upon the hands of the Naz'a-rite, after *the hair of* his separation is shaven:

20 And the priest shall wave them *for* a wave offering before the LORD: this *is* holy for the priest, with the wave breast and heave shoulder: and after that the Naz'a-rite may drink wine.

21 This *is* the law of the Naz'a-rite who hath vowed, *and of* his offering unto the LORD for his separation, beside *that* that his hand shall get: according to the vow which he vowed, so he must do after the law of his separation.

22 ¶ And the LORD spake unto Mo'ses, saying,

23 Speak unto Aar'on and unto his sons, saying, On this wise ye shall bless the children of Is'ra-el, saying unto them,

24 The LORD bless thee, and keep thee:

25 The LORD make his face shine upon thee, and be gracious unto thee:

26 The LORD lift up his countenance upon thee, and give thee peace.

27 And they shall put my name upon the children of Is'ra-el; and I will bless them.

7

AND it came to pass on the day that Mo'ses had fully set up the tabernacle, and had anointed it, and sanctified it, and all the instruments thereof, both the altar and all the vessels thereof, and had anointed them, and sanctified them;

2 That the princes of Is'ra-el, heads of the house of their fathers, who *were* the princes of the tribes, and were over them that were numbered, offered:

3 And they brought their offering before the LORD, six covered wagons, and twelve oxen; a wagon for two of the princes, and for each one an ox: and they brought them before the tabernacle.

4 And the LORD spake unto Mo'ses, saying,

5 Take *it* of them, that they may be to do the service of the tabernacle of the congregation; and thou shalt give them unto the Le'vites, to every man according to his service.

6 And Mo'ses took the wagons and the oxen, and gave them unto the Le'vites.

7 Two wagons and four oxen he gave unto the sons of Ger'shon, according to their service:

8 And four wagons and eight oxen he gave unto the sons of Me-ra'ri, according unto their service, under the hand of Ith'a-mar the son of Aar'on the priest.

9 But unto the sons of Ko'hath he gave none: because the service of the sanctuary belonging unto them *was that* they should bear upon their shoulders.

10 ¶ And the princes offered for dedicating of the altar in the day that it was anointed, even the princes offered their offering before the altar.

11 And the LORD said unto Mo'ses, They shall offer their offering, each prince on his day, for the dedicating of the altar.

12 ¶ And he that offered his offering the first day was Nah'shon the son of Am-min'a-dab, of the tribe of Ju'dah:

13 And his offering *was* one silver charger, the weight thereof *was* an hundred and thirty *shekels*, one silver bowl of seventy shekels, after the shekel of the sanctuary; both of them *were* full of fine flour mingled with oil for a meat offering:

14 One spoon of ten *shekels* of gold, full of incense:

15 One young bullock, one ram, one lamb of the first year, for a burnt offering:

16 One kid of the goats for a sin offering:

17 And for a sacrifice of peace offerings, two oxen, five rams, five he goats, five lambs of the first year: this *was* the offering of Nah'shon the son of Am-min'a-dab.

18 ¶ On the second day Ne-than'e-el the son of Zu'ar, prince of Is'sa-char, did offer:

19 He offered *for* his offering one silver charger, the weight whereof *was* an hundred and thirty *shekels*, one silver bowl of seventy shekels, after the shekel of the sanctuary; both of them full of fine flour mingled with oil for a meat offering:

20 One spoon of gold of ten *shekels*, full of incense:

21 One young bullock, one ram, one lamb of the first year, for a burnt offering:

22 One kid of the goats for a sin offering:

23 And for a sacrifice of peace offerings, two oxen, five rams, five he goats, five lambs of the first year: this *was* the offering of Ne-than'e-el the son of Zu'ar.

24 ¶ On the third day E-li'ab the son of He'lon, prince of the children of Zeb'u-lun, *did offer*:

25 His offering *was* one silver charger, the weight whereof *was* an hundred and thirty *shekels*, one silver bowl of seventy shekels, after the shekel of the sanctuary; both of them full of fine flour mingled with oil for a meat offering:

26 One golden spoon of ten *shekels*, full of incense:

27 One young bullock, one ram, one lamb of the first year, for a burnt offering:

28 One kid of the goats for a sin offering:

29 And for a sacrifice of peace offerings, two oxen, five rams, five he goats, five lambs of the first year: this *was* the offering of E-li'ab the son of He'lon.

30 ¶ On the fourth day E-li'zur the son of Shed'e-ur, prince of the children of Reu'ben, *did offer*:

31 His offering *was* one silver charger of the weight of an hundred and thirty *shekels*, one

silver bowl of seventy shekels, after the shekel
of the sanctuary; both of them full of fine flour
mingled with oil for a meat offering:
32 One golden spoon of ten *shekels,* full of
incense:
33 One young bullock, one ram, one lamb of
the first year, for a burnt offering:
34 One kid of the goats for a sin offering:
35 And for a sacrifice of peace offerings, two
oxen, five rams, five he goats, five lambs of the
first year: this *was* the offering of E-li'zur the
son of Shed'e-ur.
36 ¶ On the fifth day She-lu'mi-el the son of
Zu-ri-shad'da-i, prince of the children of Sim'e-
on, *did offer:*
37 His offering *was* one silver charger, the
weight whereof *was* an hundred and thirty
shekels, one silver bowl of seventy shekels, after the shekel of the sanctuary; both of them
full of fine flour mingled with oil for a meat offering:
38 One golden spoon of ten *shekels,* full of
incense:
39 One young bullock, one ram, one lamb of
the first year, for a burnt offering:
40 One kid of the goats for a sin offering:
41 And for a sacrifice of peace offerings, two
oxen, five rams, five he goats, five lambs of the
first year: this *was* the offering of She-lu'mi-el
the son of Zu-ri-shad'da-i.
42 ¶ On the sixth day E-li'a-saph the son of
Deu'el, prince of the children of Gad, *offered:*
43 His offering *was* one silver charger of the
weight of an hundred and thirty *shekels,* a silver
bowl of seventy shekels, after the shekel of the
sanctuary; both of them full of fine flour mingled with oil for a meat offering:
44 One golden spoon of ten *shekels,* full of
incense:
45 One young bullock, one ram, one lamb of
the first year, for a burnt offering:
46 One kid of the goats for a sin offering:
47 And for a sacrifice of peace offerings, two
oxen, five rams, five he goats, five lambs of the
first year: this *was* the offering of E-li'a-saph the
son of Deu'el.
48 ¶ On the seventh day E-lish'a-ma the son
of Am-mi'hud, prince of the children of E'phra-
im, *offered:*
49 His offering *was* one silver charger, the
weight whereof *was* an hundred and thirty
shekels, one silver bowl of seventy shekels, after the shekel of the sanctuary; both of them
full of fine flour mingled with oil for a meat offering:
50 One golden spoon of ten *shekels,* full of
incense:
51 One young bullock, one ram, one lamb of
the first year, for a burnt offering:
52 One kid of the goats for a sin offering:
53 And for a sacrifice of peace offerings, two
oxen, five rams, five he goats, five lambs of the
first year: this *was* the offering of E-lish'a-ma
the son of Am-mi'hud.
54 ¶ On the eighth day *offered* Ga-ma'li-el
the son of Pe-dah'zur, prince of the children of
Ma-nas'seh:
55 His offering *was* one silver charger of the
weight of an hundred and thirty *shekels,* one
silver bowl of seventy shekels, after the shekel
of the sanctuary; both of them full of fine flour
mingled with oil for a meat offering:
56 One golden spoon of ten *shekels,* full of
incense:
57 One young bullock, one ram, one lamb of
the first year, for a burnt offering:
58 One kid of the goats for a sin offering:
59 And for a sacrifice of peace offerings, two
oxen, five rams, five he goats, five lambs of the
first year: this *was* the offering of Ga-ma'li-el
the son of Pe-dah'zur.
60 ¶ On the ninth day Ab'i-dan the son of
Gid-e-o'ni, prince of the children of Ben'ja-min,
offered:
61 His offering *was* one silver charger, the
weight whereof *was* an hundred and thirty
shekels, one silver bowl of seventy shekels, after the shekel of the sanctuary; both of them
full of fine flour mingled with oil for a meat offering:
62 One golden spoon of ten *shekels,* full of
incense:
63 One young bullock, one ram, one lamb of
the first year, for a burnt offering:
64 One kid of the goats for a sin offering:
65 And for a sacrifice of peace offerings, two
oxen, five rams, five he goats, five lambs of the
first year: this *was* the offering of Ab'i-dan the
son of Gid-e-o'ni.
66 ¶ On the tenth day A-hi-e'zer the son of
Am-mi-shad'da-i, prince of the children of Dan,
offered:
67 His offering *was* one silver charger, the
weight whereof *was* an hundred and thirty
shekels, one silver bowl of seventy shekels, after the shekel of the sanctuary; both of them
full of fine flour mingled with oil for a meat offering:
68 One golden spoon of ten *shekels,* full of
incense:
69 One young bullock, one ram, one lamb of
the first year, for a burnt offering:
70 One kid of the goats for a sin offering:
71 And for a sacrifice of peace offerings, two
oxen, five rams, five he goats, five lambs of the
first year: this *was* the offering of A-hi-e'zer the
son of Am-mi-shad'da-i.
72 ¶ On the eleventh day Pa'gi-el the son of
Oc'ran, prince of the children of Ash'er, *offered:*
73 His offering *was* one silver charger, the
weight whereof *was* an hundred and thirty
shekels, one silver bowl of seventy shekels, after the shekel of the sanctuary; both of them
full of fine flour mingled with oil for a meat offering:
74 One golden spoon of ten *shekels,* full of
incense:
75 One young bullock, one ram, one lamb of
the first year, for a burnt offering:
76 One kid of the goats for a sin offering:
77 And for a sacrifice of peace offerings, two
oxen, five rams, five he goats, five lambs of the
first year: this *was* the offering of Pa'gi-el the
son of Oc'ran.
78 ¶ On the twelfth day A-hi'ra the son of
E'nan, prince of the children of Naph'ta-li, *offered:*
79 His offering *was* one silver charger, the
weight whereof *was* an hundred and thirty
shekels, one silver bowl of seventy shekels, after the shekel of the sanctuary; both of them
full of fine flour mingled with oil for a meat offering:
80 One golden spoon of ten *shekels,* full of
incense:
81 One young bullock, one ram, one lamb of
the first year, for a burnt offering:
82 One kid of the goats for a sin offering:
83 And for a sacrifice of peace offerings, two
oxen, five rams, five he goats, five lambs of the
first year: this *was* the offering of A-hi'ra the
son of E'nan.
84 This *was* the dedication of the altar, in the
day when it was anointed, by the princes of Is'-

ra-el: twelve chargers of silver, twelve silver bowls, twelve spoons of gold:

85 Each charger of silver *weighing* an hundred and thirty *shekels*, each bowl seventy: all the silver vessels *weighed* two thousand and four hundred *shekels*, after the shekel of the sanctuary:

86 The golden spoons *were* twelve, full of incense, *weighing* ten *shekels* apiece, after the shekel of the sanctuary: all the gold of the spoons *was* an hundred and twenty *shekels*.

87 All the oxen for the burnt offering *were* twelve bullocks, the rams twelve, the lambs of the first year twelve, with their meat offering: and the kids of the goats for sin offering twelve.

88 And all the oxen for the sacrifice of the peace offerings *were* twenty and four bullocks, the rams sixty, the he goats sixty, the lambs of the first year sixty. This *was* the dedication of the altar, after that it was anointed.

89 And when Mo'ses was gone into the tabernacle of the congregation to speak with him, then he heard the voice of one speaking unto him from off the mercy seat that *was* upon the ark of testimony, from between the two cherubims: and he spake unto him.

8 AND the LORD spake unto Mo'ses, saying,

2 Speak unto Aar'on, and say unto him, When thou lightest the lamps, the seven lamps shall give light over against the candlestick.

3 And Aar'on did so; he lighted the lamps thereof over against the candlestick, as the LORD commanded Mo'ses.

4 And this work of the candlestick *was of* beaten gold, unto the shaft thereof, unto the flowers thereof, *was* beaten work: according unto the pattern which the LORD had shewed Mo'ses, so he made the candlestick.

5 ¶ And the LORD spake unto Mo'ses, saying,

6 Take the Le'vites from among the children of Is'ra-el, and cleanse them.

7 And thus shalt thou do unto them, to cleanse them: Sprinkle water of purifying upon them, and let them shave all their flesh, and let them wash their clothes, and *so* make themselves clean.

8 Then let them take a young bullock with his meat offering, *even* fine flour mingled with oil, and another young bullock shalt thou take for a sin offering.

9 And thou shalt bring the Le'vites before the tabernacle of the congregation: and thou shalt gather the whole assembly of the children of Is'ra-el together:

10 And thou shalt bring the Le'vites before the LORD: and the children of Is'ra-el shall put their hands upon the Le'vites:

11 And Aar'on shall offer the Le'vites before the LORD *for* an offering of the children of Is'ra-el, that they may execute the service of the LORD.

12 And the Le'vites shall lay their hands upon the heads of the bullocks: and thou shalt offer the one *for* a sin offering, and the other *for* a burnt offering, unto the LORD, to make an atonement for the Le'vites.

13 And thou shalt set the Le'vites before Aar'on, and before his sons, and offer them *for* an offering unto the LORD.

14 Thus shalt thou separate the Le'vites from among the children of Is'ra-el: and the Le'vites shall be mine.

15 And after that shall the Le'vites go in to do the service of the tabernacle of the congregation: and thou shalt cleanse them, and offer them *for* an offering.

16 For they *are* wholly given unto me from among the children of Is'ra-el; instead of such as open every womb, *even instead of* the firstborn of all the children of Is'ra-el, have I taken them unto me.

17 For all the firstborn of the children of Is'ra-el *are* mine, *both* man and beast: on the day that I smote every firstborn in the land of E'gypt I sanctified them for myself.

18 And I have taken the Le'vites for all the firstborn of the children of Is'ra-el.

19 And I have given the Le'vites *as* a gift to Aar'on and to his sons from among the children of Is'ra-el, to do the service of the children of Is'ra-el in the tabernacle of the congregation, and to make an atonement for the children of Is'ra-el: that there be no plague among the children of Is'ra-el, when the children of Is'ra-el come nigh unto the sanctuary.

20 And Mo'ses, and Aar'on, and all the congregation of the children of Is'ra-el, did to the Le'vites according unto all that the LORD commanded Mo'ses concerning the Le'vites, so did the children of Is'ra-el unto them.

21 And the Le'vites were purified, and they washed their clothes; and Aar'on offered them *as* an offering before the LORD; and Aar'on made an atonement for them to cleanse them.

22 And after that went the Le'vites in to do their service in the tabernacle of the congregation before Aar'on, and before his sons: as the LORD had commanded Mo'ses concerning the Le'vites, so did they unto them.

23 ¶ And the LORD spake unto Mo'ses, saying,

24 This *is it* that *belongeth* unto the Le'vites: from twenty and five years old and upward they shall go in to wait upon the service of the tabernacle of the congregation:

25 And from the age of fifty years they shall cease waiting upon the service *thereof*, and shall serve no more:

26 But shall minister with their brethren in the tabernacle of the congregation, to keep the charge, and shall do no service. Thus shalt thou do unto the Le'vites touching their charge.

9 AND the LORD spake unto Mo'ses in the wilderness of Si'nai, in the first month of the second year after they were come out of the land of E'gypt, saying,

2 Let the children of Is'ra-el also keep the passover at his appointed season.

3 In the fourteenth day of this month, at even, ye shall keep it in his appointed season: according to all the rites of it, and according to all the ceremonies thereof, shall ye keep it.

4 And Mo'ses spake unto the children of Is'ra-el, that they should keep the passover.

5 And they kept the passover on the fourteenth day of the first month at even in the wilderness of Si'nai: according to all that the LORD commanded Mo'ses, so did the children of Is'ra-el.

6 ¶ And there were certain men, who were defiled by the dead body of a man, that they could not keep the passover on that day: and they came before Mo'ses and before Aar'on on that day:

7 And those men said unto him, We *are* defiled by the dead body of a man: wherefore are we kept back, that we may not offer an offering of the LORD in his appointed season among the children of Is'ra-el?

8 And Mo'ses said unto them, Stand still, and I will hear what the LORD will command concerning you.

9 ¶ And the LORD spake unto Mo'ses, saying,
10 Speak unto the children of Is'ra-el, saying,
If any man of you or of your posterity shall be
unclean by reason of a dead body, or *be* in a
journey afar off, yet he shall keep the passover
unto the LORD.
11 The fourteenth day of the second month
at even they shall keep it, *and* eat it with unleavened bread and bitter *herbs*.
12 They shall leave none of it unto the morning, nor break any bone of it: according to all
the ordinances of the passover they shall keep
it.
13 But the man that *is* clean, and is not in a
journey, and forbeareth to keep the passover,
even the same soul shall be cut off from among
his people: because he brought not the offering
of the LORD in his appointed season, that man
shall bear his sin.
14 And if a stranger shall sojourn among
you, and will keep the passover unto the LORD;
according to the ordinance of the passover, and
according to the manner thereof, so shall he do:
ye shall have one ordinance, both for the stranger, and for him that was born in the land.
15 ¶ And on the day that the tabernacle was
reared up the cloud covered the tabernacle,
namely, the tent of the testimony: and at even
there was upon the tabernacle as it were the
appearance of fire, until the morning.
16 So it was alway: the cloud covered it *by
day*, and the appearance of fire by night.
17 And when the cloud was taken up from
the tabernacle, then after that the children of
Is'ra-el journeyed: and in the place where the
cloud abode, there the children of Is'ra-el
pitched their tents.
18 At the commandment of the LORD the
children of Is'ra-el journeyed, and at the commandment of the LORD they pitched: as long as
the cloud abode upon the tabernacle they rested
in their tents.
19 And when the cloud tarried long upon the
tabernacle many days, then the children of Is'-
ra-el kept the charge of the LORD, and journeyed not.
20 And *so* it was, when the cloud was a few
days upon the tabernacle; according to the
commandment of the LORD they abode in their
tents, and according to the commandment of
the LORD they journeyed.
21 And *so* it was, when the cloud abode from
even unto the morning, and *that* the cloud was
taken up in the morning, then they journeyed:
whether *it was* by day or by night that the cloud
was taken up, they journeyed.
22 Or *whether it were* two days, or a month,
or a year, that the cloud tarried upon the tabernacle, remaining thereon, the children of Is'ra-el
abode in their tents, and journeyed not: but
when it was taken up, they journeyed.
23 At the commandment of the LORD they
rested in the tents, and at the commandment of
the LORD they journeyed: they kept the charge
of the LORD, at the commandment of the LORD
by the hand of Mo'ses.

10 AND the LORD spake unto Mo'ses, saying,
2 Make thee two trumpets of silver; of a
whole piece shalt thou make them: that thou
mayest use them for the calling of the assembly, and for the journeying of the camps.
3 And when they shall blow with them, all
the assembly shall assemble themselves to thee
at the door of the tabernacle of the congregation.
4 And if they blow *but* with one *trumpet*,
then the princes, *which are* heads of the thousands of Is'ra-el, shall gather themselves unto
thee.
5 When ye blow an alarm, then the camps
that lie on the east parts shall go forward.
6 When ye blow an alarm the second time,
then the camps that lie on the south side shall
take their journey: they shall blow an alarm for
their journeys.
7 But when the congregation is to be gathered together, ye shall blow, but ye shall not
sound an alarm.
8 And the sons of Aar'on, the priests, shall
blow with the trumpets; and they shall be to
you for an ordinance for ever throughout your
generations.
9 And if ye go to war in your land against the
enemy that oppresseth you, then ye shall blow
an alarm with the trumpets; and ye shall be remembered before the LORD your God, and ye
shall be saved from your enemies.
10 Also in the day of your gladness, and in
your solemn days, and in the beginnings of your
months, ye shall blow with the trumpets over
your burnt offerings, and over the sacrifices of
your peace offerings; that they may be to you
for a memorial before your God: I *am* the LORD
your God.
11 ¶ And it came to pass on the twentieth
day of the second month, in the second year,
that the cloud was taken up from off the tabernacle of the testimony.
12 And the children of Is'ra-el took their
journeys out of the wilderness of Si'nai; and the
cloud rested in the wilderness of Pa'ran.
13 And they first took their journey according to the commandment of the LORD by the
hand of Mo'ses.
14 ¶ In the first *place* went the standard of
the camp of the children of Ju'dah according to
their armies: and over his host *was* Nah'shon
the son of Am-min'a-dab.
15 And over the host of the tribe of the children of Is'sa-char *was* Ne-than'e-el the son of
Zu'ar.
16 And over the host of the tribe of the children of Zeb'u-lun *was* E-li'ab the son of He'lon.
17 And the tabernacle was taken down; and
the sons of Ger'shon and the sons of Me-ra'ri
set forward, bearing the tabernacle.
18 ¶ And the standard of the camp of Reu'-
ben set forward according to their armies: and
over his host *was* E-li'zur the son of Shed'e-ur.
19 And over the host of the tribe of the children of Sim'e-on *was* She-lu'mi-el the son of
Zu-ri-shad'da-i.
20 And over the host of the tribe of the children of Gad *was* E-li'a-saph the son of Deu'el.
21 And the Ko'hath-ites set forward, bearing
the sanctuary: and *the other* did set up the tabernacle against they came.
22 ¶ And the standard of the camp of the
children of E'phra-im set forward according to
their armies: and over his host *was* E-lish'a-ma
the son of Am-mi'hud.
23 And over the host of the tribe of the children of Ma-nas'seh *was* Ga-ma'li-el the son of
Pe-dah'zur.
24 And over the host of the tribe of the children of Ben'ja-min *was* Ab'i-dan the son of Gid-
e-o'ni.
25 ¶ And the standard of the camp of the
children of Dan set forward, *which was* the rereward of all the camps throughout their hosts:
and over his host *was* A-hi-e'zer the son of Am-
mi-shad'da-i.

26 And over the host of the tribe of the children of Ash'er *was* Pa'gi-el the son of Oc'ran.
27 And over the host of the tribe of the children of Naph'ta-li *was* A-hi'ra the son of E'nan.
28 Thus *were* the journeyings of the children
of Is'ra-el according to their armies, when they
set forward.
29 ¶ And Mo'ses said unto Ho-bab, the son
of Ra-gu'el the Mid'i-an-ite, Mo'ses' father in
law, We are journeying unto the place of which
the LORD said, I will give it you: come thou with
us, and we will do thee good: for the LORD hath
spoken good concerning Is'ra-el.
30 And he said unto him, I will not go; but I
will depart to mine own land, and to my kindred.
31 And he said, Leave us not, I pray thee; forasmuch as thou knowest how we are to encamp
in the wilderness, and thou mayest be to us instead of eyes.
32 And it shall be, if thou go with us, yea, it
shall be, that what goodness the LORD shall do
unto us, the same will we do unto thee.
33 ¶ And they departed from the mount of
the LORD three days' journey: and the ark of the
covenant of the LORD went before them in the
three days' journey, to search out a resting
place for them.
34 And the cloud of the LORD *was* upon them
by day, when they went out of the camp.
35 And it came to pass, when the ark set forward, that Mo'ses said, Rise up, LORD, and let
thine enemies be scattered; and let them that
hate thee flee before thee.
36 And when it rested, he said, Return, O
LORD, unto the many thousands of Is'ra-el.

11 AND *when* the people complained, it
displeased the LORD: and the LORD
heard *it;* and his anger was kindled; and the fire
of the LORD burnt among them, and consumed
them that were in the uttermost parts of the
camp.
2 And the people cried unto Mo'ses; and
when Mo'ses prayed unto the LORD, the fire was
quenched.
3 And he called the name of the place Tab'e-
rah: because the fire of the LORD burnt among
them.
4 ¶ And the mixt multitude that *was* among
them fell a lusting: and the children of Is'ra-el
also wept again, and said, Who shall give us
flesh to eat?
5 We remember the fish, which we did eat in
E'gypt freely; the cucumbers, and the melons,
and the leeks, and the onions, and the garlick:
6 But now our soul *is* dried away: *there is*
nothing at all, beside this manna, *before* our
eyes.
7 And the manna *was* as coriander seed, and
the colour thereof as the colour of bdellium.
8 *And* the people went about, and gathered
it, and ground *it* in mills, or beat *it* in a mortar,
and baked *it* in pans, and made cakes of it: and
the taste of it was as the taste of fresh oil.
9 And when the dew fell upon the camp in
the night, the manna fell upon it.
10 ¶ Then Mo'ses heard the people weep
throughout their families, every man in the
door of his tent: and the anger of the LORD was
kindled greatly; Mo'ses also was displeased.
11 And Mo'ses said unto the LORD, Wherefore hast thou afflicted thy servant? and wherefore have I not found favour in thy sight, that
thou layest the burden of all this people upon
me?
12 Have I conceived all this people? have I
begotten them, that thou shouldest say unto
me, Carry them in thy bosom, as a nursing father beareth the sucking child, unto the land
which thou swarest unto their fathers?
13 Whence should I have flesh to give unto
all this people? for they weep unto me, saying,
Give us flesh, that we may eat.
14 I am not able to bear all this people alone,
because *it is* too heavy for me.
15 And if thou deal thus with me, kill me, I
pray thee, out of hand, if I have found favour in
thy sight; and let me not see my wretchedness.
16 ¶ And the LORD said unto Mo'ses, Gather
unto me seventy men of the elders of Is'ra-el,
whom thou knowest to be the elders of the people, and officers over them; and bring them unto
the tabernacle of the congregation, that they
may stand there with thee.
17 And I will come down and talk with thee
there: and I will take of the spirit which *is* upon
thee, and will put *it* upon them; and they shall
bear the burden of the people with thee, that
thou bear *it* not thyself alone.
18 And say thou unto the people, Sanctify
yourselves against to morrow, and ye shall eat
flesh: for ye have wept in the ears of the LORD,
saying, Who shall give us flesh to eat? for *it was*
well with us in E'gypt: therefore the LORD will
give you flesh, and ye shall eat.
19 Ye shall not eat one day, nor two days,
nor five days, neither ten days, nor twenty days;
20 *But* even a whole month, until it come out
at your nostrils, and it be loathsome unto you:
because that ye have despised the LORD which
is among you, and have wept before him, saying, Why came we forth out of E'gypt?
21 And Mo'ses said, The people, among
whom I *am, are* six hundred thousand footmen;
and thou hast said, I will give them flesh, that
they may eat a whole month.
22 Shall the flocks and the herds be slain for
them, to suffice them? or shall all the fish of the
sea be gathered together for them, to suffice
them?
23 And the LORD said unto Mo'ses, Is the
LORD's hand waxed short? thou shalt see now
whether my word shall come to pass unto thee
or not.
24 ¶ And Mo'ses went out, and told the people the words of the LORD, and gathered the
seventy men of the elders of the people, and set
them round about the tabernacle.
25 And the LORD came down in a cloud, and
spake unto him, and took of the spirit that *was*
upon him, and gave *it* unto the seventy elders:
and it came to pass, *that,* when the spirit rested
upon them, they prophesied, and did not cease.
26 But there remained two *of the* men in the
camp, the name of the one *was* El'dad, and the
name of the other Me'dad: and the spirit rested
upon them; and they *were* of them that were
written, but went not out unto the tabernacle:
and they prophesied in the camp.
27 And there ran a young man, and told Mo'-
ses, and said, El'dad and Me'dad do prophesy in
the camp.
28 And Josh'u-a the son of Nun, the servant
of Mo'ses, *one* of his young men, answered and
said, My lord Mo'ses, forbid them.
29 And Mo'ses said unto him, Enviest thou
for my sake? would God that all the LORD's people were prophets, *and* that the LORD would put
his spirit upon them!
30 And Mo'ses gat him into the camp, he and
the elders of Is'ra-el.
31 ¶ And there went forth a wind from the
LORD, and brought quails from the sea, and let

them fall by the camp, as it were a day's journey on this side, and as it were a day's journey
on the other side, round about the camp, and as
it were two cubits *high* upon the face of the
earth.
32 And the people stood up all that day, and
all *that* night, and all the next day, and they
gathered the quails: he that gathered least gathered ten homers: and they spread *them* all
abroad for themselves round about the camp.
33 And while the flesh *was* yet between their
teeth, ere it was chewed, the wrath of the LORD
was kindled against the people, and the LORD
smote the people with a very great plague.
34 And he called the name of that place Kib'-
roth–hat-ta'a-vah: because there they buried
the people that lusted.
35 *And* the people journeyed from Kib'roth-
hat-ta'a-vah unto Ha-ze'roth; and abode at Ha-
ze'roth.

12 AND Mir'i-am and Aar'on spake against
Mo'ses because of the E-thi-o'pi-an
woman whom he had married: for he had married an E-thi-o'pi-an woman.
2 And they said, Hath the LORD indeed spoken only by Mo'ses? hath he not spoken also by
us? And the LORD heard *it*.
3 (Now the man Mo'ses *was* very meek,
above all the men which *were* upon the face of
the earth.)
4 And the LORD spake suddenly unto Mo'ses,
and unto Aar'on, and unto Mir'i-am, Come out
ye three unto the tabernacle of the congregation. And they three came out.
5 And the LORD came down in the pillar of
the cloud, and stood *in* the door of the tabernacle, and called Aar'on and Mir'i-am: and they
both came forth.
6 And he said, Hear now my words: If there
be a prophet among you, *I* the LORD will make
myself known unto him in a vision, *and* will
speak unto him in a dream.
7 My servant Mo'ses *is* not so, who *is* faithful
in all mine house.
8 With him will I speak mouth to mouth,
even apparently, and not in dark speeches; and
the similitude of the LORD shall he behold:
wherefore then were ye not afraid to speak
against my servant Mo'ses?
9 And the anger of the LORD was kindled
against them; and he departed.
10 And the cloud departed from off the tabernacle; and, behold, Mir'i-am *became* leprous,
white as snow: and Aar'on looked upon Mir'i-
am, and, behold, *she was* leprous.
11 And Aar'on said unto Mo'ses, Alas, my
lord, I beseech thee, lay not the sin upon us,
wherein we have done foolishly, and wherein
we have sinned.
12 Let her not be as one dead, of whom the
flesh is half consumed when he cometh out of
his mother's womb.
13 And Mo'ses cried unto the LORD, saying,
Heal her now, O God, I beseech thee.
14 ¶ And the LORD said unto Mo'ses, If her
father had but spit in her face, should she not be
ashamed seven days? let her be shut out from
the camp seven days, and after that let her be
received in *again*.
15 And Mir'i-am was shut out from the camp
seven days: and the people journeyed not till
Mir'i-am was brought in *again*.
16 And afterward the people removed from
Ha-ze'roth, and pitched in the wilderness of Pa'-
ran.

13 AND the LORD spake unto Mo'ses, saying,
2 Send thou men, that they may search the
land of Ca'naan, which I give unto the children
of Is'ra-el: of every tribe of their fathers shall ye
send a man, every one a ruler among them.
3 And Mo'ses by the commandment of the
LORD sent them from the wilderness of Pa'ran:
all those men *were* heads of the children of Is'-
ra-el.
4 And these *were* their names: of the tribe of
Reu'ben, Sham-mu'a the son of Zac'cur.
5 Of the tribe of Sim'e-on, Sha'phat the son
of Ho'ri.
6 Of the tribe of Ju'dah, Ca'leb the son of Je-
phun'neh.
7 Of the tribe of Is'sa-char, I'gal the son of
Jo'seph.
8 Of the tribe of E'phra-im, O-she'a the son of
Nun.
9 Of the tribe of Ben'ja-min, Pal'ti the son of
Ra'phu.
10 Of the tribe of Zeb'u-lun, Gad'di-el the son
of So'di.
11 Of the tribe of Jo'seph, *namely*, of the
tribe of Ma-nas'seh, Gad'di the son of Su'si.
12 Of the tribe of Dan, Am'mi-el the son of
Ge-mal'li.
13 Of the tribe of Ash'er, Se'thur the son of
Mi'chael.
14 Of the tribe of Naph'ta-li, Nah'bi the son
of Voph'si.
15 Of the tribe of Gad, Ge-u'el the son of Ma'-
chi.
16 These *are* the names of the men which
Mo'ses sent to spy out the land. And Mo'ses
called O-she'a the son of Nun Je-hosh'u-a.
17 ¶ And Mo'ses sent them to spy out the
land of Ca'naan, and said unto them, Get you up
this *way* southward, and go up into the mountain:
18 And see the land, what it *is*; and the people that dwelleth therein, whether they *be*
strong or weak, few or many;
19 And what the land *is* that they dwell in,
whether it *be* good or bad; and what cities *they*
be that they dwell in, whether in tents, or in
strong holds;
20 And what the land *is*, whether it *be* fat or
lean, whether there be wood therein, or not.
And be ye of good courage, and bring of the
fruit of the land. Now the time *was* the time of
the firstripe grapes.
21 ¶ So they went up, and searched the land
from the wilderness of Zin unto Re'hob, as men
come to Ha'math.
22 And they ascended by the south, and
came unto He'bron; where A-hi'man, She'shai,
and Tal'mai, the children of A'nak, *were*. (Now
He'bron was built seven years before Zo'an in
E'gypt.)
23 And they came unto the brook of Esh'col,
and cut down from thence a branch with one
cluster of grapes, and they bare it between two
upon a staff; and *they brought* of the pomegranates, and of the figs.
24 The place was called the brook Esh'col,
because of the cluster of grapes which the children of Is'ra-el cut down from thence.
25 And they returned from searching of the
land after forty days.
26 ¶ And they went and came to Mo'ses, and
to Aar'on, and to all the congregation of the
children of Is'ra-el, unto the wilderness of Pa'-
ran, to Ka'desh; and brought back word unto
them, and unto all the congregation, and
shewed them the fruit of the land.

27 And they told him, and said, We came
unto the land whither thou sentest us, and
surely it floweth with milk and honey; and this
is the fruit of it.
28 Nevertheless the people *be* strong that
dwell in the land, and the cities *are* walled, *and*
very great: and moreover we saw the children
of A'nak there.
29 The Am'a-lek-ites dwell in the land of the
south: and the Hit'tites, and the Jeb'u-sites, and
the Am'or-ites, dwell in the mountains: and the
Ca'naan-ites dwell by the sea, and by the coast
of Jor'dan.
30 And Ca'leb stilled the people before Mo'-
ses, and said, Let us go up at once, and possess
it; for we are well able to overcome it.
31 But the men that went up with him said,
We be not able to go up against the people; for
they *are* stronger than we.
32 And they brought up an evil report of the
land which they had searched unto the children
of Is'ra-el, saying, The land, through which we
have gone to search it, *is* a land that eateth up
the inhabitants thereof; and all the people that
we saw in it *are* men of a great stature.
33 And there we saw the giants, the sons of
A'nak, *which come* of the giants: and we were
in our own sight as grasshoppers, and so we
were in their sight.

14 AND all the congregation lifted up their
voice, and cried; and the people wept
that night.
2 And all the children of Is'ra-el murmured
against Mo'ses and against Aar'on: and the
whole congregation said unto them, Would God
that we had died in the land of E'gypt! or would
God we had died in this wilderness!
3 And wherefore hath the LORD brought us
unto this land, to fall by the sword, that our
wives and our children should be a prey? were
it not better for us to return into E'gypt?
4 And they said one to another, Let us make
a captain, and let us return into E'gypt.
5 Then Mo'ses and Aar'on fell on their faces
before all the assembly of the congregation of
the children of Is'ra-el.
6 ¶ And Josh'u-a the son of Nun, and Ca'leb
the son of Je-phun'neh, *which were* of them that
searched the land, rent their clothes:
7 And they spake unto all the company of the
children of Is'ra-el, saying, The land, which we
passed through to search it, *is* an exceeding
good land.
8 If the LORD delight in us, then he will bring
us into this land, and give it us; a land which
floweth with milk and honey.
9 Only rebel not ye against the LORD, neither
fear ye the people of the land; for they *are* bread
for us: their defence is departed from them, and
the LORD *is* with us: fear them not.
10 But all the congregation bade stone them
with stones. And the glory of the LORD appeared in the tabernacle of the congregation before all the children of Is'ra-el.
11 ¶ And the LORD said unto Mo'ses, How
long will this people provoke me? and how long
will it be ere they believe me, for all the signs
which I have shewed among them?
12 I will smite them with the pestilence, and
disinherit them, and will make of thee a greater
nation and mightier than they.
13 ¶ And Mo'ses said unto the LORD, Then
the E-gyptians shall hear *it*, (for thou broughtest up this people in thy might from among
them;)
14 And they will tell *it* to the inhabitants of
this land: *for* they have heard that thou LORD
art among this people, that thou LORD art seen
face to face, and *that* thy cloud standeth over
them, and *that* thou goest before them, by day
time in a pillar of a cloud, and in a pillar of fire
by night.
15 ¶ Now *if* thou shalt kill *all* this people as
one man, then the nations which have heard the
fame of thee will speak, saying,
16 Because the LORD was not able to bring
this people into the land which he sware unto
them, therefore he hath slain them in the wilderness.
17 And now, I beseech thee, let the power of
my LORD be great, according as thou hast spoken, saying,
18 The LORD *is* longsuffering, and of great
mercy, forgiving iniquity and transgression,
and by no means clearing *the guilty*, visiting the
iniquity of the fathers upon the children unto
the third and fourth *generation*.
19 Pardon, I beseech thee, the iniquity of this
people according unto the greatness of thy mercy, and as thou hast forgiven this people, from
E'gypt even until now.
20 And the LORD said, I have pardoned according to thy word:
21 But *as* truly *as* I live, all the earth shall be
filled with the glory of the LORD.
22 Because all those men which have seen
my glory, and my miracles, which I did in E'-
gypt and in the wilderness, and have tempted
me now these ten times, and have not hearkened to my voice;
23 Surely they shall not see the land which I
sware unto their fathers, neither shall any of
them that provoked me see it:
24 But my servant Ca'leb, because he had another spirit with him, and hath followed me fully, him will I bring into the land whereinto he
went; and his seed shall possess it.
25 (Now the Am'a-lek-ites and the Ca'naan-
ites dwelt in the valley.) To morrow turn you,
and get you into the wilderness by the way of
the Red sea.
26 ¶ And the LORD spake unto Mo'ses and
unto Aar'on, saying,
27 How long *shall I bear with* this evil congregation, which murmur against me? I have
heard the murmurings of the children of Is'ra-
el, which they murmur against me.
28 Say unto them, *As truly as* I live, saith the
LORD, as ye have spoken in mine ears, so will I
do to you:
29 Your carcases shall fall in this wilderness;
and all that were numbered of you, according to
your whole number, from twenty years old and
upward, which have murmured against me,
30 Doubtless ye shall not come into the land,
concerning which I sware to make you dwell
therein, save Ca'leb the son of Je-phun'neh, and
Josh'u-a the son of Nun.
31 But your little ones, which ye said should
be a prey, them will I bring in, and they shall
know the land which ye have despised.
32 But *as for* you, your carcases, they shall
fall in this wilderness.
33 And your children shall wander in the wilderness forty years, and bear your whoredoms,
until your carcases be wasted in the wilderness.
34 After the number of the days in which ye
searched the land, *even* forty days, each day for
a year, shall ye bear your iniquities, *even* forty
years, and ye shall know my breach of promise.
35 I the LORD have said, I will surely do it
unto all this evil congregation, that are gathered

together against me: in this wilderness they shall be consumed, and there they shall die.

36 And the men, which Mo'ses sent to search the land, who returned, and made all the congregation to murmur against him, by bringing up a slander upon the land,

37 Even those men that did bring up the evil report upon the land, died by the plague before the LORD.

38 But Josh'u-a the son of Nun, and Ca'leb the son of Je-phun'neh, *which were* of the men that went to search the land, lived *still*.

39 And Mo'ses told these sayings unto all the children of Is'ra-el: and the people mourned greatly.

40 ¶ And they rose up early in the morning, and gat them up into the top of the mountain, saying, Lo, we *be here*, and will go up unto the place which the LORD hath promised: for we have sinned.

41 And Mo'ses said, Wherefore now do ye transgress the commandment of the LORD? but it shall not prosper.

42 Go not up, for the LORD *is* not among you; that ye be not smitten before your enemies.

43 For the Am'a-lek-ites and the Ca'naan-ites *are* there before you, and ye shall fall by the sword: because ye are turned away from the LORD, therefore the LORD will not be with you.

44 But they presumed to go up unto the hill top: nevertheless the ark of the covenant of the LORD, and Mo'ses, departed not out of the camp.

45 Then the Am'a-lek-ites came down, and the Ca'naan-ites which dwelt in that hill, and smote them, and discomfited them, *even* unto Hor'mah.

15 AND the LORD spake unto Mo'ses, saying,

2 Speak unto the children of Is'ra-el, and say unto them, When ye be come into the land of your habitations, which I give unto you,

3 And will make an offering by fire unto the LORD, a burnt offering, or a sacrifice in performing a vow, or in a freewill offering, or in your solemn feasts, to make a sweet savour unto the LORD, of the herd, or of the flock:

4 Then shall he that offereth his offering unto the LORD bring a meat offering of a tenth deal of flour mingled with the fourth *part* of an hin of oil.

5 And the fourth *part* of an hin of wine for a drink offering shalt thou prepare with the burnt offering or sacrifice, for one lamb.

6 Or for a ram, thou shalt prepare *for* a meat offering two tenth deals of flour mingled with the third *part* of an hin of oil.

7 And for a drink offering thou shalt offer the third *part* of an hin of wine, *for* a sweet savour unto the LORD.

8 And when thou preparest a bullock *for* a burnt offering, or *for* a sacrifice in performing a vow, or peace offerings unto the LORD:

9 Then shall he bring with a bullock a meat offering of three tenth deals of flour mingled with half an hin of oil.

10 And thou shalt bring for a drink offering half an hin of wine, *for* an offering made by fire, of a sweet savour unto the LORD.

11 Thus shall it be done for one bullock, or for one ram, or for a lamb, or a kid.

12 According to the number that ye shall prepare, so shall ye do to every one according to their number.

13 All that are born of the country shall do these things after this manner, in offering an offering made by fire, of a sweet savour unto the LORD.

14 And if a stranger sojourn with you, or whosoever *be* among you in your generations, and will offer an offering made by fire, of a sweet savour unto the LORD; as ye do, so he shall do.

15 One ordinance *shall be both* for you of the congregation, and also for the stranger that sojourneth *with you*, an ordinance for ever in your generations: as ye *are*, so shall the stranger be before the LORD.

16 One law and one manner shall be for you, and for the stranger that sojourneth with you.

17 ¶ And the LORD spake unto Mo'ses, saying,

18 Speak unto the children of Is'ra-el, and say unto them, When ye come into the land whither I bring you,

19 Then it shall be, that, when ye eat of the bread of the land, ye shall offer up an heave offering unto the LORD.

20 Ye shall offer up a cake of the first of your dough *for* an heave offering: as *ye do* the heave offering of the threshingfloor, so shall ye heave it.

21 Of the first of your dough ye shall give unto the LORD an heave offering in your generations.

22 ¶ And if ye have erred, and not observed all these commandments, which the LORD hath spoken unto Mo'ses,

23 *Even* all that the LORD hath commanded you by the hand of Mo'ses, from the day that the LORD commanded Mo'ses, and henceforward among your generations;

24 Then it shall be, if *ought* be committed by ignorance without the knowledge of the congregation, that all the congregation shall offer one young bullock for a burnt offering, for a sweet savour unto the LORD, with his meat offering, and his drink offering, according to the manner, and one kid of the goats for a sin offering.

25 And the priest shall make an atonement for all the congregation of the children of Is'ra-el, and it shall be forgiven them; for it *is* ignorance: and they shall bring their offering, a sacrifice made by fire unto the LORD, and their sin offering before the LORD, for their ignorance:

26 And it shall be forgiven all the congregation of the children of Is'ra-el, and the stranger that sojourneth among them; seeing all the people *were* in ignorance.

27 ¶ And if any soul sin through ignorance, then he shall bring a she goat of the first year for a sin offering.

28 And the priest shall make an atonement for the soul that sinneth ignorantly, when he sinneth by ignorance before the LORD, to make an atonement for him; and it shall be forgiven him.

29 Ye shall have one law for him that sinneth through ignorance, *both for* him that is born among the children of Is'ra-el, and for the stranger that sojourneth among them.

30 ¶ But the soul that doeth *ought* presumptuously, *whether he be* born in the land, or a stranger, the same reproacheth the LORD; and that soul shall be cut off from among his people.

31 Because he hath despised the word of the LORD, and hath broken his commandment, that soul shall utterly be cut off; his iniquity *shall be* upon him.

32 ¶ And while the children of Is'ra-el were in the wilderness, they found a man that gathered sticks upon the sabbath day.

33 And they that found him gathering sticks

brought him unto Mo'ses and Aar'on, and unto
all the congregation.
34 And they put him in ward, because it was
not declared what should be done to him.
35 And the LORD said unto Mo'ses, The man
shall be surely put to death: all the congregation shall stone him with stones without the
camp.
36 And all the congregation brought him
without the camp, and stoned him with stones,
and he died; as the LORD commanded Mo'ses.
37 ¶ And the LORD spake unto Mo'ses, saying,
38 Speak unto the children of Is'ra-el, and
bid them that they make them fringes in the
borders of their garments throughout their generations, and that they put upon the fringe of
the borders a ribband of blue:
39 And it shall be unto you for a fringe, that
ye may look upon it, and remember all the commandments of the LORD, and do them; and that
ye seek not after your own heart and your own
eyes, after which ye use to go a whoring:
40 That ye may remember, and do all my
commandments, and be holy unto your God.
41 I *am* the LORD your God, which brought
you out of the land of E'gypt, to be your God: I
am the LORD your God.

16 NOW Ko'rah, the son of Iz'har, the son
of Ko'hath, the son of Le'vi, and Da'than
and A-bi'ram, the sons of E-li'ab, and On, the
son of Pe'leth, sons of Reu'ben, took *men:*
2 And they rose up before Mo'ses, with certain of the children of Is'ra-el, two hundred and
fifty princes of the assembly, famous in the congregation, men of renown:
3 And they gathered themselves together
against Mo'ses and against Aar'on, and said
unto them, *Ye take* too much upon you, seeing
all the congregation *are* holy, every one of
them, and the LORD *is* among them: wherefore
then lift ye up yourselves above the congregation of the LORD?
4 And when Mo'ses heard *it*, he fell upon his
face:
5 And he spake unto Ko'rah and unto all his
company, saying, Even to morrow the LORD will
shew who *are* his, and *who is* holy; and will
cause *him* to come near unto him: even *him*
whom he hath chosen will he cause to come
near unto him.
6 This do; Take you censers, Ko'rah, and all
his company;
7 And put fire therein, and put incense in
them before the LORD to morrow: and it shall be
that the man whom the LORD doth choose, he
shall be holy: *ye take* too much upon you, ye
sons of Le'vi.
8 And Mo'ses said unto Ko'rah, Hear, I pray
you, ye sons of Le'vi:
9 *Seemeth it but* a small thing unto you, that
the God of Is'ra-el hath separated you from the
congregation of Is'ra-el, to bring you near to
himself to do the service of the tabernacle of
the LORD, and to stand before the congregation
to minister unto them?
10 And he hath brought thee near *to him*,
and all thy brethren the sons of Le'vi with thee:
and seek ye the priesthood also?
11 For which cause *both* thou and all thy
company *are* gathered together against the
LORD: and what *is* Aar'on, that ye murmur
against him?
12 ¶ And Mo'ses sent to call Da'than and A-
bi'ram, the sons of E-li'ab: which said, We will
not come up:
13 *Is it* a small thing that thou hast brought
us up out of a land that floweth with milk and
honey, to kill us in the wilderness, except thou
make thyself altogether a prince over us?
14 Moreover thou hast not brought us into a
land that floweth with milk and honey, or given
us inheritance of fields and vineyards: wilt thou
put out the eyes of these men? we will not come
up.
15 And Mo'ses was very wroth, and said
unto the LORD, Respect not thou their offering: I
have not taken one ass from them, neither have
I hurt one of them.
16 And Mo'ses said unto Ko'rah, Be thou and
all thy company before the LORD, thou, and
they, and Aar'on, to morrow:
17 And take every man his censer, and put
incense in them, and bring ye before the LORD
every man his censer, two hundred and fifty
censers; thou also, and Aar'on, each *of you* his
censer.
18 And they took every man his censer, and
put fire in them, and laid incense thereon, and
stood in the door of the tabernacle of the congregation with Mo'ses and Aar'on.
19 And Ko'rah gathered all the congregation
against them unto the door of the tabernacle of
the congregation: and the glory of the LORD appeared unto all the congregation.
20 And the LORD spake unto Mo'ses and unto
Aar'on, saying,
21 Separate yourselves from among this congregation, that I may consume them in a moment.
22 And they fell upon their faces, and said, O
God, the God of the spirits of all flesh, shall one
man sin, and wilt thou be wroth with all the
congregation?
23 ¶ And the LORD spake unto Mo'ses, saying,
24 Speak unto the congregation, saying, Get
you up from about the tabernacle of Ko'rah,
Da'than, and A-bi'ram.
25 And Mo'ses rose up and went unto Da'-
than and A-bi'ram; and the elders of Is'ra-el followed him.
26 And he spake unto the congregation, saying, Depart, I pray you, from the tents of these
wicked men, and touch nothing of theirs, lest ye
be consumed in all their sins.
27 So they gat up from the tabernacle of Ko'-
rah, Da'than, and A-bi'ram, on every side: and
Da'than and A-bi'ram came out, and stood in
the door of their tents, and their wives, and
their sons, and their little children.
28 And Mo'ses said, Hereby ye shall know
that the LORD hath sent me to do all these
works; for *I have* not *done them* of mine own
mind.
29 If these men die the common death of all
men, or if they be visited after the visitation of
all men; *then* the LORD hath not sent me.
30 But if the LORD make a new thing, and the
earth open her mouth, and swallow them up,
with all that *appertain* unto them, and they go
down quick into the pit; then ye shall understand that these men have provoked the LORD.
31 ¶ And it came to pass, as he had made an
end of speaking all these words, that the ground
clave asunder that *was* under them:
32 And the earth opened her mouth, and
swallowed them up, and their houses, and all
the men that *appertained* unto Ko'rah, and all
their goods.
33 They, and all that *appertained* to them,
went down alive into the pit, and the earth

closed upon them: and they perished from
among the congregation.
34 And all Is′ra-el that *were* round about
them fled at the cry of them: for they said, Lest
the earth swallow us up *also*.
35 And there came out a fire from the LORD,
and consumed the two hundred and fifty men
that offered incense.
36 ¶ And the LORD spake unto Mo′ses, saying,
37 Speak unto E-le-a′zar the son of Aar′on
the priest, that he take up the censers out of the
burning, and scatter thou the fire yonder; for
they are hallowed.
38 The censers of these sinners against their
own souls, let them make them broad plates *for*
a covering of the altar: for they offered them
before the LORD, therefore they are hallowed:
and they shall be a sign unto the children of
Is′ra-el.
39 And E-le-a′zar the priest took the brasen
censers, wherewith they that were burnt had
offered; and they were made broad *plates for* a
covering of the altar:
40 *To be* a memorial unto the children of Is′-
ra-el, that no stranger, which *is* not of the seed
of Aar′on, come near to offer incense before the
LORD; that he be not as Ko′rah, and as his company: as the LORD said to him by the hand of
Mo′ses.
41 ¶ But on the morrow all the congregation
of the children of Is′ra-el murmured against
Mo′ses and against Aar′on, saying, Ye have
killed the people of the LORD.
42 And it came to pass, when the congregation was gathered against Mo′ses and against
Aar′on, that they looked toward the tabernacle
of the congregation: and, behold, the cloud covered it, and the glory of the LORD appeared.
43 And Mo′ses and Aar′on came before the
tabernacle of the congregation.
44 ¶ And the LORD spake unto Mo′ses, saying,
45 Get you up from among this congregation,
that I may consume them as in a moment. And
they fell upon their faces.
46 ¶ And Mo′ses said unto Aar′on, Take a
censer, and put fire therein from off the altar,
and put on incense, and go quickly unto the
congregation, and make an atonement for
them: for there is wrath gone out from the
LORD; the plague is begun.
47 And Aar′on took as Mo′ses commanded,
and ran into the midst of the congregation; and,
behold, the plague was begun among the people: and he put on incense, and made an atonement for the people.
48 And he stood between the dead and the
living; and the plague was stayed.
49 Now they that died in the plague were
fourteen thousand and seven hundred, beside
them that died about the matter of Ko′rah.
50 And Aar′on returned unto Mo′ses unto the
door of the tabernacle of the congregation: and
the plague was stayed.

17

AND the LORD spake unto Mo′ses, saying,
2 Speak unto the children of Is′ra-el, and
take of every one of them a rod according to the
house of *their* fathers, of all their princes according to the house of their fathers twelve
rods: write thou every man's name upon his
rod.
3 And thou shalt write Aar′on's name upon
the rod of Le′vi: for one rod *shall be* for the
head of the house of their fathers.
4 And thou shalt lay them up in the tabernacle of the congregation before the testimony,
where I will meet with you.
5 And it shall come to pass, *that* the man's
rod, whom I shall choose, shall blossom: and I
will make to cease from me the murmurings of
the children of Is′ra-el, whereby they murmur
against you.
6 ¶ And Mo′ses spake unto the children of
Is′ra-el, and every one of their princes gave him
a rod apiece, for each prince one, according to
their fathers' houses, *even* twelve rods: and the
rod of Aar′on *was* among their rods.
7 And Mo′ses laid up the rods before the
LORD in the tabernacle of witness.
8 And it came to pass, that on the morrow
Mo′ses went into the tabernacle of witness; and,
behold, the rod of Aar′on for the house of Le′vi
was budded, and brought forth buds, and
bloomed blossoms, and yielded almonds.
9 And Mo′ses brought out all the rods from
before the LORD unto all the children of Is′ra-el:
and they looked, and took every man his rod.
10 ¶ And the LORD said unto Mo′ses, Bring
Aar′on's rod again before the testimony, to be
kept for a token against the rebels; and thou
shalt quite take away their murmurings from
me, that they die not.
11 And Mo′ses did *so*: as the LORD commanded him, so did he.
12 And the children of Is′ra-el spake unto
Mo′ses, saying, Behold, we die, we perish, we
all perish.
13 Whosoever cometh any thing near unto
the tabernacle of the LORD shall die: shall we be
consumed with dying?

18

AND the LORD said unto Aar′on, Thou
and thy sons and thy father's house with
thee shall bear the iniquity of the sanctuary:
and thou and thy sons with thee shall bear the
iniquity of your priesthood.
2 And thy brethren also of the tribe of Le′vi,
the tribe of thy father, bring thou with thee,
that they may be joined unto thee, and minister
unto thee: but thou and thy sons with thee *shall
minister* before the tabernacle of witness.
3 And they shall keep thy charge, and the
charge of all the tabernacle: only they shall not
come nigh the vessels of the sanctuary and the
altar, that neither they, nor ye also, die.
4 And they shall be joined unto thee, and
keep the charge of the tabernacle of the congregation, for all the service of the tabernacle: and
a stranger shall not come nigh unto you.
5 And ye shall keep the charge of the sanctuary, and the charge of the altar: that there be no
wrath any more upon the children of Is′ra-el.
6 And I, behold, I have taken your brethren
the Le′vites from among the children of Is′ra-el:
to you *they are* given *as* a gift for the LORD, to
do the service of the tabernacle of the congregation.
7 Therefore thou and thy sons with thee shall
keep your priest's office for every thing of the
altar, and within the veil; and ye shall serve: I
have given your priest's office *unto you as* a
service of gift: and the stranger that cometh
nigh shall be put to death.
8 ¶ And the LORD spake unto Aar′on, Behold, I also have given thee the charge of mine
heave offerings of all the hallowed things of the
children of Is′ra-el; unto thee have I given them
by reason of the anointing, and to thy sons, by
an ordinance for ever.
9 This shall be thine of the most holy things,
reserved from the fire: every oblation of theirs,

every meat offering of theirs, and every sin offering of theirs, and every trespass offering of theirs, which they shall render unto me, *shall be* most holy for thee and for thy sons.

10 In the most holy *place* shalt thou eat it; every male shall eat it: it shall be holy unto thee.

11 And this *is* thine; the heave offering of their gift, with all the wave offerings of the children of Is′ra-el: I have given them unto thee, and to thy sons and to thy daughters with thee, by a statute for ever: every one that is clean in thy house shall eat of it.

12 All the best of the oil, and all the best of the wine, and of the wheat, the firstfruits of them which they shall offer unto the LORD, them have I given thee.

13 *And* whatsoever is first ripe in the land, which they shall bring unto the LORD, shall be thine; every one that is clean in thine house shall eat *of* it.

14 Every thing devoted in Is′ra-el shall be thine.

15 Every thing that openeth the matrix in all flesh, which they bring unto the LORD, *whether it be* of men or beasts, shall be thine: nevertheless the firstborn of man shalt thou surely redeem, and the firstling of unclean beasts shalt thou redeem.

16 And those that are to be redeemed from a month old shalt thou redeem, according to thine estimation, for the money of five shekels, after the shekel of the sanctuary, which *is* twenty gerahs.

17 But the firstling of a cow, or the firstling of a sheep, or the firstling of a goat, thou shalt not redeem; they *are* holy: thou shalt sprinkle their blood upon the altar, and shalt burn their fat *for* an offering made by fire, for a sweet savour unto the LORD.

18 And the flesh of them shall be thine, as the wave breast and as the right shoulder are thine.

19 All the heave offerings of the holy things, which the children of Is′ra-el offer unto the LORD, have I given thee, and thy sons and thy daughters with thee, by a statute for ever: it *is* a covenant of salt for ever before the LORD unto thee and to thy seed with thee.

20 ¶ And the LORD spake unto Aar′on, Thou shalt have no inheritance in their land, neither shalt thou have any part among them: I *am* thy part and thine inheritance among the children of Is′ra-el.

21 And, behold, I have given the children of Le′vi all the tenth in Is′ra-el for an inheritance, for their service which they serve, *even* the service of the tabernacle of the congregation.

22 Neither must the children of Is′ra-el henceforth come nigh the tabernacle of the congregation, lest they bear sin, and die.

23 But the Le′vites shall do the service of the tabernacle of the congregation, and they shall bear their iniquity: *it shall be* a statute for ever throughout your generations, that among the children of Is′ra-el they have no inheritance.

24 But the tithes of the children of Is′ra-el, which they offer *as* an heave offering unto the LORD, I have given to the Le′vites to inherit: therefore I have said unto them, Among the children of Is′ra-el they shall have no inheritance.

25 ¶ And the LORD spake unto Mo′ses, saying,

26 Thus speak unto the Le′vites, and say unto them, When ye take of the children of Is′ra-el the tithes which I have given you from them for your inheritance, then ye shall offer up an heave offering of it for the LORD, *even* a tenth *part* of the tithe.

27 And *this* your heave offering shall be reckoned unto you, as though *it were* the corn of the threshingfloor, and as the fulness of the winepress.

28 Thus ye also shall offer an heave offering unto the LORD of all your tithes, which ye receive of the children of Is′ra-el; and ye shall give thereof the LORD's heave offering to Aar′on the priest.

29 Out of all your gifts ye shall offer every heave offering of the LORD, of all the best thereof, *even* the hallowed part thereof out of it.

30 Therefore thou shalt say unto them, When ye have heaved the best thereof from it, then it shall be counted unto the Le′vites as the increase of the threshingfloor, and as the increase of the winepress.

31 And ye shall eat it in every place, ye and your households: for it *is* your reward for your service in the tabernacle of the congregation.

32 And ye shall bear no sin by reason of it, when ye have heaved from it the best of it: neither shall ye pollute the holy things of the children of Is′ra-el, lest ye die.

19 AND the LORD spake unto Mo′ses and unto Aar′on, saying,

2 This *is* the ordinance of the law which the LORD hath commanded, saying, Speak unto the children of Is′ra-el, that they bring thee a red heifer without spot, wherein *is* no blemish, *and* upon which never came yoke:

3 And ye shall give her unto E-le-a′zar the priest, that he may bring her forth without the camp, and *one* shall slay her before his face:

4 And E-le-a′zar the priest shall take of her blood with his finger, and sprinkle of her blood directly before the tabernacle of the congregation seven times:

5 And *one* shall burn the heifer in his sight; her skin, and her flesh, and her blood, with her dung, shall he burn:

6 And the priest shall take cedar wood, and hyssop, and scarlet, and cast *it* into the midst of the burning of the heifer.

7 Then the priest shall wash his clothes, and he shall bathe his flesh in water, and afterward he shall come into the camp, and the priest shall be unclean until the even.

8 And he that burneth her shall wash his clothes in water, and bathe his flesh in water, and shall be unclean until the even.

9 And a man *that is* clean shall gather up the ashes of the heifer, and lay *them* up without the camp in a clean place, and it shall be kept for the congregation of the children of Is′ra-el for a water of separation: it *is* a purification for sin.

10 And he that gathereth the ashes of the heifer shall wash his clothes, and be unclean until the even: and it shall be unto the children of Is′ra-el, and unto the stranger that sojourneth among them, for a statute for ever.

11 ¶ He that toucheth the dead body of any man shall be unclean seven days.

12 He shall purify himself with it on the third day, and on the seventh day he shall be clean: but if he purify not himself the third day, then the seventh day he shall not be clean.

13 Whosoever toucheth the dead body of any man that is dead, and purifieth not himself, defileth the tabernacle of the LORD; and that soul shall be cut off from Is′ra-el: because the water of separation was not sprinkled upon him, he shall be unclean; his uncleanness *is* yet upon him.

14 This *is* the law, when a man dieth in a tent: all that come into the tent, and all that *is* in the tent, shall be unclean seven days.

15 And every open vessel, which hath no covering bound upon it, *is* unclean.

16 And whosoever toucheth one that is slain with a sword in the open fields, or a dead body, or a bone of a man, or a grave, shall be unclean seven days.

17 And for an unclean *person* they shall take of the ashes of the burnt heifer of purification for sin, and running water shall be put thereto in a vessel:

18 And a clean person shall take hyssop, and dip *it* in the water, and sprinkle *it* upon the tent, and upon all the vessels, and upon the persons that were there, and upon him that touched a bone, or one slain, or one dead, or a grave:

19 And the clean *person* shall sprinkle upon the unclean on the third day, and on the seventh day: and on the seventh day he shall purify himself, and wash his clothes, and bathe himself in water, and shall be clean at even.

20 But the man that shall be unclean, and shall not purify himself, that soul shall be cut off from among the congregation, because he hath defiled the sanctuary of the LORD: the water of separation hath not been sprinkled upon him; he *is* unclean.

21 And it shall be a perpetual statute unto them, that he that sprinkleth the water of separation shall wash his clothes; and he that toucheth the water of separation shall be unclean until even.

22 And whatsoever the unclean *person* toucheth shall be unclean; and the soul that toucheth *it* shall be unclean until even.

20 THEN came the children of Is′ra-el, *even* the whole congregation, into the desert of Zin in the first month: and the people abode in Ka′desh; and Mir′i-am died there, and was buried there.

2 And there was no water for the congregation: and they gathered themselves together against Mo′ses and against Aar′on.

3 And the people chode with Mo′ses, and spake, saying, Would God that we had died when our brethren died before the LORD!

4 And why have ye brought up the congregation of the LORD into this wilderness, that we and our cattle should die there?

5 And wherefore have ye made us to come up out of E′gypt, to bring us in unto this evil place? it *is* no place of seed, or of figs, or of vines, or of pomegranates; neither *is* there any water to drink.

6 And Mo′ses and Aar′on went from the presence of the assembly unto the door of the tabernacle of the congregation, and they fell upon their faces: and the glory of the LORD appeared unto them.

7 ¶ And the LORD spake unto Mo′ses, saying,

8 Take the rod, and gather thou the assembly together, thou, and Aar′on thy brother, and speak ye unto the rock before their eyes; and it shall give forth his water, and thou shalt bring forth to them water out of the rock: so thou shalt give the congregation and their beasts drink.

9 And Mo′ses took the rod from before the LORD, as he commanded him.

10 And Mo′ses and Aar′on gathered the congregation together before the rock, and he said unto them, Hear now, ye rebels; must we fetch you water out of this rock?

11 And Mo′ses lifted up his hand, and with his rod he smote the rock twice: and the water came out abundantly, and the congregation drank, and their beasts *also*.

12 ¶ And the LORD spake unto Mo′ses and Aar′on, Because ye believed me not, to sanctify me in the eyes of the children of Is′ra-el, therefore ye shall not bring this congregation into the land which I have given them.

13 This *is* the water of Mer′i-bah; because the children of Is′ra-el strove with the LORD, and he was sanctified in them.

14 ¶ And Mo′ses sent messengers from Ka′desh unto the king of E′dom, Thus saith thy brother Is′ra-el, Thou knowest all the travail that hath befallen us:

15 How our fathers went down into E′gypt, and we have dwelt in E′gypt a long time; and the E-gyptians vexed us, and our fathers:

16 And when we cried unto the LORD, he heard our voice, and sent an angel, and hath brought us forth out of E′gypt: and, behold, we *are* in Ka′desh, a city in the uttermost of thy border:

17 Let us pass, I pray thee, through thy country: we will not pass through the fields, or through the vineyards, neither will we drink *of* the water of the wells: we will go by the king's *high* way, we will not turn to the right hand nor to the left, until we have passed thy borders.

18 And E′dom said unto him, Thou shalt not pass by me, lest I come out against thee with the sword.

19 And the children of Is′ra-el said unto him, We will go by the high way: and if I and my cattle drink of thy water, then I will pay for it: I will only, without *doing* any thing *else*, go through on my feet.

20 And he said, Thou shalt not go through. And E′dom came out against him with much people, and with a strong hand.

21 Thus E′dom refused to give Is′ra-el passage through his border: wherefore Is′ra-el turned away from him.

22 ¶ And the children of Is′ra-el, *even* the whole congregation, journeyed from Ka′desh, and came unto mount Hor.

23 And the LORD spake unto Mo′ses and Aar′on in mount Hor, by the coast of the land of E′dom, saying,

24 Aar′on shall be gathered unto his people: for he shall not enter into the land which I have given unto the children of Is′ra-el, because ye rebelled against my word at the water of Mer′i-bah.

25 Take Aar′on and E-le-a′zar his son, and bring them up unto mount Hor:

26 And strip Aar′on of his garments, and put them upon E-le-a′zar his son: and Aar′on shall be gathered *unto his people*, and shall die there.

27 And Mo′ses did as the LORD commanded: and they went up into mount Hor in the sight of all the congregation.

28 And Mo′ses stripped Aar′on of his garments, and put them upon E-le-a′zar his son; and Aar′on died there in the top of the mount: and Mo′ses and E-le-a′zar came down from the mount.

29 And when all the congregation saw that Aar′on was dead, they mourned for Aar′on thirty days, *even* all the house of Is′ra-el.

21 AND *when* king A′rad the Ca′naan-ite, which dwelt in the south, heard tell that Is′ra-el came by the way of the spies; then he fought against Is′ra-el, and took *some* of them prisoners.

2 And Is′ra-el vowed a vow unto the LORD,

and said, If thou wilt indeed deliver this people into my hand, then I will utterly destroy their cities.

3 And the LORD hearkened to the voice of Is'ra-el, and delivered up the Ca'naan-ites; and they utterly destroyed them and their cities: and he called the name of the place Hor'mah.

4 ¶ And they journeyed from mount Hor by the way of the Red sea, to compass the land of E'dom: and the soul of the people was much discouraged because of the way.

5 And the people spake against God, and against Mo'ses, Wherefore have ye brought us up out of E'gypt to die in the wilderness? for *there is* no bread, neither *is there any* water; and our soul loatheth this light bread.

6 And the LORD sent fiery serpents among the people, and they bit the people; and much people of Is'ra-el died.

7 ¶ Therefore the people came to Mo'ses, and said, We have sinned, for we have spoken against the LORD, and against thee; pray unto the LORD, that he take away the serpents from us. And Mo'ses prayed for the people.

8 And the LORD said unto Mo'ses, Make thee a fiery serpent, and set it upon a pole: and it shall come to pass, that every one that is bitten, when he looketh upon it, shall live.

9 And Mo'ses made a serpent of brass, and put it upon a pole, and it came to pass, that if a serpent had bitten any man, when he beheld the serpent of brass, he lived.

10 ¶ And the children of Is'ra-el set forward, and pitched in O'both.

11 And they journeyed from O'both, and pitched at Ij'e-ab'a-rim, in the wilderness which *is* before Mo'ab, toward the sunrising.

12 ¶ From thence they removed, and pitched in the valley of Za'red.

13 From thence they removed, and pitched on the other side of Ar'non, which *is* in the wilderness that cometh out of the coasts of the Am'or-ites: for Ar'non *is* the border of Mo'ab, between Mo'ab and the Am'or-ites.

14 Wherefore it is said in the book of the wars of the LORD, What he did in the Red sea, and in the brooks of Ar'non,

15 And at the stream of the brooks that goeth down to the dwelling of Ar, and lieth upon the border of Mo'ab.

16 And from thence *they went* to Be'er: that *is* the well whereof the LORD spake unto Mo'ses, Gather the people together, and I will give them water.

17 ¶ Then Is'ra-el sang this song, Spring up, O well; sing ye unto it:

18 The princes digged the well, the nobles of the people digged it, by *the direction of* the lawgiver, with their staves. And from the wilderness *they went* to Mat'ta-nah:

19 And from Mat'ta-nah to Na-ha'li-el: and from Na-ha'li-el to Ba'moth:

20 And from Ba'moth *in* the valley, that *is* in the country of Mo'ab, to the top of Pis'gah, which looketh toward Jesh'i-mon.

21 ¶ And Is'ra-el sent messengers unto Si'hon king of the Am'or-ites, saying,

22 Let me pass through thy land: we will not turn into the fields, or into the vineyards; we will not drink *of* the waters of the well: *but* we will go along by the king's *high* way, until we be past thy borders.

23 And Si'hon would not suffer Is'ra-el to pass through his border: but Si'hon gathered all his people together, and went out against Is'ra-el into the wilderness: and he came to Ja'haz, and fought against Is'ra-el.

24 And Is'ra-el smote him with the edge of the sword, and possessed his land from Ar'non unto Jab'bok, even unto the children of Am'mon: for the border of the children of Am'mon *was* strong.

25 And Is'ra-el took all these cities: and Is'ra-el dwelt in all the cities of the Am'or-ites, in Hesh'bon, and in all the villages thereof.

26 For Hesh'bon *was* the city of Si'hon the king of the Am'or-ites, who had fought against the former king of Mo'ab, and taken all his land out of his hand, even unto Ar'non.

27 Wherefore they that speak in proverbs say, Come into Hesh'bon, let the city of Si'hon be built and prepared:

28 For there is a fire gone out of Hesh'bon, a flame from the city of Si'hon: it hath consumed Ar of Mo'ab, *and* the lords of the high places of Ar'non.

29 Woe to thee, Mo'ab! thou art undone, O people of Che'mosh: he hath given his sons that escaped, and his daughters, into captivity unto Si'hon king of the Am'or-ites.

30 We have shot at them; Hesh'bon is perished even unto Di'bon, and we have laid them waste even unto No'phah, which *reacheth* unto Med'e-ba.

31 ¶ Thus Is'ra-el dwelt in the land of the Am'or-ites.

32 And Mo'ses sent to spy out Ja-a'zer, and they took the villages thereof, and drove out the Am'or-ites that *were* there.

33 ¶ And they turned and went up by the way of Ba'shan: and Og the king of Ba'shan went out against them, he, and all his people, to the battle at Ed're-i.

34 And the LORD said unto Mo'ses, Fear him not: for I have delivered him into thy hand, and all his people, and his land; and thou shalt do to him as thou didst unto Si'hon king of the Am'or-ites, which dwelt at Hesh'bon.

35 So they smote him, and his sons, and all his people, until there was none left him alive: and they possessed his land.

22 AND the children of Is'ra-el set forward, and pitched in the plains of Mo'ab on this side Jor'dan *by* Jer'i-cho.

2 ¶ And Ba'lak the son of Zip'por saw all that Is'ra-el had done to the Am'or-ites.

3 And Mo'ab was sore afraid of the people, because they *were* many: and Mo'ab was distressed because of the children of Is'ra-el.

4 And Mo'ab said unto the elders of Mid'i-an, Now shall this company lick up all *that are* round about us, as the ox licketh up the grass of the field. And Ba'lak the son of Zip'por *was* king of the Mo'ab-ites at that time.

5 He sent messengers therefore unto Ba'laam the son of Be'or to Pe'thor, which *is* by the river of the land of the children of his people, to call him, saying, Behold, there is a people come out from E'gypt: behold, they cover the face of the earth, and they abide over against me:

6 Come now therefore, I pray thee, curse me this people; for they *are* too mighty for me: peradventure I shall prevail, *that* we may smite them, and *that* I may drive them out of the land: for I wot that he whom thou blessest *is* blessed, and he whom thou cursest is cursed.

7 And the elders of Mo'ab and the elders of Mid'i-an departed with the rewards of divination in their hand; and they came unto Ba'laam, and spake unto him the words of Ba'lak.

8 And he said unto them, Lodge here this night, and I will bring you word again, as the

LORD shall speak unto me: and the princes of
Mo'ab abode with Ba'laam.
9 And God came unto Ba'laam, and said,
What men *are* these with thee?
10 And Ba'laam said unto God, Ba'lak the
son of Zip'por, king of Mo'ab, hath sent unto
me, *saying*,
11 Behold, *there is* a people come out of E'-
gypt, which covereth the face of the earth:
come now, curse me them; peradventure I shall
be able to overcome them, and drive them out.
12 And God said unto Ba'laam, Thou shalt
not go with them; thou shalt not curse the people: for they *are* blessed.
13 And Ba'laam rose up in the morning, and
said unto the princes of Ba'lak, Get you into
your land: for the LORD refuseth to give me
leave to go with you.
14 And the princes of Mo'ab rose up, and
they went unto Ba'lak, and said, Ba'laam refuseth to come with us.
15 ¶ And Ba'lak sent yet again princes,
more, and more honourable than they.
16 And they came to Ba'laam, and said to
him, Thus saith Ba'lak the son of Zip'por, Let
nothing, I pray thee, hinder thee from coming
unto me:
17 For I will promote thee unto very great
honour, and I will do whatsoever thou sayest
unto me: come therefore, I pray thee, curse me
this people.
18 And Ba'laam answered and said unto the
servants of Ba'lak, If Ba'lak would give me his
house full of silver and gold, I cannot go beyond
the word of the LORD my God, to do less or
more.
19 Now therefore, I pray you, tarry ye also
here this night, that I may know what the LORD
will say unto me more.
20 And God came unto Ba'laam at night, and
said unto him, If the men come to call thee, rise
up, *and* go with them; but yet the word which I
shall say unto thee, that shalt thou do.
21 And Ba'laam rose up in the morning, and
saddled his ass, and went with the princes of
Mo'ab.
22 ¶ And God's anger was kindled because
he went: and the angel of the LORD stood in the
way for an adversary against him. Now he was
riding upon his ass, and his two servants *were*
with him.
23 And the ass saw the angel of the LORD
standing in the way, and his sword drawn in his
hand: and the ass turned aside out of the way,
and went into the field: and Ba'laam smote the
ass, to turn her into the way.
24 But the angel of the LORD stood in a path
of the vineyards, a wall *being* on this side, and a
wall on that side.
25 And when the ass saw the angel of the
LORD, she thrust herself unto the wall, and
crushed Ba'laam's foot against the wall: and he
smote her again.
26 And the angel of the LORD went further,
and stood in a narrow place, where *was* no way
to turn either to the right hand or to the left.
27 And when the ass saw the angel of the
LORD, she fell down under Ba'laam: and Ba'-
laam's anger was kindled, and he smote the ass
with a staff.
28 And the LORD opened the mouth of the
ass, and she said unto Ba'laam, What have I
done unto thee, that thou hast smitten me these
three times?
29 And Ba'laam said unto the ass, Because
thou hast mocked me: I would there were a
sword in mine hand, for now would I kill thee.
30 And the ass said unto Ba'laam, *Am* not I
thine ass, upon which thou hast ridden ever
since *I was* thine unto this day? was I ever wont
to do so unto thee? And he said, Nay.
31 Then the LORD opened the eyes of Ba'-
laam, and he saw the angel of the LORD standing in the way, and his sword drawn in his
hand: and he bowed down his head, and fell flat
on his face.
32 And the angel of the LORD said unto him,
Wherefore hast thou smitten thine ass these
three times? behold, I went out to withstand
thee, because *thy* way is perverse before me:
33 And the ass saw me, and turned from me
these three times: unless she had turned from
me, surely now also I had slain thee, and saved
her alive.
34 And Ba'laam said unto the angel of the
LORD, I have sinned; for I knew not that thou
stoodest in the way against me: now therefore,
if it displease thee, I will get me back again.
35 And the angel of the LORD said unto Ba'-
laam, Go with the men: but only the word that I
shall speak unto thee, that thou shalt speak. So
Ba'laam went with the princes of Ba'lak.
36 ¶ And when Ba'lak heard that Ba'laam
was come, he went out to meet him unto a city
of Mo'ab, which *is* in the border of Ar'non,
which *is* in the utmost coast.
37 And Ba'lak said unto Ba'laam, Did I not
earnestly send unto thee to call thee? wherefore
camest thou not unto me? am I not able indeed
to promote thee to honour?
38 And Ba'laam said unto Ba'lak, Lo, I am
come unto thee: have I now any power at all to
say any thing? the word that God putteth in my
mouth, that shall I speak.
39 And Ba'laam went with Ba'lak, and they
came unto Kir'jath-hu'zoth.
40 And Ba'lak offered oxen and sheep, and
sent to Ba'laam, and to the princes that *were*
with him.
41 And it came to pass on the morrow, that
Ba'lak took Ba'laam, and brought him up into
the high places of Ba'al, that thence he might
see the utmost *part* of the people.

23 AND Ba'laam said unto Ba'lak, Build me
here seven altars, and prepare me here
seven oxen and seven rams.
2 And Ba'lak did as Ba'laam had spoken; and
Ba'lak and Ba'laam offered on *every* altar a bullock and a ram.
3 And Ba'laam said unto Ba'lak, Stand by thy
burnt offering, and I will go: peradventure the
LORD will come to meet me: and whatsoever he
sheweth me I will tell thee. And he went to an
high place.
4 And God met Ba'laam: and he said unto
him, I have prepared seven altars, and I have
offered upon *every* altar a bullock and a ram.
5 And the LORD put a word in Ba'laam's
mouth, and said, Return unto Ba'lak, and thus
thou shalt speak.
6 And he returned unto him, and, lo, he stood
by his burnt sacrifice, he, and all the princes of
Mo'ab.
7 And he took up his parable, and said, Ba'-
lak the king of Mo'ab hath brought me from A'-
ram, out of the mountains of the east, *saying*,
Come, curse me Ja'cob, and come, defy Is'ra-el.
8 How shall I curse, whom God hath not
cursed? or how shall I defy, *whom* the LORD
hath not defied?
9 For from the top of the rocks I see him, and
from the hills I behold him: lo, the people shall

dwell alone, and shall not be reckoned among
the nations.
10 Who can count the dust of Ja'cob, and the
number of the fourth *part* of Is'ra-el? Let me die
the death of the righteous, and let my last end
be like his!
11 And Ba'lak said unto Ba'laam, What hast
thou done unto me? I took thee to curse mine
enemies, and, behold, thou hast blessed *them*
altogether.
12 And he answered and said, Must I not
take heed to speak that which the LORD hath
put in my mouth?
13 And Ba'lak said unto him, Come, I pray
thee, with me unto another place, from whence
thou mayest see them: thou shalt see but the
utmost part of them, and shalt not see them all:
and curse me them from thence.
14 ¶ And he brought him into the field of
Zo'phim, to the top of Pisgah, and built seven
altars, and offered a bullock and a ram on *every*
altar.
15 And he said unto Ba'lak, Stand here by
thy burnt offering, while I meet *the LORD* yonder.
16 And the LORD met Ba'laam, and put a
word in his mouth, and said, Go again unto Ba'-
lak, and say thus.
17 And when he came to him, behold, he
stood by his burnt offering, and the princes of
Mo'ab with him. And Ba'lak said unto him,
What hath the LORD spoken?
18 And he took up his parable, and said, Rise
up, Ba'lak, and hear; hearken unto me, thou son
of Zip'por:
19 God *is* not a man, that he should lie; neither the son of man, that he should repent: hath
he said, and shall he not do *it?* or hath he spoken, and shall he not make it good?
20 Behold, I have received *commandment* to
bless: and he hath blessed; and I cannot reverse
it.
21 He hath not beheld iniquity in Ja'cob, neither hath he seen perverseness in Is'ra-el: the
LORD his God *is* with him, and the shout of a
king *is* among them.
22 God brought them out of E'gypt; he hath
as it were the strength of an unicorn.
23 Surely *there is* no enchantment against
Ja'cob, neither *is there* any divination against
Is'ra-el: according to this time it shall be said of
Ja'cob and of Is'ra-el, What hath God wrought!
24 Behold, the people shall rise up as a great
lion, and lift up himself as a young lion: he shall
not lie down until he eat *of* the prey, and drink
the blood of the slain.
25 ¶ And Ba'lak said unto Ba'laam, Neither
curse them at all, nor bless them at all.
26 But Ba'laam answered and said unto Ba'-
lak, Told not I thee, saying, All that the LORD
speaketh, that I must do?
27 ¶ And Ba'lak said unto Ba'laam, Come, I
pray thee, I will bring thee unto another place;
peradventure it will please God that thou mayest curse me them from thence.
28 And Ba'lak brought Ba'laam unto the top
of Pe'or, that looketh toward Jesh'i-mon.
29 And Ba'laam said unto Ba'lak, Build me
here seven altars, and prepare me here seven
bullocks and seven rams.
30 And Ba'lak did as Ba'laam had said, and
offered a bullock and a ram on *every* altar.

24 AND when Ba'laam saw that it pleased
the LORD to bless Is'ra-el, he went not,
as at other times, to seek for enchantments, but
he set his face toward the wilderness.
2 And Ba'laam lifted up his eyes, and he saw
Is'ra-el abiding *in his tents* according to their
tribes; and the spirit of God came upon him.
3 And he took up his parable, and said, Ba'-
laam the son of Be'or hath said, and the man
whose eyes are open hath said:
4 He hath said, which heard the words of
God, which saw the vision of the Almighty, falling *into a trance,* but having his eyes open:
5 How goodly are thy tents, O Ja'cob, *and*
thy tabernacles, O Is'ra-el!
6 As the valleys are they spread forth, as gardens by the river's side, as the trees of lign aloes
which the LORD hath planted, *and* as cedar
trees beside the waters.
7 He shall pour the water out of his buckets,
and his seed *shall be* in many waters, and his
king shall be higher than A'gag, and his kingdom shall be exalted.
8 God brought him forth out of E'gypt; he
hath as it were the strength of an unicorn: he
shall eat up the nations his enemies, and shall
break their bones, and pierce *them* through
with his arrows.
9 He couched, he lay down as a lion, and as a
great lion: who shall stir him up? Blessed *is* he
that blesseth thee, and cursed *is* he that curseth
thee.
10 ¶ And Ba'lak's anger was kindled against
Ba'laam, and he smote his hands together: and
Ba'lak said unto Ba'laam, I called thee to curse
mine enemies, and, behold, thou hast altogether
blessed *them* these three times.
11 Therefore now flee thou to thy place: I
thought to promote thee unto great honour; but,
lo, the LORD hath kept thee back from honour.
12 And Ba'laam said unto Ba'lak, Spake I not
also to thy messengers which thou sentest unto
me, saying,
13 If Ba'lak would give me his house full of
silver and gold, I cannot go beyond the commandment of the LORD, to do *either* good or bad
of mine own mind; *but* what the LORD saith,
that will I speak?
14 And now, behold, I go unto my people:
come *therefore, and* I will advertise thee what
this people shall do to thy people in the latter
days.
15 ¶ And he took up his parable, and said,
Ba'laam the son of Be'or hath said, and the man
whose eyes are open hath said:
16 He hath said, which heard the words of
God, and knew the knowledge of the most
High, *which* saw the vision of the Almighty,
falling *into a trance,* but having his eyes open:
17 I shall see him, but not now: I shall behold
him, but not nigh: there shall come a Star out of
Ja'cob, and a Sceptre shall rise out of Is'ra-el,
and shall smite the corners of Mo'ab, and destroy all the children of Sheth.
18 And E'dom shall be a possession, Se'ir
also shall be a possession for his enemies; and
Is'ra-el shall do valiantly.
19 Out of Ja'cob shall come he that shall
have dominion, and shall destroy him that remaineth of the city.
20 ¶ And when he looked on Am'a-lek, he
took up his parable, and said, Am'a-lek *was* the
first of the nations; but his latter end *shall be*
that he perish for ever.
21 And he looked on the Ken'ites, and took
up his parable, and said, Strong is thy dwellingplace, and thou puttest thy nest in a rock.
22 Nevertheless the Kenite shall be wasted,
until As'shur shall carry thee away captive.
23 And he took up his parable, and said,
Alas, who shall live when God doeth this!

24 And ships *shall come* from the coast of
Chit'tim, and shall afflict As'shur, and shall afflict E'ber, and he also shall perish for ever.
25 And Ba'laam rose up, and went and returned to his place: and Ba'lak also went his
way.

25 AND Is'ra-el abode in Shit'tim, and the
people began to commit whoredom with
the daughters of Mo'ab.
2 And they called the people unto the sacrifices of their gods: and the people did eat, and
bowed down to their gods.
3 And Is'ra-el joined himself unto Ba'al–pe'-
or: and the anger of the LORD was kindled
against Is'ra-el.
4 And the LORD said unto Mo'ses, Take all
the heads of the people, and hang them up before the LORD against the sun, that the fierce
anger of the LORD may be turned away from
Is'ra-el.
5 And Mo'ses said unto the judges of Is'ra-el,
Slay ye every one his men that were joined unto
Ba'al–pe'or.
6 ¶ And, behold, one of the children of Is'ra-
el came and brought unto his brethen a Mid'i-
an-it-ish woman in the sight of Mo'ses, and in
the sight of all the congregation of the children
of Is'ra-el, who *were* weeping *before* the door of
the tabernacle of the congregation.
7 And when Phin'e-has, the son of E-le-a'zar,
the son of Aar'on the priest, saw *it,* he rose up
from among the congregation, and took a javelin in his hand;
8 And he went after the man of Is'ra-el into
the tent, and thrust both of them through, the
man of Is'ra-el, and the woman through her belly. So the plague was stayed from the children
of Is'ra-el.
9 And those that died in the plague were
twenty and four thousand.
10 ¶ And the LORD spake unto Mo'ses, saying,
11 Phin'e-has, the son of E-le-a'zar, the son of
Aar'on the priest, hath turned my wrath away
from the children of Is'ra-el, while he was zealous for my sake among them, that I consumed
not the children of Is'ra-el in my jealousy.
12 Wherefore say, Behold, I give unto him
my covenant of peace:
13 And he shall have it, and his seed after
him, *even* the covenant of an everlasting priesthood; because he was zealous for his God, and
made an atonement for the children of Is'ra-el.
14 Now the name of the Is'ra-el-ite that was
slain, *even* that was slain with the Mid'i-an-it-
ish woman, *was* Zim'ri, the son of Sa'lu, a
prince of a chief house among the Sim'e-on-ites.
15 And the name of the Mid'i-an-it-ish
woman that was slain *was* Coz'bi, the daughter
of Zur; he *was* head over a people, *and* of a
chief house in Mid'i-an.
16 ¶ And the LORD spake unto Mo'ses, saying,
17 Vex the Mid'i-an-ites, and smite them:
18 For they vex you with their wiles, wherewith they have beguiled you in the matter of
Pe'or, and in the matter of Coz'bi, the daughter
of a prince of Mid'i-an, their sister, which was
slain in the day of the plague for Pe'or's sake.

26 AND it came to pass after the plague,
that the LORD spake unto Mo'ses and
unto E-le-a'zar the son of Aar'on the priest, saying,
2 Take the sum of all the congregation of the
children of Is'ra-el, from twenty years old and
upward, throughout their fathers' house, all
that are able to go to war in Is'ra-el.
3 And Mo'ses and E-le-a'zar the priest spake
with them in the plains of Mo'ab by Jor'dan
near Jer'i-cho, saying,
4 *Take the sum of the people,* from twenty
years old and upward; as the LORD commanded
Mo'ses and the children of Is'ra-el, which went
forth out of the land of E'gypt.
5 ¶ Reu'ben, the eldest son of Is'ra-el: the
children of Reu'ben; Ha'noch, *of whom cometh*
the family of the Ha'noch-ites: of Pal'lu, the
family of the Pal'lu-ites:
6 Of Hez'ron, the family of the Hez'ron-ites:
of Car'mi, the family of the Car'mites.
7 These *are* the families of the Reu'ben-ites:
and they that were numbered of them were
forty and three thousand and seven hundred
and thirty.
8 And the sons of Pal'lu; E-li'ab.
9 And the sons of E-li'ab; Ne-mu'el, and Da'-
than, and A-bi'ram. This *is that* Da'than and A-
bi'ram, *which were* famous in the congregation,
who strove against Mo'ses and against Aar'on
in the company of Ko'rah, when they strove
against the LORD:
10 And the earth opened her mouth, and
swallowed them up together with Ko'rah, when
that company died, what time the fire devoured
two hundred and fifty men: and they became a
sign.
11 Notwithstanding the children of Ko'rah
died not.
12 ¶ The sons of Sim'e-on after their families: of Ne-mu'el, the family of the Ne-mu'el-
ites: of Ja'min, the family of the Ja'min-ites: of
Ja'chin, the family of the Ja'chin-ites:
13 Of Ze'rah, the family of the Zar'hites: of
Sha'ul, the family of the Sha'ul-ites.
14 These *are* the families of the Sim'e-on-
ites, twenty and two thousand and two hundred.
15 ¶ The children of Gad after their families:
of Ze'phon, the family of the Ze'phon-ites: of
Hag'gi, the family of the Hag'gites: of Shu'ni,
the family of the Shu'nites:
16 Of Oz'ni, the family of the Oz'nites: of E'-
ri, the family of the E'rites:
17 Of A'rod, the family of the A'rod-ites: of
A-re'li, the family of the A-re'lites.
18 These *are* the families of the children of
Gad according to those that were numbered of
them, forty thousand and five hundred.
19 ¶ The sons of Ju'dah *were* Er and O'nan:
and Er and O'nan died in the land of Ca'naan.
20 And the sons of Ju'dah after their families
were; of She'lah, the family of the She'lan-ites:
of Pha'rez, the family of the Phar'zites: of Ze'-
rah, the family of the Zar'hites.
21 And the sons of Pha'rez were; of Hez'ron,
the family of the Hez'ron-ites: of Ha'mul, the
family of the Ha'mul-ites.
22 These *are* the families of Ju'dah according
to those that were numbered of them, threescore and sixteen thousand and five hundred.
23 ¶ *Of* the sons of Is'sa-char after their families: *of* To'la, the family of the To'la-ites: of Pu'-
a, the family of the Pu'nites:
24 Of Jash'ub, the family of the Jash'ub-ites:
of Shim'ron, the family of the Shim'ron-ites.
25 These *are* the families of Is'sa-char according to those that were numbered of them,
threescore and four thousand and three hundred.
26 ¶ *Of* the sons of Zeb'u-lun after their families: of Se'red, the family of the Sar'dites: of

E'lon, the family of the E'lon-ites: of Jah'le-el,
the family of the Jah'le-el-ites.
27 These *are* the families of the Zeb'u-lun-
ites according to those that were numbered of
them, threescore thousand and five hundred.
28 ¶ The sons of Jo'seph after their families
were Ma-nas'seh and E'phra-im.
29 Of the sons of Ma-nas'seh: of Ma'chir, the
family of the Ma'chir-ites: and Ma'chir begat
Gil'e-ad: of Gil'e-ad *come* the family of the Gil'-
e-ad-ites.
30 These *are* the sons of Gil'e-ad: *of* Je-e'zer,
the family of the Je-e'zer-ites: of He'lek, the
family of the He'lek-ites:
31 And *of* As'ri-el, the family of the As'ri-el-
ites: and *of* Shechem, the family of the She'-
chem-ites:
32 And *of* She-mi'da, the family of the She-
mi'da-ites: and *of* He'pher, the family of the
He'pher-ites.
33 ¶ And Ze-lo'phe-had the son of He'pher
had no sons, but daughters: and the names of
the daughters of Ze-lo'phe-had *were* Mah'lah,
and No'ah, Hog'lah, Mil'cah, and Tir'zah.
34 These *are* the families of Ma-nas'seh, and
those that were numbered of them, fifty and
two thousand and seven hundred.
35 ¶ These *are* the sons of E'phra-im after
their families: of Shu'the-lah, the family of the
Shu'thal-hites: of Be'cher, the family of the
Bach'rites: of Ta'han, the family of the Ta'han-
ites.
36 And these *are* the sons of Shu'the-lah: of
E'ran, the family of the E'ran-ites.
37 These *are* the families of the sons of E'-
phra-im according to those that were numbered
of them, thirty and two thousand and five hundred. These *are* the sons of Jo'seph after their
families.
38 ¶ The sons of Ben'ja-min after their families: of Be'la, the family of the Be'la-ites: of
Ash'bel, the family of the Ash'bel-ites: of A-hi'-
ram, the family of the A-hi'ram-ites:
39 Of Shu'pham, the family of the Shu'pham-
ites: of Hu'pham, the family of the Hu'pham-
ites.
40 And the sons of Be'la were Ard and Na'a-
man: *of Ard*, the family of the Ard'ites: *and* of
Na'a-man, the family of the Na'a-mites.
41 These *are* the sons of Ben'ja-min after
their families: and they that were numbered of
them *were* forty and five thousand and six hundred.
42 ¶ These *are* the sons of Dan after their
families: of Shu'ham, the family of the Shu'-
ham-ites. These *are* the families of Dan after
their families.
43 All the families of the Shu'ham-ites, according to those that were numbered of them,
were threescore and four thousand and four
hundred.
44 ¶ *Of* the children of Ash'er after their
families: of Jim'na, the family of the Jim'nites:
of Jes'u-i, the family of the Jes'u-ites: of Be-ri'-
ah, the family of the Be-ri'tes.
45 Of the sons of Be-ri'ah: of He'ber, the family of the He'ber-ites: of Mal'chi-el, the family of
the Mal'chi-el-ites.
46 And the name of the daughter of Ash'er
was Sa'rah.
47 These *are* the families of the sons of Ash'-
er according to those that were numbered of
them; *who were* fifty and three thousand and
four hundred.
48 ¶ *Of* the sons of Naph'ta-li after their
families: of Jah'ze-el, the family of the Jah'ze-
el-ites: of Gu'ni, the family of the Gu'nites:
49 Of Je'zer, the family of the Je'zer-ites: of
Shil'lem, the family of the Shil'lem-ites.
50 These *are* the families of Naph'ta-li according to their families: and they that were
numbered of them *were* forty and five thousand
and four hundred.
51 These *were* the numbered of the children
of Is'ra-el, six hundred thousand and a thousand seven hundred and thirty.
52 ¶ And the LORD spake unto Mo'ses, saying,
53 Unto these the land shall be divided for an
inheritance according to the number of names.
54 To many thou shalt give the more inheritance, and to few thou shalt give the less inheritance: to every one shall his inheritance be giv-
en according to those that were numbered of
him.
55 Notwithstanding the land shall be divided
by lot: according to the names of the tribes of
their fathers they shall inherit.
56 According to the lot shall the possession
thereof be divided between many and few.
57 ¶ And these *are* they that were numbered
of the Le'vites after their families: of Ger'shon,
the family of the Ger'shon-ites: of Ko'hath, the
family of the Ko'hath-ites: of Me-ra'ri, the family of the Me-ra'rites.
58 These *are* the families of the Le'vites: the
family of the Lib'nites, the family of the He'-
bron-ites, the family of the Mah'lites, the family
of the Mu'shites, the family of the Ko'rath-ites.
And Ko'hath begat Am'ram.
59 And the name of Am'ram's wife *was*
Joch'e-bed, the daughter of Le'vi, whom *her
mother* bare to Le'vi in E'gypt: and she bare
unto Am'ram Aar'on and Mo'ses, and Mir'i-am
their sister.
60 And unto Aar'on was born Na'dab, and A-
bi'hu, E-le-a'zar, and Ith'a-mar.
61 And Na'dab and A-bi'hu died, when they
offered strange fire before the LORD.
62 And those that were numbered of them
were twenty and three thousand, all males from
a month old and upward: for they were not
numbered among the children of Is'ra-el, because there was no inheritance given them
among the children of Is'ra-el.
63 ¶ These *are* they that were numbered by
Mo'ses and E-le-a'zar the priest, who numbered
the children of Is'ra-el in the plains of Mo'ab by
Jor'dan *near* Jer'i-cho.
64 But among these there was not a man of
them whom Mo'ses and Aar'on the priest numbered, when they numbered the children of Is'-
ra-el in the wilderness of Si'nai.
65 For the LORD had said of them, They shall
surely die in the wilderness. And there was not
left a man of them, save Ca'leb the son of Je-
phun'neh, and Josh'u-a the son of Nun.

27 THEN came the daughters of Ze-lo'phe-
had, the son of He'pher, the son of Gil'e-
ad, the son of Ma'chir, the son of Ma-nas'seh, of
the families of Ma-nas'seh the son of Jo'seph:
and these *are* the names of his daughters; Mah'-
lah, No'ah, and Hog'lah, and Mil'cah, and Tir'-
zah.
2 And they stood before Mo'ses, and before
E-le-a'zar the priest, and before the princes and
all the congregation, *by* the door of the tabernacle of the congregation, saying,
3 Our father died in the wilderness, and he
was not in the company of them that gathered
themselves together against the LORD in the
company of Ko'rah; but died in his own sin, and
had no sons.

4 Why should the name of our father be done
away from among his family, because he hath
no son? Give unto us *therefore* a possession
among the brethren of our father.
5 And Mo'ses brought their cause before the
LORD.
6 ¶ And the LORD spake unto Mo'ses, saying,
7 The daughters of Ze-lo'phe-had speak
right: thou shalt surely give them a possession
of an inheritance among their father's brethren;
and thou shalt cause the inheritance of their father to pass unto them.
8 And thou shalt speak unto the children of
Is'ra-el, saying, If a man die, and have no son,
then ye shall cause his inheritance to pass unto
his daughter.
9 And if he have no daughter, then ye shall
give his inheritance unto his brethren.
10 And if he have no brethren, then ye shall
give his inheritance unto his father's brethren.
11 And if his father have no brethren, then ye
shall give his inheritance unto his kinsman that
is next to him of his family, and he shall possess
it: and it shall be unto the children of Is'ra-el a
statute of judgment, as the LORD commanded
Mo'ses.
12 ¶ And the LORD said unto Mo'ses, Get
thee up into this mount Ab'a-rim, and see the
land which I have given unto the children of
Is'ra-el.
13 And when thou hast seen it, thou also
shalt be gathered unto thy people, as Aar'on thy
brother was gathered.
14 For ye rebelled against my commandment
in the desert of Zin, in the strife of the congregation, to sanctify me at the water before their
eyes: that *is* the water of Mer'i-bah in Ka'desh
in the wilderness of Zin.
15 ¶ And Mo'ses spake unto the LORD, saying,
16 Let the LORD, the God of the spirits of all
flesh, set a man over the congregation,
17 Which may go out before them, and
which may go in before them, and which may
lead them out, and which may bring them in;
that the congregation of the LORD be not as
sheep which have no shepherd.
18 ¶ And the LORD said unto Mo'ses, Take
thee Josh'u-a the son of Nun, a man in whom *is*
the spirit, and lay thine hand upon him;
19 And set him before E-le-a'zar the priest,
and before all the congregation; and give him a
charge in their sight.
20 And thou shalt put *some* of thine honour
upon him, that all the congregation of the children of Is'ra-el may be obedient.
21 And he shall stand before E-le-a'zar the
priest, who shall ask *counsel* for him after the
judgment of U'rim before the LORD: at his word
shall they go out, and at his word they shall
come in, *both* he, and all the children of Is'ra-el
with him, even all the congregation.
22 And Mo'ses did as the LORD commanded
him: and he took Josh'u-a, and set him before E-le-a'zar the priest, and before all the congregation:
23 And he laid his hands upon him, and gave
him a charge, as the LORD commanded by the
hand of Mo'ses.

28 AND the LORD spake unto Mo'ses, saying,
2 Command the children of Is'ra-el, and say
unto them, My offering, *and* my bread for my
sacrifices made by fire, *for* a sweet savour unto
me, shall ye observe to offer unto me in their
due season.
3 And thou shalt say unto them, This *is* the
offering made by fire which ye shall offer unto
the LORD; two lambs of the first year without
spot day by day, *for* a continual burnt offering.
4 The one lamb shalt thou offer in the morning, and the other lamb shalt thou offer at even;
5 And a tenth *part* of an ephah of flour for a
meat offering, mingled with the fourth *part* of
an hin of beaten oil.
6 *It is* a continual burnt offering, which was
ordained in mount Si'nai for a sweet savour, a
sacrifice made by fire unto the LORD.
7 And the drink offering thereof *shall be* the
fourth *part* of an hin for the one lamb: in the
holy *place* shalt thou cause the strong wine to
be poured unto the LORD *for* a drink offering.
8 And the other lamb shalt thou offer at
even: as the meat offering of the morning, and
as the drink offering thereof, thou shalt offer *it*,
a sacrifice made by fire, of a sweet savour unto
the LORD.
9 ¶ And on the sabbath day two lambs of the
first year without spot, and two tenth deals of
flour *for* a meat offering, mingled with oil, and
the drink offering thereof:
10 *This is* the burnt offering of every sabbath, beside the continual burnt offering, and
his drink offering.
11 ¶ And in the beginnings of your months
ye shall offer a burnt offering unto the LORD;
two young bullocks, and one ram, seven lambs
of the first year without spot;
12 And three tenth deals of flour *for* a meat
offering, mingled with oil, for one bullock; and
two tenth deals of flour *for* a meat offering,
mingled with oil, for one ram;
13 And a several tenth deal of flour mingled
with oil *for* a meat offering unto one lamb; *for* a
burnt offering of a sweet savour, a sacrifice
made by fire unto the LORD.
14 And their drink offerings shall be half an
hin of wine unto a bullock, and the third *part* of
an hin unto a ram, and a fourth *part* of an hin
unto a lamb: this *is* the burnt offering of every
month throughout the months of the year.
15 And one kid of the goats for a sin offering
unto the LORD shall be offered, beside the continual burnt offering, and his drink offering.
16 And in the fourteenth day of the first
month *is* the passover of the LORD.
17 And in the fifteenth day of this month *is*
the feast: seven days shall unleavened bread be
eaten.
18 In the first day *shall be* an holy convocation; ye shall do no manner of servile work
therein:
19 But ye shall offer a sacrifice made by fire
for a burnt offering unto the LORD; two young
bullocks, and one ram, and seven lambs of the
first year: they shall be unto you without blemish:
20 And their meat offering *shall be of* flour
mingled with oil: three tenth deals shall ye offer
for a bullock, and two tenth deals for a ram;
21 A several tenth deal shalt thou offer for
every lamb, throughout the seven lambs:
22 And one goat *for* a sin offering, to make
an atonement for you.
23 Ye shall offer these beside the burnt offering in the morning, which *is* for a continual
burnt offering.
24 After this manner ye shall offer daily,
throughout the seven days, the meat of the sacrifice made by fire, of a sweet savour unto the
LORD: it shall be offered beside the continual
burnt offering, and his drink offering.
25 And on the seventh day ye shall have an

holy convocation; ye shall do no servile work.
26 ¶ Also in the day of the firstfruits, when
ye bring a new meat offering unto the LORD,
after your weeks *be out*, ye shall have an holy
convocation; ye shall do no servile work:
27 But ye shall offer the burnt offering for a
sweet savour unto the LORD; two young bullocks, one ram, seven lambs of the first year;
28 And their meat offering of flour mingled
with oil, three tenth deals unto one bullock, two
tenth deals unto one ram,
29 A several tenth deal unto one lamb,
throughout the seven lambs;
30 *And* one kid of the goats, to make an
atonement for you.
31 Ye shall offer *them* beside the continual
burnt offering, and his meat offering, (they shall
be unto you without blemish) and their drink
offerings.

29 AND in the seventh month, on the first
day of the month, ye shall have an holy
convocation; ye shall do no servile work: it is a
day of blowing the trumpets unto you.
2 And ye shall offer a burnt offering for a
sweet savour unto the LORD; one young bullock,
one ram, *and* seven lambs of the first year without blemish:
3 And their meat offering *shall be of* flour
mingled with oil, three tenth deals for a bullock,
and two tenth deals for a ram,
4 And one tenth deal for one lamb, throughout the seven lambs:
5 And one kid of the goats *for* a sin offering,
to make an atonement for you:
6 Beside the burnt offering of the month, and
his meat offering, and the daily burnt offering,
and his meat offering, and their drink offerings,
according unto their manner, for a sweet savour, a sacrifice made by fire unto the LORD.
7 ¶ And ye shall have on the tenth *day* of
this seventh month an holy convocation; and ye
shall afflict your souls: ye shall not do any work
therein.
8 But ye shall offer a burnt offering unto the
LORD *for* a sweet savour; one young bullock,
one ram, *and* seven lambs of the first year; they
shall be unto you without blemish:
9 And their meat offering *shall be of* flour
mingled with oil, three tenth deals to a bullock,
and two tenth deals to one ram,
10 A several tenth deal for one lamb,
throughout the seven lambs:
11 One kid of the goats *for* a sin offering; beside the sin offering of atonement, and the continual burnt offering, and the meat offering of it,
and their drink offerings.
12 ¶ And on the fifteenth day of the seventh
month ye shall have an holy convocation; ye
shall do no servile work, and ye shall keep a
feast unto the LORD seven days:
13 And ye shall offer a burnt offering, a sacrifice made by fire, of a sweet savour unto the
LORD; thirteen young bullocks, two rams, *and*
fourteen lambs of the first year; they shall be
without blemish:
14 And their meat offering *shall be of* flour
mingled with oil, three tenth deals unto every
bullock of the thirteen bullocks, two tenth deals
to each ram of the two rams,
15 And a several tenth deal to each lamb of
the fourteen lambs:
16 And one kid of the goats *for* a sin offering;
beside the continual burnt offering, his meat offering, and his drink offering.
17 ¶ And on the second day *ye shall offer*
twelve young bullocks, two rams, fourteen
lambs of the first year without spot:
18 And their meat offering and their drink offerings for the bullocks, for the rams, and for
the lambs, *shall be* according to their number,
after the manner:
19 And one kid of the goats *for* a sin offering;
beside the continual burnt offering, and the
meat offering thereof, and their drink offerings.
20 ¶ And on the third day eleven bullocks,
two rams, fourteen lambs of the first year without blemish;
21 And their meat offering and their drink offerings for the bullocks, for the rams, and for
the lambs, *shall be* according to their number,
after the manner:
22 And one goat *for* a sin offering; beside the
continual burnt offering, and his meat offering,
and his drink offering.
23 ¶ And on the fourth day ten bullocks, two
rams, *and* fourteen lambs of the first year without blemish:
24 Their meat offering and their drink offerings for the bullocks, for the rams, and for the
lambs, *shall be* according to their number, after
the manner:
25 And one kid of the goats *for* a sin offering;
beside the continual burnt offering, his meat offering, and his drink offering.
26 ¶ And on the fifth day nine bullocks, two
rams, *and* fourteen lambs of the first year without spot:
27 And their meat offering and their drink offerings for the bullocks, for the rams, and for
the lambs, *shall be* according to their number,
after the manner:
28 And one goat *for* a sin offering; beside the
continual burnt offering, and his meat offering,
and his drink offering.
29 ¶ And on the sixth day eight bullocks,
two rams, *and* fourteen lambs of the first year
without blemish:
30 And their meat offering and their drink offerings for the bullocks, for the rams, and for
the lambs, *shall be* according to their number,
after the manner:
31 And one goat *for* a sin offering; beside the
continual burnt offering, his meat offering, and
his drink offering.
32 ¶ And on the seventh day seven bullocks,
two rams, *and* fourteen lambs of the first year
without blemish:
33 And their meat offering and their drink offerings for the bullocks, for the rams, and for
the lambs, *shall be* according to their number,
after the manner:
34 And one goat *for* a sin offering; beside the
continual burnt offering, his meat offering, and
his drink offering.
35 ¶ On the eighth day ye shall have a solemn assembly: ye shall do no servile work
therein:
36 But ye shall offer a burnt offering, a sacrifice made by fire, of a sweet savour unto the
LORD: one bullock, one ram, seven lambs of the
first year without blemish:
37 Their meat offering and their drink offerings for the bullock, for the ram, and for the
lambs, *shall be* according to their number, after
the manner:
38 And one goat *for* a sin offering; beside the
continual burnt offering, and his meat offering,
and his drink offering.
39 These *things* ye shall do unto the LORD in
your set feasts, beside your vows, and your
freewill offerings, for your burnt offerings, and

for your meat offerings, and for your drink offerings, and for your peace offerings.

40 And Mo'ses told the children of Is'ra-el according to all that the LORD commanded Mo'ses.

30 AND Mo'ses spake unto the heads of the tribes concerning the children of Is'ra-el, saying, This *is* the thing which the LORD hath commanded.

2 If a man vow a vow unto the LORD, or swear an oath to bind his soul with a bond; he shall not break his word, he shall do according to all that proceedeth out of his mouth.

3 If a woman also vow a vow unto the LORD, and bind *herself* by a bond, *being* in her father's house in her youth;

4 And her father hear her vow, and her bond wherewith she hath bound her soul, and her father shall hold his peace at her: then all her vows shall stand, and every bond wherewith she hath bound her soul shall stand.

5 But if her father disallow her in the day that he heareth; not any of her vows, or of her bonds wherewith she hath bound her soul, shall stand: and the LORD shall forgive her, because her father disallowed her.

6 And if she had at all an husband, when she vowed, or uttered ought out of her lips, wherewith she bound her soul;

7 And her husband heard *it,* and held his peace at her in the day that he heard *it:* then her vows shall stand, and her bonds wherewith she bound her soul shall stand.

8 But if her husband disallowed her on the day that he heard *it;* then he shall make her vow which she vowed, and that which she uttered with her lips, wherewith she bound her soul, of none effect: and the LORD shall forgive her.

9 But every vow of a widow, and of her that is divorced, wherewith they have bound their souls, shall stand against her.

10 And if she vowed in her husband's house, or bound her soul by a bond with an oath;

11 And her husband heard *it,* and held his peace at her, *and* disallowed her not: then all her vows shall stand, and every bond wherewith she bound her soul shall stand.

12 But if her husband hath utterly made them void on the day he heard *them; then* whatsoever proceeded out of her lips concerning her vows, or concerning the bond of her soul, shall not stand: her husband hath made them void; and the LORD shall forgive her.

13 Every vow, and every binding oath to afflict the soul, her husband may establish it, or her husband may make it void.

14 But if her husband altogether hold his peace at her from day to day; then he establisheth all her vows, or all her bonds, which *are* upon her: he confirmeth them, because he held his peace at her in the day that he heard *them.*

15 But if he shall any ways make them void after that he hath heard *them;* then he shall bear her iniquity.

16 These *are* the statutes, which the LORD commanded Mo'ses, between a man and his wife, between the father and his daughter, *being yet* in her youth in her father's house.

31 AND the LORD spake unto Mo'ses, saying,

2 Avenge the children of Is'ra-el of the Mid'i-an-ites: afterward shalt thou be gathered unto thy people.

3 And Mo'ses spake unto the people, saying, Arm some of yourselves unto the war, and let them go against the Mid'i-an-ites, and avenge the LORD of Mid'i-an.

4 Of every tribe a thousand, throughout all the tribes of Is'ra-el, shall ye send to the war.

5 So there were delivered out of the thousands of Is'ra-el, a thousand of *every* tribe, twelve thousand armed for war.

6 And Mo'ses sent them to the war, a thousand of *every* tribe, them and Phin'e-has the son of E-le-a'zar the priest, to the war, with the holy instruments, and the trumpets to blow in his hand.

7 And they warred against the Mid'i-an-ites, as the LORD commanded Mo'ses; and they slew all the males.

8 And they slew the kings of Mid'i-an, beside the rest of them that were slain; *namely,* E'vi, and Re'kem, and Zur, and Hur, and Re'ba, five kings of Mid'i-an: Ba'laam also the son of Be'or they slew with the sword.

9 And the children of Is'ra-el took *all* the women of Mid'i-an captives, and their little ones, and took the spoil of all their cattle, and all their flocks, and all their goods.

10 And they burnt all their cities wherein they dwelt, and all their goodly castles, with fire.

11 And they took all the spoil, and all the prey, *both* of men and of beasts.

12 And they brought the captives, and the prey, and the spoil, unto Mo'ses, and E-le-a'zar the priest, and unto the congregation of the children of Is'ra-el, unto the camp at the plains of Mo'ab, which *are* by Jor'dan *near* Jer'i-cho.

13 ¶ And Mo'ses, and E-le-a'zar the priest, and all the princes of the congregation, went forth to meet them without the camp.

14 And Mo'ses was wroth with the officers of the host, *with* the captains over thousands, and captains over hundreds, which came from the battle.

15 And Mo'ses said unto them, Have ye saved all the women alive?

16 Behold, these caused the children of Is'ra-el, through the counsel of Ba'laam, to commit trespass against the LORD in the matter of Pe'or, and there was a plague among the congregation of the LORD.

17 Now therefore kill every male among the little ones, and kill every woman that hath known man by lying with him.

18 But all the women children, that have not known a man by lying with him, keep alive for yourselves.

19 And do ye abide without the camp seven days: whosoever hath killed any person, and whosoever hath touched any slain, purify *both* yourselves and your captives on the third day, and on the seventh day.

20 And purify all *your* raiment, and all that is made of skins, and all work of goats' *hair,* and all things made of wood.

21 ¶ And E-le-a'zar the priest said unto the men of war which went to the battle, This *is* the ordinance of the law which the LORD commanded Mo'ses;

22 Only the gold, and the silver, the brass, the iron, the tin, and the lead,

23 Every thing that may abide the fire, ye shall make *it* go through the fire, and it shall be clean: nevertheless it shall be purified with the water of separation: and all that abideth not the fire ye shall make go through the water.

24 And ye shall wash your clothes on the seventh day, and ye shall be clean, and afterward ye shall come into the camp.

25 ¶ And the LORD spake unto Mo'ses, saying,

26 Take the sum of the prey that was taken, *both* of man and of beast, thou, and E-le-a'zar the priest, and the chief fathers of the congregation:

27 And divide the prey into two parts; between them that took the war upon them, who went out to battle, and between all the congregation:

28 And levy a tribute unto the LORD of the men of war which went out to battle: one soul of five hundred, *both* of the persons, and of the beeves, and of the asses, and of the sheep:

29 Take *it* of their half, and give *it* unto E-le-a'zar the priest, *for* an heave offering of the LORD.

30 And of the children of Is'ra-el's half, thou shalt take one portion of fifty, of the persons, of the beeves, of the asses, and of the flocks, of all manner of beasts, and give them unto the Le'vites, which keep the charge of the tabernacle of the LORD.

31 And Mo'ses and E-le-a'zar the priest did as the LORD commanded Mo'ses.

32 And the booty, *being* the rest of the prey which the men of war had caught, was six hundred thousand and seventy thousand and five thousand sheep,

33 And threescore and twelve thousand beeves,

34 And threescore and one thousand asses,

35 And thirty and two thousand persons in all, of women that had not known man by lying with him.

36 And the half, *which was* the portion of them that went out to war, was in number three hundred thousand and seven and thirty thousand and five hundred sheep:

37 And the LORD's tribute of the sheep was six hundred and threescore and fifteen.

38 And the beeves *were* thirty and six thousand; of which the LORD's tribute *was* threescore and twelve.

39 And the asses *were* thirty thousand and five hundred; of which the LORD's tribute *was* threescore and one.

40 And the persons *were* sixteen thousand; of which the LORD's tribute *was* thirty and two persons.

41 And Mo'ses gave the tribute, *which was* the LORD's heave offering, unto E-le-a'zar the priest, as the LORD commanded Mo'ses.

42 And of the children of Is'ra-el's half, which Mo'ses divided from the men that warred,

43 (Now the half *that pertained unto* the congregation was three hundred thousand and thirty thousand *and* seven thousand and five hundred sheep,

44 And thirty and six thousand beeves,

45 And thirty thousand asses and five hundred,

46 And sixteen thousand persons;)

47 Even of the children of Is'ra-el's half, Mo'ses took one portion of fifty, *both* of man and of beast, and gave them unto the Le'vites, which kept the charge of the tabernacle of the LORD; as the LORD commanded Mo'ses.

48 ¶ And the officers which *were* over thousands of the host, the captains of thousands, and captains of hundreds, came near unto Mo'ses:

49 And they said unto Mo'ses, Thy servants have taken the sum of the men of war which *are* under our charge, and there lacketh not one man of us.

50 We have therefore brought an oblation for the LORD, what every man hath gotten, of jewels of gold, chains, and bracelets, rings, earrings, and tablets, to make an atonement for our souls before the LORD.

51 And Mo'ses and E-le-a'zar the priest took the gold of them, *even* all wrought jewels.

52 And all the gold of the offering that they offered up to the LORD, of the captains of thousands, and of the captains of hundreds, was sixteen thousand seven hundred and fifty shekels.

53 (*For* the men of war had taken spoil, every man for himself.)

54 And Mo'ses and E-le-a'zar the priest took the gold of the captains of thousands and of hundreds, and brought it into the tabernacle of the congregation, *for* a memorial for the children of Is'ra-el before the LORD.

32 NOW the children of Reu'ben and the children of Gad had a very great multitude of cattle: and when they saw the land of Ja'zer, and the land of Gil'e-ad, that, behold, the place *was* a place for cattle;

2 The children of Gad and the children of Reu'ben came and spake unto Mo'ses, and to E-le-a'zar the priest, and unto the princes of the congregation, saying,

3 At'a-roth, and Di'bon, and Ja'zer, and Nim'rah, and Hesh'bon, and E-le-a'leh, and She'bam, and Ne'bo, and Be'on,

4 *Even* the country which the LORD smote before the congregation of Is'ra-el, *is* a land for cattle, and thy servants have cattle:

5 Wherefore, said they, if we have found grace in thy sight, let this land be given unto thy servants for a possession, *and* bring us not over Jor'dan.

6 ¶ And Mo'ses said unto the children of Gad and to the children of Reu'ben, Shall your brethren go to war, and shall ye sit here?

7 And wherefore discourage ye the heart of the children of Is'ra-el from going over into the land which the LORD hath given them?

8 Thus did your fathers, when I sent them from Ka'desh-bar'ne-a to see the land.

9 For when they went up unto the valley of Esh'col, and saw the land, they discouraged the heart of the children of Is'ra-el, that they should not go into the land which the LORD had given them.

10 And the LORD's anger was kindled the same time, and he sware, saying,

11 Surely none of the men that came up out of E'gypt, from twenty years old and upward, shall see the land which I sware unto A'braham, unto I'saac, and unto Ja'cob; because they have not wholly followed me:

12 Save Ca'leb the son of Je-phun'neh the Kenez-ite, and Josh'u-a the son of Nun: for they have wholly followed the LORD.

13 And the LORD's anger was kindled against Is'ra-el, and he made them wander in the wilderness forty years, until all the generation, that had done evil in the sight of the LORD, was consumed.

14 And, behold, ye are risen up in your fathers' stead, an increase of sinful men, to augment yet the fierce anger of the LORD toward Is'ra-el.

15 For if ye turn away from after him, he will yet again leave them in the wilderness; and ye shall destroy all this people.

16 ¶ And they came near unto him, and said, We will build sheepfolds here for our cattle, and cities for our little ones:

17 But we ourselves will go ready armed be-

fore the children of Is'ra-el, until we have
brought them unto their place: and our little
ones shall dwell in the fenced cities because of
the inhabitants of the land.
18 We will not return unto our houses, until
the children of Is'ra-el have inherited every man
his inheritance.
19 For we will not inherit with them on yonder side Jor'dan, or forward; because our inheritance is fallen to us on this side Jor'dan eastward.
20 ¶ And Mo'ses said unto them, If ye will do
this thing, if ye will go armed before the LORD
to war,
21 And will go all of you armed over Jor'dan
before the LORD, until he hath driven out his
enemies from before him,
22 And the land be subdued before the LORD:
then afterward ye shall return, and be guiltless
before the LORD, and before Is'ra-el; and this
land shall be your possession before the LORD.
23 But if ye will not do so, behold, ye have
sinned against the LORD: and be sure your sin
will find you out.
24 Build you cities for your little ones, and
folds for your sheep; and do that which hath
proceeded out of your mouth.
25 And the children of Gad and the children
of Reu'ben spake unto Mo'ses, saying, Thy servants will do as my lord commandeth.
26 Our little ones, our wives, our flocks, and
all our cattle, shall be there in the cities of Gil'e-
ad:
27 But thy servants will pass over, every man
armed for war, before the LORD to battle, as my
lord saith.
28 So concerning them Mo'ses commanded
E-le-a'zar the priest, and Josh'u-a the son of
Nun, and the chief fathers of the tribes of the
children of Is'ra-el:
29 And Mo'ses said unto them, If the children of Gad and the children of Reu'ben will
pass with you over Jor'dan, every man armed to
battle, before the LORD, and the land shall be
subdued before you; then ye shall give them the
land of Gil'e-ad for a possession:
30 But if they will not pass over with you
armed, they shall have possessions among you
in the land of Ca'naan.
31 And the children of Gad and the children
of Reu'ben answered, saying, As the LORD hath
said unto thy servants, so will we do.
32 We will pass over armed before the LORD
into the land of Ca'naan, that the possession of
our inheritance on this side Jor'dan *may be*
ours.
33 And Mo'ses gave unto them, *even* to the
children of Gad, and to the children of Reu'ben,
and unto half the tribe of Ma-nas'seh the son of
Jo'seph, the kingdom of Si'hon king of the Am'-
or-ites, and the kingdom of Og king of Ba'shan,
the land, with the cities thereof in the coasts,
even the cities of the country round about.
34 ¶ And the children of Gad built Di'bon,
and At'a-roth, and Ar'o-er,
35 And At'roth, Sho'phan, and Ja-a'zer, and
Jog'-be-hah,
36 And Beth-nim'rah, and Beth-ha'ran,
fenced cities: and folds for sheep.
37 And the children of Reu'ben built Hesh'-
bon, and E-le-a'leh, and Kir-jath-a'im,
38 And Ne'bo, and Ba'al-me'on, (their names
being changed,) and Shib'mah: and gave other
names unto the cities which they builded.
39 And the children of Ma'chir the son of
Ma-nas'seh went to Gil'e-ad, and took it, and
dispossessed the Am'or-ite which *was* in it.
40 And Mo'ses gave Gil'e-ad unto Ma'chir
the son of Ma-nas'seh; and he dwelt therein.
41 And Ja'ir the son of Ma-nas'seh went and
took the small towns thereof, and called them
Ha'voth-ja'ir.
42 And No'bah went and took Ke'nath, and
the villages thereof, and called it No'bah, after
his own name.

33 THESE *are* the journeys of the children
of Is'ra-el, which went forth out of the
land of E'gypt with their armies under the hand
of Mo'ses and Aar'on.
2 And Mo'ses wrote their goings out according to their journeys by the commandment of
the LORD: and these *are* their journeys according to their goings out.
3 And they departed from Ra-me'ses in the
first month, on the fifteenth day of the first
month; on the morrow after the passover the
children of Is'ra-el went out with an high hand
in the sight of all the Egyptians
4 For the E-gyptians buried all *their* firstborn, which the LORD had smitten among them:
upon their gods also the LORD executed judgments.
5 And the children of Is'ra-el removed from
Ra-me'ses, and pitched in Suc'coth.
6 And they departed from Suc'coth, and
pitched in E'tham, which *is* in the edge of the
wilderness.
7 And they removed from E'tham, and
turned again unto Pi-ha-hi'roth, which *is* before
Ba'al-ze'phon: and they pitched before Mig'dol.
8 And they departed from before Pi-ha-hi'-
roth, and passed through the midst of the sea
into the wilderness, and went three days' journey in the wilderness of E'tham, and pitched in
Ma'rah.
9 And they removed from Ma'rah, and came
unto E'lim: and in E'lim *were* twelve fountains
of water, and threescore and ten palm trees;
and they pitched there.
10 And they removed from E'lim, and encamped by the Red sea.
11 And they removed from the Red sea, and
encamped in the wilderness of Sin.
12 And they took their journey out of the wilderness of Sin, and encamped in Doph'kah.
13 And they departed from Doph'kah, and
encamped in A'lush.
14 And they removed from A'lush, and encamped at Reph'i-dim, where was no water for
the people to drink.
15 And they departed from Reph'i-dim, and
pitched in the wilderness of Si'nai.
16 And they removed from the desert of Si'-
nai, and pitched at Kib'roth-hat-ta'a-vah.
17 And they departed from Kib'roth-hat-ta'-
a-vah, and encamped at Ha-ze'roth.
18 And they departed from Ha-ze'roth, and
pitched in Rith'mah.
19 And they departed from Rith'mah, and
pitched at Rim'mon-pa'rez.
20 And they departed from Rim'mon-pa'rez,
and pitched in Lib'nah.
21 And they removed from Lib'nah, and
pitched at Ris'sah.
22 And they journeyed from Ris'sah, and
pitched in Ke-hel'a-thah.
23 And they went from Ke-hel'a-thah, and
pitched in mount Sha'pher.
24 And they removed from mount Sha'pher,
and encamped in Har'a-dah.
25 And they removed from Har'a-dah, and
pitched in Mak-he'loth.

26 And they removed from Mak-he'loth, and encamped at Ta'hath.

27 And they departed from Ta'hath, and pitched at Ta'rah.

28 And they removed from Ta'rah, and pitched in Mith'cah.

29 And they went from Mith'cah, and pitched in Hash-mo'nah.

30 And they departed from Hash-mo'nah, and encamped at Mo-se'roth.

31 And they departed from Mo-se'roth, and pitched in Ben-e-ja'a-kan.

32 And they removed from Ben-e-ja'a-kan, and encamped at Hor-ha-gid'gad.

33 And they went from Hor-ha-gid'gad, and pitched in Jot'ba-thah.

34 And they removed from Jot'ba-thah, and encamped at E-bro'nah.

35 And they departed from E-bro'nah, and encamped at E'zi-on-ga'ber.

36 And they removed from E'zi-on-ga'ber, and pitched in the wilderness of Zin, which *is* Ka'desh.

37 And they removed from Ka'desh, and pitched in mount Hor, in the edge of the land of E'dom.

38 And Aar'on the priest went up into mount Hor at the commandment of the LORD, and died there, in the fortieth year after the children of Is'ra-el were come out of the land of E'gypt, in the first *day* of the fifth month.

39 And Aar'on *was* an hundred and twenty and three years old when he died in mount Hor.

40 And king A'rad the Ca'naan-ite, which dwelt in the south in the land of Ca'naan, heard of the coming of the children of Is'ra-el.

41 And they departed from mount Hor, and pitched in Zal-mo'nah.

42 And they departed from Zal-mo'nah, and pitched in Pu'non.

43 And they departed from Pu'non, and pitched in O'both.

44 And they departed from O'both, and pitched in Ij'e-ab'a-rim, in the border of Mo'ab.

45 And they departed from I'im, and pitched in Di'bon-gad.

46 And they removed from Di'bon-gad, and encamped in Al'mon-dib-la-tha'im.

47 And they removed from Al'mon-dib-la-tha'im, and pitched in the mountains of Ab'a-rim, before Ne'bo.

48 And they departed from the mountains of Ab'a-rim, and pitched in the plains of Mo'ab by Jor'dan *near* Jer'i-cho.

49 And they pitched by Jor'dan, from Beth-jes'i-moth *even* unto A'bel-shit'tim in the plains of Mo'ab.

50 ¶ And the LORD spake unto Mo'ses in the plains of Mo'ab by Jor'dan *near* Jer'i-cho, saying,

51 Speak unto the children of Is'ra-el, and say unto them, When ye are passed over Jor'dan into the land of Ca'naan;

52 Then ye shall drive out all the inhabitants of the land from before you, and destroy all their pictures, and destroy all their molten images, and quite pluck down all their high places:

53 And ye shall dispossess *the inhabitants of* the land, and dwell therein: for I have given you the land to possess it.

54 And ye shall divide the land by lot for an inheritance among your families: *and* to the more ye shall give the more inheritance, and to the fewer ye shall give the less inheritance: every man's *inheritance* shall be in the place where his lot falleth; according to the tribes of your fathers ye shall inherit.

55 But if ye will not drive out the inhabitants of the land from before you; then it shall come to pass, that those which ye let remain of them *shall be* pricks in your eyes, and thorns in your sides, and shall vex you in the land wherein ye dwell.

56 Moreover it shall come to pass, *that* I shall do unto you, as I thought to do unto them.

34 AND the LORD spake unto Mo'ses, saying,

2 Command the children of Is'ra-el, and say unto them, When ye come into the land of Ca'naan; (this *is* the land that shall fall unto you for an inheritance, *even* the land of Ca'naan with the coasts thereof:)

3 Then your south quarter shall be from the wilderness of Zin along by the coast of E'dom, and your south border shall be the outmost coast of the salt sea eastward:

4 And your border shall turn from the south to the ascent of A-krab'bim, and pass on to Zin: and the going forth thereof shall be from the south Ka'desh-bar'ne-a, and shall go on to Ha'zar-ad'dar, and pass on to Az'mon:

5 And the border shall fetch a compass from Az'mon unto the river of E'gypt, and the goings out of it shall be at the sea.

6 And *as for* the western border, ye shall even have the great sea for a border: this shall be your west border.

7 And this shall be your north border: from the great sea ye shall point out for you mount Hor:

8 From mount Hor ye shall point out *your border* unto the entrance of Ha'math; and the goings forth of the border shall be to Zedad:

9 ¶ And the border shall go on to Ziph'ron, and the goings out of it shall be at Ha'zar-e'nan: this shall be your north border.

10 And ye shall point out your east border from Ha'zar-e'nan to She'pham:

11 And the coast shall go down from She'pham to Rib'lah, on the east side of A'in; and the border shall descend, and shall reach unto the side of the sea of Chin'ne-reth eastward:

12 And the border shall go down to Jor'dan, and the goings out of it shall be at the salt sea: this shall be your land with the coasts thereof round about.

13 And Mo'ses commanded the children of Is'ra-el, saying, This *is* the land which ye shall inherit by lot, which the LORD commanded to give unto the nine tribes, and to the half tribe:

14 For the tribe of the children of Reu'ben according to the house of their fathers, and the tribe of the children of Gad according to the house of their fathers, have received *their inheritance;* and half the tribe of Ma-nas'seh have received their inheritance:

15 The two tribes and the half tribe have received their inheritance on this side Jor'dan *near* Jer'i-cho eastward, toward the sunrising.

16 And the LORD spake unto Mo'ses, saying,

17 These *are* the names of the men which shall divide the land unto you: E-le-a'zar the priest, and Josh'u-a the son of Nun.

18 And ye shall take one prince of every tribe, to divide the land by inheritance.

19 And the names of the men *are* these: Of the tribe of Ju'dah, Ca'leb the son of Je-phun'neh.

20 And of the tribe of the children of Sim'e-on, She-mu'el the son of Am-mi'hud.

21 Of the tribe of Ben'ja-min, E-li'dad the son of Chis'lon.

22 And the prince of the tribe of the children
of Dan, Buk'ki the son of Jog'li.
23 The prince of the children of Jo'seph, for
the tribe of the children of Ma-nas'seh, Han'ni-el the son of E'phod.
24 And the prince of the tribe of the children
of E'phra-im, Ke-mu'el the son of Shiph'tan.
25 And the prince of the tribe of the children
of Zeb'u-lun, E-liz'a-phan the son of Par'nach.
26 And the prince of the tribe of the children
of Is'sa-char, Pal'ti-el the son of Az'zan.
27 And the prince of the tribe of the children
of Ash'er, A-hi'hud the son of Shel'o-mi.
28 And the prince of the tribe of the children
of Naph'ta-li, Ped'a-hel the son of Am-mi'hud.
29 These *are they* whom the LORD commanded to divide the inheritance unto the children of Is'ra-el in the land of Ca'naan.

35 AND the LORD spake unto Mo'ses in the plains of Mo'ab by Jor'dan *near* Jer'i-cho, saying,
2 Command the children of Is'ra-el, that they give unto the Le'vites of the inheritance of their possession cities to dwell in; and ye shall give *also* unto the Le'vites suburbs for the cities round about them.
3 And the cities shall they have to dwell in; and the suburbs of them shall be for their cattle, and for their goods, and for all their beasts.
4 And the suburbs of the cities, which ye shall give unto the Le'vites, *shall reach* from the wall of the city and outward a thousand cubits round about.
5 And ye shall measure from without the city on the east side two thousand cubits, and on the south side two thousand cubits, and on the west side two thousand cubits, and on the north side two thousand cubits; and the city *shall be* in the midst: this shall be to them the suburbs of the cities.
6 And among the cities which ye shall give unto the Le'vites *there shall be* six cities for refuge, which ye shall appoint for the manslayer, that he may flee thither: and to them ye shall add forty and two cities.
7 *So* all the cities which ye shall give to the Le'vites *shall be* forty and eight cities: them *shall ye give* with their suburbs.
8 And the cities which ye shall give *shall be* of the possession of the children of Is'ra-el: from *them that have* many ye shall give many; but from *them that have* few ye shall give few: every one shall give of his cities unto the Le'vites according to his inheritance which he inheriteth.
9 ¶ And the LORD spake unto Mo'ses, saying,
10 Speak unto the children of Is'ra-el, and say unto them, When ye be come over Jor'dan into the land of Ca'naan;
11 Then ye shall appoint you cities to be cities of refuge for you; that the slayer may flee thither, which killeth any person at unawares.
12 And they shall be unto you cities for refuge from the avenger; that the manslayer die not, until he stand before the congregation in judgment.
13 And of these cities which ye shall give six cities shall ye have for refuge.
14 Ye shall give three cities on this side Jor'dan, and three cities shall ye give in the land of Ca'naan, *which* shall be cities of refuge.
15 These six cities shall be a refuge, *both* for the children of Is'ra-el, and for the stranger, and for the sojourner among them: that every one that killeth any person unawares may flee thither.
16 And if he smite him with an instrument of iron, so that he die, he *is* a murderer: the murderer shall surely be put to death.
17 And if he smite him with throwing a stone, wherewith he may die, and he die, he *is* a murderer: the murderer shall surely be put to death.
18 Or *if* he smite him with an hand weapon of wood, wherewith he may die, and he die, he *is* a murderer: the murderer shall surely be put to death.
19 The revenger of blood himself shall slay the murderer: when he meeteth him, he shall slay him.
20 But if he thrust him of hatred, or hurl at him by laying of wait, that he die;
21 Or in enmity smite him with his hand, that he die: he that smote *him* shall surely be put to death; *for* he *is* a murderer: the revenger of blood shall slay the murderer, when he meeteth him.
22 But if he thrust him suddenly without enmity, or have cast upon him any thing without laying of wait,
23 Or with any stone, wherewith a man may die, seeing *him* not, and cast *it* upon him, that he die, and *was* not his enemy, neither sought his harm:
24 Then the congregation shall judge between the slayer and the revenger of blood according to these judgments:
25 And the congregation shall deliver the slayer out of the hand of the revenger of blood, and the congregation shall restore him to the city of his refuge, whither he was fled: and he shall abide in it unto the death of the high priest, which was anointed with the holy oil.
26 But if the slayer shall at any time come without the border of the city of his refuge, whither he was fled;
27 And the revenger of blood find him without the borders of the city of his refuge, and the revenger of blood kill the slayer; he shall not be guilty of blood:
28 Because he should have remained in the city of his refuge until the death of the high priest: but after the death of the high priest the slayer shall return into the land of his possession.
29 So these *things* shall be for a statute of judgment unto you throughout your generations in all your dwellings.
30 Whoso killeth any person, the murderer shall be put to death by the mouth of witnesses: but one witness shall not testify against any person *to cause him* to die.
31 Moreover ye shall take no satisfaction for the life of a murderer, which *is* guilty of death: but he shall be surely put to death.
32 And ye shall take no satisfaction for him that is fled to the city of his refuge, that he should come again to dwell in the land, until the death of the priest.
33 So ye shall not pollute the land wherein ye *are*: for blood it defileth the land: and the land cannot be cleansed of the blood that is shed therein, but by the blood of him that shed it.
34 Defile not therefore the land which ye shall inhabit, wherein I dwell: for I the LORD dwell among the children of Is'ra-el.

36 AND the chief fathers of the families of the children of Gil'e-ad, the son of Ma'-chir, the son of Ma-nas'seh, of the families of the sons of Jo'seph, came near, and spake before Mo'ses, and before the princes, the chief fathers of the children of Is'ra-el:

2 And they said, The LORD commanded my
lord to give the land for an inheritance by lot to
the children of Is'ra-el: and my lord was commanded to the LORD to give the inheritance of
Ze-lo'phe-had our brother unto his daughters.
3 And if they be married to any of the sons of
the *other* tribes of the children of Is'ra-el, then
shall their inheritance be taken from the inheritance of our fathers, and shall be put to the inheritance of the tribe whereunto they are received: so shall it be taken from the lot of our
inheritance.
4 And when the jubile of the children of Is'ra-
el shall be, then shall their inheritance be put
unto the inheritance of the tribe whereunto they
are received: so shall their inheritance be taken
away from the inheritance of the tribe of our
fathers.
5 And Mo'ses commanded the children of Is'-
ra-el according to the word of the LORD, saying,
The tribe of the sons of Jo'seph hath said well.
6 This *is* the thing which the LORD doth command concerning the daughters of Ze-lo'phe-
had, saying, Let them marry to whom they
think best; only to the family of the tribe of
their father shall they marry.
7 So shall not the inheritance of the children
of Is'ra-el remove from tribe to tribe: for every
one of the children of Is'ra-el shall keep himself
to the inheritance of the tribe of his fathers.
8 And every daughter, that possesseth an inheritance in any tribe of the children of Is'ra-el,
shall be wife unto one of the family of the tribe
of her father, that the children of Is'ra-el may
enjoy every man the inheritance of his fathers.
9 Neither shall the inheritance remove from
one tribe to another tribe; but every one of the
tribes of the children of Is'ra-el shall keep himself to his own inheritance.
10 Even as the LORD commanded Mo'ses, so
did the daughters of Ze-lo'phe-had:
11 For Mah'lah, Tir'zah, and Hog'lah, and
Mil'cah, and No'ah, the daughters of Ze-lo'phe-
had, were married unto their father's brothers'
sons:
12 *And* they were married into the families
of the sons of Ma-nas'seh the son of Jo'seph,
and their inheritance remained in the tribe of
the family of their father.
13 These *are* the commandments and the
judgments, which the LORD commanded by the
hand of Mo'ses unto the children of Is'ra-el in
the plains of Mo'ab by Jor'dan *near* Jer'i-cho.

THE FIFTH BOOK OF MOSES
COMMONLY CALLED

DEUTERONOMY

1 THESE *be* the words which Mo'ses spake
unto all Is'ra-el on this side Jor'dan in the
wilderness, in the plain over against the Red
sea, between Pa'ran, and To'phel, and La'ban,
and Ha-ze'roth, and Diz'a-hab.
2 (*There are* eleven days' *journey* from Ho'-
reb by the way of mount Se'ir unto Ka'desh-
bar'ne-a.)
3 And it came to pass in the fortieth year, in
the eleventh month, on the first *day* of the
month, *that* Mo'ses spake unto the children of
Is'ra-el, according unto all that the LORD had
given him in commandment unto them;
4 After he had slain Si'hon the king of the
Am'or-ites, which dwelt in Hesh'bon, and Og
the king of Ba'shan, which dwelt at As'ta-roth
in Ed're-i:
5 On this side Jor'dan, in the land of Mo'ab,
began Mo'ses to declare this law, saying,
6 The LORD our God spake unto us in Ho'reb,
saying, Ye have dwelt long enough in this
mount:
7 Turn you, and take your journey, and go to
the mount of the Am'or-ites, and unto all *the
places* nigh thereunto, in the plain, in the hills,
and in the vale, and in the south, and by the sea
side; to the land of the Ca'naan-ites, and unto
Leb'a-non, unto the great river, the river Eu-
phra'tes.
8 Behold, I have set the land before you: go
in and possess the land which the LORD sware
unto your fathers, A'bra-ham, I'saac, and Ja'-
cob, to give unto them and to their seed after
them.
9 ¶ And I spake unto you at that time, saying, I am not able to bear you myself alone:
10 The LORD your God hath multiplied you,
and, behold, ye *are* this day as the stars of
heaven for multitude.
11 (The LORD God of your fathers make you
a thousand times so many more as ye *are*, and
bless you, as he hath promised you!)
12 How can I myself alone bear your cum-
brance, and your burden, and your strife?
13 Take you wise men, and understanding,
and known among your tribes, and I will make
them rulers over you.
14 And ye answered me, and said, The thing
which thou hast spoken *is* good *for us* to do.
15 So I took the chief of your tribes, wise
men, and known, and made them heads over
you, captains over thousands, and captains over
hundreds, and captains over fifties, and captains over tens, and officers among your tribes.
16 And I charged your judges at that time,
saying, Hear *the causes* between your brethren,
and judge righteously between *every* man and
his brother, and the stranger *that is* with him.
17 Ye shall not respect persons in judgment;
but ye shall hear the small as well as the great;
ye shall not be afraid of the face of man; for the
judgment *is* God's: and the cause that is too
hard for you, bring *it* unto me, and I will hear it.
18 And I commanded you at that time all the
things which ye should do.
19 ¶ And when we departed from Ho'reb, we
went through all that great and terrible wilderness, which ye saw by the way of the mountain
of the Am'or-ites, as the LORD our God commanded us; and we came to Ka'desh–bar'ne-a.
20 And I said unto you, Ye are come unto the
mountain of the Am'or-ites, which the LORD our
God doth give unto us.
21 Behold, the LORD thy God hath set the
land before thee: go up *and* possess *it*, as the
LORD God of thy fathers hath said unto thee;
fear not, neither be discouraged.
22 ¶ And ye came near unto me every one of
you, and said, We will send men before us, and
they shall search us out the land, and bring us
word again by what way we must go up, and
into what cities we shall come.
23 And the saying pleased me well: and I
took twelve men of you, one of a tribe:

24 And they turned and went up into the
mountain, and came unto the valley of Esh′col,
and searched it out.
25 And they took of the fruit of the land in
their hands, and brought *it* down unto us, and
brought us word again, and said, *It is* a good
land which the LORD our God doth give us.
26 Notwithstanding ye would not go up, but
rebelled against the commandment of the LORD
your God:
27 And ye murmured in your tents, and said,
Because the LORD hated us, he hath brought us
forth out of the land of E′gypt, to deliver us into
the hand of the Am′or-ites, to destroy us.
28 Whither shall we go up? our brethren
have discouraged our heart, saying, The people
is greater and taller than we; the cities *are* great
and walled up to heaven; and moreover we
have seen the sons of the An′a-kims there.
29 Then I said unto you, Dread not, neither
be afraid of them.
30 The LORD your God which goeth before
you, he shall fight for you, according to all that
he did for you in E′gypt before your eyes;
31 And in the wilderness, where thou hast
seen how that the LORD thy God bare thee, as a
man doth bear his son, in all the way that ye
went, until ye came into this place.
32 Yet in this thing ye did not believe the
LORD your God,
33 Who went in the way before you, to
search you out a place to pitch your tents *in,* in
fire by night, to shew you by what way ye
should go, and in a cloud by day.
34 And the LORD heard the voice of your
words, and was wroth, and sware, saying,
35 Surely there shall not one of these men of
this evil generation see that good land, which I
sware to give unto your fathers,
36 Save Ca′leb the son of Je-phun′neh; he
shall see it, and to him will I give the land that
he hath trodden upon, and to his children, because he hath wholly followed the LORD.
37 Also the LORD was angry with me for your
sakes, saying, Thou also shalt not go in thither.
38 *But* Josh′u-a the son of Nun, which standeth before thee, he shall go in thither: encourage him: for he shall cause Is′ra-el to inherit it.
39 Moreover your little ones, which ye said
should be a prey, and your children, which in
that day had no knowledge between good and
evil, they shall go in thither, and unto them will
I give it, and they shall possess it.
40 But *as for* you, turn you, and take your
journey into the wilderness by the way of the
Red sea.
41 Then ye answered and said unto me, We
have sinned against the LORD, we will go up and
fight, according to all that the LORD our God
commanded us. And when ye had girded on every man his weapons of war, ye were ready to
go up into the hill.
42 And the LORD said unto me, Say unto
them, Go not up, neither fight; for I *am* not
among you; lest ye be smitten before your enemies.
43 So I spake unto you; and ye would not
hear, but rebelled against the commandment of
the LORD, and went presumptuously up into the
hill.
44 And the Am′or-ites, which dwelt in that
mountain, came out against you, and chased
you, as bees do, and destroyed you in Se′ir, *even*
unto Hor′mah.
45 And ye returned and wept before the
LORD; but the LORD would not hearken to your
voice, nor give ear unto you.
46 So ye abode in Ka′desh many days, according unto the days that ye abode *there.*

2 THEN we turned, and took our journey
into the wilderness by the way of the Red
sea, as the LORD spake unto me: and we compassed mount Se′ir many days.
2 And the LORD spake unto me, saying,
3 Ye have compassed this mountain long
enough: turn you northward.
4 And command thou the people, saying, Ye
are to pass through the coast of your brethren
the children of E′sau, which dwell in Se′ir; and
they shall be afraid of you: take ye good heed
unto yourselves therefore:
5 Meddle not with them; for I will not give
you of their land, no, not so much as a foot
breadth; because I have given mount Se′ir unto
E′sau *for* a possession.
6 Ye shall buy meat of them for money, that
ye may eat; and ye shall also buy water of them
for money, that ye may drink.
7 For the LORD thy God hath blessed thee in
all the works of thy hand: he knoweth thy walking through this great wilderness: these forty
years the LORD thy God *hath been* with thee;
thou hast lacked nothing.
8 And when we passed by from our brethren
the children of E′sau, which dwelt in Se′ir,
through the way of the plain from E′lath, and
from E′zi-on–ga′ber, we turned and passed by
the way of the wilderness of Mo′ab.
9 And the LORD said unto me, Distress not
the Mo′ab-ites, neither contend with them in
battle: for I will not give thee of their land *for* a
possession; because I have given Ar unto the
children of Lot *for* a possession.
10 The E′mims dwelt therein in times past, a
people great, and many, and tall, as the An′a-
kims;
11 Which also were accounted giants, as the
An′a-kims; but the Mo′ab-ites call them E′-
mims.
12 The Ho′rims also dwelt in Se′ir beforetime; but the children of E′sau succeeded them,
when they had destroyed them from before
them, and dwelt in their stead; as Is′ra-el did
unto the land of his possession, which the LORD
gave unto them.
13 Now rise up, *said I,* and get you over the
brook Ze′red. And we went over the brook Ze′-
red.
14 And the space in which we came from
Ka′desh–bar′ne-a, until we were come over the
brook Ze′red, *was* thirty and eight years; until
all the generation of the men of war were
wasted out from among the host, as the LORD
sware unto them.
15 For indeed the hand of the LORD was
against them, to destroy them from among the
host, until they were consumed.
16 ¶ So it came to pass, when all the men of
war were consumed and dead from among the
people,
17 That the LORD spake unto me, saying,
18 Thou art to pass over through Ar, the
coast of Mo′ab, this day:
19 And *when* thou comest nigh over against
the children of Am′mon, distress them not, nor
meddle with them: for I will not give thee of the
land of the children of Am′mon *any* possession;
because I have given it unto the children of Lot
for a possession.
20 (That also was accounted a land of giants:
giants dwelt therein in old time; and the Am′-
mon-ites call them Zam-zum′mims;
21 A people great, and many, and tall, as the

An'a-kims; but the LORD destroyed them before
them; and they succeeded them, and dwelt in
their stead:
22 As he did to the children of E'sau, which
dwelt in Se'ir, when he destroyed the Ho'rims
from before them; and they succeeded them,
and dwelt in their stead even unto this day:
23 And the A'vims which dwelt in Ha-ze'rim,
even unto Az'zah, the Caph'to-rims, which
came forth out of Caph'tor, destroyed them,
and dwelt in their stead.)
24 ¶ Rise ye up, take your journey, and pass
over the river Ar'non: behold, I have given into
thine hand Si'hon the Am'or-ite, king of Hesh'-
bon, and his land: begin to possess *it*, and contend with him in battle.
25 This day will I begin to put the dread of
thee and the fear of thee upon the nations *that*
are under the whole heaven, who shall hear report of thee, and shall tremble, and be in anguish because of thee.
26 ¶ And I sent messengers out of the wilderness of Ked'e-moth unto Si'hon king of
Hesh'bon with words of peace, saying,
27 Let me pass through thy land: I will go
along by the high way, I will neither turn unto
the right hand nor to the left.
28 Thou shalt sell me meat for money, that I
may eat; and give me water for money, that I
may drink: only I will pass through on my feet;
29 (As the children of E'sau which dwell in
Se'ir, and the Mo'ab-ites which dwell in Ar, did
unto me;) until I shall pass over Jor'dan into the
land which the LORD our God giveth us.
30 But Si'hon king of Hesh'bon would not let
us pass by him: for the LORD thy God hardened
his spirit, and made his heart obstinate, that he
might deliver him into thy hand, as *appeareth*
this day.
31 And the LORD said unto me, Behold, I
have begun to give Si'hon and his land before
thee: begin to possess, that thou mayest inherit
his land.
32 Then Si'hon came out against us, he and
all his people, to fight at Ja'haz.
33 And the LORD our God delivered him before us; and we smote him, and his sons, and all
his people.
34 And we took all his cities at that time, and
utterly destroyed the men, and the women, and
the little ones, of every city, we left none to remain:
35 Only the cattle we took for a prey unto
ourselves, and the spoil of the cities which we
took.
36 From Ar'o-er, which *is* by the brink of the
river of Ar'non, and *from* the city that *is* by the
river, even unto Gil'e-ad, there was not one city
too strong for us: the LORD our God delivered
all unto us:
37 Only unto the land of the children of Am'-
mon thou camest not, *nor* unto any place of the
river Jab'bok, nor unto the cities in the mountains, nor unto whatsoever the LORD our God
forbad us.

3 THEN we turned, and went up the way to
Ba'shan: and Og the king of Ba'shan came
out against us, he and all his people, to battle at
Ed're-i.
2 And the LORD said unto me, Fear him not:
for I will deliver him, and all his people, and his
land, into thy hand; and thou shalt do unto him
as thou didst unto Si'hon king of the Am'or-ites,
which dwelt at Hesh'bon.
3 So the LORD our God delivered into our
hands Og also, the king of Ba'shan, and all his
people: and we smote him until none was left to
him remaining.
4 And we took all his cities at that time, there
was not a city which we took not from them,
threescore cities, all the region of Ar'gob, the
kingdom of Og in Ba'shan.
5 All these cities *were* fenced with high
walls, gates, and bars; beside unwalled towns a
great many.
6 And we utterly destroyed them, as we did
unto Si'hon king of Hesh'bon, utterly destroying the men, women, and children, of every
city.
7 But all the cattle, and the spoil of the cities,
we took for a prey to ourselves.
8 And we took at that time out of the hand of
the two kings of the Am'or-ites the land that
was on this side Jor'dan, from the river of Ar'-
non unto mount Her'mon;
9 (*Which* Her'mon the Si-do'ni-ans call Sir'i-
on; and the Am'or-ites call it She'nir;)
10 All the cities of the plain, and all Gil'e-ad,
and all Ba'shan, unto Sal'chah and Ed're-i, cities
of the kingdom of Og in Ba'shan.
11 For only Og king of Ba'shan remained of
the remnant of giants; behold, his bedstead *was*
a bedstead of iron; *is* it not in Rab'bath of the
children of Am'mon? nine cubits *was* the length
thereof, and four cubits the breadth of it, after
the cubit of a man.
12 And this land, *which* we possessed at that
time, from Ar'o-er, which *is* by the river Ar'non,
and half mount Gil'e-ad, and the cities thereof,
gave I unto the Reu'ben-ites and to the Gad'ites.
13 And the rest of Gil'e-ad, and all Ba'shan,
being the kingdom of Og, gave I unto the half
tribe of Ma-nas'seh; all the region of Ar'gob,
with all Ba'shan, which was called the land of
giants.
14 Ja'ir the son of Ma-nas'seh took all the
country of Ar'gob unto the coasts of Gesh'u-ri
and Ma-ach'a-thi; and called them after his own
name, Ba'shan–ha'voth–ja'ir, unto this day.
15 And I gave Gil'e-ad unto Ma'chir.
16 And unto the Reu'ben-ites and unto the
Gad'ites I gave from Gil'e-ad even unto the
river Ar'non half the valley, and the border even
unto the river Jab'bok, *which is* the border of
the children of Am'mon;
17 The plain also, and Jor'dan, and the coast
thereof, from Chin'ne-reth even unto the sea of
the plain, *even* the salt sea, under Ash'doth–
pis'gah eastward.
18 ¶ And I commanded you at that time,
saying, The LORD your God hath given you this
land to possess it: ye shall pass over armed before your brethren the children of Is'ra-el, all
that are meet for the war.
19 But your wives, and your little ones, and
your cattle, (*for* I know that ye have much cattle,) shall abide in your cities which I have given
you;
20 Until the LORD have given rest unto your
brethren, as well as unto you, and *until* they
also possess the land which the LORD your God
hath given them beyond Jor'dan: and *then* shall
ye return every man unto his possession, which
I have given you.
21 ¶ And I commanded Josh'u-a at that time,
saying, Thine eyes have seen all that the LORD
your God hath done unto these two kings: so
shall the LORD do unto all the kingdoms whither
thou passest.
22 Ye shall not fear them: for the LORD your
God he shall fight for you.
23 And I besought the LORD at that time, saying,

24 O Lord GOD, thou hast begun to shew thy servant thy greatness, and thy mighty hand: for what God *is there* in heaven or in earth, that can do according to thy works, and according to thy might?

25 I pray thee, let me go over, and see the good land that *is* beyond Jor'dan, that goodly mountain, and Leb'a-non.

26 But the LORD was wroth with me for your sakes, and would not hear me: and the LORD said unto me, Let is suffice thee; speak no more unto me of this matter.

27 Get thee up into the top of Pis'gah, and lift up thine eyes westward, and northward, and southward, and eastward, and behold *it* with thine eyes: for thou shalt not go over this Jor'-dan.

28 But charge Josh'u-a, and encourage him, and strengthen him: for he shall go over before this people, and he shall cause them to inherit the land which thou shalt see.

29 So we abode in the valley over against Beth-pe'or.

4 NOW therefore hearken, O Is'ra-el, unto the statutes and unto the judgments, which I teach you, for to do *them,* that ye may live, and go in and possess the land which the LORD God of your fathers giveth you.

2 Ye shall not add unto the word which I command you, neither shall ye diminish *ought* from it, that ye may keep the commandments of the LORD your God which I command you.

3 Your eyes have seen what the LORD did because of Ba-al-pe'or: for all the men that followed Ba-al-pe'or, the LORD thy God hath destroyed them from among you.

4 But ye that did cleave unto the LORD your God *are* alive every one of you this day.

5 Behold, I have taught you statutes and judgments, even as the LORD my God commanded me, that ye should do so in the land whither ye go to possess it.

6 Keep therefore and do *them;* for this *is* your wisdom and your understanding in the sight of the nations, which shall hear all these statutes, and say, Surely this great nation *is* a wise and understanding people.

7 For what nation *is there so* great, who *hath* God *so* nigh unto them, as the LORD our God *is* in all *things that* we call upon him for?

8 And what nation *is there so* great, that hath statutes and judgments *so* righteous as all this law, which I set before you this day?

9 Only take heed to thyself, and keep thy soul diligently, lest thou forget the things which thine eyes have seen, and lest they depart from thy heart all the days of thy life: but teach them thy sons, and thy sons' sons;

10 *Specially* the day that thou stoodest before the LORD thy God in Ho'reb, when the LORD said unto me, Gather me the people together, and I will make them hear my words, that they may learn to fear me all the days that they shall live upon the earth, and *that* they may teach their children.

11 And ye came near and stood under the mountain; and the mountain burned with fire unto the midst of heaven, with darkness, clouds, and thick darkness.

12 And the LORD spake unto you out of the midst of the fire: ye heard the voice of the words, but saw no similitude; only *ye heard* a voice.

13 And he declared unto you his covenant, which he commanded you to perform, *even* ten commandments; and he wrote them upon two tables of stone.

14 ¶ And the LORD commanded me at that time to teach you statutes and judgments, that ye might do them in the land whither ye go over to possess it.

15 Take ye therefore good heed unto yourselves; for ye saw no manner of similitude on the day *that* the LORD spake unto you in Ho'reb out of the midst of the fire:

16 Lest ye corrupt *yourselves,* and make you a graven image, the similitude of any figure, the likeness of male or female,

17 The likeness of any beast that *is* on the earth, the likeness of any winged fowl that flieth in the air,

18 The likeness of any thing that creepeth on the ground, the likeness of any fish that *is* in the waters beneath the earth:

19 And lest thou lift up thine eyes unto heaven, and when thou seest the sun, and the moon, and the stars, *even* all the host of heaven, shouldest be driven to worship them, and serve them, which the LORD thy God hath divided unto all nations under the whole heaven.

20 But the LORD hath taken you, and brought you forth out of the iron furnace, *even* out of E'gypt, to be unto him a people of inheritance, as *ye are* this day.

21 Furthermore the LORD was angry with me for your sakes, and sware that I should not go over Jor'dan, and that I should not go in unto that good land, which the LORD thy God giveth thee *for* an inheritance:

22 But I must die in this land, I must not go over Jor'dan: but ye shall go over, and possess that good land.

23 Take heed unto yourselves, lest ye forget the covenant of the LORD your God, which he made with you, and make you a graven image, *or* the likeness of any *thing,* which the LORD thy God hath forbidden thee.

24 For the LORD thy God *is* a consuming fire, *even* a jealous God.

25 ¶ When thou shalt beget children, and children's children, and ye shall have remained long in the land, and shall corrupt *yourselves,* and make a graven image, *or* the likeness of any *thing,* and shall do evil in the sight of the LORD thy God, to provoke him to anger:

26 I call heaven and earth to witness against you this day, that ye shall soon utterly perish from off the land whereunto ye go over Jor'dan to possess it; ye shall not prolong *your* days upon it, but shall utterly be destroyed.

27 And the LORD shall scatter you among the nations, and ye shall be left few in number among the heathen, whither the LORD shall lead you.

28 And there ye shall serve gods, the work of men's hands, wood and stone, which neither see, nor hear, nor eat, nor smell.

29 But if from thence thou shalt seek the LORD thy God, thou shalt find *him,* if thou seek him with all thy heart and with all thy soul.

30 When thou art in tribulation, and all these things are come upon thee, *even* in the latter days, if thou turn to the LORD thy God, and shalt be obedient unto his voice;

31 (For the LORD thy God *is* a merciful God;) he will not forsake thee, neither destroy thee, nor forget the covenant of thy fathers which he sware unto them.

32 For ask now of the days that are past, which were before thee, since the day that God created man upon the earth, and *ask* from the one side of heaven unto the other, whether

there hath been *any such thing* as this great
thing *is*, or hath been heard like it?
33 Did *ever* people hear the voice of God
speaking out of the midst of the fire, as thou
hast heard, and live?
34 Or hath God assayed to go *and* take him a
nation from the midst of *another* nation, by
temptations, by signs, and by wonders, and by
war, and by a mighty hand, and by a stretched
out arm, and by great terrors, according to all
that the LORD your God did for you in E'gypt
before your eyes?
35 Unto thee it was shewed, that thou mightest know that the LORD he *is* God; *there is* none
else beside him.
36 Out of heaven he made thee to hear his
voice, that he might instruct thee: and upon
earth he shewed thee his great fire; and thou
heardest his words out of the midst of the fire.
37 And because he loved thy fathers, therefore he chose their seed after them, and brought
thee out in his sight with his mighty power out
of E'gypt;
38 To drive out nations from before thee
greater and mightier than thou *art*, to bring
thee in, to give thee their land *for* an inheritance, as *it is* this day.
39 Know therefore this day, and consider *it*
in thine heart, that the LORD he *is* God in
heaven above, and upon the earth beneath:
there is none else.
40 Thou shalt keep therefore his statutes,
and his commandments, which I command thee
this day, that it may go well with thee, and with
thy children after thee, and that thou mayest
prolong *thy* days upon the earth, which the
LORD thy God giveth thee, for ever.
41 ¶ Then Mo'ses severed three cities on this
side Jor'dan toward the sunrising;
42 That the slayer might flee thither, which
should kill his neighbour unawares, and hated
him not in times past; and that fleeing unto one
of these cities he might live:
43 *Namely*, Be'zer in the wilderness, in the
plain country, of the Reu'ben-ites; and Ra'moth
in Gil'e-ad, of the Gad'ites; and Go'lan in Ba'-
shan, of the Ma-nas'sites.
44 ¶ And this *is* the law which Mo'ses set before the children of Is'ra-el:
45 These *are* the testimonies, and the statutes, and the judgments, which Mo'ses spake
unto the children of Is'ra-el, after they came
forth out of E'gypt,
46 On this side Jor'dan, in the valley over
against Beth-pe'or, in the land of Si'hon king of
the Am'or-ites, who dwelt at Hesh'bon, whom
Mo'ses and the children of Is'ra-el smote, after
they were come forth out of E'gypt:
47 And they possessed his land, and the land
of Og king of Ba'shan, two kings of the Am'or-
ites, which *were* on this side Jor'dan toward the
sunrising;
48 From Ar'o-er, which *is* by the bank of the
river Ar'non, even unto mount Si'on, which *is*
Her'mon,
49 And all the plain on this side Jor'dan eastward, even unto the sea of the plain, under the
springs of Pis'gah.

5 AND Mo'ses called all Is'ra-el, and said
unto them, Hear, O Is'ra-el, the statutes
and judgments which I speak in your ears this
day, that ye may learn them, and keep, and do
them.
2 The LORD our God made a covenant with
us in Ho'reb.
3 The LORD made not this covenant with our
fathers, but with us, *even* us, who *are* all of us
here alive this day.
4 The LORD talked with you face to face in
the mount out of the midst of the fire,
5 (I stood between the LORD and you at that
time, to shew you the word of the LORD: for ye
were afraid by reason of the fire, and went not
up into the mount;) saying,
6 ¶ I *am* the LORD thy God, which brought
thee out of the land of E'gypt, from the house of
bondage.
7 Thou shalt have none other gods before
me.
8 Thou shalt not make thee *any* graven
image, *or* any likeness *of any thing* that *is* in
heaven above, or that *is* in the earth beneath, or
that *is* in the waters beneath the earth:
9 Thou shalt not bow down thyself unto
them, nor serve them: for I the LORD thy God
am a jealous God, visiting the iniquity of the
fathers upon the children unto the third and
fourth *generation* of them that hate me,
10 And shewing mercy unto thousands of
them that love me and keep my commandments.
11 Thou shalt not take the name of the LORD
thy God in vain: for the LORD will not hold *him*
guiltless that taketh his name in vain.
12 Keep the sabbath day to sanctify it, as the
LORD thy God hath commanded thee.
13 Six days thou shalt labour, and do all thy
work:
14 But the seventh day *is* the sabbath of the
LORD thy God: *in it* thou shalt not do any work,
thou, nor thy son, nor thy daughter, nor thy
manservant, nor thy maidservant, nor thine ox,
nor thine ass, nor any of thy cattle, nor thy
stranger that *is* within thy gates; that thy manservant and thy maidservant may rest as well
as thou.
15 And remember that thou wast a servant in
the land of E'gypt, and *that* the LORD thy God
brought thee out thence through a mighty hand
and by a stretched out arm: therefore the LORD
thy God commanded thee to keep the sabbath
day.
16 ¶ Honour thy father and thy mother, as
the LORD thy God hath commanded thee; that
thy days may be prolonged, and that it may go
well with thee, in the land which the LORD thy
God giveth thee.
17 Thou shalt not kill.
18 Neither shalt thou commit adultery.
19 Neither shalt thou steal.
20 Neither shalt thou bear false witness
against thy neighbour.
21 Neither shalt thou desire thy neighbour's
wife, neither shalt thou covet thy neighbour's
house, his field, or his manservant, or his maidservant, his ox, or his ass, or any *thing* that *is*
thy neighbour's.
22 ¶ These words the LORD spake unto all
your assembly in the mount out of the midst of
the fire, of the cloud, and of the thick darkness,
with a great voice: and he added no more. And
he wrote them in two tables of stone, and delivered them unto me.
23 And it came to pass, when ye heard the
voice out of the midst of the darkness, (for the
mountain did burn with fire,) that ye came near
unto me, *even* all the heads of your tribes, and
your elders;
24 And ye said, Behold, the LORD our God
hath shewed us his glory and his greatness, and
we have heard his voice out of the midst of the
fire: we have seen this day that God doth talk
with man, and he liveth.

25 Now therefore why should we die? for this
great fire will consume us: if we hear the voice
of the LORD our God any more, then we shall
die.
26 For who *is there of* all flesh, that hath
heard the voice of the living God speaking out
of the midst of the fire, as we *have,* and lived?
27 Go thou near, and hear all that the LORD
our God shall say: and speak thou unto us all
that the LORD our God shall speak unto thee;
and we will hear *it,* and do *it.*
28 And the LORD heard the voice of your
words, when ye spake unto me; and the LORD
said unto me, I have heard the voice of the
words of this people, which they have spoken
unto thee: they have well said all that they have
spoken.
29 O that there were such an heart in them,
that they would fear me, and keep all my commandments always, that it might be well with
them, and with their children for ever!
30 Go say to them, Get you into your tents
again.
31 But as for thee, stand thou here by me,
and I will speak unto thee all the commandments, and the statutes, and the judgments,
which thou shalt teach them, that they may do
them in the land which I give them to possess it.
32 Ye shall observe to do therefore as the
LORD your God hath commanded you: ye shall
not turn aside to the right hand or to the left.
33 Ye shall walk in all the ways which the
LORD your God hath commanded you, that ye
may live, and *that it may be* well with you, and
that ye may prolong *your* days in the land
which ye shall possess.

6 NOW these *are* the commandments, the
statutes, and the judgments, which the
LORD your God commanded to teach you, that
ye might do *them* in the land whither ye go to
possess it:
2 That thou mightest fear the LORD thy God,
to keep all his statutes and his commandments,
which I command thee, thou, and thy son, and
thy son's son, all the days of thy life; and that
thy days may be prolonged.
3 ¶ Hear therefore, O Is'ra-el, and observe to
do *it;* that it may be well with thee, and that ye
may increase mightily, as the LORD God of thy
fathers hath promised thee, in the land that
floweth with milk and honey.
4 Hear, O Is'ra-el: the LORD our God *is* one
LORD:
5 And thou shalt love the LORD thy God with
all thine heart, and with all thy soul, and with
all thy might.
6 And these words, which I command thee
this day, shall be in thine heart:
7 And thou shalt teach them diligently unto
thy children, and shalt talk of them when thou
sittest in thine house, and when thou walkest
by the way, and when thou liest down, and
when thou risest up.
8 And thou shalt bind them for a sign upon
thine hand, and they shall be as frontlets between thine eyes.
9 And thou shalt write them upon the posts
of thy house, and on thy gates.
10 And it shall be, when the LORD thy God
shall have brought thee into the land which he
sware unto thy fathers, to A'bra-ham, to I'saac,
and to Ja'cob, to give thee great and goodly
cities, which thou buildedst not,
11 And houses full of all good *things,* which
thou filledst not, and wells digged, which thou
diggedst not, vineyards and olive trees, which
thou plantedst not; when thou shalt have eaten
and be full;
12 *Then* beware lest thou forget the LORD,
which brought thee forth out of the land of E'-
gypt, from the house of bondage.
13 Thou shalt fear the LORD thy God, and
serve him, and shalt swear by his name.
14 Ye shall not go after other gods, of the
gods of the people which *are* round about you;
15 (For the LORD thy God *is* a jealous God
among you) lest the anger of the LORD thy God
be kindled against thee, and destroy thee from
off the face of the earth.
16 ¶ Ye shall not tempt the LORD your God,
as ye tempted *him* in Mas'sah.
17 Ye shall diligently keep the commandments of the LORD your God, and his testimonies, and his statutes, which he hath commanded thee.
18 And thou shalt do *that which is* right and
good in the sight of the LORD: that it may be
well with thee, and that thou mayest go in and
possess the good land which the LORD sware
unto thy fathers,
19 To cast out all thine enemies from before
thee, as the LORD hath spoken.
20 *And* when thy son asketh thee in time to
come, saying, What *mean* the testimonies, and
the statutes, and the judgments, which the
LORD our God hath commanded you?
21 Then thou shalt say unto thy son, We
were Pha'raoh's bondmen in E'gypt; and the
LORD brought us out of E'gypt with a mighty
hand:
22 And the LORD shewed signs and wonders,
great and sore, upon E'gypt, upon Pha'raoh, and
upon all his household, before our eyes:
23 And he brought us out from thence, that
he might bring us in, to give us the land which
he sware unto our fathers.
24 And the LORD commanded us to do all
these statutes, to fear the LORD our God, for our
good always, that he might preserve us alive, as
it is at this day.
25 And it shall be our righteousness, if we
observe to do all these commandments before
the LORD our God, as he hath commanded us.

7 WHEN the LORD thy God shall bring thee
into the land whither thou goest to possess
it, and hath cast out many nations before thee,
the Hit'tites, and the Gir'ga-shites, and the Am'-
or-ites, and the Ca'naan-ites, and the Per'iz-
zites, and the Hi'vites, and the Jeb'u-sites,
seven nations greater and mightier than thou;
2 And when the LORD thy God shall deliver
them before thee; thou shalt smite them, *and*
utterly destroy them; thou shalt make no covenant with them, nor shew mercy unto them:
3 Neither shalt thou make marriages with
them; thy daughter thou shalt not give unto his
son, nor his daughter shalt thou take unto thy
son.
4 For they will turn away thy son from following me, that they may serve other gods: so
will the anger of the LORD be kindled against
you, and destroy thee suddenly.
5 But thus shall ye deal with them; ye shall
destroy their altars, and break down their images, and cut down their groves, and burn their
graven images with fire.
6 For thou *art* an holy people unto the LORD
thy God: the LORD thy God hath chosen thee to
be a special people unto himself, above all people that *are* upon the face of the earth.
7 The LORD did not set his love upon you, nor
choose you, because ye were more in number

than any people; for ye *were* the fewest of all
people:
8 But because the LORD loved you, and because he would keep the oath which he had
sworn unto your fathers, hath the LORD brought
you out with a mighty hand, and redeemed you
out of the house of bondmen, from the hand of
Pha'raoh king of E'gypt.
9 Know therefore that the LORD thy God, he
is God, the faithful God, which keepeth covenant and mercy with them that love him and
keep his commandments to a thousand generations;
10 And repayeth them that hate him to their
face, to destroy them: he will not be slack to
him that hateth him, he will repay him to his
face.
11 Thou shalt therefore keep the commandments, and the statutes, and the judgments,
which I command thee this day, to do them.
12 ¶ Wherefore it shall come to pass, if ye
hearken to these judgments, and keep, and do
them, that the LORD thy God shall keep unto
thee the covenant and the mercy which he
sware unto thy fathers:
13 And he will love thee, and bless thee, and
multiply thee: he will also bless the fruit of thy
womb, and the fruit of thy land, thy corn, and
thy wine, and thine oil, the increase of thy kine,
and the flocks of thy sheep, in the land which he
sware unto thy fathers to give thee.
14 Thou shalt be blessed above all people:
there shall not be male or female barren among
you, or among your cattle.
15 And the LORD will take away from thee all
sickness, and will put none of the evil diseases
of E'gypt, which thou knowest, upon thee; but
will lay them upon all *them* that hate thee.
16 And thou shalt consume all the people
which the LORD thy God shall deliver thee; thine
eye shall have no pity upon them: neither shalt
thou serve their gods; for that *will be* a snare
unto thee.
17 If thou shalt say in thine heart, These nations *are* more than I; how can I dispossess
them?
18 Thou shalt not be afraid of them: *but* shalt
well remember what the LORD thy God did unto
Pha'raoh, and unto all E'gypt;
19 The great temptations which thine eyes
saw, and the signs, and the wonders, and the
mighty hand, and the stretched out arm,
whereby the LORD thy God brought thee out: so
shall the LORD thy God do unto all the people of
whom thou art afraid.
20 Moreover the LORD thy God will send the
hornet among them, until they that are left, and
hide themselves from thee, be destroyed.
21 Thou shalt not be affrighted at them: for
the LORD thy God *is* among you, a mighty God
and terrible.
22 And the LORD thy God will put out those
nations before thee by little and little: thou
mayest not consume them at once, lest the
beasts of the field increase upon thee.
23 But the LORD thy God shall deliver them
unto thee, and shall destroy them with a mighty
destruction, until they be destroyed.
24 And he shall deliver their kings into thine
hand, and thou shalt destroy their name from
under heaven: there shall no man be able to
stand before thee, until thou have destroyed
them.
25 The graven images of their gods shall ye
burn with fire: thou shalt not desire the silver or
gold *that is* on them, nor take *it* unto thee, lest
thou be snared therein: for it *is* an abomination
to the LORD thy God.
26 Neither shalt thou bring an abomination
into thine house, lest thou be a cursed thing like
it: *but* thou shalt utterly detest it, and thou shalt
utterly abhor it; for it *is* a cursed thing.

8 ALL the commandments which I command thee this day shall ye observe to do,
that ye may live, and multiply, and go in and
possess the land which the LORD sware unto
your fathers.
2 And thou shalt remember all the way
which the LORD thy God led thee these forty
years in the wilderness, to humble thee, *and* to
prove thee, to know what *was* in thine heart,
whether thou wouldest keep his commandments, or no.
3 And he humbled thee, and suffered thee to
hunger, and fed thee with manna, which thou
knewest not, neither did thy fathers know; that
he might make thee know that man doth not
live by bread only, but by every *word* that proceedeth out of the mouth of the LORD doth man
live.
4 Thy raiment waxed not old upon thee, neither did thy foot swell, these forty years.
5 Thou shalt also consider in thine heart,
that, as a man chasteneth his son, *so* the LORD
thy God chasteneth thee.
6 Therefore thou shalt keep the commandments of the LORD thy God, to walk in his ways,
and to fear him.
7 For the LORD thy God bringeth thee into a
good land, a land of brooks of water, of fountains and depths that spring out of valleys and
hills;
8 A land of wheat, and barley, and vines, and
fig trees, and pomegranates; a land of oil olive,
and honey;
9 A land wherein thou shalt eat bread without scarceness, thou shalt not lack any *thing* in
it; a land whose stones *are* iron, and out of
whose hills thou mayest dig brass.
10 When thou hast eaten and art full, then
thou shalt bless the LORD thy God for the good
land which he hath given thee.
11 Beware that thou forget not the LORD thy
God, in not keeping his commandments, and his
judgments, and his statutes, which I command
thee this day:
12 Lest *when* thou hast eaten and art full,
and hast built goodly houses, and dwelt *therein;*
13 And *when* thy herds and thy flocks multiply, and thy silver and thy gold is multiplied,
and all that thou hast is multiplied;
14 Then thine heart be lifted up, and thou
forget the LORD thy God, which brought thee
forth out of the land of E'gypt, from the house
of bondage;
15 Who led thee through that great and terrible wilderness, *wherein were* fiery serpents, and
scorpions, and drought, where *there was* no water; who brought thee forth water out of the
rock of flint;
16 Who fed thee in the wilderness with manna, which thy fathers knew not, that he might
humble thee, and that he might prove thee, to
do thee good at thy latter end;
17 And thou say in thine heart, My power
and the might of *mine* hand hath gotten me this
wealth.
18 But thou shalt remember the LORD thy
God: for *it is* he that giveth thee power to get
wealth, that he may establish his covenant
which he sware unto thy fathers, as *it is* this
day.

19 And it shall be, if thou do at all forget the LORD thy God, and walk after other gods, and serve them, and worship them, I testify against you this day that ye shall surely perish.

20 As the nations which the LORD destroyeth before your face, so shall ye perish; because ye would not be obedient unto the voice of the LORD your God.

9 HEAR, O Is'ra-el: Thou *art* to pass over Jor'dan this day, to go in to possess nations greater and mightier than thyself, cities great and fenced up to heaven,

2 A people great and tall, the children of the An'a-kims, whom thou knowest, and *of whom* thou hast heard *say,* Who can stand before the children of A'nak!

3 Understand therefore this day, that the LORD thy God *is* he which goeth over before thee; *as* a consuming fire he shall destroy them, and he shall bring them down before thy face: so shalt thou drive them out, and destroy them quickly, as the LORD hath said unto thee.

4 Speak not thou in thine heart, after that the LORD thy God hath cast them out from before thee, saying, For my righteousness the LORD hath brought me in to possess this land: but for the wickedness of these nations the LORD doth drive them out from before thee.

5 Not for thy righteousness, or for the uprightness of thine heart, dost thou go to possess their land: but for the wickedness of these nations the LORD thy God doth drive them out from before thee, and that he may perform the word which the LORD sware unto thy fathers, A'bra-ham, I'saac, and Ja'cob.

6 Understand therefore, that the LORD thy God giveth thee not this good land to possess it for thy righteousness; for thou *art* a stiffnecked people.

7 ¶ Remember, *and* forget not, how thou provokedst the LORD thy God to wrath in the wilderness: from the day that thou didst depart out of the land of E'gypt, until ye came unto this place, ye have been rebellious against the LORD.

8 Also in Ho'reb ye provoked the LORD to wrath, so that the LORD was angry with you to have destroyed you.

9 When I was gone up into the mount to receive the tables of stone, *even* the tables of the covenant which the LORD made with you, then I abode in the mount forty days and forty nights, I neither did eat bread nor drink water:

10 And the LORD delivered unto me two tables of stone written with the finger of God; and on them *was written* according to all the words, which the LORD spake with you in the mount out of the midst of the fire in the day of the assembly.

11 And it came to pass at the end of forty days and forty nights, *that* the LORD gave me the two tables of stone, *even* the tables of the covenant.

12 And the LORD said unto me, Arise, get thee down quickly from hence; for thy people which thou hast brought forth out of E'gypt have corrupted *themselves;* they are quickly turned aside out of the way which I commanded them; they have made them a molten image.

13 Furthermore the LORD spake unto me, saying, I have seen this people, and, behold, it *is* a stiffnecked people:

14 Let me alone, that I may destroy them, and blot out their name from under heaven: and I will make of thee a nation mightier and greater than they.

15 So I turned and came down from the mount, and the mount burned with fire: and the two tables of the covenant *were* in my two hands.

16 And I looked, and, behold, ye had sinned against the LORD your God, *and* had made you a molten calf: ye had turned aside quickly out of the way which the LORD had commanded you.

17 And I took the two tables, and cast them out of my two hands, and brake them before your eyes.

18 And I fell down before the LORD, as at the first, forty days and forty nights: I did neither eat bread, nor drink water, because of all your sins which ye sinned, in doing wickedly in the sight of the LORD, to provoke him to anger.

19 For I was afraid of the anger and hot displeasure, wherewith the LORD was wroth against you to destroy you. But the LORD hearkened unto me at that time also.

20 And the LORD was very angry with Aar'on to have destroyed him: and I prayed for Aar'on also the same time.

21 And I took your sin, the calf which ye had made, and burnt it with fire, and stamped it, *and* ground *it* very small, *even* until it was as small as dust: and I cast the dust thereof into the brook that descended out of the mount.

22 And at Tab'e-rah, and at Mas'sah, and at Kib'roth-hat-ta'a-vah, ye provoked the LORD to wrath.

23 Likewise when the LORD sent you from Ka'desh-bar'ne-a, saying, Go up and possess the land which I have given you; then ye rebelled against the commandment of the LORD your God, and ye believed him not, nor hearkened to his voice.

24 Ye have been rebellious against the LORD from the day that I knew you.

25 Thus I fell down before the LORD forty days and forty nights, as I fell down *at the first;* because the LORD had said he would destroy you.

26 I prayed therefore unto the LORD, and said, O Lord GOD, destroy not thy people and thine inheritance, which thou hast redeemed through thy greatness, which thou hast brought forth out of E'gypt with a mighty hand.

27 Remember thy servants, A'bra-ham, I'saac, and Ja'cob; look not unto the stubbornness of this people, nor to their wickedness, nor to their sin:

28 Lest the land whence thou broughtest us out say, Because the LORD was not able to bring them into the land which he promised them, and because he hated them, he hath brought them out to slay them in the wilderness.

29 Yet they *are* thy people and thine inheritance, which thou broughtest out by thy mighty power and by thy stretched out arm.

10 AT that time the LORD said unto me, Hew thee two tables of stone like unto the first, and come up unto me into the mount, and make thee an ark of wood.

2 And I will write on the tables the words that were in the first tables which thou brakest, and thou shalt put them in the ark.

3 And I made an ark *of* shittim wood, and hewed two tables of stone like unto the first, and went up into the mount, having the two tables in mine hand.

4 And he wrote on the tables, according to the first writing, the ten commandments, which the LORD spake unto you in the mount out of the midst of the fire in the day of the assembly: and the LORD gave them unto me.

5 And I turned myself and came down from the mount, and put the tables in the ark which I had made; and there they be, as the LORD commanded me.

6 ¶ And the children of Is'ra-el took their journey from Be-e'roth of the children of Ja'a-kan to Mo-se'ra: there Aar'on died, and there he was buried, and E-le-a'zar his son ministered in the priest's office in his stead.

7 From thence they journeyed unto Gud'go-dah; and from Gud'go-dah to Jot'bath, a land of rivers of waters.

8 ¶ At that time the LORD separated the tribe of Le'vi, to bear the ark of the covenant of the LORD, to stand before the LORD, to minister unto him, and to bless in his name, unto this day.

9 Wherefore Le'vi hath no part nor inheritance with his brethren; the LORD *is* his inheritance, according as the LORD thy God promised him.

10 And I stayed in the mount, according to the first time, forty days and forty nights; and the LORD hearkened unto me at that time also, *and* the LORD would not destroy thee.

11 And the LORD said unto me, Arise, take *thy* journey before the people, that they may go in and possess the land, which I sware unto their fathers to give unto them.

12 ¶ And now, Is'ra-el, what doth the LORD thy God require of thee, but to fear the LORD thy God, to walk in all his ways, and to love him, and to serve the LORD thy God with all thy heart and with all thy soul,

13 To keep the commandments of the LORD, and his statutes, which I command thee this day for thy good?

14 Behold, the heaven and the heaven of heavens *is* the LORD's thy God, the earth *also*, with all that therein *is*.

15 Only the LORD had a delight in thy fathers to love them, and he chose their seed after them, *even* you above all people, as *it is* this day.

16 Circumcise therefore the foreskin of your heart, and be no more stiffnecked.

17 For the LORD your God *is* God of gods, and LORD of lords, a great God, a mighty, and a terrible, which regardeth not persons, nor taketh reward:

18 He doth execute the judgment of the fatherless and widow, and loveth the stranger, in giving him food and raiment.

19 Love ye therefore the stranger: for ye were strangers in the land of E'gypt.

20 Thou shalt fear the LORD thy God; him shalt thou serve, and to him shalt thou cleave, and swear by his name.

21 He *is* thy praise, and he *is* thy God, that hath done for thee these great and terrible things, which thine eyes have seen.

22 Thy fathers went down into E'gypt with threescore and ten persons; and now the LORD thy God hath made thee as the stars of heaven for multitude.

11

THEREFORE thou shalt love the LORD thy God, and keep his charge, and his statutes, and his judgments, and his commandments, alway.

2 And know ye this day: for *I speak* not with your children which have not known, and which have not seen the chastisement of the LORD your God, his greatness, his mighty hand, and his stretched out arm,

3 And his miracles, and his acts, which he did in the midst of E'gypt unto Pha'raoh the king of E'gypt, and unto all his land;

4 And what he did unto the army of E'gypt, unto their horses, and to their chariots; how he made the water of the Red sea to overflow them as they pursued after you, and *how* the LORD hath destroyed them unto this day;

5 And what he did unto you in the wilderness, until ye came into this place;

6 And what he did unto Da'than and A-bi'-ram, the sons of E-li'ab, the son of Reu'ben: how the earth opened her mouth, and swallowed them up, and their households, and their tents, and all the substance that *was* in their possession, in the midst of all Is'ra-el:

7 But your eyes have seen all the great acts of the LORD which he did.

8 Therefore shall ye keep all the commandments which I command you this day, that ye may be strong, and go in and possess the land, whither ye go to possess it;

9 And that ye may prolong *your* days in the land, which the LORD sware unto your fathers to give unto them and to their seed, a land that floweth with milk and honey.

10 ¶ For the land, whither thou goest in to possess it, *is* not as the land of E'gypt, from whence ye came out, where thou sowedst thy seed, and wateredst *it* with thy foot, as a garden of herbs:

11 But the land, whither ye go to possess it, *is* a land of hills and valleys, *and* drinketh water of the rain of heaven:

12 A land which the LORD thy God careth for: the eyes of the LORD thy God *are* always upon it, from the beginning of the year even unto the end of the year.

13 ¶ And it shall come to pass, if ye shall hearken diligently unto my commandments which I command you this day, to love the LORD your God, and to serve him with all your heart and with all your soul,

14 That I will give *you* the rain of your land in his due season, the first rain and the latter rain, that thou mayest gather in thy corn, and thy wine, and thine oil.

15 And I will send grass in thy fields for thy cattle, that thou mayest eat and be full.

16 Take heed to yourselves, that your heart be not deceived, and ye turn aside, and serve other gods, and worship them;

17 And *then* the LORD's wrath be kindled against you, and he shut up the heaven, that there be no rain, and that the land yield not her fruit; and *lest* ye perish quickly from off the good land which the LORD giveth you.

18 ¶ Therefore shall ye lay up these my words in your heart and in your soul, and bind them for a sign upon your hand, that they may be as frontlets between your eyes.

19 And ye shall teach them your children, speaking of them when thou sittest in thine house, and when thou walkest by the way, when thou liest down, and when thou risest up.

20 And thou shalt write them upon the door posts of thine house, and upon thy gates:

21 That your days may be multiplied, and the days of your children, in the land which the LORD sware unto your fathers to give them, as the days of heaven upon the earth.

22 ¶ For if ye shall diligently keep all these commandments which I command you, to do them, to love the LORD your God, to walk in all his ways, and to cleave unto him;

23 Then will the LORD drive out all these nations from before you, and ye shall possess greater nations and mightier than yourselves.

24 Every place whereon the soles of your feet shall tread shall be yours: from the wilderness and Leb'a-non, from the river, the river Eu-phra'tes, even unto the uttermost sea shall your coast be.

25 There shall no man be able to stand before you: *for* the LORD your God shall lay the fear of you and the dread of you upon all the land that ye shall tread upon, as he hath said unto you.

26 ¶ Behold, I set before you this day a blessing and a curse;

27 A blessing, if ye obey the commandments of the LORD your God, which I command you this day:

28 And a curse, if ye will not obey the commandments of the LORD your God, but turn aside out of the way which I command you this day, to go after other gods, which ye have not known.

29 And it shall come to pass, when the LORD thy God hath brought thee in unto the land whither thou goest to possess it, that thou shalt put the blessing upon mount Ger'i-zim, and the curse upon mount E'bal.

30 *Are* they not on the other side Jor'dan, by the way where the sun goeth down, in the land of the Ca'naan-ites, which dwell in the champaign over against Gil'gal, beside the plains of Mo'reh?

31 For ye shall pass over Jor'dan to go in to possess the land which the LORD your God giveth you, and ye shall possess it, and dwell therein.

32 And ye shall observe to do all the statutes and judgments which I set before you this day.

12 THESE *are* the statutes and judgments, which ye shall observe to do in the land, which the LORD God of thy fathers giveth thee to possess it, all the days that ye live upon the earth.

2 Ye shall utterly destroy all the places, wherein the nations which ye shall possess served their gods, upon the high mountains, and upon the hills, and under every green tree:

3 And ye shall overthrow their altars, and break their pillars, and burn their groves with fire; and ye shall hew down the graven images of their gods, and destroy the names of them out of that place.

4 Ye shall not do so unto the LORD your God.

5 But unto the place which the LORD your God shall choose out of all your tribes to put his name there, *even* unto his habitation shall ye seek, and thither thou shalt come:

6 And thither ye shall bring your burnt offerings, and your sacrifices, and your tithes, and heave offerings of your hand, and your vows, and your freewill offerings, and the firstlings of your herds and of your flocks:

7 And there ye shall eat before the LORD your God, and ye shall rejoice in all that ye put your hand unto, ye and your households, wherein the LORD thy God hath blessed thee.

8 Ye shall not do after all *the things* that we do here this day, every man whatsoever *is* right in his own eyes.

9 For ye are not as yet come to the rest and to the inheritance, which the LORD your God giveth you.

10 But *when* ye go over Jor'dan, and dwell in the land which the LORD your God giveth you to inherit, and *when* he giveth you rest from all your enemies round about, so that ye dwell in safety;

11 Then there shall be a place which the LORD your God shall choose to cause his name to dwell there; thither shall ye bring all that I command you; your burnt offerings, and your sacrifices, your tithes, and the heave offering of your hand, and all your choice vows which ye vow unto the LORD:

12 And ye shall rejoice before the LORD your God, ye, and your sons, and your daughters, and your menservants, and your maidservants, and the Le'vite that *is* within your gates; forasmuch as he hath no part nor inheritance with you.

13 Take heed to thyself that thou offer not thy burnt offerings in every place that thou seest:

14 But in the place which the LORD shall choose in one of thy tribes, there thou shalt offer thy burnt offerings, and there thou shalt do all that I command thee.

15 Notwithstanding thou mayest kill and eat flesh in all thy gates, whatsoever thy soul lusteth after, according to the blessing of the LORD thy God which he hath given thee: the unclean and the clean may eat thereof, as of the roebuck, and as of the hart.

16 Only ye shall not eat the blood; ye shall pour it upon the earth as water.

17 ¶ Thou mayest not eat within thy gates the tithe of thy corn, or of thy wine, or of thy oil, or the firstlings of thy herds or of thy flock, nor any of thy vows which thou vowest, nor thy freewill offerings, or heave offering of thine hand:

18 But thou must eat them before the LORD thy God in the place which the LORD thy God shall choose, thou, and thy son, and thy daughter, and thy manservant, and thy maidservant, and the Le'vite that *is* within thy gates: and thou shalt rejoice before the LORD thy God in all that thou puttest thine hands unto.

19 Take heed to thyself that thou forsake not the Le'vite as long as thou livest upon the earth.

20 ¶ When the LORD thy God shall enlarge thy border, as he hath promised thee, and thou shalt say, I will eat flesh, because thy soul longeth to eat flesh; thou mayest eat flesh, whatsoever thy soul lusteth after.

21 If the place which the LORD thy God hath chosen to put his name there be too far from thee, then thou shalt kill of thy herd and of thy flock, which the LORD hath given thee, as I have commanded thee, and thou shalt eat in thy gates whatsoever thy soul lusteth after.

22 Even as the roebuck and the hart is eaten, so thou shalt eat them: the unclean and the clean shall eat *of* them alike.

23 Only be sure that thou eat not the blood: for the blood *is* the life; and thou mayest not eat the life with the flesh.

24 Thou shalt not eat it; thou shalt pour it upon the earth as water.

25 Thou shalt not eat it; that it may go well with thee, and with thy children after thee, when thou shalt do *that which is* right in the sight of the LORD.

26 Only thy holy things which thou hast, and thy vows, thou shalt take, and go unto the place which the LORD shall choose:

27 And thou shalt offer thy burnt offerings, the flesh and the blood, upon the altar of the LORD thy God: and the blood of thy sacrifices shall be poured out upon the altar of the LORD thy God, and thou shalt eat the flesh.

28 Observe and hear all these words which I command thee, that it may go well with thee, and with thy children after thee for ever, when thou doest *that which is* good and right in the sight of the LORD thy God.

29 ¶ When the LORD thy God shall cut off the
nations from before thee, whither thou goest to
possess them, and thou succeedest them, and
dwellest in their land;
30 Take heed to thyself that thou be not
snared by following them, after that they be destroyed from before thee; and that thou enquire
not after their gods, saying, How did these nations serve their gods? even so will I do likewise.
31 Thou shalt not do so unto the LORD thy
God: for every abomination to the LORD, which
he hateth, have they done unto their gods; for
even their sons and their daughters they have
burnt in the fire to their gods.
32 What thing soever I command you, observe to do it: thou shalt not add thereto, nor
diminish from it.

13 IF there arise among you a prophet, or a
dreamer of dreams, and giveth thee a
sign or a wonder,
2 And the sign or the wonder come to pass,
whereof he spake unto thee, saying, Let us go
after other gods, which thou hast not known,
and let us serve them;
3 Thou shalt not hearken unto the words of
that prophet, or that dreamer of dreams: for the
LORD your God proveth you, to know whether
ye love the LORD your God with all your heart
and with all your soul.
4 Ye shall walk after the LORD your God, and
fear him, and keep his commandments, and
obey his voice, and ye shall serve him, and
cleave unto him.
5 And that prophet, or that dreamer of
dreams, shall be put to death; because he hath
spoken to turn *you* away from the LORD your
God, which brought you out of the land of E′-
gypt, and redeemed you out of the house of
bondage, to thrust thee out of the way which
the LORD thy God commanded thee to walk in.
So shalt thou put the evil away from the midst
of thee.
6 ¶ If thy brother, the son of thy mother, or
thy son, or thy daughter, or the wife of thy bosom, or thy friend, which *is* as thine own soul,
entice thee secretly, saying, Let us go and serve
other gods, which thou hast not known, thou,
nor thy fathers;
7 *Namely*, of the gods of the people which
are round about you, nigh unto thee, or far off
from thee, from the *one* end of the earth even
unto the *other* end of the earth;
8 Thou shalt not consent unto him, nor
hearken unto him; neither shall thine eye pity
him, neither shalt thou spare, neither shalt thou
conceal him:
9 But thou shalt surely kill him; thine hand
shall be first upon him to put him to death, and
afterwards the hand of all the people.
10 And thou shalt stone him with stones, that
he die; because he hath sought to thrust thee
away from the LORD thy God, which brought
thee out of the land of E′gypt, from the house of
bondage.
11 And all Is′ra-el shall hear, and fear, and
shall do no more any such wickedness as this is
among you.
12 ¶ If thou shalt hear *say* in one of thy
cities, which the LORD thy God hath given thee
to dwell there, saying,
13 *Certain* men, the children of Be′li-al, are
gone out from among you, and have withdrawn
the inhabitants of their city, saying, Let us go
and serve other gods, which ye have not known;
14 Then shalt thou enquire, and make search,
and ask diligently; and, behold, *if it be* truth,
and the thing certain, *that* such abomination is
wrought among you;
15 Thou shalt surely smite the inhabitants of
that city with the edge of the sword, destroying
it utterly, and all that *is* therein, and the cattle
thereof, with the edge of the sword.
16 And thou shalt gather all the spoil of it
into the midst of the street thereof, and shalt
burn with fire the city, and all the spoil thereof
every whit, for the LORD thy God: and it shall be
an heap for ever; it shall not be built again.
17 And there shall cleave nought of the
cursed thing to thine hand: that the LORD may
turn from the fierceness of his anger, and shew
thee mercy, and have compassion upon thee,
and multiply thee, as he hath sworn unto thy
fathers;
18 When thou shalt hearken to the voice of
the LORD thy God, to keep all his commandments which I command thee this day, to do
that which is right in the eyes of the LORD thy
God.

14 YE *are* the children of the LORD your
God: ye shall not cut yourselves, nor
make any baldness between your eyes for the
dead.
2 For thou *art* an holy people unto the LORD
thy God, and the LORD hath chosen thee to be a
peculiar people unto himself, above all the nations that *are* upon the earth.
3 ¶ Thou shalt not eat any abominable thing.
4 These *are* the beasts which ye shall eat: the
ox, the sheep, and the goat,
5 The hart, and the roebuck, and the fallow
deer, and the wild goat, and the pygarg, and the
wild ox, and the chamois.
6 And every beast that parteth the hoof, and
cleaveth the cleft into two claws, *and* cheweth
the cud among beasts, that ye shall eat.
7 Nevertheless these ye shall not eat of them
that chew the cud, or of them that divide the
cloven hoof; *as* the camel, and the hare, and the
coney: for they chew the cud, but divide not the
hoof; *therefore* they *are* unclean unto you.
8 And the swine, because it divideth the
hoof, yet cheweth not the cud, it *is* unclean unto
you: ye shall not eat of their flesh, nor touch
their dead carcase.
9 ¶ These ye shall eat of all that *are* in the
waters: all that have fins and scales shall ye eat:
10 And whatsoever hath not fins and scales
ye may not eat; it *is* unclean unto you.
11 ¶ *Of* all clean birds ye shall eat.
12 But these *are they* of which ye shall not
eat: the eagle, and the ossifrage, and the ospray,
13 And the glede, and the kite, and the vulture after his kind,
14 And every raven after his kind,
15 And the owl, and the night hawk, and the
cuckow, and the hawk after his kind,
16 The little owl, and the great owl, and the
swan,
17 And the pelican, and the gier eagle, and
the cormorant,
18 And the stork, and the heron after her
kind, and the lapwing, and the bat.
19 And every creeping thing that flieth *is* unclean unto you: they shall not be eaten.
20 *But of* all clean fowls ye may eat.
21 ¶ Ye shall not eat *of* any thing that dieth
of itself: thou shalt give it unto the stranger that
is in thy gates, that he may eat it; or thou mayest sell it unto an alien: for thou *art* an holy
people unto the LORD thy God. Thou shalt not
seethe a kid in his mother's milk.

22 Thou shalt truly tithe all the increase of
thy seed, that the field bringeth forth year by
year.
23 And thou shalt eat before the LORD thy
God, in the place which he shall choose to place
his name there, the tithe of thy corn, of thy
wine, and of thine oil, and the firstlings of thy
herds and of thy flocks; that thou mayest learn
to fear the LORD thy God always.
24 And if the way be too long for thee, so
that thou art not able to carry it; *or* if the place
be too far from thee, which the LORD thy God
shall choose to set his name there, when the
LORD thy God hath blessed thee:
25 Then shalt thou turn *it* into money, and
bind up the money in thine hand, and shalt go
unto the place which the LORD thy God shall
choose:
26 And thou shalt bestow that money for
whatsoever thy soul lusteth after, for oxen, or
for sheep, or for wine, or for strong drink, or for
whatsoever thy soul desireth: and thou shalt eat
there before the LORD thy God, and thou shalt
rejoice, thou, and thine household,
27 And the Le'vite that *is* within thy gates;
thou shalt not forsake him; for he hath no part
nor inheritance with thee.
28 ¶ At the end of three years thou shalt
bring forth all the tithe of thine increase the
same year, and shalt lay *it* up within thy gates:
29 And the Le'vite, (because he hath no part
nor inheritance with thee,) and the stranger,
and the fatherless, and the widow, which *are*
within thy gates, shall come, and shall eat and
be satisfied; that the LORD thy God may bless
thee in all the work of thine hand which thou
doest.

15 AT the end of *every* seven years thou
shalt make a release.
2 And this *is* the manner of the release: Every creditor that lendeth *ought* unto his neighbour shall release *it;* he shall not exact *it* of his
neighbour, or of his brother; because it is called
the LORD's release.
3 Of a foreigner thou mayest exact *it again:*
but *that* which is thine with thy brother thine
hand shall release;
4 Save when there shall be no poor among
you; for the LORD shall greatly bless thee in the
land which the LORD thy God giveth thee *for* an
inheritance to possess it:
5 Only if thou carefully hearken unto the
voice of the LORD thy God, to observe to do all
these commandments which I command thee
this day.
6 For the LORD thy God blesseth thee, as he
promised thee: and thou shalt lend unto many
nations, but thou shalt not borrow; and thou
shalt reign over many nations, but they shall
not reign over thee.
7 ¶ If there be among you a poor man of one
of thy brethren within any of thy gates in thy
land which the LORD thy God giveth thee, thou
shalt not harden thine heart, nor shut thine
hand from thy poor brother:
8 But thou shalt open thine hand wide unto
him, and shalt surely lend him sufficient for his
need, *in that* which he wanteth.
9 Beware that there be not a thought in thy
wicked heart, saying, The seventh year, the
year of release, is at hand; and thine eye be evil
against thy poor brother, and thou givest him
nought; and he cry unto the LORD against thee,
and it be sin unto thee.
10 Thou shalt surely give him, and thine
heart shall not be grieved when thou givest
unto him: because that for this thing the LORD
thy God shall bless thee in all thy works, and in
all that thou puttest thine hand unto.
11 For the poor shall never cease out of the
land: therefore I command thee, saying, Thou
shalt open thine hand wide unto thy brother, to
thy poor, and to thy needy, in thy land.
12 ¶ *And* if thy brother, an He'brew man, or
an He'brew woman, be sold unto thee, and
serve thee six years; then in the seventh year
thou shalt let him go free from thee.
13 And when thou sendest him out free from
thee, thou shalt not let him go away empty:
14 Thou shalt furnish him liberally out of thy
flock, and out of thy floor, and out of thy winepress: *of that* wherewith the LORD thy God hath
blessed thee thou shalt give unto him.
15 And thou shalt remember that thou wast
a bondman in the land of E'gypt, and the LORD
thy God redeemed thee: therefore I command
thee this thing to day.
16 And it shall be, if he say unto thee, I will
not go away from thee; because he loveth thee
and thine house, because he is well with thee;
17 Then thou shalt take an aul, and thrust *it*
through his ear unto the door, and he shall be
thy servant for ever. And also unto thy maidservant thou shalt do likewise.
18 It shall not seem hard unto thee, when
thou sendest him away free from thee; for he
hath been worth a double hired servant *to thee,*
in serving thee six years: and the LORD thy God
shall bless thee in all that thou doest.
19 ¶ All the firstling males that come of thy
herd and of thy flock thou shalt sanctify unto
the LORD thy God: thou shalt do no work with
the firstling of thy bullock, nor shear the firstling of thy sheep.
20 Thou shalt eat *it* before the LORD thy God
year by year in the place which the LORD shall
choose, thou and thy household.
21 And if there be *any* blemish therein, *as if
it be* lame, or blind, *or have* any ill blemish, thou
shalt not sacrifice it unto the LORD thy God.
22 Thou shalt eat it within thy gates: the unclean and the clean *person shall eat it* alike, as
the roebuck, and as the hart.
23 Only thou shalt not eat the blood thereof;
thou shalt pour it upon the ground as water.

16 OBSERVE the month of A'bib, and keep
the passover unto the LORD thy God: for
in the month of A'bib the LORD thy God brought
thee forth out of E'gypt by night.
2 Thou shalt therefore sacrifice the passover
unto the LORD thy God, of the flock and the
herd, in the place which the LORD shall choose
to place his name there.
3 Thou shalt eat no leavened bread with it;
seven days shalt thou eat unleavened bread
therewith, *even* the bread of affliction; for thou
camest forth out of the land of E'gypt in haste:
that thou mayest remember the day when thou
camest forth out of the land of E'gypt all the
days of thy life.
4 And there shall be no leavened bread seen
with thee in all thy coast seven days; neither
shall there *any thing* of the flesh, which thou
sacrificedst the first day at even, remain all
night until the morning.
5 Thou mayest not sacrifice the passover
within any of thy gates, which the LORD thy
God giveth thee:
6 But at the place which the LORD thy God
shall choose to place his name in, there thou
shalt sacrifice the passover at even, at the going

down of the sun, at the season that thou camest
forth out of E'gypt.
7 And thou shalt roast and eat *it* in the place
which the LORD thy God shall choose: and thou
shalt turn in the morning, and go unto thy tents.
8 Six days thou shalt eat unleavened bread:
and on the seventh day *shall be* a solemn assembly to the LORD thy God: thou shalt do no
work *therein.*
9 ¶ Seven weeks shalt thou number unto
thee: begin to number the seven weeks from
such time as thou beginnest *to put* the sickle to
the corn.
10 And thou shalt keep the feast of weeks
unto the LORD thy God with a tribute of a freewill offering of thine hand, which thou shalt
give *unto the LORD thy God,* according as the
LORD thy God hath blessed thee:
11 And thou shalt rejoice before the LORD
thy God, thou, and thy son, and thy daughter,
and thy manservant, and thy maidservant, and
the Le'vite that *is* within thy gates, and the
stranger, and the fatherless, and the widow,
that *are* among you, in the place which the
LORD thy God hath chosen to place his name
there.
12 And thou shalt remember that thou wast
a bondman in E'gypt: and thou shalt observe
and do these statutes.
13 ¶ Thou shalt observe the feast of tabernacles seven days, after that thou hast gathered in
thy corn and thy wine:
14 And thou shalt rejoice in thy feast, thou,
and thy son, and thy daughter, and thy manservant, and thy maidservant, and the Le'vite, the
stranger, and the fatherless, and the widow,
that *are* within thy gates.
15 Seven days shalt thou keep a solemn feast
unto the LORD thy God in the place which the
LORD shall choose: because the LORD thy God
shall bless thee in all thine increase, and in all
the works of thine hands, therefore thou shalt
surely rejoice.
16 ¶ Three times in a year shall all thy males
appear before the LORD thy God in the place
which he shall choose; in the feast of unleavened bread, and in the feast of weeks, and in the
feast of tabernacles: and they shall not appear
before the LORD empty:
17 Every man *shall give* as he is able, according to the blessing of the LORD thy God which
he hath given thee.
18 ¶ Judges and officers shalt thou make
thee in all thy gates, which the LORD thy God
giveth thee, throughout thy tribes: and they
shall judge the people with just judgment.
19 Thou shalt not wrest judgment; thou shalt
not respect persons, neither take a gift: for a
gift doth blind the eyes of the wise, and pervert
the words of the righteous.
20 That which is altogether just shalt thou
follow, that thou mayest live, and inherit the
land which the LORD thy God giveth thee.
21 ¶ Thou shalt not plant thee a grove of any
trees near unto the altar of the LORD thy God,
which thou shalt make thee.
22 Neither shalt thou set thee up *any* image;
which the LORD thy God hateth.

17 THOU shalt not sacrifice unto the LORD
thy God *any* bullock, or sheep, wherein
is blemish, *or* any evilfavouredness: for that *is*
an abomination unto the LORD thy God.
2 ¶ If there be found among you, within any
of thy gates which the LORD thy God giveth
thee, man or woman, that hath wrought wickedness in the sight of the LORD thy God, in
transgressing his covenant,
3 And hath gone and served other gods, and
worshipped them, either the sun, or moon, or
any of the host of heaven, which I have not
commanded;
4 And it be told thee, and thou hast heard *of
it,* and enquired diligently, and, behold, *it be*
true, *and* the thing certain, *that* such abomination is wrought in Is'ra-el:
5 Then shalt thou bring forth that man or
that woman, which have committed that
wicked thing, unto thy gates, *even* that man or
that woman, and shalt stone them with stones,
till they die.
6 At the mouth of two witnesses, or three
witnesses, shall he that is worthy of death be
put to death; *but* at the mouth of one witness he
shall not be put to death.
7 The hands of the witnesses shall be first
upon him to put him to death, and afterward
the hands of all the people. So thou shalt put
the evil away from among you.
8 ¶ If there arise a matter too hard for thee
in judgment, between blood and blood, between
plea and plea, and between stroke and stroke,
being matters of controversy within thy gates:
then shalt thou arise, and get thee up into the
place which the LORD thy God shall choose;
9 And thou shalt come unto the priests the
Le'vites, and unto the judge that shall be in
those days, and enquire; and they shall shew
thee the sentence of judgment:
10 And thou shalt do according to the sentence, which they of that place which the LORD
shall choose shall shew thee; and thou shalt observe to do according to all that they inform
thee:
11 According to the sentence of the law
which they shall teach thee, and according to
the judgment which they shall tell thee, thou
shalt do: thou shalt not decline from the sentence which they shall shew thee, *to* the right
hand, nor *to* the left.
12 And the man that will do presumptuously,
and will not hearken unto the priest that standeth to minister there before the LORD thy God,
or unto the judge, even that man shall die: and
thou shalt put away the evil from Is'ra-el.
13 And all the people shall hear, and fear,
and do no more presumptuously.
14 ¶ When thou art come unto the land
which the LORD thy God giveth thee, and shalt
possess it, and shalt dwell therein, and shalt
say, I will set a king over me, like as all the
nations that *are* about me;
15 Thou shalt in any wise set *him* king over
thee, whom the LORD thy God shall choose: *one*
from among thy brethren shalt thou set king
over thee: thou mayest not set a stranger over
thee, which *is* not thy brother.
16 But he shall not multiply horses to himself, nor cause the people to return to E'gypt, to
the end that he should multiply horses: forasmuch as the LORD hath said unto you, Ye shall
henceforth return no more that way.
17 Neither shall he multiply wives to himself,
that his heart turn not away: neither shall he
greatly multiply to himself silver and gold.
18 And it shall be, when he sitteth upon the
throne of his kingdom, that he shall write him a
copy of this law in a book out of *that which is*
before the priests the Le'vites:
19 And it shall be with him, and he shall read
therein all the days of his life: that he may learn
to fear the LORD his God, to keep all the words
of this law and these statutes, to do them:

20 That his heart be not lifted up above his brethren, and that he turn not aside from the commandment, *to* the right hand, or *to* the left: to the end that he may prolong *his* days in his kingdom, he, and his children, in the midst of Is′ra-el.

18 THE priests the Le′vites, *and* all the tribe of Le′vi, shall have no part nor inheritance with Is′ra-el: they shall eat the offerings of the LORD made by fire, and his inheritance.

2 Therefore shall they have no inheritance among their brethren: the LORD *is* their inheritance, as he hath said unto them.

3 ¶ And this shall be the priest's due from the people, from them that offer a sacrifice, whether *it be* ox or sheep; and they shall give unto the priest the shoulder, and the two cheeks, and the maw.

4 The firstfruit *also* of thy corn, of thy wine, and of thine oil, and the first of the fleece of thy sheep, shalt thou give him.

5 For the LORD thy God hath chosen him out of all thy tribes, to stand to minister in the name of the LORD, him and his sons for ever.

6 ¶ And if a Le′vite come from any of thy gates out of all Is′ra-el, where he sojourned, and come with all the desire of his mind unto the place which the LORD shall choose;

7 Then he shall minister in the name of the LORD his God, as all his brethren the Le′vites *do*, which stand there before the LORD.

8 They shall have like portions to eat, beside that which cometh of the sale of his patrimony.

9 ¶ When thou art come into the land which the LORD thy God giveth thee, thou shalt not learn to do after the abominations of those nations.

10 There shall not be found among you *any one* that maketh his son or his daughter to pass through the fire, *or* that useth divination, *or* an observer of times, or an enchanter, or a witch,

11 Or a charmer, or a consulter with familiar spirits, or a wizard, or a necromancer.

12 For all that do these things *are* an abomination unto the LORD: and because of these abominations the LORD thy God doth drive them out from before thee.

13 Thou shalt be perfect with the LORD thy God.

14 For these nations, which thou shalt possess, hearkened unto observers of times, and unto diviners: but as for thee, the LORD thy God hath not suffered thee so *to do*.

15 ¶ The LORD thy God will raise up unto thee a Prophet from the midst of thee, of thy brethren, like unto me; unto him ye shall hearken;

16 According to all that thou desiredst of the LORD thy God in Ho′reb in the day of the assembly, saying, Let me not hear again the voice of the LORD my God, neither let me see this great fire any more, that I die not.

17 And the LORD said unto me, They have well *spoken that* which they have spoken.

18 I will raise them up a Prophet from among their brethren, like unto thee, and will put my words in his mouth; and he shall speak unto them all that I shall command him.

19 And it shall come to pass, *that* whosoever will not hearken unto my words which he shall speak in my name, I will require *it* of him.

20 But the prophet, which shall presume to speak a word in my name, which I have not commanded him to speak, or that shall speak in the name of other gods, even that prophet shall die.

21 And if thou say in thine heart, How shall we know the word which the LORD hath not spoken?

22 When a prophet speaketh in the name of the LORD, if the thing follow not, nor come to pass, that *is* the thing which the LORD hath not spoken, *but* the prophet hath spoken it presumptuously: thou shalt not be afraid of him.

19 WHEN the LORD thy God hath cut off the nations, whose land the LORD thy God giveth thee, and thou succeedest them, and dwellest in their cities, and in their houses;

2 Thou shalt separate three cities for thee in the midst of thy land, which the LORD thy God giveth thee to possess it.

3 Thou shalt prepare thee a way, and divide the coasts of thy land, which the LORD thy God giveth thee to inherit, into three parts, that every slayer may flee thither.

4 ¶ And this *is* the case of the slayer, which shall flee thither, that he may live: Whoso killeth his neighbour ignorantly, whom he hated not in time past;

5 As when a man goeth into the wood with his neighbour to hew wood, and his hand fetcheth a stroke with the ax to cut down the tree, and the head slippeth from the helve, and lighteth upon his neighbour, that he die; he shall flee unto one of those cities, and live:

6 Lest the avenger of the blood pursue the slayer, while his heart is hot, and overtake him, because the way is long, and slay him; whereas he *was* not worthy of death, inasmuch as he hated him not in time past.

7 Wherefore I command thee, saying, Thou shalt separate three cities for thee.

8 And if the LORD thy God enlarge thy coast, as he hath sworn unto thy fathers, and give thee all the land which he promised to give unto thy fathers;

9 If thou shalt keep all these commandments to do them, which I command thee this day, to love the LORD thy God, and to walk ever in his ways; then shalt thou add three cities more for thee, beside these three:

10 That innocent blood be not shed in thy land, which the LORD thy God giveth thee *for* an inheritance, and *so* blood be upon thee.

11 ¶ But if any man hate his neighbour, and lie in wait for him, and rise up against him, and smite him mortally that he die, and fleeth into one of these cities:

12 Then the elders of his city shall send and fetch him thence, and deliver him into the hand of the avenger of blood, that he may die.

13 Thine eye shall not pity him, but thou shalt put away *the guilt of* innocent blood from Is′ra-el, that it may go well with thee.

14 ¶ Thou shalt not remove thy neighbour's landmark, which they of old time have set in thine inheritance, which thou shalt inherit in the land that the LORD thy God giveth thee to possess it.

15 ¶ One witness shall not rise up against a man for any iniquity, or for any sin, in any sin that he sinneth: at the mouth of two witnesses, or at the mouth of three witnesses, shall the matter be established.

16 ¶ If a false witness rise up against any man to testify against him *that which is* wrong;

17 Then both the men, between whom the controversy *is*, shall stand before the LORD, before the priests and the judges, which shall be in those days;

18 And the judges shall make diligent inquisition: and, behold, *if* the witness *be* a false witness, *and* hath testified falsely against his brother;

19 Then shall ye do unto him, as he had thought to have done unto his brother: so shalt thou put the evil away from among you.

20 And those which remain shall hear, and fear, and shall henceforth commit no more any such evil among you.

21 And thine eye shall not pity; *but* life *shall go* for life, eye for eye, tooth for tooth, hand for hand, foot for foot.

20 WHEN thou goest out to battle against thine enemies, and seest horses, and chariots, *and* a people more than thou, be not afraid of them: for the LORD thy God *is* with thee, which brought thee up out of the land of E'gypt.

2 And it shall be, when ye are come nigh unto the battle, that the priest shall approach and speak unto the people,

3 And shall say unto them, Hear, O Is'ra-el, ye approach this day unto battle against your enemies: let not your hearts faint, fear not, and do not tremble, neither be ye terrified because of them;

4 For the LORD your God *is* he that goeth with you, to fight for you against your enemies, to save you.

5 ¶ And the officers shall speak unto the people, saying, What man *is there* that hath built a new house, and hath not dedicated it? let him go and return to his house, lest he die in the battle, and another man dedicate it.

6 And what man *is he* that hath planted a vineyard, and hath not *yet* eaten of it? let him *also* go and return unto his house, lest he die in the battle, and another man eat of it.

7 And what man *is there* that hath betrothed a wife, and hath not taken her? let him go and return unto his house, lest he die in the battle, and another man take her.

8 And the officers shall speak further unto the people, and they shall say, What man *is there that is* fearful and fainthearted? let him go and return unto his house, lest his brethren's heart faint as well as his heart.

9 And it shall be, when the officers have made an end of speaking unto the people, that they shall make captains of the armies to lead the people.

10 ¶ When thou comest nigh unto a city to fight against it, then proclaim peace unto it.

11 And it shall be, if it make thee answer of peace, and open unto thee, then it shall be, *that* all the people *that is* found therein shall be tributaries unto thee, and they shall serve thee.

12 And if it will make no peace with thee, but will make war against thee, then thou shalt besiege it:

13 And when the LORD thy God hath delivered it into thine hands, thou shalt smite every male thereof with the edge of the sword:

14 But the women, and the little ones, and the cattle, and all that is in the city, *even* all the spoil thereof, shalt thou take unto thyself; and thou shalt eat the spoil of thine enemies, which the LORD thy God hath given thee.

15 Thus shalt thou do unto all the cities *which are* very far off from thee, which *are* not of the cities of these nations.

16 But of the cities of these people, which the LORD thy God doth give thee *for* an inheritance, thou shalt save alive nothing that breatheth:

17 But thou shalt utterly destroy them; *namely,* the Hit'tites, and the Am'or-ites, the Ca'naan-ites, and the Per'iz-zites, the Hi'vites, and the Jeb'u-sites; as the LORD thy God hath commanded thee:

18 That they teach you not to do after all their abominations, which they have done unto their gods; so should ye sin against the LORD your God.

19 ¶ When thou shalt besiege a city a long time, in making war against it to take it, thou shalt not destroy the trees thereof by forcing an ax against them: for thou mayest eat of them, and thou shalt not cut them down (for the tree of the field *is* man's *life*) to employ *them* in the siege:

20 Only the trees which thou knowest that they *be* not trees for meat, thou shalt destroy and cut them down; and thou shalt build bulwarks against the city that maketh war with thee, until it be subdued.

21 IF *one* be found slain in the land which the LORD thy God giveth thee to possess it, lying in the field, *and* it be not known who hath slain him:

2 Then thy elders and thy judges shall come forth, and they shall measure unto the cities which *are* round about him that is slain:

3 And it shall be, *that* the city *which is* next unto the slain man, even the elders of that city shall take an heifer, which hath not been wrought with, *and* which hath not drawn in the yoke;

4 And the elders of that city shall bring down the heifer unto a rough valley, which is neither eared nor sown, and shall strike off the heifer's neck there in the valley:

5 And the priests the sons of Le'vi shall come near; for them the LORD thy God hath chosen to minister unto him, and to bless in the name of the LORD; and by their word shall every controversy and every stroke be *tried:*

6 And all the elders of that city, *that are* next unto the slain *man,* shall wash their hands over the heifer that is beheaded in the valley:

7 And they shall answer and say, Our hands have not shed this blood, neither have our eyes seen *it.*

8 Be merciful, O LORD, unto thy people Is'ra-el, whom thou hast redeemed, and lay not innocent blood unto thy people of Is'ra-el's charge. And the blood shall be forgiven them.

9 So shalt thou put away the *guilt of* innocent blood from among you, when thou shalt do *that which is* right in the sight of the LORD.

10 ¶ When thou goest forth to war against thine enemies, and the LORD thy God hath delivered them into thine hands, and thou hast taken them captive,

11 And seest among the captives a beautiful woman, and hast a desire unto her, that thou wouldest have her to thy wife;

12 Then thou shalt bring her home to thine house; and she shall shave her head, and pare her nails;

13 And she shall put the raiment of her captivity from off her, and shall remain in thine house, and bewail her father and her mother a full month: and after that thou shalt go in unto her, and be her husband, and she shall be thy wife.

14 And it shall be, if thou have no delight in her, then thou shalt let her go whither she will; but thou shalt not sell her at all for money, thou shalt not make merchandise of her, because thou hast humbled her.

15 ¶ If a man have two wives, one beloved,

and another hated, and they have born him children, *both* the beloved and the hated; and *if* the firstborn son be hers that was hated:

16 Then it shall be, when he maketh his sons to inherit *that* which he hath, *that* he may not make the son of the beloved firstborn before the son of the hated, *which is indeed* the firstborn:

17 But he shall acknowledge the son of the hated *for* the firstborn, by giving him a double portion of all that he hath: for he *is* the beginning of his strength; the right of the firstborn *is* his.

18 ¶ If a man have a stubborn and rebellious son, which will not obey the voice of his father, or the voice of his mother, and *that,* when they have chastened him, will not hearken unto them:

19 Then shall his father and his mother lay hold on him, and bring him out unto the elders of his city, and unto the gate of his place;

20 And they shall say unto the elders of his city, This our son *is* stubborn and rebellious, he will not obey our voice; *he is* a glutton, and a drunkard.

21 And all the men of his city shall stone him with stones, that he die: so shalt thou put evil away from among you; and all Is′ra-el shall hear, and fear.

22 ¶ And if a man have committed a sin worthy of death, and he be to be put to death, and thou hang him on a tree:

23 His body shall not remain all night upon the tree, but thou shalt in any wise bury him that day; (for he that is hanged *is* accursed of God;) that thy land be not defiled, which the LORD thy God giveth thee *for* an inheritance.

22 THOU shalt not see thy brother's ox or his sheep go astray, and hide thyself from them: thou shalt in any case bring them again unto thy brother.

2 And if thy brother *be* not nigh unto thee, or if thou know him not, then thou shalt bring it unto thine own house, and it shall be with thee until thy brother seek after it, and thou shalt restore it to him again.

3 In like manner shalt thou do with his ass; and so shalt thou do with his raiment; and with all lost thing of thy brother's, which he hath lost, and thou hast found, shalt thou do likewise: thou mayest not hide thyself.

4 ¶ Thou shalt not see thy brother's ass or his ox fall down by the way, and hide thyself from them: thou shalt surely help him to lift *them* up again.

5 ¶ The woman shall not wear that which pertaineth unto a man, neither shall a man put on a woman's garment: for all that do so *are* abomination unto the LORD thy God.

6 ¶ If a bird's nest chance to be before thee in the way in any tree, or on the ground, *whether they be* young ones, or eggs, and the dam sitting upon the young, or upon the eggs, thou shalt not take the dam with the young:

7 *But* thou shalt in any wise let the dam go, and take the young to thee; that it may be well with thee, and *that* thou mayest prolong *thy* days.

8 ¶ When thou buildest a new house, then thou shalt make a battlement for thy roof, that thou bring not blood upon thine house, if any man fall from thence.

9 ¶ Thou shalt not sow thy vineyard with divers seeds: lest the fruit of thy seed which thou hast sown, and the fruit of thy vineyard, be defiled.

10 ¶ Thou shalt not plow with an ox and an ass together.

11 ¶ Thou shalt not wear a garment of divers sorts, *as* of woollen and linen together.

12 ¶ Thou shalt make thee fringes upon the four quarters of thy vesture, wherewith thou coverest *thyself.*

13 ¶ If any man take a wife, and go in unto her, and hate her,

14 And give occasions of speech against her, and bring up an evil name upon her, and say, I took this woman, and when I came to her, I found her not a maid:

15 Then shall the father of the damsel, and her mother, take and bring forth *the tokens of* the damsel's virginity unto the elders of the city in the gate:

16 And the damsel's father shall say unto the elders, I gave my daughter unto this man to wife, and he hateth her;

17 And, lo, he hath given occasions of speech *against her,* saying, I found not thy daughter a maid; and yet these *are the tokens of* my daughter's virginity. And they shall spread the cloth before the elders of the city.

18 And the elders of that city shall take that man and chastise him;

19 And they shall amerce him in an hundred *shekels* of silver, and give *them* unto the father of the damsel, because he hath brought up an evil name upon a virgin of Is′ra-el: and she shall be his wife; he may not put her away all his days.

20 But if this thing be true, *and the tokens of* virginity be not found for the damsel:

21 Then they shall bring out the damsel to the door of her father's house, and the men of her city shall stone her with stones that she die: because she hath wrought folly in Is′ra-el, to play the whore in her father's house: so shalt thou put evil away from among you.

22 ¶ If a man be found lying with a woman married to an husband, then they shall both of them die, *both* the man that lay with the woman, and the woman: so shalt thou put away evil from Is′ra-el.

23 ¶ If a damsel *that is* a virgin be betrothed unto an husband, and a man find her in the city, and lie with her;

24 Then ye shall bring them both out unto the gate of that city, and ye shall stone them with stones that they die; the damsel, because she cried not, *being* in the city; and the man, because he hath humbled his neighbour's wife: so thou shalt put away evil from among you.

25 ¶ But if a man find a betrothed damsel in the field, and the man force her, and lie with her: then the man only that lay with her shall die:

26 But unto the damsel thou shalt do nothing; *there is* in the damsel no sin *worthy* of death: for as when a man riseth against his neighbour, and slayeth him, even so *is* this matter:

27 For he found her in the field, *and* the betrothed damsel cried, and *there was* none to save her.

28 ¶ If a man find a damsel *that is* a virgin, which is not betrothed, and lay hold on her, and lie with her, and they be found;

29 Then the man that lay with her shall give unto the damsel's father fifty *shekels* of silver, and she shall be his wife; because he hath humbled her, he may not put her away all his days.

30 ¶ A man shall not take his father's wife, nor discover his father's skirt.

23 HE that is wounded in the stones, or
hath his privy member cut off, shall not
enter into the congregation of the LORD.
2 A bastard shall not enter into the congregation of the LORD; even to his tenth generation
shall he not enter into the congregation of the
LORD.
3 An Am'mon-ite or Mo'ab-ite shall not enter
into the congregation of the LORD; even to their
tenth generation shall they not enter into the
congregation of the LORD for ever:
4 Because they met you not with bread and
with water in the way, when ye came forth out
of E'gypt; and because they hired against thee
Ba'laam the son of Be'or of Pe'thor of Mes-o-po-
ta'mi-a, to curse thee.
5 Nevertheless the LORD thy God would not
hearken unto Ba'laam; but the LORD thy God
turned the curse into a blessing unto thee, because the LORD thy God loved thee.
6 Thou shalt not seek their peace nor their
prosperity all thy days for ever.
7 ¶ Thou shalt not abhor an E'dom-ite; for he
is thy brother: thou shalt not abhor an E-gyp'-
tian; because thou wast a stranger in his land.
8 The children that are begotten of them
shall enter into the congregation of the LORD in
their third generation.
9 ¶ When the host goeth forth against thine
enemies, then keep thee from every wicked
thing.
10 ¶ If there be among you any man, that is
not clean by reason of uncleanness that chanc-
eth him by night, then shall he go abroad out of
the camp, he shall not come within the camp:
11 But it shall be, when evening cometh on,
he shall wash *himself* with water: and when the
sun is down, he shall come into the camp *again*.
12 ¶ Thou shalt have a place also without
the camp, whither thou shalt go forth abroad:
13 And thou shalt have a paddle upon thy
weapon; and it shall be, when thou wilt ease
thyself abroad, thou shalt dig therewith, and
shalt turn back and cover that which cometh
from thee:
14 For the LORD thy God walketh in the
midst of thy camp, to deliver thee, and to give
up thine enemies before thee; therefore shall
thy camp be holy: that he see no unclean thing
in thee, and turn away from thee.
15 ¶ Thou shalt not deliver unto his master
the servant which is escaped from his master
unto thee:
16 He shall dwell with thee, *even* among you,
in that place which he shall choose in one of thy
gates, where it liketh him best: thou shalt not
oppress him.
17 ¶ There shall be no whore of the daughters of Is'ra-el, nor a sodomite of the sons of
Is'ra-el.
18 Thou shalt not bring the hire of a whore,
or the price of a dog, into the house of the LORD
thy God for any vow: for even both these *are*
abomination unto the LORD thy God.
19 ¶ Thou shalt not lend upon usury to thy
brother; usury of money, usury of victuals,
usury of any thing that is lent upon usury:
20 Unto a stranger thou mayest lend upon
usury; but unto thy brother thou shalt not lend
upon usury: that the LORD thy God may bless
thee in all that thou settest thine hand to in the
land whither thou goest to possess it.
21 ¶ When thou shalt vow a vow unto the
LORD thy God, thou shalt not slack to pay it: for
the LORD thy God will surely require it of thee;
and it would be sin in thee.
22 But if thou shalt forbear to vow, it shall be
no sin in thee.
23 That which is gone out of thy lips thou
shalt keep and perform; *even* a freewill offering,
according as thou hast vowed unto the LORD
thy God, which thou hast promised with thy
mouth.
24 ¶ When thou comest into thy neighbour's
vineyard, then thou mayest eat grapes thy fill at
thine own pleasure; but thou shalt not put *any*
in thy vessel.
25 When thou comest into the standing corn
of thy neighbour, then thou mayest pluck the
ears with thine hand; but thou shalt not move a
sickle unto thy neighbour's standing corn.

24 WHEN a man hath taken a wife, and
married her, and it come to pass that
she find no favour in his eyes, because he hath
found some uncleanness in her: then let him
write her a bill of divorcement, and give *it* in
her hand, and send her out of his house.
2 And when she is departed out of his house,
she may go and be another man's *wife*.
3 And *if* the latter husband hate her, and
write her a bill of divorcement, and giveth *it* in
her hand, and sendeth her out of his house; or if
the latter husband die, which took her *to be* his
wife;
4 Her former husband, which sent her away,
may not take her again to be his wife, after that
she is defiled; for that *is* abomination before the
LORD: and thou shalt not cause the land to sin,
which the LORD thy God giveth thee *for* an inheritance.
5 ¶ When a man hath taken a new wife, he
shall not go out to war, neither shall he be
charged with any business: *but* he shall be free
at home one year, and shall cheer up his wife
which he hath taken.
6 ¶ No man shall take the nether or the upper millstone to pledge: for he taketh *a man's*
life to pledge.
7 ¶ If a man be found stealing any of his
brethren of the children of Is'ra-el, and maketh
merchandise of him, or selleth him; then that
thief shall die; and thou shalt put evil away
from among you.
8 ¶ Take heed in the plague of leprosy, that
thou observe diligently, and do according to all
that the priests the Le'vites shall teach you: as I
commanded them, *so* ye shall observe to do.
9 Remember what the LORD thy God did
unto Mir'i-am by the way, after that ye were
come forth out of E'gypt.
10 ¶ When thou dost lend thy brother any
thing, thou shalt not go into his house to fetch
his pledge.
11 Thou shalt stand abroad, and the man to
whom thou dost lend shall bring out the pledge
abroad unto thee.
12 And if the man *be* poor, thou shalt not
sleep with his pledge:
13 In any case thou shalt deliver him the
pledge again when the sun goeth down, that he
may sleep in his own raiment, and bless thee:
and it shall be righteousness unto thee before
the LORD thy God.
14 ¶ Thou shalt not oppress an hired servant
that is poor and needy, *whether he be* of thy
brethren, or of thy strangers that *are* in thy land
within thy gates:
15 At his day thou shalt give *him* his hire,
neither shall the sun go down upon it; for he *is*
poor, and setteth his heart upon it: lest he cry
against thee unto the LORD, and it be sin unto
thee.

16 The fathers shall not be put to death for the children, neither shall the children be put to death for the fathers: every man shall be put to death for his own sin.

17 ¶ Thou shalt not pervert the judgment of the stranger, *nor* of the fatherless; nor take a widow's raiment to pledge:

18 But thou shalt remember that thou wast a bondman in E'gypt, and the LORD thy God redeemed thee thence: therefore I command thee to do this thing.

19 ¶ When thou cuttest down thine harvest in thy field, and hast forgot a sheaf in the field, thou shalt not go again to fetch it: it shall be for the stranger, for the fatherless, and for the widow: that the LORD thy God may bless thee in all the work of thine hands.

20 When thou beatest thine olive tree, thou shalt not go over the boughs again: it shall be for the stranger, for the fatherless, and for the widow.

21 When thou gatherest the grapes of thy vineyard, thou shalt not glean *it* afterward: it shall be for the stranger, for the fatherless, and for the widow.

22 And thou shalt remember that thou wast a bondman in the land of E'gypt: therefore I command thee to do this thing.

25 IF there be a controversy between men, and they come unto judgment, that *the judges* may judge them; then they shall justify the righteous, and condemn the wicked.

2 And it shall be, if the wicked man *be* worthy to be beaten, that the judge shall cause him to lie down, and to be beaten before his face, according to his fault, by a certain number.

3 Forty stripes he may give him, *and* not exceed: lest, *if* he should exceed, and beat him above these with many stripes, then thy brother should seem vile unto thee.

4 ¶ Thou shalt not muzzle the ox when he treadeth out *the corn.*

5 ¶ If brethren dwell together, and one of them die, and have no child, the wife of the dead shall not marry without unto a stranger: her husband's brother shall go in unto her, and take her to him to wife, and perform the duty of an husband's brother unto her.

6 And it shall be, *that* the firstborn which she beareth shall succeed in the name of his brother *which* is dead, that his name be not put out of Is'ra-el.

7 And if the man like not to take his brother's wife, then let his brother's wife go up to the gate unto the elders, and say, My husband's brother refuseth to raise up unto his brother a name in Is'ra-el, he will not perform the duty of my husband's brother.

8 Then the elders of his city shall call him, and speak unto him: and *if* he stand *to it,* and say, I like not to take her;

9 Then shall his brother's wife come unto him in the presence of the elders, and loose his shoe from off his foot, and spit in his face, and shall answer and say, So shall it be done unto that man that will not build up his brother's house.

10 And his name shall be called in Is'ra-el, The house of him that hath his shoe loosed.

11 ¶ When men strive together one with another, and the wife of the one draweth near for to deliver her husband out of the hand of him that smiteth him, and putteth forth her hand, and taketh him by the secrets:

12 Then thou shalt cut off her hand, thine eye shall not pity *her.*

13 ¶ Thou shalt not have in thy bag divers weights, a great and a small.

14 Thou shalt not have in thine house divers measures, a great and a small.

15 *But* thou shalt have a perfect and just weight, a perfect and just measure shalt thou have: that thy days may be lengthened in the land which the LORD thy God giveth thee.

16 For all that do such things, *and* all that do unrighteously, *are* an abomination unto the LORD thy God.

17 ¶ Remember what Am'a-lek did unto thee by the way, when ye were come forth out of E'gypt;

18 How he met thee by the way, and smote the hindmost of thee, *even* all *that were* feeble behind thee, when thou *wast* faint and weary; and he feared not God.

19 Therefore it shall be, when the LORD thy God hath given thee rest from all thine enemies round about, in the land which the LORD thy God giveth thee *for* an inheritance to possess it, *that* thou shalt blot out the remembrance of Am'a-lek from under heaven; thou shalt not forget *it.*

26 AND it shall be, when thou *art* come in unto the land which the LORD thy God giveth thee *for* an inheritance, and possessest it, and dwellest therein;

2 That thou shalt take of the first of all the fruit of the earth, which thou shalt bring of thy land that the LORD thy God giveth thee, and shalt put *it* in a basket, and shalt go unto the place which the LORD thy God shall choose to place his name there.

3 And thou shalt go unto the priest that shall be in those days, and say unto him, I profess this day unto the LORD thy God, that I am come unto the country which the LORD sware unto our fathers for to give us.

4 And the priest shall take the basket out of thine hand, and set it down before the altar of the LORD thy God.

5 And thou shalt speak and say before the LORD thy God, A Syr'i-an ready to perish *was* my father, and he went down into E'gypt, and sojourned there with a few, and became there a nation, great, mighty, and populous:

6 And the E-gyptians evil entreated us, and afflicted us, and laid upon us hard bondage:

7 And when we cried unto the LORD God of our fathers, the LORD heard our voice, and looked on our affliction, and our labour, and our oppression:

8 And the LORD brought us forth out of E'gypt with a mighty hand, and with an outstretched arm, and with great terribleness, and with signs, and with wonders:

9 And he hath brought us into this place, and hath given us this land, *even* a land that floweth with milk and honey.

10 And now, behold, I have brought the firstfruits of the land, which thou, O LORD, hast given me. And thou shalt set it before the LORD thy God, and worship before the LORD thy God:

11 And thou shalt rejoice in every good *thing* which the LORD thy God hath given unto thee, and unto thine house, thou, and the Le'vite, and the stranger that *is* among you.

12 ¶ When thou hast made an end of tithing all the tithes of thine increase the third year, *which is* the year of tithing, and hast given *it* unto the Le'vite, the stranger, the fatherless, and the widow, that they may eat within thy gates, and be filled;

13 Then thou shalt say before the LORD thy

God, I have brought away the hallowed things out of *mine* house, and also have given them unto the Le'vite, and unto the stranger, to the fatherless, and to the widow, according to all thy commandments which thou hast commanded me: I have not transgressed thy commandments, neither have I forgotten *them:*

14 I have not eaten thereof in my mourning, neither have I taken away *ought* thereof for *any* unclean *use*, nor given *ought* thereof for the dead: *but* I have hearkened to the voice of the LORD my God, *and* have done according to all that thou hast commanded me.

15 Look down from thy holy habitation, from heaven, and bless thy people Is'ra-el, and the land which thou hast given us, as thou swarest unto our fathers, a land that floweth with milk and honey.

16 ¶ This day the LORD thy God hath commanded thee to do these statutes and judgments: thou shalt therefore keep and do them with all thine heart, and with all thy soul.

17 Thou hast avouched the LORD this day to be thy God, and to walk in his ways, and to keep his statutes, and his commandments, and his judgments, and to hearken unto his voice:

18 And the LORD hath avouched thee this day to be his peculiar people, as he hath promised thee, and that *thou* shouldest keep all his commandments;

19 And to make thee high above all nations which he hath made, in praise, and in name, and in honour; and that thou mayest be an holy people unto the LORD thy God, as he hath spoken.

27 AND Mo'ses with the elders of Is'ra-el commanded the people, saying, Keep all the commandments which I command you this day.

2 And it shall be on the day when ye shall pass over Jor'dan unto the land which the LORD thy God giveth thee, that thou shalt set thee up great stones, and plaister them with plaister:

3 And thou shalt write upon them all the words of this law, when thou art passed over, that thou mayest go in unto the land which the LORD thy God giveth thee, a land that floweth with milk and honey; as the LORD God of thy fathers hath promised thee.

4 Therefore it shall be when ye be gone over Jor'dan, *that* ye shall set up these stones, which I command you this day, in mount E'bal, and thou shalt plaister them with plaister.

5 And there shalt thou build an altar unto the LORD thy God, an altar of stones: thou shalt not lift up *any* iron *tool* upon them.

6 Thou shalt build the altar of the LORD thy God of whole stones: and thou shalt offer burnt offerings thereon unto the LORD thy God:

7 And thou shalt offer peace offerings, and shalt eat there, and rejoice before the LORD thy God.

8 And thou shalt write upon the stones all the words of this law very plainly.

9 ¶ And Mo'ses and the priests the Le'vites spake unto all Is'ra-el, saying, Take heed, and hearken, O Is'ra-el; this day thou art become the people of the LORD thy God.

10 Thou shalt therefore obey the voice of the LORD thy God, and do his commandments and his statutes, which I command thee this day.

11 ¶ And Mo'ses charged the people the same day, saying,

12 These shall stand upon mount Ger'i-zim to bless the people, when ye are come over Jor'dan; Sim'e-on, and Le'vi, and Ju'dah, and Is'sachar, and Jo'seph, and Ben'ja-min:

13 And these shall stand upon mount E'bal to curse; Reu'ben, Gad, and Ash'er, and Zeb'u-lun, Dan, and Naph'ta-li.

14 ¶ And the Le'vites shall speak, and say unto all the men of Is'ra-el with a loud voice,

15 Cursed *be* the man that maketh *any* graven or molten image, an abomination unto the LORD, the work of the hands of the craftsman, and putteth *it* in *a* secret *place.* And all the people shall answer and say, Amen.

16 Cursed *be* he that setteth light by his father or his mother. And all the people shall say, Amen.

17 Cursed *be* he that removeth his neighbour's landmark. And all the people shall say, Amen.

18 Cursed *be* he that maketh the blind to wander out of the way. And all the people shall say, Amen.

19 Cursed *be* he that perverteth the judgment of the stranger, fatherless, and widow. And all the people shall say, Amen.

20 Cursed *be* he that lieth with his father's wife; because he uncovereth his father's skirt. And all the people shall say, Amen.

21 Cursed *be* he that lieth with any manner of beast. And all the people shall say, Amen.

22 Cursed *be* he that lieth with his sister, the daughter of his father, or the daughter of his mother. And all the people shall say, Amen.

23 Cursed *be* he that lieth with his mother in law. And all the people shall say, Amen.

24 Cursed *be* he that smiteth his neighbour secretly. And all the people shall say, Amen.

25 Cursed *be* he that taketh reward to slay an innocent person. And all the people shall say, Amen.

26 Cursed *be* he that confirmeth not *all* the words of this law to do them. And all the people shall say, Amen.

28 AND it shall come to pass, if thou shalt hearken diligently unto the voice of the LORD thy God, to observe *and* to do all his commandments which I command thee this day, that the LORD thy God will set thee on high above all nations of the earth:

2 And all these blessings shall come on thee, and overtake thee, if thou shalt hearken unto the voice of the LORD thy God.

3 Blessed *shalt* thou *be* in the city, and blessed *shalt* thou *be* in the field.

4 Blessed *shall be* the fruit of thy body, and the fruit of thy ground, and the fruit of thy cattle, the increase of thy kine, and the flocks of thy sheep.

5 Blessed *shall be* thy basket and thy store.

6 Blessed *shalt* thou *be* when thou comest in, and blessed *shalt* thou *be* when thou goest out.

7 The LORD shall cause thine enemies that rise up against thee to be smitten before thy face: they shall come out against thee one way, and flee before thee seven ways.

8 The LORD shall command the blessing upon thee in thy storehouses, and in all that thou settest thine hand unto; and he shall bless thee in the land which the LORD thy God giveth thee.

9 The LORD shall establish thee an holy people unto himself, as he hath sworn unto thee, if thou shalt keep the commandments of the LORD thy God, and walk in his ways.

10 And all people of the earth shall see that thou art called by the name of the LORD; and they shall be afraid of thee.

11 And the LORD shall make thee plenteous

in goods, in the fruit of thy body, and in the fruit
of thy cattle, and in the fruit of thy ground, in
the land which the LORD sware unto thy fathers
to give thee.
12 The LORD shall open unto thee his good
treasure, the heaven to give the rain unto thy
land in his season, and to bless all the work of
thine hand: and thou shalt lend unto many nations, and thou shalt not borrow.
13 And the LORD shall make thee the head,
and not the tail; and thou shalt be above only,
and thou shalt not be beneath; if that thou
hearken unto the commandments of the LORD
thy God, which I command thee this day, to observe and to do *them:*
14 And thou shalt not go aside from any of
the words which I command thee this day, *to*
the right hand, or *to* the left, to go after other
gods to serve them.
15 ¶ But it shall come to pass, if thou wilt
not hearken unto the voice of the LORD thy God,
to observe to do all his commandments and his
statutes which I command thee this day; that all
these curses shall come upon thee, and overtake thee:
16 Cursed *shalt* thou *be* in the city, and
cursed *shalt* thou *be* in the field.
17 Cursed *shall be* thy basket and thy store.
18 Cursed *shall be* the fruit of thy body, and
the fruit of thy land, the increase of thy kine,
and the flocks of thy sheep.
19 Cursed *shalt* thou *be* when thou comest
in, and cursed *shalt* thou *be* when thou goest
out.
20 The LORD shall send upon thee cursing,
vexation, and rebuke, in all that thou settest
thine hand unto for to do, until thou be destroyed, and until thou perish quickly; because
of the wickedness of thy doings, whereby thou
hast forsaken me.
21 The LORD shall make the pestilence cleave
unto thee, until he have consumed thee from off
the land, whither thou goest to possess it.
22 The LORD shall smite thee with a consumption, and with a fever, and with an inflammation, and with an extreme burning, and with
the sword, and with blasting, and with mildew;
and they shall pursue thee until thou perish.
23 And thy heaven that *is* over thy head shall
be brass, and the earth that *is* under thee *shall
be* iron.
24 The LORD shall make the rain of thy land
powder and dust: from heaven shall it come
down upon thee, until thou be destroyed.
25 The LORD shall cause thee to be smitten
before thine enemies: thou shalt go out one way
against them, and flee seven ways before them:
and shalt be removed into all the kingdoms of
the earth.
26 And thy carcase shall be meat unto all
fowls of the air, and unto the beasts of the
earth, and no man shall fray *them* away.
27 The LORD will smite thee with the botch of
E'gypt, and with the emerods, and with the
scab, and with the itch, whereof thou canst not
be healed.
28 The LORD shall smite thee with madness,
and blindness, and astonishment of heart:
29 And thou shalt grope at noonday, as the
blind gropeth in darkness, and thou shalt not
prosper in thy ways: and thou shalt be only oppressed and spoiled evermore, and no man shall
save *thee.*
30 Thou shalt betroth a wife, and another
man shall lie with her: thou shalt build an
house, and thou shalt not dwell therein: thou
shalt plant a vineyard, and shalt not gather the
grapes thereof.
31 Thine ox *shall be* slain before thine eyes,
and thou shalt not eat thereof: thine ass *shall be*
violently taken away from before thy face, and
shall not be restored to thee: thy sheep *shall be*
given unto thine enemies, and thou shalt have
none to rescue *them.*
32 Thy sons and thy daughters *shall be* given
unto another people, and thine eyes shall look,
and fail *with longing* for them all the day long:
and *there shall be* no might in thine hand.
33 The fruit of thy land, and all thy labours,
shall a nation which thou knowest not eat up;
and thou shalt be only oppressed and crushed
alway:
34 So that thou shalt be mad for the sight of
thine eyes which thou shalt see.
35 The LORD shall smite thee in the knees,
and in the legs, with a sore botch that cannot be
healed, from the sole of thy foot unto the top of
thy head.
36 The LORD shall bring thee, and thy king
which thou shalt set over thee, unto a nation
which neither thou nor thy fathers have known;
and there shalt thou serve other gods, wood and
stone.
37 And thou shalt become an astonishment,
a proverb, and a byword, among all nations
whither the LORD shall lead thee.
38 Thou shalt carry much seed out into the
field, and shalt gather *but* little in; for the locust
shall consume it.
39 Thou shalt plant vineyards, and dress
them, but shalt neither drink *of* the wine, nor
gather *the grapes;* for the worms shall eat them.
40 Thou shalt have olive trees throughout all
thy coasts, but thou shalt not anoint *thyself*
with the oil; for thine olive shall cast *his fruit.*
41 Thou shalt beget sons and daughters, but
thou shalt not enjoy them; for they shall go into
captivity.
42 All thy trees and fruit of thy land shall the
locust consume.
43 The stranger that *is* within thee shall get
up above thee very high; and thou shalt come
down very low.
44 He shall lend to thee, and thou shalt not
lend to him: he shall be the head, and thou shalt
be the tail.
45 Moreover all these curses shall come
upon thee, and shall pursue thee, and overtake
thee, till thou be destroyed; because thou hear-
kenedst not unto the voice of the LORD thy God,
to keep his commandments and his statutes
which he commanded thee:
46 And they shall be upon thee for a sign and
for a wonder, and upon thy seed for ever.
47 Because thou servedst not the LORD thy
God with joyfulness, and with gladness of
heart, for the abundance of all *things;*
48 Therefore shalt thou serve thine enemies
which the LORD shall send against thee, in hunger, and in thirst, and in nakedness, and in want
of all *things:* and he shall put a yoke of iron
upon thy neck, until he have destroyed thee.
49 The LORD shall bring a nation against thee
from far, from the end of the earth, *as swift* as
the eagle flieth; a nation whose tongue thou
shalt not understand;
50 A nation of fierce countenance, which
shall not regard the person of the old, nor shew
favour to the young:
51 And he shall eat the fruit of thy cattle, and
the fruit of thy land, until thou be destroyed:
which *also* shall not leave thee *either* corn,

wine, or oil, *or* the increase of thy kine, or flocks
of thy sheep, until he have destroyed thee.
52 And he shall besiege thee in all thy gates,
until thy high and fenced walls come down,
wherein thou trustedst, throughout all thy land:
and he shall besiege thee in all thy gates
throughout all thy land, which the LORD thy
God hath given thee.
53 And thou shalt eat the fruit of thine own
body, the flesh of thy sons and of thy daughters,
which the LORD thy God hath given thee, in the
siege, and in the straitness, wherewith thine enemies shall distress thee:
54 *So that* the man *that is* tender among you,
and very delicate, his eye shall be evil toward
his brother, and toward the wife of his bosom,
and toward the remnant of his children which
he shall leave:
55 So that he will not give to any of them of
the flesh of his children whom he shall eat: because he hath nothing left him in the siege, and
in the straitness, wherewith thine enemies shall
distress thee in all thy gates.
56 The tender and delicate woman among
you, which would not adventure to set the sole
of her foot upon the ground for delicateness and
tenderness, her eye shall be evil toward the husband of her bosom, and toward her son, and
toward her daughter,
57 And toward her young one that cometh
out from between her feet, and toward her children which she shall bear: for she shall eat
them for want of all *things* secretly in the siege
and straitness, wherewith thine enemy shall
distress thee in thy gates.
58 If thou wilt not observe to do all the
words of this law that are written in this book,
that thou mayest fear this glorious and fearful
name, THE LORD THY GOD;
59 Then the LORD will make thy plagues
wonderful, and the plagues of thy seed, *even*
great plagues, and of long continuance, and
sore sicknesses, and of long continuance.
60 Moreover he will bring upon thee all the
diseases of E'gypt, which thou wast afraid of;
and they shall cleave unto thee.
61 Also every sickness, and every plague,
which *is* not written in the book of this law,
them will the LORD bring upon thee, until thou
be destroyed.
62 And ye shall be left few in number,
whereas ye were as the stars of heaven for multitude; because thou wouldest not obey the
voice of the LORD thy God.
63 And it shall come to pass, *that* as the
LORD rejoiced over you to do you good, and to
multiply you; so the LORD will rejoice over you
to destroy you, and to bring you to nought; and
ye shall be plucked from off the land whither
thou goest to possess it.
64 And the LORD shall scatter thee among all
people, from the one end of the earth even unto
the other; and there thou shalt serve other gods,
which neither thou nor thy fathers have known,
even wood and stone.
65 And among these nations shalt thou find
no ease, neither shall the sole of the foot have
rest: but the LORD shall give thee there a trembling heart, and failing of eyes, and sorrow of
mind:
66 And thy life shall hang in doubt before
thee; and thou shalt fear day and night, and
shalt have none assurance of thy life:
67 In the morning thou shalt say, Would God
it were even! and at even thou shalt say, Would
God it were morning! for the fear of thine heart
wherewith thou shalt fear, and for the sight of
thine eyes which thou shalt see.
68 And the LORD shall bring thee into E'gypt
again with ships, by the way whereof I spake
unto thee, Thou shalt see it no more again: and
there ye shall be sold unto your enemies for
bondmen and bondwomen, and no man shall
buy *you*.

29 THESE *are* the words of the covenant,
which the LORD commanded Mo'ses to
make with the children of Is'ra-el in the land of
Mo'ab, beside the covenant which he made with
them in Ho'reb.
2 ¶ And Mo'ses called unto all Is'ra-el, and
said unto them, Ye have seen all that the LORD
did before your eyes in the land of E'gypt unto
Pha'raoh, and unto all his servants, and unto all
his land;
3 The great temptations which thine eyes
have seen, the signs, and those great miracles:
4 Yet the LORD hath not given you an heart
to perceive, and eyes to see, and ears to hear,
unto this day.
5 And I have led you forty years in the wilderness: your clothes are not waxen old upon
you, and thy shoe is not waxen old upon thy
foot.
6 Ye have not eaten bread, neither have ye
drunk wine or strong drink: that ye might know
that I *am* the LORD your God.
7 And when ye came unto this place, Si'hon
the king of Hesh'bon, and Og the king of Ba'-
shan, came out against us unto battle, and we
smote them:
8 And we took their land, and gave it for an
inheritance unto the Reu'ben-ites, and to the
Gad'ites, and to the half tribe of Ma-nas'seh.
9 Keep therefore the words of this covenant,
and do them, that ye may prosper in all that ye
do.
10 ¶ Ye stand this day all of you before the
LORD your God; your captains of your tribes,
your elders, and your officers, *with* all the men
of Is'ra-el,
11 Your little ones, your wives, and thy
stranger that *is* in thy camp, from the hewer of
thy wood unto the drawer of thy water:
12 That thou shouldest enter into covenant
with the LORD thy God, and into his oath, which
the LORD thy God maketh with thee this day:
13 That he may establish thee to day for a
people unto himself, and *that* he may be unto
thee a God, as he hath said unto thee, and as he
hath sworn unto thy fathers, to A'bra-ham, to
I'saac, and to Ja'cob.
14 Neither with you only do I make this covenant and this oath;
15 But with *him* that standeth here with us
this day before the LORD our God, and also with
him that *is* not here with us this day:
16 (For ye know how we have dwelt in the
land of E'gypt; and how we came through the
nations which ye passed by;
17 And ye have seen their abominations, and
their idols, wood and stone, silver and gold,
which *were* among them:)
18 Lest there should be among you man, or
woman, or family, or tribe, whose heart turneth
away this day from the LORD our God, to go *and*
serve the gods of these nations; lest there
should be among you a root that beareth gall
and wormwood;
19 And it come to pass, when he heareth the
words of this curse, that he bless himself in his
heart, saying, I shall have peace, though I walk

in the imagination of mine heart, to add drunkenness to thirst:
20 The LORD will not spare him, but then the
anger of the LORD and his jealousy shall smoke
against that man, and all the curses that are
written in this book shall lie upon him, and the
LORD shall blot out his name from under
heaven.
21 And the LORD shall separate him unto evil
out of all the tribes of Is′ra-el, according to all
the curses of the covenant that are written in
this book of the law:
22 So that the generation to come of your
children that shall rise up after you, and the
stranger that shall come from a far land, shall
say, when they see the plagues of the land, and
the sicknesses which the LORD hath laid upon it;
23 *And that* the whole land thereof *is* brimstone, and salt, *and* burning, *that* it is not sown,
nor beareth, nor any grass groweth therein, like
the overthrow of Sod′om, and Go-mor′rah, Ad′-
mah, and Ze-bo′im, which the LORD overthrew
in his anger, and in his wrath:
24 Even all nations shall say, Wherefore hath
the LORD done thus unto this land? what *meaneth* the heat of this great anger?
25 Then men shall say, Because they have
forsaken the covenant of the LORD God of their
fathers, which he made with them when he
brought them forth out of the land of E′gypt:
26 For they went and served other gods, and
worshipped them, gods whom they knew not,
and *whom* he had not given unto them:
27 And the anger of the LORD was kindled
against this land, to bring upon it all the curses
that are written in this book:
28 And the LORD rooted them out of their
land in anger, and in wrath, and in great indignation, and cast them into another land, as *it is*
this day.
29 The secret *things belong* unto the LORD
our God: but those *things which are* revealed
belong unto us and to our children for ever, that
we may do all the words of this law.

30 AND it shall come to pass, when all
these things are come upon thee, the
blessing and the curse, which I have set before
thee, and thou shalt call *them* to mind among
all the nations, whither the LORD thy God hath
driven thee,
2 And shalt return unto the LORD thy God,
and shalt obey his voice according to all that I
command thee this day, thou and thy children,
with all thine heart, and with all thy soul;
3 That then the LORD thy God will turn thy
captivity, and have compassion upon thee, and
will return and gather thee from all the nations,
whither the LORD thy God hath scattered thee.
4 If *any* of thine be driven out unto the outmost *parts* of heaven, from thence will the
LORD thy God gather thee, and from thence will
he fetch thee:
5 And the LORD thy God will bring thee into
the land which thy fathers possessed, and thou
shalt possess it; and he will do thee good, and
multiply thee above thy fathers.
6 And the LORD thy God will circumcise
thine heart, and the heart of thy seed, to love
the LORD thy God with all thine heart, and with
all thy soul, that thou mayest live.
7 And the LORD thy God will put all these
curses upon thine enemies, and on them that
hate thee, which persecuted thee.
8 And thou shalt return and obey the voice of
the LORD, and do all his commandments which I
command thee this day.
9 And the LORD thy God will make thee plenteous in every work of thine hand, in the fruit of
thy body, and in the fruit of thy cattle, and in
the fruit of thy land, for good: for the LORD will
again rejoice over thee for good, as he rejoiced
over thy fathers:
10 If thou shalt hearken unto the voice of the
LORD thy God, to keep his commandments and
his statutes which are written in this book of
the law, *and* if thou turn unto the LORD thy God
with all thine heart, and with all thy soul.
11 ¶ For this commandment which I command thee this day, it *is* not hidden from thee,
neither *is* it far off.
12 It *is* not in heaven, that thou shouldest
say, Who shall go up for us to heaven, and bring
it unto us, that we may hear it, and do it?
13 Neither *is* it beyond the sea, that thou
shouldest say, Who shall go over the sea for us,
and bring it unto us, that we may hear it, and do
it?
14 But the word *is* very nigh unto thee, in thy
mouth, and in thy heart, that thou mayest do it.
15 ¶ See, I have set before thee this day life
and good, and death and evil;
16 In that I command thee this day to love
the LORD thy God, to walk in his ways, and to
keep his commandments and his statutes and
his judgments, that thou mayest live and multiply: and the LORD thy God shall bless thee in the
land whither thou goest to possess it.
17 But if thine heart turn away, so that thou
wilt not hear, but shalt be drawn away, and
worship other gods, and serve them;
18 I denounce unto you this day, that ye shall
surely perish, *and that* ye shall not prolong
your days upon the land, whither thou passest
over Jor′dan to go to possess it.
19 I call heaven and earth to record this day
against you, *that* I have set before you life and
death, blessing and cursing: therefore choose
life, that both thou and thy seed may live:
20 That thou mayest love the LORD thy God,
and that thou mayest obey his voice, and that
thou mayest cleave unto him: for he *is* thy life,
and the length of thy days: that thou mayest
dwell in the land which the LORD sware unto
thy fathers, to A′bra-ham, to I′saac, and to Ja′-
cob, to give them.

31 AND Mo′ses went and spake these
words unto all Is′ra-el.
2 And he said unto them, I *am* an hundred
and twenty years old this day; I can no more go
out and come in: also the LORD hath said unto
me, Thou shalt not go over this Jor′dan.
3 The LORD thy God, he will go over before
thee, *and* he will destroy these nations from before thee, and thou shalt possess them: *and*
Josh′u-a, he shall go over before thee, as the
LORD hath said.
4 And the LORD shall do unto them as he did
to Si′hon and to Og, kings of the Am′or-ites, and
unto the land of them, whom he destroyed.
5 And the LORD shall give them up before
your face, that ye may do unto them according
unto all the commandments which I have commanded you.
6 Be strong and of a good courage, fear not,
nor be afraid of them: for the LORD thy God, he
it is that doth go with thee; he will not fail thee,
nor forsake thee.
7 ¶ And Mo′ses called unto Josh′u-a, and
said unto him in the sight of all Is′ra-el, Be
strong and of a good courage: for thou must go
with this people unto the land which the LORD

hath sworn unto their fathers to give them; and
thou shalt cause them to inherit it.
8 And the LORD, he *it is* that doth go before
thee; he will be with thee, he will not fail thee,
neither forsake thee: fear not, neither be dismayed.
9 ¶ And Mo'ses wrote this law, and delivered
it unto the priests the sons of Le'vi, which bare
the ark of the covenant of the LORD, and unto
all the elders of Is'ra-el.
10 And Mo'ses commanded them, saying, At
the end of *every* seven years, in the solemnity of
the year of release, in the feast of tabernacles,
11 When all Is'ra-el is come to appear before
the LORD thy God in the place which he shall
choose, thou shalt read this law before all Is'ra-
el in their hearing.
12 Gather the people together, men, and
women, and children, and thy stranger that *is*
within thy gates, that they may hear, and that
they may learn, and fear the LORD your God,
and observe to do all the words of this law:
13 And *that* their children, which have not
known *any thing*, may hear, and learn to fear
the LORD your God, as long as ye live in the land
whither ye go over Jor'dan to possess it.
14 ¶ And the LORD said unto Mo'ses, Behold,
thy days approach that thou must die: call
Josh'u-a, and present yourselves in the tabernacle of the congregation, that I may give him a
charge. And Mo'ses and Josh'u-a went, and presented themselves in the tabernacle of the congregation.
15 And the LORD appeared in the tabernacle
in a pillar of a cloud: and the pillar of the cloud
stood over the door of the tabernacle.
16 ¶ And the LORD said unto Mo'ses, Behold,
thou shalt sleep with thy fathers; and this people will rise up, and go a whoring after the gods
of the strangers of the land, whither they go *to
be* among them, and will forsake me, and break
my covenant which I have made with them.
17 Then my anger shall be kindled against
them in that day, and I will forsake them, and I
will hide my face from them, and they shall be
devoured, and many evils and troubles shall befall them; so that they will say in that day, Are
not these evils come upon us, because our God
is not among us?
18 And I will surely hide my face in that day
for all the evils which they shall have wrought,
in that they are turned unto other gods.
19 Now therefore write ye this song for you,
and teach it the children of Is'ra-el: put it in
their mouths, that this song may be a witness
for me against the children of Is'ra-el.
20 For when I shall have brought them into
the land which I sware unto their fathers, that
floweth with milk and honey; and they shall
have eaten and filled themselves, and waxen
fat; then will they turn unto other gods, and
serve them, and provoke me, and break my covenant.
21 And it shall come to pass, when many
evils and troubles are befallen them, that this
song shall testify against them as a witness; for
it shall not be forgotten out of the mouths of
their seed: for I know their imagination which
they go about, even now, before I have brought
them into the land which I sware.
22 ¶ Mo'ses therefore wrote this song the
same day, and taught it the children of Is'ra-el.
23 And he gave Josh'u-a the son of Nun a
charge, and said, Be strong and of a good courage: for thou shalt bring the children of Is'ra-el
into the land which I sware unto them: and I
will be with thee.
24 ¶ And it came to pass, when Mo'ses had
made an end of writing the words of this law in
a book, until they were finished,
25 That Mo'ses commanded the Le'vites,
which bare the ark of the covenant of the LORD,
saying,
26 Take this book of the law, and put it in the
side of the ark of the covenant of the LORD your
God, that it may be there for a witness against
thee.
27 For I know thy rebellion, and thy stiff
neck: behold, while I am yet alive with you this
day, ye have been rebellious against the LORD;
and how much more after my death?
28 ¶ Gather unto me all the elders of your
tribes, and your officers, that I may speak these
words in their ears, and call heaven and earth to
record against them.
29 For I know that after my death ye will utterly corrupt *yourselves*, and turn aside from
the way which I have commanded you; and evil
will befall you in the latter days; because ye will
do evil in the sight of the LORD, to provoke him
to anger through the work of your hands.
30 And Mo'ses spake in the ears of all the
congregation of Is'ra-el the words of this song,
until they were ended.

32 GIVE ear, O ye heavens, and I will
speak; and hear, O earth, the words of
my mouth.
2 My doctrine shall drop as the rain, my
speech shall distil as the dew, as the small rain
upon the tender herb, and as the showers upon
the grass:
3 Because I will publish the name of the
LORD: ascribe ye greatness unto our GOD.
4 *He is* the Rock, his work *is* perfect: for all
his ways *are* judgment: a God of truth and without iniquity, just and right *is* he.
5 They have corrupted themselves, their spot
is not *the spot* of his children: *they are* a perverse and crooked generation.
6 Do ye thus requite the LORD, O foolish people and unwise? *is* not he thy father *that* hath
bought thee? hath he not made thee, and established thee?
7 ¶ Remember the days of old, consider the
years of many generations: ask thy father, and
he will shew thee; thy elders, and they will tell
thee.
8 When the most High divided to the nations
their inheritance, when he separated the sons of
Ad'am, he set the bounds of the people according to the number of the children of Is'ra-el.
9 For the LORD's portion *is* his people; Ja'cob
is the lot of his inheritance.
10 He found him in a desert land, and in the
waste howling wilderness; he led him about, he
instructed him, he kept him as the apple of his
eye.
11 As an eagle stirreth up her nest, fluttereth
over her young, spreadeth abroad her wings,
taketh them, beareth them on her wings:
12 *So* the LORD alone did lead him, and *there
was* no strange god with him.
13 He made him ride on the high places of
the earth, that he might eat the increase of the
fields; and he made him to suck honey out of
the rock, and oil out of the flinty rock;
14 Butter of kine, and milk of sheep, with fat
of lambs, and rams of the breed of Ba'shan, and
goats, with the fat of kidneys of wheat; and
thou didst drink the pure blood of the grape.
15 ¶ But Jeshu-run waxed fat, and kicked:
thou art waxen fat, thou art grown thick, thou
art covered *with fatness;* then he forsook God

which made him, and lightly esteemed the Rock
of his salvation.
16 They provoked him to jealousy with
strange *gods*, with abominations provoked they
him to anger.
17 They sacrificed unto devils, not to God; to
gods whom they knew not, to new *gods that*
came newly up, whom your fathers feared not.
18 Of the Rock *that* begat thee thou art un-
mindful, and hast forgotten God that formed
thee.
19 And when the LORD saw *it*, he abhorred
them, because of the provoking of his sons, and
of his daughters.
20 And he said, I will hide my face from
them, I will see what their end *shall be:* for they
are a very froward generation, children in
whom *is* no faith.
21 They have moved me to jealousy with
that which is not God; they have provoked me
to anger with their vanities: and I will move
them to jealousy with *those which are* not a
people; I will provoke them to anger with a foolish nation.
22 For a fire is kindled in mine anger, and
shall burn unto the lowest hell, and shall consume the earth with her increase, and set on fire
the foundations of the mountains.
23 I will heap mischiefs upon them; I will
spend mine arrows upon them.
24 *They shall be* burnt with hunger, and devoured with burning heat, and with bitter destruction: I will also send the teeth of beasts
upon them, with the poison of serpents of the
dust.
25 The sword without, and terror within,
shall destroy both the young man and the virgin, the suckling *also* with the man of gray
hairs.
26 I said, I would scatter them into corners, I
would make the remembrance of them to cease
from among men:
27 Were it not that I feared the wrath of the
enemy, lest their adversaries should behave
themselves strangely, *and* lest they should say,
Our hand *is* high, and the LORD hath not done
all this.
28 For they *are* a nation void of counsel, neither *is there any* understanding in them.
29 O that they were wise, *that* they understood this, *that* they would consider their latter
end!
30 How should one chase a thousand, and
two put ten thousand to flight, except their
Rock had sold them, and the LORD had shut
them up?
31 For their rock *is* not as our Rock, even our
enemies themselves *being* judges.
32 For their vine *is* of the vine of Sod'om, and
of the fields of Go-mor'rah: their grapes *are*
grapes of gall, their clusters *are* bitter:
33 Their wine *is* the poison of dragons, and
the cruel venom of asps.
34 *Is* not this laid up in store with me, *and*
sealed up among my treasures?
35 To me *belongeth* vengeance, and recompence; their foot shall slide in *due* time: for the
day of their calamity *is* at hand, and the things
that shall come upon them make haste.
36 For the LORD shall judge his people, and
repent himself for his servants, when he seeth
that *their* power is gone, and *there is* none shut
up, or left.
37 And he shall say, Where *are* their gods,
their rock in whom they trusted,
38 Which did eat the fat of their sacrifices,
and drank the wine of their drink offerings? let
them rise up and help you, *and* be your protec-
tion.
39 See now that I, *even* I, *am* he, and *there is*
no god with me: I kill, and I make alive; I
wound, and I heal: neither *is there any* that can
deliver out of my hand.
40 For I lift up my hand to heaven, and say, I
live for ever.
41 If I whet my glittering sword, and mine
hand take hold on judgment; I will render vengeance to mine enemies, and will reward them
that hate me.
42 I will make mine arrows drunk with
blood, and my sword shall devour flesh; *and*
that with the blood of the slain and of the captives, from the beginning of revenges upon the
enemy.
43 Rejoice, O ye nations, *with* his people: for
he will avenge the blood of his servants, and
will render vengeance to his adversaries, and
will be merciful unto his land, *and* to his people.
44 ¶ And Mo'ses came and spake all the
words of this song in the ears of the people, he,
and Ho-she'a the son of Nun.
45 And Mo'ses made an end of speaking all
these words to all Is'ra-el:
46 And he said unto them, Set your hearts
unto all the words which I testify among you
this day, which ye shall command your children
to observe to do, all the words of the law.
47 For it *is* not a vain thing for you; because
it *is* your life: and through this thing ye shall
prolong *your* days in the land, whither ye go
over Jor'dan to possess it.
48 And the LORD spake unto Mo'ses that selfsame day, saying,
49 Get thee up into this mountain Ab'a-rim,
unto mount Ne'bo, which *is* in the land of Mo'-
ab, that *is* over against Jer'i-cho; and behold the
land of Ca'naan, which I give unto the children
of Is'ra-el for a possession:
50 And die in the mount whither thou goest
up, and be gathered unto thy people; as Aar'on
thy brother died in mount Hor, and was gathered unto his people:
51 Because ye trespassed against me among
the children of Is'ra-el at the waters of Mer'i-
bah–Ka'desh, in the wilderness of Zin; because
ye sanctified me not in the midst of the children
of Is'ra-el.
52 Yet thou shalt see the land before *thee:*
but thou shalt not go thither unto the land
which I give the children of Is'ra-el.

33 AND this *is* the blessing, wherewith
Mo'ses the man of God blessed the children of Is'ra-el before his death.
2 And he said, The LORD came from Si'nai,
and rose up from Se'ir unto them; he shined
forth from mount Pa'ran, and he came with ten
thousands of saints: from his right hand *went* a
fiery law for them.
3 Yea, he loved the people; all his saints *are*
in thy hand: and they sat down at thy feet; *every*
one shall receive of thy words.
4 Mo'ses commanded us a law, *even* the inheritance of the congregation of Ja'cob.
5 And he was king in Jeshu-run, when the
heads of the people *and* the tribes of Is'ra-el
were gathered together.
6 ¶ Let Reu'ben live, and not die; and let *not*
his men be few.
7 ¶ And this *is the blessing* of Ju'dah: and he
said, Hear, LORD, the voice of Ju'dah, and bring
him unto his people: let his hands be sufficient
for him; and be thou an help *to him* from his
enemies.

8 ¶ And of Le′vi he said, *Let* thy Thum′mim and thy U′rim *be* with thy holy one, whom thou didst prove at Mas′sah, *and with* whom thou didst strive at the waters of Mer′i-bah;

9 Who said unto his father and to his mother, I have not seen him; neither did he acknowledge his brethren, nor knew his own children: for they have observed thy word, and kept thy covenant.

10 They shall teach Ja′cob thy judgments, and Is′ra-el thy law: they shall put incense before thee, and whole burnt sacrifice upon thine altar.

11 Bless, LORD, his substance, and accept the work of his hands: smite through the loins of them that rise against him, and of them that hate him, that they rise not again.

12 ¶ *And* of Ben′ja-min he said, The beloved of the LORD shall dwell in safety by him; *and the LORD* shall cover him all the day long, and he shall dwell between his shoulders.

13 ¶ And of Jo′seph he said, Blessed of the LORD *be* his land, for the precious things of heaven, for the dew, and for the deep that coucheth beneath,

14 And for the precious fruits *brought forth* by the sun, and for the precious things put forth by the moon,

15 And for the chief things of the ancient mountains, and for the precious things of the lasting hills,

16 And for the precious things of the earth and fulness thereof, and *for* the good will of him that dwelt in the bush: let *the blessing* come upon the head of Jo′seph, and upon the top of the head of him *that was* separated from his brethren.

17 His glory *is like* the firstling of his bullock, and his horns *are like* the horns of unicorns: with them he shall push the people together to the ends of the earth: and they *are* the ten thousands of E′phra-im, and they *are* the thousands of Ma-nas′seh.

18 ¶ And of Zeb′u-lun he said, Rejoice, Zeb′-u-lun, in thy going out; and, Is′sa-char, in thy tents.

19 They shall call the people unto the mountain; there they shall offer sacrifices of righteousness: for they shall suck *of* the abundance of the seas, and *of* treasures hid in the sand.

20 ¶ And of Gad he said, Blessed *be* he that enlargeth Gad: he dwelleth as a lion, and teareth the arm with the crown of the head.

21 And he provided the first part for himself, because there, *in* a portion of the lawgiver, *was he* seated; and he came with the heads of the people, he executed the justice of the LORD, and his judgments with Is′ra-el.

22 ¶ And of Dan he said, Dan *is* a lion's whelp: he shall leap from Ba′shan.

23 ¶ And of Naph′ta-li he said, O Naph′ta-li, satisfied with favour, and full with the blessing of the LORD: possess thou the west and the south.

24 ¶ And of Ash′er he said, *Let* Ash′er *be* blessed with children; let him be acceptable to his brethren, and let him dip his foot in oil.

25 Thy shoes *shall be* iron and brass; and as thy days, *so shall* thy strength *be.*

26 ¶ *There is* none like unto the God of Je-shu-run, *who* rideth upon the heaven in thy help, and in his excellency on the sky.

27 The eternal God *is thy* refuge, and underneath *are* the everlasting arms: and he shall thrust out the enemy from before thee; and shall say, Destroy *them.*

28 Is′ra-el then shall dwell in safety alone: the fountain of Ja′cob *shall be* upon a land of corn and wine; also his heavens shall drop down dew.

29 Happy *art* thou, O Is′ra-el: who *is* like unto thee, O people saved by the LORD, the shield of thy help, and who *is* the sword of thy excellency! and thine enemies shall be found liars unto thee; and thou shalt tread upon their high places.

34 AND Mo′ses went up from the plains of Mo′ab unto the mountain of Ne′bo, to the top of Pis′gah, that *is* over against Jer′i-cho. And the LORD shewed him all the land of Gil′e-ad, unto Dan,

2 And all Naph′ta-li, and the land of E′phra-im, and Ma-nas′seh, and all the land of Ju′dah, unto the utmost sea,

3 And the south, and the plain of the valley of Jer′i-cho, the city of palm trees, unto Zo′ar.

4 And the LORD said unto him, This *is* the land which I sware unto A′bra-ham, unto I′saac, and unto Ja′cob, saying, I will give it unto thy seed: I have caused thee to see *it* with thine eyes, but thou shalt not go over thither.

5 ¶ So Mo′ses the servant of the LORD died there in the land of Mo′ab, according to the word of the LORD.

6 And he buried him in a valley in the land of Mo′ab, over against Beth-pe′or: but no man knoweth of his sepulchre unto this day.

7 ¶ And Mo′ses *was* an hundred and twenty years old when he died: his eye was not dim, nor his natural force abated.

8 ¶ And the children of Is′ra-el wept for Mo′-ses in the plains of Mo′ab thirty days: so the days of weeping *and* mourning for Mo′ses were ended.

9 ¶ And Josh′u-a the son of Nun was full of the spirit of wisdom; for Mo′ses had laid his hands upon him: and the children of Is′ra-el hearkened unto him, and did as the LORD commanded Mo′ses.

10 ¶ And there arose not a prophet since in Is′ra-el like unto Mo′ses, whom the LORD knew face to face,

11 In all the signs and the wonders, which the LORD sent him to do in the land of E′gypt to Pha′raoh, and to all his servants, and to all his land,

12 And in all that mighty hand, and in all the great terror which Mo′ses shewed in the sight of all Is′ra-el.

THE BOOK OF

JOSHUA

1 NOW after the death of Mo'ses the servant
of the LORD it came to pass, that the LORD
spake unto Josh'u-a the son of Nun, Mo'ses'
minister, saying,
2 Mo'ses my servant is dead; now therefore
arise, go over this Jor'dan, thou, and all this
people, unto the land which I do give to them,
even to the children of Is'ra-el.
3 Every place that the sole of your foot shall
tread upon, that have I given unto you, as I said
unto Mo'ses.
4 From the wilderness and this Leb'a-non
even unto the great river, the river Eu-phra'tes,
all the land of the Hit'tites, and unto the great
sea toward the going down of the sun, shall be
your coast.
5 There shall not any man be able to stand
before thee all the days of thy life: as I was with
Mo'ses, *so* I will be with thee: I will not fail thee,
nor forsake thee.
6 Be strong and of a good courage: for unto
this people shalt thou divide for an inheritance
the land, which I sware unto their fathers to
give them.
7 Only be thou strong and very courageous,
that thou mayest observe to do according to all
the law, which Mo'ses my servant commanded
thee: turn not from it *to* the right hand or *to* the
left, that thou mayest prosper whithersoever
thou goest.
8 This book of the law shall not depart out of
thy mouth; but thou shalt meditate therein day
and night, that thou mayest observe to do according to all that is written therein: for then
thou shalt make thy way prosperous, and then
thou shalt have good success.
9 Have not I commanded thee? Be strong and
of a good courage; be not afraid, neither be thou
dismayed: for the LORD thy God *is* with thee
whithersoever thou goest.
10 ¶ Then Josh'u-a commanded the officers
of the people, saying,
11 Pass through the host, and command the
people, saying, Prepare you victuals; for within
three days ye shall pass over this Jor'dan, to go
in to possess the land, which the LORD your God
giveth you to possess it.
12 ¶ And to the Reu'ben-ites, and to the
Gad'ites, and to half the tribe of Ma-nas'seh,
spake Josh'u-a, saying,
13 Remember the word which Mo'ses the
servant of the LORD commanded you, saying,
The LORD your God hath given you rest, and
hath given you this land.
14 Your wives, your little ones, and your cattle, shall remain in the land which Mo'ses gave
you on this side Jor'dan; but ye shall pass before your brethren armed, all the mighty men of
valour, and help them;
15 Until the LORD have given your brethren
rest, as *he hath given* you, and they also have
possessed the land which the LORD your God
giveth them: then ye shall return unto the land
of your possession, and enjoy it, which Mo'ses
the LORD's servant gave you on this side Jor'-
dan toward the sunrising.
16 ¶ And they answered Josh'u-a, saying, All
that thou commandest us we will do, and
whithersoever thou sendest us, we will go.
17 According as we hearkened unto Mo'ses
in all things, so will we hearken unto thee: only
the LORD thy God be with thee, as he was with
Mo'ses.
18 Whosoever *he be* that doth rebel against
thy commandment, and will not hearken unto
thy words in all that thou commandest him, he
shall be put to death: only be strong and of a
good courage.

2 AND Josh'u-a the son of Nun sent out of
Shit'tim two men to spy secretly, saying,
Go view the land, even Jer'i-cho. And they
went, and came into an harlot's house, named
Ra'hab, and lodged there.
2 And it was told the king of Jer'i-cho, saying, Behold, there came men in hither to night
of the children of Is'ra-el to search out the country.
3 And the king of Jer'i-cho sent unto Ra'hab,
saying, Bring forth the men that are come to
thee, which are entered into thine house: for
they be come to search out all the country.
4 And the woman took the two men, and hid
them, and said thus, There came men unto me,
but I wist not whence they *were*:
5 And it came to pass *about the time* of shut-
ting of the gate, when it was dark, that the men
went out: whither the men went I wot not: pursue after them quickly; for ye shall overtake
them.
6 But she had brought them up to the roof of
the house, and hid them with the stalks of flax,
which she had laid in order upon the roof.
7 And the men pursued after them the way
to Jor'dan unto the fords: and as soon as they
which pursued after them were gone out, they
shut the gate.
8 ¶ And before they were laid down, she
came up unto them upon the roof;
9 And she said unto the men, I know that the
LORD hath given you the land, and that your
terror is fallen upon us, and that all the inhabitants of the land faint because of you.
10 For we have heard how the LORD dried up
the water of the Red sea for you, when ye came
out of E'gypt; and what ye did unto the two
kings of the Am'or-ites, that *were* on the other
side Jor'dan, Si'hon and Og, whom ye utterly
destroyed.
11 And as soon as we had heard *these things*,
our hearts did melt, neither did there remain
any more courage in any man, because of you:
for the LORD your God, he *is* God in heaven
above, and in earth beneath.
12 Now therefore, I pray you, swear unto me
by the LORD, since I have shewed you kindness,
that ye will also shew kindness unto my father's
house, and give me a true token:
13 And *that* ye will save alive my father, and
my mother, and my brethren, and my sisters,
and all that they have, and deliver our lives
from death.
14 And the men answered her, Our life for
yours, if ye utter not this our business. And it
shall be, when the LORD hath given us the land,
that we will deal kindly and truly with thee.
15 Then she let them down by a cord through
the window: for her house *was* upon the town
wall, and she dwelt upon the wall.
16 And she said unto them, Get you to the
mountain, lest the pursuers meet you; and hide
yourselves there three days, until the pursuers

be returned: and afterward may ye go your way.

17 And the men said unto her, We *will be* blameless of this thine oath which thou hast made us swear.

18 Behold, *when* we come into the land, thou shalt bind this line of scarlet thread in the window which thou didst let us down by: and thou shalt bring thy father, and thy mother, and thy brethren, and all thy father's household, home unto thee.

19 And it shall be, *that* whosoever shall go out of the doors of thy house into the street, his blood *shall be* upon his head, and we *will be* guiltless: and whosoever shall be with thee in the house, his blood *shall be* on our head, if *any* hand be upon him.

20 And if thou utter this our business, then we will be quit of thine oath which thou hast made us to swear.

21 And she said, According unto your words, so *be* it. And she sent them away, and they departed: and she bound the scarlet line in the window.

22 And they went, and came unto the mountain, and abode there three days, until the pursuers were returned: and the pursuers sought *them* throughout all the way, but found *them* not.

23 ¶ So the two men returned, and descended from the mountain, and passed over, and came to Josh'u-a the son of Nun, and told him all *things* that befell them:

24 And they said unto Josh'u-a, Truly the LORD hath delivered into our hands all the land; for even all the inhabitants of the country do faint because of us.

3 AND Josh'u-a rose early in the morning; and they removed from Shit'tim, and came to Jor'dan, he and all the children of Is'ra-el, and lodged there before they passed over.

2 And it came to pass after three days, that the officers went through the host;

3 And they commanded the people, saying, When ye see the ark of the covenant of the LORD your God, and the priests the Le'vites bearing it, then ye shall remove from your place, and go after it.

4 Yet there shall be a space between you and it, about two thousand cubits by measure: come not near unto it, that ye may know the way by which ye must go: for ye have not passed *this* way heretofore.

5 And Josh'u-a said unto the people, Sanctify yourselves: for to morrow the LORD will do wonders among you.

6 And Josh'u-a spake unto the priests, saying, Take up the ark of the covenant, and pass over before the people. And they took up the ark of the covenant, and went before the people.

7 ¶ And the LORD said unto Josh'u-a, This day will I begin to magnify thee in the sight of all Is'ra-el, that they may know that, as I was with Mo'ses, *so* I will be with thee.

8 And thou shalt command the priests that bear the ark of the covenant, saying, When ye are come to the brink of the water of Jor'dan, ye shall stand still in Jor'dan.

9 ¶ And Josh'u-a said unto the children of Is'ra-el, Come hither, and hear the words of the LORD your God.

10 And Josh'u-a said, Hereby ye shall know that the living God *is* among you, and *that* he will without fail drive out from before you the Ca'naan-ites, and the Hit'tites, and the Hi'vites, and the Per'iz-zites, and the Gir'ga-shites, and the Am'or-ites, and the Jeb'u-sites.

11 Behold, the ark of the covenant of the LORD of all the earth passeth over before you into Jor'dan.

12 Now therefore take you twelve men out of the tribes of Is'ra-el, out of every tribe a man.

13 And it shall come to pass, as soon as the soles of the feet of the priests that bear the ark of the LORD, the Lord of all the earth, shall rest in the waters of Jor'dan, *that* the waters of Jor'dan shall be cut off *from* the waters that come down from above; and they shall stand upon an heap.

14 ¶ And it came to pass, when the people removed from their tents, to pass over Jor'dan, and the priests bearing the ark of the covenant before the people;

15 And as they that bare the ark were come unto Jor'dan, and the feet of the priests that bare the ark were dipped in the brim of the water, (for Jor'dan overfloweth all his banks all the time of harvest,)

16 That the waters which came down from above stood *and* rose up upon an heap very far from the city Ad'am, that *is* beside Zar'e-tan: and those that came down toward the sea of the plain, *even* the salt sea, failed, *and* were cut off: and the people passed over right against Jer'i-cho.

17 And the priests that bare the ark of the covenant of the LORD stood firm on dry ground in the midst of Jor'dan, and all the Is'ra-el-ites passed over on dry ground, until all the people were passed clean over Jor'dan.

4 AND it came to pass, when all the people were clean passed over Jor'dan, that the LORD spake unto Josh'u-a, saying,

2 Take you twelve men out of the people, out of every tribe a man,

3 And command ye them, saying, Take you hence out of the midst of Jor'dan, out of the place where the priests' feet stood firm, twelve stones, and ye shall carry them over with you, and leave them in the lodging place, where ye shall lodge this night.

4 Then Josh'u-a called the twelve men, whom he had prepared of the children of Is'ra-el, out of every tribe a man:

5 And Josh'u-a said unto them, Pass over before the ark of the LORD your God into the midst of Jor'dan, and take you up every man of you a stone upon his shoulder, according unto the number of the tribes of the children of Is'ra-el:

6 That this may be a sign among you, *that* when your children ask *their fathers* in time to come, saying, What *mean* ye by these stones?

7 Then ye shall answer them, That the waters of Jor'dan were cut off before the ark of the covenant of the LORD; when it passed over Jor'dan, the waters of Jor'dan were cut off: and these stones shall be for a memorial unto the children of Is'ra-el for ever.

8 And the children of Is'ra-el did so as Josh'u-a commanded, and took up twelve stones out of the midst of Jor'dan, as the LORD spake unto Josh'u-a, according to the number of the tribes of the children of Is'ra-el, and carried them over with them unto the place where they lodged, and laid them down there.

9 And Josh'u-a set up twelve stones in the midst of Jor'dan, in the place where the feet of the priests which bare the ark of the covenant stood: and they are there unto this day.

10 ¶ For the priests which bare the ark stood

in the midst of Jor'dan, until every thing was finished that the LORD commanded Josh'u-a to speak unto the people, according to all that Mo'ses commanded Josh'u-a: and the people hasted and passed over.

11 And it came to pass, when all the people were clean passed over, that the ark of the LORD passed over, and the priests, in the presence of the people.

12 And the children of Reu'ben, and the children of Gad, and half the tribe of Ma-nas'seh, passed over armed before the children of Is'ra-el, as Mo'ses spake unto them:

13 About forty thousand prepared for war passed over before the LORD unto battle, to the plains of Jer'i-cho.

14 ¶ On that day the LORD magnified Josh'u-a in the sight of all Is'ra-el; and they feared him, as they feared Mo'ses, all the days of his life.

15 And the LORD spake unto Josh'u-a, saying,

16 Command the priests that bear the ark of the testimony, that they come up out of Jor'dan.

17 Josh'u-a therefore commanded the priests, saying, Come ye up out of Jor'dan.

18 And it came to pass, when the priests that bare the ark of the covenant of the LORD were come up out of the midst of Jor'dan, *and* the soles of the priests' feet were lifted up unto the dry land, that the waters of Jor'dan returned unto their place, and flowed over all his banks, as *they did* before.

19 ¶ And the people came up out of Jor'dan on the tenth *day* of the first month, and encamped in Gil'gal, in the east border of Jer'i-cho.

20 And those twelve stones, which they took out of Jor'dan, did Josh'u-a pitch in Gil'gal.

21 And he spake unto the children of Is'ra-el, saying, When your children shall ask their fathers in time to come, saying, What *mean* these stones?

22 Then ye shall let your children know, saying, Is'ra-el came over this Jor'dan on dry land.

23 For the LORD your God dried up the waters of Jor'dan from before you, until ye were passed over, as the LORD your God did to the Red sea, which he dried up from before us, until we were gone over:

24 That all the people of the earth might know the hand of the LORD, that it *is* mighty: that ye might fear the LORD your God for ever.

5 AND it came to pass, when all the kings of the Am'or-ites, which *were* on the side of Jor'dan westward, and all the kings of the Ca'naan-ites, which *were* by the sea, heard that the LORD had dried up the waters of Jor'dan from before the children of Is'ra-el, until we were passed over, that their heart melted, neither was there spirit in them any more, because of the children of Is'ra-el.

2 ¶ At that time the LORD said unto Josh'u-a, Make thee sharp knives, and circumcise again the children of Is'ra-el the second time.

3 And Josh'u-a made him sharp knives, and circumcised the children of Is'ra-el at the hill of the foreskins.

4 And this *is* the cause why Josh'u-a did circumcise: All the people that came out of E'gypt, *that were* males, *even* all the men of war, died in the wilderness by the way, after they came out of E'gypt.

5 Now all the people that came out were circumcised: but all the people *that were* born in the wilderness by the way as they came forth out of E'gypt, *them* they had not circumcised.

6 For the children of Is'ra-el walked forty years in the wilderness, till all the people *that were* men of war, which came out of E'gypt, were consumed, because they obeyed not the voice of the LORD: unto whom the LORD sware that he would not shew them the land, which the LORD sware unto their fathers that he would give us, a land that floweth with milk and honey.

7 And their children, *whom* he raised up in their stead, them Josh'u-a circumcised: for they were uncircumcised, because they had not circumcised them by the way.

8 And it came to pass, when they had done circumcising all the people, that they abode in their places in the camp, till they were whole.

9 And the LORD said unto Josh'u-a, This day have I rolled away the reproach of E'gypt from off you. Wherefore the name of the place is called Gil'gal unto this day.

10 ¶ And the children of Is'ra-el encamped in Gil'gal, and kept the passover on the fourteenth day of the month at even in the plains of Jer'i-cho.

11 And they did eat of the old corn of the land on the morrow after the passover, unleavened cakes, and parched *corn* in the selfsame day.

12 ¶ And the manna ceased on the morrow after they had eaten of the old corn of the land; neither had the children of Is'ra-el manna any more; but they did eat of the fruit of the land of Ca'naan that year.

13 ¶ And it came to pass, when Josh'u-a was by Jer'i-cho, that he lifted up his eyes and looked, and, behold, there stood a man over against him with his sword drawn in his hand: and Josh'u-a went unto him, and said unto him, *Art* thou for us, or for our adversaries?

14 And he said, Nay; but *as* captain of the host of the LORD am I now come. And Josh'u-a fell on his face to the earth, and did worship, and said unto him, What saith my lord unto his servant?

15 And the captain of the LORD's host said unto Josh'u-a, Loose thy shoe from off thy foot; for the place whereon thou standest *is* holy. And Josh'u-a did so.

6 NOW Jer'i-cho was straitly shut up because of the children of Is'ra-el: none went out, and none came in.

2 And the LORD said unto Josh'u-a, See, I have given into thine hand Jer'i-cho, and the king thereof, *and* the mighty men of valour.

3 And ye shall compass the city, all *ye* men of war, *and* go round about the city once. Thus shalt thou do six days.

4 And seven priests shall bear before the ark seven trumpets of rams' horns: and the seventh day ye shall compass the city seven times, and the priests shall blow with the trumpets.

5 And it shall come to pass, that when they make a long *blast* with the ram's horn, *and* when ye hear the sound of the trumpet, all the people shall shout with a great shout; and the wall of the city shall fall down flat, and the people shall ascend up every man straight before him.

6 ¶ And Josh'u-a the son of Nun called the priests, and said unto them, Take up the ark of the covenant, and let seven priests bear seven trumpets of rams' horns before the ark of the LORD.

7 And he said unto the people, Pass dn, and compass the city, and let him that is armed pass on before the ark of the LORD.

8 ¶ And it came to pass, when Josh'u-a had

spoken unto the people, that the seven priests
bearing the seven trumpets of rams' horns
passed on before the LORD, and blew with the
trumpets: and the ark of the covenant of the
LORD followed them.
9 ¶ And the armed men went before the
priests that blew with the trumpets, and the rereward came after the ark, *the priests* going on,
and blowing with the trumpets.
10 And Josh'u-a had commanded the people,
saying, Ye shall not shout, nor make any noise
with your voice, neither shall *any* word proceed
out of your mouth, until the day I bid you shout;
then shall ye shout.
11 So the ark of the LORD compassed the
city, going about *it* once: and they came into the
camp, and lodged in the camp.
12 ¶ And Josh'u-a rose early in the morning,
and the priests took up the ark of the LORD.
13 And seven priests bearing seven trumpets
of rams' horns before the ark of the LORD went
on continually, and blew with the trumpets: and
the armed men went before them; but the rereward came after the ark of the LORD, *the priests*
going on, and blowing with the trumpets.
14 And the second day they compassed the
city once, and returned into the camp: so they
did six days.
15 And it came to pass on the seventh day,
that they rose early about the dawning of the
day, and compassed the city after the same
manner seven times: only on that day they compassed the city seven times.
16 And it came to pass at the seventh time,
when the priests blew with the trumpets, Josh'-
u-a said unto the people, Shout; for the LORD
hath given you the city.
17 ¶ And the city shall be accursed, *even* it,
and all that *are* therein, to the LORD: only Ra'-
hab the harlot shall live, she and all that *are*
with her in the house, because she hid the messengers that we sent.
18 And ye, in any wise keep *yourselves* from
the accursed thing, lest ye make *yourselves* accursed, when ye take of the accursed thing, and
make the camp of Is'ra-el a curse, and trouble
it.
19 But all the silver, and gold, and vessels of
brass and iron, *are* consecrated unto the LORD:
they shall come into the treasury of the LORD.
20 So the people shouted when *the priests*
blew with the trumpets: and it came to pass,
when the people heard the sound of the trumpet, and the people shouted with a great shout,
that the wall fell down flat, so that the people
went up into the city, every man straight before
him, and they took the city.
21 And they utterly destroyed all that *was* in
the city, both man and woman, young and old,
and ox, and sheep, and ass, with the edge of the
sword.
22 But Josh'u-a had said unto the two men
that had spied out the country, Go into the harlot's house, and bring out thence the woman,
and all that she hath, as ye sware unto her.
23 And the young men that were spies went
in, and brought out Ra'hab, and her father, and
her mother, and her brethren, and all that she
had; and they brought out all her kindred, and
left them without the camp of Is'ra-el.
24 And they burnt the city with fire, and all
that *was* therein: only the silver, and the gold,
and the vessels of brass and of iron, they put
into the treasury of the house of the LORD.
25 And Josh'u-a saved Ra'hab the harlot
alive, and her father's household, and all that
she had; and she dwelleth in Is'ra-el *even* unto
this day; because she hid the messengers,
which Josh'u-a sent to spy out Jer'i-cho.
26 ¶ And Josh'u-a adjured *them* at that time,
saying, Cursed *be* the man before the LORD, that
riseth up and buildeth this city Jer'i-cho: he
shall lay the foundation thereof in his firstborn,
and in his youngest *son* shall he set up the gates
of it.
27 So the LORD was with Josh'u-a; and his
fame was *noised* throughout all the country.

7 BUT the children of Is'ra-el committed a
trespass in the accursed thing: for A'chan,
the son of Car'mi, the son of Zab'di, the son of
Ze'rah, of the tribe of Ju'dah, took of the accursed thing: and the anger of the LORD was
kindled against the children of Is'ra-el.
2 And Josh'u-a sent men from Jer'i-cho to A'-
i, which *is* beside Beth–a'ven, on the east side of
Beth'–el, and spake unto them, saying, Go up
and view the country. And the men went up and
viewed A'i.
3 And they returned to Josh'u-a, and said
unto him, Let not all the people go up; but let
about two or three thousand men go up and
smite A'i; *and* make not all the people to labour
thither; for they *are but* few.
4 So there went up thither of the people
about three thousand men: and they fled before
the men of A'i.
5 And the men of A'i smote of them about
thirty and six men: for they chased them *from*
before the gate *even* unto Sheb'a-rim, and
smote them in the going down: wherefore the
hearts of the people melted, and became as water.
6 ¶ And Josh'u-a rent his clothes, and fell to
the earth upon his face before the ark of the
LORD until the eventide, he and the elders of
Is'ra-el, and put dust upon their heads.
7 And Josh'u-a said, Alas, O Lord GOD,
wherefore hast thou at all brought this people
over Jor'dan, to deliver us into the hand of the
Am'or-ites, to destroy us? would to God we had
been content, and dwelt on the other side Jor'-
dan!
8 O Lord, what shall I say, when Is'ra-el turneth their backs before their enemies!
9 For the Ca'naan-ites and all the inhabitants
of the land shall hear *of it,* and shall environ us
round, and cut off our name from the earth: and
what wilt thou do unto thy great name?
10 ¶ And the LORD said unto Josh'u-a, Get
thee up; wherefore liest thou thus upon thy
face?
11 Is'ra-el hath sinned, and they have also
transgressed my covenant which I commanded
them: for they have even taken of the accursed
thing, and have also stolen, and dissembled
also, and they have put *it* even among their own
stuff.
12 Therefore the children of Is'ra-el could not
stand before their enemies, *but* turned *their*
backs before their enemies, because they were
accursed: neither will I be with you any more,
except ye destroy the accursed from among
you.
13 Up, sanctify the people, and say, Sanctify
yourselves against to morrow: for thus saith the
LORD God of Is'ra-el, *There is* an accursed thing
in the midst of thee, O Is'ra-el: thou canst not
stand before thine enemies, until ye take away
the accursed thing from among you.
14 In the morning therefore ye shall be
brought according to your tribes: and it shall
be, *that* the tribe which the LORD taketh shall
come according to the families *thereof:* and the

family which the LORD shall take shall come by
households; and the household which the LORD
shall take shall come man by man.
15 And it shall be, *that* he that is taken with
the accursed thing shall be burnt with fire, he
and all that he hath: because he hath transgressed the covenant of the LORD, and because
he hath wrought folly in Is'ra-el.
16 ¶ So Josh'u-a rose up early in the morning, and brought Is'ra-el by their tribes; and the
tribe of Ju'dah was taken:
17 And he brought the family of Ju'dah; and
he took the family of the Zar'hites: and he
brought the family of the Zar'hites man by man;
and Zab'di was taken:
18 And he brought his household man by
man; and A'chan, the son of Car'mi, the son of
Zab'di, the son of Ze'rah, of the tribe of Ju'dah,
was taken.
19 And Josh'u-a said unto A'chan, My son,
give, I pray thee, glory to the LORD God of Is'ra-
el, and make confession unto him; and tell me
now what thou hast done; hide *it* not from me.
20 And A'chan answered Josh'u-a, and said,
Indeed I have sinned against the LORD God of
Is'ra-el, and thus and thus have I done:
21 When I saw among the spoils a goodly
Bab'y-lo-nish garment, and two hundred shekels of silver, and a wedge of gold of fifty shekels
weight, then I coveted them, and took them;
and, behold, they *are* hid in the earth in the
midst of my tent, and the silver under it.
22 ¶ So Josh'u-a sent messengers, and they
ran unto the tent; and, behold, *it was* hid in his
tent, and the silver under it.
23 And they took them out of the midst of
the tent, and brought them unto Josh'u-a, and
unto all the children of Is'ra-el, and laid them
out before the LORD.
24 And Josh'u-a, and all Is'ra-el with him,
took A'chan the son of Ze'rah, and the silver,
and the garment, and the wedge of gold, and his
sons, and his daughters, and his oxen, and his
asses, and his sheep, and his tent, and all that
he had: and they brought them unto the valley
of A'chor.
25 And Josh'u-a said, Why hast thou troubled us? the LORD shall trouble thee this day.
And all Is'ra-el stoned him with stones, and
burned them with fire, after they had stoned
them with stones.
26 And they raised over him a great heap of
stones unto this day. So the LORD turned from
the fierceness of his anger. Wherefore the name
of that place was called, The valley of A'chor,
unto this day.

8 AND the LORD said unto Josh'u-a, Fear
not, neither be thou dismayed: take all the
people of war with thee, and arise, go up to A'i:
see, I have given into thy hand the king of A'i,
and his people, and his city, and his land:
2 And thou shalt do to A'i and her king as
thou didst unto Jer'i-cho and her king: only the
spoil thereof, and the cattle thereof, shall ye
take for a prey unto yourselves: lay thee an ambush for the city behind it.
3 ¶ So Josh'u-a arose, and all the people of
war, to go up against A'i: and Josh'u-a chose
out thirty thousand mighty men of valour, and
sent them away by night.
4 And he commanded them, saying, Behold,
ye shall lie in wait against the city, *even* behind
the city: go not very far from the city, but be ye
all ready:
5 And I, and all the people that *are* with me,
will approach unto the city: and it shall come to
pass, when they come out against us, as at the
first, that we will flee before them,
6 (For they will come out after us) till we
have drawn them from the city; for they will
say, They flee before us, as at the first: therefore
we will flee before them.
7 Then ye shall rise up from the ambush, and
seize upon the city: for the LORD your God will
deliver it into your hand.
8 And it shall be, when ye have taken the
city, *that* ye shall set the city on fire: according
to the commandment of the LORD shall ye do.
See, I have commanded you.
9 ¶ Josh'u-a therefore sent them forth: and
they went to lie in ambush, and abode between
Beth'-el and A'i, on the west side of A'i: but
Josh'u-a lodged that night among the people.
10 And Josh'u-a rose up early in the morning,
and numbered the people, and went up, he and
the elders of Is'ra-el, before the people to A'i.
11 And all the people, *even the people* of war
that *were* with him, went up, and drew nigh,
and came before the city, and pitched on the
north side of A'i: now *there was* a valley between them and A'i.
12 And he took about five thousand men, and
set them to lie in ambush between Beth'-el and
A'i, on the west side of the city.
13 And when they had set the people, *even*
all the host that *was* on the north of the city,
and their liers in wait on the west of the city,
Josh'u-a went that night into the midst of the
valley.
14 ¶ And it came to pass, when the king of
A'i saw *it*, that they hasted and rose up early,
and the men of the city went out against Is'ra-el
to battle, he and all his people, at a time appointed, before the plain; but he wist not that
there were liers in ambush against him behind
the city.
15 And Josh'u-a and all Is'ra-el made as if
they were beaten before them, and fled by the
way of the wilderness.
16 And all the people that *were* in A'i were
called together to pursue after them: and they
pursued after Josh'u-a, and were drawn away
from the city.
17 And there was not a man left in A'i or
Beth'-el, that went not out after Is'ra-el: and
they left the city open, and pursued after Is'ra-
el.
18 And the LORD said unto Josh'u-a, Stretch
out the spear that *is* in thy hand toward A'i; for
I will give it into thine hand. And Josh'u-a
stretched out the spear that *he had* in his hand
toward the city.
19 And the ambush arose quickly out of their
place, and they ran as soon as he had stretched
out his hand: and they entered into the city, and
took it, and hasted and set the city on fire.
20 And when the men of A'i looked behind
them, they saw, and, behold, the smoke of the
city ascended up to heaven, and they had no
power to flee this way or that way: and the people that fled to the wilderness turned back upon
the pursuers.
21 And when Josh'u-a and all Is'ra-el saw
that the ambush had taken the city, and that the
smoke of the city ascended, then they turned
again, and slew the men of A'i.
22 And the other issued out of the city
against them; so they were in the midst of Is'ra-
el, some on this side, and some on that side: and
they smote them, so that they let none of them
remain or escape.
23 And the king of A'i they took alive, and
brought him to Josh'u-a.

24 And it came to pass, when Is'ra-el had made an end of slaying all the inhabitants of A'i in the field, in the wilderness wherein they chased them, and when they were all fallen on the edge of the sword, until they were consumed, that all the Is'ra-el-ites returned unto A'i, and smote it with the edge of the sword.

25 And *so* it was, *that* all that fell that day, both of men and women, *were* twelve thousand, *even* all the men of A'i.

26 For Josh'u-a drew not his hand back, wherewith he stretched out the spear, until he had utterly destroyed all the inhabitants of A'i.

27 Only the cattle and the spoil of that city Is'ra-el took for a prey unto themselves, according unto the word of the LORD which he commanded Josh'u-a.

28 And Josh'u-a burnt A'i, and made it an heap for ever, *even* a desolation unto this day.

29 And the king of A'i he hanged on a tree until eventide: and as soon as the sun was down, Josh'u-a commanded that they should take his carcase down from the tree, and cast it at the entering of the gate of the city, and raise thereon a great heap of stones, *that remaineth* unto this day.

30 ¶ Then Josh'u-a built an altar unto the LORD God of Is'ra-el in mount E'bal,

31 As Mo'ses the servant of the LORD commanded the children of Is'ra-el, as it is written in the book of the law of Mo'ses, an altar of whole stones, over which no man hath lift up *any* iron; and they offered thereon burnt offerings unto the LORD, and sacrificed peace offerings.

32 ¶ And he wrote there upon the stones a copy of the law of Mo'ses, which he wrote in the presence of the children of Is'ra-el.

33 And all Is'ra-el, and their elders, and officers, and their judges, stood on this side the ark and on that side before the priests the Le'vites, which bare the ark of the covenant of the LORD, as well the stranger, as he that was born among them; half of them over against mount Ger'i-zim, and half of them over against mount E'bal; as Mo'ses the servant of the LORD had commanded before, that they should bless the people of Is'ra-el.

34 And afterward he read all the words of the law, the blessings and cursings, according to all that is written in the book of the law.

35 There was not a word of all that Mo'ses commanded, which Josh'u-a read not before all the congregation of Is'ra-el, with the women, and the little ones, and the strangers that were conversant among them.

9 AND it came to pass, when all the kings which *were* on this side Jor'dan, in the hills, and in the valleys, and in all the coasts of the great sea over against Leb'a-non, the Hit'tite, and the Am'or-ite, the Ca'naan-ite, the Per'iz-zite, the Hi'vite, and the Jeb'u-site, heard *thereof*:

2 That they gathered themselves together, to fight with Josh'u-a and with Is'ra-el, with one accord.

3 ¶ And when the inhabitants of Gib'e-on heard what Josh'u-a had done unto Jer'i-cho and to A'i,

4 They did work wilily, and went and made as if they had been ambassadors, and took old sacks upon their asses, and wine bottles, old, and rent, and bound up;

5 And old shoes and clouted upon their feet, and old garments upon them; and all the bread of their provision was dry *and* mouldy.

6 And they went to Josh'u-a unto the camp at Gil'gal, and said unto him, and to the men of Is'ra-el, We be come from a far country: now therefore make ye a league with us.

7 And the men of Is'ra-el said unto the Hi'vites, Peradventure ye dwell among us; and how shall we make a league with you?

8 And they said unto Josh'u-a, We *are* thy servants. And Josh'u-a said unto them, Who *are* ye? and from whence come ye?

9 And they said unto him, From a very far country thy servants are come because of the name of the LORD thy God: for we have heard the fame of him, and all that he did in E'gypt,

10 And all that he did to the two kings of the Am'or-ites, that *were* beyond Jor'dan, to Si'hon king of Hesh'bon, and to Og king of Ba'shan, which *was* at Ash'ta-roth.

11 Wherefore our elders and all the inhabitants of our country spake to us, saying, Take victuals with you for the journey, and go to meet them, and say unto them, We *are* your servants: therefore now make ye a league with us.

12 This our bread we took hot *for* our provision out of our houses on the day we came forth to go unto you; but now, behold, it is dry, and it is mouldy:

13 And these bottles of wine, which we filled, *were* new; and, behold, they be rent: and these our garments and our shoes are become old by reason of the very long journey.

14 And the men took of their victuals, and asked not *counsel* at the mouth of the LORD.

15 And Josh'u-a made peace with them, and made a league with them, to let them live: and the princes of the congregation sware unto them.

16 ¶ And it came to pass at the end of three days after they had made a league with them, that they heard that they *were* their neighbours, and *that* they dwelt among them.

17 And the children of Is'ra-el journeyed, and came unto their cities on the third day. Now their cities *were* Gib'e-on, and Che-phi'rah, and Be-e'roth, and Kir'jath-je'a-rim.

18 And the children of Is'ra-el smote them not, because the princes of the congregation had sworn unto them by the LORD God of Is'ra-el. And all the congregation murmured against the princes.

19 But all the princes said unto all the congregation, We have sworn unto them by the LORD God of Is'ra-el: now therefore we may not touch them.

20 This we will do to them; we will even let them live, lest wrath be upon us, because of the oath which we sware unto them.

21 And the princes said unto them, Let them live; but let them be hewers of wood and drawers of water unto all the congregation; as the princes had promised them.

22 ¶ And Josh'u-a called for them, and he spake unto them, saying, Wherefore have ye beguiled us, saying, We *are* very far from you; when ye dwell among us?

23 Now therefore ye *are* cursed, and there shall none of you be freed from being bondmen, and hewers of wood and drawers of water for the house of my God.

24 And they answered Josh'u-a, and said, Because it was certainly told thy servants, how that the LORD thy God commanded his servant Mo'ses to give you all the land, and to destroy all the inhabitants of the land from before you, therefore we were sore afraid of our lives because of you, and have done this thing.

25 And now, behold, we *are* in thine hand: as it seemeth good and right unto thee to do unto us, do.

26 And so did he unto them, and delivered them out of the hand of the children of Is'ra-el, that they slew them not.

27 And Josh'u-a made them that day hewers of wood and drawers of water for the congregation, and for the altar of the LORD, even unto this day, in the place which he should choose.

10 NOW it came to pass, when A-don'i-ze'dec king of Je-ru'sa-lem had heard how Josh'u-a had taken A'i, and had utterly destroyed it; as he had done to Jer'i-cho and her king, so he had done to A'i and her king; and how the inhabitants of Gib'e-on had made peace with Is'ra-el, and were among them;

2 That they feared greatly, because Gib'e-on *was* a great city, as one of the royal cities, and because it *was* greater than A'i, and all the men thereof *were* mighty.

3 Wherefore A-don'i-ze'dec king of Je-ru'salem sent unto Ho'ham king of He'bron, and unto Pi'ram king of Jar'muth, and unto Ja-phi'a king of La'chish, and unto De'bir king of Eg'lon, saying,

4 Come up unto me, and help me, that we may smite Gib'e-on: for it hath made peace with Josh'u-a and with the children of Is'ra-el.

5 Therefore the five kings of the Am'or-ites, the king of Je-ru'sa-lem, the king of He'bron, the king of Jar'muth, the king of La'chish, the king of Eg'lon, gathered themselves together, and went up, they and all their hosts, and encamped before Gib'e-on, and made war against it.

6 ¶ And the men of Gib'e-on sent unto Josh'u-a to the camp to Gil'gal, saying, Slack not thy hand from thy servants; come up to us quickly, and save us, and help us: for all the kings of the Am'or-ites that dwell in the mountains are gathered together against us.

7 So Josh'u-a ascended from Gil'gal, he, and all the people of war with him, and all the mighty men of valour.

8 ¶ And the LORD said unto Josh'u-a, Fear them not: for I have delivered them into thine hand; there shall not a man of them stand before thee.

9 Josh'u-a therefore came unto them suddenly, *and* went up from Gil'gal all night.

10 And the LORD discomfited them before Is'ra-el, and slew them with a great slaughter at Gib'e-on, and chased them along the way that goeth up to Beth-ho'ron, and smote them to A-ze'kah, and unto Mak-ke'dah.

11 And it came to pass, as they fled from before Is'ra-el, *and* were in the going down to Beth-ho'ron, that the LORD cast down great stones from heaven upon them unto A-ze'kah, and they died: *they were* more which died with hailstones than *they* whom the children of Is'ra-el slew with the sword.

12 ¶ Then spake Josh'u-a to the LORD in the day when the LORD delivered up the Am'or-ites before the children of Is'ra-el, and he said in the sight of Is'ra-el, Sun, stand thou still upon Gib'e-on; and thou, Moon, in the valley of Aj'a-lon.

13 And the sun stood still, and the moon stayed, until the people had avenged themselves upon their enemies. *Is* not this written in the book of Ja'sher? So the sun stood still in the midst of heaven, and hasted not to go down about a whole day.

14 And there was no day like that before it or after it, that the LORD hearkened unto the voice of a man: for the LORD fought for Is'ra-el.

15 ¶ And Josh'u-a returned, and all Is'ra-el with him, unto the camp to Gil'gal.

16 But these five kings fled, and hid themselves in a cave at Mak-ke'dah.

17 And it was told Josh'u-a, saying, The five kings are found hid in a cave at Mak-ke'dah.

18 And Josh'u-a said, Roll great stones upon the mouth of the cave, and set men by it for to keep them:

19 And stay ye not, *but* pursue after your enemies, and smite the hindmost of them; suffer them not to enter into their cities: for the LORD your God hath delivered them into your hand.

20 And it came to pass, when Josh'u-a and the children of Is'ra-el had made an end of slaying them with a very great slaughter, till they were consumed, that the rest *which* remained of them entered into fenced cities.

21 And all the people returned to the camp to Josh'u-a at Mak-ke'dah in peace: none moved his tongue against any of the children of Is'ra-el.

22 Then said Josh'u-a, Open the mouth of the cave, and bring out those five kings unto me out of the cave.

23 And they did so, and brought forth those five kings unto him out of the cave, the king of Je-ru'sa-lem, the king of He'bron, the king of Jar'muth, the king of La'chish, *and* the king of Eg'lon.

24 And it came to pass, when they brought out those kings unto Josh'u-a, that Josh'u-a called for all the men of Is'ra-el, and said unto the captains of the men of war which went with him, Come near, put your feet upon the necks of these kings. And they came near, and put their feet upon the necks of them.

25 And Josh'u-a said unto them, Fear not, nor be dismayed, be strong and of good courage: for thus shall the LORD do to all your enemies against whom ye fight.

26 And afterward Josh'u-a smote them, and slew them, and hanged them on five trees: and they were hanging upon the trees until the evening.

27 And it came to pass at the time of the going down of the sun, *that* Josh'u-a commanded, and they took them down off the trees, and cast them into the cave wherein they had been hid, and laid great stones in the cave's mouth, *which remain* until this very day.

28 ¶ And that day Josh'u-a took Mak-ke'dah, and smote it with the edge of the sword, and the king thereof he utterly destroyed, them, and all the souls that *were* therein; he let none remain: and he did to the king of Mak-ke'dah as he did unto the king of Jer'i-cho.

29 Then Josh'u-a passed from Mak-ke'dah, and all Is'ra-el with him, unto Lib'nah, and fought against Lib'nah:

30 And the LORD delivered it also, and the king thereof, into the hand of Is'ra-el; and he smote it with the edge of the sword, and all the souls that *were* therein; he let none remain in it; but did unto the king thereof as he did unto the king of Jer'i-cho.

31 ¶ And Josh'u-a passed from Lib'nah, and all Is'ra-el with him, unto La'chish, and encamped against it, and fought against it:

32 And the LORD delivered La'chish into the hand of Is'ra-el, which took it on the second day, and smote it with the edge of the sword, and all the souls that *were* therein, according to all that he had done to Lib'nah.

33 ¶ Then Ho'ram king of Ge'zer came up to

help La'chish; and Josh'u-a smote him and his people, until he had left him none remaining.

34 ¶ And from La'chish Josh'u-a passed unto Eg'lon, and all Is'ra-el with him; and they encamped against it, and fought against it:

35 And they took it on that day, and smote it with the edge of the sword, and all the souls that *were* therein he utterly destroyed that day, according to all that he had done to La'chish.

36 And Josh'u-a went up from Eg'lon, and all Is'ra-el with him, unto He'bron; and they fought against it:

37 And they took it, and smote it with the edge of the sword, and the king thereof, and all the cities thereof, and all the souls that *were* therein; he left none remaining, according to all that he had done to Eg'lon; but destroyed it utterly, and all the souls that *were* therein.

38 ¶ And Josh'u-a returned, and all Is'ra-el with him, to De'bir; and fought against it:

39 And he took it, and the king thereof, and all the cities thereof; and they smote them with the edge of the sword, and utterly destroyed all the souls that *were* therein; he left none remaining: as he had done to He'bron, so he did to De'bir, and to the king thereof; as he had done also to Lib'nah, and to her king.

40 ¶ So Josh'u-a smote all the country of the hills, and of the south, and of the vale, and of the springs, and all their kings: he left none remaining, but utterly destroyed all that breathed, as the LORD God of Is'ra-el commanded.

41 And Josh'u-a smote them from Ka'desh-bar'ne-a even unto Ga'za, and all the country of Go'shen, even unto Gib'e-on.

42 And all these kings and their land did Josh'u-a take at one time, because the LORD God of Is'ra-el fought for Is'ra-el.

43 And Josh'u-a returned, and all Is'ra-el with him, unto the camp to Gil'gal.

11 AND it came to pass, when Ja'bin king of Ha'zor had heard *those things*, that he sent to Jo'bab king of Ma'don, and to the king of Shim'ron, and to the king of Ach'shaph,

2 And to the kings that *were* on the north of the mountains, and of the plains south of Chin'-ne-roth, and in the valley, and in the borders of Dor on the west,

3 *And to* the Ca'naan-ite on the east and on the west, and *to* the Am'or-ite, and the Hit'tite, and the Per'iz-zite, and the Jeb'u-site in the mountains, and *to* the Hi'vite under Her'mon in the land of Miz'peh.

4 And they went out, they and all their hosts with them, much people, even as the sand that *is* upon the sea shore in multitude, with horses and chariots very many.

5 And when all these kings were met together, they came and pitched together at the waters of Me'rom, to fight against Is'ra-el.

6 ¶ And the LORD said unto Josh'u-a, Be not afraid because of them: for to morrow about this time will I deliver them up all slain before Is'ra-el: thou shalt hough their horses, and burn their chariots with fire.

7 So Josh'u-a came, and all the people of war with him, against them by the waters of Me'-rom suddenly; and they fell upon them.

8 And the LORD delivered them into the hand of Is'ra-el, who smote them, and chased them unto great Zi'don, and unto Mis're-photh-ma'-im, and unto the valley of Miz'peh eastward; and they smote them, until they left them none remaining.

9 And Josh'u-a did unto them as the LORD bade him: he houghed their horses, and burnt their chariots with fire.

10 ¶ And Josh'u-a at that time turned back, and took Ha'zor, and smote the king thereof with the sword: for Ha'zor beforetime was the head of all those kingdoms.

11 And they smote all the souls that *were* therein with the edge of the sword, utterly destroying *them*: there was not any left to breathe: and he burnt Ha'zor with fire.

12 And all the cities of those kings, and all the kings of them, did Josh'u-a take, and smote them with the edge of the sword, *and* he utterly destroyed them, as Mo'ses the servant of the LORD commanded.

13 But *as for* the cities that stood still in their strength, Is'ra-el burned none of them, save Ha'zor only; *that* did Josh'u-a burn.

14 And all the spoil of these cities, and the cattle, the children of Is'ra-el took for a prey unto themselves; but every man they smote with the edge of the sword, until they had destroyed them, neither left they any to breathe.

15 ¶ As the LORD commanded Mo'ses his servant, so did Mo'ses command Josh'u-a, and so did Josh'u-a; he left nothing undone of all that the LORD commanded Mo'ses.

16 So Josh'u-a took all that land, the hills, and all the south country, and all the land of Go'shen, and the valley, and the plain, and the mountain of Is'ra-el, and the valley of the same;

17 *Even* from the mount Ha'lak, that goeth up to Se'ir, even unto Ba'al-gad in the valley of Leb'a-non under mount Her'mon: and all their kings he took, and smote them, and slew them.

18 Josh'u-a made war a long time with all those kings.

19 There was not a city that made peace with the children of Is'ra-el, save the Hi'vites the inhabitants of Gib'e-on: all *other* they took in battle.

20 For it was of the LORD to harden their hearts, that they should come against Is'ra-el in battle, that he might destroy them utterly, *and* that they might have no favour, but that he might destroy them, as the LORD commanded Mo'ses.

21 ¶ And at that time came Josh'u-a, and cut off the An'a-kims from the mountains, from He'bron, from De'bir, from A'nab, and from all the mountains of Ju'dah, and from all the mountains of Is'ra-el: Josh'u-a destroyed them utterly with their cities.

22 There was none of the An'a-kims left in the land of the children of Is'ra-el: only in Ga'za, in Gath, and in Ash'dod, there remained.

23 So Josh'u-a took the whole land, according to all that the LORD said unto Mo'ses; and Josh'u-a gave it for an inheritance unto Is'ra-el according to their divisions by their tribes. And the land rested from war.

12 NOW these *are* the kings of the land, which the children of Is'ra-el smote, and possessed their land on the other side Jor'dan toward the rising of the sun, from the river Ar'-non unto mount Her'mon, and all the plain on the east:

2 Si'hon king of the Am'or-ites, who dwelt in Hesh'bon, *and* ruled from Ar'o-er, which *is* upon the bank of the river Ar'non, and from the middle of the river, and from half Gil'e-ad, even unto the river Jab'bok, *which is* the border of the children of Am'mon;

3 And from the plain to the sea of Chin'ne-roth on the east, and unto the sea of the plain, *even* the salt sea on the east, the way to Beth-

jesh'i-moth; and from the south, under Ash'-
doth-pis'gah:
4 ¶ And the coast of Og king of Ba'shan,
which was of the remnant of the giants, that
dwelt at Ash'ta-roth and at Ed're-i,
5 And reigned in mount Her'mon, and in Sal'-
cah, and in all Ba'shan, unto the border of the
Gesh'u-rites and the Ma-ach'a-thites, and half
Gil'e-ad, the border of Si'hon king of Hesh'bon.
6 Them did Mo'ses the servant of the LORD
and the children of Is'ra-el smite: and Mo'ses
the servant of the LORD gave it *for* a possession
unto the Reu'ben-ites, and the Gad'ites, and the
half tribe of Ma-nas'seh.
7 ¶ And these *are* the kings of the country
which Josh'u-a and the children of Is'ra-el
smote on this side Jor'dan on the west, from
Ba'al-gad in the valley of Leb'a-non even unto
the mount Ha'lak, that goeth up to Se'ir; which
Josh'u-a gave unto the tribes of Is'ra-el *for* a
possession according to their divisions;
8 In the mountains, and in the valleys, and in
the plains, and in the springs, and in the wilderness, and in the south country; the Hit'tites, the
Am'or-ites, and the Ca'naan-ites, the Per'iz-
zites, the Hi'vites, and the Jeb'u-sites:
9 ¶ The king of Jer'i-cho, one; the king of A'i,
which *is* beside Beth'-el, one;
10 The king of Je-ru'sa-lem, one; the king of
He'bron, one;
11 The king of Jar'muth, one; the king of La'-
chish, one;
12 The king of Eg'lon, one; the king of Ge'zer,
one;
13 The king of De'bir, one; the king of Ge'der,
one;
14 The king of Hor'mah, one; the king of A'-
rad, one;
15 The king of Lib'nah, one; the king of A-
dul'lam, one;
16 The king of Mak-ke'dah, one; the king of
Beth'-el, one;
17 The king of Tap'pu-ah, one; the king of
He'pher, one;
18 The king of A'phek, one; the king of La-
shar'on, one;
19 The king of Ma'don, one; the king of Ha'-
zor, one;
20 The king of Shim'ron-me'ron, one; the
king of Ach'shaph, one;
21 The king of Ta'a-nach, one; the king of
Me-gid'do, one;
22 The king of Ke'desh, one; the king of Jok'-
ne-am of Car'mel, one;
23 The king of Dor in the coast of Dor, one;
the king of the nations of Gil'gal, one;
24 The king of Tir'zah, one: all the kings
thirty and one.

13 NOW Josh'u-a was old *and* stricken in
years; and the LORD said unto him, Thou
art old *and* stricken in years, and there remaineth yet very much land to be possessed.
2 This *is* the land that yet remaineth: all the
borders of the Phi-lis'tines, and all Gesh'u-ri,
3 From Si'hor, which *is* before E'gypt, even
unto the borders of Ek'ron northward, *which* is
counted to the Ca'naan-ite: five lords of the Phi-
lis'tines; the Ga'zath-ites, and the Ash'doth-ites,
the Esh'ka-lon-ites, the Git'tites, and the Ek'ron-
ites; also the A'vites:
4 From the south, all the land of the Ca'naan-
ites, and Me-a'rah that *is* beside the Si-do'ni-
ans, unto A'phek, to the borders of the Am'or-
ites:
5 And the land of the Gib'lites, and all Leb'a-
non, toward the sunrising, from Ba'al-gad under mount Her'mon unto the entering into Ha'-
math.
6 All the inhabitants of the hill country from
Leb'a-non unto Mis're-photh-ma'im, *and* all the
Si-do'ni-ans, them will I drive out from before
the children of Is'ra-el: only divide thou it by lot
unto the Is'ra-el-ites for an inheritance, as I
have commanded thee.
7 Now therefore divide this land for an inheritance unto the nine tribes, and the half tribe of
Ma-nas'seh,
8 With whom the Reu'ben-ites and the Gad'-
ites have received their inheritance, which Mo'-
ses gave them, beyond Jor'dan eastward, *even*
as Mo'ses the servant of the LORD gave them;
9 From Ar'o-er, that *is* upon the bank of the
river Ar'non, and the city that *is* in the midst of
the river, and all the plain of Med'e-ba unto Di'-
bon;
10 And all the cities of Si'hon king of the
Am'or-ites, which reigned in Hesh'bon, unto the
border of the children of Am'mon;
11 And Gil'e-ad, and the border of the Gesh'-
u-rites and Ma-ach'a-thites, and all mount Her'-
mon, and all Ba'shan unto Sal'cah;
12 All the kingdom of Og in Ba'shan, which
reigned in Ash'ta-roth and in Ed're-i, who remained of the remnant of the giants: for these
did Mo'ses smite, and cast them out.
13 Nevertheless the children of Is'ra-el expelled not the Gesh'u-rites, nor the Ma-ach'a-
thites: but the Gesh'u-rites and the Ma-ach'a-
thites dwell among the Is'ra-el-ites until this
day.
14 Only unto the tribe of Le'vi he gave none
inheritance; the sacrifices of the LORD God of
Is'ra-el made by fire *are* their inheritance, as he
said unto them.
15 ¶ And Mo'ses gave unto the tribe of the
children of Reu'ben *inheritance* according to
their families.
16 And their coast was from Ar'o-er, that *is*
on the bank of the river Ar'non, and the city
that *is* in the midst of the river, and all the plain
by Med'e-ba;
17 Hesh'bon, and all her cities that *are* in the
plain; Di'bon, and Ba'moth-ba'al, and Beth-ba'-
al-me'on,
18 And Ja-ha'za, and Ked'e-moth, and
Meph'a-ath,
19 And Kir-jath-a'im, and Sib'mah, and Za'-
reth-sha'har in the mount of the valley,
20 And Beth-pe'or, and Ash'doth-pis'gah,
and Beth-jesh'i-moth,
21 And all the cities of the plain, and all the
kingdom of Si'hon king of the Am'or-ites, which
reigned in Hesh'bon, whom Mo'ses smote with
the princes of Mid'i-an, E'vi, and Re'kem, and
Zur, and Hur, and Re'ba, *which were* dukes of
Si'hon, dwelling in the country.
22 ¶ Ba'laam also the son of Be'or, the sooth-
sayer, did the children of Is'ra-el slay with the
sword among them that were slain by them.
23 And the border of the children of Reu'ben
was Jor'dan, and the border *thereof*. This *was*
the inheritance of the children of Reu'ben after
their families, the cities and the villages thereof.
24 And Mo'ses gave *inheritance* unto the
tribe of Gad, *even* unto the children of Gad according to their families.
25 And their coast was Ja'zer, and all the
cities of Gil'e-ad, and half the land of the children of Am'mon, unto Ar'o-er that *is* before
Rab'bah;
26 And from Hesh'bon unto Ra'math-miz'-
peh, and Bet'o-nim; and from Ma-ha-na'im unto
the border of De'bir;

27 And in the valley, Beth–a'ram, and Beth–nim'rah, and Suc'coth, and Za'phon, the rest of the kingdom of Si'hon king of Hesh'bon, Jor'dan and *his* border, *even* unto the edge of the sea of Chin'ne-reth on the other side Jor'dan eastward.

28 This *is* the inheritance of the children of Gad after their families, the cities, and their villages.

29 ¶ And Mo'ses gave *inheritance* unto the half tribe of Ma-nas'seh: and *this* was *the possession* of the half tribe of the children of Ma-nas'seh by their families.

30 And their coast was from Ma-ha-na'im, all Ba'shan, all the kingdom of Og king of Ba'shan, and all the towns of Ja'ir, which *are* in Ba'shan, threescore cities:

31 And half Gil'e-ad, and Ash'ta-roth, and Ed're-i, cities of the kingdom of Og in Ba'shan, *were pertaining* unto the children of Ma'chir the son of Ma-nas'seh, *even* to the one half of the children of Ma'chir by their families.

32 These *are the countries* which Mo'ses did distribute for inheritance in the plains of Mo'ab, on the other side Jor'dan, by Jer'i-cho, eastward.

33 But unto the tribe of Le'vi Mo'ses gave not *any* inheritance: the LORD God of Is'ra-el *was* their inheritance, as he said unto them.

14 AND these *are the countries* which the children of Is'ra-el inherited in the land of Ca'naan, which E-le-a'zar the priest, and Josh'u-a the son of Nun, and the heads of the fathers of the tribes of the children of Is'ra-el, distributed for inheritance to them.

2 By lot *was* their inheritance, as the LORD commanded by the hand of Mo'ses, for the nine tribes, and *for* the half tribe.

3 For Mo'ses had given the inheritance of two tribes and an half tribe on the other side Jor'dan: but unto the Le'vites he gave none inheritance among them.

4 For the children of Jo'seph were two tribes, Ma-nas'seh and E'phra-im: therefore they gave no part unto the Le'vites in the land, save cities to dwell *in*, with their suburbs for their cattle and for their substance.

5 As the LORD commanded Mo'ses, so the children of Is'ra-el did, and they divided the land.

6 ¶ Then the children of Ju'dah came unto Josh'u-a in Gil'gal: and Ca'leb the son of Je-phun'neh the Ken'ez-ite said unto him, Thou knowest the thing that the LORD said unto Mo'ses the man of God concerning me and thee in Ka'desh–bar'ne-a.

7 Forty years old *was* I when Mo'ses the servant of the LORD sent me from Ka'desh–bar'ne-a to espy out the land; and I brought him word again as *it was* in mine heart.

8 Nevertheless my brethren that went up with me made the heart of the people melt: but I wholly followed the LORD my God.

9 And Mo'ses sware on that day, saying, Surely the land whereon thy feet have trodden shall be thine inheritance, and thy children's for ever, because thou hast wholly followed the LORD my God.

10 And now, behold, the LORD hath kept me alive, as he said, these forty and five years, even since the LORD spake this word unto Mo'ses, while *the children of* Is'ra-el wandered in the wilderness: and now, lo, I *am* this day fourscore and five years old.

11 As yet I *am as* strong this day as *I was* in the day that Mo'ses sent me: as my strength *was* then, even so *is* my strength now, for war, both to go out, and to come in.

12 Now therefore give me this mountain, whereof the LORD spake in that day; for thou heardest in that day how the An'a-kims *were* there, and *that* the cities *were* great *and* fenced: if so be the LORD *will be* with me, then I shall be able to drive them out, as the LORD said.

13 And Josh'u-a blessed him, and gave unto Ca'leb the son of Je-phun'neh He'bron for an inheritance.

14 He'bron therefore became the inheritance of Ca'leb the son of Je-phun'neh the Ken'ez-ite unto this day, because that he wholly followed the LORD God of Is'ra-el.

15 And the name of He'bron before *was* Kir'jath–ar'ba; *which Ar'ba was* a great man among the An'a-kims. And the land had rest from war.

15 *THIS* then was the lot of the tribe of the children of Ju'dah by their families; *even* to the border of E'dom the wilderness of Zin southward *was* the uttermost part of the south coast.

2 And their south border was from the shore of the salt sea, from the bay that looketh southward:

3 And it went out to the south side to Ma-al'eh–a-crab'bim, and passed along to Zin, and ascended up on the south side unto Ka'desh–bar'ne-a, and passed along to Hez'ron, and went up to A'dar, and fetched a compass to Kar'ka-a:

4 *From thence* it passed toward Az'mon, and went out unto the river of E'gypt; and the goings out of that coast were at the sea: this shall be your south coast.

5 And the east border *was* the salt sea, *even* unto the end of Jor'dan. And *their* border in the north quarter *was* from the bay of the sea at the uttermost part of Jor'dan:

6 And the border went up to Beth–hog'la, and passed along by the north of Beth–ar'a-bah; and the border went up to the stone of Bo'han the son of Reu'ben:

7 And the border went up toward De'bir from the valley of A'chor, and so northward, looking toward Gil'gal, that *is* before the going up to A-dum'mim, which *is* on the south side of the river: and the border passed toward the waters of En–she'mesh, and the goings out thereof were at En–ro'gel:

8 And the border went up by the valley of the son of Hin'nom unto the south side of the Jeb'u-site; the same *is* Je-ru'sa-lem: and the border went up to the top of the mountain that *lieth* before the valley of Hin'nom westward, which *is* at the end of the valley of the giants northward:

9 And the border was drawn from the top of the hill unto the fountain of the water of Neph'to-ah, and went out to the cities of mount E'phron; and the border was drawn to Ba'al-ah, which *is* Kir'jath–je'a-rim:

10 And the border compassed from Ba'al-ah westward unto mount Se'ir, and passed along unto the side of mount Je'a-rim, which *is* Ches'a-lon, on the north side, and went down to Beth–she'mesh, and passed on to Tim'nah:

11 And the border went out unto the side of Ek'ron northward: and the border was drawn to Shi'cron, and passed along to mount Ba'al-ah, and went out unto Jab'ne-el; and the goings out of the border were at the sea.

12 And the west border *was* to the great sea, and the coast *thereof*. This *is* the coast of the children of Ju'dah round about according to their families.

13 ¶ And unto Ca'leb the son of Je-phun'neh he gave a part among the children of Ju'dah, according to the commandment of the LORD to Josh'u-a, *even* the city of Ar'ba the father of A'nak, which *city is* He'bron.

14 And Ca'leb drove thence the three sons of A'nak, She'shai, and A-hi'man, and Tal'mai, the children of A'nak.

15 And he went up thence to the inhabitants of De'bir: and the name of De'bir before *was* Kir'jath-se'pher.

16 ¶ And Ca'leb said, He that smiteth Kir'jath-se'pher, and taketh it, to him will I give Ach'sah my daughter to wife.

17 And Oth'ni-el the son of Ke'naz, the brother of Ca'leb, took it: and he gave him Ach'sah his daughter to wife.

18 And it came to pass, as she came *unto him*, that she moved him to ask of her father a field: and she lighted off *her* ass; and Ca'leb said unto her, What wouldest thou?

19 Who answered, Give me a blessing; for thou hast given me a south land; give me also springs of water. And he gave her the upper springs, and the nether springs.

20 This *is* the inheritance of the tribe of the children of Ju'dah according to their families.

21 And the uttermost cities of the tribe of the children of Ju'dah toward the coast of E'dom southward were Kab'ze-el, and E'der, and Ja'gur,

22 And Ki'nah, and Di-mo'nah, and Ad'a-dah,

23 And Ke'desh, and Ha'zor, and Ith'nan,

24 Ziph, and Te'lem, and Be'a-loth,

25 And Ha'zor, Ha-dat'tah, and Ke'ri-oth, *and* Hez'ron, which *is* Ha'zor,

26 A'mam, and She'ma, and Mol'a-dah,

27 And Ha'zar-gad'dah, and Hesh'mon, and Beth-pa'let,

28 And Ha'zar-shu'al, and Be'er-she'ba, and Biz-joth'jah,

29 Ba'al-ah, and I'im, and A'zem,

30 And El'to-lad, and Che'sil, and Hor'mah,

31 And Zik'lag, and Mad-man'nah, and San-san'nah,

32 And Leb'a-oth, and Shil'him, and A'in, and Rim'mon: all the cities *are* twenty and nine, with their villages:

33 *And* in the valley, Esh'ta-ol, and Zo're-ah, and Ash'nah,

34 And Za-no'ah, and En-gan'nim, Tap'pu-ah, and E'nam,

35 Jar'muth, and A-dul'lam, So'coh, and A-ze'kah,

36 And Shar-a'im, and Ad-i-tha'im, and Ge-de'rah, and Ged-e-roth-a'im; fourteen cities with their villages:

37 Ze'nan, and Had'a-shah, and Mig'dal-gad,

38 And Dil'e-an, and Miz'peh, and Jok'the-el,

39 La'chish, and Boz'kath, and Eg'lon,

40 And Cab'bon, and Lah'mam, and Kith'lish,

41 And Ge-de'roth, Beth-da'gon, and Na'a-mah, and Mak-ke'dah; sixteen cities with their villages:

42 Lib'nah, and E'ther, and A'shan,

43 And Jiph'tah, and Ash'nah, and Ne'zib,

44 And Kei'lah, and Ach'zib, and Ma-re'shah; nine cities with their villages:

45 Ek'ron, with her towns and her villages:

46 From Ek'ron even unto the sea, all that *lay* near Ash'dod, with their villages:

47 Ash'dod with her towns and her villages, Ga'za with her towns and her villages, unto the river of E'gypt, and the great sea, and the border *thereof:*

48 ¶ And in the mountains, Sha'mir, and Jat'tir, and So'coh,

49 And Dan'nah, and Kir'jath-san'nah, which *is* De'bir,

50 And A'nab, and Esh'te-moh, and A'nim,

51 And Go'shen, and Ho'lon, and Gi'loh; eleven cities with their villages:

52 A'rab, and Du'mah, and E'she-an,

53 And Ja'num, and Beth-tap'pu-ah, and A-phe'kah,

54 And Hum'tah, and Kir'jath-ar'ba, which *is* He'bron, and Zi'or; nine cities with their villages:

55 Ma'on, Car'mel, and Ziph, and Jut'tah,

56 And Jez're-el, and Jok'de-am, and Za-no'ah,

57 Cain, Gib'e-ah, and Tim'nah; ten cities with their villages:

58 Hal'hul, Beth'-zur, and Ge'dor,

59 And Ma'a-rath, and Beth-a'noth, and El'te-kon; six cities with their villages:

60 Kir'jath-ba'al, which *is* Kir'jath-je'a-rim, and Rab'bah; two cities with their villages:

61 In the wilderness, Beth-ar'a-bah, Mid'din, and Sec'a-cah,

62 And Nib'shan, and the city of Salt, and En-ge'di; six cities with their villages.

63 ¶ As for the Jeb'u-sites the inhabitants of Je-ru'sa-lem, the children of Ju'dah could not drive them out: but the Jeb'u-sites dwell with the children of Ju'dah at Je-ru'sa-lem unto this day.

16 AND the lot of the children of Jo'seph fell from Jor'dan by Jer'i-cho, unto the water of Jer'i-cho on the east, to the wilderness that goeth up from Jer'i-cho throughout mount Beth'-el,

2 And goeth out from Beth'-el to Luz, and passeth along unto the borders of Ar'chi to At'a-roth,

3 And goeth down westward to the coast of Japh-le'ti, unto the coast of Beth-ho'ron the nether, and to Ge'zer: and the goings out thereof are at the sea.

4 So the children of Jo'seph, Ma-nas'seh and E'phra-im, took their inheritance.

5 ¶ And the border of the children of E'phra-im according to their families was *thus:* even the border of their inheritance on the east side was At'a-roth-ad'dar, unto Beth-ho'ron the upper;

6 And the border went out toward the sea to Mich'me-thah on the north side; and the border went about eastward unto Ta'a-nath-shi'loh, and passed by it on the east to Ja-no'hah;

7 And it went down from Ja-no'hah to At'a-roth, and to Na'a-rath, and came to Jer'i-cho, and went out at Jor'dan.

8 The border went out from Tap'pu-ah westward unto the river Ka'nah; and the goings out thereof were at the sea. This *is* the inheritance of the tribe of the children of E'phra-im by their families.

9 And the separate cities for the children of E'phra-im *were* among the inheritance of the children of Ma-nas'seh, all the cities with their villages.

10 And they drave not out the Ca'naan-ites that dwelt in Ge'zer: but the Ca'naan-ites dwell among the E'phra-im-ites unto this day, and serve under tribute.

17 THERE was also a lot for the tribe of Ma-nas'seh; for he *was* the firstborn of Jo'seph; *to wit,* for Ma'chir the firstborn of Ma-nas'seh, the father of Gil'e-ad: because he was a

man of war, therefore he had Gil'e-ad and Ba'shan.

2 There was also *a lot* for the rest of the children of Ma-nas'seh by their families; for the children of A-bi-e'zer, and for the children of He'lek, and for the children of As'ri-el, and for the children of She'chem, and for the children of He'pher, and for the children of She-mi'da: these *were* the male children of Ma-nas'seh the son of Jo'seph by their families.

3 ¶ But Ze-lo'phe-had, the son of He'pher, the son of Gil'e-ad, the son of Ma'chir, the son of Ma-nas'seh, had no sons, but daughters: and these *are* the names of his daughters, Mah'lah, and No'ah, Hog'lah, Mil'cah, and Tir'zah.

4 And they came near before E-le-a'zar the priest, and before Josh'u-a the son of Nun, and before the princes, saying, The LORD commanded Mo'ses to give us an inheritance among our brethren. Therefore according to the commandment of the LORD he gave them an inheritance among the brethren of their father.

5 And there fell ten portions to Ma-nas'seh, beside the land of Gil'e-ad and Ba'shan, which *were* on the other side Jor'dan;

6 Because the daughters of Ma-nas'seh had an inheritance among his sons: and the rest of Ma-nas'seh's sons had the land of Gil'e-ad.

7 ¶ And the coast of Ma-nas'seh was from Ash'er to Mich'me-thah, that *lieth* before She'chem; and the border went along on the right hand unto the inhabitants of En-tap'pu-ah.

8 *Now* Ma-nas'seh had the land of Tap'pu-ah: but Tap'pu-ah on the border of Ma-nas'seh *belonged* to the children of E'phra-im;

9 And the coast descended unto the river Ka'nah, southward of the river: these cities of E'phra-im *are* among the cities of Ma-nas'seh: the coast of Ma-nas'seh also *was* on the north side of the river, and the outgoings of it were at the sea:

10 Southward *it was* E'phra-im's, and northward *it was* Ma-nas'seh's, and the sea is his border; and they met together in Ash'er on the north, and in Is'sa-char on the east.

11 And Ma-nas'seh had in Is'sa-char and in Ash'er Beth-she'an and her towns, and Ib'le-am and her towns, and the inhabitants of Dor and her towns, and the inhabitants of En'-dor and her towns, and the inhabitants of Ta'a-nach and her towns, and the inhabitants of Me-gid'do and her towns, *even* three countries.

12 Yet the children of Ma-nas'seh could not drive out *the inhabitants of* those cities; but the Ca'naan-ites would dwell in that land.

13 Yet it came to pass, when the children of Is'ra-el were waxen strong, that they put the Ca'naan-ites to tribute; but did not utterly drive them out.

14 And the children of Jo'seph spake unto Josh'u-a, saying, Why hast thou given me *but* one lot and one portion to inherit, seeing I *am* a great people, forasmuch as the LORD hath blessed me hitherto?

15 And Josh'u-a answered them, If thou *be* a great people, *then* get thee up to the wood *country,* and cut down for thyself there in the land of the Per'iz-zites and of the giants, if mount E'phra-im be too narrow for thee.

16 And the children of Jo'seph said, The hill is not enough for us: and all the Ca'naan-ites that dwell in the land of the valley have chariots of iron, *both they* who *are* of Beth-she'an and her towns, and *they* who *are* of the valley of Jez're-el.

17 And Josh'u-a spake unto the house of Jo'seph, *even* to E'phra-im and to Ma-nas'seh, saying, Thou *art* a great people, and hast great power: thou shalt not have one lot *only:*

18 But the mountain shall be thine; for it *is* a wood, and thou shalt cut it down: and the outgoings of it shall be thine: for thou shalt drive out the Ca'naan-ites, though they have iron chariots, *and* though they *be* strong.

18 AND the whole congregation of the children of Is'ra-el assembled together at Shi'loh, and set up the tabernacle of the congregation there. And the land was subdued before them.

2 And there remained among the children of Is'ra-el seven tribes, which had not yet received their inheritance.

3 And Josh'u-a said unto the children of Is'ra-el, How long *are* ye slack to go to possess the land, which the LORD God of your fathers hath given you?

4 Give out from among you three men for *each* tribe: and I will send them, and they shall rise, and go through the land, and describe it according to the inheritance of them; and they shall come *again* to me.

5 And they shall divide it into seven parts: Ju'dah shall abide in their coast on the south, and the house of Jo'seph shall abide in their coasts on the north.

6 Ye shall therefore describe the land *into* seven parts, and bring *the description* hither to me, that I may cast lots for you here before the LORD our God.

7 But the Le'vites have no part among you; for the priesthood of the LORD *is* their inheritance: and Gad, and Reu'ben, and half the tribe of Ma-nas'seh, have received their inheritance beyond Jor'dan on the east, which Mo'ses the servant of the LORD gave them.

8 ¶ And the men arose, and went away: and Josh'u-a charged them that went to describe the land, saying, Go and walk through the land, and describe it, and come again to me, that I may here cast lots for you before the LORD in Shi'loh.

9 And the men went and passed through the land, and described it by cities into seven parts in a book, and came *again* to Josh'u-a to the host at Shi'loh.

10 ¶ And Josh'u-a cast lots for them in Shi'loh before the LORD: and there Josh'u-a divided the land unto the children of Is'ra-el according to their divisions.

11 ¶ And the lot of the tribe of the children of Ben'ja-min came up according to their families: and the coast of their lot came forth between the children of Ju'dah and the children of Jo'seph.

12 And their border on the north side was from Jor'dan; and the border went up to the side of Jer'i-cho on the north side, and went up through the mountains westward; and the goings out thereof were at the wilderness of Beth-a'ven.

13 And the border went over from thence toward Luz, to the side of Luz, which *is* Beth'-el, southward; and the border descended to At'-a-roth-a'dar, near the hill that *lieth* on the south side of the nether Beth-ho'ron.

14 And the border was drawn *thence,* and compassed the corner of the sea southward, from the hill that *lieth* before Beth-ho'ron southward; and the goings out thereof were at Kir'jath-ba'al, which *is* Kir'jath-je'a-rim, a city of the children of Ju'dah: this *was* the west quarter.

15 And the south quarter *was* from the end of Kir'jath-je'a-rim, and the border went out on

the west, and went out to the well of waters of
Neph'to-ah:
16 And the border came down to the end of
the mountain that *lieth* before the valley of the
son of Hin'nom, *and* which *is* in the valley of
the giants on the north, and descended to the
valley of Hin'nom, to the side of Je-bu'si on the
south, and descended to En–ro'gel,
17 And was drawn from the north, and went
forth to En–she'mesh, and went forth toward
Gel'i-loth, which *is* over against the going up of
A-dum'mim, and descended to the stone of Bo'-
han the son of Reu'ben,
18 And passed along toward the side over
against Ar'a-bah northward, and went down
unto Ar'a-bah:
19 And the border passed along to the side of
Beth–hog'lah northward: and the outgoings of
the border were at the north bay of the salt sea
at the south end of Jor'dan: this *was* the south
coast.
20 And Jor'dan was the border of it on the
east side. This *was* the inheritance of the children of Ben'ja-min, by the coasts thereof round
about, according to their families.
21 Now the cities of the tribe of the children
of Ben'ja-min according to their families were
Jer'i-cho, and Beth–hog'lah, and the valley of
Ke'ziz,
22 And Beth–ar'a-bah, and Zem-a-ra'im, and
Beth'–el,
23 And A'vim, and Pa'rah, and Oph'rah,
24 And Che'phar–ha-am'mo-nai, and Oph'ni,
and Ga'ba; twelve cities with their villages:
25 Gib'e-on, and Ra'mah, and Be-e'roth,
26 And Miz'peh, and Che-phi'rah, and Mo'-
zah,
27 And Re'kem, and Ir'pe-el, and Tar'a-lah,
28 And Ze'lah, E'leph, and Je-bu'si, which *is*
Je-ru'sa-lem, Gib'e-ath, *and* Kir'jath; fourteen
cities with their villages. This *is* the inheritance
of the children of Ben'ja-min according to their
families.

19 AND the second lot came forth to Sim'-
e-on, *even* for the tribe of the children of
Sim'e-on according to their families: and their
inheritance was within the inheritance of the
children of Ju'dah.
2 And they had in their inheritance Be'er-
she'ba, and She'ba, and Mol'a-dah,
3 And Ha'zar–shu'al, and Ba'lah, and A'zem,
4 And El'to-lad, and Be'thul, and Hor'mah,
5 And Zik'lag, and Beth–mar'ca-both, and
Ha'zar–su'sah,
6 And Beth–leb'a-oth, and Sha-ru'hen; thirteen cities and their villages:
7 A'in, Rem'mon, and E'ther, and A'shan;
four cities and their villages:
8 And all the villages that *were* round about
these cities to Ba'al-ath–be'er, Ra'math of the
south. This *is* the inheritance of the tribe of the
children of Sim'e-on according to their families.
9 Out of the portion of the children of Ju'dah
was the inheritance of the children of Sim'e-on:
for the part of the children of Ju'dah was too
much for them: therefore the children of Sim'e-
on had their inheritance within the inheritance
of them.
10 ¶ And the third lot came up for the children of Zeb'u-lun according to their families:
and the border of their inheritance was unto
Sa'rid:
11 And their border went up toward the sea,
and Mar'a-lah, and reached to Dab'ba-sheth,
and reached to the river that *is* before Jok'ne-
am;
12 And turned from Sa'rid eastward toward
the sunrising unto the border of Chis'loth–ta'-
bor, and then goeth out to Dab'e-rath, and
goeth up to Ja-phi'a,
13 And from thence passeth on along on the
east to Git'tah–he'pher, to It'tah–ka'zin, and
goeth out to Rem'mon–meth'o-ar to Ne-ah;
14 And the border compasseth it on the
north side to Han'na-thon: and the outgoings
thereof are in the valley of Jiph'thah–el:
15 And Kat'tath, and Na-hal'lal, and Shim'-
ron, and I-da'lah, and Beth'–le-hem: twelve
cities with their villages.
16 This *is* the inheritance of the children of
Zeb'u-lun according to their families, these
cities with their villages.
17 ¶ *And* the fourth lot came out to Is'sa-
char, for the children of Is'sa-char according to
their families.
18 And their border was toward Jez're-el,
and Che-sul'loth, and Shu'nem,
19 And Haph-ra'im, and Shi'hon, and An-a-
ha'rath,
20 And Rab'bith, and Kish'i-on, and A'bez,
21 And Re'meth, and En–gan'nim, and En-
had'dah, and Beth–paz'zez;
22 And the coast reacheth to Ta'bor, and
Sha-haz'i-mah, and Beth–she'mesh; and the
outgoings of their border were at Jor'dan: sixteen cities with their villages.
23 This *is* the inheritance of the tribe of the
children of Is'sa-char according to their families, the cities and their villages.
24 ¶ And the fifth lot came out for the tribe
of the children of Ash'er according to their families.
25 And their border was Hel'kath, and Ha'li,
and Be'ten, and Ach'shaph,
26 And A-lam'me-lech, and A'mad, and Mi'-
she-al; and reacheth to Car'mel westward, and
to Shi'hor–lib'nath;
27 And turneth toward the sunrising to
Beth–da'gon, and reacheth to Zeb'u-lun, and to
the valley of Jiph'thah–el toward the north side
of Beth–e'mek, and Ne'i-el, and goeth out to
Ca'bul on the left hand,
28 And He'bron, and Re'hob, and Ham'mon,
and Ka'nah, *even* unto great Zi'don;
29 And *then* the coast turneth to Ra'mah,
and to the strong city Tyre; and the coast turneth to Ho'sah; and the outgoings thereof are at
the sea from the coast to Ach'zib:
30 Um'mah also, and A'phek, and Re'hob:
twenty and two cities with their villages.
31 This *is* the inheritance of the tribe of the
children of Ash'er according to their families,
these cities with their villages.
32 ¶ The sixth lot came out to the children of
Naph'ta-li *even* for the children of Naph'ta-li according to their families.
33 And their coast was from He'leph, from
Al'lon to Za-a-nan'nim, and Ad'a-mi, Ne'keb,
and Jab'ne-el, unto La'kum; and the outgoings
thereof were at Jor'dan:
34 And *then* the coast turneth westward to
Az'noth–ta'bor, and goeth out from thence to
Huk'kok, and reacheth to Zeb'u-lun on the
south side, and reacheth to Ash'er on the west
side, and to Ju'dah upon Jor'dan toward the
sunrising.
35 And the fenced cities *are* Zid'dim, Zer,
and Ham'math, Rak'kath, and Chin'ne-reth,
36 And Ad'a-mah, and Ra'mah, and Ha'zor,
37 And Ke'desh, and Ed're-i, and En–ha'zor,
38 And I'ron, and Mig'dal–el, Ho'rem, and
Beth–a'nath, and Beth–she'mesh; nineteen
cities with their villages.

39 This *is* the inheritance of the tribe of the children of Naph'ta-li according to their families, the cities and their villages.

40 ¶ *And* the seventh lot came out for the tribe of the children of Dan according to their families.

41 And the coast of their inheritance was Zo'rah, and Esh'ta-ol, and Ir-she'mesh,

42 And Sha-al-ab'bin, and Aj'a-lon, and Jeth'lah,

43 And E'lon, and Thim'na-thah, and Ek'ron,

44 And El'te-keh, and Gib'be-thon, and Ba'al-ath,

45 And Je'hud, and Ben'e–be'rak, and Gath–rim'mon,

46 And Me–jar'kon, and Rak'kon, with the border before Ja'pho.

47 And the coast of the children of Dan went out *too little* for them: therefore the children of Dan went up to fight against Le'shem, and took it, and smote it with the edge of the sword, and possessed it, and dwelt therein, and called Le'shem, Dan, after the name of Dan their father.

48 This *is* the inheritance of the tribe of the children of Dan according to their families, these cities with their villages.

49 ¶ When they had made an end of dividing the land for inheritance by their coasts, the children of Is'ra-el gave an inheritance to Josh'u-a the son of Nun among them:

50 According to the word of the LORD they gave him the city which he asked, *even* Tim'nath–se'rah in mount E'phra-im: and he built the city, and dwelt therein.

51 These *are* the inheritances, which E-le-a'zar the priest, and Josh'u-a the son of Nun, and the heads of the fathers of the tribes of the children of Is'ra-el, divided for an inheritance by lot in Shi'loh before the LORD, at the door of the tabernacle of the congregation. So they made an end of dividing the country.

20

THE LORD also spake unto Josh'u-a, saying,

2 Speak to the children of Is'ra-el, saying, Appoint out for you cities of refuge, whereof I spake unto you by the hand of Mo'ses:

3 That the slayer that killeth *any* person unawares *and* unwittingly may flee thither: and they shall be your refuge from the avenger of blood.

4 And when he that doth flee unto one of those cities shall stand at the entering of the gate of the city, and shall declare his cause in the ears of the elders of that city, they shall take him into the city unto them, and give him a place, that he may dwell among them.

5 And if the avenger of blood pursue after him, then they shall not deliver the slayer up into his hand; because he smote his neighbour unwittingly, and hated him not beforetime.

6 And he shall dwell in that city, until he stand before the congregation for judgment, *and* until the death of the high priest that shall be in those days: then shall the slayer return, and come unto his own city, and unto his own house, unto the city from whence he fled.

7 ¶ And they appointed Ke'desh in Gal'i-lee in mount Naph'ta-li, and She'chem in mount E'phra-im, and Kir'jath–ar'ba, which *is* He'bron, in the mountain of Ju'dah.

8 And on the other side Jor'dan by Jer'i-cho eastward, they assigned Be'zer in the wilderness upon the plain out of the tribe of Reu'ben, and Ra'moth in Gil'e-ad out of the tribe of Gad, and Go'lan in Ba'shan out of the tribe of Ma-nas'seh.

9 These were the cities appointed for all the children of Is'ra-el, and for the stranger that sojourneth among them, that whosoever killeth *any* person at unawares might flee thither, and not die by the hand of the avenger of blood, until he stood before the congregation.

21

THEN came near the heads of the fathers of the Le'vites unto E-le-a'zar the priest, and unto Josh'u-a the son of Nun, and unto the heads of the fathers of the tribes of the children of Is'ra-el;

2 And they spake unto them at Shi'loh in the land of Ca'naan, saying, The LORD commanded by the hand of Mo'ses to give us cities to dwell in, with the suburbs thereof for our cattle.

3 And the children of Is'ra-el gave unto the Le'vites out of their inheritance, at the commandment of the LORD, these cities and their suburbs.

4 And the lot came out for the families of the Ko'hath-ites: and the children of Aar'on the priest, *which were* of the Le'vites, had by lot out of the tribe of Ju'dah, and out of the tribe of Sim'e-on, and out of the tribe of Ben'ja-min, thirteen cities.

5 And the rest of the children of Ko'hath *had* by lot out of the families of the tribe of E'phra-im, and out of the tribe of Dan, and out of the half tribe of Ma-nas'seh, ten cities.

6 And the children of Ger'shon *had* by lot out of the families of the tribe of Is'sa-char, and out of the tribe of Ash'er, and out of the tribe of Naph'ta-li, and out of the half tribe of Ma-nas'seh in Ba'shan, thirteen cities.

7 The children of Me-ra'ri by their families *had* out of the tribe of Reu'ben, and out of the tribe of Gad, and out of the tribe of Zeb'u-lun, twelve cities.

8 And the children of Is'ra-el gave by lot unto the Le'vites these cities with their suburbs, as the LORD commanded by the hand of Mo'ses.

9 ¶ And they gave out of the tribe of the children of Ju'dah, and out of the tribe of the children of Sim'e-on, these cities which are *here* mentioned by name,

10 Which the children of Aar'on, *being* of the families of the Ko'hath-ites, *who were* of the children of Le'vi, had: for theirs was the first lot.

11 And they gave them the city of Ar'ba the father of A'nak, which *city is* He'bron, in the hill *country* of Ju'dah, with the suburbs thereof round about it.

12 But the fields of the city, and the villages thereof, gave they to Ca'leb the son of Je-phun'neh for his possession.

13 ¶ Thus they gave to the children of Aar'on the priest He'bron with her suburbs, *to be* a city of refuge for the slayer; and Lib'nah with her suburbs,

14 And Jat'tir with her suburbs, and Esh-te-mo'a with her suburbs,

15 And Ho'lon with her suburbs, and De'bir with her suburbs,

16 And A'in with her suburbs, and Jut'tah with her suburbs, *and* Beth–she'mesh with her suburbs; nine cities out of those two tribes.

17 And out of the tribe of Ben'ja-min, Gib'e-on with her suburbs, Ge'ba with her suburbs,

18 An'a-thoth with her suburbs, and Al'mon with her suburbs; four cities.

19 All the cities of the children of Aar'on, the priests, *were* thirteen cities with their suburbs.

20 ¶ And the families of the children of Ko'hath, the Le'vites which remained of the chil-

dren of Ko'hath, even they had the cities of
their lot out of the tribe of E'phra-im.
21 For they gave them She'chem with her
suburbs in mount E'phra-im, *to be* a city of refuge for the slayer; and Ge'zer with her suburbs,
22 And Kib'za-im with her suburbs, and
Beth-ho'ron with her suburbs; four cities.
23 And out of the tribe of Dan, El'te-keh with
her suburbs, Gib'be-thon with her suburbs,
24 Aij'a-lon with her suburbs, Gath-rim'mon
with her suburbs; four cities.
25 And out of the half tribe of Ma-nas'seh,
Ta'nach with her suburbs, and Gath-rim'mon
with her suburbs; two cities.
26 All the cities *were* ten with their suburbs
for the families of the children of Ko'hath that
remained.
27 ¶ And unto the children of Ger'shon, of
the families of the Le'vites, out of the *other* half
tribe of Ma-nas'seh *they gave* Go'lan in Ba'shan
with her suburbs, *to be* a city of refuge for the
slayer; and Be-esh'-te-rah with her suburbs;
two cities.
28 And out of the tribe of Is'sa-char, Ki'shon
with her suburbs, Dab'a-reh with her suburbs,
29 Jar'muth with her suburbs, En-gan'nim
with her suburbs; four cities.
30 And out of the tribe of Ash'er, Mi'shal
with her suburbs, Ab'don with her suburbs,
31 Hel'kath with her suburbs, and Re'hob
with her suburbs; four cities.
32 And out of the tribe of Naph'ta-li, Ke'desh
in Gal'i-lee with her suburbs, *to be* a city of refuge for the slayer; and Ham'moth-dor with her
suburbs, and Kar'tan with her suburbs; three
cities.
33 All the cities of the Ger'shon-ites according to their families *were* thirteen cities with
their suburbs.
34 ¶ And unto the families of the children of
Me-ra'ri, the rest of the Le'vites, out of the tribe
of Zeb'u-lun, Jok'ne-am with her suburbs, and
Kar'tah with her suburbs,
35 Dim'nah with her suburbs, Na'ha-lal with
her suburbs; four cities.
36 And out of the tribe of Reu'ben, Be'zer
with her suburbs, and Ja-ha'zah with her suburbs,
37 Ked'e-moth with her suburbs, and Meph'-
a-ath with her suburbs; four cities.
38 And out of the tribe of Gad, Ra'moth in
Gil'e-ad with her suburbs, *to be* a city of refuge
for the slayer; and Ma-ha-na'im with her suburbs,
39 Hesh'bon with her suburbs, Ja'zer with
her suburbs; four cities in all.
40 So all the cities for the children of Me-ra'ri
by their families, which were remaining of the
families of the Le'vites, were *by* their lot twelve
cities.
41 All the cities of the Le'vites within the
possession of the children of Is'ra-el *were* forty
and eight cities with their suburbs.
42 These cities were every one with their
suburbs round about them: thus *were* all these
cities.
43 ¶ And the LORD gave unto Is'ra-el all the
land which he sware to give unto their fathers;
and they possessed it, and dwelt therein.
44 And the LORD gave them rest round
about, according to all that he sware unto their
fathers: and there stood not a man of all their
enemies before them; the LORD delivered all
their enemies into their hand.
45 There failed not ought of any good thing
which the LORD had spoken unto the house of
Is'ra-el; all came to pass.

22 THEN Josh'u-a called the Reu'ben-ites,
and the Gad'ites, and the half tribe of
Ma-nas'seh,
2 And said unto them, Ye have kept all that
Mo'ses the servant of the LORD commanded
you, and have obeyed my voice in all that I
commanded you:
3 Ye have not left your brethren these many
days unto this day, but have kept the charge of
the commandment of the LORD your God.
4 And now the LORD your God hath given
rest unto your brethren, as he promised them:
therefore now return ye, and get you unto your
tents, *and* unto the land of your possession,
which Mo'ses the servant of the LORD gave you
on the other side Jor'dan.
5 But take diligent heed to do the commandment and the law, which Mo'ses the servant of
the LORD charged you, to love the LORD your
God, and to walk in all his ways, and to keep his
commandments, and to cleave unto him, and to
serve him with all your heart and with all your
soul.
6 So Josh'u-a blessed them, and sent them
away: and they went unto their tents.
7 ¶ Now to the *one* half of the tribe of Ma-
nas'seh Mo'ses had given *possession* in Ba'shan:
but unto the *other* half thereof gave Josh'u-a
among their brethren on this side Jor'dan westward. And when Josh'u-a sent them away also
unto their tents, then he blessed them,
8 And he spake unto them, saying, Return
with much riches unto your tents, and with very
much cattle, with silver, and with gold, and
with brass, and with iron, and with very much
raiment: divide the spoil of your enemies with
your brethren.
9 ¶ And the children of Reu'ben and the children of Gad and the half tribe of Ma-nas'seh
returned, and departed from the children of Is'-
ra-el out of Shi'loh, which *is* in the land of Ca'-
naan, to go unto the country of Gil'e-ad, to the
land of their possession, whereof they were
possessed, according to the word of the LORD
by the hand of Mo'ses.
10 ¶ And when they came unto the borders
of Jor'dan, that *are* in the land of Ca'naan, the
children of Reu'ben and the children of Gad and
the half tribe of Ma-nas'seh built there an altar
by Jor'dan, a great altar to see to.
11 ¶ And the children of Is'ra-el heard say,
Behold, the children of Reu'ben and the children of Gad and the half tribe of Ma-nas'seh
have built an altar over against the land of Ca'-
naan, in the borders of Jor'dan, at the passage
of the children of Is'ra-el.
12 And when the children of Is'ra-el heard *of
it*, the whole congregation of the children of Is'-
ra-el gathered themselves together at Shi'loh, to
go up to war against them.
13 And the children of Is'ra-el sent unto the
children of Reu'ben, and to the children of Gad,
and to the half tribe of Ma-nas'seh, into the land
of Gil'e-ad, Phin'e-has the son of E-le-a'zar the
priest.
14 And with him ten princes, of each chief
house a prince throughout all the tribes of Is'ra-
el; and each one *was* an head of the house of
their fathers among the thousands of Is'ra-el.
15 ¶ And they came unto the children of
Reu'ben, and to the children of Gad, and to the
half tribe of Ma-nas'seh, unto the land of Gil'e-
ad, and they spake with them, saying,
16 Thus saith the whole congregation of the
LORD, What trespass *is* this that ye have committed against the God of Is'ra-el, to turn away
this day from following the LORD, in that ye

have builded you an altar, that ye might rebel
this day against the LORD?
17 *Is* the iniquity of Pe'or too little for us,
from which we are not cleansed until this day,
although there was a plague in the congregation
of the LORD,
18 But that ye must turn away this day from
following the LORD? and it will be, *seeing* ye
rebel to day against the LORD, that to morrow
he will be wroth with the whole congregation of
Is'ra-el.
19 Notwithstanding, if the land of your possession *be* unclean, *then* pass ye over unto the
land of the possession of the LORD, wherein the
LORD's tabernacle dwelleth, and take possession among us: but rebel not against the LORD,
nor rebel against us, in building you an altar
beside the altar of the LORD our God.
20 Did not A'chan the son of Ze'rah commit a
trespass in the accursed thing, and wrath fell on
all the congregation of Is'ra-el? and that man
perished not alone in his iniquity.
21 ¶ Then the children of Reu'ben and the
children of Gad and the half tribe of Ma-nas'seh
answered, and said unto the heads of the thousands of Is'ra-el,
22 The LORD God of gods, the LORD God of
gods, he knoweth, and Is'ra-el he shall know; if
it be in rebellion, or if in transgression against
the LORD, (save us not this day,)
23 That we have built us an altar to turn from
following the LORD, or if to offer thereon burnt
offering or meat offering, or if to offer peace
offerings thereon, let the LORD himself require
it;
24 And if we have not *rather* done it for fear
of *this* thing, saying, In time to come your children might speak unto our children, saying,
What have ye to do with the LORD God of Is'ra-
el?
25 For the LORD hath made Jor'dan a border
between us and you, ye children of Reu'ben and
children of Gad; ye have no part in the LORD: so
shall your children make our children cease
from fearing the LORD.
26 Therefore we said, Let us now prepare to
build us an altar, not for burnt offering, nor for
sacrifice:
27 But *that* it *may be* a witness between us,
and you, and our generations after us, that we
might do the service of the LORD before him
with our burnt offerings, and with our sacrifices, and with our peace offerings; that your
children may not say to our children in time to
come, Ye have no part in the LORD.
28 Therefore said we, that it shall be, when
they should *so* say to us or to our generations in
time to come, that we may say *again*, Behold
the pattern of the altar of the LORD, which our
fathers made, not for burnt offerings, nor for
sacrifices; but it *is* a witness between us and
you.
29 God forbid that we should rebel against
the LORD, and turn this day from following the
LORD, to build an altar for burnt offerings, for
meat offerings, or for sacrifices, beside the altar
of the LORD our God that *is* before his tabernacle.
30 ¶ And when Phin'e-has the priest, and the
princes of the congregation and heads of the
thousands of Is'ra-el which *were* with him,
heard the words that the children of Reu'ben
and the children of Gad and the children of Ma-
nas'seh spake, it pleased them.
31 And Phin'e-has the son of E-le-a'zar the
priest said unto the children of Reu'ben, and to
the children of Gad, and to the children of Ma-
nas'seh, This day we perceive that the LORD *is*
among us, because ye have not committed this
trespass against the LORD: now ye have delivered the children of Is'ra-el out of the hand of
the LORD.
32 ¶ And Phin'e-has the son of E-le-a'zar the
priest, and the princes, returned from the children of Reu'ben, and from the children of Gad,
out of the land of Gil'e-ad, unto the land of Ca'-
naan, to the children of Is'ra-el, and brought
them word again.
33 And the thing pleased the children of Is'-
ra-el; and the children of Is'ra-el blessed God,
and did not intend to go up against them in battle, to destroy the land wherein the children of
Reu'ben and Gad dwelt.
34 And the children of Reu'ben and the children of Gad called the altar *Ed:* for it *shall be* a
witness between us that the LORD *is* God.

23 AND it came to pass a long time after
that the LORD had given rest unto Is'ra-
el from all their enemies round about, that
Josh'u-a waxed old *and* stricken in age.
2 And Josh'u-a called for all Is'ra-el, *and* for
their elders, and for their heads, and for their
judges, and for their officers, and said unto
them, I am old *and* stricken in age:
3 And ye have seen all that the LORD your
God hath done unto all these nations because of
you; for the LORD your God *is* he that hath
fought for you.
4 Behold, I have divided unto you by lot
these nations that remain, to be an inheritance
for your tribes, from Jor'dan, with all the nations that I have cut off, even unto the great sea
westward.
5 And the LORD your God, he shall expel
them from before you, and drive them from out
of your sight; and ye shall possess their land, as
the LORD your God hath promised unto you.
6 Be ye therefore very courageous to keep
and to do all that is written in the book of the
law of Mo'ses, that ye turn not aside therefrom
to the right hand or *to* the left;
7 That ye come not among these nations,
these that remain among you; neither make
mention of the name of their gods, nor cause to
swear *by them*, neither serve them, nor bow
yourselves unto them:
8 But cleave unto the LORD your God, as ye
have done unto this day.
9 For the LORD hath driven out from before
you great nations and strong: but *as for* you, no
man hath been able to stand before you unto
this day.
10 One man of you shall chase a thousand:
for the LORD your God, he *it is* that fighteth for
you, as he hath promised you.
11 Take good heed therefore unto yourselves, that ye love the LORD your God.
12 Else if ye do in any wise go back, and
cleave unto the remnant of these nations, *even*
these that remain among you, and shall make
marriages with them, and go in unto them, and
they to you:
13 Know for a certainty that the LORD your
God will no more drive out *any of* these nations
from before you; but they shall be snares and
traps unto you, and scourges in your sides, and
thorns in your eyes, until ye perish from off this
good land which the LORD your God hath given
you.
14 And, behold, this day I *am* going the way
of all the earth: and ye know in all your hearts
and in all your souls, that not one thing hath
failed of all the good things which the LORD

your God spake concerning you; all are come to pass unto you, *and* not one thing hath failed thereof.

15 Therefore it shall come to pass, *that* as all good things are come upon you, which the LORD your God promised you; so shall the LORD bring upon you all evil things, until he have destroyed you from off this good land which the LORD your God hath given you.

16 When ye have transgressed the covenant of the LORD your God, which he commanded you, and have gone and served other gods, and bowed yourselves to them; then shall the anger of the LORD be kindled against you, and ye shall perish quickly from off the good land which he hath given unto you.

24 AND Josh'u-a gathered all the tribes of Is'ra-el to She'chem, and called for the elders of Is'ra-el, and for their heads, and for their judges, and for their officers; and they presented themselves before God.

2 And Josh'u-a said unto all the people, Thus saith the LORD God of Is'ra-el, Your fathers dwelt on the other side of the flood in old time, *even* Te'rah, the father of A'bra-ham, and the father of Na'chor: and they served other gods.

3 And I took your father A'bra-ham from the other side of the flood, and led him throughout all the land of Ca'naan, and multiplied his seed, and gave him I'saac.

4 And I gave unto I'saac Ja'cob and E'sau: and I gave unto E'sau mount Se'ir, to possess it; but Ja'cob and his children went down into E'-gypt.

5 I sent Mo'ses also and Aar'on, and I plagued E'gypt, according to that which I did among them: and afterward I brought you out.

6 And I brought your fathers out of E'gypt: and ye came unto the sea; and the E-gyp'tians pursued after your fathers with chariots and horsemen unto the Red sea.

7 And when they cried unto the LORD, he put darkness between you and the E-gyp'tians, and brought the sea upon them, and covered them; and your eyes have seen what I have done in E'gypt: and ye dwelt in the wilderness a long season.

8 And I brought you into the land of the Am'-or-ites, which dwelt on the other side Jor'dan; and they fought with you: and I gave them into your hand, that ye might possess their land; and I destroyed them from before you.

9 Then Ba'lak the son of Zip'por, king of Mo'-ab, arose and warred against Is'ra-el, and sent and called Ba'laam the son of Be'or to curse you:

10 But I would not hearken unto Ba'laam; therefore he blessed you still: so I delivered you out of his hand.

11 And ye went over Jor'dan, and came unto Jer'i-cho: and the men of Jer'i-cho fought against you, the Am'or-ites, and the Per'iz-zites, and the Ca'naan-ites, and the Hit'tites, and the Gir'ga-shites, the Hi'vites, and the Jeb'u-sites; and I delivered them into your hand.

12 And I sent the hornet before you, which drave them out from before you, *even* the two kings of the Am'or-ites; *but* not with thy sword, nor with thy bow.

13 And I have given you a land for which ye did not labour, and cities which ye built not, and ye dwell in them; of the vineyards and oliveyards which ye planted not do ye eat.

14 ¶ Now therefore fear the LORD, and serve him in sincerity and in truth: and put away the gods which your fathers served on the other side of the flood, and in E'gypt; and serve ye the LORD.

15 And if it seem evil unto you to serve the LORD, choose you this day whom ye will serve; whether the gods which your fathers served that *were* on the other side of the flood, or the gods of the Am'or-ites, in whose land ye dwell: but as for me and my house, we will serve the LORD.

16 And the people answered and said, God forbid that we should forsake the LORD, to serve other gods;

17 For the LORD our God, he *it is* that brought us up and our fathers out of the land of E'gypt, from the house of bondage, and which did those great signs in our sight, and preserved us in all the way wherein we went, and among all the people through whom we passed:

18 And the LORD drave out from before us all the people, even the Am'or-ites which dwelt in the land: *therefore* will we also serve the LORD; for he *is* our God.

19 And Josh'u-a said unto the people, Ye cannot serve the LORD: for he *is* an holy God; he *is* a jealous God; he will not forgive your transgressions nor your sins.

20 If ye forsake the LORD, and serve strange gods, then he will turn and do you hurt, and consume you, after that he hath done you good.

21 And the people said unto Josh'u-a, Nay; but we will serve the LORD.

22 And Josh'u-a said unto the people, Ye *are* witnesses against yourselves that ye have chosen you the LORD, to serve him. And they said, *We are* witnesses.

23 Now therefore put away, *said he*, the strange gods which *are* among you, and incline your heart unto the LORD God of Is'ra-el.

24 And the people said unto Josh'u-a, The LORD our God will we serve, and his voice will we obey.

25 So Josh'u-a made a covenant with the people that day, and set them a statute and an ordinance in She'chem.

26 ¶ And Josh'u-a wrote these words in the book of the law of God, and took a great stone, and set it up there under an oak, that *was* by the sanctuary of the LORD.

27 And Josh'u-a said unto all the people, Behold, this stone shall be a witness unto us; for it hath heard all the words of the LORD which he spake unto us: it shall be therefore a witness unto you, lest ye deny your God.

28 So Josh'u-a let the people depart, every man unto his inheritance.

29 ¶ And it came to pass after these things, that Josh'u-a the son of Nun, the servant of the LORD, died, *being* an hundred and ten years old.

30 And they buried him in the border of his inheritance in Tim'nath–se'rah, which *is* in mount E'phra-im, on the north side of the hill of Ga'ash.

31 And Is'ra-el served the LORD all the days of Josh'u-a, and all the days of the elders that overlived Josh'u-a, and which had known all the works of the LORD, that he had done for Is'ra-el.

32 ¶ And the bones of Jo'seph, which the children of Is'ra-el brought up out of E'gypt, buried they in She'chem, in a parcel of ground which Ja'cob bought of the sons of Ha'mor the father of She'chem for an hundred pieces of silver: and it became the inheritance of the children of Jo'seph.

33 And E-le-a'zar the son of Aar'on died; and they buried him in a hill *that pertained to* Phin'-e-has his son, which was given him in mount E'phra-im.

THE BOOK OF

JUDGES

1 NOW after the death of Josh'u-a it came to pass, that the children of Is'ra-el asked the LORD, saying, Who shall go up for us against the Ca'naan-ites first, to fight against them?

2 And the LORD said, Ju'dah shall go up: behold, I have delivered the land into his hand.

3 And Ju'dah said unto Sim'e-on his brother, Come up with me into my lot, that we may fight against the Ca'naan-ites; and I likewise will go with thee into thy lot. So Sim'e-on went with him.

4 And Ju'dah went up; and the LORD delivered the Ca'naan-ites and the Per'iz-zites into their hand: and they slew of them in Be'zek ten thousand men.

5 And they found A-don'i–be'zek in Be'zek: and they fought against him, and they slew the Ca'naan-ites and the Per'iz-zites.

6 But A-don'i–be'zek fled; and they pursued after him, and caught him, and cut off his thumbs and his great toes.

7 And A-don'i–be'zek said, Threescore and ten kings, having their thumbs and their great toes cut off, gathered *their meat* under my table: as I have done, so God hath requited me. And they brought him to Je-ru'sa-lem, and there he died.

8 Now the children of Ju'dah had fought against Je-ru'sa-lem, and had taken it, and smitten it with the edge of the sword, and set the city on fire.

9 ¶ And afterward the children of Ju'dah went down to fight against the Ca'naan-ites, that dwelt in the mountain, and in the south, and in the valley.

10 And Ju'dah went against the Ca'naan-ites that dwelt in He'bron: (now the name of He'bron before *was* Kir'jath–ar'ba:) and they slew She'shai, and A-hi'man, and Tal'mai.

11 And from thence he went against the inhabitants of De'bir: and the name of De'bir before *was* Kir'jath–se'pher:

12 And Ca'leb said, He that smiteth Kir'jath–se'pher, and taketh it, to him will I give Ach'sah my daughter to wife.

13 And Oth'ni-el the son of Ke'naz, Ca'leb's younger brother, took it: and he gave him Ach'sah his daughter to wife.

14 And it came to pass, when she came *to him*, that she moved him to ask of her father a field; and she lighted from off *her* ass; and Ca'leb said unto her, What wilt thou?

15 And she said unto him, Give me a blessing: for thou hast given me a south land; give me also springs of water. And Ca'leb gave her the upper springs and the nether springs.

16 ¶ And the children of the Ken'ite, Mo'ses' father in law, went up out of the city of palm trees with the children of Ju'dah into the wilderness of Ju'dah, which *lieth* in the south of A'rad; and they went and dwelt among the people.

17 And Ju'dah went with Sim'e-on his brother, and they slew the Ca'naan-ites that inhabited Ze'phath, and utterly destroyed it. And the name of the city was called Hor'mah.

18 Also Ju'dah took Ga'za with the coast thereof, and As'ke-lon with the coast thereof, and Ek'ron with the coast thereof.

19 And the LORD was with Ju'dah; and he drave out *the inhabitants of* the mountain; but could not drive out the inhabitants of the valley, because they had chariots of iron.

20 And they gave He'bron unto Ca'leb, as Mo'ses said: and he expelled thence the three sons of A'nak.

21 And the children of Ben'ja-min did not drive out the Jeb'u-sites that inhabited Je-ru'salem; but the Jeb'u-sites dwell with the children of Ben'ja-min in Je-ru'sa-lem unto this day.

22 ¶ And the house of Jo'seph, they also went up against Beth'–el: and the LORD *was* with them.

23 And the house of Jo'seph sent to descry Beth'–el. (Now the name of the city before *was* Luz.)

24 And the spies saw a man come forth out of the city, and they said unto him, Shew us, we pray thee, the entrance into the city, and we will shew thee mercy.

25 And when he shewed them the entrance into the city, they smote the city with the edge of the sword; but they let go the man and all his family.

26 And the man went into the land of the Hit'tites, and built a city, and called the name thereof Luz: which *is* the name thereof unto this day.

27 ¶ Neither did Ma-nas'seh drive out *the inhabitants of* Beth–she'an and her towns, nor Ta'a-nach and her towns, nor the inhabitants of Dor and her towns, nor the inhabitants of Ib'le-am and her towns, nor the inhabitants of Megid'do and her towns: but the Ca'naan-ites would dwell in that land.

28 And it came to pass, when Is'ra-el was strong, that they put the Ca'naan-ites to tribute, and did not utterly drive them out.

29 ¶ Neither did E'phra-im drive out the Ca'naan-ites that dwelt in Ge'zer; but the Ca'naan-ites dwelt in Ge'zer among them.

30 ¶ Neither did Zeb'u-lun drive out the inhabitants of Kit'ron, nor the inhabitants of Na'ha-lol; but the Ca'naan-ites dwelt among them, and became tributaries.

31 ¶ Neither did Ash'er drive out the inhabitants of Ac'cho, nor the inhabitants of Zi'don, nor of Ah'lab, nor of Ach'zib, nor of Hel'bah, nor of A'phik, nor of Re'hob:

32 But the Ash'er-ites dwelt among the Ca'naan-ites, the inhabitants of the land: for they did not drive them out.

33 ¶ Neither did Naph'ta-li drive out the inhabitants of Beth–she'mesh, nor the inhabitants of Beth–a'nath; but he dwelt among the Ca'naan-ites, the inhabitants of the land: nevertheless the inhabitants of Beth–she'mesh and of Beth–a'nath became tributaries unto them.

34 And the Am'or-ites forced the children of Dan into the mountain: for they would not suffer them to come down to the valley:

35 But the Am'or-ites would dwell in mount He'res in Aij'a-lon, and in Sha-al'bim: yet the hand of the house of Jo'seph prevailed, so that they became tributaries.

36 And the coast of the Am'or-ites *was* from the going up to A-krab'bim, from the rock, and upward.

2 AND an angel of the LORD came up from Gil'gal to Bo'chim, and said, I made you to go up out of E'gypt, and have brought you unto

the land which I sware unto your fathers; and I
said, I will never break my covenant with you.
2 And ye shall make no league with the inhabitants of this land; ye shall throw down their
altars: but ye have not obeyed my voice: why
have ye done this?
3 Wherefore I also said, I will not drive them
out from before you; but they shall be *as thorns*
in your sides, and their gods shall be a snare
unto you.
4 And it came to pass, when the angel of the
LORD spake these words unto all the children of
Is'ra-el, that the people lifted up their voice, and
wept.
5 And they called the name of that place Bo'-
chim: and they sacrificed there unto the LORD.
6 ¶ And when Josh'u-a had let the people go,
the children of Is'ra-el went every man unto his
inheritance to possess the land.
7 And the people served the LORD all the
days of Josh'u-a, and all the days of the elders
that outlived Josh'u-a, who had seen all the
great works of the LORD, that he did for Is'ra-el.
8 And Josh'u-a the son of Nun, the servant of
the LORD, died, *being* an hundred and ten years
old.
9 And they buried him in the border of his
inheritance in Tim'nath-he'res, in the mount of
E'phra-im, on the north side of the hill Ga'ash.
10 And also all that generation were gathered unto their fathers: and there arose another
generation after them, which knew not the
LORD, nor yet the works which he had done for
Is'ra-el.
11¶ And the children of Is'ra-el did evil in the
sight of the LORD, and served Ba'al-im:
12 And they forsook the LORD God of their
fathers, which brought them out of the land of
E'gypt, and followed other gods, of the gods of
the people that *were* round about them, and
bowed themselves unto them, and provoked the
LORD to anger.
13 And they forsook the LORD, and served
Ba'al and Ash'ta-roth.
14 ¶ And the anger of the LORD was hot
against Is'ra-el, and he delivered them into the
hands of spoilers that spoiled them, and he sold
them into the hands of their enemies round
about, so that they could not any longer stand
before their enemies.
15 Whithersoever they went out, the hand of
the LORD was against them for evil, as the LORD
had said, and as the LORD had sworn unto them:
and they were greatly distressed.
16 ¶ Nevertheless the LORD raised up
judges, which delivered them out of the hand of
those that spoiled them.
17 And yet they would not hearken unto
their judges, but they went a whoring after other gods, and bowed themselves unto them: they
turned quickly out of the way which their fathers walked in, obeying the commandments of
the LORD; *but* they did not so.
18 And when the LORD raised them up
judges, then the LORD was with the judge, and
delivered them out of the hand of their enemies
all the days of the judge: for it repented the
LORD because of their groanings by reason of
them that oppressed them and vexed them.
19 And it came to pass, when the judge was
dead, *that* they returned, and corrupted *themselves* more than their fathers, in following other gods to serve them, and to bow down unto
them; they ceased not from their own doings,
nor from their stubborn way.
20 ¶ And the anger of the LORD was hot
against Is'ra-el; and he said, Because that this
people hath transgressed my covenant which I
commanded their fathers, and have not hearkened unto my voice;
21 I also will not henceforth drive out any
from before them of the nations which Josh'u-a
left when he died:
22 That through them I may prove Is'ra-el,
whether they will keep the way of the LORD to
walk therein, as their fathers did keep *it*, or not.
23 Therefore the LORD left those nations,
without driving them out hastily; neither delivered he them into the hand of Josh'u-a.

3 NOW these *are* the nations which the
LORD left, to prove Is'ra-el by them, *even*
as many *of Is'ra-el* as had not known all the
wars of Ca'naan;
2 Only that the generations of the children of
Is'ra-el might know, to teach them war, at the
least such as before knew nothing thereof;
3 *Namely*, five lords of the Phi-lis'tines, and
all the Ca'naan-ites, and the Si-do'ni-ans, and
the Hi'vites that dwelt in mount Leb'a-non,
from mount Ba'al-her'mon unto the entering in
of Ha'math.
4 And they were to prove Is'ra-el by them, to
know whether they would hearken unto the
commandments of the LORD, which he commanded their fathers by the hand of Mo'ses.
5 ¶ And the children of Is'ra-el dwelt among
the Ca'naan-ites, Hit'tites, and Am'or-ites, and
Per'iz-zites, and Hi'vites, and Jeb'u-sites:
6 And they took their daughters to be their
wives, and gave their daughters to their sons,
and served their gods.
7 And the children of Is'ra-el did evil in the
sight of the LORD, and forgat the LORD their
God, and served Ba'al-im and the groves.
8 ¶ Therefore the anger of the LORD was hot
against Is'ra-el, and he sold them into the hand
of Chu'shan-rish-a-tha'im king of Mes-o-po-ta'-
mi-a: and the children of Is'ra-el served Chu'-
shan-rish-a-tha'im eight years.
9 And when the children of Is'ra-el cried unto
the LORD, the LORD raised up a deliverer to the
children of Is'ra-el, who delivered them, *even*
Oth'ni-el the son of Ke'naz, Ca'leb's younger
brother.
10 And the Spirit of the LORD came upon
him, and he judged Is'ra-el, and went out to
war: and the LORD delivered Chu'shan-rish-a-
tha'im king of Mes-o-po-ta'mi-a into his hand;
and his hand prevailed against Chu'shan-rish-
a-tha'im.
11 And the land had rest forty years. And
Oth'ni-el the son of Ke'naz died.
12 ¶ And the children of Is'ra-el did evil
again in the sight of the LORD: and the LORD
strengthened Eg'lon the king of Mo'ab against
Is'ra-el, because they had done evil in the sight
of the LORD.
13 And he gathered unto him the children of
Am'mon and Am'a-lek, and went and smote Is'-
ra-el, and possessed the city of palm trees.
14 So the children of Is'ra-el served Eg'lon
the king of Mo'ab eighteen years.
15 But when the children of Is'ra-el cried
unto the LORD, the LORD raised them up a deliverer, E'hud the son of Ge'ra, a Ben'ja-mite, a
man lefthanded: and by him the children of Is'-
ra-el sent a present unto Eg'lon the king of Mo'-
ab.
16 But E'hud made him a dagger which had
two edges, of a cubit length; and he did gird it
under his raiment upon his right thigh.
17 And he brought the present unto Eg'lon
king of Mo'ab: and Eg'lon *was* a very fat man.

18 And when he had made an end to offer the
present, he sent away the people that bare the
present.
19 But he himself turned again from the
quarries that *were* by Gil'gal, and said, I have a
secret errand unto thee, O king: who said, Keep
silence. And all that stood by him went out
from him.
20 And E'hud came unto him; and he was sitting in a summer parlour, which he had for himself alone. And E'hud said, I have a message
from God unto thee. And he arose out of *his*
seat.
21 And E'hud put forth his left hand, and
took the dagger from his right thigh, and thrust
it into his belly:
22 And the haft also went in after the blade;
and the fat closed upon the blade, so that he
could not draw the dagger out of his belly; and
the dirt came out.
23 Then E'hud went forth through the porch,
and shut the doors of the parlour upon him, and
locked them.
24 When he was gone out, his servants came;
and when they saw that, behold, the doors of
the parlour *were* locked, they said, Surely he
covereth his feet in his summer chamber.
25 And they tarried till they were ashamed:
and, behold, he opened not the doors of the parlour; therefore they took a key, and opened
them: and, behold, their lord *was* fallen down
dead on the earth.
26 And E'hud escaped while they tarried, and
passed beyond the quarries, and escaped unto
Se'i-rath.
27 And it came to pass, when he was come,
that he blew a trumpet in the mountain of E'-
phra-im, and the children of Is'ra-el went down
with him from the mount, and he before them.
28 And he said unto them, Follow after me:
for the LORD hath delivered your enemies the
Mo'ab-ites into your hand. And they went down
after him, and took the fords of Jor'dan toward
Mo'ab, and suffered not a man to pass over.
29 And they slew of Mo'ab at that time about
ten thousand men, all lusty, and all men of valour; and there escaped not a man.
30 So Mo'ab was subdued that day under the
hand of Is'ra-el. And the land had rest fourscore
years.
31 ¶ And after him was Sham'gar the son of
A'nath, which slew of the Phi-lis'tines six hundred men with an ox goad: and he also delivered Is'ra-el.

4 AND the children of Is'ra-el again did evil
in the sight of the LORD, when E'hud was
dead.
2 And the LORD sold them into the hand of
Ja'bin king of Ca'naan, that reigned in Ha'zor;
the captain of whose host *was* Sis'e-ra, which
dwelt in Ha-ro'sheth of the Gen'tiles.
3 And the children of Is'ra-el cried unto the
LORD: for he had nine hundred chariots of iron;
and twenty years he mightily oppressed the
children of Is'ra-el.
4 ¶ And Deb'o-rah, a prophetess, the wife of
Lap'i-doth, she judged Is'ra-el at that time.
5 And she dwelt under the palm tree of Deb'-
o-rah between Ra'mah and Beth'-el in mount
E'phra-im: and the children of Is'ra-el came up
to her for judgment.
6 And she sent and called Ba'rak the son of
A-bin'o-am out of Ke'desh-naph'ta-li, and said
unto him, Hath not the LORD God of Is'ra-el
commanded, *saying,* Go and draw toward
mount Ta'bor, and take with thee ten thousand
men of the children of Naph'ta-li and of the children of Zeb'u-lun?
7 And I will draw unto thee to the river Ki'-
shon Sis'e-ra, the captain of Ja'bin's army, with
his chariots and his multitude; and I will deliver
him into thine hand.
8 And Ba'rak said unto her, If thou wilt go
with me, then I will go: but if thou wilt not go
with me, *then* I will not go.
9 And she said, I will surely go with thee:
notwithstanding the journey that thou takest
shall not be for thine honour; for the LORD shall
sell Sis'e-ra into the hand of a woman. And
Deb'o-rah arose, and went with Ba'rak to Ke'-
desh.
10 ¶ And Ba'rak called Zeb'u-lun and Naph'-
ta-li to Ke'desh; and he went up with ten thousand men at his feet: and Deb'o-rah went up
with him.
11 Now He'ber the Ken'ite, *which was* of the
children of Ho'bab the father in law of Mo'ses,
had severed himself from the Ken'ites, and
pitched his tent unto the plain of Za-a-na'im,
which *is* by Ke'desh.
12 And they shewed Sis'e-ra that Ba'rak the
son of A-bin'o-am was gone up to mount Ta'-
bor.
13 And Sis'e-ra gathered together all his
chariots, *even* nine hundred chariots of iron,
and all the people that *were* with him, from Ha-
ro'sheth of the Gen'tiles unto the river of Ki'-
shon.
14 And Deb'o-rah said unto Ba'rak, Up; for
this *is* the day in which the LORD hath delivered
Sis'e-ra into thine hand: is not the LORD gone
out before thee? So Ba'rak went down from
mount Ta'bor, and ten thousand men after him.
15 And the LORD discomfited Sis'e-ra, and all
his chariots, and all *his* host, with the edge of
the sword before Ba'rak; so that Sis'e-ra lighted
down off *his* chariot, and fled away on his feet.
16 But Ba'rak pursued after the chariots, and
after the host, unto Ha-ro'sheth of the Gen'tiles:
and all the host of Sis'e-ra fell upon the edge of
the sword; *and* there was not a man left.
17 Howbeit Sis'e-ra fled away on his feet to
the tent of Ja'el the wife of He'ber the Ken'ite:
for *there was* peace between Ja'bin the king of
Ha'zor and the house of He'ber the Ken'ite.
18 ¶ And Ja'el went out to meet Sis'e-ra, and
said unto him, Turn in, my lord, turn in to me;
fear not. And when he had turned in unto her
into the tent, she covered him with a mantle.
19 And he said unto her, Give me, I pray
thee, a little water to drink; for I am thirsty.
And she opened a bottle of milk, and gave him
drink, and covered him.
20 Again he said unto her, Stand in the door
of the tent, and it shall be, when any man doth
come and enquire of thee, and say, Is there any
man here? that thou shalt say, No.
21 Then Ja'el He'ber's wife took a nail of the
tent, and took an hammer in her hand, and went
softly unto him, and smote the nail into his temples, and fastened it into the ground: for he was
fast asleep and weary. So he died.
22 And, behold, as Ba'rak pursued Sis'e-ra,
Ja'el came out to meet him, and said unto him,
Come, and I will shew thee the man whom thou
seekest. And when he came into her *tent,* behold, Sis'e-ra lay dead, and the nail *was* in his
temples.
23 So God subdued on that day Ja'bin the
king of Ca'naan before the children of Is'ra-el.
24 And the hand of the children of Is'ra-el
prospered, and prevailed against Ja'bin the king

of Ca'naan, until they had destroyed Ja'bin king of Ca'naan.

5 THEN sang Deb'o-rah and Ba'rak the son of A-bin'o-am on that day, saying,

2 Praise ye the LORD for the avenging of Is'-ra-el, when the people willingly offered themselves.

3 Hear, O ye kings; give ear, O ye princes; I, *even* I, will sing unto the LORD; I will sing *praise* to the LORD God of Is'ra-el.

4 LORD, when thou wentest out of Se'ir, when thou marchedst out of the field of E'dom, the earth trembled, and the heavens dropped, the clouds also dropped water.

5 The mountains melted from before the LORD, *even* that Si'nai from before the LORD God of Is'ra-el.

6 In the days of Sham'gar the son of A'nath, in the days of Ja'el, the highways were unoccupied, and the travellers walked through byways.

7 *The inhabitants of* the villages ceased, they ceased in Is'ra-el, until that I Deb'o-rah arose, that I arose a mother in Is'ra-el.

8 They chose new gods; then *was* war in the gates: was there a shield or spear seen among forty thousand in Is'ra-el?

9 My heart *is* toward the governors of Is'ra-el, that offered themselves willingly among the people. Bless ye the LORD.

10 Speak, ye that ride on white asses, ye that sit in judgment, and walk by the way.

11 *They that are delivered* from the noise of archers in the places of drawing water, there shall they rehearse the righteous acts of the LORD, *even* the righteous acts *toward the inhabitants* of his villages in Is'ra-el: then shall the people of the LORD go down to the gates.

12 Awake, awake, Deb'o-rah: awake, awake, utter a song: arise, Ba'rak, and lead thy captivity captive, thou son of A-bin'o-am.

13 Then he made him that remaineth have dominion over the nobles among the people: the LORD made me have dominion over the mighty.

14 Out of E'phra-im *was there* a root of them against Am'a-lek; after thee, Ben'ja-min, among thy people; out of Ma'chir came down governors, and out of Zeb'u-lun they that handle the pen of the writer.

15 And the princes of Is'sa-char *were* with Deb'o-rah; even Is'sa-char, and also Ba'rak: he was sent on foot into the valley. For the divisions of Reu'ben *there were* great thoughts of heart.

16 Why abodest thou among the sheepfolds, to hear the bleatings of the flocks? For the divisions of Reu'ben *there were* great searchings of heart.

17 Gil'e-ad abode beyond Jor'dan: and why did Dan remain in ships? Ash'er continued on the sea shore, and abode in his breaches.

18 Zeb'u-lun and Naph'ta-li *were* a people *that* jeoparded their lives unto the death in the high places of the field.

19 The kings came *and* fought, then fought the kings of Ca'naan in Ta'a-nach by the waters of Me-gid'do; they took no gain of money.

20 They fought from heaven; the stars in their courses fought against Sis'e-ra.

21 The river of Ki'shon swept them away, that ancient river, the river Ki'shon. O my soul, thou hast trodden down strength.

22 Then were the horsehoofs broken by the means of the pransings, the pransings of their mighty ones.

23 Curse ye Me'roz, said the angel of the LORD, curse ye bitterly the inhabitants thereof; because they came not to the help of the LORD, to the help of the LORD against the mighty.

24 Blessed above women shall Ja'el the wife of He'ber the Ken'ite be, blessed shall she be above women in the tent.

25 He asked water, *and* she gave *him* milk; she brought forth butter in a lordly dish.

26 She put her hand to the nail, and her right hand to the workmen's hammer; and with the hammer she smote Sis'e-ra, she smote off his head, when she had pierced and stricken through his temples.

27 At her feet he bowed, he fell, he lay down: at her feet he bowed, he fell: where he bowed, there he fell down dead.

28 The mother of Sis'e-ra looked out at a window, and cried through the lattice, Why is his chariot *so* long in coming? why tarry the wheels of his chariots?

29 Her wise ladies answered her, yea, she returned answer to herself,

30 Have they not sped? have they *not* divided the prey; to every man a damsel *or* two; to Sis'e-ra a prey of divers colours, a prey of divers colours of needlework, of divers colours of needlework on both sides, *meet* for the necks of *them that take* the spoil?

31 So let all thine enemies perish, O LORD: but *let* them that love him *be* as the sun when he goeth forth in his might. And the land had rest forty years.

6 AND the children of Is'ra-el did evil in the sight of the LORD: and the LORD delivered them into the hand of Mid'i-an seven years.

2 And the hand of Mid'i-an prevailed against Is'ra-el: *and* because of the Mid'i-an-ites the children of Is'ra-el made them the dens which *are* in the mountains, and caves, and strong holds.

3 And *so* it was, when Is'ra-el had sown, that the Mid'i-an-ites came up, and the Am'a-lek-ites, and the children of the east, even they came up against them;

4 And they encamped against them, and destroyed the increase of the earth, till thou come unto Ga'za, and left no sustenance for Is'ra-el, neither sheep, nor ox, nor ass.

5 For they came up with their cattle and their tents, and they came as grasshoppers for multitude; *for* both they and their camels were without number: and they entered into the land to destroy it.

6 And Is'ra-el was greatly impoverished because of the Mid'i-an-ites; and the children of Is'ra-el cried unto the LORD.

7 ¶ And it came to pass, when the children of Is'ra-el cried unto the LORD because of the Mid'i-an-ites,

8 That the LORD sent a prophet unto the children of Is'ra-el, which said unto them, Thus saith the LORD God of Is'ra-el, I brought you up from E'gypt, and brought you forth out of the house of bondage;

9 And I delivered you out of the hand of the E-gyp'tians, and out of the hand of all that oppressed you, and drave them out from before you, and gave you their land;

10 And I said unto you, I *am* the LORD your God; fear not the gods of the Am'or-ites, in whose land ye dwell: but ye have not obeyed my voice.

11 ¶ And there came an angel of the LORD, and sat under an oak which *was* in Oph'rah, that *pertained* unto Jo'ash the A'bi–ez'rite: and

his son Gid'e-on threshed wheat by the winepress, to hide *it* from the Mid'i-an-ites.
12 And the angel of the LORD appeared unto
him, and said unto him, The LORD *is* with thee,
thou mighty man of valour.
13 And Gid'e-on said unto him, Oh my Lord,
if the LORD be with us, why then is all this befallen us? and where *be* all his miracles which
our fathers told us of, saying, Did not the LORD
bring us up from E'gypt? but now the LORD hath
forsaken us, and delivered us into the hands of
the Mid'i-an-ites.
14 And the LORD looked upon him, and said,
Go in this thy might, and thou shalt save Is'ra-el
from the hand of the Mid'i-an-ites: have not I
sent thee?
15 And he said unto him, Oh my Lord,
wherewith shall I save Is'ra-el? behold, my family *is* poor in Ma-nas'seh, and I *am* the least in
my father's house.
16 And the LORD said unto him, Surely I will
be with thee, and thou shalt smite the Mid'i-an-
ites as one man.
17 And he said unto him, If now I have found
grace in thy sight, then shew me a sign that
thou talkest with me.
18 Depart not hence, I pray thee, until I come
unto thee, and bring forth my present, and set *it*
before thee. And he said, I will tarry until thou
come again.
19 ¶ And Gid'e-on went in, and made ready
a kid, and unleavened cakes of an ephah of
flour: the flesh he put in a basket, and he put the
broth in a pot, and brought *it* out unto him under the oak, and presented *it*.
20 And the angel of God said unto him, Take
the flesh and the unleavened cakes, and lay
them upon this rock, and pour out the broth.
And he did so.
21 ¶ Then the angel of the LORD put forth the
end of the staff that *was* in his hand, and
touched the flesh and the unleavened cakes;
and there rose up fire out of the rock, and consumed the flesh and the unleavened cakes.
Then the angel of the LORD departed out of his
sight.
22 And when Gid'e-on perceived that he *was*
an angel of the LORD, Gid'e-on said, Alas, O
Lord GOD! for because I have seen an angel of
the LORD face to face.
23 And the LORD said unto him, Peace *be*
unto thee; fear not: thou shalt not die.
24 Then Gid'e-on built an altar there unto the
LORD, and called it Je-ho'vah–sha'lom: unto this
day it *is* yet in Oph'rah of the A'bi-ez'rites.
25 ¶ And it came to pass the same night,
that the LORD said unto him, Take thy father's
young bullock, even the second bullock of
seven years old, and throw down the altar of
Ba'al that thy father hath, and cut down the
grove that *is* by it:
26 And build an altar unto the LORD thy God
upon the top of this rock, in the ordered place,
and take the second bullock, and offer a burnt
sacrifice with the wood of the grove which thou
shalt cut down.
27 Then Gid'e-on took ten men of his servants, and did as the LORD had said unto him:
and *so* it was, because he feared his father's
household, and the men of the city, that he
could not do *it* by day, that he did *it* by night.
28 ¶ And when the men of the city arose early in the morning, behold, the altar of Ba'al was
cast down, and the grove was cut down that
was by it, and the second bullock was offered
upon the altar *that was* built.
29 And they said one to another, Who hath
done this thing? And when they enquired and
asked, they said, Gid'e-on the son of Jo'ash hath
done this thing.
30 Then the men of the city said unto Jo'ash,
Bring out thy son, that he may die: because he
hath cast down the altar of Ba'al, and because
he hath cut down the grove that *was* by it.
31 And Jo'ash said unto all that stood against
him, Will ye plead for Ba'al? will ye save him?
he that will plead for him, let him be put to
death whilst *it is yet* morning: if he *be* a god, let
him plead for himself, because *one* hath cast
down his altar.
32 Therefore on that day he called him Je-
rub'ba-al, saying, Let Ba'al plead against him,
because he hath thrown down his altar.
33 ¶ Then all the Mid'i-an-ites and the Am'a-
lek-ites and the children of the east were gathered together, and went over, and pitched in the
valley of Jez're-el.
34 But the Spirit of the LORD came upon
Gid'e-on, and he blew a trumpet; and A'bi–e'zer
was gathered after him.
35 And he sent messengers throughout all
Ma-nas'seh; who also was gathered after him:
and he sent messengers unto Ash'er, and unto
Zeb'u-lun, and unto Naph'ta-li; and they came
up to meet them.
36 ¶ And Gid'e-on said unto God, If thou wilt
save Is'ra-el by mine hand, as thou hast said,
37 Behold, I will put a fleece of wool in the
floor; *and* if the dew be on the fleece only, and *it*
be dry upon all the earth *beside*, then shall I
know that thou wilt save Is'ra-el by mine hand,
as thou hast said.
38 And it was so: for he rose up early on the
morrow, and thrust the fleece together, and
wringed the dew out of the fleece, a bowl full of
water.
39 And Gid'e-on said unto God, Let not thine
anger be hot against me, and I will speak but
this once: let me prove, I pray thee, but this
once with the fleece; let it now be dry only upon
the fleece, and upon all the ground let there be
dew.
40 And God did so that night: for it was dry
upon the fleece only, and there was dew on all
the ground.

7 THEN Je-rub'ba-al, who *is* Gid'e-on, and
all the people that *were* with him, rose up
early, and pitched beside the well of Ha'rod: so
that the host of the Mid'i-an-ites were on the
north side of them, by the hill of Mo'reh, in the
valley.
2 And the LORD said unto Gid'e-on, The people that *are* with thee *are* too many for me to
give the Mid'i-an-ites into their hands, lest Is'ra-
el vaunt themselves against me, saying, Mine
own hand hath saved me.
3 Now therefore go to, proclaim in the ears
of the people, saying, Whosoever *is* fearful and
afraid, let him return and depart early from
mount Gil'e-ad. And there returned of the people twenty and two thousand; and there remained ten thousand.
4 And the LORD said unto Gid'e-on, The people *are* yet *too* many; bring them down unto the
water, and I will try them for thee there: and it
shall be, *that* of whom I say unto thee, This
shall go with thee, the same shall go with thee;
and of whomsoever I say unto thee, This shall
not go with thee, the same shall not go.
5 So he brought down the people unto the
water: and the LORD said unto Gid'e-on, Every
one that lappeth of the water with his tongue,
as a dog lappeth, him shalt thou set by himself;

likewise every one that boweth down upon his
knees to drink.
6 And the number of them that lapped, *putting* their hand to their mouth, were three hundred men: but all the rest of the people bowed
down upon their knees to drink water.
7 And the LORD said unto Gid'e-on, By the
three hundred men that lapped will I save you,
and deliver the Mid'i-an-ites into thine hand:
and let all the *other* people go every man unto
his place.
8 So the people took victuals in their hand,
and their trumpets: and he sent all *the rest of*
Is'ra-el every man unto his tent, and retained
those three hundred men: and the host of Mid'i-
an was beneath him in the valley.
9 ¶ And it came to pass the same night, that
the LORD said unto him, Arise, get thee down
unto the host; for I have delivered it into thine
hand.
10 But if thou fear to go down, go thou with
Phu'rah thy servant down to the host:
11 And thou shalt hear what they say; and
afterward shall thine hands be strengthened to
go down unto the host. Then went he down
with Phu'rah his servant unto the outside of the
armed men that *were* in the host.
12 And the Mid'i-an-ites and the Am'a-lek-
ites and all the children of the east lay along in
the valley like grasshoppers for multitude; and
their camels *were* without number, as the sand
by the sea side for multitude.
13 And when Gid'e-on was come, behold,
there was a man that told a dream unto his fellow, and said, Behold, I dreamed a dream, and,
lo, a cake of barley bread tumbled into the host
of Mid'i-an, and came unto a tent, and smote it
that it fell, and overturned it, that the tent lay
along.
14 And his fellow answered and said, This *is*
nothing else save the sword of Gid'e-on the son
of Jo'ash, a man of Is'ra-el: *for* into his hand
hath God delivered Mid'i-an, and all the host.
15 ¶ And it was *so,* when Gid'e-on heard the
telling of the dream, and the interpretation
thereof, that he worshipped, and returned into
the host of Is'ra-el, and said, Arise; for the LORD
hath delivered into your hand the host of Mid'i-
an.
16 And he divided the three hundred men
into three companies, and he put a trumpet in
every man's hand, with empty pitchers, and
lamps within the pitchers.
17 And he said unto them, Look on me, and
do likewise: and, behold, when I come to the
outside of the camp, it shall be *that,* as I do, so
shall ye do.
18 When I blow with a trumpet, I and all that
are with me, then blow ye the trumpets also on
every side of all the camp, and say, *The sword*
of the LORD, and of Gid'e-on.
19 ¶ So Gid'e-on, and the hundred men that
were with him, came unto the outside of the
camp in the beginning of the middle watch; and
they had but newly set the watch: and they
blew the trumpets, and brake the pitchers that
were in their hands.
20 And the three companies blew the trumpets, and brake the pitchers, and held the lamps
in their left hands, and the trumpets in their
right hands to blow *withal:* and they cried, The
sword of the LORD, and of Gid'e-on.
21 And they stood every man in his place
round about the camp: and all the host ran, and
cried, and fled.
22 And the three hundred blew the trumpets,
and the LORD set every man's sword against his
fellow, even throughout all the host: and the
host fled to Beth-shit'tah in Zer'e-rath, *and* to
the border of A'bel-me-ho'lah, unto Tab'bath.
23 And the men of Is'ra-el gathered themselves together out of Naph'ta-li, and out of
Ash'er, and out of all Ma-nas'seh, and pursued
after the Mid'i-an-ites.
24 ¶ And Gid'e-on sent messengers throughout all mount E'phra-im, saying, Come down
against the Mid'i-an-ites, and take before them
the waters unto Beth-ba'rah and Jor'dan. Then
all the men of E'phra-im gathered themselves
together, and took the waters unto Beth-ba'rah
and Jor'dan.
25 And they took two princes of the Mid'i-
an-ites, O'reb and Ze'eb; and they slew O'reb
upon the rock O'reb, and Ze'eb they slew at the
winepress of Ze'eb, and pursued Mid'i-an, and
brought the heads of O'reb and Ze'eb to Gid'e-
on on the other side Jor'dan.

8 AND the men of E'phra-im said unto him,
Why hast thou served us thus, that thou
calledst us not, when thou wentest to fight with
the Mid'i-an-ites? And they did chide with him
sharply.
2 And he said unto them, What have I done
now in comparison of you? *Is* not the gleaning
of the grapes of E'phra-im better than the vintage of A'bi-e'zer?
3 God hath delivered into your hands the
princes of Mid'i-an, O'reb and Ze'eb: and what
was I able to do in comparison of you? Then
their anger was abated toward him, when he
had said that.
4 ¶ And Gid'e-on came to Jor'dan, *and*
passed over, he, and the three hundred men
that *were* with him, faint, yet pursuing *them.*
5 And he said unto the men of Suc'coth,
Give, I pray you, loaves of bread unto the people that follow me; for they *be* faint, and I am
pursuing after Ze'bah and Zal-mun'na, kings of
Mid'i-an.
6 ¶ And the princes of Suc'coth said, *Are* the
hands of Ze'bah and Zal-mun'na now in thine
hand, that we should give bread unto thine
army?
7 And Gid'e-on said, Therefore when the
LORD hath delivered Ze'bah and Zal-mun'na
into mine hand, then I will tear your flesh with
the thorns of the wilderness and with briers.
8 ¶ And he went up thence to Pe-nu'el, and
spake unto them likewise: and the men of Pe-
nu'el answered him as the men of Suc'coth had
answered *him.*
9 And he spake also unto the men of Pe-nu'-
el, saying, When I come again in peace, I will
break down this tower.
10 ¶ Now Ze'bah and Zal-mun'na *were* in
Kar'kor, and their hosts with them, about fifteen thousand *men,* all that were left of all the
hosts of the children of the east: for there fell an
hundred and twenty thousand men that drew
sword.
11 ¶ And Gid'e-on went up by the way of
them that dwelt in tents on the east of No'bah
and Jog'be-hah, and smote the host: for the host
was secure.
12 And when Ze'bah and Zal-mun'na fled, he
pursued after them, and took the two kings of
Mid'i-an, Ze'bah and Zal-mun'na, and discomfited all the host.
13 ¶ And Gid'e-on the son of Jo'ash returned
from battle before the sun *was up,*
14 And caught a young man of the men of
Suc'coth, and enquired of him: and he de-

scribed unto him the princes of Suc'coth, and
the elders thereof, *even* threescore and seventeen men.
15 And he came unto the men of Suc'coth,
and said, Behold Ze'bah and Zal-mun'na, with
whom ye did upbraid me, saying, *Are* the hands
of Ze'bah and Zal-mun'na now in thine hand,
that we should give bread unto thy men *that*
are weary?
16 And he took the elders of the city, and
thorns of the wilderness and briers, and with
them he taught the men of Suc'coth.
17 And he beat down the tower of Pe-nu'el,
and slew the men of the city.
18 ¶ Then said he unto Ze'bah and Zal-mun'-
na, What manner of men *were they* whom ye
slew at Ta'bor? And they answered, As thou
art, so *were* they; each one resembled the children of a king.
19 And he said, They *were* my brethren, *even*
the sons of my mother: *as* the LORD liveth, if ye
had saved them alive, I would not slay you.
20 And he said unto Je'ther his firstborn, Up,
and slay them. But the youth drew not his
sword: for he feared, because he *was* yet a
youth.
21 Then Ze'bah and Zal-mun'na said, Rise
thou, and fall upon us: for as the man *is, so is*
his strength. And Gid'e-on arose, and slew Ze'-
bah and Zal-mun'na, and took away the ornaments that *were* on their camels' necks.
22 ¶ Then the men of Is'ra-el said unto Gid'e-
on, Rule thou over us, both thou, and thy son,
and thy son's son also: for thou hast delivered
us from the hand of Mid'i-an.
23 And Gid'e-on said unto them, I will not
rule over you, neither shall my son rule over
you: the LORD shall rule over you.
24 ¶ And Gid'e-on said unto them, I would
desire a request of you, that ye would give me
every man the earrings of his prey. (For they
had golden earrings, because they *were* Ish'ma-
el-ites.)
25 And they answered, We will willingly give
them. And they spread a garment, and did cast
therein every man the earrings of his prey.
26 And the weight of the golden earrings that
he requested was a thousand and seven hundred *shekels* of gold; beside ornaments, and col-
lars, and purple raiment that *was* on the kings
of Mid'i-an, and beside the chains that *were*
about their camels' necks.
27 And Gid'e-on made an ephod thereof, and
put it in his city, *even* in Oph'rah: and all Is'ra-el
went thither a whoring after it: which thing became a snare unto Gid'e-on, and to his house.
28 ¶ Thus was Mid'i-an subdued before the
children of Is'ra-el, so that they lifted up their
heads no more. And the country was in quietness forty years in the days of Gid'e-on.
29 ¶ And Je-rub'ba-al the son of Jo'ash went
and dwelt in his own house.
30 And Gid'e-on had threescore and ten sons
of his body begotten: for he had many wives.
31 And his concubine that *was* in She'chem,
she also bare him a son, whose name he called
A-bim'e-lech.
32 ¶ And Gid'e-on the son of Jo'ash died in a
good old age, and was buried in the sepulchre
of Jo'ash his father, in Oph'rah of the A'bi-ez'-
rites.
33 And it came to pass, as soon as Gid'e-on
was dead, that the children of Is'ra-el turned
again, and went a whoring after Ba'al-im, and
made Ba'al-be'rith their god.
34 And the children of Is'ra-el remembered
not the LORD their God, who had delivered
them out of the hands of all their enemies on
every side:
35 Neither shewed they kindness to the
house of Je-rub'ba-al, *namely*, Gid'e-on, according to all the goodness which he had shewed
unto Is'ra-el.

9 AND A-bim'e-lech the son of Je-rub'ba-al
went to She'chem unto his mother's brethren, and communed with them, and with all the
family of the house of his mother's father, saying,
2 Speak, I pray you, in the ears of all the men
of She'chem, Whether *is* better for you, either
that all the sons of Je-rub'ba-al, *which are*
threescore and ten persons, reign over you, or
that one reign over you? remember also that I
am your bone and your flesh.
3 And his mother's brethren spake of him in
the ears of all the men of She'chem all these
words: and their hearts inclined to follow A-
bim'e-lech; for they said, He *is* our brother.
4 And they gave him threescore and ten
pieces of silver out of the house of Ba'al-be'rith,
wherewith A-bim'e-lech hired vain and light
persons, which followed him.
5 And he went unto his father's house at
Oph'rah, and slew his brethren the sons of Je-
rub'ba-al, *being* threescore and ten persons,
upon one stone: notwithstanding yet Jo'tham
the youngest son of Je-rub'ba-al was left; for he
hid himself.
6 And all the men of She'chem gathered together, and all the house of Mil'lo, and went,
and made A-bim'e-lech king, by the plain of the
pillar that *was* in She'chem.
7 ¶ And when they told *it* to Jo'tham, he
went and stood in the top of mount Ger'i-zim,
and lifted up his voice, and cried, and said unto
them, Hearken unto me, ye men of She'chem,
that God may hearken unto you.
8 The trees went forth *on a time* to anoint a
king over them; and they said unto the olive
tree, Reign thou over us.
9 But the olive tree said unto them, Should I
leave my fatness, wherewith by me they honour
God and man, and go to be promoted over the
trees?
10 And the trees said to the fig tree, Come
thou, *and* reign over us.
11 But the fig tree said unto them, Should I
forsake my sweetness, and my good fruit, and
go to be promoted over the trees?
12 Then said the trees unto the vine, Come
thou, *and* reign over us.
13 And the vine said unto them, Should I
leave my wine, which cheereth God and man,
and go to be promoted over the trees?
14 Then said all the trees unto the bramble,
Come thou, *and* reign over us.
15 And the bramble said unto the trees, If in
truth ye anoint me king over you, *then* come
and put your trust in my shadow: and if not, let
fire come out of the bramble, and devour the
cedars of Leb'a-non.
16 Now therefore, if ye have done truly and
sincerely, in that ye have made A-bim'e-lech
king, and if ye have dealt well with Je-rub'ba-al
and his house, and have done unto him according to the deserving of his hands;
17 (For my father fought for you, and adven-
tured his life far, and delivered you out of the
hand of Mid'i-an:
18 And ye are risen up against my father's
house this day, and have slain his sons, threescore and ten persons, upon one stone, and
have made A-bim'e-lech, the son of his maidser-

vant, king over the men of She'chem, because
he *is* your brother;)
19 If ye then have dealt truly and sincerely
with Je-rub'ba-al and with his house this day,
then rejoice ye in A-bim'e-lech, and let him also
rejoice in you:
20 But if not, let fire come out from A-bim'e-
lech, and devour the men of She'chem, and the
house of Mil'lo; and let fire come out from the
men of She'chem, and from the house of Mil'lo,
and devour A-bim'e-lech.
21 And Jo'tham ran away, and fled, and went
to Be'er, and dwelt there, for fear of A-bim'e-
lech his brother.
22 ¶ When A-bim'e-lech had reigned three
years over Is'ra-el,
23 Then God sent an evil spirit between A-
bim'e-lech and the men of She'chem; and the
men of She'chem dealt treacherously with A-
bim'e-lech:
24 That the cruelty *done* to the threescore
and ten sons of Je-rub'ba-al might come, and
their blood be laid upon A-bim'e-lech their
brother, which slew them; and upon the men of
She'chem, which aided him in the killing of his
brethren.
25 And the men of She'chem set liers in wait
for him in the top of the mountains, and they
robbed all that came along that way by them:
and it was told A-bim'e-lech.
26 And Ga'al the son of E'bed came with his
brethren, and went over to She'chem: and the
men of She'chem put their confidence in him.
27 And they went out into the fields, and
gathered their vineyards, and trode *the grapes,*
and made merry, and went into the house of
their god, and did eat and drink, and cursed A-
bim'e-lech.
28 And Ga'al the son of E'bed said, Who *is* A-
bim'e-lech, and who *is* She'chem, that we
should serve him? *is* not *he* the son of Je-rub'ba-
al? and Ze'bul his officer? serve the men of Ha'-
mor the father of She'chem: for why should we
serve him?
29 And would to God this people were under
my hand! then would I remove A-bim'e-lech.
And he said to A-bim'e-lech, Increase thine
army, and come out.
30 ¶ And when Ze'bul the ruler of the city
heard the words of Ga'al the son of E'bed, his
anger was kindled.
31 And he sent messengers unto A-bim'e-
lech privily, saying, Behold, Ga'al the son of E'-
bed and his brethren be come to She'chem; and,
behold, they fortify the city against thee.
32 Now therefore up by night, thou and the
people that *is* with thee, and lie in wait in the
field:
33 And it shall be, *that* in the morning, as
soon as the sun is up, thou shalt rise early, and
set upon the city: and, behold, *when* he and the
people that *is* with him come out against thee,
then mayest thou do to them as thou shalt find
occasion.
34 ¶ And A-bim'e-lech rose up, and all the
people that *were* with him, by night, and they
laid wait against She'chem in four companies.
35 And Ga'al the son of E'bed went out, and
stood in the entering of the gate of the city: and
A-bim'e-lech rose up, and the people that *were*
with him, from lying in wait.
36 And when Ga'al saw the people, he said to
Ze'bul, Behold, there come people down from
the top of the mountains. And Ze'bul said unto
him, Thou seest the shadow of the mountains as
if they were men.
37 And Ga'al spake again and said, See there
come people down by the middle of the land,
and another company come along by the plain
of Me-on'e-nim.
38 Then said Ze'bul unto him, Where *is* now
thy mouth, wherewith thou saidst, Who *is* A-
bim'e-lech, that we should serve him? *is* not this
the people that thou hast despised? go out, I
pray now, and fight with them.
39 And Ga'al went out before the men of
She'chem, and fought with A-bim'e-lech.
40 And A-bim'e-lech chased him, and he fled
before him, and many were overthrown *and*
wounded, *even* unto the entering of the gate.
41 And A-bim'e-lech dwelt at A-ru'mah: and
Ze'bul thrust out Ga'al and his brethren, that
they should not dwell in She'chem.
42 And it came to pass on the morrow, that
the people went out into the field; and they told
A-bim'e-lech.
43 And he took the people, and divided them
into three companies, and laid wait in the field,
and looked, and, behold, the people *were* come
forth out of the city; and he rose up against
them, and smote them.
44 And A-bim'e-lech, and the company that
was with him, rushed forward, and stood in the
entering of the gate of the city: and the two *other* companies ran upon all *the people* that *were*
in the fields, and slew them.
45 And A-bim'e-lech fought against the city
all that day; and he took the city, and slew the
people that *was* therein, and beat down the city,
and sowed it with salt.
46 ¶ And when all the men of the tower of
She'chem heard *that,* they entered into an hold
of the house of the god Be'rith.
47 And it was told A-bim'e-lech, that all the
men of the tower of She'chem were gathered
together.
48 And A-bim'e-lech gat him up to mount
Zal'mon, he and all the people that *were* with
him; and A-bim'e-lech took an ax in his hand,
and cut down a bough from the trees, and took
it, and laid *it* on his shoulder, and said unto the
people that *were* with him, What ye have seen
me do, make haste, *and* do as I *have done.*
49 And all the people likewise cut down every man his bough, and followed A-bim'e-lech,
and put *them* to the hold, and set the hold on
fire upon them; so that all the men of the tower
of She'chem died also, about a thousand men
and women.
50 ¶ Then went A-bim'e-lech to The'bez, and
encamped against The'bez, and took it.
51 But there was a strong tower within the
city, and thither fled all the men and women,
and all they of the city, and shut *it* to them, and
gat them up to the top of the tower.
52 And A-bim'e-lech came unto the tower,
and fought against it, and went hard unto the
door of the tower to burn it with fire.
53 And a certain woman cast a piece of a
millstone upon A-bim'e-lech's head, and all to
brake his skull.
54 Then he called hastily unto the young man
his armourbearer, and said unto him, Draw thy
sword, and slay me, that men say not of me, A
woman slew him. And his young man thrust
him through, and he died.
55 And when the men of Is'ra-el saw that A-
bim'e-lech was dead, they departed every man
unto his place.
56 ¶ Thus God rendered the wickedness of
A-bim'e-lech, which he did unto his father, in
slaying his seventy brethren:
57 And all the evil of the men of She'chem
did God render upon their heads: and upon

them came the curse of Jo'tham the son of Je-rub'ba-al.

10 AND after A-bim'e-lech there arose to defend Is'ra-el To'la the son of Pu'ah, the son of Do'do, a man of Is'sa-char; and he dwelt in Sha'mir in mount E'phra-im.

2 And he judged Is'ra-el twenty and three years, and died, and was buried in Sha'mir.

3 ¶ And after him arose Ja'ir, a Gil'e-ad-ite, and judged Is'ra-el twenty and two years.

4 And he had thirty sons that rode on thirty ass colts, and they had thirty cities, which are called Ha'voth–ja'ir unto this day, which *are* in the land of Gil'e-ad.

5 And Ja'ir died, and was buried in Ca'mon.

6 ¶ And the children of Is'ra-el did evil again in the sight of the LORD, and served Ba'al-im, and Ash'ta-roth, and the gods of Syr'i-a, and the gods of Zi'don, and the gods of Mo'ab, and the gods of the children of Am'mon, and the gods of the Phi-lis'tines, and forsook the LORD, and served not him.

7 And the anger of the LORD was hot against Is'ra-el, and he sold them into the hands of the Phi-lis'tines, and into the hands of the children of Am'mon.

8 And that year they vexed and oppressed the children of Is'ra-el: eighteen years, all the children of Is'ra-el that *were* on the other side Jor'dan in the land of the Am'or-ites, which *is* in Gil'e-ad.

9 Moreover the children of Am'mon passed over Jor'dan to fight also against Ju'dah, and against Ben'ja-min, and against the house of E'phra-im; so that Is'ra-el was sore distressed.

10 ¶ And the children of Is'ra-el cried unto the LORD, saying, We have sinned against thee, both because we have forsaken our God, and also served Ba'al-im.

11 And the LORD said unto the children of Is'ra-el, *Did* not *I deliver you* from the E-gyp'tians, and from the Am'or-ites, from the children of Am'mon, and from the Phi-lis'tines?

12 The Zi-do'ni-ans also, and the Am'a-lek-ites, and the Ma'on-ites, did oppress you; and ye cried to me, and I delivered you out of their hand.

13 Yet ye have forsaken me, and served other gods: wherefore I will deliver you no more.

14 Go and cry unto the gods which ye have chosen; let them deliver you in the time of your tribulation.

15 ¶ And the children of Is'ra-el said unto the LORD, We have sinned: do thou unto us whatsoever seemeth good unto thee; deliver us only, we pray thee, this day.

16 And they put away the strange gods from among them, and served the LORD: and his soul was grieved for the misery of Is'ra-el.

17 Then the children of Am'mon were gathered together, and encamped in Gil'e-ad. And the children of Is'ra-el assembled themselves together, and encamped in Miz'peh.

18 And the people *and* princes of Gil'e-ad said one to another, What man *is he* that will begin to fight against the children of Am'mon? he shall be head over all the inhabitants of Gil'e-ad.

11 NOW Jeph'thah the Gil'e-ad-ite was a mighty man of valour, and he *was* the son of an harlot: and Gil'e-ad begat Jeph'thah.

2 And Gil'e-ad's wife bare him sons; and his wife's sons grew up, and they thrust out Jeph'thah, and said unto him, Thou shalt not inherit in our father's house; for thou *art* the son of a strange woman.

3 Then Jeph'thah fled from his brethren, and dwelt in the land of Tob: and there were gathered vain men to Jeph'thah, and went out with him.

4 ¶ And it came to pass in process of time, that the children of Am'mon made war against Is'ra-el.

5 And it was so, that when the children of Am'mon made war against Is'ra-el, the elders of Gil'e-ad went to fetch Jeph'thah out of the land of Tob:

6 And they said unto Jeph'thah, Come, and be our captain, that we may fight with the children of Am'mon.

7 And Jeph'thah said unto the elders of Gil'e-ad, Did not ye hate me, and expel me out of my father's house? and why are ye come unto me now when ye are in distress?

8 And the elders of Gil'e-ad said unto Jeph'thah, Therefore we turn again to thee now, that thou mayest go with us, and fight against the children of Am'mon, and be our head over all the inhabitants of Gil'e-ad.

9 And Jeph'thah said unto the elders of Gil'e-ad, If ye bring me home again to fight against the children of Am'mon, and the LORD deliver them before me, shall I be your head?

10 And the elders of Gil'e-ad said unto Jeph'thah, the LORD be witness between us, if we do not so according to thy words.

11 Then Jeph'thah went with the elders of Gil'e-ad, and the people made him head and captain over them: and Jeph'thah uttered all his words before the LORD in Miz'peh.

12 ¶ And Jeph'thah sent messengers unto the king of the children of Am'mon, saying, What hast thou to do with me, that thou art come against me to fight in my land?

13 And the king of the children of Am'mon answered unto the messengers of Jeph'thah, Because Is'ra-el took away my land, when they came up out of E'gypt, from Ar'non even unto Jab'bok, and unto Jor'dan: now therefore restore those *lands* again peaceably.

14 And Jeph'thah sent messengers again unto the king of the children of Am'mon:

15 And said unto him, Thus saith Jeph'thah, Is'ra-el took not away the land of Mo'ab, nor the land of the children of Am'mon:

16 But when Is'ra-el came up from E'gypt, and walked through the wilderness unto the Red sea, and came to Ka'desh;

17 Then Is'ra-el sent messengers unto the king of E'dom, saying, Let me, I pray thee, pass through thy land: but the king of E'dom would not hearken *thereto*. And in like manner they sent unto the king of Mo'ab: but he would not *consent:* and Is'ra-el abode in Ka'desh.

18 Then they went along through the wilderness, and compassed the land of E'dom, and the land of Mo'ab, and came by the east side of the land of Mo'ab, and pitched on the other side of Ar'non, but came not within the border of Mo'ab: for Ar'non *was* the border of Mo'ab.

19 And Is'ra-el sent messengers unto Si'hon king of the Am'or-ites, the king of Hesh'bon; and Is'ra-el said unto him, Let us pass, we pray thee, through thy land into my place.

20 But Si'hon trusted not Is'ra-el to pass through his coast: but Si'hon gathered all his people together, and pitched in Ja'haz, and fought against Is'ra-el.

21 And the LORD God of Is'ra-el delivered Si'hon and all his people into the hand of Is'ra-el, and they smote them: so Is'ra-el possessed all

the land of the Am'or-ites, the inhabitants of
that country.
22 And they possessed all the coasts of the
Am'or-ites, from Ar'non even unto Jab'bok, and
from the wilderness even unto Jor'dan.
23 So now the LORD God of Is'ra-el hath dispossessed the Am'or-ites from before his people
Is'ra-el, and shouldest thou possess it?
24 Wilt not thou possess that which Che'-
mosh thy god giveth thee to possess? So whomsoever the LORD our God shall drive out from
before us, them will we possess.
25 And now *art* thou any thing better than
Ba'lak the son of Zip'por, king of Mo'ab? did he
ever strive against Is'ra-el, or did he ever fight
against them,
26 While Is'ra-el dwelt in Hesh'bon and her
towns, and in Ar'o-er and her towns, and in all
the cities that *be* along by the coasts of Ar'non,
three hundred years? why therefore did ye not
recover *them* within that time?
27 Wherefore I have not sinned against thee,
but thou doest me wrong to war against me: the
LORD the Judge be judge this day between the
children of Is'ra-el and the children of Am'mon.
28 Howbeit the king of the children of Am'-
mon hearkened not unto the words of Jeph'thah
which he sent him.
29 ¶ Then the Spirit of the LORD came upon
Jeph'thah, and he passed over Gil'e-ad, and Ma-
nas'seh, and passed over Miz'peh of Gil'e-ad,
and from Miz'peh of Gil'e-ad he passed over
unto the children of Am'mon.
30 And Jeph'thah vowed a vow unto the
LORD, and said, If thou shalt without fail deliver
the children of Am'mon into mine hands,
31 Then it shall be, that whatsoever cometh
forth of the doors of my house to meet me,
when I return in peace from the children of
Am'mon, shall surely be the LORD's, and I will
offer it up for a burnt offering.
32 ¶ So Jeph'thah passed over unto the children of Am'mon to fight against them; and the
LORD delivered them into his hands.
33 And he smote them from Ar'o-er, even till
thou come to Min'nith, *even* twenty cities, and
unto the plain of the vineyards, with a very
great slaughter. Thus the children of Am'mon
were subdued before the children of Is'ra-el.
34 ¶ And Jeph'thah came to Miz'peh unto
his house, and, behold, his daughter came out
to meet him with timbrels and with dances: and
she *was his* only child; beside her he had neither
son nor daughter.
35 And it came to pass, when he saw her,
that he rent his clothes, and said, Alas, my
daughter! thou hast brought me very low, and
thou art one of them that trouble me: for I have
opened my mouth unto the LORD, and I cannot
go back.
36 And she said unto him, My father, *if* thou
hast opened thy mouth unto the LORD, do to me
according to that which hath proceeded out of
thy mouth; forasmuch as the LORD hath taken
vengeance for thee of thine enemies, *even* of the
children of Am'mon.
37 And she said unto her father, Let this
thing be done for me: let me alone two months,
that I may go up and down upon the mountains,
and bewail my virginity, I and my fellows.
38 And he said, Go. And he sent her away *for*
two months: and she went with her companions, and bewailed her virginity upon the mountains.
39 And it came to pass at the end of two
months, that she returned unto her father, who
did with her *according* to his vow which he had
vowed: and she knew no man. And it was a custom in Is'ra-el,
40 *That* the daughters of Is'ra-el went yearly
to lament the daughter of Jeph'thah the Gil'e-
ad-ite four days in a year.

12 AND the men of E'phra-im gathered
themselves together, and went northward, and said unto Jeph'thah, Wherefore
passedst thou over to fight against the children
of Am'mon, and didst not call us to go with
thee? we will burn thine house upon thee with
fire.
2 And Jeph'thah said unto them, I and my
people were at great strife with the children of
Am'mon; and when I called you, ye delivered
me not out of their hands.
3 And when I saw that ye delivered *me* not, I
put my life in my hands, and passed over
against the children of Am'mon, and the LORD
delivered them into my hand: wherefore then
are ye come up unto me this day, to fight
against me?
4 Then Jeph'thah gathered together all the
men of Gil'e-ad, and fought with E'phra-im: and
the men of Gil'e-ad smote E'phra-im, because
they said, Ye Gil'e-ad-ites *are* fugitives of E'-
phra-im among the E'phra-im-ites, *and* among
the Ma-nas'sites.
5 And the Gil'e-ad-ites took the passages of
Jor'dan before the E'phra-im-ites: and it was *so*,
that when those E'phra-im-ites which were escaped said, Let me go over; that the men of Gil'-
e-ad said unto him, *Art* thou an E'phra-im-ite? If
he said, Nay;
6 Then said they unto him, Say now Shib'bo-
leth: and he said Sib'bo-leth: for he could not
frame to pronounce *it* right. Then they took
him, and slew him at the passages of Jor'dan:
and there fell at that time of the E'phra-im-ites
forty and two thousand.
7 And Jeph'thah judged Is'ra-el six years.
Then died Jeph'thah the Gil'e-ad-ite, and was
buried in *one of* the cities of Gil'e-ad.
8 ¶ And after him Ib'zan of Beth'-le-hem
judged Is'ra-el.
9 And he had thirty sons, and thirty daughters, *whom* he sent abroad, and took in thirty
daughters from abroad for his sons. And he
judged Is'ra-el seven years.
10 Then died Ib'zan, and was buried at Beth'-
-le-hem.
11 ¶ And after him E'lon, a Zeb'u-lon-ite,
judged Is'ra-el; and he judged Is'ra-el ten years.
12 And E'lon the Zeb'u-lon-ite died, and was
buried in Aij'a-lon in the country of Zeb'u-lun.
13 ¶ And after him Ab'don the son of Hil'lel,
a Pir'a-thon-ite, judged Is'ra-el.
14 And he had forty sons and thirty nephews, that rode on threescore and ten ass colts:
and he judged Is'ra-el eight years.
15 And Ab'don the son of Hil'lel the Pir'a-
thon-ite died, and was buried in Pir'a-thon in
the land of E'phra-im, in the mount of the Am'a-
lek-ites.

13 AND the children of Is'ra-el did evil
again in the sight of the LORD; and the
LORD delivered them into the hand of the Phi-
lis'tines forty years.
2 ¶ And there was a certain man of Zo'rah,
of the family of the Dan'ites, whose name *was*
Ma-no'ah; and his wife *was* barren, and bare
not.
3 And the angel of the LORD appeared unto
the woman, and said unto her, Behold now,

thou *art* barren, and bearest not: but thou shalt conceive, and bear a son.

4 Now therefore beware, I pray thee, and drink not wine nor strong drink, and eat not any unclean *thing:*

5 For, lo, thou shalt conceive, and bear a son; and no razor shall come on his head: for the child shall be a Naz'a-rite unto God from the womb: and he shall begin to deliver Is'ra-el out of the hand of the Phi-lis'tines.

6 ¶ Then the woman came and told her husband, saying, A man of God came unto me, and his countenance *was* like the countenance of an angel of God, very terrible: but I asked him not whence he *was,* neither told he me his name:

7 But he said unto me, Behold, thou shalt conceive, and bear a son; and now drink no wine nor strong drink, neither eat any unclean *thing:* for the child shall be a Naz'a-rite to God from the womb to the day of his death.

8 ¶ Then Ma-no'ah intreated the LORD, and said, O my Lord, let the man of God which thou didst send come again unto us, and teach us what we shall do unto the child that shall be born.

9 And God hearkened to the voice of Ma-no'ah; and the angel of God came again unto the woman as she sat in the field: but Ma-no'ah her husband *was* not with her.

10 And the woman made haste, and ran, and shewed her husband, and said unto him, Behold, the man hath appeared unto me, that came unto me the *other* day.

11 And Ma-no'ah arose, and went after his wife, and came to the man, and said unto him, *Art* thou the man that spakest unto the woman? And he said, I *am.*

12 And Ma-no'ah said, Now let thy words come to pass. How shall we order the child, and *how* shall we do unto him?

13 And the angel of the LORD said unto Ma-no'ah, Of all that I said unto the woman let her beware.

14 She may not eat of any *thing* that cometh of the vine, neither let her drink wine or strong drink, nor eat any unclean *thing:* all that I commanded her let her observe.

15 ¶ And Ma-no'ah said unto the angel of the LORD, I pray thee, let us detain thee, until we shall have made ready a kid for thee.

16 And the angel of the LORD said unto Ma-no'ah, Though thou detain me, I will not eat of thy bread: and if thou wilt offer a burnt offering, thou must offer it unto the LORD. For Ma-no'ah knew not that he *was* an angel of the LORD.

17 And Ma-no'ah said unto the angel of the LORD, What *is* thy name, that when thy sayings come to pass we may do thee honour?

18 And the angel of the LORD said unto him, Why askest thou thus after my name, seeing it *is* secret?

19 So Ma-no'ah took a kid with a meat offering, and offered *it* upon a rock unto the LORD: and *the angel* did wonderously; and Ma-no'ah and his wife looked on.

20 For it came to pass, when the flame went up toward heaven from off the altar, that the angel of the LORD ascended in the flame of the altar. And Ma-no'ah and his wife looked on *it,* and fell on their faces to the ground.

21 But the angel of the LORD did no more appear to Ma-no'ah and to his wife. Then Ma-no'ah knew that he *was* an angel of the LORD.

22 And Ma-no'ah said unto his wife, We shall surely die, because we have seen God.

23 But his wife said unto him, If the LORD were pleased to kill us, he would not have received a burnt offering and a meat offering at our hands, neither would he have shewed us all these *things,* nor would as at this time have told us *such things* as these.

24 ¶ And the woman bare a son, and called his name Sam'son: and the child grew, and the LORD blessed him.

25 And the Spirit of the LORD began to move him at times in the camp of Dan between Zo'rah and Esh'ta-ol.

14

AND Sam'son went down to Tim'nath, and saw a woman in Tim'nath of the daughters of the Phi-lis'tines.

2 And he came up, and told his father and his mother, and said, I have seen a woman in Tim'nath of the daughters of the Phi-lis'tines: now therefore get her for me to wife.

3 Then his father and his mother said unto him, *Is there* never a woman among the daughters of thy brethren, or among all my people, that thou goest to take a wife of the uncircumcised Phi-lis'tines? And Sam'son said unto his father, Get her for me; for she pleaseth me well.

4 But his father and his mother knew not that it *was* of the LORD, that he sought an occasion against the Phi-lis'tines: for at that time the Phi-lis'tines had dominion over Is'ra-el.

5 ¶ Then went Sam'son down, and his father and his mother, to Tim'nath, and came to the vineyards of Tim'nath: and, behold, a young lion roared against him.

6 And the Spirit of the LORD came mightily upon him, and he rent him as he would have rent a kid, and *he had* nothing in his hand: but he told not his father or his mother what he had done.

7 And he went down, and talked with the woman; and she pleased Sam'son well.

8 ¶ And after a time he returned to take her, and he turned aside to see the carcase of the lion: and, behold, *there was* a swarm of bees and honey in the carcase of the lion.

9 And he took thereof in his hands, and went on eating, and came to his father and mother, and he gave them, and they did eat: but he told not them that he had taken the honey out of the carcase of the lion.

10 ¶ So his father went down unto the woman: and Sam'son made there a feast; for so used the young men to do.

11 And it came to pass, when they saw him, that they brought thirty companions to be with him.

12 ¶ And Sam'son said unto them, I will now put forth a riddle unto you: if ye can certainly declare it me within the seven days of the feast, and find *it* out, then I will give you thirty sheets and thirty change of garments:

13 But if ye cannot declare *it* me, then shall ye give me thirty sheets and thirty change of garments. And they said unto him, Put forth thy riddle, that we may hear it.

14 And he said unto them, Out of the eater came forth meat, and out of the strong came forth sweetness. And they could not in three days expound the riddle.

15 And it came to pass on the seventh day, that they said unto Sam'son's wife, Entice thy husband, that he may declare unto us the riddle, lest we burn thee and thy father's house with fire: have ye called us to take that we have? *is it* not *so?*

16 And Sam'son's wife wept before him, and said, Thou dost but hate me, and lovest me not: thou hast put forth a riddle unto the children of my people, and hast not told *it* me. And he said

unto her, Behold, I have not told *it* my father nor my mother, and shall I tell *it* thee?

17 And she wept before him the seven days, while their feast lasted: and it came to pass on the seventh day, that he told her, because she lay sore upon him: and she told the riddle to the children of her people.

18 And the men of the city said unto him on the seventh day before the sun went down, What *is* sweeter than honey? and what *is* stronger than a lion? And he said unto them, If ye had not plowed with my heifer, ye had not found out my riddle.

19 ¶ And the Spirit of the LORD came upon him and he went down to Ash'ke-lon, and slew thirty men of them, and took their spoil, and gave change of garments unto them which expounded the riddle. And his anger was kindled, and he went up to his father's house.

20 But Sam'son's wife was *given* to his companion, whom he had used as his friend.

15 BUT it came to pass within a while after, in the time of wheat harvest, that Sam'son visited his wife with a kid; and he said, I will go in to my wife into the chamber. But her father would not suffer him to go in.

2 And her father said, I verily thought that thou hadst utterly hated her; therefore I gave her to thy companion: *is* not her younger sister fairer than she? take her, I pray thee, instead of her.

3 ¶ And Sam'son said concerning them, Now shall I be more blameless than the Phi-lis'tines, though I do them a displeasure.

4 And Sam'son went and caught three hundred foxes, and took firebrands, and turned tail to tail, and put a firebrand in the midst between two tails.

5 And when he had set the brands on fire, he let *them* go into the standing corn of the Phi-lis'tines, and burnt up both the shocks, and also the standing corn, with the vineyards *and* olives.

6 ¶ Then the Phi-lis'tines said, Who hath done this? And they answered, Sam'son, the son in law of the Tim'nite, because he had taken his wife, and given her to his companion. And the Phi-lis'tines came up, and burnt her and her father with fire.

7 ¶ And Sam'son said unto them, Though ye have done this, yet will I be avenged of you, and after that I will cease.

8 And he smote them hip and thigh with a great slaughter: and he went down and dwelt in the top of the rock E'tam.

9 ¶ Then the Phi-lis'tines went up, and pitched in Ju'dah, and spread themselves in Le'hi.

10 And the men of Ju'dah said, Why are ye come up against us? And they answered, To bind Sam'son are we come up, to do to him as he hath done to us.

11 Then three thousand men of Ju'dah went to the top of the rock E'tam, and said to Sam'son, Knowest thou not that the Phi-lis'tines *are* rulers over us? what *is* this *that* thou hast done unto us? And he said unto them, As they did unto me, so have I done unto them.

12 And they said unto him, We are come down to bind thee, that we may deliver thee into the hand of the Phi-lis'tines. And Sam'son said unto them, Swear unto me, that ye will not fall upon me yourselves.

13 And they spake unto him, saying, No; but we will bind thee fast, and deliver thee into their hand: but surely we will not kill thee. And they bound him with two new cords, and brought him up from the rock.

14 ¶ *And* when he came unto Le'hi, the Phi-lis'tines shouted against him: and the Spirit of the LORD came mightily upon him, and the cords that *were* upon his arms became as flax that was burnt with fire, and his bands loosed from off his hands.

15 And he found a new jawbone of an ass, and put forth his hand, and took it, and slew a thousand men therewith.

16 And Sam'son said, With the jawbone of an ass, heaps upon heaps, with the jaw of an ass have I slain a thousand men.

17 And it came to pass, when he had made an end of speaking, that he cast away the jawbone out of his hand, and called that place Ra'-math–le'hi.

18 ¶ And he was sore athirst, and called on the LORD, and said, Thou hast given this great deliverance into the hand of thy servant: and now shall I die for thirst, and fall into the hand of the uncircumcised?

19 But God clave an hollow place that *was* in the jaw, and there came water thereout; and when he had drunk, his spirit came again, and he revived: wherefore he called the name thereof En–hak'ko-re, which *is* in Le'hi unto this day.

20 And he judged Is'ra-el in the days of the Phi-lis'tines twenty years.

16 THEN went Sam'son to Ga'za, and saw there an harlot, and went in unto her.

2 *And it was told* the Ga'zites, saying, Sam'son is come hither. And they compassed *him* in, and laid wait for him all night in the gate of the city, and were quiet all the night, saying, In the morning, when it is day, we shall kill him.

3 And Sam'son lay till midnight, and arose at midnight, and took the doors of the gate of the city, and the two posts, and went away with them, bar and all, and put *them* upon his shoulders, and carried them up to the top of an hill that *is* before He'bron.

4 ¶ And it came to pass afterward, that he loved a woman in the valley of So'rek, whose name *was* De-li'lah.

5 And the lords of the Phi-lis'tines came up unto her, and said unto her, Entice him, and see wherein his great strength *lieth*, and by what *means* we may prevail against him, that we may bind him to afflict him: and we will give thee every one of us eleven hundred *pieces* of silver.

6 ¶ And De-li'lah said to Sam'son, Tell me, I pray thee, wherein thy great strength *lieth*, and wherewith thou mightest be bound to afflict thee.

7 And Sam'son said unto her, If they bind me with seven green withs that were never dried, then shall I be weak, and be as another man.

8 Then the lords of the Phi-lis'tines brought up to her seven green withs which had not been dried, and she bound him with them.

9 Now *there were* men lying in wait, abiding with her in the chamber. And she said unto him, The Phi-lis'tines *be* upon thee, Sam'son. And he brake the withs, as a thread of tow is broken when it toucheth the fire. So his strength was not known.

10 And De-li'lah said unto Sam'son, Behold, thou hast mocked me, and told me lies: now tell me, I pray thee, wherewith thou mightest be bound.

11 And he said unto her, If they bind me fast

with new ropes that never were occupied, then
shall I be weak, and be as another man.
12 De-li'lah therefore took new ropes, and
bound him therewith, and said unto him, The
Phi-lis'tines *be* upon thee, Sam'son. And *there*
were liers in wait abiding in the chamber. And
he brake them from off his arms like a thread.
13 And De-li'lah said unto Sam'son, Hitherto
thou hast mocked me, and told me lies: tell me
wherewith thou mightest be bound. And he said
unto her, If thou weavest the seven locks of my
head with the web.
14 And she fastened *it* with the pin, and said
unto him, The Phi-lis'tines *be* upon thee, Sam'-
son. And he awaked out of his sleep, and went
away with the pin of the beam, and with the
web.
15 ¶ And she said unto him, How canst thou
say, I love thee, when thine heart *is* not with
me? thou hast mocked me these three times,
and hast not told me wherein thy great strength
lieth.
16 And it came to pass, when she pressed
him daily with her words, and urged him, so
that his soul was vexed unto death;
17 That he told her all his heart, and said
unto her, There hath not come a razor upon
mine head; for I *have been* a Naz'a-rite unto
God from my mother's womb: if I be shaven,
then my strength will go from me, and I shall
become weak, and be like any *other* man.
18 And when De-li'lah saw that he had told
her all his heart, she sent and called for the
lords of the Phi-lis'tines, saying, Come up this
once, for he hath shewed me all his heart. Then
the lords of the Phi-lis'tines came up unto her,
and brought money in their hand.
19 And she made him sleep upon her knees;
and she called for a man, and she caused him to
shave off the seven locks of his head; and she
began to afflict him, and his strength went from
him.
20 And she said, The Phi-lis'tines *be* upon
thee, Sam'son. And he awoke out of his sleep,
and said, I will go out as at other times before,
and shake myself. And he wist not that the
LORD was departed from him.
21 ¶ But the Phi-lis'tines took him, and put
out his eyes, and brought him down to Ga'za,
and bound him with fetters of brass; and he did
grind in the prison house.
22 Howbeit the hair of his head began to
grow again after he was shaven.
23 Then the lords of the Phi-lis'tines gathered
them together for to offer a great sacrifice unto
Da'gon their god, and to rejoice: for they said,
Our god hath delivered Sam'son our enemy into
our hand.
24 And when the people saw him, they
praised their god: for they said, Our god hath
delivered into our hands our enemy, and the destroyer of our country, which slew many of us.
25 And it came to pass, when their hearts
were merry, that they said, Call for Sam'son,
that he may make us sport. And they called for
Sam'son out of the prison house; and he made
them sport: and they set him between the pillars.
26 And Sam'son said unto the lad that held
him by the hand, Suffer me that I may feel the
pillars whereupon the house standeth, that I
may lean upon them.
27 Now the house was full of men and
women; and all the lords of the Phi-lis'tines
were there; and *there were* upon the roof about
three thousand men and women, that beheld
while Sam'son made sport.
28 And Sam'son called unto the LORD, and
said, O Lord GOD, remember me, I pray thee,
and strengthen me, I pray thee, only this once,
O God, that I may be at once avenged of the
Phi-lis'tines for my two eyes.
29 And Sam'son took hold of the two middle
pillars upon which the house stood, and on
which it was borne up, of the one with his right
hand, and of the other with his left.
30 And Sam'son said, Let me die with the
Phi-lis'tines. And he bowed himself with *all his*
might; and the house fell upon the lords, and
upon all the people that *were* therein. So the
dead which he slew at his death were more than
they which he slew in his life.
31 Then his brethren and all the house of his
father came down, and took him, and brought
him up, and buried him between Zo'rah and
Esh'ta-ol in the buryingplace of Ma-no'ah his father. And he judged Is'ra-el twenty years.

17 AND there was a man of mount E'phra-
im, whose name *was* Mi'cah.
2 And he said unto his mother, The eleven
hundred *shekels* of silver that were taken from
thee, about which thou cursedst, and spakest of
also in mine ears, behold, the silver *is* with me;
I took it. And his mother said, Blessed *be thou*
of the LORD, my son.
3 And when he had restored the eleven hundred *shekels* of silver to his mother, his mother
said, I had wholly dedicated the silver unto the
LORD from my hand for my son, to make a
graven image and a molten image: now therefore I will restore it unto thee.
4 Yet he restored the money unto his mother;
and his mother took two hundred *shekels* of silver, and gave them to the founder, who made
thereof a graven image and a molten image:
and they were in the house of Mi'cah.
5 And the man Mi'cah had an house of gods,
and made an ephod, and teraphim, and consecrated one of his sons, who became his priest.
6 In those days *there was* no king in Is'ra-el,
but every man did *that which was* right in his
own eyes.
7 ¶ And there was a young man out of Beth'-
-le-hem-ju'dah of the family of Ju'dah, who
was a Le'vite, and he sojourned there.
8 And the man departed out of the city from
Beth'-le-hem-ju'dah to sojourn where he could
find *a place:* and he came to mount E'phra-im
to the house of Mi'cah, as he journeyed.
9 And Mi'cah said unto him, Whence comest
thou? And he said unto him, I *am* a Le'vite of
Beth'-le-hem-ju'dah, and I go to sojourn where
I may find *a place*.
10 And Mi'cah said unto him, Dwell with me,
and be unto me a father and a priest, and I will
give thee ten *shekels* of silver by the year, and a
suit of apparel, and thy victuals. So the Le'vite
went in.
11 And the Le'vite was content to dwell with
the man; and the young man was unto him as
one of his sons.
12 And Mi'cah consecrated the Le'vite; and
the young man became his priest, and was in
the house of Mi'cah.
13 Then said Mi'cah, Now know I that the
LORD will do me good, seeing I have a Le'vite to
my priest.

18 IN those days *there was* no king in Is'ra-
el: and in those days the tribe of the
Dan'ites sought them an inheritance to dwell in;
for unto that day *all their* inheritance had not
fallen unto them among the tribes of Is'ra-el.

2 And the children of Dan sent of their family
five men from their coasts, men of valour, from
Zo'rah, and from Esh'ta-ol, to spy out the land,
and to search it; and they said unto them, Go,
search the land: who when they came to mount
E'phra-im to the house of Mi'cah, they lodged
there.
3 When they *were* by the house of Mi'cah,
they knew the voice of the young man the Le'-
vite: and they turned in thither, and said unto
him, Who brought thee hither? and what makest thou in this *place?* and what hast thou here?
4 And he said unto them, Thus and thus dealeth Mi'cah with me, and hath hired me, and I
am his priest.
5 And they said unto him, Ask counsel, we
pray thee, of God, that we may know whether
our way which we go shall be prosperous.
6 And the priest said unto them, Go in peace:
before the LORD *is* your way wherein ye go.
7 ¶ Then the five men departed, and came to
La'ish, and saw the people that *were* therein,
how they dwelt careless, after the manner of
the Zi-do'ni-ans, quiet and secure; and *there
was* no magistrate in the land, that might put
them to shame in *any* thing; and they *were* far
from the Zi-do'ni-ans, and had no business with
any man.
8 And they came unto their brethren to Zo'-
rah and Esh'ta-ol: and their brethren said unto
them, What *say* ye?
9 And they said, Arise, that we may go up
against them: for we have seen the land, and,
behold, it *is* very good: and *are* ye still? be not
slothful to go, *and* to enter to possess the land.
10 When ye go, ye shall come unto a people
secure, and to a large land: for God hath given it
into your hands; a place where *there is* no want
of any thing that *is* in the earth.
11 ¶ And there went from thence of the family of the Dan'ites, out of Zo'rah and out of Esh'-
ta-ol, six hundred men appointed with weapons
of war.
12 And they went up, and pitched in Kir'-
jath-je'a-rim, in Ju'dah: wherefore they called
that place Ma'ha-neh-dan unto this day: behold, *it is* behind Kir'jath-je'a-rim.
13 And they passed thence unto mount E'-
phra-im, and came unto the house of Mi'cah.
14 ¶ Then answered the five men that went
to spy out the country of La'ish, and said unto
their brethren, Do ye know that there is in these
houses an ephod, and teraphim, and a graven
image, and a molten image? now therefore consider what ye have to do.
15 And they turned thitherward, and came to
the house of the young man the Le'vite, *even*
unto the house of Mi'cah, and saluted him.
16 And the six hundred men appointed with
their weapons of war, which *were* of the children of Dan, stood by the entering of the gate.
17 And the five men that went to spy out the
land went up, *and* came in thither, *and* took the
graven image, and the ephod, and the teraphim,
and the molten image: and the priest stood in
the entering of the gate with the six hundred
men *that were* appointed with weapons of war.
18 And these went into Mi'cah's house, and
fetched the carved image, the ephod, and the
teraphim, and the molten image. Then said the
priest unto them, What do ye?
19 And they said unto him, Hold thy peace,
lay thine hand upon thy mouth, and go with us,
and be to us a father and a priest: *is it* better for
thee to be a priest unto the house of one man, or
that thou be a priest unto a tribe and a family in
Is'ra-el?
20 And the priest's heart was glad, and he
took the ephod, and the teraphim, and the
graven image, and went in the midst of the people.
21 So they turned and departed, and put the
little ones and the cattle and the carriage before
them.
22 ¶ *And* when they were a good way from
the house of Mi'cah, the men that *were* in the
houses near to Mi'cah's house were gathered
together, and overtook the children of Dan.
23 And they cried unto the children of Dan.
And they turned their faces, and said unto Mi'-
cah, What aileth thee, that thou comest with
such a company?
24 And he said, Ye have taken away my gods
which I made, and the priest, and ye are gone
away: and what have I more? and what *is* this
that ye say unto me, What aileth thee?
25 And the children of Dan said unto him,
Let not thy voice be heard among us, lest angry
fellows run upon thee, and thou lose thy life,
with the lives of thy household.
26 And the children of Dan went their way:
and when Mi'cah saw that they *were* too strong
for him, he turned and went back unto his
house.
27 And they took *the things* which Mi'cah
had made, and the priest which he had, and
came unto La'ish, unto a people *that were* at
quiet and secure: and they smote them with the
edge of the sword, and burnt the city with fire.
28 And *there was* no deliverer, because it
was far from Zi'don, and they had no business
with *any* man; and it was in the valley that *lieth*
by Beth-re'hob. And they built a city, and dwelt
therein.
29 And they called the name of the city Dan,
after the name of Dan their father, who was
born unto Is'ra-el: howbeit the name of the city
was La'ish at the first.
30 ¶ And the children of Dan set up the
graven image: and Jon'a-than, the son of Ger'-
shom, the son of Ma-nas'seh, he and his sons
were priests to the tribe of Dan until the day of
the captivity of the land.
31 And they set them up Mi'cah's graven
image, which he made, all the time that the
house of God was in Shi'loh.

19 AND it came to pass in those days,
when *there was* no king in Is'ra-el, that
there was a certain Le'vite sojourning on the
side of mount E'phra-im, who took to him a
concubine out of Beth'-le-hem-ju'dah.
2 And his concubine played the whore
against him, and went away from him unto her
father's house to Beth'-le-hem-ju'dah, and was
there four whole months.
3 And her husband arose, and went after her,
to speak friendly unto her, *and* to bring her
again, having her servant with him, and a couple of asses: and she brought him into her father's house: and when the father of the damsel
saw him, he rejoiced to meet him.
4 And his father in law, the damsel's father,
retained him; and he abode with him three
days: so they did eat and drink, and lodged
there.
5 ¶ And it came to pass on the fourth day,
when they arose early in the morning, that he
rose up to depart: and the damsel's father said
unto his son in law, Comfort thine heart with a
morsel of bread, and afterward go your way.
6 And they sat down, and did eat and drink
both of them together: for the damsel's father

had said unto the man, Be content, I pray thee, and tarry all night, and let thine heart be merry.

7 And when the man rose up to depart, his father in law urged him: therefore he lodged there again.

8 And he arose early in the morning on the fifth day to depart: and the damsel's father said, Comfort thine heart, I pray thee. And they tarried until afternoon, and they did eat both of them.

9 And when the man rose up to depart, he, and his concubine, and his servant, his father in law, the damsel's father, said unto him, Behold, now the day draweth toward evening, I pray you tarry all night: behold, the day groweth to an end, lodge here, that thine heart may be merry; and to morrow get you early on your way, that thou mayest go home.

10 But the man would not tarry that night, but he rose up and departed, and came over against Je'bus, which *is* Je-ru'sa-lem; and *there were* with him two asses saddled, his concubine also *was* with him.

11 *And* when they *were* by Je'bus, the day was far spent; and the servant said unto his master, Come, I pray thee, and let us turn in into this city of the Jeb'u-sites, and lodge in it.

12 And his master said unto him, We will not turn aside hither into the city of a stranger, that *is* not of the children of Is'ra-el; we will pass over to Gib'e-ah.

13 And he said unto his servant, Come, and let us draw near to one of these places to lodge all night, in Gib'e-ah, or in Ra'mah.

14 And they passed on and went their way; and the sun went down upon them *when they were* by Gib'e-ah, which *belongeth* to Ben'ja-min.

15 And they turned aside thither, to go in *and* to lodge in Gib'e-ah: and when he went in, he sat him down in a street of the city: for *there was* no man that took them into his house to lodging.

16 ¶ And, behold, there came an old man from his work out of the field at even, which *was* also of mount E'phra-im; and he sojourned in Gib'e-ah: but the men of the place *were* Ben'ja-mites.

17 And when he had lifted up his eyes, he saw a wayfaring man in the street of the city: and the old man said, Whither goest thou? and whence comest thou?

18 And he said unto him, We *are* passing from Beth'-le-hem-ju'dah toward the side of mount E'phra-im; from thence *am* I: and I went to Beth'-le-hem-ju'dah, but I *am now* going to the house of the LORD; and there *is* no man that receiveth me to house.

19 Yet there is both straw and provender for our asses; and there is bread and wine also for me, and for thy handmaid, and for the young man *which is* with thy servants: *there is* no want of any thing.

20 And the old man said, Peace *be* with thee; howsoever *let* all thy wants *lie* upon me; only lodge not in the street.

21 So he brought him into his house, and gave provender unto the asses: and they washed their feet, and did eat and drink.

22 ¶ *Now* as they were making their hearts merry, behold, the men of the city, certain sons of Be'li-al, beset the house round about, *and* beat at the door, and spake to the master of the house, the old man, saying, Bring forth the man that came into thine house, that we may know him.

23 And the man, the master of the house, went out unto them, and said unto them, Nay, my brethren, *nay*, I pray you, do not *so* wickedly; seeing that this man is come into mine house, do not this folly.

24 Behold, *here is* my daughter a maiden, and his concubine; them I will bring out now, and humble ye them, and do with them what seemeth good unto you: but unto this man do not so vile a thing.

25 But the men would not hearken to him: so the man took his concubine, and brought her forth unto them; and they knew her, and abused her all the night until the morning: and when the day began to spring, they let her go.

26 Then came the woman in the dawning of the day, and fell down at the door of the man's house where her lord *was*, till it was light.

27 And her lord rose up in the morning, and opened the doors of the house, and went out to go his way: and, behold, the woman his concubine was fallen down *at* the door of the house, and her hands *were* upon the threshold.

28 And he said unto her, Up, and let us be going. But none answered. Then the man took her *up* upon an ass, and the man rose up, and gat him unto his place.

29 ¶ And when he was come into his house, he took a knife, and laid hold on his concubine, and divided her, *together* with her bones, into twelve pieces, and sent her into all the coasts of Is'ra-el.

30 And it was so, that all that saw it said, There was no such deed done nor seen from the day that the children of Is'ra-el came up out of the land of E'gypt unto this day: consider of it, take advice, and speak *your minds*.

20 THEN all the children of Is'ra-el went out, and the congregation was gathered together as one man, from Dan even to Be'er-she'ba, with the land of Gil'e-ad, unto the LORD in Miz'peh.

2 And the chief of all the people, *even* of all the tribes of Is'ra-el, presented themselves in the assembly of the people of God, four hundred thousand footmen that drew sword.

3 (Now the children of Ben'ja-min heard that the children of Is'ra-el were gone up to Miz'peh.) Then said the children of Is'ra-el, Tell *us*, how was this wickedness?

4 And the Le'vite, the husband of the woman that was slain, answered and said, I came into Gib'e-ah that *belongeth* to Ben'ja-min, I and my concubine, to lodge.

5 And the men of Gib'e-ah rose against me, and beset the house round about upon me by night, *and* thought to have slain me: and my concubine have they forced, that she is dead.

6 And I took my concubine, and cut her in pieces, and sent her throughout all the country of the inheritance of Is'ra-el: for they have committed lewdness and folly in Is'ra-el.

7 Behold, ye *are* all children of Is'ra-el; give here your advice and counsel.

8 ¶ And all the people arose as one man, saying, We will not any *of us* go to his tent, neither will we any *of us* turn into his house.

9 But now this *shall be* the thing which we will do to Gib'e-ah; *we will go up* by lot against it;

10 And we will take ten men of an hundred throughout all the tribes of Is'ra-el, and an hundred of a thousand, and a thousand out of ten thousand, to fetch victual for the people, that they may do, when they come to Gib'e-ah of Ben'ja-min, according to all the folly that they have wrought in Is'ra-el.

11 So all the men of Is′ra-el were gathered against the city, knit together as one man.

12 ¶ And the tribes of Is′ra-el sent men through all the tribe of Ben′ja-min, saying, What wickedness *is* this that is done among you?

13 Now therefore, deliver *us* the men, the children of Be′li-al, which *are* in Gib′e-ah, that we may put them to death, and put away evil from Is′ra-el. But the children of Ben′ja-min would not hearken to the voice of their brethren the children of Is′ra-el:

14 But the children of Ben′ja-min gathered themselves together out of the cities unto Gib′e-ah, to go out to battle against the children of Is′ra-el.

15 And the children of Ben′ja-min were numbered at that time out of the cities twenty and six thousand men that drew sword, beside the inhabitants of Gib′e-ah, which were numbered seven hundred chosen men.

16 Among all this people *there were* seven hundred chosen men lefthanded; every one could sling stones at an hair *breadth*, and not miss.

17 And the men of Is′ra-el, beside Ben′ja-min, were numbered four hundred thousand men that drew sword: all these *were* men of war.

18 ¶ And the children of Is′ra-el arose, and went up to the house of God, and asked counsel of God, and said, Which of us shall go up first to the battle against the children of Ben′ja-min? And the LORD said, Ju′dah *shall go up* first.

19 And the children of Is′ra-el rose up in the morning, and encamped against Gib′e-ah.

20 And the men of Is′ra-el went out to battle against Ben′ja-min; and the men of Is′ra-el put themselves in array to fight against them at Gib′e-ah.

21 And the children of Ben′ja-min came forth out of Gib′e-ah, and destroyed down to the ground of the Is′ra-el-ites that day twenty and two thousand men.

22 And the people the men of Is′ra-el encouraged themselves, and set their battle again in array in the place where they put themselves in array the first day.

23 (And the children of Is′ra-el went up and wept before the LORD until even, and asked counsel of the LORD, saying, Shall I go up again to battle against the children of Ben′ja-min my brother? And the LORD said, Go up against him.)

24 And the children of Is′ra-el came near against the children of Ben′ja-min the second day.

25 And Ben′ja-min went forth against them out of Gib′e-ah the second day, and destroyed down to the ground of the children of Is′ra-el again eighteen thousand men; all these drew the sword.

26 ¶ Then all the children of Is′ra-el, and all the people, went up, and came unto the house of God, and wept, and sat there before the LORD, and fasted that day until even, and offered burnt offerings and peace offerings before the LORD.

27 And the children of Is′ra-el enquired of the LORD, (for the ark of the covenant of God *was* there in those days,

28 And Phin′e-has, the son of E-le-a′zar, the son of Aar′on, stood before it in those days,) saying, Shall I yet again go out to battle against the children of Ben′ja-min my brother, or shall I cease? And the LORD said, Go up; for to-morrow I will deliver them into thine hand.

29 And Is′ra-el set liers in wait round about Gib′e-ah.

30 And the children of Is′ra-el went up against the children of Ben′ja-min on the third day, and put themselves in array against Gib′e-ah, as at other times.

31 And the children of Ben′ja-min went out against the people, *and* were drawn away from the city; and they began to smite of the people, *and* kill, as at other times, in the highways, of which one goeth up to the house of God, and the other to Gib′e-ah in the field, about thirty men of Is′ra-el.

32 And the children of Ben′ja-min said, They *are* smitten down before us, as at the first. But the children of Is′ra-el said, Let us flee, and draw them from the city unto the highways.

33 And all the men of Is′ra-el rose up out of their place, and put themselves in array at Ba′al–ta′mar: and the liers in wait of Is′ra-el came forth out of their places, *even* out of the meadows of Gib′e-ah.

34 And there came against Gib′e-ah ten thousand chosen men out of all Is′ra-el, and the battle was sore: but they knew not that evil *was* near them.

35 And the LORD smote Ben′ja-min before Is′ra-el: and the children of Is′ra-el destroyed of the Ben′ja-mites that day twenty and five thousand and an hundred men: all these drew the sword.

36 So the children of Ben′ja-min saw that they were smitten: for the men of Is′ra-el gave place to the Ben′ja-mites, because they trusted unto the liers in wait which they had set beside Gib′e-ah.

37 And the liers in wait hasted, and rushed upon Gib′e-ah; and the liers in wait drew *themselves* along, and smote all the city with the edge of the sword.

38 Now there was an appointed sign between the men of Is′ra-el and the liers in wait, that they should make a great flame with smoke rise up out of the city.

39 And when the men of Is′ra-el retired in the battle, Ben′ja-min began to smite *and* kill of the men of Is′ra-el about thirty persons: for they said, Surely they are smitten down before us, as *in* the first battle.

40 But when the flame began to arise up out of the city with a pillar of smoke, the Ben′ja-mites looked behind them, and, behold, the flame of the city ascended up to heaven.

41 And when the men of Is′ra-el turned again, the men of Ben′ja-min were amazed: for they saw that evil was come upon them.

42 Therefore they turned *their backs* before the men of Is′ra-el unto the way of the wilderness; but the battle overtook them; and them which *came* out of the cities they destroyed in the midst of them.

43 *Thus* they inclosed the Ben′ja-mites round about, *and* chased them, *and* trode them down with ease over against Gib′e-ah toward the sunrising.

44 And there fell of Ben′ja-min eighteen thousand men; all these *were* men of valour.

45 And they turned and fled toward the wilderness unto the rock of Rim′mon: and they gleaned of them in the highways five thousand men; and pursued hard after them unto Gi′dom, and slew two thousand men of them.

46 So that all which fell that day of Ben′ja-min were twenty and five thousand men that drew the sword; all these *were* men of valour.

47 But six hundred men turned and fled to

the wilderness unto the rock Rim'mon, and abode in the rock Rim'mon four months.

48 And the men of Is'ra-el turned again upon the children of Ben'ja-min, and smote them with the edge of the sword, as well the men of *every* city, as the beast, and all that came to hand: also they set on fire all the cities that they came to.

21 NOW the men of Is'ra-el had sworn in Miz'peh, saying, There shall not any of us give his daughter unto Ben'ja-min to wife.

2 And the people came to the house of God, and abode there till even before God, and lifted up their voices, and wept sore;

3 And said, O LORD God of Is'ra-el, why is this come to pass in Is'ra-el, that there should be to day one tribe lacking in Is'ra-el?

4 And it came to pass on the morrow, that the people rose early, and built there an altar, and offered burnt offerings and peace offerings.

5 And the children of Is'ra-el said, Who *is there* among all the tribes of Is'ra-el that came not up with the congregation unto the LORD? For they had made a great oath concerning him that came not up to the LORD to Miz'peh, saying, He shall surely be put to death.

6 And the children of Is'ra-el repented them for Ben'ja-min their brother, and said, There is one tribe cut off from Is'ra-el this day.

7 How shall we do for wives for them that remain, seeing we have sworn by the LORD that we will not give them of our daughters to wives?

8 ¶ And they said, What one *is there* of the tribes of Is'ra-el that came not up to Miz'peh to the LORD? And, behold, there came none to the camp from Ja'besh–gil'e-ad to the assembly.

9 For the people were numbered, and, behold, *there were* none of the inhabitants of Ja'besh–gil'e-ad there.

10 And the congregation sent thither twelve thousand men of the valiantest, and commanded them, saying, Go and smite the inhabitants of Ja'besh–gil'e-ad with the edge of the sword, with the women and the children.

11 And this *is* the thing that ye shall do, Ye shall utterly destroy every male, and every woman that hath lain by man.

12 And they found among the inhabitants of Ja'besh–gil'e-ad four hundred young virgins, that had known no man by lying with any male: and they brought them unto the camp to Shi'loh, which *is* in the land of Ca'naan.

13 And the whole congregation sent *some* to speak to the children of Ben'ja-min that *were* in the rock Rim'mon, and to call peaceably unto them.

14 And Ben'ja-min came again at that time; and they gave them wives which they had saved alive of the women of Ja'besh–gil'e-ad: and yet so they sufficed them not.

15 And the people repented them for Ben'ja-min, because that the LORD had made a breach in the tribes of Is'ra-el.

16 ¶ Then the elders of the congregation said, How shall we do for wives for them that remain, seeing the women are destroyed out of Ben'ja-min?

17 And they said, *There must be* an inheritance for them that be escaped of Ben'ja-min, that a tribe be not destroyed out of Is'ra-el.

18 Howbeit we may not give them wives of our daughters: for the children of Is'ra-el have sworn, saying, Cursed *be* he that giveth a wife to Ben'ja-min.

19 Then they said, Behold, *there is* a feast of the LORD in Shi'loh yearly *in a place* which *is* on the north side of Beth'–el, on the east side of the highway that goeth up from Beth'–el to She'-chem, and on the south of Le'bo-nah.

20 Therefore they commanded the children of Ben'ja-min, saying, Go and lie in wait in the vineyards;

21 And see, and, behold, if the daughters of Shi'loh come out to dance in dances, then come ye out of the vineyards, and catch you every man his wife of the daughters of Shi'loh, and go to the land of Ben'ja-min.

22 And it shall be, when their fathers or their brethren come unto us to complain, that we will say unto them, Be favourable unto them for our sakes: because we reserved not to each man his wife in the war: for ye did not give unto them at this time, *that* ye should be guilty.

23 And the children of Ben'ja-min did so, and took *them* wives, according to their number, of them that danced, whom they caught: and they went and returned unto their inheritance, and repaired the cities, and dwelt in them.

24 And the children of Is'ra-el departed thence at that time, every man to his tribe and to his family, and they went out from thence every man to his inheritance.

25 In those days *there was* no king in Is'ra-el: every man did *that which was* right in his own eyes.

THE BOOK OF

RUTH

1 NOW it came to pass in the days when the judges ruled, that there was a famine in the land. And a certain man of Beth'–le-hem–ju'dah went to sojourn in the country of Mo'ab, he, and his wife, and his two sons.

2 And the name of the man *was* E-lim'e-lech, and the name of his wife Na-o'mi, and the name of his two sons Mah'lon and Chil'i-on, Eph'rath-ites of Beth'–le-hem–ju'dah. And they came into the country of Mo'ab, and continued there.

3 And E-lim'e-lech Na-o'mi's husband died; and she was left, and her two sons.

4 And they took them wives of the women of Mo'ab; the name of the one *was* Or'pah, and the name of the other Ruth: and they dwelled there about ten years.

5 And Mah'lon and Chil'i-on died also both of them; and the woman was left of her two sons and her husband.

6 ¶ Then she arose with her daughters in law, that she might return from the country of Mo'ab: for she had heard in the country of Mo'-ab how that the LORD had visited his people in giving them bread.

7 Wherefore she went forth out of the place where she was, and her two daughters in law with her; and they went on the way to return unto the land of Ju'dah.

8 And Na-o'mi said unto her two daughters

in law, Go, return each to her mother's house:
the LORD deal kindly with you, as ye have dealt
with the dead, and with me.
9 The LORD grant you that ye may find rest,
each *of you* in the house of her husband. Then
she kissed them; and they lifted up their voice,
and wept.
10 And they said unto her, Surely we will return with thee unto thy people.
11 And Na-o'mi said, Turn again, my daughters: why will ye go with me? *are* there yet *any*
more sons in my womb, that they may be your
husbands?
12 Turn again, my daughters, go *your way;*
for I am too old to have an husband. If I should
say, I have hope, *if* I should have an husband
also to night, and should also bear sons;
13 Would ye tarry for them till they were
grown? would ye stay for them from having
husbands? nay, my daughters; for it grieveth
me much for your sakes that the hand of the
LORD is gone out against me.
14 And they lifted up their voice, and wept
again: and Or'pah kissed her mother in law; but
Ruth clave unto her.
15 And she said, Behold, thy sister in law is
gone back unto her people, and unto her gods:
return thou after thy sister in law.
16 And Ruth said, Intreat me not to leave
thee, *or* to return from following after thee: for
whither thou goest, I will go; and where thou
lodgest, I will lodge: thy people *shall be* my people, and thy God my God:
17 Where thou diest, will I die, and there will
I be buried: the LORD do so to me, and more
also, *if ought* but death part thee and me.
18 When she saw that she was stedfastly
minded to go with her, then she left speaking
unto her.
19 ¶ So they two went until they came to
Beth'-le-hem. And it came to pass, when they
were come to Beth'-le-hem, that all the city was
moved about them, and they said, *Is* this Na-
o'mi?
20 And she said unto them, Call me not Na-
o'mi, call me Ma'ra: for the Almighty hath dealt
very bitterly with me.
21 I went out full, and the LORD hath brought
me home again empty: why *then* call ye me Na-
o'mi, seeing the LORD hath testified against me,
and the Almighty hath afflicted me?
22 So Na-o'mi returned, and Ruth the Mo'ab-
it-ess, her daughter in law, with her, which returned out of the country of Mo'ab: and they
came to Beth'-le-hem in the beginning of barley
harvest.

2 AND Na-o'mi had a kinsman of her husband's, a mighty man of wealth, of the
family of E-lim'e-lech; and his name *was* Bo'az.
2 And Ruth the Mo'ab-it-ess said unto Na-o'-
mi, Let me now go to the field, and glean ears of
corn after *him* in whose sight I shall find grace.
And she said unto her, Go, my daughter.
3 And she went, and came, and gleaned in
the field after the reapers: and her hap was to
light on a part of the field *belonging* unto Bo'az,
who *was* of the kindred of E-lim'e-lech.
4 ¶ And, behold, Bo'az came from Beth'-le-
hem, and said unto the reapers, The LORD *be*
with you. And they answered him, The LORD
bless thee.
5 Then said Bo'az unto his servant that was
set over the reapers, Whose damsel *is* this?
6 And the servant that was set over the reapers answered and said, It *is* the Mo'ab-it-ish
damsel that came back with Na-o'mi out of the
country of Mo'ab:
7 And she said, I pray you, let me glean and
gather after the reapers among the sheaves: so
she came, and hath continued even from the
morning until now, that she tarried a little in the
house.
8 Then said Bo'az unto Ruth, Hearest thou
not, my daughter? Go not to glean in another
field, neither go from hence, but abide here fast
by my maidens:
9 *Let* thine eyes *be* on the field that they do
reap, and go thou after them: have I not
charged the young men that they shall not
touch thee? and when thou art athirst, go unto
the vessels, and drink of *that* which the young
men have drawn.
10 Then she fell on her face, and bowed herself to the ground, and said unto him, Why have
I found grace in thine eyes, that thou shouldest
take knowledge of me, seeing I *am* a stranger?
11 And Bo'az answered and said unto her, It
hath fully been shewed me, all that thou hast
done unto thy mother in law since the death of
thine husband: and *how* thou hast left thy father and thy mother, and the land of thy nativity, and art come unto a people which thou
knewest not heretofore.
12 The LORD recompense thy work, and a full
reward be given thee of the LORD God of Is'ra-
el, under whose wings thou art come to trust.
13 Then she said, Let me find favour in thy
sight, my lord; for that thou hast comforted me,
and for that thou hast spoken friendly unto
thine handmaid, though I be not like unto one of
thine handmaidens.
14 And Bo'az said unto her, At mealtime
come thou hither, and eat of the bread, and dip
thy morsel in the vinegar. And she sat beside
the reapers: and he reached her parched *corn,*
and she did eat, and was sufficed, and left.
15 And when she was risen up to glean, Bo'-
az commanded his young men, saying, Let her
glean even among the sheaves, and reproach
her not:
16 And let fall also *some* of the handfuls of
purpose for her, and leave *them,* that she may
glean *them,* and rebuke her not.
17 So she gleaned in the field until even, and
beat out that she had gleaned: and it was about
an ephah of barley.
18 ¶ And she took *it* up, and went into the
city: and her mother in law saw what she had
gleaned: and she brought forth, and gave to her
that she had reserved after she was sufficed.
19 And her mother in law said unto her,
Where hast thou gleaned to day? and where
wroughtest thou? blessed be he that did take
knowledge of thee. And she shewed her mother
in law with whom she had wrought, and said,
The man's name with whom I wrought to day *is*
Bo'az.
20 And Na-o'mi said unto her daughter in
law, Blessed *be* he of the LORD, who hath not
left off his kindness to the living and to the
dead. And Na-o'mi said unto her, The man *is*
near of kin unto us, one of our next kinsmen.
21 And Ruth the Mo'ab-it-ess said, He said
unto me also, Thou shalt keep fast by my young
men, until they have ended all my harvest.
22 And Na-o'mi said unto Ruth her daughter
in law, *It is* good, my daughter, that thou go out
with his maidens, that they meet thee not in any
other field.
23 So she kept fast by the maidens of Bo'az
to glean unto the end of barley harvest and of

wheat harvest; and dwelt with her mother in law.

3 THEN Na-o′mi her mother in law said unto her, My daughter, shall I not seek rest for thee, that it may be well with thee?

2 And now *is* not Bo′az of our kindred, with whose maidens thou wast? Behold, he winnoweth barley to night in the threshingfloor.

3 Wash thyself therefore, and anoint thee, and put thy raiment upon thee, and get thee down to the floor: *but* make not thyself known unto the man, until he shall have done eating and drinking.

4 And it shall be, when he lieth down, that thou shalt mark the place where he shall lie, and thou shalt go in, and uncover his feet, and lay thee down; and he will tell thee what thou shalt do.

5 And she said unto her, All that thou sayest unto me I will do.

6 ¶ And she went down unto the floor, and did according to all that her mother in law bade her.

7 And when Bo′az had eaten and drunk, and his heart was merry, he went to lie down at the end of the heap of corn: and she came softly, and uncovered his feet, and laid her down.

8 ¶ And it came to pass at midnight, that the man was afraid, and turned himself: and, behold, a woman lay at his feet.

9 And he said, Who *art* thou? And she answered, I *am* Ruth thine handmaid: spread therefore thy skirt over thine handmaid; for thou *art* a near kinsman.

10 And he said, Blessed *be* thou of the LORD, my daughter: *for* thou hast shewed more kindness in the latter end than at the beginning, inasmuch as thou followedst not young men, whether poor or rich.

11 And now, my daughter, fear not; I will do to thee all that thou requirest: for all the city of my people doth know that thou *art* a virtuous woman.

12 And now it is true that I *am thy* near kinsman: howbeit there is a kinsman nearer than I.

13 Tarry this night, and it shall be in the morning, *that* if he will perform unto thee the part of a kinsman, well; let him do the kinsman's part: but if he will not do the part of a kinsman to thee, then will I do the part of a kinsman to thee, *as* the LORD liveth: lie down until the morning.

14 ¶ And she lay at his feet until the morning: and she rose up before one could know another. And he said, Let it not be known that a woman came into the floor.

15 Also he said, Bring the veil that *thou hast* upon thee, and hold it. And when she held it, he measured six *measures* of barley, and laid *it* on her: and she went into the city.

16 And when she came to her mother in law, she said, Who *art* thou, my daughter? And she told her all that the man had done to her.

17 And she said, These six *measures* of barley gave he me; for he said to me, Go not empty unto thy mother in law.

18 Then said she, Sit still, my daughter, until thou know how the matter will fall: for the man will not be in rest, until he have finished the thing this day.

4 THEN went Bo′az up to the gate, and sat him down there: and, behold, the kinsman of whom Bo′az spake came by; unto whom he said, Ho, such a one! turn aside, sit down here. And he turned aside, and sat down.

2 And he took ten men of the elders of the city, and said, Sit ye down here. And they sat down.

3 And he said unto the kinsman, Na-o′mi, that is come again out of the country of Mo′ab, selleth a parcel of land, which *was* our brother E-lim′e-lech's:

4 And I thought to advertise thee, saying, Buy *it* before the inhabitants, and before the elders of my people. If thou wilt redeem *it*, redeem *it*: but if thou wilt not redeem *it*, *then* tell me, that I may know: for *there is* none to redeem *it* beside thee; and I *am* after thee. And he said, I will redeem *it*.

5 Then said Bo′az, What day thou buyest the field of the hand of Na-o′mi, thou must buy *it* also of Ruth the Mo′ab-it-ess, the wife of the dead, to raise up the name of the dead upon his inheritance.

6 ¶ And the kinsman said, I cannot redeem *it* for myself, lest I mar mine own inheritance: redeem thou my right to thyself; for I cannot redeem *it*.

7 Now this *was the manner* in former time in Is′ra-el concerning redeeming and concerning changing, for to confirm all things; a man plucked off his shoe, and gave *it* to his neighbour: and this *was* a testimony in Is′ra-el.

8 Therefore the kinsman said unto Bo′az, Buy *it* for thee. So he drew off his shoe.

9 ¶ And Bo′az said unto the elders, and *unto* all the people, Ye *are* witnesses this day, that I have bought all that *was* E-lim′e-lech's, and all that *was* Chil′i-on's and Mah′lon's, of the hand of Na-o′mi.

10 Moreover Ruth the Mo′ab-it-ess, the wife of Mah′lon, have I purchased to be my wife, to raise up the name of the dead upon his inheritance, that the name of the dead be not cut off from among his brethren, and from the gate of his place: ye *are* witnesses this day.

11 And all the people that *were* in the gate, and the elders, said, *We are* witnesses. The LORD make the woman that is come into thine house like Ra′chel and like Le′ah, which two did build the house of Is′ra-el: and do thou worthily in Eph′ra-tah, and be famous in Beth′-le-hem:

12 And let thy house be like the house of Pha′rez, whom Ta′mar bare unto Ju′dah, of the seed which the LORD shall give thee of this young woman.

13 ¶ So Bo′az took Ruth, and she was his wife: and when he went in unto her, the LORD gave her conception, and she bare a son.

14 And the women said unto Na-o′mi, Blessed *be* the LORD, which hath not left thee this day without a kinsman, that his name may be famous in Is′ra-el.

15 And he shall be unto thee a restorer of *thy* life, and a nourisher of thine old age: for thy daughter in law, which loveth thee, which is better to thee than seven sons, hath born him.

16 And Na-o′mi took the child, and laid it in her bosom, and became nurse unto it.

17 And the women her neighbours gave it a name, saying, There is a son born to Na-o′mi; and they called his name O′bed: he *is* the father of Jes′se, the father of Da′vid.

18 ¶ Now these *are* the generations of Pha′rez: Pha′rez begat Hez′ron,

19 And Hez′ron begat Ram, and Ram begat Am-min′a-dab,

20 And Am-min′a-dab begat Nah′shon, and Nah′shon begat Sal′mon,

21 And Sal′mon begat Bo′az, and Bo′az begat O′bed,

22 And O′bed begat Jes′se, and Jes′se begat Da′vid.

THE FIRST BOOK OF

SAMUEL

1

1 NOW there was a certain man of Ra-math-a'im-zo'phim, of mount E'phra-im, and his name *was* El'ka-nah, the son of Jer'o-ham, the son of E-li'hu, the son of To'hu, the son of Zuph, an Eph'rath-ite:

2 And he had two wives; the name of the one *was* Han'nah, and the name of the other Pe-nin'nah: and Pe-nin'nah had children, but Han'nah had no children.

3 And this man went up out of his city yearly to worship and to sacrifice unto the LORD of hosts in Shi'loh: And the two sons of E'li, Hoph'ni and Phin'e-has, the priests of the LORD, *were* there.

4 ¶ And when the time was that El'ka-nah offered, he gave to Pe-nin'nah his wife, and to all her sons and her daughters, portions:

5 But unto Han'nah he gave a worthy portion; for he loved Han'nah: but the LORD had shut up her womb.

6 And her adversary also provoked her sore, for to make her fret, because the LORD had shut up her womb.

7 And *as* he did so year by year, when she went up to the house of the LORD, so she provoked her; therefore she wept, and did not eat.

8 Then said El'ka-nah her husband to her, Han'nah, why weepest thou? and why eatest thou not? and why is thy heart grieved? *am* not I better to thee than ten sons?

9 ¶ So Han'nah rose up after they had eaten in Shi'loh, and after they had drunk. Now E'li the priest sat upon a seat by a post of the temple of the LORD.

10 And she *was* in bitterness of soul, and prayed unto the LORD, and wept sore.

11 And she vowed a vow, and said, O LORD of hosts, if thou wilt indeed look on the affliction of thine handmaid, and remember me, and not forget thine handmaid, but wilt give unto thine handmaid a man child, then I will give him unto the LORD all the days of his life, and there shall no razor come upon his head.

12 And it came to pass, as she continued praying before the LORD, that E'li marked her mouth.

13 Now Han'nah, she spake in her heart; only her lips moved, but her voice was not heard: therefore E'li thought she had been drunken.

14 And E'li said unto her, How long wilt thou be drunken? put away thy wine from thee.

15 And Han'nah answered and said, No, my lord, I *am* a woman of a sorrowful spirit: I have drunk neither wine nor strong drink, but have poured out my soul before the LORD.

16 Count not thine handmaid for a daughter of Be'li-al: for out of the abundance of my complaint and grief have I spoken hitherto.

17 Then E'li answered and said, Go in peace: and the God of Is'ra-el grant *thee* thy petition that thou hast asked of him.

18 And she said, Let thine handmaid find grace in thy sight. So the woman went her way, and did eat, and her countenance was no more *sad*.

19 ¶ And they rose up in the morning early, and worshipped before the LORD, and returned, and came to their house to Ra'mah: and El'ka-nah knew Han'nah his wife; and the LORD remembered her.

20 Wherefore it came to pass, when the time was come about after Han'nah had conceived, that she bare a son, and called his name Sam'u-el, *saying*, Because I have asked him of the LORD.

21 And the man El'ka-nah, and all his house, went up to offer unto the LORD the yearly sacrifice, and his vow.

22 But Han'nah went not up; for she said unto her husband, *I will not go up* until the child be weaned, and *then* I will bring him, that he may appear before the LORD, and there abide for ever.

23 And El'ka-nah her husband said unto her, Do what seemeth thee good; tarry until thou have weaned him; only the LORD establish his word. So the woman abode, and gave her son suck until she weaned him.

24 ¶ And when she had weaned him, she took him up with her, with three bullocks, and one ephah of flour, and a bottle of wine, and brought him unto the house of the LORD in Shi'loh: and the child *was* young.

25 And they slew a bullock, and brought the child to E'li.

26 And she said, Oh my lord, *as* thy soul liveth, my lord, I *am* the woman that stood by thee here, praying unto the LORD.

27 For this child I prayed; and the LORD hath given me my petition which I asked of him:

28 Therefore also I have lent him to the LORD; as long as he liveth he shall be lent to the LORD. And he worshipped the LORD there.

2

2 AND Han'nah prayed, and said, My heart rejoiceth in the LORD, mine horn is exalted in the LORD: my mouth is enlarged over mine enemies; because I rejoice in thy salvation.

2 *There is* none holy as the LORD: for *there is* none beside thee: neither *is there* any rock like our God.

3 Talk no more so exceeding proudly; let *not* arrogancy come out of your mouth: for the LORD *is* a God of knowledge, and by him actions are weighed.

4 The bows of the mighty men *are* broken, and they that stumbled are girded with strength.

5 *They that were* full have hired out themselves for bread; and *they that were* hungry ceased: so that the barren hath born seven; and she that hath many children is waxed feeble.

6 The LORD killeth, and maketh alive: he bringeth down to the grave, and bringeth up.

7 The LORD maketh poor, and maketh rich: he bringeth low, and lifteth up.

8 He raiseth up the poor out of the dust, *and* lifteth up the beggar from the dunghill, to set *them* among princes, and to make them inherit the throne of glory: for the pillars of the earth *are* the LORD's, and he hath set the world upon them.

9 He will keep the feet of his saints, and the wicked shall be silent in darkness; for by strength shall no man prevail.

10 The adversaries of the LORD shall be broken to pieces; out of heaven shall he thunder upon them: the LORD shall judge the ends of the earth; and he shall give strength unto his king, and exalt the horn of his anointed.

11 And El'ka-nah went to Ra'mah to his house. And the child did minister unto the LORD before E'li the priest.

12 ¶ Now the sons of E'li *were* sons of Be'li-al; they knew not the LORD.

13 And the priest's custom with the people *was, that,* when any man offered sacrifice, the priest's servant came, while the flesh was in seething, with a fleshhook of three teeth in his hand;

14 And he struck *it* into the pan, or kettle, or caldron, or pot; all that the fleshhook brought up the priest took for himself. So they did in Shi'loh unto all the Is'ra-el-ites that came thither.

15 Also before they burnt the fat, the priest's servant came, and said to the man that sacrificed, Give flesh to roast for the priest; for he will not have sodden flesh of thee, but raw.

16 And *if* any man said unto him, Let them not fail to burn the fat presently, and *then* take *as much* as thy soul desireth; then he would answer him, *Nay;* but thou shalt give *it me* now: and if not, I will take *it* by force.

17 Wherefore the sin of the young men was very great before the LORD: for men abhorred the offering of the LORD.

18 ¶ But Sam'u-el ministered before the LORD, *being* a child, girded with a linen ephod.

19 Moreover his mother made him a little coat, and brought *it* to him from year to year, when she came up with her husband to offer the yearly sacrifice.

20 ¶ And E'li blessed El'ka-nah and his wife, and said, The LORD give thee seed of this woman for the loan which is lent to the LORD. And they went unto their own home.

21 And the LORD visited Han'nah, so that she conceived, and bare three sons and two daughters. And the child Sam'u-el grew before the LORD.

22 ¶ Now E'li was very old, and heard all that his sons did unto all Is'ra-el; and how they lay with the women that assembled *at* the door of the tabernacle of the congregation.

23 And he said unto them, Why do ye such things? for I hear of your evil dealings by all this people.

24 Nay, my sons; for *it is* no good report that I hear: ye make the LORD's people to transgress.

25 If one man sin against another, the judge shall judge him: but if a man sin against the LORD, who shall intreat for him? Notwithstanding they hearkened not unto the voice of their father, because the LORD would slay them.

26 And the child Sam'u-el grew on, and was in favour both with the LORD, and also with men.

27 ¶ And there came a man of God unto E'li, and said unto him, Thus saith the LORD, Did I plainly appear unto the house of thy father, when they were in E'gypt in Pha'raoh's house?

28 And did I choose him out of all the tribes of Is'ra-el *to be* my priest, to offer upon mine altar, to burn incense, to wear an ephod before me? and did I give unto the house of thy father all the offerings made by fire of the children of Is'ra-el?

29 Wherefore kick ye at my sacrifice and at mine offering, which I have commanded *in my* habitation; and honourest thy sons above me, to make yourselves fat with the chiefest of all the offerings of Is'ra-el my people?

30 Wherefore the LORD God of Is'ra-el saith, I said indeed *that* thy house, and the house of thy father, should walk before me for ever: but now the LORD saith, Be it far from me; for them that honour me I will honour, and they that despise me shall be lightly esteemed.

31 Behold, the days come, that I will cut off thine arm, and the arm of thy father's house, that there shall not be an old man in thine house.

32 And thou shalt see an enemy *in my* habitation, in all *the wealth* which God shall give Is'ra-el: and there shall not be an old man in thine house for ever.

33 And the man of thine, *whom* I shall not cut off from mine altar, *shall be* to consume thine eyes, and to grieve thine heart: and all the increase of thine house shall die in the flower of their age.

34 And this *shall be* a sign unto thee, that shall come upon thy sons, on Hoph'ni and Phin'-e-has; in one day they shall die both of them.

35 And I will raise me up a faithful priest, *that* shall do according to *that* which *is* in mine heart and in my mind: and I will build him a sure house; and he shall walk before mine anointed for ever.

36 And it shall come to pass, *that* every one that is left in thine house shall come *and* crouch to him for a piece of silver and a morsel of bread, and shall say, Put me, I pray thee, into one of the priests' offices, that I may eat a piece of bread.

3 AND the child Sam'u-el ministered unto the LORD before E'li. And the word of the LORD was precious in those days; *there was* no open vision.

2 And it came to pass at that time, when E'li *was* laid down in his place, and his eyes began to wax dim, *that* he could not see;

3 And ere the lamp of God went out in the temple of the LORD, where the ark of God *was,* and Sam'u-el was laid down *to sleep;*

4 That the LORD called Sam'u-el: and he answered, Here *am* I.

5 And he ran unto E'li, and said, Here *am* I; for thou calledst me. And he said, I called not; lie down again. And he went and lay down.

6 And the LORD called yet again, Sam'u-el. And Sam'u-el arose and went to E'li, and said, Here *am* I; for thou didst call me. And he answered, I called not, my son; lie down again.

7 Now Sam'u-el did not yet know the LORD, neither was the word of the LORD yet revealed unto him.

8 And the LORD called Sam'u-el again the third time. And he arose and went to E'li, and said, Here *am* I; for thou didst call me. And E'li perceived that the LORD had called the child.

9 Therefore E'li said unto Sam'u-el, Go, lie down: and it shall be, if he call thee, that thou shalt say, Speak, LORD; for thy servant heareth. So Sam'u-el went and lay down in his place.

10 And the LORD came, and stood, and called as at other times, Sam'u-el, Sam'u-el. Then Sam'u-el answered, Speak; for thy servant heareth.

11 ¶ And the LORD said to Sam'u-el, Behold, I will do a thing in Is'ra-el, at which both the ears of every one that heareth it shall tingle.

12 In that day I will perform against E'li all *things* which I have spoken concerning his house: when I begin, I will also make an end.

13 For I have told him that I will judge his house for ever for the iniquity which he knoweth; because his sons made themselves vile, and he restrained them not.

14 And therefore I have sworn unto the house of E'li, that the iniquity of E'li's house shall not be purged with sacrifice nor offering for ever.

15 ¶ And Sam'u-el lay until the morning, and

opened the doors of the house of the LORD. And Sam'u-el feared to shew E'li the vision.

16 Then E'li called Sam'u-el, and said, Sam'u-el, my son. And he answered, Here *am* I.

17 And he said, What *is* the thing that *the* LORD hath said unto thee? I pray thee hide *it* not from me: God do so to thee, and more also, if thou hide *any* thing from me of all the things that he said unto thee.

18 And Sam'u-el told him every whit, and hid nothing from him. And he said, It *is* the LORD: let him do what seemeth him good.

19 ¶ And Sam'u-el grew, and the LORD was with him, and did let none of his words fall to the ground.

20 And all Is'ra-el from Dan even to Be'er-she'ba knew that Sam'u-el *was* established *to be* a prophet of the LORD.

21 And the LORD appeared again in Shi'loh: for the LORD revealed himself to Sam'u-el in Shi'loh by the word of the LORD.

4 AND the word of Sam'u-el came to all Is'ra-el. Now Is'ra-el went out against the Phi-lis'tines to battle, and pitched beside Eb'en-e'zer: and the Phi-lis'tines pitched in A'phek.

2 And the Phi-lis'tines put themselves in array against Is'ra-el: and when they joined battle, Is'ra-el was smitten before the Phi-lis'tines: and they slew of the army in the field about four thousand men.

3 ¶ And when the people were come into the camp, the elders of Is'ra-el said, Wherefore hath the LORD smitten us to day before the Phi-lis'tines? Let us fetch the ark of the covenant of the LORD out of Shi'loh unto us, that, when it cometh among us, it may save us out of the hand of our enemies.

4 So the people sent to Shi'loh, that they might bring from thence the ark of the covenant of the LORD of hosts, which dwelleth *between* the cherubims: and the two sons of E'li, Hoph'ni and Phin'e-has, *were* there with the ark of the covenant of God.

5 And when the ark of the covenant of the LORD came into the camp, all Is'ra-el shouted with a great shout, so that the earth rang again.

6 And when the Phi-lis'tines heard the noise of the shout, they said, What *meaneth* the noise of this great shout in the camp of the He'brews? And they understood that the ark of the LORD was come into the camp.

7 And the Phi-lis'tines were afraid, for they said, God is come into the camp. And they said, Woe unto us! for there hath not been such a thing heretofore.

8 Woe unto us! who shall deliver us out of the hand of these mighty Gods? these *are* the Gods that smote the E-gyp'tians with all the plagues in the wilderness.

9 Be strong, and quit yourselves like men, O ye Phi-lis'tines, that ye be not servants unto the He'brews, as they have been to you: quit yourselves like men, and fight.

10 ¶ And the Phi-lis'tines fought, and Is'ra-el was smitten, and they fled every man into his tent: and there was a very great slaughter; for there fell of Is'ra-el thirty thousand footmen.

11 And the ark of God was taken; and the two sons of E'li, Hoph'ni and Phin'e-has, were slain.

12 ¶ And there ran a man of Ben'ja-min out of the army, and came to Shi'loh the same day with his clothes rent, and with earth upon his head.

13 And when he came, lo, E'li sat upon a seat by the wayside watching: for his heart trembled for the ark of God. And when the man came into the city, and told *it*, all the city cried out.

14 And when E'li heard the noise of the crying, he said, What *meaneth* the noise of this tumult? And the man came in hastily, and told E'li.

15 Now E'li was ninety and eight years old; and his eyes were dim, that he could not see.

16 And the man said unto E'li, I *am* he that came out of the army, and I fled to day out of the army. And he said, What is there done, my son?

17 And the messenger answered and said, Is'ra-el is fled before the Phi-lis'tines, and there hath been also a great slaughter among the people, and thy two sons also, Hoph'ni and Phin'e-has, are dead, and the ark of God is taken.

18 And it came to pass, when he made mention of the ark of God, that he fell from off the seat backward by the side of the gate, and his neck brake, and he died: for he was an old man, and heavy. And he had judged Is'ra-el forty years.

19 ¶ And his daughter in law, Phin'e-has' wife, was with child, *near* to be delivered: and when she heard the tidings that the ark of God was taken, and that her father in law and her husband were dead, she bowed herself and travailed; for her pains came upon her.

20 And about the time of her death the women that stood by her said unto her, Fear not; for thou hast born a son. But she answered not, neither did she regard *it*.

21 And she named the child I'-cha-bod, saying, The glory is departed from Is'ra-el: because the ark of God was taken, and because of her father in law and her husband.

22 And she said, The glory is departed from Is'ra-el: for the ark of God is taken.

5 AND the Phi-lis'tines took the ark of God, and brought it from Eb'en-e'zer unto Ash'dod.

2 When the Phi-lis'tines took the ark of God, they brought it into the house of Da'gon, and set it by Da'gon.

3 ¶ And when they of Ash'dod arose early on the morrow, behold, Da'gon *was* fallen upon his face to the earth before the ark of the LORD. And they took Da'gon, and set him in his place again.

4 And when they arose early on the morrow morning, behold, Da'gon *was* fallen upon his face to the ground before the ark of the LORD; and the head of Da'gon and both the palms of his hands *were* cut off upon the threshold; only *the stump of* Da'gon was left to him.

5 Therefore neither the priests of Da'gon, nor any that come into Da'gon's house, tread on the threshold of Da'gon in Ash'dod unto this day.

6 But the hand of the LORD was heavy upon them of Ash'dod, and he destroyed them, and smote them with emerods, *even* Ash'dod and the coasts thereof.

7 And when the men of Ash'dod saw that *it was* so, they said, The ark of the God of Is'ra-el shall not abide with us: for his hand is sore upon us, and upon Da'gon our god.

8 They sent therefore and gathered all the lords of the Phi-lis'tines unto them, and said, What shall we do with the ark of the God of Is'ra-el? And they answered, Let the ark of the God of Is'ra-el be carried about unto Gath. And they carried the ark of the God of Is'ra-el about *thither*.

9 And it was so, that, after they had carried it about, the hand of the LORD was against the

city with a very great destruction: and he smote
the men of the city, both small and great, and
they had emerods in their secret parts.
10 ¶ Therefore they sent the ark of God to
Ek'ron. And it came to pass, as the ark of God
came to Ek'ron, that the Ek'ron-ites cried out,
saying, They have brought about the ark of the
God of Is'ra-el to us, to slay us and our people.
11 So they sent and gathered together all the
lords of the Phi-lis'tines, and said, Send away
the ark of the God of Is'ra-el, and let it go again
to his own place, that it slay us not, and our
people: for there was a deadly destruction
throughout all the city; the hand of God was
very heavy there.
12 And the men that died not were smitten
with the emerods: and the cry of the city went
up to heaven.

6 AND the ark of the LORD was in the country of the Phi-lis'tines seven months.
2 And the Phi-lis'tines called for the priests
and the diviners, saying, What shall we do to
the ark of the LORD? tell us wherewith we shall
send it to his place.
3 And they said, If ye send away the ark of
the God of Is'ra-el, send it not empty; but in any
wise return him a trespass offering: then ye
shall be healed, and it shall be known to you
why his hand is not removed from you.
4 Then said they, What *shall be* the trespass
offering which we shall return to him? They answered, Five golden emerods, and five golden
mice, *according to* the number of the lords of
the Phi-lis'tines: for one plague *was* on you all,
and on your lords.
5 Wherefore ye shall make images of your
emerods, and images of your mice that mar the
land; and ye shall give glory unto the God of
Is'ra-el: peradventure he will lighten his hand
from off you, and from off your gods, and from
off your land.
6 Wherefore then do ye harden your hearts,
as the E-gyp'tians and Pha'raoh hardened their
hearts? when he had wrought wonderfully
among them, did they not let the people go, and
they departed?
7 Now therefore make a new cart, and take
two milch kine, on which there hath come no
yoke, and tie the kine to the cart, and bring
their calves home from them:
8 And take the ark of the LORD, and lay it
upon the cart; and put the jewels of gold, which
ye return him *for* a trespass offering, in a coffer
by the side thereof; and send it away, that it
may go.
9 And see, if it goeth up by the way of his
own coast to Beth-she'mesh, *then* he hath done
us this great evil: but if not, then we shall know
that *it is* not his hand *that* smote us; it *was* a
chance *that* happened to us.
10 ¶ And the men did so; and took two milch
kine, and tied them to the cart, and shut up
their calves at home:
11 And they laid the ark of the LORD upon
the cart, and the coffer with the mice of gold
and the images of their emerods.
12 And the kine took the straight way to the
way of Beth-she'mesh, *and* went along the
highway, lowing as they went, and turned not
aside *to* the right hand or *to* the left; and the
lords of the Phi-lis'tines went after them unto
the border of Beth-she'mesh.
13 And *they of* Beth-she'mesh *were* reaping
their wheat harvest in the valley: and they lifted
up their eyes, and saw the ark, and rejoiced to
see *it*.
14 And the cart came into the field of Josh'u-
a, a Beth-she'mite, and stood there, where *there*
was a great stone: and they clave the wood of
the cart, and offered the kine a burnt offering
unto the LORD.
15 And the Le'vites took down the ark of the
LORD, and the coffer that *was* with it, wherein
the jewels of gold *were*, and put *them* on the
great stone: and the men of Beth-she'mesh offered burnt offerings and sacrificed sacrifices
the same day unto the LORD.
16 And when the five lords of the Phi-lis'tines
had seen *it*, they returned to Ek'ron the same
day.
17 And these *are* the golden emerods which
the Phi-lis'tines returned *for* a trespass offering
unto the LORD; for Ash'dod one, for Ga'za one,
for As'ke-lon one, for Gath one, for Ek'ron one;
18 And the golden mice, *according to* the
number of all the cities of the Phi-lis'tines *be-*
longing to the five lords, *both* of fenced cities,
and of country villages, even unto the great
stone of A'bel, whereon they set down the ark
of the LORD: *which stone remaineth* unto this
day in the field of Josh'u-a, the Beth-she'mite.
19 ¶ And he smote the men of Beth-she'-
mesh, because they had looked into the ark of
the LORD, even he smote of the people fifty
thousand and threescore and ten men: and the
people lamented, because the LORD had smitten
many of the people with a great slaughter.
20 And the men of Beth-she'mesh said, Who
is able to stand before this holy LORD God? and
to whom shall he go up from us?
21 ¶ And they sent messengers to the inhabitants of Kir'jath-je'a-rim, saying, The Phi-lis'-
tines have brought again the ark of the LORD;
come ye down, *and* fetch it up to you.

7 AND the men of Kir'jath-je'a-rim came,
and fetched up the ark of the LORD, and
brought it into the house of A-bin'a-dab in the
hill, and sanctified E-le-a'zar his son to keep the
ark of the LORD.
2 And it came to pass, while the ark abode in
Kir'jath-je'a-rim, that the time was long; for it
was twenty years: and all the house of Is'ra-el
lamented after the LORD.
3 ¶ And Sam'u-el spake unto all the house of
Is'ra-el, saying, If ye do return unto the LORD
with all your hearts, *then* put away the strange
gods and Ash'ta-roth from among you, and prepare your hearts unto the LORD, and serve him
only: and he will deliver you out of the hand of
the Phi-lis'tines.
4 Then the children of Is'ra-el did put away
Ba'al-im and Ash'ta-roth, and served the LORD
only.
5 And Sam'u-el said, Gather all Is'ra-el to
Miz'peh, and I will pray for you unto the LORD.
6 And they gathered together to Miz'peh,
and drew water, and poured *it* out before the
LORD, and fasted on that day, and said there,
We have sinned against the LORD. And Sam'u-el
judged the children of Is'ra-el in Miz'peh.
7 And when the Phi-lis'tines heard that the
children of Is'ra-el were gathered together to
Miz'peh, the lords of the Phi-lis'tines went up
against Is'ra-el. And when the children of Is'ra-
el heard *it*, they were afraid of the Phi-lis'tines.
8 And the children of Is'ra-el said to Sam'u-
el, Cease not to cry unto the LORD our God for
us, that he will save us out of the hand of the
Phi-lis'tines.
9 ¶ And Sam'u-el took a sucking lamb, and
offered *it for* a burnt offering wholly unto the

LORD: and Sam'u-el cried unto the LORD for Is'-
ra-el; and the LORD heard him.
10 And as Sam'u-el was offering up the burnt
offering, the Phi-lis'tines drew near to battle
against Is'ra-el: but the LORD thundered with a
great thunder on that day upon the Phi-lis'tines,
and discomfited them; and they were smitten
before Is'ra-el.
11 And the men of Is'ra-el went out of Miz'-
peh, and pursued the Phi-lis'tines, and smote
them, until *they came* under Beth'-car.
12 Then Sam'u-el took a stone, and set *it* between Miz'peh and Shen, and called the name
of it Eb'en-e'zer, saying, Hitherto hath the LORD
helped us.
13 ¶ So the Phi-lis'tines were subdued, and
they came no more into the coast of Is'ra-el:
and the hand of the LORD was against the Phi-
lis'tines all the days of Sam'u-el.
14 And the cities which the Phi-lis'tines had
taken from Is'ra-el were restored to Is'ra-el,
from Ek'ron even unto Gath; and the coasts
thereof did Is'ra-el deliver out of the hands of
the Phi-lis'tines. And there was peace between
Is'ra-el and the Am'or-ites.
15 And Sam'u-el judged Is'ra-el all the days
of his life.
16 And he went from year to year in circuit
to Beth'-el, and Gil'gal, and Miz'peh, and
judged Is'ra-el in all those places.
17 And his return *was* to Ra'mah; for there
was his house; and there he judged Is'ra-el; and
there he built an altar unto the LORD.

8 AND it came to pass, when Sam'u-el was
old, that he made his sons judges over Is'-
ra-el.
2 Now the name of his firstborn was Jo'el;
and the name of his second, A-bi'ah: *they were*
judges in Be'er-she'ba.
3 And his sons walked not in his ways, but
turned aside after lucre, and took bribes, and
perverted judgment.
4 Then all the elders of Is'ra-el gathered
themselves together, and came to Sam'u-el
unto Ra'mah,
5 And said unto him, Behold, thou art old,
and thy sons walk not in thy ways: now make
us a king to judge us like all the nations.
6 ¶ But the thing displeased Sam'u-el, when
they said, Give us a king to judge us. And Sam'-
u-el prayed unto the LORD.
7 And the LORD said unto Sam'u-el, Hearken
unto the voice of the people in all that they say
unto thee: for they have not rejected thee, but
they have rejected me, that I should not reign
over them.
8 According to all the works which they have
done since the day that I brought them up out
of E'gypt even unto this day, wherewith they
have forsaken me, and served other gods, so do
they also unto thee.
9 Now therefore hearken unto their voice:
howbeit yet protest solemnly unto them, and
shew them the manner of the king that shall
reign over them.
10 ¶ And Sam'u-el told all the words of the
LORD unto the people that asked of him a king.
11 And he said, This will be the manner of
the king that shall reign over you: He will take
your sons, and appoint *them* for himself, for his
chariots, and *to be* his horsemen; and *some*
shall run before his chariots.
12 And he will appoint him captains over
thousands, and captains over fifties; and *will set*
them to ear his ground, and to reap his harvest,
and to make his instruments of war, and instruments of his chariots.
13 And he will take your daughters *to be* con-
fectionaries, and *to be* cooks, and *to be* bakers.
14 And he will take your fields, and your
vineyards, and your oliveyards, *even* the best *of*
them, and give *them* to his servants.
15 And he will take the tenth of your seed,
and of your vineyards, and give to his officers,
and to his servants.
16 And he will take your menservants, and
your maidservants, and your goodliest young
men, and your asses, and put *them* to his work.
17 He will take the tenth of your sheep: and
ye shall be his servants.
18 And ye shall cry out in that day because
of your king which ye shall have chosen you;
and the LORD will not hear you in that day.
19 ¶ Nevertheless the people refused to obey
the voice of Sam'u-el; and they said, Nay; but
we will have a king over us;
20 That we also may be like all the nations;
and that our king may judge us, and go out before us, and fight our battles.
21 And Sam'u-el heard all the words of the
people, and he rehearsed them in the ears of the
LORD.
22 And the LORD said to Sam'u-el, Hearken
unto their voice, and make them a king. And
Sam'u-el said unto the men of Is'ra-el, Go ye
every man unto his city.

9 NOW there was a man of Ben'ja-min,
whose name *was* Kish, the son of A-bi'el,
the son of Ze'ror, the son of Be-cho'rath, the son
of A-phi'ah, a Ben'ja-mite, a mighty man of
power.
2 And he had a son, whose name *was* Saul, a
choice young man, and a goodly: and *there was*
not among the children of Is'ra-el a goodlier
person than he: from his shoulders and upward
he was higher than any of the people.
3 And the asses of Kish Saul's father were
lost. And Kish said to Saul his son, Take now
one of the servants with thee, and arise, go seek
the asses.
4 And he passed through mount E'phra-im,
and passed through the land of Shal'i-sha, but
they found *them* not: then they passed through
the land of Sha'lim, and *there they were* not:
and he passed through the land of the Ben'ja-
mites, but they found *them* not.
5 *And* when they were come to the land of
Zuph, Saul said to his servant that *was* with
him, Come, and let us return; lest my father
leave *caring* for the asses, and take thought for
us.
6 And he said unto him, Behold now, *there is*
in this city a man of God, and *he is* an honourable man; all that he saith cometh surely to
pass: now let us go thither; peradventure he can
shew us our way that we should go.
7 Then said Saul to his servant, But, behold,
if we go, what shall we bring the man? for the
bread is spent in our vessels, and *there is* not a
present to bring to the man of God: what have
we?
8 And the servant answered Saul again, and
said, Behold, I have here at hand the fourth part
of a shekel of silver: *that* will I give to the man
of God, to tell us our way.
9 (Beforetime in Is'ra-el, when a man went to
enquire of God, thus he spake, Come, and let us
go to the seer: for *he that is* now *called* a
Prophet was beforetime called a Seer.)
10 Then said Saul to his servant, Well said;

come, let us go. So they went unto the city
where the man of God *was*.
11 ¶ *And* as they went up the hill to the city,
they found young maidens going out to draw
water, and said unto them, Is the seer here?
12 And they answered them, and said, He is;
behold, *he is* before you: make haste now, for
he came to day to the city; for *there is* a sacrifice of the people to day in the high place:
13 As soon as ye be come into the city, ye
shall straightway find him, before he go up to
the high place to eat: for the people will not eat
until he come, because he doth bless the sacrifice; *and* afterwards they eat that be bidden.
Now therefore get you up; for about this time
ye shall find him.
14 And they went up into the city: *and* when
they were come into the city, behold, Sam'u-el
came out against them, for to go up to the high
place.
15 ¶ Now the LORD had told Sam'u-el in his
ear a day before Saul came, saying,
16 To morrow about this time I will send
thee a man out of the land of Ben'ja-min, and
thou shalt anoint him *to be* captain over my
people Is'ra-el, that he may save my people out
of the hand of the Phi-lis'tines: for I have looked
upon my people, because their cry is come unto
me.
17 And when Sam'u-el saw Saul, the LORD
said unto him, Behold the man whom I spake to
thee of! this same shall reign over my people.
18 Then Saul drew near to Sam'u-el in the
gate, and said, Tell me, I pray thee, where the
seer's house *is*.
19 And Sam'u-el answered Saul, and said, I
am the seer: go up before me unto the high
place; for ye shall eat with me to day, and to
morrow I will let thee go, and will tell thee all
that *is* in thine heart.
20 And as for thine asses that were lost three
days ago, set not thy mind on them; for they are
found. And on whom *is* all the desire of Is'ra-el?
Is it not on thee, and on all thy father's house?
21 And Saul answered and said, *Am* not I a
Ben'ja-mite, of the smallest of the tribes of Is'-
ra-el? and my family the least of all the families
of the tribe of Ben'ja-min? wherefore then
speakest thou so to me?
22 And Sam'u-el took Saul and his servant,
and brought them into the parlour, and made
them sit in the chiefest place among them that
were bidden, which *were* about thirty persons.
23 And Sam'u-el said unto the cook, Bring
the portion which I gave thee, of which I said
unto thee, Set it by thee.
24 And the cook took up the shoulder, and
that which *was* upon it, and set *it* before Saul.
And *Sam'u-el* said, Behold that which is left! set
it before thee, *and* eat: for unto this time hath it
been kept for thee since I said, I have invited
the people. So Saul did eat with Sam'u-el that
day.
25 ¶ And when they were come down from
the high place into the city, *Sam'u-el* communed with Saul upon the top of the house.
26 And they arose early: and it came to pass
about the spring of the day, that Sam'u-el called
Saul to the top of the house, saying, Up, that I
may send thee away. And Saul arose, and they
went out both of them, he and Sam'u-el,
abroad.
27 *And* as they were going down to the end
of the city, Sam'u-el said to Saul, Bid the servant pass on before us, (and he passed on,) but
stand thou still a while, that I may shew thee
the word of God.

10 THEN Sam'u-el took a vial of oil, and
poured *it* upon his head, and kissed him,
and said, *Is it* not because the LORD hath
anointed thee *to be* captain over his inheritance?
2 When thou art departed from me to day,
then thou shalt find two men by Ra'chel's sepulchre in the border of Ben'ja-min at Zel'zah; and
they will say unto thee, The asses which thou
wentest to seek are found: and, lo, thy father
hath left the care of the asses, and sorroweth
for you, saying, What shall I do for my son?
3 Then shalt thou go on forward from thence,
and thou shalt come to the plain of Ta'bor, and
there shall meet thee three men going up to God
to Beth'-el, one carrying three kids, and another carrying three loaves of bread, and another carrying a bottle of wine:
4 And they will salute thee, and give thee
two *loaves* of bread; which thou shalt receive of
their hands.
5 After that thou shalt come to the hill of
God, where *is* the garrison of the Phi-lis'tines:
and it shall come to pass, when thou art come
thither to the city, that thou shalt meet a company of prophets coming down from the high
place with a psaltery, and a tabret, and a pipe,
and a harp, before them; and they shall prophesy:
6 And the Spirit of the LORD will come upon
thee, and thou shalt prophesy with them, and
shalt be turned into another man.
7 And let it be, when these signs are come
unto thee, *that* thou do as occasion serve thee;
for God *is* with thee.
8 And thou shalt go down before me to Gil'-
gal; and, behold, I will come down unto thee, to
offer burnt offerings, *and* to sacrifice sacrifices
of peace offerings: seven days shalt thou tarry,
till I come to thee, and shew thee what thou
shalt do.
9 ¶ And it was *so*, that when he had turned
his back to go from Sam'u-el, God gave him another heart: and all those signs came to pass
that day.
10 And when they came thither to the hill,
behold, a company of prophets met him; and
the Spirit of God came upon him, and he prophesied among them.
11 And it came to pass, when all that knew
him beforetime saw that, behold, he prophesied
among the prophets, then the people said one to
another, What *is* this *that* is come unto the son
of Kish? *Is* Saul also among the prophets?
12 And one of the same place answered and
said, But who *is* their father? Therefore it became a proverb, *Is* Saul also among the prophets?
13 And when he had made an end of prophesying, he came to the high place.
14 ¶ And Saul's uncle said unto him and to
his servant, Whither went ye? And he said, To
seek the asses: and when we saw that *they were*
no where, we came to Sam'u-el.
15 And Saul's uncle said, Tell me, I pray
thee, what Sam'u-el said unto you.
16 And Saul said unto his uncle, He told us
plainly that the asses were found. But of the
matter of the kingdom, whereof Sam'u-el
spake, he told him not.
17 ¶ And Sam'u-el called the people together
unto the LORD to Miz'peh;
18 And said unto the children of Is'ra-el,
Thus saith the LORD God of Is'ra-el, I brought
up Is'ra-el out of E'gypt, and delivered you out
of the hand of the E-gyp'tians, and out of the

hand of all kingdoms, *and* of them that oppressed you:
19 And ye have this day rejected your God,
who himself saved you out of all your adversities and your tribulations; and ye have said unto
him, *Nay,* but set a king over us. Now therefore
present yourselves before the LORD by your
tribes, and by your thousands.
20 And when Sam'u-el had caused all the
tribes of Is'ra-el to come near, the tribe of Ben'-
ja-min was taken.
21 When he had caused the tribe of Ben'ja-
min to come near by their families, the family
of Ma'tri was taken, and Saul the son of Kish
was taken: and when they sought him, he could
not be found.
22 Therefore they enquired of the LORD further, if the man should yet come thither. And
the LORD answered, Behold, he hath hid himself
among the stuff.
23 And they ran and fetched him thence: and
when he stood among the people, he was higher
than any of the people from his shoulders and
upward.
24 And Sam'u-el said to all the people, See ye
him whom the LORD hath chosen, that *there is*
none like him among all the people? And all the
people shouted, and said, God save the king.
25 Then Sam'u-el told the people the manner
of the kingdom, and wrote *it* in a book, and laid
it up before the LORD. And Sam'u-el sent all the
people away, every man to his house.
26 ¶ And Saul also went home to Gib'e-ah;
and there went with him a band of men, whose
hearts God had touched.
27 But the children of Be'li-al said, How shall
this man save us? And they despised him, and
brought him no presents. But he held his peace.

11 THEN Na'hash the Am'mon-ite came
up, and encamped against Ja'besh-gil'e-
ad: and all the men of Ja'besh said unto Na'-
hash, Make a covenant with us, and we will
serve thee.
2 And Na'hash the Am'mon-ite answered
them, On this *condition* will I make *a covenant*
with you, that I may thrust out all your right
eyes, and lay it *for* a reproach upon all Is'ra-el.
3 And the elders of Ja'besh said unto him,
Give us seven days' respite, that we may send
messengers unto all the coasts of Is'ra-el: and
then, if *there be* no man to save us, we will
come out to thee.
4 ¶ Then came the messengers to Gib'e-ah of
Saul, and told the tidings in the ears of the people: and all the people lifted up their voices, and
wept.
5 And, behold, Saul came after the herd out
of the field; and Saul said, What *aileth* the people that they weep? And they told him the tidings of the men of Ja'besh.
6 And the Spirit of God came upon Saul
when he heard those tidings, and his anger was
kindled greatly.
7 And he took a yoke of oxen, and hewed
them in pieces, and sent *them* throughout all
the coasts of Is'ra-el by the hands of messengers, saying, Whosoever cometh not forth after
Saul and after Sam'u-el, so shall it be done unto
his oxen. And the fear of the LORD fell on the
people, and they came out with one consent.
8 And when he numbered them in Be'zek,
the children of Is'ra-el were three hundred thousand, and the men of Ju'dah thirty thousand.
9 And they said unto the messengers that
came, Thus shall ye say unto the men of Ja'-
besh-gil'e-ad, To morrow, by *that time* the sun
be hot, ye shall have help. And the messengers
came and shewed *it* to the men of Ja'besh; and
they were glad.
10 Therefore the men of Ja'besh said, To
morrow we will come out unto you, and ye shall
do with us all that seemeth good unto you.
11 And it was *so* on the morrow, that Saul
put the people in three companies; and they
came into the midst of the host in the morning
watch, and slew the Am'mon-ites until the heat
of the day: and it came to pass, that they which
remained were scattered, so that two of them
were not left together.
12 ¶ And the people said unto Sam'u-el,
Who *is* he that said, Shall Saul reign over us?
bring the men, that we may put them to death.
13 And Saul said, There shall not a man be
put to death this day: for to day the LORD hath
wrought salvation in Is'ra-el.
14 Then said Sam'u-el to the people, Come,
and let us go to Gil'gal, and renew the kingdom
there.
15 And all the people went to Gil'gal; and
there they made Saul king before the LORD in
Gil'gal; and there they sacrificed sacrifices of
peace offerings before the LORD; and there Saul
and all the men of Is'ra-el rejoiced greatly.

12 AND Sam'u-el said unto all Is'ra-el, Behold, I have hearkened unto your voice
in all that ye said unto me, and have made a
king over you.
2 And now, behold, the king walketh before
you: and I am old and grayheaded; and, behold,
my sons *are* with you: and I have walked before
you from my childhood unto this day.
3 Behold, here I *am:* witness against me before the LORD, and before his anointed: whose
ox have I taken? or whose ass have I taken? or
whom have I defrauded? whom have I oppressed? or of whose hand have I received *any*
bribe to blind mine eyes therewith? and I will
restore it you.
4 And they said, Thou hast not defrauded us,
nor oppressed us, neither hast thou taken ought
of any man's hand.
5 And he said unto them, The LORD *is* witness against you, and his anointed *is* witness
this day, that ye have not found ought in my
hand. And they answered, *He is* witness.
6 ¶ And Sam'u-el said unto the people, *It is*
the LORD that advanced Mo'ses and Aar'on, and
that brought your fathers up out of the land of
E'gypt.
7 Now therefore stand still, that I may reason
with you before the LORD of all the righteous
acts of the LORD, which he did to you and to
your fathers.
8 When Ja'cob was come into E'gypt, and
your fathers cried unto the LORD, then the LORD
sent Mo'ses and Aar'on, which brought forth
your fathers out of E'gypt, and made them
dwell in this place.
9 And when they forgat the LORD their God,
he sold them into the hand of Sis'e-ra, captain
of the host of Ha'zor, and into the hand of the
Phi-lis'tines, and into the hand of the king of
Mo'ab, and they fought against them.
10 And they cried unto the LORD, and said,
We have sinned, because we have forsaken the
LORD, and have served Ba'al-im and Ash'ta-
roth: but now deliver us out of the hand of our
enemies, and we will serve thee.
11 And the LORD sent Je-rub'ba-al, and Be'-
dan, and Jeph'thah, and Sam'u-el, and delivered
you out of the hand of your enemies on every
side, and ye dwelled safe.

12 And when ye saw that Na'hash the king of
the children of Am'mon came against you, ye
said unto me, Nay; but a king shall reign over
us: when the LORD your God *was* your king.
13 Now therefore behold the king whom ye
have chosen, *and* whom ye have desired! and,
behold, the LORD hath set a king over you.
14 If ye will fear the LORD, and serve him,
and obey his voice, and not rebel against the
commandment of the LORD, then shall both ye
and also the king that reigneth over you continue following the LORD your God:
15 But if ye will not obey the voice of the
LORD, but rebel against the commandment of
the LORD, then shall the hand of the LORD be
against you, as *it was* against your fathers.
16 ¶ Now therefore stand and see this great
thing, which the LORD will do before your eyes.
17 *Is it* not wheat harvest to-day? I will call
unto the LORD, and he shall send thunder and
rain; that ye may perceive and see that your
wickedness *is* great, which ye have done in the
sight of the LORD, in asking you a king.
18 So Sam'u-el called unto the LORD; and the
LORD sent thunder and rain that day: and all the
people greatly feared the LORD and Sam'u-el.
19 And all the people said unto Sam'u-el,
Pray for thy servants unto the LORD thy God,
that we die not: for we have added unto all our
sins *this* evil, to ask us a king.
20 ¶ And Sam'u-el said unto the people, Fear
not: ye have done all this wickedness: yet turn
not aside from following the LORD, but serve
the LORD with all your heart;
21 And turn ye not aside: for *then should ye*
go after vain *things*, which cannot profit nor deliver; for they *are* vain.
22 For the LORD will not forsake his people
for his great name's sake: because it hath
pleased the LORD to make you his people.
23 Moreover as for me, God forbid that I
should sin against the LORD in ceasing to pray
for you: but I will teach you the good and the
right way:
24 Only fear the LORD, and serve him in truth
with all your heart: for consider how great
things he hath done for you.
25 But if ye shall still do wickedly, ye shall be
consumed, both ye and your king.

13 SAUL reigned one year; and when he
had reigned two years over Is'ra-el,
2 Saul chose him three thousand *men* of Is'-
ra-el; *whereof* two thousand were with Saul in
Mich'mash and in mount Beth'-el, and a thousand were with Jon'a-than in Gib'e-ah of Ben'ja-
min: and the rest of the people he sent every
man to his tent.
3 And Jon'a-than smote the garrison of the
Phi-lis'tines that *was* in Ge'ba, and the Phi-lis'-
tines heard *of it*. And Saul blew the trumpet
throughout all the land, saying, Let the He'-
brews hear.
4 And all Is'ra-el heard say *that* Saul had
smitten a garrison of the Phi-lis'tines, and *that*
Is'ra-el also was had in abomination with the
Phi-lis'tines. And the people were called together after Saul to Gil'gal.
5 ¶ And the Phi-lis'tines gathered themselves together to fight with Is'ra-el, thirty thousand chariots, and six thousand horsemen, and
people as the sand which *is* on the sea shore in
multitude: and they came up, and pitched in
Mich'mash, eastward from Beth-a'ven.
6 When the men of Is'ra-el saw that they
were in a strait, (for the people were distressed,) then the people did hide themselves in
caves, and in thickets, and in rocks, and in high
places, and in pits.
7 And *some of* the He'brews went over Jor'-
dan to the land of Gad and Gil'e-ad. As for Saul,
he *was* yet in Gil'gal, and all the people followed him trembling.
8 ¶ And he tarried seven days, according to
the set time that Sam'u-el *had appointed*: but
Sam'u-el came not to Gil'gal; and the people
were scattered from him.
9 And Saul said, Bring hither a burnt offering
to me, and peace offerings. And he offered the
burnt offering.
10 And it came to pass, that as soon as he
had made an end of offering the burnt offering,
behold, Sam'u-el came; and Saul went out to
meet him, that he might salute him.
11 ¶ And Sam'u-el said, What hast thou
done? And Saul said, Because I saw that the
people were scattered from me, and *that* thou
camest not within the days appointed, and *that*
the Phi-lis'tines gathered themselves together
at Mich'mash;
12 Therefore said I, The Phi-lis'tines will
come down now upon me to Gil'gal, and I have
not made supplication unto the LORD: I forced
myself therefore, and offered a burnt offering.
13 And Sam'u-el said to Saul, Thou hast done
foolishly: thou hast not kept the commandment
of the LORD thy God, which he commanded
thee: for now would the LORD have established
thy kingdom upon Is'ra-el for ever.
14 But now thy kingdom shall not continue:
the LORD hath sought him a man after his own
heart, and the LORD hath commanded him *to be*
captain over his people, because thou hast not
kept *that* which the LORD commanded thee.
15 And Sam'u-el arose, and gat him up from
Gil'gal unto Gib'e-ah of Ben'ja-min. And Saul
numbered the people *that were* present with
him, about six hundred men.
16 And Saul, and Jon'a-than his son, and the
people *that were* present with them, abode in
Gib'e-ah of Ben'ja-min: but the Phi-lis'tines encamped in Mich'mash.
17 ¶ And the spoilers came out of the camp
of the Phi-lis'tines in three companies: one company turned unto the way *that leadeth to* Oph'-
rah, unto the land of Shu'al:
18 And another company turned the way *to*
Beth-ho'ron: and another company turned *to*
the way of the border that looketh to the valley
of Ze-bo'im toward the wilderness.
19 ¶ Now there was no smith found throughout all the land of Is'ra-el: for the Phi-lis'tines
said, Lest the He'brews make *them* swords or
spears:
20 But all the Is'ra-el-ites went down to the
Phi-lis'tines, to sharpen every man his share,
and his coulter, and his ax, and his mattock.
21 Yet they had a file for the mattocks, and
for the coulters, and for the forks, and for the
axes, and to sharpen the goads.
22 So it came to pass in the day of battle,
that there was neither sword nor spear found in
the hand of any of the people that *were* with
Saul and Jon'a-than: but with Saul and with
Jon'a-than his son was there found.
23 And the garrison of the Phi-lis'tines went
out to the passage of Mich'mash.

14 NOW it came to pass upon a day, that
Jon'a-than the son of Saul said unto the
young man that bare his armour, Come, and let
us go over to the Phi-lis'tines' garrison, that *is*
on the other side. But he told not his father.
2 And Saul tarried in the uttermost part of

Gib′e-ah under a pomegranate tree which *is* in Mig′ron: and the people that *were* with him *were* about six hundred men;

3 And A-hi′ah, the son of A-hi′tub, I–chabod's brother, the son of Phin′e-has, the son of E′li, the LORD's priest in Shi′loh, wearing an ephod. And the people knew not that Jon′a-than was gone.

4 ¶ And between the passages, by which Jon′a-than sought to go over unto the Phi-lis′-tines' garrison, *there was* a sharp rock on the one side, and a sharp rock on the other side: and the name of one *was* Bo′zez, and the name of the other Se′neh.

5 The forefront of the one *was* situate northward over against Mich′mash, and the other southward over against Gib′e-ah.

6 And Jon′a-than said to the young man that bare his armour, Come, and let us go over unto the garrison of these uncircumcised: it may be that the LORD will work for us: for *there is* no restraint to the LORD to save by many or by few.

7 And his armourbearer said unto him, Do all that *is* in thine heart: turn thee; behold, I *am* with thee according to thy heart.

8 Then said Jon′a-than, Behold, we will pass over unto *these* men, and we will discover ourselves unto them.

9 If they say thus unto us, Tarry until we come to you; then we will stand still in our place, and will not go up unto them.

10 But if they say thus, Come up unto us; then we will go up: for the LORD hath delivered them into our hand: and this *shall be* a sign unto us.

11 And both of them discovered themselves unto the garrison of the Phi-lis′tines: and the Phi-lis′tines said, Behold, the He′brews come forth out of the holes where they had hid themselves.

12 And the men of the garrison answered Jon′a-than and his armourbearer, and said, Come up to us, and we will shew you a thing. And Jon′a-than said unto his armourbearer, Come up after me: for the LORD hath delivered them into the hand of Is′ra-el.

13 And Jon′a-than climbed up upon his hands and upon his feet, and his armourbearer after him: and they fell before Jon′a-than; and his armourbearer slew after him.

14 And that first slaughter, which Jon′a-than and his armourbearer made, was about twenty men, within as it were an half acre of land, *which* a yoke *of oxen might plow.*

15 And there was trembling in the host, in the field, and among all the people: the garrison, and the spoilers, they also trembled, and the earth quaked: so it was a very great trembling.

16 And the watchmen of Saul in Gib′e-ah of Ben′ja-min looked; and, behold, the multitude melted away, and they went on beating down *one another.*

17 Then said Saul unto the people that *were* with him, Number now, and see who is gone from us. And when they had numbered, behold, Jon′a-than and his armourbearer *were* not *there.*

18 And Saul said unto A-hi′ah, Bring hither the ark of God. For the ark of God was at that time with the children of Is′ra-el.

19 ¶ And it came to pass, while Saul talked unto the priest, that the noise that *was* in the host of the Phi-lis′tines went on and increased: and Saul said unto the priest, Withdraw thine hand.

20 And Saul and all the people that *were* with him assembled themselves, and they came to the battle: and, behold, every man's sword was against his fellow, *and there was* a very great discomfiture.

21 Moreover the He′brews *that* were with the Phi-lis′tines before that time, which went up with them into the camp *from the country* round about, even they also *turned* to be with the Is′ra-el-ites that *were* with Saul and Jon′a-than.

22 Likewise all the men of Is′ra-el which had hid themselves in mount E′phra-im, *when* they heard that the Phi-lis′tines fled, even they also followed hard after them in the battle.

23 So the LORD saved Is′ra-el that day: and the battle passed over unto Beth–a′ven.

24 ¶ And the men of Is′ra-el were distressed that day: for Saul had adjured the people, saying, Cursed *be* the man that eateth *any* food until evening, that I may be avenged on mine enemies. So none of the people tasted *any* food.

25 And all *they of* the land came to a wood; and there was honey upon the ground.

26 And when the people were come into the wood, behold, the honey dropped; but no man put his hand to his mouth: for the people feared the oath.

27 But Jon′a-than heard not when his father charged the people with the oath: wherefore he put forth the end of the rod that *was* in his hand, and dipped it in an honeycomb, and put his hand to his mouth; and his eyes were enlightened.

28 Then answered one of the people, and said, Thy father straitly charged the people with an oath, saying, Cursed *be* the man that eateth *any* food this day. And the people were faint.

29 Then said Jon′a-than, My father hath troubled the land: see, I pray you, how mine eyes have been enlightened, because I tasted a little of this honey.

30 How much more, if haply the people had eaten freely to day of the spoil of their enemies which they found? for had there not been now a much greater slaughter among the Phi-lis′tines?

31 And they smote the Phi-lis′tines that day from Mich′mash to Aij′a-lon: and the people were very faint.

32 And the people flew upon the spoil, and took sheep, and oxen, and calves, and slew *them* on the ground: and the people did eat *them* with the blood.

33 ¶ Then they told Saul, saying, Behold, the people sin against the LORD, in that they eat with the blood. And he said, Ye have transgressed: roll a great stone unto me this day.

34 And Saul said, Disperse yourselves among the people, and say unto them, Bring me hither every man his ox, and every man his sheep, and slay *them* here, and eat; and sin not against the LORD in eating with the blood. And all the people brought every man his ox with him that night, and slew *them* there.

35 And Saul built an altar unto the LORD: the same was the first altar that he built unto the LORD.

36 ¶ And Saul said, Let us go down after the Phi-lis′tines by night, and spoil them until the morning light, and let us not leave a man of them. And they said, Do whatsoever seemeth good unto thee. Then said the priest, Let us draw near hither unto God.

37 And Saul asked counsel of God, Shall I go down after the Phi-lis′tines? wilt thou deliver them into the hand of Is′ra-el? But he answered him not that day.

38 And Saul said, Draw ye near hither, all the chief of the people: and know and see wherein this sin hath been this day.

39 For, *as* the LORD liveth, which saveth Is'ra-el, though it be in Jon'a-than my son, he shall surely die. But *there was* not a man among all the people *that* answered him.

40 Then said he unto all Is'ra-el, Be ye on one side, and I and Jon'a-than my son will be on the other side. And the people said unto Saul, Do what seemeth good unto thee.

41 Therefore Saul said unto the LORD God of Is'ra-el, Give a perfect *lot.* And Saul and Jon'a-than were taken: but the people escaped.

42 And Saul said, Cast *lots* between me and Jon'a-than my son. And Jon'a-than was taken.

43 Then Saul said to Jon'a-than, Tell me what thou hast done. And Jon'a-than told him, and said, I did but taste a little honey with the end of the rod that *was* in mine hand, *and,* lo, I must die.

44 And Saul answered, God do so and more also: for thou shalt surely die, Jon'a-than.

45 And the people said unto Saul, Shall Jon'a-than die, who hath wrought this great salvation in Is'ra-el? God forbid: *as* the LORD liveth, there shall not one hair of his head fall to the ground; for he hath wrought with God this day. So the people rescued Jon'a-than, that he died not.

46 Then Saul went up from following the Phi-lis'tines: and the Phi-lis'tines went to their own place.

47 ¶ So Saul took the kingdom over Is'ra-el, and fought against all his enemies on every side, against Mo'ab, and against the children of Am'mon, and against E'dom, and against the kings of Zo'bah, and against the Phi-lis'tines: and whithersoever he turned himself, he vexed *them.*

48 And he gathered an host, and smote the Am'a-lek-ites, and delivered Is'ra-el out of the hands of them that spoiled them.

49 Now the sons of Saul were Jon'a-than, and Ish'u-i, and Mel'chi-shu'a: and the names of his two daughters *were these;* the name of the firstborn Me'rab, and the name of the younger Mi'chal:

50 And the name of Saul's wife *was* A-hin'o-am, the daughter of A-him'a-az: and the name of the captain of his host *was* Ab'ner, the son of Ner, Saul's uncle.

51 And Kish *was* the father of Saul; and Ner the father of Ab'ner *was* the son of A-bi'el.

52 And there was sore war against the Phi-lis'tines all the days of Saul: and when Saul saw any strong man, or any valiant man, he took him unto him.

15

SAM'U-EL also said unto Saul, The LORD sent me to anoint thee *to be* king over his people, over Is'ra-el: now therefore hearken thou unto the voice of the words of the LORD.

2 Thus saith the LORD of hosts, I remember *that* which Am'a-lek did to Is'ra-el, how he laid *wait* for him in the way, when he came up from E'gypt.

3 Now go and smite Am'a-lek, and utterly destroy all that they have, and spare them not; but slay both man and woman, infant and suckling, ox and sheep, camel and ass.

4 And Saul gathered the people together, and numbered them in Tel'a-im, two hundred thousand footmen, and ten thousand men of Ju'dah.

5 And Saul came to a city of Am'a-lek, and laid wait in the valley.

6 ¶ And Saul said unto the Ken'ites, Go, depart, get you down from among the Am'a-lek-ites, lest I destroy you with them: for ye shewed kindness to all the children of Is'ra-el, when they came up out of E'gypt. So the Ken'ites departed from among the Am'a-lek-ites.

7 And Saul smote the Am'a-lek-ites from Hav'i-lah *until* thou comest to Shur, that *is* over against E'gypt.

8 And he took A'gag the king of the Am'a-lek-ites alive, and utterly destroyed all the people with the edge of the sword.

9 But Saul and the people spared A'gag, and the best of the sheep, and of the oxen, and of the fatlings, and the lambs, and all *that was* good, and would not utterly destroy them: but every thing *that was* vile and refuse, that they destroyed utterly.

10 ¶ Then came the word of the LORD unto Sam'u-el, saying,

11 It repenteth me that I have set up Saul *to be* king: for he is turned back from following me, and hath not performed my commandments. And it grieved Sam'u-el; and he cried unto the LORD all night.

12 And when Sam'u-el rose early to meet Saul in the morning, it was told Sam'u-el, saying, Saul came to Car'mel, and, behold, he set him up a place, and is gone about, and passed on, and gone down to Gil'gal.

13 And Sam'u-el came to Saul: and Saul said unto him, Blessed *be* thou of the LORD: I have performed the commandment of the LORD.

14 And Sam'u-el said, What *meaneth* then this bleating of the sheep in mine ears, and the lowing of the oxen which I hear?

15 And Saul said, They have brought them from the Am'a-lek-ites: for the people spared the best of the sheep and of the oxen, to sacrifice unto the LORD thy God; and the rest we have utterly destroyed.

16 Then Sam'u-el said unto Saul, Stay, and I will tell thee what the LORD hath said to me this night. And he said unto him, Say on.

17 And Sam'u-el said, When thou *wast* little in thine own sight, *wast* thou not *made* the head of the tribes of Is'ra-el, and the LORD anointed thee king over Is'ra-el?

18 And the LORD sent thee on a journey, and said, Go and utterly destroy the sinners the Am'a-lek-ites, and fight against them until they be consumed.

19 Wherefore then didst thou not obey the voice of the LORD, but didst fly upon the spoil, and didst evil in the sight of the LORD?

20 And Saul said unto Sam'u-el, Yea, I have obeyed the voice of the LORD, and have gone the way which the LORD sent me, and have brought A'gag the king of Am'a-lek, and have utterly destroyed the Am'a-lek-ites.

21 But the people took of the spoil, sheep and oxen, the chief of the things which should have been utterly destroyed, to sacrifice unto the LORD thy God in Gil'gal.

22 And Sam'u-el said, Hath the LORD *as great* delight in burnt offerings and sacrifices, as in obeying the voice of the LORD? Behold, to obey *is* better than sacrifice, *and* to hearken than the fat of rams.

23 For rebellion *is as* the sin of witchcraft, and stubbornness *is as* iniquity and idolatry. Because thou hast rejected the word of the LORD, he hath also rejected thee from *being* king.

24 ¶ And Saul said unto Sam'u-el, I have sinned: for I have transgressed the command-

ment of the LORD, and thy words: because I
feared the people, and obeyed their voice.
25 Now therefore, I pray thee, pardon my
sin, and turn again with me, that I may worship
the LORD.
26 And Sam'u-el said unto Saul, I will not return with thee: for thou hast rejected the word
of the LORD, and the LORD hath rejected thee
from being king over Is'ra-el.
27 And as Sam'u-el turned about to go away,
he laid hold upon the skirt of his mantle, and it
rent.
28 And Sam'u-el said unto him, The LORD
hath rent the kingdom of Is'ra-el from thee this
day, and hath given it to a neighbour of thine,
that is better than thou.
29 And also the Strength of Is'ra-el will not
lie nor repent: for he *is* not a man, that he
should repent.
30 Then he said, I have sinned: *yet* honour
me now, I pray thee, before the elders of my
people, and before Is'ra-el, and turn again with
me, that I may worship the LORD thy God.
31 So Sam'u-el turned again after Saul; and
Saul worshipped the LORD.
32 ¶ Then said Sam'u-el, Bring ye hither to
me A'gag the king of the Am'a-lek-ites. And A'-
gag came unto him delicately. And A'gag said,
Surely the bitterness of death is past.
33 And Sam'u-el said, As thy sword hath
made women childless, so shall thy mother be
childless among women. And Sam'u-el hewed
A'gag in pieces before the LORD in Gil'gal.
34 ¶ Then Sam'u-el went to Ra'mah; and
Saul went up to his house to Gib'e-ah of Saul.
35 And Sam'u-el came no more to see Saul
until the day of his death: nevertheless Sam'u-el
mourned for Saul: and the LORD repented that
he had made Saul king over Is'ra-el.

16 AND the LORD said unto Sam'u-el, How
long wilt thou mourn for Saul, seeing I
have rejected him from reigning over Is'ra-el?
fill thine horn with oil, and go, I will send thee
to Jes'se the Beth'-le-hem-ite: for I have provided me a king among his sons.
2 And Sam'u-el said, How can I go? if Saul
hear *it*, he will kill me. And the LORD said, Take
an heifer with thee, and say, I am come to sacrifice to the LORD.
3 And call Jes'se to the sacrifice, and I will
shew thee what thou shalt do: and thou shalt
anoint unto me *him* whom I name unto thee.
4 And Sam'u-el did that which the LORD
spake, and came to Beth'-le-hem. And the elders of the town trembled at his coming, and
said, Comest thou peaceably?
5 And he said, Peaceably: I am come to sacrifice unto the LORD: sanctify yourselves, and
come with me to the sacrifice. And he sanctified
Jes'se and his sons, and called them to the sacrifice.
6 ¶ And it came to pass, when they were
come, that he looked on E-li'ab, and said, Surely
the LORD's anointed *is* before him.
7 But the LORD said unto Sam'u-el, Look not
on his countenance, or on the height of his stature; because I have refused him: for *the LORD
seeth* not as man seeth; for man looketh on the
outward appearance, but the LORD looketh on
the heart.
8 Then Jes'se called A-bin'a-dab, and made
him pass before Sam'u-el. And he said, Neither
hath the LORD chosen this.
9 Then Jes'se made Sham'mah to pass by.
And he said, Neither hath the LORD chosen this.
10 Again, Jes'se made seven of his sons to
pass before Sam'u-el. And Sam'u-el said unto
Jes'se, The LORD hath not chosen these.
11 And Sam'u-el said unto Jes'se, Are here
all *thy* children? And he said, There remaineth
yet the youngest, and, behold, he keepeth the
sheep. And Sam'u-el said unto Jes'se, Send and
fetch him: for we will not sit down till he come
hither.
12 And he sent, and brought him in. Now he
was ruddy, *and* withal of a beautiful countenance, and goodly to look to. And the LORD
said, Arise, anoint him: for this *is* he.
13 Then Sam'u-el took the horn of oil, and
anointed him in the midst of his brethren: and
the Spirit of the LORD came upon Da'vid from
that day forward. So Sam'u-el rose up, and
went to Ra'mah.
14 ¶ But the Spirit of the LORD departed
from Saul, and an evil spirit from the LORD
troubled him.
15 And Saul's servants said unto him, Behold
now, an evil spirit from God troubleth thee.
16 Let our lord now command thy servants,
which are before thee, to seek out a man, *who is*
a cunning player on an harp: and it shall come
to pass, when the evil spirit from God is upon
thee, that he shall play with his hand, and thou
shalt be well.
17 And Saul said unto his servants, Provide
me now a man that can play well, and bring *him*
to me.
18 Then answered one of the servants, and
said, Behold, I have seen a son of Jes'se the
Beth'-le-hem-ite, *that is* cunning in playing, and
a mighty valiant man, and a man of war, and
prudent in matters, and a comely person, and
the LORD *is* with him.
19 ¶ Wherefore Saul sent messengers unto
Jes'se, and said, Send me Da'vid thy son, which
is with the sheep.
20 And Jes'se took an ass *laden* with bread,
and a bottle of wine, and a kid, and sent *them*
by Da'vid his son unto Saul.
21 And Da'vid came to Saul, and stood before him: and he loved him greatly; and he became his armourbearer.
22 And Saul sent to Jes'se, saying, Let Da'-
vid, I pray thee, stand before me; for he hath
found favour in my sight.
23 And it came to pass, when the *evil* spirit
from God was upon Saul, that Da'vid took an
harp, and played with his hand: so Saul was refreshed, and was well, and the evil spirit departed from him.

17 NOW the Phi-lis'tines gathered together
their armies to battle, and were gathered together at Sho'choh, which *belongeth* to
Ju'dah, and pitched between Sho'choh and A-
ze'kah, in E'phes-dam'mim.
2 And Saul and the men of Is'ra-el were gathered together, and pitched by the valley of E'-
lah, and set the battle in array against the Phi-
lis'tines.
3 And the Phi-lis'tines stood on a mountain
on the one side, and Is'ra-el stood on a mountain on the other side: and *there was* a valley
between them.
4 ¶ And there went out a champion out of
the camp of the Phi-lis'tines, named Go-li'ath,
of Gath, whose height *was* six cubits and a
span.
5 And *he had* an helmet of brass upon his
head, and he *was* armed with a coat of mail;
and the weight of the coat *was* five thousand
shekels of brass.

6 And *he had* greaves of brass upon his legs, and a target of brass between his shoulders.

7 And the staff of his spear *was* like a weaver's beam; and his spear's head *weighed* six hundred shekels of iron: and one bearing a shield went before him.

8 And he stood and cried unto the armies of Is'ra-el, and said unto them, Why are ye come out to set *your* battle in array? *am* not I a Phi-lis'tine, and ye servants to Saul? choose you a man for you, and let him come down to me.

9 If he be able to fight with me, and to kill me, then will we be your servants: but if I prevail against him, and kill him, then shall ye be our servants, and serve us.

10 And the Phi-lis'tine said, I defy the armies of Is'ra-el this day; give me a man, that we may fight together.

11 When Saul and all Is'ra-el heard those words of the Phi-lis'tine, they were dismayed, and greatly afraid.

12 ¶ Now Da'vid *was* the son of that Eph'-rath-ite of Beth'-le-hem-ju'dah, whose name *was* Jes'se; and he had eight sons: and the man went among men *for* an old man in the days of Saul.

13 And the three eldest sons of Jes'se went *and* followed Saul to the battle: and the names of his three sons that went to the battle *were* E-li'ab the firstborn, and next unto him A-bin'a-dab, and the third Sham'mah.

14 And Da'vid *was* the youngest: and the three eldest followed Saul.

15 But Da'vid went and returned from Saul to feed his father's sheep at Beth'-le-hem.

16 And the Phi-lis'tine drew near morning and evening, and presented himself forty days.

17 And Jes'se said unto Da'vid his son, Take now for thy brethren an ephah of this parched *corn,* and these ten loaves, and run to the camp to thy brethren;

18 And carry these ten cheeses unto the captain of *their* thousand, and look how thy brethren fare, and take their pledge.

19 Now Saul, and they, and all the men of Is'ra-el, *were* in the valley of E'lah, fighting with the Phi-lis'tines.

20 ¶ And Da'vid rose up early in the morning, and left the sheep with a keeper, and took, and went, as Jes'se had commanded him; and he came to the trench, as the host was going forth to the fight, and shouted for the battle.

21 For Is'ra-el and the Phi-lis'tines had put the battle in array, army against army.

22 And Da'vid left his carriage in the hand of the keeper of the carriage, and ran into the army, and came and saluted his brethren.

23 And as he talked with them, behold, there came up the champion, the Phi-lis'tine of Gath, Go-li'ath by name, out of the armies of the Phi-lis'tines, and spake according to the same words: and Da'vid heard *them.*

24 And all the men of Is'ra-el, when they saw the man, fled from him, and were sore afraid.

25 And the men of Is'ra-el said, Have ye seen this man that is come up? surely to defy Is'ra-el is he come up: and it shall be, *that* the man who killeth him, the king will enrich him with great riches, and will give him his daughter, and make his father's house free in Is'ra-el.

26 And Da'vid spake to the men that stood by him, saying, What shall be done to the man that killeth this Phi-lis'tine, and taketh away the reproach from Is'ra-el? for who *is* this uncircumcised Phi-lis'tine, that he should defy the armies of the living God?

27 And the people answered him after this manner, saying, So shall it be done to the man that killeth him.

28 ¶ And E-li'ab his eldest brother heard when he spake unto the men; and E-li'ab's anger was kindled against Da'vid, and he said, Why camest thou down hither? and with whom hast thou left those few sheep in the wilderness? I know thy pride, and the naughtiness of thine heart; for thou art come down that thou mightest see the battle.

29 And Da'vid said, What have I now done? *Is there* not a cause?

30 ¶ And he turned from him toward another, and spake after the same manner: and the people answered him again after the former manner.

31 And when the words were heard which Da'vid spake, they rehearsed *them* before Saul: and he sent for him.

32 ¶ And Da'vid said to Saul, Let no man's heart fail because of him; thy servant will go and fight with this Phi-lis'tine.

33 And Saul said to Da'vid, Thou art not able to go against this Phi-lis'tine to fight with him: for thou *art but* a youth, and he a man of war from his youth.

34 And Da'vid said unto Saul, Thy servant kept his father's sheep, and there came a lion, and a bear, and took a lamb out of the flock:

35 And I went out after him, and smote him, and delivered *it* out of his mouth: and when he arose against me, I caught *him* by his beard, and smote him, and slew him.

36 Thy servant slew both the lion and the bear: and this uncircumcised Phi-lis'tine shall be as one of them, seeing he hath defied the armies of the living God.

37 Da'vid said moreover, The LORD that delivered me out of the paw of the lion, and out of the paw of the bear, he will deliver me out of the hand of this Phi-lis'tine. And Saul said unto Da'vid, Go, and the LORD be with thee.

38 ¶ And Saul armed Da'vid with his armour, and he put an helmet of brass upon his head; also he armed him with a coat of mail.

39 And Da'vid girded his sword upon his armour, and he assayed to go; for he had not proved *it.* And Da'vid said unto Saul, I cannot go with these; for I have not proved *them.* And Da'vid put them off him.

40 And he took his staff in his hand, and chose him five smooth stones out of the brook, and put them in a shepherd's bag which he had, even in a scrip; and his sling *was* in his hand: and he drew near to the Phi-lis'tine.

41 And the Phi-lis'tine came on and drew near unto Da'vid; and the man that bare the shield *went* before him.

42 And when the Phi-lis'tine looked about, and saw Da'vid, he disdained him: for he was *but* a youth, and ruddy, and of a fair countenance.

43 And the Phi-lis'tine said unto Da'vid, *Am* I a dog, that thou comest to me with staves? And the Phi-lis'tine cursed Da'vid by his gods.

44 And the Phi-lis'tine said to Da'vid, Come to me, and I will give thy flesh unto the fowls of the air, and to the beasts of the field.

45 Then said Da'vid to the Phi-lis'tine, Thou comest to me with a sword, and with a spear, and with a shield: but I come to thee in the name of the LORD of hosts, the God of the armies of Is'ra-el, whom thou hast defied.

46 This day will the LORD deliver thee into mine hand; and I will smite thee, and take thine head from thee; and I will give the carcases of the host of the Phi-lis'tines this day unto the

fowls of the air, and to the wild beasts of the
earth; that all the earth may know that there is
a God in Is'ra-el.
47 And all this assembly shall know that the
LORD saveth not with sword and spear: for the
battle *is* the LORD's, and he will give you into
our hands.
48 And it came to pass, when the Phi-lis'tine
arose, and came and drew nigh to meet Da'vid,
that Da'vid hasted, and ran toward the army to
meet the Phi-lis'tine.
49 And Da'vid put his hand in his bag, and
took thence a stone, and slang *it*, and smote the
Phi-lis'tine in his forehead, that the stone sunk
into his forehead; and he fell upon his face to
the earth.
50 So Da'vid prevailed over the Phi-lis'tine
with a sling and with a stone, and smote the
Phi-lis'tine, and slew him; but *there was* no
sword in the hand of Da'vid.
51 Therefore Da'vid ran, and stood upon the
Phi-lis'tine, and took his sword, and drew it out
of the sheath thereof, and slew him, and cut off
his head therewith. And when the Phi-lis'tines
saw their champion was dead, they fled.
52 And the men of Is'ra-el and of Ju'dah
arose, and shouted, and pursued the Phi-lis'-
tines, until thou come to the valley, and to the
gates of Ek'ron. And the wounded of the Phi-
lis'tines fell down by the way to Sha-a-ra'im,
even unto Gath, and unto Ek'ron.
53 And the children of Is'ra-el returned from
chasing after the Phi-lis'tines, and they spoiled
their tents.
54 And Da'vid took the head of the Phi-lis'-
tine, and brought it to Je-ru'sa-lem; but he put
his armour in his tent.
55 ¶ And when Saul saw Da'vid go forth
against the Phi-lis'tine, he said unto Ab'ner, the
captain of the host, Ab'ner, whose son *is* this
youth? And Ab'ner said, *As* thy soul liveth, O
king, I cannot tell.
56 And the king said, Enquire thou whose
son the stripling *is*.
57 And as Da'vid returned from the slaughter
of the Phi-lis'tine, Ab'ner took him, and brought
him before Saul with the head of the Phi-lis'tine
in his hand.
58 And Saul said to him, Whose son *art* thou,
thou young man? And Da'vid answered, *I am*
the son of thy servant Jes'se the Beth'-le-hem-
ite.

18

AND it came to pass, when he had made
an end of speaking unto Saul, that the
soul of Jon'a-than was knit with the soul of Da'-
vid, and Jon'a-than loved him as his own soul.
2 And Saul took him that day, and would let
him go no more home to his father's house.
3 Then Jon'a-than and Da'vid made a covenant, because he loved him as his own soul.
4 And Jon'a-than stripped himself of the robe
that *was* upon him, and gave it to Da'vid, and
his garments, even to his sword, and to his bow,
and to his girdle.
5 ¶ And Da'vid went out whithersoever Saul
sent him, *and* behaved himself wisely: and Saul
set him over the men of war, and he was accepted in the sight of all the people, and also in
the sight of Saul's servants.
6 And it came to pass as they came, when
Da'vid was returned from the slaughter of the
Phi-lis'tine, that the women came out of all
cities of Is'ra-el, singing and dancing, to meet
king Saul, with tabrets, with joy, and with instruments of musick.
7 And the women answered *one another* as
they played, and said, Saul hath slain his thousands, and Da'vid his ten thousands.
8 And Saul was very wroth, and the saying
displeased him; and he said, They have ascribed
unto Da'vid ten thousands, and to me they have
ascribed *but* thousands: and *what* can he have
more but the kingdom?
9 And Saul eyed Da'vid from that day and
forward.
10 ¶ And it came to pass on the morrow,
that the evil spirit from God came upon Saul,
and he prophesied in the midst of the house:
and Da'vid played with his hand, as at other
times: and *there was* a javelin in Saul's hand.
11 And Saul cast the javelin; for he said, I
will smite Da'vid even to the wall *with it*. And
Da'vid avoided out of his presence twice.
12 ¶ And Saul was afraid of Da'vid, because
the LORD was with him, and was departed from
Saul.
13 Therefore Saul removed him from him,
and made him his captain over a thousand; and
he went out and came in before the people.
14 And Da'vid behaved himself wisely in all
his ways; and the LORD *was* with him.
15 Wherefore when Saul saw that he behaved himself very wisely, he was afraid of
him.
16 But all Is'ra-el and Ju'dah loved Da'vid,
because he went out and came in before them.
17 ¶ And Saul said to Da'vid, Behold my elder daughter Me'rab, her will I give thee to
wife: only be thou valiant for me, and fight the
LORD's battles. For Saul said, Let not mine hand
be upon him, but let the hand of the Phi-lis'tines
be upon him.
18 And Da'vid said unto Saul, Who *am* I? and
what *is* my life, *or* my father's family in Is'ra-el,
that I should be son in law to the king?
19 But it came to pass at the time when Me'-
rab Saul's daughter should have been given to
Da'vid, that she was given unto A'dri-el the Me-
hol'ath-ite to wife.
20 And Mi'chal Saul's daughter loved Da'vid:
and they told Saul, and the thing pleased him.
21 And Saul said, I will give him her, that she
may be a snare to him, and that the hand of the
Phi-lis'tines may be against him. Wherefore
Saul said to Da'vid, Thou shalt this day be my
son in law in *the one of* the twain.
22 ¶ And Saul commanded his servants, *saying*, Commune with Da'vid secretly, and say,
Behold, the king hath delight in thee, and all his
servants love thee: now therefore be the king's
son in law.
23 And Saul's servants spake those words in
the ears of Da'vid. And Da'vid said, Seemeth it
to you *a* light *thing* to be a king's son in law,
seeing that I *am* a poor man, and lightly esteemed?
24 And the servants of Saul told him, saying,
On this manner spake Da'vid.
25 And Saul said, Thus shall ye say to Da'vid,
The king desireth not any dowry, but an hundred foreskins of the Phi-lis'tines, to be avenged
of the king's enemies. But Saul thought to make
Da'vid fall by the hand of the Phi-lis'tines.
26 And when his servants told Da'vid these
words, it pleased Da'vid well to be the king's
son in law: and the days were not expired.
27 Wherefore Da'vid arose and went, he and
his men, and slew of the Phi-lis'tines two hundred men; and Da'vid brought their foreskins,
and they gave them in full tale to the king, that
he might be the king's son in law. And Saul
gave him Mi'chal his daughter to wife.
28 ¶ And Saul saw and knew that the LORD

was with Da'vid, and *that* Mi'chal Saul's daughter loved him.
29 And Saul was yet the more afraid of Da'vid; and Saul became Da'vid's enemy continually.
30 Then the princes of the Phi-lis'tines went forth: and it came to pass, after they went forth, *that* Da'vid behaved himself more wisely than all the servants of Saul; so that his name was much set by.

19 AND Saul spake to Jon'a-than his son, and to all his servants, that they should kill Da'vid.
2 But Jon'a-than Saul's son delighted much in Da'vid: and Jon'a-than told Da'vid, saying, Saul my father seeketh to kill thee: now therefore, I pray thee, take heed to thyself until the morning, and abide in a secret *place*, and hide thyself:
3 And I will go out and stand beside my father in the field where thou *art*, and I will commune with my father of thee; and what I see, that I will tell thee.
4 ¶ And Jon'a-than spake good of Da'vid unto Saul his father, and said unto him, Let not the king sin against his servant, against Da'vid; because he hath not sinned against thee, and because his works *have been* to thee-ward very good:
5 For he did put his life in his hand, and slew the Phi-lis'tine, and the LORD wrought a great salvation for all Is'ra-el: thou sawest *it*, and didst rejoice: wherefore then wilt thou sin against innocent blood, to slay Da'vid without a cause?
6 And Saul hearkened unto the voice of Jon'a-than: and Saul sware, *As* the LORD liveth, he shall not be slain.
7 And Jon'a-than called Da'vid, and Jon'a-than shewed him all those things. And Jon'a-than brought Da'vid to Saul, and he was in his presence, as in times past.
8 ¶ And there was war again: and Da'vid went out, and fought with the Phi-lis'tines, and slew them with a great slaughter; and they fled from him.
9 And the evil spirit from the LORD was upon Saul, as he sat in his house with his javelin in his hand: and Da'vid played with *his* hand.
10 And Saul sought to smite Da'vid even to the wall with the javelin; but he slipped away out of Saul's presence, and he smote the javelin into the wall: and Da'vid fled, and escaped that night.
11 Saul also sent messengers unto Da'vid's house, to watch him, and to slay him in the morning: and Mi'chal Da'vid's wife told him, saying, If thou save not thy life to night, to morrow thou shalt be slain.
12 ¶ So Mi'chal let Da'vid down through a window: and he went, and fled, and escaped.
13 And Mi'chal took an image, and laid *it* in the bed, and put a pillow of goats' *hair* for his bolster, and covered *it* with a cloth.
14 And when Saul sent messengers to take Da'vid, she said, He *is* sick.
15 And Saul sent the messengers *again* to see Da'vid, saying, Bring him up to me in the bed, that I may slay him.
16 And when the messengers were come in, behold, *there was* an image in the bed, with a pillow of goats' *hair* for his bolster.
17 And Saul said unto Mi'chal, Why hast thou deceived me so, and sent away mine enemy, that he is escaped? And Mi'chal answered Saul, He said unto me, Let me go; why should I kill thee?
18 ¶ So Da'vid fled, and escaped, and came to Sam'u-el to Ra'mah, and told him all that Saul had done to him. And he and Sam'u-el went and dwelt in Na'ioth.
19 And it was told Saul, saying, Behold, Da'vid *is* at Na'ioth in Ra'mah.
20 And Saul sent messengers to take Da'vid: and when they saw the company of the prophets prophesying, and Sam'u-el standing *as* appointed over them, the Spirit of God was upon the messengers of Saul, and they also prophesied.
21 And when it was told Saul, he sent other messengers, and they prophesied likewise. And Saul sent messengers again the third time, and they prophesied also.
22 Then went he also to Ra'mah, and came to a great well that *is* in Se'chu: and he asked and said, Where *are* Sam'u-el and Da'vid? And *one* said, Behold, *they be* at Na'ioth in Ra'mah.
23 And he went thither to Na'ioth in Ra'mah: and the Spirit of God was upon him also, and he went on, and prophesied, until he came to Na'ioth in Ra'mah.
24 And he stripped off his clothes also, and prophesied before Sam'u-el in like manner, and lay down naked all that day and all that night. Wherefore they say, *Is* Saul also among the prophets?

20 AND Da'vid fled from Na'ioth in Ra'mah, and came and said before Jon'a-than, What have I done? what *is* mine iniquity? and what *is* my sin before thy father, that he seeketh my life?
2 And he said unto him, God forbid; thou shalt not die: behold, my father will do nothing either great or small, but that he will shew it me: and why should my father hide this thing from me? it *is* not *so*.
3 And Da'vid sware moreover, and said, Thy father certainly knoweth that I have found grace in thine eyes; and he saith, Let not Jon'a-than know this, lest he be grieved: but truly *as* the LORD liveth, and *as* thy soul liveth, *there is* but a step between me and death.
4 Then said Jon'a-than unto Da'vid, Whatsoever thy soul desireth, I will even do *it* for thee.
5 And Da'vid said unto Jon'a-than, Behold, to morrow *is* the new moon, and I should not fail to sit with the king at meat: but let me go, that I may hide myself in the field unto the third *day* at even.
6 If thy father at all miss me, then say, Da'vid earnestly asked *leave* of me that he might run to Beth'-le-hem his city: for *there is* a yearly sacrifice there for all the family.
7 If he say thus, *It is* well; thy servant shall have peace: but if he be very wroth, *then* be sure that evil is determined by him.
8 Therefore thou shalt deal kindly with thy servant; for thou hast brought thy servant into a covenant of the LORD with thee: notwithstanding, if there be in me iniquity, slay me thyself; for why shouldest thou bring me to thy father?
9 And Jon'a-than said, Far be it from thee: for if I knew certainly that evil were determined by my father to come upon thee, then would not I tell it thee?
10 Then said Da'vid to Jon'a-than, Who shall tell me? or what *if* thy father answer thee roughly?
11 ¶ And Jon'a-than said unto Da'vid, Come, and let us go out into the field. And they went out both of them into the field.

12 And Jon'a-than said unto Da'vid, O LORD
God of Is'ra-el, when I have sounded my father
about to morrow any time, *or* the third *day*,
and, behold, *if there be* good toward Da'vid, and
I then send not unto thee, and shew it thee;
13 The LORD do so and much more to Jon'a-
than: but if it please my father *to do* thee evil,
then I will shew it thee, and send thee away,
that thou mayest go in peace: and the LORD be
with thee, as he hath been with my father.
14 And thou shalt not only while yet I live
shew me the kindness of the LORD, that I die
not:
15 But *also* thou shalt not cut off thy kindness from my house for ever: no, not when the
LORD hath cut off the enemies of Da'vid every
one from the face of the earth.
16 So Jon'a-than made *a covenant* with the
house of Da'vid, *saying*, Let the LORD even require *it* at the hand of Da'vid's enemies.
17 And Jon'a-than caused Da'vid to swear
again, because he loved him: for he loved him
as he loved his own soul.
18 Then Jon'a-than said to Da'vid, To morrow *is* the new moon: and thou shalt be missed,
because thy seat will be empty.
19 And *when* thou hast stayed three days,
then thou shalt go down quickly, and come to
the place where thou didst hide thyself when
the business was *in hand*, and shalt remain by
the stone E'zel.
20 And I will shoot three arrows on the side
thereof, as though I shot at a mark.
21 And, behold, I will send a lad, *saying*, Go,
find out the arrows. If I expressly say unto the
lad, Behold, the arrows *are* on this side of thee,
take them; then come thou: for *there is* peace to
thee, and no hurt; *as* the LORD liveth.
22 But if I say thus unto the young man, Behold, the arrows *are* beyond thee; go thy way:
for the LORD hath sent thee away.
23 And *as touching* the matter which thou
and I have spoken of, behold, the LORD *be* between thee and me for ever.
24 ¶ So Da'vid hid himself in the field: and
when the new moon was come, the king sat him
down to eat meat.
25 And the king sat upon his seat, as at other
times, *even* upon a seat by the wall: and Jon'a-
than arose, and Ab'ner sat by Saul's side, and
Da'vid's place was empty.
26 Nevertheless Saul spake not any thing
that day: for he thought, Something hath befall-
en him, he *is* not clean; surely he *is* not clean.
27 And it came to pass on the morrow, *which
was* the second *day* of the month, that Da'vid's
place was empty: and Saul said unto Jon'a-than
his son, Wherefore cometh not the son of Jes'se
to meat, neither yesterday, nor to day?
28 And Jon'a-than answered Saul, Da'vid
earnestly asked *leave* of me *to go* to Beth'-le-
hem:
29 And he said, Let me go, I pray thee; for
our family hath a sacrifice in the city; and my
brother, he hath commanded me *to be there*:
and now, if I have found favour in thine eyes,
let me get away, I pray thee, and see my brethren. Therefore he cometh not unto the king's
table.
30 Then Saul's anger was kindled against
Jon'a-than, and he said unto him, Thou son of
the perverse rebellious *woman*, do not I know
that thou hast chosen the son of Jes'se to thine
own confusion, and unto the confusion of thy
mother's nakedness?
31 For as long as the son of Jes'se liveth upon
the ground, thou shalt not be established, nor
thy kingdom. Wherefore now send and fetch
him unto me, for he shall surely die.
32 And Jon'a-than answered Saul his father,
and said unto him, Wherefore shall he be slain?
what hath he done?
33 And Saul cast a javelin at him to smite
him: whereby Jon'a-than knew that it was determined of his father to slay Da'vid.
34 So Jon'a-than arose from the table in
fierce anger, and did eat no meat the second
day of the month: for he was grieved for Da'vid,
because his father had done him shame.
35 ¶ And it came to pass in the morning, that
Jon'a-than went out into the field at the time
appointed with Da'vid, and a little lad with him.
36 And he said unto his lad, Run, find out
now the arrows which I shoot. *And* as the lad
ran, he shot an arrow beyond him.
37 And when the lad was come to the place
of the arrow which Jon'a-than had shot, Jon'a-
than cried after the lad, and said, *Is* not the arrow beyond thee?
38 And Jon'a-than cried after the lad, Make
speed, haste, stay not. And Jon'a-than's lad
gathered up the arrows, and came to his master.
39 But the lad knew not any thing: only Jon'-
a-than and Da'vid knew the matter.
40 And Jon'a-than gave his artillery unto his
lad, and said unto him, Go, carry *them* to the
city.
41 ¶ *And* as soon as the lad was gone, Da'vid
arose out of *a place* toward the south, and fell
on his face to the ground, and bowed himself
three times: and they kissed one another, and
wept one with another, until Da'vid exceeded.
42 And Jon'a-than said to Da'vid, Go in
peace, forasmuch as we have sworn both of us
in the name of the LORD, saying, The LORD be
between me and thee, and between my seed
and thy seed for ever. And he arose and departed: and Jon'a-than went into the city.

21 THEN came Da'vid to Nob to A-him'e-
lech the priest: and A-him'e-lech was
afraid at the meeting of Da'vid, and said unto
him, Why *art* thou alone, and no man with
thee?
2 And Da'vid said unto A-him'e-lech the
priest, The king hath commanded me a business, and hath said unto me, Let no man know
any thing of the business whereabout I send
thee, and what I have commanded thee: and I
have appointed *my* servants to such and such a
place.
3 Now therefore what is under thine hand?
give *me* five *loaves of* bread in mine hand, or
what there is present.
4 And the priest answered Da'vid, and said,
There is no common bread under mine hand,
but there is hallowed bread; if the young men
have kept themselves at least from women.
5 And Da'vid answered the priest, and said
unto him, Of a truth women *have been* kept
from us about these three days, since I came
out, and the vessels of the young men are holy,
and *the bread is* in a manner common, yea,
though it were sanctified this day in the vessel.
6 So the priest gave him hallowed *bread*: for
there was no bread there but the shewbread,
that was taken from before the LORD, to put hot
bread in the day when it was taken away.
7 Now a certain man of the servants of Saul
was there that day, detained before the LORD;
and his name *was* Do'eg, an E'dom-ite, the
chiefest of the herdmen that *belonged* to Saul.
8 ¶ And Da'vid said unto A-him'e-lech, And

is there not here under thine hand spear or sword? for I have neither brought my sword nor my weapons with me, because the king's business required haste.

9 And the priest said, The sword of Go-li'ath the Phi-lis'tine, whom thou slewest in the valley of E'lah, behold, it *is here* wrapped in a cloth behind the ephod: if thou wilt take that, take *it*: for *there is* no other save that here. And Da'vid said, *There is* none like that; give it me.

10 ¶ And Da'vid arose, and fled that day for fear of Saul, and went to A'chish the king of Gath.

11 And the servants of A'chish said unto him, *Is* not this Da'vid the king of the land? did they not sing one to another of him in dances, saying, Saul hath slain his thousands, and Da'vid his ten thousands?

12 And Da'vid laid up these words in his heart, and was sore afraid of A'chish the king of Gath.

13 And he changed his behaviour before them, and feigned himself mad in their hands, and scrabbled on the doors of the gate, and let his spittle fall down upon his beard.

14 Then said A'chish unto his servants, Lo, ye see the man is mad: wherefore *then* have ye brought him to me?

15 Have I need of mad men, that ye have brought this *fellow* to play the mad man in my presence? shall this *fellow* come into my house?

22 DA'VID therefore departed thence, and escaped to the cave A-dul'lam: and when his brethren and all his father's house heard *it*, they went down thither to him.

2 And every one *that was* in distress, and every one that *was* in debt, and every one *that was* discontented, gathered themselves unto him; and he became a captain over them: and there were with him about four hundred men.

3 ¶ And Da'vid went thence to Miz'peh of Mo'ab: and he said unto the king of Mo'ab, Let my father and my mother, I pray thee, come forth, *and be* with you, till I know what God will do for me.

4 And he brought them before the king of Mo'ab: and they dwelt with him all the while that Da'vid was in the hold.

5 ¶ And the prophet Gad said unto Da'vid, Abide not in the hold; depart, and get thee into the land of Ju'dah. Then Da'vid departed, and came into the forest of Ha'reth.

6 ¶ When Saul heard that Da'vid was discovered, and the men that *were* with him, (now Saul abode in Gib'e-ah under a tree in Ra'mah, having his spear in his hand, and all his servants *were* standing about him;)

7 Then Saul said unto his servants that stood about him, Hear now, ye Ben'ja-mites; will the son of Jes'se give every one of you fields and vineyards, *and* make you all captains of thousands, and captains of hundreds;

8 That all of you have conspired against me, and *there is* none that sheweth me that my son hath made a league with the son of Jes'se, and *there is* none of you that is sorry for me, or sheweth unto me that my son hath stirred up my servant against me, to lie in wait, as at this day?

9 ¶ Then answered Do'eg the E'dom-ite, which was set over the servants of Saul, and said, I saw the son of Jes'se coming to Nob, to A-him'e-lech the son of A-hi'tub.

10 And he enquired of the LORD for him, and gave him victuals, and gave him the sword of Go-li'ath the Phi-lis'tine.

11 Then the king sent to call A-him'e-lech the priest, the son of A-hi'tub, and all his father's house, the priests that *were* in Nob: and they came all of them to the king.

12 And Saul said, Hear now, thou son of A-hi'tub. And he answered, Here I *am*, my lord.

13 And Saul said unto him, Why have ye conspired against me, thou and the son of Jes'se, in that thou hast given him bread, and a sword, and hast enquired of God for him, that he should rise against me, to lie in wait, as at this day?

14 Then A-him'e-lech answered the king, and said, And who *is so* faithful among all thy servants as Da'vid, which is the king's son in law, and goeth at thy bidding, and is honourable in thine house?

15 Did I then begin to enquire of God for him? be it far from me: let not the king impute *any* thing unto his servant, *nor* to all the house of my father: for thy servant knew nothing of all this, less or more.

16 And the king said, Thou shalt surely die, A-him'e-lech, thou, and all thy father's house.

17 ¶ And the king said unto the footmen that stood about him, Turn, and slay the priests of the LORD; because their hand also *is* with Da'vid, and because they knew when he fled, and did not shew it to me. But the servants of the king would not put forth their hand to fall upon the priests of the LORD.

18 And the king said to Do'eg, Turn thou, and fall upon the priests. And Do'eg the E'dom-ite turned, and he fell upon the priests, and slew on that day fourscore and five persons that did wear a linen ephod.

19 And Nob, the city of the priests, smote he with the edge of the sword, both men and women, children and sucklings, and oxen, and asses, and sheep, with the edge of the sword.

20 ¶ And one of the sons of A-him'e-lech the son of A-hi'tub, named A-bi'a-thar, escaped, and fled after Da'vid.

21 And A-bi'a-thar shewed Da'vid that Saul had slain the LORD's priests.

22 And Da'vid said unto A-bi'a-thar, I knew *it* that day, when Do'eg the E'dom-ite *was* there, that he would surely tell Saul: I have occasioned *the death* of all the persons of thy father's house.

23 Abide thou with me, fear not: for he that seeketh my life seeketh thy life: but with me thou *shalt be* in safeguard.

23 THEN they told Da'vid, saying, Behold, the Phi-lis'tines fight against Kei'lah, and they rob the threshingfloors.

2 Therefore Da'vid enquired of the LORD, saying, Shall I go and smite these Phi-lis'tines? And the LORD said unto Da'vid, Go, and smite the Phi-lis'tines, and save Kei'lah.

3 And Da'vid's men said unto him, Behold, we be afraid here in Ju'dah: how much more then if we come to Kei'lah against the armies of the Phi-lis'tines?

4 Then Da'vid enquired of the LORD yet again. And the LORD answered him and said, Arise, go down to Kei'lah; for I will deliver the Phi-lis'tines into thine hand.

5 So Da'vid and his men went to Kei'lah, and fought with the Phi-lis'tines, and brought away their cattle, and smote them with a great slaughter. So Da'vid saved the inhabitants of Kei'lah.

6 And it came to pass, when A-bi'a-thar the son of A-him'e-lech fled to Da'vid to Kei'lah, *that* he came down *with* an ephod in his hand.

7 ¶ And it was told Saul that Da'vid was come to Kei'lah. And Saul said, God hath delivered him into mine hand; for he is shut in, by entering into a town that hath gates and bars.

8 And Saul called all the people together to war, to go down to Kei'lah, to besiege Da'vid and his men.

9 ¶ And Da'vid knew that Saul secretly practised mischief against him; and he said to A-bi'a-thar the priest, Bring hither the ephod.

10 Then said Da'vid, O LORD God of Is'ra-el, thy servant hath certainly heard that Saul seeketh to come to Kei'lah, to destroy the city for my sake.

11 Will the men of Kei'lah deliver me up into his hand? will Saul come down, as thy servant hath heard? O LORD God of Is'ra-el, I beseech thee, tell thy servant. And the LORD said, He will come down.

12 Then said Da'vid, Will the men of Kei'lah deliver me and my men into the hand of Saul? And the LORD said, They will deliver *thee* up.

13 ¶ Then Da'vid and his men, *which were* about six hundred, arose and departed out of Kei'lah, and went whithersoever they could go. And it was told Saul that Da'vid was escaped from Kei'lah; and he forbare to go forth.

14 And Da'vid abode in the wilderness in strong holds, and remained in a mountain in the wilderness of Ziph. And Saul sought him every day, but God delivered him not into his hand.

15 And Da'vid saw that Saul was come out to seek his life: and Da'vid *was* in the wilderness of Ziph in a wood.

16 ¶ And Jon'a-than Saul's son arose, and went to Da'vid into the wood, and strengthened his hand in God.

17 And he said unto him, Fear not: for the hand of Saul my father shall not find thee; and thou shalt be king over Is'ra-el, and I shall be next unto thee; and that also Saul my father knoweth.

18 And they two made a covenant before the LORD: and Da'vid abode in the wood, and Jon'a-than went to his house.

19 ¶ Then came up the Ziph'ites to Saul to Gib'e-ah, saying, Doth not Da'vid hide himself with us in strong holds in the wood, in the hill of Hach'i-lah, which *is* on the south of Jesh'i-mon?

20 Now therefore, O king, come down according to all the desire of thy soul to come down; and our part *shall be* to deliver him into the king's hand.

21 And Saul said, Blessed *be* ye of the LORD; for ye have compassion on me.

22 Go, I pray you, prepare yet, and know and see his place where his haunt is, *and* who hath seen him there: for it is told me *that* he dealeth very subtilly.

23 See therefore, and take knowledge of all the lurking places where he hideth himself, and come ye again to me with the certainty, and I will go with you: and it shall come to pass, if he be in the land, that I will search him out throughout all the thousands of Ju'dah.

24 And they arose, and went to Ziph before Saul: but Da'vid and his men *were* in the wilderness of Ma'on, in the plain on the south of Jesh'i-mon.

25 Saul also and his men went to seek *him*. And they told Da'vid: wherefore he came down into a rock, and abode in the wilderness of Ma'on. And when Saul heard *that*, he pursued after Da'vid in the wilderness of Ma'on.

26 And Saul went on this side of the mountain, and Da'vid and his men on that side of the mountain: and Da'vid made haste to get away for fear of Saul; for Saul and his men compassed Da'vid and his men round about to take them.

27 ¶ But there came a messenger unto Saul, saying, Haste thee, and come; for the Phi-lis'tines have invaded the land.

28 Wherefore Saul returned from pursuing after Da'vid, and went against the Phi-lis'tines: therefore they called that place Se'la-ham-mah-le'koth.

29 ¶ And Da'vid went up from thence, and dwelt in strong holds at En-ge'di.

24 AND it came to pass, when Saul was returned from following the Phi-lis'tines, that it was told him, saying, Behold, Da'vid *is* in the wilderness of En-ge'di.

2 Then Saul took three thousand chosen men out of all Is'ra-el, and went to seek Da'vid and his men upon the rocks of the wild goats.

3 And he came to the sheepcotes by the way, where *was* a cave; and Saul went in to cover his feet: and Da'vid and his men remained in the sides of the cave.

4 And the men of Da'vid said unto him, Behold the day of which the LORD said unto thee, Behold, I will deliver thine enemy into thine hand, that thou mayest do to him as it shall seem good unto thee. Then Da'vid arose, and cut off the skirt of Saul's robe privily.

5 And it came to pass afterward, that Da'vid's heart smote him, because he had cut off Saul's skirt.

6 And he said unto his men, The LORD forbid that I should do this thing unto my master, the LORD's anointed, to stretch forth mine hand against him, seeing he *is* the anointed of the LORD.

7 So Da'vid stayed his servants with these words, and suffered them not to rise against Saul. But Saul rose up out of the cave, and went on *his* way.

8 Da'vid also arose afterward, and went out of the cave, and cried after Saul, saying, My lord the king. And when Saul looked behind him, Da'vid stooped with his face to the earth, and bowed himself.

9 ¶ And Da'vid said to Saul, Wherefore hearest thou men's words, saying, Behold, Da'vid seeketh thy hurt?

10 Behold, this day thine eyes have seen how that the LORD had delivered thee to day into mine hand in the cave: and *some* bade *me* kill thee: but *mine eye* spared thee; and I said, I will not put forth mine hand against my lord; for he *is* the LORD's anointed.

11 Moreover, my father, see, yea, see the skirt of thy robe in my hand: for in that I cut off the skirt of thy robe, and killed thee not, know thou and see that *there is* neither evil nor transgression in mine hand, and I have not sinned against thee; yet thou huntest my soul to take it.

12 The LORD judge between me and thee, and the LORD avenge me of thee: but mine hand shall not be upon thee.

13 As saith the proverb of the ancients, Wickedness proceedeth from the wicked: but mine hand shall not be upon thee.

14 After whom is the king of Is'ra-el come out? after whom dost thou pursue? after a dead dog, after a flea.

15 The LORD therefore be judge, and judge between me and thee, and see, and plead my cause, and deliver me out of thine hand.

16 ¶ And it came to pass, when Da'vid had made an end of speaking these words unto Saul, that Saul said, *Is* this thy voice, my son

Da′vid? And Saul lifted up his voice, and wept.
17 And he said to Da′vid, Thou *art* more
righteous than I: for thou hast rewarded me
good, whereas I have rewarded thee evil.
18 And thou hast shewed this day how that
thou hast dealt well with me: forasmuch as
when the LORD had delivered me into thine
hand, thou killedst me not.
19 For if a man find his enemy, will he let
him go well away? wherefore the LORD reward
thee good for that thou hast done unto me this
day.
20 And now, behold, I know well that thou
shalt surely be king, and that the kingdom of
Is′ra-el shall be established in thine hand.
21 Swear now therefore unto me by the
LORD, that thou wilt not cut off my seed after
me, and that thou wilt not destroy my name out
of my father's house.
22 And Da′vid sware unto Saul. And Saul
went home; but Da′vid and his men gat them up
unto the hold.

25 AND Sam′u-el died; and all the Is′ra-el-
ites were gathered together, and lamented him, and buried him in his house at Ra′-
mah. And Da′vid arose, and went down to the
wilderness of Pa′ran.
2 And *there was* a man in Ma′on, whose possessions *were* in Car′mel; and the man *was* very
great, and he had three thousand sheep, and a
thousand goats: and he was shearing his sheep
in Car′mel.
3 Now the name of the man *was* Na′bal; and
the name of his wife Ab′i-gail: and *she was* a
woman of good understanding, and of a beautiful countenance: but the man *was* churlish and
evil in his doings; and he *was* of the house of
Ca′leb.
4 ¶ And Da′vid heard in the wilderness that
Na′bal did shear his sheep.
5 And Da′vid sent out ten young men, and
Da′vid said unto the young men, Get you up to
Car′mel, and go to Na′bal, and greet him in my
name:
6 And thus shall ye say to him that liveth *in
prosperity,* Peace *be* both to thee, and peace *be*
to thine house, and peace *be* unto all that thou
hast.
7 And now I have heard that thou hast shearers: now thy shepherds which were with us, we
hurt them not, neither was there ought missing
unto them, all the while they were in Car′mel.
8 Ask thy young men, and they will shew
thee. Wherefore let the young men find favour
in thine eyes: for we come in a good day: give, I
pray thee, whatsoever cometh to thine hand
unto thy servants, and to thy son Da′vid.
9 And when Da′vid's young men came, they
spake to Na′bal according to all those words in
the name of Da′vid, and ceased.
10 ¶ And Na′bal answered Da′vid's servants,
and said, Who *is* Da′vid? and who *is* the son of
Jes′se? there be many servants now a days that
break away every man from his master.
11 Shall I then take my bread, and my water,
and my flesh that I have killed for my shearers,
and give *it* unto men, whom I know not whence
they *be?*
12 So Da′vid's young men turned their way,
and went again, and came and told him all
those sayings.
13 And Da′vid said unto his men, Gird ye on
every man his sword. And they girded on every
man his sword; and Da′vid also girded on his
sword: and there went up after Da′vid about
four hundred men; and two hundred abode by
the stuff.
14 ¶ But one of the young men told Ab′i-gail,
Na′bal's wife, saying, Behold, Da′vid sent messengers out of the wilderness to salute our master; and he railed on them.
15 But the men *were* very good unto us, and
we were not hurt, neither missed we any thing,
as long as we were conversant with them, when
we were in the fields:
16 They were a wall unto us both by night
and day, all the while we were with them keeping the sheep.
17 Now therefore know and consider what
thou wilt do; for evil is determined against our
master, and against all his household: for he *is
such* a son of Be′li-al, that *a man* cannot speak
to him.
18 ¶ Then Ab′i-gail made haste, and took
two hundred loaves, and two bottles of wine,
and five sheep ready dressed, and five measures
of parched *corn,* and an hundred clusters of raisins, and two hundred cakes of figs, and laid
them on asses.
19 And she said unto her servants, Go on before me; behold, I come after you. But she told
not her husband Na′bal.
20 And it was *so, as* she rode on the ass, that
she came down by the covert of the hill, and,
behold, Da′vid and his men came down against
her; and she met them.
21 Now Da′vid had said, Surely in vain have I
kept all that this *fellow* hath in the wilderness,
so that nothing was missed of all that *pertained*
unto him: and he hath requited me evil for
good.
22 So and more also do God unto the enemies of Da′vid, if I leave of all that *pertain* to
him by the morning light any that pisseth
against the wall.
23 And when Ab′i-gail saw Da′vid, she
hasted, and lighted off the ass, and fell before
Da′vid on her face, and bowed herself to the
ground,
24 And fell at his feet, and said, Upon me, my
lord, *upon* me *let this* iniquity *be:* and let thine
handmaid, I pray thee, speak in thine audience,
and hear the words of thine handmaid.
25 Let not my lord, I pray thee, regard this
man of Be′li-al, *even* Na′bal: for as his name *is,*
so *is* he; Na′bal *is* his name, and folly *is* with
him: but I thine handmaid saw not the young
men of my lord, whom thou didst send.
26 Now therefore, my lord, *as* the LORD liveth, and *as* thy soul liveth, seeing the LORD hath
withholden thee from coming to *shed* blood,
and from avenging thyself with thine own hand,
now let thine enemies, and they that seek evil to
my lord, be as Na′bal.
27 And now this blessing which thine handmaid hath brought unto my lord, let it even be
given unto the young men that follow my lord.
28 I pray thee, forgive the trespass of thine
handmaid: for the LORD will certainly make my
lord a sure house; because my lord fighteth the
battles of the LORD, and evil hath not been
found in thee *all* thy days.
29 Yet a man is risen to pursue thee, and to
seek thy soul: but the soul of my lord shall be
bound in the bundle of life with the LORD thy
God; and the souls of thine enemies, them shall
he sling out, *as out* of the middle of a sling.
30 And it shall come to pass, when the LORD
shall have done to my lord according to all the
good that he hath spoken concerning thee, and
shall have appointed thee ruler over Is′ra-el;
31 That this shall be no grief unto thee, nor

offence of heart unto my lord, either that thou
hast shed blood causeless, or that my lord hath
avenged himself: but when the LORD shall have
dealt well with my lord, then remember thine
handmaid.
32 ¶ And Da'vid said to Ab'i-gail, Blessed *be*
the LORD God of Is'ra-el, which sent thee this
day to meet me:
33 And blessed *be* thy advice, and blessed *be*
thou, which hast kept me this day from coming
to *shed* blood, and from avenging myself with
mine own hand.
34 For in very deed, *as* the LORD God of Is'ra-
el liveth, which hath kept me back from hurting
thee, except thou hadst hasted and come to
meet me, surely there had not been left unto
Na'bal by the morning light any that pisseth
against the wall.
35 So Da'vid received of her hand *that* which
she had brought him, and said unto her, Go up
in peace to thine house; see, I have hearkened
to thy voice, and have accepted thy person.
36 ¶ And Ab'i-gail came to Na'bal; and, behold, he held a feast in his house, like the feast
of a king; and Na'bal's heart *was* merry within
him, for he *was* very drunken: wherefore she
told him nothing, less or more, until the morning light.
37 But it came to pass in the morning, when
the wine was gone out of Na'bal, and his wife
had told him these things, that his heart died
within him, and he became *as* a stone.
38 And it came to pass about ten days *after*,
that the LORD smote Na'bal, that he died.
39 ¶ And when Da'vid heard that Na'bal was
dead, he said, Blessed *be* the LORD, that hath
pleaded the cause of my reproach from the
hand of Na'bal, and hath kept his servant from
evil: for the LORD hath returned the wickedness
of Na'bal upon his own head. And Da'vid sent
and communed with Ab'i-gail, to take her to
him to wife.
40 And when the servants of Da'vid were
come to Ab'i-gail to Car'mel, they spake unto
her, saying, Da'vid sent us unto thee, to take
thee to him to wife.
41 And she arose, and bowed herself on *her*
face to the earth, and said, Behold, *let* thine
handmaid *be* a servant to wash the feet of the
servants of my lord.
42 And Ab'i-gail hasted, and arose, and rode
upon an ass, with five damsels of hers that went
after her; and she went after the messengers of
Da'vid, and became his wife.
43 Da'vid also took A-hin'o-am of Jez're-el;
and they were also both of them his wives.
44 ¶ But Saul had given Mi'chal his daughter, Da'vid's wife, to Phal'ti the son of La'ish,
which *was* of Gal'lim.

26 AND the Ziph'ites came unto Saul to
Gib'e-ah, saying, Doth not Da'vid hide
himself in the hill of Hach'i-lah, *which is* before
Jesh'i-mon?
2 Then Saul arose, and went down to the wilderness of Ziph, having three thousand chosen
men of Is'ra-el with him, to seek Da'vid in the
wilderness of Ziph.
3 And Saul pitched in the hill of Hach'i-lah,
which *is* before Jesh'i-mon, by the way. But
Da'vid abode in the wilderness, and he saw that
Saul came after him into the wilderness.
4 Da'vid therefore sent out spies, and understood that Saul was come in very deed.
5 ¶ And Da'vid arose, and came to the place
where Saul had pitched: and Da'vid beheld the
place where Saul lay, and Ab'ner the son of
Ner, the captain of his host: and Saul lay in the
trench, and the people pitched round about
him.
6 Then answered Da'vid and said to A-him'e-
lech the Hit'tite, and to A-bish'a-i the son of
Zer-u-i'ah, brother to Jo'ab, saying, Who will go
down with me to Saul to the camp? And A-
bish'a-i said, I will go down with thee.
7 So Da'vid and A-bish'a-i came to the people by night: and, behold, Saul lay sleeping
within the trench, and his spear stuck in the
ground at his bolster: but Ab'ner and the people
lay round about him.
8 Then said A-bish'a-i to Da'vid, God hath
delivered thine enemy into thine hand this day:
now therefore let me smite him, I pray thee,
with the spear even to the earth at once, and I
will not *smite* him the second time.
9 And Da'vid said to A-bish'a-i, Destroy him
not: for who can stretch forth his hand against
the LORD's anointed, and be guiltless?
10 Da'vid said furthermore, *As* the LORD liveth, the LORD shall smite him; or his day shall
come to die; or he shall descend into battle, and
perish.
11 The LORD forbid that I should stretch
forth mine hand against the LORD's anointed:
but, I pray thee, take thou now the spear that *is*
at his bolster, and the cruse of water, and let us
go.
12 So Da'vid took the spear and the cruse of
water from Saul's bolster; and they gat them
away, and no man saw *it*, nor knew *it*, neither
awaked: for they *were* all asleep; because a
deep sleep from the LORD was fallen upon them.
13 ¶ Then Da'vid went over to the other side,
and stood on the top of an hill afar off; a great
space *being* between them:
14 And Da'vid cried to the people, and to
Ab'ner the son of Ner, saying, Answerest thou
not, Ab'ner? Then Ab'ner answered and said,
Who *art* thou *that* criest to the king?
15 And Da'vid said to Ab'ner, *Art* not thou a
valiant man? and who *is* like to thee in Is'ra-el?
wherefore then hast thou not kept thy lord the
king? for there came one of the people in to destroy the king thy lord.
16 This thing *is* not good that thou hast done.
As the LORD liveth, ye *are* worthy to die, because ye have not kept your master, the LORD's
anointed. And now see where the king's spear
is, and the cruse of water that *was* at his bolster.
17 And Saul knew Da'vid's voice, and said, *Is*
this thy voice, my son Da'vid? And Da'vid said,
It is my voice, my lord, O king.
18 And he said, Wherefore doth my lord thus
pursue after his servant? for what have I done?
or what evil *is* in mine hand?
19 Now therefore, I pray thee, let my lord the
king hear the words of his servant. If the LORD
have stirred thee up against me, let him accept
an offering; but if *they be* the children of men,
cursed *be* they before the LORD; for they have
driven me out this day from abiding in the inheritance of the LORD, saying, Go, serve other
gods.
20 Now therefore, let not my blood fall to the
earth before the face of the LORD: for the king
of Is'ra-el is come out to seek a flea, as when
one doth hunt a partridge in the mountains.
21 ¶ Then said Saul, I have sinned: return,
my son Da'vid: for I will no more do thee harm,
because my soul was precious in thine eyes this
day: behold, I have played the fool, and have
erred exceedingly.
22 And Da'vid answered and said, Behold the

king's spear! and let one of the young men come over and fetch it.

23 The LORD render to every man his righteousness and his faithfulness: for the LORD delivered thee into *my* hand to day, but I would not stretch forth mine hand against the LORD's anointed.

24 And, behold, as thy life was much set by this day in mine eyes, so let my life be much set by in the eyes of the LORD, and let him deliver me out of all tribulation.

25 Then Saul said to Da′vid, Blessed *be* thou, my son Da′vid: thou shalt both do great *things*, and also shalt still prevail. So Da′vid went on his way, and Saul returned to his place.

27 AND Da′vid said in his heart, I shall now perish one day by the hand of Saul: *there is* nothing better for me than that I should speedily escape into the land of the Phi-lis′tines; and Saul shall despair of me, to seek me any more in any coast of Is′ra-el: so shall I escape out of his hand.

2 And Da′vid arose, and he passed over with the six hundred men that *were* with him unto A′chish, the son of Ma′och, king of Gath.

3 And Da′vid dwelt with A′chish at Gath, he and his men, every man with his household, *even* Da′vid with his two wives, A-hin′o-am the Jez′re-el-it-ess, and Ab′i-gail the Car′mel-it-ess, Na′bal's wife.

4 And it was told Saul that Da′vid was fled to Gath: and he sought no more again for him.

5 ¶ And Da′vid said unto A′chish, If I have now found grace in thine eyes, let them give me a place in some town in the country, that I may dwell there: for why should thy servant dwell in the royal city with thee?

6 Then A′chish gave him Zik′lag that day: wherefore Zik′lag pertaineth unto the kings of Ju′dah unto this day.

7 And the time that Da′vid dwelt in the country of the Phi-lis′tines was a full year and four months.

8 ¶ And Da′vid and his men went up, and invaded the Gesh′u-rites, and the Gez′rites, and the Am′a-lek-ites: for those *nations were* of old the inhabitants of the land, as thou goest to Shur, even unto the land of E′gypt.

9 And Da′vid smote the land, and left neither man nor woman alive, and took away the sheep, and the oxen, and the asses, and the camels, and the apparel, and returned, and came to A′chish.

10 And A′chish said, Whither have ye made a road to day? And Da′vid said, Against the south of Ju′dah, and against the south of the Je-rah′me-el-ites, and against the south of the Ken′ites.

11 And Da′vid saved neither man nor woman alive, to bring *tidings* to Gath, saying, Lest they should tell on us, saying, So did Da′vid, and so *will be* his manner all the while he dwelleth in the country of the Phi-lis′tines.

12 And A′chish believed Da′vid, saying, He hath made his people Is′ra-el utterly to abhor him; therefore he shall be my servant for ever.

28 AND it came to pass in those days, that the Phi-lis′tines gathered their armies together for warfare, to fight with Is′ra-el. And A′chish said unto Da′vid, Know thou assuredly, that thou shalt go out with me to battle, thou and thy men.

2 And Da′vid said to A′chish, Surely thou shalt know what thy servant can do. And A′chish said to Da′vid, Therefore will I make thee keeper of mine head for ever.

3 ¶ Now Sam′u-el was dead, and all Is′ra-el had lamented him, and buried him in Ra′mah, even in his own city. And Saul had put away those that had familiar spirits, and the wizards, out of the land.

4 And the Phi-lis′tines gathered themselves together, and came and pitched in Shu′nem: and Saul gathered all Is′ra-el together, and they pitched in Gil-bo′a.

5 And when Saul saw the host of the Phi-lis′tines, he was afraid, and his heart greatly trembled.

6 And when Saul enquired of the LORD, the LORD answered him not, neither by dreams, nor by U′rim, nor by prophets.

7 ¶ Then said Saul unto his servants, Seek me a woman that hath a familiar spirit, that I may go to her, and enquire of her. And his servants said to him, Behold, *there is* a woman that hath a familiar spirit at En′-dor.

8 And Saul disguised himself, and put on other raiment, and he went, and two men with him, and they came to the woman by night: and he said, I pray thee, divine unto me by the familiar spirit, and bring me *him* up, whom I shall name unto thee.

9 And the woman said unto him, Behold, thou knowest what Saul hath done, how he hath cut off those that have familiar spirits, and the wizards, out of the land: wherefore then layest thou a snare for my life, to cause me to die?

10 And Saul sware to her by the LORD, saying, *As* the LORD liveth, there shall no punishment happen to thee for this thing.

11 Then said the woman, Whom shall I bring up unto thee? And he said, Bring me up Sam′u-el.

12 And when the woman saw Sam′u-el, she cried with a loud voice: and the woman spake to Saul, saying, Why hast thou deceived me? for thou *art* Saul.

13 And the king said unto her, Be not afraid: for what sawest thou? And the woman said unto Saul, I saw gods ascending out of the earth.

14 And he said unto her, What form *is* he of? And she said, An old man cometh up; and he *is* covered with a mantle. And Saul perceived that it *was* Sam′u-el, and he stooped with *his* face to the ground, and bowed himself.

15 ¶ And Sam′u-el said to Saul, Why hast thou disquieted me, to bring me up? And Saul answered, I am sore distressed; for the Phi-lis′tines make war against me, and God is departed from me, and answereth me no more, neither by prophets, nor by dreams: therefore I have called thee, that thou mayest make known unto me what I shall do.

16 Then said Sam′u-el, Wherefore then dost thou ask of me, seeing the LORD is departed from thee, and is become thine enemy?

17 And the LORD hath done to him, as he spake by me: for the LORD hath rent the kingdom out of thine hand, and given it to thy neighbour, *even* to Da′vid:

18 Because thou obeyedst not the voice of the LORD, nor executedst his fierce wrath upon Am′a-lek, therefore hath the LORD done this thing unto thee this day.

19 Moreover the LORD will also deliver Is′ra-el with thee into the hand of the Phi-lis′tines: and to morrow *shalt* thou and thy sons *be* with me: the LORD also shall deliver the host of Is′ra-el into the hand of the Phi-lis′tines.

20 Then Saul fell straightway all along on the

earth, and was sore afraid, because of the words of Sam'u-el: and there was no strength in him; for he had eaten no bread all the day, nor all the night.

21 ¶ And the woman came unto Saul, and saw that he was sore troubled, and said unto him, Behold, thine handmaid hath obeyed thy voice, and I have put my life in my hand, and have hearkened unto thy words which thou spakest unto me.

22 Now therefore, I pray thee, hearken thou also unto the voice of thine handmaid, and let me set a morsel of bread before thee; and eat, that thou mayest have strength, when thou goest on thy way.

23 But he refused, and said, I will not eat. But his servants, together with the woman, compelled him; and he hearkened unto their voice. So he arose from the earth, and sat upon the bed.

24 And the woman had a fat calf in the house; and she hasted, and killed it, and took flour, and kneaded *it*, and did bake unleavened bread thereof:

25 And she brought *it* before Saul, and before his servants; and they did eat. Then they rose up, and went away that night.

29 NOW the Phi-lis'tines gathered together all their armies to A'phek: and the Is'ra-el-ites pitched by a fountain which *is* in Jez're-el.

2 And the lords of the Phi-lis'tines passed on by hundreds, and by thousands: but Da'vid and his men passed on in the rereward with A'chish.

3 Then said the princes of the Phi-lis'tines, What *do* these He'brews *here?* And A'chish said unto the princes of the Phi-lis'tines, *Is* not this Da'vid, the servant of Saul the king of Is'ra-el, which hath been with me these days, or these years, and I have found no fault in him since he fell *unto me* unto this day?

4 And the princes of the Phi-lis'tines were wroth with him; and the princes of the Phi-lis'tines said unto him, Make this fellow return, that he may go again to his place which thou hast appointed him, and let him not go down with us to battle, lest in the battle he be an adversary to us: for wherewith should he reconcile himself unto his master? *should it* not *be* with the heads of these men?

5 *Is* not this Da'vid, of whom they sang one to another in dances, saying, Saul slew his thousands, and Da'vid his ten thousands?

6 ¶ Then A'chish called Da'vid, and said unto him, Surely, *as* the LORD liveth, thou hast been upright, and thy going out and thy coming in with me in the host *is* good in my sight: for I have not found evil in thee since the day of thy coming unto me unto this day: nevertheless the lords favour thee not.

7 Wherefore now return, and go in peace, that thou displease not the lords of the Phi-lis'tines.

8 ¶ And Da'vid said unto A'chish, But what have I done? and what hast thou found in thy servant so long as I have been with thee unto this day, that I may not go fight against the enemies of my lord the king?

9 And A'chish answered and said to Da'vid, I know that thou *art* good in my sight, as an angel of God: notwithstanding the princes of the Phi-lis'tines have said, He shall not go up with us to the battle.

10 Wherefore now rise up early in the morning with thy master's servants that are come with thee: and as soon as ye be up early in the morning, and have light, depart.

11 So Da'vid and his men rose up early to depart in the morning, to return into the land of the Phi-lis'tines. And the Phi-lis'tines went up to Jez're-el.

30 AND it came to pass, when Da'vid and his men were come to Zik'lag on the third day, that the Am'a-lek-ites had invaded the south, and Zik'lag, and smitten Zik'lag, and burned it with fire;

2 And had taken the women captives, that *were* therein: they slew not any, either great or small, but carried *them* away, and went on their way.

3 ¶ So Da'vid and his men came to the city, and, behold, *it was* burned with fire; and their wives, and their sons, and their daughters, were taken captives.

4 Then Da'vid and the people that *were* with him lifted up their voice and wept, until they had no more power to weep.

5 And Da'vid's two wives were taken captives, A-hin'o-am the Jez're-el-it-ess, and Ab'i-gail the wife of Na'bal the Car'mel-ite.

6 And Da'vid was greatly distressed; for the people spake of stoning him, because the soul of all the people was grieved, every man for his sons and for his daughters: but Da'vid encouraged himself in the LORD his God.

7 And Da'vid said to A-bi'a-thar the priest, A-him'e-lech's son, I pray thee, bring me hither the ephod. And A-bi'a-thar brought thither the ephod to Da'vid.

8 And Da'vid enquired at the LORD, saying, Shall I pursue after this troop? shall I overtake them? And he answered him, Pursue: for thou shalt surely overtake *them*, and without fail recover *all*.

9 So Da'vid went, he and the six hundred men that *were* with him, and came to the brook Be'sor, where those that were left behind stayed.

10 But Da'vid pursued, he and four hundred men: for two hundred abode behind, which were so faint that they could not go over the brook Be'sor.

11 ¶ And they found an E-gyp'tian in the field, and brought him to Da'vid, and gave him bread, and he did eat; and they made him drink water;

12 And they gave him a piece of a cake of figs, and two clusters of raisins: and when he had eaten, his spirit came again to him: for he had eaten no bread, nor drunk *any* water, three days and three nights.

13 And Da'vid said unto him, To whom *belongest* thou? and whence *art* thou? And he said, I *am* a young man of E'gypt, servant to an Am'a-lek-ite; and my master left me, because three days agone I fell sick.

14 We made an invasion *upon* the south of the Cher'eth-ites, and upon *the coast* which *belongeth* to Ju'dah, and upon the south of Ca'leb; and we burned Zik'lag with fire.

15 And Da'vid said to him, Canst thou bring me down to this company? And he said, Swear unto me by God, that thou wilt neither kill me, nor deliver me into the hands of my master, and I will bring thee down to this company.

16 ¶ And when he had brought him down, behold, *they were* spread abroad upon all the earth, eating and drinking, and dancing, because of all the great spoil that they had taken out of the land of the Phi-lis'tines, and out of the land of Ju'dah.

17 And Da'vid smote them from the twilight
even unto the evening of the next day: and
there escaped not a man of them, save four
hundred young men, which rode upon camels,
and fled.
18 And Da'vid recovered all that the Am'a-
lek-ites had carried away: and Da'vid rescued
his two wives.
19 And there was nothing lacking to them,
neither small nor great, neither sons nor daughters, neither spoil, nor any *thing* that they had
taken to them: Da'vid recovered all.
20 And Da'vid took all the flocks and the
herds, *which* they drave before those *other* cattle, and said, This *is* Da'vid's spoil.
21 ¶ And Da'vid came to the two hundred
men, which were so faint that they could not
follow Da'vid, whom they had made also to
abide at the brook Be'sor: and they went forth
to meet Da'vid, and to meet the people that
were with him: and when Da'vid came near to
the people, he saluted them.
22 Then answered all the wicked men and
men of Be'li-al, of those that went with Da'vid,
and said, Because they went not with us, we
will not give them *ought* of the spoil that we
have recovered, save to every man his wife and
his children, that they may lead *them* away, and
depart.
23 Then said Da'vid, Ye shall not do so, my
brethren, with that which the LORD hath given
us, who hath preserved us, and delivered the
company that came against us into our hand.
24 For who will hearken unto you in this
matter? but as his part *is* that goeth down to the
battle, so *shall* his part *be* that tarrieth by the
stuff: they shall part alike.
25 And it was *so* from that day forward, that
he made it a statute and an ordinance for Is'ra-
el unto this day.
26 ¶ And when Da'vid came to Zik'lag, he
sent of the spoil unto the elders of Ju'dah, *even*
to his friends, saying, Behold a present for you
of the spoil of the enemies of the LORD;
27 To *them* which *were* in Beth'-el, and to
them which *were* in south Ra'moth, and to *them*
which *were* in Jat'tir,
28 And to *them* which *were* in Ar'o-er, and to
them which *were* in Siph'moth, and to *them*
which *were* in Esh-te-mo'a,
29 And to *them* which *were* in Ra'chal, and to
them which *were* in the cities of the Je-rah'me-
el-ites, and to *them* which *were* in the cities of
the Ken'ites,
30 And to *them* which *were* in Hor'mah, and
to *them* which *were* in Chor-a'shan, and to *them*
which *were* in A'thach,
31 And to *them* which *were* in He'bron, and
to all the places where Da'vid himself and his
men were wont to haunt.

31 NOW the Phi-lis'tines fought against Is'-
ra-el: and the men of Is'ra-el fled from
before the Phi-lis'tines, and fell down slain in
mount Gil-bo'a.
2 And the Phi-lis'tines followed hard upon
Saul and upon his sons; and the Phi-lis'tines
slew Jon'a-than, and A-bin'a-dab, and Mel'chi-
shu'a, Saul's sons.
3 And the battle went sore against Saul, and
the archers hit him; and he was sore wounded
of the archers.
4 Then said Saul unto his armourbearer,
Draw thy sword, and thrust me through therewith; lest these uncircumcised come and thrust
me through, and abuse me. But his armourbearer would not; for he was sore afraid. Therefore
Saul took a sword, and fell upon it.
5 And when his armourbearer saw that Saul
was dead, he fell likewise upon his sword, and
died with him.
6 So Saul died, and his three sons, and his
armourbearer, and all his men, that same day
together.
7 ¶ And when the men of Is'ra-el that *were*
on the other side of the valley, and *they* that
were on the other side Jor'dan, saw that the
men of Is'ra-el fled, and that Saul and his sons
were dead, they forsook the cities, and fled; and
the Phi-lis'tines came and dwelt in them.
8 And it came to pass on the morrow, when
the Phi-lis'tines came to strip the slain, that
they found Saul and his three sons fallen in
mount Gil-bo'a.
9 And they cut off his head, and stripped off
his armour, and sent into the land of the Phi-
lis'tines round about, to publish *it in* the house
of their idols, and among the people.
10 And they put his armour in the house of
Ash'ta-roth: and they fastened his body to the
wall of Beth'-shan.
11 ¶ And when the inhabitants of Ja'besh-
gil'e-ad heard of that which the Phi-lis'tines had
done to Saul;
12 All the valiant men arose, and went all
night, and took the body of Saul and the bodies
of his sons from the wall of Beth'-shan, and
came to Ja'besh, and burnt them there.
13 And they took their bones, and buried
them under a tree at Ja'besh, and fasted seven
days.

THE SECOND BOOK OF

SAMUEL

1 NOW it came to pass after the death of
Saul, when Da'vid was returned from the
slaughter of the Am'a-lek-ites, and Da'vid had
abode two days in Zik'lag;
2 It came even to pass on the third day, that,
behold, a man came out of the camp from Saul
with his clothes rent, and earth upon his head:
and *so* it was, when he came to Da'vid, that he
fell to the earth, and did obeisance.
3 And Da'vid said unto him, From whence
comest thou? And he said unto him, Out of the
camp of Is'ra-el am I escaped.
4 And Da'vid said unto him, How went the
matter? I pray thee, tell me. And he answered,
That the people are fled from the battle, and
many of the people also are fallen and dead;
and Saul and Jon'a-than his son are dead also.
5 And Da'vid said unto the young man that
told him, How knowest thou that Saul and Jon'-
a-than his son be dead?
6 And the young man that told him said, As I
happened by chance upon mount Gil-bo'a, behold, Saul leaned upon his spear; and, lo, the
chariots and horsemen followed hard after him.
7 And when he looked behind him, he saw
me, and called unto me. And I answered, Here
am I.

8 And he said unto me, Who *art* thou? And I
answered him, I *am* an Am'a-lek-ite.
9 He said unto me again, Stand, I pray thee,
upon me, and slay me: for anguish is come upon
me, because my life *is* yet whole in me.
10 So I stood upon him, and slew him, because I was sure that he could not live after that
he was fallen: and I took the crown that *was*
upon his head, and the bracelet that *was* on his
arm, and have brought them hither unto my
lord.
11 Then Da'vid took hold on his clothes, and
rent them; and likewise all the men that *were*
with him:
12 And they mourned, and wept, and fasted
until even, for Saul, and for Jon'a-than his son,
and for the people of the LORD, and for the
house of Is'ra-el; because they were fallen by
the sword.
13 ¶ And Da'vid said unto the young man
that told him, Whence *art* thou? And he answered, I *am* the son of a stranger, an Am'a-lek-
ite.
14 And Da'vid said unto him, How wast thou
not afraid to stretch forth thine hand to destroy
the LORD's anointed?
15 And Da'vid called one of the young men,
and said, Go near, *and* fall upon him. And he
smote him that he died.
16 And Da'vid said unto him, Thy blood *be*
upon thy head; for thy mouth hath testified
against thee, saying, I have slain the LORD's
anointed.
17 ¶ And Da'vid lamented with this lamentation over Saul and over Jon'a-than his son:
18 (Also he bade them teach the children of
Ju'dah *the use of* the bow: behold, *it is* written
in the book of Ja'sher.)
19 The beauty of Is'ra-el is slain upon thy
high places: how are the mighty fallen!
20 Tell *it* not in Gath, publish *it* not in the
streets of As'ke-lon; lest the daughters of the
Phi-lis'tines rejoice, lest the daughters of the
uncircumcised triumph.
21 Ye mountains of Gil-bo'a, *let there be* no
dew, neither *let there be* rain, upon you, nor
fields of offerings: for there the shield of the
mighty is vilely cast away, the shield of Saul, *as
though he had* not *been* anointed with oil.
22 From the blood of the slain, from the fat
of the mighty, the bow of Jon'a-than turned not
back, and the sword of Saul returned not empty.
23 Saul and Jon'a-than *were* lovely and
pleasant in their lives, and in their death they
were not divided: they were swifter than eagles,
they were stronger than lions.
24 Ye daughters of Is'ra-el, weep over Saul,
who clothed you in scarlet, with *other* delights,
who put on ornaments of gold upon your apparel.
25 How are the mighty fallen in the midst of
the battle! O Jon'a-than, *thou wast* slain in thine
high places.
26 I am distressed for thee, my brother Jon'a-
than: very pleasant hast thou been unto me: thy
love to me was wonderful, passing the love of
women.
27 How are the mighty fallen, and the weapons of war perished!

2 AND it came to pass after this, that Da'vid
enquired of the LORD, saying, Shall I go up
into any of the cities of Ju'dah? And the LORD
said unto him, Go up. And Da'vid said, Whither
shall I go up? And he said, Unto He'bron.
2 So Da'vid went up thither, and his two
wives also, A-hin'o-am the Jez're-el-it-ess, and
Ab'i-gail Na'bal's wife the Car'mel-ite.
3 And his men that *were* with him did Da'vid
bring up, every man with his household: and
they dwelt in the cities of He'bron.
4 And the men of Ju'dah came, and there
they anointed Da'vid king over the house of Ju'-
dah. And they told Da'vid, saying, *That* the men
of Ja'besh-gil'e-ad *were they* that buried Saul.
5 ¶ And Da'vid sent messengers unto the
men of Ja'besh-gil'e-ad, and said unto them,
Blessed *be* ye of the LORD, that ye have shewed
this kindness unto your lord, *even* unto Saul,
and have buried him.
6 And now the LORD shew kindness and
truth unto you: and I also will requite you this
kindness, because ye have done this thing.
7 Therefore now let your hands be
strengthened, and be ye valiant: for your master Saul is dead, and also the house of Ju'dah
have anointed me king over them.
8 ¶ But Ab'ner the son of Ner, captain of
Saul's host, took Ish-bo'sheth the son of Saul,
and brought him over to Ma-ha-na'im;
9 And made him king over Gil'e-ad, and over
the Ash'ur-ites, and over Jez're-el, and over E'-
phra-im, and over Ben'ja-min, and over all Is'ra-
el.
10 Ish-bo'sheth Saul's son *was* forty years
old when he began to reign over Is'ra-el, and
reigned two years. But the house of Ju'dah followed Da'vid.
11 And the time that Da'vid was king in He'-
bron over the house of Ju'dah was seven years
and six months.
12 ¶ And Ab'ner the son of Ner, and the servants of Ish-bo'sheth the son of Saul, went out
from Ma-ha-na'im to Gib'e-on.
13 And Jo'ab the son of Zer-u-i'ah, and the
servants of Da'vid, went out, and met together
by the pool of Gib'e-on: and they sat down, the
one on the one side of the pool, and the other on
the other side of the pool.
14 And Ab'ner said to Jo'ab, Let the young
men now arise, and play before us. And Jo'ab
said, Let them arise.
15 Then there arose and went over by number twelve of Ben'ja-min, which *pertained* to
Ish-bo'sheth the son of Saul, and twelve of the
servants of Da'vid.
16 And they caught every one his fellow by
the head, and *thrust* his sword in his fellow's
side; so they fell down together: wherefore that
place was called Hel'kath-haz'zu-rim, which *is*
in Gib'e-on.
17 And there was a very sore battle that day;
and Ab'ner was beaten, and the men of Is'ra-el,
before the servants of Da'vid.
18 ¶ And there were three sons of Zer-u-i'ah
there, Jo'ab, and A-bish'a-i, and A'sa-hel: and
A'sa-hel *was as* light of foot as a wild roe.
19 And A'sa-hel pursued after Ab'ner; and in
going he turned not to the right hand nor to the
left from following Ab'ner.
20 Then Ab'ner looked behind him, and said,
Art thou A'sa-hel? And he answered, I *am*.
21 And Ab'ner said to him, Turn thee aside to
thy right hand or to thy left, and lay thee hold
on one of the young men, and take thee his armour. But A'sa-hel would not turn aside from
following of him.
22 And Ab'ner said again to A'sa-hel, Turn
thee aside from following me: wherefore should
I smite thee to the ground? how then should I
hold up my face to Jo'ab thy brother?
23 Howbeit he refused to turn aside: wherefore Ab'ner with the hinder end of the spear

smote him under the fifth *rib,* that the spear
came out behind him; and he fell down there,
and died in the same place: and it came to pass,
that as many as came to the place where A'sa-
hel fell down and died stood still.
24 Jo'ab also and A-bish'a-i pursued after
Ab'ner: and the sun went down when they were
come to the hill of Am'mah, that *lieth* before
Gi'ah by the way of the wilderness of Gib'e-on.
25 ¶ And the children of Ben'ja-min gathered themselves together after Ab'ner, and became one troop, and stood on the top of an hill.
26 Then Ab'ner called to Jo'ab, and said,
Shall the sword devour for ever? knowest thou
not that it will be bitterness in the latter end?
how long shall it be then, ere thou bid the people return from following their brethren?
27 And Jo'ab said, *As* God liveth, unless thou
hadst spoken, surely then in the morning the
people had gone up every one from following
his brother.
28 So Jo'ab blew a trumpet, and all the people stood still, and pursued after Is'ra-el no
more, neither fought they any more.
29 And Ab'ner and his men walked all that
night through the plain, and passed over Jor'-
dan, and went through all Bith'ron, and they
came to Ma-ha-na'im.
30 And Jo'ab returned from following Ab'-
ner: and when he had gathered all the people
together, there lacked of Da'vid's servants nineteen men and A'sa-hel.
31 But the servants of Da'vid had smitten of
Ben'ja-min, and of Ab'ner's men, *so that* three
hundred and threescore men died.
32 ¶ And they took up A'sa-hel, and buried
him in the sepulchre of his father, which *was in*
Beth'-le-hem. And Jo'ab and his men went all
night, and they came to He'bron at break of
day.

3 NOW there was long war between the
house of Saul and the house of Da'vid: but
Da'vid waxed stronger and stronger, and the
house of Saul waxed weaker and weaker.
2 ¶ And unto Da'vid were sons born in He'-
bron: and his firstborn was Am'non, of A-hin'o-
am the Jez're-el-it-ess;
3 And his second, Chil'e-ab, of Ab'i-gail the
wife of Na'bal the Car'mel-ite; and the third,
Ab'sa-lom the son of Ma'a-cah the daughter of
Tal'mai king of Ge'shur;
4 And the fourth, Ad-o-ni'jah the son of
Hag'gith; and the fifth, Sheph-a-ti'ah the son of
Ab'i-tal;
5 And the sixth, Ith're-am, by Eg'lah Da'vid's
wife. These were born to Da'vid in He'bron.
6 ¶ And it came to pass, while there was war
between the house of Saul and the house of Da'-
vid, that Ab'ner made himself strong for the
house of Saul.
7 And Saul had a concubine, whose name
was Riz'pah, the daughter of A-i'ah: and *Ish-
bo'sheth* said to Ab'ner, Wherefore hast thou
gone in unto my father's concubine?
8 Then was Ab'ner very wroth for the words
of Ish-bo'sheth, and said, *Am* I a dog's head,
which against Ju'dah do shew kindness this day
unto the house of Saul thy father, to his brethren, and to his friends, and have not delivered
thee into the hand of Da'vid, that thou chargest
me to day with a fault concerning this woman?
9 So do God to Ab'ner, and more also, except, as the LORD hath sworn to Da'vid, even so
I do to him;
10 To translate the kingdom from the house
of Saul, and to set up the throne of Da'vid over
Is'ra-el and over Ju'dah, from Dan even to Be'-
er-she'ba.
11 And he could not answer Ab'ner a word
again, because he feared him.
12 ¶ And Ab'ner sent messengers to Da'vid
on his behalf, saying, Whose *is* the land? saying
also, Make thy league with me, and, behold, my
hand *shall be* with thee, to bring about all Is'ra-
el unto thee.
13 ¶ And he said, Well; I will make a league
with thee: but one thing I require of thee, that
is, Thou shalt not see my face, except thou first
bring Mi'chal Saul's daughter, when thou comest to see my face.
14 And Da'vid sent messengers to Ish-bo'-
sheth Saul's son, saying, Deliver *me* my wife
Mi'chal, which I espoused to me for an hundred
foreskins of the Phi-lis'tines.
15 And Ish-bo'sheth sent, and took her from
her husband, *even* from Phal'ti-el the son of La'-
ish.
16 And her husband went with her along
weeping behind her to Ba-hu'rim. Then said
Ab'ner unto him, Go, return. And he returned.
17 ¶ And Ab'ner had communication with
the elders of Is'ra-el, saying, Ye sought for Da'-
vid in times past *to be* king over you:
18 Now then do *it:* for the LORD hath spoken
of Da'vid, saying, By the hand of my servant
Da'vid I will save my people Is'ra-el out of the
hand of the Phi-lis'tines, and out of the hand of
all their enemies.
19 And Ab'ner also spake in the ears of Ben'-
ja-min: and Ab'ner went also to speak in the
ears of Da'vid in He'bron all that seemed good
to Is'ra-el, and that seemed good to the whole
house of Ben'ja-min.
20 So Ab'ner came to Da'vid to He'bron, and
twenty men with him. And Da'vid made Ab'ner
and the men that *were* with him a feast.
21 And Ab'ner said unto Da'vid, I will arise
and go, and will gather all Is'ra-el unto my lord
the king, that they may make a league with
thee, and that thou mayest reign over all that
thine heart desireth. And Da'vid sent Ab'ner
away; and he went in peace.
22 ¶ And, behold, the servants of Da'vid and
Jo'ab came from *pursuing* a troop, and brought
in a great spoil with them: but Ab'ner *was* not
with Da'vid in He'bron; for he had sent him
away, and he was gone in peace.
23 When Jo'ab and all the host that *was* with
him were come, they told Jo'ab, saying, Ab'ner
the son of Ner came to the king, and he hath
sent him away, and he is gone in peace.
24 Then Jo'ab came to the king, and said,
What hast thou done? behold, Ab'ner came
unto thee; why *is* it *that* thou hast sent him
away, and he is quite gone?
25 Thou knowest Ab'ner the son of Ner, that
he came to deceive thee, and to know thy going
out and thy coming in, and to know all that thou
doest.
26 And when Jo'ab was come out from Da'-
vid, he sent messengers after Ab'ner, which
brought him again from the well of Si'rah: but
Da'vid knew *it* not.
27 And when Ab'ner was returned to He'-
bron, Jo'ab took him aside in the gate to speak
with him quietly, and smote him there under
the fifth *rib,* that he died, for the blood of A'sa-
hel his brother.
28 ¶ And afterward when Da'vid heard *it,* he
said, I and my kingdom *are* guiltless before the
LORD for ever, from the blood of Ab'ner the son
of Ner:
29 Let it rest on the head of Jo'ab, and on all

his father's house; and let there not fail from the
house of Jo'ab one that hath an issue, or that is
a leper, or that leaneth on a staff, or that falleth
on the sword, or that lacketh bread.
30 So Jo'ab and A-bish'a-i his brother slew
Ab'ner, because he had slain their brother A'sa-
hel at Gib'e-on in the battle.
31 ¶ And Da'vid said to Jo'ab, and to all the
people that *were* with him, Rend your clothes,
and gird you with sackcloth, and mourn before
Ab'ner. And king Da'vid *himself* followed the
bier.
32 And they buried Ab'ner in He'bron: and
the king lifted up his voice, and wept at the
grave of Ab'ner; and all the people wept.
33 And the king lamented over Ab'ner, and
said, Died Ab'ner as a fool dieth?
34 Thy hands *were* not bound, nor thy feet
put into fetters: as a man falleth before wicked
men, *so* fellest thou. And all the people wept
again over him.
35 And when all the people came to cause
Da'vid to eat meat while it was yet day, Da'vid
sware, saying, So do God to me, and more also,
if I taste bread, or ought else, till the sun be
down.
36 And all the people took notice *of it*, and it
pleased them: as whatsoever the king did
pleased all the people.
37 For all the people and all Is'ra-el understood that day that it was not of the king to slay
Ab'ner the son of Ner.
38 And the king said unto his servants, Know
ye not that there is a prince and a great man
fallen this day in Is'ra-el?
39 And I *am* this day weak, though anointed
king; and these men the sons of Zer-u-i'ah *be*
too hard for me: the LORD shall reward the doer
of evil according to his wickedness.

4 AND when Saul's son heard that Ab'ner
was dead in He'bron, his hands were feeble, and all the Is'ra-el-ites were troubled.
2 And Saul's son had two men *that were* captains of bands: the name of the one *was* Ba'a-
nah, and the name of the other Re'chab, the
sons of Rim'mon a Be-e'roth-ite, of the children
of Ben'ja-min: (for Be-e'roth also was reckoned
to Ben'ja-min.
3 And the Be-e'roth-ites fled to Git'ta-im, and
were sojourners there until this day.)
4 And Jon'a-than, Saul's son, had a son *that
was* lame of *his* feet. He was five years old
when the tidings came of Saul and Jon'a-than
out of Jez're-el, and his nurse took him up, and
fled: and it came to pass, as she made haste to
flee, that he fell, and became lame. And his
name *was* Me-phib'o-sheth.
5 And the sons of Rim'mon the Be-e'roth-ite,
Re'chab and Ba'a-nah, went, and came about
the heat of the day to the house of Ish-bo'sheth,
who lay on a bed at noon.
6 And they came thither into the midst of the
house, *as though* they would have fetched
wheat; and they smote him under the fifth *rib*:
and Re'chab and Ba'a-nah his brother escaped.
7 For when they came into the house, he lay
on his bed in his bedchamber, and they smote
him, and slew him, and beheaded him, and took
his head, and gat them away through the plain
all night.
8 And they brought the head of Ish-bo'sheth
unto Da'vid to He'bron, and said to the king,
Behold the head of Ish-bo'sheth the son of Saul
thine enemy, which sought thy life; and the
LORD hath avenged my lord the king this day of
Saul, and of his seed.
9 ¶ And Da'vid answered Re'chab and Ba'a-
nah his brother, the sons of Rim'mon the Be-
e'roth-ite, and said unto them, *As* the LORD liveth, who hath redeemed my soul out of all adversity,
10 When one told me, saying, Behold, Saul is
dead, thinking to have brought good tidings, I
took hold of him, and slew him in Zik'lag, who
thought that I would have given him a reward
for his tidings:
11 How much more, when wicked men have
slain a righteous person in his own house upon
his bed? shall I not therefore now require his
blood of your hand, and take you away from the
earth?
12 And Da'vid commanded his young men,
and they slew them, and cut off their hands and
their feet, and hanged *them* up over the pool in
He'bron. But they took the head of Ish-bo'-
sheth, and buried *it* in the sepulchre of Ab'ner
in He'bron.

5 THEN came all the tribes of Is'ra-el to Da'-
vid unto He'bron, and spake, saying, Behold, we *are* thy bone and thy flesh.
2 Also in time past, when Saul was king over
us, thou wast he that leddest out and broughtest in Is'ra-el: and the LORD said to thee, Thou
shalt feed my people Is'ra-el, and thou shalt be
a captain over Is'ra-el.
3 So all the elders of Is'ra-el came to the king
to He'bron; and king Da'vid made a league with
them in He'bron before the LORD: and they
anointed Da'vid king over Is'ra-el.
4 ¶ Da'vid *was* thirty years old when he began to reign, *and* he reigned forty years.
5 In He'bron he reigned over Ju'dah seven
years and six months: and in Je-ru'sa-lem he
reigned thirty and three years over all Is'ra-el
and Ju'dah.
6 ¶ And the king and his men went to Je-
ru'sa-lem unto the Jeb'u-sites, the inhabitants
of the land: which spake unto Da'vid, saying,
Except thou take away the blind and the lame,
thou shalt not come in hither: thinking, Da'vid
cannot come in hither.
7 Nevertheless Da'vid took the strong hold of
Zi'on: the same *is* the city of Da'vid.
8 And Da'vid said on that day, Whosoever
getteth up to the gutter, and smiteth the Jeb'u-
sites, and the lame and the blind, *that are* hated
of Da'vid's soul, *he shall be chief and captain*.
Wherefore they said, The blind and the lame
shall not come into the house.
9 So Da'vid dwelt in the fort, and called it the
city of Da'vid. And Da'vid built round about
from Mil'lo and inward.
10 And Da'vid went on, and grew great, and
the LORD God of hosts *was* with him.
11 ¶ And Hi'ram king of Tyre sent messengers to Da'vid, and cedar trees, and carpenters,
and masons: and they built Da'vid an house.
12 And Da'vid perceived that the LORD had
established him king over Is'ra-el, and that he
had exalted his kingdom for his people Is'ra-el's
sake.
13 ¶ And Da'vid took *him* more concubines
and wives out of Je-ru'sa-lem, after he was
come from He'bron: and there were yet sons
and daughters born to Da'vid.
14 And these *be* the names of those that were
born unto him in Je-ru'sa-lem; Sham-mu'ah,
and Sho'bab, and Na'than, and Sol'o-mon,
15 Ib'har also, and El-i-shu'a, and Ne'pheg,
and Ja-phi'a,
16 And E-lish'a-ma, and E-li'a-da, and E-
liph'a-let.

17 ¶ But when the Phi-lis′tines heard that they had anointed Da′vid king over Is′ra-el, all the Phi-lis′tines came up to seek Da′vid; and Da′vid heard *of it,* and went down to the hold.

18 The Phi-lis′tines also came and spread themselves in the valley of Reph′a-im.

19 And Da′vid enquired of the LORD, saying, Shall I go up to the Phi-lis′tines? wilt thou deliver them into mine hand? And the LORD said unto Da′vid, Go up: for I will doubtless deliver the Phi-lis′tines into thine hand.

20 And Da′vid came to Ba′al–per′a-zim, and Da′vid smote them there, and said, The LORD hath broken forth upon mine enemies before me, as the breach of waters. Therefore he called the name of that place Ba′al–per′a-zim.

21 And there they left their images, and Da′vid and his men burned them.

22 ¶ And the Phi-lis′tines came up yet again, and spread themselves in the valley of Reph′a-im.

23 And when Da′vid enquired of the LORD, he said, Thou shalt not go up; *but* fetch a compass behind them, and come upon them over against the mulberry trees.

24 And let it be, when thou hearest the sound of a going in the tops of the mulberry trees, that then thou shalt bestir thyself: for then shall the LORD go out before thee, to smite the host of the Phi-lis′tines.

25 And Da′vid did so, as the LORD had commanded him; and smote the Phi-lis′tines from Ge′ba until thou come to Ga′zer.

6 AGAIN, Da′vid gathered together all *the* chosen *men* of Is′ra-el, thirty thousand.

2 And Da′vid arose, and went with all the people that *were* with him from Ba′a-le of Ju′dah, to bring up from thence the ark of God, whose name is called by the name of the LORD of hosts that dwelleth *between* the cherubims.

3 And they set the ark of God upon a new cart, and brought it out of the house of A-bin′a-dab that *was* in Gib′e-ah: and Uz′zah and A-hi′o, the sons of A-bin′a-dab, drave the new cart.

4 And they brought it out of the house of A-bin′a-dab which *was* at Gib′e-ah, accompanying the ark of God: and A-hi′o went before the ark.

5 And Da′vid and all the house of Is′ra-el played before the LORD on all manner of *instruments made of* fir wood, even on harps, and on psalteries, and on timbrels, and on cornets, and on cymbals.

6 ¶ And when they came to Na′chon's threshingfloor, Uz′zah put forth *his hand* to the ark of God, and took hold of it; for the oxen shook *it.*

7 And the anger of the LORD was kindled against Uz′zah; and God smote him there for *his* error; and there he died by the ark of God.

8 And Da′vid was displeased, because the LORD had made a breach upon Uz′zah: and he called the name of the place Pe′rez–uz′zah to this day.

9 And Da′vid was afraid of the LORD that day, and said, How shall the ark of the LORD come to me?

10 So Da′vid would not remove the ark of the LORD unto him into the city of Da′vid: but Da′vid carried it aside into the house of O′bed–e′dom the Git′tite.

11 And the ark of the LORD continued in the house of O′bed–e′dom the Git′tite three months: and the LORD blessed O′bed–e′dom, and all his household.

12 ¶ And it was told king Da′vid, saying, The LORD hath blessed the house of O′bed–e′dom, and all that *pertaineth* unto him, because of the ark of God. So Da′vid went and brought up the ark of God from the house of O′bed–e′dom into the city of Da′vid with gladness.

13 And it was *so,* that when they that bare the ark of the LORD had gone six paces, he sacrificed oxen and fatlings.

14 And Da′vid danced before the LORD with all *his* might; and Da′vid *was* girded with a linen ephod.

15 So Da′vid and all the house of Is′ra-el brought up the ark of the LORD with shouting, and with the sound of the trumpet.

16 And as the ark of the LORD came into the city of Da′vid, Mi′chal Saul's daughter looked through a window, and saw king Da′vid leaping and dancing before the LORD; and she despised him in her heart.

17 ¶ And they brought in the ark of the LORD, and set it in his place, in the midst of the tabernacle that Da′vid had pitched for it: and Da′vid offered burnt offerings and peace offerings before the LORD.

18 And as soon as Da′vid had made an end of offering burnt offerings and peace offerings, he blessed the people in the name of the LORD of hosts.

19 And he dealt among all the people, *even* among the whole multitude of Is′ra-el, as well to the women as men, to every one a cake of bread, and a good piece *of flesh,* and a flagon *of wine.* So all the people departed every one to his house.

20 ¶ Then Da′vid returned to bless his household. And Mi′chal the daughter of Saul came out to meet Da′vid, and said, How glorious was the king of Is′ra-el to day, who uncovered himself to day in the eyes of the handmaids of his servants, as one of the vain fellows shamelessly uncovereth himself!

21 And Da′vid said unto Mi′chal, *It was* before the LORD, which chose me before thy father, and before all his house, to appoint me ruler over the people of the LORD, over Is′ra-el: therefore will I play before the LORD.

22 And I will yet be more vile than thus, and will be base in mine own sight: and of the maidservants which thou hast spoken of, of them shall I be had in honour.

23 Therefore Mi′chal the daughter of Saul had no child unto the day of her death.

7 AND it came to pass, when the king sat in his house, and the LORD had given him rest round about from all his enemies;

2 That the king said unto Na′than the prophet, See now, I dwell in an house of cedar, but the ark of God dwelleth within curtains.

3 And Na′than said to the king, Go, do all that *is* in thine heart; for the LORD *is* with thee.

4 ¶ And it came to pass that night, that the word of the LORD came unto Na′than, saying,

5 Go and tell my servant Da′vid, Thus saith the LORD, Shalt thou build me an house for me to dwell in?

6 Whereas I have not dwelt in *any* house since the time that I brought up the children of Is′ra-el out of E′gypt, even to this day, but have walked in a tent and in a tabernacle.

7 In all *the places* wherein I have walked with all the children of Is′ra-el spake I a word with any of the tribes of Is′ra-el, whom I commanded to feed my people Is′ra-el, saying, Why build ye not me an house of cedar?

8 Now therefore so shalt thou say unto my servant Da′vid, Thus saith the LORD of hosts, I

took thee from the sheepcote, from following the sheep, to be ruler over my people, over Is'-ra-el:

9 And I was with thee whithersoever thou wentest, and have cut off all thine enemies out of thy sight, and have made thee a great name, like unto the name of the great *men* that *are* in the earth.

10 Moreover I will appoint a place for my people Is'ra-el, and will plant them, that they may dwell in a place of their own, and move no more; neither shall the children of wickedness afflict them any more, as beforetime,

11 And as since the time that I commanded judges *to be* over my people Is'ra-el, and have caused thee to rest from all thine enemies. Also the LORD telleth thee that he will make thee an house.

12 ¶ And when thy days be fulfilled, and thou shalt sleep with thy fathers, I will set up thy seed after thee, which shall proceed out of thy bowels, and I will establish his kingdom.

13 He shall build an house for my name, and I will stablish the throne of his kingdom for ever.

14 I will be his father, and he shall be my son. If he commit iniquity, I will chasten him with the rod of men, and with the stripes of the children of men:

15 But my mercy shall not depart away from him, as I took *it* from Saul, whom I put away before thee.

16 And thine house and thy kingdom shall be established for ever before thee: thy throne shall be established for ever.

17 According to all these words, and according to all this vision, so did Na'than speak unto Da'vid.

18 ¶ Then went king Da'vid in, and sat before the LORD, and he said, Who *am* I, O Lord GOD? and what *is* my house, that thou hast brought me hitherto?

19 And this was yet a small thing in thy sight, O Lord GOD; but thou hast spoken also of thy servant's house for a great while to come. And *is* this the manner of man, O Lord GOD?

20 And what can Da'vid say more unto thee? for thou, Lord GOD, knowest thy servant.

21 For thy word's sake, and according to thine own heart, hast thou done all these great things, to make thy servant know *them*.

22 Wherefore thou art great, O LORD God: for *there is* none like thee, neither *is there any* God beside thee, according to all that we have heard with our ears.

23 And what one nation in the earth *is* like thy people, *even* like Is'ra-el, whom God went to redeem for a people to himself, and to make him a name, and to do for you great things and terrible, for thy land, before thy people, which thou redeemedst to thee from E'gypt, *from* the nations and their gods?

24 For thou hast confirmed to thyself thy people Is'ra-el *to be* a people unto thee for ever: and thou, LORD, art become their God.

25 And now, O LORD God, the word that thou hast spoken concerning thy servant, and concerning his house, establish *it* for ever, and do as thou hast said.

26 And let thy name be magnified for ever, saying, The LORD of hosts *is* the God over Is'ra-el: and let the house of thy servant Da'vid be established before thee.

27 For thou, O LORD of hosts, God of Is'ra-el, hast revealed to thy servant, saying, I will build thee an house: therefore hath thy servant found in his heart to pray this prayer unto thee.

28 And now, O Lord GOD, thou *art* that God, and thy words be true, and thou hast promised this goodness unto thy servant:

29 Therefore now let it please thee to bless the house of thy servant, that it may continue for ever before thee: for thou, O Lord GOD, hast spoken *it:* and with thy blessing let the house of thy servant be blessed for ever.

8 AND after this it came to pass, that Da'vid smote the Phi-lis'tines, and subdued them: and Da'vid took Me'theg-am'mah out of the hand of the Phi-lis'tines.

2 And he smote Mo'ab, and measured them with a line, casting them down to the ground; even with two lines measured he to put to death, and with one full line to keep alive. And *so* the Mo'ab-ites became Da'vid's servants, *and* brought gifts.

3 ¶ Da'vid smote also Had-ad-e'zer, the son of Re'hob, king of Zo'bah, as he went to recover his border at the river Eu-phra'tes.

4 And Da'vid took from him a thousand *chariots,* and seven hundred horsemen, and twenty thousand footmen: and Da'vid houghed all the chariot *horses,* but reserved of them *for* an hundred chariots.

5 And when the Syr'i-ans of Da-mas'cus came to succour Had-ad-e'zer king of Zo'bah, Da'vid slew of the Syr'i-ans two and twenty thousand men.

6 Then Da'vid put garrisons in Syr'i-a of Da-mas'cus: and the Syr'i-ans became servants to Da'vid, *and* brought gifts. And the LORD preserved Da'vid whithersoever he went.

7 And Da'vid took the shields of gold that were on the servants of Had-ad-e'zer, and brought them to Je-ru'sa-lem.

8 And from Be'tah, and from Ber'o-thai, cities of Had-ad-e'zer, king Da'vid took exceeding much brass.

9 ¶ When To'i king of Ha'math heard that Da'vid had smitten all the host of Had-ad-e'zer,

10 Then To'i sent Jo'ram his son unto king Da'vid, to salute him, and to bless him, because he had fought against Had-ad-e'zer, and smitten him: for Had-ad-e'zer had wars with To'i. And *Jo'ram* brought with him vessels of silver, and vessels of gold, and vessels of brass:

11 Which also king Da'vid did dedicate unto the LORD, with the silver and gold that he had dedicated of all nations which he subdued;

12 Of Syr'i-a, and of Mo'ab, and of the children of Am'mon, and of the Phi-lis'tines, and of Am'a-lek, and of the spoil of Had-ad-e'zer, son of Re'hob, king of Zo'bah.

13 And Da'vid gat *him* a name when he returned from smiting of the Syr'i-ans in the valley of salt, *being* eighteen thousand *men*.

14 ¶ And he put garrisons in E'dom; throughout all E'dom put he garrisons, and all they of E'dom became Da'vid's servants. And the LORD preserved Da'vid whithersoever he went.

15 And Da'vid reigned over all Is'ra-el; and Da'vid executed judgment and justice unto all his people.

16 And Jo'ab the son of Zer-u-i'ah *was* over the host; and Je-hosh'a-phat the son of A-hi'lud *was* recorder;

17 And Za'dok the son of A-hi'tub, and A-him'e-lech the son of A-bi'a-thar, *were* the priests; and Ser-a-i'ah *was* the scribe;

18 And Be-na'iah the son of Je-hoi'a-da *was over* both the Cher'eth-ites and the Pe'leth-ites; and Da'vid's sons were chief rulers.

9 AND Da'vid said, Is there yet any that is left of the house of Saul, that I may shew him kindness for Jon'a-than's sake?

2 And *there was* of the house of Saul a servant whose name *was* Zi'ba. And when they had called him unto Da'vid, the king said unto him, *Art* thou Zi'ba? And he said, Thy servant *is he.*

3 And the king said, *Is* there not yet any of the house of Saul, that I may shew the kindness of God unto him? And Zi'ba said unto the king, Jon'a-than hath yet a son, *which is* lame on *his* feet.

4 And the king said unto him, Where *is* he? And Zi'ba said unto the king, Behold, he *is* in the house of Ma'chir, the son of Am'mi-el, in Lo–de'bar.

5 ¶ Then king Da'vid sent, and fetched him out of the house of Ma'chir, the son of Am'mi-el, from Lo–de'bar.

6 Now when Me-phib'o-sheth, the son of Jon'a-than, the son of Saul, was come unto Da'vid, he fell on his face, and did reverence. And Da'vid said, Me-phib'o-sheth. And he answered, Behold thy servant!

7 ¶ And Da'vid said unto him, Fear not: for I will surely shew thee kindness for Jon'a-than thy father's sake, and will restore thee all the land of Saul thy father; and thou shalt eat bread at my table continually.

8 And he bowed himself, and said, What *is* thy servant, that thou shouldest look upon such a dead dog as I *am?*

9 ¶ Then the king called to Zi'ba, Saul's servant, and said unto him, I have given unto thy master's son all that pertained to Saul and to all his house.

10 Thou therefore, and thy sons, and thy servants, shall till the land for him, and thou shalt bring in *the fruits,* that thy master's son may have food to eat: but Me-phib'o-sheth thy master's son shall eat bread alway at my table. Now Zi'ba had fifteen sons and twenty servants.

11 Then said Zi'ba unto the king, According to all that my lord the king hath commanded his servant, so shall thy servant do. As for Me-phib'o-sheth, *said the king,* he shall eat at my table, as one of the king's sons.

12 And Me-phib'o-sheth had a young son, whose name *was* Mi'cha. And all that dwelt in the house of Zi'ba *were* servants unto Me-phib'o-sheth.

13 So Me-phib'o-sheth dwelt in Je-ru'sa-lem: for he did eat continually at the king's table; and was lame on both his feet.

10 AND it came to pass after this, that the king of the children of Am'mon died, and Ha'nun his son reigned in his stead.

2 Then said Da'vid, I will shew kindness unto Ha'nun the son of Na'hash, as his father shewed kindness unto me. And Da'vid sent to comfort him by the hand of his servants for his father. And Da'vid's servants came into the land of the children of Am'mon.

3 And the princes of the children of Am'mon said unto Ha'nun their lord, Thinkest thou that Da'vid doth honour thy father, that he hath sent comforters unto thee? hath not Da'vid *rather* sent his servants unto thee, to search the city, and to spy it out, and to overthrow it?

4 Wherefore Ha'nun took Da'vid's servants, and shaved off the one half of their beards, and cut off their garments in the middle, *even* to their buttocks, and sent them away.

5 When they told *it* unto Da'vid, he sent to meet them, because the men were greatly ashamed: and the king said, Tarry at Jer'i-cho until your beards be grown, and *then* return.

6 ¶ And when the children of Am'mon saw that they stank before Da'vid, the children of Am'mon sent and hired the Syr'i-ans of Beth–re'hob, and the Syr'i-ans of Zo'ba, twenty thousand footmen, and of king Ma'a-cah a thousand men, and of Ish'–tob twelve thousand men.

7 And when Da'vid heard of *it,* he sent Jo'ab, and all the host of the mighty men.

8 And the children of Am'mon came out, and put the battle in array at the entering in of the gate: and the Syr'i-ans of Zo'ba, and of Re'hob, and Ish'–tob, and Ma'a-cah, *were* by themselves in the field.

9 When Jo'ab saw that the front of the battle was against him before and behind, he chose of all the choice *men* of Is'ra-el, and put *them* in array against the Syr'i-ans:

10 And the rest of the people he delivered into the hand of A-bish'a-i his brother, that he might put *them* in array against the children of Am'mon.

11 And he said, If the Syr'i-ans be too strong for me, then thou shalt help me: but if the children of Am'mon be too strong for thee, then I will come and help thee.

12 Be of good courage, and let us play the men for our people, and for the cities of our God: and the LORD do that which seemeth him good.

13 And Jo'ab drew nigh, and the people that *were* with him, unto the battle against the Syr'i-ans: and they fled before him.

14 And when the children of Am'mon saw that the Syr'i-ans were fled, then fled they also before A-bish'a-i, and entered into the city. So Jo'ab returned from the children of Am'mon, and came to Je-ru'sa-lem.

15 ¶ And when the Syr'i-ans saw that they were smitten before Is'ra-el, they gathered themselves together.

16 And Had-ar-e'zer sent, and brought out the Syr'i-ans that *were* beyond the river: and they came to He'lam; and Sho'bach the captain of the host of Had-ar-e'zer *went* before them.

17 And when it was told Da'vid, he gathered all Is'ra-el together, and passed over Jor'dan, and came to He'lam. And the Syr'i-ans set themselves in array against Da'vid, and fought with him.

18 And the Syr'i-ans fled before Is'ra-el; and Da'vid slew *the men of* seven hundred chariots of the Syr'i-ans, and forty thousand horsemen, and smote Sho'bach the captain of their host, who died there.

19 And when all the kings *that were* servants to Had-ar-e'zer saw that they were smitten before Is'ra-el, they made peace with Is'ra-el, and served them. So the Syr'i-ans feared to help the children of Am'mon any more.

11 AND it came to pass, after the year was expired, at the time when kings go forth *to battle,* that Da'vid sent Jo'ab, and his servants with him, and all Is'ra-el; and they destroyed the children of Am'mon, and besieged Rab'bah. But Da'vid tarried still at Je-ru'sa-lem.

2 ¶ And it came to pass in an eveningtide, that Da'vid arose from off his bed, and walked upon the roof of the king's house: and from the roof he saw a woman washing herself; and the woman *was* very beautiful to look upon.

3 And Da'vid sent and enquired after the woman. And *one* said, *Is* not this Bath'–she-ba, the daughter of E-li'am, the wife of U-ri'ah the Hit'tite?

4 And Da'vid sent messengers, and took her; and she came in unto him, and he lay with her; for she was purified from her uncleanness: and she returned unto her house.

5 And the woman conceived, and sent and told Da'vid, and said, I *am* with child.

6 ¶ And Da'vid sent to Jo'ab, *saying*, Send me U-ri'ah the Hit'tite. And Jo'ab sent U-ri'ah to Da'vid.

7 And when U-ri'ah was come unto him, Da'vid demanded *of him* how Jo'ab did, and how the people did, and how the war prospered.

8 And Da'vid said to U-ri'ah, Go down to thy house, and wash thy feet. And U-ri'ah departed out of the king's house, and there followed him a mess *of meat* from the king.

9 But U-ri'ah slept at the door of the king's house, with all the servants of his lord, and went not down to his house.

10 And when they had told Da'vid, saying, U-ri'ah went not down unto his house, Da'vid said unto U-ri'ah, Camest thou not from *thy* journey? why *then* didst thou not go down unto thine house?

11 And U-ri'ah said unto Da'vid, The ark, and Is'ra-el, and Ju'dah, abide in tents; and my lord Jo'ab, and the servants of my lord, are encamped in the open fields; shall I then go into mine house, to eat and to drink, and to lie with my wife? *as* thou livest, and *as* thy soul liveth, I will not do this thing.

12 And Da'vid said to U-ri'ah, Tarry here to day also, and to morrow I will let thee depart. So U-ri'ah abode in Je-ru'sa-lem that day, and the morrow.

13 And when Da'vid had called him, he did eat and drink before him; and he made him drunk: and at even he went out to lie on his bed with the servants of his lord, but went not down to his house.

14 ¶ And it came to pass in the morning, that Da'vid wrote a letter to Jo'ab, and sent *it* by the hand of U-ri'ah.

15 And he wrote in the letter, saying, Set ye U-ri'ah in the forefront of the hottest battle, and retire ye from him, that he may be smitten, and die.

16 And it came to pass, when Jo'ab observed the city, that he assigned U-ri'ah unto a place where he knew that valiant men *were*.

17 And the men of the city went out, and fought with Jo'ab: and there fell *some* of the people of the servants of Da'vid; and U-ri'ah the Hit'tite died also.

18 ¶ Then Jo'ab sent and told Da'vid all the things concerning the war;

19 And charged the messenger, saying, When thou hast made an end of telling the matters of the war unto the king,

20 And if so be that the king's wrath arise, and he say unto thee, Wherefore approached ye so nigh unto the city when ye did fight? knew ye not that they would shoot from the wall?

21 Who smote A-bim'e-lech the son of Je-rub'be-sheth? did not a woman cast a piece of a millstone upon him from the wall, that he died in The'bez? why went ye nigh the wall? then say thou, Thy servant U-ri'ah the Hit'tite is dead also.

22 ¶ So the messenger went, and came and shewed Da'vid all that Jo'ab had sent him for.

23 And the messenger said unto Da'vid, Surely the men prevailed against us, and came out unto us into the field, and we were upon them even unto the entering of the gate.

24 And the shooters shot from off the wall upon thy servants; and *some* of the king's servants be dead, and thy servant U-ri'ah the Hit'tite is dead also.

25 Then Da'vid said unto the messenger, Thus shalt thou say unto Jo'ab, Let not this thing displease thee, for the sword devoureth one as well as another: make thy battle more strong against the city, and overthrow it: and encourage thou him.

26 ¶ And when the wife of U-ri'ah heard that U-ri'ah her husband was dead, she mourned for her husband.

27 And when the mourning was past, Da'vid sent and fetched her to his house, and she became his wife, and bare him a son. But the thing that Da'vid had done displeased the LORD.

12 AND the LORD sent Na'than unto Da'vid. And he came unto him, and said unto him, There were two men in one city; the one rich, and the other poor.

2 The rich *man* had exceeding many flocks and herds:

3 But the poor *man* had nothing, save one little ewe lamb, which he had bought and nourished up: and it grew up together with him, and with his children; it did eat of his own meat, and drank of his own cup, and lay in his bosom, and was unto him as a daughter.

4 And there came a traveller unto the rich man, and he spared to take of his own flock and of his own herd, to dress for the wayfaring man that was come unto him; but took the poor man's lamb, and dressed it for the man that was come to him.

5 And Da'vid's anger was greatly kindled against the man; and he said to Na'than, *As* the LORD liveth, the man that hath done this *thing* shall surely die:

6 And he shall restore the lamb fourfold, because he did this thing, and because he had no pity.

7 ¶ And Na'than said to Da'vid, Thou *art* the man. Thus saith the LORD God of Is'ra-el, I anointed thee king over Is'ra-el, and I delivered thee out of the hand of Saul;

8 And I gave thee thy master's house, and thy master's wives into thy bosom, and gave thee the house of Is'ra-el and of Ju'dah; and if *that had been* too little, I would moreover have given unto thee such and such things.

9 Wherefore hast thou despised the commandment of the LORD, to do evil in his sight? thou hast killed U-ri'ah the Hit'tite with the sword, and hast taken his wife *to be* thy wife, and hast slain him with the sword of the children of Am'mon.

10 Now therefore the sword shall never depart from thine house; because thou hast despised me, and hast taken the wife of U-ri'ah the Hit'tite to be thy wife.

11 Thus saith the LORD, Behold, I will raise up evil against thee out of thine own house, and I will take thy wives before thine eyes, and give *them* unto thy neighbour, and he shall lie with thy wives in the sight of this sun.

12 For thou didst *it* secretly: but I will do this thing before all Is'ra-el, and before the sun.

13 And Da'vid said unto Na'than, I have sinned against the LORD. And Na'than said unto Da'vid, The LORD also hath put away thy sin; thou shalt not die.

14 Howbeit, because by this deed thou hast given great occasion to the enemies of the LORD to blaspheme, the child also *that is* born unto thee shall surely die.

15 ¶ And Na'than departed unto his house.

And the LORD struck the child that U-ri'ah's
wife bare unto Da'vid, and it was very sick.
16 Da'vid therefore besought God for the
child; and Da'vid fasted, and went in, and lay all
night upon the earth.
17 And the elders of his house arose, *and
went* to him, to raise him up from the earth: but
he would not, neither did he eat bread with
them.
18 And it came to pass on the seventh day,
that the child died. And the servants of Da'vid
feared to tell him that the child was dead: for
they said, Behold, while the child was yet alive,
we spake unto him, and he would not hearken
unto our voice: how will he then vex himself, if
we tell him that the child is dead?
19 But when Da'vid saw that his servants
whispered, Da'vid perceived that the child was
dead: therefore Da'vid said unto his servants, Is
the child dead? And they said, He is dead.
20 Then Da'vid arose from the earth, and
washed, and anointed *himself,* and changed his
apparel, and came into the house of the LORD,
and worshipped: then he came to his own
house; and when he required, they set bread before him, and he did eat.
21 Then said his servants unto him, What
thing *is* this that thou hast done? thou didst fast
and weep for the child, *while it was* alive; but
when the child was dead, thou didst rise and eat
bread.
22 And he said, While the child was yet alive,
I fasted and wept: for I said, Who can tell
whether GOD will be gracious to me, that the
child may live?
23 But now he is dead, wherefore should I
fast? can I bring him back again? I shall go to
him, but he shall not return to me.
24 ¶ And Da'vid comforted Bath'-she-ba his
wife, and went in unto her, and lay with her:
and she bare a son, and he called his name Sol'-
o-mon: and the LORD loved him.
25 And he sent by the hand of Na'than the
prophet; and he called his name Jed-i-di'ah, because of the LORD.
26 ¶ And Jo'ab fought against Rab'bah of
the children of Am'mon, and took the royal city.
27 And Jo'ab sent messengers to Da'vid, and
said, I have fought against Rab'bah, and have
taken the city of waters.
28 Now therefore gather the rest of the people together, and encamp against the city, and
take it: lest I take the city, and it be called after
my name.
29 And Da'vid gathered all the people together, and went to Rab'bah, and fought against
it, and took it.
30 And he took their king's crown from off
his head, the weight whereof *was* a talent of
gold with the precious stones: and it was *set* on
Da'vid's head. And he brought forth the spoil of
the city in great abundance.
31 And he brought forth the people that *were*
therein, and put *them* under saws, and under
harrows of iron, and under axes of iron, and
made them pass through the brickkiln: and thus
did he unto all the cities of the children of Am'-
mon. So Da'vid and all the people returned unto
Je-ru'sa-lem.

13 AND it came to pass after this, that Ab'-
sa-lom the son of Da'vid had a fair sister, whose name *was* Ta'mar; and Am'non the
son of Da'vid loved her.
2 And Am'non was so vexed, that he fell sick
for his sister Ta'mar; for she *was* a virgin; and
Am'non thought it hard for him to do any thing
to her.
3 But Am'non had a friend, whose name *was*
Jon'a-dab, the son of Shim'e-ah Da'vid's
brother: and Jon'a-dab *was* a very subtil man.
4 And he said unto him, Why *art* thou, *being*
the king's son, lean from day to day? wilt thou
not tell me? And Am'non said unto him, I love
Ta'mar, my brother Ab'sa-lom's sister.
5 And Jon'a-dab said unto him, Lay thee
down on thy bed, and make thyself sick: and
when thy father cometh to see thee, say unto
him, I pray thee, Let my sister Ta'mar come,
and give me meat, and dress the meat in my
sight, that I may see *it,* and eat *it* at her hand.
6 ¶ So Am'non lay down, and made himself
sick: and when the king was come to see him,
Am'non said unto the king, I pray thee, let Ta'-
mar my sister come, and make me a couple of
cakes in my sight, that I may eat at her hand.
7 Then Da'vid sent home to Ta'mar, saying,
Go now to thy brother Am'non's house, and
dress him meat.
8 So Ta'mar went to her brother Am'non's
house; and he was laid down. And she took
flour, and kneaded *it,* and made cakes in his
sight, and did bake the cakes.
9 And she took a pan, and poured *them* out
before him; but he refused to eat. And Am'non
said, Have out all men from me. And they went
out every man from him.
10 And Am'non said unto Ta'mar, Bring the
meat into the chamber, that I may eat of thine
hand. And Ta'mar took the cakes which she had
made, and brought *them* into the chamber to
Am'non her brother.
11 And when she had brought *them* unto him
to eat, he took hold of her, and said unto her,
Come lie with me, my sister.
12 And she answered him, Nay, my brother,
do not force me; for no such thing ought to be
done in Is'ra-el: do not thou this folly.
13 And I, whither shall I cause my shame to
go? and as for thee, thou shalt be as one of the
fools in Is'ra-el. Now therefore, I pray thee,
speak unto the king; for he will not withhold me
from thee.
14 Howbeit he would not hearken unto her
voice: but, being stronger than she, forced her,
and lay with her.
15 ¶ Then Am'non hated her exceedingly; so
that the hatred wherewith he hated her *was*
greater than the love wherewith he had loved
her. And Am'non said unto her, Arise, be gone.
16 And she said unto him, *There is* no cause:
this evil in sending me away *is* greater than the
other that thou didst unto me. But he would not
hearken unto her.
17 Then he called his servant that ministered
unto him, and said, Put now this *woman* out
from me, and bolt the door after her.
18 And *she had* a garment of divers colours
upon her: for with such robes were the king's
daughters *that were* virgins apparelled. Then
his servant brought her out, and bolted the door
after her.
19 ¶ And Ta'mar put ashes on her head, and
rent her garment of divers colours that *was* on
her, and laid her hand on her head, and went on
crying.
20 And Ab'sa-lom her brother said unto her,
Hath Am'non thy brother been with thee? but
hold now thy peace, my sister: he *is* thy brother;
regard not this thing. So Ta'mar remained desolate in her brother Ab'sa-lom's house.
21 ¶ But when king Da'vid heard of all these
things, he was very wroth.

22 And Ab'sa-lom spake unto his brother
Am'non neither good nor bad: for Ab'sa-lom
hated Am'non, because he had forced his sister
Ta'mar.
23 ¶ And it came to pass after two full years,
that Ab'sa-lom had sheepshearers in Ba'al–ha'-
zor, which *is* beside E'phra-im: and Ab'sa-lom
invited all the king's sons.
24 And Ab'sa-lom came to the king, and said,
Behold now, thy servant hath sheepshearers; let
the king, I beseech thee, and his servants go
with thy servant.
25 And the king said to Ab'sa-lom, Nay, my
son, let us not all now go, lest we be chargeable
unto thee. And he pressed him: howbeit he
would not go, but blessed him.
26 Then said Ab'sa-lom, If not, I pray thee,
let my brother Am'non go with us. And the king
said unto him, Why should he go with thee?
27 But Ab'sa-lom pressed him, that he let
Am'non and all the king's sons go with him.
28 ¶ Now Ab'sa-lom had commanded his
servants, saying, Mark ye now when Am'non's
heart is merry with wine, and when I say unto
you, Smite Am'non; then kill him, fear not: have
not I commanded you? be courageous, and be
valiant.
29 And the servants of Ab'sa-lom did unto
Am'non as Ab'sa-lom had commanded. Then all
the king's sons arose, and every man gat him up
upon his mule, and fled.
30 ¶ And it came to pass, while they were in
the way, that tidings came to Da'vid, saying,
Ab'sa-lom hath slain all the king's sons, and
there is not one of them left.
31 Then the king arose, and tare his garments, and lay on the earth; and all his servants
stood by with their clothes rent.
32 And Jon'a-dab, the son of Shim'e-ah Da'-
vid's brother, answered and said, Let not my
lord suppose *that* they have slain all the young
men the king's sons; for Am'non only is dead:
for by the appointment of Ab'sa-lom this hath
been determined from the day that he forced
his sister Ta'mar.
33 Now therefore let not my lord the king
take the thing to his heart, to think that all the
king's sons are dead: for Am'non only is dead.
34 But Ab'sa-lom fled. And the young man
that kept the watch lifted up his eyes, and
looked, and, behold, there came much people
by the way of the hill side behind him.
35 And Jon'a-dab said unto the king, Behold,
the king's sons come: as thy servant said, so it
is.
36 And it came to pass, as soon as he had
made an end of speaking, that, behold, the
king's sons came, and lifted up their voice and
wept: and the king also and all his servants
wept very sore.
37 ¶ But Ab'sa-lom fled, and went to Tal'-
mai, the son of Am-mi'hud, king of Ge'shur.
And *Da'vid* mourned for his son every day.
38 So Ab'sa-lom fled, and went to Ge'shur,
and was there three years.
39 And *the soul of* king Da'vid longed to go
forth unto Ab'sa-lom: for he was comforted
concerning Am'non, seeing he was dead.

14 NOW Jo'ab the son of Zer-u-i'ah perceived that the king's heart *was* toward
Ab'sa-lom.
2 And Jo'ab sent to Te-ko'ah, and fetched
thence a wise woman, and said unto her, I pray
thee, feign thyself to be a mourner, and put on
now mourning apparel, and anoint not thyself
with oil, but be as a woman that had a long time
mourned for the dead:
3 And come to the king, and speak on this
manner unto him. So Jo'ab put the words in her
mouth.
4 ¶ And when the woman of Te-ko'ah spake
to the king, she fell on her face to the ground,
and did obeisance, and said, Help, O king.
5 And the king said unto her, What aileth
thee? And she answered, I *am* indeed a widow
woman, and mine husband is dead.
6 And thy handmaid had two sons, and they
two strove together in the field, and *there was*
none to part them, but the one smote the other,
and slew him.
7 And, behold, the whole family is risen
against thine handmaid, and they said, Deliver
him that smote his brother, that we may kill
him, for the life of his brother whom he slew;
and we will destroy the heir also: and so they
shall quench my coal which is left, and shall not
leave to my husband *neither* name nor remainder upon the earth.
8 And the king said unto the woman, Go to
thine house, and I will give charge concerning
thee.
9 And the woman of Te-ko'ah said unto the
king, My lord, O king, the iniquity *be* on me,
and on my father's house: and the king and his
throne *be* guiltless.
10 And the king said, Whosoever saith *ought*
unto thee, bring him to me, and he shall not
touch thee any more.
11 Then said she, I pray thee, let the king remember the LORD thy God, that thou wouldest
not suffer the revengers of blood to destroy any
more, lest they destroy my son. And he said, *As*
the LORD liveth, there shall not one hair of thy
son fall to the earth.
12 Then the woman said, Let thine handmaid, I pray thee, speak *one* word unto my lord
the king. And he said, Say on.
13 And the woman said, Wherefore then hast
thou thought such a thing against the people of
God? for the king doth speak this thing as one
which is faulty, in that the king doth not fetch
home again his banished.
14 For we must needs die, and *are* as water
spilt on the ground, which cannot be gathered
up again; neither doth God respect *any* person:
yet doth he devise means, that his banished be
not expelled from him.
15 Now therefore that I am come to speak of
this thing unto my lord the king, *it is* because
the people have made me afraid: and thy handmaid said, I will now speak unto the king; it
may be that the king will perform the request of
his handmaid.
16 For the king will hear, to deliver his handmaid out of the hand of the man *that would*
destroy me and my son together out of the inheritance of God.
17 Then thine handmaid said, The word of
my lord the king shall now be comfortable: for
as an angel of God, so *is* my lord the king to
discern good and bad: therefore the LORD thy
God will be with thee.
18 Then the king answered and said unto the
woman, Hide not from me, I pray thee, the
thing that I shall ask thee. And the woman said,
Let my lord the king now speak.
19 And the king said, *Is not* the hand of Jo'ab
with thee in all this? And the woman answered
and said, *As* thy soul liveth, my lord the king,
none can turn to the right hand or to the left
from ought that my lord the king hath spoken:
for thy servant Jo'ab, he bade me, and he put all

these words in the mouth of thine handmaid:

20 To fetch about this form of speech hath thy servant Jo'ab done this thing: and my lord *is* wise, according to the wisdom of an angel of God, to know all *things* that *are* in the earth.

21 ¶ And the king said unto Jo'ab, Behold now, I have done this thing: go therefore, bring the young man Ab'sa-lom again.

22 And Jo'ab fell to the ground on his face, and bowed himself, and thanked the king: and Jo'ab said, To day thy servant knoweth that I have found grace in thy sight, my lord, O king, in that the king hath fulfilled the request of his servant.

23 So Jo'ab arose and went to Ge'shur, and brought Ab'sa-lom to Je-ru'sa-lem.

24 And the king said, Let him turn to his own house, and let him not see my face. So Ab'sa-lom returned to his own house, and saw not the king's face.

25¶ But in all Is'ra-el there was none to be so much praised as Ab'sa-lom for his beauty: from the sole of his foot even to the crown of his head there was no blemish in him.

26 And when he polled his head, (for it was at every year's end that he polled *it:* because *the hair* was heavy on him, therefore he polled it:) he weighed the hair of his head at two hundred shekels after the king's weight.

27 And unto Ab'sa-lom there were born three sons, and one daughter, whose name *was* Ta'mar: she was a woman of a fair countenance.

28 ¶ So Ab'sa-lom dwelt two full years in Je-ru'sa-lem, and saw not the king's face.

29 Therefore Ab'sa-lom sent for Jo'ab, to have sent him to the king; but he would not come to him: and when he sent again the second time, he would not come.

30 Therefore he said unto his servants, See, Jo'ab's field is near mine, and he hath barley there; go and set it on fire. And Ab'sa-lom's servants set the field on fire.

31 Then Jo'ab arose, and came to Ab'sa-lom unto *his* house, and said unto him, Wherefore have thy servants set my field on fire?

32 And Ab'sa-lom answered Jo'ab, Behold, I sent unto thee, saying, Come hither, that I may send thee to the king, to say, Wherefore am I come from Ge'shur? *it had been* good for me *to have been* there still: now therefore let me see the king's face; and if there be *any* iniquity in me, let him kill me.

33 So Jo'ab came to the king, and told him: and when he had called for Ab'sa-lom, he came to the king, and bowed himself on his face to the ground before the king: and the king kissed Ab'sa-lom.

15 AND it came to pass after this, that Ab'sa-lom prepared him chariots and horses, and fifty men to run before him.

2 And Ab'sa-lom rose up early, and stood beside the way of the gate: and it was *so,* that when any man that had a controversy came to the king for judgment, then Ab'sa-lom called unto him, and said, Of what city *art* thou? And he said, Thy servant *is* of one of the tribes of Is'ra-el.

3 And Ab'sa-lom said unto him, See, thy matters *are* good and right; but *there is* no man *deputed* of the king to hear thee.

4 Ab'sa-lom said moreover, Oh that I were made judge in the land, that every man which hath any suit or cause might come unto me, and I would do him justice!

5 And it was *so,* that when any man came nigh *to him* to do him obeisance, he put forth his hand, and took him, and kissed him.

6 And on this manner did Ab'sa-lom to all Is'ra-el that came to the king for judgment: so Ab'sa-lom stole the hearts of the men of Is'ra-el.

7 ¶ And it came to pass after forty years, that Ab'sa-lom said unto the king, I pray thee, let me go and pay my vow, which I have vowed unto the LORD, in He'bron.

8 For thy servant vowed a vow while I abode at Ge'shur in Syr'i-a, saying, If the LORD shall bring me again indeed to Je-ru'sa-lem, then I will serve the LORD.

9 And the king said unto him, Go in peace. So he arose, and went to He'bron.

10 ¶ But Ab'sa-lom sent spies throughout all the tribes of Is'ra-el, saying, As soon as ye hear the sound of the trumpet, then ye shall say, Ab'sa-lom reigneth in He'bron.

11 And with Ab'sa-lom went two hundred men out of Je-ru'sa-lem, *that were* called; and they went in their simplicity, and they knew not any thing.

12 And Ab'sa-lom sent for A-hith'o-phel the Gi'lo-nite, Da'vid's counsellor, from his city, *even* from Gi'loh, while he offered sacrifices. And the conspiracy was strong; for the people increased continually with Ab'sa-lom.

13 ¶ And there came a messenger to Da'vid, saying, The hearts of the men of Is'ra-el are after Ab'sa-lom.

14 And Da'vid said unto all his servants that *were* with him at Je-ru'sa-lem, Arise, and let us flee; for we shall not *else* escape from Ab'sa-lom: make speed to depart, lest he overtake us suddenly, and bring evil upon us, and smite the city with the edge of the sword.

15 And the king's servants said unto the king, Behold, thy servants *are ready to do* whatsoever my lord the king shall appoint.

16 And the king went forth, and all his household after him. And the king left ten women, *which were* concubines, to keep the house.

17 And the king went forth, and all the people after him, and tarried in a place that was far off.

18 And all his servants passed on beside him; and all the Cher'eth-ites, and all the Pe'leth-ites, and all the Git'tites, six hundred men which came after him from Gath, passed on before the king.

19 ¶ Then said the king to It'ta-i the Git'tite, Wherefore goest thou also with us? return to thy place, and abide with the king: for thou *art* a stranger, and also an exile.

20 Whereas thou camest *but* yesterday, should I this day make thee go up and down with us? seeing I go whither I may, return thou, and take back thy brethren: mercy and truth *be* with thee.

21 And It'ta-i answered the king, and said, *As* the LORD liveth, and *as* my lord the king liveth, surely in what place my lord the king shall be, whether in death or life, even there also will thy servant be.

22 And Da'vid said to It'ta-i, Go and pass over. And It'ta-i the Git'tite passed over, and all his men, and all the little ones that *were* with him.

23 And all the country wept with a loud voice, and all the people passed over: the king also himself passed over the brook Kid'ron, and all the people passed over, toward the way of the wilderness.

24 ¶ And lo Za'dok also, and all the Le'vites *were* with him, bearing the ark of the covenant

of God: and they set down the ark of God; and A-bi'a-thar went up, until all the people had done passing out of the city.

25 And the king said unto Za'dok, Carry back the ark of God into the city: if I shall find favour in the eyes of the LORD, he will bring me again, and shew me *both* it, and his habitation:

26 But if he thus say, I have no delight in thee; behold, *here am* I, let him do to me as seemeth good unto him.

27 The king said also unto Za'dok the priest, *Art not* thou a seer? return into the city in peace, and your two sons with you, A-him'a-az thy son, and Jon'a-than the son of A-bi'a-thar.

28 See, I will tarry in the plain of the wilderness, until there come word from you to certify me.

29 Za'dok therefore and A-bi'a-thar carried the ark of God again to Je-ru'sa-lem: and they tarried there.

30 ¶ And Da'vid went up by the ascent of *mount* Ol'i-vet, and wept as he went up, and had his head covered, and he went barefoot: and all the people that *was* with him covered every man his head, and they went up, weeping as they went up.

31 ¶ And *one* told Da'vid, saying, A-hith'o-phel *is* among the conspirators with Ab'sa-lom. And Da'vid said, O LORD, I pray thee, turn the counsel of A-hith'o-phel into foolishness.

32 ¶ And it came to pass, that *when* Da'vid was come to the top *of the mount,* where he worshipped God, behold, Hu'shai the Ar'chite came to meet him with his coat rent, and earth upon his head:

33 Unto whom Da'vid said, If thou passest on with me, then thou shalt be a burden unto me:

34 But if thou return to the city, and say unto Ab'sa-lom, I will be thy servant, O king; *as* I *have been* thy father's servant hitherto, so *will* I now also *be* thy servant: then mayest thou for me defeat the counsel of A-hith'o-phel.

35 And *hast thou* not there with thee Za'dok and A-bi'a-thar the priests? therefore it shall be, *that* what thing soever thou shalt hear out of the king's house, thou shalt tell *it* to Za'dok and A-bi'a-thar the priests.

36 Behold, *they have* there with them their two sons, A-him'a-az Za'dok's *son,* and Jon'a-than A-bi'a-thar's *son;* and by them ye shall send unto me every thing that ye can hear.

37 So Hu'shai Da'vid's friend came into the city, and Ab'sa-lom came into Je-ru'sa-lem.

16 AND when Da'vid was a little past the top *of the hill,* behold, Zi'ba the servant of Me-phib'o-sheth met him, with a couple of asses saddled, and upon them two hundred *loaves* of bread, and an hundred bunches of raisins, and an hundred of summer fruits, and a bottle of wine.

2 And the king said unto Zi'ba, What meanest thou by these? And Zi'ba said, The asses *be* for the king's household to ride on; and the bread and summer fruit for the young men to eat; and the wine, that such as be faint in the wilderness may drink.

3 And the king said, And where *is* thy master's son? And Zi'ba said unto the king, Behold, he abideth at Je-ru'sa-lem: for he said, To day shall the house of Is'ra-el restore me the kingdom of my father.

4 Then said the king to Zi'ba, Behold, thine *are* all that *pertained* unto Me-phib'o-sheth. And Zi'ba said, I humbly beseech thee *that* I may find grace in thy sight, my lord, O king.

5 ¶ And when king Da'vid came to Ba-hu'rim, behold, thence came out a man of the family of the house of Saul, whose name *was* Shim'e-i, the son of Ge'ra: he came forth, and cursed still as he came.

6 And he cast stones at Da'vid, and at all the servants of king Da'vid: and all the people and all the mighty men *were* on his right hand and on his left.

7 And thus said Shim'e-i when he cursed, Come out, come out, thou bloody man, and thou man of Be'li-al:

8 The LORD hath returned upon thee all the blood of the house of Saul, in whose stead thou hast reigned; and the LORD hath delivered the kingdom into the hand of Ab'sa-lom thy son: and, behold, thou *art taken* in thy mischief, because thou *art* a bloody man.

9 ¶ Then said A-bish'a-i the son of Zer-u-i'ah unto the king, Why should this dead dog curse my lord the king? let me go over, I pray thee, and take off his head.

10 And the king said, What have I to do with you, ye sons of Zer-u-i'ah? so let him curse, because the LORD hath said unto him, Curse Da'vid. Who shall then say, Wherefore hast thou done so?

11 And Da'vid said to A-bish'a-i, and to all his servants, Behold, my son, which came forth of my bowels, seeketh my life: how much more now *may this* Ben'ja-mite *do it?* let him alone, and let him curse; for the LORD hath bidden him.

12 It may be that the LORD will look on mine affliction, and that the LORD will requite me good for his cursing this day.

13 And as Da'vid and his men went by the way, Shim'e-i went along on the hill's side over against him, and cursed as he went, and threw stones at him, and cast dust.

14 And the king, and all the people that *were* with him, came weary, and refreshed themselves there.

15 ¶ And Ab'sa-lom, and all the people the men of Is'ra-el, came to Je-ru'sa-lem, and A-hith'o-phel with him.

16 And it came to pass, when Hu'shai the Ar'chite, Da'vid's friend, was come unto Ab'sa-lom, that Hu'shai said unto Ab'sa-lom, God save the king, God save the king.

17 And Ab'sa-lom said to Hu'shai, *Is* this thy kindness to thy friend? why wentest thou not with thy friend?

18 And Hu'shai said unto Ab'sa-lom, Nay; but whom the LORD, and this people, and all the men of Is'ra-el, choose, his will I be, and with him will I abide.

19 And again, whom should I serve? *should I* not *serve* in the presence of his son? as I have served in thy father's presence, so will I be in thy presence.

20 ¶ Then said Ab'sa-lom to A-hith'o-phel, Give counsel among you what we shall do.

21 And A-hith'o-phel said unto Ab'sa-lom, Go in unto thy father's concubines, which he hath left to keep the house; and all Is'ra-el shall hear that thou art abhorred of thy father: then shall the hands of all that *are* with thee be strong.

22 So they spread Ab'sa-lom a tent upon the top of the house; and Ab'sa-lom went in unto his father's concubines in the sight of all Is'ra-el.

23 And the counsel of A-hith'o-phel, which he counselled in those days, *was* as if a man had enquired at the oracle of God: so *was* all the counsel of A-hith'o-phel both with Da'vid and with Ab'sa-lom.

17 MOREOVER A-hith'o-phel said unto
Ab'sa-lom, Let me now choose out
twelve thousand men, and I will arise and pursue after Da'vid this night:
2 And I will come upon him while he *is*
weary and weak handed, and will make him
afraid: and all the people that *are* with him shall
flee; and I will smite the king only:
3 And I will bring back all the people unto
thee: the man whom thou seekest *is* as if all
returned: *so* all the people shall be in peace.
4 And the saying pleased Ab'sa-lom well,
and all the elders of Is'ra-el.
5 Then said Ab'sa-lom, Call now Hu'shai the
Ar'chite also, and let us hear likewise what he
saith.
6 And when Hu'shai was come to Ab'sa-lom,
Ab'sa-lom spake unto him, saying, A-hith'o-
phel hath spoken after this manner: shall we do
after his saying? if not; speak thou.
7 And Hu'shai said unto Ab'sa-lom, The
counsel that A-hith'o-phel hath given *is* not
good at this time.
8 For, said Hu'shai, thou knowest thy father
and his men, that they *be* mighty men, and they
be chafed in their minds, as a bear robbed of her
whelps in the field: and thy father *is* a man of
war, and will not lodge with the people.
9 Behold, he is hid now in some pit, or in
some *other* place: and it will come to pass,
when some of them be overthrown at the first,
that whosoever heareth it will say, There is a
slaughter among the people that follow Ab'sa-
lom.
10 And he also *that is* valiant, whose heart *is*
as the heart of a lion, shall utterly melt: for all
Is'ra-el knoweth that thy father *is* a mighty
man, and *they* which *be* with him *are* valiant
men.
11 Therefore I counsel that all Is'ra-el be generally gathered unto thee, from Dan even to Be'-
er–she'ba, as the sand that *is* by the sea for multitude; and that thou go to battle in thine own
person.
12 So shall we come upon him in some place
where he shall be found, and we will light upon
him as the dew falleth on the ground: and of
him and of all the men that *are* with him there
shall not be left so much as one.
13 Moreover, if he be gotten into a city, then
shall all Is'ra-el bring ropes to that city, and we
will draw it into the river, until there be not one
small stone found there.
14 And Ab'sa-lom and all the men of Is'ra-el
said, The counsel of Hu'shai the Ar'chite *is* better than the counsel of A-hith'o-phel. For the
LORD had appointed to defeat the good counsel
of A-hith'o-phel, to the intent that the LORD
might bring evil upon Ab'sa-lom.
15 ¶ Then said Hu'shai unto Za'dok and to
A-bi'a-thar the priests, Thus and thus did A-
hith'o-phel counsel Ab'sa-lom and the elders of
Is'ra-el; and thus and thus have I counselled.
16 Now therefore send quickly, and tell Da'-
vid, saying, Lodge not this night in the plains of
the wilderness, but speedily pass over; lest the
king be swallowed up, and all the people that
are with him.
17 Now Jon'a-than and A-him'a-az stayed by
En–ro'gel; for they might not be seen to come
into the city: and a wench went and told them;
and they went and told king Da'vid.
18 Nevertheless a lad saw them, and told
Ab'sa-lom: but they went both of them away
quickly, and came to a man's house in Ba-hu'-
rim, which had a well in his court; whither they
went down.
19 And the woman took and spread a covering over the well's mouth, and spread ground
corn thereon; and the thing was not known.
20 And when Ab'sa-lom's servants came to
the woman to the house, they said, Where *is* A-
him'a-az and Jon'a-than? And the woman said
unto them, They be gone over the brook of water. And when they had sought and could not
find *them*, they returned to Je-ru'sa-lem.
21 And it came to pass, after they were departed, that they came up out of the well, and
went and told king Da'vid, and said unto Da'vid,
Arise, and pass quickly over the water: for thus
hath A-hith'o-phel counselled against you.
22 Then Da'vid arose, and all the people that
were with him, and they passed over Jor'dan:
by the morning light there lacked not one of
them that was not gone over Jor'dan.
23 ¶ And when A-hith'o-phel saw that his
counsel was not followed, he saddled *his* ass,
and arose, and gat him home to his house, to his
city, and put his household in order, and hanged
himself, and died, and was buried in the sepulchre of his father.
24 Then Da'vid came to Ma-ha-na'im. And
Ab'sa-lom passed over Jor'dan, he and all the
men of Is'ra-el with him.
25 ¶ And Ab'sa-lom made Am'a-sa captain
of the host instead of Jo'ab: which Am'a-sa *was*
a man's son, whose name *was* Ith'ra an Is'ra-el-
ite, that went in to Ab'i-gail the daughter of Na'-
hash, sister to Zer-u-i'ah Jo'ab's mother.
26 So Is'ra-el and Ab'sa-lom pitched in the
land of Gil'e-ad.
27 ¶ And it came to pass, when Da'vid was
come to Ma-ha-na'im, that Sho'bi the son of
Na'hash of Rab'bah of the children of Am'mon,
and Ma'chir the son of Am'mi-el of Lo-de'bar,
and Bar-zil'la-i the Gil'e-ad-ite of Ro-ge'lim,
28 Brought beds, and basons, and earthen
vessels, and wheat, and barley, and flour, and
parched *corn*, and beans, and lentiles, and
parched *pulse*,
29 And honey, and butter, and sheep, and
cheese of kine, for Da'vid, and for the people
that *were* with him, to eat: for they said, The
people *is* hungry, and weary, and thirsty, in the
wilderness.

18 AND Da'vid numbered the people that
were with him, and set captains of thousands and captains of hundreds over them.
2 And Da'vid sent forth a third part of the
people under the hand of Jo'ab, and a third part
under the hand of A-bish'a-i the son of Zer-u-
i'ah, Jo'ab's brother, and a third part under the
hand of It'ta-i the Git'tite. And the king said
unto the people, I will surely go forth with you
myself also.
3 But the people answered, Thou shalt not go
forth: for if we flee away, they will not care for
us; neither if half of us die, will they care for us:
but now *thou art* worth ten thousand of us:
therefore now *it is* better that thou succour us
out of the city.
4 And the king said unto them, What seemeth you best I will do. And the king stood by the
gate side, and all the people came out by hundreds and by thousands.
5 And the king commanded Jo'ab and A-
bish'a-i and It'ta-i, saying, *Deal* gently for my
sake with the young man, *even* with Ab'sa-lom.
And all the people heard when the king gave all
the captains charge concerning Ab'sa-lom.
6 ¶ So the people went out into the field
against Is'ra-el: and the battle was in the wood
of E'phra-im;

7 Where the people of Is′ra-el were slain before the servants of Da′vid, and there was there
a great slaughter that day of twenty thousand
men.
8 For the battle was there scattered over the
face of all the country: and the wood devoured
more people that day than the sword devoured.
9 ¶ And Ab′sa-lom met the servants of Da′-
vid. And Ab′sa-lom rode upon a mule, and the
mule went under the thick boughs of a great
oak, and his head caught hold of the oak, and he
was taken up between the heaven and the
earth; and the mule that *was* under him went
away.
10 And a certain man saw *it*, and told Jo′ab,
and said, Behold, I saw Ab′sa-lom hanged in an
oak.
11 And Jo′ab said unto the man that told
him, And, behold, thou sawest *him*, and why
didst thou not smite him there to the ground?
and I would have given thee ten *shekels* of silver, and a girdle.
12 And the man said unto Jo′ab, Though I
should receive a thousand *shekels* of silver in
mine hand, *yet* would I not put forth mine hand
against the king's son: for in our hearing the
king charged thee and A-bish′a-i and It′ta-i, saying, Beware that none *touch* the young man
Ab′sa-lom.
13 Otherwise I should have wrought falsehood against mine own life: for there is no matter hid from the king, and thou thyself wouldest
have set thyself against *me.*
14 Then said Jo′ab, I may not tarry thus with
thee. And he took three darts in his hand, and
thrust them through the heart of Ab′sa-lom,
while he *was* yet alive in the midst of the oak.
15 And ten young men that bare Jo′ab's armour compassed about and smote Ab′sa-lom,
and slew him.
16 And Jo′ab blew the trumpet, and the people returned from pursuing after Is′ra-el: for
Jo′ab held back the people.
17 And they took Ab′sa-lom, and cast him
into a great pit in the wood, and laid a very
great heap of stones upon him: and all Is′ra-el
fled every one to his tent.
18 ¶ Now Ab′sa-lom in his lifetime had
taken and reared up for himself a pillar, which
is in the king's dale: for he said, I have no son to
keep my name in remembrance: and he called
the pillar after his own name: and it is called
unto this day, Ab′sa-lom's place.
19 ¶ Then said A-him′a-az the son of Za′dok,
Let me now run, and bear the king tidings, how
that the LORD hath avenged him of his enemies.
20 And Jo′ab said unto him, Thou shalt not
bear tidings this day, but thou shalt bear tidings
another day: but this day thou shalt bear no tidings, because the king's son is dead.
21 Then said Jo′ab to Cu′shi, Go tell the king
what thou hast seen. And Cu′shi bowed himself
unto Jo′ab, and ran.
22 Then said A-him′a-az the son of Za′dok
yet again to Jo′ab, But howsoever, let me, I pray
thee, also run after Cu′shi. And Jo′ab said,
Wherefore wilt thou run, my son, seeing that
thou hast no tidings ready?
23 But howsoever, *said he,* let me run. And
he said unto him, Run. Then A-him′a-az ran by
the way of the plain, and overran Cu′shi.
24 And Da′vid sat between the two gates:
and the watchman went up to the roof over the
gate unto the wall, and lifted up his eyes, and
looked, and behold a man running alone.
25 And the watchman cried, and told the
king. And the king said, If he *be* alone, *there is*
tidings in his mouth. And he came apace, and
drew near.
26 And the watchman saw another man running: and the watchman called unto the porter,
and said, Behold *another* man running alone.
And the king said, He also bringeth tidings.
27 And the watchman said, Me thinketh the
running of the foremost is like the running of A-
him′a-az the son of Za′dok. And the king said,
He *is* a good man, and cometh with good tidings.
28 And A-him′a-az called, and said unto the
king, All is well. And he fell down to the earth
upon his face before the king, and said, Blessed
be the LORD thy God, which hath delivered up
the men that lifted up their hand against my
lord the king.
29 And the king said, Is the young man Ab′-
sa-lom safe? And A-him′a-az answered, When
Jo′ab sent the king's servant, and *me* thy servant, I saw a great tumult, but I knew not what
it was.
30 And the king said *unto him,* Turn aside,
and stand here. And he turned aside, and stood
still.
31 And, behold, Cu′shi came; and Cu′shi
said, Tidings, my lord the king: for the LORD
hath avenged thee this day of all them that rose
up against thee.
32 And the king said unto Cu′shi, *Is* the
young man Ab′sa-lom safe? And Cu′shi answered, The enemies of my lord the king, and
all that rise against thee to do *thee* hurt, be as
that young man *is.*
33 ¶ And the king was much moved, and
went up to the chamber over the gate, and
wept: and as he went, thus he said, O my son
Ab′sa-lom, my son, my son Ab′sa-lom! would
God I had died for thee, O Ab′sa-lom, my son,
my son!

19 AND it was told Jo′ab, Behold, the king
weepeth and mourneth for Ab′sa-lom.
2 And the victory that day was *turned* into
mourning unto all the people: for the people
heard say that day how the king was grieved for
his son.
3 And the people gat them by stealth that
day into the city, as people being ashamed steal
away when they flee in battle.
4 But the king covered his face, and the king
cried with a loud voice, O my son Ab′sa-lom, O
Ab′sa-lom, my son, my son!
5 And Jo′ab came into the house to the king,
and said, Thou hast shamed this day the faces
of all thy servants, which this day have saved
thy life, and the lives of thy sons and of thy
daughters, and the lives of thy wives, and the
lives of thy concubines;
6 In that thou lovest thine enemies, and hatest thy friends. For thou hast declared this day,
that thou regardest neither princes nor servants: for this day I perceive, that if Ab′sa-lom
had lived, and all we had died this day, then it
had pleased thee well.
7 Now therefore arise, go forth, and speak
comfortably unto thy servants: for I swear by
the LORD, if thou go not forth, there will not
tarry one with thee this night: and that will be
worse unto thee than all the evil that befell thee
from thy youth until now.
8 Then the king arose, and sat in the gate.
And they told unto all the people, saying, Behold, the king doth sit in the gate. And all the
people came before the king: for Is′ra-el had
fled every man to his tent.
9 ¶ And all the people were at strife through-

out all the tribes of Is'ra-el, saying, The king saved us out of the hand of our enemies, and he delivered us out of the hand of the Phi-lis'tines; and now he is fled out of the land for Ab'sa-lom.

10 And Ab'sa-lom, whom we anointed over us, is dead in battle. Now therefore why speak ye not a word of bringing the king back?

11 ¶ And king Da'vid sent to Za'dok and to A-bi'a-thar the priests, saying, Speak unto the elders of Ju'dah, saying, Why are ye the last to bring the king back to his house? seeing the speech of all Is'ra-el is come to the king, *even* to his house.

12 Ye *are* my brethren, ye *are* my bones and my flesh: wherefore then are ye the last to bring back the king?

13 And say ye to Am'a-sa, *Art* thou not of my bone, and of my flesh? God do so to me, and more also, if thou be not captain of the host before me continually in the room of Jo'ab.

14 And he bowed the heart of all the men of Ju'dah, even as *the heart of* one man; so that they sent *this word* unto the king, Return thou, and all thy servants.

15 So the king returned, and came to Jor'dan. And Ju'dah came to Gil'gal, to go to meet the king, to conduct the king over Jor'dan.

16 ¶ And Shim'e-i the son of Ge'ra, a Ben'ja-mite, which *was* of Ba-hu'rim, hasted and came down with the men of Ju'dah to meet king Da'-vid.

17 And *there were* a thousand men of Ben'ja-min with him, and Zi'ba the servant of the house of Saul, and his fifteen sons and his twenty servants with him; and they went over Jor'dan before the king.

18 And there went over a ferry boat to carry over the king's household, and to do what he thought good. And Shim'e-i the son of Ge'ra fell down before the king, as he was come over Jor'-dan;

19 And said unto the king, Let not my lord impute iniquity unto me, neither do thou re-member that which thy servant did perversely the day that my lord the king went out of Je-ru'sa-lem, that the king should take it to his heart.

20 For thy servant doth know that I have sinned: therefore, behold, I am come the first this day of all the house of Jo'seph to go down to meet my lord the king.

21 But A-bish'a-i the son of Zer-u-i'ah an-swered and said, Shall not Shim'e-i be put to death for this, because he cursed the LORD's anointed?

22 And Da'vid said, What have I to do with you, ye sons of Zer-u-i'ah, that ye should this day be adversaries unto me? shall there any man be put to death this day in Is'ra-el? for do not I know that I *am* this day king over Is'ra-el?

23 Therefore the king said unto Shim'e-i, Thou shalt not die. And the king sware unto him.

24 ¶ And Me-phib'o-sheth the son of Saul came down to meet the king, and had neither dressed his feet, nor trimmed his beard, nor washed his clothes, from the day the king de-parted until the day he came *again* in peace.

25 And it came to pass, when he was come to Je-ru'sa-lem to meet the king, that the king said unto him, Wherefore wentest not thou with me, Me-phib'o-sheth?

26 And he answered, My lord, O king, my servant deceived me: for thy servant said, I will saddle me an ass, that I may ride thereon, and go to the king; because thy servant *is* lame.

27 And he hath slandered thy servant unto my lord the king; but my lord the king *is* as an angel of God: do therefore *what is* good in thine eyes.

28 For all *of* my father's house were but dead men before my lord the king: yet didst thou set thy servant among them that did eat at thine own table. What right therefore have I yet to cry any more unto the king?

29 And the king said unto him, Why speakest thou any more of thy matters? I have said, Thou and Zi'ba divide the land.

30 And Me-phib'o-sheth said unto the king, Yea, let him take all, forasmuch as my lord the king is come again in peace unto his own house.

31 ¶ And Bar-zil'la-i the Gil'e-ad-ite came down from Ro-ge'lim, and went over Jor'dan with the king, to conduct him over Jor'dan.

32 Now Bar-zil'la-i was a very aged man, *even* fourscore years old: and he had provided the king of sustenance while he lay at Ma-ha-na'im; for he *was* a very great man.

33 And the king said unto Bar-zil'la-i, Come thou over with me, and I will feed thee with me in Je-ru'sa-lem.

34 And Bar-zil'la-i said unto the king, How long have I to live, that I should go up with the king unto Je-ru'sa-lem?

35 I *am* this day fourscore years old: *and* can I discern between good and evil? can thy ser-vant taste what I eat or what I drink? can I hear any more the voice of singing men and singing women? wherefore then should thy servant be yet a burden unto my lord the king?

36 Thy servant will go a little way over Jor'-dan with the king: and why should the king rec-ompense it me with such a reward?

37 Let thy servant, I pray thee, turn back again, that I may die in mine own city, *and be buried* by the grave of my father and of my mother. But behold thy servant Chim'ham; let him go over with my lord the king; and do to him what shall seem good unto thee.

38 And the king answered, Chim'ham shall go over with me, and I will do to him that which shall seem good unto thee: and whatsoever thou shalt require of me, *that* will I do for thee.

39 And all the people went over Jor'dan. And when the king was come over, the king kissed Bar-zil'la-i, and blessed him; and he returned unto his own place.

40 Then the king went on to Gil'gal, and Chim'ham went on with him: and all the people of Ju'dah conducted the king, and also half the people of Is'ra-el.

41 ¶ And, behold, all the men of Is'ra-el came to the king, and said unto the king, Why have our brethren the men of Ju'dah stolen thee away, and have brought the king, and his household, and all Da'vid's men with him, over Jor'dan?

42 And all the men of Ju'dah answered the men of Is'ra-el, Because the king *is* near of kin to us: wherefore then be ye angry for this mat-ter? have we eaten at all of the king's *cost?* or hath he given us any gift?

43 And the men of Is'ra-el answered the men of Ju'dah, and said, We have ten parts in the king, and we have also more *right* in Da'vid than ye: why then did ye despise us, that our advice should not be first had in bringing back our king? And the words of the men of Ju'dah were fiercer than the words of the men of Is'ra-el.

20 AND there happened to be there a man of Be'li-al, whose name *was* She'ba, the son of Bich'ri, a Ben'ja-mite: and he blew a

trumpet, and said, We have no part in Da'vid, neither have we inheritance in the son of Jes'se: every man to his tents, O Is'ra-el.

2 So every man of Is'ra-el went up from after Da'vid, *and* followed She'ba the son of Bich'ri: but the men of Ju'dah clave unto their king, from Jor'dan even to Je-ru'sa-lem.

3 ¶ And Da'vid came to his house at Je-ru'sa-lem; and the king took the ten women *his* concubines, whom he had left to keep the house, and put them in ward, and fed them, but went not in unto them. So they were shut up unto the day of their death, living in widowhood.

4 ¶ Then said the king to Am'a-sa, Assemble me the men of Ju'dah within three days, and be thou here present.

5 So Am'a-sa went to assemble *the men of* Ju'dah: but he tarried longer than the set time which he had appointed him.

6 And Da'vid said to A-bish'a-i, Now shall She'ba the son of Bich'ri do us more harm than *did* Ab'sa-lom: take thou thy lord's servants, and pursue after him, lest he get him fenced cities, and escape us.

7 And there went out after him Jo'ab's men, and the Cher'eth-ites, and the Pe'leth-ites, and all the mighty men: and they went out of Je-ru'sa-lem, to pursue after She'ba the son of Bich'ri.

8 When they *were* at the great stone which *is* in Gib'e-on, Am'a-sa went before them. And Jo'ab's garment that he had put on was girded unto him, and upon it a girdle *with* a sword fastened upon his loins in the sheath thereof; and as he went forth it fell out.

9 And Jo'ab said to Am'a-sa, *Art* thou in health, my brother? And Jo'ab took Am'a-sa by the beard with the right hand to kiss him.

10 But Am'a-sa took no heed to the sword that *was* in Jo'ab's hand: so he smote him therewith in the fifth *rib,* and shed out his bowels to the ground, and struck him not again; and he died. So Jo'ab and A-bish'a-i his brother pursued after She'ba the son of Bich'ri.

11 And one of Jo'ab's men stood by him, and said, He that favoureth Jo'ab, and he that *is* for Da'vid, *let him go* after Jo'ab.

12 And Am'a-sa wallowed in blood in the midst of the highway. And when the man saw that all the people stood still, he removed Am'a-sa out of the highway into the field, and cast a cloth upon him, when he saw that every one that came by him stood still.

13 When he was removed out of the highway, all the people went on after Jo'ab, to pursue after She'ba the son of Bich'ri.

14 ¶ And he went through all the tribes of Is'ra-el unto A'bel, and to Beth–ma'a-chah, and all the Be'rites: and they were gathered together, and went also after him.

15 And they came and besieged him in A'bel of Beth–ma'a-chah, and they cast up a bank against the city, and it stood in the trench: and all the people that *were* with Jo'ab battered the wall, to throw it down.

16 ¶ Then cried a wise woman out of the city, Hear, hear; say, I pray you, unto Jo'ab, Come near hither, that I may speak with thee.

17 And when he was come near unto her, the woman said, *Art* thou Jo'ab? And he answered, I *am he.* Then she said unto him, Hear the words of thine handmaid. And he answered, I do hear.

18 Then she spake, saying, They were wont to speak in old time, saying, They shall surely ask *counsel* at A'bel: and so they ended *the matter.*

19 I *am one of them that are* peaceable *and* faithful in Is'ra-el: thou seekest to destroy a city and a mother in Is'ra-el: why wilt thou swallow up the inheritance of the LORD?

20 And Jo'ab answered and said, Far be it, far be it from me, that I should swallow up or destroy.

21 The matter *is* not so: but a man of mount E'phra-im, She'ba the son of Bich'ri by name, hath lifted up his hand against the king, *even* against Da'vid: deliver him only, and I will depart from the city. And the woman said unto Jo'ab, Behold, his head shall be thrown to thee over the wall.

22 Then the woman went unto all the people in her wisdom. And they cut off the head of She'ba the son of Bich'ri, and cast *it* out to Jo'ab. And he blew a trumpet, and they retired from the city, every man to his tent. And Jo'ab returned to Je-ru'sa-lem unto the king.

23 ¶ Now Jo'ab *was* over all the host of Is'ra-el: and Be-na'iah the son of Je-hoi'a-da *was* over the Cher'eth-ites and over the Pe'leth-ites:

24 And A-do'ram *was* over the tribute: and Je-hosh'a-phat the son of A-hi'lud *was* recorder:

25 And She'va *was* scribe: and Za'dok and A-bi'a-thar *were* the priests:

26 And I'ra also the Ja'ir-ite was a chief ruler about Da'vid.

21 THEN there was a famine in the days of Da'vid three years, year after year; and Da'vid enquired of the LORD. And the LORD answered, *It is* for Saul, and for *his* bloody house, because he slew the Gib'e-on-ites.

2 And the king called the Gib'e-on-ites, and said unto them; (now the Gib'e-on-ites *were* not of the children of Is'ra-el, but of the remnant of the Am'or-ites; and the children of Is'ra-el had sworn unto them: and Saul sought to slay them in his zeal to the children of Is'ra-el and Ju'dah.)

3 Wherefore Da'vid said unto the Gib'e-on-ites, What shall I do for you? and wherewith shall I make the atonement, that ye may bless the inheritance of the LORD?

4 And the Gib'e-on-ites said unto him, We will have no silver nor gold of Saul, nor of his house; neither for us shalt thou kill any man in Is'ra-el. And he said, What ye shall say, *that* will I do for you.

5 And they answered the king, The man that consumed us, and that devised against us *that* we should be destroyed from remaining in any of the coasts of Is'ra-el,

6 Let seven men of his sons be delivered unto us, and we will hang them up unto the LORD in Gib'e-ah of Saul, *whom* the LORD did choose. And the king said, I will give *them.*

7 But the king spared Me-phib'o-sheth, the son of Jon'a-than the son of Saul, because of the LORD's oath that *was* between them, between Da'vid and Jon'a-than the son of Saul.

8 But the king took the two sons of Riz'pah the daughter of A-i'ah, whom she bare unto Saul, Ar-mo'ni and Me-phib'o-sheth; and the five sons of Mi'chal the daughter of Saul, whom she brought up for A'dri-el the son of Bar-zil'la-i the Me-hol'ath-ite:

9 And he delivered them into the hands of the Gib'e-on-ites, and they hanged them in the hill before the LORD: and they fell *all* seven together, and were put to death in the days of harvest, in the first *days,* in the beginning of barley harvest.

10 ¶ And Riz'pah the daughter of A-i'ah took

sackcloth, and spread it for her upon the rock,
from the beginning of harvest until water
dropped upon them out of heaven, and suffered
neither the birds of the air to rest on them by
day, nor the beasts of the field by night.
11 And it was told Da'vid what Riz'pah the
daughter of A-i'ah, the concubine of Saul, had
done.
12 ¶ And Da'vid went and took the bones of
Saul and the bones of Jon'a-than his son from
the men of Ja'besh-gil'e-ad, which had stolen
them from the street of Beth'-shan, where the
Phi-lis'tines had hanged them, when the Phi-lis'-
tines had slain Saul in Gil-bo'a:
13 And he brought up from thence the bones
of Saul and the bones of Jon'a-than his son; and
they gathered the bones of them that were
hanged.
14 And the bones of Saul and Jon'a-than his
son buried they in the country of Ben'ja-min in
Ze'lah, in the sepulchre of Kish his father: and
they performed all that the king commanded.
And after that God was intreated for the land.
15 ¶ Moreover the Phi-lis'tines had yet war
again with Is'ra-el; and Da'vid went down, and
his servants with him, and fought against the
Phi-lis'tines: and Da'vid waxed faint.
16 And Ish'bi-be'nob, which *was* of the sons
of the giant, the weight of whose spear *weighed*
three hundred *shekels* of brass in weight, he
being girded with a new *sword*, thought to have
slain Da'vid.
17 But A-bish'a-i the son of Zer-u-i'ah suc-
coured him, and smote the Phi-lis'tine, and
killed him. Then the men of Da'vid sware unto
him, saying, Thou shalt go no more out with us
to battle, that thou quench not the light of Is'ra-
el.
18 And it came to pass after this, that there
was again a battle with the Phi-lis'tines at Gob:
then Sib'be-chai the Hu'shath-ite slew Saph,
which *was* of the sons of the giant.
19 And there was again a battle in Gob with
the Phi-lis'tines, where El-ha'nan the son of Ja-
ar'e-or'e-gim, a Beth'-le-hem-ite, slew *the*
brother of Go-li'ath the Git'tite, the staff of
whose spear *was* like a weaver's beam.
20 And there was yet a battle in Gath, where
was a man of *great* stature, that had on every
hand six fingers, and on every foot six toes, four
and twenty in number; and he also was born to
the giant.
21 And when he defied Is'ra-el, Jon'a-than
the son of Shim'e-ah the brother of Da'vid slew
him.
22 These four were born to the giant in Gath,
and fell by the hand of Da'vid, and by the hand
of his servants.

22 AND Da'vid spake unto the LORD the
words of this song in the day *that* the
LORD had delivered him out of the hand of all
his enemies, and out of the hand of Saul:
2 And he said, The LORD *is* my rock, and my
fortress, and my deliverer;
3 The God of my rock; in him will I trust: *he*
is my shield, and the horn of my salvation, my
high tower, and my refuge, my saviour; thou
savest me from violence.
4 I will call on the LORD, *who is* worthy to be
praised: so shall I be saved from mine enemies.
5 When the waves of death compassed me,
the floods of ungodly men made me afraid;
6 The sorrows of hell compassed me about;
the snares of death prevented me;
7 In my distress I called upon the LORD, and
cried to my God: and he did hear my voice out
of his temple, and my cry *did enter* into his ears.
8 Then the earth shook and trembled; the
foundations of heaven moved and shook, because he was wroth.
9 There went up a smoke out of his nostrils,
and fire out of his mouth devoured: coals were
kindled by it.
10 He bowed the heavens also, and came
down; and darkness *was* under his feet.
11 And he rode upon a cherub, and did fly:
and he was seen upon the wings of the wind.
12 And he made darkness pavilions round
about him, dark waters, *and* thick clouds of the
skies.
13 Through the brightness before him were
coals of fire kindled.
14 The LORD thundered from heaven, and the
most High uttered his voice.
15 And he sent out arrows, and scattered
them; lightning, and discomfited them.
16 And the channels of the sea appeared, the
foundations of the world were discovered, at
the rebuking of the LORD, at the blast of the
breath of his nostrils.
17 He sent from above, he took me; he drew
me out of many waters;
18 He delivered me from my strong enemy,
and from them that hated me: for they were too
strong for me.
19 They prevented me in the day of my calamity: but the LORD was my stay.
20 He brought me forth also into a large
place: he delivered me, because he delighted in
me.
21 The LORD rewarded me according to my
righteousness: according to the cleanness of my
hands hath he recompensed me.
22 For I have kept the ways of the LORD, and
have not wickedly departed from my God.
23 For all his judgments *were* before me: and
as for his statutes, I did not depart from them.
24 I was also upright before him, and have
kept myself from mine iniquity.
25 Therefore the LORD hath recompensed me
according to my righteousness; according to my
cleanness in his eye sight.
26 With the merciful thou wilt shew thyself
merciful, *and* with the upright man thou wilt
shew thyself upright.
27 With the pure thou wilt shew thyself pure;
and with the froward thou wilt shew thyself unsavoury.
28 And the afflicted people thou wilt save:
but thine eyes *are* upon the haughty, *that* thou
mayest bring *them* down.
29 For thou *art* my lamp, O LORD: and the
LORD will lighten my darkness.
30 For by thee I have run through a troop: by
my God have I leaped over a wall.
31 *As for* God, his way *is* perfect; the word of
the LORD *is* tried: he *is* a buckler to all them that
trust in him.
32 For who *is* God, save the LORD? and who
is a rock, save our God?
33 God *is* my strength *and* power: and he
maketh my way perfect.
34 He maketh my feet like hinds' *feet:* and
setteth me upon my high places.
35 He teacheth my hands to war; so that a
bow of steel is broken by mine arms.
36 Thou hast also given me the shield of thy
salvation: and thy gentleness hath made me
great.
37 Thou hast enlarged my steps under me; so
that my feet did not slip.
38 I have pursued mine enemies, and de-

stroyed them; and turned not again until I had consumed them.

39 And I have consumed them, and wounded them, that they could not arise: yea, they are fallen under my feet.

40 For thou hast girded me with strength to battle: them that rose up against me hast thou subdued under me.

41 Thou hast also given me the necks of mine enemies, that I might destroy them that hate me.

42 They looked, but *there was* none to save; *even* unto the LORD, but he answered them not.

43 Then did I beat them as small as the dust of the earth, I did stamp them as the mire of the street, *and* did spread them abroad.

44 Thou also hast delivered me from the strivings of my people, thou hast kept me *to be* head of the heathen: a people *which* I knew not shall serve me.

45 Strangers shall submit themselves unto me: as soon as they hear, they shall be obedient unto me.

46 Strangers shall fade away, and they shall be afraid out of their close places.

47 The LORD liveth; and blessed *be* my rock; and exalted be the God of the rock of my salvation.

48 It *is* God that avengeth me, and that bringeth down the people under me,

49 And that bringeth me forth from mine enemies: thou also hast lifted me up on high above them that rose up against me: thou hast delivered me from the violent man.

50 Therefore I will give thanks unto thee, O LORD, among the heathen, and I will sing praises unto thy name.

51 *He is* the tower of salvation for his king: and sheweth mercy to his anointed, unto Da'vid, and to his seed for evermore.

23 NOW these *be* the last words of Da'vid. Da'vid the son of Jes'se said, and the man *who was* raised up on high, the anointed of the God of Ja'cob, and the sweet psalmist of Is'ra-el, said,

2 The Spirit of the LORD spake by me, and his word *was* in my tongue.

3 The God of Is'ra-el said, the Rock of Is'ra-el spake to me, He that ruleth over men *must be* just, ruling in the fear of God.

4 And *he shall be* as the light of the morning, *when* the sun riseth, *even* a morning without clouds; *as* the tender grass *springing* out of the earth by clear shining after rain.

5 Although my house *be* not so with God; yet he hath made with me an everlasting covenant, ordered in all *things*, and sure: for *this is* all my salvation, and all *my* desire, although he make *it* not to grow.

6 ¶ But *the sons* of Be'li-al *shall be* all of them as thorns thrust away, because they cannot be taken with hands:

7 But the man *that* shall touch them must be fenced with iron and the staff of a spear; and they shall be utterly burned with fire in the *same* place.

8 ¶ These *be* the names of the mighty men whom Da'vid had: The Tach'mo-nite that sat in the seat, chief among the captains; the same *was* Ad'i-no the Ez'nite: *he lift up his spear* against eight hundred, whom he slew at one time.

9 And after him *was* E-le-a'zar the son of Do'do the A-ho'hite, *one* of the three mighty men with Da'vid, when they defied the Phi-lis'tines *that* were there gathered together to battle, and the men of Is'ra-el were gone away:

10 He arose, and smote the Phi-lis'tines until his hand was weary, and his hand clave unto the sword: and the LORD wrought a great victory that day; and the people returned after him only to spoil.

11 And after him *was* Sham'mah the son of Ag'e-e the Ha'ra-rite. And the Phi-lis'tines were gathered together into a troop, where was a piece of ground full of lentiles: and the people fled from the Phi-lis'tines.

12 But he stood in the midst of the ground, and defended it, and slew the Phi-lis'tines: and the LORD wrought a great victory.

13 And three of the thirty chief went down, and came to Da'vid in the harvest time unto the cave of A-dul'lam: and the troop of the Phi-lis'tines pitched in the valley of Reph'a-im.

14 And Da'vid *was* then in an hold, and the garrison of the Phi-lis'tines *was* then *in* Beth'-le-hem.

15 And Da'vid longed, and said, Oh that one would give me drink of the water of the well of Beth'-le-hem, which *is* by the gate!

16 And the three mighty men brake through the host of the Phi-lis'tines, and drew water out of the well of Beth'-le-hem, that *was* by the gate, and took *it*, and brought *it* to Da'vid: nevertheless he would not drink thereof, but poured it out unto the LORD.

17 And he said, Be it far from me, O LORD, that I should do this: *is not this* the blood of the men that went in jeopardy of their lives? therefore he would not drink it. These things did these three mighty men.

18 And A-bish'a-i, the brother of Jo'ab, the son of Zer-u-i'ah, was chief among three. And he lifted up his spear against three hundred, *and* slew *them*, and had the name among three.

19 Was he not most honourable of three? therefore he was their captain: howbeit he attained not unto the *first* three.

20 And Be-na'iah the son of Je-hoi'a-da, the son of a valiant man, of Kab'ze-el, who had done many acts, he slew two lionlike men of Mo'ab: he went down also and slew a lion in the midst of a pit in time of snow:

21 And he slew an E-gyp'tian, a goodly man: and the E-gyp'tian had a spear in his hand; but he went down to him with a staff, and plucked the spear out of the E-gyp'tian's hand, and slew him with his own spear.

22 These *things* did Be-na'iah the son of Je-hoi'a-da, and had the name among three mighty men.

23 He was more honourable than the thirty, but he attained not to the *first* three. And Da'vid set him over his guard.

24 A'sa-hel the brother of Jo'ab *was* one of the thirty; El-ha'nan the son of Do'do of Beth'-le-hem,

25 Sham'mah the Ha'rod-ite, El'i-ka the Ha'rod-ite,

26 He'lez the Pal'tite, I'ra the son of Ik'kesh the Te-ko'ite,

27 A-bi-e'zer the An'e-thoth-ite, Me-bun'nai the Hu'shath-ite,

28 Zal'mon the A-ho'hite, Ma-har'a-i the Ne-toph'a-thite,

29 He'leb the son of Ba'a-nah, a Ne-toph'a-thite, It'ta-i the son of Ri'bai out of Gib'e-ah of the children of Ben'ja-min,

30 Be-na'iah the Pir'a-thon-ite, Hid'da-i of the brooks of Ga'ash,

31 A'bi-al'bon the Ar'bath-ite, Az'ma-veth the Bar-hu'mite,

32 E-li'ah-ba the Sha-al'bo-nite, of the sons of
Ja'shen, Jon'a-than,
33 Sham'mah the Ha'ra-rite, A-hi'am the son
of Sha'rar the Ha'ra-rite,
34 E-liph'e-let the son of A-has'ba-i, the son
of the Ma-ach'a-thite, E-li'am the son of A-hith'-
o-phel the Gi'lo-nite,
35 Hez'ra-i the Car'mel-ite, Pa'a-rai the Ar'-
bite,
36 I'gal the son of Na'than of Zo'bah, Ba'ni
the Gad'ite,
37 Ze'lek the Am'mon-ite, Na'ha-ri the Be-e'-
roth-ite, armourbearer to Jo'ab the son of Zer-
u-i'ah,
38 I'ra an Ith'rite, Ga'reb an Ith'rite,
39 U-ri'ah the Hit'tite: thirty and seven in all.

24 AND again the anger of the LORD was
kindled against Is'ra-el, and he moved
Da'vid against them to say, Go, number Is'ra-el
and Ju'dah.
2 For the king said to Jo'ab the captain of the
host, which *was* with him, Go now through all
the tribes of Is'ra-el, from Dan even to Be'er-
she'ba, and number ye people, that I may know
the number of the people.
3 And Jo'ab said unto the king, Now the
LORD thy God add unto the people, how many
soever they be, an hundredfold, and that the
eyes of my lord the king may see *it:* but why
doth my lord the king delight in this thing?
4 Notwithstanding the king's word prevailed
against Jo'ab, and against the captains of the
host. And Jo'ab and the captains of the host
went out from the presence of the king, to number the people of Is'ra-el.
5 ¶ And they passed over Jor'dan, and
pitched in Ar'o-er, on the right side of the city
that *lieth* in the midst of the river of Gad, and
toward Ja'zer:
6 Then they came to Gil'e-ad, and to the land
of Tah'tim-hod'shi; and they came to Dan-ja'-
an, and about to Zi'don,
7 And came to the strong hold of Tyre, and to
all the cities of the Hi'vites, and of the Ca'naan-
ites: and they went out to the south of Ju'dah,
even to Be'er-she'ba.
8 So when they had gone through all the
land, they came to Je-ru'sa-lem at the end of
nine months and twenty days.
9 And Jo'ab gave up the sum of the number
of the people unto the king: and there were in
Is'ra-el eight hundred thousand vailant men
that drew the sword; and the men of Ju'dah
were five hundred thousand men.
10 ¶ And Da'vid's heart smote him after that
he had numbered the people. And Da'vid said
unto the LORD, I have sinned greatly in that I
have done: and now, I beseech thee, O LORD,
take away the iniquity of thy servant; for I have
done very foolishly.
11 For when Da'vid was up in the morning,
the word of the LORD came unto the prophet
Gad, Da'vid's seer, saying,
12 Go and say unto Da'vid, Thus saith the
LORD, I offer thee three *things;* choose thee one
of them, that I may *do it* unto thee.
13 So Gad came to Da'vid, and told him, and
said unto him, Shall seven years of famine
come unto thee in thy land? or wilt thou flee
three months before thine enemies, while they
pursue thee? or that there be three days' pestilence in thy land? now advise, and see what answer I shall return to him that sent me.
14 And Da'vid said unto Gad, I am in a great
strait: let us fall now into the hand of the LORD;
for his mercies *are* great: and let me not fall into
the hand of man.
15 ¶ So the LORD sent a pestilence upon Is'-
ra-el from the morning even to the time appointed: and there died of the people from Dan
even to Be'er-she'ba seventy thousand men.
16 And when the angel stretched out his
hand upon Je-ru'sa-lem to destroy it, the LORD
repented him of the evil, and said to the angel
that destroyed the people, It is enough: stay
now thine hand. And the angel of the LORD was
by the threshingplace of A-rau'nah the Jeb'u-
site.
17 And Da'vid spake unto the LORD when he
saw the angel that smote the people, and said,
Lo, I have sinned, and I have done wickedly:
but these sheep, what have they done? let thine
hand, I pray thee, be against me, and against
my father's house.
18 ¶ And Gad came that day to Da'vid, and
said unto him, Go up, rear an altar unto the
LORD in the threshingfloor of A-rau'nah the
Jeb'u-site.
19 And Da'vid, according to the saying of
Gad, went up as the LORD commanded.
20 And A-rau'nah looked, and saw the king
and his servants coming on toward him: and A-
rau'nah went out, and bowed himself before the
king on his face upon the ground.
21 And A-rau'nah said, Wherefore is my lord
the king come to his servant? And Da'vid said,
To buy the threshingfloor of thee, to build an
altar unto the LORD, that the plague may be
stayed from the people.
22 And A-rau'nah said unto Da'vid, Let my
lord the king take and offer up what *seemeth*
good unto him: behold, *here be* oxen for burnt
sacrifice, and threshing instruments and *other*
instruments of the oxen for wood.
23 All these *things* did A-rau'nah, *as* a king,
give unto the king. And A-rau'nah said unto the
king, The LORD thy God accept thee.
24 And the king said unto A-rau'nah, Nay;
but I will surely buy *it* of thee at a price: neither
will I offer burnt offerings unto the LORD my
God of that which doth cost me nothing. So
Da'vid bought the threshingfloor and the oxen
for fifty shekels of silver.
25 And Da'vid built there an altar unto the
LORD, and offered burnt offerings and peace offerings. So the LORD was intreated for the land,
and the plague was stayed from Is'ra-el.

THE FIRST BOOK OF THE

KINGS

1 NOW king Da'vid was old *and* stricken in
years; and they covered him with clothes,
but he gat no heat.
2 Wherefore his servants said unto him, Let
there be sought for my lord the king a young
virgin: and let her stand before the king, and let
her cherish him, and let her lie in thy bosom,
that my lord the king may get heat.
3 So they sought for a fair damsel throughout all the coasts of Is'ra-el, and found Ab'i-

shag a Shu'nam-mite, and brought her to the
king.
4 And the damsel *was* very fair, and cher-
ished the king, and ministered to him: but the
king knew her not.
5 ¶ Then Ad-o-ni'jah the son of Hag'gith exalted himself, saying, I will be king: and he prepared him chariots and horsemen, and fifty men
to run before him.
6 And his father had not displeased him at
any time in saying, Why hast thou done so? and
he also *was a* very goodly *man;* and *his mother*
bare him after Ab'sa-lom.
7 And he conferred with Jo'ab the son of Zer-
u-i'ah, and with A-bi'a-thar the priest: and they
following Ad-o-ni'jah helped *him.*
8 But Za'dok the priest, and Be-na'iah the
son of Je-hoi'a-da, and Na'than the prophet, and
Shim'e-i, and Re'i, and the mighty men which
belonged to Da'vid, were not with Ad-o-ni'jah.
9 And Ad-o-ni'jah slew sheep and oxen and
fat cattle by the stone of Zo'he-leth, which *is* by
En-ro'gel, and called all his brethren the king's
sons, and all the men of Ju'dah the king's servants:
10 But Na'than the prophet, and Be-na'iah,
and the mighty men, and Sol'o-mon his brother,
he called not.
11 ¶ Wherefore Na'than spake unto Bath'-
she-ba the mother of Sol'o-mon, saying, Hast
thou not heard that Ad-o-ni'jah the son of Hag'-
gith doth reign, and Da'vid our lord knoweth *it*
not?
12 Now therefore come, let me, I pray thee,
give thee counsel, that thou mayest save thine
own life, and the life of thy son Sol'o-mon.
13 Go and get thee in unto king Da'vid, and
say unto him, Didst not thou, my lord, O king,
swear unto thine handmaid, saying, Assuredly
Sol'o-mon thy son shall reign after me, and he
shall sit upon my throne? why then doth Ad-o-
ni'jah reign?
14 Behold, while thou yet talkest there with
the king, I also will come in after thee, and confirm thy words.
15 ¶ And Bath'-she-ba went in unto the king
into the chamber: and the king was very old;
and Ab'i-shag the Shu'nam-mite ministered
unto the king.
16 And Bath'-she-ba bowed, and did obeisance unto the king. And the king said, What
wouldest thou?
17 And she said unto him, My lord, thou
swarest by the LORD thy God unto thine handmaid, *saying,* Assuredly Sol'o-mon thy son shall
reign after me, and he shall sit upon my throne.
18 And now, behold, Ad-o-ni'jah reigneth;
and now, my lord the king, thou knowest *it* not:
19 And he hath slain oxen and fat cattle and
sheep in abundance, and hath called all the sons
of the king, and A-bi'a-thar the priest, and Jo'ab
the captain of the host: but Sol'o-mon thy servant hath he not called.
20 And thou, my lord, O king, the eyes of all
Is'ra-el *are* upon thee, that thou shouldest tell
them who shall sit on the throne of my lord the
king after him.
21 Otherwise it shall come to pass, when my
lord the king shall sleep with his fathers, that I
and my son Sol'o-mon shall be counted offend-
ers.
22 ¶ And, lo, while she yet talked with the
king, Na'than the prophet also came in.
23 And they told the king, saying, Behold
Na'than the prophet. And when he was come in
before the king, he bowed himself before the
king with his face to the ground.
24 And Na'than said, My lord, O king, hast
thou said, Ad-o-ni'jah shall reign after me, and
he shall sit upon my throne?
25 For he is gone down this day, and hath
slain oxen and fat cattle and sheep in abundance, and hath called all the king's sons, and
the captains of the host, and A-bi'a-thar the
priest; and, behold, they eat and drink before
him, and say, God save king Ad-o-ni'jah.
26 But me, *even* me thy servant, and Za'dok
the priest, and Be-na'iah the son of Je-hoi'a-da,
and thy servant Sol'o-mon, hath he not called.
27 Is this thing done by my lord the king, and
thou hast not shewed *it* unto thy servant, who
should sit on the throne of my lord the king after him?
28 ¶ Then king Da'vid answered and said,
Call me Bath'-she-ba. And she came into the
king's presence, and stood before the king.
29 And the king sware, and said, *As* the LORD
liveth, that hath redeemed my soul out of all
distress,
30 Even as I sware unto thee by the LORD
God of Is'ra-el, saying, Assuredly Sol'o-mon thy
son shall reign after me, and he shall sit upon
my throne in my stead; even so will I certainly
do this day.
31 Then Bath'-she-ba bowed with *her* face to
the earth, and did reverence to the king, and
said, Let my lord king Da'vid live for ever.
32 ¶ And king Da'vid said, Call me Za'dok
the priest, and Na'than the prophet, and Be-na'-
iah the son of Je-hoi'a-da. And they came before the king.
33 The king also said unto them, Take with
you the servants of your lord, and cause Sol'o-
mon my son to ride upon mine own mule, and
bring him down to Gi'hon:
34 And let Za'dok the priest and Na'than the
prophet anoint him there king over Is'ra-el: and
blow ye with the trumpet, and say, God save
king Sol'o-mon.
35 Then ye shall come up after him, that he
may come and sit upon my throne; for he shall
be king in my stead: and I have appointed him
to be ruler over Is'ra-el and over Ju'dah.
36 And Be-na'iah the son of Je-hoi'a-da answered the king, and said, Amen: the LORD God
of my lord the king say so *too.*
37 As the LORD hath been with my lord the
king even so be he with Sol'o-mon, and make
his throne greater than the throne of my lord
king Da'vid.
38 So Za'dok the priest, and Na'than the
prophet, and Be-na'iah the son of Je-hoi'a-da,
and the Cher'eth-ites, and the Pe'leth-ites, went
down, and caused Sol'o-mon to ride upon king
Da'vid's mule, and brought him to Gi'hon.
39 And Za'dok the priest took an horn of oil
out of the tabernacle, and anointed Sol'o-mon.
And they blew the trumpet; and all the people
said, God save king Sol'o-mon.
40 And all the people came up after him, and
the people piped with pipes, and rejoiced with
great joy, so that the earth rent with the sound
of them.
41 ¶ And Ad-o-ni'jah and all the guests that
were with him heard *it* as they had made an end
of eating. And when Jo'ab heard the sound of
the trumpet, he said, Wherefore *is this* noise of
the city being in an uproar?
42 And while he yet spake, behold, Jon'a-
than the son of A-bi'a-thar the priest came: and
Ad-o-ni'jah said unto him, Come in; for thou *art*
a valiant man, and bringest good tidings.
43 And Jon'a-than answered and said to Ad-

o-ni'jah, Verily our lord king Da'vid hath made Sol'o-mon king.

44 And the king hath sent with him Za'dok the priest, and Na'than the prophet, and Be-na'-iah the son of Je-hoi'a-da, and the Cher'eth-ites, and the Pe'leth-ites, and they have caused him to ride upon the king's mule:

45 And Za'dok the priest and Na'than the prophet have anointed him king in Gi'hon: and they are come up from thence rejoicing, so that the city rang again. This *is* the noise that ye have heard.

46 And also Sol'o-mon sitteth on the throne of the kingdom.

47 And moreover the king's servants came to bless our lord king Da'vid, saying, God make the name of Sol'o-mon better than thy name, and make his throne greater than thy throne. And the king bowed himself upon the bed.

48 And also thus said the king, Blessed *be* the LORD God of Is'ra-el, which hath given *one* to sit on my throne this day, mine eyes even seeing *it*.

49 And all the guests that *were* with Ad-o-ni'jah were afraid, and rose up, and went every man his way.

50 ¶ And Ad-o-ni'jah feared because of Sol'-o-mon, and arose, and went, and caught hold on the horns of the altar.

51 And it was told Sol'o-mon, saying, Behold, Ad-o-ni'jah feareth king Sol'o-mon: for, lo, he hath caught hold on the horns of the altar, saying, Let king Sol'o-mon swear unto me to day that he will not slay his servant with the sword.

52 And Sol'o-mon said, If he will shew himself a worthy man, there shall not an hair of him fall to the earth: but if wickedness shall be found in him, he shall die.

53 So king Sol'o-mon sent, and they brought him down from the altar. And he came and bowed himself to king Sol'o-mon: and Sol'o-mon said unto him, Go to thine house.

2 NOW the days of Da'vid drew nigh that he should die; and he charged Sol'o-mon his son, saying,

2 I go the way of all the earth: be thou strong therefore, and shew thyself a man;

3 And keep the charge of the LORD thy God, to walk in his ways, to keep his statutes, and his commandments, and his judgments, and his testimonies, as it is written in the law of Mo'ses, that thou mayest prosper in all that thou doest, and whithersoever thou turnest thyself:

4 That the LORD may continue his word which he spake concerning me, saying, If thy children take heed to their way, to walk before me in truth with all their heart and with all their soul, there shall not fail thee (said he) a man on the throne of Is'ra-el.

5 Moreover thou knowest also what Jo'ab the son of Zer-u-i'ah did to me, *and* what he did to the two captains of the hosts of Is'ra-el, unto Ab'ner the son of Ner, and unto Am'a-sa the son of Je'ther, whom he slew, and shed the blood of war in peace, and put the blood of war upon his girdle that *was* about his loins, and in his shoes that *were* on his feet.

6 Do therefore according to thy wisdom, and let not his hoar head go down to the grave in peace.

7 But shew kindness unto the sons of Bar-zil'la-i the Gil'e-ad-ite, and let them be of those that eat at thy table: for so they came to me when I fled because of Ab'sa-lom thy brother.

8 And, behold, *thou hast* with thee Shim'e-i the son of Ge'ra, a Ben'ja-mite of Ba-hu'rim, which cursed me with a grievous curse in the day when I went to Ma-ha-na'im: but he came down to meet me at Jor'dan, and I sware to him by the LORD, saying, I will not put thee to death with the sword.

9 Now therefore hold him not guiltless: for thou *art* a wise man, and knowest what thou oughtest to do unto him; but his hoar head bring thou down to the grave with blood.

10 So Da'vid slept with his fathers, and was buried in the city of Da'vid.

11 And the days that Da'vid reigned over Is'-ra-el *were* forty years: seven years reigned he in He'bron, and thirty and three years reigned he in Je-ru'sa-lem.

12 ¶ Then sat Sol'o-mon upon the throne of Da'vid his father; and his kingdom was established greatly.

13 ¶ And Ad-o-ni'jah the son of Hag'gith came to Bath'-she-ba the mother of Sol'o-mon. And she said, Comest thou peaceably? And he said, Peaceably.

14 He said moreover, I have somewhat to say unto thee. And she said, Say on.

15 And he said, Thou knowest that the kingdom was mine, and *that* all Is'ra-el set their faces on me, that I should reign: howbeit the kingdom is turned about, and is become my brother's: for it was his from the LORD.

16 And now I ask one petition of thee, deny me not. And she said unto him, Say on.

17 And he said, Speak, I pray thee, unto Sol'-o-mon the king, (for he will not say thee nay,) that he give me Ab'i-shag the Shu'nam-mite to wife.

18 And Bath'-she-ba said, Well; I will speak for thee unto the king.

19 ¶ Bath'-she-ba therefore went unto king Sol'o-mon, to speak unto him for Ad-o-ni'jah. And the king rose up to meet her, and bowed himself unto her, and sat down on his throne, and caused a seat to be set for the king's mother; and she sat on his right hand.

20 Then she said, I desire one small petition of thee; *I pray thee,* say me not nay. And the king said unto her, Ask on, my mother: for I will not say thee nay.

21 And she said, Let Ab'i-shag the Shu'nam-mite be given to Ad-o-ni'jah thy brother to wife.

22 And king Sol'o-mon answered and said unto his mother, And why dost thou ask Ab'i-shag the Shu'nam-mite for Ad-o-ni'jah? ask for him the kingdom also; for he *is* mine elder brother; even for him, and for A-bi'a-thar the priest, and for Jo'ab the son of Zer-u-i'ah.

23 Then king Sol'o-mon sware by the LORD, saying, God do so to me, and more also, if Ad-o-ni'jah have not spoken this word against his own life.

24 Now therefore, *as* the LORD liveth, which hath established me, and set me on the throne of Da'vid my father, and who hath made me an house, as he promised, Ad-o-ni'jah shall be put to death this day.

25 And king Sol'o-mon sent by the hand of Be-na'iah the son of Je-hoi'a-da; and he fell upon him that he died.

26 ¶ And unto A-bi'a-thar the priest said the king, Get thee to An'a-thoth, unto thine own fields; for thou *art* worthy of death: but I will not at this time put thee to death, because thou barest the ark of the Lord GOD before Da'vid my father, and because thou hast been afflicted in all wherein my father was afflicted.

27 So Sol'o-mon thrust out A-bi'a-thar from being priest unto the LORD; that he might fulfil the word of the LORD, which he spake concerning the house of E'li in Shi'loh.

28 ¶ Then tidings came to Jo′ab: for Jo′ab had turned after Ad-o-ni′jah, though he turned not after Ab′sa-lom. And Jo′ab fled unto the tabernacle of the LORD, and caught hold on the horns of the altar.

29 And it was told king Sol′o-mon that Jo′ab was fled unto the tabernacle of the LORD; and, behold, *he is* by the altar. Then Sol′o-mon sent Be-na′iah the son of Je-hoi′a-da, saying, Go, fall upon him.

30 And Be-na′iah came to the tabernacle of the LORD, and said unto him, Thus saith the king, Come forth. And he said, Nay: but I will die here. And Be-na′iah brought the king word again, saying, Thus said Jo′ab, and thus he answered me.

31 And the king said unto him, Do as he hath said, and fall upon him, and bury him; that thou mayest take away the innocent blood, which Jo′ab shed, from me, and from the house of my father.

32 And the LORD shall return his blood upon his own head, who fell upon two men more righteous and better than he, and slew them with the sword, my father Da′vid not knowing *thereof, to wit,* Ab′ner the son of Ner, captain of the host of Is′ra-el, and Am′a-sa the son of Je′-ther, captain of the host of Ju′dah.

33 Their blood shall therefore return upon the head of Jo′ab, and upon the head of his seed for ever: but upon Da′vid, and upon his seed, and upon his house, and upon his throne, shall there be peace for ever from the LORD.

34 So Be-na′iah the son of Je-hoi′a-da went up, and fell upon him, and slew him: and he was buried in his own house in the wilderness.

35 ¶ And the king put Be-na′iah the son of Je-hoi′a-da in his room over the host: and Za′-dok the priest did the king put in the room of A-bi′a-thar.

36 ¶ And the king sent and called for Shim′e-i, and said unto him, Build thee an house in Je-ru′sa-lem, and dwell there, and go not forth thence any whither.

37 For it shall be, *that* on the day thou goest out, and passest over the brook Kid′ron, thou shalt know for certain that thou shalt surely die: thy blood shall be upon thine own head.

38 And Shim′e-i said unto the king, The saying *is* good: as my lord the king hath said, so will thy servant do. And Shim′e-i dwelt in Je-ru′sa-lem many days.

39 And it came to pass at the end of three years, that two of the servants of Shim′e-i ran away unto A′chish son of Ma′a-chah king of Gath. And they told Shim′e-i, saying, Behold, thy servants *be* in Gath.

40 And Shim′e-i arose, and saddled his ass, and went to Gath to A′chish to seek his servants: and Shim′e-i went, and brought his servants from Gath.

41 And it was told Sol′o-mon that Shim′e-i had gone from Je-ru′sa-lem to Gath, and was come again.

42 And the king sent and called for Shim′e-i, and said unto him, Did I not make thee to swear by the LORD, and protested unto thee, saying, Know for a certain, on the day thou goest out, and walkest abroad any whither, that thou shalt surely die? and thou saidst unto me, The word *that* I have heard *is* good.

43 Why then hast thou not kept the oath of the LORD, and the commandment that I have charged thee with?

44 The king said moreover to Shim′e-i, Thou knowest all the wickedness which thine heart is privy to, that thou didst to Da′vid my father: therefore the LORD shall return thy wickedness upon thine own head;

45 And king Sol′o-mon *shall be* blessed, and the throne of Da′vid shall be established before the LORD for ever.

46 So the king commanded Be-na′iah the son of Je-hoi′a-da; which went out, and fell upon him, that he died. And the kingdom was established in the hand of Sol′o-mon.

3 AND Sol′o-mon made affinity with Pha′-raoh king of E′gypt, and took Pha′raoh's daughter, and brought her into the city of Da′-vid, until he had made an end of building his own house, and the house of the LORD, and the wall of Je-ru′sa-lem round about.

2 Only the people sacrificed in high places, because there was no house built unto the name of the LORD, until those days.

3 And Sol′o-mon loved the LORD, walking in the statutes of Da′vid his father: only he sacrificed and burnt incense in high places.

4 And the king went to Gib′e-on to sacrifice there; for that *was* the great high place: a thousand burnt offerings did Sol′o-mon offer upon that altar.

5 ¶ In Gib′e-on the LORD appeared to Sol′o-mon in a dream by night: and God said, Ask what I shall give thee.

6 And Sol′o-mon said, Thou hast shewed unto thy servant Da′vid my father great mercy, according as he walked before thee in truth, and in righteousness, and in uprightness of heart with thee; and thou hast kept for him this great kindness, that thou hast given him a son to sit on his throne, as *it is* this day.

7 And now, O LORD my God, thou hast made thy servant king instead of Da′vid my father: and I *am but* a little child: I know not *how* to go out or come in.

8 And thy servant *is* in the midst of thy people which thou hast chosen, a great people, that cannot be numbered nor counted for multitude.

9 Give therefore thy servant an understanding heart to judge thy people, that I may discern between good and bad: for who is able to judge this thy so great a people?

10 And the speech pleased the LORD, that Sol′o-mon had asked this thing.

11 And God said unto him, Because thou hast asked this thing, and hast not asked for thyself long life; neither hast asked riches for thyself, nor hast asked the life of thine enemies; but hast asked for thyself understanding to discern judgment;

12 Behold, I have done according to thy words: lo, I have given thee a wise and an understanding heart; so that there was none like thee before thee, neither after thee shall any arise like unto thee.

13 And I have also given thee that which thou hast not asked, both riches, and honour: so that there shall not be any among the kings like unto thee all thy days.

14 And if thou wilt walk in my ways, to keep my statutes and my commandments, as thy father Da′vid did walk, then I will lengthen thy days.

15 And Sol′o-mon awoke; and, behold, *it was* a dream. And he came to Je-ru′sa-lem, and stood before the ark of the covenant of the LORD, and offered up burnt offerings, and offered peace offerings, and made a feast to all his servants.

16 ¶ Then came there two women, *that were* harlots, unto the king, and stood before him.

17 And the one woman said, O my lord, I and

this woman dwell in one house; and I was delivered of a child with her in the house.

18 And it came to pass the third day after that I was delivered, that this woman was delivered also: and we *were* together; *there was* no stranger with us in the house, save we two in the house.

19 And this woman's child died in the night; because she overlaid it.

20 And she arose at midnight, and took my son from beside me, while thine handmaid slept, and laid it in her bosom, and laid her dead child in my bosom.

21 And when I rose in the morning to give my child suck, behold, it was dead: but when I had considered it in the morning, behold, it was not my son, which I did bear.

22 And the other woman said, Nay; but the living *is* my son, and the dead *is* thy son. And this said, No; but the dead *is* thy son, and the living *is* my son. Thus they spake before the king.

23 Then said the king, The one saith, This *is* my son that liveth, and thy son *is* the dead: and the other saith, Nay; but thy son *is* the dead, and my son *is* the living.

24 And the king said, Bring me a sword. And they brought a sword before the king.

25 And the king said, Divide the living child in two, and give half to the one, and half to the other.

26 Then spake the woman whose the living child *was* unto the king, for her bowels yearned upon her son, and she said, O my lord, give her the living child, and in no wise slay it. But the other said, Let it be neither mine nor thine, *but* divide *it*.

27 Then the king answered and said, Give her the living child, and in no wise slay it: she *is* the mother thereof.

28 And all Is'ra-el heard of the judgment which the king had judged; and they feared the king: for they saw that the wisdom of God *was* in him, to do judgment.

4 SO king Sol'o-mon was king over all Is'ra-el.

2 And these *were* the princes which he had; Az-a-ri'ah the son of Za'dok the priest,

3 El-i-ho'reph and A-hi'ah, the sons of Shi'sha, scribes; Je-hosh'a-phat the son of A-hi'lud, the recorder.

4 And Be-na'iah the son of Je-hoi'a-da *was* over the host: and Za'dok and A-bi'a-thar *were* the priests:

5 And Az-a-ri'ah the son of Na'than *was* over the officers: and Za'bud the son of Na'than *was* principal officer, *and* the king's friend:

6 And A-hi'shar *was* over the household: and Ad-o-ni'ram the son of Ab'da *was* over the tribute.

7 ¶ And Sol'o-mon had twelve officers over all Is'ra-el, which provided victuals for the king and his household: each man his month in a year made provision.

8 And these *are* their names: The son of Hur, in mount E'phra-im:

9 The son of De'kar, in Ma'kaz, and in Sha-al'bim, and Beth–she'mesh, and E'lon–beth–ha'-nan:

10 The son of He'sed, in Ar'u-both; to him *pertained* So'choh, and all the land of He'pher:

11 The son of A-bin'a-dab, in all the region of Dor; which had Ta'phath the daughter of Sol'o-mon to wife:

12 Ba'a-na the son of A-hi'lud; *to him pertained* Ta'a-nach and Me-gid'do, and all Beth–she'an, which *is* by Zar'ta-nah beneath Jez're-el, from Beth–she'an to A'bel–me-ho'lah, *even* unto *the place that is* beyond Jok'ne-am:

13 The son of Ge'ber, in Ra'moth–gil'e-ad; to him *pertained* the towns of Ja'ir the son of Ma-nas'seh, which *are* in Gil'e-ad; to him *also pertained* the region of Ar'gob, which *is* in Ba'shan, threescore great cities with walls and brasen bars:

14 A-hin'a-dab the son of Id'do *had* Ma-ha-na'im:

15 A-him'a-az *was* in Naph'ta-li; he also took Bas'math the daughter of Sol'o-mon to wife:

16 Ba'a-nah the son of Hu'shai *was* in Ash'er and in A'loth:

17 Je-hosh'a-phat the son of Par'u-ah, in Is'-sa-char:

18 Shim'e-i the son of E'lah, in Ben'ja-min:

19 Ge'ber the son of U'ri *was* in the country of Gil'e-ad, *in* the country of Si'hon king of the Am'or-ites, and of Og king of Ba'shan; and *he was* the only officer which *was* in the land.

20 ¶ Ju'dah and Is'ra-el *were* many, as the sand which *is* by the sea in multitude, eating and drinking, and making merry.

21 And Sol'o-mon reigned over all kingdoms from the river unto the land of the Phi-lis'tines, and unto the border of E'gypt: they brought presents, and served Sol'o-mon all the days of his life.

22 ¶ And Sol'o-mon's provision for one day was thirty measures of fine flour, and threescore measures of meal,

23 Ten fat oxen, and twenty oxen out of the pastures, and an hundred sheep, beside harts, and roebucks, and fallowdeer, and fatted fowl.

24 For he had dominion over all *the region* on this side the river, from Tiph'sah even to Az'-zah, over all the kings on this side the river: and he had peace on all sides round about him.

25 And Ju'dah and Is'ra-el dwelt safely, every man under his vine and under his fig tree, from Dan even to Be'er–she'ba, all the days of Sol'o-mon.

26 ¶ And Sol'o-mon had forty thousand stalls of horses for his chariots, and twelve thousand horsemen.

27 And those officers provided victual for king Sol'o-mon, and for all that came unto king Sol'o-mon's table, every man in his month: they lacked nothing.

28 Barley also and straw for the horses and dromedaries brought they unto the place where *the officers* were, every man according to his charge.

29 ¶ And God gave Sol'o-mon wisdom and understanding exceeding much, and largeness of heart, even as the sand that *is* on the sea shore.

30 And Sol'o-mon's wisdom excelled the wisdom of all the children of the east country, and all the wisdom of E'gypt.

31 For he was wiser than all men; than E'-than the Ez'ra-hite, and He'man, and Chal'col, and Dar'da, the sons of Ma'hol: and his fame was in all nations round about.

32 And he spake three thousand proverbs: and his songs were a thousand and five.

33 And he spake of trees, from the cedar tree that *is* in Leb'a-non even unto the hyssop that springeth out of the wall: he spake also of beasts, and of fowl, and of creeping things, and of fishes.

34 And there came of all people to hear the wisdom of Sol'o-mon, from all kings of the earth, which had heard of his wisdom.

5 AND Hi'ram king of Tyre sent his servants
unto Sol'o-mon; for he had heard that they
had anointed him king in the room of his father:
for Hi'ram was ever a lover of Da'vid.
2 And Sol'o-mon sent to Hi'ram, saying,
3 Thou knowest how that Da'vid my father
could not build an house unto the name of the
LORD his God for the wars which were about
him on every side, until the LORD put them under the soles of his feet.
4 But now the LORD my God hath given me
rest on every side, *so that there is* neither adversary nor evil occurrent.
5 And, behold, I purpose to build an house
unto the name of the LORD my God, as the LORD
spake unto Da'vid my father, saying, Thy son,
whom I will set upon thy throne in thy room, he
shall build an house unto my name.
6 Now therefore command thou that they
hew me cedar trees out of Leb'a-non; and my
servants shall be with thy servants: and unto
thee will I give hire for thy servants according
to all that thou shalt appoint: for thou knowest
that *there is* not among us any that can skill to
hew timber like unto the Si-do'ni-ans.
7 ¶ And it came to pass, when Hi'ram heard
the words of Sol'o-mon, that he rejoiced
greatly, and said, Blessed *be* the LORD this day,
which hath given unto Da'vid a wise son over
this great people.
8 And Hi'ram sent to Sol'o-mon, saying, I
have considered the things which thou sentest
to me for: *and* I will do all thy desire concerning
timber of cedar, and concerning timber of fir.
9 My servants shall bring *them* down from
Leb'a-non unto the sea: and I will convey them
by sea in floats unto the place that thou shalt
appoint me, and will cause them to be discharged there, and thou shalt receive *them*: and
thou shalt accomplish my desire, in giving food
for my household.
10 So Hi'ram gave Sol'o-mon cedar trees and
fir trees *according to* all his desire.
11 And Sol'o-mon gave Hi'ram twenty thousand measures of wheat *for* food to his household, and twenty measures of pure oil: thus
gave Sol'o-mon to Hi'ram year by year.
12 And the LORD gave Sol'o-mon wisdom, as
he promised him: and there was peace between
Hi'ram and Sol'o-mon; and they two made a
league together.
13 ¶ And king Sol'o-mon raised a levy out of
all Is'ra-el; and the levy was thirty thousand
men.
14 And he sent them to Leb'a-non, ten thousand a month by courses: a month they were in
Leb'a-non, *and* two months at home: and Ad-o-ni'ram *was* over the levy.
15 And Sol'o-mon had threescore and ten
thousand that bare burdens, and fourscore
thousand hewers in the mountains;
16 Beside the chief of Sol'o-mon's officers
which *were* over the work, three thousand and
three hundred, which ruled over the people that
wrought in the work.
17 And the king commanded, and they
brought great stones, costly stones, *and* hewed
stones to lay the foundation of the house.
18 And Sol'o-mon's builders and Hi'ram's
builders did hew *them*, and the stonesquarers:
so they prepared timber and stones to build the
house.

6 AND it came to pass in the four hundred
and eightieth year after the children of Is'ra-el were come out of the land of E'gypt, in the
fourth year of Sol'o-mon's reign over Is'ra-el, in
the month Zif, which *is* the second month, that
he began to build the house of the LORD.
2 And the house which king Sol'o-mon built
for the LORD, the length thereof *was* threescore
cubits, and the breadth thereof twenty *cubits*,
and the height thereof thirty cubits.
3 And the porch before the temple of the
house, twenty cubits *was* the length thereof, according to the breadth of the house; *and* ten cubits *was* the breadth thereof before the house.
4 And for the house he made windows of
narrow lights.
5 ¶ And against the wall of the house he
built chambers round about, *against* the walls
of the house round about, *both* of the temple
and of the oracle: and he made chambers round
about:
6 The nethermost chamber *was* five cubits
broad, and the middle *was* six cubits broad, and
the third *was* seven cubits broad: for without *in
the wall* of the house he made narrowed rests
round about, that *the beams* should not be fastened in the walls of the house.
7 And the house, when it was in building,
was built of stone made ready before it was
brought thither: so that there was neither hammer nor ax *nor* any tool of iron heard in the
house, while it was in building.
8 The door for the middle chamber *was* in
the right side of the house: and they went up
with winding stairs into the middle *chamber*,
and out of the middle into the third.
9 So he built the house, and finished it; and
covered the house with beams and boards of
cedar.
10 And *then* he built chambers against all the
house, five cubits high: and they rested on the
house with timber of cedar.
11 ¶ And the word of the LORD came to Sol'o-mon, saying,
12 *Concerning* this house which thou art in
building, if thou wilt walk in my statutes, and
execute my judgments, and keep all my commandments to walk in them; then will I perform
my word with thee, which I spake unto Da'vid
thy father:
13 And I will dwell among the children of Is'ra-el, and will not forsake my people Is'ra-el.
14 So Sol'o-mon built the house, and finished
it.
15 And he built the walls of the house within
with boards of cedar, both the floor of the
house, and the walls of the ceiling: *and* he covered *them* on the inside with wood, and covered
the floor of the house with planks of fir.
16 And he built twenty cubits on the sides of
the house, both the floor and the walls with
boards of cedar: he even built *them* for it
within, *even* for the oracle, *even* for the most
holy *place*.
17 And the house, that *is*, the temple before
it, was forty cubits *long*.
18 And the cedar of the house within *was*
carved with knops and open flowers: all *was* cedar; there was no stone seen.
19 And the oracle he prepared in the house
within, to set there the ark of the covenant of
the LORD.
20 And the oracle in the forepart *was* twenty
cubits in length, and twenty cubits in breadth,
and twenty cubits in the height thereof: and he
overlaid it with pure gold; and *so* covered the
altar *which was of* cedar.
21 So Sol'o-mon overlaid the house within
with pure gold: and he made a partition by the
chains of gold before the oracle; and he overlaid
it with gold.

22 And the whole house he overlaid with gold, until he had finished all the house: also the whole altar that *was* by the oracle he overlaid with gold.

23 ¶ And within the oracle he made two cherubims *of* olive tree, *each* ten cubits high.

24 And five cubits *was* the one wing of the cherub, and five cubits the other wing of the cherub: from the uttermost part of the one wing unto the uttermost part of the other *were* ten cubits.

25 And the other cherub *was* ten cubits: both the cherubims *were* of one measure and one size.

26 The height of the one cherub *was* ten cubits, and so *was it* of the other cherub.

27 And he set the cherubims within the inner house: and they stretched forth the wings of the cherubims, so that the wing of the one touched the *one* wall, and the wing of the other cherub touched the other wall; and their wings touched one another in the midst of the house.

28 And he overlaid the cherubims with gold.

29 And he carved all the walls of the house round about with carved figures of cherubims and palm trees and open flowers, within and without.

30 And the floor of the house he overlaid with gold, within and without.

31 ¶ And for the entering of the oracle he made doors *of* olive tree: the lintel *and* side posts *were* a fifth part *of the wall.*

32 The two doors also *were of* olive tree; and he carved upon them carvings of cherubims and palm trees and open flowers, and overlaid *them* with gold, and spread gold upon the cherubims, and upon the palm trees.

33 So also made he for the door of the temple posts *of* olive tree, a fourth part *of the wall.*

34 And the two doors *were of* fir tree: the two leaves of the one door *were* folding, and the two leaves of the other door *were* folding.

35 And he carved *thereon* cherubims and palm trees and open flowers: and covered *them* with gold fitted upon the carved work.

36 ¶ And he built the inner court with three rows of hewed stone, and a row of cedar beams.

37 ¶ In the fourth year was the foundation of the house of the LORD laid, in the month Zif:

38 And in the eleventh year, in the month Bul, which *is* the eighth month, was the house finished throughout all the parts thereof, and according to all the fashion of it. So was he seven years in building it.

7

BUT Sol'o-mon was building his own house thirteen years, and he finished all his house.

2 ¶ He built also the house of the forest of Leb'a-non; the length thereof *was* an hundred cubits, and the breadth thereof fifty cubits, and the height thereof thirty cubits, upon four rows of cedar pillars, with cedar beams upon the pillars.

3 And *it was* covered with cedar above upon the beams, that *lay* on forty five pillars, fifteen *in* a row.

4 And *there were* windows *in* three rows, and light *was* against light *in* three ranks.

5 And all the doors and posts *were* square, with the windows: and light *was* against light *in* three ranks.

6 ¶ And he made a porch of pillars; the length thereof *was* fifty cubits, and the breadth thereof thirty cubits: and the porch *was* before them: and the *other* pillars and the thick beam *were* before them.

7 ¶ Then he made a porch for the throne where he might judge, *even* the porch of judgment: and *it was* covered with cedar from one side of the floor to the other.

8 ¶ And his house where he dwelt *had* another court within the porch, *which* was of the like work. Sol'o-mon made also an house for Pha'raoh's daughter, whom he had taken *to wife,* like unto this porch.

9 All these *were of* costly stones, according to the measures of hewed stones, sawed with saws, within and without, even from the foundation unto the coping, and *so* on the outside toward the great court.

10 And the foundation *was of* costly stones, even great stones, stones of ten cubits, and stones of eight cubits.

11 And above *were* costly stones, after the measures of hewed stones, and cedars.

12 And the great court round about *was* with three rows of hewed stones, and a row of cedar beams, both for the inner court of the house of the LORD, and for the porch of the house.

13 ¶ And king Sol'o-mon sent and fetched Hi'ram out of Tyre.

14 He *was* a widow's son of the tribe of Naph'ta-li, and his father *was* a man of Tyre, a worker in brass: and he was filled with wisdom, and understanding, and cunning to work all works in brass. And he came to king Sol'o-mon, and wrought all his work.

15 For he cast two pillars of brass, of eighteen cubits high apiece: and a line of twelve cubits did compass either of them about.

16 And he made two chapiters *of* molten brass, to set upon the tops of the pillars: the height of the one chapiter *was* five cubits, and the height of the other chapiter *was* five cubits:

17 *And* nets of checker work, and wreaths of chain work, for the chapiters which *were* upon the top of the pillars; seven for the one chapiter, and seven for the other chapiter.

18 And he made the pillars, and two rows round about upon the one network, to cover the chapiters that *were* upon the top, with pomegranates: and so did he for the other chapiter.

19 And the chapiters that *were* upon the top of the pillars *were* of lily work in the porch, four cubits.

20 And the chapiters upon the two pillars *had pomegranates* also above, over against the belly which *was* by the network: and the pomegranates *were* two hundred in rows round about upon the other chapiter.

21 And he set up the pillars in the porch of the temple: and he set up the right pillar, and called the name thereof Ja'chin: and he set up the left pillar, and called the name thereof Bo'-az.

22 And upon the top of the pillars *was* lily work: so was the work of the pillars finished.

23 ¶ And he made a molten sea, ten cubits from the one brim to the other: *it was* round all about, and his height *was* five cubits: and a line of thirty cubits did compass it round about.

24 And under the brim of it round about *there were* knops compassing it, ten in a cubit, compassing the sea round about: the knops *were* cast in two rows, when it was cast.

25 It stood upon twelve oxen, three looking toward the north, and three looking toward the west, and three looking toward the south, and three looking toward the east: and the sea *was set* above upon them, and all their hinder parts *were* inward.

26 And it *was* an hand breadth thick, and the brim thereof was wrought like the brim of a

cup, with flowers of lilies: it contained two
thousand baths.
27 ¶ And he made ten bases of brass; four
cubits *was* the length of one base, and four cubits the breadth thereof, and three cubits the
height of it.
28 And the work of the bases *was* on this
manner: they had borders, and the borders
were between the ledges:
29 And on the borders that *were* between the
ledges *were* lions, oxen, and cherubims: and
upon the ledges *there was* a base above: and
beneath the lions and oxen *were* certain additions made of thin work.
30 And every base had four brasen wheels,
and plates of brass: and the four corners thereof
had undersetters: under the laver *were* undersetters molten, at the side of every addition.
31 And the mouth of it within the chapiter
and above *was* a cubit: but the mouth thereof
was round *after* the work of the base, a cubit
and an half: and also upon the mouth of it *were*
gravings with their borders, foursquare, not
round.
32 And under the borders *were* four wheels;
and the axletrees of the wheels *were joined* to
the base: and the height of a wheel *was* a cubit
and half a cubit.
33 And the work of the wheels *was* like the
work of a chariot wheel: their axletrees, and
their naves, and their felloes, and their spokes,
were all molten.
34 And *there were* four undersetters to the
four corners of one base: *and* the undersetters
were of the very base itself.
35 And in the top of the base *was there* a
round compass of half a cubit high: and on the
top of the base the ledges thereof and the borders thereof *were* of the same.
36 For on the plates of the ledges thereof,
and on the borders thereof, he graved cherubims, lions, and palm trees, according to the
proportion of every one, and additions round
about.
37 After this *manner* he made the ten bases:
all of them had one casting, one measure, *and*
one size.
38 ¶ Then made he ten lavers of brass: one
laver contained forty baths: *and* every laver
was four cubits: *and* upon every one of the ten
bases one laver.
39 And he put five bases on the right side of
the house, and five on the left side of the house:
and he set the sea on the right side of the house
eastward over against the south.
40 ¶ And Hi'ram made the lavers, and the
shovels, and the basons. So Hi'ram made an
end of doing all the work that he made king
Sol'o-mon for the house of the LORD:
41 The two pillars, and the *two* bowls of the
chapiters that *were* on the top of the two pillars;
and the two networks, to cover the two bowls
of the chapiters which *were* upon the top of the
pillars;
42 And four hundred pomegranates for the
two networks, *even* two rows of pomegranates
for one network, to cover the two bowls of the
chapiters that *were* upon the pillars;
43 And the ten bases, and ten lavers on the
bases;
44 And one sea, and twelve oxen under the
sea;
45 And the pots, and the shovels, and the basons: and all these vessels, which Hi'ram made
to king Sol'o-mon for the house of the LORD,
were of bright brass.
46 In the plain of Jor'dan did the king cast
them, in the clay ground between Suc'coth and
Zar'than.
47 And Sol'o-mon left all the vessels *un-
weighed,* because they were exceeding many:
neither was the weight of the brass found out.
48 And Sol'o-mon made all the vessels that
pertained unto the house of the LORD: the altar
of gold, and the table of gold, whereupon the
shewbread *was,*
49 And the candlesticks of pure gold, five on
the right *side,* and five on the left, before the
oracle, with the flowers, and the lamps, and the
tongs *of* gold,
50 And the bowls, and the snuffers, and the
basons, and the spoons, and the censers *of* pure
gold; and the hinges *of* gold, *both* for the doors
of the inner house, the most holy *place, and* for
the doors of the house, *to wit,* of the temple.
51 So was ended all the work that king Sol'o-
mon made for the house of the LORD. And Sol'o-
mon brought in the things which Da'vid his father had dedicated; *even* the silver, and the
gold, and the vessels, did he put among the
treasures of the house of the LORD.

8 THEN Sol'o-mon assembled the elders of
Is'ra-el, and all the heads of the tribes, the
chief of the fathers of the children of Is'ra-el,
unto king Sol'o-mon in Je-ru'sa-lem, that they
might bring up the ark of the covenant of the
LORD out of the city of Da'vid, which *is* Zi'on.
2 And all the men of Is'ra-el assembled themselves unto king Sol'o-mon at the feast in the
month Eth'a-nim, which *is* the seventh month.
3 And all the elders of Is'ra-el came, and the
priests took up the ark.
4 And they brought up the ark of the LORD,
and the tabernacle of the congregation, and all
the holy vessels that *were* in the tabernacle,
even those did the priests and the Le'vites bring
up.
5 And king Sol'o-mon, and all the congregation of Is'ra-el, that were assembled unto him,
were with him before the ark, sacrificing sheep
and oxen, that could not be told nor numbered
for multitude.
6 And the priests brought in the ark of the
covenant of the LORD unto his place, into the
oracle of the house, to the most holy *place, even*
under the wings of the cherubims.
7 For the cherubims spread forth *their* two
wings over the place of the ark, and the cherubims covered the ark and the staves thereof
above.
8 And they drew out the staves, that the ends
of the staves were seen out in the holy *place*
before the oracle, and they were not seen without: and there they are unto this day.
9 *There was* nothing in the ark save the two
tables of stone, which Mo'ses put there at Ho'-
reb, when the LORD made *a covenant* with the
children of Is'ra-el, when they came out of the
land of E'gypt.
10 And it came to pass, when the priests
were come out of the holy *place,* that the cloud
filled the house of the LORD,
11 So that the priests could not stand to minister because of the cloud: for the glory of the
LORD had filled the house of the LORD.
12 ¶ Then spake Sol'o-mon, The LORD said
that he would dwell in the thick darkness.
13 I have surely built thee an house to dwell
in, a settled place for thee to abide in for ever.
14 And the king turned his face about, and
blessed all the congregation of Is'ra-el: (and all
the congregation of Is'ra-el stood;)
15 And he said, Blessed *be* the LORD God of

Is'ra-el, which spake with his mouth unto Da'vid my father, and hath with his hand fulfilled *it*, saying,

16 Since the day that I brought forth my people Is'ra-el out of E'gypt, I chose no city out of all the tribes of Is'ra-el to build an house, that my name might be therein; but I chose Da'vid to be over my people Is'ra-el.

17 And it was in the heart of Da'vid my father to build an house for the name of the LORD God of Is'ra-el.

18 And the LORD said unto Da'vid my father, Whereas it was in thine heart to build an house unto my name, thou didst well that it was in thine heart.

19 Nevertheless thou shalt not build the house; but thy son that shall come forth out of thy loins, he shall build the house unto my name.

20 And the LORD hath performed his word that he spake, and I am risen up in the room of Da'vid my father, and sit on the throne of Is'ra-el, as the LORD promised, and have built an house for the name of the LORD God of Is'ra-el.

21 And I have set there a place for the ark, wherein *is* the covenant of the LORD, which he made with our fathers, when he brought them out of the land of E'gypt.

22 ¶ And Sol'o-mon stood before the altar of the LORD in the presence of all the congregation of Is'ra-el, and spread forth his hands toward heaven:

23 And he said, LORD God of Is'ra-el, *there is* no God like thee, in heaven above, or on earth beneath, who keepest covenant and mercy with thy servants that walk before thee with all their heart:

24 Who hast kept with thy servant Da'vid my father that thou promisedst him: thou spakest also with thy mouth, and has fulfilled *it* with thine hand, as *it is* this day.

25 Therefore now, LORD God of Is'ra-el, keep with thy servant Da'vid my father that thou promisedst him, saying, There shall not fail thee a man in my sight to sit on the throne of Is'ra-el; so that thy children take heed to their way, that they walk before me as thou hast walked before me.

26 And now, O God of Is'ra-el, let thy word, I pray thee, be verified, which thou spakest unto thy servant Da'vid my father.

27 But will God indeed dwell on the earth? behold, the heaven and heaven of heavens cannot contain thee; how much less this house that I have builded?

28 Yet have thou respect unto the prayer of thy servant, and to his supplication, O LORD my God, to hearken unto the cry and to the prayer, which thy servant prayeth before thee to day:

29 That thine eyes may be open toward this house night and day, *even* toward the place of which thou hast said, My name shall be there: that thou mayest hearken unto the prayer which thy servant shall make toward this place.

30 And hearken thou to the supplication of thy servant, and of thy people Is'ra-el, when they shall pray toward this place: and hear thou in heaven thy dwelling place: and when thou hearest, forgive.

31 ¶ If any man trespass against his neighbour, and an oath be laid upon him to cause him to swear, and the oath come before thine altar in this house:

32 Then hear thou in heaven, and do, and judge thy servants, condemning the wicked, to bring his way upon his head; and justifying the righteous, to give him according to his righteousness.

33 ¶ When thy people Is'ra-el be smitten down before the enemy, because they have sinned against thee, and shall turn again to thee, and confess thy name, and pray, and make supplication unto thee in this house:

34 Then hear thou in heaven, and forgive the sin of thy people Is'ra-el, and bring them again unto the land which thou gavest unto their fathers.

35 ¶ When heaven is shut up, and there is no rain, because they have sinned against thee; if they pray toward this place, and confess thy name, and turn from their sin, when thou afflictest them:

36 Then hear thou in heaven, and forgive the sin of thy servants, and of thy people Is'ra-el, that thou teach them the good way wherein they should walk, and give rain upon thy land, which thou hast given to thy people for an inheritance.

37 ¶ If there be in the land famine, if there be pestilence, blasting, mildew, locust, *or* if there be caterpiller; if their enemy besiege them in the land of their cities; whatsoever plague, whatsoever sickness *there be*;

38 What prayer and supplication soever be *made* by any man, *or* by all thy people Is'ra-el, which shall know every man the plague of his own heart, and spread forth his hands toward this house:

39 Then hear thou in heaven thy dwelling place, and forgive, and do, and give to every man according to his ways, whose heart thou knowest; (for thou, *even* thou only, knowest the hearts of all the children of men;)

40 That they may fear thee all the days that they live in the land which thou gavest unto our fathers.

41 Moreover concerning a stranger, that *is* not of thy people Is'ra-el, but cometh out of a far country for thy name's sake;

42 (For they shall hear of thy great name, and of thy strong hand, and of thy stretched out arm:) when he shall come and pray toward this house;

43 Hear thou in heaven thy dwelling place, and do according to all that the stranger calleth to thee for: that all people of the earth may know thy name, to fear thee, as *do* thy people Is'ra-el; and that they may know that this house, which I have builded, is called by thy name.

44 ¶ If thy people go out to battle against their enemy, whithersoever thou shalt send them, and shall pray unto the LORD toward the city which thou hast chosen, and *toward* the house that I have built for thy name:

45 Then hear thou in heaven their prayer and their supplication, and maintain their cause.

46 If they sin against thee, (for *there is* no man that sinneth not,) and thou be angry with them, and deliver them to the enemy, so that they carry them away captives unto the land of the enemy, far or near;

47 *Yet* if they shall bethink themselves in the land whither they were carried captives, and repent, and make supplication unto thee in the land of them that carried them captives, saying, We have sinned, and have done perversely, we have committed wickedness;

48 And *so* return unto thee with all their heart, and with all their soul, in the land of their enemies, which led them away captive, and pray unto thee toward their land, which thou gavest unto their fathers, the city which thou

hast chosen, and the house which I have built
for thy name:
49 Then hear thou their prayer and their supplication in heaven thy dwelling place, and
maintain their cause,
50 And forgive thy people that have sinned
against thee, and all their transgressions
wherein they have transgressed against thee,
and give them compassion before them who
carried them captive, that they may have compassion on them:
51 For they *be* thy people, and thine inheritance, which thou broughtest forth out of E'-
gypt, from the midst of the furnace of iron:
52 That thine eyes may be open unto the supplication of thy servant, and unto the supplication of thy people Is'ra-el, to hearken unto them
in all that they call for unto thee.
53 For thou didst separate them from among
all the people of the earth, *to be* thine inheritance, as thou spakest by the hand of Mo'ses
thy servant, when thou broughtest our fathers
out of E'gypt, O Lord GOD.
54 And it was *so,* that when Sol'o-mon had
made an end of praying all this prayer and supplication unto the LORD, he arose from before
the altar of the LORD, from kneeling on his
knees with his hands spread up to heaven.
55 And he stood, and blessed all the congregation of Is'ra-el with a loud voice, saying,
56 Blessed *be* the LORD, that hath given rest
unto his people Is'ra-el, according to all that he
promised: there hath not failed one word of all
his good promise, which he promised by the
hand of Mo'ses his servant.
57 The LORD our God be with us, as he was
with our fathers: let him not leave us, nor forsake us:
58 That he may incline our hearts unto him,
to walk in all his ways, and to keep his commandments, and his statutes, and his judgments, which he commanded our fathers.
59 And let these my words, wherewith I have
made supplication before the LORD, be nigh
unto the LORD our God day and night, that he
maintain the cause of his servant, and the cause
of his people Is'ra-el at all times, as the matter
shall require:
60 That all the people of the earth may know
that the LORD *is* God, *and that there is* none
else.
61 Let your heart therefore be perfect with
the LORD our God, to walk in his statutes, and
to keep his commandments, as at this day.
62 ¶ And the king, and all Is'ra-el with him,
offered sacrifice before the LORD.
63 And Sol'o-mon offered a sacrifice of peace
offerings, which he offered unto the LORD, two
and twenty thousand oxen, and an hundred and
twenty thousand sheep. So the king and all the
children of Is'ra-el dedicated the house of the
LORD.
64 The same day did the king hallow the middle of the court that *was* before the house of the
LORD: for there he offered burnt offerings, and
meat offerings, and the fat of the peace offerings: because the brasen altar that *was* before
the LORD *was* too little to receive the burnt offerings, and meat offerings, and the fat of the
peace offerings.
65 And at that time Sol'o-mon held a feast,
and all Is'ra-el with him, a great congregation,
from the entering in of Ha'math unto the river
of E'gypt, before the LORD our God, seven days
and seven days, *even* fourteen days.
66 On the eighth day he sent the people
away: and they blessed the king, and went unto
their tents joyful and glad of heart for all the
goodness that the LORD had done for Da'vid his
servant, and for Is'ra-el his people.

9 AND it came to pass, when Sol'o-mon had
finished the building of the house of the
LORD, and the king's house, and all Sol'o-mon's
desire which he was pleased to do,
2 That the LORD appeared to Sol'o-mon the
second time, as he had appeared unto him at
Gib'e-on.
3 And the LORD said unto him, I have heard
thy prayer and thy supplication, that thou hast
made before me: I have hallowed this house,
which thou hast built, to put my name there for
ever; and mine eyes and mine heart shall be
there perpetually.
4 And if thou wilt walk before me, as Da'vid
thy father walked, in integrity of heart, and in
uprightness, to do according to all that I have
commanded thee, *and* wilt keep my statutes
and my judgments:
5 Then I will establish the throne of thy kingdom upon Is'ra-el for ever, as I promised to Da'-
vid thy father, saying, There shall not fail thee a
man upon the throne of Is'ra-el.
6 *But* if ye shall at all turn from following
me, ye or your children, and will not keep my
commandments *and* my statutes which I have
set before you, but go and serve other gods, and
worship them:
7 Then will I cut off Is'ra-el out of the land
which I have given them; and this house, which
I have hallowed for my name, will I cast out of
my sight; and Is'ra-el shall be a proverb and a
byword among all people:
8 And at this house, *which* is high, every one
that passeth by it shall be astonished, and shall
hiss; and they shall say, Why hath the LORD
done thus unto this land, and to this house?
9 And they shall answer, Because they forsook the LORD their God, who brought forth
their fathers out of the land of E'gypt, and have
taken hold upon other gods, and have worshipped them, and served them: therefore hath
the LORD brought upon them all this evil.
10 ¶ And it came to pass at the end of
twenty years, when Sol'o-mon had built the two
houses, the house of the LORD, and the king's
house,
11 (*Now* Hi'ram the king of Tyre had furnished Sol'o-mon with cedar trees and fir trees,
and with gold, according to all his desire,) that
then king Sol'o-mon gave Hi'ram twenty cities
in the land of Gal'i-lee.
12 And Hi'ram came out from Tyre to see the
cities which Sol'o-mon had given him; and they
pleased him not.
13 And he said, What cities *are* these which
thou hast given me, my brother? And he called
them the land of Ca'bul unto this day.
14 And Hi'ram sent to the king sixscore talents of gold.
15 ¶ And this *is* the reason of the levy which
king Sol'o-mon raised; for to build the house of
the LORD, and his own house, and Mil'lo, and
the wall of Je-ru'sa-lem, and Ha'zor, and Me-
gid'do, and Ge'zer.
16 *For* Pha'raoh king of E'gypt had gone up,
and taken Ge'zer, and burnt it with fire, and
slain the Ca'naan-ites that dwelt in the city, and
given it *for* a present unto his daughter, Sol'o-
mon's wife.
17 And Sol'o-mon built Ge'zer, and Beth-ho'-
ron the nether,
18 And Ba'al-ath, and Tad'mor in the wilderness, in the land,

19 And all the cities of store that Sol'o-mon
had, and cities for his chariots, and cities for his
horsemen, and that which Sol'o-mon desired to
build in Je-ru'sa-lem, and in Leb'a-non, and in
all the land of his dominion.
20 *And* all the people *that were* left of the
Am'or-ites, Hit'tites, Per'iz-zites, Hi'vites, and
Jeb'u-sites, which *were* not of the children of
Is'ra-el,
21 Their children that were left after them in
the land, whom the children of Is'ra-el also
were not able utterly to destroy, upon those did
Solomon levy a tribute of bondservice unto this
day.
22 But of the children of Is'ra-el did Sol'o-
mon make no bondmen: but they *were* men of
war, and his servants, and his princes, and his
captains, and rulers of his chariots, and his
horsemen.
23 These *were* the chief of the officers that
were over Sol'o-mon's work, five hundred and
fifty, which bare rule over the people that
wrought in the work.
24 ¶ But Pha'raoh's daughter came up out of
the city of Da'vid unto her house which *Sol'o-*
mon had built for her: then did he build Mil'lo.
25 ¶ And three times in a year did Sol'o-mon
offer burnt offerings and peace offerings upon
the altar which he built unto the LORD, and he
burnt incense upon the altar that *was* before the
LORD. So he finished the house.
26 ¶ And king Sol'o-mon made a navy of
ships in E'zi-on–ge'ber, which *is* beside E'loth,
on the shore of the Red sea, in the land of E'-
dom.
27 And Hi'ram sent in the navy his servants,
shipmen that had knowledge of the sea, with
the servants of Sol'o-mon.
28 And they came to O'phir, and fetched
from thence gold, four hundred and twenty talents, and brought *it* to king Sol'o-mon.

10 AND when the queen of She'ba heard of
the fame of Sol'o-mon concerning the
name of the LORD, she came to prove him with
hard questions.
2 And she came to Je-ru'sa-lem with a very
great train, with camels that bare spices, and
very much gold, and precious stones: and when
she was come to Sol'o-mon, she communed
with him of all that was in her heart.
3 And Sol'o-mon told her all her questions:
there was not *any* thing hid from the king,
which he told her not.
4 And when the queen of She'ba had seen all
Sol'o-mon's wisdom, and the house that he had
built,
5 And the meat of his table, and the sitting of
his servants, and the attendance of his ministers, and their apparel, and his cupbearers, and
his ascent by which he went up unto the house
of the LORD; there was no more spirit in her.
6 And she said to the king, It was a true report that I heard in mine own land of thy acts
and of thy wisdom.
7 Howbeit I believed not the words, until I
came, and mine eyes had seen *it:* and, behold,
the half was not told me: thy wisdom and prosperity exceedeth the fame which I heard.
8 Happy *are* thy men, happy *are* these thy
servants, which stand continually before thee,
and that hear thy wisdom.
9 Blessed be the LORD thy God, which delighted in thee, to set thee on the throne of Is'ra-
el: because the LORD loved Is'ra-el for ever,
therefore made he thee king, to do judgment
and justice.
10 And she gave the king an hundred and
twenty talents of gold, and of spices very great
store, and precious stones: there came no more
such abundance of spices as these which the
queen of She'ba gave to king Sol'o-mon.
11 And the navy also of Hi'ram, that brought
gold from O'phir, brought in from O'phir great
plenty of almug trees, and precious stones.
12 And the king made of the almug trees pillars for the house of the LORD, and for the king's
house, harps also and psalteries for singers:
there came no such almug trees, nor were seen
unto this day.
13 And king Sol'o-mon gave unto the queen
of She'ba all her desire, whatsoever she asked,
beside *that* which Sol'o-mon gave her of his
royal bounty. So she turned and went to her
own country, she and her servants.
14 ¶ Now the weight of gold that came to
Sol'o-mon in one year was six hundred threescore and six talents of gold,
15 Beside *that he had* of the merchantmen,
and of the traffick of the spice merchants, and
of all the kings of A-ra'bi-a, and of the governors of the country.
16 ¶ And king Sol'o-mon made two hundred
targets *of* beaten gold: six hundred *shekels* of
gold went to one target.
17 And *he made* three hundred shields *of*
beaten gold; three pound of gold went to one
shield: and the king put them in the house of the
forest of Leb'a-non.
18 ¶ Moreover the king made a great throne
of ivory, and overlaid it with the best gold.
19 The throne had six steps, and the top of
the throne *was* round behind: and *there were*
stays on either side on the place of the seat, and
two lions stood beside the stays.
20 And twelve lions stood there on the one
side and on the other upon the six steps: there
was not the like made in any kingdom.
21 ¶ And all king Sol'o-mon's drinking vessels *were of* gold, and all the vessels of the
house of the forest of Leb'a-non *were of* pure
gold; none *were of* silver: it was nothing accounted of in the days of Sol'o-mon.
22 For the king had at sea a navy of Thar'-
shish with the navy of Hi'ram: once in three
years came the navy of Thar'shish, bringing
gold, and silver, ivory, and apes, and peacocks.
23 So king Sol'o-mon exceeded all the kings
of the earth for riches and for wisdom.
24 ¶ And all the earth sought to Sol'o-mon,
to hear his wisdom, which God had put in his
heart.
25 And they brought every man his present,
vessels of silver, and vessels of gold, and garments, and armour, and spices, horses, and
mules, a rate year by year.
26 ¶ And Sol'o-mon gathered together chariots and horsemen: and he had a thousand and
four hundred chariots, and twelve thousand
horsemen, whom he bestowed in the cities for
chariots, and with the king at Je-ru'sa-lem.
27 And the king made silver *to be* in Je-ru'sa-
lem as stones, and cedars made he *to be* as the
sycomore trees that *are* in the vale, for abundance.
28 ¶ And Sol'o-mon had horses brought out
of E'gypt, and linen yarn: the king's merchants
received the linen yarn at a price.
29 And a chariot came up and went out of
E'gypt for six hundred *shekels* of silver, and an
horse for an hundred and fifty: and so for all the
kings of the Hit'tites, and for the kings of Syr'i-
a, did they bring *them* out by their means.

11 BUT king Sol'o-mon loved many strange women, together with the daughter of Pha'raoh, women of the Mo'ab-ites, Am'mon-ites, E'dom-ites, Zi-do'ni-ans, *and* Hit'tites;

2 Of the nations *concerning* which the LORD said unto the children of Is'ra-el, Ye shall not go in to them, neither shall they come in unto you: *for* surely they will turn away your heart after their gods: Sol'o-mon clave unto these in love.

3 And he had seven hundred wives, princesses, and three hundred concubines: and his wives turned away his heart.

4 For it came to pass, when Sol'o-mon was old, *that* his wives turned away his heart after other gods: and his heart was not perfect with the LORD his God, as *was* the heart of Da'vid his father.

5 For Sol'o-mon went after Ash'to-reth the goddess of the Zi-do'ni-ans, and after Mil'com the abomination of the Am'mon-ites.

6 And Sol'o-mon did evil in the sight of the LORD, and went not fully after the LORD, as *did* Da'vid his father.

7 Then did Sol'o-mon build an high place for Che'mosh, the abomination of Mo'ab, in the hill that *is* before Je-ru'sa-lem, and for Mo'lech, the abomination of the children of Am'mon.

8 And likewise did he for all his strange wives, which burnt incense and sacrificed unto their gods.

9 ¶ And the LORD was angry with Sol'o-mon, because his heart was turned from the LORD God of Is'ra-el, which had appeared unto him twice,

10 And had commanded him concerning this thing, that he should not go after other gods: but he kept not that which the LORD commanded.

11 Wherefore the LORD said unto Sol'o-mon, Forasmuch as this is done of thee, and thou hast not kept my covenant and my statutes, which I have commanded thee, I will surely rend the kingdom from thee, and will give it to thy servant.

12 Notwithstanding in thy days I will not do it for Da'vid thy father's sake: *but* I will rend it out of the hand of thy son.

13 Howbeit I will not rend away all the kingdom; *but* will give one tribe to thy son for Da'vid my servant's sake, and for Je-ru'sa-lem's sake which I have chosen.

14 ¶ And the LORD stirred up an adversary unto Sol'o-mon, Ha'dad the E'dom-ite: he *was* of the king's seed in E'dom.

15 For it came to pass, when Da'vid was in E'dom, and Jo'ab the captain of the host was gone up to bury the slain, after he had smitten every male in E'dom;

16 (For six months did Jo'ab remain there with all Is'ra-el, until he had cut off every male in E'dom:)

17 That Ha'dad fled, he and certain E'domites of his father's servants with him, to go into E'gypt; Ha'dad *being* yet a little child.

18 And they arose out of Mid'i-an, and came to Pa'ran: and they took men with them out of Pa'ran, and they came to E'gypt, unto Pha'raoh king of E'gypt; which gave him an house, and appointed him victuals, and gave him land.

19 And Ha'dad found great favour in the sight of Pha'raoh, so that he gave him to wife the sister of his own wife, the sister of Tah'pen-es the queen.

20 And the sister of Tah'pen-es bare him Ge-nu'bath his son, whom Tah'pen-es weaned in Pha'raoh's house: and Ge-nu'bath was in Pha'raoh's household among the sons of Pha'raoh.

21 And when Ha'dad heard in E'gypt that Da'vid slept with his fathers, and that Jo'ab the captain of the host was dead, Ha'dad said to Pha'raoh, Let me depart, that I may go to mine own country.

22 Then Pha'raoh said unto him, But what hast thou lacked with me, that, behold, thou seekest to go to thine own country? And he answered, Nothing: howbeit let me go in any wise.

23 ¶ And God stirred him up *another* adversary, Re'zon the son of E-li'a-dah, which fled from his lord Had-ad-e'zer king of Zo'bah:

24 And he gathered men unto him, and became captain over a band, when Da'vid slew them *of Zo'bah:* and they went to Da-mas'cus, and dwelt therein, and reigned in Da-mas'cus.

25 And he was an adversary to Is'ra-el all the days of Sol'o-mon, beside the mischief that Ha'dad *did:* and he abhorred Is'ra-el, and reigned over Syr'i-a.

26 ¶ And Jer-o-bo'am the son of Ne'bat, an Eph'rath-ite of Zer'e-da, Sol'o-mon's servant, whose mother's name *was* Ze-ru'ah, a widow woman, even he lifted up *his* hand against the king.

27 And this *was* the cause that he lifted up *his* hand against the king: Sol'o-mon built Mil'lo, *and* repaired the breaches of the city of Da'vid his father.

28 And the man Jer-o-bo'am *was* a mighty man of valour: and Sol'o-mon seeing the young man that he was industrious, he made him ruler over all the charge of the house of Jo'seph.

29 And it came to pass at that time when Jer-o-bo'am went out of Je-ru'sa-lem, that the prophet A-hi'jah the Shi'lo-nite found him in the way; and he had clad himself with a new garment; and they two *were* alone in the field:

30 And A-hi'jah caught the new garment that *was* on him, and rent it *in* twelve pieces:

31 And he said to Jer-o-bo'am, Take thee ten pieces: for thus saith the LORD, the God of Is'ra-el, Behold, I will rend the kingdom out of the hand of Sol'o-mon, and will give ten tribes to thee:

32 (But he shall have one tribe for my servant Da'vid's sake, and for Je-ru'sa-lem's sake, the city which I have chosen out of all the tribes of Is'ra-el:)

33 Because that they have forsaken me, and have worshipped Ash'to-reth the goddess of the Zi-do'ni-ans, Che'mosh the god of the Mo'ab-ites, and Mil'com the god of the children of Am'mon, and have not walked in my ways, to do *that which is* right in mine eyes, and *to keep* my statutes and my judgments, as *did* Da'vid his father.

34 Howbeit I will not take the whole kingdom out of his hand: but I will make him prince all the days of his life for Da'vid my servant's sake, whom I chose, because he kept my commandments and my statutes:

35 But I will take the kingdom out of his son's hand, and will give it unto thee, *even* ten tribes.

36 And unto his son will I give one tribe, that Da'vid my servant may have a light alway before me in Je-ru'sa-lem, the city which I have chosen me to put my name there.

37 And I will take thee, and thou shalt reign according to all that thy soul desireth, and shalt be king over Is'ra-el.

38 And it shall be, if thou wilt hearken unto all that I command thee, and wilt walk in my ways, and do *that is* right in my sight, to keep my statutes and my commandments, as Da'vid

my servant did; that I will be with thee, and
build thee a sure house, as I built for Da'vid,
and will give Is'ra-el unto thee.
39 And I will for this afflict the seed of Da'-
vid, but not for ever.
40 Sol'o-mon sought therefore to kill Jer-o-
bo'am. And Jer-o-bo'am arose, and fled into E'-
gypt, unto Shi'shak king of E'gypt, and was in
E'gypt until the death of Sol'o-mon.
41 ¶ And the rest of the acts of Sol'o-mon,
and all that he did, and his wisdom, *are* they not
written in the book of the acts of Sol'o-mon?
42 And the time that Sol'o-mon reigned in Je-
ru'sa-lem over all Is'ra-el *was* forty years.
43 And Sol'o-mon slept with his fathers, and
was buried in the city of Da'vid his father: and
Re-ho-bo'am his son reigned in his stead.

12 AND Re-ho-bo'am went to She'chem:
for all Is'ra-el were come to She'chem to
make him king.
2 And it came to pass, when Jer-o-bo'am the
son of Ne'bat, who was yet in E'gypt, heard *of*
it, (for he was fled from the presence of king
Sol'o-mon, and Jer-o-bo'am dwelt in E'gypt;)
3 That they sent and called him. And Jer-o-
bo'am and all the congregation of Is'ra-el came,
and spake unto Re-ho-bo'am, saying,
4 Thy father made our yoke grievous: now
therefore make thou the grievous service of thy
father, and his heavy yoke which he put upon
us, lighter, and we will serve thee.
5 And he said unto them, Depart yet *for*
three days, then come again to me. And the
people departed.
6 ¶ And king Re-ho-bo'am consulted with
the old men, that stood before Sol'o-mon his father while he yet lived, and said, How do ye
advise that I may answer this people?
7 And they spake unto him, saying, If thou
wilt be a servant unto this people this day, and
wilt serve them, and answer them, and speak
good words to them, then they will be thy servants for ever.
8 But he forsook the counsel of the old men,
which they had given him, and consulted with
the young men that were grown up with him,
and which stood before him:
9 And he said unto them, What counsel give
ye that we may answer this people, who have
spoken to me, saying, Make the yoke which thy
father did put upon us lighter?
10 And the young men that were grown up
with him spake unto him, saying, Thus shalt
thou speak unto this people that spake unto
thee, saying, Thy father made our yoke heavy,
but make thou *it* lighter unto us; thus shalt thou
say unto them, My little *finger* shall be thicker
than my father's loins.
11 And now whereas my father did lade you
with a heavy yoke, I will add to your yoke: my
father hath chastised you with whips, but I will
chastise you with scorpions.
12 ¶ So Jer-o-bo'am and all the people came
to Re-ho-bo'am the third day, as the king had
appointed, saying, Come to me again the third
day.
13 And the king answered the people
roughly, and forsook the old men's counsel that
they gave him;
14 And spake to them after the counsel of
the young men, saying, My father made your
yoke heavy, and I will add to your yoke: my
father *also* chastised you with whips, but I will
chastise you with scorpions.
15 Wherefore the king hearkened not unto
the people; for the cause was from the LORD,
that he might perform his saying, which the
LORD spake by A-hi'jah the Shi'lo-nite unto Jer-
o-bo'am the son of Ne'bat.
16 ¶ So when all Is'ra-el saw that the king
hearkened not unto them, the people answered
the king, saying, What portion have we in Da'-
vid? neither *have we* inheritance in the son of
Jes'se: to your tents, O Is'ra-el: now see to thine
own house, Da'vid. So Is'ra-el departed unto
their tents.
17 But *as for* the children of Is'ra-el which
dwelt in the cities of Ju'dah, Re-ho-bo'am
reigned over them.
18 Then king Re-ho-bo'am sent A-do'ram,
who *was* over the tribute; and all Is'ra-el stoned
him with stones, that he died. Therefore king
Re-ho-bo'am made speed to get him up to his
chariot, to flee to Je-ru'sa-lem.
19 So Is'ra-el rebelled against the house of
Da'vid unto this day.
20 And it came to pass, when all Is'ra-el
heard that Jer-o-bo'am was come again, that
they sent and called him unto the congregation,
and made him king over all Is'ra-el: there was
none that followed the house of Da'vid, but the
tribe of Ju'dah only.
21 ¶ And when Re-ho-bo'am was come to
Je-ru'sa-lem, he assembled all the house of Ju'-
dah, with the tribe of Ben'ja-min, an hundred
and fourscore thousand chosen men, which
were warriors, to fight against the house of Is'-
ra-el, to bring the kingdom again to Re-ho-bo'-
am the son of Sol'o-mon.
22 But the word of God came unto Shem-a-
i'ah the man of God, saying,
23 Speak unto Re-ho-bo'am, the son of Sol'o-
mon, king of Ju'dah, and unto all the house of
Ju'dah and Ben'ja-min, and to the remnant of
the people, saying,
24 Thus saith the LORD, Ye shall not go up,
nor fight against your brethren the children of
Is'ra-el: return every man to his house; for this
thing is from me. They hearkened therefore to
the word of the LORD, and returned to depart,
according to the word of the LORD.
25 ¶ Then Jer-o-bo'am built She'chem in
mount E'phra-im, and dwelt therein; and went
out from thence, and built Pe-nu'el.
26 And Jer-o-bo'am said in his heart, Now
shall the kingdom return to the house of Da'vid:
27 If this people go up to do sacrifice in the
house of the LORD at Je-ru'sa-lem, then shall the
heart of this people turn again unto their lord,
even unto Re-ho-bo'am king of Ju'dah, and they
shall kill me, and go again to Re-ho-bo'am king
of Ju'dah.
28 Whereupon the king took counsel, and
made two calves *of* gold, and said unto them, It
is too much for you to go up to Je-ru'sa-lem:
behold thy gods, O Is'ra-el, which brought thee
up out of the land of E'gypt.
29 And he set the one in Beth'-el, and the
other put he in Dan.
30 And this thing became a sin: for the people went *to worship* before the one, *even* unto
Dan.
31 And he made an house of high places, and
made priests of the lowest of the people, which
were not of the sons of Le'vi.
32 And Jer-o-bo'am ordained a feast in the
eighth month, on the fifteenth day of the month,
like unto the feast that *is* in Ju'dah, and he offered upon the altar. So did he in Beth'-el, sacrificing unto the calves that he had made: and he
placed in Beth'-el the priests of the high places
which he had made.
33 So he offered upon the altar which he had

made in Beth'-el the fifteenth day of the eighth
month, *even* in the month which he had devised
of his own heart; and ordained a feast unto the
children of Is'ra-el: and he offered upon the altar, and burnt incense.

13

AND, behold, there came a man of God
out of Ju'dah by the word of the LORD
unto Beth'-el: and Jer-o-bo'am stood by the altar to burn incense.
2 And he cried against the altar in the word
of the LORD, and said, O altar, altar, thus saith
the LORD; Behold, a child shall be born unto the
house of Da'vid, Jo-si'ah by name; and upon
thee shall he offer the priests of the high places
that burn incense upon thee, and men's bones
shall be burnt upon thee.
3 And he gave a sign the same day, saying,
This *is* the sign which the LORD hath spoken;
Behold, the altar shall be rent, and the ashes
that *are* upon it shall be poured out.
4 And it came to pass, when king Jer-o-bo'-
am heard the saying of the man of God, which
had cried against the altar in Beth'-el, that he
put forth his hand from the altar, saying, Lay
hold on him. And his hand, which he put forth
against him, dried up, so that he could not pull
it in again to him.
5 The altar also was rent, and the ashes
poured out from the altar, according to the sign
which the man of God had given by the word of
the LORD.
6 And the king answered and said unto the
man of God, Intreat now the face of the LORD
thy God, and pray for me, that my hand may be
restored me again. And the man of God besought the LORD, and the king's hand was restored him again, and became as *it was* before.
7 And the king said unto the man of God,
Come home with me, and refresh thyself, and I
will give thee a reward.
8 And the man of God said unto the king, If
thou wilt give me half thine house, I will not go
in with thee, neither will I eat bread nor drink
water in this place:
9 For so was it charged me by the word of
the LORD, saying, Eat no bread, nor drink water,
nor turn again by the same way that thou camest.
10 So he went another way, and returned not
by the way that he came to Beth'-el.
11 ¶ Now there dwelt an old prophet in
Beth'-el; and his sons came and told him all the
works that the man of God had done that day in
Beth'-el: the words which he had spoken unto
the king, them they told also to their father.
12 And their father said unto them, What
way went he? For his sons had seen what way
the man of God went, which came from Ju'dah.
13 And he said unto his sons, Saddle me the
ass. So they saddled him the ass: and he rode
thereon,
14 And went after the man of God, and found
him sitting under an oak: and he said unto him,
Art thou the man of God that camest from Ju'-
dah? And he said, I *am*.
15 Then he said unto him, Come home with
me, and eat bread.
16 And he said, I may not return with thee,
nor go in with thee: neither will I eat bread nor
drink water with thee in this place:
17 For it was said to me by the word of the
LORD, Thou shalt eat no bread nor drink water
there, nor turn again to go by the way that thou
camest.
18 He said unto him, I *am* a prophet also as
thou *art:* and an angel spake unto me by the
word of the LORD, saying, Bring him back with
thee into thine house, that he may eat bread and
drink water. *But* he lied unto him.
19 So he went back with him, and did eat
bread in his house, and drank water.
20 ¶ And it came to pass, as they sat at the
table, that the word of the LORD came unto the
prophet that brought him back:
21 And he cried unto the man of God that
came from Ju'dah, saying, Thus saith the LORD,
Forasmuch as thou hast disobeyed the mouth of
the LORD, and hast not kept the commandment
which the LORD thy God commanded thee,
22 But camest back, and hast eaten bread
and drunk water in the place, of the which *the*
LORD did say to thee, Eat no bread, and drink no
water; thy carcase shall not come unto the sepulchre of thy fathers.
23 ¶ And it came to pass, after he had eaten
bread, and after he had drunk, that he saddled
for him the ass, *to wit*, for the prophet whom he
had brought back.
24 And when he was gone, a lion met him by
the way, and slew him: and his carcase was cast
in the way, and the ass stood by it, the lion also
stood by the carcase.
25 And, behold, men passed by, and saw the
carcase cast in the way, and the lion standing
by the carcase: and they came and told *it* in the
city where the old prophet dwelt.
26 And when the prophet that brought him
back from the way heard *thereof*, he said, It *is*
the man of God, who was disobedient unto the
word of the LORD: therefore the LORD hath delivered him unto the lion, which hath torn him,
and slain him, according to the word of the
LORD, which he spake unto him.
27 And he spake to his sons, saying, Saddle
me the ass. And they saddled *him*.
28 And he went and found his carcase cast in
the way, and the ass and the lion standing by
the carcase: the lion had not eaten the carcase,
nor torn the ass.
29 And the prophet took up the carcase of
the man of God, and laid it upon the ass, and
brought it back: and the old prophet came to
the city, to mourn and to bury him.
30 And he laid his carcase in his own grave;
and they mourned over him, *saying*, Alas, my
brother!
31 And it came to pass, after he had buried
him, that he spake to his sons, saying, When I
am dead, then bury me in the sepulchre
wherein the man of God *is* buried; lay my bones
beside his bones:
32 For the saying which he cried by the word
of the LORD against the altar in Beth'-el, and
against all the houses of the high places which
are in the cities of Sa-ma'ri-a, shall surely come
to pass.
33 ¶ After this thing Jer-o-bo'am returned
not from his evil way, but made again of the
lowest of the people priests of the high places:
whosoever would, he consecrated him, and he
became *one* of the priests of the high places.
34 And this thing became sin unto the house
of Jer-o-bo'am, even to cut *it* off, and to destroy
it from off the face of the earth.

14

AT that time A-bi'jah the son of Jer-o-
bo'am fell sick.
2 And Jer-o-bo'am said to his wife, Arise, I
pray thee, and disguise thyself, that thou be not
known to be the wife of Jer-o-bo'am; and get
thee to Shi'loh: behold, there *is* A-hi'jah the
prophet, which told me that *I should be* king
over this people.

3 And take with thee ten loaves, and cracknels, and a cruse of honey, and go to him: he shall tell thee what shall become of the child.

4 And Jer-o-bo'am's wife did so, and arose, and went to Shi'loh, and came to the house of A-hi'jah. But A-hi'jah could not see; for his eyes were set by reason of his age.

5 ¶ And the LORD said unto A-hi'jah, Behold, the wife of Jer-o-bo'am cometh to ask a thing of thee for her son; for he *is* sick: thus and thus shalt thou say unto her: for it shall be, when she cometh in, that she shall feign herself *to be* another *woman.*

6 And it was *so,* when A-hi'jah heard the sound of her feet, as she came in at the door, that he said, Come in, thou wife of Jer-o-bo'am; why feignest thou thyself *to be* another? for I *am* sent to thee *with* heavy *tidings.*

7 Go, tell Jer-o-bo'am, Thus saith the LORD God of Is'ra-el, Forasmuch as I exalted thee from among the people, and made thee prince over my people Is'ra-el,

8 And rent the kingdom away from the house of Da'vid, and gave it thee: and *yet* thou hast not been as my servant Da'vid, who kept my commandments, and who followed me with all his heart, to do *that* only *which was* right in mine eyes;

9 But hast done evil above all that were before thee: for thou hast gone and made thee other gods, and molten images, to provoke me to anger, and hast cast me behind thy back:

10 Therefore, behold, I will bring evil upon the house of Jer-o-bo'am, and will cut off from Jer-o-bo'am him that pisseth against the wall, *and* him that is shut up and left in Is'ra-el, and will take away the remnant of the house of Jer-o-bo'am, as a man taketh away dung, till it be all gone.

11 Him that dieth of Jer-o-bo'am in the city shall the dogs eat; and him that dieth in the field shall the fowls of the air eat: for the LORD hath spoken *it.*

12 Arise thou therefore, get thee to thine own house: *and* when thy feet enter into the city, the child shall die.

13 And all Is'ra-el shall mourn for him, and bury him: for he only of Jer-o-bo'am shall come to the grave, because in him there is found *some* good thing toward the LORD God of Is'ra-el in the house of Jer-o-bo'am.

14 Moreover the LORD shall raise him up a king over Is'ra-el, who shall cut off the house of Jer-o-bo'am that day: but what? even now.

15 For the LORD shall smite Is'ra-el, as a reed is shaken in the water, and he shall root up Is'ra-el out of this good land, which he gave to their fathers, and shall scatter them beyond the river, because they have made their groves, provoking the LORD to anger.

16 And he shall give Is'ra-el up because of the sins of Jer-o-bo'am, who did sin, and who made Is'ra-el to sin.

17 ¶ And Jer-o-bo'am's wife arose, and departed, and came to Tir'zah: *and* when she came to the threshold of the door, the child died;

18 And they buried him; and all Is'ra-el mourned for him, according to the word of the LORD, which he spake by the hand of his servant A-hi'jah the prophet.

19 And the rest of the acts of Jer-o-bo'am, how he warred, and how he reigned, behold, they *are* written in the book of the chronicles of the kings of Is'ra-el.

20 And the days which Jer-o-bo'am reigned *were* two and twenty years: and he slept with his fathers, and Na'dab his son reigned in his stead.

21 ¶ And Re-ho-bo'am the son of Sol'o-mon reigned in Ju'dah. Re-ho-bo'am *was* forty and one years old when he began to reign, and he reigned seventeen years in Je-ru'sa-lem, the city which the LORD did choose out of all the tribes of Is'ra-el, to put his name there. And his mother's name *was* Na'a-mah an Am'mon-it-ess.

22 And Ju'dah did evil in the sight of the LORD, and they provoked him to jealousy with their sins which they had committed, above all that their fathers had done.

23 For they also built them high places, and images, and groves, on every high hill, and under every green tree.

24 And there were also sodomites in the land: *and* they did according to all the abominations of the nations which the LORD cast out before the children of Is'ra-el.

25 ¶ And it came to pass in the fifth year of king Re-ho-bo'am, *that* Shi'shak king of E'gypt came up against Je-ru'sa-lem:

26 And he took away the treasures of the house of the LORD, and the treasures of the king's house; he even took away all: and he took away all the shields of gold which Sol'o-mon had made.

27 And king Re-ho-bo'am made in their stead brasen shields, and committed *them* unto the hands of the chief of the guard, which kept the door of the king's house.

28 And it was *so,* when the king went into the house of the LORD, that the guard bare them, and brought them back into the guard chamber.

29 ¶ Now the rest of the acts of Re-ho-bo'am, and all that he did, *are* they not written in the book of the chronicles of the kings of Ju'dah?

30 And there was war between Re-ho-bo'am and Jer-o-bo'am all *their* days.

31 And Re-ho-bo'am slept with his fathers, and was buried with his fathers in the city of Da'vid. And his mother's name *was* Na'a-mah an Am'mon-it-ess. And A-bi'jam his son reigned in his stead.

15 NOW in the eighteenth year of king Jer-o-bo'am the son of Ne'bat reigned A-bi'jam over Ju'dah.

2 Three years reigned he in Je-ru'sa-lem. And his mother's name *was* Ma'a-chah, the daughter of A-bish'a-lom.

3 And he walked in all the sins of his father, which he had done before him: and his heart was not perfect with the LORD his God, as the heart of Da'vid his father.

4 Nevertheless for Da'vid's sake did the LORD his God give him a lamp in Je-ru'sa-lem, to set up his son after him, and to establish Je-ru'sa-lem:

5 Because Da'vid did *that which was* right in the eyes of the LORD, and turned not aside from any *thing* that he commanded him all the days of his life, save only in the matter of U-ri'ah the Hit'tite.

6 And there was war between Re-ho-bo'am and Jer-o-bo'am all the days of his life.

7 Now the rest of the acts of A-bi'jam, and all that he did, *are* they not written in the book of the chronicles of the kings of Ju'dah? And there was war between A-bi'jam and Jer-o-bo'am.

8 And A-bi'jam slept with his fathers; and they buried him in the city of Da'vid: and A'sa his son reigned in his stead.

9 ¶ And in the twentieth year of Jer-o-bo'am
king of Is'ra-el reigned A'sa over Ju'dah.
10 And forty and one years reigned he in Je-
ru'sa-lem. And his mother's name *was* Ma'a-
chah, the daughter of A-bish'a-lom.
11 And A'sa did *that which was* right in the
eyes of the LORD, as *did* Da'vid his father.
12 And he took away the sodomites out of
the land, and removed all the idols that his fathers had made.
13 And also Ma'a-chah his mother, even her
he removed from *being* queen, because she had
made an idol in a grove; and A'sa destroyed her
idol, and burnt *it* by the brook Kid'ron.
14 But the high places were not removed:
nevertheless A'sa's heart was perfect with the
LORD all his days.
15 And he brought in the things which his
father had dedicated, and the things which himself had dedicated, into the house of the LORD,
silver, and gold, and vessels.
16 ¶ And there was war between A'sa and
Ba'a-sha king of Is'ra-el all their days.
17 And Ba'a-sha king of Is'ra-el went up
against Ju'dah, and built Ra'mah, that he might
not suffer any to go out or come in to A'sa king
of Ju'dah.
18 Then A'sa took all the silver and the gold
that were left in the treasures of the house of
the LORD, and the treasures of the king's house,
and delivered them into the hand of his servants: and king A'sa sent them to Ben-ha'dad,
the son of Tab'ri-mon, the son of He'zi-on, king
of Syr'i-a, that dwelt at Da-mas'cus, saying,
19 *There is* a league between me and thee,
and between my father and thy father: behold, I
have sent unto thee a present of silver and gold;
come and break thy league with Ba'a-sha king
of Is'ra-el, that he may depart from me.
20 So Ben-ha'dad hearkened unto king A'sa,
and sent the captains of the hosts which he had
against the cities of Is'ra-el, and smote I'jon,
and Dan, and A'bel-beth-ma'a-chah, and all
Cin'ne-roth, with all the land of Naph'ta-li.
21 And it came to pass, when Ba'a-sha heard
thereof, that he left off building of Ra'mah, and
dwelt in Tir'zah.
22 Then king A'sa made a proclamation
throughout all Ju'dah; none *was* exempted: and
they took away the stones of Ra'mah, and the
timber thereof, wherewith Ba'a-sha had
builded; and king A'sa built with them Ge'ba of
Ben'ja-min, and Miz'pah.
23 The rest of all the acts of A'sa, and all his
might, and all that he did, and the cities which
he built, *are* they not written in the book of the
chronicles of the kings of Ju'dah? Nevertheless
in the time of his old age he was diseased in his
feet.
24 And A'sa slept with his fathers, and was
buried with his fathers in the city of Da'vid his
father: and Je-hosh'a-phat his son reigned in his
stead.
25 ¶ And Na'dab the son of Jer-o-bo'am began to reign over Is'ra-el in the second year of
A'sa king of Ju'dah, and reigned over Is'ra-el
two years.
26 And he did evil in the sight of the LORD,
and walked in the way of his father, and in his
sin wherewith he made Is'ra-el to sin.
27 ¶ And Ba'a-sha the son of A-hi'jah, of the
house of Is'sa-char, conspired against him; and
Ba'a-sha smote him at Gib'be-thon, which *belonged* to the Phi-lis'tines; for Na'dab and all Is'-
ra-el laid siege to Gib'be-thon.
28 Even in the third year of A'sa king of Ju'-
dah did Ba'a-sha slay him, and reigned in his
stead.
29 And it came to pass, when he reigned,
that he smote all the house of Jer-o-bo'am; he
left not to Jer-o-bo'am any that breathed, until
he had destroyed him, according unto the saying of the LORD, which he spake by his servant
A-hi'jah the Shi'lo-nite:
30 Because of the sins of Jer-o-bo'am which
he sinned, and which he made Is'ra-el sin, by his
provocation wherewith he provoked the LORD
God of Is'ra-el to anger.
31 ¶ Now the rest of the acts of Na'dab, and
all that he did, *are* they not written in the book
of the chronicles of the kings of Is'ra-el?
32 And there was war between A'sa and Ba'-
a-sha king of Is'ra-el all their days.
33 In the third year of A'sa king of Ju'dah
began Ba'a-sha the son of A-hi'jah to reign over
all Is'ra-el in Tir'zah, twenty and four years.
34 And he did evil in the sight of the LORD,
and walked in the way of Jer-o-bo'am, and in
his sin wherewith he made Is'ra-el to sin.

16 THEN the word of the LORD came to Je'-
hu the son of Ha-na'ni against Ba'a-sha,
saying,
2 Forasmuch as I exalted thee out of the
dust, and made thee prince over my people Is'-
ra-el; and thou hast walked in the way of Jer-o-
bo'am, and hast made my people Is'ra-el to sin,
to provoke me to anger with their sins;
3 Behold, I will take away the posterity of
Ba'a-sha, and the posterity of his house; and
will make thy house like the house of Jer-o-bo'-
am the son of Ne'bat.
4 Him that dieth of Ba'a-sha in the city shall
the dogs eat; and him that dieth of his in the
fields shall the fowls of the air eat.
5 Now the rest of the acts of Ba'a-sha, and
what he did, and his might, *are* they not written
in the book of the chronicles of the kings of Is'-
ra-el?
6 So Ba'a-sha slept with his fathers, and was
buried in Tir'zah: and E'lah his son reigned in
his stead.
7 And also by the hand of the prophet Je'hu
the son of Ha-na'ni came the word of the LORD
against Ba'a-sha, and against his house, even
for all the evil that he did in the sight of the
LORD, in provoking him to anger with the work
of his hands, in being like the house of Jer-o-
bo'am; and because he killed him.
8 ¶ In the twenty and sixth year of A'sa king
of Ju'dah began E'lah the son of Ba'a-sha to
reign over Is'ra-el in Tir'zah, two years.
9 And his servant Zim'ri, captain of half *his*
chariots, conspired against him, as he was in
Tir'zah, drinking himself drunk in the house of
Ar'za steward of *his* house in Tir'zah.
10 And Zim'ri went in and smote him, and
killed him, in the twenty and seventh year of
A'sa king of Ju'dah, and reigned in his stead.
11 ¶ And it came to pass, when he began to
reign, as soon as he sat on his throne, *that* he
slew all the house of Ba'a-sha he left him not
one that pisseth against a wall, neither of his
kinsfolks, nor of his friends.
12 Thus did Zim'ri destroy all the house of
Ba'a-sha, according to the word of the LORD,
which he spake against Ba'a-sha by Je'hu the
prophet,
13 For all the sins of Ba'a-sha, and the sins of
E'lah his son, by which they sinned, and by
which they made Is'ra-el to sin, in provoking
the LORD God of Is'ra-el to anger with their
vanities.

14 Now the rest of the acts of E'lah, and all that he did, *are* they not written in the book of the chronicles of the kings of Is'ra-el?

15 ¶ In the twenty and seventh year of A'sa king of Ju'dah did Zim'ri reign seven days in Tir'zah. And the people *were* encamped against Gib'be-thon, which *belonged* to the Phi-lis'tines.

16 And the people *that were* encamped heard say, Zim'ri hath conspired, and hath also slain the king: wherefore all Is'ra-el made Om'ri, the captain of the host, king over Is'ra-el that day in the camp.

17 And Om'ri went up from Gib'be-thon, and all Is'ra-el with him, and they besieged Tir'zah.

18 And it came to pass, when Zim'ri saw that the city was taken, that he went into the palace of the king's house, and burnt the king's house over him with fire, and died,

19 For his sins which he sinned in doing evil in the sight of the LORD, in walking in the way of Jer-o-bo'am, and in his sin which he did, to make Is'ra-el to sin.

20 Now the rest of the acts of Zim'ri, and his treason that he wrought, *are* they not written in the book of the chronicles of the kings of Is'ra-el?

21 ¶ Then were the people of Is'ra-el divided into two parts: half of the people followed Tib'ni the son of Gi'nath, to make him king; and half followed Om'ri.

22 But the people that followed Om'ri prevailed against the people that followed Tib'ni the son of Gi'nath: so Tib'ni died, and Om'ri reigned.

23 ¶ In the thirty and first year of A'sa king of Ju'dah began Om'ri to reign over Is'ra-el, twelve years: six years reigned he in Tir'zah.

24 And he bought the hill Sa-ma'ri-a of She'mer for two talents of silver, and built on the hill, and called the name of the city which he built, after the name of She'mer, owner of the hill, Sa-ma'ri-a.

25 ¶ But Om'ri wrought evil in the eyes of the LORD, and did worse than all that *were* before him.

26 For he walked in all the way of Jer-o-bo'am the son of Ne'bat, and in his sin wherewith he made Is'ra-el to sin, to provoke the LORD God of Is'ra-el to anger with their vanities.

27 Now the rest of the acts of Om'ri which he did, and his might that he shewed, *are* they not written in the book of the chronicles of the kings of Is'ra-el?

28 So Om'ri slept with his fathers, and was buried in Sa-ma'ri-a: and A'hab his son reigned in his stead.

29 ¶ And in the thirty and eighth year of A'sa king of Ju'dah began A'hab the son of Om'ri to reign over Is'ra-el: and A'hab the son of Om'ri reigned over Is'ra-el in Sa-ma'ri-a twenty and two years.

30 And A'hab the son of Om'ri did evil in the sight of the LORD above all that *were* before him.

31 And it came to pass, as if it had been a light thing for him to walk in the sins of Jer-o-bo'am the son of Ne'bat, that he took to wife Jez'e-bel the daughter of Eth'ba-al king of the Zi-do'ni-ans, and went and served Ba'al, and worshipped him.

32 And he reared up an altar for Ba'al in the house of Ba'al, which he had built in Sa-ma'ri-a.

33 And A'hab made a grove; and A'hab did more to provoke the LORD God of Is'ra-el to anger than all the kings of Is'ra-el that were before him.

34 ¶ In his days did Hi'el the Beth'-el-ite build Jer'i-cho: he laid the foundation thereof in A-bi'ram his firstborn, and set up the gates thereof in his youngest *son* Se'gub, according to the word of the LORD, which he spake by Josh'u-a the son of Nun.

17

AND E-li'jah the Tish'bite, *who was* of the inhabitants of Gil'e-ad, said unto A'hab, *As* the LORD God of Is'ra-el liveth, before whom I stand, there shall not be dew nor rain these years, but according to my word.

2 And the word of the LORD came unto him, saying,

3 Get thee hence, and turn thee eastward, and hide thyself by the brook Che'rith, that *is* before Jor'dan.

4 And it shall be, *that* thou shalt drink of the brook; and I have commanded the ravens to feed thee there.

5 So he went and did according unto the word of the LORD: for he went and dwelt by the brook Che'rith, that *is* before Jor'dan.

6 And the ravens brought him bread and flesh in the morning, and bread and flesh in the evening; and he drank of the brook.

7 And it came to pass, after a while, that the brook dried up, because there had been no rain in the land.

8 ¶ And the word of the LORD came unto him, saying,

9 Arise, get thee to Zar'e-phath, which *belongeth* to Zi'don, and dwell there: behold, I have commanded a widow woman there to sustain thee.

10 So he arose and went to Zar'e-phath. And when he came to the gate of the city, behold, the widow woman *was* there gathering of sticks: and he called to her, and said, Fetch me, I pray thee, a little water in a vessel, that I may drink.

11 And as she was going to fetch *it*, he called to her, and said, Bring me, I pray thee, a morsel of bread in thine hand.

12 And she said, *As* the LORD thy God liveth, I have not a cake, but an handful of meal in a barrel, and a little oil in a cruse: and, behold, I *am* gathering two sticks, that I may go in and dress it for me and my son, that we may eat it, and die.

13 And E-li'jah said unto her, Fear not; go *and* do as thou hast said: but make me thereof a little cake first, and bring *it* unto me, and after make for thee and for thy son.

14 For thus saith the LORD God of Is'ra-el, The barrel of meal shall not waste, neither shall the cruse of oil fail, until the day *that* the LORD sendeth rain upon the earth.

15 And she went and did according to the saying of E-li'jah: and she, and he, and her house, did eat *many* days.

16 *And* the barrel of meal wasted not, neither did the cruse of oil fail, according to the word of the LORD, which he spake by E-li'jah.

17 ¶ And it came to pass after these things, *that* the son of the woman, the mistress of the house, fell sick; and his sickness was so sore, that there was no breath left in him.

18 And she said unto E-li'jah, What have I to do with thee, O thou man of God? art thou come unto me to call my sin to remembrance, and to slay my son?

19 And he said unto her, Give me thy son. And he took him out of her bosom, and carried him up into a loft, where he abode, and laid him upon his own bed.

20 And he cried unto the LORD, and said, O LORD my God, hast thou also brought evil upon

the widow with whom I sojourn, by slaying her
son?
21 And he stretched himself upon the child
three times, and cried unto the LORD, and said,
O LORD my God, I pray thee, let this child's soul
come into him again.
22 And the LORD heard the voice of E-li'jah;
and the soul of the child came into him again,
and he revived.
23 And E-li'jah took the child, and brought
him down out of the chamber into the house,
and delivered him unto his mother: and E-li'jah
said, See, thy son liveth.
24 ¶ And the woman said to E-li'jah, Now by
this I know that thou *art* a man of God, *and* that
the word of the LORD in thy mouth *is* truth.

18 AND it came to pass *after* many days,
that the word of the LORD came to E-
li'jah in the third year, saying, Go, shew thyself
unto A'hab; and I will send rain upon the earth.
2 And E-li'jah went to shew himself unto A'-
hab. And *there was* a sore famine in Sa-ma'ri-a.
3 And A'hab called O-ba-di'ah, which *was*
the governor of *his* house. (Now O-ba-di'ah
feared the LORD greatly:
4 For it was *so,* when Jez'e-bel cut off the
prophets of the LORD, that O-ba-di'ah took an
hundred prophets, and hid them by fifty in a
cave, and fed them with bread and water.)
5 And A'hab said unto O-ba-di'ah, Go into
the land, unto all fountains of water, and unto
all brooks: peradventure we may find grass to
save the horses and mules alive, that we lose
not all the beasts.
6 So they divided the land between them to
pass throughout it: A'hab went one way by himself, and O-ba-di'ah went another way by himself.
7 ¶ And as O-ba-di'ah was in the way, behold, E-li'jah met him: and he knew him, and
fell on his face, and said, *Art* thou that my lord
E-li'jah?
8 And he answered him, I *am:* go, tell thy
lord, Behold, E-li'jah *is here.*
9 And he said, What have I sinned, that thou
wouldest deliver thy servant into the hand of
A'hab, to slay me?
10 *As* the LORD thy God liveth, there is no
nation or kingdom, whither my lord hath not
sent to seek thee: and when they said, *He is* not
there; he took an oath of the kingdom and nation, that they found thee not.
11 And now thou sayest, Go, tell thy lord, Behold, E-li'jah *is here.*
12 And it shall come to pass, *as soon as* I am
gone from thee, that the Spirit of the LORD shall
carry thee whither I know not; and *so* when I
come and tell A'hab, and he cannot find thee, he
shall slay me: but I thy servant fear the LORD
from my youth.
13 Was it not told my lord what I did when
Jez'e-bel slew the prophets of the LORD, how I
hid an hundred men of the LORD's prophets by
fifty in a cave, and fed them with bread and
water?
14 And now thou sayest, Go, tell thy lord, Behold, E-li'jah *is here:* and he shall slay me.
15 And E-li'jah said, *As* the LORD of hosts liveth, before whom I stand, I will surely shew
myself unto him to day.
16 So O-ba-di'ah went to meet A'hab, and
told him: and A'hab went to meet E-li'jah.
17 ¶ And it came to pass, when A'hab saw E-
li'jah, that A'hab said unto him, *Art* thou he that
troubleth Is'ra-el?
18 And he answered, I have not troubled Is'-
ra-el; but thou, and thy father's house, in that ye
have forsaken the commandments of the LORD,
and thou hast followed Ba'al-im.
19 Now therefore send, *and* gather to me all
Is'ra-el unto mount Car'mel, and the prophets
of Ba'al four hundred and fifty, and the prophets of the groves four hundred, which eat at
Jez'e-bel's table.
20 So A'hab sent unto all the children of Is'-
ra-el, and gathered the prophets together unto
mount Car'mel.
21 And E-li'jah came unto all the people, and
said, How long halt ye between two opinions? if
the LORD *be* God, follow him: but if Ba'al, *then*
follow him. And the people answered him not a
word.
22 Then said E-li'jah unto the people, I, *even*
I only, remain a prophet of the LORD; but Ba'al's
prophets *are* four hundred and fifty men.
23 Let them therefore give us two bullocks;
and let them choose one bullock for themselves,
and cut it in pieces, and lay *it* on wood, and put
no fire *under:* and I will dress the other bullock,
and lay *it* on wood, and put no fire *under:*
24 And call ye on the name of your gods, and
I will call on the name of the LORD: and the God
that answereth by fire, let him be God. And all
the people answered and said, It is well spoken.
25 And E-li'jah said unto the prophets of Ba'-
al, Choose you one bullock for yourselves, and
dress *it* first; for ye *are* many; and call on the
name of your gods, but put no fire *under.*
26 And they took the bullock which was giv-
en them, and they dressed *it,* and called on the
name of Ba'al from morning even until noon,
saying, O Ba'al, hear us. But *there was* no voice,
nor any that answered. And they leaped upon
the altar which was made.
27 And it came to pass at noon, that E-li'jah
mocked them, and said, Cry aloud: for he *is* a
god; either he is talking, or he is pursuing, or he
is in a journey, *or* peradventure he sleepeth, and
must be awaked.
28 And they cried aloud, and cut themselves
after their manner with knives and lancets, till
the blood gushed out upon them.
29 And it came to pass, when midday was
past, and they prophesied until the *time* of the
offering of the *evening* sacrifice, that *there was*
neither voice, nor any to answer, nor any that
regarded.
30 And E-li'jah said unto all the people,
Come near unto me. And all the people came
near unto him. And he repaired the altar of the
LORD *that was* broken down.
31 And E-li'jah took twelve stones, according
to the number of the tribes of the sons of Ja'-
cob, unto whom the word of the LORD came,
saying, Is'ra-el shall be thy name:
32 And with the stones he built an altar in
the name of the LORD: and he made a trench
about the altar, as great as would contain two
measures of seed.
33 And he put the wood in order, and cut the
bullock in pieces, and laid *him* on the wood, and
said, Fill four barrels with water, and pour *it* on
the burnt sacrifice, and on the wood.
34 And he said, Do *it* the second time. And
they did *it* the second time. And he said, Do *it*
the third time. And they did *it* the third time.
35 And the water ran round about the altar;
and he filled the trench also with water.
36 And it came to pass at *the time of* the offering of the *evening* sacrifice, that E-li'jah the
prophet came near, and said, LORD God of A'-
bra-ham, I'saac, and of Is'ra-el, let it be known
this day that thou *art* God in Is'ra-el, and *that* I

am thy servant, and *that* I have done all these
things at thy word.
37 Hear me, O LORD, hear me, that this people may know that thou *art* the LORD God, and
that thou hast turned their heart back again.
38 Then the fire of the LORD fell, and consumed the burnt sacrifice, and the wood, and
the stones, and the dust, and licked up the water that *was* in the trench.
39 And when all the people saw *it*, they fell
on their faces: and they said, The LORD, he *is*
the God; the LORD, he *is* the God.
40 And E-li'jah said unto them, Take the
prophets of Ba'al; let not one of them escape.
And they took them: and E-li'jah brought them
down to the brook Ki'shon, and slew them
there.
41 ¶ And E-li'jah said unto A'hab, Get thee
up, eat and drink; for *there is* a sound of abundance of rain.
42 So A'hab went up to eat and to drink. And
E-li'jah went up to the top of Car'mel; and he
cast himself down upon the earth, and put his
face between his knees,
43 And said to his servant, Go up now, look
toward the sea. And he went up, and looked,
and said, *There is* nothing. And he said, Go
again seven times.
44 And it came to pass at the seventh time,
that he said, Behold, there ariseth a little cloud
out of the sea, like a man's hand. And he said,
Go up, say unto A'hab, Prepare *thy chariot*, and
get thee down, that the rain stop thee not.
45 And it came to pass in the mean while,
that the heaven was black with clouds and
wind, and there was a great rain. And A'hab
rode, and went to Jez're-el.
46 And the hand of the LORD was on E-li'jah;
and he girded up his loins, and ran before A'hab
to the entrance of Jez're-el.

19 AND A'hab told Jez'e-bel all that E-li'-
jah had done, and withal how he had
slain all the prophets with the sword.
2 Then Jez'e-bel sent a messenger unto E-li'-
jah, saying, So let the gods do *to me*, and more
also, if I make not thy life as the life of one of
them by to morrow about this time.
3 And when he saw *that*, he arose, and went
for his life, and came to Be'er-she'ba, which *belongeth* to Ju'dah, and left his servant there.
4 ¶ But he himself went a day's journey into
the wilderness, and came and sat down under a
juniper tree: and he requested for himself that
he might die; and said, It is enough; now, O
LORD, take away my life; for I *am* not better
than my fathers.
5 And as he lay and slept under a juniper
tree, behold, then an angel touched him, and
said unto him, Arise *and* eat.
6 And he looked, and, behold, *there was* a
cake baken on the coals, and a cruse of water at
his head. And he did eat and drink, and laid him
down again.
7 And the angel of the LORD came again the
second time, and touched him, and said, Arise
and eat; because the journey *is* too great for
thee.
8 And he arose, and did eat and drink, and
went in the strength of that meat forty days and
forty nights unto Ho'reb the mount of God.
9 ¶ And he came thither unto a cave, and
lodged there; and, behold, the word of the LORD
came to him, and he said unto him, What doest
thou here, E-li'jah?
10 And he said, I have been very jealous for
the LORD God of hosts: for the children of Is'ra-
el have forsaken thy covenant, thrown down
thine altars, and slain thy prophets with the
sword; and I, *even* I only, am left; and they seek
my life, to take it away.
11 And he said, Go forth, and stand upon the
mount before the LORD. And, behold, the LORD
passed by, and a great and strong wind rent the
mountains, and brake in pieces the rocks before
the LORD; *but* the LORD *was* not in the wind: and
after the wind an earthquake; *but* the LORD *was*
not in the earthquake:
12 And after the earthquake a fire; *but* the
LORD *was* not in the fire: and after the fire a still
small voice.
13 And it was *so*, when E-li'jah heard *it*, that
he wrapped his face in his mantle, and went
out, and stood in the entering in of the cave.
And, behold, *there came* a voice unto him, and
said, What doest thou here, E-li'jah?
14 And he said, I have been very jealous for
the LORD God of hosts: because the children of
Is'ra-el have forsaken thy covenant, thrown
down thine altars, and slain thy prophets with
the sword; and I, *even* I only, am left; and they
seek my life, to take it away.
15 And the LORD said unto him, Go, return
on thy way to the wilderness of Da-mas'cus:
and when thou comest, anoint Haz'a-el *to be*
king over Syr'i-a:
16 And Je'hu the son of Nim'shi shalt thou
anoint *to be* king over Is'ra-el: and E-li'sha the
son of Sha'phat of A'bel-me-ho'lah shalt thou
anoint *to be* prophet in thy room.
17 And it shall come to pass, *that* him that
escapeth the sword of Haz'a-el shall Je'hu slay:
and him that escapeth from the sword of Je'hu
shall E-li'sha slay.
18 Yet I have left *me* seven thousand in Is'ra-
el, all the knees which have not bowed unto Ba'-
al, and every mouth which hath not kissed him.
19 ¶ So he departed thence, and found E-li'-
sha the son of Sha'phat, who *was* plowing *with*
twelve yoke *of oxen* before him, and he with
the twelfth: and E-li'jah passed by him, and cast
his mantle upon him.
20 And he left the oxen, and ran after E-li'-
jah, and said, Let me, I pray thee, kiss my father
and my mother, and *then* I will follow thee. And
he said unto him, Go back again: for what have
I done to thee?
21 And he returned back from him, and took
a yoke of oxen, and slew them, and boiled their
flesh with the instruments of the oxen, and gave
unto the people, and they did eat. Then he
arose, and went after E-li'jah, and ministered
unto him.

20 AND Ben-ha'dad the king of Syr'i-a
gathered all his host together: and *there
were* thirty and two kings with him, and horses,
and chariots: and he went up and besieged Sa-
ma'ri-a, and warred against it.
2 And he sent messengers to A'hab king of
Is'ra-el into the city, and said unto him, Thus
saith Ben-ha'dad,
3 Thy silver and thy gold *is* mine; thy wives
also and thy children, *even* the goodliest, *are*
mine.
4 And the king of Is'ra-el answered and said,
My lord, O king, according to thy saying, I *am*
thine, and all that I have.
5 And the messengers came again, and said,
Thus speaketh Ben-ha'dad, saying, Although I
have sent unto thee, saying, Thou shalt deliver
me thy silver, and thy gold, and thy wives, and
thy children;
6 Yet I will send my servants unto thee to

morrow about this time, and they shall search
thine house, and the houses of thy servants; and
it shall be, *that* whatsoever is pleasant in thine
eyes, they shall put *it* in their hand, and take *it*
away.
7 Then the king of Is'ra-el called all the elders
of the land, and said, Mark, I pray you, and see
how this *man* seeketh mischief: for he sent unto
me for my wives, and for my children, and for
my silver, and for my gold; and I denied him
not.
8 And all the elders and all the people said
unto him, Hearken not *unto him,* nor consent.
9 Wherefore he said unto the messengers of
Ben-ha'dad, Tell my lord the king, All that thou
didst send for to thy servant at the first I will
do: but this thing I may not do. And the messengers departed, and brought him word again.
10 And Ben-ha'dad sent unto him, and said,
The gods do so unto me, and more also, if the
dust of Sa-ma'ri-a shall suffice for handfuls for
all the people that follow me.
11 And the king of Is'ra-el answered and
said, Tell *him,* Let not him that girdeth on *his
harness* boast himself as he that putteth it off.
12 And it came to pass, when *Ben-ha'dad*
heard this message, as he *was* drinking, he and
the kings in the pavilions, that he said unto his
servants, Set *yourselves in array.* And they set
themselves in array against the city.
13 ¶ And, behold, there came a prophet unto
A'hab king of Is'ra-el, saying, Thus saith the
LORD, Hast thou seen all this great multitude?
behold, I will deliver it into thine hand this day;
and thou shalt know that I *am* the LORD.
14 And A'hab said, By whom? And he said,
Thus saith the LORD, *Even* by the young men of
the princes of the provinces. Then he said, Who
shall order the battle? And he answered, Thou.
15 Then he numbered the young men of the
princes of the provinces, and they were two
hundred and thirty two: and after them he numbered all the people, *even* all the children of Is'-
ra-el, *being* seven thousand.
16 And they went out at noon. But Ben-ha'-
dad *was* drinking himself drunk in the pavilions, he and the kings, the thirty and two kings
that helped him.
17 And the young men of the princes of the
provinces went out first; and Ben-ha'dad sent
out, and they told him, saying, There are men
come out of Sa-ma'ri-a.
18 And he said, Whether they be come out
for peace, take them alive; or whether they be
come out for war, take them alive.
19 So these young men of the princes of the
provinces came out of the city, and the army
which followed them.
20 And they slew every one his man: and the
Syr'i-ans fled; and Is'ra-el pursued them: and
Ben-ha'dad the king of Syr'i-a escaped on an
horse with the horsemen.
21 And the king of Is'ra-el went out, and
smote the horses and chariots, and slew the
Syr'i-ans with a great slaughter.
22 ¶ And the prophet came to the king of Is'-
ra-el, and said unto him, Go, strengthen thyself,
and mark, and see what thou doest: for at the
return of the year the king of Syr'i-a will come
up against thee.
23 And the servants of the king of Syr'i-a
said unto him, Their gods *are* gods of the hills;
therefore they were stronger than we; but let us
fight against them in the plain, and surely we
shall be stronger than they.
24 And do this thing, Take the kings away,
every man out of his place, and put captains in
their rooms:
25 And number thee an army, like the army
that thou hast lost, horse for horse, and chariot
for chariot: and we will fight against them in
the plain, *and* surely we shall be stronger than
they. And he hearkened unto their voice, and
did so.
26 And it came to pass at the return of the
year, that Ben-ha'dad numbered the Syr'i-ans,
and went up to A'phek, to fight against Is'ra-el.
27 And the children of Is'ra-el were numbered, and were all present, and went against
them: and the children of Is'ra-el pitched before
them like two little flocks of kids; but the Syr'i-
ans filled the country.
28 ¶ And there came a man of God, and
spake unto the king of Is'ra-el, and said, Thus
saith the LORD, Because the Syr'i-ans have said,
The LORD *is* God of the hills, but he *is* not God
of the valleys, therefore will I deliver all this
great multitude into thine hand, and ye shall
know that I *am* the LORD.
29 And they pitched one over against the
other seven days. And *so* it was, that in the seventh day the battle was joined: and the children
of Is'ra-el slew of the Syr'i-ans an hundred
thousand footmen in one day.
30 But the rest fled to A'phek, into the city;
and *there* a wall fell upon twenty and seven
thousand of the men *that were* left. And Ben-
ha'dad fled, and came into the city, into an inner
chamber.
31 ¶ And his servants said unto him, Behold
now, we have heard that the kings of the house
of Is'ra-el *are* merciful kings: let us, I pray thee,
put sackcloth on our loins, and ropes upon our
heads, and go out to the king of Is'ra-el: peradventure he will save thy life.
32 So they girded sackcloth on their loins,
and *put* ropes on their heads, and came to the
king of Is'ra-el, and said, Thy servant Ben-ha'-
dad saith, I pray thee, let me live. And he said,
Is he yet alive? he *is* my brother.
33 Now the men did diligently observe
whether *any thing would come* from him, and
did hastily catch *it:* and they said, Thy brother
Ben-ha'dad. Then he said, Go ye, bring him.
Then Ben-ha'dad came forth to him; and he
caused him to come up into the chariot.
34 And *Ben-ha'dad* said unto him, The cities,
which my father took from thy father, I will restore; and thou shalt make streets for thee in
Da-mas'cus, as my father made in Sa-ma'ri-a.
Then *said A'hab,* I will send thee away with this
covenant. So he made a covenant with him, and
sent him away.
35 ¶ And a certain man of the sons of the
prophets said unto his neighbour in the word of
the LORD, Smite me, I pray thee. And the man
refused to smite him.
36 Then said he unto him, Because thou hast
not obeyed the voice of the LORD, behold, as
soon as thou art departed from me, a lion shall
slay thee. And as soon as he was departed from
him, a lion found him, and slew him.
37 Then he found another man, and said,
Smite me, I pray thee. And the man smote him,
so that in smiting he wounded *him.*
38 So the prophet departed, and waited for
the king by the way, and disguised himself with
ashes upon his face.
39 And as the king passed by, he cried unto
the king: and he said, Thy servant went out into
the midst of the battle; and, behold, a man
turned aside, and brought a man unto me, and
said, Keep this man:if by any means he be miss-

ing, then shall thy life be for his life, or else thou
shalt pay a talent of silver.
40 And as thy servant was busy here and
there, he was gone. And the king of Is'ra-el said
unto him, So *shall* thy judgment *be:* thyself hast
decided *it.*
41 And he hasted, and took the ashes away
from his face; and the king of Is'ra-el discerned
him that he *was* of the prophets.
42 And he said unto him, Thus saith the
LORD, Because thou hast let go out of *thy* hand
a man whom I appointed to utter destruction,
therefore thy life shall go for his life, and thy
people for his people.
43 And the king of Is'ra-el went to his house
heavy and displeased, and came to Sa-ma'ri-a.

21 AND it came to pass after these things,
that Na'both the Jez're-el-ite had a vineyard, which *was* in Jez're-el, hard by the palace
of A'hab king of Sa-ma'ri-a.
2 And A'hab spake unto Na'both, saying,
Give me thy vineyard, that I may have it for a
garden of herbs, because it *is* near unto my
house: and I will give thee for it a better vineyard than it; *or,* if it seem good to thee, I will
give thee the worth of it in money.
3 And Na'both said to A'hab, The LORD forbid it me, that I should give the inheritance of
my fathers unto thee.
4 And A'hab came into his house heavy and
displeased because of the word which Na'both
the Jez're-el-ite had spoken to him: for he had
said, I will not give thee the inheritance of my
fathers. And he laid him down upon his bed,
and turned away his face, and would eat no
bread.
5 ¶ But Jez'e-bel his wife came to him, and
said unto him, Why is thy spirit so sad, that
thou eatest no bread?
6 And he said unto her, Because I spake unto
Na'both the Jez're-el-ite, and said unto him,
Give me thy vineyard for money; or else, if it
please thee, I will give thee *another* vineyard
for it: and he answered, I will not give thee my
vineyard.
7 And Jez'e-bel his wife said unto him, Dost
thou now govern the kingdom of Is'ra-el? arise,
and eat bread, and let thine heart be merry: I
will give thee the vineyard of Na'both the Jez'-
re-el-ite.
8 So she wrote letters in A'hab's name, and
sealed *them* with his seal, and sent the letters
unto the elders and to the nobles that *were* in
his city, dwelling with Na'both.
9 And she wrote in the letters, saying, Proclaim a fast, and set Na'both on high among the
people:
10 And set two men, sons of Be'li-al, before
him, to bear witness against him, saying, Thou
didst blaspheme God and the king. And *then*
carry him out, and stone him, that he may die.
11 And the men of his city, *even* the elders
and the nobles who were the inhabitants in his
city, did as Jez'e-bel had sent unto them, *and* as
it *was* written in the letters which she had sent
unto them.
12 They proclaimed a fast, and set Na'both
on high among the people.
13 And there came in two men, children of
Be'li-al, and sat before him: and the men of Be'-
li-al witnessed against him, *even* against Na'-
both, in the presence of the people, saying, Na'-
both did blaspheme God and the king. Then
they carried him forth out of the city, and
stoned him with stones, that he died.
14 Then they sent to Jez'e-bel, saying, Na'-
both is stoned, and is dead.
15 ¶ And it came to pass, when Jez'e-bel
heard that Na'both was stoned, and was dead,
that Jez'e-bel said to A'hab, Arise, take possession of the vineyard of Na'both the Jez're-el-ite,
which he refused to give thee for money: for
Na'both is not alive, but dead.
16 And it came to pass, when A'hab heard
that Na'both was dead, that A'hab rose up to go
down to the vineyard of Na'both the Jez're-el-
ite, to take possession of it.
17 ¶ And the word of the LORD came to E-
li'jah the Tish'bite, saying,
18 Arise, go down to meet A'hab king of Is'-
ra-el, which *is* in Sa-ma'ri-a: behold, *he is* in the
vineyard of Na'both, whither he is gone down
to possess it.
19 And thou shalt speak unto him, saying,
Thus saith the LORD, Hast thou killed, and also
taken possession? And thou shalt speak unto
him, saying, Thus saith the LORD, In the place
where dogs licked the blood of Na'both shall
dogs lick thy blood, even thine.
20 And A'hab said to E-li'jah, Hast thou
found me, O mine enemy? And he answered, I
have found *thee:* because thou hast sold thyself
to work evil in the sight of the LORD.
21 Behold, I will bring evil upon thee, and
will take away thy posterity, and will cut off
from A'hab him that pisseth against the wall,
and him that is shut up and left in Is'ra-el,
22 And will make thine house like the house
of Jer-o-bo'am the son of Ne'bat, and like the
house of Ba'a-sha the son of A-hi'jah, for the
provocation wherewith thou hast provoked *me*
to anger, and made Is'ra-el to sin.
23 And of Jez'e-bel also spake the LORD, saying, The dogs shall eat Jez'e-bel by the wall of
Jez're-el.
24 Him that dieth of A'hab in the city the
dogs shall eat; and him that dieth in the field
shall the fowls of the air eat.
25 ¶ But there was none like unto A'hab,
which did sell himself to work wickedness in
the sight of the LORD, whom Jez'e-bel his wife
stirred up.
26 And he did very abominably in following
idols, according to all *things* as did the Am'or-
ites, whom the LORD cast out before the children of Is'ra-el.
27 And it came to pass, when A'hab heard
those words, that he rent his clothes, and put
sackcloth upon his flesh, and fasted, and lay in
sackcloth, and went softly.
28 And the word of the LORD came to E-li'jah
the Tish'bite, saying,
29 Seest thou how A'hab humbleth himself
before me? because he humbleth himself before
me, I will not bring the evil in his days: *but* in
his son's days will I bring the evil upon his
house.

22 AND they continued three years without war between Syr'i-a and Is'ra-el.
2 And it came to pass in the third year, that
Je-hosh'a-phat the king of Ju'dah came down to
the king of Is'ra-el.
3 And the king of Is'ra-el said unto his servants, Know ye that Ra'moth in Gil'e-ad *is* ours,
and we *be* still, *and* take it not out of the hand
of the king of Syr'i-a?
4 And he said unto Je-hosh'a-phat, Wilt thou
go with me to battle to Ra'moth-gil'e-ad? And
Je-hosh'a-phat said to the king of Is'ra-el, I *am*
as thou *art,* my people as thy people, my horses
as thy horses.

5 And Je-hosh'a-phat said unto the king of Is'ra-el, Enquire, I pray thee, at the word of the LORD to day.

6 Then the king of Is'ra-el gathered the prophets together, about four hundred men, and said unto them, Shall I go against Ra'moth-gil'e-ad to battle, or shall I forbear? And they said, Go up; for the LORD shall deliver *it* into the hand of the king.

7 And Je-hosh'a-phat said, *Is there* not here a prophet of the LORD besides, that we might enquire of him?

8 And the king of Is'ra-el said unto Je-hosh'a-phat, *There is* yet one man, Mi-ca'iah the son of Im'lah, by whom we may enquire of the LORD: but I hate him; for he doth not prophesy good concerning me, but evil. And Je-hosh'a-phat said, Let not the king say so.

9 Then the king of Is'ra-el called an officer, and said, Hasten *hither* Mi-ca'iah the son of Im'lah.

10 And the king of Is'ra-el and Je-hosh'a-phat the king of Ju'dah sat each on his throne, having put on their robes, in a void place in the entrance of the gate of Sa-ma'ri-a; and all the prophets prophesied before them.

11 And Zed-e-ki'ah the son of Che-na'a-nah made him horns of iron: and he said, Thus saith the LORD, With these shalt thou push the Syr'i-ans, until thou have consumed them.

12 And all the prophets prophesied so, saying, Go up to Ra'moth-gil'e-ad, and prosper: for the LORD shall deliver *it* into the king's hand.

13 And the messenger that was gone to call Mi-ca'iah spake unto him, saying, Behold now, the words of the prophets *declare* good unto the king with one mouth: let thy word, I pray thee, be like the word of one of them, and speak *that which is* good.

14 And Mi-ca'iah said, *As* the LORD liveth, what the LORD saith unto me, that will I speak.

15 ¶ So he came to the king. And the king said unto him, Mi-ca'iah, shall we go against Ra'moth-gil'e-ad to battle, or shall we forbear? And he answered him, Go, and prosper: for the LORD shall deliver *it* into the hand of the king.

16 And the king said unto him, How many times shall I adjure thee that thou tell me nothing but *that which is* true in the name of the LORD?

17 And he said, I saw all Is'ra-el scattered upon the hills, as sheep that have not a shepherd: and the LORD said, These have no master: let them return every man to his house in peace.

18 And the king of Is'ra-el said unto Je-hosh'a-phat, Did I not tell thee that he would prophesy no good concerning me, but evil?

19 And he said, Hear thou therefore the word of the LORD: I saw the LORD sitting on his throne, and all the host of heaven standing by him on his right hand and on his left.

20 And the LORD said, Who shall persuade A'hab, that he may go up and fall at Ra'moth-gil'e-ad? And one said on this manner, and another said on that manner.

21 And there came forth a spirit, and stood before the LORD, and said, I will persuade him.

22 And the LORD said unto him, Wherewith? And he said, I will go forth, and I will be a lying spirit in the mouth of all his prophets. And he said, Thou shalt persuade *him,* and prevail also: go forth, and do so.

23 Now therefore, behold, the LORD hath put a lying spirit in the mouth of all these thy prophets, and the LORD hath spoken evil concerning thee.

24 But Zed-e-ki'ah the son of Che-na'a-nah went near, and smote Mi-ca'iah on the cheek, and said, Which way went the Spirit of the LORD from me to speak unto thee?

25 And Mi-ca'iah said, Behold, thou shalt see in that day, when thou shalt go into an inner chamber to hide thyself.

26 And the king of Is'ra-el said, Take Mi-ca'iah, and carry him back unto A'mon the governor of the city, and to Jo'ash the king's son;

27 And say, Thus saith the king, Put this *fellow* in the prison, and feed him with bread of affliction and with water of affliction, until I come in peace.

28 And Mi-ca'iah said, If thou return at all in peace, the LORD hath not spoken by me. And he said, Hearken, O people, every one of you.

29 So the king of Is'ra-el and Je-hosh'a-phat the king of Ju'dah went up to Ra'moth-gil'e-ad.

30 And the king of Is'ra-el said unto Je-hosh'a-phat, I will disguise myself, and enter into the battle; but put thou on thy robes. And the king of Is'ra-el disguised himself, and went into the battle.

31 But the king of Syr'i-a commanded his thirty and two captains that had rule over his chariots, saying, Fight neither with small nor great, save only with the king of Is'ra-el.

32 And it came to pass, when the captains of the chariots saw Je-hosh'a-phat, that they said, Surely it *is* the king of Is'ra-el. And they turned aside to fight against him: and Je-hosh'a-phat cried out.

33 And it came to pass, when the captains of the chariots perceived that it *was* not the king of Is'ra-el, that they turned back from pursuing him.

34 And a *certain* man drew a bow at a venture, and smote the king of Is'ra-el between the joints of the harness: wherefore he said unto the driver of his chariot, Turn thine hand, and carry me out of the host; for I am wounded.

35 And the battle increased that day: and the king was stayed up in his chariot against the Syr'i-ans, and died at even: and the blood ran out of the wound into the midst of the chariot.

36 And there went a proclamation throughout the host about the going down of the sun, saying, Every man to his city, and every man to his own country.

37 ¶ So the king died, and was brought to Sa-ma'ri-a; and they buried the king in Sa-ma'ri-a.

38 And *one* washed the chariot in the pool of Sa-ma'ri-a; and the dogs licked up his blood; and they washed his armour; according unto the word of the LORD which he spake.

39 Now the rest of the acts of A'hab, and all that he did, and the ivory house which he made, and all the cities that he built, *are* they not written in the book of the chronicles of the kings of Is'ra-el?

40 So A'hab slept with his fathers; and A-ha-zi'ah his son reigned in his stead.

41 ¶ And Je-hosh'a-phat the son of A'sa began to reign over Ju'dah in the fourth year of A'hab king of Is'ra-el.

42 Je-hosh'a-phat *was* thirty and five years old when he began to reign; and he reigned twenty and five years in Je-ru'sa-lem. And his mother's name *was* A-zu'bah the daughter of Shil'hi.

43 And he walked in all the ways of A'sa his father; he turned not aside from it, doing *that which was* right in the eyes of the LORD: nevertheless the high places were not taken away; *for* the people offered and burnt incense yet in the high places.

44 And Je-hosh'a-phat made peace with the king of Is'ra-el.

45 Now the rest of the acts of Je-hosh'a-phat, and his might that he shewed, and how he warred, *are* they not written in the book of the chronicles of the kings of Ju'dah?

46 And the remnant of the sodomites, which remained in the days of his father A'sa, he took out of the land.

47 *There was* then no king in E'dom: a deputy *was* king.

48 Je-hosh'a-phat made ships of Thar'shish to go to O'phir for gold: but they went not; for the ships were broken at E'zi-on-ge'ber.

49 Then said A-ha-zi'ah the son of A'hab unto Je-hosh'a-phat, Let my servants go with thy servants in the ships. But Je-hosh'a-phat would not.

50 ¶ And Je-hosh'a-phat slept with his fathers, and was buried with his fathers in the city of Da'vid his father: and Je-ho'ram his son reigned in his stead.

51 ¶ A-ha-zi'ah the son of A'hab began to reign over Is'ra-el in Sa-ma'ri-a the seventeenth year of Je-hosh'a-phat king of Ju'dah, and reigned two years over Is'ra-el.

52 And he did evil in the sight of the LORD, and walked in the way of his father, and in the way of his mother, and in the way of Jer-o-bo'-am the son of Ne'bat, who made Is'ra-el to sin:

53 For he served Ba'al, and worshipped him, and provoked to anger the LORD God of Is'ra-el, according to all that his father had done.

THE SECOND BOOK OF THE

KINGS

1 THEN Mo'ab rebelled against Is'ra-el after the death of A'hab.

2 And A-ha-zi'ah fell down through a lattice in his upper chamber that *was* in Sa-ma'ri-a, and was sick: and he sent messengers, and said unto them, Go, enquire of Ba'al-ze'bub the god of Ek'ron whether I shall recover of this disease.

3 But the angel of the LORD said to E-li'jah the Tish'bite, Arise, go up to meet the messengers of the king of Sa-ma'ri-a, and say unto them, *Is it* not because *there is* not a God in Is'ra-el, *that* ye go to enquire of Ba'al-ze'bub the god of Ek'ron?

4 Now therefore thus saith the LORD, Thou shalt not come down from that bed on which thou art gone up, but shalt surely die. And E-li'jah departed.

5 ¶ And when the messengers turned back unto him, he said unto them, Why are ye now turned back?

6 And they said unto him, There came a man up to meet us, and said unto us, Go, turn again unto the king that sent you, and say unto him, Thus saith the LORD, *Is it* not because *there is* not a God in Is'ra-el, *that* thou sendest to enquire of Ba'al-ze'bub the god of Ek'ron? therefore thou shalt not come down from that bed on which thou art gone up, but shalt surely die.

7 And he said unto them, What manner of man *was he* which came up to meet you, and told you these words?

8 And they answered him, *He was* an hairy man, and girt with a girdle of leather about his loins. And he said, It *is* E-li'jah the Tish'bite.

9 Then the king sent unto him a captain of fifty with his fifty. And he went up to him: and, behold, he sat on the top of an hill. And he spake unto him, Thou man of God, the king hath said, Come down.

10 And E-li'jah answered and said to the captain of fifty, If I *be* a man of God, then let fire come down from heaven, and consume thee and thy fifty. And there came down fire from heaven, and consumed him and his fifty.

11 Again also he sent unto him another captain of fifty with his fifty. And he answered and said unto him, O man of God, thus hath the king said, Come down quickly.

12 And E-li'jah answered and said unto them, If I *be* a man of God, let fire come down from heaven, and consume thee and thy fifty. And the fire of God came down from heaven, and consumed him and his fifty.

13 ¶ And he sent again a captain of the third fifty with his fifty. And the third captain of fifty went up, and came and fell on his knees before E-li'jah, and besought him, and said unto him, O man of God, I pray thee, let my life, and the life of these fifty thy servants, be precious in thy sight.

14 Behold, there came fire down from heaven, and burnt up the two captains of the former fifties with their fifties: therefore let my life now be precious in thy sight.

15 And the angel of the LORD said unto E-li'jah, Go down with him: be not afraid of him. And he arose, and went down with him unto the king.

16 And he said unto him, Thus saith the LORD, Forasmuch as thou hast sent messengers to enquire of Ba'al-ze'bub the god of Ek'ron, *is it* not because *there is* no God in Is'ra-el to enquire of his word? therefore thou shalt not come down off that bed on which thou art gone up, but shalt surely die.

17 ¶ So he died according to the word of the LORD which E-li'jah had spoken. And Je-ho'ram reigned in his stead in the second year of Je-ho'ram the son of Je-hosh'a-phat king of Ju'dah; because he had no son.

18 Now the rest of the acts of A-ha-zi'ah which he did, *are* they not written in the book of the chronicles of the kings of Is'ra-el?

2 AND it came to pass, when the LORD would take up E-li'jah into heaven by a whirlwind, that E-li'jah went with E-li'sha from Gil'gal.

2 And E-li'jah said unto E-li'sha, Tarry here, I pray thee; for the LORD hath sent me to Beth'-el. And E-li'sha said *unto him, As* the LORD liveth, and *as* thy soul liveth, I will not leave thee. So they went down to Beth'-el.

3 And the sons of the prophets that *were* at Beth'-el came forth to E-li'sha, and said unto him, Knowest thou that the LORD will take away thy master from thy head to day? And he said, Yea, I know *it;* hold ye your peace.

4 And E-li'jah said unto him, E-li'sha, tarry here, I pray thee; for the LORD hath sent me to Jer'i-cho. And he said, *As* the LORD liveth, and *as* thy soul liveth, I will not leave thee. So they came to Jer'i-cho.

5 And the sons of the prophets that *were* at Jer'i-cho came to E-li'sha, and said unto him, Knowest thou that the LORD will take away thy master from thy head to day? And he answered, Yea, I know *it:* hold ye your peace.

6 And E-li'jah said unto him, Tarry, I pray thee, here; for the LORD hath sent me to Jor'dan. And he said, *As* the LORD liveth, and *as* thy soul liveth, I will not leave thee. And they two went on.

7 And fifty men of the sons of the prophets went, and stood to view afar off: and they two stood by Jor'dan.

8 And E-li'jah took his mantle, and wrapped *it* together, and smote the waters, and they were divided hither and thither, so that they two went over on dry ground.

9 ¶ And it came to pass, when they were gone over, that E-li'jah said unto E-li'sha, Ask what I shall do for thee, before I be taken away from thee. And E-li'sha said, I pray thee, let a double portion of thy spirit be upon me.

10 And he said, Thou hast asked a hard thing: *nevertheless,* if thou see me *when I am* taken from thee, it shall be so unto thee; but if not, it shall not be *so.*

11 And it came to pass, as they still went on, and talked, that, behold, *there appeared* a chariot of fire, and horses of fire, and parted them both asunder; and E-li'jah went up by a whirlwind into heaven.

12 ¶ And E-li'sha saw *it,* and he cried, My father, my father, the chariot of Is'ra-el, and the horsemen thereof. And he saw him no more: and he took hold of his own clothes, and rent them in two pieces.

13 He took up also the mantle of E-li'jah that fell from him, and went back and stood by the bank of Jor'dan;

14 And he took the mantle of E-li'jah that fell from him, and smote the waters, and said, Where *is* the LORD God of E-li'jah? and when he also had smitten the waters, they parted hither and thither: and E-li'sha went over.

15 And when the sons of the prophets which *were* to view at Jer'i-cho saw him, they said, The spirit of E-li'jah doth rest on E-li'sha. And they came to meet him, and bowed themselves to the ground before him.

16 ¶ And they said unto him, Behold now, there be with thy servants fifty strong men; let them go, we pray thee, and seek thy master: lest peradventure the Spirit of the LORD hath taken him up, and cast him upon some mountain, or into some valley. And he said, Ye shall not send.

17 And when they urged him till he was ashamed, he said, Send. They sent therefore fifty men; and they sought three days, but found him not.

18 And when they came again to him, (for he tarried at Jer'i-cho,) he said unto them, Did I not say unto you, Go not?

19 ¶ And the men of the city said unto E-li'sha, Behold, I pray thee, the situation of this city *is* pleasant, as my lord seeth: but the water *is* naught, and the ground barren.

20 And he said, Bring me a new cruse, and put salt therein. And they brought *it* to him.

21 And he went forth unto the spring of the waters, and cast the salt in there, and said, Thus saith the LORD, I have healed these waters; there shall not be from thence any more death or barren *land.*

22 So the waters were healed unto this day, according to the saying of E-li'sha which he spake.

23 ¶ And he went up from thence unto Beth'-el: and as he was going up by the way, there came forth little children out of the city, and mocked him, and said unto him, Go up, thou bald head; go up, thou bald head.

24 And he turned back, and looked on them, and cursed them in the name of the LORD. And there came forth two she bears out of the wood, and tare forty and two children of them.

25 And he went from thence to mount Car'mel, and from thence he returned to Sa-ma'ri-a.

3

NOW Je-ho'ram the son of A'hab began to reign over Is'ra-el in Sa-ma'ri-a the eighteenth year of Je-hosh'a-phat king of Ju'dah, and reigned twelve years.

2 And he wrought evil in the sight of the LORD; but not like his father, and like his mother: for he put away the image of Ba'al that his father had made.

3 Nevertheless he cleaved unto the sins of Jer-o-bo'am the son of Ne'bat, which made Is'ra-el to sin; he departed not therefrom.

4 ¶ And Me'sha king of Mo'ab was a sheepmaster, and rendered unto the king of Is'ra-el an hundred thousand lambs, and an hundred thousand rams, with the wool.

5 But it came to pass, when A'hab was dead, that the king of Mo'ab rebelled against the king of Is'ra-el.

6 ¶ And king Je-ho'ram went out of Sa-ma'ri-a the same time, and numbered all Is'ra-el.

7 And he went and sent to Je-hosh'a-phat the king of Ju'dah, saying, The king of Mo'ab hath rebelled against me: wilt thou go with me against Mo'ab to battle? And he said, I will go up: I *am* as thou *art,* my people as thy people, *and* my horses as thy horses.

8 And he said, Which way shall we go up? And he answered, The way through the wilderness of E'dom.

9 So the king of Is'ra-el went, and the king of Ju'dah, and the king of E'dom: and they fetched a compass of seven days' journey: and there was no water for the host, and for the cattle that followed them.

10 And the king of Is'ra-el said, Alas! that the LORD hath called these three kings together, to deliver them into the hand of Mo'ab!

11 But Je-hosh'a-phat said, *Is there* not here a prophet of the LORD, that we may enquire of the LORD by him? And one of the king of Is'ra-el's servants answered and said, Here *is* E-li'sha the son of Sha'phat, which poured water on the hands of E-li'jah.

12 And Je-hosh'a-phat said, The word of the LORD is with him. So the king of Is'ra-el and Je-hosh'a-phat and the king of E'dom went down to him.

13 And E-li'sha said unto the king of Is'ra-el, What have I to do with thee? get thee to the prophets of thy father, and to the prophets of thy mother. And the king of Is'ra-el said unto him, Nay: for the LORD hath called these three kings together, to deliver them into the hand of Mo'ab.

14 And E-li'sha said, *As* the LORD of hosts liveth, before whom I stand, surely, were it not that I regard the presence of Je-hosh'a-phat the king of Ju'dah, I would not look toward thee, nor see thee.

15 But now bring me a minstrel. And it came to pass, when the minstrel played, that the hand of the LORD came upon him.

16 And he said, Thus saith the LORD, Make this valley full of ditches.

17 For thus saith the LORD, Ye shall not see

wind, neither shall ye see rain; yet that valley
shall be filled with water, that ye may drink,
both ye, and your cattle, and your beasts.
18 And this is *but* a light thing in the sight of
the LORD: he will deliver the Mo'ab-ites also
into your hand.
19 And ye shall smite every fenced city, and
every choice city, and shall fell every good tree,
and stop all wells of water, and mar every good
piece of land with stones.
20 And it came to pass in the morning, when
the meat offering was offered, that, behold,
there came water by the way of E'dom, and the
country was filled with water.
21 ¶ And when all the Mo'ab-ites heard that
the kings were come up to fight against them,
they gathered all that were able to put on armour, and upward, and stood in the border.
22 And they rose up early in the morning,
and the sun shone upon the water, and the Mo'-
ab-ites saw the water on the other side *as* red as
blood:
23 And they said, This *is* blood: the kings are
surely slain, and they have smitten one another:
now therefore, Mo'ab, to the spoil.
24 And when they came to the camp of Is'ra-
el, the Is'ra-el-ites rose up and smote the Mo'ab-
ites, so that they fled before them: but they
went forward smiting the Mo'ab-ites, even in
their country.
25 And they beat down the cities, and on every good piece of land cast every man his stone,
and filled it; and they stopped all the wells of
water, and felled all the good trees: only in Kir-
har'a-seth left they the stones thereof; howbeit
the slingers went about *it*, and smote it.
26 ¶ And when the king of Mo'ab saw that
the battle was too sore for him, he took with
him seven hundred men that drew swords, to
break through *even* unto the king of E'dom: but
they could not.
27 Then he took his eldest son that should
have reigned in his stead, and offered him *for* a
burnt offering upon the wall. And there was
great indignation against Is'ra-el: and they departed from him, and returned to *their own*
land.

4 NOW there cried a certain woman of the
wives of the sons of the prophets unto E-
li'sha, saying, Thy servant my husband is dead;
and thou knowest that thy servant did fear the
LORD: and the creditor is come to take unto him
my two sons to be bondmen.
2 And E-li'sha said unto her, What shall I do
for thee? tell me, what hast thou in the house?
And she said, Thine handmaid hath not any
thing in the house, save a pot of oil.
3 Then he said, Go, borrow thee vessels
abroad of all thy neighbours, *even* empty vessels; borrow not a few.
4 And when thou art come in, thou shalt shut
the door upon thee and upon thy sons, and shalt
pour out into all those vessels, and thou shalt
set aside that which is full.
5 So she went from him, and shut the door
upon her and upon her sons, who brought *the*
vessels to her; and she poured out.
6 And it came to pass, when the vessels were
full, that she said unto her son, Bring me yet a
vessel. And he said unto her, *There is* not a vessel more. And the oil stayed.
7 Then she came and told the man of God.
And he said, Go, sell the oil, and pay thy debt,
and live thou and thy children of the rest.
8 ¶ And it fell on a day, that E-li'sha passed
to Shu'nem, where *was* a great woman; and she
constrained him to eat bread. And *so* it was,
that as oft as he passed by, he turned in thither
to eat bread.
9 And she said unto her husband, Behold
now, I perceive that this *is* an holy man of God,
which passeth by us continually.
10 Let us make a little chamber, I pray thee,
on the wall; and let us set for him there a bed,
and a table, and a stool, and a candlestick: and
it shall be, when he cometh to us, that he shall
turn in thither.
11 And it fell on a day, that he came thither,
and he turned into the chamber, and lay there.
12 And he said to Ge-ha'zi his servant, Call
this Shu'nam-mite. And when he had called her,
she stood before him.
13 And he said unto him, Say now unto her,
Behold, thou hast been careful for us with all
this care; what *is* to be done for thee? wouldest
thou be spoken for to the king, or to the captain
of the host? And she answered, I dwell among
mine own people.
14 And he said, What then *is* to be done for
her? And Ge-ha'zi answered, Verily she hath no
child, and her husband is old.
15 And he said, Call her. And when he had
called her, she stood in the door.
16 And he said, About this season, according
to the time of life, thou shalt embrace a son.
And she said, Nay, my lord, *thou* man of God,
do not lie unto thine handmaid.
17 And the woman conceived, and bare a son
at that season that E-li'sha had said unto her,
according to the time of life.
18 ¶ And when the child was grown, it fell
on a day, that he went out to his father to the
reapers.
19 And he said unto his father, My head, my
head. And he said to a lad, Carry him to his
mother.
20 And when he had taken him, and brought
him to his mother, he sat on her knees till noon,
and *then* died.
21 And she went up, and laid him on the bed
of the man of God, and shut *the door* upon him,
and went out.
22 And she called unto her husband, and
said, Send me, I pray thee, one of the young
men, and one of the asses, that I may run to the
man of God, and come again.
23 And he said, Wherefore wilt thou go to
him to day? *it is* neither new moon, nor sabbath. And she said, *It shall be* well.
24 Then she saddled an ass, and said to her
servant, Drive, and go forward; slack not *thy*
riding for me, except I bid thee.
25 So she went and came unto the man of
God to mount Car'mel. And it came to pass,
when the man of God saw her afar off, that he
said to Ge-ha'zi his servant, Behold, *yonder is*
that Shu'nam-mite:
26 Run now, I pray thee, to meet her, and say
unto her, *Is it* well with thee? *is it* well with thy
husband? *is it* well with the child? And she answered, *It is* well.
27 And when she came to the man of God to
the hill, she caught him by the feet: but Ge-ha'zi
came near to thrust her away. And the man of
God said, Let her alone; for her soul *is* vexed
within her: and the LORD hath hid *it* from me,
and hath not told me.
28 Then she said, Did I desire a son of my
lord? did I not say, Do not deceive me?
29 Then he said to Ge-ha'zi, Gird up thy
loins, and take my staff in thine hand, and go
thy way: if thou meet any man, salute him not;

and if any salute thee, answer him not again:
and lay my staff upon the face of the child.
30 And the mother of the child said, *As* the
LORD liveth, and *as* thy soul liveth, I will not
leave thee. And he arose, and followed her.
31 And Ge-ha′zi passed on before them, and
laid the staff upon the face of the child; but
there was neither voice, nor hearing. Wherefore
he went again to meet him, and told him, saying, The child is not awaked.
32 And when E-li′sha was come into the
house, behold, the child was dead, *and* laid
upon his bed.
33 He went in therefore, and shut the door
upon them twain, and prayed unto the LORD.
34 And he went up, and lay upon the child,
and put his mouth upon his mouth, and his eyes
upon his eyes, and his hands upon his hands:
and he stretched himself upon the child; and the
flesh of the child waxed warm.
35 Then he returned, and walked in the
house to and fro; and went up, and stretched
himself upon him: and the child sneezed seven
times, and the child opened his eyes.
36 And he called Ge-ha′zi, and said, Call this
Shu′nam-mite. So he called her. And when she
was come in unto him, he said, Take up thy son.
37 Then she went in, and fell at his feet, and
bowed herself to the ground, and took up her
son, and went out.
38 ¶ And E-li′sha came again to Gil′gal: and
there was a dearth in the land; and the sons of
the prophets *were* sitting before him: and he
said unto his servant, Set on the great pot, and
seethe pottage for the sons of the prophets.
39 And one went out into the field to gather
herbs, and found a wild vine, and gathered
thereof wild gourds his lap full, and came and
shred *them* into the pot of pottage: for they
knew *them* not.
40 So they poured out for the men to eat.
And it came to pass, as they were eating of the
pottage that they cried out, and said, O *thou*
man of God, *there is* death in the pot. And they
could not eat *thereof.*
41 But he said, Then bring meal. And he cast
it into the pot; and he said, Pour out for the
people, that they may eat. And there was no
harm in the pot.
42 ¶ And there came a man from Ba′al–shal′-
i-sha, and brought the man of God bread of the
first-fruits, twenty loaves of barley, and full
ears of corn in the husk thereof. And he said,
Give unto the people, that they may eat.
43 And his servitor said, What, should I set
this before an hundred men? He said again,
Give the people, that they may eat: for thus
saith the LORD, They shall eat, and shall leave
thereof.
44 So he set *it* before them, and they did eat,
and left *thereof,* according to the word of the
LORD.

5 NOW Na′a-man, captain of the host of the
king of Syr′i-a, was a great man with his
master, and honourable, because by him the
LORD had given deliverance unto Syr′i-a: he was
also a mighty man in valour, *but he was* a leper.
2 And the Syr′i-ans had gone out by companies, and had brought away captive out of the
land of Is′ra-el a little maid; and she waited on
Na′a-man's wife.
3 And she said unto her mistress, Would God
my lord *were* with the prophet that *is* in Sa-
ma′ri-a! for he would recover him of his leprosy.
4 And *one* went in, and told his lord, saying,
Thus and thus said the maid that *is* of the land
of Is′ra-el.
5 And the king of Syr′i-a said, Go to, go, and
I will send a letter unto the king of Is′ra-el. And
he departed, and took with him ten talents of
silver, and six thousand *pieces* of gold, and ten
changes of raiment.
6 And he brought the letter to the king of Is′-
ra-el, saying, Now when this letter is come unto
thee, behold, I have *therewith* sent Na′a-man
my servant to thee, that thou mayest recover
him of his leprosy.
7 And it came to pass, when the king of Is′ra-
el had read the letter, that he rent his clothes,
and said, *Am* I God, to kill and to make alive,
that this man doth send unto me to recover a
man of his leprosy? wherefore consider, I pray
you, and see how he seeketh a quarrel against
me.
8 ¶ And it was *so,* when E-li′sha the man of
God had heard that the king of Is′ra-el had rent
his clothes, that he sent to the king, saying,
Wherefore hast thou rent thy clothes? let him
come now to me, and he shall know that there
is a prophet in Is′ra-el.
9 So Na′a-man came with his horses and
with his chariot, and stood at the door of the
house of E-li′sha.
10 And E-li′sha sent a messenger unto him,
saying, Go and wash in Jor′dan seven times,
and thy flesh shall come again to thee, and thou
shalt be clean.
11 But Na′a-man was wroth, and went away,
and said, Behold, I thought, He will surely come
out to me, and stand, and call on the name of
the LORD his God, and strike his hand over the
place, and recover the leper.
12 *Are* not Ab′a-na and Phar′par, rivers of
Da-mas′cus, better than all the waters of Is′ra-
el? may I not wash in them, and be clean? So he
turned and went away in a rage.
13 And his servants came near, and spake
unto him, and said, My father, *if* the prophet
had bid thee *do some* great thing, wouldest thou
not have done *it?* how much rather then, when
he saith to thee, Wash, and be clean?
14 Then went he down, and dipped himself
seven times in Jor′dan, according to the saying
of the man of God: and his flesh came again like
unto the flesh of a little child, and he was clean.
15 ¶ And he returned to the man of God, he
and all his company, and came, and stood before him: and he said, Behold, now I know that
there is no God in all the earth, but in Is′ra-el:
now therefore, I pray thee, take a blessing of
thy servant.
16 But he said, *As* the LORD liveth, before
whom I stand, I will receive none. And he urged
him to take *it;* but he refused.
17 And Na′a-man said, Shall there not then, I
pray thee, be given to thy servant two mules'
burden of earth? for thy servant will henceforth
offer neither burnt offering nor sacrifice unto
other gods, but unto the LORD.
18 In this thing the LORD pardon thy servant,
that when my master goeth into the house of
Rim′mon to worship there, and he leaneth on
my hand, and I bow myself in the house of
Rim′mon: when I bow down myself in the
house of Rim′mon, the LORD pardon thy servant
in this thing.
19 And he said unto him, Go in peace. So he
departed from him a little way.
20 ¶ But Ge-ha′zi, the servant of E-li′sha the
man of God, said, Behold, my master hath
spared Na′a-man this Syr′i-an, in not receiving
at his hands that which he brought: but, *as* the

LORD liveth, I will run after him, and take somewhat of him.
21 So Ge-ha'zi followed after Na'a-man. And
when Na'a-man saw *him* running after him, he
lighted down from the chariot to meet him, and
said, *Is* all well?
22 And he said, All *is* well. My master hath
sent me, saying, Behold, even now there be
come to me from mount E'phra-im two young
men of the sons of the prophets: give them, I
pray thee, a talent of silver, and two changes of
garments.
23 And Na'a-man said, Be content, take two
talents. And he urged him, and bound two talents of silver in two bags, with two changes of
garments, and laid *them* upon two of his servants; and they bare *them* before him.
24 And when he came to the tower, he took
them from their hand, and bestowed *them* in
the house: and he let the men go, and they departed.
25 But he went in, and stood before his master. And E-li'sha said unto him, Whence *comest
thou,* Ge-ha'zi? And he said, Thy servant went
no whither.
26 And he said unto him, Went not mine
heart *with thee,* when the man turned again
from his chariot to meet thee? *Is it* a time to
receive money, and to receive garments, and
oliveyards, and vineyards, and sheep, and oxen,
and menservants, and maidservants?
27 The leprosy therefore of Na'a-man shall
cleave unto thee, and unto thy seed for ever.
And he went out from his presence a leper *as
white* as snow.

6 AND the sons of the prophets said unto E-
li'sha, Behold now, the place where we
dwell with thee is too strait for us.
2 Let us go, we pray thee, unto Jor'dan, and
take thence every man a beam, and let us make
us a place there, where we may dwell. And he
answered, Go ye.
3 And one said, Be content, I pray thee, and
go with thy servants. And he answered, I will
go.
4 So he went with them. And when they
came to Jor'dan, they cut down wood.
5 But as one was felling a beam, the ax head
fell into the water: and he cried, and said, Alas,
master! for it was borrowed.
6 And the man of God said, Where fell it?
And he shewed him the place. And he cut down
a stick, and cast *it* in thither; and the iron did
swim.
7 Therefore said he, Take *it* up to thee. And
he put out his hand, and took it.
8 ¶ Then the king of Syr'i-a warred against
Is'ra-el, and took counsel with his servants, saying, In such and such a place *shall be* my camp.
9 And the man of God sent unto the king of
Is'ra-el, saying, Beware that thou pass not such
a place; for thither the Syr'i-ans are come down.
10 And the king of Is'ra-el sent to the place
which the man of God told him and warned him
of, and saved himself there, not once nor twice.
11 Therefore the heart of the king of Syr'i-a
was sore troubled for this thing; and he called
his servants, and said unto them, Will ye not
shew me which of us *is* for the king of Is'ra-el?
12 And one of his servants said, None, my
lord, O king: but E-li'sha, the prophet that *is* in
Is'ra-el, telleth the king of Is'ra-el the words
that thou speakest in thy bedchamber.
13 ¶ And he said, Go and spy where he *is,*
that I may send and fetch him. And it was told
him, saying, Behold, *he is* in Do'than.
14 Therefore sent he thither horses, and
chariots, and a great host: and they came by
night, and compassed the city about.
15 And when the servant of the man of God
was risen early, and gone forth, behold, an host
compassed the city both with horses and chariots. And his servant said unto him, Alas, my
master! how shall we do?
16 And he answered, Fear not: for they that
be with us *are* more than they that *be* with
them.
17 And E-li'sha prayed, and said, LORD, I
pray thee, open his eyes, that he may see. And
the LORD opened the eyes of the young man;
and he saw: and, behold, the mountain *was* full
of horses and chariots of fire round about E-
li'sha.
18 And when they came down to him, E-li'-
sha prayed unto the LORD, and said, Smite this
people, I pray thee, with blindness. And he
smote them with blindness according to the
word of E-li'sha.
19 ¶ And E-li'sha said unto them, This *is* not
the way, neither *is* this the city: follow me, and
I will bring you to the man whom ye seek. But
he led them to Sa-ma'ri-a.
20 And it came to pass, when they were
come into Sa-ma'ri-a, that E-li'sha said, LORD,
open the eyes of these *men,* that they may see.
And the LORD opened their eyes, and they saw;
and, behold, *they were* in the midst of Sa-ma'ri-
a.
21 And the king of Is'ra-el said unto E-li'sha,
when he saw them, My father, shall I smite
them? shall I smite *them?*
22 And he answered, Thou shalt not smite
them: wouldest thou smite those whom thou
hast taken captive with thy sword and with thy
bow? set bread and water before them, that
they may eat and drink, and go to their master.
23 And he prepared great provision for them:
and when they had eaten and drunk, he sent
them away, and they went to their master. So
the bands of Syr'i-a came no more into the land
of Is'ra-el.
24 ¶ And it came to pass after this, that Ben-
ha'dad king of Syr'i-a gathered all his host, and
went up, and besieged Sa-ma'ri-a.
25 And there was a great famine in Sa-ma'ri-
a: and, behold, they besieged it, until an ass's
head was *sold* for fourscore *pieces* of silver, and
the fourth part of a cab of dove's dung for five
pieces of silver.
26 And as the king of Is'ra-el was passing by
upon the wall, there cried a woman unto him,
saying, Help, my lord, O king.
27 And he said, If the LORD do not help thee,
whence shall I help thee? out of the barnfloor,
or out of the winepress?
28 And the king said unto her, What aileth
thee? And she answered, This woman said unto
me, Give thy son, that we may eat him to day,
and we will eat my son to morrow.
29 So we boiled my son, and did eat him: and
I said unto her on the next day, Give thy son,
that we may eat him: and she hath hid her son.
30 ¶ And it came to pass, when the king
heard the words of the woman, that he rent his
clothes; and he passed by upon the wall, and
the people looked, and, behold, *he had* sackcloth within upon his flesh.
31 Then he said, God do so and more also to
me, if the head of E-li'sha the son of Sha'phat
shall stand on him this day.
32 But E-li'sha sat in his house, and the elders sat with him; and *the king* sent a man from
before him: but ere the messenger came to him,

he said to the elders, See ye how this son of a
murderer hath sent to take away mine head?
look, when the messenger cometh, shut the
door, and hold him fast at the door: *is* not the
sound of his master's feet behind him?
33 And while he yet talked with them, behold, the messenger came down unto him: and
he said, Behold, this evil *is* of the LORD; what
should I wait for the LORD any longer?

7 THEN E-li'sha said, Hear ye the word of
the LORD; Thus saith the LORD, To morrow
about this time *shall* a measure of fine flour *be*
sold for a shekel, and two measures of barley
for a shekel, in the gate of Sa-ma'ri-a.
2 Then a lord on whose hand the king leaned
answered the man of God, and said, Behold, *if*
the LORD would make windows in heaven,
might this thing be? And he said, Behold, thou
shalt see *it* with thine eyes, but shalt not eat
thereof.
3 ¶ And there were four leprous men at the
entering in of the gate: and they said one to another, Why sit we here until we die?
4 If we say, We will enter into the city, then
the famine *is* in the city, and we shall die there:
and if we sit still here, we die also. Now therefore come, and let us fall unto the host of the
Syr'i-ans: if they save us alive, we shall live; and
if they kill us, we shall but die.
5 And they rose up in the twilight, to go unto
the camp of the Syr'i-ans: and when they were
come to the uttermost part of the camp of Syr'i-
a, behold, *there was* no man there.
6 For the LORD had made the host of the Syr'-
i-ans to hear a noise of chariots, and a noise of
horses, *even* the noise of a great host: and they
said one to another, Lo, the king of Is'ra-el hath
hired against us the kings of the Hit'tites, and
the kings of the E-gyp'tians, to come upon us.
7 Wherefore they arose and fled in the twilight, and left their tents, and their horses, and
their asses, even the camp as it *was*, and fled for
their life.
8 And when these lepers came to the uttermost part of the camp, they went into one tent,
and did eat and drink, and carried thence silver,
and gold, and raiment, and went and hid *it;* and
came again, and entered into another tent, and
carried thence *also*, and went and hid *it*.
9 Then they said one to another, We do not
well: this day *is* a day of good tidings, and we
hold our peace: if we tarry till the morning light,
some mischief will come upon us: now therefore come, that we may go and tell the king's
household.
10 So they came and called unto the porter of
the city: and they told them, saying, We came
to the camp of the Syr'i-ans, and, behold, *there*
was no man there, neither voice of man, but
horses tied, and asses tied, and the tents as they
were.
11 And he called the porters; and they told *it*
to the king's house within.
12 ¶ And the king arose in the night, and
said unto his servants, I will now shew you
what the Syr'i-ans have done to us. They know
that we *be* hungry; therefore are they gone out
of the camp to hide themselves in the field, saying, When they come out of the city, we shall
catch them alive, and get into the city.
13 And one of his servants answered and
said, Let *some* take, I pray thee, five of the
horses that remain, which are left in the city,
(behold, they *are* as all the multitude of Is'ra-el
that are left in it: behold, *I say*, they *are* even as
all the multitude of the Is'ra-el-ites that are consumed:) and let us send and see.
14 They took therefore two chariot horses;
and the king sent after the host of the Syr'i-ans,
saying, Go and see.
15 And they went after them unto Jor'dan:
and, lo, all the way *was* full of garments and
vessels, which the Syr'i-ans had cast away in
their haste. And the messengers returned, and
told the king.
16 And the people went out, and spoiled the
tents of the Syr'i-ans. So a measure of fine flour
was *sold* for a shekel, and two measures of barley for a shekel, according to the word of the
LORD.
17 ¶ And the king appointed the lord on
whose hand he leaned to have the charge of the
gate: and the people trode upon him in the gate,
and he died, as the man of God had said, who
spake when the king came down to him.
18 And it came to pass as the man of God
had spoken to the king, saying, Two measures
of barley for a shekel, and a measure of fine
flour for a shekel, shall be to morrow about this
time in the gate of Sa-ma'ri-a:
19 And that lord answered the man of God,
and said, Now, behold, *if* the LORD should make
windows in heaven, might such a thing be? And
he said, Behold, thou shalt see it with thine
eyes, but shalt not eat thereof.
20 And so it fell out unto him: for the people
trode upon him in the gate, and he died.

8 THEN spake E-li'sha unto the woman,
whose son he had restored to life, saying,
Arise, and go thou and thine household, and sojourn wheresoever thou canst sojourn: for the
LORD hath called for a famine; and it shall also
come upon the land seven years.
2 And the woman arose, and did after the
saying of the man of God: and she went with
her household, and sojourned in the land of the
Phi-lis'tines seven years.
3 And it came to pass at the seven years' end,
that the woman returned out of the land of the
Phi-lis'tines: and she went forth to cry unto the
king for her house and for her land.
4 And the king talked with Ge-ha'zi the servant of the man of God, saying, Tell me, I pray
thee, all the great things that E-li'sha hath done.
5 And it came to pass, as he was telling the
king how he had restored a dead body to life,
that, behold, the woman, whose son he had restored to life, cried to the king for her house and
for her land. And Ge-ha'zi said, My lord, O king,
this *is* the woman, and this *is* her son, whom E-
li'sha restored to life.
6 And when the king asked the woman, she
told him. So the king appointed unto her a certain officer, saying, Restore all that *was* hers,
and all the fruits of the field since the day that
she left the land, even until now.
7 ¶ And E-li'sha came to Da-mas'cus; and
Ben–ha'dad the king of Syr'i-a was sick; and it
was told him, saying, The man of God is come
hither.
8 And the king said unto Haz'a-el, Take a
present in thine hand, and go, meet the man of
God, and enquire of the LORD by him, saying,
Shall I recover of this disease?
9 So Haz'a-el went to meet him, and took a
present with him, even of every good thing of
Da-mas'cus, forty camels' burden, and came
and stood before him, and said, Thy son Ben–
ha'dad king of Syr'i-a hath sent me to thee, saying, Shall I recover of this disease?
10 And E-li'sha said unto him, Go, say unto

him, Thou mayest certainly recover: howbeit the LORD hath shewed me that he shall surely die.

11 And he settled his countenance stedfastly, until he was ashamed: and the man of God wept.

12 And Haz'a-el said, Why weepeth my lord? And he answered, Because I know the evil that thou wilt do unto the children of Is'ra-el: their strong holds wilt thou set on fire, and their young men wilt thou slay with the sword, and wilt dash their children, and rip up their women with child.

13 And Haz'a-el said, But what, *is* thy servant a dog, that he should do this great thing? And E-li'sha answered, The LORD hath shewed me that thou *shalt be* king over Syr'i-a.

14 So he departed from E-li'sha, and came to his master; who said to him, What said E-li'sha to thee? And he answered, He told me *that* thou shouldest surely recover.

15 And it came to pass on the morrow, that he took a thick cloth, and dipped *it* in water, and spread *it* on his face, so that he died: and Haz'a-el reigned in his stead.

16 ¶ And in the fifth year of Jo'ram the son of A'hab king of Is'ra-el, Je-hosh'a-phat *being* then king of Ju'dah, Je-ho'ram the son of Je-hosh'a-phat king of Ju'dah began to reign.

17 Thirty and two years old was he when he began to reign; and he reigned eight years in Je-ru'sa-lem.

18 And he walked in the way of the kings of Is'ra-el, as did the house of A'hab: for the daughter of A'hab was his wife: and he did evil in the sight of the LORD.

19 Yet the LORD would not destroy Ju'dah for Da'vid his servant's sake, as he promised him to give him alway a light, *and* to his children.

20 ¶ In his days E'dom revolted from under the hand of Ju'dah, and made a king over themselves.

21 So Jo'ram went over to Za'ir, and all the chariots with him: and he rose by night, and smote the E'dom-ites which compassed him about, and the captains of the chariots: and the people fled into their tents.

22 Yet E'dom revolted from under the hand of Ju'dah unto this day. Then Lib'nah revolted at the same time.

23 And the rest of the acts of Jo'ram, and all that he did, *are* they not written in the book of the chronicles of the kings of Ju'dah?

24 And Jo'ram slept with his fathers, and was buried with his fathers in the city of Da'vid: and A-ha-zi'ah his son reigned in his stead.

25 ¶ In the twelfth year of Jo'ram the son of A'hab king of Is'ra-el did A-ha-zi'ah the son of Je-ho'ram king of Ju'dah begin to reign.

26 Two and twenty years old *was* A-ha-zi'ah when he began to reign; and he reigned one year in Je-ru'sa-lem. And his mother's name *was* Ath-a-li'ah, the daughter of Om'ri king of Is'ra-el.

27 And he walked in the way of the house of A'hab, and did evil in the sight of the LORD, as *did* the house of A'hab: for he *was* the son in law of the house of A'hab.

28 ¶ And he went with Jo'ram the son of A'hab to the war against Haz'a-el king of Syr'i-a in Ra'moth-gil'e-ad; and the Syr'i-ans wounded Jo'ram.

29 And king Jo'ram went back to be healed in Jez're-el of the wounds which the Syr'i-ans had given him at Ra'mah, when he fought against Haz'a-el king of Syr'i-a. And A-ha-zi'ah the son of Je-ho'ram king of Ju'dah went down to see Jo'ram the son of A'hab in Jez're-el, because he was sick.

9 AND E-li'sha the prophet called one of the children of the prophets, and said unto him, Gird up thy loins, and take this box of oil in thine hand, and go to Ra'moth-gil'e-ad:

2 And when thou comest thither, look out there Je'hu the son of Je-hosh'a-phat the son of Nim'shi, and go in, and make him arise up from among his brethren, and carry him to an inner chamber;

3 Then take the box of oil, and pour *it* on his head, and say, Thus saith the LORD, I have anointed thee king over Is'ra-el. Then open the door, and flee, and tarry not.

4 ¶ So the young man, *even* the young man the prophet, went to Ra'moth-gil'e-ad.

5 And when he came, behold, the captains of the host *were* sitting; and he said, I have an errand to thee, O captain. And Je'hu said, Unto which of all us? And he said, To thee, O captain.

6 And he arose, and went into the house; and he poured the oil on his head, and said unto him, Thus saith the LORD God of Is'ra-el, I have anointed thee king over the people of the LORD, *even* over Is'ra-el.

7 And thou shalt smite the house of A'hab thy master, that I may avenge the blood of my servants the prophets, and the blood of all the servants of the LORD, at the hand of Jez'e-bel.

8 For the whole house of A'hab shall perish: and I will cut off from A'hab him that pisseth against the wall, and him that is shut up and left in Is'ra-el:

9 And I will make the house of A'hab like the house of Jer-o-bo'am the son of Ne'bat, and like the house of Ba'a-sha the son of A-hi'jah:

10 And the dogs shall eat Jez'e-bel in the portion of Jez're-el, and *there shall be* none to bury *her*. And he opened the door, and fled.

11 ¶ Then Je'hu came forth to the servants of his lord: and *one* said unto him, *Is* all well? wherefore came this mad *fellow* to thee? And he said unto them, Ye know the man, and his communication.

12 And they said, *It is* false; tell us now. And he said, Thus and thus spake he to me, saying, Thus saith the LORD, I have anointed thee king over Is'ra-el.

13 Then they hasted, and took every man his garment, and put *it* under him on the top of the stairs, and blew with trumpets, saying, Je'hu is king.

14 So Je'hu the son of Je-hosh'a-phat the son of Nim'shi conspired against Jo'ram. (Now Jo'ram had kept Ra'moth-gil'e-ad, he and all Is'ra-el, because of Haz'a-el king of Syr'i-a.

15 But king Jo'ram was returned to be healed in Jez're-el of the wounds which the Syr'i-ans had given him, when he fought with Haz'a-el king of Syr'i-a.) And Je'hu said, If it be your minds, *then* let none go forth *nor* escape out of the city to go to tell *it* in Jez're-el.

16 So Je'hu rode in a chariot, and went to Jez're-el; for Jo'ram lay there. And A-ha-zi'ah king of Ju'dah was come down to see Jo'ram.

17 And there stood a watchman on the tower in Jez're-el, and he spied the company of Je'hu as he came, and said, I see a company. And Jo'ram said, Take an horseman, and send to meet them, and let him say, *Is it* peace?

18 So there went one on horseback to meet him, and said, Thus saith the king, *Is it* peace? And Je'hu said, What hast thou to do with peace? turn thee behind me. And the watchman

told, saying, The messenger came to them, but he cometh not again.

19 Then he sent out a second on horseback, which came to them, and said, Thus saith the king, *Is it* peace? And Je'hu answered, What hast thou to do with peace? turn thee behind me.

20 And the watchman told, saying, He came even unto them, and cometh not again: and the driving *is* like the driving of Je'hu the son of Nim'shi; for he driveth furiously.

21 And Jo'ram said, Make ready. And his chariot was made ready. And Jo'ram king of Is'-ra-el and A-ha-zi'ah king of Ju'dah went out, each in his chariot, and they went out against Je'hu, and met him in the portion of Na'both the Jez're-el-ite.

22 And it came to pass, when Jo'ram saw Je'-hu, that he said, *Is it* peace, Je'hu? And he answered, What peace, so long as the whoredoms of thy mother Jez'e-bel and her witchcrafts *are so* many?

23 And Jo'ram turned his hands, and fled, and said to A-ha-zi'ah, *There is* treachery, O A-ha-zi'ah.

24 And Je'hu drew a bow with his full strength, and smote Je-ho'ram between his arms, and the arrow went out at his heart, and he sunk down in his chariot.

25 Then said Je'hu to Bid'kar his captain, Take up, *and* cast him in the portion of the field of Na'both the Jez're-el-ite: for remember how that, when I and thou rode together after A'hab his father, the LORD laid this burden upon him;

26 Surely I have seen yesterday the blood of Na'both, and the blood of his sons, saith the LORD; and I will requite thee in this plat, saith the LORD. Now therefore take *and* cast him into the plat *of ground,* according to the word of the LORD.

27 ¶ But when A-ha-zi'ah the king of Ju'dah saw *this,* he fled by the way of the garden house. And Je'hu followed after him, and said, Smite him also in the chariot. *And they did so* at the going up to Gur, which *is* by Ib'le-am. And he fled to Me-gid'do, and died there.

28 And his servants carried him in a chariot to Je-ru'sa-lem, and buried him in his sepulchre with his fathers in the city of Da'vid.

29 And in the eleventh year of Jo'ram the son of A'hab began A-ha-zi'ah to reign over Ju'dah.

30 ¶ And when Je'hu was come to Jez're-el, Jez'e-bel heard *of it;* and she painted her face, and tired her head, and looked out at a window.

31 And as Je'hu entered in at the gate, she said, *Had* Zim'ri peace, who slew his master?

32 And he lifted up his face to the window, and said, Who *is* on my side? who? And there looked out to him two *or* three eunuchs.

33 And he said, Throw her down. So they threw her down: and *some* of her blood was sprinkled on the wall, and on the horses: and he trode her under foot.

34 And when he was come in, he did eat and drink, and said, Go, see now this cursed *woman,* and bury her: for she *is* a king's daughter.

35 And they went to bury her: but they found no more of her than the skull, and the feet, and the palms of *her* hands.

36 Wherefore they came again, and told him. And he said, This *is* the word of the LORD, which he spake by his servant E-li'jah the Tish'-bite, saying, In the portion of Jez're-el shall dogs eat the flesh of Jez'e-bel:

37 And the carcase of Jez'e-bel shall be as dung upon the face of the field in the portion of Jez're-el; *so* that they shall not say, This *is* Jez'-e-bel.

10 AND A'hab had seventy sons in Sa-ma'-ri-a. And Je'hu wrote letters, and sent to Sa-ma'ri-a, unto the rulers of Jez're-el, to the elders, and to them that brought up A'hab's *children,* saying,

2 Now as soon as this letter cometh to you, seeing your master's sons *are* with you, and *there are* with you chariots and horses, a fenced city also, and armour;

3 Look even out the best and meetest of your master's sons, and set *him* on his father's throne, and fight for your master's house.

4 But they were exceedingly afraid, and said, Behold, two kings stood not before him: how then shall we stand?

5 And he that *was* over the house, and he that *was* over the city, the elders also, and the bringers up *of the children,* sent to Je'hu, saying, We *are* thy servants, and will do all that thou shalt bid us; we will not make any king: do thou *that which is* good in thine eyes.

6 Then he wrote a letter the second time to them, saying, If ye *be* mine, and *if* ye will hearken unto my voice, take ye the heads of the men your master's sons, and come to me to Jez're-el by to morrow this time. Now the king's sons, *being* seventy persons, *were* with the great men of the city, which brought them up.

7 And it came to pass, when the letter came to them, that they took the king's sons, and slew seventy persons, and put their heads in baskets, and sent him *them* to Jez're-el.

8 ¶ And there came a messenger, and told him, saying, They have brought the heads of the king's sons. And he said, Lay ye them in two heaps at the entering in of the gate until the morning.

9 And it came to pass in the morning, that he went out, and stood, and said to all the people, Ye *be* righteous: behold, I conspired against my master, and slew him: but who slew all these?

10 Know now that there shall fall unto the earth nothing of the word of the LORD, which the LORD spake concerning the house of A'hab: for the LORD hath done *that* which he spake by his servant E-li'jah.

11 So Je'hu slew all that remained of the house of A'hab in Jez're-el, and all his great men, and his kinsfolks, and his priests, until he left him none remaining.

12 ¶ And he arose and departed, and came to Sa-ma'ri-a. *And* as he *was* at the shearing house in the way,

13 Je'hu met with the brethren of A-ha-zi'ah king of Ju'dah, and said, Who *are* ye? And they answered, We *are* the brethren of A-ha-zi'ah; and we go down to salute the children of the king and the children of the queen.

14 And he said, Take them alive. And they took them alive, and slew them at the pit of the shearing house, *even* two and forty men; neither left he any of them.

15 ¶ And when he was departed thence, he lighted on Je-hon'a-dab the son of Re'chab *coming* to meet him: and he saluted him, and said to him, Is thine heart right, as my heart *is* with thy heart? And Je-hon'a-dab answered, It is. If it be, give *me* thine hand. And he gave *him* his hand; and he took him up to him into the chariot.

16 And he said, Come with me, and see my zeal for the LORD. So they made him ride in his chariot.

17 And when he came to Sa-ma'ri-a, he slew all that remained unto A'hab in Sa-ma'ri-a, till

he had destroyed him, according to the saying
of the LORD, which he spake to E-li'jah.
18 ¶ And Je'hu gathered all the people together, and said unto them, A'hab served Ba'al
a little; *but* Je'hu shall serve him much.
19 Now therefore call unto me all the prophets of Ba'al, all his servants, and all his priests; let none be wanting: for I have a great sacrifice *to do* to Ba'al; whosoever shall be wanting, he shall not live. But Je'hu did *it* in subtilty, to the intent that he might destroy the worshippers of Ba'al.
20 And Je'hu said, Proclaim a solemn assembly for Ba'al. And they proclaimed *it*.
21 And Je'hu sent through all Is'ra-el: and all the worshippers of Ba'al came, so that there was not a man left that came not. And they came into the house of Ba'al; and the house of Ba'al was full from one end to another.
22 And he said unto him that *was* over the vestry, Bring forth vestments for all the worshippers of Ba'al. And he brought them forth vestments.
23 And Je'hu went, and Je-hon'a-dab the son of Re'chab, into the house of Ba'al, and said unto the worshippers of Ba'al, Search, and look that there be here with you none of the servants of the LORD, but the worshippers of Ba'al only.
24 And when they went in to offer sacrifices and burnt offerings, Je'hu appointed fourscore men without, and said, *If* any of the men whom I have brought into your hands escape, *he that letteth him go*, his life *shall be* for the life of him.
25 And it came to pass, as soon as he had made an end of offering the burnt offering, that Je'hu said to the guard and to the captains, Go in, *and* slay them; let none come forth. And they smote them with the edge of the sword; and the guard and the captains cast *them* out, and went to the city of the house of Ba'al.
26 And they brought forth the images out of the house of Ba'al, and burned them.
27 And they brake down the image of Ba'al, and brake down the house of Ba'al, and made it a draught house unto this day.
28 Thus Je'hu destroyed Ba'al out of Is'ra-el.
29 ¶ Howbeit *from* the sins of Jer-o-bo'am the son of Ne'bat, who made Is'ra-el to sin, Je'hu departed not from after them, *to wit*, the golden calves that *were* in Beth'-el, and that *were* in Dan.
30 And the LORD said unto Je'hu, Because thou hast done well in executing *that which is* right in mine eyes, *and* hast done unto the house of A'hab according to all that *was* in mine heart, thy children of the fourth *generation* shall sit on the throne of Is'ra-el.
31 But Je'hu took no heed to walk in the law of the LORD God of Is'ra-el with all his heart: for he departed not from the sins of Jer-o-bo'am, which made Is'ra-el to sin.
32 ¶ In those days the LORD began to cut Is'ra-el short: and Haz'a-el smote them in all the coasts of Is'ra-el;
33 From Jor'dan eastward, all the land of Gil'e-ad, the Gad'ites, and the Reu'ben-ites, and the Ma-nas'sites, from Ar'o-er, which *is* by the river Ar'non, even Gil'e-ad and Ba'shan.
34 Now the rest of the acts of Je'hu, and all that he did, and all his might, *are* they not written in the book of the chronicles of the kings of Is'ra-el?
35 And Je'hu slept with his fathers: and they buried him in Sa-ma'ri-a. And Je-ho'a-haz his son reigned in his stead.
36 And the time that Je'hu reigned over Is'ra-el in Sa-ma'ri-a *was* twenty and eight years.

11 AND when Ath-a-li'ah the mother of A-ha-zi'ah saw that her son was dead, she arose and destroyed all the seed royal.
2 But Je-hosh'e-ba, the daughter of king Jo'-ram, sister of A-ha-zi'ah, took Jo'ash the son of A-ha-zi'ah, and stole him from among the king's sons *which were* slain; and they hid him, *even* him and his nurse, in the bedchamber from Ath-a-li'ah, so that he was not slain.
3 And he was with her hid in the house of the LORD six years. And Ath-a-li'ah did reign over the land.
4 ¶ And the seventh year Je-hoi'a-da sent and fetched the rulers over hundreds, with the captains and the guard, and brought them to him into the house of the LORD, and made a covenant with them, and took an oath of them in the house of the LORD, and shewed them the king's son.
5 And he commanded them, saying, This *is* the thing that ye shall do; A third part of you that enter in on the sabbath shall even be keepers of the watch of the king's house;
6 And a third part *shall be* at the gate of Sur; and a third part at the gate behind the guard: so shall ye keep the watch of the house, that it be not broken down.
7 And two parts of all you that go forth on the sabbath, even they shall keep the watch of the house of the LORD about the king.
8 And ye shall compass the king round about, every man with his weapons in his hand: and he that cometh within the ranges, let him be slain: and be ye with the king as he goeth out and as he cometh in.
9 And the captains over the hundreds did according to all *things* that Je-hoi'a-da the priest commanded: and they took every man his men that were to come in on the sabbath, with them that should go out on the sabbath, and came to Je-hoi'a-da the priest.
10 And to the captains over hundreds did the priest give king Da'vid's spears and shields, that *were* in the temple of the LORD.
11 And the guard stood, every man with his weapons in his hand, round about the king, from the right corner of the temple to the left corner of the temple, *along* by the altar and the temple.
12 And he brought forth the king's son, and put the crown upon him, and *gave him* the testimony; and they made him king, and anointed him; and they clapped their hands, and said, God save the king.
13 ¶ And when Ath-a-li'ah heard the noise of the guard *and* of the people, she came to the people into the temple of the LORD.
14 And when she looked, behold, the king stood by a pillar, as the manner *was*, and the princes and the trumpeters by the king, and all the people of the land rejoiced, and blew with trumpets: and Ath-a-li'ah rent her clothes, and cried, Treason, Treason.
15 But Je-hoi'a-da the priest commanded the captains of the hundreds, the officers of the host, and said unto them, Have her forth without the ranges: and him that followeth her kill with the sword. For the priest had said, Let her not be slain in the house of the LORD.
16 And they laid hands on her; and she went by the way by the which the horses came into the king's house: and there was she slain.
17 ¶ And Je-hoi'a-da made a covenant between the LORD and the king and the people,

that they should be the LORD's people; between
the king also and the people.
18 And all the people of the land went into
the house of Ba'al, and brake it down; his altars
and his images brake they in pieces thoroughly,
and slew Mat'tan the priest of Ba'al before the
altars. And the priest appointed officers over
the house of the LORD.
19 And he took the rulers over hundreds, and
the captains, and the guard, and all the people
of the land; and they brought down the king
from the house of the LORD, and came by the
way of the gate of the guard to the king's house.
And he sat on the throne of the kings.
20 And all the people of the land rejoiced,
and the city was in quiet: and they slew Ath-a-
li'ah with the sword *beside* the king's house.
21 Seven years old *was* Je-ho'ash when he
began to reign.

12 IN the seventh year of Je'hu Je-ho'ash
began to reign; and forty years reigned
he in Je-ru'sa-lem. And his mother's name *was*
Zib'i-ah of Be'er-she'ba.
2 And Je-ho'ash did *that which was* right in
the sight of the LORD all his days wherein Je-
hoi'a-da the priest instructed him.
3 But the high places were not taken away:
the people still sacrificed and burnt incense in
the high places.
4 ¶ And Je-ho'ash said to the priests, All the
money of the dedicated things that is brought
into the house of the LORD, *even* the money of
every one that passeth *the account*, the money
that every man is set at, *and* all the money that
cometh into any man's heart to bring into the
house of the LORD,
5 Let the priests take *it* to them, every man
of his acquaintance: and let them repair the
breaches of the house, wheresoever any breach
shall be found.
6 But it was *so*, *that* in the three and twentieth year of king Je-ho'ash the priests had not
repaired the breaches of the house.
7 Then king Je-ho'ash called for Je-hoi'a-da
the priest, and the *other* priests, and said unto
them, Why repair ye not the breaches of the
house? now therefore receive no *more* money of
your acquaintance, but deliver it for the
breaches of the house.
8 And the priests consented to receive no
more money of the people, neither to repair the
breaches of the house.
9 But Je-hoi'a-da the priest took a chest, and
bored a hole in the lid of it, and set it beside the
altar, on the right side as one cometh into the
house of the LORD: and the priests that kept the
door put therein all the money *that was* brought
into the house of the LORD.
10 And it was *so*, when they saw that *there
was* much money in the chest, that the king's
scribe and the high priest came up, and they put
up in bags, and told the money that was found
in the house of the LORD.
11 And they gave the money, being told, into
the hands of them that did the work, that had
the oversight of the house of the LORD: and they
laid it out to the carpenters and builders, that
wrought upon the house of the LORD,
12 And to masons, and hewers of stone, and
to buy timber and hewed stone to repair the
breaches of the house of the LORD, and for all
that was laid out for the house to repair *it*.
13 Howbeit there were not made for the
house of the LORD bowls of silver, snuffers, basons, trumpets, any vessels of gold, or vessels
of silver, of the money *that was* brought into
the house of the LORD:
14 But they gave that to the workmen, and
repaired therewith the house of the LORD.
15 Moreover they reckoned not with the
men, into whose hand they delivered the money
to be bestowed on workmen: for they dealt
faithfully.
16 The trespass money and sin money was
not brought into the house of the LORD: it was
the priests'.
17 ¶ Then Haz'a-el king of Syr'i-a went up,
and fought against Gath, and took it: and Haz'a-
el set his face to go up to Je-ru'sa-lem.
18 And Je-ho'ash king of Ju'dah took all the
hallowed things that Je-hosh'a-phat, and Je-ho'-
ram, and A-ha-zi'ah, his fathers, kings of Ju'-
dah, had dedicated, and his own hallowed
things, and all the gold *that was* found in the
treasures of the house of the LORD, and in the
king's house, and sent *it* to Haz'a-el king of
Syr'i-a: and he went away from Je-ru'sa-lem.
19 ¶ And the rest of the acts of Jo'ash, and
all that he did, *are* they not written in the book
of the chronicles of the kings of Ju'dah?
20 And his servants arose, and made a conspiracy, and slew Jo'ash in the house of Mil'lo,
which goeth down to Sil'la.
21 For Joz'a-char the son of Shim'e-ath, and
Je-hoz'a-bad the son of Sho'mer, his servants,
smote him, and he died; and they buried him
with his fathers in the city of Da'vid: and Am-a-
zi'ah his son reigned in his stead.

13 IN the three and twentieth year of Jo'-
ash the son of A-ha-zi'ah king of Ju'dah
Je-ho'a-haz the son of Je'hu began to reign over
Is'ra-el in Sa-ma'ri-a, *and reigned* seventeen
years.
2 And he did *that which was* evil in the sight
of the LORD, and followed the sins of Jer-o-bo'-
am the son of Ne'bat, which made Is'ra-el to sin;
he departed not therefrom.
3 ¶ And the anger of the LORD was kindled
against Is'ra-el, and he delivered them into the
hand of Haz'a-el king of Syr'i-a, and into the
hand of Ben-ha'dad the son of Haz'a-el, all *their*
days.
4 And Je-ho'a-haz besought the LORD, and
the LORD hearkened unto him: for he saw the
oppression of Is'ra-el, because the king of Syr'i-
a oppressed them.
5 (And the LORD gave Is'ra-el a saviour, so
that they went out from under the hand of the
Syr'i-ans: and the children of Is'ra-el dwelt in
their tents, as beforetime.
6 Nevertheless they departed not from the
sins of the house of Jer-o-bo'am, who made Is'-
ra-el sin, *but* walked therein: and there remained the grove also in Sa-ma'ri-a.)
7 Neither did he leave of the people to Je-
ho'a-haz but fifty horsemen, and ten chariots,
and ten thousand footmen; for the king of Syr'i-
a had destroyed them, and had made them like
the dust by threshing.
8 ¶ Now the rest of the acts of Je-ho'a-haz,
and all that he did, and his might, *are* they not
written in the book of the chronicles of the
kings of Is'ra-el?
9 And Je-ho'a-haz slept with his fathers; and
they buried him in Sa-ma'ri-a: and Jo'ash his
son reigned in his stead.
10 ¶ In the thirty and seventh year of Jo'ash
king of Ju'dah began Je-ho'ash the son of Je-
ho'a-haz to reign over Is'ra-el in Sa-ma'ri-a, *and
reigned* sixteen years.
11 And he did *that which was* evil in the

sight of the LORD; he departed not from all the
sins of Jer-o-bo'am the son of Ne'bat, who made
Is'ra-el sin: *but* he walked therein.
12 And the rest of the acts of Jo'ash, and all
that he did, and his might wherewith he fought
against Am-a-zi'ah king of Ju'dah, *are* they not
written in the book of the chronicles of the
kings of Is'ra-el?
13 And Jo'ash slept with his fathers; and Jer-
o-bo'am sat upon his throne: and Jo'ash was
buried in Sa-ma'ri-a with the kings of Is'ra-el.
14 ¶ Now E-li'sha was fallen sick of his sickness whereof he died. And Jo'ash the king of
Is'ra-el came down unto him, and wept over his
face, and said, O my father, my father, the
chariot of Is'ra-el, and the horsemen thereof.
15 And E-li'sha said unto him, Take bow and
arrows. And he took unto him bow and arrows.
16 And he said to the king of Is'ra-el, Put
thine hand upon the bow. And he put his hand
upon it: and E-li'sha put his hands upon the
king's hands.
17 And he said, Open the window eastward.
And he opened *it.* Then E-li'sha said, Shoot.
And he shot. And he said, The arrow of the
LORD's deliverance, and the arrow of deliverance from Syr'i-a: for thou shalt smite the Syr'i-
ans in A'phek, till thou have consumed *them.*
18 And he said, Take the arrows. And he
took *them.* And he said unto the king of Is'ra-el,
Smite upon the ground. And he smote thrice,
and stayed.
19 And the man of God was wroth with him,
and said, Thou shouldest have smitten five or
six times; then hadst thou smitten Syr'i-a till
thou hadst consumed *it:* whereas now thou
shalt smite Syr'i-a *but* thrice.
20 ¶ And E-li'sha died, and they buried him.
And the bands of the Mo'ab-ites invaded the
land at the coming in of the year.
21 And it came to pass, as they were burying
a man, that, behold, they spied a band *of men;*
and they cast the man into the sepulchre of E-
li'sha: and when the man was let down, and
touched the bones of E-li'sha, he revived, and
stood up on his feet.
22 ¶ But Haz'a-el king of Syr'i-a oppressed
Is'ra-el all the days of Je-ho'a-haz.
23 And the LORD was gracious unto them,
and had compassion on them, and had respect
unto them, because of his covenant with A'bra-
ham, I'saac, and Ja'cob, and would not destroy
them, neither cast he them from his presence as
yet.
24 So Haz'a-el king of Syr'i-a died; and Ben–
ha'dad his son reigned in his stead.
25 And Je-ho'ash the son of Je-ho'a-haz took
again out of the hand of Ben–ha'dad the son of
Haz'a-el the cities, which he had taken out of
the hand of Je-ho'a-haz his father by war. Three
times did Jo'ash beat him, and recovered the
cities of Is'ra-el.

14 IN the second year of Jo'ash son of Je-
ho'a-haz king of Is'ra-el reigned Am-a-
zi'ah the son of Jo'ash king of Ju'dah.
2 He was twenty and five years old when he
began to reign, and reigned twenty and nine
years in Je-ru'sa-lem. And his mother's name
was Je-ho-ad'dan of Je-ru'sa-lem.
3 And he did *that which was* right in the
sight of the LORD, yet not like Da'vid his father:
he did according to all things as Jo'ash his father did.
4 Howbeit the high places were not taken
away: as yet the people did sacrifice and burnt
incense on the high places.
5 ¶ And it came to pass, as soon as the kingdom was confirmed in his hand, that he slew his
servants which had slain the king his father.
6 But the children of the murderers he slew
not: according unto that which is written in the
book of the law of Mo'ses, wherein the LORD
commanded, saying, The fathers shall not be
put to death for the children, nor the children be
put to death for the fathers; but every man shall
be put to death for his own sin.
7 He slew of E'dom in the valley of salt ten
thousand, and took Se'lah by war, and called
the name of it Jok'the-el unto this day.
8 ¶ Then Am-a-zi'ah sent messengers to Je-
ho'ash, the son of Je-ho'a-haz son of Je'hu, king
of Is'ra-el, saying, Come, let us look one another
in the face.
9 And Je-ho'ash the king of Is'ra-el sent to
Am-a-zi'ah king of Ju'dah, saying, The thistle
that *was* in Leb'a-non sent to the cedar that *was*
in Leb'a-non, saying, Give thy daughter to my
son to wife: and there passed by a wild beast
that *was* in Leb'a-non, and trode down the thistle.
10 Thou hast indeed smitten E'dom, and
thine heart hath lifted thee up: glory *of this,* and
tarry at home: for why shouldest thou meddle
to *thy* hurt, that thou shouldest fall, *even* thou,
and Ju'dah with thee?
11 But Am-a-zi'ah would not hear. Therefore
Je-ho'ash king of Is'ra-el went up; and he and
Am-a-zi'ah king of Ju'dah looked one another in
the face at Beth–she'mesh, which *belongeth* to
Ju'dah.
12 And Ju'dah was put to the worse before
Is'ra-el; and they fled every man to their tents.
13 And Je-ho'ash king of Is'ra-el took Am-a-
zi'ah king of Ju'dah, the son of Je-ho'ash the son
of A-ha-zi'ah, at Beth–she'mesh, and came to
Je-ru'sa-lem, and brake down the wall of Je-ru'-
sa-lem from the gate of E'phra-im unto the corner gate, four hundred cubits.
14 And he took all the gold and silver, and all
the vessels that were found in the house of the
LORD, and in the treasures of the king's house,
and hostages, and returned to Sa-ma'ri-a.
15 ¶ Now the rest of the acts of Je-ho'ash
which he did, and his might, and how he fought
with Am-a-zi'ah king of Ju'dah, *are* they not
written in the book of the chronicles of the
kings of Is'ra-el?
16 And Je-ho'ash slept with his fathers, and
was buried in Sa-ma'ri-a with the kings of Is'ra-
el; and Jer-o-bo'am his son reigned in his stead.
17 ¶ And Am-a-zi'ah the son of Jo'ash king
of Ju'dah lived after the death of Je-ho'ash son
of Je-ho'a-haz king of Is'ra-el fifteen years.
18 And the rest of the acts of Am-a-zi'ah, *are*
they not written in the book of the chronicles of
the kings of Ju'dah?
19 Now they made a conspiracy against him
in Je-ru'sa-lem: and he fled to La'chish; but they
sent after him to La'chish, and slew him there.
20 And they brought him on horses: and he
was buried at Je-ru'sa-lem with his fathers in
the city of Da'vid.
21 ¶ And all the people of Ju'dah took Az-a-
ri'ah, which *was* sixteen years old, and made
him king instead of his father Am-a-zi'ah.
22 He built E'lath, and restored it to Ju'dah,
after that the king slept with his fathers.
23 ¶ In the fifteenth year of Am-a-zi'ah the
son of Jo'ash king of Ju'dah Jer-o-bo'am the son
of Jo'ash king of Is'ra-el began to reign in Sa-
ma'ri-a, *and reigned* forty and one years.
24 And he did *that which was* evil in the
sight of the LORD: he departed not from all the

sins of Jer-o-bo'am the son of Ne'bat, who made
Is'ra-el to sin.
25 He restored the coast of Is'ra-el from the
entering of Ha'math unto the sea of the plain,
according to the word of the LORD God of Is'ra-
el, which he spake by the hand of his servant
Jo'nah, the son of A-mit'ta-i, the prophet, which
was of Gath–he'pher.
26 For the LORD saw the affliction of Is'ra-el,
that it was very bitter: for *there was* not any
shut up, nor any left, nor any helper for Is'ra-el.
27 And the LORD said not that he would blot
out the name of Is'ra-el from under heaven: but
he saved them by the hand of Jer-o-bo'am the
son of Jo'ash.
28 ¶ Now the rest of the acts of Jer-o-bo'am,
and all that he did, and his might, how he
warred, and how he recovered Da-mas'cus, and
Ha'math, *which belonged* to Ju'dah, for Is'ra-el,
are they not written in the book of the chronicles of the kings of Is'ra-el?
29 And Jer-o-bo'am slept with his fathers,
even with the kings of Is'ra-el; and Zach-a-ri'ah
his son reigned in his stead.

15 IN the twenty and seventh year of Jer-o-
bo'am king of Is'ra-el began Az-a-ri'ah
son of Am-a-zi'ah king of Ju'dah to reign.
2 Sixteen years old was he when he began to
reign, and he reigned two and fifty years in Je-
ru'sa-lem. And his mother's name *was* Jech-o-
li'ah of Je-ru'sa-lem.
3 And he did *that which was* right in the
sight of the LORD, according to all that his father Am-a-zi'ah had done;
4 Save that the high places were not removed: the people sacrificed and burnt incense
still on the high places.
5 ¶ And the LORD smote the king, so that he
was a leper unto the day of his death, and dwelt
in a several house. And Jo'tham the king's son
was over the house, judging the people of the
land.
6 And the rest of the acts of Az-a-ri'ah, and
all that he did, *are* they not written in the book
of the chronicles of the kings of Ju'dah?
7 So Az-a-ri'ah slept with his fathers; and
they buried him with his fathers in the city of
Da'vid: and Jo'tham his son reigned in his stead.
8 ¶ In the thirty and eighth year of Az-a-ri'ah
king of Ju'dah did Zach-a-ri'ah the son of Jer-o-
bo'am reign over Is'ra-el in Sa-ma'ri-a six
months.
9 And he did *that which was* evil in the sight
of the LORD, as his fathers had done: he departed not from the sins of Jer-o-bo'am the son
of Ne'bat, who made Is'ra-el to sin.
10 And Shal'lum the son of Ja'besh conspired
against him, and smote him before the people,
and slew him, and reigned in his stead.
11 And the rest of the acts of Zach-a-ri'ah,
behold, they *are* written in the book of the
chronicles of the kings of Is'ra-el.
12 This *was* the word of the LORD which he
spake unto Je'hu, saying, Thy sons shall sit on
the throne of Is'ra-el unto the fourth *generation*.
And so it came to pass.
13 ¶ Shal'lum the son of Ja'besh began to
reign in the nine and thirtieth year of Uz-zi'ah
king of Ju'dah; and he reigned a full month in
Sa-ma'ri-a.
14 For Men'a-hem the son of Ga'di went up
from Tir'zah, and came to Sa-ma'ri-a, and
smote Shal'lum the son of Ja'besh in Sa-ma'ri-a,
and slew him, and reigned in his stead.
15 And the rest of the acts of Shal'lum, and
his conspiracy which he made, behold, they *are*
written in the book of the chronicles of the
kings of Is'ra-el.
16 ¶ Then Men'a-hem smote Tiph'sah, and
all that *were* therein, and the coasts thereof
from Tir'zah: because they opened not *to him*,
therefore he smote *it: and* all the women
therein that were with child he ripped up.
17 In the nine and thirtieth year of Az-a-ri'ah
king of Ju'dah began Men'a-hem the son of Ga'-
di to reign over Is'ra-el, *and reigned* ten years in
Sa-ma'ri-a.
18 And he did *that which was* evil in the
sight of the LORD: he departed not all his days
from the sins of Jer-o-bo'am the son of Ne'bat,
who made Is'ra-el to sin.
19 *And* Pul the king of As-syr'i-a came
against the land: and Men'a-hem gave Pul a
thousand talents of silver, that his hand might
be with him to confirm the kingdom in his hand.
20 And Men'a-hem exacted the money of Is'-
ra-el, *even* of all the mighty men of wealth, of
each man fifty shekels of silver, to give to the
king of As-syr'i-a. So the king of As-syr'i-a
turned back, and stayed not there in the land.
21 ¶ And the rest of the acts of Men'a-hem,
and all that he did, *are* they not written in the
book of the chronicles of the kings of Is'ra-el?
22 And Men'a-hem slept with his fathers;
and Pek-a-hi'ah his son reigned in his stead.
23 ¶ In the fiftieth year of Az-a-ri'ah king of
Ju'dah Pek-a-hi'ah the son of Men'a-hem began
to reign over Is'ra-el in Sa-ma'ri-a, *and reigned*
two years.
24 And he did *that which was* evil in the
sight of the LORD: he departed not from the sins
of Jer-o-bo'am the son of Ne'bat, who made Is'-
ra-el to sin.
25 But Pe'kah the son of Rem-a-li'ah, a captain of his, conspired against him, and smote
him in Sa-ma'ri-a, in the palace of the king's
house, with Ar'gob and A-ri'eh, and with him
fifty men of the Gil'e-ad-ites: and he killed him,
and reigned in his room.
26 And the rest of the acts of Pek-a-hi'ah,
and all that he did, behold, they *are* written in
the book of the chronicles of the kings of Is'ra-
el.
27 ¶ In the two and fiftieth year of Az-a-ri'ah
king of Ju'dah Pe'kah the son of Rem-a-li'ah began to reign over Is'ra-el in Sa-ma'ri-a, *and
reigned* twenty years.
28 And he did *that which was* evil in the
sight of the LORD: he departed not from the sins
of Jer-o-bo'am the son of Ne'bat, who made Is'-
ra-el to sin.
29 In the days of Pe'kah king of Is'ra-el came
Tig'lath–pi-le'ser king of As-syr'i-a, and took I'-
jon, and A'bel–beth–ma'a-chah, and Ja-no'ah,
and Ke'desh, and Ha'zor, and Gil'e-ad, and Gal'-
i-lee, all the land of Naph'ta-li, and carried them
captive to As-syr'i-a.
30 And Ho-she'a the son of E'lah made a conspiracy against Pe'kah the son of Rem-a-li'ah,
and smote him, and slew him, and reigned in his
stead, in the twentieth year of Jo'tham the son
of Uz-zi'ah.
31 And the rest of the acts of Pe'kah, and all
that he did, behold, they *are* written in the book
of the chronicles of the kings of Is'ra-el.
32 ¶ In the second year of Pe'kah the son of
Rem-a-li'ah king of Is'ra-el began Jo'tham the
son of Uz-zi'ah king of Ju'dah to reign.
33 Five and twenty years old was he when he
began to reign, and he reigned sixteen years in
Je-ru'sa-lem. And his mother's name *was* Je-
ru'sha, the daughter of Za'dok.
34 And he did *that which was* right in the

sight of the LORD: he did according to all that
his father Uz-zi'ah had done.
35 ¶ Howbeit the high places were not removed: the people sacrificed and burned incense still in the high places. He built the higher
gate of the house of the LORD.
36 ¶ Now the rest of the acts of Jo'tham, and
all that he did, *are* they not written in the book
of the chronicles of the kings of Ju'dah?
37 In those days the LORD began to send
against Ju'dah Re'zin the king of Syr'i-a, and
Pe'kah the son of Rem-a-li'ah.
38 And Jo'tham slept with his fathers, and
was buried with his fathers in the city of Da'vid
his father: and A'haz his son reigned in his
stead.

16 IN the seventeenth year of Pe'kah the
son of Rem-a-li'ah A'haz the son of Jo'-
tham king of Ju'dah began to reign.
2 Twenty years old *was* A'haz when he began to reign, and reigned sixteen years in Je-
ru'sa-lem, and did not *that which was* right in
the sight of the LORD his God, like Da'vid his
father.
3 But he walked in the way of the kings of
Is'ra-el, yea, and made his son to pass through
the fire, according to the abominations of the
heathen, whom the LORD cast out from before
the children of Is'ra-el.
4 And he sacrificed and burnt incense in the
high places, and on the hills, and under every
green tree.
5 ¶ Then Re'zin king of Syr'i-a and Pe'kah
son of Rem-a-li'ah king of Is'ra-el came up to
Je-ru'sa-lem to war: and they besieged A'haz,
but could not overcome *him*.
6 At that time Re'zin king of Syr'i-a recovered E'lath to Syr'i-a, and drave the Jews from
E'lath: and the Syr'i-ans came to E'lath, and
dwelt there unto this day.
7 So A'haz sent messengers to Tig'lath-pi-
le'ser king of As-syr'i-a, saying, I *am* thy servant and thy son: come up, and save me out of
the hand of the king of Syr'i-a, and out of the
hand of the king of Is'ra-el, which rise up
against me.
8 And A'haz took the silver and gold that
was found in the house of the LORD, and in the
treasures of the king's house, and sent *it for* a
present to the king of As-syr'i-a.
9 And the king of As-syr'i-a hearkened unto
him: for the king of As-syr'i-a went up against
Da-mas'cus, and took it, and carried *the people*
of it captive to Kir, and slew Re'zin.
10 ¶ And king A'haz went to Da-mas'cus to
meet Tig'lath-pi-le'ser king of As-syr'i-a, and
saw an altar that *was* at Da-mas'cus: and king
A'haz sent to U-ri'jah the priest the fashion of
the altar, and the pattern of it, according to all
the workmanship thereof.
11 And U-ri'jah the priest built an altar according to all that king A'haz had sent from Da-
mas'cus: so U-ri'jah the priest made *it* against
king A'haz came from Da-mas'cus.
12 And when the king was come from Da-
mas'cus, the king saw the altar: and the king
approached to the altar, and offered thereon.
13 And he burnt his burnt offering and his
meat offering, and poured his drink offering,
and sprinkled the blood of his peace offerings,
upon the altar.
14 And he brought also the brasen altar,
which *was* before the LORD, from the forefront
of the house, from between the altar and the
house of the LORD, and put it on the north side
of the altar.
15 And king A'haz commanded U-ri'jah the
priest, saying, Upon the great altar burn the
morning burnt offering, and the evening meat
offering, and the king's burnt sacrifice, and his
meat offering, with the burnt offering of all the
people of the land, and their meat offering, and
their drink offerings; and sprinkle upon it all the
blood of the burnt offering, and all the blood of
the sacrifice: and the brasen altar shall be for
me to enquire *by*.
16 Thus did U-ri'jah the priest, according to
all that king A'haz commanded.
17 ¶ And king A'haz cut off the borders of
the bases, and removed the laver from off them;
and took down the sea from off the brasen oxen
that *were* under it, and put it upon a pavement
of stones.
18 And the covert for the sabbath that they
had built in the house, and the king's entry
without, turned he from the house of the LORD
for the king of As-syr'i-a.
19 ¶ Now the rest of the acts of A'haz which
he did, *are* they not written in the book of the
chronicles of the kings of Ju'dah?
20 And A'haz slept with his fathers, and was
buried with his fathers in the city of Da'vid: and
Hez-e-ki'ah his son reigned in his stead.

17 IN the twelfth year of A'haz king of Ju'-
dah began Ho-she'a the son of E'lah to
reign in Sa-ma'ri-a over Is'ra-el nine years.
2 And he did *that which was* evil in the sight
of the LORD, but not as the kings of Is'ra-el that
were before him.
3 ¶ Against him came up Shal-man-e'ser
king of As-syr'i-a; and Ho-she'a became his servant, and gave him presents.
4 And the king of As-syr'i-a found conspiracy in Ho-she'a: for he had sent messengers to
So king of E'gypt, and brought no present to the
king of As-syr'i-a, as *he had done* year by year:
therefore the king of As-syr'i-a shut him up, and
bound him in prison.
5 ¶ Then the king of As-syr'i-a came up
throughout all the land, and went up to Sa-ma'-
ri-a, and besieged it three years.
6 ¶ In the ninth year of Ho-she'a the king of
As-syr'i-a took Sa-ma'ri-a, and carried Is'ra-el
away into As-syr'i-a, and placed them in Ha'lah
and in Ha'bor *by* the river of Go'zan, and in the
cities of the Medes.
7 For *so* it was, that the children of Is'ra-el
had sinned against the LORD their God, which
had brought them up out of the land of E'gypt,
from under the hand of Pha'raoh king of E'gypt,
and had feared other gods,
8 And walked in the statutes of the heathen,
whom the LORD cast out from before the children of Is'ra-el, and of the kings of Is'ra-el,
which they had made.
9 And the children of Is'ra-el did secretly
those things that *were* not right against the
LORD their God, and they built them high places
in all their cities, from the tower of the watchmen to the fenced city.
10 And they set them up images and groves
in every high hill, and under every green tree:
11 And there they burnt incense in all the
high places, as *did* the heathen whom the LORD
carried away before them; and wrought wicked
things to provoke the LORD to anger:
12 For they served idols, whereof the LORD
had said unto them, Ye shall not do this thing.
13 Yet the LORD testified against Is'ra-el, and
against Ju'dah, by all the prophets, *and by* all
the seers, saying, Turn ye from your evil ways,
and keep my commandments *and* my statutes,

according to all the law which I commanded
your fathers, and which I sent to you by my
servants the prophets.
14 Notwithstanding they would not hear, but
hardened their necks, like to the neck of their
fathers, that did not believe in the LORD their
God.
15 And they rejected his statutes, and his
covenant that he made with their fathers, and
his testimonies which he testified against them;
and they followed vanity, and became vain, and
went after the heathen that *were* round about
them, *concerning* whom the LORD had charged
them, that they should not do like them.
16 And they left all the commandments of
the LORD their God, and made them molten images, *even* two calves, and made a grove, and
worshipped all the host of heaven, and served
Ba'al.
17 And they caused their sons and their
daughters to pass through the fire, and used
divination and enchantments, and sold themselves to do evil in the sight of the LORD, to
provoke him to anger.
18 Therefore the LORD was very angry with
Is'ra-el, and removed them out of his sight:
there was none left but the tribe of Ju'dah only.
19 Also Ju'dah kept not the commandments
of the LORD their God, but walked in the statutes of Is'ra-el which they made.
20 And the LORD rejected all the seed of Is'-
ra-el, and afflicted them, and delivered them
into the hand of spoilers, until he had cast them
out of his sight.
21 For he rent Is'ra-el from the house of Da'-
vid; and they made Jer-o-bo'am the son of Ne'-
bat king: and Jer-o-bo'am drave Is'ra-el from
following the LORD, and made them sin a great
sin.
22 For the children of Is'ra-el walked in all
the sins of Jer-o-bo'am which he did; they departed not from them;
23 Until the LORD removed Is'ra-el out of his
sight, as he had said by all his servants the
prophets. So was Is'ra-el carried away out of
their own land to As-syr'i-a unto this day.
24 ¶ And the king of As-syr'i-a brought *men*
from Bab'y-lon, and from Cu'thah, and from A'-
va, and from Ha'math, and from Seph-ar-va'im,
and placed *them* in the cities of Sa-ma'ri-a instead of the children of Is'ra-el: and they possessed Sa-ma'ri-a, and dwelt in the cities
thereof.
25 And *so* it was at the beginning of their
dwelling there, *that* they feared not the LORD:
therefore the LORD sent lions among them,
which slew *some* of them.
26 Wherefore they spake to the king of As-
syr'i-a, saying, The nations which thou hast removed, and placed in the cities of Sa-ma'ri-a,
know not the manner of the God of the land:
therefore he hath sent lions among them, and,
behold, they slay them, because they know not
the manner of the God of the land.
27 Then the king of As-syr'i-a commanded,
saying, Carry thither one of the priests whom
ye brought from thence; and let them go and
dwell there, and let him teach them the manner
of the God of the land.
28 Then one of the priests whom they had
carried away from Sa-ma'ri-a came and dwelt
in Beth'-el, and taught them how they should
fear the LORD.
29 Howbeit every nation made gods of their
own, and put *them* in the houses of the high
places which the Sa-mar'i-tans had made, every
nation in their cities wherein they dwelt.
30 And the men of Bab'y-lon made Suc'coth-
be'noth, and the men of Cuth made Ner'gal, and
the men of Ha'math made Ash'i-ma,
31 And the A'vites made Nib'haz and Tar'-
tak, and the Seph'ar-vites burnt their children
in fire to A-dram'me-lech and A-nam'me-lech,
the gods of Seph-ar-va'im.
32 So they feared the LORD, and made unto
themselves of the lowest of them priests of the
high places, which sacrificed for them in the
houses of the high places.
33 They feared the LORD, and served their
own gods, after the manner of the nations
whom they carried away from thence.
34 Unto this day they do after the former
manners: they fear not the LORD, neither do
they after their statutes, or after their ordinances, or after the law and commandment
which the LORD commanded the children of Ja'-
cob, whom he named Is'ra-el;
35 With whom the LORD had made a covenant, and charged them, saying, Ye shall not
fear other gods, nor bow yourselves to them,
nor serve them, nor sacrifice to them:
36 But the LORD, who brought you up out of
the land of E'gypt with great power and a
stretched out arm, him shall ye fear, and him
shall ye worship, and to him shall ye do sacrifice.
37 And the statutes, and the ordinances, and
the law, and the commandment, which he
wrote for you, ye shall observe to do for evermore; and ye shall not fear other gods.
38 And the covenant that I have made with
you ye shall not forget; neither shall ye fear other gods.
39 But the LORD your God ye shall fear; and
he shall deliver you out of the hand of all your
enemies.
40 Howbeit they did not hearken, but they
did after their former manner.
41 So these nations feared the LORD, and
served their graven images, both their children,
and their children's children: as did their fathers, so do they unto this day.

18 NOW it came to pass in the third year of
Ho-she'a son of E'lah king of Is'ra-el,
that Hez-e-ki'ah the son of A'haz king of Ju'dah
began to reign.
2 Twenty and five years old was he when he
began to reign; and he reigned twenty and nine
years in Je-ru'sa-lem. His mother's name also
was A'bi, the daughter of Zach-a-ri'ah.
3 And he did *that which was* right in the
sight of the LORD, according to all that Da'vid
his father did.
4 ¶ He removed the high places, and brake
the images, and cut down the groves, and brake
in pieces the brasen serpent that Mo'ses had
made: for unto those days the children of Is'ra-
el did burn incense to it: and he called it Ne-
hush'tan.
5 He trusted in the LORD God of Is'ra-el; so
that after him was none like him among all the
kings of Ju'dah, nor *any* that were before him.
6 For he clave to the LORD, *and* departed not
from following him, but kept his commandments, which the LORD commanded Mo'ses.
7 And the LORD was with him; *and* he prospered whithersoever he went forth: and he rebelled against the king of As-syr'i-a, and served
him not.
8 He smote the Phi-lis'tines, *even* unto Ga'za,
and the borders thereof, from the tower of the
watchmen to the fenced city.
9 ¶ And it came to pass in the fourth year of

king Hez-e-ki'ah, which *was* the seventh year of Ho-she'a son of E'lah king of Is'ra-el, *that* Shal-man-e'ser king of As-syr'i-a came up against Sa-ma'ri-a, and besieged it.

10 And at the end of three years they took it: *even* in the sixth year of Hez-e-ki'ah, that *is* the ninth year of Ho-she'a king of Is'ra-el, Sa-ma'ri-a was taken.

11 And the king of As-syr'i-a did carry away Is'ra-el unto As-syr'i-a, and put them in Ha'lah and in Ha'bor *by* the river of Go'zan, and in the cities of the Medes:

12 Because they obeyed not the voice of the LORD their God, but transgressed his covenant, *and* all that Mo'ses the servant of the LORD commanded, and would not hear *them*, nor do *them*.

13 ¶ Now in the fourteenth year of king Hez-e-ki'ah did Sen-nach'e-rib king of As-syr'i-a come up against all the fenced cities of Ju'dah, and took them.

14 And Hez-e-ki'ah king of Ju'dah sent to the king of As-syr'i-a to La'chish, saying, I have offended; return from me: that which thou puttest on me will I bear. And the king of As-syr'i-a appointed unto Hez-e-ki'ah king of Ju'dah three hundred talents of silver and thirty talents of gold.

15 And Hez-e-ki'ah gave *him* all the silver that was found in the house of the LORD, and in the treasures of the king's house.

16 At that time did Hez-e-ki'ah cut off *the gold from* the doors of the temple of the LORD, and *from* the pillars which Hez-e-ki'ah king of Ju'dah had overlaid, and gave it to the king of As-syr'i-a.

17 ¶ And the king of As-syr'i-a sent Tar'tan and Rab'sa-ris and Rab'-sha-keh from La'chish to king Hez-e-ki'ah with a great host against Je-ru'sa-lem. And they went up and came to Je-ru'sa-lem. And when they were come up, they came and stood by the conduit of the upper pool, which *is* in the highway of the fuller's field.

18 And when they had called to the king, there came out to them E-li'a-kim the son of Hil-ki'ah, which *was* over the household, and Sheb'na the scribe, and Jo'ah the son of A'saph the recorder.

19 And Rab'-sha-keh said unto them, Speak ye now to Hez-e-ki'ah, Thus saith the great king, the king of As-syr'i-a, What confidence *is* this wherein thou trustest?

20 Thou sayest, (but *they are but* vain words,) *I have* counsel and strength for the war. Now on whom dost thou trust, that thou rebellest against me?

21 Now, behold, thou trustest upon the staff of this bruised reed, *even* upon E'gypt, on which if a man lean, it will go into his hand, and pierce it: so *is* Pha'raoh king of E'gypt unto all that trust on him.

22 But if ye say unto me, We trust in the LORD our God: *is* not that he, whose high places and whose altars Hez-e-ki'ah hath taken away, and hath said to Ju'dah and Je-ru'sa-lem, Ye shall worship before this altar in Je-ru'sa-lem?

23 Now therefore, I pray thee, give pledges to my lord the king of As-syr'i-a, and I will deliver thee two thousand horses, if thou be able on thy part to set riders upon them.

24 How then wilt thou turn away the face of one captain of the least of my master's servants, and put thy trust on E'gypt for chariots and for horsemen?

25 Am I now come up without the LORD against this place to destroy it? The LORD said to me, Go up against this land, and destroy it.

26 Then said E-li'a-kim the son of Hil-ki'ah, and Sheb'na, and Jo'ah, unto Rab'-sha-keh, Speak, I pray thee, to thy servants in the Syr'i-an language; for we understand *it:* and talk not with us in the Jews' language in the ears of the people that *are* on the wall.

27 But Rab'-sha-keh said unto them, Hath my master sent me to thy master, and to thee, to speak these words? *hath he* not *sent me* to the men which sit on the wall, that they may eat their own dung, and drink their own piss with you?

28 Then Rab'-sha-keh stood and cried with a loud voice in the Jews' language, and spake, saying, Hear the word of the great king, the king of As-syr'i-a:

29 Thus saith the king, Let not Hez-e-ki'ah deceive you: for he shall not be able to deliver you out of his hand:

30 Neither let Hez-e-ki'ah make you trust in the LORD, saying, The LORD will surely deliver us, and this city shall not be delivered into the hand of the king of As-syr'i-a.

31 Hearken not to Hez-e-ki'ah: for thus saith the king of As-syr'i-a, Make *an agreement* with me by a present, and come out to me, and *then* eat ye every man of his own vine, and every one of his fig tree, and drink ye every one the waters of his cistern:

32 Until I come and take you away to a land like your own land, a land of corn and wine, a land of bread and vineyards, a land of oil olive and of honey, that ye may live, and not die: and hearken not unto Hez-e-ki'ah, when he persuadeth you, saying, The LORD will deliver us.

33 Hath any of the gods of the nations delivered at all his land out of the hand of the king of As-syr'i-a?

34 Where *are* the gods of Ha'math, and of Ar'pad? where *are* the gods of Seph-ar-va'im, He'na, and I'vah? have they delivered Sa-ma'ri-a out of mine hand?

35 Who *are* they among all the gods of the countries, that have delivered their country out of mine hand, that the LORD should deliver Je-ru'sa-lem out of mine hand?

36 But the people held their peace, and answered him not a word: for the king's commandment was, saying, Answer him not.

37 Then came E-li'a-kim the son of Hil-ki'ah, which *was* over the household, and Sheb'na the scribe, and Jo'ah the son of A'saph the recorder, to Hez-e-ki'ah with *their* clothes rent, and told him the words of Rab'-sha-keh.

19 AND it came to pass, when king Hez-e-ki'ah heard *it,* that he rent his clothes, and covered himself with sackcloth, and went into the house of the LORD.

2 And he sent E-li'a-kim, which *was* over the household, and Sheb'na the scribe, and the elders of the priests, covered with sackcloth, to I-sa'iah the prophet the son of A'moz.

3 And they said unto him, Thus saith Hez-e-ki'ah, This day *is* a day of trouble, and of rebuke, and blasphemy: for the children are come to the birth, and *there is* not strength to bring forth.

4 It may be the LORD thy God will hear all the words of Rab'-sha-keh, whom the king of As-syr'i-a his master hath sent to reproach the living God; and will reprove the words which the LORD thy God hath heard: wherefore lift up *thy* prayer for the remnant that are left.

5 So the servants of king Hez-e-ki'ah came to I-sa'iah.

6 ¶ And I-sa'iah said unto them, Thus shall ye say to your master, Thus saith the LORD, Be not afraid of the words which thou hast heard, with which the servants of the king of As-syr'i-a have blasphemed me.

7 Behold, I will send a blast upon him, and he shall hear a rumour, and shall return to his own land; and I will cause him to fall by the sword in his own land.

8 ¶ So Rab'-sha-keh returned, and found the king of As-syr'i-a warring against Lib'nah: for he had heard that he was departed from La'-chish.

9 And when he heard say of Tir'ha-kah king of E-thi-o'pi-a, Behold, he is come out to fight against thee: he sent messengers again unto Hez-e-ki'ah, saying,

10 Thus shall ye speak to Hez-e-ki'ah king of Ju'dah, saying, Let not thy God in whom thou trustest deceive thee, saying, Je-ru'sa-lem shall not be delivered into the hand of the king of As-syr'i-a.

11 Behold, thou hast heard what the kings of As-syr'i-a have done to all lands, by destroying them utterly: and shalt thou be delivered?

12 Have the gods of the nations delivered them which my fathers have destroyed; *as* Go'-zan, and Ha'ran, and Re'zeph, and the children of E'den which *were* in The-la'sar?

13 Where *is* the king of Ha'math, and the king of Ar'pad, and the king of the city of Seph-ar-va'im, of He'na, and I'vah?

14 ¶ And Hez-e-ki'ah received the letter of the hand of the messengers, and read it: and Hez-e-ki'ah went up into the house of the LORD, and spread it before the LORD.

15 And Hez-e-ki'ah prayed before the LORD, and said, O LORD God of Is'ra-el, which dwellest *between* the cherubims, thou art the God, *even* thou alone, of all the kingdoms of the earth; thou hast made heaven and earth.

16 LORD, bow down thine ear, and hear: open, LORD, thine eyes, and see: and hear the words of Sen-nach'e-rib, which hath sent him to reproach the living God.

17 Of a truth, LORD, the kings of As-syr'i-a have destroyed the nations and their lands,

18 And have cast their gods into the fire: for they *were* no gods, but the work of men's hands, wood and stone: therefore they have destroyed them.

19 Now therefore, O LORD our God, I beseech thee, save thou us out of his hand, that all the kingdoms of the earth may know that thou *art* the LORD God, *even* thou only.

20 ¶ Then I-sa'iah the son of A'moz sent to Hez-e-ki'ah, saying, Thus saith the LORD God of Is'ra-el, *That* which thou hast prayed to me against Sen-nach'e-rib king of As-syr'i-a I have heard.

21 This *is* the word that the LORD hath spoken concerning him; The virgin the daughter of Zi'on hath despised thee, *and* laughed thee to scorn; the daughter of Je-ru'sa-lem hath shaken her head at thee.

22 Whom hast thou reproached and blasphemed? and against whom hast thou exalted *thy* voice, and lifted up thine eyes on high? *even* against the Holy *One* of Is'ra-el.

23 By thy messengers thou hast reproached the LORD, and hast said, With the multitude of my chariots I am come up to the height of the mountains, to the sides of Leb'a-non, and will cut down the tall cedar trees thereof, *and* the choice fir trees thereof: and I will enter into the lodgings of his borders, *and into* the forest of his Car'mel.

24 I have digged and drunk strange waters, and with the sole of my feet have I dried up all the rivers of besieged places.

25 Hast thou not heard long ago *how* I have done it, *and* of ancient times that I have formed it? now have I brought it to pass, that thou shouldest be to lay waste fenced cities *into* ruinous heaps.

26 Therefore their inhabitants were of small power, they were dismayed and confounded; they were *as* the grass of the field, and *as* the green herb, *as* the grass on the house tops, and *as corn* blasted before it be grown up.

27 But I know thy abode, and thy going out, and thy coming in, and thy rage against me.

28 Because thy rage against me and thy tumult is come up into mine ears, therefore I will put my hook in thy nose, and my bridle in thy lips, and I will turn thee back by the way by which thou camest.

29 And this *shall be* a sign unto thee, Ye shall eat this year such things as grow of themselves, and in the second year that which springeth of the same; and in the third year sow ye, and reap, and plant vineyards, and eat the fruits thereof.

30 And the remnant that is escaped of the house of Ju'dah shall yet again take root downward, and bear fruit upward.

31 For out of Je-ru'sa-lem shall go forth a remnant, and they that escape out of mount Zi'-on: the zeal of the LORD *of hosts* shall do this.

32 Therefore thus saith the LORD concerning the king of As-syr'i-a, He shall not come into this city, nor shoot an arrow there, nor come before it with shield, nor cast a bank against it.

33 By the way that he came, by the same shall he return, and shall not come into this city, saith the LORD.

34 For I will defend this city, to save it, for mine own sake, and for my servant Da'vid's sake.

35 ¶ And it came to pass that night, that the angel of the LORD went out, and smote in the camp of the As-syr'i-ans an hundred fourscore and five thousand: and when they arose early in the morning, behold, they *were* all dead corpses.

36 So Sen-nach'e-rib king of As-syr'i-a departed, and went and returned, and dwelt at Nin'e-veh.

37 And it came to pass, as he was worshipping in the house of Nis'roch his god, that A-dram'me-lech and Sha-re'zer his sons smote him with the sword: and they escaped into the land of Ar-me'ni-a. And E'sar-had'don his son reigned in his stead.

20 IN those days was Hez-e-ki'ah sick unto death. And the prophet I-sa'iah the son of A'moz came to him, and said unto him, Thus saith the LORD, Set thine house in order; for thou shalt die, and not live.

2 Then he turned his face to the wall, and prayed unto the LORD, saying,

3 I beseech thee, O LORD, remember now how I have walked before thee in truth and with a perfect heart, and have done *that which is* good in thy sight. And Hez-e-ki'ah wept sore.

4 And it came to pass, afore I-sa'iah was gone out into the middle court, that the word of the LORD came to him, saying,

5 Turn again, and tell Hez-e-ki'ah the captain of my people, Thus saith the LORD, the God of Da'vid thy father, I have heard thy prayer, I have seen thy tears: behold, I will heal thee: on

the third day thou shalt go up unto the house of the LORD.

6 And I will add unto thy days fifteen years; and I will deliver thee and this city out of the hand of the king of As-syr'i-a; and I will defend this city for mine own sake, and for my servant Da'vid's sake.

7 And I-sa'iah said, Take a lump of figs. And they took and laid *it* on the boil, and he recovered.

8 ¶ And Hez-e-ki'ah said unto I-sa'iah, What *shall be* the sign that the LORD will heal me, and that I shall go up into the house of the LORD the third day?

9 And I-sa'iah said, This sign shalt thou have of the LORD, that the LORD will do the thing that he hath spoken: shall the shadow go forward ten degrees, or go back ten degrees?

10 And Hez-e-ki'ah answered, It is a light thing for the shadow to go down ten degrees: nay, but let the shadow return backward ten degrees.

11 And I-sa'iah the prophet cried unto the LORD: and he brought the shadow ten degrees backward, by which it had gone down in the dial of A'haz.

12 ¶ At that time Be-ro'dach–bal'a-dan, the son of Bal'a-dan, king of Bab'y-lon, sent letters and a present unto Hez-e-ki'ah: for he had heard that Hez-e-ki'ah had been sick.

13 And Hez-e-ki'ah hearkened unto them, and shewed them all the house of his precious things, the silver, and the gold, and the spices, and the precious ointment, and *all* the house of his armour, and all that was found in his treasures: there was nothing in his house, nor in all his dominion, that Hez-e-ki'ah shewed them not.

14 ¶ Then came I-sa'iah the prophet unto king Hez-e-ki'ah, and said unto him, What said these men? and from whence came they unto thee? And Hez-e-ki'ah said, They are come from a far country, *even* from Bab'y-lon.

15 And he said, What have they seen in thine house? And Hez-e-ki'ah answered, All *the things* that *are* in mine house have they seen: there is nothing among my treasures that I have not shewed them.

16 And I-sa'iah said unto Hez-e-ki'ah, Hear the word of the LORD.

17 Behold, the days come, that all that *is* in thine house, and that which thy fathers have laid up in store unto this day, shall be carried into Bab'y-lon: nothing shall be left, saith the LORD.

18 And of thy sons that shall issue from thee, which thou shalt beget, shall they take away; and they shall be eunuchs in the palace of the king of Bab'y-lon.

19 Then said Hez-e-ki'ah unto I-sa'iah, Good *is* the word of the LORD which thou hast spoken. And he said, *Is it* not *good*, if peace and truth be in my days?

20 ¶ And the rest of the acts of Hez-e-ki'ah, and all his might, and how he made a pool, and a conduit, and brought water into the city, *are* they not written in the book of the chronicles of the kings of Ju'dah?

21 And Hez-e-ki'ah slept with his fathers: and Ma-nas'seh his son reigned in his stead.

21 MA-NAS'SEH *was* twelve years old when he began to reign, and reigned fifty and five years in Je-ru'sa-lem. And his mother's name *was* Heph'zi–bah.

2 And he did *that which was* evil in the sight of the LORD, after the abominations of the heathen, whom the LORD cast out before the children of Is'ra-el.

3 For he built up again the high places which Hez-e-ki'ah his father had destroyed; and he reared up altars for Ba'al, and made a grove, as did A'hab king of Is'ra-el; and worshipped all the host of heaven, and served them.

4 And he built altars in the house of the LORD, of which the LORD said, In Je-ru'sa-lem will I put my name.

5 And he built altars for all the host of heaven in the two courts of the house of the LORD.

6 And he made his son pass through the fire, and observed times, and used enchantments, and dealt with familiar spirits and wizards: he wrought much wickedness in the sight of the LORD, to provoke *him* to anger.

7 And he set a graven image of the grove that he had made in the house, of which the LORD said to Da'vid, and to Sol'o-mon his son, In this house, and in Je-ru'sa-lem, which I have chosen out of all tribes of Is'ra-el, will I put my name for ever:

8 Neither will I make the feet of Is'ra-el move any more out of the land which I gave their fathers; only if they will observe to do according to all that I have commanded them, and according to all the law that my servant Mo'ses commanded them.

9 But they hearkened not: and Ma-nas'seh seduced them to do more evil than did the nations whom the LORD destroyed before the children of Is'ra-el.

10 ¶ And the LORD spake by his servants the prophets, saying,

11 Because Ma-nas'seh king of Ju'dah hath done these abominations, *and* hath done wickedly above all that the Am'or-ites did, which *were* before him, and hath made Ju'dah also to sin with his idols:

12 Therefore thus saith the LORD God of Is'ra-el, Behold, I *am* bringing *such* evil upon Je-ru'sa-lem and Ju'dah, that whosoever heareth of it, both his ears shall tingle.

13 And I will stretch over Je-ru'sa-lem the line of Sa-ma'ri-a, and the plummet of the house of A'hab: and I will wipe Je-ru'sa-lem as *a man* wipeth a dish, wiping *it*, and turning *it* upside down.

14 And I will forsake the remnant of mine inheritance, and deliver them into the hand of their enemies; and they shall become a prey and a spoil to all their enemies;

15 Because they have done *that which was* evil in my sight, and have provoked me to anger, since the day their fathers came forth out of E'gypt, even unto this day.

16 Moreover Ma-nas'seh shed innocent blood very much, till he had filled Je-ru'sa-lem from one end to another; beside his sin wherewith he made Ju'dah to sin, in doing *that which was* evil in the sight of the LORD.

17 ¶ Now the rest of the acts of Ma-nas'seh, and all that he did, and his sin that he sinned, *are* they not written in the book of the chronicles of the kings of Ju'dah?

18 And Ma-nas'seh slept with his fathers, and was buried in the garden of his own house, in the garden of Uz'za: and A'mon his son reigned in his stead.

19 ¶ A'mon *was* twenty and two years old when he began to reign, and he reigned two years in Je-ru'sa-lem. And his mother's name *was* Me-shul'le-meth, the daughter of Ha'ruz of Jot'bah.

20 And he did *that which was* evil in the sight of the LORD, as his father Ma-nas'seh did.

21 And he walked in all the way that his father walked in, and served the idols that his father served, and worshipped them:

22 And he forsook the LORD God of his fathers, and walked not in the way of the LORD.

23 ¶ And the servants of A'mon conspired against him, and slew the king in his own house.

24 And the people of the land slew all them that had conspired against king A'mon; and the people of the land made Jo-si'ah his son king in his stead.

25 Now the rest of the acts of A'mon which he did, *are* they not written in the book of the chronicles of the kings of Ju'dah?

26 And he was buried in his sepulchre in the garden of Uz'za: and Jo-si'ah his son reigned in his stead.

22

JO-SI'AH *was* eight years old when he began to reign, and he reigned thirty and one years in Je-ru'sa-lem. And his mother's name *was* Je-di'dah, the daughter of Ad-a-i'ah of Bos'cath.

2 And he did *that which was* right in the sight of the LORD, and walked in all the way of Da'vid his father, and turned not aside to the right hand or to the left.

3 ¶ And it came to pass in the eighteenth year of king Jo-si'ah, *that* the king sent Sha'phan the son of Az-a-li'ah, the son of Me-shul'lam, the scribe, to the house of the LORD, saying,

4 Go up to Hil-ki'ah the high priest, that he may sum the silver which is brought into the house of the LORD, which the keepers of the door have gathered of the people:

5 And let them deliver it into the hand of the doers of the work, that have the oversight of the house of the LORD: and let them give it to the doers of the work which *is* in the house of the LORD, to repair the breaches of the house,

6 Unto carpenters, and builders, and masons, and to buy timber and hewn stone to repair the house.

7 Howbeit there was no reckoning made with them of the money that was delivered into their hand, because they dealt faithfully.

8 ¶ And Hil-ki'ah the high priest said unto Sha'phan the scribe, I have found the book of the law in the house of the LORD. And Hil-ki'ah gave the book to Sha'phan, and he read it.

9 And Sha'phan the scribe came to the king, and brought the king word again, and said, Thy servants have gathered the money that was found in the house, and have delivered it into the hand of them that do the work, that have the oversight of the house of the LORD.

10 And Sha'phan the scribe shewed the king, saying, Hil-ki'ah the priest hath delivered me a book. And Sha'phan read it before the king.

11 And it came to pass, when the king had heard the words of the book of the law, that he rent his clothes.

12 And the king commanded Hil-ki'ah the priest, and A-hi'kam the son of Sha'phan, and Ach'bor the son of Mi-cha'iah, and Sha'phan the scribe, and A-sa-hi'ah a servant of the king's, saying,

13 Go ye, enquire of the LORD for me, and for the people, and for all Ju'dah, concerning the words of this book that is found: for great *is* the wrath of the LORD that is kindled against us, because our fathers have not hearkened unto the words of this book, to do according unto all that which is written concerning us.

14 So Hil-ki'ah the priest, and A-hi'kam, and Ach'bor, and Sha'phan, and A-sa-hi'ah, went unto Hul'dah the prophetess, the wife of Shal'lum the son of Tik'vah, the son of Har'has, keeper of the wardrobe; (now she dwelt in Je-ru'sa-lem in the college;) and they communed with her.

15 ¶ And she said to them, Thus saith the LORD God of Is'ra-el, Tell the man that sent you to me,

16 Thus saith the LORD, Behold, I will bring evil upon this place, and upon the inhabitants thereof, *even* all the words of the book which the king of Ju'dah hath read:

17 Because they have forsaken me, and have burned incense unto other gods, that they might provoke me to anger with all the works of their hands; therefore my wrath shall be kindled against this place, and shall not be quenched.

18 But to the king of Ju'dah which sent you to enquire of the LORD, thus shall ye say to him, Thus saith the LORD God of Is'ra-el, *As touching* the words which thou hast heard;

19 Because thine heart was tender, and thou hast humbled thyself before the LORD, when thou heardest what I spake against this place, and against the inhabitants thereof, that they should become a desolation and a curse, and hast rent thy clothes, and wept before me; I also have heard *thee,* saith the LORD.

20 Behold therefore, I will gather thee unto thy fathers, and thou shalt be gathered into thy grave in peace; and thine eyes shall not see all the evil which I will bring upon this place. And they brought the king word again.

23

AND the king sent, and they gathered unto him all the elders of Ju'dah and of Je-ru'sa-lem.

2 And the king went up into the house of the LORD, and all the men of Ju'dah and all the inhabitants of Je-ru'sa-lem with him, and the priests, and the prophets, and all the people, both small and great: and he read in their ears all the words of the book of the covenant which was found in the house of the LORD.

3 ¶ And the king stood by a pillar, and made a covenant before the LORD, to walk after the LORD, and to keep his commandments and his testimonies and his statutes with all *their* heart and all *their* soul, to perform the words of this covenant that were written in this book. And all the people stood to the covenant.

4 And the king commanded Hil-ki'ah the high priest, and the priests of the second order, and the keepers of the door, to bring forth out of the temple of the LORD all the vessels that were made for Ba'al, and for the grove, and for all the host of heaven: and he burned them without Je-ru'sa-lem in the fields of Kid'ron, and carried the ashes of them unto Beth'–el.

5 And he put down the idolatrous priests, whom the kings of Ju'dah had ordained to burn incense in the high places in the cities of Ju'dah, and in the places round about Je-ru'sa-lem; them also that burned incense unto Ba'al, to the sun, and to the moon, and to the planets, and to all the host of heaven.

6 And he brought out the grove from the house of the LORD, without Je-ru'sa-lem, unto the brook Kid'ron, and burned it at the brook Kid'ron, and stamped *it* small to powder, and cast the powder thereof upon the graves of the children of the people.

7 And he brake down the houses of the sodomites, that *were* by the house of the LORD, where the women wove hangings for the grove.

8 And he brought all the priests out of the cities of Ju'dah, and defiled the high places where the priests had burned incense, from Ge'ba to Be'er–she'ba, and brake down the high places of the gates that *were* in the entering in of the gate of Josh'u-a the governor of the city, which *were* on a man's left hand at the gate of the city.

9 Nevertheless the priests of the high places came not up to the altar of the LORD in Je-ru'sa-lem, but they did eat of the unleavened bread among their brethren.

10 And he defiled To'pheth, which *is* in the valley of the children of Hin'nom, that no man might make his son or his daughter to pass through the fire to Mo'lech.

11 And he took away the horses that the kings of Ju'dah had given to the sun, at the entering in of the house of the LORD, by the chamber of Na'than–me'lech the chamberlain, which *was* in the suburbs, and burned the chariots of the sun with fire.

12 And the altars that *were* on the top of the upper chamber of A'haz, which the kings of Ju'dah had made, and the altars which Ma-nas'seh had made in the two courts of the house of the LORD, did the king beat down, and brake *them* down from thence, and cast the dust of them into the brook Kid'ron.

13 And the high places that *were* before Je-ru'sa-lem, which *were* on the right hand of the mount of corruption, which Sol'o-mon the king of Is'ra-el had builded for Ash'to-reth the abomination of the Zi-do'ni-ans, and for Che'mosh the abomination of the Mo'ab-ites, and for Mil'com the abomination of the children of Am'mon, did the king defile.

14 And he brake in pieces the images, and cut down the groves, and filled their places with the bones of men.

15 ¶ Moreover the altar that *was* at Beth'–el, *and* the high place which Jer-o-bo'am the son of Ne'bat, who made Is'ra-el to sin, had made, both that altar and the high place he brake down, and burned the high place, *and* stamped *it* small to powder, and burned the grove.

16 And as Jo-si'ah turned himself, he spied the sepulchres that *were* there in the mount, and sent, and took the bones out of the sepulchres, and burned *them* upon the altar, and polluted it, according to the word of the LORD which the man of God proclaimed, who proclaimed these words.

17 Then he said, What title *is* that that I see? And the men of the city told him, *It is* the sepulchre of the man of God, which came from Ju'dah, and proclaimed these things that thou hast done against the altar of Beth'–el.

18 And he said, Let him alone; let no man move his bones. So they let his bones alone, with the bones of the prophet that came out of Sa-ma'ri-a.

19 And all the houses also of the high places that *were* in the cities of Sa-ma'ri-a, which the kings of Is'ra-el had made to provoke *the LORD* to anger, Jo-si'ah took away, and did to them according to all the acts that he had done in Beth'–el.

20 And he slew all the priests of the high places that *were* there upon the altars, and burned men's bones upon them, and returned to Je-ru'sa-lem.

21 ¶ And the king commanded all the people, saying, Keep the passover unto the LORD your God, as *it is* written in the book of this covenant.

22 Surely there was not holden such a passover from the days of the judges that judged Is'ra-el, nor in all the days of the kings of Is'ra-el, nor of the kings of Ju'dah;

23 But in the eighteenth year of king Jo-si'ah, *wherein* this passover was holden to the LORD in Je-ru'sa-lem.

24 ¶ Moreover, the *workers with* familiar spirits, and the wizards, and the images, and the idols, and all the abominations that were spied in the land of Ju'dah and in Je-ru'sa-lem, did Jo-si'ah put away, that he might perform the words of the law which were written in the book that Hil-ki'ah the priest found in the house of the LORD.

25 And like unto him was there no king before him, that turned to the LORD with all his heart, and with all his soul, and with all his might, according to all the law of Mo'ses; neither after him arose there *any* like him.

26 ¶ Notwithstanding the LORD turned not from the fierceness of his great wrath, wherewith his anger was kindled against Ju'dah, because of all the provocations that Ma-nas'seh had provoked him withal.

27 And the LORD said, I will remove Ju'dah also out of my sight, as I have removed Is'ra-el, and will cast off this city Je-ru'sa-lem which I have chosen, and the house of which I said, My name shall be there.

28 Now the rest of the acts of Jo-si'ah, and all that he did, *are* they not written in the book of the chronicles of the kings of Ju'dah?

29 ¶ In his days Pha'raoh–ne'choh king of E'gypt went up against the king of As-syr'i-a to the river Eu-phra'tes: and king Jo-si'ah went against him; and he slew him at Me-gid'do, when he had seen him.

30 And his servants carried him in a chariot dead from Me-gid'do, and brought him to Je-ru'sa-lem, and buried him in his own sepulchre. And the people of the land took Je-ho'a-haz the son of Jo-si'ah, and anointed him, and made him king in his father's stead.

31 ¶ Je-ho'a-haz *was* twenty and three years old when he began to reign; and he reigned three months in Je-ru'sa-lem. And his mother's name *was* Ha-mu'tal, the daughter of Jer-e-mi'ah of Lib'nah.

32 And he did *that which was* evil in the sight of the LORD, according to all that his fathers had done.

33 And Pha'raoh–ne'choh put him in bands at Rib'lah in the land of Ha'math, that he might not reign in Je-ru'sa-lem; and put the land to a tribute of an hundred talents of silver, and a talent of gold.

34 And Pha'raoh–ne'choh made E-li'a-kim the son of Jo-si'ah king in the room of Jo-si'ah his father, and turned his name to Je-hoi'a-kim, and took Je-ho'a-haz away: and he came to E'gypt, and died there.

35 And Je-hoi'a-kim gave the silver and the gold to Pha'raoh; but he taxed the land to give the money according to the commandment of Pha'raoh: he exacted the silver and the gold of the people of the land, of every one according to his taxation, to give *it* unto Pha'raoh–ne'choh.

36 ¶ Je-hoi'a-kim *was* twenty and five years old when he began to reign; and he reigned eleven years in Je-ru'sa-lem. And his mother's name *was* Ze-bu'dah, the daughter of Pe-da'iah of Ru'mah.

37 And he did *that which was* evil in the

sight of the LORD, according to all that his fathers had done.

24 IN his days Neb-u-chad-nez'zar king of
Bab'y-lon came up, and Je-hoi'a-kim became his servant three years: then he turned
and rebelled against him.
2 And the LORD sent against him bands of
the Chal'dees, and bands of the Syr'i-ans, and
bands of the Mo'ab-ites, and bands of the children of Am'mon, and sent them against Ju'dah
to destroy it, according to the word of the LORD,
which he spake by his servants the prophets.
3 Surely at the commandment of the LORD
came *this* upon Ju'dah, to remove *them* out of
his sight, for the sins of Ma-nas'seh, according
to all that he did;
4 And also for the innocent blood that he
shed: for he filled Je-ru'sa-lem with innocent
blood; which the LORD would not pardon.
5 ¶ Now the rest of the acts of Je-hoi'a-kim,
and all that he did, *are* they not written in the
book of the chronicles of the kings of Ju'dah?
6 So Je-hoi'a-kim slept with his fathers: and
Je-hoi'a-chin his son reigned in his stead.
7 And the king of E'gypt came not again any
more out of his land: for the king of Bab'y-lon
had taken from the river of E'gypt unto the
river Eu-phra'tes all that pertained to the king
of E'gypt.
8 ¶ Je-hoi'a-chin *was* eighteen years old
when he began to reign, and he reigned in Je-
ru'sa-lem three months. And his mother's name
was Ne-hush'ta, the daughter of El'na-than of
Je-ru'sa-lem.
9 And he did *that which was* evil in the sight
of the LORD, according to all that his father had
done.
10 ¶ At that time the servants of Neb-u-
chad-nez'zar king of Bab'y-lon came up against
Je-ru'sa-lem, and the city was besieged.
11 And Neb-u-chad-nez'zar king of Bab'y-lon
came against the city, and his servants did besiege it.
12 And Je-hoi'a-chin the king of Ju'dah went
out to the king of Bab'y-lon, he, and his mother,
and his servants, and his princes, and his officers: and the king of Bab'y-lon took him in the
eighth year of his reign.
13 And he carried out thence all the treasures of the house of the LORD, and the treasures of the king's house, and cut in pieces all
the vessels of gold which Sol'o-mon king of Is'-
ra-el had made in the temple of the LORD, as the
LORD had said.
14 And he carried away all Je-ru'sa-lem, and
all the princes, and all the mighty men of valour, *even* ten thousand captives, and all the
craftsmen and smiths: none remained, save the
poorest sort of the people of the land.
15 And he carried away Je-hoi'a-chin to
Bab'y-lon, and the king's mother, and the king's
wives, and his officers, and the mighty of the
land, *those* carried he into captivity from Je-ru'-
sa-lem to Bab'y-lon.
16 And all the men of might, *even* seven
thousand, and craftsmen and smiths a thousand, all *that were* strong *and* apt for war, even
them the king of Bab'y-lon brought captive to
Bab'y-lon.
17 ¶ And the king of Bab'y-lon made Mat-ta-
ni'ah his father's brother king in his stead, and
changed his name to Zed-e-ki'ah.
18 Zed-e-ki'ah *was* twenty and one years old
when he began to reign, and he reigned eleven
years in Je-ru'sa-lem. And his mother's name
was Ha-mu'tal, the daughter of Jer-e-mi'ah of
Lib'nah.
19 And he did *that which was* evil in the
sight of the LORD, according to all that Je-hoi'a-
kim had done.
20 For through the anger of the LORD it came
to pass in Je-ru'sa-lem and Ju'dah, until he had
cast them out from his presence, that Zed-e-ki'-
ah rebelled against the king of Bab'y-lon.

25 AND it came to pass in the ninth year of
his reign, in the tenth month, in the
tenth *day* of the month, *that* Neb-u-chad-nez'-
zar king of Bab'y-lon came, he, and all his host,
against Je-ru'sa-lem, and pitched against it; and
they built forts against it round about.
2 And the city was besieged unto the eleventh year of king Zed-e-ki'ah.
3 And on the ninth *day* of the *fourth* month
the famine prevailed in the city, and there was
no bread for the people of the land.
4 ¶ And the city was broken up, and all the
men of war *fled* by night by the way of the gate
between two walls, which *is* by the king's garden: (now the Chal'dees *were* against the city
round about:) and *the king* went the way
toward the plain.
5 And the army of the Chal'dees pursued after the king, and overtook him in the plains of
Jer'i-cho: and all his army was scattered from
him.
6 So they took the king, and brought him up
to the king of Bab'y-lon to Rib'lah; and they
gave judgment upon him.
7 And they slew the sons of Zed-e-ki'ah before his eyes, and put out the eyes of Zed-e-
ki'ah, and bound him with fetters of brass, and
carried him to Bab'y-lon.
8 ¶ And in the fifth month, on the seventh
day of the month, which *is* the nineteenth year
of king Neb-u-chad-nez'zar king of Bab'y-lon,
came Neb'u-zar–a'dan, captain of the guard, a
servant of the king of Bab'y-lon, unto Je-ru'sa-
lem:
9 And he burnt the house of the LORD, and
the king's house, and all the houses of Je-ru'sa-
lem, and every great *man's* house burnt he with
fire.
10 And all the army of the Chal'dees, that
were with the captain of the guard, brake down
the walls of Je-ru'sa-lem round about.
11 Now the rest of the people *that were* left
in the city, and the fugitives that fell away to
the king of Bab'y-lon, with the remnant of the
multitude, did Neb'u-zar–a'dan the captain of
the guard carry away.
12 But the captain of the guard left of the
poor of the land *to be* vinedressers and husbandmen.
13 And the pillars of brass that *were* in the
house of the LORD, and the bases, and the brasen sea that *was* in the house of the LORD, did
the Chal'dees break in pieces, and carried the
brass of them to Bab'y-lon.
14 And the pots, and the shovels, and the
snuffers, and the spoons, and all the vessels of
brass wherewith they ministered, took they
away.
15 And the firepans, and the bowls, *and* such
things as *were* of gold, *in* gold, and of silver, *in*
silver, the captain of the guard took away.
16 The two pillars, one sea, and the bases
which Sol'o-mon had made for the house of the
LORD; the brass of all these vessels was without
weight.
17 The height of the one pillar *was* eighteen

cubits, and the chapiter upon it *was* brass: and
the height of the chapiter three cubits; and the
wreathen work, and pomegranates upon the
chapiter round about, all of brass: and like unto
these had the second pillar with wreathen
work.
18 ¶ And the captain of the guard took Ser-
a-i'ah the chief priest, and Zeph-a-ni'ah the second priest, and the three keepers of the door:
19 And out of the city he took an officer that
was set over the men of war, and five men of
them that were in the king's presence, which
were found in the city, and the principal scribe
of the host, which mustered the people of the
land, and threescore men of the people of the
land *that were* found in the city:
20 And Neb'u-zar–a'dan captain of the guard
took these, and brought them to the king of
Bab'y-lon to Rib'lah:
21 And the king of Bab'y-lon smote them,
and slew them at Rib'lah in the land of Ha'-
math. So Ju'dah was carried away out of their
land.
22 ¶ And *as for* the people that remained in
the land of Ju'dah, whom Neb-u-chad-nez'zar
king of Bab'y-lon had left, even over them he
made Ged-a-li'ah the son of A-hi'kam, the son
of Sha'phan, ruler.
23 And when all the captains of the armies,
they and their men, heard that the king of Bab'-
y-lon had made Ged-a-li'ah governor, there
came to Ged-a-li'ah to Miz'pah, even Ish'ma-el
the son of Neth-a-ni'ah, and Jo-ha'nan the son
of Ca-re'ah, and Ser-a-i'ah the son of Tan'hu-
meth the Ne-toph'a-thite, and Ja-az-a-ni'ah the
son of a Ma-ach'a-thite, they and their men.
24 And Ged-a-li'ah sware to them, and to
their men, and said unto them, Fear not to be
the servants of the Chal'dees: dwell in the land,
and serve the king of Bab'y-lon; and it shall be
well with you.
25 But it came to pass in the seventh month,
that Ish'ma-el the son of Neth-a-ni'ah, the son
of E-lish'a-ma, of the seed royal, came, and ten
men with him, and smote Ged-a-li'ah, that he
died, and the Jews and the Chal'dees that were
with him at Miz'pah.
26 And all the people, both small and great,
and the captains of the armies, arose, and came
to E'gypt: for they were afraid of the Chal'dees.
27 ¶ And it came to pass in the seven and
thirtieth year of the captivity of Je-hoi'a-chin
king of Ju'dah, in the twelfth month, on the
seven and twentieth *day* of the month, *that* E'-
vil-me-ro'dach king of Bab'y-lon in the year
that he began to reign did lift up the head of Je-
hoi'a-chin king of Ju'dah out of prison;
28 And he spake kindly to him, and set his
throne above the throne of the kings that *were*
with him in Bab'y-lon;
29 And changed his prison garments: and he
did eat bread continually before him all the
days of his life.
30 And his allowance *was* a continual allowance given him of the king, a daily rate for every day, all the days of his life.

THE FIRST BOOK OF THE

CHRONICLES

1 AD'AM, Sheth, E'nosh,
2 Ke'nan, Ma-ha'la-le-el, Je'red,
3 He'noch, Me-thu'se-lah, La'mech,
4 No'ah, Shem, Ham, and Ja'pheth.
5 ¶ The sons of Ja'pheth; Go'mer, and Ma'-
gog, and Mad'a-i, and Ja'van, and Tu'bal, and
Me'shech, and Ti'ras.
6 And the sons of Go'mer; Ash'che-naz, and
Ri'phath, and To-gar'mah.
7 And the sons of Ja'van; E-li'shah, and Tar'-
shish, Kit'tim, and Dod'a-nim.
8 ¶ The sons of Ham; Cush, and Miz'ra-im,
Put, and Ca'naan.
9 And the sons of Cush; Se'ba, and Hav'i-lah,
and Sab'ta, and Ra'a-mah, and Sab'te-cha. And
the sons of Ra'a-mah; She'ba, and De'dan.
10 And Cush begat Nim'rod: he began to be
mighty upon the earth.
11 And Miz'ra-im begat Lu'dim, and An'a-
mim, and Le'ha-bim, and Naph'tu-him,
12 And Path-ru'sim, and Cas'lu-him, (of
whom came the Phi-lis'tines,) and Caph'tho-
rim.
13 And Ca'naan begat Zi'don his firstborn,
and Heth,
14 The Jeb'u-site also, and the Am'or-ite, and
the Gir'ga-shite,
15 And the Hi'vite, and the Ark'ite, and the
Sin'ite,
16 And the Ar'vad-ite, and the Zem'a-rite,
and the Ha'math-ite.
17 ¶ The sons of Shem; E'lam, and Assh'ur,
and Ar-phax'ad, and Lud, and A'ram, and Uz,
and Hul, and Ge'ther, and Me'shech.
18 And Ar-phax'ad begat She'lah, and She'-
lah begat E'ber.
19 And unto E'ber were born two sons: the
name of the one *was* Pe'leg; because in his days
the earth was divided: and his brother's name
was Jok'tan.
20 And Jok'tan begat Al-mo'dad, and She'-
leph, and Ha'zar–ma'veth, and Je'rah,
21 Ha-do'ram also, and U'zal, and Dik'lah,
22 And E'bal, and A-bim'a-el, and She'ba,
23 And O'phir, and Hav'i-lah, and Jo'bab. All
these *were* the sons of Jok'tan.
24 ¶ Shem, Ar-phax'ad, She'lah,
25 E'ber, Pe'leg, Re'u,
26 Se'rug, Na'hor, Te'rah,
27 A'bram; the same *is* A'bra-ham.
28 The sons of A'bra-ham; I'saac, and Ish'-
ma-el.
29 ¶ These *are* their generations: The firstborn of Ish'ma-el, Ne-ba'ioth; then Ke'dar, and
Ad'be-el, and Mib'sam,
30 Mish'ma, and Du'mah, Mas'sa, Ha'dad,
and Te'ma,
31 Je'tur, Na'phish, and Ked'e-mah. These
are the sons of Ish'ma-el.
32 ¶ Now the sons of Ke-tu'rah, A'bra-ham's
concubine: she bare Zim'ran, and Jok'shan, and
Me'dan, and Mid'i-an, and Ish'bak, and Shu'ah.
And the sons of Jok'shan; She'ba, and De'dan.
33 And the sons of Mid'i-an; E'phah, and E'-
pher, and He'noch, and A-bi'da, and El'da-ah.
All these *are* the sons of Ke-tu'rah.
34 And A'bra-ham begat I'saac. The sons of
I'saac; E'sau and Is'ra-el.
35 ¶ The son's of E'sau; El'i-phaz, Reu'el,
and Je'ush, and Ja-a'lam, and Ko'rah.
36 The sons of El'i-phaz; Te'man, and O'mar,

Ze'phi, and Ga'tam, Ke'naz, and Tim'na, and
Am'a-lek.
37 The sons of Reu'el; Na'hath, Ze'rah,
Sham'mah, and Miz'zah.
38 And the sons of Se'ir; Lo'tan, and Sho'bal,
and Zib'e-on, and A'nah, and Di'shon, and E'-
zar, and Di'shan.
39 And the sons of Lo'tan; Ho'ri, and Ho'-
mam: and Tim'na *was* Lo'tan's sister.
40 The sons of Sho'bal; A-li'an, and Man'a-
hath, and E'bal, She'phi, and O'nam. And the
sons of Zib'e-on; A-i'ah, and A'nah.
41 The sons of A'nah; Di'shon. And the sons
of Di'shon; Am'ram, and Esh'ban, and Ith'ran,
and Che'ran.
42 The sons of E'zer; Bil'han, and Za'van,
and Ja'kan. The sons of Di'shan; Uz, and A'ran.
43 ¶ Now these *are* the kings that reigned in
the land of E'dom before *any* king reigned over
the children of Is'ra-el; Be'la the son of Be'or:
and the name of his city *was* Din'ha-bah.
44 And when Be'la was dead, Jo'bab the son
of Ze'rah of Boz'rah reigned in his stead.
45 And when Jo'bab was dead, Hu'sham of
the land of the Te'man-ites reigned in his stead.
46 And when Hu'sham was dead, Ha'dad the
son of Be'dad, which smote Mid'i-an in the field
of Mo'ab, reigned in his stead: and the name of
his city *was* A'vith.
47 And when Ha'dad was dead, Sam'lah of
Mas're-kah reigned in his stead.
48 And when Sam'lah was dead, Sha'ul of
Re-ho'both by the river reigned in his stead.
49 And when Sha'ul was dead, Ba'al-ha'nan
the son of Ach'bor reigned in his stead.
50 And when Ba'al-ha'nan was dead, Ha'dad
reigned in his stead: and the name of his city
was Pa'i; and his wife's name *was* Me-het'a-bel,
the daughter of Ma'tred, the daughter of Mez'a-
hab.
51 ¶ Ha'dad died also. And the dukes of E'-
dom were; duke Tim'nah, duke A-li'ah, duke
Je'theth,
52 Duke A-ho-lib'a-mah, duke E'lah, duke
Pi'non,
53 Duke Ke'naz, duke Te'man, duke Mib'zar,
54 Duke Mag'di-el, duke I'ram. These *are* the
dukes of E'dom.

2 THESE *are* the sons of Is'ra-el; Reu'ben,
Sim'e-on, Le'vi, and Ju'dah, Is'sa-char, and
Zeb'u-lun,
2 Dan, Jo'seph, and Ben'ja-min, Naph'ta-li,
Gad, and Ash'er.
3 ¶ The sons of Ju'dah; Er, and O'nan, and
She'lah: *which* three were born unto him of the
daughter of Shu'a the Ca'naan-it-ess. And Er,
the firstborn of Ju'dah, was evil in the sight of
the LORD; and he slew him.
4 And Ta'mar his daughter in law bare him
Pha'rez and Ze'rah. All the sons of Ju'dah *were*
five.
5 The sons of Pha'rez; Hez'ron, and Ha'mul.
6 And the sons of Ze'rah; Zim'ri, and E'than,
and He'man, and Cal'col, and Da'ra: five of
them in all.
7 And the sons of Car'mi; A'char, the trou-
bler of Is'ra-el, who transgressed in the thing
accursed.
8 And the sons of E'than; Az-a-ri'ah.
9 The sons also of Hez'ron, that were born
unto him; Je-rah'me-el, and Ram, and Che-lu'-
bai.
10 And Ram begat Am-min'a-dab; and Am-
min'a-dab begat Nah'shon, prince of the children of Ju'dah;
11 And Nah'shon begat Sal'ma, and Sal'ma
begat Bo'az,
12 And Bo'az begat O'bed, and O'bed begat
Jes'se,
13 ¶ And Jes'se begat his firstborn E-li'ab,
and A-bin'a-dab the second, and Shim'ma the
third,
14 Ne-than'e-el the fourth, Rad'da-i the fifth,
15 O'zem the sixth, Da'vid the seventh:
16 Whose sisters *were* Zer-u-i'ah, and Ab'i-
gail. And the sons of Zer-u-i'ah; A-bish'a-i, and
Jo'ab, and A'sa-hel, three.
17 And Ab'i-gail bare Am'a-sa: and the father of Am'a-sa *was* Je'ther the Ish'me-el-ite.
18 ¶ And Ca'leb the son of Hez'ron begat
children of A-zu'bah *his* wife, and of Je'ri-oth:
her sons *are* these; Je'sher, and Sho'bab, and
Ar'don.
19 And when A-zu'bah was dead, Ca'leb took
unto him Eph'rath, which bare him Hur.
20 And Hur begat U'ri, and U'ri begat Be-
zal'e-el.
21 ¶ And afterward Hez'ron went in to the
daughter of Ma'chir the father of Gil'e-ad,
whom he married when he *was* threescore
years old; and she bare him Se'gub.
22 And Se'gub begat Ja'ir, who had three and
twenty cities in the land of Gil'e-ad.
23 And he took Ge'shur, and A'ram, with the
towns of Ja'ir, from them, with Ke'nath, and the
towns thereof, *even* threescore cities. All these
belonged to the sons of Ma'chir the father of
Gil'e-ad.
24 And after that Hez'ron was dead in Ca'-
leb-eph'ra-tah, then A-bi'ah Hez'ron's wife bare
him Ash'ur the father of Te-ko'a.
25 ¶ And the sons of Je-rah'me-el the firstborn of Hez'ron were, Ram the firstborn, and
Bu'nah, and O'ren, and O'zem, *and* A-hi'jah.
26 Je-rah'me-el had also another wife, whose
name *was* At'a-rah; she *was* the mother of O'-
nam.
27 And the sons of Ram the firstborn of Je-
rah'me-el were, Ma'az, and Ja'min, and E'ker.
28 And the sons of O'nam were, Sham'ma-i,
and Ja'da. And the sons of Sham'ma-i; Na'dab
and Ab'i-shur.
29 And the name of the wife of Ab'i-shur *was*
Ab-i-ha'il, and she bare him Ah'ban, and Mo'lid.
30 And the sons of Na'dab; Se'led, and Ap'-
pa-im: but Se'led died without children.
31 And the sons of Ap'pa-im; Ish'i. And the
sons of Ish'i; She'shan. And the children of
She'shan; Ah'lai.
32 And the sons of Ja'da the brother of
Sham'ma-i; Je'ther, and Jon'a-than: and Je'ther
died without children.
33 And the sons of Jon'a-than; Pe'leth, and
Za'za. These were the sons of Je-rah'me-el.
34 ¶ Now She'shan had no sons, but daughters. And She'shan had a servant, an E-gyp'tian,
whose name *was* Jar'ha.
35 And She'shan gave his daughter to Jar'ha
his servant to wife; and she bare him At'tai.
36 And At'tai begat Na'than, and Na'than begat Za'bad,
37 And Za'bad begat Eph'lal, and Eph'lal begat O'bed.
38 And O'bed begat Je'hu, and Je'hu begat
Az-a-ri'ah,
39 And Az-a-ri'ah begat He'lez, and He'lez
begat E-le'a-sah,
40 And E-le'a-sah begat Si-sam'a-i, and Si-
sam'a-i begat Shal'lum,
41 And Shal'lum begat Jek-a-mi'ah, and Jek-
a-mi'ah begat E-lish'a-ma.
42 ¶ Now the sons of Ca'leb the brother of

Je-rah'me-el *were,* Me'sha his firstborn, which
was the father of Ziph; and the sons of Ma-re'-
shah the father of He'bron.
43 And the sons of He'bron; Ko'rah, and
Tap'pu-ah, and Re'kem, and She'ma.
44 And She'ma begat Ra'ham, the father of
Jor'ko-am: and Re'kem begat Sham'ma-i.
45 And the son of Sham'ma-i *was* Ma'on: and
Ma'on *was* the father of Beth'-zur.
46 And E'phah, Ca'leb's concubine, bare Ha'-
ran, and Mo'za, and Ga'zez: and Ha'ran begat
Ga'zez.
47 And the sons of Jah'da-i; Re'gem, and Jo'-
tham, and Ge'sham, and Pe'let, and E'phah, and
Sha'aph.
48 Ma'a-chah, Ca'leb's concubine, bare She'-
ber, and Tir'ha-nah.
49 She bare also Sha'aph the father of Mad-
man'nah, She'va the father of Mach'be-nah, and
the father of Gib'e-a: and the daughter of Ca'leb
was Ach'sa.
50 ¶ These were the sons of Ca'leb the son of
Hur, the firstborn of Eph'ra-tah; Sho'bal the father of Kir'jath-je'a-rim,
51 Sal'ma the father of Beth'-le-hem, Ha'-
reph the father of Beth-ga'der.
52 And Sho'bal the father of Kir'jath-je'a-
rim had sons; Har'o-eh, *and* half of the Ma-na'-
heth-ites.
53 And the families of Kir'jath-je'a-rim; the
Ith'rites, and the Pu'hites, and the Shu'math-
ites, and the Mish'ra-ites; of them came the Za'-
re-ath-ites, and the Esh'ta-ul-ites.
54 The sons of Sal'ma; Beth'-le-hem, and the
Ne-toph'a-thites, At'a-roth, the house of Jo'ab,
and half of the Ma-na'heth-ites, the Zo'rites.
55 And the families of the scribes which
dwelt at Ja'bez; the Ti'rath-ites, the Shim'e-ath-
ites, *and* Su'chath-ites. These *are* the Ken'ites
that came of He'math, the father of the house of
Re'chab.

3 NOW these were the sons of Da'vid, which
were born unto him in He'bron; the firstborn Am'non, of A-hin'o-am the Jez're-el-it-ess;
the second Dan'iel, of Ab'i-gail the Car'mel-it-
ess:
2 The third, Ab'sa-lom the son of Ma'a-chah
the daughter of Tal'mai king of Ge'shur: the
fourth, Ad-o-ni'jah the son of Hag'gith:
3 The fifth, Sheph-a-ti'ah of Ab'i-tal: the
sixth, Ith're-am by Eg'lah his wife.
4 *These* six were born unto him in He'bron;
and there he reigned seven years and six
months: and in Je-ru'sa-lem he reigned thirty
and three years.
5 And these were born unto him in Je-ru'sa-
lem; Shim'e-a, and Sho'bab, and Na'than, and
Sol'o-mon, four, of Bath'-shu-a the daughter of
Am'mi-el:
6 Ib'har also, and E-lish'a-ma, and E-liph'e-
let,
7 And No'gah, and Ne'pheg, and Ja-phi'a,
8 And E-lish'a-ma, and E-li'a-da, and E-liph'-
e-let, nine.
9 *These were* all the sons of Da'vid, beside
the sons of the concubines, and Ta'mar their
sister.
10 ¶ And Sol'o-mon's son *was* Re-ho-bo'am,
A-bi'a his son, A'sa his son, Je-hosh'a-phat his
son,
11 Jo'ram his son, A-ha-zi'ah his son, Jo'ash
his son,
12 Am-a-zi'ah his son, Az-a-ri'ah his son, Jo'-
tham his son,
13 A'haz his son, Hez-e-ki'ah his son, Ma-
nas'seh his son,
14 A'mon his son, Jo-si'ah his son.
15 And the sons of Jo-si'ah *were,* the firstborn Jo-ha'nan, the second Je-hoi'a-kim, the
third Zed-e-ki'ah, the fourth Shal'lum.
16 And the sons of Je-hoi'a-kim: Jec-o-ni'ah
his son, Zed-e-ki'ah his son.
17 ¶ And the sons of Jec-o-ni'ah; As'sir, Sa-
la'-thi-el his son,
18 Mal-chi'ram also, and Pe-da'iah, and She-
na'zar, Jec-a-mi'ah, Hosh'a-ma, and Ned-a-bi'-
ah.
19 And the sons of Pe-da'iah *were,* Ze-rub'-
ba-bel, and Shim'e-i: and the sons of Ze-rub'ba-
bel; Me-shul'lam, and Han-a-ni'ah, and Shel'o-
mith their sister:
20 And Ha-shu'bah, and O'hel, and Ber-e-
chi'ah, and Has-a-di'ah, Ju'shab-he'sed, five.
21 And the sons of Han-a-ni'ah; Pel-a-ti'ah,
and Je-sa'iah: the sons of Reph-a-i'ah, the sons
of Ar'nan, the sons of O-ba-di'ah, the sons of
Shech-a-ni'ah.
22 And the sons of Shech-a-ni'ah; Shem-a-i'-
ah: and the sons of Shem-a-i'ah; Hat'tush, and
Ig'e-al, and Ba-ri'ah, and Ne-a-ri'ah, and Sha'-
phat, six.
23 And the sons of Ne-a-ri'ah; El-i-o-e'na-i,
and Hez-e-ki'ah, and Az'ri-kam, three.
24 And the sons of El-i-o-e'na-i *were,* Hod-a-
i'ah, and E-li'a-shib, and Pel-a-i'ah, and Ak'kub,
and Jo-ha'nan, and Dal-a-i'ah, and An-a'ni,
seven.

4 THE sons of Ju'dah; Pha'rez, Hez'ron, and
Car'mi, and Hur, and Sho'bal.
2 And Re-a-i'ah the son of Sho'bal begat Ja'-
hath; and Ja'hath begat A-hu'ma-i, and La'had.
These *are* the families of the Zo'rath-ites.
3 And these *were of* the father of E'tam; Jez'-
re-el, and Ish'ma, and Id'bash: and the name of
their sister *was* Haz-e-lel-po'ni:
4 And Pe-nu'el the father of Ge'dor, and E'zer
the father of Hu'shah. These *are* the sons of
Hur, the firstborn of Eph'ra-tah, the father of
Beth'-le-hem.
5 ¶ And Ash'ur the father of Te-ko'a had two
wives, He'lah and Na'a-rah.
6 And Na'a-rah bare him A-hu'zam, and He'-
pher, and Tem'e-ni, and Ha-a-hash'ta-ri. These
were the sons of Na'a-rah.
7 And the sons of He'lah *were,* Ze'reth, and
Jez'o-ar, and Eth-nan.
8 And Coz begat A'nub, and Zo-be'bah, and
the families of A-har'hel the son of Ha'rum.
9 ¶ And Ja'bez was more honourable than
his brethren: and his mother called his name
Ja'bez, saying, Because I bare him with sorrow.
10 And Ja'bez called on the God of Is'ra-el,
saying, Oh that thou wouldest bless me indeed,
and enlarge my coast, and that thine hand
might be with me, and that thou wouldest keep
me from evil, that it may not grieve me! And
God granted him that which he requested.
11 ¶ And Che'lub the brother of Shu'ah begat Me'hir, which *was* the father of Esh'ton.
12 And Esh'ton begat Beth-ra'pha, and Pa-
se'ah, and Te-hin'nah the father of Ir-na'hash.
These *are* the men of Re'chah.
13 And the sons of Ke'naz; Oth'ni-el, and
Ser-a-i'ah: and the sons of Oth'ni-el; Ha'thath.
14 And Me-on'o-thai begat Oph'rah: and Ser-
a-i'ah begat Jo'ab, the father of the valley of
Char'a-shim; for they were craftsmen.
15 And the sons of Ca'leb the son of Je-
phun'neh; I'ru, E'lah, and Na'am: and the sons
of E'lah, even Ke'naz.
16 And the sons of Je-ha-le'le-el; Ziph, and
Zi'phah, Tir'i-a, and A-sa're-el.

17 And the sons of Ez′ra *were,* Je′ther, and Me′red, and E′pher, and Ja′lon: and she bare Mir′i-am, and Sham′ma-i, and Ish′bah the father of Esh-te-mo′a.

18 And his wife Je-hu-di′jah bare Je′red the father of Ge′dor, and He′ber the father of So′-cho, and Je-ku′thi-el the father of Za-no′ah. And these *are* the sons of Bith′i-ah the daughter of Pha′raoh, which Me′red took.

19 And the sons of *his* wife Ho-di′ah the sister of Na′ham, the father of Kei′lah the Gar′-mite, and Esh-te-mo′a the Ma-ach′a-thite.

20 And the sons of Shi′mon *were,* Am′non, and Rin′nah, Ben–ha′nan, and Ti′lon. And the sons of Ish′i *were,* Zo′heth, and Ben–zo′heth.

21 ¶ The sons of She′lah the son of Ju′dah *were,* Er the father of Le′cah, and La′a-dah the father of Ma-re′shah, and the families of the house of them that wrought fine linen, of the house of Ash-be′a,

22 And Jo′kim, and the men of Cho′ze-ba, and Jo′ash, and Sa′raph, who had the dominion in Mo′ab, and Jash′u-bi–le′hem. And *these are* ancient things.

23 These *were* the potters, and those that dwelt among plants and hedges: there they dwelt with the king for his work.

24 ¶ The sons of Sim′e-on *were,* Ne-mu′el, and Ja′min, Ja′rib, Ze′rah, *and* Sha′ul:

25 Shal′lum his son, Mib′sam his son, Mish′-ma his son.

26 And the sons of Mish′ma; Ha-mu′el his son, Zac′chur his son, Shim′e-i his son.

27 And Shim′e-i had sixteen sons and six daughters; but his brethren had not many children, neither did all their family multiply, like to the children of Ju′dah.

28 And they dwelt at Be′er–she′ba, and Mol′-a-dah, and Ha′zar–shu′al,

29 And at Bil′hah, and at E′zem, and at To′-lad,

30 And at Beth-u′el, and at Hor′mah, and at Zik′lag,

31 And at Beth–mar′ca-both, and Ha′zar–su′-sim, and at Beth–bir′e-i, and at Sha-a-ra′im. These *were* their cities unto the reign of Da′vid.

32 And their villages *were,* E′tam, and A′in, Rim′mon, and To′chen, and A′shan, five cities:

33 And all their villages that *were* round about the same cities, unto Ba′al. These *were* their habitations, and their genealogy.

34 And Me-sho′bab, and Jam′lech, and Jo′-shah the son of Am-a-zi′ah,

35 And Jo′el, and Je′hu the son of Jos-i-bi′ah, the son of Ser-a-i′ah, the son of A′si-el,

36 And El-i-o-e′na-i, and Ja-ak′o-bah, and Jesh-o-ha-i′ah, and A-sa-i′ah, and A-di′el, and Je-sim′i-el, and Be-na′iah,

37 And Zi′za the son of Shi′phi, the son of Al′lon, the son of Je-da′iah, the son of Shim′ri, the son of Shem-a-i′ah;

38 These mentioned by *their* names *were* princes in their families: and the house of their fathers increased greatly.

39 ¶ And they went to the entrance of Ge′-dor, *even* unto the east side of the valley, to seek pasture for their flocks.

40 And they found fat pasture and good, and the land *was* wide, and quiet, and peaceable; for *they* of Ham had dwelt there of old.

41 And these written by name came in the days of Hez-e-ki′ah king of Ju′dah, and smote their tents, and the habitations that were found there, and destroyed them utterly unto this day, and dwelt in their rooms: because *there was* pasture there for their flocks.

42 And *some* of them, *even* of the sons of Sim′e-on, five hundred men, went to mount Se′-ir, having for their captains Pel-a-ti′ah, and Ne-a-ri′ah, and Reph-a-i′ah, and Uz′zi-el, the sons of Ish′i.

43 And they smote the rest of the Am′a-lek-ites that were escaped, and dwelt there unto this day.

5 NOW the sons of Reu′ben the firstborn of Is′ra-el, (for he *was* the firstborn; but, forasmuch as he defiled his father's bed, his birthright was given unto the sons of Jo′seph the son of Is′ra-el: and the genealogy is not to be reckoned after the birthright.

2 For Ju′dah prevailed above his brethren, and of him *came* the chief ruler; but the birthright *was* Jo′seph's:)

3 The sons, *I say,* of Reu′ben the firstborn of Is′ra-el *were,* Ha′noch, and Pal′lu, Hez′ron, and Car′mi.

4 The sons of Jo′el; Shem-a-i′ah his son, Gog his son, Shim′e-i his son,

5 Mi′cah his son, Re-a-i′a his son, Ba′al his son,

6 Be-e′rah his son, whom Til′gath–pil-ne′ser king of As-syr′i-a carried away *captive:* he *was* prince of the Reu′ben-ites.

7 And his brethren by their families, when the genealogy of their generations was reckoned, *were* the chief, Je-i′el, and Zech-a-ri′ah,

8 And Be′la the son of A′zaz, the son of She′-ma, the son of Jo′el, who dwelt in Ar′o-er, even unto Ne′bo and Ba′al–me′on:

9 And eastward he inhabited unto the entering in of the wilderness from the river Eu-phra′-tes: because their cattle were multiplied in the land of Gil′e-ad.

10 And in the days of Saul they made war with the Ha′gar-ites, who fell by their hand: and they dwelt in their tents throughout all the east *land* of Gil′e-ad.

11 ¶ And the children of Gad dwelt over against them, in the land of Ba′shan unto Sal′-cah:

12 Jo′el the chief, and Sha′pham the next, and Ja-a′nai, and Sha′phat in Ba′shan.

13 And their brethren of the house of their fathers *were,* Mi′chael, and Me-shul′lam, and She′ba, and Jo′ra-i, and Ja′chan, and Zi′a, and He′ber, seven.

14 These *are* the children of Ab-i-ha′il the son of Hu′ri, the son of Ja-ro′ah, the son of Gil′-e-ad, the son of Mi′chael, the son of Je-shish′a-i, the son of Jah′do, the son of Buz;

15 A′hi the son of Ab′di-el, the son of Gu′ni, chief of the house of their fathers.

16 And they dwelt in Gil′e-ad in Ba′shan, and in her towns, and in all the suburbs of Shar′on, upon their borders.

17 All these were reckoned by genealogies in the days of Jo′tham king of Ju′dah, and in the days of Jer-o-bo′am king of Is′ra-el.

18 ¶ The sons of Reu′ben, and the Gad′ites, and half the tribe of Ma-nas′seh, of valiant men, men able to bear buckler and sword, and to shoot with bow, and skilful in war, *were* four and forty thousand seven hundred and threescore, that went out to war.

19 And they made war with the Ha′gar-ites, with Je′tur, and Ne′phish, and No′dab.

20 And they were helped against them, and the Ha′gar-ites were delivered into their hand, and all that *were* with them: for they cried to God in the battle, and he was intreated of them; because they put their trust in him.

21 And they took away their cattle; of their camels fifty thousand, and of sheep two hun-

dred and fifty thousand, and of asses two thousand, and of men an hundred thousand.
22 For there fell down many slain, because
the war *was* of God. And they dwelt in their
steads until the captivity.
23 ¶ And the children of the half tribe of Ma-
nas'seh dwelt in the land: they increased from
Ba'shan unto Ba'al-her'mon and Se'nir, and
unto mount Her'mon.
24 And these *were* the heads of the house of
their fathers, even E'pher, and Ish'i, and E-li'el,
and Az'ri-el, and Jer-e-mi'ah, and Hod-a-vi'ah,
and Jah'di-el, mighty men of valour, famous
men, *and* heads of the house of their fathers.
25 ¶ And they transgressed against the God
of their fathers, and went a whoring after the
gods of the people of the land, whom God destroyed before them.
26 And the God of Is'ra-el stirred up the
spirit of Pul king of As-syr'i-a, and the spirit of
Til'gath-pil-ne'ser king of As-syr'i-a, and he
carried them away, even the Reu'ben-ites, and
the Gad'ites, and the half tribe of Ma-nas'seh,
and brought them unto Ha'lah, and Ha'bor, and
Ha'ra, and to the river Go'zan, unto this day.

6 THE sons of Le'vi; Ger'shon, Ko'hath, and
Me-ra'ri.
2 And the sons of Ko'hath; Am'ram, Iz'har,
and He'bron, and Uz'zi-el.
3 And the children of Am'ram; Aar'on, and
Mo'ses, and Mir'i-am. The sons also of Aar'on;
Na'dab, and A-bi'hu, E-le-a'zar, and Ith'a-mar.
4 ¶ E-le-a'zar begat Phin'e-has, Phin'e-has
begat A-bish'u-a,
5 And A-bish'u-a begat Buk'ki, and Buk'ki
begat Uz'zi,
6 And Uz'zi begat Zer-a-hi'ah, and Zer-a-hi'-
ah begat Me-ra'ioth,
7 Me-ra'ioth begat Am-a-ri'ah, and Am-a-ri'-
ah begat A-hi'tub,
8 And A-hi'tub begat Za'dok, and Za'dok begat A-him'a-az,
9 And A-him'a-az begat Az-a-ri'ah, and Az-a-
ri'ah begat Jo-ha'nan,
10 And Jo-ha'nan begat Az-a-ri'ah, (he *it is*
that executed the priest's office in the temple
that Sol'o-mon built in Je-ru'sa-lem:)
11 And Az-a-ri'ah begat Am-a-ri'ah, and Am-
a-ri'ah begat A-hi'tub,
12 And A-hi'tub begat Za'dok, and Za'dok
begat Shal'lum,
13 And Shal'lum begat Hil-ki'ah, and Hil-ki'-
ah begat Az-a-ri'ah,
14 And Az-a-ri'ah begat Ser-a-i'ah, and Ser-
a-i'ah begat Je-hoz'a-dak,
15 And Je-hoz'a-dak went *into captivity,*
when the LORD carried away Ju'dah and Je-ru'-
sa-lem by the hand of Neb-u-chad-nez'zar.
16 ¶ The sons of Le'vi; Ger'shom, Ko'hath,
and Me-ra'ri.
17 And these *be* the names of the sons of
Ger'shom; Lib'ni, and Shim'e-i.
18 And the sons of Ko'hath *were,* Am'ram,
and Iz'har, and He'bron, and Uz'zi-el.
19 The sons of Me-ra'ri; Mah'li, and Mu'shi.
And these *are* the families of the Le'vites according to their fathers.
20 Of Ger'shom; Lib'ni his son, Ja'hath his
son, Zim'mah his son,
21 Jo'ah his son, Id'do his son, Ze'rah his son,
Je-at'e-rai his son.
22 The sons of Ko'hath; Am-min'a-dab his
son, Ko'rah his son, As'sir his son,
23 El'ka-nah his son, and E-bi'a-saph his son,
and As'sir his son,
24 Ta'hath his son, U'ri-el his son, Uz-zi'ah
his son, and Sha'ul his son.
25 And the sons of El'ka-nah; A-mas'a-i, and
A-hi'moth.
26 *As for* El'ka-nah: the sons of El'ka-nah;
Zo'phai his son, and Na'hath his son,
27 E-li'ab his son, Jer'o-ham his son, El'ka-
nah his son.
28 And the sons of Sam'u-el; the firstborn
Vash'ni, and A-bi'ah.
29 The sons of Me-ra'ri; Mah'li, Lib'ni his
son, Shim'e-i his son, Uz'za his son,
30 Shim'e-a his son, Hag-gi'ah his son, A-sa-
i'ah his son.
31 And these *are they* whom Da'vid set over
the service of song in the house of the LORD,
after that the ark had rest.
32 And they ministered before the dwelling
place of the tabernacle of the congregation with
singing, until Sol'o-mon had built the house of
the LORD in Je-ru'sa-lem: and *then* they waited
on their office according to their order.
33 And these *are* they that waited with their
children. Of the sons of the Ko'hath-ites: He'-
man a singer, the son of Jo'el, the son of She-
mu'el,
34 The son of El'ka-nah, the son of Jer'o-
ham, the son of E-li'el, the son of To'ah,
35 The son of Zuph, the son of El'ka-nah, the
son of Ma'hath, the son of A-mas'a-i,
36 The son of El'ka-nah, the son of Jo'el, the
son of Az-a-ri'ah, the son of Zeph-a-ni'ah,
37 The son of Ta'hath, the son of As'sir, the
son of E-bi'a-saph, the son of Ko'rah,
38 The son of Iz'har, the son of Ko'hath, the
son of Le'vi, the son of Is'ra-el.
39 And his brother A'saph, who stood on his
right hand, *even* A'saph the son of Ber-a-chi'ah,
the son of Shim'e-a,
40 The son of Mi'chael, the son of Ba-a-se'-
iah, the son of Mal-chi'ah,
41 The son of Eth'ni, the son of Ze'rah, the
son of Ad-a-i'ah,
42 The son of E'than, the son of Zim'mah, the
son of Shim'e-i,
43 The son of Ja'hath, the son of Ger'shom,
the son of Le'vi.
44 And their brethren the sons of Me-ra'ri
stood on the left hand: E'than the son of Kish'i,
the son of Ab'di, the son of Mal'luch,
45 The son of Hash-a-bi'ah, the son of Am-a-
zi'ah, the son of Hil-ki'ah,
46 The son of Am'zi, the son of Ba'ni, the son
of Sha'mer,
47 The son of Mah'li, the son of Mu'shi, the
son of Me-ra'ri, the son of Le'vi.
48 Their brethren also the Le'vites *were* appointed unto all manner of service of the tabernacle of the house of God.
49 ¶ But Aar'on and his sons offered upon
the altar of the burnt offering, and on the altar
of incense, *and were appointed* for all the work
of the *place* most holy, and to make an atonement for Is'ra-el, according to all that Mo'ses
the servant of God had commanded.
50 And these *are* the sons of Aar'on; E-le-a'-
zar his son, Phin'e-has his son, A-bish'u-a his
son,
51 Buk'ki his son, Uz'zi his son, Zer-a-hi'ah
his son,
52 Me-ra'ioth his son, Am-a-ri'ah his son, A-
hi'tub his son,
53 Za'dok his son, A-him'a-az his son.
54 ¶ Now these *are* their dwelling places
throughout their castles in their coasts, of the
sons of Aar'on, of the families of the Ko'hath-
ites: for theirs was the lot.

55 And they gave them He'bron in the land of Ju'dah, and the suburbs thereof round about it.

56 But the fields of the city, and the villages thereof, they gave to Ca'leb the son of Je-phun'-neh.

57 And to the sons of Aar'on they gave the cities of Ju'dah, *namely*, He'bron, *the city* of refuge, and Lib'nah with her suburbs, and Jat'-tir, and Esh-te-mo'a, with their suburbs,

58 And Hi'len with her suburbs, De'bir with her suburbs,

59 And A'shan with her suburbs, and Beth-she'mesh with her suburbs:

60 And out of the tribe of Ben'ja-min; Ge'ba with her suburbs, and Al'e-meth with her suburbs, and An'a-thoth with her suburbs. All their cities throughout their families *were* thirteen cities.

61 And unto the sons of Ko'hath, *which were* left of the family of that tribe, *were cities given* out of the half tribe, *namely, out of* the half *tribe* of Ma-nas'seh, by lot, ten cities.

62 And to the sons of Ger'shom throughout their families out of the tribe of Is'sa-char, and out of the tribe of Ash'er, and out of the tribe of Ma-nas'seh in Ba'shan, thirteen cities.

63 Unto the sons of Me-ra'ri *were given* by lot, throughout their families, out of the tribe of Reu'ben, and out of the tribe of Gad, and out of the tribe of Zeb'u-lun, twelve cities.

64 And the children of Is'ra-el gave to the Le'vites *these* cities with their suburbs.

65 And they gave by lot out of the tribe of the children of Ju'dah, and out of the tribe of the children of Sim'e-on, and out of the tribe of the children of Ben'ja-min, these cities, which are called by *their* names.

66 And *the residue* of the families of the sons of Ko'hath had cities of their coasts out of the tribe of E'phra-im.

67 And they gave unto them, *of* the cities of refuge, Shechem in mount E'phra-im with her suburbs; *they gave* also Ge'zer with her suburbs,

68 And Jok'me-am with her suburbs, and Beth-ho'ron with her suburbs.

69 And Aij'a-lon with her suburbs, and Gath-rim'mon with her suburbs:

70 And out of the half tribe of Ma-nas'seh; A'ner with her suburbs, and Bil'e-am with her suburbs, for the family of the remnant of the sons of Ko'hath.

71 Unto the sons of Ger'shom *were given* out of the family of the half tribe of Ma-nas'seh, Go'lan in Ba'shan with her suburbs, and Ash'ta-roth with her suburbs:

72 And out of the tribe of Is'sa-char; Ke'desh with her suburbs, Dab'e-rath with her suburbs,

73 And Ra'moth with her suburbs, and A'-nem with her suburbs:

74 And out of the tribe of Ash'er; Ma'shal with her suburbs, and Ab'don with her suburbs,

75 And Hu'kok with her suburbs, and Re'hob with her suburbs:

76 And out of the tribe of Naph'ta-li; Ke'desh in Gal'i-lee with her suburbs, and Ham'mon with her suburbs, and Kir-jath-a'im with her suburbs.

77 Unto the rest of the children of Me-ra'ri *were given* out of the tribe of Zeb'u-lun, Rim'-mon with her suburbs, Ta'bor with her suburbs:

78 And on the other side Jor'dan by Jer'i-cho, on the east side of Jor'dan, *were given them* out of the tribe of Reu'ben, Be'zer in the wilderness with her suburbs, and Jah'zah with her suburbs,

79 Ked'e-moth also with her suburbs, and Meph'a-ath with her suburbs:

80 And out of the tribe of Gad; Ra'moth in Gil'e-ad with her suburbs, and Ma-ha-na'im with her suburbs,

81 And Hesh'bon with her suburbs, and Ja'-zer with her suburbs.

7 NOW the sons of Is'sa-char *were*, To'la, and Pu'ah, Jash'ub, and Shim'rom, four.

2 And the sons of To'la; Uz'zi, and Reph-a-i'ah, and Je'ri-el, and Jah'ma-i, and Jib'sam, and She-mu'el, heads of their father's house, *to wit*, of To'la: *they were* valiant men of might in their generations; whose number *was* in the days of Da'vid two and twenty thousand and six hundred.

3 And the sons of Uz'zi; Iz-ra-hi'ah: and the sons of Iz-ra-hi'ah; Mi'chael, and O-ba-di'ah, and Jo'el, Ish-i'ah, five: all of them chief men.

4 And with them, by their generations, after the house of their fathers, *were* bands of soldiers for war, six and thirty thousand *men*: for they had many wives and sons.

5 And their brethren among all the families of Is'sa-char *were* valiant men of might, reckoned in all by their genealogies fourscore and seven thousand.

6 ¶ *The sons* of Ben'ja-min; Be'la, and Be'-cher, and Je-di'a-el, three.

7 And the sons of Be'la; Ez'bon, and Uz'zi, and Uz'zi-el, and Jer'i-moth, and I'ri, five; heads of the house of *their* fathers, mighty men of valour; and were reckoned by their genealogies twenty and two thousand and thirty and four.

8 And the sons of Be'cher; Ze-mi'ra, and Jo'-ash, and E-li-e'zer, and El-i-o-e'na-i, and Om'ri, and Jer'i-moth, and A-bi'ah, and An'a-thoth, and Al'a-meth. All these *are* the sons of Be'cher.

9 And the number of them, after their genealogy by their generations, heads of the house of their fathers, mighty men of valour, *was* twenty thousand and two hundred.

10 The sons also of Je-di'a-el; Bil'han: and the sons of Bil'han; Je'ush, and Ben'ja-min, and E'-hud, and Che-na'a-nah, and Ze'than, and Thar'-shish, and A-hish'a-har.

11 All these the sons of Je-di'a-el, by the heads of their fathers, mighty men of valour, *were* seventeen thousand and two hundred *soldiers*, fit to go out for war *and* battle.

12 Shup'pim also, and Hup'pim, the children of Ir, *and* Hu'shim, the sons of A'her.

13 ¶ The sons of Naph'ta-li; Jah'zi-el, and Gu'ni, and Je'zer, and Shal'lum, the sons of Bil'-hah.

14 ¶ The sons of Ma-nas'seh; Ash'ri-el, whom she bare: (*but* his concubine the A'ram-it-ess bare Ma'chir the father of Gil'e-ad:

15 And Ma'chir took to wife *the sister* of Hup'pim and Shup'pim, whose sister's name *was* Ma'a-chah;) and the name of the second *was* Ze-lo'phe-had: and Ze-lo'phe-had had daughters.

16 And Ma'a-chah the wife of Ma'chir bare a son, and she called his name Pe'resh; and the name of his brother *was* She'resh; and his sons *were* U'lam and Ra'kem.

17 And the sons of U'lam; Be'dan. These *were* the sons of Gil'e-ad, the son of Ma'chir, the son of Ma-nas'seh.

18 And his sister Ham-mol'e-keth bare I'-shod, and A-bi-e'zer, and Ma-ha'lah.

19 And the sons of She-mi'dah were, A-hi'an, and She'chem, and Lik'hi, and A'ni-am.

20 ¶ And the sons of E'phra-im; Shu'the-lah,

and Be'red his son, and Ta'hath his son, and El'-
a-dah his son, and Ta'hath his son,
21 ¶ And Za'bad his son, and Shu'the-lah his
son, and E'zer, and E'le-ad, whom the men of
Gath *that were* born in *that* land slew, because
they came down to take away their cattle.
22 And E'phra-im their father mourned many
days, and his brethren came to comfort him.
23 ¶ And when he went in to his wife, she
conceived, and bare a son, and he called his
name Be-ri'ah, because it went evil with his
house.
24 (And his daughter *was* She'rah, who built
Beth–ho'ron the nether, and the upper, and Uz'-
zen–she'rah.)
25 And Re'phah *was* his son, also Re'sheph,
and Te'lah his son, and Ta'han his son,
26 La'a-dan his son, Am-mi'hud his son, E-
lish'a-ma his son,
27 Non his son, Je-hosh'u-ah his son.
28 ¶ And their possessions and habitations
were, Beth'–el and the towns thereof, and eastward Na'a-ran, and westward Ge'zer, with the
towns thereof; She'chem also and the towns
thereof, unto Ga'za and the towns thereof:
29 And by the borders of the children of Ma-
nas'seh, Beth–she'an and her towns, Ta'a-nach
and her towns, Me-gid'do and her towns, Dor
and her towns. In these dwelt the children of
Jo'seph the son of Is'ra-el.
30 ¶ The sons of Ash'er; Im'nah, and Is'u-ah,
and Ish'u-ai, and Be-ri'ah, and Se'rah their sister.
31 And the sons of Be-ri'ah; He'ber, and Mal'-
chi-el, who *is* the father of Bir'za-vith.
32 And He'ber begat Japh'let, and Sho'mer,
and Ho'tham, and Shu'a their sister.
33 And the sons of Japh'let; Pa'sach, and
Bim'hal, and Ash'vath. These *are* the children of
Japh'let.
34 And the sons of Sha'mer; A'hi, and Roh'-
gah, Je-hub'bah, and A'ram.
35 And the sons of his brother He'lem; Zo'-
phah, and Im'na, and She'lesh, and A'mal.
36 The sons of Zo'phah; Su'ah, and Har'ne-
pher, and Shu'al, and Be'ri, and Im'rah,
37 Be'zer, and Hod, and Sham'ma, and Shil'-
shah, and Ith'ran, and Be-e'ra.
38 And the sons of Je'ther; Je-phun'neh, and
Pis'pah, and A'ra.
39 And the sons of Ul'la; A'rah, and Han'i-el,
and Re-zi'a.
40 All these *were* the children of Ash'er,
heads of *their* father's house, choice *and* mighty
men of valour, chief of the princes. And the
number throughout the genealogy of them that
were apt to the war *and* to battle *was* twenty
and six thousand men.

8 NOW Ben'ja-min begat Be'la his firstborn,
Ash'bel the second, and A-har'ah the third,
2 No'hah the fourth, and Ra'pha the fifth.
3 And the sons of Be'la were, Ad'dar, and
Ge'ra, and A-bi'hud,
4 And A-bish'u-a, and Na'a-man, and A-ho'-
ah,
5 And Ge'ra, and She-phu'phan, and Hu'ram.
6 And these *are* the sons of E'hud: these are
the heads of the fathers of the inhabitants of
Ge'ba, and they removed them to Man'a-hath:
7 And Na'a-man, and A-hi'ah, and Ge'ra, he
removed them, and begat Uz'za, and A-hi'hud.
8 And Sha-ha-ra'im begat *children* in the
country of Mo'ab, after he had sent them away;
Hu'shim and Ba'a-ra *were* his wives.
9 And he begat of Ho'desh his wife, Jo'bab,
and Zib'i-a, and Me'sha, and Mal'cham,
10 And Je'uz, and Shach-i'a and Mir'ma.
These *were* his sons, heads of the fathers.
11 And of Hu'shim he begat Ab'i-tub, and El'-
pa-al.
12 The sons of El'pa-al; E'ber, and Mi'sham,
and Sha'med, who built O'no, and Lod, with the
towns thereof:
13 Be-ri'ah also, and She'ma, who *were*
heads of the fathers of the inhabitants of Aij'a-
lon, who drove away the inhabitants of Gath:
14 And A-hi'o, Sha'shak, and Jer'e-moth,
15 And Zeb-a-di'ah, and A'rad, and A'der,
16 And Mi'chael, and Is'pah, and Jo'ha, the
sons of Be-ri'ah;
17 And Zeb-a-di'ah, and Me-shul'lam, and
Hez'e-ki, and He'ber,
18 Ish'me-rai also, and Jez-li'ah, and Jo'bab,
the sons of El'pa-al;
19 And Ja'kim, and Zich'ri, and Zab'di,
20 And E-li-e'na-i, and Zil'thai, and E-li'el,
21 And Ad-a-i'ah, and Ber-a-i'ah, and Shim'-
rath, the sons of Shim'hi;
22 And Ish'pan, and He'ber, and E-li'el,
23 And Ab'don, and Zich'ri, and Ha'nan,
24 And Han-a-ni'ah, and E'lam, and An-to-
thi'jah,
25 And Iph-e-de'iah, and Pe-nu'el, the sons of
Sha'shak:
26 And Sham-she-ra'i, and She-ha-ri'ah, and
Ath-a-li'ah,
27 And Jar'e-si'ah, and E-li'ah, and Zich'ri,
the sons of Jer'o-ham.
28 These *were* heads of the fathers, by their
generations, chief *men*. These dwelt in Je-ru'sa-
lem.
29 And at Gib'e-on dwelt the father of Gib'e-
on; whose wife's name *was* Ma'a-chah:
30 And his firstborn son Ab'don, and Zur,
and Kish, and Ba'al, and Na'dab,
31 And Ge'dor, and A-hi'o, and Za'cher.
32 And Mik'loth begat Shim'e-ah. And these
also dwelt with their brethren in Je-ru'sa-lem,
over against them.
33 ¶ And Ner begat Kish, and Kish begat
Saul, and Saul begat Jon'a-than, and Mal-chi-
shu'a, and A-bin'a-dab, and Esh-ba'al.
34 And the son of Jon'a-than *was* Mer'ib–ba'-
al: and Mer'ib–ba'al begat Mi'cah.
35 And the sons of Mi'cah *were,* Pi'thon, and
Me'lech, and Ta're-a, and A'haz.
36 And A'haz begat Je-ho'a-dah; and Je-ho'a-
dah begat Al'e-meth, and Az'ma-veth, and
Zim'ri; and Zim'ri begat Mo'za,
37 And Mo'za begat Bin'e-a: Ra'pha *was* his
son, E-le'a-sah his son, A'zel his son:
38 And A'zel had six sons, whose names *are*
these, Az'ri-kam, Boch'e-ru, and Ish'ma-el, and
She-a-ri'ah, and O-ba-di'ah, and Ha'nan. All
these *were* the sons of A'zel.
39 And the sons of E'shek his brother *were,*
U'lam his firstborn, Je'nush the second, and E-
liph'e-let the third.
40 And the sons of U'lam were mighty men
of valour, archers, and had many sons, and
sons' sons, an hundred and fifty. All these *are* of
the sons of Ben'ja-min.

9 SO all Is'ra-el were reckoned by genealogies; and, behold, they *were* written in the
book of the kings of Is'ra-el and Ju'dah, *who*
were carried away to Bab'y-lon for their transgression.
2 ¶ Now the first inhabitants that *dwelt* in
their possessions in their cities *were,* the Is'ra-
el-ites, the priests, Le'vites, and the Neth'i-
nims.
3 And in Je-ru'sa-lem dwelt of the children of

Ju'dah, and of the children of Ben'ja-min, and of
the children of E'phra-im, and Ma-nas'seh;
4 U'tha-i the son of Am-mi'hud, the son of
Om'ri, the son of Im'ri, the son of Ba'ni, of the
children of Pha'rez the son of Ju'dah.
5 And of the Shi'lo-nites; A-sa-i'ah the firstborn, and his sons.
6 And of the sons of Ze'rah; Je-u'el, and their
brethren, six hundred and ninety.
7 And of the sons of Ben'ja-min; Sal'lu the
son of Me-shul'lam, the son of Hod-a-vi'ah, the
son of Has-e-nu'ah,
8 And Ib-ne'iah the son of Jer'o-ham, and E'-
lah the son of Uz'zi, the son of Mich'ri, and Me-
shul'lam the son of Sheph-a-thi'ah, the son of
Re-u'el, the son of Ib-ni'jah;
9 And their brethren, according to their generations, nine hundred and fifty and six. All
these men *were* chief of the fathers in the house
of their fathers.
10 ¶ And of the priests; Je-da'iah, and Je-
hoi'a-rib, and Ja'chin,
11 And Az-a-ri'ah the son of Hil-ki'ah, the
son of Me-shul'lam, the son of Za'dok, the son
of Me-ra'ioth, the son of A-hi'tub, the ruler of
the house of God;
12 And Ad-a-i'ah the son of Jer'o-ham, the
son of Pash'ur, the son of Mal-chi'jah, and Ma-
as'i-ai the son of A-di'el, the son of Jah'ze-rah,
the son of Me-shul'lam, the son of Me-shil'le-
mith, the son of Im'mer;
13 And their brethren, heads of the house of
their fathers, a thousand and seven hundred
and threescore; very able men for the work of
the service of the house of God.
14 And of the Le'vites; Shem-a-i'ah the son of
Has'shub, the son of Az'ri-kam, the son of
Hash-a-bi'ah, of the sons of Me-ra'ri;
15 And Bak-bak'kar, He'resh, and Ga'lal, and
Mat-ta-ni'ah, the son of Mi'cah, the son of Zich'-
ri, the son of A'saph;
16 And O-ba-di'ah the son of Shem-a-i'ah,
the son of Ga'lal, the son of Jed'u-thun, and Ber-
e-chi'ah the son of A'sa, the son of El'ka-nah,
that dwelt in the villages of the Ne-toph'a-
thites.
17 And the porters *were*, Shal'lum, and Ak'-
kub, and Tal'mon, and A-hi'man, and their
brethren: Shal'lum *was* the chief;
18 Who hitherto *waited* in the king's gate
eastward: they *were* porters in the companies of
the children of Le'vi.
19 And Shal'lum the son of Ko're, the son of
E-bi'a-saph, the son of Ko'rah, and his brethren,
of the house of his father, the Ko'rah-ites, *were*
over the work of the service, keepers of the
gates of the tabernacle: and their fathers, *being*
over the host of the LORD, *were* keepers of the
entry.
20 And Phin'e-has the son of E-le-a'zar was
the ruler over them in time past, *and* the LORD
was with him.
21 *And* Zech-a-ri'ah the son of Me-shel-e-mi'-
ah *was* porter of the door of the tabernacle of
the congregation.
22 All these *which were* chosen to be porters
in the gates *were* two hundred and twelve.
These were reckoned by their genealogy in their
villages, whom Da'vid and Sam'u-el the seer did
ordain in their set office.
23 So they and their children *had* the oversight of the gates of the house of the LORD,
namely, the house of the tabernacle, by wards.
24 In four quarters were the porters, toward
the east, west, north, and south.
25 And their brethren, *which were* in their
villages, *were* to come after seven days from
time to time with them.
26 For these Le'vites, the four chief porters,
were in *their* set office, and were over the chambers and treasuries of the house of God.
27 ¶ And they lodged round about the house
of God, because the charge *was* upon them, and
the opening thereof every morning *pertained* to
them.
28 And *certain* of them had the charge of the
ministering vessels, that they should bring
them in and out by tale.
29 *Some* of them also *were* appointed to
oversee the vessels, and all the instruments of
the sanctuary, and the fine flour, and the wine,
and the oil, and the frankincense, and the
spices.
30 And *some* of the sons of the priests made
the ointment of the spices.
31 And Mat-ti-thi'ah, *one* of the Le'vites, who
was the firstborn of Shal'lum the Ko'rah-ite,
had the set office over the things that were
made in the pans.
32 And *other* of their brethren, of the sons of
the Ko'hath-ites, *were* over the shewbread, to
prepare *it* every sabbath.
33 And these *are* the singers, chief of the fathers of the Le'vites, *who remaining* in the
chambers *were* free: for they were employed in
that work day and night.
34 These chief fathers of the Le'vites *were*
chief throughout their generations; these dwelt
at Je-ru'sa-lem.
35 ¶ And in Gib'e-on dwelt the father of
Gib'e-on, Je-hi'el, whose wife's name *was* Ma'a-
chah:
36 And his firstborn son Ab'don, then Zur,
and Kish, and Ba'al, and Ner, and Na'dab,
37 And Ge'dor, and A-hi'o, and Zech-a-ri'ah,
and Mik'loth.
38 And Mik'loth begat Shim'e-am. And they
also dwelt with their brethren at Je-ru'sa-lem,
over against their brethren.
39 And Ner begat Kish; and Kish begat Saul;
and Saul begat Jon'a-than, and Mal-chi-shu'a,
and A-bin'a-dab, and Esh–ba'al.
40 And the son of Jon'a-than *was* Mer'ib–ba'-
al: and Mer'ib–ba'al begat Mi'cah.
41 And the sons of Mi'cah *were*, Pi'thon, and
Me'lech, and Tah-re'a, *and A'haz*.
42 And A'haz begat Ja'rah; and Ja'rah begat
Al'e-meth, and Az'ma-veth, and Zim'ri; and
Zim'ri begat Mo'za;
43 And Mo'za begat Bin'e-a; and Reph-a-i'ah
his son, E-le'a-sah his son, A'zel his son.
44 And A'zel had six sons, whose names *are*
these, Az'ri-kam, Boch'e-ru, and Ish'ma-el, and
She-a-ri'ah, and O-ba-di'ah, and Ha'nan: these
were the sons of A'zel.

10 NOW the Phi-lis'tines fought against Is'-
ra-el; and the men of Is'ra-el fled from
before the Phi-lis'tines, and fell down slain in
mount Gil-bo'a.
2 And the Phi-lis'tines followed hard after
Saul, and after his sons; and the Phi-lis'tines
slew Jon'a-than, and A-bin'a-dab, and Mal-chi-
shu'a, the sons of Saul.
3 And the battle went sore against Saul, and
the archers hit him, and he was wounded of the
archers.
4 Then said Saul to his armourbearer, Draw
thy sword, and thrust me through therewith;
lest these uncircumcised come and abuse me.
But his armourbearer would not; for he was
sore afraid. So Saul took a sword, and fell upon
it.

5 And when his armourbearer saw that Saul
was dead, he fell likewise on the sword, and
died.
6 So Saul died, and his three sons, and all his
house died together.
7 And when all the men of Is'ra-el that *were*
in the valley saw that they fled, and that Saul
and his sons were dead, then they forsook their
cities, and fled: and the Phi-lis'tines came and
dwelt in them.
8 ¶ And it came to pass on the morrow,
when the Phi-lis'tines came to strip the slain,
that they found Saul and his sons fallen in
mount Gil-bo'a.
9 And when they had stripped him, they took
his head, and his armour, and sent into the land
of the Phi-lis'tines round about, to carry tidings
unto their idols, and to the people.
10 And they put his armour in the house of
their gods, and fastened his head in the temple
of Da'gon.
11 ¶ And when all Ja'besh-gil'e-ad heard all
that the Phi-lis'tines had done to Saul,
12 They arose, all the valiant men, and took
away the body of Saul, and the bodies of his
sons, and brought them to Ja'besh, and buried
their bones under the oak in Ja'besh, and fasted
seven days.
13 ¶ So Saul died for his transgression
which he committed against the LORD, *even*
against the word of the LORD, which he kept
not, and also for asking *counsel* of *one that had*
a familiar spirit, to enquire *of it;*
14 And enquired not of the LORD: therefore
he slew him, and turned the kingdom unto Da'-
vid the son of Jes'se.

11 THEN all Is'ra-el gathered themselves
to Da'vid unto He'bron, saying, Behold,
we *are* thy bone and thy flesh.
2 And moreover in time past, even when
Saul was king, thou *wast* he that leddest out
and broughtest in Is'ra-el: and the LORD thy
God said unto thee, Thou shalt feed my people
Is'ra-el, and thou shalt be ruler over my people
Is'ra-el.
3 Therefore came all the elders of Is'ra-el to
the king to He'bron; and Da'vid made a covenant with them in He'bron before the LORD;
and they anointed Da'vid king over Is'ra-el, according to the word of the LORD by Sam'u-el.
4 ¶ And Da'vid and all Is'ra-el went to Je-
ru'sa-lem, which *is* Je'bus; where the Jeb'u-sites
were, the inhabitants of the land.
5 And the inhabitants of Je'bus said to Da'-
vid, Thou shalt not come hither. Nevertheless
Da'vid took the castle of Zi'on, which *is* the city
of Da'vid.
6 And Da'vid said, Whosoever smiteth the
Jeb'u-sites first shall be chief and captain. So
Jo'ab the son of Zer-u-i'ah went first up, and
was chief.
7 And Da'vid dwelt in the castle; therefore
they called it the city of Da'vid.
8 And he built the city round about, even
from Mil'lo round about: and Jo'ab repaired the
rest of the city.
9 So Da'vid waxed greater and greater: for
the LORD of hosts *was* with him.
10 ¶ These also *are* the chief of the mighty
men whom Da'vid had, who strengthened
themselves with him in his kingdom, *and* with
all Is'ra-el, to make him king, according to the
word of the LORD concerning Is'ra-el.
11 And this *is* the number of the mighty men
whom Da'vid had; Ja-sho'be-am, an Hach'mo-
nite, the chief of the captains: he lifted up his
spear against three hundred slain *by him* at one
time.
12 And after him *was* E-le-a'zar the son of
Do'do, the A-ho'hite, who *was one* of the three
mighties.
13 He was with Da'vid at Pas-dam'mim, and
there the Phi-lis'tines were gathered together to
battle, where was a parcel of ground full of barley; and the people fled from before the Phi-lis'-
tines.
14 And they set themselves in the midst of
that parcel, and delivered it, and slew the Phi-
lis'tines; and the LORD saved *them* by a great
deliverance.
15 ¶ Now three of the thirty captains went
down to the rock to Da'vid, into the cave of A-
dul'lam; and the host of the Phi-lis'tines encamped in the valley of Reph'a-im.
16 And Da'vid *was* then in the hold, and the
Phi-lis'tines' garrison *was* then at Beth'-le-hem.
17 And Da'vid longed, and said, Oh that one
would give me drink of the water of the well of
Beth'-le-hem, that *is* at the gate!
18 And the three brake through the host of
the Phi-lis'tines, and drew water out of the well
of Beth'-le-hem, that *was* by the gate, and took
it, and brought *it* to Da'vid: but Da'vid would
not drink *of* it, but poured it out to the LORD,
19 And said, My God forbid it me, that I
should do this thing: shall I drink the blood of
these men that have put their lives in jeopardy?
for with *the jeopardy of* their lives they brought
it. Therefore he would not drink it. These things
did these three mightiest.
20 ¶ And A-bish'a-i the brother of Jo'ab, he
was chief of the three: for lifting up his spear
against three hundred, he slew *them*, and had a
name among the three.
21 Of the three, he was more honourable
than the two; for he was their captain: howbeit
he attained not to the *first* three.
22 Be-na'iah the son of Je-hoi'a-da, the son of
a valiant man of Kab'ze-el, who had done many
acts; he slew two lionlike men of Mo'ab: also he
went down and slew a lion in a pit in a snowy
day.
23 And he slew an E-gyp'tian, a man of *great*
stature, five cubits high; and in the E-gyp'tian's
hand *was* a spear like a weaver's beam; and he
went down to him with a staff, and plucked the
spear out of the E-gyp'tian's hand, and slew him
with his own spear.
24 These *things* did Be-na'iah the son of Je-
hoi'a-da, and had the name among the three
mighties.
25 Behold, he was honourable among the
thirty, but attained not to the *first* three: and
Da'vid set him over his guard.
26 ¶ Also the valiant men of the armies
were, A'sa-hel the brother of Jo'ab, El-ha'nan
the son of Do'do of Beth'-le-hem,
27 Sham'moth the Ha'ro-rite, He'lez the Pel'-
o-nite,
28 I'ra the son of Ik'kesh the Te-ko'ite, A-bi-
e'zer the An'toth-ite,
29 Sib'be-cai the Hu'shath-ite, I'lai the A-ho'-
hite,
30 Ma-har'a-i the Ne-toph'a-thite, He'led the
son of Ba'a-nah the Ne-toph'a-thite,
31 Ith'a-i the son of Ri'bai of Gib'e-ah, *that*
pertained to the children of Ben'ja-min, Be-na'-
iah the Pir'a-thon-ite,
32 Hu'rai of the brooks of Ga'ash, A-bi'el the
Ar'bath-ite,
33 Az'ma-veth the Ba-ha'rum-ite, E-li'ah-ba
the Sha-al'bo-nite,

34 The sons of Ha'shem the Gi'zo-nite, Jon'a-
than the son of Sha'ge the Ha'ra-rite,
35 A-hi'am the son of Sa'car the Ha'ra-rite,
El'i-phal the son of Ur,
36 He'pher the Mech'e-rath-ite, A-hi'jah the
Pel'o-nite,
37 Hez'ro the Car'mel-ite, Na'a-rai the son of
Ez'ba-i,
38 Jo'el the brother of Na'than, Mib'har the
son of Hag-ge'ri,
39 Ze'lek the Am'mon-ite, Na-har'a-i the Be'-
roth-ite, the armourbearer of Jo'ab the son of
Zer-u-i'ah,
40 I'ra the Ith'rite, Ga'reb the Ith'rite,
41 U-ri'ah the Hit'tite, Za'bad the son of Ah'-
lai,
42 Ad'i-na the son of Shi'za the Reu'ben-ite, a
captain of the Reu'ben-ites, and thirty with him,
43 Ha'nan the son of Ma'a-chah, and Josh'a-
phat the Mith'nite,
44 Uz-zi'a the Ash'te-rath-ite, Sha'ma and Je-
hi'el the sons of Ho'than the Ar'o-er-ite,
45 Je-di'a-el the son of Shim'ri, and Jo'ha his
brother, the Ti'zite,
46 E-li'el the Ma'ha-vite, and Jer'i-bai, and
Josh-a-vi'ah, the sons of El'na-am, and Ith'mah
the Mo'ab-ite,
47 E-li'el, and O'bed, and Ja'si-el the Mes'o-
ba-ite.

12 NOW these *are* they that came to Da'-
vid to Zik'lag, while he yet kept himself
close because of Saul the son of Kish: and they
were among the mighty men, helpers of the
war.
2 *They were* armed with bows, and could use
both the right hand and the left in *hurling*
stones and *shooting* arrows out of a bow, *even*
of Saul's brethren of Ben'ja-min.
3 The chief *was* A-hi-e'zer, then Jo'ash, the
sons of She-ma'ah the Gib'e-ath-ite; and Je'zi-el,
and Pe'let, the sons of Az'ma-veth; and Ber'a-
chah, and Je'hu the An'toth-ite,
4 And Is-ma-i'ah the Gib'e-on-ite, a mighty
man among the thirty, and over the thirty; and
Jer-e-mi'ah, and Ja-ha'zi-el, and Jo-ha'nan, and
Jos'a-bad the Ged'e-rath-ite,
5 E-lu'za-i, and Jer'i-moth, and Be-a-li'ah,
and Shem-a-ri'ah, and Sheph-a-ti'ah the Har'u-
phite,
6 El'ka-nah, and Je-si'ah, and A-zar'e-el, and
Jo-e'zer, and Ja-sho'be-am, the Kor'hites,
7 And Jo-e'lah, and Zeb-a-di'ah, the sons of
Jer'o-ham of Ge'dor.
8 And of the Gad'ites there separated themselves unto Da'vid into the hold to the wilderness men of might, *and* men of war *fit* for the
battle, that could handle shield and buckler,
whose faces *were like* the faces of lions, and
were as swift as the roes upon the mountains;
9 E'zer the first, O-ba-di'ah the second, E-li'-
ab the third,
10 Mish-man'nah the fourth, Jer-e-mi'ah the
fifth,
11 At'tai the sixth, E-li'el the seventh,
12 Jo-ha'nan the eighth, El'za-bad the ninth,
13 Jer-e-mi'ah the tenth, Mach'ba-nai the
eleventh.
14 These *were* of the sons of Gad, captains of
the host: one of the least *was* over an hundred,
and the greatest over a thousand.
15 These *are* they that went over Jor'dan in
the first month, when it had overflown all his
banks; and they put to flight all *them* of the valleys, *both* toward the east, and toward the west.
16 And there came of the children of Ben'ja-
min and Ju'dah to the hold unto Da'vid.
17 And Da'vid went out to meet them, and
answered and said unto them, If ye be come
peaceably unto me to help me, mine heart shall
be knit unto you: but if *ye be come* to betray me
to mine enemies, seeing *there is* no wrong in
mine hands, the God of our fathers look
thereon, and rebuke *it.*
18 Then the spirit came upon A-mas'a-i, *who
was* chief of the captains, *and he said,* Thine *are
we,* Da'vid, and on thy side, thou son of Jes'se:
peace, peace *be* unto thee, and peace *be* to thine
helpers; for thy God helpeth thee. Then Da'vid
received them, and made them captains of the
band.
19 And there fell *some* of Ma-nas'seh to Da'-
vid, when he came with the Phi-lis'tines against
Saul to battle: but they helped them not: for the
lords of the Phi-lis'tines upon advisement sent
him away, saying, He will fall to his master Saul
to *the jeopardy of* our heads.
20 As he went to Zik'lag, there fell to him of
Ma-nas'seh, Ad'nah, and Joz'a-bad, and Je-di'a-
el, and Mi'chael, and Joz'a-bad, and E-li'hu, and
Zil'thai, captains of the thousands that *were* of
Ma-nas'seh.
21 And they helped Da'vid against the band
of the rovers: for they *were* all mighty men of
valour, and were captains in the host.
22 For at *that* time day by day there came to
Da'vid to help him, until *it was* a great host, like
the host of God.
23 ¶ And these *are* the numbers of the bands
that were ready armed to the war, *and* came to
Da'vid to He'bron, to turn the kingdom of Saul
to him, according to the word of the LORD.
24 The children of Ju'dah that bare shield
and spear *were* six thousand and eight hundred,
ready armed to the war.
25 Of the children of Sim'e-on, mighty men
of valour for the war, seven thousand and one
hundred.
26 Of the children of Le'vi four thousand and
six hundred.
27 And Je-hoi'a-da *was* the leader of the
Aar'on-ites, and with him *were* three thousand
and seven hundred;
28 And Za'dok, a young man mighty of valour, and of his father's house twenty and two
captains.
29 And of the children of Ben'ja-min, the kindred of Saul, three thousand: for hitherto the
greatest part of them had kept the ward of the
house of Saul.
30 And of the children of E'phra-im twenty
thousand and eight hundred, mighty men of
valour, famous throughout the house of their
fathers.
31 And of the half tribe of Ma-nas'seh eighteen thousand, which were expressed by name,
to come and make Da'vid king.
32 And of the children of Is'sa-char, *which
were men* that had understanding of the times,
to know what Is'ra-el ought to do; the heads of
them *were* two hundred; and all their brethren
were at their commandment.
33 Of Zeb'u-lun, such as went forth to battle,
expert in war, with all instruments of war, fifty
thousand, which could keep rank: *they were* not
of double heart.
34 And of Naph'ta-li a thousand captains,
and with them with shield and spear thirty and
seven thousand.
35 And of the Dan'ites expert in war twenty
and eight thousand and six hundred.
36 And of Ash'er, such as went forth to battle, expert in war, forty thousand.
37 And on the other side of Jor'dan, of the

Reu′ben-ites, and the Gad′ites, and of the half tribe of Ma-nas′seh, with all manner of instruments of war for the battle, an hundred and twenty thousand.

38 All these men of war, that could keep rank, came with a perfect heart to He′bron, to make Da′vid king over all Is′ra-el: and all the rest also of Is′ra-el *were* of one heart to make Da′vid king.

39 And there they were with Da′vid three days, eating and drinking: for their brethren had prepared for them.

40 Moreover they that were nigh them, *even* unto Is′sa-char and Zeb′u-lun and Naph′ta-li, brought bread on asses, and on camels, and on mules, and on oxen, *and* meat, meal, cakes of figs, and bunches of raisins, and wine, and oil, and oxen, and sheep abundantly: for *there was* joy in Is′ra-el.

13 AND Da′vid consulted with the captains of thousands and hundreds, *and* with every leader.

2 And Da′vid said unto all the congregation of Is′ra-el, If *it seem* good unto you, and *that it be* of the LORD our God, let us send abroad unto our brethren every where, *that are* left in all the land of Is′ra-el, and with them *also* to the priests and Le′vites *which are* in their cities *and* suburbs, that they may gather themselves unto us:

3 And let us bring again the ark of our God to us: for we enquired not at it in the days of Saul.

4 And all the congregation said that they would do so: for the thing was right in the eyes of all the people.

5 So Da′vid gathered all Is′ra-el together, from Shi′hor of E′gypt even unto the entering of He′math, to bring the ark of God from Kir′jath–je′a-rim.

6 And Da′vid went up, and all Is′ra-el, to Ba′al-ah, *that is*, to Kir′jath–je′a-rim, which *belonged* to Ju′dah, to bring up thence the ark of God the LORD, that dwelleth *between* the cherubims, whose name is called *on it*.

7 And they carried the ark of God in a new cart out of the house of A-bin′a-dab: and Uz′za and A-hi′o drave the cart.

8 And Da′vid and all Is′ra-el played before God with all *their* might, and with singing, and with harps, and with psalteries, and with timbrels, and with cymbals, and with trumpets.

9 ¶ And when they came unto the threshingfloor of Chi′don, Uz′za put forth his hand to hold the ark; for the oxen stumbled.

10 And the anger of the LORD was kindled against Uz′za, and he smote him, because he put his hand to the ark: and there he died before God.

11 And Da′vid was displeased, because the LORD had made a breach upon Uz′za: wherefore that place is called Pe′rez–uz′za to this day.

12 And Da′vid was afraid of God that day, saying, How shall I bring the ark of God *home* to me?

13 So Da′vid brought not the ark *home* to himself to the city of Da′vid, but carried it aside into the house of O′bed–e′dom the Git′tite.

14 And the ark of God remained with the family of O′bed–e′dom in his house three months. And the LORD blessed the house of O′bed–e′dom, and all that he had.

14 NOW Hi′ram king of Tyre sent messengers to Da′vid, and timber of cedars, with masons and carpenters, to build him an house.

2 And Da′vid perceived that the LORD had confirmed him king over Is′ra-el, for his kingdom was lifted up on high, because of his people Is′ra-el.

3 ¶ And Da′vid took more wives at Je-ru′sa-lem: and Da′vid begat more sons and daughters.

4 Now these *are* the names of *his* children which he had in Je-ru′sa-lem; Sham-mu′a, and Sho′bab, Na′than, and Sol′o-mon,

5 And Ib′har, and El-i-shu′a, and El′pa-let,

6 And No′gah, and Ne′pheg, and Ja-phi′a,

7 And E-lish′a-ma, and Be-el-i′a-da, and E-liph′a-let.

8 ¶ And when the Phi-lis′tines heard that Da′vid was anointed king over all Is′ra-el, all the Phi-lis′tines went up to seek Da′vid. And Da′vid heard *of it*, and went out against them.

9 And the Phi-lis′tines came and spread themselves in the valley of Reph′a-im.

10 And Da′vid enquired of God, saying, Shall I go up against the Phi-lis′tines? And wilt thou deliver them into mine hand? And the LORD said unto him, Go up; for I will deliver them into thine hand.

11 So they came up to Ba′al–per′a-zim; and Da′vid smote them there. Then Da′vid said, God hath broken in upon mine enemies by mine hand like the breaking forth of waters: therefore they called the name of that place Ba′al–per′a-zim.

12 And when they had left their gods there, Da′vid gave a commandment, and they were burned with fire.

13 And the Phi-lis′tines yet again spread themselves abroad in the valley.

14 Therefore Da′vid enquired again of God; and God said unto him, Go not up after them; turn away from them, and come upon them over against the mulberry trees.

15 And it shall be, when thou shalt hear a sound of going in the tops of the mulberry trees, *that* then thou shalt go out to battle: for God is gone forth before thee to smite the host of the Phi-lis′tines.

16 Da′vid therefore did as God commanded him: and they smote the host of the Phi-lis′tines from Gib′e-on even to Ga′zer.

17 And the fame of Da′vid went out into all lands; and the LORD brought the fear of him upon all nations.

15 AND *Da′vid* made him houses in the city of Da′vid, and prepared a place for the ark of God, and pitched for it a tent.

2 Then Da′vid said, None ought to carry the ark of God but the Le′vites: for them hath the LORD chosen to carry the ark of God, and to minister unto him for ever.

3 And Da′vid gathered all Is′ra-el together to Je-ru′sa-lem, to bring up the ark of the LORD unto his place, which he had prepared for it.

4 And Da′vid assembled the children of Aar′on, and the Le′vites:

5 Of the sons of Ko′hath; U′ri-el the chief, and his brethren an hundred and twenty:

6 Of the sons of Me-ra′ri; A-sa-i′ah the chief, and his brethren two hundred and twenty:

7 Of the sons of Ger′shom; Jo′el the chief, and his brethren an hundred and thirty:

8 Of the sons of E-liz′a-phan; Shem-a-i′ah the chief, and his brethren two hundred:

9 Of the sons of He′bron; E-li′el the chief, and his brethren fourscore:

10 Of the sons of Uz′zi-el; Am-min′a-dab the chief, and his brethren an hundred and twelve.

11 And Da′vid called for Za′dok and A-bi′a-

thar the priests, and for the Le'vites, for U'ri-el, A-sa-i'ah, and Jo'el, Shem-a-i'ah, and E-li'el, and Am-min'a-dab,

12 And said unto them, Ye *are* the chief of the fathers of the Le'vites: sanctify yourselves, *both* ye and your brethren, that ye may bring up the ark of the LORD God of Is'ra-el unto *the place that* I have prepared for it.

13 For because ye *did it* not at the first, the LORD our God made a breach upon us, for that we sought him not after the due order.

14 So the priests and the Le'vites sanctified themselves to bring up the ark of the LORD God of Is'ra-el.

15 And the children of the Le'vites bare the ark of God upon their shoulders with the staves thereon, as Mo'ses commanded according to the word of the LORD.

16 And Da'vid spake to the chief of the Le'vites to appoint their brethren *to be* the singers with instruments of musick, psalteries and harps and cymbals, sounding, by lifting up the voice with joy.

17 So the Le'vites appointed He'man the son of Jo'el; and of his brethren, A'saph the son of Ber-e-chi'ah; and of the sons of Me-ra'ri their brethren, E'than the son of Kush-a'iah;

18 And with them their brethren of the second *degree,* Zech-a-ri'ah, Ben, and Ja-a'zi-el, and She-mir'a-moth, and Je-hi'el, and Un'ni, E-li'ab, and Be-na'iah, and Ma-a-se'iah, and Mat-ti-thi'ah, and E-liph'e-leh, and Mik-ne'iah, and O'bed–e'dom, and Je-i'el, the porters.

19 So the singers, He'man, A'saph, and E'than, *were appointed* to sound with cymbals of brass;

20 And Zech-a-ri'ah, and A'zi-el, and She-mir'a-moth, and Je-hi'el, and Un'ni, and E-li'ab, and Ma-a-se'iah, and Be-na'iah, with psalteries on Al'a-moth;

21 And Mat-ti-thi'ah, and E-liph'e-leh, and Mik-ne'iah, and O'bed–e'dom, and Je-i'el, and Az-a-zi'ah, with harps on the Shem'i-nith to excel.

22 And Chen-a-ni'ah, chief of the Le'vites, *was* for song: he instructed about the song, because he *was* skilful.

23 And Ber-e-chi'ah and El'ka-nah *were* doorkeepers for the ark.

24 And Sheb-a-ni'ah, and Je-hosh'a-phat, and Ne-than'e-el, and A-mas'a-i, and Zech-a-ri'ah, and Be-na'iah, and E-li-e'zer, the priests, did blow with the trumpets before the ark of God: and O'bed–e'dom and Je-hi'ah *were* doorkeepers for the ark.

25 ¶ So Da'vid, and the elders of Is'ra-el, and the captains over thousands, went to bring up the ark of the covenant of the LORD out of the house of O'bed–e'dom with joy.

26 And it came to pass, when God helped the Le'vites that bare the ark of the covenant of the LORD, that they offered seven bullocks and seven rams.

27 And Da'vid *was* clothed with a robe of fine linen, and all the Le'vites that bare the ark, and the singers, and Chen-a-ni'ah the master of the song with the singers: Da'vid also *had* upon him an ephod of linen.

28 Thus all Is'ra-el brought up the ark of the covenant of the LORD with shouting, and with sound of the cornet, and with trumpets, and with cymbals, making a noise with psalteries and harps.

29 ¶ And it came to pass, *as* the ark of the covenant of the LORD came to the city of Da'vid, that Mi'chal the daughter of Saul looking out at a window saw king Da'vid dancing and playing: and she despised him in her heart.

16

SO they brought the ark of God, and set it in the midst of the tent that Da'vid had pitched for it: and they offered burnt sacrifices and peace offerings before God.

2 And when Da'vid had made an end of offering the burnt offerings and the peace offerings, he blessed the people in the name of the LORD.

3 And he dealt to every one of Is'ra-el, both man and woman, to every one a loaf of bread, and a good piece of flesh, and a flagon *of wine.*

4 ¶ And he appointed *certain* of the Le'vites to minister before the ark of the LORD, and to record, and to thank and praise the LORD God of Is'ra-el:

5 A'saph the chief, and next to him Zech-a-ri'ah, Je-i'el, and She-mir'a-moth, and Je-hi'el, and Mat-ti-thi'ah, and E-li'ab, and Be-na'iah, and O'bed–e'dom: and Je-i'el with psalteries and with harps; but A'saph made a sound with cymbals;

6 Be-na'iah also and Ja-ha'zi-el the priests with trumpets continually before the ark of the covenant of God.

7 ¶ Then on that day Da'vid delivered first *this psalm* to thank the LORD into the hand of A'saph and his brethren.

8 Give thanks unto the LORD, call upon his name, make known his deeds among the people.

9 Sing unto him, sing psalms unto him, talk ye of all his wondrous works.

10 Glory ye in his holy name: let the heart of them rejoice that seek the LORD.

11 Seek the LORD and his strength, seek his face continually.

12 Remember his marvellous works that he hath done, his wonders, and the judgments of his mouth;

13 O ye seed of Is'ra-el his servant, ye children of Ja'cob, his chosen ones.

14 He *is* the LORD our God; his judgments *are* in all the earth.

15 Be ye mindful always of his covenant; the word *which* he commanded to a thousand generations;

16 *Even of the covenant* which he made with A'bra-ham, and of his oath unto I'saac;

17 And hath confirmed the same to Ja'cob for a law, *and* to Is'ra-el *for* an everlasting covenant,

18 Saying, Unto thee will I give the land of Ca'naan, the lot of your inheritance;

19 When ye were but few, even a few, and strangers in it.

20 And *when* they went from nation to nation, and from *one* kingdom to another people;

21 He suffered no man to do them wrong: yea, he reproved kings for their sakes,

22 *Saying,* Touch not mine anointed, and do my prophets no harm.

23 Sing unto the LORD, all the earth; shew forth from day to day his salvation.

24 Declare his glory among the heathen; his marvellous works among all nations.

25 For great *is* the LORD, and greatly to be praised: he also *is* to be feared above all gods.

26 For all the gods of the people *are* idols: but the LORD made the heavens.

27 Glory and honour *are* in his presence; strength and gladness *are* in his place.

28 Give unto the LORD, ye kindreds of the people, give unto the LORD glory and strength.

29 Give unto the LORD the glory *due* unto his

name: bring an offering, and come before him:
worship the LORD in the beauty of holiness.
30 Fear before him, all the earth: the world
also shall be stable, that it be not moved.
31 Let the heavens be glad, and let the earth
rejoice: and let *men* say among the nations, The
LORD reigneth.
32 Let the sea roar, and the fulness thereof:
let the fields rejoice, and all that *is* therein.
33 Then shall the trees of the wood sing out
at the presence of the LORD, because he cometh
to judge the earth.
34 O give thanks unto the LORD; for *he is*
good; for his mercy *endureth* for ever.
35 And say ye, Save us, O God of our salvation, and gather us together, and deliver us
from the heathen, that we may give thanks to
thy holy name, *and* glory in thy praise.
36 Blessed *be* the LORD God of Is'ra-el for
ever and ever. And all the people said, Amen,
and praised the LORD.
37 ¶ So he left there before the ark of the
covenant of the LORD A'saph and his brethren,
to minister before the ark continually, as every
day's work required:
38 And O'bed-e'dom with their brethren,
threescore and eight; O'bed-e'dom also the son
of Jed'u-thun and Ho'sah *to be* porters:
39 And Za'dok the priest, and his brethren
the priests, before the tabernacle of the LORD in
the high place that *was* at Gib'e-on,
40 To offer burnt offerings unto the LORD
upon the altar of the burnt offering continually
morning and evening, and *to do* according to all
that is written in the law of the LORD, which he
commanded Is'ra-el;
41 And with them He'man and Jed'u-thun,
and the rest that were chosen, who were expressed by name, to give thanks to the LORD,
because his mercy *endureth* for ever;
42 And with them He'man and Jed'u-thun
with trumpets and cymbals for those that
should make a sound, and with musical instruments of God. And the sons of Jed'u-thun *were*
porters.
43 And all the people departed every man to
his house: and Da'vid returned to bless his
house.

17 NOW it came to pass, as Da'vid sat in
his house, that Da'vid said to Na'than
the prophet, Lo, I dwell in an house of cedars,
but the ark of the covenant of the LORD *remaineth* under curtains.
2 Then Na'than said unto Da'vid, Do all that
is in thine heart; for God *is* with thee.
3 ¶ And it came to pass the same night, that
the word of God came to Na'than, saying,
4 Go and tell Da'vid my servant, Thus saith
the LORD, Thou shalt not build me an house to
dwell in:
5 For I have not dwelt in an house since the
day that I brought up Is'ra-el unto this day; but
have gone from tent to tent, and from *one* tabernacle *to another*.
6 Wheresoever I have walked with all Is'ra-
el, spake I a word to any of the judges of Is'ra-
el, whom I commanded to feed my people, saying, Why have ye not built me an house of cedars?
7 Now therefore thus shalt thou say unto my
servant Da'vid, Thus saith the LORD of hosts, I
took thee from the sheepcote, *even* from following the sheep, that thou shouldest be ruler over
my people Is'ra-el:
8 And I have been with thee whithersoever
thou hast walked, and have cut off all thine enemies from before thee, and have made thee a
name like the name of the great men that *are* in
the earth.
9 Also I will ordain a place for my people Is'-
ra-el, and will plant them, and they shall dwell
in their place, and shall be moved no more; neither shall the children of wickedness waste
them any more, as at the beginning,
10 And since the time that I commanded
judges *to be* over my people Is'ra-el. Moreover I
will subdue all thine enemies. Furthermore I tell
thee that the LORD will build thee an house.
11 ¶ And it shall come to pass, when thy
days be expired that thou must go *to be* with
thy fathers, that I will raise up thy seed after
thee, which shall be of thy sons; and I will establish his kingdom.
12 He shall build me an house, and I will
stablish his throne for ever.
13 I will be his father, and he shall be my
son: and I will not take my mercy away from
him, as I took *it* from *him* that was before thee:
14 But I will settle him in mine house and in
my kingdom for ever: and his throne shall be
established for evermore.
15 According to all these words, and according to all this vision, so did Na'than speak unto
Da'vid.
16 ¶ And Da'vid the king came and sat before the LORD, and said, Who *am* I, O LORD
God, and what *is* mine house, that thou hast
brought me hitherto?
17 And *yet* this was a small thing in thine
eyes, O God; for thou hast *also* spoken of thy
servant's house for a great while to come, and
hast regarded me according to the estate of a
man of high degree, O LORD God.
18 What can Da'vid *speak* more to thee for
the honour of thy servant? for thou knowest thy
servant.
19 O LORD, for thy servant's sake, and according to thine own heart, hast thou done all
this greatness, in making known all *these* great
things.
20 O LORD, *there is*, none like thee, neither *is
there any* God beside thee, according to all that
we have heard with our ears.
21 And what one nation in the earth *is* like
thy people Is'ra-el, whom God went to redeem
to be his own people, to make thee a name of
greatness and terribleness, by driving out nations from before thy people, whom thou hast
redeemed out of E'gypt?
22 For thy people Is'ra-el didst thou make
thine own people for ever; and thou, LORD, becamest their God.
23 Therefore now, LORD, let the thing that
thou hast spoken concerning thy servant and
concerning his house be established for ever,
and do as thou hast said.
24 Let it even be established, that thy name
may be magnified for ever, saying, The LORD of
hosts *is* the God of Is'ra-el, *even* a God to Is'ra-
el: and *let* the house of Da'vid thy servant *be*
established before thee.
25 For thou, O my God, hast told thy servant
that thou wilt build him an house: therefore thy
servant hath found *in his heart* to pray before
thee.
26 And now, LORD, thou art God, and hast
promised this goodness unto thy servant:
27 Now therefore let it please thee to bless
the house of thy servant, that it may be before
thee for ever: for thou blessest, O LORD, and *it
shall be* blessed for ever.

18 NOW after this it came to pass, that Da′vid smote the Phi-lis′tines, and subdued them, and took Gath and her towns out of the hand of the Phi-lis′tines.

2 And he smote Mo′ab; and the Mo′ab-ites became Da′vid's servants, *and* brought gifts.

3 ¶ And Da′vid smote Had-ar-e′zer king of Zo′bah unto Ha′math, as he went to stablish his dominion by the river Eu-phra′tes.

4 And Da′vid took from him a thousand chariots, and seven thousand horsemen, and twenty thousand footmen: Da′vid also houghed all the chariot *horses*, but reserved of them an hundred chariots.

5 And when the Syr′i-ans of Da-mas′cus came to help Had-ar-e′zer king of Zo′bah, Da′vid slew of the Syr′i-ans two and twenty thousand men.

6 Then Da′vid put *garrisons* in Syr′i–a–da-mas′cus; and the Syr′i-ans became Da′vid's servants, *and* brought gifts. Thus the LORD preserved Da′vid whithersoever he went.

7 And Da′vid took the shields of gold that were on the servants of Had-ar-e′zer, and brought them to Je-ru′sa-lem.

8 Likewise from Tib′hath, and from Chun, cities of Had-ar-e′zer, brought Da′vid very much brass, wherewith Sol′o-mon made the brasen sea, and the pillars, and the vessels of brass.

9 ¶ Now when To′u king of Ha′math heard how Da′vid had smitten all the host of Had-ar-e′zer king of Zo′bah;

10 He sent Ha-do′ram his son to king Da′vid, to enquire of his welfare, and to congratulate him, because he had fought against Had-ar-e′zer, and smitten him; (for Had-ar-e′zer had war with To′u;) and *with him* all manner of vessels of gold and silver and brass.

11 ¶ Them also king Da′vid dedicated unto the LORD, with the silver and the gold that he brought from all *these* nations; from E′dom, and from Mo′ab, and from the children of Am′mon, and from the Phi-lis′tines, and from Am′a-lek.

12 Moreover A-bish′a-i the son of Zer-u-i′ah slew of the E′dom-ites in the valley of salt eighteen thousand.

13 ¶ And he put garrisons in E′dom; and all the E′dom-ites became Da′vid's servants. Thus the LORD preserved Da′vid whithersoever he went.

14 ¶ So Da′vid reigned over all Is′ra-el, and executed judgment and justice among all his people.

15 And Jo′ab the son of Zer-u-i′ah *was* over the host; and Je-hosh′a-phat the son of A-hi′lud, recorder.

16 And Za′dok the son of A-hi′tub, and A-bim′e-lech the son of A-bi′a-thar, *were* the priests; and Shav′sha was scribe;

17 And Be-na′iah the son of Je-hoi′a-da *was* over the Cher′eth-ites and the Pe′leth-ites; and the sons of Da′vid *were* chief about the king.

19 NOW it came to pass after this, that Na′hash the king of the children of Am′mon died, and his son reigned in his stead.

2 And Da′vid said, I will shew kindness unto Ha′nun the son of Na′hash, because his father shewed kindness to me. And Da′vid sent messengers to comfort him concerning his father. So the servants of Da′vid came into the land of the children of Am′mon to Ha′nun, to comfort him.

3 But the princes of the children of Am′mon said to Ha′nun, Thinkest thou that Da′vid doth honour thy father, that he hath sent comforters unto thee? are not his servants come unto thee for to search, and to overthrow, and to spy out the land?

4 Wherefore Ha′nun took Da′vid's servants, and shaved them, and cut off their garments in the midst hard by their buttocks, and sent them away.

5 Then there went *certain*, and told Da′vid how the men were served. And he sent to meet them: for the men were greatly ashamed. And the king said, Tarry at Jer′i-cho until your beards be grown, and *then* return.

6 ¶ And when the children of Am′mon saw that they had made themselves odious to Da′vid, Ha′nun and the children of Am′mon sent a thousand talents of silver to hire them chariots and horsemen out of Mes-o-po-ta′mi-a, and out of Syr′i-a–ma′a-chah, and out of Zo′bah.

7 So they hired thirty and two thousand chariots, and the king of Ma′a-chah and his people; who came and pitched before Med′e-ba. And the children of Am′mon gathered themselves together from their cities, and came to battle.

8 And when Da′vid heard *of it,* he sent Jo′ab, and all the host of the mighty men.

9 And the children of Am′mon came out, and put the battle in array before the gate of the city: and the kings that were come *were* by themselves in the field.

10 Now when Jo′ab saw that the battle was set against him before and behind, he chose out of all the choice of Is′ra-el, and put *them* in array against the Syr′i-ans.

11 And the rest of the people he delivered unto the hand of A-bish′a-i his brother, and they set *themselves* in array against the children of Am′mon.

12 And he said, If the Syr′i-ans be too strong for me, then thou shalt help me: but if the children of Am′mon be too strong for thee, then I will help thee.

13 Be of good courage, and let us behave ourselves valiantly for our people, and for the cities of our God: and let the LORD do *that which is* good in his sight.

14 So Jo′ab and the people that *were* with him drew nigh before the Syr′i-ans unto the battle; and they fled before him.

15 And when the children of Am′mon saw that the Syr′i-ans were fled, they likewise fled before A-bish′a-i his brother, and entered into the city. Then Jo′ab came to Je-ru′sa-lem.

16 ¶ And when the Syr′i-ans saw that they were put to the worse before Is′ra-el, they sent messengers, and drew forth the Syr′i-ans that *were* beyond the river: and Sho′phach the captain of the host of Had-ar-e′zer *went* before them.

17 And it was told Da′vid; and he gathered all Is′ra-el, and passed over Jor′dan, and came upon them, and set *the battle* in array against them. So when Da′vid had put the battle in array against the Syr′i-ans, they fought with him.

18 But the Syr′i-ans fled before Is′ra-el; and Da′vid slew of the Syr′i-ans seven thousand *men which fought in* chariots, and forty thousand footmen, and killed Sho′phach the captain of the host.

19 And when the servants of Had-ar-e′zer saw that they were put to the worse before Is′ra-el, they made peace with Da′vid, and became his servants: neither would the Syr′i-ans help the children of Am′mon any more.

20 AND it came to pass, that after the year was expired, at the time that kings go

out *to battle,* Jo'ab led forth the power of the
army, and wasted the country of the children of
Am'mon, and came and beseiged Rab'bah. But
Da'vid tarried at Je-ru'sa-lem. And Jo'ab smote
Rab'bah, and destroyed it.
2 And Da'vid took the crown of their king
from off his head, and found it to weigh a talent
of gold, and *there were* precious stones in it;
and it was set upon Da'vid's head: and he
brought also exceeding much spoil out of the
city.
3 And he brought out the people that *were* in
it, and cut *them* with saws, and with harrows of
iron, and with axes. Even so dealt Da'vid with
all the cities of the children of Am'mon. And
Da'vid and all the people returned to Je-ru'sa-
lem.
4 ¶ And it came to pass after this, that there
arose war at Ge'zer with the Phi-lis'tines; at
which time Sib'be-chai the Hu'shath-ite slew
Sip'pai, *that was* of the children of the giant:
and they were subdued.
5 And there was war again with the Phi-lis'-
tines; and El-ha'nan the son of Ja'ir slew Lah'mi
the brother of Go-li'ath the Git'tite, whose spear
staff *was* like a weaver's beam.
6 And yet again there was war at Gath,
where was a man of *great* stature, whose fingers and toes *were* four and twenty, six *on each
hand,* and six *on each foot:* and he also was the
son of the giant.
7 But when he defied Is'ra-el, Jon'a-than the
son of Shim'e-a Da'vid's brother slew him.
8 These were born unto the giant in Gath;
and they fell by the hand of Da'vid, and by the
hand of his servants.

21 AND Sa'tan stood up against Is'ra-el,
and provoked Da'vid to number Is'ra-el.
2 And Da'vid said to Jo'ab and to the rulers
of the people, Go, number Is'ra-el from Be'er-
she'ba even to Dan; and bring the number of
them to me, that I may know *it.*
3 And Jo'ab answered, The LORD make his
people an hundred times so many more as they
be: but, my lord the king, *are* they not all my
lord's servants? why then doth my lord require
this thing? why will he be a cause of trespass to
Is'ra-el?
4 Nevertheless the king's word prevailed
against Jo'ab. Wherefore Jo'ab departed, and
went throughout all Is'ra-el, and came to Je-ru'-
sa-lem.
5 ¶ And Jo'ab gave the sum of the number of
the people unto Da'vid. And all *they of* Is'ra-el
were a thousand thousand and an hundred
thousand men that drew sword: and Ju'dah *was*
four hundred threescore and ten thousand men
that drew sword.
6 But Le'vi and Ben'ja-min counted he not
among them: for the king's word was abominable to Jo'ab.
7 And God was displeased with this thing;
therefore he smote Is'ra-el.
8 And Da'vid said unto God, I have sinned
greatly, because I have done this thing: but
now, I beseech thee, do away the iniquity of thy
servant; for I have done very foolishly.
9 ¶ And the LORD spake unto Gad, Da'vid's
seer, saying,
10 Go and tell Da'vid, saying, Thus saith the
LORD, I offer thee three *things:* choose thee one
of them, that I may do *it* unto thee.
11 So Gad came to Da'vid, and said unto
him, Thus saith the LORD, Choose thee
12 Either three years' famine; or three
months to be destroyed before thy foes, while
that the sword of thine enemies overtaketh
thee; or else three days the sword of the LORD,
even the pestilence, in the land, and the angel of
the LORD destroying throughout all the coasts
of Is'ra-el. Now therefore advise thyself what
word I shall bring again to him that sent me.
13 And Da'vid said unto Gad, I am in a great
strait: let me fall now into the hand of the LORD;
for very great *are* his mercies: but let me not
fall into the hand of man.
14 ¶ So the LORD sent pestilence upon Is'ra-
el: and there fell of Is'ra-el seventy thousand
men.
15 And God sent an angel unto Je-ru'sa-lem
to destroy it: and as he was destroying, the
LORD beheld, and he repented him of the evil,
and said to the angel that destroyed, It is
enough, stay now thine hand. And the angel of
the LORD stood by the threshingfloor of Or'nan
the Jeb'u-site.
16 And Da'vid lifted up his eyes, and saw the
angel of the LORD stand between the earth and
the heaven, having a drawn sword in his hand
stretched out over Je-ru'sa-lem. Then Da'vid
and the elders *of Is'ra-el, who were* clothed in
sackcloth, fell upon their faces.
17 And Da'vid said unto God, *Is it* not I *that*
commanded the people to be numbered? even I
it is that have sinned and done evil indeed; but
as for these sheep, what have they done? let
thine hand, I pray thee, O LORD my God, be on
me, and on my father's house; but not on thy
people, that they should be plagued.
18 ¶ Then the angel of the LORD commanded
Gad to say to Da'vid, that Da'vid should go up,
and set up an altar unto the LORD in the threshingfloor of Or'nan the Jeb'u-site.
19 And Da'vid went up at the saying of Gad,
which he spake in the name of the LORD.
20 And Or'nan turned back, and saw the angel; and his four sons with him hid themselves.
Now Or'nan was threshing wheat.
21 And as Da'vid came to Or'nan, Or'nan
looked and saw Da'vid, and went out of the
threshingfloor, and bowed himself to Da'vid
with *his* face to the ground.
22 Then Da'vid said to Or'nan, Grant me the
place of *this* threshingfloor, that I may build an
altar therein unto the LORD: thou shalt grant it
me for the full price: that the plague may be
stayed from the people.
23 And Or'nan said unto Da'vid, Take *it* to
thee, and let my lord the king do *that which is*
good in his eyes: lo, I give *thee* the oxen *also*
for burnt offerings, and the threshing instruments for wood, and the wheat for the meat offering; I give it all.
24 And king Da'vid said to Or'nan, Nay; but I
will verily buy it for the full price: for I will not
take *that* which *is* thine for the LORD, nor offer
burnt offerings without cost.
25 So Da'vid gave to Or'nan for the place six
hundred shekels of gold by weight.
26 And Da'vid built there an altar unto the
LORD, and offered burnt offerings and peace offerings, and called upon the LORD; and he answered him from heaven by fire upon the altar
of burnt offering.
27 And the LORD commanded the angel; and
he put up his sword again into the sheath
thereof.
28 ¶ At that time when Da'vid saw that the
LORD had answered him in the threshingfloor of
Or'nan the Jeb'u-site, then he sacrificed there.
29 For the tabernacle of the LORD, which
Mo'ses made in the wilderness, and the altar of

the burnt offering, *were* at that season in the high place at Gib′e-on.

30 But Da′vid could not go before it to enquire of God: for he was afraid because of the sword of the angel of the LORD.

22 THEN Da′vid said, This *is* the house of the LORD God, and this *is* the altar of the burnt offering for Is′ra-el.

2 And Da′vid commanded to gather together the strangers that *were* in the land of Is′ra-el; and he set masons to hew wrought stones to build the house of God.

3 And Da′vid prepared iron in abundance for the nails for the doors of the gates, and for the joinings; and brass in abundance without weight;

4 Also cedar trees in abundance: for the Zi-do′ni-ans and they of Tyre brought much cedar wood to Da′vid.

5 And Da′vid said, Sol′o-mon my son *is* young and tender, and the house *that is* to be builded for the LORD *must be* exceeding magnifical, of fame and of glory throughout all countries: I will *therefore* now make preparation for it. So Da′vid prepared abundantly before his death.

6 ¶ Then he called for Sol′o-mon his son, and charged him to build an house for the LORD God of Is′ra-el.

7 And Da′vid said to Sol′o-mon, My son, as for me, it was in my mind to build an house unto the name of the LORD my God:

8 But the word of the LORD came to me, saying, Thou hast shed blood abundantly, and hast made great wars: thou shalt not build an house unto my name, because thou hast shed much blood upon the earth in my sight.

9 Behold, a son shall be born to thee, who shall be a man of rest; and I will give him rest from all his enemies round about: for his name shall be Sol′o-mon, and I will give peace and quietness unto Is′ra-el in his days.

10 He shall build an house for my name; and he shall be my son, and I *will be* his father; and I will establish the throne of his kingdom over Is′ra-el for ever.

11 Now, my son, the LORD be with thee; and prosper thou, and build the house of the LORD thy God, as he hath said of thee.

12 Only the LORD give thee wisdom and understanding, and give thee charge concerning Is′ra-el, that thou mayest keep the law of the LORD thy God.

13 Then shalt thou prosper, if thou takest heed to fulfil the statutes and judgments which the LORD charged Mo′ses with concerning Is′ra-el: be strong, and of good courage; dread not, nor be dismayed.

14 Now, behold, in my trouble I have prepared for the house of the LORD an hundred thousand talents of gold, and a thousand thousand talents of silver; and of brass and iron without weight; for it is in abundance: timber also and stone have I prepared; and thou mayest add thereto.

15 Moreover *there are* workmen with thee in abundance, hewers and workers of stone and timber, and all manner of cunning men for every manner of work.

16 Of the gold, the silver, and the brass, and the iron, *there is* no number. Arise *therefore,* and be doing, and the LORD be with thee.

17 ¶ Da′vid also commanded all the princes of Is′ra-el to help Sol′o-mon his son, *saying,*

18 *Is* not the LORD your God with you? and hath he *not* given you rest on every side? for he hath given the inhabitants of the land into mine hand; and the land is subdued before the LORD, and before his people.

19 Now set your heart and your soul to seek the LORD your God; arise therefore, and build ye the sanctuary of the LORD God, to bring the ark of the covenant of the LORD, and the holy vessels of God, into the house that is to be built to the name of the LORD.

23 SO when Da′vid was old and full of days, he made Sol′o-mon his son king over Is′ra-el.

2 ¶ And he gathered together all the princes of Is′ra-el, with the priests and the Le′vites.

3 Now the Le′vites were numbered from the age of thirty years and upward: and their number by their polls, man by man, was thirty and eight thousand.

4 Of which, twenty and four thousand *were* to set forward the work of the house of the LORD; and six thousand *were* officers and judges:

5 Moreover four thousand *were* porters; and four thousand praised the LORD with the instruments which I made, *said Da′vid,* to praise *therewith.*

6 And Da′vid divided them into courses among the sons of Le′vi, *namely,* Ger′shon, Ko′hath, and Me-ra′ri.

7 ¶ Of the Ger′shon-ites *were,* La′a-dan, and Shim′e-i.

8 The sons of La′a-dan; the chief *was* Je-hi′el, and Ze′tham, and Jo′el, three.

9 The sons of Shim′e-i; Shel′o-mith, and Ha′zi-el, and Ha′ran, three. These *were* the chief of the fathers of La′a-dan.

10 And the sons of Shim′e-i *were,* Ja′hath, Zi′na, and Je′ush, and Be-ri′ah. These four *were* the sons of Shim′e-i.

11 And Ja′hath was the chief, and Zi′zah the second: but Je′ush and Be-ri′ah had not many sons; therefore they were in one reckoning, according to *their* father's house.

12 ¶ The sons of Ko′hath; Am′ram, Iz′har, He′bron, and Uz′zi-el, four.

13 The sons of Am′ram; Aar′on and Mo′ses: and Aar′on was separated, that he should sanctify the most holy things, he and his sons for ever, to burn incense before the LORD, to minister unto him, and to bless in his name for ever.

14 Now *concerning* Mo′ses the man of God, his sons were named of the tribe of Le′vi.

15 The sons of Mo′ses *were,* Ger′shom, and E-li-e′zer.

16 Of the sons of Ger′shom, Sheb′u-el *was* the chief.

17 And the sons of E-li-e′zer *were,* Re-ha-bi′ah the chief. And E-li-e′zer had none other sons; but the sons of Re-ha-bi′ah were very many.

18 Of the sons of Iz′har; Shel′o-mith the chief.

19 Of the sons of He′bron; Je-ri′ah the first, Am-a-ri′ah the second, Ja-ha′zi-el the third, and Jek-a-me′am the fourth.

20 Of the sons of Uz′zi-el; Mi′cah the first, and Je-si′ah the second.

21 ¶ The sons of Me-ra′ri; Mah′li, and Mu′shi. The sons of Mah′li; E-le-a′zar, and Kish.

22 And E-le-a′zar died, and had no sons, but daughters: and their brethren the sons of Kish took them.

23 The sons of Mu′shi; Mah′li, and E′der, and Jer′e-moth, three.

24 ¶ These *were* the sons of Le′vi after the house of their fathers; *even* the chief of the fathers, as they were counted by number of

names by their polls, that did the work for the
service of the house of the LORD, from the age
of twenty years and upward.
25 For Da'vid said, The LORD God of Is'ra-el
hath given rest unto his people, that they may
dwell in Je-ru'sa-lem for ever:
26 And also unto the Le'vites; they shall no
more carry the tabernacle, nor any vessels of it
for the service thereof.
27 For by the last words of Da'vid the Le'-
vites *were* numbered from twenty years old and
above:
28 Because their office *was* to wait on the
sons of Aar'on for the service of the house of
the LORD, in the courts, and in the chambers,
and in the purifying of all holy things, and the
work of the service of the house of God;
29 Both for the shewbread, and for the fine
flour for meat offering, and for the unleavened
cakes, and for *that which is baked in* the pan,
and for that which is fried, and for all manner of
measure and size;
30 And to stand every morning to thank and
praise the LORD, and likewise at even;
31 And to offer all burnt sacrifices unto the
LORD in the sabbaths, in the new moons, and on
the set feasts, by number, according to the order commanded unto them, continually before
the LORD:
32 And that they should keep the charge of
the tabernacle of the congregation, and the
charge of the holy *place*, and the charge of the
sons of Aar'on their brethren, in the service of
the house of the LORD.

24 NOW *these are* the divisions of the sons
of Aar'on. The sons of Aar'on; Na'dab,
and A-bi'hu, E-le-a'zar, and Ith'a-mar.
2 But Na'dab and A-bi'hu died before their
father, and had no children: therefore E-le-a'zar
and Ith'a-mar executed the priest's office.
3 And Da'vid distributed them, both Za'dok
of the sons of E-le-a'zar, and A-him'e-lech of the
sons of Ith'a-mar, according to their offices in
their service.
4 And there were more chief men found of
the sons of E-le-a'zar than of the sons of Ith'a-
mar; and *thus* were they divided. Among the
sons of E-le-a'zar *there were* sixteen chief men
of the house of *their* fathers, and eight among
the sons of Ith'a-mar according to the house of
their fathers.
5 Thus were they divided by lot, one sort
with another; for the governors of the sanctuary, and governors *of the house* of God, were of
the sons of E-le-a'zar, and of the sons of Ith'a-
mar.
6 And Shem-a-i'ah the son of Ne-than'e-el
the scribe, *one* of the Le'vites, wrote them before the king, and the princes, and Za'dok the
priest, and A-him'e-lech the son of A-bi'a-thar,
and *before* the chief of the fathers of the priests
and Le'vites: one principal household being
taken for E-le-a'zar, and *one* taken for Ith'a-
mar.
7 Now the first lot came forth to Je-hoi'a-rib,
the second to Je-da'iah.
8 The third to Ha'rim, the fourth to Se-o'rim,
9 The fifth to Mal-chi'jah, the sixth to Mij'a-
min,
10 The seventh to Hak'koz, the eighth to A-
bi'jah,
11 The ninth to Jesh'u-ah, the tenth to Shech-
a-ni'ah,
12 The eleventh to E-li'a-shib, the twelfth to
Ja'kim,
13 The thirteenth to Hup'pah, the fourteenth
to Je'sheb'e-ab,
14 The fifteenth to Bil'gah, the sixteenth to
Im'mer,
15 The seventeenth to He'zir, the eighteenth
to Aph'ses,
16 The nineteenth to Peth-a-hi'ah, the twentieth to Je-hez'e-kel,
17 The one and twentieth to Ja'chin, the two
and twentieth to Ga'mul,
18 The three and twentieth to Del-a-i'ah, the
four and twentieth to Ma-a-zi'ah.
19 These *were* the orderings of them in their
service to come into the house of the LORD, according to their manner, under Aar'on their father, as the LORD God of Is'ra-el had commanded him.
20 ¶ And the rest of the sons of Le'vi *were
these:* Of the sons of Am'ram; Shu'ba-el: of the
sons of Shu'ba-el; Jeh-de'iah.
21 Concerning Re-ha-bi'ah: of the sons of Re-
ha-bi'ah, the first *was* Issh-i'ah.
22 Of the Iz'har-ites; Shel'o-moth: of the sons
of Shel'o-moth; Ja'hath.
23 And the sons of *He'bron;* Je-ri'ah *the first,*
Am-a-ri'ah the second, Ja-ha'zi-el the third, Jek-
a-me'am the fourth.
24 *Of* the sons of Uz'zi-el; Mi'chah: of the
sons of Mi'chah; Sha'mir.
25 The brother of Mi'chah *was* Issh-i'ah: of
the sons of Issh-i'ah; Zech-a-ri'ah.
26 The sons of Me-ra'ri *were* Mah'li and Mu'-
shi: the sons of Ja-a-zi'ah; Be'no.
27 ¶ The sons of Me-ra'ri by Ja-a-zi'ah; Be'-
no, and Sho'ham, and Zac'cur, and Ib'ri.
28 Of Mah'li *came* E-le-a'zar, who had no
sons.
29 Concerning Kish: the son of Kish *was* Je-
rah'me-el.
30 The sons also of Mu'shi; Mah'li, and E'der,
and Jer'i-moth. These *were* the sons of the Le'-
vites after the house of their fathers.
31 These likewise cast lots over against their
brethren the sons of Aar'on in the presence of
Da'vid the king, and Za'dok, and A-him'e-lech,
and the chief of the fathers of the priests and
Le'vites, even the principal fathers over against
their younger brethren.

25 MOREOVER Da'vid and the captains of
the host separated to the service of the
sons of A'saph, and of He'man, and of Jed'u-
thun, who should prophesy with harps, with
psalteries, and with cymbals: and the number
of the workmen according to their service was:
2 Of the sons of A'saph; Zac'cur, and Jo'seph,
and Neth-a-ni'ah, and As-a-re'lah, the sons of
A'saph under the hands of A'saph, which
prophesied according to the order of the king.
3 Of Jed'u-thun: the sons of Jed'u-thun; Ged-
a-li'ah, and Ze'ri, and Je-sha'iah, Hash-a-bi'ah,
and Mat-ti-thi'ah, six, under the hands of their
father Jed'u-thun, who prophesied with a harp,
to give thanks and to praise the LORD.
4 Of He'man: the sons of He'man; Buk-ki'ah,
Mat-ta-ni'ah, Uz'zi-el, Sheb'u-el, and Jer'i-moth,
Han-a-ni'ah, Ha-na'ni, E-li'a-thah, Gid-dal'ti,
and Ro-mam'ti–e'zer, Josh-bek'a-shah, Mal'lo-
thi, Ho'thir, *and* Ma-ha'zi-oth:
5 All these *were* the sons of He'man the
king's seer in the words of God, to lift up the
horn. And God gave to He'man fourteen sons
and three daughters.
6 All these *were* under the hands of their father for song *in* the house of the LORD, with
cymbals, psalteries, and harps, for the service

of the house of God, according to the king's order to A'saph, Jed'u-thun, and He'man.

7 So the number of them, with their brethren that were instructed in the songs of the LORD, *even* all that were cunning, was two hundred fourscore and eight.

8 ¶ And they cast lots, ward against *ward,* as well the small as the great, the teacher as the scholar.

9 Now the first lot came forth for A'saph to Jo'seph: the second to Ged-a-li'ah, who with his brethren and sons *were* twelve:

10 The third to Zac'cur, *he,* his sons, and his brethren, *were* twelve:

11 The fourth to Iz'ri, *he,* his sons, and his brethren, *were* twelve:

12 The fifth to Neth-a-ni'ah, *he,* his sons, and his brethren, *were* twelve:

13 The sixth to Buk-ki'ah, *he,* his sons, and his brethren, *were* twelve:

14 The seventh to Je-shar'e-lah, *he,* his sons, and his brethren, *were* twelve:

15 The eighth to Je-sha'iah, *he,* his sons, and his brethren, *were* twelve:

16 The ninth to Mat-ta-ni'ah, *he,* his sons, and his brethren, *were* twelve:

17 The tenth to Shim'e-i, *he,* his sons, and his brethren, *were* twelve:

18 The eleventh to A-zar'e-el, *he,* his sons, and his brethren, *were* twelve:

19 The twelfth to Hash-a-bi'ah, *he,* his sons, and his brethren, *were* twelve:

20 The thirteenth to Shu'ba-el, *he,* his sons, and his brethren, *were* twelve:

21 The fourteenth to Mat-ti-thi'ah, *he,* his sons, and his brethren, *were* twelve:

22 The fifteenth to Jer'e-moth, *he,* his sons, and his brethren, *were* twelve:

23 The sixteenth to Han-a-ni'ah, *he,* his sons, and his brethren, *were* twelve:

24 The seventeenth to Josh-bek'a-shah, *he,* his sons, and his brethren, *were* twelve:

25 The eighteenth to Ha-na'ni, *he,* his sons, and his brethren, *were* twelve:

26 The nineteenth to Mal'lo-thi, *he,* his sons, and his brethren, *were* twelve:

27 The twentieth to E-li'a-thah, *he,* his sons, and his brethren, *were* twelve:

28 The one and twentieth to Ho'thir, *he,* his sons, and his brethren, *were* twelve:

29 The two and twentieth to Gid-dal'ti, *he,* his sons, and his brethren, *were* twelve:

30 The three and twentieth to Ma-ha'zi-oth, *he,* his sons, and his brethren, *were* twelve:

31 The four and twentieth to Ro-mam'ti–e'zer, *he,* his sons, and his brethren, *were* twelve.

26

CONCERNING the divisions of the porters: Of the Kor'hites *was* Me-shel-e-mi'ah the son of Ko're, of the sons of A'saph.

2 And the sons of Me-shel-e-mi'ah *were,* Zech-a-ri'ah the firstborn, Je-di'a-el the second, Zeb-a-di'ah the third, Jath'ni-el the fourth,

3 E'lam the fifth, Je-ho-ha'nan the sixth, El-i-o-e'na-i the seventh.

4 Moreover the sons of O'bed–e'dom *were,* Shem-a-i'ah the firstborn, Je-hoz'a-bad the second, Jo'ah the third, and Sa'car the fourth, and Ne-than'e-el the fifth,

5 Am'mi-el the sixth, Is'sa-char the seventh, Pe-ul'thai the eighth: for God blessed him.

6 Also unto Shem-a-i'ah his son were sons born, that ruled throughout the house of their father: for they *were* mighty men of valour.

7 The sons of Shem-a-i'ah; Oth'ni, and Re'pha-el, and O'bed, El'za-bad, whose brethren *were* strong men, E-li'hu, and Sem-a-chi'ah.

8 All these of the sons of O'bed–e'dom: they and their sons and their brethren, able men for strength for the service, *were* threescore and two of O'bed–e'dom.

9 And Me-shel-e-mi'ah had sons and brethren, strong men, eighteen.

10 Also Ho'sah, of the children of Me-ra'ri, had sons; Sim'ri the chief, (for *though* he was not the firstborn, yet his father made him the chief;)

11 Hil-ki'ah the second, Teb-a-li'ah the third, Zech-a-ri'ah the fourth: all the sons and brethren of Ho'sah *were* thirteen.

12 Among these *were* the divisions of the porters, *even* among the chief men, *having* wards one against another, to minister in the house of the LORD.

13 ¶ And they cast lots, as well the small as the great, according to the house of their fathers, for every gate.

14 And the lot eastward fell to Shel-e-mi'ah. Then for Zech-a-ri'ah his son, a wise counsellor, they cast lots; and his lot came out northward.

15 To O'bed–e'dom southward; and to his sons the house of A-sup'pim.

16 To Shup'pim and Ho'sah *the lot came forth* westward, with the gate Shal'le-cheth, by the causeway of the going up, ward against ward.

17 Eastward *were* six Le'vites, northward four a day, southward four a day, and toward A-sup'pim two *and* two.

18 At Par'bar westward, four at the causeway, *and* two at Par'bar.

19 These *are* the divisions of the porters among the sons of Ko're, and among the sons of Me-ra'ri.

20 ¶ And of the Le'vites, A-hi'jah *was* over the treasures of the house of God, and over the treasures of the dedicated things.

21 *As concerning* the sons of La'a-dan; the sons of the Ger'shon-ite La'a-dan, chief fathers, *even* of La'a-dan the Ger'shon-ite, *were* Je-hi'e-li.

22 The sons of Je-hi'e-li; Ze'tham, and Jo'el his brother, *which were* over the treasures of the house of the LORD.

23 Of the Am'ram-ites, *and* the Iz'har-ites, the He'bron-ites, *and* the Uz'zi-el-ites:

24 And Sheb'u-el the son of Ger'shom, the son of Mo'ses, *was* ruler of the treasures.

25 And his brethren by E-li-e'zer; Re-ha-bi'ah his son, and Je-sha'iah his son, and Jo'ram his son, and Zich'ri his son, and Shel'o-mith his son.

26 Which Shel'o-mith and his brethren *were* over all the treasures of the dedicated things, which Da'vid the king, and the chief fathers, the captains over thousands and hundreds, and the captains of the host, had dedicated.

27 Out of the spoils won in battles did they dedicate to maintain the house of the LORD.

28 And all that Sam'u-el the seer, and Saul the son of Kish, and Ab'ner the son of Ner, and Jo'ab the son of Zer-u-i'ah, had dedicated; *and* whosoever had dedicated *any thing, it was* under the hand of Shel'o-mith, and of his brethren.

29 ¶ Of the Iz'har-ites, Chen-a-ni'ah and his sons *were* for the outward business over Is'ra-el, for officers and judges.

30 *And* of the He'bron-ites, Hash-a-bi'ah and his brethren, men of valour, a thousand and seven hundred, *were* officers among them of Is'ra-el on this side Jor'dan westward in all the business of the LORD, and in the service of the king.

31 Among the He'bron-ites *was* Je-ri'jah the

chief, *even* among the He'bron-ites, according
to the generations of his fathers. In the fortieth
year of the reign of Da'vid they were sought for,
and there were found among them mighty men
of valour at Ja'zer of Gil'e-ad.
32 And his brethren, men of valour, *were* two
thousand and seven hundred chief fathers,
whom king Da'vid made rulers over the Reu'-
ben-ites, the Gad'ites, and the half tribe of Ma-
nas'seh, for every matter pertaining to God, and
affairs of the king.

27 NOW the children of Is'ra-el after their
number, *to wit,* the chief fathers and
captains of thousands and hundreds, and their
officers that served the king in any matter of the
courses, which came in and went out month by
month throughout all the months of the year, of
every course *were* twenty and four thousand.
2 Over the first course for the first month
was Ja-sho'be-am the son of Zab'di-el: and in
his course *were* twenty and four thousand.
3 Of the children of Pe'rez *was* the chief of all
the captains of the host for the first month.
4 And over the course of the second month
was Dod'a-i an A-ho'hite, and of his course *was*
Mik'loth also the ruler: in his course likewise
were twenty and four thousand.
5 The third captain of the host for the third
month *was* Be-na'iah the son of Je-hoi'a-da, a
chief priest: and in his course *were* twenty and
four thousand.
6 This *is that* Be-na'iah, *who was* mighty
among the thirty, and above the thirty: and in
his course *was* Am-miz'a-bad his son.
7 The fourth *captain* for the fourth month
was A'sa-hel the brother of Jo'ab, and Zeb-a-
di'ah his son after him: and in his course *were*
twenty and four thousand.
8 The fifth captain for the fifth month *was*
Sham'huth the Iz'ra-hite: and in his course *were*
twenty and four thousand.
9 The sixth *captain* for the sixth month *was*
I'ra the son of Ik'kesh the Te-ko'ite: and in his
course *were* twenty and four thousand.
10 The seventh *captain* for the seventh
month *was* He'lez the Pel'o-nite, of the children
of E'phra-im: and in his course *were* twenty and
four thousand.
11 The eighth *captain* for the eighth month
was Sib'be-cai the Hu'shath-ite, of the Zar'-
hites: and in his course *were* twenty and four
thousand.
12 The ninth *captain* for the ninth month
was A-bi-e'zer the An'e-toth-ite, of the Ben'ja-
mites: and in his course *were* twenty and four
thousand.
13 The tenth *captain* for the tenth month
was Ma-har'a-i the Ne-toph'a-thite, of the Zar'-
hites: and in his course *were* twenty and four
thousand.
14 The eleventh *captain* for the eleventh
month *was* Be-na'iah the Pir'a-thon-ite, of the
children of E'phra-im: and in his course *were*
twenty and four thousand.
15 The twelfth *captain* for the twelfth month
was Hel'da-i the Ne-toph'a-thite, of Oth'ni-el:
and in his course *were* twenty and four thousand.
16 ¶ Furthermore over the tribes of Is'ra-el:
the ruler of the Reu'ben-ites *was* E-li-e'zer the
son of Zich'ri: of the Sim'e-on-ites, Sheph-a-ti'-
ah the son of Ma'a-chah:
17 Of the Le'vites, Hash-a-bi'ah the son of
Ke-mu'el: of the Aar'on-ites, Za'dok:
18 Of Ju'dah, E-li'hu, *one* of the brethren of
Da'vid: of Is'sa-char, Om'ri the son of Mi'chael:
19 Of Zeb'u-lun, Ish-ma-i'ah the son of O-ba-
di'ah: of Naph'ta-li, Jer'i-moth the son of Az'ri-
el:
20 Of the children of E'phra-im, Ho-she'a the
son of Az-a-zi'ah: of the half tribe of Ma-nas'-
seh, Jo'el the son of Pe-da'iah:
21 Of the half *tribe* of Ma-nas'seh in Gil'e-ad,
Id'do the son of Zech-a-ri'ah: of Ben'ja-min, Ja-
a'si-el the son of Ab'ner:
22 Of Dan, A-zar'e-el the son of Jer'o-ham.
These *were* the princes of the tribes of Is'ra-el.
23 ¶ But Da'vid took not the number of them
from twenty years old and under: because the
LORD had said he would increase Is'ra-el like to
the stars of the heavens.
24 Jo'ab the son of Zer-u-i'ah began to number, but he finished not, because there fell
wrath for it against Is'ra-el; neither was the
number put in the account of the chronicles of
king Da'vid.
25 ¶ And over the king's treasures *was* Az'-
ma-veth the son of A-di'el: and over the storehouses in the fields, in the cities, and in the villages, and in the castles, *was* Je-hon'a-than the
son of Uz-zi'ah:
26 And over them that did the work of the
field for tillage of the ground *was* Ez'ri the son
of Che'lub:
27 And over the vineyards *was* Shim'e-i the
Ra'math-ite: over the increase of the vineyards
for the wine cellars *was* Zab'di the Shiph'mite:
28 And over the olive trees and the sycomore
trees that *were* in the low plains *was* Ba'al–ha'-
nan the Ged'e-rite: and over the cellars of oil
was Jo'ash:
29 And over the herds that fed in Shar'on
was Shit'ra-i the Shar'on-ite: and over the herds
that were in the valleys *was* Sha'phat the son of
Ad'la-i:
30 Over the camels also *was* O'bil the Ish'-
ma-el-ite: and over the asses *was* Jeh-de'iah the
Me-ron'-o-thite:
31 And over the flocks *was* Ja'ziz the Ha'ger-
ite. All these *were* the rulers of the substance
which *was* king Da'vid's.
32 Also Jon'a-than Da'vid's uncle was a
counsellor, a wise man, and a scribe: and Je-
hi'el the son of Hach'mo-ni *was* with the king's
sons:
33 And A-hith'o-phel *was* the king's counsellor: and Hu'shai the Ar'chite *was* the king's
companion:
34 And after A-hith'o-phel *was* Je-hoi'a-da
the son of Be-na'iah, and A-bi'a-thar: and the
general of the king's army *was* Jo'ab.

28 AND Da'vid assembled all the princes
of Is'ra-el, the princes of the tribes, and
the captains of the companies that ministered
to the king by course, and the captains over the
thousands, and captains over the hundreds, and
the stewards over all the substance and possession of the king, and of his sons, with the officers, and with the mighty men, and with all the
valiant men, unto Je-ru'sa-lem.
2 Then Da'vid the king stood up upon his
feet, and said, Hear me, my brethren, and my
people: *As for me,* I *had* in mine heart to build
an house of rest for the ark of the covenant of
the LORD, and for the footstool of our God, and
had made ready for the building:
3 But God said unto me, Thou shalt not build
an house for my name, because thou *hast been*
a man of war, and hast shed blood.
4 Howbeit the LORD God of Is'ra-el chose me
before all the house of my father to be king over
Is'ra-el for ever: for he hath chosen Ju'dah *to be*

the ruler; and of the house of Ju'dah, the house
of my father; and among the sons of my father
he liked me to make *me* king over all Is'ra-el:
5 And of all my sons, (for the LORD hath giv-
en me many sons,) he hath chosen Sol'o-mon
my son to sit upon the throne of the kingdom of
the LORD over Is'ra-el.
6 And he said unto me, Sol'o-mon thy son, he
shall build my house and my courts: for I have
chosen him *to be* my son, and I will be his father.
7 Moreover I will establish his kingdom for
ever, if he be constant to do my commandments
and my judgments, as at this day.
8 Now therefore in the sight of all Is'ra-el the
congregation of the LORD, and in the audience
of our God, keep and seek for all the commandments of the LORD your God: that ye may possess this good land, and leave *it* for an inheritance for your children after you for ever.
9 ¶ And thou, Sol'o-mon my son, know thou
the God of thy father, and serve him with a perfect heart and with a willing mind: for the LORD
searcheth all hearts, and understandeth all the
imaginations of the thoughts: if thou seek him,
he will be found of thee; but if thou forsake him,
he will cast thee off for ever.
10 Take heed now; for the LORD hath chosen
thee to build an house for the sanctuary: be
strong, and do *it*.
11 ¶ Then Da'vid gave to Sol'o-mon his son
the pattern of the porch, and of the houses
thereof, and of the treasuries thereof, and of the
upper chambers thereof, and of the inner par-
lours thereof, and of the place of the mercy
seat,
12 And the pattern of all that he had by the
spirit, of the courts of the house of the LORD,
and of all the chambers round about, of the
treasuries of the house of God, and of the treasuries of the dedicated things:
13 Also for the courses of the priests and the
Le'vites, and for all the work of the service of
the house of the LORD, and for all the vessels of
service in the house of the LORD.
14 *He gave* of gold by weight for *things* of
gold, for all instruments of all manner of service; *silver also* for all instruments of silver by
weight, for all instruments of every kind of service:
15 Even the weight for the candlesticks of
gold, and for their lamps of gold, by weight for
every candlestick, and for the lamps thereof:
and for the candlesticks of silver by weight,
both for the candlestick, and *also* for the lamps
thereof, according to the use of every candlestick.
16 And by weight *he gave* gold for the tables
of shewbread, for every table; and *likewise* silver for the tables of silver:
17 Also pure gold for the fleshhooks, and the
bowls, and the cups: and for the golden basons
he gave gold by weight for every bason; and
likewise silver by weight for every bason of silver:
18 And for the altar of incense refined gold
by weight; and gold for the pattern of the
chariot of the cherubims, that spread out *their*
wings, and covered the ark of the covenant of
the LORD.
19 All *this, said Da'vid,* the LORD made me
understand in writing by *his* hand upon me,
even all the works of this pattern.
20 And Da'vid said to Sol'o-mon his son, Be
strong and of good courage, and do *it:* fear not,
nor be dismayed: for the LORD God, *even* my
God, *will be* with thee; he will not fail thee, nor
forsake thee, until thou hast finished all the
work for the service of the house of the LORD.
21 And, behold, the courses of the priests
and the Le'vites, *even they shall be with thee* for
all the service of the house of God: and *there*
shall be with thee for all manner of workmanship every willing skilful man, for any manner
of service: also the princes and all the people
will be wholly at thy commandment.

29 FURTHERMORE Da'vid the king said
unto all the congregation, Sol'o-mon my
son, whom alone God hath chosen, *is yet* young
and tender, and the work *is* great: for the palace
is not for man, but for the LORD God.
2 Now I have prepared with all my might for
the house of my God the gold for *things to be*
made of gold, and the silver for *things* of silver,
and the brass for *things* of brass, the iron for
things of iron, and wood for *things* of wood;
onyx stones, and *stones* to be set, glistering
stones, and of divers colours, and all manner of
precious stones, and marble stones in abundance.
3 Moreover, because I have set my affection
to the house of my God, I have of mine own
proper good, of gold and silver, *which* I have
given to the house of my God, over and above
all that I have prepared for the holy house,
4 *Even* three thousand talents of gold, of the
gold of O'phir, and seven thousand talents of
refined silver, to overlay the walls of the houses
withal:
5 The gold for *things* of gold, and the silver
for *things* of silver, and for all manner of work
to be made by the hands of artificers. And who
then is willing to consecrate his service this day
unto the LORD?
6 ¶ Then the chief of the fathers and princes
of the tribes of Is'ra-el, and the captains of thousands and of hundreds, with the rulers of the
king's work, offered willingly,
7 And gave for the service of the house of
God of gold five thousand talents and ten thousand drams, and of silver ten thousand talents,
and of brass eighteen thousand talents, and one
hundred thousand talents of iron.
8 And they with whom *precious* stones were
found gave *them* to the treasure of the house of
the LORD, by the hand of Je-hi'el the Ger'shon-
ite.
9 Then the people rejoiced, for that they offered willingly, because with perfect heart they
offered willingly to the LORD: and Da'vid the
king also rejoiced with great joy.
10 ¶ Wherefore Da'vid blessed the LORD before all the congregation: and Da'vid said,
Blessed *be* thou, LORD God of Is'ra-el our father,
for ever and ever.
11 Thine, O LORD, *is* the greatness, and the
power, and the glory, and the victory, and the
majesty: for all *that is* in the heaven and in the
earth *is thine;* thine *is* the kingdom, O LORD,
and thou art exalted as head above all.
12 Both riches and honour *come* of thee, and
thou reignest over all; and in thine hand *is*
power and might; and in thine hand *it is* to
make great, and to give strength unto all.
13 Now therefore, our God, we thank thee,
and praise thy glorious name.
14 But who *am* I, and what *is* my people, that
we should be able to offer so willingly after this
sort? for all things *come* of thee, and of thine
own have we given thee.
15 For we *are* strangers before thee, and sojourners, as *were* all our fathers: our days on

the earth *are* as a shadow, and *there is* none abiding.

16 O LORD our God, all this store that we have prepared to build thee an house for thine holy name *cometh* of thine hand, and *is* all thine own.

17 I know also, my God, that thou triest the heart, and hast pleasure in uprightness. As for me, in the uprightness of mine heart I have willingly offered all these things: and now have I seen with joy thy people, which are present here, to offer willingly unto thee.

18 O LORD God of A'bra-ham, I'saac, and of Is'ra-el, our fathers, keep this for ever in the imagination of the thoughts of the heart of thy people, and prepare their heart unto thee:

19 And give unto Sol'o-mon my son a perfect heart, to keep thy commandments, thy testimonies, and thy statutes, and to do all *these things*, and to build the palace, *for* the which I have made provision.

20 ¶ And Da'vid said to all the congregation, Now bless the LORD your God. And all the congregation blessed the LORD God of their fathers, and bowed down their heads, and worshipped the LORD, and the king.

21 And they sacrificed sacrifices unto the LORD, and offered burnt offerings unto the LORD, on the morrow after that day, *even* a thousand bullocks, a thousand rams, *and* a thousand lambs, with their drink offerings, and sacrifices in abundance for all Is'ra-el:

22 And did eat and drink before the LORD on that day with great gladness. And they made Sol'o-mon the son of Da'vid king the second time, and anointed *him* unto the LORD *to be* the chief governor, and Za'dok *to be* priest.

23 Then Sol'o-mon sat on the throne of the LORD as king instead of Da'vid his father, and prospered; and all Is'ra-el obeyed him.

24 And all the princes, and the mighty men, and all the sons likewise of king Da'vid, submitted themselves unto Sol'o-mon the king.

25 And the LORD magnified Sol'o-mon exceedingly in the sight of all Is'ra-el, and bestowed upon him *such* royal majesty as had not been on any king before him in Is'ra-el.

26 ¶ Thus Da'vid the son of Jes'se reigned over all Is'ra-el.

27 And the time that he reigned over Is'ra-el *was* forty years; seven years reigned he in He'bron, and thirty and three *years* reigned he in Je-ru'sa-lem.

28 And he died in a good old age, full of days, riches, and honour: and Sol'o-mon his son reigned in his stead.

29 Now the acts of Da'vid the king, first and last, behold, they *are* written in the book of Sam'u-el the seer, and in the book of Na'than the prophet, and in the book of Gad the seer,

30 With all his reign and his might, and the times that went over him, and over Is'ra-el, and over all the kingdoms of the countries.

THE SECOND BOOK OF THE

CHRONICLES

1 AND Sol'o-mon the son of Da'vid was strengthened in his kingdom, and the LORD his God *was* with him, and magnified him exceedingly.

2 Then Sol'o-mon spake unto all Is'ra-el, to the captains of thousands and of hundreds, and to the judges, and to every governor in all Is'ra-el, the chief of the fathers.

3 So Sol'o-mon, and all the congregation with him, went to the high place that *was* at Gib'e-on; for there was the tabernacle of the congregation of God, which Mo'ses the servant of the LORD had made in the wilderness.

4 But the ark of God had Da'vid brought up from Kir'jath-je'a-rim to *the place which* Da'vid had prepared for it: for he had pitched a tent for it at Je-ru'sa-lem.

5 Moreover the brasen altar, that Be-zal'e-el the son of U'ri, the son of Hur had made, he put before the tabernacle of the LORD: and Sol'o-mon and the congregation sought unto it.

6 And Sol'o-mon went up thither to the brasen altar before the LORD, which *was* at the tabernacle of the congregation, and offered a thousand burnt offerings upon it.

7 ¶ In that night did God appear unto Sol'o-mon, and said unto him, Ask what I shall give thee.

8 And Sol'o-mon said unto God, Thou hast shewed great mercy unto Da'vid my father, and hast made me to reign in his stead.

9 Now, O LORD God, let thy promise unto Da'vid my father be established: for thou hast made me king over a people like the dust of the earth in multitude.

10 Give me now wisdom and knowledge, that I may go out and come in before this people: for who can judge this thy people, *that is so* great?

11 And God said to Sol'o-mon, Because this was in thine heart, and thou hast not asked riches, wealth, or honour, nor the life of thine enemies, neither yet hast asked long life; but hast asked wisdom and knowledge for thyself, that thou mayest judge my people, over whom I have made thee king:

12 Wisdom and knowledge *is* granted unto thee; and I will give thee riches, and wealth, and honour, such as none of the kings have had that *have been* before thee, neither shall there any after thee have the like.

13 ¶ Then Sol'o-mon came *from his journey* to the high place that *was* at Gib'e-on to Je-ru'sa-lem, from before the tabernacle of the congregation, and reigned over Is'ra-el.

14 And Sol'o-mon gathered chariots and horsemen: and he had a thousand and four hundred chariots, and twelve thousand horsemen, which he placed in the chariot cities, and with the king at Je-ru'sa-lem.

15 And the king made silver and gold at Je-ru'sa-lem *as plenteous* as stones, and cedar trees made he as the sycomore trees that *are* in the vale for abundance.

16 And Sol'o-mon had horses brought out of E'gypt, and linen yarn: the king's merchants received the linen yarn at a price.

17 And they fetched up, and brought forth out of E'gypt a chariot for six hundred *shekels* of silver, and an horse for an hundred and fifty: and so brought they out *horses* for all the kings of the Hit'tites, and for the kings of Syr'i-a, by their means.

2 AND Sol'o-mon determined to build an house for the name of the LORD, and an house for his kingdom.

2 And Sol'o-mon told out threescore and ten thousand men to bear burdens, and fourscore thousand to hew in the mountain, and three thousand and six hundred to oversee them.

3 ¶ And Sol'o-mon sent to Hu'ram the king of Tyre, saying, As thou didst deal with Da'vid my father, and didst send him cedars to build him an house to dwell therein, *even so deal with me.*

4 Behold, I build an house to the name of the LORD my God, to dedicate *it* to him, *and* to burn before him sweet incense, and for the continual shewbread, and for the burnt offerings morning and evening, on the sabbaths, and on the new moons, and on the solemn feasts of the LORD our God. This *is an ordinance* for ever to Is'ra-el.

5 And the house which I build *is* great: for great *is* our God above all gods.

6 But who is able to build him an house, seeing the heaven and heaven of heavens cannot contain him? who *am* I then, that I should build him an house, save only to burn sacrifice before him?

7 Send me now therefore a man cunning to work in gold, and in silver, and in brass, and in iron, and in purple, and crimson, and blue, and that can skill to grave with the cunning men that *are* with me in Ju'dah and in Je-ru'sa-lem, whom Da'vid my father did provide.

8 Send me also cedar trees, fir trees, and algum trees, out of Leb'a-non: for I know that thy servants can skill to cut timber in Leb'a-non; and, behold, my servants *shall be* with thy servants,

9 Even to prepare me timber in abundance: for the house which I am about to build *shall be* wonderful great.

10 And, behold, I will give to thy servants, the hewers that cut timber, twenty thousand measures of beaten wheat, and twenty thousand measures of barley, and twenty thousand baths of wine, and twenty thousand baths of oil.

11 ¶ Then Hu'ram the king of Tyre answered in writing, which he sent to Sol'o-mon, Because the LORD hath loved his people, he hath made thee king over them.

12 Hu'ram said moreover, Blessed *be* the LORD God of Is'ra-el, that made heaven and earth, who hath given to Da'vid the king a wise son, endued with prudence and understanding, that might build an house for the LORD, and an house for his kingdom.

13 And now I have sent a cunning man, endued with understanding, of Hu'ram my father's,

14 The son of a woman of the daughters of Dan, and his father *was* a man of Tyre, skilful to work in gold, and in silver, in brass, in iron, in stone, and in timber, in purple, in blue, and in fine linen, and in crimson; also to grave any manner of graving, and to find out every device which shall be put to him, with thy cunning men, and with the cunning men of my lord Da'vid thy father.

15 Now therefore the wheat, and the barley, the oil, and the wine, which my lord hath spoken of, let him send unto his servants:

16 And we will cut wood out of Leb'a-non, as much as thou shalt need: and we will bring it to thee in floats by sea to Jop'pa; and thou shalt carry it up to Je-ru'sa-lem.

17 ¶ And Sol'o-mon numbered all the strangers that *were* in the land of Is'ra-el, after the numbering wherewith Da'vid his father had numbered them; and they were found an hundred and fifty thousand and three thousand and six hundred.

18 And he set threescore and ten thousand of them *to be* bearers of burdens, and fourscore thousand *to be* hewers in the mountain, and three thousand and six hundred overseers to set the people a work.

3 THEN Sol'o-mon began to build the house of the LORD at Je-ru'sa-lem in mount Mo-ri'ah, where *the LORD* appeared unto Da'vid his father, in the place that Da'vid had prepared in the threshingfloor of Or'nan the Jeb'u-site.

2 And he began to build in the second *day* of the second month, in the fourth year of his reign.

3 ¶ Now these *are the things wherein* Sol'o-mon was instructed for the building of the house of God. The length by cubits after the first measure *was* threescore cubits, and the breadth twenty cubits.

4 And the porch that *was* in the front *of the house,* the length *of it was* according to the breadth of the house, twenty cubits, and the height *was* an hundred and twenty: and he overlaid it within with pure gold.

5 And the greater house he cieled with fir tree, which he overlaid with fine gold, and set thereon palm trees and chains.

6 And he garnished the house with precious stones for beauty: and the gold *was* gold of Par-va'im.

7 He overlaid also the house, the beams, the posts, and the walls thereof, and the doors thereof, with gold; and graved cherubims on the walls.

8 And he made the most holy house, the length whereof *was* according to the breadth of the house, twenty cubits, and the breadth thereof twenty cubits: and he overlaid it with fine gold, *amounting* to six hundred talents.

9 And the weight of the nails *was* fifty shekels of gold. And he overlaid the upper chambers with gold.

10 And in the most holy house he made two cherubims of image work, and overlaid them with gold.

11 ¶ And the wings of the cherubims *were* twenty cubits long: one wing *of the one cherub was* five cubits, reaching to the wall of the house: and the other wing *was likewise* five cubits, reaching to the wing of the other cherub.

12 And *one* wing of the other cherub *was* five cubits, reaching to the wall of the house: and the other wing *was* five cubits *also,* joining to the wing of the other cherub.

13 The wings of these cherubims spread themselves forth twenty cubits: and they stood on their feet, and their faces *were* inward.

14 ¶ And he made the veil *of* blue, and purple, and crimson, and fine linen, and wrought cherubims thereon.

15 Also he made before the house two pillars of thirty and five cubits high, and the chapiter that *was* on the top of each of them *was* five cubits.

16 And he made chains, *as* in the oracle, and put *them* on the heads of the pillars; and made an hundred pomegranates, and put *them* on the chains.

17 And he reared up the pillars before the temple, one on the right hand, and the other on the left; and called the name of that on the right hand Ja'chin, and the name of that on the left Bo'az.

4 MOREOVER he made an altar of brass, twenty cubits the length thereof, and twenty cubits the breadth thereof, and ten cubits the height thereof.

2 ¶ Also he made a molten sea of ten cubits from brim to brim, round in compass, and five cubits the height thereof; and a line of thirty cubits did compass it round about.

3 And under it *was* the similitude of oxen, which did compass it round about: ten in a cubit, compassing the sea round about. Two rows of oxen *were* cast, when it was cast.

4 It stood upon twelve oxen, three looking toward the north, and three looking toward the west, and three looking toward the south, and three looking toward the east: and the sea *was set* above upon them, and all their hinder parts *were* inward.

5 And the thickness of it *was* an handbreadth, and the brim of it like the work of the brim of a cup, with flowers of lilies; *and* it received and held three thousand baths.

6 ¶ He made also ten lavers, and put five on the right hand, and five on the left, to wash in them: such things as they offered for the burnt offering they washed in them; but the sea *was* for the priests to wash in.

7 And he made ten candlesticks of gold according to their form, and set *them* in the temple, five on the right hand, and five on the left.

8 He made also ten tables, and placed *them* in the temple, five on the right side, and five on the left. And he made an hundred basons of gold.

9 ¶ Furthermore he made the court of the priests, and the great court, and doors for the court, and overlaid the doors of them with brass.

10 And he set the sea on the right side of the east end, over against the south.

11 And Hu'ram made the pots, and the shovels, and the basons. And Hu'ram finished the work that he was to make for king Sol'o-mon for the house of God;

12 *To wit,* the two pillars, and the pommels, and the chapiters *which were* on the top of the two pillars, and the two wreaths to cover the two pommels of the chapiters which *were* on the top of the pillars;

13 And four hundred pomegranates on the two wreaths; two rows of pomegranates on each wreath, to cover the two pommels of the chapiters which *were* upon the pillars.

14 He made also bases, and lavers made he upon the bases;

15 One sea, and twelve oxen under it.

16 The pots also, and the shovels, and the fleshhooks, and all their instruments, did Hu'ram his father make to king Sol'o-mon for the house of the LORD of bright brass.

17 In the plain of Jor'dan did the king cast them, in the clay ground between Suc'coth and Ze-red'a-thah.

18 Thus Sol'o-mon made all these vessels in great abundance: for the weight of the brass could not be found out.

19 ¶ And Sol'o-mon made all the vessels that *were for* the house of God, the golden altar also, and the tables whereon the shewbread *was set;*

20 Moreover the candlesticks with their lamps, that they should burn after the manner before the oracle, of pure gold;

21 And the flowers, and the lamps, and the tongs, *made he of* gold, *and* that perfect gold;

22 And the snuffers, and the basons, and the spoons, and the censers, *of* pure gold: and the entry of the house, the inner doors thereof for the most holy *place*, and the doors of the house of the temple, *were of* gold.

5 THUS all the work that Sol'o-mon made for the house of the LORD was finished: and Sol'o-mon brought in *all* the things that Da'vid his father had dedicated; and the silver, and the gold, and all the instruments, put he among the treasures of the house of God.

2 ¶ Then Sol'o-mon assembled the elders of Is'ra-el, and all the heads of the tribes, the chief of the fathers of the children of Is'ra-el, unto Je-ru'sa-lem, to bring up the ark of the covenant of the LORD out of the city of Da'vid, which *is* Zi'-on.

3 Wherefore all the men of Is'ra-el assembled themselves unto the king in the feast which *was* in the seventh month.

4 And all the elders of Is'ra-el came; and the Le'vites took up the ark.

5 And they brought up the ark, and the tabernacle of the congregation, and all the holy vessels that *were* in the tabernacle, these did the priests *and* the Le'vites bring up.

6 Also king Sol'o-mon, and all the congregation of Is'ra-el that were assembled unto him before the ark, sacrificed sheep and oxen, which could not be told nor numbered for multitude.

7 And the priests brought in the ark of the covenant of the LORD unto his place, to the oracle of the house, into the most holy *place, even* under the wings of the cherubims:

8 For the cherubims spread forth *their* wings over the place of the ark, and the cherubims covered the ark and the staves thereof above.

9 And they drew out the staves *of the ark,* that the ends of the staves were seen from the ark before the oracle; but they were not seen without. And there it is unto this day.

10 *There was* nothing in the ark save the two tables which Mo'ses put *therein* at Ho'reb, when the LORD made *a covenant* with the children of Is'ra-el, when they came out of E'gypt.

11 ¶ And it came to pass, when the priests were come out of the holy *place:* (for all the priests *that were* present were sanctified, *and* did not *then* wait by course:

12 Also the Le'vites *which were* the singers, all of them of A'saph, of He'man, of Jed'u-thun, with their sons and their brethren, *being* arrayed in white linen, having cymbals and psalteries and harps, stood at the east end of the altar, and with them an hundred and twenty priests sounding with trumpets:)

13 It came even to pass, as the trumpeters and singers *were* as one, to make one sound to be heard in praising and thanking the LORD; and when they lifted up *their* voice with the trumpets and cymbals and instruments of musick, and praised the LORD, *saying,* For *he is* good; for his mercy *endureth* for ever: that *then* the house was filled with a cloud, *even* the house of the LORD;

14 So that the priests could not stand to minister by reason of the cloud: for the glory of the LORD had filled the house of God.

6 THEN said Sol'o-mon, The LORD hath said that he would dwell in the thick darkness.

2 But I have built an house of habitation for thee, and a place for thy dwelling for ever.

3 And the king turned his face, and blessed the whole congregation of Is'ra-el: and all the congregation of Is'ra-el stood.

4 And he said, Blessed *be* the LORD God of Is'ra-el, who hath with his hands fulfilled *that*

which he spake with his mouth to my father Da'vid, saying,

5 Since the day that I brought forth my people out of the land of E'gypt I chose no city among all the tribes of Is'ra-el to build an house in, that my name might be there; neither chose I any man to be a ruler over my people Is'ra-el:

6 But I have chosen Je-ru'sa-lem, that my name might be there; and have chosen Da'vid to be over my people Is'ra-el.

7 Now it was in the heart of Da'vid my father to build an house for the name of the LORD God of Is'ra-el.

8 But the LORD said to Da'vid my father, Forasmuch as it was in thine heart to build an house for my name, thou didst well in that it was in thine heart:

9 Notwithstanding thou shalt not build the house; but thy son which shall come forth out of thy loins, he shall build the house for my name.

10 The LORD therefore hath performed his word that he hath spoken: for I am risen up in the room of Da'vid my father, and am set on the throne of Is'ra-el, as the LORD promised, and have built the house for the name of the LORD God of Is'ra-el.

11 And in it have I put the ark, wherein *is* the covenant of the LORD, that he made with the children of Is'ra-el.

12 ¶ And he stood before the altar of the LORD in the presence of all the congregation of Is'ra-el, and spread forth his hands:

13 For Sol'o-mon had made a brasen scaffold, of five cubits long, and five cubits broad, and three cubits high, and had set it in the midst of the court: and upon it he stood, and kneeled down upon his knees before all the congregation of Is'ra-el, and spread forth his hands toward heaven,

14 And said, O LORD God of Is'ra-el, *there is* no God like thee in the heaven, nor in the earth; which keepest covenant, and *shewest* mercy unto thy servants, that walk before thee with all their hearts:

15 Thou which hast kept with thy servant Da'vid my father that which thou hast promised him; and spakest with thy mouth, and hast fulfilled *it* with thine hand, as *it is* this day.

16 Now therefore, O LORD God of Is'ra-el, keep with thy servant Da'vid my father that which thou hast promised him, saying, There shall not fail thee a man in my sight to sit upon the throne of Is'ra-el; yet so that thy children take heed to their way to walk in my law, as thou hast walked before me.

17 Now then, O LORD God of Is'ra-el, let thy word be verified, which thou hast spoken unto thy servant Da'vid.

18 But will God in very deed dwell with men on the earth? behold, heaven and the heaven of heavens cannot contain thee; how much less this house which I have built!

19 Have respect therefore to the prayer of thy servant, and to his supplication, O LORD my God, to hearken unto the cry and the prayer which thy servant prayeth before thee:

20 That thine eyes may be open upon this house day and night, upon the place whereof thou hast said that thou wouldest put thy name there; to hearken unto the prayer which thy servant prayeth toward this place.

21 Hearken therefore unto the supplications of thy servant, and of thy people Is'ra-el, which they shall make toward this place: hear thou from thy dwelling place, *even* from heaven; and when thou hearest, forgive.

22 ¶ If a man sin against his neighbour, and an oath be laid upon him to make him swear, and the oath come before thine altar in this house;

23 Then hear thou from heaven, and do, and judge thy servants, by requiting the wicked, by recompensing his way upon his own head; and by justifying the righteous, by giving him according to his righteousness.

24 ¶ And if thy people Is'ra-el be put to the worse before the enemy, because they have sinned against thee; and shall return and confess thy name, and pray and make supplication before thee in this house;

25 Then hear thou from the heavens, and forgive the sin of thy people Is'ra-el, and bring them again unto the land which thou gavest to them and to their fathers.

26 ¶ When the heaven is shut up, and there is no rain, because they have sinned against thee; *yet* if they pray toward this place, and confess thy name, and turn from their sin, when thou dost afflict them;

27 Then hear thou from heaven, and forgive the sin of thy servants, and of thy people Is'ra-el, when thou hast taught them the good way, wherein they should walk; and send rain upon thy land, which thou hast given unto thy people for an inheritance.

28 ¶ If there be dearth in the land, if there be pestilence, if there be blasting, or mildew, locusts, or caterpillers; if their enemies besiege them in the cities of their land; whatsoever sore or whatsoever sickness *there be:*

29 *Then* what prayer *or* what supplication soever shall be made of any man, or of all thy people Is'ra-el, when every one shall know his own sore and his own grief, and shall spread forth his hands in this house:

30 Then hear thou from heaven thy dwelling place, and forgive, and render unto every man according unto all his ways, whose heart thou knowest; (for thou only knowest the hearts of the children of men:)

31 That they may fear thee, to walk in thy ways, so long as they live in the land which thou gavest unto our fathers.

32 ¶ Moreover concerning the stranger, which is not of thy people Is'ra-el, but is come from a far country for thy great name's sake, and thy mighty hand, and thy stretched out arm; if they come and pray in this house;

33 Then hear thou from the heavens, *even* from thy dwelling place, and do according to all that the stranger calleth to thee for; that all people of the earth may know thy name, and fear thee, as *doth* thy people Is'ra-el, and may know that this house which I have built is called by thy name.

34 If thy people go out to war against their enemies by the way that thou shalt send them, and they pray unto thee toward this city which thou hast chosen, and the house which I have built for thy name;

35 Then hear thou from the heavens their prayer and their supplication, and maintain their cause.

36 If they sin against thee, (for *there is* no man which sinneth not,) and thou be angry with them, and deliver them over before *their* enemies, and they carry them away captives unto a land far off or near;

37 Yet *if* they bethink themselves in the land whither they are carried captive, and turn and pray unto thee in the land of their captivity, saying, We have sinned, we have done amiss, and have dealt wickedly;

38 If they return to thee with all their heart
and with all their soul in the land of their captivity, whither they have carried them captives,
and pray toward their land, which thou gavest
unto their fathers, and *toward* the city which
thou hast chosen, and toward the house which I
have built for thy name:
39 Then hear thou from the heavens, *even*
from thy dwelling place, their prayer and their
supplications, and maintain their cause, and
forgive thy people which have sinned against
thee.
40 Now, my God, let, I beseech thee, thine
eyes be open, and *let* thine ears *be* attent unto
the prayer *that is made* in this place.
41 Now therefore arise, O LORD God, into thy
resting place, thou, and the ark of thy strength:
let thy priests, O LORD God, be clothed with salvation, and let thy saints rejoice in goodness.
42 O LORD God, turn not away the face of
thine anointed: remember the mercies of Da'vid
thy servant.

7 NOW when Sol'o-mon had made an end of
praying, the fire came down from heaven,
and consumed the burnt offering and the sacrifices; and the glory of the LORD filled the house.
2 And the priests could not enter into the
house of the LORD, because the glory of the
LORD had filled the LORD's house.
3 And when all the children of Is'ra-el saw
how the fire came down, and the glory of the
LORD upon the house, they bowed themselves
with their faces to the ground upon the pavement, and worshipped, and praised the LORD,
saying, For *he is* good; for his mercy *endureth*
for ever.
4 ¶ Then the king and all the people offered
sacrifices before the LORD.
5 And king Sol'o-mon offered a sacrifice of
twenty and two thousand oxen, and an hundred
and twenty thousand sheep: so the king and all
the people dedicated the house of God.
6 And the priests waited on their offices: the
Le'vites also with instruments of musick of the
LORD, which Da'vid the king had made to praise
the LORD, because his mercy *endureth* for ever,
when Da'vid praised by their ministry; and the
priests sounded trumpets before them, and all
Is'ra-el stood.
7 Moreover Sol'o-mon hallowed the middle
of the court that *was* before the house of the
LORD: for there he offered burnt offerings, and
the fat of the peace offerings, because the brasen altar which Sol'o-mon had made was not
able to receive the burnt offerings, and the meat
offerings, and the fat.
8 ¶ Also at the same time Sol'o-mon kept the
feast seven days, and all Is'ra-el with him, a
very great congregation, from the entering in of
Ha'math unto the river of E'gypt.
9 And in the eighth day they made a solemn
assembly: for they kept the dedication of the
altar seven days, and the feast seven days.
10 And on the three and twentieth day of the
seventh month he sent the people away into
their tents, glad and merry in heart for the
goodness that the LORD had shewed unto Da'-
vid, and to Sol'o-mon, and to Is'ra-el his people.
11 Thus Sol'o-mon finished the house of the
LORD, and the king's house: and all that came
into Sol'o-mon's heart to make in the house of
the LORD, and in his own house, he prosperously effected.
12 ¶ And the LORD appeared to Sol'o-mon by
night, and said unto him, I have heard thy
prayer, and have chosen this place to myself for
an house of sacrifice.
13 If I shut up heaven that there be no rain,
or if I command the locusts to devour the land,
or if I send pestilence among my people;
14 If my people, which are called by my
name, shall humble themselves, and pray, and
seek my face, and turn from their wicked ways;
then will I hear from heaven, and will forgive
their sin, and will heal their land.
15 Now mine eyes shall be open, and mine
ears attent unto the prayer *that is made* in this
place.
16 For now have I chosen and sanctified this
house, that my name may be there for ever: and
mine eyes and mine heart shall be there perpetually.
17 And as for thee, if thou wilt walk before
me, as Da'vid thy father walked, and do according to all that I have commanded thee, and shalt
observe my statutes and my judgments;
18 Then will I stablish the throne of thy kingdom, according as I have covenanted with Da'-
vid thy father, saying, There shall not fail thee a
man *to be* ruler in Is'ra-el.
19 But if ye turn away, and forsake my statutes and my commandments, which I have set
before you, and shall go and serve other gods,
and worship them;
20 Then will I pluck them up by the roots out
of my land which I have given them; and this
house, which I have sanctified for my name, will I
cast out of my sight, and will make it *to be* a proverb and a byword among all nations.
21 And this house, which is high, shall be an
astonishment to every one that passeth by it; so
that he shall say, Why hath the LORD done thus
unto this land, and unto this house?
22 And it shall be answered, Because they
forsook the LORD God of their fathers, which
brought them forth out of the land of E'gypt,
and laid hold on other gods, and worshipped
them, and served them: therefore hath he
brought all this evil upon them.

8 AND it came to pass at the end of twenty
years, wherein Sol'o-mon had built the
house of the LORD, and his own house,
2 That the cities which Hu'ram had restored
to Sol'o-mon, Sol'o-mon built them, and caused
the children of Is'ra-el to dwell there.
3 And Sol'o-mon went to Ha'math–zo'bah,
and prevailed against it.
4 And he built Tad'mor in the wilderness,
and all the store cities, which he built in Ha'-
math.
5 Also he built Beth–ho'ron the upper, and
Beth–ho'ron the nether, fenced cities, with
walls, gates, and bars;
6 And Ba'al-ath, and all the store cities that
Sol'o-mon had, and all the chariot cities, and
the cities of the horsemen, and all that Sol'o-
mon desired to build in Je-ru'sa-lem, and in
Leb'a-non, and throughout all the land of his
dominion.
7 ¶ *As for* all the people *that were* left of the
Hit'tites, and the Am'or-ites, and the Per'iz-
zites, and the Hi'vites, and the Jeb'u-sites,
which *were* not of Is'ra-el,
8 *But* of their children, who were left after
them in the land, whom the children of Is'ra-el
consumed not, them did Sol'o-mon make to pay
tribute until this day.
9 But of the children of Is'ra-el did Sol'o-mon
make no servants for his work; but they *were*
men of war, and chief of his captains, and captains of his chariots and horsemen.

10 And these *were* the chief of king Sol'o-mon's officers, *even* two hundred and fifty, that bare rule over the people.

11 ¶ And Sol'o-mon brought up the daughter of Pha'raoh out of the city of Da'vid unto the house that he had built for her: for he said, My wife shall not dwell in the house of Da'vid king of Is'ra-el, because *the places are* holy, whereunto the ark of the LORD hath come.

12 ¶ Then Sol'o-mon offered burnt offerings unto the LORD on the altar of the LORD, which he had built before the porch,

13 Even after a certain rate every day, offering according to the commandment of Mo'ses, on the sabbaths, and on the new moons, and on the solemn feasts, three times in the year, *even* in the feast of unleavened bread, and in the feast of weeks, and in the feast of tabernacles.

14 ¶ And he appointed, according to the order of Da'vid his father, the courses of the priests to their service, and the Le'vites to their charges, to praise and minister before the priests, as the duty of every day required: the porters also by their courses at every gate: for so had Da'vid the man of God commanded.

15 And they departed not from the commandment of the king unto the priests and Le'vites concerning any matter, or concerning the treasures.

16 Now all the work of Sol'o-mon was prepared unto the day of the foundation of the house of the LORD, and until it was finished. *So* the house of the LORD was perfected.

17 ¶ Then went Sol'o-mon to E'zi-on-ge'ber, and to E'loth, at the sea side in the land of E'dom.

18 And Hu'ram sent him by the hands of his servants ships, and servants that had knowledge of the sea; and they went with the servants of Sol'o-mon to O'phir, and took thence four hundred and fifty talents of gold, and brought *them* to king Sol'o-mon.

9 AND when the queen of She'ba heard of the fame of Sol'o-mon, she came to prove Sol'o-mon with hard questions at Je-ru'sa-lem, with a very great company, and camels that bare spices, and gold in abundance, and precious stones: and when she was come to Sol'o-mon, she communed with him of all that was in her heart.

2 And Sol'o-mon told her all her questions: and there was nothing hid from Sol'o-mon which he told her not.

3 And when the queen of She'ba had seen the wisdom of Sol'o-mon, and the house that he had built,

4 And the meat of his table, and the sitting of his servants, and the attendance of his ministers, and their apparel; his cupbearers also, and their apparel; and his ascent by which he went up into the house of the LORD; there was no more spirit in her.

5 And she said to the king, *It was* a true report which I heard in mine own land of thine acts, and of thy wisdom:

6 Howbeit I believed not their words, until I came, and mine eyes had seen *it:* and, behold, the one half of the greatness of thy wisdom was not told me: *for* thou exceedest the fame that I heard.

7 Happy *are* thy men, and happy *are* these thy servants, which stand continually before thee, and hear thy wisdom.

8 Blessed be the LORD thy God, which delighted in thee to set thee on his throne, *to be* king for the LORD thy God: because thy God loved Is'ra-el, to establish them for ever, therefore made he thee king over them, to do judgment and justice.

9 And she gave the king an hundred and twenty talents of gold, and of spices great abundance, and precious stones: neither was there any such spice as the queen of She'ba gave king Sol'o-mon.

10 And the servants also of Hu'ram, and the servants of Sol'o-mon, which brought gold from O'phir, brought algum trees and precious stones.

11 And the king made *of* the algum trees terraces to the house of the LORD, and to the king's palace, and harps and psalteries for singers: and there were none such seen before in the land of Ju'dah.

12 And king Sol'o-mon gave to the queen of She'ba all her desire, whatsoever she asked, beside *that* which she had brought unto the king. So she turned, and went away to her own land, she and her servants.

13 ¶ Now the weight of gold that came to Sol'o-mon in one year was six hundred and threescore and six talents of gold;

14 Beside *that which* chapmen and merchants brought. And all the kings of A-ra'bi-a and governors of the country brought gold and silver to Sol'o-mon.

15 ¶ And king Sol'o-mon made two hundred targets *of* beaten gold: six hundred *shekels* of beaten gold went to one target.

16 And three hundred shields *made he of* beaten gold: three hundred *shekels* of gold went to one shield. And the king put them in the house of the forest of Leb'a-non.

17 Moreover the king made a great throne of ivory, and overlaid it with pure gold.

18 And *there were* six steps to the throne, with a footstool of gold, *which were* fastened to the throne, and stays on each side of the sitting place, and two lions standing by the stays:

19 And twelve lions stood there on the one side and the other upon the six steps. There was not the like made in any kingdom.

20 ¶ And all the drinking vessels of king Sol'o-mon *were of* gold, and all the vessels of the house of the forest of Leb'a-non *were of* pure gold: none *were of* silver; it was *not* any thing accounted of in the days of Sol'o-mon.

21 For the king's ships went to Tar'shish with the servants of Hu'ram: every three years once came the ships of Tar'shish bringing gold, and silver, ivory, and apes, and peacocks.

22 And king Sol'o-mon passed all the kings of the earth in riches and wisdom.

23 ¶ And all the kings of the earth sought the presence of Sol'o-mon, to hear his wisdom, that God had put in his heart.

24 And they brought every man his present, vessels of silver, and vessels of gold, and raiment, harness, and spices, horses, and mules, a rate year by year.

25 ¶ And Sol'o-mon had four thousand stalls for horses and chariots, and twelve thousand horsemen; whom he bestowed in the chariot cities, and with the king at Je-ru'sa-lem.

26 ¶ And he reigned over all the kings from the river even unto the land of the Phi-lis'tines, and to the border of E'gypt.

27 And the king made silver in Je-ru'sa-lem as stones, and cedar trees made he as the sycomore trees that *are* in the low plains in abundance.

28 And they brought unto Sol'o-mon horses out of E'gypt, and out of all lands.

29 ¶ Now the rest of the acts of Sol'o-mon,

first and last, *are* they not written in the book of
Na'than the prophet, and in the prophecy of A-
hi'jah the Shi'lo-nite, and in the visions of Id'do
the seer against Jer-o-bo'am the son of Ne'bat?
30 And Sol'o-mon reigned in Je-ru'sa-lem
over all Is'ra-el forty years.
31 And Sol'o-mon slept with his fathers, and
he was buried in the city of Da'vid his father:
and Re-ho-bo'am his son reigned in his stead.

10 AND Re-ho-bo'am went to She'chem:
for to She'chem were all Is'ra-el come to
make him king.
2 And it came to pass, when Jer-o-bo'am the
son of Ne'bat, who *was* in E'gypt, whither he
had fled from the presence of Sol'o-mon the
king, heard *it*, that Jer-o-bo'am returned out of
E'gypt.
3 And they sent and called him. So Jer-o-bo'-
am and all Is'ra-el came and spake to Re-ho-
bo'am, saying,
4 Thy father made our yoke grievous: now
therefore ease thou somewhat the grievous servitude of thy father, and his heavy yoke that he
put upon us, and we will serve thee.
5 And he said unto them, Come again unto
me after three days. And the people departed.
6 ¶ And king Re-ho-bo'am took counsel with
the old men that had stood before Sol'o-mon his
father while he yet lived, saying, What counsel
give ye *me* to return answer to this people?
7 And they spake unto him, saying, If thou be
kind to this people, and please them, and speak
good words to them, they will be thy servants
for ever.
8 But he forsook the counsel which the old
men gave him, and took counsel with the young
men that were brought up with him, that stood
before him.
9 And he said unto them, What advice give
ye that we may return answer to this people,
which have spoken to me, saying, Ease somewhat the yoke that thy father did put upon us?
10 And the young men that were brought up
with him spake unto him, saying, Thus shalt
thou answer the people that spake unto thee,
saying, Thy father made our yoke heavy, but
make thou *it* somewhat lighter for us; thus shalt
thou say unto them, My little *finger* shall be
thicker than my father's loins.
11 For whereas my father put a heavy yoke
upon you, I will put more to your yoke: my father chastised you with whips, but I *will chastise you* with scorpions.
12 So Jer-o-bo'am and all the people came to
Re-ho-bo'am on the third day, as the king bade,
saying, Come again to me on the third day.
13 And the king answered them roughly; and
king Re-ho-bo'am forsook the counsel of the old
men,
14 And answered them after the advice of
the young men, saying, My father made your
yoke heavy, but I will add thereto: my father
chastised you with whips, but I *will chastise
you* with scorpions.
15 So the king hearkened not unto the people: for the cause was of God, that the LORD
might perform his word, which he spake by the
hand of A-hi'jah the Shi'lo-nite to Jer-o-bo'am
the son of Ne'bat.
16 ¶ And when all Is'ra-el *saw* that the king
would not hearken unto them, the people answered the king, saying, What portion have we
in Da'vid? and *we have* none inheritance in the
son of Jes'se: every man to your tents, O Is'ra-
el: *and* now, Da'vid, see to thine own house. So
all Is'ra-el went to their tents.
17 But *as for* the children of Is'ra-el that
dwelt in the cities of Ju'dah, Re-ho-bo'am
reigned over them.
18 Then king Re-ho-bo'am sent Ha-do'ram
that *was* over the tribute; and the children of
Is'ra-el stoned him with stones, that he died.
But king Re-ho-bo'am made speed to get him
up to *his* chariot, to flee to Je-ru'sa-lem.
19 And Is'ra-el rebelled against the house of
Da'vid unto this day.

11 AND when Re-ho-bo'am was come to
Je-ru'sa-lem, he gathered of the house
of Ju'dah and Ben'ja-min an hundred and fourscore thousand chosen *men*, which were warriors, to fight against Is'ra-el, that he might
bring the kingdom again to Re-ho-bo'am.
2 But the word of the LORD came to Shem-a-
i'ah the man of God, saying,
3 Speak unto Re-ho-bo'am the son of Sol'o-
mon, king of Ju'dah, and to all Is'ra-el in Ju'dah
and Ben'ja-min, saying,
4 Thus saith the LORD, Ye shall not go up, nor
fight against your brethren: return every man to
his house: for this thing is done of me. And they
obeyed the words of the LORD, and returned
from going against Jer-o-bo'am.
5 ¶ And Re-ho-bo'am dwelt in Je-ru'sa-lem,
and built cities for defence in Ju'dah.
6 He built even Beth'-le-hem, and E'tam, and
Te-ko'a,
7 And Beth'-zur, and Sho'co, and A-dul'lam,
8 And Gath, and Ma-re'shah, and Ziph,
9 And Ad-o-ra'im, and La'chish, and A-ze'-
kah,
10 And Zo'rah, and Aij'a-lon, and He'bron,
which *are* in Ju'dah and in Ben'ja-min fenced
cities.
11 And he fortified the strong holds, and put
captains in them, and store of victual, and of oil
and wine.
12 And in every several city *he put* shields
and spears, and made them exceeding strong,
having Ju'dah and Ben'ja-min on his side.
13 ¶ And the priests and the Le'vites that
were in all Is'ra-el resorted to him out of all
their coasts.
14 For the Le'vites left their suburbs and
their possession, and came to Ju'dah and Je-ru'-
sa-lem: for Jer-o-bo'am and his sons had cast
them off from executing the priest's office unto
the LORD:
15 And he ordained him priests for the high
places, and for the devils, and for the calves
which he had made.
16 And after them out of all the tribes of Is'-
ra-el such as set their hearts to seek the LORD
God of Is'ra-el came to Je-ru'sa-lem, to sacrifice
unto the LORD God of their fathers.
17 So they strengthened the kingdom of Ju'-
dah, and made Re-ho-bo'am the son of Sol'o-
mon strong, three years: for three years they
walked in the way of Da'vid and Sol'o-mon.
18 ¶ And Re-ho-bo'am took him Ma'ha-lath
the daughter of Jer'i-moth the son of Da'vid to
wife, *and* Ab-i-ha'il the daughter of E-li'ab the
son of Jes'se;
19 Which bare him children; Je'ush, and
Sham-a-ri'ah, and Za'ham.
20 And after her he took Ma'a-chah the
daughter of Ab'sa-lom; which bare him A-bi'-
jah, and At'tai, and Zi'za, and Shel'o-mith.
21 And Re-ho-bo'am loved Ma'a-chah the
daughter of Ab'sa-lom above all his wives and
his concubines: (for he took eighteen wives, and
threescore concubines; and begat twenty and
eight sons, and threescore daughters.)

22 And Re-ho-bo'am made A-bi'jah the son of Ma'a-chah the chief, *to be* ruler among his brethren: for *he thought* to make him king.
23 And he dealt wisely, and dispersed of all his children throughout all the countries of Ju'dah and Ben'ja-min, unto every fenced city: and he gave them victual in abundance. And he desired many wives.

12 AND it came to pass, when Re-ho-bo'am had established the kingdom, and had strengthened himself, he forsook the law of the LORD, and all Is'ra-el with him.
2 And it came to pass, *that* in the fifth year of king Re-ho-bo'am Shi'shak king of E'gypt came up against Je-ru'sa-lem, because they had transgressed against the LORD,
3 With twelve hundred chariots, and threescore thousand horsemen: and the people *were* without number that came with him out of E'gypt; the Lu'bims, the Suk'ki-ims, and the E-thi-o'pi-ans.
4 And he took the fenced cities which *pertained* to Ju'dah, and came to Je-ru'sa-lem.
5 ¶ Then came Shem-a-i'ah the prophet to Re-ho-bo'am, and *to* the princes of Ju'dah, that were gathered together to Je-ru'sa-lem because of Shi'shak, and said unto them, Thus saith the LORD, Ye have forsaken me, and therefore have I also left you in the hand of Shi'shak.
6 Whereupon the princes of Is'ra-el and the king humbled themselves; and they said, The LORD *is* righteous.
7 And when the LORD saw that they humbled themselves, the word of the LORD came to Shem-a-i'ah, saying, They have humbled themselves; *therefore* I will not destroy them, but I will grant them some deliverance; and my wrath shall not be poured out upon Je-ru'sa-lem by the hand of Shi'shak.
8 Nevertheless they shall be his servants; that they may know my service, and the service of the kingdoms of the countries.
9 So Shi'shak king of E'gypt came up against Je-ru'sa-lem, and took away the treasures of the house of the LORD, and the treasures of the king's house; he took all: he carried away also the shields of gold which Sol'o-mon had made.
10 Instead of which king Re-ho-bo'am made shields of brass, and committed *them* to the hands of the chief of the guard, that kept the entrance of the king's house.
11 And when the king entered into the house of the LORD, the guard came and fetched them, and brought them again into the guard chamber.
12 And when he humbled himself, the wrath of the LORD turned from him, that he would not destroy *him* altogether: and also in Ju'dah things went well.
13 ¶ So king Re-ho-bo'am strengthened himself in Je-ru'sa-lem, and reigned: for Re-ho-bo'am *was* one and forty years old when he began to reign, and he reigned seventeen years in Je-ru'sa-lem, the city which the LORD had chosen out of all the tribes of Is'ra-el, to put his name there. And his mother's name *was* Na'a-mah an Am'mon-it-ess.
14 And he did evil, because he prepared not his heart to seek the LORD.
15 Now the acts of Re-ho-bo'am, first and last, *are* they not written in the book of Shem-a-i'ah the prophet, and of Id'do the seer concerning genealogies? And *there were* wars between Re-ho-bo'am and Jer-o-bo'am continually.
16 And Re-ho-bo'am slept with his fathers, and was buried in the city of Da'vid: and A-bi'jah his son reigned in his stead.

13 NOW in the eighteenth year of king Jer-o-bo'am began A-bi'jah to reign over Ju'dah.
2 He reigned three years in Je-ru'sa-lem. His mother's name also *was* Mi-cha'iah the daughter of U'ri-el of Gib'e-ah. And there was war between A-bi'jah and Jer-o-bo'am.
3 And A-bi'jah set the battle in array with an army of valiant men of war, *even* four hundred thousand chosen men: Jer-o-bo'am also set the battle in array against him with eight hundred thousand chosen men, *being* mighty men of valour.
4 ¶ And A-bi'jah stood up upon mount Zem-a-ra'im, which *is* in mount E'phra-im, and said, Hear me, thou Jer-o-bo'am, and all Is'ra-el;
5 Ought ye not to know that the LORD God of Is'ra-el gave the kingdom over Is'ra-el to Da'vid for ever, *even* to him and to his sons by a covenant of salt?
6 Yet Jer-o-bo'am the son of Ne'bat, the servant of Sol'o-mon the son of Da'vid, is risen up, and hath rebelled against his lord.
7 And there are gathered unto him vain men, the children of Be'li-al, and have strengthened themselves against Re-ho-bo'am the son of Sol'o-mon, when Re-ho-bo'am was young and tenderhearted, and could not withstand them.
8 And now ye think to withstand the kingdom of the LORD in the hand of the sons of Da'vid; and ye *be* a great multitude, and *there are* with you golden calves, which Jer-o-bo'am made you for gods.
9 Have ye not cast out the priests of the LORD, the sons of Aar'on, and the Le'vites, and have made you priests after the manner of the nations of *other* lands? so that whosoever cometh to consecrate himself with a young bullock and seven rams, *the same* may be a priest of *them that are* no gods.
10 But as for us, the LORD *is* our God, and we have not forsaken him; and the priests, which minister unto the LORD, *are* the sons of Aar'on, and the Le'vites *wait* upon *their* business:
11 And they burn unto the LORD every morning and every evening burnt sacrifices and sweet incense: the shewbread also *set they in order* upon the pure table; and the candlestick of gold with the lamps thereof, to burn every evening: for we keep the charge of the LORD our God; but ye have forsaken him.
12 And, behold, God himself *is* with us for *our* captain, and his priests with sounding trumpets to cry alarm against you. O children of Is'ra-el, fight ye not against the LORD God of your fathers; for ye shall not prosper.
13 ¶ But Jer-o-bo'am caused an ambushment to come about behind them: so they were before Ju'dah, and the ambushment *was* behind them.
14 And when Ju'dah looked back, behold, the battle *was* before and behind: and they cried unto the LORD, and the priests sounded with the trumpets.
15 Then the men of Ju'dah gave a shout: and as the men of Ju'dah shouted, it came to pass, that God smote Jer-o-bo'am and all Is'ra-el before A-bi'jah and Ju'dah.
16 And the children of Is'ra-el fled before Ju'dah: and God delivered them into their hand.
17 And A-bi'jah and his people slew them with a great slaughter: so there fell down slain of Is'ra-el five hundred thousand chosen men.
18 Thus the children of Is'ra-el were brought

under at that time, and the children of Ju'dah prevailed, because they relied upon the LORD God of their fathers.

19 And A-bi'jah pursued after Jer-o-bo'am, and took cities from him, Beth'-el with the towns thereof, and Jesh'a-nah with the towns thereof, and E'phra-in with the towns thereof.

20 Neither did Jer-o-bo'am recover strength again in the days of A-bi'jah: and the LORD struck him, and he died.

21 ¶ But A-bi'jah waxed mighty, and married fourteen wives, and begat twenty and two sons, and sixteen daughters.

22 And the rest of the acts of A-bi'jah, and his ways, and his sayings, *are* written in the story of the prophet Id'do.

14

SO A-bi'jah slept with his fathers, and they buried him in the city of Da'vid: and A'sa his son reigned in his stead. In his days the land was quiet ten years.

2 And A'sa did *that which was* good and right in the eyes of the LORD his God:

3 For he took away the altars of the strange *gods*, and the high places, and brake down the images, and cut down the groves:

4 And commanded Ju'dah to seek the LORD God of their fathers, and to do the law and the commandment.

5 Also he took away out of all the cities of Ju'dah the high places and the images: and the kingdom was quiet before him.

6 ¶ And he built fenced cities in Ju'dah: for the land had rest, and he had no war in those years; because the LORD had given him rest.

7 Therefore he said unto Ju'dah, Let us build these cities, and make about *them* walls, and towers, gates, and bars, *while* the land *is* yet before us; because we have sought the LORD our God, we have sought *him*, and he hath given us rest on every side. So they built and prospered.

8 And A'sa had an army *of men* that bare targets and spears, out of Ju'dah three hundred thousand; and out of Ben'ja-min, that bare shields and drew bows, two hundred and fourscore thousand: all these *were* mighty men of valour.

9 ¶ And there came out against them Ze'rah the E-thi-o'pi-an with an host of a thousand thousand, and three hundred chariots; and came unto Ma-re'shah.

10 Then A'sa went out against him, and they set the battle in array in the valley of Zeph'a-thah at Ma-re'shah.

11 And A'sa cried unto the LORD his God, and said, LORD, *it is* nothing with thee to help, whether with many, or with them that have no power: help us, O LORD our God; for we rest on thee, and in thy name we go against this multitude. O LORD, thou *art* our God; let not man prevail against thee.

12 So the LORD smote the E-thi-o'pi-ans before A'sa, and before Ju'dah; and the E-thi-o'pi-ans fled.

13 And A'sa and the people that *were* with him pursued them unto Ge'rar: and the E-thi-o'pi-ans were overthrown, that they could not recover themselves; for they were destroyed before the LORD, and before his host; and they carried away very much spoil.

14 And they smote all the cities round about Ge'rar; for the fear of the LORD came upon them: and they spoiled all the cities; for there was exceeding much spoil in them.

15 They smote also the tents of cattle, and carried away sheep and camels in abundance, and returned to Je-ru'sa-lem.

15

AND the Spirit of God came upon Az-a-ri'ah the son of O'ded:

2 And he went out to meet A'sa, and said unto him, Hear ye me, A'sa, and all Ju'dah and Ben'ja-min; The LORD *is* with you, while ye be with him; and if ye seek him, he will be found of you; but if ye forsake him, he will forsake you.

3 Now for a long season Is'ra-el *hath been* without the true God, and without a teaching priest, and without law.

4 But when they in their trouble did turn unto the LORD God of Is'ra-el, and sought him, he was found of them.

5 And in those times *there was* no peace to him that went out, nor to him that came in, but great vexations *were* upon all the inhabitants of the countries.

6 And nation was destroyed of nation, and city of city: for God did vex them with all adversity.

7 Be ye strong therefore, and let not your hands be weak: for your work shall be rewarded.

8 And when A'sa heard these words, and the prophecy of O'ded the prophet, he took courage, and put away the abominable idols out of all the land of Ju'dah and Ben'ja-min, and out of the cities which he had taken from mount E'-phra-im, and renewed the altar of the LORD, that *was* before the porch of the LORD.

9 And he gathered all Ju'dah and Ben'ja-min, and the strangers with them out of E'phra-im and Ma-nas'seh, and out of Sim'e-on: for they fell to him out of Is'ra-el in abundance, when they saw that the LORD his God *was* with him.

10 So they gathered themselves together at Je-ru'sa-lem in the third month, in the fifteenth year of the reign of A'sa.

11 And they offered unto the LORD the same time, of the spoil *which* they had brought, seven hundred oxen and seven thousand sheep.

12 And they entered into a covenant to seek the LORD God of their fathers with all their heart and with all their soul;

13 That whosoever would not seek the LORD God of Is'ra-el should be put to death, whether small or great, whether man or woman.

14 And they sware unto the LORD with a loud voice, and with shouting, and with trumpets, and with cornets.

15 And all Ju'dah rejoiced at the oath: for they had sworn with all their heart, and sought him with their whole desire; and he was found of them: and the LORD gave them rest round about.

16 ¶ And also *concerning* Ma'a-chah the mother of A'sa the king, he removed her from *being* queen, because she had made an idol in a grove: and A'sa cut down her idol, and stamped *it*, and burnt *it* at the brook Kid'ron.

17 But the high places were not taken away out of Is'ra-el: nevertheless the heart of A'sa was perfect all his days.

18 ¶ And he brought into the house of God the things that his father had dedicated, and that he himself had dedicated, silver, and gold, and vessels.

19 And there was no *more* war unto the five and thirtieth year of the reign of A'sa.

16

IN the six and thirtieth year of the reign of A'sa Ba'a-sha king of Is'ra-el came up against Ju'dah, and built Ra'mah, to the intent

that he might let none go out or come in to A'sa
king of Ju'dah.
2 Then A'sa brought out silver and gold out
of the treasures of the house of the LORD and of
the king's house, and sent to Ben–ha'dad king
of Syr'i-a, that dwelt at Da-mas'cus, saying,
3 *There is* a league between me and thee, as
there was between my father and thy father:
behold, I have sent thee silver and gold; go,
break thy league with Ba'a-sha king of Is'ra-el,
that he may depart from me.
4 And Ben–ha'dad hearkened unto king A'sa,
and sent the captains of his armies against the
cities of Is'ra-el; and they smote I'jon, and Dan,
and A'bel–ma'im, and all the store cities of
Naph'ta-li.
5 And it came to pass, when Ba'a-sha heard
it, that he left off building of Ra'mah, and let his
work cease.
6 Then A'sa the king took all Ju'dah; and
they carried away the stones of Ra'mah, and
the timber thereof, wherewith Ba'a-sha was
building; and he built therewith Ge'ba and Miz'-
pah.
7 ¶ And at that time Ha-na'ni the seer came
to A'sa king of Ju'dah, and said unto him, Because thou hast relied on the king of Syr'i-a,
and not relied on the LORD thy God, therefore is
the host of the king of Syr'i-a escaped out of
thine hand.
8 Were not the E-thi-o'pi-ans and the Lu'-
bims a huge host, with very many chariots and
horsemen? yet, because thou didst rely on the
LORD, he delivered them into thine hand.
9 For the eyes of the LORD run to and fro
throughout the whole earth, to shew himself
strong in the behalf of *them* whose heart *is* perfect toward him. Herein thou hast done foolishly: therefore from henceforth thou shalt have
wars.
10 Then A'sa was wroth with the seer, and
put him in a prison house; for *he was* in a rage
with him because of this *thing*. And A'sa oppressed *some* of the people the same time.
11 ¶ And, behold, the acts of A'sa, first and
last, lo, they *are* written in the book of the kings
of Ju'dah and Is'ra-el.
12 And A'sa in the thirty and ninth year of
his reign was diseased in his feet, until his disease *was* exceeding *great*: yet in his disease he
sought not to the LORD, but to the physicians.
13 ¶ And A'sa slept with his fathers, and
died in the one and fortieth year of his reign:
14 And they buried him in his own sepulchres, which he had made for himself in the city
of Da'vid, and laid him in the bed which was
filled with sweet odours and divers kinds *of
spices* prepared by the apothecaries' art: and
they made a very great burning for him.

17 AND Je-hosh'a-phat his son reigned in
his stead, and strengthened himself
against Is'ra-el.
2 And he placed forces in all the fenced cities
of Ju'dah, and set garrisons in the land of Ju'-
dah, and in the cities of E'phra-im, which A'sa
his father had taken.
3 And the LORD was with Je-hosh'a-phat, because he walked in the first ways of his father
Da'vid, and sought not unto Ba'al-im;
4 But sought to the *LORD* God of his father,
and walked in his commandments, and not after the doings of Is'ra-el.
5 Therefore the LORD stablished the kingdom
in his hand: and all Ju'dah brought to Je-hosh'a-
phat presents; and he had riches and honour in
abundance.
6 And his heart was lifted up in the ways of
the LORD: moreover he took away the high
places and groves out of Ju'dah.
7 ¶ Also in the third year of his reign he sent
to his princes, *even* to Ben–ha'il, and to O-ba-
di'ah, and to Zech-a-ri'ah, and to Ne-than'e-el,
and to Mi-cha'iah, to teach in the cities of Ju'-
dah.
8 And with them *he sent* Le'vites, *even*
Shem-a-i'ah, and Neth-a-ni'ah, and Zeb-a-di'ah,
and A'sa-hel, and She-mir'a-moth, and Je-hon'-
a-than, and Ad-o-ni'jah, and To-bi'jah, and Tob-
ad-o-ni'jah, Le'vites; and with them E-lish'a-ma
and Je-ho'ram, priests.
9 And they taught in Ju'dah, and *had* the
book of the law of the LORD with them, and
went about throughout all the cities of Ju'dah,
and taught the people.
10 ¶ And the fear of the LORD fell upon all
the kingdoms of the lands that *were* round
about Ju'dah, so that they made no war against
Je-hosh'a-phat.
11 Also *some* of the Phi-lis'tines brought Je-
hosh'a-phat presents, and tribute silver; and the
A-ra'bi-ans brought him flocks, seven thousand
and seven hundred rams, and seven thousand
and seven hundred he goats.
12 ¶ And Je-hosh'a-phat waxed great exceedingly; and he built in Ju'dah castles, and
cities of store.
13 And he had much business in the cities of
Ju'dah: and the men of war, mighty men of valour, *were* in Je-ru'sa-lem.
14 And these *are* the numbers of them according to the house of their fathers: Of Ju'dah,
the captains of thousands; Ad'nah the chief, and
with him mighty men of valour three hundred
thousand.
15 And next to him *was* Je-ho-ha'nan the
captain, and with him two hundred and fourscore thousand.
16 And next him *was* Am-a-si'ah the son of
Zich'ri, who willingly offered himself unto the
LORD; and with him two hundred thousand
mighty men of valour.
17 And of Ben'ja-min; E-li'a-da a mighty man
of valour, and with him armed men with bow
and shield two hundred thousand.
18 And next him *was* Je-hoz'a-bad, and with
him an hundred and fourscore thousand ready
prepared for the war.
19 These waited on the king, beside *those*
whom the king put in the fenced cities throughout all Ju'dah.

18 NOW Je-hosh'a-phat had riches and
honour in abundance, and joined affinity
with A'hab.
2 And after *certain* years he went down to
A'hab to Sa-ma'ri-a. And A'hab killed sheep
and oxen for him in abundance, and for the people that *he had* with him, and persuaded him to
go up *with him* to Ra'moth–gil'e-ad.
3 And A'hab king of Is'ra-el said unto Je-
hosh'a-phat king of Ju'dah, Wilt thou go with
me to Ra'moth–gil'e-ad? And he answered him,
I *am* as thou *art*, and my people as thy people;
and *we will be* with thee in the war.
4 ¶ And Je-hosh'a-phat said unto the king of
Is'ra-el, Enquire, I pray thee, at the word of the
LORD to day.
5 Therefore the king of Is'ra-el gathered together of prophets four hundred men, and said
unto them, Shall we go to Ra'moth–gil'e-ad to
battle, or shall I forbear? And they said, Go up;
for God will deliver *it* into the king's hand.
6 But Je-hosh'a-phat said, *Is there* not here a

prophet of the LORD besides, that we might enquire of him?

7 And the king of Is'ra-el said unto Je-hosh'a-phat, *There is* yet one man, by whom we may enquire of the LORD: but I hate him; for he never prophesied good unto me, but always evil: the same *is* Mi-ca'iah the son of Im'la. And Je-hosh'a-phat said, Let not the king say so.

8 And the king of Is'ra-el called for one *of his* officers, and said, Fetch quickly Mi-ca'iah the son of Im'la.

9 And the king of Is'ra-el and Je-hosh'a-phat king of Ju'dah sat either of them on his throne, clothed in *their* robes, and they sat in a void place at the entering in of the gate of Sa-ma'ri-a; and all the prophets prophesied before them.

10 And Zed-e-ki'ah the son of Che-na'a-nah had made him horns of iron, and said, Thus saith the LORD, With these thou shalt push Syr'i-a until they be consumed.

11 And all the prophets prophesied so, saying, Go up to Ra'moth-gil'e-ad, and prosper: for the LORD shall deliver *it* into the hand of the king.

12 And the messenger that went to call Mi-ca'iah spake to him, saying, Behold, the words of the prophets *declare* good to the king with one assent; let thy word therefore, I pray thee, be like one of theirs, and speak thou good.

13 And Mi-ca'iah said, *As* the LORD liveth, even what my God saith, that will I speak.

14 And when he was come to the king, the king said unto him, Mi-ca'iah, shall we go to Ra'moth-gil'e-ad to battle, or shall I forbear? And he said, Go ye up, and prosper, and they shall be delivered into your hand.

15 And the king said to him, How many times shall I adjure thee that thou say nothing but the truth to me in the name of the LORD?

16 Then he said, I did see all Is'ra-el scattered upon the mountains, as sheep that have no shepherd: and the LORD said, These have no master; let them return *therefore* every man to his house in peace.

17 And the king of Is'ra-el said to Je-hosh'a-phat, Did I not tell thee *that* he would not prophesy good unto me, but evil?

18 Again he said, Therefore hear the word of the LORD; I saw the LORD sitting upon his throne, and all the host of heaven standing on his right hand and *on* his left.

19 And the LORD said, Who shall entice A'hab king of Is'ra-el, that he may go up and fall at Ra'moth-gil'e-ad? And one spake saying after this manner, and another saying after that manner.

20 Then there came out a spirit, and stood before the LORD, and said, I will entice him. And the LORD said unto him, Wherewith?

21 And he said, I will go out, and be a lying spirit in the mouth of all his prophets. And *the LORD* said, Thou shalt entice *him,* and thou shalt also prevail: go out, and do *even* so.

22 Now therefore, behold, the LORD hath put a lying spirit in the mouth of these thy prophets, and the LORD hath spoken evil against thee.

23 Then Zed-e-ki'ah the son of Che-na'a-nah came near, and smote Mi-ca'iah upon the cheek, and said, Which way went the Spirit of the LORD from me to speak unto thee?

24 And Mi-ca'iah said, Behold, thou shalt see on that day when thou shalt go into an inner chamber to hide thyself.

25 Then the king of Is'ra-el said, Take ye Mi-ca'iah, and carry him back to A'mon the governor of the city, and to Jo'ash the king's son;

26 And say, Thus saith the king, Put this *fellow* in the prison, and feed him with bread of affliction and with water of affliction, until I return in peace.

27 And Mi-ca'iah said, If thou certainly return in peace, *then* hath not the LORD spoken by me. And he said, Hearken, all ye people.

28 So the king of Is'ra-el and Je-hosh'a-phat the king of Ju'dah went up to Ra'moth-gil'e-ad.

29 And the king of Is'ra-el said unto Je-hosh'a-phat, I will disguise myself, and will go to the battle; but put thou on thy robes. So the king of Is'ra-el disguised himself; and they went to the battle.

30 Now the king of Syr'i-a had commanded the captains of the chariots that *were* with him, saying, Fight ye not with small or great, save only with the king of Is'ra-el.

31 And it came to pass, when the captains of the chariots saw Je-hosh'a-phat, that they said, It *is* the king of Is'ra-el. Therefore they compassed about him to fight: but Je-hosh'a-phat cried out, and the LORD helped him; and God moved them *to depart* from him.

32 For it came to pass, that, when the captains of the chariots perceived that it was not the king of Is'ra-el, they turned back again from pursuing him.

33 And a *certain* man drew a bow at a venture, and smote the king of Is'ra-el between the joints of the harness: therefore he said to his chariot man, Turn thine hand, that thou mayest carry me out of the host; for I am wounded.

34 And the battle increased that day: howbeit the king of Is'ra-el stayed *himself* up in *his* chariot against the Syr'i-ans until the even: and about the time of the sun going down he died.

19 AND Je-hosh'a-phat the king of Ju'dah returned to his house in peace to Je-ru'sa-lem.

2 And Je'hu the son of Ha-na'ni the seer went out to meet him, and said to king Je-hosh'a-phat, Shouldest thou help the ungodly, and love them that hate the LORD? therefore *is* wrath upon thee from before the LORD.

3 Nevertheless there are good things found in thee, in that thou hast taken away the groves out of the land, and hast prepared thine heart to seek God.

4 And Je-hosh'a-phat dwelt at Je-ru'sa-lem: and he went out again through the people from Be'er-she'ba to mount E'phra-im, and brought them back unto the LORD God of their fathers.

5 ¶ And he set judges in the land throughout all the fenced cities of Ju'dah, city by city,

6 And said to the judges, Take heed what ye do: for ye judge not for man, but for the LORD, who *is* with you in the judgment.

7 Wherefore now let the fear of the LORD be upon you; take heed and do *it:* for *there is* no iniquity with the LORD our God, nor respect of persons, nor taking of gifts.

8 ¶ Moreover in Je-ru'sa-lem did Je-hosh'a-phat set of the Le'vites, and *of* the priests, and of the chief of the fathers of Is'ra-el, for the judgment of the LORD, and for controversies, when they returned to Je-ru'sa-lem.

9 And he charged them, saying, Thus shall ye do in the fear of the LORD, faithfully, and with a perfect heart.

10 And what cause soever shall come to you of your brethren that dwell in their cities, between blood and blood, between law and commandment, statutes and judgments, ye shall even warn them that they trespass not against the LORD, and *so* wrath come upon you, and

upon your brethren: this do, and ye shall not trespass.

11 And, behold, Am-a-ri'ah the chief priest *is* over you in all matters of the LORD; and Zeb-a-di'ah the son of Ish'ma-el, the ruler of the house of Ju'dah, for all the king's matters: also the Le'vites *shall be* officers before you. Deal courageously, and the LORD shall be with the good.

20 IT came to pass after this also, *that* the children of Mo'ab, and the children of Am'mon, and with them *other* beside the Am'mon-ites, came against Je-hosh'a-phat to battle.

2 Then there came some that told Je-hosh'a-phat, saying, There cometh a great multitude against thee from beyond the sea on this side Syr'i-a; and, behold, they *be* in Haz'a-zon-ta'mar, which *is* En-ge'di.

3 And Je-hosh'a-phat feared, and set himself to seek the LORD, and proclaimed a fast throughout all Ju'dah.

4 And Ju'dah gathered themselves together, to ask *help* of the LORD: even out of all the cities of Ju'dah they came to seek the LORD.

5 ¶ And Je-hosh'a-phat stood in the congregation of Ju'dah and Je-ru'sa-lem, in the house of the LORD, before the new court,

6 And said, O LORD God of our fathers, *art* not thou God in heaven? and rulest *not* thou over all the kingdoms of the heathen? and in thine hand *is there not* power and might, so that none is able to withstand thee?

7 *Art* not thou our God, *who* didst drive out the inhabitants of this land before thy people Is'ra-el, and gavest it to the seed of A'bra-ham thy friend for ever?

8 And they dwelt therein, and have built thee a sanctuary therein for thy name, saying,

9 If, *when* evil cometh upon us, *as* the sword, judgment, or pestilence, or famine, we stand before this house, and in thy presence, (for thy name *is* in this house,) and cry unto thee in our affliction, then thou wilt hear and help.

10 And now, behold, the children of Am'mon and Mo'ab and mount Se'ir, whom thou wouldest not let Is'ra-el invade, when they came out of the land of E'gypt, but they turned from them, and destroyed them not;

11 Behold, *I say, how* they reward us, to come to cast us out of thy possession, which thou hast given us to inherit.

12 O our God, wilt thou not judge them? for we have no might against this great company that cometh against us; neither know we what to do: but our eyes *are* upon thee.

13 And all Ju'dah stood before the LORD, with their little ones, their wives, and their children.

14 ¶ Then upon Ja-ha'zi-el the son of Zech-a-ri'ah, the son of Be-na'iah, the son of Je-i'el, the son of Mat-ta-ni'ah, a Le'vite of the sons of A'saph, came the Spirit of the LORD in the midst of the congregation;

15 And he said, Hearken ye, all Ju'dah, and ye inhabitants of Je-ru'sa-lem, and thou king Je-hosh'a-phat, Thus saith the LORD unto you, Be not afraid nor dismayed by reason of this great multitude; for the battle *is* not yours, but God's.

16 To morrow go ye down against them: behold, they come up by the cliff of Ziz; and ye shall find them at the end of the brook, before the wilderness of Jer'u-el.

17 Ye shall not *need* to fight in this *battle:* set yourselves, stand ye *still,* and see the salvation of the LORD with you, O Ju'dah and Je-ru'sa-lem: fear not, nor be dismayed; to morrow go out against them: for the LORD *will be* with you.

18 And Je-hosh'a-phat bowed his head with *his* face to the ground: and all Ju'dah and the inhabitants of Je-ru'sa-lem fell before the LORD, worshipping the LORD.

19 And the Le'vites, of the children of the Ko'hath-ites, and of the children of the Kor'hites, stood up to praise the LORD God of Is'ra-el with a loud voice on high.

20 ¶ And they rose early in the morning, and went forth into the wilderness of Te-ko'a: and as they went forth, Je-hosh'a-phat stood and said, Hear me, O Ju'dah, and ye inhabitants of Je-ru'sa-lem; Believe in the LORD your God, so shall ye be established; believe his prophets, so shall ye prosper.

21 And when he had consulted with the people, he appointed singers unto the LORD, and that should praise the beauty of holiness, as they went out before the army, and to say, Praise the LORD; for his mercy *endureth* for ever.

22 ¶ And when they began to sing and to praise, the LORD set ambushments against the children of Am'mon, Mo'ab, and mount Se'ir, which were come against Ju'dah; and they were smitten.

23 For the children of Am'mon and Mo'ab stood up against the inhabitants of mount Se'ir, utterly to slay and destroy *them:* and when they had made an end of the inhabitants of Se'ir, every one helped to destroy another.

24 And when Ju'dah came toward the watch tower in the wilderness, they looked unto the multitude, and, behold, they *were* dead bodies fallen to the earth, and none escaped.

25 And when Je-hosh'a-phat and his people came to take away the spoil of them, they found among them in abundance both riches with the dead bodies, and precious jewels, which they stripped off for themselves, more than they could carry away: and they were three days in gathering of the spoil, it was so much.

26 ¶ And on the fourth day they assembled themselves in the valley of Ber'a-chah; for there they blessed the LORD: therefore the name of the same place was called, The valley of Ber'a-chah, unto this day.

27 Then they returned, every man of Ju'dah and Je-ru'sa-lem, and Je-hosh'a-phat in the forefront of them, to go again to Je-ru'sa-lem with joy; for the LORD had made them to rejoice over their enemies.

28 And they came to Je-ru'sa-lem with psalteries and harps and trumpets unto the house of the LORD.

29 And the fear of God was on all the kingdoms of *those* countries, when they had heard that the LORD fought against the enemies of Is'ra-el.

30 So the realm of Je-hosh'a-phat was quiet: for his God gave him rest round about.

31 ¶ And Je-hosh'a-phat reigned over Ju'dah: *he was* thirty and five years old when he began to reign, and he reigned twenty and five years in Je-ru'sa-lem. And his mother's name *was* A-zu'bah the daughter of Shil'hi.

32 And he walked in the way of A'sa his father, and departed not from it, doing *that which was* right in the sight of the LORD.

33 Howbeit the high places were not taken away: for as yet the people had not prepared their hearts unto the God of their fathers.

34 Now the rest of the acts of Je-hosh'a-phat, first and last, behold, they *are* written in the book of Je'hu the son of Ha-na'ni, who *is* mentioned in the book of the kings of Is'ra-el.

35 ¶ And after this did Je-hosh'a-phat king

of Ju'dah join himself with A-ha-zi'ah king of Is'ra-el, who did very wickedly:

36 And he joined himself with him to make ships to go to Tar'shish: and they made the ships in E'zi-on-ga'ber.

37 Then E-li-e'zer the son of Dod'a-vah of Ma-re'shah prophesied against Je-hosh'a-phat, saying, Because thou hast joined thyself with A-ha-zi'ah, the LORD hath broken thy works. And the ships were broken, that they were not able to go to Tar'shish.

21 NOW Je-hosh'a-phat slept with his fathers, and was buried with his fathers in the city of Da'vid. And Je-ho'ram his son reigned in his stead.

2 And he had brethren the sons of Je-hosh'a-phat, Az-a-ri'ah, and Je-hi'el, and Zech-a-ri'ah, and Az-a-ri'ah, and Mi'chael, and Sheph-a-ti'ah: all these *were* the sons of Je-hosh'a-phat king of Is'ra-el.

3 And their father gave them great gifts of silver, and of gold, and of precious things, with fenced cities in Ju'dah: but the kingdom gave he to Je-ho'ram; because he *was* the firstborn.

4 Now when Je-ho'ram was risen up to the kingdom of his father, he strengthened himself, and slew all his brethren with the sword, and *divers* also of the princes of Is'ra-el.

5 ¶ Je-ho'ram *was* thirty and two years old when he began to reign, and he reigned eight years in Je-ru'sa-lem.

6 And he walked in the way of the kings of Is'ra-el, like as did the house of A'hab: for he had the daughter of A'hab to wife: and he wrought *that which was* evil in the eyes of the LORD.

7 Howbeit the LORD would not destroy the house of Da'vid, because of the covenant that he had made with Da'vid, and as he promised to give a light to him and to his sons for ever.

8 ¶ In his days the E'dom-ites revolted from under the dominion of Ju'dah, and made themselves a king.

9 Then Je-ho'ram went forth with his princes, and all his chariots with him: and he rose up by night, and smote the E'dom-ites which compassed him in, and the captains of the chariots.

10 So the E'dom-ites revolted from under the hand of Ju'dah unto this day. The same time *also* did Lib'nah revolt from under his hand; because he had forsaken the LORD God of his fathers.

11 Moreover he made high places in the mountains of Ju'dah, and caused the inhabitants of Je-ru'sa-lem to commit fornication, and compelled Ju'dah *thereto*.

12 ¶ And there came a writing to him from E-li'jah the prophet, saying, Thus saith the LORD God of Da'vid thy father, Because thou hast not walked in the ways of Je-hosh'a-phat thy father, nor in the ways of A'sa king of Ju'dah,

13 But hast walked in the way of the kings of Is'ra-el, and hast made Ju'dah and the inhabitants of Je-ru'sa-lem to go a whoring, like to the whoredoms of the house of A'hab, and also hast slain thy brethren of thy father's house, *which were* better than thyself:

14 Behold, with a great plague will the LORD smite thy people, and thy children, and thy wives, and all thy goods:

15 And thou *shalt have* great sickness by disease of thy bowels, until thy bowels fall out by reason of the sickness day by day.

16 ¶ Moreover the LORD stirred up against Je-ho'ram the spirit of the Phi-lis'tines, and of the A-ra'bi-ans, that *were* near the E-thi-o'pi-ans:

17 And they came up into Ju'dah, and brake into it, and carried away all the substance that was found in the king's house, and his sons also, and his wives; so that there was never a son left him, save Je-ho'a-haz, the youngest of his sons.

18 ¶ And after all this the LORD smote him in his bowels with an incurable disease.

19 And it came to pass, that in process of time, after the end of two years, his bowels fell out by reason of his sickness: so he died of sore diseases. And his people made no burning for him, like the burning of his fathers.

20 Thirty and two years old was he when he began to reign, and he reigned in Je-ru'sa-lem eight years, and departed without being desired. Howbeit they buried him in the city of Da'vid, but not in the sepulchres of the kings.

22 AND the inhabitants of Je-ru'sa-lem made A-ha-zi'ah his youngest son king in his stead: for the band of men that came with the A-ra'bi-ans to the camp had slain all the eldest. So A-ha-zi'ah the son of Je-ho'ram king of Ju'dah reigned.

2 Forty and two years old *was* A-ha-zi'ah when he began to reign, and he reigned one year in Je-ru'sa-lem. His mother's name also *was* Ath-a-li'ah the daughter of Om'ri.

3 He also walked in the ways of the house of A'hab: for his mother was his counsellor to do wickedly.

4 Wherefore he did evil in the sight of the LORD like the house of A'hab: for they were his counsellors after the death of his father to his destruction.

5 ¶ He walked also after their counsel, and went with Je-ho'ram the son of A'hab king of Is'ra-el to war against Haz'a-el king of Syr'i-a at Ra'moth-gil'e-ad: and the Syr'i-ans smote Jo'ram.

6 And he returned to be healed in Jez're-el because of the wounds which were given him at Ra'mah, when he fought with Haz'a-el king of Syr'i-a. And Az-a-ri'ah the son of Je-ho'ram king of Ju'dah went down to see Je-ho'ram the son of A'hab at Jez're-el, because he was sick.

7 And the destruction of A-ha-zi'ah was of God by coming to Jo'ram: for when he was come, he went out with Je-ho'ram against Je'hu the son of Nim'shi, whom the LORD had anointed to cut off the house of A'hab.

8 And it came to pass, that, when Je'hu was executing judgment upon the house of A'hab, and found the princes of Ju'dah, and the sons of the brethren of A-ha-zi'ah, that ministered to A-ha-zi'ah, he slew them.

9 And he sought A-ha-zi'ah: and they caught him, (for he was hid in Sa-ma'ri-a,) and brought him to Je'hu: and when they had slain him, they buried him: Because, said they, he *is* the son of Je-hosh'a-phat, who sought the LORD with all his heart. So the house of A-ha-zi'ah had no power to keep still the kingdom.

10 ¶ But when Ath-a-li'ah the mother of A-ha-zi'ah saw that her son was dead, she arose and destroyed all the seed royal of the house of Ju'dah.

11 But Je-ho-shab'e-ath, the daughter of the king, took Jo'ash the son of A-ha-zi'ah, and stole him from among the king's sons that were slain, and put him and his nurse in a bedchamber. So Je-ho-shab'e-ath, the daughter of king Je-ho'ram, the wife of Je-hoi'a-da the priest, (for

she was the sister of A-ha-zi'ah,) hid him from
Ath-a-li'ah, so that she slew him not.
12 And he was with them hid in the house of
God six years: and Ath-a-li'ah reigned over the
land.

23 AND in the seventh year Je-hoi'a-da
strengthened himself, and took the captains of hundreds, Az-a-ri'ah the son of Jer'o-
ham, and Ish'ma-el the son of Je-ho-ha'nan, and
Az-a-ri'ah the son of O'bed, and Ma-a-se'iah the
son of Ad-a-i'ah, and E-lish'a-phat the son of
Zich'ri, into covenant with him.
2 And they went about in Ju'dah, and gathered the Le'vites out of all the cities of Ju'dah,
and the chief of the fathers of Is'ra-el, and they
came to Je-ru'sa-lem.
3 And all the congregation made a covenant
with the king in the house of God. And he said
unto him, Behold, the king's son shall reign, as
the LORD hath said of the sons of Da'vid.
4 This *is* the thing that ye shall do; A third
part of you entering on the sabbath, of the
priests and of the Le'vites, *shall be* porters of
the doors;
5 And a third part *shall be* at the king's
house; and a third part at the gate of the foundation: and all the people *shall be* in the courts
of the house of the LORD.
6 But let none come into the house of the
LORD, save the priests, and they that minister of
the Le'vites; they shall go in, for they *are* holy:
but all the people shall keep the watch of the
LORD.
7 And the Le'vites shall compass the king
round about, every man with his weapons in his
hand; and whosoever *else* cometh into the
house, he shall be put to death: but be ye with
the king when he cometh in, and when he goeth
out.
8 So the Le'vites and all Ju'dah did according
to all things that Je-hoi'a-da the priest had commanded, and took every man his men that were
to come in on the sabbath:, with them that were
to go *out* on the sabbath: for Je-hoi'a-da the
priest dismissed not the courses.
9 Moreover Je-hoi'a-da the priest delivered
to the captains of hundreds spears, and bucklers, and shields, that *had been* king Da'vid's,
which *were* in the house of God.
10 And he set all the people, every man having his weapon in his hand, from the right side
of the temple to the left side of the temple,
along by the altar and the temple, by the king
round about.
11 Then they brought out the king's son, and
put upon him the crown, and *gave him* the testimony, and made him king. And Je-hoi'a-da and
his sons anointed him, and said, God save the
king.
12 ¶ Now when Ath-a-li'ah heard the noise
of the people running and praising the king, she
came to the people into the house of the LORD:
13 And she looked, and, behold, the king
stood at his pillar at the entering in, and the
princes and the trumpets by the king: and all
the people of the land rejoiced, and sounded
with trumpets, also the singers with instruments of musick, and such as taught to sing
praise. Then Ath-a-li'ah rent her clothes, and
said, Treason, Treason.
14 Then Je-hoi'a-da the priest brought out
the captains of hundreds that were set over the
host, and said unto them, Have her forth of the
ranges: and whoso followeth her, let him be
slain with the sword. For the priest said, Slay
her not in the house of the LORD.
15 So they laid hands on her; and when she
was come to the entering of the horse gate by
the king's house, they slew her there.
16 ¶ And Je-hoi'a-da made a covenant between him, and between all the people, and between the king, that they should be the LORD's
people.
17 Then all the people went to the house of
Ba'al, and brake it down, and brake his altars
and his images in pieces, and slew Mat'tan the
priest of Ba'al before the altars.
18 Also Je-hoi'a-da appointed the offices of
the house of the LORD by the hand of the priests
the Le'vites, whom Da'vid had distributed in the
house of the LORD, to offer the burnt offerings
of the LORD, as *it is* written in the law of Mo'ses,
with rejoicing and with singing, *as it was ordained* by Da'vid.
19 And he set the porters at the gates of the
house of the LORD, that none *which was* unclean in any thing should enter in.
20 And he took the captains of hundreds, and
the nobles, and the governors of the people, and
all the people of the land, and brought down the
king from the house of the LORD: and they came
through the high gate into the king's house, and
set the king upon the throne of the kingdom.
21 And all the people of the land rejoiced:
and the city was quiet, after that they had slain
Ath-a-li'ah with the sword.

24 JO'ASH *was* seven years old when he
began to reign, and he reigned forty
years in Je-ru'sa-lem. His mother's name also
was Zib'i-ah of Be'er–she'ba.
2 And Jo'ash did *that which was* right in the
sight of the LORD all the days of Je-hoi'a-da the
priest.
3 And Je-hoi'a-da took for him two wives;
and he begat sons and daughters.
4 ¶ And it came to pass after this, *that* Jo'-
ash was minded to repair the house of the LORD.
5 And he gathered together the priests and
the Le'vites, and said to them, Go out unto the
cities of Ju'dah, and gather of all Is'ra-el money
to repair the house of your God from year to
year, and see that ye hasten the matter. Howbeit the Le'vites hastened *it* not.
6 And the king called for Je-hoi'a-da the
chief, and said unto him, Why hast thou not required of the Le'vites to bring in out of Ju'dah
and out of Je-ru'sa-lem the collection, *according to the commandment* of Mo'ses the servant
of the LORD, and of the congregation of Is'ra-el,
for the tabernacle of witness?
7 For the sons of Ath-a-li'ah, that wicked
woman, had broken up the house of God; and
also all the dedicated things of the house of the
LORD did they bestow upon Ba'al-im.
8 And at the king's commandment they
made a chest, and set it without at the gate of
the house of the LORD.
9 And they made a proclamation through
Ju'dah and Je-ru'sa-lem, to bring in to the LORD
the collection *that* Mo'ses the servant of God
laid upon Is'ra-el in the wilderness.
10 And all the princes and all the people rejoiced, and brought in, and cast into the chest,
until they had made an end.
11 Now it came to pass, that at what time the
chest was brought unto the king's office by the
hand of the Le'vites, and when they saw that
there was much money, the king's scribe and
the high priest's officer came and emptied the
chest, and took it, and carried it to his place
again. Thus they did day by day, and gathered
money in abundance.

12 And the king and Je-hoi'a-da gave it to such as did the work of the service of the house of the LORD, and hired masons and carpenters to repair the house of the LORD, and also such as wrought iron and brass to mend the house of the LORD.

13 So the workmen wrought, and the work was perfected by them, and they set the house of God in his state, and strengthened it.

14 And when they had finished *it,* they brought the rest of the money before the king and Je-hoi'a-da, whereof were made vessels for the house of the LORD, *even* vessels to minister, and to offer *withal,* and spoons, and vessels of gold and silver. And they offered burnt offerings in the house of the LORD continually all the days of Je-hoi'a-da.

15 ¶ But Je-hoi'a-da waxed old, and was full of days when he died; an hundred and thirty years old *was he* when he died.

16 And they buried him in the city of Da'vid among the kings, because he had done good in Is'ra-el, both toward God, and toward his house.

17 Now after the death of Je-hoi'a-da came the princes of Ju'dah, and made obeisance to the king. Then the king hearkened unto them.

18 And they left the house of the LORD God of their fathers, and served groves and idols: and wrath came upon Ju'dah and Je-ru'sa-lem for this their trespass.

19 Yet he sent prophets to them, to bring them again unto the LORD; and they testified against them: but they would not give ear.

20 And the Spirit of God came upon Zech-a-ri'ah the son of Je-hoi'a-da the priest, which stood above the people, and said unto them, Thus saith God, Why transgress ye the commandments of the LORD, that ye cannot prosper? because ye have forsaken the LORD, he hath also forsaken you.

21 And they conspired against him, and stoned him with stones at the commandment of the king in the court of the house of the LORD.

22 Thus Jo'ash the king remembered not the kindness which Je-hoi'a-da his father had done to him, but slew his son. And when he died, he said, The LORD look upon *it,* and require *it.*

23 ¶ And it came to pass at the end of the year, *that* the host of Syr'i-a came up against him: and they came to Ju'dah and Je-ru'sa-lem, and destroyed all the princes of the people from among the people, and sent all the spoil of them unto the king of Da-mas'cus.

24 For the army of the Syr'i-ans came with a small company of men, and the LORD delivered a very great host into their hand, because they had forsaken the LORD God of their fathers. So they executed judgment against Jo'ash.

25 And when they were departed from him, (for they left him in great diseases,) his own servants conspired against him for the blood of the sons of Je-hoi'a-da the priest, and slew him on his bed, and he died: and they buried him in the city of Da'vid, but they buried him not in the sepulchres of the kings.

26 And these are they that conspired against him; Za'bad the son of Shim'e-ath an Am'mon-it-ess, and Je-hoz'a-bad the son of Shim'rith a Mo'ab-it-ess.

27 ¶ Now *concerning* his sons, and the greatness of the burdens *laid* upon him, and the repairing of the house of God, behold, they *are* written in the story of the book of the kings. And Am-a-zi'ah his son reigned in his stead.

25 AM-A-ZI'AH *was* twenty and five years old *when* he began to reign, and he reigned twenty and nine years in Je-ru'sa-lem. And his mother's name *was* Je-ho-ad'dan of Je-ru'sa-lem.

2 And he did *that which was* right in the sight of the LORD, but not with a perfect heart.

3 ¶ Now it came to pass, when the kingdom was established to him, that he slew his servants that had killed the king his father.

4 But he slew not their children, but *did* as *it is* written in the law in the book of Mo'ses, where the LORD commanded, saying, The fathers shall not die for the children, neither shall the children die for the fathers, but every man shall die for his own sin.

5 ¶ Moreover Am-a-zi'ah gathered Ju'dah together, and made them captains over thousands, and captains over hundreds, according to the houses of *their* fathers, throughout all Ju'dah and Ben'ja-min: and he numbered them from twenty years old and above, and found them three hundred thousand choice *men, able* to go forth to war, that could handle spear and shield.

6 He hired also an hundred thousand mighty men of valour out of Is'ra-el for an hundred talents of silver.

7 But there came a man of God to him, saying, O king, let not the army of Is'ra-el go with thee; for the LORD *is* not with Is'ra-el, *to wit, with* all the children of E'phra-im.

8 But if thou wilt go, do *it,* be strong for the battle: God shall make thee fall before the enemy: for God hath power to help, and to cast down.

9 And Am-a-zi'ah said to the man of God, But what shall we do for the hundred talents which I have given to the army of Is'ra-el? And the man of God answered, The LORD is able to give thee much more than this.

10 Then Am-a-zi'ah separated them, *to wit,* the army that was come to him out of E'phra-im, to go home again: wherefore their anger was greatly kindled against Ju'dah, and they returned home in great anger.

11 ¶ And Am-a-zi'ah strengthened himself, and led forth his people, and went to the valley of salt, and smote of the children of Se'ir ten thousand.

12 And *other* ten thousand *left* alive did the children of Ju'dah carry away captive, and brought them unto the top of the rock, and cast them down from the top of the rock, that they all were broken in pieces.

13 ¶ But the soldiers of the army which Am-a-zi'ah sent back, that they should not go with him to battle, fell upon the cities of Ju'dah, from Sa-ma'ri-a even unto Beth–ho'ron, and smote three thousand of them, and took much spoil.

14 ¶ Now it came to pass, after that Am-a-zi'ah was come from the slaughter of the E'-dom-ites, that he brought the gods of the children of Se'ir, and set them up *to be* his gods, and bowed down himself before them, and burned incense unto them.

15 Wherefore the anger of the LORD was kindled against Am-a-zi'ah, and he sent unto him a prophet, which said unto him, Why hast thou sought after the gods of the people, which could not deliver their own people out of thine hand?

16 And it came to pass, as he talked with him, that *the king* said unto him, Art thou made of the king's counsel? forbear; why shouldest thou be smitten? Then the prophet forbare, and said, I know that God hath determined to de-

stroy thee, because thou hast done this, and
hast not hearkened unto my counsel.
17 ¶ Then Am-a-zi'ah king of Ju'dah took advice, and sent to Jo'ash, the son of Je-ho'a-haz,
the son of Je'hu, king of Is'ra-el, saying, Come,
let us see one another in the face.
18 And Jo'ash king of Is'ra-el sent to Am-a-
zi'ah king of Ju'dah, saying, The thistle that *was*
in Leb'a-non sent to the cedar that *was* in Leb'a-
non, saying, Give thy daughter to my son to
wife: and there passed by a wild beast that *was*
in Leb'a-non, and trode down the thistle.
19 Thou sayest, Lo, thou hast smitten the E'-
dom-ites; and thine heart lifteth thee up to
boast: abide now at home; why shouldest thou
meddle to *thine* hurt, that thou shouldest fall,
even thou, and Ju'dah with thee?
20 But Am-a-zi'ah would not hear; for it
came of God, that he might deliver them into
the hand *of their enemies,* because they sought
after the gods of E'dom.
21 So Jo'ash the king of Is'ra-el went up; and
they saw one another in the face, *both* he and
Am-a-zi'ah king of Ju'dah, at Beth-she'mesh,
which *belongeth* to Ju'dah.
22 And Ju'dah was put to the worse before
Is'ra-el, and they fled every man to his tent.
23 And Jo'ash the king of Is'ra-el took Am-a-
zi'ah king of Ju'dah, the son of Jo'ash, the son of
Je-ho'a-haz, at Beth-she'mesh, and brought him
to Je-ru'sa-lem, and brake down the wall of Je-
ru'sa-lem from the gate of E'phra-im to the corner gate, four hundred cubits.
24 And *he took* all the gold and the silver,
and all the vessels that were found in the house
of God with O'bed-e'dom, and the treasures of
the king's house, the hostages also, and returned to Sa-ma'ri-a.
25 ¶ And Am-a-zi'ah the son of Jo'ash king
of Ju'dah lived after the death of Jo'ash son of
Je-ho'a-haz king of Is'ra-el fifteen years.
26 Now the rest of the acts of Am-a-zi'ah,
first and last, behold, *are* they not written in the
book of the kings of Ju'dah and Is'ra-el?
27 ¶ Now after the time that Am-a-zi'ah did
turn away from following the LORD they made a
conspiracy against him in Je-ru'sa-lem; and he
fled to La'chish: but they sent to La'chish after
him, and slew him there.
28 And they brought him upon horses, and
buried him with his fathers in the city of Ju'dah.

26

THEN all the people of Ju'dah took Uz-
zi'ah, who *was* sixteen years old, and
made him king in the room of his father Am-a-
zi'ah.
2 He built E'loth, and restored it to Ju'dah,
after that the king slept with his fathers.
3 Sixteen years old *was* Uz-zi'ah when he began to reign, and he reigned fifty and two years
in Je-ru'sa-lem. His mother's name also *was*
Jec-o-li'ah of Je-ru'sa-lem.
4 And he did *that which was* right in the
sight of the LORD, according to all that his father Am-a-zi'ah did.
5 And he sought God in the days of Zech-a-
ri'ah, who had understanding in the visions of
God: and as long as he sought the LORD, God
made him to prosper.
6 And he went forth and warred against the
Phi-lis'tines, and brake down the wall of Gath,
and the wall of Jab'neh, and the wall of Ash'-
dod, and built cities about Ash'dod, and among
the Phi-lis'tines.
7 And God helped him against the Phi-lis'-
tines, and against the A-ra'bi-ans that dwelt in
Gur-ba'al, and the Me-hu'nims.
8 And the Am'mon-ites gave gifts to Uz-zi'-
ah: and his name spread abroad *even* to the entering in of E'gypt; for he strengthened *himself*
exceedingly.
9 Moreover Uz-zi'ah built towers in Je-ru'sa-
lem at the corner gate, and at the valley gate,
and at the turning *of the wall,* and fortified
them.
10 Also he built towers in the desert, and
digged many wells: for he had much cattle, both
in the low country, and in the plains: husbandmen *also,* and vine dressers in the mountains,
and in Car'mel: for he loved husbandry.
11 Moreover Uz-zi'ah had an host of fighting
men, that went out to war by bands, according
to the number of their account by the hand of
Je-i'el the scribe and Ma-a-se'iah the ruler, under the hand of Han-a-ni'ah, *one* of the king's
captains.
12 The whole number of the chief of the fathers of the mighty men of valour *were* two
thousand and six hundred.
13 And under their hand *was* an army, three
hundred thousand and seven thousand and five
hundred, that made war with mighty power, to
help the king against the enemy.
14 And Uz-zi'ah prepared for them throughout all the host shields, and spears, and helmets, and habergeons, and bows, and slings *to
cast* stones.
15 And he made in Je-ru'sa-lem engines, in-
vented by cunning men, to be on the towers and
upon the bulwarks, to shoot arrows and great
stones withal. And his name spread far abroad;
for he was marvellously helped, till he was
strong.
16 ¶ But when he was strong, his heart was
lifted up to *his* destruction: for he transgressed
against the LORD his God, and went into the
temple of the LORD to burn incense upon the
altar of incense.
17 And Az-a-ri'ah the priest went in after
him, and with him fourscore priests of the
LORD, *that were* valiant men:
18 And they withstood Uz-zi'ah the king, and
said unto him, *It appertaineth* not unto thee,
Uz-zi'ah, to burn incense unto the LORD, but to
the priests the sons of Aar'on, that are consecrated to burn incense: go out of the sanctuary;
for thou hast trespassed; neither *shall it be* for
thine honour from the LORD God.
19 Then Uz-zi'ah was wroth, and *had* a censer in his hand to burn incense: and while he
was wroth with the priests, the leprosy even
rose up in his forehead before the priests in the
house of the LORD, from beside the incense altar.
20 And Az-a-ri'ah the chief priest, and all the
priests, looked upon him, and, behold, he *was*
leprous in his forehead, and they thrust him out
from thence; yea, himself hasted also to go out,
because the LORD had smitten him.
21 And Uz-zi'ah the king was a leper unto
the day of his death, and dwelt in a several
house, *being* a leper; for he was cut off from the
house of the LORD: and Jo'tham his son *was*
over the king's house, judging the people of the
land.
22 ¶ Now the rest of the acts of Uz-zi'ah,
first and last, did I-sa'iah the prophet, the son of
A'moz, write.
23 So Uz-zi'ah slept with his fathers, and
they buried him with his fathers in the field of
the burial which *belonged* to the kings; for they
said, He *is* a leper: and Jo'tham his son reigned
in his stead.

27 JO'THAM *was* twenty and five years old when he began to reign, and he reigned sixteen years in Je-ru'sa-lem. His mother's name also *was* Je-ru'-shah, the daughter of Za'-dok.

2 And he did *that which was* right in the sight of the LORD, according to all that his father Uz-zi'ah did: howbeit he entered not into the temple of the LORD. And the people did yet corruptly.

3 He built the high gate of the house of the LORD, and on the wall of O'phel he built much.

4 Moreover he built cities in the mountains of Ju'dah, and in the forests he built castles and towers.

5 ¶ He fought also with the king of the Am'-mon-ites, and prevailed against them. And the children of Am'mon gave him the same year an hundred talents of silver, and ten thousand measures of wheat, and ten thousand of barley. So much did the children of Am'mon pay unto him, both the second year, and the third.

6 So Jo'tham became mighty, because he prepared his ways before the LORD his God.

7 ¶ Now the rest of the acts of Jo'tham, and all his wars, and his ways, lo, they *are* written in the book of the kings of Is'ra-el and Ju'dah.

8 He was five and twenty years old when he began to reign, and reigned sixteen years in Je-ru'sa-lem.

9 ¶ And Jo'tham slept with his fathers, and they buried him in the city of Da'vid: and A'haz his son reigned in his stead.

28 AHAZ *was* twenty years old when he began to reign, and he reigned sixteen years in Je-ru'sa-lem: but he did not *that which was* right in the sight of the LORD, like Da'vid his father:

2 For he walked in the ways of the kings of Is'ra-el, and made also molten images for Ba'al-im.

3 Moreover he burnt incense in the valley of the son of Hin'nom, and burnt his children in the fire, after the abominations of the heathen whom the LORD had cast out before the children of Is'ra-el.

4 He sacrificed also and burnt incense in the high places, and on the hills, and under every green tree.

5 Wherefore the LORD his God delivered him into the hand of the king of Syr'i-a; and they smote him, and carried away a great multitude of them captives, and brought *them* to Da-mas'-cus. And he was also delivered into the hand of the king of Is'ra-el, who smote him with a great slaughter.

6 ¶ For Pe'kah the son of Rem-a-li'ah slew in Ju'dah an hundred and twenty thousand in one day, *which were* all valiant men; because they had forsaken the LORD God of their fathers.

7 And Zich'ri, a mighty man of E'phra-im, slew Ma-a-se'iah the king's son, and Az'ri-kam the governor of the house, and El'ka-nah *that was* next to the king.

8 And the children of Is'ra-el carried away captive of their brethren two hundred thousand, women, sons, and daughters, and took also away much spoil from them, and brought the spoil to Sa-ma'ri-a.

9 But a prophet of the LORD was there, whose name *was* O'ded: and he went out before the host that came to Sa-ma'ri-a, and said unto them, Behold, because the LORD God of your fathers was wroth with Ju'dah, he hath delivered them into your hand, and ye have slain them in a rage *that* reacheth up unto heaven.

10 And now ye purpose to keep under the children of Ju'dah and Je-ru'sa-lem for bondmen and bondwomen unto you: *but are there* not with you, even with you, sins against the LORD your God?

11 Now hear me therefore, and deliver the captives again, which ye have taken captive of your brethren: for the fierce wrath of the LORD *is* upon you.

12 Then certain of the heads of the children of E'phra-im, Az-a-ri'ah the son of Jo-ha'nan, Ber-e-chi'ah the son of Me-shil'le-moth, and Je-hiz-ki'ah the son of Shal'lum, and Am'a-sa the son of Had'la-i, stood up against them that came from the war,

13 And said unto them, Ye shall not bring in the captives hither: for whereas we have offended against the LORD *already,* ye intend to add *more* to our sins and to our trespass: for our trespass is great, and *there is* fierce wrath against Is'ra-el.

14 So the armed men left the captives and the spoil before the princes and all the congregation.

15 And the men which were expressed by name rose up, and took the captives, and with the spoil clothed all that were naked among them, and arrayed them, and shod them, and gave them to eat and to drink, and anointed them, and carried all the feeble of them upon asses, and brought them to Jer'i-cho, the city of palm trees, to their brethren: then they returned to Sa-ma'ri-a.

16 ¶ At that time did king A'haz send unto the kings of As-syr'i-a to help him.

17 For again the E'dom-ites had come and smitten Ju'dah, and carried away captives.

18 The Phi-lis'tines also had invaded the cities of the low country, and of the south of Ju'dah, and had taken Beth–she'mesh, and Aj'a-lon, and Ge-de'roth, and Sho'cho with the villages thereof, and Tim'nah with the villages thereof, Gim'zo also and the villages thereof: and they dwelt there.

19 For the LORD brought Ju'dah low because of A'haz king of Is'ra-el; for he made Ju'dah naked, and transgressed sore against the LORD.

20 And Til'gath–pil-ne'ser king of As-syr'i-a came unto him, and distressed him, but strengthened him not.

21 For A'haz took away a portion *out* of the house of the LORD, and *out* of the house of the king, and of the princes, and gave *it* unto the king of As-syr'i-a: but he helped him not.

22 ¶ And in the time of his distress did he trespass yet more against the LORD: this *is that* king A'haz.

23 For he sacrificed unto the gods of Da-mas'cus, which smote him: and he said, Because the gods of the kings of Syr'i-a help them, *therefore* will I sacrifice to them, that they may help me. But they were the ruin of him, and of all Is'ra-el.

24 And A'haz gathered together the vessels of the house of God, and cut in pieces the vessels of the house of God, and shut up the doors of the house of the LORD, and he made him altars in every corner of Je-ru'sa-lem.

25 And in every several city of Ju'dah he made high places to burn incense unto other gods, and provoked to anger the LORD God of his fathers.

26 ¶ Now the rest of his acts and of all his ways, first and last, behold, they *are* written in the book of the kings of Ju'dah and Is'ra-el.

27 And A'haz slept with his fathers, and they buried him in the city, *even* in Je-ru'sa-lem: but

they brought him not into the sepulchres of the kings of Is'ra-el: and Hez-e-ki'ah his son reigned in his stead.

29 HEZ-E-KI'AH began to reign *when he was* five and twenty years old, and he reigned nine and twenty years in Je-ru'sa-lem. And his mother's name *was* A-bi'jah, the daughter of Zech-a-ri'ah.

2 And he did *that which was* right in the sight of the LORD, according to all that Da'vid his father had done.

3 ¶ He in the first year of his reign, in the first month, opened the doors of the house of the LORD, and repaired them.

4 And he brought in the priests and the Le'vites, and gathered them together into the east street,

5 And said unto them, Hear me, ye Le'vites, sanctify now yourselves, and sanctify the house of the LORD God of your fathers, and carry forth the filthiness out of the holy *place*.

6 For our fathers have trespassed, and done *that which was* evil in the eyes of the LORD our God, and have forsaken him, and have turned away their faces from the habitation of the LORD, and turned *their* backs.

7 Also they have shut up the doors of the porch, and put out the lamps, and have not burned incense nor offered burnt offerings in the holy *place* unto the God of Is'ra-el.

8 Wherefore the wrath of the LORD was upon Ju'dah and Je-ru'sa-lem, and he hath delivered them to trouble, to astonishment, and to hissing, as ye see with your eyes.

9 For, lo, our fathers have fallen by the sword, and our sons and our daughters and our wives *are* in captivity for this.

10 Now *it is* in mine heart to make a covenant with the LORD God of Is'ra-el, that his fierce wrath may turn away from us.

11 My sons, be not now negligent: for the LORD hath chosen you to stand before him, to serve him, and that ye should minister unto him, and burn incense.

12 ¶ Then the Le'vites arose, Ma'hath the son of A-mas'a-i, and Jo'el the son of Az-a-ri'ah, of the sons of the Ko'hath-ites: and of the sons of Me-ra'ri, Kish the son of Ab'di, and Az-a-ri'ah the son of Je-hal'e-lel: and of the Ger'shon-ites; Jo'ah the son of Zim'mah, and E'den the son of Jo'ah:

13 And of the sons of El'za-phan; Shim'ri, and Je-i'el: and of the sons of A'saph; Zech-a-ri'ah, and Mat-ta-ni'ah:

14 And of the sons of He'man; Je-hi'el, and Shim'e-i: and of the sons of Jed'u-thun; Shem-a-i'ah, and Uz'zi-el.

15 And they gathered their brethren, and sanctified themselves, and came, according to the commandment of the king, by the words of the LORD, to cleanse the house of the LORD.

16 And the priests went into the inner part of the house of the LORD, to cleanse *it,* and brought out all the uncleanness that they found in the temple of the LORD into the court of the house of the LORD. And the Le'vites took *it,* to carry *it* out abroad into the brook Kid'ron.

17 Now they began on the first *day* of the first month to sanctify, and on the eighth day of the month came they to the porch of the LORD: so they sanctified the house of the LORD in eight days; and in the sixteenth day of the first month they made an end.

18 Then they went in to Hez-e-ki'ah the king, and said, We have cleansed all the house of the LORD, and the altar of burnt offering, with all the vessels thereof, and the shewbread table, with all the vessels thereof.

19 Moreover all the vessels, which king A'haz in his reign did cast away in his transgression, have we prepared and sanctified, and, behold, they *are* before the altar of the LORD.

20 ¶ Then Hez-e-ki'ah the king rose early, and gathered the rulers of the city, and went up to the house of the LORD.

21 And they brought seven bullocks, and seven rams, and seven lambs, and seven he goats, for a sin offering for the kingdom, and for the sanctuary, and for Ju'dah. And he commanded the priests the sons of Aar'on to offer *them* on the altar of the LORD.

22 So they killed the bullocks, and the priests received the blood, and sprinkled *it* on the altar: likewise, when they had killed the rams, they sprinkled the blood upon the altar: they killed also the lambs, and they sprinkled the blood upon the altar.

23 And they brought forth the he goats *for* the sin offering before the king and the congregation; and they laid their hands upon them:

24 And the priests killed them, and they made reconciliation with their blood upon the altar, to make an atonement for all Is'ra-el: for the king commanded *that* the burnt offering and the sin offering *should be made* for all Is'ra-el.

25 And he set the Le'vites in the house of the LORD with cymbals, with psalteries, and with harps, according to the commandment of Da'vid, and of Gad the king's seer, and Na'than the prophet: for *so was* the commandment of the LORD by his prophets.

26 And the Le'vites stood with the instruments of Da'vid, and the priests with the trumpets.

27 And Hez-e-ki'ah commanded to offer the burnt offering upon the altar. And when the burnt offering began, the song of the LORD began *also* with the trumpets, and with the instruments *ordained* by Da'vid king of Is'ra-el.

28 And all the congregation worshipped, and the singers sang, and the trumpeters sounded: *and* all *this continued* until the burnt offering was finished.

29 And when they had made an end of offering, the king and all that were present with him bowed themselves, and worshipped.

30 Moreover Hez-e-ki'ah the king and the princes commanded the Le'vites to sing praise unto the LORD with the words of Da'vid, and of A'saph the seer. And they sang praises with gladness, and they bowed their heads and worshipped.

31 Then Hez-e-ki'ah answered and said, Now ye have consecrated yourselves unto the LORD, come near and bring sacrifices and thank offerings into the house of the LORD. And the congregation brought in sacrifices and thank offerings; and as many as were of a free heart burnt offerings.

32 And the number of the burnt offerings, which the congregation brought, was threescore and ten bullocks, an hundred rams, *and* two hundred lambs: all these *were* for a burnt offering to the LORD.

33 And the consecrated things *were* six hundred oxen and three thousand sheep.

34 But the priests were too few, so that they could not flay all the burnt offerings: wherefore their brethren the Le'vites did help them, till the work was ended, and until the *other* priests had sanctified themselves: for the Le'vites *were*

more upright in heart to sanctify themselves
than the priests.
35 And also the burnt offerings *were* in abundance, with the fat of the peace offerings, and
the drink offerings for *every* burnt offering. So
the service of the house of the LORD was set in
order.
36 And Hez-e-ki'ah rejoiced, and all the people, that God had prepared the people: for the
thing was *done* suddenly.

30 AND Hez-e-ki'ah sent to all Is'ra-el and
Ju'dah, and wrote letters also to E'phra-
im and Ma-nas'seh, that they should come to
the house of the LORD at Je-ru'sa-lem, to keep
the passover unto the LORD God of Is'ra-el.
2 For the king had taken counsel, and his
princes, and all the congregation in Je-ru'sa-
lem, to keep the passover in the second month.
3 For they could not keep it at that time, because the priests had not sanctified themselves
sufficiently, neither had the people gathered
themselves together to Je-ru'sa-lem.
4 And the thing pleased the king and all the
congregation.
5 So they established a decree to make proclamation throughout all Is'ra-el, from Be'er-
she'ba even to Dan, that they should come to
keep the passover unto the LORD God of Is'ra-el
at Je-ru'sa-lem: for they had not done *it* of a
long *time in such sort* as it was written.
6 So the posts went with the letters from the
king and his princes throughout all Is'ra-el and
Ju'dah, and according to the commandment of
the king, saying, Ye children of Is'ra-el, turn
again unto the LORD God of A'bra-ham, I'saac,
and Is'ra-el, and he will return to the remnant of
you, that are escaped out of the hand of the
kings of As-syr'i-a.
7 And be not ye like your fathers, and like
your brethren, which trespassed against the
LORD God of their fathers, *who* therefore gave
them up to desolation, as ye see.
8 Now be ye not stiffnecked, as your fathers
were, but yield yourselves unto the LORD, and
enter into his sanctuary, which he hath sanctified for ever: and serve the LORD your God, that
the fierceness of his wrath may turn away from
you.
9 For if ye turn again unto the LORD, your
brethren and your children *shall find* compassion before them that lead them captive, so that
they shall come again into this land: for the
LORD your God *is* gracious and merciful, and
will not turn away *his* face from you, if ye return unto him.
10 So the posts passed from city to city
through the country of E'phra-im and Ma-nas'-
seh even unto Zeb'u-lun: but they laughed them
to scorn, and mocked them.
11 Nevertheless divers of Ash'er and Ma-
nas'seh and of Zeb'u-lun humbled themselves,
and came to Je-ru'sa-lem.
12 Also in Ju'dah the hand of God was to
give them one heart to do the commandment of
the king and of the princes, by the word of the
LORD.
13 ¶ And there assembled at Je-ru'sa-lem
much people to keep the feast of unleavened
bread in the second month, a very great congregation.
14 And they arose and took away the altars
that *were* in Je-ru'sa-lem, and all the altars for
incense took they away, and cast *them* into the
brook Kid'ron.
15 Then they killed the passover on the fourteenth *day* of the second month: and the priests
and the Le'vites were ashamed, and sanctified
themselves, and brought in the burnt offerings
into the house of the LORD.
16 And they stood in their place after their
manner, according to the law of Mo'ses the man
of God: the priests sprinkled the blood, *which
they received* of the hand of the Le'vites.
17 For *there were* many in the congregation
that were not sanctified: therefore the Le'vites
had the charge of the killing of the passovers
for every one *that was* not clean, to sanctify
them unto the LORD.
18 For a multitude of the people, *even* many
of E'phra-im, and Ma-nas'seh, Is'sa-char, and
Zeb'u-lun, had not cleansed themselves, yet did
they eat the passover otherwise than it was
written. But Hez-e-ki'ah prayed for them, saying, The good LORD pardon every one
19 *That* prepareth his heart to seek God, the
LORD God of his fathers, though *he be* not
cleansed according to the purification of the
sanctuary.
20 And the LORD hearkened to Hez-e-ki'ah,
and healed the people.
21 And the children of Is'ra-el that were present at Je-ru'sa-lem, kept the feast of unleavened bread seven days with great gladness: and
the Le'vites and the priests praised the LORD
day by day, *singing* with loud instruments unto
the LORD.
22 And Hez-e-ki'ah spake comfortably unto
all the Le'vites that taught the good knowledge
of the LORD: and they did eat throughout the
feast seven days, offering peace offerings, and
making confession to the LORD God of their fathers.
23 And the whole assembly took counsel to
keep other seven days: and they kept *other*
seven days with gladness.
24 For Hez-e-ki'ah king of Ju'dah did give to
the congregation a thousand bullocks and seven
thousand sheep; and the princes gave to the
congregation a thousand bullocks and ten thousand sheep: and a great number of priests sanctified themselves.
25 And all the congregation of Ju'dah, with
the priests and the Le'vites, and all the congregation that came out of Is'ra-el, and the strangers that came out of the land of Is'ra-el, and that
dwelt in Ju'dah, rejoiced.
26 So there was great joy in Je-ru'sa-lem: for
since the time of Sol'o-mon the son of Da'vid
king of Is'ra-el *there was* not the like in Je-ru'sa-
lem.
27 ¶ Then the priests the Le'vites arose and
blessed the people: and their voice was heard,
and their prayer came *up* to his holy dwelling
place, *even* unto heaven.

31 NOW when all this was finished, all Is'-
ra-el that were present went out to the
cities of Ju'dah, and brake the images in pieces,
and cut down the groves, and threw down the
high places and the altars out of all Ju'dah and
Ben'ja-min, in E'phra-im also and Ma-nas'seh,
until they had utterly destroyed them all. Then
all the children of Is'ra-el returned, every man
to his possession, into their own cities.
2 ¶ And Hez-e-ki'ah appointed the courses
of the priests and the Le'vites after their
courses, every man according to his service, the
priests and Le'vites for burnt offerings and for
peace offerings, to minister, and to give thanks,
and to praise in the gates of the tents of the
LORD.
3 *He appointed* also the king's portion of his
substance for the burnt offerings, *to wit,* for the

morning and evening burnt offerings, and the
burnt offerings for the sabbaths, and for the
new moons, and for the set feasts, as *it is* written in the law of the LORD.
4 Moreover he commanded the people that
dwelt in Je-ru'sa-lem to give the portion of the
priests and the Le'vites, that they might be encouraged in the law of the LORD.
5 ¶ And as soon as the commandment came
abroad, the children of Is'ra-el brought in abundance the firstfruits of corn, wine, and oil, and
honey, and of all the increase of the field; and
the tithe of all *things* brought they in abundantly.
6 And *concerning* the children of Is'ra-el and
Ju'dah, that dwelt in the cities of Ju'dah, they
also brought in the tithe of oxen and sheep, and
the tithe of holy things which were consecrated
unto the LORD their God, and laid *them* by
heaps.
7 In the third month they began to lay the
foundation of the heaps, and finished *them* in
the seventh month.
8 And when Hez-e-ki'ah and the princes
came and saw the heaps, they blessed the LORD,
and his people Is'ra-el.
9 Then Hez-e-ki'ah questioned with the
priests and the Le'vites concerning the heaps.
10 And Az-a-ri'ah the chief priest of the
house of Za'dok answered him, and said, Since
the people began to bring the offerings into the
house of the LORD, we have had enough to eat,
and have left plenty: for the LORD hath blessed
his people; and that which is left *is* this great
store.
11 ¶ Then Hez-e-ki'ah commanded to prepare chambers in the house of the LORD; and
they prepared *them*,
12 And brought in the offerings and the
tithes and the dedicated *things* faithfully: over
which Con-o-ni'ah the Le'vite *was* ruler, and
Shim'e-i his brother *was* the next.
13 And Je-hi'el, and Az-a-zi'ah, and Na'hath,
and A'sa-hel, and Jer'i-moth, and Joz'a-bad, and
E-li'el, and Is-ma-chi'ah, and Ma'hath, and Be-
na'iah, *were* overseers under the hand of Con-o-
ni'ah and Shim'e-i his brother, at the commandment of Hez-e-ki'ah the king, and Az-a-ri'ah the
ruler of the house of God.
14 And Ko're the son of Im'nah the Le'vite,
the porter toward the east, *was* over the freewill offerings of God, to distribute the oblations
of the LORD, and the most holy things.
15 And next him *were* E'den, and Mi-ni'a-
min, and Jesh'u-a, and Shem-a-i'ah, Am-a-ri'ah,
and Shec-a-ni'ah, in the cities of the priests, in
their set office, to give to their brethren by
courses, as well to the great as to the small:
16 Beside their genealogy of males, from
three years old and upward, *even* unto every
one that entereth into the house of the LORD, his
daily portion for their service in their charges
according to their courses;
17 Both to the genealogy of the priests by the
house of their fathers, and the Le'vites from
twenty years old and upward, in their charges
by their courses;
18 And to the genealogy of all their little
ones, their wives, and their sons, and their
daughters, through all the congregation: for in
their set office they sanctified themselves in
holiness:
19 Also of the sons of Aar'on the priests,
which were in the fields of the suburbs of their
cities, in every several city, the men that were
expressed by name, to give portions to all the
males among the priests, and to all that were
reckoned by genealogies among the Le'vites.
20 ¶ And thus did Hez-e-ki'ah throughout all
Ju'dah, and wrought *that which was* good and
right and truth before the LORD his God.
21 And in every work that he began in the
service of the house of God, and in the law, and
in the commandments, to seek his God, he did *it*
with all his heart, and prospered.

32 AFTER these things, and the establishment thereof, Sen-nach'e-rib king of As-
syr'i-a came, and entered into Ju'dah, and encamped against the fenced cities, and thought
to win them for himself.
2 And when Hez-e-ki'ah saw that Sen-nach'-
e-rib was come, and that he was purposed to
fight against Je-ru'sa-lem,
3 He took counsel with his princes and his
mighty men to stop the waters of the fountains
which *were* without the city: and they did help
him.
4 So there was gathered much people together, who stopped all the fountains, and the
brook that ran through the midst of the land,
saying, Why should the kings of As-syr'i-a
come, and find much water?
5 Also he strengthened himself, and built up
all the wall that was broken, and raised *it* up to
the towers, and another wall without, and repaired Mil'lo *in* the city of Da'vid, and made
darts and shields in abundance.
6 And he set captains of war over the people,
and gathered them together to him in the street
of the gate of the city, and spake comfortably to
them, saying,
7 Be strong and courageous, be not afraid
nor dismayed for the king of As-syr'i-a, nor for
all the multitude that *is* with him: for *there be*
more with us than with him:
8 With him *is* an arm of flesh; but with us *is*
the LORD our God to help us, and to fight our
battles. And the people rested themselves upon
the words of Hez-e-ki'ah king of Ju'dah.
9 ¶ After this did Sen-nach'e-rib king of As-
syr'i-a send his servants to Je-ru'sa-lem, (but he
himself laid siege against La'chish, and all his
power with him,) unto Hez-e-ki'ah king of Ju'-
dah, and unto all Ju'dah that *were* at Je-ru'sa-
lem, saying,
10 Thus saith Sen-nach'e-rib king of As-syr'i-
a, Whereon do ye trust, that ye abide in the
siege in Je-ru'sa-lem?
11 Doth not Hez-e-ki'ah persuade you to give
over yourselves to die by famine and by thirst,
saying, The LORD our God shall deliver us out of
the hand of the king of As-syr'i-a?
12 Hath not the same Hez-e-ki'ah taken
away his high places and his altars, and commanded Ju'dah and Je-ru'sa-lem, saying, Ye
shall worship before one altar, and burn incense
upon it?
13 Know ye not what I and my fathers have
done unto all the people of *other* lands? were
the gods of the nations of those lands any ways
able to deliver their lands out of mine hand?
14 Who *was there* among all the gods of
those nations that my fathers utterly destroyed,
that could deliver his people out of mine hand,
that your God should be able to deliver you out
of mine hand?
15 Now therefore let not Hez-e-ki'ah deceive
you, nor persuade you on this manner, neither
yet believe him: for no god of any nation or
kingdom was able to deliver his people out of
mine hand, and out of the hand of my fathers:

how much less shall your God deliver you out of mine hand?

16 And his servants spake yet *more* against the LORD God, and against his servant Hez-e-ki'ah.

17 He wrote also letters to rail on the LORD God of Is'ra-el, and to speak against him, saying, As the gods of the nations of *other* lands have not delivered their people out of mine hand, so shall not the God of Hez-e-ki'ah deliver his people out of mine hand.

18 Then they cried with a loud voice in the Jews' speech unto the people of Je-ru'sa-lem that *were* on the wall, to affright them, and to trouble them; that they might take the city.

19 And they spake against the God of Je-ru'sa-lem, as against the gods of the people of the earth, *which were* the work of the hands of man.

20 And for this *cause* Hez-e-ki'ah the king, and the prophet I-sa'iah the son of A'moz, prayed and cried to heaven.

21 ¶ And the LORD sent an angel, which cut off all the mighty men of valour, and the leaders and captains in the camp of the king of As-syr'i-a. So he returned with shame of face to his own land. And when he was come into the house of his god, they that came forth of his own bowels slew him there with the sword.

22 Thus the LORD saved Hez-e-ki'ah and the inhabitants of Je-ru'sa-lem from the hand of Sen-nach'e-rib the king of As-syr'i-a, and from the hand of all *other*, and guided them on every side.

23 And many brought gifts unto the LORD to Je-ru'sa-lem, and presents to Hez-e-ki'ah king of Ju'dah: so that he was magnified in the sight of all nations from thenceforth.

24 ¶ In those days Hez-e-ki'ah was sick to the death, and prayed unto the LORD: and he spake unto him, and he gave him a sign.

25 But Hez-e-ki'ah rendered not again according to the benefit *done* unto him; for his heart was lifted up: therefore there was wrath upon him, and upon Ju'dah and Je-ru'sa-lem.

26 Notwithstanding Hez-e-ki'ah humbled himself for the pride of his heart, *both* he and the inhabitants of Je-ru'sa-lem, so that the wrath of the LORD came not upon them in the days of Hez-e-ki'ah.

27 ¶ And Hez-e-ki'ah had exceeding much riches and honour: and he made himself treasuries for silver, and for gold, and for precious stones, and for spices, and for shields, and for all manner of pleasant jewels;

28 Storehouses also for the increase of corn, and wine, and oil; and stalls for all manner of beasts, and cotes for flocks.

29 Moreover he provided him cities, and possessions of flocks and herds in abundance: for God had given him substance very much.

30 This same Hez-e-ki'ah also stopped the upper watercourse of Gi'hon, and brought it straight down to the west side of the city of Da'vid. And Hez-e-ki'ah prospered in all his works.

31 ¶ Howbeit in *the business of* the ambassadors of the princes of Bab'y-lon, who sent unto him to enquire of the wonder that was *done* in the land, God left him, to try him, that he might know all *that was* in his heart.

32 ¶ Now the rest of the acts of Hez-e-ki'ah, and his goodness, behold, they *are* written in the vision of I-sa'iah the prophet, the son of A'moz, *and* in the book of the kings of Ju'dah and Is'ra-el.

33 And Hez-e-ki'ah slept with his fathers, and they buried him in the chiefest of the sepulchres of the sons of Da'vid: and all Ju'dah and the inhabitants of Je-ru'sa-lem did him honour at his death. And Ma-nas'seh his son reigned in his stead.

33 MA-NAS'SEH *was* twelve years old when he began to reign, and he reigned fifty and five years in Je-ru'sa-lem:

2 But did *that which was* evil in the sight of the LORD, like unto the abominations of the heathen, whom the LORD had cast out before the children of Is'ra-el.

3 ¶ For he built again the high places which Hez-e-ki'ah his father had broken down, and he reared up altars for Ba'al-im, and made groves, and worshipped all the host of heaven, and served them.

4 Also he built altars in the house of the LORD, whereof the LORD had said, In Je-ru'sa-lem shall my name be for ever.

5 And he built altars for all the host of heaven in the two courts of the house of the LORD.

6 And he caused his children to pass through the fire in the valley of the son of Hin'nom: also he observed times, and used enchantments, and used witchcraft, and dealt with a familiar spirit, and with wizards: he wrought much evil in the sight of the LORD, to provoke him to anger.

7 And he set a carved image, the idol which he had made, in the house of God, of which God had said to Da'vid and to Sol'o-mon his son, In this house, and in Je-ru'sa-lem, which I have chosen before all the tribes of Is'ra-el, will I put my name for ever:

8 Neither will I any more remove the foot of Is'ra-el from out of the land which I have appointed for your fathers; so that they will take heed to do all that I have commanded them, according to the whole law and the statutes and the ordinances by the hand of Mo'ses.

9 So Ma-nas'seh made Ju'dah and the inhabitants of Je-ru'sa-lem to err, *and* to do worse than the heathen, whom the LORD had destroyed before the children of Is'ra-el.

10 And the LORD spake to Ma-nas'seh, and to his people: but they would not hearken.

11 ¶ Wherefore the LORD brought upon them the captains of the host of the king of As-syr'i-a, which took Ma-nas'seh among the thorns, and bound him with fetters, and carried him to Bab'y-lon.

12 And when he was in affliction, he besought the LORD his God, and humbled himself greatly before the God of his fathers,

13 And prayed unto him: and he was intreated of him, and heard his supplication, and brought him again to Je-ru'sa-lem into his kingdom. Then Ma-nas'seh knew that the LORD he *was* God.

14 Now after this he built a wall without the city of Da'vid, on the west side of Gi'hon, in the valley, even to the entering in at the fish gate, and compassed about O'phel, and raised it up a very great height, and put captains of war in all the fenced cities of Ju'dah.

15 And he took away the strange gods, and the idol out of the house of the LORD, and all the altars that he had built in the mount of the house of the LORD, and in Je-ru'sa-lem, and cast *them* out of the city.

16 And he repaired the altar of the LORD, and sacrificed thereon peace offerings and thank offerings, and commanded Ju'dah to serve the LORD God of Is'ra-el.

17 Nevertheless the people did sacrifice still

in the high places, *yet* unto the LORD their God
only.
18 ¶ Now the rest of the acts of Ma-nas'seh,
and his prayer unto his God, and the words of
the seers that spake to him in the name of the
LORD God of Is'ra-el, behold, they *are written* in
the book of the kings of Is'ra-el.
19 His prayer also, and *how God* was intreated of him, and all his sins, and his trespass,
and the places wherein he built high places, and
set up groves and graven images, before he was
humbled: behold, they *are* written among the
sayings of the seers.
20 ¶ So Ma-nas'seh slept with his fathers,
and they buried him in his own house: and A'-
mon his son reigned in his stead.
21 ¶ A'mon *was* two and twenty years old
when he began to reign, and reigned two years
in Je-ru'sa-lem.
22 But he did *that which was* evil in the sight
of the LORD, as did Ma-nas'seh his father: for
A'mon sacrificed unto all the carved images
which Ma-nas'seh his father had made, and
served them;
23 And humbled not himself before the
LORD, as Ma-nas'seh his father had humbled
himself; but A'mon trespassed more and more.
24 And his servants conspired against him,
and slew him in his own house.
25 ¶ But the people of the land slew all them
that had conspired against king A'mon; and the
people of the land made Jo-si'ah his son king in
his stead.

34 JO-SI'AH *was* eight years old when he
began to reign, and he reigned in Je-ru'-
sa-lem one and thirty years.
2 And he did *that which was* right in the
sight of the LORD, and walked in the ways of
Da'vid his father, and declined *neither* to the
right hand, nor to the left.
3 ¶ For in the eighth year of his reign, while
he was yet young, he began to seek after the
God of Da'vid his father: and in the twelfth year
he began to purge Ju'dah and Je-ru'sa-lem from
the high places, and the groves, and the carved
images, and the molten images.
4 And they brake down the altars of Ba'al-im
in his presence; and the images, that *were* on
high above them, he cut down; and the groves,
and the carved images, and the molten images,
he brake in pieces, and made dust *of them,* and
strowed *it* upon the graves of them that had
sacrificed unto them.
5 And he burnt the bones of the priests upon
their altars, and cleansed Ju'dah and Je-ru'sa-
lem.
6 And *so did he* in the cities of Ma-nas'seh,
and E'phra-im, and Sim'e-on, even unto Naph'-
ta-li, with their mattocks round about.
7 And when he had broken down the altars
and the groves, and had beaten the graven images into powder, and cut down all the idols
throughout all the land of Is'ra-el, he returned
to Je-ru'sa-lem.
8 ¶ Now in the eighteenth year of his reign,
when he had purged the land, and the house, he
sent Sha'phan the son of Az-a-li'ah, and Ma-a-
se'iah the governor of the city, and Jo'ah the
son of Jo'a-haz the recorder, to repair the house
of the LORD his God.
9 And when they came to Hil-ki'ah the high
priest, they delivered the money that was
brought into the house of God, which the Le'-
vites that kept the doors had gathered of the
hand of Ma-nas'seh and E'phra-im, and of all
the remnant of Is'ra-el, and of all Ju'dah and
Ben'ja-min; and they returned to Je-ru'sa-lem.
10 And they put *it* in the hand of the workmen that had the oversight of the house of the
LORD, and they gave it to the workmen that
wrought in the house of the LORD, to repair and
amend the house:
11 Even to the artificers and builders gave
they *it,* to buy hewn stone, and timber for cou-
plings, and to floor the houses which the kings
of Ju'dah had destroyed.
12 And the men did the work faithfully: and
the overseers of them *were* Ja'hath and O-ba-
di'ah, the Le'vites, of the sons of Me-ra'ri; and
Zech-a-ri'ah and Me-shul'lam, of the sons of the
Ko'hath-ites, to set *it* forward; and *other of* the
Le'vites, all that could skill of instruments of
musick.
13 Also *they were* over the bearers of burdens, and *were* overseers of all that wrought the
work in any manner of service: and of the Le'-
vites *there were* scribes, and officers, and porters.
14 ¶ And when they brought out the money
that was brought into the house of the LORD,
Hil-ki'ah the priest found a book of the law of
the LORD *given* by Mo'ses.
15 And Hil-ki'ah answered and said to Sha'-
phan the scribe, I have found the book of the
law in the house of the LORD. And Hil-ki'ah delivered the book to Sha'phan.
16 And Sha'phan carried the book to the
king, and brought the king word back again,
saying, All that was committed to thy servants,
they do *it.*
17 And they have gathered together the
money that was found in the house of the LORD,
and have delivered it into the hand of the overseers, and to the hand of the workmen.
18 Then Sha'phan the scribe told the king,
saying, Hil-ki'ah the priest hath given me a
book. And Sha'phan read it before the king.
19 And it came to pass, when the king had
heard the words of the law, that he rent his
clothes.
20 And the king commanded Hil-ki'ah, and
A-hi'kam the son of Sha'phan, and Ab'don the
son of Mi'cah, and Sha'phan the scribe, and A-
sa-i'ah a servant of the king's, saying,
21 Go, enquire of the LORD for me, and for
them that are left in Is'ra-el and in Ju'dah, concerning the words of the book that is found: for
great *is* the wrath of the LORD that is poured out
upon us, because our fathers have not kept the
word of the LORD, to do after all that is written
in this book.
22 And Hil-ki'ah, and *they* that the king *had
appointed,* went to Hul'dah the prophetess, the
wife of Shal'lum the son of Tik'vath, the son of
Has'rah, keeper of the wardrobe; (now she
dwelt in Je-ru'sa-lem in the college:) and they
spake to her to that *effect.*
23 ¶ And she answered them, Thus saith the
LORD God of Is'ra-el, Tell ye the man that sent
you to me,
24 Thus saith the LORD, Behold, I will bring
evil upon this place, and upon the inhabitants
thereof, *even* all the curses that are written in
the book which they have read before the king
of Ju'dah:
25 Because they have forsaken me, and have
burned incense unto other gods, that they might
provoke me to anger with all the works of their
hands; therefore my wrath shall be poured out
upon this place, and shall not be quenched.
26 And as for the king of Ju'dah, who sent
you to enquire of the LORD, so shall ye say unto

him, Thus saith the LORD God of Is'ra-el *con-*
cerning the words which thou hast heard;
27 Because thine heart was tender, and thou
didst humble thyself before God, when thou
heardest his words against this place, and
against the inhabitants thereof, and humbledst
thyself before me, and didst rend thy clothes,
and weep before me; I have even heard *thee*
also, saith the LORD.
28 Behold, I will gather thee to thy fathers,
and thou shalt be gathered to thy grave in
peace, neither shall thine eyes see all the evil
that I will bring upon this place, and upon the
inhabitants of the same. So they brought the
king word again.
29 ¶ Then the king sent and gathered together all the elders of Ju'dah and Je-ru'sa-lem.
30 And the king went up into the house of
the LORD, and all the men of Ju'dah, and the
inhabitants of Je-ru'sa-lem, and the priests, and
the Le'vites, and all the people, great and small:
and he read in their ears all the words of the
book of the covenant that was found in the
house of the LORD.
31 And the king stood in his place, and made
a covenant before the LORD, to walk after the
LORD, and to keep his commandments, and his
testimonies, and his statutes, with all his heart,
and with all his soul, to perform the words of
the covenant which are written in this book.
32 And he caused all that were present in Je-
ru'sa-lem and Ben'ja-min to stand *to it*. And the
inhabitants of Je-ru'sa-lem did according to the
covenant of God, the God of their fathers.
33 And Jo-si'ah took away all the abominations out of all the countries that *pertained* to
the children of Is'ra-el, and made all that were
present in Is'ra-el to serve, *even* to serve the
LORD their God. *And* all his days they departed
not from following the LORD, the God of their
fathers.

35 MOREOVER Jo-si'ah kept a passover
unto the LORD in Je-ru'sa-lem: and they
killed the passover on the fourteenth *day* of the
first month.
2 And he set the priests in their charges, and
encouraged them to the service of the house of
the LORD,
3 And said unto the Le'vites that taught all
Is'ra-el, which were holy unto the LORD, Put the
holy ark in the house which Sol'o-mon the son
of Da'vid king of Is'ra-el did build; *it shall* not
be a burden upon *your* shoulders: serve now the
LORD your God, and his people Is'ra-el,
4 And prepare *yourselves* by the houses of
your fathers, after your courses, according to
the writing of Da'vid king of Is'ra-el, and according to the writing of Sol'o-mon his son.
5 And stand in the holy *place* according to
the divisions of the families of the fathers of
your brethren the people, and *after* the division
of the families of the Le'vites.
6 So kill the passover, and sanctify yourselves, and prepare your brethren, that *they*
may do according to the word of the LORD by
the hand of Mo'ses.
7 And Jo-si'ah gave to the people, of the
flock, lambs and kids, all for the passover offerings, for all that were present, to the number of
thirty thousand, and three thousand bullocks:
these *were* of the king's substance.
8 And his princes gave willingly unto the
people, to the priests, and to the Le'vites: Hil-
ki'ah and Zech-a-ri'ah and Je-hi'el, rulers of the
house of God, gave unto the priests for the
passover offerings two thousand and six hundred *small cattle*, and three hundred oxen.
9 Con-a-ni'ah also, and Shem-a-i'ah and Ne-
than'e-el, his brethren, and Hash-a-bi'ah and Je-
i'el and Joz'a-bad, chief of the Le'vites, gave
unto the Le'vites for passover offerings five
thousand *small cattle*, and five hundred oxen.
10 So the service was prepared, and the
priests stood in their place, and the Le'vites in
their courses, according to the king's commandment.
11 And they killed the passover, and the
priests sprinkled *the blood* from their hands,
and the Le'vites flayed *them*.
12 And they removed the burnt offerings,
that they might give according to the divisions
of the families of the people, to offer unto the
LORD, as *it is* written in the book of Mo'ses. And
so *did they* with the oxen.
13 And they roasted the passover with fire
according to the ordinance: but the *other* holy
offerings sod they in pots, and in caldrons, and
in pans, and divided *them* speedily among all
the people.
14 And afterward they made ready for themselves, and for the priests: because the priests
the sons of Aar'on *were busied* in offering of
burnt offerings and the fat until night; therefore
the Le'vites prepared for themselves, and for
the priests the sons of Aar'on.
15 And the singers the sons of A'saph *were* in
their place, according to the commandment of
Da'vid, and A'saph, and He'man, and Jed'u-
thun the king's seer; and the porters *waited* at
every gate; they might not depart from their
service; for their brethren the Le'vites prepared
for them.
16 So all the service of the LORD was prepared the same day, to keep the passover, and
to offer burnt offerings upon the altar of the
LORD, according to the commandment of king
Jo-si'ah.
17 And the children of Is'ra-el that were present kept the passover at that time, and the
feast of unleavened bread seven days.
18 And there was no passover like to that
kept in Is'ra-el from the days of Sam'u-el the
prophet; neither did all the kings of Is'ra-el keep
such a passover as Jo-si'ah kept, and the
priests, and the Le'vites, and all Ju'dah and Is'-
ra-el that were present, and the inhabitants of
Je-ru'sa-lem.
19 In the eighteenth year of the reign of Jo-
si'ah was this passover kept.
20 ¶ After all this, when Jo-si'ah had prepared the temple, Ne'cho king of E'gypt came
up to fight against Char'che-mish by Eu-phra'-
tes: and Jo-si'ah went out against him.
21 But he sent ambassadors to him, saying,
What have I to do with thee, thou king of Ju'-
dah? *I come* not against thee this day, but
against the house wherewith I have war: for
God commanded me to make haste: forbear
thee from *meddling with* God, who *is* with me,
that he destroy thee not.
22 Nevertheless Jo-si'ah would not turn his
face from him, but disguised himself, that he
might fight with him, and hearkened not unto
the words of Ne'cho from the mouth of God,
and came to fight in the valley of Me-gid'do.
23 And the archers shot at king Jo-si'ah; and
the king said to his servants, Have me away; for
I am sore wounded.
24 His servants therefore took him out of
that chariot, and put him in the second chariot
that he had; and they brought him to Je-ru'sa-
lem, and he died, and was buried in *one of* the

sepulchres of his fathers. And all Ju'dah and Je-
ru'sa-lem mourned for Jo-si'ah.
25 ¶ And Jer-e-mi'ah lamented for Jo-si'ah:
and all the singing men and the singing women
spake of Jo-si'ah in their lamentations to this
day, and made them an ordinance in Is'ra-el:
and, behold, they *are* written in the lamentations.
26 Now the rest of the acts of Jo-si'ah, and
his goodness, according to *that which was* written in the law of the LORD,
27 And his deeds, first and last, behold, they
are written in the book of the kings of Is'ra-el
and Ju'dah.

36 THEN the people of the land took Je-
ho'a-haz the son of Jo-si'ah, and made
him king in his father's stead in Je-ru'sa-lem.
2 Je-ho'a-haz *was* twenty and three years old
when he began to reign, and he reigned three
months in Je-ru'sa-lem.
3 And the king of E'gypt put him down at Je-
ru'sa-lem, and condemned the land in an hundred talents of silver and a talent of gold.
4 And the king of E'gypt made E-li'a-kim his
brother king over Ju'dah and Je-ru'sa-lem, and
turned his name to Je-hoi'a-kim. And Ne'cho
took Je-ho'a-haz his brother, and carried him to
E'gypt.
5 ¶ Je-hoi'a-kim *was* twenty and five years
old when he began to reign, and he reigned
eleven years in Je-ru'sa-lem: and he did *that*
which was evil in the sight of the LORD his God.
6 Against him came up Neb-u-chad-nez'zar
king of Bab'y-lon, and bound him in fetters, to
carry him to Bab'y-lon.
7 Neb-u-chad-nez'zar also carried of the vessels of the house of the LORD to Bab'y-lon, and
put them in his temple at Bab'y-lon.
8 Now the rest of the acts of Je-hoi'a-kim,
and his abominations which he did, and that
which was found in him, behold, they *are* written in the book of the kings of Is'ra-el and Ju'-
dah: and Je-hoi'a-chin his son reigned in his
stead.
9 ¶ Je-hoi'a-chin *was* eight years old when
he began to reign, and he reigned three months
and ten days in Je-ru'sa-lem: and he did *that*
which was evil in the sight of the LORD.
10 And when the year was expired, king
Neb-u-chad-nez'zar sent, and brought him to
Bab'y-lon, with the goodly vessels of the house
of the LORD, and made Zed-e-ki'ah his brother
king over Ju'dah and Je-ru'sa-lem.
11 ¶ Zed-e-ki'ah *was* one and twenty years
old when he began to reign, and reigned eleven
years in Je-ru'sa-lem.
12 And he did *that which was* evil in the
sight of the LORD his God, *and* humbled not
himself before Jer-e-mi'ah the prophet *speaking*
from the mouth of the LORD.
13 And he also rebelled against king Neb-u-
chad-nez'zar, who had made him swear by God:
but he stiffened his neck, and hardened his
heart from turning unto the LORD God of Is'ra-
el.
14 ¶ Moreover all the chief of the priests,
and the people, transgressed very much after
all the abominations of the heathen; and polluted the house of the LORD which he had hallowed in Je-ru'sa-lem.
15 And the LORD God of their fathers sent to
them by his messengers, rising up betimes, and
sending; because he had compassion on his
people, and on his dwelling place:
16 But they mocked the messengers of God,
and despised his words, and misused his prophets, until the wrath of the LORD arose against
his people, till *there was* no remedy.
17 Therefore he brought upon them the king
of the Chal'dees, who slew their young men
with the sword in the house of their sanctuary,
and had no compassion upon young man or
maiden, old man, or him that stooped for age:
he gave *them* all into his hand.
18 And all the vessels of the house of God,
great and small, and the treasures of the house
of the LORD, and the treasures of the king, and
of his princes; all *these* he brought to Bab'y-lon.
19 And they burnt the house of God, and
brake down the wall of Je-ru'sa-lem, and burnt
all the palaces thereof with fire, and destroyed
all the goodly vessels thereof.
20 And them that had escaped from the
sword carried he away to Bab'y-lon; where they
were servants to him and his sons until the
reign of the kingdom of Per'sia:
21 To fulfil the word of the LORD by the
mouth of Jer-e-mi'ah, until the land had en-
joyed her sabbaths: *for* as long as she lay desolate she kept sabbath, to fulfil threescore and
ten years.
22 ¶ Now in the first year of Cy'rus king of
Per'sia, that the word of the LORD *spoken* by the
mouth of Jer-e-mi'ah might be accomplished,
the LORD stirred up the spirit of Cy'rus king of
Per'sia, that he made a proclamation throughout all his kingdom, and *put it* also in writing,
saying,
23 Thus saith Cy'rus king of Per'sia, All the
kingdoms of the earth hath the LORD God of
heaven given me; and he hath charged me to
build him an house in Je-ru'sa-lem, which *is* in
Ju'dah. Who *is there* among you of all his people? The LORD his God *be* with him, and let him
go up.

THE BOOK OF

EZRA

1 NOW in the first year of Cy'rus king of
Per'sia, that the word of the LORD by the
mouth of Jer-e-mi'ah might be fulfilled, the
LORD stirred up the spirit of Cy'rus king of Per'-
sia, that he made a proclamation throughout all
his kingdom, and *put it* also in writing, saying,
2 Thus saith Cy'rus king of Per'sia, The LORD
God of heaven hath given me all the kingdoms
of the earth; and he hath charged me to build
him an house at Je-ru'sa-lem, which *is* in Ju'-
dah.
3 Who *is there* among you of all his people?
his God be with him, and let him go up to Je-
ru'sa-lem, which *is* in Ju'dah, and build the
house of the LORD God of Is'ra-el, (he *is* the
God,) which *is* in Je-ru'sa-lem.
4 And whosoever remaineth in any place
where he sojourneth, let the men of his place
help him with silver, and with gold, and with
goods, and with beasts, beside the freewill offering for the house of God that *is* in Je-ru'sa-
lem.

5 ¶ Then rose up the chief of the fathers of Ju'dah and Ben'ja-min, and the priests, and the Le'vites, with all *them* whose spirit God had raised, to go up to build the house of the LORD which *is* in Je-ru'sa-lem.

6 And all they that *were* about them strengthened their hands with vessels of silver, with gold, with goods, and with beasts, and with precious things, beside all *that* was willingly offered.

7 ¶ Also Cy'rus the king brought forth the vessels of the house of the LORD, which Neb-u-chad-nez'zar had brought forth out of Je-ru'sa-lem, and had put them in the house of his gods;

8 Even those did Cy'rus king of Per'sia bring forth by the hand of Mith're-dath the treasurer, and numbered them unto Shesh-baz'zar, the prince of Ju'dah.

9 And this *is* the number of them: thirty chargers of gold, a thousand chargers of silver, nine and twenty knives,

10 Thirty basons of gold, silver basons of a second *sort* four hundred and ten, *and* other vessels a thousand.

11 All the vessels of gold and of silver *were* five thousand and four hundred. All *these* did Shesh-baz'zar bring up with *them of* the captivity that were brought up from Bab'y-lon unto Je-ru'sa-lem.

2 NOW these *are* the children of the province that went up out of the captivity, of those which had been carried away, whom Neb-u-chad-nez'zar the king of Bab'y-lon had carried away unto Bab'y-lon, and came again unto Je-ru'sa-lem and Ju'dah, every one unto his city;

2 Which came with Ze-rub'ba-bel: Jesh'u-a, Ne-he-mi'ah, Ser-a-i'ah, Re-el-a'iah, Mor'de-cai, Bil'shan, Miz'par, Big'va-i, Re'hum, Ba'a-nah. The number of the men of the people of Is'ra-el:

3 The children of Pa'rosh, two thousand an hundred seventy and two.

4 The children of Sheph-a-ti'ah, three hundred seventy and two.

5 The children of A'rah, seven hundred seventy and five.

6 The children of Pa'hath-mo'ab, of the children of Jesh'u-a *and* Jo'ab, two thousand eight hundred and twelve.

7 The children of E'lam, a thousand two hundred fifty and four.

8 The children of Zat'tu, nine hundred forty and five.

9 The children of Zac'ca-i, seven hundred and threescore.

10 The children of Ba'ni, six hundred forty and two.

11 The children of Beb'a-i; six hundred twenty and three.

12 The children of Az'gad, a thousand two hundred twenty and two.

13 The children of A-don'i-kam, six hundred sixty and six.

14 The children of Big'va-i, two thousand fifty and six.

15 The children of A'din, four hundred fifty and four.

16 The children of A'ter of Hez-e-ki'ah, ninety and eight.

17 The children of Be'zai, three hundred twenty and three.

18 The children of Jo'rah, an hundred and twelve.

19 The children of Ha'shum, two hundred twenty and three.

20 The children of Gib'bar, ninety and five.

21 The children of Beth'-le-hem, an hundred twenty and three.

22 The men of Ne-to'phah, fifty and six.

23 The men of An'a-thoth, an hundred twenty and eight.

24 The children of Az'ma-veth, forty and two.

25 The children of Kir'jath-a'rim, Che-phi'rah, and Be-e'roth, seven hundred and forty and three.

26 The children of Ra'mah and Ga'ba, six hundred twenty and one.

27 The men of Mich'mas, an hundred twenty and two.

28 The men of Beth'-el and A'i, two hundred twenty and three.

29 The children of Ne'bo, fifty and two.

30 The children of Mag'bish, an hundred fifty and six.

31 The children of the other E'lam, a thousand two hundred fifty and four.

32 The children of Ha'rim, three hundred and twenty.

33 The children of Lod, Ha'did, and O'no, seven hundred twenty and five.

34 The children of Jer'i-cho, three hundred forty and five.

35 The children of Se-na'ah, three thousand and six hundred and thirty.

36 ¶ The priests: the children of Je-da'iah, of the house of Jesh'u-a, nine hundred seventy and three.

37 The children of Im'mer, a thousand fifty and two.

38 The children of Pash'ur, a thousand two hundred forty and seven.

39 The children of Ha'rim, a thousand and seventeen.

40 ¶ The Le'vites: the children of Jesh'u-a and Kad'mi-el, of the children of Hod-a-vi'ah, seventy and four.

41 ¶ The singers: the children of A'saph, an hundred twenty and eight.

42 ¶ The children of the porters: the children of Shal'lum, the children of A'ter, the children of Tal'mon, the children of Ak'kub, the children of Hat'i-ta, the children of Sho'ba-i, *in* all an hundred thirty and nine.

43 ¶ The Neth'i-nims: the children of Zi'ha, the children of Ha-su'pha, the children of Tab'ba-oth,

44 The children of Ke'ros, the children of Si'a-ha, the children of Pa'don,

45 The children of Leb'a-nah, the children of Hag'a-bah, the children of Ak'kub,

46 The children of Ha'gab, the children of Shal'ma-i, the children of Ha'nan,

47 The children of Gid'del, the children of Ga'har, the children of Re-a-i'ah,

48 The children of Re'zin, the children of Ne-ko'da, the children of Gaz'zam,

49 The children of Uz'za, the children of Pa-se'ah, the children of Be'sai,

50 The children of As'nah, the children of Me-hu'nim, the children of Ne-phu'sim,

51 The children of Bak'buk, the children of Ha-ku'pha, the children of Har'hur,

52 The children of Baz'luth, the children of Me-hi'da, the children of Har'sha,

53 The children of Bar'kos, the children of Sis'e-ra, the children of Tha'mah,

54 The children of Ne-zi'ah, the children of Hat'i-pha.

55 ¶ The children of Sol'o-mon's servants: the children of So'ta-i, the children of Soph'e-reth, the children of Pe-ru'da,

56 The children of Ja-a'lah, the children of
Dar'kon, the children of Gid'del,
57 The children of Sheph-a-ti'ah, the children
of Hat'til, the children of Poch'e-reth of Ze-ba'-
im, the children of A'mi.
58 All the Neth'i-nims, and the children of
Sol'o-mon's servants, *were* three hundred
ninety and two.
59 And these *were* they which went up from
Tel–me'lah, Tel–har'sa, Che'rub, Ad'dan, *and*
Im'mer: but they could not shew their father's
house, and their seed, whether they *were* of Is'-
ra-el:
60 The children of Del-a-i'ah, the children of
To-bi'ah, the children of Ne-ko'da, six hundred
fifty and two.
61 ¶ And of the children of the priests: the
children of Ha-ba'iah, the children of Koz, the
children of Bar-zil'la-i; which took a wife of the
daughters of Bar-zil'la-i the Gil'e-ad-ite, and
was called after their name:
62 These sought their register *among* those
that were reckoned by genealogy, but they
were not found: therefore were they, as polluted, put from the priesthood.
63 And the Tir'sha-tha said unto them, that
they should not eat of the most holy things, till
there stood up a priest with U'rim and with
Thum'mim.
64 ¶ The whole congregation together *was*
forty and two thousand three hundred *and*
threescore,
65 Beside their servants and their maids, of
whom *there were* seven thousand three hundred thirty and seven: and *there were* among
them two hundred singing men and singing
women.
66 Their horses *were* seven hundred thirty
and six; their mules, two hundred forty and five;
67 Their camels, four hundred thirty and five;
their asses, six thousand seven hundred and
twenty.
68 ¶ And *some* of the chief of the fathers,
when they came to the house of the LORD which
is at Je-ru'sa-lem, offered freely for the house of
God to set it up in his place:
69 They gave after their ability unto the treasure of the work threescore and one thousand
drams of gold, and five thousand pound of silver, and one hundred priests' garments.
70 So the priests, and the Le'vites, and *some*
of the people, and the singers, and the porters,
and the Neth'i-nims, dwelt in their cities, and all
Is'ra-el in their cities.

3 AND when the seventh month was come,
and the children of Is'ra-el *were* in the
cities, the people gathered themselves together
as one man to Je-ru'sa-lem.
2 Then stood up Jesh'u-a the son of Joz'a-
dak, and his brethren the priests, and Ze-rub'-
ba-bel the son of She-al'ti-el, and his brethren,
and builded the altar of the God of Is'ra-el, to
offer burnt offerings thereon, as *it is* written in
the law of Mo'ses the man of God.
3 And they set the altar upon his bases; for
fear *was* upon them because of the people of
those countries: and they offered burnt offerings thereon unto the LORD, *even* burnt offerings morning and evening.
4 They kept also the feast of tabernacles, as
it is written, and *offered* the daily burnt offerings by number, according to the custom, as the
duty of every day required;
5 And afterward *offered* the continual burnt
offering, both of the new moons, and of all the
set feasts of the LORD that were consecrated,
and of every one that willingly offered a freewill
offering unto the LORD.
6 From the first day of the seventh month began they to offer burnt offerings unto the LORD.
But the foundation of the temple of the LORD
was not *yet* laid.
7 They gave money also unto the masons,
and to the carpenters; and meat, and drink, and
oil, unto them of Zi'don, and to them of Tyre, to
bring cedar trees from Leb'a-non to the sea of
Jop'pa, according to the grant that they had of
Cy'rus king of Per'sia.
8 ¶ Now in the second year of their coming
unto the house of God at Je-ru'sa-lem, in the
second month, began Ze-rub'ba-bel the son of
She-al'ti-el, and Jesh'u-a the son of Joz'a-dak,
and the remnant of their brethren the priests
and the Le'vites, and all they that were come
out of the captivity unto Je-ru'sa-lem; and appointed the Le'vites, from twenty years old and
upward, to set forward the work of the house of
the LORD.
9 Then stood Jesh'u-a *with* his sons and his
brethren, Kad'mi-el and his sons, the sons of
Ju'dah, together, to set forward the workmen in
the house of God: the sons of Hen'a-dad, *with*
their sons and their brethren the Le'vites.
10 And when the builders laid the foundation
of the temple of the LORD, they set the priests in
their apparel with trumpets, and the Le'vites
the sons of A'saph with cymbals, to praise the
LORD, after the ordinance of Da'vid king of Is'-
ra-el.
11 And they sang together by course in praising and giving thanks unto the LORD; because
he is good, for his mercy *endureth* for ever
toward Is'ra-el. And all the people shouted with
a great shout, when they praised the LORD, because the foundation of the house of the LORD
was laid.
12 But many of the priests and Le'vites and
chief of the fathers, *who were* ancient men, that
had seen the first house, when the foundation of
this house was laid before their eyes, wept with
a loud voice; and many shouted aloud for joy;
13 So that the people could not discern the
noise of the shout of joy from the noise of the
weeping of the people: for the people shouted
with a loud shout, and the noise was heard afar
off.

4 NOW when the adversaries of Ju'dah and
Ben'ja-min heard that the children of the
captivity builded the temple unto the LORD God
of Is'ra-el;
2 Then they came to Ze-rub'ba-bel, and to
the chief of the fathers, and said unto them, Let
us build with you: for we seek your God, as ye
do; and we do sacrifice unto him since the days
of E'sar–had'don king of As'sur, which brought
us up hither.
3 But Ze-rub'ba-bel, and Jesh'u-a, and the
rest of the chief of the fathers of Is'ra-el, said
unto them, Ye have nothing to do with us to
build an house unto our God; but we ourselves
together will build unto the LORD God of Is'ra-
el, as king Cy'rus the king of Per'sia hath commanded us.
4 Then the people of the land weakened the
hands of the people of Ju'dah, and troubled
them in building,
5 And hired counsellors against them, to
frustrate their purpose, all the days of Cy'rus
king of Per'sia, even until the reign of Da-ri'us
king of Per'sia.
6 And in the reign of A-has-u-e'rus, in the beginning of his reign, wrote they *unto him* an

accusation against the inhabitants of Ju'dah
and Je-ru'sa-lem.
7 ¶ And in the days of Ar-tax-erx'es wrote
Bish'lam, Mith're-dath, Ta'be-el, and the rest of
their companions, unto Ar-tax-erx'es king of
Per'sia; and the writing of the letter *was* written
in the Syr'i-an tongue, and interpreted in the
Syr'i-an tongue.
8 Re'hum the chancellor and Shim'shai the
scribe wrote a letter against Je-ru'sa-lem to Ar-
tax-erx'es the king in this sort:
9 Then *wrote* Re'hum the chancellor, and
Shim'shai the scribe, and the rest of their companions; the Di'na-ites, the A-phar'sath-chites,
the Tar'pel-ites, the A-phar'sites, the Ar'che-
vites, the Bab-y-lo'ni-ans, the Su'san-chites, the
De-ha'vites, *and* the E'lam-ites,
10 And the rest of the nations whom the
great and noble As-nap'per brought over, and
set in the cities of Sa-ma'ri-a, and the rest *that*
are on this side the river, and at such a time.
11 ¶ This *is* the copy of the letter that they
sent unto him, *even* unto Ar-tax-erx'es the king;
Thy servants the men on this side the river, and
at such a time.
12 Be it known unto the king, that the Jews
which came up from thee to us are come unto
Je-ru'sa-lem, building the rebellious and the bad
city, and have set up the walls *thereof*, and
joined the foundations.
13 Be it known now unto the king, that, if
this city be builded, and the walls set up *again*,
then will they not pay toll, tribute, and custom,
and *so* thou shalt endamage the revenue of the
kings.
14 Now because we have maintenance from
the king's palace, and it was not meet for us to
see the king's dishonour, therefore have we
sent and certified the king;
15 That search may be made in the book of
the records of thy fathers: so shalt thou find in
the book of the records, and know that this city
is a rebellious city, and hurtful unto kings and
provinces, and that they have moved sedition
within the same of old time: for which cause
was this city destroyed.
16 We certify the king that, if this city be
builded *again*, and the walls thereof set up, by
this means thou shalt have no portion on this
side the river.
17 ¶ *Then* sent the king an answer unto Re'-
hum the chancellor, and *to* Shim'shai the scribe,
and *to* the rest of their companions that dwell in
Sa-ma'ri-a, and *unto* the rest beyond the river,
Peace, and at such a time.
18 The letter which ye sent unto us hath been
plainly read before me.
19 And I commanded, and search hath been
made, and it is found that this city of old time
hath made insurrection against kings, and *that*
rebellion and sedition have been made therein.
20 There have been mighty kings also over
Je-ru'sa-lem, which have ruled over all *coun-*
tries beyond the river; and toll, tribute, and custom, was paid unto them.
21 Give ye now commandment to cause
these men to cease, and that this city be not
builded, until *another* commandment shall be
given from me.
22 Take heed now that ye fail not to do this:
why should damage grow to the hurt of the
kings?
23 ¶ Now when the copy of king Ar-tax-erx'-
es' letter *was* read before Re'hum, and Shim'-
shai the scribe, and their companions, they
went up in haste to Je-ru'sa-lem unto the Jews,
and made them to cease by force and power.
24 Then ceased the work of the house of God
which *is* at Je-ru'sa-lem. So it ceased unto the
second year of the reign of Da-ri'us king of Per'-
sia.

5 THEN the prophets, Hag'ga-i the prophet,
and Zech-a-ri'ah the son of Id'do, prophesied unto the Jews that *were* in Ju'dah and Je-
ru'sa-lem in the name of the God of Is'ra-el,
even unto them.
2 Then rose up Ze-rub'ba-bel the son of She-
al'ti-el, and Jesh'u-a the son of Joz'a-dak, and
began to build the house of God which *is* at Je-
ru'sa-lem: and with them *were* the prophets of
God helping them.
3 ¶ At the same time came to them Tatnai,
governor on this side the river, and She'thar-
boz'na-i, and their companions, and said thus
unto them, Who hath commanded you to build
this house, and to make up this wall?
4 Then said we unto them after this manner,
What are the names of the men that make this
building?
5 But the eye of their God was upon the elders of the Jews that they could not cause them
to cease, till the matter came to Da-ri'us: and
then they returned answer by letter concerning
this *matter*.
6 ¶ The copy of the letter that Tat'na-i, governor on this side the river, and She'thar-boz'-
na-i, and his companions the A-phar'sach-ites,
which *were* on this side the river, sent unto Da-
ri'us the king:
7 They sent a letter unto him, wherein was
written thus; Unto Da-ri'us the king, all peace.
8 Be it known unto the king, that we went
into the province of Ju-de'a, to the house of the
great God, which is builded with great stones,
and timber is laid in the walls, and this work
goeth fast on, and prospereth in their hands.
9 Then asked we those elders, *and* said unto
them thus, Who commanded you to build this
house, and to make up these walls?
10 We asked their names also, to certify
thee, that we might write the names of the men
that *were* the chief of them.
11 And thus they returned us answer, saying,
We are the servants of the God of heaven and
earth, and build the house that was builded
these many years ago, which a great king of
Is'ra-el builded and set up.
12 But after that our fathers had provoked
the God of heaven unto wrath, he gave them
into the hand of Neb-u-chad-nez'zar the king of
Bab'y-lon, the Chal-de'an, who destroyed this
house, and carried the people away into Bab'y-
lon.
13 But in the first year of Cy'rus the king of
Bab'y-lon *the same* king Cy'rus made a decree
to build this house of God.
14 And the vessels also of gold and silver of
the house of God, which Neb-u-chad-nez'zar
took out of the temple that *was* in Je-ru'sa-lem,
and brought them into the temple of Bab'y-lon,
those did Cy'rus the king take out of the temple
of Bab'y-lon, and they were delivered unto *one*,
whose name *was* Shesh-baz'zar, whom he had
made governor;
15 And said unto him, Take these vessels, go,
carry them into the temple that *is* in Je-ru'sa-
lem, and let the house of God be builded in his
place.
16 Then came the same Shesh-baz'zar, *and*
laid the foundation of the house of God which *is*
in Je-ru'sa-lem: and since that time even until
now hath it been in building, and *yet* it is not
finished.

17 Now therefore, if *it seem* good to the king,
let there be search made in the king's treasure
house, which *is* there at Bab'y-lon, whether it be
so, that a decree was made of Cy'rus the king to
build this house of God at Je-ru'sa-lem, and let
the king send his pleasure to us concerning this
matter.

6 THEN Da-ri'us the king made a decree,
and search was made in the house of the
rolls, where the treasures were laid up in Bab'y-
lon.
2 And there was found at Ach'me-tha, in the
palace that *is* in the province of the Medes, a
roll, and therein *was* a record thus written:
3 In the first year of Cy'rus the king *the same*
Cy'rus the king made a decree *concerning* the
house of God at Je-ru'sa-lem, Let the house be
builded, the place where they offered sacrifices,
and let the foundations thereof be strongly laid;
the height thereof threescore cubits, *and* the
breadth thereof threescore cubits;
4 *With* three rows of great stones, and a row
of new timber: and let the expenses be given
out of the king's house:
5 And also let the golden and silver vessels of
the house of God, which Neb-u-chad-nez'zar
took forth out of the temple which *is* at Je-ru'-
sa-lem, and brought unto Bab'y-lon, be restored, and brought again unto the temple
which *is* at Je-ru'sa-lem, *every one* to his place,
and place *them* in the house of God.
6 Now *therefore*, Tat'na-i, governor beyond
the river, She'thar–boz'na-i, and your companions the A-phar'sach-ites, which *are* beyond the
river, be ye far from thence:
7 Let the work of this house of God alone; let
the governor of the Jews and the elders of the
Jews build this house of God in his place.
8 Moreover I make a decree what ye shall do
to the elders of these Jews for the building of
this house of God: that of the king's goods, *even*
of the tribute beyond the river, forthwith expenses be given unto these men, that they be
not hindered.
9 And that which they have need of, both
young bullocks, and rams, and lambs, for the
burnt offerings of the God of heaven, wheat,
salt, wine, and oil, according to the appointment of the priests which *are* at Je-ru'sa-lem,
let it be given them day by day without fail:
10 That they may offer sacrifices of sweet
savours unto the God of heaven, and pray for
the life of the king, and of his sons.
11 Also I have made a decree, that whosoever shall alter this word, let timber be pulled
down from his house, and being set up, let him
be hanged thereon; and let his house be made a
dunghill for this.
12 And the God that hath caused his name to
dwell there destroy all kings and people, that
shall put to their hand to alter *and* to destroy
this house of God which *is* at Je-ru'sa-lem. I Da-
ri'us have made a decree; let it be done with
speed.
13 ¶ Then Tat'na-i, governor on this side the
river, She'thar–boz'na-i, and their companions,
according to that which Da-ri'us the king had
sent, so they did speedily.
14 And the elders of the Jews builded, and
they prospered through the prophesying of
Hag'ga-i the prophet and Zech-a-ri'ah the son of
Id'do. And they builded, and finished *it*, according to the commandment of the God of Is'ra-el,
and according to the commandment of Cy'rus,
and Da-ri'us, and Ar-tax-erx'es king of Per'sia.
15 And this house was finished on the third
day of the month A'dar, which was in the sixth
year of the reign of Da-ri'us the king.
16 ¶ And the children of Is'ra-el, the priests,
and the Le'vites, and the rest of the children of
the captivity, kept the dedication of this house
of God with joy,
17 And offered at the dedication of this
house of God an hundred bullocks, two hundred
rams, four hundred lambs; and for a sin offering
for all Is'ra-el, twelve he goats, according to the
number of the tribes of Is'ra-el.
18 And they set the priests in their divisions,
and the Le'vites in their courses, for the service
of God, which *is* at Je-ru'sa-lem; as it is written
in the book of Mo'ses.
19 And the children of the captivity kept the
passover upon the fourteenth *day* of the first
month.
20 For the priests and the Le'vites were purified together, all of them *were* pure, and killed
the passover for all the children of the captivity,
and for their brethren the priests, and for themselves.
21 And the children of Is'ra-el, which were
come again out of captivity, and all such as had
separated themselves unto them from the filthiness of the heathen of the land, to seek the
LORD God of Is'ra-el, did eat,
22 And kept the feast of unleavened bread
seven days with joy: for the LORD had made
them joyful, and turned the heart of the king of
As-syr'i-a unto them, to strengthen their hands
in the work of the house of God, the God of
Is'ra-el.

7 NOW after these things, in the reign of Ar-
tax-erx'es king of Per'sia, Ez'ra the son of
Ser-a-i'ah, the son of Az-a-ri'ah, the son of Hil-
ki'ah,
2 The son of Shal'lum, the son of Za'dok, the
son of A-hi'tub,
3 The son of Am-a-ri'ah, the son of Az-a-ri'-
ah, the son of Me-ra'ioth,
4 The son of Zer-a-hi'ah, the son of Uz'zi, the
son of Buk'ki,
5 The son of A-bish'u-a, the son of Phin'e-
has, the son of E-le-a'zar, the son of Aar'on the
chief priest
6 This Ez'ra went up from Bab'y-lon; and he
was a ready scribe in the law of Mo'ses, which
the LORD God of Is'ra-el had given: and the king
granted him all his request, according to the
hand of the LORD his God upon him.
7 And there went up *some* of the children of
Is'ra-el, and of the priests, and the Le'vites, and
the singers, and the porters, and the Neth'i-
nims, unto Je-ru'sa-lem, in the seventh year of
Ar-tax-erx'es the king.
8 And he came to Je-ru'sa-lem in the fifth
month, which *was* in the seventh year of the
king.
9 For upon the first *day* of the first month
began he to go up from Bab'y-lon, and on the
first *day* of the fifth month came he to Je-ru'sa-
lem, according to the good hand of his God
upon him.
10 For Ez'ra had prepared his heart to seek
the law of the LORD, and to do *it*, and to teach in
Is'ra-el statutes and judgments.
11 ¶ Now this *is* the copy of the letter that
the king Ar-tax-erx'es gave unto Ez'ra the
priest, the scribe, *even* a scribe of the words of
the commandments of the LORD, and of his statutes to Is'ra-el.
12 Ar-tax-erx'es, king of kings, unto Ez'ra
the priest, a scribe of the law of the God of
heaven, perfect *peace*, and at such a time.

13 I make a decree, that all they of the people
of Is′ra-el, and *of* his priests and Le′vites, in my
realm, which are minded of their own freewill
to go up to Je-ru′sa-lem, go with thee.
14 Forasmuch as thou art sent of the king,
and of his seven counsellors, to enquire concerning Ju′dah and Je-ru′sa-lem, according to
the law of thy God which *is* in thine hand;
15 And to carry the silver and gold, which
the king and his counsellors have freely offered
unto the God of Is′ra-el, whose habitation *is* in
Je-ru′sa-lem,
16 And all the silver and gold that thou canst
find in all the province of Bab′y-lon, with the
freewill offering of the people, and of the
priests, offering willingly for the house of their
God which *is* in Je-ru′sa-lem:
17 That thou mayest buy speedily with this
money bullocks, rams, lambs, with their meat
offerings and their drink offerings, and offer
them upon the altar of the house of your God
which *is* in Je-ru′sa-lem.
18 And whatsoever shall seem good to thee,
and to thy brethren, to do with the rest of the
silver and the gold, that do after the will of your
God.
19 The vessels also that are given thee for the
service of the house of thy God, *those* deliver
thou before the God of Je-ru′sa-lem.
20 And whatsoever more shall be needful for
the house of thy God, which thou shalt have
occasion to bestow, bestow *it* out of the king's
treasure house.
21 And I, *even* I Ar-tax-erx′es the king, do
make a decree to all the treasurers which *are*
beyond the river, that whatsoever Ez′ra the
priest, the scribe of the law of the God of
heaven, shall require of you, it be done speedily,
22 Unto an hundred talents of silver, and to
an hundred measures of wheat, and to an hundred baths of wine, and to an hundred baths of
oil, and salt without prescribing *how much.*
23 Whatsoever is commanded by the God of
heaven, let it be diligently done for the house of
the God of heaven: for why should there be
wrath against the realm of the king and his
sons?
24 Also we certify you, that touching any of
the priests and Le′vites, singers, porters, Neth′i-
nims, or ministers of this house of God, it shall
not be lawful to impose toll, tribute, or custom,
upon them.
25 And thou, Ez′ra, after the wisdom of thy
God, that *is* in thine hand, set magistrates and
judges, which may judge all the people that *are*
beyond the river, all such as know the laws of
thy God; and teach ye them that know *them*
not.
26 And whosoever will not do the law of thy
God, and the law of the king, let judgment be
executed speedily upon him, whether *it be* unto
death, or to banishment, or to confiscation of
goods, or to imprisonment.
27 ¶ Blessed *be* the LORD God of our fathers,
which hath put *such a thing* as this in the king's
heart, to beautify the house of the LORD which
is in Je-ru′sa-lem:
28 And hath extended mercy unto me before
the king, and his counsellors, and before all the
king's mighty princes. And I was strengthened
as the hand of the LORD my God *was* upon me,
and I gathered together out of Is′ra-el chief men
to go up with me.

8 THESE *are* now the chief of their fathers,
and *this is* the genealogy of them that went
up with me from Bab′y-lon, in the reign of Ar-
tax-erx′es the king.
2 Of the sons of Phin′e-has; Ger′shom: of the
sons of Ith′a-mar; Dan′iel: of the sons of Da′vid;
Hat′tush.
3 Of the sons of Shech-a-ni′ah, of the sons of
Pha′rosh; Zech-a-ri′ah: and with him were reckoned by genealogy of the males an hundred and
fifty.
4 Of the sons of Pa′hath–mo′ab; El-i-ho-e′na-
i the son of Zer-a-hi′ah, and with him two hundred males.
5 Of the sons of Shech-a-ni′ah; the son of Ja-
ha′zi-el, and with him three hundred males.
6 Of the sons also of A′din; E′bed the son of
Jon′a-than, and with him fifty males.
7 And of the sons of E′lam; Je-sha′iah the son
of Ath-a-li′ah, and with him seventy males.
8 And of the sons of Sheph-a-ti′ah; Zeb-a-di′-
ah the son of Mi′chael, and with him fourscore
males.
9 Of the sons of Jo′ab; O-ba-di′ah the son of
Je-hi′el, and with him two hundred and eighteen males.
10 And of the sons of Shel′o-mith; the son of
Jos-i-phi′ah, and with him an hundred and
threescore males.
11 And of the sons of Beb′a-i; Zech-a-ri′ah
the son of Beb′a-i, and with him twenty and
eight males.
12 And of the sons of Az′gad; Jo-ha′nan the
son of Hak′ka-tan, and with him an hundred
and ten males.
13 And of the last sons of A-don′i-kam,
whose names *are* these, E-liph′e-let, Je-i′el, and
Shem-a-i′ah, and with them threescore males.
14 Of the sons also of Big′va-i; U′tha-i, and
Zab′bud, and with them seventy males.
15 ¶ And I gathered them together to the
river that runneth to A-ha′va; and there abode
we in tents three days: and I viewed the people,
and the priests, and found there none of the
sons of Le′vi.
16 Then sent I for E-li-e′zer, for A′ri-el, for
Shem-a-i′ah, and for El′na-than, and for Ja′rib,
and for El′na-than, and for Na′than, and for
Zech-a-ri′ah, and for Me-shul′lam, chief men;
also for Joi′a-rib, and for El′na-than, men of understanding.
17 And I sent them with commandment unto
Id′do the chief at the place Ca-siph′i-a, and I
told them what they should say unto Id′do, *and*
to his brethren the Neth′i-nims, at the place Ca-
siph′i-a, that they should bring unto us ministers for the house of our God.
18 And by the good hand of our God upon us
they brought us a man of understanding, of the
sons of Mah′li, the son of Le′vi, the son of Is′ra-
el; and Sher-e-bi′ah, with his sons and his brethren, eighteen;
19 And Hash-a-bi′ah, and with him Je-sha′-
iah of the sons of Me-ra′ri, his brethren and
their sons, twenty;
20 Also of the Neth′i-nims, whom Da′vid and
the princes had appointed for the service of the
Le′vites, two hundred and twenty Neth′i-nims:
all of them were expressed by name.
21 ¶ Then I proclaimed a fast there, at the
river of A-ha′va, that we might afflict ourselves
before our God, to seek of him a right way for
us, and for our little ones, and for all our substance.
22 For I was ashamed to require of the king a
band of soldiers and horsemen to help us
against the enemy in the way: because we had
spoken unto the king, saying, The hand of our
God *is* upon all them for good that seek him;

but his power and his wrath *is* against all them that forsake him.

23 So we fasted and besought our God for this: and he was intreated of us.

24 ¶ Then I separated twelve of the chief of the priests, Sher-e-bi'ah, Hash-a-bi'ah, and ten of their brethren with them,

25 And weighed unto them the silver, and the gold, and the vessels, *even* the offering of the house of our God, which the king, and his counsellors, and his lords, and all Is'ra-el *there* present, had offered:

26 I even weighed unto their hand six hundred and fifty talents of silver, and silver vessels an hundred talents, *and* of gold an hundred talents;

27 Also twenty basons of gold, of a thousand drams; and two vessels of fine copper, precious as gold.

28 And I said unto them, Ye *are* holy unto the LORD; the vessels *are* holy also; and the silver and the gold *are* a freewill offering unto the LORD God of your fathers.

29 Watch ye, and keep *them*, until ye weigh *them* before the chief of the priests and the Le'vites, and chief of the fathers of Is'ra-el, at Je-ru'sa-lem, in the chambers of the house of the LORD.

30 So took the priests and the Le'vites the weight of the silver, and the gold, and the vessels, to bring *them* to Je-ru'sa-lem unto the house of our God.

31 ¶ Then we departed from the river of A-ha'va on the twelfth *day* of the first month, to go unto Je-ru'sa-lem: and the hand of our God was upon us, and he delivered us from the hand of the enemy, and of such as lay in wait by the way.

32 And we came to Je-ru'sa-lem, and abode there three days.

33 ¶ Now on the fourth day was the silver and the gold and the vessels weighed in the house of our God by the hand of Mer'e-moth the son of U-ri'ah the priest; and with him was E-le-a'zar the son of Phin'e-has; and with them *was* Joz'a-bad the son of Jesh'u-a, and No-a-di'ah the son of Bin'nu-i, Le'vites;

34 By number *and* by weight of every one: and all the weight was written at that time.

35 *Also* the children of those that had been carried away, which were come out of the captivity, offered burnt offerings unto the God of Is'ra-el, twelve bullocks for all Is'ra-el, ninety and six rams, seventy and seven lambs, twelve he goats *for* a sin offering: all *this was* a burnt offering unto the LORD.

36 ¶ And they delivered the king's commissions unto the king's lieutenants, and to the governors on this side the river: and they furthered the people, and the house of God.

9 NOW when these things were done, the princes came to me, saying, The people of Is'ra-el, and the priests, and the Le'vites, have not separated themselves from the people of the lands, *doing* according to their abominations, *even* of the Ca'naan-ites, the Hit'tites, the Per'iz-zites, the Jeb'u-sites, the Am'mon-ites, the Mo'ab-ites, the E-gyptians, and the Am'or-ites.

2 For they have taken of their daughters for themselves, and for their sons: so that the holy seed have mingled themselves with the people of *those* lands: yea, the hand of the princes and rulers hath been chief in this trespass.

3 And when I heard this thing, I rent my garment and my mantle, and plucked off the hair of my head and of my beard, and sat down astonied.

4 Then were assembled unto me every one that trembled at the words of the God of Is'ra-el, because of the transgression of those that had been carried away; and I sat astonied until the evening sacrifice.

5 ¶ And at the evening sacrifice I arose up from my heaviness; and having rent my garment and my mantle, I fell upon my knees, and spread out my hands unto the LORD my God,

6 And said, O my God, I am ashamed and blush to lift up my face to thee, my God: for our iniquities are increased over *our* head, and our trespass is grown up unto the heavens.

7 Since the days of our fathers *have* we *been* in a great trespass unto this day; and for our iniquities have we, our kings, *and* our priests, been delivered into the hand of the kings of the lands, to the sword, to captivity, and to a spoil, and to confusion of face, as *it is* this day.

8 And now for a little space grace hath been *shewed* from the LORD our God, to leave us a remnant to escape, and to give us a nail in his holy place, that our God may lighten our eyes, and give us a little reviving in our bondage.

9 For we *were* bondmen; yet our God hath not forsaken us in our bondage, but hath extended mercy unto us in the sight of the kings of Per'sia, to give us a reviving, to set up the house of our God, and to repair the desolations thereof, and to give us a wall in Ju'dah and in Je-ru'sa-lem.

10 And now, O our God, what shall we say after this? for we have forsaken thy commandments,

11 Which thou hast commanded by thy servants the prophets, saying, The land, unto which ye go to possess it, is an unclean land with the filthiness of the people of the lands, with their abominations, which have filled it from one end to another with their uncleanness.

12 Now therefore give not your daughters unto their sons, neither take their daughters unto your sons, nor seek their peace or their wealth for ever: that ye may be strong, and eat the good of the land, and leave *it* for an inheritance to your children for ever.

13 And after all that is come upon us for our evil deeds, and for our great trespass, seeing that thou our God hast punished us less than our iniquities *deserve*, and hast given us *such* deliverance as this;

14 Should we again break thy commandments, and join in affinity with the people of these abominations? wouldest not thou be angry with us till thou hadst consumed *us*, so that *there should be* no remnant nor escaping?

15 O LORD God of Is'ra-el, thou *art* righteous: for we remain yet escaped, as *it is* this day: behold, we *are* before thee in our trespasses: for we cannot stand before thee because of this.

10 NOW when Ez'ra had prayed, and when he had confessed, weeping and casting himself down before the house of God, there assembled unto him out of Is'ra-el a very great congregation of men and women and children: for the people wept very sore.

2 And Shech-a'ni'ah the son of Je-hi'el, *one* of the sons of E'lam, answered and said unto Ez'ra, We have trespassed against our God, and have taken strange wives of the people of the land: yet now there is hope in Is'ra-el concerning this thing.

3 Now therefore let us make a covenant with our God to put away all the wives, and such as

are born of them, according to the counsel of my lord, and of those that tremble at the commandment of our God; and let it be done according to the law.

4 Arise; for *this* matter *belongeth* unto thee: we also *will be* with thee: be of good courage, and do *it*.

5 Then arose Ez′ra, and made the chief priests, the Le′vites, and all Is′ra-el, to swear that they should do according to this word. And they sware.

6 ¶ Then Ez′ra rose up from before the house of God, and went into the chamber of Jo-ha′nan the son of E-li′a-shib: and *when* he came thither, he did eat no bread, nor drink water: for he mourned because of the transgression of them that had been carried away.

7 And they made proclamation throughout Ju′dah and Je-ru′sa-lem unto all the children of the captivity, that they should gather themselves together unto Je-ru′sa-lem;

8 And that whosoever would not come within three days, according to the counsel of the princes and the elders, all his substance should be forfeited, and himself separated from the congregation of those that had been carried away.

9 ¶ Then all the men of Ju′dah and Ben′jamin gathered themselves together unto Je-ru′sa-lem within three days. It *was* the ninth month, on the twentieth *day* of the month; and all the people sat in the street of the house of God, trembling because of *this* matter, and for the great rain.

10 And Ez′ra the priest stood up, and said unto them, Ye have transgressed, and have taken strange wives, to increase the trespass of Is′ra-el.

11 Now therefore make confession unto the LORD God of your fathers, and do his pleasure: and separate yourselves from the people of the land, and from the strange wives.

12 Then all the congregation answered and said with a loud voice, As thou hast said, so must we do.

13 But the people *are* many, and *it is* a time of much rain, and we are not able to stand without, neither *is this* a work of one day or two: for we are many that have transgressed in this thing.

14 Let now our rulers of all the congregation stand, and let all them which have taken strange wives in our cities come at appointed times, and with them the elders of every city, and the judges thereof, until the fierce wrath of our God for this matter be turned from us.

15 ¶ Only Jon′a-than the son of A′sa-hel and Ja-ha-zi′ah the son of Tik′vah were employed about this *matter*: and Me-shul′lam and Shab-beth′a-i the Le′vite helped them.

16 And the children of the captivity did so. And Ez′ra the priest, *with* certain chief of the fathers, after the house of their fathers, and all of them by *their* names, were separated, and sat down in the first day of the tenth month to examine the matter.

17 And they made an end with all the men that had taken strange wives by the first day of the first month.

18 ¶ And among the sons of the priests there were found that had taken strange wives: *namely*, of the sons of Jesh′u-a the son of Joz′a-dak, and his brethren; Ma-a-se′iah, and E-li-e′zer, and Ja′rib, and Ged-a-li′ah.

19 And they gave their hands that they would put away their wives; and *being* guilty, *they offered* a ram of the flock for their trespass.

20 And of the sons of Im′mer; Ha-na′ni, and Zeb-a-di′ah.

21 And of the sons of Ha′rim; Ma-a-se′iah, and E-li′jah, and Shem-a-i′ah, and Je-hi′el, and Uz-zi′ah.

22 And of the sons of Pash′ur; El-i-o-e′na-i, Ma-a-se′iah, Ish′ma-el, Ne-than′e-el, Joz′a-bad, and El′-a-sah.

23 Also of the Le′vites; Joz′a-bad, and Shim′e-i, and Ke-la′iah, (the same *is* Kel′i-ta,) Peth-a-hi′ah, Ju′dah, and E-li-e′zer.

24 Of the singers also; E-li′a-shib: and of the porters; Shal′lum, and Te′lem, and U′ri.

25 Moreover of Is′ra-el: of the sons of Pa′rosh; Ra-mi′ah, and Je-zi′ah, and Mal-chi′ah, and Mi′a-min, and E-le-a′zar, and Mal-chi′jah, and Be-na′iah.

26 And of the sons of E′lam; Mat-ta-ni′ah, Zech-a-ri′ah, and Je-hi′el, and Ab′di, and Jer′e-moth, and E-li′ah.

27 And of the sons of Zat′tu; El-i-o-e′na-i, E-li′a-shib, Mat-ta-ni′ah, and Jer′e-moth, and Za′bad, and A-zi′za.

28 Of the sons of Beb′a-i; Je-ho-ha′nan, Han-a-ni′ah, Zab′bai, *and* Ath′lai.

29 And of the sons of Ba′ni; Me-shul′lam, Mal′luch, and Ad-a-i′ah, Jash′ub, and She′al, and Ra′moth.

30 And of the sons of Pa′hath–mo′ab; Ad′na, and Che′lal, Be-na′iah, Ma-a-se′iah, Mat-ta-ni′ah, Be-zal′e-el, and Bin′nu-i, and Ma-nas′seh.

31 And *of* the sons of Ha′rim; E-li-e′zer, Ish-i′jah, Mal-chi′ah, Shem-a-i′ah, Shim′e-on,

32 Ben′ja-min, Mal′luch, *and* Shem-a-ri′ah.

33 Of the sons of Ha′shum; Mat-te-na′i, Mat′ta-thah, Za′bad, E-liph′e-let, Jer′e-mai, Ma-nas′seh, *and* Shim′e-i.

34 Of the sons of Ba′ni, Ma-ad′ai, Am′ram, and U′el,

35 Be-na′iah, Be-de′iah, Chel′luh,

36 Va-ni′ah, Mer′e-moth, E-li′a-shib,

37 Mat-ta-ni′ah, Mat-te-na′i, and Ja′a-sau,

38 And Ba′ni, and Bin′nu-i, Shim′e-i,

39 And Shel-e-mi′ah, and Na′than, and Ad-a-i′ah,

40 Mach-na-de′bai, Shash′a-i, Shar′a-i,

41 A-zar′e-el, and Shel-e-mi′ah, Shem-a-ri′ah,

42 Shal′lum, Am-a-ri′ah, *and* Jo′seph.

43 Of the sons of Ne′bo; Je-i′el, Mat-ti-thi′ah, Za′bad, Ze-bi′na, Ja-da′u, and Jo′el, Be-na′iah.

44 All these had taken strange wives: and *some* of them had wives by whom they had children.

THE BOOK OF

NEHEMIAH

1 THE words of Ne-he-mi'ah the son of Hach-a-li'ah. And it came to pass in the month Chis'leu, in the twentieth year, as I was in Shu'shan the palace,

2 That Ha-na'ni, one of my brethren, came, he and *certain* men of Ju'dah; and I asked them concerning the Jews that had escaped, which were left of the captivity, and concerning Je-ru'sa-lem.

3 And they said unto me, The remnant that are left of the captivity there in the province *are* in great affliction and reproach: the wall of Je-ru'sa-lem also *is* broken down, and the gates thereof are burned with fire.

4 ¶ And it came to pass, when I heard these words, that I sat down and wept, and mourned *certain* days, and fasted, and prayed before the God of heaven,

5 And said, I beseech thee, O LORD God of heaven, the great and terrible God, that keepeth covenant and mercy for them that love him and observe his commandments:

6 Let thine ear now be attentive, and thine eyes open, that thou mayest hear the prayer of thy servant, which I pray before thee now, day and night, for the children of Is'ra-el thy servants, and confess the sins of the children of Is'ra-el, which we have sinned against thee: both I and my father's house have sinned.

7 We have dealt very corruptly against thee, and have not kept the commandments, nor the statutes, nor the judgments, which thou commandedst thy servant Mo'ses.

8 Remember, I beseech thee, the word that thou commandedst thy servant Mo'ses, saying, *If* ye transgress, I will scatter you abroad among the nations:

9 But *if* ye turn unto me, and keep my commandments, and do them; though there were of you cast out unto the uttermost part of the heaven, *yet* will I gather them from thence, and will bring them unto the place that I have chosen to set my name there.

10 Now these *are* thy servants and thy people, whom thou hast redeemed by thy great power, and by thy strong hand.

11 O Lord, I beseech thee, let now thine ear be attentive to the prayer of thy servant, and to the prayer of thy servants, who desire to fear thy name: and prosper, I pray thee, thy servant this day, and grant him mercy in the sight of this man. For I was the king's cupbearer.

2 AND it came to pass in the month Ni'san, in the twentieth year of Ar-tax-erx'es the king, *that* wine *was* before him: and I took up the wine, and gave *it* unto the king. Now I had not been *beforetime* sad in his presence.

2 Wherefore the king said unto me, Why *is* thy countenance sad, seeing thou *art* not sick? this *is* nothing *else* but sorrow of heart. Then I was very sore afraid,

3 And said unto the king, Let the king live for ever: why should not my countenance be sad, when the city, the place of my fathers' sepulchres, *lieth* waste, and the gates thereof are consumed with fire?

4 Then the king said unto me, For what dost thou make request? So I prayed to the God of heaven.

5 And I said unto the king, If it please the king, and if thy servant have found favour in thy sight, that thou wouldest send me unto Ju'dah, unto the city of my fathers' sepulchres, that I may build it.

6 And the king said unto me, (the queen also sitting by him,) For how long shall thy journey be? and when wilt thou return? So it pleased the king to send me; and I set him a time.

7 Moreover I said unto the king, If it please the king, let letters be given me to the governors beyond the river, that they may convey me over till I come into Ju'dah;

8 And a letter unto A'saph the keeper of the king's forest, that he may give me timber to make beams for the gates of the palace which *appertained* to the house, and for the wall of the city, and for the house that I shall enter into. And the king granted me, according to the good hand of my God upon me.

9 ¶ Then I came to the governors beyond the river, and gave them the king's letters. Now the king had sent captains of the army and horsemen with me.

10 When San-bal'lat the Hor'o-nite, and To-bi'ah the servant, the Am'mon-ite, heard *of it*, it grieved them exceedingly that there was come a man to seek the welfare of the children of Is'-ra-el.

11 So I came to Je-ru'sa-lem, and was there three days.

12 ¶ And I arose in the night, I and some few men with me; neither told I *any* man what my God had put in my heart to do at Je-ru'sa-lem: neither *was there any* beast with me, save the beast that I rode upon.

13 And I went out by night by the gate of the valley, even before the dragon well, and to the dung port, and viewed the walls of Je-ru'sa-lem, which were broken down, and the gates thereof were consumed with fire.

14 Then I went on to the gate of the fountain, and to the king's pool: but *there was* no place for the beast *that was* under me to pass.

15 Then went I up in the night by the brook, and viewed the wall, and turned back, and entered by the gate of the valley, and *so* returned.

16 And the rulers knew not whither I went, or what I did; neither had I as yet told *it* to the Jews, nor to the priests, nor to the nobles, nor to the rulers, nor to the rest that did the work.

17 ¶ Then said I unto them, Ye see the distress that we *are* in, how Je-ru'sa-lem *lieth* waste, and the gates thereof are burned with fire: come, and let us build up the wall of Je-ru'sa-lem, that we be no more a reproach.

18 Then I told them of the hand of my God which was good upon me; as also the king's words that he had spoken unto me. And they said, Let us rise up and build. So they strengthened their hands for *this* good *work*.

19 But when San-bal'lat the Hor'o-nite, and To-bi'ah the servant, the Am'mon-ite, and Ge'-shem the A-ra'bi-an, heard *it*, they laughed us to scorn, and despised us, and said, What *is* this thing that ye do? will ye rebel against the king?

20 Then answered I them, and said unto them, The God of heaven, he will prosper us; therefore we his servants will arise and build: but ye have no portion, nor right, nor memorial, in Je-ru'sa-lem.

3 THEN E-li'a-shib the high priest rose up with his brethren the priests, and they

builded the sheep gate; they sanctified it, and set up the doors of it; even unto the tower of Me'ah they sanctified it, unto the tower of Ha-nan'e-el.

2 And next unto him builded the men of Jer'i-cho. And next to them builded Zac'cur the son of Im'ri.

3 But the fish gate did the sons of Has-se-na'ah build, who *also* laid the beams thereof, and set up the doors thereof, the locks thereof, and the bars thereof.

4 And next unto them repaired Mer'e-moth the son of U-ri'jah, the son of Koz. And next unto them repaired Me-shul'lam the son of Ber-e-chi'ah, the son of Me-shez'a-be-el. And next unto them repaired Za'dok the son of Ba'a-na.

5 And next unto them the Te-ko'ites repaired; but their nobles put not their necks to the work of their Lord.

6 Moreover the old gate repaired Je-hoi'a-da the son of Pa-se'ah, and Me-shul'lam the son of Bes-o-de'iah; they laid the beams thereof, and set up the doors thereof, and the locks thereof, and the bars thereof.

7 And next unto them repaired Mel-a-ti'ah the Gib'e-on-ite, and Ja'don the Me-ron'o-thite, the men of Gib'e-on, and of Miz'pah, unto the throne of the governor on this side the river.

8 Next unto him repaired Uz'zi-el the son of Har-ha-i'ah, of the goldsmiths. Next unto him also repaired Han-a-ni'ah the son of *one of* the apothecaries, and they fortified Je-ru'sa-lem unto the broad wall.

9 And next unto them repaired Reph-a-i'ah the son of Hur, the ruler of the half part of Je-ru'sa-lem.

10 And next unto them repaired Je-da'iah the son of Ha-ru'maph, even over against his house. And next unto him repaired Hat'tush the son of Hash-ab-ni'ah.

11 Mal-chi'jah the son of Ha'rim, and Ha'-shub the son of Pa'hath–mo'ab, repaired the other piece, and the tower of the furnaces.

12 And next unto him repaired Shal'lum the son of Ha-lo'hesh, the ruler of the half part of Je-ru'sa-lem, he and his daughters.

13 The valley gate repaired Ha'nun, and the inhabitants of Za-no'ah; they built it, and set up the doors thereof, the locks thereof, and the bars thereof, and a thousand cubits on the wall unto the dung gate.

14 But the dung gate repaired Mal-chi'ah the son of Re'chab, the ruler of part of Beth–hac'ce-rem; he built it, and set up the doors thereof, the locks thereof, and the bars thereof.

15 But the gate of the fountain repaired Shal'lun the son of Col–ho'zeh, the ruler of part of Miz'pah; he built it, and covered it, and set up the doors thereof, the locks thereof, and the bars thereof, and the wall of the pool of Si-lo'ah by the king's garden, and unto the stairs that go down from the city of Da'vid.

16 After him repaired Ne-he-mi'ah the son of Az'buk, the ruler of the half part of Beth'–zur, unto *the place* over against the sepulchres of Da'vid, and to the pool that was made, and unto the house of the mighty.

17 After him repaired the Le'vites, Re'hum the son of Ba'ni. Next unto him repaired Hash-a-bi'ah, the ruler of the half part of Kei'lah, in his part.

18 After him repaired their brethren, Bav'a-i the son of Hen'a-dad, the ruler of the half part of Kei'lah.

19 And next to him repaired E'zer the son of Jesh'u-a, the ruler of Miz'pah, another piece over against the going up to the armoury at the turning *of the wall*.

20 After him Ba'ruch the son of Zab'bai earnestly repaired the other piece, from the turning *of the wall* unto the door of the house of E-li'a-shib the high priest.

21 After him repaired Mer'e-moth the son of U-ri'jah the son of Koz another piece, from the door of the house of E-li'a-shib even to the end of the house of E-li'a-shib.

22 And after him repaired the priests, the men of the plain.

23 After him repaired Ben'ja-min and Ha'-shub over against their house. After him repaired Az-a-ri'ah the son of Ma-a-se'iah the son of An-a-ni'ah by his house.

24 After him repaired Bin'nu-i the son of Hen'a-dad another piece, from the house of Az-a-ri'ah unto the turning *of the wall*, even unto the corner.

25 Pa'lal the son of U'za-i, over against the turning *of the wall*, and the tower which lieth out from the king's high house, that *was* by the court of the prison. After him Pe-da'iah the son of Pa'rosh.

26 Moreover the Neth'i-nims dwelt in O'phel, unto *the place* over against the water gate toward the east, and the tower that lieth out.

27 After them the Te-ko'ites repaired another piece, over against the great tower that lieth out, even unto the wall of O'phel.

28 From above the horse gate repaired the priests, every one over against his house.

29 After them repaired Za'dok the son of Im'-mer over against his house. After him repaired also Shem-a-i'ah the son of Shech-a-ni'ah, the keeper of the east gate.

30 After him repaired Han-a-ni'ah the son of Shel-e-mi'ah, and Ha'nun the sixth son of Za'-laph, another piece. After him repaired Me-shul'lam the son of Ber-e-chi'ah over against his chamber.

31 After him repaired Mal-chi'ah the goldsmith's son unto the place of the Neth'i-nims, and of the merchants, over against the gate Miph'kad, and to the going up of the corner.

32 And between the going up of the corner unto the sheep gate repaired the goldsmiths and the merchants.

4

BUT it came to pass, that when San-bal'lat heard that we builded the wall, he was wroth, and took great indignation, and mocked the Jews.

2 And he spake before his brethren and the army of Sa-ma'ri-a, and said, What do these feeble Jews? will they fortify themselves? will they sacrifice? will they make an end in a day? will they revive the stones out of the heaps of the rubbish which are burned?

3 Now To-bi'ah the Am'mon-ite *was* by him, and he said, Even that which they build, if a fox go up, he shall even break down their stone wall.

4 Hear, O our God; for we are despised: and turn their reproach upon their own head, and give them for a prey in the land of captivity:

5 And cover not their iniquity, and let not their sin be blotted out from before thee: for they have provoked *thee* to anger before the builders.

6 So built we the wall; and all the wall was joined together unto the half thereof: for the people had a mind to work.

7 ¶ But it came to pass, *that* when San-bal'-lat, and To-bi'ah, and the A-ra'bi-ans, and the Am'mon-ites, and the Ash'dod-ites, heard that

the walls of Je-ru'sa-lem were made up, *and* that the breaches began to be stopped, then they were very wroth,

8 And conspired all of them together to come *and* to fight against Je-ru'sa-lem, and to hinder it.

9 Nevertheless we made our prayer unto our God, and set a watch against them day and night, because of them.

10 And Ju'dah said, The strength of the bearers of burdens is decayed, and *there is* much rubbish; so that we are not able to build the wall.

11 And our adversaries said, They shall not know, neither see, till we come in the midst among them, and slay them, and cause the work to cease.

12 And it came to pass, that when the Jews which dwelt by them came, they said unto us ten times, From all places whence ye shall return unto us *they will be upon you.*

13 ¶ Therefore set I in the lower places behind the wall, *and* on the higher places, I even set the people after their families with their swords, their spears, and their bows.

14 And I looked, and rose up, and said unto the nobles, and to the rulers, and to the rest of the people, Be not ye afraid of them: remember the LORD, *which is* great and terrible, and fight for your brethren, your sons, and your daughters, your wives, and your houses.

15 And it came to pass, when our enemies heard that it was known unto us, and God had brought their counsel to nought, that we returned all of us to the wall, every one unto his work.

16 And it came to pass from that time forth, *that* the half of my servants wrought in the work, and the other half of them held both the spears, the shields, and the bows, and the habergeons; and the rulers *were* behind all the house of Ju'dah.

17 They which builded on the wall, and they that bare burdens, with those that laded, *every one* with one of his hands wrought in the work, and with the other *hand* held a weapon.

18 For the builders, every one had his sword girded by his side, and *so* builded. And he that sounded the trumpet *was* by me.

19 ¶ And I said unto the nobles, and to the rulers, and to the rest of the people, The work *is* great and large, and we are separated upon the wall, one far from another.

20 In what place *therefore* ye hear the sound of the trumpet, resort ye thither unto us: our God shall fight for us.

21 So we laboured in the work: and half of them held the spears from the rising of the morning till the stars appeared.

22 Likewise at the same time said I unto the people, Let every one with his servant lodge within Je-ru'sa-lem, that in the night they may be a guard to us, and labour on the day.

23 So neither I, nor my brethren, nor my servants, nor the men of the guard which followed me, none of us put off our clothes, *saving that* every one put them off for washing.

5 AND there was a great cry of the people and of their wives against their brethren the Jews.

2 For there were that said, We, our sons, and our daughters, *are* many: therefore we take up corn *for them,* that we may eat, and live.

3 *Some* also there were that said, We have mortgaged our lands, vineyards, and houses, that we might buy corn, because of the dearth.

4 There were also that said, We have borrowed money for the king's tribute, *and that upon* our lands and vineyards.

5 Yet now our flesh *is* as the flesh of our brethren, our children as their children: and, lo, we bring into bondage our sons and our daughters to be servants, and *some* of our daughters are brought unto bondage *already:* neither *is it* in our power *to redeem them;* for other men have our lands and vineyards.

6 ¶ And I was very angry when I heard their cry and these words.

7 Then I consulted with myself, and I rebuked the nobles, and the rulers, and said unto them, Ye exact usury, every one of his brother. And I set a great assembly against them.

8 And I said unto them, We after our ability have redeemed our brethren the Jews, which were sold unto the heathen; and will ye even sell your brethren? or shall they be sold unto us? Then held they their peace, and found nothing *to answer.*

9 Also I said, It *is* not good that ye do: ought ye not to walk in the fear of our God because of the reproach of the heathen our enemies?

10 I likewise, *and* my brethren, and my servants, might exact of them money and corn: I pray you, let us leave off this usury.

11 Restore, I pray you, to them, even this day, their lands, their vineyards, their oliveyards, and their houses, also the hundredth *part* of the money, and of the corn, the wine, and the oil, that ye exact of them.

12 Then said they, We will restore *them,* and will require nothing of them; so will we do as thou sayest. Then I called the priests, and took an oath of them, that they should do according to this promise.

13 Also I shook my lap, and said, So God shake out every man from his house, and from his labour, that performeth not this promise, even thus be he shaken out, and emptied. And all the congregation said, Amen, and praised the LORD. And the people did according to this promise.

14 ¶ Moreover from the time that I was appointed to be their governor in the land of Ju'dah, from the twentieth year even unto the two and thirtieth year of Ar-tax-erx'es the king, *that is,* twelve years, I and my brethren have not eaten the bread of the governor.

15 But the former governors that *had been* before me were chargeable unto the people, and had taken of them bread and wine, beside forty shekels of silver; yea, even their servants bare rule over the people: but so did not I, because of the fear of God.

16 Yea, also I continued in the work of this wall, neither bought we any land: and all my servants *were* gathered thither unto the work.

17 Moreover *there were* at my table an hundred and fifty of the Jews and rulers, beside those that came unto us from among the heathen that *are* about us.

18 Now *that* which was prepared *for me* daily *was* one ox *and* six choice sheep; also fowls were prepared for me, and once in ten days store of all sorts of wine: yet for all this required not I the bread of the governor, because the bondage was heavy upon this people.

19 Think upon me, my God, for good, *according* to all that I have done for this people.

6 NOW it came to pass, when San-bal'lat, and To-bi'ah, and Ge'shem the A-ra'bi-an, and the rest of our enemies, heard that I had builded the wall, and *that* there was no breach

left therein; (though at that time I had not set
up the doors upon the gates;)
2 That San-bal'lat and Ge'shem sent unto me,
saying, Come, let us meet together in *some one*
of the villages in the plain of O'no. But they
thought to do me mischief.
3 And I sent messengers unto them, saying, I
am doing a great work, so that I cannot come
down: why should the work cease, whilst I
leave it, and come down to you?
4 Yet they sent unto me four times after this
sort; and I answered them after the same manner.
5 Then sent San-bal'lat his servant unto me
in like manner the fifth time with an open letter
in his hand;
6 Wherein *was* written, It is reported among
the heathen, and Gash'mu saith *it, that* thou
and the Jews think to rebel: for which cause
thou buildest the wall, that thou mayest be their
king, according to these words.
7 And thou hast also appointed prophets to
preach of thee at Je-ru'sa-lem, saying, *There is* a
king in Ju'dah: and now shall it be reported to
the king according to these words. Come now
therefore, and let us take counsel together.
8 Then I sent unto him, saying, There are no
such things done as thou sayest, but thou feignest them out of thine own heart.
9 For they all made us afraid, saying, Their
hands shall be weakened from the work, that it
be not done. Now therefore, *O God,* strengthen
my hands.
10 Afterward I came unto the house of
Shem-a-i'ah the son of Del-a-i'ah the son of Me-
het'a-beel, who *was* shut up; and he said, Let us
meet together in the house of God, within the
temple, and let us shut the doors of the temple:
for they will come to slay thee; yea, in the night
will they come to slay thee.
11 And I said, Should such a man as I flee?
and who *is there,* that, *being* as I *am,* would go
into the temple to save his life? I will not go in.
12 And, lo, I perceived that God had not sent
him; but that he pronounced this prophecy
against me: for To-bi'ah and San-bal'lat had
hired him.
13 Therefore *was* he hired, that I should be
afraid, and do so, and sin, and *that* they might
have *matter* for an evil report, that they might
reproach me.
14 My God, think thou upon To-bi'ah and
San-bal'lat according to these their works, and
on the prophetess No-a-di'ah, and the rest of
the prophets, that would have put me in fear.
15 ¶ So the wall was finished in the twenty
and fifth *day of the month* E'lul, in fifty and two
days.
16 And it came to pass, that when all our enemies heard *thereof,* and all the heathen that
were about us saw *these things,* they were much
cast down in their own eyes: for they perceived
that this work was wrought of our God.
17 ¶ Moreover in those days the nobles of
Ju'dah sent many letters unto To-bi'ah, and *the*
letters of To-bi'ah came unto them.
18 For *there were* many in Ju'dah sworn unto
him, because he *was* the son in law of Shech-a-
ni'ah the son of A'rah; and his son Jo-ha'nan
had taken the daughter of Me-shul'lam the son
of Ber-e-chi'ah.
19 Also they reported his good deeds before
me, and uttered my words to him. *And* To-bi'ah
sent letters to put me in fear.

7 NOW it came to pass, when the wall was
built, and I had set up the doors, and the
porters and the singers and the Le'vites were
appointed,
2 That I gave my brother Ha-na'ni, and Han-
a-ni'ah the ruler of the palace, charge over Je-
ru'sa-lem: for he *was* a faithful man, and feared
God above many.
3 And I said unto them, Let not the gates of
Je-ru'sa-lem be opened until the sun be hot; and
while they stand by, let them shut the doors,
and bar *them:* and appoint watches of the inhabitants of Je-ru'sa-lem, every one in his
watch, and every one *to be* over against his
house.
4 Now the city *was* large and great: but the
people *were* few therein, and the houses *were*
not builded.
5 ¶ And my God put into mine heart to
gather together the nobles, and the rulers, and
the people, that they might be reckoned by genealogy. And I found a register of the genealogy
of them which came up at the first, and found
written therein,
6 These *are* the children of the province, that
went up out of the captivity, of those that had
been carried away, whom Neb-u-chad-nez'zar
the king of Bab'y-lon had carried away, and
came again to Je-ru'sa-lem and to Ju'dah, every
one unto his city;
7 Who came with Ze-rub'ba-bel, Jesh'u-a,
Ne-he-mi'ah, Az-a-ri'ah, Ra-a-mi'ah, Na-ham'a-
ni, Mor'de-cai, Bil'shan, Mis'pe-reth, Big'va-i,
Ne'hum, Ba'a-nah. The number, *I say,* of the
men of the people of Is'ra-el *was this;*
8 The children of Pa'rosh, two thousand an
hundred seventy and two.
9 The children of Sheph-a-ti'ah, three hundred seventy and two.
10 The children of A'rah, six hundred fifty
and two.
11 The children of Pa'hath-mo'ab, of the
chiildren of Jesh'u-a and Jo'ab, two thousand
and eight hundred *and* eighteen.
12 The children of E'lam, a thousand two
hundred fifty and four.
13 The children of Zat'tu, eight hundred forty
and five.
14 The children of Zac'ca-i, seven hundred
and threescore.
15 The children of Bin'nu-i, six hundred forty
and eight.
16 The children of Beb'a-i, six hundred
twenty and eight.
17 The children of Az'gad, two thousand
three hundred twenty and two.
18 The children of A-don'i-kam, six hundred
threescore and seven.
19 The children of Big'va-i, two thousand
threescore and seven.
20 The children of A'din, six hundred fifty
and five.
21 The children of A'ter of Hez-e-ki'ah,
ninety and eight.
22 The children of Ha'shum, three hundred
twenty and eight.
23 The children of Be'zai, three hundred
twenty and four.
24 The children of Ha'riph, an hundred and
twelve.
25 The children of Gib'e-on, ninety and five.
26 The men of Beth'-le-hem and Ne-to'phah,
an hundred fourscore and eight.
27 The men of An'a-thoth, an hundred
twenty and eight.
28 The men of Beth-az'ma-veth, forty and
two.
29 The men of Kir'jath-je'a-rim, Che-phi'rah,
and Be-e'roth, seven hundred forty and three.

30 The men of Ra'mah and Ga'ba, six hundred twenty and one.
31 The men of Mich'mas, an hundred and
twenty and two.
32 The men of Beth'-el and A'i, an hundred
twenty and three.
33 The men of the other Ne'bo, fifty and two.
34 The children of the other E'lam, a thousand two hundred fifty and four.
35 The children of Ha'rim, three hundred and
twenty.
36 The children of Jer'i-cho, three hundred
forty and five.
37 The children of Lod, Ha'did, and O'no,
seven hundred twenty and one.
38 The children of Se-na'ah, three thousand
nine hundred and thirty.
39 ¶ The priests: the children of Je-da'iah, of
the house of Jesh'u-a, nine hundred seventy and
three.
40 The children of Im'mer, a thousand fifty
and two.
41 The children of Pash'ur, a thousand two
hundred forty and seven.
42 The children of Ha'rim, a thousand and
seventeen.
43 ¶ The Le'vites: the children of Jesh'u-a, of
Kad'mi-el, *and* of the children of Ho-de'vah,
seventy and four.
44 ¶ The singers: the children of A'saph, an
hundred forty and eight.
45 ¶ The porters: the children of Shal'lum,
the children of A'ter, the children of Tal'mon,
the children of Ak'kub, the children of Hat'i-ta,
the children of Sho'ba-i, an hundred thirty and
eight.
46 ¶ The Neth'i-nims: the children of Zi'ha,
the children of Ha-su'pha, the children of Tab'-
ba-oth,
47 The children of Ke'ros, the children of Si'-
a, the children of Pa'don,
48 The children of Leb'a-na, the children of
Hag'a-ba, the children of Shal'ma-i,
49 The children of Ha'nan, the children of
Gid'del, the children of Ga'har,
50 The children of Re-a-i'ah, the children of
Re'zin, the children of Ne-ko'da,
51 The children of Gaz'zam, the children of
Uz'za, the children of Pha-se'ah,
52 The children of Be'sai, the children of Me-
u'nim, the children of Ne-phish'e-sim,
53 The children of Bak'buk, the children of
Ha-ku'pha, the children of Har'hur,
54 The children of Baz'lith, the children of
Me-hi'da, the children of Har'sha,
55 The children of Bar'kos, the children of
Sis'e-ra, the children of Ta'mah,
56 The children of Ne-zi'ah, the children of
Hat'i-pha.
57 ¶ The children of Sol'o-mon's servants:
the children of So'ta-i, the children of Soph'e-
reth, the children of Pe-ri'da,
58 The children of Ja-a'la, the children of
Dar'kon, the children of Gid'del,
59 The children of Sheph-a-ti'ah, the children
of Hat'til, the children of Poch'e-reth of Ze-ba'-
im, the children of A'mon.
60 All the Neth'i-nims, and the children of
Sol'o-mon's servants, *were* three hundred
ninety and two.
61 And these *were* they which went up *also*
from Tel-me'lah, Tel-ha-re'sha, Che'rub, Ad'-
don, and Im'mer: but they could not shew their
father's house, nor their seed, whether they
were of Is'ra-el.
62 The children of Del-a-i'ah, the children of
To-bi'ah, the children of Ne-ko'da, six hundred
forty and two.
63 ¶ And of the priests: the children of Ha-
ba'iah, the children of Koz, the children of Bar-
zil'la-i, which took *one* of the daughters of Bar-
zil'la-i the Gil'e-ad-ite to wife, and was called
after their name.
64 These sought their register *among* those
that were reckoned by genealogy, but it was not
found: therefore were they, as polluted, put
from the priesthood.
65 And the Tir'sha-tha said unto them, that
they should not eat of the most holy things, till
there stood *up* a priest with U'rim and Thum'-
mim.
66 ¶ The whole congregation together *was*
forty and two thousand three hundred and
threescore,
67 Beside their manservants and their maidservants, of whom *there were* seven thousand
three hundred thirty and seven: and they had
two hundred forty and five singing men and
singing women.
68 Their horses, seven hundred thirty and
six: their mules, two hundred forty and five:
69 *Their* camels, four hundred thirty and
five: six thousand seven hundred and twenty
asses.
70 ¶ And some of the chief of the fathers
gave unto the work. The Tir'sha-tha gave to the
treasure a thousand drams of gold, fifty basons,
five hundred and thirty priests' garments.
71 And *some* of the chief of the fathers gave
to the treasure of the work twenty thousand
drams of gold, and two thousand and two hundred pound of silver.
72 And *that* which the rest of the people
gave *was* twenty thousand drams of gold, and
two thousand pound of silver, and threescore
and seven priests' garments.
73 So the priests, and the Le'vites, and the
porters, and the singers, and *some* of the people, and the Neth'i-nims, and all Is'ra-el, dwelt
in their cities; and when the seventh month
came, the children of Is'ra-el *were* in their cities.

8 AND all the people gathered themselves
together as one man into the street that
was before the water gate; and they spake unto
Ez'ra the scribe to bring the book of the law of
Mo'ses, which the LORD had commanded to Is'-
ra-el.
2 And Ez'ra the priest brought the law before
the congregation both of men and women, and
all that could hear with understanding, upon
the first day of the seventh month.
3 And he read therein before the street that
was before the water gate from the morning until midday, before the men and the women, and
those that could understand; and the ears of all
the people *were attentive* unto the book of the
law.
4 And Ez'ra the scribe stood upon a pulpit of
wood, which they had made for the purpose;
and beside him stood Mat-ti-thi'ah, and She'ma,
and An-a-i'ah, and U-ri'jah, and Hil-ki'ah, and
Ma-a-se'iah, on his right hand; and on his left
hand, Pe-da'iah, and Mish'a-el, and Mal-chi'ah,
and Ha'shum, and Hash-bad'a-na, Zech-a-ri'ah,
and Me-shul'lam.
5 And Ez'ra opened the book in the sight of
all the people; (for he was above all the people;)
and when he opened it, all the people stood up:
6 And Ez'ra blessed the LORD, the great God.
And all the people answered, Amen, Amen,
with lifting up their hands: and they bowed

their heads, and worshipped the LORD with
their faces to the ground.
7 Also Jesh'u-a, and Ba'ni, and Sher-e-bi'ah,
Ja'min, Ak'kub, Shab-beth'a-i, Ho-di'jah, Ma-a-
se'iah, Kel'i-ta, Az-a-ri'ah, Joz'a-bad, Ha'nan,
Pel-a-i'ah, and the Le'vites, caused the people to
understand the law: and the people *stood* in
their place.
8 So they read in the book in the law of God
distinctly, and gave the sense, and caused *them*
to understand the reading.
9 ¶ And Ne-he-mi'ah, which *is* the Tir'sha-
tha, and Ez'ra the priest the scribe, and the Le'-
vites that taught the people, said unto all the
people, This day *is* holy unto the LORD your
God; mourn not, nor weep. For all the people
wept, when they heard the words of the law.
10 Then he said unto them, Go your way, eat
the fat, and drink the sweet, and send portions
unto them for whom nothing is prepared: for
this day *is* holy unto our Lord: neither be ye
sorry; for the joy of the LORD is your strength.
11 So the Le'vites stilled all the people, saying, Hold your peace, for the day *is* holy; neither
be ye grieved.
12 And all the people went their way to eat,
and to drink, and to send portions, and to make
great mirth, because they had understood the
words that were declared unto them.
13 ¶ And on the second day were gathered
together the chief of the fathers of all the people, the priests, and the Le'vites, unto Ez'ra the
scribe, even to understand the words of the law.
14 And they found written in the law which
the LORD had commanded by Mo'ses, that the
children of Is'ra-el should dwell in booths in the
feast of the seventh month:
15 And that they should publish and proclaim in all their cities, and in Je-ru'sa-lem, saying, Go forth unto the mount, and fetch olive
branches, and pine branches, and myrtle
branches, and palm branches, and branches of
thick trees, to make booths, as *it is* written.
16 ¶ So the people went forth, and brought
them, and made themselves booths, every one
upon the roof of his house, and in their courts,
and in the courts of the house of God, and in the
street of the water gate, and in the street of the
gate of E'phra-im.
17 And all the congregation of them that
were come again out of the captivity made
booths, and sat under the booths: for since the
days of Jesh'u-a the son of Nun unto that day
had not the children of Is'ra-el done so. And
there was very great gladness.
18 Also day by day, from the first day unto
the last day, he read in the book of the law of
God. And they kept the feast seven days; and
on the eighth day *was* a solemn assembly, according unto the manner.

9 NOW in the twenty and fourth day of this
month the children of Is'ra-el were assembled with fasting, and with sackclothes, and
earth upon them.
2 And the seed of Is'ra-el separated themselves from all strangers, and stood and confessed their sins, and the iniquities of their fathers.
3 And they stood up in their place, and read
in the book of the law of the LORD their God *one*
fourth part of the day; and *another* fourth part
they confessed, and worshipped the LORD their
God.
4 ¶ Then stood up upon the stairs, of the Le'-
vites, Jesh'u-a, and Ba'ni, Kad'mi-el, Sheb-a-ni'-
ah, Bun'ni, Sher-e-bi'ah, Ba'ni, *and* Chen'a-ni,
and cried with a loud voice unto the LORD their
God.
5 Then the Le'vites, Jesh'u-a, and Kad'mi-el,
Ba'ni, Hash-ab-ni'ah, Sher-e-bi'ah, Ho-di'jah,
Sheb-a-ni'ah, *and* Peth-a-hi'ah, said, Stand up
and bless the LORD your God for ever and ever:
and blessed be thy glorious name, which is exalted above all blessing and praise.
6 Thou, *even* thou, *art* LORD alone; thou hast
made heaven, the heaven of heavens, with all
their host, the earth, and all *things* that *are*
therein, the seas, and all that *is* therein, and
thou preservest them all; and the host of heaven
worshippeth thee.
7 Thou *art* the LORD the God, who didst
choose A'bram, and broughtest him forth out of
Ur of the Chal'dees, and gavest him the name of
A'bra-ham;
8 And foundest his heart faithful before thee,
and madest a covenant with him to give the
land of the Ca'naan-ites, the Hit'tites, the Am'-
or-ites, and the Per'iz-zites, and the Jeb'u-sites,
and the Gir'ga-shites, to give *it, I say*, to his
seed, and hast performed thy words; for thou
art righteous:
9 And didst see the affliction of our fathers in
E'gypt, and heardest their cry by the Red sea;
10 And shewedst signs and wonders upon
Pha'raoh, and on all his servants, and on all the
people of his land: for thou knewest that they
dealt proudly against them. So didst thou get
thee a name, as *it is* this day.
11 And thou didst divide the sea before
them, so that they went through the midst of
the sea on the dry land; and their persecutors
thou threwest into the deeps, as a stone into the
mighty waters.
12 Moreover thou leddest them in the day by
a cloudy pillar; and in the night by a pillar of
fire, to give them light in the way wherein they
should go.
13 Thou camest down also upon mount Si'-
nai, and spakest with them from heaven, and
gavest them right judgments, and true laws,
good statutes and commandments:
14 And madest known unto them thy holy
sabbath, and commandedst them precepts,
statutes, and laws, by the hand of Mo'ses thy
servant:
15 And gavest them bread from heaven for
their hunger, and broughtest forth water for
them out of the rock for their thirst, and promisedst them that they should go in to possess
the land which thou hadst sworn to give them.
16 But they and our fathers dealt proudly,
and hardened their necks, and hearkened not to
thy commandments,
17 And refused to obey, neither were mindful
of thy wonders that thou didst among them; but
hardened their necks, and in their rebellion appointed a captain to return to their bondage:
but thou *art* a God ready to pardon, gracious
and merciful, slow to anger, and of great kindness, and forsookest them not.
18 Yea, when they had made them a molten
calf, and said, This *is* thy God that brought thee
up out of E'gypt, and had wrought great provocations;
19 Yet thou in thy manifold mercies forsookest them not in the wilderness: the pillar of the
cloud departed not from them by day, to lead
them in the way; neither the pillar of fire by
night, to shew them light, and the way wherein
they should go.
20 Thou gavest also thy good spirit to instruct them, and withheldest not thy manna

from their mouth, and gavest them water for
their thirst.
21 Yea, forty years didst thou sustain them
in the wilderness, *so that* they lacked nothing;
their clothes waxed not old, and their feet
swelled not.
22 Moreover thou gavest them kingdoms and
nations, and didst divide them into corners: so
they possessed the land of Si'hon, and the land
of the king of Hesh'bon, and the land of Og king
of Ba'shan.
23 Their children also multipliedst thou as
the stars of heaven, and broughtest them into
the land, concerning which thou hadst promised to their fathers, that they should go in to
possess *it*.
24 So the children went in and possessed the
land, and thou subduedst before them the inhabitants of the land, the Ca'naan-ites, and gavest them into their hands, with their kings, and
the people of the land, that they might do with
them as they would.
25 And they took strong cities, and a fat
land, and possessed houses full of all goods,
wells digged, vineyards, and oliveyards, and
fruit trees in abundance: so they did eat, and
were filled, and became fat, and delighted
themselves in thy great goodness.
26 Nevertheless they were disobedient, and
rebelled against thee, and cast thy law behind
their backs, and slew thy prophets which testified against them to turn them to thee, and they
wrought great provocations.
27 Therefore thou deliveredst them into the
hand of their enemies, who vexed them: and in
the time of their trouble, when they cried unto
thee, thou heardest *them* from heaven; and according to thy manifold mercies thou gavest
them saviours, who saved them out of the hand
of their enemies.
28 But after they had rest, they did evil again
before thee: therefore leftest thou them in the
hand of their enemies, so that they had the dominion over them: yet when they returned, and
cried unto thee, thou heardest *them* from
heaven; and many times didst thou deliver
them according to thy mercies;
29 And testifiedst against them, that thou
mightest bring them again unto thy law: yet
they dealt proudly, and hearkened not unto thy
commandments, but sinned against thy judgments, (which if a man do, he shall live in
them;) and withdrew the shoulder, and hardened their neck, and would not hear.
30 Yet many years didst thou forbear them,
and testifiedst against them by thy spirit in thy
prophets: yet would they not give ear: therefore
gavest thou them into the hand of the people of
the lands.
31 Nevertheless for thy great mercies' sake
thou didst not utterly consume them, nor forsake them; for thou *art* a gracious and merciful
God.
32 Now therefore, our God, the great, the
mighty, and the terrible God, who keepest covenant and mercy, let not all the trouble seem
little before thee, that hath come upon us, on
our kings, on our princes, and on our priests,
and on our prophets, and on our fathers, and on
all thy people, since the time of the kings of As-
syr'i-a unto this day.
33 Howbeit thou *art* just in all that is brought
upon us; for thou hast done right, but we have
done wickedly:
34 Neither have our kings, our princes, our
priests, nor our fathers, kept thy law, nor hearkened unto thy commandments and thy testimonies, wherewith thou didst testify against them.
35 For they have not served thee in their
kingdom, and in thy great goodness that thou
gavest them, and in the large and fat land which
thou gavest before them, neither turned they
from their wicked works.
36 Behold, we *are* servants this day, and *for*
the land that thou gavest unto our fathers to eat
the fruit thereof and the good thereof, behold,
we *are* servants in it:
37 And it yieldeth much increase unto the
kings whom thou hast set over us because of
our sins: also they have dominion over our bodies, and over our cattle, at their pleasure, and
we *are* in great distress.
38 And because of all this we make a sure
covenant, and write *it;* and our princes, Le'-
vites, *and* priests, seal *unto it*.

10 NOW those that sealed *were*, Ne-he-mi'-
ah, the Tir'sha-tha, the son of Hach-a-
li'ah, and Zid-ki'jah,
2 Ser-a-i'ah, Az-a-ri'ah, Jer-e-mi'ah,
3 Pash'ur, Am-a-ri'ah, Mal-chi'jah,
4 Hat'tush, Sheb-a-ni'ah, Mal'luch,
5 Ha'rim, Mer'e-moth, O-ba-di'ah,
6 Dan'iel, Gin'ne-thon, Ba'ruch,
7 Me-shul'lam, A-bi'jah, Mij'a-min,
8 Ma-a-zi'ah, Bil'ga-i, Shem-a-i'ah: these
were the priests.
9 And the Le'vites: both Jesh'u-a the son of
Az-a-ni'ah, Bin'nu-i of the sons of Hen'a-dad,
Kad'mi-el;
10 And their brethren, Sheb-a-ni'ah, Ho-di'-
jah, Kel'i-ta, Pel-a-i'ah, Ha'nan,
11 Mi'cha, Re'hob, Hash-a-bi'ah,
12 Zac'cur, Sher-e-bi'ah, Sheb-a-ni'ah,
13 Ho-di'jah, Ba'ni, Ben'i-nu.
14 The chief of the people; Pa'rosh, Pa'hath-
mo'ab, E'lam, Zat'thu, Ba'ni,
15 Bun'ni, Az'gad, Beb'a-i,
16 Ad-o-ni'jah, Big'va-i, A'din,
17 A'ter, Hiz-ki'jah, Az'zur,
18 Ho-di'jah, Ha'shum, Be'zai,
19 Ha'riph, An'a-thoth, Neb'a-i,
20 Mag'pi-ash, Me-shul'lam, He'zir,
21 Me-shez'a-be-el, Za'dok, Jad-du'a,
22 Pel-a-ti'ah, Ha'nan, An-a-i'ah,
23 Ho-she'a, Han-a-ni'ah, Ha'shub,
24 Hal-lo'hesh, Pil'e-ha, Sho'bek,
25 Re'hum, Ha-shab'nah, Ma-a-se'iah,
26 And A-hi'jah, Ha'nan, A'nan,
27 Mal'luch, Ha'rim, Ba'a-nah.
28 ¶ And the rest of the people, the priests,
the Le'vites, the porters, the singers, the Neth'i-
nims, and all they that had separated themselves from the people of the lands unto the law
of God, their wives, their sons, and their daughters, every one having knowledge, and having
understanding;
29 They clave to their brethren, their nobles,
and entered into a curse, and into an oath, to
walk in God's law, which was given by Mo'ses
the servant of God, and to observe and do all
the commandments of the LORD our Lord, and
his judgments and his statutes;
30 And that we would not give our daughters
unto the people of the land, nor take their
daughters for our sons:
31 And *if* the people of the land bring ware
or any victuals on the sabbath day to sell, *that*
we would not buy it of them on the sabbath, or
on the holy day: and *that* we would leave the
seventh year, and the exaction of every debt.
32 Also we made ordinances for us, to

charge ourselves yearly with the third part of a
shekel for the service of the house of our God;
33 For the shewbread, and for the continual
meat offering, and for the continual burnt offering, of the sabbaths, of the new moons, for the
set feasts, and for the holy *things,* and for the
sin offerings to make an atonement for Is'ra-el,
and *for* all the work of the house of our God.
34 And we cast the lots among the priests,
the Le'vites, and the people, for the wood offering, to bring *it* into the house of our God, after
the houses of our fathers, at times appointed
year by year, to burn upon the altar of the LORD
our God, as *it is* written in the law:
35 And to bring the firstfruits of our ground,
and the firstfruits of all fruit of all trees, year by
year, unto the house of the LORD:
36 Also the firstborn of our sons, and of our
cattle, as *it is* written in the law, and the firstlings of our herds and of our flocks, to bring to
the house of our God, unto the priests that minister in the house of our God:
37 And *that* we should bring the firstfruits of
our dough, and our offerings, and the fruit of all
manner of trees, of wine and of oil, unto the
priests, to the chambers of the house of our
God; and the tithes of our ground unto the Le'-
vites, that the same Le'vites might have the
tithes in all the cities of our tillage.
38 And the priest the son of Aar'on shall be
with the Le'vites, when the Le'vites take tithes:
and the Le'vites shall bring up the tithe of the
tithes unto the house of our God, to the chambers, into the treasure house.
39 For the children of Is'ra-el and the children of Le'vi shall bring the offering of the corn,
of the new wine, and the oil, unto the chambers,
where *are* the vessels of the sanctuary, and the
priests that minister, and the porters, and the
singers: and we will not forsake the house of
our God.

11 AND the rulers of the people dwelt at
Je-ru'sa-lem: the rest of the people also
cast lots, to bring one of ten to dwell in Je-ru'sa-
lem the holy city, and nine parts *to dwell* in *other* cities.
2 And the people blessed all the men, that
willingly offered themselves to dwell at Je-ru'-
sa-lem.
3 ¶ Now these *are* the chief of the province
that dwelt in Je-ru'sa-lem: but in the cities of
Ju'dah dwelt every one in his possession in their
cities, *to wit,* Is'ra-el, the priests, and the Le'-
vites, and the Neth'i-nims, and the children of
Sol'o-mon's servants.
4 And at Je-ru'sa-lem dwelt *certain* of the
children of Ju'dah, and of the children of Ben'ja-
min. Of the children of Ju'dah; Ath-a-i'ah the
son of Uz-zi'ah, the son of Zech-a-ri'ah, the son
of Am-a-ri'ah, the son of Sheph-a-ti'ah, the son
of Ma-ha'la-le-el, of the children of Pe'rez;
5 And Ma-a-se'iah the son of Ba'ruch, the son
of Col-ho'zeh, the son of Ha-za'iah, the son of
Ad-a-i'ah, the son of Joi'a-rib, the son of Zech-a-
ri'ah, the son of Shi-lo'ni.
6 All the sons of Pe'rez that dwelt at Je-ru'sa-
lem *were* four hundred threescore and eight valiant men.
7 And these *are* the sons of Ben'ja-min; Sal'lu
the son of Me-shul'lam, the son of Jo'ed, the son
of Pe-da'iah, the son of Kol-a-i'ah, the son of
Ma-a-se'iah, the son of Ith'i-el, the son of Je-sa'-
iah.
8 And after him Gab'ba-i, Sal'la-i, nine hundred twenty and eight.
9 And Jo'el the son of Zich'ri *was* their overseer: and Ju'dah the son of Se-nu'ah *was* second
over the city.
10 Of the priests: Je-da'iah the son of Joi'a-
rib, Ja'chin.
11 Ser-a-i'ah the son of Hil-ki'ah, the son of
Me-shul'lam, the son of Za'dok, the son of Me-
ra'ioth, the son of A-hi'tub, *was* the ruler of the
house of God.
12 And their brethren that did the work of
the house *were* eight hundred twenty and two:
and Ad-a-i'ah the son of Jer'o-ham, the son of
Pel-a-li'ah, the son of Am'zi, the son of Zech-a-
ri'ah, the son of Pash'ur, the son of Mal-chi'ah,
13 And his brethren, chief of the fathers, two
hundred forty and two: and A-mash'a-i the son
of A-zar'e-el, the son of A-has'a-i, the son of
Me-shil'le-moth, the son of Im'mer,
14 And their brethren, mighty men of valour,
an hundred twenty and eight: and their overseer *was* Zab'di-el, the son of *one of* the great
men.
15 Also of the Le'vites: Shem-a-i'ah the son
of Ha'shub, the son of Az'ri-kam, the son of
Hash-a-bi'ah, the son of Bun'ni;
16 And Shab-beth'a-i and Joz'a-bad, of the
chief of the Le'vites, *had* the oversight of the
outward business of the house of God.
17 And Mat-ta-ni'ah the son of Mi'cha, the
son of Zab'di, the son of A'saph, *was* the principal to begin the thanksgiving in prayer: and
Bak-buk-i'ah the second among his brethren,
and Ab'da the son of Sham-mu'a, the son of
Ga'lal, the son of Jed'u-thun.
18 All the Le'vites in the holy city *were* two
hundred fourscore and four.
19 Moreover the porters, Ak'kub, Tal'mon,
and their brethren that kept the gates, *were* an
hundred seventy and two.
20 ¶ And the residue of Is'ra-el, of the
priests, *and* the Le'vites, *were* in all the cities of
Ju'dah, every one in his inheritance.
21 But the Neth'i-nims dwelt in O'phel: and
Zi'ha and Gis'pa *were* over the Neth'i-nims.
22 The overseer also of the Le'vites at Je-ru'-
sa-lem *was* Uz'zi the son of Ba'ni, the son of
Hash-a-bi'ah, the son of Mat-ta-ni'ah, the son of
Mi'cha. Of the sons of A'saph, the singers *were*
over the business of the house of God.
23 For *it was* the king's commandment concerning them, that a certain portion should be
for the singers, due for every day.
24 And Peth-a-hi'ah the son of Me-shez'a-be-
el, of the children of Ze'rah the son of Ju'dah,
was at the king's hand in all matters concerning
the people.
25 And for the villages, with their fields,
some of the children of Ju'dah dwelt at Kir'-
jath-ar'ba, and *in* the villages thereof, and at
Di'bon, and *in* the villages thereof, and at Je-
kab'ze-el, and *in* the villages thereof,
26 And at Jesh'u-a, and at Mol'a-dah, and at
Beth-phe'let,
27 And at Ha'zar-shu'al, and at Be'er-she'ba,
and *in* the villages thereof,
28 And at Zik'lag, and at Mek'o-nah, and in
the villages thereof,
29 And at En-rim'mon, and at Za're-ah, and
at Jar'muth,
30 Za-no'ah, A-dul'lam, and *in* their villages,
at La'chish, and the fields thereof, at A-ze'kah,
and *in* the villages thereof. And they dwelt from
Be'er-she'ba unto the valley of Hin'nom.
31 The children also of Ben'ja-min from Ge'-
ba *dwelt* at Mich'mash, and A-i'ja, and Beth'-el,
and *in* their villages,
32 *And* at An'a-thoth, Nob, An-a-ni'ah,
33 Ha'zor, Ra'mah, Git'ta-im,

34 Ha'did, Ze-bo'im, Ne-bal'lat,
35 Lod, and O'no, the valley of craftsmen.
36 And of the Le'vites *were* divisions *in* Ju'-
dah, *and* in Ben'ja-min.

12 NOW these *are* the priests and the Le'-
vites that went up with Ze-rub'ba-bel
the son of She-al'ti-el, and Jesh'u-a: Ser-a-i'ah,
Jer-e-mi'ah, Ez'ra,
2 Am-a-ri'ah, Mal'luch, Hat'tush,
3 Shech-a-ni'ah, Re'hum, Mer'e-moth,
4 Id'do, Gin'ne-tho, A-bi'jah,
5 Mi'a-min, Ma-a-di'ah, Bil'gah,
6 Shem-a-i'ah, and Joi'a-rib, Je-da'iah,
7 Sal'lu, A'mok, Hil-ki'ah, Je-da'iah. These
were the chief of the priests and of their brethren in the days of Jesh'u-a.
8 Moreover the Le'vites: Jesh'u-a, Bin'nu-i,
Kad'mi-el, Sher-e-bi'ah, Ju'dah, *and* Mat-ta-ni'-
ah, *which was* over the thanksgiving, he and his
brethren.
9 Also Bak-buk-i'ah and Un'ni, their brethren, *were* over against them in the watches.
10 ¶ And Jesh'u-a begat Joi'a-kim, Joi'a-kim
also begat E-li'a-shib, and E-li'a-shib begat Joi'-
a-da,
11 And Joi'a-da begat Jon'a-than, and Jon'a-
than begat Jad-du'a.
12 And in the days of Joi'a-kim were priests,
the chief of the fathers: of Ser-a-i'ah, Mer-a-i'-
ah; of Jer-e-mi'ah, Han-a-ni'ah;
13 Of Ez'ra, Me-shul'lam; of Am-a-ri'ah, Je-
ho-ha'nan;
14 Of Mel'i-cu, Jon'a-than; of Sheb-a-ni'ah,
Jo'seph;
15 Of Ha'rim, Ad'na; of Me-ra'ioth, Hel'ka-i;
16 Of Id'do, Zech-a-ri'ah; of Gin'ne-thon, Me-
shul'lam;
17 Of A-bi'jah, Zich'ri; of Mi-ni'a-min, of Mo-
a-di'ah, Pil'tai;
18 Of Bil'gah, Sham-mu'a; of Shem-a-i'ah, Je-
hon'a-than;
19 And of Joi'a-rib, Mat-te-na'i; of Je-da'iah,
Uz'zi;
20 Of Sal'la-i, Kal'la-i; of A'mok, E'ber;
21 Of Hil-ki'ah, Hash-a-bi'ah; of Je-da'iah,
Ne-than'e-el.
22 ¶ The Le'vites in the days of E-li'a-shib,
Joi'a-da, and Jo-ha'nan, and Jad-du'a, *were* recorded chief of the fathers: also the priests, to
the reign of Da-ri'us the Per'sian.
23 The sons of Le'vi, the chief of the fathers,
were written in the book of the chronicles, even
until the days of Jo-ha'nan the son of E-li'a-shib.
24 And the chief of the Le'vites: Hash-a-bi'-
ah, Sher-e-bi'ah, and Jesh'u-a the son of Kad'-
mi-el, with their brethren over against them, to
praise *and* to give thanks, according to the
commandment of Da'vid the man of God, ward
over against ward.
25 Mat-ta-ni'ah, and Bak-buk-i'ah, O-ba-di'-
ah, Me-shul'lam, Tal'mon, Ak'kub, *were* porters
keeping the ward at the thresholds of the gates.
26 These *were* in the days of Joi'a-kim the
son of Jesh'u-a, the son of Joz'a-dak, and in the
days of Ne-he-mi'ah the governor, and of Ez'ra
the priest, the scribe.
27 ¶ And at the dedication of the wall of Je-
ru'sa-lem they sought the Le'vites out of all
their places, to bring them to Je-ru'sa-lem, to
keep the dedication with gladness, both with
thanksgivings, and with singing, *with* cymbals,
psalteries, and with harps.
28 And the sons of the singers gathered
themselves together, both out of the plain country round about Je-ru'sa-lem, and from the villages of Ne-toph'a-thi;
29 Also from the house of Gil'gal, and out of
the fields of Ge'ba and Az'ma-veth: for the singers had builded them villages round about Je-
ru'sa-lem.
30 And the priests and the Le'vites purified
themselves, and purified the people, and the
gates, and the wall.
31 Then I brought up the princes of Ju'dah
upon the wall, and appointed two great *companies of them that gave* thanks, *whereof one*
went on the right hand upon the wall toward
the dung gate:
32 And after them went Hosh-a-i'ah, and half
of the princes of Ju'dah,
33 And Az-a-ri'ah, Ez'ra, and Me-shul'lam,
34 Ju'dah, and Ben'ja-min, and Shem-a-i'ah,
and Jer-e-mi'ah,
35 And *certain* of the priests' sons with
trumpets; *namely*, Zech-a-ri'ah the son of Jon'a-
than, the son of Shem-a-i'ah, the son of Mat-ta-
ni'ah, the son of Mi-cha'iah, the son of Zac'cur,
the son of A'saph:
36 And his brethren, Shem-a-i'ah, and A-zar'-
a-el, Mil-a-la'i, Gil'a-lai, Ma-a'i, Ne-than'e-el,
and Ju'dah, Ha-na'ni, with the musical instruments of Da'vid the man of God, and Ez'ra the
scribe before them.
37 And at the fountain gate, which was over
against them, they went up by the stairs of the
city of Da'vid, at the going up of the wall, above
the house of Da'vid, even unto the water gate
eastward.
38 And the other *company of them that gave*
thanks went over against *them*, and I after
them, and the half of the people upon the wall,
from beyond the tower of the furnaces even
unto the broad wall;
39 And from above the gate of E'phra-im,
and above the old gate, and above the fish gate,
and the tower of Ha-nan'e-el, and the tower of
Me'ah, even unto the sheep gate: and they stood
still in the prison gate.
40 So stood the two *companies of them that
gave* thanks in the house of God, and I, and the
half of the rulers with me:
41 And the priests; E-li'a-kim, Ma-a-se'iah,
Mi-ni'a-min, Mi-cha'iah, El-i-o-e'na-i, Zech-a-ri'-
ah, *and* Han-a-ni'ah, with trumpets;
42 And Ma-a-se'iah, and Shem-a-i'ah, and E-
le-a'zar, and Uz'zi, and Je-ho-ha'nan, and Mal-
chi'jah, and E'lam, and E'zer. And the singers
sang loud, with Jez-ra-hi'ah *their* overseer.
43 Also that day they offered great sacrifices,
and rejoiced: for God had made them rejoice
with great joy: the wives also and the children
rejoiced: so that the joy of Je-ru'sa-lem was
heard even afar off.
44 ¶ And at that time were some appointed
over the chambers for the treasures, for the offerings, for the firstfruits, and for the tithes, to
gather into them out of the fields of the cities
the portions of the law for the priests and Le'-
vites: for Ju'dah rejoiced for the priests and for
the Le'vites that waited.
45 And both the singers and the porters kept
the ward of their God, and the ward of the purification, according to the commandment of Da'-
vid, *and* of Sol'o-mon his son.
46 For in the days of Da'vid and A'saph of
old *there were* chief of the singers, and songs of
praise and thanksgiving unto God.
47 And all Is'ra-el in the days of Ze-rub'ba-
bel, and in the days of Ne-he-mi'ah, gave the
portions of the singers and the porters, every
day his portion: and they sanctified *holy things*
unto the Le'vites; and the Le'vites sanctified
them unto the children of Aar'on.

13 ON that day they read in the book of Mo'-
ses in the audience of the people; and
therein was found written, that the Am'mon-ite
and the Mo'ab-ite should not come into the congregation of God for ever;
2 Because they met not the children of Is'ra-
el with bread and with water, but hired Ba'laam
against them, that he should curse them: howbeit our God turned the curse into a blessing.
3 Now it came to pass, when they had heard
the law, that they separated from Is'ra-el all the
mixed multitude.
4 ¶ And before this, E-li'a-shib the priest,
having the oversight of the chamber of the
house of our God, *was* allied unto To-bi'ah:
5 And he had prepared for him a great chamber, where aforetime they laid the meat offerings, the frankincense, and the vessels, and the
tithes of the corn, the new wine, and the oil,
which was commanded *to be given* to the Le'-
vites, and the singers, and the porters; and the
offerings of the priests.
6 But in all this *time* was not I at Je-ru'sa-
lem: for in the two and thirtieth year of Ar-tax-
erx'es king of Bab'y-lon came I unto the king,
and after certain days obtained I leave of the
king:
7 And I came to Je-ru'sa-lem, and understood of the evil that E-li'a-shib did for To-bi'ah,
in preparing him a chamber in the courts of the
house of God.
8 And it grieved me sore: therefore I cast
forth all the household stuff of To-bi'ah out of
the chamber.
9 Then I commanded, and they cleansed the
chambers: and thither brought I again the vessels of the house of God, with the meat offering
and the frankincense.
10 ¶ And I perceived that the portions of the
Le'vites had not been given *them:* for the Le'-
vites and the singers, that did the work, were
fled every one to his field.
11 Then contended I with the rulers, and
said, Why is the house of God forsaken? And I
gathered them together, and set them in their
place.
12 Then brought all Ju'dah the tithe of the
corn and the new wine and the oil unto the treasuries.
13 And I made treasurers over the treasuries,
Shel-e-mi'ah the priest, and Za'dok the scribe,
and of the Le'vites, Pe-da'iah: and next to them
was Ha'nan the son of Zac'cur, the son of Mat-
ta-ni'ah: for they were counted faithful, and
their office *was* to distribute unto their brethren.
14 Remember me, O my God, concerning
this, and wipe not out my good deeds that I
have done for the house of my God, and for the
offices thereof.
15 ¶ In those days saw I in Ju'dah *some*
treading wine presses on the sabbath, and
bringing in sheaves, and lading asses; as also
wine, grapes, and figs, and all *manner of* burdens, which they brought into Je-ru'sa-lem on
the sabbath day: and I testified *against them* in
the day wherein they sold victuals.
16 There dwelt men of Tyre also therein,
which brought fish, and all manner of ware, and
sold on the sabbath unto the children of Ju'dah,
and in Je-ru'sa-lem.
17 Then I contended with the nobles of Ju'-
dah, and said unto them, What evil thing *is* this
that ye do, and profane the sabbath day?
18 Did not your fathers thus, and did not our
God bring all this evil upon us, and upon this
city? yet ye bring more wrath upon Is'ra-el by
profaning the sabbath.
19 And it came to pass, that when the gates
of Je-ru'sa-lem began to be dark before the sabbath, I commanded that the gates should be
shut, and charged that they should not be
opened till after the sabbath: and *some* of my
servants set I at the gates, *that* there should no
burden be brought in on the sabbath day.
20 So the merchants and sellers of all kind of
ware lodged without Je-ru'sa-lem once or twice.
21 Then I testified against them, and said
unto them, Why lodge ye about the wall? if ye
do *so* again, I will lay hands on you. From that
time forth came they no *more* on the sabbath.
22 And I commanded the Le'vites that they
should cleanse themselves, and *that* they
should come *and* keep the gates, to sanctify the
sabbath day. Remember me, O my God, *concerning* this also, and spare me according to the
greatness of thy mercy.
23 ¶ In those days also saw I Jews *that* had
married wives of Ash'dod, of Am'mon, *and* of
Mo'ab:
24 And their children spake half in the
speech of Ash'dod, and could not speak in the
Jews' language, but according to the language
of each people.
25 And I contended with them, and cursed
them, and smote certain of them, and plucked
off their hair, and made them swear by God,
saying, Ye shall not give your daughters unto
their sons, nor take their daughters unto your
sons, or for yourselves.
26 Did not Sol'o-mon king of Is'ra-el sin by
these things? yet among many nations was
there no king like him, who was beloved of his
God, and God made him king over all Is'ra-el:
nevertheless even him did outlandish women
cause to sin.
27 Shall we then hearken unto you to do all
this great evil, to transgress against our God in
marrying strange wives?
28 And *one* of the sons of Joi'a-da, the son of
E-li'a-shib the high priest, *was* son in law to
San-bal'lat the Hor'o-nite: therefore I chased
him from me.
29 Remember them, O my God, because they
have defiled the priesthood, and the covenant of
the priesthood, and of the Le'vites.
30 Thus cleansed I them from all strangers,
and appointed the wards of the priests and the
Le'vites, every one in his business;
31 And for the wood offering, at times appointed, and for the firstfruits. Remember me,
O my God, for good.

THE BOOK OF

ESTHER

1 NOW it came to pass in the days of A-has-
u-e'rus, (this *is* A-has-u-e'rus which
reigned, from Ind'ia even unto E-thi-o'pi-a, *over*
an hundred and seven and twenty provinces:)
2 *That* in those days, when the king A-has-u-
e'rus sat on the throne of his kingdom, which
was in Shu'shan the palace,
3 In the third year of his reign, he made a
feast unto all his princes and his servants; the
power of Per'sia and Me'di-a, the nobles and
princes of the provinces, *being* before him:
4 When he shewed the riches of his glorious
kingdom and the honour of his excellent majesty many days, *even* an hundred and fourscore
days.
5 And when these days were expired, the
king made a feast unto all the people that were
present in Shu'shan the palace, both unto great
and small, seven days, in the court of the garden of the king's palace;
6 *Where were* white, green, and blue, *hangings,* fastened with cords of fine linen and purple to silver rings and pillars of marble: the
beds *were of* gold and silver, upon a pavement
of red, and blue, and white, and black, marble.
7 And they gave *them* drink in vessels of
gold, (the vessels being diverse one from another,) and royal wine in abundance, according
to the state of the king.
8 And the drinking *was* according to the law;
none did compel: for so the king had appointed
to all the officers of his house, that they should
do according to every man's pleasure.
9 Also Vash'ti the queen made a feast for the
women *in* the royal house which *belonged* to
king A-has-u-e'rus.
10 ¶ On the seventh day, when the heart of
the king was merry with wine, he commanded
Me-hu'man, Biz'tha, Har-bo'na, Big'tha, and A-
bag'tha, Ze'thar, and Car'cas, the seven chamberlains that served in the presence of A-has-u-
e'rus the king,
11 To bring Vash'ti the queen before the king
with the crown royal, to shew the people and
the princes her beauty: for she *was* fair to look
on.
12 But the queen Vash'ti refused to come at
the king's commandment by *his* chamberlains:
therefore was the king very wroth, and his anger burned in him.
13 ¶ Then the king said to the wise men,
which knew the times, (for so *was* the king's
manner toward all that knew law and judgment:
14 And the next unto him *was* Car-she'na,
She'thar, Ad'ma-tha, Tar'shish, Me'res, Mar'se-
na, *and* Me-mu'can, the seven princes of Per'sia
and Me'di-a, which saw the king's face, *and*
which sat the first in the kingdom;)
15 What shall we do unto the queen Vash'ti
according to law, because she hath not performed the commandment of the king A-has-u-
e'rus by the chamberlains?
16 And Me-mu'can answered before the king
and the princes, Vash'ti the queen hath not
done wrong to the king only, but also to all the
princes, and to all the people that *are* in all the
provinces of the king A-has-u-e'rus.
17 For *this* deed of the queen shall come
abroad unto all women, so that they shall despise their husbands in their eyes, when it shall
be reported, The king A-has-u-e'rus commanded Vash'ti the queen to be brought in before him, but she came not.
18 *Likewise* shall the ladies of Per'sia and
Me'di-a say this day unto all the king's princes,
which have heard of the deed of the queen.
Thus *shall there arise* too much contempt and
wrath.
19 If it please the king, let there go a royal
commandment from him, and let it be written
among the laws of the Per'sians and the Medes,
that it be not altered, That Vash'ti come no
more before king A-has-u-e'rus; and let the king
give her royal estate unto another that is better
than she.
20 And when the king's decree which he
shall make shall be published throughout all his
empire, (for it is great,) all the wives shall give
to their husbands honour, both to great and
small.
21 And the saying pleased the king and the
princes; and the king did according to the word
of Me-mu'can:
22 For he sent letters into all the king's provinces, into every province according to the writing thereof, and to every people after their language, that every man should bear rule in his
own house, and that *it* should be published according to the language of every people.

2 AFTER these things, when the wrath of
king A-has-u-e'rus was appeased, he remembered Vash'ti, and what she had done, and
what was decreed against her.
2 Then said the king's servants that ministered unto him, Let there be fair young virgins
sought for the king:
3 And let the king appoint officers in all the
provinces of his kingdom, that they may gather
together all the fair young virgins unto Shu'-
shan the palace, to the house of the women,
unto the custody of He'ge the king's chamberlain, keeper of the women; and let their things
for purification be given *them:*
4 And let the maiden which pleaseth the king
be queen instead of Vash'ti. And the thing
pleased the king; and he did so.
5 ¶ *Now* in Shu'shan the palace there was a
certain Jew, whose name *was* Mor'de-cai, the
son of Ja'ir, the son of Shim'e-i, the son of Kish,
a Ben'ja-mite;
6 Who had been carried away from Je-ru'sa-
lem with the captivity which had been carried
away with Jec-o-ni'ah king of Ju'dah, whom
Neb-u-chad-nez'zar the king of Bab'y-lon had
carried away.
7 And he brought up Ha-das'sah, that *is,* Es'-
ther, his uncle's daughter: for she had neither
father nor mother, and the maid *was* fair and
beautiful; whom Mor'de-cai, when her father
and mother were dead, took for his own daughter.
8 ¶ So it came to pass, when the king's commandment and his decree was heard, and when
many maidens were gathered together unto
Shu'shan the palace, to the custody of Heg'a-i,
that Es'ther was brought also unto the king's
house, to the custody of Heg'a-i, keeper of the
women.
9 And the maiden pleased him, and she obtained kindness of him; and he speedily gave
her her things for purification, with such things

as belonged to her, and seven maidens, *which were* meet to be given her, out of the king's house: and he preferred her and her maids unto the best *place* of the house of the women.

10 Es'ther had not shewed her people nor her kindred: for Mor'de-cai had charged her that she should not shew *it*.

11 And Mor'de-cai walked every day before the court of the women's house, to know how Es'ther did, and what should become of her.

12 ¶ Now when every maid's turn was come to go in to king A-has-u-e'rus, after that she had been twelve months, according to the manner of the women, (for so were the days of their purifications accomplished, *to wit,* six months with oil of myrrh, and six months with sweet odours, and with *other* things for the purifying of the women;)

13 Then thus came *every* maiden unto the king; whatsoever she desired was given her to go with her out of the house of the women unto the king's house.

14 In the evening she went, and on the morrow she returned into the second house of the women, to the custody of Sha-ash'gaz, the king's chamberlain, which kept the concubines: she came in unto the king no more, except the king delighted in her, and that she were called by name.

15 ¶ Now when the turn of Es'ther, the daughter of Ab-i-ha'il the uncle of Mor'de-cai, who had taken her for his daughter, was come to go in unto the king, she required nothing but what Heg'a-i the king's chamberlain, the keeper of the women, appointed. And Es'ther obtained favour in the sight of all them that looked upon her.

16 So Es'ther was taken unto king A-has-u-e'rus into his house royal in the tenth month, which *is* the month Te'beth, in the seventh year of his reign.

17 And the king loved Es'ther above all the women, and she obtained grace and favour in his sight more than all the virgins; so that he set the royal crown upon her head, and made her queen instead of Vash'ti.

18 Then the king made a great feast unto all his princes and his servants, *even* Es'ther's feast; and he made a release to the provinces, and gave gifts, according to the state of the king.

19 And when the virgins were gathered together the second time, then Mor'de-cai sat in the king's gate.

20 Es'ther had not *yet* shewed her kindred nor her people; as Mor'de-cai had charged her: for Es'ther did the commandment of Mor'de-cai, like as when she was brought up with him.

21 ¶ In those days, while Mor'de-cai sat in the king's gate, two of the king's chamberlains, Big'than and Te'resh, of those which kept the door, were wroth, and sought to lay hand on the king A-has-u-e'rus.

22 And the thing was known to Mor'de-cai, who told *it* unto Es'ther the queen; and Es'ther certified the king *thereof* in Mor'de-cai's name.

23 And when inquisition was made of the matter, it was found out; therefore they were both hanged on a tree: and it was written in the book of the chronicles before the king.

3 AFTER these things did king A-has-u-e'rus promote Ha'man the son of Ham-med'a-tha the A'gag-ite, and advanced him, and set his seat above all the princes that *were* with him.

2 And all the king's servants, that *were* in the king's gate, bowed, and reverenced Ha'man: for the king had so commanded concerning him. But Mor'de-cai bowed not, nor did *him* reverence.

3 Then the king's servants, which *were* in the king's gate, said unto Mor'de-cai, Why transgressest thou the king's commandment?

4 Now it came to pass, when they spake daily unto him, and he hearkened not unto them, that they told Ha'man, to see whether Mor'de-cai's matters would stand: for he had told them that he *was* a Jew.

5 And when Ha'man saw that Mor'de-cai bowed not, nor did him reverence, then was Ha'man full of wrath.

6 And he thought scorn to lay hands on Mor'de-cai alone; for they had shewed him the people of Mor'de-cai: wherefore Ha'man sought to destroy all the Jews that *were* throughout the whole kingdom of A-has-u-e'rus, *even* the people of Mor'de-cai.

7 ¶ In the first month, that *is*, the month Ni'san, in the twelfth year of king A-has-u-e'rus, they cast Pur, that *is,* the lot, before Ha'man from day to day, and from month to month, *to* the twelfth *month,* that *is,* the month A'dar.

8 ¶ And Ha'man said unto king A-has-u-e'rus, There is a certain people scattered abroad and dispersed among the people in all the provinces of thy kingdom; and their laws *are* diverse from all people; neither keep they the king's laws: therefore it *is* not for the king's profit to suffer them.

9 If it please the king, let it be written that they may be destroyed: and I will pay ten thousand talents of silver to the hands of those that have the charge of the business, to bring *it* into the king's treasuries.

10 And the king took his ring from his hand, and gave it unto Ha'man the son of Ham-med'a-tha the A'gag-ite, the Jews' enemy.

11 And the king said unto Ha'man, The silver *is* given to thee, the people also, to do with them as it seemeth good to thee.

12 Then were the king's scribes called on the thirteenth day of the first month, and there was written according to all that Ha'man had commanded unto the king's lieutenants, and to the governors that *were* over every province, and to the rulers of every people of every province according to the writing thereof, and *to* every people after their language; in the name of king A-has-u-e'rus was it written, and sealed with the king's ring.

13 And the letters were sent by posts into all the king's provinces, to destroy, to kill, and to cause to perish, all Jews, both young and old, little children and women, in one day, *even* upon the thirteenth *day* of the twelfth month, which *is* the month A'dar, and *to take* the spoil of them for a prey.

14 The copy of the writing for a commandment to be given in every province was published unto all people, that they should be ready against that day.

15 The posts went out, being hastened by the king's commandment, and the decree was given in Shu'shan the palace. And the king and Ha'man sat down to drink; but the city Shu'shan was perplexed.

4 WHEN Mor'de-cai perceived all that was done, Mor'de-cai rent his clothes, and put on sackcloth with ashes, and went out into the midst of the city, and cried with a loud and a bitter cry;

2 And came even before the king's gate: for

none *might* enter into the king's gate clothed
with sackcloth.
3 And in every province, whithersoever the
king's commandment and his decree came,
there was great mourning among the Jews, and
fasting, and weeping, and wailing; and many
lay in sackcloth and ashes.
4 ¶ So Es'ther's maids and her chamberlains
came and told *it* her. Then was the queen exceedingly grieved; and she sent raiment to
clothe Mor'de-cai, and to take away his sackcloth from him: but he received *it* not.
5 Then called Es'ther for Ha'tach, *one* of the
king's chamberlains, whom he had appointed to
attend upon her, and gave him a commandment
to Mor'de-cai, to know what it *was*, and why it
was.
6 So Ha'tach went forth to Mor'de-cai unto
the street of the city, which *was* before the
king's gate.
7 And Mor'de-cai told him of all that had
happened unto him, and of the sum of the money that Ha'man had promised to pay to the
king's treasuries for the Jews, to destroy them.
8 Also he gave him the copy of the writing of
the decree that was given at Shu'shan to destroy them, to shew *it* unto Es'ther, and to declare *it* unto her, and to charge her that she
should go in unto the king, to make supplication
unto him, and to make request before him for
her people.
9 And Ha'tach came and told Es'ther the
words of Mor'de-cai.
10 ¶ Again Es'ther spake unto Ha'tach, and
gave him commandment unto Mor'de-cai;
11 All the king's servants, and the people of
the king's provinces, do know, that whosoever,
whether man or woman, shall come unto the
king into the inner court, who is not called,
there is one law of his to put *him* to death, except such to whom the king shall hold out the
golden sceptre, that he may live: but I have not
been called to come in unto the king these
thirty days.
12 And they told to Mor'de-cai Es'ther's
words.
13 Then Mor'de-cai commanded to answer
Es'ther, Think not with thyself that thou shalt
escape in the king's house, more than all the
Jews.
14 For if thou altogether holdest thy peace at
this time, *then* shall there enlargement and deliverance arise to the Jews from another place;
but thou and thy father's house shall be destroyed: and who knoweth whether thou art
come to the kingdom for *such* a time as this?
15 ¶ Then Es'ther bade *them* return Mor'de-
cai *this answer*,
16 Go, gather together all the Jews that are
present in Shu'shan, and fast ye for me, and neither eat nor drink three days, night or day: I
also and my maidens will fast likewise; and so
will I go in unto the king, which *is* not according
to the law: and if I perish, I perish.
17 So Mor'de-cai went his way, and did according to all that Es'ther had commanded him.

5 NOW it came to pass on the third day, that
Es'ther put on *her* royal *apparel*, and
stood in the inner court of the king's house,
over against the king's house: and the king sat
upon his royal throne in the royal house, over
against the gate of the house.
2 And it was so, when the king saw Es'ther
the queen standing in the court, *that* she obtained favour in his sight: and the king held out
to Es'ther the golden sceptre that *was* in his
hand. So Es'ther drew near, and touched the top
of the sceptre.
3 Then said the king unto her, What wilt
thou, queen Es'ther? and what *is* thy request? it
shall be even given thee to the half of the kingdom.
4 And Es'ther answered, If *it seem* good unto
the king, let the king and Ha'man come this day
unto the banquet that I have prepared for him.
5 Then the king said, Cause Ha'man to make
haste, that he may do as Es'ther hath said. So
the king and Ha'man came to the banquet that
Es'ther had prepared.
6 ¶ And the king said unto Es'ther at the
banquet of wine, What *is* thy petition? and it
shall be granted thee: and what *is* thy request?
even to the half of the kingdom it shall be performed.
7 Then answered Es'ther, and said, My petition and my request *is;*
8 If I have found favour in the sight of the
king, and if it please the king to grant my petition, and to perform my request, let the king
and Ha'man come to the banquet that I shall
prepare for them, and I will do to morrow as the
king hath said.
9 ¶ Then went Ha'man forth that day joyful
and with a glad heart: but when Ha'man saw
Mor'de-cai in the king's gate, that he stood not
up, nor moved for him, he was full of indignation against Mor'de-cai.
10 Nevertheless Ha'man refrained himself:
and when he came home, he sent and called for
his friends, and Ze'resh his wife.
11 And Ha'man told them of the glory of his
riches, and the multitude of his children, and all
the things wherein the king had promoted him,
and how he had advanced him above the
princes and servants of the king.
12 Ha'man said moreover, Yea, Es'ther the
queen did let no man come in with the king
unto the banquet that she had prepared but myself; and to morrow am I invited unto her also
with the king.
13 Yet all this availeth me nothing, so long as
I see Mor'de-cai the Jew sitting at the king's
gate.
14 ¶ Then said Ze'resh his wife and all his
friends unto him, Let a gallows be made of fifty
cubits high, and to morrow speak thou unto the
king that Mor'de-cai may be hanged thereon:
then go thou in merrily with the king unto the
banquet. And the thing pleased Ha'man; and he
caused the gallows to be made.

6 ON that night could not the king sleep, and
he commanded to bring the book of records of the chronicles; and they were read before the king.
2 And it was found written, that Mor'de-cai
had told of Big'tha-na and Te'resh, two of the
king's chamberlains, the keepers of the door,
who sought to lay hand on the king A-has-u-
e'rus.
3 And the king said, What honour and dignity hath been done to Mor'de-cai for this? Then
said the king's servants that ministered unto
him, There is nothing done for him.
4 ¶ And the king said, Who *is* in the court?
Now Ha'man was come into the outward court
of the king's house, to speak unto the king to
hang Mor'de-cai on the gallows that he had prepared for him.
5 And the king's servants said unto him, Behold, Ha'man standeth in the court. And the
king said, Let him come in.
6 So Ha'man came in. And the king said unto

him, What shall be done unto the man whom
the king delighteth to honour? Now Ha'man
thought in his heart, To whom would the king
delight to do honour more than to myself?
7 And Ha'man answered the king, For the
man whom the king delighteth to honour,
8 Let the royal apparel be brought which the
king *useth* to wear, and the horse that the king
rideth upon, and the crown royal which is set
upon his head:
9 And let this apparel and horse be delivered
to the hand of one of the king's most noble
princes, that they may array the man *withal*
whom the king delighteth to honour, and bring
him on horseback through the street of the city,
and proclaim before him, Thus shall it be done
to the man whom the king delighteth to honour.
10 Then the king said to Ha'man, Make
haste, *and* take the apparel and the horse, as
thou hast said, and do even so to Mor'de-cai the
Jew, that sitteth at the king's gate: let nothing
fail of all that thou hast spoken.
11 Then took Ha'man the apparel and the
horse, and arrayed Mor'de-cai, and brought him
on horseback through the street of the city, and
proclaimed before him, Thus shall it be done
unto the man whom the king delighteth to honour.
12 ¶ And Mor'de-cai came again to the
king's gate. But Ha'man hasted to his house
mourning, and having his head covered.
13 And Ha'man told Ze'resh his wife and all
his friends every *thing* that had befallen him.
Then said his wise men and Ze'resh his wife
unto him, If Mor'de-cai *be* of the seed of the
Jews, before whom thou hast begun to fall, thou
shalt not prevail against him, but shalt surely
fall before him.
14 And while they *were* yet talking with him,
came the king's chamberlains, and hasted to
bring Ha'man unto the banquet that Es'ther had
prepared.

7 SO the king and Ha'man came to banquet
with Es'ther the queen.
2 And the king said again unto Es'ther on the
second day at the banquet of wine, What *is* thy
petition, queen Es'ther? and it shall be granted
thee: and what *is* thy request? and it shall be
performed, *even* to the half of the kingdom.
3 Then Es'ther the queen answered and said,
If I have found favour in thy sight, O king, and
if it please the king, let my life be given me at
my petition, and my people at my request:
4 For we are sold, I and my people, to be destroyed, to be slain, and to perish. But if we had
been sold for bondmen and bondwomen, I had
held my tongue, although the enemy could not
countervail the king's damage.
5 ¶ Then the king A-has-u-e'rus answered
and said unto Es'ther the queen, Who is he, and
where is he, that durst presume in his heart to
do so?
6 And Es'ther said, The adversary and enemy
is this wicked Ha'man. Then Ha'man was afraid
before the king and the queen.
7 ¶ And the king arising from the banquet of
wine in his wrath *went* into the palace garden:
and Ha'man stood up to make request for his
life to Es'ther the queen; for he saw that there
was evil determined against him by the king.
8 Then the king returned out of the palace
garden into the place of the banquet of wine;
and Ha'man was fallen upon the bed whereon
Es'ther *was*. Then said the king, Will he force
the queen also before me in the house? As the
word went out of the king's mouth, they covered Ha'man's face.
9 And Har-bo'nah, one of the chamberlains,
said before the king, Behold also, the gallows
fifty cubits high, which Ha'man had made for
Mor'de-cai, who had spoken good for the king,
standeth in the house of Ha'man. Then the king
said, Hang him thereon.
10 So they hanged Ha'man on the gallows
that he had prepared for Mor'de-cai. Then was
the king's wrath pacified.

8 ON that day did the king A-has-u-e'rus
give the house of Ha'man the Jews' enemy
unto Es'ther the queen. And Mor'de-cai came
before the king; for Es'ther had told what he
was unto her.
2 And the king took off his ring, which he
had taken from Ha'man, and gave it unto Mor'-
de-cai. And Es'ther set Mor'de-cai over the
house of Ha'man.
3 ¶ And Es'ther spake yet again before the
king, and fell down at his feet, and besought
him with tears to put away the mischief of Ha'-
man the A'gag-ite, and his device that he had
devised against the Jews.
4 Then the king held out the golden sceptre
toward Es'ther. So Es'ther arose, and stood before the king,
5 And said, If it please the king, and if I have
found favour in his sight, and the thing *seem*
right before the king, and I *be* pleasing in his
eyes, let it be written to reverse the letters devised by Ha'man the son of Ham-med'a-tha the
A'gag-ite, which he wrote to destroy the Jews
which *are* in all the king's provinces:
6 For how can I endure to see the evil that
shall come unto my people? or how can I endure to see the destruction of my kindred?
7 ¶ Then the king A-has-u-e'rus said unto
Es'ther the queen and to Mor'de-cai the Jew,
Behold, I have given Es'ther the house of Ha'-
man, and him they have hanged upon the gallows, because he laid his hand upon the Jews.
8 Write ye also for the Jews, as it liketh you,
in the king's name, and seal *it* with the king's
ring: for the writing which is written in the
king's name, and sealed with the king's ring,
may no man reverse.
9 Then were the king's scribes called at that
time in the third month, that *is*, the month Si'-
van, on the three and twentieth *day* thereof;
and it was written according to all that Mor'de-
cai commanded unto the Jews, and to the lieutenants, and the deputies and rulers of the provinces which *are* from Ind'ia unto E-thi-o'pi-a, an
hundred twenty and seven provinces, unto every province according to the writing thereof,
and unto every people after their language, and
to the Jews according to their writing, and according to their language.
10 And he wrote in the king A-has-u-e'rus'
name, and sealed *it* with the king's ring, and
sent letters by posts on horseback, *and* riders
on mules, camels, *and* young dromedaries:
11 Wherein the king granted the Jews which
were in every city to gather themselves together, and to stand for their life, to destroy, to
slay, and to cause to perish, all the power of the
people and province that would assault them,
both little ones and women, and *to take* the
spoil of them for a prey,
12 Upon one day in all the provinces of king
A-has-u-e'rus, *namely*, upon the thirteenth *day*
of the twelfth month, which *is* the month A'dar.
13 The copy of the writing for a commandment to be given in every province *was* pub-

lished unto all people, and that the Jews should be ready against that day to avenge themselves on their enemies.

14 *So* the posts that rode upon mules *and* camels went out, being hastened and pressed on by the king's commandment. And the decree was given at Shu'shan the palace.

15 ¶ And Mor'de-cai went out from the presence of the king in royal apparel of blue and white, and with a great crown of gold, and with a garment of fine linen and purple: and the city of Shu'shan rejoiced and was glad.

16 The Jews had light, and gladness, and joy, and honour.

17 And in every province, and in every city, whithersoever the king's commandment and his decree came, the Jews had joy and gladness, a feast and a good day. And many of the people of the land became Jews; for the fear of the Jews fell upon them.

9 NOW in the twelfth month, that *is*, the month A'dar, on the thirteenth day of the same, when the king's commandment and his decree drew near to be put in execution, in the day that the enemies of the Jews hoped to have power over them, (though it was turned to the contrary, that the Jews had rule over them that hated them;)

2 The Jews gathered themselves together in their cities throughout all the provinces of the king A-has-u-e'rus, to lay hand on such as sought their hurt: and no man could withstand them; for the fear of them fell upon all people.

3 And all the rulers of the provinces, and the lieutenants, and the deputies, and officers of the king, helped the Jews; because the fear of Mor'de-cai fell upon them.

4 For Mor'de-cai *was* great in the king's house, and his fame went out throughout all the provinces: for this man Mor'de-cai waxed greater and greater.

5 Thus the Jews smote all their enemies with the stroke of the sword, and slaughter, and destruction, and did what they would unto those that hated them.

6 And in Shu'shan the palace the Jews slew and destroyed five hundred men.

7 And Par-shan'da-tha, and Dal'phon and As'pa-tha,

8 And Por'a-tha, and Ad-a-li'a, and A-rid'a-tha,

9 And Par-mash'ta, and A-ris'a-i, and A-rid'a-i, and Va-jez'a-tha,

10 The ten sons of Ha'man the son of Ham-med'a-tha, the enemy of the Jews, slew they; but on the spoil laid they not their hand.

11 On that day the number of those that were slain in Shu'shan the palace was brought before the king.

12 ¶ And the king said unto Es'ther the queen, The Jews have slain and destroyed five hundred men in Shu'shan the palace, and the ten sons of Ha'man; what have they done in the rest of the king's provinces? now what *is* thy petition? and it shall be granted thee: or what *is* thy request further? and it shall be done.

13 Then said Es'ther, If it please the king, let it be granted to the Jews which *are* in Shu'shan to do to morrow also according unto this day's decree, and let Ha'man's ten sons be hanged upon the gallows.

14 And the king commanded it so to be done: and the decree was given at Shu'shan; and they hanged Ha'man's ten sons.

15 For the Jews that *were* in Shu'shan gathered themselves together on the fourteenth day also of the month A'dar, and slew three hundred men at Shu'shan; but on the prey they laid not their hand.

16 But the other Jews that *were* in the king's provinces gathered themselves together, and stood for their lives, and had rest from their enemies, and slew of their foes seventy and five thousand, but they laid not their hands on the prey,

17 On the thirteenth day of the month A'dar; and on the fourteenth day of the same rested they, and made it a day of feasting and gladness.

18 But the Jews that *were* at Shu'shan assembled together on the thirteenth *day* thereof, and on the fourteenth thereof; and on the fifteenth *day* of the same they rested, and made it a day of feasting and gladness.

19 Therefore the Jews of the villages, that dwelt in the unwalled towns, made the fourteenth day of the month A'dar *a day of* gladness and feasting, and a good day, and of sending portions one to another.

20 ¶ And Mor'de-cai wrote these things, and sent letters unto all the Jews that *were* in all the provinces of the king A-has-u-e'rus, *both* nigh and far,

21 To stablish *this* among them, that they should keep the fourteenth day of the month A'dar, and the fifteenth day of the same, yearly,

22 As the days wherein the Jews rested from their enemies, and the month which was turned unto them from sorrow to joy, and from mourning into a good day: that they should make them days of feasting and joy, and of sending portions one to another, and gifts to the poor.

23 And the Jews undertook to do as they had begun, and as Mor'de-cai had written unto them;

24 Because Ha'man the son of Ham-med'a-tha, the A'gag-ite, the enemy of all the Jews, had devised against the Jews to destroy them, and had cast Pur, that *is*, the lot, to consume them, and to destroy them;

25 But when *Es'ther* came before the king, he commanded by letters that his wicked device, which he devised against the Jews, should return upon his own head, and that he and his sons should be hanged on the gallows.

26 Wherefore they called these days Pu'rim after the name of Pur. Therefore for all the words of this letter, and *of that* which they had seen concerning this matter, and which had come unto them,

27 The Jews ordained, and took upon them, and upon their seed, and upon all such as joined themselves unto them, so as it should not fail, that they would keep these two days according to their writing, and according to their *appointed* time every year;

28 And *that* these days *should be* remembered and kept throughout every generation, every family, every province, and every city; and *that* these days of Pu'rim should not fail from among the Jews, nor the memorial of them perish from their seed.

29 Then Es'ther the queen, the daughter of Ab-i-ha'il, and Mor'de-cai the Jew, wrote with all authority, to confirm this second letter of Pu'rim.

30 And he sent the letters unto all the Jews, to the hundred twenty and seven provinces of the kingdom of A-has-u-e'rus, *with* words of peace and truth,

31 To confirm these days of Pu'rim in their times *appointed*, according as Mor'de-cai the Jew and Es'ther the queen had enjoined them,

and as they had decreed for themselves and for their seed, the matters of the fastings and their cry.

32 And the decree of Es'ther confirmed these matters of Pu'rim; and it was written in the book.

10 AND the king A-has-u-e'rus laid a tribute upon the land, and *upon* the isles of the sea.

2 And all the acts of his power and of his might, and the declaration of the greatness of Mor'de-cai, whereunto the king advanced him, *are* they not written in the book of the chronicles of the kings of Me'di-a and Per'sia?

3 For Mor'de-cai the Jew *was* next unto king A-has-u-e'rus, and great among the Jews, and accepted of the multitude of his brethren, seeking the wealth of his people, and speaking peace to all his seed.

THE BOOK OF

JOB

1 THERE was a man in the land of Uz, whose name *was* Job: and that man was perfect and upright, and one that feared God, and eschewed evil.

2 And there were born unto him seven sons and three daughters.

3 His substance also was seven thousand sheep, and three thousand camels, and five hundred yoke of oxen, and five hundred she asses, and a very great household; so that this man was the greatest of all the men of the east.

4 And his sons went and feasted *in their* houses, every one his day; and sent and called for their three sisters to eat and to drink with them.

5 And it was so, when the days of *their* feasting were gone about, that Job sent and sanctified them, and rose up early in the morning, and offered burnt offerings *according* to the number of them all: for Job said, It may be that my sons have sinned, and cursed God in their hearts. Thus did Job continually.

6 ¶ Now there was a day when the sons of God came to present themselves before the LORD, and Sa'tan came also among them.

7 And the LORD said unto Sa'tan, Whence comest thou? Then Sa'tan answered the LORD, and said, From going to and fro in the earth, and from walking up and down in it.

8 And the LORD said unto Sa'tan, Hast thou considered my servant Job, that *there is* none like him in the earth, a perfect and an upright man, one that feareth God, and escheweth evil?

9 Then Sa'tan answered the LORD, and said, Doth Job fear God for nought?

10 Hast not thou made an hedge about him, and about his house, and about all that he hath on every side? thou hast blessed the work of his hands, and his substance is increased in the land.

11 But put forth thine hand now, and touch all that he hath, and he will curse thee to thy face.

12 And the LORD said unto Sa'tan, Behold, all that he hath *is* in thy power; only upon himself put not forth thine hand. So Sa'tan went forth from the presence of the LORD.

13 ¶ And there was a day when his sons and his daughters *were* eating and drinking wine in their eldest brother's house:

14 And there came a messenger unto Job, and said, The oxen were plowing, and the asses feeding beside them:

15 And the Sa-be'ans fell *upon them,* and took them away; yea, they have slain the servants with the edge of the sword; and I only am escaped alone to tell thee.

16 While he *was* yet speaking, there came also another, and said, The fire of God is fallen from heaven, and hath burned up the sheep, and the servants, and consumed them; and I only am escaped alone to tell thee.

17 While he *was* yet speaking, there came also another, and said, The Chal-de'ans made out three bands, and fell upon the camels, and have carried them away, yea, and slain the servants with the edge of the sword; and I only am escaped alone to tell thee.

18 While he *was* yet speaking, there came also another, and said, Thy sons and thy daughters *were* eating and drinking wine in their eldest brother's house:

19 And, behold, there came a great wind from the wilderness, and smote the four corners of the house, and it fell upon the young men, and they are dead; and I only am escaped alone to tell thee.

20 Then Job arose, and rent his mantle, and shaved his head, and fell down upon the ground, and worshipped,

21 And said, Naked came I out of my mother's womb, and naked shall I return thither: the LORD gave, and the LORD hath taken away; blessed be the name of the LORD.

22 In all this Job sinned not, nor charged God foolishly.

2 AGAIN there was a day when the sons of God came to present themselves before the LORD, and Sa'tan came also among them to present himself before the LORD.

2 And the LORD said unto Sa'tan, From whence comest thou? And Sa'tan answered the LORD, and said, From going to and fro in the earth, and from walking up and down in it.

3 And the LORD said unto Sa'tan, Hast thou considered my servant Job, that *there is* none like him in the earth, a perfect and an upright man, one that feareth God, and escheweth evil? and still he holdeth fast his integrity, although thou movedst me against him, to destroy him without cause.

4 And Sa'tan answered the LORD, and said, Skin for skin, yea, all that a man hath will he give for his life.

5 But put forth thine hand now, and touch his bone and his flesh, and he will curse thee to thy face.

6 And the LORD said unto Sa'tan, Behold, he *is* in thine hand; but save his life.

7 ¶ So went Sa'tan forth from the presence of the LORD, and smote Job with sore boils from the sole of his foot unto his crown.

8 And he took him a potsherd to scrape himself withal; and he sat down among the ashes.

9 ¶ Then said his wife unto him, Dost thou still retain thine integrity? curse God, and die.

10 But he said unto her, Thou speakest as

one of the foolish women speaketh. What? shall we receive good at the hand of God, and shall we not receive evil? In all this did not Job sin with his lips.

11 ¶ Now when Job's three friends heard of all this evil that was come upon him, they came every one from his own place; El′i-phaz the Te′man-ite, and Bil′dad the Shu′hite, and Zo′phar the Na′a-math-ite: for they had made an appointment together to come to mourn with him and to comfort him.

12 And when they lifted up their eyes afar off, and knew him not, they lifted up their voice, and wept; and they rent every one his mantle, and sprinkled dust upon their heads toward heaven.

13 So they sat down with him upon the ground seven days and seven nights, and none spake a word unto him: for they saw that *his* grief was very great.

3 AFTER this opened Job his mouth, and cursed his day.

2 And Job spake, and said,

3 Let the day perish wherein I was born, and the night *in which* it was said, There is a man child conceived.

4 Let that day be darkness; let not God regard it from above, neither let the light shine upon it.

5 Let darkness and the shadow of death stain it; let a cloud dwell upon it; let the blackness of the day terrify it.

6 *As for* that night, let darkness seize upon it; let it not be joined unto the days of the year, let it not come into the number of the months.

7 Lo, let that night be solitary, let no joyful voice come therein.

8 Let them curse it that curse the day, who are ready to raise up their mourning.

9 Let the stars of the twilight thereof be dark; let it look for light, but *have* none; neither let it see the dawning of the day:

10 Because it shut not up the doors of my *mother's* womb, nor hid sorrow from mine eyes.

11 Why died I not from the womb? *why* did I *not* give up the ghost when I came out of the belly?

12 Why did the knees prevent me? or why the breasts that I should suck?

13 For now should I have lain still and been quiet, I should have slept: then had I been at rest,

14 With kings and counsellors of the earth, which built desolate places for themselves;

15 Or with princes that had gold, who filled their houses with silver:

16 Or as an hidden untimely birth I had not been; as infants *which* never saw light.

17 There the wicked cease *from* troubling; and there the weary be at rest.

18 *There* the prisoners rest together; they hear not the voice of the oppressor.

19 The small and great are there; and the servant *is* free from his master.

20 Wherefore is light given to him that is in misery, and life unto the bitter *in* soul;

21 Which long for death, but it *cometh* not; and dig for it more than for hid treasures;

22 Which rejoice exceedingly, *and* are glad, when they can find the grave?

23 *Why is light given* to a man whose way is hid, and whom God hath hedged in?

24 For my sighing cometh before I eat, and my roarings are poured out like the waters.

25 For the thing which I greatly feared is come upon me, and that which I was afraid of is come unto me.

26 I was not in safety, neither had I rest, neither was I quiet; yet trouble came.

4 THEN El′i-phaz the Te′man-ite answered and said,

2 *If* we assay to commune with thee, wilt thou be grieved? but who can withhold himself from speaking?

3 Behold, thou hast instructed many, and thou hast strengthened the weak hands.

4 Thy words have upholden him that was falling, and thou hast strengthened the feeble knees.

5 But now it is come upon thee, and thou faintest; it toucheth thee, and thou art troubled.

6 *Is* not *this* thy fear, thy confidence, thy hope, and the uprightness of thy ways?

7 Remember, I pray thee, who *ever* perished, being innocent? or where were the righteous cut off?

8 Even as I have seen, they that plow iniquity, and sow wickedness, reap the same.

9 By the blast of God they perish, and by the breath of his nostrils are they consumed.

10 The roaring of the lion, and the voice of the fierce lion, and the teeth of the young lions, are broken.

11 The old lion perisheth for lack of prey, and the stout lion's whelps are scattered abroad.

12 Now a thing was secretly brought to me, and mine ear received a little thereof.

13 In thoughts from the visions of the night, when deep sleep falleth on men,

14 Fear came upon me, and trembling, which made all my bones to shake.

15 Then a spirit passed before my face; the hair of my flesh stood up:

16 It stood still, but I could not discern the form thereof: an image *was* before mine eyes, *there was* silence, and I heard a voice, *saying,*

17 Shall mortal man be more just than God? shall a man be more pure than his maker?

18 Behold, he put no trust in his servants; and his angels he charged with folly:

19 How much less *in* them that dwell in houses of clay, whose foundation *is* in the dust, *which* are crushed before the moth?

20 They are destroyed from morning to evening: they perish for ever without any regarding *it.*

21 Doth not their excellency *which is* in them go away? they die, even without wisdom.

5 CALL now, if there be any that will answer thee; and to which of the saints wilt thou turn?

2 For wrath killeth the foolish man, and envy slayeth the silly one.

3 I have seen the foolish taking root: but suddenly I cursed his habitation.

4 His children are far from safety, and they are crushed in the gate, neither *is there* any to deliver *them.*

5 Whose harvest the hungry eateth up, and taketh it even out of the thorns, and the robber swalloweth up their substance.

6 Although affliction cometh not forth of the dust, neither doth trouble spring out of the ground;

7 Yet man is born unto trouble, as the sparks fly upward.

8 I would seek unto God, and unto God would I commit my cause:

9 Which doeth great things and unsearchable; marvellous things without number:

10 Who giveth rain upon the earth, and sendeth waters upon the fields:
11 To set up on high those that be low; that those which mourn may be exalted to safety.
12 He disappointeth the devices of the crafty, so that their hands cannot perform *their* enterprise.
13 He taketh the wise in their own craftiness: and the counsel of the froward is carried headlong.
14 They meet with darkness in the daytime, and grope in the noonday as in the night.
15 But he saveth the poor from the sword, from their mouth, and from the hand of the mighty.
16 So the poor hath hope, and iniquity stoppeth her mouth.
17 Behold, happy *is* the man whom God correcteth: therefore despise not thou the chastening of the Almighty:
18 For he maketh sore, and bindeth up: he woundeth, and his hands make whole.
19 He shall deliver thee in six troubles: yea, in seven there shall no evil touch thee.
20 In famine he shall redeem thee from death: and in war from the power of the sword.
21 Thou shalt be hid from the scourge of the tongue: neither shalt thou be afraid of destruction when it cometh.
22 At destruction and famine thou shalt laugh: neither shalt thou be afraid of the beasts of the earth.
23 For thou shalt be in league with the stones of the field: and the beasts of the field shall be at peace with thee.
24 And thou shalt know that thy tabernacle *shall be* in peace; and thou shalt visit thy habitation, and shalt not sin.
25 Thou shalt know also that thy seed *shall be* great, and thine offspring as the grass of the earth.
26 Thou shalt come to *thy* grave in a full age, like as a shock of corn cometh in in his season.
27 Lo this, we have searched it, so it *is;* hear it, and know thou *it* for thy good.

6 BUT Job answered and said,
2 Oh that my grief were throughly weighed, and my calamity laid in the balances together!
3 For now it would be heavier than the sand of the sea: therefore my words are swallowed up.
4 For the arrows of the Almighty *are* within me, the poison whereof drinketh up my spirit: the terrors of God do set themselves in array against me.
5 Doth the wild ass bray when he hath grass? or loweth the ox over his fodder?
6 Can that which is unsavoury be eaten without salt? or is there *any* taste in the white of an egg?
7 The things *that* my soul refused to touch *are* as my sorrowful meat.
8 Oh that I might have my request; and that God would grant *me* the thing that I long for!
9 Even that it would please God to destroy me; that he would let loose his hand, and cut me off!
10 Then should I yet have comfort; yea, I would harden myself in sorrow: let him not spare; for I have not concealed the words of the Holy One.
11 What *is* my strength, that I should hope? and what *is* mine end, that I should prolong my life?
12 *Is* my strength the strength of stones? or *is* my flesh of brass?
13 *Is* not my help in me? and is wisdom driven quite from me?
14 To him that is afflicted pity *should be shewed* from his friend; but he forsaketh the fear of the Almighty.
15 My brethren have dealt deceitfully as a brook, *and* as the stream of brooks they pass away;
16 Which are blackish by reason of the ice, *and* wherein the snow is hid:
17 What time they wax warm, they vanish: when it is hot, they are consumed out of their place.
18 The paths of their way are turned aside; they go to nothing, and perish.
19 The troops of Te′ma looked, the companies of She′ba waited for them.
20 They were confounded because they had hoped; they came thither, and were ashamed.
21 For now ye are nothing; ye see *my* casting down, and are afraid.
22 Did I say, Bring unto me? or, Give a reward for me of your substance?
23 Or, Deliver me from the enemy's hand? or, Redeem me from the hand of the mighty?
24 Teach me, and I will hold my tongue: and cause me to understand wherein I have erred.
25 How forcible are right words! but what doth your arguing reprove?
26 Do ye imagine to reprove words, and the speeches of one that is desperate, *which are* as wind?
27 Yea, ye overwhelm the fatherless, and ye dig *a pit* for your friend.
28 Now therefore be content, look upon me; for *it is* evident unto you if I lie.
29 Return, I pray you, let it not be iniquity; yea, return again, my righteousness *is* in it.
30 Is there iniquity in my tongue? cannot my taste discern perverse things?

7 *IS there* not an appointed time to man upon earth? *are not* his days also like the days of an hireling?
2 As a servant earnestly desireth the shadow, and as an hireling looketh for *the reward* of his work:
3 So am I made to possess months of vanity, and wearisome nights are appointed to me.
4 When I lie down, I say, When shall I arise, and the night be gone? and I am full of tossings to and fro unto the dawning of the day.
5 My flesh is clothed with worms and clods of dust; my skin is broken, and become loathsome.
6 My days are swifter than a weaver's shuttle, and are spent without hope.
7 O remember that my life *is* wind: mine eye shall no more see good.
8 The eye of him that hath seen me shall see me no *more*: thine eyes *are* upon me, and I *am* not.
9 *As* the cloud is consumed and vanisheth away: so he that goeth down to the grave shall come up no *more*.
10 He shall return no more to his house, neither shall his place know him any more.
11 Therefore I will not refrain my mouth; I will speak in the anguish of my spirit; I will complain in the bitterness of my soul.
12 *Am* I a sea, or a whale, that thou settest a watch over me?
13 When I say, My bed shall comfort me, my couch shall ease my complaint;

14 Then thou scarest me with dreams, and terrifiest me through visions:

15 So that my soul chooseth strangling, *and* death rather than my life.

16 I loathe *it*: I would not live alway: let me alone; for my days *are* vanity.

17 What *is* man, that thou shouldest magnify him? and that thou shouldest set thine heart upon him?

18 And *that* thou shouldest visit him every morning, *and* try him every moment?

19 How long wilt thou not depart from me, nor let me alone till I swallow down my spittle?

20 I have sinned; what shall I do unto thee, O thou preserver of men? why hast thou set me as a mark against thee, so that I am a burden to myself?

21 And why dost thou not pardon my transgression, and take away mine iniquity? for now shall I sleep in the dust; and thou shalt seek me in the morning, but I *shall* not *be*.

8 THEN answered Bil'dad the Shu'hite, and said,

2 How long wilt thou speak these *things?* and *how long shall* the words of thy mouth *be like* a strong wind?

3 Doth God pervert judgment? or doth the Almighty pervert justice?

4 If thy children have sinned against him, and he have cast them away for their transgression;

5 If thou wouldest seek unto God betimes, and make thy supplication to the Almighty;

6 If thou *wert* pure and upright; surely now he would awake for thee, and make the habitation of thy righteousness prosperous.

7 Though thy beginning was small, yet thy latter end should greatly increase.

8 For enquire, I pray thee, of the former age, and prepare thyself to the search of their fathers:

9 (For we *are but of* yesterday, and know nothing, because our days upon earth *are* a shadow:)

10 Shall not they teach thee, *and* tell thee, and utter words out of their heart?

11 Can the rush grow up without mire? can the flag grow without water?

12 Whilst it *is* yet in his greenness, *and* not cut down, it withereth before any *other* herb.

13 So *are* the paths of all that forget God; and the hypocrite's hope shall perish:

14 Whose hope shall be cut off, and whose trust *shall be* a spider's web.

15 He shall lean upon his house, but it shall not stand: he shall hold it fast, but it shall not endure.

16 He *is* green before the sun, and his branch shooteth forth in his garden.

17 His roots are wrapped about the heap, *and* seeth the place of stones.

18 If he destroy him from his place, then *it* shall deny him, *saying*, I have not seen thee.

19 Behold, this *is* the joy of his way, and out of the earth shall others grow.

20 Behold, God will not cast away a perfect *man*, neither will he help the evildoers:

21 Till he fill thy mouth with laughing, and thy lips with rejoicing.

22 They that hate thee shall be clothed with shame; and the dwelling place of the wicked shall come to nought.

9 THEN Job answered and said,

2 I know *it is* so of a truth: but how should man be just with God?

3 If he will contend with him, he cannot answer him one of a thousand.

4 *He is* wise in heart, and mighty in strength: who hath hardened *himself* against him, and hath prospered?

5 Which removeth the mountains, and they know not: which overturneth them in his anger.

6 Which shaketh the earth out of her place, and the pillars thereof tremble.

7 Which commandeth the sun, and it riseth not; and sealeth up the stars.

8 Which alone spreadeth out the heavens, and treadeth upon the waves of the sea.

9 Which maketh Arc-tu'rus, O-ri'on, and Ple'-ia-des, and the chambers of the south.

10 Which doeth great things past finding out; yea, and wonders without number.

11 Lo, he goeth by me, and I see *him* not: he passeth on also, but I perceive him not.

12 Behold, he taketh away, who can hinder him? who will say unto him, What doest thou?

13 *If* God will not withdraw his anger, the proud helpers do stoop under him.

14 How much less shall I answer him, *and* choose out my words *to reason* with him?

15 Whom, though I were righteous, *yet* would I not answer, *but* I would make supplication to my judge.

16 If I had called, and he had answered me; *yet* would I not believe that he had hearkened unto my voice.

17 For he breaketh me with a tempest, and multiplieth my wounds without cause.

18 He will not suffer me to take my breath, but filleth me with bitterness.

19 If *I speak* of strength, lo, *he is* strong: and if of judgment, who shall set me a time *to plead?*

20 If I justify myself, mine own mouth shall condemn me: *if I say,* I *am* perfect, it shall also prove me perverse.

21 *Though* I *were* perfect, *yet* would I not know my soul: I would despise my life.

22 This *is* one *thing*, therefore I said *it*, He destroyeth the perfect and the wicked.

23 If the scourge slay suddenly, he will laugh at the trial of the innocent.

24 The earth is given into the hand of the wicked: he covereth the faces of the judges thereof; if not, where, *and* who *is* he?

25 Now my days are swifter than a post: they flee away, they see no good.

26 They are passed away as the swift ships: as the eagle *that* hasteth to the prey.

27 If I say, I will forget my complaint, I will leave off my heaviness, and comfort *myself*:

28 I am afraid of all my sorrows, I know that thou wilt not hold me innocent.

29 *If* I be wicked, why then labour I in vain?

30 If I wash myself with snow water, and make my hands never so clean;

31 Yet shalt thou plunge me in the ditch, and mine own clothes shall abhor me.

32 For *he is* not a man, as I *am, that* I should answer him, *and* we should come together in judgment.

33 Neither is there any daysman betwixt us, *that* might lay his hand upon us both.

34 Let him take his rod away from me, and let not his fear terrify me:

35 *Then* would I speak, and not fear him; but *it is* not so with me.

10 MY soul is weary of my life; I will leave my complaint upon myself; I will speak in the bitterness of my soul.

2 I will say unto God, Do not condemn me; shew me wherefore thou contendest with me.

3 *Is it* good unto thee that thou shouldest oppress, that thou shouldest despise the work of thine hands, and shine upon the counsel of the wicked?

4 Hast thou eyes of flesh? or seest thou as man seeth?

5 *Are* thy days as the days of man? *are* thy years as man's days,

6 That thou enquirest after mine iniquity, and searchest after my sin?

7 Thou knowest that I am not wicked; and *there is* none that can deliver out of thine hand.

8 Thine hands have made me and fashioned me together round about; yet thou dost destroy me.

9 Remember, I beseech thee, that thou hast made me as the clay; and wilt thou bring me into dust again?

10 Hast thou not poured me out as milk, and curdled me like cheese?

11 Thou hast clothed me with skin and flesh, and hast fenced me with bones and sinews.

12 Thou hast granted me life and favour, and thy visitation hath preserved my spirit.

13 And these *things* hast thou hid in thine heart: I know that this *is* with thee.

14 If I sin, then thou markest me, and thou wilt not acquit me from mine iniquity.

15 If I be wicked, woe unto me; and *if* I be righteous, *yet* will I not lift up my head. *I am* full of confusion; therefore see thou mine affliction;

16 For it increaseth. Thou huntest me as a fierce lion: and again thou shewest thyself marvellous upon me.

17 Thou renewest thy witnesses against me, and increasest thine indignation upon me; changes and war *are* against me.

18 Wherefore then hast thou brought me forth out of the womb? Oh that I had given up the ghost, and no eye had seen me!

19 I should have been as though I had not been; I should have been carried from the womb to the grave.

20 *Are* not my days few? cease *then, and* let me alone, that I may take comfort a little,

21 Before I go *whence* I shall not return, *even* to the land of darkness and the shadow of death;

22 A land of darkness, as darkness *itself; and* of the shadow of death, without any order, and *where* the light *is* as darkness.

11 THEN answered Zo'phar the Na'a-math-ite, and said,

2 Should not the multitude of words be answered? and should a man full of talk be justified?

3 Should thy lies make men hold their peace? and when thou mockest, shall no man make thee ashamed?

4 For thou hast said, My doctrine *is* pure, and I am clean in thine eyes.

5 But oh that God would speak, and open his lips against thee;

6 And that he would shew thee the secrets of wisdom, that *they are* double to that which is! Know therefore that God exacteth of thee *less* than thine iniquity *deserveth.*

7 Canst thou by searching find out God? canst thou find out the Almighty unto perfection?

8 *It is* as high as heaven; what canst thou do? deeper than hell; what canst thou know?

9 The measure thereof *is* longer than the earth, and broader than the sea.

10 If he cut off, and shut up, or gather together, then who can hinder him?

11 For he knoweth vain men: he seeth wickedness also; will he not then consider *it?*

12 For vain man would be wise, though man be born *like* a wild ass's colt.

13 If thou prepare thine heart, and stretch out thine hands toward him;

14 If iniquity *be* in thine hand, put it far away, and let not wickedness dwell in thy tabernacles.

15 For then shalt thou lift up thy face without spot; yea, thou shalt be stedfast, and shalt not fear:

16 Because thou shalt forget *thy* misery, *and* remember *it* as waters *that* pass away:

17 And *thine* age shall be clearer than the noonday; thou shalt shine forth, thou shalt be as the morning.

18 And thou shalt be secure, because there is hope; yea, thou shalt dig *about thee, and* thou shalt take thy rest in safety.

19 Also thou shalt lie down, and none shall make *thee* afraid; yea, many shall make suit unto thee.

20 But the eyes of the wicked shall fail, and they shall not escape, and their hope *shall be as* the giving up of the ghost.

12 AND Job answered and said,

2 No doubt but ye *are* the people, and wisdom shall die with you.

3 But I have understanding as well as you; I *am* not inferior to you: yea, who knoweth not such things as these?

4 I am *as* one mocked of his neighbour, who calleth upon God, and he answereth him: the just upright *man is* laughed to scorn.

5 He that is ready to slip with *his* feet *is as* a lamp despised in the thought of him that is at ease.

6 The tabernacles of robbers prosper, and they that provoke God are secure; into whose hand God bringeth *abundantly.*

7 But ask now the beasts, and they shall teach thee; and the fowls of the air, and they shall tell thee:

8 Or speak to the earth, and it shall teach thee: and the fishes of the sea shall declare unto thee.

9 Who knoweth not in all these that the hand of the LORD hath wrought this?

10 In whose hand *is* the soul of every living thing, and the breath of all mankind.

11 Doth not the ear try words? and the mouth taste his meat?

12 With the ancient *is* wisdom; and in length of days understanding.

13 With him *is* wisdom and strength, he hath counsel and understanding.

14 Behold, he breaketh down, and it cannot be built again: he shutteth up a man, and there can be no opening.

15 Behold, he withholdeth the waters, and they dry up: also he sendeth them out, and they overturn the earth.

16 With him *is* strength and wisdom: the deceived and the deceiver *are* his.

17 He leadeth counsellors away spoiled, and maketh the judges fools.

18 He looseth the bond of kings, and girdeth their loins with a girdle.

19 He leadeth princes away spoiled, and overthroweth the mighty.

20 He removeth away the speech of the

trusty, and taketh away the understanding of the aged.

21 He poureth contempt upon princes, and weakeneth the strength of the mighty.

22 He discovereth deep things out of darkness,and bringeth out to light the shadow of death.

23 He increaseth the nations, and destroyeth them: he enlargeth the nations, and straiteneth them *again*.

24 He taketh away the heart of the chief of the people of the earth, and causeth them to wander in a wilderness *where there is* no way.

25 They grope in the dark without light, and he maketh them to stagger like *a* drunken *man*.

13

LO, mine eye hath seen all *this*, mine ear hath heard and understood it.

2 What ye know, *the same* do I know also: I *am* not inferior unto you.

3 Surely I would speak to the Almighty, and I desire to reason with God.

4 But ye *are* forgers of lies, ye *are* all physicians of no value.

5 O that ye would altogether hold your peace! and it should be your wisdom.

6 Hear now my reasoning, and hearken to the pleadings of my lips.

7 Will ye speak wickedly for God? and talk deceitfully for him?

8 Will ye accept his person? will ye contend for God?

9 Is it good that he should search you out? or as one man mocketh another, do ye *so* mock him?

10 He will surely reprove you, if ye do secretly accept persons.

11 Shall not his excellency make you afraid? and his dread fall upon you?

12 Your remembrances *are* like unto ashes, your bodies to bodies of clay.

13 Hold your peace, let me alone, that I may speak, and let come on me what *will*.

14 Wherefore do I take my flesh in my teeth, and put my life in mine hand?

15 Though he slay me, yet will I trust in him: but I will maintain mine own ways before him.

16 He also *shall be* my salvation: for an hypocrite shall not come before him.

17 Hear diligently my speech, and my declaration with your ears.

18 Behold now, I have ordered *my* cause; I know that I shall be justified.

19 Who *is* he *that* will plead with me? for now, if I hold my tongue, I shall give up the ghost.

20 Only do not two *things* unto me: then will I not hide myself from thee.

21 Withdraw thine hand far from me: and let not thy dread make me afraid.

22 Then call thou, and I will answer: or let me speak, and answer thou me.

23 How many *are* mine iniquities and sins? make me to know my transgression and my sin.

24 Wherefore hidest thou thy face, and holdest me for thine enemy?

25 Wilt thou break a leaf driven to and fro? and wilt thou pursue the dry stubble?

26 For thou writest bitter things against me, and makest me to possess the iniquities of my youth.

27 Thou puttest my feet also in the stocks, and lookest narrowly unto all my paths; thou settest a print upon the heels of my feet.

28 And he, as a rotten thing, consumeth, as a garment that is moth eaten.

14

MAN *that is* born of a woman *is* of few days, and full of trouble.

2 He cometh forth like a flower, and is cut down: he fleeth also as a shadow, and continueth not.

3 And dost thou open thine eyes upon such an one, and bringest me into judgment with thee?

4 Who can bring a clean *thing* out of an unclean? not one.

5 Seeing his days *are* determined, the number of his months *are* with thee, thou hast appointed his bounds that he cannot pass:

6 Turn from him, that he may rest, till he shall accomplish, as an hireling, his day.

7 For there is hope of a tree, if it be cut down, that it will sprout again, and that the tender branch thereof will not cease.

8 Though the root thereof wax old in the earth, and the stock thereof die in the ground;

9 *Yet* through the scent of water it will bud, and bring forth boughs like a plant.

10 But man dieth, and wasteth away: yea, man giveth up the ghost, and where *is* he?

11 *As* the waters fail from the sea, and the flood decayeth and drieth up:

12 So man lieth down, and riseth not: till the heavens *be* no more, they shall not awake, nor be raised out of their sleep.

13 O that thou wouldest hide me in the grave, that thou wouldest keep me secret, until thy wrath be past, that thou wouldest appoint me a set time, and remember me!

14 If a man die, shall he live *again?* all the days of my appointed time will I wait, till my change come.

15 Thou shalt call, and I will answer thee: thou wilt have a desire to the work of thine hands.

16 For now thou numberest my steps: dost thou not watch over my sin?

17 My transgression *is* sealed up in a bag, and thou sewest up mine iniquity.

18 And surely the mountain falling cometh to nought, and the rock is removed out of his place.

19 The waters wear the stones: thou washest away the things which grow *out* of the dust of the earth; and thou destroyest the hope of man.

20 Thou prevailest for ever against him, and he passeth: thou changest his countenance, and sendest him away.

21 His sons come to honour, and he knoweth *it* not; and they are brought low, but he perceiveth *it* not of them.

22 But his flesh upon him shall have pain, and his soul within him shall mourn.

15

THEN answered El'i-phaz the Te'man-ite, and said,

2 Should a wise man utter vain knowledge, and fill his belly with the east wind?

3 Should he reason with unprofitable talk? or with speeches wherewith he can do no good?

4 Yea, thou castest off fear, and restrainest prayer before God.

5 For thy mouth uttereth thine iniquity, and thou choosest the tongue of the crafty.

6 Thine own mouth condemneth thee, and not I; yea, thine own lips testify against thee.

7 *Art* thou the first man *that* was born? or wast thou made before the hills?

8 Hast thou heard the secret of God? and dost thou restrain wisdom to thyself?

9 What knowest thou, that we know not? *what* understandest thou, which *is* not in us?

10 With us *are* both the grayheaded and very aged men, much elder than thy father.
11 *Are* the consolations of God small with thee? is there any secret thing with thee?
12 Why doth thine heart carry thee away? and what do thy eyes wink at,
13 That thou turnest thy spirit against God, and lettest *such* words go out of thy mouth?
14 What *is* man, that he should be clean? and *he which is* born of a woman, that he should be righteous?
15 Behold, he putteth no trust in his saints; yea, the heavens are not clean in his sight.
16 How much more abominable and filthy *is* man, which drinketh iniquity like water?
17 I will shew thee, hear me; and that *which* I have seen I will declare:
18 Which wise men have told from their fathers, and have not hid *it:*
19 Unto whom alone the earth was given, and no stranger passed among them.
20 The wicked man travaileth with pain all *his* days, and the number of years is hidden to the oppressor.
21 A dreadful sound *is* in his ears: in prosperity the destroyer shall come upon him.
22 He believeth not that he shall return out of darkness, and he is waited for of the sword.
23 He wandereth abroad for bread, *saying,* Where *is it?* he knoweth that the day of darkness is ready at his hand.
24 Trouble and anguish shall make him afraid; they shall prevail against him, as a king ready to the battle.
25 For he stretcheth out his hand against God, and strengtheneth himself against the Almighty.
26 He runneth upon him, *even* on *his* neck, upon the thick bosses of his bucklers:
27 Because he covereth his face with his fatness, and maketh collops of fat on *his* flanks.
28 And he dwelleth in desolate cities, *and* in houses which no man inhabiteth, which are ready to become heaps.
29 He shall not be rich, neither shall his substance continue, neither shall he prolong the perfection thereof upon the earth.
30 He shall not depart out of darkness; the flame shall dry up his branches, and by the breath of his mouth shall he go away.
31 Let not him that is deceived trust in vanity: for vanity shall be his recompence.
32 It shall be accomplished before his time, and his branch shall not be green.
33 He shall shake off his unripe grape as the vine, and shall cast off his flower as the olive.
34 For the congregation of hypocrites *shall be* desolate, and fire shall consume the tabernacles of bribery.
35 They conceive mischief, and bring forth vanity, and their belly prepareth deceit.

16 THEN Job answered and said,
2 I have heard many such things: miserable comforters *are* ye all.
3 Shall vain words have an end? or what emboldeneth thee that thou answerest?
4 I also could speak as ye *do:* if your soul were in my soul's stead, I could heap up words against you, and shake mine head at you.
5 *But* I would strengthen you with my mouth, and the moving of my lips should asswage *your grief.*
6 Though I speak, my grief is not asswaged: and *though* I forbear, what am I eased?
7 But now he hath made me weary: thou hast made desolate all my company.
8 And thou hast filled me with wrinkles, *which* is a witness *against me:* and my leanness rising up in me beareth witness to my face.
9 He teareth *me* in his wrath, who hateth me: he gnasheth upon me with his teeth; mine enemy sharpeneth his eyes upon me.
10 They have gaped upon me with their mouth; they have smitten me upon the cheek reproachfully; they have gathered themselves together against me.
11 God hath delivered me to the ungodly, and turned me over into the hands of the wicked.
12 I was at ease, but he hath broken me asunder: he hath also taken *me* by my neck, and shaken me to pieces, and set me up for his mark.
13 His archers compass me round about, he cleaveth my reins asunder, and doth not spare; he poureth out my gall upon the ground.
14 He breaketh me with breach upon breach, he runneth upon me like a giant.
15 I have sewed sackcloth upon my skin, and defiled my horn in the dust.
16 My face is foul with weeping, and on my eyelids *is* the shadow of death;
17 Not for *any* injustice in mine hands: also my prayer *is* pure.
18 O earth, cover not thou my blood, and let my cry have no place.
19 Also now, behold, my witness *is* in heaven, and my record *is* on high.
20 My friends scorn me: *but* mine eye poureth out *tears* unto God.
21 O that one might plead for a man with God, as a man *pleadeth* for his neighbour!
22 When a few years are come, then I shall go the way *whence* I shall not return.

17 MY breath is corrupt, my days are extinct, the graves *are ready* for me.
2 *Are there* not mockers with me? and doth not mine eye continue in their provocation?
3 Lay down now, put me in a surety with thee; who *is* he *that* will strike hands with me?
4 For thou hast hid their heart from understanding: therefore shalt thou not exalt *them.*
5 He that speaketh flattery to *his* friends, even the eyes of his children shall fail.
6 He hath made me also a byword of the people; and aforetime I was as a tabret.
7 Mine eye also is dim by reason of sorrow, and all my members *are* as a shadow.
8 Upright *men* shall be astonied at this, and the innocent shall stir up himself against the hypocrite.
9 The righteous also shall hold on his way, and he that hath clean hands shall be stronger and stronger.
10 But as for you all, do ye return, and come now: for I cannot find *one* wise *man* among you.
11 My days are past, my purposes are broken off, *even* the thoughts of my heart.
12 They change the night into day: the light *is* short because of darkness.
13 If I wait, the grave *is* mine house: I have made my bed in the darkness.
14 I have said to corruption, Thou *art* my father: to the worm, *Thou art* my mother, and my sister.
15 And where *is* now my hope? as for my hope, who shall see it?
16 They shall go down to the bars of the pit, when *our* rest together *is* in the dust.

18 THEN answered Bil'dad the Shu'hite, and said,

2 How long *will it be ere* ye make an end of words? mark, and afterwards we will speak.

3 Wherefore are we counted as beasts, *and* reputed vile in your sight?

4 He teareth himself in his anger: shall the earth be forsaken for thee? and shall the rock be removed out of his place?

5 Yea, the light of the wicked shall be put out, and the spark of his fire shall not shine.

6 The light shall be dark in his tabernacle, and his candle shall be put out with him.

7 The steps of his strength shall be straitened, and his own counsel shall cast him down.

8 For he is cast into a net by his own feet, and he walketh upon a snare.

9 The gin shall take *him* by the heel, *and* the robber shall prevail against him.

10 The snare *is* laid for him in the ground, and a trap for him in the way.

11 Terrors shall make him afraid on every side, and shall drive him to his feet.

12 His strength shall be hungerbitten, and destruction *shall be* ready at his side.

13 It shall devour the strength of his skin: *even* the firstborn of death shall devour his strength.

14 His confidence shall be rooted out of his tabernacle, and it shall bring him to the king of terrors.

15 It shall dwell in his tabernacle, because *it is* none of his: brimstone shall be scattered upon his habitation.

16 His roots shall be dried up beneath, and above shall his branch be cut off.

17 His remembrance shall perish from the earth, and he shall have no name in the street.

18 He shall be driven from light into darkness, and chased out of the world.

19 He shall neither have son nor nephew among his people, nor any remaining in his dwellings.

20 They that come after *him* shall be astonied at his day, as they that went before were affrighted.

21 Surely such *are* the dwellings of the wicked, and this *is* the place *of him that* knoweth not God.

19 THEN Job answered and said,

2 How long will ye vex my soul, and break me in pieces with words?

3 These ten times have ye reproached me: ye are not ashamed *that* ye make yourselves strange to me.

4 And be it indeed *that* I have erred, mine error remaineth with myself.

5 If indeed ye will magnify *yourselves* against me, and plead against me my reproach:

6 Know now that God hath overthrown me, and hath compassed me with his net.

7 Behold, I cry out of wrong, but I am not heard: I cry aloud, but *there is* no judgment.

8 He hath fenced up my way that I cannot pass, and he hath set darkness in my paths.

9 He hath stripped me of my glory, and taken the crown *from* my head.

10 He hath destroyed me on every side, and I am gone: and mine hope hath he removed like a tree.

11 He hath also kindled his wrath against me, and he counteth me unto him as *one of* his enemies.

12 His troops come together, and raise up their way against me, and encamp round about my tabernacle.

13 He hath put my brethren far from me, and mine acquaintance are verily estranged from me.

14 My kinsfolk have failed, and my familiar friends have forgotten me.

15 They that dwell in mine house, and my maids, count me for a stranger: I am an alien in their sight.

16 I called my servant, and he gave *me* no answer; I intreated him with my mouth.

17 My breath is strange to my wife, though I intreated for the children's *sake* of mine own body.

18 Yea, young children despised me; I arose, and they spake against me.

19 All my inward friends abhorred me: and they whom I loved are turned against me.

20 My bone cleaveth to my skin and to my flesh, and I am escaped with the skin of my teeth.

21 Have pity upon me, have pity upon me, O ye my friends; for the hand of God hath touched me.

22 Why do ye persecute me as God, and are not satisfied with my flesh?

23 Oh that my words were now written! oh that they were printed in a book!

24 That they were graven with an iron pen and lead in the rock for ever!

25 For I know *that* my redeemer liveth, and *that* he shall stand at the latter *day* upon the earth:

26 And *though* after my skin *worms* destroy this *body*, yet in my flesh shall I see God:

27 Whom I shall see for myself, and mine eyes shall behold, and not another; *though* my reins be consumed within me.

28 But ye should say, Why persecute we him, seeing the root of the matter is found in me?

29 Be ye afraid of the sword: for wrath *bringeth* the punishments of the sword, that ye may know *there is* a judgment.

20 THEN answered Zo'phar the Na'a-math-ite, and said,

2 Therefore do my thoughts cause me to answer, and for *this* I make haste.

3 I have heard the check of my reproach, and the spirit of my understanding causeth me to answer.

4 Knowest thou *not* this of old, since man was placed upon earth,

5 That the triumphing of the wicked *is* short, and the joy of the hypocrite *but* for a moment?

6 Though his excellency mount up to the heavens, and his head reach unto the clouds;

7 *Yet* he shall perish for ever like his own dung: they which have seen him shall say, Where *is* he?

8 He shall fly away as a dream, and shall not be found: yea, he shall be chased away as a vision of the night.

9 The eye also *which* saw him shall *see him* no more; neither shall his place any more behold him.

10 His children shall seek to please the poor, and his hands shall restore their goods.

11 His bones are full *of the sin* of his youth, which shall lie down with him in the dust.

12 Though wickedness be sweet in his mouth, *though* he hide it under his tongue;

13 *Though* he spare it, and forsake it not; but keep it still within his mouth:

14 *Yet* his meat in his bowels is turned, *it is* the gall of asps within him.

15 He hath swallowed down riches, and he

shall vomit them up again: God shall cast them
out of his belly.
16 He shall suck the poison of asps: the viper's tongue shall slay him.
17 He shall not see the rivers, the floods, the
brooks of honey and butter.
18 That which he laboured for shall he restore, and shall not swallow *it* down: according
to *his* substance *shall* the restitution *be*, and he
shall not rejoice *therein*.
19 Because he hath oppressed *and* hath forsaken the poor; *because* he hath violently taken
away an house which he builded not;
20 Surely he shall not feel quietness in his
belly, he shall not save of that which he desired.
21 There shall none of his meat be left; therefore shall no man look for his goods.
22 In the fulness of his sufficiency he shall be
in straits: every hand of the wicked shall come
upon him.
23 *When* he is about to fill his belly, *God*
shall cast the fury of his wrath upon him, and
shall rain *it* upon him while he is eating.
24 He shall flee from the iron weapon, *and*
the bow of steel shall strike him through.
25 It is drawn, and cometh out of the body;
yea, the glittering sword cometh out of his gall:
terrors *are* upon him.
26 All darkness *shall be* hid in his secret
places: a fire not blown shall consume him; it
shall go ill with him that is left in his tabernacle.
27 The heaven shall reveal his iniquity; and
the earth shall rise up against him.
28 The increase of his house shall depart,
and his goods shall flow away in the day of his
wrath.
29 This *is* the portion of a wicked man from
God, and the heritage appointed unto him by
God.

21

BUT Job answered and said,
2 Hear diligently my speech, and let
this be your consolations.
3 Suffer me that I may speak; and after that I
have spoken, mock on.
4 As for me, *is* my complaint to man? and if
it were so, why should not my spirit be troubled?
5 Mark me, and be astonished, and lay *your*
hand upon *your* mouth.
6 Even when I remember I am afraid, and
trembling taketh hold on my flesh.
7 Wherefore do the wicked live, become old,
yea, are mighty in power?
8 Their seed is established in their sight with
them, and their offspring before their eyes.
9 Their houses *are* safe from fear, neither *is*
the rod of God upon them.
10 Their bull gendereth, and faileth not; their
cow calveth, and casteth not her calf.
11 They send forth their little ones like a
flock, and their children dance.
12 They take the timbrel and harp, and rejoice at the sound of the organ.
13 They spend their days in wealth, and in a
moment go down to the grave.
14 Therefore they say unto God, Depart from
us; for we desire not the knowledge of thy
ways.
15 What *is* the Almighty, that we should
serve him? and what profit should we have, if
we pray unto him?
16 Lo, their good *is* not in their hand: the
counsel of the wicked is far from me.
17 How oft is the candle of the wicked put
out! and *how oft* cometh their destruction upon
them! *God* distributeth sorrows in his anger.
18 They are as stubble before the wind, and
as chaff that the storm carrieth away.
19 God layeth up his iniquity for his children:
he rewardeth him, and he shall know *it*.
20 His eyes shall see his destruction, and he
shall drink of the wrath of the Almighty.
21 For what pleasure *hath* he in his house after him, when the number of his months is cut
off in the midst?
22 Shall *any* teach God knowledge? seeing
he judgeth those that are high.
23 One dieth in his full strength, being
wholly at ease and quiet.
24 His breasts are full of milk, and his bones
are moistened with marrow.
25 And another dieth in the bitterness of his
soul, and never eateth with pleasure.
26 They shall lie down alike in the dust, and
the worms shall cover them.
27 Behold, I know your thoughts, and the devices *which* ye wrongfully imagine against me.
28 For ye say, Where *is* the house of the
prince? and where *are* the dwelling places of
the wicked?
29 Have ye not asked them that go by the
way? and do ye not know their tokens,
30 That the wicked is reserved to the day of
destruction? they shall be brought forth to the
day of wrath.
31 Who shall declare his way to his face? and
who shall repay him *what* he hath done?
32 Yet shall he be brought to the grave, and
shall remain in the tomb.
33 The clods of the valley shall be sweet unto
him, and every man shall draw after him, as
there are innumerable before him.
34 How then comfort ye me in vain, seeing in
your answers there remaineth falsehood?

22

THEN El'i-phaz the Te'man-ite answered and said,
2 Can a man be profitable unto God, as he
that is wise may be profitable unto himself?
3 *Is it* any pleasure to the Almighty, that thou
are righteous? or *is it* gain *to him*, that thou
makest thy ways perfect?
4 Will he reprove thee for fear of thee? will
he enter with thee into judgment?
5 *Is* not thy wickedness great? and thine iniquities infinite?
6 For thou hast taken a pledge from thy
brother for nought, and stripped the naked of
their clothing.
7 Thou hast not given water to the weary to
drink, and thou hast withholden bread from the
hungry.
8 But *as for* the mighty man, he had the
earth; and the honourable man dwelt in it.
9 Thou hast sent widows away empty, and
the arms of the fatherless have been broken.
10 Therefore snares *are* round about thee,
and sudden fear troubleth thee;
11 Or darkness, *that* thou canst not see; and
abundance of waters cover thee.
12 *Is* not God in the height of heaven? and
behold the height of the stars, how high they
are!
13 And thou sayest, How doth God know?
can he judge through the dark cloud?
14 Thick clouds *are* a covering to him, that
he seeth not; and he walketh in the circuit of
heaven.
15 Hast thou marked the old way which
wicked men have trodden?
16 Which were cut down out of time, whose
foundation was overflown with a flood:

17 Which said unto God, Depart from us: and what can the Almighty do for them?

18 Yet he filled their houses with good *things:* but the counsel of the wicked is far from me.

19 The righteous see *it,* and are glad: and the innocent laugh them to scorn.

20 Whereas our substance is not cut down, but the remnant of them the fire consumeth.

21 Acquaint now thyself with him, and be at peace: thereby good shall come unto thee.

22 Receive, I pray thee, the law from his mouth, and lay up his words in thine heart.

23 If thou return to the Almighty, thou shalt be built up, thou shalt put away iniquity far from thy tabernacles.

24 Then shalt thou lay up gold as dust, and the *gold* of O'phir as the stones of the brooks.

25 Yea, the Almighty shall be thy defence, and thou shalt have plenty of silver.

26 For then shalt thou have thy delight in the Almighty, and shalt lift up thy face unto God.

27 Thou shalt make thy prayer unto him, and he shall hear thee, and thou shalt pay thy vows.

28 Thou shalt also decree a thing, and it shall be established unto thee: and the light shall shine upon thy ways.

29 When *men* are cast down, then thou shalt say, *There is* lifting up; and he shall save the humble person.

30 He shall deliver the island of the innocent: and it is delivered by the pureness of thine hands.

23

THEN Job answered and said,

2 Even to day *is* my complaint bitter: my stroke is heavier than my groaning.

3 Oh that I knew where I might find him! *that* I might come *even* to his seat!

4 I would order *my* cause before him, and fill my mouth with arguments.

5 I would know the words *which* he would answer me, and understand what he would say unto me.

6 Will he plead against me with *his* great power? No; but he would put *strength* in me.

7 There the righteous might dispute with him; so should I be delivered for ever from my judge.

8 Behold, I go forward, but he *is* not *there:* and backward, but I cannot perceive him:

9 On the left hand, where he doth work, but I cannot behold *him:* he hideth himself on the right hand, that I cannot see *him:*

10 But he knoweth the way that I take: *when* he hath tried me, I shall come forth as gold.

11 My foot hath held his steps, his way have I kept, and not declined.

12 Neither have I gone back from the commandment of his lips; I have esteemed the words of his mouth more than my necessary *food.*

13 But he *is* in one *mind,* and who can turn him? and *what* his soul desireth, even *that* he doeth.

14 For he performeth *the thing that is* appointed for me: and many such *things are* with him.

15 Therefore am I troubled at his presence: when I consider, I am afraid of him.

16 For God maketh my heart soft and the Almighty troubleth me:

17 Because I was not cut off before the darkness, *neither* hath he covered the darkness from my face.

24

WHY, seeing times are not hidden from the Almighty, do they that know him not see his days?

2 *Some* remove the landmarks; they violently take away flocks, and feed *thereof.*

3 They drive away the ass of the fatherless, they take the widow's ox for a pledge.

4 They turn the needy out of the way: the poor of the earth hide themselves together.

5 Behold, *as* wild asses in the desert, go they forth to their work; rising betimes for a prey: the wilderness *yieldeth* food for them *and* for *their* children.

6 They reap *every one* his corn in the field: and they gather the vintage of the wicked.

7 They cause the naked to lodge without clothing, that *they have* no covering in the cold.

8 They are wet with the showers of the mountains, and embrace the rock for want of a shelter.

9 They pluck the fatherless from the breast, and take a pledge of the poor.

10 They cause *him* to go naked without clothing, and they take away the sheaf *from* the hungry;

11 *Which* make oil within their walls, *and* tread *their* winepresses, and suffer thirst.

12 Men groan from out of the city, and the soul of the wounded crieth out: yet God layeth not folly *to them.*

13 They are of those that rebel against the light; they know not the ways thereof, nor abide in the paths thereof.

14 The murderer rising with the light killeth the poor and needy, and in the night is as a thief.

15 The eye also of the adulterer waiteth for the twilight, saying, No eye shall see me: and disguiseth *his* face.

16 In the dark they dig through houses, *which* they had marked for themselves in the daytime: they know not the light.

17 For the morning *is* to them even as the shadow of death: if *one* know *them, they are in* the terrors of the shadow of death.

18 He *is* swift as the waters; their portion is cursed in the earth: he beholdeth not the way of the vineyards.

19 Drought and heat consume the snow waters: *so doth* the grave *those which* have sinned.

20 The womb shall forget him; the worm shall feed sweetly on him; he shall be no more remembered; and wickedness shall be broken as a tree.

21 He evil entreateth the barren *that* beareth not: and doeth not good to the widow.

22 He draweth also the mighty with his power: he riseth up, and no *man* is sure of life.

23 *Though* it be given him *to be* in safety, whereon he resteth; yet his eyes *are* upon their ways.

24 They are exalted for a little while, but are gone and brought low, they are taken out of the way as all *other,* and cut off as the tops of the ears of corn.

25 And if *it be* not *so* now, who will make me a liar, and make my speech nothing worth?

25

THEN answered Bil'dad the Shu'hite, and said,

2 Dominion and fear *are* with him, he maketh peace in his high places.

3 Is there any number of his armies? and upon whom doth not his light arise?

4 How then can man be justified with God? or how can he be clean *that is* born of a woman?

5 Behold even to the moon, and it shineth not; yea, the stars are not pure in his sight.

6 How much less man, *that is* a worm? and the son of man, *which is* a worm?

26 BUT Job answered and said,

2 How hast thou helped *him that is* without power? *how* savest thou the arm *that hath* no strength?

3 How hast thou counselled *him that hath* no wisdom? and *how* hast thou plentifully declared the thing as it is?

4 To whom hast thou uttered words? and whose spirit came from thee?

5 Dead *things* are formed from under the waters, and the inhabitants thereof.

6 Hell *is* naked before him, and destruction hath no covering.

7 He stretcheth out the north over the empty place, *and* hangeth the earth upon nothing.

8 He bindeth up the waters in his thick clouds; and the cloud is not rent under them.

9 He holdeth back the face of his throne, *and* spreadeth his cloud upon it.

10 He hath compassed the waters with bounds, until the day and night come to an end.

11 The pillars of heaven tremble and are astonished at his reproof.

12 He divideth the sea with his power, and by his understanding he smiteth through the proud.

13 By his spirit he hath garnished the heavens; his hand hath formed the crooked serpent.

14 Lo, these *are* parts of his ways: but how little a portion is heard of him? but the thunder of his power who can understand?

27 MOREOVER Job continued his parable, and said,

2 *As* God liveth, *who* hath taken away my judgment; and the Almighty, *who* hath vexed my soul;

3 All the while my breath *is* in me, and the spirit of God *is* in my nostrils;

4 My lips shall not speak wickedness, nor my tongue utter deceit.

5 God forbid that I should justify you: till I die I will not remove mine integrity from me.

6 My righteousness I hold fast, and will not let it go: my heart shall not reproach *me* so long as I live.

7 Let mine enemy be as the wicked, and he that riseth up against me as the unrighteous.

8 For what *is* the hope of the hypocrite, though he hath gained, when God taketh away his soul?

9 Will God hear his cry when trouble cometh upon him?

10 Will he delight himself in the Almighty? will he always call upon God?

11 I will teach you by the hand of God: *that* which *is* with the Almighty will I not conceal.

12 Behold, all ye yourselves have seen *it;* why then are ye thus altogether vain?

13 This *is* the portion of a wicked man with God, and the heritage of oppressors, *which* they shall receive of the Almighty.

14 If his children be multiplied, *it is* for the sword: and his offspring shall not be satisfied with bread.

15 Those that remain of him shall be buried in death: and his widows shall not weep.

16 Though he heap up silver as the dust, and prepare raiment as the clay;

17 He may prepare *it,* but the just shall put *it* on, and the innocent shall divide the silver.

18 He buildeth his house as a moth, and as a booth *that* the keeper maketh.

19 The rich man shall lie down, but he shall not be gathered: he openeth his eyes, and he *is* not.

20 Terrors take hold on him as waters, a tempest stealeth him away in the night.

21 The east wind carrieth him away, and he departeth: and as a storm hurleth him out of his place.

22 For *God* shall cast upon him, and not spare: he would fain flee out of his hand.

23 *Men* shall clap their hands at him, and shall hiss him out of his place.

28 SURELY there is a vein for the silver, and a place for gold *where* they fine *it.*

2 Iron is taken out of the earth, and brass *is* molten *out of* the stone.

3 He setteth an end to darkness, and searcheth out all perfection: the stones of darkness, and the shadow of death.

4 The flood breaketh out from the inhabitant; *even the waters* forgotten of the foot: they are dried up, they are gone away from men.

5 *As for* the earth, out of it cometh bread: and under it is turned up as it were fire.

6 The stones of it *are* the place of sapphires: and it hath dust of gold.

7 *There is* a path which no fowl knoweth, and which the vulture's eye hath not seen:

8 The lion's whelps have not trodden it, nor the fierce lion passed by it.

9 He putteth forth his hand upon the rock; he overturneth the mountains by the roots.

10 He cutteth out rivers among the rocks; and his eye seeth every precious thing.

11 He bindeth the floods from overflowing; and *the thing that is* hid bringeth he forth to light.

12 But where shall wisdom be found? and where *is* the place of understanding?

13 Man knoweth not the price thereof; neither is it found in the land of the living.

14 The depth saith, It *is* not in me: and the sea saith, *It is* not with me.

15 It cannot be gotten for gold, neither shall silver be weighed *for* the price thereof.

16 It cannot be valued with the gold of O'-phir, with the precious onyx, or the sapphire.

17 The gold and the crystal cannot equal it: and the exchange of it *shall not be for* jewels of fine gold.

18 No mention shall be made of coral, or of pearls: for the price of wisdom *is* above rubies.

19 The topaz of E-thi-o'pi-a shall not equal it, neither shall it be valued with pure gold.

20 Whence then cometh wisdom? and where *is* the place of understanding?

21 Seeing it is hid from the eyes of all living, and kept close from the fowls of the air.

22 Destruction and death say, We have heard the fame thereof with our ears.

23 God understandeth the way thereof, and he knoweth the place thereof.

24 For he looketh to the ends of the earth, *and* seeth under the whole heaven;

25 To make the weight for the winds; and he weigheth the waters by measure.

26 When he made a decree for the rain, and a way for the lightning of the thunder:

27 Then did he see it, and declare it; he prepared it, yea, and searched it out.

28 And unto man he said, Behold, the fear of the LORD, that *is* wisdom; and to depart from evil *is* understanding.

29 MOREOVER Job continued his parable,
and said,
2 Oh that I were as *in* months past, as *in* the
days *when* God preserved me;
3 When his candle shined upon my head, *and*
when by his light I walked *through* darkness;
4 As I was in the days of my youth, when the
secret of God *was* upon my tabernacle;
5 When the Almighty *was* yet with me, *when*
my children *were* about me;
6 When I washed my steps with butter, and
the rock poured me out rivers of oil;
7 When I went out to the gate through the
city, *when* I prepared my seat in the street!
8 The young men saw me, and hid themselves: and the aged arose, *and* stood up.
9 The princes refrained talking, and laid *their*
hand on their mouth.
10 The nobles held their peace, and their
tongue cleaved to the roof of their mouth.
11 When the ear heard *me*, then it blessed
me; and when the eye saw *me*, it gave witness
to me:
12 Because I delivered the poor that cried,
and the fatherless, and *him that had* none to
help him.
13 The blessing of him that was ready to perish came upon me: and I caused the widow's
heart to sing for joy.
14 I put on righteousness, and it clothed me:
my judgment *was* as a robe and a diadem.
15 I was eyes to the blind, and feet *was* I to
the lame.
16 I *was* a father to the poor: and the cause
which I knew not I searched out.
17 And I brake the jaws of the wicked, and
plucked the spoil out of his teeth.
18 Then I said, I shall die in my nest, and I
shall multiply *my* days as the sand.
19 My root *was* spread out by the waters,
and the dew lay all night upon my branch.
20 My glory *was* fresh in me, and my bow
was renewed in my hand.
21 Unto me *men* gave ear, and waited, and
kept silence at my counsel.
22 After my words they spake not again; and
my speech dropped upon them.
23 And they waited for me as for the rain;
and they opened their mouth wide *as* for the
latter rain.
24 *If* I laughed on them, they believed *it* not;
and the light of my countenance they cast not
down.
25 I chose out their way, and sat chief, and
dwelt as a king in the army, as one *that* comforteth the mourners.

30 BUT now *they that are* younger than I
have me in derision, whose fathers I
would have disdained to have set with the dogs
of my flock.
2 Yea, whereto *might* the strength of their
hands *profit* me, in whom old age was perished?
3 For want and famine *they were* solitary;
fleeing into the wilderness in former time desolate and waste.
4 Who cut up mallows by the bushes, and juniper roots *for* their meat.
5 They were driven forth from among *men*,
(they cried after them as *after* a thief;)
6 To dwell in the cliffs of the valleys, *in* caves
of the earth, and *in* the rocks.
7 Among the bushes they brayed; under the
nettles they were gathered together.
8 *They were* children of fools, yea, children of
base men: they were viler than the earth.
9 And now am I their song, yea, I am their
byword.
10 They abhor me, they flee far from me, and
spare not to spit in my face.
11 Because he hath loosed my cord, and afflicted me, they have also let loose the bridle
before me.
12 Upon *my* right *hand* rise the youth; they
push away my feet, and they raise up against
me the ways of their destruction.
13 They mar my path, they set forward my
calamity, they have no helper.
14 They came *upon me* as a wide breaking in
of waters: in the desolation they rolled themselves *upon me.*
15 Terrors are turned upon me: they pursue
my soul as the wind: and my welfare passeth
away as a cloud.
16 And now my soul is poured out upon me;
the days of affliction have taken hold upon me.
17 My bones are pierced in me in the night
season: and my sinews take no rest.
18 By the great force *of my disease* is my
garment changed: it bindeth me about as the
collar of my coat.
19 He hath cast me into the mire, and I am
become like dust and ashes.
20 I cry unto thee, and thou dost not hear
me: I stand up, and thou regardest me *not.*
21 Thou art become cruel to me: with thy
strong hand thou opposest thyself against me.
22 Thou liftest me up to the wind; thou causest me to ride *upon it,* and dissolvest my substance.
23 For I know *that* thou wilt bring me *to*
death, and *to* the house appointed for all living.
24 Howbeit he will not stretch out *his* hand
to the grave, though they cry in his destruction.
25 Did not I weep for him that was in trouble? was *not* my soul grieved for the poor?
26 When I looked for good, then evil came
unto me: and when I waited for light, there
came darkness.
27 My bowels boiled, and rested not: the
days of affliction prevented me.
28 I went mourning without the sun: I stood
up, *and* I cried in the congregation.
29 I am a brother to dragons, and a companion to owls.
30 My skin is black upon me, and my bones
are burned with heat.
31 My harp also is *turned* to mourning, and
my organ into the voice of them that weep.

31 I MADE a covenant with mine eyes;
why then should I think upon a maid?
2 For what portion of God *is there* from
above? and *what* inheritance of the Almighty
from on high?
3 *Is* not destruction to the wicked? and a
strange *punishment* to the workers of iniquity?
4 Doth not he see my ways, and count all my
steps?
5 If I have walked with vanity, or if my foot
hath hasted to deceit;
6 Let me be weighed in an even balance, that
God may know mine integrity.
7 If my step hath turned out of the way, and
mine heart walked after mine eyes, and if any
blot hath cleaved to mine hands;
8 *Then* let me sow, and let another eat; yea,
let my offspring be rooted out.
9 If mine heart have been deceived by a
woman, or *if* I have laid wait at my neighbour's
door;
10 *Then* let my wife grind unto another, and
let others bow down upon her.

11 For this *is* an heinous crime; yea, it *is* an
iniquity *to be punished by* the judges.
12 For it *is* a fire *that* consumeth to destruction, and would root out all mine increase.
13 If I did despise the cause of my manservant or of my maidservant, when they contended with me;
14 What then shall I do when God riseth up?
and when he visiteth, what shall I answer him?
15 Did not he that made me in the womb
make him? and did not one fashion us in the
womb?
16 If I have withheld the poor from *their* desire, or have caused the eyes of the widow to
fail;
17 Or have eaten my morsel myself alone,
and the fatherless hath not eaten thereof;
18 (For from my youth he was brought up
with me, as *with* a father, and I have guided her
from my mother's womb;)
19 If I have seen any perish for want of clothing, or any poor without covering;
20 If his loins have not blessed me, and *if* he
were *not* warmed with the fleece of my sheep;
21 If I have lifted up my hand against the fatherless, when I saw my help in the gate:
22 *Then* let mine arm fall from my shoulder
blade, and mine arm be broken from the bone.
23 For destruction *from* God *was* a terror to
me, and by reason of his highness I could not
endure.
24 If I have made gold my hope, or have said
to the fine gold, *Thou art* my confidence;
25 If I rejoiced because my wealth *was* great,
and because mine hand had gotten much;
26 If I beheld the sun when it shined, or the
moon walking *in* brightness;
27 And my heart hath been secretly enticed,
or my mouth hath kissed my hand:
28 This also *were* an iniquity *to be punished*
by the judge: for I should have denied the God
that is above.
29 If I rejoiced at the destruction of him that
hated me, or lifted up myself when evil found
him:
30 Neither have I suffered my mouth to sin
by wishing a curse to his soul.
31 If the men of my tabernacle said not, Oh
that we had of his flesh! we cannot be satisfied.
32 The stranger did not lodge in the street:
but I opened my doors to the traveller.
33 If I covered my transgressions as Ad'am,
by hiding mine iniquity in my bosom:
34 Did I fear a great multitude, or did the
contempt of families terrify me, that I kept silence, *and* went not out of the door?
35 Oh that one would hear me! behold, my
desire *is, that* the Almighty would answer me,
and *that* mine adversary had written a book.
36 Surely I would take it upon my shoulder,
and bind it *as* a crown to me.
37 I would declare unto him the number of
my steps; as a prince would I go near unto him.
38 If my land cry against me, or that the furrows likewise thereof complain;
39 If I have eaten the fruits thereof without
money, or have caused the owners therof to
lose their life:
40 Let thistles grow instead of wheat, and
cockle instead of barley. The words of Job are
ended.

32 SO these three men ceased to answer
Job, because he *was* righteous in his
own eyes.
2 Then was kindled the wrath of E-li'hu the
son of Bar'a-chel the Bu'zite, of the kindred of
Ram: against Job was his wrath kindled, because he justified himself rather than God.
3 Also against his three friends was his
wrath kindled, because they had found no answer, and *yet* had condemned Job.
4 Now E-li'hu had waited till Job had spoken,
because they *were* elder than he.
5 When E-li'hu saw that *there was* no answer
in the mouth of *these* three men, then his wrath
was kindled.
6 And E-li'hu the son of Bar'a-chel the Bu'-
zite answered and said, I *am* young, and ye *are*
very old; wherefore I was afraid, and durst not
shew you mine opinion.
7 I said, Days should speak, and multitude of
years should teach wisdom.
8 But *there is* a spirit in man: and the inspiration of the Almighty giveth them understanding.
9 Great men are not *always* wise: neither do
the aged understand judgment.
10 Therefore I said, Hearken to me; I also
will shew mine opinion.
11 Behold, I waited for your words; I gave
ear to your reasons, whilst ye searched out
what to say.
12 Yea, I attended unto you, and, behold,
there was none of you that convinced Job, *or*
that answered his words:
13 Lest ye should say, We have found out
wisdom: God thrusteth him down, not man.
14 Now he hath not directed *his* words
against me: neither will I answer him with your
speeches.
15 They were amazed, they answered no
more: they left off speaking.
16 When I had waited, (for they spake not,
but stood still, *and* answered no more;)
17 *I said,* I will answer also my part, I also
will shew mine opinion.
18 For I am full of matter, the spirit within
me constraineth me.
19 Behold, my belly *is* as wine *which* hath no
vent; it is ready to burst like new bottles.
20 I will speak, that I may be refreshed: I will
open my lips and answer.
21 Let me not, I pray you, accept any man's
person, neither let me give flattering titles unto
man.
22 For I know not to give flattering titles; *in*
so doing my maker would soon take me away.

33 WHEREFORE, Job, I pray thee, hear
my speeches, and hearken to all my
words.
2 Behold, now I have opened my mouth, my
tongue hath spoken in my mouth.
3 My words *shall be of* the uprightness of my
heart: and my lips shall utter knowledge
clearly.
4 The spirit of God hath made me, and the
breath of the Almighty hath given me life.
5 If thou canst answer me, set *thy words* in
order before me, stand up.
6 Behold, I *am* according to thy wish in
God's stead: I also am formed out of the clay.
7 Behold, my terror shall not make thee
afraid, neither shall my hand be heavy upon
thee.
8 Surely thou hast spoken in mine hearing,
and I have heard the voice of *thy* words, *saying,*
9 I am clean without transgression, I *am* innocent; neither *is there* iniquity in me.
10 Behold, he findeth occasions against me,
he counteth me for his enemy.
11 He putteth my feet in the stocks, he marketh all my paths.

12 Behold, *in* this thou art not just: I will answer thee, that God is greater than man.
13 Why dost thou strive against him? for he
giveth not account of any of his matters.
14 For God speaketh once, yea twice, *yet*
man perceiveth it not.
15 In a dream, in a vision of the night, when
deep sleep falleth upon men, in slumberings
upon the bed;
16 Then he openeth the ears of men, and
sealeth their instruction,
17 That he may withdraw man *from his* purpose, and hide pride from man.
18 He keepeth back his soul from the pit, and
his life from perishing by the sword.
19 He is chastened also with pain upon his
bed, and the multitude of his bones with strong
pain:
20 So that his life abhorreth bread, and his
soul dainty meat.
21 His flesh is consumed away, that it cannot be seen; and his bones *that* were not seen
stick out.
22 Yea, his soul draweth near unto the grave,
and his life to the destroyers.
23 If there be a messenger with him, an interpreter, one among a thousand, to shew unto
man his uprightness:
24 Then he is gracious unto him, and saith,
Deliver him from going down to the pit: I have
found a ransom.
25 His flesh shall be fresher than a child's: he
shall return to the days of his youth:
26 He shall pray unto God, and he will be favourable unto him: and he shall see his face
with joy: for he will render unto man his righteousness.
27 He looketh upon men, and *if any* say, I
have sinned, and perverted *that which was*
right, and it profited me not:
28 He will deliver his soul from going into
the pit, and his life shall see the light.
29 Lo, all these *things* worketh God oftentimes with man,
30 To bring back his soul from the pit, to be
enlightened with the light of the living.
31 Mark well, O Job, hearken unto me: hold
thy peace, and I will speak.
32 If thou hast any thing to say, answer me:
speak, for I desire to justify thee.
33 If not, hearken unto me: hold thy peace,
and I shall teach thee wisdom.

34 FURTHERMORE E-li'hu answered and
said,
2 Hear my words, O ye wise *men;* and give
ear unto me, ye that have knowledge.
3 For the ear trieth words, as the mouth tast-
eth meat.
4 Let us choose to us judgment: let us know
among ourselves what *is* good.
5 For Job hath said, I am righteous: and God
hath taken away my judgment.
6 Should I lie against my right? my wound *is*
incurable without transgression.
7 What man *is* like Job, *who* drinketh up
scorning like water?
8 Which goeth in company with the workers
of iniquity, and walketh with wicked men.
9 For he hath said, It profiteth a man nothing
that he should delight himself with God.
10 Therefore hearken unto me, ye men of understanding: far be it from God, *that he should*
do wickedness; and *from* the Almighty, *that he*
should commit iniquity.
11 For the work of a man shall he render
unto him, and cause every man to find according to *his* ways.
12 Yea, surely God will not do wickedly, neither will the Almighty pervert judgment.
13 Who hath given him a charge over the
earth? or who hath disposed the whole world?
14 If he set his heart upon man, *if* he gather
unto himself his spirit and his breath;
15 All flesh shall perish together, and man
shall turn again unto dust.
16 If now *thou hast* understanding, hear this:
hearken to the voice of my words.
17 Shall even he that hateth right govern?
and wilt thou condemn him that is most just?
18 *Is it fit* to say to a king, *Thou art* wicked?
and to princes, *Ye are* ungodly?
19 *How much less to him* that accepteth not
the persons of princes, nor regardeth the rich
more than the poor? for they all *are* the work of
his hands.
20 In a moment shall they die, and the people
shall be troubled at midnight, and pass away:
and the mighty shall be taken away without
hand.
21 For his eyes *are* upon the ways of man,
and he seeth all his goings.
22 *There is* no darkness, nor shadow of
death, where the workers of iniquity may hide
themselves.
23 For he will not lay upon man more *than*
right; that he should enter into judgment with
God.
24 He shall break in pieces mighty men without number, and set others in their stead.
25 Therefore he knoweth their works, and he
overturneth *them* in the night, so that they are
destroyed.
26 He striketh them as wicked men in the
open sight of others;
27 Because they turned back from him, and
would not consider any of his ways:
28 So that they cause the cry of the poor to
come unto him, and he heareth the cry of the
afflicted.
29 When he giveth quietness, who then can
make trouble? and when he hideth *his* face, who
then can behold him? whether *it be done*
against a nation, or against a man only:
30 That the hypocrite reign not, lest the people be ensnared.
31 Surely it is meet to be said unto God, I
have borne *chastisement,* I will not offend *any*
more:
32 *That which* I see not teach thou me: if I
have done iniquity, I will do no more.
33 *Should it be* according to thy mind? he
will recompense it, whether thou refuse, or
whether thou choose; and not I: therefore speak
what thou knowest.
34 Let men of understanding tell me, and let
a wise man hearken unto me.
35 Job hath spoken without knowledge, and
his words *were* without wisdom.
36 My desire *is that* Job may be tried unto
the end because of *his* answers for wicked men.
37 For he addeth rebellion unto his sin, he
clappeth *his hands* among us, and multiplieth
his words against God.

35 E-LI'HU spake moreover, and said,
2 Thinkest thou this to be right, *that*
thou saidst, My righteousness *is* more than
God's?
3 For thou saidst, What advantage will it be
unto thee? *and,* What profit shall I have, *if I be*
cleansed from my sin?

4 I will answer thee, and thy companions
with thee.
5 Look unto the heavens, and see; and behold
the clouds *which* are higher than thou.
6 If thou sinnest, what doest thou against
him? or *if* thy transgressions be multiplied,
what doest thou unto him?
7 If thou be righteous, what givest thou him?
or what receiveth he of thine hand?
8 Thy wickedness *may hurt* a man as thou
art; and thy righteousness *may profit* the son of
man.
9 By reason of the multitude of oppressions
they make *the oppressed* to cry: they cry out by
reason of the arm of the mighty.
10 But none saith, Where *is* God my maker,
who giveth songs in the night;
11 Who teacheth us more than the beasts of
the earth, and maketh us wiser than the fowls
of heaven?
12 There they cry, but none giveth answer,
because of the pride of evil men.
13 Surely God will not hear vanity, neither
will the Almighty regard it.
14 Although thou sayest thou shalt not see
him, *yet* judgment *is* before him; therefore trust
thou in him.
15 But now, because *it is* not *so,* he hath visited in his anger; yet he knoweth *it* not in great
extremity:
16 Therefore doth Job open his mouth in
vain; he multiplieth words without knowledge.

36 E-LI'HU also proceeded, and said,
2 Suffer me a little, and I will shew
thee that *I have* yet to speak on God's behalf.
3 I will fetch my knowledge from afar, and
will ascribe righteousness to my Maker.
4 For truly my words *shall* not *be* false: he
that is perfect in knowledge *is* with thee.
5 Behold, God *is* mighty, and despiseth not
any: he is mighty in strength *and* wisdom.
6 He preserveth not the life of the wicked:
but giveth right to the poor.
7 He withdraweth not his eyes from the
righteous: but with kings *are they* on the
throne; yea, he doth establish them for ever,
and they are exalted.
8 And if *they be* bound in fetters, *and* be
holden in cords of affliction;
9 Then he sheweth them their work, and
their transgressions that they have exceeded.
10 He openeth also their ear to discipline,
and commandeth that they return from iniquity.
11 If they obey and serve *him,* they shall
spend their days in prosperity, and their years
in pleasures.
12 But if they obey not, they shall perish by
the sword, and they shall die without knowledge.
13 But the hypocrites in heart heap up wrath:
they cry not when he bindeth them.
14 They die in youth, and their life *is* among
the unclean.
15 He delivereth the poor in his affliction,
and openeth their ears in oppression.
16 Even so would he have removed thee out
of the strait *into* a broad place, where *there is*
no straitness; and that which should be set on
thy table *should be* full of fatness.
17 But thou hast fulfilled the judgment of the
wicked: judgment and justice take hold *on thee.*
18 Because *there is* wrath, *beware* lest he
take thee away with *his* stroke: then a great
ransom cannot deliver thee.
19 Will he esteem thy riches? *no,* not gold,
nor all the forces of strength.
20 Desire not the night, when people are cut
off in their place.
21 Take heed, regard not iniquity: for this
hast thou chosen rather than affliction.
22 Behold, God exalteth by his power: who
teacheth like him?
23 Who hath enjoined him his way? or who
can say, Thou hast wrought iniquity?
24 Remember that thou magnify his work,
which men behold.
25 Every man may see it; man may behold *it*
afar off.
26 Behold, God *is* great, and we know *him*
not, neither can the number of his years be
searched out.
27 For he maketh small the drops of water:
they pour down rain according to the vapour
thereof:
28 Which the clouds do drop *and* distil upon
man abundantly.
29 Also can *any* understand the spreadings
of the clouds, *or* the noise of his tabernacle?
30 Behold, he spreadeth his light upon it, and
covereth the bottom of the sea.
31 For by them judgeth he the people; he giveth meat in abundance.
32 With clouds he covereth the light; and
commandeth it *not to shine* by *the cloud* that
cometh betwixt.
33 The noise thereof sheweth concerning it,
the cattle also concerning the vapour.

37 AT this also my heart trembleth, and is
moved out of his place.
2 Hear attentively the noise of his voice, and
the sound *that* goeth out of his mouth.
3 He directeth it under the whole heaven,
and his lightning unto the ends of the earth.
4 After it a voice roareth: he thundereth with
the voice of his excellency; and he will not stay
them when his voice is heard.
5 God thundereth marvellously with his
voice; great things doeth he, which we cannot
comprehend.
6 For he saith to the snow, Be thou *on* the
earth; likewise to the small rain, and to the
great rain of his strength.
7 He sealeth up the hand of every man; that
all men may know his work.
8 Then the beasts go into dens, and remain in
their places.
9 Out of the south cometh the whirlwind:
and cold out of the north.
10 By the breath of God frost is given: and
the breadth of the waters is straitened.
11 Also by watering he wearieth the thick
cloud: he scattereth his bright cloud:
12 And it is turned round about by his counsels: that they may do whatsoever he commandeth them upon the face of the world in the
earth.
13 He causeth it to come, whether for correction, or for his land, or for mercy.
14 Hearken unto this, O Job: stand still, and
consider the wondrous works of God.
15 Dost thou know when God disposed them,
and caused the light of his cloud to shine?
16 Dost thou know the balancings of the
clouds, the wondrous works of him which is
perfect in knowledge?
17 How thy garments *are* warm, when he
quieteth the earth by the south *wind?*
18 Hast thou with him spread out the sky,
which is strong, *and* as a molten looking glass?
19 Teach us what we shall say unto him; *for*

we cannot order *our speech* by reason of darkness.
20 Shall it be told him that I speak? if a man
speak, surely he shall be swallowed up.
21 And now *men* see not the bright light
which *is* in the clouds: but the wind passeth,
and cleanseth them.
22 Fair weather cometh out of the north:
with God *is* terrible majesty.
23 *Touching* the Almighty, we cannot find
him out: *he is* excellent in power, and in judgment, and in plenty of justice: he will not afflict.
24 Men do therefore fear him: he respecteth
not any *that are* wise of heart.

38 THEN the LORD answered Job out of the
whirlwind, and said,
2 Who *is* this that darkeneth counsel by
words without knowledge?
3 Gird up now thy loins like a man; for I will
demand of thee, and answer thou me.
4 Where wast thou when I laid the foundations of the earth? declare, if thou hast understanding.
5 Who hath laid the measures thereof, if thou
knowest? or who hath stretched the line upon
it?
6 Whereupon are the foundations thereof
fastened? or who laid the corner stone thereof;
7 When the morning stars sang together, and
all the sons of God shouted for joy?
8 Or *who* shut up the sea with doors, when it
brake forth, *as if* it had issued out of the womb?
9 When I made the cloud the garment
thereof, and thick darkness a swaddlingband
for it,
10 And brake up for it my decreed *place,* and
set bars and doors,
11 And said, Hitherto shalt thou come, but
no further: and here shall thy proud waves be
stayed?
12 Hast thou commanded the morning since
thy days; *and* caused the dayspring to know his
place;
13 That it might take hold of the ends of the
earth, that the wicked might be shaken out of
it?
14 It is turned as clay *to* the seal; and they
stand as a garment.
15 And from the wicked their light is withholden, and the high arm shall be broken.
16 Hast thou entered into the springs of the
sea? or hast thou walked in the search of the
depth?
17 Have the gates of death been opened unto
thee? or hast thou seen the doors of the shadow
of death?
18 Hast thou perceived the breadth of the
earth? declare if thou knowest it all.
19 Where *is* the way *where* light dwelleth?
and *as for* darkness, where *is* the place thereof,
20 That thou shouldest take it to the bound
thereof, and that thou shouldest know the paths
to the house thereof?
21 Knowest thou *it,* because thou wast then
born? or *because* the number of thy days *is*
great?
22 Hast thou entered into the treasures of the
snow? or hast thou seen the treasures of the
hail,
23 Which I have reserved against the time of
trouble, against the day of battle and war?
24 By what way is the light parted, *which*
scattereth the east wind upon the earth?
25 Who hath divided a watercourse for the
overflowing of waters, or a way for the lightning of thunder;
26 To cause it to rain on the earth, *where* no
man *is; on* the wilderness, wherein *there is* no
man;
27 To satisfy the desolate and waste *ground;*
and to cause the bud of the tender herb to
spring forth?
28 Hath the rain a father? or who hath begotten the drops of dew?
29 Out of whose womb came the ice? and the
hoary frost of heaven, who hath gendered it?
30 The waters are hid as *with* a stone, and
the face of the deep is frozen.
31 Canst thou bind the sweet influences of
Ple'ia-des, or loose the bands of O-ri'on?
32 Canst thou bring forth Maz'za-roth in his
season? or canst thou guide Arc-tu'rus with his
sons?
33 Knowest thou the ordinances of heaven?
canst thou set the dominion thereof in the
earth?
34 Canst thou lift up thy voice to the clouds,
that abundance of waters may cover thee?
35 Canst thou send lightnings, that they may
go, and say unto thee, Here we *are?*
36 Who hath put wisdom in the inward
parts? or who hath given understanding to the
heart?
37 Who can number the clouds in wisdom?
or who can stay the bottles of heaven,
38 When the dust groweth into hardness,
and the clods cleave fast together?
39 Wilt thou hunt the prey for the lion? or fill
the appetite of the young lions,
40 When they couch in *their* dens, *and* abide
in the covert to lie in wait?
41 Who provideth for the raven his food?
when his young ones cry unto God, they wander for lack of meat.

39 KNOWEST thou the time when the wild
goats of the rock bring forth? *or* canst
thou mark when the hinds do calve?
2 Canst thou number the months *that* they
fulfil? or knowest thou the time when they
bring forth?
3 They bow themselves, they bring forth
their young ones, they cast out their sorrows.
4 Their young ones are in good liking, they
grow up with corn; they go forth, and return not
unto them.
5 Who hath sent out the wild ass free? or
who hath loosed the bands of the wild ass?
6 Whose house I have made the wilderness,
and the barren land his dwellings.
7 He scorneth the multitude of the city, neither regardeth he the crying of the driver.
8 The range of the mountains *is* his pasture,
and he searcheth after every green thing.
9 Will the unicorn be willing to serve thee, or
abide by thy crib?
10 Canst thou bind the unicorn with his band
in the furrow? or will he harrow the valleys after thee?
11 Wilt thou trust him, because his strength
is great? or wilt thou leave thy labour to him?
12 Wilt thou believe him, that he will bring
home thy seed, and gather *it into* thy barn?
13 *Gavest thou* the goodly wings unto the
peacocks? or wings and feathers unto the os-
trich?
14 Which leaveth her eggs in the earth, and
warmeth them in dust,
15 And forgetteth that the foot may crush
them, or that the wild beast may break them.
16 She is hardened against her young ones,
as though *they were* not hers: her labour is in
vain without fear;

17 Because God hath deprived her of wisdom, neither hath he imparted to her understanding.
18 What time she lifteth up herself on high, she scorneth the horse and his rider.
19 Hast thou given the horse strength? hast thou clothed his neck with thunder?
20 Canst thou make him afraid as a grasshopper? the glory of his nostrils *is* terrible.
21 He paweth in the valley, and rejoiceth in *his* strength: he goeth on to meet the armed men.
22 He mocketh at fear, and is not affrighted; neither turneth he back from the sword.
23 The quiver rattleth against him, the glittering spear and the shield.
24 He swalloweth the ground with fierceness and rage: neither believeth he that *it is* the sound of the trumpet.
25 He saith among the trumpets, Ha, ha; and he smelleth the battle afar off, the thunder of the captains, and the shouting.
26 Doth the hawk fly by thy wisdom, *and* stretch her wings toward the south?
27 Doth the eagle mount up at thy command, and make her nest on high?
28 She dwelleth and abideth on the rock, upon the crag of the rock, and the strong place.
29 From thence she seeketh the prey, *and* her eyes behold afar off.
30 Her young ones also suck up blood: and where the slain *are,* there *is* she.

40

MOREOVER the LORD answered Job, and said,
2 Shall he that contendeth with the Almighty instruct *him?* he that reproveth God, let him answer it.
3 ¶ Then Job answered the LORD, and said,
4 Behold, I am vile; what shall I answer thee? I will lay mine hand upon my mouth.
5 Once have I spoken; but I will not answer: yea, twice; but I will proceed no further.
6 ¶ Then answered the LORD unto Job out of the whirlwind, and said,
7 Gird up thy loins now like a man: I will demand of thee, and declare thou unto me.
8 Wilt thou also disannul my judgment? wilt thou condemn me, that thou mayest be righteous?
9 Hast thou an arm like God? or canst thou thunder with a voice like him?
10 Deck thyself now *with* majesty and excellency; and array thyself with glory and beauty.
11 Cast abroad the rage of thy wrath: and behold every one *that is* proud, and abase him.
12 Look on every one *that is* proud, *and* bring him low; and tread down the wicked in their place.
13 Hide them in the dust together; *and* bind their faces in secret.
14 Then will I also confess unto thee that thine own right hand can save thee.
15 ¶ Behold now behemoth, which I made with thee; he eateth grass as an ox.
16 Lo now, his strength *is* in his loins, and his force *is* in the navel of his belly.
17 He moveth his tail like a cedar: the sinews of his stones are wrapped together.
18 His bones *are as* strong pieces of brass; his bones *are* like bars of iron.
19 He *is* the chief of the ways of God: he that made him can make his sword to approach *unto him.*
20 Surely the mountains bring him forth food, where all the beasts of the field play.
21 He lieth under the shady trees, in the covert of the reed, and fens.
22 The shady trees cover him *with* their shadow; the willows of the brook compass him about.
23 Behold, he drinketh up a river, *and* hasteth not: he trusteth that he can draw up Jor'dan into his mouth.
24 He taketh it with his eyes: *his* nose pierceth through snares.

41

CANST thou draw out leviathan with an hook? or his tongue with a cord *which* thou lettest down?
2 Canst thou put an hook into his nose? or bore his jaw through with a thorn?
3 Will he make many supplications unto thee? will he speak soft *words* unto thee?
4 Will he make a covenant with thee? wilt thou take him for a servant for ever?
5 Wilt thou play with him as *with* a bird? or wilt thou bind him for thy maidens?
6 Shall the companions make a banquet of him? shall they part him among the merchants?
7 Canst thou fill his skin with barbed irons? or his head with fish spears?
8 Lay thine hand upon him, remember the battle, do no more.
9 Behold, the hope of him is in vain: shall not *one* be cast down even at the sight of him?
10 None *is* so fierce that dare stir him up: who then is able to stand before me?
11 Who hath prevented me, that I should repay *him? whatsoever is* under the whole heaven is mine.
12 I will not conceal his parts, nor his power, nor his comely proportion.
13 Who can discover the face of his garment? *or* who can come *to him* with his double bridle?
14 Who can open the doors of his face? his teeth *are* terrible round about.
15 *His* scales *are his* pride, shut up together *as with* a close seal.
16 One is so near to another, that no air can come between them.
17 They are joined one to another, they stick together, that they cannot be sundered.
18 By his neesings a light doth shine, and his eyes *are* like the eyelids of the morning.
19 Out of his mouth go burning lamps, *and* sparks of fire leap out.
20 Out of his nostrils goeth smoke, as *out* of a seething pot or caldron.
21 His breath kindleth coals, and a flame goeth out of his mouth.
22 In his neck remaineth strength, and sorrow is turned into joy before him.
23 The flakes of his flesh are joined together: they are firm in themselves; they cannot be moved.
24 His heart is as firm as a stone; yea, as hard as a piece of the nether *millstone.*
25 When he raiseth up himself, the mighty are afraid: by reason of breakings they purify themselves.
26 The sword of him that layeth at him cannot hold: the spear, the dart, nor the habergeon.
27 He esteemeth iron as straw, *and* brass as rotten wood.
28 The arrow cannot make him flee: slingstones are turned with him into stubble.
29 Darts are counted as stubble: he laugheth at the shaking of a spear.
30 Sharp stones *are* under him: he spreadeth sharp pointed things upon the mire.

31 He maketh the deep to boil like a pot: he maketh the sea like a pot of ointment.

32 He maketh a path to shine after him; *one* would think the deep *to be* hoary.

33 Upon earth there is not his like, who is made without fear.

34 He beholdeth all high *things:* he *is* a king over all the children of pride.

42 THEN Job answered the LORD, and said,

2 I know that thou canst do every *thing,* and *that* no thought can be withholden from thee.

3 Who *is* he that hideth counsel without knowledge? therefore have I uttered that I understood not; things too wonderful for me, which I knew not.

4 Hear, I beseech thee, and I will speak: I will demand of thee, and declare thou unto me.

5 I have heard of thee by the hearing of the ear: but now mine eye seeth thee.

6 Wherefore I abhor *myself,* and repent in dust and ashes.

7 ¶ And it was *so,* that after the LORD had spoken these words unto Job, the LORD said to El'i-phaz the Te'man-ite, My wrath is kindled against thee, and against thy two friends: for ye have not spoken of me *the thing that is* right, as my servant Job *hath.*

8 Therefore take unto you now seven bullocks and seven rams, and go to my servant Job, and offer up for yourselves a burnt offering; and my servant Job shall pray for you: for him will I accept: lest I deal with you *after your* folly, in that ye have not spoken of me *the thing which is* right, like my servant Job.

9 So El'i-phaz the Te'man-ite and Bil'dad the Shu'hite *and* Zo'phar the Na'a-math-ite went, and did according as the LORD commanded them: the LORD also accepted Job.

10 And the LORD turned the captivity of Job, when he prayed for his friends: also the LORD gave Job twice as much as he had before.

11 Then came there unto him all his brethren, and all his sisters, and all they that had been of his acquaintance before, and did eat bread with him in his house: and they bemoaned him, and comforted him over all the evil that the LORD had brought upon him: every man also gave him a piece of money, and every one an earring of gold.

12 So the LORD blessed the latter end of Job more than his beginning: for he had fourteen thousand sheep, and six thousand camels, and a thousand yoke of oxen, and a thousand she asses.

13 He had also seven sons and three daughters.

14 And he called the name of the first, Je-mi'ma; and the name of the second, Ke-zi'a; and the name of the third, Ker'en-hap'puch.

15 And in all the land were no women found *so* fair as the daughters of Job: and their father gave them inheritance among their brethren.

16 After this lived Job an hundred and forty years, and saw his sons, and his sons' sons, *even* four generations.

17 So Job died, *being* old and full of days.

THE PSALMS

1 BLESSED *is* the man that walketh not in the counsel of the ungodly, nor standeth in the way of sinners, nor sitteth in the seat of the scornful.

2 But his delight *is* in the law of the LORD; and in his law doth he meditate day and night.

3 And he shall be like a tree planted by the rivers of water, that bringeth forth his fruit in his season; his leaf also shall not wither; and whatsoever he doeth shall prosper.

4 The ungodly *are* not so: but *are* like the chaff which the wind driveth away.

5 Therefore the ungodly shall not stand in the judgment, nor sinners in the congregation of the righteous.

6 For the LORD knoweth the way of the righteous: but the way of the ungodly shall perish.

2 WHY do the heathen rage, and the people imagine a vain thing?

2 The kings of the earth set themselves, and the rulers take counsel together, against the LORD, and against his anointed, *saying,*

3 Let us break their bands asunder, and cast away their cords from us.

4 He that sitteth in the heavens shall laugh: the LORD shall have them in derision.

5 Then shall he speak unto them in his wrath, and vex them in his sore displeasure.

6 Yet have I set my king upon my holy hill of Zi'on.

7 I will declare the decree: the LORD hath said unto me, Thou *art* my Son; this day have I begotten thee.

8 Ask of me, and I shall give *thee* the heathen *for* thine inheritance, and the uttermost parts of the earth *for* thy possession.

9 Thou shalt break them with a rod of iron; thou shalt dash them in pieces like a potter's vessel.

10 Be wise now therefore, O ye kings: be instructed, ye judges of the earth.

11 Serve the LORD with fear, and rejoice with trembling.

12 Kiss the Son, lest he be angry, and ye perish *from* the way, when his wrath is kindled but a little. Blessed *are* all they that put their trust in him.

A Psalm of David, when he fled from Absalom his son.

3 LORD, how are they increased that trouble me! many *are* they that rise up against me.

2 Many *there be* which say of my soul, *There is* no help for him in God. Se'lah.

3 But thou, O LORD, *art* a shield for me; my glory, and the lifter up of mine head.

4 I cried unto the LORD with my voice, and he heard me out of his holy hill. Se'lah.

5 I laid me down and slept; I awaked; for the LORD sustained me.

6 I will not be afraid of ten thousands of people, that have set *themselves* against me round about.

7 Arise, O LORD; save me, O my God: for thou hast smitten all mine enemies *upon* the cheek bone; thou hast broken the teeth of the ungodly.

8 Salvation *belongeth* unto the LORD: thy blessing *is* upon thy people. Se'lah.

To the chief Musician on Neginoth. A Psalm of David.

4 HEAR me when I call, O God of my righteousness: thou hast enlarged me *when I was* in distress; have mercy upon me, and hear my prayer.
2 O ye sons of men, how long *will ye turn* my glory into shame? *how long* will ye love vanity, *and* seek after leasing? Se'lah.
3 But know that the LORD hath set apart him that is godly for himself: the LORD will hear when I call unto him.
4 Stand in awe, and sin not: commune with your own heart upon your bed, and be still. Se'lah.
5 Offer the sacrifices of righteousness, and put your trust in the LORD.
6 *There be* many that say, Who will shew us *any* good? LORD, lift thou up the light of thy countenance upon us.
7 Thou hast put gladness in my heart, more than in the time *that* their corn and their wine increased.
8 I will both lay me down in peace, and sleep: for thou, LORD, only makest me dwell in safety.

To the chief Musician upon Nehiloth, A Psalm of David.

5 GIVE ear to my words, O LORD, consider my meditation.
2 Hearken unto the voice of my cry, my King, and my God: for unto thee will I pray.
3 My voice shalt thou hear in the morning, O LORD; in the morning will I direct *my prayer* unto thee, and will look up.
4 For thou *art* not a God that hath pleasure in wickedness: neither shall evil dwell with thee.
5 The foolish shall not stand in thy sight: thou hatest all workers of iniquity.
6 Thou shalt destroy them that speak leasing: the LORD will abhor the bloody and deceitful man.
7 But as for me, I will come *into* thy house in the multitude of thy mercy: *and* in thy fear will I worship toward thy holy temple.
8 Lead me, O LORD, in thy righteousness because of mine enemies; make thy way straight before my face.
9 For *there is* no faithfulness in their mouth; their inward part *is* very wickedness; their throat *is* an open sepulchre; they flatter with their tongue.
10 Destroy thou them, O God; let them fall by their own counsels; cast them out in the multitude of their transgressions; for they have rebelled against thee.
11 But let all those that put their trust in thee rejoice: let them ever shout for joy, because thou defendest them: let them also that love thy name be joyful in thee.
12 For thou, LORD, wilt bless the righteous; with favour wilt thou compass him as *with* a shield.

To the chief Musician on Neginoth upon Sheminith, A Psalm of David.

6 O LORD, rebuke me not in thine anger, neither chasten me in thy hot displeasure.
2 Have mercy upon me, O LORD; for I *am* weak: O LORD, heal me; for my bones are vexed.
3 My soul is also sore vexed: but thou, O LORD, how long?
4 Return, O LORD, deliver my soul: oh save me for thy mercies' sake.
5 For in death *there is* no remembrance of thee: in the grave who shall give thee thanks?
6 I am weary with my groaning; all the night make I my bed to swim; I water my couch with my tears.
7 Mine eye is consumed because of grief; it waxeth old because of all mine enemies.
8 Depart from me, all ye workers of iniquity; for the LORD hath heard the voice of my weeping.
9 The LORD hath heard my supplication; the LORD will receive my prayer.
10 Let all mine enemies be ashamed and sore vexed: let them return *and* be ashamed suddenly.

Shiggaion of David, which he sang unto the LORD, concerning the words of Cush the Benjamite.

7 O LORD my God, in thee do I put my trust: save me from all them that persecute me, and deliver me:
2 Lest he tear my soul like a lion, rending *it* in pieces, while *there is* none to deliver.
3 O LORD my God, if I have done this; if there be iniquity in my hands;
4 If I have rewarded evil unto him that was at peace with me; (yea, I have delivered him that without cause is mine enemy:)
5 Let the enemy persecute my soul, and take *it;* yea, let him tread down my life upon the earth, and lay mine honour in the dust. Se'lah.
6 Arise, O LORD, in thine anger, lift up thyself because of the rage of mine enemies: and awake for me *to* the judgment *that* thou hast commanded.
7 So shall the congregation of the people compass thee about: for their sakes therefore return thou on high.
8 The LORD shall judge the people: judge me, O LORD, according to my righteousness, and according to mine integrity *that is* in me.
9 Oh let the wickedness of the wicked come to an end; but establish the just: for the righteous God trieth the hearts and reins.
10 My defence *is* of God, which saveth the upright in heart.
11 God judgeth the righteous, and God is angry *with the wicked* every day.
12 If he turn not, he will whet his sword; he hath bent his bow, and made it ready.
13 He hath also prepared for him the instruments of death; he ordaineth his arrows against the persecutors.
14 Behold, he travaileth with iniquity, and hath conceived mischief, and brought forth falsehood.
15 He made a pit, and digged it, and is fallen into the ditch *which* he made.
16 His mischief shall return upon his own head, and his violent dealing shall come down upon his own pate.
17 I will praise the LORD according to his righteousness: and will sing praise to the name of the LORD most high.

To the chief Musician upon Gittith, A Psalm of David.

8 O LORD our Lord, how excellent *is* thy name in all the earth! who hast set thy glory above the heavens.
2 Out of the mouth of babes and sucklings hast thou ordained strength because of thine enemies that thou mightest still the enemy and the avenger.

3 When I consider thy heavens, the work of
thy fingers, the moon and the stars, which thou
hast ordained;
4 What is man, that thou art mindful of him?
and the son of man, that thou visitest him?
5 For thou hast made him a little lower than
the angels, and hast crowned him with glory
and honour.
6 Thou madest him to have dominion over
the works of thy hands; thou hast put all *things*
under his feet:
7 All sheep and oxen, yea, and the beasts of
the field;
8 The fowl of the air, and the fish of the sea,
and whatsoever passeth through the paths of
the seas.
9 O LORD our Lord, how excellent *is* thy
name in all the earth!

To the chief Musician upon Muth-labben, A Psalm of David.

9 I WILL praise *thee,* O LORD, with my
whole heart; I will shew forth all thy marvellous works.
2 I will be glad and rejoice in thee: I will sing
praise to thy name, O thou most High.
3 When mine enemies are turned back, they
shall fall and perish at thy presence.
4 For thou hast maintained my right and my
cause; thou satest in the throne judging right.
5 Thou hast rebuked the heathen, thou hast
destroyed the wicked, thou hast put out their
name for ever and ever.
6 O thou enemy, destructions are come to a
perpetual end: and thou hast destroyed cities;
their memorial is perished with them.
7 But the LORD shall endure for ever: he hath
prepared his throne for judgment.
8 And he shall judge the world in righteousness, he shall minister judgment to the people
in uprightness.
9 The LORD also will be a refuge for the oppressed, a refuge in times of trouble.
10 And they that know thy name will put
their trust in thee: for thou, LORD, hast not forsaken them that seek thee.
11 Sing praises to the LORD, which dwelleth
in Zi'on: declare among the people his doings.
12 When he maketh inquisition for blood, he
remembereth them: he forgetteth not the cry of
the humble.
13 Have mercy upon me, O LORD; consider
my trouble *which I suffer* of them that hate me,
thou that liftest me up from the gates of death:
14 That I may shew forth all thy praise in the
gates of the daughter of Zi'on: I will rejoice in
thy salvation.
15 The heathen are sunk down in the pit *that*
they made: in the net which they hid is their
own foot taken.
16 The LORD is known *by* the judgment
which he executeth: the wicked is snared in the
work of his own hands. Hig-ga'ion. Se'lah.
17 The wicked shall be turned into hell, *and*
all the nations that forget God.
18 For the needy shall not always be forgotten: the expectation of the poor shall *not* perish
for ever.
19 Arise, O LORD; let not man prevail: let the
heathen be judged in thy sight.
20 Put them in fear, O LORD: *that* the nations
may know themselves *to be but* men. Se'lah.

10 WHY standest thou afar off, O LORD?
why hidest thou *thyself* in times of trouble?
2 The wicked in *his* pride doth persecute the
poor: let them be taken in the devices that they
have imagined.
3 For the wicked boasteth of his heart's desire, and blesseth the covetous, *whom* the LORD
abhorreth.
4 The wicked through the pride of his countenance, will not seek *after God:* God *is* not in
all his thoughts.
5 His ways are always grievous; thy judgments *are* far above out of his sight: *as for* all
his enemies, he puffeth at them.
6 He hath said in his heart, I shall not be
moved: for *I shall* never *be* in adversity.
7 His mouth is full of cursing and deceit and
fraud: under his tongue *is* mischief and vanity.
8 He sitteth in the lurking places of the villages: in the secret places doth he murder the
innocent: his eyes are privily set against the
poor.
9 He lieth in wait secretly as a lion in his den:
he lieth in wait to catch the poor: he doth catch
the poor, when he draweth him into his net.
10 He croucheth, *and* humbleth himself, that
the poor may fall by his strong ones.
11 He hath said in his heart, God hath forgotten: he hideth his face; he will never see *it.*
12 Arise, O LORD; O God, lift up thine hand:
forget not the humble.
13 Wherefore doth the wicked contemn
God? he hath said in his heart, Thou wilt not
require *it.*
14 Thou hast seen *it;* for thou beholdest mischief and spite, to requite *it* with thy hand: the
poor committeth himself unto thee; thou art the
helper of the fatherless.
15 Break thou the arm of the wicked and the
evil *man:* seek out his wickedness *till* thou find
none.
16 The LORD *is* King for ever and ever: the
heathen are perished out of his land.
17 LORD, thou hast heard the desire of the
humble: thou wilt prepare their hearts, thou
wilt cause thine ear to hear:
18 To judge the fatherless and the oppressed,
that the man of the earth may no more oppress.

To the chief Musician, *A Psalm* of David.

11 IN the LORD put I my trust: how say ye
to my soul, Flee *as* a bird to your mountain?
2 For, lo, the wicked bend *their* bow, they
make ready their arrow upon the string, that
they may privily shoot at the upright in heart.
3 If the foundations be destroyed, what can
the righteous do?
4 The LORD *is* in his holy temple, the LORD's
throne *is* in heaven: his eyes behold, his eyelids
try, the children of men.
5 The LORD trieth the righteous: but the
wicked and him that loveth violence his soul
hateth.
6 Upon the wicked he shall rain snares, fire
and brimstone, and an horrible tempest: *this
shall be* the portion of their cup.
7 For the righteous LORD loveth righteousness; his countenance doth behold the upright.

To the chief Musician upon Sheminith, A Psalm of David.

12 HELP, LORD; for the godly man ceaseth;
for the faithful fail from among the children of men.
2 They speak vanity every one with his
neighbour: *with* flattering lips *and* with a double heart do they speak.

3 The LORD shall cut off all flattering lips,
and the tongue that speaketh proud things:
4 Who have said, With our tongue will we
prevail; our lips *are* our own: who *is* lord over
us?
5 For the oppression of the poor, for the sighing of the needy, now will I arise, saith the
LORD; I will set *him* in safety *from him that*
puffeth at him.
6 The words of the LORD *are* pure words: *as*
silver tried in a furnace of earth, purified seven
times.
7 Thou shalt keep them, O LORD, thou shalt
preserve them from this generation for ever.
8 The wicked walk on every side, when the
vilest men are exalted.

To the chief Musician, A Psalm of David.

13 HOW long wilt thou forget me, O LORD?
for ever? how long wilt thou hide thy
face from me?
2 How long shall I take counsel in my soul,
having sorrow in my heart daily? how long shall
mine enemy be exalted over me?
3 Consider *and* hear me, O LORD my God:
lighten mine eyes, lest I sleep the *sleep of* death;
4 Lest mine enemy say, I have prevailed
against him; *and* those that trouble me rejoice
when I am moved.
5 But I have trusted in thy mercy; my heart
shall rejoice in thy salvation.
6 I will sing unto the LORD, because he hath
dealt bountifully with me.

To the chief Musician, *A Psalm* of David.

14 THE fool hath said in his heart, *There is*
no God. They are corrupt, they have
done abominable works, *there is* none that
doeth good.
2 The LORD looked down from heaven upon
the children of men, to see if there were any
that did understand, *and* seek God.
3 They are all gone aside, they are *all* together become filthy: *there is* none that doeth
good, no, not one.
4 Have all the workers of iniquity no knowledge? who eat up my people *as* they eat bread,
and call not upon the LORD.
5 There were they in great fear: for God *is* in
the generation of the righteous.
6 Ye have shamed the counsel of the poor,
because the LORD *is* his refuge.
7 Oh that the salvation of Is′ra-el *were come*
out of Zi′on! when the LORD bringeth back the
captivity of his people, Ja′cob shall rejoice, *and*
Is′ra-el shall be glad.

A Psalm of David.

15 LORD, who shall abide in thy tabernacle? who shall dwell in thy holy hill?
2 He that walketh uprightly, and worketh
righteousness, and speaketh the truth in his
heart.
3 *He that* backbiteth not with his tongue, nor
doeth evil to his neighbour, nor taketh up a reproach against his neighbour.
4 In whose eyes a vile person is contemned;
but he honoureth them that fear the LORD. *He
that* sweareth to *his own* hurt, and changeth
not.
5 *He that* putteth not out his money to usury,
nor taketh reward against the innocent. He that
doeth these *things* shall never be moved.

Michtam of David.

16 PRESERVE me, O God: for in thee do I
put my trust.
2 O *my soul,* thou hast said unto the LORD,
Thou *art* my LORD: my goodness *extendeth* not
to thee;
3 *But* to the saints that *are* in the earth, and
to the excellent, in whom *is* all my delight.
4 Their sorrows shall be multiplied *that* hasten *after* another *god:* their drink offerings of
blood will I not offer, nor take up their names
into my lips.
5 The LORD *is* the portion of mine inheritance
and of my cup: thou maintainest my lot.
6 The lines are fallen unto me in pleasant
places; yea, I have a goodly heritage.
7 I will bless the LORD, who hath given me
counsel: my reins also instruct me in the night
seasons.
8 I have set the LORD always before me: because *he is* at my right hand, I shall not be
moved.
9 Therefore my heart is glad, and my glory
rejoiceth: my flesh also shall rest in hope.
10 For thou wilt not leave my soul in hell;
neither wilt thou suffer thine Holy One to see
corruption.
11 Thou wilt shew me the path of life: in thy
presence *is* fulness of joy; at thy right hand
there are pleasures for evermore.

A Prayer of David.

17 HEAR the right, O LORD, attend unto
my cry, give ear unto my prayer, *that
goeth* not out of feigned lips.
2 Let my sentence come forth from thy presence; let thine eyes behold the things that are
equal.
3 Thou hast proved mine heart; thou hast visited *me* in the night; thou hast tried me, *and*
shalt find nothing; I am purposed *that* my
mouth shall not transgress.
4 Concerning the works of men, by the word
of thy lips I have kept *me from* the paths of the
destroyer.
5 Hold up my goings in thy paths, *that* my
footsteps slip not.
6 I have called upon thee, for thou wilt hear
me, O God: incline thine ear unto me, *and hear*
my speech.
7 Shew thy marvellous lovingkindness, O
thou that savest by thy right hand them which
put their trust *in thee* from those that rise up
against them.
8 Keep me as the apple of the eye, hide me
under the shadow of thy wings,
9 From the wicked that oppress me, *from* my
deadly enemies, *who* compass me about.
10 They are inclosed in their own fat: with
their mouth they speak proudly.
11 They have now compassed us in our
steps: they have set their eyes bowing down to
the earth;
12 Like as a lion *that* is greedy of his prey,
and as it were a young lion lurking in secret
places.
13 Arise, O LORD, disappoint him, cast him
down: deliver my soul from the wicked, *which
is* thy sword:
14 From men *which are* thy hand, O LORD,
from men of the world, *which have* their portion in *this* life, and whose belly thou fillest with
thy hid *treasure:* they are full of children, and
leave the rest of their *substance* to their babes.

15 As for me, I will behold thy face in righteousness: I shall be satisfied, when I awake,
with thy likeness.

To the chief Musician, *A Psalm* of David, the
servant of the LORD, who spake unto the LORD
the words of this song in the day *that* the
LORD delivered him from the hand of all his
enemies, and from the hand of Saul: And he
said.

18 I WILL love thee, O LORD, my strength.
2 The LORD *is* my rock, and my fortress, and my deliverer; my God, my strength,
in whom I will trust; my buckler, and the horn
of my salvation, *and* my high tower.
3 I will call upon the LORD, *who is worthy* to
be praised: so shall I be saved from mine enemies.
4 The sorrows of death compassed me, and
the floods of ungodly men made me afraid.
5 The sorrows of hell compassed me about:
the snares of death prevented me.
6 In my distress I called upon the LORD, and
cried unto my God: he heard my voice out of his
temple, and my cry came before him, *even* into
his ears.
7 Then the earth shook and trembled; the
foundations also of the hills moved and were
shaken, because he was wroth.
8 There went up a smoke out of his nostrils,
and fire out of his mouth devoured: coals were
kindled by it.
9 He bowed the heavens also, and came
down: and darkness *was* under his feet.
10 And he rode upon a cherub, and did fly:
yea, he did fly upon the wings of the wind.
11 He made darkness his secret place; his pavilion round about him *were* dark waters *and*
thick clouds of the skies.
12 At the brightness *that was* before him his
thick clouds passed, hail *stones* and coals of
fire.
13 The LORD also thundered in the heavens,
and the Highest gave his voice; hail *stones* and
coals of fire.
14 Yea, he sent out his arrows, and scattered
them; and he shot out lightnings, and discomfited them.
15 Then the channels of waters were seen,
and the foundations of the world were discovered at thy rebuke, O LORD, at the blast of the
breath of thy nostrils.
16 He sent from above, he took me, he drew
me out of many waters.
17 He delivered me from my strong enemy,
and from them which hated me: for they were
too strong for me.
18 They prevented me in the day of my calamity: but the LORD was my stay.
19 He brought me forth also into a large
place; he delivered me, because he delighted in
me.
20 The LORD rewarded me according to my
righteousness; according to the cleanness of my
hands hath he recompensed me.
21 For I have kept the ways of the LORD, and
have not wickedly departed from my God.
22 For all his judgments *were* before me, and
I did not put away his statutes from me.
23 I was also upright before him, and I kept
myself from mine iniquity.
24 Therefore hath the LORD recompensed me
according to my righteousness, according to the
cleanness of my hands in his eyesight.
25 With the merciful thou wilt shew thyself
merciful; with an upright man thou wilt shew
thyself upright;
26 With the pure thou wilt shew thyself pure;
and with the froward thou wilt shew thyself froward.
27 For thou wilt save the afflicted people; but
wilt bring down high looks.
28 For thou wilt light my candle: the LORD
my God will enlighten my darkness.
29 For by thee I have run through a troop;
and by my God have I leaped over a wall.
30 *As for* God, his way *is* perfect: the word of
the LORD is tried: he *is* a buckler to all those
that trust in him.
31 For who *is* God save the LORD? or who *is* a
rock save our God?
32 *It is* God that girdeth me with strength,
and maketh my way perfect.
33 He maketh my feet like hinds' *feet*, and
setteth me upon my high places.
34 He teacheth my hands to war, so that a
bow of steel is broken by mine arms.
35 Thou hast also given me the shield of thy
salvation: and thy right hand hath holden me
up, and thy gentleness hath made me great.
36 Thou hast enlarged my steps under me,
that my feet did not slip.
37 I have pursued mine enemies, and overtaken them: neither did I turn again till they
were consumed.
38 I have wounded them that they were not
able to rise: they are fallen under my feet.
39 For thou hast girded me with strength
unto the battle: thou hast subdued under me
those that rose up against me.
40 Thou hast also given me the necks of mine
enemies; that I might destroy them that hate
me.
41 They cried, but *there was* none to save
them: even unto the LORD, but he answered
them not.
42 Then did I beat them small as the dust before the wind: I did cast them out as the dirt in
the streets.
43 Thou hast delivered me from the strivings
of the people; *and* thou hast made me the head
of the heathen: a people *whom* I have not
known shall serve me.
44 As soon as they hear of me, they shall
obey me: the strangers shall submit themselves
unto me.
45 The strangers shall fade away, and be
afraid out of their close places.
46 The LORD liveth; and blessed *be* my rock;
and let the God of my salvation be exalted.
47 *It is* God that avengeth me, and subdueth
the people under me.
48 He delivereth me from mine enemies: yea,
thou liftest me up above those that rise up
against me: thou hast delivered me from the
violent man.
49 Therefore will I give thanks unto thee, O
LORD, among the heathen, and sing praises unto
thy name.
50 Great deliverance giveth he to his king;
and sheweth mercy to his anointed, to Da'vid,
and to his seed for evermore.

To the chief Musician, A Psalm of David.

19 THE heavens declare the glory of God;
and the firmament sheweth his handy-
work.
2 Day unto day uttereth speech, and night
unto night sheweth knowledge.
3 *There is* no speech nor language, *where*
their voice is not heard.
4 Their line is gone out through all the earth,
and their words to the end of the world. In them
hath he set a tabernacle for the sun,

5 Which *is* as a bridegroom coming out of his chamber, *and* rejoiceth as a strong man to run a race.
6 His going forth *is* from the end of the heaven, and his circuit unto the ends of it: and there is nothing hid from the heat thereof.
7 The law of the LORD *is* perfect, converting the soul: the testimony of the LORD *is* sure, making wise the simple.
8 The statutes of the LORD *are* right, rejoicing the heart: the commandment of the LORD *is* pure, enlightening the eyes.
9 The fear of the LORD *is* clean, enduring for ever: the judgments of the LORD *are* true *and* righteous altogether.
10 More to be desired *are they* than gold, yea, than much fine gold: sweeter also than honey and the honeycomb.
11 Moreover by them is thy servant warned: *and* in keeping of them *there is* great reward.
12 Who can understand *his* errors? cleanse thou me from secret *faults.*
13 Keep back thy servant also from presumptuous *sins;* let them not have dominion over me: then shall I be upright, and I shall be innocent from the great transgression.
14 Let the words of my mouth, and the meditation of my heart, be acceptable in thy sight, O LORD, my strength, and my redeemer.

To the chief Musician, A Psalm of David.

20 THE LORD hear thee in the day of trouble; the name of the God of Ja'cob defend thee;
2 Send thee help from the sanctuary, and strengthen thee out of Zi'on;
3 Remember all thy offerings, and accept thy burnt sacrifice; Se'lah.
4 Grant thee according to thine own heart, and fulfil all thy counsel.
5 We will rejoice in thy salvation, and in the name of our God we will set up *our* banners: the LORD fulfil all thy petitions.
6 Now know I that the LORD saveth his anointed; he will hear him from his holy heaven with the saving strength of his right hand.
7 Some *trust* in chariots, and some in horses: but we will remember the name of the LORD our God.
8 They are brought down and fallen: but we are risen, and stand upright.
9 Save, LORD: let the king hear us when we call.

To the chief Musician, A Psalm of David.

21 THE king shall joy in thy strength, O LORD; and in thy salvation how greatly shall he rejoice!
2 Thou hast given him his heart's desire, and hast not withholden the request of his lips. Se'lah.
3 For thou preventest him with the blessings of goodness: thou settest a crown of pure gold on his head.
4 He asked life of thee, *and* thou gavest *it* him, *even* length of days for ever and ever.
5 His glory *is* great in thy salvation: honour and majesty hast thou laid upon him.
6 For thou hast made him most blessed for ever: thou hast made him exceeding glad with thy countenance.
7 For the king trusteth in the LORD, and through the mercy of the most High he shall not be moved.
8 Thine hand shall find out all thine enemies: thy right hand shall find out those that hate thee.
9 Thou shalt make them as a fiery oven in the time of thine anger: the LORD shall swallow them up in his wrath, and the fire shall devour them.
10 Their fruit shalt thou destroy from the earth, and their seed from among the children of men.
11 For they intended evil against thee: they imagined a mischievous device, *which* they are not able *to perform.*
12 Therefore shalt thou make them turn their back, *when* thou shalt make ready *thine arrows* upon thy strings against the face of them.
13 Be thou exalted, LORD, in thine own strength: *so* will we sing and praise thy power.

To the chief Musician upon Aijeleth Shahar, A Psalm of David.

22 MY God, my God, why hast thou forsaken me? *why art thou so* far from helping me, *and from* the words of my roaring?
2 O my God, I cry in the daytime, but thou hearest not; and in the night season, and am not silent.
3 But thou *art* holy, *O thou* that inhabitest the praises of Is'ra-el.
4 Our fathers trusted in thee: they trusted, and thou didst deliver them.
5 They cried unto thee, and were delivered: they trusted in thee, and were not confounded.
6 But I *am* a worm, and no man; a reproach of men, and despised of the people.
7 All they that see me laugh me to scorn: they shoot out the lip, they shake the head, *saying,*
8 He trusted on the LORD *that* he would deliver him: let him deliver him, seeing he delighted in him.
9 But thou *art* he that took me out of the womb: thou didst make me hope *when I was* upon my mother's breasts.
10 I was cast upon thee from the womb: thou *art* my God from my mother's belly.
11 Be not far from me; for trouble *is* near; for *there is* none to help.
12 Many bulls have compassed me: strong *bulls* of Ba'shan have beset me round.
13 They gaped upon me *with* their mouths, *as* a ravening and a roaring lion.
14 I am poured out like water, and all my bones are out of joint: my heart is like wax; it is melted in the midst of my bowels.
15 My strength is dried up like a potsherd; and my tongue cleaveth to my jaws; and thou hast brought me into the dust of death.
16 For dogs have compassed me: the assembly of the wicked have inclosed me: they pierced my hands and my feet.
17 I may tell all my bones: they look *and* stare upon me.
18 They part my garments among them, and cast lots upon my vesture.
19 But be not thou far from me, O LORD: O my strength, haste thee to help me.
20 Deliver my soul from the sword; my darling from the power of the dog.
21 Save me from the lion's mouth: for thou hast heard me from the horns of the unicorns.
22 I will declare thy name unto my brethren: in the midst of the congregation will I praise thee.
23 Ye that fear the LORD, praise him; all ye the seed of Ja'cob, glorify him; and fear him, all ye the seed of Is'ra-el.

24 For he hath not despised nor abhorred the
affliction of the afflicted; neither hath he hid his
face from him; but when he cried unto him, he
heard.
25 My praise *shall be* of thee in the great
congregation: I will pay my vows before them
that fear him.
26 The meek shall eat and be satisfied: they
shall praise the LORD that seek him: your heart
shall live for ever.
27 All the ends of the world shall remember
and turn unto the LORD: and all the kindreds of
the nations shall worship before thee.
28 For the kingdom *is* the LORD's: and he *is*
the governor among the nations.
29 All *they that be* fat upon earth shall eat
and worship: all they that go down to the dust
shall bow before him: and none can keep alive
his own soul.
30 A seed shall serve him; it shall be accounted to the Lord for a generation.
31 They shall come, and shall declare his
righteousness unto a people that shall be born,
that he hath done *this*.

A Psalm of David.

23 THE LORD *is* my shepherd; I shall not
want.
2 He maketh me to lie down in green pastures: he leadeth me beside the still waters.
3 He restoreth my soul: he leadeth me in the
paths of righteousness for his name's sake.
4 Yea, though I walk through the valley of
the shadow of death, I will fear no evil: for thou
art with me; thy rod and thy staff they comfort
me.
5 Thou preparest a table before me in the
presence of mine enemies: thou anointest my
head with oil; my cup runneth over.
6 Surely goodness and mercy shall follow me
all the days of my life: and I will dwell in the
house of the LORD for ever.

A Psalm of David.

24 THE earth *is* the LORD's, and the fulness
thereof; the world, and they that dwell
therein.
2 For he hath founded it upon the seas, and
established it upon the floods.
3 Who shall ascend into the hill of the LORD?
or who shall stand in his holy place?
4 He that hath clean hands, and a pure heart;
who hath not lifted up his soul unto vanity, nor
sworn deceitfully.
5 He shall receive the blessing from the
LORD, and righteousness from the God of his
salvation.
6 This *is* the generation of them that seek
him, that seek thy face, O Ja'cob. Se'lah.
7 Lift up your heads, O ye gates; and be ye
lift up, ye everlasting doors; and the King of
glory shall come in.
8 Who *is* this King of glory? The LORD strong
and mighty, the LORD mighty in battle.
9 Lift up your heads, O ye gates; even lift
them up, ye everlasting doors; and the King of
glory shall come in.
10 Who is this King of glory? The LORD of
hosts, he *is* the King of glory. Se'lah.

A Psalm of David.

25 UNTO thee, O LORD, do I lift up my soul.
2 O my God, I trust in thee: let me not
be ashamed, let not mine enemies triumph over
me.
3 Yea, let none that wait on thee be ashamed:
let them be ashamed which transgress without
cause.
4 Shew me thy ways, O LORD; teach me thy
paths.
5 Lead me in thy truth, and teach me: for
thou *art* the God of my salvation; on thee do I
wait all the day.
6 Remember, O LORD, thy tender mercies
and thy lovingkindnesses; for they *have been*
ever of old.
7 Remember not the sins of my youth, nor
my transgressions: according to thy mercy remember thou me for thy goodness' sake, O
LORD.
8 Good and upright *is* the LORD: therefore
will he teach sinners in the way.
9 The meek will he guide in judgment: and
the meek will he teach his way.
10 All the paths of the LORD *are* mercy and
truth unto such as keep his covenant and his
testimonies.
11 For thy name's sake, O LORD, pardon
mine iniquity; for it *is* great.
12 What man *is* he that feareth the LORD?
him shall he teach in the way *that* he shall
choose.
13 His soul shall dwell at ease; and his seed
shall inherit the earth.
14 The secret of the LORD *is* with them that
fear him; and he will shew them his covenant.
15 Mine eyes *are* ever toward the LORD; for
he shall pluck my feet out of the net.
16 Turn thee unto me, and have mercy upon
me; for I *am* desolate and afflicted.
17 The troubles of my heart are enlarged: O
bring thou me out of my distresses.
18 Look upon mine affliction and my pain;
and forgive all my sins.
19 Consider mine enemies; for they are
many; and they hate me with cruel hatred.
20 O keep my soul, and deliver me: let me
not be ashamed; for I put my trust in thee.
21 Let integrity and uprightness preserve
me; for I wait on thee.
22 Redeem Is'ra-el, O God, out of all his troubles.

A Psalm of David.

26 JUDGE me, O LORD; for I have walked
in mine integrity: I have trusted also in
the LORD; *therefore* I shall not slide.
2 Examine me, O LORD, and prove me; try
my reins and my heart.
3 For thy lovingkindness *is* before mine eyes:
and I have walked in thy truth.
4 I have not sat with vain persons, neither
will I go in with dissemblers.
5 I have hated the congregation of evildoers;
and will not sit with the wicked.
6 I will wash mine hands in innocency: so
will I compass thine altar, O LORD:
7 That I may publish with the voice of
thanksgiving, and tell of all thy wondrous
works.
8 LORD, I have loved the habitation of thy
house, and the place where thine honour dwelleth.
9 Gather not my soul with sinners, nor my
life with bloody men:
10 In whose hands *is* mischief, and their right
hand is full of bribes.
11 But as for me, I will walk in mine integrity: redeem me, and be merciful unto me.
12 My foot standeth in an even place: in the
congregations will I bless the LORD.

A Psalm of David.

27 THE LORD *is* my light and my salvation; whom shall I fear? the LORD *is* the strength of my life; of whom shall I be afraid?

2 When the wicked, *even* mine enemies and my foes, came upon me to eat up my flesh, they stumbled and fell.

3 Though an host should encamp against me, my heart shall not fear: though war should rise against me, in this *will* I *be* confident.

4 One *thing* have I desired of the LORD, that will I seek after; that I may dwell in the house of the LORD all the days of my life, to behold the beauty of the LORD, and to enquire in his temple.

5 For in the time of trouble he shall hide me in his pavilion: in the secret of his tabernacle shall he hide me; he shall set me up upon a rock.

6 And now shall mine head be lifted up above mine enemies round about me: therefore will I offer in his tabernacle sacrifices of joy; I will sing, yea, I will sing praises unto the LORD.

7 Hear, O LORD, *when* I cry with my voice: have mercy also upon me, and answer me.

8 *When thou saidst,* Seek ye my face; my heart said unto thee, Thy face, LORD, will I seek.

9 Hide not thy face *far* from me; put not thy servant away in anger: thou hast been my help; leave me not, neither forsake me, O God of my salvation.

10 When my father and my mother forsake me, then the LORD will take me up.

11 Teach me thy way, O LORD, and lead me in a plain path, because of mine enemies.

12 Deliver me not over unto the will of mine enemies: for false witnesses are risen up against me, and such as breathe out cruelty.

13 *I had fainted,* unless I had believed to see the goodness of the LORD in the land of the living.

14 Wait on the LORD: be of good courage, and he shall strengthen thine heart: wait, I say, on the LORD.

A Psalm of David.

28 UNTO thee will I cry, O LORD my rock; be not silent to me: lest, *if* thou be silent to me, I become like them that go down into the pit.

2 Hear the voice of my supplications, when I cry unto thee, when I lift up my hands toward thy holy oracle.

3 Draw me not away with the wicked, and with the workers of iniquity, which speak peace to their neighbours, but mischief *is* in their hearts.

4 Give them according to their deeds, and according to the wickedness of their endeavours: give them after the work of their hands; render to them their desert.

5 Because they regard not the works of the LORD, nor the operation of his hands, he shall destroy them, and not build them up.

6 Blessed *be* the LORD, because he hath heard the voice of my supplications.

7 The LORD *is* my strength and my shield; my heart trusted in him, and I am helped: therefore my heart greatly rejoiceth; and with my song will I praise him.

8 The LORD *is* their strength, and he *is* the saving strength of his anointed.

9 Save thy people, and bless thine inheritance: feed them also, and lift them up for ever.

A Psalm of David.

29 GIVE unto the LORD, O ye mighty, give unto the LORD glory and strength.

2 Give unto the LORD the glory due unto his name; worship the LORD in the beauty of holiness.

3 The voice of the LORD *is* upon the waters: the God of glory thundereth: the LORD *is* upon many waters.

4 The voice of the LORD *is* powerful; the voice of the LORD *is* full of majesty.

5 The voice of the LORD breaketh the cedars; yea, the LORD breaketh the cedars of Leb'a-non.

6 He maketh them also to skip like a calf; Leb'a-non and Sir'i-on like a young unicorn.

7 The voice of the LORD divideth the flames of fire.

8 The voice of the LORD shaketh the wilderness; the LORD shaketh the wilderness of Ka'desh.

9 The voice of the LORD maketh the hinds to calve, and discovereth the forests: and in his temple doth every one speak of *his* glory.

10 The LORD sitteth upon the flood; yea, the LORD sitteth King for ever.

11 The LORD will give strength unto his people; the LORD will bless his people with peace.

A Psalm *and* Song *at* the dedication of the house of David.

30 I WILL extol thee, O LORD; for thou hast lifted me up, and hast not made my foes to rejoice over me.

2 O LORD my God, I cried unto thee, and thou hast healed me.

3 O LORD, thou hast brought up my soul from the grave: thou hast kept me alive, that I should not go down to the pit.

4 Sing unto the LORD, O ye saints of his, and give thanks at the remembrance of his holiness.

5 For his anger *endureth but* a moment; in his favour *is* life: weeping may endure for a night, but joy *cometh* in the morning.

6 And in my prosperity I said, I shall never be moved.

7 LORD, by thy favour thou hast made my mountain to stand strong: thou didst hide thy face, *and* I was troubled.

8 I cried to thee, O LORD; and unto the LORD I made supplication.

9 What profit *is there* in my blood, when I go down to the pit? Shall the dust praise thee? shall it declare thy truth?

10 Hear, O LORD, and have mercy upon me: LORD, be thou my helper.

11 Thou hast turned for me my mourning into dancing: thou hast put off my sackcloth, and girded me with gladness;

12 To the end that *my* glory may sing praise to thee, and not be silent. O LORD my God, I will give thanks unto thee for ever.

To the chief Musician, A Psalm of David.

31 IN thee, O LORD, do I put my trust; let me never be ashamed: deliver me in thy righteousness.

2 Bow down thine ear to me; deliver me speedily: be thou my strong rock, for an house of defence to save me.

3 For thou *art* my rock and my fortress; therefore for thy name's sake lead me, and guide me.

4 Pull me out of the net that they have laid privily for me: for thou *art* my strength.

5 Into thine hand I commit my spirit: thou
hast redeemed me, O LORD God of truth.
6 I have hated them that regard lying vanities: but I trust in the LORD.
7 I will be glad and rejoice in thy mercy: for
thou hast considered my trouble; thou hast
known my soul in adversities;
8 And hast not shut me up into the hand of
the enemy: thou hast set my feet in a large
room.
9 Have mercy upon me, O LORD, for I am in
trouble: mine eye is consumed with grief, *yea,*
my soul and my belly.
10 For my life is spent with grief, and my
years with sighing: my strength faileth because
of mine iniquity, and my bones are consumed.
11 I was a reproach among all mine enemies,
but especially among my neighbours, and a fear
to mine acquaintance: they that did see me
without fled from me.
12 I am forgotten as a dead man out of mind:
I am like a broken vessel.
13 For I have heard the slander of many: fear
was on every side: while they took counsel together against me, they devised to take away
my life.
14 But I trusted in thee, O LORD: I said, Thou
art my God.
15 My times *are* in thy hand: deliver me from
the hands of mine enemies, and from them that
persecute me.
16 Make thy face to shine upon thy servant:
save me for thy mercies' sake.
17 Let me not be ashamed, O LORD; for I
have called upon thee: let the wicked be
ashamed, *and* let them be silent in the grave.
18 Let the lying lips be put to silence; which
speak grievous things proudly and contemptu-
ously against the righteous.
19 *Oh* how great *is* thy goodness, which thou
hast laid up for them that fear thee; *which* thou
hast wrought for them that trust in thee before
the sons of men!
20 Thou shalt hide them in the secret of thy
presence from the pride of man: thou shalt keep
them secretly in a pavilion from the strife of
tongues.
21 Blessed *be* the LORD: for he hath shewed
me his marvellous kindness in a strong city.
22 For I said in my haste, I am cut off from
before thine eyes: nevertheless thou heardest
the voice of my supplications when I cried unto
thee.
23 O love the LORD, all ye his saints: *for* the
LORD preserveth the faithful, and plentifully rewardeth the proud doer.
24 Be of good courage, and he shall
strengthen your heart, all ye that hope in the
LORD.

A Psalm of David, Maschil.

32 BLESSED *is he whose* transgression *is*
forgiven, *whose* sin *is* covered.
2 Blessed *is* the man unto whom the LORD
imputeth not iniquity, and in whose spirit *there*
is no guile.
3 When I kept silence, my bones waxed old
through my roaring all the day long.
4 For day and night thy hand was heavy
upon me: my moisture is turned into the
drought of summer. Se'lah.
5 I acknowledged my sin unto thee, and mine
iniquity have I not hid. I said, I will confess my
transgressions unto the LORD; and thou forgavest the iniquity of my sin. Se'lah.
6 For this shall every one that is godly pray
unto thee in a time when thou mayest be found:
surely in the floods of great waters they shall
not come nigh unto him.
7 Thou *art* my hiding place; thou shalt preserve me from trouble; thou shalt compass me
about with songs of deliverance. Se'lah.
8 I will instruct thee and teach thee in the
way which thou shalt go: I will guide thee with
mine eye.
9 Be ye not as the horse, *or* as the mule,
which have no understanding: whose mouth
must be held in with bit and bridle, lest they
come near unto thee.
10 Many sorrows *shall be* to the wicked: but
he that trusteth in the LORD, mercy shall compass him about.
11 Be glad in the LORD, and rejoice, ye righteous: and shout for joy, all *ye that are* upright in
heart.

33 REJOICE in the LORD, O ye righteous:
for praise is comely for the upright.
2 Praise the LORD with harp: sing unto him
with the psaltery *and* an instrument of ten
strings.
3 Sing unto him a new song; play skilfully
with a loud noise.
4 For the word of the LORD *is* right; and all
his works *are done* in truth.
5 He loveth righteousness and judgment: the
earth is full of the goodness of the LORD.
6 By the word of the LORD were the heavens
made; and all the host of them by the breath of
his mouth.
7 He gathereth the waters of the sea together
as an heap: he layeth up the depth in storehouses.
8 Let all the earth fear the LORD: let all the
inhabitants of the world stand in awe of him.
9 For he spake, and it was *done;* he commanded, and it stood fast.
10 The LORD bringeth the counsel of the heathen to nought: he maketh the devices of the
people of none effect.
11 The counsel of the LORD standeth for ever,
the thoughts of his heart to all generations.
12 Blessed *is* the nation whose God *is* the
LORD; *and* the people *whom* he hath chosen for
his own inheritance.
13 The LORD looketh from heaven; he beholdeth all the sons of men.
14 From the place of his habitation he looketh upon all the inhabitants of the earth.
15 He fashioneth their hearts alike; he considereth all their works.
16 There is no king saved by the multitude of
an host: a mighty man is not delivered by much
strength.
17 An horse *is* a vain thing for safety: neither
shall he deliver *any* by his great strength.
18 Behold, the eye of the LORD *is* upon them
that fear him, upon them that hope in his mercy;
19 To deliver their soul from death, and to
keep them alive in famine.
20 Our soul waiteth for the LORD: he *is* our
help and our shield.
21 For our heart shall rejoice in him, because
we have trusted in his holy name.
22 Let thy mercy, O LORD, be upon us, according as we hope in thee.

A Psalm of David, when he changed his
behaviour before Abimelech, who drove him
away, and he departed.

34 I WILL bless the LORD at all times: his
praise *shall* continually *be* in my mouth.

2 My soul shall make her boast in the LORD: the humble shall hear *thereof*, and be glad.

3 O magnify the LORD with me, and let us exalt his name together.

4 I sought the LORD, and he heard me, and delivered me from all my fears.

5 They looked unto him, and were lightened: and their faces were not ashamed.

6 This poor man cried, and the LORD heard *him*, and saved him out of all his troubles.

7 The angel of the LORD encampeth round about them that fear him, and delivereth them.

8 O taste and see that the LORD *is* good: blessed *is* the man *that* trusteth in him.

9 O fear the LORD, ye his saints: for *there is* no want to them that fear him.

10 The young lions do lack, and suffer hunger: but they that seek the LORD shall not want any good *thing*.

11 Come, ye children, hearken unto me: I will teach you the fear of the LORD.

12 What man *is he that* desireth life, *and* loveth *many* days, that he may see good?

13 Keep thy tongue from evil, and thy lips from speaking guile.

14 Depart from evil, and do good; seek peace, and pursue it.

15 The eyes of the LORD *are* upon the righteous, and his ears *are open* unto their cry.

16 The face of the LORD *is* against them that do evil, to cut off the remembrance of them from the earth.

17 *The righteous* cry, and the LORD heareth, and delivereth them out of all their troubles.

18 The LORD *is* nigh unto them that are of a broken heart; and saveth such as be of a contrite spirit.

19 Many *are* the afflictions of the righteous: but the LORD delivereth him out of them all.

20 He keepeth all his bones: not one of them is broken.

21 Evil shall slay the wicked: and they that hate the righteous shall be desolate.

22 The LORD redeemeth the soul of his servants: and none of them that trust in him shall be desolate.

A Psalm of David.

35 PLEAD *my cause*, O LORD, with them that strive with me: fight against them that fight against me.

2 Take hold of shield and buckler, and stand up for mine help.

3 Draw out also the spear, and stop *the way* against them that persecute me: say unto my soul, I *am* thy salvation.

4 Let them be confounded and put to shame that seek after my soul: let them be turned back and brought to confusion that devise my hurt.

5 Let them be as chaff before the wind: and let the angel of the LORD chase *them*.

6 Let their way be dark and slippery: and let the angel of the LORD persecute them.

7 For without cause have they hid for me their net *in* a pit, *which* without cause they have digged for my soul.

8 Let destruction come upon him at unawares; and let his net that he hath hid catch himself: into that very destruction let him fall.

9 And my soul shall be joyful in the LORD: it shall rejoice in his salvation.

10 All my bones shall say, LORD, who *is* like unto thee, which deliverest the poor from him that is too strong for him, yea, the poor and the needy from him that spoileth him?

11 False witnesses did rise up; they laid to my charge *things* that I knew not.

12 They rewarded me evil for good *to* the spoiling of my soul.

13 But as for me, when they were sick, my clothing *was* sackcloth: I humbled my soul with fasting; and my prayer returned into mine own bosom.

14 I behaved myself as though *he had been* my friend *or* brother: I bowed down heavily, as one that mourneth *for his* mother.

15 But in mine adversity they rejoiced, and gathered themselves together: *yea*, the abjects gathered themselves together against me, and I knew *it* not; they did tear *me*, and ceased not:

16 With hypocritical mockers in feasts, they gnashed upon me with their teeth.

17 Lord, how long wilt thou look on? rescue my soul from their destructions, my darling from the lions.

18 I will give thee thanks in the great congregation: I will praise thee among much people.

19 Let not them that are mine enemies wrongfully rejoice over me: *neither* let them wink with the eye that hate me without a cause.

20 For they speak not peace: but they devise deceitful matters against *them that are* quiet in the land.

21 Yea, they opened their mouth wide against me, *and* said, Aha, aha, our eye hath seen *it*.

22 *This* thou hast seen, O LORD: keep not silence: O Lord, be not far from me.

23 Stir up thyself, and awake to my judgment, *even* unto my cause, my God and my Lord.

24 Judge me, O LORD my God, according to thy righteousness; and let them not rejoice over me.

25 Let them not say in their hearts, Ah, so would we have it: let them not say, We have swallowed him up.

26 Let them be ashamed and brought to confusion together that rejoice at mine hurt: let them be clothed with shame and dishonour that magnify *themselves* against me.

27 Let them shout for joy, and be glad, that favour my righteous cause: yea, let them say continually, Let the LORD be magnified, which hath pleasure in the prosperity of his servant.

28 And my tongue shall speak of thy righteousness *and* of thy praise all the day long.

To the chief Musician, *A Psalm* of David the servant of the LORD.

36 THE transgression of the wicked saith within my heart, *that there is* no fear of God before his eyes.

2 For he flattereth himself in his own eyes, until his iniquity be found to be hateful.

3 The words of his mouth *are* iniquity and deceit: he hath left off to be wise, *and* to do good.

4 He deviseth mischief upon his bed; he setteth himself in a way *that is* not good; he abhorreth not evil.

5 Thy mercy, O LORD, *is* in the heavens; *and* thy faithfulness *reacheth* unto the clouds.

6 Thy righteousness *is* like the great mountains; thy judgments *are* a great deep: O LORD, thou preservest man and beast.

7 How excellent *is* thy lovingkindness, O God! therefore the children of men put their trust under the shadow of thy wings.

8 They shall be abundantly satisfied with the fatness of thy house; and thou shalt make them drink of the river of thy pleasures.

9 For with thee *is* the fountain of life: in thy
light shall we see light.
10 O continue thy lovingkindness unto them
that know thee; and thy righteousness to the
upright in heart.
11 Let not the foot of pride come against me,
and let not the hand of the wicked remove me.
12 There are the workers of iniquity fallen:
they are cast down, and shall not be able to rise.

A Psalm of David.

37 FRET not thyself because of evildoers,
neither be thou envious against the
workers of iniquity.
2 For they shall soon be cut down like the
grass, and wither as the green herb.
3 Trust in the LORD, and do good; *so* shalt
thou dwell in the land, and verily thou shalt be
fed.
4 Delight thyself also in the LORD; and he
shall give thee the desires of thine heart.
5 Commit thy way unto the LORD; trust also
in him; and he shall bring *it* to pass.
6 And he shall bring forth thy righteousness
as the light, and thy judgment as the noonday.
7 Rest in the LORD, and wait patiently for
him: fret not thyself because of him who prospereth in his way, because of the man who
bringeth wicked devices to pass.
8 Cease from anger, and forsake wrath: fret
not thyself in any wise to do evil.
9 For evildoers shall be cut off: but those that
wait upon the LORD, they shall inherit the earth.
10 For yet a little while, and the wicked *shall*
not *be:* yea, thou shalt diligently consider his
place, and it *shall* not *be.*
11 But the meek shall inherit the earth; and
shall delight themselves in the abundance of
peace.
12 The wicked plotteth against the just, and
gnasheth upon him with his teeth.
13 The Lord shall laugh at him: for he seeth
that his day is coming.
14 The wicked have drawn out the sword,
and have bent their bow, to cast down the poor
and needy, *and* to slay such as be of upright
conversation.
15 Their sword shall enter into their own
heart, and their bows shall be broken.
16 A little that a righteous man hath *is* better
than the riches of many wicked.
17 For the arms of the wicked shall be broken: but the LORD upholdeth the righteous.
18 The LORD knoweth the days of the upright: and their inheritance shall be for ever.
19 They shall not be ashamed in the evil
time: and in the days of famine they shall be
satisfied.
20 But the wicked shall perish, and the enemies of the LORD *shall be* as the fat of lambs:
they shall consume; into smoke shall they consume away.
21 The wicked borroweth, and payeth not
again: but the righteous sheweth mercy, and
giveth.
22 For *such as be* blessed of him shall inherit
the earth; and *they that be* cursed of him shall
be cut off.
23 The steps of a *good* man are ordered by
the LORD: and he delighteth in his way.
24 Though he fall, he shall not be utterly cast
down: for the LORD upholdeth *him with* his
hand.
25 I have been young, and *now* am old; yet
have I not seen the righteous forsaken, nor his
seed begging bread.
26 *He is* ever merciful, and lendeth; and his
seed *is* blessed.
27 Depart from evil, and do good; and dwell
for evermore.
28 For the LORD loveth judgment, and forsaketh not his saints; they are preserved for
ever: but the seed of the wicked shall be cut off.
29 The righteous shall inherit the land, and
dwell therein for ever.
30 The mouth of the righteous speaketh wisdom, and his tongue talketh of judgment.
31 The law of his God *is* in his heart; none of
his steps shall slide.
32 The wicked watcheth the righteous, and
seeketh to slay him.
33 The LORD will not leave him in his hand,
nor condemn him when he is judged.
34 Wait on the LORD, and keep his way, and
he shall exalt thee to inherit the land: when the
wicked are cut off, thou shalt see *it.*
35 I have seen the wicked in great power,
and spreading himself like a green bay tree.
36 Yet he passed away, and, lo, he *was* not:
yea, I sought him, but he could not be found.
37 Mark the perfect *man,* and behold the upright: for the end of *that* man *is* peace.
38 But the transgressors shall be destroyed
together: the end of the wicked shall be cut off.
39 But the salvation of the righteous *is* of the
LORD: *he is* their strength in the time of trouble.
40 And the LORD shall help them, and deliver
them: he shall deliver them from the wicked,
and save them, because they trust in him.

A Psalm of David, to bring to remembrance.

38 O LORD, rebuke me not in thy wrath:
neither chasten me in thy hot displeasure.
2 For thine arrows stick fast in me, and thy
hand presseth me sore.
3 *There is* no soundness in my flesh because
of thine anger; neither *is there any* rest in my
bones because of my sin.
4 For mine iniquities are gone over mine
head: as an heavy burden they are too heavy for
me.
5 My wounds stink *and* are corrupt because
of my foolishness.
6 I am troubled; I am bowed down greatly; I
go mourning all the day long.
7 For my loins are filled with a loathsome
disease: and *there is* no soundness in my flesh.
8 I am feeble and sore broken: I have roared
by reason of the disquietness of my heart.
9 Lord, all my desire *is* before thee; and my
groaning is not hid from thee.
10 My heart panteth, my strength faileth me:
as for the light of mine eyes, it also is gone from
me.
11 My lovers and my friends stand aloof
from my sore; and my kinsmen stand afar off.
12 They also that seek after my life lay
snares *for me:* and they that seek my hurt speak
mischievous things, and imagine deceits all the
day long.
13 But I, as a deaf *man,* heard not; and *I was*
as a dumb man *that* openeth not his mouth.
14 Thus I was as a man that heareth not, and
in whose mouth *are* no reproofs.
15 For in thee, O LORD, do I hope: thou wilt
hear, O Lord my God.
16 For I said, *Hear me,* lest *otherwise* they
should rejoice over me: when my foot slippeth,
they magnify *themselves* against me.
17 For I *am* ready to halt, and my sorrow *is*
continually before me.

18 For I will declare mine iniquity; I will be sorry for my sin.

19 But mine enemies *are* lively, *and* they are strong: and they that hate me wrongfully are multiplied.

20 They also that render evil for good are mine adversaries; because I follow *the thing that* good *is*.

21 Forsake me not, O LORD: O my God, be not far from me.

22 Make haste to help me, O Lord my salvation.

To the chief Musician, *even* to Jeduthun, A Psalm of David.

39 I SAID, I will take heed to my ways, that I sin not with my tongue: I will keep my mouth with a bridle, while the wicked is before me.

2 I was dumb with silence, I held my peace, *even* from good; and my sorrow was stirred.

3 My heart was hot within me; while I was musing the fire burned: *then* spake I with my tongue,

4 LORD, make me to know mine end, and the measure of my days, what it *is; that* I may know how frail I *am*.

5 Behold, thou hast made my days *as* an handbreadth; and mine age *is* as nothing before thee: verily every man at his best state *is* altogether vanity. Se'lah.

6 Surely every man walketh in a vain shew: surely they are disquieted in vain: he heapeth up *riches*, and knoweth not who shall gather them.

7 And now, Lord, what wait I for? my hope *is* in thee.

8 Deliver me from all my transgressions: make me not the reproach of the foolish.

9 I was dumb, I opened not my mouth; because thou didst *it*.

10 Remove thy stroke away from me: I am consumed by the blow of thine hand.

11 When thou with rebukes dost correct man for iniquity, thou makest his beauty to consume away like a moth: surely every man *is* vanity. Se'lah.

12 Hear my prayer, O LORD, and give ear unto my cry; hold not thy peace at my tears: for I *am* a stranger with thee, *and* a sojourner, as all my fathers *were*.

13 O spare me, that I may recover strength, before I go hence, and be no more.

To the chief Musician, A Psalm of David.

40 I WAITED patiently for the LORD; and he inclined unto me, and heard my cry.

2 He brought me up also out of an horrible pit, out of the miry clay, and set my feet upon a rock, *and* established my goings.

3 And he hath put a new song in my mouth, *even* praise unto our God: many shall see *it*, and fear, and shall trust in the LORD.

4 Blessed *is* that man that maketh the LORD his trust, and respecteth not the proud, nor such as turn aside to lies.

5 Many, O LORD my God, *are* thy wonderful works *which* thou hast done, and thy thoughts *which are* to us-ward: they cannot be reckoned up in order unto thee: *if* I would declare and speak *of them*, they are more than can be numbered.

6 Sacrifice and offering thou didst not desire; mine ears hast thou opened: burnt offering and sin offering hast thou not required.

7 Then said I, Lo, I come: in the volume of the book *it is* written of me,

8 I delight to do thy will, O my God: yea, thy law *is* within my heart.

9 I have preached righteousness in the great congregation: lo, I have not refrained my lips, O LORD, thou knowest.

10 I have not hid thy righteousness within my heart; I have declared thy faithfulness and thy salvation: I have not concealed thy lovingkindness and thy truth from the great congregation.

11 Withhold not thou thy tender mercies from me, O LORD: let thy lovingkindness and thy truth continually preserve me.

12 For innumerable evils have compassed me about: mine iniquities have taken hold upon me, so that I am not able to look up; they are more than the hairs of mine head: therefore my heart faileth me.

13 Be pleased, O LORD, to deliver me: O LORD, make haste to help me.

14 Let them be ashamed and confounded together that seek after my soul to destroy it; let them be driven backward and put to shame that wish me evil.

15 Let them be desolate for a reward of their shame that say unto me, Aha, aha.

16 Let all those that seek thee rejoice and be glad in thee: let such as love thy salvation say continually, The LORD be magnified.

17 But I *am* poor and needy; *yet* the Lord thinketh upon me: thou *art* my help and my deliverer; make no tarrying, O my God.

To the chief Musician, A Psalm of David.

41 BLESSED *is* he that considereth the poor: the LORD will deliver him in time of trouble.

2 The LORD will preserve him, and keep him alive; *and* he shall be blessed upon the earth: and thou wilt not deliver him unto the will of his enemies.

3 The LORD will strengthen him upon the bed of languishing: thou wilt make all his bed in his sickness.

4 I said, LORD, be merciful unto me: heal my soul; for I have sinned against thee.

5 Mine enemies speak evil of me, When shall he die, and his name perish?

6 And if he come to see *me*, he speaketh vanity: his heart gathereth iniquity to itself; *when* he goeth abroad, he telleth *it*.

7 All that hate me whisper together against me: against me do they devise my hurt.

8 An evil disease, *say they*, cleaveth fast unto him: and *now* that he lieth he shall rise up no more.

9 Yea, mine own familiar friend, in whom I trusted, which did eat of my bread, hath lifted up *his* heel against me.

10 But thou, O LORD, be merciful unto me, and raise me up, that I may requite them.

11 By this I know that thou favourest me, because mine enemy doth not triumph over me.

12 And as for me, thou upholdest me in mine integrity, and settest me before thy face for ever.

13 Blessed *be* the LORD God of Is'ra-el from everlasting, and to everlasting. Amen, and Amen.

To the chief Musician, Maschil, for the sons of Korah.

42 AS the hart panteth after the water brooks, so panteth my soul after thee, O God.

2 My soul thirsteth for God, for the living God: when shall I come and appear before God?

3 My tears have been my meat day and night, while they continually say unto me, Where *is* thy God?

4 When I remember these *things*, I pour out my soul in me: for I had gone with the multitude, I went with them to the house of God, with the voice of joy and praise, with a multitude that kept holyday.

5 Why art thou cast down, O my soul? and *why* art thou disquieted in me? hope thou in God: for I shall yet praise him *for* the help of his countenance.

6 O my God, my soul is cast down within me: therefore will I remember thee from the land of Jor′dan, and of the Her′mon-ites, from the hill Mi′zar.

7 Deep calleth unto deep at the noise of thy waterspouts: all thy waves and thy billows are gone over me.

8 *Yet* the LORD will command his lovingkindness in the daytime, and in the night his song *shall be* with me, *and* my prayer unto the God of my life.

9 I will say unto God my rock, Why hast thou forgotten me? why go I mourning because of the oppression of the enemy?

10 *As* with a sword in my bones, mine enemies reproach me; while they say daily unto me, Where *is* thy God?

11 Why art thou cast down, O my soul? and why art thou disquieted within me? hope thou in God: for I shall yet praise him, *who is* the health of my countenance, and my God.

43 JUDGE me, O God, and plead my cause against an ungodly nation: O deliver me from the deceitful and unjust man.

2 For thou *art* the God of my strength: why dost thou cast me off? why go I mourning because of the oppression of the enemy?

3 O send out thy light and thy truth: let them lead me; let them bring me unto thy holy hill, and to thy tabernacles.

4 Then will I go unto the altar of God, unto God my exceeding joy: yea, upon the harp will I praise thee, O God my God.

5 Why art thou cast down, O my soul? and why art thou disquieted within me? hope in God: for I shall yet praise him, *who is* the health of my countenance, and my God.

To the chief Musician for the sons of Korah, Maschil.

44 WE have heard with our ears, O God, our fathers have told us, *what* work thou didst in their days, in the times of old.

2 *How* thou didst drive out the heathen with thy hand, and plantedst them; *how* thou didst afflict the people, and cast them out.

3 For they got not the land in possession by their own sword, neither did their own arm save them: but thy right hand, and thine arm, and the light of thy countenance, because thou hadst a favour unto them.

4 Thou art my King, O God: command deliverances for Ja′cob.

5 Through thee will we push down our enemies: through thy name will we tread them under that rise up against us.

6 For I will not trust in my bow, neither shall my sword save me.

7 But thou hast saved us from our enemies, and hast put them to shame that hated us.

8 In God we boast all the day long, and praise thy name for ever. Se′lah.

9 But thou hast cast off, and put us to shame; and goest not forth with our armies.

10 Thou makest us to turn back from the enemy: and they which hate us spoil for themselves.

11 Thou hast given us like sheep *appointed* for meat; and hast scattered us among the heathen.

12 Thou sellest thy people for nought, and dost not increase *thy wealth* by their price.

13 Thou makest us a reproach to our neighbours, a scorn and a derision to them that are round about us.

14 Thou makest us a byword among the heathen, a shaking of the head among the people.

15 My confusion *is* continually before me, and the shame of my face hath covered me,

16 For the voice of him that reproacheth and blasphemeth; by reason of the enemy and avenger.

17 All this is come upon us; yet have we not forgotten thee, neither have we dealt falsely in thy covenant.

18 Our heart is not turned back, neither have our steps declined from thy way;

19 Though thou hast sore broken us in the place of dragons, and covered us with the shadow of death.

20 If we have forgotten the name of our God, or stretched out our hands to a strange god;

21 Shall not God search this out? for he knoweth the secrets of the heart.

22 Yea, for thy sake are we killed all the day long; we are counted as sheep for the slaughter.

23 Awake, why sleepest thou, O Lord? arise, cast *us* not off for ever.

24 Wherefore hidest thou thy face, *and* forgettest our affliction and our oppression?

25 For our soul is bowed down to the dust: our belly cleaveth unto the earth.

26 Arise for our help, and redeem us for thy mercies' sake.

To the chief Musician upon Shoshannim, for the sons of Korah, Maschil, A Song of loves.

45 MY heart is inditing a good matter: I speak of the things which I have made touching the king: my tongue *is* the pen of a ready writer.

2 Thou art fairer than the children of men: grace is poured into thy lips: therefore God hath blessed thee for ever.

3 Gird thy sword upon *thy* thigh, O *most* mighty, with thy glory and thy majesty.

4 And in thy majesty ride prosperously because of truth and meekness *and* righteousness; and thy right hand shall teach thee terrible things.

5 Thine arrows *are* sharp in the heart of the king's enemies; *whereby* the people fall under thee.

6 Thy throne, O God, *is* for ever and ever: the sceptre of thy kingdom *is* a right sceptre.

7 Thou lovest righteousness, and hatest wickedness: therefore God, thy God, hath anointed thee with the oil of gladness above thy fellows.

8 All thy garments *smell* of myrrh, and aloes, *and* cassia, out of the ivory palaces, whereby they have made thee glad.

9 Kings' daughters *were* among thy honourable women: upon thy right hand did stand the queen in gold of O′phir.

10 Hearken, O daughter, and consider, and incline thine ear; forget also thine own people, and thy father's house;

11 So shall the king greatly desire thy
beauty: for he *is* thy LORD; and worship thou
him.
12 And the daughter of Tyre *shall be there*
with a gift; *even* the rich among the people shall
intreat thy favour.
13 The king's daughter *is* all glorious within:
her clothing *is* of wrought gold.
14 She shall be brought unto the king in raiment of needlework: the virgins her companions that follow her shall be brought unto thee.
15 With gladness and rejoicing shall they be
brought: they shall enter into the king's palace.
16 Instead of thy fathers shall be thy children, whom thou mayest make princes in all the
earth.
17 I will make thy name to be remembered in
all generations: therefore shall the people praise
thee for ever and ever.

To the chief Musician for the sons of Korah, A Song upon Alamoth.

46 GOD *is* our refuge and strength, a very present help in trouble.
2 Therefore will not we fear, though the
earth be removed, and though the mountains be
carried into the midst of the sea;
3 *Though* the waters thereof roar *and* be
troubled, *though* the mountains shake with the
swelling thereof. Se'lah.
4 *There is* a river, the streams whereof shall
make glad the city of God, the holy *place* of the
tabernacles of the most High.
5 God *is* in the midst of her; she shall not be
moved: God shall help her, *and that* right early.
6 The heathen raged, the kingdoms were
moved: he uttered his voice, the earth melted.
7 The LORD of hosts *is* with us; the God of
Ja'cob *is* our refuge. Se'lah.
8 Come, behold the works of the LORD, what
desolations he hath made in the earth.
9 He maketh wars to cease unto the end of
the earth; he breaketh the bow, and cutteth the
spear in sunder; he burneth the chariot in the
fire.
10 Be still, and know that I *am* God: I will be
exalted among the heathen, I will be exalted in
the earth.
11 The LORD of hosts *is* with us; the God of
Ja'cob *is* our refuge. Se'lah.

To the chief Musician, A Psalm for the sons of Korah.

47 O CLAP your hands, all ye people; shout unto God with the voice of triumph.
2 For the LORD most high *is* terrible; *he is* a
great King over all the earth.
3 He shall subdue the people under us, and
the nations under our feet.
4 He shall choose our inheritance for us, the
excellency of Ja'cob whom he loved. Se'lah.
5 God is gone up with a shout, the LORD with
the sound of a trumpet.
6 Sing praises to God, sing praises: sing
praises unto our King, sing praises.
7 For God *is* the King of all the earth: sing ye
praises with understanding.
8 God reigneth over the heathen: God sitteth
upon the throne of his holiness.
9 The princes of the people are gathered together, *even* the people of the God of A'bra-
ham: for the shields of the earth *belong* unto
God: he is greatly exalted.

A Song *and* Psalm for the sons of Korah.

48 GREAT *is* the LORD, and greatly to be praised in the city of our God, *in* the mountain of his holiness.
2 Beautiful for situation, the joy of the whole
earth, *is* mount Zi'on, *on* the sides of the north,
the city of the great King.
3 God is known in her palaces for a refuge.
4 For, lo, the kings were assembled, they
passed by together.
5 They saw *it, and* so they marvelled; they
were troubled, *and* hasted away.
6 Fear took hold upon them there, *and* pain,
as of a woman in travail.
7 Thou breakest the ships of Tar'shish with
an east wind.
8 As we have heard, so have we seen in the
city of the LORD of hosts, in the city of our God:
God will establish it for ever. Se'lah.
9 We have thought of thy lovingkindness, O
God, in the midst of thy temple.
10 According to thy name, O God, so *is* thy
praise unto the ends of the earth: thy right hand
is full of righteousness.
11 Let mount Zi'on rejoice, let the daughters
of Ju'dah be glad, because of thy judgments.
12 Walk about Zi'on, and go round about
her: tell the towers thereof.
13 Mark ye well her bulwarks, consider her
palaces; that ye may tell *it* to the generation following.
14 For this God *is* our God for ever and ever:
he will be our guide *even* unto death.

To the chief Musician, A Psalm for the sons of Korah.

49 HEAR this, all *ye* people; give ear, all *ye* inhabitants of the world:
2 Both low and high, rich and poor, together.
3 My mouth shall speak of wisdom; and the
meditation of my heart *shall be* of understanding.
4 I will incline mine ear to a parable: I will
open my dark saying upon the harp.
5 Wherefore should I fear in the days of evil,
when the iniquity of my heels shall compass me
about?
6 They that trust in their wealth, and boast
themselves in the multitude of their riches;
7 None *of them* can by any means redeem his
brother, nor give to God a ransom for him:
8 (For the redemption of their soul *is* precious, and it ceaseth for ever:)
9 That he should still live for ever, *and* not
see corruption.
10 For he seeth *that* wise men die, likewise
the fool and the brutish person perish, and
leave their wealth to others.
11 Their inward thought *is, that* their houses
shall continue for ever, *and* their dwelling
places to all generations; they call *their* lands
after their own names.
12 Nevertheless man *being* in honour abideth
not: he is like the beasts *that* perish.
13 This their way *is* their folly: yet their posterity approve their sayings. Se'lah.
14 Like sheep they are laid in the grave;
death shall feed on them; and the upright shall
have dominion over them in the morning; and
their beauty shall consume in the grave from
their dwelling.
15 But God will redeem my soul from the
power of the grave: for he shall receive me. Se'-
lah.
16 Be not thou afraid when one is made rich,
when the glory of his house is increased;

17 For when he dieth he shall carry nothing
away: his glory shall not descend after him.
18 Though while he lived he blessed his soul:
and *men* will praise thee, when thou doest well
to thyself.
19 He shall go to the generation of his fathers; they shall never see light.
20 Man *that is* in honour, and understandeth
not, is like the beasts *that* perish.

A Psalm of Asaph.

50 THE mighty God, *even* the LORD, hath
spoken, and called the earth from the
rising of the sun unto the going down thereof.
2 Out of Zi'on, the perfection of beauty, God
hath shined.
3 Our God shall come, and shall not keep silence: a fire shall devour before him, and it shall
be very tempestuous round about him.
4 He shall call to the heavens from above,
and to the earth, that he may judge his people.
5 Gather my saints together unto me; those
that have made a covenant with me by sacrifice.
6 And the heavens shall declare his righteousness: for God *is* judge himself. Se'lah.
7 Hear, O my people, and I will speak; O Is'-
ra-el, and I will testify against thee: I *am* God,
even thy God.
8 I will not reprove thee for thy sacrifices or
thy burnt offerings, *to have been* continually before me.
9 I will take no bullock out of thy house, *nor*
he goats out of thy folds.
10 For every beast of the forest *is* mine, *and*
the cattle upon a thousand hills.
11 I know all the fowls of the mountains: and
the wild beasts of the field *are* mine.
12 If I were hungry, I would not tell thee: for
the world *is* mine, and the fulness thereof.
13 Will I eat the flesh of bulls, or drink the
blood of goats?
14 Offer unto God thanksgiving; and pay thy
vows unto the most High:
15 And call upon me in the day of trouble: I
will deliver thee, and thou shalt glorify me.
16 But unto the wicked God saith, What hast
thou to do to declare my statutes, or *that* thou
shouldest take my covenant in thy mouth?
17 Seeing thou hatest instruction, and castest my words behind thee.
18 When thou sawest a thief, then thou con-
sentedst with him, and hast been partaker with
adulterers.
19 Thou givest thy mouth to evil, and thy
tongue frameth deceit.
20 Thou sittest *and* speakest against thy
brother; thou slanderest thine own mother's
son.
21 These *things* hast thou done, and I kept
silence; thou thoughtest that I was altogether
such an one as thyself: *but* I will reprove thee,
and set *them* in order before thine eyes.
22 Now consider this, ye that forget God, lest
I tear *you* in pieces, and *there be* none to deliver.
23 Whoso offereth praise glorifieth me: and
to him that ordereth *his* conversation *aright* will
I shew the salvation of God.

To the chief Musician, A Psalm of David,
when Nathan the prophet came unto him,
after he had gone in to Bath-sheba.

51 HAVE mercy upon me, O God, according to thy lovingkindness: according
unto the multitude of thy tender mercies blot
out my transgressions.
2 Wash me throughly from mine iniquity,
and cleanse me from my sin.
3 For I acknowledge my transgressions: and
my sin *is* ever before me.
4 Against thee, thee only, have I sinned, and
done *this* evil in thy sight: that thou mightest be
justified when thou speakest, *and* be clear
when thou judgest.
5 Behold, I was shapen in iniquity; and in sin
did my mother conceive me.
6 Behold, thou desirest truth in the inward
parts: and in the hidden *part* thou shalt make
me to know wisdom.
7 Purge me with hyssop, and I shall be clean:
wash me, and I shall be whiter than snow.
8 Make me to hear joy and gladness; *that* the
bones *which* thou hast broken may rejoice.
9 Hide thy face from my sins, and blot out all
mine iniquities.
10 Create in me a clean heart, O God; and
renew a right spirit within me.
11 Cast me not away from thy presence; and
take not thy holy spirit from me.
12 Restore unto me the joy of thy salvation;
and uphold me *with thy* free spirit.
13 *Then* will I teach transgressors thy ways;
and sinners shall be converted unto thee.
14 Deliver me from bloodguiltiness, O God,
thou God of my salvation: *and* my tongue shall
sing aloud of thy righteousness.
15 O Lord, open thou my lips; and my mouth
shall shew forth thy praise.
16 For thou desirest not sacrifice; else would
I give *it:* thou delightest not in burnt offering.
17 The sacrifices of God *are* a broken spirit: a
broken and a contrite heart, O God, thou wilt
not despise.
18 Do good in thy good pleasure unto Zi'on:
build thou the walls of Je-ru'sa-lem.
19 Then shalt thou be pleased with the sacrifices of righteousness, with burnt offering and
whole burnt offering: then shall they offer bullocks upon thine altar.

To the chief Musician, Maschil, *A Psalm* of
David, when Doeg the Edomite came and told
Saul, and said unto him, David is come to the
house of Ahimelech.

52 WHY boastest thou thyself in mischief,
O mighty man? the goodness of God *endureth* continually.
2 Thy tongue deviseth mischiefs; like a sharp
razor, working deceitfully.
3 Thou lovest evil more than good; *and* lying
rather than to speak righteousness. Se'lah.
4 Thou lovest all devouring words, O *thou*
deceitful tongue.
5 God shall likewise destroy thee for ever, he
shall take thee away, and pluck thee out of *thy*
dwelling place, and root thee out of the land of
the living. Se'lah.
6 The righteous also shall see, and fear, and
shall laugh at him:
7 Lo, *this is* the man *that* made not God his
strength; but trusted in the abundance of his
riches, *and* strengthened himself in his wickedness.
8 But I *am* like a green olive tree in the house
of God: I trust in the mercy of God for ever and
ever.
9 I will praise thee for ever, because thou
hast done *it:* and I will wait on thy name; for *it
is* good before thy saints.

To the chief Musician, upon Mahalath,
Maschil, *A Psalm* of David.

53 THE fool hath said in his heart, *There is*
no God. Corrupt are they, and have
done abominable iniquity: *there is* none that
doeth good.
2 God looked down from heaven upon the
children of men, to see if there were *any* that
did understand, that did seek God.
3 Every one of them is gone back: they are
altogether become filthy; *there is* none that
doeth good, no, not one.
4 Have the workers of iniquity no knowledge? who eat up my people *as* they eat bread:
they have not called upon God.
5 There were they in great fear, *where* no
fear was: for God hath scattered the bones of
him that encampeth *against* thee: thou hast put
them to shame, because God hath despised
them.
6 Oh that the salvation of Is'ra-el *were come*
out of Zi'on! When God bringeth back the captivity of his people, Ja'cob shall rejoice *and* Is'-
ra-el shall be glad.

To the chief Musician on Neginoth, Maschil, *A
Psalm* of David, when the Ziphims came and
said to Saul, Doth not David hide himself with
us?

54 SAVE me, O God, by thy name, and
judge me by thy strength.
2 Hear my prayer, O God; give ear to the
words of my mouth.
3 For strangers are risen up against me, and
oppressors seek after my soul: they have not set
God before them. Se'lah.
4 Behold, God *is* mine helper: the Lord *is*
with them that uphold my soul.
5 He shall reward evil unto mine enemies:
cut them off in thy truth.
6 I will freely sacrifice unto thee: I will praise
thy name, O LORD; for *it is* good.
7 For he hath delivered me out of all trouble:
and mine eye hath seen *his desire* upon mine
enemies.

To the chief Musician on Neginoth, Maschil, *A
Psalm* of David.

55 GIVE ear to my prayer, O God; and hide
not thyself from my supplication.
2 Attend unto me, and hear me: I mourn in
my complaint, and make a noise;
3 Because of the voice of the enemy, because
of the oppression of the wicked: for they cast
iniquity upon me, and in wrath they hate me.
4 My heart is sore pained within me: and the
terrors of death are fallen upon me.
5 Fearfulness and trembling are come upon
me, and horror hath overwhelmed me.
6 And I said, Oh that I had wings like a dove!
for then would I fly away, and be at rest.
7 Lo, *then* would I wander far off, *and* remain in the wilderness. Se'lah.
8 I would hasten my escape from the windy
storm *and* tempest.
9 Destroy, O Lord, *and* divide their tongues:
for I have seen violence and strife in the city.
10 Day and night they go about it upon the
walls thereof: mischief also and sorrow *are* in
the midst of it.
11 Wickedness *is* in the midst thereof: deceit
and guile depart not from her streets.
12 For *it was* not an enemy *that* reproached
me; then I could have borne *it:* neither *was it* he
that hated me *that* did magnify *himself* against
me; then I would have hid myself from him:
13 But *it was* thou, a man mine equal, my
guide, and mine acquaintance.
14 We took sweet counsel together, *and*
walked unto the house of God in company.
15 Let death seize upon them, *and* let them
go down quick into hell: for wickedness *is* in
their dwellings, *and* among them.
16 As for me, I will call upon God; and the
LORD shall save me.
17 Evening, and morning, and at noon, will I
pray, and cry aloud: and he shall hear my voice.
18 He hath delivered my soul in peace from
the battle *that was* against me: for there were
many with me.
19 God shall hear, and afflict them, even he
that abideth of old. Se'lah. Because they have
no changes, therefore they fear not God.
20 He hath put forth his hands against such
as be at peace with him: he hath broken his covenant.
21 *The words* of his mouth were smoother
than butter, but war *was* in his heart: his words
were softer than oil, yet *were* they drawn
swords.
22 Cast thy burden upon the LORD, and he
shall sustain thee: he shall never suffer the
righteous to be moved.
23 But thou, O God, shalt bring them down
into the pit of destruction: bloody and deceitful
men shall not live out half their days; but I will
trust in thee.

To the chief Musician upon Jonath-elem-
rechokim, Michtam of David, when the
Philistines took him in Gath.

56 BE merciful unto me, O God: for man
would swallow me up; he fighting daily
oppresseth me.
2 Mine enemies would daily swallow *me* up:
for *they be* many that fight against me, O thou
most High.
3 What time I am afraid, I will trust in thee.
4 In God I will praise his word, in God I have
put my trust; I will not fear what flesh can do
unto me.
5 Every day they wrest my words: all their
thoughts *are* against me for evil.
6 They gather themselves together, they hide
themselves, they mark my steps, when they
wait for my soul.
7 Shall they escape by iniquity? in *thine* anger cast down the people, O God.
8 Thou tellest my wanderings: put thou my
tears into thy bottle: *are they* not in thy book?
9 When I cry *unto thee,* then shall mine enemies turn back: this I know; for God *is* for me.
10 In God will I praise *his* word: in the LORD
will I praise *his* word.
11 In God have I put my trust: I will not be
afraid what man can do unto me.
12 Thy vows *are* upon me, O God: I will render praises unto thee.
13 For thou hast delivered my soul from
death: *wilt* not *thou deliver* my feet from falling, that I may walk before God in the light of
the living?

To the chief Musician, Al-taschith, Michtam of
David, when he fled from Saul in the cave.

57 BE merciful unto me, O God, be merciful unto me: for my soul trusteth in thee:
yea, in the shadow of thy wings will I make my
refuge, until *these* calamities be overpast.

2 I will cry unto God most high; unto God
that performeth *all things* for me.
3 He shall send from heaven, and save me
from the reproach of him that would swallow
me up. Se'lah. God shall send forth his mercy
and his truth.
4 My soul *is* among lions: *and* I lie *even*
among them that are set on fire, *even* the sons
of men, whose teeth *are* spears and arrows, and
their tongue a sharp sword.
5 Be thou exalted, O God, above the heavens;
let thy glory *be* above all the earth.
6 They have prepared a net for my steps; my
soul is bowed down: they have digged a pit before me, into the midst whereof they are fallen
themselves. Se'lah.
7 My heart is fixed, O God, my heart is fixed:
I will sing and give praise.
8 Awake up, my glory; awake, psaltery and
harp: I *myself* will awake early.
9 I will praise thee, O Lord, among the people: I will sing unto thee among the nations.
10 For thy mercy *is* great unto the heavens,
and thy truth unto the clouds.
11 Be thou exalted, O God, above the heavens: *let* thy glory *be* above all the earth.

To the chief Musician, Al-taschith, Michtam of
David.

58 DO ye indeed speak righteousness, O
congregation? do ye judge uprightly, O
ye sons of men?
2 Yea, in heart ye work wickedness; ye
weigh the violence of your hands in the earth.
3 The wicked are estranged from the womb:
they go astray as soon as they be born, speaking lies.
4 Their poison *is* like the poison of a serpent:
they are like the deaf adder *that* stoppeth her
ear;
5 Which will not hearken to the voice of
charmers, charming never so wisely.
6 Break their teeth, O God, in their mouth:
break out the great teeth of the young lions, O
LORD.
7 Let them melt away as waters *which* run
continually: *when* he bendeth *his bow to shoot*
his arrows, let them be as cut in pieces.
8 As a snail *which* melteth, let *every one of*
them pass away: *like* the untimely birth of a
woman, *that* they may not see the sun.
9 Before your pots can feel the thorns, he
shall take them away as with a whirlwind, both
living, and in *his* wrath.
10 The righteous shall rejoice when he seeth
the vengeance: he shall wash his feet in the
blood of the wicked.
11 So that a man shall say, Verily *there is* a
reward for the righteous: verily he is a God that
judgeth in the earth.

To the chief Musician, Al-taschith, Michtam of
David, when Saul sent, and they watched the
house to kill him.

59 DELIVER me from mine enemies, O my
God: defend me from them that rise up
against me.
2 Deliver me from the workers of iniquity,
and save me from bloody men.
3 For, lo, they lie in wait for my soul: the
mighty are gathered against me; not *for* my
transgression, nor *for* my sin, O LORD.
4 They run and prepare themselves without
my fault: awake to help me, and behold.
5 Thou therefore, O LORD God of hosts, the
God of Is'ra-el, awake to visit all the heathen:
be not merciful to any wicked transgressors.
Se'lah.
6 They return at evening: they make a noise
like a dog, and go round about the city.
7 Behold, they belch out with their mouth:
swords *are* in their lips: for who, *say they,* doth
hear?
8 But thou, O LORD, shalt laugh at them; thou
shalt have all the heathen in derision.
9 *Because of* his strength will I wait upon
thee: for God *is* my defence.
10 The God of my mercy shall prevent me:
God shall let me see *my desire* upon mine enemies.
11 Slay them not, lest my people forget: scatter them by thy power; and bring them down, O
Lord our shield.
12 *For* the sin of their mouth *and* the words
of their lips let them even be taken in their
pride: and for cursing and lying *which* they
speak.
13 Consume *them* in wrath, consume *them,*
that they *may* not *be:* and let them know that
God ruleth in Ja'cob unto the ends of the earth.
Se'lah.
14 And at evening let them return; *and* let
them make a noise like a dog, and go round
about the city.
15 Let them wander up and down for meat,
and grudge if they be not satisfied.
16 But I will sing of thy power; yea, I will
sing aloud of thy mercy in the morning: for thou
hast been my defence and refuge in the day of
my trouble.
17 Unto thee, O my strength, will I sing: for
God *is* my defence, *and* the God of my mercy.

To the chief Musician upon Shushan-eduth,
Michtam of David, to teach; when he strove
with Aram-naharaim, and with Aram-zobah,
when Joab returned, and smote of Edom in the
valley of Salt twelve thousand.

60 O GOD, thou hast cast us off, thou hast
scattered us, thou hast been displeased;
O turn thyself to us again.
2 Thou hast made the earth to tremble; thou
hast broken it: heal the breaches thereof; for it
shaketh.
3 Thou hast shewed thy people hard things:
thou hast made us to drink the wine of astonishment.
4 Thou hast given a banner to them that fear
thee, that it may be displayed because of the
truth. Se'lah.
5 That thy beloved may be delivered; save
with thy right hand, and hear me.
6 God hath spoken in his holiness; I will rejoice, I will divide She'chem, and mete out the
valley of Suc'coth.
7 Gil'e-ad *is* mine, and Ma-nas'seh *is* mine;
E'phra-im also *is* the strength of mine head; Ju'-
dah *is* my lawgiver;
8 Mo'ab *is* my washpot: over E'dom will I
cast out my shoe: Phi-lis'tia, triumph thou because of me.
9 Who will bring me *into* the strong city?
who will lead me into E'dom?
10 *Wilt* not thou, O God, *which* hadst cast us
off? and *thou,* O God, *which* didst not go out
with our armies?
11 Give us help from trouble: for vain *is* the
help of man.
12 Through God we shall do valiantly: for he
it is that shall tread down our enemies.

To the chief Musician upon Neginah, *A Psalm*
of David.

61 HEAR my cry, O God; attend unto my
prayer.
2 From the end of the earth will I cry unto
thee, when my heart is overwhelmed: lead me
to the rock *that* is higher than I.
3 For thou hast been a shelter for me, *and* a
strong tower from the enemy.
4 I will abide in thy tabernacle for ever: I will
trust in the covert of thy wings. Se'lah.
5 For thou, O God, hast heard my vows: thou
hast given *me* the heritage of those that fear thy
name.
6 Thou wilt prolong the king's life: *and* his
years as many generations.
7 He shall abide before God for ever: O prepare mercy and truth, *which* may preserve him.
8 So will I sing praise unto thy name for ever,
that I may daily perform my vows.

To the chief Musician, to Jeduthun, A Psalm
of David.

62 TRULY my soul waiteth upon God:
from him *cometh* my salvation.
2 He only *is* my rock and my salvation; *he is*
my defence; I shall not be greatly moved.
3 How long will ye imagine mischief against
a man? ye shall be slain all of you: as a bowing
wall *shall ye be, and as* a tottering fence.
4 They only consult to cast *him* down from
his excellency: they delight in lies: they bless
with their mouth, but they curse inwardly. Se'-
lah.
5 My soul, wait thou only upon God; for my
expectation *is* from him.
6 He only *is* my rock and my salvation: *he is*
my defence; I shall not be moved.
7 In God *is* my salvation and my glory: the
rock of my strength, *and* my refuge, *is* in God.
8 Trust in him at all times; ye people, pour
out your heart before him: God *is* a refuge for
us. Se'lah.
9 Surely men of low degree *are* vanity, *and*
men of high degree *are* a lie: to be laid in the
balance, they *are* altogether *lighter* than vanity.
10 Trust not in oppression, and become not
vain in robbery: if riches increase, set not your
heart *upon them.*
11 God hath spoken once; twice have I heard
this; that power *belongeth* unto God.
12 Also unto thee, O Lord, *belongeth* mercy:
for thou renderest to every man according to
his work.

A Psalm of David, when he was in the
wilderness of Judah.

63 O GOD, thou *art* my God; early will I
seek thee: my soul thirsteth for thee, my
flesh longeth for thee in a dry and thirsty land,
where no water is;
2 To see thy power and thy glory, so *as* I
have seen thee in the sanctuary.
3 Because thy lovingkindness *is* better than
life, my lips shall praise thee.
4 Thus will I bless thee while I live: I will lift
up my hands in thy name.
5 My soul shall be satisfied as *with* marrow
and fatness; and my mouth shall praise *thee*
with joyful lips:
6 When I remember thee upon my bed, *and*
meditate on thee in the *night* watches.
7 Because thou hast been my help, therefore
in the shadow of thy wings will I rejoice.
8 My soul followeth hard after thee: thy right
hand upholdeth me.
9 But those *that* seek my soul, to destroy *it,*
shall go into the lower parts of the earth.
10 They shall fall by the sword: they shall be
a portion for foxes.
11 But the king shall rejoice in God; every
one that sweareth by him shall glory: but the
mouth of them that speak lies shall be stopped.

To the chief Musician, A Psalm of David.

64 HEAR my voice, O God, in my prayer:
preserve my life from fear of the enemy.
2 Hide me from the secret counsel of the
wicked; from the insurrection of the workers of
iniquity:
3 Who whet their tongue like a sword, *and*
bend *their bows to shoot* their arrows, *even* bitter words:
4 That they may shoot in secret at the perfect: suddenly do they shoot at him, and fear
not.
5 They encourage themselves *in* an evil matter: they commune of laying snares privily; they
say, Who shall see them?
6 They search out iniquities; they accomplish
a diligent search: both the inward *thought* of
every one *of them,* and the heart, *is* deep.
7 But God shall shoot at them *with* an arrow;
suddenly shall they be wounded.
8 So they shall make their own tongue to fall
upon themselves: all that see them shall flee
away.
9 And all men shall fear, and shall declare
the work of God; for they shall wisely consider
of his doing.
10 The righteous shall be glad in the LORD,
and shall trust in him; and all the upright in
heart shall glory.

To the chief Musician, A Psalm *and* Song of
David.

65 PRAISE waiteth for thee, O God, in Si'-
on: and unto thee shall the vow be performed:
2 O thou that hearest prayer, unto thee shall
all flesh come.
3 Iniquities prevail against me: *as for* our
transgressions, thou shalt purge them away.
4 Blessed *is the man whom* thou choosest,
and causest to approach *unto thee, that* he may
dwell in thy courts: we shall be satisfied with
the goodness of thy house, *even* of thy holy
temple.
5 *By* terrible things in righteousness wilt
thou answer us, O God of our salvation; *who art*
the confidence of all the ends of the earth, and
of them that are afar off *upon* the sea:
6 Which by his strength setteth fast the
mountains; *being* girded with power:
7 Which stilleth the noise of the seas, the
noise of their waves, and the tumult of the people.
8 They also that dwell in the uttermost parts
are afraid at thy tokens: thou makest the outgoings of the morning and evening to rejoice.
9 Thou visitest the earth, and waterest it:
thou greatly enrichest it with the river of God,
which is full of water: thou preparest them
corn, when thou hast so provided for it.
10 Thou waterest the ridges thereof abundantly: thou settlest the furrows thereof: thou
makest it soft with showers: thou blessest the
springing thereof.

11 Thou crownest the year with thy goodness; and thy paths drop fatness.
12 They drop *upon* the pastures of the wilderness: and the little hills rejoice on every side.
13 The pastures are clothed with flocks; the
valleys also are covered over with corn; they
shout for joy, they also sing.

To the chief Musician, A Song *or* Psalm.

66 MAKE a joyful noise unto God, all ye
lands:
2 Sing forth the honour of his name: make
his praise glorious.
3 Say unto God, How terrible *art thou in* thy
works! through the greatness of thy power shall
thine enemies submit themselves unto thee.
4 All the earth shall worship thee, and shall
sing unto thee; they shall sing *to* thy name. Se'-
lah.
5 Come and see the works of God: *he is* terrible *in his* doing toward the children of men.
6 He turned the sea into dry *land:* they went
through the flood on foot: there did we rejoice
in him.
7 He ruleth by his power for ever; his eyes
behold the nations: let not the rebellious exalt
themselves. Se'lah.
8 O bless our God, ye people, and make the
voice of his praise to be heard:
9 Which holdeth our soul in life, and suffereth not our feet to be moved.
10 For thou, O God, hast proved us: thou
hast tried us, as silver is tried.
11 Thou broughtest us into the net; thou
laidst affliction upon our loins.
12 Thou hast caused men to ride over our
heads; we went through fire and through water:
but thou broughtest us out into a wealthy *place.*
13 I will go into thy house with burnt offerings: I will pay thee my vows,
14 Which my lips have uttered, and my
mouth hath spoken, when I was in trouble.
15 I will offer unto thee burnt sacrifices of
fatlings, with the incense of rams; I will offer
bullocks with goats. Se'lah.
16 Come *and* hear, all ye that fear God, and I
will declare what he hath done for my soul.
17 I cried unto him with my mouth, and he
was extolled with my tongue.
18 If I regard iniquity in my heart, the Lord
will not hear *me:*
19 *But* verily God hath heard *me;* he hath attended to the voice of my prayer.
20 Blessed *be* God, which hath not turned
away my prayer, nor his mercy from me.

To the chief Musician on Neginoth, A Psalm *or* Song.

67 GOD be merciful unto us, and bless us;
and cause his face to shine upon us; Se'-
lah.
2 That thy way may be known upon earth,
thy saving health among all nations.
3 Let the people praise thee, O God; let all
the people praise thee.
4 O let the nations be glad and sing for joy:
for thou shalt judge the people righteously, and
govern the nations upon earth. Se'lah
5 Let the people praise thee, O God; let all
the people praise thee.
6 *Then* shall the earth yield her increase; *and*
God, *even* our own God, shall bless us.
7 God shall bless us; and all the ends of the
earth shall fear him.

To the chief Musician, A Psalm *or* Song of David.

68 LET God arise, let his enemies be scattered: let them also that hate him flee
before him.
2 As smoke is driven away, *so* drive *them*
away: as wax melteth before the fire, *so* let the
wicked perish at the presence of God.
3 But let the righteous be glad; let them rejoice before God: yea, let them exceedingly rejoice.
4 Sing unto God, sing praises to his name:
extol him that rideth upon the heavens by his
name JAH, and rejoice before him.
5 A father of the fatherless, and a judge of
the widows, *is* God in his holy habitation.
6 God setteth the solitary in families: he
bringeth out those which are bound with
chains: but the rebellious dwell in a dry *land.*
7 O God, when thou wentest forth before thy
people, when thou didst march through the wilderness; Se'lah:
8 The earth shook, the heavens also dropped
at the presence of God: *even* Si'nai itself *was
moved* at the presence of God, the God of Is'ra-
el.
9 Thou, O God, didst send a plentiful rain,
whereby thou didst confirm thine inheritance,
when it was weary.
10 Thy congregation hath dwelt therein:
thou, O God, hast prepared of thy goodness for
the poor.
11 The Lord gave the word: great *was* the
company of those that published *it.*
12 Kings of armies did flee apace: and she
that tarried at home divided the spoil.
13 Though ye have lien among the pots, *yet
shall ye be as* the wings of a dove covered with
silver, and her feathers with yellow gold.
14 When the Almighty scattered kings in it,
it was *white* as snow in Sal'mon.
15 The hill of God *is as* the hill of Ba'shan; an
high hill *as* the hill of Ba'shan.
16 Why leap ye, ye high hills? *this is* the hill
which God desireth to dwell in; yea, the LORD
will dwell *in it* for ever.
17 The chariots of God *are* twenty thousand,
even thousands of angels: the Lord *is* among
them, *as in* Si'nai, in the holy *place.*
18 Thou hast ascended on high, thou hast led
captivity captive: thou hast received gifts for
men; yea, *for* the rebellious also, that the LORD
God might dwell *among them.*
19 Blessed *be* the Lord, *who* daily loadeth us
with benefits, even the God of our salvation.
Se'lah.
20 *He that is* our God *is* the God of salvation;
and unto GOD the Lord *belong* the issues from
death.
21 But God shall wound the head of his enemies, *and* the hairy scalp of such an one as
goeth on still in his trespasses.
22 The Lord said, I will bring again from Ba'-
shan, I will bring *my people* again from the
depths of the sea:
23 That thy foot may be dipped in the blood
of *thine* enemies, *and* the tongue of thy dogs in
the same.
24 They have seen thy goings, O God; *even*
the goings of my God, my King, in the sanctuary.
25 The singers went before, the players on
instruments *followed* after; among *them were*
the damsels playing with timbrels.
26 Bless ye God in the congregations, *even*
the Lord, from the fountain of Is'ra-el.

27 There *is* little Ben'ja-min *with* their ruler,
the princes of Ju'dah *and* their council, the
princes of Zeb'u-lun, *and* the princes of Naph'-
ta-li.
28 Thy God hath commanded thy strength:
strengthen, O God, that which thou hast
wrought for us.
29 Because of thy temple at Je-ru'sa-lem
shall kings bring presents unto thee.
30 Rebuke the company of spearmen, the
multitude of the bulls, with the calves of the
people, *till every one* submit himself with
pieces of silver: scatter thou the people *that* delight in war.
31 Princes shall come out of E'gypt; E-thi-o'-
pi-a shall soon stretch out her hands unto God.
32 Sing unto God, ye kingdoms of the earth;
O sing praises unto the Lord; Se'lah:
33 To him that rideth upon the heavens of
heavens, *which were* of old; lo, he doth send out
his voice, *and that* a mighty voice.
34 Ascribe ye strength unto God: his excellency *is* over Is'ra-el, and his strength *is* in the
clouds.
35 O God, *thou art* terrible out of thy holy
places: the God of Is'ra-el *is* he that giveth
strength and power unto *his* people. Blessed *be*
God.

To the chief Musician upon Shoshannim, *A Psalm* of David.

69 SAVE me, O God; for the waters are
come in unto *my* soul.
2 I sink in deep mire, where *there is* no standing: I am come into deep waters, where the
floods overflow me.
3 I am weary of my crying: my throat is
dried: mine eyes fail while I wait for my God.
4 They that hate me without a cause are
more than the hairs of mine head: they that
would destroy me, *being* mine enemies wrongfully, are mighty: then I restored *that* which I
took not away.
5 O God, thou knowest my foolishness; and
my sins are not hid from thee.
6 Let not them that wait on thee, O Lord GOD
of hosts, be ashamed for my sake: let not those
that seek thee be confounded for my sake, O
God of Is'ra-el.
7 Because for thy sake I have borne reproach; shame hath covered my face.
8 I am become a stranger unto my brethren,
and an alien unto my mother's children.
9 For the zeal of thine house hath eaten me
up; and the reproaches of them that reproached
thee are fallen upon me.
10 When I wept, *and chastened* my soul with
fasting, that was to my reproach.
11 I made sackcloth also my garment; and I
became a proverb to them.
12 They that sit in the gate speak against me;
and I *was* the song of the drunkards.
13 But as for me, my prayer *is* unto thee, O
LORD, *in* an acceptable time: O God, in the multitude of thy mercy hear me, in the truth of thy
salvation.
14 Deliver me out of the mire, and let me not
sink: let me be delivered from them that hate
me, and out of the deep waters.
15 Let not the waterflood overflow me, neither let the deep swallow me up, and let not the
pit shut her mouth upon me.
16 Hear me, O LORD; for thy lovingkindness
is good: turn unto me according to the multitude of thy tender mercies.
17 And hide not thy face from thy servant;
for I am in trouble: hear me speedily.
18 Draw nigh unto my soul, *and* redeem it:
deliver me because of mine enemies.
19 Thou hast known my reproach, and my
shame, and my dishonour: mine adversaries *are*
all before thee.
20 Reproach hath broken my heart; and I am
full of heaviness: and I looked *for some* to take
pity, but *there was* none; and for comforters,
but I found none.
21 They gave me also gall for my meat; and
in my thirst they gave me vinegar to drink.
22 Let their table become a snare before
them: and *that which should have been* for *their*
welfare, *let it become* a trap.
23 Let their eyes be darkened, that they see
not; and make their loins continually to shake.
24 Pour out thine indignation upon them, and
let thy wrathful anger take hold of them.
25 Let their habitation be desolate; *and* let
none dwell in their tents.
26 For they persecute *him* whom thou hast
smitten; and they talk to the grief of those
whom thou hast wounded.
27 Add iniquity unto their iniquity: and let
them not come into thy righteousness.
28 Let them be blotted out of the book of the
living, and not be written with the righteous.
29 But I *am* poor and sorrowful: let thy salvation, O God, set me up on high.
30 I will praise the name of God with a song,
and will magnify him with thanksgiving.
31 *This* also shall please the LORD better than
an ox *or* bullock that hath horns and hoofs.
32 The humble shall see *this, and* be glad:
and your heart shall live that seek God.
33 For the LORD heareth the poor, and despiseth not his prisoners.
34 Let the heaven and earth praise him, the
seas, and every thing that moveth therein.
35 For God will save Zi'on, and will build the
cities of Ju'dah: that they may dwell there, and
have it in possession.
36 The seed also of his servants shall inherit
it: and they that love his name shall dwell
therein.

To the chief Musician, *A Psalm* of David, to bring to remembrance.

70 *MAKE haste,* O God, to deliver me;
make haste to help me, O LORD.
2 Let them be ashamed and confounded that
seek after my soul: let them be turned backward, and put to confusion, that desire my hurt.
3 Let them be turned back for a reward of
their shame that say, Aha, aha.
4 Let all those that seek thee rejoice and be
glad in thee: and let such as love thy salvation
say continually, Let God be magnified.
5 But I *am* poor and needy: make haste unto
me, O God, thou *art* my help and my deliverer;
O LORD, make no tarrying.

71 IN thee, O LORD, do I put my trust: let
me never be put to confusion.
2 Deliver me in thy righteousness, and cause
me to escape: incline thine ear unto me, and
save me.
3 Be thou my strong habitation, whereunto I
may continually resort: thou hast given commandment to save me; for thou *art* my rock and
my fortress.
4 Deliver me, O my God, out of the hand of
the wicked, out of the hand of the unrighteous
and cruel man.

5 For thou *art* my hope, O Lord GOD: *thou art* my trust from my youth.

6 By thee have I been holden up from the womb: thou art he that took me out of my mother's bowels: my praise *shall be* continually of thee.

7 I am as a wonder unto many; but thou *art* my strong refuge.

8 Let my mouth be filled *with* thy praise *and with* thy honour all the day.

9 Cast me not off in the time of old age; forsake me not when my strength faileth.

10 For mine enemies speak against me; and they that lay wait for my soul take counsel together,

11 Saying, God hath forsaken him: persecute and take him; for *there is* none to deliver *him*.

12 O God, be not far from me: O my God, make haste for my help.

13 Let them be confounded *and* consumed that are adversaries to my soul; let them be covered *with* reproach and dishonour that seek my hurt.

14 But I will hope continually, and will yet praise thee more and more.

15 My mouth shall shew forth thy righteousness *and* thy salvation all the day; for I know not the numbers *thereof*.

16 I will go in the strength of the Lord GOD: I will make mention of thy righteousness, *even* of thine only.

17 O God, thou hast taught me from my youth: and hitherto have I declared thy wondrous works.

18 Now also when I am old and grayheaded, O God, forsake me not; until I have shewed thy strength unto *this* generation, *and* thy power to every one *that* is to come.

19 Thy righteousness also, O God, *is* very high, who hast done great things: O God, who *is* like unto thee!

20 *Thou*, which hast shewed me great and sore troubles, shalt quicken me again, and shalt bring me up again from the depths of the earth.

21 Thou shalt increase my greatness, and comfort me on every side.

22 I will also praise thee with the psaltery, *even* thy truth, O my God: unto thee will I sing with the harp, O thou Holy One of Is'ra-el.

23 My lips shall greatly rejoice when I sing unto thee; and my soul, which thou hast redeemed.

24 My tongue also shall talk of thy righteousness all the day long: for they are confounded, for they are brought unto shame, that seek my hurt.

A Psalm for Solomon.

72 GIVE the king thy judgments, O God, and thy righteousness unto the king's son.

2 He shall judge thy people with righteousness, and thy poor with judgment.

3 The mountains shall bring peace to the people, and the little hills, by righteousness.

4 He shall judge the poor of the people, he shall save the children of the needy, and shall break in pieces the oppressor.

5 They shall fear thee as long as the sun and moon endure, throughout all generations.

6 He shall come down like rain upon the mown grass: as showers *that* water the earth.

7 In his days shall the righteous flourish; and abundance of peace so long as the moon endureth.

8 He shall have dominion also from sea to sea, and from the river unto the ends of the earth.

9 They that dwell in the wilderness shall bow before him; and his enemies shall lick the dust.

10 The kings of Tar'shish and of the isles shall bring presents: the kings of She'ba and Se'ba shall offer gifts.

11 Yea, all kings shall fall down before him: all nations shall serve him.

12 For he shall deliver the needy when he crieth; the poor also, and *him* that hath no helper.

13 He shall spare the poor and needy, and shall save the souls of the needy.

14 He shall redeem their soul from deceit and violence: and precious shall their blood be in his sight.

15 And he shall live, and to him shall be given of the gold of She'ba: prayer also shall be made for him continually; *and* daily shall he be praised.

16 There shall be an handful of corn in the earth upon the top of the mountains; the fruit thereof shall shake like Leb'a-non: and *they* of the city shall flourish like grass of the earth.

17 His name shall endure for ever: his name shall be continued as long as the sun: and *men* shall be blessed in him: all nations shall call him blessed.

18 Blessed *be* the LORD God, the God of Is'ra-el, who only doeth wondrous things.

19 And blessed *be* his glorious name for ever: and let the whole earth be filled *with* his glory; Amen, and Amen.

20 The prayers of Da'vid the son of Jes'se are ended.

A Psalm of Asaph.

73 TRULY God *is* good to Is'ra-el, *even* to such as are of a clean heart.

2 But as for me, my feet were almost gone; my steps had well nigh slipped.

3 For I was envious at the foolish, *when* I saw the prosperity of the wicked.

4 For *there are* no bands in their death: but their strength *is* firm.

5 They *are* not in trouble *as other* men; neither are they plagued like *other* men.

6 Therefore pride compasseth them about as a chain; violence covereth them *as* a garment.

7 Their eyes stand out with fatness: they have more than heart could wish.

8 They are corrupt, and speak wickedly *concerning* oppression: they speak loftily.

9 They set their mouth against the heavens, and their tongue walketh through the earth.

10 Therefore his people return hither: and waters of a full *cup* are wrung out to them.

11 And they say, How doth God know? and is there knowledge in the most High?

12 Behold, these *are* the ungodly, who prosper in the world; they increase *in* riches.

13 Verily I have cleansed my heart *in* vain, and washed my hands in innocency.

14 For all the day long have I been plagued, and chastened every morning.

15 If I say, I will speak thus; behold, I should offend *against* the generation of thy children.

16 When I thought to know this, it *was* too painful for me;

17 Until I went into the sanctuary of God; *then* understood I their end.

18 Surely thou didst set them in slippery places: thou castedst them down into destruction.

19 How are they *brought* into desolation, as

in a moment! they are utterly consumed with
terrors.
20 As a dream when *one* awaketh; *so*, O
Lord, when thou awakest, thou shalt despise
their image.
21 Thus my heart was grieved, and I was
pricked in my reins.
22 So foolish *was* I, and ignorant: I was *as* a
beast before thee.
23 Nevertheless I *am* continually with thee:
thou hast holden *me* by my right hand.
24 Thou shalt guide me with thy counsel, and
afterward receive me *to* glory.
25 Whom have I in heaven *but thee?* and
there is none upon earth *that* I desire beside
thee.
26 My flesh and my heart faileth: *but* God *is*
the strength of my heart, and my portion for
ever.
27 For, lo, they that are far from thee shall
perish: thou hast destroyed all them that go a
whoring from thee.
28 But *it is* good for me to draw near to God:
I have put my trust in the Lord GOD, that I may
declare all thy works.

Maschil of Asaph.

74 O GOD, why hast thou cast *us* off for
ever? *why* doth thine anger smoke
against the sheep of thy pasture?
2 Remember thy congregation, *which* thou
hast purchased of old; the rod of thine inheritance, *which* thou hast redeemed; this mount
Zi'on, wherein thou hast dwelt.
3 Lift up thy feet unto the perpetual desolations; *even* all *that* the enemy hath done wickedly in the sanctuary.
4 Thine enemies roar in the midst of thy congregations; they set up their ensigns *for* signs.
5 *A man* was famous according as he had
lifted up axes upon the thick trees.
6 But now they break down the carved work
thereof at once with axes and hammers.
7 They have cast fire into thy sanctuary, they
have defiled *by casting down* the dwelling place
of thy name to the ground.
8 They said in their hearts, Let us destroy
them together: they have burned up all the
synagogues of God in the land.
9 We see not our signs: *there is* no more any
prophet: neither *is there* among us any that
knoweth how long.
10 O God, how long shall the adversary reproach? shall the enemy blaspheme thy name
for ever?
11 Why withdrawest thou thy hand, even thy
right hand? pluck *it* out of thy bosom.
12 For God *is* my King of old, working salvation in the midst of the earth.
13 Thou didst divide the sea by thy strength:
thou brakest the heads of the dragons in the
waters.
14 Thou brakest the heads of leviathan in
pieces, *and* gavest him *to be* meat to the people
inhabiting the wilderness.
15 Thou didst cleave the fountain and the
flood: thou driedst up mighty rivers.
16 The day *is* thine, the night also *is* thine:
thou hast prepared the light and the sun.
17 Thou hast set all the borders of the earth:
thou hast made summer and winter.
18 Remember this, *that* the enemy hath reproached, O LORD, and *that* the foolish people
have blasphemed thy name.
19 O deliver not the soul of thy turtledove
unto the multitude *of the wicked:* forget not the
congregation of thy poor for ever.
20 Have respect unto the covenant: for the
dark places of the earth are full of the habitations of cruelty.
21 O let not the oppressed return ashamed:
let the poor and needy praise thy name.
22 Arise, O God, plead thine own cause: remember how the foolish man reproacheth thee
daily.
23 Forget not the voice of thine enemies: the
tumult of those that rise up against thee increaseth continually.

To the chief Musician, Al-taschith, A Psalm *or*
Song of Asaph.

75 UNTO thee, O God, do we give thanks,
unto thee do we give thanks: for *that*
thy name is near thy wondrous works declare.
2 When I shall receive the congregation I will
judge uprightly.
3 The earth and all the inhabitants thereof
are dissolved: I bear up the pillars of it. Se'lah.
4 I said unto the fools, Deal not foolishly: and
to the wicked, Lift not up the horn:
5 Lift not up your horn on high: speak *not
with* a stiff neck.
6 For promotion *cometh* neither from the
east, nor from the west, nor from the south.
7 But God *is* the judge: he putteth down one,
and setteth up another.
8 For in the hand of the LORD *there is* a cup,
and the wine is red; it is full of mixture; and he
poureth out of the same: but the dregs thereof,
all the wicked of the earth shall wring *them* out,
and drink *them*.
9 But I will declare for ever; I will sing
praises to the God of Ja'cob.
10 All the horns of the wicked also will I cut
off; *but* the horns of the righteous shall be exalted.

To the chief Musician on Neginoth, A Psalm *or*
Song of Asaph.

76 IN Ju'dah *is* God known: his name *is*
great in Is'ra-el.
2 In Sa'lem also is his tabernacle, and his
dwelling place in Zi'on.
3 There brake he the arrows of the bow, the
shield, and the sword, and the battle. Se'lah.
4 Thou *art* more glorious *and* excellent than
the mountains of prey.
5 The stouthearted are spoiled, they have
slept their sleep: and none of the men of might
have found their hands.
6 At thy rebuke, O God of Ja'cob, both the
chariot and horse are cast into a dead sleep.
7 Thou, *even* thou, *art* to be feared: and who
may stand in thy sight when once thou art angry?
8 Thou didst cause judgment to be heard
from heaven; the earth feared, and was still,
9 When God arose to judgment, to save all
the meek of the earth. Se'lah.
10 Surely the wrath of man shall praise thee:
the remainder of wrath shalt thou restrain.
11 Vow, and pay unto the LORD your God: let
all that be round about him bring presents unto
him that ought to be feared.
12 He shall cut off the spirit of princes: *he is*
terrible to the kings of the earth.

To the chief Musician, to Jeduthun, A Psalm
of Asaph.

77 I CRIED unto God with my voice, *even*
unto God with my voice; and he gave
ear unto me.

2 In the day of my trouble I sought the Lord:
my sore ran in the night, and ceased not: my
soul refused to be comforted.
3 I remembered God, and was troubled: I
complained, and my spirit was overwhelmed.
Se′lah.
4 Thou holdest mine eyes waking: I am so
troubled that I cannot speak.
5 I have considered the days of old, the years
of ancient times.
6 I call to remembrance my song in the night:
I commune with mine own heart: and my spirit
made diligent search.
7 Will the Lord cast off for ever? and will he
be favourable no more?
8 Is his mercy clean gone for ever? doth *his*
promise fail for evermore?
9 Hath God forgotten to be gracious? hath he
in anger shut up his tender mercies? Se′lah.
10 And I said, This *is* my infirmity: *but I will*
remember the years of the right hand of the
most High.
11 I will remember the works of the LORD:
surely I will remember thy wonders of old.
12 I will meditate also of all thy work, and
talk of thy doings.
13 Thy way, O God, *is* in the sanctuary: who
is so great a God as *our* God?
14 Thou *art* the God that doest wonders:
thou hast declared thy strength among the people.
15 Thou hast with *thine* arm redeemed thy
people, the sons of Ja′cob and Jo′seph. Se′lah.
16 The waters saw thee, O God, the waters
saw thee; they were afraid: the depths also
were troubled.
17 The clouds poured out water: the skies
sent out a sound: thine arrows also went
abroad.
18 The voice of thy thunder *was* in the
heaven: the lightnings lightened the world: the
earth trembled and shook.
19 Thy way *is* in the sea, and thy path in the
great waters, and thy footsteps are not known.
20 Thou leddest thy people like a flock by the
hand of Mo′ses and Aar′on.

Maschil of Asaph.

78 GIVE ear, O my people, *to* my law: incline your ears to the words of my
mouth.
2 I will open my mouth in a parable: I will
utter dark sayings of old:
3 Which we have heard and known, and our
fathers have told us.
4 We will not hide *them* from their children,
shewing to the generation to come the praises
of the LORD, and his strength, and his wonderful
works that he hath done.
5 For he established a testimony in Ja′cob,
and appointed a law in Is′ra-el, which he commanded our fathers, that they should make
them known to their children:
6 That the generation to come might know
them, even the children *which* should be born;
who should arise and declare *them* to their children:
7 That they might set their hope in God, and
not forget the works of God, but keep his commandments:
8 And might not be as their fathers, a stubborn and rebellious generation; a generation
that set not their heart aright, and whose spirit
was not stedfast with God.
9 The children of E′phra-im, *being* armed,
and carrying bows, turned back in the day of
battle.
10 They kept not the covenant of God, and
refused to walk in his law;
11 And forgat his works, and his wonders
that he had shewed them.
12 Marvellous things did he in the sight of
their fathers, in the land of E′gypt, *in* the field of
Zo′an.
13 He divided the sea, and caused them to
pass through; and he made the waters to stand
as an heap.
14 In the daytime also he led them with a
cloud, and all the night with a light of fire.
15 He clave the rocks in the wilderness, and
gave *them* drink as *out of* the great depths.
16 He brought streams also out of the rock,
and caused waters to run down like rivers.
17 And they sinned yet more against him by
provoking the most High in the wilderness.
18 And they tempted God in their heart by
asking meat for their lust.
19 Yea, they spake against God; they said,
Can God furnish a table in the wilderness?
20 Behold, he smote the rock, that the waters
gushed out, and the streams overflowed; can he
give bread also? can he provide flesh for his
people?
21 Therefore the LORD heard *this,* and was
wroth: so a fire was kindled against Ja′cob, and
anger also came up against Is′ra-el;
22 Because they believed not in God, and
trusted not in his salvation:
23 Though he had commanded the clouds
from above, and opened the doors of heaven,
24 And had rained down manna upon them
to eat, and had given them of the corn of
heaven.
25 Man did eat angels' food: he sent them
meat to the full.
26 He caused an east wind to blow in the
heaven: and by his power he brought in the
south wind.
27 He rained flesh also upon them as dust,
and feathered fowls like as the sand of the sea:
28 And he let *it* fall in the midst of their
camp, round about their habitations.
29 So they did eat, and were well filled: for
he gave them their own desire;
30 They were not estranged from their lust.
But while their meat *was* yet in their mouths,
31 The wrath of God came upon them, and
slew the fattest of them, and smote down the
chosen *men* of Is′ra-el.
32 For all this they sinned still, and believed
not for his wondrous works.
33 Therefore their days did he consume in
vanity, and their years in trouble.
34 When he slew them, then they sought
him: and they returned and enquired early after
God.
35 And they remembered that God *was* their
rock, and the high God their redeemer.
36 Nevertheless they did flatter him with
their mouth, and they lied unto him with their
tongues.
37 For their heart was not right with him,
neither were they stedfast in his covenant.
38 But he, *being* full of compassion, forgave
their iniquity, and destroyed *them* not: yea,
many a time turned he his anger away, and did
not stir up all his wrath.
39 For he remembered that they *were but*
flesh; a wind that passeth away, and cometh not
again.
40 How oft did they provoke him in the wilderness, *and* grieve him in the desert!

41 Yea, they turned back and tempted God,
and limited the Holy One of Is′ra-el.
42 They remembered not his hand, *nor* the
day when he delivered them from the enemy.
43 How he had wrought his signs in E′gypt,
and his wonders in the field of Zo′an:
44 And had turned their rivers into blood;
and their floods, that they could not drink.
45 He sent divers sorts of flies among them,
which devoured them; and frogs, which destroyed them.
46 He gave also their increase unto the caterpiller, and their labour unto the locust.
47 He destroyed their vines with hail, and
their sycomore trees with frost.
48 He gave up their cattle also to the hail,
and their flocks to hot thunderbolts.
49 He cast upon them the fierceness of his
anger, wrath, and indignation, and trouble, by
sending evil angels *among them.*
50 He made a way to his anger; he spared not
their soul from death, but gave their life over to
the pestilence;
51 And smote all the firstborn in E′gypt; the
chief of *their* strength in the tabernacles of
Ham:
52 But made his own people to go forth like
sheep, and guided them in the wilderness like a
flock.
53 And he led them on safely, so that they
feared not: but the sea overwhelmed their enemies.
54 And he brought them to the border of his
sanctuary, *even to* this mountain, *which* his
right hand had purchased.
55 He cast out the heathen also before them,
and divided them an inheritance by line, and
made the tribes of Is′ra-el to dwell in their tents.
56 Yet they tempted and provoked the most
high God, and kept not his testimonies:
57 But turned back, and dealt unfaithfully
like their fathers: they were turned aside like a
deceitful bow.
58 For they provoked him to anger with their
high places, and moved him to jealousy with
their graven images.
59 When God heard *this,* he was wroth, and
greatly abhorred Is′ra-el:
60 So that he forsook the tabernacle of Shi′-
loh, the tent *which* he placed among men;
61 And delivered his strength into captivity,
and his glory into the enemy's hand.
62 He gave his people over also unto the
sword; and was wroth with his inheritance.
63 The fire consumed their young men; and
their maidens were not given to marriage.
64 Their priests fell by the sword; and their
widows made no lamentation.
65 Then the Lord awaked as one out of sleep,
and like a mighty man that shouteth by reason
of wine.
66 And he smote his enemies in the hinder
parts: he put them to a perpetual reproach.
67 Moreover he refused the tabernacle of Jo′-
seph, and chose not the tribe of E′phra-im:
68 But chose the tribe of Ju′dah, the mount
Zi′on which he loved.
69 And he built his sanctuary like high *palaces,* like the earth which he hath established
for ever.
70 He chose Da′vid also his servant, and took
him from the sheepfolds:
71 From following the ewes great with young
he brought him to feed Ja′cob his people, and
Is′ra-el his inheritance.
72 So he fed them according to the integrity
of his heart; and guided them by the skilfulness
of his hands.

A Psalm of Asaph.

79 O GOD, the heathen are come into thine
inheritance; thy holy temple have they
defiled; they have laid Je-ru′sa-lem on heaps.
2 The dead bodies of thy servants have they
given *to be* meat unto the fowls of the heaven,
the flesh of thy saints unto the beasts of the
earth.
3 Their blood have they shed like water
round about Je-ru′sa-lem; and *there was* none
to bury *them.*
4 We are become a reproach to our neighbours, a scorn and derision to them that are
round about us.
5 How long, LORD? wilt thou be angry for
ever? shall thy jealousy burn like fire?
6 Pour out thy wrath upon the heathen that
have not known thee, and upon the kingdoms
that have not called upon thy name.
7 For they have devoured Ja′cob, and laid
waste his dwelling place.
8 O remember not against us former iniquities: let thy tender mercies speedily prevent us:
for we are brought very low.
9 Help us, O God of our salvation, for the glory of thy name: and deliver us, and purge away
our sins, for thy name's sake.
10 Wherefore should the heathen say, Where
is their God? let him be known among the heathen in our sight *by* the revenging of the blood
of thy servants *which is* shed.
11 Let the sighing of the prisoner come before thee; according to the greatness of thy
power preserve thou those that are appointed
to die;
12 And render unto our neighbours sevenfold into their bosom their reproach, wherewith
they have reproached thee, O Lord.
13 So we thy people and sheep of thy pasture
will give thee thanks for ever: we will shew
forth thy praise to all generations.

To the chief Musician upon Shoshannim-
eduth, A Psalm of Asaph.

80 GIVE ear, O Shepherd of Is′ra-el, thou
that leadest Jo′seph like a flock; thou
that dwellest *between* the cherubims, shine
forth.
2 Before E′phra-im and Ben′ja-min and Ma-
nas′seh stir up thy strength, and come *and* save
us.
3 Turn us again, O God, and cause thy face to
shine; and we shall be saved.
4 O LORD God of hosts, how long wilt thou be
angry against the prayer of thy people?
5 Thou feedest them with the bread of tears;
and givest them tears to drink in great measure.
6 Thou makest us a strife unto our neighbours: and our enemies laugh among themselves.
7 Turn us again, O God of hosts, and cause
thy face to shine; and we shall be saved.
8 Thou hast brought a vine out of E′gypt:
thou hast cast out the heathen, and planted it.
9 Thou preparedst *room* before it, and didst
cause it to take deep root, and it filled the land.
10 The hills were covered with the shadow of
it, and the boughs thereof *were like* the goodly
cedars.
11 She sent out her boughs unto the sea, and
her branches unto the river.
12 Why hast thou *then* broken down her

hedges, so that all they which pass by the way
do pluck her?
13 The boar out of the wood doth waste it,
and the wild beast of the field doth devour it.
14 Return, we beseech thee, O God of hosts:
look down from heaven, and behold, and visit
this vine;
15 And the vineyard which thy right hand
hath planted, and the branch *that* thou madest
strong for thyself.
16 *It is* burned with fire, *it is* cut down: they
perish at the rebuke of thy countenance.
17 Let thy hand be upon the man of thy right
hand, upon the son of man *whom* thou madest
strong for thyself.
18 So will not we go back from thee: quicken
us, and we will call upon thy name.
19 Turn us again, O LORD God of hosts, cause
thy face to shine; and we shall be saved.

To the chief Musician upon Gittith, *A Psalm* of Asaph.

81 SING aloud unto God our strength:
make a joyful noise unto the God of Ja'-
cob.
2 Take a psalm, and bring hither the timbrel,
the pleasant harp with the psaltery.
3 Blow up the trumpet in the new moon, in
the time appointed, on our solemn feast day.
4 For this *was* a statute for Is'ra-el, *and* a law
of the God of Ja'cob.
5 This he ordained in Jo'seph *for* a testimony,
when he went out through the land of E'gypt:
where I heard a language *that* I understood not.
6 I removed his shoulder from the burden:
his hands were delivered from the pots.
7 Thou calledst in trouble, and I delivered
thee; I answered thee in the secret place of
thunder: I proved thee at the waters of Meribah.
Se'lah.
8 Hear, O my people, and I will testify unto
thee: O Is'ra-el, if thou wilt hearken unto me;
9 There shall no strange god be in thee; neither shalt thou worship any strange god.
10 I *am* the LORD thy God, which brought
thee out of the land of E'gypt: open thy mouth
wide, and I will fill it.
11 But my people would not hearken to my
voice; and Is'ra-el would none of me.
12 So I gave them up unto their own hearts'
lust: *and* they walked in their own counsels.
13 Oh that my people had hearkened unto
me, *and* Is'ra-el had walked in my ways!
14 I should soon have subdued their enemies,
and turned my hand against their adversaries.
15 The haters of the LORD should have submitted themselves unto him: but their time
should have endured for ever.
16 He should have fed them also with the finest of the wheat: and with honey out of the rock
should I have satisfied thee.

A Psalm of Asaph.

82 GOD standeth in the congregation of
the mighty; he judgeth among the gods.
2 How long will ye judge unjustly, and accept the persons of the wicked? Se'lah.
3 Defend the poor and fatherless: do justice
to the afflicted and needy.
4 Deliver the poor and needy: rid *them* out of
the hand of the wicked.
5 They know not, neither will they understand; they walk on in darkness: all the foundations of the earth are out of course.
6 I have said, Ye *are* gods; and all of you *are*
children of the most High.
7 But ye shall die like men, and fall like one
of the princes.
8 Arise, O God, judge the earth: for thou
shalt inherit all nations.

A Song *or* Psalm of Asaph.

83 KEEP not thou silence, O God: hold not
thy peace, and be not still, O God.
2 For, lo, thine enemies make a tumult: and
they that hate thee have lifted up the head.
3 They have taken crafty counsel against thy
people, and consulted against thy hidden ones.
4 They have said, Come, and let us cut them
off from *being* a nation; that the name of Is'ra-el
may be no more in remembrance.
5 For they have consulted together with one
consent: they are confederate against thee:
6 The tabernacles of E'dom, and the Ish'ma-
el-ites; of Mo'ab, and the Ha'gar-enes;
7 Ge'bal, and Am'mon, and Am'a-lek; the
Phi-lis'tines with the inhabitants of Tyre;
8 As'sur also is joined with them: they have
holpen the children of Lot. Se'lah.
9 Do unto them as *unto* the Mid'i-an-ites; as
to Sis'e-ra, as *to* Ja'bin, at the brook of Ki'son:
10 *Which* perished at En'-dor: they became
as dung for the earth.
11 Make their nobles like O'reb, and like Ze'-
eb: yea, all their princes as Ze'bah, and as Zal-
mun'na:
12 Who said, Let us take to ourselves the
houses of God in possession.
13 O my God, make them like a wheel; as the
stubble before the wind.
14 As the fire burneth a wood, and as the
flame setteth the mountains on fire;
15 So persecute them with thy tempest, and
make them afraid with thy storm.
16 Fill their faces with shame; that they may
seek thy name, O LORD.
17 Let them be confounded and troubled for
ever; yea, let them be put to shame, and perish:
18 That *men* may know that thou, whose
name alone *is* JE-HO'VAH, *art* the most high
over all the earth.

To the chief Musician upon Gittith, A Psalm for the sons of Korah.

84 HOW amiable *are* thy tabernacles, O
LORD of hosts!
2 My soul longeth, yea, even fainteth for the
courts of the LORD: my heart and my flesh
crieth out for the living God.
3 Yea, the sparrow hath found an house, and
the swallow a nest for herself, where she may
lay her young, *even* thine altars, O LORD of
hosts, my King, and my God.
4 Blessed *are* they that dwell in thy house:
they will be still praising thee. Se'lah.
5 Blessed *is* the man whose strength *is* in
thee; in whose heart *are* the ways *of them.*
6 *Who* passing through the valley of Ba'ca
make it a well; the rain also filleth the pools.
7 They go from strength to strength, *every
one of them* in Zi'on appeareth before God.
8 O LORD God of hosts, hear my prayer: give
ear, O God of Ja'cob. Se'lah.
9 Behold, O God our shield, and look upon
the face of thine anointed.
10 For a day in thy courts *is* better than a
thousand. I had rather be a doorkeeper in the
house of my God, than to dwell in the tents of
wickedness.
11 For the LORD God *is* a sun and shield: the
LORD will give grace and glory: no good *thing*

will he withhold from them that walk uprightly.
12 O LORD of hosts, blessed *is* the man that
trusteth in thee.

To the chief Musician, A Psalm for the sons of
Korah.

85 LORD, thou hast been favourable unto
thy land: thou hast brought back the
captivity of Ja'cob.
2 Thou hast forgiven the iniquity of thy people, thou hast covered all their sin. Se'lah.
3 Thou hast taken away all thy wrath: thou
hast turned *thyself* from the fierceness of thine
anger.
4 Turn us, O God of our salvation, and cause
thine anger toward us to cease.
5 Wilt thou be angry with us for ever? wilt
thou draw out thine anger to all generations?
6 Wilt thou not revive us again: that thy people may rejoice in thee?
7 Shew us thy mercy, O LORD, and grant us
thy salvation.
8 I will hear what God the LORD will speak:
for he will speak peace unto his people, and to
his saints: but let them not turn again to folly.
9 Surely his salvation *is* nigh them that fear
him; that glory may dwell in our land.
10 Mercy and truth are met together; righteousness and peace have kissed *each other.*
11 Truth shall spring out of the earth; and
righteousness shall look down from heaven.
12 Yea, the LORD shall give *that which is*
good; and our land shall yield her increase.
13 Righteousness shall go before him; and
shall set *us* in the way of his steps.

A Prayer of David.

86 BOW down thine ear, O LORD, hear me:
for I *am* poor and needy.
2 Preserve my soul; for I *am* holy: O thou my
God, save thy servant that trusteth in thee.
3 Be merciful unto me, O Lord: for I cry unto
thee daily.
4 Rejoice the soul of thy servant: for unto
thee, O Lord, do I lift up my soul.
5 For thou, Lord, *art* good, and ready to forgive; and plenteous in mercy unto all them that
call upon thee.
6 Give ear, O LORD, unto my prayer; and attend to the voice of my supplications.
7 In the day of my trouble I will call upon
thee: for thou wilt answer me.
8 Among the gods *there is* none like unto
thee, O Lord; neither *are there any works* like
unto thy works.
9 All nations whom thou hast made shall
come and worship before thee, O Lord; and
shall glorify thy name.
10 For thou *art* great, and doest wondrous
things: thou *art* God alone.
11 Teach me thy way, O LORD; I will walk in
thy truth: unite my heart to fear thy name.
12 I will praise thee, O Lord my God, with all
my heart: and I will glorify thy name for evermore.
13 For great *is* thy mercy toward me: and
thou hast delivered my soul from the lowest
hell.
14 O God, the proud are risen against me,
and the assemblies of violent *men* have sought
after my soul; and have not set thee before
them.
15 But thou, O Lord, *art* a God full of compassion, and gracious, longsuffering, and plenteous in mercy and truth.
16 O turn unto me, and have mercy upon me;
give thy strength unto thy servant, and save the
son of thine handmaid.
17 Shew me a token for good; that they
which hate me may see *it*, and be ashamed: because thou, LORD, hast holpen me, and comforted me.

A Psalm *or* Song for the sons of Korah.

87 HIS foundation *is* in the holy mountains.
2 The LORD loveth the gates of Zi'on
more than all the dwellings of Ja'cob.
3 Glorious things are spoken of thee, O city
of God. Se'lah.
4 I will make mention of Ra'hab and Bab'y-
lon to them that know me: behold Phi-lis'tia,
and Tyre, with E-thi-o'pi-a; this *man* was born
there.
5 And of Zi'on it shall be said, This and that
man was born in her: and the highest himself
shall establish her.
6 The LORD shall count, when he writeth up
the people, *that* this *man* was born there. Se'-
lah.
7 As well the singers as the players on instruments *shall be there:* all my springs *are* in thee.

A Song *or* Psalm for the sons of Korah, to the
chief Musician upon Mahalath Leannoth,
Maschil of Heman the Ezrahite.

88 O LORD God of my salvation, I have
cried day *and* night before thee:
2 Let my prayer come before thee: incline
thine ear unto my cry;
3 For my soul is full of troubles: and my life
draweth nigh unto the grave.
4 I am counted with them that go down into
the pit: I am as a man *that hath* no strength:
5 Free among the dead, like the slain that lie
in the grave, whom thou rememberest no more:
and they are cut off from thy hand.
6 Thou hast laid me in the lowest pit, in darkness, in the deeps.
7 Thy wrath lieth hard upon me, and thou
hast afflicted *me* with all thy waves. Se'lah.
8 Thou hast put away mine acquaintance far
from me; thou hast made me an abomination
unto them: *I am* shut up, and I cannot come
forth.
9 Mine eye mourneth by reason of affliction:
LORD, I have called daily upon thee, I have
stretched out my hands unto thee.
10 Wilt thou shew wonders to the dead? shall
the dead arise *and* praise thee? Se'lah.
11 Shall thy lovingkindness be declared in
the grave? *or* thy faithfulness in destruction?
12 Shall thy wonders be known in the dark?
and thy righteousness in the land of forgetful-
ness?
13 But unto thee have I cried, O LORD; and in
the morning shall my prayer prevent thee.
14 LORD, why castest thou off my soul? *why*
hidest thou thy face from me?
15 I *am* afflicted and ready to die from *my*
youth up: *while* I suffer thy terrors I am dis-
tracted.
16 Thy fierce wrath goeth over me; thy terrors have cut me off.
17 They came round about me daily like water; they compassed me about together.
18 Lover and friend hast thou put far from
me, *and* mine acquaintance into darkness.

Maschil of Ethan the Ezrahite.

89 I WILL sing of the mercies of the LORD
for ever: with my mouth will I make
known thy faithfulness to all generations.

2 For I have said, Mercy shall be built up for
ever; thy faithfulness shalt thou establish in the
very heavens.
3 I have made a covenant with my chosen, I
have sworn unto Da'vid my servant,
4 Thy seed will I establish for ever, and build
up thy throne to all generations. Se'lah.
5 And the heavens shall praise thy wonders,
O LORD: thy faithfulness also in the congregation of the saints.
6 For who in the heaven can be compared
unto the LORD? *who* among the sons of the
mighty can be likened unto the LORD?
7 God is greatly to be feared in the assembly
of the saints, and to be had in reverence of all
them that are about him.
8 O LORD God of hosts, who *is* a strong LORD
like unto thee? or to thy faithfulness round
about thee?
9 Thou rulest the raging of the sea: when the
waves thereof arise, thou stillest them.
10 Thou hast broken Ra'hab in pieces, as one
that is slain; thou hast scattered thine enemies
with thy strong arm.
11 The heavens *are* thine, the earth also *is*
thine: *as for* the world and the fulness thereof,
thou hast founded them.
12 The north and the south thou hast created
them: Ta'bor and Her'mon shall rejoice in thy
name.
13 Thou hast a mighty arm: strong is thy
hand, *and* high is thy right hand.
14 Justice and judgment *are* the habitation of
thy throne: mercy and truth shall go before thy
face.
15 Blessed *is* the people that know the joyful
sound: they shall walk, O LORD, in the light of
thy countenance.
16 In thy name shall they rejoice all the day:
and in thy righteousness shall they be exalted.
17 For thou *art* the glory of their strength:
and in thy favour our horn shall be exalted.
18 For the LORD *is* our defence; and the Holy
One of Is'ra-el *is* our king.
19 Then thou spakest in vision to thy holy
one, and saidst, I have laid help upon *one that is*
mighty; I have exalted *one* chosen out of the
people.
20 I have found Da'vid my servant; with my
holy oil have I anointed him:
21 With whom my hand shall be established:
mine arm also shall strengthen him.
22 The enemy shall not exact upon him; nor
the son of wickedness afflict him.
23 And I will beat down his foes before his
face, and plague them that hate him.
24 But my faithfulness and my mercy *shall
be* with him: and in my name shall his horn be
exalted.
25 I will set his hand also in the sea, and his
right hand in the rivers.
26 He shall cry unto me, Thou *art* my father,
my God, and the rock of my salvation.
27 Also I will make him *my* firstborn, higher
than the kings of the earth.
28 My mercy will I keep for him for evermore, and my covenant shall stand fast with
him.
29 His seed also will I make *to endure* for
ever, and his throne as the days of heaven.
30 If his children forsake my law, and walk
not in my judgments;
31 If they break my statutes, and keep not
my commandments;
32 Then will I visit their transgression with
the rod, and their iniquity with stripes.
33 Nevertheless my lovingkindness will I not
utterly take from him, nor suffer my faithfulness to fail.
34 My covenant will I not break, nor alter the
thing that is gone out of my lips.
35 Once have I sworn by my holiness that I
will not lie unto Da'vid.
36 His seed shall endure for ever, and his
throne as the sun before me.
37 It shall be established for ever as the
moon, and *as* a faithful witness in heaven. Se'-
lah.
38 But thou hast cast off and abhorred, thou
hast been wroth with thine anointed.
39 Thou hast made void the covenant of thy
servant: thou hast profaned his crown *by casting it* to the ground.
40 Thou hast broken down all his hedges;
thou hast brought his strong holds to ruin.
41 All that pass by the way spoil him: he is a
reproach to his neighbours.
42 Thou hast set up the right hand of his adversaries; thou hast made all his enemies to rejoice.
43 Thou hast also turned the edge of his
sword, and hast not made him to stand in the
battle.
44 Thou hast made his glory to cease, and
cast his throne down to the ground.
45 The days of his youth hast thou shortened: thou hast covered him with shame. Se'-
lah.
46 How long, LORD? wilt thou hide thyself for
ever? shall thy wrath burn like fire?
47 Remember how short my time is: wherefore hast thou made all men in vain?
48 What man *is he that* liveth, and shall not
see death? shall he deliver his soul from the
hand of the grave? Se'lah.
49 Lord, where *are* thy former lovingkindnesses, *which* thou swarest unto Da'vid in thy
truth?
50 Remember, Lord, the reproach of thy servants; *how* I do bear in my bosom *the reproach
of* all the mighty people;
51 Wherewith thine enemies have reproached, O LORD; wherewith they have reproached the footsteps of thine anointed.
52 Blessed *be* the LORD for evermore. Amen,
and Amen.

A Prayer of Moses the man of God.

90 LORD, thou hast been our dwelling
place in all generations.
2 Before the mountains were brought forth,
or ever thou hadst formed the earth and the
world, even from everlasting to everlasting,
thou *art* God.
3 Thou turnest man to destruction; and sayest, Return, ye children of men.
4 For a thousand years in thy sight *are but* as
yesterday when it is past, and *as* a watch in the
night.
5 Thou carriest them away as with a flood;
they are *as* a sleep: in the morning *they are* like
grass *which* groweth up.
6 In the morning it flourisheth, and groweth
up; in the evening it is cut down, and withereth.
7 For we are consumed by thine anger, and
by thy wrath are we troubled.
8 Thou hast set our iniquities before thee, our
secret *sins* in the light of thy countenance.
9 For all our days are passed away in thy
wrath: we spend our years as a tale *that is told*.
10 The days of our years *are* threescore years
and ten; and if by reason of strength *they be*

fourscore years, yet *is* their strength labour and
sorrow; for it is soon cut off, and we fly away.
11 Who knoweth the power of thine anger?
even according to thy fear, *so is* thy wrath.
12 So teach *us* to number our days, that we
may apply *our* hearts unto wisdom.
13 Return, O LORD, how long? and let it repent thee concerning thy servants.
14 O satisfy us early with thy mercy; that we
may rejoice and be glad all our days.
15 Make us glad according to the days
wherein thou hast afflicted us, *and* the years
wherein we have seen evil.
16 Let thy work appear unto thy servants,
and thy glory unto their children.
17 And let the beauty of the LORD our God be
upon us: and establish thou the work of our
hands upon us; yea, the work of our hands establish thou it.

91 HE that dwelleth in the secret place of the most High shall abide under the shadow of the Almighty.
2 I will say of the LORD, *He is* my refuge and
my fortress: my God; in him will I trust.
3 Surely he shall deliver thee from the snare
of the fowler, *and* from the noisome pestilence.
4 He shall cover thee with his feathers, and
under his wings shalt thou trust: his truth *shall
be thy* shield and buckler.
5 Thou shalt not be afraid for the terror by
night; *nor* for the arrow *that* flieth by day;
6 *Nor* for the pestilence *that* walketh in darkness; *nor* for the destruction *that* wasteth at noonday.
7 A thousand shall fall at thy side, and ten
thousand at thy right hand; *but* it shall not
come nigh thee.
8 Only with thine eyes shalt thou behold and
see the reward of the wicked.
9 Because thou hast made the LORD, *which is*
my refuge, *even* the most High, thy habitation;
10 There shall no evil befall thee, neither
shall any plague come nigh thy dwelling.
11 For he shall give his angels charge over
thee, to keep thee in all thy ways.
12 They shall bear thee up in *their* hands, lest
thou dash thy foot against a stone.
13 Thou shalt tread upon the lion and adder:
the young lion and the dragon shalt thou trample under feet.
14 Because he hath set his love upon me,
therefore will I deliver him: I will set him on
high, because he hath known my name.
15 He shall call upon me, and I will answer
him: I *will be* with him in trouble; I will deliver
him, and honour him.
16 With long life will I satisfy him, and shew
him my salvation.

A Psalm *or* Song for the sabbath day.

92 *IT is a* good *thing* to give thanks unto the LORD, and to sing praises unto thy name, O most High:
2 To shew forth thy lovingkindness in the
morning, and thy faithfulness every night,
3 Upon an instrument of ten strings, and
upon the psaltery; upon the harp with a solemn
sound.
4 For thou, Lord, hast made me glad through
thy work: I will triumph in the works of thy
hands.
5 O LORD, how great are thy works! *and* thy
thoughts are very deep.
6 A brutish man knoweth not; neither doth a
fool understand this.
7 When the wicked spring as the grass, and
when all the workers of iniquity do flourish; *it is*
that they shall be destroyed for ever:
8 But thou, LORD, *art most* high for evermore.
9 For, lo, thine enemies, O LORD, for, lo, thine
enemies shall perish; all the workers of iniquity
shall be scattered.
10 But my horn shalt thou exalt like *the horn
of* an unicorn: I shall be anointed with fresh oil.
11 Mine eye also shall see *my desire* on mine
enemies, *and* mine ears shall hear *my desire* of
the wicked that rise up against me.
12 The righteous shall flourish like the palm
tree: he shall grow like a cedar in Leb'a-non.
13 Those that be planted in the house of the
LORD shall flourish in the courts of our God.
14 They shall still bring forth fruit in old age;
they shall be fat and flourishing;
15 To shew that the LORD *is* upright: *he is* my
rock, and *there is* no unrighteousness in him.

93 THE LORD reigneth, he is clothed with majesty; the LORD is clothed with strength, *wherewith* he hath girded himself: the world also is stablished, that it cannot be moved.
2 Thy throne *is* established of old: thou *art*
from everlasting.
3 The floods have lifted up, O LORD, the
floods have lifted up their voice; the floods lift
up their waves.
4 The LORD on high *is* mightier than the noise
of many waters, *yea, than* the mighty waves of
the sea.
5 Thy testimonies are very sure: holiness becometh thine house, O LORD, for ever.

94 O LORD God, to whom vengeance belongeth; O God, to whom vengeance belongeth, shew thyself.
2 Lift up thyself, thou judge of the earth: render a reward to the proud.
3 LORD, how long shall the wicked, how long
shall the wicked triumph?
4 *How long* shall they utter *and* speak hard
things? *and* all the workers of iniquity boast
themselves?
5 They break in pieces thy people, O LORD,
and afflict thine heritage.
6 They slay the widow and the stranger, and
murder the fatherless.
7 Yet they say, The LORD shall not see, neither shall the God of Ja'cob regard *it*.
8 Understand, ye brutish among the people:
and *ye* fools, when will ye be wise?
9 He that planted the ear, shall he not hear?
he that formed the eye, shall he not see?
10 He that chastiseth the heathen, shall not
he correct? he that teacheth man knowledge,
shall not he know?
11 The LORD knoweth the thoughts of man,
that they *are* vanity.
12 Blessed *is* the man whom thou chastenest,
O LORD, and teachest him out of thy law;
13 That thou mayest give him rest from the
days of adversity, until the pit be digged for the
wicked.
14 For the LORD will not cast off his people,
neither will he forsake his inheritance.
15 But judgment shall return unto righteousness: and all the upright in heart shall follow it.
16 Who will rise up for me against the evildoers? *or* who will stand up for me against the
workers of iniquity?
17 Unless the LORD *had been* my help, my
soul had almost dwelt in silence.

18 When I said, My foot slippeth; thy mercy,
O LORD, held me up.
19 In the multitude of my thoughts within
me thy comforts delight my soul.
20 Shall the throne of iniquity have fellowship with thee, which frameth mischief by a
law?
21 They gather themselves together against
the soul of the righteous, and condemn the innocent blood.
22 But the LORD is my defence; and my God
is the rock of my refuge.
23 And he shall bring upon them their own
iniquity, and shall cut them off in their own
wickedness; *yea*, the LORD our God shall cut
them off.

95 O COME, let us sing unto the LORD: let
us make a joyful noise to the rock of our
salvation.
2 Let us come before his presence with
thanksgiving, and make a joyful noise unto him
with psalms.
3 For the LORD *is* a great God, and a great
King above all gods.
4 In his hand *are* the deep places of the earth:
the strength of the hills *is* his also.
5 The sea *is* his, and he made it: and his
hands formed the dry *land*.
6 O come, let us worship and bow down: let
us kneel before the LORD our maker.
7 For he *is* our God; and we *are* the people of
his pasture, and the sheep of his hand. To day if
ye will hear his voice,
8 Harden not your heart, as in the provocation, *and* as *in* the day of temptation in the wilderness:
9 When your fathers tempted me, proved
me, and saw my work.
10 Forty years long was I grieved with *this*
generation, and said, It *is* a people that do err in
their heart, and they have not known my ways:
11 Unto whom I sware in my wrath that they
should not enter into my rest.

96 O SING unto the LORD a new song: sing
unto the LORD, all the earth.
2 Sing unto the LORD, bless his name; shew
forth his salvation from day to day.
3 Declare his glory among the heathen, his
wonders among all people.
4 For the LORD *is* great, and greatly to be
praised: he *is* to be feared above all gods.
5 For all the gods of the nations *are* idols: but
the LORD made the heavens.
6 Honour and majesty *are* before him:
strength and beauty *are* in his sanctuary.
7 Give unto the LORD, O ye kindreds of the
people, give unto the LORD glory and strength.
8 Give unto the LORD the glory *due unto* his
name: bring an offering, and come into his
courts.
9 O worship the LORD in the beauty of holiness: fear before him, all the earth.
10 Say among the heathen *that* the LORD
reigneth: the world also shall be established
that it shall not be moved: he shall judge the
people righteously.
11 Let the heavens rejoice, and let the earth
be glad; let the sea roar, and the fulness thereof.
12 Let the field be joyful, and all that *is*
therein: then shall all the trees of the wood rejoice
13 Before the LORD: for he cometh, for he
cometh to judge the earth: he shall judge the
world with righteousness, and the people with
his truth.

97 THE LORD reigneth; let the earth rejoice;
let the multitude of isles be glad *thereof*.
2 Clouds and darkness *are* round about him:
righteousness and judgment *are* the habitation
of his throne.
3 A fire goeth before him, and burneth up his
enemies round about.
4 His lightnings enlightened the world: the
earth saw, and trembled.
5 The hills melted like wax at the presence of
the LORD, at the presence of the LORD of the
whole earth.
6 The heavens declare his righteousness, and
all the people see his glory.
7 Confounded be all they that serve graven
images, that boast themselves of idols: worship
him, all *ye* gods.
8 Zi'on heard, and was glad; and the daughters of Ju'dah rejoiced because of thy judgments, O LORD.
9 For thou, LORD, *art* high above all the
earth: thou art exalted far above all gods.
10 Ye that love the LORD, hate evil: he preserveth the souls of his saints; he delivereth
them out of the hand of the wicked.
11 Light is sown for the righteous, and gladness for the upright in heart.
12 Rejoice in the LORD, ye righteous; and
give thanks at the remembrance of his holiness.

A Psalm.

98 O SING unto the LORD a new song; for
he hath done marvellous things: his
right hand, and his holy arm, hath gotten him
the victory.
2 The LORD hath made known his salvation:
his righteousness hath he openly shewed in the
sight of the heathen.
3 He hath remembered his mercy and his
truth toward the house of Is'ra-el: all the ends
of the earth have seen the salvation of our God.
4 Make a joyful noise unto the LORD, all the
earth: make a loud noise, and rejoice, and sing
praise.
5 Sing unto the LORD with the harp; with the
harp, and the voice of a psalm.
6 With trumpets and sound of cornet make a
joyful noise before the LORD, the King.
7 Let the sea roar, and the fulness thereof;
the world, and they that dwell therein.
8 Let the floods clap *their* hands: let the hills
be joyful together
9 Before the LORD; for he cometh to judge
the earth: with righteousness shall he judge the
world, and the people with equity.

99 THE LORD reigneth; let the people tremble: he sitteth *between* the cherubims;
let the earth be moved.
2 The LORD *is* great in Zi'on; and he *is* high
above all the people.
3 Let them praise thy great and terrible
name; *for* it *is* holy.
4 The king's strength also loveth judgment;
thou dost establish equity, thou executest judgment and righteousness in Ja'cob.
5 Exalt ye the LORD our God, and worship at
his footstool; *for* he *is* holy.
6 Mo'ses and Aar'on among his priests, and
Sam'u-el among them that call upon his name;
they called upon the LORD, and he answered
them.
7 He spake unto them in the cloudy pillar:
they kept his testimonies, and the ordinance
that he gave them.
8 Thou answeredst them, O LORD our God:

thou wast a God that forgavest them, though
thou tookest vengeance of their inventions.
9 Exalt the LORD our God, and worship at his
holy hill; for the LORD our God *is* holy.

A Psalm of praise.

100 MAKE a joyful noise unto the LORD,
all ye lands.
2 Serve the LORD with gladness: come before
his presence with singing.
3 Know ye that the LORD he *is* God: *it is* he
that hath made us, and not we ourselves; *we are*
his people, and the sheep of his pasture.
4 Enter into his gates with thanksgiving, *and*
into his courts with praise: be thankful unto
him, *and* bless his name.
5 For the LORD *is* good; his mercy *is* everlasting; and his truth *endureth* to all generations.

A Psalm of David.

101 I WILL sing of mercy and judgment:
unto thee, O LORD, will I sing.
2 I will behave myself wisely in a perfect
way. O when wilt thou come unto me? I will
walk within my house with a perfect heart.
3 I will set no wicked thing before mine eyes:
I hate the work of them that turn aside; *it* shall
not cleave to me.
4 A froward heart shall depart from me: I
will not know a wicked *person*.
5 Whoso privily slandereth his neighbour,
him will I cut off: him that hath an high look
and a proud heart will not I suffer.
6 Mine eyes *shall be* upon the faithful of the
land, that they may dwell with me: he that
walketh in a perfect way, he shall serve me.
7 He that worketh deceit shall not dwell
within my house: he that telleth lies shall not
tarry in my sight.
8 I will early destroy all the wicked of the
land; that I may cut off all wicked doers from
the city of the LORD.

A Prayer of the afflicted, when he is
overwhelmed, and poureth out his complaint
before the LORD.

102 HEAR my prayer, O LORD, and let my
cry come unto thee.
2 Hide not thy face from me in the day *when*
I am in trouble; incline thine ear unto me: in the
day *when* I call answer me speedily.
3 For my days are consumed like smoke, and
my bones are burned as an hearth.
4 My heart is smitten, and withered like
grass; so that I forget to eat my bread.
5 By reason of the voice of my groaning my
bones cleave to my skin.
6 I am like a pelican of the wilderness: I am
like an owl of the desert.
7 I watch, and am as a sparrow alone upon
the house top.
8 Mine enemies reproach me all the day; *and*
they that are mad against me are sworn against
me.
9 For I have eaten ashes like bread, and mingled my drink with weeping,
10 Because of thine indignation and thy
wrath: for thou hast lifted me up, and cast me
down.
11 My days *are* like a shadow that declineth;
and I am withered like grass.
12 But thou, O LORD, shalt endure for ever;
and thy remembrance unto all generations.
13 Thou shalt arise, *and* have mercy upon
Zi'on: for the time to favour her, yea, the set
time, is come.
14 For thy servants take pleasure in her
stones, and favour the dust thereof.
15 So the heathen shall fear the name of the
LORD, and all the kings of the earth thy glory.
16 When the LORD shall build up Zi'on, he
shall appear in his glory.
17 He will regard the prayer of the destitute,
and not despise their prayer.
18 This shall be written for the generation to
come: and the people which shall be created
shall praise the LORD.
19 For he hath looked down from the height
of his sanctuary; from heaven did the LORD behold the earth;
20 To hear the groaning of the prisoner; to
loose those that are appointed to death;
21 To declare the name of the LORD in Zi'on,
and his praise in Je-ru'sa-lem;
22 When the people are gathered together,
and the kingdoms, to serve the LORD.
23 He weakened my strength in the way; he
shortened my days.
24 I said, O my God, take me not away in the
midst of my days: thy years *are* throughout all
generations.
25 Of old hast thou laid the foundation of the
earth: and the heavens *are* the work of thy
hands.
26 They shall perish, but thou shalt endure:
yea, all of them shall wax old like a garment; as
a vesture shalt thou change them, and they
shall be changed:
27 But thou *art* the same, and thy years shall
have no end.
28 The children of thy servants shall continue, and their seed shall be established before
thee.

A Psalm of David.

103 BLESS the LORD, O my soul: and all
that is within me, *bless* his holy
name.
2 Bless the LORD, O my soul, and forget not
all his benefits:
3 Who forgiveth all thine iniquities; who
healeth all thy diseases;
4 Who redeemeth thy life from destruction;
who crowneth thee with lovingkindness and
tender mercies;
5 Who satisfieth thy mouth with good *things;*
so that thy youth is renewed like the eagle's.
6 The LORD executeth righteousness and
judgment for all that are oppressed.
7 He made known his ways unto Mo'ses, his
acts unto the children of Is'ra-el.
8 The LORD *is* merciful and gracious, slow to
anger, and plenteous in mercy.
9 He will not always chide: neither will he
keep *his anger* for ever.
10 He hath not dealt with us after our sins;
nor rewarded us according to our iniquities.
11 For as the heaven is high above the earth,
so great is his mercy toward them that fear him.
12 As far as the east is from the west, *so* far
hath he removed our transgressions from us.
13 Like as a father pitieth *his* children, *so* the
LORD pitieth them that fear him.
14 For he knoweth our frame; he remembereth that we *are* dust.
15 *As for* man, his days *are* as grass: as a
flower of the field, so he flourisheth.
16 For the wind passeth over it, and it is

gone; and the place thereof shall know it no more.

17 But the mercy of the LORD *is* from everlasting to everlasting upon them that fear him, and his righteousness unto children's children;

18 To such as keep his covenant, and to those that remember his commandments to do them.

19 The LORD hath prepared his throne in the heavens; and his kingdom ruleth over all.

20 Bless the LORD, ye his angels, that excel in strength, that do his commandments, hearkening unto the voice of his word.

21 Bless ye the LORD, all *ye* his hosts; *ye* ministers of his, that do his pleasure.

22 Bless the LORD, all his works in all places of his dominion: bless the LORD, O my soul.

104 BLESS the LORD, O my soul. O LORD my God, thou art very great; thou art clothed with honour and majesty.

2 Who coverest *thyself* with light as *with* a garment: who stretchest out the heavens like a curtain:

3 Who layeth the beams of his chambers in the waters: who maketh the clouds his chariot: who walketh upon the wings of the wind:

4 Who maketh his angels spirits; his ministers a flaming fire:

5 *Who* laid the foundations of the earth, *that* it should not be removed for ever.

6 Thou coveredst it with the deep as *with* a garment: the waters stood above the mountains.

7 At thy rebuke they fled; at the voice of thy thunder they hasted away.

8 They go up by the mountains; they go down by the valleys unto the place which thou hast founded for them.

9 Thou hast set a bound that they may not pass over; that they turn not again to cover the earth.

10 He sendeth the springs into the valleys, *which* run among the hills.

11 They give drink to every beast of the field: the wild asses quench their thirst.

12 By them shall the fowls of the heaven have their habitation, *which* sing among the branches.

13 He watereth the hills from his chambers: the earth is satisfied with the fruit of thy works.

14 He causeth the grass to grow for the cattle, and herb for the service of man: that he may bring forth food out of the earth;

15 And wine *that* maketh glad the heart of man, *and* oil to make *his* face to shine, and bread *which* strengtheneth man's heart.

16 The trees of the LORD are full *of sap;* the cedars of Leb′a-non, which he hath planted;

17 Where the birds make their nests: *as for* the stork, the fir trees *are* her house.

18 The high hills *are* a refuge for the wild goats; *and* the rocks for the conies.

19 He appointed the moon for seasons: the sun knoweth his going down.

20 Thou makest darkness, and it is night: wherein all the beasts of the forest do creep *forth.*

21 The young lions roar after their prey, and seek their meat from God.

22 The sun ariseth, they gather themselves together, and lay them down in their dens.

23 Man goeth forth unto his work and to his labour until the evening.

24 O LORD, how manifold are thy works! in wisdom hast thou made them all: the earth is full of thy riches.

25 *So is* this great and wide sea, wherein *are* things creeping innumerable, both small and great beasts.

26 There go the ships: *there is* that leviathan, *whom* thou hast made to play therein.

27 These wait all upon thee; that thou mayest give *them* their meat in due season.

28 *That* thou givest them they gather: thou openest thine hand, they are filled with good.

29 Thou hidest thy face, they are troubled: thou takest away their breath, they die, and return to their dust.

30 Thou sendest forth thy spirit, they are created: and thou renewest the face of the earth.

31 The glory of the LORD shall endure for ever: the LORD shall rejoice in his works.

32 He looketh on the earth, and it trembleth: he toucheth the hills, and they smoke.

33 I will sing unto the LORD as long as I live: I will sing praise to my God while I have my being.

34 My meditation of him shall be sweet: I will be glad in the LORD.

35 Let the sinners be consumed out of the earth, and let the wicked be no more. Bless thou the LORD, O my soul. Praise ye the LORD.

105 O GIVE thanks unto the LORD; call upon his name: make known his deeds among the people.

2 Sing unto him, sing psalms unto him: talk ye of all his wondrous works.

3 Glory ye in his holy name: let the heart of them rejoice that seek the LORD.

4 Seek the LORD, and his strength: seek his face evermore.

5 Remember his marvellous works that he hath done; his wonders, and the judgments of his mouth;

6 O ye seed of A′bra-ham his servant, ye children of Ja′cob his chosen.

7 He *is* the LORD our God: his judgments *are* in all the earth.

8 He hath remembered his covenant for ever, the word *which* he commanded to a thousand generations.

9 Which *covenant* he made with A′bra-ham, and his oath unto I′saac;

10 And confirmed the same unto Ja′cob for a law, *and* to Is′ra-el *for* an everlasting covenant:

11 Saying, Unto thee will I give the land of Ca′naan the lot of your inheritance:

12 When they were *but* a few men in number; yea, very few, and strangers in it.

13 When they went from one nation to another, from *one* kingdom to another people;

14 He suffered no man to do them wrong: yea, he reproved kings for their sakes;

15 *Saying,* Touch not mine anointed, and do my prophets no harm.

16 Moreover he called for a famine upon the land: he brake the whole staff of bread.

17 He sent a man before them, *even* Jo′seph, *who* was sold for a servant:

18 Whose feet they hurt with fetters: he was laid in iron:

19 Until the time that his word came: the word of the LORD tried him.

20 The king sent and loosed him; *even* the ruler of the people, and let him go free.

21 He made him lord of his house, and ruler of all his substance:

22 To bind his princes at his pleasure; and teach his senators wisdom.

23 Is′ra-el also came into E′gypt; and Ja′cob sojourned in the land of Ham.

24 And he increased his people greatly; and
made them stronger than their enemies.
25 He turned their heart to hate his people, to
deal subtilly with his servants.
26 He sent Mo′ses his servant; *and* Aar′on
whom he had chosen.
27 They shewed his signs among them, and
wonders in the land of Ham.
28 He sent darkness, and made it dark; and
they rebelled not against his word.
29 He turned their waters into blood, and
slew their fish.
30 Their land brought forth frogs in abundance, in the chambers of their kings.
31 He spake, and there came divers sorts of
flies, *and* lice in all their coasts.
32 He gave them hail for rain, *and* flaming
fire in their land.
33 He smote their vines also and their fig
trees; and brake the trees of their coasts.
34 He spake, and the locusts came, and caterpillers, and that without number,
35 And did eat up all the herbs in their land,
and devoured the fruit of their ground.
36 He smote also all the firstborn in their
land, the chief of all their strength.
37 He brought them forth also with silver
and gold: and *there was* not one feeble *person*
among their tribes.
38 E′gypt was glad when they departed: for
the fear of them fell upon them.
39 He spread a cloud for a covering; and fire
to give light in the night.
40 *The people* asked, and he brought quails,
and satisfied them with the bread of heaven.
41 He opened the rock, and the waters
gushed out; they ran in the dry places *like* a
river.
42 For he remembered his holy promise, *and*
A′bra-ham his servant.
43 And he brought forth his people with joy,
and his chosen with gladness:
44 And gave them the lands of the heathen:
and they inherited the labour of the people;
45 That they might observe his statutes, and
keep his laws. Praise ye the LORD.

106 PRAISE ye the LORD. O give thanks
unto the LORD; for *he is* good: for his
mercy *endureth* for ever.
2 Who can utter the mighty acts of the LORD?
who can shew forth all his praise?
3 Blessed *are* they that keep judgment, *and*
he that doeth righteousness at all times.
4 Remember me, O LORD, with the favour
that thou bearest unto thy people: O visit me
with thy salvation;
5 That I may see the good of thy chosen, that
I may rejoice in the gladness of thy nation, that
I may glory with thine inheritance.
6 We have sinned with our fathers, we have
committed iniquity, we have done wickedly.
7 Our fathers understood not thy wonders in
E′gypt; they remembered not the multitude of
thy mercies; but provoked *him* at the sea, *even*
at the Red sea.
8 Nevertheless he saved them for his name's
sake, that he might make his mighty power to
be known.
9 He rebuked the Red sea also, and it was
dried up: so he led them through the depths, as
through the wilderness.
10 And he saved them from the hand of him
that hated *them*, and redeemed them from the
hand of the enemy.
11 And the waters covered their enemies:
there was not one of them left.
12 Then believed they his words; they sang
his praise.
13 They soon forgat his works; they waited
not for his counsel:
14 But lusted exceedingly in the wilderness,
and tempted God in the desert.
15 And he gave them their request; but sent
leanness into their soul.
16 They envied Mo′ses also in the camp, *and*
Aar′on the saint of the LORD.
17 The earth opened and swallowed up Da′-
than, and covered the company of A-bi′ram.
18 And a fire was kindled in their company;
the flame burned up the wicked.
19 They made a calf in Ho′reb, and worshipped the molten image.
20 Thus they changed their glory into the similitude of an ox that eateth grass.
21 They forgat God their saviour, which had
done great things in E′gypt;
22 Wondrous works in the land of Ham, *and*
terrible things by the Red sea.
23 Therefore he said that he would destroy
them, had not Mo′ses his chosen stood before
him in the breach, to turn away his wrath, lest
he should destroy *them*.
24 Yea, they despised the pleasant land, they
believed not his word:
25 But murmured in their tents, *and* hearkened not unto the voice of the LORD.
26 Therefore he lifted up his hand against
them, to overthrow them in the wilderness:
27 To overthrow their seed also among the
nations, and to scatter them in the lands.
28 They joined themselves also unto Ba′al-
pe′or, and ate the sacrifices of the dead.
29 Thus they provoked *him* to anger with
their inventions: and the plague brake in upon
them.
30 Then stood up Phin′e-has, and executed
judgment: and *so* the plague was stayed.
31 And that was counted unto him for righteousness unto all generations for evermore.
32 They angered *him* also at the waters of
strife, so that it went ill with Mo′ses for their
sakes:
33 Because they provoked his spirit, so that
he spake unadvisedly with his lips.
34 They did not destroy the nations, concerning whom the LORD commanded them:
35 But were mingled among the heathen, and
learned their works.
36 And they served their idols: which were a
snare unto them.
37 Yea, they sacrificed their sons and their
daughters unto devils,
38 And shed innocent blood, *even* the blood
of their sons and of their daughters, whom they
sacrificed unto the idols of Ca′naan: and the
land was polluted with blood.
39 Thus were they defiled with their own
works, and went a whoring with their own inventions.
40 Therefore was the wrath of the LORD kindled against his people, insomuch that he abhorred his own inheritance.
41 And he gave them into the hand of the
heathen; and they that hated them ruled over
them.
42 Their enemies also oppressed them, and
they were brought into subjection under their
hand.
43 Many times did he deliver them; but they
provoked *him* with their counsel, and were
brought low for their iniquity.
44 Nevertheless he regarded their affliction,
when he heard their cry:

45 And he remembered for them his covenant, and repented according to the multitude
of his mercies.
46 He made them also to be pitied of all
those that carried them captives.
47 Save us, O LORD our God, and gather us
from among the heathen, to give thanks unto
thy holy name, *and* to triumph in thy praise.
48 Blessed *be* the LORD God of Is′ra-el from
everlasting to everlasting: and let all the people
say. Amen. Praise ye the LORD.

107

O GIVE thanks unto the LORD, for *he*
is good: for his mercy *endureth* for
ever.
2 Let the redeemed of the LORD say *so*,
whom he hath redeemed from the hand of the
enemy;
3 And gathered them out of the lands, from
the east, and from the west, from the north, and
from the south.
4 They wandered in the wilderness in a solitary way; they found no city to dwell in.
5 Hungry and thirsty, their soul fainted in
them.
6 Then they cried unto the LORD in their trouble, *and* he delivered them out of their distresses.
7 And he led them forth by the right way,
that they might go to a city of habitation.
8 Oh that *men* would praise the LORD *for* his
goodness, and *for* his wonderful works to the
children of men!
9 For he satisfieth the longing soul, and filleth the hungry soul with goodness.
10 Such as sit in darkness and in the shadow
of death, *being* bound in affliction and iron;
11 Because they rebelled against the words
of God, and contemned the counsel of the most
High:
12 Therefore he brought down their heart
with labour; they fell down, and *there was* none
to help.
13 Then they cried unto the LORD in their
trouble, *and* he saved them out of their distresses.
14 He brought them out of darkness and the
shadow of death, and brake their bands in sunder.
15 Oh that *men* would praise the LORD *for* his
goodness, and *for* his wonderful works to the
children of men!
16 For he hath broken the gates of brass, and
cut the bars of iron in sunder.
17 Fools because of their transgression, and
because of their iniquities, are afflicted.
18 Their soul abhorreth all manner of meat;
and they draw near unto the gates of death.
19 Then they cry unto the LORD in their trouble, *and* he saveth them out of their distresses.
20 He sent his word, and healed them, and
delivered *them* from their destructions.
21 Oh that *men* would praise the LORD *for* his
goodness, and *for* his wonderful works to the
children of men!
22 And let them sacrifice the sacrifices of
thanksgiving, and declare his works with rejoicing.
23 They that go down to the sea in ships, that
do business in great waters;
24 These see the works of the LORD, and his
wonders in the deep.
25 For he commandeth, and raiseth the
stormy wind, which lifteth up the waves
thereof.
26 They mount up to the heaven, they go
down again to the depths: their soul is melted
because of trouble.
27 They reel to and fro, and stagger like a
drunken man, and are at their wit's end.
28 Then they cry unto the LORD in their trouble, and he bringeth them out of their distresses.
29 He maketh the storm a calm, so that the
waves thereof are still.
30 Then are they glad because they be quiet;
so he bringeth them unto their desired haven.
31 Oh that *men* would praise the LORD *for* his
goodness, and *for* his wonderful works to the
children of men!
32 Let them exalt him also in the congregation of the people, and praise him in the assembly of the elders.
33 He turneth rivers into a wilderness, and
the watersprings into dry ground;
34 A fruitful land into barrenness, for the
wickedness of them that dwell therein.
35 He turneth the wilderness into a standing
water, and dry ground into watersprings.
36 And there he maketh the hungry to dwell,
that they may prepare a city for habitation;
37 And sow the fields, and plant vineyards,
which may yield fruits of increase.
38 He blesseth them also, so that they are
multiplied greatly; and suffereth not their cattle
to decrease.
39 Again, they are minished and brought low
through oppression, affliction, and sorrow.
40 He poureth contempt upon princes, and
causeth them to wander in the wilderness,
where there is no way.
41 Yet setteth he the poor on high from affliction, and maketh *him* families like a flock.
42 The righteous shall see *it*, and rejoice: and
all iniquity shall stop her mouth.
43 Whoso *is* wise, and will observe these
things, even they shall understand the lovingkindness of the LORD.

A Song *or* Psalm of David.

108

O GOD, my heart is fixed; I will sing
and give praise, even with my glory.
2 Awake, psaltery and harp: I *myself* will
awake early.
3 I will praise thee, O LORD, among the people: and I will sing praises unto thee among the
nations.
4 For thy mercy *is* great above the heavens:
and thy truth *reacheth* unto the clouds.
5 Be thou exalted, O God, above the heavens:
and thy glory above all the earth;
6 That thy beloved may be delivered: save
with thy right hand, and answer me.
7 God hath spoken in his holiness; I will rejoice, I will divide She′chem, and mete out the
valley of Suc′coth.
8 Gil′e-ad *is* mine; Ma-nas′seh *is* mine; E′-
phra-im also *is* the strength of mine head; Ju′-
dah *is* my lawgiver;
9 Mo′ab *is* my washpot: over E′dom will I
cast out my shoe; over Phi-lis′tia will I triumph.
10 Who will bring me into the strong city?
who will lead me into E′dom?
11 *Wilt* not *thou*, O God, *who* hast cast us
off? and wilt not thou, O God, go forth with our
hosts?
12 Give us help from trouble: for vain *is* the
help of man.
13 Through God we shall do valiantly: for he
it is that shall tread down our enemies.

To the chief Musician, A Psalm of David.

109 HOLD not thy peace, O God of my
praise;
2 For the mouth of the wicked and the mouth
of the deceitful are opened against me: they
have spoken against me with a lying tongue.
3 They compassed me about also with words
of hatred; and fought against me without a
cause.
4 For my love they are my adversaries: but I
give myself unto prayer.
5 And they have rewarded me evil for good,
and hatred for my love.
6 Set thou a wicked man over him: and let
Sa'tan stand at his right hand.
7 When he shall be judged, let him be condemned: and let his prayer become sin.
8 Let his days be few; *and* let another take
his office.
9 Let his children be fatherless, and his wife
a widow.
10 Let his children be continually vagabonds,
and beg: let them seek *their bread* also out of
their desolate places.
11 Let the extortioner catch all that he hath;
and let the strangers spoil his labour.
12 Let there be none to extend mercy unto
him: neither let there be any to favour his fatherless children.
13 Let his posterity be cut off; *and* in the generation following let their name be blotted out.
14 Let the iniquity of his fathers be remembered with the LORD; and let not the sin of his
mother be blotted out.
15 Let them be before the LORD continually,
that he may cut off the memory of them from
the earth.
16 Because that he remembered not to shew
mercy, but persecuted the poor and needy man,
that he might even slay the broken in heart.
17 As he loved cursing, so let it come unto
him: as he delighted not in blessing, so let it be
far from him.
18 As he clothed himself with cursing like as
with his garment, so let it come into his bowels
like water, and like oil into his bones.
19 Let it be unto him as the garment *which*
covereth him, and for a girdle wherewith he is
girded continually.
20 *Let* this *be* the reward of mine adversaries
from the LORD, and of them that speak evil
against my soul.
21 But do thou for me, O GOD the Lord, for
thy name's sake: because thy mercy *is* good, deliver thou me.
22 For I *am* poor and needy, and my heart is
wounded within me.
23 I am gone like the shadow when it declineth: I am tossed up and down as the locust.
24 My knees are weak through fasting; and
my flesh faileth of fatness.
25 I became also a reproach unto them: *when*
they looked upon me they shaked their heads.
26 Help me, O LORD my God: O save me according to thy mercy:
27 That they may know that this *is* thy hand;
that thou, LORD, hast done it.
28 Let them curse, but bless thou: when they
arise, let them be ashamed; but let thy servant
rejoice.
29 Let mine adversaries be clothed with
shame, and let them cover themselves with
their own confusion, as with a mantle.
30 I will greatly praise the LORD with my
mouth; yea, I will praise him among the multitude.
31 For he shall stand at the right hand of the
poor, to save *him* from those that condemn his
soul.

A Psalm of David.

110 THE LORD said unto my Lord, Sit
thou at my right hand, until I make
thine enemies thy footstool.
2 The LORD shall send the rod of thy strength
out of Zi'on: rule thou in the midst of thine enemies.
3 Thy people *shall be* willing in the day of thy
power, in the beauties of holiness from the
womb of the morning: thou hast the dew of thy
youth.
4 The LORD hath sworn, and will not repent,
Thou *art* a priest for ever after the order of Mel-
chiz'e-dek.
5 The Lord at thy right hand shall strike
through kings in the day of his wrath.
6 He shall judge among the heathen, he shall
fill *the places* with the dead bodies; he shall
wound the heads over many countries.
7 He shall drink of the brook in the way:
therefore shall he lift up the head.

111 PRAISE ye the LORD. I will praise the
LORD with *my* whole heart, in the assembly of the upright, and *in* the congregation.
2 The works of the LORD *are* great, sought
out of all them that have pleasure therein.
3 His work *is* honourable and glorious: and
his righteousness endureth for ever.
4 He hath made his wonderful works to be
remembered: the LORD *is* gracious and full of
compassion.
5 He hath given meat unto them that fear
him: he will ever be mindful of his covenant.
6 He hath shewed his people the power of his
works, that he may give them the heritage of
the heathen.
7 The works of his hands *are* verity and judgment; all his commandments *are* sure.
8 They stand fast for ever and ever, *and are*
done in truth and uprightness.
9 He sent redemption unto his people: he
hath commanded his covenant for ever: holy
and reverend *is* his name.
10 The fear of the LORD *is* the beginning of
wisdom: a good understanding have all they
that do *his commandments:* his praise endureth
for ever.

112 PRAISE ye the LORD. Blessed *is* the
man *that* feareth the LORD, *that* delighteth greatly in his commandments.
2 His seed shall be mighty upon earth: the
generation of the upright shall be blessed.
3 Wealth and riches *shall be* in his house:
and his righteousness endureth for ever.
4 Unto the upright there ariseth light in the
darkness: *he is* gracious, and full of compassion, and righteous.
5 A good man sheweth favour, and lendeth:
he will guide his affairs with discretion.
6 Surely he shall not be moved for ever: the
righteous shall be in everlasting remembrance.
7 He shall not be afraid of evil tidings: his
heart is fixed, trusting in the LORD.
8 His heart *is* established, he shall not be
afraid, until he see *his desire* upon his enemies.
9 He hath dispersed, he hath given to the
poor; his righteousness endureth for ever; his
horn shall be exalted with honour.
10 The wicked shall see *it,* and be grieved; he

shall gnash with his teeth, and melt away: the
desire of the wicked shall perish.

113 PRAISE ye the LORD. Praise, O ye
servants of the LORD, praise the name
of the LORD.
2 Blessed be the name of the LORD from this
time forth and for evermore.
3 From the rising of the sun unto the going
down of the same the LORD's name *is* to be
praised.
4 The LORD *is* high above all nations, *and* his
glory above the heavens.
5 Who *is* like unto the LORD our God, who
dwelleth on high,
6 Who humbleth *himself* to behold *the things*
that are in heaven, and in the earth!
7 He raiseth up the poor out of the dust, *and*
lifteth the needy out of the dunghill;
8 That he may set *him* with princes, *even*
with the princes of his people.
9 He maketh the barren woman to keep
house, *and to be* a joyful mother of children.
Praise ye the LORD.

114 WHEN Is'ra-el went out of E'gypt,
the house of Ja'cob from a people of
strange language;
2 Ju'dah was his sanctuary, *and* Is'ra-el his
dominion.
3 The sea saw *it*, and fled: Jor'dan was driven
back.
4 The mountains skipped like rams, *and* the
little hills like lambs.
5 What *ailed* thee, O thou sea, that thou fleddest? thou Jor'dan, *that* thou wast driven back?
6 Ye mountains, *that* ye skipped like rams;
and ye little hills, like lambs?
7 Tremble, thou earth, at the presence of the
Lord, at the presence of the God of Ja'cob;
8 Which turned the rock *into* a standing water, the flint into a fountain of waters.

115 NOT unto us, O LORD, not unto us,
but unto thy name give glory, for thy
mercy, *and* for thy truth's sake.
2 Wherefore should the heathen say, Where
is now their God?
3 But our God *is* in the heavens: he hath done
whatsoever he hath pleased.
4 Their idols *are* silver and gold, the work of
men's hands.
5 They have mouths, but they speak not:
eyes have they, but they see not:
6 They have ears, but they hear not: noses
have they, but they smell not:
7 They have hands, but they handle not: feet
have they, but they walk not: neither speak
they through their throat.
8 They that make them are like unto them; *so*
is every one that trusteth in them.
9 O Is'ra-el, trust thou in the LORD: he *is* their
help and their shield.
10 O house of Aar'on, trust in the LORD: he *is*
their help and their shield.
11 Ye that fear the LORD, trust in the LORD:
he *is* their help and their shield.
12 The LORD hath been mindful of us: he will
bless *us;* he will bless the house of Is'ra-el; he
will bless the house of Aar'on.
13 He will bless them that fear the LORD,
both small and great.
14 The LORD shall increase you more and
more, you and your children.
15 Ye *are* blessed of the LORD which made
heaven and earth.
16 The heaven, *even* the heavens, *are* the
LORD's: but the earth hath he given to the children of men.
17 The dead praise not the LORD, neither any
that go down into silence.
18 But we will bless the LORD from this time
forth and for evermore. Praise the LORD.

116 I LOVE the LORD, because he hath
heard my voice *and* my supplications.
2 Because he hath inclined his ear unto me,
therefore will I call upon *him* as long as I live.
3 The sorrows of death compassed me, and
the pains of hell gat hold upon me: I found trouble and sorrow.
4 Then called I upon the name of the LORD; O
LORD, I beseech thee, deliver my soul.
5 Gracious *is* the LORD, and righteous; yea,
our God *is* merciful.
6 The LORD preserveth the simple: I was
brought low, and he helped me.
7 Return unto thy rest, O my soul; for the
LORD hath dealt bountifully with thee.
8 For thou hast delivered my soul from
death, mine eyes from tears, *and* my feet from
falling.
9 I will walk before the LORD in the land of
the living.
10 I believed, therefore have I spoken: I was
greatly afflicted:
11 I said in my haste, All men *are* liars.
12 What shall I render unto the LORD *for* all
his benefits toward me?
13 I will take the cup of salvation, and call
upon the name of the LORD.
14 I will pay my vows unto the LORD now in
the presence of all his people.
15 Precious in the sight of the LORD *is* the
death of his saints.
16 O LORD, truly I *am* thy servant; I *am* thy
servant, *and* the son of thine handmaid: thou
hast loosed my bonds.
17 I will offer to thee the sacrifice of thanksgiving, and will call upon the name of the LORD.
18 I will pay my vows unto the LORD now in
the presence of all his people,
19 In the courts of the LORD's house, in the
midst of thee, O Je-ru'sa-lem. Praise ye the
LORD.

117 O PRAISE the LORD, all ye nations:
praise him, all ye people.
2 For his merciful kindness is great toward
us: and the truth of the LORD *endureth* for ever.
Praise ye the LORD.

118 O GIVE thanks unto the LORD; for *he*
is good: because his mercy *endureth*
for ever.
2 Let Is'ra-el now say, that his mercy *endur-*
eth for ever.
3 Let the house of Aar'on now say, that his
mercy *endureth* for ever.
4 Let them now that fear the LORD say, that
his mercy *endureth* for ever.
5 I called upon the LORD in distress: the LORD
answered me, *and set me* in a large place.
6 The LORD *is* on my side; I will not fear:
what can man do unto me?
7 The LORD taketh my part with them that
help me: therefore shall I see *my desire* upon
them that hate me.
8 *It is* better to trust in the LORD than to put
confidence in man.
9 *It is* better to trust in the LORD than to put
confidence in princes.

10 All nations compassed me about: but in
the name of the LORD will I destroy them.
11 They compassed me about; yea, they compassed me about: but in the name of the LORD I
will destroy them.
12 They compassed me about like bees; they
are quenched as the fire of thorns: for in the
name of the LORD I will destroy them.
13 Thou hast thrust sore at me that I might
fall: but the LORD helped me.
14 The LORD *is* my strength and song, and is
become my salvation.
15 The voice of rejoicing and salvation *is* in
the tabernacles of the righteous: the right hand
of the LORD doeth valiantly.
16 The right hand of the LORD is exalted: the
right hand of the LORD doeth valiantly.
17 I shall not die, but live, and declare the
works of the LORD.
18 The LORD hath chastened me sore: but he
hath not given me over unto death.
19 Open to me the gates of righteousness: I
will go into them, *and* I will praise the LORD:
20 This gate of the LORD, into which the
righteous shall enter.
21 I will praise thee: for thou hast heard me,
and art become my salvation.
22 The stone *which* the builders refused is
become the head *stone* of the corner.
23 This is the LORD's doing; it *is* marvellous
in our eyes.
24 This *is* the day *which* the LORD hath made;
we will rejoice and be glad in it.
25 Save now, I beseech thee, O LORD: O
LORD, I beseech thee, send now prosperity.
26 Blessed *be* he that cometh in the name of
the LORD: we have blessed you out of the house
of the LORD.
27 God *is* the LORD, which hath shewed us
light: bind the sacrifice with cords, *even* unto
the horns of the altar.
28 Thou *art* my God, and I will praise thee:
thou art my God, I will exalt thee.
29 O give thanks unto the LORD; for *he is*
good: for his mercy *endureth* for ever.

ALEPH.

119 BLESSED *are* the undefiled in the
way, who walk in the law of the
LORD.
2 Blessed *are* they that keep his testimonies,
and that seek him with the whole heart.
3 They also do no iniquity: they walk in his
ways.
4 Thou hast commanded *us* to keep thy precepts diligently.
5 O that my ways were directed to keep thy
statutes!
6 Then shall I not be ashamed, when I have
respect unto all thy commandments.
7 I will praise thee with uprightness of heart,
when I shall have learned thy righteous judgments.
8 I will keep thy statutes: O forsake me not
utterly.

BETH.

9 Wherewithal shall a young man cleanse his
way? by taking heed *thereto* according to thy
word.
10 With my whole heart have I sought thee:
O let me not wander from thy commandments.
11 Thy word have I hid in mine heart, that I
might not sin against thee.
12 Blessed *art* thou, O LORD: teach me thy
statutes.
13 With my lips have I declared all the judgments of thy mouth.
14 I have rejoiced in the way of thy testimonies, as *much as* in all riches.
15 I will meditate in thy precepts, and have
respect unto thy ways.
16 I will delight myself in thy statutes: I will
not forget thy word.

GIMEL.

17 Deal bountifully with thy servant, *that* I
may live, and keep thy word.
18 Open thou mine eyes, that I may behold
wondrous things out of thy law.
19 I *am* a stranger in the earth: hide not thy
commandments from me.
20 My soul breaketh for the longing *that it*
hath unto thy judgments at all times.
21 Thou hast rebuked the proud *that are*
cursed, which do err from thy commandments.
22 Remove from me reproach and contempt;
for I have kept thy testimonies.
23 Princes also did sit *and* speak against me:
but thy servant did meditate in thy statutes.
24 Thy testimonies also *are* my delight *and*
my counsellors.

DALETH.

25 My soul cleaveth unto the dust: quicken
thou me according to thy word.
26 I have declared my ways, and thou heardest me: teach me thy statutes.
27 Make me to understand the way of thy
precepts: so shall I talk of thy wondrous works.
28 My soul melteth for heaviness: strengthen
thou me according unto thy word.
29 Remove from me the way of lying: and
grant me thy law graciously.
30 I have chosen the way of truth: thy judgments have I laid *before me.*
31 I have stuck unto thy testimonies: O
LORD, put me not to shame.
32 I will run the way of thy commandments,
when thou shalt enlarge my heart.

HE.

33 Teach me, O LORD, the way of thy statutes; and I shall keep it *unto* the end.
34 Give me understanding, and I shall keep
thy law; yea, I shall observe it with *my* whole
heart.
35 Make me to go in the path of thy commandments; for therein do I delight.
36 Incline my heart unto thy testimonies, and
not to covetousness.
37 Turn away mine eyes from beholding vanity; *and* quicken thou me in thy way.
38 Stablish thy word unto thy servant, who *is*
devoted to thy fear.
39 Turn away my reproach which I fear: for
thy judgments *are* good.
40 Behold, I have longed after thy precepts:
quicken me in thy righteousness.

VAU.

41 Let thy mercies come also unto me, O
LORD, *even* thy salvation, according to thy
word.
42 So shall I have wherewith to answer him
that reproacheth me: for I trust in thy word.
43 And take not the word of truth utterly out
of my mouth; for I have hoped in thy judgments.
44 So shall I keep thy law continually for
ever and ever.
45 And I will walk at liberty: for I seek thy
precepts.

46 I will speak of thy testimonies also before
kings, and will not be ashamed.
47 And I will delight myself in thy commandments, which I have loved.
48 My hands also will I lift up unto thy commandments, which I have loved; and I will
meditate in thy statutes.

ZAIN.

49 Remember the word unto thy servant,
upon which thou hast caused me to hope.
50 This *is* my comfort in my affliction: for thy
word hath quickened me.
51 The proud have had me greatly in derision: *yet* have I not declined from thy law.
52 I remembered thy judgments of old, O
LORD; and have comforted myself.
53 Horror hath taken hold upon me because
of the wicked that forsake thy law.
54 Thy statutes have been my songs in the
house of my pilgrimage.
55 I have remembered thy name, O LORD, in
the night, and have kept thy law.
56 This I had, because I kept thy precepts.

CHETH.

57 *Thou art* my portion, O LORD: I have said
that I would keep thy words.
58 I intreated thy favour with *my* whole
heart: be merciful unto me according to thy
word.
59 I thought on my ways, and turned my feet
unto thy testimonies.
60 I made haste, and delayed not to keep thy
commandments.
61 The bands of the wicked have robbed me:
but I have not forgotten thy law.
62 At midnight I will rise to give thanks unto
thee because of thy righteous judgments.
63 I *am* a companion of all *them* that fear
thee, and of them that keep thy precepts.
64 The earth, O LORD, is full of thy mercy:
teach me thy statutes.

TETH.

65 Thou hast dealt well with thy servant, O
LORD, according unto thy word.
66 Teach me good judgment and knowledge:
for I have believed thy commandments.
67 Before I was afflicted I went astray: but
now have I kept thy word.
68 Thou *art* good, and doest good; teach me
thy statutes.
69 The proud have forged a lie against me:
but I will keep thy precepts with *my* whole
heart.
70 Their heart is as fat as grease; *but* I delight in thy law.
71 *It is* good for me that I have been afflicted;
that I might learn thy statutes.
72 The law of thy mouth *is* better unto me
than thousands of gold and silver.

JOD.

73 Thy hands have made me and fashioned
me: give me understanding, that I may learn thy
commandments.
74 They that fear thee will be glad when they
see me; because I have hoped in thy word.
75 I know, O LORD, that thy judgments *are*
right, and *that* thou in faithfulness hast afflicted
me.
76 Let, I pray thee, thy merciful kindness be
for my comfort, according to thy word unto thy
servant.
77 Let thy tender mercies come unto me,
that I may live: for thy law *is* my delight.
78 Let the proud be ashamed; for they dealt
perversely with me without a cause: *but* I will
meditate in thy precepts.
79 Let those that fear thee turn unto me, and
those that have known thy testimonies.
80 Let my heart be sound in thy statutes; that
I be not ashamed.

CAPH.

81 My soul fainteth for thy salvation: *but* I
hope in thy word.
82 Mine eyes fail for thy word, saying, When
wilt thou comfort me?
83 For I am become like a bottle in the
smoke; *yet* do I not forget thy statutes.
84 How many *are* the days of thy servant?
when wilt thou execute judgment on them that
persecute me?
85 The proud have digged pits for me, which
are not after thy law.
86 All thy commandments *are* faithful: they
persecute me wrongfully; help thou me.
87 They had almost consumed me upon
earth; but I forsook not thy precepts.
88 Quicken me after thy lovingkindness; so
shall I keep the testimony of thy mouth.

LAMED.

89 For ever, O LORD, thy word is settled in
heaven.
90 Thy faithfulness *is* unto all generations:
thou hast established the earth, and it abideth.
91 They continue this day according to thine
ordinances: for all *are* thy servants.
92 Unless thy law *had been* my delights, I
should then have perished in mine affliction.
93 I will never forget thy precepts: for with
them thou hast quickened me.
94 I *am* thine, save me; for I have sought thy
precepts.
95 The wicked have waited for me to destroy
me: *but* I will consider thy testimonies.
96 I have seen an end of all perfection: *but*
thy commandment *is* exceeding broad.

MEM.

97 O how love I thy law! it *is* my meditation
all the day.
98 Thou through thy commandments hast
made me wiser than mine enemies: for they *are*
ever with me.
99 I have more understanding than all my
teachers: for thy testimonies *are* my meditation.
100 I understand more than the ancients, because I keep thy precepts.
101 I have refrained my feet from every evil
way, that I might keep thy word.
102 I have not departed from thy judgments:
for thou hast taught me.
103 How sweet are thy words unto my taste!
yea, sweeter than honey to my mouth!
104 Through thy precepts I get understanding: therefore I hate every false way.

NUN.

105 Thy word *is* a lamp unto my feet, and a
light unto my path.
106 I have sworn, and I will perform *it*, that I
will keep thy righteous judgments.
107 I am afflicted very much: quicken me, O
LORD, according unto thy word.
108 Accept, I beseech thee, the freewill offerings of my mouth, O LORD, and teach me thy
judgments.
109 My soul *is* continually in my hand: yet do
I not forget thy law.

110 The wicked have laid a snare for me: yet I erred not from thy precepts.

111 Thy testimonies have I taken as an heritage for ever: for they *are* the rejoicing of my heart.

112 I have inclined mine heart to perform thy statutes alway, *even unto* the end.

SAMECH.

113 I hate *vain* thoughts: but thy law do I love.

114 Thou *art* my hiding place and my shield: I hope in thy word.

115 Depart from me, ye evildoers: for I will keep the commandments of my God.

116 Uphold me according unto thy word, that I may live: and let me not be ashamed of my hope.

117 Hold thou me up, and I shall be safe: and I will have respect unto thy statutes continually.

118 Thou hast trodden down all them that err from thy statutes: for their deceit *is* falsehood.

119 Thou puttest away all the wicked of the earth *like* dross: therefore I love thy testimonies.

120 My flesh trembleth for fear of thee; and I am afraid of thy judgments.

AIN.

121 I have done judgment and justice: leave me not to mine oppressors.

122 Be surety for thy servant for good: let not the proud oppress me.

123 Mine eyes fail for thy salvation, and for the word of thy righteousness.

124 Deal with thy servant according unto thy mercy, and teach me thy statutes.

125 I *am* thy servant; give me understanding, that I may know thy testimonies.

126 *It is* time for *thee*, LORD, to work: *for* they have made void thy law.

127 Therefore I love thy commandments above gold; yea, above fine gold.

128 Therefore I esteem all *thy* precepts *concerning* all *things to be* right; *and* I hate every false way.

PE.

129 Thy testimonies *are* wonderful: therefore doth my soul keep them.

130 The entrance of thy words giveth light; it giveth understanding unto the simple.

131 I opened my mouth, and panted: for I longed for thy commandments.

132 Look thou upon me, and be merciful unto me, as thou usest to do unto those that love thy name.

133 Order my steps in thy word: and let not any iniquity have dominion over me.

134 Deliver me from the oppression of man: so will I keep thy precepts.

135 Make thy face to shine upon thy servant; and teach me thy statutes.

136 Rivers of waters run down mine eyes, because they keep not thy law.

TZADDI.

137 Righteous *art* thou, O LORD, and upright *are* thy judgments.

138 Thy testimonies *that* thou hast commanded *are* righteous and very faithful.

139 My zeal hath consumed me, because mine enemies have forgotten thy words.

140 Thy word *is* very pure: therefore thy servant loveth it.

141 I *am* small and despised: *yet* do not I forget thy precepts.

142 Thy righteousness *is* an everlasting righteousness, and thy law *is* the truth.

143 Trouble and anguish have taken hold on me: *yet* thy commandments *are* my delights.

144 The righteousness of thy testimonies *is* everlasting: give me understanding, and I shall live.

KOPH.

145 I cried with *my* whole heart; hear me, O LORD: I will keep thy statutes.

146 I cried unto thee; save me, and I shall keep thy testimonies.

147 I prevented the dawning of the morning, and cried: I hoped in thy word.

148 Mine eyes prevent the *night* watches, that I might meditate in thy word.

149 Hear my voice according unto thy lovingkindness: O LORD, quicken me according to thy judgment.

150 They draw nigh that follow after mischief: they are far from thy law.

151 Thou *art* near, O LORD; and all thy commandments *are* truth.

152 Concerning thy testimonies, I have known of old that thou hast founded them for ever.

RESH.

153 Consider mine affliction, and deliver me: for I do not forget thy law.

154 Plead my cause, and deliver me: quicken me according to thy word.

155 Salvation *is* far from the wicked: for they seek not thy statutes.

156 Great *are* thy tender mercies, O LORD: quicken me according to thy judgments.

157 Many *are* my persecutors and mine enemies; *yet* do I not decline from thy testimonies.

158 I beheld the transgressors, and was grieved; because they kept not thy word.

159 Consider how I love thy precepts: quicken me, O LORD, according to thy lovingkindness.

160 Thy word *is* true *from* the beginning: and every one of thy righteous judgments *endureth* for ever.

SCHIN.

161 Princes have persecuted me without a cause: but my heart standeth in awe of thy word.

162 I rejoice at thy word, as one that findeth great spoil.

163 I hate and abhor lying: *but* thy law do I love.

164 Seven times a day do I praise thee because of thy righteous judgments.

165 Great peace have they which love thy law: and nothing shall offend them.

166 LORD, I have hoped for thy salvation, and done thy commandments.

167 My soul hath kept thy testimonies; and I love them exceedingly.

168 I have kept thy precepts and thy testimonies: for all my ways *are* before thee.

TAU.

169 Let my cry come near before thee, O LORD: give me understanding according to thy word.

170 Let my supplication come before thee: deliver me according to thy word.

171 My lips shall utter praise, when thou hast taught me thy statutes.

172 My tongue shall speak of thy word: for
all thy commandments *are* righteousness.
173 Let thine hand help me; for I have chosen
thy precepts.
174 I have longed for thy salvation, O LORD;
and thy law *is* my delight.
175 Let my soul live, and it shall praise thee;
and let thy judgments help me.
176 I have gone astray like a lost sheep; seek
thy servant; for I do not forget thy commandments.

A Song of degrees.

120 IN my distress I cried unto the LORD,
and he heard me.
2 Deliver my soul, O LORD, from lying lips,
and from a deceitful tongue.
3 What shall be given unto thee? or what
shall be done unto thee, thou false tongue?
4 Sharp arrows of the mighty, with coals of
juniper.
5 Woe is me, that I sojourn in Me'sech, *that* I
dwell in the tents of Ke'dar!
6 My soul hath long dwelt with him that hateth peace.
7 I *am for* peace: but when I speak, they *are*
for war.

A Song of degrees.

121 I WILL lift up mine eyes unto the
hills, from whence cometh my help.
2 My help *cometh* from the LORD, which
made heaven and earth.
3 He will not suffer thy foot to be moved: he
that keepeth thee will not slumber.
4 Behold, he that keepeth Is'ra-el shall neither slumber nor sleep.
5 The LORD *is* thy keeper: the LORD *is* thy
shade upon thy right hand.
6 The sun shall not smite thee by day, nor the
moon by night.
7 The LORD shall preserve thee from all evil:
he shall preserve thy soul.
8 The LORD shall preserve thy going out and
thy coming in from this time forth, and even for
evermore.

A Song of degrees of David.

122 I WAS glad when they said unto me,
Let us go into the house of the LORD.
2 Our feet shall stand within thy gates, O Je-
ru'sa-lem.
3 Je-ru'sa-lem is builded as a city that is
compact together:
4 Whither the tribes go up, the tribes of the
LORD, unto the testimony of Is'ra-el, to give
thanks unto the name of the LORD.
5 For there are set thrones of judgment, the
thrones of the house of Da'vid.
6 Pray for the peace of Je-ru'sa-lem: they
shall prosper that love thee.
7 Peace be within thy walls, *and* prosperity
within thy palaces.
8 For my brethren and companions' sakes, I
will now say, Peace *be* within thee.
9 Because of the house of the LORD our God I
will seek thy good.

A Song of degrees.

123 UNTO thee lift I up mine eyes, O thou
that dwellest in the heavens.
2 Behold, as the eyes of servants *look* unto
the hand of their masters, *and* as the eyes of a
maiden unto the hand of her mistress; so our
eyes *wait* upon the LORD our God, until that he
have mercy upon us.
3 Have mercy upon us, O LORD, have mercy
upon us: for we are exceedingly filled with contempt.
4 Our soul is exceedingly filled with the
scorning of those that are at ease, *and* with the
contempt of the proud.

A Song of degrees of David.

124 IF *it had not been* the LORD who was
on our side, now may Is'ra-el say;
2 If *it had not been* the LORD who was on our
side, when men rose up against us:
3 Then they had swallowed us up quick,
when their wrath was kindled against us:
4 Then the waters had overwhelmed us, the
stream had gone over our soul:
5 Then the proud waters had gone over our
soul.
6 Blessed *be* the LORD, who hath not given us
as a prey to their teeth.
7 Our soul is escaped as a bird out of the
snare of the fowlers: the snare is broken, and
we are escaped.
8 Our help *is* in the name of the LORD, who
made heaven and earth.

A Song of degrees.

125 THEY that trust in the LORD *shall be*
as mount Zi'on, *which* cannot be removed, *but* abideth for ever.
2 *As* the mountains *are* round about Je-ru'sa-
lem, so the LORD *is* round about his people from
henceforth even for ever.
3 For the rod of the wicked shall not rest
upon the lot of the righteous; lest the righteous
put forth their hands unto iniquity.
4 Do good, O LORD, unto *those that be* good,
and to *them that are* upright in their hearts.
5 As for such as turn aside unto their
crooked ways, the LORD shall lead them forth
with the workers of iniquity: *but* peace *shall be*
upon Is'ra-el.

A Song of degrees.

126 WHEN the LORD turned again the
captivity of Zi'on, we were like them
that dream.
2 Then was our mouth filled with laughter,
and our tongue with singing: then said they
among the heathen, The LORD hath done great
things for them.
3 The LORD hath done great things for us;
whereof we are glad.
4 Turn again our captivity, O LORD, as the
streams in the south.
5 They that sow in tears shall reap in joy.
6 He that goeth forth and weepeth, bearing
precious seed, shall doubtless come again with
rejoicing, bringing his sheaves *with him.*

A Song of degrees *for Solomon.

127 EXCEPT the LORD build the house,
they labour in vain that build it: except the LORD keep the city, the watchman
waketh *but* in vain.
2 *It is* vain for you to rise up early, to sit up
late, to eat the bread of sorrows: *for* so he giveth his beloved sleep.
3 Lo, children *are* an heritage of the LORD:
and the fruit of the womb *is his* reward.

4 As arrows *are* in the hand of a mighty man;
so *are* children of the youth.
5 Happy *is* the man that hath his quiver full
of them: they shall not be ashamed, but they
shall speak with the enemies in the gate.

A Song of degrees.

128 BLESSED *is* every one that feareth
the LORD; that walketh in his ways.
2 For thou shalt eat the labour of thine
hands: happy *shalt* thou *be,* and *it shall be* well
with thee.
3 Thy wife *shall be* as a fruitful vine by the
sides of thine house: thy children like olive
plants round about thy table.
4 Behold, that thus shall the man be blessed
that feareth the LORD.
5 The LORD shall bless thee out of Zi'on: and
thou shalt see the good of Je-ru'sa-lem all the
days of thy life.
6 Yea, thou shalt see thy children's children,
and peace upon Is'ra-el.

A Song of degrees.

129 MANY a time have they afflicted me
from my youth, may Is'ra-el now say:
2 Many a time have they afflicted me from
my youth: yet they have not prevailed against
me.
3 The plowers plowed upon my back: they
made long their furrows.
4 The LORD *is* righteous: he hath cut asunder
the cords of the wicked.
5 Let them all be confounded and turned
back that hate Zi'on.
6 Let them be as the grass *upon* the house
tops, which withereth afore it groweth up:
7 Wherewith the mower filleth not his hand;
nor he that bindeth sheaves his bosom.
8 Neither do they which go by say, The blessing of the LORD *be* upon you: we bless you in the
name of the LORD.

A Song of degrees.

130 OUT of the depths have I cried unto
thee, O LORD.
2 Lord, hear my voice: let thine ears be attentive to the voice of my supplications.
3 If thou, LORD, shouldest mark iniquities, O
Lord, who shall stand?
4 But *there is* forgiveness with thee, that
thou mayest be feared.
5 I wait for the LORD, my soul doth wait, and
in his word do I hope.
6 My soul *waiteth* for the Lord more than
they that watch for the morning: *I say, more
than* they that watch for the morning.
7 Let Is'ra-el hope in the LORD: for with the
LORD *there is* mercy, and with him *is* plenteous
redemption.
8 And he shall redeem Is'ra-el from all his iniquities.

A Song of degrees of David.

131 LORD, my heart is not haughty, nor
mine eyes lofty: neither do I exercise
myself in great matters, or in things too high for
me.
2 Surely I have behaved and quieted myself,
as a child that is weaned of his mother: my soul
is even as a weaned child.
3 Let Is'ra-el hope in the LORD from henceforth and for ever.

A Song of degrees.

132 LORD, remember Da'vid, *and* all his
afflictions:
2 How he sware unto the LORD, *and* vowed
unto the mighty *God* of Ja'cob;
3 Surely I will not come into the tabernacle
of my house, nor go up into my bed;
4 I will not give sleep to mine eyes, *or* slumber to mine eyelids,
5 Until I find out a place for the LORD, an
habitation for the mighty *God* of Ja'cob.
6 Lo, we heard of it at Eph'ra-tah: we found it
in the fields of the wood.
7 We will go into his tabernacles: we will
worship at his footstool.
8 Arise, O LORD, into thy rest; thou, and the
ark of thy strength.
9 Let thy priests be clothed with righteousness; and let thy saints shout for joy.
10 For thy servant Da'vid's sake turn not
away the face of thine anointed.
11 The LORD hath sworn *in* truth unto Da'vid;
he will not turn from it; Of the fruit of thy body
will I set upon thy throne.
12 If thy children will keep my covenant and
my testimony that I shall teach them, their children shall also sit upon thy throne for evermore.
13 For the LORD hath chosen Zi'on; he hath
desired *it* for his habitation.
14 This *is* my rest for ever: here will I dwell;
for I have desired it.
15 I will abundantly bless her provision: I
will satisfy her poor with bread.
16 I will also clothe her priests with salvation: and her saints shall shout aloud for joy.
17 There will I make the horn of Da'vid to
bud: I have ordained a lamp for mine anointed.
18 His enemies will I clothe with shame: but
upon himself shall his crown flourish.

A Song of degrees of David.

133 BEHOLD, how good and how pleasant *it is* for brethren to dwell together
in unity!
2 *It is* like the precious ointment upon the
head, that ran down upon the beard, *even* Aar'-
on's beard: that went down to the skirts of his
garments;
3 As the dew of Her'mon, *and as the dew*
that descended upon the mountains of Zi'on: for
there the LORD commanded the blessing, *even*
life for evermore.

A Song of degrees.

134 BEHOLD, bless ye the LORD, all *ye*
servants of the LORD, which by night
stand in the house of the LORD.
2 Lift up your hands *in* the sanctuary, and
bless the LORD.
3 The LORD that made heaven and earth
bless thee out of Zi'on.

135 PRAISE ye the LORD. Praise ye the
name of the LORD; praise *him,* O ye
servants of the LORD.
2 Ye that stand in the house of the LORD, in
the courts of the house of our God,
3 Praise the LORD; for the LORD *is* good: sing
praises unto his name; for *it is* pleasant.
4 For the LORD hath chosen Ja'cob unto himself, *and* Is'ra-el for his peculiar treasure.
5 For I know that the LORD *is* great, and *that*
our Lord *is* above all gods.

6 Whatsoever the LORD pleased, *that* did he in heaven, and in earth, in the seas, and all deep places.

7 He causeth the vapours to ascend from the ends of the earth; he maketh lightnings for the rain; he bringeth the wind out of his treasuries.

8 Who smote the firstborn of E′gypt, both of man and beast.

9 *Who* sent tokens and wonders into the midst of thee, O E′gypt, upon Pha′raoh, and upon all his servants.

10 Who smote great nations, and slew mighty kings;

11 Si′hon king of the Am′or-ites, and Og king of Ba′shan, and all the kingdoms of Ca′naan:

12 And gave their land *for* an heritage, an heritage unto Is′ra-el his people.

13 Thy name, O LORD, *endureth* for ever; *and* thy memorial, O LORD, throughout all generations.

14 For the LORD will judge his people, and he will repent himself concerning his servants.

15 The idols of the heathen *are* silver and gold, the work of men's hands.

16 They have mouths, but they speak not; eyes have they, but they see not;

17 They have ears, but they hear not; neither is there *any* breath in their mouths.

18 They that make them are like unto them: *so is* every one that trusteth in them.

19 Bless the LORD, O house of Is′ra-el: bless the LORD, O house of Aar′on:

20 Bless the LORD, O house of Le′vi: ye that fear the LORD, bless the LORD.

21 Blessed be the LORD out of Zi′on, which dwelleth at Je-ru′sa-lem. Praise ye the LORD.

136

O GIVE thanks unto the LORD; for *he is* good: for his mercy *endureth* for ever.

2 O give thanks unto the God of gods: for his mercy *endureth* for ever.

3 O give thanks to the Lord of lords: for his mercy *endureth* for ever.

4 To him who alone doeth great wonders: for his mercy *endureth* for ever.

5 To him that by wisdom made the heavens: for his mercy *endureth* for ever.

6 To him that stretched out the earth above the waters: for his mercy *endureth* for ever.

7 To him that made great lights: for his mercy *endureth* for ever:

8 The sun to rule by day: for his mercy *endureth* for ever:

9 The moon and stars to rule by night: for his mercy *endureth* for ever.

10 To him that smote E′gypt in their firstborn: for his mercy *endureth* for ever:

11 And brought out Is′ra-el from among them: for his mercy *endureth* for ever.

12 With a strong hand, and with a stretched out arm: for his mercy *endureth* for ever.

13 To him which divided the Red sea into parts: for his mercy *endureth* for ever:

14 And made Is′ra-el to pass through the midst of it: for his mercy *endureth* for ever:

15 But overthrew Pha′raoh and his host in the Red sea: for his mercy *endureth* for ever.

16 To him which led his people through the wilderness: for his mercy *endureth* for ever.

17 To him which smote great kings: for his mercy *endureth* for ever:

18 And slew famous kings: for his mercy *endureth* for ever:

19 Si′hon king of the Am′or-ites: for his mercy *endureth* for ever:

20 And Og the king of Ba′shan: for his mercy *endureth* for ever:

21 And gave their land for an heritage: for his mercy *endureth* for ever:

22 *Even* an heritage unto Is′ra-el his servant: for his mercy *endureth* for ever.

23 Who remembered us in our low estate: for his mercy *endureth* for ever.

24 And hath redeemed us from our enemies: for his mercy *endureth* for ever.

25 Who giveth food to all flesh: for his mercy *endureth* for ever.

26 O give thanks unto the God of heaven: for his mercy *endureth* for ever.

137

BY the rivers of Bab′y-lon, there we sat down, yea, we wept, when we remembered Zi′on.

2 We hanged our harps upon the willows in the midst thereof.

3 For there they that carried us away captive required of us a song; and they that wasted us *required of us* mirth, *saying*, Sing us *one* of the songs of Zi′on.

4 How shall we sing the LORD's song in a strange land?

5 If I forget thee, O Je-ru′sa-lem, let my right hand forget *her cunning*.

6 If I do not remember thee, let my tongue cleave to the roof of my mouth; if I prefer not Je-ru′sa-lem above my chief joy.

7 Remember, O LORD, the children of E′dom in the day of Je-ru′sa-lem; who said, Rase *it*, rase *it, even* to the foundation thereof.

8 O daughter of Bab′y-lon, who art to be destroyed; happy *shall he be*, that rewardeth thee as thou hast served us.

9 Happy *shall he be*, that taketh and dasheth thy little ones against the stones.

A Psalm of David.

138

I WILL praise thee with my whole heart: before the gods will I sing praise unto thee.

2 I will worship toward thy holy temple, and praise thy name for thy lovingkindness and for thy truth: for thou hast magnified thy word above all thy name.

3 In the day when I cried thou answeredst me, *and* strengthenedst me *with* strength in my soul.

4 All the kings of the earth shall praise thee, O LORD, when they hear the words of thy mouth.

5 Yea, they shall sing in the ways of the LORD: for great *is* the glory of the LORD.

6 Though the LORD *be* high, yet hath he respect unto the lowly: but the proud he knoweth afar off.

7 Though I walk in the midst of trouble, thou wilt revive me: thou shalt stretch forth thine hand against the wrath of mine enemies, and thy right hand shall save me.

8 The LORD will perfect *that which* concerneth me: thy mercy, O LORD, *endureth* for ever: forsake not the works of thine own hands.

To the chief Musician, A Psalm of David.

139

O LORD, thou hast searched me, and known *me*.

2 Thou knowest my downsitting and mine uprising, thou understandest my thought afar off.

3 Thou compassest my path and my lying down, and art acquainted *with* all my ways.

4 For *there is* not a word in my tongue, *but,*
lo, O LORD, thou knowest it altogether.
5 Thou hast beset me behind and before, and
laid thine hand upon me.
6 *Such* knowledge *is* too wonderful for me; it
is high, I cannot *attain* unto it.
7 Whither shall I go from thy spirit? or
whither shall I flee from thy presence?
8 If I ascend up into heaven, thou *art* there: if
I make my bed in hell, behold, thou *art there.*
9 *If* I take the wings of the morning, *and*
dwell in the uttermost parts of the sea;
10 Even there shall thy hand lead me, and
thy right hand shall hold me.
11 If I say, Surely the darkness shall cover
me; even the night shall be light about me.
12 Yea, the darkness hideth not from thee;
but the night shineth as the day: the darkness
and the light *are* both alike *to thee.*
13 For thou hast possessed my reins: thou
hast covered me in my mother's womb.
14 I will praise thee; for I am fearfully *and*
wonderfully made: marvellous *are* thy works;
and *that* my soul knoweth right well.
15 My substance was not hid from thee,
when I was made in secret, *and* curiously
wrought in the lowest parts of the earth.
16 Thine eyes did see my substance, yet
being unperfect; and in thy book all *my mem-*
bers were written, *which* in continuance were
fashioned, when *as yet there was* none of them.
17 How precious also are thy thoughts unto
me, O God! how great is the sum of them!
18 *If* I should count them, they are more in
number than the sand: when I awake, I am still
with thee.
19 Surely thou wilt slay the wicked, O God:
depart from me therefore, ye bloody men.
20 For they speak against thee wickedly, *and*
thine enemies take *thy name* in vain.
21 Do not I hate them, O LORD, that hate
thee? and am not I grieved with those that rise
up against thee?
22 I hate them with perfect hatred: I count
them mine enemies.
23 Search me, O God, and know my heart:
try me, and know my thoughts:
24 And see if *there be any* wicked way in me,
and lead me in the way everlasting.

To the chief Musician, A Psalm of David.

140 DELIVER me, O LORD from the evil
man: preserve me from the violent
man;
2 Which imagine mischiefs in *their* heart;
continually are they gathered together *for* war.
3 They have sharpened their tongues like a
serpent; adders' poison *is* under their lips. Se'-
lah.
4 Keep me, O LORD, from the hands of the
wicked; preserve me from the violent man; who
have purposed to overthrow my goings.
5 The proud have hid a snare for me, and
cords; they have spread a net by the wayside;
they have set gins for me. Se'lah.
6 I said unto the LORD, Thou *art* my God:
hear the voice of my supplications, O LORD.
7 O GOD the Lord, the strength of my salvation, thou hast covered my head in the day of
battle.
8 Grant not, O LORD, the desires of the
wicked: further not his wicked device; *lest* they
exalt themselves. Se'lah.
9 *As for* the head of those that compass me
about, let the mischief of their own lips cover
them.
10 Let burning coals fall upon them: let them
be cast into the fire; into deep pits, that they
rise not up again.
11 Let not an evil speaker be established in
the earth: evil shall hunt the violent man to
overthrow *him.*
12 I know that the LORD will maintain the
cause of the afflicted, *and* the right of the poor.
13 Surely the righteous shall give thanks
unto thy name: the upright shall dwell in thy
presence.

A Psalm of David.

141 LORD, I cry unto thee: make haste
unto me; give ear unto my voice,
when I cry unto thee.
2 Let my prayer be set forth before thee *as*
incense; *and* the lifting up of my hands *as* the
evening sacrifice.
3 Set a watch, O LORD, before my mouth;
keep the door of my lips.
4 Incline not my heart to *any* evil thing, to
practise wicked works with men that work iniquity: and let me not eat of their dainties.
5 Let the righteous smite me; *it shall be* a
kindness: and let him reprove me; *it shall be* an
excellent oil, *which* shall not break my head: for
yet my prayer also *shall be* in their calamities.
6 When their judges are overthrown in stony
places, they shall hear my words; for they are
sweet.
7 Our bones are scattered at the grave's
mouth, as when one cutteth and cleaveth *wood*
upon the earth.
8 But mine eyes *are* unto thee, O GOD the
Lord: in thee is my trust; leave not my soul destitute.
9 Keep me from the snares *which* they have
laid for me, and the gins of the workers of iniquity.
10 Let the wicked fall into their own nets,
whilst that I withal escape.

*Maschil of David; A Prayer when he was in
the cave.

142 I CRIED unto the LORD with my
voice; with my voice unto the LORD
did I make my supplication.
2 I poured out my complaint before him; I
shewed before him my trouble.
3 When my spirit was overwhelmed within
me, then thou knewest my path. In the way
wherein I walked have they privily laid a snare
for me.
4 I looked on *my* right hand, and beheld, but
there was no man that would know me: refuge
failed me; no man cared for my soul.
5 I cried unto thee, O LORD: I said, Thou *art*
my refuge *and* my portion in the land of the
living.
6 Attend unto my cry; for I am brought very
low: deliver me from my persecutors; for they
are stronger than I.
7 Bring my soul out of prison, that I may
praise thy name: the righteous shall compass
me about; for thou shalt deal bountifully with
me.

A Psalm of David.

143 HEAR my prayer, O LORD, give ear to
my supplications: in thy faithfulness
answer me, *and* in thy righteousness.
2 And enter not into judgment with thy servant: for in thy sight shall no man living be justified.

3 For the enemy hath persecuted my soul; he
hath smitten my life down to the ground; he
hath made me to dwell in darkness, as those
that have been long dead.
4 Therefore is my spirit overwhelmed within
me; my heart within me is desolate.
5 I remember the days of old; I meditate on
all thy works; I muse on the work of thy hands.
6 I stretch forth my hands unto thee: my soul
thirsteth after thee, as a thirsty land. Se'lah.
7 Hear me speedily, O LORD: my spirit
faileth: hide not thy face from me, lest I be like
unto them that go down into the pit.
8 Cause me to hear thy lovingkindness in the
morning; for in thee do I trust: cause me to
know the way wherein I should walk; for I lift
up my soul unto thee.
9 Deliver me, O LORD, from mine enemies: I
flee unto thee to hide me.
10 Teach me to do thy will; for thou *art* my
God: thy spirit *is* good; lead me into the land of
uprightness.
11 Quicken me, O LORD, for thy name's sake:
for thy righteousness' sake bring my soul out of
trouble.
12 And of thy mercy cut off mine enemies,
and destroy all them that afflict my soul: for I
am thy servant.

A Psalm of David.

144 BLESSED *be* the LORD my strength,
which teacheth my hands to war, *and*
my fingers to fight:
2 My goodness, and my fortress; my high
tower, and my deliverer; my shield, and *he* in
whom I trust; who subdueth my people under
me.
3 LORD, what *is* man, that thou takest knowledge of him! *or* the son of man, that thou makest account of him!
4 Man is like to vanity: his days *are* as a
shadow that passeth away.
5 Bow thy heavens, O LORD, and come down:
touch the mountains, and they shall smoke.
6 Cast forth lightning, and scatter them:
shoot out thine arrows, and destroy them.
7 Send thine hand from above; rid me, and
deliver me out of great waters, from the hand of
strange children;
8 Whose mouth speaketh vanity, and their
right hand *is* a right hand of falsehood.
9 I will sing a new song unto thee, O God:
upon a psaltery *and* an instrument of ten
strings will I sing praises unto thee.
10 *It is he* that giveth salvation unto kings:
who delivereth Da'vid his servant from the
hurtful sword.
11 Rid me, and deliver me from the hand of
strange children, whose mouth speaketh vanity,
and their right hand *is* a right hand of falsehood:
12 That our sons *may be* as plants grown up
in their youth; *that* our daughters *may be* as
corner stones, polished *after* the similitude of a
palace:
13 *That* our garners *may be* full, affording all
manner of store: *that* our sheep may bring forth
thousands and ten thousands in our streets:
14 *That* our oxen *may be* strong to labour;
that there be no breaking in, nor going out; that
there be no complaining in our streets.
15 Happy *is that* people, that is in such a
case: *yea,* happy *is that* people, whose God *is*
the LORD.

David's *Psalm* of praise.

145 I WILL extol thee, my God, O king;
and I will bless thy name for ever and
ever.
2 Every day will I bless thee; and I will praise
thy name for ever and ever.
3 Great *is* the LORD, and greatly to be
praised; and his greatness *is* unsearchable.
4 One generation shall praise thy works to
another, and shall declare thy mighty acts.
5 I will speak of the glorious honour of thy
majesty, and of thy wondrous works.
6 And *men* shall speak of the might of thy
terrible acts: and I will declare thy greatness.
7 They shall abundantly utter the memory of
thy great goodness, and shall sing of thy righteousness.
8 The LORD *is* gracious, and full of compassion; slow to anger, and of great mercy.
9 The LORD *is* good to all: and his tender mercies *are* over all his works.
10 All thy works shall praise thee, O LORD;
and thy saints shall bless thee.
11 They shall speak of the glory of thy kingdom, and talk of thy power;
12 To make known to the sons of men his
mighty acts, and the glorious majesty of his
kingdom.
13 Thy kingdom *is* an everlasting kingdom,
and thy dominion *endureth* throughout all generations.
14 The LORD upholdeth all that fall, and raiseth up all *those that be* bowed down.
15 The eyes of all wait upon thee; and thou
givest them their meat in due season.
16 Thou openest thine hand, and satisfiest
the desire of every living thing.
17 The LORD *is* righteous in all his ways, and
holy in all his works.
18 The LORD *is* nigh unto all them that call
upon him, to all that call upon him in truth.
19 He will fulfil the desire of them that fear
him: he also will hear their cry, and will save
them.
20 The LORD preserveth all them that love
him: but all the wicked will he destroy.
21 My mouth shall speak the praise of the
LORD: and let all flesh bless his holy name for
ever and ever.

146 PRAISE ye the LORD. Praise the
LORD, O my soul.
2 While I live will I praise the LORD: I will
sing praises unto my God while I have any
being.
3 Put not your trust in princes, *nor* in the son
of man, in whom *there is* no help.
4 His breath goeth forth, he returneth to his
earth; in that very day his thoughts perish.
5 Happy *is he* that *hath* the God of Ja'cob for
his help, whose hope *is* in the LORD his God:
6 Which made heaven, and earth, the sea,
and all that therein *is:* which keepeth truth for
ever:
7 Which executeth judgment for the oppressed: which giveth food to the hungry. The
LORD looseth the prisoners:
8 The LORD openeth *the eyes of* the blind: the
LORD raiseth them that are bowed down: the
LORD loveth the righteous.
9 The LORD preserveth the strangers; he re-
lieveth the fatherless and widow: but the way of
the wicked he turneth upside down.
10 The LORD shall reign for ever, *even* thy
God, O Zi'on, unto all generations. Praise ye the
LORD.

147 PRAISE ye the LORD: for *it is* good to
sing praises unto our God; for *it is*
pleasant; *and* praise is comely.
2 The LORD doth build up Je-ru'sa-lem: he
gathereth together the outcasts of Is'ra-el.
3 He healeth the broken in heart, and bindeth
up their wounds.
4 He telleth the number of the stars; he calleth them all by *their* names.
5 Great *is* our Lord, and of great power: his
understanding *is* infinite.
6 The LORD lifteth up the meek: he casteth
the wicked down to the ground.
7 Sing unto the LORD with thanksgiving; sing
praise upon the harp unto our God:
8 Who covereth the heaven with clouds, who
prepareth rain for the earth, who maketh grass
to grow upon the mountains.
9 He giveth to the beast his food, *and* to the
young ravens which cry.
10 He delighteth not in the strength of the
horse: he taketh not pleasure in the legs of a
man.
11 The LORD taketh pleasure in them that
fear him, in those that hope in his mercy.
12 Praise the LORD, O Je-ru'sa-lem; praise
thy God, O Zi'on.
13 For he hath strengthened the bars of thy
gates; he hath blessed thy children within thee.
14 He maketh peace *in* thy borders, *and* filleth thee with the finest of the wheat.
15 He sendeth forth his commandment *upon*
earth: his word runneth very swiftly.
16 He giveth snow like wool: he scattereth
the hoarfrost like ashes.
17 He casteth forth his ice like morsels: who
can stand before his cold?
18 He sendeth out his word, and melteth
them: he causeth his wind to blow, *and* the waters flow.
19 He sheweth his word unto Ja'cob, his statutes and his judgments unto Is'ra-el.
20 He hath not dealt so with any nation: and
as for his judgments, they have not known
them. Praise ye the LORD.

148 PRAISE ye the LORD. Praise ye the
LORD from the heavens: praise him in
the heights.
2 Praise ye him, all his angels: praise ye him,
all his hosts.
3 Praise ye him, sun and moon: praise him,
all ye stars of light.
4 Praise him, ye heavens of heavens, and ye
waters that *be* above the heavens.
5 Let them praise the name of the LORD: for
he commanded, and they were created.
6 He hath also stablished them for ever and
ever: he hath made a decree which shall not
pass.
7 Praise the LORD from the earth, ye dragons,
and all deeps:
8 Fire, and hail; snow, and vapours; stormy
wind fulfilling his word:
9 Mountains, and all hills; fruitful trees, and
all cedars:
10 Beasts, and all cattle; creeping things, and
flying fowl:
11 Kings of the earth, and all people; princes,
and all judges of the earth:
12 Both young men, and maidens; old men,
and children:
13 Let them praise the name of the LORD: for
his name alone is excellent; his glory *is* above
the earth and heaven.
14 He also exalteth the horn of his people,
the praise of all his saints; *even* of the children
of Is'ra-el, a people near unto him. Praise ye the
LORD.

149 PRAISE ye the LORD. Sing unto the
LORD a new song, *and* his praise in
the congregation of saints.
2 Let Is'ra-el rejoice in him that made him:
let the children of Zi'on be joyful in their King.
3 Let them praise his name in the dance: let
them sing praises unto him with the timbrel and
harp.
4 For the LORD taketh pleasure in his people:
he will beautify the meek with salvation.
5 Let the saints be joyful in glory: let them
sing aloud upon their beds.
6 *Let* the high *praises* of God *be* in their
mouth, and a twoedged sword in their hand;
7 To execute vengeance upon the heathen,
and punishments upon the people;
8 To bind their kings with chains, and their
nobles with fetters of iron;
9 To execute upon them the judgment written: this honour have all his saints. Praise ye the
LORD.

150 PRAISE ye the LORD. Praise God in
his sanctuary: praise him in the firmament of his power.
2 Praise him for his mighty acts: praise him
according to his excellent greatness.
3 Praise him with the sound of the trumpet:
praise him with the psaltery and harp.
4 Praise him with the timbrel and dance:
praise him with stringed instruments and or-
gans.
5 Praise him upon the loud cymbals: praise
him upon the high sounding cymbals.
6 Let every thing that hath breath praise the
LORD. Praise ye the LORD.

THE PROVERBS

1 THE proverbs of Sol'o-mon the son of Da'-
vid, king of Is'ra-el;
2 To know wisdom and instruction; to perceive the words of understanding;
3 To receive the instruction of wisdom, justice, and judgment, and equity;
4 To give subtilty to the simple, to the young
man knowledge and discretion.
5 A wise *man* will hear, and will increase
learning; and a man of understanding shall attain unto wise counsels:
6 To understand a proverb, and the interpretation; the words of the wise, and their dark
sayings.
7 ¶ The fear of the LORD *is* the beginning of
knowledge: *but* fools despise wisdom and instruction.
8 My son, hear the instruction of thy father,
and forsake not the law of thy mother:
9 For they *shall be* an ornament of grace
unto thy head, and chains about thy neck.
10 ¶ My son, if sinners entice thee, consent
thou not.
11 If they say, Come with us, let us lay wait

for blood, let us lurk privily for the innocent
without cause:
12 Let us swallow them up alive as the grave;
and whole, as those that go down into the pit:
13 We shall find all precious substance, we
shall fill our houses with spoil:
14 Cast in thy lot among us; let us all have
one purse:
15 My son, walk not thou in the way with
them; refrain thy foot from their path:
16 For their feet run to evil, and make haste
to shed blood.
17 Surely in vain the net is spread in the
sight of any bird.
18 And they lay wait for their *own* blood;
they lurk privily for their *own* lives.
19 So *are* the ways of every one that is
greedy of gain; *which* taketh away the life of
the owners thereof.
20 ¶ Wisdom crieth without; she uttereth
her voice in the streets:
21 She crieth in the chief place of concourse,
in the openings of the gates: in the city she uttereth her words, *saying*,
22 How long, ye simple ones, will ye love
simplicity? and the scorners delight in their
scorning, and fools hate knowledge?
23 Turn you at my reproof: behold, I will
pour out my spirit unto you, I will make known
my words unto you.
24 ¶ Because I have called, and ye refused; I
have stretched out my hand, and no man regarded;
25 But ye have set at nought all my counsel,
and would none of my reproof:
26 I also will laugh at your calamity; I will
mock when your fear cometh;
27 When your fear cometh as desolation, and
your destruction cometh as a whirlwind; when
distress and anguish cometh upon you.
28 Then shall they call upon me, but I will
not answer; they shall seek me early, but they
shall not find me:
29 For that they hated knowledge, and did
not choose the fear of the LORD:
30 They would none of my counsel: they despised all my reproof.
31 Therefore shall they eat of the fruit of
their own way, and be filled with their own devices.
32 For the turning away of the simple shall
slay them, and the prosperity of fools shall destroy them.
33 But whoso hearkeneth unto me shall
dwell safely, and shall be quiet from fear of evil.

2 MY son, if thou wilt receive my words, and
hide my commandments with thee;
2 So that thou incline thine ear unto wisdom,
and apply thine heart to understanding;
3 Yea, if thou criest after knowledge, *and*
liftest up thy voice for understanding;
4 If thou seekest her as silver, and searchest
for her as *for* hid treasures;
5 Then shalt thou understand the fear of the
LORD, and find the knowledge of God.
6 For the LORD giveth wisdom: out of his
mouth *cometh* knowledge and understanding.
7 He layeth up sound wisdom for the righteous: *he is* a buckler to them that walk uprightly.
8 He keepeth the paths of judgment, and preserveth the way of his saints.
9 Then shalt thou understand righteousness,
and judgment, and equity; *yea*, every good
path.
10 ¶ When wisdom entereth into thine heart,
and knowledge is pleasant unto thy soul;
11 Discretion shall preserve thee, understanding shall keep thee:
12 To deliver thee from the way of the evil
man, from the man that speaketh froward
things;
13 Who leave the paths of uprightness, to
walk in the ways of darkness;
14 Who rejoice to do evil, *and* delight in the
frowardness of the wicked;
15 Whose ways *are* crooked, and *they* froward in their paths:
16 To deliver thee from the strange woman,
even from the stranger *which* flattereth with
her words;
17 Which forsaketh the guide of her youth,
and forgetteth the covenant of her God.
18 For her house inclineth unto death, and
her paths unto the dead.
19 None that go unto her return again, neither take they hold of the paths of life.
20 That thou mayest walk in the way of good
men, and keep the paths of the righteous.
21 For the upright shall dwell in the land, and
the perfect shall remain in it.
22 But the wicked shall be cut off from the
earth, and the transgressors shall be rooted out
of it.

3 MY son, forget not my law; but let thine
heart keep my commandments:
2 For length of days, and long life, and peace,
shall they add to thee.
3 Let not mercy and truth forsake thee: bind
them about thy neck; write them upon the table
of thine heart:
4 So shalt thou find favour and good understanding in the sight of God and man.
5 ¶ Trust in the LORD with all thine heart;
and lean not unto thine own understanding.
6 In all thy ways acknowledge him, and he
shall direct thy paths.
7 ¶ Be not wise in thine own eyes: fear the
LORD, and depart from evil.
8 It shall be health to thy navel, and marrow
to thy bones.
9 Honour the LORD with thy substance, and
with the firstfruits of all thine increase:
10 So shall thy barns be filled with plenty,
and thy presses shall burst out with new wine.
11 ¶ My son, despise not the chastening of
the LORD; neither be weary of his correction:
12 For whom the LORD loveth he correcteth;
even as a father the son *in whom* he delighteth.
13 ¶ Happy *is* the man *that* findeth wisdom,
and the man *that* getteth understanding.
14 For the merchandise of it *is* better than
the merchandise of silver, and the gain thereof
than fine gold.
15 She *is* more precious than rubies: and all
the things thou canst desire are not to be compared unto her.
16 Length of days *is* in her right hand; *and* in
her left hand riches and honour.
17 Her ways *are* ways of pleasantness, and
all her paths *are* peace.
18 She *is* a tree of life to them that lay hold
upon her: and happy *is every one* that retaineth
her.
19 The LORD by wisdom hath founded the
earth; by understanding hath he established the
heavens.
20 By his knowledge the depths are broken
up, and the clouds drop down the dew.
21 ¶ My son, let not them depart from thine
eyes: keep sound wisdom and discretion:

22 So shall they be life unto thy soul, and
grace to thy neck.
23 Then shalt thou walk in thy way safely,
and thy foot shall not stumble.
24 When thou liest down, thou shalt not be
afraid: yea, thou shalt lie down, and thy sleep
shall be sweet.
25 Be not afraid of sudden fear, neither of the
desolation of the wicked, when it cometh.
26 For the LORD shall be thy confidence, and
shall keep thy foot from being taken.
27 ¶ Withhold not good from them to whom
it is due, when it is in the power of thine hand to
do *it*.
28 Say not unto thy neighbour, Go, and come
again, and to morrow I will give; when thou
hast it by thee.
29 Devise not evil against thy neighbour, seeing he dwelleth securely by thee.
30 ¶ Strive not with a man without cause, if
he have done thee no harm.
31 ¶ Envy thou not the oppressor, and
choose none of his ways.
32 For the froward *is* abomination to the
LORD: but his secret *is* with the righteous.
33 ¶ The curse of the LORD *is* in the house of
the wicked: but he blesseth the habitation of the
just.
34 Surely he scorneth the scorners: but he
giveth grace unto the lowly.
35 The wise shall inherit glory: but shame
shall be the promotion of fools.

4 HEAR, ye children, the instruction of a father, and attend to know understanding.
2 For I give you good doctrine, forsake ye not
my law.
3 For I was my father's son, tender and only
beloved in the sight of my mother.
4 He taught me also, and said unto me, Let
thine heart retain my words: keep my commandments, and live.
5 Get wisdom, get understanding: forget *it*
not; neither decline from the words of my
mouth.
6 Forsake her not, and she shall preserve
thee: love her, and she shall keep thee.
7 Wisdom *is* the principal thing; *therefore* get
wisdom: and with all thy getting get understanding.
8 Exalt her, and she shall promote thee: she
shall bring thee to honour, when thou dost embrace her.
9 She shall give to thine head an ornament of
grace: a crown of glory shall she deliver to thee.
10 Hear, O my son, and receive my sayings;
and the years of thy life shall be many.
11 I have taught thee in the way of wisdom; I
have led thee in right paths.
12 When thou goest, thy steps shall not be
straitened; and when thou runnest, thou shalt
not stumble.
13 Take fast hold of instruction; let *her* not
go: keep her; for she *is* thy life.
14 ¶ Enter not into the path of the wicked,
and go not in the way of evil *men*.
15 Avoid it, pass not by it, turn from it, and
pass away.
16 For they sleep not, except they have done
mischief; and their sleep is taken away, unless
they cause *some* to fall.
17 For they eat the bread of wickedness, and
drink the wine of violence.
18 But the path of the just *is* as the shining
light, that shineth more and more unto the perfect day.
19 The way of the wicked *is* as darkness:
they know not at what they stumble.
20 ¶ My son, attend to my words; incline
thine ear unto my sayings.
21 Let them not depart from thine eyes; keep
them in the midst of thine heart.
22 For they *are* life unto those that find them,
and health to all their flesh.
23 ¶ Keep thy heart with all diligence; for
out of it *are* the issues of life.
24 Put away from thee a froward mouth, and
perverse lips put far from thee.
25 Let thine eyes look right on, and let thine
eyelids look straight before thee.
26 Ponder the path of thy feet, and let all thy
ways be established.
27 Turn not to the right hand nor to the left:
remove thy foot from evil.

5 MY son, attend unto my wisdom, *and* bow
thine ear to my understanding:
2 That thou mayest regard discretion, and
that thy lips may keep knowledge.
3 ¶ For the lips of a strange woman drop *as*
an honeycomb, and her mouth *is* smoother than
oil:
4 But her end is bitter as wormwood, sharp
as a twoedged sword.
5 Her feet go down to death; her steps take
hold on hell.
6 Lest thou shouldest ponder the path of life,
her ways are moveable, *that* thou canst not
know *them*.
7 Hear me now therefore, O ye children, and
depart not from the words of my mouth.
8 Remove thy way far from her, and come
not nigh the door of her house:
9 Lest thou give thine honour unto others,
and thy years unto the cruel:
10 Lest strangers be filled with thy wealth;
and thy labours *be* in the house of a stranger;
11 And thou mourn at the last, when thy
flesh and thy body are consumed,
12 And say, How have I hated instruction,
and my heart despised reproof;
13 And have not obeyed the voice of my
teachers, nor inclined mine ear to them that instructed me!
14 I was almost in all evil in the midst of the
congregation and assembly.
15 ¶ Drink waters out of thine own cistern,
and running waters out of thine own well.
16 Let thy fountains be dispersed abroad,
and rivers of waters in the streets.
17 Let them be only thine own, and not
strangers' with thee.
18 Let thy fountain be blessed: and rejoice
with the wife of thy youth.
19 *Let her be as* the loving hind and pleasant
roe; let her breasts satisfy thee at all times; and
be thou ravished always with her love.
20 And why wilt thou, my son, be ravished
with a strange woman, and embrace the bosom
of a stranger?
21 For the ways of man *are* before the eyes
of the LORD, and he pondereth all his goings.
22 ¶ His own iniquities shall take the wicked
himself, and he shall be holden with the cords
of his sins.
23 He shall die without instruction; and in
the greatness of his folly he shall go astray.

6 MY son, if thou be surety for thy friend, *if*
thou hast stricken thy hand with a stranger,
2 Thou art snared with the words of thy

mouth, thou art taken with the words of thy
mouth.
3 Do this now, my son, and deliver thyself,
when thou art come into the hand of thy friend;
go, humble thyself, and make sure thy friend.
4 Give not sleep to thine eyes, nor slumber to
thine eyelids.
5 Deliver thyself as a roe from the hand *of
the hunter,* and as a bird from the hand of the
fowler.
6 ¶ Go to the ant, thou sluggard; consider
her ways, and be wise:
7 Which having no guide, overseer, or ruler,
8 Provideth her meat in the summer, *and*
gathereth her food in the harvest.
9 How long wilt thou sleep, O sluggard?
when wilt thou arise out of thy sleep?
10 *Yet* a little sleep, a little slumber, a little
folding of the hands to sleep:
11 So shall thy poverty come as one that
travelleth, and thy want as an armed man.
12 ¶ A naughty person, a wicked man, walketh with a froward mouth.
13 He winketh with his eyes, he speaketh
with his feet, he teacheth with his fingers;
14 Frowardness *is* in his heart, he deviseth
mischief continually; he soweth discord.
15 Therefore shall his calamity come suddenly; suddenly shall he be broken without
remedy.
16 ¶ These six *things* doth the LORD hate:
yea, seven *are* an abomination unto him:
17 A proud look, a lying tongue, and hands
that shed innocent blood,
18 An heart that deviseth wicked imaginations, feet that be swift in running to mischief,
19 A false witness *that* speaketh lies, and he
that soweth discord among brethren.
20 ¶ My son, keep thy father's commandment, and forsake not the law of thy mother:
21 Bind them continually upon thine heart,
and tie them about thy neck.
22 When thou goest, it shall lead thee; when
thou sleepest, it shall keep thee; and *when* thou
awakest, it shall talk with thee.
23 For the commandment *is* a lamp; and the
law *is* light; and reproofs of instruction *are* the
way of life:
24 To keep thee from the evil woman, from
the flattery of the tongue of a strange woman.
25 Lust not after her beauty in thine heart;
neither let her take thee with her eyelids.
26 For by means of a whorish woman *a man
is brought* to a piece of bread: and the adulteress will hunt for the precious life.
27 Can a man take fire in his bosom, and his
clothes not be burned?
28 Can one go upon hot coals, and his feet
not be burned?
29 So he that goeth in to his neighbour's
wife; whosoever toucheth her shall not be innocent.
30 *Men* do not despise a thief, if he steal to
satisfy his soul when he is hungry;
31 But *if* he be found, he shall restore sevenfold; he shall give all the substance of his house.
32 *But* whoso committeth adultery with a
woman lacketh understanding: he *that* doeth it
destroyeth his own soul.
33 A wound and dishonour shall he get; and
his reproach shall not be wiped away.
34 For jealousy *is* the rage of a man: therefore he will not spare in the day of vengeance.
35 He will not regard any ransom; neither
will he rest content, though thou givest many
gifts.

7 MY son, keep my words, and lay up my
commandments with thee.
2 Keep my commandments, and live; and my
law as the apple of thine eye.
3 Bind them upon thy fingers, write them
upon the table of thine heart.
4 Say unto wisdom, Thou *art* my sister; and
call understanding *thy* kinswoman:
5 That they may keep thee from the strange
woman, from the stranger *which* flattereth with
her words.
6 ¶ For at the window of my house I looked
through my casement,
7 And beheld among the simple ones, I discerned among the youths, a young man void of
understanding,
8 Passing through the street near her corner;
and he went the way to her house,
9 In the twilight, in the evening, in the black
and dark night:
10 And, behold, there met him a woman *with*
the attire of an harlot, and subtil of heart.
11 (She *is* loud and stubborn; her feet abide
not in her house:
12 Now *is she* without, now in the streets,
and lieth in wait at every corner.)
13 So she caught him, and kissed him, *and*
with an impudent face said unto him,
14 *I have* peace offerings with me; this day
have I payed my vows.
15 Therefore came I forth to meet thee, diligently to seek thy face, and I have found thee.
16 I have decked my bed with coverings of
tapestry, with carved *works,* with fine linen of
E'gypt.
17 I have perfumed my bed with myrrh,
aloes, and cinnamon.
18 Come, let us take our fill of love until the
morning: let us solace ourselves with loves.
19 For the goodman *is* not at home, he is
gone a long journey:
20 He hath taken a bag of money with him,
and will come home at the day appointed.
21 With her much fair speech she caused
him to yield, with the flattering of her lips she
forced him.
22 He goeth after her straightway, as an ox
goeth to the slaughter, or as a fool to the correction of the stocks;
23 Till a dart strike through his liver; as a
bird hasteth to the snare, and knoweth not that
it *is* for his life.
24 ¶ Hearken unto me now therefore, O ye
children, and attend to the words of my mouth.
25 Let not thine heart decline to her ways, go
not astray in her paths.
26 For she hath cast down many wounded:
yea, many strong *men* have been slain by her.
27 Her house *is* the way to hell, going down
to the chambers of death.

8 DOTH not wisdom cry? and understanding
put forth her voice?
2 She standeth in the top of high places, by
the way in the places of the paths.
3 She crieth at the gates, at the entry of the
city, at the coming in at the doors.
4 Unto you, O men, I call; and my voice *is* to
the sons of man.
5 O ye simple, understand wisdom: and, ye
fools, be ye of an understanding heart.
6 Hear; for I will speak of excellent things;
and the opening of my lips *shall be* right things.
7 For my mouth shall speak truth; and wickedness *is* an abomination to my lips.
8 All the words of my mouth *are* in right-

eousness; *there is* nothing froward or perverse in them.

9 They *are* all plain to him that understandeth, and right to them that find knowledge.

10 Receive my instruction, and not silver; and knowledge rather than choice gold.

11 For wisdom *is* better than rubies; and all the things that may be desired are not to be compared to it.

12 I wisdom dwell with prudence, and find out knowledge of witty inventions.

13 The fear of the LORD *is* to hate evil: pride, and arrogancy, and the evil way, and the froward mouth, do I hate.

14 Counsel *is* mine, and sound wisdom: I *am* understanding; I have strength.

15 By me kings reign, and princes decree justice.

16 By me princes rule, and nobles, *even* all the judges of the earth.

17 I love them that love me; and those that seek me early shall find me.

18 Riches and honour *are* with me; *yea*, durable riches and righteousness.

19 My fruit *is* better than gold, yea, than fine gold; and my revenue than choice silver.

20 I lead in the way of righteousness, in the midst of the paths of judgment:

21 That I may cause those that love me to inherit substance; and I will fill their treasures.

22 The LORD possessed me in the beginning of his way, before his works of old.

23 I was set up from everlasting, from the beginning, or ever the earth was.

24 When *there were* no depths, I was brought forth; when *there were* no fountains abounding with water.

25 Before the mountains were settled, before the hills was I brought forth:

26 While as yet he had not made the earth, nor the fields, nor the highest part of the dust of the world.

27 When he prepared the heavens, I *was* there: when he set a compass upon the face of the depth:

28 When he established the clouds above: when he strengthened the fountains of the deep:

29 When he gave to the sea his decree, that the waters should not pass his commandment: when he appointed the foundations of the earth:

30 Then I was by him, *as* one brought up *with him:* and I was daily *his* delight, rejoicing always before him;

31 Rejoicing in the habitable part of his earth; and my delights *were* with the sons of men.

32 Now therefore hearken unto me, O ye children: for blessed *are they that* keep my ways.

33 Hear instruction, and be wise, and refuse it not.

34 Blessed *is* the man that heareth me, watching daily at my gates, waiting at the posts of my doors.

35 For whoso findeth me findeth life, and shall obtain favour of the LORD.

36 But he that sinneth against me wrongeth his own soul: all they that hate me love death.

9 WISDOM hath builded her house, she hath hewn out her seven pillars:

2 She hath killed her beasts; she hath mingled her wine; she hath also furnished her table.

3 She hath sent forth her maidens: she crieth upon the highest places of the city,

4 Whoso *is* simple, let him turn in hither: *as for* him that wanteth understanding, she saith to him,

5 Come, eat of my bread, and drink of the wine *which* I have mingled.

6 Forsake the foolish, and live; and go in the way of understanding.

7 He that reproveth a scorner getteth to himself shame: and he that rebuketh a wicked *man getteth* himself a blot.

8 Reprove not a scorner, lest he hate thee: rebuke a wise man, and he will love thee.

9 Give *instruction* to a wise *man*, and he will be yet wiser: teach a just *man*, and he will increase in learning.

10 The fear of the LORD *is* the beginning of wisdom: and the knowledge of the holy *is* understanding.

11 For by me thy days shall be multiplied, and the years of thy life shall be increased.

12 If thou be wise, thou shalt be wise for thyself: but *if* thou scornest, thou alone shalt bear *it*.

13 ¶ A foolish woman *is* clamorous: *she is* simple, and knoweth nothing.

14 For she sitteth at the door of her house, on a seat in the high places of the city,

15 To call passengers who go right on their ways:

16 Whoso *is* simple, let him turn in hither: and *as for* him that wanteth understanding, she saith to him,

17 Stolen waters are sweet, and bread *eaten* in secret is pleasant.

18 But he knoweth not that the dead *are* there; *and that* her guests *are* in the depths of hell.

10 THE proverbs of Sol'o-mon. A wise son maketh a glad father: but a foolish son *is* the heaviness of his mother.

2 Treasures of wickedness profit nothing: but righteousness delivereth from death.

3 The LORD will not suffer the soul of the righteous to famish: but he casteth away the substance of the wicked.

4 He becometh poor that dealeth *with* a slack hand: but the hand of the diligent maketh rich.

5 He that gathereth in summer *is* a wise son: *but* he that sleepeth in harvest *is* a son that causeth shame.

6 Blessings *are* upon the head of the just: but violence covereth the mouth of the wicked.

7 The memory of the just *is* blessed: but the name of the wicked shall rot.

8 The wise in heart will receive commandments: but a prating fool shall fall.

9 He that walketh uprightly walketh surely: but he that perverteth his ways shall be known.

10 He that winketh with the eye causeth sorrow: but a prating fool shall fall.

11 The mouth of a righteous *man is* a well of life: but violence covereth the mouth of the wicked.

12 Hatred stirreth up strifes: but love covereth all sins.

13 In the lips of him that hath understanding wisdom is found: but a rod *is* for the back of him that is void of understanding.

14 Wise *men* lay up knowledge: but the mouth of the foolish *is* near destruction.

15 The rich man's wealth *is* his strong city: the destruction of the poor *is* their poverty.

16 The labour of the righteous *tendeth* to life: the fruit of the wicked to sin.

17 He *is in* the way of life that keepeth instruction: but he that refuseth reproof erreth.

18 He that hideth hatred *with* lying lips, and
he that uttereth a slander, *is* a fool.
19 In the multitude of words there wanteth
not sin: but he that refraineth his lips *is* wise.
20 The tongue of the just *is as* choice silver:
the heart of the wicked *is* little worth.
21 The lips of the righteous feed many: but
fools die for want of wisdom.
22 The blessing of the LORD, it maketh rich,
and he addeth no sorrow with it.
23 *It is* as sport to a fool to do mischief: but a
man of understanding hath wisdom.
24 The fear of the wicked, it shall come upon
him: but the desire of the righteous shall be
granted.
25 As the whirlwind passeth, so *is* the
wicked no *more:* but the righteous *is* an everlasting foundation.
26 As vinegar to the teeth, and as smoke to
the eyes, so *is* the sluggard to them that send
him.
27 The fear of the LORD prolongeth days: but
the years of the wicked shall be shortened.
28 The hope of the righteous *shall be* gladness: but the expectation of the wicked shall
perish.
29 The way of the LORD *is* strength to the upright: but destruction *shall be* to the workers of
iniquity.
30 The righteous shall never be removed: but
the wicked shall not inhabit the earth.
31 The mouth of the just bringeth forth wisdom: but the froward tongue shall be cut out.
32 The lips of the righteous know what is acceptable: but the mouth of the wicked *speaketh*
frowardness.

11 A FALSE balance *is* abomination to the
LORD: but a just weight *is* his delight.
2 *When* pride cometh, then cometh shame:
but with the lowly *is* wisdom.
3 The integrity of the upright shall guide
them: but the perverseness of transgressors
shall destroy them.
4 Riches profit not in the day of wrath: but
righteousness delivereth from death.
5 The righteousness of the perfect shall direct his way: but the wicked shall fall by his
own wickedness.
6 The righteousness of the upright shall deliver them: but transgressors shall be taken in
their own naughtiness.
7 When a wicked man dieth, *his* expectation
shall perish: and the hope of unjust *men* perisheth.
8 The righteous is delivered out of trouble,
and the wicked cometh in his stead.
9 An hypocrite with *his* mouth destroyeth his
neighbour: but through knowledge shall the
just be delivered.
10 When it goeth well with the righteous, the
city rejoiceth: and when the wicked perish,
there is shouting.
11 By the blessing of the upright the city is
exalted: but it is overthrown by the mouth of
the wicked.
12 He that is void of wisdom despiseth his
neighbour: but a man of understanding holdeth
his peace.
13 A talebearer revealeth secrets: but he that
is of a faithful spirit concealeth the matter.
14 Where no counsel *is,* the people fall: but
in the multitude of counsellors *there is* safety.
15 He that is surety for a stranger shall smart
for it: and he that hateth suretiship is sure.
16 A gracious woman retaineth honour: and
strong *men* retain riches.
17 The merciful man doeth good to his own
soul: but *he that is* cruel troubleth his own flesh.
18 The wicked worketh a deceitful work: but
to him that soweth righteousness *shall be* a sure
reward.
19 As righteousness *tendeth* to life: so he
that pursueth evil *pursueth it* to his own death.
20 They that are of a froward heart *are*
abomination to the LORD: but *such as are* upright in *their* way *are* his delight.
21 *Though* hand *join* in hand, the wicked
shall not be unpunished: but the seed of the
righteous shall be delivered.
22 *As* a jewel of gold in a swine's snout, *so is*
a fair woman which is without discretion.
23 The desire of the righteous *is* only good:
but the expectation of the wicked *is* wrath.
24 There is that scattereth, and yet increaseth; and *there is* that withholdeth more than is
meet, but *it tendeth* to poverty.
25 The liberal soul shall be made fat: and he
that watereth shall be watered also himself.
26 He that withholdeth corn, the people shall
curse him: but blessing *shall be* upon the head
of him that selleth *it.*
27 He that diligently seeketh good procureth
favour: but he that seeketh mischief, it shall
come unto him.
28 He that trusteth in his riches shall fall: but
the righteous shall flourish as a branch.
29 He that troubleth his own house shall inherit the wind: and the fool *shall be* servant to
the wise of heart.
30 The fruit of the righteous *is* a tree of life;
and he that winneth souls *is* wise.
31 Behold, the righteous shall be recompensed in the earth: much more the wicked and
the sinner.

12 WHOSO loveth instruction loveth
knowledge: but he that hateth reproof *is*
brutish.
2 A good *man* obtaineth favour of the LORD:
but a man of wicked devices will he condemn.
3 A man shall not be established by wickedness: but the root of the righteous shall not be
moved.
4 A virtuous woman *is* a crown to her husband: but she that maketh ashamed *is* as rottenness in his bones.
5 The thoughts of the righteous *are* right: *but*
the counsels of the wicked *are* deceit.
6 The words of the wicked *are* to lie in wait
for blood: but the mouth of the upright shall
deliver them.
7 The wicked are overthrown, and *are* not:
but the house of the righteous shall stand.
8 A man shall be commended according to
his wisdom: but he that is of a perverse heart
shall be despised.
9 *He that is* despised, and hath a servant, *is*
better than he that honoureth himself, and lacketh bread.
10 A righteous *man* regardeth the life of his
beast: but the tender mercies of the wicked *are*
cruel.
11 He that tilleth his land shall be satisfied
with bread: but he that followeth vain *persons*
is void of understanding.
12 The wicked desireth the net of evil *men:*
but the root of the righteous yieldeth *fruit.*
13 The wicked is snared by the transgression
of *his* lips: but the just shall come out of trouble.
14 A man shall be satisfied with good by the
fruit of *his* mouth: and the recompence of a
man's hands shall be rendered unto him.

15 The way of a fool *is* right in his own eyes: but he that hearkeneth unto counsel *is* wise.
16 A fool's wrath is presently known: but a prudent *man* covereth shame.
17 *He that* speaketh truth sheweth forth righteousness: but a false witness deceit.
18 There is that speaketh like the piercings of a sword: but the tongue of the wise *is* health.
19 The lip of truth shall be established for ever: but a lying tongue *is* but for a moment.
20 Deceit *is* in the heart of them that imagine evil: but to the counsellors of peace *is* joy.
21 There shall no evil happen to the just: but the wicked shall be filled with mischief.
22 Lying lips *are* abomination to the LORD: but they that deal truly *are* his delight.
23 A prudent man concealeth knowledge: but the heart of fools proclaimeth foolishness.
24 The hand of the diligent shall bear rule: but the slothful shall be under tribute.
25 Heaviness in the heart of man maketh it stoop: but a good word maketh it glad.
26 The righteous *is* more excellent than his neighbour: but the way of the wicked seduceth them.
27 The slothful *man* roasteth not that which he took in hunting: but the substance of a diligent man *is* precious.
28 In the way of righteousness *is* life; and *in* the pathway *thereof there is* no death.

13 A WISE son *heareth* his father's instruction: but a scorner heareth not rebuke.
2 A man shall eat good by the fruit of *his* mouth: but the soul of the transgressors *shall eat* violence.
3 He that keepeth his mouth keepeth his life: *but* he that openeth wide his lips shall have destruction.
4 The soul of the sluggard desireth, and *hath* nothing: but the soul of the diligent shall be made fat.
5 A righteous *man* hateth lying: but a wicked *man* is loathsome, and cometh to shame.
6 Righteousness keepeth *him that is* upright in the way: but wickedness overthroweth the sinner.
7 There is that maketh himself rich, yet *hath* nothing: *there is* that maketh himself poor, yet *hath* great riches.
8 The ransom of a man's life *are* his riches: but the poor heareth not rebuke.
9 The light of the righteous rejoiceth: but the lamp of the wicked shall be put out.
10 Only by pride cometh contention: but with the well advised *is* wisdom.
11 Wealth *gotten* by vanity shall be diminished: but he that gathereth by labour shall increase.
12 Hope deferred maketh the heart sick: but *when* the desire cometh, *it is* a tree of life.
13 Whoso despiseth the word shall be destroyed: but he that feareth the commandment shall be rewarded.
14 The law of the wise *is* a fountain of life, to depart from the snares of death.
15 Good understanding giveth favour: but the way of transgressors *is* hard.
16 Every prudent *man* dealeth with knowledge: but a fool layeth open *his* folly.
17 A wicked messenger falleth into mischief: but a faithful ambassador *is* health.
18 Poverty and shame *shall be to* him that refuseth instruction: but he that regardeth reproof shall be honoured.
19 The desire accomplished is sweet to the soul: but *it is* abomination to fools to depart from evil.
20 He that walketh with wise *men* shall be wise: but a companion of fools shall be destroyed.
21 Evil pursueth sinners: but to the righteous good shall be repayed.
22 A good *man* leaveth an inheritance to his children's children: and the wealth of the sinner *is* laid up for the just.
23 Much food *is in* the tillage of the poor: but there is *that is* destroyed for want of judgment.
24 He that spareth his rod hateth his son: but he that loveth him chasteneth him betimes.
25 The righteous eateth to the satisfying of his soul: but the belly of the wicked shall want.

14 EVERY wise woman buildeth her house: but the foolish plucketh it down with her hands.
2 He that walketh in his uprightness feareth the LORD: but *he that is* perverse in his ways despiseth him.
3 In the mouth of the foolish *is* a rod of pride: but the lips of the wise shall preserve them.
4 Where no oxen *are*, the crib *is* clean: but much increase *is* by the strength of the ox.
5 A faithful witness will not lie: but a false witness will utter lies.
6 A scorner seeketh wisdom, and *findeth it* not: but knowledge *is* easy unto him that understandeth.
7 Go from the presence of a foolish man, when thou perceivest not *in him* the lips of knowledge.
8 The wisdom of the prudent is to understand his way: but the folly of fools *is* deceit.
9 Fools make a mock at sin: but among the righteous *there is* favour.
10 The heart knoweth his own bitterness; and a stranger doth not intermeddle with his joy.
11 The house of the wicked shall be overthrown: but the tabernacle of the upright shall flourish.
12 There is a way which seemeth right unto a man, but the end thereof *are* the ways of death.
13 Even in laughter the heart is sorrowful; and the end of that mirth *is* heaviness.
14 The backslider in heart shall be filled with his own ways: and a good man *shall be satisfied* from himself.
15 The simple believeth every word: but the prudent *man* looketh well to his going.
16 A wise *man* feareth, and departeth from evil: but the fool rageth, and is confident.
17 *He that is* soon angry dealeth foolishly: and a man of wicked devices is hated.
18 The simple inherit folly: but the prudent are crowned with knowledge.
19 The evil bow before the good; and the wicked at the gates of the righteous.
20 The poor is hated even of his own neighbour: but the rich *hath* many friends.
21 He that despiseth his neighbour sinneth: but he that hath mercy on the poor, happy *is* he.
22 Do they not err that devise evil? but mercy and truth *shall be* to them that devise good.
23 In all labour there is profit: but the talk of the lips *tendeth* only to penury.
24 The crown of the wise *is* their riches: *but* the foolishness of fools *is* folly.
25 A true witness delivereth souls: but a deceitful *witness* speaketh lies.
26 In the fear of the LORD *is* strong confidence: and his children shall have a place of refuge.

27 The fear of the LORD *is* a fountain of life,
to depart from the snares of death.
28 In the multitude of people *is* the king's
honour: but in the want of people *is* the destruction of the prince.
29 *He that is* slow to wrath *is* of great understanding: but *he that is* hasty of spirit exalteth
folly.
30 A sound heart *is* the life of the flesh: but
envy the rottenness of the bones.
31 He that oppresseth the poor reproacheth
his Maker: but he that honoureth him hath mercy on the poor.
32 The wicked is driven away in his wickedness: but the righteous hath hope in his death.
33 Wisdom resteth in the heart of him that
hath understanding: but *that which is* in the
midst of fools is made known.
34 Righteousness exalteth a nation: but sin *is*
a reproach to any people.
35 The king's favour *is* toward a wise servant: but his wrath *is against* him that causeth
shame.

15 A SOFT answer turneth away wrath:
but grievous words stir up anger.
2 The tongue of the wise useth knowledge
aright: but the mouth of fools poureth out foolishness.
3 The eyes of the LORD *are* in every place,
beholding the evil and the good.
4 A wholesome tongue *is* a tree of life: but
perverseness therein *is* a breach in the spirit.
5 A fool despiseth his father's instruction:
but he that regardeth reproof is prudent.
6 In the house of the righteous *is* much treasure: but in the revenues of the wicked is trouble.
7 The lips of the wise disperse knowledge:
but the heart of the foolish *doeth* not so.
8 The sacrifice of the wicked *is* an abomination to the LORD: but the prayer of the upright *is*
his delight.
9 The way of the wicked *is* an abomination
unto the LORD: but he loveth him that followeth
after righteousness.
10 Correction *is* grievous unto him that forsaketh the way: *and* he that hateth reproof shall
die.
11 Hell and destruction *are* before the LORD:
how much more then the hearts of the children
of men?
12 A scorner loveth not one that reproveth
him: neither will he go unto the wise.
13 A merry heart maketh a cheerful countenance: but by sorrow of the heart the spirit is
broken.
14 The heart of him that hath understanding
seeketh knowledge: but the mouth of fools
feedeth on foolishness.
15 All the days of the afflicted *are* evil: but he
that is of a merry heart *hath* a continual feast.
16 Better *is* little with the fear of the LORD
than great treasure and trouble therewith.
17 Better *is* a dinner of herbs where love is,
than a stalled ox and hatred therewith.
18 A wrathful man stirreth up strife: but *he
that is* slow to anger appeaseth strife.
19 The way of the slothful *man is* as an
hedge of thorns: but the way of the righteous *is*
made plain.
20 A wise son maketh a glad father: but a
foolish man despiseth his mother.
21 Folly *is* joy to *him that is* destitute of wisdom: but a man of understanding walketh uprightly.
22 Without counsel purposes are disap-
pointed: but in the multitude of counsellors
they are established.
23 A man hath joy by the answer of his
mouth: and a word *spoken* in due season, how
good *is it!*
24 The way of life *is* above to the wise, that
he may depart from hell beneath.
25 The LORD will destroy the house of the
proud: but he will establish the border of the
widow.
26 The thoughts of the wicked *are* an abomination to the LORD: but *the words* of the pure
are pleasant words.
27 He that is greedy of gain troubleth his
own house; but he that hateth gifts shall live.
28 The heart of the righteous studieth to answer: but the mouth of the wicked poureth out
evil things.
29 The LORD *is* far from the wicked: but he
heareth the prayer of the righteous.
30 The light of the eyes rejoiceth the heart:
and a good report maketh the bones fat.
31 The ear that heareth the reproof of life
abideth among the wise.
32 He that refuseth instruction despiseth his
own soul: but he that heareth reproof getteth
understanding.
33 The fear of the LORD *is* the instruction of
wisdom; and before honour *is* humility.

16 THE preparations of the heart in man,
and the answer of the tongue, *is* from
the LORD.
2 All the ways of a man *are* clean in his own
eyes; but the LORD weigheth the spirits.
3 Commit thy works unto the LORD, and thy
thoughts shall be established.
4 The LORD hath made all *things* for himself:
yea, even the wicked for the day of evil.
5 Every one *that is* proud in heart *is* an
abomination to the LORD: *though* hand *join* in
hand, he shall not be unpunished.
6 By mercy and truth iniquity is purged: and
by the fear of the LORD *men* depart from evil.
7 When a man's ways please the LORD, he
maketh even his enemies to be at peace with
him.
8 Better *is* a little with righteousness than
great revenues without right.
9 A man's heart deviseth his way: but the
LORD directeth his steps.
10 A divine sentence *is* in the lips of the king:
his mouth transgresseth not in judgment.
11 A just weight and balance *are* the LORD's:
all the weights of the bag *are* his work.
12 *It is* an abomination to kings to commit
wickedness: for the throne is established by
righteousness.
13 Righteous lips *are* the delight of kings;
and they love him that speaketh right.
14 The wrath of a king *is as* messengers of
death: but a wise man will pacify it.
15 In the light of the king's countenance *is*
life; and his favour *is* as a cloud of the latter
rain.
16 How much better *is it* to get wisdom than
gold! and to get understanding rather to be chosen than silver!
17 The highway of the upright *is* to depart
from evil: he that keepeth his way preserveth
his soul.
18 Pride *goeth* before destruction, and an
haughty spirit before a fall.
19 Better *it is to be* of an humble spirit with
the lowly, than to divide the spoil with the
proud.
20 He that handleth a matter wisely shall

find good: and whoso trusteth in the LORD, happy *is* he.
21 The wise in heart shall be called prudent:
and the sweetness of the lips increaseth learning.
22 Understanding *is* a wellspring of life unto
him that hath it: but the instruction of fools *is*
folly.
23 The heart of the wise teacheth his mouth,
and addeth learning to his lips.
24 Pleasant words *are as* an honeycomb,
sweet to the soul, and health to the bones.
25 There is a way that seemeth right unto a
man, but the end thereof *are* the ways of death.
26 He that laboureth laboureth for himself;
for his mouth craveth it of him.
27 An ungodly man diggeth up evil: and in
his lips *there is* as a burning fire.
28 A froward man soweth strife: and a whis-
perer separateth chief friends.
29 A violent man enticeth his neighbour, and
leadeth him into the way *that is* not good.
30 He shutteth his eyes to devise froward
things: moving his lips he bringeth evil to pass.
31 The hoary head *is* a crown of glory, *if* it be
found in the way of righteousness.
32 *He that is* slow to anger *is* better than the
mighty; and he that ruleth his spirit than he that
taketh a city.
33 The lot is cast into the lap; but the whole
disposing thereof *is* of the LORD.

17 BETTER *is* a dry morsel, and quietness
therewith, than an house full of sacrifices *with* strife.
2 A wise servant shall have rule over a son
that causeth shame, and shall have part of the
inheritance among the brethren.
3 The fining pot *is* for silver, and the furnace
for gold: but the LORD trieth the hearts.
4 A wicked doer giveth heed to false lips;
and a liar giveth ear to a naughty tongue.
5 Whoso mocketh the poor reproacheth his
Maker: *and* he that is glad at calamities shall
not be unpunished.
6 Children's children *are* the crown of old
men; and the glory of children *are* their fathers.
7 Excellent speech becometh not a fool:
much less do lying lips a prince.
8 A gift *is as* a precious stone in the eyes of
him that hath it: whithersoever it turneth, it
prospereth.
9 He that covereth a transgression seeketh
love; but he that repeateth a matter separateth
very friends.
10 A reproof entereth more into a wise man
than an hundred stripes into a fool.
11 An evil *man* seeketh only rebellion: therefore a cruel messenger shall be sent against
him.
12 Let a bear robbed of her whelps meet a
man, rather than a fool in his folly.
13 Whoso rewardeth evil for good, evil shall
not depart from his house.
14 The beginning of strife *is as* when one letteth out water: therefore leave off contention,
before it be meddled with.
15 He that justifieth the wicked, and he that
condemneth the just, even they both *are* abomination to the LORD.
16 Wherefore *is there* a price in the hand of a
fool to get wisdom, seeing *he hath* no heart *to
it?*
17 A friend loveth at all times, and a brother
is born for adversity.
18 A man void of understanding striketh
hands, *and* becometh surety in the presence of
his friend.
19 He loveth transgression that loveth strife:
and he that exalteth his gate seeketh destruction.
20 He that hath a froward heart findeth no
good: and he that hath a perverse tongue falleth
into mischief.
21 He that begetteth a fool *doeth it* to his sorrow: and the father of a fool hath no joy.
22 A merry heart doeth good *like* a medicine:
but a broken spirit drieth the bones.
23 A wicked *man* taketh a gift out of the bosom to pervert the ways of judgment.
24 Wisdom *is* before him that hath understanding; but the eyes of a fool *are* in the ends
of the earth.
25 A foolish son *is* a grief to his father, and
bitterness to her that bare him.
26 Also to punish the just *is* not good, *nor* to
strike princes for equity.
27 He that hath knowledge spareth his
words: *and* a man of understanding is of an excellent spirit.
28 Even a fool, when he holdeth his peace, is
counted wise: *and* he that shutteth his lips *is*
esteemed a man of understanding.

18 THROUGH desire a man, having separated himself, seeketh *and* intermed-
dleth with all wisdom.
2 A fool hath no delight in understanding,
but that his heart may discover itself.
3 When the wicked cometh, *then* cometh
also contempt, and with ignominy reproach.
4 The words of a man's mouth *are as* deep
waters, *and* the wellspring of wisdom *as* a flowing brook.
5 *It is* not good to accept the person of the
wicked, to overthrow the righteous in judgment.
6 A fool's lips enter into contention, and his
mouth calleth for strokes.
7 A fool's mouth *is* his destruction, and his
lips *are* the snare of his soul.
8 The words of a talebearer *are* as wounds,
and they go down into the innermost parts of
the belly.
9 He also that is slothful in his work is
brother to him that is a great waster.
10 The name of the LORD *is* a strong tower:
the righteous runneth into it, and is safe.
11 The rich man's wealth *is* his strong city,
and as an high wall in his own conceit.
12 Before destruction the heart of man is
haughty, and before honour *is* humility.
13 He that answereth a matter before he
heareth *it*, it *is* folly and shame unto him.
14 The spirit of a man will sustain his infirmity; but a wounded spirit who can bear?
15 The heart of the prudent getteth knowledge; and the ear of the wise seeketh knowledge.
16 A man's gift maketh room for him, and
bringeth him before great men.
17 *He that is* first in his own cause *seemeth*
just; but his neighbour cometh and searcheth
him.
18 The lot causeth contentions to cease, and
parteth between the mighty.
19 A brother offended *is harder to be won*
than a strong city: and *their* contentions *are* like
the bars of a castle.
20 A man's belly shall be satisfied with the
fruit of his mouth; *and* with the increase of his
lips shall he be filled.
21 Death and life *are* in the power of the

tongue: and they that love it shall eat the fruit thereof.

22 *Whoso* findeth a wife findeth a good *thing*, and obtaineth favour of the LORD.

23 The poor useth intreaties; but the rich answereth roughly.

24 A man *that hath* friends must shew himself friendly: and there is a friend *that* sticketh closer than a brother.

19

BETTER *is* the poor that walketh in his integrity, than *he that is* perverse in his lips, and is a fool.

2 Also, *that* the soul *be* without knowledge, *it is* not good; and he that hasteth with *his* feet sinneth.

3 The foolishness of man perverteth his way: and his heart fretteth against the LORD.

4 Wealth maketh many friends; but the poor is separated from his neighbour.

5 A false witness shall not be unpunished, and *he that* speaketh lies shall not escape.

6 Many will intreat the favour of the prince: and every man *is* a friend to him that giveth gifts.

7 All the brethren of the poor do hate him: how much more do his friends go far from him? he pursueth *them with* words, *yet* they *are* wanting *to him*.

8 He that getteth wisdom loveth his own soul: he that keepeth understanding shall find good.

9 A false witness shall not be unpunished, and *he that* speaketh lies shall perish.

10 Delight is not seemly for a fool; much less for a servant to have rule over princes.

11 The discretion of a man deferreth his anger; and *it is* his glory to pass over a transgression.

12 The king's wrath *is* as the roaring of a lion; but his favour *is* as dew upon the grass.

13 A foolish son *is* the calamity of his father: and the contentions of a wife *are* a continual dropping.

14 House and riches *are* the inheritance of fathers: and a prudent wife *is* from the LORD.

15 Slothfulness casteth into a deep sleep; and an idle soul shall suffer hunger.

16 He that keepeth the commandment keepeth his own soul; *but* he that despiseth his ways shall die.

17 He that hath pity upon the poor lendeth unto the LORD; and that which he hath given will he pay him again.

18 Chasten thy son while there is hope, and let not thy soul spare for his crying.

19 A man of great wrath shall suffer punishment: for if thou deliver *him*, yet thou must do it again.

20 Hear counsel, and receive instruction, that thou mayest be wise in thy latter end.

21 *There are* many devices in a man's heart; nevertheless the counsel of the LORD, that shall stand.

22 The desire of a man *is* his kindness: and a poor man *is* better than a liar.

23 The fear of the LORD *tendeth* to life: and *he that hath it* shall abide satisfied; he shall not be visited with evil.

24 A slothful *man* hideth his hand in *his* bosom, and will not so much as bring it to his mouth again.

25 Smite a scorner, and the simple will beware: and reprove one that hath understanding, *and* he will understand knowledge.

26 He that wasteth *his* father, *and* chaseth away *his* mother, *is* a son that causeth shame, and bringeth reproach.

27 Cease, my son, to hear the instruction *that causeth* to err from the words of knowledge.

28 An ungodly witness scorneth judgment: and the mouth of the wicked devoureth iniquity.

29 Judgments are prepared for scorners, and stripes for the back of fools.

20

WINE *is* a mocker, strong drink *is* raging: and whosoever is deceived thereby is not wise.

2 The fear of a king *is* as the roaring of a lion: *whoso* provoketh him to anger sinneth *against* his own soul.

3 *It is* an honour for a man to cease from strife: but every fool will be meddling.

4 The sluggard will not plow by reason of the cold; *therefore* shall he beg in harvest, and *have* nothing.

5 Counsel in the heart of man *is like* deep water; but a man of understanding will draw it out.

6 Most men will proclaim every one his own goodness: but a faithful man who can find?

7 The just *man* walketh in his integrity: his children *are* blessed after him.

8 A king that sitteth in the throne of judgment scattereth away all evil with his eyes.

9 Who can say, I have made my heart clean, I am pure from my sin?

10 Divers weights, *and* divers measures, both of them *are* alike abomination to the LORD.

11 Even a child is known by his doings, whether his work *be* pure, and whether *it be* right.

12 The hearing ear, and the seeing eye, the LORD hath made even both of them.

13 Love not sleep, lest thou come to poverty; open thine eyes, *and* thou shalt be satisfied with bread.

14 *It is* naught, *it is* naught, saith the buyer: but when he is gone his way, then he boasteth.

15 There is gold, and a multitude of rubies: but the lips of knowledge *are* a precious jewel.

16 Take his garment that is surety *for* a stranger: and take a pledge of him for a strange woman.

17 Bread of deceit *is* sweet to a man; but afterwards his mouth shall be filled with gravel.

18 *Every* purpose is established by counsel: and with good advice make war.

19 He that goeth about *as* a talebearer revealeth secrets: therefore meddle not with him that flattereth with his lips.

20 Whoso curseth his father or his mother, his lamp shall be put out in obscure darkness.

21 An inheritance *may be* gotten hastily at the beginning; but the end thereof shall not be blessed.

22 Say not thou, I will recompense evil; *but* wait on the LORD, and he shall save thee.

23 Divers weights *are* an abomination unto the LORD; and a false balance *is* not good.

24 Man's goings *are* of the LORD; how can a man then understand his own way?

25 *It is* a snare to the man *who* devoureth *that which is* holy, and after vows to make enquiry.

26 A wise king scattereth the wicked, and bringeth the wheel over them.

27 The spirit of man *is* the candle of the LORD, searching all the inward parts of the belly.

28 Mercy and truth preserve the king: and his throne is upholden by mercy.

29 The glory of young men *is* their strength: and the beauty of old men *is* the gray head.

30 The blueness of a wound cleanseth away evil: so *do* stripes the inward parts of the belly.

21 THE king's heart *is* in the hand of the LORD, *as* the rivers of water: he turneth it whithersoever he will.

2 Every way of a man *is* right in his own eyes: but the LORD pondereth the hearts.

3 To do justice and judgment *is* more acceptable to the LORD than sacrifice.

4 An high look, and a proud heart, *and* the plowing of the wicked, *is* sin.

5 The thoughts of the diligent *tend* only to plenteousness; but of every one *that is* hasty only to want.

6 The getting of treasures by a lying tongue *is* a vanity tossed to and fro of them that seek death.

7 The robbery of the wicked shall destroy them; because they refuse to do judgment.

8 The way of man *is* froward and strange: but *as for* the pure, his work *is* right.

9 *It is* better to dwell in a corner of the house top, than with a brawling woman in a wide house.

10 The soul of the wicked desireth evil: his neighbour findeth no favour in his eyes.

11 When the scorner is punished, the simple is made wise: and when the wise is instructed, he receiveth knowledge.

12 The righteous *man* wisely considereth the house of the wicked: *but God* overthroweth the wicked for *their* wickedness.

13 Whoso stoppeth his ears at the cry of the poor, he also shall cry himself, but shall not be heard.

14 A gift in secret pacifieth anger: and a reward in the bosom strong wrath.

15 *It is* joy to the just to do judgment: but destruction *shall be* to the workers of iniquity.

16 The man that wandereth out of the way of understanding shall remain in the congregation of the dead.

17 He that loveth pleasure *shall be* a poor man: he that loveth wine and oil shall not be rich.

18 The wicked *shall be* a ransom for the righteous, and the transgressor for the upright.

19 *It is* better to dwell in the wilderness, than with a contentious and an angry woman.

20 *There is* treasure to be desired and oil in the dwelling of the wise; but a foolish man spendeth it up.

21 He that followeth after righteousness and mercy findeth life, righteousness, and honour.

22 A wise *man* scaleth the city of the mighty, and casteth down the strength of the confidence thereof.

23 Whoso keepeth his mouth and his tongue keepeth his soul from troubles.

24 Proud *and* haughty scorner *is* his name, who dealeth in proud wrath.

25 The desire of the slothful killeth him; for his hands refuse to labour.

26 He coveteth greedily all the day long: but the righteous giveth and spareth not.

27 The sacrifice of the wicked *is* abomination: how much more, *when* he bringeth it with a wicked mind?

28 A false witness shall perish: but the man that heareth speaketh constantly.

29 A wicked man hardeneth his face: but *as for* the upright, he directeth his way.

30 *There is* no wisdom nor understanding nor counsel against the LORD.

31 The horse *is* prepared against the day of battle: but safety *is* of the LORD.

22 A *GOOD* name *is* rather to be chosen than great riches, *and* loving favour rather than silver and gold.

2 The rich and poor meet together: the LORD *is* the maker of them all.

3 A prudent *man* forseeth the evil, and hideth himself: but the simple pass on, and are punished.

4 By humility *and* the fear of the LORD *are* riches, and honour, and life.

5 Thorns *and* snares *are* in the way of the froward: he that doth keep his soul shall be far from them.

6 Train up a child in the way he should go: and when he is old, he will not depart from it.

7 The rich ruleth over the poor, and the borrower *is* servant to the lender.

8 He that soweth iniquity shall reap vanity: and the rod of his anger shall fail.

9 He that hath a bountiful eye shall be blessed; for he giveth of his bread to the poor.

10 Cast out the scorner, and contention shall go out; yea, strife and reproach shall cease.

11 He that loveth pureness of heart, *for* the grace of his lips the king *shall be* his friend.

12 The eyes of the LORD preserve knowledge, and he overthroweth the words of the transgressor.

13 The slothful *man* saith, *There is* a lion without, I shall be slain in the streets.

14 The mouth of strange women *is* a deep pit: he that is abhorred of the LORD shall fall therein.

15 Foolishness *is* bound in the heart of a child; *but* the rod of correction shall drive it far from him.

16 He that oppresseth the poor to increase his *riches, and* he that giveth to the rich, *shall* surely *come* to want.

17 Bow down thine ear, and hear the words of the wise, and apply thine heart unto my knowledge.

18 For *it is* a pleasant thing if thou keep them within thee; they shall withal be fitted in thy lips.

19 That thy trust may be in the LORD, I have made known to thee this day, even to thee.

20 Have not I written to thee excellent things in counsels and knowledge,

21 That I might make thee know the certainty of the words of truth; that thou mightest answer the words of truth to them that send unto thee?

22 Rob not the poor, because he *is* poor: neither oppress the afflicted in the gate:

23 For the LORD will plead their cause, and spoil the soul of those that spoiled them.

24 Make no friendship with an angry man; and with a furious man thou shalt not go:

25 Lest thou learn his ways, and get a snare to thy soul.

26 Be not thou *one* of them that strike hands, *or* of them that are sureties for debts.

27 If thou hast nothing to pay, why should he take away thy bed from under thee?

28 Remove not the ancient landmark, which thy fathers have set.

29 Seest thou a man diligent in his business? he shall stand before kings; he shall not stand before mean *men*.

23 WHEN thou sittest to eat with a ruler,
consider diligently what *is* before thee:
2 And put a knife to thy throat, if thou *be* a
man given to appetite.
3 Be not desirous of his dainties: for they *are*
deceitful meat.
4 Labour not to be rich: cease from thine
own wisdom.
5 Wilt thou set thine eyes upon that which is
not? for *riches* certainly make themselves
wings; they fly away as an eagle toward heaven.
6 Eat thou not the bread of *him that hath* an
evil eye, neither desire thou his dainty meats:
7 For as he thinketh in his heart, so *is* he: Eat
and drink, saith he to thee; but his heart *is* not
with thee.
8 The morsel *which* thou hast eaten shalt
thou vomit up, and lose thy sweet words.
9 Speak not in the ears of a fool: for he will
despise the wisdom of thy words.
10 Remove not the old landmark; and enter
not into the fields of the fatherless:
11 For their redeemer *is* mighty; he shall
plead their cause with thee.
12 Apply thine heart unto instruction, and
thine ears to the words of knowledge.
13 Withhold not correction from the child:
for *if* thou beatest him with the rod, he shall not
die.
14 Thou shalt beat him with the rod, and
shalt deliver his soul from hell.
15 My son, if thine heart be wise, my heart
shall rejoice, even mine.
16 Yea, my reins shall rejoice, when thy lips
speak right things.
17 Let not thine heart envy sinners: but *be
thou* in the fear of the LORD all the day long.
18 For surely there is an end; and thine expectation shall not be cut off.
19 Hear thou, my son, and be wise, and guide
thine heart in the way.
20 Be not among winebibbers; among riotous
eaters of flesh:
21 For the drunkard and the glutton shall
come to poverty: and drowsiness shall clothe *a
man* with rags.
22 Hearken unto thy father that begat thee,
and despise not thy mother when she is old.
23 Buy the truth, and sell *it* not; *also* wisdom,
and instruction, and understanding.
24 The father of the righteous shall greatly
rejoice: and he that begetteth a wise *child* shall
have joy of him.
25 Thy father and thy mother shall be glad,
and she that bare thee shall rejoice.
26 My son, give me thine heart, and let thine
eyes observe my ways.
27 For a whore *is* a deep ditch; and a strange
woman *is* a narrow pit.
28 She also lieth in wait as *for* a prey, and
increaseth the transgressors among men.
29 Who hath woe? who hath sorrow? who
hath contentions? who hath babbling? who hath
wounds without cause? who hath redness of
eyes?
30 They that tarry long at the wine; they that
go to seek mixed wine.
31 Look not thou upon the wine when it is
red, when it giveth his colour in the cup, *when* it
moveth itself aright.
32 At the last it biteth like a serpent, and
stingeth like an adder.
33 Thine eyes shall behold strange women,
and thine heart shall utter perverse things.
34 Yea, thou shalt be as he that lieth down in
the midst of the sea, or as he that lieth upon the
top of a mast.
35 They have stricken me, *shalt thou say,
and* I was not sick; they have beaten me, *and* I
felt *it* not: when shall I awake? I will seek it yet
again.

24 BE not thou envious against evil men,
neither desire to be with them.
2 For their heart studieth destruction, and
their lips talk of mischief.
3 Through wisdom is an house builded; and
by understanding it is established:
4 And by knowledge shall the chambers be
filled with all precious and pleasant riches.
5 A wise man *is* strong; yea, a man of knowledge increaseth strength.
6 For by wise counsel thou shalt make thy
war: and in multitude of counsellors *there is*
safety.
7 Wisdom *is* too high for a fool: he openeth
not his mouth in the gate.
8 He that deviseth to do evil shall be called a
mischievous person.
9 The thought of foolishness *is* sin: and the
scorner *is* an abomination to men.
10 *If* thou faint in the day of adversity, thy
strength *is* small.
11 If thou forbear to deliver *them that are*
drawn unto death, and *those that are* ready to
be slain;
12 If thou sayest, Behold, we knew it not;
doth not he that pondereth the heart consider
it? and he that keepeth thy soul, doth *not* he
know *it?* and shall *not* he render to *every* man
according to his works?
13 My son, eat thou honey, because *it is*
good; and the honeycomb, *which is* sweet to thy
taste:
14 So *shall* the knowledge of wisdom *be* unto
thy soul: when thou hast found *it,* then there
shall be a reward, and thy expectation shall not
be cut off.
15 Lay not wait, O wicked *man,* against the
dwelling of the righteous; spoil not his resting
place:
16 For a just *man* falleth seven times, and
riseth up again: but the wicked shall fall into
mischief.
17 Rejoice not when thine enemy falleth, and
let not thine heart be glad when he stumbleth:
18 Lest the LORD see *it,* and it displease him,
and he turn away his wrath from him.
19 Fret not thyself because of evil *men,* neither be thou envious at the wicked;
20 For there shall be no reward to the evil
man; the candle of the wicked shall be put out.
21 My son, fear thou the LORD and the king:
and meddle not with them that are given to
change:
22 For their calamity shall rise suddenly; and
who knoweth the ruin of them both?
23 These *things* also *belong* to the wise. *It is*
not good to have respect of persons in judgment.
24 He that saith unto the wicked, Thou *art*
righteous; him shall the people curse, nations
shall abhor him:
25 But to them that rebuke *him* shall be delight, and a good blessing shall come upon
them.
26 *Every man* shall kiss *his* lips that giveth a
right answer.
27 Prepare thy work without, and make it fit
for thyself in the field; and afterwards build
thine house.
28 Be not a witness against thy neighbour
without cause; and deceive *not* with thy lips.
29 Say not, I will do so to him as he hath

done to me: I will render to the man according
to his work.
30 I went by the field of the slothful, and by
the vineyard of the man void of understanding;
31 And, lo, it was all grown over with thorns,
and nettles had covered the face thereof, and
the stone wall thereof was broken down.
32 Then I saw, *and* considered *it* well: I
looked upon *it, and* received instruction.
33 *Yet* a little sleep, a little slumber, a little
folding of the hands to sleep:
34 So shall thy poverty come *as* one that
travelleth; and thy want as an armed man.

25 THESE *are* also proverbs of Sol'o-mon,
which the men of Hez-e-ki'ah king of
Ju'dah copied out.
2 *It is* the glory of God to conceal a thing: but
the honour of kings *is* to search out a matter.
3 The heaven for height, and the earth for
depth, and the heart of kings *is* unsearchable.
4 Take away the dross from the silver, and
there shall come forth a vessel for the finer.
5 Take away the wicked *from* before the
king, and his throne shall be established in
righteousness.
6 Put not forth thyself in the presence of the
king, and stand not in the place of great *men:*
7 For better *it is* that it be said unto thee,
Come up hither; than that thou shouldest be put
lower in the presence of the prince whom thine
eyes have seen.
8 Go not forth hastily to strive, lest *thou
know not* what to do in the end thereof, when
thy neighbour hath put thee to shame.
9 Debate thy cause with thy neighbour *himself;* and discover not a secret to another:
10 Lest he that heareth *it* put thee to shame,
and thine infamy turn not away.
11 A word fitly spoken *is like* apples of gold
in pictures of silver.
12 *As* an earring of gold, and an ornament of
fine gold, *so is* a wise reprover upon an obedient
ear.
13 As the cold of snow in the time of harvest,
so is a faithful messenger to them that send
him: for he refresheth the soul of his masters.
14 Whoso boasteth himself of a false gift *is
like* clouds and wind without rain.
15 By long forbearing is a prince persuaded,
and a soft tongue breaketh the bone.
16 Hast thou found honey? eat so much as is
sufficient for thee, lest thou be filled therewith,
and vomit it.
17 Withdraw thy foot from thy neighbour's
house; lest he be weary of thee, and *so* hate
thee.
18 A man that beareth false witness against
his neighbour *is* a maul, and a sword, and a
sharp arrow.
19 Confidence in an unfaithful man in time of
trouble *is like* a broken tooth, and a foot out of
joint.
20 *As* he that taketh away a garment in cold
weather, *and as* vinegar upon nitre, so *is* he that
singeth songs to an heavy heart.
21 If thine enemy be hungry, give him bread
to eat; and if he be thirsty, give him water to
drink:
22 For thou shalt heap coals of fire upon his
head, and the LORD shall reward thee.
23 The north wind driveth away rain: so *doth*
an angry countenance a backbiting tongue.
24 *It is* better to dwell in the corner of the
house top, than with a brawling woman and in a
wide house.
25 *As* cold waters to a thirsty soul, so *is* good
news from a far country.
26 A righteous man falling down before the
wicked *is as* a troubled fountain, and a corrupt
spring.
27 *It is* not good to eat much honey: so *for
men* to search their own glory *is not* glory.
28 He that *hath* no rule over his own spirit *is
like* a city *that is* broken down, *and* without
walls.

26 AS snow in summer, and as rain in harvest, so honour is not seemly for a fool.
2 As the bird by wandering, as the swallow
by flying, so the curse causeless shall not come.
3 A whip for the horse, a bridle for the ass,
and a rod for the fool's back.
4 Answer not a fool according to his folly,
lest thou also be like unto him.
5 Answer a fool according to his folly, lest he
be wise in his own conceit.
6 He that sendeth a message by the hand of a
fool cutteth off the feet, *and* drinketh damage.
7 The legs of the lame are not equal: so *is* a
parable in the mouth of fools.
8 As he that bindeth a stone in a sling, so *is*
he that giveth honour to a fool.
9 *As* a thorn goeth up into the hand of a
drunkard, so *is* a parable in the mouth of fools.
10 The great *God* that formed all *things* both
rewardeth the fool, and rewardeth transgressors.
11 As a dog returneth to his vomit, *so* a fool
returneth to his folly.
12 Seest thou a man wise in his own conceit?
there is more hope of a fool than of him.
13 The slothful *man* saith, *There is* a lion in
the way; a lion *is* in the streets.
14 *As* the door turneth upon his hinges, so
doth the slothful upon his bed.
15 The slothful hideth his hand in *his* bosom;
it grieveth him to bring it again to his mouth.
16 The sluggard *is* wiser in his own conceit
than seven men that can render a reason.
17 He that passeth by, *and* meddleth with
strife *belonging* not to him, *is like* one that taketh a dog by the ears.
18 As a mad *man* who casteth firebrands, arrows, and death,
19 So *is* the man *that* deceiveth his neighbour, and saith, Am not I in sport?
20 Where no wood is, *there* the fire goeth
out: so where *there is* no talebearer, the strife
ceaseth.
21 *As* coals *are* to burning coals, and wood to
fire; so *is* a contentious man to kindle strife.
22 The words of a talebearer *are* as wounds,
and they go down into the innermost parts of
the belly.
23 Burning lips and a wicked heart *are like* a
potsherd covered with silver dross.
24 He that hateth dissembleth with his lips,
and layeth up deceit within him;
25 When he speaketh fair, believe him not:
for *there are* seven abominations in his heart.
26 *Whose* hatred is covered by deceit, his
wickedness shall be shewed before the *whole*
congregation.
27 Whoso diggeth a pit shall fall therein: and
he that rolleth a stone, it will return upon him.
28 A lying tongue hateth *those that are* afflicted by it; and a flattering mouth worketh
ruin.

27 BOAST not thyself of to morrow; for
thou knowest not what a day may bring
forth.

2 Let another man praise thee, and not thine
own mouth; a stranger, and not thine own lips.
3 A stone *is* heavy, and the sand weighty; but
a fool's wrath *is* heavier than them both.
4 Wrath *is* cruel, and anger *is* outrageous;
but who *is* able to stand before envy?
5 Open rebuke *is* better than secret love.
6 Faithful *are* the wounds of a friend; but the
kisses of an enemy *are* deceitful.
7 The full soul loatheth an honeycomb; but to
the hungry soul every bitter thing is sweet.
8 As a bird that wandereth from her nest, so
is a man that wandereth from his place.
9 Ointment and perfume rejoice the heart: so
doth the sweetness of a man's friend by hearty
counsel.
10 Thine own friend, and thy father's friend,
forsake not; neither go into thy brother's house
in the day of thy calamity: *for* better *is* a neighbour *that is* near than a brother far off.
11 My son, be wise, and make my heart glad,
that I may answer him that reproacheth me.
12 A prudent *man* foreseeth the evil, *and*
hideth himself; *but* the simple pass on, *and* are
punished.
13 Take his garment that is surety for a
stranger, and take a pledge of him for a strange
woman.
14 He that blesseth his friend with a loud
voice, rising early in the morning, it shall be
counted a curse to him.
15 A continual dropping in a very rainy day
and a contentious woman are alike.
16 Whosoever hideth her hideth the wind,
and the ointment of his right hand, *which* bewrayeth *itself*.
17 Iron sharpeneth iron; so a man sharpeneth
the countenance of his friend.
18 Whoso keepeth the fig tree shall eat the
fruit thereof: so he that waiteth on his master
shall be honoured.
19 As in water face *answereth* to face, so the
heart of man to man.
20 Hell and destruction are never full; so the
eyes of man are never satisfied.
21 *As* the fining pot for silver, and the furnace for gold; so *is* a man to his praise.
22 Though thou shouldest bray a fool in a
mortar among wheat with a pestle, *yet* will not
his foolishness depart from him.
23 Be thou diligent to know the state of thy
flocks, *and* look well to thy herds.
24 For riches *are* not for ever: and doth the
crown *endure* to every generation?
25 The hay appeareth, and the tender grass
sheweth itself, and herbs of the mountains are
gathered.
26 The lambs *are* for thy clothing, and the
goats *are* the price of the field.
27 And *thou shalt have* goats' milk enough
for thy food, for the food of thy household, and
for the maintenance for thy maidens.

28 THE wicked flee when no man pursueth: but the righteous are bold as a lion.
2 For the transgression of a land many *are*
the princes thereof: but by a man of understanding *and* knowledge the state *thereof* shall
be prolonged.
3 A poor man that oppresseth the poor *is like*
a sweeping rain which leaveth no food.
4 They that forsake the law praise the
wicked: but such as keep the law contend with
them.
5 Evil men understand not judgment: but
they that seek the LORD understand all *things*.
6 Better *is* the poor that walketh in his uprightness, than *he that is* perverse *in his* ways,
though he *be* rich.
7 Whoso keepeth the law *is* a wise son: but
he that is a companion of riotous *men* shameth
his father.
8 He that by usury and unjust gain increaseth his substance, he shall gather it for him that
will pity the poor.
9 He that turneth away his ear from hearing
the law, even his prayer *shall be* abomination.
10 Whoso causeth the righteous to go astray
in an evil way, he shall fall himself into his own
pit: but the upright shall have good *things* in
possession.
11 The rich man *is* wise in his own conceit;
but the poor that hath understanding searcheth
him out.
12 When righteous *men* do rejoice, *there is*
great glory: but when the wicked rise, a man is
hidden.
13 He that covereth his sins shall not prosper: but whoso confesseth and forsaketh *them*
shall have mercy.
14 Happy *is* the man that feareth alway: but
he that hardeneth his heart shall fall into mischief.
15 *As* a roaring lion, and a ranging bear; *so is*
a wicked ruler over the poor people.
16 The prince that wanteth understanding *is*
also a great oppressor: *but* he that hateth covetousness shall prolong *his* days.
17 A man that doeth violence to the blood of
any person shall flee to the pit; let no man stay
him.
18 Whoso walketh uprightly shall be saved:
but *he that is* perverse *in his* ways shall fall at
once.
19 He that tilleth his land shall have plenty of
bread: but he that followeth after vain *persons*
shall have poverty enough.
20 A faithful man shall abound with blessings: but he that maketh haste to be rich shall
not be innocent.
21 To have respect of persons *is* not good: for
for a piece of bread *that* man will transgress.
22 He that hasteth to be rich *hath* an evil eye,
and considereth not that poverty shall come
upon him.
23 He that rebuketh a man afterwards shall
find more favour than he that flattereth with the
tongue.
24 Whoso robbeth his father or his mother,
and saith, *It is* no transgression; the same *is* the
companion of a destroyer.
25 He that is of a proud heart stirreth up
strife: but he that putteth his trust in the LORD
shall be made fat.
26 He that trusteth in his own heart is a fool:
but whoso walketh wisely, he shall be delivered.
27 He that giveth unto the poor shall not
lack: but he that hideth his eyes shall have
many a curse.
28 When the wicked rise, men hide themselves: but when they perish, the righteous increase.

29 HE, that being often reproved hardeneth *his* neck, shall suddenly be destroyed, and that without remedy.
2 When the righteous are in authority, the
people rejoice: but when the wicked beareth
rule, the people mourn.
3 Whoso loveth wisdom rejoiceth his father:
but he that keepeth company with harlots
spendeth *his* substance.

4 The king by judgment establisheth the land: but he that receiveth gifts overthroweth it.

5 A man that flattereth his neighbour spreadeth a net for his feet.

6 In the transgression of an evil man *there is* a snare: but the righteous doth sing and rejoice.

7 The righteous considereth the cause of the poor: *but* the wicked regardeth not to know *it*.

8 Scornful men bring a city into a snare: but wise *men* turn away wrath.

9 *If* a wise man contendeth with a foolish man, whether he rage or laugh, *there is* no rest.

10 The bloodthirsty hate the upright: but the just seek his soul.

11 A fool uttereth all his mind: but a wise *man* keepeth it in till afterwards.

12 If a ruler hearken to lies, all his servants *are* wicked.

13 The poor and the deceitful man meet together: the LORD lighteneth both their eyes.

14 The king that faithfully judgeth the poor, his throne shall be established for ever.

15 The rod and reproof give wisdom: but a child left *to himself* bringeth his mother to shame.

16 When the wicked are multiplied, transgression increaseth: but the righteous shall see their fall.

17 Correct thy son, and he shall give thee rest; yea, he shall give delight unto thy soul.

18 Where *there is* no vision, the people perish: but he that keepeth the law, happy *is* he.

19 A servant will not be corrected by words: for though he understand he will not answer.

20 Seest thou a man *that is* hasty in his words? *there is* more hope of a fool than of him.

21 He that delicately bringeth up his servant from a child shall have him become *his* son at the length.

22 An angry man stirreth up strife, and a furious man aboundeth in transgression.

23 A man's pride shall bring him low: but honour shall uphold the humble in spirit.

24 Whoso is partner with a thief hateth his own soul: he heareth cursing, and bewrayeth *it* not.

25 The fear of man bringeth a snare: but whoso putteth his trust in the LORD shall be safe.

26 Many seek the ruler's favour; but *every* man's judgment *cometh* from the LORD.

27 An unjust man *is* an abomination to the just: and *he that is* upright in the way *is* abomination to the wicked.

30 THE words of A'gur the son of Ja'keh, *even* the prophecy: the man spake unto Ith'i-el, even unto Ith'i-el and U'cal,

2 Surely I *am* more brutish than *any* man, and have not the understanding of a man.

3 I neither learned wisdom, nor have the knowledge of the holy.

4 Who hath ascended up into heaven, or descended? who hath gathered the wind in his fists? who hath bound the waters in a garment? who hath established all the ends of the earth? what *is* his name, and what *is* his son's name, if thou canst tell?

5 Every word of God *is* pure: he *is* a shield unto them that put their trust in him.

6 Add thou not unto his words, lest he reprove thee, and thou be found a liar.

7 Two *things* have I required of thee; deny me *them* not before I die:

8 Remove far from me vanity and lies: give me neither poverty nor riches; feed me with food convenient for me:

9 Lest I be full, and deny *thee*, and say, Who *is* the LORD? or lest I be poor, and steal, and take the name of my God *in vain*.

10 Accuse not a servant unto his master, lest he curse thee, and thou be found guilty.

11 *There is* a generation *that* curseth their father, and doth not bless their mother.

12 *There is* a generation *that are* pure in their own eyes, and *yet* is not washed from their filthiness.

13 *There is* a generation, O how lofty are their eyes! and their eyelids are lifted up.

14 *There is* a generation, whose teeth *are as* swords, and their jaw teeth *as* knives, to devour the poor from off the earth, and the needy from *among* men.

15 The horseleach hath two daughters, *crying*, Give, give. There are three *things that* are never satisfied, *yea*, four *things* say not, *It is* enough:

16 The grave; and the barren womb; the earth *that* is not filled with water; and the fire *that* saith not, *It is* enough.

17 The eye *that* mocketh at *his* father, and despiseth to obey *his* mother, the ravens of the valley shall pick it out, and the young eagles shall eat it.

18 There be three *things which* are too wonderful for me, yea, four which I know not:

19 The way of an eagle in the air; the way of a serpent upon a rock; the way of a ship in the midst of the sea; and the way of a man with a maid.

20 Such *is* the way of an adulterous woman; she eateth, and wipeth her mouth, and saith, I have done no wickedness.

21 For three *things* the earth is disquieted, and for four *which* it cannot bear:

22 For a servant when he reigneth; and a fool when he is filled with meat;

23 For an odious *woman* when she is married; and an handmaid that is heir to her mistress.

24 There be four *things which are* little upon the earth, but they *are* exceeding wise:

25 The ants *are* a people not strong, yet they prepare their meat in the summer;

26 The conies *are but* a feeble folk, yet make they their houses in the rocks;

27 The locusts have no king, yet go they forth all of them by bands;

28 The spider taketh hold with her hands, and is in kings' palaces.

29 There be three *things* which go well, yea, four are comely in going:

30 A lion *which is* strongest among beasts, and turneth not away for any;

31 A greyhound; an he goat also; and a king, against whom *there is* no rising up.

32 If thou hast done foolishly in lifting up thyself, or if thou hast thought evil, *lay* thine hand upon thy mouth.

33 Surely the churning of milk bringeth forth butter, and the wringing of the nose bringeth forth blood: so the forcing of wrath bringeth forth strife.

31 THE words of king Lem'u-el, the prophecy that his mother taught him.

2 What, my son? and what, the son of my womb? and what, the son of my vows?

3 Give not thy strength unto women, nor thy ways to that which destroyeth kings.

4 *It is* not for kings, O Lem'u-el, *it is* not for kings to drink wine; nor for princes strong drink:

5 Lest they drink, and forget the law, and pervert the judgment of any of the afflicted.
6 Give strong drink unto him that is ready to perish, and wine unto those that be of heavy hearts.
7 Let him drink, and forget his poverty, and remember his misery no more.
8 Open thy mouth for the dumb in the cause of all such as are appointed to destruction.
9 Open thy mouth, judge righteously, and plead the cause of the poor and needy.
10 ¶ Who can find a virtuous woman? for her price *is* far above rubies.
11 The heart of her husband doth safely trust in her, so that he shall have no need of spoil.
12 She will do him good and not evil all the days of her life.
13 She seeketh wool, and flax, and worketh willingly with her hands.
14 She is like the merchants' ships; she bringeth her food from afar.
15 She riseth also while it is yet night, and giveth meat to her household, and a portion to her maidens.
16 She considereth a field, and buyeth it: with the fruit of her hands she planteth a vineyard.
17 She girdeth her loins with strength, and strengtheneth her arms.
18 She perceiveth that her merchandise *is* good: her candle goeth not out by night.
19 She layeth her hands to the spindle, and her hands hold the distaff.
20 She stretcheth out her hand to the poor; yea, she reacheth forth her hands to the needy.
21 She is not afraid of the snow for her household: for all her household *are* clothed with scarlet.
22 She maketh herself coverings of tapestry; her clothing *is* silk and purple.
23 Her husband is known in the gates, when he sitteth among the elders of the land.
24 She maketh fine linen, and selleth *it;* and delivereth girdles unto the merchant.
25 Strength and honour *are* her clothing; and she shall rejoice in time to come.
26 She openeth her mouth with wisdom; and in her tongue *is* the law of kindness.
27 She looketh well to the ways of her household, and eateth not the bread of idleness.
28 Her children arise up, and call her blessed; her husband *also,* and he praiseth her.
29 Many daughters have done virtuously, but thou excellest them all.
30 Favour *is* deceitful, and beauty *is* vain: *but* a woman *that* feareth the LORD, she shall be praised.
31 Give her of the fruit of her hands; and let her own works praise her in the gates.

ECCLESIASTES

OR, THE PREACHER

1 THE words of the Preacher, the son of Da'vid, king in Je-ru'sa-lem.
2 Vanity of vanities, saith the Preacher, vanity of vanities; all *is* vanity.
3 What profit hath a man of all his labour which he taketh under the sun?
4 *One* generation passeth away, and *another* generation cometh: but the earth abideth for ever.
5 The sun also ariseth, and the sun goeth down, and hasteth to his place where he arose.
6 The wind goeth toward the south, and turneth about unto the north; it whirleth about continually, and the wind returneth again according to his circuits.
7 All the rivers run into the sea; yet the sea *is* not full; unto the place from whence the rivers come, thither they return again.
8 All things *are* full of labour; man cannot utter *it:* the eye is not satisfied with seeing, nor the ear filled with hearing.
9 The thing that hath been, it *is that* which shall be; and that which is done *is* that which shall be done: and *there is* no new *thing* under the sun.
10 Is there *any* thing whereof it may be said, See, this *is* new? it hath been already of old time, which was before us.
11 *There is* no remembrance of former *things;* neither shall there be *any* remembrance of *things* that are to come with *those* that shall come after.
12 ¶ I the Preacher was king over Is'ra-el in Je-ru'sa-lem.
13 And I gave my heart to seek and search out by wisdom concerning all *things* that are done under heaven: this sore travail hath God given to the sons of man to be exercised therewith.
14 I have seen all the works that are done under the sun; and, behold, all *is* vanity and vexation of spirit.
15 *That which is* crooked cannot be made straight: and that which is wanting cannot be numbered.
16 I communed with mine own heart, saying, Lo, I am come to great estate, and have gotten more wisdom than all *they* that have been before me in Je-ru'sa-lem: yea, my heart had great experience of wisdom and knowledge.
17 And I gave my heart to know wisdom, and to know madness and folly: I perceived that this also is vexation of spirit.
18 For in much wisdom *is* much grief: and he that increaseth knowledge increaseth sorrow.

2 I SAID in mine heart, Go to now, I will prove thee with mirth, therefore enjoy pleasure: and, behold, this also *is* vanity.
2 I said of laughter, *It is* mad: and of mirth, What doeth it?
3 I sought in mine heart to give myself unto wine, yet acquainting mine heart with wisdom; and to lay hold on folly, till I might see what *was* that good for the sons of men, which they should do under the heaven all the days of their life.
4 I made me great works; I builded me houses; I planted me vineyards:
5 I made me gardens and orchards, and I planted trees in them of all *kind of* fruits:
6 I made me pools of water, to water therewith the wood that bringeth forth trees:
7 I got *me* servants and maidens, and had servants born in my house; also I had great possessions of great and small cattle above all that were in Je-ru'sa-lem before me:
8 I gathered me also silver and gold, and the

peculiar treasure of kings and of the provinces: I gat me men singers and women singers, and the delights of the sons of men, *as* musical instruments, and that of all sorts.

9 So I was great, and increased more than all that were before me in Je-ru′sa-lem: also my wisdom remained with me.

10 And whatsoever mine eyes desired I kept not from them, I withheld not my heart from any joy; for my heart rejoiced in all my labour: and this was my portion of all my labour.

11 Then I looked on all the works that my hands had wrought, and on the labour that I had laboured to do: and, behold, all *was* vanity and vexation of spirit, and *there was* no profit under the sun.

12 ¶ And I turned myself to behold wisdom, and madness, and folly: for what *can* the man *do* that cometh after the king? *even* that which hath been already done.

13 Then I saw that wisdom excelleth folly, as far as light excelleth darkness.

14 The wise man's eyes *are* in his head; but the fool walketh in darkness: and I myself perceived also that one event happeneth to them all.

15 Then said I in my heart, As it happeneth to the fool, so it happeneth even to me; and why was I then more wise? Then I said in my heart, that this also *is* vanity.

16 For *there is* no remembrance of the wise more than of the fool for ever; seeing that which now *is* in the days to come shall all be forgotten. And how dieth the wise *man?* as the fool.

17 Therefore I hated life; because the work that is wrought under the sun *is* grievous unto me: for all *is* vanity and vexation of spirit.

18 ¶ Yea, I hated all my labour which I had taken under the sun: because I should leave it unto the man that shall be after me.

19 And who knoweth whether he shall be a wise *man* or a fool? yet shall he have rule over all my labour wherein I have laboured, and wherein I have shewed myself wise under the sun. This *is* also vanity.

20 Therefore I went about to cause my heart to despair of all the labour which I took under the sun.

21 For there is a man whose labour *is* in wisdom, and in knowledge, and in equity; yet to a man that hath not laboured therein shall he leave it *for* his portion. This also *is* vanity and a great evil.

22 For what hath man of all his labour, and of the vexation of his heart, wherein he hath laboured under the sun?

23 For all his days *are* sorrows, and his travail grief; yea, his heart taketh not rest in the night. This is also vanity.

24 ¶ *There is* nothing better for a man, *than* that he should eat and drink, and *that* he should make his soul enjoy good in his labour. This also I saw, that it *was* from the hand of God.

25 For who can eat, or who else can hasten *hereunto,* more than I?

26 For *God* giveth to a man that *is* good in his sight wisdom, and knowledge, and joy: but to the sinner he giveth travail, to gather and to heap up, that he may give to *him that is* good before God. This also *is* vanity and vexation of spirit.

3 TO every *thing there is* a season, and a time to every purpose under the heaven:

2 A time to be born, and a time to die; a time to plant, and a time to pluck up *that which is* planted;

3 A time to kill, and a time to heal; a time to break down, and a time to build up;

4 A time to weep, and a time to laugh; a time to mourn, and a time to dance;

5 A time to cast away stones, and a time to gather stones together; a time to embrace, and a time to refrain from embracing;

6 A time to get, and a time to lose; a time to keep, and a time to cast away;

7 A time to rend, and a time to sew; a time to keep silence, and a time to speak;

8 A time to love, and a time to hate; a time of war, and a time of peace.

9 What profit hath he that worketh in that wherein he laboureth?

10 I have seen the travail, which God hath given to the sons of men to be exercised in it.

11 He hath made every *thing* beautiful in his time: also he hath set the world in their heart, so that no man can find out the work that God maketh from the beginning to the end.

12 I know that *there is* no good in them, but for *a man* to rejoice, and to do good in his life.

13 And also that every man should eat and drink, and enjoy the good of all his labour, it *is* the gift of God.

14 I know that, whatsoever God doeth, it shall be for ever: nothing can be put to it, nor any thing taken from it: and God doeth *it,* that *men* should fear before him.

15 That which hath been is now; and that which is to be hath already been; and God requireth that which is past.

16 ¶ And moreover I saw under the sun the place of judgment, *that* wickedness *was* there; and the place of righteousness, *that* iniquity *was* there.

17 I said in mine heart, God shall judge the righteous and the wicked: for *there is* a time there for every purpose and for every work.

18 I said in mine heart concerning the estate of the sons of men, that God might manifest them, and that they might see that they themselves are beasts.

19 For that which befalleth the sons of men befalleth beasts; even one thing befalleth them: as the one dieth, so dieth the other; yea, they have all one breath; so that a man hath no preeminence above a beast: for all *is* vanity.

20 All go unto one place; all are of the dust, and all turn to dust again.

21 Who knoweth the spirit of man that goeth upward, and the spirit of the beast that goeth downward to the earth?

22 Wherefore I perceive that *there is* nothing better, than that a man should rejoice in his own works; for that *is* his portion: for who shall bring him to see what shall be after him?

4 SO I returned, and considered all the oppressions that are done under the sun: and behold the tears of *such as were* oppressed, and they had no comforter; and on the side of their oppressors *there was* power; but they had no comforter.

2 Wherefore I praised the dead which are already dead more than the living which are yet alive.

3 Yea, better *is he* than both they, which hath not yet been, who hath not seen the evil work that is done under the sun.

4 ¶ Again, I considered all travail, and every right work, that for this a man is envied of his neighbour. This *is* also vanity and vexation of spirit.

5 The fool foldeth his hands together, and eateth his own flesh.

6 Better *is* an handful *with* quietness, than both the hands full *with* travail and vexation of spirit.

7 ¶ Then I returned, and I saw vanity under the sun.

8 There is one *alone*, and *there is* not a second; yea, he hath neither child nor brother: yet *is there* no end of all his labour; neither is his eye satisfied with riches; neither *saith he,* For whom do I labour, and bereave my soul of good? This *is* also vanity, yea, it *is* a sore travail.

9 ¶ Two *are* better than one; because they have a good reward for their labour.

10 For if they fall, the one will lift up his fellow: but woe to him *that is* alone when he falleth; for *he hath* not another to help him up.

11 Again, if two lie together, then they have heat: but how can one be warm *alone?*

12 And if one prevail against him, two shall withstand him; and a threefold cord is not quickly broken.

13 ¶ Better *is* a poor and a wise child than an old and foolish king, who will no more be admonished.

14 For out of prison he cometh to reign; whereas also *he that is* born in his kingdom becometh poor.

15 I considered all the living which walk under the sun, with the second child that shall stand up in his stead.

16 *There is* no end of all the people, *even* of all that have been before them: they also that come after shall not rejoice in him. Surely this also *is* vanity and vexation of spirit.

5 KEEP thy foot when thou goest to the house of God, and be more ready to hear, than to give the sacrifice of fools: for they consider not that they do evil.

2 Be not rash with thy mouth, and let not thine heart be hasty to utter *any* thing before God: for God *is* in heaven, and thou upon earth: therefore let thy words be few.

3 For a dream cometh through the multitude of business; and a fool's voice *is known* by multitude of words.

4 When thou vowest a vow unto God, defer not to pay it; for *he hath* no pleasure in fools: pay that which thou hast vowed.

5 Better *is it* that thou shouldest not vow, than that thou shouldest vow and not pay.

6 Suffer not thy mouth to cause thy flesh to sin; neither say thou before the angel, that it *was* an error: wherefore should God be angry at thy voice, and destroy the work of thine hands?

7 For in the multitude of dreams and many words *there are* also *divers* vanities: but fear thou God.

8 ¶ If thou seest the oppression of the poor, and violent perverting of judgment and justice in a province, marvel not at the matter: for *he that is* higher than the highest regardeth; and *there be* higher than they.

9 ¶ Moreover the profit of the earth is for all: the king *himself* is served by the field.

10 He that loveth silver shall not be satisfied with silver; nor he that loveth abundance with increase: this *is* also vanity.

11 When goods increase, they are increased that eat them: and what good *is there* to the owners thereof, saving the beholding *of them* with their eyes?

12 The sleep of a labouring man *is* sweet, whether he eat little or much: but the abundance of the rich will not suffer him to sleep.

13 There is a sore evil *which* I have seen under the sun, *namely,* riches kept for the owners thereof to their hurt.

14 But those riches perish by evil travail: and he begetteth a son, and *there is* nothing in his hand.

15 As he came forth of his mother's womb, naked shall he return to go as he came, and shall take nothing of his labour, which he may carry away in his hand.

16 And this also *is* a sore evil, *that* in all points as he came, so shall he go: and what profit hath he that hath laboured for the wind?

17 All his days also he eateth in darkness, and *he hath* much sorrow and wrath with his sickness.

18 ¶ Behold *that* which I have seen: *it is* good and comely *for one* to eat and to drink, and to enjoy the good of all his labour that he taketh under the sun all the days of his life, which God giveth him: for it *is* his portion.

19 Every man also to whom God hath given riches and wealth, and hath given him power to eat thereof, and to take his portion, and to rejoice in his labour; this *is* the gift of God.

20 For he shall not much remember the days of his life; because God answereth *him* in the joy of his heart.

6 THERE is an evil which I have seen under the sun, and it *is* common among men:

2 A man to whom God hath given riches, wealth, and honour, so that he wanteth nothing for his soul of all that he desireth, yet God giveth him not power to eat thereof, but a stranger eateth it: this *is* vanity, and it *is* an evil disease.

3 ¶ If a man beget an hundred *children,* and live many years, so that the days of his years be many, and his soul be not filled with good, and also *that* he have no burial; I say, *that* an untimely birth *is* better than he.

4 For he cometh in with vanity, and departeth in darkness, and his name shall be covered with darkness.

5 Moreover he hath not seen the sun, nor known *any thing:* this hath more rest than the other.

6 ¶ Yea, though he live a thousand years twice *told,* yet hath he seen no good: do not all go to one place?

7 All the labour of man *is* for his mouth, and yet the appetite is not filled.

8 For what hath the wise more than the fool? what hath the poor, that knoweth to walk before the living?

9 ¶ Better *is* the sight of the eyes than the wandering of the desire: this *is* also vanity and vexation of spirit.

10 That which hath been is named already, and it is known that it *is* man: neither may he contend with him that is mightier than he.

11 ¶ Seeing there be many things that increase vanity, what *is* man the better?

12 For who knoweth what *is* good for man in *this* life, all the days of his vain life which he spendeth as a shadow? for who can tell a man what shall be after him under the sun?

7 A GOOD name *is* better than precious ointment; and the day of death than the day of one's birth.

2 ¶ *It is* better to go to the house of mourning, than to go to the house of feasting: for that *is* the end of all men; and the living will lay *it* to his heart.

3 Sorrow *is* better than laughter: for by the

sadness of the countenance the heart is made better.

4 The heart of the wise *is* in the house of mourning; but the heart of fools *is* in the house of mirth.

5 *It is* better to hear the rebuke of the wise, than for a man to hear the song of fools.

6 For as the crackling of thorns under a pot, so *is* the laughter of the fool: this also *is* vanity.

7 ¶ Surely oppression maketh a wise man mad; and a gift destroyeth the heart.

8 Better *is* the end of a thing than the beginning thereof: *and* the patient in spirit *is* better than the proud in spirit.

9 Be not hasty in thy spirit to be angry: for anger resteth in the bosom of fools.

10 Say not thou, What is *the cause* that the former days were better than these? for thou dost not enquire wisely concerning this.

11 ¶ Wisdom *is* good with an inheritance: and *by it there is* profit to them that see the sun.

12 For wisdom *is* a defence, *and* money *is* a defence: but the excellency of knowledge *is, that* wisdom giveth life to them that have it.

13 Consider the work of God: for who can make *that* straight, which he hath made crooked?

14 In the day of prosperity be joyful, but in the day of adversity consider: God also hath set the one over against the other, to the end that man should find nothing after him.

15 All *things* have I seen in the days of my vanity: there is a just *man* that perisheth in his righteousness, and there is a wicked *man* that prolongeth *his life* in his wickedness.

16 Be not righteous over much; neither make thyself over wise: why shouldest thou destroy thyself?

17 Be not over much wicked, neither be thou foolish: why shouldest thou die before thy time?

18 *It is* good that thou shouldest take hold of this; yea, also from this withdraw not thine hand: for he that feareth God shall come forth of them all.

19 Wisdom strengtheneth the wise more than ten mighty *men* which are in the city.

20 For *there is* not a just man upon earth, that doeth good, and sinneth not.

21 Also take no heed unto all words that are spoken; lest thou hear thy servant curse thee:

22 For oftentimes also thine own heart knoweth that thou thyself likewise hast cursed others.

23 ¶ All this have I proved by wisdom: I said, I will be wise; but it *was* far from me.

24 That which is far off, and exceeding deep, who can find it out?

25 I applied mine heart to know, and to search, and to seek out wisdom, and the reason *of things,* and to know the wickedness of folly, even of foolishness *and* madness:

26 And I find more bitter than death the woman, whose heart *is* snares and nets, *and* her hands *as* bands: whoso pleaseth God shall escape from her; but the sinner shall be taken by her.

27 Behold, this have I found, saith the preacher, *counting* one by one, to find out the account:

28 Which yet my soul seeketh, but I find not: one man among a thousand have I found; but a woman among all those have I not found.

29 Lo, this only have I found, that God hath made man upright; but they have sought out many inventions.

8 WHO *is* as the wise *man?* and who knoweth the interpretation of a thing? a man's wisdom maketh his face to shine, and the boldness of his face shall be changed.

2 I *counsel thee* to keep the king's commandment, and *that* in regard of the oath of God.

3 Be not hasty to go out of his sight: stand not in an evil thing; for he doeth whatsoever pleaseth him.

4 Where the word of a king *is, there is* power: and who may say unto him, What doest thou?

5 Whoso keepeth the commandment shall feel no evil thing: and a wise man's heart discerneth both time and judgment.

6 ¶ Because to every purpose there is time and judgment, therefore the misery of man *is* great upon him.

7 For he knoweth not that which shall be: for who can tell him when it shall be?

8 *There is* no man that hath power over the spirit to retain the spirit; neither *hath he* power in the day of death: and *there is* no discharge in *that* war; neither shall wickedness deliver those that are given to it.

9 All this have I seen, and applied my heart unto every work that is done under the sun: *there is* a time wherein one man ruleth over another to his own hurt.

10 And so I saw the wicked buried, who had come and gone from the place of the holy, and they were forgotten in the city where they had so done: this *is* also vanity.

11 Because sentence against an evil work is not executed speedily, therefore the heart of the sons of men is fully set in them to do evil.

12 ¶ Though a sinner do evil an hundred times, and his *days* be prolonged, yet surely I know that it shall be well with them that fear God, which fear before him:

13 But it shall not be well with the wicked, neither shall he prolong *his* days, *which are* as a shadow; because he feareth not before God.

14 There is a vanity which is done upon the earth; that there be just *men,* unto whom it happeneth according to the work of the wicked; again, there be wicked *men,* to whom it happeneth according to the work of the righteous: I said that this also *is* vanity.

15 Then I commended mirth, because a man hath no better thing under the sun, than to eat, and to drink, and to be merry: for that shall abide with him of his labour the days of his life, which God giveth him under the sun.

16 ¶ When I applied mine heart to know wisdom, and to see the business that is done upon the earth: (for also *there is that* neither day nor night seeth sleep with his eyes:)

17 Then I beheld all the work of God, that a man cannot find out the work that is done under the sun: because though a man labour to seek *it* out, yet he shall not find *it:* yea farther; though a wise *man* think to know *it,* yet shall he not be able to find *it.*

9 FOR all this I considered in my heart even to declare all this, that the righteous, and the wise, and their works, *are* in the hand of God: no man knoweth either love or hatred *by* all *that is* before them.

2 All *things come* alike to all: *there is* one event to the righteous, and to the wicked; to the good and to the clean, and to the unclean; to him that sacrificeth, and to him that sacrificeth not: as *is* the good, so *is* the sinner; *and* he that sweareth, as *he* that feareth an oath.

3 This *is* an evil among all *things* that are

done under the sun, that *there is* one event unto
all: yea, also the heart of the sons of men is full
of evil, and madness *is* in their heart while they
live, and after that *they go* to the dead.
4 ¶ For to him that is joined to all the living
there is hope: for a living dog is better than a
dead lion.
5 For the living know that they shall die: but
the dead know not any thing, neither have they
any more a reward; for the memory of them is
forgotten.
6 Also their love, and their hatred, and their
envy, is now perished; neither have they any
more a portion for ever in any *thing* that is done
under the sun.
7 ¶ Go thy way, eat thy bread with joy, and
drink thy wine with a merry heart; for God now
accepteth thy works.
8 Let thy garments be always white; and let
thy head lack no ointment.
9 Live joyfully with the wife whom thou lovest all the days of the life of thy vanity, which
he hath given thee under the sun, all the days of
thy vanity: for that *is* thy portion in *this* life, and
in thy labour which thou takest under the sun.
10 Whatsoever thy hand findeth to do, do *it*
with thy might; for *there is* no work, nor device,
nor knowledge, nor wisdom, in the grave,
whither thou goest.
11 ¶ I returned, and saw under the sun, that
the race *is* not to the swift, nor the battle to the
strong, neither yet bread to the wise, nor yet
riches to men of understanding, nor yet favour
to men of skill; but time and chance happeneth
to them all.
12 For man also knoweth not his time: as the
fishes that are taken in an evil net, and as the
birds that are caught in the snare; so *are* the
sons of men snared in an evil time, when it falleth suddenly upon them.
13 ¶ This wisdom have I seen also under the
sun, and it *seemed* great unto me:
14 *There was* a little city, and few men within
it; and there came a great king against it, and
besieged it, and built great bulwarks against it:
15 Now there was found in it a poor wise
man, and he by his wisdom delivered the city;
yet no man remembered that same poor man.
16 Then said I, Wisdom *is* better than
strength: nevertheless the poor man's wisdom
is despised, and his words are not heard.
17 The words of wise *men are* heard in quiet
more than the cry of him that ruleth among
fools.
18 Wisdom *is* better than weapons of war:
but one sinner destroyeth much good.

10 DEAD flies cause the ointment of the
apothecary to send forth a stinking savour: *so doth* a little folly him that is in reputation for wisdom *and* honour.
2 A wise man's heart *is* at his right hand; but
a fool's heart at his left.
3 Yea also, when he that is a fool walketh by
the way, his wisdom faileth *him*, and he saith to
every one *that* he *is* a fool.
4 If the spirit of the ruler rise up against thee,
leave not thy place; for yielding pacifieth great
offences.
5 There is an evil *which* I have seen under
the sun, as an error *which* proceedeth from the
ruler:
6 Folly is set in great dignity, and the rich sit
in low place.
7 I have seen servants upon horses, and
princes walking as servants upon the earth.
8 He that diggeth a pit shall fall into it; and
whoso breaketh an hedge, a serpent shall bite
him.
9 Whoso removeth stones shall be hurt
therewith; *and* he that cleaveth wood shall be
endangered thereby.
10 If the iron be blunt, and he do not whet
the edge, then must he put to more strength:
but wisdom *is* profitable to direct.
11 Surely the serpent will bite without enchantment; and a babbler is no better.
12 The words of a wise man's mouth *are* gracious; but the lips of a fool will swallow up himself.
13 The beginning of the words of his mouth
is foolishness: and the end of his talk *is* mischievous madness.
14 A fool also is full of words: a man cannot
tell what shall be; and what shall be after him,
who can tell him?
15 The labour of the foolish wearieth every
one of them, because he knoweth not how to go
to the city.
16 ¶ Woe to thee, O land, when thy king *is* a
child, and thy princes eat in the morning!
17 Blessed *art* thou, O land, when thy king *is*
the son of nobles, and thy princes eat in due
season, for strength, and not for drunkenness!
18 ¶ By much slothfulness the building decayeth; and through idleness of the hands the
house droppeth through.
19 ¶ A feast is made for laughter, and wine
maketh merry: but money answereth all *things*.
20 ¶ Curse not the king, no not in thy
thought; and curse not the rich in thy bedchamber: for a bird of the air shall carry the
voice, and that which hath wings shall tell the
matter.

11 CAST thy bread upon the waters: for
thou shalt find it after many days.
2 Give a portion to seven, and also to eight;
for thou knowest not what evil shall be upon
the earth.
3 If the clouds be full of rain, they empty
themselves upon the earth: and if the tree fall
toward the south, or toward the north, in the
place where the tree falleth, there it shall be.
4 He that observeth the wind shall not sow;
and he that regardeth the clouds shall not reap.
5 As thou knowest not what *is* the way of the
spirit, *nor* how the bones *do grow* in the womb
of her that is with child: even so thou knowest
not the works of God who maketh all.
6 In the morning sow thy seed, and in the
evening withhold not thine hand: for thou
knowest not whether shall prosper, either this
or that, or whether they both *shall be* alike
good.
7 ¶ Truly the light *is* sweet, and a pleasant
thing it is for the eyes to behold the sun:
8 But if a man live many years, *and* rejoice in
them all; yet let him remember the days of
darkness; for they shall be many. All that cometh *is* vanity.
9 ¶ Rejoice, O young man, in thy youth; and
let thy heart cheer thee in the days of thy youth,
and walk in the ways of thine heart, and in the
sight of thine eyes: but know thou, that for all
these *things* God will bring thee into judgment.
10 Therefore remove sorrow from thy heart,
and put away evil from thy flesh: for childhood
and youth *are* vanity.

12 REMEMBER now thy Creator in the
days of thy youth, while the evil days
come not, nor the years draw nigh, when thou
shalt say, I have no pleasure in them;

2 While the sun, or the light, or the moon, or
the stars, be not darkened, nor the clouds return after the rain:
3 In the day when the keepers of the house
shall tremble, and the strong men shall bow
themselves, and the grinders cease because
they are few, and those that look out of the windows be darkened,
4 And the doors shall be shut in the streets,
when the sound of the grinding is low, and he
shall rise up at the voice of the bird, and all the
daughters of musick shall be brought low;
5 Also *when* they shall be afraid of *that*
which is high, and fears *shall be* in the way, and
the almond tree shall flourish, and the grasshopper shall be a burden, and desire shall fail:
because man goeth to his long home, and the
mourners go about the streets:
6 Or ever the silver cord be loosed, or the
golden bowl be broken, or the pitcher be broken
at the fountain, or the wheel broken at the cistern.
7 Then shall the dust return to the earth as it
was: and the spirit shall return unto God who
gave it.
8 ¶ Vanity of vanities, saith the preacher; all
is vanity.
9 And moreover, because the preacher was
wise, he still taught the people knowledge; yea,
he gave good heed, and sought out, *and* set in
order many proverbs.
10 The preacher sought to find out acceptable words: and *that which was* written *was* upright, *even* words of truth.
11 The words of the wise *are* as goads, and
as nails fastened *by* the masters of assemblies,
which are given from one shepherd.
12 And further, by these, my son, be admonished: of making many books *there is* no end;
and much study *is* a weariness of the flesh.
13 ¶ Let us hear the conclusion of the whole
matter: Fear God, and keep his commandments: for this *is* the whole *duty* of man.
14 For God shall bring every work into judgment, with every secret thing, whether *it be*
good, or whether *it be* evil.

THE SONG OF SOLOMON

1 THE song of songs, which *is* Sol'o-mon's.
2 Let him kiss me with the kisses of his
mouth: for thy love *is* better than wine.
3 Because of the savour of thy good ointments thy name *is as* ointment poured forth,
therefore do the virgins love thee.
4 Draw me, we will run after thee: the king
hath brought me into his chambers: we will be
glad and rejoice in thee, we will remember thy
love more than wine: the upright love thee.
5 I *am* black, but comely, O ye daughters of
Je-ru'sa-lem, as the tents of Ke'dar, as the curtains of Sol'o-mon.
6 Look not upon me, because I *am* black, because the sun hath looked upon me: my mother's children were angry with me; they made
me the keeper of the vineyards; *but* mine own
vineyard have I not kept.
7 Tell me, O thou whom my soul loveth,
where thou feedest, where thou makest *thy*
flock to rest at noon: for why should I be as one
that turneth aside by the flocks of thy companions?
8 ¶ If thou know not, O thou fairest among
women, go thy way forth by the footsteps of the
flock, and feed thy kids beside the shepherds'
tents.
9 I have compared thee, O my love, to a company of horses in Pha'raoh's chariots.
10 Thy cheeks are comely with rows *of jew-*
els, thy neck with chains *of gold.*
11 We will make thee borders of gold with
studs of silver.
12 ¶ While the king *sitteth* at his table, my
spikenard sendeth forth the smell thereof.
13 A bundle of myrrh *is* my wellbeloved unto
me; he shall lie all night betwixt my breasts.
14 My beloved *is* unto me *as* a cluster of
camphire in the vineyards of En–ge'di.
15 Behold, thou *art* fair, my love; behold,
thou *art* fair; thou *hast* doves' eyes.
16 Behold, thou *art* fair, my beloved, yea,
pleasant: also our bed *is* green.
17 The beams of our house *are* cedar, *and*
our rafters of fir.

2 I *AM* the rose of Shar'on, *and* the lily of the
valleys.
2 As the lily among thorns, so *is* my love
among the daughters.
3 As the apple tree among the trees of the
wood, so *is* my beloved among the sons. I sat
down under his shadow with great delight, and
his fruit *was* sweet to my taste.
4 He brought me to the banqueting house,
and his banner over me *was* love.
5 Stay me with flagons, comfort me with apples: for I *am* sick of love.
6 His left hand *is* under my head, and his
right hand doth embrace me.
7 I charge you, O ye daughters of Je-ru'sa-
lem, by the roes, and by the hinds of the field,
that ye stir not up, nor awake *my* love, till he
please.
8 ¶ The voice of my beloved! behold, he
cometh leaping upon the mountains, skipping
upon the hills.
9 My beloved is like a roe or a young hart:
behold, he standeth behind our wall, he looketh
forth at the windows, shewing himself through
the lattice.
10 My beloved spake, and said unto me, Rise
up, my love, my fair one, and come away.
11 For, lo, the winter is past, the rain is over
and gone;
12 The flowers appear on the earth; the time
of the singing *of birds* is come, and the voice of
the turtle is heard in our land;
13 The fig tree putteth forth her green figs,
and the vines *with* the tender grape give a *good*
smell. Arise, my love, my fair one, and come
away.
14 ¶ O my dove, *that art* in the clefts of the
rock, in the secret *places* of the stairs, let me
see thy countenance, let me hear thy voice; for
sweet *is* thy voice, and thy countenance *is*
comely.
15 Take us the foxes, the little foxes, that
spoil the vines: for our vines *have* tender
grapes.
16 ¶ My beloved *is* mine, and I *am* his: he
feedeth among the lilies.
17 Until the day break, and the shadows flee
away, turn, my beloved, and be thou like a roe
or a young hart upon the mountains of Be'ther.

3 BY night on my bed I sought him whom
my soul loveth: I sought him, but I found
him not.
2 I will rise now, and go about the city in the
streets, and in the broad ways I will seek him
whom my soul loveth: I sought him, but I found
him not.
3 The watchmen that go about the city found
me: *to whom I said,* Saw ye him whom my soul
loveth?
4 *It was* but a little that I passed from them,
but I found him whom my soul loveth: I held
him, and would not let him go, until I had
brought him into my mother's house, and into
the chamber of her that conceived me.
5 I charge you, O ye daughters of Je-ru′sa-
lem, by the roes, and by the hinds of the field,
that ye stir not up, nor awake *my* love, till he
please.
6 ¶ Who *is* this that cometh out of the wilderness like pillars of smoke, perfumed with
myrrh and frankincense, with all powders of
the merchant?
7 Behold his bed, which *is* Sol′o-mon's; threescore valiant men *are* about it, of the valiant of
Is′ra-el.
8 They all hold swords, *being* expert in war:
every man *hath* his sword upon his thigh because of fear in the night.
9 King Sol′o-mon made himself a chariot of
the wood of Leb′a-non.
10 He made the pillars thereof *of* silver, the
bottom thereof *of* gold, the covering of it *of* purple, the midst thereof being paved *with* love, for
the daughters of Je-ru′sa-lem.
11 Go forth, O ye daughters of Zi′on, and behold king Sol′o-mon with the crown wherewith
his mother crowned him in the day of his espousals, and in the day of the gladness of his
heart.

4 BEHOLD, thou *art* fair, my love; behold,
thou *art* fair; thou *hast* doves' eyes within
thy locks: thy hair *is* as a flock of goats, that
appear from mount Gil′e-ad.
2 Thy teeth *are* like a flock *of sheep that are*
even shorn, which came up from the washing;
whereof every one bear twins, and none *is* barren among them.
3 Thy lips *are* like a thread of scarlet, and thy
speech *is* comely: thy temples *are* like a piece of
a pomegranate within thy locks.
4 Thy neck *is* like the tower of Da′vid builded
for an armoury, whereon there hang a thousand
bucklers, all shields of mighty men.
5 Thy two breasts *are* like two young roes
that are twins, which feed among the lilies.
6 Until the day break, and the shadows flee
away, I will get me to the mountain of myrrh,
and to the hill of frankincense.
7 Thou *art* all fair, my love; *there is* no spot in
thee.
8 ¶ Come with me from Leb′a-non, *my*
spouse, with me from Leb′a-non: look from the
top of Am′a-na, from the top of She′nir and
Her′mon, from the lions' dens, from the mountains of the leopards.
9 Thou hast ravished my heart, my sister, *my*
spouse; thou hast ravished my heart with one of
thine eyes, with one chain of thy neck.
10 How fair is thy love, my sister, *my* spouse!
how much better is thy love than wine! and the
smell of thine ointments than all spices!
11 Thy lips, O *my* spouse, drop *as* the honeycomb: honey and milk *are* under thy tongue;
and the smell of thy garments *is* like the smell
of Leb′a-non.
12 A garden inclosed *is* my sister, *my* spouse;
a spring shut up, a fountain sealed.
13 Thy plants *are* an orchard of pomegranates, with pleasant fruits; camphire, with spikenard,
14 Spikenard and saffron; calamus and cinnamon, with all trees of frankincense; myrrh
and aloes, with all the chief spices:
15 A fountain of gardens, a well of living waters, and streams from Leb′a-non.
16 ¶ Awake, O north wind; and come, thou
south; blow upon my garden, *that* the spices
thereof may flow out. Let my beloved come into
his garden, and eat his pleasant fruits.

5 I AM come into my garden, my sister, *my*
spouse: I have gathered my myrrh with my
spice; I have eaten my honeycomb with my
honey; I have drunk my wine with my milk: eat,
O friends; drink, yea, drink abundantly, O beloved.
2 ¶ I sleep, but my heart waketh: *it is* the
voice of my beloved that knocketh, *saying,*
Open to me, my sister, my love, my dove, my
undefiled: for my head is filled with dew, *and*
my locks with the drops of the night.
3 I have put off my coat; how shall I put it
on? I have washed my feet; how shall I defile
them?
4 My beloved put in his hand by the hole *of*
the door, and my bowels were moved for him.
5 I rose up to open to my beloved; and my
hands dropped *with* myrrh, and my fingers *with*
sweet smelling myrrh, upon the handles of the
lock.
6 I opened to my beloved; but my beloved
had withdrawn himself, *and* was gone: my soul
failed when he spake: I sought him, but I could
not find him; I called him, but he gave me no
answer.
7 The watchmen that went about the city
found me, they smote me, they wounded me;
the keepers of the walls took away my veil from
me.
8 I charge you, O daughters of Je-ru′sa-lem,
if ye find my beloved, that ye tell him, that I *am*
sick of love.
9 ¶ What *is* thy beloved more than *another*
beloved, O thou fairest among women? what *is*
thy beloved more than *another* beloved, that
thou dost so charge us?
10 My beloved *is* white and ruddy, the
chiefest among ten thousand.
11 His head *is as* the most fine gold, his locks
are bushy, *and* black as a raven.
12 His eyes *are* as *the eyes* of doves by the
rivers of waters, washed with milk, *and* fitly
set.
13 His cheeks *are* as a bed of spices, *as* sweet
flowers: his lips *like* lilies, dropping sweet
smelling myrrh.
14 His hands *are as* gold rings set with the
beryl: his belly *is as* bright ivory overlaid *with*
sapphires.
15 His legs *are as* pillars of marble, set upon
sockets of fine gold: his countenance *is* as Leb′-
a-non, excellent as the cedars.
16 His mouth *is* most sweet: yea, he *is* altogether lovely. This *is* my beloved, and this *is* my
friend, O daughters of Je-ru′sa-lem.

6 WHITHER is thy beloved gone, O thou
fairest among women? whither is thy beloved turned aside? that we may seek him with
thee.
2 My beloved is gone down into his garden,

to the beds of spices, to feed in the gardens, and
to gather lilies.
3 I *am* my beloved's, and my beloved *is*
mine: he feedeth among the lilies.
4 ¶ Thou *art* beautiful, O my love, as Tir'zah,
comely as Je-ru'sa-lem, terrible as *an army*
with banners.
5 Turn away thine eyes from me, for they
have overcome me: thy hair *is* as a flock of
goats that appear from Gil'e-ad.
6 Thy teeth *are* as a flock of sheep which go
up from the washing, whereof every one beareth twins, and *there is* not one barren among
them.
7 As a piece of a pomegranate *are* thy temples within thy locks.
8 There are threescore queens, and fourscore
concubines, and virgins without number.
9 My dove, my undefiled is *but* one; she *is* the
only one of her mother, she *is* the choice *one* of
her that bare her. The daughters saw her, and
blessed her; *yea*, the queens and the concubines, and they praised her.
10 ¶ Who *is* she *that* looketh forth as the
morning, fair as the moon, clear as the sun, *and*
terrible as *an army* with banners?
11 I went down into the garden of nuts to see
the fruits of the valley, *and* to see whether the
vine flourished, *and* the pomegranates budded.
12 Or ever I was aware, my soul made me
like the chariots of Am-mi'-na-dib.
13 Return, return, O Shu'lam-ite; return, return, that we may look upon thee. What will ye
see in the Shu'lam-ite? As it were the company
of two armies.

7 HOW beautiful are thy feet with shoes, O
prince's daughter! the joints of thy thighs
are like jewels, the work of the hands of a cunning workman.
2 Thy navel *is like* a round goblet, *which*
wanteth not liquor: thy belly *is like* an heap of
wheat set about with lilies.
3 Thy two breasts *are* like two young roes
that are twins.
4 Thy neck *is* as a tower of ivory; thine eyes
like the fishpools in Hesh'bon, by the gate of
Bath-rab'bim: thy nose *is* as the tower of Leb'a-
non which looketh toward Da-mas'cus.
5 Thine head upon thee *is* like Car'mel, and
the hair of thine head like purple; the king *is*
held in the galleries.
6 How fair and how pleasant art thou, O
love, for delights!
7 This thy stature is like to a palm tree, and
thy breasts to clusters *of grapes*.
8 I said, I will go up to the palm tree, I will
take hold of the boughs thereof: now also thy
breasts shall be as clusters of the vine, and the
smell of thy nose like apples;
9 And the roof of thy mouth like the best
wine for my beloved, that goeth *down* sweetly,
causing the lips of those that are asleep to
speak.
10 ¶ I *am* my beloved's, and his desire *is*
toward me.
11 Come, my beloved, let us go forth into the
field; let us lodge in the villages.
12 Let us get up early to the vineyards; let us
see if the vine flourish, *whether* the tender
grape appear, *and* the pomegranates bud forth:
there will I give thee my loves.
13 The mandrakes give a smell, and at our
gates *are* all manner of pleasant *fruits*, new and
old, *which* I have laid up for thee, O my beloved.

8 O THAT thou *wert* as my brother, that
sucked the breasts of my mother! *when* I
should find thee without, I would kiss thee; yea,
I should not be despised.
2 I would lead thee, *and* bring thee into my
mother's house, *who* would instruct me: I
would cause thee to drink of spiced wine of the
juice of my pomegranate.
3 His left hand *should be* under my head, and
his right hand should embrace me.
4 I charge you, O daughters of Je-ru'sa-lem,
that ye stir not up, nor awake *my* love, until he
please.
5 Who *is* this that cometh up from the wilderness, leaning upon her beloved? I raised thee
up under the apple tree: there thy mother
brought thee forth: there she brought thee forth
that bare thee.
6 ¶ Set me as a seal upon thine heart, as a
seal upon thine arm: for love *is* strong as death;
jealousy *is* cruel as the grave: the coals thereof
are coals of fire, *which hath* a most vehement
flame.
7 Many waters cannot quench love, neither
can the floods drown it: if a man would give all
the substance of his house for love, it would utterly be contemned.
8 ¶ We have a little sister, and she hath no
breasts: what shall we do for our sister in the
day when she shall be spoken for?
9 If she *be* a wall, we will build upon her a
palace of silver: and if she *be* a door, we will
inclose her with boards of cedar.
10 I *am* a wall, and my breasts like towers:
then was I in his eyes as one that found favour.
11 Sol'o-mon had a vineyard at Ba'al-ha'-
mon; he let out the vineyard unto keepers; every one for the fruit thereof was to bring a thousand *pieces* of silver.
12 My vineyard, which *is* mine, *is* before me:
thou, O Sol'o-mon, *must have* a thousand, and
those that keep the fruit thereof two hundred.
13 Thou that dwellest in the gardens, the
companions hearken to thy voice: cause me to
hear *it*.
14 ¶ Make haste, my beloved, and be thou
like to a roe or to a young hart upon the mountains of spices.

THE BOOK OF

ISAIAH

1 THE vision of I-sa'iah the son of A'moz,
which he saw concerning Ju'dah and Je-
ru'sa-lem in the days of Uz-zi'ah, Jo'tham, A'-
haz, *and* Hez-e-ki'ah, kings of Ju'dah.
2 Hear, O heavens, and give ear, O earth: for
the LORD hath spoken, I have nourished and
brought up children, and they have rebelled
against me.
3 The ox knoweth his owner, and the ass his
master's crib: *but* Is'ra-el doth not know, my
people doth not consider.
4 Ah sinful nation, a people laden with iniq-

uity, a seed of evildoers, children that are corrupters: they have forsaken the LORD, they have provoked the Holy One of Is'ra-el unto anger, they are gone away backward.
5 ¶ Why should ye be stricken any more? ye will revolt more and more: the whole head is sick, and the whole heart faint.
6 From the sole of the foot even unto the head *there is* no soundness in it; *but* wounds, and bruises, and putrifying sores: they have not been closed, neither bound up, neither mollified with ointment.
7 Your country *is* desolate, your cities *are* burned with fire: your land, strangers devour it in your presence, and *it is* desolate, as overthrown by strangers.
8 And the daughter of Zi'on is left as a cottage in a vineyard, as a lodge in a garden of cucumbers, as a besieged city.
9 Except the LORD of hosts had left unto us a very small remnant, we should have been as Sod'om, *and* we should have been like unto Gomor'rah.
10 ¶ Hear the word of the LORD, ye rulers of Sod'om; give ear unto the law of our God, ye people of Go-mor'rah.
11 To what purpose *is* the multitude of your sacrifices unto me? saith the LORD: I am full of the burnt offerings of rams, and the fat of fed beasts; and I delight not in the blood of bullocks, or of lambs, or of he goats.
12 When ye come to appear before me, who hath required this at your hand, to tread my courts?
13 Bring no more vain oblations; incense is an abomination unto me; the new moons and sabbaths, the calling of assemblies, I cannot away with; *it is* iniquity, even the solemn meeting.
14 Your new moons and your appointed feasts my soul hateth: they are a trouble unto me; I am weary to bear *them*.
15 And when ye spread forth your hands, I will hide mine eyes from you: yea, when ye make many prayers, I will not hear: your hands are full of blood.
16 ¶ Wash you, make you clean; put away the evil of your doings from before mine eyes; cease to do evil;
17 Learn to do well; seek judgment, relieve the oppressed, judge the fatherless, plead for the widow.
18 Come now, and let us reason together, saith the LORD: though your sins be as scarlet, they shall be as white as snow; though they be red like crimson, they shall be as wool.
19 If ye be willing and obedient, ye shall eat the good of the land:
20 But if ye refuse and rebel, ye shall be devoured with the sword: for the mouth of the LORD hath spoken *it*.
21 ¶ How is the faithful city become an harlot! it was full of judgment; righteousness lodged in it; but now murderers.
22 Thy silver is become dross, thy wine mixed with water:
23 Thy princes *are* rebellious, and companions of thieves: every one loveth gifts, and followeth after rewards: they judge not the fatherless, neither doth the cause of the widow come unto them.
24 Therefore saith the Lord, the LORD of hosts, the mighty One of Is'ra-el, Ah, I will ease me of mine adversaries, and avenge me of mine enemies:
25 ¶ And I will turn my hand upon thee, and purely purge away thy dross, and take away all thy tin:
26 And I will restore thy judges as at the first, and thy counsellors as at the beginning: afterward thou shalt be called, The city of righteousness, the faithful city.
27 Zi'on shall be redeemed with judgment, and her converts with righteousness.
28 ¶ And the destruction of the transgressors and of the sinners *shall be* together, and they that forsake the LORD shall be consumed.
29 For they shall be ashamed of the oaks which ye have desired, and ye shall be confounded for the gardens that ye have chosen.
30 For ye shall be as an oak whose leaf fadeth, and as a garden that hath no water.
31 And the strong shall be as tow, and the maker of it as a spark, and they shall both burn together, and none shall quench *them*.

2 THE word that I-sa'iah the son of A'moz saw concerning Ju'dah and Je-ru'sa-lem.
2 And it shall come to pass in the last days, *that* the mountain of the LORD's house shall be established in the top of the mountains, and shall be exalted above the hills; and all nations shall flow unto it.
3 And many people shall go and say, Come ye, and let us go up to the mountain of the LORD, to the house of the God of Ja'cob; and he will teach us of his ways, and we will walk in his paths: for out of Zi'on shall go forth the law, and the word of the LORD from Je-ru'sa-lem.
4 And he shall judge among the nations, and shall rebuke many people: and they shall beat their swords into plowshares, and their spears into pruninghooks: nation shall not lift up sword against nation, neither shall they learn war any more.
5 O house of Ja'cob, come ye, and let us walk in the light of the LORD.
6 ¶ Therefore thou hast forsaken thy people the house of Ja'cob, because they be replenished from the east, and *are* soothsayers like the Phi-lis'tines, and they please themselves in the children of strangers.
7 Their land also is full of silver and gold, neither *is there any* end of their treasures; their land is also full of horses, neither *is there any* end of their chariots:
8 Their land also is full of idols; they worship the work of their own hands, that which their own fingers have made:
9 And the mean man boweth down, and the great man humbleth himself: therefore forgive them not.
10 ¶ Enter into the rock, and hide thee in the dust, for fear of the LORD, and for the glory of his majesty.
11 The lofty looks of man shall be humbled, and the haughtiness of men shall be bowed down, and the LORD alone shall be exalted in that day.
12 For the day of the LORD of hosts *shall be* upon every *one that is* proud and lofty, and upon every *one that is* lifted up; and he shall be brought low:
13 And upon all the cedars of Leb'a-non, *that are* high and lifted up, and upon all the oaks of Ba'shan,
14 And upon all the high mountains, and upon all the hills *that are* lifted up,
15 And upon every high tower, and upon every fenced wall,
16 And upon all the ships of Tar'shish, and upon all pleasant pictures.
17 And the loftiness of man shall be bowed

down, and the haughtiness of men shall be made low: and the LORD alone shall be exalted in that day.

18 And the idols he shall utterly abolish.

19 And they shall go into the holes of the rocks, and into the caves of the earth, for fear of the LORD, and for the glory of his majesty, when he ariseth to shake terribly the earth.

20 In that day a man shall cast his idols of silver, and his idols of gold, which they made *each one* for himself to worship, to the moles and to the bats;

21 To go into the clefts of the rocks, and into the tops of the ragged rocks, for fear of the LORD, and for the glory of his majesty, when he ariseth to shake terribly the earth.

22 Cease ye from man, whose breath *is* in his nostrils: for wherein is he to be accounted of?

3 FOR, behold, the Lord, the LORD of hosts, doth take away from Je-ru'sa-lem and from Ju'dah the stay and the staff, the whole stay of bread, and the whole stay of water,

2 The mighty man, and the man of war, the judge, and the prophet, and the prudent, and the ancient,

3 The captain of fifty, and the honourable man, and the counsellor, and the cunning artificer, and the eloquent orator.

4 And I will give children *to be* their princes, and babes shall rule over them.

5 And the people shall be oppressed, every one by another, and every one by his neighbour: the child shall behave himself proudly against the ancient, and the base against the honourable.

6 When a man shall take hold of his brother of the house of his father, *saying*, Thou hast clothing, be thou our ruler, and *let* this ruin *be* under thy hand:

7 In that day shall he swear, saying, I will not be an healer; for in my house *is* neither bread nor clothing: make me not a ruler of the people.

8 For Je-ru'sa-lem is ruined, and Ju'dah is fallen: because their tongue and their doings *are* against the LORD, to provoke the eyes of his glory.

9 ¶ The shew of their countenance doth witness against them; and they declare their sin as Sod'om, they hide *it* not. Woe unto their soul! for they have rewarded evil unto themselves.

10 Say ye to the righteous, that *it shall be* well *with him:* for they shall eat the fruit of their doings.

11 Woe unto the wicked! *it shall be* ill *with him:* for the reward of his hands shall be given him.

12 ¶ *As for* my people, children *are* their oppressors, and women rule over them. O my people, they which lead thee cause *thee* to err, and destroy the way of thy paths.

13 The LORD standeth up to plead, and standeth to judge the people.

14 The LORD will enter into judgment with the ancients of his people, and the princes thereof: for ye have eaten up the vineyard; the spoil of the poor *is* in your houses.

15 What mean ye *that* ye beat my people to pieces, and grind the faces of the poor? saith the Lord GOD of hosts.

16 ¶ Moreover the LORD saith, Because the daughters of Zi'on are haughty, and walk with stretched forth necks and wanton eyes, walking and mincing *as* they go, and making a tinkling with their feet:

17 Therefore the Lord will smite with a scab the crown of the head of the daughters of Zi'on, and the LORD will discover their secret parts.

18 In that day the Lord will take away the bravery of *their* tinkling ornaments *about their feet*, and *their* cauls, and *their* round tires like the moon,

19 The chains, and the bracelets, and the mufflers,

20 The bonnets, and the ornaments of the legs, and the headbands, and the tablets, and the earrings,

21 The rings, and nose jewels,

22 The changeable suits of apparel, and the mantles, and the wimples, and the crisping pins,

23 The glasses, and the fine linen, and the hoods, and the vails.

24 And it shall come to pass, *that* instead of sweet smell there shall be stink; and instead of a girdle a rent; and instead of well set hair baldness; and instead of a stomacher a girding of sackcloth; *and* burning instead of beauty.

25 Thy men shall fall by the sword, and thy mighty in the war.

26 And her gates shall lament and mourn; and she *being* desolate shall sit upon the ground.

4 AND in that day seven women shall take hold of one man, saying, We will eat our own bread, and wear our own apparel: only let us be called by thy name, to take away our reproach.

2 In that day shall the branch of the LORD be beautiful and glorious, and the fruit of the earth *shall be* excellent and comely for them that are escaped of Is'ra-el.

3 And it shall come to pass, *that he that is* left in Zi'on, and *he that* remaineth in Je-ru'salem, shall be called holy, *even* every one that is written among the living in Je-ru'sa-lem:

4 When the Lord shall have washed away the filth of the daughters of Zi'on, and shall have purged the blood of Je-ru'sa-lem from the midst thereof by the spirit of judgment, and by the spirit of burning.

5 And the LORD will create upon every dwelling place of mount Zi'on, and upon her assemblies, a cloud and smoke by day, and the shining of a flaming fire by night: for upon all the glory *shall be* a defence.

6 And there shall be a tabernacle for a shadow in the daytime from the heat, and for a place of refuge, and for a covert from storm and from rain.

5 NOW will I sing to my wellbeloved a song of my beloved touching his vineyard. My wellbeloved hath a vineyard in a very fruitful hill:

2 And he fenced it, and gathered out the stones thereof, and planted it with the choicest vine, and built a tower in the midst of it, and also made a winepress therein: and he looked that it should bring forth grapes, and it brought forth wild grapes.

3 And now, O inhabitants of Je-ru'sa-lem, and men of Ju'dah, judge, I pray you, betwixt me and my vineyard.

4 What could have been done more to my vineyard, that I have not done in it? wherefore, when I looked that it should bring forth grapes, brought it forth wild grapes?

5 And now go to; I will tell you what I will do to my vineyard: I will take away the hedge thereof, and it shall be eaten up; *and* break down the wall thereof, and it shall be trodden down:

6 And I will lay it waste: it shall not be pruned, nor digged; but there shall come up briers and thorns: I will also command the clouds that they rain no rain upon it.

7 For the vineyard of the LORD of hosts *is* the house of Is'ra-el, and the men of Ju'dah his pleasant plant: and he looked for judgment, but behold oppression; for righteousness, but behold a cry.

8 ¶ Woe unto them that join house to house, *that* lay field to field, till *there be* no place, that they may be placed alone in the midst of the earth!

9 In mine ears *said* the LORD of hosts, Of a truth many houses shall be desolate, *even* great and fair, without inhabitant.

10 Yea, ten acres of vineyard shall yield one bath, and the seed of an homer shall yield an ephah.

11 ¶ Woe unto them that rise up early in the morning, *that* they may follow strong drink; that continue until night, *till* wine inflame them!

12 And the harp, and the viol, the tabret, and pipe, and wine, are in their feasts: but they regard not the work of the LORD, neither consider the operation of his hands.

13 ¶ Therefore my people are gone into captivity, because *they have* no knowledge: and their honourable men *are* famished, and their multitude dried up with thirst.

14 Therefore hell hath enlarged herself, and opened her mouth without measure: and their glory, and their multitude, and their pomp, and he that rejoiceth, shall descend into it.

15 And the mean man shall be brought down, and the mighty man shall be humbled, and the eyes of the lofty shall be humbled:

16 But the LORD of hosts shall be exalted in judgment, and God that is holy shall be sanctified in righteousness.

17 Then shall the lambs feed after their manner, and the waste places of the fat ones shall strangers eat.

18 Woe unto them that draw iniquity with cords of vanity, and sin as it were with a cart rope:

19 That say, Let him make speed, *and* hasten his work, that we may see *it:* and let the counsel of the Holy One of Is'ra-el draw nigh and come, that we may know *it!*

20 ¶ Woe unto them that call evil good, and good evil; that put darkness for light, and light for darkness; that put bitter for sweet, and sweet for bitter!

21 Woe unto *them that are* wise in their own eyes, and prudent in their own sight!

22 Woe unto *them that are* mighty to drink wine, and men of strength to mingle strong drink:

23 Which justify the wicked for reward, and take away the righteousness of the righteous from him!

24 Therefore as the fire devoureth the stubble, and the flame consumeth the chaff, *so* their root shall be as rottenness, and their blossom shall go up as dust: because they have cast away the law of the LORD of hosts, and despised the word of the Holy One of Is'ra-el.

25 Therefore is the anger of the LORD kindled against his people, and he hath stretched forth his hand against them, and hath smitten them: and the hills did tremble, and their carcases *were* torn in the midst of the streets. For all this his anger is not turned away, but his hand *is* stretched out still.

26 ¶ And he will lift up an ensign to the nations from far, and will hiss unto them from the end of the earth: and, behold, they shall come with speed swiftly:

27 None shall be weary nor stumble among them; none shall slumber nor sleep; neither shall the girdle of their loins be loosed, nor the latchet of their shoes be broken:

28 Whose arrows *are* sharp, and all their bows bent, their horses' hoofs shall be counted like flint, and their wheels like a whirlwind:

29 Their roaring *shall be* like a lion, they shall roar like young lions: yea, they shall roar, and lay hold of the prey, and shall carry *it* away safe, and none shall deliver *it.*

30 And in that day they shall roar against them like the roaring of the sea: and if *one* look unto the land, behold darkness *and* sorrow, and the light is darkened in the heavens thereof.

6 IN the year that king Uz-zi'ah died I saw also the Lord sitting upon a throne, high and lifted up, and his train filled the temple.

2 Above it stood the seraphims: each one had six wings; with twain he covered his face, and with twain he covered his feet, and with twain he did fly.

3 And one cried unto another, and said, Holy, holy, holy, *is* the LORD of hosts: the whole earth *is* full of his glory.

4 And the posts of the door moved at the voice of him that cried, and the house was filled with smoke.

5 ¶ Then said I, Woe *is* me! for I am undone; because I *am* a man of unclean lips, and I dwell in the midst of a people of unclean lips: for mine eyes have seen the King, the LORD of hosts.

6 Then flew one of the seraphims unto me, having a live coal in his hand, *which* he had taken with the tongs from off the altar:

7 And he laid *it* upon my mouth, and said, Lo, this hath touched thy lips; and thine iniquity is taken away, and thy sin purged.

8 Also I heard the voice of the Lord, saying, Whom shall I send, and who will go for us? Then said I, Here *am* I; send me.

9 ¶ And he said, Go, and tell this people, Hear ye indeed, but understand not; and see ye indeed, but perceive not.

10 Make the heart of this people fat, and make their ears heavy, and shut their eyes; lest they see with their eyes, and hear with their ears, and understand with their heart, and convert, and be healed.

11 Then said I, Lord, how long? And he answered, Until the cities be wasted without inhabitant, and the houses without man, and the land be utterly desolate,

12 And the LORD have removed men far away, and *there be* a great forsaking in the midst of the land.

13 ¶ But yet in it *shall be* a tenth, and *it* shall return, and shall be eaten: as a teil tree, and as an oak, whose substance *is* in them, when they cast *their leaves: so* the holy seed *shall be* the substance thereof.

7 AND it came to pass in the days of A'haz the son of Jo'tham, the son of Uz-zi'ah, king of Ju'dah, *that* Re'zin the king of Syr'i-a, and Pe'kah the son of Rem-a-li'ah, king of Is'ra-el, went up toward Je-ru'sa-lem to war against it, but could not prevail against it.

2 And it was told the house of Da'vid, saying, Syr'i-a is confederate with E'phra-im. And his heart was moved, and the heart of his people, as the trees of the wood are moved with the wind.

3 Then said the LORD unto I-sa'iah, Go forth now to meet A'haz, thou, and She'ar-ja'shub

thy son, at the end of the conduit of the upper pool in the highway of the fuller's field;

4 And say unto him, Take heed, and be quiet; fear not, neither be fainthearted for the two tails of these smoking firebrands, for the fierce anger of Re'zin with Syr'i-a, and of the son of Rem-a-li'ah.

5 Because Syr'i-a, E'phra-im, and the son of Rem-a-li'ah, have taken evil counsel against thee, saying,

6 Let us go up against Ju'dah, and vex it, and let us make a breach therein for us, and set a king in the midst of it, *even* the son of Ta'be-al:

7 Thus saith the Lord GOD, It shall not stand, neither shall it come to pass.

8 For the head of Syr'i-a *is* Da-mas'cus, and the head of Da-mas'cus *is* Re'zin; and within threescore and five years shall E'phra-im be broken, that it be not a people.

9 And the head of E'phra-im *is* Sa-ma'ri-a, and the head of Sa-ma'ri-a *is* Rem-a-li'ah's son. If ye will not believe, surely ye shall not be established.

10 ¶ Moreover the LORD spake again unto A'haz, saying,

11 Ask thee a sign of the LORD thy God; ask it either in the depth, or in the height above.

12 But A'haz said, I will not ask, neither will I tempt the LORD.

13 And he said, Hear ye now, O house of Da'vid; *Is it* a small thing for you to weary men, but will ye weary my God also?

14 Therefore the Lord himself shall give you a sign; Behold, a virgin shall conceive, and bear a son, and shall call his name Im-man'u-el.

15 Butter and honey shall he eat, that he may know to refuse the evil, and choose the good.

16 For before the child shall know to refuse the evil, and choose the good, the land that thou abhorrest shall be forsaken of both her kings.

17 ¶ The LORD shall bring upon thee, and upon thy people, and upon thy father's house, days that have not come, from the day that E'phra-im departed from Ju'dah; *even* the king of As-syr'i-a.

18 And it shall come to pass in that day, *that* the LORD shall hiss for the fly that *is* in the uttermost part of the rivers of E'gypt, and for the bee that *is* in the land of As-syr'i-a.

19 And they shall come, and shall rest all of them in the desolate valleys, and in the holes of the rocks, and upon all thorns, and upon all bushes.

20 In the same day shall the Lord shave with a razor that is hired, *namely,* by them beyond the river, by the king of As-syr'i-a, the head, and the hair of the feet: and it shall also consume the beard.

21 And it shall come to pass in that day, *that* a man shall nourish a young cow, and two sheep;

22 And it shall come to pass, for the abundance of milk *that* they shall give he shall eat butter: for butter and honey shall every one eat that is left in the land.

23 And it shall come to pass in that day, *that* every place shall be, where there were a thousand vines at a thousand silverlings, it shall *even* be for briers and thorns.

24 With arrows and with bows shall *men* come thither; because all the land shall become briers and thorns.

25 And *on* all hills that shall be digged with the mattock, there shall not come thither the fear of briers and thorns: but it shall be for the sending forth of oxen, and for the treading of lesser cattle.

8 MOREOVER the LORD said unto me, Take thee a great roll, and write in it with a man's pen concerning Ma'her-shal'al-hash'-baz.

2 And I took unto me faithful witnesses to record, U-ri'ah the priest, and Zech-a-ri'ah the son of Je-ber-e-chi'ah.

3 And I went unto the prophetess; and she conceived, and bare a son. Then said the LORD to me, Call his name Ma'her-shal'al-hash'-baz.

4 For before the child shall have knowledge to cry, My father, and my mother, the riches of Da-mas'cus and the spoil of Sa-ma'ri-a shall be taken away before the king of As-syr'i-a.

5 ¶ The LORD spake also unto me again, saying,

6 Forasmuch as this people refuseth the waters of Shi-lo'ah that go softly, and rejoice in Re'zin and Rem-a-li'ah's son;

7 Now therefore, behold, the Lord bringeth up upon them the waters of the river, strong and many, *even* the king of As-syr'i-a, and all his glory: and he shall come up over all his channels, and go over all his banks:

8 And he shall pass through Ju'dah; he shall overflow and go over, he shall reach *even* to the neck; and the stretching out of his wings shall fill the breadth of thy land, O Im-man'u-el.

9 ¶ Associate yourselves, O ye people, and ye shall be broken in pieces; and give ear, all ye of far countries: gird yourselves, and ye shall be broken in pieces; gird yourselves, and ye shall be broken in pieces.

10 Take counsel together, and it shall come to nought; speak the word, and it shall not stand: for God *is* with us.

11 ¶ For the LORD spake thus to me with a strong hand, and instructed me that I should not walk in the way of this people, saying,

12 Say ye not, A confederacy, to all *them to* whom this people shall say, A confederacy; neither fear ye their fear, nor be afraid.

13 Sanctify the LORD of hosts himself; and *let* him *be* your fear, and *let* him *be* your dread.

14 And he shall be for a sanctuary; but for a stone of stumbling and for a rock of offence to both the houses of Is'ra-el, for a gin and for a snare to the inhabitants of Je-ru'sa-lem.

15 And many among them shall stumble, and fall, and be broken, and be snared, and be taken.

16 Bind up the testimony, seal the law among my disciples.

17 And I will wait upon the LORD, that hideth his face from the house of Ja'cob, and I will look for him.

18 Behold, I and the children whom the LORD hath given me *are* for signs and for wonders in Is'ra-el from the LORD of hosts, which dwelleth in mount Zi'on.

19 ¶ And when they shall say unto you, Seek unto them that have familiar spirits, and unto wizards that peep, and that mutter: should not a people seek unto their God? for the living to the dead?

20 To the law and to the testimony: if they speak not according to this word, *it is* because *there is* no light in them.

21 And they shall pass through it, hardly bestead and hungry: and it shall come to pass, that when they shall be hungry, they shall fret themselves, and curse their king and their God, and look upward.

22 And they shall look unto the earth; and behold trouble and darkness, dimness of anguish; and *they shall be* driven to darkness.

9 NEVERTHELESS the dimness *shall* not *be*
such as *was* in her vexation, when at the
first he lightly afflicted the land of Zeb'u-lun
and the land of Naph'ta-li, and afterward did
more grievously afflict *her by* the way of the
sea, beyond Jor'dan, in Gal'i-lee of the nations.
2 The people that walked in darkness have
seen a great light: they that dwell in the land of
the shadow of death, upon them hath the light
shined.
3 Thou hast multiplied the nation, *and* not increased the joy: they joy before thee according
to the joy in harvest, *and* as *men* rejoice when
they divide the spoil.
4 For thou hast broken the yoke of his burden, and the staff of his shoulder, the rod of his
oppressor, as in the day of Mid'i-an.
5 For every battle of the warrior *is* with confused noise, and garments rolled in blood; but
this shall be with burning *and* fuel of fire.
6 For unto us a child is born, unto us a son is
given: and the government shall be upon his
shoulder: and his name shall be called Wonderful, Counsellor, The mighty God, The everlasting Father, The Prince of Peace.
7 Of the increase of *his* government and
peace *there shall be* no end, upon the throne of
Da'vid, and upon his kingdom, to order it, and
to establish it with judgment and with justice
from henceforth even for ever. The zeal of the
LORD of hosts will perform this.
8 ¶ The Lord sent a word into Ja'cob, and it
hath lighted upon Is'ra-el.
9 And all the people shall know, *even* E'phra-
im and the inhabitant of Sa-ma'ri-a, that say in
the pride and stoutness of heart,
10 The bricks are fallen down, but we will
build with hewn stones: the sycomores are cut
down, but we will change *them into* cedars.
11 Therefore the LORD shall set up the adversaries of Re'zin against him, and join his enemies together;
12 The Syr'i-ans before, and the Phi-lis'tines
behind; and they shall devour Is'ra-el with open
mouth. For all this his anger is not turned away,
but his hand *is* stretched out still.
13 ¶ For the people turneth not unto him
that smiteth them, neither do they seek the
LORD of hosts.
14 Therefore the LORD will cut off from Is'ra-
el head and tail, branch and rush, in one day.
15 The ancient and honourable, he *is* the
head; and the prophet that teacheth lies, he *is*
the tail.
16 For the leaders of this people cause *them*
to err; and *they that are* led of them *are* destroyed.
17 Therefore the Lord shall have no joy in
their young men, neither shall have mercy on
their fatherless and widows: for every one *is* an
hypocrite and an evildoer, and every mouth
speaketh folly. For all this his anger is not
turned away, but his hand *is* stretched out still.
18 ¶ For wickedness burneth as the fire: it
shall devour the briers and thorns, and shall
kindle in the thickets of the forest, and they
shall mount up *like* the lifting up of smoke.
19 Through the wrath of the LORD of hosts is
the land darkened, and the people shall be as
the fuel of the fire: no man shall spare his
brother.
20 And he shall snatch on the right hand, and
be hungry; and he shall eat on the left hand, and
they shall not be satisfied: they shall eat every
man the flesh of his own arm:
21 Ma-nas'seh, E'phra-im; and E'phra-im,
Ma-nas'seh: *and* they together *shall be* against
Ju'dah. For all this his anger is not turned away,
but his hand *is* stretched out still.

10 WOE unto them that decree unrighteous decrees, and that write grievousness *which* they have prescribed;
2 To turn aside the needy from judgment,
and to take away the right from the poor of my
people, that widows may be their prey, and *that*
they may rob the fatherless!
3 And what will ye do in the day of visitation,
and in the desolation *which* shall come from
far? to whom will ye flee for help? and where
will ye leave your glory?
4 Without me they shall bow down under the
prisoners, and they shall fall under the slain.
For all this his anger is not turned away, but his
hand *is* stretched out still.
5 ¶ O As-syr'i-an, the rod of mine anger, and
the staff in their hand is mine indignation.
6 I will send him against an hypocritical nation, and against the people of my wrath will I
give him a charge, to take the spoil, and to take
the prey, and to tread them down like the mire
of the streets.
7 Howbeit he meaneth not so, neither doth
his heart think so; but *it is* in his heart to destroy and cut off nations not a few.
8 For he saith, *Are* not my princes altogether
kings?
9 *Is* not Cal'no as Car'che-mish? *is* not Ha'-
math as Ar'pad? *is* not Sa-ma'ri-a as Da-mas'-
cus?
10 As my hand hath found the kingdoms of
the idols, and whose graven images did excel
them of Je-ru'sa-lem and of Sa-ma'ri-a;
11 Shall I not, as I have done unto Sa-ma'ri-a
and her idols, so do to Je-ru'sa-lem and her
idols?
12 Wherefore it shall come to pass, *that*
when the Lord hath performed his whole work
upon mount Zi'on and on Je-ru'sa-lem, I will
punish the fruit of the stout heart of the king of
As-syr'i-a, and the glory of his high looks.
13 For he saith, By the strength of my hand I
have done *it*, and by my wisdom; for I am prudent: and I have removed the bounds of the
people, and have robbed their treasures, and I
have put down the inhabitants like a valiant
man:
14 And my hand hath found as a nest the
riches of the people: and as one gathereth eggs
that are left, have I gathered all the earth; and
there was none that moved the wing, or opened
the mouth, or peeped.
15 Shall the ax boast itself against him that
heweth therewith? *or* shall the saw magnify itself against him that shaketh it? as if the rod
should shake *itself* against them that lift it up,
or as if the staff should lift up *itself, as if it were*
no wood.
16 Therefore shall the Lord, the Lord of
hosts, send among his fat ones leanness; and
under his glory he shall kindle a burning like
the burning of a fire.
17 And the light of Is'ra-el shall be for a fire,
and his Holy One for a flame: and it shall burn
and devour his thorns and his briers in one day;
18 And shall consume the glory of his forest,
and of his fruitful field, both soul and body: and
they shall be as when a standardbearer fainteth.
19 And the rest of the trees of his forest shall
be few, that a child may write them.
20 ¶ And it shall come to pass in that day,
that the remnant of Is'ra-el, and such as are escaped of the house of Ja'cob, shall no more
again stay upon him that smote them; but shall

stay upon the LORD, the Holy One of Is'ra-el, in truth.

21 The remnant shall return, *even* the remnant of Ja'cob, unto the mighty God.

22 For though thy people Is'ra-el be as the sand of the sea, *yet* a remnant of them shall return: the consumption decreed shall overflow with righteousness.

23 For the Lord GOD of hosts shall make a consumption, even determined, in the midst of all the land.

24 ¶ Therefore thus saith the Lord GOD of hosts, O my people that dwellest in Zi'on, be not afraid of the As-syr'i-an: he shall smite thee with a rod, and shall lift up his staff against thee, after the manner of E'gypt.

25 For yet a very little while, and the indignation shall cease, and mine anger in their destruction.

26 And the LORD of hosts shall stir up a scourge for him according to the slaughter of Mid'i-an at the rock of O'reb: and *as* his rod *was* upon the sea, so shall he lift it up after the manner of E'gypt.

27 And it shall come to pass in that day, *that* his burden shall be taken away from off thy shoulder, and his yoke from off thy neck, and the yoke shall be destroyed because of the anointing.

28 He is come to A-i'ath, he is passed to Mig'ron; at Mich'mash he hath laid up his carriages:

29 They are gone over the passage: they have taken up their lodging at Ge'ba; Ra'mah is afraid; Gib'e-ah of Saul is fled.

30 Lift up thy voice, O daughter of Gal'lim: cause it to be heard unto La'ish, O poor An'a-thoth.

31 Mad-me'nah is removed; the inhabitants of Ge'bim gather themselves to flee.

32 As yet shall he remain at Nob that day: he shall shake his hand *against* the mount of the daughter of Zi'on, the hill of Je-ru'sa-lem.

33 Behold, the Lord, the LORD of hosts, shall lop the bough with terror: and the high ones of stature *shall be* hewn down, and the haughty shall be humbled.

34 And he shall cut down the thickets of the forest with iron, and Leb'a-non shall fall by a mighty one.

11 AND there shall come forth a rod out of the stem of Jes'se, and a Branch shall grow out of his roots:

2 And the spirit of the LORD shall rest upon him, the spirit of wisdom and understanding, the spirit of counsel and might, the spirit of knowledge and of the fear of the LORD;

3 And shall make him of quick understanding in the fear of the LORD: and he shall not judge after the sight of his eyes, neither reprove after the hearing of his ears:

4 But with righteousness shall he judge the poor, and reprove with equity for the meek of the earth: and he shall smite the earth with the rod of his mouth, and with the breath of his lips shall he slay the wicked.

5 And righteousness shall be the girdle of his loins, and faithfulness the girdle of his reins.

6 The wolf also shall dwell with the lamb, and the leopard shall lie down with the kid; and the calf and the young lion and the fatling together; and a little child shall lead them.

7 And the cow and the bear shall feed; their young ones shall lie down together: and the lion shall eat straw like the ox.

8 And the sucking child shall play on the hole of the asp, and the weaned child shall put his hand on the cockatrice' den.

9 They shall not hurt nor destroy in all my holy mountain: for the earth shall be full of the knowledge of the LORD, as the waters cover the sea.

10 ¶ And in that day there shall be a root of Jes'se, which shall stand for an ensign of the people; to it shall the Gen-tiles seek: and his rest shall be glorious.

11 And it shall come to pass in that day, *that* the Lord shall set his hand again the second time to recover the remnant of his people, which shall be left, from As-syr'i-a, and from E'gypt, and from Path'ros, and from Cush, and from E'lam, and from Shi'nar, and from Ha'math, and from the islands of the sea.

12 And he shall set up an ensign for the nations, and shall assemble the outcasts of Is'ra-el, and gather together the dispersed of Ju'dah from the four corners of the earth.

13 The envy also of E'phra-im shall depart, and the adversaries of Ju'dah shall be cut off: E'phra-im shall not envy Ju'dah, and Ju'dah shall not vex E'phra-im.

14 But they shall fly upon the shoulders of the Phi-lis'tines toward the west; they shall spoil them of the east together: they shall lay their hand upon E'dom and Mo'ab; and the children of Am'mon shall obey them.

15 And the LORD shall utterly destroy the tongue of the E-gyp'tian sea; and with his mighty wind shall he shake his hand over the river, and shall smite it in the seven streams, and make *men* go over dryshod.

16 And there shall be an highway for the remnant of his people, which shall be left, from As-syr'i-a; like as it was to Is'ra-el in the day that he came up out of the land of E'gypt.

12 AND in that day thou shalt say, O LORD, I will praise thee: though thou wast angry with me, thine anger is turned away, and thou comfortedst me.

2 Behold, God *is* my salvation; I will trust, and not be afraid: for the LORD JE-HO'VAH *is* my strength and *my* song; he also is become my salvation.

3 Therefore with joy shall ye draw water out of the wells of salvation.

4 And in that day shall ye say, Praise the LORD, call upon his name, declare his doings among the people, make mention that his name is exalted.

5 Sing unto the LORD; for he hath done excellent things: this *is* known in all the earth.

6 Cry out and shout, thou inhabitant of Zi'on: for great *is* the Holy One of Is'ra-el in the midst of thee.

13 THE burden of Bab'y-lon, which I-sa'iah the son of A'moz did see.

2 Lift ye up a banner upon the high mountain, exalt the voice unto them, shake the hand, that they may go into the gates of the nobles.

3 I have commanded my sanctified ones, I have also called my mighty ones for mine anger, *even* them that rejoice in my highness.

4 The noise of a multitude in the mountains, like as of a great people; a tumultuous noise of the kingdoms of nations gathered together: the LORD of hosts mustereth the host of the battle.

5 They come from a far country, from the end of heaven, *even* the LORD, and the weapons of his indignation, to destroy the whole land.

6 ¶ Howl ye; for the day of the LORD *is* at

hand; it shall come as a destruction from the Almighty.

7 Therefore shall all hands be faint, and every man's heart shall melt:

8 And they shall be afraid: pangs and sorrows shall take hold of them; they shall be in pain as a woman that travaileth: they shall be amazed one at another; their faces *shall be as* flames.

9 Behold, the day of the LORD cometh, cruel both with wrath and fierce anger, to lay the land desolate: and he shall destroy the sinners thereof out of it.

10 For the stars of heaven and the constellations thereof shall not give their light: the sun shall be darkened in his going forth, and the moon shall not cause her light to shine.

11 And I will punish the world for *their* evil, and the wicked for their iniquity; and I will cause the arrogancy of the proud to cease, and will lay low the haughtiness of the terrible.

12 I will make a man more precious than fine gold; even a man than the golden wedge of O'phir.

13 Therefore I will shake the heavens, and the earth shall remove out of her place, in the wrath of the LORD of hosts, and in the day of his fierce anger.

14 And it shall be as the chased roe, and as a sheep that no man taketh up: they shall every man turn to his own people, and flee every one into his own land.

15 Every one that is found shall be thrust through; and every one that is joined *unto them* shall fall by the sword.

16 Their children also shall be dashed to pieces before their eyes; their houses shall be spoiled, and their wives ravished.

17 Behold, I will stir up the Medes against them, which shall not regard silver; and *as for* gold, they shall not delight in it.

18 *Their* bows also shall dash the young men to pieces; and they shall have no pity on the fruit of the womb; their eye shall not spare children.

19 ¶ And Bab'y-lon, the glory of kingdoms, the beauty of the Chal'dees' excellency, shall be as when God overthrew Sod'om and Go-mor'rah.

20 It shall never be inhabited, neither shall it be dwelt in from generation to generation: neither shall the A-ra'bi-an pitch tent there; neither shall the shepherds make their fold there.

21 But wild beasts of the desert shall lie there; and their houses shall be full of doleful creatures; and owls shall dwell there, and satyrs shall dance there.

22 And the wild beasts of the islands shall cry in their desolate houses, and dragons in *their* pleasant palaces: and her time *is* near to come, and her days shall not be prolonged.

14 FOR the LORD will have mercy on Ja'cob, and will yet choose Is'ra-el, and set them in their own land: and the strangers shall be joined with them, and they shall cleave to the house of Ja'cob.

2 And the people shall take them, and bring them to their place: and the house of Is'ra-el shall possess them in the land of the LORD for servants and handmaids: and they shall take them captives, whose captives they were; and they shall rule over their oppressors.

3 And it shall come to pass in the day that the LORD shall give thee rest from thy sorrow, and from thy fear, and from the hard bondage wherein thou wast made to serve,

4 ¶ That thou shalt take up this proverb against the king of Bab'y-lon, and say, How hath the oppressor ceased! the golden city ceased!

5 The LORD hath broken the staff of the wicked, *and* the sceptre of the rulers.

6 He who smote the people in wrath with a continual stroke, he that ruled the nations in anger, is persecuted, *and* none hindereth.

7 The whole earth is at rest, *and* is quiet: they break forth into singing.

8 Yea, the fir trees rejoice at thee, *and* the cedars of Leb'a-non, *saying,* Since thou art laid down, no feller is come up against us.

9 Hell from beneath is moved for thee to meet *thee* at thy coming: it stirreth up the dead for thee, *even* all the chief ones of the earth; it hath raised up from their thrones all the kings of the nations.

10 All they shall speak and say unto thee, Art thou also become weak as we? art thou become like unto us?

11 Thy pomp is brought down to the grave, *and* the noise of thy viols: the worm is spread under thee, and the worms cover thee.

12 How art thou fallen from heaven, O Lu'cifer, son of the morning! *how* art thou cut down to the ground, which didst weaken the nations!

13 For thou hast said in thine heart, I will ascend into heaven, I will exalt my throne above the stars of God: I will sit also upon the mount of the congregation, in the sides of the north:

14 I will ascend above the heights of the clouds; I will be like the most High.

15 Yet thou shalt be brought down to hell, to the sides of the pit.

16 They that see thee shall narrowly look upon thee, *and* consider thee, *saying, Is* this the man that made the earth to tremble, that did shake kingdoms;

17 *That* made the world as a wilderness, and destroyed the cities thereof; *that* opened not the house of his prisoners?

18 All the kings of the nations, *even* all of them, lie in glory, every one in his own house.

19 But thou art cast out of thy grave like an abominable branch, *and as* the raiment of those that are slain, thrust through with a sword, that go down to the stones of the pit; as a carcase trodden under feet.

20 Thou shalt not be joined with them in burial, because thou hast destroyed thy land, *and* slain thy people: the seed of evildoers shall never be renowned.

21 Prepare slaughter for his children for the iniquity of their fathers; that they do not rise, nor possess the land, nor fill the face of the world with cities.

22 For I will rise up against them, saith the LORD of hosts, and cut off from Bab'y-lon the name, and remnant, and son, and nephew, saith the LORD.

23 I will also make it a possession for the bittern, and pools of water: and I will sweep it with the besom of destruction, saith the LORD of hosts.

24 ¶ The LORD of hosts hath sworn, saying, Surely as I have thought, so shall it come to pass; and as I have purposed, *so* shall it stand:

25 That I will break the As-syr'i-an in my land, and upon my mountains tread him under foot: then shall his yoke depart from off them, and his burden depart from off their shoulders.

26 This *is* the purpose that is purposed upon the whole earth: and this *is* the hand that is stretched out upon all the nations.

27 For the LORD of hosts hath purposed, and

who shall disannul *it?* and his hand *is* stretched
out, and who shall turn it back?
28 In the year that king A'haz died was this
burden.
29 ¶ Rejoice not thou, whole Pal-es-ti'na, because the rod of him that smote thee is broken:
for out of the serpent's root shall come forth a
cockatrice, and his fruit *shall be* a fiery flying
serpent.
30 And the firstborn of the poor shall feed,
and the needy shall lie down in safety: and I will
kill thy root with famine, and he shall slay thy
remnant.
31 Howl, O gate; cry, O city; thou, whole Pal-
es-ti'na, *art* dissolved: for there shall come from
the north a smoke, and none *shall be* alone in
his appointed times.
32 What shall *one* then answer the messengers of the nation? That the LORD hath founded
Zi'on, and the poor of his people shall trust in it.

15 THE burden of Mo'ab. Because in the
night Ar of Mo'ab is laid waste, *and*
brought to silence; because in the night Kir of
Mo'ab is laid waste, *and* brought to silence;
2 He is gone up to Ba'jith, and to Di'bon, the
high places, to weep: Mo'ab shall howl over
Ne'bo, and over Med'e-ba: on all their heads
shall be baldness, *and* every beard cut off.
3 In their streets they shall gird themselves
with sackcloth: on the tops of their houses, and
in their streets, every one shall howl, weeping
abundantly.
4 And Hesh'bon shall cry, and E-le-a'leh:
their voice shall be heard *even* unto Ja'haz:
therefore the armed soldiers of Mo'ab shall cry
out; his life shall be grievous unto him.
5 My heart shall cry out for Mo'ab; his fugitives *shall flee* unto Zo'ar, an heifer of three
years old: for by the mounting up of Lu'hith
with weeping shall they go it up; for in the way
of Hor-o-na'im they shall raise up a cry of destruction.
6 For the waters of Nim'rim shall be desolate: for the hay is withered away, the grass
faileth, there is no green thing.
7 Therefore the abundance they have gotten,
and that which they have laid up, shall they carry away to the brook of the willows.
8 For the cry is gone round about the borders
of Mo'ab; the howling thereof unto Eg'la-im,
and the howling thereof unto Be'er–e'lim.
9 For the waters of Di'mon shall be full of
blood: for I will bring more upon Di'mon, lions
upon him that escapeth of Mo'ab, and upon the
remnant of the land.

16 SEND ye the lamb to the ruler of the
land from Se'la to the wilderness, unto
the mount of the daughter of Zi'on.
2 For it shall be, *that*, as a wandering bird
cast out of the nest, *so* the daughters of Mo'ab
shall be at the fords of Ar'non.
3 Take counsel, execute judgment; make thy
shadow as the night in the midst of the noonday; hide the outcasts; bewray not him that
wandereth.
4 Let mine outcasts dwell with thee, Mo'ab;
be thou a covert to them from the face of the
spoiler: for the extortioner is at an end, the
spoiler ceaseth, the oppressors are consumed
out of the land.
5 And in mercy shall the throne be established: and he shall sit upon it in truth in the
tabernacle of Da'vid, judging, and seeking judgment, and hasting righteousness.
6 ¶ We have heard of the pride of Mo'ab; *he*
is very proud: *even* of his haughtiness, and his
pride, and his wrath: *but* his lies *shall* not *be* so.
7 Therefore shall Mo'ab howl for Mo'ab, ev-
ery one shall howl: for the foundations of Kir–
har'e-seth shall ye mourn; surely *they are*
stricken.
8 For the fields of Hesh'bon languish, *and* the
vine of Sib'mah: the lords of the heathen have
broken down the principal plants thereof, they
are come *even* unto Ja'zer, they wandered
through the wilderness: her branches are
stretched out, they are gone over the sea.
9 ¶ Therefore I will bewail with the weeping
of Ja'zer the vine of Sib'mah: I will water thee
with my tears, O Hesh'bon, and E-le-a'leh: for
the shouting for thy summer fruits and for thy
harvest is fallen.
10 And gladness is taken away, and joy out
of the plentiful field; and in the vineyards there
shall be no singing, neither shall there be shouting: the treaders shall tread out no wine in *their*
presses; I have made *their vintage* shouting to
cease.
11 Wherefore my bowels shall sound like an
harp for Mo'ab, and mine inward parts for Kir–
ha'resh.
12 ¶ And it shall come to pass, when it is
seen that Mo'ab is weary on the high place, that
he shall come to his sanctuary to pray; but he
shall not prevail.
13 This *is* the word that the LORD hath spoken concerning Mo'ab since that time.
14 But now the LORD hath spoken, saying,
Within three years, as the years of an hireling,
and the glory of Mo'ab shall be contemned,
with all that great multitude; and the remnant
shall be very small *and* feeble.

17 THE burden of Da-mas'cus. Behold, Da-
mas'cus is taken away from *being* a city,
and it shall be a ruinous heap.
2 The cities of Ar'o-er *are* forsaken: they
shall be for flocks, which shall lie down, and
none shall make *them* afraid.
3 The fortress also shall cease from E'phra-
im, and the kingdom from Da-mas'cus, and the
remnant of Syr'i-a: they shall be as the glory of
the children of Is'ra-el, saith the LORD of hosts.
4 And in that day it shall come to pass, *that*
the glory of Ja'cob shall be made thin, and the
fatness of his flesh shall wax lean.
5 And it shall be as when the harvestman
gathereth the corn, and reapeth the ears with
his arm; and it shall be as he that gathereth ears
in the valley of Reph'a-im.
6 ¶ Yet gleaning grapes shall be left in it, as
the shaking of an olive tree, two *or* three berries
in the top of the uppermost bough, four *or* five
in the outmost fruitful branches thereof, saith
the LORD God of Is'ra-el.
7 At that day shall a man look to his Maker,
and his eyes shall have respect to the Holy One
of Is'ra-el.
8 And he shall not look to the altars, the
work of his hands, neither shall respect *that*
which his fingers have made, either the groves,
or the images.
9 ¶ In that day shall his strong cities be as a
forsaken bough, and an uppermost branch,
which they left because of the children of Is'ra-
el: and there shall be desolation.
10 Because thou hast forgotten the God of
thy salvation, and hast not been mindful of the
rock of thy strength, therefore shalt thou plant
pleasant plants, and shalt set it with strange
slips:
11 In the day shalt thou make thy plant to

grow, and in the morning shalt thou make thy seed to flourish: *but* the harvest *shall be* a heap in the day of grief and of desperate sorrow.

12 ¶ Woe to the multitude of many people, *which* make a noise like the noise of the seas; and to the rushing of nations, *that* make a rushing like the rushing of mighty waters!

13 The nations shall rush like the rushing of many waters: but *God* shall rebuke them, and they shall flee far off, and shall be chased as the chaff of the mountains before the wind, and like a rolling thing before the whirlwind.

14 And behold at eveningtide trouble; *and* before the morning he *is* not. This *is* the portion of them that spoil us, and the lot of them that rob us.

18 WOE to the land shadowing with wings, which *is* beyond the rivers of E-thi-o′pi-a:

2 That sendeth ambassadors by the sea, even in vessels of bulrushes upon the waters, *saying*, Go, ye swift messengers, to a nation scattered and peeled, to a people terrible from their beginning hitherto; a nation meted out and trodden down, whose land the rivers have spoiled!

3 All ye inhabitants of the world, and dwellers on the earth, see ye, when he lifteth up an ensign on the mountains; and when he bloweth a trumpet, hear ye.

4 For so the LORD said unto me, I will take my rest, and I will consider in my dwelling place like a clear heat upon herbs, *and* like a cloud of dew in the heat of harvest.

5 For afore the harvest, when the bud is perfect, and the sour grape is ripening in the flower, he shall both cut off the sprigs with pruning hooks, and take away *and* cut down the branches.

6 They shall be left together unto the fowls of the mountains, and to the beasts of the earth: and the fowls shall summer upon them, and all the beasts of the earth shall winter upon them.

7 ¶ In that time shall the present be brought unto the LORD of hosts of a people scattered and peeled, and from a people terrible from their beginning hitherto; a nation meted out and trodden under foot, whose land the rivers have spoiled, to the place of the name of the LORD of hosts, the mount Zi′on.

19 THE burden of E′gypt. Behold, the LORD rideth upon a swift cloud, and shall come into E′gypt: and the idols of E′gypt shall be moved at his presence, and the heart of E′gypt shall melt in the midst of it.

2 And I will set the E-gyp′tians against the E-gyp′tians: and they shall fight every one against his brother, and every one against his neighbour; city against city, *and* kingdom against kingdom.

3 And the spirit of E′gypt shall fail in the midst thereof; and I will destroy the counsel thereof: and they shall seek to the idols, and to the charmers, and to them that have familiar spirits, and to the wizards.

4 And the E-gyp′tians will I give over into the hand of a cruel lord; and a fierce king shall rule over them, saith the Lord, the LORD of hosts.

5 And the waters shall fail from the sea, and the river shall be wasted and dried up.

6 And they shall turn the rivers far away; *and* the brooks of defence shall be emptied and dried up: the reeds and flags shall wither.

7 The paper reeds by the brooks, by the mouth of the brooks, and every thing sown by the brooks, shall wither, be driven away, and be no *more*.

8 The fishers also shall mourn, and all they that cast angle into the brooks shall lament, and they that spread nets upon the waters shall languish.

9 Moreover they that work in fine flax, and they that weave networks, shall be confounded.

10 And they shall be broken in the purposes thereof, all that make sluices *and* ponds for fish.

11 ¶ Surely the princes of Zo′an *are* fools, the counsel of the wise counsellors of Pha′raoh is become brutish: how say ye unto Pha′raoh, I *am* the son of the wise, the son of ancient kings?

12 Where *are* they? where *are* thy wise *men?* and let them tell thee now, and let them know what the LORD of hosts hath purposed upon E′gypt.

13 The princes of Zo′an are become fools, the princes of Noph are deceived; they have also seduced E′gypt, *even they that are* the stay of the tribes thereof.

14 The LORD hath mingled a perverse spirit in the midst thereof: and they have caused E′gypt to err in every work thereof, as a drunken *man* staggereth in his vomit.

15 Neither shall there be *any* work for E′gypt, which the head or tail, branch or rush, may do.

16 In that day shall E′gypt be like unto women: and it shall be afraid and fear because of the shaking of the hand of the LORD of hosts, which he shaketh over it.

17 And the land of Ju′dah shall be a terror unto E′gypt, every one that maketh mention thereof shall be afraid in himself, because of the counsel of the LORD of hosts, which he hath determined against it.

18 ¶ In that day shall five cities in the land of E′gypt speak the language of Ca′naan, and swear to the LORD of hosts; one shall be called, The city of destruction.

19 In that day shall there be an altar to the LORD in the midst of the land of E′gypt, and a pillar at the border thereof to the LORD.

20 And it shall be for a sign and for a witness unto the LORD of hosts in the land of E′gypt: for they shall cry unto the LORD because of the oppressors, and he shall send them a saviour, and a great one, and he shall deliver them.

21 And the LORD shall be known to E′gypt, and the E-gyp′tians shall know the LORD in that day, and shall do sacrifice and oblation; yea, they shall vow a vow unto the LORD, and perform *it*.

22 And the LORD shall smite E′gypt: he shall smite and heal *it:* and they shall return *even* to the LORD, and he shall be intreated of them, and shall heal them.

23 ¶ In that day shall there be a highway out of E′gypt to As-syr′i-a, and the As-syr′i-an shall come into E′gypt, and the E-gyp′tian into As-syr′i-a, and the E-gyp′tians shall serve with the As-syr′i-ans.

24 In that day shall Is′ra-el be the third with E′gypt and with As-syr′i-a, *even* a blessing in the midst of the land:

25 Whom the LORD of hosts shall bless, saying, Blessed *be* E′gypt my people, and As-syr′i-a the work of my hands, and Is′ra-el mine inheritance.

20 IN the year that Tar′tan came unto Ash′dod, (when Sar′gon the king of As-syr′i-a sent him,) and fought against Ash′dod, and took it;

2 At the same time spake the LORD by I-sa'-
iah the son of A'moz, saying, Go and loose the
sackcloth from off thy loins, and put off thy
shoe from thy foot. And he did so, walking
naked and barefoot.
3 And the LORD said, Like as my servant I-
sa'iah hath walked naked and barefoot three
years *for* a sign and wonder upon E'gypt and
upon E-thi-o'pi-a;
4 So shall the king of As-syr'i-a lead away
the E-gyp'tians prisoners, and the E-thi-o'pi-ans
captives, young and old, naked and barefoot,
even with *their* buttocks uncovered, to the
shame of E'gypt.
5 And they shall be afraid and ashamed of E-
thi-o'pi-a their expectation, and of E'gypt their
glory.
6 And the inhabitant of this isle shall say in
that day, Behold, such *is* our expectation,
whither we flee for help to be delivered from
the king of As-syr'i-a: and how shall we escape?

21 THE burden of the desert of the sea. As
whirlwinds in the south pass through; *so*
it cometh from the desert, from a terrible land.
2 A grievous vision is declared unto me; the
treacherous dealer dealeth treacherously, and
the spoiler spoileth. Go up, O E'lam: besiege, O
Me'di-a; all the sighing thereof have I made to
cease.
3 Therefore are my loins filled with pain:
pangs have taken hold upon me, as the pangs of
a woman that travaileth: I was bowed down at
the hearing *of it;* I was dismayed at the seeing
of it.
4 My heart panted, fearfulness affrighted me:
the night of my pleasure hath he turned into
fear unto me.
5 Prepare the table, watch in the watchtower, eat, drink: arise, ye princes, *and* anoint
the shield.
6 For thus hath the Lord said unto me, Go,
set a watchman, let him declare what he seeth.
7 And he saw a chariot *with* a couple of
horsemen, a chariot of asses, *and* a chariot of
camels; and he hearkened diligently with much
heed:
8 And he cried, A lion: My lord, I stand continually upon the watchtower in the daytime,
and I am set in my ward whole nights:
9 And, behold, here cometh a chariot of men,
with a couple of horsemen. And he answered
and said, Bab'y-lon is fallen, is fallen; and all the
graven images of her gods he hath broken unto
the ground.
10 O my threshing, and the corn of my floor:
that which I have heard of the LORD of hosts,
the God of Is'ra-el, have I declared unto you.
11 ¶ The burden of Du'mah. He calleth to me
out of Se'ir, Watchman, what of the night?
Watchman, what of the night?
12 The watchman said, The morning cometh,
and also the night: if ye will enquire, enquire ye:
return, come.
13 ¶ The burden upon A-ra'bi-a. In the forest
in A-ra'bi-a shall ye lodge, O ye travelling companies of Ded'a-nim.
14 The inhabitants of the land of Tema
brought water to him that was thirsty, they prevented with their bread him that fled.
15 For they fled from the swords, from the
drawn sword, and from the bent bow, and from
the grievousness of war.
16 For thus hath the Lord said unto me,
Within a year, according to the years of an hireling, and all the glory of Ke'dar shall fail:
17 And the residue of the number of archers,
the mighty men of the children of Ke'dar, shall
be diminished: for the LORD God of Is'ra-el hath
spoken *it.*

22 THE burden of the valley of vision.
What aileth thee now, that thou art
wholly gone up to the house tops?
2 Thou that art full of stirs, a tumultuous
city, a joyous city: thy slain *men are* not slain
with the sword, nor dead in battle.
3 All thy rulers are fled together, they are
bound by the archers: all that are found in thee
are bound together, *which* have fled from far.
4 Therefore said I, Look away from me; I will
weep bitterly, labour not to comfort me, because of the spoiling of the daughter of my people.
5 For *it is* a day of trouble, and of treading
down, and of perplexity by the Lord GOD of
hosts in the valley of vision, breaking down the
walls, and of crying to the mountains.
6 And E'lam bare the quiver with chariots of
men *and* horsemen, and Kir uncovered the
shield.
7 And it shall come to pass, *that* thy choicest
valleys shall be full of chariots, and the horsemen shall set themselves in array at the gate.
8 ¶ And he discovered the covering of Ju'-
dah, and thou didst look in that day to the armour of the house of the forest.
9 Ye have seen also the breaches of the city
of Da'vid, that they are many: and ye gathered
together the waters of the lower pool.
10 And ye have numbered the houses of Je-
ru'sa-lem, and the houses have ye broken down
to fortify the wall.
11 Ye made also a ditch between the two
walls for the water of the old pool: but ye have
not looked unto the maker thereof, neither had
respect unto him that fashioned it long ago.
12 And in that day did the Lord GOD of hosts
call to weeping, and to mourning, and to baldness, and to girding with sackcloth:
13 And behold joy and gladness, slaying
oxen, and killing sheep, eating flesh, and drinking wine: let us eat and drink; for to morrow we
shall die.
14 And it was revealed in mine ears by the
LORD of hosts, Surely this iniquity shall not be
purged from you till ye die, saith the Lord GOD
of hosts.
15 ¶ Thus saith the Lord GOD of hosts, Go,
get thee unto this treasurer, *even* unto Sheb'na,
which *is* over the house, *and say,*
16 What hast thou here? and whom hast thou
here, that thou hast hewed thee out a sepulchre
here, *as* he that heweth him out a sepulchre on
high, *and* that graveth an habitation for himself
in a rock?
17 Behold, the LORD will carry thee away
with a mighty captivity, and will surely cover
thee.
18 He will surely violently turn and toss thee
like a ball into a large country: there shalt thou
die, and there the chariots of thy glory *shall be*
the shame of thy lord's house.
19 And I will drive thee from thy station, and
from thy state shall he pull thee down.
20 ¶ And it shall come to pass in that day,
that I will call my servant E-li'a-kim the son of
Hil-ki'ah:
21 And I will clothe him with thy robe, and
strengthen him with thy girdle, and I will commit thy government into his hand: and he shall
be a father to the inhabitants of Je-ru'sa-lem,
and to the house of Ju'dah.
22 And the key of the house of Da'vid will I

lay upon his shoulder; so he shall open, and none shall shut; and he shall shut, and none shall open.
23 And I will fasten him as a nail in a sure place; and he shall be for a glorious throne to his father's house.
24 And they shall hang upon him all the glory of his father's house, the offspring and the issue, all vessels of small quantity, from the vessels of cups, even to all the vessels of flagons.
25 In that day, saith the LORD of hosts, shall the nail that is fastened in the sure place be removed, and be cut down, and fall; and the burden that *was* upon it shall be cut off: for the LORD hath spoken *it*.

23 THE burden of Tyre. Howl, ye ships of Tar'shish; for it is laid waste, so that there is no house, no entering in: from the land of Chit'tim it is revealed to them.
2 Be still, ye inhabitants of the isle; thou whom the merchants of Zi'don, that pass over the sea, have replenished.
3 And by great waters the seed of Si'hor, the harvest of the river, *is* her revenue; and she is a mart of nations.
4 Be thou ashamed, O Zi'don: for the sea hath spoken, *even* the strength of the sea, saying, I travail not, nor bring forth children, neither do I nourish up young men, *nor* bring up virgins.
5 As at the report concerning E'gypt, *so* shall they be sorely pained at the report of Tyre.
6 Pass ye over to Tar'shish; howl, ye inhabitants of the isle.
7 *Is* this your joyous *city*, whose antiquity *is* of ancient days? her own feet shall carry her afar off to sojourn.
8 Who hath taken this counsel against Tyre, the crowning *city*, whose merchants *are* princes, whose traffickers *are* the honourable of the earth?
9 The LORD of hosts hath purposed it, to stain the pride of all glory, *and* to bring into contempt all the honourable of the earth.
10 Pass through thy land as a river, O daughter of Tar'shish: *there is* no more strength.
11 He stretched out his hand over the sea, he shook the kingdoms: the LORD hath given a commandment against the merchant *city*, to destroy the strong holds thereof.
12 And he said, Thou shalt no more rejoice, O thou oppressed virgin, daughter of Zi'don: arise, pass over to Chit'tim; there also shalt thou have no rest.
13 Behold the land of the Chal-de'ans; this people was not, *till* the As-syr'i-an founded it for them that dwell in the wilderness: they set up the towers thereof, they raised up the palaces thereof; *and* he brought it to ruin.
14 Howl, ye ships of Tar'shish: for your strength is laid waste.
15 And it shall come to pass in that day, that Tyre shall be forgotten seventy years, according to the days of one king: after the end of seventy years shall Tyre sing as an harlot.
16 Take an harp, go about the city, thou harlot that hast been forgotten; make sweet melody, sing many songs, that thou mayest be remembered.
17 ¶ And it shall come to pass after the end of seventy years, that the LORD will visit Tyre, and she shall turn to her hire, and shall commit fornication with all the kingdoms of the world upon the face of the earth.
18 And her merchandise and her hire shall be holiness to the LORD: it shall not be treasured nor laid up; for her merchandise shall be for them that dwell before the LORD, to eat sufficiently, and for durable clothing.

24 BEHOLD, the LORD maketh the earth empty, and maketh it waste, and turneth it upside down, and scattereth abroad the inhabitants thereof.
2 And it shall be, as with the people, so with the priest; as with the servant, so with his master; as with the maid, so with her mistress; as with the buyer, so with the seller; as with the lender, so with the borrower; as with the taker of usury, so with the giver of usury to him.
3 The land shall be utterly emptied, and utterly spoiled: for the LORD hath spoken this word.
4 The earth mourneth *and* fadeth away, the world languisheth *and* fadeth away, the haughty people of the earth do languish.
5 The earth also is defiled under the inhabitants thereof; because they have transgressed the laws, changed the ordinance, broken the everlasting covenant.
6 Therefore hath the curse devoured the earth, and they that dwell therein are desolate: therefore the inhabitants of the earth are burned, and few men left.
7 The new wine mourneth, the vine languisheth, all the merryhearted do sigh.
8 The mirth of tabrets ceaseth, the noise of them that rejoice endeth, the joy of the harp ceaseth.
9 They shall not drink wine with a song; strong drink shall be bitter to them that drink it.
10 The city of confusion is broken down: every house is shut up, that no man may come in.
11 *There is* a crying for wine in the streets; all joy is darkened, the mirth of the land is gone.
12 In the city is left desolation, and the gate is smitten with destruction.
13 ¶ When thus it shall be in the midst of the land among the people, *there shall be* as the shaking of an olive tree, *and* as the gleaning grapes when the vintage is done.
14 They shall lift up their voice, they shall sing for the majesty of the LORD, they shall cry aloud from the sea.
15 Wherefore glorify ye the LORD in the fires, *even* the name of the LORD God of Is'ra-el in the isles of the sea.
16 ¶ From the uttermost part of the earth have we heard songs, *even* glory to the righteous. But I said, My leanness, my leanness, woe unto me! the treacherous dealers have dealt treacherously; yea, the treacherous dealers have dealt very treacherously.
17 Fear, and the pit, and the snare, *are* upon thee, O inhabitant of the earth.
18 And it shall come to pass, *that* he who fleeth from the noise of the fear shall fall into the pit; and he that cometh up out of the midst of the pit shall be taken in the snare: for the windows from on high are open, and the foundations of the earth do shake.
19 The earth is utterly broken down, the earth is clean dissolved, the earth is moved exceedingly.
20 The earth shall reel to and fro like a drunkard, and shall be removed like a cottage; and the transgression thereof shall be heavy upon it; and it shall fall, and not rise again.
21 And it shall come to pass in that day, *that* the LORD shall punish the host of the high ones *that are* on high, and the kings of the earth upon the earth.

22 And they shall be gathered together, *as*
prisoners are gathered in the pit, and shall be
shut up in the prison, and after many days shall
they be visited.
23 Then the moon shall be confounded, and
the sun ashamed, when the LORD of hosts shall
reign in mount Zi'on, and in Je-ru'sa-lem, and
before his ancients gloriously.

25 O LORD, thou *art* my God; I will exalt
thee, I will praise thy name; for thou
hast done wonderful *things; thy* counsels of old
are faithfulness *and* truth.
2 For thou hast made of a city an heap; *of* a
defenced city a ruin: a palace of strangers to be
no city; it shall never be built.
3 Therefore shall the strong people glorify
thee, the city of the terrible nations shall fear
thee.
4 For thou hast been a strength to the poor, a
strength to the needy in his distress, a refuge
from the storm, a shadow from the heat, when
the blast of the terrible ones *is* as a storm
against the wall.
5 Thou shalt bring down the noise of strangers, as the heat in a dry place; *even* the heat
with the shadow of a cloud: the branch of the
terrible ones shall be brought low.
6 ¶ And in this mountain shall the LORD of
hosts make unto all people a feast of fat things,
a feast of wines on the lees, of fat things full of
marrow, of wines on the lees well refined.
7 And he will destroy in this mountain the
face of the covering cast over all people, and
the veil that is spread over all nations.
8 He will swallow up death in victory; and
the Lord GOD will wipe away tears from off all
faces; and the rebuke of his people shall he take
away from off all the earth: for the LORD hath
spoken *it*.
9 ¶ And it shall be said in that day, Lo, this *is*
our God; we have waited for him, and he will
save us: this *is* the LORD; we have waited for
him, we will be glad and rejoice in his salvation.
10 For in this mountain shall the hand of the
LORD rest, and Mo'ab shall be trodden down under him, even as straw is trodden down for the
dunghill.
11 And he shall spread forth his hands in the
midst of them, as he that swimmeth spreadeth
forth *his hands* to swim: and he shall bring
down their pride together with the spoils of
their hands.
12 And the fortress of the high fort of thy
walls shall he bring down, lay low, *and* bring to
the ground, *even* to the dust.

26 IN that day shall this song be sung in
the land of Ju'dah; We have a strong
city; salvation will *God* appoint *for* walls and
bulwarks.
2 Open ye the gates, that the righteous nation which keepeth the truth may enter in.
3 Thou wilt keep *him* in perfect peace, *whose*
mind *is* stayed *on thee:* because he trusteth in
thee.
4 Trust ye in the LORD for ever: for in the
LORD JE-HO'VAH *is* everlasting strength:
5 ¶ For he bringeth down them that dwell on
high; the lofty city, he layeth it low; he layeth it
low, *even* to the ground; he bringeth it *even* to
the dust.
6 The foot shall tread it down, *even* the feet
of the poor, *and* the steps of the needy.
7 The way of the just *is* uprightness: thou,
most upright, dost weigh the path of the just.
8 Yea, in the way of thy judgments, O LORD,
have we waited for thee; the desire of *our* soul
is to thy name, and to the remembrance of thee.
9 With my soul have I desired thee in the
night; yea, with my spirit within me will I seek
thee early: for when thy judgments *are* in the
earth, the inhabitants of the world will learn
righteousness.
10 Let favour be shewed to the wicked, *yet*
will he not learn righteousness: in the land of
uprightness will he deal unjustly, and will not
behold the majesty of the LORD.
11 LORD, *when* thy hand is lifted up, they will
not see: *but* they shall see, and be ashamed for
their envy at the people; yea, the fire of thine
enemies shall devour them.
12 ¶ LORD, thou wilt ordain peace for us: for
thou also hast wrought all our works in us.
13 O LORD our God, *other* lords beside thee
have had dominion over us: *but* by thee only
will we make mention of thy name.
14 *They are* dead, they shall not live; *they are*
deceased, they shall not rise: therefore hast
thou visited and destroyed them, and made all
their memory to perish.
15 Thou hast increased the nation, O LORD,
thou hast increased the nation: thou art glorified: thou hadst removed *it* far *unto* all the ends
of the earth.
16 LORD, in trouble have they visited thee,
they poured out a prayer *when* thy chastening
was upon them.
17 Like as a woman with child, *that* draweth
near the time of her delivery, is in pain, *and*
crieth out in her pangs; so have we been in thy
sight, O LORD.
18 We have been with child, we have been in
pain, we have as it were brought forth wind; we
have not wrought any deliverance in the earth;
neither have the inhabitants of the world fallen.
19 Thy dead *men* shall live, *together with* my
dead body shall they arise. Awake and sing, ye
that dwell in dust: for thy dew *is as* the dew of
herbs, and the earth shall cast out the dead.
20 ¶ Come, my people, enter thou into thy
chambers, and shut thy doors about thee: hide
thyself as it were for a little moment, until the
indignation be overpast.
21 For, behold, the LORD cometh out of his
place to punish the inhabitants of the earth for
their iniquity: the earth also shall disclose her
blood, and shall no more cover her slain.

27 IN that day the LORD with his sore and
great and strong sword shall punish leviathan the piercing serpent, even leviathan
that crooked serpent; and he shall slay the
dragon that *is* in the sea.
2 In that day sing ye unto her, A vineyard of
red wine.
3 I the LORD do keep it; I will water it every
moment: lest *any* hurt it, I will keep it night and
day.
4 Fury *is* not in me: who would set the briers
and thorns against me in battle? I would go
through them, I would burn them together.
5 Or let him take hold of my strength, *that* he
may make peace with me; *and* he shall make
peace with me.
6 He shall cause them that come of Ja'cob to
take root: Is'ra-el shall blossom and bud, and fill
the face of the world with fruit.
7 ¶ Hath he smitten him, as he smote those
that smote him? *or* is he slain according to the
slaughter of them that are slain by him?
8 In measure, when it shooteth forth, thou
wilt debate with it: he stayeth his rough wind in
the day of the east wind.

9 By this therefore shall the iniquity of Ja'cob be purged; and this *is* all the fruit to take away his sin; when he maketh all the stones of the altar as chalkstones that are beaten in sunder, the groves and images shall not stand up.

10 Yet the defenced city *shall be* desolate, *and* the habitation forsaken, and left like a wilderness: there shall the calf feed, and there shall he lie down, and consume the branches thereof.

11 When the boughs thereof are withered, they shall be broken off: the women come, *and* set them on fire: for it *is* a people of no understanding: therefore he that made them will not have mercy on them, and he that formed them will shew them no favour.

12 ¶ And it shall come to pass in that day, *that* the LORD shall beat off from the channel of the river unto the stream of E'gypt, and ye shall be gathered one by one, O ye children of Is'ra-el.

13 And it shall come to pass in that day, *that* the great trumpet shall be blown, and they shall come which were ready to perish in the land of As-syr'i-a, and the outcasts in the land of E'gypt, and shall worship the LORD in the holy mount at Je-ru'sa-lem.

28 WOE to the crown of pride, to the drunkards of E'phra-im, whose glorious beauty *is* a fading flower, which *are* on the head of the fat valleys of them that are overcome with wine!

2 Behold, the Lord hath a mighty and strong one, *which* as a tempest of hail *and* a destroying storm, as a flood of mighty waters overflowing, shall cast down to the earth with the hand.

3 The crown of pride, the drunkards of E'phra-im, shall be trodden under feet:

4 And the glorious beauty, which *is* on the head of the fat valley, shall be a fading flower, *and* as the hasty fruit before the summer; which *when* he that looketh upon it seeth, while it is yet in his hand he eateth it up.

5 ¶ In that day shall the LORD of hosts be for a crown of glory, and for a diadem of beauty, unto the residue of his people,

6 And for a spirit of judgment to him that sitteth in judgment, and for strength to them that turn the battle to the gate.

7 ¶ But they also have erred through wine, and through strong drink are out of the way; the priest and the prophet have erred through strong drink, they are swallowed up of wine, they are out of the way through strong drink; they err in vision, they stumble *in* judgment.

8 For all tables are full of vomit *and* filthiness, *so that there is* no place *clean.*

9 ¶ Whom shall he teach knowledge? and whom shall he make to understand doctrine? *them that are* weaned from the milk, *and* drawn from the breasts.

10 For precept *must be* upon precept, precept upon precept; line upon line, line upon line; here a little *and* there a little:

11 For with stammering lips and another tongue will he speak to this people.

12 To whom he said, This *is* the rest *wherewith* ye may cause the weary to rest; and this *is* the refreshing: yet they would not hear.

13 But the word of the LORD was unto them precept upon precept, precept upon precept; line upon line, line upon line; here a little, *and* there a little; that they might go, and fall backward, and be broken, and snared, and taken.

14 ¶ Wherefore hear the word of the LORD, ye scornful men, that rule this people which *is* in Je-ru'sa-lem.

15 Because ye have said, We have made a covenant with death, and with hell are we at agreement; when the overflowing scourge shall pass through, it shall not come unto us: for we have made lies our refuge, and under falsehood have we hid ourselves:

16 ¶ Therefore thus saith the Lord GOD, Behold, I lay in Zi'on for a foundation a stone, a tried stone, a precious corner *stone,* a sure foundation: he that believeth shall not make haste.

17 Judgment also will I lay to the line, and righteousness to the plummet: and the hail shall sweep away the refuge of lies, and the waters shall overflow the hiding place.

18 ¶ And your covenant with death shall be disannulled, and your agreement with hell shall not stand; when the overflowing scourge shall pass through, then ye shall be trodden down by it.

19 From the time that it goeth forth it shall take you: for morning by morning shall it pass over, by day and by night: and it shall be a vexation only *to* understand the report.

20 For the bed is shorter than that *a man* can stretch himself *on it:* and the covering narrower than that he can wrap himself *in it.*

21 For the LORD shall rise up as *in* mount Per'a-zim, he shall be wroth as *in* the valley of Gib'e-on, that he may do his work, his strange work; and bring to pass his act, his strange act.

22 Now therefore be ye not mockers, lest your bands be made strong: for I have heard from the Lord GOD of hosts a consumption, even determined upon the whole earth.

23 ¶ Give ye ear, and hear my voice; hearken, and hear my speech.

24 Doth the plowman plow all day to sow? doth he open and break the clods of his ground?

25 When he hath made plain the face thereof, doth he not cast abroad the fitches, and scatter the cummin, and cast in the principal wheat and the appointed barley and the rie in their place?

26 For his God doth instruct him to discretion, *and* doth teach him.

27 For the fitches are not threshed with a threshing instrument, neither is a cart wheel turned about upon the cummin; but the fitches are beaten out with a staff, and the cummin with a rod.

28 Bread *corn* is bruised; because he will not ever be threshing it, nor break *it with* the wheel of his cart, nor bruise it *with* his horsemen.

29 This also cometh forth from the LORD of hosts, *which* is wonderful in counsel, *and* excellent in working.

29 WOE to A'ri-el, to A'ri-el, the city *where* Da'vid dwelt! add ye year to year; let them kill sacrifices.

2 Yet I will distress A'ri-el, and there shall be heaviness and sorrow: and it shall be unto me as A'ri-el.

3 And I will camp against thee round about, and will lay siege against thee with a mount, and I will raise forts against thee.

4 And thou shalt be brought down, *and* shalt speak out of the ground, and thy speech shall be low out of the dust, and thy voice shall be, as of one that hath a familiar spirit, out of the ground, and thy speech shall whisper out of the dust.

5 Moreover the multitude of thy strangers shall be like small dust, and the multitude of the

terrible ones *shall be* as chaff that passeth away: yea, it shall be at an instant suddenly.

6 Thou shalt be visited of the LORD of hosts with thunder, and with earthquake, and great noise, with storm and tempest, and the flame of devouring fire.

7 ¶ And the multitude of all the nations that fight against A'ri-el, even all that fight against her and her munition, and that distress her, shall be as a dream of a night vision.

8 It shall even be as when an hungry *man* dreameth, and, behold, he eateth; but he awaketh, and his soul is empty: or as when a thirsty man dreameth, and, behold, he drinketh; but he awaketh, and, behold, *he is* faint, and his soul hath appetite: so shall the multitude of all the nations be, that fight against mount Zi'on.

9 ¶ Stay yourselves, and wonder; cry ye out, and cry: they are drunken, but not with wine; they stagger, but not with strong drink.

10 For the LORD hath poured out upon you the spirit of deep sleep, and hath closed your eyes: the prophets and your rulers, the seers hath he covered.

11 And the vision of all is become unto you as the words of a book that is sealed, which *men* deliver to one that is learned, saying, Read this, I pray thee: and he saith, I cannot; for it *is* sealed:

12 And the book is delivered to him that is not learned, saying, Read this, I pray thee: and he saith, I am not learned.

13 ¶ Wherefore the Lord said, Forasmuch as this people draw near *me* with their mouth, and with their lips do honour me, but have removed their heart far from me, and their fear toward me is taught by the precept of men:

14 Therefore, behold, I will proceed to do a marvellous work among this people, *even* a marvellous work and a wonder: for the wisdom of their wise *men* shall perish, and the understanding of their prudent *men* shall be hid.

15 Woe unto them that seek deep to hide their counsel from the LORD, and their works are in the dark, and they say, Who seeth us? and who knoweth us?

16 Surely your turning of things upside down shall be esteemed as the potter's clay: for shall the work say of him that made it, He made me not? or shall the thing framed say of him that framed it, He had no understanding?

17 *Is* it not yet a very little while, and Leb'anon shall be turned into a fruitful field, and the fruitful field shall be esteemed as a forest?

18 ¶ And in that day shall the deaf hear the words of the book, and the eyes of the blind shall see out of obscurity, and out of darkness.

19 The meek also shall increase *their* joy in the LORD, and the poor among men shall rejoice in the Holy One of Is'ra-el.

20 For the terrible one is brought to nought, and the scorner is consumed, and all that watch for iniquity are cut off:

21 That make a man an offender for a word, and lay a snare for him that reproveth in the gate, and turn aside the just for a thing of nought.

22 Therefore thus saith the LORD, who redeemed A'bra-ham, concerning the house of Ja'cob, Ja'cob shall not now be ashamed, neither shall his face now wax pale.

23 But when he seeth his children, the work of mine hands, in the midst of him, they shall sanctify my name, and sanctify the Holy One of Ja'cob, and shall fear the God of Is'ra-el.

24 They also that erred in spirit shall come to understanding, and they that murmured shall learn doctrine.

30 WOE to the rebellious children, saith the LORD, that take counsel, but not of me; and that cover with a covering, but not of my spirit, that they may add sin to sin:

2 That walk to go down into E'gypt, and have not asked at my mouth; to strengthen themselves in the strength of Pha'raoh, and to trust in the shadow of E'gypt!

3 Therefore shall the strength of Pha'raoh be your shame, and the trust in the shadow of E'gypt *your* confusion.

4 For his princes were at Zo'an, and his ambassadors came to Ha'nes.

5 They were all ashamed of a people *that* could not profit them, nor be an help nor profit, but a shame, and also a reproach.

6 The burden of the beasts of the south: into the land of trouble and anguish, from whence *come* the young and old lion, the viper and fiery flying serpent, they will carry their riches upon the shoulders of young asses, and their treasures upon the bunches of camels, to a people *that* shall not profit *them*.

7 For the E-gyp'tians shall help in vain, and to no purpose: therefore have I cried concerning this, Their strength *is* to sit still.

8 ¶ Now go, write it before them in a table, and note it in a book, that it may be for the time to come for ever and ever:

9 That this *is* a rebellious people, lying children, children *that* will not hear the law of the LORD:

10 Which say to the seers, See not; and to the prophets, Prophesy not unto us right things, speak unto us smooth things, prophesy deceits:

11 Get you out of the way, turn aside out of the path, cause the Holy One of Is'ra-el to cease from before us.

12 Wherefore thus saith the Holy One of Is'ra-el, Because ye despise this word, and trust in oppression and perverseness, and stay thereon:

13 Therefore this iniquity shall be to you as a breach ready to fall, swelling out in a high wall, whose breaking cometh suddenly at an instant.

14 And he shall break it as the breaking of the potters' vessel that is broken in pieces; he shall not spare: so that there shall not be found in the bursting of it a sherd to take fire from the hearth, or to take water *withal* out of the pit.

15 For thus saith the Lord GOD, the Holy One of Is'ra-el; In returning and rest shall ye be saved; in quietness and in confidence shall be your strength: and ye would not.

16 But ye said, No; for we will flee upon horses; therefore shall ye flee: and, We will ride upon the swift; therefore shall they that pursue you be swift.

17 One thousand *shall flee* at the rebuke of one; at the rebuke of five shall ye flee: till ye be left as a beacon upon the top of a mountain, and as an ensign on an hill.

18 ¶ And therefore will the LORD wait, that he may be gracious unto you, and therefore will he be exalted, that he may have mercy upon you: for the LORD *is* a God of judgment: blessed *are* all they that wait for him.

19 For the people shall dwell in Zi'on at Jeru'sa-lem: thou shalt weep no more: he will be very gracious unto thee at the voice of thy cry; when he shall hear it, he will answer thee.

20 And *though* the LORD give you the bread of adversity, and the water of affliction, yet shall not thy teachers be removed into a corner any more, but thine eyes shall see thy teachers:

21 And thine ears shall hear a word behind
thee, saying, This *is* the way, walk ye in it, when
ye turn to the right hand, and when ye turn to
the left.
22 Ye shall defile also the covering of thy
graven images of silver, and the ornament of
thy molten images of gold: thou shalt cast them
away as a menstruous cloth; thou shalt say unto
it, Get thee hence.
23 Then shall he give the rain of thy seed,
that thou shalt sow the ground withal; and
bread of the increase of the earth, and it shall be
fat and plenteous: in that day shall thy cattle
feed in large pastures.
24 The oxen likewise and the young asses
that ear the ground shall eat clean provender,
which hath been winnowed with the shovel and
with the fan.
25 And there shall be upon every high mountain, and upon every high hill, rivers *and*
streams of waters in the day of the great
slaughter, when the towers fall.
26 Moreover the light of the moon shall be as
the light of the sun, and the light of the sun shall
be sevenfold, as the light of seven days, in the
day that the LORD bindeth up the breach of his
people, and healeth the stroke of their wound.
27 ¶ Behold, the name of the LORD cometh
from far, burning *with* his anger, and the burden *therof is* heavy: his lips are full of indignation, and his tongue as a devouring fire:
28 And his breath, as an overflowing stream,
shall reach to the midst of the neck, to sift the
nations with the sieve of vanity: and *there shall
be* a bridle in the jaws of the people, causing
them to err.
29 Ye shall have a song, as in the night *when*
a holy solemnity is kept; and gladness of heart,
as when one goeth with a pipe to come into the
mountain of the LORD, to the mighty One of Is′-
ra-el.
30 And the LORD shall cause his glorious
voice to be heard, and shall shew the lighting
down of his arm, with the indignation of *his* anger, and *with* the flame of a devouring fire, *with*
scattering, and tempest, and hailstones.
31 For through the voice of the LORD shalt
the As-syr′i-an be beaten down, *which* smote
with a rod.
32 And *in* every place where the grounded
staff shall pass, which the LORD shall lay upon
him, *it* shall be with tabrets and harps: and in
battles of shaking will he fight with it.
33 For To′phet *is* ordained of old; yea, for the
king it is prepared; he hath made *it* deep *and*
large: the pile thereof *is* fire and much wood;
the breath of the LORD, like a stream of brimstone, doth kindle it.

31

WOE to them that go down to E′gypt for
help; and stay on horses, and trust in
chariots, because *they are* many; and in horsemen, because they are very strong; but they
look not unto the Holy One of Is′ra-el, neither
seek the LORD!
2 Yet he also *is* wise, and will bring evil, and
will not call back his words: but will arise
against the house of the evildoers, and against
the help of them that work iniquity.
3 Now the E-gyp′tians *are* men, and not God;
and their horses flesh, and not spirit. When the
LORD shall stretch out his hand, both he that
helpeth shall fall, and he that is holpen shall fall
down, and they all shall fail together.
4 For thus hath the LORD spoken unto me,
Like as the lion and the young lion roaring on
his prey, when a multitude of shepherds is
called forth against him, *he* will not be afraid of
their voice, nor abase himself for the noise of
them: so shall the LORD of hosts come down to
fight for mount Zi′on, and for the hill thereof.
5 As birds flying, so will the LORD of hosts
defend Je-ru′sa-lem; defending also he will deliver *it; and* passing over he will preserve *it.*
6 ¶ Turn ye unto *him from* whom the children of Is′ra-el have deeply revolted.
7 For in that day every man shall cast away
his idols of silver, and his idols of gold, which
your own hands have made unto you *for* a sin.
8 ¶ Then shall the As-syr′i-an fall with the
sword, not of a mighty man; and the sword, not
of a mean man, shall devour him: but he shall
flee from the sword, and his young men shall be
discomfited.
9 And he shall pass over to his strong hold
for fear, and his princes shall be afraid of the
ensign, saith the LORD, whose fire *is* in Zi′on,
and his furnace in Je-ru′sa-lem.

32

BEHOLD, a king shall reign in righteousness, and princes shall rule in judgment.
2 And a man shall be as an hiding place from
the wind, and a covert from the tempest; as rivers of water in a dry place, as the shadow of a
great rock in a weary land.
3 And the eyes of them that see shall not be
dim, and the ears of them that hear shall heark-
en.
4 The heart also of the rash shall understand
knowledge, and the tongue of the stammerers
shall be ready to speak plainly.
5 The vile person shall be no more called liberal, nor the churl said *to be* bountiful.
6 For the vile person will speak villany, and
his heart will work iniquity, to practise hypocrisy, and to utter error against the LORD, to
make empty the soul of the hungry, and he will
cause the drink of the thirsty to fail.
7 The instruments also of the churl *are* evil:
he deviseth wicked devices to destroy the poor
with lying words, even when the needy speaketh right.
8 But the liberal deviseth liberal things; and
by liberal things shall he stand.
9 ¶ Rise up, ye women that are at ease; hear
my voice, ye careless daughters; give ear unto
my speech.
10 Many days and years shall ye be troubled,
ye careless women: for the vintage shall fail,
the gathering shall not come.
11 Tremble, ye women that are at ease; be
troubled, ye careless ones: strip you, and make
you bare, and gird *sackcloth* upon *your* loins.
12 They shall lament for the teats, for the
pleasant fields, for the fruitful vine.
13 Upon the land of my people shall come up
thorns *and* briers; yea, upon all the houses of
joy *in* the joyous city:
14 Because the palaces shall be forsaken; the
multitude of the city shall be left; the forts and
towers shall be for dens for ever, a joy of wild
asses, a pasture of flocks;
15 Until the spirit be poured upon us from on
high, and the wilderness be a fruitful field, and
the fruitful field be counted for a forest.
16 Then judgment shall dwell in the wilderness, and righteousness remain in the fruitful
field.
17 And the work of righteousness shall be
peace; and the effect of righteousness quietness
and assurance for ever.
18 And my people shall dwell in a peaceable

habitation, and in sure dwellings, and in quiet resting places;

19 When it shall hail, coming down on the forest; and the city shall be low in a low place.

20 Blessed *are* ye that sow beside all waters, that send forth *thither* the feet of the ox and the ass.

33 WOE to thee that spoilest, and thou *wast* not spoiled; and dealest treacherously, and they dealt not treacherously with thee! when thou shalt cease to spoil, thou shalt be spoiled; *and* when thou shalt make an end to deal treacherously, they shall deal treacherously with thee.

2 O LORD, be gracious unto us; we have waited for thee: be thou their arm every morning, our salvation also in the time of trouble.

3 At the noise of the tumult the people fled; at the lifting up of thyself the nations were scattered.

4 And your spoil shall be gathered *like* the gathering of the caterpiller: as the running to and fro of locusts shall he run upon them.

5 The LORD is exalted; for he dwelleth on high: he hath filled Zi'on with judgment and righteousness.

6 And wisdom and knowledge shall be the stability of thy times, *and* strength of salvation: the fear of the LORD *is* his treasure.

7 Behold, their valiant ones shall cry without: the ambassadors of peace shall weep bitterly.

8 The highways lie waste, the wayfaring man ceaseth: he hath broken the covenant, he hath despised the cities, he regardeth no man.

9 The earth mourneth *and* languisheth: Leb'-a-non is ashamed *and* hewn down: Shar'on is like a wilderness; and Ba'shan and Car'mel shake off *their fruits*.

10 Now will I rise, saith the LORD; now will I be exalted; now will I lift up myself.

11 Ye shall conceive chaff, ye shall bring forth stubble: your breath, *as* fire, shall devour you.

12 And the people shall be *as* the burnings of lime: *as* thorns cut up shall they be burned in the fire.

13 ¶ Hear, ye *that are* far off, what I have done; and, ye *that are* near, acknowledge my might.

14 The sinners in Zi'on are afraid; fearfulness hath surprised the hypocrites. Who among us shall dwell with the devouring fire? who among us shall dwell with everlasting burnings?

15 He that walketh righteously, and speaketh uprightly; he that despiseth the gain of oppressions, that shaketh his hands from holding of bribes, that stoppeth his ears from hearing of blood, and shutteth his eyes from seeing evil;

16 He shall dwell on high: his place of defence *shall be* the munitions of rocks: bread shall be given him; his waters *shall be* sure.

17 Thine eyes shall see the king in his beauty: they shall behold the land that is very far off.

18 Thine heart shall meditate terror. Where *is* the scribe? where *is* the receiver? where *is* he that counted the towers?

19 Thou shalt not see a fierce people, a people of a deeper speech than thou canst perceive; of a stammering tongue, *that thou canst* not understand.

20 Look upon Zi'on, the city of our solemnities: thine eyes shall see Je-ru'sa-lem a quiet habitation, a tabernacle *that* shall not be taken down; not one of the stakes thereof shall ever be removed, neither shall any of the cords thereof be broken.

21 But there the glorious LORD *will be* unto us a place of broad rivers *and* streams; wherein shall go no galley with oars, neither shall gallant ship pass thereby.

22 For the LORD *is* our judge, the LORD *is* our lawgiver, the LORD *is* our king; he will save us.

23 Thy tacklings are loosed; they could not well strengthen their mast, they could not spread the sail: then is the prey of a great spoil divided; the lame take the prey.

24 And the inhabitant shall not say, I am sick: the people that dwell therein *shall be* forgiven *their* iniquity.

34 COME near, ye nations, to hear; and hearken, ye people: let the earth hear, and all that is therein; the world, and all things that come forth of it.

2 For the indignation of the LORD *is* upon all nations, and *his* fury upon all their armies: he hath utterly destroyed them, he hath delivered them to the slaughter.

3 Their slain also shall be cast out, and their stink shall come up out of their carcases, and the mountains shall be melted with their blood.

4 And all the host of heaven shall be dissolved, and the heavens shall be rolled together as a scroll: and all their host shall fall down, as the leaf falleth off from the vine, and as a falling *fig* from the fig tree.

5 For my sword shall be bathed in heaven: behold, it shall come down upon I-du-me'a, and upon the people of my curse, to judgment.

6 The sword of the LORD is filled with blood, it is made fat with fatness, *and* with the blood of lambs and goats, with the fat of the kidneys of rams: for the LORD hath a sacrifice in Boz'-rah, and a great slaughter in the land of I-du-me'a.

7 And the unicorns shall come down with them, and the bullocks with the bulls; and their land shall be soaked with blood, and their dust made fat with fatness.

8 For *it is* the day of the LORD's vengeance, *and* the year of recompences for the controversy of Zi'on.

9 And the streams thereof shall be turned into pitch, and the dust thereof into brimstone, and the land thereof shall become burning pitch.

10 It shall not be quenched night nor day; the smoke thereof shall go up for ever: from generation to generation it shall lie waste; none shall pass through it for ever and ever.

11 ¶ But the cormorant and the bittern shall possess it; the owl also and the raven shall dwell in it: and he shall stretch out upon it the line of confusion, and the stones of emptiness.

12 They shall call the nobles thereof to the kingdom, but none *shall be* there, and all her princes shall be nothing.

13 And thorns shall come up in her palaces, nettles and brambles in the fortresses thereof: and it shall be an habitation of dragons, *and* a court for owls.

14 The wild beasts of the desert shall also meet with the wild beasts of the island, and the satyr shall cry to his fellow; the screech owl also shall rest there, and find for herself a place of rest.

15 There shall the great owl make her nest, and lay, and hatch, and gather under her shadow: there shall the vultures also be gathered, every one with her mate.

16 ¶ Seek ye out of the book of the LORD, and read: no one of these shall fail, none shall want her mate: for my mouth it hath com-

manded, and his spirit it hath gathered them.
17 And he hath cast the lot for them, and his
hand hath divided it unto them by line: they
shall possess it for ever, from generation to generation shall they dwell therein.

35 THE wilderness and the solitary place
shall be glad for them; and the desert
shall rejoice, and blossom as the rose.
2 It shall blossom abundantly, and rejoice
even with joy and singing: the glory of Leb′a-non shall be given unto it, the excellency of
Car′mel and Shar′on, they shall see the glory of
the LORD, *and* the excellency of our God.
3 ¶ Strengthen ye the weak hands, and confirm the feeble knees.
4 Say to them *that are* of a fearful heart, Be
strong, fear not: behold, your God will come
with vengeance, *even* God *with* a recompence;
he will come and save you.
5 Then the eyes of the blind shall be opened,
and the ears of the deaf shall be unstopped.
6 Then shall the lame *man* leap as an hart,
and the tongue of the dumb sing: for in the wilderness shall waters break out, and streams in
the desert.
7 And the parched ground shall become a
pool, and the thirsty land springs of water: in
the habitation of dragons, where each lay, *shall
be* grass with reeds and rushes.
8 And an highway shall be there, and a way,
and it shall be called The way of holiness; the
unclean shall not pass over it; but it *shall be* for
those: the wayfaring men, though fools, shall
not err *therein.*
9 No lion shall be there, nor *any* ravenous
beast shall go up thereon, it shall not be found
there; but the redeemed shall walk *there:*
10 And the ransomed of the LORD shall return, and come to Zi′on with songs and everlasting joy upon their heads: they shall obtain
joy and gladness, and sorrow and sighing shall
flee away.

36 NOW it came to pass in the fourteenth
year of king Hez-e-ki′ah, *that* Sen-nach′e-rib king of As-syr′i-a came up against all the
defenced cities of Ju′dah, and took them.
2 And the king of As-syr′i-a sent Rab′sha-keh
from La′chish to Je-ru′sa-lem unto king Hez-e-ki′ah with a great army. And he stood by the
conduit of the upper pool in the highway of the
fuller's field.
3 Then came forth unto him E-li′a-kim, Hil-ki′ah's son, which was over the house, and
Sheb′na the scribe, and Jo′ah, A′saph's son, the
recorder.
4 ¶ And Rab′sha-keh said unto them, Say ye
now to Hez-e-ki′ah, Thus saith the great king,
the king of As-syr′i-a, What confidence *is* this
wherein thou trustest?
5 I say, *sayest thou,* (but *they are but* vain
words) *I have* counsel and strength for war:
now on whom dost thou trust, that thou rebellest against me?
6 Lo, thou trustest in the staff of this broken
reed, on E′gypt; whereon if a man lean, it will
go into his hand, and pierce it: so *is* Pha′raoh
king of E′gypt to all that trust in him.
7 But if thou say to me, We trust in the LORD
our God: *is it* not he, whose high places and
whose altars Hez-e-ki′ah hath taken away, and
said to Ju′dah and to Je-ru′sa-lem, Ye shall worship before this altar?
8 Now therefore give pledges, I pray thee, to
my master the king of As-syr′i-a, and I will give
thee two thousand horses, if thou be able on thy
part to set riders upon them.
9 How then wilt thou turn away the face of
one captain of the least of my master's servants, and put thy trust on E′gypt for chariots
and for horsemen?
10 And am I now come up without the LORD
against this land to destroy it? the LORD said
unto me, Go up against this land, and destroy it.
11 ¶ Then said E-li′a-ki′m and Sheb′na and
Jo′ah unto Rab′sha-keh, Speak, I pray thee,
unto thy servants in the Syr′i-an language; for
we understand *it:* and speak not to us in the
Jews' language, in the ears of the people that
are on the wall.
12 ¶ But Rab′sha-keh said, Hath my master
sent me to thy master and to thee to speak
these words? *hath he* not *sent me* to the men
that sit upon the wall, that they may eat their
own dung, and drink their own piss with you?
13 Then Rab′sha-keh stood, and cried with a
loud voice in the Jews' language, and said, Hear
ye the words of the great king, the king of As-syr′i-a.
14 Thus saith the king, Let not Hez-e-ki′ah
deceive you: for he shall not be able to deliver
you.
15 Neither let Hez-e-ki′ah make you trust in
the LORD, saying, The LORD will surely deliver
us: this city shall not be delivered into the hand
of the king of As-syr′i-a.
16 Hearken not to Hez-e-ki′ah: for thus saith
the king of As-syr′i-a, Make *an agreement* with
me *by* a present, and come out to me: and eat ye
every one of his vine, and every one of his fig
tree, and drink ye every one the waters of his
own cistern;
17 Until I come and take you away to a land
like your own land, a land of corn and wine, a
land of bread and vineyards.
18 *Beware* lest Hez-e-ki′ah persuade you,
saying, The LORD will deliver us. Hath any of
the gods of the nations delivered his land out of
the hand of the king of As-syr′i-a?
19 Where *are* the gods of Ha′math and Ar-phad? where *are* the gods of Seph-ar-va′im? and
have they delivered Sa-ma′ri-a out of my hand?
20 Who *are they* among all the gods of these
lands, that have delivered their land out of my
hand, that the LORD should deliver Je-ru′sa-lem
out of my hand?
21 But they held their peace, and answered
him not a word: for the king's commandment
was, saying, Answer him not.
22 ¶ Then came E-li′a-kim, the son of Hil-ki′ah, that *was* over the household, and Sheb′na
the scribe, and Jo′ah, the son of A′saph, the recorder to Hez-e-ki′ah with *their* clothes rent,
and told him the words of Rab′sha-keh.

37 AND it came to pass, when king Hez-e-ki′ah heard *it,* that he rent his clothes,
and covered himself with sackcloth, and went
into the house of the LORD.
2 And he sent E-li′a-kim, who *was* over the
household, and Sheb′na the scribe, and the elders of the priests covered with sackcloth, unto
I-sa′iah the prophet the son of A′moz.
3 And they said unto him, Thus saith Hez-e-ki′ah, This day *is* a day of trouble, and of rebuke, and of blasphemy: for the children are
come to the birth, and *there is* not strength to
bring forth.
4 It may be the LORD thy God will hear the
words of Rab′sha-keh, whom the king of As-syr′i-a his master hath sent to reproach the living God, and will reprove the words which the

LORD thy God hath heard: wherefore lift up *thy*
prayer for the remnant that is left.
5 So the servants of king Hez-e-ki'ah came to
I-sa'iah.
6 ¶ And I-sa'iah said unto them, Thus shall
ye say unto your master, Thus saith the LORD,
Be not afraid of the words that thou hast heard,
wherewith the servants of the king of As-syr'i-a
have blasphemed me.
7 Behold, I will send a blast upon him, and he
shall hear a rumour, and return to his own land;
and I will cause him to fall by the sword in his
own land.
8 ¶ So Rab'sha-keh returned, and found the
king of As-syr'i-a warring against Lib'nah: for
he had heard that he was departed from La'-
chish.
9 And he heard say concerning Tir'ha-kah
king of E-thi-o'pi-a, He is come forth to make
war with thee. And when he heard *it*, he sent
messengers to Hez-e-ki'ah, saying,
10 Thus shall ye speak to Hez-e-ki'ah king of
Ju'dah, saying, Let not thy God, in whom thou
trustest, deceive thee, saying, Je-ru'sa-lem shall
not be given into the hand of the king of As-
syr'i-a.
11 Behold, thou hast heard what the kings of
As-syr'i-a have done to all lands by destroying
them utterly; and shalt thou be delivered?
12 Have the gods of the nations delivered
them which my fathers have destroyed, *as* Go'-
zan, and Ha'ran, and Re'zeph, and the children
of E'den which *were* in Te-las'sar?
13 Where *is* the king of Ha'math, and the
king of Ar'phad, and the king of the city of
Seph-ar-va'im, He'na, and I'vah?
14 ¶ And Hez-e-ki'ah received the letter
from the hand of the messengers, and read it:
and Hez-e-ki'ah went up unto the house of the
LORD, and spread it before the LORD.
15 And Hez-e-ki'ah prayed unto the LORD,
saying,
16 O LORD of hosts, God of Is'ra-el, that
dwellest *between* the cherubims, thou *art* the
God, *even* thou alone, of all the kingdoms of the
earth: thou hast made heaven and earth.
17 Incline thine ear, O LORD, and hear; open
thine eyes, O LORD, and see: and hear all the
words of Sen-nach'e-rib, which hath sent to reproach the living God.
18 Of a truth, LORD, the kings of As-syr'i-a
have laid waste all the nations, and their countries,
19 And have cast their gods into the fire: for
they *were* no gods, but the work of men's
hands, wood and stone: therefore they have destroyed them.
20 Now therefore, O LORD our God, save us
from his hand, that all the kingdoms of the
earth may know that thou *art* the LORD, *even*
thou only.
21 ¶ Then I-sa'iah the son of A'moz sent
unto Hez-e-ki'ah, saying, Thus saith the LORD
God of Is'ra-el, Whereas thou hast prayed to me
against Sen-nach'e-rib king of As-syr'i-a:
22 This *is* the word which the LORD hath spoken concerning him; The virgin, the daughter of
Zi'on, hath despised thee, *and* laughed thee to
scorn; the daughter of Je-ru'sa-lem hath shaken
her head at thee.
23 Whom hast thou reproached and blasphemed? and against whom hast thou exalted
thy voice, and lifted up thine eyes on high? *even*
against the Holy One of Is'ra-el.
24 By thy servants hast thou reproached the
Lord, and hast said, By the multitude of my
chariots am I come up to the height of the
mountains, to the sides of Leb'a-non; and I will
cut down the tall cedars thereof, *and* the choice
fir trees thereof: and I will enter into the height
of his border, *and* the forest of his Car'mel.
25 I have digged, and drunk water; and with
the sole of my feet have I dried up all the rivers
of the besieged places.
26 Hast thou not heard long ago, *how* I have
done it; *and* of ancient times, that I have
formed it? now have I brought it to pass, that
thou shouldest be to lay waste defenced cities
into ruinous heaps.
27 Therefore their inhabitants *were* of small
power, they were dismayed and confounded:
they were *as* the grass of the field, and *as* the
green herb, *as* the grass on the house tops, and
as corn blasted before it be grown up.
28 But I know thy abode, and thy going out,
and thy coming in, and thy rage against me.
29 Because thy rage against me, and thy tumult, is come up into mine ears, therefore will I
put my hook in thy nose, and my bridle in thy
lips, and I will turn thee back by the way by
which thou camest.
30 And this *shall be* a sign unto thee, Ye shall
eat *this* year such as groweth of itself; and the
second year that which springeth of the same:
and in the third year sow ye, and reap, and
plant vineyards, and eat the fruit thereof.
31 And the remnant that is escaped of the
house of Ju'dah shall again take root downward, and bear fruit upward:
32 For out of Je-ru'sa-lem shall go forth a
remnant, and they that escape out of mount Zi'-
on: the zeal of the LORD of hosts shall do this.
33 Therefore thus saith the LORD concerning
the king of As-syr'i-a, He shall not come into
this city, nor shoot an arrow there, nor come
before it with shields, nor cast a bank against it.
34 By the way that he came, by the same
shall he return, and shall not come into this city,
saith the LORD.
35 For I will defend this city to save it for
mine own sake, and for my servant Da'vid's
sake.
36 Then the angel of the LORD went forth,
and smote in the camp of the As-syr'i-ans a
hundred and fourscore and five thousand: and
when they arose early in the morning, behold,
they *were* all dead corpses.
37 ¶ So Sen-nach'e-rib king of As-syr'i-a departed, and went and returned, and dwelt at
Nin'e-veh.
38 And it came to pass, as he was worshipping in the house of Nis'roch his god, that A-
dram'me-lech and Sha-re'zer his sons smote
him with the sword; and they escaped into the
land of Ar-me'ni-a: and E'sar-had'don his son
reigned in his stead.

38 IN those days was Hez-e-ki'ah sick unto
death. And I-sa'iah the prophet the son
of A'moz came unto him, and said unto him,
Thus saith the LORD, Set thine house in order:
for thou shalt die, and not live.
2 Then Hez-e-ki'ah turned his face toward
the wall, and prayed unto the LORD,
3 And said, Remember now, O LORD, I beseech thee, how I have walked before thee in
truth and with a perfect heart, and have done
that which is good in thy sight. And Hez-e-ki'ah
wept sore.
4 ¶ Then came the word of the LORD to I-
sa'iah, saying,
5 Go, and say to Hez-e-ki'ah, Thus saith the
LORD, the God of Da'vid thy father, I have heard

thy prayer, I have seen thy tears: behold, I will add unto thy days fifteen years.

6 And I will deliver thee and this city out of the hand of the king of As-syr'i-a: and I will defend this city.

7 And this *shall be* a sign unto thee from the LORD, that the LORD will do this thing that he hath spoken;

8 Behold, I will bring again the shadow of the degrees, which is gone down in the sun dial of A'haz, ten degrees backward. So the sun returned ten degrees, by which degrees it was gone down.

9 ¶ The writing of Hez-e-ki'ah king of Ju'dah, when he had been sick, and was recovered of his sickness:

10 I said in the cutting off of my days, I shall go to the gates of the grave: I am deprived of the residue of my years.

11 I said, I shall not see the LORD, *even* the LORD, in the land of the living: I shall behold man no more with the inhabitants of the world.

12 Mine age is departed, and is removed from me as a shepherd's tent: I have cut off like a weaver my life: he will cut me off with pining sickness: from day *even* to night wilt thou make an end of me.

13 I reckoned till morning, *that*, as a lion, so will he break all my bones: from day *even* to night wilt thou make an end of me.

14 Like a crane *or* a swallow, so did I chatter: I did mourn as a dove: mine eyes fail *with looking* upward: O LORD, I am oppressed; undertake for me.

15 What shall I say? he hath both spoken unto me, and himself hath done *it*; I shall go softly all my years in the bitterness of my soul.

16 O Lord, by these *things men* live, and in all these *things is* the life of my spirit: so wilt thou recover me, and make me to live.

17 Behold, for peace I had great bitterness: but thou hast in love to my soul *delivered it* from the pit of corruption: for thou hast cast all my sins behind thy back.

18 For the grave cannot praise thee, death can *not* celebrate thee: they that go down into the pit cannot hope for thy truth.

19 The living, the living, he shall praise thee, as I *do* this day: the father to the children shall make known thy truth.

20 The LORD *was ready* to save me: therefore we will sing my songs to the stringed instruments all the days of our life in the house of the LORD.

21 For I-sa'iah had said, Let them take a lump of figs, and lay *it* for a plaister upon the boil, and he shall recover.

22 Hez-e-ki'ah also had said What *is* the sign that I shall go up to the house of the LORD?

39 AT that time Me-ro'dach–bal'a-dan, the son of Bal'a-dan, king of Bab'y-lon, sent letters and a present to Hez-e-ki'ah: for he had heard that he had been sick, and was recovered.

2 And Hez-e-ki'ah was glad of them, and shewed them the house of his precious things, the silver, and the gold, and the spices, and the precious ointment, and all the house of his armour, and all that was found in his treasures: there was nothing in his house, nor in all his dominion, that Hez-e-ki'ah shewed them not.

3 ¶ Then came I-sa'iah the prophet unto king Hez-e-ki'ah, and said unto him, What said these men? and from whence came they unto thee? And Hez-e-ki'ah said, They are come from a far country unto me, *even* from Bab'y-lon.

4 Then said he, What have they seen in thine house? And Hez-e-ki'ah answered, All that *is* in mine house have they seen: there is nothing among my treasures that I have not shewed them.

5 Then said I-sa'iah to Hez-e-ki'ah, Hear the word of the LORD of hosts:

6 Behold, the days come, that all that *is* in thine house, and *that* which thy fathers have laid up in store until this day, shall be carried to Bab'y-lon: nothing shall be left, saith the LORD.

7 And of thy sons that shall issue from thee, which thou shalt beget, shall they take away; and they shall be eunuchs in the palace of the king of Bab'y-lon.

8 Then said Hez-e-ki'ah to I-sa'iah, Good *is* the word of the LORD which thou hast spoken. He said moreover, For there shall be peace and truth in my days.

40 COMFORT ye, comfort ye my people, saith your God.

2 Speak ye comfortably to Je-ru'sa-lem, and cry unto her, that her warfare is accomplished, that her iniquity is pardoned: for she hath received of the LORD's hand double for all her sins.

3 ¶ The voice of him that crieth in the wilderness, Prepare ye the way of the LORD, make straight in the desert a highway for our God.

4 Every valley shall be exalted, and every mountain and hill shall be made low: and the crooked shall be made straight, and the rough places plain:

5 And the glory of the LORD shall be revealed, and all flesh shall see *it* together: for the mouth of the LORD hath spoken *it*.

6 The voice said, Cry. And he said, What shall I cry? All flesh *is* grass, and all the goodliness thereof *is* as the flower of the field:

7 The grass withereth, the flower fadeth: because the spirit of the LORD bloweth upon it: surely the people *is* grass.

8 The grass withereth, the flower fadeth: but the word of our God shall stand for ever.

9 ¶ O Zi'on, that bringest good tidings, get thee up into the high mountain; O Je-ru'sa-lem, that bringest good tidings, lift up thy voice with strength; lift *it* up, be not afraid; say unto the cities of Ju'dah, Behold your God!

10 Behold, the Lord GOD will come with strong *hand*, and his arm shall rule for him: behold, his reward *is* with him, and his work before him.

11 He shall feed his flock like a shepherd: he shall gather the lambs with his arm, and carry *them* in his bosom, *and* shall gently lead those that are with young.

12 ¶ Who hath measured the waters in the hollow of his hand, and meted out heaven with the span, and comprehended the dust of the earth in a measure, and weighed the mountains in scales, and the hills in a balance?

13 Who hath directed the Spirit of the LORD, or *being* his counsellor hath taught him?

14 With whom took he counsel, and *who* instructed him, and taught him in the path of judgment, and taught him knowledge, and shewed to him the way of understanding?

15 Behold, the nations *are* as a drop of a bucket, and are counted as the small dust of the balance: behold, he taketh up the isles as a very little thing.

16 And Leb'a-non *is* not sufficient to burn, nor the beasts thereof sufficient for a burnt offering.

17 All nations before him *are* as nothing; and

they are counted to him less than nothing, and
vanity.
18 ¶ To whom then will ye liken God? or
what likeness will ye compare unto him?
19 The workman melteth a graven image,
and the goldsmith spreadeth it over with gold,
and casteth silver chains.
20 He that *is* so impoverished that he hath no
oblation chooseth a tree *that* will not rot; he
seeketh unto him a cunning workman to prepare a graven image, *that* shall not be moved.
21 Have ye not known? have ye not heard?
hath it not been told you from the beginning?
have ye not understood from the foundations of
the earth?
22 *It is* he that sitteth upon the circle of the
earth, and the inhabitants thereof *are* as grasshoppers; that stretcheth out the heavens as a
curtain, and spreadeth them out as a tent to
dwell in:
23 That bringeth the princes to nothing; he
maketh the judges of the earth as vanity.
24 Yea, they shall not be planted; yea, they
shall not be sown: yea, their stock shall not take
root in the earth: and he shall also blow upon
them, and they shall wither, and the whirlwind
shall take them away as stubble.
25 To whom then will ye liken me, or shall I
be equal? saith the Holy One.
26 Lift up your eyes on high, and behold who
hath created these *things,* that bringeth out
their host by number: he calleth them all by
names by the greatness of his might, for that *he
is* strong in power; not one faileth.
27 Why sayest thou, O Ja'cob, and speakest,
O Is'ra-el, My way is hid from the LORD, and my
judgment is passed over from my God?
28 ¶ Hast thou not known? hast thou not
heard, *that* the everlasting God, the LORD, the
Creator of the ends of the earth, fainteth not,
neither is weary? *there is* no searching of his
understanding.
29 He giveth power to the faint; and to *them
that have* no might he increaseth strength.
30 Even the youths shall faint and be weary,
and the young men shall utterly fall:
31 But they that wait upon the LORD shall renew *their* strength; they shall mount up with
wings as eagles; they shall run, and not be
weary; *and* they shall walk, and not faint.

41 KEEP silence before me, O islands; and
let the people renew *their* strength: let
them come near; then let them speak: let us
come near together to judgment.
2 Who raised up the righteous *man* from the
east, called him to his foot, gave the nations before him, and made *him* rule over kings? he
gave *them* as the dust to his sword, *and* as
driven stubble to his bow.
3 He pursued them, *and* passed safely; *even*
by the way *that* he had not gone with his feet.
4 Who hath wrought and done *it,* calling the
generations from the beginning? I the LORD, the
first, and with the last; I *am* he.
5 The isles saw *it,* and feared; the ends of the
earth were afraid, drew near, and came.
6 They helped every one his neighbour; and
every one said to his brother, Be of good courage.
7 So the carpenter encouraged the goldsmith, *and* he that smootheth *with* the hammer
him that smote the anvil, saying, It *is* ready for
the sodering: and he fastened it with nails, *that*
it should not be moved.
8 But thou, Is'ra-el, *art* my servant, Ja'cob
whom I have chosen, the seed of A'bra-ham my
friend.
9 *Thou* whom I have taken from the ends of
the earth, and called thee from the chief men
thereof, and said unto thee, Thou *art* my servant; I have chosen thee, and not cast thee
away.
10 ¶ Fear thou not; for I *am* with thee: be not
dismayed; for I *am* thy God: I will strengthen
thee; yea, I will help thee; yea, I will uphold thee
with the right hand of my righteousness.
11 Behold, all they that were incensed
against thee shall be ashamed and confounded:
they shall be as nothing; and they that strive
with thee shall perish.
12 Thou shalt seek them, and shalt not find
them, *even* them that contended with thee: they
that war against thee shall be as nothing, and as
a thing of nought.
13 For I the LORD thy God will hold thy right
hand, saying unto thee, Fear not; I will help
thee.
14 Fear not, thou worm Ja'cob, *and* ye men
of Is'ra-el; I will help thee, saith the LORD, and
thy redeemer, the Holy One of Is'ra-el.
15 Behold, I will make thee a new sharp
threshing instrument having teeth: thou shalt
thresh the mountains, and beat *them* small, and
shalt make the hills as chaff.
16 Thou shalt fan them, and the wind shall
carry them away, and the whirlwind shall scatter them: and thou shalt rejoice in the LORD,
and shalt glory in the Holy One of Is'ra-el.
17 *When* the poor and needy seek water, and
there is none, *and* their tongue faileth for thirst,
I the LORD will hear them, *I* the God of Is'ra-el
will not forsake them.
18 I will open rivers in high places, and fountains in the midst of the valleys: I will make the
wilderness a pool of water, and the dry land
springs of water.
19 I will plant in the wilderness the cedar,
the shittah tree, and the myrtle, and the oil tree;
I will set in the desert the fir tree, *and* the pine,
and the box tree together:
20 That they may see, and know, and consider, and understand together, that the hand of
the LORD hath done this, and the Holy One of
Is'ra-el hath created it.
21 Produce your cause, saith the LORD; bring
forth your strong *reasons,* saith the King of Ja'-
cob.
22 Let them bring *them* forth, and shew us
what shall happen: let them shew the former
things, what they *be,* that we may consider
them, and know the latter end of them; or declare us things for to come.
23 Shew the things that are to come hereafter, that we may know that ye *are* gods; yea, do
good, or do evil, that we may be dismayed, and
behold *it* together.
24 Behold, ye *are* of nothing, and your work
of nought: an abomination *is he that* chooseth
you.
25 I have raised up *one* from the north, and
he shall come: from the rising of the sun shall
he call upon my name: and he shall come upon
princes as *upon* morter, and as the potter treadeth clay.
26 Who hath declared from the beginning,
that we may know? and beforetime, that we
may say, *He is* righteous? yea, *there is* none that
sheweth, yea, *there is* none that declareth, yea,
there is none that heareth your words.
27 The first *shall say* to Zi'on, Behold, behold
them: and I will give to Je-ru'sa-lem one that
bringeth good tidings.

28 For I beheld, and *there was* no man; even
among them, and *there was* no counsellor, that,
when I asked of them, could answer a word.
29 Behold, they *are* all vanity; their works
are nothing: their molten images *are* wind and
confusion.

42 BEHOLD my servant, whom I uphold;
mine elect, *in whom* my soul delighteth;
I have put my spirit upon him: he shall bring
forth judgment to the Gen′tiles.
2 He shall not cry, nor lift up, nor cause his
voice to be heard in the street.
3 A bruised reed shall he not break, and the
smoking flax shall he not quench: he shall bring
forth judgment unto truth.
4 He shall not fail nor be discouraged, till he
have set judgment in the earth: and the isles
shall wait for his law.
5 ¶ Thus saith God the LORD, he that created
the heavens, and stretched them out; he that
spread forth the earth, and that which cometh
out of it; he that giveth breath unto the people
upon it, and spirit to them that walk therein:
6 I the LORD have called thee in righteousness, and will hold thine hand, and will keep
thee, and give thee for a covenant of the people,
for a light of the Gen′tiles;
7 To open the blind eyes, to bring out the
prisoners from the prison, *and* them that sit in
darkness out of the prison house.
8 I *am* the LORD: that *is* my name: and my
glory will I not give to another, neither my
praise to graven images.
9 Behold, the former things are come to pass,
and new things do I declare: before they spring
forth I tell you of them.
10 Sing unto the LORD a new song, *and* his
praise from the end of the earth, ye that go
down to the sea, and all that is therein; the isles,
and the inhabitants thereof.
11 Let the wilderness and the cities thereof
lift up *their voice*, the villages *that* Ke′dar doth
inhabit: let the inhabitants of the rock sing, let
them shout from the top of the mountains.
12 Let them give glory unto the LORD, and
declare his praise in the islands.
13 The LORD shall go forth as a mighty man,
he shall stir up jealousy like a man of war: he
shall cry, yea, roar; he shall prevail against his
enemies.
14 I have long time holden my peace; I have
been still, *and* refrained myself: *now* will I cry
like a travailing woman; I will destroy and devour at once.
15 I will make waste mountains and hills,
and dry up all their herbs; and I will make the
rivers islands, and I will dry up the pools.
16 And I will bring the blind by a way *that*
they knew not; I will lead them in paths *that*
they have not known: I will make darkness light
before them, and crooked things straight. These
things will I do unto them, and not forsake
them.
17 ¶ They shall be turned back, they shall be
greatly ashamed, that trust in graven images,
that say to the molten images, Ye *are* our gods.
18 Hear, ye deaf; and look, ye blind, that ye
may see.
19 Who *is* blind, but my servant? or deaf, as
my messenger *that* I sent? who *is* blind as *he*
that is perfect, and blind as the LORD's servant?
20 Seeing many things, but thou observest
not; opening the ears, but he heareth not.
21 The LORD is well pleased for his righteousness' sake; he will magnify the law, and make *it*
honourable.
22 But this *is* a people robbed and spoiled;
they are all of them snared in holes, and they
are hid in prison houses: they are for a prey,
and none delivereth; for a spoil, and none saith,
Restore.
23 Who among you will give ear to this? *who*
will hearken and hear for the time to come?
24 Who gave Ja′cob for a spoil, and Is′ra-el to
the robbers? did not the LORD, he against whom
we have sinned? for they would not walk in his
ways, neither were they obedient unto his law.
25 Therefore he hath poured upon him the
fury of his anger, and the strength of battle: and
it hath set him on fire round about, yet he knew
not; and it burned him, yet he laid *it* not to
heart.

43 BUT now thus saith the LORD that created thee, O Ja′cob, and he that formed
thee, O Is′ra-el, Fear not: for I have redeemed
thee, I have called *thee* by thy name; thou *art*
mine.
2 When thou passest through the waters, I
will be with thee; and through the rivers, they
shall not overflow thee: when thou walkest
through the fire, thou shalt not be burned; neither shall the flame kindle upon thee.
3 For I *am* the LORD thy God, the Holy One
of Is′ra-el, thy Saviour: I gave E′gypt *for* thy
ransom, E-thi-o′pi-a and Se′ba for thee.
4 Since thou wast precious in my sight, thou
hast been honourable, and I have loved thee:
therefore will I give men for thee, and people
for thy life.
5 Fear not: for I *am* with thee: I will bring thy
seed from the east, and gather thee from the
west;
6 I will say to the north, Give up; and to the
south, Keep not back: bring my sons from far,
and my daughters from the ends of the earth;
7 *Even* every one that is called by my name:
for I have created him for my glory, I have
formed him; yea, I have made him.
8 ¶ Bring forth the blind people that have
eyes, and the deaf that have ears.
9 Let all the nations be gathered together,
and let the people be assembled: who among
them can declare this, and shew us former
things? let them bring forth their witnesses,
that they may be justified: or let them hear, and
say, *It is* truth.
10 Ye *are* my witnesses, saith the LORD, and
my servant whom I have chosen: that ye may
know and believe me, and understand that I *am*
he: before me there was no God formed, neither
shall there be after me.
11 I, *even* I, *am* the LORD; and beside me
there is no saviour.
12 I have declared, and have saved, and I
have shewed, when *there was* no strange *god*
among you: therefore ye *are* my witnesses,
saith the LORD, that I *am* God.
13 Yea, before the day *was* I *am* he; and
there is none that can deliver out of my hand: I
will work, and who shall let it?
14 ¶ Thus saith the LORD, your redeemer, the
Holy One of Is′ra-el; For your sake I have sent
to Bab′y-lon, and have brought down all their
nobles, and the Chal-de′ans, whose cry *is* in the
ships.
15 I *am* the LORD, your Holy One, the creator
of Is′ra-el, your King.
16 Thus saith the LORD, which maketh a way
in the sea, and a path in the mighty waters;
17 Which bringeth forth the chariot and
horse, the army and the power; they shall lie

down together, they shall not rise: they are extinct, they are quenched as tow.

18 ¶ Remember ye not the former things, neither consider the things of old.

19 Behold, I will do a new thing; now it shall spring forth; shall ye not know it? I will even make a way in the wilderness, *and* rivers in the desert.

20 The beast of the field shall honour me, the dragons and the owls: because I give waters in the wilderness, *and* rivers in the desert, to give drink to my people, my chosen.

21 This people have I formed for myself; they shall shew forth my praise.

22 ¶ But thou hast not called upon me, O Ja′cob; but thou hast been weary of me, O Is′ra-el.

23 Thou hast not brought me the small cattle of thy burnt offerings; neither hast thou honoured me with thy sacrifices. I have not caused thee to serve with an offering, nor wearied thee with incense.

24 Thou hast bought me no sweet cane with money, neither hast thou filled me with the fat of thy sacrifices: but thou hast made me to serve with thy sins, thou hast wearied me with thine iniquities.

25 I, *even* I, *am* he that blotteth out thy transgressions for mine own sake, and will not remember thy sins.

26 Put me in remembrance: let us plead together: declare thou, that thou mayest be justified.

27 Thy first father hath sinned, and thy teachers have transgressed against me.

28 Therefore I have profaned the princes of the sanctuary, and have given Ja′cob to the curse, and Is′ra-el to reproaches.

44 YET now hear, O Ja′cob my servant; and Is′ra-el, whom I have chosen:

2 Thus saith the LORD that made thee, and formed thee from the womb, *which* will help thee; Fear not, O Ja′cob, my servant; and thou, Jes′u-run, whom I have chosen.

3 For I will pour water upon him that is thirsty, and floods upon the dry ground: I will pour my spirit upon thy seed, and my blessing upon thine offspring:

4 And they shall spring up *as* among the grass, as willows by the water courses.

5 One shall say, I *am* the LORD's; and another shall call *himself* by the name of Ja′cob; and another shall subscribe *with* his hand unto the LORD, and surname *himself* by the name of Is′ra-el.

6 Thus saith the LORD the King of Is′ra-el, and his redeemer the LORD of hosts; I *am* the first, and I *am* the last; and beside me *there is* no God.

7 And who, as I, shall call, and shall declare it, and set it in order for me, since I appointed the ancient people? and the things that are coming, and shall come, let them shew unto them.

8 Fear ye not, neither be afraid: have not I told thee from that time, and have declared *it?* ye *are* even my witnesses. Is there a God beside me? yea, *there is* no God; I know not *any.*

9 ¶ They that make a graven image *are* all of them vanity; and their delectable things shall not profit; and they *are* their own witnesses; they see not, nor know; that they may be ashamed.

10 Who hath formed a god, or molten a graven image *that* is profitable for nothing?

11 Behold, all his fellows shall be ashamed: and the workmen, they *are* of men: let them all be gathered together, let them stand up; *yet* they shall fear, *and* they shall be ashamed together.

12 The smith with the tongs both worketh in the coals, and fashioneth it with hammers, and worketh it with the strength of his arms: yea, he is hungry, and his strength faileth: he drinketh no water, and is faint.

13 The carpenter stretcheth out *his* rule; he marketh it out with a line; he fitteth it with planes, and he marketh it out with the compass, and maketh it after the figure of a man, according to the beauty of a man; that it may remain in the house.

14 He heweth him down cedars, and taketh the cypress and the oak, which he strengtheneth for himself among the trees of the forest: he planteth an ash, and the rain doth nourish *it.*

15 Then shall it be for a man to burn: for he will take thereof, and warm himself; yea, he kindleth *it,* and baketh bread; yea, he maketh a god, and worshippeth *it;* he maketh it a graven image, and falleth down thereto.

16 He burneth part thereof in the fire; with part thereof he eateth flesh; he roasteth roast, and is satisfied: yea, he warmeth *himself,* and saith, Aha, I am warm, I have seen the fire:

17 And the residue thereof he maketh a god, *even* his graven image: he falleth down unto it, and worshippeth *it,* and prayeth unto it, and saith, Deliver me; for thou *art* my god.

18 They have not known nor understood: for he hath shut their eyes, that they cannot see; *and* their hearts, that they cannot understand.

19 And none considereth in his heart, neither *is there* knowledge nor understanding to say, I have burned part of it in the fire; yea, also I have baked bread upon the coals thereof; I have roasted flesh, and eaten *it:* and shall I make the residue thereof an abomination? shall I fall down to the stock of a tree?

20 He feedeth on ashes: a deceived heart hath turned him aside, that he cannot deliver his soul, nor say, *Is there* not a lie in my right hand?

21 ¶ Remember these, O Ja′cob and Is′ra-el; for thou *art* my servant: I have formed thee; thou *art* my servant: O Is′ra-el, thou shalt not be forgotten of me.

22 I have blotted out, as a thick cloud, thy transgressions, and, as a cloud, thy sins: return unto me; for I have redeemed thee.

23 Sing, O ye heavens; for the LORD hath done *it:* shout, ye lower parts of the earth: break forth into singing, ye mountains, O forest, and every tree therein: for the LORD hath redeemed Ja′cob, and glorified himself in Is′ra-el.

24 Thus saith the LORD, thy redeemer, and he that formed thee from the womb, I *am* the LORD that maketh all *things;* that stretcheth forth the heavens alone; that spreadeth abroad the earth by myself;

25 That frustrateth the tokens of the liars, and maketh diviners mad; that turneth wise *men* backward, and maketh their knowledge foolish;

26 That confirmeth the word of his servant, and performeth the counsel of his messengers; that saith to Je-ru′sa-lem, Thou shalt be inhabited; and to the cities of Ju′dah, Ye shall be built, and I will raise up the decayed places thereof:

27 That saith to the deep, Be dry, and I will dry up thy rivers:

28 That saith of Cy′rus, *He is* my shepherd, and shall perform all my pleasure: even saying to Je-ru′sa-lem, Thou shalt be built; and to the temple, Thy foundation shall be laid.

45 THUS saith the LORD to his anointed, to
Cy'rus, whose right hand I have holden,
to subdue nations before him; and I will loose
the loins of kings, to open before him the two
leaved gates; and the gates shall not be shut;
2 I will go before thee, and make the crooked
places straight: I will break in pieces the gates
of brass, and cut in sunder the bars of iron:
3 And I will give thee the treasures of darkness, and hidden riches of secret places, that
thou mayest know that I, the LORD which call
thee by thy name, *am* the God of Is'ra-el.
4 For Ja'cob my servant's sake, and Is'ra-el
mine elect, I have even called thee by thy name:
I have surnamed thee, though thou hast not
known me.
5 ¶ I *am* the LORD, and *there is* none else,
there is no God beside me: I girded thee, though
thou hast not known me:
6 That they may know from the rising of the
sun, and from the west, that *there is* none beside me. I *am* the LORD, and *there is* none else.
7 I form the light, and create darkness: I
make peace, and create evil: I the LORD do all
these *things*.
8 Drop down, ye heavens, from above, and
let the skies pour down righteousness: let the
earth open, and let them bring forth salvation,
and let righteousness spring up together; I the
LORD have created it.
9 Woe unto him that striveth with his Maker!
Let the potsherd *strive* with the potsherds of the
earth. Shall the clay say to him that fashioneth
it, What makest thou? or thy work, He hath no
hands?
10 Woe unto him that saith unto *his* father,
What begettest thou? or to the woman, What
hast thou brought forth?
11 Thus saith the LORD, the Holy One of Is'-
ra-el, and his Maker, Ask me of things to come
concerning my sons, and concerning the work
of my hands command ye me.
12 I have made the earth, and created man
upon it: I, *even* my hands, have stretched out
the heavens, and all their host have I commanded.
13 I have raised him up in righteousness, and
I will direct all his ways: he shall build my city,
and he shall let go my captives, not for price nor
reward, saith the LORD of hosts.
14 Thus saith the LORD, The labour of E'gypt,
and merchandise of E-thi-o'pi-a and of the Sa-
be'ans, men of stature, shall come over unto
thee, and they shall be thine: they shall come
after thee; in chains they shall come over, and
they shall fall down unto thee, they shall make
supplication unto thee, *saying*, Surely God *is* in
thee; and *there is* none else, *there is* no God.
15 Verily thou *art* a God that hidest thyself,
O God of Is'ra-el, the Saviour.
16 They shall be ashamed, and also confounded, all of them: they shall go to confusion
together *that are* makers of idols.
17 *But* Is'ra-el shall be saved in the LORD
with an everlasting salvation: ye shall not be
ashamed nor confounded world without end.
18 For thus saith the LORD that created the
heavens; God himself that formed the earth and
made it; he hath established it, he created it not
in vain, he formed it to be inhabited: I *am* the
LORD; and *there is* none else.
19 I have not spoken in secret, in a dark
place of the earth: I said not unto the seed of
Ja'cob, Seek ye me in vain: I the LORD speak
righteousness, I declare things that are right.
20 ¶ Assemble yourselves and come; draw
near together, ye *that are* escaped of the nations: they have no knowledge that set up the
wood of their graven image, and pray unto a
god *that* cannot save.
21 Tell ye, and bring *them* near; yea, let them
take counsel together: who hath declared this
from ancient time? *who* hath told it from that
time? *have* not I the LORD? and *there is* no God
else beside me; a just God and a Saviour; *there
is* none beside me.
22 Look unto me, and be ye saved, all the
ends of the earth: for I *am* God, and *there is*
none else.
23 I have sworn by myself, the word is gone
out of my mouth *in* righteousness, and shall not
return, That unto me every knee shall bow, every tongue shall swear.
24 Surely, shall *one* say, in the LORD have I
righteousness and strength: *even* to him shall
men come; and all that are incensed against
him shall be ashamed.
25 In the LORD shall all the seed of Is'ra-el be
justified, and shall glory.

46 BEL boweth down, Ne'bo stoopeth,
their idols were upon the beasts, and
upon the cattle: your carriages *were* heavy load-
en; *they are* a burden to the weary *beast*.
2 They stoop, they bow down together; they
could not deliver the burden, but themselves
are gone into captivity.
3 ¶ Hearken unto me, O house of Ja'cob, and
all the remnant of the house of Is'ra-el, which
are borne *by me* from the belly, which are carried from the womb:
4 And *even* to *your* old age I *am* he; and *even*
to hoar hairs will I carry *you*: I have made, and
I will bear; even I will carry, and will deliver
you.
5 ¶ To whom will ye liken me, and make *me*
equal, and compare me, that we may be like?
6 They lavish gold out of the bag, and weigh
silver in the balance, *and* hire a goldsmith; and
he maketh it a god: they fall down, yea, they
worship.
7 They bear him upon the shoulder, they carry him, and set him in his place, and he standeth; from his place shall he not remove: yea,
one shall cry unto him, yet can he not answer,
nor save him out of his trouble.
8 Remember this, and shew yourselves men:
bring *it* again to mind, O ye transgressors.
9 Remember the former things of old: for I
am God, and *there is* none else; *I am* God, and
there is none like me,
10 Declaring the end from the beginning, and
from ancient times *the things* that are not *yet*
done, saying, My counsel shall stand, and I will
do all my pleasure:
11 Calling a ravenous bird from the east, the
man that executeth my counsel from a far
country: yea, I have spoken *it*, I will also bring
it to pass; I have purposed *it*, I will also do it.
12 ¶ Hearken unto me, ye stouthearted, that
are far from righteousness:
13 I bring near my righteousness; it shall not
be far off, and my salvation shall not tarry: and
I will place salvation in Zi'on for Is'ra-el my glory.

47 COME down, and sit in the dust, O virgin daughter of Bab'y-lon, sit on the
ground: *there is* no throne, O daughter of the
Chal-de'ans: for thou shalt no more be called
tender and delicate.
2 Take the millstones, and grind meal; uncover thy locks, make bare the leg, uncover the
thigh, pass over the rivers.

3 Thy nakedness shall be uncovered, yea, thy shame shall be seen: I will take vengeance, and I will not meet *thee as* a man.

4 *As for* our redeemer, the LORD of hosts *is* his name, the Holy One of Is′ra-el.

5 Sit thou silent, and get thee into darkness, O daughter of the Chal-de′ans: for thou shalt no more be called, The lady of kingdoms.

6 ¶ I was wroth with my people, I have polluted mine inheritance, and given them into thine hand: thou didst shew them no mercy; upon the ancient hast thou very heavily laid thy yoke.

7 ¶ And thou saidst, I shall be a lady for ever: *so* that thou didst not lay these *things* to thy heart, neither didst remember the latter end of it.

8 Therefore hear now this, *thou that art* given to pleasures, that dwellest carelessly, that sayest in thine heart, I *am*, and none else beside me; I shall not sit *as* a widow, neither shall I know the loss of children:

9 But these two *things* shall come to thee in a moment in one day, the loss of children, and widowhood: they shall come upon thee in their perfection for the multitude of thy sorceries, *and* for the great abundance of thine enchantments.

10 ¶ For thou hast trusted in thy wickedness: thou hast said, None seeth me. Thy wisdom and thy knowledge, it hath perverted thee; and thou hast said in thine heart, I *am*, and none else beside me.

11 ¶ Therefore shall evil come upon thee; thou shalt not know from whence it riseth: and mischief shall fall upon thee; thou shalt not be able to put it off: and desolation shall come upon thee suddenly, *which* thou shalt not know.

12 Stand now with thine enchantments, and with the multitude of thy sorceries, wherein thou hast laboured from thy youth; if so be thou shalt be able to profit, if so be thou mayest prevail.

13 Thou art wearied in the multitude of thy counsels. Let now the astrologers, the stargazers, the monthly prognosticators, stand up, and save thee from *these things* that shall come upon thee.

14 Behold, they shall be as stubble; the fire shall burn them; they shall not deliver themselves from the power of the flame: *there shall* not *be* a coal to warm at, *nor* fire to sit before it.

15 Thus shall they be unto thee with whom thou hast laboured, *even* thy merchants, from thy youth: they shall wander every one to his quarter; none shall save thee.

48 HEAR ye this, O house of Ja′cob, which are called by the name of Is′ra-el, and are come forth out of the waters of Ju′dah, which swear by the name of the LORD, and make mention of the God of Is′ra-el, *but* not in truth, nor in righteousness.

2 For they call themselves of the holy city, and stay themselves upon the God of Is′ra-el; The LORD of hosts *is* his name.

3 I have declared the former things from the beginning; and they went forth out of my mouth, and I shewed them; I did *them* suddenly, and they came to pass.

4 Because I knew that thou *art* obstinate, and thy neck *is* an iron sinew, and thy brow brass;

5 I have even from the beginning declared *it* to thee; before it came to pass I shewed *it* thee: lest thou shouldest say, Mine idol hath done them, and my graven image, and my molten image, hath commanded them.

6 Thou hast heard, see all this; and will not ye declare *it?* I have shewed thee new things from this time, even hidden things, and thou didst not know them.

7 They are created now, and not from the beginning; even before the day when thou heardest them not; lest thou shouldest say, Behold, I knew them.

8 Yea, thou heardest not; yea, thou knewest not; yea, from that time *that* thine ear was not opened: for I knew that thou wouldest deal very treacherously, and wast called a transgressor from the womb.

9 ¶ For my name's sake will I defer mine anger, and for my praise will I refrain for thee, that I cut thee not off.

10 Behold, I have refined thee, but not with silver; I have chosen thee in the furnace of affliction.

11 For mine own sake, *even* for mine own sake, will I do *it:* for how should *my name* be polluted? and I will not give my glory unto another.

12 ¶ Hearken unto me, O Ja′cob and Is′ra-el, my called; I *am* he; I *am* the first, I also *am* the last.

13 Mine hand also hath laid the foundation of the earth, and my right hand hath spanned the heavens: *when* I call unto them, they stand up together.

14 All ye, assemble yourselves, and hear; which among them hath declared these *things?* The LORD hath loved him: he will do his pleasure on Bab′y-lon, and his arm *shall be on* the Chal-de′ans.

15 I, *even* I, have spoken; yea, I have called him: I have brought him, and he shall make his way prosperous.

16 ¶ Come ye near unto me, hear ye this; I have not spoken in secret from the beginning; from the time that it was, there *am* I: and now the Lord GOD, and his Spirit, hath sent me.

17 Thus saith the LORD, thy redeemer, the Holy One of Is′ra-el; I *am* the LORD thy God which teacheth thee to profit, which leadeth thee by the way *that* thou shouldest go.

18 O that thou hadst hearkened to my commandments! then had thy peace been as a river, and thy righteousness as the waves of the sea:

19 Thy seed also had been as the sand, and the offspring of thy bowels like the gravel thereof; his name should not have been cut off nor destroyed from before me.

20 ¶ Go ye forth of Bab′y-lon, flee ye from the Chal-de′ans, with a voice of singing declare ye, tell this, utter it *even* to the end of the earth; say ye, The LORD hath redeemed his servant Ja′cob.

21 And they thirsted not *when* he led them through the deserts: he caused the waters to flow out of the rock for them: he clave the rock also, and the waters gushed out.

22 *There is* no peace, saith the LORD, unto the wicked.

49 LISTEN O isles, unto me; and hearken, ye people, from far; The LORD hath called me from the womb; from the bowels of my mother hath he made mention of my name.

2 And he hath made my mouth like a sharp sword; in the shadow of his hand hath he hid me, and made me a polished shaft; in his quiver hath he hid me;

3 And said unto me, Thou *art* my servant, O Is′ra-el, in whom I will be glorified.

4 Then I said, I have laboured in vain, I have spent my strength for nought, and in vain: *yet*

surely my judgment *is* with the LORD, and my work with my God.

5 ¶ And now, saith the LORD that formed me from the womb *to be* his servant, to bring Ja'cob again to him, Though Is'ra-el be not gathered, yet shall I be glorious in the eyes of the LORD, and my God shall be my strength.

6 And he said, It is a light thing that thou shouldest be my servant to raise up the tribes of Ja'cob, and to restore the preserved of Is'ra-el: I will also give thee for a light to the Gen'tiles, that thou mayest be my salvation unto the end of the earth.

7 Thus saith the LORD, the Redeemer of Is'ra-el, *and* his Holy One, to him whom man despiseth, to him whom the nation abhorreth, to a servant of rulers, Kings shall see and arise, princes also shall worship, because of the LORD that is faithful, *and* the Holy One of Is'ra-el, and he shall choose thee.

8 Thus saith the LORD, In an acceptable time have I heard thee, and in a day of salvation have I helped thee: and I will preserve thee, and give thee for a covenant of the people, to establish the earth, to cause to inherit the desolate heritages;

9 That thou mayest say to the prisoners, Go forth; to them that *are* in darkness, Shew yourselves. They shall feed in the ways, and their pastures *shall be* in all high places.

10 They shall not hunger nor thirst; neither shall the heat nor sun smite them: for he that hath mercy on them shall lead them, even by the springs of water shall he guide them.

11 And I will make all my mountains a way, and my highways shall be exalted.

12 Behold, these shall come from far: and, lo, these from the north and from the west; and these from the land of Si'nim.

13 ¶ Sing, O heavens; and be joyful, O earth; and break forth into singing, O mountains: for the LORD hath comforted his people, and will have mercy upon his afflicted.

14 But Zi'on said, The LORD hath forsaken me, and my Lord hath forgotten me.

15 Can a woman forget her sucking child, that she should not have compassion on the son of her womb? yea, they may forget, yet will I not forget thee.

16 Behold, I have graven thee upon the palms of *my* hands; thy walls *are* continually before me.

17 Thy children shall make haste; thy destroyers and they that made thee waste shall go forth of thee.

18 ¶ Lift up thine eyes round about, and behold: all these gather themselves together, *and* come to thee. *As* I live, saith the LORD, thou shalt surely clothe thee with them all, as with an ornament, and bind them *on thee,* as a bride *doeth.*

19 For thy waste and thy desolate places, and the land of thy destruction, shall even now be too narrow by reason of the inhabitants, and they that swallowed thee up shall be far away.

20 The children which thou shalt have, after thou hast lost the other, shall say again in thine ears, The place *is* too strait for me: give place to me that I may dwell.

21 Then shalt thou say in thine heart, Who hath begotten me these, seeing I have lost my children, and am desolate, a captive, and removing to and fro? and who hath brought up these? Behold, I was left alone; these, where *had* they *been?*

22 Thus saith the Lord GOD, Behold, I will lift up mine hand to the Gen'tiles, and set up my standard to the people: and they shall bring thy sons in *their* arms, and thy daughters shall be carried upon *their* shoulders.

23 And kings shall be thy nursing fathers, and their queens thy nursing mothers: they shall bow down to thee with *their* face toward the earth, and lick up the dust of thy feet; and thou shalt know that I *am* the LORD: for they shall not be ashamed that wait for me.

24 ¶ Shall the prey be taken from the mighty, or the lawful captive delivered?

25 But thus saith the LORD, Even the captives of the mighty shall be taken away, and the prey of the terrible shall be delivered: for I will contend with him that contendeth with thee, and I will save thy children.

26 And I will feed them that oppress thee with their own flesh; and they shall be drunken with their own blood, as with sweet wine: and all flesh shall know that I the LORD *am* thy Saviour and thy Redeemer, the mighty One of Ja'cob.

50

THUS saith the LORD, Where *is* the bill of your mother's divorcement, whom I have put away? or which of my creditors *is it* to whom I have sold you? Behold, for your iniquities have ye sold yourselves, and for your transgressions is your mother put away.

2 Wherefore, when I came, *was there* no man? when I called, *was there* none to answer? Is my hand shortened at all, that it cannot redeem? or have I no power to deliver? behold, at my rebuke I dry up the sea, I make the rivers a wilderness: their fish stinketh, because *there is* no water, and dieth for thirst.

3 I clothe the heavens with blackness, and I make sackcloth their covering.

4 The Lord GOD hath given me the tongue of the learned, that I should know how to speak a word in season to *him that is* weary: he wakeneth morning by morning, he wakeneth mine ear to hear as the learned.

5 ¶ The Lord GOD hath opened mine ear, and I was not rebellious, neither turned away back.

6 I gave my back to the smiters, and my cheeks to them that plucked off the hair: I hid not my face from shame and spitting.

7 ¶ For the Lord GOD will help me; therefore shall I not be confounded: therefore have I set my face like a flint, and I know that I shall not be ashamed.

8 *He is* near that justifieth me; who will contend with me? let us stand together: who *is* mine adversary? let him come near to me.

9 Behold, the Lord GOD will help me; who *is* he *that* shall condemn me? lo, they all shall wax old as a garment; the moth shall eat them up.

10 ¶ Who *is* among you that feareth the LORD, that obeyeth the voice of his servant, that walketh *in* darkness, and hath no light? let him trust in the name of the LORD, and stay upon his God.

11 Behold, all ye that kindle a fire, that compass *yourselves* about with sparks: walk in the light of your fire, and in the sparks *that* ye have kindled. This shall ye have of mine hand; ye shall lie down in sorrow.

51

HEARKEN to me, ye that follow after righteousness, ye that seek the LORD: look unto the rock *whence* ye are hewn, and to the hole of the pit *whence* ye are digged.

2 Look unto A'bra-ham your father, and unto Sa'rah *that* bare you: for I called him alone, and blessed him, and increased him.

3 For the LORD shall comfort Zi'on: he will

comfort all her waste places; and he will make
her wilderness like E'den, and her desert like
the garden of the LORD; joy and gladness shall
be found therein, thanksgiving, and the voice of
melody.
4 ¶ Hearken unto me, my people; and give
ear unto me, O my nation: for a law shall proceed from me, and I will make my judgment to
rest for a light of the people.
5 My righteousness *is* near; my salvation is
gone forth, and mine arms shall judge the people; the isles shall wait upon me, and on mine
arm shall they trust.
6 Lift up your eyes to the heavens, and look
upon the earth beneath: for the heavens shall
vanish away like smoke, and the earth shall
wax old like a garment, and they that dwell
therein shall die in like manner: but my salvation shall be for ever, and my righteousness
shall not be abolished.
7 ¶ Hearken unto me, ye that know righteousness, the people in whose heart *is* my law;
fear ye not the reproach of men, neither be ye
afraid of their revilings.
8 For the moth shall eat them up like a garment, and the worm shall eat them like wool:
but my righteousness shall be for ever, and my
salvation from generation to generation.
9 ¶ Awake, awake, put on strength, O arm of
the LORD; awake, as in the ancient days, in the
generations of old. *Art* thou not it that hath cut
Ra'hab, *and* wounded the dragon?
10 *Art* thou not it which hath dried the sea,
the waters of the great deep; that hath made the
depths of the sea a way for the ransomed to
pass over?
11 Therefore the redeemed of the LORD shall
return, and come with singing unto Zi'on; and
everlasting joy *shall be* upon their head: they
shall obtain gladness and joy; *and* sorrow and
mourning shall flee away.
12 I, *even* I, *am* he that comforteth you: who
art thou, that thou shouldest be afraid of a man
that shall die, and of the son of man *which* shall
be made *as* grass;
13 And forgettest the LORD thy maker, that
hath stretched forth the heavens, and laid the
foundations of the earth; and hast feared continually every day because of the fury of the
oppressor, as if he were ready to destroy? and
where *is* the fury of the oppressor?
14 The captive exile hasteneth that he may
be loosed, and that he should not die in the pit,
nor that his bread should fail.
15 But I *am* the LORD thy God, that divided
the sea, whose waves roared: The LORD of hosts
is his name.
16 And I have put my words in thy mouth,
and I have covered thee in the shadow of mine
hand, that I may plant the heavens, and lay the
foundations of the earth, and say unto Zi'on,
Thou *art* my people.
17 ¶ Awake, awake, stand up, O Je-ru'sa-
lem, which hast drunk at the hand of the LORD
the cup of his fury; thou hast drunken the dregs
of the cup of trembling, *and* wrung *them* out.
18 *There is* none to guide her among all the
sons *whom* she hath brought forth; neither *is
there any* that taketh her by the hand of all the
sons *that* she hath brought up.
19 These two *things* are come unto thee; who
shall be sorry for thee? desolation, and destruction, and the famine, and the sword: by whom
shall I comfort thee?
20 Thy sons have fainted, they lie at the head
of all the streets, as a wild bull in a net: they are
full of the fury of the LORD, the rebuke of thy
God.
21 ¶ Therefore hear now this, thou afflicted,
and drunken, but not with wine:
22 Thus saith thy Lord the LORD, and thy
God *that* pleadeth the cause of his people, Behold, I have taken out of thine hand the cup of
trembling, *even* the dregs of the cup of my fury;
thou shalt no more drink it again:
23 But I will put it into the hand of them that
afflict thee; which have said to thy soul, Bow
down, that we may go over: and thou hast laid
thy body as the ground, and as the street, to
them that went over.

52 AWAKE, awake; put on thy strength, O
Zi'on; put on thy beautiful garments, O
Je-ru'sa-lem, the holy city: for henceforth there
shall no more come into thee the uncircumcised
and the unclean.
2 Shake thyself from the dust; arise, *and* sit
down, O Je-ru'sa-lem: loose thyself from the
bands of thy neck, O captive daughter of Zi'on.
3 For thus saith the LORD, Ye have sold yourselves for nought; and ye shall be redeemed
without money.
4 For thus saith the Lord GOD, My people
went down aforetime into E'gypt to sojourn
there; and the As-syr'i-an oppressed them without cause.
5 Now therefore, what have I here, saith the
LORD, that my people is taken away for nought?
they that rule over them make them to howl,
saith the LORD; and my name continually every
day *is* blasphemed.
6 Therefore my people shall know my name:
therefore *they shall know* in that day that I *am*
he that doth speak: behold, *it is* I.
7 ¶ How beautiful upon the mountains are
the feet of him that bringeth good tidings, that
publisheth peace; that bringeth good tidings of
good, that publisheth salvation; that saith unto
Zi'on, Thy God reigneth!
8 Thy watchmen shall lift up the voice; with
the voice together shall they sing: for they shall
see eye to eye, when the LORD shall bring again
Zi'on.
9 ¶ Break forth into joy, sing together, ye
waste places of Je-ru'sa-lem: for the LORD hath
comforted his people, he hath redeemed Je-ru'-
sa-lem.
10 The LORD hath made bare his holy arm in
the eyes of all the nations; and all the ends of
the earth shall see the salvation of our God.
11 ¶ Depart ye, depart ye, go ye out from
thence, touch no unclean *thing;* go ye out of the
midst of her; be ye clean, that bear the vessels
of the LORD.
12 For ye shall not go out with haste, nor go
by flight: for the LORD will go before you; and
the God of Is'ra-el *will be* your rereward.
13 ¶ Behold, my servant shall deal pru-
dently, he shall be exalted and extolled, and be
very high.
14 As many were astonied at thee; his visage
was so marred more than any man, and his
form more than the sons of men:
15 So shall he sprinkle many nations; the
kings shall shut their mouths at him: for *that*
which had not been told them shall they see;
and *that* which they had not heard shall they
consider.

53 WHO hath believed our report? and to
whom is the arm of the LORD revealed?
2 For he shall grow up before him as a tender
plant, and as a root out of a dry ground: he hath

no form nor comeliness; and when we shall see
him, *there is* no beauty that we should desire
him.
3 He is despised and rejected of men; a man
of sorrows, and acquainted with grief: and we
hid as it were *our* faces from him; he was despised, and we esteemed him not.
4 ¶ Surely he hath borne our griefs, and carried our sorrows: yet we did esteem him
stricken, smitten of God, and afflicted.
5 But he *was* wounded for our transgressions, *he was* bruised for our iniquities: the
chastisement of our peace *was* upon him; and
with his stripes we are healed.
6 All we like sheep have gone astray; we
have turned every one to his own way; and the
LORD hath laid on him the iniquity of us all.
7 He was oppressed, and he was afflicted, yet
he opened not his mouth: he is brought as a
lamb to the slaughter, and as a sheep before her
shearers is dumb, so he openeth not his mouth.
8 He was taken from prison and from judgment: and who shall declare his generation? for
he was cut off out of the land of the living: for
the transgression of my people was he stricken.
9 And he made his grave with the wicked,
and with the rich in his death; because he had
done no violence, neither *was any* deceit in his
mouth.
10 ¶ Yet it pleased the LORD to bruise him;
he hath put *him* to grief: when thou shalt make
his soul an offering for sin, he shall see *his* seed,
he shall prolong *his* days, and the pleasure of
the LORD shall prosper in his hand.
11 He shall see of the travail of his soul, *and*
shall be satisfied: by his knowledge shall my
righteous servant justify many; for he shall bear
their iniquities.
12 Therefore will I divide him *a portion* with
the great, and he shall divide the spoil with the
strong; because he hath poured out his soul
unto death: and he was numbered with the
transgressors; and he bare the sin of many, and
made intercession for the transgressors.

54 SING, O barren, thou *that* didst not
bear; break forth into singing, and cry
aloud, thou *that* didst not travail with child: for
more *are* the children of the desolate than the
children of the married wife, saith the LORD.
2 Enlarge the place of thy tent, and let them
stretch forth the curtains of thine habitations:
spare not, lengthen thy cords, and strengthen
thy stakes;
3 For thou shalt break forth on the right hand
and on the left; and thy seed shall inherit the
Gen'tiles, and make the desolate cities to be inhabited.
4 Fear not; for thou shalt not be ashamed:
neither be thou confounded; for thou shalt not
be put to shame: for thou shalt forget the shame
of thy youth, and shalt not remember the reproach of thy widowhood any more.
5 For thy Maker *is* thine husband; the LORD
of hosts *is* his name; and thy Redeemer the
Holy One of Is'ra-el; The God of the whole earth
shall he be called.
6 For the LORD hath called thee as a woman
forsaken and grieved in spirit, and a wife of
youth, when thou wast refused, saith thy God.
7 For a small moment have I forsaken thee;
but with great mercies will I gather thee.
8 In a little wrath I hid my face from thee for
a moment; but with everlasting kindness will I
have mercy on thee, saith the LORD thy Redeemer.
9 For this *is as* the waters of No'ah unto me:
for *as* I have sworn that the waters of No'ah
should no more go over the earth; so have I
sworn that I would not be wroth with thee, nor
rebuke thee.
10 For the mountains shall depart, and the
hills be removed; but my kindness shall not depart from thee, neither shall the covenant of my
peace be removed, saith the LORD that hath
mercy on thee.
11 ¶ O thou afflicted, tossed with tempest,
and not comforted, behold, I will lay thy stones
with fair colours, and lay thy foundations with
sapphires.
12 And I will make thy windows of agates,
and thy gates of carbuncles, and all thy borders
of pleasant stones.
13 And all thy children *shall be* taught of the
LORD; and great *shall be* the peace of thy children.
14 In righteousness shalt thou be established: thou shalt be far from oppression; for
thou shalt not fear: and from terror; for it shall
not come near thee.
15 Behold, they shall surely gather together,
but not by me: whosoever shall gather together
against thee shall fall for thy sake.
16 Behold, I have created the smith that
bloweth the coals in the fire, and that bringeth
forth an instrument for his work; and I have
created the waster to destroy.
17 ¶ No weapon that is formed against thee
shall prosper; and every tongue *that* shall rise
against thee in judgment thou shalt condemn.
This *is* the heritage of the servants of the LORD,
and their righteousness *is* of me, saith the LORD.

55 HO, every one that thirsteth, come ye to
the waters, and he that hath no money;
come ye, buy, and eat; yea, come, buy wine and
milk without money and without price.
2 Wherefore do ye spend money for *that
which is* not bread? and your labour for *that
which* satisfieth not? hearken diligently unto
me, and eat ye *that which is* good, and let your
soul delight itself in fatness.
3 Incline your ear, and come unto me: hear,
and your soul shall live; and I will make an
everlasting covenant with you, *even* the sure
mercies of Da'vid.
4 Behold, I have given him *for* a witness to
the people, a leader and commander to the people.
5 Behold, thou shalt call a nation *that* thou
knowest not, and nations *that* knew not thee
shall run unto thee because of the LORD thy
God, and for the Holy One of Is'ra-el; for he
hath glorified thee.
6 ¶ Seek ye the LORD while he may be found,
call ye upon him while he is near:
7 Let the wicked forsake his way, and the unrighteous man his thoughts: and let him return
unto the LORD, and he will have mercy upon
him; and to our God, for he will abundantly pardon.
8 ¶ For my thoughts *are* not your thoughts,
neither *are* your ways my ways, saith the LORD.
9 For *as* the heavens are higher than the
earth, so are my ways higher than your ways,
and my thoughts than your thoughts.
10 For as the rain cometh down, and the
snow from heaven, and returneth not thither,
but watereth the earth, and maketh it bring
forth and bud, that it may give seed to the
sower, and bread to the eater:
11 So shall my word be that goeth forth out
of my mouth: it shall not return unto me void,
but it shall accomplish that which I please, and

it shall prosper *in the thing* whereto I sent it.
12 For ye shall go out with joy, and be led
forth with peace: the mountains and the hills
shall break forth before you into singing, and all
the trees of the field shall clap *their* hands.
13 Instead of the thorn shall come up the fir
tree, and instead of the brier shall come up the
myrtle tree: and it shall be to the LORD for a
name, for an everlasting sign *that* shall not be
cut off.

56 THUS saith the LORD, Keep ye judgment, and do justice: for my salvation *is*
near to come, and my righteousness to be revealed.
2 Blessed *is* the man *that* doeth this, and the
son of man *that* layeth hold on it; that keepeth
the sabbath from polluting it, and keepeth his
hand from doing any evil.
3 ¶ Neither let the son of the stranger, that
hath joined himself to the LORD, speak, saying,
The LORD hath utterly separated me from his
people: neither let the eunuch say, Behold, I *am*
a dry tree.
4 For thus saith the LORD unto the eunuchs
that keep my sabbaths, and choose *the things*
that please me, and take hold of my covenant;
5 Even unto them will I give in mine house
and within my walls a place and a name better
than of sons and of daughters: I will give them
an everlasting name, that shall not be cut off.
6 Also the sons of the stranger, that join
themselves to the LORD, to serve him, and to
love the name of the LORD, to be his servants,
every one that keepeth the sabbath from polluting it, and taketh hold of my covenant;
7 Even them will I bring to my holy mountain, and make them joyful in my house of
prayer: their burnt offerings and their sacrifices
shall be accepted upon mine altar; for mine
house shall be called an house of prayer for all
people.
8 The Lord GOD which gathereth the outcasts
of Is'ra-el saith, Yet will I gather *others* to him,
beside those that are gathered unto him.
9 ¶ All ye beasts of the field, come to devour,
yea, all ye beasts in the forest.
10 His watchmen *are* blind: they are all ignorant, they *are* all dumb dogs, they cannot bark;
sleeping, lying down, loving to slumber.
11 Yea, *they are* greedy dogs *which* can never have enough, and they *are* shepherds *that*
cannot understand: they all look to their own
way, every one for his gain, from his quarter.
12 Come ye, *say they,* I will fetch wine, and
we will fill ourselves with strong drink; and to
morrow shall be as this day, *and* much more
abundant.

57 THE righteous perisheth, and no man
layeth *it* to heart: and merciful men *are*
taken away, none considering that the righteous is taken away from the evil *to come.*
2 He shall enter into peace: they shall rest in
their beds, *each one* walking *in* his uprightness.
3 ¶ But draw near hither, ye sons of the sor-
ceress, the seed of the adulterer and the whore.
4 Against whom do ye sport yourselves?
against whom make ye a wide mouth, *and* draw
out the tongue? *are* ye not children of transgression, a seed of falsehood,
5 Enflaming yourselves with idols under every green tree, slaying the children in the valleys under the clifts of the rocks?
6 Among the smooth *stones* of the stream *is*
thy portion; they, they *are* thy lot: even to them
hast thou poured a drink offering, thou hast offered a meat offering. Should I receive comfort
in these?
7 Upon a lofty and high mountain hast thou
set thy bed: even thither wentest thou up to offer sacrifice.
8 Behind the doors also and the posts hast
thou set up thy remembrance: for thou hast discovered *thyself to another* than me, and art
gone up; thou hast enlarged thy bed, and made
thee *a covenant* with them; thou lovedst their
bed where thou sawest *it.*
9 And thou wentest to the king with ointment, and didst increase thy perfumes, and
didst send thy messengers far off, and didst de-
base *thyself even* unto hell.
10 Thou art wearied in the greatness of thy
way; *yet* saidst thou not, There is no hope: thou
hast found the life of thine hand; therefore thou
wast not grieved.
11 And of whom hast thou been afraid or
feared, that thou hast lied, and hast not remembered me, nor laid *it* to thy heart? have not I
held my peace even of old, and thou fearest me
not?
12 I will declare thy righteousness, and thy
works; for they shall not profit thee.
13 ¶ When thou criest, let thy companies deliver thee; but the wind shall carry them all
away; vanity shall take *them:* but he that putteth his trust in me shall possess the land, and
shall inherit my holy mountain;
14 And shall say, Cast ye up, cast ye up, prepare the way, take up the stumblingblock out of
the way of my people.
15 For thus saith the high and lofty One that
inhabiteth eternity, whose name *is* Holy; I dwell
in the high and holy *place,* with him also *that is*
of a contrite and humble spirit, to revive the
spirit of the humble, and to revive the heart of
the contrite ones.
16 For I will not contend for ever, neither
will I be always wroth: for the spirit should fail
before me, and the souls *which* I have made.
17 For the iniquity of his covetousness was I
wroth, and smote him: I hid me, and was wroth,
and he went on frowardly in the way of his
heart.
18 I have seen his ways, and will heal him: I
will lead him also, and restore comforts unto
him and to his mourners.
19 I create the fruit of the lips; Peace, peace
to *him that is* far off, and to *him that is* near,
saith the LORD; and I will heal him.
20 But the wicked *are* like the troubled sea,
when it cannot rest, whose waters cast up mire
and dirt.
21 *There is* no peace, saith my God, to the
wicked.

58 CRY aloud, spare not, lift up thy voice
like a trumpet, and shew my people
their transgression, and the house of Ja'cob
their sins.
2 Yet they seek me daily, and delight to
know my ways, as a nation that did righteousness, and forsook not the ordinance of their
God: they ask of me the ordinances of justice;
they take delight in approaching to God.
3 ¶ Wherefore have we fasted, *say they,* and
thou seest not? *wherefore* have we afflicted our
soul, and thou takest no knowledge? Behold, in
the day of your fast ye find pleasure, and exact
all your labours.
4 Behold, ye fast for strife and debate, and to
smite with the fist of wickedness: ye shall not
fast as *ye do this* day, to make your voice to be
heard on high.

5 Is it such a fast that I have chosen? a day
for a man to afflict his soul? *is it* to bow down
his head as a bulrush, and to spread sackcloth
and ashes *under him?* wilt thou call this a fast,
and an acceptable day to the LORD?
6 *Is* not this the fast that I have chosen? to
loose the bands of wickedness, to undo the
heavy burdens, and to let the oppressed go free,
and that ye break every yoke?
7 *Is it* not to deal thy bread to the hungry,
and that thou bring the poor that are cast out to
thy house? when thou seest the naked, that
thou cover him; and that thou hide not thyself
from thine own flesh?
8 ¶ Then shall thy light break forth as the
morning, and thine health shall spring forth
speedily: and thy righteousness shall go before
thee: the glory of the LORD shall be thy rereward.
9 Then shalt thou call, and the LORD shall answer; thou shalt cry, and he shall say, Here I
am. If thou take away from the midst of thee
the yoke, the putting forth of the finger, and
speaking vanity;
10 And *if* thou draw out thy soul to the hungry, and satisfy the afflicted soul; then shall thy
light rise in obscurity, and thy darkness *be* as
the noon day:
11 And the LORD shall guide thee continually,
and satisfy thy soul in drought, and make fat
thy bones: and thou shalt be like a watered garden, and like a spring of water, whose waters
fail not.
12 And *they that shall be* of thee shall build
the old waste places: thou shalt raise up the
foundations of many generations; and thou
shalt be called, The repairer of the breach, The
restorer of paths to dwell in.
13 ¶ If thou turn away thy foot from the sabbath, *from* doing thy pleasure on my holy day;
and call the sabbath a delight, the holy of the
LORD, honourable; and shalt honour him, not
doing thine own ways, nor finding thine own
pleasure, nor speaking *thine own* words:
14 Then shalt thou delight thyself in the
LORD; and I will cause thee to ride upon the
high places of the earth, and feed thee with the
heritage of Ja'cob thy father: for the mouth of
the LORD hath spoken *it*.

59

BEHOLD, the LORD's hand is not shortened, that it cannot save; neither his ear
heavy, that it cannot hear:
2 But your iniquities have separated between
you and your God, and your sins have hid *his*
face from you, that he will not hear.
3 For your hands are defiled with blood, and
your fingers with iniquity; your lips have spoken lies, your tongue hath muttered perverseness.
4 None calleth for justice, nor *any* pleadeth
for truth: they trust in vanity, and speak lies;
they conceive mischief, and bring forth iniquity.
5 They hatch cockatrice' eggs, and weave the
spider's web: he that eateth of their eggs dieth,
and that which is crushed breaketh out into a
viper.
6 Their webs shall not become garments, neither shall they cover themselves with their
works: their works *are* works of iniquity, and
the act of violence *is* in their hands.
7 Their feet run to evil, and they make haste
to shed innocent blood: their thoughts *are*
thoughts of iniquity; wasting and destruction
are in their paths.
8 The way of peace they know not; and *there*
is no judgment in their goings: they have made
them crooked paths: whosoever goeth therein
shall not know peace.
9 ¶ Therefore is judgment far from us, neither doth justice overtake us: we wait for light,
but behold obscurity; for brightness, *but* we
walk in darkness.
10 We grope for the wall like the blind, and
we grope as if *we had* no eyes: we stumble at
noon day as in the night; *we are* in desolate
places as dead *men*.
11 We roar all like bears, and mourn sore
like doves: we look for judgment, but *there is*
none; for salvation, *but* it is far off from us.
12 For our transgressions are multiplied before thee, and our sins testify against us: for our
transgressions *are* with us; and *as for* our iniquities, we know them;
13 In transgressing and lying against the
LORD, and departing away from our God,
speaking oppression and revolt, conceiving and
uttering from the heart words of falsehood.
14 And judgment is turned away backward,
and justice standeth afar off: for truth is fallen
in the street, and equity cannot enter.
15 Yea, truth faileth; and he *that* departeth
from evil maketh himself a prey: and the LORD
saw *it*, and it displeased him that *there was* no
judgment.
16 ¶ And he saw that *there was* no man, and
wondered that *there was* no intercessor: therefore his arm brought salvation unto him; and
his righteousness, it sustained him.
17 For he put on righteousness as a breastplate, and an helmet of salvation upon his head;
and he put on the garments of vengeance *for*
clothing, and was clad with zeal as a cloke.
18 According to *their* deeds, accordingly he
will repay, fury to his adversaries, recompence
to his enemies; to the islands he will repay recompence.
19 So shall they fear the name of the LORD
from the west, and his glory from the rising of
the sun. When the enemy shall come in like a
flood, the Spirit of the LORD shall lift up a standard against him.
20 ¶ And the Redeemer shall come to Zi'on,
and unto them that turn from transgression in
Ja'cob, saith the LORD.
21 As for me, this *is* my covenant with them,
saith the LORD; My spirit that *is* upon thee, and
my words which I have put in thy mouth, shall
not depart out of thy mouth, nor out of the
mouth of thy seed, nor out of the mouth of thy
seed's seed, saith the LORD, from henceforth
and for ever.

60

ARISE, shine; for thy light is come, and
the glory of the LORD is risen upon thee.
2 For, behold, the darkness shall cover the
earth, and gross darkness the people: but the
LORD shall arise upon thee, and his glory shall
be seen upon thee.
3 And the Gen'tiles shall come to thy light,
and kings to the brightness of thy rising.
4 Lift up thine eyes round about, and see: all
they gather themselves together, they come to
thee: thy sons shall come from far, and thy
daughters shall be nursed at *thy* side.
5 Then thou shalt see, and flow together, and
thine heart shall fear, and be enlarged; because
the abundance of the sea shall be converted
unto thee, the forces of the Gen'tiles shall come
unto thee.
6 The multitude of camels shall cover thee,
the dromedaries of Mid'i-an and E'phah; all
they from She'ba shall come: they shall bring

gold and incense; and they shall shew forth the praises of the LORD.

7 All the flocks of Ke'dar shall be gathered together unto thee, the rams of Ne-ba'ioth shall minister unto thee: they shall come up with acceptance on mine altar, and I will glorify the house of my glory.

8 Who *are* these *that* fly as a cloud, and as the doves to their windows?

9 Surely the isles shall wait for me, and the ships of Tar'shish first, to bring thy sons from far, their silver and their gold with them, unto the name of the LORD thy God, and to the Holy One of Is'ra-el, because he hath glorified thee.

10 And the sons of strangers shall build up thy walls, and their kings shall minister unto thee: for in my wrath I smote thee, but in my favour have I had mercy on thee.

11 Therefore thy gates shall be open continually; they shall not be shut day nor night; that *men* may bring unto thee the forces of the Gen'tiles, and *that* their kings *may be* brought.

12 For the nation and kingdom that will not serve thee shall perish; yea, *those* nations shall be utterly wasted.

13 The glory of Leb'a-non shall come unto thee, the fir tree, the pine tree, and the box together, to beautify the place of my sanctuary; and I will make the place of my feet glorious.

14 The sons also of them that afflicted thee shall come bending unto thee; and all they that despised thee shall bow themselves down at the soles of thy feet; and they shall call thee, The city of the LORD, The Zi'on of the Holy One of Is'ra-el.

15 Whereas thou hast been forsaken and hated, so that no man went through *thee*, I will make thee an eternal excellency, a joy of many generations.

16 Thou shalt also suck the milk of the Gen'tiles, and shalt suck the breast of kings: and thou shalt know that I the LORD *am* thy Saviour and thy Redeemer, the mighty One of Ja'cob.

17 For brass I will bring gold, and for iron I will bring silver, and for wood brass, and for stones iron: I will also make thy officers peace, and thine exactors righteousness.

18 Violence shall no more be heard in thy land, wasting nor destruction within thy borders; but thou shalt call thy walls Salvation, and thy gates Praise.

19 The sun shall be no more thy light by day; neither for brightness shall the moon give light unto thee: but the LORD shall be unto thee an everlasting light, and thy God thy glory.

20 Thy sun shall no more go down; neither shall thy moon withdraw itself: for the LORD shall be thine everlasting light, and the days of thy mourning shall be ended.

21 Thy people also *shall be* all righteous: they shall inherit the land for ever, the branch of my planting, the work of my hands, that I may be glorified.

22 A little one shall become a thousand, and a small one a strong nation: I the LORD will hasten it in his time.

61 THE Spirit of the Lord GOD *is* upon me; because the LORD hath anointed me to preach good tidings unto the meek; he hath sent me to bind up the brokenhearted, to proclaim liberty to the captives, and the opening of the prison to *them that are* bound;

2 To proclaim the acceptable year of the LORD, and the day of vengeance of our God; to comfort all that mourn;

3 To appoint unto them that mourn in Zi'on, to give unto them beauty for ashes, the oil of joy for mourning, the garment of praise for the spirit of heaviness; that they might be called trees of righteousness, the planting of the LORD, that he might be glorified.

4 ¶ And they shall build the old wastes, they shall raise up the former desolations, and they shall repair the waste cities, the desolations of many generations.

5 And strangers shall stand and feed your flocks, and the sons of the alien *shall be* your plowmen and your vinedressers.

6 But ye shall be named the Priests of the LORD: *men* shall call you the Ministers of our God: ye shall eat the riches of the Gen'tiles, and in their glory shall ye boast yourselves.

7 ¶ For your shame *ye shall have* double; and *for* confusion they shall rejoice in their portion: therefore in their land they shall possess the double: everlasting joy shall be unto them.

8 For I the LORD love judgment, I hate robbery for burnt offering; and I will direct their work in truth, and I will make an everlasting covenant with them.

9 And their seed shall be known among the Gen'tiles, and their offspring among the people: all that see them shall acknowledge them, that they *are* the seed *which* the LORD hath blessed.

10 I will greatly rejoice in the LORD, my soul shall be joyful in my God; for he hath clothed me with the garments of salvation, he hath covered me with the robe of righteousness, as a bridegroom decketh *himself* with ornaments, and as a bride adorneth *herself* with her jewels.

11 For as the earth bringeth forth her bud, and as the garden causeth the things that are sown in it to spring forth; so the Lord GOD will cause righteousness and praise to spring forth before all the nations.

62 FOR Zi'on's sake will I not hold my peace, and for Je-ru'sa-lem's sake I will not rest, until the righteousness thereof go forth as brightness, and the salvation thereof as a lamp *that* burneth.

2 And the Gen'tiles shall see thy righteousness, and all kings thy glory: and thou shalt be called by a new name, which the mouth of the LORD shall name.

3 Thou shalt also be a crown of glory in the hand of the LORD, and a royal diadem in the hand of thy God.

4 Thou shalt no more be termed Forsaken; neither shall thy land any more be termed Desolate: but thou shalt be called Heph'zi-bah, and thy land Beu'lah: for the LORD delighteth in thee, and thy land shall be married.

5 ¶ For *as* a young man marrieth a virgin, *so* shall thy sons marry thee: and *as* the bridegroom rejoiceth over the bride, *so* shall thy God rejoice over thee.

6 I have set watchmen upon thy walls, O Je-ru'sa-lem, *which* shall never hold their peace day nor night: ye that make mention of the LORD, keep not silence,

7 And give him no rest, till he establish, and till he make Je-ru'sa-lem a praise in the earth.

8 The LORD hath sworn by his right hand, and by the arm of his strength, Surely I will no more give thy corn *to be* meat for thine enemies; and the sons of the stranger shall not drink thy wine, for the which thou hast laboured:

9 But they that have gathered it shall eat it, and praise the LORD; and they that have brought it together shall drink it in the courts of my holiness.

10 ¶ Go through, go through the gates; prepare ye the way of the people; cast up, cast up the highway; gather out the stones; lift up a standard for the people.

11 Behold, the LORD hath proclaimed unto the end of the world, Say ye to the daughter of Zi'on, Behold, thy salvation cometh; behold, his reward *is* with him, and his work before him.

12 And they shall call them, The holy people, The redeemed of the LORD: and thou shalt be called, Sought out, A city not forsaken.

63 WHO *is* this that cometh from E'dom, with dyed garments from Boz'rah? this *that is* glorious in his apparel, travelling in the greatness of his strength? I that speak in righteousness, mighty to save.

2 Wherefore *art thou* red in thine apparel, and thy garments like him that treadeth in the winefat?

3 I have trodden the winepress alone; and of the people *there was* none with me: for I will tread them in mine anger, and trample them in my fury; and their blood shall be sprinkled upon my garments, and I will stain all my raiment.

4 For the day of vengeance *is* in mine heart, and the year of my redeemed is come.

5 And I looked, and *there was* none to help; and I wondered that *there was* none to uphold: therefore mine own arm brought salvation unto me; and my fury, it upheld me.

6 And I will tread down the people in mine anger, and make them drunk in my fury, and I will bring down their strength to the earth.

7 ¶ I will mention the lovingkindnesses of the LORD, *and* the praises of the LORD, according to all that the LORD hath bestowed on us, and the great goodness toward the house of Is'ra-el, which he hath bestowed on them according to his mercies, and according to the multitude of his lovingkindnesses.

8 For he said, Surely they *are* my people, children *that* will not lie: so he was their Saviour.

9 In all their affliction he was afflicted, and the angel of his presence saved them: in his love and in his pity he redeemed them; and he bare them, and carried them all the days of old.

10 ¶ But they rebelled, and vexed his holy Spirit: therefore he was turned to be their enemy, *and* he fought against them.

11 Then he remembered the days of old, Mo'ses, *and* his people, *saying,* Where *is* he that brought them up out of the sea with the shepherd of his flock? where *is* he that put his holy Spirit within him?

12 That led *them* by the right hand of Mo'ses with his glorious arm, dividing the water before them, to make himself an everlasting name?

13 That led them through the deep, as an horse in the wilderness, *that* they should not stumble?

14 As a beast goeth down into the valley, the Spirit of the LORD caused him to rest: so didst thou lead thy people, to make thyself a glorious name.

15 ¶ Look down from heaven, and behold from the habitation of thy holiness and of thy glory: where *is* thy zeal and thy strength, the sounding of thy bowels and of thy mercies toward me? are they restrained?

16 Doubtless thou *art* our father, though A'bra-ham be ignorant of us, and Is'ra-el acknowledge us not: thou, O LORD, *art* our father, our redeemer; thy name *is* from everlasting.

17 ¶ O LORD, why hast thou made us to err from thy ways, *and* hardened our hearts from thy fear? Return for thy servants' sake, the tribes of thine inheritance.

18 The people of thy holiness have possessed *it* but a little while: our adversaries have trodden down thy sanctuary.

19 We are *thine:* thou never barest rule over them; they were not called by thy name.

64 OH that thou wouldest rend the heavens, that thou wouldest come down, that the mountains might flow down at thy presence,

2 As *when* the melting fire burneth, the fire causeth the waters to boil, to make thy name known to thine adversaries, *that* the nations may tremble at thy presence!

3 When thou didst terrible things *which* we looked not for, thou camest down, the mountains flowed down at thy presence.

4 For since the beginning of the world *men* have not heard, nor perceived by the ear, neither hath the eye seen, O God, beside thee, *what* he hath prepared for him that waiteth for him.

5 Thou meetest him that rejoiceth and worketh righteousness, *those that* remember thee in thy ways: behold, thou art wroth; for we have sinned: in those is continuance, and we shall be saved.

6 But we are all as an unclean *thing,* and all our righteousnesses *are* as filthy rags; and we all do fade as a leaf; and our iniquities, like the wind, have taken us away.

7 And *there is* none that calleth upon thy name, that stirreth up himself to take hold of thee: for thou hast hid thy face from us, and hast consumed us, because of our iniquities.

8 But now, O LORD, thou *art* our father; we *are* the clay, and thou our potter; and we all *are* the work of thy hand.

9 ¶ Be not wroth very sore, O LORD, neither remember iniquity for ever: behold, see, we beseech thee, we *are* all thy people.

10 Thy holy cities are a wilderness, Zi'on is a wilderness, Je-ru'sa-lem a desolation.

11 Our holy and our beautiful house, where our fathers praised thee, is burned up with fire: and all our pleasant things are laid waste.

12 Wilt thou refrain thyself for these *things,* O LORD? wilt thou hold thy peace, and afflict us very sore?

65 I AM sought of *them that* asked not *for me;* I am found of *them that* sought me not: I said, Behold me, behold me, unto a nation *that* was not called by my name.

2 I have spread out my hands all the day unto a rebellious people, which walketh in a way *that was* not good, after their own thoughts;

3 A people that provoketh me to anger continually to my face; that sacrificeth in gardens, and burneth incense upon altars of brick;

4 Which remain among the graves, and lodge in the monuments, which eat swine's flesh, and broth of abominable *things is in* their vessels;

5 Which say, Stand by thyself, come not near to me; for I am holier than thou. These *are* a smoke in my nose, a fire that burneth all the day.

6 Behold, *it is* written before me: I will not keep silence, but will recompense, even recompense into their bosom,

7 Your iniquities, and the iniquities of your fathers together, saith the LORD, which have burned incense upon the mountains, and blasphemed me upon the hills: therefore will I measure their former work into their bosom.

8 ¶ Thus saith the LORD, As the new wine is found in the cluster, and *one* saith, Destroy it not; for a blessing *is* in it: so will I do for my servants' sakes, that I may not destroy them all.

9 And I will bring forth a seed out of Ja′cob, and out of Ju′dah an inheritor of my mountains: and mine elect shall inherit it, and my servants shall dwell there.

10 And Shar′on shall be a fold of flocks, and the valley of A′chor a place for the herds to lie down in, for my people that have sought me.

11 ¶ But ye *are* they that forsake the LORD, that forget my holy mountain, that prepare a table for that troop, and that furnish the drink offering unto that number.

12 Therefore will I number you to the sword, and ye shall all bow down to the slaughter: because when I called, ye did not answer; when I spake, ye did not hear; but did evil before mine eyes, and did choose *that* wherein I delighted not.

13 Therefore thus saith the Lord GOD, Behold, my servants shall eat, but ye shall be hungry: behold, my servants shall drink, but ye shall be thirsty: behold, my servants shall rejoice, but ye shall be ashamed:

14 Behold, my servants shall sing for joy of heart, but ye shall cry for sorrow of heart, and shall howl for vexation of spirit.

15 And ye shall leave your name for a curse unto my chosen: for the Lord GOD shall slay thee, and call his servants by another name:

16 That he who blesseth himself in the earth shall bless himself in the God of truth; and he that sweareth in the earth shall swear by the God of truth; because the former troubles are forgotten, and because they are hid from mine eyes.

17 ¶ For, behold, I create new heavens and a new earth: and the former shall not be remembered, nor come into mind.

18 But be ye glad and rejoice for ever *in that* which I create: for, behold, I create Je-ru′sa-lem a rejoicing, and her people a joy.

19 And I will rejoice in Je-ru′sa-lem, and joy in my people: and the voice of weeping shall be no more heard in her, nor the voice of crying.

20 There shall be no more thence an infant of days, nor an old man that hath not filled his days: for the child shall die an hundred years old; but the sinner *being* an hundred years old shall be accursed.

21 And they shall build houses, and inhabit *them;* and they shall plant vineyards, and eat the fruit of them.

22 They shall not build, and another inhabit; they shall not plant, and another eat: for as the days of a tree *are* the days of my people, and mine elect shall long enjoy the work of their hands.

23 They shall not labour in vain, nor bring forth for trouble; for they *are* the seed of the blessed of the LORD, and their offspring with them.

24 And it shall come to pass, that before they call, I will answer; and while they are yet speaking, I will hear.

25 The wolf and the lamb shall feed together, and the lion shall eat straw like the bullock: and dust *shall be* the serpent's meat. They shall not hurt nor destroy in all my holy mountain, saith the LORD.

66 THUS saith the LORD, The heaven *is* my throne, and the earth *is* my footstool: where *is* the house that ye build unto me? and where *is* the place of my rest?

2 For all those *things* hath mine hand made, and all those *things* have been, saith the LORD: but to this *man* will I look, *even* to *him that is* poor and of a contrite spirit, and trembleth at my word.

3 He that killeth an ox *is as if* he slew a man; he that sacrificeth a lamb, *as if* he cut off a dog's neck; he that offereth an oblation, *as if he offered* swine's blood; he that burneth incense, *as if* he blessed an idol. Yea, they have chosen their own ways, and their soul delighteth in their abominations.

4 I also will choose their delusions, and will bring their fears upon them; because when I called, none did answer; when I spake, they did not hear: but they did evil before mine eyes, and chose *that* in which I delighted not.

5 ¶ Hear the word of the LORD, ye that tremble at his word; Your brethren that hated you, that cast you out for my name's sake, said, Let the LORD be glorified: but he shall appear to your joy, and they shall be ashamed.

6 A voice of noise from the city, a voice from the temple, a voice of the LORD that rendereth recompence to his enemies.

7 Before she travailed, she brought forth; before her pain came, she was delivered of a man child.

8 Who hath heard such a thing? who hath seen such things? Shall the earth be made to bring forth in one day? *or* shall a nation be born at once? for as soon as Zi′on travailed, she brought forth her children.

9 Shall I bring to the birth, and not cause to bring forth? saith the LORD: shall I cause to bring forth, and shut *the womb?* saith thy God.

10 Rejoice ye with Je-ru′sa-lem, and be glad with her, all ye that love her: rejoice for joy with her, all ye that mourn for her:

11 That ye may suck, and be satisfied with the breasts of her consolations; that ye may milk out, and be delighted with the abundance of her glory.

12 For thus saith the LORD, Behold I will extend peace to her like a river, and the glory of the Gen′tiles like a flowing stream: then shall ye suck, ye shall be borne upon *her* sides, and be dandled upon *her* knees.

13 As one whom his mother comforteth, so will I comfort you; and ye shall be comforted in Je-ru′sa-lem.

14 And when ye see *this,* your heart shall rejoice, and your bones shall flourish like an herb: and the hand of the LORD shall be known toward his servants, and *his* indignation toward his enemies.

15 For, behold, the LORD will come with fire, and with his chariots like a whirlwind, to render his anger with fury, and his rebuke with flames of fire.

16 For by fire and by his sword will the LORD plead with all flesh: and the slain of the LORD shall be many.

17 They that sanctify themselves, and purify themselves in the gardens, behind one *tree* in the midst, eating swine's flesh, and the abomination, and the mouse, shall be consumed together, saith the LORD.

18 For I *know* their works and their thoughts: it shall come, that I will gather all nations and tongues; and they shall come, and see my glory.

19 And I will set a sign among them, and I will send those that escape of them unto the nations, *to* Tar′shish, Pul, and Lud, that draw the bow, *to* Tu′bal, and Ja′van, *to* the isles afar off, that have not heard my fame, neither have

seen my glory; and they shall declare my glory among the Gen'tiles.

20 And they shall bring all your brethren *for* an offering unto the LORD out of all nations upon horses, and in chariots, and in litters, and upon mules, and upon swift beasts, to my holy mountain Je-ru'sa-lem, saith the LORD, as the children of Is'ra-el bring an offering in a clean vessel into the house of the LORD.

21 And I will also take of them for priests *and* for Le'vites, saith the LORD.

22 For as the new heavens and the new earth, which I will make, shall remain before me, saith the LORD, so shall your seed and your name remain.

23 And it shall come to pass, *that* from one new moon to another, and from one sabbath to another, shall all flesh come to worship before me, saith the LORD.

24 And they shall go forth, and look upon the carcases of the men that have transgressed against me: for their worm shall not die, neither shall their fire be quenched; and they shall be an abhorring unto all flesh.

THE BOOK OF

JEREMIAH

1 THE words of Jer-e-mi'ah the son of Hil-ki'ah, of the priests that *were* in An'a-thoth in the land of Ben'ja-min:

2 To whom the word of the LORD came in the days of Jo-si'ah the son of A'mon king of Ju'dah, in the thirteenth year of his reign.

3 It came also in the days of Je-hoi'a-kim the son of Jo-si'ah king of Ju'dah, unto the end of the eleventh year of Zed-e-ki'ah the son of Jo-si'ah king of Ju'dah, unto the carrying away of Je-ru'sa-lem captive in the fifth month.

4 Then the word of the LORD came unto me, saying,

5 Before I formed thee in the belly I knew thee; and before thou camest forth out of the womb I sanctified thee, *and* I ordained thee a prophet unto the nations.

6 Then said I, Ah, Lord GOD! behold, I cannot speak: for I *am* a child.

7 ¶ But the LORD said unto me, Say not, I *am* a child: for thou shalt go to all that I shall send thee, and whatsoever I command thee thou shalt speak.

8 Be not afraid of their faces: for I *am* with thee to deliver thee, saith the LORD.

9 Then the LORD put forth his hand, and touched my mouth. And the LORD said unto me, Behold, I have put my words in thy mouth.

10 See, I have this day set thee over the nations and over the kingdoms, to root out, and to pull down, and to destroy, and to throw down, to build, and to plant.

11 ¶ Moreover the word of the LORD came unto me, saying, Jer-e-mi'ah, what seest thou? And I said, I see a rod of an almond tree.

12 Then said the LORD unto me, Thou hast well seen: for I will hasten my word to perform it.

13 And the word of the LORD came unto me the second time, saying, What seest thou? And I said, I see a seething pot; and the face thereof *is* toward the north.

14 Then the LORD said unto me, Out of the north an evil shall break forth upon all the inhabitants of the land.

15 For, lo, I will call all the families of the kingdoms of the north, saith the LORD; and they shall come, and they shall set every one his throne at the entering of the gates of Je-ru'sa-lem, and against all the walls thereof round about, and against all the cities of Ju'dah.

16 And I will utter my judgments against them touching all their wickedness, who have forsaken me, and have burned incense unto other gods, and worshipped the works of their own hands.

17 ¶ Thou therefore gird up thy loins, and arise, and speak unto them all that I command thee: be not dismayed at their faces, lest I confound thee before them.

18 For, behold, I have made thee this day a defenced city, and an iron pillar, and brasen walls against the whole land, against the kings of Ju'dah, against the princes thereof, against the priests thereof, and against the people of the land.

19 And they shall fight against thee; but they shall not prevail against thee; for I *am* with thee, saith the LORD, to deliver thee.

2 MOREOVER the word of the LORD came to me, saying,

2 Go and cry in the ears of Je-ru'sa-lem, saying, Thus saith the LORD; I remember thee, the kindness of thy youth, the love of thine espousals, when thou wentest after me in the wilderness, in a land *that was* not sown.

3 Is'ra-el *was* holiness unto the LORD, *and* the firstfruits of his increase: all that devour him shall offend; evil shall come upon them, saith the LORD.

4 Hear ye the word of the LORD, O house of Ja'cob, and all the families of the house of Is'ra-el:

5 ¶ Thus saith the LORD, What iniquity have your fathers found in me, that they are gone far from me, and have walked after vanity, and are become vain?

6 Neither said they, Where *is* the LORD that brought us up out of the land of E'gypt, that led us through the wilderness, through a land of deserts and of pits, through a land of drought, and of the shadow of death, through a land that no man passed through, and where no man dwelt?

7 And I brought you into a plentiful country, to eat the fruit thereof and the goodness thereof; but when ye entered, ye defiled my land, and made mine heritage an abomination.

8 The priests said not, Where *is* the LORD? and they that handle the law knew me not: the pastors also transgressed against me, and the prophets prophesied by Ba'al, and walked after *things that* do not profit.

9 ¶ Wherefore I will yet plead with you, saith the LORD, and with your children's children will I plead.

10 For pass over the isles of Chit'tim, and see; and send unto Ke'dar, and consider diligently, and see if there be such a thing.

11 Hath a nation changed *their* gods, which *are* yet no gods? but my people have changed their glory for *that which* doth not profit.

12 Be astonished, O ye heavens, at this, and be horribly afraid, be ye very desolate, saith the LORD.

13 For my people have committed two evils; they have forsaken me the fountain of living waters, *and* hewed them out cisterns, broken cisterns, that can hold no water.

14 ¶ *Is* Is′ra-el a servant? *is* he a homeborn *slave?* why is he spoiled?

15 The young lions roared upon him, *and* yelled, and they made his land waste: his cities are burned without inhabitant.

16 Also the children of Noph and Ta′hap′a-nes have broken the crown of thy head.

17 Hast thou not procured this unto thyself, in that thou hast forsaken the LORD thy God, when he led thee by the way?

18 And now what hast thou to do in the way of E′gypt, to drink the waters of Si′hor? or what hast thou to do in the way of As-syr′i-a, to drink the waters of the river?

19 Thine own wickedness shall correct thee, and thy backslidings shall reprove thee: know therefore and see that *it is* an evil *thing* and bitter, that thou hast forsaken the LORD thy God, and that my fear *is* not in thee, saith the Lord GOD of hosts.

20 ¶ For of old time I have broken thy yoke, *and* burst thy bands; and thou saidst, I will not transgress; when upon every high hill and under every green tree thou wanderest, playing the harlot.

21 Yet I had planted thee a noble vine, wholly a right seed: how then art thou turned into the degenerate plant of a strange vine unto me?

22 For though thou wash thee with nitre, and take thee much sope, *yet* thine iniquity is marked before me, saith the Lord GOD.

23 How canst thou say, I am not polluted, I have not gone after Ba′al-im? see thy way in the valley, know what thou hast done: *thou art* a swift dromedary traversing her ways;

24 A wild ass used to the wilderness, *that* snuffeth up the wind at her pleasure; in her occasion who can turn her away? all they that seek her will not weary themselves; in her month they shall find her.

25 Withhold thy foot from being unshod, and thy throat from thirst: but thou saidst, There is no hope: no; for I have loved strangers, and after them will I go.

26 As the thief is ashamed when he is found, so is the house of Is′ra-el ashamed; they, their kings, their princes, and their priests, and their prophets,

27 Saying to a stock, Thou *art* my father; and to a stone, Thou hast brought me forth: for they have turned *their* back unto me, and not *their* face: but in the time of their trouble they will say, Arise, and save us.

28 But where *are* thy gods that thou hast made thee? let them arise, if they can save thee in the time of thy trouble: for *according to* the number of thy cities are thy gods, O Ju′dah.

29 Wherefore will ye plead with me? ye all have transgressed against me, saith the LORD.

30 In vain have I smitten your children; they received no correction: your own sword hath devoured your prophets, like a destroying lion.

31 ¶ O generation, see ye the word of the LORD. Have I been a wilderness unto Is′ra-el? a land of darkness? wherefore say my people, We are lords; we will come no more unto thee?

32 Can a maid forget her ornaments, *or* a bride her attire? yet my people have forgotten me days without number.

33 Why trimmest thou thy way to seek love? therefore hast thou also taught the wicked ones thy ways.

34 Also in thy skirts is found the blood of the souls of the poor innocents: I have not found it by secret search, but upon all these.

35 Yet thou sayest, Because I am innocent, surely his anger shall turn from me. Behold, I will plead with thee, because thou sayest, I have not sinned.

36 Why gaddest thou about so much to change thy way? thou also shalt be ashamed of E′gypt, as thou wast ashamed of As-syr′i-a.

37 Yea, thou shalt go forth from him, and thine hands upon thine head: for the LORD hath rejected thy confidences, and thou shalt not prosper in them.

3 THEY say, If a man put away his wife, and she go from him, and become another man's, shall he return unto her again? shall not that land be greatly polluted? but thou hast played the harlot with many lovers; yet return again to me, saith the LORD.

2 Lift up thine eyes unto the high places, and see where thou hast not been lien with. In the ways hast thou sat for them, as the A-ra′bi-an in the wilderness; and thou hast polluted the land with thy whoredoms and with thy wickedness.

3 Therefore the showers have been withholden, and there hath been no latter rain; and thou hadst a whore's forehead, thou refusedst to be ashamed.

4 Wilt thou not from this time cry unto me, My father, thou *art* the guide of my youth?

5 Will he reserve *his anger* for ever? will he keep *it* to the end? Behold, thou hast spoken and done evil things as thou couldest.

6 ¶ The LORD said also unto me in the days of Jo-si′ah the king, Hast thou seen *that* which backsliding Is′ra-el hath done? she is gone up upon every high mountain and under every green tree, and there hath played the harlot.

7 And I said after she had done all these *things*, Turn thou unto me. But she returned not. And her treacherous sister Ju′dah saw *it*.

8 And I saw, when for all the causes whereby backsliding Is′ra-el committed adultery I had put her away, and given her a bill of divorce; yet her treacherous sister Ju′dah feared not, but went and played the harlot also.

9 And it came to pass through the lightness of her whoredom, that she defiled the land, and committed adultery with stones and with stocks.

10 And yet for all this her treacherous sister Ju′dah hath not turned unto me with her whole heart, but feignedly, saith the LORD.

11 And the LORD said unto me, The backsliding Is′ra-el hath justified herself more than treacherous Ju′dah.

12 ¶ Go and proclaim these words toward the north, and say, Return, thou backsliding Is′ra-el, saith the LORD; *and* I will not cause mine anger to fall upon you: for I *am* merciful, saith the LORD, *and* I will not keep *anger* for ever.

13 Only acknowledge thine iniquity, that thou hast transgressed against the LORD thy God, and hast scattered thy ways to the strangers under every green tree, and ye have not obeyed my voice, saith the LORD.

14 Turn, O backsliding children, saith the LORD; for I am married unto you: and I will take you one of a city, and two of a family, and I will bring you to Zi′on:

15 And I will give you pastors according to

mine heart, which shall feed you with knowledge and understanding.

16 And it shall come to pass, when ye be multiplied and increased in the land, in those days, saith the LORD, they shall say no more, The ark of the covenant of the LORD: neither shall it come to mind: neither shall they remember it; neither shall they visit *it;* neither shall *that* be done any more.

17 At that time they shall call Je-ru'sa-lem the throne of the LORD; and all the nations shall be gathered unto it, to the name of the LORD, to Je-ru'sa-lem: neither shall they walk any more after the imagination of their evil heart.

18 In those days the house of Ju'dah shall walk with the house of Is'ra-el, and they shall come together out of the land of the north to the land that I have given for an inheritance unto your fathers.

19 But I said, How shall I put thee among the children, and give thee a pleasant land, a goodly heritage of the hosts of nations? and I said, Thou shalt call me, My father; and shalt not turn away from me.

20 ¶ Surely *as* a wife treacherously departeth from her husband, so have ye dealt treacherously with me, O house of Is'ra-el, saith the LORD.

21 A voice was heard upon the high places, weeping *and* supplications of the children of Is'ra-el: for they have perverted their way, *and* they have forgotten the LORD their God.

22 Return, ye backsliding children, *and* I will heal your backslidings. Behold, we come unto thee; for thou *art* the LORD our God.

23 Truly in vain *is salvation hoped for* from the hills, *and from* the multitude of mountains: truly in the LORD our God *is* the salvation of Is'ra-el.

24 For shame hath devoured the labour of our fathers from our youth; their flocks and their herds, their sons and their daughters.

25 We lie down in our shame, and our confusion covereth us: for we have sinned against the LORD our God, we and our fathers, from our youth even unto this day, and have not obeyed the voice of the LORD our God.

4

IF thou wilt return, O Is'ra-el, saith the LORD, return unto me: and if thou wilt put away thine abominations out of my sight, then shalt thou not remove.

2 And thou shalt swear, The LORD liveth, in truth, in judgment, and in righteousness; and the nations shall bless themselves in him, and in him shall they glory.

3 ¶ For thus saith the LORD to the men of Ju'dah and Je-ru'sa-lem, Break up your fallow ground, and sow not among thorns.

4 Circumcise yourselves to the LORD, and take away the foreskins of your heart, ye men of Ju'dah and inhabitants of Je-ru'sa-lem: lest my fury come forth like fire, and burn that none can quench *it,* because of the evil of your doings.

5 Declare ye in Ju'dah, and publish in Je-ru'sa-lem; and say, Blow ye the trumpet in the land: cry, gather together, and say, Assemble yourselves, and let us go into the defenced cities.

6 Set up the standard toward Zi'on: retire, stay not: for I will bring evil from the north, and a great destruction.

7 The lion is come up from his thicket, and the destroyer of the Gen-tiles is on his way; he is gone forth from his place to make thy land desolate; *and* thy cities shall be laid waste, without an inhabitant.

8 For this gird you with sackcloth, lament and howl: for the fierce anger of the LORD is not turned back from us.

9 And it shall come to pass at that day, saith the LORD, *that* the heart of the king shall perish, and the heart of the princes; and the priests shall be astonished, and the prophets shall wonder.

10 Then said I, Ah, Lord GOD! surely thou hast greatly deceived this people and Je-ru'sa-lem, saying, Ye shall have peace; whereas the sword reacheth unto the soul.

11 At that time shall it be said to this people and to Je-ru'sa-lem, A dry wind of the high places in the wilderness toward the daughter of my people, not to fan, nor to cleanse,

12 *Even* a full wind from those *places* shall come unto me: now also will I give sentence against them.

13 Behold, he shall come up as clouds, and his chariots *shall be* as a whirlwind: his horses are swifter than eagles. Woe unto us! for we are spoiled.

14 O Je-ru'sa-lem, wash thine heart from wickedness, that thou mayest be saved. How long shall thy vain thoughts lodge within thee?

15 For a voice declareth from Dan, and publisheth affliction from mount E'phra-im.

16 Make ye mention to the nations; behold, publish against Je-ru'sa-lem, *that* watchers come from a far country, and give out their voice against the cities of Ju'dah.

17 As keepers of a field, are they against her round about; because she hath been rebellious against me, saith the LORD.

18 Thy way and thy doings have procured these *things* unto thee; this *is* thy wickedness, because it is bitter, because it reacheth unto thine heart.

19 ¶ My bowels, my bowels! I am pained at my very heart; my heart maketh a noise in me; I cannot hold my peace, because thou hast heard, O my soul, the sound of the trumpet, the alarm of war.

20 Destruction upon destruction is cried; for the whole land is spoiled: suddenly are my tents spoiled, *and* my curtains in a moment.

21 How long shall I see the standard, *and* hear the sound of the trumpet?

22 For my people *is* foolish, they have not known me; they *are* sottish children, and they have none understanding: they *are* wise to do evil, but to do good they have no knowledge.

23 I beheld the earth, and, lo, *it was* without form, and void; and the heavens, and they *had* no light.

24 I beheld the mountains, and, lo, they trembled, and all the hills moved lightly.

25 I beheld, and, lo, *there was* no man, and all the birds of the heavens were fled.

26 I beheld, and, lo, the fruitful place *was* a wilderness, and all the cities thereof were broken down at the presence of the LORD, *and* by his fierce anger.

27 For thus hath the LORD said, The whole land shall be desolate; yet will I not make a full end.

28 For this shall the earth mourn, and the heavens above be black: because I have spoken *it,* I have purposed *it,* and will not repent, neither will I turn back from it.

29 The whole city shall flee for the noise of the horsemen and bowmen; they shall go into thickets, and climb up upon the rocks: every

city *shall be* forsaken, and not a man dwell
therein.
30 And *when* thou *art* spoiled, what wilt thou
do? Though thou clothest thyself with crimson,
though thou deckest thee with ornaments of
gold, though thou rentest thy face with paint-
ing, in vain shalt thou make thyself fair; *thy* lovers will despise thee, they will seek thy life.
31 For I have heard a voice as of a woman in
travail, *and* the anguish as of her that bringeth
forth her first child, the voice of the daughter of
Zi'on, *that* bewaileth herself, *that* spreadeth her
hands, *saying,* Woe *is* me now! for my soul is
wearied because of murderers.

5 RUN ye to and fro through the streets of
Je-ru'sa-lem, and see now, and know, and
seek in the broad places thereof, if ye can find a
man, if there be *any* that executeth judgment,
that seeketh the truth; and I will pardon it.
2 And though they say, The LORD liveth;
surely they swear falsely.
3 O LORD, *are* not thine eyes upon the truth?
thou hast stricken them, but they have not
grieved; thou hast consumed them, *but* they
have refused to receive correction: they have
made their faces harder than a rock; they have
refused to return.
4 Therefore I said, Surely these *are* poor;
they are foolish: for they know not the way of
the LORD, *nor* the judgment of their God.
5 I will get me unto the great men, and will
speak unto them; for they have known the way
of the LORD, *and* the judgment of their God: but
these have altogether broken the yoke, *and*
burst the bonds.
6 Wherefore a lion out of the forest shall slay
them, *and* a wolf of the evenings shall spoil
them, a leopard shall watch over their cities:
every one that goeth out thence shall be torn in
pieces: because their transgressions are many,
and their backslidings are increased.
7 ¶ How shall I pardon thee for this? thy
children have forsaken me, and sworn by *them*
that are no gods: when I had fed them to the
full, they then committed adultery, and assembled themselves by troops in the harlots'
houses.
8 They were *as* fed horses in the morning:
every one neighed after his neighbour's wife.
9 Shall I not visit for these *things*? saith the
LORD: and shall not my soul be avenged on such
a nation as this?
10 ¶ Go ye up upon her walls, and destroy;
but make not a full end: take away her battle-
ments; for they *are* not the LORD'S.
11 For the house of Is'ra-el and the house of
Ju'dah have dealt very treacherously against
me, saith the LORD.
12 They have belied the LORD, and said, *It is*
not he; neither shall evil come upon us; neither
shall we see sword nor famine:
13 And the prophets shall become wind, and
the word *is* not in them: thus shall it be done
unto them.
14 Wherefore thus saith the LORD God of
hosts, Because ye speak this word, behold, I
will make my words in thy mouth fire, and this
people wood, and it shall devour them.
15 Lo, I will bring a nation upon you from
far, O house of Is'ra-el, saith the LORD: it *is* a
mighty nation, it *is* an ancient nation, a nation
whose language thou knowest not, neither understandest what they say.
16 Their quiver *is* as an open sepulchre, they
are all mighty men.
17 And they shall eat up thine harvest, and
thy bread, *which* thy sons and thy daughters
should eat: they shall eat up thy flocks and
thine herds: they shall eat up thy vines and thy
fig trees: they shall impoverish thy fenced
cities, wherein thou trustedst, with the sword.
18 Nevertheless in those days, saith the
LORD, I will not make a full end with you.
19 ¶ And it shall come to pass, when ye shall
say, Wherefore doeth the LORD our God all
these *things* unto us? then shalt thou answer
them, Like as ye have forsaken me, and served
strange gods in your land, so shall ye serve
strangers in a land *that is* not yours.
20 Declare this in the house of Ja'cob, and
publish it in Ju'dah, saying,
21 Hear now this, O foolish people, and without understanding; which have eyes, and see
not; which have ears, and hear not:
22 Fear ye not me? saith the LORD: will ye
not tremble at my presence, which have placed
the sand *for* the bound of the sea by a perpetual
decree, that it cannot pass it: and though the
waves thereof toss themselves, yet can they not
prevail; though they roar, yet can they not pass
over it?
23 But this people hath a revolting and a rebellious heart; they are revolted and gone.
24 Neither say they in their heart, Let us now
fear the LORD our God, that giveth rain, both
the former and the latter, in his season: he re-
serveth unto us the appointed weeks of the harvest.
25 ¶ Your iniquities have turned away these
things, and your sins have withholden good
things from you.
26 For among my people are found wicked
men: they lay wait, as he that setteth snares;
they set a trap, they catch men.
27 As a cage is full of birds, so *are* their
houses full of deceit: therefore they are become
great, and waxen rich.
28 They are waxen fat, they shine: yea, they
overpass the deeds of the wicked: they judge
not the cause, the cause of the fatherless, yet
they prosper; and the right of the needy do they
not judge.
29 Shall I not visit for these *things?* saith the
LORD: shall not my soul be avenged on such a
nation as this?
30 ¶ A wonderful and horrible thing is committed in the land;
31 The prophets prophesy falsely, and the
priests bear rule by their means; and my people
love *to have it* so: and what will ye do in the end
thereof?

6 O YE children of Ben'ja-min, gather yourselves to flee out of the midst of Je-ru'sa-
lem, and blow the trumpet in Te-ko'a, and set
up a sign of fire in Beth–hac'ce-rem: for evil appeareth out of the north, and great destruction.
2 I have likened the daughter of Zi'on to a
comely and delicate *woman.*
3 The shepherds with their flocks shall come
unto her; they shall pitch *their* tents against her
round about; they shall feed every one in his
place.
4 Prepare ye war against her; arise, and let us
go up at noon. Woe unto us! for the day goeth
away, for the shadows of the evening are
stretched out.
5 Arise, and let us go by night, and let us destroy her palaces.
6 ¶ For thus hath the LORD of hosts said,
Hew ye down trees, and cast a mount against
Je-ru'sa-lem: this *is* the city to be visited; she *is*
wholly oppression in the midst of her.

7 As a fountain casteth out her waters, so she casteth out her wickedness: violence and spoil is heard in her; before me continually *is* grief and wounds.

8 Be thou instructed, O Je-ru'sa-lem, lest my soul depart from thee; lest I make thee desolate, a land not inhabited.

9 ¶ Thus saith the LORD of hosts, They shall throughly glean the remnant of Is'ra-el as a vine: turn back thine hand as a grapegatherer into the baskets.

10 To whom shall I speak, and give warning, that they may hear? behold, their ear *is* uncircumcised, and they cannot hearken: behold, the word of the LORD is unto them a reproach; they have no delight in it.

11 Therefore I am full of the fury of the LORD; I am weary with holding in: I will pour it out upon the children abroad, and upon the assembly of young men together: for even the husband with the wife shall be taken, the aged with *him that is* full of days.

12 And their houses shall be turned unto others, *with their* fields and wives together: for I will stretch out my hand upon the inhabitants of the land, saith the LORD.

13 For from the least of them even unto the greatest of them every one *is* given to covetousness; and from the prophet even unto the priest every one dealeth falsely.

14 They have healed also the hurt *of the daughter* of my people slightly, saying, Peace, peace; when *there is* no peace.

15 Were they ashamed when they had committed abomination? nay, they were not at all ashamed, neither could they blush: therefore they shall fall among them that fall: at the time *that* I visit them they shall be cast down, saith the LORD.

16 Thus saith the LORD, Stand ye in the ways, and see, and ask for the old paths, where *is* the good way, and walk therein, and ye shall find rest for your souls. But they said, We will not walk *therein*.

17 Also I set watchmen over you, *saying*, Hearken to the sound of the trumpet. But they said, We will not hearken.

18 ¶ Therefore hear, ye nations, and know, O congregation, what *is* among them.

19 Hear, O earth: behold, I will bring evil upon this people, *even* the fruit of their thoughts, because they have not hearkened unto my words, nor to my law, but rejected it.

20 To what purpose cometh there to me incense from She'ba, and the sweet cane from a far country? your burnt offerings *are* not acceptable, nor your sacrifices sweet unto me.

21 Therefore thus saith the LORD, Behold, I will lay stumblingblocks before this people, and the fathers and the sons together shall fall upon them; the neighbour and his friend shall perish.

22 Thus saith the LORD, Behold, a people cometh from the north country, and a great nation shall be raised from the sides of the earth.

23 They shall lay hold on bow and spear; they *are* cruel, and have no mercy; their voice roareth like the sea; and they ride upon horses, set in array as men for war against thee, O daughter of Zi'on.

24 We have heard the fame thereof: our hands wax feeble: anguish hath taken hold of us, *and* pain, as of a woman in travail.

25 Go not forth into the field, nor walk by the way; for the sword of the enemy *and* fear *is* on every side.

26 ¶ O daughter of my people, gird *thee* with sackcloth, and wallow thyself in ashes: make thee mourning, *as for* an only son, most bitter lamentation: for the spoiler shall suddenly come upon us.

27 I have set thee *for* a tower *and* a fortress among my people, that thou mayest know and try their way.

28 They *are* all grievous revolters, walking with slanders: *they are* brass and iron; they *are* all corrupters.

29 The bellows are burned, the lead is consumed of the fire; the founder melteth in vain: for the wicked are not plucked away.

30 Reprobate silver shall *men* call them, because the LORD hath rejected them.

7

THE word that came to Jer-e-mi'ah from the LORD, saying,

2 Stand in the gate of the LORD's house, and proclaim there this word, and say, Hear the word of the LORD, all *ye of* Ju'dah, that enter in at these gates to worship the LORD.

3 Thus saith the LORD of hosts, the God of Is'ra-el, Amend your ways and your doings, and I will cause you to dwell in this place.

4 Trust ye not in lying words, saying, The temple of the LORD, The temple of the LORD, The temple of the LORD, *are* these.

5 For if ye throughly amend your ways and your doings; if ye throughly execute judgment between a man and his neighbour;

6 *If* ye oppress not the stranger, the fatherless, and the widow, and shed not innocent blood in this place, neither walk after other gods to your hurt:

7 Then will I cause you to dwell in this place, in the land that I gave to your fathers, for ever and ever.

8 ¶ Behold, ye trust in lying words, that cannot profit.

9 Will ye steal, murder, and commit adultery, and swear falsely, and burn incense unto Ba'al, and walk after other gods whom ye know not;

10 And come and stand before me in this house, which is called by my name, and say, We are delivered to do all these abominations?

11 Is this house, which is called by my name, become a den of robbers in your eyes? Behold, even I have seen *it*, saith the LORD.

12 But go ye now unto my place which *was* in Shi'loh, where I set my name at the first, and see what I did to it for the wickedness of my people Is'ra-el.

13 And now, because ye have done all these works, saith the LORD, and I spake unto you, rising up early and speaking, but ye heard not; and I called you, but ye answered not;

14 Therefore will I do unto *this* house, which is called by my name, wherein ye trust, and unto the place which I gave to you and to your fathers, as I have done to Shi'loh.

15 And I will cast you out of my sight, as I have cast out all your brethren, *even* the whole seed of E'phra-im.

16 Therefore pray not thou for this people, neither lift up cry nor prayer for them, neither make intercession to me: for I will not hear thee.

17 ¶ Seest thou not what they do in the cities of Ju'dah and in the streets of Je-ru'sa-lem?

18 The children gather wood, and the fathers kindle the fire, and the women knead *their* dough, to make cakes to the queen of heaven, and to pour out drink offerings unto other gods, that they may provoke me to anger.

19 Do they provoke me to anger? saith the

LORD: *do they* not *provoke* themselves to the confusion of their own faces?

20 Therefore thus saith the Lord GOD; Behold, mine anger and my fury shall be poured out upon this place, upon man, and upon beast, and upon the trees of the field, and upon the fruit of the ground; and it shall burn, and shall not be quenched.

21 ¶ Thus saith the LORD of hosts, the God of Is'ra-el; Put your burnt offerings unto your sacrifices, and eat flesh.

22 For I spake not unto your fathers, nor commanded them in the day that I brought them out of the land of E'gypt, concerning burnt offerings or sacrifices:

23 But this thing commanded I them, saying, Obey my voice, and I will be your God, and ye shall be my people: and walk ye in all the ways that I have commanded you, that it may be well unto you.

24 But they hearkened not, nor inclined their ear, but walked in the counsels *and* in the imagination of their evil heart, and went backward, and not forward.

25 Since the day that your fathers came forth out of the land of E'gypt unto this day I have even sent unto you all my servants the prophets, daily rising up early and sending *them:*

26 Yet they hearkened not unto me, nor inclined their ear, but hardened their neck: they did worse than their fathers.

27 Therefore thou shalt speak all these words unto them; but they will not hearken to thee: thou shalt also call unto them; but they will not answer thee.

28 But thou shalt say unto them, This *is* a nation that obeyeth not the voice of the LORD their God, nor receiveth correction: truth is perished, and is cut off from their mouth.

29 ¶ Cut off thine hair, *O Je-ru'sa-lem,* and cast *it* away, and take up a lamentation on high places; for the LORD hath rejected and forsaken the generation of his wrath.

30 For the children of Ju'dah have done evil in my sight, saith the LORD: they have set their abominations in the house which is called by my name, to pollute it.

31 And they have built the high places of To'-phet, which *is* in the valley of the son of Hin'-nom, to burn their sons and their daughters in the fire; which I commanded *them* not, neither came it into my heart.

32 ¶ Therefore, behold, the days come, saith the LORD, that it shall no more be called To'-phet, nor the valley of the son of Hin'nom, but the valley of slaughter: for they shall bury in To'phet, till there be no place.

33 And the carcases of this people shall be meat for the fowls of the heaven, and for the beasts of the earth; and none shall fray *them* away.

34 Then will I cause to cease from the cities of Ju'dah, and from the streets of Je-ru'sa-lem, the voice of mirth, and the voice of gladness, the voice of the bridegroom, and the voice of the bride: for the land shall be desolate.

8 AT that time, saith the LORD, they shall bring out the bones of the kings of Ju'dah, and the bones of his princes, and the bones of the priests, and the bones of the prophets, and the bones of the inhabitants of Je-ru'sa-lem, out of their graves:

2 And they shall spread them before the sun, and the moon, and all the host of heaven, whom they have loved, and whom they have served, and after whom they have walked, and whom they have sought, and whom they have worshipped: they shall not be gathered, nor be buried; they shall be for dung upon the face of the earth.

3 And death shall be chosen rather than life by all the residue of them that remain of this evil family, which remain in all the places whither I have driven them, saith the LORD of hosts.

4 ¶ Moreover thou shalt say unto them, Thus saith the LORD; Shall they fall, and not arise? shall he turn away, and not return?

5 Why *then* is this people of Je-ru'sa-lem slidden back by a perpetual backsliding? they hold fast deceit, they refuse to return.

6 I hearkened and heard, *but* they spake not aright: no man repented him of his wickedness, saying, What have I done? every one turned to his course, as the horse rusheth into the battle.

7 Yea, the stork in the heaven knoweth her appointed times; and the turtle and the crane and the swallow observe the time of their coming; but my people know not the judgment of the LORD.

8 How do ye say, We *are* wise, and the law of the LORD *is* with us? Lo, certainly in vain made he *it;* the pen of the scribes *is* in vain.

9 The wise *men* are ashamed, they are dismayed and taken: lo, they have rejected the word of the LORD; and what wisdom *is* in them?

10 Therefore will I give their wives unto others, *and* their fields to them that shall inherit *them:* for every one from the least even unto the greatest is given to covetousness, from the prophet even unto the priest every one dealeth falsely.

11 For they have healed the hurt of the daughter of my people slightly, saying, Peace, peace; when *there is* no peace.

12 Were they ashamed when they had committed abomination? nay, they were not at all ashamed, neither could they blush: therefore shall they fall among them that fall: in the time of their visitation they shall be cast down, saith the LORD.

13 ¶ I will surely consume them, saith the LORD: *there shall be* no grapes on the vine, nor figs on the fig tree, and the leaf shall fade; and *the things that* I have given them shall pass away from them.

14 Why do we sit still? assemble yourselves, and let us enter into the defenced cities, and let us be silent there: for the LORD our God hath put us to silence, and given us water of gall to drink, because we have sinned against the LORD.

15 We looked for peace, but no good *came; and* for a time of health, and behold trouble!

16 The snorting of his horses was heard from Dan: the whole land trembled at the sound of the neighing of his strong ones; for they are come, and have devoured the land, and all that is in it; the city, and those that dwell therein.

17 For, behold, I will send serpents, cockatrices, among you, which *will* not *be* charmed, and they shall bite you, saith the LORD.

18 ¶ *When* I would comfort myself against sorrow, my heart *is* faint in me.

19 Behold the voice of the cry of the daughter of my people because of them that dwell in a far country: *Is* not the LORD in Zi'on? *is* not her king in her? Why have they provoked me to anger with their graven images, *and* with strange vanities?

20 The harvest is past, the summer is ended, and we are not saved.

21 For the hurt of the daughter of my people

am I hurt; I am black; astonishment hath taken hold on me.

22 *Is there* no balm in Gil'e-ad; *is there* no physician there? why then is not the health of the daughter of my people recovered?

9 OH that my head were waters, and mine eyes a fountain of tears, that I might weep day and night for the slain of the daughter of my people!

2 Oh that I had in the wilderness a lodging place of wayfaring men; that I might leave my people, and go from them! for they *be* all adulterers, an assembly of treacherous men.

3 And they bend their tongues *like* their bow *for* lies: but they are not valiant for the truth upon the earth; for they proceed from evil to evil, and they know not me, saith the LORD.

4 Take ye heed every one of his neighbour, and trust ye not in any brother: for every brother will utterly supplant, and every neighbour will walk with slanders.

5 And they will deceive every one his neighbour, and will not speak the truth: they have taught their tongue to speak lies, *and* weary themselves to commit iniquity.

6 Thine habitation *is* in the midst of deceit; through deceit they refuse to know me, saith the LORD.

7 Therefore thus saith the LORD of hosts, Behold, I will melt them, and try them; for how shall I do for the daughter of my people?

8 Their tongue *is as* an arrow shot out; it speaketh deceit: *one* speaketh peaceably to his neighbour with his mouth, but in heart he layeth his wait.

9 ¶ Shall I not visit them for these *things?* saith the LORD: shall not my soul be avenged on such a nation as this?

10 For the mountains will I take up a weeping and wailing, and for the habitations of the wilderness a lamentation, because they are burned up, so that none can pass through *them;* neither can *men* hear the voice of the cattle; both the fowl of the heavens and the beast are fled; they are gone.

11 And I will make Je-ru'sa-lem heaps, *and* a den of dragons; and I will make the cities of Ju'dah desolate, without an inhabitant.

12 ¶ Who *is* the wise man, that may understand this? and *who is he* to whom the mouth of the LORD hath spoken, that he may declare it, for what the land perisheth *and* is burned up like a wilderness, that none passeth through?

13 And the LORD saith, Because they have forsaken my law which I set before them, and have not obeyed my voice, neither walked therein;

14 But have walked after the imagination of their own heart, and after Ba'al-im, which their fathers taught them:

15 Therefore thus saith the LORD of hosts, the God of Is'ra-el; Behold, I will feed them, *even* this people, with wormwood, and give them water of gall to drink.

16 I will scatter them also among the heathen, whom neither they nor their fathers have known: and I will send a sword after them, till I have consumed them.

17 ¶ Thus saith the LORD of hosts, Consider ye, and call for the mourning women, that they may come; and send for cunning *women,* that they may come:

18 And let them make haste, and take up a wailing for us, that our eyes may run down with tears, and our eyelids gush out with waters.

19 For a voice of wailing is heard out of Zi'on, How are we spoiled! we are greatly confounded, because we have forsaken the land, because our dwellings have cast *us* out.

20 Yet hear the word of the LORD, O ye women, and let your ear receive the word of his mouth, and teach your daughters wailing, and every one her neighbour lamentation.

21 For death is come up into our windows, *and* is entered into our palaces, to cut off the children from without, *and* the young men from the streets.

22 Speak, Thus saith the LORD, Even the carcases of men shall fall as dung upon the open field, and as the handful after the harvestman, and none shall gather *them.*

23 ¶ Thus saith the LORD, Let not the wise *man* glory in his wisdom, neither let the mighty *man* glory in his might, let not the rich *man* glory in his riches:

24 But let him that glorieth glory in this, that he understandeth and knoweth me, that I *am* the LORD which exercise lovingkindness, judgment, and righteousness, in the earth: for in these *things* I delight, saith the LORD.

25 ¶ Behold, the days come, saith the LORD, that I will punish all *them which are* circumcised with the uncircumcised;

26 E'gypt, and Ju'dah, and E'dom, and the children of Am'mon, and Mo'ab, and all *that are* in the utmost corners, that dwell in the wilderness: for all *these* nations *are* uncircumcised, and all the house of Is'ra-el *are* uncircumcised in the heart.

10 HEAR ye the word which the LORD speaketh unto you, O house of Is'ra-el:

2 Thus saith the LORD, Learn not the way of the heathen, and be not dismayed at the signs of heaven, for the heathen are dismayed at them.

3 For the customs of the people *are* vain: for *one* cutteth a tree out of the forest, the work of the hands of the workman, with the ax.

4 They deck it with silver and with gold; they fasten it with nails and with hammers, that it move not.

5 They *are* upright as the palm tree, but speak not: they must needs be borne, because they cannot go. Be not afraid of them; for they cannot do evil, neither also *is it* in them to do good.

6 Forasmuch as *there is* none like unto thee, O LORD; thou *art* great, and thy name *is* great in might.

7 Who would not fear thee, O King of nations? for to thee doth it appertain: forasmuch as among all the wise *men* of the nations, and in all their kingdoms, *there is* none like unto thee.

8 But they are altogether brutish and foolish: the stock *is* a doctrine of vanities.

9 Silver spread into plates is brought from Tar'shish, and gold from U'phaz, the work of the workman, and of the hands of the founder: blue and purple *is* their clothing: they *are* all the work of cunning *men.*

10 But the LORD *is* the true God, he *is* the living God, and an everlasting king: at his wrath the earth shall tremble, and the nations shall not be able to abide his indignation.

11 Thus shall ye say unto them, The gods that have not made the heavens and the earth, *even* they shall perish from the earth, and from under these heavens.

12 He hath made the earth by his power, he hath established the world by his wisdom, and hath stretched out the heavens by his discretion.

13 When he uttereth his voice, *there is* a multitude of waters in the heavens, and he causeth the vapours to ascend from the ends of the earth; he maketh lightnings with rain, and bringeth forth the wind out of his treasures.

14 Every man is brutish in *his* knowledge: every founder is confounded by the graven image: for his molten image *is* falsehood, and *there is* no breath in them.

15 They *are* vanity, *and* the work of errors: in the time of their visitation they shall perish.

16 The portion of Ja'cob *is* not like them: for he *is* the former of all *things;* and Is'ra-el *is* the rod of his inheritance: The LORD of hosts *is* his name.

17 ¶ Gather up thy wares out of the land, O inhabitant of the fortress.

18 For thus saith the LORD, Behold, I will sling out the inhabitants of the land at this once, and will distress them, that they may find *it so*.

19 ¶ Woe is me for my hurt! my wound is grievous: but I said, Truly this *is* a grief, and I must bear it.

20 My tabernacle is spoiled, and all my cords are broken: my children are gone forth of me, and they *are* not: *there is* none to stretch forth my tent any more, and to set up my curtains.

21 For the pastors are become brutish, and have not sought the LORD: therefore they shall not prosper, and all their flocks shall be scattered.

22 Behold, the noise of the bruit is come, and a great commotion out of the north country, to make the cities of Ju'dah desolate, *and* a den of dragons.

23 ¶ O LORD, I know that the way of man *is* not in himself: *it is* not in man that walketh to direct his steps.

24 O LORD, correct me, but with judgment; not in thine anger, lest thou bring me to nothing.

25 Pour out thy fury upon the heathen that know thee not, and upon the families that call not on thy name: for they have eaten up Ja'cob, and devoured him, and consumed him, and have made his habitation desolate.

11 THE word that came to Jer-e-mi'ah from the LORD, saying,

2 Hear ye the words of this covenant, and speak unto the men of Ju'dah, and to the inhabitants of Je-ru'sa-lem;

3 And say thou unto them, Thus saith the LORD God of Is'ra-el; Cursed *be* the man that obeyeth not the words of this covenant,

4 Which I commanded your fathers in the day *that* I brought them forth out of the land of E'gypt, from the iron furnace, saying, Obey my voice, and do them, according to all which I command you: so shall ye be my people, and I will be your God:

5 That I may perform the oath which I have sworn unto your fathers, to give them a land flowing with milk and honey, as *it is* this day. Then answered I, and said, So be it, O LORD.

6 Then the LORD said unto me, Proclaim all these words in the cities of Ju'dah, and in the streets of Je-ru'sa-lem, saying, Hear ye the words of this covenant, and do them.

7 For I earnestly protested unto your fathers in the day *that* I brought them up out of the land of E'gypt, *even* unto this day, rising early and protesting, saying, Obey my voice.

8 Yet they obeyed not, nor inclined their ear, but walked every one in the imagination of their evil heart: therefore I will bring upon them all the words of this covenant, which I commanded *them* to do; but they did *them* not.

9 And the LORD said unto me, A conspiracy is found among the men of Ju'dah, and among the inhabitants of Je-ru'sa-lem.

10 They are turned back to the iniquities of their forefathers, which refused to hear my words; and they went after other gods to serve them: the house of Is'ra-el and the house of Ju'dah have broken my covenant which I made with their fathers.

11 ¶ Therefore thus saith the LORD, Behold, I will bring evil upon them, which they shall not be able to escape; and though they shall cry unto me, I will not hearken unto them.

12 Then shall the cities of Ju'dah and inhabitants of Je-ru'sa-lem go, and cry unto the gods unto whom they offer incense: but they shall not save them at all in the time of their trouble.

13 For *according to* the number of thy cities were thy gods, O Ju'dah; and *according to* the number of the streets of Je-ru'sa-lem have ye set up altars to *that* shameful thing, *even* altars to burn incense unto Ba'al.

14 Therefore pray not thou for this people, neither lift up a cry or prayer for them: for I will not hear *them* in the time that they cry unto me for their trouble.

15 What hath my beloved to do in mine house, *seeing* she hath wrought lewdness with many, and the holy flesh is passed from thee? when thou doest evil, then thou rejoicest.

16 The LORD called thy name, A green olive tree, fair, *and* of goodly fruit: with the noise of a great tumult he hath kindled fire upon it, and the branches of it are broken.

17 For the LORD of hosts, that planted thee, hath pronounced evil against thee, for the evil of the house of Is'ra-el and of the house of Ju'dah, which they have done against themselves to provoke me to anger in offering incense unto Ba'al.

18 ¶ And the LORD hath given me knowledge *of it,* and I know *it:* then thou shewedst me their doings.

19 But I *was* like a lamb *or* an ox *that* is brought to the slaughter; and I knew not that they had devised devices against me, *saying,* Let us destroy the tree with the fruit thereof, and let us cut him off from the land of the living, that his name may be no more remembered.

20 But, O LORD of hosts, that judgest righteously, that triest the reins and the heart, let me see thy vengeance on them: for unto thee have I revealed my cause.

21 Therefore thus saith the LORD of the men of An'a-thoth, that seek thy life, saying, Prophesy not in the name of the LORD, that thou die not by our hand:

22 Therefore thus saith the LORD of hosts, Behold, I will punish them: the young men shall die by the sword; their sons and their daughters shall die by famine:

23 And there shall be no remnant of them: for I will bring evil upon the men of An'a-thoth, *even* the year of their visitation.

12 RIGHTEOUS *art* thou, O LORD, when I plead with thee: yet let me talk with thee of *thy* judgments: Wherefore doth the way of the wicked prosper? *wherefore* are all they happy that deal very treacherously?

2 Thou hast planted them, yea, they have taken root: they grow, yea, they bring forth fruit: thou *art* near in their mouth, and far from their reins.

3 But thou, O LORD, knowest me: thou hast seen me, and tried mine heart toward thee: pull them out like sheep for the slaughter, and prepare them for the day of slaughter.

4 How long shall the land mourn, and the herbs of every field wither, for the wickedness of them that dwell therein? the beasts are consumed, and the birds; because they said, He shall not see our last end.

5 ¶ If thou hast run with the footmen, and they have wearied thee, then how canst thou contend with horses? and *if* in the land of peace, *wherein* thou trustedst, *they wearied thee,* then how wilt thou do in the swelling of Jor'dan?

6 For even thy brethren, and the house of thy father, even they have dealt treacherously with thee; yea, they have called a multitude after thee: believe them not, though they speak fair words unto thee.

7 ¶ I have forsaken mine house, I have left mine heritage; I have given the dearly beloved of my soul into the hand of her enemies.

8 Mine heritage is unto me as a lion in the forest; it crieth out against me: therefore have I hated it.

9 Mine heritage *is* unto me *as* a speckled bird, the birds round about *are* against her; come ye, assemble all the beasts of the field, come to devour.

10 Many pastors have destroyed my vineyard, they have trodden my portion under foot, they have made my pleasant portion a desolate wilderness.

11 They have made it desolate, *and being* desolate it mourneth unto me; the whole land is made desolate, because no man layeth *it* to heart.

12 The spoilers are come upon all high places through the wilderness: for the sword of the LORD shall devour from the *one* end of the land even to the *other* end of the land: no flesh shall have peace.

13 They have sown wheat, but shall reap thorns: they have put themselves to pain, *but* shall not profit: and they shall be ashamed of your revenues because of the fierce anger of the LORD.

14 ¶ Thus saith the LORD against all mine evil neighbours, that touch the inheritance which I have caused my people Is'ra-el to inherit; Behold, I will pluck them out of their land, and pluck out the house of Ju'dah from among them.

15 And it shall come to pass, after that I have plucked them out I will return, and have compassion on them, and will bring them again, every man to his heritage, and every man to his land.

16 And it shall come to pass, if they will diligently learn the ways of my people, to swear by my name, The LORD liveth; as they taught my people to swear by Ba'al; then shall they be built in the midst of my people.

17 But if they will not obey, I will utterly pluck up and destroy that nation, saith the LORD.

13 THUS saith the LORD unto me, Go and get thee a linen girdle, and put it upon thy loins, and put it not in water.

2 So I got a girdle according to the word of the LORD, and put *it* on my loins.

3 And the word of the LORD came unto me the second time, saying,

4 Take the girdle that thou hast got, which *is* upon thy loins, and arise, go to Eu-phra'tes, and hide it there in a hole of the rock.

5 So I went, and hid it by Eu-phra'tes, as the LORD commanded me.

6 And it came to pass after many days, that the LORD said unto me, Arise, go to Eu-phra'tes, and take the girdle from thence, which I commanded thee to hide there.

7 Then I went to Eu-phra'tes, and digged, and took the girdle from the place where I had hid it: and, behold, the girdle was marred, it was profitable for nothing.

8 Then the word of the LORD came unto me, saying,

9 Thus saith the LORD, After this manner will I mar the pride of Ju'dah, and the great pride of Je-ru'sa-lem.

10 This evil people, which refuse to hear my words, which walk in the imagination of their heart, and walk after other gods, to serve them, and to worship them, shall even be as this girdle, which is good for nothing.

11 For as the girdle cleaveth to the loins of a man, so have I caused to cleave unto me the whole house of Is'ra-el and the whole house of Ju'dah, saith the LORD; that they might be unto me for a people, and for a name, and for a praise, and for a glory: but they would not hear.

12 ¶ Therefore thou shalt speak unto them this word; Thus saith the LORD God of Is'ra-el, Every bottle shall be filled with wine: and they shall say unto thee, Do we not certainly know that every bottle shall be filled with wine?

13 Then shalt thou say unto them, Thus saith the LORD, Behold, I will fill all the inhabitants of this land, even the kings that sit upon Da'vid's throne, and the priests, and the prophets, and all the inhabitants of Je-ru'sa-lem, with drunkenness.

14 And I will dash them one against another, even the fathers and the sons together, saith the LORD: I will not pity, nor spare, nor have mercy, but destroy them.

15 ¶ Hear ye, and give ear; be not proud: for the LORD hath spoken.

16 Give glory to the LORD your God, before he cause darkness, and before your feet stumble upon the dark mountains, and, while ye look for light, he turn it into the shadow of death, *and* make *it* gross darkness.

17 But if ye will not hear it, my soul shall weep in secret places for *your* pride; and mine eye shall weep sore, and run down with tears, because the LORD's flock is carried away captive.

18 Say unto the king and to the queen, Humble yourselves, sit down: for your principalities shall come down, *even* the crown of your glory.

19 The cities of the south shall be shut up, and none shall open *them:* Ju'dah shall be carried away captive all of it, it shall be wholly carried away captive.

20 Lift up your eyes, and behold them that come from the north: where *is* the flock *that* was given thee, thy beautiful flock?

21 What wilt thou say when he shall punish thee? for thou hast taught them *to be* captains, *and* as chief over thee: shall not sorrows take thee, as a woman in travail?

22 ¶ And if thou say in thine heart, Wherefore come these things upon me? For the greatness of thine iniquity are thy skirts discovered, *and* thy heels made bare.

23 Can the E-thi-o'pi-an change his skin, or the leopard his spots? *then* may ye also do good, that are accustomed to do evil.

24 Therefore will I scatter them as the stub-

ble that passeth away by the wind of the wilderness.

25 This *is* thy lot, the portion of thy measures from me, saith the LORD; because thou hast forgotten me, and trusted in falsehood.

26 Therefore will I discover thy skirts upon thy face, that thy shame may appear.

27 I have seen thine adulteries, and thy neighings, the lewdness of thy whoredom, *and* thine abominations on the hills in the fields. Woe unto thee, O Je-ru'sa-lem! wilt thou not be made clean? when *shall it* once *be?*

14 THE word of the LORD that came to Jer-e-mi'ah concerning the dearth.

2 Ju'dah mourneth, and the gates thereof languish; they are black unto the ground; and the cry of Je-ru'sa-lem is gone up.

3 And their nobles have sent their little ones to the waters: they came to the pits, *and* found no water; they returned with their vessels empty; they were ashamed and confounded, and covered their heads.

4 Because the ground is chapt, for there was no rain in the earth, the plowmen were ashamed, they covered their heads.

5 Yea, the hind also calved in the field, and forsook *it*, because there was no grass.

6 And the wild asses did stand in the high places, they snuffed up the wind like dragons; their eyes did fail, because *there was* no grass.

7 ¶ O LORD, though our iniquities testify against us, do thou *it* for thy name's sake: for our backslidings are many; we have sinned against thee.

8 O the hope of Is'ra-el, the saviour thereof in time of trouble, why shouldest thou be as a stranger in the land, and as a wayfaring man *that* turneth aside to tarry for a night?

9 Why shouldest thou be as a man astonied, as a mighty man *that* cannot save? yet thou, O LORD, *art* in the midst of us, and we are called by thy name; leave us not.

10 ¶ Thus saith the LORD unto this people, Thus have they loved to wander, they have not refrained their feet, therefore the LORD doth not accept them; he will now remember their iniquity, and visit their sins.

11 Then said the LORD unto me, Pray not for this people for *their* good.

12 When they fast, I will not hear their cry; and when they offer burnt offering and an oblation, I will not accept them: but I will consume them by the sword, and by the famine, and by the pestilence.

13 ¶ Then said I, Ah, Lord GOD! behold, the prophets say unto them, Ye shall not see the sword, neither shall ye have famine; but I will give you assured peace in this place.

14 Then the LORD said unto me, The prophets prophesy lies in my name: I sent them not, neither have I commanded them, neither spake unto them: they prophesy unto you a false vision and divination, and a thing of nought, and the deceit of their heart.

15 Therefore thus saith the LORD concerning the prophets that prophesy in my name, and I sent them not, yet they say, Sword and famine shall not be in this land; By sword and famine shall those prophets be consumed.

16 And the people to whom they prophesy shall be cast out in the streets of Je-ru'sa-lem because of the famine and the sword; and they shall have none to bury them, them, their wives, nor their sons, nor their daughters: for I will pour their wickedness upon them.

17 ¶ Therefore thou shalt say this word unto them; Let mine eyes run down with tears night and day, and let them not cease: for the virgin daughter of my people is broken with a great breach, with a very grievous blow.

18 If I go forth into the field, then behold the slain with the sword! and if I enter into the city, then behold them that are sick with famine! yea, both the prophet and the priest go about into a land that they know not.

19 Hast thou utterly rejected Ju'dah? hath thy soul loathed Zi'on? why hast thou smitten us, and *there is* no healing for us? we looked for peace, and *there is* no good; and for the time of healing, and behold trouble!

20 We acknowledge, O LORD, our wickedness, *and* the iniquity of our fathers: for we have sinned against thee.

21 Do not abhor *us*, for thy name's sake, do not disgrace the throne of thy glory: remember, break not thy covenant with us.

22 Are there *any* among the vanities of the Gen'tiles that can cause rain? or can the heavens give showers? *art* not thou he, O LORD our God? therefore we will wait upon thee: for thou hast made all these *things*.

15 THEN said the LORD unto me, Though Mo'ses and Sam'u-el stood before me, *yet* my mind *could* not *be* toward this people: cast *them* out of my sight, and let them go forth.

2 And it shall come to pass, if they say unto thee, Whither shall we go forth? then thou shalt tell them, Thus saith the LORD; Such as *are* for death, to death; and such as *are* for the sword, to the sword; and such as *are* for the famine, to the famine; and such as *are* for the captivity, to the captivity.

3 And I will appoint over them four kinds, saith the LORD: the sword to slay, and the dogs to tear, and the fowls of the heaven, and the beasts of the earth, to devour and destroy.

4 And I will cause them to be removed into all kingdoms of the earth, because of Ma-nas'seh the son of Hez-e-ki'ah king of Ju'dah, for *that* which he did in Je-ru'sa-lem.

5 For who shall have pity upon thee, O Je-ru'sa-lem? or who shall bemoan thee? or who shall go aside to ask how thou doest?

6 Thou hast forsaken me, saith the LORD, thou art gone backward: therefore will I stretch out my hand against thee, and destroy thee; I am weary with repenting.

7 And I will fan them with a fan in the gates of the land; I will bereave *them* of children, I will destroy my people, *since* they return not from their ways.

8 Their widows are increased to me above the sand of the seas: I have brought upon them against the mother of the young men a spoiler at noonday: I have caused *him* to fall upon it suddenly, and terrors upon the city.

9 She that hath borne seven languisheth: she hath given up the ghost; her sun is gone down while *it was* yet day: she hath been ashamed and confounded: and the residue of them will I deliver to the sword before their enemies, saith the LORD.

10 ¶ Woe is me, my mother, that thou hast borne me a man of strife and a man of contention to the whole earth! I have neither lent on usury, nor men have lent to me on usury; *yet* every one of them doth curse me.

11 The LORD said, Verily it shall be well with thy remnant; verily I will cause the enemy to entreat thee *well* in the time of evil and in the time of affliction.

12 Shall iron break the northern iron and the steel?

13 Thy substance and thy treasures will I give to the spoil without price, and *that* for all thy sins, even in all thy borders.

14 And I will make *thee* to pass with thine enemies into a land *which* thou knowest not: for a fire is kindled in mine anger, *which* shall burn upon you.

15 ¶ O LORD, thou knowest: remember me, and visit me, and revenge me of my persecutors; take me not away in thy longsuffering: know that for thy sake I have suffered rebuke.

16 Thy words were found, and I did eat them; and thy word was unto me the joy and rejoicing of mine heart: for I am called by thy name, O LORD God of hosts.

17 I sat not in the assembly of the mockers, nor rejoiced; I sat alone because of thy hand: for thou hast filled me with indignation.

18 Why is my pain perpetual, and my wound incurable, *which* refuseth to be healed? wilt thou be altogether unto me as a liar, *and as* waters *that* fail?

19 ¶ Therefore thus saith the LORD, If thou return, then will I bring thee again, *and* thou shalt stand before me: and if thou take forth the precious from the vile, thou shalt be as my mouth: let them return unto thee; but return not thou unto them.

20 And I will make thee unto this people a fenced brasen wall: and they shall fight against thee, but they shall not prevail against thee: for I *am* with thee to save thee and to deliver thee, saith the LORD.

21 And I will deliver thee out of the hand of the wicked, and I will redeem thee out of the hand of the terrible.

16 THE word of the LORD came also unto me, saying,

2 Thou shalt not take thee a wife, neither shalt thou have sons or daughters in this place.

3 For thus saith the LORD concerning the sons and concerning the daughters that are born in this place, and concerning their mothers that bare them, and concerning their fathers that begat them in this land;

4 They shall die of grievous deaths; they shall not be lamented; neither shall they be buried; *but* they shall be as dung upon the face of the earth: and they shall be consumed by the sword, and by famine; and their carcases shall be meat for the fowls of heaven, and for the beasts of the earth.

5 For thus saith the LORD, Enter not into the house of mourning, neither go to lament nor bemoan them: for I have taken away my peace from this people, saith the LORD, *even* lovingkindness and mercies.

6 Both the great and the small shall die in this land: they shall not be buried, neither shall *men* lament for them, nor cut themselves, nor make themselves bald for them:

7 Neither shall *men* tear *themselves* for them in mourning, to comfort them for the dead; neither shall *men* give them the cup of consolation to drink for their father or for their mother.

8 Thou shalt not also go into the house of feasting, to sit with them to eat and to drink.

9 For thus saith the LORD of hosts, the God of Is′ra-el; Behold, I will cause to cease out of this place in your eyes, and in your days, the voice of mirth, and the voice of gladness, the voice of the bridegroom, and the voice of the bride.

10 ¶ And it shall come to pass, when thou shalt shew this people all these words, and they shall say unto thee, Wherefore hath the LORD pronounced all this great evil against us? or what *is* our iniquity? or what *is* our sin that we have committed against the LORD our God?

11 Then shalt thou say unto them, Because your fathers have forsaken me, saith the LORD, and have walked after other gods, and have served them, and have worshipped them, and have forsaken me, and have not kept my law;

12 And ye have done worse than your fathers; for, behold, ye walk every one after the imagination of his evil heart, that they may not hearken unto me:

13 Therefore will I cast you out of this land into a land that ye know not, *neither* ye nor your fathers; and there shall ye serve other gods day and night; where I will not shew you favour.

14 ¶ Therefore, behold, the days come, saith the LORD, that it shall no more be said, The LORD liveth, that brought up the children of Is′ra-el out of the land of E′gypt;

15 But, The LORD liveth, that brought up the children of Is′ra-el from the land of the north, and from all the lands whither he had driven them: and I will bring them again into their land that I gave unto their fathers.

16 ¶ Behold, I will send for many fishers, saith the LORD, and they shall fish them; and after will I send for many hunters, and they shall hunt them from every mountain, and from every hill, and out of the holes of the rocks.

17 For mine eyes *are* upon all their ways: they are not hid from my face, neither is their iniquity hid from mine eyes.

18 And first I will recompense their iniquity and their sin double; because they have defiled my land, they have filled mine inheritance with the carcases of their detestable and abominable things.

19 O LORD, my strength, and my fortress, and my refuge in the day of affliction, the Gen′tiles shall come unto thee from the ends of the earth, and shall say, Surely our fathers have inherited lies, vanity, and *things* wherein *there is* no profit.

20 Shall a man make gods unto himself, and they *are* no gods?

21 Therefore, behold, I will this once cause them to know, I will cause them to know mine hand and my might; and they shall know that my name *is* The LORD.

17 THE sin of Ju′dah *is* written with a pen of iron, *and* with the point of a diamond: *it is* graven upon the table of their heart, and upon the horns of your altars;

2 Whilst their children remember their altars and their groves by the green trees upon the high hills.

3 O my mountain in the field, I will give thy substance *and* all thy treasures to the spoil, *and* thy high places for sin, throughout all thy borders.

4 And thou, even thyself, shalt discontinue from thine heritage that I gave thee; and I will cause thee to serve thine enemies in the land which thou knowest not: for ye have kindled a fire in mine anger, *which* shall burn for ever.

5 ¶ Thus saith the LORD; Cursed *be* the man that trusteth in man, and maketh flesh his arm, and whose heart departeth from the LORD.

6 For he shall be like the heath in the desert, and shall not see when good cometh; but shall inhabit the parched places in the wilderness, *in* a salt land and not inhabited.

7 Blessed *is* the man that trusteth in the LORD, and whose hope the LORD is.

8 For he shall be as a tree planted by the waters, and *that* spreadeth out her roots by the river, and shall not see when heat cometh, but her leaf shall be green; and shall not be careful in the year of drought, neither shall cease from yielding fruit.

9 ¶ The heart *is* deceitful above all *things*, and desperately wicked: who can know it?

10 I the LORD search the heart, *I* try the reins, even to give every man according to his ways, *and* according to the fruit of his doings.

11 *As* the partridge sitteth *on eggs*, and hatcheth *them* not; *so* he that getteth riches, and not by right, shall leave them in the midst of his days, and at his end shall be a fool.

12 ¶ A glorious high throne from the beginning *is* the place of our sanctuary.

13 O LORD, the hope of Is'ra-el, all that forsake thee shall be ashamed, *and* they that depart from me shall be written in the earth, because they have forsaken the LORD, the fountain of living waters.

14 Heal me, O LORD, and I shall be healed; save me, and I shall be saved: for thou *art* my praise.

15 ¶ Behold, they say unto me, Where *is* the word of the LORD? let it come now.

16 As for me, I have not hastened from *being* a pastor to follow thee: neither have I desired the woeful day; thou knowest: that which came out of my lips was *right* before thee.

17 Be not a terror unto me: thou *art* my hope in the day of evil.

18 Let them be confounded that persecute me, but let not me be confounded: let them be dismayed, but let not me be dismayed: bring upon them the day of evil, and destroy them with double destruction.

19 ¶ Thus said the LORD unto me; Go and stand in the gate of the children of the people, whereby the kings of Ju'dah come in, and by the which they go out, and in all the gates of Je-ru'sa-lem;

20 And say unto them, Hear ye the word of the LORD, ye kings of Ju'dah, and all Ju'dah, and all the inhabitants of Je-ru'sa-lem, that enter in by these gates:

21 Thus saith the LORD; Take heed to yourselves, and bear no burden on the sabbath day, nor bring *it* in by the gates of Je-ru'sa-lem;

22 Neither carry forth a burden out of your houses on the sabbath day, neither do ye any work, but hallow ye the sabbath day, as I commanded your fathers.

23 But they obeyed not, neither inclined their ear, but made their neck stiff, that they might not hear, nor receive instruction.

24 And it shall come to pass, if ye diligently hearken unto me, saith the LORD, to bring in no burden through the gates of this city on the sabbath day, but hallow the sabbath day, to do no work therein;

25 Then shall there enter into the gates of this city kings and princes sitting upon the throne of Da'vid, riding in chariots and on horses, they, and their princes, the men of Ju'dah, and the inhabitants of Je-ru'sa-lem: and this city shall remain for ever.

26 And they shall come from the cities of Ju'dah, and from the places about Je-ru'sa-lem, and from the land of Ben'ja-min, and from the plain, and from the mountains, and from the south, bringing burnt offerings, and sacrifices, and meat offerings, and incense, and bringing sacrifices of praise, unto the house of the LORD.

27 But if ye will not hearken unto me to hallow the sabbath day, and not to bear a burden, even entering in at the gates of Je-ru'sa-lem on the sabbath day; then will I kindle a fire in the gates thereof, and it shall devour the palaces of Je-ru'sa-lem, and it shall not be quenched.

18 THE word which came to Jer-e-mi'ah from the LORD, saying,

2 Arise, and go down to the potter's house, and there I will cause thee to hear my words.

3 Then I went down to the potter's house, and, behold, he wrought a work on the wheels.

4 And the vessel that he made of clay was marred in the hand of the potter: so he made it again another vessel, as seemed good to the potter to make *it*.

5 Then the word of the LORD came to me, saying,

6 O house of Is'ra-el, cannot I do with you as this potter? saith the LORD. Behold, as the clay *is* in the potter's hand, so *are* ye in mine hand, O house of Is'ra-el.

7 At *what* instant I shall speak concerning a nation, and concerning a kingdom, to pluck up, and to pull down, and to destroy *it;*

8 If that nation, against whom I have pronounced, turn from their evil, I will repent of the evil that I thought to do unto them.

9 And *at what* instant I shall speak concerning a nation, and concerning a kingdom, to build and to plant *it;*

10 If it do evil in my sight, that it obey not my voice, then I will repent of the good, wherewith I said I would benefit them.

11 ¶ Now therefore go to, speak to the men of Ju'dah, and to the inhabitants of Je-ru'sa-lem, saying, Thus saith the LORD; Behold, I frame evil against you, and devise a device against you: return ye now every one from his evil way, and make your ways and your doings good.

12 And they said, There is no hope: but we will walk after our own devices, and we will every one do the imagination of his evil heart.

13 Therefore thus saith the LORD; Ask ye now among the heathen, who hath heard such things: the virgin of Is'ra-el hath done a very horrible thing.

14 Will *a man* leave the snow of Leb'a-non *which cometh* from the rock of the field? *or* shall the cold flowing waters that come from another place be forsaken?

15 Because my people hath forgotten me, they have burned incense to vanity, and they have caused them to stumble in their ways *from* the ancient paths, to walk in paths, *in* a way not cast up;

16 To make their land desolate, *and* a perpetual hissing; every one that passeth thereby shall be astonished, and wag his head.

17 I will scatter them as with an east wind, before the enemy; I will shew them the back, and not the face, in the day of their calamity.

18 ¶ Then said they, Come, and let us devise devices against Jer-e-mi'ah; for the law shall not perish from the priest, nor counsel from the wise, nor the word from the prophet. Come, and let us smite him with the tongue, and let us not give heed to any of his words.

19 Give heed to me, O LORD, and hearken to the voice of them that contend with me.

20 Shall evil be recompensed for good? for they have digged a pit for my soul. Remember that I stood before thee to speak good for them, *and* to turn away thy wrath from them.

21 Therefore deliver up their children to the

famine, and pour out their *blood* by the force of the sword; and let their wives be bereaved of their children, and *be* widows; and let their men be put to death; *let* their young men *be* slain by the sword in battle.

22 Let a cry be heard from their houses, when thou shalt bring a troop suddenly upon them: for they have digged a pit to take me, and hid snares for my feet.

23 Yet, LORD, thou knowest all their counsel against me to slay *me:* forgive not their iniquity, neither blot out their sin from thy sight, but let them be overthrown before thee; deal *thus* with them in the time of thine anger.

19 THUS saith the LORD, Go and get a potter's earthen bottle, and *take* of the ancients of the people, and of the ancients of the priests;

2 And go forth unto the valley of the son of Hin'nom, which *is* by the entry of the east gate, and proclaim there the words that I shall tell thee,

3 And say, Hear ye the word of the LORD, O kings of Ju'dah, and inhabitants of Je-ru'sa-lem; Thus saith the LORD of hosts, the God of Is'ra-el; Behold, I will bring evil upon this place, the which whosoever heareth, his ears shall tingle.

4 Because they have forsaken me, and have estranged this place, and have burned incense in it unto other gods, whom neither they nor their fathers have known, nor the kings of Ju'dah, and have filled this place with the blood of innocents;

5 They have built also the high places of Ba'al, to burn their sons with fire *for* burnt offerings unto Ba'al, which I commanded not, nor spake *it,* neither came *it* into my mind:

6 Therefore, behold, the days come, saith the LORD, that this place shall no more be called To'phet, nor The valley of the son of Hin'nom, but The valley of slaughter.

7 And I will make void the counsel of Ju'dah and Je-ru'sa-lem in this place; and I will cause them to fall by the sword before their enemies, and by the hands of them that seek their lives: and their carcases will I give to be meat for the fowls of the heaven, and for the beasts of the earth.

8 And I will make this city desolate, and an hissing; every one that passeth thereby shall be astonished and hiss because of all the plagues thereof.

9 And I will cause them to eat the flesh of their sons and the flesh of their daughters, and they shall eat every one the flesh of his friend in the siege and straitness, wherewith their enemies, and they that seek their lives, shall straiten them.

10 Then shalt thou break the bottle in the sight of the men that go with thee,

11 And shalt say unto them, Thus saith the LORD of hosts; Even so will I break this people and this city as *one* breaketh a potter's vessel, that cannot be made whole again: and they shall bury *them* in To'phet, till *there be* no place to bury.

12 Thus will I do unto this place, saith the LORD, and to the inhabitants thereof, and *even* make this city as To'phet:

13 And the houses of Je-ru'sa-lem, and the houses of the kings of Ju'dah, shall be defiled as the place of To'phet, because of all the houses upon whose roofs they have burned incense unto all the host of heaven, and have poured out drink offerings unto other gods.

14 Then came Jer-e-mi'ah from To'phet, whither the LORD had sent him to prophesy; and he stood in the court of the LORD's house; and said to all the people,

15 Thus saith the LORD of hosts, the God of Is'ra-el; Behold, I will bring upon this city and upon all her towns all the evil that I have pronounced against it, because they have hardened their necks, that they might not hear my words.

20 NOW Pash'ur the son of Im'mer the priest, who *was* also chief governor in the house of the LORD, heard that Jer-e-mi'ah prophesied these things.

2 Then Pash'ur smote Jer-e-mi'ah the prophet, and put him in the stocks that *were* in the high gate of Ben'ja-min, which *was* by the house of the LORD.

3 And it came to pass on the morrow, that Pash'ur brought forth Jer-e-mi'ah out of the stocks. Then said Jer-e-mi'ah unto him, The LORD hath not called thy name Pash'ur, but Ma'gor-mis'sa-bib.

4 For thus saith the LORD, Behold, I will make thee a terror to thyself, and to all thy friends: and they shall fall by the sword of their enemies, and thine eyes shall behold *it:* and I will give all Ju'dah into the hand of the king of Bab'y-lon, and he shall carry them captive into Bab'y-lon, and shall slay them with the sword.

5 Moreover I will deliver all the strength of this city, and all the labours thereof, and all the precious things thereof, and all the treasures of the kings of Ju'dah will I give into the hand of their enemies, which shall spoil them, and take them, and carry them to Bab'y-lon.

6 And thou, Pash'ur, and all that dwell in thine house shall go into captivity: and thou shalt come to Bab'y-lon, and there thou shalt die, and shalt be buried there, thou, and all thy friends, to whom thou hast prophesied lies.

7 ¶ O LORD, thou hast deceived me, and I was deceived: thou art stronger than I, and hast prevailed: I am in derision daily, every one mocketh me.

8 For since I spake, I cried out, I cried violence and spoil; because the word of the LORD was made a reproach unto me, and a derision, daily.

9 Then I said, I will not make mention of him, nor speak any more in his name. But *his word* was in mine heart as a burning fire shut up in my bones, and I was weary with forbearing, and I could not *stay.*

10 ¶ For I heard the defaming of many, fear on every side. Report, *say they,* and we will report it. All my familiars watched for my halting, *saying,* Peradventure he will be enticed, and we shall prevail against him, and we shall take our revenge on him.

11 But the LORD *is* with me as a mighty terrible one: therefore my persecutors shall stumble, and they shall not prevail: they shall be greatly ashamed; for they shall not prosper: *their* everlasting confusion shall never be forgotten.

12 But, O LORD of hosts, that triest the righteous, *and* seest the reins and the heart, let me see thy vengeance on them: for unto thee have I opened my cause.

13 Sing unto the LORD, praise ye the LORD: for he hath delivered the soul of the poor from the hand of evildoers.

14 ¶ Cursed *be* the day wherein I was born: let not the day wherein my mother bare me be blessed.

15 Cursed *be* the man who brought tidings to

my father, saying, A man child is born unto
thee; making him very glad.
16 And let that man be as the cities which
the LORD overthrew, and repented not: and let
him hear the cry in the morning, and the shouting at noontide;
17 Because he slew me not from the womb;
or that my mother might have been my grave,
and her womb *to be* always great *with me.*
18 Wherefore came I forth out of the womb
to see labour and sorrow, that my days should
be consumed with shame?

21 THE word which came unto Jer-e-mi'ah
from the LORD, when king Zed-e-ki'ah
sent unto him Pash'ur the son of Mel-chi'ah,
and Zeph-a-ni'ah the son of Ma-a-se'iah the
priest, saying,
2 Enquire, I pray thee, of the LORD for us; for
Neb-u-chad-rez'zar king of Bab'y-lon maketh
war against us; if so be that the LORD will deal
with us according to all his wondrous works,
that he may go up from us.
3 ¶ Then said Jer-e-mi'ah unto them, Thus
shall ye say to Zed-e-ki'ah:
4 Thus saith the LORD God of Is'ra-el; Behold,
I will turn back the weapons of war that *are* in
your hands, wherewith ye fight against the king
of Bab'y-lon, and *against* the Chal-de'ans,
which besiege you without the walls, and I will
assemble them into the midst of this city.
5 And I myself will fight against you with an
outstretched hand and with a strong arm, even
in anger, and in fury, and in great wrath.
6 And I will smite the inhabitants of this city,
both man and beast: they shall die of a great
pestilence.
7 And afterward, saith the LORD, I will deliver Zed-e-ki'ah king of Ju'dah, and his servants, and the people, and such as are left in
this city from the pestilence, from the sword,
and from the famine, into the hand of Neb-u-
chad-rez'zar king of Bab'y-lon, and into the
hand of their enemies, and into the hand of
those that seek their life: and he shall smite
them with the edge of the sword; he shall not
spare them, neither have pity, nor have mercy.
8 ¶ And unto this people thou shalt say,
Thus saith the LORD; Behold, I set before you
the way of life, and the way of death.
9 He that abideth in this city shall die by the
sword, and by the famine, and by the pestilence: but he that goeth out, and falleth to the
Chal-de'ans that besiege you, he shall live, and
his life shall be unto him for a prey.
10 For I have set my face against this city for
evil, and not for good, saith the LORD: it shall be
given into the hand of the king of Bab'y-lon, and
he shall burn it with fire.
11 ¶ And touching the house of the king of
Ju'dah, *say,* Hear ye the word of the LORD;
12 O house of Da'vid, thus saith the LORD;
Execute judgment in the morning, and deliver
him that is spoiled out of the hand of the oppressor, lest my fury go out like fire, and burn
that none can quench *it,* because of the evil of
your doings.
13 Behold, I *am* against thee, O inhabitant of
the valley, *and* rock of the plain, saith the LORD;
which say, Who shall come down against us? or
who shall enter into our habitations?
14 But I will punish you according to the
fruit of your doings, saith the LORD: and I will
kindle a fire in the forest thereof, and it shall
devour all things round about it.

22 THUS saith the LORD; Go down to the
house of the king of Ju'dah, and speak
there this word,
2 And say, Hear the word of the LORD, O
king of Ju'dah, that sittest upon the throne of
Da'vid, thou, and thy servants, and thy people
that enter in by these gates:
3 Thus saith the LORD; Execute ye judgment
and righteousness, and deliver the spoiled out
of the hand of the oppressor: and do no wrong,
do no violence to the stranger, the fatherless,
nor the widow, neither shed innocent blood in
this place.
4 For if ye do this thing indeed, then shall
there enter in by the gates of this house kings
sitting upon the throne of Da'vid, riding in
chariots and on horses, he, and his servants,
and his people.
5 But if ye will not hear these words, I swear
by myself, saith the LORD, that this house shall
become a desolation.
6 For thus saith the LORD unto the king's
house of Ju'dah; Thou *art* Gil'e-ad unto me, *and*
the head of Leb'a-non: *yet* surely I will make
thee a wilderness, *and* cities *which* are not inhabited.
7 And I will prepare destroyers against thee,
every one with his weapons: and they shall cut
down thy choice cedars, and cast *them* into the
fire.
8 And many nations shall pass by this city,
and they shall say every man to his neighbour,
Wherefore hath the LORD done thus unto this
great city?
9 Then they shall answer, Because they have
forsaken the covenant of the LORD their God,
and worshipped other gods, and served them.
10 ¶ Weep ye not for the dead, neither bemoan him: *but* weep sore for him that goeth
away: for he shall return no more, nor see his
native country.
11 For thus saith the LORD touching Shal'lum
the son of Jo-si'ah king of Ju'dah, which reigned
instead of Jo-si'ah his father, which went forth
out of this place; He shall not return thither any
more:
12 But he shall die in the place whither they
have led him captive, and shall see this land no
more.
13 ¶ Woe unto him that buildeth his house
by unrighteousness, and his chambers by
wrong; *that* useth his neighbour's service without wages, and giveth him not for his work;
14 That saith, I will build me a wide house
and large chambers, and cutteth him out windows; and *it is* cieled with cedar, and painted
with vermilion.
15 Shalt thou reign, because thou closest *thyself* in cedar? did not thy father eat and drink,
and do judgment and justice, *and* then *it was*
well with him?
16 He judged the cause of the poor and
needy; then *it was* well *with him: was* not this
to know me? saith the LORD.
17 But thine eyes and thine heart *are* not but
for thy covetousness, and for to shed innocent
blood, and for oppression, and for violence, to
do *it.*
18 Therefore thus saith the LORD concerning
Je-hoi'a-kim the son of Jo-si'ah king of Ju'dah;
They shall not lament for him, *saying,* Ah my
brother! or, Ah sister! they shall not lament for
him, *saying,* Ah lord! or, Ah his glory!
19 He shall be buried with the burial of an
ass, drawn and cast forth beyond the gates of
Je-ru'sa-lem.
20 ¶ Go up to Leb'a-non, and cry; and lift up

thy voice in Ba′shan, and cry from the passages: for all thy lovers are destroyed.

21 I spake unto thee in thy prosperity; *but* thou saidst, I will not hear. This *hath been* thy manner from thy youth, that thou obeyedst not my voice.

22 The wind shall eat up all thy pastors, and thy lovers shall go into captivity: surely then shalt thou be ashamed and confounded for all thy wickedness.

23 O inhabitant of Leb′a-non, that makest thy nest in the cedars, how gracious shalt thou be when pangs come upon thee, the pain as of a woman in travail!

24 *As* I live, saith the LORD, though Co-ni′ah the son of Je-hoi′a-kim king of Ju′dah were the signet upon my right hand, yet would I pluck thee thence;

25 And I will give thee into the hand of them that seek thy life, and into the hand *of them* whose face thou fearest, even into the hand of Neb-u-chad-rez′zar king of Bab′y-lon, and into the hand of the Chal-de′ans.

26 And I will cast thee out, and thy mother that bare thee, into another country, where ye were not born; and there shall ye die.

27 But to the land whereunto they desire to return, thither shall they not return.

28 *Is* this man Co-ni′ah a despised broken idol? *is he* a vessel wherein *is* no pleasure? wherefore are they cast out, he and his seed, and are cast into a land which they know not?

29 O earth, earth, earth, hear the word of the LORD.

30 Thus saith the LORD, Write ye this man childless, a man *that* shall not prosper in his days: for no man of his seed shall prosper, sitting upon the throne of Da′vid, and ruling any more in Ju′dah.

23 WOE be unto the pastors that destroy and scatter the sheep of my pasture! saith the LORD.

2 Therefore thus saith the LORD God of Is′ra-el against the pastors that feed my people; Ye have scattered my flock, and driven them away, and have not visited them: behold, I will visit upon you the evil of your doings, saith the LORD.

3 And I will gather the remnant of my flock out of all countries whither I have driven them, and will bring them again to their folds; and they shall be fruitful and increase.

4 And I will set up shepherds over them which shall feed them: and they shall fear no more, nor be dismayed, neither shall they be lacking, saith the LORD.

5 ¶ Behold, the days come, saith the LORD, that I will raise unto Da′vid a righteous Branch, and a King shall reign and prosper, and shall execute judgment and justice in the earth.

6 In his days Ju′dah shall be saved, and Is′ra-el shall dwell safely: and this *is* his name whereby he shall be called, THE LORD OUR RIGHTEOUSNESS.

7 Therefore, behold, the days come, saith the LORD, that they shall no more say, The LORD liveth, which brought up the children of Is′ra-el out of the land of E′gypt;

8 But, The LORD liveth, which brought up and which led the seed of the house of Is′ra-el out of the north country, and from all countries whither I had driven them; and they shall dwell in their own land.

9 ¶ Mine heart within me is broken because of the prophets; all my bones shake; I am like a drunken man, and like a man whom wine hath overcome, because of the LORD, and because of the words of his holiness.

10 For the land is full of adulterers; for because of swearing the land mourneth; the pleasant places of the wilderness are dried up, and their course is evil, and their force *is* not right.

11 For both prophet and priest are profane; yea, in my house have I found their wickedness, saith the LORD.

12 Wherefore their way shall be unto them as slippery *ways* in the darkness: they shall be driven on, and fall therein: for I will bring evil upon them, *even* the year of their visitation, saith the LORD.

13 And I have seen folly in the prophets of Sa-ma′ri-a; they prophesied in Ba′al, and caused my people Is′ra-el to err.

14 I have seen also in the prophets of Je-ru′-sa-lem an horrible thing: they commit adultery, and walk in lies: they strengthen also the hands of evildoers, that none doth return from his wickedness: they are all of them unto me as Sod′om, and the inhabitants thereof as Go-mor′rah.

15 Therefore thus saith the LORD of hosts concerning the prophets; Behold, I will feed them with wormwood, and make them drink the water of gall: for from the prophets of Je-ru′sa-lem is profaneness gone forth into all the land.

16 Thus saith the LORD of hosts, Hearken not unto the words of the prophets that prophesy unto you: they make you vain: they speak a vision of their own heart, *and* not out of the mouth of the LORD.

17 They say still unto them that despise me, The LORD hath said, Ye shall have peace; and they say unto every one that walketh after the imagination of his own heart, No evil shall come upon you.

18 For who hath stood in the counsel of the LORD, and hath perceived and heard his word? who hath marked his word, and heard *it?*

19 Behold, a whirlwind of the LORD is gone forth in fury, even a grievous whirlwind: it shall fall grievously upon the head of the wicked.

20 The anger of the LORD shall not return, until he have executed, and till he have performed the thoughts of his heart: in the latter days ye shall consider it perfectly.

21 I have not sent these prophets, yet they ran: I have not spoken to them, yet they prophesied.

22 But if they had stood in my counsel, and had caused my people to hear my words, then they should have turned them from their evil way, and from the evil of their doings.

23 *Am* I a God at hand, saith the LORD, and not a God afar off?

24 Can any hide himself in secret places that I shall not see him? saith the LORD. Do not I fill heaven and earth? saith the LORD.

25 I have heard what the prophets said, that prophesy lies in my name, saying, I have dreamed, I have dreamed.

26 How long shall *this* be in the heart of the prophets that prophesy lies? yea, *they are* prophets of the deceit of their own heart;

27 Which think to cause my people to forget my name by their dreams which they tell every man to his neighbour, as their fathers have forgotten my name for Ba′al.

28 The prophet that hath a dream, let him tell a dream; and he that hath my word, let him speak my word faithfully. What *is* the chaff to the wheat? saith the LORD.

29 *Is* not my word like as a fire? saith the

LORD; and like a hammer *that* breaketh the rock
in pieces?
30 Therefore, behold, I *am* against the prophets, saith the LORD, that steal my words every
one from his neighbour.
31 Behold, I *am* against the prophets, saith
the LORD, that use their tongues, and say, He
saith.
32 Behold, I *am* against them that prophesy
false dreams, saith the LORD, and do tell them,
and cause my people to err by their lies, and by
their lightness; yet I sent them not, nor commanded them: therefore they shall not profit
this people at all, saith the LORD.
33 ¶ And when this people, or the prophet,
or a priest, shall ask thee, saying, What *is* the
burden of the LORD? thou shalt then say unto
them, What burden? I will even forsake you,
saith the LORD.
34 And *as for* the prophet, and the priest, and
the people, that shall say, The burden of the
LORD, I will even punish that man and his
house.
35 Thus shall ye say every one to his neighbour, and every one to his brother, What hath
the LORD answered? and, What hath the LORD
spoken?
36 And the burden of the LORD shall ye mention no more: for every man's word shall be his
burden; for ye have perverted the words of the
living God, of the LORD of hosts our God.
37 Thus shalt thou say to the prophet, What
hath the LORD answered thee? and, What hath
the LORD spoken?
38 But since ye say, The burden of the LORD;
therefore thus saith the LORD; Because ye say
this word, The burden of the LORD, and I have
sent unto you, saying, Ye shall not say, The burden of the LORD;
39 Therefore, behold, I, even I, will utterly
forget you, and I will forsake you, and the city
that I gave you and your fathers, *and cast you*
out of my presence:
40 And I will bring an everlasting reproach
upon you, and a perpetual shame, which shall
not be forgotten.

24

THE LORD shewed me, and, behold, two
baskets of figs *were* set before the temple of the LORD, after that Neb-u-chad-rez'zar
king of Bab'y-lon had carried away captive Jec-
o-ni'ah the son of Je-hoi'a-kim king of Ju'dah,
and the princes of Ju'dah, with the carpenters
and smiths, from Je-ru'sa-lem, and had brought
them to Bab'y-lon.
2 One basket *had* very good figs, *even* like
the figs *that are* first ripe: and the other basket
had very naughty figs, which could not be eat-
en, they were so bad.
3 Then said the LORD unto me, What seest
thou, Jer-e-mi'ah? And I said, Figs; the good
figs, very good; and the evil, very evil, that cannot be eaten, they are so evil.
4 ¶ Again the word of the LORD came unto
me, saying,
5 Thus saith the LORD, the God of Is'ra-el;
Like these good figs, so will I acknowledge
them that are carried away captive of Ju'dah,
whom I have sent out of this place into the land
of the Chal-de'ans for *their* good.
6 For I will set mine eyes upon them for
good, and I will bring them again to this land:
and I will build them, and not pull *them* down;
and I will plant them, and not pluck *them* up.
7 And I will give them an heart to know me,
that I *am* the LORD: and they shall be my people, and I will be their God: for they shall return
unto me with their whole heart.
8 ¶ And as the evil figs, which cannot be eat-
en, they are so evil; surely thus saith the LORD,
So will I give Zed-e-ki'ah the king of Ju'dah,
and his princes, and the residue of Je-ru'sa-lem,
that remain in this land, and them that dwell in
the land of E'gypt:
9 And I will deliver them to be removed into
all the kingdoms of the earth for *their* hurt, *to
be* a reproach and a proverb, a taunt and a
curse, in all places whither I shall drive them.
10 And I will send the sword, the famine, and
the pestilence, among them, till they be consumed from off the land that I gave unto them
and to their fathers.

25

THE word that came to Jer-e-mi'ah concerning all the people of Ju'dah in the
fourth year of Je-hoi'a-kim the son of Jo-si'ah
king of Ju'dah, that *was* the first year of Neb-u-
chad-rez'zar king of Bab'y-lon;
2 The which Jer-e-mi'ah the prophet spake
unto all the people of Ju'dah, and to all the inhabitants of Je-ru'sa-lem, saying,
3 From the thirteenth year of Jo-si'ah the son
of A'mon king of Ju'dah, even unto this day,
that *is* the three and twentieth year, the word of
the LORD hath come unto me, and I have spoken
unto you, rising early and speaking; but ye have
not hearkened.
4 And the LORD hath sent unto you all his
servants the prophets, rising early and sending
them; but ye have not hearkened, nor inclined
your ear to hear.
5 They said, Turn ye again now every one
from his evil way, and from the evil of your doings, and dwell in the land that the LORD hath
given unto you and to your fathers for ever and
ever:
6 And go not after other gods to serve them,
and to worship them, and provoke me not to
anger with the works of your hands; and I will
do you no hurt.
7 Yet ye have not hearkened unto me, saith
the LORD; that ye might provoke me to anger
with the works of your hands to your own hurt.
8 ¶ Therefore thus saith the LORD of hosts;
Because ye have not heard my words,
9 Behold, I will send and take all the families
of the north, saith the LORD, and Neb-u-chad-
rez'zar the king of Bab'y-lon, my servant, and
will bring them against this land, and against
the inhabitants thereof, and against all these
nations round about, and will utterly destroy
them, and make them an astonishment, and an
hissing, and perpetual desolations.
10 Moreover I will take from them the voice
of mirth, and the voice of gladness, the voice of
the bridegroom, and the voice of the bride, the
sound of the millstones, and the light of the candle.
11 And this whole land shall be a desolation,
and an astonishment; and these nations shall
serve the king of Bab'y-lon seventy years.
12 ¶ And it shall come to pass, when seventy
years are accomplished, *that* I will punish the
king of Bab'y-lon, and that nation, saith the
LORD, for their iniquity, and the land of the
Chal-de'ans, and will make it perpetual desolations.
13 And I will bring upon that land all my
words which I have pronounced against it, *even*
all that is written in this book, which Jer-e-mi'-
ah hath prophesied against all the nations.
14 For many nations and great kings shall
serve themselves of them also: and I will rec-

ompense them according to their deeds, and according to the works of their own hands.
15 ¶ For thus saith the LORD God of Is'ra-el
unto me; Take the wine cup of this fury at my
hand, and cause all the nations, to whom I send
thee, to drink it.
16 And they shall drink, and be moved, and
be mad, because of the sword that I will send
among them.
17 Then took I the cup at the LORD's hand,
and made all the nations to drink, unto whom
the LORD had sent me:
18 *To wit,* Je-ru'sa-lem, and the cities of Ju'-
dah, and the kings thereof, and the princes
thereof, to make them a desolation, an astonishment, an hissing, and a curse; as *it is* this day;
19 Pha'raoh king of E'gypt, and his servants,
and his princes, and all his people;
20 And all the mingled people, and all the
kings of the land of Uz, and all the kings of the
land of the Phi-lis'tines, and Ash'ke-lon, and
Az'zah, and Ek'ron, and the remnant of Ash'-
dod,
21 E'dom, and Mo'ab, and the children of
Am'mon,
22 And all the kings of Ty'rus, and all the
kings of Zi'don, and the kings of the isles which
are beyond the sea,
23 De'dan, and Te'ma, and Buz, and all *that*
are in the utmost corners,
24 And all the kings of A-ra'bi-a, and all the
kings of the mingled people that dwell in the
desert,
25 And all the kings of Zim'ri, and all the
kings of E'lam, and all the kings of the Medes,
26 And all the kings of the north, far and
near, one with another, and all the kingdoms of
the world, which *are* upon the face of the earth:
and the king of She'shach shall drink after
them.
27 Therefore thou shalt say unto them, Thus
saith the LORD of hosts, the God of Is'ra-el;
Drink ye, and be drunken, and spue, and fall,
and rise no more, because of the sword which I
will send among you.
28 And it shall be, if they refuse to take the
cup at thine hand to drink, then shalt thou say
unto them, Thus saith the LORD of hosts; Ye
shall certainly drink.
29 For, lo, I begin to bring evil on the city
which is called by my name, and should ye be
utterly unpunished? Ye shall not be unpunished: for I will call for a sword upon all the
inhabitants of the earth, saith the LORD of hosts.
30 Therefore prophesy thou against them all
these words, and say unto them, The LORD shall
roar from on high, and utter his voice from his
holy habitation; he shall mightily roar upon his
habitation; he shall give a shout, as they that
tread *the grapes,* against all the inhabitants of
the earth.
31 A noise shall come *even* to the ends of the
earth; for the LORD hath a controversy with the
nations, he will plead with all flesh; he will give
them *that are* wicked to the sword, saith the
LORD.
32 Thus saith the LORD of hosts, Behold, evil
shall go forth from nation to nation, and a great
whirlwind shall be raised up from the coasts of
the earth.
33 And the slain of the LORD shall be at that
day from *one* end of the earth even unto the
other end of the earth: they shall not be lamented, neither gathered, nor buried; they shall
be dung upon the ground.
34 ¶ Howl, ye shepherds, and cry; and wallow yourselves *in the ashes,* ye principal of the
flock: for the days of your slaughter and of your
dispersions are accomplished; and ye shall fall
like a pleasant vessel.
35 And the shepherds shall have no way to
flee, nor the principal of the flock to escape.
36 A voice of the cry of the shepherds, and
an howling of the principal of the flock, *shall be*
heard: for the LORD hath spoiled their pasture.
37 And the peaceable habitations are cut
down because of the fierce anger of the LORD.
38 He hath forsaken his covert, as the lion:
for their land is desolate because of the fierceness of the oppressor, and because of his fierce
anger.

26 IN the beginning of the reign of Je-hoi'a-
kim the son of Jo-si'ah king of Ju'dah
came this word from the LORD, saying,
2 Thus saith the LORD; Stand in the court of
the LORD's house, and speak unto all the cities
of Ju'dah, which come to worship in the LORD's
house, all the words that I command thee to
speak unto them; diminish not a word:
3 If so be they will hearken, and turn every
man from his evil way, that I may repent me of
the evil, which I purpose to do unto them because of the evil of their doings.
4 And thou shalt say unto them, Thus saith
the LORD; If ye will not hearken to me, to walk
in my law, which I have set before you,
5 To hearken to the words of my servants the
prophets, whom I sent unto you, both rising up
early, and sending *them,* but ye have not hearkened;
6 Then will I make this house like Shi'loh,
and will make this city a curse to all the nations
of the earth.
7 So the priests and the prophets and all the
people heard Jer-e-mi'ah speaking these words
in the house of the LORD.
8 ¶ Now it came to pass, when Jer-e-mi'ah
had made an end of speaking all that the LORD
had commanded *him* to speak unto all the people, that the priests and the prophets and all the
people took him, saying, Thou shalt surely die.
9 Why hast thou prophesied in the name of
the LORD, saying, This house shall be like Shi'-
loh, and this city shall be desolate without an
inhabitant? And all the people were gathered
against Jer-e-mi'ah in the house of the LORD.
10 ¶ When the princes of Ju'dah heard these
things, then they came up from the king's house
unto the house of the LORD, and sat down in the
entry of the new gate of the LORD's *house.*
11 Then spake the priests and the prophets
unto the princes and to all the people, saying,
This man *is* worthy to die; for he hath prophesied against this city, as ye have heard with
your ears.
12 ¶ Then spake Jer-e-mi'ah unto all the
princes and to all the people, saying, The LORD
sent me to prophesy against this house and
against this city all the words that ye have
heard.
13 Therefore now amend your ways and your
doings, and obey the voice of the LORD your
God; and the LORD will repent him of the evil
that he hath pronounced against you.
14 As for me, behold, I *am* in your hand: do
with me as seemeth good and meet unto you.
15 But know ye for certain, that if ye put me
to death, ye shall surely bring innocent blood
upon yourselves, and upon this city, and upon
the inhabitants thereof: for of a truth the LORD
hath sent me unto you to speak all these words
in your ears.
16 ¶ Then said the princes and all the people

unto the priests and to the prophets; This man *is* not worthy to die: for he hath spoken to us in the name of the LORD our God.

17 Then rose up certain of the elders of the land, and spake to all the assembly of the people, saying,

18 Mi'cah the Mo'ras-thite prophesied in the days of Hez-e-ki'ah king of Ju'dah, and spake to all the people of Ju'dah, saying, Thus saith the LORD of hosts; Zi'on shall be plowed *like* a field, and Je-ru'sa-lem shall become heaps, and the mountain of the house as the high places of a forest.

19 Did Hez-e-ki'ah king of Ju'dah and all Ju'dah put him at all to death? did he not fear the LORD, and besought the LORD, and the LORD repented him of the evil which he had pronounced against them? Thus might we procure great evil against our souls.

20 And there was also a man that prophesied in the name of the LORD, U-ri'jah the son of Shem-a-i'ah of Kir'jath–je'a-rim, who prophesied against this city and against this land according to all the words of Jer-e-mi'ah:

21 And when Je-hoi'a-kim the king, with all his mighty men, and all the princes, heard his words, the king sought to put him to death: but when U-ri'jah heard it, he was afraid, and fled, and went into E'gypt;

22 And Je-hoi'a-kim the king sent men into E'gypt, *namely,* El'na-than the son of Ach'bor, and *certain* men with him into E'gypt.

23 And they fetched forth U-ri'jah out of E'gypt, and brought him unto Je-hoi'a-kim the king; who slew him with the sword, and cast his dead body into the graves of the common people.

24 Nevertheless the hand of A-hi'kam the son of Sha'phan was with Jer-e-mi'ah, that they should not give him into the hand of the people to put him to death.

27 IN the beginning of the reign of Je-hoi'a-kim the son of Jo-si'ah king of Ju'dah came this word unto Jer-e-mi'ah from the LORD, saying,

2 Thus saith the LORD to me; Make thee bonds and yokes, and put them upon thy neck,

3 And send them to the king of E'dom, and to the king of Mo'ab, and to the king of the Am'mon-ites, and to the king of Ty'rus, and to the king of Zi'don, by the hand of the messengers which come to Je-ru'sa-lem unto Zed-e-ki'ah king of Ju'dah;

4 And command them to say unto their masters, Thus saith the LORD of hosts, the God of Is'ra-el; Thus shall ye say unto your masters;

5 I have made the earth, the man and the beast that *are* upon the ground, by my great power and by my outstretched arm, and have given it unto whom it seemed meet unto me.

6 And now have I given all these lands into the hand of Neb-u-chad-nez'zar the king of Bab'y-lon, my servant; and the beasts of the field have I given him also to serve him.

7 And all nations shall serve him, and his son, and his son's son, until the very time of his land come: and then many nations and great kings shall serve themselves of him.

8 And it shall come to pass, *that* the nation and kingdom which will not serve the same Neb-u-chad-nez'zar the king of Bab'y-lon, and that will not put their neck under the yoke of the king of Bab'y-lon, that nation will I punish, saith the LORD, with the sword, and with the famine, and with the pestilence, until I have consumed them by his hand.

9 Therefore hearken not ye to your prophets, nor to your diviners, nor to your dreamers, nor to your enchanters, nor to your sorcerers, which speak unto you, saying, Ye shall not serve the king of Bab'y-lon:

10 For they prophesy a lie unto you, to remove you far from your land; and that I should drive you out, and ye should perish.

11 But the nations that bring their neck under the yoke of the king of Bab'y-lon, and serve him, those will I let remain still in their own land, saith the LORD; and they shall till it, and dwell therein.

12 ¶ I spake also to Zed-e-ki'ah king of Ju'dah according to all these words, saying, Bring your necks under the yoke of the king of Bab'y-lon, and serve him and his people, and live.

13 Why will ye die, thou and thy people, by the sword, by the famine, and by the pestilence, as the LORD hath spoken against the nation that will not serve the king of Bab'y-lon?

14 Therefore hearken not unto the words of the prophets that speak unto you, saying, Ye shall not serve the king of Bab'y-lon: for they prophesy a lie unto you.

15 For I have not sent them, saith the LORD, yet they prophesy a lie in my name; that I might drive you out, and that ye might perish, ye, and the prophets that prophesy unto you.

16 Also I spake to the priests and to all this people, saying, Thus saith the LORD; Hearken not to the words of your prophets that prophesy unto you, saying, Behold, the vessels of the LORD's house shall now shortly be brought again from Bab'y-lon: for they prophesy a lie unto you.

17 Hearken not unto them; serve the king of Bab'y-lon, and live: wherefore should this city be laid waste?

18 But if they *be* prophets, and if the word of the LORD be with them, let them now make intercession to the LORD of hosts, that the vessels which are left in the house of the LORD, and *in* the house of the king of Ju'dah, and at Je-ru'sa-lem, go not to Bab'y-lon.

19 ¶ For thus saith the LORD of hosts concerning the pillars, and concerning the sea, and concerning the bases, and concerning the residue of the vessels that remain in this city,

20 Which Neb-u-chad-nez'zar king of Bab'y-lon took not, when he carried away captive Jec-o-ni'ah the son of Je-hoi'a-kim king of Ju'dah from Je-ru'sa-lem to Bab'y-lon, and all the nobles of Ju'dah and Je-ru'sa-lem;

21 Yea, thus saith the LORD of hosts, the God of Is'ra-el, concerning the vessels that remain *in* the house of the LORD, and *in* the house of the king of Ju'dah and of Je-ru'sa-lem;

22 They shall be carried to Bab'y-lon, and there shall they be until the day that I visit them, saith the LORD; then will I bring them up, and restore them to this place.

28 AND it came to pass the same year, in the beginning of the reign of Zed-e-ki'ah king of Ju'dah, in the fourth year, *and* in the fifth month, *that* Han-a-ni'ah the son of A'zur the prophet, which *was* of Gib'e-on, spake unto me in the house of the LORD, in the presence of the priests and of all the people, saying,

2 Thus speaketh the LORD of hosts, the God of Is'ra-el, saying, I have broken the yoke of the king of Bab'y-lon.

3 Within two full years will I bring again into this place all the vessels of the LORD's house, that Neb-u-chad-nez'zar king of Bab'y-lon took

away from this place, and carried them to Bab'-
y-lon:
4 And I will bring again to this place Jec-o-
ni'ah the son of Je-hoi'a-kim king of Ju'dah,
with all the captives of Ju'dah, that went into
Bab'y-lon, saith the LORD: for I will break the
yoke of the king of Bab'y-lon.
5 ¶ Then the prophet Jer-e-mi'ah said unto
the prophet Han-a-ni'ah in the presence of the
priests, and in the presence of all the people
that stood in the house of the LORD,
6 Even the prophet Jer-e-mi'ah said, Amen:
the LORD do so: the LORD perform thy words
which thou hast prophesied, to bring again the
vessels of the LORD's house, and all that is carried away captive, from Bab'y-lon into this
place.
7 Nevertheless hear thou now this word that
I speak in thine ears, and in the ears of all the
people;
8 The prophets that have been before me and
before thee of old prophesied both against
many countries, and against great kingdoms, of
war, and of evil, and of pestilence.
9 The prophet which prophesieth of peace,
when the word of the prophet shall come to
pass, *then* shall the prophet be known, that the
LORD hath truly sent him.
10 ¶ Then Han-a-ni'ah the prophet took the
yoke from off the prophet Jer-e-mi'ah's neck,
and brake it.
11 And Han-a-ni'ah spake in the presence of
all the people, saying, Thus saith the LORD;
Even so will I break the yoke of Neb-u-chad-
nez'zar king of Bab'y-lon from the neck of all
nations within the space of two full years. And
the prophet Jer-e-mi'ah went his way.
12 ¶ Then the word of the LORD came unto
Jer-e-mi'ah *the prophet,* after that Han-a-ni'ah
the prophet had broken the yoke from off the
neck of the prophet Jer-e-mi'ah, saying,
13 Go and tell Han-a-ni'ah, saying, Thus saith
the LORD; Thou hast broken the yokes of wood;
but thou shalt make for them yokes of iron.
14 For thus saith the LORD of hosts, the God
of Is'ra-el; I have put a yoke of iron upon the
neck of all these nations, that they may serve
Neb-u-chad-nez'zar king of Bab'y-lon; and they
shall serve him: and I have given him the beasts
of the field also.
15 ¶ Then said the prophet Jer-e-mi'ah unto
Han-a-ni'ah the prophet, Hear now, Han-a-ni'-
ah; The LORD hath not sent thee; but thou makest this people to trust in a lie.
16 Therefore thus saith the LORD; Behold, I
will cast thee from off the face of the earth: this
year thou shalt die, because thou hast taught
rebellion against the LORD.
17 So Han-a-ni'ah the prophet died the same
year in the seventh month.

29 NOW these *are* the words of the letter
that Jer-e-mi'ah the prophet sent from
Je-ru'sa-lem unto the residue of the elders
which were carried away captives, and to the
priests, and to the prophets, and to all the people whom Neb-u-chad-nez'zar had carried away
captive from Je-ru'sa-lem to Bab'y-lon;
2 (After that Jec-o-ni'ah the king, and the
queen, and the eunuchs, the princes of Ju'dah
and Je-ru'sa-lem, and the carpenters, and the
smiths, were departed from Je-ru'sa-lem;)
3 By the hand of El'-a-sah the son of Sha'-
phan, and Gem-a-ri'ah the son of Hil-ki'ah,
(whom Zed-e-ki'ah king of Ju'dah sent unto
Bab'y-lon to Neb-u-chad-nez'zar king of Bab'y-
lon) saying,
4 Thus saith the LORD of hosts, the God of
Is'ra-el, unto all that are carried away captives,
whom I have caused to be carried away from
Je-ru'sa-lem unto Bab'y-lon;
5 Build ye houses, and dwell *in them;* and
plant gardens, and eat the fruit of them;
6 Take ye wives, and beget sons and daughters; and take wives for your sons, and give
your daughters to husbands, that they may bear
sons and daughters; that ye may be increased
there, and not diminished.
7 And seek the peace of the city whither I
have caused you to be carried away captives,
and pray unto the LORD for it: for in the peace
thereof shall ye have peace.
8 ¶ For thus saith the LORD of hosts, the God
of Is'ra-el; Let not your prophets and your diviners, that *be* in the midst of you, deceive you,
neither hearken to your dreams which ye cause
to be dreamed.
9 For they prophesy falsely unto you in my
name: I have not sent them, saith the LORD.
10 ¶ For thus saith the LORD, That after seventy years be accomplished at Bab'y-lon I will
visit you, and perform my good word toward
you, in causing you to return to this place.
11 For I know the thoughts that I think
toward you, saith the LORD, thoughts of peace,
and not of evil, to give you an expected end.
12 Then shall ye call upon me, and ye shall
go and pray unto me, and I will hearken unto
you.
13 And ye shall seek me, and find *me,* when
ye shall search for me with all your heart.
14 And I will be found of you, saith the LORD:
and I will turn away your captivity, and I will
gather you from all the nations, and from all the
places whither I have driven you, saith the
LORD; and I will bring you again into the place
whence I caused you to be carried away captive.
15 ¶ Because ye have said, The LORD hath
raised us up prophets in Bab'y-lon;
16 *Know* that thus saith the LORD of the king
that sitteth upon the throne of Da'vid, and of all
the people that dwelleth in this city, *and* of your
brethren that are not gone forth with you into
captivity;
17 Thus saith the LORD of hosts; Behold, I
will send upon them the sword, the famine, and
the pestilence, and will make them like vile figs,
that cannot be eaten, they are so evil.
18 And I will persecute them with the sword,
with the famine, and with the pestilence, and
will deliver them to be removed to all the kingdoms of the earth, to be a curse, and an astonishment, and an hissing, and a reproach, among
all the nations whither I have driven them:
19 Because they have not hearkened to my
words, saith the LORD, which I sent unto them
by my servants the prophets, rising up early
and sending *them;* but ye would not hear, saith
the LORD.
20 ¶ Hear ye therefore the word of the LORD,
all ye of the captivity, whom I have sent from
Je-ru'sa-lem to Bab'y-lon:
21 Thus saith the LORD of hosts, the God of
Is'ra-el, of A'hab the son of Kol-a-i'ah, and of
Zed-e-ki'ah the son of Ma-a-se'iah, which
prophesy a lie unto you in my name; Behold, I
will deliver them into the hand of Neb-u-chad-
rez'zar king of Bab'y-lon; and he shall slay them
before your eyes;
22 And of them shall be taken up a curse by
all the captivity of Ju'dah which *are* in Bab'y-
lon, saying, The LORD make thee like Zed-e-ki'-

ah and like A'hab, whom the king of Bab'y-lon
roasted in the fire;
23 Because they have committed villany in
Is'ra-el, and have committed adultery with their
neighbours' wives, and have spoken lying
words in my name, which I have not commanded them; even I know, and *am* a witness,
saith the LORD.
24 ¶ *Thus* shalt thou also speak to Shem-a-
i'ah the Ne-hel'a-mite, saying,
25 Thus speaketh the LORD of hosts, the God
of Is'ra-el, saying, Because thou hast sent letters in thy name unto all the people that *are* at
Je-ru'sa-lem, and to Zeph-a-ni'ah the son of Ma-
a-se'iah the priest, and to all the priests, saying,
26 The LORD hath made thee priest in the
stead of Je-hoi'a-da the priest, that ye should be
officers in the house of the LORD, for every man
that is mad, and maketh himself a prophet, that
thou shouldest put him in prison, and in the
stocks.
27 Now therefore why hast thou not reproved Jer-e-mi'ah of An'a-thoth, which maketh himself a prophet to you?
28 For therefore he sent unto us *in* Bab'y-lon,
saying, This *captivity is* long: build ye houses,
and dwell *in them;* and plant gardens, and eat
the fruit of them.
29 And Zeph-a-ni'ah the priest read this letter in the ears of Jer-e-mi'ah the prophet.
30 ¶ Then came the word of the LORD unto
Jer-e-mi'ah, saying,
31 Send to all them of the captivity, saying,
Thus saith the LORD concerning Shem-a-i'ah the
Ne-hel'a-mite; Because that Shem-a-i'ah hath
prophesied unto you, and I sent him not, and he
caused you to trust in a lie:
32 Therefore thus saith the LORD; Behold, I
will punish Shem-a-i'ah the Ne-hel'a-mite, and
his seed: he shall not have a man to dwell
among this people; neither shall he behold the
good that I will do for my people, saith the
LORD; because he hath taught rebellion against
the LORD.

30 THE word that came to Jer-e-mi'ah
from the LORD, saying,
2 Thus speaketh the LORD God of Is'ra-el,
saying, Write thee all the words that I have spoken unto thee in a book.
3 For, lo, the days come, saith the LORD, that
I will bring again the captivity of my people Is'-
ra-el and Ju'dah, saith the LORD: and I will
cause them to return to the land that I gave to
their fathers, and they shall possess it.
4 ¶ And these *are* the words that the LORD
spake concerning Is'ra-el and concerning Ju'-
dah.
5 For thus saith the LORD; We have heard a
voice of trembling, of fear, and not of peace.
6 Ask ye now, and see whether a man doth
travail with child? wherefore do I see every
man with his hands on his loins, as a woman in
travail, and all faces are turned into paleness?
7 Alas! for that day *is* great, so that none *is*
like it: it *is* even the time of Ja'cob's trouble; but
he shall be saved out of it.
8 For it shall come to pass in that day, saith
the LORD of hosts, *that* I will break his yoke
from off thy neck, and will burst thy bonds, and
strangers shall no more serve themselves of
him:
9 But they shall serve the LORD their God,
and Da'vid their king, whom I will raise up unto
them.
10 ¶ Therefore fear thou not, O my servant
Ja'cob, saith the LORD; neither be dismayed, O
Is'ra-el: for, lo, I will save thee from afar, and
thy seed from the land of their captivity; and
Ja'cob shall return, and shall be in rest, and be
quiet, and none shall make *him* afraid.
11 For I *am* with thee, saith the LORD, to save
thee: though I make a full end of all nations
whither I have scattered thee, yet will I not
make a full end of thee: but I will correct thee in
measure, and will not leave thee altogether unpunished.
12 For thus saith the LORD, Thy bruise *is* incurable, *and* thy wound *is* grievous.
13 *There is* none to plead thy cause, that thou
mayest be bound up: thou hast no healing medicines.
14 All thy lovers have forgotten thee; they
seek thee not; for I have wounded thee with the
wound of an enemy, with the chastisement of a
cruel one, for the multitude of thine iniquity;
because thy sins were increased.
15 Why criest thou for thine affliction? thy
sorrow *is* incurable for the multitude of thine
iniquity: *because* thy sins were increased, I
have done these things unto thee.
16 Therefore all they that devour thee shall
be devoured; and all thine adversaries, every
one of them, shall go into captivity; and they
that spoil thee shall be a spoil, and all that prey
upon thee will I give for a prey.
17 For I will restore health unto thee, and I
will heal thee of thy wounds, saith the LORD;
because they called thee an Outcast, *saying,*
This *is* Zi'on, whom no man seeketh after.
18 ¶ Thus saith the LORD; Behold, I will bring
again the captivity of Ja'cob's tents, and have
mercy on his dwellingplaces; and the city shall
be builded upon her own heap, and the palace
shall remain after the manner thereof.
19 And out of them shall proceed thanksgiving and the voice of them that make merry: and
I will multiply them, and they shall not be few; I
will also glorify them, and they shall not be
small.
20 Their children also shall be as aforetime,
and their congregation shall be established before me, and I will punish all that oppress them.
21 And their nobles shall be of themselves,
and their governor shall proceed from the midst
of them; and I will cause him to draw near, and
he shall approach unto me: for who *is* this that
engaged his heart to approach unto me? saith
the LORD.
22 And ye shall be my people, and I will be
your God.
23 Behold, the whirlwind of the LORD goeth
forth with fury, a continuing whirlwind: it shall
fall with pain upon the head of the wicked.
24 The fierce anger of the LORD shall not return, until he have done *it,* and until he have
performed the intents of his heart: in the latter
days ye shall consider it.

31 AT the same time, saith the LORD, will I
be the God of all the families of Is'ra-el,
and they shall be my people.
2 Thus saith the LORD, The people *which*
were left of the sword found grace in the wilderness; *even* Is'ra-el, when I went to cause him to
rest.
3 The LORD hath appeared of old unto me,
saying, Yea, I have loved thee with an everlasting love: therefore with lovingkindness have
I drawn thee.
4 Again I will build thee, and thou shalt be
built, O virgin of Is'ra-el: thou shalt again be
adorned with thy tabrets, and shalt go forth in
the dances of them that make merry.

5 Thou shalt yet plant vines upon the mountains of Sa-ma'ri-a: the planters shall plant, and
shall eat *them* as common things.
6 For there shall be a day, *that* the watchmen
upon the mount E'phra-im shall cry, Arise ye,
and let us go up to Zi'on unto the LORD our God.
7 For thus saith the LORD; Sing with gladness
for Ja'cob, and shout among the chief of the nations: publish ye, praise ye, and say, O LORD,
save thy people, the remnant of Is'ra-el.
8 Behold, I will bring them from the north
country, and gather them from the coasts of the
earth, *and* with them the blind and the lame,
the woman with child and her that travaileth
with child together: a great company shall return thither.
9 They shall come with weeping, and with
supplications will I lead them: I will cause them
to walk by the rivers of waters in a straight
way, wherein they shall not stumble: for I am a
father to Is'ra-el, and E'phra-im *is* my firstborn.
10 ¶ Hear the word of the LORD, O ye nations, and declare *it* in the isles afar off, and say,
He that scattered Is'ra-el will gather him, and
keep him, as a shepherd *doth* his flock.
11 For the LORD hath redeemed Ja'cob, and
ransomed him from the hand of *him that was*
stronger than he.
12 Therefore they shall come and sing in the
height of Zi'on, and shall flow together to the
goodness of the LORD, for wheat, and for wine,
and for oil, and for the young of the flock and of
the herd: and their soul shall be as a watered
garden; and they shall not sorrow any more at
all.
13 Then shall the virgin rejoice in the dance,
both young men and old together: for I will turn
their mourning into joy, and will comfort them,
and make them rejoice from their sorrow.
14 And I will satiate the soul of the priests
with fatness, and my people shall be satisfied
with my goodness, saith the LORD.
15 ¶ Thus saith the LORD; A voice was heard
in Ra'mah, lamentation, *and* bitter weeping;
Ra'hel weeping for her children refused to be
comforted for her children, because they *were*
not.
16 Thus saith the LORD; Refrain thy voice
from weeping, and thine eyes from tears: for
thy work shall be rewarded, saith the LORD; and
they shall come again from the land of the enemy.
17 And there is hope in thine end, saith the
LORD, that thy children shall come again to
their own border.
18 ¶ I have surely heard E'phra-im bemoan-
ing himself *thus;* Thou hast chastised me, and I
was chastised, as a bullock unaccustomed *to
the yoke:* turn thou me, and I shall be turned;
for thou *art* the LORD my God.
19 Surely after that I was turned, I repented;
and after that I was instructed, I smote upon
my thigh: I was ashamed, yea, even confounded, because I did bear the reproach of my
youth.
20 *Is* E'phra-im my dear son? *is he* a pleasant
child? for since I spake against him, I do earnestly remember him still: therefore my bowels
are troubled for him; I will surely have mercy
upon him, saith the LORD.
21 Set thee up waymarks, make thee high
heaps: set thine heart toward the highway, *even*
the way *which* thou wentest: turn again, O virgin of Is'ra-el, turn again to these thy cities.
22 ¶ How long wilt thou go about, O thou
backsliding daughter? for the LORD hath created a new thing in the earth, A woman shall
compass a man.
23 Thus saith the LORD of hosts, the God of
Is'ra-el; As yet they shall use this speech in the
land of Ju'dah and in the cities thereof, when I
shall bring again their captivity; The LORD bless
thee, O habitation of justice, *and* mountain of
holiness.
24 And there shall dwell in Ju'dah itself, and
in all the cities thereof together, husbandmen,
and they *that* go forth with flocks.
25 For I have satiated the weary soul, and I
have replenished every sorrowful soul.
26 Upon this I awaked, and beheld; and my
sleep was sweet unto me.
27 ¶ Behold, the days come, saith the LORD,
that I will sow the house of Is'ra-el and the
house of Ju'dah with the seed of man, and with
the seed of beast.
28 And it shall come to pass, *that* like as I
have watched over them, to pluck up, and to
break down, and to throw down, and to destroy,
and to afflict; so will I watch over them, to
build, and to plant, saith the LORD.
29 In those days they shall say no more, The
fathers have eaten a sour grape, and the children's teeth are set on edge.
30 But every one shall die for his own iniquity: every man that eateth the sour grape, his
teeth shall be set on edge.
31 ¶ Behold, the days come, saith the LORD,
that I will make a new covenant with the house
of Is'ra-el, and with the house of Ju'dah:
32 Not according to the covenant that I made
with their fathers in the day *that* I took them by
the hand to bring them out of the land of E'gypt;
which my covenant they brake, although I was
an husband unto them, saith the LORD:
33 But this *shall be* the covenant that I will
make with the house of Is'ra-el; After those
days, saith the LORD, I will put my law in their
inward parts, and write it in their hearts; and
will be their God, and they shall be my people.
34 And they shall teach no more every man
his neighbour, and every man his brother, saying, Know the LORD: for they shall all know me,
from the least of them unto the greatest of
them, saith the LORD: for I will forgive their iniquity, and I will remember their sin no more.
35 ¶ Thus saith the LORD, which giveth the
sun for a light by day, *and* the ordinances of the
moon and of the stars for a light by night, which
divideth the sea when the waves thereof roar;
The LORD of hosts *is* his name:
36 If those ordinances depart from before
me, saith the LORD, *then* the seed of Is'ra-el also
shall cease from being a nation before me for
ever.
37 Thus saith the LORD; If heaven above can
be measured, and the foundations of the earth
searched out beneath, I will also cast off all the
seed of Is'ra-el for all that they have done, saith
the LORD.
38 ¶ Behold, the days come, saith the LORD,
that the city shall be built to the LORD from the
tower of Ha-nan'e-el unto the gate of the corner.
39 And the measuring line shall yet go forth
over against it upon the hill Ga'reb, and shall
compass about to Go'ath.
40 And the whole valley of the dead bodies,
and of the ashes, and all the fields unto the
brook of Kid'ron, unto the corner of the horse
gate toward the east, *shall be* holy unto the
LORD; it shall not be plucked up, nor thrown
down any more for ever.

32 THE word that came to Jer-e-mi'ah from the LORD in the tenth year of Zed-e-ki'ah king of Ju'dah, which *was* the eighteenth year of Neb-u-chad-rez'zar.

2 For then the king of Bab'y-lon's army besieged Je-ru'sa-lem: and Jer-e-mi'ah the prophet was shut up in the court of the prison, which *was* in the king of Ju'dah's house.

3 For Zed-e-ki'ah king of Ju'dah had shut him up, saying, Wherefore dost thou prophesy, and say, Thus saith the LORD, Behold, I will give this city into the hand of the king of Bab'y-lon, and he shall take it;

4 And Zed-e-ki'ah king of Ju'dah shall not escape out of the hand of the Chal-de'ans, but shall surely be delivered into the hand of the king of Bab'y-lon, and shall speak with him mouth to mouth, and his eyes shall behold his eyes;

5 And he shall lead Zed-e-ki'ah to Bab'y-lon, and there shall he be until I visit him, saith the LORD: though ye fight with the Chal-de'ans, ye shall not prosper.

6 ¶ And Jer-e-mi'ah said, The word of the LORD came unto me, saying,

7 Behold, Ha-nam'e-el the son of Shal'lum thine uncle shall come unto thee, saying, Buy thee my field that *is* in An'a-thoth: for the right of redemption *is* thine to buy *it*.

8 So Ha-nam'e-el mine uncle's son came to me in the court of the prison according to the word of the LORD, and said unto me, Buy my field, I pray thee, that *is* in An'a-thoth, which *is* in the country of Ben'ja-min: for the right of inheritance *is* thine, and the redemption *is* thine; buy *it* for thyself. Then I knew that this *was* the word of the LORD.

9 And I bought the field of Ha-nam'e-el my uncle's son, that *was* in An'a-thoth, and weighed him the money, *even* seventeen shekels of silver.

10 And I subscribed the evidence, and sealed *it*, and took witnesses, and weighed *him* the money in the balances.

11 So I took the evidence of the purchase, *both* that which was sealed *according* to the law and custom, and that which was open:

12 And I gave the evidence of the purchase unto Ba'ruch the son of Ne-ri'ah, the son of Ma-a-se'iah, in the sight of Ha-nam'e-el mine uncle's *son*, and in the presence of the witnesses that subscribed the book of the purchase, before all the Jews that sat in the court of the prison.

13 ¶ And I charged Ba'ruch before them, saying,

14 Thus saith the LORD of hosts, the God of Is'ra-el; Take these evidences, this evidence of the purchase, both which is sealed, and this evidence which is open; and put them in an earthen vessel, that they may continue many days.

15 For thus saith the LORD of hosts, the God of Is'ra-el; Houses and fields and vineyards shall be possessed again in this land.

16 ¶ Now when I had delivered the evidence of the purchase unto Ba'ruch the son of Ne-ri'ah, I prayed unto the LORD, saying,

17 Ah Lord GOD! behold, thou hast made the heaven and the earth by thy great power and stretched out arm, *and* there is nothing too hard for thee:

18 Thou shewest lovingkindness unto thousands, and recompensest the iniquity of the fathers into the bosom of their children after them: the Great, the Mighty God, the LORD of hosts, *is* his name,

19 Great in counsel, and mighty in work: for thine eyes *are* open upon all the ways of the sons of men: to give every one according to his ways, and according to the fruit of his doings:

20 Which hast set signs and wonders in the land of E'gypt, *even* unto this day, and in Is'ra-el, and among *other* men; and hast made thee a name, as at this day;

21 And hast brought forth thy people Is'ra-el out of the land of E'gypt with signs, and with wonders, and with a strong hand, and with a stretched out arm, and with great terror;

22 And hast given them this land, which thou didst swear to their fathers to give them, a land flowing with milk and honey;

23 And they came in, and possessed it; but they obeyed not thy voice, neither walked in thy law; they have done nothing of all that thou commandedst them to do: therefore thou hast caused all this evil to come upon them:

24 Behold the mounts, they are come unto the city to take it; and the city is given into the hand of the Chal-de'ans, that fight against it, because of the sword, and of the famine, and of the pestilence: and what thou hast spoken is come to pass; and, behold, thou seest *it*.

25 And thou hast said unto me, O Lord GOD, Buy thee the field for money, and take witnesses; for the city is given into the hand of the Chal-de'ans.

26 ¶ Then came the word of the LORD unto Jer-e-mi'ah, saying,

27 Behold, I *am* the LORD, the God of all flesh: is there any thing too hard for me?

28 Therefore thus saith the LORD; Behold, I will give this city into the hand of the Chal-de'ans, and into the hand of Neb-u-chad-rez'zar king of Bab'y-lon, and he shall take it:

29 And the Chal-de'ans, that fight against this city, shall come and set fire on this city, and burn it with the houses, upon whose roofs they have offered incense unto Ba'al, and poured out drink offerings unto other gods, to provoke me to anger.

30 For the children of Is'ra-el and the children of Ju'dah have only done evil before me from their youth: for the children of Is'ra-el have only provoked me to anger with the work of their hands, saith the LORD.

31 For this city hath been to me *as* a provocation of mine anger and of my fury from the day that they built it even unto this day; that I should remove it from before my face,

32 Because of all the evil of the children of Is'ra-el and of the children of Ju'dah, which they have done to provoke me to anger, they, their kings, their princes, their priests, and their prophets, and the men of Ju'dah, and the inhabitants of Je-ru'sa-lem.

33 And they have turned unto me the back, and not the face: though I taught them, rising up early and teaching *them*, yet they have not hearkened to receive instruction.

34 But they set their abominations in the house, which is called by my name, to defile it.

35 And they built the high places of Ba'al, which *are* in the valley of the son of Hin'nom, to cause their sons and their daughters to pass through *the fire* unto Mo'lech; which I commanded them not, neither came it into my mind, that they should do this abomination, to cause Ju'dah to sin.

36 ¶ And now therefore thus saith the LORD, the God of Is'ra-el, concerning this city, whereof ye say, It shall be delivered into the hand of the king of Bab'y-lon by the sword, and by the famine, and by the pestilence;

37 Behold, I will gather them out of all countries, whither I have driven them in mine anger,
and in my fury, and in great wrath; and I will
bring them again unto this place, and I will
cause them to dwell safely:
38 And they shall be my people, and I will be
their God:
39 And I will give them one heart, and one
way, that they may fear me for ever, for the
good of them, and of their children after them:
40 And I will make an everlasting covenant
with them, that I will not turn away from them,
to do them good; but I will put my fear in their
hearts, that they shall not depart from me.
41 Yea, I will rejoice over them to do them
good, and I will plant them in this land assuredly with my whole heart and with my
whole soul.
42 For thus saith the LORD; Like as I have
brought all this great evil upon this people, so
will I bring upon them all the good that I have
promised them.
43 And fields shall be bought in this land,
whereof ye say, *It is* desolate without man or
beast; it is given into the hand of the Chal-de'-
ans.
44 Men shall buy fields for money, and subscribe evidences, and seal *them*, and take witnesses in the land of Ben'ja-min, and in the
places about Je-ru'sa-lem, and in the cities of
Ju'dah, and in the cities of the mountains, and
in the cities of the valley, and in the cities of the
south: for I will cause their captivity to return,
saith the LORD.

33 MOREOVER the word of the LORD
came unto Jer-e-mi'ah the second time,
while he was yet shut up in the court of the
prison, saying,
2 Thus saith the LORD the maker thereof, the
LORD that formed it, to establish it; the LORD *is*
his name;
3 Call unto me, and I will answer thee, and
shew thee great and mighty things, which thou
knowest not.
4 For thus saith the LORD, the God of Is'ra-el,
concerning the houses of this city, and concerning the houses of the kings of Ju'dah, which are
thrown down by the mounts, and by the sword;
5 They come to fight with the Chal-de'ans,
but *it is* to fill them with the dead bodies of
men, whom I have slain in mine anger and in
my fury, and for all whose wickedness I have
hid my face from this city.
6 Behold, I will bring it health and cure, and I
will cure them, and will reveal unto them the
abundance of peace and truth.
7 And I will cause the captivity of Ju'dah and
the captivity of Is'ra-el to return, and will build
them, as at the first.
8 And I will cleanse them from all their iniquity, whereby they have sinned against me; and
I will pardon all their iniquities, whereby they
have sinned, and whereby they have transgressed against me.
9 ¶ And it shall be to me a name of joy, a
praise and an honour before all the nations of
the earth, which shall hear all the good that I do
unto them: and they shall fear and tremble for
all the goodness and for all the prosperity that I
procure unto it.
10 Thus saith the LORD; Again there shall be
heard in this place, which ye say *shall be* desolate without man and without beast, *even* in the
cities of Ju'dah, and in the streets of Je-ru'sa-
lem, that are desolate, without man, and without inhabitant, and without beast,
11 The voice of joy, and the voice of gladness, the voice of the bridegroom, and the voice
of the bride, the voice of them that shall say,
Praise the LORD of hosts: for the LORD *is* good;
for his mercy *endureth* for ever: *and* of them
that shall bring the sacrifice of praise into the
house of the LORD. For I will cause to return the
captivity of the land, as at the first, saith the
LORD.
12 Thus saith the LORD of hosts; Again in this
place, which is desolate without man and without beast, and in all the cities thereof, shall be
an habitation of shepherds causing *their* flocks
to lie down.
13 In the cities of the mountains, in the cities
of the vale, and in the cities of the south, and in
the land of Ben'ja-min, and in the places about
Je-ru'sa-lem, and in the cities of Ju'dah, shall
the flocks pass again under the hands of him
that telleth *them*, saith the LORD.
14 Behold, the days come, saith the LORD,
that I will perform that good thing which I have
promised unto the house of Is'ra-el and to the
house of Ju'dah.
15 ¶ In those days, and at that time, will I
cause the Branch of righteousness to grow up
unto Da'vid; and he shall execute judgment and
righteousness in the land.
16 In those days shall Ju'dah be saved, and
Je-ru'sa-lem shall dwell safely: and this *is the
name* wherewith she shall be called, The LORD
our righteousness.
17 ¶ For thus saith the LORD; Da'vid shall
never want a man to sit upon the throne of the
house of Is'ra-el;
18 Neither shall the priests the Le'vites want
a man before me to offer burnt offerings, and to
kindle meat offerings, and to do sacrifice continually.
19 ¶ And the word of the LORD came unto
Jer-e-mi'ah, saying,
20 Thus saith the LORD; If ye can break my
covenant of the day, and my covenant of the
night, and that there should not be day and
night in their season;
21 *Then* may also my covenant be broken
with Da'vid my servant, that he should not have
a son to reign upon his throne; and with the
Le'vites the priests, my ministers.
22 As the host of heaven cannot be numbered, neither the sand of the sea measured: so
will I multiply the seed of Da'vid my servant,
and the Le'vites that minister unto me.
23 Moreover the word of the LORD came to
Jer-e-mi'ah, saying,
24 Considerest thou not what this people
have spoken, saying, The two families which
the LORD hath chosen, he hath even cast them
off? thus they have despised my people, that
they should be no more a nation before them.
25 Thus saith the LORD; If my covenant *be*
not with day and night, *and if* I have not appointed the ordinances of heaven and earth;
26 Then will I cast away the seed of Ja'cob,
and Da'vid my servant, *so* that I will not take
any of his seed *to be* rulers over the seed of
A'bra-ham, I'saac, and Ja'cob: for I will cause
their captivity to return, and have mercy on
them.

34 THE word which came unto Jer-e-mi'ah
from the LORD, when Neb-u-chad-nez'-
zar king of Bab'y-lon, and all his army, and all
the kingdoms of the earth of his dominion, and
all the people, fought against Je-ru'sa-lem, and
against all the cities thereof, saying,
2 Thus saith the LORD, the God of Is'ra-el; Go

and speak to Zed-e-ki'ah king of Ju'dah, and tell him, Thus saith the LORD; Behold, I will give this city into the hand of the king of Bab'y-lon, and he shall burn it with fire:

3 And thou shalt not escape out of his hand, but shalt surely be taken, and delivered into his hand; and thine eyes shall behold the eyes of the king of Bab'y-lon, and he shall speak with thee mouth to mouth, and thou shalt go to Bab'y-lon.

4 Yet hear the word of the LORD, O Zed-e-ki'ah king of Ju'dah; Thus saith the LORD of thee, Thou shalt not die by the sword:

5 *But* thou shalt die in peace: and with the burnings of thy fathers, the former kings which were before thee, so shall they burn *odours* for thee; and they will lament thee, *saying*, Ah lord! for I have pronounced the word, saith the LORD.

6 Then Jer-e-mi'ah the prophet spake all these words unto Zed-e-ki'ah king of Ju'dah in Je-ru'sa-lem,

7 When the king of Bab'y-lon's army fought against Je-ru'sa-lem, and against all the cities of Ju'dah that were left, against La'chish, and against A-ze'kah: for these defenced cities remained of the cities of Ju'dah.

8 ¶ *This is* the word that came unto Jer-e-mi'ah from the LORD, after that the king Zed-e-ki'ah had made a covenant with all the people which *were* at Je-ru'sa-lem, to proclaim liberty unto them;

9 That every man should let his manservant, and every man his maidservant, *being* an He'brew or an He'brew-ess, go free; that none should serve himself of them, *to wit*, of a Jew his brother.

10 Now when all the princes, and all the people, which had entered into the covenant, heard that every one should let his manservant, and every one his maidservant, go free, that none should serve themselves of them any more, then they obeyed, and let *them* go.

11 But afterward they turned, and caused the servants and the handmaids, whom they had let go free, to return, and brought them into subjection for servants and for handmaids.

12 ¶ Therefore the word of the LORD came to Jer-e-mi'ah from the LORD, saying,

13 Thus saith the LORD, the God of Is'ra-el; I made a covenant with your fathers in the day that I brought them forth out of the land of E'gypt, out of the house of bondmen, saying,

14 At the end of seven years let ye go every man his brother an He'brew, which hath been sold unto thee; and when he hath served thee six years, thou shalt let him go free from thee: but your fathers hearkened not unto me, neither inclined their ear.

15 And ye were now turned, and had done right in my sight, in proclaiming liberty every man to his neighbour; and ye had made a covenant before me in the house which is called by my name:

16 But ye turned and polluted my name, and caused every man his servant, and every man his handmaid, whom he had set at liberty at their pleasure, to return, and brought them into subjection, to be unto you for servants and for handmaids.

17 Therefore thus saith the LORD; Ye have not hearkened unto me, in proclaiming liberty, every one to his brother, and every man to his neighbour: behold, I proclaim a liberty for you, saith the LORD, to the sword, to the pestilence, and to the famine; and I will make you to be removed into all the kingdoms of the earth.

18 And I will give the men that have transgressed my covenant, which have not performed the words of the covenant which they had made before me, when they cut the calf in twain, and passed between the parts thereof,

19 The princes of Ju'dah, and the princes of Je-ru'sa-lem, the eunuchs, and the priests, and all the people of the land, which passed between the parts of the calf;

20 I will even give them into the hand of their enemies, and into the hand of them that seek their life: and their dead bodies shall be for meat unto the fowls of the heaven, and to the beasts of the earth.

21 And Zed-e-ki'ah king of Ju'dah and his princes will I give into the hand of their enemies, and into the hand of them that seek their life, and into the hand of the king of Bab'y-lon's army, which are gone up from you.

22 Behold, I will command, saith the LORD, and cause them to return to this city; and they shall fight against it, and take it, and burn it with fire: and I will make the cities of Ju'dah a desolation without an inhabitant.

35 THE word which came unto Jer-e-mi'ah from the LORD in the days of Je-hoi'a-kim the son of Jo-si'ah king of Ju'dah, saying,

2 Go unto the house of the Re'chab-ites, and speak unto them, and bring them into the house of the LORD, into one of the chambers, and give them wine to drink.

3 Then I took Ja-az-a-ni'ah the son of Jer-e-mi'ah, the son of Hab-a-zi-ni'ah, and his brethren, and all his sons, and the whole house of the Re'chab-ites;

4 And I brought them into the house of the LORD, into the chamber of the sons of Ha'nan, the son of Ig-da-li'ah, a man of God, which *was* by the chamber of the princes, which *was* above the chamber of Ma-a-se'iah the son of Shal'lum, the keeper of the door:

5 And I set before the sons of the house of the Re'chab-ites pots full of wine, and cups, and I said unto them, Drink ye wine.

6 But they said, We will drink no wine: for Jon'a-dab the son of Re'chab our father commanded us, saying, Ye shall drink no wine, *neither* ye, nor your sons for ever:

7 Neither shall ye build house, nor sow seed, nor plant vineyard, nor have *any*: but all your days ye shall dwell in tents; that ye may live many days in the land where ye *be* strangers.

8 Thus have we obeyed the voice of Jon'a-dab the son of Re'chab our father in all that he hath charged us, to drink no wine all our days, we, our wives, our sons, nor our daughters;

9 Nor to build houses for us to dwell in: neither have we vineyard, nor field, nor seed:

10 But we have dwelt in tents, and have obeyed, and done according to all that Jon'a-dab our father commanded us.

11 But it came to pass, when Neb-u-chad-rez'zar king of Bab'y-lon came up into the land, that we said, Come, and let us go to Je-ru'sa-lem for fear of the army of the Chal-de'ans, and for fear of the army of the Syr'i-ans: so we dwell at Je-ru'sa-lem.

12 ¶ Then came the word of the LORD unto Jer-e-mi'ah, saying,

13 Thus saith the LORD of hosts, the God of Is'ra-el; Go and tell the men of Ju'dah and the inhabitants of Je-ru'sa-lem, Will ye not receive instruction to hearken to my words? saith the LORD.

14 The words of Jon'a-dab the son of Re'chab, that he commanded his sons not to drink wine, are performed; for unto this day they

drink none, but obey their father's commandment: notwithstanding I have spoken unto you, rising early and speaking; but ye hearkened not unto me.

15 I have sent also unto you all my servants the prophets, rising up early and sending *them*, saying, Return ye now every man from his evil way, and amend your doings, and go not after other gods to serve them, and ye shall dwell in the land which I have given to you and to your fathers: but ye have not inclined your ear, nor hearkened unto me.

16 Because the sons of Jon'a-dab the son of Re'chab have performed the commandment of their father, which he commanded them; but this people hath not hearkened unto me:

17 Therefore thus saith the LORD God of hosts, the God of Is'ra-el; Behold, I will bring upon Ju'dah and upon all the inhabitants of Je-ru'sa-lem all the evil that I have pronounced against them: because I have spoken unto them, but they have not heard; and I have called unto them, but they have not answered.

18 ¶ And Jer-e-mi'ah said unto the house of the Re'chab-ites, Thus saith the LORD of hosts, the God of Is'ra-el; Because ye have obeyed the commandment of Jon'a-dab your father, and kept all his precepts, and done according unto all that he hath commanded you:

19 Therefore thus saith the LORD of hosts, the God of Is'ra-el; Jon'a-dab the son of Re'chab shall not want a man to stand before me for ever.

36 AND it came to pass in the fourth year of Je-hoi'a-kim the son of Jo-si'ah king of Ju'dah, *that* this word came unto Jer-e-mi'ah from the LORD, saying,

2 Take thee a roll of a book, and write therein all the words that I have spoken unto thee against Is'ra-el, and against Ju'dah, and against all the nations, from the day I spake unto thee, from the days of Jo-si'ah, even unto this day.

3 It may be that the house of Ju'dah will hear all the evil which I purpose to do unto them; that they may return every man from his evil way; that I may forgive their iniquity and their sin.

4 Then Jer-e-mi'ah called Ba'ruch the son of Ne-ri'ah: and Ba'ruch wrote from the mouth of Jer-e-mi'ah all the words of the LORD, which he had spoken unto him, upon a roll of a book.

5 And Jer-e-mi'ah commanded Ba'ruch, saying, I *am* shut up; I cannot go into the house of the LORD:

6 Therefore go thou, and read in the roll, which thou hast written from my mouth, the words of the LORD in the ears of the people in the LORD's house upon the fasting day: and also thou shalt read them in the ears of all Ju'dah that come out of their cities.

7 It may be they will present their supplication before the LORD, and will return every one from his evil way: for great *is* the anger and the fury that the LORD hath pronounced against this people.

8 And Ba'ruch the son of Ne-ri'ah did according to all that Jer-e-mi'ah the prophet commanded him, reading in the book the words of the LORD in the LORD's house.

9 And it came to pass in the fifth year of Je-hoi'a-kim the son of Jo-si'ah king of Ju'dah, in the ninth month, *that* they proclaimed a fast before the LORD to all the people in Je-ru'sa-lem, and to all the people that came from the cities of Ju'dah unto Je-ru'sa-lem.

10 Then read Ba'ruch in the book the words of Jer-e-mi'ah in the house of the LORD, in the chamber of Gem-a-ri'ah the son of Sha'phan the scribe, in the higher court, at the entry of the new gate of the LORD's house, in the ears of all the people.

11 ¶ When Mi-cha'iah the son of Gem-a-ri'ah, the son of Sha'phan, had heard out of the book all the words of the LORD,

12 Then he went down into the king's house, into the scribe's chamber: and, lo, all the princes sat there, *even* E-lish'a-ma the scribe, and Del-a-i'ah the son of Shem-a-i'ah, and El'na-than the son of Ach'bor, and Gem-a-ri'ah the son of Sha'phan, and Zed-e-ki'ah the son of Han-a-ni'ah, and all the princes.

13 Then Mi-cha'iah declared unto them all the words that he had heard, when Ba'ruch read the book in the ears of the people.

14 Therefore all the princes sent Je-hu'di the son of Neth-a-ni'ah, the son of Shel-e-mi'ah, the son of Cu'shi, unto Ba'ruch, saying, Take in thine hand the roll wherein thou hast read in the ears of the people, and come. So Ba'ruch the son of Ne-ri'ah took the roll in his hand, and came unto them.

15 And they said unto him, Sit down now, and read it in our ears. So Ba'ruch read *it* in their ears.

16 Now it came to pass, when they had heard all the words, they were afraid both one and other, and said unto Ba'ruch, We will surely tell the king of all these words.

17 And they asked Ba'ruch, saying, Tell us now, How didst thou write all these words at his mouth?

18 Then Ba'ruch answered them, He pronounced all these words unto me with his mouth, and I wrote *them* with ink in the book.

19 Then said the princes unto Ba'ruch, Go, hide thee, thou and Jer-e-mi'ah; and let no man know where ye be.

20 ¶ And they went in to the king into the court, but they laid up the roll in the chamber of E-lish'a-ma the scribe, and told all the words in the ears of the king.

21 So the king sent Je-hu'di to fetch the roll: and he took it out of E-lish'a-ma the scribe's chamber. And Je-hu'di read it in the ears of the king, and in the ears of all the princes which stood beside the king.

22 Now the king sat in the winterhouse in the ninth month: and *there was a fire* on the hearth burning before him.

23 And it came to pass, *that* when Je-hu'di had read three or four leaves, he cut it with the penknife, and cast *it* into the fire that *was* on the hearth, until all the roll was consumed in the fire that *was* on the hearth.

24 Yet they were not afraid, nor rent their garments, *neither* the king, nor any of his servants that heard all these words.

25 Nevertheless El'na-than and Del-a-i'ah and Gem-a-ri'ah had made intercession to the king that he would not burn the roll: but he would not hear them.

26 But the king commanded Je-rah'me-el the son of Ham'me-lech, and Ser-a-i'ah the son of Az'ri-el, and Shel-e-mi'ah the son of Ab'de-el, to take Ba'ruch the scribe and Jer-e-mi'ah the prophet: but the LORD hid them.

27 ¶ Then the word of the LORD came to Jer-e-mi'ah, after that the king had burned the roll, and the words which Ba'ruch wrote at the mouth of Jer-e-mi'ah, saying,

28 Take thee again another roll, and write in it all the former words that were in the first roll,

which Je-hoi'a-kim the king of Ju'dah hath
burned.
29 And thou shalt say to Je-hoi'a-kim king of
Ju'dah, Thus saith the LORD; Thou hast burned
this roll, saying, Why hast thou written therein,
saying, The king of Bab'y-lon shall certainly
come and destroy this land, and shall cause to
cease from thence man and beast?
30 Therefore thus saith the LORD of Je-hoi'a-
kim king of Ju'dah; He shall have none to sit
upon the throne of Da'vid: and his dead body
shall be cast out in the day to the heat, and in
the night to the frost.
31 And I will punish him and his seed and his
servants for their iniquity; and I will bring upon
them, and upon the inhabitants of Je-ru'sa-lem,
and upon the men of Ju'dah, all the evil that I
have pronounced against them; but they hearkened not.
32 ¶ Then took Jer-e-mi'ah another roll, and
gave it to Ba'ruch the scribe, the son of Ne-ri'-
ah; who wrote therein from the mouth of Jer-e-
mi'ah all the words of the book which Je-hoi'a-
kim king of Ju'dah had burned in the fire: and
there were added besides unto them many like
words.

37 AND king Zed-e-ki'ah the son of Jo-si'-
ah reigned instead of Co-ni'ah the son of
Je-hoi'a-kim, whom Neb-u-chad-rez'zar king of
Bab'y-lon made king in the land of Ju'dah.
2 But neither he, nor his servants, nor the
people of the land, did hearken unto the words
of the LORD, which he spake by the prophet Jer-
e-mi'ah.
3 And Zed-e-ki'ah the king sent Je'hu-cal the
son of Shel-e-mi'ah and Zeph-a-ni'ah the son of
Ma-a-se'iah the priest to the prophet Jer-e-mi'-
ah, saying, Pray now unto the LORD our God for
us.
4 Now Jer-e-mi'ah came in and went out
among the people: for they had not put him into
prison.
5 Then Pha'raoh's army was come forth out
of E'gypt: and when the Chal-de'ans that besieged Je-ru'sa-lem heard tidings of them, they
departed from Je-ru'sa-lem.
6 ¶ Then came the word of the LORD unto
the prophet Jer-e-mi'ah, saying,
7 Thus saith the LORD, the God of Is'ra-el;
Thus shall ye say to the king of Ju'dah, that sent
you unto me to enquire of me; Behold, Pha'-
raoh's army, which is come forth to help you,
shall return to E'gypt into their own land.
8 And the Chal-de'ans shall come again, and
fight against this city, and take it, and burn it
with fire.
9 Thus saith the LORD; Deceive not yourselves, saying, The Chal-de'ans shall surely depart from us: for they shall not depart.
10 For though ye had smitten the whole
army of the Chal-de'ans that fight against you,
and there remained *but* wounded men among
them, *yet* should they rise up every man in his
tent, and burn this city with fire.
11 ¶ And it came to pass, that when the
army of the Chal-de'ans was broken up from Je-
ru'sa-lem for fear of Pha'raoh's army,
12 Then Jer-e-mi'ah went forth out of Je-ru'-
sa-lem to go into the land of Ben'ja-min, to
separate himself thence in the midst of the people.
13 And when he was in the gate of Ben'ja-
min, a captain of the ward *was* there, whose
name *was* I-ri'jah, the son of Shel-e-mi'ah, the
son of Han-a-ni'ah; and he took Jer-e-mi'ah the
prophet, saying, Thou fallest away to the Chal-
de'ans.
14 Then said Jer-e-mi'ah, *It is* false; I fall not
away to the Chal-de'ans. But he hearkened not
to him: so I-ri'jah took Jer-e-mi'ah, and brought
him to the princes.
15 Wherefore the princes were wroth with
Jer-e-mi'ah, and smote him, and put him in
prison in the house of Jon'a-than the scribe: for
they had made that the prison.
16 ¶ When Jer-e-mi'ah was entered into the
dungeon, and into the cabins, and Jer-e-mi'ah
had remained there many days;
17 Then Zed-e-ki'ah the king sent, and took
him out: and the king asked him secretly in his
house, and said, Is there *any* word from the
LORD? And Jer-e-mi'ah said, There is: for, said
he, thou shalt be delivered into the hand of the
king of Bab'y-lon.
18 Moreover Jer-e-mi'ah said unto king Zed-
e-ki'ah, What have I offended against thee, or
against thy servants, or against this people, that
ye have put me in prison?
19 Where *are* now your prophets which
prophesied unto you, saying, The king of Bab'y-
lon shall not come against you, nor against this
land?
20 Therefore hear now, I pray thee, O my
lord the king: let my supplication, I pray thee,
be accepted before thee; that thou cause me not
to return to the house of Jon'a-than the scribe,
lest I die there.
21 Then Zed-e-ki'ah the king commanded
that they should commit Jer-e-mi'ah into the
court of the prison, and that they should give
him daily a piece of bread out of the bakers'
street, until all the bread in the city were spent.
Thus Jer-e-mi'ah remained in the court of the
prison.

38 THEN Sheph-a-ti'ah the son of Mat'tan,
and Ged-a-li'ah the son of Pash'ur, and
Ju'cal the son of Shel-e-mi'ah, and Pash'ur the
son of Mal-chi'ah, heard the words that Jer-e-
mi'ah had spoken unto all the people, saying,
2 Thus saith the LORD, He that remaineth in
this city shall die by the sword, by the famine,
and by the pestilence: but he that goeth forth to
the Chal-de'ans shall live; for he shall have his
life for a prey, and shall live.
3 Thus saith the LORD, This city shall surely
be given into the hand of the king of Bab'y-lon's
army, which shall take it.
4 Therefore the princes said unto the king,
We beseech thee, let this man be put to death:
for thus he weakeneth the hands of the men of
war that remain in this city, and the hands of all
the people, in speaking such words unto them:
for this man seeketh not the welfare of this people, but the hurt.
5 Then Zed-e-ki'ah the king said, Behold, he
is in your hand: for the king *is* not *he that* can
do *any* thing against you.
6 Then took they Jer-e-mi'ah, and cast him
into the dungeon of Mal-chi'ah the son of Ham'-
me-lech, that *was* in the court of the prison: and
they let down Jer-e-mi'ah with cords. And in
the dungeon *there was* no water, but mire: so
Jer-e-mi'ah sunk in the mire.
7 ¶ Now when E'bed-me'lech the E-thi-o'pi-
an, one of the eunuchs which was in the king's
house, heard that they had put Jer-e-mi'ah in
the dungeon; the king then sitting in the gate of
Ben'ja-min;
8 E'bed-me'lech went forth out of the king's
house, and spake to the king, saying,
9 My lord the king, these men have done evil

in all that they have done to Jer-e-mi'ah the prophet, whom they have cast into the dungeon; and he is like to die for hunger in the place where he is: for *there is* no more bread in the city.

10 Then the king commanded E'bed-me'lech the E-thi-o'pi-an, saying, Take from hence thirty men with thee, and take up Jer-e-mi'ah the prophet out of the dungeon, before he die.

11 So E'bed-me'lech took the men with him, and went into the house of the king under the treasury, and took thence old cast clouts and old rotten rags, and let them down by cords into the dungeon to Jer-e-mi'ah.

12 And E'bed-me'lech the E-thi-o'pi-an said unto Jer-e-mi'ah, Put now *these* old cast clouts and rotten rags under thine armholes under the cords. And Jer-e-mi'ah did so.

13 So they drew up Jer-e-mi'ah with cords, and took him up out of the dungeon: and Jer-e-mi'ah remained in the court of the prison.

14 ¶ Then Zed-e-ki'ah the king sent, and took Jer-e-mi'ah the prophet unto him into the third entry that *is* in the house of the LORD: and the king said unto Jer-e-mi'ah, I will ask thee a thing; hide nothing from me.

15 Then Jer-e-mi'ah said unto Zed-e-ki'ah, If I declare *it* unto thee, wilt thou not surely put me to death? and if I give thee counsel, wilt thou not hearken unto me?

16 So Zed-e-ki'ah the king sware secretly unto Jer-e-mi'ah, saying, *As* the LORD liveth, that made us this soul, I will not put thee to death, neither will I give thee into the hand of these men that seek thy life.

17 Then said Jer-e-mi'ah unto Zed-e-ki'ah, Thus saith the LORD, the God of hosts, the God of Is'ra-el; If thou wilt assuredly go forth unto the king of Bab'y-lon's princes, then thy soul shall live, and this city shall not be burned with fire; and thou shalt live, and thine house:

18 But if thou wilt not go forth to the king of Bab'y-lon's princes, then shall this city be given into the hand of the Chal-de'ans, and they shall burn it with fire, and thou shalt not escape out of their hand.

19 And Zed-e-ki'ah the king said unto Jer-e-mi'ah, I am afraid of the Jews that are fallen to the Chal-de'ans, lest they deliver me into their hand, and they mock me.

20 But Jer-e-mi'ah said, They shall not deliver *thee.* Obey, I beseech thee, the voice of the LORD, which I speak unto thee: so it shall be well unto thee, and thy soul shall live.

21 But if thou refuse to go forth, this *is* the word that the LORD hath shewed me:

22 And, behold, all the women that are left in the king of Ju'dah's house *shall be* brought forth to the king of Bab'y-lon's princes, and those *women* shall say, Thy friends have set thee on, and have prevailed against thee: thy feet are sunk in the mire, *and* they are turned away back.

23 So they shall bring out all thy wives and thy children to the Chal-de'ans: and thou shalt not escape out of their hand, but shalt be taken by the hand of the king of Bab'y-lon: and thou shalt cause this city to be burned with fire.

24 ¶ Then said Zed-e-ki'ah unto Jer-e-mi'ah, Let no man know of these words, and thou shalt not die.

25 But if the princes hear that I have talked with thee, and they come unto thee, and say unto thee, Declare unto us now what thou hast said unto the king, hide it not from us, and we will not put thee to death; also what the king said unto thee:

26 Then thou shalt say unto them, I presented my supplication before the king, that he would not cause me to return to Jon'a-than's house, to die there.

27 Then came all the princes unto Jer-e-mi'ah, and asked him: and he told them according to all these words that the king had commanded. So they left off speaking with him; for the matter was not perceived.

28 So Jer-e-mi'ah abode in the court of the prison until the day that Je-ru'sa-lem was taken: and he was *there* when Je-ru'sa-lem was taken.

39 IN the ninth year of Zed-e-ki'ah king of Ju'dah, in the tenth month, came Neb-u-chad-rez'zar king of Bab'y-lon and all his army against Je-ru'sa-lem, and they besieged it.

2 *And* in the eleventh year of Zed-e-ki'ah, in the fourth month, the ninth *day* of the month, the city was broken up.

3 And all the princes of the king of Bab'y-lon came in, and sat in the middle gate, *even* Ner'gal-sha-re'zer, Sam'gar-ne'bo, Sar-se'chim, Rab'-sa-ris, Ner'gal-sha-re'zer, Rab'-mag, with all the residue of the princes of the king of Bab'y-lon.

4 ¶ And it came to pass, *that* when Zed-e-ki'ah the king of Ju'dah saw them, and all the men of war, then they fled, and went forth out of the city by night, by the way of the king's garden, by the gate betwixt the two walls: and he went out the way of the plain.

5 But the Chal-de'ans' army pursued after them, and overtook Zed-e-ki'ah in the plains of Jer'i-cho: and when they had taken him, they brought him up to Neb-u-chad-nez'zar king of Bab'y-lon to Rib'lah in the land of Ha'math, where he gave judgment upon him.

6 Then the king of Bab'y-lon slew the sons of Zed-e-ki'ah in Rib'lah before his eyes: also the king of Bab'y-lon slew all the nobles of Ju'dah.

7 Moreover he put out Zed-e-ki'ah's eyes, and bound him with chains, to carry him to Bab'y-lon.

8 ¶ And the Chal-de'ans burned the king's house, and the houses of the people, with fire, and brake down the walls of Je-ru'sa-lem.

9 Then Neb'u-zar-a'dan the captain of the guard carried away captive into Bab'y-lon the remnant of the people that remained in the city, and those that fell away, that fell to him, with the rest of the people that remained.

10 But Neb'u-zar-a'dan the captain of the guard left of the poor of the people, which had nothing, in the land of Ju'dah, and gave them vineyards and fields at the same time.

11 ¶ Now Neb-u-chad-rez'zar king of Bab'y-lon gave charge concerning Jer-e-mi'ah to Neb'-u-zar-a'dan the captain of the guard, saying,

12 Take him, and look well to him, and do him no harm; but do unto him even as he shall say unto thee.

13 So Neb'u-zar-a'dan the captain of the guard sent, and Neb-u-shas'ban, Rab'-sa-ris, and Ner'gal-sha-re'zer, Rab'-mag, and all the king of Bab'y-lon's princes;

14 Even they sent, and took Jer-e-mi'ah out of the court of the prison, and committed him unto Ged-a-li'ah the son of A-hi'kam the son of Sha'phan, that he should carry him home: so he dwelt among the people.

15 ¶ Now the word of the LORD came unto Jer-e-mi'ah, while he was shut up in the court of the prison, saying,

16 Go and speak to E'bed-me'lech the E-thi-o'pi-an, saying, Thus saith the LORD of hosts,

the God of Is'ra-el; Behold, I will bring my
words upon this city for evil, and not for good;
and they shall be *accomplished* in that day before thee.
17 But I will deliver thee in that day, saith
the LORD: and thou shalt not be given into the
hand of the men of whom thou *art* afraid.
18 For I will surely deliver thee, and thou
shalt not fall by the sword, but thy life shall be
for a prey unto thee: because thou hast put thy
trust in me, saith the LORD.

40 THE word that came to Jer-e-mi'ah
from the LORD, after that Neb'u-zar-a'-
dan the captain of the guard had let him go
from Ra'mah, when he had taken him being
bound in chains among all that were carried
away captive of Je-ru'sa-lem and Ju'dah, which
were carried away captive unto Bab'y-lon.
2 And the captain of the guard took Jer-e-
mi'ah, and said unto him, The LORD thy God
hath pronounced this evil upon this place.
3 Now the LORD hath brought *it*, and done
according as he hath said: because ye have
sinned against the LORD, and have not obeyed
his voice, therefore this thing is come upon you.
4 And now, behold, I loose thee this day from
the chains which *were* upon thine hand. If it
seem good unto thee to come with me into
Bab'y-lon, come; and I will look well unto thee:
but if it seem ill unto thee to come with me into
Bab'y-lon, forbear: behold, all the land *is* before
thee: whither it seemeth good and convenient
for thee to go, thither go.
5 Now while he was not yet gone back, *he*
said, Go back also to Ged-a-li'ah the son of A-
hi'kam the son of Sha'phan, whom the king of
Bab'y-lon hath made governor over the cities of
Ju'dah, and dwell with him among the people:
or go wheresoever it seemeth convenient unto
thee to go. So the captain of the guard gave him
victuals and a reward, and let him go.
6 Then went Jer-e-mi'ah unto Ged-a-li'ah the
son of A-hi'kam to Miz'pah; and dwelt with him
among the people that were left in the land.
7 ¶ Now when all the captains of the forces
which *were* in the fields, *even* they and their
men, heard that the king of Bab'y-lon had made
Ged-a-li'ah the son of A-hi'kam governor in the
land, and had committed unto him men, and
women, and children, and of the poor of the
land, of them that were not carried away captive to Bab'y-lon;
8 Then they came to Ged-a-li'ah to Miz'pah,
even Ish'ma-el the son of Neth-a-ni'ah, and Jo-
ha'nan and Jon'a-than the sons of Ka-re'ah, and
Ser-a-i'ah the son of Tan'hu-meth, and the sons
of E'phai the Ne-toph'a-thite, and Jez-a-ni'ah
the son of a Ma-ach'a-thite, they and their men.
9 And Ged-a-li'ah the son of A-hi'kam the
son of Sha'phan sware unto them and to their
men, saying, Fear not to serve the Chal-de'ans:
dwell in the land, and serve the king of Bab'y-
lon, and it shall be well with you.
10 As for me, behold, I will dwell at Miz'pah,
to serve the Chal-de'ans, which will come unto
us: but ye, gather ye wine, and summer fruits,
and oil, and put *them* in your vessels, and dwell
in your cities that ye have taken.
11 Likewise when all the Jews that *were* in
Mo'ab, and among the Am'mon-ites, and in E'-
dom, and that *were* in all the countries, heard
that the king of Bab'y-lon had left a remnant of
Ju'dah, and that he had set over them Ged-a-
li'ah the son of A-hi'kam the son of Sha'phan;
12 Even all the Jews returned out of all
places whither they were driven, and came to
the land of Ju'dah, to Ged-a-li'ah, unto Miz'pah,
and gathered wine and summer fruits very
much.
13 ¶ Moreover Jo-ha'nan the son of Ka-re'-
ah, and all the captains of the forces that *were*
in the fields, came to Ged-a-li'ah to Miz'pah,
14 And said unto him, Dost thou certainly
know that Ba'a-lis the king of the Am'mon-ites
hath sent Ish'ma-el the son of Neth-a-ni'ah to
slay thee? But Ged-a-li'ah the son of A-hi'kam
believed them not.
15 Then Jo-ha'nan the son of Ka-re'ah spake
to Ged-a-li'ah in Miz'pah secretly, saying, Let
me go, I pray thee, and I will slay Ish'ma-el the
son of Neth-a-ni'ah, and no man shall know *it*:
wherefore should he slay thee, that all the Jews
which are gathered unto thee should be scattered, and the remnant in Ju'dah perish?
16 But Ged-a-li'ah the son of A-hi'kam said
unto Jo-ha'nan the son of Ka-re'ah, Thou shalt
not do this thing: for thou speakest falsely of
Ish'ma-el.

41 NOW it came to pass in the seventh
month, *that* Ish'ma-el the son of Neth-a-
ni'ah the son of E-lish'a-ma, of the seed royal,
and the princes of the king, even ten men with
him, came unto Ged-a-li'ah the son of A-hi'kam
to Miz'pah; and there they did eat bread together in Miz'pah.
2 Then arose Ish'ma-el the son of Neth-a-ni'-
ah, and the ten men that were with him, and
smote Ged-a-li'ah the son of A-hi'kam the son
of Sha'phan with the sword, and slew him,
whom the king of Bab'y-lon had made governor
over the land.
3 Ish'ma-el also slew all the Jews that were
with him, *even* with Ged-a-li'ah, at Miz'pah, and
the Chal-de'ans that were found there, *and* the
men of war.
4 And it came to pass the second day after he
had slain Ged-a-li'ah, and no man knew *it*,
5 That there came certain from She'chem,
from Shi'loh, and from Sa-ma'ri-a, *even* fourscore men, having their beards shaven, and
their clothes rent, and having cut themselves,
with offerings and incense in their hand, to
bring *them* to the house of the LORD.
6 And Ish'ma-el the son of Neth-a-ni'ah went
forth from Miz'pah to meet them, weeping all
along as he went: and it came to pass, as he met
them, he said unto them, Come to Ged-a-li'ah
the son of A-hi'kam.
7 And it was *so*, when they came into the
midst of the city, that Ish'ma-el the son of Neth-
a-ni'ah slew them, *and cast them* into the midst
of the pit, he, and the men that *were* with him.
8 But ten men were found among them that
said unto Ish'ma-el, Slay us not: for we have
treasures in the field, of wheat, and of barley,
and of oil, and of honey. So he forbare, and slew
them not among their brethren.
9 Now the pit wherein Ish'ma-el had cast all
the dead bodies of the men, whom he had slain
because of Ged-a-li'ah, *was* it which A'sa the
king had made for fear of Ba'a-sha king of Is'ra-
el: *and* Ish'ma-el the son of Neth-a-ni'ah filled it
with *them that were* slain.
10 Then Ish'ma-el carried away captive all
the residue of the people that *were* in Miz'pah,
even the king's daughters, and all the people
that remained in Miz'pah, whom Neb'u-zar-a'-
dan the captain of the guard had committed to
Ged-a-li'ah the son of A-hi'kam: and Ish'ma-el
the son of Neth-a-ni'ah carried them away captive, and departed to go over to the Am'mon-
ites.

11 ¶ But when Jo-ha'nan the son of Ka-re'ah,
and all the captains of the forces that *were* with
him, heard of all the evil that Ish'ma-el the son
of Neth-a-ni'ah had done,
12 Then they took all the men, and went to
fight with Ish'ma-el the son of Neth-a-ni'ah, and
found him by the great waters that *are* in Gib'e-
on.
13 Now it came to pass, *that* when all the
people which *were* with Ish'ma-el saw Jo-ha'-
nan the son of Ka-re'ah, and all the captains of
the forces that *were* with him, then they were
glad.
14 So all the people that Ish'ma-el had carried away captive from Miz'pah cast about and
returned, and went unto Jo-ha'nan the son of
Ka-re'ah.
15 But Ish'ma-el the son of Neth-a-ni'ah escaped from Jo-ha'nan with eight men, and went
to the Am'mon-ites.
16 Then took Jo-ha'nan the son of Ka-re'ah,
and all the captains of the forces that *were* with
him, all the remnant of the people whom he had
recovered from Ish'ma-el the son of Neth-a-ni'-
ah, from Miz'pah, after *that* he had slain Ged-a-
li'ah the son of A-hi'kam, *even* mighty men of
war, and the women, and the children, and the
eunuchs, whom he had brought again from
Gib'e-on:
17 And they departed, and dwelt in the habitation of Chim'ham, which is by Beth'-le-hem,
to go to enter into E'gypt,
18 Because of the Chal-de'ans: for they were
afraid of them, because Ish'ma-el the son of
Neth-a-ni'ah had slain Ged-a-li'ah the son of A-
hi'kam, whom the king of Bab'y-lon made governor in the land.

42 THEN all the captains of the forces, and
Jo-ha'nan the son of Ka-re'ah, and Jez-
a-ni'ah the son of Hosh-a-i'ah, and all the people
from the least even unto the greatest, came
near,
2 And said unto Jer-e-mi'ah the prophet, Let,
we beseech thee, our supplication be accepted
before thee, and pray for us unto the LORD thy
God, *even* for all this remnant; (for we are left
but a few of many, as thine eyes do behold us:)
3 That the LORD thy God may shew us the
way wherein we may walk, and the thing that
we may do.
4 Then Jer-e-mi'ah the prophet said unto
them, I have heard *you;* behold, I will pray unto
the LORD your God according to your words;
and it shall come to pass, *that* whatsoever thing
the LORD shall answer you, I will declare *it* unto
you; I will keep nothing back from you.
5 Then they said to Jer-e-mi'ah, The LORD be
a true and faithful witness between us, if we do
not even according to all things for the which
the LORD thy God shall send thee to us.
6 Whether *it be* good, or whether *it be* evil,
we will obey the voice of the LORD our God, to
whom we send thee; that it may be well with us,
when we obey the voice of the LORD our God.
7 ¶ And it came to pass after ten days, that
the word of the LORD came unto Jer-e-mi'ah.
8 Then called he Jo-ha'nan the son of Ka-re'-
ah, and all the captains of the forces which *were*
with him, and all the people from the least even
to the greatest,
9 And said unto them, Thus saith the LORD,
the God of Is'ra-el, unto whom ye sent me to
present your supplication before him;
10 If ye will still abide in this land, then will I
build you, and not pull *you* down, and I will
plant you, and not pluck *you* up: for I repent me
of the evil that I have done unto you.
11 Be not afraid of the king of Bab'y-lon, of
whom ye are afraid; be not afraid of him, saith
the LORD: for I *am* with you to save you, and to
deliver you from his hand.
12 And I will shew mercies unto you, that he
may have mercy upon you, and cause you to
return to your own land.
13 ¶ But if ye say, We will not dwell in this
land, neither obey the voice of the LORD your
God,
14 Saying, No; but we will go into the land of
E'gypt, where we shall see no war, nor hear the
sound of the trumpet, nor have hunger of bread;
and there will we dwell:
15 And now therefore hear the word of the
LORD, ye remnant of Ju'dah; Thus saith the
LORD of hosts, the God of Is'ra-el; If ye wholly
set your faces to enter into E'gypt, and go to
sojourn there;
16 Then it shall come to pass, *that* the sword,
which ye feared, shall overtake you there in the
land of E'gypt, and the famine, whereof ye were
afraid, shall follow close after you there in E'-
gypt; and there ye shall die.
17 So shall it be with all the men that set
their faces to go into E'gypt to sojourn there;
they shall die by the sword, by the famine, and
by the pestilence: and none of them shall remain or escape from the evil that I will bring
upon them.
18 For thus saith the LORD of hosts, the God
of Is'ra-el; As mine anger and my fury hath
been poured forth upon the inhabitants of Je-
ru'sa-lem; so shall my fury be poured forth
upon you, when ye shall enter into E'gypt: and
ye shall be an execration, and an astonishment,
and a curse, and a reproach; and ye shall see
this place no more.
19 ¶ The LORD hath said concerning you, O
ye remnant of Ju'dah; Go ye not into E'gypt:
know certainly that I have admonished you this
day.
20 For ye dissembled in your hearts, when ye
sent me unto the LORD your God, saying, Pray
for us unto the LORD our God; and according
unto all that the LORD our God shall say, so declare unto us, and we will do *it.*
21 And *now* I have this day declared *it* to
you; but ye have not obeyed the voice of the
LORD your God, nor any *thing* for the which he
hath sent me unto you.
22 Now therefore know certainly that ye
shall die by the sword, by the famine, and by
the pestilence, in the place whither ye desire to
go *and* to sojourn.

43 AND it came to pass, *that* when Jer-e-
mi'ah had made an end of speaking unto
all the people all the words of the LORD their
God, for which the LORD their God had sent him
to them, *even* all these words,
2 Then spake Az-a-ri'ah the son of Hosh-a-
i'ah, and Jo-ha'nan the son of Ka-re'ah, and all
the proud men, saying unto Jer-e-mi'ah, Thou
speakest falsely: the LORD our God hath not
sent thee to say, Go not into E'gypt to sojourn
there:
3 But Ba'ruch the son of Ne-ri'ah setteth thee
on against us, for to deliver us into the hand of
the Chal-de'ans, that they might put us to
death, and carry us away captives into Bab'y-
lon.
4 So Jo-ha'nan the son of Ka-re'ah, and all
the captains of the forces, and all the people,

obeyed not the voice of the LORD, to dwell in
the land of Ju'dah.
5 But Jo-ha'nan the son of Ka-re'ah, and all
the captains of the forces, took all the remnant
of Ju'dah, that were returned from all nations,
whither they had been driven, to dwell in the
land of Ju'dah;
6 *Even* men, and women, and children, and
the king's daughters, and every person that
Neb'u-zar-a'dan the captain of the guard had
left with Ged-a-li'ah the son of A-hi'kam the son
of Sha'phan, and Jer-e-mi'ah the prophet, and
Ba'ruch the son of Ne-ri'ah.
7 So they came into the land of E'gypt: for
they obeyed not the voice of the LORD: thus
came they *even* to Tah'pan-hes.
8 ¶ Then came the word of the LORD unto
Jer-e-mi'ah in Tah'pan-hes, saying,
9 Take great stones in thine hand, and hide
them in the clay in the brickkiln, which *is* at the
entry of Pha'raoh's house in Tah'pan-hes, in the
sight of the men of Ju'dah;
10 And say unto them, Thus saith the LORD
of hosts, the God of Is'ra-el; Behold, I will send
and take Neb-u-chad-rez'zar the king of Bab'y-
lon, my servant, and will set his throne upon
these stones that I have hid; and he shall spread
his royal pavilion over them.
11 And when he cometh, he shall smite the
land of E'gypt, *and deliver* such *as are* for death
to death; and such *as are* for captivity to captivity; and such *as are* for the sword to the sword.
12 And I will kindle a fire in the houses of the
gods of E'gypt; and he shall burn them, and carry them away captives: and he shall array himself with the land of E'gypt, as a shepherd putteth on his garment; and he shall go forth from
thence in peace.
13 He shall break also the images of Beth-
she'mesh, that *is* in the land of E'gypt; and the
houses of the gods of the E-gyp'tians shall he
burn with fire.

44 THE word that came to Jer-e-mi'ah concerning all the Jews which dwell in the
land of E'gypt, which dwell at Mig'dol, and at
Tah'pan-hes, and at Noph, and in the country of
Path'ros, saying,
2 Thus saith the LORD of hosts, the God of
Is'ra-el; Ye have seen all the evil that I have
brought upon Je-ru'sa-lem, and upon all the
cities of Ju'dah; and, behold, this day they *are* a
desolation, and no man dwelleth therein,
3 Because of their wickedness which they
have committed to provoke me to anger, in that
they went to burn incense, *and* to serve other
gods, whom they knew not, *neither* they, ye,
nor your fathers.
4 Howbeit I sent unto you all my servants the
prophets, rising early and sending *them*, saying,
Oh, do not this abominable thing that I hate.
5 But they hearkened not, nor inclined their
ear to turn from their wickedness, to burn no
incense unto other gods.
6 Wherefore my fury and mine anger was
poured forth, and was kindled in the cities of
Ju'dah and in the streets of Je-ru'sa-lem; and
they are wasted *and* desolate, as at this day.
7 Therefore now thus saith the LORD, the
God of hosts, the God of Is'ra-el; Wherefore
commit ye *this* great evil against your souls, to
cut off from you man and woman, child and
suckling, out of Ju'dah, to leave you none to remain;
8 In that ye provoke me unto wrath with the
works of your hands, burning incense unto other gods in the land of E'gypt, whither ye be
gone to dwell, that ye might cut yourselves off,
and that ye might be a curse and a reproach
among all the nations of the earth?
9 Have ye forgotten the wickedness of your
fathers, and the wickedness of the kings of Ju'-
dah, and the wickedness of their wives, and
your own wickedness, and the wickedness of
your wives, which they have committed in the
land of Ju'dah, and in the streets of Je-ru'sa-
lem?
10 They are not humbled *even* unto this day,
neither have they feared, nor walked in my law,
nor in my statutes, that I set before you and
before your fathers.
11 ¶ Therefore thus saith the LORD of hosts,
the God of Is'ra-el; Behold, I will set my face
against you for evil, and to cut off all Ju'dah.
12 And I will take the remnant of Ju'dah, that
have set their faces to go into the land of E'gypt
to sojourn there, and they shall all be consumed, *and* fall in the land of E'gypt; they shall
even be consumed by the sword *and* by the
famine: they shall die, from the least even unto
the greatest, by the sword and by the famine:
and they shall be an execration, *and* an astonishment, and a curse, and a reproach.
13 For I will punish them that dwell in the
land of E'gypt, as I have punished Je-ru'sa-lem,
by the sword, by the famine, and by the pestilence:
14 So that none of the remnant of Ju'dah,
which are gone into the land of E'gypt to sojourn there, shall escape or remain, that they
should return into the land of Ju'dah, to the
which they have a desire to return to dwell
there: for none shall return but such as shall
escape.
15 ¶ Then all the men which knew that their
wives had burned incense unto other gods, and
all the women that stood by, a great multitude,
even all the people that dwelt in the land of E'-
gypt, in Path'ros, answered Jer-e-mi'ah, saying,
16 *As for* the word that thou hast spoken
unto us in the name of the LORD, we will not
hearken unto thee.
17 But we will certainly do whatsoever thing
goeth forth out of our own mouth, to burn incense unto the queen of heaven, and to pour out
drink offerings unto her, as we have done, we
and our fathers, our kings, and our princes, in
the cities of Ju'dah, and in the streets of Je-ru'-
sa-lem: for *then* had we plenty of victuals, and
were well, and saw no evil.
18 But since we left off to burn incense to the
queen of heaven, and to pour out drink offerings unto her, we have wanted all *things*, and
have been consumed by the sword and by the
famine.
19 And when we burned incense to the queen
of heaven, and poured out drink offerings unto
her, did we make her cakes to worship her, and
pour out drink offerings unto her, without our
men?
20 ¶ Then Jer-e-mi'ah said unto all the people, to the men, and to the women, and to all the
people which had given him *that* answer, saying,
21 The incense that ye burned in the cities of
Ju'dah, and in the streets of Je-ru'sa-lem, ye,
and your fathers, your kings, and your princes,
and the people of the land, did not the LORD
remember them, and came it *not* into his mind?
22 So that the LORD could no longer bear, because of the evil of your doings, *and* because of
the abominations which ye have committed;
therefore is your land a desolation, and an as-

tonishment, and a curse, without an inhabitant, as at this day.

23 Because ye have burned incense, and because ye have sinned against the LORD, and have not obeyed the voice of the LORD, nor walked in his law, nor in his statutes, nor in his testimonies; therefore this evil is happened unto you, as at this day.

24 Moreover Jer-e-mi′ah said unto all the people, and to all the women, Hear the word of the LORD, all Ju′dah that *are* in the land of E′gypt:

25 Thus saith the LORD of hosts, the God of Is′ra-el, saying; Ye and your wives have both spoken with your mouths, and fulfilled with your hand, saying, We will surely perform our vows that we have vowed, to burn incense to the queen of heaven, and to pour out drink offerings unto her: ye will surely accomplish your vows, and surely perform your vows.

26 Therefore hear ye the word of the LORD, all Ju′dah that dwell in the land of E′gypt; Behold, I have sworn by my great name, saith the LORD, that my name shall no more be named in the mouth of any man of Ju′dah in all the land of E′gypt, saying, The Lord GOD liveth.

27 Behold, I will watch over them for evil, and not for good: and all the men of Ju′dah that *are* in the land of E′gypt shall be consumed by the sword and by the famine, until there be an end of them.

28 Yet a small number that escape the sword shall return out of the land of E′gypt into the land of Ju′dah, and all the remnant of Ju′dah, that are gone into the land of E′gypt to sojourn there, shall know whose words shall stand, mine, or theirs.

29 ¶ And this *shall be* a sign unto you, saith the LORD, that I will punish you in this place, that ye may know that my words shall surely stand against you for evil:

30 Thus saith the LORD; Behold, I will give Pha′raoh–hoph′ra king of E′gypt into the hand of his enemies, and into the hand of them that seek his life; as I gave Zed-e-ki′ah king of Ju′dah into the hand of Neb-u-chad-rez′zar king of Bab′y-lon, his enemy, and that sought his life.

45 THE word that Jer-e-mi′ah the prophet spake unto Ba′ruch the son of Ne-ri′ah, when he had written these words in a book at the mouth of Jer-e-mi′ah, in the fourth year of Je-hoi′a-kim the son of Jo-si′ah king of Ju′dah, saying,

2 Thus saith the LORD, the God of Is′ra-el, unto thee, O Ba′ruch;

3 Thou didst say, Woe is me now! for the LORD hath added grief to my sorrow; I fainted in my sighing, and I find no rest.

4 ¶ Thus shalt thou say unto him, The LORD saith thus; Behold, *that* which I have built will I break down, and that which I have planted I will pluck up, even this whole land.

5 And seekest thou great things for thyself? seek *them* not: for, behold, I will bring evil upon all flesh, saith the LORD: but thy life will I give unto thee for a prey in all places whither thou goest.

46 THE word of the LORD which came to Jer-e-mi′ah the prophet against the Gen′tiles;

2 Against E′gypt, against the army of Pha′raoh–ne′cho king of E′gypt, which was by the river Eu-phra′tes in Car′che-mish, which Neb′u-chad-rez′zar king of Bab′y-lon smote in the fourth year of Je-hoi′a-kim the son of Jo-si′ah king of Ju′dah.

3 Order ye the buckler and shield, and draw near to battle.

4 Harness the horses; and get up, ye horsemen, and stand forth with *your* helmets; furbish the spears, *and* put on the brigandines.

5 Wherefore have I seen them dismayed *and* turned away back? and their mighty ones are beaten down, and are fled apace, and look not back: *for* fear *was* round about, saith the LORD.

6 Let not the swift flee away, nor the mighty man escape; they shall stumble, and fall toward the north by the river Eu-phra′tes.

7 Who *is* this *that* cometh up as a flood, whose waters are moved as the rivers?

8 E′gypt riseth up like a flood, and *his* waters are moved like the rivers; and he saith, I will go up, *and* will cover the earth; I will destroy the city and the inhabitants thereof.

9 Come up, ye horses; and rage, ye chariots; and let the mighty men come forth; the E-thi-o′pi-ans and the Lib′y-ans, that handle the shield; and the Lyd′i-ans, that handle *and* bend the bow.

10 For this *is* the day of the Lord GOD of hosts, a day of vengeance, that he may avenge him of his adversaries: and the sword shall devour, and it shall be satiate and made drunk with their blood: for the Lord GOD of hosts hath a sacrifice in the north country by the river Eu-phra′tes.

11 Go up into Gil′e-ad, and take balm, O virgin, the daughter of E′gypt: in vain shalt thou use many medicines; *for* thou shalt not be cured.

12 The nations have heard of thy shame, and thy cry hath filled the land: for the mighty man hath stumbled against the mighty, *and* they are fallen both together.

13 ¶ The word that the LORD spake to Jer-e-mi′ah the prophet, how Neb-u-chad-rez′zar king of Bab′y-lon should come *and* smite the land of E′gypt.

14 Declare ye in E′gypt, and publish in Mig′dol, and publish in Noph and in Tah′pan-hes: say ye, Stand fast, and prepare thee; for the sword shall devour round about thee.

15 Why are thy valiant *men* swept away? they stood not, because the LORD did drive them.

16 He made many to fall, yea, one fell upon another: and they said, Arise, and let us go again to our own people, and to the land of our nativity, from the oppressing sword.

17 They did cry there, Pha′raoh king of E′gypt *is but* a noise; he hath passed the time appointed.

18 *As* I live, saith the King, whose name *is* the LORD of hosts, Surely as Ta′bor *is* among the mountains, and as Car′mel by the sea, *so* shall he come.

19 O thou daughter dwelling in E′gypt, furnish thyself to go into captivity: for Noph shall be waste and desolate without an inhabitant.

20 E′gypt *is like* a very fair heifer, *but* destruction cometh; it cometh out of the north.

21 Also her hired men *are* in the midst of her like fatted bullocks; for they also are turned back, *and* are fled away together: they did not stand, because the day of their calamity was come upon them, *and* the time of their visitation.

22 The voice thereof shall go like a serpent; for they shall march with an army, and come against her with axes, as hewers of wood.

23 They shall cut down her forest, saith the

LORD, though it cannot be searched; because
they are more than the grasshoppers, and *are*
innumerable.
24 The daughter of E'gypt shall be confounded; she shall be delivered into the hand of
the people of the north.
25 The LORD of hosts, the God of Is'ra-el,
saith; Behold, I will punish the multitude of No,
and Pha'raoh, and E'gypt, with their gods, and
their kings; even Pha'raoh, and *all* them that
trust in him:
26 And I will deliver them into the hand of
those that seek their lives, and into the hand of
Neb-u-chad-rez'zar king of Bab'y-lon, and into
the hand of his servants: and afterward it shall
be inhabited, as in the days of old, saith the
LORD.
27 ¶ But fear not thou, O my servant Ja'cob,
and be not dismayed, O Is'ra-el: for, behold, I
will save thee from afar off, and thy seed from
the land of their captivity; and Ja'cob shall return, and be in rest and at ease, and none shall
make *him* afraid.
28 Fear thou not, O Ja'cob my servant, saith
the LORD: for I *am* with thee; for I will make a
full end of all the nations whither I have driven
thee: but I will not make a full end of thee, but
correct thee in measure; yet will I not leave thee
wholly unpunished.

47 THE word of the LORD that came to Jer-
e-mi'ah the prophet against the Phi-lis'-
tines, before that Pha'raoh smote Ga'za.
2 Thus saith the LORD; Behold, waters rise up
out of the north, and shall be an overflowing
flood, and shall overflow the land, and all that is
therein; the city, and them that dwell therein:
then the men shall cry, and all the inhabitants
of the land shall howl.
3 At the noise of the stamping of the hoofs of
his strong *horses*, at the rushing of his chariots,
and at the rumbling of his wheels, the fathers
shall not look back to *their* children for feeble-
ness of hands;
4 Because of the day that cometh to spoil all
the Phi-lis'tines, *and* to cut off from Ty'rus and
Zi'don every helper that remaineth: for the
LORD will spoil the Phi-lis'tines, the remnant of
the country of Caph'tor.
5 Baldness is come upon Ga'za; Ash'ke-lon is
cut off *with* the remnant of their valley: how
long wilt thou cut thyself?
6 O thou sword of the LORD, how long *will it*
be ere thou be quiet? put up thyself into thy
scabbard, rest, and be still.
7 How can it be quiet, seeing the LORD hath
given it a charge against Ash'ke-lon, and
against the sea shore? there hath he appointed
it.

48 AGAINST Mo'ab thus saith the LORD of
hosts, the God of Is'ra-el; Woe unto Ne'-
bo! for it is spoiled: Kir-i-a-tha'im is confounded
and taken: Mis'gab is confounded and dismayed.
2 *There shall be* no more praise of Mo'ab: in
Hesh'bon they have devised evil against it;
come, and let us cut it off from *being* a nation.
Also thou shalt be cut down, O Mad'men; the
sword shall pursue thee.
3 A voice of crying *shall be* from Hor-o-na'-
im, spoiling and great destruction.
4 Mo'ab is destroyed; her little ones have
caused a cry to be heard.
5 For in the going up of Lu'hith continual
weeping shall go up; for in the going down of
Hor-o-na'im the enemies have heard a cry of
destruction.
6 Flee, save your lives, and be like the heath
in the wilderness.
7 ¶ For because thou hast trusted in thy
works and in thy treasures, thou shalt also be
taken: and Che'mosh shall go forth into captivity *with* his priests and his princes together.
8 And the spoiler shall come upon every city,
and no city shall escape: the valley also shall
perish, and the plain shall be destroyed, as the
LORD hath spoken.
9 Give wings unto Mo'ab, that it may flee and
get away: for the cities thereof shall be desolate, without any to dwell therein.
10 Cursed *be* he that doeth the work of the
LORD deceitfully, and cursed *be* he that keepeth
back his sword from blood.
11 ¶ Mo'ab hath been at ease from his youth,
and he hath settled on his lees, and hath not
been emptied from vessel to vessel, neither
hath he gone into captivity: therefore his taste
remained in him, and his scent is not changed.
12 Therefore, behold, the days come, saith
the LORD, that I will send unto him wanderers,
that shall cause him to wander, and shall empty
his vessels and break their bottles.
13 And Mo'ab shall be ashamed of Che'-
mosh, as the house of Is'ra-el was ashamed of
Beth'-el their confidence.
14 ¶ How say ye, We *are* mighty and strong
men for the war?
15 Mo'ab is spoiled, and gone up *out of* her
cities, and his chosen young men are gone
down to the slaughter, saith the King, whose
name *is* the LORD of hosts.
16 The calamity of Mo'ab *is* near to come,
and his affliction hasteth fast.
17 All ye that are about him, bemoan him;
and all ye that know his name, say, How is the
strong staff broken, *and* the beautiful rod!
18 Thou daughter that dost inhabit Di'bon,
come down from *thy* glory, and sit in thirst; for
the spoiler of Mo'ab shall come upon thee, *and*
he shall destroy thy strong holds.
19 O inhabitant of Ar'o-er, stand by the way,
and espy; ask him that fleeth, and her that escapeth, *and* say, What is done?
20 Mo'ab is confounded; for it is broken
down: howl and cry; tell ye it in Ar'non, that
Mo'ab is spoiled,
21 And judgment is come upon the plain
country; upon Ho'lon, and upon Ja-ha'zah, and
upon Meph'a-ath,
22 And upon Di'bon, and upon Ne'bo, and
upon Beth-dib-la-tha'im,
23 And upon Kir-i-a-tha'im, and upon Beth-
ga'mul, and upon Beth-me'on,
24 And upon Ke'ri-oth, and upon Boz'rah,
and upon all the cities of the land of Mo'ab, far
or near.
25 The horn of Mo'ab is cut off, and his arm
is broken, saith the LORD.
26 ¶ Make ye him drunken: for he magnified
himself against the LORD: Mo'ab also shall wallow in his vomit, and he also shall be in derision.
27 For was not Is'ra-el a derision unto thee?
was he found among thieves? for since thou
spakest of him, thou skippedst for joy.
28 O ye that dwell in Mo'ab, leave the cities,
and dwell in the rock, and be like the dove *that*
maketh her nest in the sides of the hole's
mouth.
29 We have heard the pride of Mo'ab, (he is
exceeding proud) his loftiness, and his arro-

gancy, and his pride, and the haughtiness of his heart.

30 I know his wrath, saith the LORD; but *it shall* not *be* so; his lies shall not so effect *it*.

31 Therefore will I howl for Mo'ab, and I will cry out for all Mo'ab; *mine heart* shall mourn for the men of Kir–he'res.

32 O vine of Sib'mah, I will weep for thee with the weeping of Ja'zer: thy plants are gone over the sea, they reach *even* to the sea of Ja'-zer: the spoiler is fallen upon thy summer fruits and upon thy vintage.

33 And joy and gladness is taken from the plentiful field, and from the land of Mo'ab; and I have caused wine to fail from the winepresses: none shall tread with shouting; *their* shouting *shall be* no shouting.

34 From the cry of Hesh'bon *even* unto E-le-a'leh, *and even* unto Ja'haz, have they uttered their voice, from Zo'ar *even* unto Hor-o-na'im, *as* an heifer of three years old: for the waters also of Nim'rim shall be desolate.

35 Moreover I will cause to cease in Mo'ab, saith the LORD, him that offereth in the high places, and him that burneth incense to his gods.

36 Therefore mine heart shall sound for Mo'-ab like pipes, and mine heart shall sound like pipes for the men of Kir–he'res: because the riches *that* he hath gotten are perished.

37 For every head *shall be* bald, and every beard clipped: upon all the hands *shall be* cuttings, and upon the loins sackcloth.

38 *There shall be* lamentation generally upon all the house tops of Mo'ab and in the streets thereof: for I have broken Mo'ab like a vessel wherein *is* no pleasure, saith the LORD.

39 They shall howl, *saying,* How is it broken down! how hath Mo'ab turned the back with shame! so shall Mo'ab be a derision and a dismaying to all them about him.

40 For thus saith the LORD; Behold, he shall fly as an eagle, and shall spread his wings over Mo'ab.

41 Ke'ri-oth is taken, and the strong holds are surprised, and the mighty men's hearts in Mo'ab at that day shall be as the heart of a woman in her pangs.

42 And Mo'ab shall be destroyed from *being* a people, because he hath magnified *himself* against the LORD.

43 Fear, and the pit, and the snare, *shall be* upon thee, O inhabitant of Mo'ab, saith the LORD.

44 He that fleeth from the fear shall fall into the pit; and he that getteth up out of the pit shall be taken in the snare: for I will bring upon it, *even* upon Mo'ab, the year of their visitation, saith the LORD.

45 They that fled stood under the shadow of Hesh'bon because of the force: but a fire shall come forth out of Hesh'bon, and a flame from the midst of Si'hon, and shall devour the corner of Mo'ab, and the crown of the head of the tumultuous ones.

46 Woe be unto thee, O Mo'ab! the people of Che'mosh perisheth: for thy sons are taken captives, and thy daughters captives.

47 ¶ Yet will I bring again the captivity of Mo'ab in the latter days, saith the LORD. Thus far *is* the judgment of Mo'ab.

49 CONCERNING the Am'mon-ites, thus saith the LORD; Hath Is'ra-el no sons? hath he no heir? why *then* doth their king inherit Gad, and his people dwell in his cities?

2 Therefore, behold, the days come, saith the LORD, that I will cause an alarm of war to be heard in Rab'bah of the Am'mon-ites; and it shall be a desolate heap, and her daughters shall be burned with fire: then shall Is'ra-el be heir unto them that were his heirs, saith the LORD.

3 Howl, O Hesh'bon, for A'i is spoiled: cry, ye daughters of Rab'bah, gird you with sackcloth; lament, and run to and fro by the hedges; for their king shall go into captivity, *and* his priests and his princes together.

4 Wherefore gloriest thou in the valleys, thy flowing valley, O backsliding daughter? that trusted in her treasures, *saying,* Who shall come unto me?

5 Behold, I will bring a fear upon thee, saith the Lord GOD of hosts, from all those that be about thee; and ye shall be driven out every man right forth; and none shall gather up him that wandereth.

6 And afterward I will bring again the captivity of the children of Am'mon, saith the LORD.

7 ¶ Concerning E'dom, thus saith the LORD of hosts; *Is* wisdom no more in Te'man? is counsel perished from the prudent? is their wisdom vanished?

8 Flee ye, turn back, dwell deep, O inhabitants of De'dan; for I will bring the calamity of E'sau upon him, the time *that* I will visit him.

9 If grapegatherers come to thee, would they not leave *some* gleaning grapes? if thieves by night, they will destroy till they have enough.

10 But I have made E'sau bare, I have uncovered his secret places, and he shall not be able to hide himself: his seed is spoiled, and his brethren, and his neighbours, and he *is* not.

11 Leave thy fatherless children, I will preserve *them* alive; and let thy widows trust in me.

12 For thus saith the LORD; Behold, they whose judgment *was* not to drink of the cup have assuredly drunken; and *art* thou he *that* shall altogether go unpunished? thou shalt not go unpunished, but thou shalt surely drink *of it*.

13 For I have sworn by myself, saith the LORD, that Boz'rah shall become a desolation, a reproach, a waste, and a curse; and all the cities thereof shall be perpetual wastes.

14 I have heard a rumour from the LORD, and an ambassador is sent unto the heathen, *saying,* Gather ye together, and come against her, and rise up to the battle.

15 For, lo, I will make thee small among the heathen, *and* despised among men.

16 Thy terribleness hath deceived thee, *and* the pride of thine heart, O thou that dwellest in the clefts of the rock, that holdest the height of the hill: though thou shouldest make thy nest as high as the eagle, I will bring thee down from thence, saith the LORD.

17 Also E'dom shall be a desolation: every one that goeth by it shall be astonished, and shall hiss at all the plagues thereof.

18 As in the overthrow of Sod'om and Go-mor'rah and the neighbour *cities* thereof, saith the LORD, no man shall abide there, neither shall a son of man dwell in it.

19 Behold, he shall come up like a lion from the swelling of Jor'dan against the habitation of the strong: but I will suddenly make him run away from her: and who *is* a chosen *man, that* I may appoint over her? for who *is* like me? and who will appoint me the time? and who *is* that shepherd that will stand before me?

20 Therefore hear the counsel of the LORD, that he hath taken against E'dom; and his purposes, that he hath purposed against the inhabi-

tants of Te'man: Surely the least of the flock shall draw them out: surely he shall make their habitations desolate with them.

21 The earth is moved at the noise of their fall, at the cry the noise thereof was heard in the Red sea.

22 Behold, he shall come up and fly as the eagle, and spread his wings over Boz'rah: and at that day shall the heart of the mighty men of E'dom be as the heart of a woman in her pangs.

23 ¶ Concerning Da-mas'cus. Ha'math is confounded, and Ar'pad: for they have heard evil tidings: they are fainthearted; *there is* sorrow on the sea; it cannot be quiet.

24 Da-mas'cus is waxed feeble, *and* turneth herself to flee, and fear hath seized on *her*: anguish and sorrows have taken her, as a woman in travail.

25 How is the city of praise not left, the city of my joy!

26 Therefore her young men shall fall in her streets, and all the men of war shall be cut off in that day, saith the LORD of hosts.

27 And I will kindle a fire in the wall of Damas'cus, and it shall consume the palaces of Ben–ha'dad.

28 ¶ Concerning Ke'dar, and concerning the kingdoms of Ha'zor, which Neb-u-chad-rez'zar king of Bab'y-lon shall smite, thus saith the LORD; Arise ye, go up to Ke'dar, and spoil the men of the east.

29 Their tents and their flocks shall they take away: they shall take to themselves their curtains, and all their vessels, and their camels; and they shall cry unto them, Fear *is* on every side.

30 ¶ Flee, get you far off, dwell deep, O ye inhabitants of Ha'zor, saith the LORD; for Neb-u-chad-rez'zar king of Bab'y-lon hath taken counsel against you, and hath conceived a purpose against you.

31 Arise, get you up unto the wealthy nation, that dwelleth without care, saith the LORD, which have neither gates nor bars, *which* dwell alone.

32 And their camels shall be a booty, and the multitude of their cattle a spoil: and I will scatter into all winds them *that are* in the utmost corners; and I will bring their calamity from all sides thereof, saith the LORD.

33 And Ha'zor shall be a dwelling for dragons, *and* a desolation for ever: there shall no man abide there, nor *any* son of man dwell in it.

34 ¶ The word of the LORD that came to Jere-mi'ah the prophet against E'lam in the beginning of the reign of Zed-e-ki'ah king of Ju'dah, saying,

35 Thus saith the LORD of hosts; Behold, I will break the bow of E'lam, the chief of their might.

36 And upon E'lam will I bring the four winds from the four quarters of heaven, and will scatter them toward all those winds; and there shall be no nation whither the outcasts of E'lam shall not come.

37 For I will cause E'lam to be dismayed before their enemies, and before them that seek their life: and I will bring evil upon them, *even* my fierce anger, saith the LORD; and I will send the sword after them, till I have consumed them:

38 And I will set my throne in E'lam, and will destroy from thence the king and the princes, saith the LORD.

39 ¶ But it shall come to pass in the latter days, *that* I will bring again the captivity of E'lam, saith the LORD.

50

THE word that the LORD spake against Bab'y-lon *and* against the land of the Chal-de'ans by Jer-e-mi'ah the prophet.

2 Declare ye among the nations, and publish, and set up a standard; publish, *and* conceal not: say, Bab'y-lon is taken, Bel is confounded, Mero'dach is broken in pieces; her idols are confounded, her images are broken in pieces.

3 For out of the north there cometh up a nation against her, which shall make her land desolate, and none shall dwell therein: they shall remove, they shall depart, both man and beast.

4 ¶ In those days, and in that time, saith the LORD, the children of Is'ra-el shall come, they and the children of Ju'dah together, going and weeping: they shall go, and seek the LORD their God.

5 They shall ask the way to Zi'on with their faces thitherward, *saying*, Come, and let us join ourselves to the LORD in a perpetual covenant *that* shall not be forgotten.

6 My people hath been lost sheep: their shepherds have caused them to go astray, they have turned them away *on* the mountains: they have gone from mountain to hill, they have forgotten their restingplace.

7 All that found them have devoured them: and their adversaries said, We offend not, because they have sinned against the LORD, the habitation of justice, even the LORD, the hope of their fathers.

8 Remove out of the midst of Bab'y-lon, and go forth out of the land of the Chal-de'ans, and be as the he goats before the flocks.

9 ¶ For, lo, I will raise and cause to come up against Bab'y-lon an assembly of great nations from the north country: and they shall set themselves in array against her; from thence she shall be taken: their arrows *shall be* as of a mighty expert man; none shall return in vain.

10 And Chal-de'a shall be a spoil: all that spoil her shall be satisfied, saith the LORD.

11 Because ye were glad, because ye rejoiced, O ye destroyers of mine heritage, because ye are grown fat as the heifer at grass, and bellow as bulls;

12 Your mother shall be sore confounded; she that bare you shall be ashamed: behold, the hindermost of the nations *shall be* a wilderness, a dry land, and a desert.

13 Because of the wrath of the LORD it shall not be inhabited, but it shall be wholly desolate: every one that goeth by Bab'y-lon shall be astonished, and hiss at all her plagues.

14 Put yourselves in array against Bab'y-lon round about: all ye that bend the bow, shoot at her, spare no arrows: for she hath sinned against the LORD.

15 Shout against her round about: she hath given her hand: her foundations are fallen, her walls are thrown down: for it *is* the vengeance of the LORD: take vengeance upon her; as she hath done, do unto her.

16 Cut off the sower from Bab'y-lon, and him that handleth the sickle in the time of harvest: for fear of the oppressing sword they shall turn every one to his people, and they shall flee every one to his own land.

17 ¶ Israel *is* a scattered sheep; the lions have driven *him* away: first the king of As-syr'i-a hath devoured him; and last this Neb-u-chad-rez'zar king of Bab'y-lon hath broken his bones.

18 Therefore thus saith the LORD of hosts, the God of Is'ra-el; Behold, I will punish the king of Bab'y-lon and his land, as I have punished the king of As-syr'i-a.

19 And I will bring Is′ra-el again to his habitation, and he shall feed on Car′mel and Ba′-
shan, and his soul shall be satisfied upon mount
E′phra-im and Gil′e-ad.
20 In those days, and in that time, saith the
LORD, the iniquity of Is′ra-el shall be sought for,
and *there shall be* none; and the sins of Ju′dah,
and they shall not be found: for I will pardon
them whom I reserve.
21 ¶ Go up against the land of Mer-a-tha′im,
even against it, and against the inhabitants of
Pe′kod: waste and utterly destroy after them,
saith the LORD, and do according to all that I
have commanded thee.
22 A sound of battle *is* in the land, and of
great destruction.
23 How is the hammer of the whole earth cut
asunder and broken! how is Bab′y-lon become a
desolation among the nations!
24 I have laid a snare for thee, and thou art
also taken, O Bab′y-lon, and thou wast not
aware: thou art found, and also caught, because
thou hast striven against the LORD.
25 The LORD hath opened his armoury, and
hath brought forth the weapons of his indignation: for this *is* the work of the Lord GOD of
hosts in the land of the Chal-de′ans.
26 Come against her from the utmost border,
open her storehouses: cast her up as heaps, and
destroy her utterly: let nothing of her be left.
27 Slay all her bullocks; let them go down to
the slaughter: woe unto them! for their day is
come, the time of their visitation.
28 The voice of them that flee and escape out
of the land of Bab′y-lon, to declare in Zi′on the
vengeance of the LORD our God, the vengeance
of his temple.
29 Call together the archers against Bab′y-
lon: all ye that bend the bow, camp against it
round about; let none thereof escape: recompense her according to her work; according to
all that she hath done, do unto her: for she hath
been proud against the LORD, against the Holy
One of Is′ra-el.
30 Therefore shall her young men fall in the
streets, and all her men of war shall be cut off in
that day, saith the LORD.
31 Behold, I *am* against thee, *O thou* most
proud, saith the Lord GOD of hosts: for thy day
is come, the time *that* I will visit thee.
32 And the most proud shall stumble and
fall, and none shall raise him up: and I will kindle a fire in his cities, and it shall devour all
round about him.
33 ¶ Thus saith the LORD of hosts; The children of Is′ra-el and the children of Ju′dah *were*
oppressed together: and all that took them captives held them fast; they refused to let them
go.
34 Their Redeemer *is* strong; the LORD of
hosts *is* his name: he shall throughly plead their
cause, that he may give rest to the land, and
disquiet the inhabitants of Bab′y-lon.
35 ¶ A sword *is* upon the Chal-de′ans, saith
the LORD, and upon the inhabitants of Bab′y-
lon, and upon her princes, and upon her wise
men.
36 A sword *is* upon the liars; and they shall
dote: a sword *is* upon her mighty men; and they
shall be dismayed.
37 A sword *is* upon their horses, and upon
their chariots, and upon all the mingled people
that *are* in the midst of her; and they shall become as women: a sword *is* upon her treasures;
and they shall be robbed.
38 A drought *is* upon her waters; and they
shall be dried up: for it *is* the land of graven
images, and they are mad upon *their* idols.
39 Therefore the wild beasts of the desert
with the wild beasts of the islands shall dwell
there, and the owls shall dwell therein: and it
shall be no more inhabited for ever; neither
shall it be dwelt in from generation to generation.
40 As God overthrew Sod′om and Go-mor′-
rah and the neighbour *cities* thereof, saith the
LORD; *so* shall no man abide there, neither shall
any son of man dwell therein.
41 Behold, a people shall come from the
north, and a great nation, and many kings shall
be raised up from the coasts of the earth.
42 They shall hold the bow and the lance:
they *are* cruel, and will not shew mercy: their
voice shall roar like the sea, and they shall ride
upon horses, *every one* put in array, like a man
to the battle, against thee, O daughter of Bab′y-
lon.
43 The king of Bab′y-lon hath heard the report of them, and his hands waxed feeble: anguish took hold of him, *and* pangs as of a
woman in travail.
44 Behold, he shall come up like a lion from
the swelling of Jor′dan unto the habitation of
the strong: but I will make them suddenly run
away from her: and who *is* a chosen *man, that* I
may appoint over her? for who *is* like me? and
who will appoint me the time? and who *is* that
shepherd that will stand before me?
45 Therefore hear ye the counsel of the LORD,
that he hath taken against Bab′y-lon; and his
purposes, that he hath purposed against the
land of the Chal-de′ans: Surely the least of the
flock shall draw them out: surely he shall make
their habitation desolate with them.
46 At the noise of the taking of Bab′y-lon the
earth is moved, and the cry is heard among the
nations.

51 THUS saith the LORD; Behold, I will
raise up against Bab′y-lon, and against
them that dwell in the midst of them that rise
up against me, a destroying wind;
2 And will send unto Bab′y-lon fanners, that
shall fan her, and shall empty her land: for in
the day of trouble they shall be against her
round about.
3 Against *him that* bendeth let the archer
bend his bow, and against *him that* lifteth himself up in his brigandine: and spare ye not her
young men; destroy ye utterly all her host.
4 Thus the slain shall fall in the land of the
Chal-de′ans, and *they that are* thrust through in
her streets.
5 For Is′ra-el *hath* not *been* forsaken, nor Ju′-
dah of his God, of the LORD of hosts; though
their land was filled with sin against the Holy
One of Is′ra-el.
6 Flee out of the midst of Bab′y-lon, and deliver every man his soul: be not cut off in her
iniquity; for this *is* the time of the LORD's vengeance; he will render unto her a recompence.
7 Bab′y-lon *hath been* a golden cup in the
LORD's hand, that made all the earth drunken:
the nations have drunken of her wine; therefore
the nations are mad.
8 Bab′y-lon is suddenly fallen and destroyed:
howl for her; take balm for her pain, if so be she
may be healed.
9 We would have healed Bab′y-lon, but she is
not healed: forsake her, and let us go every one
into his own country: for her judgment reacheth unto heaven, and is lifted up *even* to the
skies.

10 The LORD hath brought forth our righteousness: come, and let us declare in Zi'on the
work of the LORD our God.
11 Make bright the arrows; gather the
shields: the LORD hath raised up the spirit of the
kings of the Medes: for his device *is* against
Bab'y-lon, to destroy it; because it *is* the vengeance of the LORD, the vengeance of his temple.
12 Set up the standard upon the walls of
Bab'y-lon, make the watch strong, set up the
watchmen, prepare the ambushes: for the LORD
hath both devised and done that which he
spake against the inhabitants of Bab'y-lon.
13 O thou that dwellest upon many waters,
abundant in treasures, thine end is come, *and*
the measure of thy covetousness.
14 The LORD of hosts hath sworn by himself,
saying, Surely I will fill thee with men, as with
caterpillers; and they shall lift up a shout
against thee.
15 He hath made the earth by his power, he
hath established the world by his wisdom, and
hath stretched out the heaven by his understanding.
16 When he uttereth *his* voice, *there is* a multitude of waters in the heavens; and he causeth
the vapours to ascend from the ends of the
earth: he maketh lightnings with rain, and
bringeth forth the wind out of his treasures.
17 Every man is brutish by *his* knowledge;
every founder is confounded by the graven
image: for his molten image *is* falsehood, and
there is no breath in them.
18 They *are* vanity, the work of errors: in the
time of their visitation they shall perish.
19 The portion of Ja'cob *is* not like them; for
he *is* the former of all things: and *Is'ra-el is* the
rod of his inheritance: the LORD of hosts *is* his
name.
20 Thou *art* my battle ax *and* weapons of
war: for with thee will I break in pieces the nations, and with thee will I destroy kingdoms;
21 And with thee will I break in pieces the
horse and his rider; and with thee will I break in
pieces the chariot and his rider;
22 With thee also will I break in pieces man
and woman; and with thee will I break in pieces
old and young; and with thee will I break in
pieces the young man and the maid;
23 I will also break in pieces with thee the
shepherd and his flock; and with thee will I
break in pieces the husbandman and his yoke of
oxen; and with thee will I break in pieces captains and rulers.
24 And I will render unto Bab'y-lon and to all
the inhabitants of Chal-de'a all their evil that
they have done in Zi'on in your sight, saith the
LORD.
25 Behold, I *am* against thee, O destroying
mountain, saith the LORD, which destroyest all
the earth: and I will stretch out mine hand upon
thee, and roll thee down from the rocks, and
will make thee a burnt mountain.
26 And they shall not take of thee a stone for
a corner, nor a stone for foundations; but thou
shalt be desolate for ever, saith the LORD.
27 Set ye up a standard in the land, blow the
trumpet among the nations, prepare the nations
against her, call together against her the kingdoms of Ar'a-rat, Min'ni, and Ash'che-naz; appoint a captain against her; cause the horses to
come up as the rough caterpillers.
28 Prepare against her the nations with the
kings of the Medes, the captains thereof, and all
the rulers thereof, and all the land of his dominion.
29 And the land shall tremble and sorrow:
for every purpose of the LORD shall be performed against Bab'y-lon, to make the land of
Bab'y-lon a desolation without an inhabitant.
30 The mighty men of Bab'y-lon have for-
born to fight, they have remained in *their* holds:
their might hath failed; they became as women:
they have burned her dwellingplaces; her bars
are broken.
31 One post shall run to meet another, and
one messenger to meet another, to shew the
king of Bab'y-lon that his city is taken at *one*
end,
32 And that the passages are stopped, and
the reeds they have burned with fire, and the
men of war are affrighted.
33 For thus saith the LORD of hosts, the God
of Is'ra-el; The daughter of Bab'y-lon *is* like a
threshingfloor, *it is* time to thresh her: yet a little while, and the time of her harvest shall
come.
34 Neb-u-chad-rez'zar the king of Bab'y-lon
hath devoured me, he hath crushed me, he hath
made me an empty vessel, he hath swallowed
me up like a dragon, he hath filled his belly with
my delicates, he hath cast me out.
35 The violence done to me and to my flesh
be upon Bab'y-lon, shall the inhabitant of Zi'on
say; and my blood upon the inhabitants of Chal-
de'a, shall Je-ru'sa-lem say.
36 Therefore thus saith the LORD; Behold, I
will plead thy cause, and take vengeance for
thee; and I will dry up her sea, and make her
springs dry.
37 And Bab'y-lon shall become heaps, a
dwellingplace for dragons, an astonishment,
and an hissing, without an inhabitant.
38 They shall roar together like lions: they
shall yell as lions' whelps.
39 In their heat I will make their feasts, and I
will make them drunken, that they may rejoice,
and sleep a perpetual sleep, and not wake, saith
the LORD.
40 I will bring them down like lambs to the
slaughter, like rams with he goats.
41 How is She'shach taken! and how is the
praise of the whole earth surprised! how is
Bab'y-lon become an astonishment among the
nations!
42 The sea is come up upon Bab'y-lon: she is
covered with the multitude of the waves
thereof.
43 Her cities are a desolation, a dry land, and
a wilderness, a land wherein no man dwelleth,
neither doth *any* son of man pass thereby.
44 And I will punish Bel in Bab'y-lon, and I
will bring forth out of his mouth that which he
hath swallowed up: and the nations shall not
flow together any more unto him: yea, the wall
of Bab'y-lon shall fall.
45 My people, go ye out of the midst of her,
and deliver ye every man his soul from the
fierce anger of the LORD.
46 And lest your heart faint, and ye fear for
the rumour that shall be heard in the land; a
rumour shall both come *one* year, and after that
in *another* year *shall come* a rumour, and violence in the land, ruler against ruler.
47 Therefore, behold, the days come, that I
will do judgment upon the graven images of
Bab'y-lon: and her whole land shall be confounded, and all her slain shall fall in the midst
of her.
48 Then the heaven and the earth, and all
that *is* therein, shall sing for Bab'y-lon: for the
spoilers shall come unto her from the north,
saith the LORD.

49 As Bab'y-lon *hath caused* the slain of Is'ra-el to fall, so at Bab'y-lon shall fall the slain of all the earth.

50 Ye that have escaped the sword, go away, stand not still: remember the LORD afar off, and let Je-ru'sa-lem come into your mind.

51 We are confounded, because we have heard reproach: shame hath covered our faces: for strangers are come into the sanctuaries of the LORD's house.

52 Wherefore, behold, the days come, saith the LORD, that I will do judgment upon her graven images: and through all her land the wounded shall groan.

53 Though Bab'y-lon should mount up to heaven, and though she should fortify the height of her strength, *yet* from me shall spoilers come unto her, saith the LORD.

54 A sound of a cry *cometh* from Bab'y-lon, and great destruction from the land of the Chal-de'ans:

55 Because the LORD hath spoiled Bab'y-lon, and destroyed out of her the great voice; when her waves do roar like great waters, a noise of their voice is uttered:

56 Because the spoiler is come upon her, *even* upon Bab'y-lon, and her mighty men are taken, every one of their bows is broken: for the LORD God of recompences shall surely requite.

57 And I will make drunk her princes, and her wise *men*, her captains, and her rulers, and her mighty men: and they shall sleep a perpetual sleep, and not wake, saith the King, whose name *is* the LORD of hosts.

58 Thus saith the LORD of hosts; The broad walls of Bab'y-lon shall be utterly broken, and her high gates shall be burned with fire; and the people shall labour in vain, and the folk in the fire, and they shall be weary.

59 ¶ The word which Jer-e-mi'ah the prophet commanded Ser-a-i'ah the son of Ne-ri'ah, the son of Ma-a-se'iah, when he went with Zed-e-ki'ah the king of Ju'dah into Bab'y-lon in the fourth year of his reign. And *this* Ser-a-i'ah *was* a quiet prince.

60 So Jer-e-mi'ah wrote in a book all the evil that should come upon Bab'y-lon, *even* all these words that are written against Bab'y-lon.

61 And Jer-e-mi'ah said to Ser-a-i'ah, When thou comest to Bab'y-lon, and shalt see, and shalt read all these words;

62 Then shalt thou say, O LORD, thou hast spoken against this place, to cut it off, that none shall remain in it, neither man nor beast, but that it shall be desolate for ever.

63 And it shall be, when thou hast made an end of reading this book, *that* thou shalt bind a stone to it, and cast it into the midst of Eu-phra'tes:

64 And thou shalt say, Thus shall Bab'y-lon sink, and shall not rise from the evil that I will bring upon her: and they shall be weary. Thus far *are* the words of Jer-e-mi'ah.

52

ZED-E-KI'AH *was* one and twenty years old when he began to reign, and he reigned eleven years in Je-ru'sa-lem. And his mother's name *was* Ha-mu'tal the daughter of Jer-e-mi'ah of Lib'nah.

2 And he did *that which was* evil in the eyes of the LORD, according to all that Je-hoi'a-kim had done.

3 For through the anger of the LORD it came to pass in Je-ru'sa-lem and Ju'dah, till he had cast them out from his presence, that Zed-e-ki'ah rebelled against the king of Bab'y-lon.

4 ¶ And it came to pass in the ninth year of his reign, in the tenth month, in the tenth *day* of the month, *that* Neb-u-chad-rez'zar king of Bab'y-lon came, he and all his army, against Je-ru'sa-lem, and pitched against it, and built forts against it round about.

5 So the city was besieged unto the eleventh year of king Zed-e-ki'ah.

6 And in the fourth month, in the ninth *day* of the month, the famine was sore in the city, so that there was no bread for the people of the land.

7 Then the city was broken up and all the men of war fled, and went forth out of the city by night by the way of the gate between the two walls, which *was* by the king's garden; (now the Chal-de'ans *were* by the city round about:) and they went by the way of the plain.

8 ¶ But the army of the Chal-de'ans pursued after the king, and overtook Zed-e-ki'ah in the plains of Jer'i-cho; and all his army was scattered from him.

9 Then they took the king, and carried him up unto the king of Bab'y-lon to Rib'lah in the land of Ha'math; where he gave judgment upon him.

10 And the king of Bab'y-lon slew the sons of Zed-e-ki'ah before his eyes: he slew also all the princes of Ju'dah in Rib'lah.

11 Then he put out the eyes of Zed-e-ki'ah; and the king of Bab'y-lon bound him in chains, and carried him to Bab'y-lon, and put him in prison till the day of his death.

12 ¶ Now in the fifth month, in the tenth *day* of the month, which *was* the nineteenth year of Neb-u-chad-rez'zar king of Bab'y-lon, came Neb'u-zar–a'dan, captain of the guard, *which* served the king of Bab'y-lon, into Je-ru'sa-lem,

13 And burned the house of the LORD, and the king's house; and all the houses of Je-ru'sa-lem, and all the houses of the great *men*, burned he with fire:

14 And all the army of the Chal-de'ans, that *were* with the captain of the guard, brake down all the walls of Je-ru'sa-lem round about.

15 Then Neb'u-zar–a'dan the captain of the guard carried away captive *certain* of the poor of the people, and the residue of the people that remained in the city, and those that fell away, that fell to the king of Bab'y-lon, and the rest of the multitude.

16 But Neb'u-zar–a'dan the captain of the guard left *certain* of the poor of the land for vinedressers and for husbandmen.

17 Also the pillars of brass that *were* in the house of the LORD, and the bases, and the brasen sea that *was* in the house of the LORD, the Chal-de'ans brake, and carried all the brass of them to Bab'y-lon.

18 The caldrons also, and the shovels, and the snuffers, and the bowls, and the spoons, and all the vessels of brass wherewith they ministered, took they away.

19 And the basons, and the firepans, and the bowls, and the caldrons, and the candlesticks, and the spoons, and the cups; *that* which *was* of gold *in* gold, and *that* which *was* of silver *in* silver, took the captain of the guard away.

20 The two pillars, one sea, and twelve brasen bulls that *were* under the bases, which king Sol'o-mon had made in the house of the LORD: the brass of all these vessels was without weight.

21 And *concerning* the pillars, the height of one pillar *was* eighteen cubits; and a fillet of twelve cubits did compass it; and the thickness thereof *was* four fingers: *it was* hollow.

22 And a chapiter of brass *was* upon it; and the height of one chapiter *was* five cubits, with network and pomegranates upon the chapiters round about, all *of* brass. The second pillar also and the pomegranates *were* like unto these.

23 And there were ninety and six pomegranates on a side; *and* all the pomegranates upon the network *were* an hundred round about.

24 ¶ And the captain of the guard took Se-ra-i'ah the chief priest, and Zeph-a-ni'ah the second priest, and the three keepers of the door:

25 He took also out of the city an eunuch, which had the charge of the men of war; and seven men of them that were near the king's person, which were found in the city; and the principal scribe of the host, who mustered the people of the land; and threescore men of the people of the land, that were found in the midst of the city.

26 So Neb'u-zar-a'dan the captain of the guard took them, and brought them to the king of Bab'y-lon to Rib'lah.

27 And the king of Bab'y-lon smote them, and put them to death in Rib'lah in the land of Ha'math. Thus Ju'dah was carried away captive out of his own land.

28 This *is* the people whom Neb-u-chad-rez'-zar carried away captive: in the seventh year three thousand Jews and three and twenty:

29 In the eighteenth year of Neb-u-chad-rez'-zar he carried away captive from Je-ru'sa-lem eight hundred thirty and two persons:

30 In the three and twentieth year of Neb-u-chad-rez'zar Neb'u-zar-a'dan the captain of the guard carried away captive of the Jews seven hundred forty and five persons: all the persons *were* four thousand and six hundred.

31 ¶ And it came to pass in the seven and thirtieth year of the captivity of Je-hoi'a-chin king of Ju'dah, in the twelfth month, in the five and twentieth *day* of the month, *that* E'vil-me-ro'dach king of Bab'y-lon in the *first* year of his reign lifted up the head of Je-hoi'a-chin king of Ju'dah, and brought him forth out of prison,

32 And spake kindly unto him, and set his throne above the throne of the kings that *were* with him in Bab'y-lon,

33 And changed his prison garments: and he did continually eat bread before him all the days of his life.

34 And *for* his diet, there was a continual diet given him of the king of Bab'y-lon, every day a portion until the day of his death, all the days of his life.

THE LAMENTATIONS

OF JEREMIAH

1 HOW doth the city sit solitary, *that was* full of people! *how* is she become as a widow! she *that was* great among the nations, *and* princess among the provinces, *how* is she become tributary!

2 She weepeth sore in the night, and her tears *are* on her cheeks: among all her lovers she hath none to comfort *her:* all her friends have dealt treacherously with her, they are become her enemies.

3 Ju'dah is gone into captivity because of affliction, and because of great servitude: she dwelleth among the heathen, she findeth no rest: all her persecutors overtook her between the straits.

4 The ways of Zi'on do mourn, because none come to the solemn feasts: all her gates are desolate: her priests sigh, her virgins are afflicted, and she *is* in bitterness.

5 Her adversaries are the chief, her enemies prosper; for the LORD hath afflicted her for the multitude of her transgressions: her children are gone into captivity before the enemy.

6 And from the daughter of Zi'on all her beauty is departed: her princes are become like harts *that* find no pasture, and they are gone without strength before the pursuer.

7 Je-ru'sa-lem remembered in the days of her affliction and of her miseries all her pleasant things that she had in the days of old, when her people fell into the hand of the enemy, and none did help her: the adversaries saw her, *and* did mock at her sabbaths.

8 Je-ru'sa-lem hath grievously sinned; therefore she is removed: all that honoured her despise her, because they have seen her nakedness: yea, she sigheth, and turneth backward.

9 Her filthiness *is* in her skirts; she remembereth not her last end; therefore she came down wonderfully: she had no comforter. O LORD, behold my affliction: for the enemy hath magnified *himself.*

10 The adversary hath spread out his hand upon all her pleasant things: for she hath seen *that* the heathen entered into her sanctuary, whom thou didst command *that* they should not enter into thy congregation.

11 All her people sigh, they seek bread; they have given their pleasant things for meat to relieve the soul: see, O LORD, and consider; for I am become vile.

12 ¶ *Is it* nothing to you, all ye that pass by? behold, and see if there be any sorrow like unto my sorrow, which is done unto me, wherewith the LORD hath afflicted *me* in the day of his fierce anger.

13 From above hath he sent fire into my bones, and it prevaileth against them: he hath spread a net for my feet, he hath turned me back: he hath made me desolate *and* faint all the day.

14 The yoke of my transgressions is bound by his hand: they are wreathed, *and* come up upon my neck: he hath made my strength to fall, the Lord hath delivered me into *their* hands, *from whom* I am not able to rise up.

15 The Lord hath trodden under foot all my mighty *men* in the midst of me: he hath called an assembly against me to crush my young men: the Lord hath trodden the virgin, the daughter of Ju'dah, *as* in a winepress.

16 For these *things* I weep; mine eye, mine eye runneth down with water, because the comforter that should relieve my soul is far from me: my children are desolate, because the enemy prevailed.

17 Zi'on spreadeth forth her hands, *and there is* none to comfort her: the LORD hath commanded concerning Ja'cob, *that* his adversaries *should be* round about him: Je-ru'sa-lem is as a menstruous woman among them.

18 ¶ The LORD is righteous; for I have rebelled against his commandment: hear, I pray

you, all people, and behold my sorrow: my virgins and my young men are gone into captivity.
19 I called for my lovers, *but* they deceived
me: my priests and mine elders gave up the
ghost in the city, while they sought their meat
to relieve their souls.
20 Behold, O LORD; for I *am* in distress: my
bowels are troubled; mine heart is turned
within me; for I have grievously rebelled:
abroad the sword bereaveth, at home *there is* as
death.
21 They have heard that I sigh: *there is* none
to comfort me: all mine enemies have heard of
my trouble; they are glad that thou hast done *it:*
thou wilt bring the day *that* thou hast called,
and they shall be like unto me.
22 Let all their wickedness come before thee;
and do unto them, as thou hast done unto me
for all my transgressions: for my sighs *are*
many, and my heart *is* faint.

2 HOW hath the Lord covered the daughter
of Zi'on with a cloud in his anger, *and* cast
down from heaven unto the earth the beauty of
Is'ra-el, and remembered not his footstool in the
day of his anger!
2 The Lord hath swallowed up all the habitations of Ja'cob, and hath not pitied: he hath
thrown down in his wrath the strong holds of
the daughter of Ju'dah; he hath brought *them*
down to the ground: he hath polluted the kingdom and the princes thereof.
3 He hath cut off in *his* fierce anger all the
horn of Is'ra-el: he hath drawn back his right
hand from before the enemy, and he burned
against Ja'cob like a flaming fire, *which* devoureth round about.
4 He hath bent his bow like an enemy: he
stood with his right hand as an adversary, and
slew all *that were* pleasant to the eye in the tabernacle of the daughter of Zi'on: he poured out
his fury like fire.
5 The Lord was as an enemy: he hath swallowed up Is'ra-el, he hath swallowed up all her
palaces: he hath destroyed his strong holds, and
hath increased in the daughter of Ju'dah
mourning and lamentation.
6 And he hath violently taken away his tabernacle, as *if it were of* a garden: he hath destroyed his places of the assembly: the LORD
hath caused the solemn feasts and sabbaths to
be forgotten in Zi'on, and hath despised in the
indignation of his anger the king and the priest.
7 The Lord hath cast off his altar, he hath abhorred his sanctuary, he hath given up into the
hand of the enemy the walls of her palaces; they
have made a noise in the house of the LORD, as
in the day of a solemn feast.
8 The LORD hath purposed to destroy the
wall of the daughter of Zi'on: he hath stretched
out a line, he hath not withdrawn his hand from
destroying: therefore he made the rampart and
the wall to lament; they languished together.
9 Her gates are sunk into the ground; he hath
destroyed and broken her bars: her king and
her princes *are* among the Gen'tiles: the law *is*
no *more;* her prophets also find no vision from
the LORD.
10 The elders of the daughter of Zi'on sit
upon the ground, *and* keep silence: they have
cast up dust upon their heads; they have girded
themselves with sackcloth: the virgins of Je-ru'-
sa-lem hang down their heads to the ground.
11 Mine eyes do fail with tears, my bowels
are troubled, my liver is poured upon the earth,
for the destruction of the daughter of my people; because the children and the sucklings
swoon in the streets of the city.
12 They say to their mothers, Where *is* corn
and wine? when they swooned as the wounded
in the streets of the city, when their soul was
poured out into their mothers' bosom.
13 What thing shall I take to witness for
thee? what thing shall I liken to thee, O daughter of Je-ru'sa-lem? what shall I equal to thee,
that I may comfort thee, O virgin daughter of
Zi'on? for thy breach *is* great like the sea: who
can heal thee?
14 Thy prophets have seen vain and foolish
things for thee: and they have not discovered
thine iniquity, to turn away thy captivity; but
have seen for thee false burdens and causes of
banishment.
15 All that pass by clap *their* hands at thee;
they hiss and wag their head at the daughter of
Je-ru'sa-lem, *saying, Is* this the city that *men*
call The perfection of beauty, The joy of the
whole earth?
16 All thine enemies have opened their
mouth against thee: they hiss and gnash the
teeth: they say, We have swallowed *her* up: certainly this *is* the day that we looked for; we
have found, we have seen *it.*
17 The LORD hath done *that* which he had devised; he hath fulfilled his word that he had
commanded in the days of old: he hath thrown
down, and hath not pitied: and he hath caused
thine enemy to rejoice over thee, he hath set up
the horn of thine adversaries.
18 Their heart cried unto the Lord, O wall of
the daughter of Zi'on, let tears run down like a
river day and night: give thyself no rest; let not
the apple of thine eye cease.
19 Arise, cry out in the night: in the beginning of the watches pour out thine heart like
water before the face of the Lord: lift up thy
hands toward him for the life of thy young children, that faint for hunger in the top of every
street.
20 ¶ Behold, O LORD, and consider to whom
thou hast done this. Shall the women eat their
fruit, *and* children of a span long? shall the
priest and the prophet be slain in the sanctuary
of the Lord?
21 The young and the old lie on the ground in
the streets: my virgins and my young men are
fallen by the sword; thou hast slain *them* in the
day of thine anger; thou hast killed, *and* not
pitied.
22 Thou hast called as in a solemn day my
terrors round about, so that in the day of the
LORD's anger none escaped nor remained: those
that I have swaddled and brought up hath mine
enemy consumed.

3 I *AM* the man *that* hath seen affliction by
the rod of his wrath.
2 He hath led me, and brought *me into* darkness, but not *into* light.
3 Surely against me is he turned; he turneth
his hand *against me* all the day.
4 My flesh and my skin hath he made old; he
hath broken my bones.
5 He hath builded against me, and compassed *me* with gall and travail.
6 He hath set me in dark places, as *they that
be* dead of old.
7 He hath hedged me about, that I cannot get
out: he hath made my chain heavy.
8 Also when I cry and shout, he shutteth out
my prayer.
9 He hath inclosed my ways with hewn
stone, he hath made my paths crooked.

10 He *was* unto me *as* a bear lying in wait, *and as* a lion in secret places.
11 He hath turned aside my ways, and pulled me in pieces: he hath made me desolate.
12 He hath bent his bow, and set me as a mark for the arrow.
13 He hath caused the arrows of his quiver to enter into my reins.
14 I was a derision to all my people; *and* their song all the day.
15 He hath filled me with bitterness, he hath made me drunken with wormwood.
16 He hath also broken my teeth with gravel stones, he hath covered me with ashes.
17 And thou hast removed my soul far off from peace: I forgat prosperity.
18 And I said, My strength and my hope is perished from the LORD:
19 Remembering mine affliction and my misery, the wormwood and the gall.
20 My soul hath *them* still in remembrance, and is humbled in me.
21 This I recall to my mind, therefore have I hope.
22 ¶ *It is of* the LORD's mercies that we are not consumed, because his compassions fail not.
23 *They are* new every morning: great *is* thy faithfulness.
24 The LORD *is* my portion, saith my soul; therefore will I hope in him.
25 The LORD *is* good unto them that wait for him, to the soul *that* seeketh him.
26 *It is* good that *a man* should both hope and quietly wait for the salvation of the LORD.
27 *It is* good for a man that he bear the yoke in his youth.
28 He sitteth alone and keepeth silence, because he hath borne *it* upon him.
29 He putteth his mouth in the dust; if so be there may be hope.
30 He giveth *his* cheek to him that smiteth him: he is filled full with reproach.
31 For the Lord will not cast off for ever:
32 But though he cause grief, yet will he have compassion according to the multitude of his mercies.
33 For he doth not afflict willingly nor grieve the children of men.
34 To crush under his feet all the prisoners of the earth,
35 To turn aside the right of a man before the face of the most High,
36 To subvert a man in his cause, the Lord approveth not.
37 ¶ Who *is* he *that* saith, and it cometh to pass, *when* the Lord commandeth *it* not?
38 Out of the mouth of the most High proceedeth not evil and good?
39 Wherefore doth a living man complain, a man for the punishment of his sins?
40 Let us search and try our ways, and turn again to the LORD.
41 Let us lift up our heart with *our* hands unto God in the heavens.
42 We have transgressed and have rebelled: thou hast not pardoned.
43 Thou hast covered with anger, and persecuted us: thou hast slain, thou hast not pitied.
44 Thou hast covered thyself with a cloud, that *our* prayer should not pass through.
45 Thou hast made us *as* the offscouring and refuse in the midst of the people.
46 All our enemies have opened their mouths against us.
47 Fear and a snare is come upon us, desolation and destruction.
48 Mine eye runneth down with rivers of water for the destruction of the daughter of my people.
49 Mine eye trickleth down, and ceaseth not, without any intermission,
50 Till the LORD look down, and behold from heaven.
51 Mine eye affecteth mine heart because of all the daughters of my city.
52 Mine enemies chased me sore, like a bird, without cause.
53 They have cut off my life in the dungeon, and cast a stone upon me.
54 Waters flowed over mine head; *then* I said, I am cut off.
55 ¶ I called upon thy name, O LORD, out of the low dungeon.
56 Thou hast heard my voice: hide not thine ear at my breathing, at my cry.
57 Thou drewest near in the day *that* I called upon thee: thou saidst, Fear not.
58 O Lord, thou hast pleaded the causes of my soul; thou hast redeemed my life.
59 O LORD, thou hast seen my wrong: judge thou my cause.
60 Thou hast seen all their vengeance *and* all their imaginations against me.
61 Thou hast heard their reproach, O LORD, *and* all their imaginations against me;
62 The lips of those that rose up against me, and their device against me all the day.
63 Behold their sitting down, and their rising up; I *am* their musick.
64 ¶ Render unto them a recompence, O LORD, according to the work of their hands.
65 Give them sorrow of heart, thy curse unto them.
66 Persecute and destroy them in anger from under the heavens of the LORD.

4 HOW is the gold become dim! *how* is the most fine gold changed! the stones of the sanctuary are poured out in the top of every street.
2 The precious sons of Zi'on, comparable to fine gold, how are they esteemed as earthen pitchers, the work of the hands of the potter!
3 Even the sea monsters draw out the breast, they give suck to their young ones: the daughter of my people *is become* cruel, like the ostriches in the wilderness.
4 The tongue of the sucking child cleaveth to the roof of his mouth for thirst: the young children ask bread, *and* no man breaketh *it* unto them.
5 They that did feed delicately are desolate in the streets: they that were brought up in scarlet embrace dunghills.
6 For the punishment of the iniquity of the daughter of my people is greater than the punishment of the sin of Sod'om, that was overthrown as in a moment, and no hands stayed on her.
7 Her Naz'a-rites were purer than snow, they were whiter than milk, they were more ruddy in body than rubies, their polishing *was* of sapphire:
8 Their visage is blacker than a coal; they are not known in the streets: their skin cleaveth to their bones; it is withered, it is become like a stick.
9 *They that be* slain with the sword are better than *they that be* slain with hunger: for these pine away, stricken through for *want of* the fruits of the field.

10 The hands of the pitiful women have sodden their own children: they were their meat in
the destruction of the daughter of my people.
11 The LORD hath accomplished his fury; he
hath poured out his fierce anger, and hath kindled a fire in Zi'on, and it hath devoured the
foundations thereof.
12 The kings of the earth, and all the inhabitants of the world, would not have believed that
the adversary and the enemy should have entered into the gates of Je-ru'sa-lem.
13 ¶ For the sins of her prophets, *and* the iniquities of her priests, that have shed the blood
of the just in the midst of her,
14 They have wandered *as* blind *men* in the
streets, they have polluted themselves with
blood, so that men could not touch their garments.
15 They cried unto them, Depart ye; *it is* unclean; depart, depart, touch not: when they fled
away and wandered, they said among the heathen, They shall no more sojourn *there*.
16 The anger of the LORD hath divided them;
he will no more regard them: they respected not
the persons of the priests, they favoured not the
elders.
17 As for us, our eyes as yet failed for our
vain help: in our watching we have watched for
a nation *that* could not save *us*.
18 They hunt our steps, that we cannot go in
our streets: our end is near, our days are fulfilled; for our end is come.
19 Our persecutors are swifter than the eagles of the heaven: they pursued us upon the
mountains, they laid wait for us in the wilderness.
20 The breath of our nostrils, the anointed of
the LORD, was taken in their pits, of whom we
said, Under his shadow we shall live among the
heathen.
21 ¶ Rejoice and be glad, O daughter of E'-
dom, that dwellest in the land of Uz; the cup
also shall pass through unto thee: thou shalt be
drunken, and shalt make thyself naked.
22 ¶ The punishment of thine iniquity is accomplished, O daughter of Zi'on; he will no
more carry thee away into captivity: he will
visit thine iniquity, O daughter of E'dom; he will
discover thy sins.

5 REMEMBER, O LORD, what is come upon
us: consider, and behold our reproach.
2 Our inheritance is turned to strangers, our
houses to aliens.
3 We are orphans and fatherless, our mothers *are* as widows.
4 We have drunken our water for money; our
wood is sold unto us.
5 Our necks *are* under persecution: we labour, *and* have no rest.
6 We have given the hand to the E-gyp'tians,
and to the As-syr'i-ans, to be satisfied with
bread.
7 Our fathers have sinned, *and are* not; and
we have borne their iniquities.
8 Servants have ruled over us: *there is* none
that doth deliver *us* out of their hand.
9 We gat our bread with *the peril of* our lives
because of the sword of the wilderness.
10 Our skin was black like an oven because
of the terrible famine.
11 They ravished the women in Zi'on, *and*
the maids in the cities of Ju'dah.
12 Princes are hanged up by their hand: the
faces of elders were not honoured.
13 They took the young men to grind, and
the children fell under the wood.
14 The elders have ceased from the gate, the
young men from their musick.
15 The joy of our heart is ceased; our dance
is turned into mourning.
16 The crown is fallen *from* our head: woe
unto us, that we have sinned!
17 For this our heart is faint; for these *things*
our eyes are dim.
18 Because of the mountain of Zi'on, which
is desolate, the foxes walk upon it.
19 Thou, O LORD, remainest for ever; thy
throne from generation to generation.
20 Wherefore dost thou forget us for ever,
and forsake us so long time?
21 Turn thou us unto thee, O LORD, and we
shall be turned; renew our days as of old.
22 But thou hast utterly rejected us; thou art
very wroth against us.

THE BOOK OF

EZEKIEL

1 NOW it came to pass in the thirtieth year,
in the fourth *month*, in the fifth *day* of the
month, as I *was* among the captives by the river
of Che'bar, *that* the heavens were opened, and I
saw visions of God.
2 In the fifth *day* of the month, which *was*
the fifth year of king Je-hoi'a-chin's captivity,
3 The word of the LORD came expressly unto
E-ze'ki-el the priest, the son of Bu'zi, in the land
of the Chal-de'ans by the river Che'bar; and the
hand of the LORD was there upon him.
4 ¶ And I looked, and, behold, a whirlwind
came out of the north, a great cloud, and a fire
infolding itself, and a brightness *was* about it,
and out of the midst thereof as the colour of
amber, out of the midst of the fire.
5 Also out of the midst thereof *came* the likeness of four living creatures. And this *was* their
appearance; they had the likeness of a man.
6 And every one had four faces, and every
one had four wings.
7 And their feet *were* straight feet; and the
sole of their feet *was* like the sole of a calf's
foot: and they sparkled like the colour of bur-
nished brass.
8 And *they had* the hands of a man under
their wings on their four sides; and they four
had their faces and their wings.
9 Their wings *were* joined one to another;
they turned not when they went; they went every one straight forward.
10 As for the likeness of their faces, they four
had the face of a man, and the face of a lion, on
the right side: and they four had the face of an
ox on the left side; they four also had the face of
an eagle.
11 Thus *were* their faces: and their wings
were stretched upward; two *wings* of every one
were joined one to another, and two covered
their bodies.
12 And they went every one straight forward: whither the spirit was to go, they went;
and they turned not when they went.
13 As for the likeness of the living creatures,

their appearance *was* like burning coals of fire, *and* like the appearance of lamps: it went up and down among the living creatures; and the fire was bright, and out of the fire went forth lightning.

14 And the living creatures ran and returned as the appearance of a flash of lightning.

15 ¶ Now as I beheld the living creatures, behold one wheel upon the earth by the living creatures, with his four faces.

16 The appearance of the wheels and their work *was* like unto the colour of a beryl: and they four had one likeness: and their appearance and their work *was* as it were a wheel in the middle of a wheel.

17 When they went, they went upon their four sides: *and* they turned not when they went.

18 As for their rings, they were so high that they were dreadful; and their rings *were* full of eyes round about them four.

19 And when the living creatures went, the wheels went by them: and when the living creatures were lifted up from the earth, the wheels were lifted up.

20 Whithersoever the spirit was to go, they went, thither *was their* spirit to go; and the wheels were lifted up over against them: for the spirit of the living creature *was* in the wheels.

21 When those went, *these* went; and when those stood, *these* stood; and when those were lifted up from the earth, the wheels were lifted up over against them: for the spirit of the living creature *was* in the wheels.

22 And the likeness of the firmament upon the heads of the living creature *was* as the colour of the terrible crystal, stretched forth over their heads above.

23 And under the firmament *were* their wings straight, the one toward the other: every one had two, which covered on this side, and every one had two, which covered on that side, their bodies.

24 And when they went, I heard the noise of their wings, like the noise of great waters, as the voice of the Almighty, the voice of speech, as the noise of an host: when they stood, they let down their wings.

25 And there was a voice from the firmament that *was* over their heads, when they stood, *and* had let down their wings.

26 ¶ And above the firmament that *was* over their heads *was* the likeness of a throne, as the appearance of a sapphire stone: and upon the likeness of the throne *was* the likeness as the appearance of a man above upon it.

27 And I saw as the colour of amber, as the appearance of fire round about within it, from the appearance of his loins even upward, and from the appearance of his loins even downward, I saw as it were the appearance of fire, and it had brightness round about.

28 As the appearance of the bow that is in the cloud in the day of rain, so *was* the appearance of the brightness round about. This *was* the appearance of the likeness of the glory of the LORD. And when I saw *it,* I fell upon my face, and I heard a voice of one that spake.

2 AND he said unto me, Son of man, stand upon thy feet, and I will speak unto thee.

2 And the spirit entered into me when he spake unto me, and set me upon my feet, that I heard him that spake unto me.

3 And he said unto me, Son of man, I send thee to the children of Is'ra-el, to a rebellious nation that hath rebelled against me: they and their fathers have transgressed against me, *even* unto this very day.

4 For *they are* impudent children and stiffhearted. I do send thee unto them; and thou shalt say unto them, Thus saith the Lord GOD.

5 And they, whether they will hear, or whether they will forbear, (for they *are* a rebellious house,) yet shall know that there hath been a prophet among them.

6 ¶ And thou, son of man, be not afraid of them, neither be afraid of their words, though briers and thorns *be* with thee, and thou dost dwell among scorpions: be not afraid of their words, nor be dismayed at their looks, though they *be* a rebellious house.

7 And thou shalt speak my words unto them, whether they will hear, or whether they will forbear: for they *are* most rebellious.

8 But thou, son of man, hear what I say unto thee; Be not thou rebellious like that rebellious house: open thy mouth, and eat that I give thee.

9 ¶ And when I looked, behold, an hand *was* sent unto me; and, lo, a roll of a book *was* therein;

10 And he spread it before me; and it *was* written within and without: and *there was* written therein lamentations, and mourning, and woe.

3 MOREOVER he said unto me, Son of man, eat that thou findest; eat this roll, and go speak unto the house of Is'ra-el.

2 So I opened my mouth, and he caused me to eat that roll.

3 And he said unto me, Son of man, cause thy belly to eat, and fill thy bowels with this roll that I give thee. Then did I eat *it;* and it was in my mouth as honey for sweetness.

4 ¶ And he said unto me, Son of man, go, get thee unto the house of Is'ra-el, and speak with my words unto them.

5 For thou *art* not sent to a people of a strange speech and of an hard language, *but* to the house of Is'ra-el;

6 Not to many people of a strange speech and of an hard language, whose words thou canst not understand. Surely, had I sent thee to them, they would have hearkened unto thee.

7 But the house of Is'ra-el will not hearken unto thee; for they will not hearken unto me: for all the house of Is'ra-el *are* impudent and hardhearted.

8 Behold, I have made thy face strong against their faces, and thy forehead strong against their foreheads.

9 As an adamant harder than flint have I made thy forehead: fear them not, neither be dismayed at their looks, though they *be* a rebellious house.

10 Moreover he said unto me, Son of man, all my words that I shall speak unto thee receive in thine heart, and hear with thine ears.

11 And go, get thee to them of the captivity, unto the children of thy people, and speak unto them, and tell them, Thus saith the Lord GOD; whether they will hear, or whether they will forbear.

12 Then the spirit took me up, and I heard behind me a voice of a great rushing, *saying,* Blessed *be* the glory of the LORD from his place.

13 *I heard* also the noise of the wings of the living creatures that touched one another, and the noise of the wheels over against them, and a noise of a great rushing.

14 So the spirit lifted me up, and took me away, and I went in bitterness, in the heat of my

spirit; but the hand of the LORD was strong
upon me.
15 ¶ Then I came to them of the captivity at
Tel–a′bib, that dwelt by the river of Che′bar,
and I sat where they sat, and remained there
astonished among them seven days.
16 And it came to pass at the end of seven
days, that the word of the LORD came unto me,
saying,
17 Son of man, I have made thee a watchman
unto the house of Is′ra-el: therefore hear the
word at my mouth, and give them warning
from me.
18 When I say unto the wicked, Thou shalt
surely die; and thou givest him not warning, nor
speakest to warn the wicked from his wicked
way, to save his life; the same wicked *man* shall
die in his iniquity; but his blood will I require at
thine hand.
19 Yet if thou warn the wicked, and he turn
not from his wickedness, nor from his wicked
way, he shall die in his iniquity; but thou hast
delivered thy soul.
20 Again, When a righteous *man* doth turn
from his righteousness, and commit iniquity,
and I lay a stumblingblock before him, he shall
die: because thou hast not given him warning,
he shall die in his sin, and his righteousness
which he hath done shall not be remembered;
but his blood will I require at thine hand.
21 Nevertheless if thou warn the righteous
man, that the righteous sin not, and he doth not
sin, he shall surely live, because he is warned;
also thou hast delivered thy soul.
22 ¶ And the hand of the LORD was there
upon me; and he said unto me, Arise, go forth
into the plain, and I will there talk with thee.
23 Then I arose, and went forth into the
plain: and, behold, the glory of the LORD stood
there, as the glory which I saw by the river of
Che′bar: and I fell on my face.
24 Then the spirit entered into me, and set
me upon my feet, and spake with me, and said
unto me, Go, shut thyself within thine house.
25 But thou, O son of man, behold, they shall
put bands upon thee, and shall bind thee with
them, and thou shalt not go out among them:
26 And I will make thy tongue cleave to the
roof of thy mouth, that thou shalt be dumb, and
shalt not be to them a reprover: for they *are* a
rebellious house.
27 But when I speak with thee, I will open
thy mouth, and thou shalt say unto them, Thus
saith the Lord GOD; He that heareth, let him
hear; and he that forbeareth, let him forbear:
for they *are* a rebellious house.

4 THOU also, son of man, take thee a tile,
and lay it before thee, and pourtray upon it
the city, *even* Je-ru′sa-lem:
2 And lay siege against it, and build a fort
against it, and cast a mount against it; set the
camp also against it, and set *battering* rams
against it round about.
3 Moreover take thou unto thee an iron pan,
and set it *for* a wall of iron between thee and
the city: and set thy face against it, and it shall
be besieged, and thou shalt lay siege against it.
This *shall be* a sign to the house of Is′ra-el.
4 Lie thou also upon thy left side, and lay the
iniquity of the house of Is′ra-el upon it: *according*
to the number of the days that thou shalt lie
upon it thou shalt bear their iniquity.
5 For I have laid upon thee the years of their
iniquity, according to the number of the days,
three hundred and ninety days: so shalt thou
bear the iniquity of the house of Is′ra-el.
6 And when thou hast accomplished them,
lie again on thy right side, and thou shalt bear
the iniquity of the house of Ju′dah forty days: I
have appointed thee each day for a year.
7 Therefore thou shalt set thy face toward
the siege of Je-ru′sa-lem, and thine arm *shall be*
uncovered, and thou shalt prophesy against it.
8 And, behold, I will lay bands upon thee,
and thou shalt not turn thee from one side to
another, till thou hast ended the days of thy
siege.
9 ¶ Take thou also unto thee wheat, and barley,
and beans, and lentiles, and millet, and
fitches, and put them in one vessel, and make
thee bread thereof, *according* to the number of
the days that thou shalt lie upon thy side, three
hundred and ninety days shalt thou eat thereof.
10 And thy meat which thou shalt eat *shall
be* by weight, twenty shekels a day: from time
to time shalt thou eat it.
11 Thou shalt drink also water by measure,
the sixth part of an hin: from time to time shalt
thou drink.
12 And thou shalt eat it *as* barley cakes, and
thou shalt bake it with dung that cometh out of
man, in their sight.
13 And the LORD said, Even thus shall the
children of Is′ra-el eat their defiled bread
among the Gen′tiles, whither I will drive them.
14 Then said I, Ah Lord GOD! behold, my soul
hath not been polluted: for from my youth up
even till now have I not eaten of that which
dieth of itself, or is torn in pieces; neither came
there abominable flesh into my mouth.
15 Then he said unto me, Lo, I have given
thee cow's dung for man's dung, and thou shalt
prepare thy bread therewith.
16 Moreover he said unto me, Son of man,
behold, I will break the staff of bread in Je-ru′-
sa-lem: and they shall eat bread by weight, and
with care; and they shall drink water by measure,
and with astonishment:
17 That they may want bread and water, and
be astonied one with another, and consume
away for their iniquity.

5 AND thou, son of man, take thee a sharp
knife, take thee a barber's razor, and cause
it to pass upon thine head and upon thy beard:
then take thee balances to weigh, and divide the
hair.
2 Thou shalt burn with fire a third part in the
midst of the city, when the days of the siege are
fulfilled: and thou shalt take a third part, *and*
smite about it with a knife: and a third part thou
shalt scatter in the wind; and I will draw out a
sword after them.
3 Thou shalt also take thereof a few in number,
and bind them in thy skirts.
4 Then take of them again, and cast them
into the midst of the fire, and burn them in the
fire; *for* thereof shall a fire come forth into all
the house of Is′ra-el.
5 ¶ Thus saith the Lord GOD; This *is* Je-ru′salem:
I have set it in the midst of the nations and
countries *that are* round about her.
6 And she hath changed my judgments into
wickedness more than the nations, and my statutes
more than the countries that *are* round
about her: for they have refused my judgments
and my statutes, they have not walked in them.
7 Therefore thus saith the Lord GOD; Because
ye multiplied more than the nations that *are*
round about you, *and* have not walked in my
statutes, neither have kept my judgments, neither
have done according to the judgments of
the nations that *are* round about you;

8 Therefore thus saith the Lord GOD; Behold,
I, even I, *am* against thee, and will execute
judgments in the midst of thee in the sight of
the nations.
9 And I will do in thee that which I have not
done, and whereunto I will not do any more the
like, because of all thine abominations.
10 Therefore the fathers shall eat the sons in
the midst of thee, and the sons shall eat their
fathers; and I will execute judgments in thee,
and the whole remnant of thee will I scatter into
all the winds.
11 Wherefore, *as* I live, saith the Lord GOD;
Surely, because thou hast defiled my sanctuary
with all thy detestable things, and with all thine
abominations, therefore will I also diminish
thee; neither shall mine eye spare, neither will I
have any pity.
12 ¶ A third part of thee shall die with the
pestilence, and with famine shall they be consumed in the midst of thee: and a third part
shall fall by the sword round about thee; and I
will scatter a third part into all the winds, and I
will draw out a sword after them.
13 Thus shall mine anger be accomplished,
and I will cause my fury to rest upon them, and
I will be comforted: and they shall know that I
the LORD have spoken *it* in my zeal, when I
have accomplished my fury in them.
14 Moreover I will make thee waste, and a
reproach among the nations that *are* round
about thee, in the sight of all that pass by.
15 So it shall be a reproach and a taunt, an
instruction and an astonishment unto the nations that *are* round about thee, when I shall
execute judgments in thee in anger and in fury
and in furious rebukes. I the LORD have spoken
it.
16 When I shall send upon them the evil arrows of famine, which shall be for *their* destruction, *and* which I will send to destroy you: and I
will increase the famine upon you, and will
break your staff of bread:
17 So will I send upon you famine and evil
beasts, and they shall bereave thee; and pestilence and blood shall pass through thee; and I
will bring the sword upon thee. I the LORD have
spoken *it.*

6 AND the word of the LORD came unto me,
saying,
2 Son of man, set thy face toward the mountains of Is'ra-el, and prophesy against them,
3 And say, Ye mountains of Is'ra-el, hear the
word of the Lord GOD; Thus saith the Lord GOD
to the mountains, and to the hills, to the rivers,
and to the valleys; Behold, I, *even* I, will bring a
sword upon you, and I will destroy your high
places.
4 And your altars shall be desolate, and your
images shall be broken: and I will cast down
your slain *men* before your idols.
5 And I will lay the dead carcases of the children of Is'ra-el before their idols; and I will scatter your bones round about your altars.
6 In all your dwellingplaces the cities shall be
laid waste, and the high places shall be desolate; that your altars may be laid waste and
made desolate, and your idols may be broken
and cease, and your images may be cut down,
and your works may be abolished.
7 And the slain shall fall in the midst of you,
and ye shall know that I *am* the LORD.
8 ¶ Yet will I leave a remnant, that ye may
have *some* that shall escape the sword among
the nations, when ye shall be scattered through
the countries.
9 And they that escape of you shall remember me among the nations whither they shall be
carried captives, because I am broken with
their whorish heart, which hath departed from
me, and with their eyes, which go a whoring
after their idols: and they shall loathe themselves for the evils which they have committed
in all their abominations.
10 And they shall know that I *am* the LORD,
and that I have not said in vain that I would do
this evil unto them.
11 ¶ Thus saith the Lord GOD; Smite with
thine hand, and stamp with thy foot, and say,
Alas for all the evil abominations of the house
of Is'ra-el! for they shall fall by the sword, by
the famine, and by the pestilence.
12 He that is far off shall die of the pestilence; and he that is near shall fall by the sword;
and he that remaineth and is besieged shall die
by the famine: thus will I accomplish my fury
upon them.
13 Then shall ye know that I *am* the LORD,
when their slain *men* shall be among their idols
round about their altars, upon every high hill, in
all the tops of the mountains, and under every
green tree, and under every thick oak, the place
where they did offer sweet savour to all their
idols.
14 So will I stretch out my hand upon them,
and make the land desolate, yea, more desolate
than the wilderness toward Dib'lath, in all their
habitations: and they shall know that I *am* the
LORD.

7 MOREOVER the word of the LORD came
unto me, saying,
2 Also, thou son of man, thus saith the Lord
GOD unto the land of Is'ra-el; An end, the end is
come upon the four corners of the land.
3 Now *is* the end *come* upon thee, and I will
send mine anger upon thee, and will judge thee
according to thy ways, and will recompense
upon thee all thine abominations.
4 And mine eye shall not spare thee, neither
will I have pity: but I will recompense thy ways
upon thee, and thine abominations shall be in
the midst of thee: and ye shall know that I *am*
the LORD.
5 Thus saith the Lord GOD; An evil, an only
evil, behold, is come.
6 An end is come, the end is come: it watcheth for thee; behold, it is come.
7 The morning is come unto thee, O thou that
dwellest in the land: the time is come, the day
of trouble *is* near, and not the sounding again of
the mountains.
8 Now will I shortly pour out my fury upon
thee, and accomplish mine anger upon thee:
and I will judge thee according to thy ways, and
will recompense thee for all thine abominations.
9 And mine eye shall not spare, neither will I
have pity: I will recompense thee according to
thy ways and thine abominations *that* are in the
midst of thee; and ye shall know that I *am* the
LORD that smiteth.
10 Behold the day, behold, it is come: the
morning is gone forth; the rod hath blossomed,
pride hath budded.
11 Violence is risen up into a rod of wickedness: none of them *shall remain,* nor of their
multitude, nor of any of theirs: neither *shall
there be* wailing for them.
12 The time is come, the day draweth near:
let not the buyer rejoice, nor the seller mourn:
for wrath *is* upon all the multitude thereof.
13 For the seller shall not return to that

which is sold, although they were yet alive: for
the vision *is* touching the whole multitude
thereof, *which* shall not return; neither shall
any strengthen himself in the iniquity of his life.
14 They have blown the trumpet, even to
make all ready; but none goeth to the battle: for
my wrath *is* upon all the multitude thereof.
15 The sword *is* without, and the pestilence
and the famine within: he that *is* in the field
shall die with the sword; and he that *is* in the
city, famine and pestilence shall devour him.
16 ¶ But they that escape of them shall escape,
and shall be on the mountains like doves
of the valleys, all of them mourning, every one
for his iniquity.
17 All hands shall be feeble, and all knees
shall be weak *as* water.
18 They shall also gird *themselves* with sackcloth,
and horror shall cover them; and shame
shall be upon all faces, and baldness upon all
their heads.
19 They shall cast their silver in the streets,
and their gold shall be removed: their silver and
their gold shall not be able to deliver them in
the day of the wrath of the LORD: they shall not
satisfy their souls, neither fill their bowels: because
it is the stumblingblock of their iniquity.
20 ¶ As for the beauty of his ornament, he
set it in majesty: but they made the images of
their abominations *and* of their detestable
things therein: therefore have I set it far from
them.
21 And I will give it into the hands of the
strangers for a prey, and to the wicked of the
earth for a spoil; and they shall pollute it.
22 My face will I turn also from them, and
they shall pollute my secret *place:* for the robbers
shall enter into it, and defile it.
23 ¶ Make a chain: for the land is full of
bloody crimes, and the city is full of violence.
24 Wherefore I will bring the worst of the
heathen, and they shall possess their houses: I
will also make the pomp of the strong to cease;
and their holy places shall be defiled.
25 Destruction cometh; and they shall seek
peace, and *there shall be* none.
26 Mischief shall come upon mischief, and
rumour shall be upon rumour; then shall they
seek a vision of the prophet; but the law shall
perish from the priest, and counsel from the ancients.
27 The king shall mourn, and the prince shall
be clothed with desolation, and the hands of the
people of the land shall be troubled: I will do
unto them after their way, and according to
their deserts will I judge them; and they shall
know that I *am* the LORD.

8 AND it came to pass in the sixth year, in
the sixth *month,* in the fifth *day* of the
month, *as* I sat in mine house, and the elders of
Ju'dah sat before me, that the hand of the Lord
GOD fell there upon me.
2 Then I beheld, and lo a likeness as the appearance
of fire: from the appearance of his
loins even downward, fire; and from his loins
even upward, as the appearance of brightness,
as the colour of amber.
3 And he put forth the form of an hand, and
took me by a lock of mine head; and the spirit
lifted me up between the earth and the heaven,
and brought me in the visions of God to Je-ru'-sa-lem,
to the door of the inner gate that looketh
toward the north; where *was* the seat of the
image of jealousy, which provoketh to jealousy.
4 And, behold, the glory of the God of Is'ra-el
was there, according to the vision that I saw in
the plain.
5 ¶ Then said he unto me, Son of man, lift up
thine eyes now the way toward the north. So I
lifted up mine eyes the way toward the north,
and behold northward at the gate of the altar
this image of jealousy in the entry.
6 He said furthermore unto me, Son of man,
seest thou what they do? *even* the great abominations
that the house of Is'ra-el committeth
here, that I should go far off from my sanctuary?
but turn thee yet again, *and* thou shalt see
greater abominations.
7 ¶ And he brought me to the door of the
court; and when I looked, behold a hole in the
wall.
8 Then said he unto me, Son of man, dig now
in the wall: and when I had digged in the wall,
behold a door.
9 And he said unto me, Go in, and behold the
wicked abominations that they do here.
10 So I went in and saw; and behold every
form of creeping things, and abominable
beasts, and all the idols of the house of Is'ra-el,
pourtrayed upon the wall round about.
11 And there stood before them seventy men
of the ancients of the house of Is'ra-el, and in
the midst of them stood Ja-az-a-ni'ah the son of
Sha'phan, with every man his censer in his
hand; and a thick cloud of incense went up.
12 Then said he unto me, Son of man, hast
thou seen what the ancients of the house of Is'-ra-el
do in the dark, every man in the chambers
of his imagery? for they say, The LORD seeth us
not; the LORD hath forsaken the earth.
13 ¶ He said also unto me, Turn thee yet
again, *and* thou shalt see greater abominations
that they do.
14 Then he brought me to the door of the
gate of the LORD's house which *was* toward the
north; and, behold, there sat women weeping
for Tam'muz.
15 ¶ Then said he unto me, Hast thou seen
this, O son of man? turn thee yet again, *and*
thou shalt see greater abominations than these.
16 And he brought me into the inner court of
the LORD's house, and behold, at the door of the
temple of the LORD, between the porch and the
altar, *were* about five and twenty men, with
their backs toward the temple of the LORD, and
their faces toward the east; and they worshipped
the sun toward the east.
17 ¶ Then he said unto me, Hast thou seen
this, O son of man? Is it a light thing to the
house of Ju'dah that they commit the abominations
which they commit here? for they have
filled the land with violence, and have returned
to provoke me to anger: and, lo, they put the
branch to their nose.
18 Therefore will I also deal in fury: mine eye
shall not spare, neither will I have pity: and
though they cry in mine ears with a loud voice,
yet will I not hear them.

9 HE cried also in mine ears with a loud
voice, saying, Cause them that have
charge over the city to draw near, even every
man *with* his destroying weapon in his hand.
2 And, behold, six men came from the way of
the higher gate, which lieth toward the north,
and every man a slaughter weapon in his hand;
and one man among them *was* clothed with linen,
with a writer's inkhorn by his side: and they
went in, and stood beside the brasen altar.
3 And the glory of the God of Is'ra-el was
gone up from the cherub, whereupon he was, to
the threshold of the house. And he called to the

man clothed with linen, which *had* the writer's
inkhorn by his side;
4 And the LORD said unto him, Go through
the midst of the city, through the midst of Je-
ru'sa-lem, and set a mark upon the foreheads of
the men that sigh and that cry for all the abominations that be done in the midst thereof.
5 ¶ And to the others he said in mine hearing, Go ye after him through the city, and smite:
let not your eye spare, neither have ye pity:
6 Slay utterly old *and* young, both maids,
and little children, and women: but come not
near any man upon whom *is* the mark; and begin at my sanctuary. Then they began at the
ancient men which *were* before the house.
7 And he said unto them, Defile the house,
and fill the courts with the slain: go ye forth.
And they went forth, and slew in the city.
8 ¶ And it came to pass, while they were
slaying them, and I was left, that I fell upon my
face, and cried, and said, Ah Lord GOD! wilt
thou destroy all the residue of Is'ra-el in thy
pouring out of thy fury upon Je-ru'sa-lem?
9 Then said he unto me, The iniquity of the
house of Is'ra-el and Ju'dah *is* exceeding great,
and the land is full of blood, and the city full of
perverseness: for they say, The LORD hath forsaken the earth, and the LORD seeth not.
10 And as for me also, mine eye shall not
spare, neither will I have pity, *but* I will recompense their way upon their head.
11 And, behold, the man clothed with linen,
which *had* the inkhorn by his side, reported the
matter, saying, I have done as thou hast commanded me.

10 THEN I looked, and, behold, in the firmament that was above the head of the
cherubims there appeared over them as it were
a sapphire stone, as the appearance of the likeness of a throne.
2 And he spake unto the man clothed with
linen, and said, Go in between the wheels, *even*
under the cherub, and fill thine hand with coals
of fire from between the cherubims, and scatter
them over the city. And he went in in my sight.
3 Now the cherubims stood on the right side
of the house, when the man went in; and the
cloud filled the inner court.
4 Then the glory of the LORD went up from
the cherub, *and stood* over the threshold of the
house; and the house was filled with the cloud,
and the court was full of the brightness of the
LORD's glory.
5 And the sound of the cherubims' wings
was heard *even* to the outer court, as the voice
of the Almighty God when he speaketh.
6 And it came to pass, *that* when he had
commanded the man clothed with linen, saying,
Take fire from between the wheels, from between the cherubims; then he went in, and
stood beside the wheels.
7 And *one* cherub stretched forth his hand
from between the cherubims unto the fire that
was between the cherubims, and took *thereof,*
and put *it* into the hands of *him that was*
clothed with linen: who took *it,* and went out.
8 ¶ And there appeared in the cherubims the
form of a man's hand under their wings.
9 And when I looked, behold the four wheels
by the cherubims, one wheel by one cherub,
and another wheel by another cherub: and the
appearance of the wheels *was* as the colour of a
beryl stone.
10 And *as for* their appearances, they four
had one likeness, as if a wheel had been in the
midst of a wheel.
11 When they went, they went upon their
four sides; they turned not as they went, but to
the place whither the head looked they followed
it; they turned not as they went.
12 And their whole body, and their backs,
and their hands, and their wings, and the
wheels, *were* full of eyes round about, *even* the
wheels that they four had.
13 As for the wheels, it was cried unto them
in my hearing, O wheel.
14 And every one had four faces: the first
face *was* the face of a cherub, and the second
face *was* the face of a man, and the third the
face of a lion, and the fourth the face of an
eagle.
15 And the cherubims were lifted up. This *is*
the living creature that I saw by the river of
Che'bar.
16 And when the cherubims went, the
wheels went by them: and when the cherubims
lifted up their wings to mount up from the
earth, the same wheels also turned not from beside them.
17 When they stood, *these* stood; and when
they were lifted up, *these* lifted up themselves
also: for the spirit of the living creature *was* in
them.
18 Then the glory of the LORD departed from
off the threshold of the house, and stood over
the cherubims.
19 And the cherubims lifted up their wings,
and mounted up from the earth in my sight:
when they went out, the wheels also *were* beside them, and *every one* stood at the door of
the east gate of the LORD's house; and the glory
of the God of Is'ra-el *was* over them above.
20 This *is* the living creature that I saw under
the God of Is'ra-el by the river of Che'bar; and I
knew that they *were* the cherubims.
21 Every one had four faces apiece, and every one four wings; and the likeness of the
hands of a man *was* under their wings.
22 And the likeness of their faces *was* the
same faces which I saw by the river of Che'bar,
their appearances and themselves: they went
every one straight forward.

11 MOREOVER the spirit lifted me up, and
brought me unto the east gate of the
LORD's house, which looketh eastward: and behold at the door of the gate five and twenty
men; among whom I saw Ja-az-a-ni'ah the son
of A'zur, and Pel-a-ti'ah the son of Be-na'iah,
princes of the people.
2 Then said he unto me, Son of man, these
are the men that devise mischief, and give
wicked counsel in this city:
3 Which say, *It is* not near; let us build
houses: this *city is* the caldron, and we *be* the
flesh.
4 ¶ Therefore prophesy against them, prophesy, O son of man.
5 And the Spirit of the LORD fell upon me,
and said unto me, Speak; Thus saith the LORD;
Thus have ye said, O house of Is'ra-el: for I
know the things that come into your mind, *every one of* them.
6 Ye have multiplied your slain in this city,
and ye have filled the streets thereof with the
slain.
7 Therefore thus saith the Lord GOD; Your
slain whom ye have laid in the midst of it, they
are the flesh, and this *city is* the caldron: but I
will bring you forth out of the midst of it.
8 Ye have feared the sword; and I will bring a
sword upon you, saith the Lord GOD.
9 And I will bring you out of the midst

thereof, and deliver you into the hands of strangers, and will execute judgments among you.

10 Ye shall fall by the sword; I will judge you in the border of Is′ra-el; and ye shall know that I *am* the LORD.

11 This *city* shall not be your caldron, neither shall ye be the flesh in the midst thereof; *but* I will judge you in the border of Is′ra-el:

12 And ye shall know that I *am* the LORD: for ye have not walked in my statutes, neither executed my judgments, but have done after the manners of the heathen that *are* round about you.

13 ¶ And it came to pass, when I prophesied, that Pel-a-ti′ah the son of Be-na′iah died. Then fell I down upon my face, and cried with a loud voice, and said, Ah Lord GOD! wilt thou make a full end of the remnant of Is′ra-el?

14 Again the word of the LORD came unto me, saying,

15 Son of man, thy brethren, *even* thy brethren, the men of thy kindred, and all the house of Is′ra-el wholly, *are* they unto whom the inhabitants of Je-ru′sa-lem have said, Get you far from the LORD: unto us is this land given in possession.

16 Therefore say, Thus saith the Lord GOD; Although I have cast them far off among the heathen, and although I have scattered them among the countries, yet will I be to them as a little sanctuary in the countries where they shall come.

17 Therefore say, Thus saith the Lord GOD; I will even gather you from the people, and assemble you out of the countries where ye have been scattered, and I will give you the land of Is′ra-el.

18 And they shall come thither, and they shall take away all the detestable things thereof and all the abominations thereof from thence.

19 And I will give them one heart, and I will put a new spirit within you; and I will take the stony heart out of their flesh, and will give them an heart of flesh:

20 That they may walk in my statutes, and keep mine ordinances, and do them: and they shall be my people, and I will be their God.

21 But *as for them* whose heart walketh after the heart of their detestable things and their abominations, I will recompense their way upon their own heads, saith the Lord GOD.

22 ¶ Then did the cherubims lift up their wings, and the wheels beside them; and the glory of the God of Is′ra-el *was* over them above.

23 And the glory of the LORD went up from the midst of the city, and stood upon the mountain which *is* on the east side of the city.

24 ¶ Afterwards the spirit took me up, and brought me in a vision by the Spirit of God into Chal-de′a, to them of the captivity. So the vision that I had seen went up from me.

25 Then I spake unto them of the captivity all the things that the LORD had shewed me.

12

THE word of the LORD also came unto me, saying,

2 Son of man, thou dwellest in the midst of a rebellious house, which have eyes to see, and see not; they have ears to hear, and hear not: for they *are* a rebellious house.

3 Therefore, thou son of man, prepare thee stuff for removing, and remove by day in their sight; and thou shalt remove from thy place to another place in their sight: it may be they will consider, though they *be* a rebellious house.

4 Then shalt thou bring forth thy stuff by day in their sight, as stuff for removing: and thou shalt go forth at even in their sight, as they that go forth into captivity.

5 Dig thou through the wall in their sight, and carry out thereby.

6 In their sight shalt thou bear *it* upon *thy* shoulders, *and* carry *it* forth in the twilight: thou shalt cover thy face, that thou see not the ground: for I have set thee *for* a sign unto the house of Is′ra-el.

7 And I did so as I was commanded: I brought forth my stuff by day, as stuff for captivity, and in the even I digged through the wall with mine hand; I brought *it* forth in the twilight, *and* I bare *it* upon *my* shoulder in their sight.

8 ¶ And in the morning came the word of the LORD unto me, saying,

9 Son of man, hath not the house of Is′ra-el, the rebellious house, said unto thee, What doest thou?

10 Say thou unto them, Thus saith the Lord GOD; This burden *concerneth* the prince in Je-ru′sa-lem, and all the house of Is′ra-el that *are* among them.

11 Say, I *am* your sign: like as I have done, so shall it be done unto them: they shall remove *and* go into captivity.

12 And the prince that *is* among them shall bear upon *his* shoulder in the twilight, and shall go forth: they shall dig through the wall to carry out thereby: he shall cover his face, that he see not the ground with *his* eyes.

13 My net also will I spread upon him, and he shall be taken in my snare: and I will bring him to Bab′y-lon *to* the land of the Chal-de′ans; yet shall he not see it, though he shall die there.

14 And I will scatter toward every wind all that *are* about him to help him, and all his bands; and I will draw out the sword after them.

15 And they shall know that I *am* the LORD, when I shall scatter them among the nations, and disperse them in the countries.

16 But I will leave a few men of them from the sword, from the famine, and from the pestilence; that they may declare all their abominations among the heathen whither they come; and they shall know that I *am* the LORD.

17 ¶ Moreover the word of the LORD came to me, saying,

18 Son of man, eat thy bread with quaking, and drink thy water with trembling and with carefulness;

19 And say unto the people of the land, Thus saith the Lord GOD of the inhabitants of Je-ru′sa-lem, *and* of the land of Is′ra-el; They shall eat their bread with carefulness, and drink their water with astonishment, that her land may be desolate from all that is therein, because of the violence of all them that dwell therein.

20 And the cities that are inhabited shall be laid waste, and the land shall be desolate; and ye shall know that I *am* the LORD.

21 ¶ And the word of the LORD came unto me, saying,

22 Son of man, what *is* that proverb *that* ye have in the land of Is′ra-el, saying, The days are prolonged, and every vision faileth?

23 Tell them therefore, Thus saith the Lord GOD; I will make this proverb to cease, and they shall no more use it as a proverb in Is′ra-el; but say unto them, The days are at hand, and the effect of every vision.

24 For there shall be no more any vain vision nor flattering divination within the house of Is′ra-el.

25 For I *am* the LORD: I will speak, and the
word that I shall speak shall come to pass; it
shall be no more prolonged: for in your days, O
rebellious house, will I say the word, and will
perform it, saith the Lord GOD.
26 ¶ Again the word of the LORD came to
me, saying,
27 Son of man, behold, *they of* the house of
Is'ra-el say, The vision that he seeth *is* for many
days *to come,* and he prophesieth of the times
that are far off.
28 Therefore say unto them, Thus saith the
Lord GOD; There shall none of my words be prolonged any more, but the word which I have
spoken shall be done, saith the Lord GOD.

13 AND the word of the LORD came unto
me, saying,
2 Son of man, prophesy against the prophets
of Is'ra-el that prophesy, and say thou unto
them that prophesy out of their own hearts,
Hear ye the word of the LORD:
3 Thus saith the Lord GOD; Woe unto the
foolish prophets, that follow their own spirit,
and have seen nothing!
4 O Is'ra-el, thy prophets are like the foxes in
the deserts.
5 Ye have not gone up into the gaps, neither
made up the hedge for the house of Is'ra-el to
stand in the battle in the day of the LORD.
6 They have seen vanity and lying divination,
saying, The LORD saith: and the LORD hath not
sent them: and they have made *others* to hope
that they would confirm the word.
7 Have ye not seen a vain vision, and have ye
not spoken a lying divination, whereas ye say,
The LORD saith *it;* albeit I have not spoken?
8 Therefore thus saith the Lord GOD; Because
ye have spoken vanity, and seen lies, therefore,
behold, I *am* against you, saith the Lord GOD.
9 And mine hand shall be upon the prophets
that see vanity, and that divine lies: they shall
not be in the assembly of my people, neither
shall they be written in the writing of the house
of Is'ra-el, neither shall they enter into the land
of Is'ra-el; and ye shall know that I *am* the Lord
GOD.
10 ¶ Because, even because they have seduced my people, saying, Peace; and *there was*
no peace; and one built up a wall, and, lo, others
daubed it with untempered *morter:*
11 Say unto them which daub *it* with untempered *morter,* that it shall fall: there shall be an
overflowing shower; and ye, O great hailstones,
shall fall; and a stormy wind shall rend *it.*
12 Lo, when the wall is fallen, shall it not be
said unto you, Where *is* the daubing wherewith
ye have daubed *it?*
13 Therefore thus saith the Lord GOD; I will
even rend *it* with a stormy wind in my fury; and
there shall be an overflowing shower in mine
anger, and great hailstones in *my* fury to consume *it.*
14 So will I break down the wall that ye have
daubed with untempered *morter,* and bring it
down to the ground, so that the foundation
thereof shall be discovered, and it shall fall, and
ye shall be consumed in the midst thereof: and
ye shall know that I *am* the LORD.
15 Thus will I accomplish my wrath upon the
wall, and upon them that have daubed it with
untempered *morter,* and will say unto you, The
wall *is* no *more,* neither they that daubed it;
16 *To wit,* the prophets of Is'ra-el which
prophesy concerning Je-ru'sa-lem, and which
see visions of peace for her, and *there is* no
peace, saith the Lord GOD.
17 ¶ Likewise, thou son of man, set thy face
against the daughters of thy people, which
prophesy out of their own heart; and prophesy
thou against them,
18 And say, Thus saith the Lord GOD; Woe to
the *women* that sew pillows to all armholes,
and make kerchiefs upon the head of every stature to hunt souls! Will ye hunt the souls of my
people, and will ye save the souls alive *that*
come unto you?
19 And will ye pollute me among my people
for handfuls of barley and for pieces of bread,
to slay the souls that should not die, and to save
the souls alive that should not live, by your
lying to my people that hear *your* lies?
20 Wherefore thus saith the Lord GOD; Behold, I *am* against your pillows, wherewith ye
there hunt the souls to make *them* fly, and I will
tear them from your arms, and will let the souls
go, *even* the souls that ye hunt to make *them*
fly.
21 Your kerchiefs also will I tear, and deliver
my people out of your hand, and they shall be
no more in your hand to be hunted; and ye shall
know that I *am* the LORD.
22 Because with lies ye have made the heart
of the righteous sad, whom I have not made
sad; and strengthened the hands of the wicked,
that he should not return from his wicked way,
by promising him life:
23 Therefore ye shall see no more vanity, nor
divine divinations: for I will deliver my people
out of your hand: and ye shall know that I *am*
the LORD.

14 THEN came certain of the elders of Is'-
ra-el unto me, and sat before me.
2 And the word of the LORD came unto me,
saying,
3 Son of man, these men have set up their
idols in their heart, and put the stumblingblock
of their iniquity before their face: should I be
enquired of at all by them?
4 Therefore speak unto them, and say unto
them, Thus saith the Lord GOD; Every man of
the house of Is'ra-el that setteth up his idols in
his heart, and putteth the stumblingblock of his
iniquity before his face, and cometh to the
prophet; I the LORD will answer him that cometh according to the multitude of his idols;
5 That I may take the house of Is'ra-el in
their own heart, because they are all estranged
from me through their idols.
6 ¶ Therefore say unto the house of Is'ra-el,
Thus saith the Lord GOD; Repent, and turn
yourselves from your idols; and turn away your
faces from all your abominations.
7 For every one of the house of Is'ra-el, or of
the stranger that sojourneth in Is'ra-el, which
separateth himself from me, and setteth up his
idols in his heart, and putteth the stumblingblock of his iniquity before his face, and cometh
to a prophet to enquire of him concerning me; I
the LORD will answer him by myself:
8 And I will set my face against that man,
and will make him a sign and a proverb, and I
will cut him off from the midst of my people;
and ye shall know that I *am* the LORD.
9 And if the prophet be deceived when he
hath spoken a thing, I the LORD have deceived
that prophet, and I will stretch out my hand
upon him, and will destroy him from the midst
of my people Is'ra-el.
10 And they shall bear the punishment of
their iniquity: the punishment of the prophet
shall be even as the punishment of him that
seeketh *unto him;*

11 That the house of Is'ra-el may go no more astray from me, neither be polluted any more with all their transgressions; but that they may be my people, and I may be their God, saith the Lord GOD.

12 ¶ The word of the LORD came again to me, saying,

13 Son of man, when the land sinneth against me by trespassing grievously, then will I stretch out mine hand upon it, and will break the staff of the bread thereof, and will send famine upon it, and will cut off man and beast from it:

14 Though these three men, No'ah, Dan'iel, and Job, were in it, they should deliver *but* their own souls by their righteousness, saith the Lord GOD.

15 ¶ If I cause noisome beasts to pass through the land, and they spoil it, so that it be desolate, that no man may pass through because of the beasts:

16 *Though* these three men *were* in it, *as* I live, saith the Lord GOD, they shall deliver neither sons nor daughters; they only shall be delivered, but the land shall be desolate.

17 ¶ Or *if* I bring a sword upon that land, and say, Sword, go through the land; so that I cut off man and beast from it:

18 Though these three men *were* in it, *as* I live, saith the Lord GOD, they shall deliver neither sons nor daughters, but they only shall be delivered themselves.

19 ¶ Or *if* I send a pestilence into that land, and pour out my fury upon it in blood, to cut off from it man and beast:

20 Though No'ah, Dan'iel, and Job, *were* in it, *as* I live, saith the Lord GOD, they shall deliver neither son nor daughter; they shall *but* deliver their own souls by their righteousness.

21 For thus saith the Lord GOD; How much more when I send my four sore judgments upon Je-ru'sa-lem, the sword, and the famine, and the noisome beast, and the pestilence, to cut off from it man and beast?

22 ¶ Yet, behold, therein shall be left a remnant that shall be brought forth, *both* sons and daughters: behold, they shall come forth unto you, and ye shall see their way and their doings: and ye shall be comforted concerning the evil that I have brought upon Je-ru'sa-lem, *even* concerning all that I have brought upon it.

23 And they shall comfort you, when ye see their ways and their doings: and ye shall know that I have not done without cause all that I have done in it, saith the Lord GOD.

15 AND the word of the LORD came unto me, saying,

2 Son of man, What is the vine tree more than any tree, *or than* a branch which is among the trees of the forest?

3 Shall wood be taken thereof to do any work? or will *men* take a pin of it to hang any vessel thereon?

4 Behold, it is cast into the fire for fuel; the fire devoureth both the ends of it, and the midst of it is burned. Is it meet for *any* work?

5 Behold, when it was whole, it was meet for no work: how much less shall it be meet yet for *any* work, when the fire hath devoured it, and it is burned?

6 ¶ Therefore thus saith the Lord GOD; As the vine tree among the trees of the forest, which I have given to the fire for fuel, so will I give the inhabitants of Je-ru'sa-lem.

7 And I will set my face against them; they shall go out from *one* fire, and *another* fire shall devour them; and ye shall know that I *am* the LORD, when I set my face against them.

8 And I will make the land desolate, because they have committed a trespass, saith the Lord GOD.

16 AGAIN the word of the LORD came unto me, saying,

2 Son of man, cause Je-ru'sa-lem to know her abominations,

3 And say, Thus saith the Lord GOD unto Je-ru'sa-lem; Thy birth and thy nativity *is* of the land of Ca'naan; thy father *was* an Am'or-ite, and thy mother an Hit'tite.

4 And *as for* thy nativity, in the day thou wast born thy navel was not cut, neither wast thou washed in water to supple *thee;* thou wast not salted at all, nor swaddled at all.

5 None eye pitied thee, to do any of these unto thee, to have compassion upon thee; but thou wast cast out in the open field, to the loathing of thy person, in the day that thou wast born.

6 ¶ And when I passed by thee, and saw thee polluted in thine own blood, I said unto thee *when thou wast* in thy blood, Live; yea, I said unto thee *when thou wast* in thy blood, Live.

7 I have caused thee to multiply as the bud of the field, and thou hast increased and waxen great, and thou art come to excellent ornaments: *thy* breasts are fashioned, and thine hair is grown, whereas thou *wast* naked and bare.

8 Now when I passed by thee, and looked upon thee, behold, thy time *was* the time of love; and I spread my skirt over thee, and covered thy nakedness: yea, I sware unto thee, and entered into a covenant with thee, saith the Lord GOD, and thou becamest mine.

9 Then washed I thee with water; yea, I throughly washed away thy blood from thee, and I anointed thee with oil.

10 I clothed thee also with broidered work, and shod thee with badgers' skin, and I girded thee about with fine linen, and I covered thee with silk.

11 I decked thee also with ornaments, and I put bracelets upon thy hands, and a chain on thy neck.

12 And I put a jewel on thy forehead, and earrings in thine ears, and a beautiful crown upon thine head.

13 Thus wast thou decked with gold and silver; and thy raiment *was of* fine linen, and silk, and broidered work; thou didst eat fine flour, and honey, and oil: and thou wast exceeding beautiful, and thou didst prosper into a kingdom.

14 And thy renown went forth among the heathen for thy beauty: for it *was* perfect through my comeliness, which I had put upon thee, saith the Lord GOD.

15 ¶ But thou didst trust in thine own beauty, and playedst the harlot because of thy renown, and pouredst out thy fornications on every one that passed by; his it was.

16 And of thy garments thou didst take, and deckedst thy high places with divers colours, and playedst the harlot thereupon: *the like things* shall not come, neither shall it be so.

17 Thou hast also taken thy fair jewels of my gold and of my silver, which I had given thee, and madest to thyself images of men, and didst commit whoredom with them,

18 And tookest thy broidered garments, and coveredst them: and thou hast set mine oil and mine incense before them.

19 My meat also which I gave thee, fine flour,

and oil, and honey, *wherewith* I fed thee, thou
hast even set it before them for a sweet savour:
and *thus* it was, saith the Lord GOD.
20 Moreover thou hast taken thy sons and
thy daughters, whom thou hast borne unto me,
and these hast thou sacrificed unto them to be
devoured. *Is this* of thy whoredoms a small
matter,
21 That thou hast slain my children, and delivered them to cause them to pass through *the*
fire for them?
22 And in all thine abominations and thy
whoredoms thou hast not remembered the days
of thy youth, when thou wast naked and bare,
and wast polluted in thy blood.
23 And it came to pass after all thy wickedness, (woe, woe unto thee! saith the Lord GOD;)
24 *That* thou hast also built unto thee an eminent place, and hast made thee an high place in
every street.
25 Thou hast built thy high place at every
head of the way, and hast made thy beauty to
be abhorred, and hast opened thy feet to every
one that passed by, and multiplied thy whoredoms.
26 Thou hast also committed fornication
with the E-gyp'tians thy neighbours, great of
flesh; and hast increased thy whoredoms, to
provoke me to anger.
27 Behold, therefore I have stretched out my
hand over thee, and have diminished thine ordi-
nary *food*, and delivered thee unto the will of
them that hate thee, the daughters of the Phi-
lis'tines, which are ashamed of thy lewd way.
28 Thou hast played the whore also with the
As-syr'i-ans, because thou wast unsatiable; yea,
thou hast played the harlot with them, and yet
couldest not be satisfied.
29 Thou hast moreover multiplied thy fornication in the land of Ca'naan unto Chal-de'a;
and yet thou wast not satisfied herewith.
30 How weak is thine heart, saith the Lord
GOD, seeing thou doest all these *things*, the
work of an imperious whorish woman;
31 In that thou buildest thine eminent place
in the head of every way, and makest thine high
place in every street; and hast not been as an
harlot, in that thou scornest hire;
32 *But as* a wife that committeth adultery,
which taketh strangers instead of her husband!
33 They give gifts to all whores: but thou givest thy gifts to all thy lovers, and hirest them,
that they may come unto thee on every side for
thy whoredom.
34 And the contrary is in thee from *other*
women in thy whoredoms, whereas none followeth thee to commit whoredoms: and in that
thou givest a reward, and no reward is given
unto thee, therefore thou art contrary.
35 ¶ Wherefore, O harlot, hear the word of
the LORD:
36 Thus saith the Lord GOD; Because thy
filthiness was poured out, and thy nakedness
discovered through thy whoredoms with thy
lovers, and with all the idols of thy abominations, and by the blood of thy children, which
thou didst give unto them;
37 Behold, therefore I will gather all thy lovers, with whom thou hast taken pleasure, and
all *them* that thou hast loved, with all *them* that
thou hast hated; I will even gather them round
about against thee, and will discover thy nakedness unto them, that they may see all thy nakedness.
38 And I will judge thee, as women that
break wedlock and shed blood are judged; and I
will give thee blood in fury and jealousy.
39 And I will also give thee into their hand,
and they shall throw down thine eminent place,
and shall break down thy high places; they shall
strip thee also of thy clothes, and shall take thy
fair jewels, and leave thee naked and bare.
40 They shall also bring up a company
against thee, and they shall stone thee with
stones, and thrust thee through with their
swords.
41 And they shall burn thine houses with fire,
and execute judgments upon thee in the sight of
many women: and I will cause thee to cease
from playing the harlot, and thou also shalt give
no hire any more.
42 So will I make my fury toward thee to
rest, and my jealousy shall depart from thee,
and I will be quiet, and will be no more angry.
43 Because thou hast not remembered the
days of thy youth, but hast fretted me in all
these *things;* behold, therefore I also will recompense thy way upon *thine* head, saith the
Lord GOD: and thou shalt not commit this lewdness above all thine abominations.
44 ¶ Behold, every one that useth proverbs
shall use *this* proverb against thee, saying, As *is*
the mother, *so is* her daughter.
45 Thou *art* thy mother's daughter, that
loatheth her husband and her children; and
thou *art* the sister of thy sisters, which loathed
their husbands and their children: your mother
was an Hit'tite, and your father an Am'or-ite.
46 And thine elder sister *is* Sa-ma'ri-a, she
and her daughters that dwell at thy left hand:
and thy younger sister, that dwelleth at thy
right hand, *is* Sod'om and her daughters.
47 Yet hast thou not walked after their ways,
nor done after their abominations: but, as *if*
that were a very little *thing*, thou wast corrupted more than they in all thy ways.
48 *As* I live, saith the Lord GOD, Sod'om thy
sister hath not done, she nor her daughters, as
thou hast done, thou and thy daughters.
49 Behold, this was the iniquity of thy sister
Sod'om, pride, fulness of bread, and abundance
of idleness was in her and in her daughters, neither did she strengthen the hand of the poor
and needy.
50 And they were haughty, and committed
abomination before me: therefore I took them
away as I saw *good*.
51 Neither hath Sa-ma'ri-a committed half of
thy sins; but thou hast multiplied thine abominations more than they, and hast justified thy
sisters in all thine abominations which thou
hast done.
52 Thou also, which hast judged thy sisters,
bear thine own shame for thy sins that thou
hast committed more abominable than they:
they are more righteous than thou: yea, be thou
confounded also, and bear thy shame, in that
thou hast justified thy sisters.
53 When I shall bring again their captivity,
the captivity of Sod'om and her daughters, and
the captivity of Sa-ma'ri-a and her daughters,
then *will I bring again* the captivity of thy captives in the midst of them:
54 That thou mayest bear thine own shame,
and mayest be confounded in all that thou hast
done, in that thou art a comfort unto them.
55 When thy sisters, Sod'om and her daughters, shall return to their former estate, and Sa-
ma'ri-a and her daughters shall return to their
former estate, then thou and thy daughters
shall return to your former estate.
56 For thy sister Sod'om was not mentioned
by thy mouth in the day of thy pride,
57 Before thy wickedness was discovered, as

at the time of *thy* reproach of the daughters of
Syr'i-a, and all *that are* round about her, the
daughters of the Phi-lis'tines, which despise
thee round about.
58 Thou hast borne thy lewdness and thine
abominations, saith the LORD.
59 For thus saith the Lord GOD; I will even
deal with thee as thou hast done, which hast
despised the oath in breaking the covenant.
60 ¶ Nevertheless I will remember my covenant with thee in the days of thy youth, and I
will establish unto thee an everlasting covenant.
61 Then thou shalt remember thy ways, and
be ashamed, when thou shalt receive thy sisters, thine elder and thy younger: and I will give
them unto thee for daughters, but not by thy
covenant.
62 And I will establish my covenant with
thee; and thou shalt know that I *am* the LORD:
63 That thou mayest remember, and be confounded, and never open thy mouth any more
because of thy shame, when I am pacified
toward thee for all that thou hast done, saith
the Lord GOD.

17 AND the word of the LORD came unto
me, saying,
2 Son of man, put forth a riddle, and speak a
parable unto the house of Is'ra-el;
3 And say, Thus saith the Lord GOD; A great
eagle with great wings, longwinged, full of
feathers, which had divers colours, came unto
Leb'a-non, and took the highest branch of the
cedar:
4 He cropped off the top of his young twigs,
and carried it into a land of traffick; he set it in a
city of merchants.
5 He took also of the seed of the land, and
planted it in a fruitful field; he placed *it* by great
waters, *and* set it *as* a willow tree.
6 And it grew, and became a spreading vine
of low stature, whose branches turned toward
him, and the roots thereof were under him: so it
became a vine, and brought forth branches, and
shot forth sprigs.
7 There was also another great eagle with
great wings and many feathers: and, behold,
this vine did bend her roots toward him, and
shot forth her branches toward him, that he
might water it by the furrows of her plantation.
8 It was planted in a good soil by great waters, that it might bring forth branches, and that
it might bear fruit, that it might be a goodly
vine.
9 Say thou, Thus saith the Lord GOD; Shall it
prosper? shall he not pull up the roots thereof,
and cut off the fruit thereof, that it wither? it
shall wither in all the leaves of her spring, even
without great power or many people to pluck it
up by the roots thereof.
10 Yea, behold, *being* planted, shall it prosper? shall it not utterly wither, when the east
wind toucheth it? it shall wither in the furrows
where it grew.
11 ¶ Moreover the word of the LORD came
unto me, saying,
12 Say now to the rebellious house, Know ye
not what these *things mean?* tell *them,* Behold,
the king of Bab'y-lon is come to Je-ru'sa-lem,
and hath taken the king thereof, and the princes
thereof, and led them with him to Bab'y-lon;
13 And hath taken of the king's seed, and
made a covenant with him, and hath taken an
oath of him: he hath also taken the mighty of
the land:
14 That the kingdom might be base, that it
might not lift itself up, *but* that by keeping of
his covenant it might stand.
15 But he rebelled against him in sending his
ambassadors into E'gypt, that they might give
him horses and much people. Shall he prosper?
shall he escape that doeth such *things?* or shall
he break the covenant, and be delivered?
16 *As* I live, saith the Lord GOD, surely in the
place *where* the king *dwelleth* that made him
king, whose oath he despised, and whose covenant he brake, *even* with him in the midst of
Bab'y-lon he shall die.
17 Neither shall Pha'raoh with *his* mighty
army and great company make for him in the
war, by casting up mounts, and building forts,
to cut off many persons:
18 Seeing he despised the oath by breaking
the covenant, when, lo, he had given his hand,
and hath done all these *things,* he shall not escape.
19 Therefore thus saith the Lord GOD; *As* I
live, surely mine oath that he hath despised,
and my covenant that he hath broken, even it
will I recompense upon his own head.
20 And I will spread my net upon him, and he
shall be taken in my snare, and I will bring him
to Bab'y-lon, and will plead with him there for
his trespass that he hath trespassed against me.
21 And all his fugitives with all his bands
shall fall by the sword, and they that remain
shall be scattered toward all winds: and ye shall
know that I the LORD have spoken *it.*
22 ¶ Thus saith the Lord GOD; I will also take
of the highest branch of the high cedar, and will
set *it:* I will crop off from the top of his young
twigs a tender one, and will plant *it* upon an
high mountain and eminent:
23 In the mountain of the height of Is'ra-el
will I plant it; and it shall bring forth boughs,
and bear fruit, and be a goodly cedar: and under
it shall dwell all fowl of every wing; in the
shadow of the branches thereof shall they
dwell.
24 And all the trees of the field shall know
that I the LORD have brought down the high
tree, have exalted the low tree, have dried up
the green tree, and have made the dry tree to
flourish: I the LORD have spoken and have done
it.

18 THE word of the LORD came unto me
again, saying,
2 What mean ye, that ye use this proverb
concerning the land of Is'ra-el, saying, The fathers have eaten sour grapes, and the children's
teeth are set on edge?
3 *As* I live, saith the Lord GOD, ye shall not
have *occasion* any more to use this proverb in
Is'ra-el.
4 Behold, all souls are mine; as the soul of the
father, so also the soul of the son is mine: the
soul that sinneth, it shall die.
5 ¶ But if a man be just, and do that which is
lawful and right,
6 *And* hath not eaten upon the mountains,
neither hath lifted up his eyes to the idols of the
house of Is'ra-el, neither hath defiled his neighbour's wife, neither hath come near to a menstruous woman,
7 And hath not oppressed any, *but* hath restored to the debtor his pledge, hath spoiled
none by violence, hath given his bread to the
hungry, and hath covered the naked with a garment;
8 He *that* hath not given forth upon usury,
neither hath taken any increase, *that* hath with-

drawn his hand from iniquity, hath executed true judgment between man and man,

9 Hath walked in my statutes, and hath kept my judgments, to deal truly; he *is* just, he shall surely live, saith the Lord GOD.

10 ¶ If he beget a son *that is* a robber, a shedder of blood, and *that* doeth the like to *any* one of these *things*,

11 And that doeth not any of those *duties*, but even hath eaten upon the mountains, and defiled his neighbour's wife,

12 Hath oppressed the poor and needy, hath spoiled by violence, hath not restored the pledge, and hath lifted up his eyes to the idols, hath committed abomination,

13 Hath given forth upon usury, and hath taken increase: shall he then live? he shall not live: he hath done all these abominations; he shall surely die; his blood shall be upon him.

14 ¶ Now, lo, *if* he beget a son, that seeth all his father's sins which he hath done, and considereth, and doeth not such like,

15 *That* hath not eaten upon the mountains, neither hath lifted up his eyes to the idols of the house of Is'ra-el, hath not defiled his neighbour's wife,

16 Neither hath oppressed any, hath not withholden the pledge, neither hath spoiled by violence, *but* hath given his bread to the hungry, and hath covered the naked with a garment,

17 *That* hath taken off his hand from the poor, *that* hath not received usury nor increase, hath executed my judgments, hath walked in my statutes; he shall not die for the iniquity of his father, he shall surely live.

18 *As for* his father, because he cruelly oppressed, spoiled his brother by violence, and did *that* which *is* not good among his people, lo, even he shall die in his iniquity.

19 ¶ Yet say ye, Why? doth not the son bear the iniquity of the father? When the son hath done that which is lawful and right, *and* hath kept all my statutes, and hath done them, he shall surely live.

20 The soul that sinneth, it shall die. The son shall not bear the iniquity of the father, neither shall the father bear the iniquity of the son: the righteousness of the righteous shall be upon him, and the wickedness of the wicked shall be upon him.

21 But if the wicked will turn from all his sins that he hath committed, and keep all my statutes, and do that which is lawful and right, he shall surely live, he shall not die.

22 All his transgressions that he hath committed, they shall not be mentioned unto him: in his righteousness that he hath done he shall live.

23 Have I any pleasure at all that the wicked should die? saith the Lord GOD: *and* not that he should return from his ways, and live?

24 ¶ But when the righteous turneth away from his righteousness, and committeth iniquity, *and* doeth according to all the abominations that the wicked *man* doeth, shall he live? All his righteousness that he hath done shall not be mentioned: in his trespass that he hath trespassed, and in his sin that he hath sinned, in them shall he die.

25 ¶ Yet ye say, The way of the Lord is not equal. Hear now, O house of Is'ra-el; Is not my way equal? are not your ways unequal?

26 When a righteous *man* turneth away from his righteousness, and committeth iniquity, and dieth in them; for his iniquity that he hath done shall he die.

27 Again, when the wicked *man* turneth away from his wickedness that he hath committed, and doeth that which is lawful and right, he shall save his soul alive.

28 Because he considereth, and turneth away from all his transgressions that he hath committed, he shall surely live, he shall not die.

29 Yet saith the house of Is'ra-el, The way of the Lord is not equal. O house of Is'ra-el, are not my ways equal? are not your ways unequal?

30 Therefore I will judge you, O house of Is'ra-el, every one according to his ways, saith the Lord GOD. Repent, and turn *yourselves* from all your transgressions; so iniquity shall not be your ruin.

31 ¶ Cast away from you all your transgressions, whereby ye have transgressed; and make you a new heart and a new spirit: for why will ye die, O house of Is'ra-el?

32 For I have no pleasure in the death of him that dieth, saith the Lord GOD: wherefore turn *yourselves*, and live ye.

19

MOREOVER take thou up a lamentation for the princes of Is'ra-el,

2 And say, What *is* thy mother? A lioness: she lay down among lions, she nourished her whelps among young lions.

3 And she brought up one of her whelps: it became a young lion, and it learned to catch the prey; it devoured men.

4 The nations also heard of him; he was taken in their pit, and they brought him with chains unto the land of E'gypt.

5 Now when she saw that she had waited, *and* her hope was lost, then she took another of her whelps, *and* made him a young lion.

6 And he went up and down among the lions, he became a young lion, and learned to catch the prey, *and* devoured men.

7 And he knew their desolate palaces, and he laid waste their cities; and the land was desolate, and the fulness thereof, by the noise of his roaring.

8 Then the nations set against him on every side from the provinces, and spread their net over him: he was taken in their pit.

9 And they put him in ward in chains, and brought him to the king of Bab'y-lon: they brought him into holes, that his voice should no more be heard upon the mountains of Is'ra-el.

10 ¶ Thy mother *is* like a vine in thy blood, planted by the waters: she was fruitful and full of branches by reason of many waters.

11 And she had strong rods for the sceptres of them that bare rule, and her stature was exalted among the thick branches, and she appeared in her height with the multitude of her branches.

12 But she was plucked up in fury, she was cast down to the ground, and the east wind dried up her fruit: her strong rods were broken and withered; the fire consumed them.

13 And now she *is* planted in the wilderness, in a dry and thirsty ground.

14 And fire is gone out of a rod of her branches, *which* hath devoured her fruit, so that she hath no strong rod *to be* a sceptre to rule. This *is* a lamentation, and shall be for a lamentation.

20

AND it came to pass in the seventh year, in the fifth *month*, the tenth *day* of the month, *that* certain of the elders of Is'ra-el came to enquire of the LORD, and sat before me.

2 Then came the word of the LORD unto me, saying,

3 Son of man, speak unto the elders of Is'ra-
el, and say unto them, Thus saith the Lord GOD;
Are ye come to enquire of me? *As* I live, saith
the Lord GOD, I will not be enquired of by you.
4 Wilt thou judge them, son of man, wilt
thou judge *them?* cause them to know the
abominations of their fathers:
5 ¶ And say unto them, Thus saith the Lord
GOD; In the day when I chose Is'ra-el, and lifted
up mine hand unto the seed of the house of Ja'-
cob, and made myself known unto them in the
land of E'gypt, when I lifted up mine hand unto
them, saying, I *am* the LORD your God;
6 In the day *that* I lifted up mine hand unto
them, to bring them forth of the land of E'gypt
into a land that I had espied for them, flowing
with milk and honey, which *is* the glory of all
lands:
7 Then said I unto them, Cast ye away every
man the abominations of his eyes, and defile
not yourselves with the idols of E'gypt: I *am* the
LORD your God.
8 But they rebelled against me, and would
not hearken unto me: they did not every man
cast away the abominations of their eyes, neither did they forsake the idols of E'gypt: then I
said, I will pour out my fury upon them, to accomplish my anger against them in the midst of
the land of E'gypt.
9 But I wrought for my name's sake, that it
should not be polluted before the heathen,
among whom they *were,* in whose sight I made
myself known unto them, in bringing them
forth out of the land of E'gypt.
10 ¶ Wherefore I caused them to go forth
out of the land of E'gypt, and brought them into
the wilderness.
11 And I gave them my statutes, and shewed
them my judgments, which *if* a man do, he shall
even live in them.
12 Moreover also I gave them my sabbaths,
to be a sign between me and them, that they
might know that I *am* the LORD that sanctify
them.
13 But the house of Is'ra-el rebelled against
me in the wilderness: they walked not in my
statutes, and they despised my judgments,
which *if* a man do, he shall even live in them;
and my sabbaths they greatly polluted: then I
said, I would pour out my fury upon them in the
wilderness, to consume them.
14 But I wrought for my name's sake, that it
should not be polluted before the heathen, in
whose sight I brought them out.
15 Yet also I lifted up my hand unto them in
the wilderness, that I would not bring them into
the land which I had given *them,* flowing with
milk and honey, which *is* the glory of all lands;
16 Because they despised my judgments, and
walked not in my statutes, but polluted my sabbaths: for their heart went after their idols.
17 Nevertheless mine eye spared them from
destroying them, neither did I make an end of
them in the wilderness.
18 But I said unto their children in the wilderness, Walk ye not in the statutes of your fathers, neither observe their judgments, nor defile yourselves with their idols:
19 I *am* the LORD your God; walk in my statutes, and keep my judgments, and do them;
20 And hallow my sabbaths; and they shall
be a sign between me and you, that ye may
know that I *am* the LORD your God.
21 Notwithstanding the children rebelled
against me: they walked not in my statutes, neither kept my judgments to do them, which *if* a
man do, he shall even live in them; they polluted my sabbaths: then I said, I would pour out
my fury upon them, to accomplish my anger
against them in the wilderness.
22 Nevertheless I withdrew mine hand, and
wrought for my name's sake, that it should not
be polluted in the sight of the heathen, in whose
sight I brought them forth.
23 I lifted up mine hand unto them also in the
wilderness, that I would scatter them among
the heathen, and disperse them through the
countries;
24 Because they had not executed my judgments, but had despised my statutes, and had
polluted my sabbaths, and their eyes were after
their fathers' idols.
25 Wherefore I gave them also statutes *that*
were not good, and judgments whereby they
should not live;
26 And I polluted them in their own gifts, in
that they caused to pass through *the fire* all that
openeth the womb, that I might make them
desolate, to the end that they might know that I
am the LORD.
27 ¶ Therefore, son of man, speak unto the
house of Is'ra-el, and say unto them, Thus saith
the Lord GOD; Yet in this your fathers have
blasphemed me, in that they have committed a
trespass against me.
28 *For* when I had brought them into the
land, *for* the which I lifted up mine hand to give
it to them, then they saw every high hill, and all
the thick trees, and they offered there their sacrifices, and there they presented the provocation of their offering: there also they made their
sweet savour, and poured out there their drink
offerings.
29 Then I said unto them, What *is* the high
place whereunto ye go? And the name thereof is
called Ba'mah unto this day.
30 Wherefore say unto the house of Is'ra-el,
Thus saith the Lord GOD; Are ye polluted after
the manner of your fathers? and commit ye
whoredom after their abominations?
31 For when ye offer your gifts, when ye
make your sons to pass through the fire, ye pollute yourselves with all your idols, even unto
this day: and shall I be enquired of by you, O
house of Is'ra-el? *As* I live, saith the Lord GOD, I
will not be enquired of by you.
32 And that which cometh into your mind
shall not be at all, that ye say, We will be as the
heathen, as the families of the countries, to
serve wood and stone.
33 ¶ *As* I live, saith the Lord GOD, surely
with a mighty hand, and with a stretched out
arm, and with fury poured out, will I rule over
you:
34 And I will bring you out from the people,
and will gather you out of the countries wherein
ye are scattered, with a mighty hand, and with
a stretched out arm, and with fury poured out.
35 And I will bring you into the wilderness of
the people, and there will I plead with you face
to face.
36 Like as I pleaded with your fathers in the
wilderness of the land of E'gypt, so will I plead
with you, saith the Lord GOD.
37 And I will cause you to pass under the
rod, and I will bring you into the bond of the
covenant:
38 And I will purge out from among you the
rebels, and them that transgress against me: I
will bring them forth out of the country where
they sojourn, and they shall not enter into the
land of Is'ra-el: and ye shall know that I *am* the
LORD.
39 As for you, O house of Is'ra-el, thus saith

the Lord GOD; Go ye, serve ye every one his
idols, and hereafter *also*, if ye will not hearken
unto me: but pollute ye my holy name no more
with your gifts, and with your idols.
40 For in mine holy mountain, in the mountain of the height of Is'ra-el, saith the Lord GOD,
there shall all the house of Is'ra-el, all of them in
the land, serve me: there will I accept them, and
there will I require your offerings, and the firstfruits of your oblations, with all your holy
things.
41 I will accept you with your sweet savour,
when I bring you out from the people, and
gather you out of the countries wherein ye have
been scattered; and I will be sanctified in you
before the heathen.
42 And ye shall know that I *am* the LORD,
when I shall bring you into the land of Is'ra-el,
into the country *for* the which I lifted up mine
hand to give it to your fathers.
43 And there shall ye remember your ways,
and all your doings, wherein ye have been defiled; and ye shall loathe yourselves in your own
sight for all your evils that ye have committed.
44 And ye shall know that I *am* the LORD,
when I have wrought with you for my name's
sake, not according to your wicked ways, nor
according to your corrupt doings, O ye house of
Is'ra-el, saith the Lord GOD.
45 ¶ Moreover the word of the LORD came
unto me, saying,
46 Son of man, set thy face toward the south,
and drop *thy word* toward the south, and
prophesy against the forest of the south field;
47 And say to the forest of the south, Hear
the word of the LORD; Thus saith the Lord GOD;
Behold, I will kindle a fire in thee, and it shall
devour every green tree in thee, and every dry
tree: the flaming flame shall not be quenched,
and all faces from the south to the north shall
be burned therein.
48 And all flesh shall see that I the LORD have
kindled it: it shall not be quenched.
49 Then said I, Ah Lord GOD! they say of me,
Doth he not speak parables?

21 AND the word of the LORD came unto
me, saying,
2 Son of man, set thy face toward Je-ru'sa-
lem, and drop *thy word* toward the holy places,
and prophesy against the land of Is'ra-el,
3 And say to the land of Is'ra-el, Thus saith
the LORD; Behold, I *am* against thee, and will
draw forth my sword out of his sheath, and will
cut off from thee the righteous and the wicked.
4 Seeing then that I will cut off from thee the
righteous and the wicked, therefore shall my
sword go forth out of his sheath against all flesh
from the south to the north:
5 That all flesh may know that I the LORD
have drawn forth my sword out of his sheath: it
shall not return any more.
6 Sigh therefore, thou son of man, with the
breaking of *thy* loins; and with bitterness sigh
before their eyes.
7 And it shall be, when they say unto thee,
Wherefore sighest thou? that thou shalt answer,
For the tidings; because it cometh: and every
heart shall melt, and all hands shall be feeble,
and every spirit shall faint, and all knees shall
be weak *as* water: behold, it cometh, and shall
be brought to pass, saith the Lord GOD.
8 ¶ Again the word of the LORD came unto
me, saying,
9 Son of man, prophesy, and say, Thus saith
the LORD; Say, A sword, a sword is sharpened,
and also furbished:
10 It is sharpened to make a sore slaughter; it
is furbished that it may glitter: should we then
make mirth? it contemneth the rod of my son,
as every tree.
11 And he hath given it to be furbished, that
it may be handled: this sword is sharpened, and
it is furbished, to give it into the hand of the
slayer.
12 Cry and howl, son of man: for it shall be
upon my people, it *shall be* upon all the princes
of Is'ra-el: terrors by reason of the sword shall
be upon my people: smite therefore upon *thy*
thigh.
13 Because *it is* a trial, and what if *the sword*
contemn even the rod? it shall be no *more*, saith
the LORD God.
14 Thou therefore, son of man, prophesy, and
smite *thine* hands together, and let the sword
be doubled the third time, the sword of the
slain: it *is* the sword of the great *men that are*
slain, which entereth into their privy chambers.
15 I have set the point of the sword against
all their gates, that *their* heart may faint, and
their ruins be multiplied: ah! *it is* made bright, *it*
is wrapped up for the slaughter.
16 Go thee one way or other, *either* on the
right hand, *or* on the left, whithersoever thy
face *is* set.
17 I will also smite mine hands together, and
I will cause my fury to rest: I the LORD have
said *it*.
18 ¶ The word of the LORD came unto me
again, saying,
19 Also, thou son of man, appoint thee two
ways, that the sword of the king of Bab'y-lon
may come: both twain shall come forth out of
one land: and choose thou a place, choose *it* at
the head of the way to the city.
20 Appoint a way, that the sword may come
to Rab'bath of the Am'mon-ites, and to Ju'dah
in Je-ru'sa-lem the defenced.
21 For the king of Bab'y-lon stood at the
parting of the way, at the head of the two ways,
to use divination: he made *his* arrows bright, he
consulted with images, he looked in the liver.
22 At his right hand was the divination for
Je-ru'sa-lem, to appoint captains, to open the
mouth in the slaughter, to lift up the voice with
shouting, to appoint *battering* rams against the
gates, to cast a mount, *and* to build a fort.
23 And it shall be unto them as a false divination in their sight, to them that have sworn
oaths: but he will call to remembrance the iniquity, that they may be taken.
24 Therefore thus saith the Lord GOD; Because ye have made your iniquity to be remembered, in that your transgressions are discovered, so that in all your doings your sins do
appear; because, *I say*, that ye are come to remembrance, ye shall be taken with the hand.
25 ¶ And thou, profane wicked prince of Is'-
ra-el, whose day is come, when iniquity *shall*
have an end,
26 Thus saith the Lord GOD; Remove the diadem, and take off the crown: this *shall* not *be*
the same: exalt *him that is* low, and abase *him*
that is high.
27 I will overturn, overturn, overturn, it: and
it shall be no *more*, until he come whose right it
is; and I will give it *him*.
28 ¶ And thou, son of man, prophesy and
say, Thus saith the Lord GOD concerning the
Am'mon-ites, and concerning their reproach;
even say thou, The sword, the sword *is* drawn:
for the slaughter *it is* furbished, to consume because of the glittering:
29 Whiles they see vanity unto thee, whiles

they divine a lie unto thee, to bring thee upon the necks of *them that are* slain, of the wicked, whose day is come, when their iniquity *shall have* an end.

30 Shall I cause *it* to return into his sheath? I will judge thee in the place where thou wast created, in the land of thy nativity.

31 And I will pour out mine indignation upon thee, I will blow against thee in the fire of my wrath, and deliver thee into the hand of brutish men, *and* skilful to destroy.

32 Thou shalt be for fuel to the fire; thy blood shall be in the midst of the land; thou shalt be no *more* remembered: for I the LORD have spoken *it*.

22

MOREOVER the word of the LORD came unto me, saying,

2 Now, thou son of man, wilt thou judge, wilt thou judge the bloody city? yea, thou shalt shew her all her abominations.

3 Then say thou, Thus saith the Lord GOD, The city sheddeth blood in the midst of it, that her time may come, and maketh idols against herself to defile herself.

4 Thou art become guilty in thy blood that thou hast shed; and hast defiled thyself in thine idols which thou hast made; and thou hast caused thy days to draw near, and art come *even* unto thy years: therefore have I made thee a reproach unto the heathen, and a mocking to all countries.

5 *Those that be* near, and *those that be* far from thee, shall mock thee, *which art* infamous *and* much vexed.

6 Behold, the princes of Is'ra-el, every one were in thee to their power to shed blood.

7 In thee have they set light by father and mother: in the midst of thee have they dealt by oppression with the stranger: in thee have they vexed the fatherless and the widow.

8 Thou hast despised mine holy things, and hast profaned my sabbaths.

9 In thee are men that carry tales to shed blood: and in thee they eat upon the mountains: in the midst of thee they commit lewdness.

10 In thee have they discovered their fathers' nakedness: in thee have they humbled her that was set apart for pollution.

11 And one hath committed abomination with his neighbour's wife; and another hath lewdly defiled his daughter in law; and another in thee hath humbled his sister, his father's daughter.

12 In thee have they taken gifts to shed blood; thou hast taken usury and increase, and thou hast greedily gained of thy neighbours by extortion, and hast forgotten me, saith the Lord GOD.

13 ¶ Behold, therefore I have smitten mine hand at thy dishonest gain which thou hast made, and at thy blood which hath been in the midst of thee.

14 Can thine heart endure, or can thine hands be strong, in the days that I shall deal with thee? I the LORD have spoken *it*, and will do *it*.

15 And I will scatter thee among the heathen, and disperse thee in the countries, and will consume thy filthiness out of thee.

16 And thou shalt take thine inheritance in thyself in the sight of the heathen, and thou shalt know that I *am* the LORD.

17 And the word of the LORD came unto me, saying,

18 Son of man, the house of Is'ra-el is to me become dross: all they *are* brass, and tin, and iron, and lead, in the midst of the furnace; they are *even* the dross of silver.

19 Therefore thus saith the Lord GOD; Because ye are all become dross, behold, therefore I will gather you into the midst of Je-ru'sa-lem.

20 *As* they gather silver, and brass, and iron, and lead, and tin, into the midst of the furnace, to blow the fire upon it, to melt *it;* so will I gather *you* in mine anger and in my fury, and I will leave *you there*, and melt you.

21 Yea, I will gather you, and blow upon you in the fire of my wrath, and ye shall be melted in the midst thereof.

22 As silver is melted in the midst of the furnace, so shall ye be melted in the midst thereof; and ye shall know that I the LORD have poured out my fury upon you.

23 ¶ And the word of the LORD came unto me, saying,

24 Son of man, say unto her, Thou *art* the land that is not cleansed, nor rained upon in the day of indignation.

25 *There is* a conspiracy of her prophets in the midst thereof, like a roaring lion ravening the prey; they have devoured souls; they have taken the treasure and precious things; they have made her many widows in the midst thereof.

26 Her priests have violated my law, and have profaned mine holy things: they have put no difference between the holy and profane, neither have they shewed *difference* between the unclean and the clean, and have hid their eyes from my sabbaths, and I am profaned among them.

27 Her princes in the midst thereof *are* like wolves ravening the prey, to shed blood, *and* to destroy souls, to get dishonest gain.

28 And her prophets have daubed them with untempered *morter*, seeing vanity, and divining lies unto them, saying, Thus saith the Lord GOD, when the LORD hath not spoken.

29 The people of the land have used oppression, and exercised robbery, and have vexed the poor and needy: yea, they have oppressed the stranger wrongfully.

30 And I sought for a man among them, that should make up the hedge, and stand in the gap before me for the land, that I should not destroy it: but I found none.

31 Therefore have I poured out mine indignation upon them; I have consumed them with the fire of my wrath: their own way have I recompensed upon their heads, saith the Lord GOD.

23

THE word of the LORD came again unto me, saying,

2 Son of man, there were two women, the daughters of one mother:

3 And they committed whoredoms in E'gypt; they committed whoredoms in their youth: there were their breasts pressed, and there they bruised the teats of their virginity.

4 And the names of them *were* A-ho'lah the elder, and A-hol'i-bah her sister: and they were mine, and they bare sons and daughters. Thus *were* their names; Sa-ma'ri-a *is* A-ho'lah, and Je-ru'sa-lem A-hol'i-bah.

5 And A-ho'lah played the harlot when she was mine; and she doted on her lovers, on the As-syr'i-ans *her* neighbours,

6 *Which were* clothed with blue, captains and rulers, all of them desirable young men, horsemen riding upon horses.

7 Thus she committed her whoredoms with them, with all them *that were* the chosen men

of As-syr′i-a, and with all on whom she doted: with all their idols she defiled herself.

8 Neither left she her whoredoms *brought* from E′gypt: for in her youth they lay with her, and they bruised the breasts of her virginity, and poured their whoredom upon her.

9 Wherefore I have delivered her into the hand of her lovers, into the hand of the As-syr′i-ans, upon whom she doted.

10 These discovered her nakedness: they took her sons and her daughters, and slew her with the sword: and she became famous among women; for they had executed judgment upon her.

11 And when her sister A-hol′i-bah saw *this*, she was more corrupt in her inordinate love than she, and in her whoredoms more than her sister in *her* whoredoms.

12 She doted upon the As-syr′i-ans *her* neighbours, captains and rulers clothed most gorgeously, horsemen riding upon horses, all of them desirable young men.

13 Then I saw that she was defiled, *that* they *took* both one way,

14 And *that* she increased her whoredoms: for when she saw men pourtrayed upon the wall, the images of the Chal-de′ans pourtrayed with vermilion,

15 Girded with girdles upon their loins, exceeding in dyed attire upon their heads, all of them princes to look to, after the manner of the Bab-y-lo′ni-ans of Chal-de′a, the land of their nativity:

16 And as soon as she saw them with her eyes, she doted upon them, and sent messengers unto them into Chal-de′a.

17 And the Bab-y-lo′ni-ans came to her into the bed of love, and they defiled her with their whoredom, and she was polluted with them, and her mind was alienated from them.

18 So she discovered her whoredoms, and discovered her nakedness: then my mind was alienated from her, like as my mind was alienated from her sister.

19 Yet she multiplied her whoredoms, in calling to remembrance the days of her youth, wherein she had played the harlot in the land of E′gypt.

20 For she doted upon their paramours, whose flesh *is as* the flesh of asses, and whose issue *is like* the issue of horses.

21 Thus thou calledst to remembrance the lewdness of thy youth, in bruising thy teats by the E-gyp′tians for the paps of thy youth.

22 ¶ Therefore, O A-hol′i-bah, thus saith the Lord GOD; Behold, I will raise up thy lovers against thee, from whom thy mind is alienated, and I will bring them against thee on every side;

23 The Bab-y-lo′ni-ans, and all the Chal-de′-ans, Pe′kod, and Sho′a, and Ko′a, *and* all the As-syr′i-ans with them: all of them desirable young men, captains and rulers, great lords and renowned, all of them riding upon horses.

24 And they shall come against thee with chariots, wagons, and wheels, and with an assembly of people, *which* shall set against thee buckler and shield and helmet round about: and I will set judgment before them, and they shall judge thee according to their judgments.

25 And I will set my jealousy against thee, and they shall deal furiously with thee: they shall take away thy nose and thine ears; and thy remnant shall fall by the sword: they shall take thy sons and thy daughters; and thy residue shall be devoured by the fire.

26 They shall also strip thee out of thy clothes, and take away thy fair jewels.

27 Thus will I make thy lewdness to cease from thee, and thy whoredom *brought* from the land of E′gypt: so that thou shalt not lift up thine eyes unto them, nor remember E′gypt any more.

28 For thus saith the Lord GOD; Behold, I will deliver thee into the hand *of them* whom thou hatest, into the hand *of them* from whom thy mind is alienated:

29 And they shall deal with thee hatefully, and shall take away all thy labour, and shall leave thee naked and bare: and the nakedness of thy whoredoms shall be discovered, both thy lewdness and thy whoredoms.

30 I will do these *things* unto thee, because thou hast gone a whoring after the heathen, *and* because thou art polluted with their idols.

31 Thou hast walked in the way of thy sister; therefore will I give her cup into thine hand.

32 Thus saith the Lord GOD; Thou shalt drink of thy sister's cup deep and large: thou shalt be laughed to scorn and had in derision; it containeth much.

33 Thou shalt be filled with drunkenness and sorrow, with the cup of astonishment and desolation, with the cup of thy sister Sa-ma′ri-a.

34 Thou shalt even drink it and suck *it* out, and thou shalt break the sherds thereof, and pluck off thine own breasts: for I have spoken *it*, saith the Lord GOD.

35 Therefore thus saith the Lord GOD; Because thou hast forgotten me, and cast me behind thy back, therefore bear thou also thy lewdness and thy whoredoms.

36 ¶ The LORD said moreover unto me; Son of man, wilt thou judge A-ho′lah and A-hol′i-bah? yea, declare unto them their abominations;

37 That they have committed adultery, and blood *is* in their hands, and with their idols have they committed adultery, and have also caused their sons, whom they bare unto me, to pass for them through *the fire*, to devour *them*.

38 Moreover this they have done unto me: they have defiled my sanctuary in the same day, and have profaned my sabbaths.

39 For when they had slain their children to their idols, then they came the same day into my sanctuary to profane it; and, lo, thus have they done in the midst of mine house.

40 And furthermore, that ye have sent for men to come from far, unto whom a messenger *was* sent; and, lo, they came: for whom thou didst wash thyself, paintedst thy eyes, and deckedst thyself with ornaments,

41 And satest upon a stately bed, and a table prepared before it, whereupon thou hast set mine incense and mine oil.

42 And a voice of a multitude being at ease *was* with her: and with the men of the common sort *were* brought Sa-be′ans from the wilderness, which put bracelets upon their hands, and beautiful crowns upon their heads.

43 Then said I unto *her that was* old in adulteries, Will they now commit whoredoms with her, and she *with them?*

44 Yet they went in unto her, as they go in unto a woman that playeth the harlot: so went they in unto A-ho′lah and unto A-hol′i-bah, the lewd women.

45 ¶ And the righteous men, they shall judge them after the manner of adulteresses, and after the manner of women that shed blood; because they *are* adulteresses, and blood *is* in their hands.

46 For thus saith the Lord GOD; I will bring

up a company upon them, and will give them to be removed and spoiled.

47 And the company shall stone them with stones, and dispatch them with their swords; they shall slay their sons and their daughters, and burn up their houses with fire.

48 Thus will I cause lewdness to cease out of the land, that all women may be taught not to do after your lewdness.

49 And they shall recompense your lewdness upon you, and ye shall bear the sins of your idols: and ye shall know that I *am* the Lord GOD.

24 AGAIN in the ninth year, in the tenth month, in the tenth *day* of the month, the word of the LORD came unto me, saying,

2 Son of man, write thee the name of the day, *even* of this same day: the king of Bab'y-lon set himself against Je-ru'sa-lem this same day.

3 And utter a parable unto the rebellious house, and say unto them, Thus saith the Lord GOD; Set on a pot, set *it* on, and also pour water into it:

4 Gather the pieces thereof into it, *even* every good piece, the thigh, and the shoulder; fill *it* with the choice bones.

5 Take the choice of the flock, and burn also the bones under it, *and* make it boil well, and let them seethe the bones of it therein.

6 ¶ Wherefore thus saith the Lord GOD; Woe to the bloody city, to the pot whose scum *is* therein, and whose scum is not gone out of it! bring it out piece by piece; let no lot fall upon it.

7 For her blood is in the midst of her; she set it upon the top of a rock; she poured it not upon the ground, to cover it with dust;

8 That it might cause fury to come up to take vengeance; I have set her blood upon the top of a rock, that it should not be covered.

9 Therefore thus saith the Lord GOD; Woe to the bloody city! I will even make the pile for fire great.

10 Heap on wood, kindle the fire, consume the flesh, and spice it well, and let the bones be burned.

11 Then set it empty upon the coals thereof, that the brass of it may be hot, and may burn, and *that* the filthiness of it may be molten in it, *that* the scum of it may be consumed.

12 She hath wearied *herself* with lies, and her great scum went not forth out of her: her scum *shall be* in the fire.

13 In thy filthiness *is* lewdness: because I have purged thee, and thou wast not purged, thou shalt not be purged from thy filthiness any more, till I have caused my fury to rest upon thee.

14 I the LORD have spoken *it:* it shall come to pass, and I will do *it;* I will not go back, neither will I spare, neither will I repent; according to thy ways, and according to thy doings, shall they judge thee, saith the Lord GOD.

15 ¶ Also the word of the LORD came unto me, saying,

16 Son of man, behold, I take away from thee the desire of thine eyes with a stroke: yet neither shalt thou mourn nor weep, neither shall thy tears run down.

17 Forbear to cry, make no mourning for the dead, bind the tire of thine head upon thee, and put on thy shoes upon thy feet, and cover not *thy* lips, and eat not the bread of men.

18 So I spake unto the people in the morning: and at even my wife died; and I did in the morning as I was commanded.

19 ¶ And the people said unto me, Wilt thou not tell us what these *things are* to us, that thou doest *so?*

20 Then I answered them, The word of the LORD came unto me, saying,

21 Speak unto the house of Is'ra-el, Thus saith the Lord GOD; Behold, I will profane my sanctuary, the excellency of your strength, the desire of your eyes, and that which your soul pitieth; and your sons and your daughters whom ye have left shall fall by the sword.

22 And ye shall do as I have done: ye shall not cover *your* lips, nor eat the bread of men.

23 And your tires *shall be* upon your heads, and your shoes upon your feet: ye shall not mourn nor weep; but ye shall pine away for your iniquities, and mourn one toward another.

24 Thus E-ze'ki-el is unto you a sign: according to all that he hath done shall ye do: and when this cometh, ye shall know that I *am* the Lord GOD.

25 Also, thou son of man, *shall it* not *be* in the day when I take from them their strength, the joy of their glory, the desire of their eyes, and that whereupon they set their minds, their sons and their daughters,

26 *That* he that escapeth in that day shall come unto thee, to cause *thee* to hear *it* with *thine* ears?

27 In that day shall thy mouth be opened to him which is escaped, and thou shalt speak, and be no more dumb: and thou shalt be a sign unto them; and they shall know that I *am* the LORD.

25 THE word of the LORD came again unto me, saying,

2 Son of man, set thy face against the Am'mon-ites, and prophesy against them;

3 And say unto the Am'mon-ites, Hear the word of the Lord GOD; Thus saith the Lord GOD; Because thou saidst, Aha, against my sanctuary, when it was profaned; and against the land of Is'ra-el, when it was desolate; and against the house of Ju'dah, when they went into captivity;

4 Behold, therefore I will deliver thee to the men of the east for a possession, and they shall set their palaces in thee, and make their dwellings in thee: they shall eat thy fruit, and they shall drink thy milk.

5 And I will make Rab'bah a stable for camels, and the Am'mon-ites a couching place for flocks: and ye shall know that I *am* the LORD.

6 For thus saith the Lord GOD; Because thou hast clapped *thine* hands, and stamped with the feet, and rejoiced in heart with all thy despite against the land of Is'ra-el;

7 Behold, therefore I will stretch out mine hand upon thee, and will deliver thee for a spoil to the heathen; and I will cut thee off from the people, and I will cause thee to perish out of the countries: I will destroy thee; and thou shalt know that I *am* the LORD.

8 ¶ Thus saith the Lord GOD; Because that Mo'ab and Se'ir do say, Behold, the house of Ju'dah *is* like unto all the heathen;

9 Therefore, behold, I will open the side of Mo'ab from the cities, from his cities *which are* on his frontiers, the glory of the country, Beth–jesh'i-moth, Ba'al–me'on, and Kir-i-a-tha'im,

10 Unto the men of the east with the Am'mon-ites, and will give them in possession, that the Am'mon-ites may not be remembered among the nations.

11 And I will execute judgments upon Mo'ab; and they shall know that I *am* the LORD.

12 ¶ Thus saith the Lord GOD; Because that E'dom hath dealt against the house of Ju'dah by

taking vengeance, and hath greatly offended,
and revenged himself upon them;
13 Therefore thus saith the Lord GOD; I will
also stretch out mine hand upon E'dom, and
will cut off man and beast from it; and I will
make it desolate from Te'man; and they of De'-
dan shall fall by the sword.
14 And I will lay my vengeance upon E'dom
by the hand of my people Is'ra-el: and they shall
do in E'dom according to mine anger and according to my fury; and they shall know my
vengeance, saith the Lord GOD.
15 ¶ Thus saith the Lord GOD; Because the
Phi-lis'tines have dealt by revenge, and have
taken vengeance with a despiteful heart, to destroy *it* for the old hatred;
16 Therefore thus saith the Lord GOD; Behold, I will stretch out mine hand upon the Phi-
lis'tines, and I will cut off the Cher'eth-ims, and
destroy the remnant of the sea coast.
17 And I will execute great vengeance upon
them with furious rebukes; and they shall know
that I *am* the LORD, when I shall lay my vengeance upon them.

26 AND it came to pass in the eleventh
year, in the first *day* of the month, *that*
the word of the LORD came unto me, saying,
2 Son of man, because that Ty'rus hath said
against Je-ru'sa-lem, Aha, she is broken *that*
was the gates of the people: she is turned unto
me: I shall be replenished, *now* she is laid
waste:
3 Therefore thus saith the Lord GOD; Behold,
I *am* against thee, O Ty'rus, and will cause
many nations to come up against thee, as the
sea causeth his waves to come up.
4 And they shall destroy the walls of Ty'rus,
and break down her towers: I will also scrape
her dust from her, and make her like the top of
a rock.
5 It shall be *a place for* the spreading of nets
in the midst of the sea: for I have spoken *it*,
saith the Lord GOD: and it shall become a spoil
to the nations.
6 And her daughters which *are* in the field
shall be slain by the sword; and they shall know
that I *am* the LORD.
7 ¶ For thus saith the Lord GOD; Behold, I
will bring upon Ty'rus Neb-u-chad-rez'zar king
of Bab'y-lon, a king of kings, from the north,
with horses, and with chariots, and with horsemen, and companies, and much people.
8 He shall slay with the sword thy daughters
in the field: and he shall make a fort against
thee, and cast a mount against thee, and lift up
the buckler against thee.
9 And he shall set engines of war against thy
walls, and with his axes he shall break down
thy towers.
10 By reason of the abundance of his horses
their dust shall cover thee: thy walls shall shake
at the noise of the horsemen, and of the wheels,
and of the chariots, when he shall enter into thy
gates, as men enter into a city wherein is made
a breach.
11 With the hoofs of his horses shall he tread
down all thy streets: he shall slay thy people by
the sword, and thy strong garrisons shall go
down to the ground.
12 And they shall make a spoil of thy riches,
and make a prey of thy merchandise: and they
shall break down thy walls, and destroy thy
pleasant houses: and they shall lay thy stones
and thy timber and thy dust in the midst of the
water.
13 And I will cause the noise of thy songs to
cease; and the sound of thy harps shall be no
more heard.
14 And I will make thee like the top of a
rock: thou shalt be *a place* to spread nets upon;
thou shalt be built no more: for I the LORD have
spoken *it*, saith the Lord GOD.
15 ¶ Thus saith the Lord GOD to Ty'rus; Shall
not the isles shake at the sound of thy fall, when
the wounded cry, when the slaughter is made in
the midst of thee?
16 Then all the princes of the sea shall come
down from their thrones, and lay away their
robes, and put off their broidered garments:
they shall clothe themselves with trembling;
they shall sit upon the ground, and shall tremble at *every* moment, and be astonished at thee.
17 And they shall take up a lamentation for
thee, and say to thee, How art thou destroyed,
that wast inhabited of seafaring men, the renowned city, which wast strong in the sea, she
and her inhabitants, which cause their terror *to*
be on all that haunt it!
18 Now shall the isles tremble in the day of
thy fall; yea, the isles that *are* in the sea shall be
troubled at thy departure.
19 For thus saith the Lord GOD; When I shall
make thee a desolate city, like the cities that are
not inhabited; when I shall bring up the deep
upon thee, and great waters shall cover thee;
20 When I shall bring thee down with them
that descend into the pit, with the people of old
time, and shall set thee in the low parts of the
earth, in places desolate of old, with them that
go down to the pit, that thou be not inhabited;
and I shall set glory in the land of the living;
21 I will make thee a terror, and thou *shalt be*
no *more:* though thou be sought for, yet shalt
thou never be found again, saith the Lord GOD.

27 THE word of the LORD came again unto
me, saying,
2 Now, thou son of man, take up a lamentation for Ty'rus;
3 And say unto Ty'rus, O thou that art situate
at the entry of the sea, *which art* a merchant of
the people for many isles, Thus saith the Lord
GOD; O Ty'rus, thou hast said, I *am* of perfect
beauty.
4 Thy borders *are* in the midst of the seas,
thy builders have perfected thy beauty.
5 They have made all thy *ship* boards of fir
trees of Se'nir: they have taken cedars from
Leb'a-non to make masts for thee.
6 *Of* the oaks of Ba'shan have they made
thine oars; the company of the Ash'ur-ites have
made thy benches *of* ivory, *brought* out of the
isles of Chit'tim.
7 Fine linen with broidered work from E'gypt
was that which thou spreadest forth to be thy
sail; blue and purple from the isles of E-li'shah
was that which covered thee.
8 The inhabitants of Zi'don and Ar'vad were
thy mariners: thy wise *men*, O Ty'rus, *that* were
in thee, were thy pilots.
9 The ancients of Ge'bal and the wise *men*
thereof were in thee thy calkers: all the ships of
the sea with their mariners were in thee to occupy thy merchandise.
10 They of Per'sia and of Lud and of Phut
were in thine army, thy men of war: they
hanged the shield and helmet in thee; they set
forth thy comeliness.
11 The men of Ar'vad with thine army *were*
upon thy walls round about, and the Gam'ma-
dims were in thy towers: they hanged their
shields upon thy walls round about; they have
made thy beauty perfect.

12 Tar'shish *was* thy merchant by reason of the multitude of all *kind of* riches; with silver, iron, tin, and lead, they traded in thy fairs.

13 Ja'van, Tu'bal, and Me'shech, they *were* thy merchants: they traded the persons of men and vessels of brass in thy market.

14 They of the house of To-gar'mah traded in thy fairs with horses and horsemen and mules.

15 The men of De'dan *were* thy merchants; many isles *were* the merchandise of thine hand: they brought thee *for* a present horns of ivory and ebony.

16 Syr'i-a *was* thy merchant by reason of the multitude of the wares of thy making: they occupied in thy fairs with emeralds, purple, and broidered work, and fine linen, and coral, and agate.

17 Ju'dah, and the land of Is'ra-el, they *were* thy merchants: they traded in thy market wheat of Min'nith, and Pan'nag, and honey, and oil, and balm.

18 Da-mas'cus *was* thy merchant in the multitude of the wares of thy making, for the multitude of all riches; in the wine of Hel'bon, and white wool.

19 Dan also and Ja'van going to and fro occupied in thy fairs: bright iron, cassia, and calamus, were in thy market.

20 De'dan *was* thy merchant in precious clothes for chariots.

21 A-ra'bi-a, and all the princes of Ke'dar, they occupied with thee in lambs, and rams, and goats: in these *were they* thy merchants.

22 The merchants of She'ba and Ra'a-mah, they *were* thy merchants: they occupied in thy fairs with chief of all spices, and with all precious stones, and gold.

23 Ha'ran, and Can'neh, and E'den, the merchants of She'ba, Assh'ur, *and* Chil'mad, *were* thy merchants.

24 These *were* thy merchants in all sorts *of things*, in blue clothes, and broidered work, and in chests of rich apparel, bound with cords, and made of cedar, among thy merchandise.

25 The ships of Tar'shish did sing of thee in thy market: and thou wast replenished, and made very glorious in the midst of the seas.

26 ¶ Thy rowers have brought thee into great waters: the east wind hath broken thee in the midst of the seas.

27 Thy riches, and thy fairs, thy merchandise, thy mariners, and thy pilots, thy calkers, and the occupiers of thy merchandise, and all thy men of war, that *are* in thee, and in all thy company which *is* in the midst of thee, shall fall into the midst of the seas in the day of thy ruin.

28 The suburbs shall shake at the sound of the cry of thy pilots.

29 And all that handle the oar, the mariners, *and* all the pilots of the sea, shall come down from their ships, they shall stand upon the land;

30 And shall cause their voice to be heard against thee, and shall cry bitterly, and shall cast up dust upon their heads, they shall wallow themselves in the ashes:

31 And they shall make themselves utterly bald for thee, and gird them with sackcloth, and they shall weep for thee with bitterness of heart *and* bitter wailing.

32 And in their wailing they shall take up a lamentation for thee, and lament over thee, *saying*, What *city is* like Ty'rus, like the destroyed in the midst of the sea?

33 When thy wares went forth out of the seas, thou filledst many people; thou didst enrich the kings of the earth with the multitude of thy riches and of thy merchandise.

34 In the time *when* thou shalt be broken by the seas in the depths of the waters thy merchandise and all thy company in the midst of thee shall fall.

35 All the inhabitants of the isles shall be astonished at thee, and their kings shall be sore afraid, they shall be troubled in *their* countenance.

36 The merchants among the people shall hiss at thee; thou shalt be a terror, and never *shalt be* any more.

28

THE word of the LORD came again unto me, saying,

2 Son of man, say unto the prince of Ty'rus, Thus saith the Lord GOD; Because thine heart *is* lifted up, and thou hast said, I *am* a God, I sit *in* the seat of God, in the midst of the seas; yet thou *art* a man, and not God, though thou set thine heart as the heart of God:

3 Behold, thou *art* wiser than Dan'iel; there is no secret that they can hide from thee:

4 With thy wisdom and with thine understanding thou hast gotten thee riches, and hast gotten gold and silver into thy treasures:

5 By thy great wisdom *and* by thy traffick hast thou increased thy riches, and thine heart is lifted up because of thy riches:

6 Therefore thus saith the Lord GOD; Because thou hast set thine heart as the heart of God;

7 Behold, therefore I will bring strangers upon thee, the terrible of the nations: and they shall draw their swords against the beauty of thy wisdom, and they shall defile thy brightness.

8 They shall bring thee down to the pit, and thou shalt die the deaths of *them that are* slain in the midst of the seas.

9 Wilt thou yet say before him that slayeth thee, I *am* God? but thou *shalt be* a man, and no God, in the hand of him that slayeth thee.

10 Thou shalt die the deaths of the uncircumcised by the hand of strangers: for I have spoken *it*, saith the Lord GOD.

11 ¶ Moreover the word of the LORD came unto me, saying,

12 Son of man, take up a lamentation upon the king of Ty'rus, and say unto him, Thus saith the Lord GOD; Thou sealest up the sum, full of wisdom, and perfect in beauty.

13 Thou hast been in E'den the garden of God; every precious stone *was* thy covering, the sardius, topaz, and the diamond, the beryl, the onyx, and the jasper, the sapphire, the emerald, and the carbuncle, and gold: the workmanship of thy tabrets and of thy pipes was prepared in thee in the day that thou wast created.

14 Thou *art* the anointed cherub that covereth; and I have set thee *so*: thou wast upon the holy mountain of God; thou hast walked up and down in the midst of the stones of fire.

15 Thou *wast* perfect in thy ways from the day that thou wast created, till iniquity was found in thee.

16 By the multitude of thy merchandise they have filled the midst of thee with violence, and thou hast sinned: therefore I will cast thee as profane out of the mountain of God: and I will destroy thee, O covering cherub, from the midst of the stones of fire.

17 Thine heart was lifted up because of thy beauty, thou hast corrupted thy wisdom by reason of thy brightness: I will cast thee to the ground, I will lay thee before kings, that they may behold thee.

18 Thou hast defiled thy sanctuaries by the multitude of thine iniquities, by the iniquity of

thy traffick; therefore will I bring forth a fire from the midst of thee, it shall devour thee, and I will bring thee to ashes upon the earth in the sight of all them that behold thee.

19 All they that know thee among the people shall be astonished at thee: thou shalt be a terror, and never *shalt* thou *be* any more.

20 ¶ Again the word of the LORD came unto me, saying,

21 Son of man, set thy face against Zi'don, and prophesy against it,

22 And say, Thus saith the Lord GOD; Behold, I *am* against thee, O Zi'don; and I will be glorified in the midst of thee: and they shall know that I *am* the LORD, when I shall have executed judgments in her, and shall be sanctified in her.

23 For I will send into her pestilence, and blood into her streets; and the wounded shall be judged in the midst of her by the sword upon her on every side; and they shall know that I *am* the LORD.

24 ¶ And there shall be no more a pricking brier unto the house of Is'ra-el, nor *any* grieving thorn of all *that are* round about them, that despised them; and they shall know that I *am* the Lord GOD.

25 Thus saith the Lord GOD; When I shall have gathered the house of Is'ra-el from the people among whom they are scattered, and shall be sanctified in them in the sight of the heathen, then shall they dwell in their land that I have given to my servant Ja'cob.

26 And they shall dwell safely therein, and shall build houses, and plant vineyards; yea, they shall dwell with confidence, when I have executed judgments upon all those that despise them round about them; and they shall know that I *am* the LORD their God.

29

IN the tenth year, in the tenth *month*, in the twelfth *day* of the month, the word of the LORD came unto me, saying,

2 Son of man, set thy face against Pha'raoh king of E'gypt, and prophesy against him, and against all E'gypt:

3 Speak, and say, Thus saith the Lord GOD; Behold, I *am* against thee, Pha'raoh king of E'gypt, the great dragon that lieth in the midst of his rivers, which hath said, My river *is* mine own, and I have made *it* for myself.

4 But I will put hooks in thy jaws, and I will cause the fish of thy rivers to stick unto thy scales, and I will bring thee up out of the midst of thy rivers, and all the fish of thy rivers shall stick unto thy scales.

5 And I will leave thee *thrown* into the wilderness, thee and all the fish of thy rivers: thou shalt fall upon the open fields; thou shalt not be brought together, nor gathered: I have given thee for meat to the beasts of the field and to the fowls of the heaven.

6 And all the inhabitants of E'gypt shall know that I *am* the LORD, because they have been a staff of reed to the house of Is'ra-el.

7 When they took hold of thee by thy hand, thou didst break, and rend all their shoulder: and when they leaned upon thee, thou brakest, and madest all their loins to be at a stand.

8 ¶ Therefore thus saith the Lord GOD; Behold, I will bring a sword upon thee, and cut off man and beast out of thee.

9 And the land of E'gypt shall be desolate and waste; and they shall know that I *am* the LORD: because he hath said, The river *is* mine, and I have made *it*.

10 Behold, therefore I *am* against thee, and against thy rivers, and I will make the land of E'gypt utterly waste *and* desolate, from the tower of Sy-e'ne even unto the border of E-thi-o'pi-a.

11 No foot of man shall pass through it, nor foot of beast shall pass through it, neither shall it be inhabited forty years.

12 And I will make the land of E'gypt desolate in the midst of the countries *that are* desolate, and her cities among the cities *that are* laid waste shall be desolate forty years: and I will scatter the E-gyp'tians among the nations, and will disperse them through the countries.

13 ¶ Yet thus saith the Lord GOD; At the end of forty years will I gather the E-gyp'tians from the people whither they were scattered:

14 And I will bring again the captivity of E'gypt, and will cause them to return *into* the land of Path'ros, into the land of their habitation; and they shall be there a base kingdom.

15 It shall be the basest of the kingdoms; neither shall it exalt itself any more above the nations: for I will diminish them, that they shall no more rule over the nations.

16 And it shall be no more the confidence of the house of Is'ra-el, which bringeth *their* iniquity to remembrance, when they shall look after them: but they shall know that I *am* the Lord GOD.

17 ¶ And it came to pass in the seven and twentieth year, in the first *month*, in the first *day* of the month, the word of the LORD came unto me, saying,

18 Son of man, Neb-u-chad-rez'zar king of Bab'y-lon caused his army to serve a great service against Ty'rus: every head *was* made bald, and every shoulder *was* peeled: yet had he no wages, nor his army, for Ty'rus, for the service that he had served against it:

19 Therefore thus saith the Lord GOD; Behold, I will give the land of E'gypt unto Neb-u-chad-rez'zar king of Bab'y-lon; and he shall take her multitude, and take her spoil, and take her prey; and it shall be the wages for his army.

20 I have given him the land of E'gypt *for* his labour wherewith he served against it, because they wrought for me, saith the Lord GOD.

21 ¶ In that day will I cause the horn of the house of Is'ra-el to bud forth, and I will give thee the opening of the mouth in the midst of them; and they shall know that I *am* the LORD.

30

THE word of the LORD came again unto me, saying,

2 Son of man, prophesy and say, Thus saith the Lord GOD; Howl ye, Woe worth the day!

3 For the day *is* near, even the day of the LORD *is* near, a cloudy day; it shall be the time of the heathen.

4 And the sword shall come upon E'gypt, and great pain shall be in E-thi-o'pi-a, when the slain shall fall in E'gypt, and they shall take away her multitude, and her foundations shall be broken down.

5 E-thi-o'pi-a, and Lib'y-a, and Lyd'i-a, and all the mingled people, and Chub, and the men of the land that is in league, shall fall with them by the sword.

6 Thus saith the LORD; They also that uphold E'gypt shall fall; and the pride of her power shall come down: from the tower of Sy-e'ne shall they fall in it by the sword, saith the Lord GOD.

7 And they shall be desolate in the midst of the countries *that are* desolate, and her cities shall be in the midst of the cities *that are* wasted.

8 And they shall know that I *am* the LORD,

when I have set a fire in E'gypt, and *when* all
her helpers shall be destroyed.
9 In that day shall messengers go forth from
me in ships to make the careless E-thi-o'pi-ans
afraid, and great pain shall come upon them, as
in the day of E'gypt: for, lo, it cometh.
10 Thus saith the Lord GOD; I will also make
the multitude of E'gypt to cease by the hand of
Neb-u-chad-rez'zar king of Bab'y-lon.
11 He and his people with him, the terrible of
the nations, shall be brought to destroy the
land: and they shall draw their swords against
E'gypt, and fill the land with the slain.
12 And I will make the rivers dry, and sell
the land into the hand of the wicked: and I will
make the land waste, and all that is therein, by
the hand of strangers: I the LORD have spoken
it.
13 Thus saith the Lord GOD; I will also destroy the idols, and I will cause *their* images to
cease out of Noph; and there shall be no more a
prince of the land of E'gypt: and I will put a fear
in the land of E'gypt.
14 And I will make Path'ros desolate, and
will set fire in Zo'an, and will execute judgments in No.
15 And I will pour my fury upon Sin, the
strength of E'gypt; and I will cut off the multitude of No.
16 And I will set fire in E'gypt: Sin shall have
great pain, and No shall be rent asunder, and
Noph *shall have* distresses daily.
17 The young men of A'ven and of Pi-be'seth
shall fall by the sword: and these *cities* shall go
into captivity.
18 At Te-haph'ne-hes also the day shall be
darkened, when I shall break there the yokes of
E'gypt: and the pomp of her strength shall
cease in her: as for her, a cloud shall cover her,
and her daughters shall go into captivity.
19 Thus will I execute judgments in E'gypt:
and they shall know that I *am* the LORD.
20 ¶ And it came to pass in the eleventh
year, in the first *month,* in the seventh *day* of
the month, *that* the word of the LORD came
unto me, saying,
21 Son of man, I have broken the arm of
Pha'raoh king of E'gypt; and, lo, it shall not be
bound up to be healed, to put a roller to bind it,
to make it strong to hold the sword.
22 Therefore thus saith the Lord GOD; Behold, I *am* against Pha'raoh king of E'gypt, and
will break his arms, the strong, and that which
was broken; and I will cause the sword to fall
out of his hand.
23 And I will scatter the E-gyp'tians among
the nations, and will disperse them through the
countries.
24 And I will strengthen the arms of the king
of Bab'y-lon, and put my sword in his hand: but
I will break Pha'raoh's arms, and he shall groan
before him with the groanings of a deadly
wounded *man.*
25 But I will strengthen the arms of the king
of Bab'y-lon, and the arms of Pha'raoh shall fall
down; and they shall know that I *am* the LORD,
when I shall put my sword into the hand of the
king of Bab'y-lon, and he shall stretch it out
upon the land of E'gypt.
26 And I will scatter the E-gyp'tians among
the nations, and disperse them among the countries; and they shall know that I *am* the LORD.

31 AND it came to pass in the eleventh
year, in the third *month,* in the first *day*
of the month, *that* the word of the LORD came
unto me, saying,
2 Son of man, speak unto Pha'raoh king of
E'gypt, and to his multitude; Whom art thou
like in thy greatness?
3 ¶ Behold, the As-syr'i-an *was* a cedar in
Leb'a-non with fair branches, and with a shadowing shroud, and of an high stature; and his
top was among the thick boughs.
4 The waters made him great, the deep set
him up on high with her rivers running round
about his plants, and sent out her little rivers
unto all the trees of the field.
5 Therefore his height was exalted above all
the trees of the field, and his boughs were multiplied, and his branches became long because
of the multitude of waters, when he shot forth.
6 All the fowls of heaven made their nests in
his boughs, and under his branches did all the
beasts of the field bring forth their young, and
under his shadow dwelt all great nations.
7 Thus was he fair in his greatness, in the
length of his branches: for his root was by great
waters.
8 The cedars in the garden of God could not
hide him: the fir trees were not like his boughs,
and the chesnut trees were not like his
branches; nor any tree in the garden of God was
like unto him in his beauty.
9 I have made him fair by the multitude of
his branches: so that all the trees of E'den, that
were in the garden of God, envied him.
10 ¶ Therefore thus saith the Lord GOD; Because thou hast lifted up thyself in height, and
he hath shot up his top among the thick boughs,
and his heart is lifted up in his height;
11 I have therefore delivered him into the
hand of the mighty one of the heathen; he shall
surely deal with him: I have driven him out for
his wickedness.
12 And strangers, the terrible of the nations,
have cut him off, and have left him: upon the
mountains and in all the valleys his branches
are fallen, and his boughs are broken by all the
rivers of the land; and all the people of the earth
are gone down from his shadow, and have left
him.
13 Upon his ruin shall all the fowls of the
heaven remain, and all the beasts of the field
shall be upon his branches:
14 To the end that none of all the trees by the
waters exalt themselves for their height, neither
shoot up their top among the thick boughs, neither their trees stand up in their height, all that
drink water: for they are all delivered unto
death, to the nether parts of the earth, in the
midst of the children of men, with them that go
down to the pit.
15 Thus saith the Lord GOD; In the day when
he went down to the grave I caused a mourning:
I covered the deep for him, and I restrained the
floods thereof, and the great waters were
stayed: and I caused Leb'a-non to mourn for
him, and all the trees of the field fainted for
him.
16 I made the nations to shake at the sound
of his fall, when I cast him down to hell with
them that descend into the pit: and all the trees
of E'den, the choice and best of Leb'a-non, all
that drink water, shall be comforted in the
nether parts of the earth.
17 They also went down into hell with him
unto *them that be* slain with the sword; and
they that were his arm, *that* dwelt under his
shadow in the midst of the heathen.
18 ¶ To whom art thou thus like in glory and
in greatness among the trees of E'den? yet shalt
thou be brought down with the trees of E'den
unto the nether parts of the earth: thou shalt lie

in the midst of the uncircumcised with *them*
that be slain by the sword. This is Pha'raoh and
all his multitude, saith the Lord GOD.

32 AND it came to pass in the twelfth year,
in the twelfth month, in the first *day* of
the month, *that* the word of the LORD came
unto me, saying,
2 Son of man, take up a lamentation for Pha'-
raoh king of E'gypt, and say unto him, Thou art
like a young lion of the nations, and thou *art* as
a whale in the seas: and thou camest forth with
thy rivers, and troubledst the waters with thy
feet, and fouledst their rivers.
3 Thus saith the Lord GOD; I will therefore
spread out my net over thee with a company of
many people; and they shall bring thee up in my
net.
4 Then will I leave thee upon the land, I will
cast thee forth upon the open field, and will
cause all the fowls of the heaven to remain
upon thee, and I will fill the beasts of the whole
earth with thee.
5 And I will lay thy flesh upon the mountains, and fill the valleys with thy height.
6 I will also water with thy blood the land
wherein thou swimmest, *even* to the mountains;
and the rivers shall be full of thee.
7 And when I shall put thee out, I will cover
the heaven, and make the stars thereof dark; I
will cover the sun with a cloud, and the moon
shall not give her light.
8 All the bright lights of heaven will I make
dark over thee, and set darkness upon thy land,
saith the Lord GOD.
9 I will also vex the hearts of many people,
when I shall bring thy destruction among the
nations, into the countries which thou hast not
known.
10 Yea, I will make many people amazed at
thee, and their kings shall be horribly afraid for
thee, when I shall brandish my sword before
them; and they shall tremble at *every* moment,
every man for his own life, in the day of thy fall.
11 ¶ For thus saith the Lord GOD; The sword
of the king of Bab'y-lon shall come upon thee.
12 By the swords of the mighty will I cause
thy multitude to fall, the terrible of the nations,
all of them: and they shall spoil the pomp of
E'gypt, and all the multitude thereof shall be
destroyed.
13 I will destroy also all the beasts thereof
from beside the great waters; neither shall the
foot of man trouble them any more, nor the
hoofs of beasts trouble them.
14 Then will I make their waters deep, and
cause their rivers to run like oil, saith the Lord
GOD.
15 When I shall make the land of E'gypt
desolate, and the country shall be destitute of
that whereof it was full, when I shall smite all
them that dwell therein, then shall they know
that I *am* the LORD.
16 This *is* the lamentation wherewith they
shall lament her: the daughters of the nations
shall lament her: they shall lament for her, *even*
for E'gypt, and for all her multitude, saith the
Lord GOD.
17 ¶ It came to pass also in the twelfth year,
in the fifteenth *day* of the month, *that* the word
of the LORD came unto me, saying,
18 Son of man, wail for the multitude of E'-
gypt, and cast them down, *even* her, and the
daughters of the famous nations, unto the
nether parts of the earth, with them that go
down into the pit.
19 Whom dost thou pass in beauty? go down,
and be thou laid with the uncircumcised.
20 They shall fall in the midst of *them that*
are slain by the sword: she is delivered to the
sword: draw her and all her multitudes.
21 The strong among the mighty shall speak
to him out of the midst of hell with them that
help him: they are gone down, they lie uncircumcised, slain by the sword.
22 Assh'ur *is* there and all her company: his
graves *are* about him: all of them slain, fallen
by the sword:
23 Whose graves are set in the sides of the
pit, and her company is round about her grave:
all of them slain, fallen by the sword, which
caused terror in the land of the living.
24 There *is* E'lam and all her multitude round
about her grave, all of them slain, fallen by the
sword, which are gone down uncircumcised
into the nether parts of the earth, which caused
their terror in the land of the living; yet have
they borne their shame with them that go down
to the pit.
25 They have set her a bed in the midst of the
slain with all her multitude: her graves *are*
round about him: all of them uncircumcised,
slain by the sword: though their terror was
caused in the land of the living, yet have they
borne their shame with them that go down to
the pit: he is put in the midst of *them that be*
slain.
26 There *is* Me'shech, Tu'bal, and all her multitude: her graves *are* round about him: all of
them uncircumcised, slain by the sword, though
they caused their terror in the land of the living.
27 And they shall not lie with the mighty *that*
are fallen of the uncircumcised, which are gone
down to hell with their weapons of war: and
they have laid their swords under their heads,
but their iniquities shall be upon their bones,
though *they were* the terror of the mighty in the
land of the living.
28 Yea, thou shalt be broken in the midst of
the uncircumcised, and shalt lie with *them that*
are slain with the sword.
29 There *is* E'dom, her kings, and all her
princes, which with their might are laid by *them*
that were slain by the sword: they shall lie with
the uncircumcised, and with them that go down
to the pit.
30 There *be* the princes of the north, all of
them, and all the Zi-do'ni-ans, which are gone
down with the slain; with their terror they are
ashamed of their might; and they lie uncircumcised with *them that be* slain by the sword, and
bear their shame with them that go down to the
pit.
31 Pha'raoh shall see them, and shall be comforted over all his multitude, *even* Pha'raoh and
all his army slain by the sword, saith the Lord
GOD.
32 For I have caused my terror in the land of
the living: and he shall be laid in the midst of
the uncircumcised with *them that are* slain with
the sword, *even* Pha'raoh and all his multitude,
saith the Lord GOD.

33 AGAIN the word of the LORD came unto
me, saying,
2 Son of man, speak to the children of thy
people, and say unto them, When I bring the
sword upon a land, if the people of the land take
a man of their coasts, and set him for their
watchman:
3 If when he seeth the sword come upon the
land, he blow the trumpet, and warn the people;
4 Then whosoever heareth the sound of the

trumpet, and taketh not warning; if the sword come, and take him away, his blood shall be upon his own head.

5 He heard the sound of the trumpet, and took not warning; his blood shall be upon him. But he that taketh warning shall deliver his soul.

6 But if the watchman see the sword come, and blow not the trumpet, and the people be not warned; if the sword come, and take *any* person from among them, he is taken away in his iniquity; but his blood will I require at the watchman's hand.

7 ¶ So thou, O son of man, I have set thee a watchman unto the house of Is'ra-el; therefore thou shalt hear the word at my mouth, and warn them from me.

8 When I say unto the wicked, O wicked *man*, thou shalt surely die; if thou dost not speak to warn the wicked from his way, that wicked *man* shall die in his iniquity; but his blood will I require at thine hand.

9 Nevertheless, if thou warn the wicked of his way to turn from it; if he do not turn from his way, he shall die in his iniquity; but thou hast delivered thy soul.

10 Therefore, O thou son of man, speak unto the house of Is'ra-el; Thus ye speak, saying, If our transgressions and our sins *be* upon us, and we pine away in them, how should we then live?

11 Say unto them, *As* I live, saith the Lord GOD, I have no pleasure in the death of the wicked; but that the wicked turn from his way and live: turn ye, turn ye from your evil ways; for why will ye die, O house of Is'ra-el?

12 Therefore, thou son of man, say unto the children of thy people, The righteousness of the righteous shall not deliver him in the day of his transgression: as for the wickedness of the wicked, he shall not fall thereby in the day that he turneth from his wickedness; neither shall the righteous be able to live for his *righteousness* in the day that he sinneth.

13 When I shall say to the righteous, *that* he shall surely live; if he trust to his own righteousness, and commit iniquity, all his righteousnesses shall not be remembered; but for his iniquity that he hath committed, he shall die for it.

14 Again, when I say unto the wicked, Thou shalt surely die; if he turn from his sin, and do that which is lawful and right;

15 *If* the wicked restore the pledge, give again that he had robbed, walk in the statutes of life, without committing iniquity; he shall surely live, he shall not die.

16 None of his sins that he hath committed shall be mentioned unto him: he hath done that which is lawful and right; he shall surely live.

17 ¶ Yet the children of thy people say, The way of the Lord is not equal: but as for them, their way is not equal.

18 When the righteous turneth from his righteousness, and committeth iniquity, he shall even die thereby.

19 But if the wicked turn from his wickedness, and do that which is lawful and right, he shall live thereby.

20 ¶ Yet ye say, The way of the Lord is not equal. O ye house of Is'ra-el, I will judge you every one after his ways.

21 ¶ And it came to pass in the twelfth year of our captivity, in the tenth *month*, in the fifth *day* of the month, *that* one that had escaped out of Je-ru'sa-lem came unto me, saying, The city is smitten.

22 Now the hand of the LORD was upon me in the evening, afore he that was escaped came; and had opened my mouth, until he came to me in the morning; and my mouth was opened, and I was no more dumb.

23 Then the word of the LORD came unto me, saying,

24 Son of man, they that inhabit those wastes of the land of Is'ra-el speak, saying, A'-bra-ham was one, and he inherited the land: but we *are* many; the land is given us for inheritance.

25 Wherefore say unto them, Thus saith the Lord GOD; Ye eat with the blood, and lift up your eyes toward your idols, and shed blood: and shall ye possess the land?

26 Ye stand upon your sword, ye work abomination, and ye defile every one his neighbour's wife: and shall ye possess the land?

27 Say thou thus unto them, Thus saith the Lord GOD; *As* I live, surely they that *are* in the wastes shall fall by the sword, and him that *is* in the open field will I give to the beasts to be devoured, and they that *be* in the forts and in the caves shall die of the pestilence.

28 For I will lay the land most desolate, and the pomp of her strength shall cease; and the mountains of Is'ra-el shall be desolate, that none shall pass through.

29 Then shall they know that I *am* the LORD, when I have laid the land most desolate because of all their abominations which they have committed.

30 ¶ Also, thou son of man, the children of thy people still are talking against thee by the walls and in the doors of the houses, and speak one to another, every one to his brother, saying, Come, I pray you, and hear what is the word that cometh forth from the LORD.

31 And they come unto thee as the people cometh, and they sit before thee *as* my people, and they hear thy words, but they will not do them: for with their mouth they shew much love, *but* their heart goeth after their covetousness.

32 And, lo, thou *art* unto them as a very lovely song of one that hath a pleasant voice, and can play well on an instrument: for they hear thy words, but they do them not.

33 And when this cometh to pass, (lo, it will come,) then shall they know that a prophet hath been among them.

34 AND the word of the LORD came unto me, saying,

2 Son of man, prophesy against the shepherds of Is'ra-el, prophesy, and say unto them, Thus saith the Lord GOD unto the shepherds; Woe *be* to the shepherds of Is'ra-el that do feed themselves! should not the shepherds feed the flocks?

3 Ye eat the fat, and ye clothe you with the wool, ye kill them that are fed: *but* ye feed not the flock.

4 The diseased have ye not strengthened, neither have ye healed that which was sick, neither have ye bound up *that which was* broken, neither have ye brought again that which was driven away, neither have ye sought that which was lost; but with force and with cruelty have ye ruled them.

5 And they were scattered, because *there is* no shepherd: and they became meat to all the beasts of the field, when they were scattered.

6 My sheep wandered through all the mountains, and upon every high hill: yea, my flock

was scattered upon all the face of the earth, and
none did search or seek *after them.*
7 ¶ Therefore, ye shepherds, hear the word
of the LORD;
8 *As* I live, saith the Lord GOD, surely because my flock became a prey, and my flock
became meat to every beast of the field, because *there was* no shepherd, neither did my
shepherds search for my flock, but the shepherds fed themselves, and fed not my flock;
9 Therefore, O ye shepherds, hear the word
of the LORD;
10 Thus saith the Lord GOD; Behold, I *am*
against the shepherds; and I will require my
flock at their hand, and cause them to cease
from feeding the flock; neither shall the shepherds feed themselves any more; for I will deliver my flock from their mouth, that they may
not be meat for them.
11 ¶ For thus saith the Lord GOD; Behold, I,
even I, will both search my sheep, and seek
them out.
12 As a shepherd seeketh out his flock in the
day that he is among his sheep *that are* scattered; so will I seek out my sheep, and will deliver them out of all places where they have
been scattered in the cloudy and dark day.
13 And I will bring them out from the people,
and gather them from the countries, and will
bring them to their own land, and feed them
upon the mountains of Is'ra-el by the rivers, and
in all the inhabited places of the country.
14 I will feed them in a good pasture, and
upon the high mountains of Is'ra-el shall their
fold be: there shall they lie in a good fold, and *in*
a fat pasture shall they feed upon the mountains of Is'ra-el.
15 I will feed my flock, and I will cause them
to lie down, saith the Lord GOD.
16 I will seek that which was lost, and bring
again that which was driven away, and will
bind up *that which was* broken, and will
strengthen that which was sick: but I will destroy the fat and the strong; I will feed them
with judgment.
17 And *as for* you, O my flock, thus saith the
Lord GOD; Behold, I judge between cattle and
cattle, between the rams and the he goats.
18 *Seemeth it* a small thing unto you to have
eaten up the good pasture, but ye must tread
down with your feet the residue of your pastures? and to have drunk of the deep waters,
but ye must foul the residue with your feet?
19 And *as for* my flock, they eat that which
ye have trodden with your feet; and they drink
that which ye have fouled with your feet.
20 ¶ Therefore thus saith the Lord GOD unto
them; Behold, I, *even* I, will judge between the
fat cattle and between the lean cattle.
21 Because ye have thrust with side and with
shoulder, and pushed all the diseased with your
horns, till ye have scattered them abroad;
22 Therefore will I save my flock, and they
shall no more be a prey; and I will judge between cattle and cattle.
23 And I will set up one shepherd over them,
and he shall feed them, *even* my servant Da'vid;
he shall feed them, and he shall be their shepherd.
24 And I the LORD will be their God, and my
servant Da'vid a prince among them; I the LORD
have spoken *it.*
25 And I will make with them a covenant of
peace, and will cause the evil beasts to cease
out of the land: and they shall dwell safely in
the wilderness, and sleep in the woods.
26 And I will make them and the places
round about my hill a blessing; and I will cause
the shower to come down in his season; there
shall be showers of blessing.
27 And the tree of the field shall yield her
fruit, and the earth shall yield her increase, and
they shall be safe in their land, and shall know
that I *am* the LORD, when I have broken the
bands of their yoke, and delivered them out of
the hand of those that served themselves of
them.
28 And they shall no more be a prey to the
heathen, neither shall the beast of the land devour them; but they shall dwell safely, and none
shall make *them* afraid.
29 And I will raise up for them a plant of renown, and they shall be no more consumed
with hunger in the land, neither bear the shame
of the heathen any more.
30 Thus shall they know that I the LORD their
God *am* with them, and *that* they, *even* the
house of Is'ra-el, *are* my people, saith the Lord
GOD.
31 And ye my flock, the flock of my pasture,
are men, *and* I *am* your God, saith the Lord
GOD.

35

MOREOVER the word of the LORD
came unto me, saying,
2 Son of man, set thy face against mount Se'-
ir, and prophesy against it,
3 And say unto it, Thus saith the Lord GOD;
Behold, O mount Se'ir, I *am* against thee, and I
will stretch out mine hand against thee, and I
will make thee most desolate.
4 I will lay thy cities waste, and thou shalt be
desolate, and thou shalt know that I *am* the
LORD.
5 Because thou hast had a perpetual hatred,
and hast shed *the blood of* the children of Is'ra-
el by the force of the sword in the time of their
calamity, in the time *that their* iniquity *had* an
end:
6 Therefore, *as* I live, saith the Lord GOD, I
will prepare thee unto blood, and blood shall
pursue thee: sith thou hast not hated blood,
even blood shall pursue thee.
7 Thus will I make mount Se'ir most desolate, and cut off from it him that passeth out
and him that returneth.
8 And I will fill his mountains with his slain
men: in thy hills, and in thy valleys, and in all
thy rivers, shall they fall that are slain with the
sword.
9 I will make thee perpetual desolations, and
thy cities shall not return: and ye shall know
that I *am* the LORD.
10 Because thou hast said, These two nations
and these two countries shall be mine, and we
will possess it; whereas the LORD was there:
11 Therefore, *as* I live, saith the Lord GOD, I
will even do according to thine anger, and according to thine envy which thou hast used out
of thy hatred against them; and I will make myself known among them, when I have judged
thee.
12 And thou shalt know that I *am* the LORD,
and that I have heard all thy blasphemies which
thou hast spoken against the mountains of Is'-
ra-el, saying, They are laid desolate, they are
given us to consume.
13 Thus with your mouth ye have boasted
against me, and have multiplied your words
against me: I have heard *them.*
14 Thus saith the Lord GOD; When the whole
earth rejoiceth, I will make thee desolate.
15 As thou didst rejoice at the inheritance of
the house of Is'ra-el, because it was desolate, so

will I do unto thee: thou shalt be desolate, O
mount Se'ir, and all I-du-me'a, *even* all of it: and
they shall know that I *am* the LORD.

36 ALSO, thou son of man, prophesy unto
the mountains of Is'ra-el, and say, Ye
mountains of Is'ra-el, hear the word of the
LORD:
2 Thus saith the Lord GOD; Because the enemy hath said against you, Aha, even the ancient
high places are ours in possession:
3 Therefore prophesy and say, Thus saith the
Lord GOD; Because they have made *you* desolate, and swallowed you up on every side, that
ye might be a possession unto the residue of the
heathen, and ye are taken up in the lips of talkers, and *are* an infamy of the people:
4 Therefore, ye mountains of Is'ra-el, hear
the word of the Lord GOD; Thus saith the Lord
GOD to the mountains, and to the hills, to the
rivers, and to the valleys, to the desolate
wastes, and to the cities that are forsaken,
which became a prey and derision to the residue of the heathen that *are* round about;
5 Therefore thus saith the Lord GOD; Surely
in the fire of my jealousy have I spoken against
the residue of the heathen, and against all I-du-
me'a, which have appointed my land into their
possession with the joy of all *their* heart, with
despiteful minds, to cast it out for a prey.
6 Prophesy therefore concerning the land of
Is'ra-el, and say unto the mountains, and to the
hills, to the rivers, and to the valleys, Thus saith
the Lord GOD; Behold, I have spoken in my jealousy and in my fury, because ye have borne the
shame of the heathen:
7 Therefore thus saith the Lord GOD; I have
lifted up mine hand, Surely the heathen that *are*
about you, they shall bear their shame.
8 ¶ But ye, O mountains of Is'ra-el, ye shall
shoot forth your branches, and yield your fruit
to my people of Is'ra-el: for they are at hand to
come.
9 For, behold, I *am* for you, and I will turn
unto you, and ye shall be tilled and sown:
10 And I will multiply men upon you, all the
house of Is'ra-el, *even* all of it: and the cities
shall be inhabited, and the wastes shall be
builded:
11 And I will multiply upon you man and
beast; and they shall increase and bring fruit:
and I will settle you after your old estates, and
will do better *unto you* than at your beginnings:
and ye shall know that I *am* the LORD.
12 Yea, I will cause men to walk upon you,
even my people Is'ra-el; and they shall possess
thee, and thou shalt be their inheritance, and
thou shalt no more henceforth bereave them *of*
men.
13 Thus saith the Lord GOD; Because they
say unto you, Thou *land* devourest up men, and
hast bereaved thy nations;
14 Therefore thou shalt devour men no more,
neither bereave thy nations any more, saith the
Lord GOD.
15 Neither will I cause *men* to hear in thee
the shame of the heathen any more, neither
shalt thou bear the reproach of the people any
more, neither shalt thou cause thy nations to
fall any more, saith the Lord GOD.
16 ¶ Moreover the word of the LORD came
unto me, saying,
17 Son of man, when the house of Is'ra-el
dwelt in their own land, they defiled it by their
own way and by their doings: their way was
before me as the uncleanness of a removed
woman.
18 Wherefore I poured my fury upon them
for the blood that they had shed upon the land,
and for their idols *wherewith* they had polluted
it:
19 And I scattered them among the heathen,
and they were dispersed through the countries:
according to their way and according to their
doings I judged them.
20 And when they entered unto the heathen,
whither they went, they profaned my holy
name, when they said to them, These *are* the
people of the LORD, and are gone forth out of
his land.
21 ¶ But I had pity for mine holy name,
which the house of Is'ra-el had profaned among
the heathen, whither they went.
22 Therefore say unto the house of Is'ra-el,
Thus saith the Lord GOD; I do not *this* for your
sakes, O house of Is'ra-el, but for mine holy
name's sake, which ye have profaned among
the heathen, whither ye went.
23 And I will sanctify my great name, which
was profaned among the heathen, which ye
have profaned in the midst of them; and the
heathen shall know that I *am* the LORD, saith
the Lord GOD, when I shall be sanctified in you
before their eyes.
24 For I will take you from among the heathen, and gather you out of all countries, and
will bring you into your own land.
25 ¶ Then will I sprinkle clean water upon
you, and ye shall be clean: from all your filthiness, and from all your idols, will I cleanse you.
26 A new heart also will I give you, and a
new spirit will I put within you: and I will take
away the stony heart out of your flesh, and I
will give you an heart of flesh.
27 And I will put my spirit within you, and
cause you to walk in my statutes, and ye shall
keep my judgments, and do *them.*
28 And ye shall dwell in the land that I gave
to your fathers; and ye shall be my people, and I
will be your God.
29 I will also save you from all your unclean-
nesses: and I will call for the corn, and will increase it, and lay no famine upon you.
30 And I will multiply the fruit of the tree,
and the increase of the field, that ye shall receive no more reproach of famine among the
heathen.
31 Then shall ye remember your own evil
ways, and your doings that *were* not good, and
shall loathe yourselves in your own sight for
your iniquities and for your abominations.
32 Not for your sakes do I *this,* saith the Lord
GOD, be it known unto you: be ashamed and
confounded for your own ways, O house of Is'-
ra-el.
33 Thus saith the Lord GOD; In the day that I
shall have cleansed you from all your iniquities
I will also cause *you* to dwell in the cities, and
the wastes shall be builded.
34 And the desolate land shall be tilled,
whereas it lay desolate in the sight of all that
passed by.
35 And they shall say, This land that was
desolate is become like the garden of E'den; and
the waste and desolate and ruined cities *are be-*
come fenced, *and* are inhabited.
36 Then the heathen that are left round about
you shall know that I the LORD build the ruined
places, and plant that that was desolate: I the
LORD have spoken *it,* and I will do *it.*
37 Thus saith the Lord GOD; I will yet *for* this
be enquired of by the house of Is'ra-el, to do *it*
for them; I will increase them with men like a
flock.

38 As the holy flock, as the flock of Je-ru'sa-lem in her solemn feasts; so shall the waste cities be filled with flocks of men: and they shall know that I *am* the LORD.

37 THE hand of the LORD was upon me, and carried me out in the spirit of the LORD, and set me down in the midst of the valley which *was* full of bones,

2 And caused me to pass by them round about: and, behold, *there were* very many in the open valley; and, lo, *they were* very dry.

3 And he said unto me, Son of man, can these bones live? And I answered, O Lord GOD, thou knowest.

4 Again he said unto me, Prophesy upon these bones, and say unto them, O ye dry bones, hear the word of the LORD.

5 Thus saith the Lord GOD unto these bones; Behold, I will cause breath to enter into you, and ye shall live:

6 And I will lay sinews upon you, and will bring up flesh upon you, and cover you with skin, and put breath in you, and ye shall live; and ye shall know that I *am* the LORD.

7 So I prophesied as I was commanded: and as I prophesied, there was a noise, and behold a shaking, and the bones came together, bone to his bone.

8 And when I beheld, lo, the sinews and the flesh came up upon them, and the skin covered them above: but *there was* no breath in them.

9 Then said he unto me, Prophesy unto the wind, prophesy, son of man, and say to the wind, Thus saith the Lord GOD; Come from the four winds, O breath, and breathe upon these slain, that they may live.

10 So I prophesied as he commanded me, and the breath came into them, and they lived, and stood up upon their feet, an exceeding great army.

11 ¶ Then he said unto me, Son of man, these bones are the whole house of Is'ra-el: behold, they say, Our bones are dried, and our hope is lost: we are cut off for our parts.

12 Therefore prophesy and say unto them, Thus saith the Lord GOD; Behold, O my people, I will open your graves, and cause you to come up out of your graves, and bring you into the land of Is'ra-el.

13 And ye shall know that I *am* the LORD, when I have opened your graves, O my people, and brought you up out of your graves,

14 And shall put my spirit in you, and ye shall live, and I shall place you in your own land: then shall ye know that I the LORD have spoken *it*, and performed *it*, saith the LORD.

15 ¶ The word of the LORD came again unto me, saying,

16 Moreover, thou son of man, take thee one stick, and write upon it, For Ju'dah, and for the children of Is'ra-el his companions: then take another stick, and write upon it, For Jo'seph, the stick of E'phra-im, and *for* all the house of Is'ra-el his companions:

17 And join them one to another into one stick; and they shall become one in thine hand.

18 ¶ And when the children of thy people shall speak unto thee, saying, Wilt thou not shew us what thou *meanest* by these?

19 Say unto them, Thus saith the Lord GOD; Behold, I will take the stick of Jo'seph, which *is* in the hand of E'phra-im, and the tribes of Is'ra-el his fellows, and will put them with him, *even* with the stick of Ju'dah, and make them one stick, and they shall be one in mine hand.

20 ¶ And the sticks whereon thou writest shall be in thine hand before their eyes.

21 And say unto them, Thus saith the Lord GOD; Behold, I will take the children of Is'ra-el from among the heathen, whither they be gone, and will gather them on every side, and bring them into their own land:

22 And I will make them one nation in the land upon the mountains of Is'ra-el; and one king shall be king to them all: and they shall be no more two nations, neither shall they be divided into two kingdoms any more at all:

23 Neither shall they defile themselves any more with their idols, nor with their detestable things, nor with any of their transgressions: but I will save them out of all their dwellingplaces, wherein they have sinned, and will cleanse them: so shall they be my people, and I will be their God.

24 And Da'vid my servant *shall be* king over them; and they all shall have one shepherd: they shall also walk in my judgments, and observe my statutes, and do them.

25 And they shall dwell in the land that I have given unto Ja'cob my servant, wherein your fathers have dwelt; and they shall dwell therein, *even* they, and their children, and their children's children for ever: and my servant Da'vid *shall be* their prince for ever.

26 Moreover I will make a covenant of peace with them; it shall be an everlasting covenant with them: and I will place them, and multiply them, and will set my sanctuary in the midst of them for evermore.

27 My tabernacle also shall be with them: yea, I will be their God, and they shall be my people.

28 And the heathen shall know that I the LORD do sanctify Is'ra-el, when my sanctuary shall be in the midst of them for evermore.

38 AND the word of the LORD came unto me, saying,

2 Son of man, set thy face against Gog, the land of Ma'gog, the chief prince of Me'shech and Tu'bal, and prophesy against him,

3 And say, Thus saith the Lord GOD; Behold, I *am* against thee, O Gog, the chief prince of Me'shech and Tu'bal:

4 And I will turn thee back, and put hooks into thy jaws, and I will bring thee forth, and all thine army, horses and horsemen, all of them clothed with all sorts *of armour, even* a great company *with* bucklers and shields, all of them handling swords:

5 Per'sia, E-thi-o'pi-a, and Lib'y-a with them; all of them with shield and helmet:

6 Go'mer, and all his bands; the house of To-gar'mah of the north quarters, and all his bands: *and* many people with thee.

7 Be thou prepared, and prepare for thyself, thou, and all thy company that are assembled unto thee, and be thou a guard unto them.

8 ¶ After many days thou shalt be visited: in the latter years thou shalt come into the land *that is* brought back from the sword, *and is* gathered out of many people, against the mountains of Is'ra-el, which have been always waste: but it is brought forth out of the nations, and they shall dwell safely all of them.

9 Thou shalt ascend and come like a storm, thou shalt be like a cloud to cover the land, thou, and all thy bands, and many people with thee.

10 Thus saith the Lord GOD; It shall also come to pass, *that* at the same time shall things

come into thy mind, and thou shalt think an evil
thought:
11 And thou shalt say, I will go up to the land
of unwalled villages; I will go to them that are
at rest, that dwell safely, all of them dwelling
without walls, and having neither bars nor
gates,
12 To take a spoil, and to take a prey; to turn
thine hand upon the desolate places *that are*
now inhabited, and upon the people *that are*
gathered out of the nations, which have gotten
cattle and goods, that dwell in the midst of the
land.
13 She'ba, and De'dan, and the merchants of
Tar'shish, with all the young lions thereof, shall
say unto thee, Art thou come to take a spoil?
hast thou gathered thy company to take a prey?
to carry away silver and gold, to take away cattle and goods, to take a great spoil?
14 ¶ Therefore, son of man, prophesy and
say unto Gog, Thus saith the Lord God; In that
day when my people of Is'ra-el dwelleth safely,
shalt thou not know *it?*
15 And thou shalt come from thy place out of
the north parts, thou, and many people with
thee, all of them riding upon horses, a great
company, and a mighty army:
16 And thou shalt come up against my people of Is'ra-el, as a cloud to cover the land; it
shall be in the latter days, and I will bring thee
against my land, that the heathen may know
me, when I shall be sanctified in thee, O Gog,
before their eyes.
17 Thus saith the Lord God; *Art* thou he of
whom I have spoken in old time by my servants
the prophets of Is'ra-el, which prophesied in
those days *many* years that I would bring thee
against them?
18 And it shall come to pass at the same time
when Gog shall come against the land of Is'ra-
el, saith the Lord God, *that* my fury shall come
up in my face.
19 For in my jealousy *and* in the fire of my
wrath have I spoken, Surely in that day there
shall be a great shaking in the land of Is'ra-el;
20 So that the fishes of the sea, and the fowls
of the heaven, and the beasts of the field, and all
creeping things that creep upon the earth, and
all the men that *are* upon the face of the earth,
shall shake at my presence, and the mountains
shall be thrown down, and the steep places
shall fall, and every wall shall fall to the ground.
21 And I will call for a sword against him
throughout all my mountains, saith the Lord
God: every man's sword shall be against his
brother.
22 And I will plead against him with pestilence and with blood; and I will rain upon him,
and upon his bands, and upon the many people
that *are* with him, an overflowing rain, and
great hailstones, fire, and brimstone.
23 Thus will I magnify myself, and sanctify
myself; and I will be known in the eyes of many
nations, and they shall know that I *am* the
Lord.

39 THEREFORE, thou son of man, prophesy against Gog, and say, Thus saith the
Lord God; Behold, I *am* against thee, O Gog, the
chief prince of Me'shech and Tu'bal:
2 And I will turn thee back, and leave but the
sixth part of thee, and will cause thee to come
up from the north parts, and will bring thee
upon the mountains of Is'ra-el:
3 And I will smite thy bow out of thy left
hand, and will cause thine arrows to fall out of
thy right hand.
4 Thou shalt fall upon the mountains of Is'ra-
el, thou, and all thy bands, and the people that
is with thee: I will give thee unto the ravenous
birds of every sort, and *to* the beasts of the field
to be devoured.
5 Thou shalt fall upon the open field: for I
have spoken *it*, saith the Lord God.
6 And I will send a fire on Ma'gog, and
among them that dwell carelessly in the isles:
and they shall know that I *am* the Lord.
7 So will I make my holy name known in the
midst of my people Is'ra-el; and I will not *let*
them pollute my holy name any more: and the
heathen shall know that I *am* the Lord, the
Holy One in Is'ra-el.
8 ¶ Behold, it is come, and it is done, saith
the Lord God; this *is* the day whereof I have
spoken.
9 And they that dwell in the cities of Is'ra-el
shall go forth, and shall set on fire and burn the
weapons, both the shields and the bucklers, the
bows and the arrows, and the handstaves, and
the spears, and they shall burn them with fire
seven years:
10 So that they shall take no wood out of the
field, neither cut down *any* out of the forests;
for they shall burn the weapons with fire: and
they shall spoil those that spoiled them, and rob
those that robbed them, saith the Lord God.
11 ¶ And it shall come to pass in that day,
that I will give unto Gog a place there of graves
in Is'ra-el, the valley of the passengers on the
east of the sea: and it shall stop the *noses* of the
passengers: and there shall they bury Gog and
all his multitude: and they shall call *it* The valley of Ha'mon-gog.
12 And seven months shall the house of Is'ra-
el be burying of them, that they may cleanse the
land.
13 Yea, all the people of the land shall bury
them; and it shall be to them a renown the day
that I shall be glorified, saith the Lord God.
14 And they shall sever out men of continual
employment, passing through the land to bury
with the passengers those that remain upon the
face of the earth, to cleanse it: after the end of
seven months shall they search.
15 And the passengers *that* pass through the
land, when *any* seeth a man's bone, then shall
he set up a sign by it, till the buriers have buried
it in the valley of Ha'mon-gog.
16 And also the name of the city *shall be* Ha-
mo'nah. Thus shall they cleanse the land.
17 ¶ And, thou son of man, thus saith the
Lord God; Speak unto every feathered fowl,
and to every beast of the field, Assemble yourselves, and come; gather yourselves on every
side to my sacrifice that I do sacrifice for you,
even a great sacrifice upon the mountains of Is'-
ra-el, that ye may eat flesh, and drink blood.
18 Ye shall eat the flesh of the mighty, and
drink the blood of the princes of the earth, of
rams, of lambs, and of goats, of bullocks, all of
them fatlings of Ba'shan.
19 And ye shall eat fat till ye be full, and
drink blood till ye be drunken, of my sacrifice
which I have sacrificed for you.
20 Thus ye shall be filled at my table with
horses and chariots, with mighty men, and with
all men of war, saith the Lord God.
21 And I will set my glory among the heathen, and all the heathen shall see my judgment
that I have executed, and my hand that I have
laid upon them.
22 So the house of Is'ra-el shall know that I
am the Lord their God from that day and forward.

23 ¶ And the heathen shall know that the
house of Is′ra-el went into captivity for their iniquity: because they trespassed against me,
therefore hid I my face from them, and gave
them into the hand of their enemies: so fell they
all by the sword.
24 According to their uncleanness and according to their transgressions have I done unto
them, and hid my face from them.
25 Therefore thus saith the Lord GOD; Now
will I bring again the captivity of Ja′cob, and
have mercy upon the whole house of Is′ra-el,
and will be jealous for my holy name;
26 After that they have borne their shame,
and all their trespasses whereby they have trespassed against me, when they dwelt safely in
their land, and none made *them* afraid.
27 When I have brought them again from the
people, and gathered them out of their enemies′
lands, and am sanctified in them in the sight of
many nations;
28 Then shall they know that I *am* the LORD
their God, which caused them to be led into
captivity among the heathen: but I have gathered them unto their own land, and have left
none of them any more there.
29 Neither will I hide my face any more from
them: for I have poured out my spirit upon the
house of Is′ra-el, saith the Lord GOD.

40 IN the five and twentieth year of our
captivity, in the beginning of the year, in
the tenth *day* of the month, in the fourteenth
year after that the city was smitten, in the selfsame day the hand of the LORD was upon me,
and brought me thither.
2 In the visions of God brought he me into
the land of Is′ra-el, and set me upon a very high
mountain, by which *was* as the frame of a city
on the south.
3 And he brought me thither, and, behold,
there was a man, whose appearance *was* like
the appearance of brass, with a line of flax in
his hand, and a measuring reed; and he stood in
the gate.
4 And the man said unto me, Son of man,
behold with thine eyes, and hear with thine
ears, and set thine heart upon all that I shall
shew thee; for to the intent that I might shew
them unto thee *art* thou brought hither: declare
all that thou seest to the house of Is′ra-el.
5 And behold a wall on the outside of the
house round about, and in the man′s hand a
measuring reed of six cubits *long* by the cubit
and an hand breadth: so he measured the
breadth of the building, one reed; and the
height, one reed.
6 ¶ Then came he unto the gate which looketh toward the east, and went up the stairs
thereof, and measured the threshold of the gate,
which was one reed broad; and the other
threshold *of the gate, which was* one reed
broad.
7 And *every* little chamber *was* one reed
long, and one reed broad; and between the little
chambers *were* five cubits; and the threshold of
the gate by the porch of the gate within *was* one
reed.
8 He measured also the porch of the gate
within, one reed.
9 Then measured he the porch of the gate,
eight cubits; and the posts thereof, two cubits;
and the porch of the gate *was* inward.
10 And the little chambers of the gate eastward *were* three on this side, and three on that
side; they three *were* of one measure: and the
posts had one measure on this side and on that
side.
11 And he measured the breadth of the entry
of the gate, ten cubits; *and* the length of the
gate, thirteen cubits.
12 The space also before the little chambers
was one cubit *on this side,* and the space *was*
one cubit on that side: and the little chambers
were six cubits on this side, and six cubits on
that side.
13 He measured then the gate from the roof
of *one* little chamber to the roof of another: the
breadth *was* five and twenty cubits, door
against door.
14 He made also posts of threescore cubits,
even unto the post of the court round about the
gate.
15 And from the face of the gate of the entrance unto the face of the porch of the inner
gate *were* fifty cubits.
16 And *there were* narrow windows to the little chambers, and to their posts within the gate
round about, and likewise to the arches: and
windows *were* round about inward: and upon
each post *were* palm trees.
17 Then brought he me into the outward
court, and, lo, *there were* chambers, and a pavement made for the court round about: thirty
chambers *were* upon the pavement.
18 And the pavement by the side of the gates
over against the length of the gates *was* the
lower pavement.
19 Then he measured the breadth from the
forefront of the lower gate unto the forefront of
the inner court without, an hundred cubits eastward and northward.
20 ¶ And the gate of the outward court that
looked toward the north, he measured the
length thereof, and the breadth thereof.
21 And the little chambers thereof *were* three
on this side and three on that side; and the posts
thereof and the arches thereof were after the
measure of the first gate: the length thereof *was*
fifty cubits, and the breadth five and twenty cubits.
22 And their windows, and their arches, and
their palm trees, *were* after the measure of the
gate that looketh toward the east; and they
went up unto it by seven steps; and the arches
thereof *were* before them.
23 And the gate of the inner court *was* over
against the gate toward the north, and toward
the east; and he measured from gate to gate an
hundred cubits.
24 ¶ After that he brought me toward the
south, and behold a gate toward the south: and
he measured the posts thereof and the arches
thereof according to these measures.
25 And *there were* windows in it and in the
arches thereof round about, like those windows: the length *was* fifty cubits, and the
breadth five and twenty cubits.
26 And *there were* seven steps to go up to it,
and the arches thereof *were* before them: and it
had palm trees, one on this side, and another on
that side, upon the posts thereof.
27 And *there was* a gate in the inner court
toward the south: and he measured from gate
to gate toward the south an hundred cubits.
28 And he brought me to the inner court by
the south gate: and he measured the south gate
according to these measures;
29 And the little chambers thereof, and the
posts thereof, and the arches thereof, according
to these measures: and *there were* windows in it
and in the arches thereof round about: *it was*

fifty cubits long, and five and twenty cubits broad.

30 And the arches round about *were* five and twenty cubits long, and five cubits broad.

31 And the arches thereof *were* toward the utter court; and palm trees *were* upon the posts thereof: and the going up to it *had* eight steps.

32 ¶ And he brought me into the inner court toward the east: and he measured the gate according to these measures.

33 And the little chambers thereof, and the posts thereof, and the arches thereof, *were* according to these measures: and *there were* windows therein and in the arches thereof round about: *it was* fifty cubits long, and five and twenty cubits broad.

34 And the arches thereof *were* toward the outward court; and palm trees *were* upon the posts thereof, on this side, and on that side: and the going up to it *had* eight steps.

35 ¶ And he brought me to the north gate, and measured *it* according to these measures;

36 The little chambers thereof, the posts thereof, and the arches thereof, and the windows to it round about: the length *was* fifty cubits, and the breadth five and twenty cubits.

37 And the posts thereof *were* toward the utter court; and palm trees *were* upon the posts thereof, on this side, and on that side: and the going up to it *had* eight steps.

38 And the chambers and the entries thereof *were* by the posts of the gates, where they washed the burnt offering.

39 ¶ And in the porch of the gate *were* two tables on this side, and two tables on that side, to slay thereon the burnt offering and the sin offering and the trespass offering.

40 And at the side without, as one goeth up to the entry of the north gate, *were* two tables; and on the other side, which *was* at the porch of the gate, *were* two tables.

41 Four tables *were* on this side, and four tables on that side, by the side of the gate; eight tables, whereupon they slew *their sacrifices*.

42 And the four tables *were* of hewn stone for the burnt offering, of a cubit and an half long, and a cubit and an half broad, and one cubit high: whereupon also they laid the instruments wherewith they slew the burnt offering and the sacrifice.

43 And within *were* hooks, an hand broad, fastened round about: and upon the tables *was* the flesh of the offering.

44 ¶ And without the inner gate *were* the chambers of the singers in the inner court, which *was* at the side of the north gate; and their prospect *was* toward the south: one at the side of the east gate *having* the prospect toward the north.

45 And he said unto me, This chamber, whose prospect *is* toward the south, *is* for the priests, the keepers of the charge of the house.

46 And the chamber whose prospect *is* toward the north *is* for the priests, the keepers of the charge of the altar: these *are* the sons of Za'dok among the sons of Le'vi, which come near to the LORD to minister unto him.

47 So he measured the court, an hundred cubits long, and an hundred cubits broad, foursquare; and the altar *that was* before the house.

48 ¶ And he brought me to the porch of the house, and measured *each* post of the porch, five cubits on this side, and five cubits on that side: and the breadth of the gate *was* three cubits on this side, and three cubits on that side.

49 The length of the porch *was* twenty cubits, and the breadth eleven cubits; and *he brought me* by the steps whereby they went up to it: and *there were* pillars by the posts, one on this side, and another on that side.

41 AFTERWARD he brought me to the temple, and measured the posts, six cubits broad on the one side, and six cubits broad on the other side, *which was* the breadth of the tabernacle.

2 And the breadth of the door *was* ten cubits; and the sides of the door *were* five cubits on the one side, and five cubits on the other side: and he measured the length thereof, forty cubits: and the breadth, twenty cubits.

3 Then went he inward, and measured the post of the door, two cubits; and the door, six cubits; and the breadth of the door, seven cubits.

4 So he measured the length thereof, twenty cubits; and the breadth, twenty cubits, before the temple: and he said unto me, This *is* the most holy *place*.

5 After he measured the wall of the house, six cubits; and the breadth of *every* side chamber, four cubits, round about the house on every side.

6 And the side chambers *were* three, one over another, and thirty in order; and they entered into the wall which *was* of the house for the side chambers round about, that they might have hold, but they had not hold in the wall of the house.

7 And *there was* an enlarging, and a winding about still upward to the side chambers: for the winding about of the house went still upward round about the house: therefore the breadth of the house *was still* upward, and so increased *from* the lowest *chamber* to the highest by the midst.

8 I saw also the height of the house round about: the foundations of the side chambers *were* a full reed of six great cubits.

9 The thickness of the wall, which *was* for the side chamber without, *was* five cubits: and *that* which *was* left *was* the place of the side chambers that *were* within.

10 And between the chambers *was* the wideness of twenty cubits round about the house on every side.

11 And the doors of the side chambers *were* toward *the place that was* left, one door toward the north, and another door toward the south: and the breadth of the place that was left *was* five cubits round about.

12 Now the building that *was* before the separate place at the end toward the west *was* seventy cubits broad; and the wall of the building *was* five cubits thick round about, and the length thereof ninety cubits.

13 So he measured the house, an hundred cubits long; and the separate place, and the building, with the walls thereof, an hundred cubits long;

14 Also the breadth of the face of the house, and of the separate place toward the east, an hundred cubits.

15 And he measured the length of the building over against the separate place which *was* behind it, and the galleries thereof on the one side and on the other side, an hundred cubits, with the inner temple, and the porches of the court;

16 The door posts, and the narrow windows, and the galleries round about on their three stories, over against the door, cieled with wood round about, and from the ground up to the windows, and the windows *were* covered;

17 To that above the door, even unto the inner house, and without, and by all the wall
round about within and without, by measure.
18 And *it was* made with cherubims and
palm trees, so that a palm tree *was* between a
cherub and a cherub; and *every* cherub had two
faces;
19 So that the face of a man *was* toward the
palm tree on the one side, and the face of a
young lion toward the palm tree on the other
side: *it was* made through all the house round
about.
20 From the ground unto above the door
were cherubims and palm trees made, and *on*
the wall of the temple.
21 The posts of the temple *were* squared, *and*
the face of the sanctuary; the appearance *of the*
one as the appearance *of the other.*
22 The altar of wood *was* three cubits high,
and the length thereof two cubits; and the corners thereof, and the length thereof, and the
walls thereof, *were* of wood: and he said unto
me, This *is* the table that *is* before the LORD.
23 And the temple and the sanctuary had
two doors.
24 And the doors had two leaves *apiece,* two
turning leaves; two *leaves* for the one door, and
two leaves for the other *door.*
25 And *there were* made on them, on the
doors of the temple, cherubims and palm trees,
like as *were* made upon the walls; and *there*
were thick planks upon the face of the porch
without.
26 And *there were* narrow windows and
palm trees on the one side and on the other
side, on the sides of the porch, and *upon* the
side chambers of the house, and thick planks.

42 THEN he brought me forth into the utter court, the way toward the north: and
he brought me into the chamber that *was* over
against the separate place, and which *was* before the building toward the north.
2 Before the length of an hundred cubits *was*
the north door, and the breadth *was* fifty cubits.
3 Over against the twenty *cubits* which *were*
for the inner court, and over against the pavement which *was* for the utter court, *was* gallery
against gallery in three *stories.*
4 And before the chambers *was* a walk of ten
cubits breadth inward, a way of one cubit; and
their doors toward the north.
5 Now the upper chambers *were* shorter: for
the galleries were higher than these, than the
lower, and than the middlemost of the building.
6 For they *were* in three *stories,* but had not
pillars as the pillars of the courts: therefore *the*
building was straitened more than the lowest
and the middlemost from the ground.
7 And the wall that *was* without over against
the chambers, toward the utter court on the
forepart of the chambers, the length thereof
was fifty cubits.
8 For the length of the chambers that *were* in
the utter court *was* fifty cubits: and, lo, before
the temple *were* an hundred cubits.
9 And from under these chambers *was* the
entry on the east side, as one goeth into them
from the utter court.
10 The chambers *were* in the thickness of the
wall of the court toward the east, over against
the separate place, and over against the building.
11 And the way before them *was* like the appearance of the chambers which *were* toward
the north, as long as they, *and* as broad as they:
and all their goings out *were* both according to
their fashions, and according to their doors.
12 And according to the doors of the chambers that *were* toward the south *was* a door in
the head of the way, *even* the way directly before the wall toward the east, as one entereth
into them.
13 ¶ Then said he unto me, The north chambers *and* the south chambers, which *are* before
the separate place, they *be* holy chambers,
where the priests that approach unto the LORD
shall eat the most holy things: there shall they
lay the most holy things, and the meat offering,
and the sin offering, and the trespass offering;
for the place *is* holy.
14 When the priests enter therein, then shall
they not go out of the holy *place* into the utter
court, but there they shall lay their garments
wherein they minister; for they *are* holy; and
shall put on other garments, and shall approach
to *those things* which *are* for the people.
15 Now when he had made an end of measuring the inner house, he brought me forth
toward the gate whose prospect *is* toward the
east, and measured it round about.
16 He measured the east side with the measuring reed, five hundred reeds, with the measuring reed round about.
17 He measured the north side, five hundred
reeds, with the measuring reed round about.
18 He measured the south side, five hundred
reeds, with the measuring reed.
19 ¶ He turned about to the west side, *and*
measured five hundred reeds with the measuring reed.
20 He measured it by the four sides: it had a
wall round about, five hundred *reeds* long, and
five hundred broad, to make a separation between the sanctuary and the profane place.

43 AFTERWARD he brought me to the
gate, *even* the gate that looketh toward
the east:
2 And, behold, the glory of the God of Is'ra-el
came from the way of the east: and his voice
was like a noise of many waters: and the earth
shined with his glory.
3 And *it was* according to the appearance of
the vision which I saw, *even* according to the
vision that I saw when I came to destroy the
city: and the visions *were* like the vision that I
saw by the river Che'bar; and I fell upon my
face.
4 And the glory of the LORD came into the
house by the way of the gate whose prospect *is*
toward the east.
5 So the spirit took me up, and brought me
into the inner court; and, behold, the glory of
the LORD filled the house.
6 And I heard *him* speaking unto me out of
the house; and the man stood by me.
7 ¶ And he said unto me, Son of man, the
place of my throne, and the place of the soles of
my feet, where I will dwell in the midst of the
children of Is'ra-el for ever, and my holy name,
shall the house of Is'ra-el no more defile, *neither*
they, nor their kings, by their whoredom, nor by
the carcases of their kings in their high places.
8 In their setting of their threshold by my
thresholds, and their post by my posts, and the
wall between me and them, they have even defiled my holy name by their abominations that
they have committed: wherefore I have consumed them in mine anger.
9 Now let them put away their whoredom,
and the carcases of their kings, far from me,
and I will dwell in the midst of them for ever.

10 ¶ Thou son of man, shew the house to the
house of Is'ra-el, that they may be ashamed of
their iniquities: and let them measure the pattern.
11 And if they be ashamed of all that they
have done, shew them the form of the house,
and the fashion thereof, and the goings out
thereof, and the comings in thereof, and all the
forms thereof, and all the ordinances thereof,
and all the forms thereof, and all the laws
thereof: and write *it* in their sight, that they
may keep the whole form thereof, and all the
ordinances thereof, and do them.
12 This *is* the law of the house; Upon the top
of the mountain the whole limit thereof round
about *shall be* most holy. Behold, this *is* the law
of the house.
13 ¶ And these *are* the measures of the altar
after the cubits: The cubit *is* a cubit and an
hand breadth; even the bottom *shall be* a cubit,
and the breadth a cubit, and the border thereof
by the edge thereof round about *shall be* a span:
and this *shall be* the higher place of the altar.
14 And from the bottom *upon* the ground
even to the lower settle *shall be* two cubits, and
the breadth one cubit; and from the lesser settle
even to the greater settle *shall be* four cubits,
and the breadth *one* cubit.
15 So the altar *shall be* four cubits; and from
the altar and upward *shall be* four horns.
16 And the altar *shall be* twelve *cubits* long,
twelve broad, square in the four squares
thereof.
17 And the settle *shall be* fourteen *cubits*
long and fourteen broad in the four squares
thereof; and the border about it *shall be* half a
cubit; and the bottom thereof *shall be* a cubit
about; and his stairs shall look toward the east.
18 ¶ And he said unto me, Son of man, thus
saith the Lord GOD; These *are* the ordinances of
the altar in the day when they shall make it, to
offer burnt offerings thereon, and to sprinkle
blood thereon.
19 And thou shalt give to the priests the Le'-
vites that be of the seed of Za'dok, which approach unto me, to minister unto me, saith the
Lord GOD, a young bullock for a sin offering.
20 And thou shalt take of the blood thereof,
and put *it* on the four horns of it, and on the
four corners of the settle, and upon the border
round about: thus shalt thou cleanse and purge
it.
21 Thou shalt take the bullock also of the sin
offering, and he shall burn it in the appointed
place of the house, without the sanctuary.
22 And on the second day thou shalt offer a
kid of the goats without blemish for a sin offering; and they shall cleanse the altar, as they did
cleanse *it* with the bullock.
23 When thou hast made an end of cleansing
it, thou shalt offer a young bullock without
blemish, and a ram out of the flock without
blemish.
24 And thou shalt offer them before the
LORD, and the priests shall cast salt upon them,
and they shall offer them up *for* a burnt offering
unto the LORD.
25 Seven days shalt thou prepare every day a
goat *for* a sin offering: they shall also prepare a
young bullock, and a ram out of the flock, without blemish.
26 Seven days shall they purge the altar and
purify it; and they shall consecrate themselves.
27 And when these days are expired, it shall
be, *that* upon the eighth day, and *so* forward,
the priests shall make your burnt offerings
upon the altar, and your peace offerings; and I
will accept you, saith the Lord GOD.

44

THEN he brought me back the way of
the gate of the outward sanctuary which
looketh toward the east; and it *was* shut.
2 Then said the LORD unto me; This gate shall
be shut, it shall not be opened, and no man shall
enter in by it; because the LORD, the God of Is'-
ra-el, hath entered in by it, therefore it shall be
shut.
3 *It is* for the prince; the prince, he shall sit in
it to eat bread before the LORD; he shall enter by
the way of the porch of *that* gate, and shall go
out by the way of the same.
4 ¶ Then brought he me the way of the north
gate before the house: and I looked, and, behold, the glory of the LORD filled the house of
the LORD: and I fell upon my face.
5 And the LORD said unto me, Son of man,
mark well, and behold with thine eyes, and hear
with thine ears all that I say unto thee concerning all the ordinances of the house of the LORD,
and all the laws thereof; and mark well the entering in of the house, with every going forth of
the sanctuary.
6 And thou shalt say to the rebellious, *even*
to the house of Is'ra-el, Thus saith the Lord
GOD; O ye house of Is'ra-el, let it suffice you of
all your abominations,
7 In that ye have brought *into my sanctuary*
strangers, uncircumcised in heart, and uncircumcised in flesh, to be in my sanctuary, to pollute it, *even* my house, when ye offer my bread,
the fat and the blood, and they have broken my
covenant because of all your abominations.
8 And ye have not kept the charge of mine
holy things: but ye have set keepers of my
charge in my sanctuary for yourselves.
9 ¶ Thus saith the Lord GOD; No stranger,
uncircumcised in heart, nor uncircumcised in
flesh, shall enter into my sanctuary, of any
stranger that *is* among the children of Is'ra-el.
10 And the Le'vites that are gone away far
from me, when Is'ra-el went astray, which went
astray away from me after their idols; they shall
even bear their iniquity.
11 Yet they shall be ministers in my sanctuary, *having* charge at the gates of the house,
and ministering to the house: they shall slay the
burnt offering and the sacrifice for the people,
and they shall stand before them to minister
unto them.
12 Because they ministered unto them before
their idols, and caused the house of Is'ra-el to
fall into iniquity; therefore have I lifted up mine
hand against them, saith the Lord GOD, and
they shall bear their iniquity.
13 And they shall not come near unto me, to
do the office of a priest unto me, nor to come
near to any of my holy things, in the most holy
place: but they shall bear their shame, and their
abominations which they have committed.
14 But I will make them keepers of the
charge of the house, for all the service thereof,
and for all that shall be done therein.
15 ¶ But the priests the Le'vites, the sons of
Za'dok, that kept the charge of my sanctuary
when the children of Is'ra-el went astray from
me, they shall come near to me to minister unto
me, and they shall stand before me to offer unto
me the fat and the blood, saith the Lord GOD:
16 They shall enter into my sanctuary, and
they shall come near to my table, to minister
unto me, and they shall keep my charge.
17 ¶ And it shall come to pass, *that* when
they enter in at the gates of the inner court,

they shall be clothed with linen garments; and no wool shall come upon them, whiles they minister in the gates of the inner court, and within.

18 They shall have linen bonnets upon their heads, and shall have linen breeches upon their loins; they shall not gird *themselves* with any thing that causeth sweat.

19 And when they go forth into the utter court, *even* into the utter court to the people, they shall put off their garments wherein they ministered, and lay them in the holy chambers, and they shall put on other garments; and they shall not sanctify the people with their garments.

20 Neither shall they shave their heads, nor suffer their locks to grow long; they shall only poll their heads.

21 Neither shall any priest drink wine, when they enter into the inner court.

22 Neither shall they take for their wives a widow, nor her that is put away: but they shall take maidens of the seed of the house of Is′ra-el, or a widow that had a priest before.

23 And they shall teach my people *the difference* between the holy and profane, and cause them to discern between the unclean and the clean.

24 And in controversy they shall stand in judgment; *and* they shall judge it according to my judgments: and they shall keep my laws and my statutes in all mine assemblies; and they shall hallow my sabbaths.

25 And they shall come at no dead person to defile themselves: but for father, or for mother, or for son, or for daughter, for brother, or for sister that hath had no husband, they may defile themselves.

26 And after he is cleansed, they shall reckon unto him seven days.

27 And in the day that he goeth into the sanctuary, unto the inner court, to minister in the sanctuary, he shall offer his sin offering, saith the Lord GOD.

28 And it shall be unto them for an inheritance: I *am* their inheritance: and ye shall give them no possession in Is′ra-el: I *am* their possession.

29 They shall eat the meat offering, and the sin offering, and the trespass offering; and every dedicated thing in Is′ra-el shall be theirs.

30 And the first of all the firstfruits of all *things,* and every oblation of all, of every *sort* of your oblations, shall be the priest's: ye shall also give unto the priest the first of your dough, that he may cause the blessing to rest in thine house.

31 The priests shall not eat of any thing that is dead of itself, or torn, whether it be fowl or beast.

45

MOREOVER, when ye shall divide by lot the land for inheritance, ye shall offer an oblation unto the LORD, an holy portion of the land: the length *shall be* the length of five and twenty thousand *reeds,* and the breadth *shall be* ten thousand. This *shall be* holy in all the borders thereof round about.

2 Of this there shall be for the sanctuary five hundred *in length,* with five hundred *in breadth,* square round about; and fifty cubits round about for the suburbs thereof.

3 And of this measure shalt thou measure the length of five and twenty thousand, and the breadth of ten thousand: and in it shall be the sanctuary *and* the most holy *place.*

4 The holy *portion* of the land shall be for the priests the ministers of the sanctuary, which shall come near to minister unto the LORD: and it shall be a place for their houses, and an holy place for the sanctuary.

5 And the five and twenty thousand of length, and the ten thousand of breadth, shall also the Le′vites, the ministers of the house, have for themselves, for a possession for twenty chambers.

6 ¶ And ye shall appoint the possession of the city five thousand broad, and five and twenty thousand long, over against the oblation of the holy *portion:* it shall be for the whole house of Is′ra-el.

7 ¶ And a *portion shall be* for the prince on the one side and on the other side of the oblation of the holy *portion,* and of the possession of the city, before the oblation of the holy *portion,* and before the possession of the city, from the west side westward, and from the east side eastward: and the length *shall be* over against one of the portions, from the west border unto the east border.

8 In the land shall be his possession in Is′ra-el: and my princes shall no more oppress my people; and *the rest of* the land shall they give to the house of Is′ra-el according to their tribes.

9 ¶ Thus saith the Lord GOD; Let it suffice you, O princes of Is′ra-el: remove violence and spoil, and execute judgment and justice, take away your exactions from my people, saith the Lord GOD.

10 Ye shall have just balances, and a just ephah, and a just bath.

11 The ephah and the bath shall be of one measure, that the bath may contain the tenth part of an homer, and the ephah the tenth part of an homer: the measure thereof shall be after the homer.

12 And the shekel *shall be* twenty gerahs: twenty shekels, five and twenty shekels, fifteen shekels, shall be your maneh.

13 This *is* the oblation that ye shall offer; the sixth part of an ephah of an homer of wheat, and ye shall give the sixth part of an ephah of an homer of barley:

14 Concerning the ordinance of oil, the bath of oil, *ye shall offer* the tenth part of a bath out of the cor, *which is* an homer of ten baths; for ten baths *are* an homer:

15 And one lamb out of the flock, out of two hundred, out of the fat pastures of Is′ra-el; for a meat offering, and for a burnt offering, and for peace offerings, to make reconciliation for them, saith the Lord GOD.

16 All the people of the land shall give this oblation for the prince in Is′ra-el.

17 And it shall be the prince's part *to give* burnt offerings, and meat offerings, and drink offerings, in the feasts, and in the new moons, and in the sabbaths, in all solemnities of the house of Is′ra-el: he shall prepare the sin offering, and the meat offering, and the burnt offering, and the peace offerings, to make reconciliation for the house of Is′ra-el.

18 Thus saith the Lord GOD; In the first *month,* in the first *day* of the month, thou shalt take a young bullock without blemish, and cleanse the sanctuary:

19 And the priest shall take of the blood of the sin offering, and put *it* upon the posts of the house, and upon the four corners of the settle of the altar, and upon the posts of the gate of the inner court.

20 And so thou shalt do the seventh *day* of the month for every one that erreth, and for *him that is* simple: so shall ye reconcile the house.

21 In the first *month*, in the fourteenth day of
the month, ye shall have the passover, a feast of
seven days; unleavened bread shall be eaten.
22 And upon that day shall the prince prepare for himself and for all the people of the
land a bullock *for* a sin offering.
23 And seven days of the feast he shall prepare a burnt offering to the LORD, seven bullocks and seven rams without blemish daily the
seven days; and a kid of the goats daily *for* a sin
offering.
24 And he shall prepare a meat offering of an
ephah for a bullock, and an ephah for a ram,
and an hin of oil for an ephah.
25 In the seventh *month*, in the fifteenth day
of the month, shall he do the like in the feast of
the seven days, according to the sin offering,
according to the burnt offering, and according
to the meat offering, and according to the oil.

46 THUS saith the Lord GOD; The gate of
the inner court that looketh toward the
east shall be shut the six working days; but on
the sabbath it shall be opened, and in the day of
the new moon it shall be opened.
2 And the prince shall enter by the way of
the porch of *that* gate without, and shall stand
by the post of the gate, and the priests shall
prepare his burnt offering and his peace offerings, and he shall worship at the threshold of
the gate: then he shall go forth; but the gate
shall not be shut until the evening.
3 Likewise the people of the land shall worship at the door of this gate before the LORD in
the sabbaths and in the new moons.
4 And the burnt offering that the prince shall
offer unto the LORD in the sabbath day *shall be*
six lambs without blemish, and a ram without
blemish.
5 And the meat offering *shall be* an ephah for
a ram, and the meat offering for the lambs as he
shall be able to give, and an hin of oil to an
ephah.
6 And in the day of the new moon *it shall be*
a young bullock without blemish, and six
lambs, and a ram: they shall be without blemish.
7 And he shall prepare a meat offering, an
ephah for a bullock, and an ephah for a ram,
and for the lambs according as his hand shall
attain unto, and an hin of oil to an ephah.
8 And when the prince shall enter, he shall
go in by the way of the porch of *that* gate, and
he shall go forth by the way thereof.
9 ¶ But when the people of the land shall
come before the LORD in the solemn feasts, he
that entereth in by the way of the north gate to
worship shall go out by the way of the south
gate; and he that entereth by the way of the
south gate shall go forth by the way of the north
gate: he shall not return by the way of the gate
whereby he came in, but shall go forth over
against it.
10 And the prince in the midst of them, when
they go in, shall go in; and when they go forth,
shall go forth.
11 And in the feasts and in the solemnities
the meat offering shall be an ephah to a bullock,
and an ephah to a ram, and to the lambs as he is
able to give, and an hin of oil to an ephah.
12 Now when the prince shall prepare a voluntary burnt offering or peace offerings volun-
tarily unto the LORD, *one* shall then open him
the gate that looketh toward the east, and he
shall prepare his burnt offering and his peace
offerings, as he did on the sabbath day: then he
shall go forth; and after his going forth *one* shall
shut the gate.
13 Thou shalt daily prepare a burnt offering
unto the LORD *of* a lamb of the first year without blemish: thou shalt prepare it every morning.
14 And thou shalt prepare a meat offering for
it every morning, the sixth part of an ephah,
and the third part of an hin of oil, to temper
with the fine flour; a meat offering continually
by a perpetual ordinance unto the LORD.
15 Thus shall they prepare the lamb, and the
meat offering, and the oil, every morning *for* a
continual burnt offering.
16 ¶ Thus saith the Lord GOD; If the prince
give a gift unto any of his sons, the inheritance
thereof shall be his sons'; it *shall be* their possession by inheritance.
17 But if he give a gift of his inheritance to
one of his servants, then it shall be his to the
year of liberty; after it shall return to the prince:
but his inheritance shall be his sons' for them.
18 Moreover the prince shall not take of the
people's inheritance by oppression, to thrust
them out of their possession; *but* he shall give
his sons inheritance out of his own possession:
that my people be not scattered every man
from his possession.
19 ¶ After he brought me through the entry,
which *was* at the side of the gate, into the holy
chambers of the priests, which looked toward
the north: and, behold, there *was* a place on the
two sides westward.
20 Then said he unto me, This *is* the place
where the priests shall boil the trespass offering
and the sin offering, where they shall bake the
meat offering; that they bear *them* not out into
the utter court, to sanctify the people.
21 Then he brought me forth into the utter
court, and caused me to pass by the four corners of the court; and, behold, in every corner of
the court *there was* a court.
22 In the four corners of the court *there were*
courts joined of forty *cubits* long and thirty
broad: these four corners *were* of one measure.
23 And *there was* a row *of building* round
about in them, round about them four, and *it
was* made with boiling places under the rows
round about.
24 Then said he unto me, These *are* the
places of them that boil, where the ministers of
the house shall boil the sacrifice of the people.

47 AFTERWARD he brought me again
unto the door of the house; and, behold,
waters issued out from under the threshold of
the house eastward: for the forefront of the
house *stood toward* the east, and the waters
came down from under from the right side of
the house, at the south *side* of the altar.
2 Then brought he me out of the way of the
gate northward, and led me about the way
without unto the utter gate by the way that
looketh eastward; and, behold, there ran out
waters on the right side.
3 And when the man that had the line in his
hand went forth eastward, he measured a thousand cubits, and he brought me through the waters; the waters *were* to the ancles.
4 Again he measured a thousand, and
brought me through the waters; the waters
were to the knees. Again he measured a thousand, and brought me through; the waters *were*
to the loins.
5 Afterward he measured a thousand; *and it
was* a river that I could not pass over: for the

waters were risen, waters to swim in, a river that could not be passed over.

6 ¶ And he said unto me, Son of man, hast thou seen *this?* Then he brought me, and caused me to return to the brink of the river.

7 Now when I had returned, behold, at the bank of the river *were* very many trees on the one side and on the other.

8 Then said he unto me, These waters issue out toward the east country, and go down into the desert, and go into the sea: *which being* brought forth into the sea, the waters shall be healed.

9 And it shall come to pass, *that* every thing that liveth, which moveth, whithersoever the rivers shall come, shall live: and there shall be a very great multitude of fish, because these waters shall come thither: for they shall be healed; and every thing shall live whither the river cometh.

10 And it shall come to pass, *that* the fishers shall stand upon it from En–ge'di even unto En–eg'la-im; they shall be a *place* to spread forth nets; their fish shall be according to their kinds, as the fish of the great sea, exceeding many.

11 But the miry places thereof and the marishes thereof shall not be healed; they shall be given to salt.

12 And by the river upon the bank thereof, on this side and on that side, shall grow all trees for meat, whose leaf shall not fade, neither shall the fruit thereof be consumed: it shall bring forth new fruit according to his months, because their waters they issued out of the sanctuary: and the fruit thereof shall be for meat, and the leaf thereof for medicine.

13 ¶ Thus saith the Lord GOD; This *shall be* the border, whereby ye shall inherit the land according to the twelve tribes of Is'ra-el: Jo'seph *shall have two* portions.

14 And ye shall inherit it, one as well as another: *concerning* the which I lifted up mine hand to give it unto your fathers: and this land shall fall unto you for inheritance.

15 And this *shall be* the border of the land toward the north side, from the great sea, the way of Heth'lon, as men go to Ze'dad;

16 Ha'math, Be-ro'thah, Sib'ra-im, which *is* between the border of Da-mas'cus and the border of Ha'math; Ha'zar–hat'ti-con, which *is* by the coast of Hau'ran.

17 And the border from the sea shall be Ha'zar–e'nan, the border of Da-mas'cus, and the north northward, and the border of Ha'math. And *this is* the north side.

18 And the east side ye shall measure from Hau'ran, and from Da-mas'cus, and from Gil'e-ad, and from the land of Is'ra-el *by* Jor'dan, from the border unto the east sea. And *this is* the east side.

19 And the south side southward, from Ta'mar *even* to the waters of strife *in* Ka'desh, the river to the great sea. And *this is* the south side southward.

20 The west side also *shall be* the great sea from the border, till a man come over against Ha'math. This *is* the west side.

21 So shall ye divide this land unto you according to the tribes of Is'ra-el.

22 ¶ And it shall come to pass, *that* ye shall divide it by lot for an inheritance unto you, and to the strangers that sojourn among you, which shall beget children among you: and they shall be unto you as born in the country among the children of Is'ra-el; they shall have inheritance with you among the tribes of Is'ra-el.

23 And it shall come to pass, *that* in what tribe the stranger sojourneth, there shall ye give *him* his inheritance, saith the Lord GOD.

48 NOW these *are* the names of the tribes. From the north end to the coast of the way of Heth'lon, as one goeth to Ha'math, Ha'zar–e'nan, the border of Da-mas'cus northward, to the coast of Ha'math; for these are his sides east *and* west; a *portion for* Dan.

2 And by the border of Dan, from the east side unto the west side, a *portion for* Ash'er.

3 And by the border of Ash'er, from the east side even unto the west side, a *portion for* Naph'ta-li.

4 And by the border of Naph'ta-li, from the east side unto the west side, a *portion for* Ma-nas'seh.

5 And by the border of Ma-nas'seh, from the east side unto the west side, a *portion for* E'phra-im.

6 And by the border of E'phra-im, from the east side even unto the west side, a *portion for* Reu'ben.

7 And by the border of Reu'ben, from the east side unto the west side, a *portion for* Ju'dah.

8 ¶ And by the border of Ju'dah, from the east side unto the west side, shall be the offering which ye shall offer of five and twenty thousand *reeds in* breadth, and *in* length as one of the *other* parts, from the east side unto the west side: and the sanctuary shall be in the midst of it.

9 The oblation that ye shall offer unto the LORD *shall be* of five and twenty thousand in length, and of ten thousand in breadth.

10 And for them, *even* for the priests, shall be *this* holy oblation; toward the north five and twenty thousand *in length*, and toward the west ten thousand in breadth, and toward the east ten thousand in breadth, and toward the south five and twenty thousand in length: and the sanctuary of the LORD shall be in the midst thereof.

11 *It shall be* for the priests that are sanctified of the sons of Za'dok; which have kept my charge, which went not astray when the children of Is'ra-el went astray, as the Le'vites went astray.

12 And *this* oblation of the land that is offered shall be unto them a thing most holy by the border of the Le'vites.

13 And over against the border of the priests the Le'vites *shall have* five and twenty thousand in length, and ten thousand in breadth: all the length *shall be* five and twenty thousand, and the breadth ten thousand.

14 And they shall not sell of it, neither exchange, nor alienate the firstfruits of the land: for *it is* holy unto the LORD.

15 ¶ And the five thousand, that are left in the breadth over against the five and twenty thousand, shall be a profane *place* for the city, for dwelling, and for suburbs: and the city shall be in the midst thereof.

16 And these *shall be* the measures thereof; the north side four thousand and five hundred, and the south side four thousand and five hundred, and on the east side four thousand and five hundred, and the west side four thousand and five hundred.

17 And the suburbs of the city shall be toward the north two hundred and fifty, and toward the south two hundred and fifty, and toward the east two hundred and fifty, and toward the west two hundred and fifty.

18 And the residue in length over against the oblation of the holy *portion shall be* ten thousand eastward, and ten thousand westward: and it shall be over against the oblation of the holy *portion;* and the increase thereof shall be for food unto them that serve the city.

19 And they that serve the city shall serve it out of all the tribes of Is'ra-el.

20 All the oblation *shall be* five and twenty thousand by five and twenty thousand: ye shall offer the holy oblation foursquare, with the possession of the city.

21 ¶ And the residue *shall be* for the prince, on the one side and on the other of the holy oblation, and of the possession of the city, over against the five and twenty thousand of the oblation toward the east border, and westward over against the five and twenty thousand toward the west border, over against the portions for the prince: and it shall be the holy oblation; and the sanctuary of the house *shall be* in the midst thereof.

22 Moreover from the possession of the Le'vites, and from the possession of the city, *being* in the midst *of that* which is the prince's, between the border of Ju'dah and the border of Ben'ja-min, shall be for the prince.

23 As for the rest of the tribes, from the east side unto the west side, Ben'ja-min *shall have* a *portion.*

24 And by the border of Ben'ja-min, from the east side unto the west side, Sim'e-on *shall have* a *portion.*

25 And by the border of Sim'e-on, from the east side unto the west side, Is'sa-char a *portion.*

26 And by the border of Is'sa-char, from the east side unto the west side, Zeb'u-lun a *portion.*

27 And by the border of Zeb'u-lun, from the east side unto the west side, Gad a *portion.*

28 And by the border of Gad at the south side southward, the border shall be even from Ta'mar *unto* the waters of strife *in* Ka'desh, *and* to the river toward the great sea.

29 This *is* the land which ye shall divide by lot unto the tribes of Is'ra-el for inheritance, and these *are* their portions, saith the Lord GOD.

30 ¶ And these *are* the goings out of the city on the north side, four thousand and five hundred measures.

31 And the gates of the city *shall be* after the names of the tribes of Is'ra-el: three gates northward; one gate of Reu'ben, one gate of Ju'dah, one gate of Le'vi.

32 And at the east side four thousand and five hundred: and three gates; and one gate of Jo'seph, one gate of Ben'ja-min, one gate of Dan.

33 And at the south side four thousand and five hundred measures: and three gates; one gate of Sim'e-on, one gate of Is'sa-char, one gate of Zeb'u-lun.

34 At the west side four thousand and five hundred, *with* their three gates; one gate of Gad, one gate of Ash'er, one gate of Naph'ta-li.

35 *It was* round about eighteen thousand *measures:* and the name of the city from *that* day *shall be,* The LORD *is* there.

THE BOOK OF

DANIEL

1 IN the third year of the reign of Je-hoi'a-kim king of Ju'dah came Neb-u-chad-nez'zar king of Bab'y-lon unto Je-ru'sa-lem, and besieged it.

2 And the Lord gave Je-hoi'a-kim king of Ju'dah into his hand, with part of the vessels of the house of God: which he carried into the land of Shi'nar to the house of his god; and he brought the vessels into the treasure house of his god.

3 ¶ And the king spake unto Ash'pe-naz the master of his eunuchs, that he should bring *certain* of the children of Is'ra-el, and of the king's seed, and of the princes;

4 Children in whom *was* no blemish, but well favoured, and skilful in all wisdom, and cunning in knowledge, and understanding science, and such as *had* ability in them to stand in the king's palace, and whom they might teach the learning and the tongue of the Chal-de'ans.

5 And the king appointed them a daily provision of the king's meat, and of the wine which he drank: so nourishing them three years, that at the end thereof they might stand before the king.

6 Now among these were of the children of Ju'dah, Dan'iel, Han-a-ni'ah, Mish'a-el, and Az-a-ri'ah:

7 Unto whom the prince of the eunuchs gave names: for he gave unto Dan'iel *the name* of Bel-te-shaz'zar; and to Han-a-ni'ah, of Sha'drach; and to Mish'a-el, of Me'shach; and to Az-a-ri'ah, of A-bed'–ne-go.

8 ¶ But Dan'iel purposed in his heart that he would not defile himself with the portion of the king's meat, nor with the wine which he drank: therefore he requested of the prince of the eunuchs that he might not defile himself.

9 Now God had brought Dan'iel into favour and tender love with the prince of the eunuchs.

10 And the prince of the eunuchs said unto Dan'iel, I fear my lord the king, who hath appointed your meat and your drink: for why should he see your faces worse liking than the children which *are* of your sort? then shall ye make *me* endanger my head to the king.

11 Then said Dan'iel to Mel'zar, whom the prince of the eunuchs had set over Dan'iel, Han-a-ni'ah, Mish'a-el, and Az-a-ri'ah,

12 Prove thy servants, I beseech thee, ten days; and let them give us pulse to eat, and water to drink.

13 Then let our countenances be looked upon before thee, and the countenance of the children that eat of the portion of the king's meat: and as thou seest, deal with thy servants.

14 So he consented to them in this matter, and proved them ten days.

15 And at the end of ten days their countenances appeared fairer and fatter in flesh than all the children which did eat the portion of the king's meat.

16 Thus Mel'zar took away the portion of their meat, and the wine that they should drink; and gave them pulse.

17 ¶ As for these four children, God gave them knowledge and skill in all learning and wisdom: and Dan'iel had understanding in all visions and dreams.

18 Now at the end of the days that the king
had said he should bring them in, then the
prince of the eunuchs brought them in before
Neb-u-chad-nez'zar.
19 And the king communed with them; and
among them all was found none like Dan'iel,
Han-a-ni'ah, Mish'a-el, and Az-a-ri'ah: therefore
stood they before the king.
20 And in all matters of wisdom *and* understanding, that the king enquired of them, he
found them ten times better than all the magicians *and* astrologers that *were* in all his realm.
21 And Dan'iel continued *even* unto the first
year of king Cy'rus.

2 AND in the second year of the reign of
Neb-u-chad-nez'zar Neb-u-chad-nez'zar
dreamed dreams, wherewith his spirit was troubled, and his sleep brake from him.
2 Then the king commanded to call the magicians, and the astrologers, and the sorcerers,
and the Chal-de'ans, for to shew the king his
dreams. So they came and stood before the
king.
3 And the king said unto them, I have
dreamed a dream, and my spirit was troubled to
know the dream.
4 Then spake the Chal-de'ans to the king in
Syr'i-ack, O king, live for ever: tell thy servants
the dream, and we will shew the interpretation.
5 The king answered and said to the Chal-
de'ans, The thing is gone from me: if ye will not
make known unto me the dream, with the interpretation thereof, ye shall be cut in pieces, and
your houses shall be made a dunghill.
6 But if ye shew the dream, and the interpretation thereof, ye shall receive of me gifts and
rewards and great honour: therefore shew me
the dream, and the interpretation thereof.
7 They answered again and said, Let the king
tell his servants the dream, and we will shew
the interpretation of it.
8 The king answered and said, I know of certainty that ye would gain the time, because ye
see the thing is gone from me.
9 But if ye will not make known unto me the
dream, *there is but* one decree for you: for ye
have prepared lying and corrupt words to speak
before me, till the time be changed: therefore
tell me the dream, and I shall know that ye can
shew me the interpretation thereof.
10 ¶ The Chal-de'ans answered before the
king, and said, There is not a man upon the
earth that can shew the king's matter: therefore
there is no king, lord, nor ruler, *that* asked such
things at any magician, or astrologer, or Chal-
de'an.
11 And *it is* a rare thing that the king requireth, and there is none other that can shew it
before the king, except the gods, whose dwelling is not with flesh.
12 For this cause the king was angry and
very furious, and commanded to destroy all the
wise *men* of Bab'y-lon.
13 And the decree went forth that the wise
men should be slain; and they sought Dan'iel
and his fellows to be slain.
14 ¶ Then Dan'iel answered with counsel
and wisdom to A'ri-och the captain of the king's
guard, which was gone forth to slay the wise
men of Bab'y-lon:
15 He answered and said to A'ri-och the
king's captain, Why *is* the decree *so* hasty from
the king? Then A'ri-och made the thing known
to Dan'iel.
16 Then Dan'iel went in, and desired of the
king that he would give him time, and that he
would shew the king the interpretation.
17 Then Dan'iel went to his house, and made
the thing known to Han-a-ni'ah, Mish'a-el, and
Az-a-ri'ah, his companions:
18 That they would desire mercies of the God
of heaven concerning this secret; that Dan'iel
and his fellows should not perish with the rest
of the wise *men* of Bab'y-lon.
19 ¶ Then was the secret revealed unto Dan'-
iel in a night vision. Then Dan'iel blessed the
God of heaven.
20 Dan'iel answered and said, Blessed be the
name of God for ever and ever: for wisdom and
might are his:
21 And he changeth the times and the seasons: he removeth kings, and setteth up kings:
he giveth wisdom unto the wise, and knowledge
to them that know understanding:
22 He revealeth the deep and secret things:
he knoweth what *is* in the darkness, and the
light dwelleth with him.
23 I thank thee, and praise thee, O thou God
of my fathers, who hast given me wisdom and
might, and hast made known unto me now
what we desired of thee: for thou hast *now*
made known unto us the king's matter.
24 ¶ Therefore Dan'iel went in unto A'ri-och,
whom the king had ordained to destroy the
wise *men* of Bab'y-lon: he went and said thus
unto him; Destroy not the wise *men* of Bab'y-
lon: bring me in before the king, and I will shew
unto the king the interpretation.
25 Then A'ri-och brought in Dan'iel before
the king in haste, and said thus unto him, I have
found a man of the captives of Ju'dah, that will
make known unto the king the interpretation.
26 The king answered and said to Dan'iel,
whose name *was* Bel-te-shaz'zar, Art thou able
to make known unto me the dream which I
have seen, and the interpretation thereof?
27 Dan'iel answered in the presence of the
king, and said, The secret which the king hath
demanded cannot the wise *men*, the astrologers, the magicians, the soothsayers, shew unto
the king;
28 But there is a God in heaven that revealeth secrets, and maketh known to the king Neb-
u-chad-nez'zar what shall be in the latter days.
Thy dream, and the visions of thy head upon
thy bed, are these;
29 As for thee, O king, thy thoughts came
into thy mind upon thy bed, what should come
to pass hereafter: and he that revealeth secrets
maketh known to thee what shall come to pass.
30 But as for me, this secret is not revealed
to me for *any* wisdom that I have more than
any living, but for *their* sakes that shall make
known the interpretation to the king, and that
thou mightest know the thoughts of thy heart.
31 ¶ Thou, O king, sawest, and behold a
great image. This great image, whose brightness *was* excellent, stood before thee; and the
form thereof *was* terrible.
32 This image's head *was* of fine gold, his
breast and his arms of silver, his belly and his
thighs of brass,
33 His legs of iron, his feet part of iron and
part of clay.
34 Thou sawest till that a stone was cut out
without hands, which smote the image upon his
feet *that were* of iron and clay, and brake them
to pieces.
35 Then was the iron, the clay, the brass, the
silver, and the gold, broken to pieces together,
and became like the chaff of the summer
threshingfloors; and the wind carried them

away, that no place was found for them: and the stone that smote the image became a great mountain, and filled the whole earth.

36 ¶ This *is* the dream; and we will tell the interpretation thereof before the king.

37 Thou, O king, *art* a king of kings: for the God of heaven hath given thee a kingdom, power, and strength, and glory.

38 And wheresoever the children of men dwell, the beasts of the field and the fowls of the heaven hath he given into thine hand, and hath made thee ruler over them all. Thou *art* this head of gold.

39 And after thee shall arise another kingdom inferior to thee, and another third kingdom of brass, which shall bear rule over all the earth.

40 And the fourth kingdom shall be strong as iron: forasmuch as iron breaketh in pieces and subdueth all *things:* and as iron that breaketh all these, shall it break in pieces and bruise.

41 And whereas thou sawest the feet and toes, part of potters' clay, and part of iron, the kingdom shall be divided; but there shall be in it of the strength of the iron, forasmuch as thou sawest the iron mixed with miry clay.

42 And *as* the toes of the feet *were* part of iron, and part of clay, *so* the kingdom shall be partly strong, and partly broken.

43 And whereas thou sawest iron mixed with miry clay, they shall mingle themselves with the seed of men: but they shall not cleave one to another, even as iron is not mixed with clay.

44 And in the days of these kings shall the God of heaven set up a kingdom, which shall never be destroyed: and the kingdom shall not be left to other people, *but* it shall break in pieces and consume all these kingdoms, and it shall stand for ever.

45 Forasmuch as thou sawest that the stone was cut out of the mountain without hands, and that it brake in pieces the iron, the brass, the clay, the silver, and the gold; the great God hath made known to the king what shall come to pass hereafter: and the dream *is* certain, and the interpretation thereof sure.

46 ¶ Then the king Neb-u-chad-nez'zar fell upon his face, and worshipped Dan'iel, and commanded that they should offer an oblation and sweet odours unto him.

47 The king answered unto Dan'iel, and said, Of a truth *it is,* that your God *is* a God of gods, and a Lord of kings, and a revealer of secrets, seeing thou couldest reveal this secret.

48 Then the king made Dan'iel a great man, and gave him many great gifts, and made him ruler over the whole province of Bab'y-lon, and chief of the governors over all the wise *men* of Bab'y-lon.

49 Then Dan'iel requested of the king, and he set Sha'drach, Me'shach, and A-bed'-ne-go, over the affairs of the province of Bab'y-lon: but Dan'iel *sat* in the gate of the king.

3 NEB-CHAD-NEZ'ZAR the king made an image of gold, whose height *was* threescore cubits, *and* the breadth thereof six cubits: he set it up in the plain of Du'ra, in the province of Bab'y-lon.

2 Then Neb-u-chad-nez'zar the king sent to gather together the princes, the governors, and the captains, the judges, the treasurers, the counsellors, the sheriffs, and all the rulers of the provinces, to come to the dedication of the image which Neb-u-chad-nez'zar the king had set up.

3 Then the princes, the governors, and captains, the judges, the treasurers, the counsellors, the sheriffs, and all the rulers of the provinces, were gathered together unto the dedication of the image that Neb-u-chad-nez'zar the king had set up; and they stood before the image that Neb-u-chad-nez'zar had set up.

4 Then an herald cried aloud, To you it is commanded, O people, nations, and languages,

5 *That* at what time ye hear the sound of the cornet, flute, harp, sackbut, psaltery, dulcimer, and all kinds of musick, ye fall down and worship the golden image that Neb-u-chad-nez'zar the king hath set up:

6 And whoso falleth not down and worshippeth shall the same hour be cast into the midst of a burning fiery furnace.

7 Therefore at that time, when all the people heard the sound of the cornet, flute, harp, sackbut, psaltery, and all kinds of musick, all the people, the nations, and the languages, fell down *and* worshipped the golden image that Neb-u-chad-nez'zar the king had set up.

8 ¶ Wherefore at that time certain Chal-de'ans came near, and accused the Jews.

9 They spake and said to the king Neb-u-chad-nez'zar, O king, live for ever.

10 Thou, O king, hast made a decree, that every man that shall hear the sound of the cornet, flute, harp, sackbut, psaltery, and dulcimer, and all kinds of musick, shall fall down and worship the golden image:

11 And whoso falleth not down and worshippeth, *that* he should be cast into the midst of a burning fiery furnace.

12 There are certain Jews whom thou hast set over the affairs of the province of Bab'y-lon, Sha'drach, Me'shach, and A-bed'-ne-go; these men, O king, have not regarded thee: they serve not thy gods, nor worship the golden image which thou hast set up.

13 ¶ Then Neb-u-chad-nez'zar in *his* rage and fury commanded to bring Sha'drach, Me'shach, and A-bed'-ne-go. Then they brought these men before the king.

14 Neb-u-chad-nez'zar spake and said unto them, *Is it* true, O Sha'drach, Me'shach, and A-bed'-nego, do not ye serve my gods, nor worship the golden image which I have set up?

15 Now if ye be ready that at what time ye hear the sound of the cornet, flute, harp, sackbut, psaltery, and dulcimer, and all kinds of musick, ye fall down and worship the image which I have made; *well:* but if ye worship not, ye shall be cast the same hour into the midst of a burning fiery furnace; and who *is* that God that shall deliver you out of my hands?

16 Sha'drach, Me'shach, and A-bed'-ne-go, answered and said to the king, O Neb-u-chad-nez'zar, we *are* not careful to answer thee in this matter.

17 If it be *so,* our God whom we serve is able to deliver us from the burning fiery furnace, and he will deliver *us* out of thine hand, O king.

18 But if not, be it known unto thee, O king, that we will not serve thy gods, nor worship the golden image which thou hast set up.

19 ¶ Then was Neb-u-chad-nez'zar full of fury, and the form of his visage was changed against Sha'drach, Me'shach, and A-bed'-ne-go: *therefore* he spake, and commanded that they should heat the furnace one seven times more than it was wont to be heated.

20 And he commanded the most mighty men that *were* in his army to bind Sha'drach, Me'shach, and A-bed'-ne-go, *and* to cast *them* into the burning fiery furnace.

21 Then these men were bound in their coats, their hosen, and their hats, and their *other* gar-

ments, and were cast into the midst of the burning fiery furnace.

22 Therefore because the king's commandment was urgent, and the furnace exceeding hot, the flame of the fire slew those men that took up Sha'drach, Me'shach, and A-bed'-ne-go.

23 And these three men, Sha'drach, Me'-shach, and A-bed'-ne-go, fell down bound into the midst of the burning fiery furnace.

24 Then Neb-u-chad-nez'zar the king was astonied, and rose up in haste, *and* spake, and said unto his counsellors, Did not we cast three men bound into the midst of the fire? They answered and said unto the king, True, O king.

25 He answered and said, Lo, I see four men loose, walking in the midst of the fire, and they have no hurt; and the form of the fourth is like the Son of God.

26 ¶ Then Neb-u-chad-nez'zar came near to the mouth of the burning fiery furnace, *and* spake, and said, Sha'drach, Me'shach, and A-bed'-ne-go, ye servants of the most high God, come forth, and come *hither*. Then Sha'drach, Me'shach, and A-bed'-ne-go, came forth of the midst of the fire.

27 And the princes, governors, and captains, and the king's counsellors, being gathered together saw these men, upon whose bodies the fire had no power, nor was an hair of their head singed, neither were their coats changed, nor the smell of fire had passed on them.

28 *Then* Neb-u-chad-nez'zar spake, and said, Blessed *be* the God of Sha'drach, Me'shach,and A-bed'-ne-go, who hath sent his angel, and delivered his servants that trusted in him, and have changed the king's word, and yielded their bodies, that they might not serve nor worship any god, except their own God.

29 Therefore I make a decree, That every people, nation, and language, which speak any thing amiss against the God of Sha'drach, Me'-shach, and A-bed'-ne-go, shall be cut in pieces, and their houses shall be made a dunghill: because there is no other God that can deliver after this sort.

30 Then the king promoted Sha'drach, Me'-shach, and A-bed'-ne-go, in the province of Bab'y-lon.

4 NEB-CHAD-NEZ'ZAR the king, unto all people, nations, and languages, that dwell in all the earth; Peace be multiplied unto you.

2 I thought it good to shew the signs and wonders that the high God hath wrought toward me.

3 How great *are* his signs! and how mighty *are* his wonders! his kingdom *is* an everlasting kingdom, and his dominion *is* from generation to generation.

4 ¶ I Neb-u-chad-nez'zar was at rest in mine house, and flourishing in my palace:

5 I saw a dream which made me afraid, and the thoughts upon my bed and the visions of my head troubled me.

6 Therefore made I a decree to bring in all the wise *men* of Bab'y-lon before me, that they might make known unto me the interpretation of the dream.

7 Then came in the magicians, the astrologers, the Chal-de'ans, and the soothsayers: and I told the dream before them; but they did not make known unto me the interpretation thereof.

8 ¶ But at the last Dan'iel came in before me, whose name *was* Bel-te-shaz'zar, according to the name of my god, and in whom *is* the spirit of the holy gods: and before him I told the dream, *saying*,

9 O Bel-te-shaz'zar, master of the magicians, because I know that the spirit of the holy gods *is* in thee, and no secret troubleth thee, tell me the visions of my dream that I have seen, and the interpretation thereof.

10 Thus *were* the visions of mine head in my bed; I saw, and behold a tree in the midst of the earth, and the height thereof *was* great.

11 The tree grew, and was strong, and the height thereof reached unto heaven, and the sight thereof to the end of all the earth:

12 The leaves thereof *were* fair, and the fruit thereof much, and in it *was* meat for all: the beasts of the field had shadow under it, and the fowls of the heaven dwelt in the boughs thereof, and all flesh was fed of it.

13 I saw in the visions of my head upon my bed, and, behold, a watcher and an holy one came down from heaven;

14 He cried aloud, and said thus, Hew down the tree, and cut off his branches, shake off his leaves, and scatter his fruit: let the beasts get away from under it, and the fowls from his branches:

15 Nevertheless leave the stump of his roots in the earth, even with a band of iron and brass, in the tender grass of the field; and let it be wet with the dew of heaven, and *let* his portion *be* with the beasts in the grass of the earth:

16 Let his heart be changed from man's, and let a beast's heart be given unto him; and let seven times pass over him.

17 This matter *is* by the decree of the watchers, and the demand by the word of the holy ones: to the intent that the living may know that the most High ruleth in the kingdom of men, and giveth it to whomsoever he will, and setteth up over it the basest of men.

18 This dream I king Neb-u-chad-nez'zar have seen. Now thou, O Bel-te-shaz'zar, declare the interpretation thereof, forasmuch as all the wise *men* of my kingdom are not able to make known unto me the interpretation: but thou *art* able; for the spirit of the holy gods *is* in thee.

19 ¶ Then Dan'iel, whose name *was* Bel-te-shaz'zar, was astonied for one hour, and his thoughts troubled him. The king spake, and said, Bel-te-shaz'zar, let not the dream, or the interpretation thereof, trouble thee. Bel-te-shaz'zar answered and said, My lord, the dream *be* to them that hate thee, and the interpretation thereof to thine enemies.

20 The tree that thou sawest, which grew, and was strong, whose height reached unto the heaven, and the sight thereof to all the earth;

21 Whose leaves *were* fair, and the fruit thereof much, and in it *was* meat for all; under which the beasts of the field dwelt, and upon whose branches the fowls of the heaven had their habitation:

22 It *is* thou, O king, that art grown and become strong: for thy greatness is grown, and reacheth unto heaven, and thy dominion to the end of the earth.

23 And whereas the king saw a watcher and an holy one coming down from heaven, and saying, Hew the tree down, and destroy it; yet leave the stump of the roots thereof in the earth, even with a band of iron and brass, in the tender grass of the field; and let it be wet with the dew of heaven, and *let* his portion *be* with the beasts of the field, till seven times pass over him;

24 This *is* the interpretation, O king, and this

is the decree of the most High, which is come
upon my lord the king:
25 That they shall drive thee from men, and
thy dwelling shall be with the beasts of the
field, and they shall make thee to eat grass as
oxen, and they shall wet thee with the dew of
heaven, and seven times shall pass over thee,
till thou know that the most High ruleth in the
kingdom of men, and giveth it to whomsoever
he will.
26 And whereas they commanded to leave
the stump of the tree roots; thy kingdom shall
be sure unto thee, after that thou shalt have
known that the heavens do rule.
27 Wherefore, O king, let my counsel be acceptable unto thee, and break off thy sins by
righteousness, and thine iniquities by shewing
mercy to the poor; if it may be a lengthening of
thy tranquillity.
28 ¶ All this came upon the king Neb-u-
chad-nez'zar.
29 At the end of twelve months he walked in
the palace of the kingdom of Bab'y-lon.
30 The king spake, and said, Is not this great
Bab'y-lon, that I have built for the house of the
kingdom by the might of my power, and for the
honour of my majesty?
31 While the word *was* in the king's mouth,
there fell a voice from heaven, *saying*, O king
Neb-u-chad-nez'zar, to thee it is spoken; The
kingdom is departed from thee.
32 And they shall drive thee from men, and
thy dwelling *shall be* with the beasts of the
field: they shall make thee to eat grass as oxen,
and seven times shall pass over thee, until thou
know that the most High ruleth in the kingdom
of men, and giveth it to whomsoever he will.
33 The same hour was the thing fulfilled
upon Neb-u-chad-nez'zar: and he was driven
from men, and did eat grass as oxen, and his
body was wet with the dew of heaven, till his
hairs were grown like eagles' *feathers*, and his
nails like birds' *claws*.
34 And at the end of the days I Neb-u-chad-
nez'zar lifted up mine eyes unto heaven, and
mine understanding returned unto me, and I
blessed the most High, and I praised and honoured him that liveth for ever, whose dominion
is an everlasting dominion, and his kingdom *is*
from generation to generation:
35 And all the inhabitants of the earth *are*
reputed as nothing: and he doeth according to
his will in the army of heaven, and *among* the
inhabitants of the earth: and none can stay his
hand, or say unto him, What doest thou?
36 At the same time my reason returned unto
me; and for the glory of my kingdom, mine honour and brightness returned unto me; and my
counsellors and my lords sought unto me; and I
was established in my kingdom, and excellent
majesty was added unto me.
37 Now I Neb-u-chad-nez'zar praise and extol and honour the King of heaven, all whose
works *are* truth, and his ways judgment: and
those that walk in pride he is able to abase.

5 BEL-SHAZ'ZAR the king made a great
feast to a thousand of his lords, and drank
wine before the thousand.
2 Bel-shaz'zar, whiles he tasted the wine,
commanded to bring the golden and silver vessels which his father Neb-u-chad-nez'zar had
taken out of the temple which *was* in Je-ru'sa-
lem; that the king, and his princes, his wives,
and his concubines, might drink therein.
3 Then they brought the golden vessels that
were taken out of the temple of the house of
God which *was* at Je-ru'sa-lem; and the king,
and his princes, his wives, and his concubines,
drank in them.
4 They drank wine, and praised the gods of
gold, and of silver, of brass, of iron, of wood,
and of stone.
5 ¶ In the same hour came forth fingers of a
man's hand, and wrote over against the candlestick upon the plaister of the wall of the king's
palace: and the king saw the part of the hand
that wrote.
6 Then the king's countenance was changed,
and his thoughts troubled him, so that the joints
of his loins were loosed, and his knees smote
one against another.
7 The king cried aloud to bring in the astrologers, the Chal-de'ans, and the soothsayers. *And*
the king spake, and said to the wise *men* of
Bab'y-lon, Whosoever shall read this writing,
and shew me the interpretation thereof, shall be
clothed with scarlet, and *have* a chain of gold
about his neck, and shall be the third ruler in
the kingdom.
8 Then came in all the king's wise *men:* but
they could not read the writing, nor make
known to the king the interpretation thereof.
9 Then was king Bel-shaz'zar greatly troubled, and his countenance was changed in him,
and his lords were astonied.
10 ¶ *Now* the queen by reason of the words
of the king and his lords came into the banquet
house: *and* the queen spake and said, O king,
live for ever: let not thy thoughts trouble thee,
nor let thy countenance be changed:
11 There is a man in thy kingdom, in whom *is*
the spirit of the holy gods; and in the days of
thy father light and understanding and wisdom,
like the wisdom of the gods, was found in him;
whom the king Neb-u-chad-nez'zar thy father,
the king, *I say*, thy father, made master of the
magicians, astrologers, Chal-de'ans, *and* soothsayers;
12 Forasmuch as an excellent spirit, and
knowledge, and understanding, interpreting of
dreams, and shewing of hard sentences, and
dissolving of doubts, were found in the same
Dan'iel, whom the king named Bel-te-shaz'zar:
now let Dan'iel be called, and he will shew the
interpretation.
13 Then was Dan'iel brought in before the
king. *And* the king spake and said unto Dan'iel,
Art thou that Dan'iel, which *art* of the children
of the captivity of Ju'dah, whom the king my
father brought out of Jew'ry?
14 I have even heard of thee, that the spirit of
the gods *is* in thee, and *that* light and understanding and excellent wisdom is found in thee.
15 And now the wise *men*, the astrologers,
have been brought in before me, that they
should read this writing, and make known unto
me the interpretation thereof: but they could
not shew the interpretation of the thing:
16 And I have heard of thee, that thou canst
make interpretations, and dissolve doubts: now
if thou canst read the writing, and make known
to me the interpretation thereof, thou shalt be
clothed with scarlet, and *have* a chain of gold
about thy neck, and shalt be the third ruler in
the kingdom.
17 ¶ Then Dan'iel answered and said before
the king, Let thy gifts be to thyself, and give thy
rewards to another; yet I will read the writing
unto the king, and make known to him the interpretation.
18 O thou king, the most high God gave Neb-
u-chad-nez'zar thy father a kingdom, and majesty, and glory, and honour:

19 And for the majesty that he gave him, all people, nations, and languages, trembled and feared before him: whom he would he slew; and whom he would he kept alive; and whom he would he set up; and whom he would he put down.

20 But when his heart was lifted up, and his mind hardened in pride, he was deposed from his kingly throne, and they took his glory from him:

21 And he was driven from the sons of men; and his heart was made like the beasts, and his dwelling *was* with the wild asses: they fed him with grass like oxen, and his body was wet with the dew of heaven; till he knew that the most high God ruled in the kingdom of men, and *that* he appointeth over it whomsoever he will.

22 And thou his son, O Bel-shaz′zar, hast not humbled thine heart, though thou knewest all this;

23 But hast lifted up thyself against the Lord of heaven; and they have brought the vessels of his house before thee, and thou, and thy lords, thy wives, and thy concubines, have drunk wine in them; and thou hast praised the gods of silver, and gold, of brass, iron, wood, and stone, which see not, nor hear, nor know: and the God in whose hand thy breath *is*, and whose *are* all thy ways, hast thou not glorified:

24 Then was the part of the hand sent from him; and this writing was written.

25 ¶ And this *is* the writing that was written, ME′NE, ME′NE, TE′KEL, U-PHAR′SIN.

26 This *is* the interpretation of the thing: ME′NE; God hath numbered thy kingdom, and finished it.

27 TE′KEL; Thou art weighed in the balances, and art found wanting.

28 PE′RES; Thy kingdom is divided, and given to the Medes and Per′sians.

29 Then commanded Bel-shaz′zar, and they clothed Dan′iel with scarlet, and *put* a chain of gold about his neck, and made a proclamation concerning him, that he should be the third ruler in the kingdom.

30 ¶ In that night was Bel-shaz′zar the king of the Chal-de′ans slain.

31 And Da-ri′us the Me′di-an took the kingdom, *being* about threescore and two years old.

6 IT pleased Da-ri′us to set over the kingdom an hundred and twenty princes, which should be over the whole kingdom;

2 And over these three presidents; of whom Dan′iel *was* first: that the princes might give accounts unto them, and the king should have no damage.

3 Then this Dan′iel was preferred above the presidents and princes, because an excellent spirit *was* in him; and the king thought to set him over the whole realm.

4 ¶ Then the presidents and princes sought to find occasion against Dan′iel concerning the kingdom; but they could find none occasion nor fault; forasmuch as he *was* faithful, neither was there any error or fault found in him.

5 Then said these men, We shall not find any occasion against this Dan′iel, except we find *it* against him concerning the law of his God.

6 Then these presidents and princes assembled together to the king, and said thus unto him, King Da-ri′us, live for ever.

7 All the presidents of the kingdom, the governors, and the princes, the counsellors, and the captains, have consulted together to establish a royal statute, and to make a firm decree, that whosoever shall ask a petition of any God or man for thirty days, save of thee, O king, he shall be cast into the den of lions.

8 Now, O king, establish the decree, and sign the writing, that it be not changed, according to the law of the Medes and Per′sians, which altereth not.

9 Wherefore king Da-ri′us signed the writing and the decree.

10 ¶ Now when Dan′iel knew that the writing was signed, he went into his house; and his windows being open in his chamber toward Je-ru′sa-lem, he kneeled upon his knees three times a day, and prayed, and gave thanks before his God, as he did aforetime.

11 Then these men assembled, and found Dan′iel praying and making supplication before his God.

12 Then they came near, and spake before the king concerning the king's decree; Hast thou not signed a decree, that every man that shall ask *a petition* of any God or man within thirty days, save of thee, O king, shall be cast into the den of lions? The king answered and said, The thing *is* true, according to the law of the Medes and Per′sians, which altereth not.

13 Then answered they and said before the king, That Dan′iel, which *is* of the children of the captivity of Ju′dah, regardeth not thee, O king, nor the decree that thou hast signed, but maketh his petition three times a day.

14 Then the king, when he heard *these* words, was sore displeased with himself, and set *his* heart on Dan′iel to deliver him: and he laboured till the going down of the sun to deliver him.

15 Then these men assembled unto the king, and said unto the king, Know, O king, that the law of the Medes and Per′sians *is*, That no decree nor statute which the king establisheth may be changed.

16 Then the king commanded, and they brought Dan′iel, and cast *him* into the den of lions. *Now* the king spake and said unto Dan′iel, Thy God whom thou servest continually, he will deliver thee.

17 And a stone was brought, and laid upon the mouth of the den; and the king sealed it with his own signet, and with the signet of his lords; that the purpose might not be changed concerning Dan′iel.

18 ¶ Then the king went to his palace, and passed the night fasting: neither were instruments of musick brought before him: and his sleep went from him.

19 Then the king arose very early in the morning, and went in haste unto the den of lions.

20 And when he came to the den, he cried with a lamentable voice unto Dan′iel: *and* the king spake and said to Dan′iel, O Dan′iel, servant of the living God, is thy God, whom thou servest continually, able to deliver thee from the lions?

21 Then said Dan′iel unto the king, O king, live for ever.

22 My God hath sent his angel, and hath shut the lions' mouths, that they have not hurt me: forasmuch as before him innocency was found in me; and also before thee, O king, have I done no hurt.

23 Then was the king exceeding glad for him, and commanded that they should take Dan′iel up out of the den. So Dan′iel was taken up out of the den, and no manner of hurt was found upon him, because he believed in his God.

24 ¶ And the king commanded, and they brought those men which had accused Dan′iel,

and they cast *them* into the den of lions, them,
their children, and their wives; and the lions
had the mastery of them, and brake all their
bones in pieces or ever they came at the bottom
of the den.
25 ¶ Then king Da-ri'us wrote unto all people, nations, and languages, that dwell in all the
earth; Peace be multiplied unto you.
26 I make a decree, That in every dominion
of my kingdom men tremble and fear before the
God of Dan'iel: for he *is* the living God, and
stedfast for ever, and his kingdom *that* which
shall not be destroyed, and his dominion *shall*
be even unto the end.
27 He delivereth and rescueth, and he worketh signs and wonders in heaven and in earth,
who hath delivered Dan'iel from the power of
the lions.
28 So this Dan'iel prospered in the reign of
Da-ri'us, and in the reign of Cy'rus the Per'sian.

7 IN the first year of Bel-shaz'zar king of
Bab'y-lon Dan'iel had a dream and visions
of his head upon his bed: then he wrote the
dream, *and* told the sum of the matters.
2 Dan'iel spake and said, I saw in my vision
by night, and, behold, the four winds of the
heaven strove upon the great sea.
3 And four great beasts came up from the
sea, diverse one from another.
4 The first *was* like a lion, and had eagle's
wings: I beheld till the wings thereof were
plucked, and it was lifted up from the earth, and
made stand upon the feet as a man, and a man's
heart was given to it.
5 And behold another beast, a second, like to
a bear, and it raised up itself on one side, and *it*
had three ribs in the mouth of it between the
teeth of it: and they said thus unto it, Arise, devour much flesh.
6 After this I beheld, and lo another, like a
leopard, which had upon the back of it four
wings of a fowl; the beast had also four heads;
and dominion was given to it.
7 After this I saw in the night visions, and
behold a fourth beast, dreadful and terrible, and
strong exceedingly; and it had great iron teeth:
it devoured and brake in pieces, and stamped
the residue with the feet of it: and it *was* diverse
from all the beasts that *were* before it; and it
had ten horns.
8 I considered the horns, and, behold, there
came up among them another little horn, before
whom there were three of the first horns
plucked up by the roots: and, behold, in this
horn *were* eyes like the eyes of man, and a
mouth speaking great things.
9 ¶ I beheld till the thrones were cast down,
and the Ancient of days did sit, whose garment
was white as snow, and the hair of his head like
the pure wool: his throne *was like* the fiery
flame, *and* his wheels *as* burning fire.
10 A fiery stream issued and came forth from
before him: thousand thousands ministered
unto him, and ten thousand times ten thousand
stood before him: the judgment was set, and
the books were opened.
11 I beheld then because of the voice of the
great words which the horn spake: I beheld
even till the beast was slain, and his body destroyed, and given to the burning flame.
12 As concerning the rest of the beasts, they
had their dominion taken away: yet their lives
were prolonged for a season and time.
13 I saw in the night visions, and, behold, *one*
like the Son of man came with the clouds of
heaven, and came to the Ancient of days, and
they brought him near before him.
14 And there was given him dominion, and
glory, and a kingdom, that all people, nations,
and languages, should serve him: his dominion
is an everlasting dominion, which shall not pass
away, and his kingdom *that* which shall not be
destroyed.
15 ¶ I Dan'iel was grieved in my spirit in the
midst of *my* body, and the visions of my head
troubled me.
16 I came near unto one of them that stood
by, and asked him the truth of all this. So he
told me, and made me know the interpretation
of the things.
17 These great beasts, which are four, *are*
four kings, *which* shall arise out of the earth.
18 But the saints of the most High shall take
the kingdom, and possess the kingdom for ever,
even for ever and ever.
19 Then I would know the truth of the fourth
beast, which was diverse from all the others,
exceeding dreadful, whose teeth *were of* iron,
and his nails *of* brass; *which* devoured, brake in
pieces, and stamped the residue with his feet;
20 And of the ten horns that *were* in his head,
and *of* the other which came up, and before
whom three fell; even *of* that horn that had
eyes, and a mouth that spake very great things,
whose look *was* more stout than his fellows.
21 I beheld, and the same horn made war
with the saints, and prevailed against them;
22 Until the Ancient of days came, and judgment was given to the saints of the most High;
and the time came that the saints possessed the
kingdom.
23 Thus he said, The fourth beast shall be the
fourth kingdom upon earth, which shall be diverse from all kingdoms, and shall devour the
whole earth, and shall tread it down, and break
it in pieces.
24 And the ten horns out of this kingdom *are*
ten kings *that* shall arise: and another shall rise
after them; and he shall be diverse from the
first, and he shall subdue three kings.
25 And he shall speak *great* words against
the most High, and shall wear out the saints of
the most High, and think to change times and
laws: and they shall be given into his hand until
a time and times and the dividing of time.
26 But the judgment shall sit, and they shall
take away his dominion, to consume and to destroy *it* unto the end.
27 And the kingdom and dominion, and the
greatness of the kingdom under the whole
heaven, shall be given to the people of the
saints of the most High, whose kingdom *is* an
everlasting kingdom, and all dominions shall
serve and obey him.
28 Hitherto *is* the end of the matter. As for
me Dan'iel, my cogitations much troubled me,
and my countenance changed in me: but I kept
the matter in my heart.

8 IN the third year of the reign of king Bel-
shaz'zar a vision appeared unto me, *even*
unto me Dan'iel, after that which appeared unto
me at the first.
2 And I saw in a vision; and it came to pass,
when I saw, that I *was* at Shu'shan *in* the palace, which *is* in the province of E'lam; and I saw
in a vision, and I was by the river of U'la-i.
3 Then I lifted up mine eyes, and saw, and
behold, there stood before the river a ram
which had *two* horns: and the *two* horns *were*
high; but one *was* higher than the other, and the
higher came up last.

4 I saw the ram pushing westward, and northward, and southward; so that no beasts might stand before him, neither *was there any* that could deliver out of his hand; but he did according to his will, and became great.

5 And as I was considering, behold, an he goat came from the west on the face of the whole earth, and touched not the ground: and the goat *had* a notable horn between his eyes.

6 And he came to the ram that had *two* horns, which I had seen standing before the river, and ran unto him in the fury of his power.

7 And I saw him come close unto the ram, and he was moved with choler against him, and smote the ram, and brake his two horns: and there was no power in the ram to stand before him, but he cast him down to the ground, and stamped upon him: and there was none that could deliver the ram out of his hand.

8 Therefore the he goat waxed very great: and when he was strong, the great horn was broken; and for it came up four notable ones toward the four winds of heaven.

9 And out of one of them came forth a little horn, which waxed exceeding great, toward the south, and toward the east, and toward the pleasant *land*.

10 And it waxed great, *even* to the host of heaven; and it cast down *some* of the host and of the stars to the ground, and stamped upon them.

11 Yea, he magnified *himself* even to the prince of the host, and by him the daily *sacrifice* was taken away, and the place of his sanctuary was cast down.

12 And an host was given *him* against the daily *sacrifice* by reason of transgression, and it cast down the truth to the ground; and it practised, and prospered.

13 ¶ Then I heard one saint speaking, and another saint said unto that certain *saint* which spake, How long *shall be* the vision *concerning* the daily *sacrifice*, and the transgression of desolation, to give both the sanctuary and the host to be trodden under foot?

14 And he said unto me, Unto two thousand and three hundred days; then shall the sanctuary be cleansed.

15 ¶ And it came to pass, when I, *even* I Dan'iel, had seen the vision, and sought for the meaning, then, behold, there stood before me as the appearance of a man.

16 And I heard a man's voice between *the banks of* U'la-i, which called, and said, Ga'bri-el, make this *man* to understand the vision.

17 So he came near where I stood: and when he came, I was afraid, and fell upon my face: but he said unto me, Understand, O son of man: for at the time of the end *shall be* the vision.

18 Now as he was speaking with me, I was in a deep sleep on my face toward the ground: but he touched me, and set me upright.

19 And he said, Behold, I will make thee know what shall be in the last end of the indignation: for at the time appointed the end *shall be*.

20 The ram which thou sawest having *two* horns *are* the kings of Me'di-a and Per'sia.

21 And the rough goat *is* the king of Gre'cia: and the great horn that *is* between his eyes *is* the first king.

22 Now that being broken, whereas four stood up for it, four kingdoms shall stand up out of the nation, but not in his power.

23 And in the latter time of their kingdom, when the transgressors are come to the full, a king of fierce countenance, and understanding dark sentences, shall stand up.

24 And his power shall be mighty, but not by his own power: and he shall destroy wonderfully, and shall prosper, and practise, and shall destroy the mighty and the holy people.

25 And through his policy also he shall cause craft to prosper in his hand; and he shall magnify *himself* in his heart, and by peace shall destroy many: he shall also stand up against the Prince of princes; but he shall be broken without hand.

26 And the vision of the evening and the morning which was told *is* true: wherefore shut thou up the vision; for it *shall be* for many days.

27 And I Dan'iel fainted, and was sick *certain* days; afterward I rose up, and did the king's business; and I was astonished at the vision, but none understood *it*.

9 IN the first year of Da-ri'us the son of A-has-u-e'rus, of the seed of the Medes, which was made king over the realm of the Chal-de'ans;

2 In the first year of his reign I Dan'iel understood by books the number of the years, whereof the word of the LORD came to Jer-e-mi'ah the prophet, that he would accomplish seventy years in the desolations of Je-ru'sa-lem.

3 ¶ And I set my face unto the Lord God, to seek by prayer and supplications, with fasting, and sackcloth, and ashes:

4 And I prayed unto the LORD my God, and made my confession, and said, O Lord, the great and dreadful God, keeping the covenant and mercy to them that love him, and to them that keep his commandments;

5 We have sinned, and have committed iniquity, and have done wickedly, and have rebelled, even by departing from thy precepts and from thy judgments:

6 Neither have we hearkened unto thy servants the prophets, which spake in thy name to our kings, our princes, and our fathers, and to all the people of the land.

7 O Lord, righteousness *belongeth* unto thee, but unto us confusion of faces, as at this day; to the men of Ju'dah, and to the inhabitants of Je-ru'sa-lem, and unto all Is'ra-el, *that are* near, and *that are* far off, through all the countries whither thou hast driven them, because of their trespass that they have trespassed against thee.

8 O Lord, to us *belongeth* confusion of face, to our kings, to our princes, and to our fathers, because we have sinned against thee.

9 To the Lord our God *belong* mercies and forgivenesses, though we have rebelled against him;

10 Neither have we obeyed the voice of the LORD our God, to walk in his laws, which he set before us by his servants the prophets.

11 Yea, all Is'ra-el have transgressed thy law, even by departing, that they might not obey thy voice; therefore the curse is poured upon us, and the oath that *is* written in the law of Mo'ses the servant of God, because we have sinned against him.

12 And he hath confirmed his words, which he spake against us, and against our judges that judged us, by bringing upon us a great evil: for under the whole heaven hath not been done as hath been done upon Je-ru'sa-lem.

13 As *it is* written in the law of Mo'ses, all this evil is come upon us: yet made we not our prayer before the LORD our God, that we might turn from our iniquities, and understand thy truth.

14 Therefore hath the LORD watched upon
the evil, and brought it upon us: for the LORD
our God *is* righteous in all his works which he
doeth: for we obeyed not his voice.
15 And now, O Lord our God, that hast
brought thy people forth out of the land of E'-
gypt with a mighty hand, and hast gotten thee
renown, as at this day; we have sinned, we have
done wickedly.
16 ¶ O Lord, according to all thy righteousness, I beseech thee, let thine anger and thy
fury be turned away from thy city Je-ru'sa-lem,
thy holy mountain: because for our sins, and for
the iniquities of our fathers, Je-ru'sa-lem and
thy people *are become* a reproach to all *that are*
about us.
17 Now therefore, O our God, hear the
prayer of thy servant, and his supplications,
and cause thy face to shine upon thy sanctuary
that is desolate, for the Lord's sake.
18 O my God, incline thine ear, and hear;
open thine eyes, and behold our desolations,
and the city which is called by thy name: for we
do not present our supplications before thee for
our righteousnesses, but for thy great mercies.
19 O Lord, hear; O Lord, forgive; O Lord,
hearken and do; defer not, for thine own sake,
O my God: for thy city and thy people are called
by thy name.
20 ¶ And whiles I *was* speaking, and praying, and confessing my sin and the sin of my
people Is'ra-el, and presenting my supplication
before the LORD my God for the holy mountain
of my God;
21 Yea, whiles I *was* speaking in prayer, even
the man Ga'bri-el, whom I had seen in the vision at the beginning, being caused to fly
swiftly, touched me about the time of the evening oblation.
22 And he informed *me,* and talked with me,
and said, O Dan'iel, I am now come forth to give
thee skill and understanding.
23 At the beginning of thy supplications the
commandment came forth, and I am come to
shew *thee;* for thou *art* greatly beloved: therefore understand the matter, and consider the vision.
24 Seventy weeks are determined upon thy
people and upon thy holy city, to finish the
transgression, and to make an end of sins, and
to make reconciliation for iniquity, and to bring
in everlasting righteousness, and to seal up the
vision and prophecy, and to anoint the most
Holy.
25 Know therefore and understand, *that*
from the going forth of the commandment to
restore and to build Je-ru'sa-lem unto the Mes-
si'ah the Prince *shall be* seven weeks, and
threescore and two weeks: the street shall be
built again, and the wall, even in troublous
times.
26 And after threescore and two weeks shall
Mes-si'ah be cut off, but not for himself: and the
people of the prince that shall come shall destroy the city and the sanctuary; and the end
thereof *shall be* with a flood, and unto the end
of the war desolations are determined.
27 And he shall confirm the covenant with
many for one week: and in the midst of the
week he shall cause the sacrifice and the oblation to cease, and for the overspreading of
abominations he shall make *it* desolate, even
until the consummation, and that determined
shall be poured upon the desolate.

10 IN the third year of Cy'rus king of Per'-
sia a thing was revealed unto Dan'iel,
whose name was called Bel-te-shaz'zar; and the
thing *was* true, but the time appointed *was*
long: and he understood the thing, and had understanding of the vision.
2 In those days I Dan'iel was mourning three
full weeks.
3 I ate no pleasant bread, neither came flesh
nor wine in my mouth, neither did I anoint myself at all, till three whole weeks were fulfilled.
4 And in the four and twentieth day of the
first month, as I was by the side of the great
river, which *is* Hid'de-kel;
5 Then I lifted up mine eyes, and looked, and
behold a certain man clothed in linen, whose
loins *were* girded with fine gold of U'phaz:
6 His body also *was* like the beryl, and his
face as the appearance of lightning, and his
eyes as lamps of fire, and his arms and his feet
like in colour to polished brass, and the voice of
his words like the voice of a multitude.
7 And I Dan'iel alone saw the vision: for the
men that were with me saw not the vision; but a
great quaking fell upon them, so that they fled
to hide themselves.
8 Therefore I was left alone, and saw this
great vision, and there remained no strength in
me: for my comeliness was turned in me into
corruption, and I retained no strength.
9 Yet heard I the voice of his words: and
when I heard the voice of his words, then was I
in a deep sleep on my face, and my face toward
the ground.
10 ¶ And, behold, an hand touched me,
which set me upon my knees and *upon* the
palms of my hands.
11 And he said unto me, O Dan'iel, a man
greatly beloved, understand the words that I
speak unto thee, and stand upright: for unto
thee am I now sent. And when he had spoken
this word unto me, I stood trembling.
12 Then said he unto me, Fear not, Dan'iel:
for from the first day that thou didst set thine
heart to understand, and to chasten thyself before thy God, thy words were heard, and I am
come for thy words.
13 But the prince of the kingdom of Per'sia
withstood me one and twenty days: but, lo, Mi'-
chael, one of the chief princes, came to help me;
and I remained there with the kings of Per'sia.
14 Now I am come to make thee understand
what shall befall thy people in the latter days:
for yet the vision *is* for *many* days.
15 And when he had spoken such words unto
me, I set my face toward the ground, and I became dumb.
16 And, behold, *one* like the similitude of the
sons of men touched my lips: then I opened my
mouth, and spake, and said unto him that stood
before me, O my lord, by the vision my sorrows
are turned upon me, and I have retained no
strength.
17 For how can the servant of this my lord
talk with this my lord? for as for me, straightway there remained no strength in me, neither
is there breath left in me.
18 Then there came again and touched me
one like the appearance of a man, and he
strengthened me,
19 And said, O man greatly beloved, fear not:
peace *be* unto thee, be strong, yea, be strong.
And when he had spoken unto me, I was
strengthened, and said, Let my lord speak; for
thou hast strengthened me.
20 Then said he, Knowest thou wherefore I
come unto thee? and now will I return to fight
with the prince of Per'sia: and when I am gone
forth, lo, the prince of Gre'cia shall come.

21 But I will shew thee that which is noted in the scripture of truth: and *there is* none that holdeth with me in these things, but Mi'chael your prince.

11 ALSO I in the first year of Da-ri'us the Mede, *even* I, stood to confirm and to strengthen him.

2 And now will I shew thee the truth. Behold, there shall stand up yet three kings in Per'sia; and the fourth shall be far richer than *they* all: and by his strength through his riches he shall stir up all against the realm of Gre'cia.

3 And a mighty king shall stand up, that shall rule with great dominion, and do according to his will.

4 And when he shall stand up, his kingdom shall be broken, and shall be divided toward the four winds of heaven; and not to his posterity, nor according to his dominion which he ruled: for his kingdom shall be plucked up, even for others beside those.

5 ¶ And the king of the south shall be strong, and *one* of his princes; and he shall be strong above him, and have dominion; his dominion *shall be* a great dominion.

6 And in the end of years they shall join themselves together; for the king's daughter of the south shall come to the king of the north to make an agreement: but she shall not retain the power of the arm; neither shall he stand, nor his arm: but she shall be given up, and they that brought her, and he that begat her, and he that strengthened her in *these* times.

7 But out of a branch of her roots shall *one* stand up in his estate, which shall come with an army, and shall enter into the fortress of the king of the north, and shall deal against them, and shall prevail:

8 And shall also carry captives into E'gypt their gods, with their princes, *and* with their precious vessels of silver and of gold; and he shall continue *more* years than the king of the north.

9 So the king of the south shall come into *his* kingdom, and shall return into his own land.

10 But his sons shall be stirred up, and shall assemble a multitude of great forces: and *one* shall certainly come, and overflow, and pass through: then shall he return, and be stirred up, *even* to his fortress.

11 And the king of the south shall be moved with choler, and shall come forth and fight with him, *even* with the king of the north: and he shall set forth a great multitude; but the multitude shall be given into his hand.

12 *And* when he hath taken away the multitude, his heart shall be lifted up; and he shall cast down *many* ten thousands: but he shall not be strengthened *by it*.

13 For the king of the north shall return, and shall set forth a multitude greater than the former, and shall certainly come after certain years with a great army and with much riches.

14 And in those times there shall many stand up against the king of the south: also the robbers of thy people shall exalt themselves to establish the vision; but they shall fall.

15 So the king of the north shall come, and cast up a mount, and take the most fenced cities: and the arms of the south shall not withstand, neither his chosen people, neither *shall there be any* strength to withstand.

16 But he that cometh against him shall do according to his own will, and none shall stand before him: and he shall stand in the glorious land, which by his hand shall be consumed.

17 He shall also set his face to enter with the strength of his whole kingdom, and upright ones with him; thus shall he do: and he shall give him the daughter of women, corrupting her: but she shall not stand *on his side*, neither be for him.

18 After this shall he turn his face unto the isles, and shall take many: but a prince for his own behalf shall cause the reproach offered by him to cease; without his own reproach he shall cause *it* to turn upon him.

19 Then he shall turn his face toward the fort of his own land: but he shall stumble and fall, and not be found.

20 Then shall stand up in his estate a raiser of taxes *in* the glory of the kingdom: but within few days he shall be destroyed, neither in anger, nor in battle.

21 And in his estate shall stand up a vile person, to whom they shall not give the honour of the kingdom: but he shall come in peaceably, and obtain the kingdom by flatteries.

22 And with the arms of a flood shall they be overflown from before him, and shall be broken; yea, also the prince of the covenant.

23 And after the league *made* with him he shall work deceitfully: for he shall come up, and shall become strong with a small people.

24 He shall enter peaceably even upon the fattest places of the province; and he shall do *that* which his fathers have not done, nor his fathers' fathers; he shall scatter among them the prey, and spoil, and riches: *yea*, and he shall forecast his devices against the strong holds, even for a time.

25 And he shall stir up his power and his courage against the king of the south with a great army; and the king of the south shall be stirred up to battle with a very great and mighty army; but he shall not stand: for they shall forecast devices against him.

26 Yea, they that feed of the portion of his meat shall destroy him, and his army shall overflow: and many shall fall down slain.

27 And both these kings' hearts *shall be* to do mischief, and they shall speak lies at one table; but it shall not prosper: for yet the end *shall be* at the time appointed.

28 Then shall he return into his land with great riches; and his heart *shall be* against the holy covenant; and he shall do *exploits*, and return to his own land.

29 At the time appointed he shall return, and come toward the south; but it shall not be as the former, or as the latter.

30 ¶ For the ships of Chit'tim shall come against him: therefore he shall be grieved, and return, and have indignation against the holy covenant: so shall he do; he shall even return, and have intelligence with them that forsake the holy covenant.

31 And arms shall stand on his part, and they shall pollute the sanctuary of strength, and shall take away the daily *sacrifice*, and they shall place the abomination that maketh desolate.

32 And such as do wickedly against the covenant shall he corrupt by flatteries: but the people that do know their God shall be strong, and do *exploits*.

33 And they that understand among the people shall instruct many : yet they shall fall by the sword, and by flame, by captivity, and by spoil, *many* days.

34 Now when they shall fall, they shall be holpen with a little help: but many shall cleave to them with flatteries.

35 And *some* of them of understanding shall fall, to try them, and to purge, and to make *them* white, *even* to the time of the end: because *it is* yet for a time appointed.

36 And the king shall do according to his will; and he shall exalt himself, and magnify himself above every god, and shall speak marvellous things against the God of gods, and shall prosper till the indignation be accomplished: for that that is determined shall be done.

37 Neither shall he regard the God of his fathers, nor the desire of women, nor regard any god: for he shall magnify himself above all.

38 But in his estate shall he honour the God of forces: and a god whom his fathers knew not shall he honour with gold, and silver, and with precious stones, and pleasant things.

39 Thus shall he do in the most strong holds with a strange god, whom he shall acknowledge *and* increase with glory: and he shall cause them to rule over many, and shall divide the land for gain.

40 And at the time of the end shall the king of the south push at him: and the king of the north shall come against him like a whirlwind, with chariots, and with horsemen, and with many ships; and he shall enter into the countries, and shall overflow and pass over.

41 He shall enter also into the glorious land, and many *countries* shall be overthrown: but these shall escape out of his hand, *even* E'dom, and Mo'ab, and the chief of the children of Am'mon.

42 He shall stretch forth his hand also upon the countries: and the land of E'gypt shall not escape.

43 But he shall have power over the treasures of gold and of silver, and over all the precious things of E'gypt: and the Lib'y-ans and the E-thi-o'pi-ans *shall be* at his steps.

44 But tidings out of the east and out of the north shall trouble him: therefore he shall go forth with great fury to destroy, and utterly to make away many.

45 And he shall plant the tabernacles of his palace between the seas in the glorious holy mountain; yet he shall come to his end, and none shall help him.

12 AND at that time shall Mi'chael stand up, the great prince which standeth for the children of thy people: and there shall be a time of trouble, such as never was since there was a nation *even* to that same time: and at that time thy people shall be delivered, every one that shall be found written in the book.

2 And many of them that sleep in the dust of the earth shall awake, some to everlasting life, and some to shame *and* everlasting contempt.

3 And they that be wise shall shine as the brightness of the firmament; and they that turn many to righteousness as the stars for ever and ever.

4 But thou, O Dan'iel, shut up the words, and seal the book, *even* to the time of the end: many shall run to and fro, and knowledge shall be increased.

5 ¶ Then I Dan'iel looked, and, behold, there stood other two, the one on this side of the bank of the river, and the other on that side of the bank of the river.

6 And *one* said to the man clothed in linen, which *was* upon the waters of the river, How long *shall it be to* the end of these wonders?

7 And I heard the man clothed in linen, which *was* upon the waters of the river, when he held up his right hand and his left hand unto heaven, and sware by him that liveth for ever that *it shall be* for a time, times, and an half; and when he shall have accomplished to scatter the power of the holy people, all these *things* shall be finished.

8 And I heard, but I understood not : then said I, O my Lord, what *shall be* the end of these *things?*

9 And he said, Go thy way, Dan'iel: for the words *are* closed up and sealed till the time of the end.

10 Many shall be purified, and made white, and tried; but the wicked shall do wickedly: and none of the wicked shall understand; but the wise shall understand.

11 And from the time *that* the daily *sacrifice* shall be taken away, and the abomination that maketh desolate set up, *there shall be* a thousand two hundred and ninety days.

12 Blessed *is* he that waiteth, and cometh to the thousand three hundred and five and thirty days.

13 But go thou thy way till the end *be:* for thou shalt rest, and stand in thy lot at the end of the days.

THE BOOK OF

HOSEA

1 THE word of the LORD that came unto Ho-se'a, the son of Be-e'ri, in the days of Uz-zi'ah, Jo'tham, A'haz, *and* Hez-e-ki'ah, kings of Ju'dah, and in the days of Jer-o-bo'am the son of Jo'ash, king of Is'ra-el.

2 The beginning of the word of the LORD by Ho-se'a. And the LORD said to Ho-se'a, Go, take unto thee a wife of whoredoms and children of whoredoms: for the land hath committed great whoredom, *departing* from the LORD.

3 So he went and took Go'mer the daughter of Dib'la-im; which conceived, and bare him a son.

4 And the LORD said unto him, Call his name Jez're-el; for yet a little *while*, and I will avenge the blood of Jez're-el upon the house of Je'hu, and will cause to cease the kingdom of the house of Is'ra-el.

5 And it shall come to pass at that day, that I will break the bow of Is'ra-el in the valley of Jez're-el.

6 ¶ And she conceived again, and bare a daughter. And *God* said unto him, Call her name Lo-ru'ha-mah: for I will no more have mercy upon the house of Is'ra-el; but I will utterly take them away.

7 But I will have mercy upon the house of Ju'dah, and will save them by the LORD their God, and will not save them by bow, nor by sword, nor by battle, by horses, nor by horsemen.

8 ¶ Now when she had weaned Lo-ru'ha-mah, she conceived, and bare a son.

9 Then said *God*, Call his name Lo-am'mi: for ye *are* not my people, and I will not be your *God*.

10 ¶ Yet the number of the children of Is′ra-
el shall be as the sand of the sea, which cannot
be measured nor numbered; and it shall come
to pass, *that* in the place where it was said unto
them, Ye *are* not my people, *there* it shall be
said unto them, *Ye are* the sons of the living
God.
11 Then shall the children of Ju′dah and the
children of Is′ra-el be gathered together, and
appoint themselves one head, and they shall
come up out of the land: for great *shall be* the
day of Jez′re-el.

2 SAY ye unto your brethren, Am′mi; and to
your sisters, Ru′ha-mah.
2 Plead with your mother, plead: for she *is*
not my wife, neither *am* I her husband: let her
therefore put away her whoredoms out of her
sight, and her adulteries from between her
breasts;
3 Lest I strip her naked, and set her as in the
day that she was born, and make her as a wilderness, and set her like a dry land, and slay her
with thirst.
4 And I will not have mercy upon her children; for they *be* the children of whoredoms.
5 For their mother hath played the harlot:
she that conceived them hath done shamefully:
for she said, I will go after my lovers, that give
me my bread and my water, my wool and my
flax, mine oil and my drink.
6 ¶ Therefore, behold, I will hedge up thy
way with thorns, and make a wall, that she
shall not find her paths.
7 And she shall follow after her lovers, but
she shall not overtake them; and she shall seek
them, but shall not find *them:* then shall she
say, I will go and return to my first husband; for
then *was it* better with me than now.
8 For she did not know that I gave her corn,
and wine, and oil, and multiplied her silver and
gold, *which* they prepared for Ba′al.
9 Therefore will I return, and take away my
corn in the time thereof, and my wine in the
season thereof, and will recover my wool and
my flax *given* to cover her nakedness.
10 And now will I discover her lewdness in
the sight of her lovers, and none shall deliver
her out of mine hand.
11 I will also cause all her mirth to cease, her
feast days, her new moons, and her sabbaths,
and all her solemn feasts.
12 And I will destroy her vines and her fig
trees, whereof she hath said, These *are* my rewards that my lovers have given me: and I will
make them a forest, and the beasts of the field
shall eat them.
13 And I will visit upon her the days of Ba′al-
im, wherein she burned incense to them, and
she decked herself with her earrings and her
jewels, and she went after her lovers, and forgat me, saith the LORD.
14 ¶ Therefore, behold, I will allure her, and
bring her into the wilderness, and speak comfortably unto her.
15 And I will give her her vineyards from
thence, and the valley of A′chor for a door of
hope: and she shall sing there, as in the days of
her youth, and as in the day when she came up
out of the land of E′gypt.
16 And it shall be at that day, saith the LORD,
that thou shalt call me Ish′i; and shalt call me
no more Ba′al-i.
17 For I will take away the names of Ba′al-im
out of her mouth, and they shall no more be
remembered by their name.
18 And in that day will I make a covenant for
them with the beasts of the field, and with the
fowls of heaven, and *with* the creeping things of
the ground: and I will break the bow and the
sword and the battle out of the earth, and will
make them to lie down safely.
19 And I will betroth thee unto me for ever;
yea, I will betroth thee unto me in righteousness, and in judgment, and in lovingkindness,
and in mercies.
20 I will even betroth thee unto me in faithfulness: and thou shalt know the LORD.
21 And it shall come to pass in that day, I
will hear, saith the LORD, I will hear the heavens, and they shall hear the earth;
22 And the earth shall hear the corn, and the
wine, and the oil; and they shall hear Jez′re-el.
23 And I will sow her unto me in the earth;
and I will have mercy upon her that had not
obtained mercy; and I will say to *them which*
were not my people, Thou *art* my people; and
they shall say, *Thou art* my God.

3 THEN said the LORD unto me, Go yet, love
a woman beloved of *her* friend, yet an
adulteress, according to the love of the LORD
toward the children of Is′ra-el, who look to other gods, and love flagons of wine.
2 So I bought her to me for fifteen *pieces* of
silver, and *for* an homer of barley, and an half
homer of barley:
3 And I said unto her, Thou shalt abide for
me many days; thou shalt not play the harlot,
and thou shalt not be for *another* man: so *will* I
also *be* for thee.
4 For the children of Is′ra-el shall abide many
days without a king, and without a prince, and
without a sacrifice, and without an image, and
without an ephod, and *without* teraphim:
5 Afterward shall the children of Is′ra-el return, and seek the LORD their God, and Da′vid
their king; and shall fear the LORD and his goodness in the latter days.

4 HEAR the word of the LORD, ye children of
Is′ra-el: for the LORD hath a controversy
with the inhabitants of the land, because *there*
is no truth, nor mercy, nor knowledge of God in
the land.
2 By swearing, and lying, and killing, and
stealing, and committing adultery, they break
out, and blood toucheth blood.
3 Therefore shall the land mourn, and every
one that dwelleth therein shall languish, with
the beasts of the field, and with the fowls of
heaven; yea, the fishes of the sea also shall be
taken away.
4 Yet let no man strive, nor reprove another:
for thy people *are* as they that strive with the
priest.
5 Therefore shalt thou fall in the day, and the
prophet also shall fall with thee in the night,
and I will destroy thy mother.
6 ¶ My people are destroyed for lack of
knowledge: because thou hast rejected knowledge, I will also reject thee, that thou shalt be
no priest to me: seeing thou hast forgotten the
law of thy God, I will also forget thy children.
7 As they were increased, so they sinned
against me: *therefore* will I change their glory
into shame.
8 They eat up the sin of my people, and they
set their heart on their iniquity.
9 And there shall be, like people, like priest:
and I will punish them for their ways, and reward them their doings.
10 For they shall eat, and not have enough:
they shall commit whoredom, and shall not in-

crease: because they have left off to take heed to the LORD.

11 Whoredom and wine and new wine take away the heart.

12 ¶ My people ask counsel at their stocks, and their staff declareth unto them: for the spirit of whoredoms hath caused *them* to err, and they have gone a whoring from under their God.

13 They sacrifice upon the tops of the mountains, and burn incense upon the hills, under oaks and poplars and elms, because the shadow thereof *is* good: therefore your daughters shall commit whoredom, and your spouses shall commit adultery.

14 I will not punish your daughters when they commit whoredom, nor your spouses when they commit adultery: for themselves are separated with whores, and they sacrifice with harlots: therefore the people *that* doth not understand shall fall.

15 ¶ Though thou, Is′ra-el, play the harlot, *yet* let not Ju′dah offend; and come not ye unto Gil′gal, neither go ye up to Beth–a′ven, nor swear, The LORD liveth.

16 For Is′ra-el slideth back as a backsliding heifer: now the LORD will feed them as a lamb in a large place.

17 E′phra-im *is* joined to idols: let him alone.

18 Their drink is sour: they have committed whoredom continually: her rulers *with* shame do love, Give ye.

19 The wind hath bound her up in her wings, and they shall be ashamed because of their sacrifices.

5 HEAR ye this, O priests; and hearken, ye house of Is′ra-el; and give ye ear, O house of the king; for judgment *is* toward you, because ye have been a snare on Miz′pah, and a net spread upon Ta′bor.

2 And the revolters are profound to make slaughter, though I *have been* a rebuker of them all.

3 I know E′phra-im, and Is′ra-el is not hid from me: for now, O E′phra-im, thou committest whoredom, *and* Is′ra-el is defiled.

4 They will not frame their doings to turn unto their God: for the spirit of whoredoms *is* in the midst of them, and they have not known the LORD.

5 And the pride of Is′ra-el doth testify to his face: therefore shall Is′ra-el and E′phra-im fall in their iniquity; Ju′dah also shall fall with them.

6 They shall go with their flocks and with their herds to seek the LORD; but they shall not find *him;* he hath withdrawn himself from them.

7 They have dealt treacherously against the LORD: for they have begotten strange children: now shall a month devour them with their portions.

8 Blow ye the cornet in Gib′e-ah, *and* the trumpet in Ra′mah: cry aloud *at* Beth–a′ven, after thee, O Ben′ja-min.

9 E′phra-im shall be desolate in the day of rebuke: among the tribes of Is′ra-el have I made known that which shall surely be.

10 The princes of Ju′dah were like them that remove the bound: *therefore* I will pour out my wrath upon them like water.

11 E′phra-im *is* oppressed *and* broken in judgment, because he willingly walked after the commandment.

12 Therefore *will* I *be* unto E′phra-im as a moth, and to the house of Ju′dah as rottenness.

13 When E′phra-im saw his sickness, and Ju′dah *saw* his wound, then went E′phra-im to the As-syr′i-an, and sent to king Ja′reb: yet could he not heal you, nor cure you of your wound.

14 For I *will be* unto E′phra-im as a lion, and as a young lion to the house of Ju′dah: I, *even* I, will tear and go away; I will take away, and none shall rescue *him.*

15 ¶ I will go *and* return to my place, till they acknowledge their offence, and seek my face: in their affliction they will seek me early.

6 COME, and let us return unto the LORD: for he hath torn, and he will heal us; he hath smitten, and he will bind us up.

2 After two days will he revive us: in the third day he will raise us up, and we shall live in his sight.

3 Then shall we know, *if* we follow on to know the LORD: his going forth is prepared as the morning; and he shall come unto us as the rain, as the latter *and* former rain unto the earth.

4 ¶ O E′phra-im, what shall I do unto thee? O Ju′dah, what shall I do unto thee? for your goodness *is* as a morning cloud, and as the early dew it goeth away.

5 Therefore have I hewed *them* by the prophets; I have slain them by the words of my mouth: and thy judgments *are as* the light *that* goeth forth.

6 For I desired mercy, and not sacrifice; and the knowledge of God more than burnt offerings.

7 But they like men have transgressed the covenant: there have they dealt treacherously against me.

8 Gil′e-ad *is* a city of them that work iniquity, *and is* polluted with blood.

9 And as troops of robbers wait for a man, *so* the company of priests murder in the way by consent: for they commit lewdness.

10 I have seen an horrible thing in the house of Is′ra-el: there *is* the whoredom of E′phra-im, Is′ra-el is defiled.

11 Also, O Ju′dah, he hath set an harvest for thee, when I returned the captivity of my people.

7 WHEN I would have healed Is′ra-el, then the iniquity of E′phra-im was discovered, and the wickedness of Sa-ma′ri-a: for they commit falsehood; and the thief cometh in, *and* the troop of robbers spoileth without.

2 And they consider not in their hearts *that* I remember all their wickedness: now their own doings have beset them about; they are before my face.

3 They make the king glad with their wickedness, and the princes with their lies.

4 They *are* all adulterers, as an oven heated by the baker, *who* ceaseth from raising after he hath kneaded the dough, until it be leavened.

5 In the day of our king the princes have made *him* sick with bottles of wine; he stretched out his hand with scorners.

6 For they have made ready their heart like an oven, whiles they lie in wait: their baker sleepeth all the night; in the morning it burneth as a flaming fire.

7 They are all hot as an oven, and have devoured their judges; all their kings are fallen: *there is* none among them that calleth unto me.

8 E′phra-im, he hath mixed himself among the people; E′phra-im is a cake not turned.

9 Strangers have devoured his strength, and
he knoweth *it* not: yea, gray hairs are here and
there upon him, yet he knoweth not.
10 And the pride of Is'ra-el testifieth to his
face: and they do not return to the LORD their
God, nor seek him for all this.
11 ¶ E'phra-im also is like a silly dove without heart: they call to E'gypt, they go to As-
syr'i-a.
12 When they shall go, I will spread my net
upon them; I will bring them down as the fowls
of the heaven; I will chastise them, as their congregation hath heard.
13 Woe unto them! for they have fled from
me: destruction unto them! because they have
transgressed against me: though I have redeemed them, yet they have spoken lies against
me.
14 And they have not cried unto me with
their heart, when they howled upon their beds:
they assemble themselves for corn and wine,
and they rebel against me.
15 Though I have bound *and* strengthened
their arms, yet do they imagine mischief
against me.
16 They return, *but* not to the most High:
they are like a deceitful bow: their princes shall
fall by the sword for the rage of their tongue:
this *shall be* their derision in the land of E'gypt.

8 SET the trumpet to thy mouth. *He shall*
come as an eagle against the house of the
LORD, because they have transgressed my covenant, and trespassed against my law.
2 Is'ra-el shall cry unto me, My God, we
know thee.
3 Is'ra-el hath cast off *the thing that is* good:
the enemy shall pursue him.
4 They have set up kings, but not by me: they
have made princes, and I knew *it* not: of their
silver and their gold have they made them idols,
that they may be cut off.
5 ¶ Thy calf, O Sa-ma'ri-a, hath cast *thee* off;
mine anger is kindled against them: how long
will it be ere they attain to innocency?
6 For from Is'ra-el *was* it also: the workman
made it; therefore it *is* not God: but the calf of
Sa-ma'ri-a shall be broken in pieces.
7 For they have sown the wind, and they
shall reap the whirlwind: it hath no stalk: the
bud shall yield no meal: if so be it yield, the
strangers shall swallow it up.
8 Is'ra-el is swallowed up: now shall they be
among the Gen'tiles as a vessel wherein *is* no
pleasure.
9 For they are gone up to As-syr'i-a, a wild
ass alone by himself: E'phra-im hath hired lovers.
10 Yea, though they have hired among the
nations, now will I gather them, and they shall
sorrow a little for the burden of the king of
princes.
11 Because E'phra-im hath made many altars
to sin, altars shall be unto him to sin.
12 I have written to him the great things of
my law, *but* they were counted as a strange
thing.
13 They sacrifice flesh *for* the sacrifices of
mine offerings, and eat *it; but* the LORD accepteth them not; now will he remember their iniquity, and visit their sins: they shall return to E'-
gypt.
14 For Is'ra-el hath forgotten his Maker, and
buildeth temples; and Ju'dah hath multiplied
fenced cities: but I will send a fire upon his
cities, and it shall devour the palaces thereof.

9 REJOICE not, O Is'ra-el, for joy, as *other*
people: for thou hast gone a whoring from
thy God, thou hast loved a reward upon every
cornfloor.
2 The floor and the winepress shall not feed
them, and the new wine shall fail in her.
3 They shall not dwell in the LORD's land; but
E'phra-im shall return to E'gypt, and they shall
eat unclean *things* in As-syr'i-a.
4 They shall not offer wine *offerings* to the
LORD, neither shall they be pleasing unto him:
their sacrifices *shall be* unto them as the bread
of mourners; all that eat thereof shall be polluted: for their bread for their soul shall not
come into the house of the LORD.
5 What will ye do in the solemn day, and in
the day of the feast of the LORD?
6 For, lo, they are gone because of destruction: E'gypt shall gather them up, Mem'phis
shall bury them: the pleasant *places* for their
silver, nettles shall possess them: thorns *shall*
be in their tabernacles.
7 The days of visitation are come, the days of
recompence are come; Is'ra-el shall know *it:* the
prophet *is* a fool, the spiritual man *is* mad, for
the multitude of thine iniquity, and the great
hatred.
8 The watchman of E'phra-im *was* with my
God: *but* the prophet *is* a snare of a fowler in all
his ways, *and* hatred in the house of his God.
9 They have deeply corrupted *themselves,* as
in the days of Gib'e-ah: *therefore* he will remember their iniquity, he will visit their sins.
10 I found Is'ra-el like grapes in the wilderness; I saw your fathers as the firstripe in the fig
tree at her first time: *but* they went to Ba'al-pe'-
or, and separated themselves unto *that* shame;
and *their* abominations were according as they
loved.
11 *As for* E'phra-im, their glory shall fly
away like a bird, from the birth, and from the
womb, and from the conception.
12 Though they bring up their children, yet
will I bereave them, *that there shall* not *be* a
man *left:* yea, woe also to them when I depart
from them!
13 E'phra-im, as I saw Ty'rus, *is* planted in a
pleasant place: but E'phra-im shall bring forth
his children to the murderer.
14 Give them, O LORD: what wilt thou give?
give them a miscarrying womb and dry breasts.
15 All their wickedness *is* in Gil'gal: for there
I hated them: for the wickedness of their doings
I will drive them out of mine house, I will love
them no more: all their princes *are* revolters.
16 E'phra-im is smitten, their root is dried
up, they shall bear no fruit: yea, though they
bring forth, yet will I slay *even* the beloved *fruit*
of their womb.
17 My God will cast them away, because
they did not hearken unto him: and they shall
be wanderers among the nations.

10 IS'RA-EL *is* an empty vine, he bringeth
forth fruit unto himself: according to the
multitude of his fruit he hath increased the altars; according to the goodness of his land they
have made goodly images.
2 Their heart is divided; now shall they be
found faulty: he shall break down their altars,
he shall spoil their images.
3 For now they shall say, We have no king,
because we feared not the LORD; what then
should a king do to us?
4 They have spoken words, swearing falsely
in making a covenant: thus judgment springeth
up as hemlock in the furrows of the field.

5 The inhabitants of Sa-ma′ri-a shall fear because of the calves of Beth–a′ven: for the people thereof shall mourn over it, and the priests thereof *that* rejoiced on it, for the glory thereof, because it is departed from it.

6 It shall be also carried unto As-syr′i-a *for* a present to king Ja′reb: E′phra-im shall receive shame, and Is′ra-el shall be ashamed of his own counsel.

7 *As for* Sa-ma′ri-a, her king is cut off as the foam upon the water.

8 The high places also of A′ven, the sin of Is′ra-el, shall be destroyed: the thorn and the thistle shall come up on their altars; and they shall say to the mountains, Cover us; and to the hills, Fall on us.

9 O Is′ra-el, thou hast sinned from the days of Gib′e-ah: there they stood: the battle in Gib′-e-ah against the children of iniquity did not overtake them.

10 *It is* in my desire that I should chastise them; and the people shall be gathered against them, when they shall bind themselves in their two furrows.

11 And E′phra-im *is as* an heifer *that is* taught, *and* loveth to tread out *the corn;* but I passed over upon her fair neck: I will make E′-phra-im to ride; Ju′dah shall plow, *and* Ja′cob shall break his clods.

12 Sow to yourselves in righteousness, reap in mercy; break up your fallow ground: for *it is* time to seek the LORD, till he come and rain righteousness upon you.

13 Ye have plowed wickedness, ye have reaped iniquity; ye have eaten the fruit of lies: because thou didst trust in thy way, in the multitude of thy mighty men.

14 Therefore shall a tumult arise among thy people, and all thy fortresses shall be spoiled, as Shal′man spoiled Beth–ar′bel in the day of battle: the mother was dashed in pieces upon *her* children.

15 So shall Beth′–el do unto you because of your great wickedness: in a morning shall the king of Is′ra-el utterly be cut off.

11 WHEN Is′ra-el *was* a child, then I loved him, and called my son out of E′gypt.

2 *As* they called them, so they went from them: they sacrificed unto Ba′al-im, and burned incense to graven images.

3 I taught E′phra-im also to go, taking them by their arms; but they knew not that I healed them.

4 I drew them with cords of a man, with bands of love: and I was to them as they that take off the yoke on their jaws, and I laid meat unto them.

5 ¶ He shall not return into the land of E′-gypt, but the As-syr′i-an shall be his king, because they refused to return.

6 And the sword shall abide on his cities, and shall consume his branches, and devour *them,* because of their own counsels.

7 And my people are bent to backsliding from me: though they called them to the most High, none at all would exalt *him.*

8 How shall I give thee up, E′phra-im? *how* shall I deliver thee, Is′ra-el? how shall I make thee as Ad′-mah? *how* shall I set thee as Ze-bo′im? mine heart is turned within me, my repentings are kindled together.

9 I will not execute the fierceness of mine anger, I will not return to destroy E′phra-im: for I *am* God, and not man; the Holy One in the midst of thee: and I will not enter into the city.

10 They shall walk after the LORD: he shall roar like a lion: when he shall roar, then the children shall tremble from the west.

11 They shall tremble as a bird out of E′gypt, and as a dove out of the land of As-syr′i-a: and I will place them in their houses, saith the LORD.

12 E′phra-im compasseth me about with lies, and the house of Is′ra-el with deceit: but Ju′dah yet ruleth with God, and is faithful with the saints.

12 E′PHRA-IM feedeth on wind, and followeth after the east wind: he daily increaseth lies and desolation; and they do make a covenant with the As-syr′i-ans, and oil is carried into E′gypt.

2 The LORD hath also a controversy with Ju′-dah, and will punish Ja′cob according to his ways; according to his doings will he recompense him.

3 ¶ He took his brother by the heel in the womb, and by his strength he had power with God:

4 Yea, he had power over the angel, and prevailed: he wept, and made supplication unto him: he found him *in* Beth′–el, and there he spake with us;

5 Even the LORD God of hosts; the LORD *is* his memorial.

6 Therefore turn thou to thy God: keep mercy and judgment, and wait on thy God continually.

7 ¶ *He is* a merchant, the balances of deceit *are* in his hand: he loveth to oppress.

8 And E′phra-im said, Yet I am become rich, I have found me out substance: *in* all my labours they shall find none iniquity in me that *were* sin.

9 And I *that am* the LORD thy God from the land of E′gypt will yet make thee to dwell in tabernacles, as in the days of the solemn feast.

10 I have also spoken by the prophets, and I have multiplied visions, and used similitudes, by the ministry of the prophets.

11 *Is there* iniquity *in* Gil′e-ad? surely they are vanity: they sacrifice bullocks in Gil′gal; yea, their altars *are* as heaps in the furrows of the fields.

12 And Ja′cob fled into the country of Syr′i-a, and Is′ra-el served for a wife, and for a wife he kept *sheep.*

13 And by a prophet the LORD brought Is′ra-el out of E′gypt, and by a prophet was he preserved.

14 E′phra-im provoked *him* to anger most bitterly: therefore shall he leave his blood upon him, and his reproach shall his LORD return unto him.

13 WHEN E′phra-im spake trembling, he exalted himself in Is′ra-el; but when he offended in Ba′al, he died.

2 And now they sin more and more, and have made them molten images of their silver, *and* idols according to their own understanding, all of it the work of the craftsmen: they say of them, Let the men that sacrifice kiss the calves.

3 Therefore they shall be as the morning cloud, and as the early dew that passeth away, as the chaff *that* is driven with the whirlwind out of the floor, and as the smoke out of the chimney.

4 Yet I *am* the LORD thy God from the land of E′gypt and thou shalt know no god but me: for *there is* no saviour beside me.

5 ¶ I did know thee in the wilderness, in the land of great drought.

6 According to their pasture, so were they

filled; they were filled, and their heart was exalted; therefore have they forgotten me.

7 Therefore I will be unto them as a lion: as a leopard by the way will I observe *them:*

8 I will meet them as a bear *that is* bereaved *of her whelps,* and will rend the caul of their heart, and there will I devour them like a lion: the wild beast shall tear them.

9 ¶ O Is′ra-el, thou hast destroyed thyself; but in me *is* thine help.

10 I will be thy king: where *is any other* that may save thee in all thy cities? and thy judges of whom thou saidst, Give me a king and princes?

11 I gave thee a king in mine anger, and took *him* away in my wrath.

12 The iniquity of E′phra-im *is* bound up; his sin *is* hid.

13 The sorrows of a travailing woman shall come upon him: he *is* an unwise son; for he should not stay long in *the place of* the breaking forth of children.

14 I will ransom them from the power of the grave; I will redeem them from death: O death, I will be thy plagues; O grave, I will be thy destruction: repentance shall be hid from mine eyes.

15 ¶ Though he be fruitful among *his* brethren, an east wind shall come, the wind of the LORD shall come up from the wilderness, and his spring shall become dry, and his fountain shall be dried up: he shall spoil the treasure of all pleasant vessels.

16 Sa-ma′ri-a shall become desolate; for she hath rebelled against her God: they shall fall by the sword: their infants shall be dashed in pieces, and their women with child shall be ripped up.

14 O IS′RA-EL, return unto the LORD thy God; for thou hast fallen by thine iniquity.

2 Take with you words, and turn to the LORD: say unto him, Take away all iniquity, and receive *us* graciously: so will we render the calves of our lips.

3 Assh′ur shall not save us; we will not ride upon horses: neither will we say any more to the work of our hands, *Ye are* our gods: for in thee the fatherless findeth mercy.

4 ¶ I will heal their backsliding, I will love them freely: for mine anger is turned away from him.

5 I will be as the dew unto Is′ra-el: he shall grow as the lily, and cast forth his roots as Leb′a-non.

6 His branches shall spread, and his beauty shall be as the olive tree, and his smell as Leb′a-non.

7 They that dwell under his shadow shall return; they shall revive *as* the corn, and grow as the vine: the scent thereof *shall be* as the wine of Leb′a-non.

8 E′phra-im *shall say,* What have I to do any more with idols? I have heard *him,* and observed him: I *am* like a green fir tree. From me is thy fruit found.

9 Who *is* wise, and he shall understand these *things?* prudent, and he shall know them? for the ways of the LORD *are* right, and the just shall walk in them: but the transgressors shall fall therein.

THE BOOK OF

JOEL

1 THE word of the LORD that came to Jo′el the son of Pe-thu′el.

2 Hear this, ye old men, and give ear, all ye inhabitants of the land. Hath this been in your days, or even in the days of your fathers?

3 Tell ye your children of it, and *let* your children *tell* their children, and their children another generation.

4 That which the palmerworm hath left hath the locust eaten; and that which the locust hath left hath the cankerworm eaten; and that which the cankerworm hath left hath the caterpiller eaten.

5 Awake, ye drunkards, and weep; and howl, all ye drinkers of wine, because of the new wine; for it is cut off from your mouth.

6 For a nation is come up upon my land, strong, and without number, whose teeth *are* the teeth of a lion, and he hath the cheek teeth of a great lion.

7 He hath laid my vine waste, and barked my fig tree: he hath made it clean bare, and cast *it* away; the branches thereof are made white.

8 ¶ Lament like a virgin girded with sackcloth for the husband of her youth.

9 The meat offering and the drink offering is cut off from the house of the LORD; the priests, the LORD's ministers, mourn.

10 The field is wasted, the land mourneth; for the corn is wasted: the new wine is dried up, the oil languisheth.

11 Be ye ashamed, O ye husbandmen; howl, O ye vinedressers, for the wheat and for the barley; because the harvest of the field is perished.

12 The vine is dried up, and the fig tree languisheth; the pomegranate tree, the palm tree also, and the apple tree, *even* all the trees of the field, are withered: because joy is withered away from the sons of men.

13 Gird yourselves, and lament, ye priests: howl, ye ministers of the altar: come, lie all night in sackcloth, ye ministers of my God: for the meat offering and the drink offering is withholden from the house of your God.

14 ¶ Sanctify ye a fast, call a solemn assembly, gather the elders *and* all the inhabitants of the land *into* the house of the LORD your God, and cry unto the LORD,

15 Alas for the day! for the day of the LORD *is* at hand, and as a destruction from the Almighty shall it come.

16 Is not the meat cut off before our eyes, *yea,* joy and gladness from the house of our God?

17 The seed is rotten under their clods, the garners are laid desolate, the barns are broken down; for the corn is withered.

18 How do the beasts groan! the herds of cattle are perplexed, because they have no pasture; yea, the flocks of sheep are made desolate.

19 O LORD, to thee will I cry: for the fire hath devoured the pastures of the wilderness, and the flame hath burned all the trees of the field.

20 The beasts of the field cry also unto thee:
for the rivers of waters are dried up, and the fire
hath devoured the pastures of the wilderness.

2 BLOW ye the trumpet in Zi'on, and sound
an alarm in my holy mountain: let all the
inhabitants of the land tremble: for the day of
the LORD cometh, for *it is* nigh at hand;
2 A day of darkness and of gloominess, a day
of clouds and of thick darkness, as the morning
spread upon the mountains: a great people and
a strong; there hath not been ever the like, neither shall be any more after it, *even* to the years
of many generations.
3 A fire devoureth before them; and behind
them a flame burneth: the land *is* as the garden
of E'den before them, and behind them a desolate wilderness; yea, and nothing shall escape
them.
4 The appearance of them *is* as the appearance of horses; and as horsemen, so shall they
run.
5 Like the noise of chariots on the tops of
mountains shall they leap, like the noise of a
flame of fire that devoureth the stubble, as a
strong people set in battle array.
6 Before their face the people shall be much
pained: all faces shall gather blackness.
7 They shall run like mighty men; they shall
climb the wall like men of war; and they shall
march every one on his ways, and they shall not
break their ranks:
8 Neither shall one thrust another; they shall
walk every one in his path: and *when* they fall
upon the sword, they shall not be wounded.
9 They shall run to and fro in the city; they
shall run upon the wall, they shall climb up
upon the houses; they shall enter in at the windows like a thief.
10 The earth shall quake before them; the
heavens shall tremble: the sun and the moon
shall be dark, and the stars shall withdraw their
shining:
11 And the LORD shall utter his voice before
his army: for his camp *is* very great: for *he is*
strong that executeth his word: for the day of
the LORD *is* great and very terrible; and who can
abide it?
12 ¶ Therefore also now, saith the LORD,
turn ye *even* to me with all your heart, and with
fasting, and with weeping, and with mourning.
13 And rend your heart, and not your garments, and turn unto the LORD your God: for he
is gracious and merciful, slow to anger, and of
great kindness, and repenteth him of the evil.
14 Who knoweth *if* he will return and repent,
and leave a blessing behind him; *even* a meat
offering and a drink offering unto the LORD your
God?
15 ¶ Blow the trumpet in Zi'on, sanctify a
fast, call a solemn assembly:
16 Gather the people, sanctify the congregation, assemble the elders, gather the children,
and those that suck the breasts: let the bridegroom go forth of his chamber, and the bride
out of her closet.
17 Let the priests, the ministers of the LORD,
weep between the porch and the altar, and let
them say, Spare thy people, O LORD, and give
not thine heritage to reproach, that the heathen
should rule over them: wherefore should they
say among the people, Where *is* their God?
18 ¶ Then will the LORD be jealous for his
land, and pity his people.
19 Yea, the LORD will answer and say unto
his people, Behold, I will send you corn, and
wine, and oil, and ye shall be satisfied therewith: and I will no more make you a reproach
among the heathen:
20 But I will remove far off from you the
northern *army*, and will drive him into a land
barren and desolate, with his face toward the
east sea, and his hinder part toward the utmost
sea, and his stink shall come up, and his ill savour shall come up, because he hath done great
things.
21 ¶ Fear not, O land; be glad and rejoice:
for the LORD will do great things.
22 Be not afraid, ye beasts of the field: for the
pastures of the wilderness do spring, for the
tree beareth her fruit, the fig tree and the vine
do yield their strength.
23 Be glad then, ye children of Zi'on, and rejoice in the LORD your God: for he hath given
you the former rain moderately, and he will
cause to come down for you the rain, the former rain, and the latter rain in the first *month*.
24 And the floors shall be full of wheat, and
the fats shall overflow with wine and oil.
25 And I will restore to you the years that the
locust hath eaten, the cankerworm, and the caterpiller, and the palmerworm, my great army
which I sent among you.
26 And ye shall eat in plenty, and be satisfied, and praise the name of the LORD your God,
that hath dealt wondrously with you: and my
people shall never be ashamed.
27 And ye shall know that I *am* in the midst
of Is'ra-el, and *that* I *am* the LORD your God,
and none else: and my people shall never be
ashamed.
28 ¶ And it shall come to pass afterward,
that I will pour out my spirit upon all flesh; and
your sons and your daughters shall prophesy,
your old men shall dream dreams, your young
men shall see visions:
29 And also upon the servants and upon the
handmaids in those days will I pour out my
spirit.
30 And I will shew wonders in the heavens
and in the earth, blood, and fire, and pillars of
smoke.
31 The sun shall be turned into darkness, and
the moon into blood, before the great and the
terrible day of the LORD come.
32 And it shall come to pass, *that* whosoever
shall call on the name of the LORD shall be delivered: for in mount Zi'on and in Je-ru'sa-lem
shall be deliverance, as the LORD hath said, and
in the remnant whom the LORD shall call.

3 FOR, behold, in those days, and in that
time, when I shall bring again the captivity
of Ju'dah and Je-ru'sa-lem,
2 I will also gather all nations, and will bring
them down into the valley of Je-hosh'a-phat,
and will plead with them there for my people
and *for* my heritage Is'ra-el, whom they have
scattered among the nations, and parted my
land.
3 And they have cast lots for my people; and
have given a boy for an harlot, and sold a girl
for wine, that they might drink.
4 Yea, and what have ye to do with me, O
Tyre, and Zi'don, and all the coasts of Pal'es-
tine? will ye render me a recompence? and if ye
recompense me, swiftly *and* speedily will I return your recompence upon your own head;
5 Because ye have taken my silver and my
gold, and have carried into your temples my
goodly pleasant things:
6 The children also of Ju'dah and the chil-

dren of Je-ru'sa-lem have ye sold unto the Gre'-cians, that ye might remove them far from their border.

7 Behold, I will raise them out of the place whither ye have sold them, and will return your recompence upon your own head:

8 And I will sell your sons and your daughters into the hand of the children of Ju'dah, and they shall sell them to the Sa-be'ans, to a people far off: for the LORD hath spoken *it*.

9 ¶ Proclaim ye this among the Gen'tiles; Prepare war, wake up the mighty men, let all the men of war draw near; let them come up:

10 Beat your plowshares into swords, and your pruninghooks into spears: let the weak say, I *am* strong.

11 Assemble yourselves, and come, all ye heathen, and gather yourselves together round about: thither cause thy mighty ones to come down, O LORD.

12 Let the heathen be wakened, and come up to the valley of Je-hosh'a-phat: for there will I sit to judge all the heathen round about.

13 Put ye in the sickle, for the harvest is ripe: come, get you down; for the press is full, the fats overflow; for their wickedness *is* great.

14 Multitudes, multitudes in the valley of decision: for the day of the LORD *is* near in the valley of decision.

15 The sun and the moon shall be darkened, and the stars shall withdraw their shining.

16 The LORD also shall roar out of Zi'on, and utter his voice from Je-ru'sa-lem; and the heavens and the earth shall shake: but the LORD *will be* the hope of his people, and the strength of the children of Is'ra-el.

17 So shall ye know that I *am* the LORD your God dwelling in Zi'on, my holy mountain: then shall Je-ru'sa-lem be holy, and there shall no strangers pass through her any more.

18 ¶ And it shall come to pass in that day, *that* the mountains shall drop down new wine, and the hills shall flow with milk, and all the rivers of Ju'dah shall flow with waters, and a fountain shall come forth of the house of the LORD, and shall water the valley of Shit'tim.

19 E'gypt shall be a desolation, and E'dom shall be a desolate wilderness, for the violence *against* the children of Ju'dah, because they have shed innocent blood in their land.

20 But Ju'dah shall dwell for ever, and Je-ru'-sa-lem from generation to generation.

21 For I will cleanse their blood *that* I have not cleansed: for the LORD dwelleth in Zi'on.

THE BOOK OF

AMOS

1 THE words of A'mos, who was among the herdmen of Te-ko'a, which he saw concerning Is'ra-el in the days of Uz-zi'ah king of Ju'dah, and in the days of Jer-o-bo'am the son of Jo'ash king of Is'ra-el, two years before the earthquake.

2 And he said, The LORD will roar from Zi'on, and utter his voice from Je-ru'sa-lem; and the habitations of the shepherds shall mourn, and the top of Car'mel shall wither.

3 Thus saith the LORD; For three transgressions of Da-mas'cus, and for four, I will not turn away *the punishment* thereof; because they have threshed Gil'e-ad with threshing instruments of iron:

4 But I will send a fire into the house of Haz'-a-el, which shall devour the palaces of Ben-ha'-dad.

5 I will break also the bar of Da-mas'cus, and cut off the inhabitant from the plain of A'ven, and him that holdeth the sceptre from the house of E'den: and the people of Syr'i-a shall go into captivity unto Kir, saith the LORD.

6 ¶ Thus saith the LORD; For three transgressions of Ga'za, and for four, I will not turn away *the punishment* thereof; because they carried away captive the whole captivity, to deliver *them* up to E'dom:

7 But I will send a fire on the wall of Ga'za, which shall devour the palaces thereof:

8 And I will cut off the inhabitant from Ash'-dod, and him that holdeth the sceptre from Ash'ke-lon, and I will turn mine hand against Ek'ron: and the remnant of the Phi-lis'tines shall perish, saith the Lord GOD.

9 ¶ Thus saith the LORD; For three transgressions of Ty'rus, and for four, I will not turn away *the punishment* thereof; because they delivered up the whole captivity to E'dom, and remembered not the brotherly covenant:

10 But I will send a fire on the wall of Ty'rus, which shall devour the palaces thereof.

11 ¶ Thus saith the LORD; For three transgressions of E'dom, and for four, I will not turn away *the punishment* thereof; because he did pursue his brother with the sword, and did cast off all pity, and his anger did tear perpetually, and he kept his wrath for ever:

12 But I will send a fire upon Te'man, which shall devour the palaces of Boz'rah.

13 ¶ Thus saith the LORD; For three transgressions of the children of Am'mon, and for four, I will not turn away *the punishment* thereof; because they have ripped up the women with child of Gil'e-ad, that they might enlarge their border:

14 But I will kindle a fire in the wall of Rab'-bah, and it shall devour the palaces thereof, with shouting in the day of battle, with a tempest in the day of the whirlwind:

15 And their king shall go into captivity, he and his princes together, saith the LORD.

2 THUS saith the LORD; For three transgressions of Mo'ab, and for four, I will not turn away *the punishment* thereof; because he burned the bones of the king of E'dom into lime:

2 But I will send a fire upon Mo'ab, and it shall devour the palaces of Kir'i-oth: and Mo'ab shall die with tumult, with shouting, *and* with the sound of the trumpet:

3 And I will cut off the judge from the midst thereof, and will slay all the princes thereof with him, saith the LORD.

4 ¶ Thus saith the LORD; For three transgressions of Ju'dah, and for four, I will not turn away *the punishment* thereof; because they have despised the law of the LORD, and have not kept his commandments, and their lies caused them to err, after the which their fathers have walked:

5 But I will send a fire upon Ju'dah, and it shall devour the palaces of Je-ru'sa-lem.

6 ¶ Thus saith the LORD; For three transgressions of Is'ra-el, and for four, I will not turn
away *the punishment* thereof; because they
sold the righteous for silver, and the poor for a
pair of shoes;
7 That pant after the dust of the earth on the
head of the poor, and turn aside the way of the
meek: and a man and his father will go in unto
the *same* maid, to profane my holy name:
8 And they lay *themselves* down upon
clothes laid to pledge by every altar, and they
drink the wine of the condemned *in* the house
of their god.
9 ¶ Yet destroyed I the Am'or-ite before
them, whose height *was* like the height of the
cedars, and he *was* strong as the oaks; yet I destroyed his fruit from above, and his roots from
beneath.
10 Also I brought you up from the land of
E'gypt, and led you forty years through the wilderness, to possess the land of the Am'or-ite.
11 And I raised up of your sons for prophets,
and of your young men for Naz'a-rites. *Is it* not
even thus, O ye children of Is'ra-el? saith the
LORD.
12 But ye gave the Naz'a-rites wine to drink;
and commanded the prophets, saying, Prophesy
not.
13 Behold, I am pressed under you, as a cart
is pressed *that is* full of sheaves.
14 Therefore the flight shall perish from the
swift, and the strong shall not strengthen his
force, neither shall the mighty deliver himself:
15 Neither shall he stand that handleth the
bow; and *he that is* swift of foot shall not deliver *himself:* neither shall he that rideth the
horse deliver himself.
16 And *he that is* courageous among the
mighty shall flee away naked in that day, saith
the LORD.

3 HEAR this word that the LORD hath spoken against you, O children of Is'ra-el,
against the whole family which I brought up
from the land of E'gypt, saying,
2 You only have I known of all the families of
the earth: therefore I will punish you for all
your iniquities.
3 Can two walk together, except they be
agreed?
4 Will a lion roar in the forest, when he hath
no prey? will a young lion cry out of his den, if
he have taken nothing?
5 Can a bird fall in a snare upon the earth,
where no gin *is* for him? shall *one* take up a
snare from the earth, and have taken nothing at
all?
6 Shall a trumpet be blown in the city, and
the people not be afraid? shall there be evil in a
city, and the LORD hath not done *it?*
7 Surely the Lord GOD will do nothing, but he
revealeth his secret unto his servants the prophets.
8 The lion hath roared, who will not fear? the
Lord GOD hath spoken, who can but prophesy?
9 ¶ Publish in the palaces of Ash'dod, and in
the palaces in the land of E'gypt, and say, Assemble yourselves upon the mountains of Sa-
ma'ri-a, and behold the great tumults in the
midst thereof, and the oppressed in the midst
thereof.
10 For they know not to do right, saith the
LORD, who store up violence and robbery in
their palaces.
11 Therefore thus saith the Lord GOD; An adversary *there shall be* even round about the
land; and he shall bring down thy strength from
thee, and thy palaces shall be spoiled.
12 Thus saith the LORD; As the shepherd taketh out of the mouth of the lion two legs, or a
piece of an ear; so shall the children of Is'ra-el
be taken out that dwell in Sa-ma'ri-a in the corner of a bed, and in Da-mas'cus *in* a couch.
13 Hear ye, and testify in the house of Ja'cob,
saith the Lord GOD, the God of hosts,
14 That in the day that I shall visit the transgressions of Is'ra-el upon him I will also visit
the altars of Beth'-el: and the horns of the altar
shall be cut off, and fall to the ground.
15 And I will smite the winter house with the
summer house; and the houses of ivory shall
perish, and the great houses shall have an end,
saith the LORD.

4 HEAR this word, ye kine of Ba'shan, that
are in the mountain of Sa-ma'ri-a, which
oppress the poor, which crush the needy, which
say to their masters, Bring, and let us drink.
2 The Lord GOD hath sworn by his holiness,
that, lo, the days shall come upon you, that he
will take you away with hooks, and your posterity with fishhooks.
3 And ye shall go out at the breaches, every
cow at that which is before her; and ye shall
cast *them* into the palace, saith the LORD.
4 ¶ Come to Beth'-el, and transgress; at Gil'-
gal multiply transgression; and bring your sacrifices every morning, *and* your tithes after
three years:
5 And offer a sacrifice of thanksgiving with
leaven, and proclaim *and* publish the free offerings: for this liketh you, O ye children of Is'ra-
el, saith the Lord GOD.
6 ¶ And I also have given you cleanness of
teeth in all your cities, and want of bread in all
your places: yet have ye not returned unto me,
saith the LORD.
7 And also I have withholden the rain from
you, when *there were* yet three months to the
harvest: and I caused it to rain upon one city,
and caused it not to rain upon another city: one
piece was rained upon, and the piece whereupon it rained not withered.
8 So two *or* three cities wandered unto one
city, to drink water; but they were not satisfied:
yet have ye not returned unto me, saith the
LORD.
9 I have smitten you with blasting and mildew: when your gardens and your vineyards
and your fig trees and your olive trees increased, the palmerworm devoured *them:* yet
have ye not returned unto me, saith the LORD.
10 I have sent among you the pestilence after
the manner of E'gypt: your young men have I
slain with the sword, and have taken away your
horses; and I have made the stink of your
camps to come up unto your nostrils: yet have
ye not returned unto me, saith the LORD.
11 I have overthrown *some* of you, as God
overthrew Sod'om and Go-mor'rah, and ye
were as a firebrand plucked out of the burning:
yet have ye not returned unto me, saith the
LORD.
12 Therefore thus will I do unto thee, O Is'ra-
el: *and* because I will do this unto thee, prepare
to meet thy God, O Is'ra-el.
13 For, lo, he that formeth the mountains,
and createth the wind, and declareth unto man
what *is* his thought, that maketh the morning
darkness, and treadeth upon the high places of
the earth, The LORD, The God of hosts, *is* his
name.

5 HEAR ye this word which I take up against you, *even* a lamentation, O house of Is'ra-el.

2 The virgin of Is'ra-el is fallen; she shall no more rise: she is forsaken upon her land; *there is* none to raise her up.

3 For thus saith the Lord GOD; The city that went out *by* a thousand shall leave an hundred, and that which went forth *by* an hundred shall leave ten, to the house of Is'ra-el.

4 ¶ For thus saith the LORD unto the house of Is'ra-el, Seek ye me, and ye shall live:

5 But seek not Beth'-el, nor enter into Gil'gal, and pass not to Be'er-she'ba: for Gil'gal shall surely go into captivity, and Beth'-el shall come to nought.

6 Seek the LORD, and ye shall live; lest he break out like fire in the house of Jo'seph, and devour *it,* and *there be* none to quench *it* in Beth'-el.

7 Ye who turn judgment to wormwood, and leave off righteousness in the earth,

8 *Seek him* that maketh the seven stars and O-ri'on, and turneth the shadow of death into the morning, and maketh the day dark with night: that calleth for the waters of the sea, and poureth them out upon the face of the earth: The LORD *is* his name:

9 That strengtheneth the spoiled against the strong, so that the spoiled shall come against the fortress.

10 They hate him that rebuketh in the gate, and they abhor him that speaketh uprightly.

11 Forasmuch therefore as your treading *is* upon the poor, and ye take from him burdens of wheat: ye have built houses of hewn stone, but ye shall not dwell in them; ye have planted pleasant vineyards, but ye shall not drink wine of them.

12 For I know your manifold transgressions and your mighty sins: they afflict the just, they take a bribe, and they turn aside the poor in the gate *from their right.*

13 Therefore the prudent shall keep silence in that time; for it *is* an evil time.

14 Seek good, and not evil, that ye may live: and so the LORD, the God of hosts, shall be with you, as ye have spoken.

15 Hate the evil, and love the good, and establish judgment in the gate: it may be that the LORD God of hosts will be gracious unto the remnant of Jo'seph.

16 Therefore the LORD, the God of hosts, the Lord, saith thus; Wailing *shall be* in all streets; and they shall say in all the highways, Alas! alas! and they shall call the husbandman to mourning, and such as are skilful of lamentation to wailing.

17 And in all vineyards *shall be* wailing: for I will pass through thee, saith the LORD.

18 Woe unto you that desire the day of the LORD! to what end *is* it for you? the day of the LORD *is* darkness, and not light.

19 As if a man did flee from a lion, and a bear met him; or went into the house, and leaned his hand on the wall, and a serpent bit him.

20 *Shall* not the day of the LORD *be* darkness, and not light? even very dark, and no brightness in it?

21 ¶ I hate, I despise your feast days, and I will not smell in your solemn assemblies.

22 Though ye offer me burnt offerings and your meat offerings, I will not accept *them:* neither will I regard the peace offerings of your fat beasts.

23 Take thou away from me the noise of thy songs; for I will not hear the melody of thy viols.

24 But let judgment run down as waters, and righteousness as a mighty stream.

25 Have ye offered unto me sacrifices and offerings in the wilderness forty years, O house of Is'ra-el?

26 But ye have borne the tabernacle of your Mo'loch and Chi'un your images, the star of your god, which ye made to yourselves.

27 Therefore will I cause you to go into captivity beyond Da-mas'cus, saith the LORD, whose name *is* The God of hosts.

6 WOE to them *that are* at ease in Zi'on, and trust in the mountain of Sa-ma'ri-a, *which are* named chief of the nations, to whom the house of Is'ra-el came!

2 Pass ye unto Cal'neh, and see; and from thence go ye to Ha'math the great: then go down to Gath of the Phi-lis'tines: *be they* better than these kingdoms? or their border greater than your border?

3 Ye that put far away the evil day, and cause the seat of violence to come near;

4 That lie upon beds of ivory, and stretch themselves upon their couches, and eat the lambs out of the flock, and the calves out of the midst of the stall;

5 That chant to the sound of the viol, *and* invent to themselves instruments of musick like Da'vid;

6 That drink wine in bowls, and anoint themselves with the chief ointments: but they are not grieved for the affliction of Jo'seph.

7 ¶ Therefore now shall they go captive with the first that go captive, and the banquet of them that stretched themselves shall be removed.

8 The Lord GOD hath sworn by himself, saith the LORD the God of hosts, I abhor the excellency of Ja'cob, and hate his palaces: therefore will I deliver up the city with all that is therein.

9 And it shall come to pass, if there remain ten men in one house, that they shall die.

10 And a man's uncle shall take him up, and he that burneth him, to bring out the bones out of the house, and shall say unto him that *is* by the sides of the house, *Is there* yet *any* with thee? and he shall say, No. Then shall he say, Hold thy tongue: for we may not make mention of the name of the LORD.

11 For, behold, the LORD commandeth, and he will smite the great house with breaches, and the little house with clefts.

12 ¶ Shall horses run upon the rock? will *one* plow *there* with oxen? for ye have turned judgment into gall, and the fruit of righteousness into hemlock:

13 Ye which rejoice in a thing of nought, which say, Have we not taken to us horns by our own strength?

14 But, behold, I will raise up against you a nation, O house of Is'ra-el, saith the LORD the God of hosts; and they shall afflict you from the entering in of He'math unto the river of the wilderness.

7 THUS hath the Lord GOD shewed unto me; and, behold, he formed grasshoppers in the beginning of the shooting up of the latter growth; and, lo, *it was* the latter growth after the king's mowings.

2 And it came to pass, *that* when they had made an end of eating the grass of the land, then I said, O Lord GOD, forgive, I beseech thee: by whom shall Ja'cob arise? for he *is* small.

3 The LORD repented for this: It shall not be,
saith the LORD.
4 ¶ Thus hath the Lord GOD shewed unto
me: and, behold, the Lord GOD called to contend by fire, and it devoured the great deep, and
did eat up a part.
5 Then said I, O Lord GOD, cease, I beseech
thee: by whom shall Ja'cob arise? for he *is*
small.
6 The LORD repented for this: This also shall
not be, saith the Lord GOD.
7 ¶ Thus he shewed me: and, behold, the
Lord stood upon a wall *made* by a plumbline,
with a plumbline in his hand.
8 And the LORD said unto me, A'mos, what
seest thou? And I said, A plumbline. Then said
the Lord, Behold, I will set a plumbline in the
midst of my people Is'ra-el: I will not again pass
by them any more:
9 And the high places of I'saac shall be desolate, and the sanctuaries of Is'ra-el shall be laid
waste; and I will rise against the house of Jer-o-
bo'am with the sword.
10 ¶ Then Am-a-zi'ah the priest of Beth'–el
sent to Jer-o-bo'am king of Is'ra-el, saying, A'-
mos hath conspired against thee in the midst of
the house of Is'ra-el: the land is not able to bear
all his words.
11 For thus A'mos saith, Jer-o-bo'am shall
die by the sword, and Is'ra-el shall surely be led
away captive out of their own land.
12 Also Am-a-zi'ah said unto A'mos, O thou
seer, go, flee thee away into the land of Ju'dah,
and there eat bread, and prophesy there:
13 But prophesy not again any more at Beth'-
–el: for it *is* the king's chapel, and it *is* the king's
court.
14 ¶ Then answered A'mos, and said to Am-
a-zi'ah, I *was* no prophet, neither *was* I a prophet's son; but I *was* an herdman, and a gatherer
of sycomore fruit:
15 And the LORD took me as I followed the
flock, and the LORD said unto me, Go, prophesy
unto my people Is'ra-el.
16 ¶ Now therefore hear thou the word of
the LORD: Thou sayest, Prophesy not against Is'-
ra-el, and drop not *thy word* against the house
of I'saac.
17 Therefore thus saith the LORD; Thy wife
shall be an harlot in the city, and thy sons and
thy daughters shall fall by the sword, and thy
land shall be divided by line; and thou shalt die
in a polluted land: and Is'ra-el shall surely go
into captivity forth of his land.

8 THUS hath the Lord GOD shewed unto me:
and behold a basket of summer fruit.
2 And he said, A'mos, what seest thou? And I
said, A basket of summer fruit. Then said the
LORD unto me, The end is come upon my people
of Is'ra-el; I will not again pass by them any
more.
3 And the songs of the temple shall be howl-
ings in that day, saith the Lord GOD: *there shall
be* many dead bodies in every place; they shall
cast *them* forth with silence.
4 ¶ Hear this, O ye that swallow up the
needy, even to make the poor of the land to fail,
5 Saying, When will the new moon be gone,
that we may sell corn? and the sabbath, that we
may set forth wheat, making the ephah small,
and the shekel great, and falsifying the balances
by deceit?
6 That we may buy the poor for silver, and
the needy for a pair of shoes; *yea,* and sell the
refuse of the wheat?
7 The LORD hath sworn by the excellency of
Ja'cob, Surely I will never forget any of their
works.
8 Shall not the land tremble for this, and every one mourn that dwelleth therein? and it
shall rise up wholly as a flood; and it shall be
cast out and drowned, as *by* the flood of E'gypt.
9 And it shall come to pass in that day, saith
the Lord GOD, that I will cause the sun to go
down at noon, and I will darken the earth in the
clear day:
10 And I will turn your feasts into mourning,
and all your songs into lamentation; and I will
bring up sackcloth upon all loins, and baldness
upon every head; and I will make it as the
mourning of an only *son,* and the end thereof as
a bitter day.
11 ¶ Behold, the days come, saith the Lord
GOD, that I will send a famine in the land, not a
famine of bread, nor a thirst for water, but of
hearing the words of the LORD:
12 And they shall wander from sea to sea,
and from the north even to the east, they shall
run to and fro to seek the word of the LORD, and
shall not find *it.*
13 In that day shall the fair virgins and young
men faint for thirst.
14 They that swear by the sin of Sa-ma'ri-a,
and say, Thy god, O Dan, liveth; and, The manner of Be'er–she'ba liveth; even they shall fall,
and never rise up again.

9 I SAW the Lord standing upon the altar:
and he said, Smite the lintel of the door,
that the posts may shake: and cut them in the
head, all of them; and I will slay the last of them
with the sword: he that fleeth of them shall not
flee away, and he that escapeth of them shall
not be delivered.
2 Though they dig into hell, thence shall
mine hand take them; though they climb up to
heaven, thence will I bring them down:
3 And though they hide themselves in the top
of Car'mel, I will search and take them out
thence; and though they be hid from my sight in
the bottom of the sea, thence will I command
the serpent, and he shall bite them:
4 And though they go into captivity before
their enemies, thence will I command the
sword, and it shall slay them: and I will set
mine eyes upon them for evil, and not for good.
5 And the Lord GOD of hosts *is* he that toucheth the land, and it shall melt, and all that dwell
therein shall mourn: and it shall rise up wholly
like a flood; and shall be drowned, as *by* the
flood of E'gypt.
6 *It is* he that buildeth his stories in the
heaven, and hath founded his troop in the earth;
he that calleth for the waters of the sea, and
poureth them out upon the face of the earth:
The LORD *is* his name.
7 *Are* ye not as children of the E-thi-o'pi-ans
unto me, O children of Is'ra-el? saith the LORD.
Have not I brought up Is'ra-el out of the land of
E'gypt? and the Phi-lis'tines from Caph'tor, and
the Syr'i-ans from Kir?
8 Behold, the eyes of the Lord GOD *are* upon
the sinful kingdom, and I will destroy it from off
the face of the earth; saving that I will not utterly destroy the house of Ja'cob, saith the LORD.
9 For, lo, I will command, and I will sift the
house of Is'ra-el among all nations, like as *corn*
is sifted in a sieve, yet shall not the least grain
fall upon the earth.
10 All the sinners of my people shall die by
the sword, which say, The evil shall not overtake nor prevent us.
11 ¶ In that day will I raise up the tabernacle

of Da′vid that is fallen, and close up the breaches thereof; and I will raise up his ruins, and I will build it as in the days of old:

12 That they may possess the remnant of E′dom, and of all the heathen, which are called by my name, saith the LORD that doeth this.

13 Behold, the days come, saith the LORD, that the plowman shall overtake the reaper, and the treader of grapes him that soweth seed; and the mountains shall drop sweet wine, and all the hills shall melt.

14 And I will bring again the captivity of my people of Is′ra-el, and they shall build the waste cities, and inhabit *them;* and they shall plant vineyards, and drink the wine thereof; they shall also make gardens, and eat the fruit of them.

15 And I will plant them upon their land, and they shall no more be pulled up out of their land which I have given them, saith the LORD thy God.

THE BOOK OF

OBADIAH

THE vision of O-ba-di′ah. Thus saith the Lord GOD concerning E′dom; We have heard a rumour from the LORD, and an ambassador is sent among the heathen, Arise ye, and let us rise up against her in battle.

2 Behold, I have made thee small among the heathen: thou art greatly despised.

3 ¶ The pride of thine heart hath deceived thee, thou that dwellest in the clefts of the rock, whose habitation *is* high; that saith in his heart, Who shall bring me down to the ground?

4 Though thou exalt *thyself* as the eagle, and though thou set thy nest among the stars, thence will I bring thee down, saith the LORD.

5 If thieves came to thee, if robbers by night, (how art thou cut off!) would they not have stolen till they had enough? if the grapegatherers came to thee, would they not leave *some* grapes?

6 How are *the things* of E′sau searched out! *how* are his hidden things sought up!

7 All the men of thy confederacy have brought thee *even* to the border: the men that were at peace with thee have deceived thee, *and* prevailed against thee; *they that eat* thy bread have laid a wound under thee: *there is* none understanding in him.

8 Shall I not in that day, saith the LORD, even destroy the wise *men* out of E′dom, and understanding out of the mount of E′sau?

9 And thy mighty *men,* O Te′man, shall be dismayed, to the end that every one of the mount of E′sau may be cut off by slaughter.

10 ¶ For *thy* violence against thy brother Ja′cob shame shall cover thee, and thou shalt be cut off for ever.

11 In the day that thou stoodest on the other side, in the day that the strangers carried away captive his forces, and foreigners entered into his gates, and cast lots upon Je-ru′sa-lem, even thou *wast* as one of them.

12 But thou shouldest not have looked on the day of thy brother in the day that he became a stranger; neither shouldest thou have rejoiced over the children of Ju′dah in the day of their destruction; neither shouldest thou have spoken proudly in the day of distress.

13 Thou shouldest not have entered into the gate of my people in the day of their calamity; yea, thou shouldest not have looked on their affliction in the day of their calamity, nor have laid *hands* on their substance in the day of their calamity;

14 Neither shouldest thou have stood in the crossway, to cut off those of his that did escape; neither shouldest thou have delivered up those of his that did remain in the day of distress.

15 For the day of the LORD *is* near upon all the heathen: as thou hast done, it shall be done unto thee: thy reward shall return upon thine own head.

16 For as ye have drunk upon my holy mountain, *so* shall all the heathen drink continually, yea, they shall drink, and they shall swallow down, and they shall be as though they had not been.

17 ¶ But upon mount Zi′on shall be deliverance, and there shall be holiness; and the house of Ja′cob shall possess their possessions.

18 And the house of Ja′cob shall be a fire, and the house of Jo′seph a flame, and the house of E′sau for stubble, and they shall kindle in them, and devour them; and there shall not be *any* remaining of the house of E′sau; for the LORD hath spoken *it.*

19 And *they of* the south shall possess the mount of E′sau; and *they of* the plain the Phi-lis′tines: and they shall possess the fields of E′phra-im, and the fields of Sa-ma′ri-a: and Ben′ja-min *shall possess* Gil′e-ad.

20 And the captivity of this host of the children of Is′ra-el *shall possess* that of the Ca′naan-ites, *even* unto Zar′e-phath; and the captivity of Je-ru′sa-lem, which *is* in Seph′a-rad, shall possess the cities of the south.

21 And saviours shall come up on mount Zi′on to judge the mount of E′sau; and the kingdom shall be the LORD's.

THE BOOK OF

JONAH

1 NOW the word of the LORD came unto Jo′nah the son of A-mit′ta-i, saying,

2 Arise, go to Nin′e-veh, that great city, and cry against it; for their wickedness is come up before me.

3 But Jo′nah rose up to flee unto Tar′shish from the presence of the LORD, and went down to Jop′pa; and he found a ship going to Tar′shish: so he paid the fare thereof, and went down into it, to go with them unto Tar′shish from the presence of the LORD.

4 ¶ But the LORD sent out a great wind into the sea, and there was a mighty tempest in the sea, so that the ship was like to be broken.

5 Then the mariners were afraid, and cried every man unto his god, and cast forth the wares that *were* in the ship into the sea, to lighten *it* of them. But Jo'nah was gone down into the sides of the ship; and he lay, and was fast asleep.

6 So the shipmaster came to him, and said unto him, What meanest thou, O sleeper? arise, call upon thy God, if so be that God will think upon us, that we perish not.

7 And they said every one to his fellow, Come, and let us cast lots, that we may know for whose cause this evil *is* upon us. So they cast lots, and the lot fell upon Jo'nah.

8 Then said they unto him, Tell us, we pray thee, for whose cause this evil *is* upon us; What *is* thine occupation? and whence comest thou? what *is* thy country? and of what people *art* thou?

9 And he said unto them, I *am* an He'brew; and I fear the LORD, the God of heaven, which hath made the sea and the dry *land*.

10 Then were the men exceedingly afraid, and said unto him, Why hast thou done this? For the men knew that he fled from the presence of the LORD, because he had told them.

11 ¶ Then said they unto him, What shall we do unto thee, that the sea may be calm unto us? for the sea wrought, and was tempestuous.

12 And he said unto them, Take me up, and cast me forth into the sea; so shall the sea be calm unto you: for I know that for my sake this great tempest *is* upon you.

13 Nevertheless the men rowed hard to bring *it* to the land; but they could not: for the sea wrought, and was tempestuous against them.

14 Wherefore they cried unto the LORD, and said, We beseech thee, O LORD, we beseech thee, let us not perish for this man's life, and lay not upon us innocent blood: for thou, O LORD, hast done as it pleased thee.

15 So they took up Jo'nah, and cast him forth into the sea: and the sea ceased from her raging.

16 Then the men feared the LORD exceedingly, and offered a sacrifice unto the LORD, and made vows.

17 ¶ Now the LORD had prepared a great fish to swallow up Jo'nah. And Jo'nah was in the belly of the fish three days and three nights.

2

THEN Jo'nah prayed unto the LORD his God out of the fish's belly,

2 And said, I cried by reason of mine affliction unto the LORD, and he heard me; out of the belly of hell cried I, *and* thou heardest my voice.

3 For thou hadst cast me into the deep, in the midst of the seas; and the floods compassed me about: all thy billows and thy waves passed over me.

4 Then I said, I am cast out of thy sight; yet I will look again toward thy holy temple.

5 The waters compassed me about, *even* to the soul: the depth closed me round about, the weeds were wrapped about my head.

6 I went down to the bottoms of the mountains; the earth with her bars *was* about me for ever: yet hast thou brought up my life from corruption, O LORD my God.

7 When my soul fainted within me I remembered the LORD: and my prayer came in unto thee, into thine holy temple.

8 They that observe lying vanities forsake their own mercy.

9 But I will sacrifice unto thee with the voice of thanksgiving; I will pay *that* that I have vowed. Salvation *is* of the LORD.

10 ¶ And the LORD spake unto the fish, and it vomited out Jo'nah upon the dry *land*.

3

AND the word of the LORD came unto Jo'nah the second time, saying,

2 Arise, go unto Nin'e-veh, that great city, and preach unto it the preaching that I bid thee.

3 So Jo'nah arose, and went unto Nin'e-veh, according to the word of the LORD. Now Nin'e-veh was an exceeding great city of three days' journey.

4 And Jo'nah began to enter into the city a day's journey, and he cried, and said, Yet forty days, and Nin'e-veh shall be overthrown.

5 ¶ So the people of Nin'e-veh believed God, and proclaimed a fast, and put on sackcloth, from the greatest of them even to the least of them.

6 For word came unto the king of Nin'e-veh, and he arose from his throne, and he laid his robe from him, and covered *him* with sackcloth, and sat in ashes.

7 And he caused *it* to be proclaimed and published through Nin'e-veh by the decree of the king and his nobles, saying, Let neither man nor beast, herd nor flock, taste any thing: let them not feed, nor drink water:

8 But let man and beast be covered with sackcloth, and cry mightily unto God: yea, let them turn every one from his evil way, and from the violence that *is* in their hands.

9 Who can tell *if* God will turn and repent, and turn away from his fierce anger, that we perish not?

10 ¶ And God saw their works, that they turned from their evil way; and God repented of the evil, that he had said that he would do unto them; and he did *it* not.

4

BUT it displeased Jo'nah exceedingly, and he was very angry.

2 And he prayed unto the LORD, and said, I pray thee, O LORD, *was* not this my saying, when I was yet in my country? Therefore I fled before unto Tar'shish: for I knew that thou *art* a gracious God, and merciful, slow to anger, and of great kindness, and repentest thee of the evil.

3 Therefore now, O LORD, take, I beseech thee, my life from me; for *it is* better for me to die than to live.

4 ¶ Then said the LORD, Doest thou well to be angry?

5 So Jo'nah went out of the city, and sat on the east side of the city, and there made him a booth, and sat under it in the shadow, till he might see what would become of the city.

6 And the LORD God prepared a gourd, and made *it* to come up over Jo'nah, that it might be a shadow over his head, to deliver him from his grief. So Jo'nah was exceeding glad of the gourd.

7 But God prepared a worm when the morning rose the next day, and it smote the gourd that it withered.

8 And it came to pass, when the sun did arise, that God prepared a vehement east wind; and the sun beat upon the head of Jo'nah, that he fainted, and wished in himself to die, and said, *It is* better for me to die than to live.

9 And God said to Jo'nah, Doest thou well to be angry for the gourd? And he said, I do well to be angry, *even* unto death.

10 Then said the LORD, Thou hast had pity on

the gourd, for the which thou hast not laboured, neither madest it grow; which came up in a night, and perished in a night:

11 And should not I spare Nin'e-veh, that great city, wherein are more than sixscore thousand persons that cannot discern between their right hand and their left hand; and *also* much cattle?

THE BOOK OF

MICAH

1 THE word of the LORD that came to Mi'cah the Mo'ras-thite in the days of Jo'tham, A'-haz, *and* Hez-e-ki'ah, kings of Ju'dah, which he saw concerning Sa-ma'ri-a and Je-ru'sa-lem.

2 Hear, all ye people; hearken, O earth, and all that therein is: and let the Lord GOD be witness against you, the Lord from his holy temple.

3 For, behold, the LORD cometh forth out of his place, and will come down, and tread upon the high places of the earth.

4 And the mountains shall be molten under him, and the valleys shall be cleft, as wax before the fire, *and* as the waters *that are* poured down a steep place.

5 For the transgression of Ja'cob *is* all this, and for the sins of the house of Is'ra-el. What *is* the transgression of Ja'cob? *is it* not Sa-ma'ri-a? and what *are* the high places of Ju'dah? *are they* not Je-ru'sa-lem?

6 Therefore I will make Sa-ma'ri-a as an heap of the field, *and* as plantings of a vineyard: and I will pour down the stones thereof into the valley, and I will discover the foundations thereof.

7 And all the graven images thereof shall be beaten to pieces, and all the hires thereof shall be burned with the fire, and all the idols thereof will I lay desolate: for she gathered *it* of the hire of an harlot, and they shall return to the hire of an harlot.

8 Therefore I will wail and howl, I will go stripped and naked: I will make a wailing like the dragons, and mourning as the owls.

9 For her wound *is* incurable; for it is come unto Ju'dah; he is come unto the gate of my people, *even* to Je-ru'sa-lem.

10 ¶ Declare ye *it* not at Gath, weep ye not at all: in the house of Aph'rah roll thyself in the dust.

11 Pass ye away, thou inhabitant of Saph'ir, having thy shame naked: the inhabitant of Za'a-nan came not forth in the mourning of Beth–e'-zel; he shall receive of you his standing.

12 For the inhabitant of Ma'roth waited carefully for good: but evil came down from the LORD unto the gate of Je-ru'sa-lem.

13 O thou inhabitant of La'chish, bind the chariot to the swift beast: she *is* the beginning of the sin to the daughter of Zi'on: for the transgressions of Is'ra-el were found in thee.

14 Therefore shalt thou give presents to Mor'esh-eth–gath: the houses of Ach'zib *shall be* a lie to the kings of Is'ra-el.

15 Yet will I bring an heir unto thee, O inhabitant of Ma-re'shah: he shall come unto A-dul'lam the glory of Is'ra-el.

16 Make thee bald, and poll thee for thy delicate children; enlarge thy baldness as the eagle; for they are gone into captivity from thee.

2 WOE to them that devise iniquity, and work evil upon their beds! when the morning is light, they practise it, because it is in the power of their hand.

2 And they covet fields, and take *them* by violence; and houses, and take *them* away: so they oppress a man and his house, even a man and his heritage.

3 Therefore thus saith the LORD; Behold, against this family do I devise an evil, from which ye shall not remove your necks; neither shall ye go haughtily: for this time *is* evil.

4 ¶ In that day shall *one* take up a parable against you, and lament with a doleful lamentation, *and* say, We be utterly spoiled: he hath changed the portion of my people: how hath he removed *it* from me! turning away he hath divided our fields.

5 Therefore thou shalt have none that shall cast a cord by lot in the congregation of the LORD.

6 Prophesy ye not, *say they to them that* prophesy: they shall not prophesy to them, *that* they shall not take shame.

7 ¶ O *thou that art* named the house of Ja'-cob, is the spirit of the LORD straitened? *are* these his doings? do not my words do good to him that walketh uprightly?

8 Even of late my people is risen up as an enemy: ye pull off the robe with the garment from them that pass by securely as men averse from war.

9 The women of my people have ye cast out from their pleasant houses; from their children have ye taken away my glory for ever.

10 Arise ye, and depart; for this *is* not *your* rest: because it is polluted, it shall destroy *you*, even with a sore destruction.

11 If a man walking in the spirit and falsehood do lie, *saying*, I will prophesy unto thee of wine and of strong drink; he shall even be the prophet of this people.

12 ¶ I will surely assemble, O Ja'cob, all of thee; I will surely gather the remnant of Is'ra-el; I will put them together as the sheep of Boz'rah, as the flock in the midst of their fold: they shall make great noise by reason of *the multitude of* men.

13 The breaker is come up before them: they have broken up, and have passed through the gate, and are gone out by it: and their king shall pass before them, and the LORD on the head of them.

3 AND I said, Hear, I pray you, O heads of Ja'cob, and ye princes of the house of Is'ra-el; *Is it* not for you to know judgment?

2 Who hate the good, and love the evil; who pluck off their skin from off them, and their flesh from off their bones;

3 Who also eat the flesh of my people, and flay their skin from off them; and they break their bones, and chop them in pieces, as for the pot, and as flesh within the caldron.

4 Then shall they cry unto the LORD, but he will not hear them: he will even hide his face from them at that time, as they have behaved themselves ill in their doings.

5 ¶ Thus saith the LORD concerning the prophets that make my people err, that bite with their teeth, and cry, Peace; and he that

putteth not into their mouths, they even prepare war against him.

6 Therefore night *shall be* unto you, that ye shall not have a vision; and it shall be dark unto you, that ye shall not divine; and the sun shall go down over the prophets, and the day shall be dark over them.

7 Then shall the seers be ashamed, and the diviners confounded: yea, they shall all cover their lips; for *there is* no answer of God.

8 ¶ But truly I am full of power by the spirit of the LORD, and of judgment, and of might, to declare unto Ja′cob his transgression, and to Is′-ra-el his sin.

9 Hear this, I pray you, ye heads of the house of Ja′cob, and princes of the house of Is′ra-el, that abhor judgment, and pervert all equity.

10 They build up Zi′on with blood, and Je-ru′sa-lem with iniquity.

11 The heads thereof judge for reward, and the priests thereof teach for hire, and the prophets thereof divine for money: yet will they lean upon the LORD, and say, *Is* not the LORD among us? none evil can come upon us.

12 Therefore shall Zi′on for your sake be plowed *as* a field, and Je-ru′sa-lem shall become heaps, and the mountain of the house as the high places of the forest.

4 BUT in the last days it shall come to pass, *that* the mountain of the house of the LORD shall be established in the top of the mountains, and it shall be exalted above the hills; and people shall flow unto it.

2 And many nations shall come, and say, Come, and let us go up to the mountain of the LORD, and to the house of the God of Ja′cob; and he will teach us of his ways, and we will walk in his paths: for the law shall go forth of Zi′on, and the word of the LORD from Je-ru′sa-lem.

3 ¶ And he shall judge among many people, and rebuke strong nations afar off; and they shall beat their swords into plowshares, and their spears into pruninghooks: nation shall not lift up a sword against nation, neither shall they learn war any more.

4 But they shall sit every man under his vine and under his fig tree; and none shall make *them* afraid: for the mouth of the LORD of hosts hath spoken *it*.

5 For all people will walk every one in the name of his god, and we will walk in the name of the LORD our God for ever and ever.

6 In that day, saith the LORD, will I assemble her that halteth, and I will gather her that is driven out, and her that I have afflicted;

7 And I will make her that halted a remnant, and her that was cast far off a strong nation: and the LORD shall reign over them in mount Zi′on from henceforth, even for ever.

8 ¶ And thou, O tower of the flock, the strong hold of the daughter of Zi′on, unto thee shall it come, even the first dominion; the kingdom shall come to the daughter of Je-ru′sa-lem.

9 Now why dost thou cry out aloud? *is there* no king in thee? is thy counsellor perished? for pangs have taken thee as a woman in travail.

10 Be in pain, and labour to bring forth, O daughter of Zi′on, like a woman in travail: for now shalt thou go forth out of the city, and thou shalt dwell in the field, and thou shalt go *even* to Bab′y-lon; there shalt thou be delivered; there the LORD shall redeem thee from the hand of thine enemies.

11 ¶ Now also many nations are gathered against thee, that say, Let her be defiled, and let our eye look upon Zi′on.

12 But they know not the thoughts of the LORD, neither understand they his counsel: for he shall gather them as the sheaves into the floor.

13 Arise and thresh, O daughter of Zi′on: for I will make thine horn iron, and I will make thy hoofs brass: and thou shalt beat in pieces many people: and I will consecrate their gain unto the LORD, and their substance unto the Lord of the whole earth.

5 NOW gather thyself in troops, O daughter of troops: he hath laid siege against us: they shall smite the judge of Is′ra-el with a rod upon the cheek.

2 But thou, Beth′-le-hem Eph′ra-tah, *though* thou be little among the thousands of Ju′dah, *yet* out of thee shall he come forth unto me *that is* to be ruler in Is′ra-el; whose goings forth *have been* from of old, from everlasting.

3 Therefore will he give them up, until the time *that* she which travaileth hath brought forth: then the remnant of his brethren shall return unto the children of Is′ra-el.

4 ¶ And he shall stand and feed in the strength of the LORD, in the majesty of the name of the LORD his God; and they shall abide: for now shall he be great unto the ends of the earth.

5 And this *man* shall be the peace, when the As-syr′i-an shall come into our land: and when he shall tread in our palaces, then shall we raise against him seven shepherds, and eight principal men.

6 And they shall waste the land of As-syr′i-a with the sword, and the land of Nim′rod in the entrances thereof: thus shall he deliver *us* from the As-syr′i-an, when he cometh into our land, and when he treadeth within our borders.

7 And the remnant of Ja′cob shall be in the midst of many people as a dew from the LORD, as the showers upon the grass, that tarrieth not for man, nor waiteth for the sons of men.

8 ¶ And the remnant of Ja′cob shall be among the Gen′tiles in the midst of many people as a lion among the beasts of the forest, as a young lion among the flocks of sheep: who, if he go through, both treadeth down, and teareth in pieces, and none can deliver.

9 Thine hand shall be lifted up upon thine adversaries, and all thine enemies shall be cut off.

10 And it shall come to pass in that day, saith the LORD, that I will cut off thy horses out of the midst of thee, and I will destroy thy chariots:

11 And I will cut off the cities of thy land, and throw down all thy strong holds:

12 And I will cut off witchcrafts out of thine hand; and thou shalt have no *more* soothsayers:

13 Thy graven images also will I cut off, and thy standing images out of the midst of thee; and thou shalt no more worship the work of thine hands.

14 And I will pluck up thy groves out of the midst of thee: so will I destroy thy cities.

15 And I will execute vengeance in anger and fury upon the heathen, such as they have not heard.

6 HEAR ye now what the LORD saith; Arise, contend thou before the mountains, and let the hills hear thy voice.

2 Hear ye, O mountains, the LORD's controversy, and ye strong foundations of the earth: for the LORD hath a controversy with his people, and he will plead with Is′ra-el.

3 O my people, what have I done unto thee? and wherein have I wearied thee? testify against me.

4 For I brought thee up out of the land of E'gypt, and redeemed thee out of the house of servants; and I sent before thee Mo'ses, Aar'on, and Mir'i-am.

5 O my people, remember now what Ba'lak king of Mo'ab consulted, and what Ba'laam the son of Be'or answered him from Shit'tim unto Gil'gal; that ye may know the righteousness of the LORD.

6 ¶ Wherewith shall I come before the LORD, *and* bow myself before the high God? shall I come before him with burnt offerings, with calves of a year old?

7 Will the LORD be pleased with thousands of rams, *or* with ten thousands of rivers of oil? shall I give my firstborn *for* my transgression, the fruit of my body *for* the sin of my soul?

8 He hath shewed thee, O man, what *is* good; and what doth the LORD require of thee, but to do justly, and to love mercy, and to walk humbly with thy God?

9 The LORD's voice crieth unto the city, and *the man of* wisdom shall see thy name: hear ye the rod, and who hath appointed it.

10 ¶ Are there yet the treasures of wickedness in the house of the wicked, and the scant measure *that is* abominable?

11 Shall I count *them* pure with the wicked balances, and with the bag of deceitful weights?

12 For the rich men thereof are full of violence, and the inhabitants thereof have spoken lies, and their tongue *is* deceitful in their mouth.

13 Therefore also will I make *thee* sick in smiting thee, in making *thee* desolate because of thy sins.

14 Thou shalt eat, but not be satisfied; and thy casting down *shall be* in the midst of thee; and thou shalt take hold, but shalt not deliver; and *that* which thou deliverest will I give up to the sword.

15 Thou shalt sow, but thou shalt not reap; thou shalt tread the olives, but thou shalt not anoint thee with oil; and sweet wine, but shalt not drink wine.

16 ¶ For the statutes of Om'ri are kept, and all the works of the house of A'hab, and ye walk in their counsels; that I should make thee a desolation, and the inhabitants thereof an hissing: therefore ye shall bear the reproach of my people.

7 WOE is me! for I am as when they have gathered the summer fruits, as the grapegleanings of the vintage: *there is* no cluster to eat: my soul desired the firstripe fruit.

2 The good *man* is perished out of the earth: and *there is* none upright among men: they all lie in wait for blood; they hunt every man his brother with a net.

3 ¶ That they may do evil with both hands earnestly, the prince asketh, and the judge *asketh* for a reward; and the great *man*, he uttereth his mischievous desire: so they wrap it up.

4 The best of them *is* as a brier: the most upright *is sharper* than a thorn hedge: the day of thy watchmen *and* thy visitation cometh; now shall be their perplexity.

5 ¶ Trust ye not in a friend, put ye not confidence in a guide: keep the doors of thy mouth from her that lieth in thy bosom.

6 For the son dishonoureth the father, the daughter riseth up against her mother, the daughter in law against her mother in law; a man's enemies *are* the men of his own house.

7 Therefore I will look unto the LORD; I will wait for the God of my salvation: my God will hear me.

8 ¶ Rejoice not against me, O mine enemy: when I fall, I shall arise; when I sit in darkness, the LORD *shall be* a light unto me.

9 I will bear the indignation of the LORD, because I have sinned against him, until he plead my cause, and execute judgment for me: he will bring me forth to the light, *and* I shall behold his righteousness.

10 Then *she that is* mine enemy shall see *it*, and shame shall cover her which said unto me, Where is the LORD thy God? mine eyes shall behold her: now shall she be trodden down as the mire of the streets.

11 *In* the day that thy walls are to be built, *in* that day shall the decree be far removed.

12 *In* that day *also* he shall come even to thee from As-syr'i-a, and *from* the fortified cities, and from the fortress even to the river, and from sea to sea, and *from* mountain to mountain.

13 Notwithstanding the land shall be desolate because of them that dwell therein, for the fruit of their doings.

14 ¶ Feed thy people with thy rod, the flock of thine heritage, which dwell solitarily *in* the wood, in the midst of Car'mel: let them feed *in* Ba'shan and Gil'e-ad, as in the days of old.

15 According to the days of thy coming out of the land of E'gypt will I shew unto him marvellous *things*.

16 ¶ The nations shall see and be confounded at all their might: they shall lay *their* hand upon *their* mouth, their ears shall be deaf.

17 They shall lick the dust like a serpent, they shall move out of their holes like worms of the earth: they shall be afraid of the LORD our God, and shall fear because of thee.

18 Who *is* a God like unto thee, that pardoneth iniquity, and passeth by the transgression of the remnant of his heritage? he retaineth not his anger for ever, because he delighteth *in* mercy.

19 He will turn again, he will have compassion upon us; he will subdue our iniquities; and thou wilt cast all their sins into the depths of the sea.

20 Thou wilt perform the truth to Ja'cob, *and* the mercy to A'bra-ham, which thou hast sworn unto our fathers from the days of old.

THE BOOK OF

NAHUM

1 THE burden of Nin'e-veh. The book of the
vision of Na'hum the El'kosh-ite.
2 God *is* jealous, and the LORD revengeth; the
LORD revengeth, and *is* furious; the LORD will
take vengeance on his adversaries, and he re-
serveth *wrath* for his enemies.
3 The LORD *is* slow to anger, and great in
power, and will not at all acquit *the wicked:* the
LORD *hath* his way in the whirlwind and in the
storm, and the clouds *are* the dust of his feet.
4 He rebuketh the sea, and maketh it dry,
and drieth up all the rivers: Ba'shan languisheth, and Car'mel, and the flower of Leb'a-non
languisheth.
5 The mountains quake at him, and the hills
melt, and the earth is burned at his presence,
yea, the world, and all that dwell therein.
6 Who can stand before his indignation? and
who can abide in the fierceness of his anger? his
fury is poured out like fire, and the rocks are
thrown down by him.
7 The LORD *is* good, a strong hold in the day
of trouble; and he knoweth them that trust in
him.
8 But with an overrunning flood he will make
an utter end of the place thereof, and darkness
shall pursue his enemies.
9 What do ye imagine against the LORD? he
will make an utter end: affliction shall not rise
up the second time.
10 For while *they be* folden together *as*
thorns, and while they are drunken *as* drunkards, they shall be devoured as stubble fully
dry.
11 There is *one* come out of thee, that imag-
ineth evil against the LORD, a wicked counsellor.
12 Thus saith the LORD; Though *they be*
quiet, and likewise many, yet thus shall they be
cut down, when he shall pass through. Though I
have afflicted thee, I will afflict thee no more.
13 For now will I break his yoke from off
thee and will burst thy bonds in sunder.
14 And the LORD hath given a commandment
concerning thee, *that* no more of thy name be
sown: out of the house of thy gods will I cut off
the graven image and the molten image: I will
make thy grave; for thou art vile.
15 Behold upon the mountains the feet of
him that bringeth good tidings, that publisheth
peace! O Ju'dah, keep thy solemn feasts, perform thy vows: for the wicked shall no more
pass through thee; he is utterly cut off.

2 HE that dasheth in pieces is come up before thy face: keep the munition, watch the
way, make *thy* loins strong, fortify *thy* power
mightily.
2 For the LORD hath turned away the excellency of Ja'cob, as the excellency of Is'ra-el: for
the emptiers have emptied them out, and
marred their vine branches.
3 The shield of his mighty men is made red,
the valiant men *are* in scarlet: the chariots *shall
be* with flaming torches in the day of his preparation, and the fir trees shall be terribly shaken.
4 The chariots shall rage in the streets, they
shall justle one against another in the broad
ways: they shall seem like torches, they shall
run like the lightnings.
5 He shall recount his worthies: they shall
stumble in their walk; they shall make haste to
the wall thereof, and the defence shall be prepared.
6 The gates of the rivers shall be opened, and
the palace shall be dissolved.
7 And Huz'zab shall be led away captive, she
shall be brought up, and her maids shall lead
her as with the voice of doves, tabering upon
their breasts.
8 But Nin'e-veh *is* of old like a pool of water:
yet they shall flee away. Stand, stand, *shall they
cry;* but none shall look back.
9 Take ye the spoil of silver, take the spoil of
gold: for *there is* none end of the store *and* glory
out of all the pleasant furniture.
10 She is empty, and void, and waste: and
the heart melteth, and the knees smite together,
and much pain *is* in all loins, and the faces of
them all gather blackness.
11 Where *is* the dwelling of the lions, and the
feedingplace of the young lions, where the lion,
even the old lion, walked, *and* the lion's whelp,
and none made *them* afraid?
12 The lion did tear in pieces enough for his
whelps, and strangled for his lionesses, and
filled his holes with prey, and his dens with ravin.
13 Behold, I *am* against thee, saith the LORD
of hosts, and I will burn her chariots in the
smoke, and the sword shall devour thy young
lions: and I will cut off thy prey from the earth,
and the voice of thy messengers shall no more
be heard.

3 WOE to the bloody city! it *is* all full of lies
and robbery; the prey departeth not;
2 The noise of a whip, and the noise of the
rattling of the wheels, and of the pransing
horses, and of the jumping chariots.
3 The horseman lifteth up both the bright
sword and the glittering spear: and *there is* a
multitude of slain, and a great number of carcases; and *there is* none end of *their* corpses;
they stumble upon their corpses:
4 Because of the multitude of the whoredoms
of the wellfavoured harlot, the mistress of
witchcrafts, that selleth nations through her
whoredoms, and families through her witchcrafts.
5 Behold, I *am* against thee, saith the LORD of
hosts; and I will discover thy skirts upon thy
face, and I will shew the nations thy nakedness,
and the kingdoms thy shame.
6 And I will cast abominable filth upon thee,
and make thee vile, and will set thee as a gazingstock.
7 And it shall come to pass, *that* all they that
look upon thee shall flee from thee, and say,
Nin'e-veh is laid waste: who will bemoan her?
whence shall I seek comforters for thee?
8 Art thou better than populous No, that was
situate among the rivers, *that had* the waters
round about it, whose rampart *was* the sea, *and*
her wall *was* from the sea?
9 E-thi-o'pi-a and E'gypt *were* her strength,
and *it was* infinite; Put and Lu'bim were thy
helpers.
10 Yet *was* she carried away, she went into
captivity: her young children also were dashed
in pieces at the top of all the streets: and they
cast lots for her honourable men, and all her
great men were bound in chains.
11 Thou also shalt be drunken: thou shalt be

hid, thou also shalt seek strength because of the
enemy.
12 All thy strong holds *shall be like* fig trees
with the firstripe figs: if they be shaken, they
shall even fall into the mouth of the eater.
13 Behold, thy people in the midst of thee *are*
women: the gates of thy land shall be set wide
open unto thine enemies: the fire shall devour
thy bars.
14 Draw thee waters for the siege, fortify thy
strong holds: go into clay, and tread the morter,
make strong the brickkiln.
15 There shall the fire devour thee; the sword
shall cut thee off, it shall eat thee up like the
cankerworm: make thyself many as the cankerworm, make thyself many as the locusts.
16 Thou hast multiplied thy merchants above
the stars of heaven: the cankerworm spoileth,
and fleeth away.
17 Thy crowned *are* as the locusts, and thy
captains as the great grasshoppers, which camp
in the hedges in the cold day, *but* when the sun
ariseth they flee away, and their place is not
known where they *are*.
18 Thy shepherds slumber, O king of As-syr'-
i-a: thy nobles shall dwell *in the dust:* thy people is scattered upon the mountains, and no
man gathereth *them*.
19 *There is* no healing of thy bruise; thy
wound is grievous: all that hear the bruit of thee
shall clap the hands over thee: for upon whom
hath not thy wickedness passed continually?

THE BOOK OF

HABAKKUK

1 THE burden which Ha-bak'kuk the
prophet did see.
2 O LORD, how long shall I cry, and thou wilt
not hear! *even* cry out unto thee *of* violence, and
thou wilt not save!
3 Why dost thou shew me iniquity, and cause
me to behold grievance? for spoiling and violence *are* before me: and there are *that* raise up
strife and contention.
4 Therefore the law is slacked, and judgment
doth never go forth: for the wicked doth compass about the righteous; therefore wrong judgment proceedeth.
5 ¶ Behold ye among the heathen, and regard, and wonder marvellously: for *I* will work
a work in your days, *which* ye will not believe,
though it be told *you*.
6 For, lo, I raise up the Chal-de'ans, *that* bitter and hasty nation, which shall march through
the breadth of the land, to possess the dwellingplaces *that are* not theirs.
7 They *are* terrible and dreadful: their judgment and their dignity shall proceed of themselves.
8 Their horses also are swifter than the leopards, and are more fierce than the evening
wolves: and their horsemen shall spread themselves, and their horsemen shall come from far;
they shall fly as the eagle *that* hasteth to eat.
9 They shall come all for violence: their faces
shall sup up *as* the east wind, and they shall
gather the captivity as the sand.
10 And they shall scoff at the kings, and the
princes shall be a scorn unto them: they shall
deride every strong hold; for they shall heap
dust, and take it.
11 Then shall *his* mind change, and he shall
pass over, and offend, *imputing* this his power
unto his god.
12 ¶ *Art* thou not from everlasting, O LORD
my God, mine Holy One? we shall not die. O
LORD, thou hast ordained them for judgment;
and, O mighty God, thou hast established them
for correction.
13 *Thou art* of purer eyes than to behold evil,
and canst not look on iniquity: wherefore lookest thou upon them that deal treacherously, *and*
holdest thy tongue when the wicked devoureth
the man that is more righteous than he?
14 And makest men as the fishes of the sea,
as the creeping things, *that have* no ruler over
them?
15 They take up all of them with the angle,
they catch them in their net, and gather them in
their drag: therefore they rejoice and are glad.
16 Therefore they sacrifice unto their net,
and burn incense unto their drag; because by
them their portion *is* fat, and their meat plenteous.
17 Shall they therefore empty their net, and
not spare continually to slay the nations?

2 I WILL stand upon my watch, and set me
upon the tower, and will watch to see what
he will say unto me, and what I shall answer
when I am reproved.
2 And the LORD answered me, and said,
Write the vision, and make *it* plain upon tables,
that he may run that readeth it.
3 For the vision *is* yet for an appointed time,
but at the end it shall speak, and not lie: though
it tarry, wait for it; because it will surely come,
it will not tarry.
4 Behold, his soul *which* is lifted up is not
upright in him: but the just shall live by his
faith.
5 ¶ Yea also, because he transgresseth by
wine, *he is* a proud man, neither keepeth at
home, who enlargeth his desire as hell, and *is* as
death, and cannot be satisfied, but gathereth
unto him all nations, and heapeth unto him all
people:
6 Shall not all these take up a parable against
him, and a taunting proverb against him, and
say, Woe to him that increaseth *that which is*
not his! how long? and to him that ladeth himself with thick clay!
7 Shall they not rise up suddenly that shall
bite thee, and awake that shall vex thee, and
thou shalt be for booties unto them?
8 Because thou hast spoiled many nations,
all the remnant of the people shall spoil thee;
because of men's blood, and *for* the violence of
the land, of the city, and of all that dwell
therein.
9 ¶ Woe to him that coveteth an evil covetousness to his house, that he may set his nest
on high, that he may be delivered from the
power of evil!
10 Thou hast consulted shame to thy house
by cutting off many people, and hast sinned
against thy soul.
11 For the stone shall cry out of the wall, and
the beam out of the timber shall answer it.
12 ¶ Woe to him that buildeth a town with
blood, and stablisheth a city by iniquity!

13 Behold, *is it* not of the LORD of hosts that the people shall labour in the very fire, and the people shall weary themselves for very vanity?

14 For the earth shall be filled with the knowledge of the glory of the LORD, as the waters cover the sea.

15 ¶ Woe unto him that giveth his neighbour drink, that puttest thy bottle to *him*, and makest *him* drunken also, that thou mayest look on their nakedness!

16 Thou art filled with shame for glory: drink thou also, and let thy foreskin be uncovered: the cup of the LORD's right hand shall be turned unto thee, and shameful spewing *shall be* on thy glory.

17 For the violence of Leb'a-non shall cover thee, and the spoil of beasts, *which* made them afraid, because of men's blood, and for the violence of the land, of the city, and of all that dwell therein.

18 ¶ What profiteth the graven image that the maker thereof hath graven it; the molten image, and a teacher of lies, that the maker of his work trusteth therein, to make dumb idols?

19 Woe unto him that saith to the wood, Awake; to the dumb stone, Arise, it shall teach! Behold, it *is* laid over with gold and silver, and *there is* no breath at all in the midst of it.

20 But the LORD *is* in his holy temple: let all the earth keep silence before him.

3 A PRAYER of Ha-bak'kuk the prophet upon Shi-gi'o-noth.

2 O LORD, I have heard thy speech, *and* was afraid: O LORD, revive thy work in the midst of the years, in the midst of the years make known; in wrath remember mercy.

3 God came from Te'man, and the Holy One from mount Pa'ran. Se'lah. His glory covered the heavens, and the earth was full of his praise.

4 And *his* brightness was as the light; he had horns *coming* out of his hand: and there *was* the hiding of his power.

5 Before him went the pestilence, and burning coals went forth at his feet.

6 He stood, and measured the earth: he beheld, and drove asunder the nations; and the everlasting mountains were scattered, the perpetual hills did bow: his ways *are* everlasting.

7 I saw the tents of Cu'shan in affliction: *and* the curtains of the land of Mid'i-an did tremble.

8 Was the LORD displeased against the rivers? *was* thine anger against the rivers? *was* thy wrath against the sea, that thou didst ride upon thine horses *and* thy chariots of salvation?

9 Thy bow was made quite naked, *according* to the oaths of the tribes, *even thy* word. Se'lah. Thou didst cleave the earth with rivers.

10 The mountains saw thee, *and* they trembled: the overflowing of the water passed by: the deep uttered his voice, *and* lifted up his hands on high.

11 The sun *and* moon stood still in their habitation: at the light of thine arrows they went, *and* at the shining of thy glittering spear.

12 Thou didst march through the land in indignation, thou didst thresh the heathen in anger.

13 Thou wentest forth for the salvation of thy people, *even* for salvation with thine anointed; thou woundedst the head out of the house of the wicked, by discovering the foundation unto the neck. Se'lah.

14 Thou didst strike through with his staves the head of his villages: they came out as a whirlwind to scatter me: their rejoicing *was* as to devour the poor secretly.

15 Thou didst walk through the sea with thine horses, *through* the heap of great waters.

16 When I heard, my belly trembled; my lips quivered at the voice: rottenness entered into my bones, and I trembled in myself, that I might rest in the day of trouble: when he cometh up unto the people, he will invade them with his troops.

17 ¶ Although the fig tree shall not blossom, neither *shall* fruit *be* in the vines; the labour of the olive shall fail, and the fields shall yield no meat; the flock shall be cut off from the fold, and *there shall be* no herd in the stalls:

18 Yet I will rejoice in the LORD, I will joy in the God of my salvation.

19 The LORD God *is* my strength, and he will make my feet like hinds' *feet*, and he will make me to walk upon mine high places. To the chief singer on my stringed instruments.

THE BOOK OF

ZEPHANIAH

1 THE word of the LORD which came unto Zeph-a-ni'ah the son of Cu'shi, the son of Ged-a-li'ah, the son of Am-a-ri'ah, the son of Hiz-ki'ah, in the days of Jo-si'ah the son of A'-mon, king of Ju'dah.

2 I will utterly consume all *things* from off the land, saith the LORD.

3 I will consume man and beast; I will consume the fowls of the heaven, and the fishes of the sea, and the stumblingblocks with the wicked; and I will cut off man from off the land, saith the LORD.

4 I will also stretch out mine hand upon Ju'-dah, and upon all the inhabitants of Je-ru'salem; and I will cut off the remnant of Ba'al from this place, *and* the name of the Chem'a-rims with the priests;

5 And them that worship the host of heaven upon the house tops; and them that worship *and* that swear by the LORD, and that swear by Mal'cham;

6 And them that are turned back from the LORD; and *those* that have not sought the LORD, nor enquired for him.

7 Hold thy peace at the presence of the Lord GOD: for the day of the LORD *is* at hand: for the LORD hath prepared a sacrifice, he hath bid his guests.

8 And it shall come to pass in the day of the LORD's sacrifice, that I will punish the princes, and the king's children, and all such as are clothed with strange apparel.

9 In the same day also will I punish all those that leap on the threshold, which fill their masters' houses with violence and deceit.

10 And it shall come to pass in that day, saith the LORD, *that there shall be* the noise of a cry from the fish gate, and an howling from the second, and a great crashing from the hills.

11 Howl, ye inhabitants of Mak'tesh, for all the merchant people are cut down; all they that bear silver are cut off.

12 And it shall come to pass at that time, *that* I will search Je-ru'sa-lem with candles, and punish the men that are settled on their lees: that say in their heart, The LORD will not do good, neither will he do evil.

13 Therefore their goods shall become a booty, and their houses a desolation: they shall also build houses, but not inhabit *them;* and they shall plant vineyards, but not drink the wine thereof.

14 The great day of the LORD *is* near, *it is* near, and hasteth greatly, *even* the voice of the day of the LORD: the mighty man shall cry there bitterly.

15 That day *is* a day of wrath, a day of trouble and distress, a day of wasteness and desolation, a day of darkness and gloominess, a day of clouds and thick darkness,

16 A day of the trumpet and alarm against the fenced cities, and against the high towers.

17 And I will bring distress upon men, that they shall walk like blind men, because they have sinned against the LORD: and their blood shall be poured out as dust, and their flesh as the dung.

18 Neither their silver nor their gold shall be able to deliver them in the day of the LORD's wrath; but the whole land shall be devoured by the fire of his jealousy: for he shall make even a speedy riddance of all them that dwell in the land.

2 GATHER yourselves together, yea, gather together, O nation not desired;

2 Before the decree bring forth, *before* the day pass as the chaff, before the fierce anger of the LORD come upon you, before the day of the LORD's anger come upon you.

3 Seek ye the LORD, all ye meek of the earth, which have wrought his judgment; seek righteousness, seek meekness: it may be ye shall be hid in the day of the LORD's anger.

4 ¶ For Ga'za shall be forsaken, and Ash'ke-lon a desolation: they shall drive out Ash'dod at the noon day, and Ek'ron shall be rooted up.

5 Woe unto the inhabitants of the sea coast, the nation of the Cher'eth-ites! the word of the LORD *is* against you; O Ca'naan, the land of the Phi-lis'tines, I will even destroy thee, that there shall be no inhabitant.

6 And the sea coast shall be dwellings *and* cottages for shepherds, and folds for flocks.

7 And the coast shall be for the remnant of the house of Ju'dah; they shall feed thereupon: in the houses of Ash'ke-lon shall they lie down in the evening: for the LORD their God shall visit them, and turn away their captivity.

8 ¶ I have heard the reproach of Mo'ab, and the revilings of the children of Am'mon, whereby they have reproached my people, and magnified *themselves* against their border.

9 Therefore *as* I live, saith the LORD of hosts, the God of Is'ra-el, Surely Mo'ab shall be as Sod'om, and the children of Am'mon as Go-mor'rah, *even* the breeding of nettles, and saltpits, and a perpetual desolation: the residue of my people shall spoil them, and the remnant of my people shall possess them.

10 This shall they have for their pride, because they have reproached and magnified *themselves* against the people of the LORD of hosts.

11 The LORD *will be* terrible unto them: for he will famish all the gods of the earth; and *men* shall worship him, every one from his place, *even* all the isles of the heathen.

12 ¶ Ye E-thi-o'pi-ans also, ye *shall be* slain by my sword.

13 And he will stretch out his hand against the north, and destroy As-syr'i-a; and will make Nin'e-veh a desolation, *and* dry like a wilderness.

14 And flocks shall lie down in the midst of her, all the beasts of the nations: both the cormorant and the bittern shall lodge in the upper lintels of it; *their* voice shall sing in the windows; desolation *shall be* in the thresholds: for he shall uncover the cedar work.

15 This *is* the rejoicing city that dwelt carelessly, that said in her heart, I *am*, and *there is* none beside me: how is she become a desolation, a place for beasts to lie down in! every one that passeth by her shall hiss, *and* wag his hand.

3 WOE to her that is filthy and polluted, to the oppressing city!

2 She obeyed not the voice; she received not correction; she trusted not in the LORD; she drew not near to her God.

3 Her princes within her *are* roaring lions; her judges *are* evening wolves; they gnaw not the bones till the morrow.

4 Her prophets *are* light *and* treacherous persons: her priests have polluted the sanctuary, they have done violence to the law.

5 The just LORD *is* in the midst thereof; he will not do iniquity: every morning doth he bring his judgment to light, he faileth not; but the unjust knoweth no shame.

6 I have cut off the nations: their towers are desolate; I made their streets waste, that none passeth by: their cities are destroyed, so that there is no man, that there is none inhabitant.

7 I said, Surely thou wilt fear me, thou wilt receive instruction; so their dwelling should not be cut off, howsoever I punished them: but they rose early, *and* corrupted all their doings.

8 ¶ Therefore wait ye upon me, saith the LORD, until the day that I rise up to the prey: for my determination *is* to gather the nations, that I may assemble the kingdoms, to pour upon them mine indignation, *even* all my fierce anger: for all the earth shall be devoured with the fire of my jealousy.

9 For then will I turn to the people a pure language, that they may all call upon the name of the LORD, to serve him with one consent.

10 From beyond the rivers of E-thi-o'pi-a my suppliants, *even* the daughter of my dispersed, shall bring mine offering.

11 In that day shalt thou not be ashamed for all thy doings, wherein thou hast transgressed against me: for then I will take away out of the midst of thee them that rejoice in thy pride, and thou shalt no more be haughty because of my holy mountain.

12 I will also leave in the midst of thee an afflicted and poor people, and they shall trust in the name of the LORD.

13 The remnant of Is'ra-el shall not do iniquity, nor speak lies; neither shall a deceitful tongue be found in their mouth: for they shall feed and lie down, and none shall make *them* afraid.

14 ¶ Sing, O daughter of Zi'on; shout, O Is'-ra-el; be glad and rejoice with all the heart, O daughter of Je-ru'sa-lem.

15 The LORD hath taken away thy judgments, he hath cast out thine enemy: the king of Is'ra-el, *even* the LORD, *is* in the midst of thee: thou shalt not see evil any more.

16 In that day it shall be said to Je-ru'sa-lem,
Fear thou not: *and to* Zi'on, Let not thine hands
be slack.
17 The LORD thy God in the midst of thee *is*
mighty; he will save, he will rejoice over thee
with joy; he will rest in his love, he will joy over
thee with singing.
18 I will gather *them that are* sorrowful for
the solemn assembly, *who* are of thee, *to whom*
the reproach of it *was* a burden.
19 Behold, at that time I will undo all that
afflict thee: and I will save her that halteth, and
gather her that was driven out; and I will get
them praise and fame in every land where they
have been put to shame.
20 At that time will I bring you *again*, even in
the time that I gather you: for I will make you a
name and a praise among all people of the
earth, when I turn back your captivity before
your eyes, saith the LORD.

THE BOOK OF

HAGGAI

1 IN the second year of Da-ri'us the king, in
the sixth month, in the first day of the
month, came the word of the LORD by Hag'ga-i
the prophet unto Ze-rub'ba-bel the son of She-
al'ti-el, governor of Ju'dah, and to Josh'u-a the
son of Jos'e-dech, the high priest, saying,
2 Thus speaketh the LORD of hosts, saying,
This people say, The time is not come, the time
that the LORD's house should be built.
3 Then came the word of the LORD by Hag'-
ga-i the prophet, saying,
4 *Is it* time for you, O ye, to dwell in your
cieled houses, and this house *lie* waste?
5 Now therefore thus saith the LORD of hosts;
Consider your ways.
6 Ye have sown much, and bring in little; ye
eat, but ye have not enough; ye drink, but ye are
not filled with drink; ye clothe you, but there is
none warm; and he that earneth wages earneth
wages *to put it* into a bag with holes.
7 ¶ Thus saith the LORD of hosts; Consider
your ways.
8 Go up to the mountain, and bring wood,
and build the house; and I will take pleasure in
it, and I will be glorified, saith the LORD.
9 Ye looked for much, and, lo, *it came* to little; and when ye brought *it* home, I did blow
upon it. Why? saith the LORD of hosts. Because
of mine house that *is* waste, and ye run every
man unto his own house.
10 Therefore the heaven over you is stayed
from dew, and the earth is stayed *from* her
fruit.
11 And I called for a drought upon the land,
and upon the mountains, and upon the corn,
and upon the new wine, and upon the oil, and
upon *that* which the ground bringeth forth, and
upon men, and upon cattle, and upon all the labour of the hands.
12 ¶ Then Ze-rub'ba-bel the son of She-al'ti-
el, and Josh'u-a the son of Jos'e-dech, the high
priest, with all the remnant of the people,
obeyed the voice of the LORD their God, and the
words of Hag'ga-i the prophet, as the LORD their
God had sent him, and the people did fear before the LORD.
13 Then spake Hag'ga-i the LORD's messenger in the LORD's message unto the people, saying, I *am* with you, saith the LORD.
14 And the LORD stirred up the spirit of Ze-
rub'ba-bel the son of She-al'ti-el, governor of
Ju'dah, and the spirit of Josh'u-a the son of Jos'-
e-dech, the high priest, and the spirit of all the
remnant of the people; and they came and did
work in the house of the LORD of hosts, their
God,
15 In the four and twentieth day of the sixth
month, in the second year of Da-ri'us the king.

2 IN the seventh *month*, in the one and
twentieth *day* of the month, came the
word of the LORD by the prophet Hag'ga-i, saying,
2 Speak now to Ze-rub'ba-bel the son of She-
al'ti-el, governor of Ju'dah, and to Josh'u-a the
son of Jos'e-dech, the high priest, and to the
residue of the people, saying,
3 Who *is* left among you that saw this house
in her first glory? and how do ye see it now? *is it*
not in your eyes in comparison of it as nothing?
4 Yet now be strong, O Ze-rub'ba-bel, saith
the LORD; and be strong, O Josh'u-a, son of Jos'-
e-dech, the high priest; and be strong, all ye
people of the land, saith the LORD, and work:
for I *am* with you, saith the LORD of hosts:
5 *According to* the word that I covenanted
with you when ye came out of E'gypt, so my
spirit remaineth among you: fear ye not.
6 For thus saith the LORD of hosts; Yet once,
it *is* a little while, and I will shake the heavens,
and the earth, and the sea, and the dry *land;*
7 And I will shake all nations, and the desire
of all nations shall come: and I will fill this
house with glory, saith the LORD of hosts.
8 The silver *is* mine, and the gold *is* mine,
saith the LORD of hosts.
9 The glory of this latter house shall be
greater than of the former, saith the LORD of
hosts: and in this place will I give peace, saith
the LORD of hosts.
10 ¶ In the four and twentieth *day* of the
ninth *month*, in the second year of Da-ri'us,
came the word of the LORD by Hag'ga-i the
prophet, saying,
11 Thus saith the LORD of hosts; Ask now the
priests *concerning* the law, saying,
12 If one bear holy flesh in the skirt of his
garment, and with his skirt do touch bread, or
pottage, or wine, or oil, or any meat, shall it be
holy? And the priests answered and said, No.
13 Then said Hag'ga-i, If *one that is* unclean
by a dead body touch any of these, shall it be
unclean? And the priests answered and said, It
shall be unclean.
14 Then answered Hag'ga-i, and said, So *is*
this people, and so *is* this nation before me,
saith the LORD; and so *is* every work of their
hands; and that which they offer there *is* unclean.
15 And now, I pray you, consider from this
day and upward, from before a stone was laid
upon a stone in the temple of the LORD:
16 Since those *days* were, when *one* came to
an heap of twenty *measures*, there were *but*
ten: when *one* came to the pressfat for to draw
out fifty *vessels* out of the press, there were *but*
twenty

17 I smote you with blasting and with mildew and with hail in all the labours of your
hands; yet ye *turned* not to me, saith the LORD.
18 Consider now from this day and upward,
from the four and twentieth day of the ninth
month, even from the day that the foundation
of the LORD's temple was laid, consider *it*.
19 Is the seed yet in the barn? yea, as yet the
vine, and the fig tree, and the pomegranate, and
the olive tree, hath not brought forth: from this
day will I bless *you*.
20 ¶ And again the word of the LORD came
unto Hag'ga-i in the four and twentieth *day* of
the month, saying,
21 Speak to Ze-rub'ba-bel, governor of Ju'-
dah, saying, I will shake the heavens and the
earth;
22 And I will overthrow the throne of kingdoms, and I will destroy the strength of the
kingdoms of the heathen; and I will overthrow
the chariots, and those that ride in them; and
the horses and their riders shall come down, every one by the sword of his brother.
23 In that day, saith the LORD of hosts, will I
take thee, O Ze-rub'ba-bel, my servant, the son
of She-al'ti-el, saith the LORD, and will make
thee as a signet: for I have chosen thee, saith
the LORD of hosts.

THE BOOK OF

ZECHARIAH

1 IN the eighth month, in the second year of
Da-ri'us, came the word of the LORD unto
Zech-a-ri'ah, the son of Ber-e-chi'ah, the son of
Id'do the prophet, saying,
2 The LORD hath been sore displeased with
your fathers.
3 Therefore say thou unto them, Thus saith
the LORD of hosts; Turn ye unto me, saith the
LORD of hosts, and I will turn unto you, saith the
LORD of hosts.
4 Be ye not as your fathers, unto whom the
former prophets have cried, saying, Thus saith
the LORD of hosts; Turn ye now from your evil
ways, and *from* your evil doings: but they did
not hear, nor hearken unto me, saith the LORD.
5 Your fathers, where *are* they? and the
prophets, do they live for ever?
6 But my words and my statutes, which I
commanded my servants the prophets, did they
not take hold of your fathers? and they returned
and said, Like as the LORD of hosts thought to
do unto us, according to our ways, and according to our doings, so hath he dealt with us.
7 ¶ Upon the four and twentieth day of the
eleventh month, which *is* the month Se'bat, in
the second year of Da-ri'us, came the word of
the LORD unto Zech-a-ri'ah, the son of Ber-e-
chi'ah, the son of Id'do the prophet, saying,
8 I saw by night, and behold a man riding
upon a red horse, and he stood among the myrtle trees that *were* in the bottom; and behind
him *were there* red horses, speckled, and white.
9 Then said I, O my lord, what *are* these?
And the angel that talked with me said unto me,
I will shew thee what these *be*.
10 And the man that stood among the myrtle
trees answered and said, These *are they* whom
the LORD hath sent to walk to and fro through
the earth.
11 And they answered the angel of the LORD
that stood among the myrtle trees, and said, We
have walked to and fro through the earth, and,
behold, all the earth sitteth still, and is at rest.
12 ¶ Then the angel of the LORD answered
and said, O LORD of hosts, how long wilt thou
not have mercy on Je-ru'sa-lem and on the
cities of Ju'dah, against which thou hast had indignation these threescore and ten years?
13 And the LORD answered the angel that
talked with me *with* good words *and* comfortable words.
14 So the angel that communed with me said
unto me, Cry thou, saying, Thus saith the LORD
of hosts; I am jealous for Je-ru'sa-lem and for
Zi'on with a great jealousy.
15 And I am very sore displeased with the
heathen *that are* at ease: for I was but a little
displeased, and they helped forward the affliction.
16 Therefore thus saith the LORD; I am returned to Je-ru'sa-lem with mercies: my house
shall be built in it, saith the LORD of hosts, and a
line shall be stretched forth upon Je-ru'sa-lem.
17 Cry yet, saying, Thus saith the LORD of
hosts; My cities through prosperity shall yet be
spread abroad; and the LORD shall yet comfort
Zi'on, and shall yet choose Je-ru'sa-lem.
18 ¶ Then lifted I up mine eyes, and saw, and
behold four horns.
19 And I said unto the angel that talked with
me, What *be* these? And he answered me, These
are the horns which have scattered Ju'dah, Is'-
ra-el, and Je-ru'sa-lem.
20 And the LORD shewed me four carpenters.
21 Then said I, What come these to do? And
he spake, saying, These *are* the horns which
have scattered Ju'dah, so that no man did lift up
his head: but these are come to fray them, to
cast out the horns of the Gen'tiles, which lifted
up *their* horn over the land of Ju'dah to scatter
it.

2 I LIFTED up mine eyes again, and looked,
and behold a man with a measuring line in
his hand.
2 Then said I, Whither goest thou? And he
said unto me, To measure Je-ru'sa-lem, to see
what *is* the breadth thereof, and what *is* the
length thereof.
3 And, behold, the angel that talked with me
went forth, and another angel went out to meet
him,
4 And said unto him, Run, speak to this
young man, saying, Je-ru'sa-lem shall be inhabited *as* towns without walls for the multitude of
men and cattle therein:
5 For I, saith the LORD, will be unto her a
wall of fire round about, and will be the glory in
the midst of her.
6 ¶ Ho, ho, *come forth,* and flee from the
land of the north, saith the LORD: for I have
spread you abroad as the four winds of the
heaven, saith the LORD.
7 Deliver thyself, O Zi'on, that dwellest *with*
the daughter of Bab'y-lon.
8 For thus saith the LORD of hosts; After the
glory hath he sent me unto the nations which
spoiled you: for he that toucheth you toucheth
the apple of his eye.
9 For, behold, I will shake mine hand upon
them, and they shall be a spoil to their servants:

and ye shall know that the LORD of hosts hath sent me.

10 ¶ Sing and rejoice, O daughter of Zi'on: for, lo, I come, and I will dwell in the midst of thee, saith the LORD.

11 And many nations shall be joined to the LORD in that day, and shall be my people: and I will dwell in the midst of thee, and thou shalt know that the LORD of hosts hath sent me unto thee.

12 And the LORD shall inherit Ju'dah his portion in the holy land, and shall choose Je-ru'sa-lem again.

13 Be silent, O all flesh, before the LORD: for he is raised up out of his holy habitation.

3 AND he shewed me Josh'u-a the high priest standing before the angel of the LORD, and Sa'tan standing at his right hand to resist him.

2 And the LORD said unto Sa'tan, The LORD rebuke thee, O Sa'tan; even the LORD that hath chosen Je-ru'sa-lem rebuke thee: *is* not this a brand plucked out of the fire?

3 Now Josh'u-a was clothed with filthy garments, and stood before the angel.

4 And he answered and spake unto those that stood before him, saying, Take away the filthy garments from him. And unto him he said, Behold, I have caused thine iniquity to pass from thee, and I will clothe thee with change of raiment.

5 And I said, Let them set a fair mitre upon his head. So they set a fair mitre upon his head, and clothed him with garments. And the angel of the LORD stood by.

6 And the angel of the LORD protested unto Josh'u-a, saying,

7 Thus saith the LORD of hosts; If thou wilt walk in my ways, and if thou wilt keep my charge, then thou shalt also judge my house, and shalt also keep my courts, and I will give thee places to walk among these that stand by.

8 Hear now, O Josh'u-a the high priest, thou, and thy fellows that sit before thee: for they *are* men wondered at: for, behold, I will bring forth my servant the BRANCH.

9 For behold the stone that I have laid before Josh'u-a; upon one stone *shall be* seven eyes: behold, I will engrave the graving thereof, saith the LORD of hosts, and I will remove the iniquity of that land in one day.

10 In that day, saith the LORD of hosts, shall ye call every man his neighbour under the vine and under the fig tree.

4 AND the angel that talked with me came again, and waked me, as a man that is wakened out of his sleep,

2 And said unto me, What seest thou? And I said, I have looked, and behold a candlestick all *of* gold, with a bowl upon the top of it, and his seven lamps thereon, and seven pipes to the seven lamps, which *are* upon the top thereof:

3 And two olive trees by it, one upon the right *side* of the bowl, and the other upon the left *side* thereof.

4 So I answered and spake to the angel that talked with me, saying, What *are* these, my lord?

5 Then the angel that talked with me answered and said unto me, Knowest thou not what these be? And I said, No, my lord.

6 Then he answered and spake unto me, saying, This *is* the word of the LORD unto Ze-rub'-ba-bel, saying, Not by might, nor by power, but by my spirit, saith the LORD of hosts.

7 Who *art* thou, O great mountain? before Ze-rub'ba-bel *thou shalt become* a plain: and he shall bring forth the headstone *thereof with* shoutings, *crying*, Grace, grace unto it.

8 Moreover the word of the LORD came unto me, saying,

9 The hands of Ze-rub'ba-bel have laid the foundation of this house; his hands shall also finish it; and thou shalt know that the LORD of hosts hath sent me unto you.

10 For who hath despised the day of small things? for they shall rejoice, and shall see the plummet in the hand of Ze-rub'ba-bel *with* those seven; they *are* the eyes of the LORD, which run to and fro through the whole earth.

11 ¶ Then answered I, and said unto him, What *are* these two olive trees upon the right *side* of the candlestick and upon the left *side* thereof?

12 And I answered again, and said unto him, What *be these* two olive branches which through the two golden pipes empty the golden *oil* out of themselves?

13 And he answered me and said, Knowest thou not what these *be?* And I said, No, my lord.

14 Then said he, These *are* the two anointed ones, that stand by the Lord of the whole earth.

5 THEN I turned, and lifted up mine eyes, and looked, and behold a flying roll.

2 And he said unto me, What seest thou? And I answered, I see a flying roll; the length thereof *is* twenty cubits, and the breadth thereof ten cubits.

3 Then said he unto me, This *is* the curse that goeth forth over the face of the whole earth: for every one that stealeth shall be cut off *as* on this side according to it; and every one that sweareth shall be cut off *as* on that side according to it.

4 I will bring it forth, saith the LORD of hosts, and it shall enter into the house of the thief, and into the house of him that sweareth falsely by my name, and it shall remain in the midst of his house, and shall consume it with the timber thereof and the stones thereof.

5 ¶ Then the angel that talked with me went forth, and said unto me, Lift up now thine eyes, and see what *is* this that goeth forth.

6 And I said, What *is* it? And he said, This *is* an ephah that goeth forth. He said moreover, This *is* their resemblance through all the earth.

7 And, behold, there was lifted up a talent of lead: and this *is* a woman that sitteth in the midst of the ephah.

8 And he said, This *is* wickedness. And he cast it into the midst of the ephah; and he cast the weight of lead upon the mouth thereof.

9 Then lifted I up mine eyes, and looked, and, behold, there came out two women, and the wind *was* in their wings; for they had wings like the wings of a stork: and they lifted up the ephah between the earth and the heaven.

10 Then said I to the angel that talked with me, Whither do these bear the ephah?

11 And he said unto me, To build it an house in the land of Shi'nar: and it shall be established, and set there upon her own base.

6 AND I turned, and lifted up mine eyes, and looked, and, behold, there came four chariots out from between two mountains; and the mountains *were* mountains of brass.

2 In the first chariot *were* red horses; and in the second chariot black horses;

3 And in the third chariot white horses; and in the fourth chariot grisled and bay horses.

4 Then I answered and said unto the angel
that talked with me, What *are* these, my lord?
5 And the angel answered and said unto me,
These *are* the four spirits of the heavens, which
go forth from standing before the Lord of all the
earth.
6 The black horses which *are* therein go forth
into the north country; and the white go forth
after them; and the grisled go forth toward the
south country.
7 And the bay went forth, and sought to go
that they might walk to and fro through the
earth: and he said, Get you hence, walk to and
fro through the earth. So they walked to and fro
through the earth.
8 Then cried he upon me, and spake unto me,
saying, Behold, these that go toward the north
country have quieted my spirit in the north
country.
9 ¶ And the word of the LORD came unto me,
saying,
10 Take of *them of* the captivity, *even* of
Hel′da-i, of To-bi′jah, and of Je-da′iah, which
are come from Bab′y-lon, and come thou the
same day, and go into the house of Jo-si′ah the
son of Zeph-a-ni′ah;
11 Then take silver and gold, and make
crowns, and set *them* upon the head of Josh′u-a
the son of Jos′e-dech, the high priest;
12 And speak unto him, saying, Thus speaketh the LORD of hosts, saying, Behold the man
whose name *is* The BRANCH; and he shall
grow up out of his place, and he shall build the
temple of the LORD:
13 Even he shall build the temple of the
LORD; and he shall bear the glory, and shall sit
and rule upon his throne; and he shall be a
priest upon his throne: and the counsel of peace
shall be between them both.
14 And the crowns shall be to He′lem, and to
To-bi′jah, and to Je-da′iah, and to Hen the son
of Zeph-a-ni′ah, for a memorial in the temple of
the LORD.
15 And they *that are* far off shall come and
build in the temple of the LORD, and ye shall
know that the LORD of hosts hath sent me unto
you. And *this* shall come to pass, if ye will diligently obey the voice of the LORD your God.

7 AND it came to pass in the fourth year of
king Da-ri′us, *that* the word of the LORD
came unto Zech-a-ri′ah in the fourth *day* of the
ninth month, *even* in Chis′leu;
2 When they had sent unto the house of God
She-re′zer and Re′gem-me′lech, and their men,
to pray before the LORD,
3 *And* to speak unto the priests which *were*
in the house of the LORD of hosts, and to the
prophets, saying, Should I weep in the fifth
month, separating myself, as I have done these
so many years?
4 ¶ Then came the word of the LORD of hosts
unto me, saying,
5 Speak unto all the people of the land, and
to the priests, saying, When ye fasted and
mourned in the fifth and seventh *month,* even
those seventy years, did ye at all fast unto me,
even to me?
6 And when ye did eat, and when ye did
drink, did not ye eat *for yourselves,* and drink
for yourselves?
7 *Should ye* not *hear* the words which the
LORD hath cried by the former prophets, when
Je-ru′sa-lem was inhabited and in prosperity,
and the cities thereof round about her, when
men inhabited the south and the plain?

8 ¶ And the word of the LORD came unto
Zech-a-ri′ah, saying,
9 Thus speaketh the LORD of hosts, saying,
Execute true judgment, and shew mercy and
compassions every man to his brother:
10 And oppress not the widow, nor the fatherless, the stranger, nor the poor; and let none
of you imagine evil against his brother in your
heart.
11 But they refused to hearken, and pulled
away the shoulder, and stopped their ears, that
they should not hear.
12 Yea, they made their hearts *as* an adamant stone, lest they should hear the law, and
the words which the LORD of hosts hath sent in
his spirit by the former prophets: therefore
came a great wrath from the LORD of hosts.
13 Therefore it is come to pass, *that* as he
cried, and they would not hear; so they cried,
and I would not hear, saith the LORD of hosts:
14 But I scattered them with a whirlwind
among all the nations whom they knew not.
Thus the land was desolate after them, that no
man passed through nor returned: for they laid
the pleasant land desolate.

8 AGAIN the word of the LORD of hosts
came *to me,* saying,
2 Thus saith the LORD of hosts; I was jealous
for Zi′on with great jealousy, and I was jealous
for her with great fury.
3 Thus saith the LORD; I am returned unto
Zi′on, and will dwell in the midst of Je-ru′sa-
lem: and Je-ru′sa-lem shall be called a city of
truth; and the mountain of the LORD of hosts the
holy mountain.
4 Thus saith the LORD of hosts; There shall
yet old men and old women dwell in the streets
of Je-ru′sa-lem, and every man with his staff in
his hand for very age.
5 And the streets of the city shall be full of
boys and girls playing in the streets thereof.
6 Thus saith the LORD of hosts; If it be marvellous in the eyes of the remnant of this people
in these days, should it also be marvellous in
mine eyes? saith the LORD of hosts.
7 Thus saith the LORD of hosts; Behold, I will
save my people from the east country, and from
the west country;
8 And I will bring them, and they shall dwell
in the midst of Je-ru′sa-lem: and they shall be
my people, and I will be their God, in truth and
in righteousness.
9 ¶ Thus saith the LORD of hosts; Let your
hands be strong, ye that hear in these days
these words by the mouth of the prophets,
which *were* in the day *that* the foundation of the
house of the LORD of hosts was laid, that the
temple might be built.
10 For before these days there was no hire
for man, nor any hire for beast; neither *was
there any* peace to him that went out or came in
because of the affliction: for I set all men every
one against his neighbour.
11 But now I *will* not *be* unto the residue of
this people as in the former days, saith the LORD
of hosts.
12 For the seed *shall be* prosperous; the vine
shall give her fruit, and the ground shall give
her increase, and the heavens shall give their
dew; and I will cause the remnant of this people
to possess all these *things.*
13 And it shall come to pass, *that* as ye were
a curse among the heathen, O house of Ju′dah,
and house of Is′ra-el; so will I save you, and ye
shall be a blessing: fear not, *but* let your hands
be strong.

14 For thus saith the LORD of hosts; As I
thought to punish you, when your fathers provoked me to wrath, saith the LORD of hosts, and
I repented not:
15 So again have I thought in these days to
do well unto Je-ru'sa-lem and to the house of
Ju'dah: fear ye not.
16 ¶ These *are* the things that ye shall do;
Speak ye every man the truth to his neighbour;
execute the judgment of truth and peace in
your gates:
17 And let none of you imagine evil in your
hearts against his neighbour; and love no false
oath: for all these *are things* that I hate, saith
the LORD.
18 ¶ And the word of the LORD of hosts
came unto me, saying,
19 Thus saith the LORD of hosts; The fast of
the fourth *month*, and the fast of the fifth, and
the fast of the seventh, and the fast of the tenth,
shall be to the house of Ju'dah joy and gladness,
and cheerful feasts; therefore love the truth and
peace.
20 Thus saith the LORD of hosts; *It shall* yet
come to pass, that there shall come people, and
the inhabitants of many cities:
21 And the inhabitants of one *city* shall go to
another, saying, Let us go speedily to pray before the LORD, and to seek the LORD of hosts: I
will go also.
22 Yea, many people and strong nations shall
come to seek the LORD of hosts in Je-ru'sa-lem,
and to pray before the LORD.
23 Thus saith the LORD of hosts; In those
days *it shall come to pass*, that ten men shall
take hold out of all languages of the nations,
even shall take hold of the skirt of him that is a
Jew, saying, We will go with you: for we have
heard *that* God *is* with you.

9 THE burden of the word of the LORD in the
land of Ha'drach, and Da-mas'cus *shall be*
the rest thereof: when the eyes of man, as of all
the tribes of Is'ra-el, *shall be* toward the LORD.
2 And Ha'math also shall border thereby;
Ty'rus, and Zi'don, though it be very wise.
3 And Ty'rus did build herself a strong hold,
and heaped up silver as the dust, and fine gold
as the mire of the streets.
4 Behold, the Lord will cast her out, and he
will smite her power in the sea; and she shall be
devoured with fire.
5 Ash'ke-lon shall see *it*, and fear; Ga'za also
shall see it, and be very sorrowful, and Ek'ron;
for her expectation shall be ashamed; and the
king shall perish from Ga'za, and Ash'ke-lon
shall not be inhabited.
6 And a bastard shall dwell in Ash'dod, and I
will cut off the pride of the Phi-lis'tines.
7 And I will take away his blood out of his
mouth, and his abominations from between his
teeth: but he that remaineth, even he, *shall be*
for our God, and he shall be as a governor in
Ju'dah, and Ek'ron as a Jeb'u-site.
8 And I will encamp about mine house because of the army, because of him that passeth
by, and because of him that returneth: and no
oppressor shall pass through them any more:
for now have I seen with mine eyes.
9 ¶ Rejoice greatly, O daughter of Zi'on;
shout, O daughter of Je-ru'sa-lem: behold, thy
King cometh unto thee: he *is* just, and having
salvation; lowly, and riding upon an ass, and
upon a colt the foal of an ass.
10 And I will cut off the chariot from E'phra-
im, and the horse from Je-ru'sa-lem, and the
battle bow shall be cut off: and he shall speak
peace unto the heathen: and his dominion *shall
be* from sea *even* to sea, and from the river *even*
to the ends of the earth.
11 As for thee also, by the blood of thy covenant I have sent forth thy prisoners out of the
pit wherein *is* no water.
12 ¶ Turn you to the strong hold, ye prisoners of hope: even to day do I declare *that* I will
render double unto thee;
13 When I have bent Ju'dah for me, filled the
bow with E'phra-im, and raised up thy sons, O
Zi'on, against thy sons, O Greece, and made
thee as the sword of a mighty man.
14 And the LORD shall be seen over them,
and his arrow shall go forth as the lightning:
and the Lord GOD shall blow the trumpet, and
shall go with whirlwinds of the south.
15 The LORD of hosts shall defend them; and
they shall devour, and subdue with sling stones;
and they shall drink, *and* make a noise as
through wine; and they shall be filled like
bowls, *and* as the corners of the altar.
16 And the LORD their God shall save them in
that day as the flock of his people: for *they shall
be as* the stones of a crown, lifted up as an ensign upon his land.
17 For how great *is* his goodness, and how
great *is* his beauty! corn shall make the young
men cheerful, and new wine the maids.

10 ASK ye of the LORD rain in the time of
the latter rain; *so* the LORD shall make
bright clouds, and give them showers of rain, to
every one grass in the field.
2 For the idols have spoken vanity, and the
diviners have seen a lie, and have told false
dreams; they comfort in vain: therefore they
went their way as a flock, they were troubled,
because *there was* no shepherd.
3 Mine anger was kindled against the shepherds, and I punished the goats: for the LORD of
hosts hath visited his flock the house of Ju'dah,
and hath made them as his goodly horse in the
battle.
4 Out of him came forth the corner, out of
him the nail, out of him the battle bow, out of
him every oppressor together.
5 ¶ And they shall be as mighty *men*, which
tread down *their enemies* in the mire of the
streets in the battle: and they shall fight, because the LORD *is* with them, and the riders on
horses shall be confounded.
6 And I will strengthen the house of Ju'dah,
and I will save the house of Jo'seph, and I will
bring them again to place them; for I have mercy upon them: and they shall be as though I had
not cast them off: for I *am* the LORD their God,
and will hear them.
7 And *they of* E'phra-im shall be like a
mighty *man*, and their heart shall rejoice as
through wine: yea, their children shall see *it*,
and be glad; their heart shall rejoice in the
LORD.
8 I will hiss for them, and gather them; for I
have redeemed them: and they shall increase as
they have increased.
9 And I will sow them among the people: and
they shall remember me in far countries; and
they shall live with their children, and turn
again.
10 I will bring them again also out of the land
of E'gypt, and gather them out of As-syr'i-a;
and I will bring them into the land of Gil'e-ad
and Leb'a-non; and *place* shall not be found for
them.
11 And he shall pass through the sea with affliction, and shall smite the waves in the sea,

and all the deeps of the river shall dry up: and the pride of As-syr'i-a shall be brought down, and the sceptre of E'gypt shall depart away.

12 And I will strengthen them in the LORD; and they shall walk up and down in his name, saith the LORD.

11 OPEN thy doors, O Leb'a-non, that the fire may devour thy cedars.

2 Howl, fir tree; for the cedar is fallen; because the mighty are spoiled: howl, O ye oaks of Ba'shan; for the forest of the vintage is come down.

3 ¶ *There is* a voice of the howling of the shepherds; for their glory is spoiled: a voice of the roaring of young lions; for the pride of Jor'dan is spoiled.

4 Thus saith the LORD my God; Feed the flock of the slaughter;

5 Whose possessors slay them, and hold themselves not guilty: and they that sell them say, Blessed *be* the LORD; for I am rich: and their own shepherds pity them not.

6 For I will no more pity the inhabitants of the land, saith the LORD: but, lo, I will deliver the men every one into his neighbour's hand, and into the hand of his king: and they shall smite the land, and out of their hand I will not deliver *them*.

7 And I will feed the flock of slaughter, *even* you, O poor of the flock. And I took unto me two staves; the one I called Beauty, and the other I called Bands; and I fed the flock.

8 Three shepherds also I cut off in one month; and my soul loathed them, and their soul also abhorred me.

9 Then said I, I will not feed you: that that dieth, let it die; and that that is to be cut off, let it be cut off; and let the rest eat every one the flesh of another.

10 ¶ And I took my staff, *even* Beauty, and cut it asunder, that I might break my covenant which I had made with all the people.

11 And it was broken in that day: and so the poor of the flock that waited upon me knew that it *was* the word of the LORD.

12 And I said unto them, If ye think good, give *me* my price; and if not, forbear. So they weighed for my price thirty *pieces* of silver.

13 And the LORD said unto me, Cast it unto the potter: a goodly price that I was prised at of them. And I took the thirty *pieces* of silver, and cast them to the potter in the house of the LORD.

14 Then I cut asunder mine other staff, *even* Bands, that I might break the brotherhood between Ju'dah and Is'ra-el.

15 ¶ And the LORD said unto me, Take unto thee yet the instruments of a foolish shepherd.

16 For, lo, I will raise up a shepherd in the land, *which* shall not visit those that be cut off, neither shall seek the young one, nor heal that that is broken, nor feed that that standeth still: but he shall eat the flesh of the fat, and tear their claws in pieces.

17 Woe to the idol shepherd that leaveth the flock! the sword *shall be* upon his arm, and upon his right eye: his arm shall be clean dried up, and his right eye shall be utterly darkened.

12 THE burden of the word of the LORD for Is'ra-el, saith the LORD, which stretcheth forth the heavens, and layeth the foundation of the earth, and formeth the spirit of man within him.

2 Behold, I will make Je-ru'sa-lem a cup of trembling unto all the people round about, when they shall be in the siege both against Ju'dah *and* against Je-ru'sa-lem.

3 ¶ And in that day will I make Je-ru'sa-lem a burdensome stone for all people: all that burden themselves with it shall be cut in pieces, though all the people of the earth be gathered together against it.

4 In that day, saith the LORD, I will smite every horse with astonishment, and his rider with madness: and I will open mine eyes upon the house of Ju'dah, and will smite every horse of the people with blindness.

5 And the governors of Ju'dah shall say in their heart, The inhabitants of Je-ru'sa-lem *shall be* my strength in the LORD of hosts their God.

6 ¶ In that day will I make the governors of Ju'dah like an hearth of fire among the wood, and like a torch of fire in a sheaf; and they shall devour all the people round about, on the right hand and on the left: and Je-ru'sa-lem shall be inhabited again in her own place, *even* in Je-ru'sa-lem.

7 The LORD also shall save the tents of Ju'dah first, that the glory of the house of Da'vid and the glory of the inhabitants of Je-ru'sa-lem do not magnify *themselves* against Ju'dah.

8 In that day shall the LORD defend the inhabitants of Je-ru'sa-lem; and he that is feeble among them at that day shall be as Da'vid; and the house of Da'vid *shall be* as God, as the angel of the LORD before them.

9 ¶ And it shall come to pass in that day, *that* I will seek to destroy all the nations that come against Je-ru'sa-lem.

10 And I will pour upon the house of Da'vid, and upon the inhabitants of Je-ru'sa-lem, the spirit of grace and of supplications: and they shall look upon me whom they have pierced, and they shall mourn for him, as one mourneth for *his* only *son*, and shall be in bitterness for him, as one that is in bitterness for *his* firstborn.

11 In that day shall there be a great mourning in Je-ru'sa-lem, as the mourning of Ha-dad-rim'mon in the valley of Me-gid'don.

12 And the land shall mourn, every family apart; the family of the house of Da'vid apart, and their wives apart; the family of the house of Na'than apart, and their wives apart;

13 The family of the house of Le'vi apart, and their wives apart; the family of Shim'e-i apart, and their wives apart;

14 All the families that remain, every family apart, and their wives apart.

13 IN that day there shall be a fountain opened to the house of Da'vid and to the inhabitants of Je-ru'sa-lem for sin and for uncleanness.

2 ¶ And it shall come to pass in that day, saith the LORD of hosts, *that* I will cut off the names of the idols out of the land, and they shall no more be remembered: and also I will cause the prophets and the unclean spirit to pass out of the land.

3 And it shall come to pass, *that* when any shall yet prophesy, then his father and his mother that begat him shall say unto him, Thou shalt not live; for thou speakest lies in the name of the LORD: and his father and his mother that begat him shall thrust him through when he prophesieth.

4 And it shall come to pass in that day, *that* the prophets shall be ashamed every one of his vision, when he hath prophesied; neither shall they wear a rough garment to deceive:

5 But he shall say, I *am* no prophet, I *am* an husbandman; for man taught me to keep cattle from my youth.

6 And *one* shall say unto him, What *are* these wounds in thine hands? Then he shall answer, *Those* with which I was wounded *in* the house of my friends.

7 ¶ Awake, O sword, against my shepherd, and against the man *that is* my fellow, saith the LORD of hosts: smite the shepherd, and the sheep shall be scattered: and I will turn mine hand upon the little ones.

8 And it shall come to pass, *that* in all the land, saith the LORD, two parts therein shall be cut off *and* die; but the third shall be left therein.

9 And I will bring the third part through the fire, and will refine them as silver is refined, and will try them as gold is tried: they shall call on my name, and I will hear them: I will say, It *is* my people: and they shall say, The LORD *is* my God.

14 BEHOLD, the day of the LORD cometh, and thy spoil shall be divided in the midst of thee.

2 For I will gather all nations against Je-ru'-sa-lem to battle; and the city shall be taken, and the houses rifled, and the women ravished; and half of the city shall go forth into captivity, and the residue of the people shall not be cut off from the city.

3 Then shall the LORD go forth, and fight against those nations, as when he fought in the day of battle.

4 ¶ And his feet shall stand in that day upon the mount of Ol'ives, which *is* before Je-ru'sa-lem on the east, and the mount of Ol'ives shall cleave in the midst thereof toward the east and toward the west, *and there shall be* a very great valley; and half of the mountain shall remove toward the north, and half of it toward the south.

5 And ye shall flee *to* the valley of the mountains; for the valley of the mountains shall reach unto A'zal: yea, ye shall flee, like as ye fled from before the earthquake in the days of Uz-zi'ah king of Ju'dah: and the LORD my God shall come, *and* all the saints with thee.

6 And it shall come to pass in that day, *that* the light shall not be clear, *nor* dark:

7 But it shall be one day which shall be known to the LORD, not day, nor night: but it shall come to pass, *that* at evening time it shall be light.

8 And it shall be in that day, *that* living waters shall go out from Je-ru'sa-lem; half of them toward the former sea, and half of them toward the hinder sea: in summer and in winter shall it be.

9 And the LORD shall be king over all the earth: in that day shall there be one LORD, and his name one.

10 All the land shall be turned as a plain from Ge'ba to Rim'mon south of Je-ru'sa-lem: and it shall be lifted up, and inhabited in her place, from Ben'ja-min's gate unto the place of the first gate, unto the corner gate, and *from* the tower of Ha-nan'e-el unto the king's winepresses.

11 And *men* shall dwell in it, and there shall be no more utter destruction; but Je-ru'sa-lem shall be safely inhabited.

12 ¶ And this shall be the plague wherewith the LORD will smite all the people that have fought against Je-ru'sa-lem; Their flesh shall consume away while they stand upon their feet, and their eyes shall consume away in their holes, and their tongue shall consume away in their mouth.

13 And it shall come to pass in that day, *that* a great tumult from the LORD shall be among them; and they shall lay hold every one on the hand of his neighbour, and his hand shall rise up against the hand of his neighbour.

14 And Ju'dah also shall fight at Je-ru'sa-lem; and the wealth of all the heathen round about shall be gathered together, gold, and silver, and apparel, in great abundance.

15 And so shall be the plague of the horse, of the mule, of the camel, and of the ass, and of all the beasts that shall be in these tents, as this plague.

16 ¶ And it shall come to pass, *that* every one that is left of all the nations which came against Je-ru'sa-lem shall even go up from year to year to worship the King, the LORD of hosts, and to keep the feast of tabernacles.

17 And it shall be, *that* whoso will not come up of *all* the families of the earth unto Je-ru'sa-lem to worship the King, the LORD of hosts, even upon them shall be no rain.

18 And if the family of E'gypt go not up, and come not, that *have* no *rain;* there shall be the plague, wherewith the LORD will smite the heathen that come not up to keep the feast of tabernacles.

19 This shall be the punishment of E'gypt, and the punishment of all nations that come not up to keep the feast of tabernacles.

20 ¶ In that day shall there be upon the bells of the horses, HOLINESS UNTO THE LORD; and the pots in the LORD's house shall be like the bowls before the altar.

21 Yea, every pot in Je-ru'sa-lem and in Ju'-dah shall be holiness unto the LORD of hosts: and all they that sacrifice shall come and take of them, and seethe therein: and in that day there shall be no more the Ca'naan-ite in the house of the LORD of hosts.

THE BOOK OF

MALACHI

1 THE burden of the word of the LORD to Is'-ra-el by Mal'a-chi.

2 I have loved you, saith the LORD. Yet ye say, Wherein hast thou loved us? *Was* not E'sau Ja'cob's brother? saith the LORD: yet I loved Ja'-cob,

3 And I hated E'sau, and laid his mountains and his heritage waste for the dragons of the wilderness.

4 Whereas E'dom saith, We are impoverished, but we will return and build the desolate places; thus saith the LORD of hosts, They shall build, but I will throw down; and they shall call them, The border of wickedness, and, The people against whom the LORD hath indignation for ever.

5 And your eyes shall see, and ye shall say, The LORD will be magnified from the border of Is'ra-el.

6 ¶ A son honoureth *his* father, and a ser-

vant his master: if then I *be* a father, where *is*
mine honour? and if I *be* a master, where *is* my
fear? saith the LORD of hosts unto you, O
priests, that despise my name. And ye say,
Wherein have we despised thy name?
7 Ye offer polluted bread upon mine altar;
and ye say, Wherein have we polluted thee? In
that ye say, The table of the LORD *is* contemptible.
8 And if ye offer the blind for sacrifice, *is it*
not evil? and if ye offer the lame and sick, *is it*
not evil? offer it now unto thy governor; will he
be pleased with thee, or accept thy person?
saith the LORD of hosts.
9 And now, I pray you, beseech God that he
will be gracious unto us: this hath been by your
means: will he regard your persons? saith the
LORD of hosts.
10 Who *is there* even among you that would
shut the doors *for nought?* neither do ye kindle
fire on mine altar for nought. I have no pleasure
in you, saith the LORD of hosts, neither will I
accept an offering at your hand.
11 For from the rising of the sun even unto
the going down of the same my name *shall be*
great among the Gen'tiles; and in every place
incense *shall be* offered unto my name, and a
pure offering: for my name *shall be* great
among the heathen, saith the LORD of hosts.
12 ¶ But ye have profaned it, in that ye say,
The table of the LORD *is* polluted; and the fruit
thereof, *even* his meat, *is* contemptible.
13 Ye said also, Behold, what a weariness *is*
it! and ye have snuffed at it, saith the LORD of
hosts; and ye brought *that which was* torn, and
the lame, and the sick; thus ye brought an offering:
should I accept this of your hand? saith the
LORD.
14 But cursed *be* the deceiver, which hath in
his flock a male, and voweth, and sacrificeth
unto the Lord a corrupt thing: for I *am* a great
King, saith the LORD of hosts, and my name *is*
dreadful among the heathen.

2 AND now, O ye priests, this commandment *is* for you.
2 If ye will not hear, and if ye will not lay *it* to
heart, to give glory unto my name, saith the
LORD of hosts, I will even send a curse upon
you, and I will curse your blessings: yea, I have
cursed them already, because ye do not lay *it* to
heart.
3 Behold, I will corrupt your seed, and
spread dung upon your faces, *even* the dung of
your solemn feasts; and *one* shall take you
away with it.
4 And ye shall know that I have sent this
commandment unto you, that my covenant
might be with Le'vi, saith the LORD of hosts.
5 My covenant was with him of life and
peace; and I gave them to him *for* the fear
wherewith he feared me, and was afraid before
my name.
6 The law of truth was in his mouth, and iniquity
was not found in his lips: he walked with
me in peace and equity, and did turn many
away from iniquity.
7 For the priest's lips should keep knowledge,
and they should seek the law at his
mouth: for he *is* the messenger of the LORD of
hosts.
8 But ye are departed out of the way; ye have
caused many to stumble at the law; ye have corrupted
the covenant of Le'vi, saith the LORD of
hosts.
9 Therefore have I also made you contemptible
and base before all the people, according as
ye have not kept my ways, but have been partial
in the law.
10 Have we not all one father? hath not one
God created us? why do we deal treacherously
every man against his brother, by profaning the
covenant of our fathers?
11 ¶ Ju'dah hath dealt treacherously, and an
abomination is committed in Is'ra-el and in Jeru'sa-lem;
for Ju'dah hath profaned the holiness
of the LORD which he loved, and hath married
the daughter of a strange god.
12 The LORD will cut off the man that doeth
this, the master and the scholar, out of the tabernacles
of Ja'cob, and him that offereth an offering
unto the LORD of hosts.
13 And this have ye done again, covering the
altar of the LORD with tears, with weeping, and
with crying out, insomuch that he regardeth not
the offering any more, or receiveth *it* with good
will at your hand.
14 ¶ Yet ye say, Wherefore? Because the
LORD hath been witness between thee and the
wife of thy youth, against whom thou hast dealt
treacherously: yet *is* she thy companion, and
the wife of thy covenant.
15 And did not he make one? Yet had he the
residue of the spirit. And wherefore one? That
he might seek a godly seed. Therefore take heed
to your spirit, and let none deal treacherously
against the wife of his youth.
16 For the LORD, the God of Is'ra-el, saith
that he hateth putting away: for *one* covereth
violence with his garment, saith the LORD of
hosts: therefore take heed to your spirit, that ye
deal not treacherously.
17 ¶ Ye have wearied the LORD with your
words. Yet ye say, Wherein have we wearied
him? When ye say, Every one that doeth evil *is*
good in the sight of the LORD, and he delighteth
in them; or, Where *is* the God of judgment?

3 BEHOLD, I will send my messenger, and
he shall prepare the way before me: and
the Lord, whom ye seek, shall suddenly come to
his temple, even the messenger of the covenant,
whom ye delight in: behold, he shall come, saith
the LORD of hosts.
2 But who may abide the day of his coming?
and who shall stand when he appeareth? for he
is like a refiner's fire, and like fullers' sope:
3 And he shall sit *as* a refiner and purifier of
silver: and he shall purify the sons of Le'vi, and
purge them as gold and silver, that they may
offer unto the LORD an offering in righteousness.
4 Then shall the offering of Ju'dah and Jeru'sa-lem
be pleasant unto the LORD, as in the
days of old, and as in former years.
5 And I will come near to you to judgment;
and I will be a swift witness against the sorcerers,
and against the adulterers, and against
false swearers, and against those that oppress
the hireling in *his* wages, the widow, and the
fatherless, and that turn aside the stranger *from*
his right, and fear not me, saith the LORD of
hosts.
6 For I *am* the LORD, I change not; therefore
ye sons of Ja'cob are not consumed.
7 ¶ Even from the days of your fathers ye
are gone away from mine ordinances, and have
not kept *them.* Return unto me, and I will return
unto you, saith the LORD of hosts. But ye said,
Wherein shall we return?
8 ¶ Will a man rob God? Yet ye have robbed
me. But ye say, Wherein have we robbed thee?
In tithes and offerings.

9 Ye *are* cursed with a curse: for ye have
robbed me, *even* this whole nation.
10 Bring ye all the tithes into the storehouse,
that there may be meat in mine house, and
prove me now herewith, saith the LORD of
hosts, if I will not open you the windows of
heaven, and pour you out a blessing, that *there*
shall not *be room* enough *to receive it*.
11 And I will rebuke the devourer for your
sakes, and he shall not destroy the fruits of your
ground; neither shall your vine cast her fruit before the time in the field, saith the LORD of
hosts.
12 And all nations shall call you blessed: for
ye shall be a delightsome land, saith the LORD
of hosts.
13 ¶ Your words have been stout against
me, saith the LORD. Yet ye say, What have we
spoken *so much* against thee?
14 Ye have said, It *is* vain to serve God: and
what profit *is it* that we have kept his ordinance, and that we have walked mournfully before the LORD of hosts?
15 And now we call the proud happy; yea,
they that work wickedness are set up; yea, *they*
that tempt God are even delivered.
16 ¶ Then they that feared the LORD spake
often one to another: and the LORD hearkened,
and heard *it*, and a book of remembrance was
written before him for them that feared the
LORD, and that thought upon his name.
17 And they shall be mine, saith the LORD of
hosts, in that day when I make up my jewels;
and I will spare them, as a man spareth his own
son that serveth him.
18 Then shall ye return, and discern between
the righteous and the wicked, between him that
serveth God and him that serveth him not.

4 FOR, behold, the day cometh, that shall
burn as an oven; and all the proud, yea,
and all that do wickedly, shall be stubble: and
the day that cometh shall burn them up, saith
the LORD of hosts, that it shall leave them neither root nor branch.
2 ¶ But unto you that fear my name shall the
Sun of righteousness arise with healing in his
wings; and ye shall go forth, and grow up as
calves of the stall.
3 And ye shall tread down the wicked; for
they shall be ashes under the soles of your feet
in the day that I shall do *this*, saith the LORD of
hosts.
4 ¶ Remember ye the law of Mo'ses my servant, which I commanded unto him in Ho'reb
for all Is'ra-el, *with* the statutes and judgments.
5 ¶ Behold, I will send you E-li'jah the
prophet before the coming of the great and
dreadful day of the LORD:
6 And he shall turn the heart of the fathers to
the children, and the heart of the children to
their fathers, lest I come and smite the earth
with a curse.

THE END OF THE OLD TESTAMENT.

THE NEW TESTAMENT

HERE'S HOPE

Tucked away in each of our minds is a picture of the future. This picture ranges from bright and colorful to dark and foreboding—from hope to hopelessness. In a contemporary play, hope is defined as "the feeling you have that the feeling you have isn't permanent."

This kind of hope is but a shadow of the robust hope that God has for you. Solid hope is anchored firmly in reality.

The road to hope begins by facing the truth about ourselves. *"For all have sinned, and come short of the glory of God (Romans 3:23)."* The first step to hope is recognizing not just that all have sinned but that I have sinned.

Our world is awash in hopelessness as a result of sin. *"For the wages of sin is death; but the gift of God is eternal life through Jesus Christ our Lord (Romans 6:23)."* In this verse God sets before us two vastly different futures: death or eternal life.

God paid a huge personal price to give us this choice so that eternal death was not inevitable. *"For when we were yet without strength, in due time Christ died for the ungodly...But God commendeth his love toward us, in that, while we were yet sinners, Christ died for us (Romans 5:6,8)."*

The choice is yours. *"That if thou shalt confess with thy mouth the Lord Jesus, and shalt believe in thine heart that God hath raised him from the dead, thou shalt be saved. For with the heart man believeth unto righteousness; and with the mouth confession is made unto salvation...For whosoever shall call upon the name of the Lord shall be saved (Romans 10:9,10,13)."*

If you have acknowledged your sin and have accepted the gift of forgiveness and eternal life Christ offers you through His death, here's how God describes your relationship with him: *"Therefore being justified by faith, we have peace with God through our Lord Jesus Christ: by whom we also have access by faith into this grace wherein we stand and rejoice in the hope of the glory of God (Romans 5:1–2)."*

Whereas before, sin was your cruel taskmaster, paying death as wages, now Christ is your gracious Lord giving you peace and hope—both now and forever. One of your first acts of obedience to Christ is to follow him in baptism. *"Therefore we are buried with him by baptism into death: that like as Christ was raised up from the dead by the glory of the Father, even so we also should walk in newness of life (Romans 6:4)."*

You will now want to know God better through prayer, Bible study, and fellowship with other Christians as a member of a church that honors Christ and His Word. *"For whatsoever things were written aforetime were written for our learning, that we through patience and comfort of the scriptures might have hope. Now the God of patience and consolation grant you to be likeminded one toward another according to Christ Jesus: That ye may with one mind and one mouth glorify God, even the Father of our Lord Jesus Christ (Romans 15:4–6)."*

THE GOSPEL ACCORDING TO

MATTHEW

1 THE book of the generation of Je'sus
Christ, the son of Da'vid, the son of A'bra-
ham.
2 A'bra-ham begat I'saac; and I'saac begat
Ja'cob; and Ja'cob begat Ju'das and his brethren;
3 And Ju'das begat Pha'res and Za'ra of Tha'-
mar; and Pha'res, begat Es'rom; and Es'rom begat A'ram;
4 And A'ram begat A-min'a-dab; and A-min'-
a-dab begat Na-as'son; and Na-as'son begat
Sal'mon;
5 And Sal'mon begat Bo'oz of Ra'chab; and
Bo'oz begat O'bed of Ruth; and O'bed begat
Jes'se;
6 And Jes'se begat Da'vid the king; and Da'-
vid the king begat Sol'o-mon of her *that had
been the wife* of U-ri'as;
7 And Sol'o-mon begat Ro-bo'am; and Ro-
bo'am begat A-bi'a; and A-bi'a begat A'sa;
8 And A'sa begat Jos'a-phat; and Jos'a-phat
begat Jo'ram; and Jo'ram begat O-zi'as;
9 And O-zi'as begat Jo'a-tham; and Jo'a-
tham begat A'chaz; and A'chaz begat Ez-e-ki'-
as;
10 And Ez-e-ki'as begat Ma-nas'ses; and Ma-
nas'ses begat A'mon; and A'mon begat Jo-si'as;
11 And Jo-si'as begat Jech-o-ni'as and his
brethren, about the time they were carried
away to Bab'y-lon:
12 And after they were brought to Bab'y-lon,
Jech-o-ni'as begat Sa-la'thi-el; and Sa-la'thi-el
begat Zo-rob'a-bel;
13 And Zo-rob'a-bel begat A-bi'ud; and A-bi'-
ud begat E-li'a-kim; and E-li'a-kim begat A'zor;
14 And A'zor begat Sa'doc; and Sa'doc begat
A'chim; and A'chim begat E-li'ud;
15 And E-li'ud begat E-le-a'zar; and E-le-a'-
zar begat Mat'than; and Mat'than begat Ja'cob;
16 And Ja'cob begat Jo'seph the husband of
Ma'ry, of whom was born Je'sus, who is called
Christ.
17 So all the generations from A'bra-ham to
Da'vid *are* fourteen generations; and from Da'-
vid until the carrying away into Bab'y-lon *are*
fourteen generations; and from the carrying
away into Bab'y-lon unto Christ *are* fourteen
generations.
18 ¶ Now the birth of Je'sus Christ was on
this wise: When as his mother Ma'ry was espoused to Jo'seph, before they came together,
she was found with child of the Ho'ly Ghost.
19 Then Jo'seph her husband, being a just
man, and not willing to make her a publick example, was minded to put her away privily.
20 But while he thought on these things, behold, the angel of the Lord appeared unto him
in a dream, saying, Jo'seph, thou son of Da'vid,
fear not to take unto thee Ma'ry thy wife: for
that which is conceived in her is of the Ho'ly
Ghost.
21 And she shall bring forth a son, and thou
shalt call his name JE'SUS: for he shall save his
people from their sins.
22 Now all this was done, that it might be
fulfilled which was spoken of the Lord by the
prophet, saying,
23 Behold, a virgin shall be with child, and
shall bring forth a son, and they shall call his
name Em-man'u-el, which being interpreted is,
God with us.
24 Then Jo'seph being raised from sleep did
as the angel of the Lord had bidden him, and
took unto him his wife:
25 And knew her not till she had brought
forth her firstborn son: and he called his name
JE'SUS.

2 NOW when Je'sus was born in Beth'le-hem
of Ju-dæ'a in the days of Her'od the king,
behold, there came wise men from the east to
Je-ru'sa-lem,
2 Saying, Where is he that is born King of the
Jews? for we have seen his star in the east, and
are come to worship him.
3 When Her'od the king had heard *these
things*, he was troubled, and all Je-ru'sa-lem
with him.
4 And when he had gathered all the chief
priests and scribes of the people together, he
demanded of them where Christ should be
born.
5 And they said unto him, In Beth'le-hem of
Ju-dæ'a: for thus it is written by the prophet,
6 And thou Beth'le-hem, *in* the land of Ju'da,
art not the least among the princes of Ju'da: for
out of thee shall come a Governor, that shall
rule my people Is'ra-el.
7 Then Her'od, when he had privily called the
wise men, enquired of them diligently what
time the star appeared.
8 And he sent them to Beth'le-hem, and said,
Go and search diligently for the young child;
and when ye have found *him*, bring me word
again, that I may come and worship him also.
9 When they had heard the king, they departed; and, lo, the star, which they saw in the
east, went before them, till it came and stood
over where the young child was.
10 When they saw the star, they rejoiced
with exceeding great joy.
11 ¶ And when they were come into the
house, they saw the young child with Ma'ry his
mother, and fell down, and worshipped him:
and when they had opened their treasures, they
presented unto him gifts; gold, frankincense,
and myrrh.
12 And being warned of God in a dream that
they should not return to Her'od, they departed
into their own country another way.
13 And when they were departed, behold,
the angel of the Lord appeareth to Jo'seph in a
dream, saying, Arise, and take the young child
and his mother, and flee into E'gypt; and be
thou there until I bring thee word: for Her'od
will seek the young child to destroy him.
14 When he arose, he took the young child
and his mother by night, and departed into E'-
gypt:
15 And was there until the death of Her'od:
that it might be fulfilled which was spoken of
the Lord by the prophet, saying, Out of E'gypt
have I called my son.
16 ¶ Then Her'od, when he saw that he was
mocked of the wise men, was exceeding wroth,
and sent forth, and slew all the children that
were in Beth'le-hem, and in all the coasts
thereof, from two years old and under, according to the time which he had diligently enquired
of the wise men.
17 Then was fulfilled that which was spoken
by Jer'e-my the prophet, saying,
18 In Ra'ma was there a voice heard, lamentation, and weeping, and great mourning, Ra'-

chel weeping *for* her children, and would not be
comforted, because they are not.
19 ¶ But when Her'od was dead, behold, an
angel of the Lord appeareth in a dream to Jo'-
seph in E'gypt,
20 Saying, Arise, and take the young child
and his mother, and go into the land of Is'ra-el:
for they are dead which sought the young
child's life.
21 And he arose, and took the young child
and his mother, and came into the land of Is'ra-
el.
22 But when he heard that Ar-che-la'us did
reign in Ju-dæ'a in the room of his father Her'-
od, he was afraid to go thither: notwithstanding, being warned of God in a dream, he turned
aside into the parts of Gal'i-lee:
23 And he came and dwelt in a city called
Naz'a-reth: that it might be fulfilled which was
spoken by the prophets, He shall be called a
Naz'a-rene.

3

IN those days came John the Bap'tist,
preaching in the wilderness of Ju-dæ'a,
2 And saying, Repent ye: for the kingdom of
heaven is at hand.
3 For this is he that was spoken of by the
prophet E-sa'ias, saying, The voice of one crying in the wilderness, Prepare ye the way of the
Lord, make his paths straight.
4 And the same John had his raiment of camel's hair, and a leathern girdle about his loins;
and his meat was locusts and wild honey.
5 Then went out to him Je-ru'sa-lem, and all
Ju-dæ'a, and all the region round about Jor'dan,
6 And were baptized of him in Jor'dan, confessing their sins.
7 ¶ But when he saw many of the Phar'i-sees
and Sad'du-cees come to his baptism, he said
unto them, O generation of vipers, who hath
warned you to flee from the wrath to come?
8 Bring forth therefore fruits meet for repentance:
9 And think not to say within yourselves, We
have A'bra-ham to *our* father: for I say unto
you, that God is able of these stones to raise up
children unto A'bra-ham.
10 And now also the ax is laid unto the root
of the trees: therefore every tree which bringeth
not forth good fruit is hewn down, and cast into
the fire.
11 I indeed baptize you with water unto repentance: but he that cometh after me is mightier than I, whose shoes I am not worthy to bear:
he shall baptize you with the Ho'ly Ghost, and
with fire:
12 Whose fan *is* in his hand, and he will
throughly purge his floor, and gather his wheat
into the garner; but he will burn up the chaff
with unquenchable fire.
13 ¶ Then cometh Je'sus from Gal'i-lee to
Jor'dan unto John, to be baptized of him.
14 But John forbad him, saying, I have need
to be baptized of thee, and comest thou to me?
15 And Je'sus answering said unto him, Suffer *it to be so* now: for thus it becometh us to
fulfill all righteousness. Then he suffered him.
16 And Je'sus, when he was baptized, went
up straightway out of the water: and, lo, the
heavens were opened unto him, and he saw the
Spirit of God descending like a dove, and lighting upon him:
17 And lo a voice from heaven, saying, This
is my beloved Son, in whom I am well pleased.

4

THEN was Je'sus led up of the spirit into
the wilderness to be tempted of the devil.
2 And when he had fasted forty days and
forty nights, he was afterward an hungred.
3 And when the tempter came to him, he
said, If thou be the Son of God, command that
these stones be made bread.
4 But he answered and said, It is written,
Man shall not live by bread alone, but by every
word that proceedeth out of the mouth of God.
5 Then the devil taketh him up into the holy
city, and setteth him on a pinnacle of the temple,
6 And saith unto him, If thou be the Son of
God, cast thyself down: for it is written, He
shall give his angels charge concerning thee:
and in *their* hands they shall bear thee up, lest
at any time thou dash thy foot against a stone.
7 Je'sus said unto him, It is written again,
Thou shalt not tempt the Lord thy God.
8 Again, the devil taketh him up into an exceeding high mountain, and sheweth him all the
kingdoms of the world, and the glory of them;
9 And saith unto him, All these things will I
give thee, if thou wilt fall down and worship
me.
10 Then saith Je'sus unto him, Get thee
hence, Sa'tan: for it is written, Thou shalt worship the Lord thy God, and him only shalt thou
serve.
11 Then the devil leaveth him, and, behold,
angels came and ministered unto him.
12 ¶ Now when Je'sus had heard that John
was cast into prison, he departed into Gal'i-lee;
13 And leaving Naz'a-reth, he came and
dwelt in Ca-per'na-um, which is upon the sea
coast, in the borders of Zab'u-lon and Neph'tha-
lim:
14 That it might be fulfilled which was spoken by E-sa'ias the prophet, saying,
15 The land of Zab'u-lon, and the land of
Neph'tha-lim, *by* the way of the sea, beyond
Jor'dan, Gal'i-lee of the Gen'tiles;
16 The people which sat in darkness saw
great light; and to them which sat in the region
and shadow of death light is sprung up.
17 ¶ From that time Je'sus began to preach,
and to say, Repent: for the kingdom of heaven
is at hand.
18 ¶ And Je'sus, walking by the sea of Gal'i-
lee, saw two brethren, Si'mon called Pe'ter, and
Andrew his brother, casting a net into the sea:
for they were fishers.
19 And he saith unto them, Follow me, and I
will make you fishers of men.
20 And they straightway left *their* nets, and
followed him.
21 And going on from thence, he saw other
two brethren, James *the son* of Zeb'e-dee, and
John his brother, in a ship with Zeb'e-dee their
father, mending their nets; and he called them.
22 And they immediately left the ship and
their father, and followed him.
23 ¶ And Je'sus went about all Gal'i-lee,
teaching in their synagogues, and preaching the
gospel of the kingdom, and healing all manner
of sickness and all manner of disease among
the people.
24 And his fame went throughout all Syr'i-a:
and they brought unto him all sick people that
were taken with divers diseases and torments,
and those which were possessed with devils,
and those which were lunatick, and those that
had the palsy; and he healed them.
25 And there followed him great multitudes
of people from Gal'i-lee, and *from* De-cap'o-lis,
and *from* Je-ru'sa-lem, and *from* Ju-dæ'a, and
from beyond Jor'dan.

5 AND seeing the multitudes, he went up
into a mountain: and when he was set, his
disciples came unto him:
2 And he opened his mouth, and taught
them, saying,
3 Blessed *are* the poor in spirit: for theirs is
the kingdom of heaven.
4 Blessed *are* they that mourn: for they shall
be comforted.
5 Blessed *are* the meek: for they shall inherit
the earth.
6 Blessed *are* they which do hunger and
thirst after righteousness: for they shall be
filled.
7 Blessed *are* the merciful: for they shall obtain mercy.
8 Blessed *are* the pure in heart: for they shall
see God.
9 Blessed *are* the peacemakers: for they shall
be called the children of God.
10 Blessed *are* they which are persecuted for
righteousness' sake: for theirs is the kingdom of
heaven.
11 Blessed are ye, when *men* shall revile you,
and persecute *you*, and shall say all manner of
evil against you falsely, for my sake.
12 Rejoice, and be exceeding glad: for great
is your reward in heaven: for so persecuted
they the prophets which were before you.
13 ¶ Ye are the salt of the earth: but if the
salt have lost his savour, wherewith shall it be
salted? it is thenceforth good for nothing, but to
be cast out, and to be trodden under foot of
men.
14 Ye are the light of the world. A city that is
set on an hill cannot be hid.
15 Neither do men light a candle, and put it
under a bushel, but on a candlestick; and it giveth light unto all that are in the house.
16 Let your light so shine before men, that
they may see your good works, and glorify your
Father which is in heaven.
17 ¶ Think not that I am come to destroy the
law, or the prophets: I am not come to destroy,
but to fulfill.
18 For verily I say unto you, Till heaven and
earth pass, one jot or one tittle shall in no wise
pass from the law, till all be fulfilled.
19 Whosoever therefore shall break one of
these least commandments, and shall teach
men so, he shall be called the least in the kingdom of heaven: but whosoever shall do and
teach *them*, the same shall be called great in the
kingdom of heaven.
20 For I say unto you, That except your
righteousness shall exceed *the righteousness* of
the scribes and Phar'i-sees, ye shall in no case
enter into the kingdom of heaven.
21 ¶ Ye have heard that it was said by them
of old time, Thou shalt not kill; and whosoever
shall kill shall be in danger of the judgment:
22 But I say unto you, That whosoever is angry with his brother without a cause shall be in
danger of the judgment: and whosoever shall
say to his brother, Raca, shall be in danger of
the council: but whosoever shall say, Thou fool,
shall be in danger of hell fire.
23 Therefore if thou bring thy gift to the altar, and there rememberest that thy brother
hath ought against thee;
24 Leave there thy gift before the altar, and
go thy way; first be reconciled to thy brother,
and then come and offer thy gift.
25 Agree with thine adversary quickly,
whiles thou art in the way with him; lest at any
time the adversary deliver thee to the judge,
and the judge deliver thee to the officer, and
thou be cast into prison.
26 Verily I say unto thee, Thou shalt by no
means come out thence, till thou hast paid the
uttermost farthing.
27 ¶ Ye have heard that it was said by them
of old time, Thou shalt not commit adultery:
28 But I say unto you, That whosoever looketh on a woman to lust after her hath committed adultery with her already in his heart.
29 And if thy right eye offend thee, pluck it
out, and cast *it* from thee: for it is profitable for
thee that one of thy members should perish,
and not *that* thy whole body should be cast into
hell.
30 And if thy right hand offend thee, cut it
off, and cast *it* from thee: for it is profitable for
thee that one of thy members should perish,
and not *that* thy whole body should be cast into
hell.
31 It hath been said, Whosoever shall put
away his wife, let him give her a writing of divorcement:
32 But I say unto you, That whosoever shall
put away his wife, saving for the cause of fornication, causeth her to commit adultery: and
whosoever shall marry her that is divorced
committeth adultery.
33 ¶ Again, ye have heard that it hath been
said by them of old time, Thou shalt not for-
swear thyself, but shalt perform unto the Lord
thine oaths:
34 But I say unto you, Swear not at all; neither by heaven; for it is God's throne:
35 Nor by the earth; for it is his footstool:
neither by Je-ru'sa-lem; for it is the city of the
great King.
36 Neither shalt thou swear by thy head, because thou canst not make one hair white or
black.
37 But let your communication be, Yea, yea;
Nay, nay: for whatsoever is more than these
cometh of evil.
38 ¶ Ye have heard that it hath been said, An
eye for an eye, and a tooth for a tooth:
39 But I say unto you, That ye resist not evil:
but whosoever shall smite thee on thy right
cheek, turn to him the other also.
40 And if any man will sue thee at the law,
and take away thy coat, let him have *thy* cloke
also.
41 And whosoever shall compel thee to go a
mile, go with him twain.
42 Give to him that asketh thee, and from
him that would borrow of thee turn not thou
away.
43 ¶ Ye have heard that it hath been said,
Thou shalt love thy neighbour, and hate thine
enemy.
44 But I say unto you, Love your enemies,
bless them that curse you, do good to them that
hate you, and pray for them which despitefully
use you, and persecute you;
45 That ye may be the children of your Father which is in heaven: for he maketh his sun
to rise on the evil and on the good, and sendeth
rain on the just and on the unjust.
46 For if ye love them which love you, what
reward have ye? do not even the publicans the
same?
47 And if ye salute your brethren only, what
do ye more *than others*? do not even the publicans so?
48 Be ye therefore perfect, even as your Father which is in heaven is perfect.

6 TAKE heed that ye do not your alms before men, to be seen of them: otherwise ye
have no reward of your Father which is in
heaven.
2 Therefore when thou doest *thine* alms, do
not sound a trumpet before thee, as the hypocrites do in the synagogues and in the streets,
that they may have glory of men. Verily I say
unto you, They have their reward.
3 But when thou doest alms, let not thy left
hand know what thy right hand doeth:
4 That thine alms may be in secret: and thy
Father which seeth in secret himself shall reward thee openly.
5 ¶ And when thou prayest, thou shalt not
be as the hypocrites *are:* for they love to pray
standing in the synagogues and in the corners
of the streets, that they may be seen of men.
Verily I say unto you, They have their reward.
6 But thou, when thou prayest, enter into thy
closet, and when thou hast shut thy door, pray
to thy Father which is in secret; and thy Father
which seeth in secret shall reward thee openly.
7 But when ye pray, use not vain repetitions,
as the heathen *do:* for they think that they shall
be heard for their much speaking.
8 Be not ye therefore like unto them: for your
Father knoweth what things ye have need of,
before ye ask him.
9 After this manner therefore pray ye: Our
Father which art in heaven, Hallowed be thy
name.
10 Thy kingdom come. Thy will be done in
earth, as *it is* in heaven.
11 Give us this day our daily bread.
12 And forgive us our debts, as we forgive
our debtors.
13 And lead us not into temptation, but deliver us from evil: For thine is the kingdom, and
the power, and the glory, for ever. Amen.
14 For if ye forgive men their trespasses,
your heavenly Father will also forgive you:
15 But if ye forgive not men their trespasses,
neither will your Father forgive your trespasses.
16 ¶ Moreover when ye fast, be not, as the
hypocrites, of a sad countenance: for they dis-
figure their faces, that they may appear unto
men to fast. Verily I say unto you, They have
their reward.
17 But thou, when thou fastest, anoint thine
head, and wash thy face;
18 That thou appear not unto men to fast, but
unto thy Father which is in secret: and thy Father, which seeth in secret, shall reward thee
openly.
19 ¶ Lay not up for yourselves treasures
upon earth, where moth and rust doth corrupt,
and where thieves break through and steal:
20 But lay up for yourselves treasures in
heaven, where neither moth nor rust doth corrupt, and where thieves do not break through
nor steal:
21 For where your treasure is, there will your
heart be also.
22 The light of the body is the eye: if therefore thine eye be single, thy whole body shall be
full of light.
23 But if thine eye be evil, thy whole body
shall be full of darkness. If therefore the light
that is in thee be darkness, how great *is* that
darkness!
24 ¶ No man can serve two masters: for either he will hate the one, and love the other; or
else he will hold to the one, and despise the other. Ye cannot serve God and mammon.
25 Therefore I say unto you, Take no thought
for your life, what ye shall eat, or what ye shall
drink; nor yet for your body, what ye shall put
on. Is not the life more than meat, and the body
than raiment?
26 Behold the fowls of the air: for they sow
not, neither do they reap, nor gather into barns;
yet your heavenly Father feedeth them. Are ye
not much better than they?
27 Which of you by taking thought can add
one cubit unto his stature?
28 And why take ye thought for raiment?
Consider the lilies of the field, how they grow;
they toil not, neither do they spin:
29 And yet I say unto you, That even Sol'o-
mon in all his glory was not arrayed like one of
these.
30 Wherefore, if God so clothe the grass of
the field, which to day is, and to morrow is cast
into the oven, *shall he* not much more *clothe*
you, O ye of little faith?
31 Therefore take no thought, saying, What
shall we eat? or, What shall we drink? or,
Wherewithal shall we be clothed?
32 (For after all these things do the Gen'tiles
seek:) for your heavenly Father knoweth that
ye have need of all these things.
33 But seek ye first the kingdom of God, and
his righteousness; and all these things shall be
added unto you.
34 Take therefore no thought for the morrow: for the morrow shall take thought for the
things of itself. Sufficient unto the day *is* the
evil thereof.

7 JUDGE not, that ye be not judged.
2 For with what judgment ye judge, ye
shall be judged: and with what measure ye
mete, it shall be measured to you again.
3 And why beholdest thou the mote that is in
thy brother's eye, but considerest not the beam
that is in thine own eye?
4 Or how wilt thou say to thy brother, Let me
pull out the mote out of thine eye; and, behold,
a beam *is* in thine own eye?
5 Thou hypocrite, first cast out the beam out
of thine own eye; and then shalt thou see clearly
to cast out the mote out of thy brother's eye.
6 ¶ Give not that which is holy unto the
dogs, neither cast ye your pearls before swine,
lest they trample them under their feet, and
turn again and rend you.
7 ¶ Ask, and it shall be given you; seek, and
ye shall find; knock, and it shall be opened unto
you:
8 For every one that asketh receiveth; and he
that seeketh findeth; and to him that knocketh
it shall be opened.
9 Or what man is there of you, whom if his
son ask bread, will he give him a stone?
10 Or if he ask a fish, will he give him a serpent?
11 If ye then, being evil, know how to give
good gifts unto your children, how much more
shall your Father which is in heaven give good
things to them that ask him?
12 Therefore all things whatsoever ye would
that men should do to you, do ye even so to
them: for this is the law and the prophets.
13 ¶ Enter ye in at the strait gate: for wide *is*
the gate, and broad *is* the way, that leadeth to
destruction, and many there be which go in
thereat:
14 Because strait *is* the gate, and narrow *is*
the way, which leadeth unto life, and few there
be that find it.
15 ¶ Beware of false prophets, which come

to you in sheep's clothing, but inwardly they are
ravening wolves.
16 Ye shall know them by their fruits. Do
men gather grapes of thorns, or figs of thistles?
17 Even so every good tree bringeth forth
good fruit; but a corrupt tree bringeth forth evil
fruit.
18 A good tree cannot bring forth evil fruit,
neither *can* a corrupt tree bring forth good fruit.
19 Every tree that bringeth not forth good
fruit is hewn down, and cast into the fire.
20 Wherefore by their fruits ye shall know
them.
21 ¶ Not every one that saith unto me, Lord,
Lord, shall enter into the kingdom of heaven;
but he that doeth the will of my Father which is
in heaven.
22 Many will say to me in that day, Lord,
Lord, have we not prophesied in thy name? and
in thy name have cast out devils? and in thy
name done many wonderful works?
23 And then will I profess unto them, I never
knew you: depart from me, ye that work iniquity.
24 ¶ Therefore whosoever heareth these sayings of mine, and doeth them, I will liken him
unto a wise man, which built his house upon a
rock:
25 And the rain descended, and the floods
came, and the winds blew, and beat upon that
house; and it fell not: for it was founded upon a
rock.
26 And every one that heareth these sayings
of mine, and doeth them not, shall be likened
unto a foolish man, which built his house upon
the sand:
27 And the rain descended, and the floods
came, and the winds blew, and beat upon that
house; and it fell and great was the fall of it.
28 And it came to pass, when Je'sus had
ended these sayings, the people were astonished at his doctrine:
29 For he taught them as *one* having authority, and not as the scribes.

8 WHEN he was come down from the mountain, great multitudes followed him.
2 And, behold, there came a leper and worshipped him, saying, Lord, if thou wilt, thou
canst make me clean.
3 And Je'sus put forth *his* hand, and touched
him, saying, I will; be thou clean. And immediately his leprosy was cleansed.
4 And Je'sus saith unto him, See thou tell no
man; but go thy way, shew thyself to the priest,
and offer the gift that Mo'ses commanded, for a
testimony unto them.
5 ¶ And when Je'sus was entered into Ca-
per'na-um, there came unto him a centurion,
beseeching him,
6 And saying, Lord, my servant lieth at home
sick of the palsy, grievously tormented.
7 And Je'sus saith unto him, I will come and
heal him.
8 The centurion answered and said, Lord, I
am not worthy that thou shouldest come under
my roof: but speak the word only, and my servant shall be healed.
9 For I am a man under authority, having soldiers under me; and I say to this *man,* Go, and
he goeth; and to another, Come, and he cometh;
and to my servant, Do this, and he doeth *it.*
10 When Je'sus heard *it,* he marvelled, and
said to them that followed, Verily I say unto
you, I have not found so great faith, no, not in
Is'ra-el.
11 And I say unto you, That many shall come
from the east and west, and shall sit down with
A'bra-ham, and I'saac, and Ja'cob, in the kingdom of heaven.
12 But the children of the kingdom shall be
cast out into outer darkness: there shall be
weeping and gnashing of teeth.
13 And Je'sus said unto the centurion, Go thy
way; and as thou hast believed, *so* be it done
unto thee. And his servant was healed in the
selfsame hour.
14 ¶ And when Je'sus was come into Pe'ter's
house, he saw his wife's mother laid, and sick of
a fever.
15 And he touched her hand, and the fever
left her: and she arose, and ministered unto
them.
16 ¶ When the even was come, they brought
unto him many that were possessed with devils:
and he cast out the spirits with *his* word, and
healed all that were sick:
17 That it might be fulfilled which was spoken by E-sa'ias the prophet, saying, Himself
took our infirmities, and bare *our* sicknesses.
18 ¶ Now when Je'sus saw great multitudes
about him, he gave commandment to depart
unto the other side.
19 And a certain scribe came, and said unto
him, Master, I will follow thee whithersoever
thou goest.
20 And Je'sus saith unto him, The foxes have
holes, and the birds of the air *have* nests; but
the Son of man hath not where to lay *his* head.
21 And another of his disciples said unto
him, Lord, suffer me first to go and bury my
father.
22 But Je'sus said unto him, Follow me; and
let the dead bury their dead.
23 ¶ And when he was entered into a ship,
his disciples followed him.
24 And, behold, there arose a great tempest
in the sea, insomuch that the ship was covered
with the waves: but he was asleep.
25 And his disciples came to *him,* and awoke
him, saying, Lord, save us: we perish.
26 And he saith unto them, Why are ye fearful, O ye of little faith? Then he arose, and rebuked the winds and the sea; and there was a
great calm.
27 But the men marvelled, saying, What
manner of man is this, that even the winds and
the sea obey him!
28 ¶ And when he was come to the other
side into the country of the Ger'ge-senes, there
met him two possessed with devils, coming out
of the tombs, exceeding fierce, so that no man
might pass by that way.
29 And, behold, they cried out, saying, What
have we to do with thee, Je'sus, thou Son of
God? art thou come hither to torment us before
the time?
30 And there was a good way off from them
an herd of many swine feeding.
31 So the devils besought him, saying, If
thou cast us out, suffer us to go away into the
herd of swine.
32 And he said unto them, Go. And when
they were come out, they went into the herd of
swine: and, behold, the whole herd of swine ran
violently down a steep place into the sea, and
perished in the waters.
33 And they that kept them fled, and went
their ways into the city, and told every thing,
and what was befallen to the possessed of the
devils.
34 And, behold, the whole city came out to
meet Je'sus: and when they saw him, they be-

sought *him* that he would depart out of their coasts.

9 AND he entered into a ship, and passed over, and came into his own city.

2 And, behold, they brought to him a man sick of the palsy, lying on a bed: and Je'sus seeing their faith said unto the sick of the palsy; Son, be of good cheer; thy sins be forgiven thee.

3 And, behold, certain of the scribes said within themselves, This *man* blasphemeth.

4 And Je'sus knowing their thoughts said, Wherefore think ye evil in your hearts?

5 For whether is easier, to say, *Thy* sins be forgiven thee; or to say, Arise, and walk?

6 But that ye may know that the Son of man hath power on earth to forgive sins, (then saith he to the sick of the palsy,) Arise, take up thy bed, and go unto thine house.

7 And he arose, and departed to his house.

8 But when the multitudes saw *it*, they marvelled, and glorified God, which had given such power unto men.

9 ¶ And as Je'sus passed forth from thence, he saw a man, named Mat'thew, sitting at the receipt of custom: and he saith unto him, Follow me. And he arose, and followed him.

10 ¶ And it came to pass, as Je'sus sat at meat in the house, behold, many publicans and sinners came and sat down with him and his disciples.

11 And when the Phar'i-sees saw *it*, they said unto his disciples, Why eateth your Master with publicans and sinners?

12 But when Je'sus heard *that*, he said unto them, They that be whole need not a physician, but they that are sick.

13 But go ye and learn what *that* meaneth, I will have mercy, and not sacrifice: for I am not come to call the righteous, but sinners to repentance.

14 ¶ Then came to him the disciples of John, saying, Why do we and the Phar'i-sees fast oft, but thy disciples fast not?

15 And Je'sus said unto them, Can the children of the bridechamber mourn, as long as the bridegroom is with them? but the days will come, when the bridegroom shall be taken from them, and then shall they fast.

16 No man putteth a piece of new cloth unto an old garment, for that which is put in to fill it up taketh from the garment, and the rent is made worse.

17 Neither do men put new wine into old bottles: else the bottles break, and the wine runneth out, and the bottles perish: but they put new wine into new bottles, and both are preserved.

18 ¶ While he spake these things unto them, behold, there came a certain ruler, and worshipped him, saying, My daughter is even now dead: but come and lay thy hand upon her, and she shall live.

19 And Je'sus arose, and followed him, and *so did* his disciples.

20 ¶ And, behold, a woman, which was diseased with an issue of blood twelve years, came behind *him*, and touched the hem of his garment:

21 For she said within herself, If I may but touch his garment, I shall be whole.

22 But Je'sus turned him about, and when he saw her, he said, Daughter, be of good comfort; thy faith hath made thee whole. And the woman was made whole from that hour.

23 And when Je'sus came into the ruler's house, and saw the minstrels and the people making a noise,

24 He said unto them, Give place: for the maid is not dead, but sleepeth. And they laughed him to scorn.

25 But when the people were put forth, he went in, and took her by the hand, and the maid arose.

26 And the fame hereof went abroad into all that land.

27 ¶ And when Je'sus departed thence, two blind men followed him, crying, and saying, *Thou* son of Da'vid, have mercy on us.

28 And when he was come into the house, the blind men came to him: and Je'sus saith unto them, Believe ye that I am able to do this? They said unto him, Yea, Lord.

29 Then touched he their eyes, saying According to your faith be it unto you.

30 And their eyes were opened; and Je'sus straitly charged them, saying, See *that* no man know *it*.

31 But they, when they were departed, spread abroad his fame in all that country.

32 ¶ As they went out, behold, they brought to him a dumb man possessed with a devil.

33 And when the devil was cast out, the dumb spake: and the multitudes marvelled, saying, It was never so seen in Is'ra-el.

34 But the Phar'i-sees said, He casteth out devils through the prince of the devils.

35 And Je'sus went about all the cities and villages, teaching in their synagogues, and preaching the gospel of the kingdom, and healing every sickness and every disease among the people.

36 ¶ But when he saw the multitudes, he was moved with compassion on them, because they fainted, and were scattered abroad, as sheep having no shepherd.

37 Then saith he unto his disciples, The harvest truly *is* plenteous, but the labourers *are* few;

38 Pray ye therefore the Lord of the harvest, that he will send forth labourers into his harvest

10 AND when he had called unto *him* his twelve disciples, he gave them power *against* unclean spirits, to cast them out, and to heal all manner of sickness and all manner of disease.

2 Now the names of the twelve apostles are these; The first, Si'mon, who is called Pe'ter, and Andrew his brother; James *the son* of Zeb'e-dee, and John his brother;

3 Phil'ip, and Bar-thol'o-mew; Thom'as, and Mat'thew the publican; James *the son* of Alphæ'us, and Leb-bæ'us, whose surname was Thad-dæ'us;

4 Si'mon the Ca'naan-ite, and Ju'das Is-car'i-ot, who also betrayed him.

5 These twelve Je'sus sent forth, and commanded them, saying, Go not into the way of the Gen'tiles, and into *any* city of the Sa-mar'i-tans enter ye not:

6 But go rather to the lost sheep of the house of Is'ra-el.

7 And as ye go, preach, saying, The kingdom of heaven is at hand.

8 Heal the sick, cleanse the lepers, raise the dead, cast out devils: freely ye have received, freely give.

9 Provide neither gold, nor silver, nor brass in your purses,

10 Nor scrip for *your* journey, neither two

coats, neither shoes, nor yet staves: for the
workman is worthy of his meat.
11 And into whatsoever city or town ye shall
enter, enquire who in it is worthy; and there
abide till ye go thence.
12 And when ye come into an house, salute
it.
13 And if the house be worthy, let your peace
come upon it: but if it be not worthy, let your
peace return to you.
14 And whosoever shall not receive you, nor
hear your words, when ye depart out of that
house or city, shake off the dust of your feet.
15 Verily I say unto you, It shall be more tolerable for the land of Sod'om and Go-mor'rha in
the day of judgment, than for that city.
16 ¶ Behold, I send you forth as sheep in the
midst of wolves: be ye therefore wise as serpents, and harmless as doves.
17 But beware of men: for they will deliver
you up to the councils, and they will scourge
you in their synagogues;
18 And ye shall be brought before governors
and kings for my sake, for a testimony against
them and the Gen'tiles.
19 But when they deliver you up, take no
thought how or what ye shall speak: for it shall
be given you in that same hour what ye shall
speak.
20 For it is not ye that speak, but the Spirit of
your Father which speaketh in you.
21 And the brother shall deliver up the
brother to death, and the father the child: and
the children shall rise up against *their* parents,
and cause them to be put to death.
22 And ye shall be hated of all *men* for my
name's sake: but he that endureth to the end
shall be saved.
23 But when they persecute you in this city,
flee ye into another: for verily I say unto you,
Ye shall not have gone over the cities of Is'ra-el,
till the Son of man be come.
24 The disciple is not above *his* master, nor
the servant above his lord.
25 It is enough for the disciple that he be as
his master, and the servant as his lord. If they
have called the master of the house Be'el'ze-
bub, how much more *shall they call* them of his
household?
26 Fear them not therefore: for there is nothing covered, that shall not be revealed; and hid,
that shall not be known.
27 What I tell you in darkness, *that* speak ye
in light: and what ye hear in the ear, *that* preach
ye upon the house tops.
28 And fear not them which kill the body,
but are not able to kill the soul: but rather fear
him which is able to destroy both soul and body
in hell.
29 Are not two sparrows sold for a farthing?
and one of them shall not fall on the ground
without your Father.
30 But the very hairs of your head are all
numbered.
31 Fear ye not therefore, ye are of more
value than many sparrows.
32 Whosoever therefore shall confess me before men, him will I confess also before my Father which is in heaven.
33 But whosoever shall deny me before men,
him will I also deny before my Father which is
in heaven.
34 Think not that I am come to send peace on
earth: I came not to send peace, but a sword.
35 For I am come to set a man at variance
against his father, and the daughter against her
mother, and the daughter in law against her
mother in law.
36 And a man's foes *shall be* they of his own
household.
37 He that loveth father or mother more than
me is not worthy of me: and he that loveth son
or daughter more than me is not worthy of me.
38 And he that taketh not his cross, and followeth after me, is not worthy of me.
39 He that findeth his life shall lose it: and he
that loseth his life for my sake shall find it.
40 ¶ He that receiveth you receiveth me, and
he that receiveth me receiveth him that sent
me.
41 He that receiveth a prophet in the name of
a prophet shall receive a prophet's reward; and
he that receiveth a righteous man in the name
of a righteous man shall receive a righteous
man's reward.
42 And whosoever shall give to drink unto
one of these little ones a cup of cold *water* only
in the name of a disciple, verily I say unto you,
he shall in no wise lose his reward.

11 AND it came to pass, when Je'sus had
made an end of commanding his twelve
disciples, he departed thence to teach and to
preach in their cities.
2 Now when John had heard in the prison the
works of Christ, he sent two of his disciples,
3 And said unto him, Art thou he that should
come, or do we look for another?
4 Je'sus answered and said unto them, Go
and shew John again those things which ye do
hear and see:
5 The blind receive their sight, and the lame
walk, the lepers are cleansed, and the deaf hear,
the dead are raised up, and the poor have the
gospel preached to them.
6 And blessed is *he*, whosoever shall not be
offended in me.
7 ¶ And as they departed, Je'sus began to
say unto the multitudes concerning John, What
went ye out into the wilderness to see? A reed
shaken with the wind?
8 But what went ye out for to see? A man
clothed in soft raiment? behold, they that wear
soft *clothing* are in kings' houses.
9 But what went ye out for to see? A
prophet? yea, I say unto you, and more than a
prophet.
10 For this is *he*, of whom it is written, Behold, I send my messenger before thy face,
which shall prepare thy way before thee.
11 Verily I say unto you, Among them that
are born of women there hath not risen a
greater than John the Bap'tist: notwithstanding
he that is least in the kingdom of heaven is
greater than he.
12 And from the days of John the Bap'tist until now the kingdom of heaven suffereth violence, and the violent take it by force.
13 For all the prophets and the law prophesied until John.
14 And if ye will receive *it*, this is E-li'as,
which was for to come.
15 He that hath ears to hear, let him hear.
16 ¶ But whereunto shall I liken this generation? It is like unto children sitting in the markets, and calling unto their fellows,
17 And saying, We have piped unto you, and
ye have not danced; we have mourned unto
you, and ye have not lamented.
18 For John came neither eating nor drinking, and they say, He hath a devil.
19 The Son of man came eating and drinking,
and they say, Behold a man gluttonous, and a

winebibber, a friend of publicans and sinners.
But wisdom is justified of her children.
20 ¶ Then began he to upbraid the cities
wherein most of his mighty works were done,
because they repented not:
21 Woe unto thee, Cho-ra'zin! woe unto thee,
Beth-sa'i-da! for if the mighty works, which
were done in you, had been done in Tyre and
Si'don, they would have repented long ago in
sackcloth and ashes.
22 But I say unto you, It shall be more tolerable for Tyre and Si'don at the day of judgment,
than for you.
23 And thou, Ca-per'na-um, which art exalted unto heaven, shalt be brought down to
hell: for if the mighty works, which have been
done in thee, had been done in Sod'om, it would
have remained until this day.
24 But I say unto you, That it shall be more
tolerable for the land of Sod'om in the day of
judgment, than for thee.
25 ¶ At that time Je'sus answered and said, I
thank thee, O Father, Lord of heaven and earth,
because thou hast hid these things from the
wise and prudent, and hast revealed them unto
babes.
26 Even so, Father: for so it seemed good in
thy sight.
27 All things are delivered unto me of my Father: and no man knoweth the Son, but the Father; neither knoweth any man the Father, save
the Son, and *he* to whomsoever the Son will reveal *him*.
28 ¶ Come unto me, all *ye* that labour and
are heavy laden, and I will give you rest.
29 Take my yoke upon you, and learn of me;
for I am meek and lowly in heart: and ye shall
find rest unto your souls.
30 For my yoke *is* easy, and my burden is
light.

12 AT that time Je'sus went on the sabbath
day through the corn; and his disciples
were an hungred, and began to pluck the ears of
corn, and to eat.
2 But when the Phar'i-sees saw *it*, they said
unto him, Behold, thy disciples do that which is
not lawful to do upon the sabbath day.
3 But he said unto them, Have ye not read
what Da'vid did, when he was an hungred, and
they that were with him;
4 How he entered into the house of God, and
did eat the shewbread, which was not lawful for
him to eat, neither for them which were with
him, but only for the priests?
5 Or have ye not read in the law, how that on
the sabbath days the priests in the temple profane the sabbath, and are blameless?
6 But I say unto you, That in this place is *one*
greater than the temple.
7 But if ye had known what *this* meaneth, I
will have mercy, and not sacrifice, ye would not
have condemned the guiltless.
8 For the Son of man is Lord even of the sabbath day.
9 And when he was departed thence, he went
into their synagogue:
10 ¶ And, behold, there was a man which
had *his* hand withered. And they asked him,
saying, Is it lawful to heal on the sabbath days?
that they might accuse him.
11 And he said unto them, What man shall
there be among you, that shall have one sheep,
and if it fall into a pit on the sabbath day, will
he not lay hold on it, and lift *it* out?
12 How much then is a man better than a
sheep? Wherefore it is lawful to do well on the
sabbath days.
13 Then saith he to the man, Stretch forth
thine hand. And he stretched *it* forth; and it was
restored whole, like as the other.
14 ¶ Then the Phar'i-sees went out, and held
a council against him, how they might destroy
him.
15 But when Je'sus knew *it*, he withdrew
himself from thence: and great multitudes followed him, and he healed them all;
16 And charged them that they should not
make him known:
17 That it might be fulfilled which was spoken by E-sa'ias the prophet, saying,
18 Behold my servant, whom I have chosen;
my beloved, in whom my soul is well pleased: I
will put my spirit upon him, and he shall shew
judgment to the Gen'tiles.
19 He shall not strive, nor cry; neither shall
any man hear his voice in the streets.
20 A bruised reed shall he not break, and
smoking flax shall he not quench, till he send
forth judgment unto victory.
21 And in his name shall the Gen'tiles trust.
22 ¶ Then was brought unto him one possessed with a devil, blind, and dumb: and he
healed him, insomuch that the blind and dumb
both spake and saw.
23 And all the people were amazed, and said,
Is not this the son of Da'vid?
24 But when the Phar'i-sees heard *it*, they
said, This *fellow* doth not cast out devils, but by
Be'el'ze-bub the prince of the devils.
25 And Je'sus knew their thoughts, and said
unto them, Every kingdom divided against itself is brought to desolation; and every city or
house divided against itself shall not stand:
26 And if Sa'tan cast out Sa'tan, he is divided
against himself; how shall then his kingdom
stand?
27 And if I by Be'el'ze-bub cast out devils, by
whom do your children cast *them* out? therefore they shall be your judges.
28 But if I cast out devils by the Spirit of
God, then the kingdom of God is come unto
you.
29 Or else how can one enter into a strong
man's house, and spoil his goods, except he first
bind the strong man? and then he will spoil his
house.
30 He that is not with me is against me; and
he that gathereth not with me scattereth
abroad.
31 ¶ Wherefore I say unto you, All manner
of sin and blasphemy shall be forgiven unto
men: but the blasphemy *against* the *Ho'ly*
Ghost shall not be forgiven unto men.
32 And whosoever speaketh a word against
the Son of man, it shall be forgiven him: but
whosoever speaketh against the Ho'ly Ghost, it
shall not be forgiven him, neither in this world,
neither in the *world* to come.
33 Either make the tree good, and his fruit
good; or else make the tree corrupt, and his
fruit corrupt: for the tree is known by *his* fruit.
34 O generation of vipers, how can ye, being
evil, speak good things? for out of the abundance of the heart the mouth speaketh.
35 A good man out of the good treasure of
the heart bringeth forth good things: and an evil
man out of the evil treasure bringeth forth evil
things.
36 But I say unto you, That every idle word
that men shall speak, they shall give account
thereof in the day of judgment.

37 For by thy words thou shalt be justified, and by thy words thou shalt be condemned.

38 ¶ Then certain of the scribes and of the Phar'i-sees answered, saying, Master, we would see a sign from thee.

39 But he answered and said unto them, An evil and adulterous generation seeketh after a sign; and there shall no sign be given to it, but the sign of the prophet Jo'nas:

40 For as Jo'nas was three days and three nights in the whale's belly; so shall the Son of man be three days and three nights in the heart of the earth.

41 The men of Nin'e-veh shall rise in judgment with this generation, and shall condemn it: because they repented at the preaching of Jo'nas; and, behold, a greater than Jo'nas *is* here.

42 The queen of the south shall rise up in the judgment with this generation, and shall condemn it: for she came from the uttermost parts of the earth to hear the wisdom of Sol'o-mon; and, behold, a greater than Sol'o-mon *is* here.

43 When the unclean spirit is gone out of a man, he walketh through dry places, seeking rest, and findeth none.

44 Then he saith, I will return into my house from whence I came out; and when he is come, he findeth *it* empty, swept, and garnished.

45 Then goeth he, and taketh with himself seven other spirits more wicked than himself, and they enter in and dwell there: and the last *state* of that man is worse than the first. Even so shall it be also unto this wicked generation.

46 ¶ While he yet talked to the people, behold, *his* mother and his brethren stood without, desiring to speak with him.

47 Then one said unto him, Behold, thy mother and thy brethren stand without, desiring to speak with thee.

48 But he answered and said unto him that told him, Who is my mother? and who are my brethren?

49 And he stretched forth his hand toward his disciples, and said, Behold my mother and my brethren!

50 For whosoever shall do the will of my Father which is in heaven, the same is my brother, and sister, and mother.

13 THE same day went Je'sus out of the house, and sat by the sea side.

2 And great multitudes were gathered together unto him, so that he went into a ship, and sat; and the whole multitude stood on the shore.

3 And he spake many things unto them in parables, saying, Behold, a sower went forth to sow;

4 And when he sowed, some *seeds* fell by the way side, and the fowls came and devoured them up:

5 Some fell upon stony places, where they had not much earth: and forthwith they sprung up, because they had no deepness of earth:

6 And when the sun was up, they were scorched; and because they had no root, they withered away.

7 And some fell among thorns; and the thorns sprung up, and choked them:

8 But other fell into good ground, and brought forth fruit, some an hundredfold, some sixtyfold, some thirtyfold.

9 Who hath ears to hear, let him hear.

10 And the disciples came, and said unto him, Why speakest thou unto them in parables?

11 He answered and said unto them, Because it is given unto you to know the mysteries of the kingdom of heaven, but to them it is not given.

12 For whosoever hath, to him shall be given, and he shall have more abundance: but whosoever hath not, from him shall be taken away even that he hath.

13 Therefore speak I to them in parables: because they seeing see not; and hearing they hear not, neither do they understand.

14 And in them is fulfilled the prophecy of E-sa'ias, which saith, By hearing ye shall hear, and shall not understand; and seeing ye shall see, and shall not perceive:

15 For this people's heart is waxed gross, and *their ears* are dull of hearing, and their eyes they have closed; lest at any time they should see with *their* eyes, and hear with *their* ears, and should understand with *their* heart, and should be converted, and I should heal them.

16 But blessed *are* your eyes, for they see: and your ears, for they hear.

17 For verily I say unto you, That many prophets and righteous *men* have desired to see *those things* which ye see, and have not seen *them;* and to hear *those things* which ye hear, and have not heard *them.*

18 ¶ Hear ye therefore the parable of the sower.

19 When any one heareth the word of the kingdom, and understandeth *it* not, then cometh the wicked *one,* and catcheth away that which was sown in his heart. This is he which received seed by the way side.

20 But he that received the seed into stony places, the same is he that heareth the word, and anon with joy receiveth it;

21 Yet hath he not root in himself, but dureth for a while: for when tribulation or persecution ariseth because of the word, by and by he is offended.

22 He also that received seed among the thorns is he that heareth the word; and the care of this world, and the deceitfulness of riches, choke the word, and he becometh unfruitful.

23 But he that received seed into the good ground is he that heareth the word, and understandeth *it;* which also beareth fruit, and bringeth forth, some an hundredfold, some sixty, some thirty.

24 ¶ Another parable put he forth unto them, saying, The kingdom of heaven is likened unto a man which sowed good seed in his field:

25 But while men slept, his enemy came and sowed tares among the wheat, and went his way.

26 But when the blade was sprung up, and brought forth fruit, then appeared the tares also.

27 So the servants of the householder came and said unto him, Sir, didst not thou sow good seed in thy field? from whence then hath it tares?

28 He said unto them, An enemy hath done this. The servants said unto him, Wilt thou then that we go and gather them up?

29 But he said, Nay; lest while ye gather up the tares, ye root up also the wheat with them.

30 Let both grow together until the harvest: and in the time of harvest I will say to the reapers, Gather ye together first the tares, and bind them in bundles to burn them: but gather the wheat into my barn.

31 ¶ Another parable put he forth unto them, saying, The kingdom of heaven is like a grain of mustard seed, which a man took, and sowed in his field:

32 Which indeed is the least of all seeds: but

when it is grown, it is the greatest among herbs,
and becometh a tree, so that the birds of the air
come and lodge in the branches thereof.
33 ¶ Another parable spake he unto them;
The kingdom of heaven is like unto leaven,
which a woman took, and hid in three measures
of meal, till the whole was leavened.
34 All these things spake Je'sus unto the
multitude in parables; and without a parable
spake he not unto them:
35 That it might be fulfilled which was spoken by the prophet, saying, I will open my
mouth in parables; I will utter things which
have been kept secret from the foundation of
the world.
36 Then Je'sus sent the multitude away, and
went into the house: and his disciples came
unto him, saying, Declare unto us the parable of
the tares of the field.
37 He answered and said unto them, He that
soweth the good seed is the Son of man;
38 The field is the world; the good seed are
the children of the kingdom; but the tares are
the children of the wicked *one;*
39 The enemy that sowed them is the devil;
the harvest is the end of the world; and the
reapers are the angels.
40 As therefore the tares are gathered and
burned in the fire; so shall it be in the end of this
world.
41 The Son of man shall send forth his angels, and they shall gather out of his kingdom
all things that offend, and them which do iniquity;
42 And shall cast them into a furnace of fire:
there shall be wailing and gnashing of teeth.
43 Then shall the righteous shine forth as the
sun in the kingdom of their Father. Who hath
ears to hear, let him hear.
44 ¶ Again, the kingdom of heaven is like
unto treasure hid in a field; the which when a
man hath found, he hideth, and for joy thereof
goeth and selleth all that he hath, and buyeth
that field.
45 ¶ Again, the kingdom of heaven is like
unto a merchant man, seeking goodly pearls:
46 Who, when he had found one pearl of
great price, went and sold all that he had, and
bought it.
47 ¶ Again, the kingdom of heaven is like
unto a net, that was cast into the sea, and gathered of every kind:
48 Which, when it was full, they drew to
shore, and sat down, and gathered the good into
vessels, but cast the bad away.
49 So shall it be at the end of the world: the
angels shall come forth, and sever the wicked
from among the just,
50 And shall cast them into the furnace of
fire: there shall be wailing and gnashing of
teeth.
51 Je'sus saith unto them, Have ye understood all these things? They say unto him, Yea,
Lord.
52 Then said he unto them, Therefore every
scribe *which is* instructed unto the kingdom of
heaven is like unto a man *that is* an householder, which bringeth forth out of his treasure
things new and old.
53 ¶ And it came to pass, *that* when Je'sus
had finished these parables, he departed thence.
54 And when he was come into his own
country, he taught them in their synagogue, insomuch that they were astonished, and said,
Whence hath this *man* this wisdom, and *these*
mighty works?
55 Is not this the carpenter's son? is not his
mother called Ma'ry? and his brethren, James,
and Jo'ses, and Si'mon, and Ju'das?
56 And his sisters, are they not all with us?
Whence then hath this *man* all these things?
57 And they were offended in him. But Je'sus
said unto them, A prophet is not without honour, save in his own country, and in his own
house.
58 And he did not many mighty works there
because of their unbelief.

14 AT that time Her'od the tetrarch heard
of the fame of Je'sus,
2 And said unto his servants, This is John the
Bap'tist; he is risen from the dead; and therefore mighty works do shew forth themselves in
him.
3 ¶ For Her'od had laid hold on John, and
bound him, and put *him* in prison for He-ro'di-
as' sake, his brother Phil'ip's wife.
4 For John said unto him, It is not lawful for
thee to have her.
5 And when he would have put him to death,
he feared the multitude, because they counted
him as a prophet.
6 But when Her'od's birthday was kept, the
daughter of He-ro'di-as danced before them,
and pleased Her'od.
7 Whereupon he promised with an oath to
give her whatsoever she would ask.
8 And she, being before instructed of her
mother, said, Give me here John Bap'tist's head
in a charger.
9 And the king was sorry: nevertheless for
the oath's sake, and them which sat with him at
meat, he commanded *it* to be given *her.*
10 And he sent, and beheaded John in the
prison.
11 And his head was brought in a charger,
and given to the damsel: and she brought *it* to
her mother.
12 And his disciples came, and took up the
body, and buried it, and went and told Je'sus.
13 ¶ When Je'sus heard *of it,* he departed
thence by ship into a desert place apart: and
when the people had heard *thereof,* they followed him on foot out of the cities.
14 And Je'sus went forth, and saw a great
multitude, and was moved with compassion
toward them, and he healed their sick.
15 ¶ And when it was evening, his disciples
came to him, saying, This is a desert place, and
the time is now past; send the multitude away,
that they may go into the villages, and buy
themselves victuals.
16 But Je'sus said unto them, They need not
depart; give ye them to eat.
17 And they say unto him, We have here but
five loaves, and two fishes.
18 He said, Bring them hither to me.
19 And he commanded the multitude to sit
down on the grass, and took the five loaves, and
the two fishes, and looking up to heaven, he
blessed, and brake, and gave the loaves to *his*
disciples, and the disciples to the multitude.
20 And they did all eat, and were filled: and
they took up of the fragments that remained
twelve baskets full.
21 And they that had eaten were about five
thousand men, beside women and children.
22 ¶ And straightway Je'sus constrained his
disciples to get into a ship, and to go before him
unto the other side, while he sent the multitudes away.
23 And when he had sent the multitudes
away, he went up into a mountain apart to pray:

and when the evening was come, he was there
alone.
24 But the ship was now in the midst of the
sea, tossed with waves: for the wind was contrary.
25 And in the fourth watch of the night Je'-
sus went unto them, walking on the sea.
26 And when the disciples saw him walking
on the sea, they were troubled, saying, It is a
spirit; and they cried out for fear.
27 But straightway Je'sus spake unto them,
saying, Be of good cheer; it is I; be not afraid.
28 And Pe'ter answered him and said, Lord,
if it be thou, bid me come unto thee on the water.
29 And he said, Come. And when Pe'ter was
come down out of the ship, he walked on the
water, to go to Je'sus.
30 But when he saw the wind boisterous, he
was afraid; and beginning to sink, he cried, saying, Lord, save me.
31 And immediately Je'sus stretched forth
his hand, and caught him, and said unto him, O
thou of little faith, wherefore didst thou doubt?
32 And when they were come into the ship,
the wind ceased.
33 Then they that were in the ship came and
worshipped him, saying, Of a truth thou art the
Son of God.
34 ¶ And when they were gone over, they
came into the land of Gen-nes'a-ret.
35 And when the men of that place had
knowledge of him, they sent out into all that
country round about, and brought unto him all
that were diseased;
36 And besought him that they might only
touch the hem of his garment: and as many as
touched were made perfectly whole.

15 THEN came to Je'sus scribes and Phar'i-
sees, which were of Je-ru'sa-lem, saying,
2 Why do thy disciples transgress the tradition of the elders? for they wash not their hands
when they eat bread.
3 But he answered and said unto them, Why
do ye also transgress the commandment of God
by your tradition?
4 For God commanded, saying, Honour thy
father and mother: and, He that curseth father
or mother, let him die the death.
5 But ye say, Whosoever shall say to *his* father or *his* mother, *It is* a gift, by whatsoever
thou mightest be profited by me;
6 And honour not his father or his mother, *he
shall be free*. Thus have ye made the commandment of God of none effect by your tradition.
7 *Ye* hypocrites, well did E-sa'ias prophesy of
you, saying,
8 This people draweth nigh unto me with
their mouth, and honoureth me with *their* lips;
but their heart is far from me.
9 But in vain they do worship me, teaching
for doctrines the commandments of men.
10 ¶ And he called the multitude, and said
unto them, Hear, and understand:
11 Not that which goeth into the mouth defileth a man; but that which cometh out of the
mouth, this defileth a man.
12 Then came his disciples, and said unto
him, Knowest thou that the Phar'i-sees were offended, after they heard this saying?
13 But he answered and said, Every plant,
which my heavenly Father hath not planted,
shall be rooted up.
14 Let them alone: they be blind leaders of
the blind. And if the blind lead the blind, both
shall fall into the ditch.
15 Then answered Pe'ter and said unto him,
Declare unto us this parable.
16 And Je'sus said, Are ye also yet without
understanding?
17 Do not ye yet understand, that whatsoever entereth in at the mouth goeth into the belly, and is cast out into the draught?
18 But those things which proceed out of the
mouth come forth from the heart; and they defile the man.
19 For out of the heart proceed evil thoughts,
murders, adulteries, fornications, thefts, false
witness, blasphemies:
20 These are *the things* which defile a man:
but to eat with unwashen hands defileth not a
man.
21 ¶ Then Je'sus went thence, and departed
into the coasts of Tyre and Si'don.
22 And, behold, a woman of Ca'naan came
out of the same coasts, and cried unto him, saying, Have mercy on me, O Lord, *thou* son of
Da'vid; my daughter is grievously vexed with a
devil.
23 But he answered her not a word. And his
disciples came and besought him, saying, Send
her away; for she crieth after us.
24 But he answered and said, I am not sent
but unto the lost sheep of the house of Is'ra-el.
25 Then came she and worshipped him, saying Lord, help me.
26 But he answered and said, It is not meet
to take the children's bread, and to cast *it* to
dogs.
27 And she said, Truth, Lord: yet the dogs
eat of the crumbs which fall from their masters'
table.
28 Then Je'sus answered and said unto her,
O woman, great *is* thy faith: be it unto thee even
as thou wilt. And her daughter was made whole
from that very hour.
29 And Je'sus departed from thence, and
came nigh unto the sea of Gal'i-lee; and went up
into a mountain, and sat down there.
30 And great multitudes came unto him, having with them *those that were* lame, blind,
dumb, maimed, and many others, and cast
them down at Je'sus' feet; and he healed them:
31 Insomuch that the multitude wondered,
when they saw the dumb to speak, the maimed
to be whole, the lame to walk, and the blind to
see: and they glorified the God of Is'ra-el.
32 ¶ Then Je'sus called his disciples *unto
him*, and said, I have compassion on the multitude, because they continue with me now three
days, and have nothing to eat: and I will not
send them away fasting, lest they faint in the
way.
33 And his disciples say unto him, Whence
should we have so much bread in the wilderness, as to fill so great a multitude?
34 And Je'sus saith unto them, How many
loaves have ye? And they said, Seven, and a few
little fishes.
35 And he commanded the multitude to sit
down on the ground.
36 And he took the seven loaves and the
fishes, and gave thanks, and brake *them*, and
gave to his disciples, and the disciples to the
multitude.
37 And they did all eat, and were filled: and
they took up of the broken *meat* that was left
seven baskets full.
38 And they that did eat were four thousand
men, beside women and children.

39 And he sent away the multitude, and took ship, and came into the coasts of Mag'da-la.

16 THE Phar'i-sees also with the Sad'du-cees came, and tempting desired him that he would shew them a sign from heaven.

2 He answered and said unto them, When it is evening, ye say, *It will be* fair weather: for the sky is red.

3 And in the morning, *It will be* foul weather to day: for the sky is red and lowring. O *ye* hypocrites, ye can discern the face of the sky; but can ye not *discern* the signs of the times?

4 A wicked and adulterous generation seeketh after a sign; and there shall no sign be given unto it, but the sign of the prophet Jo'nas. And he left them, and departed.

5 And when his disciples were come to the other side, they had forgotten to take bread.

6 ¶ Then Je'sus said unto them, Take heed and beware of the leaven of the Phar'i-sees and of the Sad'du-cees.

7 And they reasoned among themselves, saying, *It is* because we have taken no bread.

8 *Which* when Je'sus perceived, he said unto them, O ye of little faith, why reason ye among yourselves, because ye have brought no bread?

9 Do ye not yet understand, neither remember the five loaves of the five thousand, and how many baskets ye took up?

10 Neither the seven loaves of the four thousand, and how many baskets ye took up?

11 How is it that ye do not undertand that I spake *it* not to you concerning bread, that ye should beware of the leaven of the Phar'i-sees and of the Sad'du-cees?

12 Then understood they how that he bade *them* not beware of the leaven of bread, but of the doctrine of the Phar'i-sees and of the Sad'du-cees.

13 ¶ When Je'sus came into the coasts of Cæs-a-re'a Phi-lip'pi, he asked his disciples, saying, Whom do men say that I the Son of man am?

14 And they said, Some *say that thou art* John the Bap'tist: some, E-li'as; and others, Jer-e-mi'as, or one of the prophets.

15 He saith unto them, But whom say ye that I am?

16 And Si'mon Pe'ter answered and said, Thou art the Christ, the Son of the living God.

17 And Je'sus answered and said unto him, Blessed art thou, Si'mon Bar-jo'na: for flesh and blood hath not revealed *it* unto thee, but my Father which is in heaven.

18 And I say also unto thee, That thou art Pe'ter, and upon this rock I will build my church; and the gates of hell shall not prevail against it.

19 And I will give unto thee the keys of the kingdom of heaven: and whatsoever thou shalt bind on earth shall be bound in heaven: and whatsoever thou shalt loose on earth shall be loosed in heaven.

20 Then charged he his disciples that they should tell no man that he was Je'sus the Christ.

21 ¶ From that time forth began Je'sus to shew unto his disciples, how that he must go unto Je-ru'sa-lem, and suffer many things of the elders and chief priests and scribes, and be killed, and be raised again the third day.

22 Then Pe'ter took him, and began to rebuke him, saying, Be it far from thee, Lord: this shall not be unto thee.

23 But he turned, and said unto Pe'ter, Get thee behind me, Sa'tan: thou art an offence unto me: for thou savourest not the things that be of God, but those that be of men.

24 ¶ Then said Je'sus unto his disciples, If any *man* will come after me, let him deny himself, and take up his cross, and follow me.

25 For whosoever will save his life shall lose it: and whosoever will lose his life for my sake shall find it.

26 For what is a man profited, if he shall gain the whole world, and lose his own soul? or what shall a man give in exchange for his soul?

27 For the Son of man shall come in the glory of his Father with his angels; and then he shall reward every man according to his works.

28 Verily I say unto you, There be some standing here, which shall not taste of death, till they see the Son of man coming in his kingdom.

17 AND after six days Je'sus taketh Pe'ter, James, and John his brother, and bringeth them up into an high mountain apart,

2 And was transfigured before them: and his face did shine as the sun, and his raiment was white as the light.

3 And, behold, there appeared unto them Mo'ses and E-li'as talking with him.

4 Then answered Pe'ter, and said unto Je'sus, Lord, it is good for us to be here: if thou wilt, let us make here three tabernacles; one for thee, and one for Mo'ses, and one for E-li'as.

5 While he yet spake, behold, a bright cloud overshadowed them: and behold a voice out of the cloud, which said, This is my beloved Son, in whom I am well pleased; hear ye him.

6 And when the disciples heard *it,* they fell on their face, and were sore afraid.

7 And Je'sus came and touched them, and said, Arise, and be not afraid.

8 And when they had lifted up their eyes, they saw no man, save Je'sus only.

9 And as they came down from the mountain, Je'sus charged them, saying, Tell the vision to no man, until the Son of man be risen again from the dead.

10 And his disciples asked him, saying, Why then say the scribes that E-li'as must first come?

11 And Je'sus answered and said unto them, E-li'as truly shall first come, and restore all things.

12 But I say unto you, That E-li'as is come already, and they knew him not, but have done unto him whatsoever they listed. Likewise shall also the Son of man suffer of them.

13 Then the disciples understood that he spake unto them of John the Bap'tist.

14 ¶ And when they were come to the multitude, there came to him a *certain* man, kneeling down to him, and saying,

15 Lord, have mercy on my son: for he is lunatick, and sore vexed: for ofttimes he falleth into the fire, and oft into the water.

16 And I brought him to thy disciples, and they could not cure him.

17 Then Je'sus answered and said, O faithless and perverse generation, how long shall I be with you? how long shall I suffer you? bring him hither to me.

18 And Je'sus rebuked the devil; and he departed out of him: and the child was cured from that very hour.

19 Then came the disciples to Je'sus apart, and said, Why could not we cast him out?

20 And Je'sus said unto them, Because of your unbelief: for verily I say unto you, If ye have faith as a grain of mustard seed, ye shall say unto this mountain, Remove hence to yon-

der place; and it shall remove; and nothing shall be impossible unto you.

21 Howbeit this kind goeth not out but by prayer and fasting.

22 ¶ **And while they abode in Gal′i-lee, Je′sus said unto them,** The Son of man shall be betrayed into the hands of men:

23 And they shall kill him, and the third day he shall be raised again. **And they were exceeding sorry.**

24 ¶ **And when they were come to Ca-per′na-um, they that received tribute *money* came to Pe′ter, and said, Doth not your master pay tribute?**

25 **He saith, Yes. And when he was come into the house, Je′sus prevented him, saying,** What thinkest thou, Si′mon? of whom do the kings of the earth take custom or tribute? of their own children, or of strangers?

26 **Pe′ter saith unto him, Of strangers. Je′sus saith unto him,** Then are the children free.

27 Notwithstanding, lest we should offend them, go thou to the sea, and cast an hook, and take up the fish that first cometh up; and when thou hast opened his mouth, thou shalt find a piece of money: that take, and give unto them for me and thee.

18 **AT the same time came the disciples unto Je′sus, saying, Who is the greatest in the kingdom of heaven?**

2 **And Je′sus called a little child unto him, and set him in the midst of them,**

3 **And said,** Verily I say unto you, Except ye be converted, and become as little children, ye shall not enter into the kingdom of heaven.

4 Whosoever therefore shall humble himself as this little child, the same is greatest in the kingdom of heaven.

5 And whoso shall receive one such little child in my name receiveth me.

6 But whoso shall offend one of these little ones which believe in me, it were better for him that a millstone were hanged about his neck, and *that* he were drowned in the depth of the sea.

7 ¶ Woe unto the world because of offences! for it must needs be that offences come; but woe to that man by whom the offence cometh!

8 Wherefore if thy hand or thy foot offend thee, cut them off, and cast *them* from thee: it is better for thee to enter into life halt or maimed, rather than having two hands or two feet to be cast into everlasting fire.

9 And if thine eye offend thee, pluck it out, and cast *it* from thee: it is better for thee to enter into life with one eye, rather than having two eyes to be cast into hell fire.

10 Take heed that ye despise not one of these little ones; for I say unto you, That in heaven their angels do always behold the face of my Father which is in heaven.

11 For the Son of man is come to save that which was lost.

12 How think ye? if a man have an hundred sheep, and one of them be gone astray, doth he not leave the ninety and nine, and goeth into the mountains, and seeketh that which is gone astray?

13 And if so be that he find it, verily I say unto you, he rejoiceth more of that *sheep*, than of the ninety and nine which went not astray.

14 Even so it is not the will of your Father which is in heaven, that one of these little ones should perish.

15 ¶ Moreover if thy brother shall trespass against thee, go and tell him his fault between thee and him alone: if he shall hear thee, thou hast gained thy brother.

16 But if he will not hear *thee, then* take with thee one or two more, that in the mouth of two or three witnesses every word may be established.

17 And if he shall neglect to hear them, tell *it* unto the church: but if he neglect to hear the church, let him be unto thee as an heathen man and a publican.

18 Verily I say unto you, Whatsoever ye shall bind on earth shall be bound in heaven: and whatsoever ye shall loose on earth shall be loosed in heaven.

19 Again I say unto you, That if two of you shall agree on earth as touching any thing that they shall ask, it shall be done for them of my Father which is in heaven.

20 For where two or three are gathered together in my name, there am I in the midst of them.

21 ¶ **Then came Pe′ter to him, and said, Lord, how oft shall my brother sin against me, and I forgive him? till seven times?**

22 **Je′sus saith unto him,** I say not unto thee, Until seven times: but, Until seventy times seven.

23 ¶ Therefore is the kingdom of heaven likened unto a certain king, which would take account of his servants.

24 And when he had begun to reckon, one was brought unto him, which owed him ten thousand talents.

25 But forasmuch as he had not to pay, his lord commanded him to be sold, and his wife, and children, and all that he had, and payment to be made.

26 The servant therefore fell down, and worshipped him, saying, Lord, have patience with me, and I will pay thee all.

27 Then the lord of that servant was moved with compassion, and loosed him, and forgave him the debt.

28 But the same servant went out, and found one of his fellowservants, which owed him an hundred pence: and he laid hands on him, and took *him* by the throat, saying, Pay me that thou owest.

29 And his fellowservant fell down at his feet, and besought him, saying, Have patience with me, and I will pay thee all.

30 And he would not: but went and cast him into prison, till he should pay the debt.

31 So when his fellowservants saw what was done, they were very sorry, and came and told unto their lord all that was done.

32 Then his lord, after that he had called him, said unto him, O thou wicked servant, I forgave thee all that debt, because thou desiredst me:

33 Shouldest not thou also have had compassion on thy fellowservant, even as I had pity on thee?

34 And his lord was wroth, and delivered him to the tormentors, till he should pay all that was due unto him.

35 So likewise shall my heavenly Father do also unto you, if ye from your hearts forgive not every one his brother their trespasses.

19 **AND it came to pass, *that* when Je′sus had finished these sayings, he departed from Gal′i-lee, and came into the coasts of Judæ′a beyond Jor′dan;**

2 **And great multitudes followed him; and he healed them there.**

3 ¶ **The Phar′i-sees also came unto him, tempting him, and saying unto him, Is it lawful**

for a man to put away his wife for every cause?
4 And he answered and said unto them, Have
ye not read, that he which made *them* at the
beginning made them male and female,
5 And said, For this cause shall a man leave
father and mother, and shall cleave to his wife:
and they twain shall be one flesh?
6 Wherefore they are no more twain, but one
flesh. What therefore God hath joined together,
let not man put asunder.
7 They say unto him, Why did Mo'ses then
command to give a writing of divorcement, and
to put her away?
8 He saith unto them, Mo'ses because of the
hardness of your hearts suffered you to put
away your wives: but from the beginning it was
not so.
9 And I say unto you, Whosoever shall put
away his wife, except *it be* for fornication, and
shall marry another, committeth adultery: and
whoso marrieth her which is put away doth
commit adultery.
10 ¶ His disciples say unto him, If the case of
the man be so with *his* wife, it is not good to
marry.
11 But he said unto them, All *men* cannot receive this saying, save *they* to whom it is given.
12 For there are some eunuchs, which were
so born from *their* mother's womb: and there
are some eunuchs, which were made eunuchs
of men: and there be eunuchs, which have made
themselves eunuchs for the kingdom of heav-
en's sake. He that is able to receive *it*, let him
receive *it*.
13 ¶ Then were there brought unto him little
children, that he should put *his* hands on them,
and pray: and the disciples rebuked them.
14 But Je'sus said, Suffer little children, and
forbid them not, to come unto me: for of such is
the kingdom of heaven.
15 And he laid *his* hands on them, and departed thence.
16 ¶ And, behold, one came and said unto
him, Good Master, what good thing shall I do,
that I may have eternal life?
17 And he said unto him, Why callest thou
me good? *there is* none good but one, *that is*,
God: but if thou wilt enter into life, keep the
commandments.
18 He saith unto him, Which? Je'sus said,
Thou shalt do no murder, Thou shalt not commit adultery, Thou shalt not steal, Thou shalt
not bear false witness,
19 Honour thy father and *thy* mother: and,
Thou shalt love thy neighbour as thyself.
20 The young man saith unto him, All these
things have I kept from my youth up: what lack
I yet?
21 Je'sus said unto him, If thou wilt be perfect, go *and* sell that thou hast, and give to the
poor, and thou shalt have treasure in heaven:
and come *and* follow me.
22 But when the young man heard that saying, he went away sorrowful: for he had great
possessions.
23 ¶ Then said Je'sus unto his disciples, Verily I say unto you, That a rich man shall hardly
enter into the kingdom of heaven.
24 And again I say unto you, It is easier for a
camel to go through the eye of a needle, than
for a rich man to enter into the kingdom of God.
25 When his disciples heard *it*, they were exceedingly amazed, saying, Who then can be
saved?
26 But Je'sus beheld *them*, and said unto
them, With men this is impossible; but with
God all things are possible.
27 ¶ Then answered Pe'ter and said unto
him, Behold, we have forsaken all, and followed
thee; what shall we have therefore?
28 And Je'sus said unto them, Verily I say
unto you, That ye which have followed me, in
the regeneration when the Son of man shall sit
in the throne of his glory, ye also shall sit upon
twelve thrones, judging the twelve tribes of Is'-
ra-el.
29 And every one that hath forsaken houses,
or brethren, or sisters, or father, or mother, or
wife, or children, or lands, for my name's sake,
shall receive an hundredfold, and shall inherit
everlasting life.
30 But many *that are* first shall be last; and
the last *shall be* first.

20 FOR the kingdom of heaven is like unto
a man *that is* an householder, which
went out early in the morning to hire labourers
into his vineyard.
2 And when he had agreed with the labourers for a penny a day, he sent them into his
vineyard.
3 And he went out about the third hour, and
saw others standing idle in the marketplace,
4 And said unto them; Go ye also into the
vineyard, and whatsoever is right I will give
you. And they went their way.
5 Again he went out about the sixth and
ninth hour, and did likewise.
6 And about the eleventh hour he went out,
and found others standing idle, and saith unto
them, Why stand ye here all the day idle?
7 They say unto him, Because no man hath
hired us. He saith unto them, Go ye also into the
vineyard; and whatsoever is right, *that* shall ye
receive.
8 So when even was come, the lord of the
vineyard saith unto his steward, Call the labourers, and give them *their* hire, beginning
from the last unto the first.
9 And when they came that *were hired* about
the eleventh hour, they received every man a
penny.
10 But when the first came, they supposed
that they should have received more; and they
likewise received every man a penny.
11 And when they had received *it*, they murmured against the goodman of the house,
12 Saying, These last have wrought *but* one
hour, and thou hast made them equal unto us,
which have borne the burden and heat of the
day.
13 But he answered one of them, and said,
Friend, I do thee no wrong: didst not thou agree
with me for a penny?
14 Take *that* thine *is*, and go thy way: I will
give unto this last, even as unto thee.
15 Is it not lawful for me to do what I will
with mine own? Is thine eye evil, because I am
good?
16 So the last shall be first, and the first last:
for many be called, but few chosen.
17 ¶ And Je'sus going up to Je-ru'sa-lem
took the twelve disciples apart in the way, and
said unto them,
18 Behold, we go up to Je-ru'sa-lem; and the
Son of man shall be betrayed unto the chief
priests and unto the scribes, and they shall condemn him to death,
19 And shall deliver him to the Gen'tiles to
mock, and to scourge, and to crucify *him*: and
the third day he shall rise again.
20 ¶ Then came to him the mother of Zeb'e-
dee's children with her sons, worshipping *him*,
and desiring a certain thing of him.

21 And he said unto her, What wilt thou? She
saith unto him, Grant that these my two sons
may sit, the one on thy right hand, and the other
on the left in thy kingdom.
22 But Je'sus answered and said, Ye know
not what ye ask. Are ye able to drink of the cup
that I shall drink of, and to be baptized with the
baptism that I am baptized with? They say unto
him, We are able.
23 And he saith unto them, Ye shall drink indeed of my cup, and be baptized with the baptism that I am baptized with: but to sit on my
right hand, and on my left, is not mine to give,
but *it shall be given to them* for whom it is prepared of my Father.
24 And when the ten heard *it*, they were
moved with indignation against the two brethren.
25 But Je'sus called them *unto him*, and said,
Ye know that the princes of the Gen'tiles exercise dominion over them, and they that are
great exercise authority upon them.
26 But it shall not be so among you: but whosoever will be great among you, let him be your
minister;
27 And whosoever will be chief among you,
let him be your servant:
28 Even as the Son of man came not to be
ministered unto, but to minister, and to give his
life a ransom for many.
29 And as they departed from Jer'i-cho, a
great multitude followed him.
30 ¶ And, behold, two blind men sitting by
the way side, when they heard that Je'sus
passed by, cried out, saying, Have mercy on us,
O Lord, *thou* son of Da'vid.
31 And the multitude rebuked them, because
they should hold their peace: but they cried the
more, saying, Have mercy on us, O Lord, *thou*
son of Da'vid.
32 And Je'sus stood still, and called them,
and said, What will ye that I shall do unto you?
33 They say unto him, Lord, that our eyes
may be opened.
34 So Je'sus had compassion *on them*, and
touched their eyes: and immediately their eyes
received sight, and they followed him.

21 AND when they drew nigh unto Je-ru'-
sa-lem, and were come to Beth'pha-ge,
unto the mount of Ol'ives, then sent Je'sus two
disciples,
2 Saying unto them, Go into the village over
against you, and straightway ye shall find an
ass tied, and a colt with her: loose *them*, and
bring *them* unto me.
3 And if any *man* say ought unto you, ye
shall say, The Lord hath need of them; and
straightway he will send them.
4 All this was done, that it might be fulfilled
which was spoken by the prophet, saying,
5 Tell ye the daughter of Si'on, Behold, thy
King cometh unto thee, meek, and sitting upon
an ass, and a colt the foal of an ass.
6 And the disciples went, and did as Je'sus
commanded them,
7 And brought the ass, and the colt, and put
on them their clothes, and they set *him* thereon.
8 And a very great multitude spread their
garments in the way; others cut down branches
from the trees, and strawed *them* in the way.
9 And the multitudes that went before, and
that followed, cried, saying, Ho-san'na to the
son of Da'vid: Blessed *is* he that cometh in the
name of the Lord; Ho-san'na in the highest.
10 And when he was come into Je-ru'sa-lem,
all the city was moved, saying, Who is this?
11 And the multitude said, This is Je'sus the
prophet of Naz'a-reth of Gal'i-lee.
12 ¶ And Je'sus went into the temple of God,
and cast out all them that sold and bought in
the temple, and overthrew the tables of the
moneychangers, and the seats of them that sold
doves,
13 And said unto them, It is written, My
house shall be called the house of prayer; but ye
have made it a den of thieves.
14 And the blind and the lame came to him in
the temple; and he healed them.
15 And when the chief priests and scribes
saw the wonderful things that he did, and the
children crying in the temple, and saying, Ho-
san'na to the son of Da'vid; they were sore displeased,
16 And said unto him, Hearest thou what
these say? And Je'sus saith unto them, Yea;
have ye never read, Out of the mouth of babes
and sucklings thou hast perfected praise?
17 ¶ And he left them, and went out of the
city into Beth'a-ny; and he lodged there.
18 Now in the morning as he returned into
the city, he hungered.
19 And when he saw a fig tree in the way, he
came to it, and found nothing thereon, but
leaves only, and said unto it, Let no fruit grow
on thee henceforward for ever. And presently
the fig tree withered away.
20 And when the disciples saw *it*, they marvelled, saying, How soon is the fig tree withered
away!
21 Je'sus answered and said unto them, Verily I say unto you, If ye have faith, and doubt
not, ye shall not only do this *which is done* to
the fig tree, but also if ye shall say unto this
mountain, Be thou removed, and be thou cast
into the sea; it shall be done.
22 And all things, whatsoever ye shall ask in
prayer, believing, ye shall receive.
23 ¶ And when he was come into the temple,
the chief priests and the elders of the people
came unto him as he was teaching, and said, By
what authority doest thou these things? and
who gave thee this authority?
24 And Je'sus answered and said unto them,
I also will ask you one thing, which if ye tell me,
I in like wise will tell you by what authority I do
these things.
25 The baptism of John, whence was it? from
heaven, or of men? And they reasoned with
themselves, saying, If we shall say, From
heaven; he will say unto us, Why did ye not
then believe him?
26 But if we shall say, Of men; we fear the
people; for all hold John as a prophet.
27 And they answered Je'sus, and said, We
cannot tell. And he said unto them, Neither tell
I you by what authority I do these things.
28 ¶ But what think ye? A *certain* man had
two sons; and he came to the first, and said,
Son, go work to day in my vineyard.
29 He answered and said, I will not: but afterward he repented, and went.
30 And he came to the second, and said likewise. And he answered and said, I *go*, sir: and
went not.
31 Whether of them twain did the will of *his*
father? They say unto him, The first. Je'sus
saith unto them, Verily I say unto you, That the
publicans and the harlots go into the kingdom
of God before you.
32 For John came unto you in the way of
righteousness, and ye believed him not: but the
publicans and the harlots believed him: and ye,

when ye had seen *it,* repented not afterward,
that ye might believe him.
33 ¶ Hear another parable: There was a certain householder, which planted a vineyard, and
hedged it round about, and digged a winepress
in it, and built a tower, and let it out to husbandmen, and went into a far country:
34 And when the time of the fruit drew near,
he sent his servants to the husbandmen, that
they might receive the fruits of it.
35 And the husbandmen took his servants,
and beat one, and killed another, and stoned another.
36 Again, he sent other servants more than
the first: and they did unto them likewise.
37 But last of all he sent unto them his son,
saying, They will reverence my son.
38 But when the husbandmen saw the son,
they said among themselves, This is the heir;
come, let us kill him, and let us seize on his
inheritance.
39 And they caught him, and cast *him* out of
the vineyard, and slew *him.*
40 When the lord therefore of the vineyard
cometh, what will he do unto those husbandmen?
41 They say unto him, He will miserably destroy those wicked men, and will let out *his*
vineyard unto other husbandmen, which shall
render him the fruits in their seasons.
42 Je'sus saith unto them, Did ye never read
in the scriptures, The stone which the builders
rejected, the same is become the head of the
corner: this is the Lord's doing, and it is marvellous in our eyes?
43 Therefore say I unto you, The kingdom of
God shall be taken from you, and given to a
nation bringing forth the fruits thereof.
44 And whosoever shall fall on this stone
shall be broken: but on whomsoever it shall fall,
it will grind him to powder.
45 And when the chief priests and Phar'i-
sees had heard his parables, they perceived that
he spake of them.
46 But when they sought to lay hands on
him, they feared the multitude, because they
took him for a prophet.

22 AND Je'sus answered and spake unto
them again by parables, and said,
2 The kingdom of heaven is like unto a certain king, which made a marriage for his son,
3 And sent forth his servants to call them
that were bidden to the wedding: and they
would not come.
4 Again, he sent forth other servants, saying,
Tell them which are bidden, Behold, I have prepared my dinner: my oxen and *my* fatlings *are*
killed, and all things *are* ready: come unto the
marriage.
5 But they made light of *it,* and went their
ways, one to his farm, another to his merchandise:
6 And the remnant took his servants, and entreated *them* spitefully, and slew *them.*
7 But when the king heard *thereof,* he was
wroth: and he sent forth his armies, and destroyed those murderers, and burned up their
city.
8 Then saith he to his servants, The wedding
is ready, but they which were bidden were not
worthy.
9 Go ye therefore into the highways, and as
many as ye shall find, bid to the marriage.
10 So those servants went out into the highways, and gathered together all as many as they
found, both bad and good: and the wedding was
furnished with guests.
11 ¶ And when the king came in to see the
guests, he saw there a man which had not on a
wedding garment:
12 And he saith unto him, Friend, how camest thou in hither not having a wedding garment? And he was speechless.
13 Then said the king to the servants, Bind
him hand and foot, and take him away, and cast
him into outer darkness; there shall be weeping
and gnashing of teeth.
14 For many are called, but few *are* chosen.
15 ¶ Then went the Phar'i-sees, and took
counsel how they might entangle him in *his*
talk.
16 And they sent out unto him their disciples
with the He-ro'di-ans, saying, Master, we know
that thou art true, and teachest the way of God
in truth, neither carest thou for any *man:* for
thou regardest not the person of men.
17 Tell us therefore, What thinkest thou? Is it
lawful to give tribute unto Cæ'sar, or not?
18 But Je'sus perceived their wickedness,
and said, Why tempt ye me, *ye* hypocrites?
19 Shew me the tribute money. And they
brought unto him a penny.
20 And he saith unto them, Whose *is* this
image and superscription?
21 They say unto him, Cæ'sar's. Then saith
he unto them, Render therefore unto Cæ'sar the
things which are Cæ'sar's; and unto God the
things that are God's.
22 When they had heard *these words,* they
marvelled, and left him, and went their way.
23 ¶ The same day came to him the Sad'du-
cees, which say that there is no resurrection,
and asked him,
24 Saying, Master, Mo'ses said, If a man die,
having no children, his brother shall marry his
wife, and raise up seed unto his brother.
25 Now there were with us seven brethren:
and the first, when he had married a wife, deceased, and, having no issue, left his wife unto
his brother:
26 Likewise the second also, and the third,
unto the seventh.
27 And last of all the woman died also.
28 Therefore in the resurrection whose wife
shall she be of the seven? for they all had her.
29 Je'sus answered and said unto them, Ye
do err, not knowing the scriptures, nor the
power of God.
30 For in the resurrection they neither marry, nor are given in marriage, but are as the angels of God in heaven.
31 But as touching the resurrection of the
dead, have ye not read that which was spoken
unto you by God, saying,
32 I am the God of A'bra-ham, and the God
of I'saac, and the God of Ja'cob? God is not the
God of the dead, but of the living.
33 And when the multitude heard *this,* they
were astonished at his doctrine.
34 ¶ But when the Phar'i-sees had heard that
he had put the Sad'du-cees to silence, they were
gathered together.
35 Then one of them, *which was* a lawyer,
asked *him a question,* tempting him, and saying,
36 Master, which *is* the great commandment
in the law?
37 Je'sus said unto him, Thou shalt love the
Lord thy God with all thy heart, and with all thy
soul, and with all thy mind.
38 This is the first and great commandment.

39 And the second *is* like unto it, Thou shalt
love thy neighbour as thyself.
40 On these two commandments hang all the
law and the prophets.
41 ¶ While the Phar'i-sees were gathered together, Je'sus asked them,
42 Saying, What think ye of Christ? whose
son is he? They say unto him, *The son* of Da'vid.
43 He saith unto them, How then doth Da'vid
in spirit call him Lord, saying,
44 The LORD said unto my Lord, Sit thou on
my right hand, till I make thine enemies thy
footstool?
45 If Da'vid then call him Lord, how is he his
son?
46 And no man was able to answer him a
word, neither durst any *man* from that day
forth ask him any more *questions*.

23 THEN spake Je'sus to the multitude,
and to his disciples,
2 Saying, The scribes and the Phar'i-sees sit
in Mo'ses' seat:
3 All therefore whatsoever they bid you observe, *that* observe and do; but do not ye after
their works: for they say, and do not.
4 For they bind heavy burdens and grievous
to be borne, and lay *them* on men's shoulders;
but they *themselves* will not move them with
one of their fingers.
5 But all their works they do for to be seen of
men: they make broad their phylacteries, and
enlarge the borders of their garments,
6 And love the uppermost rooms at feasts,
and the chief seats in the synagogues,
7 And greetings in the markets, and to be
called of men, Rab'bi, Rab'bi.
8 But be not ye called Rab'bi: for one is your
Master, *even* Christ; and all ye are brethren.
9 And call no *man* your father upon the
earth: for one is your Father, which is in
heaven.
10 Neither be ye called masters: for one is
your Master, *even* Christ.
11 But he that is greatest among you shall be
your servant.
12 And whosoever shall exalt himself shall
be abased; and he that shall humble himself
shall be exalted.
13 ¶ But woe unto you, scribes and Phar'i-
sees, hypocrites! for ye shut up the kingdom of
heaven against men: for ye neither go in *yourselves*, neither suffer ye them that are entering
to go in.
14 Woe unto you, scribes and Phar'i-sees,
hypocrites! for ye devour widows' houses, and
for a pretence make long prayer: therefore ye
shall receive the greater damnation.
15 Woe unto you, scribes and Phar'i-sees,
hypocrites! for ye compass sea and land to
make one proselyte, and when he is made, ye
make him twofold more the child of hell than
yourselves.
16 Woe unto you, ye blind guides, which say,
Whosoever shall swear by the temple, it is
nothing; but whosoever shall swear by the gold
of the temple, he is a debtor!
17 *Ye* fools and blind: for whether is greater,
the gold, or the temple that sanctifieth the gold?
18 And, Whosoever shall swear by the altar,
it is nothing; but whosoever sweareth by the
gift that is upon it, he is guilty.
19 *Ye* fools and blind: for whether *is* greater,
the gift, or the altar that sanctifieth the gift?
20 Whoso therefore shall swear by the altar,
sweareth by it, and by all things thereon.
21 And whoso shall swear by the temple,
sweareth by it, and by him that dwelleth
therein.
22 And he that shall swear by heaven, sweareth by the throne of God, and by him that sitteth thereon.
23 Woe unto you, scribes and Phar'i-sees,
hypocrites! for ye pay tithe of mint and anise
and cummin, and have omitted the weightier
matters of the law, judgment, mercy, and faith:
these ought ye to have done, and not to leave
the other undone.
24 *Ye* blind guides, which strain at a gnat,
and swallow a camel.
25 Woe unto you, scribes and Phar'i-sees,
hypocrites! for ye make clean the outside of the
cup and of the platter, but within they are full of
extortion and excess.
26 *Thou* blind Phar'i-see, cleanse first that
which is within the cup and platter, that the
outside of them may be clean also.
27 Woe unto you, scribes and Phar'i-sees,
hypocrites! for ye are like unto whited sepulchres, which indeed appear beautiful outward,
but are within full of dead *men's* bones, and of
all uncleanness.
28 Even so ye also outwardly appear righteous unto men, but within ye are full of hypocrisy and iniquity.
29 Woe unto you, scribes and Phar'i-sees,
hypocrites! because ye build the tombs of the
prophets, and garnish the sepulchres of the
righteous,
30 And say, If we had been in the days of our
fathers, we would not have been partakers with
them in the blood of the prophets.
31 Wherefore ye be witnesses unto yourselves, that ye are the children of them which
killed the prophets.
32 Fill ye up then the measure of your fathers.
33 *Ye* serpents, *ye* generation of vipers, how
can ye escape the damnation of hell?
34 ¶ Wherefore, behold, I send unto you
prophets, and wise men, and scribes: and *some*
of them ye shall kill and crucify; and *some* of
them shall ye scourge in your synagogues, and
persecute *them* from city to city:
35 That upon you may come all the righteous
blood shed upon the earth, from the blood of
righteous A'bel unto the blood of Zach-a-ri'as
son of Bar-a-chi'as, whom ye slew between the
temple and the altar.
36 Verily I say unto you, All these things
shall come upon this generation.
37 O Je-ru'sa-lem, Je-ru'sa-lem, *thou* that
killest the prophets, and stonest them which are
sent unto thee, how often would I have gathered thy children together, even as a hen gathereth her chickens under *her* wings, and ye
would not!
38 Behold, your house is left unto you desolate.
39 For I say unto you, Ye shall not see me
henceforth, till ye shall say, Blessed *is* he that
cometh in the name of the Lord.

24 AND Je'sus went out, and departed
from the temple: and his disciples came
to *him* for to shew him the buildings of the temple.
2 And Je'sus said unto them, See ye not all
these things? verily I say unto you, There shall
not be left here one stone upon another, that
shall not be thrown down.
3 ¶ And as he sat upon the mount of Ol'ives,
the disciples came unto him privately, saying,
Tell us, when shall these things be? and what

shall be the sign of thy coming, and of the end of the world?

4 And Je'sus answered and said unto them, Take heed that no man deceive you.

5 For many shall come in my name, saying, I am Christ; and shall deceive many.

6 And ye shall hear of wars and rumours of wars: see that ye be not troubled: for all *these things* must come to pass, but the end is not yet.

7 For nation shall rise against nation, and kingdom against kingdom: and there shall be famines, and pestilences, and earthquakes, in divers places.

8 All these *are* the beginning of sorrows.

9 Then shall they deliver you up to be afflicted, and shall kill you: and ye shall be hated of all nations for my name's sake.

10 And then shall many be offended, and shall betray one another, and shall hate one another.

11 And many false prophets shall rise, and shall deceive many.

12 And because iniquity shall abound, the love of many shall wax cold.

13 But he that shall endure unto the end, the same shall be saved.

14 And this gospel of the kingdom shall be preached in all the world for a witness unto all nations; and then shall the end come.

15 When ye therefore shall see the abomination of desolation, spoken of by Dan'iel the prophet, stand in the holy place, (whoso readeth, let him understand:)

16 Then let them which be in Ju-dæ'a flee into the mountains:

17 Let him which is on the house top not come down to take any thing out of his house:

18 Neither let him which is in the field return back to take his clothes.

19 And woe unto them that are with child, and to them that give suck in those days!

20 But pray ye that your flight be not in the winter, neither on the sabbath day:

21 For then shall be great tribulation, such as was not since the beginning of the world to this time, no, nor ever shall be.

22 And except those days should be shortened, there should no flesh be saved: but for the elect's sake those days shall be shortened.

23 Then if any man shall say unto you, Lo, here *is* Christ, or there; believe *it* not.

24 For there shall arise false Christs, and false prophets, and shall shew great signs and wonders; insomuch that, if *it were* possible, they shall deceive the very elect.

25 Behold, I have told you before.

26 Wherefore if they shall say unto you, Behold, he is in the desert; go not forth: behold, *he is* in the secret chambers; believe *it* not.

27 For as the lightning cometh out of the east, and shineth even unto the west; so shall also the coming of the Son of man be.

28 For wheresoever the carcase is, there will the eagles be gathered together.

29 ¶ Immediately after the tribulation of those days shall the sun be darkened, and the moon shall not give her light, and the stars shall fall from heaven, and the powers of the heavens shall be shaken:

30 And then shall appear the sign of the Son of man in heaven: and then shall all the tribes of the earth mourn, and they shall see the Son of man coming in the clouds of heaven with power and great glory.

31 And he shall send his angels with a great sound of a trumpet, and they shall gather together his elect from the four winds, from one end of heaven to the other.

32 Now learn a parable of the fig tree; When his branch is yet tender, and putteth forth leaves, ye know that summer *is* nigh:

33 So likewise ye, when ye shall see all these things, know that it is near, *even* at the doors.

34 Verily I say unto you, This generation shall not pass, till all these things be fulfilled.

35 Heaven and earth shall pass away, but my words shall not pass away.

36 ¶ But of that day and hour knoweth no *man*, no, not the angels of heaven, but my Father only.

37 But as the days of No'e *were*, so shall also the coming of the Son of man be.

38 For as in the days that were before the flood they were eating and drinking, marrying and giving in marriage, until the day that No'e entered into the ark,

39 And knew not until the flood came, and took them all away; so shall also the coming of the Son of man be.

40 Then shall two be in the field; the one shall be taken, and the other left.

41 Two *women shall be* grinding at the mill; the one shall be taken, and the other left.

42 ¶ Watch therefore: for ye know not what hour your Lord doth come.

43 But know this, that if the goodman of the house had known in what watch the thief would come, he would have watched, and would not have suffered his house to be broken up.

44 Therefore be ye also ready: for in such an hour as ye think not the Son of man cometh.

45 Who then is a faithful and wise servant, whom his lord hath made ruler over his household, to give them meat in due season?

46 Blessed *is* that servant, whom his lord when he cometh shall find so doing.

47 Verily I say unto you, That he shall make him ruler over all his goods.

48 But and if that evil servant shall say in his heart, My lord delayeth his coming;

49 And shall begin to smite *his* fellowservants, and to eat and drink with the drunken;

50 The lord of that servant shall come in a day when he looketh not for *him*, and in an hour that he is not aware of,

51 And shall cut him asunder, and appoint *him* his portion with the hypocrites: there shall be weeping and gnashing of teeth.

25

THEN shall the kingdom of heaven be likened unto ten virgins, which took their lamps, and went forth to meet the bridegroom.

2 And five of them were wise, and five *were* foolish.

3 They that *were* foolish took their lamps, and took no oil with them:

4 But the wise took oil in their vessels with their lamps.

5 While the bridegroom tarried, they all slumbered and slept.

6 And at midnight there was a cry made, Behold, the bridegroom cometh; go ye out to meet him.

7 Then all those virgins arose, and trimmed their lamps.

8 And the foolish said unto the wise, Give us of your oil; for our lamps are gone out.

9 But the wise answered, saying, *Not so;* lest there be not enough for us and you: but go ye rather to them that sell, and buy for yourselves.

10 And while they went to buy, the bridegroom came; and they that were ready went in

with him to the marriage: and the door was
shut.
11 Afterward came also the other virgins,
saying, Lord, Lord, open to us.
12 But he answered and said, Verily I say
unto you, I know you not.
13 Watch therefore, for ye know neither the
day nor the hour wherein the Son of man cometh.
14 ¶ For *the kingdom of heaven is* as a man
travelling into a far country, *who* called his own
servants, and delivered unto them his goods.
15 And unto one he gave five talents, to another two, and to another one; to every man according to his several ability; and straightway
took his journey.
16 Then he that had received the five talents
went and traded with the same, and made *them*
other five talents.
17 And likewise he that *had received* two, he
also gained other two.
18 But he that had received one went and
digged in the earth, and hid his lord's money.
19 After a long time the lord of those servants cometh, and reckoneth with them.
20 And so he that had received five talents
came and brought other five talents, saying,
Lord, thou deliveredst unto me five talents: behold, I have gained beside them five talents
more.
21 His lord said unto him, Well done, *thou*
good and faithful servant: thou hast been faithful over a few things, I will make thee ruler over
many things: enter thou into the joy of thy lord.
22 He also that had received two talents
came and said, Lord, thou deliveredst unto me
two talents: behold, I have gained two other talents beside them.
23 His lord said unto him, Well done, good
and faithful servant; thou hast been faithful
over a few things, I will make thee ruler over
many things: enter thou into the joy of thy lord.
24 Then he which had received the one talent
came and said, Lord, I knew thee that thou art
an hard man, reaping where thou hast not
sown, and gathering where thou hast not
strawed:
25 And I was afraid, and went and hid thy
talent in the earth: lo, *there* thou hast *that is*
thine.
26 His lord answered and said unto him,
Thou wicked and slothful servant, thou knewest that I reap where I sowed not, and gather
where I have not strawed:
27 Thou oughtest therefore to have put my
money to the exchangers, and *then* at my coming I should have received mine own with
usury.
28 Take therefore the talent from him, and
give *it* unto him which hath ten talents.
29 For unto every one that hath shall be given, and he shall have abundance: but from him
that hath not shall be taken away even that
which he hath.
30 And cast ye the unprofitable servant into
outer darkness: there shall be weeping and
gnashing of teeth.
31 ¶ When the Son of man shall come in his
glory, and all the holy angels with him, then
shall he sit upon the throne of his glory:
32 And before him shall be gathered all nations; and he shall separate them one from another, as a shepherd divideth *his* sheep from the
goats:
33 And he shall set the sheep on his right
hand, but the goats on the left.
34 Then shall the King say unto them on his
right hand, Come, ye blessed of my Father, inherit the kingdom prepared for you from the
foundation of the world:
35 For I was an hungred, and ye gave me
meat: I was thirsty, and ye gave me drink: I was
a stranger, and ye took me in:
36 Naked, and ye clothed me: I was sick, and
ye visited me: I was in prison, and ye came unto
me.
37 Then shall the righteous answer him, saying, Lord, when saw we thee an hungred, and
fed *thee?* or thirsty, and gave *thee* drink?
38 When saw we thee a stranger, and took
thee in? or naked, and clothed *thee?*
39 Or when saw we thee sick, or in prison,
and came unto thee?
40 And the King shall answer and say unto
them, Verily I say unto you, Inasmuch as ye
have done *it* unto one of the least of these my
brethren, ye have done *it* unto me.
41 Then shall he say also unto them on the
left hand, Depart from me, ye cursed, into everlasting fire, prepared for the devil and his angels:
42 For I was an hungred, and ye gave me no
meat: I was thirsty, and ye gave me no drink:
43 I was a stranger, and ye took me not in:
naked, and ye clothed me not: sick, and in
prison, and ye visited me not.
44 Then shall they also answer him, saying,
Lord, when saw we thee an hungred, or athirst,
or a stranger, or naked, or sick, or in prison, and
did not minister unto thee?
45 Then shall he answer them, saying, Verily
I say unto you, Inasmuch as ye did *it* not to one
of the least of these, ye did *it* not to me.
46 And these shall go away into everlasting
punishment: but the righteous into life eternal.

26 AND it came to pass, when Je'sus had
finished all these sayings, he said unto
his disciples,
2 Ye know that after two days is *the feast of*
the passover, and the Son of man is betrayed to
be crucified.
3 Then assembled together the chief priests,
and the scribes, and the elders of the people,
unto the palace of the high priest, who was
called Ca'ia-phas,
4 And consulted that they might take Je'sus
by subtilty, and kill *him.*
5 But they said, Not on the feast *day,* lest
there be an uproar among the people.
6 ¶ Now when Je'sus was in Beth'a-ny, in the
house of Si'mon the leper,
7 There came unto him a woman having an
alabaster box of very precious ointment, and
poured it on his head, as he sat *at meat.*
8 But when his disciples saw *it,* they had indignation, saying, To what purpose *is* this
waste?
9 For this ointment might have been sold for
much, and given to the poor.
10 When Je'sus understood *it,* he said unto
them, Why trouble ye the woman? for she hath
wrought a good work upon me.
11 For ye have the poor always with you; but
me ye have not always.
12 For in that she hath poured this ointment
on my body, she did *it* for my burial.
13 Verily I say unto you, Wheresoever this
gospel shall be preached in the whole world,
there shall also this, that this woman hath done,
be told for a memorial of her.
14 ¶ Then one of the twelve, called Ju'das Iscar'i-ot, went unto the chief priests,
15 And said *unto them,* What will ye give

me, and I will deliver him unto you? And they
covenanted with him for thirty pieces of silver.
16 And from that time he sought opportunity
to betray him.
17 ¶ Now the first *day* of the *feast of* unleavened bread the disciples came to Je'sus, saying
unto him, Where wilt thou that we prepare for
thee to eat the passover?
18 And he said, Go into the city to such a
man, and say unto him, The Master saith, My
time is at hand; I will keep the passover at thy
house with my disciples.
19 And the disciples did as Je'sus had appointed them; and they made ready the passover.
20 Now when the even was come, he sat
down with the twelve.
21 And as they did eat, he said, Verily I say
unto you, that one of you shall betray me.
22 And they were exceeding sorrowful, and
began every one of them to say unto him, Lord,
is it I?
23 And he answered and said, He that dippeth *his* hand with me in the dish, the same
shall betray me.
24 The Son of man goeth as it is written of
him: but woe unto that man by whom the Son
of man is betrayed! it had been good for that
man if he had not been born.
25 Then Ju'das, which betrayed him, answered and said, Master, is it I? He said unto
him, Thou hast said.
26 ¶ And as they were eating, Je'sus took
bread, and blessed *it*, and brake *it*, and gave *it*
to the disciples, and said, Take, eat; this is my
body.
27 And he took the cup, and gave thanks,
and gave *it* to them, saying, Drink ye all of it;
28 For this is my blood of the new testament,
which is shed for many for the remission of
sins.
29 But I say unto you, I will not drink henceforth of this fruit of the vine, until that day
when I drink it new with you in my Father's
kingdom.
30 And when they had sung an hymn, they
went out into the mount of Ol'ives.
31 Then saith Je'sus unto them, All ye shall
be offended because of me this night: for it is
written, I will smite the shepherd, and the sheep
of the flock shall be scattered abroad.
32 But after I am risen again, I will go before
you into Gal'i-lee.
33 Pe'ter answered and said unto him,
Though all *men* shall be offended because of
thee, *yet* will I never be offended.
34 Je'sus said unto him, Verily I say unto
thee, That this night, before the cock crow, thou
shalt deny me thrice.
35 Pe'ter said unto him, Though I should die
with thee, yet will I not deny thee. Likewise also
said all the disciples.
36 ¶ Then cometh Je'sus with them unto a
place called Geth-sem'a-ne, and saith unto the
disciples, Sit ye here, while I go and pray yonder.
37 And he took with him Pe'ter and the two
sons of Zeb'e-dee, and began to be sorrowful
and very heavy.
38 Then saith he unto them, My soul is exceeding sorrowful, even unto death: tarry ye
here, and watch with me.
39 And he went a little farther, and fell on his
face, and prayed, saying, O my Father, if it be
possible, let this cup pass from me: nevertheless not as I will, but as thou *wilt*.
40 And he cometh unto the disciples, and
findeth them asleep, and saith unto Pe'ter,
What, could ye not watch with me one hour?
41 Watch and pray, that ye enter not into
temptation: the spirit indeed *is* willing, but the
flesh *is* weak.
42 He went away again the second time, and
prayed, saying, O my Father, if this cup may
not pass away from me, except I drink it, thy
will be done.
43 And he came and found them asleep
again: for their eyes were heavy.
44 And he left them, and went away again,
and prayed the third time, saying the same
words.
45 Then cometh he to his disciples, and saith
unto them, Sleep on now, and take *your* rest:
behold, the hour is at hand, and the Son of man
is betrayed into the hands of sinners.
46 Rise, let us be going: behold, he is at hand
that doth betray me.
47 ¶ And while he yet spake, lo, Ju'das, one
of the twelve, came, and with him a great multitude with swords and staves, from the chief
priests and elders of the people.
48 Now he that betrayed him gave them a
sign, saying, Whomsoever I shall kiss, that
same is he: hold him fast.
49 And forthwith he came to Je'sus, and said,
Hail, master; and kissed him.
50 And Je'sus said unto him, Friend, wherefore art thou come? Then came they, and laid
hands on Je'sus, and took him.
51 And, behold, one of them which were with
Je'sus stretched out *his* hand, and drew his
sword, and struck a servant of the high priest's,
and smote off his ear.
52 Then said Je'sus unto him, Put up again
thy sword into his place: for all they that take
the sword shall perish with the sword.
53 Thinkest thou that I cannot now pray to
my Father, and he shall presently give me more
than twelve legions of angels?
54 But how then shall the scriptures be fulfilled, that thus it must be?
55 In that same hour said Je'sus to the multitudes, Are ye come out as against a thief with
swords and staves for to take me? I sat daily
with you teaching in the temple, and ye laid no
hold on me.
56 But all this was done, that the scriptures
of the prophets might be fulfilled. Then all the
disciples forsook him, and fled.
57 ¶ And they that had laid hold on Je'sus
led *him* away to Ca'ia-phas the high priest,
where the scribes and the elders were assembled.
58 But Pe'ter followed him afar off unto the
high priest's palace, and went in, and sat with
the servants, to see the end.
59 Now the chief priests, and elders, and all
the council, sought false witness against Je'sus,
to put him to death;
60 But found none: yea, though many false
witnesses came, *yet* found they none. At the
last came two false witnesses,
61 And said, This *fellow* said, I am able to
destroy the temple of God, and to build it in
three days.
62 And the high priest arose, and said unto
him, Answerest thou nothing? what *is it which*
these witness against thee?
63 But Je'sus held his peace. And the high
priest answered and said unto him, I adjure
thee by the living God, that thou tell us whether
thou be the Christ, the Son of God.
64 Je'sus saith unto him, Thou hast said: nevertheless I say unto you, Hereafter shall ye see

the Son of man sitting on the right hand of power, and coming in the clouds of heaven.

65 Then the high priest rent his clothes, saying, He hath spoken blasphemy; what further need have we of witnesses? behold, now ye have heard his blasphemy.

66 What think ye? They answered and said, He is guilty of death.

67 Then did they spit in his face, and buffeted him; and others smote *him* with the palms of their hands,

68 Saying, Prophesy unto us, thou Christ, Who is he that smote thee?

69 ¶ Now Pe'ter sat without in the palace: and a damsel came unto him, saying, Thou also wast with Je'sus of Gal'i-lee.

70 But he denied before *them* all, saying, I know not what thou sayest.

71 And when he was gone out into the porch, another *maid* saw him, and said unto them that were there, This *fellow* was also with Je'sus of Naz'a-reth.

72 And again he denied with an oath, I do not know the man.

73 And after a while came unto *him* they that stood by, and said to Pe'ter, Surely thou also art *one* of them; for thy speech bewrayeth thee.

74 Then began he to curse and to swear, *saying*, I know not the man. And immediately the cock crew.

75 And Pe'ter remembered the word of Je'sus, which said unto him, Before the cock crow, thou shalt deny me thrice. And he went out, and wept bitterly.

27

WHEN the morning was come, all the chief priests and elders of the people took counsel against Je'sus to put him to death:

2 And when they had bound him, they led *him* away, and delivered him to Pon'ti-us Pi'late the governor.

3 ¶ Then Ju'das, which had betrayed him, when he saw that he was condemned, repented himself, and brought again the thirty pieces of silver to the chief priests and elders,

4 Saying, I have sinned in that I have betrayed the innocent blood. And they said, What *is that* to us? see thou *to that*.

5 And he cast down the pieces of silver in the temple, and departed, and went and hanged himself.

6 And the chief priests took the silver pieces, and said, It is not lawful for to put them into the treasury, because it is the price of blood.

7 And they took counsel, and bought with them the potter's field, to bury strangers in.

8 Wherefore that field was called, The field of blood, unto this day.

9 Then was fulfilled that which was spoken by Jer'e-my the prophet, saying, And they took the thirty pieces of silver, the price of him that was valued, whom they of the children of Is'ra-el did value;

10 And gave them for the potter's field, as the Lord appointed me.

11 And Je'sus stood before the governor: and the governor asked him, saying, Art thou the King of the Jews? And Je'sus said unto him, Thou sayest.

12 And when he was accused of the chief priests and elders, he answered nothing.

13 Then said Pi'late unto him, Hearest thou not how many things they witness against thee?

14 And he answered him to never a word; insomuch that the governor marvelled greatly.

15 Now at *that* feast the governor was wont to release unto the people a prisoner, whom they would.

16 And they had then a notable prisoner, called Ba-rab'bas.

17 Therefore when they were gathered together, Pi'late said unto them, Whom will ye that I release unto you? Ba-rab'bas, or Je'sus which is called Christ?

18 For he knew that for envy they had delivered him.

19 ¶ When he was set down on the judgment seat, his wife sent unto him, saying, Have thou nothing to do with that just man: for I have suffered many things this day in a dream because of him,

20 But the chief priests and elders persuaded the multitude that they should ask Ba-rab'bas, and destroy Je'sus.

21 The governor answered and said unto them, Whether of the twain will ye that I release unto you? They said, Ba-rab'bas.

22 Pi'late saith unto them, What shall I do then with Je'sus which is called Christ? *They* all say unto him, Let him be crucified.

23 And the governor said, Why, what evil hath he done? But they cried out the more, saying, Let him be crucified.

24 ¶ When Pi'late saw that he could prevail nothing, but *that* rather a tumult was made, he took water, and washed *his* hands before the multitude, saying, I am innocent of the blood of this just person: see ye *to it*.

25 Then answered all the people, and said, His blood *be* on us, and on our children.

26 ¶ Then released he Ba-rab'bas unto them: and when he had scourged Je'sus, he delivered *him* to be crucified.

27 Then the soldiers of the governor took Je'sus into the common hall, and gathered unto him the whole band *of soldiers*.

28 And they stripped him, and put on him a scarlet robe.

29 ¶ And when they had platted a crown of thorns, they put *it* upon his head, and a reed in his right hand: and they bowed the knee before him, and mocked him, saying, Hail, King of the Jews!

30 And they spit upon him, and took the reed, and smote him on the head.

31 And after that they had mocked him, they took the robe off from him, and put his own raiment on him, and led him away to crucify *him*.

32 And as they came out, they found a man of Cy-re'ne, Si'mon by name: him they compelled to bear his cross.

33 And when they were come unto a place called Gol'go-tha, that is to say, a place of a skull,

34 ¶ They gave him vinegar to drink mingled with gall: and when he had tasted *thereof*, he would not drink.

35 And they crucified him, and parted his garments, casting lots: that it might be fulfilled which was spoken by the prophet, They parted my garments among them, and upon my vesture did they cast lots.

36 And sitting down they watched him there;

37 And set up over his head his accusation written, THIS IS JE'SUS THE KING OF THE JEWS.

38 Then were there two thieves crucified with him, one on the right hand, and another on the left.

39 ¶ And they that passed by reviled him, wagging their heads,

40 And saying, Thou that destroyest the tem-

ple, and buildest *it* in three days, save thyself. If
thou be the Son of God, come down from the
cross.
41 Likewise also the chief priests mocking
him, with the scribes and elders, said,
42 He saved others; himself he cannot save.
If he be the King of Is'ra-el, let him now come
down from the cross, and we will believe him.
43 He trusted in God; let him deliver him
now, if he will have him: for he said, I am the
Son of God.
44 The thieves also, which were crucified
with him, cast the same in his teeth.
45 Now from the sixth hour there was darkness over all the land unto the ninth hour.
46 And about the ninth hour Je'sus cried
with a loud voice, saying, E'li, E'li, la'ma sa-
bach-tha'ni? that is to say, My God, my God,
why hast thou forsaken me?
47 Some of them that stood there, when they
heard *that*, said, This *man* calleth for E-li'as.
48 And straightway one of them ran, and
took a spunge, and filled *it* with vinegar, and
put *it* on a reed, and gave him to drink.
49 The rest said, Let be, let us see whether E-
li'as will come to save him.
50 ¶ Je'sus, when he had cried again with a
loud voice, yielded up the ghost.
51 And, behold, the veil of the temple was
rent in twain from the top to the bottom; and
the earth did quake, and the rocks rent;
52 And the graves were opened; and many
bodies of the saints which slept arose,
53 And came out of the graves after his resurrection, and went into the holy city, and appeared unto many.
54 Now when the centurion, and they that
were with him, watching Je'sus, saw the earthquake, and those things that were done, they
feared greatly, saying, Truly this was the Son of
God.
55 And many women were there beholding
afar off, which followed Je'sus from Gal'i-lee,
ministering unto him:
56 Among which was Ma'ry Mag-da-le'ne,
and Ma'ry the mother of James and Jo'ses, and
the mother of Zeb'e-dee's children.
57 When the even was come, there came a
rich man of Ar-i-ma-thæ'a, named Jo'seph, who
also himself was Je'sus' disciple:
58 He went to Pi'late, and begged the body of
Je'sus. Then Pi'late commanded the body to be
delivered.
59 And when Jo'seph had taken the body, he
wrapped it in a clean linen cloth,
60 And laid it in his own new tomb, which he
had hewn out in the rock: and he rolled a great
stone to the door of the sepulchre, and departed.
61 And there was Ma'ry Mag-da-le'ne, and
the other Ma'ry, sitting over against the sepulchre.
62 ¶ Now the next day, that followed the day
of the preparation, the chief priests and Phar'i-
sees came together unto Pi'late,
63 Saying, Sir, we remember that that deceiver said, while he was yet alive, After three
days I will rise again.
64 Command therefore that the sepulchre be
made sure until the third day, lest his disciples
come by night, and steal him away, and say
unto the people, He is risen from the dead: so
the last error shall be worse than the first.
65 Pi'late said unto them, Ye have a watch:
go your way, make *it* as sure as ye can.
66 So they went, and made the sepulchre
sure, sealing the stone, and setting a watch.

28 IN the end of the sabbath, as it began to
dawn toward the first *day* of the week,
came Ma'ry Mag-da-le'ne and the other Ma'ry
to see the sepulchre.
2 And, behold, there was a great earthquake:
for the angel of the Lord descended from
heaven, and came and rolled back the stone
from the door, and sat upon it.
3 His countenance was like lightning, and his
raiment white as snow:
4 And for fear of him the keepers did shake,
and became as dead *men*,
5 And the angel answered and said unto the
women, Fear not ye: for I know that ye seek
Je'sus, which was crucified.
6 He is not here: for he is risen, as he said,
Come, see the place where the Lord lay.
7 And go quickly, and tell his disciples that
he is risen from the dead; and, behold, he goeth
before you into Gal'i-lee; there shall ye see him:
lo, I have told you.
8 And they departed quickly from the sepulchre with fear and great joy; and did run to
bring his disciples word.
9 ¶ And as they went to tell his disciples, behold, Je'sus met them, saying All hail. And they
came and held him by the feet, and worshipped
him.
10 Then said Je'sus unto them, Be not afraid:
go tell my brethren that they go into Gal'i-lee,
and there shall they see me.
11 ¶ Now when they were going, behold,
some of the watch came into the city, and
shewed unto the chief priests all the things that
were done.
12 And when they were assembled with the
elders, and had taken counsel, they gave large
money unto the soldiers,
13 Saying, Say ye, His disciples came by
night, and stole him *away* while we slept.
14 And if this come to the governor's ears,
we will persuade him, and secure you.
15 So they took the money, and did as they
were taught: and this saying is commonly reported among the Jews until this day.
16 ¶ Then the eleven disciples went away
into Gal'i-lee, into a mountain where Je'sus had
appointed them.
17 And when they saw him, they worshipped
him: but some doubted.
18 And Je'sus came and spake unto them,
saying, All power is given unto me in heaven
and in earth.
19 Go ye therefore, and teach all nations,
baptizing them in the name of the Father, and
of the Son, and of the Ho'ly Ghost:
20 Teaching them to observe all things whatsoever I have commanded you: and, lo, I am
with you alway, *even* unto the end of the world.
Amen.

THE GOSPEL ACCORDING TO

MARK

1 THE beginning of the gospel of Je'sus
Christ, the Son of God;
2 As it is written in the prophets, Behold, I
send my messenger before thy face, which shall
prepare thy way before thee.
3 The voice of one crying in the wilderness,
Prepare ye the way of the Lord, make his paths
straight.
4 John did baptize in the wilderness, and
preach the baptism of repentance for the remission of sins.
5 And there went out unto him all the land of
Ju-dæ'a, and they of Je-ru'sa-lem, and were all
baptized of him in the river of Jor'dan, confessing their sins.
6 And John was clothed with camel's hair,
and with a girdle of a skin about his loins; and
he did eat locusts and wild honey;
7 And preached, saying, There cometh one
mightier than I after me, the latchet of whose
shoes I am not worthy to stoop down and unloose.
8 I indeed have baptized you with water: but
he shall baptize you with the Ho'ly Ghost.
9 And it came to pass in those days, that Je'-
sus came from Naz'a-reth of Gal'i-lee, and was
baptized of John in Jor'dan.
10 And straightway coming up out of the water, he saw the heavens opened, and the Spirit
like a dove descending upon him:
11 And there came a voice from heaven, *saying,* Thou art my beloved Son, in whom I am
well pleased.
12 And immediately the spirit driveth him
into the wilderness.
13 And he was there in the wilderness forty
days, tempted of Sa'tan; and was with the wild
beasts; and the angels ministered unto him.
14 Now after that John was put in prison, Je'-
sus came into Gal'i-lee, preaching the gospel of
the kingdom of God,
15 And saying, The time is fulfilled, and the
kingdom of God is at hand: repent ye, and believe the gospel.
16 Now as he walked by the sea of Gal'i-lee,
he saw Si'mon and Andrew his brother casting
a net into the sea: for they were fishers.
17 And Je'sus said unto them, Come ye after
me, and I will make you to become fishers of
men.
18 And straightway they forsook their nets,
and followed him.
19 And when he had gone a little farther
thence, he saw James the *son* of Zeb'e-dee, and
John his brother, who also were in the ship
mending their nets.
20 And straightway he called them: and they
left their father Zeb'e-dee in the ship with the
hired servants, and went after him.
21 And they went into Ca-per'na-um; and
straightway on the sabbath day he entered into
the synagogue, and taught.
22 And they were astonished at his doctrine:
for he taught them as one that had authority,
and not as the scribes.
23 And there was in their synagogue a man
with an unclean spirit; and he cried out,
24 Saying, Let *us* alone; what have we to do
with thee, thou Je'sus of Naz'a-reth? art thou
come to destroy us? I know thee who thou art,
the Holy One of God.
25 And Je'sus rebuked him, saying, Hold thy
peace, and come out of him.
26 And when the unclean spirit had torn him,
and cried with a loud voice, he came out of him.
27 And they were all amazed, insomuch that
they questioned among themselves, saying,
What thing is this? what new doctrine *is* this?
for with authority commandeth he even the unclean spirits, and they do obey him.
28 And immediately his fame spread abroad
throughout all the region round about Gal'i-lee.
29 And forthwith, when they were come out
of the synagogue, they entered into the house of
Si'mon and Andrew, with James and John.
30 But Si'mon's wife's mother lay sick of a
fever, and anon they tell him of her.
31 And he came and took her by the hand,
and lifted her up; and immediately the fever left
her, and she ministered unto them.
32 And at even, when the sun did set, they
brought unto him all that were diseased, and
them that were possessed with devils.
33 And all the city was gathered together at
the door.
34 And he healed many that were sick of divers diseases, and cast out many devils; and
suffered not the devils to speak, because they
knew him.
35 And in the morning, rising up a great
while before day, he went out, and departed
into a solitary place, and there prayed.
36 And Si'mon and they that were with him
followed after him.
37 And when they had found him, they said
unto him, All *men* seek for thee.
38 And he said unto them, Let us go into the
next towns, that I may preach there also: for
therefore came I forth.
39 And he preached in their synagogues
throughout all Gal'i-lee, and cast out devils.
40 And there came a leper to him, beseeching him, and kneeling down to him, and saying
unto him, If thou wilt, thou canst make me
clean.
41 And Je'sus, moved with compassion, put
forth *his* hand, and touched him, and saith unto
him, I will; be thou clean.
42 And as soon as he had spoken, immediately the leprosy departed from him, and he
was cleansed.
43 And he straitly charged him, and forthwith sent him away;
44 And saith unto him, See thou say nothing
to any man: but go thy way, shew thyself to the
priest, and offer for thy cleansing those things
which Mo'ses commanded, for a testimony unto
them.
45 But he went out, and began to publish *it*
much, and to blaze abroad the matter, insomuch that Je'sus could no more openly enter
into the city, but was without in desert places:
and they came to him from every quarter.

2 AND again he entered into Ca-per'na-um
after *some* days; and it was noised that he
was in the house.
2 And straightway many were gathered together, insomuch that there was no room to receive *them,* no, not so much as about the door:
and he preached the word unto them.
3 And they come unto him, bringing one sick
of the palsy, which was borne of four.

4 And when they could not come nigh unto
him for the press, they uncovered the roof
where he was: and when they had broken *it* up,
they let down the bed wherein the sick of the
palsy lay.
5 When Je'sus saw their faith, he said unto
the sick of the palsy, Son, thy sins be forgiven
thee.
6 But there were certain of the scribes sitting
there, and reasoning in their hearts,
7 Why doth this *man* thus speak blasphemies? who can forgive sins but God only?
8 And immediately when Je'sus perceived in
his spirit that they so reasoned within themselves, he said unto them, Why reason ye these
things in your hearts?
9 Whether is it easier to say to the sick of the
palsy, *Thy* sins be forgiven thee; or to say,
Arise, and take up thy bed, and walk?
10 But that ye may know that the Son of man
hath power on earth to forgive sins, (he saith to
the sick of the palsy,)
11 I say unto thee, Arise, and take up thy
bed, and go thy way into thine house.
12 And immediately he arose, took up the
bed, and went forth before them all; insomuch
that they were all amazed, and glorified God,
saying, We never saw it on this fashion.
13 And he went forth again by the sea side;
and all the multitude resorted unto him, and he
taught them.
14 And as he passed by, he saw Le'vi the *son*
of Al-phæ'us sitting at the receipt of custom,
and said unto him, Follow me. And he arose
and followed him.
15 And it came to pass, that, as Je'sus sat at
meat in his house, many publicans and sinners
sat also together with Je'sus and his disciples:
for there were many, and they followed him.
16 And when the scribes and Phar'i-sees saw
him eat with publicans and sinners, they said
unto his disciples, How is it that he eateth and
drinketh with publicans and sinners?
17 When Je'sus heard *it*, he saith unto them,
They that are whole have no need of the physician, but they that are sick: I came not to call
the righteous, but sinners to repentance.
18 And the disciples of John and of the Phar'-
i-sees used to fast: and they come and say unto
him, Why do the disciples of John and of the
Phar'i-sees fast, but thy disciples fast not?
19 And Je'sus said unto them, Can the children of the bridechamber fast, while the bridegroom is with them? as long as they have the
bridegroom with them, they cannot fast.
20 But the days will come, when the bridegroom shall be taken away from them, and then
shall they fast in those days.
21 No man also seweth a piece of new cloth
on an old garment: else the new piece that filled
it up taketh away from the old, and the rent is
made worse.
22 And no man putteth new wine into old
bottles: else the new wine doth burst the bottles, and the wine is spilled, and the bottles will
be marred: but new wine must be put into new
bottles.
23 And it came to pass, that he went through
the corn fields on the sabbath day; and his disciples began, as they went, to pluck the ears of
corn.
24 And the Phar'i-sees said unto him, Behold,
why do they on the sabbath day that which is
not lawful?
25 And he said unto them, Have ye never
read what Da'vid did, when he had need, and
was an hungred, he, and they that were with
him?
26 How he went into the house of God in the
days of A-bi'a-thar the high priest, and did eat
the shewbread, which is not lawful to eat but
for the priests, and gave also to them which
were with him?
27 And he said unto them, The sabbath was
made for man, and not man for the sabbath:
28 Therefore the Son of man is Lord also of
the sabbath.

3 AND he entered again into the synagogue;
and there was a man there which had a
withered hand.
2 And they watched him, whether he would
heal him on the sabbath day; that they might
accuse him.
3 And he saith unto the man which had the
withered hand, Stand forth.
4 And he saith unto them, Is it lawful to do
good on the sabbath days, or to do evil? to save
life, or to kill? But they held their peace.
5 And when he had looked round about on
them with anger, being grieved for the hardness
of their hearts, he saith unto the man, Stretch
forth thine hand. And he stretched *it* out: and
his hand was restored whole as the other.
6 And the Phar'i-sees went forth, and
straightway took counsel with the He-ro'di-ans
against him, how they might destroy him.
7 But Je'sus withdrew himself with his disciples to the sea: and a great multitude from Gal'-
i-lee followed him, and from Ju-dæ'a,
8 And from Je-ru'sa-lem, and from I-du-mæ'-
a, and *from* beyond Jor'dan; and they about
Tyre and Si'don, a great multitude, when they
had heard what great things he did, came unto
him.
9 And he spake to his disciples, that a small
ship should wait on him because of the multitude, lest they should throng him.
10 For he had healed many; insomuch that
they pressed upon him for to touch him, as
many as had plagues.
11 And unclean spirits, when they saw him,
fell down before him, and cried, saying, Thou
art the Son of God.
12 And he straitly charged them that they
should not make him known.
13 And he goeth up into a mountain, and
calleth *unto him* whom he would: and they
came unto him.
14 And he ordained twelve, that they should
be with him, and that he might send them forth
to preach,
15 And to have power to heal sicknesses, and
to cast out devils:
16 And Si'mon he surnamed Pe'ter;
17 And James the *son* of Zeb'e-dee, and John
the brother of James; and he surnamed them
Bo-an-er'ges, which is, The sons of thunder:
18 And Andrew, and Phil'ip, and Bar-thol'o-
mew, and Mat'thew, and Thom'as, and James
the *son* of Al-phæ'us, and Thad-dæ'us, and Si'-
mon the Ca'naan-ite,
19 And Ju'das Is-car'i-ot, which also betrayed him: and they went into an house.
20 And the multitude cometh together again,
so that they could not so much as eat bread.
21 And when his friends heard *of it*, they
went out to lay hold on him: for they said, He is
beside himself.
22 ¶ And the scribes which came down from
Je-ru'sa-lem said, He hath Beel'ze-bub, and by
the prince of the devils casteth he out devils.
23 And he called them *unto him*, and said

unto them in parables, How can Sa'tan cast out Sa'tan?
24 And if a kingdom be divided against itself, that kingdom cannot stand.
25 And if a house be divided against itself, that house cannot stand.
26 And if Sa'tan rise up against himself, and be divided, he cannot stand, but hath an end.
27 No man can enter into a strong man's house, and spoil his goods, except he will first bind the strong man; and then he will spoil his house.
28 Verily I say unto you, All sins shall be forgiven unto the sons of men, and blasphemies wherewith soever they shall blaspheme:
29 But he that shall blaspheme againt the Ho'ly Ghost hath never forgiveness, but is in danger of eternal damnation:
30 **Because they said, He hath an unclean spirit.**
31 ¶ **There came then his brethren and his mother, and, standing without, sent unto him, calling him.**
32 **And the multitude sat about him, and they said unto him, Behold, thy mother and thy brethren without seek for thee.**
33 **And he answered them, saying,** Who is my mother, or my brethren?
34 **And he looked round about on them which sat about him, and said,** Behold my mother and my brethren!
35 For whosoever shall do the will of God, the same is my brother, and my sister, and mother.

4 **AND he began again to teach by the sea side: and there was gathered unto him a great multitude, so that he entered into a ship, and sat in the sea; and the whole multitude was by the sea on the land.**
2 **And he taught them many things by parables, and said unto them in his doctrine,**
3 Hearken; Behold, there went out a sower to sow:
4 And it came to pass, as he sowed, some fell by the way side, and the fowls of the air came and devoured it up.
5 And some fell on stony ground, where it had not much earth; and immediately it sprang up, because it had no depth of earth:
6 But when the sun was up, it was scorched; and because it had no root, it withered away.
7 And some fell among thorns, and the thorns grew up, and choked it, and it yielded no fruit.
8 And other fell on good ground, and did yield fruit that sprang up and increased; and brought forth, some thirty, and some sixty, and some an hundred.
9 **And he said unto them,** He that hath ears to hear, let him hear.
10 **And when he was alone, they that were about him with the twelve asked of him the parable.**
11 **And he said unto them,** Unto you it is given to know the mystery of the kingdom of God: but unto them that are without, all *these* things are done in parables:
12 That seeing they may see, and not perceive; and hearing they may hear, and not understand; lest at any time they should be converted, and *their* sins should be forgiven them.
13 **And he said unto them,** Know ye not this parable? and how then will ye know all parables?
14 ¶ The sower soweth the word.
15 And these are they by the way side, where the word is sown; but when they have heard, Sa'tan cometh immediately, and taketh away the word that was sown in their hearts.
16 And these are they likewise which are sown on stony ground; who, when they have heard the word, immediately receive it with gladness;
17 And have no root in themselves, and so endure but for a time: afterward, when affliction or persecution ariseth for the word's sake, immediately they are offended.
18 And these are they which are sown among thorns; such as hear the word,
19 And the cares of this world, and the deceitfulness of riches, and the lusts of other things entering in, choke the word, and it becometh unfruitful.
20 And these are they which are sown on good ground; such as hear the word, and receive *it*, and bring forth fruit, some thirtyfold, some sixty, and some an hundred.
21 ¶ **And he said unto them,** Is a candle brought to be put under a bushel, or under a bed? and not to set on a candlestick?
22 For there is nothing hid, which shall not be manifested; neither was anything kept secret, but that it should come abroad.
23 If any man have ears to hear, let him hear.
24 **And he said unto them,** Take heed what ye hear: with what measure ye mete, it shall be measured to you: and unto you that hear shall more be given.
25 For he that hath, to him shall be given: and he that hath not, from him shall be taken even that which he hath.
26 ¶ **And he said,** So is the kingdom of God, as if a man should cast seed into the ground;
27 And should sleep, and rise night and day, and the seed should spring and grow up, he knoweth not how.
28 For the earth bringeth forth fruit of herself; first the blade, then the ear, after that the full corn in the ear.
29 But when the fruit is brought forth, immediately he putteth in the sickle, because the harvest is come.
30 ¶ **And he said,** Whereunto shall we liken the kingdom of God? or with what comparison shall we compare it?
31 *It is* like a grain of mustard seed, which, when it is sown in the earth, is less than all the seeds that be in the earth:
32 But when it is sown, it groweth up, and becometh greater than all herbs, and shooteth out great branches; so that the fowls of the air may lodge under the shadow of it.
33 **And with many such parables spake he the word unto them, as they were able to hear *it*.**
34 **But without a parable spake he not unto them: and when they were alone, he expounded all things to his disciples.**
35 **And the same day, when the even was come, he saith unto them,** Let us pass over unto the other side.
36 **And when they had sent away the multitude, they took him even as he was in the ship. And there were also with him other little ships.**
37 **And there arose a great storm of wind, and the waves beat into the ship, so that it was now full.**
38 **And he was in the hinder part of the ship, asleep on a pillow: and they awake him, and say unto him, Master, carest thou not that we perish?**
39 **And he arose, and rebuked the wind, and**

said unto the sea, Peace, be still. And the wind ceased, and there was a great calm.

40 And he said unto them, Why are ye so fearful? how is it that ye have no faith?

41 And they feared exceedingly, and said one to another, What manner of man is this, that even the wind and the sea obey him?

5 AND they came over unto the other side of the sea, into the country of the Gad'a-renes.

2 And when he was come out of the ship, immediately there met him out of the tombs a man with an unclean spirit,

3 Who had *his* dwelling among the tombs; and no man could bind him, no, not with chains:

4 Because that he had been often bound with fetters and chains, and the chains had been plucked asunder by him, and the fetters broken in pieces: neither could any *man* tame him.

5 And always, night and day, he was in the mountains, and in the tombs, crying, and cutting himself with stones.

6 But when he saw Je'sus afar off, he ran and worshipped him,

7 And cried with a loud voice, and said, What have I to do with thee, Je'sus, *thou* Son of the most high God? I adjure thee by God, that thou torment me not.

8 For he said unto him, Come out of the man, *thou* unclean spirit.

9 And he asked him, What *is* thy name? And he answered, saying, My name *is* Legion: for we are many.

10 And he besought him much that he would not send them away out of the country.

11 Now there was there nigh unto the mountains a great herd of swine feeding.

12 And all the devils besought him, saying, Send us into the swine, that we may enter into them.

13 And forthwith Je'sus gave them leave. And the unclean spirits went out, and entered into the swine: and the herd ran violently down a steep place into the sea, (they were about two thousand;) and were choked in the sea.

14 And they that fed the swine fled, and told *it* in the city, and in the country. And they went out to see what it was that was done.

15 And they come to Je'sus, and see him that was possessed with the devil, and had the legion, sitting, and clothed, and in his right mind: and they were afraid.

16 And they that saw *it* told them how it befell to him that was possessed with the devil, and *also* concerning the swine.

17 And they began to pray him to depart out of their coasts.

18 And when he was come into the ship, he that had been possessed with the devil prayed him that he might be with him.

19 Howbeit Je'sus suffered him not, but saith unto him, Go home to thy friends, and tell them how great things the Lord hath done for thee, and hath had compassion on thee.

20 And he departed, and began to publish in De-cap'o-lis how great things Je'sus had done for him: and all *men* did marvel.

21 And when Je'sus was passed over again by ship unto the other side, much people gathered unto him: and he was nigh unto the sea.

22 And, behold, there cometh one of the rulers of the synagogue, Ja-i'rus by name; and when he saw him, he fell at his feet,

23 And besought him greatly, saying, My little daughter lieth at the point of death: *I pray thee, come* and lay thy hands on her, that she may be healed; and she shall live.

24 And *Jesus* went with him; and much people followed him, and thronged him.

25 And a certain woman, which had an issue of blood twelve years,

26 And had suffered many things of many physicians, and had spent all that she had, and was nothing bettered, but rather grew worse,

27 When she had heard of Je'sus, came in the press behind, and touched his garment.

28 For she said, If I may touch but his clothes, I shall be whole.

29 And straightway the fountain of her blood was dried up; and she felt in *her* body that she was healed of that plague.

30 And Je'sus, immediately knowing in himself that virtue had gone out of him, turned him about in the press, and said, Who touched my clothes?

31 And his disciples said unto him, Thou seest the multitude thronging thee, and sayest thou, Who touched me?

32 And he looked round about to see her that had done this thing.

33 But the woman fearing and trembling, knowing what was done in her, came and fell down before him, and told him all the truth.

34 And he said unto her, Daughter, thy faith hath made thee whole; go in peace, and be whole of thy plague.

35 While he yet spake, there came from the ruler of the synagogue's *house certain* which said, Thy daughter is dead: why troublest thou the Master any further?

36 As soon as Je'sus heard the word that was spoken, he saith unto the ruler of the synagogue, Be not afraid, only believe.

37 And he suffered no man to follow him, save Pe'ter, and James, and John the brother of James.

38 And he cometh to the house of the ruler of the synagogue, and seeth the tumult, and them that wept and wailed greatly.

39 And when he was come in, he saith unto them, Why make ye this ado, and weep? the damsel is not dead, but sleepeth.

40 And they laughed him to scorn. But when he had put them all out, he taketh the father and the mother of the damsel, and them that were with him, and entereth in where the damsel was lying.

41 And he took the damsel by the hand, and said unto her, Tal'i-tha cu'mi; which is, being interpreted, Damsel, I say unto thee, arise.

42 And straightway the damsel arose, and walked; for she was *of the age* of twelve years. And they were astonished with a great astonishment.

43 And he charged them straitly that no man should know it; and commanded that something should be given her to eat.

6 AND he went out from thence, and came into his own country; and his disciples follow him.

2 And when the sabbath day was come, he began to teach in the synagogue: and many hearing *him* were astonished, saying, From whence hath this *man* these things? and what wisdom *is* this which is given unto him, that even such mighty works are wrought by his hands?

3 Is not this the carpenter, the son of Ma'ry, the brother of James, and Jo'ses, and of Ju'da, and Si'mon? and are not his sisters here with us? And they were offended at him.

4 But Je'sus said unto them, A prophet is not
without honour, but in his own country, and
among his own kin, and in his own house.
5 And he could there do no mighty work,
save that he laid his hands upon a few sick folk,
and healed *them*.
6 And he marvelled because of their unbelief.
And he went round about the villages, teaching.
7 ¶ And he called *unto him* the twelve, and
began to send them forth by two and two; and
gave them power over unclean spirits;
8 And commanded them that they should
take nothing for *their* journey, save a staff only;
no scrip, no bread, no money in *their* purse:
9 But *be* shod with sandals; and not put on
two coats.
10 And he said unto them, In what place soever ye enter into an house, there abide till ye
depart from that place.
11 And whosoever shall not receive you, nor
hear you, when ye depart thence, shake off the
dust under your feet for a testimony against
them. Verily I say unto you, It shall be more
tolerable for Sod'om and Go-mor'rha in the day
of judgment, than for that city.
12 And they went out, and preached that
men should repent.
13 And they cast out many devils, and
anointed with oil many that were sick, and
healed *them*.
14 And king Her'od heard *of him*; (for his
name was spread abroad:) and he said, That
John the Bap'tist was risen from the dead, and
therefore mighty works do shew forth themselves in him.
15 Others said, That it is E-li'as. And others
said, That it is a prophet, or as one of the prophets.
16 But when Her'od heard *thereof*, he said, It
is John, whom I beheaded: he is risen from the
dead.
17 For Her'od himself had sent forth and laid
hold upon John, and bound him in prison for
He-ro'di-as' sake, his brother Phil'ip's wife: for
he had married her.
18 For John had said unto Her'od, It is not
lawful for thee to have thy brother's wife.
19 Therefore He-ro'di-as had a quarrel
against him, and would have killed him; but she
could not:
20 For Her'od feared John, knowing that he
was a just man and an holy, and observed him;
and when he heard him, he did many things,
and heard him gladly.
21 And when a convenient day was come,
that Her'od on his birthday made a supper to
his lords, high captains, and chief *estates* of
Gal'i-lee;
22 And when the daughter of the said He-ro'-
di-as came in, and danced, and pleased Her'od
and them that sat with him, the king said unto
the damsel, Ask of me whatsoever thou wilt,
and I will give *it* thee.
23 And he sware unto her, Whatsoever thou
shalt ask of me, I will give *it* thee, unto the half
of my kingdom.
24 And she went forth, and said unto her
mother, What shall I ask? And she said, The
head of John the Bap'tist.
25 And she came in straightway with haste
unto the king, and asked, saying, I will that thou
give me by and by in a charger the head of John
the Bap'tist.
26 And the king was exceeding sorry; *yet* for
his oath's sake, and for their sakes which sat
with him, he would not reject her.
27 And immediately the king sent an execu-
tioner, and commanded his head to be brought:
and he went and beheaded him in the prison,
28 And brought his head in a charger, and
gave it to the damsel: and the damsel gave it to
her mother.
29 And when his disciples heard *of it*, they
came and took up his corpse, and laid it in a
tomb.
30 And the apostles gathered themselves together unto Je'sus, and told him all things, both
what they had done, and what they had taught.
31 And he said unto them, Come ye yourselves apart into a desert place, and rest a
while: for there were many coming and going,
and they had no leisure so much as to eat.
32 And they departed into a desert place by
ship privately.
33 And the people saw them departing, and
many knew him, and ran afoot thither out of all
cities, and outwent them, and came together
unto him.
34 And Je'sus, when he came out, saw much
people, and was moved with compassion
toward them, because they were as sheep not
having a shepherd: and he began to teach them
many things.
35 And when the day was now far spent, his
disciples came unto him, and said, This is a desert place, and now the time *is* far passed:
36 Send them away, that they may go into
the country round about, and into the villages,
and buy themselves bread: for they have nothing to eat.
37 He answered and said unto them, Give ye
them to eat. And they say unto him, Shall we go
and buy two hundred pennyworth of bread, and
give them to eat?
38 He saith unto them, How many loaves
have ye? go and see. And when they knew, they
say, Five, and two fishes.
39 And he commanded them to make all sit
down by companies upon the green grass.
40 And they sat down in ranks, by hundreds,
and by fifties.
41 And when he had taken the five loaves
and the two fishes, he looked up to heaven, and
blessed, and brake the loaves, and gave *them* to
his disciples to set before them; and the two
fishes divided he among them all.
42 And they did all eat, and were filled.
43 And they took up twelve baskets full of
the fragments, and of the fishes.
44 And they that did eat of the loaves were
about five thousand men.
45 And straightway he constrained his disciples to get into the ship, and to go to the other
side before unto Beth-sa'i-da, while he sent
away the people.
46 And when he had sent them away, he departed into a mountain to pray.
47 And when even was come, the ship was in
the midst of the sea, and he alone on the land.
48 And he saw them toiling in rowing; for the
wind was contrary unto them: and about the
fourth watch of the night he cometh unto them,
walking upon the sea, and would have passed
by them.
49 But when they saw him walking upon the
sea, they supposed it had been a spirit, and
cried out:
50 For they all saw him, and were troubled.
And immediately he talked with them, and
saith unto them, Be of good cheer: it is I; be not
afraid.
51 And he went up unto them into the ship;
and the wind ceased: and they were sore

amazed in themselves beyond measure, and wondered.

52 For they considered not *the miracle* of the loaves: for their heart was hardened.

53 And when they had passed over, they came into the land of Gen-nes'a-ret, and drew to the shore.

54 And when they were come out of the ship, straightway they knew him,

55 And ran through that whole region round about, and began to carry about in beds those that were sick, where they heard he was.

56 And whithersoever he entered, into villages, or cities, or country, they laid the sick in the streets, and besought him that they might touch if it were but the border of his garment: and as many as touched him were made whole.

7 THEN came together unto him the Phar'i-sees, and certain of the scribes, which came from Je-ru'sa-lem.

2 And when they saw some of his disciples eat bread with defiled, that is to say, with unwashen, hands, they found fault.

3 For the Phar'i-sees, and all the Jews, except they wash *their* hands oft, eat not, holding the tradition of the elders.

4 And *when they come* from the market, except they wash, they eat not. And many other things there be, which they have received to hold, *as* the washing of cups, and pots, brasen vessels, and of tables.

5 Then the Phar'i-sees and scribes asked him, Why walk not thy disciples according to the tradition of the elders, but eat bread with unwashen hands?

6 He answered and said unto them, Well hath E-sa'ias prophesied of you hypocrites, as it is written, This people honoureth me with *their* lips, but their heart is far from me.

7 Howbeit in vain do they worship me, teaching *for* doctrines the commandments of men.

8 For laying aside the commandment of God, ye hold the tradition of men, *as* the washing of pots and cups: and many other such like things ye do.

9 And he said unto them, Full well ye reject the commandment of God, that ye may keep your own tradition.

10 For Mo'ses said, Honour thy father and thy mother; and, Whoso curseth father or mother, let him die the death:

11 But ye say, If a man shall say to his father or mother, *It is* Corban, that is to say, a gift, by whatsoever thou mightest be profited by me; *he shall be free.*

12 And ye suffer him no more to do ought for his father or his mother;

13 Making the word of God of none effect through your tradition, which ye have delivered: and many such like things do ye.

14 ¶ And when he had called all the people *unto him,* he said unto them, Hearken unto me every one *of you,* and understand:

15 There is nothing from without a man, that entering into him can defile him: but the things which come out of him, those are they that defile the man.

16 If any man have ears to hear, let him hear.

17 And when he was entered into the house from the people, his disciples asked him concerning the parable.

18 And he saith unto them, Are ye so without understanding also? Do ye not perceive, that whatsoever thing from without entereth into the man, *it* cannot defile him;

19 Because it entereth not into his heart, but into the belly, and goeth out into the draught, purging all meats?

20 And he said, That which cometh out of the man, that defileth the man.

21 For from within, out of the heart of men, proceed evil thoughts, adulteries, fornications, murders,

22 Thefts, covetousness, wickedness, deceit, lasciviousness, an evil eye, blasphemy, pride, foolishness:

23 All these evil things come from within, and defile the man.

24 ¶ And from thence he arose, and went into the borders of Tyre and Si'don, and entered into an house, and would have no man know *it:* but he could not be hid.

25 For a *certain* woman, whose young daughter had an unclean spirit, heard of him, and came and fell at his feet:

26 The women was a Greek, a Sy-ro-phe-ni'-cian by nation; and she besought him that he would cast forth the devil out of her daughter.

27 But Je'sus said unto her, Let the children first be filled: for it is not meet to take the children's bread, and to cast *it* unto the dogs.

28 And she answered and said unto him, Yes, Lord: yet the dogs under the table eat of the children's crumbs.

29 And he said unto her, For this saying go thy way; the devil is gone out of thy daughter.

30 And when she was come to her house, she found the devil gone out, and her daughter laid upon the bed.

31 ¶ And again, departing from the coasts of Tyre and Si'don, he came unto the sea of Gal'i-lee, through the midst of the coasts of De-cap'o-lis.

32 And they bring unto him one that was deaf, and had an impediment in his speech; and they beseech him to put his hand upon him.

33 And he took him aside from the multitude, and put his fingers into his ears, and he spit, and touched his tongue;

34 And looking up to heaven, he sighed, and saith unto him, Eph'pha-tha, that is, Be opened.

35 And straightway his ears were opened, and the string of his tongue was loosed, and he spake plain.

36 And he charged them that they should tell no man: but the more he charged them, so much the more a great deal they published *it;*

37 And were beyond measure astonished, saying, He hath done all things well: he maketh both the deaf to hear, and the dumb to speak.

8 IN those days the multitude being very great, and having nothing to eat, Je'sus called his disciples *unto him,* and saith unto them,

2 I have compassion on the multitude, because they have now been with me three days, and have nothing to eat:

3 And if I send them away fasting to their own houses, they will faint by the way: for divers of them came from far.

4 And his disciples answered him, From whence can a man satisfy these *men* with bread here in the wilderness?

5 And he asked them, How many loaves have ye? And they said, Seven.

6 And he commanded the people to sit down on the ground: and he took the seven loaves, and gave thanks, and brake, and gave to his disciples to set before *them;* and they did set *them* before the people.

7 And they had a few small fishes: and he

blessed, and commanded to set them also before *them.*

8 So they did eat, and were filled: and they took up of the broken *meat* that was left seven baskets.

9 And they that had eaten were about four thousand: and he sent them away.

10 ¶ And straightway he entered into a ship with his disciples, and came into the parts of Dal-ma-nu'tha.

11 And the Phar'i-sees came forth, and began to question with him, seeking of him a sign from heaven, tempting him.

12 And he sighed deeply in his spirit, and saith, Why doth this generation seek after a sign? verily I say unto you, There shall no sign be given unto this generation.

13 And he left them, and entering into the ship again departed to the other side.

14 ¶ Now *the disciples* had forgotten to take bread, neither had they in the ship with them more than one loaf.

15 And he charged them, saying, Take heed, beware of the leaven of the Phar'i-sees, and *of* the leaven of Her'od.

16 And they reasoned among themselves, saying, *It is* because we have no bread.

17 And when Je'sus knew *it,* he saith unto them, Why reason ye, because ye have no bread? perceive ye not yet, neither understand? have ye your heart yet hardened?

18 Having eyes, see ye not? and having ears, hear ye not? and do ye not remember?

19 When I brake the five loaves among five thousand, how many baskets full of fragments took ye up? They say unto him, Twelve.

20 And when the seven among four thousand, how many baskets full of fragments took ye up? And they said, Seven.

21 And he said unto them, How is it that ye do not understand?

22 ¶ And he cometh to Beth-sa'i-da; and they bring a blind man unto him, and besought him to touch him.

23 And he took the blind man by the hand, and led him out of the town; and when he had spit on his eyes, and put his hands upon him, he asked him if he saw ought.

24 And he looked up, and said, I see men as trees, walking.

25 After that he put *his* hands again upon his eyes, and made him look up: and he was restored, and saw every man clearly.

26 And he sent him away to his house, saying, Neither go into the town, nor tell *it* to any in the town.

27 ¶ And Je'sus went out, and his disciples, into the towns of Cæs-a-re'a Phi-lip'pi: and by the way he asked his disciples, saying unto them, Whom do men say that I am?

28 And they answered, John the Bap'tist: but some *say,* E-li'as; and others, One of the prophets.

29 And he saith unto them, But whom say ye that I am? And Pe'ter answereth and saith unto him, Thou art the Christ.

30 And he charged them that they should tell no man of him.

31 And he began to teach them, that the Son of man must suffer many things, and be rejected of the elders, and *of* the chief priests, and scribes, and be killed, and after three days rise again.

32 And he spake that saying openly. And Pe'ter took him, and began to rebuke him.

33 But when he had turned about and looked on his disciples, he rebuked Pe'ter, saying, Get thee behind me, Sa'tan: for thou savourest not the things that be of God, but the things that be of men.

34 ¶ And when he had called the people *unto him* with his disciples also, he said unto them, Whosoever will come after me, let him deny himself, and take up his cross, and follow me.

35 For whosoever will save his life shall lose it; but whosoever shall lose his life for my sake and the gospel's, the same shall save it.

36 For what shall it profit a man, if he shall gain the whole world, and lose his own soul?

37 Or what shall a man give in exchange for his soul?

38 Whosoever therefore shall be ashamed of me and of my words in this adulterous and sinful generation; of him also shall the Son of man be ashamed, when he cometh in the glory of his Father with the holy angels.

9 AND he said unto them, Verily I say unto you, That there be some of them that stand here, which shall not taste of death, till they have seen the kingdom of God come with power.

2 ¶ And after six days Je'sus taketh *with him* Pe'ter, and James, and John, and leadeth them up into an high mountain apart by themselves: and he was transfigured before them.

3 And his raiment became shining, exceeding white as snow; so as no fuller on earth can white them.

4 And there appeared unto them E-li'as with Mo'ses: and they were talking with Je'sus.

5 And Pe'ter answered and said to Je'sus, Master, it is good for us to be here: and let us make three tabernacles; one for thee, and one for Mo'ses, and one for E-li'as.

6 For he wist not what to say; for they were sore afraid.

7 And there was a cloud that overshadowed them: and a voice came out of the cloud, saying, This is my beloved Son: hear him.

8 And suddenly, when they had looked round about, they saw no man any more, save Je'sus only with themselves.

9 And as they came down from the mountain, he charged them that they should tell no man what things they had seen, till the Son of man were risen from the dead.

10 And they kept that saying with themselves, questioning one with another what the rising from the dead should mean.

11 ¶ And they asked him, saying, Why say the scribes that E-li'as must first come?

12 And he answered and told them, E-li'as verily cometh first, and restoreth all things; and how it is written of the Son of man, that he must suffer many things, and be set at nought.

13 But I say unto you, That E-li'as is indeed come, and they have done unto him whatsoever they listed, as it is written of him.

14 ¶ And when he came to *his* disciples, he saw a great multitude about them, and the scribes questioning with them.

15 And straightway all the people, when they beheld him, were greatly amazed, and running to *him* saluted him.

16 And he asked the scribes, What question ye with them?

17 And one of the multitude answered and said, Master, I have brought unto thee my son, which hath a dumb spirit;

18 And wheresoever he taketh him, he teareth him: and he foameth, and gnasheth with his teeth, and pineth away: and I spake to thy disci-

ples that they should cast him out; and they
could not.
19 He answereth him, and saith, O faithless
generation, how long shall I be with you? how
long shall I suffer you? bring him unto me.
20 And they brought him unto him: and
when he saw him, straightway the spirit tare
him; and he fell on the ground, and wallowed
foaming.
21 And he asked his father, How long is it
ago since this came unto him? And he said, Of a
child.
22 And ofttimes it hath cast him into the fire,
and into the waters, to destroy him: but if thou
canst do any thing, have compassion on us, and
help us.
23 Je'sus said unto him, If thou canst believe,
all things *are* possible to him that believeth.
24 And straightway the father of the child
cried out, and said with tears, Lord, I believe;
help thou mine unbelief.
25 When Je'sus saw that the people came
running together, he rebuked the foul spirit,
saying unto him, *Thou* dumb and deaf spirit, I
charge thee, come out of him, and enter no
more into him.
26 And *the spirit* cried, and rent him sore,
and came out of him: and he was as one dead;
insomuch that many said, He is dead.
27 But Je'sus took him by the hand, and
lifted him up; and he arose.
28 And when he was come into the house, his
disciples asked him privately, Why could not
we cast him out?
29 And he said unto them, This kind can
come forth by nothing, but by prayer and fasting.
30 ¶ And they departed thence, and passed
through Gal'i-lee; and he would not that any
man should know *it*.
31 For he taught his disciples, and said unto
them, The Son of man is delivered into the
hands of men, and they shall kill him; and after
that he is killed, he shall rise the third day.
32 But they understood not that saying, and
were afraid to ask him.
33 ¶ And he came to Ca-per'na-um: and
being in the house he asked them, What was it
that ye disputed among yourselves by the way?
34 But they held their peace: for by the way
they had disputed among themselves, who
should be the greatest.
35 And he sat down, and called the twelve,
and saith unto them, If any man desire to be
first, *the same* shall be last of all, and servant of
all.
36 And he took a child, and set him in the
midst of them: and when he had taken him in
his arms, he said unto them,
37 Whosoever shall receive one of such children in my name, receiveth me: and whosoever
shall receive me, receiveth not me, but him that
sent me.
38 ¶ And John answered him, saying, Master, we saw one casting out devils in thy name,
and he followeth not us: and we forbad him,
because he followeth not us.
39 But Je'sus said, Forbid him not: for there
is no man which shall do a miracle in my name,
that can lightly speak evil of me.
40 For he that is not against us is on our part.
41 For whosoever shall give you a cup of water to drink in my name, because ye belong to
Christ, verily I say unto you, he shall not lose
his reward.
42 And whosoever shall offend one of *these*
little ones that believe in me, it is better for him
that a millstone were hanged about his neck,
and he were cast into the sea.
43 And if thy hand offend thee, cut it off: it is
better for thee to enter into life maimed, than
having two hands to go into hell, into the fire
that never shall be quenched:
44 Where their worm dieth not, and the fire
is not quenched.
45 And if thy foot offend thee, cut it off: it is
better for thee to enter halt into life, than having two feet to be cast into hell, into the fire that
never shall be quenched:
46 Where their worm dieth not, and the fire
is not quenched.
47 And if thine eye offend thee, pluck it out:
it is better for thee to enter into the kingdom of
God with one eye, than having two eyes to be
cast into hell fire:
48 Where their worm dieth not, and the fire
is not quenched.
49 For every one shall be salted with fire, and
every sacrifice shall be salted with salt.
50 Salt *is* good: but if the salt have lost his
saltness, wherewith will ye season it? Have salt
in yourselves, and have peace one with another.

10 AND he arose from thence, and cometh
into the coasts of Ju-dæ'a by the farther
side of Jor'dan: and the people resort unto him
again; and, as he was wont, he taught them
again.
2 ¶ And the Phar'i-sees came to him, and
asked him, Is it lawful for a man to put away *his*
wife? tempting him.
3 And he answered and said unto them,
What did Mo'ses command you?
4 And they said, Mo'ses suffered to write a
bill of divorcement, and to put *her* away.
5 And Je'sus answered and said unto them,
For the hardness of your heart he wrote you
this precept.
6 But from the beginning of the creation God
made them male and female.
7 For this cause shall a man leave his father
and mother, and cleave to his wife;
8 And they twain shall be one flesh: so then
they are no more twain, but one flesh.
9 What therefore God hath joined together,
let not man put asunder.
10 And in the house his disciples asked him
again of the same *matter*.
11 And he saith unto them, Whosoever shall
put away his wife, and marry another, committeth adultery against her.
12 And if a woman shall put away her husband, and be married to another, she committeth adultery.
13 ¶ And they brought young children to
him, that he should touch them: and *his* disciples rebuked those that brought *them*.
14 But when Je'sus saw *it*, he was much displeased, and said unto them, Suffer the little
children to come unto me, and forbid them not:
for of such is the kingdom of God.
15 Verily I say unto you, Whosoever shall not
receive the kingdom of God as a little child, he
shall not enter therein.
16 And he took them up in his arms, put *his*
hands upon them, and blessed them.
17 ¶ And when he was gone forth into the
way, there came one running, and kneeled to
him, and asked him, Good Master, what shall I
do that I may inherit eternal life?
18 And Je'sus said unto him, Why callest
thou me good? *there is* none good but one, *that
is*, God.
19 Thou knowest the commandments, Do

not commit adultery, Do not kill, Do not steal, Do not bear false witness, Defraud not, Honour thy father and mother.

20 And he answered and said unto him, Master, all these have I observed from my youth.

21 Then Je'sus beholding him loved him, and said unto him, One thing thou lackest: go thy way, sell whatsoever thou hast, and give to the poor, and thou shalt have treasure in heaven: and come, take up the cross, and follow me.

22 And he was sad at that saying, and went away grieved: for he had great possessions.

23 ¶ And Je'sus looked round about, and saith unto his disciples, How hardly shall they that have riches enter into the kingdom of God!

24 And the disciples were astonished at his words. But Je'sus answereth again, and saith unto them, Children, how hard is it for them that trust in riches to enter into the kingdom of God!

25 It is easier for a camel to go through the eye of a needle, than for a rich man to enter into the kingdom of God.

26 And they were astonished out of measure, saying among themselves, Who then can be saved?

27 And Je'sus looking upon them saith, With men *it is* impossible, but not with God: for with God all things are possible.

28 ¶ Then Pe'ter began to say unto him, Lo, we have left all, and have followed thee.

29 And Je'sus answered and said, Verily I say unto you, There is no man that hath left house, or brethren, or sisters, or father, or mother, or wife, or children, or lands, for my sake, and the gospel's,

30 But he shall receive an hundredfold now in this time, houses, and brethren, and sisters, and mothers, and children, and lands, with persecutions; and in the world to come eternal life.

31 But many *that are* first shall be last; and the last first.

32 ¶ And they were in the way going up to Je-ru'sa-lem; and Je'sus went before them: and they were amazed; and as they followed, they were afraid. And he took again the twelve, and began to tell them what things should happen unto him,

33 *Saying,* Behold, we go up to Je-ru'sa-lem; and the Son of man shall be delivered unto the chief priests, and unto the scribes; and they shall condemn him to death, and shall deliver him to the Gen'tiles:

34 And they shall mock him, and shall scourge him, and shall spit upon him, and shall kill him: and the third day he shall rise again.

35 ¶ And James and John, the sons of Zeb'e-dee, come unto him, saying, Master, we would that thou shouldest do for us whatsoever we shall desire.

36 And he said unto them, What would ye that I should do for you?

37 They said unto him, Grant unto us that we may sit, one on thy right hand, and the other on thy left hand, in thy glory.

38 But Je'sus said unto them, Ye know not what ye ask: can ye drink of the cup that I drink of? and be baptized with the baptism that I am baptized with?

39 And they said unto him, We can. And Je'sus said unto them, Ye shall indeed drink of the cup that I drink of; and with the baptism that I am baptized withal shall ye be baptized:

40 But to sit on my right hand and on my left hand is not mine to give; but *it shall be given to them* for whom it is prepared.

41 And when the ten heard *it,* they began to be much displeased with James and John.

42 But Je'sus called them *to him,* and saith unto them, Ye know that they which are accounted to rule over the Gen'tiles exercise lordship over them; and their great ones exercise authority upon them.

43 But so shall it not be among you: but whosoever will be great among you, shall be your minister:

44 And whosoever of you will be the chiefest, shall be servant of all.

45 For even the Son of man came not to be ministered unto, but to minister, and to give his life a ransom for many.

46 ¶ And they came to Jer'i-cho: and as he went out of Jer'i-cho with his disciples and a great number of people, blind Bar-ti-mæ'us, the son of Ti-mæ'us, sat by the highway side begging.

47 And when he heard that it was Je'sus of Naz'a-reth, he began to cry out, and say, Je'sus, *thou* son of Da'vid, have mercy on me.

48 And many charged him that he should hold his peace: but he cried the more a great deal, *Thou* son of Da'vid, have mercy on me.

49 And Je'sus stood still, and commanded him to be called. And they call the blind man, saying unto him, Be of good comfort, rise; he calleth thee.

50 And he, casting away his garment, rose, and came to Je'sus.

51 And Je'sus answered and said unto him, What wilt thou that I should do unto thee? The blind man said unto him, Lord, that I might receive my sight.

52 And Je'sus said unto him, Go thy way; thy faith hath made thee whole. And immediately he received his sight, and followed Je'sus in the way.

11

AND when they came nigh to Je-ru'sa-lem, unto Beth'pha-ge and Beth'a-ny, at the mount of Ol'ives, he sendeth forth two of his disciples,

2 And saith unto them, Go your way into the village over against you: and as soon as ye be entered into it, ye shall find a colt tied, whereon never man sat; loose him, and bring *him.*

3 And if any man say unto you, Why do ye this? say ye that the Lord hath need of him; and straightway he will send him hither.

4 And they went their way, and found the colt tied by the door without in a place where two ways met; and they loose him.

5 And certain of them that stood there said unto them, What do ye, loosing the colt?

6 And they said unto them even as Je'sus had commanded: and they let them go.

7 And they brought the colt to Je'sus, and cast their garments on him; and he sat upon him.

8 And many spread their garments in the way: and others cut down branches off the trees, and strawed *them* in the way.

9 And they that went before, and they that followed, cried, saying, Ho-san'na; Blessed *is* he that cometh in the name of the Lord:

10 Blessed *be* the kingdom of our father Da'vid, that cometh in the name of the Lord: Ho-san'na in the highest.

11 And Je'sus entered into Je-ru'sa-lem, and into the temple: and when he had looked round about upon all things, and now the eventide was come, he went out unto Beth'a-ny with the twelve.

12 ¶ And on the morrow, when they were come from Beth'a-ny, he was hungry:

13 And seeing a fig tree afar off having leaves, he came, if haply he might find any thing thereon: and when he came to it, he found nothing but leaves; for the time of figs was not *yet*.

14 And Je'sus answered and said unto it, No man eat fruit of thee hereafter for ever. And his disciples heard *it*.

15 ¶ And they come to Je-ru'sa-lem: and Je'-sus went into the temple, and began to cast out them that sold and bought in the temple, and overthrew the tables of the moneychangers, and the seats of them that sold doves;

16 And would not suffer that any man should carry *any* vessel through the temple.

17 And he taught, saying unto them, Is it not written, My house shall be called of all nations the house of prayer? but ye have made it a den of thieves.

18 And the scribes and chief priests heard *it*, and sought how they might destroy him: for they feared him, because all the people was astonished at his doctrine.

19 And when even was come, he went out of the city.

20 ¶ And in the morning, as they passed by, they saw the fig tree dried up from the roots.

21 And Pe'ter calling to remembrance saith unto him, Master, behold, the fig tree which thou cursedst is withered away.

22 And Je'sus answering saith unto them, Have faith in God.

23 For verily I say unto you, That whosoever shall say unto this mountain, Be thou removed, and be thou cast into the sea; and shall not doubt in his heart, but shall believe that those things which he saith shall come to pass; he shall have whatsoever he saith.

24 Therefore I say unto you, What things soever ye desire, when ye pray, believe that ye receive *them*, and ye shall have *them*.

25 And when ye stand praying, forgive, if ye have ought against any: that your Father also which is in heaven may forgive you your trespasses.

26 But if ye do not forgive, neither will your Father which is in heaven forgive your trespasses.

27 ¶ And they come again to Je-ru'sa-lem: and as he was walking in the temple, there come to him the chief priests, and the scribes, and the elders,

28 And say unto him, By what authority doest thou these things? and who gave thee this authority to do these things?

29 And Je'sus answered and said unto them, I will also ask of you one question, and answer me, and I will tell you by what authority I do these things.

30 The baptism of John, was *it* from heaven, or of men? answer me.

31 And they reasoned with themselves, saying, If we shall say, From heaven; he will say, Why then did ye not believe him?

32 But if we shall say, Of men; they feared the people: for all *men* counted John, that he was a prophet indeed.

33 And they answered and said unto Je'sus, We cannot tell. And Je'sus answering saith unto them, Neither do I tell you by what authority I do these things.

12

AND he began to speak unto them by parables. A *certain* man planted a vineyard, and set an hedge about *it*, and digged *a place for* the winefat, and built a tower, and let it out to husbandmen, and went into a far country.

2 And at the season he sent to the husbandmen a servant, that he might receive from the husbandmen of the fruit of the vineyard.

3 And they caught *him*, and beat him, and sent *him* away empty.

4 And again he sent unto them another servant; and at him they cast stones, and wounded *him* in the head, and sent *him* away shamefully handled.

5 And again he sent another; and him they killed, and many others; beating some, and killing some.

6 Having yet therefore one son, his wellbeloved, he sent him also last unto them, saying, They will reverence my son.

7 But those husbandmen said among themselves, This is the heir; come, let us kill him, and the inheritance shall be ours.

8 And they took him, and killed *him*, and cast *him* out of the vineyard.

9 What shall therefore the lord of the vineyard do? he will come and destroy the husbandmen, and will give the vineyard unto others.

10 And have ye not read this scripture; The stone which the builders rejected is become the head of the corner:

11 This was the Lord's doing, and it is marvellous in our eyes?

12 And they sought to lay hold on him, but feared the people: for they knew that he had spoken the parable against them: and they left him, and went their way.

13 ¶ And they send unto him certain of the Phar'i-sees and of the He-ro'di-ans, to catch him in *his* words.

14 And when they were come, they say unto him, Master, we know that thou art true, and carest for no man: for thou regardest not the person of men, but teachest the way of God in truth: Is it lawful to give tribute to Cæ'sar, or not?

15 Shall we give, or shall we not give? But he, knowing their hypocrisy, said unto them, Why tempt ye me? bring me a penny, that I may see *it*.

16 And they brought *it*. And he saith unto them, Whose *is* this image and superscription? And they said unto him, Cæ'sar's.

17 And Je'sus answering said unto them, Render to Cæ'sar the things that are Cæ'sar's, and to God the things that are God's. And they marvelled at him.

18 ¶ Then come unto him the Sad'du-cees, which say there is no resurrection; and they asked him, saying,

19 Master, Mo'ses wrote unto us, If a man's brother die, and leave *his* wife *behind him*, and leave no children, that his brother should take his wife, and raise up seed unto his brother.

20 Now there were seven brethren: and the first took a wife, and dying left no seed.

21 And the second took her, and died, neither left he any seed: and the third likewise.

22 And the seven had her, and left no seed: last of all the woman died also.

23 In the resurrection therefore, when they shall rise, whose wife shall she be of them? for the seven had her to wife.

24 And Je'sus answering said unto them, Do ye not therefore err, because ye know not the scriptures, neither the power of God?

25 For when they shall rise from the dead, they neither marry, nor are given in marriage; but are as the angels which are in heaven.

26 And as touching the dead, that they rise:
have ye not read in the book of Mo'ses, how in
the bush God spake unto him, saying, I *am* the
God of A'bra-ham, and the God of I'saac, and
the God of Ja'cob?
27 He is not the God of the dead, but the God
of the living: ye therefore do greatly err.
28 ¶ And one of the scribes came, and having heard them reasoning together, and perceiving that he had answered them well, asked him,
Which is the first commandment of all?
29 And Je'sus answered him, The first of all
the commandments *is*, Hear, O Is'ra-el; the
Lord our God is one Lord:
30 And thou shalt love the Lord thy God with
all thy heart, and with all thy soul, and with all
thy mind, and with all thy strength: this *is* the
first commandment.
31 And the second *is* like, *namely* this, Thou
shalt love thy neighbour as thyself. There is
none other commandment greater than these.
32 And the scribe said unto him, Well, Master, thou hast said the truth: for there is one
God; and there is none other but he:
33 And to love him with all the heart, and
with all the understanding, and with all the
soul, and with all the strength, and to love *his*
neighbour as himself, is more than all whole
burnt offerings and sacrifices.
34 And when Je'sus saw that he answered
discreetly, he said unto him, Thou art not far
from the kingdom of God. And no man after
that durst ask him *any question*.
35 ¶ And Je'sus answered and said, while he
taught in the temple, How say the scribes that
Christ is the son of Da'vid?
36 For Da'vid himself said by the Ho'ly
Ghost, The LORD said to my Lord, Sit thou on
my right hand, till I make thine enemies thy
footstool.
37 Da'vid therefore himself calleth him Lord;
and whence is he *then* his son? And the common people heard him gladly.
38 ¶ And he said unto them in his doctrine,
Beware of the scribes, which love to go in long
clothing, and *love* salutations in the market-
places,
39 And the chief seats in the synagogues,
and the uppermost rooms at feasts:
40 Which devour widows' houses, and for a
pretence make long prayers: these shall receive
greater damnation.
41 ¶ And Je'sus sat over against the treasury, and beheld how the people cast money
into the treasury: and many that were rich cast
in much.
42 And there came a certain poor widow,
and she threw in two mites, which make a farthing.
43 And he called *unto him* his disciples, and
saith unto them, Verily I say unto you, That this
poor widow hath cast more in, than all they
which have cast into the treasury:
44 For all *they* did cast in of their abundance;
but she of her want did cast in all that she had,
even all her living.

13 AND as he went out of the temple, one
of his disciples saith unto him, Master,
see what manner of stones and what buildings
are here!
2 And Je'sus answering said unto him, Seest
thou these great buildings? there shall not be
left one stone upon another, that shall not be
thrown down.
3 And as he sat upon the mount of Ol'ives
over against the temple, Pe'ter and James and
John and An'drew asked him privately,
4 Tell us, when shall these things be? and
what *shall be* the sign when all these things
shall be fulfilled?
5 And Je'sus answering them began to say,
Take heed lest any *man* deceive you:
6 For many shall come in my name, saying, I
am *Christ;* and shall deceive many.
7 And when ye shall hear of wars and rumours of wars, be ye not troubled: for *such
things* must needs be; but the end *shall* not *be*
yet.
8 For nation shall rise against nation, and
kingdom against kingdom: and there shall be
earthquakes in divers places, and there shall be
famines and troubles: these *are* the beginnings
of sorrows.
9 ¶ But take heed to yourselves: for they
shall deliver you up to councils; and in the synagogues ye shall be beaten: and ye shall be
brought before rulers and kings for my sake, for
a testimony against them.
10 And the gospel must first be published
among all nations.
11 But when they shall lead *you*, and deliver
you up, take no thought beforehand what ye
shall speak, neither do ye premeditate: but
whatsoever shall be given you in that hour, that
speak ye: for it is not ye that speak, but the
Ho'ly Ghost.
12 Now the brother shall betray the brother
to death, and the father the son; and children
shall rise up against *their* parents, and shall
cause them to be put to death.
13 And ye shall be hated of all *men* for my
name's sake: but he that shall endure unto the
end, the same shall be saved.
14 ¶ But when ye shall see the abomination
of desolation, spoken of by Dan'iel the prophet,
standing where it ought not, (let him that
readeth understand,) then let them that be in
Ju-dæ'a flee to the mountains:
15 And let him that is on the house top not go
down into the house, neither enter *therein*, to
take any thing out of his house:
16 And let him that is in the field not turn
back again for to take up his garment.
17 But woe to them that are with child, and
to them that give suck in those days!
18 And pray ye that your flight be not in the
winter.
19 For *in* those days shall be affliction, such
as was not from the beginning of the creation
which God created unto this time, neither shall
be.
20 And except that the Lord had shortened
those days, no flesh should be saved: but for the
elect's sake, whom he hath chosen, he hath
shortened the days.
21 And then if any man shall say to you, Lo,
here *is* Christ; or, lo, *he is* there; believe *him*
not:
22 For false Christs and false prophets shall
rise, and shall shew signs and wonders, to seduce, if *it were* possible, even the elect.
23 But take ye heed: behold, I have foretold
you all things.
24 ¶ But in those days, after that tribulation,
the sun shall be darkened, and the moon shall
not give her light,
25 And the stars of heaven shall fall, and the
powers that are in heaven shall be shaken.
26 And then shall they see the Son of man
coming in the clouds with great power and glory.
27 And then shall he send his angels, and

shall gather together his elect from the four winds, from the uttermost part of the earth to the uttermost part of heaven.
28 Now learn a parable of the fig tree; When her branch is yet tender, and putteth forth leaves, ye know that summer is near:
29 So ye in like manner, when ye shall see these things come to pass, know that it is nigh, *even* at the doors.
30 Verily I say unto you, that this generation shall not pass, till all these things be done.
31 Heaven and earth shall pass away: but my words shall not pass away.
32 ¶ But of that day and *that* hour knoweth no man, no, not the angels which are in heaven, neither the Son, but the Father.
33 Take ye heed, watch and pray: for ye know not when the time is.
34 *For the Son of man is* as a man taking a far journey, who left his house, and gave authority to his servants, and to every man his work, and commanded the porter to watch.
35 Watch ye therefore: for ye know not when the master of the house cometh, at even, or at midnight, or at the cockcrowing, or in the morning:
36 Lest coming suddenly he find you sleeping.
37 And what I say unto you I say unto all, Watch.

14 AFTER two days was *the feast of* the passover, and of unleavened bread: and the chief priests and the scribes sought how they might take him by craft, and put *him* to death.
2 But they said, Not on the feast *day,* lest there be an uproar of the people.
3 ¶ And being in Beth'a-ny in the house of Si'mon the leper, as he sat at meat, there came a woman having an alabaster box of ointment of spikenard very precious; and she brake the box, and poured *it* on his head.
4 And there were some that had indignation within themselves, and said, Why was this waste of the ointment made?
5 For it might have been sold for more than three hundred pence, and have been given to the poor. And they murmured against her.
6 And Je'sus said, Let her alone; why trouble ye her? she hath wrought a good work on me.
7 For ye have the poor with you always, and whensoever ye will ye may do them good: but me ye have not always.
8 She hath done what she could: she is come aforehand to anoint my body to the burying.
9 Verily I say unto you, Wheresoever this gospel shall be preached throughout the whole world, *this* also that she hath done shall be spoken of for a memorial of her.
10 ¶ And Ju'das Is-car'i-ot, one of the twelve, went unto the chief priests, to betray him unto them.
11 And when they heard *it,* they were glad, and promised to give him money. And he sought how he might conveniently betray him.
12 ¶ And the first day of unleavened bread, when they killed the passover, his disciples said unto him, Where wilt thou that we go and prepare that thou mayest eat the passover?
13 And he sendeth forth two of his disciples, and saith unto them, Go ye into the city, and there shall meet you a man bearing a pitcher of water: follow him.
14 And wheresoever he shall go in, say ye to the goodman of the house, The Master saith, Where is the guestchamber, where I shall eat the passover with my disciples?
15 And he will shew you a large upper room furnished *and* prepared: there make ready for us.
16 And his disciples went forth, and came into the city, and found as he had said unto them: and they made ready the passover.
17 And in the evening he cometh with the twelve.
18 And as they sat and did eat, Je'sus said, Verily I say unto you, One of you which eateth with me shall betray me.
19 And they began to be sorrowful, and to say unto him one by one, *Is* it I? and another *said, Is* it I?
20 And he answered and said unto them, *It is* one of the twelve, that dippeth with me in the dish.
21 The Son of man indeed goeth, as it is written of him: but woe to that man by whom the Son of man is betrayed! good were it for that man if he had never been born.
22 ¶ And as they did eat, Je'sus took bread, and blessed, and brake *it,* and gave to them, and said, Take, eat: this is my body.
23 And he took the cup, and when he had given thanks, he gave *it* to them: and they all drank of it.
24 And he said unto them, This is my blood of the new testament, which is shed for many.
25 Verily I say unto you, I will drink no more of the fruit of the vine, until that day that I drink it new in the kingdom of God.
26 ¶ And when they had sung an hymn, they went out into the mount of Ol'ives.
27 And Je'sus saith unto them, All ye shall be offended because of me this night: for it is written, I will smite the shepherd, and the sheep shall be scattered.
28 But after that I am risen, I will go before you into Gal'i-lee.
29 But Pe'ter said unto him, Although all shall be offended, yet *will* not I.
30 And Je'sus saith unto him, Verily I say unto thee, That this day, *even* in this night, before the cock crow twice, thou shalt deny me thrice.
31 But he spake the more vehemently, If I should die with thee, I will not deny thee in any wise. Likewise also said they all.
32 And they came to a place which was named Geth-sem'a-ne: and he saith to his disciples, Sit ye here, while I shall pray.
33 And he taketh with him Pe'ter and James and John, and began to be sore amazed, and to be very heavy;
34 And saith unto them, My soul is exceeding sorrowful unto death: tarry ye here, and watch.
35 And he went forward a little, and fell on the ground, and prayed that, if it were possible, the hour might pass from him.
36 And he said, Ab'ba, Father, all things *are* possible unto thee; take away this cup from me: nevertheless not what I will, but what thou wilt.
37 And he cometh, and findeth them sleeping, and saith unto Pe'ter, Si'mon, sleepest thou? couldest not thou watch one hour?
38 Watch ye and pray, lest ye enter into temptation. The spirit truly *is* ready, but the flesh *is* weak.
39 And again he went away, and prayed, and spake the same words.
40 And when he returned, he found them asleep again, (for their eyes were heavy,) neither wist they what to answer him.

41 And he cometh the third time, and saith
unto them, Sleep on now, and take *your* rest: it
is enough, the hour is come; behold, the Son of
man is betrayed into the hands of sinners.
42 Rise up, let us go; lo, he that betrayeth me
is at hand.
43 ¶ And immediately, while he yet spake,
cometh Ju'das, one of the twelve, and with him
a great mulitude with swords and staves, from
the chief priests and the scribes and the elders.
44 And he that betrayed him had given them
a token, saying, Whomsoever I shall kiss, that
same is he; take him, and lead *him* away safely.
45 And as soon as he was come, he goeth
straightway to him, and saith, Master, master;
and kissed him.
46 ¶ And they laid their hands on him, and
took him.
47 And one of them that stood by drew a
sword, and smote a servant of the high priest,
and cut off his ear.
48 And Je'sus answered and said unto them,
Are ye come out, as against a thief, with swords
and *with* staves to take me?
49 I was daily with you in the temple teaching,
and ye took me not: but the scriptures must
be fulfilled.
50 And they all forsook him, and fled.
51 And there followed him a certain young
man, having a linen cloth cast about *his* naked
body; and the young men laid hold on him:
52 And he left the linen cloth, and fled from
them naked.
53 ¶ And they led Je'sus away to the high
priest: and with him were assembled all the
chief priests and the elders and the scribes.
54 And Pe'ter followed him afar off, even
into the palace of the high priest: and he sat
with the servants, and warmed himself at the
fire.
55 And the chief priests and all the council
sought for witness against Je'sus to put him to
death; and found none.
56 For many bare false witness against him,
but their witness agreed not together.
57 And there arose certain, and bare false
witness against him, saying,
58 We heard him say, I will destroy this temple
that is made with hands, and within three
days I will build another made without hands.
59 But neither so did their witness agree together.
60 And the high priest stood up in the midst,
and asked Je'sus, saying, Answerest thou nothing?
what *is it which* these witness against
thee?
61 But he held his peace, and answered nothing.
Again the high priest asked him, and said
unto him, Art thou the Christ, the Son of the
Blessed?
62 And Je'sus said, I am: and ye shall see the
Son of man sitting on the right hand of power,
and coming in the clouds of heaven.
63 Then the high priest rent his clothes, and
saith, What need we any further witnesses?
64 Ye have heard the blasphemy: what think
ye? And they all condemned him to be guilty of
death.
65 And some began to spit on him, and to
cover his face, and to buffet him, and to say
unto him, Prophesy: and the servants did strike
him with the palms of their hands.
66 ¶ And as Pe'ter was beneath in the palace,
there cometh one of the maids of the high
priest:
67 And when she saw Pe'ter warming himself,
she looked upon him, and said, And thou
also wast with Je'sus of Naz'a-reth.
68 But he denied, saying, I know not, neither
understand I what thou sayest. And he went out
into the porch; and the cock crew.
69 And a maid saw him again, and began to
say to them that stood by, This is *one* of them.
70 And he denied it again. And a little after,
they that stood by said again to Pe'ter, Surely
thou art *one* of them: for thou art a Gal-i-læ'an,
and thy speech agreeth *thereto.*
71 But he began to curse and to swear, *saying,*
I know not this man of whom ye speak.
72 And the second time the cock crew. And
Pe'ter called to mind the word that Je'sus said
unto him, Before the cock crow twice, thou
shalt deny me thrice. And when he thought
thereon, he wept.

15 AND straightway in the morning the
chief priests held a consultation with
the elders and scribes and the whole council,
and bound Je'sus, and carried *him* away, and
delivered *him* to Pi'late.
2 And Pi'late asked him, Art thou the King of
the Jews? And he answering said unto him,
Thou sayest *it.*
3 And the chief priests accused him of many
things: but he answered nothing.
4 And Pi'late asked him again, saying, Answerest
thou nothing? behold how many things
they witness against thee.
5 But Je'sus yet answered nothing; so that
Pi'late marvelled.
6 Now at *that* feast he released unto them
one prisoner, whomsoever they desired.
7 And there was *one* named Ba-rab'bas,
which lay bound with them that had made insurrection
with him, who had committed murder
in the insurrection.
8 And the multitude crying aloud began to
desire *him to do* as he had ever done unto them.
9 But Pi'late answered them, saying, Will ye
that I release unto you the King of the Jews?
10 For he knew that the chief priests had delivered
him for envy.
11 But the chief priests moved the people,
that he should rather release Ba-rab'bas unto
them.
12 And Pi'late answered and said again unto
them, What will ye then that I shall do *unto him*
whom ye call the King of the Jews?
13 And they cried out again, Crucify him.
14 Then Pi'late said unto them, Why, what
evil hath he done? And they cried out the more
exceedingly, Crucify him.
15 ¶ And *so* Pi'late, willing to content the
people, released Ba-rab'bas unto them, and delivered
Je'sus, when he had scourged *him,* to be
crucified.
16 And the soldiers led him away into the
hall, called Præ-to'ri-um; and they call together
the whole band.
17 And they clothed him with purple, and
platted a crown of thorns, and put it about his
head,
18 And began to salute him, Hail, King of the
Jews!
19 And they smote him on the head with a
reed, and did spit upon him, and bowing *their*
knees worshipped him.
20 And when they had mocked him, they
took off the purple from him, and put his own
clothes on him, and led him out to crucify him.
21 And they compel one Si'mon a Cy-re'nian,
who passed by, coming out of the country,

the father of Al-ex-an'der and Ru'fus, to bear
his cross.
22 And they bring him unto the place Gol'go-
tha, which is, being interpreted, The place of a
skull.
23 And they gave him to drink wine mingled
with myrrh: but he received *it* not.
24 And when they had crucified him, they
parted his garments, casting lots upon them,
what every man should take.
25 And it was the third hour, and they crucified him.
26 And the superscription of his accusation
was written over, THE KING OF THE JEWS.
27 And with him they crucify two thieves;
the one on his right hand, and the other on his
left.
28 And the scripture was fulfilled, which
saith, And he was numbered with the transgressors.
29 And they that passed by railed on him,
wagging their heads, and saying, Ah, thou that
destroyest the temple, and buildest *it* in three
days,
30 Save thyself, and come down from the
cross.
31 Likewise also the chief priests mocking
said among themselves with the scribes, He
saved others; himself he cannot save.
32 Let Christ the King of Is'ra-el descend
now from the cross, that we may see and believe. And they that were crucified with him reviled him.
33 And when the sixth hour was come, there
was darkness over the whole land until the
ninth hour.
34 And at the ninth hour Je'sus cried with a
loud voice, saying, E-lo'i, E-lo'i, la'ma sa-bach-
tha'ni? which is, being interpreted, My God, my
God, why hast thou forsaken me?
35 And some of them that stood by, when
they heard *it*, said, Behold, he calleth E-li'as.
36 And one ran and filled a spunge full of vinegar, and put *it* on a reed, and gave him to
drink, saying, Let alone; let us see whether E-
li'as will come to take him down.
37 And Je'sus cried with a loud voice, and
gave up the ghost.
38 And the veil of the temple was rent in
twain from the top to the bottom.
39 ¶ And when the centurion, which stood
over against him, saw that he so cried out, and
gave up the ghost, he said, Truly this man was
the Son of God.
40 There were also women looking on afar
off: among whom was Ma'ry Mag-da-le'ne, and
Ma'ry the mother of James the less and of Jo'-
ses, and Sa-lo'me;
41 (Who also, when he was in Gal'i-lee, followed him, and ministered unto him;) and many
other women which came up with him unto Je-
ru'sa-lem.
42 ¶ And now when the even was come, because it was the preparation, that is, the day
before the sabbath,
43 Jo'seph of Ar-i-ma-thæ'a, an honourable
counsellor, which also waited for the kingdom
of God, came, and went in boldly unto Pi'late,
and craved the body of Je'sus.
44 And Pi'late marvelled if he were already
dead: and calling *unto him* the centurion, he
asked him whether he had been any while dead.
45 And when he knew *it* of the centurion, he
gave the body to Jo'seph.
46 And he bought fine linen, and took him
down, and wrapped him in the linen, and laid
him in a sepulchre which was hewn out of a
rock, and rolled a stone unto the door of the
sepulchre.
47 And Ma'ry Mag-da-le'ne and Ma'ry *the
mother* of Jo'ses beheld where he was laid.

16 AND when the sabbath was past, Ma'ry
Mag-da-le'ne, and Ma'ry the *mother* of
James, and Sa-lo'me, had bought sweet spices,
that they might come and anoint him.
2 And very early in the morning the first *day*
of the week, they came unto the sepulchre at
the rising of the sun.
3 And they said among themselves, Who
shall roll away the stone from the door of the
sepulchre?
4 And when they looked, they saw that the
stone was rolled away: for it was very great.
5 And entering into the sepulchre, they saw a
young man sitting on the right side, clothed in a
long white garment; and they were affrighted.
6 And he saith unto them, Be not affrighted:
Ye seek Je'sus of Naz'a-reth, which was crucified: he is risen; he is not here: behold the place
where they laid him.
7 But go your way, tell his disciples and Pe'-
ter that he goeth before you into Gal'i-lee: there
shall ye see him, as he said unto you.
8 And they went out quickly, and fled from
the sepulchre; for they trembled and were
amazed: neither said they any thing to any
man; for they were afraid.
9 ¶ Now when *Jesus* was risen early the first
day of the week, he appeared first to Ma'ry
Mag-da-le'ne, out of whom he had cast seven
devils.
10 *And* she went and told them that had been
with him, as they mourned and wept.
11 And they, when they had heard that he
was alive, and had been seen of her, believed
not.
12 ¶ After that he appeared in another form
unto two of them, as they walked, and went
into the country.
13 And they went and told *it* unto the residue: neither believed they them.
14 ¶ Afterward he appeared unto the eleven
as they sat at meat, and upbraided them with
their unbelief and hardness of heart, because
they believed not them which had seen him after he was risen.
15 And he said unto them, Go ye into all the
world, and preach the gospel to every creature.
16 He that believeth and is baptized shall be
saved: but he that believeth not shall be
damned.
17 And these signs shall follow them that believe; In my name shall they cast out devils;
they shall speak with new tongues;
18 They shall take up serpents; and if they
drink any deadly thing, it shall not hurt them;
they shall lay hands on the sick, and they shall
recover.
19 ¶ So then after the Lord had spoken unto
them, he was received up into heaven, and sat
on the right hand of God.
20 And they went forth, and preached every
where, the Lord working with *them*, and confirming the word with signs following. Amen.

THE GOSPEL ACCORDING TO

LUKE

1 FORASMUCH as many have taken in
hand to set forth in order a declaration of
those things which are most surely believed
among us,
2 Even as they delivered them unto us, which
from the beginning were eyewitnesses, and
ministers of the word;
3 It seemed good to me also, having had perfect understanding of all things from the very
first, to write unto thee in order, most excellent
The-oph'i-lus,
4 That thou mightest know the certainty of
those things, wherein thou hast been instructed.
5 ¶ THERE was in the days of Her'od, the
king of Ju-dæ'a, a certain priest named Zach-a-
ri'as, of the course of A-bi'a: and his wife *was* of
the daughters of Aar'on, and her name *was* E-
lis'a-beth.
6 And they were both righteous before God,
walking in all the commandments and ordinances of the Lord blameless.
7 And they had no child, because that E-lis'a-
beth was barren, and they both were *now* well
stricken in years.
8 And it came to pass, that while he executed
the priest's office before God in the order of his
course,
9 According to the custom of the priest's office, his lot was to burn incense when he went
into the temple of the Lord.
10 And the whole multitude of the people
were praying without at the time of incense.
11 And there appeared unto him an angel of
the Lord standing on the right side of the altar
of incense.
12 And when Zach-a-ri'as saw *him*, he was
troubled, and fear fell upon him.
13 But the angel said unto him, Fear not,
Zach-a-ri'as: for thy prayer is heard; and thy
wife E-lis'a-beth shall bear thee a son, and thou
shalt call his name John.
14 And thou shalt have joy and gladness; and
many shall rejoice at his birth.
15 For he shall be great in the sight of the
Lord, and shall drink neither wine nor strong
drink; and he shall be filled with the Ho'ly
Ghost, even from his mother's womb.
16 And many of the children of Is'ra-el shall
he turn to the Lord their God.
17 And he shall go before him in the spirit
and power of E-li'as, to turn the hearts of the
fathers to the children, and the disobedient to
the wisdom of the just; to make ready a people
prepared for the Lord.
18 And Zach-a-ri'as said unto the angel,
Whereby shall I know this? for I am an old man,
and my wife well stricken in years.
19 And the angel answering said unto him, I
am Ga'bri-el, that stand in the presence of God;
and am sent to speak unto thee, and to shew
thee these glad tidings.
20 And, behold, thou shalt be dumb, and not
able to speak, until the day that these things
shall be performed, because thou believest not
my words, which shall be fulfilled in their season.
21 And the people waited for Zach-a-ri'as,
and marvelled that he tarried so long in the
temple.
22 And when he came out, he could not
speak unto them: and they perceived that he
had seen a vision in the temple: for he beckoned
unto them, and remained speechless.
23 And it came to pass, that, as soon as the
days of his ministration were accomplished, he
departed to his own house.
24 And after those days his wife E-lis'a-beth
conceived, and hid herself five months, saying,
25 Thus hath the LORD dealt with me in the
days wherein he looked on *me*, to take away my
reproach among men.
26 And in the sixth month the angel Ga'bri-el
was sent from God unto a city of Gal'i-lee,
named Naz'a-reth,
27 To a virgin espoused to a man whose
name was Jo'seph, of the house of Da'vid; and
the virgin's name *was* Mary.
28 And the angel came in unto her, and said,
Hail, *thou that art* highly favoured, the Lord *is*
with thee: blessed *art* thou among women.
29 And when she saw *him*, she was troubled
at his saying, and cast in her mind what manner
of salutation this should be.
30 And the angel said unto her, Fear not,
Ma'ry: for thou hast found favour with God.
31 And, behold, thou shalt conceive in thy
womb, and bring forth a son, and shalt call his
name JE'SUS.
32 He shall be great, and shall be called the
Son of the Highest: and the Lord God shall give
unto him the throne of his father Da'vid:
33 And he shall reign over the house of Ja'-
cob for ever; and of his kingdom there shall be
no end.
34 Then said Ma'ry unto the angel, How shall
this be, seeing I know not a man?
35 And the angel answered and said unto
her, The Ho'ly Ghost shall come upon thee, and
the power of the Highest shall overshadow
thee: therefore also that holy thing which shall
be born of thee shall be called the Son of God.
36 And, behold, thy cousin E-lis'a-beth, she
hath also conceived a son in her old age: and
this is the sixth month with her, who was called
barren.
37 For with God nothing shall be impossible.
38 And Ma'ry said, Behold the handmaid of
the Lord; be it unto me according to thy word.
And the angel departed from her.
39 And Ma'ry arose in those days, and went
into the hill country with haste, into a city of
Ju'da;
40 And entered into the house of Zach-a-ri'-
as, and saluted E-lis'a-beth.
41 And it came to pass, that, when E-lis'a-
beth heard the salutation of Ma'ry, the babe
leaped in her womb; and E-lis'a-beth was filled
with the Ho'ly Ghost:
42 And she spake out with a loud voice, and
said, Blessed *art* thou among women, and
blessed *is* the fruit of thy womb.
43 And whence *is* this to me, that the mother
of my Lord should come to me?
44 For, lo, as soon as the voice of thy salutation sounded in mine ears, the babe leaped in
my womb for joy.
45 And blessed *is* she that believed: for there
shall be a performance of those things which
were told her from the Lord.
46 And Ma'ry said, My soul doth magnify the
Lord,
47 And my spirit hath rejoiced in God my
Saviour.

48 For he hath regarded the low estate of his handmaiden: for, behold, from henceforth all generations shall call me blessed.
49 For he that is mighty hath done to me great things; and holy *is* his name.
50 And his mercy *is* on them that fear him from generation to generation.
51 He hath shewed strength with his arm; he hath scattered the proud in the imagination of their hearts.
52 He hath put down the mighty from *their* seats, and exalted them of low degree.
53 He hath filled the hungry with good things; and the rich he hath sent empty away.
54 He hath holpen his servant Is′ra-el, in remembrance of *his* mercy;
55 As he spake to our fathers, to A′bra-ham, and to his seed for ever.
56 And Ma′ry abode with her about three months, and returned to her own house.
57 Now E-lis′a-beth's full time came that she should be delivered; and she brought forth a son.
58 And her neighbours and her cousins heard how the Lord had shewed great mercy upon her; and they rejoiced with her.
59 And it came to pass, that on the eighth day they came to circumcise the child; and they called him Zach-a-ri′as, after the name of his father.
60 And his mother answered and said, Not *so;* but he shall be called John.
61 And they said unto her, There is none of thy kindred that is called by this name.
62 And they made signs to his father, how he would have him called.
63 And he asked for a writing table, and wrote, saying, His name is John. And they marvelled all.
64 And his mouth was opened immediately, and his tongue *loosed,* and he spake, and praised God.
65 And fear came on all that dwelt round about them: and all these sayings were noised abroad throughout all the hill country of Ju-dæ′a.
66 And all they that heard *them* laid *them* up in their hearts, saying, What manner of child shall this be! And the hand of the Lord was with him.
67 And his father Zach-a-ri′as was filled with the Ho′ly Ghost, and prophesied, saying,
68 Blessed *be* the Lord God of Is′ra-el; for he hath visited and redeemed his people,
69 And hath raised up an horn of salvation for us in the house of his servant Da′vid;
70 As he spake by the mouth of his holy prophets, which have been since the world began:
71 That we should be saved from our enemies, and from the hand of all that hate us;
72 To perform the mercy *promised* to our fathers, and to remember his holy covenant;
73 The oath which he sware to our father A′bra-ham,
74 That he would grant unto us, that we being delivered out of the hand of our enemies might serve him without fear,
75 In holiness and righteousness before him, all the days of our life.
76 And thou, child, shalt be called the prophet of the Highest: for thou shalt go before the face of the Lord to prepare his ways;
77 To give knowledge of salvation unto his people by the remission of their sins,
78 Through the tender mercy of our God; whereby the dayspring from on high hath visited us,
79 To give light to them that sit in darkness and *in* the shadow of death, to guide our feet into the way of peace.
80 And the child grew, and waxed strong in spirit, and was in the deserts till the day of his shewing unto Is′ra-el.

2 AND it came to pass in those days, that there went out a decree from Cæ′sar Au-gus′tus, that all the world should be taxed.
2 (*And* this taxing was first made when Cy-re′ni-us was governor of Syr′i-a.)
3 And all went to be taxed, every one into his own city.
4 And Jo′seph also went up from Gal′i-lee, out of the city of Naz′a-reth, into Ju-dæ′a, unto the city of Da′vid, which is called Beth′le-hem; (because he was of the house and lineage of Da′vid:)
5 To be taxed with Ma′ry his espoused wife, being great with child.
6 And so it was, that, while they were there, the days were accomplished that she should be delivered.
7 And she brought forth her firstborn son, and wrapped him in swaddling clothes, and laid him in a manger; because there was no room for them in the inn.
8 And there were in the same country shepherds abiding in the field, keeping watch over their flock by night.
9 And, lo, the angel of the Lord came upon them, and the glory of the Lord shone round about them: and they were sore afraid.
10 And the angel said unto them, Fear not: for, behold, I bring you good tidings of great joy, which shall be to all people.
11 For unto you is born this day in the city of Da′vid a Saviour, which is Christ the Lord.
12 And this *shall be* a sign unto you; Ye shall find the babe wrapped in swaddling clothes, lying in a manger.
13 And suddenly there was with the angel a multitude of the heavenly host praising God, and saying,
14 Glory to God in the highest, and on earth peace, good will toward men.
15 And it came to pass, as the angels were gone away from them into heaven, the shepherds said one to another, Let us now go even unto Beth′le-hem, and see this thing which is come to pass, which the Lord hath made known unto us.
16 And they came with haste, and found Ma′ry, and Jo′seph, and the babe lying in a manger.
17 And when they had seen *it,* they made known abroad the saying which was told them concerning this child.
18 And all they that heard *it* wondered at those things which were told them by the shepherds.
19 But Ma′ry kept all these things, and pondered *them* in her heart.
20 And the shepherds returned, glorifying and praising God for all the things that they had heard and seen, as it was told unto them.
21 And when eight days were accomplished for the circumcising of the child, his name was called JE′SUS, which was so named of the angel before he was conceived in the womb.
22 And when the days of her purification according to the law of Mo′ses were accomplished, they brought him to Je-ru′sa-lem, to present *him* to the Lord;
23 (As it is written in the law of the Lord,

Every male that openeth the womb shall be called holy to the Lord;)

24 And to offer a sacrifice according to that which is said in the law of the Lord, A pair of turtledoves, or two young pigeons.

25 And, behold, there was a man in Je-ru'sa-lem, whose name *was* Sim'e-on; and the same man *was* just and devout, waiting for the consolation of Is'ra-el: and the Ho'ly Ghost was upon him.

26 And it was revealed unto him by the Ho'ly Ghost, that he should not see death, before he had seen the Lord's Christ.

27 And he came by the Spirit into the temple: and when the parents brought in the child Je'sus, to do for him after the custom of the law,

28 Then took he him up in his arms, and blessed God, and said,

29 Lord, now lettest thou thy servant depart in peace, according to thy word:

30 For mine eyes have seen thy salvation,

31 Which thou hast prepared before the face of all people;

32 A light to lighten the Gen'tiles, and the glory of thy people Is'ra-el.

33 And Jo'seph and his mother marvelled at those things which were spoken of him.

34 And Sim'e-on blessed them, and said unto Ma'ry his mother, Behold, this *child* is set for the fall and rising again of many in Is'ra-el; and for a sign which shall be spoken against;

35 (Yea, a sword shall pierce through thy own soul also,) that the thoughts of many hearts may be revealed.

36 And there was one An'na, a prophetess, the daughter of Phan-u'el, of the tribe of A'ser: she was of a great age, and had lived with an husband seven years from her virginity;

37 And she *was* a widow of about fourscore and four years, which departed not from the temple, but served *God* with fastings and prayers night and day.

38 And she coming in that instant gave thanks likewise unto the Lord, and spake of him to all them that looked for redemption in Je-ru'sa-lem.

39 And when they had performed all things according to the law of the Lord, they returned into Gal'i-lee, to their own city Naz'a-reth.

40 And the child grew, and waxed strong in spirit, filled with wisdom: and the grace of God was upon him.

41 Now his parents went to Je-ru'sa-lem every year at the feast of the passover.

42 And when he was twelve years old, they went up to Je-ru'sa-lem after the custom of the feast.

43 And when they had fulfilled the days, as they returned, the child Je'sus tarried behind in Je-ru'sa-lem; and Jo'seph and his mother knew not *of it*.

44 But they, supposing him to have been in the company, went a day's journey; and they sought him among *their* kinsfolk and acquaintance.

45 And when they found him not, they turned back again to Je-ru'sa-lem, seeking him.

46 And it came to pass, that after three days they found him in the temple, sitting in the midst of the doctors, both hearing them, and asking them questions.

47 And all that heard him were astonished at his understanding and answers.

48 And when they saw him, they were amazed: and his mother said unto him, Son, why hast thou thus dealt with us? behold, thy father and I have sought thee sorrowing.

49 And he said unto them, How is it that ye sought me? wist ye not that I must be about my Father's business?

50 And they understood not the saying which he spake unto them.

51 And he went down with them, and came to Naz'a-reth, and was subject unto them: but his mother kept all these sayings in her heart.

52 And Je'sus increased in wisdom and stature, and in favour with God and man.

3 NOW in the fifteenth year of the reign of Ti-be'ri-us Cæ'sar, Pon'ti-us Pi'late being governor of Ju-dæ'a, and Her'od being tetrarch of Gal'i-lee, and his brother Phil'ip tetrarch of I-tu-ræ'a and of the region of Trach-o-ni'tis, and Ly-sa'ni-as the tetrarch of Ab-i-le'ne,

2 An'nas and Ca'ia-phas being the high priests, the word of God came unto John the son of Zach-a-ri'as in the wilderness.

3 And he came into all the country about Jor'dan, preaching the baptism of repentance for the remission of sins;

4 As it is written in the book of the words of E-sa'ias the prophet, saying, The voice of one crying in the wilderness, Prepare ye the way of the Lord, make his paths straight.

5 Every valley shall be filled, and every mountain and hill shall be brought low; and the crooked shall be made straight, and the rough ways *shall be* made smooth;

6 And all flesh shall see the salvation of God.

7 Then said he to the multitude that came forth to be baptized of him, O generation of vipers, who hath warned you to flee from the wrath to come?

8 Bring forth therefore fruits worthy of repentance, and begin not to say within yourselves, We have A'bra-ham to *our* father: for I say unto you, That God is able of these stones to raise up children unto A'bra-ham.

9 And now also the ax is laid unto the root of the trees: every tree therefore which bringeth not forth good fruit is hewn down, and cast into the fire.

10 And the people asked him, saying, What shall we do then?

11 He answereth and saith unto them, He that hath two coats, let him impart to him that hath none; and he that hath meat, let him do likewise.

12 Then came also publicans to be baptized, and said unto him, Master, what shall we do?

13 And he said unto them, Exact no more than that which is appointed you.

14 And the soldiers likewise demanded of him, saying, And what shall we do? And he said unto them, Do violence to no man, neither accuse *any* falsely; and be content with your wages.

15 And as the people were in expectation, and all men mused in their hearts of John, whether he were the Christ, or not;

16 John answered, saying unto *them* all, I indeed baptize you with water; but one mightier than I cometh, the latchet of whose shoes I am not worthy to unloose: he shall baptize you with the Ho'ly Ghost and with fire:

17 Whose fan *is* in his hand, and he will throughly purge his floor, and will gather the wheat into his garner; but the chaff he will burn with fire unquenchable.

18 And many other things in his exhortation preached he unto the people.

19 But Her'od the tetrarch, being reproved by him for He-ro'di-as his brother Phil'ip's wife, and for all the evils which Her'od had done,

20 Added yet this above all, that he shut up John in prison.

21 Now when all the people were baptized, it came to pass, that Je'sus also being baptized, and praying, the heaven was opened,

22 And the Ho'ly Ghost descended in a bodily shape like a dove upon him, and a voice came from heaven, which said, Thou art my beloved Son; in thee I am well pleased.

23 And Je'sus himself began to be about thirty years of age, being (as was supposed) the son of Jo'seph, which was *the son* of He'li,

24 Which was *the son* of Mat'that, which was *the son* of Le'vi, which was *the son* of Mel'chi, which was *the son* of Jan'na, which was *the son* of Jo'seph,

25 Which was *the son* of Mat-ta-thi'as, which was *the son* of A'mos, which was *the son* of Na'um, which was *the son* of Es'li, which was *the son* of Nag'ge,

26 Which was *the son* of Ma'ath, which was *the son* of Mat-ta-thi'as, which was *the son* of Sem'e-i, which was *the son* of Jo'seph, which was *the son* of Ju'da,

27 Which was *the son* of Jo-an'na, which was *the son* of Rhe'sa, which was *the son* of Zo-rob'-a-bel, which was *the son* of Sa-la'thi-el, which was *the son* of Ne'ri,

28 Which was *the son* of Mel'chi, which was *the son* of Ad'di, which was *the son* of Co'sam, which was *the son* of El-mo'dam, which was *the son* of Er,

29 Which was *the son* of Jo'se, which was *the son* of E-li-e'zer, which was *the son* of Jo'rim, which was *the son* of Mat'that, which was *the son* of Le'vi,

30 Which was *the son* of Sim'e-on, which was *the son* of Ju'da, which was *the son* of Jo'-seph, which was *the son* of Jo'nan, which was *the son* of E-li'a-kim,

31 Which was *the son* of Me'le-a, which was *the son* of Me'nan, which was *the son* of Mat'ta-tha, which was *the son* of Na'than, which was *the son* of Da'vid,

32 Which was *the son* of Jes'se, which was *the son* of O'bed, which was *the son* of Bo'oz, which was *the son* of Sal'mon, which was *the son* of Na-as'son,

33 Which was *the son* of A-min'a-dab, which was *the son* of A'ram, which was *the son* of Es'-rom, which was *the son* of Pha'res, which was *the son* of Ju'da,

34 Which was *the son* of Ja'cob, which was *the son* of I'saac, which was *the son* of A'bra-ham, which was *the son* of Tha'ra, which was *the son* of Na'chor,

35 Which was *the son* of Sa'ruch, which was *the son* of Ra'gau, which was *the son* of Pha'lec, which was *the son* of He'ber, which was *the son* of Sa'la,

36 Which was *the son* of Ca-i'nan, which was *the son* of Ar-phax'ad, which was *the son* of Sem, which was *the son* of No'e, which was *the son* of La'mech,

37 Which was *the son* of Ma-thu'sa-la, which was *the son* of E'noch, which was *the son* of Ja'red, which was *the son* of Ma-le'le-el, which was *the son* of Ca-i'nan,

38 Which was *the son* of E'nos, which was *the son* of Seth, which was *the son* of Ad'am, which was *the son* of God.

4 AND Je'sus being full of the Ho'ly Ghost returned from Jor'dan, and was led by the Spirit into the wilderness,

2 Being forty days tempted of the devil. And in those days he did eat nothing: and when they were ended, he afterward hungered.

3 And the devil said unto him, If thou be the Son of God, command this stone that it be made bread.

4 And Je'sus answered him, saying, It is written, That man shall not live by bread alone, but by every word of God.

5 And the devil taking him up into an high mountain, shewed unto him all the kingdoms of the world in a moment of time.

6 And the devil said unto him, All this power will I give thee, and the glory of them: for that is delivered unto me; and to whomsoever I will I give it.

7 If thou therefore wilt worship me, all shall be thine.

8 And Je'sus answered and said unto him, Get thee behind me, Sa'tan: for it is written, Thou shalt worship the Lord thy God, and him only shalt thou serve.

9 And he brought him to Je-ru'sa-lem, and set him on a pinnacle of the temple, and said unto him, If thou be the Son of God, cast thyself down from hence:

10 For it is written, He shall give his angels charge over thee, to keep thee:

11 And in *their* hands they shall bear thee up, lest at any time thou dash thy foot against a stone.

12 And Je'sus answering said unto him, It is said, Thou shalt not tempt the Lord thy God.

13 And when the devil had ended all the temptation, he departed from him for a season.

14 ¶ And Je'sus returned in the power of the Spirit into Gal'i-lee: and there went out a fame of him through all the region round about.

15 And he taught in their synagogues, being glorified of all.

16 ¶ And he came to Naz'a-reth, where he had been brought up: and, as his custom was, he went into the synagogue on the sabbath day, and stood up for to read.

17 And there was delivered unto him the book of the prophet E-sa'ias. And when he had opened the book he found the place where it was written,

18 The Spirit of the Lord *is* upon me, because he hath anointed me to preach the gospel to the poor; he hath sent me to heal the brokenhearted, to preach deliverance to the captives, and recovering of sight to the blind, to set at liberty them that are bruised,

19 To preach the acceptable year of the Lord.

20 And he closed the book, and he gave *it* again to the minister, and sat down. And the eyes of all them that were in the synagogue were fastened on him.

21 And he began to say unto them, This day is this scripture fulfilled in your ears.

22 And all bare him witness, and wondered at the gracious words which proceeded out of his mouth. And they said, Is not this Jo'seph's son?

23 And he said unto them, Ye will surely say unto me this proverb, Physician, heal thyself: whatsoever we have heard done in Ca-per'na-um, do also here in thy country.

24 And he said, Verily I say unto you, No prophet is accepted in his own country.

25 But I tell you of a truth, many widows were in Is'ra-el in the days of E-li'as, when the heaven was shut up three years and six months, when great famine was throughout all the land;

26 But unto none of them was E-li'as sent, save unto Sa-rep'ta, *a city* of Si'don, unto a woman *that was* a widow.

27 And many lepers were in Is'ra-el in the
time of El-i-se'us the prophet; and none of them
was cleansed, saving Na'a-man the Syr'i-an.
28 And all they in the synagogue, when they
heard these things, were filled with wrath,
29 And rose up, and thrust him out of the
city, and led him unto the brow of the hill
whereon their city was built, that they might
cast him down headlong.
30 But he passing through the midst of them
went his way,
31 And came down to Ca-per'na-um, a city of
Gal'i-lee, and taught them on the sabbath days.
32 And they were astonished at his doctrine:
for his word was with power.
33 ¶ And in the synagogue there was a man,
which had a spirit of an unclean devil, and cried
out with a loud voice,
34 Saying, Let *us* alone; what have we to do
with thee, *thou* Je'sus of Naz'a-reth? art thou
come to destroy us? I know thee who thou art;
the Holy One of God.
35 And Je'sus rebuked him, saying, Hold thy
peace, and come out of him. And when the devil
had thrown him in the midst, he came out of
him, and hurt him not.
36 And they were all amazed, and spake
among themselves, saying, What a word *is* this!
for with authority and power he commandeth
the unclean spirits, and they come out.
37 And the fame of him went out into every
place of the country round about.
38 ¶ And he arose out of the synagogue, and
entered into Si'mon's house. And Si'mon's
wife's mother was taken with a great fever; and
they besought him for her.
39 And he stood over her, and rebuked the
fever; and it left her: and immediately she arose
and ministered unto them.
40 ¶ Now when the sun was setting, all they
that had any sick with divers diseases brought
them unto him; and he laid his hands on every
one of them, and healed them.
41 And devils also came out of many, crying
out, and saying, Thou art Christ the Son of God.
And he rebuking *them* suffered them not to
speak: for they knew that he was Christ.
42 And when it was day, he departed and
went into a desert place: and the people sought
him, and came unto him, and stayed him, that
he should not depart from them.
43 And he said unto them, I must preach the
kingdom of God to other cities also: for therefore am I sent.
44 And he preached in the synagogues of
Gal'i-lee.

5 AND it came to pass, that, as the people
pressed upon him to hear the word of God,
he stood by the lake of Gen-nes'a-ret,
2 And saw two ships standing by the lake:
but the fishermen were gone out of them, and
were washing *their* nets.
3 And he entered into one of the ships, which
was Si'mon's, and prayed him that he would
thrust out a little from the land. And he sat
down, and taught the people out of the ship.
4 Now when he had left speaking, he said
unto Si'mon, Launch out into the deep, and let
down your nets for a draught.
5 And Si'mon answering said unto him, Master, we have toiled all the night, and have taken
nothing: nevertheless at thy word I will let
down the net.
6 And when they had this done, they inclosed
a great multitude of fishes: and their net brake.
7 And they beckoned unto *their* partners,
which were in the other ship, that they should
come and help them. And they came, and filled
both the ships, so that they began to sink.
8 When Si'mon Pe'ter saw *it*, he fell down at
Je'sus' knees, saying, Depart from me; for I am
a sinful man, O Lord.
9 For he was astonished, and all that were
with him, at the draught of the fishes which
they had taken:
10 And so *was* also James, and John, the
sons of Zeb'e-dee, which were partners with Si'-
mon. And Je'sus said unto Si'mon, Fear not;
from henceforth thou shalt catch men.
11 And when they had brought their ships to
land, they forsook all, and followed him.
12 ¶ And it came to pass, when he was in a
certain city, behold a man full of leprosy: who
seeing Je'sus fell on *his* face, and besought him,
saying, Lord, if thou wilt, thou canst make me
clean.
13 And he put forth *his* hand, and touched
him, saying, I will: be thou clean. And immediately the leprosy departed from him.
14 And he charged him to tell no man: but
go, and shew thyself to the priest, and offer for
thy cleansing, according as Mo'ses commanded, for a testimony unto them.
15 But so much the more went there a fame
abroad of him: and great multitudes came together to hear, and to be healed by him of their
infirmities.
16 ¶ And he withdrew himself into the wilderness, and prayed.
17 And it came to pass on a certain day, as
he was teaching, that there were Phar'i-sees
and doctors of the law sitting by, which were
come out of every town of Gal'i-lee, and Ju-dæ'-
a, and Je-ru'sa-lem: and the power of the Lord
was *present* to heal them.
18 ¶ And, behold, men brought in a bed a
man which was taken with a palsy: and they
sought *means* to bring him in, and to lay *him*
before him.
19 And when they could not find by what
way they might bring him in because of the
multitude, they went upon the house top, and
let him down through the tiling with *his* couch
into the midst before Je'sus.
20 And when he saw their faith, he said unto
him, Man, thy sins are forgiven thee.
21 And the scribes and the Phar'i-sees began
to reason, saying, Who is this which speaketh
blasphemies? Who can forgive sins, but God
alone?
22 But when Je'sus perceived their thoughts,
he answering said unto them, What reason ye
in your hearts?
23 Whether is easier, to say, Thy sins be forgiven thee; or to say, Rise up and walk?
24 But that ye may know that the Son of man
hath power upon earth to forgive sins, (he said
unto the sick of the palsy,) I say unto thee,
Arise, and take up thy coucn, and go into thine
house.
25 And immediately he rose up before them,
and took up that whereon he lay, and departed
to his own house, glorifying God.
26 And they were all amazed, and they glorified God, and were filled with fear, saying, We
have seen strange things to day.
27 ¶ And after these things he went forth,
and saw a publican, named Le'vi, sitting at the
receipt of custom: and he said unto him, Follow
me.
28 And he left all, rose up, and followed him.
29 And Le'vi made him a great feast in his
own house: and there was a great company of

publicans and of others that sat down with them.

30 But their scribes and Phar'i-sees murmured against his disciples, saying, Why do ye eat and drink with publicans and sinners?

31 And Je'sus answering said unto them, They that are whole need not a physician; but they that are sick.

32 I came not to call the righteous, but sinners to repentance.

33 ¶ And they said unto him, Why do the disciples of John fast often, and make prayers, and likewise *the disciples* of the Phar'i-sees; but thine eat and drink?

34 And he said unto them, Can ye make the children of the bridechamber fast, while the bridegroom is with them?

35 But the days will come, when the bridegroom shall be taken away from them, and then shall they fast in those days.

36 ¶ And he spake also a parable unto them; No man putteth a piece of a new garment upon an old; if otherwise, then both the new maketh a rent, and the piece that was *taken* out of the new agreeth not with the old.

37 And no man putteth new wine into old bottles; else the new wine will burst the bottles, and be spilled, and the bottles shall perish.

38 But new wine must be put into new bottles; and both are preserved.

39 No man also having drunk old *wine* straightway desireth new: for he saith, The old is better.

6 AND it came to pass on the second sabbath after the first, that he went through the corn fields; and his disciples plucked the ears of corn, and did eat rubbing *them* in *their* hands.

2 And certain of the Phar'i-sees said unto them, Why do ye that which is not lawful to do on the sabbath days?

3 And Je'sus answering them said, Have ye not read so much as this, what Da'vid did, when himself was an hungred, and they which were with him;

4 How he went into the house of God, and did take and eat the shewbread, and gave also to them that were with him; which it is not lawful to eat but for the priests alone?

5 And he said unto them, That the Son of man is Lord also of the sabbath.

6 And it came to pass also on another sabbath, that he entered into the synagogue and taught: and there was a man whose right hand was withered.

7 And the scribes and Phar'i-sees watched him, whether he would heal on the sabbath day; that they might find an accusation against him.

8 But he knew their thoughts, and said to the man which had the withered hand, Rise up, and stand forth in the midst. And he arose and stood forth.

9 Then said Je'sus unto them, I will ask you one thing; Is it lawful on the sabbath days to do good, or to do evil? to save life, or to destroy *it?*

10 And looking round about upon them all, he said unto the man, Stretch forth thy hand. And he did so: and his hand was restored whole as the other.

11 And they were filled with madness; and communed one with another what they might do to Je'sus.

12 And it came to pass in those days, that he went out into a mountain to pray, and continued all night in prayer to God.

13 ¶ And when it was day, he called *unto him* his disciples: and of them he chose twelve, whom also he named apostles;

14 Si'mon, (whom he also named Pe'ter,) and Andrew his brother, James and John, Phil'ip and Bar-thol'o-mew,

15 Mat'thew and Thom'as, James the *son* of Al-phæ'us, and Si'mon called Ze-lo'tes,

16 And Ju'das *the brother* of James, and Ju'das Is-car'i-ot, which also was the traitor.

17 ¶ And he came down with them, and stood in the plain, and the company of his disciples, and a great multitude of people out of all Ju-dæ'a and Je-ru'sa-lem, and from the sea coast of Tyre and Si'don, which came to hear him, and to be healed of their diseases;

18 And they that were vexed with unclean spirits: and they were healed.

19 And the whole multitude sought to touch him: for there went virtue out of him, and healed *them* all.

20 ¶ And he lifted up his eyes on his disciples, and said, Blessed *be ye* poor: for yours is the kingdom of God.

21 Blessed *are ye* that hunger now: for ye shall be filled. Blessed *are ye* that weep now: for ye shall laugh.

22 Blessed are ye, when men shall hate you, and when they shall separate you *from their company,* and shall reproach *you,* and cast out your name as evil, for the Son of man's sake.

23 Rejoice ye in that day, and leap for joy: for, behold, your reward *is* great in heaven: for in the like manner did their fathers unto the prophets.

24 But woe unto you that are rich! for ye have received your consolation.

25 Woe unto you that are full! for ye shall hunger. Woe unto you that laugh now! for ye shall mourn and weep.

26 Woe unto you, when all men shall speak well of you! for so did their fathers to the false prophets.

27 ¶ But I say unto you which hear, Love your enemies, do good to them which hate you.

28 Bless them that curse you, and pray for them which despitefully use you.

29 And unto him that smiteth thee on the *one* cheek offer also the other; and him that taketh away thy cloke forbid not *to take thy* coat also.

30 Give to every man that asketh of thee; and of him that taketh away thy goods ask *them* not again.

31 And as ye would that men should do to you, do ye also to them likewise.

32 For if ye love them which love you, what thank have ye? for sinners also love those that love them.

33 And if ye do good to them which do good to you, what thank have ye? for sinners also do even the same.

34 And if ye lend *to them* of whom ye hope to receive, what thank have ye? for sinners also lend to sinners, to receive as much again.

35 But love ye your enemies, and do good, and lend, hoping for nothing again; and your reward shall be great, and ye shall be the children of the Highest: for he is kind unto the unthankful and *to* the evil.

36 Be ye therefore merciful, as your Father also is merciful.

37 Judge not, and ye shall not be judged: comdemn not, and ye shall not be condemned: forgive, and ye shall be forgiven:

38 Give, and it shall be given unto you; good measure, pressed down, and shaken together, and running over, shall men give into your bos-

om. For with the same measure that ye mete
withal it shall be measured to you again.
39 And he spake a parable unto them, Can
the blind lead the blind: shall they not both fall
into the ditch?
40 The disciple is not above his master: but
every one that is perfect shall be as his master.
41 And why beholdest thou the mote that is
in thy brother's eye, but perceivest not the
beam that is in thine own eye?
42 Either how canst thou say to thy brother,
Brother, let me pull out the mote that is in thine
eye, when thou thyself beholdest not the beam
that is in thine own eye? Thou hypocrite, cast
out first the beam out of thine own eye, and
then shalt thou see clearly to pull out the mote
that is in thy brother's eye.
43 For a good tree bringeth not forth corrupt
fruit; neither doth a corrupt tree bring forth
good fruit.
44 For every tree is known by his own fruit.
For of thorns men do not gather figs, nor of a
bramble bush gather they grapes.
45 A good man out of the good treasure of
his heart bringeth forth that which is good; and
an evil man out of the evil treasure of his heart
bringeth forth that which is evil: for of the
abundance of the heart his mouth speaketh.
46 ¶ And why call ye me, Lord, Lord, and do
not the things which I say?
47 Whosoever cometh to me, and heareth
my sayings, and doeth them, I will shew you to
whom he is like:
48 He is like a man which built an house, and
digged deep, and laid the foundation on a rock:
and when the flood arose, the stream beat vehemently upon that house, and could not shake it:
for it was founded upon a rock.
49 But he that heareth, and doeth not, is like
a man that without a foundation built an house
upon the earth; against which the stream did
beat vehemently, and immediately it fell; and
the ruin of that house was great.

7 NOW when he had ended all his sayings in
the audience of the people, he entered into
Ca-per'na-um.
2 And a certain centurion's servant, who was
dear unto him, was sick, and ready to die.
3 And when he heard of Je'sus, he sent unto
him the elders of the Jews, beseeching him that
he would come and heal his servant.
4 And when they came to Je'sus, they besought him instantly, saying, That he was worthy for whom he should do this:
5 For he loveth our nation, and he hath built
us a synagogue.
6 Then Je'sus went with them. And when he
was now not far from the house, the centurion
sent friends to him, saying unto him, Lord, trouble not thyself: for I am not worthy that thou
shouldest enter under my roof:
7 Wherefore neither thought I myself worthy
to come unto thee: but say in a word, and my
servant shall be healed.
8 For I also am a man set under authority,
having under me soldiers, and I say unto one,
Go, and he goeth; and to another, Come, and he
cometh; and to my servant, Do this, and he
doeth *it*.
9 When Je'sus heard these things, he marvelled at him, and turned him about, and said
unto the people that followed him, I say unto
you, I have not found so great faith, no, not in
Is'ra-el.
10 And they that were sent, returning to the
house, found the servant whole that had been
sick.
11 ¶ And it came to pass the day after, that
he went into a city called Na'in; and many of his
disciples went with him, and much people.
12 Now when he came nigh to the gate of the
city, behold, there was a dead man carried out,
the only son of his mother, and she was a
widow: and much people of the city was with
her.
13 And when the Lord saw her, he had compassion on her, and said unto her, Weep not.
14 And he came and touched the bier: and
they that bare *him* stood still. And he said,
Young man, I say unto thee, Arise.
15 And he that was dead sat up, and began to
speak. And he delivered him to his mother.
16 And there came a fear on all: and they glorified God, saying, That a great prophet is risen
up among us; and, That God hath visited his
people.
17 And this rumour of him went forth
throughout all Ju-dæ'a, and throughout all the
region round about.
18 And the disciples of John shewed him of
all these things.
19 ¶ And John calling *unto him* two of his
disciples sent *them* to Je'sus, saying, Art thou
he that should come? or look we for another?
20 When the men were come unto him, they
said, John Bap'tist hath sent us unto thee, saying, Art thou he that should come? or look we
for another?
21 And in that same hour he cured many of
their infirmities and plagues, and of evil spirits;
and unto many *that were* blind he gave sight.
22 Then Je'sus answering said unto them, Go
your way, and tell John what things ye have
seen and heard; how that the blind see, the lame
walk, the lepers are cleansed, the deaf hear, the
dead are raised, to the poor the gospel is
preached.
23 And blessed is *he*, whosoever shall not be
offended in me.
24 ¶ And when the messengers of John were
departed, he began to speak unto the people
concerning John, What went ye out into the
wilderness for to see? A reed shaken with the
wind?
25 But what went ye out for to see? A man
clothed in soft raiment? Behold, they which are
gorgeously apparelled, and live delicately, are
in kings' courts.
26 But what went ye out for to see? A
prophet? Yea, I say unto you, and much more
than a prophet.
27 This is *he*, of whom it is written, Behold, I
send my messenger before thy face, which shall
prepare thy way before thee.
28 For I say unto you, Among those that are
born of women there is not a greater prophet
than John the Bap'tist: but he that is least in the
kingdom of God is greater than he.
29 And all the people that heard *him*, and the
publicans, justified God, being baptized with
the baptism of John.
30 But the Phar'i-sees and lawyers rejected
the counsel of God against themselves, being
not baptized of him.
31 ¶ And the Lord said, Whereunto then
shall I liken the men of this generation? and to
what are they like?
32 They are like unto children sitting in the
marketplace, and calling one to another, and
saying, We have piped unto you, and ye have
not danced; we have mourned to you, and ye
have not wept.

33 For John the Bap'tist came neither eating bread nor drinking wine; and ye say, He hath a devil.
34 The Son of man is come eating and drinking; and ye say, Behold a gluttonous man, and a winebibber, a friend of publicans and sinners!
35 But wisdom is justified of all her children.
36 ¶ And one of the Phar'i-sees desired him that he would eat with him. And he went into the Phar'i-see's house, and sat down to meat.
37 And, behold, a woman in the city, which was a sinner, when she knew that *Je'sus* sat at meat in the Phar'i-see's house, brought an alabaster box of ointment,
38 And stood at his feet behind *him* weeping, and began to wash his feet with tears, and did wipe *them* with the hairs of her head, and kissed his feet, and anointed *them* with the ointment.
39 Now when the Phar'i-see which had bidden him saw *it*, he spake within himself, saying, This man, if he were a prophet, would have known who and what manner of woman *this is* that toucheth him: for she is a sinner.
40 And Je'sus answering said unto him, Si'mon, I have somewhat to say unto thee. And he saith, Master, say on.
41 There was a certain creditor which had two debtors: the one owed five hundred pence, and the other fifty.
42 And when they had nothing to pay, he frankly forgave them both. Tell me therefore, which of them will love him most?
43 Si'mon answered and said, I suppose that *he*, to whom he forgave most. And he said unto him, Thou hast rightly judged.
44 And he turned to the woman, and said unto Si'mon, Seest thou this woman? I entered into thine house, thou gavest me no water for my feet: but she hath washed my feet with tears, and wiped *them* with the hairs of her head.
45 Thou gavest me no kiss: but this woman since the time I came in hath not ceased to kiss my feet.
46 My head with oil thou didst not anoint: but this woman hath anointed my feet with ointment.
47 Wherefore I say unto thee, Her sins, which are many, are forgiven; for she loved much: but to whom little is forgiven, *the same* loveth little.
48 And he said unto her, Thy sins are forgiven.
49 And they that sat at meat with him began to say within themselves, Who is this that forgiveth sins also?
50 And he said to the woman, Thy faith hath saved thee; go in peace.

8 AND it came to pass afterward, that he went throughout every city and village, preaching and shewing the glad tidings of the kingdom of God: and the twelve *were* with him,
2 And certain women, which had been healed of evil spirits and infirmities, Ma'ry called Mag-da-le'ne, out of whom went seven devils,
3 And Jo-an'na the wife of Chu'za Her'od's steward, and Su-san'na, and many others, which ministered unto him of their substance.
4 ¶ And when much people were gathered together, and were come to him out of every city, he spake by a parable:
5 A sower went out to sow his seed: and as he sowed, some fell by the way side; and it was trodden down, and the fowls of the air devoured it.
6 And some fell upon a rock; and as soon as it was sprung up, it withered away, because it lacked moisture.
7 And some fell among thorns; and the thorns sprang up with it, and choked it.
8 And other fell on good ground, and sprang up, and bare fruit an hundredfold. And when he had said these things, he cried, He that hath ears to hear, let him hear.
9 And his disciples asked him, saying, What might this parable be?
10 And he said, Unto you it is given to know the mysteries of the kingdom of God: but to others in parables; that seeing they might not see, and hearing they might not understand.
11 Now the parable is this: The seed is the word of God.
12 Those by the way side are they that hear; then cometh the devil, and taketh away the word out of their hearts, lest they should believe and be saved.
13 They on the rock *are they*, which, when they hear, receive the word with joy; and these have no root, which for a while believe, and in time of temptation fall away.
14 And that which fell among thorns are they, which, when they have heard, go forth, and are choked with cares and riches and pleasures of *this* life, and bring no fruit to perfection.
15 But that on the good ground are they, which in an honest and good heart, having heard the word, keep *it*, and bring forth fruit with patience.
16 ¶ No man, when he hath lighted a candle, covereth it with a vessel, or putteth *it* under a bed; but setteth *it* on a candlestick, that they which enter in may see the light.
17 For nothing is secret, that shall not be made manifest; neither *any thing* hid, that shall not be known and come abroad.
18 Take heed therefore how ye hear: for whosoever hath, to him shall be given; and whosoever hath not, from him shall be taken even that which he seemeth to have.
19 ¶ Then came to him *his* mother and his brethren, and could not come at him for the press.
20 And it was told him *by certain* which said, Thy mother and thy brethren stand without, desiring to see thee.
21 And he answered and said unto them, My mother and my brethren are these which hear the word of God, and do it.
22 ¶ Now it came to pass on a certain day, that he went into a ship with his disciples: and he said unto them, Let us go over unto the other side of the lake. And they launched forth.
23 But as they sailed he fell asleep: and there came down a storm of wind on the lake; and they were filled *with water*, and were in jeopardy.
24 And they came to him, and awoke him, saying, Master, master, we perish. Then he arose, and rebuked the wind and the raging of the water: and they ceased, and there was a calm.
25 And he said unto them, Where is your faith? And they being afraid wondered, saying one to another, What manner of man is this! for he commandeth even the winds and water, and they obey him.
26 ¶ And they arrived at the country of the Gad'a-renes, which is over against Gal'i-lee.
27 And when he went forth to land, there

met him out of the city a certain man, which
had devils long time, and ware no clothes, neither abode in *any* house, but in the tombs.
28 When he saw Je'sus, he cried out, and fell
down before him, and with a loud voice said,
What have I to do with thee, Je'sus, *thou* Son of
God most high? I beseech thee, torment me not.
29 (For he had commanded the unclean spirit
to come out of the man. For oftentimes it had
caught him: and he was kept bound with chains
and in fetters; and he brake the bands, and was
driven of the devil into the wilderness.)
30 And Je'sus asked him, saying, What is thy
name? And he said, Legion: because many devils were entered into him.
31 And they besought him that he would not
command them to go out into the deep.
32 And there was there an herd of many
swine feeding on the mountain: and they besought him that he would suffer them to enter
into them. And he suffered them.
33 Then went the devils out of the man, and
entered into the swine: and the herd ran violently down a steep place into the lake, and
were choked.
34 When they that fed *them* saw what was
done, they fled, and went and told *it* in the city
and in the country.
35 Then they went out to see what was done;
and came to Je'sus, and found the man, out of
whom the devils departed, sitting at the feet of
Je'sus, clothed, and in his right mind: and they
were afraid.
36 They also which saw *it* told them by what
means he that was possessed of the devils was
healed.
37 ¶ Then the whole multitude of the country of the Gad'a-renes round about besought
him to depart from them; for they were taken
with great fear: and he went up into the ship,
and returned back again.
38 Now the man out of whom the devils were
departed besought him that he might be with
him: but Je'sus sent him away, saying,
39 Return to thine own house, and shew how
great things God hath done unto thee. And he
went his way, and published throughout the
whole city how great things Je'sus had done
unto him.
40 And it came to pass, that, when Je'sus
was returned, the people *gladly* received him:
for they were all waiting for him.
41 ¶ And, behold, there came a man named
Ja-irus, and he was a ruler of the synagogue:
and he fell down at Je'sus' feet, and besought
him that he would come into his house:
42 For he had one only daughter, about
twelve years of age, and she lay a dying. But as
he went the people thronged him.
43 ¶ And a woman having an issue of blood
twelve years, which had spent all her living
upon physicians, neither could be healed of any,
44 Came behind *him*, and touched the border
of his garment: and immediately her issue of
blood stanched.
45 And Je'sus said, Who touched me? When
all denied, Pe'ter and they that were with him
said, Master, the multitude throng thee and
press *thee*, and sayest thou, Who touched me?
46 And Je'sus said, Somebody hath touched
me: for I perceive that virtue is gone out of me.
47 And when the woman saw that she was
not hid, she came trembling, and falling down
before him, she declared unto him before all the
people for what cause she had touched him, and
how she was healed immediately.
48 And he said unto her, Daughter, be of
good comfort: thy faith hath made thee whole;
go in peace.
49 ¶ While he yet spake, there cometh one
from the ruler of the synagogue's *house*, saying
to him, Thy daughter is dead; trouble not the
Master.
50 But when Je'sus heard *it*, he answered
him, saying, Fear not: believe only, and she
shall be made whole.
51 And when he came into the house, he suffered no man to go in, save Pe'ter, and James,
and John, and the father and the mother of the
maiden.
52 And all wept, and bewailed her: but he
said, Weep not; she is not dead, but sleepeth.
53 And they laughed him to scorn, knowing
that she was dead.
54 And he put them all out, and took her by
the hand, and called, saying, Maid, arise.
55 And her spirit came again, and she arose
straightway: and he commanded to give her
meat.
56 And her parents were astonished: but he
charged them that they should tell no man what
was done.

9 THEN he called his twelve disciples together, and gave them power and authority over all devils, and to cure diseases.
2 And he sent them to preach the kingdom of
God, and to heal the sick.
3 And he said unto them, Take nothing for
your journey, neither staves, nor scrip, neither
bread, neither money; neither have two coats
apiece.
4 And whatsoever house ye enter into, there
abide, and thence depart.
5 And whosoever will not receive you, when
ye go out of that city, shake off the very dust
from your feet for a testimony against them.
6 And they departed, and went through the
towns, preaching the gospel, and healing every
where.
7 ¶ Now Her'od the tetrarch heard of all that
was done by him: and he was perplexed, because that it was said of some, that John was
risen from the dead;
8 And of some, that E-li'as had appeared; and
of others, that one of the old prophets was risen
again.
9 And Her'od said, John have I beheaded: but
who is this, of whom I hear such things? And he
desired to see him.
10 ¶ And the apostles, when they were returned, told him all that they had done. And he
took them, and went aside privately into a desert place belonging to the city called Beth-sa'i-
da.
11 And the people, when they knew *it*, followed him: and he received them, and spake
unto them of the kingdom of God, and healed
them that had need of healing.
12 And when the day began to wear away,
then came the twelve, and said unto him, Send
the multitude away, that they may go into the
towns and country round about, and lodge, and
get victuals: for we are here in a desert place.
13 But he said unto them, Give ye them to
eat. And they said, We have no more but five
loaves and two fishes; except we should go and
buy meat for all this people.
14 For they were about five thousand men.
And he said to his disciples, Make them sit
down by fifties in a company.
15 And they did so, and made them all sit
down.
16 Then he took the five loaves and the two

fishes, and looking up to heaven, he blessed
them, and brake, and gave to the disciples to set
before the multitude.
17 And they did eat, and were all filled: and
there was taken up of fragments that remained
to them twelve baskets.
18 ¶ And it came to pass, as he was alone
praying, his disciples were with him: and he
asked them, saying, Whom say the people that I
am?
19 They answering said, John the Bap'tist;
but some *say*, E-li'as; and others *say*, that one of
the old prophets is risen again.
20 He said unto them, But whom say ye that
I am? Pe'ter answering said, The Christ of God.
21 And he straitly charged them, and commanded *them* to tell no man that thing;
22 Saying, The Son of man must suffer many
things, and be rejected of the elders and chief
priests and scribes, and be slain, and be raised
the third day.
23 ¶ And he said to *them* all, If any *man* will
come after me, let him deny himself, and take
up his cross daily, and follow me.
24 For whosoever will save his life shall lose
it: but whosoever will lose his life for my sake,
the same shall save it.
25 For what is a man advantaged, if he gain
the whole world, and lose himself, or be cast
away?
26 For whosoever shall be ashamed of me
and of my words, of him shall the Son of man
be ashamed, when he shall come in his own glory, and *in his* Father's, and of the holy angels.
27 But I tell you of a truth, there be some
standing here, which shall not taste of death, till
they see the kingdom of God.
28 ¶ And it came to pass about an eight days
after these sayings, he took Pe'ter and John and
James, and went up into a mountain to pray.
29 And as he prayed, the fashion of his countenance was altered, and his raiment *was* white
and glistering.
30 And, behold, there talked with him two
men, which were Mo'ses and E-li'as:
31 Who appeared in glory, and spake of his
decease which he should accomplish at Je-ru'-
sa-lem.
32 But Pe'ter and they that were with him
were heavy with sleep: and when they were
awake, they saw his glory, and the two men
that stood with him.
33 And it came to pass, as they departed from
him, Pe'ter said unto Je'sus, Master, it is good for
us to be here: and let us make three tabernacles;
one for thee, and one for Mo'ses, and one for
E-li'as: not knowing what he said.
34 While he thus spake, there came a cloud,
and overshadowed them: and they feared as
they entered into the cloud.
35 And there came a voice out of the cloud,
saying, This is my beloved Son: hear him.
36 And when the voice was past, Je'sus was
found alone. And they kept *it* close, and told no
man in those days any of those things which
they had seen.
37 ¶ And it came to pass, that on the next
day, when they were come down from the hill,
much people met him.
38 And, behold, a man of the company cried
out, saying, Master, I beseech thee, look upon
my son: for he is mine only child.
39 And, lo, a spirit taketh him, and he suddenly crieth out; and it teareth him that he
foameth again, and bruising him hardly departeth from him.
40 And I besought thy disciples to cast him
out; and they could not.
41 And Je'sus answering said, O faithless
and perverse generation, how long shall I be
with you, and suffer you? Bring thy son hither.
42 And as he was yet a coming, the devil
threw him down, and tare *him*. And Je'sus rebuked the unclean spirit, and healed the child,
and delivered him again to his father.
43 ¶ And they were all amazed at the mighty
power of God. But while they wondered every
one at all things which Je'sus did, he said unto
his disciples,
44 Let these sayings sink down into your
ears: for the Son of man shall be delivered into
the hands of men.
45 But they understood not this saying, and
it was hid from them, that they perceived it not:
and they feared to ask him of that saying.
46 ¶ Then there arose a reasoning among
them, which of them should be greatest.
47 And Je'sus, perceiving the thought of
their heart, took a child, and set him by him,
48 And said unto them, Whosoever shall receive this child in my name receiveth me: and
whosoever shall receive me receiveth him that
sent me: for he that is least among you all, the
same shall be great.
49 ¶ And John answered and said, Master,
we saw one casting out devils in thy name; and
we forbad him, because he followeth not with
us.
50 And Je'sus said unto him, Forbid *him* not:
for he that is not against us is for us.
51 ¶ And it came to pass, when the time was
come that he should be received up, he stedfastly set his face to go to Je-ru'sa-lem,
52 And sent messengers before his face: and
they went, and entered into a village of the Sa-
mar'i-tans, to make ready for him.
53 And they did not receive him, because his
face was as though he would go to Je-ru'sa-lem.
54 And when his disciples James and John
saw *this*, they said, Lord, wilt thou that we
command fire to come down from heaven, and
consume them, even as E-li'as did?
55 But he turned, and rebuked them, and
said, Ye know not what manner of spirit ye are
of.
56 For the Son of man is not come to destroy
men's lives, but to save *them*. And they went to
another village.
57 ¶ And it came to pass, that, as they went
in the way, a certain *man* said unto him, Lord, I
will follow thee whithersoever thou goest.
58 And Je'sus said unto him, Foxes have
holes, and birds of the air *have* nests; but the
Son of man hath not where to lay *his* head.
59 And he said unto another, Follow me. But
he said, Lord, suffer me first to go and bury my
father.
60 Je'sus said unto him, Let the dead bury
their dead: but go thou and preach the kingdom
of God.
61 And another also said, LORD, I will follow
thee; but let me first go bid them farewell,
which are at home at my house.
62 And Je'sus said unto him, No man, having
put his hand to the plow, and looking back, is fit
for the kingdom of God.

10 AFTER these things the Lord appointed
other seventy also, and sent them two
and two before his face into every city and
place, whither he himself would come.
2 Therefore said he unto them, The harvest
truly *is* great, but the labourers *are* few: pray ye

therefore the Lord of the harvest, that he would send forth labourers into his harvest.

3 Go your ways: behold, I send you forth as lambs among wolves.

4 Carry neither purse, nor scrip, nor shoes: and salute no man by the way.

5 And into whatsoever house ye enter, first say, Peace *be* to this house.

6 And if the son of peace be there, your peace shall rest upon it: if not, it shall turn to you again.

7 And in the same house remain, eating and drinking such things as they give: for the labourer is worthy of his hire. Go not from house to house.

8 And into whatsoever city ye enter, and they receive you, eat such things as are set before you:

9 And heal the sick that are therein, and say unto them, The kingdom of God is come nigh unto you.

10 But into whatsoever city ye enter, and they receive you not, go your ways out into the streets of the same, and say,

11 Even the very dust of your city, which cleaveth on us, we do wipe off against you: notwithstanding be ye sure of this, that the kingdom of God is come nigh unto you.

12 But I say unto you, that it shall be more tolerable in that day for Sod'om, than for that city.

13 Woe unto thee, Cho-ra'zin! woe unto thee, Beth-sa'i-da! for if the mighty works had been done in Tyre and Si'don, which have been done in you, they had a great while ago repented, sitting in sackcloth and ashes.

14 But it shall be more tolerable for Tyre and Si'don at the judgment, than for you.

15 And thou Ca-per'na-um, which art exalted to heaven, shalt be thrust down to hell.

16 He that heareth you heareth me; and he that despiseth you despiseth me; and he that despiseth me despiseth him that sent me.

17 ¶ And the seventy returned again with joy, saying, Lord, even the devils are subject unto us through thy name.

18 And he said unto them, I beheld Sa'tan as lightning fall from heaven.

19 Behold, I give unto you power to tread on serpents and scorpions, and over all the power of the enemy: and nothing shall by any means hurt you.

20 Notwithstanding in this rejoice not, that the spirits are subject unto you; but rather rejoice, because your names are written in heaven.

21 ¶ In that hour Je'sus rejoiced in spirit, and said, I thank thee, O Father, Lord of heaven and earth, that thou hast hid these things from the wise and prudent, and hast revealed them unto babes: even so, Father; for so it seemed good in thy sight.

22 All things are delivered to me of my Father: and no man knoweth who the Son is, but the Father; and who the Father is, but the Son, and *he* to whom the Son will reveal *him*.

23 ¶ And he turned him unto *his* disciples, and said privately, Blessed *are* the eyes which see the things that ye see:

24 For I tell you, that many prophets and kings have desired to see those things which ye see, and have not seen *them;* and to hear those things which ye hear, and have not heard *them*.

25 ¶ And, behold, a certain lawyer stood up, and tempted him, saying, Master, what shall I do to inherit eternal life?

26 He said unto him, What is written in the law? how readest thou?

27 And he answering said, Thou shalt love the Lord thy God with all thy heart, and with all thy soul, and with all thy strength, and with all thy mind; and thy neighbour as thyself.

28 And he said unto him, Thou hast answered right; this do, and thou shalt live.

29 But he, willing to justify himself, said unto Je'sus, And who is my neighbour?

30 And Je'sus answering said, A certain *man* went down from Je-ru'sa-lem to Jer'i-cho, and fell among thieves, which stripped him of his raiment, and wounded *him*, and departed, leaving *him* half dead.

31 And by chance there came down a certain priest that way: and when he saw him, he passed by on the other side.

32 And likewise a Le'vite, when he was at the place, came and looked *on him*, and passed by on the other side.

33 But a certain Sa-mar'i-tan, as he journeyed, came where he was: and when he saw him, he had compassion *on him*.

34 And went to *him*, and bound up his wounds, pouring in oil and wine, and set him on his own beast, and brought him to an inn, and took care of him.

35 And on the morrow when he departed, he took out two pence, and gave *them* to the host, and said unto him, Take care of him; and whatsoever thou spendest more, when I come again, I will repay thee.

36 Which now of these three, thinkest thou, was neighbour unto him that fell among the thieves?

37 And he said, He that shewed mercy on him. Then said Je'sus unto him, Go, and do thou likewise.

38 ¶ Now it came to pass, as they went, that he entered into a certain village: and a certain woman named Mar'tha received him into her house.

39 And she had a sister called Ma'ry, which also sat at Je'sus' feet, and heard his word.

40 But Mar'tha was cumbered about much serving, and came to him, and said, Lord, dost thou not care that my sister hath left me to serve alone? bid her therefore that she help me.

41 And Je'sus answered and said unto her, Mar'tha, Mar'tha, thou art careful and troubled about many things:

42 But one thing is needful: and Ma'ry hath chosen that good part, which shall not be taken away from her.

11 AND it came to pass, that, as he was praying in a certain place, when he ceased, one of his disciples said unto him, Lord, teach us to pray, as John also taught his disciples.

2 And he said unto them, When ye pray, say, Our Father which art in heaven, Hallowed be thy name. Thy kingdom come. Thy will be done, as in heaven, so in earth.

3 Give us day by day our daily bread.

4 And forgive us our sins; for we also forgive every one that is indebted to us. And lead us not into temptation; but deliver us from evil.

5 And he said unto them, Which of you shall have a friend, and shall go unto him at midnight, and say unto him, Friend, lend me three loaves;

6 For a friend of mine in his journey is come to me, and I have nothing to set before him?

7 And he from within shall answer and say, Trouble me not: the door is now shut, and my

children are with me in bed; I cannot rise and
give thee.
8 I say unto you, Though he will not rise and
give him, because he is his friend, yet because
of his importunity he will rise and give him as
many as he needeth.
9 And I say unto you, Ask, and it shall be
given you; seek, and ye shall find; knock, and it
shall be opened unto you.
10 For every one that asketh receiveth; and
he that seeketh findeth; and to him that knocketh it shall be opened.
11 If a son shall ask bread of any of you that
is a father, will he give him a stone? or if *he ask*
a fish, will he for a fish give him a serpent?
12 Or if he shall ask an egg, will he offer him
a scorpion?
13 If ye then, being evil, know how to give
good gifts unto your children: how much more
shall *your* heavenly Father give the Ho'ly Spir'it
to them that ask him?
14 ¶ And he was casting out a devil, and it
was dumb. And it came to pass, when the devil
was gone out, the dumb spake; and the people
wondered.
15 But some of them said, He casteth out
devils through Be'el'ze-bub the chief of the devils.
16 And others, tempting *him*, sought of him
a sign from heaven.
17 But he, knowing their thoughts, said unto
them, Every kingdom divided against itself is
brought to desolation; and a house *divided*
against a house falleth.
18 If Sa'tan also be divided against himself,
how shall his kingdom stand? because ye say
that I cast out devils through Be'el'ze-bub.
19 And if I by Be'el'ze-bub cast out devils, by
whom do your sons cast *them* out? therefore
shall they be your judges.
20 But if I with the finger of God cast out
devils, no doubt the kingdom of God is come
upon you.
21 When a strong man armed keepeth his
palace, his goods are in peace:
22 But when a stronger than he shall come
upon him, and overcome him, he taketh from
him all his armour wherein he trusted, and
divideth his spoils.
23 He that is not with me is against me: and
he that gathereth not with me scattereth.
24 When the unclean spirit is gone out of a
man, he walketh through dry places, seeking
rest; and finding none, he saith, I will return
unto my house whence I came out.
25 And when he cometh, he findeth *it* swept
and garnished.
26 Then goeth he, and taketh *to him* seven
other spirits more wicked than himself; and
they enter in, and dwell there: and the last *state*
of that man is worse than the first.
27 ¶ And it came to pass, as he spake these
things, a certain woman of the company lifted
up her voice, and said unto him, Blessed *is* the
womb that bare thee, and the paps which thou
hast sucked.
28 But he said, Yea rather, blessed *are* they
that hear the word of God, and keep it.
29 ¶ And when the people were gathered
thick together, he began to say, This is an evil
generation: they seek a sign; and there shall no
sign be given it, but the sign of Jo'nas the
prophet.
30 For as Jo'nas was a sign unto the Nin'e-
vites, so shall also the Son of man be to this
generation.
31 The queen of the south shall rise up in the
judgment with the men of this generation, and
condemn them: for she came from the utmost
parts of the earth to hear the wisdom of Sol'o-
mon; and, behold, a greater than Sol'o-mon *is*
here.
32 The men of Nin'e-ve shall rise up in the
judgment with this generation, and shall condemn it: for they repented at the preaching of
Jo'nas; and, behold, a greater than Jo'nas *is*
here.
33 No man, when he hath lighted a candle,
putteth *it* in a secret place, neither under a
bushel, but on a candlestick, that they which
come in may see the light.
34 The light of the body is the eye: therefore
when thine eye is single, thy whole body also is
full of light; but when *thine eye* is evil, thy body
also *is* full of darkness.
35 Take heed therefore that the light which is
in thee be not darkness.
36 If thy whole body therefore *be* full of light,
having no part dark, the whole shall be full of
light, as when the bright shining of a candle
doth give thee light.
37 ¶ And as he spake, a certain Phar'i-see
besought him to dine with him: and he went in,
and sat down to meat.
38 And when the Phar'i-see saw *it*, he marvelled that he had not first washed before dinner.
39 And the Lord said unto him, Now do ye
Phar'i-sees make clean the outside of the cup
and the platter; but your inward part is full of
ravening and wickedness.
40 *Ye* fools, did not he that made that which
is without make that which is within also?
41 But rather give alms of such things as ye
have; and, behold, all things are clean unto you.
42 But woe unto you, Phar'i-sees! for ye tithe
mint and rue and all manner of herbs, and pass
over judgment and the love of God: these ought
ye to have done, and not to leave the other undone.
43 Woe unto you, Phar'i-sees! for ye love the
uppermost seats in the synagogues, and greetings in the markets.
44 Woe unto you, scribes and Phar'i-sees,
hypocrites! for ye are as graves which appear
not, and the men that walk over *them* are not
aware *of them*.
45 ¶ Then answered one of the lawyers, and
said unto him, Master, thus saying thou re-
proachest us also.
46 And he said, Woe unto you also, *ye* lawyers! for ye lade men with burdens grievous to
be borne, and ye yourselves touch not the burdens with one of your fingers.
47 Woe unto you! for ye build the sepulchres
of the prophets, and your fathers killed them.
48 Truly ye bear witness that ye allow the
deeds of your fathers: for they indeed killed
them, and ye build their sepulchres.
49 Therefore also said the wisdom of God, I
will send them prophets and apostles, and *some*
of them they shall slay and persecute:
50 That the blood of all the prophets, which
was shed from the foundation of the world, may
be required of this generation;
51 From the blood of A'bel unto the blood of
Zach-a-ri'as, which perished between the altar
and the temple: verily I say unto you, It shall be
required of this generation.
52 Woe unto you, lawyers! for ye have taken
away the key of knowledge: ye entered not in
yourselves, and them that were entering in ye
hindered.
53 And as he said these things unto them, the

scribes and the Phar'i-sees began to urge *him* vehemently, and to provoke him to speak of many things:

54 Laying wait for him, and seeking to catch something out of his mouth, that they might accuse him.

12

IN the mean time, when there were gathered together an innumerable multitude of people, insomuch that they trode one upon another, he began to say unto his disciples first of all, Beware ye of the leaven of the Phar'i-sees, which is hypocrisy.

2 For there is nothing covered, that shall not be revealed; neither hid, that shall not be known.

3 Therefore whatsoever ye have spoken in darkness shall be heard in the light; and that which ye have spoken in the ear in closets shall be proclaimed upon the house tops.

4 And I say unto you my friends, Be not afraid of them that kill the body, and after that have no more that they can do.

5 But I will forewarn you whom ye shall fear: Fear him, which after he hath killed hath power to cast into hell; yea, I say unto you, Fear him.

6 Are not five sparrows sold for two farthings, and not one of them is forgotten before God?

7 But even the very hairs of your head are all numbered. Fear not therefore: ye are of more value than many sparrows.

8 Also I say unto you, Whosoever shall confess me before men, him shall the Son of man also confess before the angels of God:

9 But he that denieth me before men shall be denied before the angels of God.

10 And whosoever shall speak a word against the Son of man, it shall be forgiven him: but unto him that blasphemeth against the Ho'ly Ghost it shall not be forgiven.

11 And when they bring you unto the synagogues, and *unto* magistrates, and powers, take ye no thought how or what thing ye shall answer, or what ye shall say:

12 For the Ho'ly Ghost shall teach you in the same hour what ye ought to say.

13 ¶ And one of the company said unto him, Master, speak to my brother, that he divide the inheritance with me.

14 And he said unto him, Man, who made me a judge or a divider over you?

15 And he said unto them, Take heed, and beware of covetousness: for a man's life consisteth not in the abundance of the things which he possesseth.

16 And he spake a parable unto them, saying, The ground of a certain rich man brought forth plentifully:

17 And he thought within himself, saying, What shall I do, because I have no room where to bestow my fruits?

18 And he said, This will I do: I will pull down my barns, and build greater; and there will I bestow all my fruits and my goods.

19 And I will say to my soul, Soul, thou hast much goods laid up for many years; take thine ease, eat, drink, *and* be merry.

20 But God said unto him, *Thou* fool, this night thy soul shall be required of thee: then whose shall those things be, which thou hast provided?

21 So *is* he that layeth up treasure for himself, and is not rich toward God.

22 ¶ And he said unto his disciples, Therefore I say unto you, Take no thought for your life, what ye shall eat; neither for the body, what ye shall put on.

23 The life is more than meat, and the body *is more* than raiment.

24 Consider the ravens: for they neither sow nor reap; which neither have storehouse nor barn; and God feedeth them: how much more are ye better than the fowls?

25 And which of you with taking thought can add to his stature one cubit?

26 If ye then be not able to do that thing which is least, why take ye thought for the rest?

27 Consider the lilies how they grow: they toil not, they spin not; and yet I say unto you, that Sol'o-mon in all his glory was not arrayed like one of these.

28 If then God so clothe the grass, which is to day in the field, and to morrow is cast into the oven; how much more *will he clothe* you, O ye of little faith?

29 And seek not ye what ye shall eat, or what ye shall drink, neither be ye of doubtful mind.

30 For all these things do the nations of the world seek after: and your Father knoweth that ye have need of these things.

31 ¶ But rather seek ye the kingdom of God; and all these things shall be added unto you.

32 Fear not, little flock; for it is your Father's good pleasure to give you the kingdom.

33 Sell that ye have, and give alms; provide yourselves bags which wax not old, a treasure in the heavens that faileth not, where no thief approacheth, neither moth corrupteth.

34 For where your treasure is, there will your heart be also.

35 Let your loins be girded about, and *your* lights burning;

36 And ye yourselves like unto men that wait for their lord, when he will return from the wedding; that when he cometh and knocketh, they may open unto him immediately.

37 Blessed *are* those servants, whom the lord when he cometh shall find watching: verily I say unto you, that he shall gird himself, and make them to sit down to meat, and will come forth and serve them.

38 And if he shall come in the second watch, or come in the third watch, and find *them* so, blessed are those servants.

39 And this know, that if the goodman of the house had known what hour the thief would come, he would have watched, and not have suffered his house to be broken through.

40 Be ye therefore ready also: for the Son of man cometh at an hour when ye think not.

41 ¶ Then Pe'ter said unto him, Lord, speakest thou this parable unto us, or even to all?

42 And the Lord said, Who then is that faithful and wise steward, whom *his* lord shall make ruler over his household, to give *them their* portion of meat in due season?

43 Blessed *is* that servant, whom his lord when he cometh shall find so doing.

44 Of a truth I say unto you, that he will make him ruler over all that he hath.

45 But and if that servant say in his heart, My lord delayeth his coming; and shall begin to beat the menservants and maidens, and to eat and drink, and to be drunken;

46 The lord of that servant will come in a day when he looketh not for *him*, and at an hour when he is not aware, and will cut him in sunder, and will appoint him his portion with the unbelievers.

47 And that servant, which knew his lord's will, and prepared not *himself*, neither did ac-

cording to his will, shall be beaten with many
stripes.
48 But he that knew not, and did commit
things worthy of stripes, shall be beaten with
few *stripes*. For unto whomsoever much is giv-
en, of him shall be much required: and to whom
men have committed much, of him they will
ask the more.
49 ¶ I am come to send fire on the earth; and
what will I, if it be already kindled?
50 But I have a baptism to be baptized with;
and how am I straitened till it be accomplished!
51 Suppose ye that I am come to give peace
on earth? I tell you, Nay; but rather division:
52 For from henceforth there shall be five in
one house divided, three against two, and two
against three.
53 The father shall be divided against the
son, and the son against the father; the mother
against the daughter, and the daughter against
the mother; the mother in law against her
daughter in law, and the daughter in law
against the mother in law.
54 ¶ **And he said also to the people,** When ye
see a cloud rise out of the west, straightway ye
say, There cometh a shower; and so it is.
55 And when *ye see* the south wind blow, ye
say, There will be heat; and it cometh to pass.
56 *Ye* hypocrites, ye can discern the face of
the sky and of the earth; but how is it that ye do
not discern this time?
57 Yea, and why even of yourselves judge ye
not what is right?
58 ¶ When thou goest with thine adversary
to the magistrate, *as thou art* in the way, give
diligence that thou mayest be delivered from
him; lest he hale thee to the judge, and the
judge deliver thee to the officer, and the officer
cast thee into prison.
59 I tell thee, thou shalt not depart thence,
till thou hast paid the very last mite.

13 **THERE were present at that season
some that told him of the Gal-i-læ'ans,
whose blood Pi'late had mingled with their sacrifices.**
2 **And Je'sus answering said unto them,** Suppose ye that these Gal-i-læ'ans were sinners
above all the Gal-i-læ'ans, because they suffered such things?
3 I tell you, Nay: but, except ye repent, ye
shall all likewise perish.
4 Or those eighteen, upon whom the tower in
Si-lo'am fell, and slew them, think ye that they
were sinners above all men that dwelt in Je-
ru'sa-lem?
5 I tell you, Nay: but, except ye repent, ye
shall all likewise perish.
6 ¶ **He spake also this parable;** A certain
man had a fig tree planted in his vineyard; and
he came and sought fruit thereon, and found
none.
7 Then said he unto the dresser of his vineyard, Behold, these three years I come seeking
fruit on this fig tree, and find none: cut it down;
why cumbereth it the ground?
8 And he answering said unto him, Lord, let
it alone this year also, till I shall dig about it,
and dung *it:*
9 And if it bear fruit, *well:* and if not, *then*
after that thou shalt cut it down.
10 **And he was teaching in one of the synagogues on the sabbath.**
11 ¶ **And, behold, there was a woman which
had a spirit of infirmity eighteen years, and was
bowed together, and could in no wise lift up
herself.**
12 **And when Je'sus saw her, he called *her to
him*, and said unto her,** Woman, thou art loosed
from thine infirmity.
13 **And he laid *his* hands on her: and immediately she was made straight, and glorified God.**
14 **And the ruler of the synagogue answered
with indignation, because that Je'sus had
healed on the sabbath day, and said unto the
people, There are six days in which men ought
to work: in them therefore come and be healed,
and not on the sabbath day.**
15 **The Lord then answered him, and said,**
Thou hypocrite, doth not each one of you on the
sabbath loose his ox or *his* ass from the stall,
and lead *him* away to watering?
16 And ought not this woman, being a
daughter of A'bra-ham, whom Sa'tan hath
bound, lo, these eighteen years, be loosed from
this bond on the sabbath day?
17 **And when he had said these things, all his
adversaries were ashamed: and all the people
rejoiced for all the glorious things that were
done by him.**
18 ¶ **Then said he,** Unto what is the kingdom
of God like? and whereunto shall I resemble it?
19 It is like a grain of mustard seed, which a
man took, and cast into his garden; and it grew,
and waxed a great tree; and the fowls of the air
lodged in the branches of it.
20 **And again he said,** Whereunto shall I liken
the kingdom of God?
21 It is like leaven, which a woman took and
hid in three measures of meal, till the whole
was leavened.
22 **And he went through the cities and villages, teaching, and journeying toward Je-ru'sa-
lem.**
23 **Then said one unto him, Lord, are there
few that be saved? And he said unto them,**
24 ¶ Strive to enter in at the strait gate: for
many, I say unto you, will seek to enter in, and
shall not be able.
25 When once the master of the house is ris-
en up, and hath shut to the door, and ye begin
to stand without, and to knock at the door, saying, Lord, Lord, open unto us; and he shall answer and say unto you, I know you not whence
ye are:
26 Then shall ye begin to say, We have eaten
and drunk in thy presence, and thou hast taught
in our streets.
27 But he shall say, I tell you, I know you not
whence ye are; depart from me, all *ye* workers
of iniquity.
28 There shall be weeping and gnashing of
teeth, when ye shall see A'bra-ham, and I'saac,
and Ja'cob, and all the prophets, in the kingdom
of God, and you *yourselves* thrust out.
29 And they shall come from the east, and
from the west, and from the north, and *from* the
south, and shall sit down in the kingdom of
God.
30 And, behold, there are last which shall be
first, and there are first which shall be last.
31 ¶ **The same day there came certain of the
Phar'i-sees, saying unto him, Get thee out, and
depart hence: for Her'od will kill thee.**
32 **And he said unto them,** Go ye, and tell
that fox, Behold, I cast out devils, and I do cures
to day and to morrow, and the third *day* I shall
be perfected.
33 Nevertheless I must walk to day, and to
morrow, and the *day* following: for it cannot be
that a prophet perish out of Je-ru'sa-lem.
34 O Je-ru'sa-lem, Je-ru'sa-lem, which killest
the prophets, and stonest them that are sent
unto thee; how often would I have gathered thy

children together, as a hen *doth gather* her brood under *her* wings, and ye would not!
35 Behold, your house is left unto you desolate: and verily I say unto you, Ye shall not see me, until *the time* come when ye shall say, Blessed *is* he that cometh in the name of the Lord.

14 AND it came to pass, as he went into the house of one of the chief Phar'i-sees to eat bread on the sabbath day, that they watched him.
2 And, behold, there was a certain man before him which had the dropsy.
3 And Je'sus answering spake unto the lawyers and Phar'i-sees, saying, Is it lawful to heal on the sabbath day?
4 And they held their peace. And he took *him*, and healed him, and let him go;
5 And answered them, saying, Which of you shall have an ass or an ox fallen into a pit, and will not straightway pull him out on the sabbath day?
6 And they could not answer him again to these things.
7 ¶ And he put forth a parable to those which were bidden, when he marked how they chose out the chief rooms; saying unto them,
8 When thou art bidden of any *man* to a wedding, sit not down in the highest room; lest a more honourable man than thou be bidden of him;
9 And he that bade thee and him come and say to thee, Give this man place; and thou begin with shame to take the lowest room.
10 But when thou art bidden, go and sit down in the lowest room; that when he that bade thee cometh, he may say unto thee, Friend, go up higher: then shalt thou have worship in the presence of them that sit at meat with thee.
11 For whosoever exalteth himself shall be abased; and he that humbleth himself shall be exalted.
12 ¶ Then said he also to him that bade him, When thou makest a dinner or a supper, call not thy friends, nor thy brethren, neither thy kinsmen, nor *thy* rich neighbours, lest they also bid thee again, and a recompence be made thee.
13 But when thou makest a feast, call the poor, the maimed, the lame, the blind;
14 And thou shalt be blessed; for they cannot recompense thee: for thou shalt be recompensed at the resurrection of the just.
15 ¶ And when one of them that sat at meat with him heard these things, he said unto him, Blessed *is* he that shall eat bread in the kingdom of God.
16 Then said he unto him, A certain man made a great supper, and bade many:
17 And sent his servant at supper time to say to them that were bidden, Come; for all things are now ready.
18 And they all with one *consent* began to make excuse. The first said unto him, I have bought a piece of ground, and I must needs go and see it: I pray thee have me excused.
19 And another said, I have bought five yoke of oxen, and I go to prove them: I pray thee have me excused.
20 And another said, I have married a wife, and therefore I cannot come.
21 So that servant came, and shewed his lord these things. Then the master of the house being angry said to his servant, Go out quickly into the streets and lanes of the city, and bring in hither the poor, and the maimed, and the halt, and the blind.
22 And the servant said, Lord, it is done as thou hast commanded, and yet there is room.
23 And the lord said unto the servant, Go out into the highways and hedges, and compel *them* to come in, that my house may be filled.
24 For I say unto you, That none of those men which were bidden shall taste of my supper.
25 ¶ And there went great multitudes with him: and he turned, and said unto them,
26 If any *man* come to me, and hate not his father, and mother, and wife, and children, and brethren, and sisters, yea, and his own life also, he cannot be my disciple.
27 And whosoever doth not bear his cross, and come after me, cannot be my disciple.
28 For which of you, intending to build a tower, sitteth not down first, and counteth the cost, whether he have *sufficient* to finish *it?*
29 Lest haply, after he hath laid the foundation, and is not able to finish *it*, all that behold *it* begin to mock him,
30 Saying, This man began to build, and was not able to finish.
31 Or what king, going to make war against another king, sitteth not down first, and consulteth whether he be able with ten thousand to meet him that cometh against him with twenty thousand?
32 Or else, while the other is yet a great way off, he sendeth an ambassage, and desireth conditions of peace.
33 So likewise, whosoever he be of you that forsaketh not all that he hath, he cannot be my disciple.
34 ¶ Salt *is* good: but if the salt have lost his savour, wherewith shall it be seasoned?
35 It is neither fit for the land, nor yet for the dunghill; *but* men cast it out. He that hath ears to hear, let him hear.

15 THEN drew near unto him all the publicans and sinners for to hear him.
2 And the Phar'i-sees and scribes murmured, saying, This man receiveth sinners, and eateth with them.
3 ¶ And he spake this parable unto them, saying,
4 What man of you, having an hundred sheep, if he lose one of them, doth not leave the ninety and nine in the wilderness, and go after that which is lost, until he find it?
5 And when he hath found *it*, he layeth *it* on his shoulders, rejoicing.
6 And when he cometh home, he calleth together *his* friends and neighbours, saying unto them, Rejoice with me; for I have found my sheep which was lost.
7 I say unto you, that likewise joy shall be in heaven over one sinner that repenteth, more than over ninety and nine just persons, which need no repentance.
8 ¶ Either what woman having ten pieces of silver, if she lose one piece, doth not light a candle, and sweep the house, and seek diligently till she find *it?*
9 And when she hath found *it*, she calleth *her* friends and *her* neighbours together, saying, Rejoice with me; for I have found the piece which I had lost.
10 Likewise, I say unto you, there is joy in the presence of the angels of God over one sinner that repenteth.
11 ¶ And he said, A certain man had two sons:

12 And the younger of them said to *his* father, Father, give me the portion of goods that falleth *to me*. And he divided unto them *his* living.

13 And not many days after the younger son gathered all together, and took his journey into a far country, and there wasted his substance with riotous living.

14 And when he had spent all, there arose a mighty famine in that land; and he began to be in want.

15 And he went and joined himself to a citizen of that country; and he sent him into his fields to feed swine.

16 And he would fain have filled his belly with the husks that the swine did eat: and no man gave unto him.

17 And when he came to himself, he said, How many hired servants of my father's have bread enough and to spare, and I perish with hunger!

18 I will arise and go to my father, and will say unto him, Father, I have sinned against heaven, and before thee.

19 And am no more worthy to be called thy son: make me as one of thy hired servants.

20 And he arose, and came to his father. But when he was yet a great way off, his father saw him, and had compassion, and ran, and fell on his neck, and kissed him.

21 And the son said unto him, Father, I have sinned against heaven, and in thy sight, and am no more worthy to be called thy son.

22 But the father said to his servants, Bring forth the best robe, and put *it* on him; and put a ring on his hand, and shoes on *his* feet:

23 And bring hither the fatted calf, and kill *it;* and let us eat, and be merry:

24 For this my son was dead, and is alive again; he was lost, and is found. And they began to be merry.

25 Now his elder son was in the field: and as he came and drew nigh to the house, he heard musick and dancing.

26 And he called one of the servants, and asked what these things meant.

27 And he said unto him, Thy brother is come; and thy father hath killed the fatted calf, because he hath received him safe and sound.

28 And he was angry, and would not go in: therefore came his father out, and intreated him.

29 And he answering said to *his* father, Lo, these many years do I serve thee, neither transgressed I at any time thy commandment: and yet thou never gavest me a kid, that I might make merry with my friends:

30 But as soon as this thy son was come, which hath devoured thy living with harlots, thou hast killed for him the fatted calf.

31 And he said unto him, Son, thou art ever with me, and all that I have is thine.

32 It was meet that we should make merry, and be glad: for this thy brother was dead, and is alive again; and was lost, and is found.

16 AND he said also unto his disciples, There was a certain rich man, which had a steward; and the same was accused unto him that he had wasted his goods.

2 And he called him, and said unto him, How is it that I hear this of thee? give an account of thy stewardship; for thou mayest be no longer steward.

3 Then the steward said within himself, What shall I do? for my lord taketh away from me the stewardship: I cannot dig; to beg I am ashamed.

4 I am resolved what to do, that, when I am put out of the stewardship, they may receive me into their houses.

5 So he called every one of his lord's debtors *unto him*, and said unto the first, How much owest thou unto my lord?

6 And he said, An hundred measures of oil. And he said unto him, Take thy bill, and sit down quickly, and write fifty.

7 Then said he to another, And how much owest thou? And he said, An hundred measures of wheat. And he said unto him, Take thy bill, and write fourscore.

8 And the lord commended the unjust steward, because he had done wisely: for the children of this world are in their generation wiser than the children of light.

9 And I say unto you, Make to yourselves friends of the mammon of unrighteousness; that, when ye fail, they may receive you into everlasting habitations.

10 He that is faithful in that which is least is faithful also in much: and he that is unjust in the least is unjust also in much.

11 If therefore ye have not been faithful in the unrighteous mammon, who will commit to your trust the true *riches?*

12 And if ye have not been faithful in that which is another man's, who shall give you that which is your own?

13 ¶ No servant can serve two masters: for either he will hate the one, and love the other; or else he will hold to the one, and despise the other. Ye cannot serve God and mammon.

14 And the Phar'i-sees also, who were covetous, heard all these things: and they derided him.

15 And he said unto them, Ye are they which justify yourselves before men; but God knoweth your hearts: for that which is highly esteemed among men is abomination in the sight of God.

16 The law and the prophets *were* until John: since that time the kingdom of God is preached, and every man presseth into it.

17 And it is easier for heaven and earth to pass, than one tittle of the law to fail.

18 Whosoever putteth away his wife, and marrieth another, committeth adultery: and whosoever marrieth her that is put away from *her* husband committeth adultery.

19 ¶ There was a certain rich man, which was clothed in purple and fine linen, and fared sumptuously every day:

20 And there was a certain beggar named Laz'a-rus, which was laid at his gate, full of sores,

21 And desiring to be fed with the crumbs which fell from the rich man's table: moreover the dogs came and licked his sores.

22 And it came to pass, that the beggar died, and was carried by the angels into A'bra-ham's bosom: the rich man also died, and was buried;

23 And in hell he lift up his eyes, being in torments, and seeth A'bra-ham afar off, and Laz'a-rus in his bosom.

24 And he cried and said, Father A'bra-ham, have mercy on me, and send Laz'a-rus, that he may dip the tip of his finger in water, and cool my tongue; for I am tormented in this flame.

25 But A'bra-ham said, Son, remember that thou in thy lifetime receivedst thy good things, and likewise Laz'a-rus evil things: but now he is comforted, and thou art tormented.

26 And beside all this, between us and you

there is a great gulf fixed: so that they which
would pass from hence to you cannot; neither
can they pass to us, that *would come* from
thence.
27 Then he said, I pray thee therefore, father,
that thou wouldest send him to my father's
house:
28 For I have five brethren; that he may testify unto them, lest they also come into this
place of torment.
29 A'bra-ham saith unto him, They have Mo'-
ses and the prophets; let them hear them.
30 And he said, Nay, father A'bra-ham: but if
one went unto them from the dead, they will
repent.
31 And he said unto him, If they hear not
Mo'ses and the prophets, neither will they be
persuaded, though one rose from the dead.

17 THEN said he unto the disciples, It is
impossible but that offences will come:
but woe *unto him*, through whom they come!
2 It were better for him that a millstone were
hanged about his neck, and he cast into the sea,
than that he should offend one of these little
ones.
3 ¶ Take heed to yourselves: If thy brother
trespass against thee, rebuke him; and if he repent, forgive him.
4 And if he trespass against thee seven times
in a day, and seven times in a day turn again to
thee, saying, I repent; thou shalt forgive him.
5 And the apostles said unto the Lord, Increase our faith.
6 And the Lord said, If ye had faith as a grain
of mustard seed, ye might say unto this syca-
mine tree, Be thou plucked up by the root, and
be thou planted in the sea; and it should obey
you.
7 But which of you, having a servant plowing
or feeding cattle, will say unto him by and by,
when he is come from the field, Go and sit down
to meat?
8 And will not rather say unto him, Make
ready wherewith I may sup, and gird thyself,
and serve me, till I have eaten and drunken; and
afterward thou shalt eat and drink?
9 Doth he thank that servant because he did
the things that were commanded him? I trow
not.
10 So likewise ye, when ye shall have done
all those things which are commanded you, say,
We are unprofitable servants: we have done
that which was our duty to do.
11 ¶ And it came to pass, as he went to Je-
ru'sa-lem, that he passed through the midst of
Sa-ma'ri-a and Gal'i-lee.
12 And as he entered into a certain village,
there met him ten men that were lepers, which
stood afar off:
13 And they lifted up *their* voices, and said,
Je'sus, Master, have mercy on us.
14 And when he saw *them*, he said unto
them, Go shew yourselves unto the priests. And
it came to pass, that, as they went, they were
cleansed.
15 And one of them, when he saw that he
was healed, turned back, and with a loud voice
glorified God,
16 And fell down on *his* face at his feet, giving him thanks: and he was a Sa-mar'i-tan.
17 And Je'sus answering said, Were there
not ten cleansed? but where *are* the nine?
18 There are not found that returned to give
glory to God, save this stranger.
19 And he said unto him, Arise, go thy way:
thy faith hath made thee whole.
20 ¶ And when he was demanded of the
Phar'i-sees, when the kingdom of God should
come, he answered them and said, The kingdom of God cometh not with observation:
21 Neither shall they say, Lo here! or, lo
there! for, behold, the kingdom of God is within
you.
22 And he said unto the disciples, The days
will come, when ye shall desire to see one of the
days of the Son of man, and ye shall not see *it*.
23 And they shall say to you, See here; or,
see there: go not after *them*, nor follow *them*.
24 For as the lightning, that lighteneth out of
the one *part* under heaven, shineth unto the
other *part* under heaven; so shall also the Son
of man be in his day.
25 But first must he suffer many things, and
be rejected of this generation.
26 And as it was in the days of No'e, so shall
it be also in the days of the Son of man.
27 They did eat, they drank, they married
wives, they were given in marriage, until the
day that No'e entered into the ark, and the flood
came, and destroyed them all.
28 Likewise also as it was in the days of Lot;
they did eat, they drank, they bought, they sold,
they planted, they builded;
29 But the same day that Lot went out of
Sod'om it rained fire and brimstone from
heaven, and destroyed *them* all.
30 Even thus shall it be in the day when the
Son of man is revealed.
31 In that day, he which shall be upon the
house top, and his stuff in the house, let him not
come down to take it away: and he that is in the
field, let him likewise not return back.
32 Remember Lot's wife.
33 Whosoever shall seek to save his life shall
lose it; and whosoever shall lose his life shall
preserve it.
34 I tell you, in that night there shall be two
men in one bed; the one shall be taken, and the
other shall be left.
35 Two *women* shall be grinding together;
the one shall be taken, and the other left.
36 Two *men* shall be in the field; the one shall
be taken, and the other left.
37 And they answered and said unto him,
Where, Lord? And he said unto them, Wheresoever the body *is*, thither will the eagles be gathered together.

18 AND he spake a parable unto them *to
this end*, that men ought always to pray,
and not to faint;
2 Saying, There was in a city a judge, which
feared not God, neither regarded man:
3 And there was a widow in that city; and
she came unto him, saying, Avenge me of mine
adversary.
4 And he would not for a while: but afterward he said within himself, Though I fear not
God, nor regard man;
5 Yet because this widow troubleth me, I will
avenge her, lest by her continual coming she
weary me.
6 And the Lord said, Hear what the unjust
judge saith.
7 And shall not God avenge his own elect,
which cry day and night unto him, though he
bear long with them?
8 I tell you that he will avenge them speedily.
Nevertheless when the Son of man cometh,
shall he find faith on the earth?
9 And he spake this parable unto certain
which trusted in themselves that they were
righteous, and despised others:

10 Two men went up into the temple to pray; the one a Phar'i-see, and the other a publican.
11 The Phar'i-see stood and prayed thus with himself, God, I thank thee, that I am not as other men *are*, extortioners, unjust, adulterers, or even as this publican.
12 I fast twice in the week, I give tithes of all that I possess.
13 And the publican, standing afar off, would not lift up so much as *his* eyes unto heaven, but smote upon his breast, saying, God be merciful to me a sinner.
14 I tell you, this man went down to his house justified *rather* than the other: for every one that exalteth himself shall be abased; and he that humbleth himself shall be exalted.
15 And they brought unto him also infants, that he would touch them: but when *his* disciples saw *it*, they rebuked them.
16 But Je'sus called them *unto him*, and said, Suffer little children to come unto me, and forbid them not: for of such is the kingdom of God.
17 Verily I say unto you, Whosoever shall not receive the kingdom of God as a little child shall in no wise enter therein.
18 And a certain ruler asked him, saying, Good Master, what shall I do to inherit eternal life?
19 And Je'sus said unto him, Why callest thou me good? none *is* good, save one, *that is*, God.
20 Thou knowest the commandments, Do not commit adultery, Do not kill, Do not steal, Do not bear false witness, Honour thy father and thy mother.
21 And he said, All these have I kept from my youth up.
22 Now when Je'sus heard these things, he said unto him, Yet lackest thou one thing: sell all that thou hast, and distribute unto the poor, and thou shalt have treasure in heaven: and come follow me.
23 And when he heard this, he was very sorrowful: for he was very rich.
24 And when Je'sus saw that he was very sorrowful, he said, How hardly shall they that have riches enter into the kingdom of God!
25 For it is easier for a camel to go through a needle's eye, than for a rich man to enter into the kingdom of God.
26 And they that heard *it* said, Who then can be saved?
27 And he said, The things which are impossible with men are possible with God.
28 Then Pe'ter said, Lo, we have left all, and followed thee.
29 And he said unto them, Verily I say unto you, There is no man that hath left house, or parents, or brethren, or wife, or children, for the kingdom of God's sake,
30 Who shall not receive manifold more in this present time, and in the world to come life everlasting.
31 ¶ Then he took *unto him* the twelve, and said unto them, Behold, we go up to Je-ru'salem, and all things that are written by the prophets concerning the Son of man shall be accomplished.
32 For he shall be delivered unto the Gen'tiles, and shall be mocked, and spitefully entreated, and spitted on:
33 And they shall scourge *him*, and put him to death: and the third day he shall rise again.
34 And they understood none of these things: and this saying was hid from them, neither knew they the things which were spoken.
35 ¶ And it came to pass, that as he was come nigh unto Jer'i-cho, a certain blind man sat by the way side begging:
36 And hearing the multitude pass by, he asked what it meant.
37 And they told him, that Je'sus of Naz'areth passeth by.
38 And he cried, saying, Je'sus, *thou* son of Da'vid, have mercy on me.
39 And they which went before rebuked him, that he should hold his peace: but he cried so much the more, *Thou* son of Da'vid, have mercy on me.
40 And Je'sus stood, and commanded him to be brought unto him: and when he was come near, he asked him,
41 Saying, What wilt thou that I shall do unto thee? And he said, Lord, that I may receive my sight.
42 And Je'sus said unto him, Receive thy sight: thy faith hath saved thee.
43 And immediately he received his sight, and followed him, glorifying God: and all the people when they saw *it*, gave praise unto God.

19

AND *Je'sus* entered and passed through Jer'i-cho.
2 And, behold, *there was* a man named Zacchæus, which was the chief among the publicans, and he was rich.
3 And he sought to see Je'sus who he was; and could not for the press, because he was little of stature.
4 And he ran before, and climbed up into a sycomore tree to see him: for he was to pass that *way*.
5 And when Je'sus came to the place, he looked up, and saw him, and said unto him, Zac-chæ'us, make haste, and come down; for to day I must abide at thy house.
6 And he made haste, and came down, and received him joyfully.
7 And when they saw *it*, they all murmured, saying, That he was gone to be guest with a man that is a sinner.
8 And Zac-chæ'us stood, and said unto the Lord; Behold, Lord, the half of my goods I give to the poor; and if I have taken any thing from any man by false accusation, I restore *him* fourfold.
9 And Je'sus said unto him, This day is salvation come to this house, forsomuch as he also is a son of A'bra-ham.
10 For the Son of man is come to seek and to save that which was lost.
11 And as they heard these things, he added and spake a parable, because he was nigh to Jeru'sa-lem, and because they thought that the kingdom of God should immediately appear.
12 He said therefore, A certain nobleman went into a far country to receive for himself a kingdom, and to return.
13 And he called his ten servants, and delivered them ten pounds, and said unto them, Occupy till I come.
14 But his citizens hated him, and sent a message after him, saying, We will not have this *man* to reign over us.
15 And it came to pass, that when he was returned, having received the kingdom, then he commanded these servants to be called unto him, to whom he had given the money, that he might know how much every man had gained by trading.
16 Then came the first, saying, Lord, thy pound hath gained ten pounds.
17 And he said unto him, Well, thou good servant: because thou hast been faithful in a

very little, have thou authority over ten cities.
18 And the second came, saying, Lord, thy
pound hath gained five pounds.
19 And he said likewise to him, Be thou also
over five cities.
20 And another came, saying, Lord, behold,
here is thy pound, which I have kept laid up in a
napkin:
21 For I feared thee, because thou art an austere man: thou takest up that thou layedst not
down, and reapest that thou didst not sow.
22 And he saith unto him, Out of thine own
mouth will I judge thee, *thou* wicked servant.
Thou knewest that I was an austere man, taking
up that I laid not down, and reaping that I did
not sow:
23 Wherefore then gavest not thou my money into the bank, that at my coming I might
have required mine own with usury?
24 And he said unto them that stood by, Take
from him the pound, and give *it* to him that
hath ten pounds.
25 (And they said unto him, Lord, he hath ten
pounds.)
26 For I say unto you, That unto every one
which hath shall be given; and from him that
hath not, even that he hath shall be taken away
from him.
27 But those mine enemies, which would not
that I should reign over them, bring hither, and
slay *them* before me.
28 ¶ And when he had thus spoken, he went
before, ascending up to Je-ru'sa-lem.
29 And it came to pass, when he was come
nigh to Beth'pha-ge and Beth'a-ny, at the mount
called *the mount* of Ol'ives, he sent two of his
disciples,
30 Saying, Go ye into the village over against
you; in the which at your entering ye shall find a
colt tied, whereon yet never man sat: loose him,
and bring *him hither*.
31 And if any man ask you, Why do ye loose
him? thus shall ye say unto him, Because the
Lord hath need of him.
32 And they that were sent went their way,
and found even as he had said unto them.
33 And as they were loosing the colt, the
owners thereof said unto them, Why loose ye
the colt?
34 And they said, The Lord hath need of him.
35 And they brought him to Je'sus: and they
cast their garments upon the colt, and they set
Je'sus thereon.
36 And as he went, they spread their clothes
in the way.
37 And when he was come nigh, even now at
the descent of the mount of Ol'ives, the whole
multitude of the disciples began to rejoice and
praise God with a loud voice for all the mighty
works that they had seen;
38 Saying, Blessed *be* the King that cometh
in the name of the Lord: peace in heaven, and
glory in the highest.
39 And some of the Phar'i-sees from among
the multitude said unto him, Master, rebuke thy
disciples.
40 And he answered and said unto them, I
tell you that, if these should hold their peace,
the stones would immediately cry out.
41 ¶ And when he was come near, he beheld
the city, and wept over it,
42 Saying, If thou hadst known, even thou, at
least in this thy day, the things *which belong*
unto thy peace! but now they are hid from thine
eyes.
43 For the days shall come upon thee, that
thine enemies shall cast a trench about thee,
and compass thee round, and keep thee in on
every side,
44 And shall lay thee even with the ground,
and thy children within thee; and they shall not
leave in thee one stone upon another; because
thou knewest not the time of thy visitation.
45 And he went into the temple, and began to
cast out them that sold therein, and them that
bought;
46 Saying unto them, It is written, My house
is the house of prayer: but ye have made it a
den of thieves.
47 And he taught daily in the temple. But the
chief priests and the scribes and the chief of the
people sought to destroy him,
48 And could not find what they might do:
for all the people were very attentive to hear
him.

20 AND it came to pass, *that* on one of
those days, as he taught the people in
the temple, and preached the gospel, the chief
priests and the scribes came upon *him* with the
elders,
2 And spake unto him, saying, Tell us, by
what authority doest thou these things? or who
is he that gave thee this authority?
3 And he answered and said unto them, I will
also ask you one thing; and answer me:
4 The baptism of John, was it from heaven,
or of men?
5 And they reasoned with themselves, saying, If we shall say, From heaven; he will say,
Why then believed ye him not?
6 But and if we say, Of men; all the people
will stone us: for they be persuaded that John
was a prophet.
7 And they answered, that they could not tell
whence *it was*.
8 And Je'sus said unto them, Neither tell I
you by what authority I do these things.
9 Then began he to speak to the people this
parable; A certain man planted a vineyard, and
let it forth to husbandmen, and went into a far
country for a long time.
10 And at the season he sent a servant to the
husbandmen, that they should give him of the
fruit of the vineyard: but the husbandmen beat
him, and sent *him* away empty.
11 And again he sent another servant: and
they beat him also, and entreated *him* shamefully, and sent *him* away empty.
12 And again he sent a third: and they
wounded him also, and cast *him* out.
13 Then said the lord of the vineyard, What
shall I do? I will send my beloved son: it may be
they will reverence *him* when they see him.
14 But when the husbandmen saw him, they
reasoned among themselves, saying, This is the
heir: come, let us kill him, that the inheritance
may be ours.
15 So they cast him out of the vineyard, and
killed *him*. What therefore shall the lord of the
vineyard do unto them?
16 He shall come and destroy these husbandmen, and shall give the vineyard to others. And
when they heard *it*, they said, God forbid.
17 And he beheld them, and said, What is
this then that is written, The stone which the
builders rejected, the same is become the head
of the corner?
18 Whosoever shall fall upon that stone shall
be broken; but on whomsoever it shall fall, it
will grind him to powder.
19 ¶ And the chief priests and the scribes the
same hour sought to lay hands on him; and they

feared the people: for they perceived that he
had spoken this parable against them.
20 And they watched *him*, and sent forth
spies, which should feign themselves just men,
that they might take hold of his words, that so
they might deliver him unto the power and authority of the governor.
21 And they asked him, saying, Master, we
know that thou sayest and teachest rightly, neither acceptest thou the person *of any*, but
teachest the way of God truly:
22 Is it lawful for us to give tribute unto Cæ'-
sar, or no?
23 But he perceived their craftiness, and said
unto them, Why tempt ye me?
24 Shew me a penny. Whose image and superscription hath it? They answered and said,
Cæ'sar's.
25 And he said unto them, Render therefore
unto Cæ'sar the things which be Cæ'sar's, and
unto God the things which be God's.
26 And they could not take hold of his words
before the people: and they marvelled at his answer, and held their peace.
27 ¶ Then came to *him* certain of the Sad'du-
cees, which deny that there is any resurrection:
and they asked him,
28 Saying, Master, Mo'ses wrote unto us, If
any man's brother die, having a wife, and he die
without children, that his brother should take
his wife, and raise up seed unto his brother.
29 There were therefore seven brethren: and
the first took a wife, and died without children.
30 And the second took her to wife, and he
died childless.
31 And the third took her; and in like manner
the seven also: and they left no children, and
died.
32 Last of all the woman died also.
33 Therefore in the resurrection whose wife
of them is she? for seven had her to wife.
34 And Je'sus answering said unto them, The
children of this world marry, and are given in
marriage:
35 But they which shall be accounted worthy
to obtain that world, and the resurrection from
the dead, neither marry, nor are given in marriage:
36 Neither can they die any more: for they
are equal unto the angels; and are the children
of God, being the children of the resurrection.
37 Now that the dead are raised, even Mo'ses
shewed at the bush, when he calleth the Lord
the God of A'bra-ham, and the God of I'saac,
and the God of Ja'cob.
38 For he is not a God of the dead, but of the
living: for all live unto him.
39 ¶ Then certain of the scribes answering
said, Master, thou hast well said.
40 And after that they durst not ask him any
question at all.
41 And he said unto them, How say they that
Christ is Da'vid's son?
42 And Da'vid himself saith in the book of
Psalms, The Lord said unto my Lord, Sit thou
on my right hand,
43 Till I make thine enemies thy footstool.
44 Da'vid therefore calleth him Lord, how is
he then his son?
45 ¶ Then in the audience of all the people
he said unto his disciples,
46 Beware of the scribes, which desire to
walk in long robes, and love greetings in the
markets, and the highest seats in the synagogues, and the chief rooms at feasts;
47 Which devour widows' houses, and for a
shew make long prayers: the same shall receive
greater damnation.

21 AND he looked up, and saw the rich
men casting their gifts into the treasury.
2 And he saw also a certain poor widow casting in thither two mites.
3 And he said, Of a truth I say unto you, that
this poor widow hath cast in more than they all:
4 For all these have of their abundance cast
in unto the offerings of God: but she of her penury hath cast in all the living that she had.
5 ¶ And as some spake of the temple, how it
was adorned with goodly stones and gifts, he
said,
6 *As for* these things which ye behold, the
days will come, in the which there shall not be
left one stone upon another, that shall not be
thrown down.
7 And they asked him, saying, Master, but
when shall these things be? and what sign *will*
there be when these things shall come to pass?
8 And he said, Take heed that ye be not deceived: for many shall come in my name, saying, I am *Christ;* and the time draweth near: go
ye not therefore after them.
9 But when ye shall hear of wars and com-
motions, be not terrified: for these things must
first come to pass; but the end *is* not by and by.
10 Then said he unto them, Nation shall rise
against nation, and kingdom against kingdom:
11 And great earthquakes shall be in divers
places, and famines, and pestilences; and fearful sights and great signs shall there be from
heaven.
12 But before all these, they shall lay their
hands on you, and persecute *you*, delivering
you up to the synagogues, and into prisons,
being brought before kings and rulers for my
name's sake.
13 And it shall turn to you for a testimony.
14 Settle *it* therefore in your hearts, not to
meditate before what ye shall answer:
15 For I will give you a mouth and wisdom,
which all your adversaries shall not be able to
gainsay nor resist.
16 And ye shall be betrayed both by parents,
and brethren, and kinsfolks, and friends; and
some of you shall they cause to be put to death.
17 And ye shall be hated of all *men* for my
name's sake.
18 But there shall not an hair of your head
perish.
19 In your patience possess ye your souls.
20 And when ye shall see Je-ru'sa-lem compassed with armies, then know that the desolation thereof is nigh.
21 Then let them which are in Ju-dæ'a flee to
the mountains; and let them which are in the
midst of it depart out; and let not them that are
in the countries enter thereinto.
22 For these be the days of vengeance, that
all things which are written may be fulfilled.
23 But woe unto them that are with child,
and to them that give suck, in those days! for
there shall be great distress in the land, and
wrath upon this people.
24 And they shall fall by the edge of the
sword, and shall be led away captive into all
nations: and Je-ru'sa-lem shall be trodden down
of the Gen'tiles, until the times of the Gen'tiles
be fulfilled.
25 ¶ And there shall be signs in the sun, and
in the moon, and in the stars; and upon the
earth distress of nations, with perplexity; the
sea and the waves roaring;
26 Men's hearts failing them for fear, and for

looking after those things which are coming on
the earth: for the powers of heaven shall be
shaken.
27 And then shall they see the Son of man
coming in a cloud with power and great glory.
28 And when these things begin to come to
pass, then look up, and lift up your heads; for
your redemption draweth nigh.
29 And he spake to them a parable; Behold
the fig tree, and all the trees;
30 When they now shoot forth, ye see and
know of your own selves that summer is now
nigh at hand.
31 So likewise ye, when ye see these things
come to pass, know ye that the kingdom of God
is nigh at hand.
32 Verily I say unto you, This generation
shall not pass away, till all be fulfilled.
33 Heaven and earth shall pass away: but my
words shall not pass away.
34 ¶ And take heed to yourselves, lest at any
time your hearts be overcharged with surfeit-
ing, and drunkenness, and cares of this life, and
so that day come upon you unawares.
35 For as a snare shall it come on all them
that dwell on the face of the whole earth.
36 Watch ye therefore, and pray always, that
ye may be accounted worthy to escape all these
things that shall come to pass, and to stand before the Son of man.
37 And in the day time he was teaching in
the temple; and at night he went out, and abode
in the mount that is called *the mount* of Ol'ives.
38 And all the people came early in the
morning to him in the temple, for to hear him.

22 NOW the feast of unleavened bread
drew nigh, which is called the Passover.
2 And the chief priests and scribes sought
how they might kill him; for they feared the
people.
3 ¶ Then entered Sa'tan into Ju'das surnamed Is-car'i-ot, being of the number of the
twelve.
4 And he went his way, and communed with
the chief priests and captains, how he might betray him unto them.
5 And they were glad, and covenanted to
give him money.
6 And he promised, and sought opportunity
to betray him unto them in the absence of the
multitude.
7 ¶ Then came the day of unleavened bread,
when the passover must be killed.
8 And he sent Pe'ter and John, saying, Go
and prepare us the passover, that we may eat.
9 And they said unto him, Where wilt thou
that we prepare?
10 And he said unto them, Behold, when ye
are entered into the city, there shall a man meet
you, bearing a pitcher of water; follow him into
the house where he entereth in.
11 And ye shall say unto the goodman of the
house, The Master saith unto thee, Where is the
guestchamber, where I shall eat the passover
with my disciples?
12 And he shall shew you a large upper room
furnished: there make ready.
13 And they went, and found as he had said
unto them: and they made ready the passover.
14 And when the hour was come, he sat
down, and the twelve apostles with him.
15 And he said unto them, With desire I have
desired to eat this passover with you before I
suffer:
16 For I say unto you, I will not any more eat
thereof, until it be fulfilled in the kingdom of
God.
17 And he took the cup, and gave thanks,
and said, Take this, and divide *it* among yourselves:
18 For I say unto you, I will not drink of the
fruit of the vine, until the kingdom of God shall
come.
19 ¶ And he took bread, and gave thanks,
and brake *it*, and gave unto them, saying, This
is my body which is given for you: this do in
remembrance of me.
20 Likewise also the cup after supper, saying, This cup *is* the new testament in my blood,
which is shed for you.
21 ¶ But, behold, the hand of him that betrayeth me *is* with me on the table.
22 And truly the Son of man goeth, as it was
determined: but woe unto that man by whom
he is betrayed!
23 And they began to enquire among themselves, which of them it was that should do this
thing.
24 ¶ And there was also a strife among
them, which of them should be accounted the
greatest.
25 And he said unto them, The kings of the
Gen'tiles exercise lordship over them; and they
that exercise authority upon them are called
benefactors.
26 But ye *shall* not *be* so: but he that is greatest among you, let him be as the younger; and
he that is chief, as he that doth serve.
27 For whether *is* greater, he that sitteth at
meat, or he that serveth? *is* not he that sitteth at
meat? but I am among you as he that serveth.
28 Ye are they which have continued with
me in my temptations.
29 And I appoint unto you a kingdom, as my
Father hath appointed unto me;
30 That ye may eat and drink at my table in
my kingdom, and sit on thrones judging the
twelve tribes of Is'ra-el.
31 ¶ And the Lord said, Si'mon, Si'mon, behold, Sa'tan hath desired *to have* you, that he
may sift *you* as wheat:
32 But I have prayed for thee, that thy faith
fail not: and when thou art converted,
strengthen thy brethren.
33 And he said unto him, Lord, I am ready to
go with thee, both into prison, and to death.
34 And he said, I tell thee, Pe'ter, the cock
shall not crow this day, before that thou shalt
thrice deny that thou knowest me.
35 And he said unto them, When I sent you
without purse, and scrip, and shoes, lacked ye
any thing? And they said, Nothing.
36 Then said he unto them, But now, he that
hath a purse, let him take *it*, and likewise *his*
scrip: and he that hath no sword, let him sell his
garment, and buy one.
37 For I say unto you, that this that is written
must yet be accomplished in me, And he was
reckoned among the transgressors: for the
things concerning me have an end.
38 And they said, Lord, behold, here *are* two
swords. And he said unto them, It is enough.
39 ¶ And he came out, and went, as he was
wont, to the mount of Ol'ives; and his disciples
also followed him.
40 And when he was at the place, he said
unto them, Pray that ye enter not into temptation.
41 And he was withdrawn from them about a
stone's cast, and kneeled down, and prayed,
42 Saying, Father, if thou be willing, remove

this cup from me: nevertheless not my will, but
thine, be done.
43 And there appeared an angel unto him
from heaven, strengthening him.
44 And being in an agony he prayed more
earnestly: and his sweat was as it were great
drops of blood falling down to the ground.
45 And when he rose up from prayer, and
was come to his disciples, he found them sleeping for sorrow,
46 And said unto them, Why sleep ye? rise
and pray, lest ye enter into temptation.
47 ¶ And while he yet spake, behold a multitude, and he that was called Ju'das, one of the
twelve, went before them, and drew near unto
Je'sus to kiss him.
48 But Je'sus said unto him, Ju'das, betrayest
thou the Son of man with a kiss?
49 When they which were about him saw
what would follow, they said unto him, Lord,
shall we smite with the sword?
50 ¶ And one of them smote the servant of
the high priest, and cut off his right ear.
51 And Je'sus answered and said, Suffer ye
thus far. And he touched his ear, and healed
him.
52 Then Je'sus said unto the chief priests,
and captains of the temple, and the elders,
which were come to him, Be ye come out, as
against a thief, with swords and staves?
53 When I was daily with you in the temple,
ye stretched forth no hands against me: but this
is your hour, and the power of darkness.
54 ¶ Then took they him, and led *him*, and
brought him into the high priest's house. And
Pe'ter followed afar off.
55 And when they had kindled a fire in the
midst of the hall, and were set down together,
Pe'ter sat down among them.
56 But a certain maid beheld him as he sat by
the fire, and earnestly looked upon him, and
said, This man was also with him.
57 And he denied him, saying, Woman, I
know him not.
58 And after a little while another saw him,
and said, Thou art also of them. And Pe'ter said,
Man, I am not.
59 And about the space of one hour after another confidently affirmed, saying, Of a truth
this *fellow* also was with him: for he is a Gal-i-
læ'an.
60 And Pe'ter said, Man, I know not what
thou sayest. And immediately, while he yet
spake, the cock crew.
61 And the Lord turned, and looked upon
Pe'ter. And Pe'ter remembered the word of the
Lord, how he had said unto him, Before the
cock crow, thou shalt deny me thrice.
62 And Pe'ter went out, and wept bitterly.
63 ¶ And the men that held Je'sus mocked
him, and smote *him*.
64 And when they had blindfolded him, they
struck him on the face, and asked him, saying,
Prophesy, who is it that smote thee?
65 And many other things blasphemously
spake they against him.
66 ¶ And as soon as it was day, the elders of
the people and the chief priests and the scribes
came together, and led him into their council,
saying,
67 Art thou the Christ? tell us. And he said
unto them, If I tell you, ye will not believe:
68 And if I also ask *you*, ye will not answer
me, nor let *me* go.
69 Hereafter shall the Son of man sit on the
right hand of the power of God.
70 Then said they all, Art thou then the Son
of God? And he said unto them, Ye say that I
am.
71 And they said, What need we any further
witness? for we ourselves have heard of his
own mouth.

23 AND the whole multitude of them
arose, and led him unto Pi'late.
2 And they began to accuse him, saying, We
found this *fellow* perverting the nation, and forbidding to give tribute to Cæ'sar, saying that he
himself is Christ a King.
3 And Pi'late asked him, saying, Art thou the
King of the Jews? And he answered him and
said, Thou sayest *it*.
4 Then said Pi'late to the chief priests and *to*
the people, I find no fault in this man.
5 And they were the more fierce, saying, He
stirreth up the people, teaching throughout all
Jew'ry, beginning from Gal'i-lee to this place.
6 When Pi'late heard of Gal'i-lee, he asked
whether the man were a Gal-i-læ'an.
7 And as soon as he knew that he belonged
unto Her'od's jurisdiction, he sent him to Her'-
od, who himself also was at Je-ru'sa-lem at that
time.
8 ¶ And when Her'od saw Je'sus, he was exceeding glad: for he was desirous to see him of
a long *season*, because he had heard many
things of him; and he hoped to have seen some
miracle done by him.
9 Then he questioned with him in many
words; but he answered him nothing.
10 And the chief priests and scribes stood
and vehemently accused him.
11 And Her'od with his men of war set him at
nought, and mocked *him*, and arrayed him in a
gorgeous robe, and sent him again to Pi'late.
12 ¶ And the same day Pi'late and Her'od
were made friends together: for before they
were at enmity between themselves.
13 ¶ And Pi'late, when he had called together the chief priests and the rulers and the
people,
14 Said unto them, Ye have brought this man
unto me, as one that perverteth the people: and,
behold, I, having examined *him* before you,
have found no fault in this man touching those
things whereof ye accuse him:
15 No, nor yet Her'od: for I sent you to him;
and, lo, nothing worthy of death is done unto
him.
16 I will therefore chastise him, and release
him.
17 (For of necessity he must release one unto
them at the feast.)
18 And they cried out all at once, saying,
Away with this *man*, and release unto us Ba-
rab'bas:
19 (Who for a certain sedition made in the
city, and for murder, was cast into prison.)
20 Pi'late therefore, willing to release Je'sus,
spake again to them.
21 But they cried, saying, Crucify *him*, crucify him.
22 And he said unto them the third time,
Why, what evil hath he done? I have found no
cause of death in him: I will therefore chastise
him, and let *him* go.
23 And they were instant with loud voices,
requiring that he might be crucified. And the
voices of them and of the chief priests prevailed.
24 And Pi'late gave sentence that it should
be as they required.
25 And he released unto them him that for
sedition and murder was cast into prison,

whom they had desired; but he delivered Je'sus to their will.

26 And as they led him away, they laid hold upon one Si'mon, a Cy-re'ni-an, coming out of the country, and on him they laid the cross, that he might bear *it* after Je'sus.

27 ¶ And there followed him a great company of people, and of women, which also bewailed and lamented him.

28 But Je'sus turning unto them said, Daughters of Je-ru'sa-lem, weep not for me, but weep for yourselves, and for your children.

29 For, behold, the days are coming, in the which they shall say, Blessed *are* the barren, and the wombs that never bare, and the paps which never gave suck.

30 Then shall they begin to say to the mountains, Fall on us; and to the hills, Cover us.

31 For if they do these things in a green tree, what shall be done in the dry?

32 And there were also two other, malefactors, led with him to be put to death.

33 And when they were come to the place, which is called Cal'va-ry, there they crucified him, and the malefactors, one on the right hand, and the other on the left.

34 ¶ Then said Je'sus, Father, forgive them; for they know not what they do. And they parted his raiment, and cast lots.

35 And the people stood beholding. And the rulers also with them derided *him*, saying, He saved others; let him save himself, if he be Christ, the chosen of God.

36 And the soldiers also mocked him, coming to him, and offering him vinegar,

37 And saying, If thou be the king of the Jews, save thyself.

38 And a superscription also was written over him in letters of Greek, and Lat'in, and He'brew, THIS IS THE KING OF THE JEWS.

39 ¶ And one of the malefactors which were hanged railed on him, saying, If thou be Christ, save thyself and us.

40 But the other answering rebuked him, saying, Dost not thou fear God, seeing thou art in the same condemnation?

41 And we indeed justly; for we receive the due reward of our deeds: but this man hath done nothing amiss.

42 And he said unto Je'sus, Lord, remember me when thou comest into thy kingdom.

43 And Je'sus said unto him, Verily I say unto thee, To day shalt thou be with me in paradise.

44 And it was about the sixth hour, and there was a darkness over all the earth until the ninth hour.

45 And the sun was darkened, and the veil of the temple was rent in the midst.

46 ¶ And when Je'sus had cried with a loud voice, he said, Father, into thy hands I commend my spirit: and having said thus, he gave up the ghost.

47 Now when the centurion saw what was done, he glorified God, saying, Certainly this was a righteous man.

48 And all the people that came together to that sight, beholding the things which were done, smote their breasts, and returned.

49 And all his acquaintance, and the women that followed him from Gal'i-lee, stood afar off, beholding these things.

50 ¶ And, behold, *there was* a man named Jo'seph, a counsellor; *and he was* a good man, and a just:

51 (The same had not consented to the counsel and deed of them;) *he was* of Ar-i-ma-thæ'a, a city of the Jews: who also himself waited for the kingdom of God.

52 This *man* went unto Pi'late, and begged the body of Je'sus.

53 And he took it down, and wrapped it in linen, and laid it in a sepulchre that was hewn in stone, wherein never man before was laid.

54 And that day was the preparation, and the sabbath drew on.

55 And the women also, which came with him from Gal'i-lee, followed after, and beheld the sepulchre, and how his body was laid.

56 And they returned, and prepared spices and ointments; and rested the sabbath day according to the commandment.

24 NOW upon the first *day* of the week, very early in the morning, they came unto the sepulchre, bringing the spices which they had prepared, and certain *others* with them.

2 And they found the stone rolled away from the sepulchre.

3 And they entered in, and found not the body of the Lord Je'sus.

4 And it came to pass, as they were much perplexed thereabout, behold, two men stood by them in shining garments:

5 And as they were afraid, and bowed down *their* faces to the earth, they said unto them, Why seek ye the living among the dead?

6 He is not here, but is risen: remember how he spake unto you when he was yet in Gal'i-lee,

7 Saying, The Son of man must be delivered into the hands of sinful men, and be crucified, and the third day rise again.

8 And they remembered his words,

9 And returned from the sepulchre, and told all these things unto the eleven, and to all the rest.

10 It was Ma'ry Mag-da-le'ne, and Jo-an'na, and Ma'ry *the mother* of James, and other *women that were* with them, which told these things unto the apostles.

11 And their words seemed to them as idle tales, and they believed them not.

12 Then arose Pe'ter, and ran unto the sepulchre; and stooping down, he beheld the linen clothes laid by themselves, and departed, wondering in himself at that which was come to pass.

13 ¶ And, behold, two of them went that same day to a village called Em'ma-us, which was from Je-ru'sa-lem *about* threescore furlongs.

14 And they talked together of all these things which had happened.

15 And it came to pass, that, while they communed *together* and reasoned, Je'sus himself drew near, and went with them.

16 But their eyes were holden that they should not know him.

17 And he said unto them, What manner of communications *are* these that ye have one to another, as ye walk, and are sad?

18 And the one of them, whose name was Cle'-o-pas, answering said unto him, Art thou only a stranger in Je-ru'sa-lem, and hast not known the things which are come to pass there in these days?

19 And he said unto them, What things? And they said unto him, Concerning Je'sus of Naz'a-reth, which was a prophet mighty in deed and word before God and all the people:

20 And how the chief priests and our rulers delivered him to be condemned to death, and have crucified him.

21 But we trusted that it had been he which
should have redeemed Is'ra-el: and beside all
this, to day is the third day since these things
were done.
22 Yea, and certain women also of our company made us astonished, which were early at
the sepulchre;
23 And when they found not his body, they
came, saying, that they had also seen a vision of
angels, which said that he was alive.
24 And certain of them which were with us
went to the sepulchre, and found *it* even so as
the women had said: but him they saw not.
25 Then he said unto them, O fools, and slow
of heart to believe all that the prophets have
spoken:
26 Ought not Christ to have suffered these
things, and to enter into his glory?
27 And beginning at Mo'ses and all the
prophets, he expounded unto them in all the
scriptures the things concerning himself.
28 And they drew nigh unto the village,
whither they went: and he made as though he
would have gone further.
29 But they constrained him, saying, Abide
with us: for it is toward evening, and the day is
far spent. And he went in to tarry with them.
30 And it came to pass, as he sat at meat
with them, he took bread, and blessed *it*, and
brake, and gave to them.
31 And their eyes were opened, and they
knew him; and he vanished out of their sight.
32 And they said one to another, Did not our
heart burn within us, while he talked with us by
the way, and while he opened to us the scriptures?
33 And they rose up the same hour, and returned to Je-ru'sa-lem, and found the eleven
gathered together, and them that were with
them,
34 Saying, The Lord is risen indeed, and hath
appeared to Si'mon.
35 And they told what things *were done* in
the way, and how he was known of them in
breaking of bread.
36 ¶ And as they thus spake, Je'sus himself
stood in the midst of them, and saith unto them,
Peace *be* unto you.
37 But they were terrified and affrighted, and
supposed that they had seen a spirit.
38 And he said unto them, Why are ye troubled? and why do thoughts arise in your hearts?
39 Behold my hands and my feet, that it is I
myself: handle me, and see; for a spirit hath not
flesh and bones, as ye see me have.
40 And when he had thus spoken, he shewed
them *his* hands and *his* feet.
41 And while they yet believed not for joy,
and wondered, he said unto them, Have ye here
any meat?
42 And they gave him a piece of a broiled
fish, and of an honeycomb.
43 And he took *it*, and did eat before them.
44 And he said unto them, These *are* the
words which I spake unto you, while I was yet
with you, that all things must be fulfilled, which
were written in the law of Mo'ses, and *in* the
prophets, and *in* the psalms, concerning me.
45 Then opened he their understanding, that
they might understand the scriptures,
46 And said unto them, Thus it is written,
and thus it behoved Christ to suffer, and to rise
from the dead the third day:
47 And that repentance and remission of sins
should be preached in his name among all nations, beginning at Je-ru'sa-lem.
48 And ye are witnesses of these things.
49 ¶ And, behold, I send the promise of my
Father upon you: but tarry ye in the city of Je-
ru'sa-lem, until ye be endued with power from
on high.
50 ¶ And he led them out as far as to Beth'a-
ny, and he lifted up his hands, and blessed
them.
51 And it came to pass, while he blessed
them, he was parted from them, and carried up
into heaven.
52 And they worshipped him, and returned
to Je-ru'sa-lem with great joy:
53 And were continually in the temple, praising and blessing God. Amen.

THE GOSPEL ACCORDING TO

JOHN

1 IN the beginning was the Word, and the
Word was with God, and the Word was
God.
2 The same was in the beginning with God.
3 All things were made by him; and without
him was not any thing made that was made.
4 In him was life; and the life was the light of
men.
5 And the light shineth in darkness; and the
darkness comprehended it not.
6 ¶ There was a man sent from God, whose
name *was* John.
7 The same came for a witness, to bear witness of the Light, that all *men* through him
might believe.
8 He was not that Light, but *was sent* to bear
witness of that Light.
9 *That* was the true Light, which lighteth every man that cometh into the world.
10 He was in the world, and the world was
made by him, and the world knew him not.
11 He came unto his own, and his own received him not.
12 But as many as received him, to them
gave he power to become the sons of GOD, *even*
to them that believe on his name:
13 Which were born, not of blood, nor of the
will of the flesh, nor of the will of man, but of
God.
14 And the Word was made flesh, and dwelt
among us, (and we beheld his glory, the glory as
of the only begotten of the Father,) full of grace
and truth.
15 ¶ John bare witness of him, and cried,
saying, This was he of whom I spake, He that
cometh after me is preferred before me: for he
was before me.
16 And of his fulness have all we received,
and grace for grace.
17 For the law was given by Mo'ses, *but*
grace and truth came by Je'sus Christ.
18 No man hath seen God at any time; the
only begotten Son, which is in the bosom of the
Father, he hath declared *him*.
19 ¶ And this is the record of John, when the

Jews sent priests and Le'vites from Je-ru'sa-lem
to ask him, Who art thou?
20 And he confessed, and denied not; but
confessed, I am not the Christ.
21 And they asked him, What then? Art thou
E-li'as? And he saith, I am not. Art thou that
prophet? And he answered, No.
22 Then said they unto him, Who art thou?
that we may give an answer to them that sent
us. What sayest thou of thyself?
23 He said, I *am* the voice of one crying in
the wilderness, Make straight the way of the
LORD, as said the prophet E-sa'ias.
24 And they which were sent were of the
Phar'i-sees.
25 And they asked him, and said unto him,
Why baptizest thou then, if thou be not that
Christ, nor E-li'as, neither that prophet?
26 John answered them, saying, I baptize
with water: but there standeth one among you,
whom ye know not;
27 He it is, who coming after me is preferred
before me, whose shoe's latchet I am not worthy to unloose.
28 These things were done in Beth-ab'a-ra
beyond Jor'dan, where John was baptizing.
29 ¶ The next day John seeth Je'sus coming
unto him, and saith, Behold the Lamb of God,
which taketh away the sin of the world.
30 This is he of whom I said, After me cometh a man which is preferred before me: for he
was before me.
31 And I knew him not: but that he should be
made manifest to Is'ra-el, therefore am I come
baptizing with water.
32 And John bare record, saying, I saw the
Spirit descending from heaven like a dove, and
it abode upon him.
33 And I knew him not: but he that sent me
to baptize with water, the same said unto me,
Upon whom thou shalt see the Spirit descending, and remaining on him, the same is he
which baptizeth with the Ho'ly Ghost.
34 And I saw, and bare record that this is the
Son of God.
35 ¶ Again the next day after John stood,
and two of his disciples;
36 And looking upon Je'sus as he walked, he
saith, Behold the Lamb of God!
37 And the two disciples heard him speak,
and they followed Je'sus.
38 Then Je'sus turned, and saw them following, and saith unto them, What seek ye? They
said unto him, Rab'bi, (which is to say, being
interpreted, Master,) where dwellest thou?
39 He saith unto them, Come and see. They
came and saw where he dwelt, and abode with
him that day: for it was about the tenth hour.
40 One of the two which heard John *speak*,
and followed him, was Andrew, Si'mon Pe'ter's
brother.
41 He first findeth his own brother Si'mon,
and saith unto him, We have found the Mes-
si'as, which is, being interpreted, the Christ.
42 And he brought him to Je'sus. And when
Je'sus beheld him, he said, Thou art Si'mon the
son of Jo'na: thou shalt be called Ce'phas,
which is by interpretation, A stone.
43 ¶ The day following Je'sus would go forth
into Gal'i-lee, and findeth Phil'ip, and saith unto
him, Follow me.
44 Now Phil'ip was of Beth-sa'i-da, the city
of Andrew and Pe'ter.
45 Phil'ip findeth Na-than'a-el, and saith unto
him, We have found him, of whom Mo'ses in
the law, and the prophets, did write, Je'sus of
Naz'a-reth, the son of Jo'seph.
46 And Na-than'a-el said unto him, Can there
any good thing come out of Naz'a-reth? Phil'ip
saith unto him, Come and see.
47 Je'sus saw Na-than'a-el coming to him,
and saith of him, Behold an Is'ra-el-ite indeed,
in whom is no guile!
48 Na-than'a-el saith unto him, Whence
knowest thou me? Je'sus answered and said
unto him, Before that Phil'ip called thee, when
thou wast under the fig tree, I saw thee.
49 Na-than'a-el answered and saith unto
him, Rab'bi, thou art the Son of God; thou art
the King of Is'ra-el.
50 Je'sus answered and said unto him, Because I said unto thee, I saw thee under the fig
tree, believest thou? thou shalt see greater
things than these.
51 And he saith unto him, Verily, verily, I say
unto you, Hereafter ye shall see heaven open,
and the angels of God ascending and descending upon the Son of man.

2 AND the third day there was a marriage in
Ca'na of Gal'i-lee; and the mother of Je'sus
was there:
2 And both Je'sus was called, and his disciples, to the marriage.
3 And when they wanted wine, the mother of
Je'sus saith unto him, They have no wine.
4 Je'sus saith unto her, Woman, what have I
to do with thee? mine hour is not yet come.
5 His mother saith unto the servants, Whatsoever he saith unto you, do *it*.
6 And there were set there six waterpots of
stone, after the manner of the purifying of the
Jews, containing two or three firkins apiece.
7 Je'sus saith unto them, Fill the waterpots
with water. And they filled them up to the brim.
8 And he saith unto them, Draw out now,
and bear unto the governor of the feast. And
they bare *it*.
9 When the ruler of the feast had tasted the
water that was made wine, and knew not
whence it was: (but the servants which drew
the water knew;) the governor of the feast
called the bridegroom,
10 And saith unto him, Every man at the beginning doth set forth good wine; and when
men have well drunk, then that which is worse:
but thou hast kept the good wine until now.
11 This beginning of miracles did Je'sus in
Ca'na of Gal'i-lee, and manifested forth his glory; and his disciples believed on him.
12 ¶ After this he went down to Ca-per'na-
um, he, and his mother, and his brethren, and
his disciples: and they continued there not
many days.
13 ¶ And the Jews' passover was at hand,
and Je'sus went up to Je-ru'sa-lem,
14 And found in the temple those that sold
oxen and sheep and doves, and the changers of
money sitting:
15 And when he had made a scourge of small
cords, he drove them all out of the temple, and
the sheep, and the oxen; and poured out the
changers' money, and overthrew the tables;
16 And said unto them that sold doves, Take
these things hence; make not my Father's house
an house of merchandise.
17 And his disciples remembered that it was
written, The zeal of thine house hath eaten me
up.
18 ¶ Then answered the Jews and said unto
him, What sign shewest thou unto us, seeing
that thou doest these things?
19 Je'sus answered and said unto them, De-

stroy this temple, and in three days I will raise
it up.
20 Then said the Jews, Forty and six years
was this temple in building, and wilt thou rear it
up in three days?
21 But he spake of the temple of his body.
22 When therefore he was risen from the
dead, his disciples remembered that he had said
this unto them; and they believed the scripture,
and the word which Je'sus had said.
23 ¶ Now when he was in Je-ru'sa-lem at the
passover, in the feast *day*, many believed in his
name, when they saw the miracles which he
did.
24 But Je'sus did not commit himself unto
them, because he knew all *men*,
25 And needed not that any should testify of
man: for he knew what was in man.

3 THERE was a man of the Phar'i-sees,
named Nic-o-de'mus, a ruler of the Jews:
2 The same came to Je'sus by night, and said
unto him, Rab'bi, we know that thou art a
teacher come from God: for no man can do
these miracles that thou doest, except God be
with him.
3 Je'sus answered and said unto him, Verily,
verily, I say unto thee, Except a man be born
again, he cannot see the kingdom of God.
4 Nic-o-de'mus saith unto him, How can a
man be born when he is old? can he enter the
second time into his mother's womb, and be
born?
5 Je'sus answered, Verily, verily, I say unto
thee, Except a man be born of water and *of* the
Spirit, he cannot enter into the kingdom of God.
6 That which is born of the flesh is flesh; and
that which is born of the Spirit is spirit.
7 Marvel not that I said unto thee, Ye must
be born again.
8 The wind bloweth where it listeth, and thou
hearest the sound thereof, but canst not tell
whence it cometh, and whither it goeth: so is
every one that is born of the Spirit.
9 Nic-o-de'mus answered and said unto him,
How can these things be?
10 Je'sus answered and said unto him, Art
thou a master of Is'ra-el, and knowest not these
things?
11 Verily, verily, I say unto thee, We speak
that we do know, and testify that we have seen;
and ye receive not our witness.
12 If I have told you earthly things, and ye
believe not, how shall ye believe, if I tell you *of*
heavenly things?
13 And no man hath ascended up to heaven,
but he that came down from heaven, *even* the
Son of man which is in heaven.
14 ¶ And as Mo'ses lifted up the serpent in
the wilderness, even so must the Son of man be
lifted up:
15 That whosoever believeth in him should
not perish, but have eternal life.
16 ¶ For God so loved the world, that he
gave his only begotten Son, that whosoever believeth in him should not perish, but have everlasting life.
17 For God sent not his Son into the world to
condemn the world; but that the world through
him might be saved.
18 ¶ He that believeth on him is not condemned: but he that believeth not is condemned
already, because he hath not believed in the
name of the only begotten Son of God.
19 And this is the condemnation, that light is
come into the world, and men loved darkness
rather than light, because their deeds were evil.
20 For every one that doeth evil hateth the
light, neither cometh to the light, lest his deeds
should be reproved.
21 But he that doeth truth cometh to the
light, that his deeds may be made manifest, that
they are wrought in God.
22 ¶ After these things came Je'sus and his
disciples into the land of Ju-dæ'a; and there he
tarried with them, and baptized.
23 ¶ And John also was baptizing in Æ'non
near to Sa'lim, because there was much water
there: and they came, and were baptized.
24 For John was not yet cast into prison.
25 ¶ Then there arose a question between
some of John's disciples and the Jews about purifying.
26 And they came unto John, and said unto
him, Rab'bi, he that was with thee beyond Jor'-
dan, to whom thou barest witness, behold, the
same baptizeth, and all *men* come to him.
27 John answered and said, A man can receive nothing, except it be given him from
heaven.
28 Ye yourselves bear me witness, that I
said, I am not the Christ, but that I am sent
before him.
29 He that hath the bride is the bridegroom:
but the friend of the bridegroom, which standeth and heareth him, rejoiceth greatly because
of the bridgroom's voice: this my joy therefore
is fulfilled.
30 He must increase, but I *must* decrease.
31 He that cometh from above is above all:
he that is of the earth is earthly, and speaketh
of the earth: he that cometh from heaven is
above all.
32 And what he hath seen and heard, that he
testifieth; and no man receiveth his testimony.
33 He that hath received his testimony hath
set to his seal that God is true.
34 For he whom God hath sent speaketh the
words of God: for God giveth not the Spirit by
measure *unto him*.
35 The Father loveth the Son, and hath given
all things into his hand.
36 He that believeth on the Son hath everlasting life: and he that believeth not the Son
shall not see life; but the wrath of God abideth
on him.

4 WHEN therefore the Lord knew how the
Phar'i-sees had heard that Je'sus made and
baptized more disciples than John,
2 (Though Je'sus himself baptized not, but
his disciples,)
3 He left Ju-dæ'a, and departed again into
Gal'i-lee.
4 And he must needs go through Sa-ma'ri-a.
5 Then cometh he to a city of Sa-ma'ri-a,
which is called Sy'char, near to the parcel of
ground that Ja'cob gave to his son Jo'seph.
6 Now Ja'cob's well was there. Je'sus therefore, being wearied with *his* journey, sat thus
on the well: *and* it was about the sixth hour.
7 There cometh a woman of Sa-ma'ri-a to
draw water: Je'sus saith unto her, Give me to
drink.
8 (For his disciples were gone away unto the
city to buy meat.)
9 Then saith the woman of Sa-ma'ri-a unto
him, How is it that thou, being a Jew, askest
drink of me, which am a woman of Sa-ma'ri-a?
for the Jews have no dealings with the Sa-mar'i-
tans.
10 Je'sus answered and said unto her, If thou
knewest the gift of God, and who it is that saith
to thee, Give me to drink; thou wouldest have

asked of him, and he would have given thee living water.

11 The woman saith unto him, Sir, thou hast nothing to draw with, and the well is deep: from whence then hast thou that living water?

12 Art thou greater than our father Ja'cob, which gave us the well, and drank thereof himself, and his children, and his cattle?

13 Je'sus answered and said unto her, Whosoever drinketh of this water shall thirst again:

14 But whosoever drinketh of the water that I shall give him shall never thirst; but the water that I shall give him shall be in him a well of water springing up into everlasting life.

15 The woman saith unto him, Sir, give me this water, that I thirst not, neither come hither to draw.

16 Je'sus saith unto her, Go, call thy husband, and come hither.

17 The woman answered and said, I have no husband. Je'sus said unto her, Thou hast well said, I have no husband:

18 For thou hast had five husbands; and he whom thou now hast is not thy husband: in that saidst thou truly.

19 The woman saith unto him, Sir, I perceive that thou art a prophet.

20 Our fathers worshipped in this mountain; and ye say, that in Je-ru'sa-lem is the place where men ought to worship.

21 Je'sus saith unto her, Woman, believe me, the hour cometh, when ye shall neither in this mountain, nor yet at Je-ru'sa-lem, worship the Father.

22 Ye worship ye know not what: we know what we worship: for salvation is of the Jews.

23 But the hour cometh, and now is, when the true worshippers shall worship the Father in spirit and in truth: for the Father seeketh such to worship him.

24 God *is* a Spirit: and they that worship him must worship *him* in spirit and in truth.

25 The woman saith unto him, I know that Mes-si'as cometh, which is called Christ: when he is come, he will tell us all things.

26 Je'sus saith unto her, I that speak unto thee am *he*.

27 ¶ And upon this came his disciples, and marvelled that he talked with the woman: yet no man said, What seekest thou? or, Why talkest thou with her?

28 The woman then left her waterpot, and went her way into the city, and saith to the men,

29 Come, see a man, which told me all things that ever I did: is not this the Christ?

30 Then they went out of the city, and came unto him.

31 ¶ In the mean while his disciples prayed him, saying, Master, eat.

32 But he said unto them, I have meat to eat that ye know not of.

33 Therefore said the disciples one to another, Hath any man brought him *ought* to eat?

34 Je'sus saith unto them, My meat is to do the will of him that sent me, and to finish his work.

35 Say not ye, There are yet four months, and *then* cometh harvest? behold, I say unto you, Lift up your eyes, and look on the fields; for they are white already to harvest.

36 And he that reapeth receiveth wages, and gathereth fruit unto life eternal: that both he that soweth and he that reapeth may rejoice together.

37 And herein is that saying true, One soweth, and another reapeth.

38 I sent you to reap that whereon ye bestowed no labour: other men laboured, and ye are entered into their labours.

39 ¶ And many of the Sa-mar'i-tans of that city believed on him for the saying of the woman, which testified, He told me all that ever I did.

40 So when the Sa-mar'i-tans were come unto him, they besought him that he would tarry with them: and he abode there two days.

41 And many more believed because of his own word;

42 And said unto the woman, Now we believe, not because of thy saying: for we have heard *him* ourselves, and know that this is indeed the Christ, the Saviour of the world.

43 ¶ Now after two days he departed thence, and went into Gal'i-lee.

44 For Je'sus himself testified, that a prophet hath no honour in his own country.

45 Then when he was come into Gal'i-lee, the Gal-i-læ'ans received him, having seen all the things that he did at Je-ru'sa-lem at the feast: for they also went unto the feast.

46 So Je'sus came again into Ca'na of Gal'i-lee, where he made the water wine. And there was a certain nobleman, whose son was sick at Ca-per'na-um.

47 When he heard that Je'sus was come out of Ju-dæ'a into Gal'i-lee, he went unto him, and besought him that he would come down, and heal his son: for he was at the point of death.

48 Then said Je'sus unto him, Except ye see signs and wonders, ye will not believe.

49 The nobleman saith unto him, Sir, come down ere my child die.

50 Je'sus saith unto him, Go thy way; thy son liveth. And the man believed the word that Je'sus had spoken unto him, and he went his way.

51 And as he was now going down, his servants met him, and told *him*, saying, Thy son liveth.

52 Then enquired he of them the hour when he began to amend. And they said unto him, Yesterday at the seventh hour the fever left him.

53 So the father knew that *it was* at the same hour, in the which Je'sus said unto him, Thy son liveth: and himself believed, and his whole house.

54 This *is* again the second miracle *that* Je'sus did, when he was come out of Ju-dæ'a into Gal'i-lee.

5 AFTER this there was a feast of the Jews; and Je'sus went up to Je-ru'sa-lem.

2 Now there is at Je-ru'sa-lem by the sheep *market* a pool, which is called in the He'brew tongue Be-thes'da, having five porches.

3 In these lay a great multitude of impotent folk, of blind, halt, withered, waiting for the moving of the water.

4 For an angel went down at a certain season into the pool, and troubled the water: whosoever then first after the troubling of the water stepped in was made whole of whatsoever disease he had.

5 And a certain man was there, which had an infirmity thirty and eight years.

6 When Je'sus saw him lie, and knew that he had been now a long time *in that case*, he saith unto him, Wilt thou be made whole?

7 The impotent man answered him, Sir, I have no man, when the water is troubled, to put me into the pool: but while I am coming, another steppeth down before me.

8 Je'sus saith unto him, Rise, take up thy
bed, and walk.
9 And immediately the man was made
whole, and took up his bed, and walked: and on
the same day was the sabbath.
10 ¶ The Jews therefore said unto him that
was cured, It is the sabbath day: it is not lawful
for thee to carry *thy* bed.
11 He answered them, He that made me
whole, the same said unto me, Take up thy bed,
and walk.
12 Then asked they him, What man is that
which said unto thee, Take up thy bed, and
walk?
13 And he that was healed wist not who it
was: for Je'sus had conveyed himself away, a
multitude being in *that* place.
14 Afterward Je'sus findeth him in the temple, and said unto him, Behold, thou art made
whole: sin no more, lest a worse thing come
unto thee.
15 The man departed, and told the Jews that
it was Je'sus, which had made him whole.
16 And therefore did the Jews persecute Je'-
sus, and sought to slay him, because he had
done these things on the sabbath day.
17 ¶ But Je'sus answered them, My Father
worketh hitherto, and I work.
18 Therefore the Jews sought the more to kill
him, because he not only had broken the sabbath, but said also that God was his Father,
making himself equal with God.
19 Then answered Je'sus and said unto them,
Verily, verily, I say unto you, The Son can do
nothing of himself, but what he seeth the Father
do: for what things soever he doeth, these also
doeth the Son likewise.
20 For the Father loveth the Son, and sheweth him all things that himself doeth: and he
will shew him greater works than these, that ye
may marvel.
21 For as the Father raiseth up the dead, and
quickeneth *them;* even so the Son quickeneth
whom he will.
22 For the Father judgeth no man, but hath
committed all judgment unto the Son:
23 That all *men* should honour the Son, even
as they honour the Father. He that honoureth
not the Son honoureth not the Father which
hath sent him.
24 Verily, verily, I say unto you, He that
heareth my word, and believeth on him that
sent me, hath everlasting life, and shall not
come into condemnation; but is passed from
death unto life.
25 Verily, verily, I say unto you, The hour is
coming, and now is, when the dead shall hear
the voice of the Son of God: and they that hear
shall live.
26 For as the Father hath life in himself; so
hath he given to the Son to have life in himself;
27 And hath given him authority to execute
judgment also, because he is the Son of man.
28 Marvel not at this: for the hour is coming,
in the which all that are in the graves shall hear
his voice,
29 And shall come forth; they that have done
good, unto the resurrection of life; and they that
have done evil, unto the resurrection of damnation.
30 I can of mine own self do nothing: as I
hear, I judge: and my judgment is just; because
I seek not mine own will, but the will of the
Father which hath sent me.
31 If I bear witness of myself, my witness is
not true.
32 ¶ There is another that beareth witness of
me; and I know that the witness which he witnesseth of me is true.
33 Ye sent unto John, and he bare witness
unto the truth.
34 But I receive not testimony from man: but
these things I say, that ye might be saved.
35 He was a burning and a shining light: and
ye were willing for a season to rejoice in his
light.
36 ¶ But I have greater witness than *that* of
John: for the works which the Father hath
given me to finish, the same works that I do,
bear witness of me, that the Father hath sent
me.
37 And the Father himself, which hath sent
me, hath borne witness of me. Ye have neither
heard his voice at any time, nor seen his shape.
38 And ye have not his word abiding in you:
for whom he hath sent, him ye believe not.
39 ¶ Search the scriptures; for in them ye
think ye have eternal life: and they are they
which testify of me.
40 And ye will not come to me, that ye might
have life.
41 I receive not honour from men.
42 But I know you, that ye have not the love
of God in you.
43 I am come in my Father's name, and ye
receive me not: if another shall come in his own
name, him ye will receive.
44 How can ye believe, which receive honour
one of another, and seek not the honour that
cometh from God only?
45 Do not think that I will accuse you to the
Father: there is *one* that accuseth you, *even*
Mo'ses, in whom ye trust.
46 For had ye believed Mo'ses, ye would
have believed me: for he wrote of me.
47 But if ye believe not his writings, how
shall ye believe my words?

6 AFTER these things Je'sus went over the
sea of Gal'i-lee, which is *the sea* of Ti-be'ri-
as.
2 And a great multitude followed him, because they saw his miracles which he did on
them that were diseased.
3 And Je'sus went up into a mountain, and
there he sat with his disciples.
4 And the passover, a feast of the Jews, was
nigh.
5 ¶ When Je'sus then lifted up *his* eyes, and
saw a great company come unto him, he saith
unto Phil'ip, Whence shall we buy bread, that
these may eat?
6 And this he said to prove him: for he himself knew what he would do.
7 Phil'ip answered him, Two hundred pennyworth of bread is not sufficient for them, that
every one of them may take a little.
8 One of his disciples, Andrew, Si'mon Pe'-
ter's brother, saith unto him,
9 There is a lad here, which hath five barley
loaves, and two small fishes: but what are they
among so many?
10 And Je'sus said, Make the men sit down.
Now there was much grass in the place. So the
men sat down, in number about five thousand.
11 And Je'sus took the loaves; and when he
had given thanks, he distributed to the disciples, and the disciples to them that were set
down; and likewise of the fishes as much as
they would.
12 When they were filled, he said unto his
disciples, Gather up the fragments that remain,
that nothing be lost.
13 Therefore they gathered *them* together,
and filled twelve baskets with the fragments of

the five barley loaves, which remained over and
above unto them that had eaten.
14 Then those men, when they had seen the
miracle that Je'sus did, said, This is of a truth
that prophet that should come into the world.
15 ¶ When Je'sus therefore perceived that
they would come and take him by force, to
make him a king, he departed again into a
mountain himself alone.
16 And when even was *now* come, his disciples went down unto the sea,
17 And entered into a ship, and went over
the sea toward Ca-per'na-um. And it was now
dark, and Je'sus was not come to them.
18 And the sea arose by reason of a great
wind that blew.
19 So when they had rowed about five and
twenty or thirty furlongs, they see Je'sus walking on the sea, and drawing nigh unto the ship:
and they were afraid.
20 But he saith unto them, It is I; be not
afraid.
21 Then they willingly received him into the
ship: and immediately the ship was at the land
whither they went.
22 ¶ The day following, when the people
which stood on the other side of the sea saw
that there was none other boat there, save that
one whereinto his disciples were entered, and
that Je'sus went not with his disciples into the
boat, but *that* his disciples were gone away
alone;
23 (Howbeit there came other boats from Ti-
be'ri-as nigh unto the place where they did eat
bread, after that the Lord had given thanks:)
24 When the people therefore saw that Je'sus
was not there, neither his disciples, they also
took shipping, and came to Ca-per'na-um, seeking for Je'sus.
25 And when they had found him on the other side of the sea, they said unto him, Rab'bi,
when camest thou hither?
26 Je'sus answered them and said, Verily,
verily, I say unto you, Ye seek me, not because
ye saw the miracles, but because ye did eat of
the loaves, and were filled.
27 Labour not for the meat which perisheth,
but for that meat which endureth unto everlasting life, which the Son of man shall give
unto you: for him hath God the Father sealed.
28 Then said they unto him, What shall we
do, that we might work the works of God?
29 Je'sus answered and said unto them, This
is the work of God, that ye believe on him
whom he hath sent.
30 They said therefore unto him, What sign
shewest thou then, that we may see, and believe thee? what dost thou work?
31 Our fathers did eat manna in the desert;
as it is written, He gave them bread from
heaven to eat.
32 Then Je'sus said unto them, Verily, verily,
I say unto you, Mo'ses gave you not that bread
from heaven; but my Father giveth you the true
bread from heaven.
33 For the bread of God is he which cometh
down from heaven, and giveth life unto the
world.
34 Then said they unto him, Lord, evermore
give us this bread.
35 And Je'sus said unto them, I am the bread
of life: he that cometh to me shall never hunger;
and he that believeth on me shall never thirst.
36 But I said unto you, That ye also have
seen me, and believe not.
37 All that the Father giveth me shall come
to me; and him that cometh to me I will in no
wise cast out.
38 For I came down from heaven, not to do
mine own will, but the will of him that sent me.
39 And this is the Father's will which hath
sent me, that of all which he hath given me I
should lose nothing, but should raise it up again
at the last day.
40 And this is the will of him that sent me,
that every one which seeth the Son, and believeth on him, may have everlasting life: and I will
raise him up at the last day.
41 The Jews then murmured at him, because
he said, I am the bread which came down from
heaven.
42 And they said, Is not this Je'sus, the son of
Jo'seph, whose father and mother we know?
how is it then that he saith, I came down from
heaven?
43 Je'sus therefore answered and said unto
them, Murmur not among yourselves.
44 No man can come to me, except the Father which hath sent me draw him: and I will
raise him up at the last day.
45 It is written in the prophets, And they
shall be all taught of God. Every man therefore
that hath heard, and hath learned of the Father,
cometh unto me.
46 Not that any man hath seen the Father,
save he which is of God, he hath seen the Father.
47 Verily, verily, I say unto you, He that believeth on me hath everlasting life.
48 I am that bread of life.
49 Your fathers did eat manna in the wilderness, and are dead.
50 This is the bread which cometh down
from heaven, that a man may eat thereof, and
not die.
51 I am the living bread which came down
from heaven: if any man eat of this bread, he
shall live for ever: and the bread that I will give
is my flesh, which I will give for the life of the
world.
52 The Jews therefore strove among themselves, saying, How can this man give us *his*
flesh to eat?
53 Then Je'sus said unto them, Verily, verily,
I say unto you, Except ye eat the flesh of the
Son of man, and drink his blood, ye have no life
in you.
54 Whoso eateth my flesh, and drinketh my
blood, hath eternal life; and I will raise him up
at the last day.
55 For my flesh is meat indeed, and my blood
is drink indeed.
56 He that eateth my flesh, and drinketh my
blood, dwelleth in me, and I in him.
57 As the living Father hath sent me, and I
live by the Father: so he that eateth me, even he
shall live by me.
58 This is that bread which came down from
heaven: not as your fathers did eat manna, and
are dead: he that eateth of this bread shall live
for ever.
59 These things said he in the synagogue, as
he taught in Ca-per'na-um.
60 Many therefore of his disciples, when they
had heard *this*, said, This is an hard saying; who
can hear it?
61 When Je'sus knew in himself that his disciples murmured at it, he said unto them, Doth
this offend you?
62 *What* and if ye shall see the Son of man
ascend up where he was before?
63 It is the spirit that quickeneth; the flesh

profiteth nothing: the words that I speak unto you, *they* are spirit, and *they* are life.

64 But there are some of you that believe not. For Je'sus knew from the beginning who they were that believed not, and who should betray him.

65 And he said, Therefore said I unto you, that no man can come unto me, except it were given unto him of my Father.

66 ¶ From that *time* many of his disciples went back, and walked no more with him.

67 Then said Je'sus unto the twelve, Will ye also go away?

68 Then Si'mon Pe'ter answered him, Lord, to whom shall we go? thou hast the words of eternal life.

69 And we believe and are sure that thou art that Christ, the Son of the living God.

70 Je'sus answered them, Have not I chosen you twelve, and one of you is a devil?

71 He spake of Ju'das Is-car'i-ot *the son* of Si'mon: for he it was that should betray him, being one of the twelve.

7

AFTER these things Je'sus walked in Gal'i-lee: for he would not walk in Jew'ry, because the Jews sought to kill him.

2 Now the Jews' feast of tabernacles was at hand.

3 His brethren therefore said unto him, Depart hence, and go into Ju-dæ'a, that thy disciples also may see the works that thou doest.

4 For *there is* no man *that* doeth any thing in secret, and he himself seeketh to be known openly. If thou do these things, shew thyself to the world.

5 For neither did his brethren believe in him.

6 Then Je'sus said unto them, My time is not yet come: but your time is alway ready.

7 The world cannot hate you; but me it hateth, because I testify of it, that the works thereof are evil.

8 Go ye up unto this feast: I go not up yet unto this feast; for my time is not yet full come.

9 When he had said these words unto them, he abode *still* in Gal'i-lee.

10 ¶ But when his brethren were gone up, then went he also up unto the feast, not openly, but as it were in secret.

11 Then the Jews sought him at the feast, and said, Where is he?

12 And there was much murmuring among the people concerning him: for some said, He is a good man: others said, Nay; but he deceiveth the people.

13 Howbeit no man spake openly of him for fear of the Jews.

14 ¶ Now about the midst of the feast Je'sus went up into the temple, and taught.

15 And the Jews marvelled, saying, How knoweth this man letters, having never learned?

16 Je'sus answered them, and said, My doctrine is not mine, but his that sent me.

17 If any man will do his will, he shall know of the doctrine, whether it be of God, or *whether* I speak of myself.

18 He that speaketh of himself seeketh his own glory: but he that seeketh his glory that sent him, the same is true, and no unrighteousness is in him.

19 Did not Mo'ses give you the law, and *yet* none of you keepeth the law? Why go ye about to kill me?

20 The people answered and said, Thou hast a devil: who goeth about to kill thee?

21 Je'sus answered and said unto them, I have done one work, and ye all marvel.

22 Mo'ses therefore gave unto you circumcision; (not because it is of Mo'ses, but of the fathers;) and ye on the sabbath day circumcise a man.

23 If a man on the sabbath day receive circumcision, that the law of Mo'ses should not be broken; are ye angry at me, because I have made a man every whit whole on the sabbath day?

24 Judge not according to the appearance, but judge righteous judgment.

25 Then said some of them of Je-ru'sa-lem, Is not this he, whom they seek to kill?

26 But, lo, he speaketh boldly, and they say nothing unto him. Do the rulers know indeed that this is the very Christ?

27 Howbeit we know this man whence he is: but when Christ cometh, no man knoweth whence he is.

28 Then cried Je'sus in the temple as he taught, saying, Ye both know me, and ye know whence I am: and I am not come of myself, but he that sent me is true, whom ye know not.

29 But I know him: for I am from him, and he hath sent me.

30 Then they sought to take him: but no man laid hands on him, because his hour was not yet come.

31 And many of the people believed on him, and said, When Christ cometh, will he do more miracles than these which this *man* hath done?

32 ¶ The Phar'i-sees heard that the people murmured such things concerning him; and the Phar'i-sees and the chief priests sent officers to take him.

33 Then said Je'sus unto them, Yet a little while am I with you, and *then* I go unto him that sent me.

34 Ye shall seek me, and shall not find *me:* and where I am, *thither* ye cannot come.

35 Then said the Jews among themselves, Whither will he go, that we shall not find him? will he go unto the dispersed among the Gen'tiles, and teach the Gen'tiles?

36 What *manner of* saying is this that he said, Ye shall seek me, and shall not find *me:* and where I am, *thither* ye cannot come?

37 In the last day, that great *day* of the feast, Je'sus stood and cried, saying, If any man thirst, let him come unto me, and drink.

38 He that believeth on me, as the scripture hath said, out of his belly shall flow rivers of living water.

39 (But this spake he of the Spirit, which they that believe on him should receive: for the Ho'ly Ghost was not yet *given:* because that Je'sus was not yet glorified.)

40 ¶ Many of the people therefore, when they heard this saying, said, Of a truth this is the Prophet.

41 Others said, This is the Christ. But some said, Shall Christ come out of Gal'i-lee?

42 Hath not the scripture said, That Christ cometh of the seed of Da'vid, and out of the town of Beth'le-hem, where Da'vid was?

43 So there was a division among the people because of him.

44 And some of them would have taken him; but no man laid hands on him.

45 ¶ Then came the officers to the chief priests and Phar'i-sees; and they said unto them, Why have ye not brought him?

46 The officers answered, Never man spake like this man.

47 Then answered them the Phar'i-sees, Are ye also deceived?

48 Have any of the rulers or of the Phar′i-
sees believed on him?
49 But this people who knoweth not the law
are cursed.
50 Nic-o-de′mus saith unto them, (he that
came to Je′sus by night, being one of them,)
51 Doth our law judge *any* man, before it
hear him, and know what he doeth?
52 They answered and said unto him, Art
thou also of Gal′i-lee? Search, and look: for out
of Gal′i-lee ariseth no prophet.
53 And every man went unto his own house.

8 JE′SUS went unto the mount of Ol′ives.
2 And early in the morning he came
again into the temple, and all the people came
unto him; and he sat down, and taught them.
3 And the scribes and Phar′i-sees brought
unto him a woman taken in adultery; and when
they had set her in the midst,
4 They say unto him, Master, this woman
was taken in adultery, in the very act.
5 Now Mo′ses in the law commanded us, that
such should be stoned: but what sayest thou?
6 This they said, tempting him, that they
might have to accuse him. But Je′sus stooped
down, and with *his* finger wrote on the ground,
as though he heard them not.
7 So when they continued asking him, he
lifted up himself, and said unto them, He that is
without sin among you, let him first cast a stone
at her.
8 And again he stooped down, and wrote on
the ground.
9 And they which heard *it*, being convicted
by *their own* conscience, went out one by one,
beginning at the eldest, *even* unto the last: and
Je′sus was left alone, and the woman standing
in the midst.
10 When Je′sus had lifted up himself, and
saw none but the woman, he said unto her,
Woman, where are those thine accusers? hath
no man condemned thee?
11 She said, No man, Lord. And Je′sus said
unto her, Neither do I condemn thee: go, and
sin no more.
12 ¶ Then spake Je′sus again unto them, saying, I am the light of the world: he that followeth me shall not walk in darkness, but shall
have the light of life.
13 The Phar′i-sees therefore said unto him,
Thou bearest record of thyself; thy record is not
true.
14 Je′sus answered and said unto them,
Though I bear record of myself, *yet* my record
is true: for I know whence I came, and whither
I go; but ye cannot tell whence I come, and
whither I go.
15 Ye judge after the flesh; I judge no man.
16 And yet if I judge, my judgment is true:
for I am not alone, but I and the Father that sent
me.
17 It is also written in your law, that the testimony of two men is true.
18 I am one that bear witness of myself, and
the Father that sent me beareth witness of me.
19 Then said they unto him, Where is thy Father? Je′sus answered, Ye neither know me, nor
my Father: if ye had known me, ye should have
known my Father also.
20 These words spake Je′sus in the treasury,
as he taught in the temple: and no man laid
hands on him; for his hour was not yet come.
21 Then said Je′sus again unto them, I go my
way, and ye shall seek me, and shall die in your
sins: whither I go, ye cannot come.
22 Then said the Jews, Will he kill himself?
because he saith, Whither I go, ye cannot come.
23 And he said unto them, Ye are from beneath; I am from above: ye are of this world; I
am not of this world.
24 I said therefore unto you, that ye shall die
in your sins: for if ye believe not that I am *he*, ye
shall die in your sins.
25 Then said they unto him, Who art thou?
And Je′sus saith unto them, Even *the same* that
I said unto you from the beginning.
26 I have many things to say and to judge of
you: but he that sent me is true; and I speak to
the world those things which I have heard of
him.
27 They understood not that he spake to
them of the Father.
28 Then said Je′sus unto them, When ye have
lifted up the Son of man, then shall ye know
that I am *he*, and *that* I do nothing of myself;
but as my Father hath taught me, I speak these
things.
29 And he that sent me is with me: the Father hath not left me alone; for I do always
those things that please him.
30 As he spake these words, many believed
on him.
31 Then said Je′sus to those Jews which believed on him, If ye continue in my word, *then*
are ye my disciples indeed;
32 And ye shall know the truth, and the truth
shall make you free.
33 ¶ They answered him, We be A′bra-ham′s
seed, and were never in bondage to any man:
how sayest thou, Ye shall be made free?
34 Je′sus answered them, Verily, verily, I say
unto you, Whosoever committeth sin is the servant of sin.
35 And the servant abideth not in the house
for ever: *but* the Son abideth ever.
36 If the Son therefore shall make you free,
ye shall be free indeed.
37 I know that ye are A′bra-ham′s seed; but
ye seek to kill me, because my word hath no
place in you.
38 I speak that which I have seen with my
Father: and ye do that which ye have seen with
your father.
39 They answered and said unto him, A′bra-
ham is our father. Je′sus saith unto them, If ye
were A′bra-ham′s children, ye would do the
works of A′bra-ham.
40 But now ye seek to kill me, a man that
hath told you the truth, which I have heard of
God: this did not A′bra-ham.
41 Ye do the deeds of your father. Then said
they to him, We be not born of fornication; we
have one Father, *even* God.
42 Je′sus said unto them, If God were your
Father, ye would love me: for I proceeded forth
and came from God; neither came I of myself,
but he sent me.
43 Why do ye not understand my speech?
even because ye cannot hear my word.
44 Ye are of *your* father the devil, and the
lusts of your father ye will do. He was a murderer from the beginning, and abode not in the
truth, because there is no truth in him. When he
speaketh a lie, he speaketh of his own: for he is
a liar, and the father of it.
45 And because I tell *you* the truth, ye believe me not.
46 Which of you convinceth me of sin? And
if I say the truth, why do ye not believe me?
47 He that is of God heareth God′s words: ye
therefore hear *them* not, because ye are not of
God.
48 Then answered the Jews, and said unto

him, Say we not well that thou art a Sa-mar'i-
tan, and hast a devil?
49 Je'sus answered, I have not a devil; but I
honour my Father, and ye do dishonour me.
50 And I seek not mine own glory: there is
one that seeketh and judgeth.
51 Verily, verily, I say unto you, If a man
keep my saying, he shall never see death.
52 Then said the Jews unto him, Now we
know that thou hast a devil. A'bra-ham is dead,
and the prophets; and thou sayest, If a man
keep my saying, he shall never taste of death.
53 Art thou greater than our father A'bra-
ham, which is dead? and the prophets are dead:
whom makest thou thyself?
54 Je'sus answered, If I honour myself, my
honour is nothing: it is my Father that honoureth me; of whom ye say, that he is your God:
55 Yet ye have not known him; but I know
him: and if I should say, I know him not, I shall
be a liar like unto you: but I know him, and
keep his saying.
56 Your father A'bra-ham rejoiced to see my
day: and he saw *it*, and was glad.
57 Then said the Jews unto him, Thou art not
yet fifty years old, and hast thou seen A'bra-
ham?
58 Je'sus said unto them, Verily, verily, I say
unto you, Before A'bra-ham was, I am.
59 Then took they up stones to cast at him:
but Je'sus hid himself, and went out of the temple, going through the midst of them, and so
passed by.

9 AND as *Je'sus* passed by, he saw a man
which was blind from *his* birth.
2 And his disciples asked him, saying, Master, who did sin, this man, or his parents, that
he was born blind?
3 Je'sus answered, Neither hath this man
sinned, nor his parents: but that the works of
God should be made manifest in him.
4 I must work the works of him that sent me,
while it is day: the night cometh, when no man
can work.
5 As long as I am in the world, I am the light
of the world.
6 When he had thus spoken, he spat on the
ground, and made clay of the spittle, and he
anointed the eyes of the blind man with the
clay,
7 And said unto him, Go wash in the pool of
Si-lo'am, (which is by interpretation, Sent.) He
went his way therefore, and washed, and came
seeing.
8 ¶ The neighbours therefore, and they
which before had seen him that he was blind,
said, Is not this he that sat and begged?
9 Some said, This is he: others *said*, He is like
him: *but* he said, I am *he*.
10 Therefore said they unto him, How were
thine eyes opened?
11 He answered and said, A man that is
called Je'sus made clay, and anointed mine
eyes, and said unto me, Go to the pool of Si-
lo'am, and wash: and I went and washed, and I
received sight.
12 Then said they unto him, Where is he? He
said, I know not.
13 ¶ They brought to the Phar'i-sees him
that aforetime was blind.
14 And it was the sabbath day when Je'sus
made the clay, and opened his eyes.
15 Then again the Phar'i-sees also asked him
how he had received his sight. He said unto
them, He put clay upon mine eyes, and I
washed, and do see.
16 Therefore said some of the Phar'i-sees,
This man is not of God, because he keepeth not
the sabbath day. Others said, How can a man
that is a sinner do such miracles? And there
was a division among them.
17 They say unto the blind man again, What
sayest thou of him, that he hath opened thine
eyes? He said, He is a prophet.
18 But the Jews did not believe concerning
him, that he had been blind, and received his
sight, until they called the parents of him that
had received his sight.
19 And they asked them, saying, Is this your
son, who ye say was born blind? how then doth
he now see?
20 His parents answered them and said, We
know that this is our son, and that he was born
blind:
21 But by what means he now seeth, we
know not; or who hath opened his eyes, we
know not: he is of age; ask him: he shall speak
for himself.
22 These *words* spake his parents, because
they feared the Jews: for the Jews had agreed
already, that if any man did confess that he was
Christ, he should be put out of the synagogue.
23 Therefore said his parents, He is of age;
ask him.
24 Then again called they the man that was
blind, and said unto him, Give God the praise:
we know that this man is a sinner.
25 He answered and said, Whether he be a
sinner *or no*, I know not: one thing I know, that,
whereas I was blind, now I see.
26 Then said they to him again, What did he
to thee? how opened he thine eyes?
27 He answered them, I have told you already, and ye did not hear: wherefore would ye
hear *it* again? will ye also be his disciples?
28 Then they reviled him, and said, Thou art
his disciple; but we are Mo'ses' disciples.
29 We know that God spake unto Mo'ses: *as
for* this *fellow*, we know not from whence he is.
30 The man answered and said unto them,
Why herein is a marvellous thing, that ye know
not from whence he is, and *yet* he hath opened
mine eyes.
31 Now we know that God heareth not sinners: but if any man be a worshippper of God,
and doeth his will, him he heareth.
32 Since the world began was it not heard
that any man opened the eyes of one that was
born blind.
33 If this man were not of God, he could do
nothing.
34 They answered and said unto him, Thou
wast altogether born in sins, and dost thou
teach us? And they cast him out.
35 Je'sus heard that they had cast him out;
and when he had found him, he said unto him,
Dost thou believe on the Son of God?
36 He answered and said, Who is he, Lord,
that I might believe on him?
37 And Je'sus said unto him, Thou hast both
seen him, and it is he that talketh with thee.
38 And he said, Lord, I believe. And he worshipped him.
39 ¶ And Je'sus said, For judgment I am
come into this world, that they which see not
might see; and that they which see might be
made blind.
40 And *some* of the Phar'i-sees which were
with him heard these words, and said unto him,
Are we blind also?
41 Je'sus said unto them, If ye were blind, ye
should have no sin: but now ye say, We see;
therefore your sin remaineth.

10 VERILY, verily, I say unto you, He that entereth not by the door into the sheepfold, but climbeth up some other way, the same is a thief and a robber.

2 But he that entereth in by the door is the shepherd of the sheep.

3 To him the porter openeth; and the sheep hear his voice: and he calleth his own sheep by name, and leadeth them out.

4 And when he putteth forth his own sheep, he goeth before them, and the sheep follow him: for they know his voice.

5 And a stranger will they not follow, but will flee from him: for they know not the voice of strangers.

6 This parable spake Je'sus unto them: but they understood not what things they were which he spake unto them.

7 Then said Je'sus unto them again, Verily, verily, I say unto you, I am the door of the sheep.

8 All that ever came before me are thieves and robbers: but the sheep did not hear them.

9 I am the door: by me if any man enter in, he shall be saved, and shall go in and out, and find pasture.

10 The thief cometh not, but for to steal, and to kill, and to destroy: I am come that they might have life, and that they might have *it* more abundantly.

11 I am the good shepherd: the good shepherd giveth his life for the sheep.

12 But he that is an hireling, and not the shepherd, whose own the sheep are not, seeth the wolf coming, and leaveth the sheep, and fleeth: and the wolf catcheth them, and scattereth the sheep.

13 The hireling fleeth, because he is an hireling, and careth not for the sheep.

14 I am the good shepherd, and know my *sheep*, and am known of mine.

15 As the Father knoweth me, even so know I the Father: and I lay down my life for the sheep.

16 And other sheep I have, which are not of this fold: them also I must bring, and they shall hear my voice; and there shall be one fold, *and* one shepherd.

17 Therefore doth my Father love me, because I lay down my life, that I might take it again.

18 No man taketh it from me, but I lay it down of myself. I have power to lay it down, and I have power to take it again. This commandment have I received of my Father.

19 ¶ There was a division therefore again among the Jews for these sayings.

20 And many of them said, He hath a devil, and is mad; why hear ye him?

21 Others said, These are not the words of him that hath a devil. Can a devil open the eyes of the blind?

22 ¶ And it was at Je-ru'sa-lem the feast of the dedication, and it was winter.

23 And Je'sus walked in the temple in Sol'o-mon's porch.

24 Then came the Jews round about him, and said unto him, How long dost thou make us to doubt? If thou be the Christ, tell us plainly.

25 Je'sus answered them, I told you, and ye believed not: the works that I do in my Father's name, they bear witness of me.

26 But ye believe not, because ye are not of my sheep, as I said unto you.

27 My sheep hear my voice, and I know them, and they follow me:

28 And I give unto them eternal life; and they shall never perish, neither shall any *man* pluck them out of my hand.

29 My Father, which gave *them* me, is greater than all; and no *man* is able to pluck *them* out of my Father's hand.

30 I and *my* Father are one.

31 Then the Jews took up stones again to stone him.

32 Je'sus answered them, Many good works have I shewed you from my Father; for which of those works do ye stone me?

33 The Jews answered him, saying, For a good work we stone thee not; but for blasphemy; and because that thou, being a man, makest thyself God.

34 Je'sus answered them, Is it not written in your law, I said, Ye are gods?

35 If he called them gods, unto whom the word of God came, and the scripture cannot be broken;

36 Say ye of him, whom the Father hath sanctified, and sent into the world, Thou blasphemest; because I said, I am the Son of God?

37 If I do not the works of my Father, believe me not.

38 But if I do, though ye believe not me, believe the works: that ye may know, and believe, that the Father *is* in me, and I in him.

39 Therefore they sought again to take him: but he escaped out of their hand,

40 And went away again beyond Jor'dan into the place where John at first baptized; and there he abode.

41 And many resorted unto him, and said, John did no miracle: but all things that John spake of this man were true.

42 And many believed on him there.

11 NOW a certain *man* was sick, *named* Laz'a-rus, of Beth'a-ny, the town of Ma'ry and her sister Mar'tha.

2 (It was *that* Ma'ry which anointed the Lord with ointment, and wiped his feet with her hair, whose brother Laz'a-rus was sick.)

3 Therefore his sisters sent unto him, saying, Lord, behold, he whom thou lovest is sick.

4 When Je'sus heard *that*, he said, This sickness is not unto death, but for the glory of God, that the Son of God might be glorified thereby.

5 Now Je'sus loved Mar'tha, and her sister, and Laz'a-rus.

6 When he had heard therefore that he was sick, he abode two days still in the same place where he was.

7 Then after that saith he to *his* disciples, Let us go into Ju-dæ'a again.

8 *His* disciples say unto him, Master, the Jews of late sought to stone thee; and goest thou thither again?

9 Je'sus answered, Are there not twelve hours in the day? If any man walk in the day, he stumbleth not, because he seeth the light of this world.

10 But if a man walk in the night, he stumbleth, because there is no light in him.

11 These things said he: and after that he saith unto them, Our friend Laz'a-rus sleepeth; but I go, that I may awake him out of sleep.

12 Then said his disciples, Lord, if he sleep, he shall do well.

13 Howbeit Je'sus spake of his death: but they thought that he had spoken of taking of rest in sleep.

14 Then said Je'sus unto them plainly, Laz'a-rus is dead.

15 And I am glad for your sakes that I was

not there, to the intent ye may believe; nevertheless let us go unto him.
16 Then said Thom'as, which is called Did'y-
mus, unto his fellowdisciples, Let us also go, that we may die with him.
17 Then when Je'sus came, he found that he had *lain* in the grave four days already.
18 Now Beth'a-ny was nigh unto Je-ru'sa-
lem, about fifteen furlongs off:
19 And many of the Jews came to Mar'tha and Ma'ry, to comfort them concerning their brother.
20 Then Mar'tha, as soon as she heard that Je'sus was coming, went and met him: but Ma'ry sat *still* in the house.
21 Then said Mar'tha unto Je'sus, Lord, if thou hadst been here, my brother had not died.
22 But I know, that even now, whatsoever thou wilt ask of God, God will give *it* thee.
23 Je'sus saith unto her, Thy brother shall rise again.
24 Mar'tha saith unto him, I know that he shall rise again in the resurrection at the last day.
25 Je'sus said unto her, I am the resurrection, and the life: he that believeth in me, though he were dead, yet shall he live:
26 And whosoever liveth and believeth in me shall never die. Believest thou this?
27 She saith unto him, Yea, Lord: I believe that thou art the Christ, the Son of God, which should come into the world.
28 And when she had so said, she went her way, and called Ma'ry her sister secretly, saying, The Master is come, and calleth for thee.
29 As soon as she heard *that,* she arose quickly, and came unto him.
30 Now Je'sus was not yet come into the town, but was in that place where Mar'tha met him.
31 The Jews then which were with her in the house, and comforted her, when they saw Ma'ry, that she rose up hastily and went out, followed her, saying, She goeth unto the grave to weep there.
32 Then when Ma'ry was come where Je'sus was, and saw him, she fell down at his feet, saying unto him, Lord, if thou hadst been here, my brother had not died.
33 When Je'sus therefore saw her weeping, and the Jews also weeping which came with her, he groaned in the spirit, and was troubled,
34 And said, Where have ye laid him? They said unto him, Lord, come and see.
35 Je'sus wept.
36 Then said the Jews, Behold how he loved him!
37 And some of them said, Could not this man, which opened the eyes of the blind, have caused that even this man should not have died?
38 Je'sus therefore again groaning in himself cometh to the grave. It was a cave, and a stone lay upon it.
39 Je'sus said, Take ye away the stone. Mar'tha, the sister of him that was dead, saith unto him, Lord, by this time he stinketh: for he hath been *dead* four days.
40 Je'sus saith unto her, Said I not unto thee, that, if thou wouldest believe, thou shouldest see the glory of God?
41 Then they took away the stone *from the place* where the dead was laid. And Je'sus lifted up *his* eyes, and said, Father, I thank thee that thou hast heard me.
42 And I knew that thou hearest me always: but because of the people which stand by I said *it,* that they may believe that thou hast sent me.
43 And when he thus had spoken, he cried with a loud voice, Laz'a-rus, come forth.
44 And he that was dead came forth, bound hand and foot with graveclothes: and his face was bound about with a napkin. Je'sus saith unto them, Loose him, and let him go.
45 Then many of the Jews which came to Ma'ry, and had seen the things which Je'sus did, believed on him.
46 But some of them went their ways to the Phar'i-sees, and told them what things Je'sus had done.
47 ¶ Then gathered the chief priests and the Phar'i-sees a council, and said, What do we? for this man doeth many miracles.
48 If we let him thus alone, all *men* will believe on him: and the Ro'mans shall come and take away both our place and nation.
49 And one of them, *named* Ca'ia-phas, being the high priest that same year, said unto them, Ye know nothing at all,
50 Nor consider that it is expedient for us, that one man should die for the people, and that the whole nation perish not.
51 And this spake he not of himself: but being high priest that year, he prophesied that Je'sus should die for that nation;
52 And not for that nation only, but that also he should gather together in one the children of God that were scattered abroad.
53 Then from that day forth they took counsel together for to put him to death.
54 Je'sus therefore walked no more openly among the Jews; but went thence unto a country near to the wilderness, into a city called E'phra-im, and there continued with his disciples.
55 ¶ And the Jews' passover was nigh at hand: and many went out of the country up to Je-ru'sa-lem before the passover, to purify themselves.
56 Then sought they for Je'sus, and spake among themselves, as they stood in the temple, What think ye, that he will not come to the feast?
57 Now both the chief priests and the Phar'i-sees had given a commandment, that, if any man knew where he were, he should shew *it,* that they might take him.

12 THEN Je'sus six days before the passover came to Beth'a-ny, where Laz'a-rus was which had been dead, whom he raised from the dead.
2 There they made him a supper; and Mar'tha served: but Laz'a-rus was one of them that sat at the table with him.
3 Then took Ma'ry a pound of ointment of spikenard, very costly, and anointed the feet of Je'sus, and wiped his feet with her hair: and the house was filled with the odour of the ointment.
4 Then saith one of his disciples, Ju'das Is-
car'i-ot, Si'mon's *son,* which should betray him,
5 Why was not this ointment sold for three hundred pence, and given to the poor?
6 This he said, not that he cared for the poor; but because he was a thief, and had the bag, and bare what was put therein.
7 Then said Je'sus, Let her alone: against the day of my burying hath she kept this.
8 For the poor always ye have with you; but me ye have not always.
9 Much people of the Jews therefore knew that he was there: and they came not for Je'sus' sake only, but that they might see Laz'a-rus also, whom he had raised from the dead.

10 ¶ But the chief priests consulted that they might put Laz'a-rus also to death;

11 Because that by reason of him many of the Jews went away, and believed on Je'sus.

12 ¶ On the next day much people that were come to the feast, when they heard that Je'sus was coming to Je-ru'sa-lem,

13 Took branches of palm trees, and went forth to meet him, and cried, Ho-san'na: Blessed *is* the King of Is'ra-el that cometh in the name of the Lord.

14 And Je'sus, when he had found a young ass, sat thereon; as it is written,

15 Fear not, daughter of Si'on: behold, thy King cometh, sitting on an ass's colt.

16 These things understood not his disciples at the first: but when Je'sus was glorified, then remembered they that these things were written of him, and *that* they had done these things unto him.

17 The people therefore that was with him when he called Laz'a-rus out of his grave, and raised him from the dead, bare record.

18 For this cause the people also met him, for that they heard that he had done this miracle.

19 The Phar'i-sees therefore said among themselves, Perceive ye how ye prevail nothing? behold, the world is gone after him.

20 ¶ And there were certain Greeks among them, that came up to worship at the feast:

21 The same came therefore to Phil'ip, which was of Beth-sa'i-da of Gal'i-lee, and desired him, saying, Sir, we would see Je'sus.

22 Phil'ip cometh and telleth An'drew: and again An'drew and Phil'ip tell Je'sus.

23 ¶ And Je'sus answered them, saying, The hour is come, that the Son of man should be glorified.

24 Verily, verily, I say unto you, Except a corn of wheat fall into the ground and die, it abideth alone: but if it die, it bringeth forth much fruit.

25 He that loveth his life shall lose it; and he that hateth his life in this world shall keep it unto life eternal.

26 If any man serve me, let him follow me; and where I am, there shall also my servant be: if any man serve me, him will *my* Father honour.

27 Now is my soul troubled; and what shall I say? Father, save me from this hour: but for this cause came I unto this hour.

28 Father, glorify thy name. Then came there a voice from heaven, *saying*, I have both glorified *it*, and will glorify *it* again.

29 The people therefore, that stood by, and heard *it*, said that it thundered: others said, An angel spake to him.

30 Je'sus answered and said, This voice came not because of me, but for your sakes.

31 Now is the judgment of this world: now shall the prince of this world be cast out.

32 And I, if I be lifted up from the earth, will draw all *men* unto me.

33 This he said, signifying what death he should die.

34 The people answered him, We have heard out of the law that Christ abideth for ever: and how sayest thou, The Son of man must be lifted up? who is this Son of man?

35 Then Je'sus said unto them, Yet a little while is the light with you. Walk while ye have the light, lest darkness come upon you: for he that walketh in darkness knoweth not whither he goeth.

36 While ye have light, believe in the light, that ye may be the children of light. These things spake Je'sus, and departed, and did hide himself from them.

37 ¶ But though he had done so many miracles before them, yet they believed not on him:

38 That the saying of E-sa'ias the prophet might be fulfilled, which he spake, Lord, who hath believed our report? and to whom hath the arm of the Lord been revealed?

39 Therefore they could not believe, because that E-sa'ias said again,

40 He hath blinded their eyes, and hardened their heart; that they should not see with *their* eyes, nor understand with *their* heart, and be converted, and I should heal them.

41 These things said E-sa'ias, when he saw his glory, and spake of him.

42 ¶ Nevertheless among the chief rulers also many believed on him; but because of the Phar'i-sees they did not confess *him*, lest they should be put out of the synagogue:

43 For they loved the praise of men more than the praise of God.

44 ¶ Je'sus cried and said, He that believeth on me, believeth not on me, but on him that sent me.

45 And he that seeth me seeth him that sent me.

46 I am come a light into the world, that whosoever believeth on me should not abide in darkness.

47 And if any man hear my words, and believe not, I judge him not: for I came not to judge the world, but to save the world.

48 He that rejecteth me, and receiveth not my words, hath one that judgeth him: the word that I have spoken, the same shall judge him in the last day.

49 For I have not spoken of myself; but the Father which sent me, he gave me a commandment, what I should say, and what I should speak.

50 And I know that his commandment is life everlasting: whatsoever I speak therefore, even as the Father said unto me, so I speak.

13 NOW before the feast of the passover, when Je'sus knew that his hour was come that he should depart out of this world unto the Father, having loved his own which were in the world, he loved them unto the end.

2 And supper being ended, the devil having now put into the heart of Ju'das Is-car'i-ot, Si'mon's *son*, to betray him;

3 Je'sus knowing that the Father had given all things into his hands, and that he was come from God, and went to God;

4 He riseth from supper, and laid aside his garments; and took a towel, and girded himself.

5 After that he poureth water into a bason, and began to wash the disciples' feet, and to wipe *them* with the towel wherewith he was girded.

6 Then cometh he to Si'mon Pe'ter: and Pe'ter saith unto him, Lord, dost thou wash my feet?

7 Je'sus answered and said unto him, What I do thou knowest not now; but thou shalt know hereafter.

8 Pe'ter saith unto him, Thou shalt never wash my feet. Je'sus answered him, If I wash thee not, thou hast no part with me.

9 Si'mon Pe'ter saith unto him, Lord, not my feet only, but also *my* hands and *my* head.

10 Je'sus saith to him, He that is washed needeth not save to wash *his* feet, but is clean every whit: and ye are clean, but not all.

11 For he knew who should betray him;
therefore said he, Ye are not all clean.
12 So after he had washed their feet, and had
taken his garments, and was set down again, he
said unto them, Know ye what I have done to
you?
13 Ye call me Master and Lord: and ye say
well; for *so* I am.
14 If I then, *your* Lord and Master, have
washed your feet; ye also ought to wash one
another's feet.
15 For I have given you an example, that ye
should do as I have done to you.
16 Verily, verily, I say unto you, The servant
is not greater than his lord; neither he that is
sent greater than he that sent him.
17 If ye know these things, happy are ye if ye
do them.
18 ¶ I speak not of you all: I know whom I
have chosen: but that the scripture may be fulfilled, He that eateth bread with me hath lifted
up his heel against me.
19 Now I tell you before it come, that, when
it is come to pass, ye may believe that I am *he*.
20 Verily, verily, I say unto you, He that receiveth whomsoever I send receiveth me; and
he that receiveth me receiveth him that sent
me.
21 When Je'sus had thus said, he was troubled in spirit, and testified, and said, Verily, verily, I say unto you, that one of you shall betray
me.
22 Then the disciples looked one on another,
doubting of whom he spake.
23 Now there was leaning on Je'sus' bosom
one of his disciples, whom Je'sus loved.
24 Si'mon Pe'ter therefore beckoned to him,
that he should ask who it should be of whom he
spake.
25 He then lying on Je'sus' breast saith unto
him, Lord, who is it?
26 Je'sus answered, He it is, to whom I shall
give a sop, when I have dipped *it*. And when he
had dipped the sop, he gave *it* to Ju'das Is-car'i-
ot, *the son* of Si'mon.
27 And after the sop Sa'tan entered into him.
Then said Je'sus unto him, That thou doest, do
quickly.
28 Now no man at the table knew for what
intent he spake this unto him.
29 For some *of them* thought, because Ju'das
had the bag, that Je'sus had said unto him, Buy
those things that we have need of against the
feast; or, that he should give something to the
poor.
30 He then having received the sop went immediately out: and it was night.
31 ¶ Therefore, when he was gone out, Je'-
sus said, Now is the Son of man glorified, and
God is glorified in him.
32 If God be glorified in him, God shall also
glorify him in himself, and shall straightway
glorify him.
33 Little children, yet a little while I am with
you. Ye shall seek me: and as I said unto the
Jews, Whither I go, ye cannot come; so now I
say to you.
34 A new commandment I give unto you,
That ye love one another; as I have loved you,
that ye also love one another.
35 By this shall all *men* know that ye are my
disciples, if ye have love one to another.
36 ¶ Si'mon Pe'ter said unto him, Lord,
whither goest thou? Je'sus answered him,
Whither I go, thou canst not follow me now; but
thou shalt follow me afterwards.
37 Pe'ter said unto him, Lord, why cannot I
follow thee now? I will lay down my life for thy
sake.
38 Je'sus answered him, Wilt thou lay down
thy life for my sake? Verily, verily, I say unto
thee, The cock shall not crow, till thou hast denied me thrice.

14 LET not your heart be troubled: ye believe in God, believe also in me.
2 In my Father's house are many mansions:
if *it were* not *so*, I would have told you. I go to
prepare a place for you.
3 And if I go and prepare a place for you, I
will come again, and receive you unto myself;
that where I am, *there* ye may be also.
4 And whither I go ye know, and the way ye
know.
5 Thom'as saith unto him, Lord, we know not
whither thou goest; and how can we know the
way?
6 Je'sus saith unto him, I am the way, the
truth, and the life: no man cometh unto the Father, but by me.
7 If ye had known me, ye should have known
my Father also: and from henceforth ye know
him, and have seen him.
8 Phil'ip saith unto him, Lord, shew us the
Father, and it sufficeth us.
9 Je'sus saith unto him, Have I been so long
time with you, and yet hast thou not known me,
Phil'ip? he that hath seen me hath seen the Father; and how sayest thou *then*, Shew us the
Father?
10 Believest thou not that I am in the Father,
and the Father in me? the words that I speak
unto you I speak not of myself: but the Father
that dwelleth in me, he doeth the works.
11 Believe me that I *am* in the Father, and
the Father in me: or else believe me for the very
works' sake.
12 Verily, verily, I say unto you, He that believeth on me, the works that I do shall he do
also; and greater *works* than these shall he do;
because I go unto my Father.
13 And whatsoever ye shall ask in my name,
that will I do, that the Father may be glorified in
the Son.
14 If ye shall ask any thing in my name, I will
do *it*.
15 ¶ If ye love me, keep my commandments.
16 And I will pray the Father, and he shall
give you another Comforter, that he may abide
with you for ever;
17 *Even* the Spirit of truth; whom the world
cannot receive, because it seeth him not, neither
knoweth him: but ye know him; for he dwelleth
with you, and shall be in you.
18 I will not leave you comfortless: I will
come to you.
19 Yet a little while, and the world seeth me
no more; but ye see me: because I live, ye shall
live also.
20 At that day ye shall know that I *am* in my
Father, and ye in me, and I in you.
21 He that hath my commandments, and
keepeth them, he it is that loveth me: and he
that loveth me shall be loved of my Father, and
I will love him, and will manifest myself to him.
22 Ju'das saith unto him, not Is-car'i-ot,
Lord, how is it that thou wilt manifest thyself
unto us, and not unto the world?
23 Je'sus answered and said unto him, If a
man love me, he will keep my words: and my
Father will love him, and we will come unto
him, and make our abode with him.
24 He that loveth me not keepeth not my

sayings: and the word which ye hear is not
mine, but the Father's which sent me.
25 These things have I spoken unto you,
being *yet* present with you.
26 But the Comforter, *which is* the Ho'ly
Ghost, whom the Father will send in my name,
he shall teach you all things, and bring all
things to your remembrance, whatsoever I have
said unto you.
27 Peace I leave with you, my peace I give
unto you: not as the world giveth, give I unto
you. Let not your heart be troubled, neither let
it be afraid.
28 Ye have heard how I said unto you, I go
away, and come *again* unto you. If ye loved me,
ye would rejoice, because I said, I go unto the
Father: for my Father is greater than I.
29 And now I have told you before it come to
pass, that, when it is come to pass, ye might
believe.
30 Hereafter I will not talk much with you:
for the prince of this world cometh, and hath
nothing in me.
31 But that the world may know that I love
the Father; and as the Father gave me commandment,
even so I do. Arise, let us go hence.

15 I AM the true vine, and my Father is the
husbandman.
2 Every branch in me that beareth not fruit
he taketh away: and every *branch* that beareth
fruit, he purgeth it, that it may bring forth more
fruit.
3 Now ye are clean through the word which I
have spoken unto you.
4 Abide in me, and I in you. As the branch
cannot bear fruit of itself, except it abide in the
vine; no more can ye, except ye abide in me.
5 I am the vine, *ye are* the branches: He that
abideth in me, and I in him, the same bringeth
forth much fruit: for without me ye can do
nothing.
6 If a man abide not in me, he is cast forth as
a branch, and is withered; and men gather
them, and cast *them* into the fire, and they are
burned.
7 If ye abide in me, and my words abide in
you, ye shall ask what ye will, and it shall be
done unto you.
8 Herein is my Father glorified, that ye bear
much fruit; so shall ye be my disciples.
9 As the Father hath loved me, so have I
loved you: continue ye in my love.
10 If ye keep my commandments, ye shall
abide in my love; even as I have kept my Father's
commandments, and abide in his love.
11 These things have I spoken unto you, that
my joy might remain in you, and *that* your joy
might be full.
12 This is my commandment, That ye love
one another, as I have loved you.
13 Greater love hath no man than this, that a
man lay down his life for his friends.
14 Ye are my friends, if ye do whatsoever I
command you.
15 Henceforth I call you not servants; for the
servant knoweth not what his lord doeth: but I
have called you friends; for all things that I
have heard of my Father I have made known
unto you.
16 Ye have not chosen me, but I have chosen
you, and ordained you, that ye should go and
bring forth fruit, and *that* your fruit should remain:
that whatsoever ye shall ask of the Father
in my name, he may give it you.
17 These things I command you, that ye love
one another.
18 If the world hate you, ye know that it
hated me before *it hated* you.
19 If ye were of the world, the world would
love his own: but because ye are not of the
world, but I have chosen you out of the world,
therefore the world hateth you.
20 Remember the word that I said unto you,
The servant is not greater than his lord. If they
have persecuted me, they will also persecute
you; if they have kept my saying, they will keep
yours also.
21 But all these things will they do unto you
for my name's sake, because they know not him
that sent me.
22 If I had not come and spoken unto them,
they had not had sin: but now they have no
cloke for their sin.
23 He that hateth me hateth my Father also.
24 If I had not done among them the works
which none other man did, they had not had
sin: but now have they both seen and hated
both me and my Father.
25 But *this cometh to pass,* that the word
might be fulfilled that is written in their law,
They hated me without a cause.
26 But when the Comforter is come, whom I
will send unto you from the Father, *even* the
Spirit of truth, which proceedeth from the Father,
he shall testify of me:
27 And ye also shall bear witness, because ye
have been with me from the beginning.

16 THESE things have I spoken unto you,
that ye should not be offended.
2 They shall put you out of the synagogues:
yea, the time cometh, that whosoever killeth
you will think that he doeth God service.
3 And these things will they do unto you, because
they have not known the Father, nor me.
4 But these things have I told you, that when
the time shall come, ye may remember that I
told you of them. And these things I said not
unto you at the beginning, because I was with
you.
5 But now I go my way to him that sent me;
and none of you asketh me, Whither goest
thou?
6 But because I have said these things unto
you, sorrow hath filled your heart.
7 Nevertheless I tell you the truth; It is expedient
for you that I go away: for if I go not
away, the Comforter will not come unto you;
but if I depart, I will send him unto you.
8 And when he is come, he will reprove the
world of sin, and of righteousness, and of judgment:
9 Of sin, because they believe not on me;
10 Of righteousness, because I go to my Father,
and ye see me no more;
11 Of judgment, because the prince of this
world is judged.
12 I have yet many things to say unto you,
but ye cannot bear them now.
13 Howbeit when he, the Spirit of truth, is
come, he will guide you into all truth: for he
shall not speak of himself; but whatsoever he
shall hear, *that* shall he speak: and he will shew
you things to come.
14 He shall glorify me: for he shall receive of
mine, and shall shew *it* unto you.
15 All things that the Father hath are mine:
therefore said I, that he shall take of mine, and
shall shew *it* unto you.
16 A little while, and ye shall not see me: and
again, a little while, and ye shall see me, because
I go to the Father.
17 Then said *some* of his disciples among

themselves, What is this that he saith unto us,
A little while, and ye shall not see me: and
again, a little while, and ye shall see me: and,
Because I go to the Father?
18 They said therefore, What is this that he
saith, A little while? we cannot tell what he
saith.
19 Now Je'sus knew that they were desirous
to ask him, and said unto them, Do ye enquire
among yourselves of that I said, A little while,
and ye shall not see me: and again, a little
while, and ye shall see me?
20 Verily, verily, I say unto you, That ye shall
weep and lament, but the world shall rejoice:
and ye shall be sorrowful, but your sorrow shall
be turned into joy.
21 A woman when she is in travail hath sorrow, because her hour is come: but as soon as
she is delivered of the child, she remembereth
no more the anguish, for joy that a man is born
into the world.
22 And ye now therefore have sorrow: but I
will see you again, and your heart shall rejoice,
and your joy no man taketh from you.
23 And in that day ye shall ask me nothing.
Verily, verily, I say unto you, Whatsoever ye
shall ask the Father in my name, he will give *it*
you.
24 Hitherto have ye asked nothing in my
name: ask, and ye shall receive, that your joy
may be full.
25 These things have I spoken unto you in
proverbs: but the time cometh, when I shall no
more speak unto you in proverbs, but I shall
shew you plainly of the Father.
26 At that day ye shall ask in my name: and I
say not unto you, that I will pray the Father for
you:
27 For the Father himself loveth you, because ye have loved me, and have believed that
I came out from God.
28 I came forth from the Father, and am
come into the world: again, I leave the world,
and go to the Father.
29 His disciples said unto him, Lo, now
speakest thou plainly, and speakest no proverb.
30 Now are we sure that thou knowest all
things, and needest not that any man should
ask thee: by this we believe that thou camest
forth from God.
31 Je'sus answered them, Do ye now believe?
32 Behold, the hour cometh, yea, is now
come, that ye shall be scattered, every man to
his own, and shall leave me alone: and yet I am
not alone, because the Father is with me.
33 These things I have spoken unto you, that
in me ye might have peace. In the world ye shall
have tribulation: but be of good cheer; I have
overcome the world.

17 THESE words spake Je'sus, and lifted
up his eyes to heaven, and said, Father,
the hour is come; glorify thy Son, that thy Son
also may glorify thee:
2 As thou hast given him power over all
flesh, that he should give eternal life to as many
as thou hast given him.
3 And this is life eternal, that they might
know thee the only true God, and Je'sus Christ
whom thou hast sent.
4 I have glorified thee on the earth: I have
finished the work which thou gavest me to do.
5 And now, O Father, glorify thou me with
thine own self with the glory which I had with
thee before the world was.
6 I have manifested thy name unto the men
which thou gavest me out of the world: thine
they were, and thou gavest them me; and they
have kept thy word.
7 Now they have known that all things whatsoever thou hast given me are of thee.
8 For I have given unto them the words
which thou gavest me; and they have received
them, and have known surely that I came out
from thee, and they have believed that thou
didst send me.
9 I pray for them: I pray not for the world,
but for them which thou hast given me; for they
are thine.
10 And all mine are thine, and thine are
mine; and I am glorified in them.
11 And now I am no more in the world, but
these are in the world, and I come to thee. Holy
Father, keep through thine own name those
whom thou hast given me, that they may be
one, as we *are.*
12 While I was with them in the world, I kept
them in thy name: those that thou gavest me I
have kept, and none of them is lost, but the son
of perdition; that the scripture might be fulfilled.
13 And now come I to thee; and these things
I speak in the world, that they might have my
joy fulfilled in themselves.
14 I have given them thy word; and the world
hath hated them, because they are not of the
world, even as I am not of the world.
15 I pray not that thou shouldest take them
out of the world, but that thou shouldest keep
them from the evil.
16 They are not of the world, even as I am
not of the world.
17 Sanctify them through thy truth: thy word
is truth.
18 As thou hast sent me into the world, even
so have I also sent them into the world.
19 And for their sakes I sanctify myself, that
they also might be sanctified through the truth.
20 Neither pray I for these alone, but for
them also which shall believe on me through
their word;
21 That they all may be one; as thou, Father,
art in me, and I in thee, that they also may be
one in us: that the world may believe that thou
hast sent me.
22 And the glory which thou gavest me I
have given them; that they may be one, even as
we are one:
23 I in them, and thou in me, that they may
be made perfect in one; and that the world may
know that thou hast sent me, and hast loved
them, as thou hast loved me.
24 Father, I will that they also, whom thou
hast given me, be with me where I am; that they
may behold my glory, which thou hast given
me: for thou lovedst me before the foundation
of the world.
25 O righteous Father, the world hath not
known thee: but I have known thee, and these
have known that thou hast sent me.
26 And I have declared unto them thy name,
and will declare *it:* that the love wherewith thou
hast loved me may be in them, and I in them.

18 WHEN Je'sus had spoken these words,
he went forth with his disciples over the
brook Ce'dron, where was a garden, into the
which he entered, and his disciples.
2 And Ju'das also, which betrayed him, knew
the place: for Je'sus ofttimes resorted thither
with his disciples.
3 Ju'das then, having received a band *of men*
and officers from the chief priests and Phar'i-

sees, cometh thither with lanterns and torches
and weapons.
4 Je'sus therefore, knowing all things that
should come upon him, went forth, and said
unto them, Whom seek ye?
5 They answered him, Je'sus of Naz'a-reth.
Je'sus saith unto them, I am *he.* And Ju'das
also, which betrayed him, stood with them.
6 As soon then as he had said unto them, I
am *he,* they went backward, and fell to the
ground.
7 Then asked he them again, Whom seek ye?
And they said, Je'sus of Naz'a-reth.
8 Je'sus answered, I have told you that I am
he: if therefore ye seek me, let these go their
way:
9 That the saying might be fulfilled, which he
spake, Of them which thou gavest me have I
lost none.
10 Then Si'mon Pe'ter having a sword drew
it, and smote the high priest's servant, and cut
off his right ear. The servant's name was Mal'-
chus.
11 Then said Je'sus unto Pe'ter, Put up thy
sword into the sheath: the cup which my Father
hath given me, shall I not drink it?
12 Then the band and the captain and officers of the Jews took Je'sus, and bound him,
13 And led him away to An'nas first; for he
was father in law to Ca'ia-phas, which was the
high priest that same year.
14 Now Ca'ia-phas was he, which gave counsel to the Jews, that it was expedient that one
man should die for the people.
15 ¶ And Si'mon Pe'ter followed Je'sus, and
so did another disciple: that disciple was known
unto the high priest, and went in with Je'sus
into the palace of the high priest.
16 But Pe'ter stood at the door without. Then
went out that other disciple, which was known
unto the high priest, and spake unto her that
kept the door, and brought in Pe'ter.
17 Then saith the damsel that kept the door
unto Pe'ter, Art not thou also *one* of this man's
disciples? He saith, I am not.
18 And the servants and officers stood there,
who had made a fire of coals; for it was cold:
and they warmed themselves: and Pe'ter stood
with them, and warmed himself.
19 ¶ The high priest then asked Je'sus of his
disciples, and of his doctrine.
20 Je'sus answered him, I spake openly to
the world; I ever taught in the synagogue, and
in the temple, whither the Jews always resort;
and in secret have I said nothing.
21 Why askest thou me? ask them which
heard me, what I have said unto them: behold,
they know what I said.
22 And when he had thus spoken, one of the
officers which stood by struck Je'sus with the
palm of his hand, saying, Answerest thou the
high priest so?
23 Je'sus answered him, If I have spoken
evil, bear witness of the evil: but if well, why
smitest thou me?
24 Now An'nas had sent him bound unto Ca'-
ia-phas the high priest.
25 And Si'mon Pe'ter stood and warmed
himself. They said therefore unto him, Art not
thou also *one* of his disciples? He denied *it,* and
said, I am not.
26 One of the servants of the high priest,
being *his* kinsman whose ear Pe'ter cut off,
saith, Did not I see thee in the garden with him?
27 Pe'ter then denied again: and immediately
the cock crew.
28 ¶ Then led they Je'sus from Ca'ia-phas
unto the hall of judgment: and it was early; and
they themselves went not into the judgment
hall, lest they should be defiled; but that they
might eat the passover.
29 Pi'late then went out unto them, and said,
What accusation bring ye against this man?
30 They answered and said unto him, If he
were not a malefactor, we would not have delivered him up unto thee.
31 Then said Pi'late unto them, Take ye him,
and judge him according to your law. The Jews
therefore said unto him, It is not lawful for us to
put any man to death:
32 That the saying of Je'sus might be fulfilled, which he spake, signifying what death he
should die.
33 Then Pi'late entered into the judgment
hall again, and called Je'sus, and said unto him,
Art thou the King of the Jews?
34 Je'sus answered him, Sayest thou this
thing of thyself, or did others tell it thee of me?
35 Pi'late answered, Am I a Jew? Thine own
nation and the chief priests have delivered thee
unto me: what hast thou done?
36 Je'sus answered, My kingdom is not of
this world: if my kingdom were of this world,
then would my servants fight, that I should not
be delivered to the Jews: but now is my kingdom not from hence.
37 Pi'late therefore said unto him, Art thou a
king then? Je'sus answered, Thou sayest that I
am a king. To this end was I born, and for this
cause came I into the world, that I should bear
witness unto the truth. Every one that is of the
truth heareth my voice.
38 Pi'late saith unto him, What is truth? And
when he had said this, he went out again unto
the Jews, and saith unto them, I find in him no
fault *at all.*
39 But ye have a custom, that I should release unto you one at the passover: will ye
therefore that I release unto you the King of the
Jews?
40 Then cried they all again, saying, Not this
man, but Ba-rab'bas. Now Ba-rab'bas was a
robber.

19

THEN Pi'late therefore took Je'sus, and
scourged *him.*
2 And the soldiers platted a crown of thorns,
and put *it* on his head, and they put on him a
purple robe,
3 And said, Hail, King of the Jews! and they
smote him with their hands.
4 Pi'late therefore went forth again, and saith
unto them, Behold, I bring him forth to you,
that ye may know that I find no fault in him.
5 Then came Je'sus forth, wearing the crown
of thorns, and the purple robe. And *Pi'late* saith
unto them, Behold the man!
6 When the chief priests therefore and officers saw him, they cried out, saying, Crucify
him, crucify *him.* Pi'late saith unto them, Take
ye him, and crucify *him:* for I find no fault in
him.
7 The Jews answered him, We have a law,
and by our law he ought to die, because he
made himself the Son of God.
8 ¶ When Pi'late therefore heard that saying,
he was the more afraid;
9 And went again into the judgment hall, and
saith unto Je'sus, Whence art thou? But Je'sus
gave him no answer.
10 Then saith Pi'late unto him, Speakest thou
not unto me? knowest thou not that I have
power to crucify thee, and have power to release thee?

11 Je'sus answered, Thou couldest have no power *at all* against me, except it were given thee from above: therefore he that delivered me unto thee hath the greater sin.

12 And from thenceforth Pi'late sought to release him: but the Jews cried out, saying, If thou let this man go, thou art not Cæ'sar's friend: whosoever maketh himself a king speaketh against Cæ'sar.

13 ¶ When Pi'late therefore heard that saying, he brought Je'sus forth, and sat down in the judgment seat in a place that is called the Pavement, but in the He'brew, Gab'ba-tha.

14 And it was the preparation of the passover, and about the sixth hour: and he saith unto the Jews, Behold your King!

15 But they cried out, Away with *him*, away with *him*, crucify him. Pi'late saith unto them, Shall I crucify your King? The chief priests answered, We have no king but Cæ'sar.

16 Then delivered he him therefore unto them to be crucified. And they took Je'sus, and led *him* away.

17 And he bearing his cross went forth into a place called *the place* of a skull, which is called in the He'brew Gol'go-tha:

18 Where they crucified him, and two other with him, on either side one, and Je'sus in the midst.

19 ¶ And Pi'late wrote a title, and put *it* on the cross. And the writing was, JE'SUS OF NAZ'A-RETH THE KING OF THE JEWS.

20 This title then read many of the Jews: for the place where Je'sus was crucified was nigh to the city: and it was written in He'brew, *and* Greek, *and* Lat'in.

21 Then said the chief priests of the Jews to Pi'late, Write not, The King of the Jews; but that he said, I am King of the Jews.

22 Pi'late answered, What I have written I have written.

23 ¶ Then the soldiers, when they had crucified Je'sus, took his garments, and made four parts, to every soldier a part; and also *his* coat: now the coat was without seam, woven from the top throughout.

24 They said therefore among themselves, Let us not rend it, but cast lots for it, whose it shall be: that the scripture might be fulfilled, which saith, They parted my raiment among them, and for my vesture they did cast lots. These things therefore the soldiers did.

25 ¶ Now there stood by the cross of Je'sus his mother, and his mother's sister, Ma'ry the *wife* of Cle'o-phas, and Ma'ry Mag-da-le'ne.

26 When Je'sus therefore saw his mother, and the disciple standing by, whom he loved, he saith unto his mother, Woman, behold thy son!

27 Then saith he to the disciple, Behold thy mother! And from that hour that disciple took her unto his own *home*.

28 ¶ After this, Je'sus knowing that all things were now accomplished, that the scripture might be fulfilled, saith, I thirst.

29 Now there was set a vessel full of vinegar: and they filled a spunge with vinegar, and put *it* upon hyssop, and put *it* to his mouth.

30 When Je'sus therefore had received the vinegar, he said, It is finished: and he bowed his head, and gave up the ghost.

31 The Jews therefore, because it was the preparation, that the bodies should not remain upon the cross on the sabbath day, (for that sabbath day was an high day,) besought Pi'late that their legs might be broken, and *that* they might be taken away.

32 Then came the soldiers, and brake the legs of the first, and of the other which was crucified with him.

33 But when they came to Je'sus, and saw that he was dead already, they brake not his legs:

34 But one of the soldiers with a spear pierced his side, and forthwith came there out blood and water.

35 And he that saw *it* bare record, and his record is true: and he knoweth that he saith true, that ye might believe.

36 For these things were done, that the scripture should be fulfilled, A bone of him shall not be broken.

37 And again another scripture saith, They shall look on him whom they pierced.

38 ¶ And after this Jo'seph of Ar-i-ma-thæ'a, being a disciple of Je'sus, but secretly for fear of the Jews, besought Pi'late that he might take away the body of Je'sus: and Pi'late gave *him* leave. He came therefore, and took the body of Je'sus.

39 And there came also Nic-o-de'mus, which at the first came to Je'sus by night, and brought a mixture of myrrh and aloes, about an hundred pound *weight*.

40 Then took they the body of Je'sus, and wound it in linen clothes with the spices, as the manner of the Jews is to bury.

41 Now in the place where he was crucified there was a garden; and in the garden a new sepulchre, wherein was never man yet laid.

42 There laid they Je'sus therefore because of the Jews' preparation *day;* for the sepulchre was nigh at hand.

20 THE first *day* of the week cometh Ma'ry Mag-da-le'ne early, when it was yet dark, unto the sepulchre, and seeth the stone taken away from the sepulchre.

2 Then she runneth, and cometh to Si'mon Pe'ter, and to the other disciple, whom Je'sus loved, and saith unto them, They have taken away the Lord out of the sepulchre, and we know not where they have laid him.

3 Pe'ter therefore went forth, and that other disciple, and came to the sepulchre.

4 So they ran both together: and the other disciple did outrun Pe'ter, and came first to the sepulchre.

5 And he stooping down, *and looking in,* saw the linen clothes lying; yet went he not in.

6 Then cometh Si'mon Pe'ter following him, and went into the sepulchre, and seeth the linen clothes lie,

7 And the napkin, that was about his head, not lying with the linen clothes, but wrapped together in a place by itself.

8 Then went in also that other disciple, which came first to the sepulchre, and he saw, and believed.

9 For as yet they knew not the scripture, that he must rise again from the dead.

10 Then the disciples went away again unto their own home.

11 ¶ But Ma'ry stood without at the sepulchre weeping: and as she wept, she stooped down, *and looked* into the sepulchre,

12 And seeth two angels in white sitting, the one at the head, and the other at the feet, where the body of Je'sus had lain.

13 And they say unto her, Woman, why weepest thou? She saith unto them, Because they have taken away my Lord, and I know not where they have laid him.

14 And when she had thus said, she turned herself back, and saw Je'sus standing, and knew not that it was Je'sus.

15 Je'sus saith unto her, Woman, why weepest thou? whom seekest thou? She, supposing
him to be the gardener, saith unto him, Sir, if
thou have borne him hence, tell me where thou
hast laid him, and I will take him away.
16 Je'sus saith unto her, Ma'ry. She turned
herself, and saith unto him, Rab-bo'ni; which is
to say, Master.
17 Je'sus saith unto her, Touch me not; for I
am not yet ascended to my Father: but go to my
brethren, and say unto them, I ascend unto my
Father, and your Father; and *to* my God, and
your God.
18 Ma'ry Mag-da-le'ne came and told the disciples that she had seen the Lord, and *that* he
had spoken these things unto her.
19 ¶ Then the same day at evening, being the
first *day* of the week, when the doors were shut
where the disciples were assembled for fear of
the Jews, came Je'sus and stood in the midst,
and saith unto them Peace *be* unto you.
20 And when he had so said, he shewed unto
them *his* hands and his side. Then were the disciples glad, when they saw the Lord.
21 Then said Je'sus to them again, Peace *be*
unto you: as *my* Father hath sent me, even so
send I you.
22 And when he had said this, he breathed on
them, and saith unto them, Receive ye the Ho'ly
Ghost:
23 Whose soever sins ye remit, they are re-
mitted unto them; *and* whose soever *sins* ye retain, they are retained.
24 ¶ But Thom'as, one of the twelve, called
Did'y-mus, was not with them when Je'sus
came.
25 The other disciples therefore said unto
him, We have seen the Lord. But he said unto
them, Except I shall see in his hands the print of
the nails, and put my finger into the print of the
nails, and thrust my hand into his side, I will not
believe.
26 ¶ And after eight days again his disciples
were within, and Thom'as with them: *then*
came Je'sus, the doors being shut, and stood in
the midst, and said, Peace *be* unto you.
27 Then saith he to Thom'as, Reach hither
thy finger, and behold my hands; and reach
hither thy hand, and thrust *it* into my side: and
be not faithless, but believing.
28 And Thom'as answered and said unto
him, My Lord and my God.
29 Je'sus saith unto him, Thom'as, because
thou hast seen me, thou hast believed: blessed
are they that have not seen, and *yet* have believed.
30 ¶ And many other signs truly did Je'sus in
the presence of his disciples, which are not
written in this book:
31 But these are written, that ye might believe that Je'sus is the Christ, the Son of God;
and that believing ye might have life through
his name.

21 AFTER these things Je'sus shewed himself again to the disciples at the sea of
Ti-be'ri-as; and on this wise shewed he *himself.*
2 There were together Si'mon Pe'ter, and
Thom'as called Did'y-mus, and Na-than'a-el of
Ca'na in Gal'i-lee, and the *sons* of Zeb'e-dee,
and two other of his disciples.
3 Si'mon Pe'ter saith unto them, I go a fish-
ing. They say unto him, We also go with thee.
They went forth, and entered into a ship immediately; and that night they caught nothing.
4 But when the morning was now come, Je'-
sus stood on the shore: but the disciples knew
not that it was Je'sus.
5 Then Je'sus saith unto them, Children,
have ye any meat? They answered him, No.
6 And he said unto them, Cast the net on the
right side of the ship, and ye shall find. They
cast therefore, and now they were not able to
draw it for the multitude of fishes.
7 Therefore that disciple whom Je'sus loved
saith unto Pe'ter, It is the Lord. Now when Si'-
mon Pe'ter heard that it was the Lord, he girt
his fisher's coat *unto him,* (for he was naked,)
and did cast himself into the sea.
8 And the other disciples came in a little
ship; (for they were not far from land, but as it
were two hundred cubits,) dragging the net
with fishes.
9 As soon then as they were come to land,
they saw a fire of coals there, and fish laid
thereon, and bread.
10 Je'sus saith unto them, Bring of the fish
which ye have now caught.
11 Si'mon Pe'ter went up, and drew the net
to land full of great fishes, an hundred and fifty
and three: and for all there were so many, yet
was not the net broken.
12 Je'sus saith unto them, Come *and* dine.
And none of the disciples durst ask him, Who
art thou? knowing that it was the Lord.
13 Je'sus then cometh, and taketh bread, and
giveth them, and fish likewise.
14 This is now the third time that Je'sus
shewed himself to his disciples, after that he
was risen from the dead.
15 ¶ So when they had dined, Je'sus saith to
Si'mon Pe'ter, Si'mon, *son* of Jo'nas, lovest thou
me more than these? He saith unto him, Yea,
Lord; thou knowest that I love thee. He saith
unto him, Feed my lambs.
16 He saith to him again the second time, Si'-
mon, *son* of Jo'nas, lovest thou me? He saith
unto him, Yea, Lord; thou knowest that I love
thee. He saith unto him, Feed my sheep.
17 He saith unto him the third time, Si'mon,
son of Jo'nas, lovest thou me? Pe'ter was
grieved because he said unto him the third time,
Lovest thou me? And he said unto him, Lord,
thou knowest all things; thou knowest that I
love thee. Je'sus saith unto him, Feed my sheep.
18 Verily, verily, I say unto thee, When thou
wast young, thou girdedst thyself, and walkedst
whither thou wouldest: but when thou shalt be
old, thou shalt stretch forth thy hands, and another shall gird thee, and carry *thee* whither
thou wouldest not.
19 This spake he, signifying by what death
he should glorify God. And when he had spoken
this, he saith unto him, Follow me.
20 Then Pe'ter, turning about, seeth the disciple whom Je'sus loved following; which also
leaned on his breast at supper, and said, Lord,
which is he that betrayeth thee?
21 Pe'ter seeing him saith to Je'sus, Lord,
and what *shall* this man *do?*
22 Je'sus saith unto him, If I will that he tarry
till I come, what *is that* to thee? follow thou me.
23 Then went this saying abroad among the
brethren, that that disciple should not die: yet
Je'sus said not unto him, He shall not die; but, If
I will that he tarry till I come, what *is that* to
thee?
24 This is the disciple which testifieth of
these things, and wrote these things: and we
know that his testimony is true.
25 And there are also many other things
which Je'sus did, the which, if they should be
written every one, I suppose that even the
world itself could not contain the books that
should be written. Amen.

THE

ACTS OF THE APOSTLES

1 THE former treatise have I made, O The-
oph'i-lus, of all that Je'sus began both to do
and teach,
2 Until the day in which he was taken up,
after that he through the Ho'ly Ghost had given
commandments unto the apostles whom he had
chosen:
3 To whom also he shewed himself alive after his passion by many infallible proofs, being
seen of them forty days, and speaking of the
things pertaining to the kingdom of God:
4 And, being assembled together with *them,*
commanded them that they should not depart
from Je-ru'sa-lem, but wait for the promise of
the Father, which, *saith he,* ye have heard of
me.
5 For John truly baptized with water; but ye
shall be baptized with the Ho'ly Ghost not
many days hence.
6 When they therefore were come together,
they asked of him, saying, Lord, wilt thou at
this time restore again the kingdom to Is'ra-el?
7 And he said unto them, It is not for you to
know the times or the seasons, which the Father hath put in his own power.
8 But ye shall receive power, after that the
Ho'ly Ghost is come upon you: and ye shall be
witnesses unto me both in Je-ru'sa-lem, and in
all Ju-dæ'a, and in Sa-ma'ri-a, and unto the uttermost part of the earth.
9 And when he had spoken these things,
while they beheld, he was taken up; and a cloud
received him out of their sight.
10 And while they looked stedfastly toward
heaven as he went up, behold, two men stood
by them in white apparel;
11 Which also said, Ye men of Gal'i-lee, why
stand ye gazing up into heaven? this same Je'-
sus, which is taken up from you into heaven,
shall so come in like manner as ye have seen
him go into heaven.
12 Then returned they unto Je-ru'sa-lem
from the mount called Ol'i-vet, which is from
Je-ru'sa-lem a sabbath day's journey.
13 And when they were come in, they went
up into an upper room, where abode both Pe'-
ter, and James, and John, and Andrew, Phil'ip,
and Thom'as, Bar-thol'o-mew, and Mat'thew,
James *the son* of Al-phæ'us, and Si'mon Ze-lo'-
tes, and Ju'das *the brother* of James.
14 These all continued with one accord in
prayer and supplication, with the women, and
Ma'ry the mother of Je'sus, and with his brethren.
15 ¶ And in those days Pe'ter stood up in the
midst of the disciples, and said, (the number of
names together were about an hundred and
twenty,)
16 Men *and* brethren, this scripture must
needs have been fulfilled, which the Ho'ly
Ghost by the mouth of Da'vid spake before concerning Ju'das, which was guide to them that
took Je'sus.
17 For he was numbered with us, and had
obtained part of this ministry.
18 Now this man purchased a field with the
reward of iniquity; and falling headlong, be
burst asunder in the midst, and all his bowels
gushed out.
19 And it was known unto all the dwellers at
Je-ru'sa-lem; insomuch as that field is called in
their proper tongue, A-cel'da-ma, that is to say,
The field of blood.
20 For it is written in the book of Psalms, Let
his habitation be desolate, and let no man dwell
therein: and his bishoprick let another take.
21 Wherefore of these men which have com-
panied with us all the time that the Lord Je'sus
went in and out among us,
22 Beginning from the baptism of John, unto
that same day that he was taken up from us,
must one be ordained to be a witness with us of
his resurrection.
23 And they appointed two, Jo'seph called
Bar'sa-bas, who was surnamed Jus'tus, and
Mat-thi'as.
24 And they prayed, and said, Thou, Lord,
which knowest the hearts of all *men,* shew
whether of these two thou hast chosen,
25 That he may take part of this ministry and
apostleship, from which Ju'das by transgression fell, that he might go to his own place.
26 And they gave forth their lots; and the lot
fell upon Mat-thi'as; and he was numbered with
the eleven apostles.

2 AND when the day of Pen'te-cost was fully
come, they were all with one accord in one
place.
2 And suddenly there came a sound from
heaven as of a rushing mighty wind, and it filled
all the house where they were sitting.
3 And there appeared unto them cloven
tongues like as of fire, and it sat upon each of
them.
4 And they were all filled with the Ho'ly
Ghost, and began to speak with other tongues,
as the Spirit gave them utterance.
5 And there were dwelling at Je-ru'sa-lem
Jews, devout men, out of every nation under
heaven.
6 Now when this was noised abroad, the
multitude came together, and were confounded,
because that every man heard them speak in his
own language.
7 And they were all amazed and marvelled,
saying one to another, Behold, are not all these
which speak Gal-i-læ'ans?
8 And how hear we every man in our own
tongue, wherein we were born?
9 Par'thi-ans, and Medes, and E'lam-ites, and
the dwellers in Mes-o-po-ta'mi-a, and in Ju-dæ'-
a, and Cap-pa-do'ci-a, in Pon'tus, and A'sia,
10 Phryg'i-a, and Pam-phyl'i-a, in E'gypt, and
in the parts of Lib'y-a about Cy-re'ne, and
strangers of Rome, Jews and proselytes,
11 Cretes and A-ra'bi-ans, we do hear them
speak in our tongues the wonderful works of
God.
12 And they were all amazed, and were in
doubt, saying one to another, What meaneth
this?
13 Others mocking said, These men are full
of new wine.
14 ¶ But Pe'ter, standing up with the eleven,
lifted up his voice, and said unto them, Ye men
of Ju-dæ'a, and all *ye* that dwell at Je-ru'sa-lem,
be this known unto you, and hearken to my
words:
15 For these are not drunken, as ye suppose,
seeing it is *but* the third hour of the day.
16 But this is that which was spoken by the
prophet Jo'el;

17 And it shall come to pass in the last days, saith God, I will pour out of my Spirit upon all flesh: and your sons and your daughters shall prophesy, and your young men shall see visions, and your old men shall dream dreams:
18 And on my servants and on my handmaidens I will pour out in those days of my Spirit; and they shall prophesy:
19 And I will shew wonders in heaven above, and signs in the earth beneath; blood, and fire, and vapour of smoke:
20 The sun shall be turned into darkness, and the moon into blood, before that great and notable day of the Lord come:
21 And it shall come to pass, *that* whosoever shall call on the name of the Lord shall be saved.
22 Ye men of Is′ra-el, hear these words; Je′sus of Naz′a-reth, a man approved of God among you by miracles and wonders and signs, which God did by him in the midst of you, as ye yourselves also know:
23 Him, being delivered by the determinate counsel and foreknowledge of God, ye have taken, and by wicked hands have crucified and slain:
24 Whom God hath raised up, having loosed the pains of death: because it was not possible that he should be holden of it.
25 For Da′vid speaketh concerning him, I foresaw the Lord always before my face, for he is on my right hand, that I should not be moved:
26 Therefore did my heart rejoice, and my tongue was glad; moreover also my flesh shall rest in hope:
27 Because thou wilt not leave my soul in hell, neither wilt thou suffer thine Holy One to see corruption.
28 Thou hast made known to me the ways of life; thou shalt make me full of joy with thy countenance.
29 Men *and* brethren, let me freely speak unto you of the patriarch Da′vid, that he is both dead and buried, and his sepulchre is with us unto this day.
30 Therefore being a prophet, and knowing that God had sworn with an oath to him, that of the fruit of his loins, according to the flesh, he would raise up Christ to sit on his throne;
31 He seeing this before spake of the resurrection of Christ, that his soul was not left in hell, neither his flesh did see corruption.
32 This Je′sus hath God raised up, whereof we all are witnesses.
33 Therefore being by the right hand of God exalted, and having received of the Father the promise of the Ho′ly Ghost, he hath shed forth this, which ye now see and hear.
34 For Da′vid is not ascended into the heavens: but he saith himself, The LORD said unto my Lord, Sit thou on my right hand,
35 Until I make thy foes thy footstool.
36 Therefore let all the house of Is′ra-el know assuredly, that God hath made that same Je′sus, whom ye have crucified, both Lord and Christ.
37 ¶ Now when they heard *this,* they were pricked in their heart, and said unto Pe′ter and to the rest of the apostles, Men *and* brethren, what shall we do?
38 Then Pe′ter said unto them, Repent, and be baptized every one of you in the name of Je′sus Christ for the remission of sins, and ye shall receive the gift of the Ho′ly Ghost.
39 For the promise is unto you, and to your children, and to all that are afar off, *even* as many as the Lord our God shall call.
40 And with many other words did he testify and exhort, saying, Save yourselves from this untoward generation.
41 ¶ Then they that gladly received his word were baptized: and the same day there were added *unto them* about three thousand souls.
42 And they continued stedfastly in the apostles' doctrine and fellowship, and in breaking of bread, and in prayers.
43 And fear came upon every soul: and many wonders and signs were done by the apostles.
44 And all that believed were together, and had all things common;
45 And sold their possessions and goods, and parted them to all *men,* as every man had need.
46 And they, continuing daily with one accord in the temple, and breaking bread from house to house, did eat their meat with gladness and singleness of heart,
47 Praising God, and having favour with all the people. And the Lord added to the church daily such as should be saved.

3 NOW Pe′ter and John went up together into the temple at the hour of prayer, *being* the ninth *hour.*
2 And a certain man lame from his mother's womb was carried, whom they laid daily at the gate of the temple which is called Beautiful, to ask alms of them that entered into the temple;
3 Who seeing Pe′ter and John about to go into the temple asked an alms.
4 And Pe′ter, fastening his eyes upon him with John, said, Look on us.
5 And he gave heed unto them, expecting to receive something of them.
6 Then Pe′ter said, Silver and gold have I none; but such as I have give I thee: In the name of Je′sus Christ of Naz′a-reth rise up and walk.
7 And he took him by the right hand, and lifted *him* up: and immediately his feet and ancle bones received strength.
8 And he leaping up stood, and walked, and entered with them into the temple, walking, and leaping, and praising God.
9 And all the people saw him walking and praising God:
10 And they knew that it was he which sat for alms at the Beautiful gate of the temple: and they were filled with wonder and amazement at that which had happened unto him.
11 And as the lame man which was healed held Pe′ter and John, all the people ran together unto them in the porch that is called Sol′o-mon's, greatly wondering.
12 ¶ And when Pe′ter saw *it,* he answered unto the people, Ye men of Is′ra-el, why marvel ye at this? or why look ye so earnestly on us, as though by our own power or holiness we had made this man to walk?
13 The God of A′bra-ham, and of I′saac, and of Ja′cob, the God of our fathers, hath glorified his Son Je′sus; whom ye delivered up, and denied him in the presence of Pi′late, when he was determined to let *him* go.
14 But ye denied the Holy One and the Just, and desired a murderer to be granted unto you;
15 And killed the Prince of life, whom God hath raised from the dead; whereof we are witnesses.
16 And his name through faith in his name hath made this man strong, whom ye see and know: yea, the faith which is by him hath given him this perfect soundness in the presence of you all.
17 And now, brethren, I wot that through ignorance ye did *it,* as *did* also your rulers.

18 But those things, which God before had shewed by the mouth of all his prophets, that Christ should suffer, he hath so fulfilled.

19 ¶ Repent ye therefore, and be converted, that your sins may be blotted out, when the times of refreshing shall come from the presence of the Lord;

20 And he shall send Je'sus Christ, which before was preached unto you:

21 Whom the heaven must receive until the times of restitution of all things, which God hath spoken by the mouth of all his holy prophets since the world began.

22 For Mo'ses truly said unto the fathers, A prophet shall the Lord your God raise up unto you of your brethren, like unto me; him shall ye hear in all things whatsoever he shall say unto you.

23 And it shall come to pass, *that* every soul, which will not hear that prophet, shall be destroyed from among the people.

24 Yea, and all the prophets from Sam'u-el and those that follow after, as many as have spoken, have likewise foretold of these days.

25 Ye are the children of the prophets, and of the covenant which God made with our fathers, saying unto A'bra-ham, And in thy seed shall all the kindreds of the earth be blessed.

26 Unto you first God, having raised up his Son Je'sus, sent him to bless you, in turning away every one of you from his iniquities.

4 AND as they spake unto the people, the priests, and the captain of the temple, and the Sad'du-cees, came upon them,

2 Being grieved that they taught the people, and preached through Je'sus the resurrection from the dead.

3 And they laid hands on them, and put *them* in hold unto the next day: for it was now eventide.

4 Howbeit many of them which heard the word believed; and the number of the men was about five thousand.

5 ¶ And it came to pass on the morrow, that their rulers, and elders, and scribes,

6 And An'nas the high priest, and Ca'ia-phas, and John, and Al-ex-an'der, and as many as were of the kindred of the high priest, were gathered together at Je-ru'sa-lem.

7 And when they had set them in the midst, they asked, By what power, or by what name, have ye done this?

8 Then Pe'ter, filled with the Ho'ly Ghost, said unto them, Ye rulers of the people, and elders of Is'ra-el,

9 If we this day be examined of the good deed done to the impotent man, by what means he is made whole;

10 Be it known unto you all, and to all the people of Is'ra-el, that by the name of Je'sus Christ of Naz'a-reth, whom ye crucified, whom God raised from the dead, *even* by him doth this man stand here before you whole.

11 This is the stone which was set at nought of you builders, which is become the head of the corner.

12 Neither is there salvation in any other: for there is none other name under heaven given among men, whereby we must be saved.

13 ¶ Now when they saw the boldness of Pe'ter and John, and perceived that they were unlearned and ignorant men, they marvelled; and they took knowledge of them, that they had been with Je'sus.

14 And beholding the man which was healed standing with them, they could say nothing against it.

15 But when they had commanded them to go aside out of the council, they conferred among themselves,

16 Saying, What shall we do to these men? for that indeed a notable miracle hath been done by them *is* manifest to all them that dwell in Je-ru'sa-lem; and we cannot deny *it*.

17 But that it spread no further among the people, let us straitly threaten them, that they speak henceforth to no man in this name.

18 And they called them, and commanded them not to speak at all nor teach in the name of Je'sus.

19 But Pe'ter and John answered and said unto them, Whether it be right in the sight of God to hearken unto you more than unto God, judge ye.

20 For we cannot but speak the things which we have seen and heard.

21 So when they had further threatened them, they let them go, finding nothing how they might punish them, because of the people: for all *men* glorified God for that which was done.

22 For the man was above forty years old, on whom this miracle of healing was shewed.

23 ¶ And being let go, they went to their own company, and reported all that the chief priests and elders had said unto them.

24 And when they heard that, they lifted up their voice to God with one accord, and said, Lord, thou *art* God, which hast made heaven, and earth, and the sea, and all that in them is:

25 Who by the mouth of thy servant Da'vid hast said, Why did the heathen rage, and the people imagine vain things?

26 The kings of the earth stood up, and the rulers were gathered together against the Lord, and against his Christ.

27 For of a truth against thy holy child Je'sus, whom thou hast anointed, both Her'od, and Pon'ti-us Pi'late, with the Gen'tiles, and the people of Is'ra-el, were gathered together,

28 For to do whatsoever thy hand and thy counsel determined before to be done.

29 And now, Lord, behold their threatenings: and grant unto thy servants, that with all boldness they may speak thy word,

30 By stretching forth thine hand to heal; and that signs and wonders may be done by the name of thy holy child Je'sus.

31 ¶ And when they had prayed, the place was shaken where they were assembled together; and they were all filled with the Ho'ly Ghost, and they spake the word of God with boldness.

32 And the multitude of them that believed were of one heart and of one soul: neither said any *of them* that ought of the things which he possessed was his own; but they had all things common.

33 And with great power gave the apostles witness of the resurrection of the Lord Je'sus: and great grace was upon them all.

34 Neither was there any among them that lacked: for as many as were possessors of lands or houses sold them, and brought the prices of the things that were sold,

35 And laid *them* down at the apostles' feet: and distribution was made unto every man according as he had need.

36 And Jo'ses, who by the apostles was surnamed Bar'na-bas, (which is, being interpreted, The son of consolation,) a Le'vite, *and* of the country of Cy'prus,

37 Having land, sold *it,* and brought the money, and laid *it* at the apostles' feet.

5 BUT a certain man named An-a-ni'as, with Sap-phi'ra his wife, sold a possession,
2 And kept back *part* of the price, his wife also being privy *to it,* and brought a certain part, and laid *it* at the apostles' feet.
3 But Pe'ter said, An-a-ni'as, why hath Sa'tan filled thine heart to lie to the Ho'ly Ghost, and to keep back *part* of the price of the land?
4 Whiles it remained, was it not thine own? and after it was sold, was it not in thine own power? why hast thou conceived this thing in thine heart? thou hast not lied unto men, but unto God.
5 And An-a-ni'as hearing these words fell down, and gave up the ghost: and great fear came on all them that heard these things.
6 And the young men arose, wound him up, and carried *him* out, and buried *him.*
7 And it was about the space of three hours after, when his wife, not knowing what was done, came in.
8 And Pe'ter answered unto her, Tell me whether ye sold the land for so much? And she said, Yea, for so much.
9 Then Pe'ter said unto her, How is it that ye have agreed together to tempt the Spirit of the Lord? behold, the feet of them which have buried thy husband *are* at the door, and shall carry thee out.
10 Then fell she down straightway at his feet, and yielded up the ghost: and the young men came in, and found her dead, and, carrying *her* forth, buried *her* by her husband.
11 And great fear came upon all the church, and upon as many as heard these things.
12 ¶ And by the hands of the apostles were many signs and wonders wrought among the people; (and they were all with one accord in Sol'o-mon's porch.
13 And of the rest durst no man join himself to them: but the people magnified them.
14 And believers were the more added to the Lord, multitudes both of men and women.)
15 Insomuch that they brought forth the sick into the streets, and laid *them* on beds of couches, that at the least the shadow of Pe'ter passing by might overshadow some of them.
16 There came also a multitude *out* of the cities round about unto Je-ru'sa-lem, bringing sick folks, and them which were vexed with unclean spirits: and they were healed every one.
17 ¶ Then the high priest rose up, and all they that were with him, (which is the sect of the Sad'du-cees,) and were filled with indignation,
18 And laid their hands on the apostles, and put them in the common prison.
19 But the angel of the Lord by night opened the prison doors, and brought them forth, and said,
20 Go, stand and speak in the temple to the people all the words of this life.
21 And when they heard *that,* they entered into the temple early in the morning, and taught. But the high priest came, and they that were with him, and called the council together, and all the senate of the children of Is'ra-el, and sent to the prison to have them brought.
22 But when the officers came, and found them not in the prison, they returned, and told,
23 Saying, The prison truly found we shut with all safety, and the keepers standing without before the doors: but when we had opened, we found no man within.
24 Now when the high priest and the captain of the temple and the chief priests heard these things, they doubted of them whereunto this would grow.
25 Then came one and told them, saying, Behold, the men whom ye put in prison are standing in the temple, and teaching the people.
26 Then went the captain with the officers, and brought them without violence: for they feared the people, lest they should have been stoned.
27 And when they had brought them, they set *them* before the council: and the high priest asked them,
28 Saying, Did not we straitly command you that ye should not teach in this name? and, behold, ye have filled Je-ru'sa-lem with your doctrine, and intend to bring this man's blood upon us.
29 ¶ Then Pe'ter and the *other* apostles answered and said, We ought to obey God rather than men.
30 The God of our fathers raised up Je'sus, whom ye slew and hanged on a tree.
31 Him hath God exalted with his right hand *to be* a Prince and a Saviour, for to give repentance to Is'ra-el, and forgiveness of sins.
32 And we are his witnesses of these things; and *so is* also the Ho'ly Ghost, whom God hath given to them that obey him.
33 ¶ When they heard *that,* they were cut *to the heart,* and took counsel to slay them.
34 Then stood there up one in the council, a Phar'i-see, named Ga-ma'li-el, a doctor of the law, had in reputation among all the people, and commanded to put the apostles forth a little space;
35 And said unto them, Ye men of Is'ra-el, take heed to yourselves what ye intend to do as touching these men.
36 For before these days rose up Theu'das, boasting himself to be somebody; to whom a number of men, about four hundred, joined themselves: who was slain; and all, as many as obeyed him, were scattered, and brought to nought.
37 After this man rose up Ju'das of Gal'i-lee in the days of the taxing, and drew away much people after him: he also perished; and all, *even* as many as obeyed him, were dispersed.
38 And now I say unto you, Refrain from these men, and let them alone: for if this counsel or this work be of men, it will come to nought:
39 But if it be of God, ye cannot overthrow it; lest haply ye be found even to fight against God.
40 And to him they agreed: and when they had called the apostles, and beaten *them,* they commanded that they should not speak in the name of Je'sus, and let them go.
41 ¶ And they departed from the presence of the council, rejoicing that they were counted worthy to suffer shame for his name.
42 And daily in the temple, and in every house, they ceased not to teach and preach Je'sus Christ.

6 AND in those days, when the number of the disciples was multiplied, there arose a murmuring of the Gre'cians against the He'brews, because their widows were neglected in the daily ministration.
2 Then the twelve called the multitude of the disciples *unto them,* and said, It is not reason that we should leave the word of God, and serve tables.
3 Wherefore, brethren, look ye out among

you seven men of honest report, full of the Ho'-
ly Ghost and wisdom, whom we may appoint
over this business.
4 But we will give ourselves continually to
prayer, and to the ministry of the word.
5 ¶ And the saying pleased the whole multitude: and they chose Ste'phen, a man full of
faith and of the Ho'ly Ghost, and Phil'ip, and
Proch'o-rus, and Ni-ca'nor, and Ti'mon, and
Par'me-nas, and Nic'o-las a proselyte of An'ti-
och:
6 Whom they set before the apostles: and
when they had prayed, they laid *their* hands on
them.
7 And the word of God increased; and the
number of the disciples multiplied in Je-ru'sa-
lem greatly; and a great company of the priests
were obedient to the faith.
8 And Ste'phen, full of faith and power, did
great wonders and miracles among the people.
9 ¶ Then there arose certain of the synagogue, which is called *the synagogue* of the
Lib'er-tines, and Cy-re'ni-ans, and Al-ex-an'dri-
ans, and of them of Ci-li'cia and of A'sia, disputing with Ste'phen.
10 And they were not able to resist the wisdom and the spirit by which he spake.
11 Then they suborned men, which said, We
have heard him speak blasphemous words
against Mo'ses, and *against* God.
12 And they stirred up the people, and the
elders, and the scribes, and came upon *him*, and
caught him, and brought *him* to the council,
13 And set up false witnesses, which said,
This man ceaseth not to speak blasphemous
words against this holy place, and the law:
14 For we have heard him say, that this Je'-
sus of Naz'a-reth shall destroy this place, and
shall change the customs which Mo'ses delivered us.
15 And all that sat in the council, looking
stedfastly on him, saw his face as it had been
the face of an angel.

7 THEN said the high priest, Are these
things so?
2 And he said, Men, brethren, and fathers,
hearken; The God of glory appeared unto our
father A'bra-ham, when he was in Mes-o-po-ta'-
mi-a, before he dwelt in Char'ran,
3 And said unto him, Get thee out of thy
country, and from thy kindred, and come into
the land which I shall shew thee.
4 Then came he out of the land of the Chal-
dæ'ans, and dwelt in Char'ran: and from thence,
when his father was dead, he removed him into
this land, wherein ye now dwell.
5 And he gave him none inheritance in it, no,
not *so much as* to set his foot on: yet he promised that he would give it to him for a possession, and to his seed after him, when *as yet* he
had no child.
6 And God spake on this wise, That his seed
should sojourn in a strange land; and that they
should bring them into bondage, and entreat
them evil four hundred years.
7 And the nation to whom they shall be in
bondage will I judge, said God: and after that
shall they come forth, and serve me in this
place.
8 And he gave him the covenant of circumcision: and so *A'bra-ham* begat I'saac, and circumcised him the eighth day; and I'saac *begat*
Ja'cob; and Ja'cob *begat* the twelve patriarchs.
9 And the patriarchs, moved with envy, sold
Jo'seph into E'gypt: but God was with him,
10 And delivered him out of all afflictions,
and gave him favour and wisdom in the sight of
Pha'raoh king of E'gypt; and he made him governor over E'gypt and all his house.
11 Now there came a dearth over all the land
of E'gypt and Cha'naan, and great affliction:
and our fathers found no sustenance.
12 But when Ja'cob heard that there was
corn in E'gypt, he sent out our fathers first.
13 And at the second *time* Jo'seph was made
known to his brethren; and Jo'seph's kindred
was made known unto Pha'raoh.
14 Then sent Jo'seph, and called his father
Ja'cob to *him*, and all his kindred, threescore
and fifteen souls.
15 So Ja'cob went down into E'gypt, and
died, he, and our fathers,
16 And were carried over into Sy'chem, and
laid in the sepulchre that A'bra-ham bought for
a sum of money of the sons of Em'mor *the father* of Sy'chem.
17 But when the time of the promise drew
nigh, which God had sworn to A'bra-ham, the
people grew and multiplied in E'gypt,
18 Till another king arose, which knew not
Jo'seph.
19 The same dealt subtilly with our kindred,
and evil entreated our fathers, so that they cast
out their young children, to the end they might
not live.
20 In which time Mo'ses was born, and was
exceeding fair, and nourished up in his father's
house three months:
21 And when he was cast out, Pha'raoh's
daughter took him up, and nourished him for
her own son.
22 And Mo'ses was learned in all the wisdom
of the E-gyp'tians, and was mighty in words
and in deeds.
23 And when he was full forty years old, it
came into his heart to visit his brethren the children of Is'ra-el.
24 And seeing one *of them* suffer wrong, he
defended *him*, and avenged him that was oppressed, and smote the E-gyp'tian:
25 For he supposed his brethren would have
understood how that God by his hand would
deliver them: but they understood not.
26 And the next day he shewed himself unto
them as they strove, and would have set them
at one again, saying, Sirs, ye are brethren; why
do ye wrong one to another?
27 But he that did his neighbour wrong
thrust him away, saying, Who made thee a ruler
and a judge over us?
28 Wilt thou kill me, as thou diddest the E-
gyp'tian yesterday?
29 Then fled Mo'ses at this saying, and was a
stranger in the land of Ma'di-an, where he begat
two sons.
30 And when forty years were expired, there
appeared to him in the wilderness of mount Si'-
na an angel of the Lord in a flame of fire in a
bush.
31 When Mo'ses saw *it*, he wondered at the
sight: and as he drew near to behold *it*, the
voice of the Lord came unto him,
32 *Saying*, I *am* the God of thy fathers, the
God of A'bra-ham, and the God of I'saac, and
the God of Ja'cob. Then Mo'ses trembled, and
durst not behold.
33 Then said the Lord to him, Put off thy
shoes from thy feet: for the place where thou
standest is holy ground.
34 I have seen, I have seen the affliction of
my people which is in E'gypt, and I have heard
their groaning, and am come down to deliver

them. And now come, I will send thee into E'-
gypt.
35 This Mo'ses whom they refused, saying,
Who made thee a ruler and a judge? the same
did God send *to be* a ruler and a deliverer by the
hand of the angel which appeared to him in the
bush.
36 He brought them out, after that he had
shewed wonders and signs in the land of E'gypt,
and in the Red sea, and in the wilderness forty
years.
37 ¶ This is that Mo'ses, which said unto the
children of Is'ra-el, A prophet shall the Lord
your God raise up unto you of your brethren,
like unto me; him shall ye hear.
38 This is he, that was in the church in the
wilderness with the angel which spake to him in
the mount Si'na, and *with* our fathers: who received the lively oracles to give unto us:
39 To whom our fathers would not obey, but
thrust *him* from them, and in their hearts
turned back again into E'gypt,
40 Saying unto Aar'on, Make us gods to go
before us: for *as for* this Mo'ses, which brought
us out of the land of E'gypt, we wot not what is
become of him.
41 And they made a calf in those days, and
offered sacrifice unto the idol, and rejoiced in
the works of their own hands.
42 Then God turned, and gave them up to
worship the host of heaven; as it is written in
the book of the prophets, O ye house of Is'ra-el,
have ye offered to me slain beasts and sacrifices
by the space of forty years in the wilderness?
43 Yea, ye took up the tabernacle of Mo'loch,
and the star of your god Rem'phan, figures
which ye made to worship them: and I will carry you away beyond Bab'y-lon.
44 Our fathers had the tabernacle of witness
in the wilderness, as he had appointed, speaking unto Mo'ses, that he should make it according to the fashion that he had seen.
45 Which also our fathers that came after
brought in with Je'sus into the possession of the
Gen'tiles, whom God drave out before the face
of our fathers, unto the days of Da'vid;
46 Who found favour before God, and desired to find a tabernacle for the God of Ja'cob.
47 But Sol'o-mon built him an house.
48 Howbeit the most High dwelleth not in
temples made with hands; as saith the prophet,
49 Heaven *is* my throne, and earth *is* my
footstool: what house will ye build me? saith
the Lord: or what *is* the place of my rest?
50 Hath not my hand made all these things?
51 ¶ Ye stiffnecked and uncircumcised in
heart and ears, ye do always resist the Ho'ly
Ghost: as your fathers *did*, so *do* ye.
52 Which of the prophets have not your fathers persecuted? and they have slain them
which shewed before of the coming of the Just
One; of whom ye have been now the betrayers
and murderers:
53 Who have received the law by the disposi-
tion of angels, and have not kept *it*.
54 ¶ When they heard these things, they
were cut to the heart, and they gnashed on him
with *their* teeth.
55 But he, being full of the Ho'ly Ghost,
looked up stedfastly into heaven, and saw the
glory of God, and Je'sus standing on the right
hand of God,
56 And said, Behold, I see the heavens
opened, and the Son of man standing on the
right hand of God.
57 Then they cried out with a loud voice, and
stopped their ears, and ran upon him with one
accord,
58 And cast *him* out of the city, and stoned
him: and the witnesses laid down their clothes
at a young man's feet, whose name was Saul.
59 And they stoned Ste'phen, calling upon
God, and saying, Lord Je'sus, receive my spirit.
60 And he kneeled down, and cried with a
loud voice, Lord, lay not this sin to their charge.
And when he had said this, he fell asleep.

8 AND Saul was consenting unto his death.
And at that time there was a great persecution against the church which was at Je-ru'-
sa-lem; and they were all scattered abroad
throughout the regions of Ju-dæ'a and Sa-ma'ri-
a, except the apostles.
2 And devout men carried Ste'phen *to his*
burial, and made great lamentation over him.
3 As for Saul, he made havock of the church,
entering into every house, and haling men and
women committed *them* to prison.
4 Therefore they that were scattered abroad
went every where preaching the word.
5 Then Phil'ip went down to the city of Sa-
ma'ri-a, and preached Christ unto them.
6 And the people with one accord gave heed
unto those things which Phil'ip spake, hearing
and seeing the miracles which he did.
7 For unclean spirits, crying with loud voice,
came out of many that were possessed *with*
them: and many taken with palsies, and that
were lame, were healed.
8 And there was great joy in that city.
9 But there was a certain man, called Si'mon,
which beforetime in the same city used sorcery,
and bewitched the people of Sa-ma'ri-a, giving
out that himself was some great one:
10 To whom they all gave heed, from the
least to the greatest, saying, This man is the
great power of God.
11 And to him they had regard, because that
of long time he had bewitched them with sorceries.
12 But when they believed Phil'ip preaching
the things concerning the kingdom of God, and
the name of Je'sus Christ, they were baptized,
both men and women.
13 Then Si'mon himself believed also: and
when he was baptized, he continued with Phil'-
ip, and wondered, beholding the miracles and
signs which were done.
14 Now when the apostles which were at Je-
ru'sa-lem heard that Sa-ma'ri-a had received
the word of God, they sent unto them Pe'ter and
John:
15 Who, when they were come down, prayed
for them, that they might receive the Ho'ly
Ghost:
16 (For as yet he was fallen upon none of
them: only they were baptized in the name of
the Lord Je'sus.)
17 Then laid they *their* hands on them, and
they received the Ho'ly Ghost.
18 And when Si'mon saw that through laying
on of the apostles' hands the Ho'ly Ghost was
given, he offered them money,
19 Saying, Give me also this power, that on
whomsoever I lay hands, he may receive the
Ho'ly Ghost.
20 But Pe'ter said unto him, Thy money perish with thee, because thou hast thought that
the gift of God may be purchased with money.
21 Thou hast neither part nor lot in this matter: for thy heart is not right in the sight of God.
22 Repent therefore of this thy wickedness,

and pray God, if perhaps the thought of thine
heart may be forgiven thee.
23 For I perceive that thou art in the gall of
bitterness, and *in* the bond of iniquity.
24 Then answered Si'mon, and said, Pray ye
to the Lord for me, that none of these things
which ye have spoken come upon me.
25 And they, when they had testified and
preached the word of the Lord, returned to Je-
ru'sa-lem, and preached the gospel in many villages of the Sa-mar'i-tans.
26 And the angel of the Lord spake unto
Phil'ip, saying, Arise, and go toward the south
unto the way that goeth down from Je-ru'sa-
lem unto Ga'za, which is desert.
27 And he rose and went: and, behold, a man
of E-thi-o'pi-a, an eunuch of great authority under Can'da-ce queen of the E-thi-o'pi-ans, who
had the charge of all her treasure, and had
come to Je-ru'sa-lem for to worship,
28 Was returning, and sitting in his chariot
read E-sa'ias the prophet.
29 Then the Spirit said unto Phil'ip, Go near,
and join thyself to this chariot.
30 And Phil'ip ran thither to *him*, and heard
him read the prophet E-sa'ias, and said, Understandest thou what thou readest?
31 And he said, How can I, except some man
should guide me? And he desired Phil'ip that he
would come up and sit with him.
32 The place of the scripture which he read
was this, He was led as a sheep to the slaughter;
and like a lamb dumb before his shearer, so
opened he not his mouth:
33 In his humiliation his judgment was taken
away: and who shall declare his generation? for
his life is taken from the earth.
34 And the eunuch answered Phil'ip, and
said, I pray thee, of whom speaketh the prophet
this? of himself, or of some other man?
35 Then Phil'ip opened his mouth, and began
at the same scripture, and preached unto him
Je'sus.
36 And as they went on *their* way, they came
unto a certain water: and the eunuch said, See,
here is water; what doth hinder me to be baptized?
37 And Phil'ip said, If thou believest with all
thine heart, thou mayest. And he answered and
said, I believe that Je'sus Christ is the Son of
God.
38 And he commanded the chariot to stand
still: and they went down both into the water,
both Phil'ip and the eunuch; and he baptized
him.
39 And when they were come up out of the
water, the Spirit of the Lord caught away Phil'-
ip, that the eunuch saw him no more: and he
went on his way rejoicing.
40 But Phil'ip was found at A-zo'tus: and
passing through he preached in all the cities, till
he came to Cæs-a-re'a.

9 AND Saul, yet breathing out threatenings
and slaughter against the disciples of the
Lord, went unto the high priest,
2 And desired of him letters to Da-mas'cus to
the synagogues, that if he found any of this
way, whether they were men or women, he
might bring them bound unto Je-ru'sa-lem.
3 And as he journeyed, he came near Da-
mas'cus: and suddenly there shined round
about him a light from heaven:
4 And he fell to the earth, and heard a voice
saying unto him, Saul, Saul, why persecutest
thou me?
5 And he said, Who art thou, Lord? And the
Lord said, I am Je'sus whom thou persecutest:
it is hard for thee to kick against the pricks.
6 And he trembling and astonished said,
Lord, what wilt thou have me to do? And the
Lord *said* unto him, Arise, and go into the city,
and it shall be told thee what thou must do.
7 And the men which journeyed with him
stood speechless, hearing a voice, but seeing no
man.
8 And Saul arose from the earth; and when
his eyes were opened, he saw no man: but they
led him by the hand, and brought *him* into Da-
mas'cus.
9 And he was three days without sight, and
neither did eat nor drink.
10 ¶ And there was a certain disciple at Da-
mas'cus, named An-a-ni'as; and to him said the
Lord in a vision, An-a-ni'as. And he said, Behold, I *am here*, Lord.
11 And the Lord *said* unto him, Arise, and go
into the street which is called Straight, and enquire in the house of Ju'das for *one* called Saul,
of Tar'sus: for, behold, he prayeth,
12 And hath seen in a vision a man named
An-a-ni'as coming in, and putting *his* hand on
him, that he might receive his sight.
13 Then An-a-ni'as answered, Lord, I have
heard by many of this man, how much evil he
hath done to thy saints at Je-ru'sa-lem:
14 And here he hath authority from the chief
priests to bind all that call on thy name.
15 But the Lord said unto him, Go thy way:
for he is a chosen vessel unto me, to bear my
name before the Gen'tiles, and kings, and the
children of Is'ra-el:
16 For I will shew him how great things he
must suffer for my name's sake.
17 And An-a-ni'as went his way, and entered
into the house; and putting his hands on him
said, Brother Saul, the Lord, *even* Je'sus, that
appeared unto thee in the way as thou camest,
hath sent me, that thou mightest receive thy
sight, and be filled with the Ho'ly Ghost.
18 And immediately there fell from his eyes
as it had been scales: and he received sight
forthwith, and arose, and was baptized.
19 And when he had received meat, he was
strengthened. Then was Saul certain days with
the disciples which were at Da-mas'cus.
20 And straightway he preached Christ in
the synagogues, that he is the Son of God.
21 But all that heard *him* were amazed, and
said; Is not this he that destroyed them which
called on this name in Je-ru'sa-lem, and came
hither for that intent, that he might bring them
bound unto the chief priests?
22 But Saul increased the more in strength,
and confounded the Jews which dwelt at Da-
mas'cus, proving that this is very Christ.
23 ¶ And after that many days were fulfilled,
the Jews took counsel to kill him:
24 But their laying await was known of Saul.
And they watched the gates day and night to
kill him.
25 Then the disciples took him by night, and
let *him* down by the wall in a basket.
26 And when Saul was come to Je-ru'sa-lem,
he assayed to join himself to the disciples: but
they were all afraid of him, and believed not
that he was a disciple.
27 But Bar'na-bas took him, and brought *him*
to the apostles, and declared unto them how he
had seen the Lord in the way, and that he had
spoken to him, and how he had preached boldly
at Da-mas'cus in the name of Je'sus.
28 And he was with them coming in and
going out at Je-ru'sa-lem.

29 And he spake boldly in the name of the Lord Je'sus, and disputed against the Gre'cians: but they went about to slay him.

30 *Which* when the brethren knew, they brought him down to Caes-a-re'a, and sent him forth to Tar'sus.

31 Then had the churches rest throughout all Ju-dæ'a and Gal'i-lee and Sa-ma'ri-a, and were edified; and walking in the fear of the Lord, and in the comfort of the Ho'ly Ghost, were multiplied.

32 ¶ And it came to pass, as Pe'ter passed throughout all *quarters*, he came down also to the saints which dwelt at Lyd'da.

33 And there he found a certain man named Æ'ne-as, which had kept his bed eight years, and was sick of the palsy.

34 And Pe'ter said unto him, Æ'ne-as, Je'sus Christ maketh thee whole: arise, and make thy bed. And he arose immediately.

35 And all that dwelt at Lyd'da and Sa'ron saw him, and turned to the Lord.

36 ¶ Now there was at Jop'pa a certain disciple named Tab'i-tha, which by interpretation is called Dor'cas: this woman was full of good works and almsdeeds which she did.

37 And it came to pass in those days, that she was sick, and died: whom when they had washed, they laid *her* in an upper chamber.

38 And forasmuch as Lyd'da was nigh to Jop'pa, and the disciples had heard that Pe'ter was there, they sent unto him two men, desiring *him* that he would not delay to come to them.

39 Then Pe'ter arose and went with them. When he was come, they brought him into the upper chamber: and all the widows stood by him weeping, and shewing the coats and garments which Dor'cas made, while she was with them.

40 But Pe'ter put them all forth, and kneeled down, and prayed; and turning *him* to the body said, Tab'i-tha, arise. And she opened her eyes: and when she saw Pe'ter, she sat up.

41 And he gave her *his* hand, and lifted her up, and when he had called the saints and widows, presented her alive.

42 And it was known throughout all Jop'pa; and many believed in the Lord.

43 And it came to pass, that he tarried many days in Jop'pa with one Si'mon a tanner.

10

THERE was a certain man in Cæs-a-re'a called Cor-ne'lius, a centurion of the band called the Ital'ian *band*,

2 A devout *man*, and one that feared God with all his house, which gave much alms to the people, and prayed to God alway.

3 He saw in a vision evidently about the ninth hour of the day an angel of God coming in to him, and saying unto him, Cor-ne'lius.

4 And when he looked on him, he was afraid, and said, What is it, Lord? And he said unto him, Thy prayers and thine alms are come up for a memorial before God.

5 And now send men to Jop'pa, and call for *one* Si'mon, whose surname is Pe'ter:

6 He lodgeth with one Si'mon a tanner, whose house is by the sea side: he shall tell thee what thou oughtest to do.

7 And when the angel which spake unto Cor-ne'lius was departed, he called two of his household servants, and a devout soldier of them that waited on him continually;

8 And when he had declared all *these* things unto them, he sent them to Jop'pa.

9 ¶ On the morrow, as they went on their journey, and drew nigh unto the city, Pe'ter went up upon the house top to pray about the sixth hour:

10 And he became very hungry, and would have eaten: but while they made ready, he fell into a trance,

11 And saw heaven opened, and a certain vessel descending unto him, as it had been a great sheet knit at the four corners, and let down to the earth:

12 Wherein were all manner of fourfooted beasts of the earth, and wild beasts, and creeping things, and fowls of the air.

13 And there came a voice to him, Rise, Pe'ter; kill, and eat.

14 But Pe'ter said, Not so, Lord; for I have never eaten any thing that is common or unclean.

15 And the voice *spake* unto him again the second time, What God hath cleansed, *that* call not thou common.

16 This was done thrice: and the vessel was received up again into heaven.

17 Now while Pe'ter doubted in himself what this vision which he had seen should mean, behold, the men which were sent from Cor-ne'lius had made enquiry for Si'mon's house, and stood before the gate,

18 And called, and asked whether Si'mon, which was surnamed Pe'ter, were lodged there.

19 ¶ While Pe'ter thought on the vision, the Spirit said unto him, Behold, three men seek thee.

20 Arise therefore, and get thee down, and go with them, doubting nothing: for I have sent them.

21 Then Pe'ter went down to the men which were sent unto him from Cor-ne'lius; and said, Behold, I am he whom ye seek: what *is* the cause wherefore ye are come?

22 And they said, Cor-ne'lius the centurion, a just man, and one that feareth God, and of good report among all the nation of the Jews, was warned from God by an holy angel to send for thee into his house, and to hear words of thee.

23 Then called he them in, and lodged *them*. And on the morrow Pe'ter went away with them, and certain brethren from Jop'pa accompanied him.

24 And the morrow after they entered into Cæs-a-re'a. And Cor-ne'lius waited for them, and had called together his kinsmen and near friends.

25 And as Pe'ter was coming in, Cor-ne'lius met him, and fell down at his feet, and worshipped *him*.

26 But Pe'ter took him up, saying, Stand up; I myself also am a man.

27 And as he talked with him, he went in, and found many that were come together.

28 And he said unto them, Ye know how that it is an unlawful thing for a man that is a Jew to keep company, or come unto one of another nation; but God hath shewed me that I should not call any man common or unclean.

29 Therefore came I *unto you* without gainsaying, as soon as I was sent for: I ask therefore for what intent ye have sent for me?

30 And Cor-ne'lius said, Four days ago I was fasting until this hour; and at the ninth hour I prayed in my house, and behold, a man stood before me in bright clothing,

31 And said, Cor-ne'lius, thy prayer is heard, and thine alms are had in remembrance in the sight of God.

32 Send therefore to Jop'pa, and call hither Si'mon, whose surname is Pe'ter; he is lodged in the house of *one* Si'mon a tanner by the sea

side: who, when he cometh, shall speak unto
thee.
33 Immediately therefore I sent to thee; and
thou hast well done that thou art come. Now
therefore are we all here present before God, to
hear all things that are commanded thee of
God.
34 ¶ Then Pe'ter opened *his* mouth, and said,
Of a truth I perceive that God is no respecter of
persons:
35 But in every nation he that feareth him,
and worketh righteousness, is accepted with
him.
36 The word which *God* sent unto the children of Is'ra-el, preaching peace by Je'sus
Christ: (he is Lord of all:)
37 That word, *I say*, ye know, which was
published throughout all Ju-dæ'a, and began
from Gal'i-lee, after the baptism which John
preached;
38 How God anointed Je'sus of Naz'a-reth
with the Ho'ly Ghost and with power: who went
about doing good, and healing all that were oppressed of the devil; for God was with him.
39 And we are witnesses of all things which
he did both in the land of the Jews, and in Je-
ru'sa-lem; whom they slew and hanged on a
tree:
40 Him God raised up the third day, and
shewed him openly;
41 Not to all the people, but unto witnesses
chosen before of God, *even* to us, who did eat
and drink with him after he rose from the dead.
42 And he commanded us to preach unto the
people, and to testify that it is he which was
ordained of God *to be* the Judge of quick and
dead.
43 To him give all the prophets witness, that
through his name whosoever believeth in him
shall receive remission of sins.
44 ¶ While Pe'ter yet spake these words, the
Ho'ly Ghost fell on all them which heard the
word.
45 And they of the circumcision which believed were astonished, as many as came with
Pe'ter, because that on the Gen'tiles also was
poured out the gift of the Ho'ly Ghost.
46 For they heard them speak with tongues,
and magnify God. Then answered Pe'ter,
47 Can any man forbid water, that these
should not be baptized, which have received the
Ho'ly Ghost as well as we?
48 And he commanded them to be baptized
in the name of the Lord. Then prayed they him
to tarry certain days.

11 AND the apostles and brethren that
were in Ju-dæ'a heard that the Gen'tiles
had also received the word of God.
2 And when Pe'ter was come up to Je-ru'sa-
lem, they that were of the circumcision contended with him,
3 Saying, Thou wentest in to men uncircumcised, and didst eat with them.
4 But Pe'ter rehearsed *the matter* from the
beginning, and expounded *it* by order unto
them, saying,
5 I was in the city of Jop'pa praying: and in a
trance I saw a vision, A certain vessel descend,
as it had been a great sheet, let down from
heaven by four corners; and it came even to me:
6 Upon the which when I had fastened mine
eyes, I considered, and saw fourfooted beasts of
the earth, and wild beasts, and creeping things,
and fowls of the air.
7 And I heard a voice saying unto me, Arise,
Pe'ter; slay and eat.
8 But I said, Not so, Lord: for nothing common or unclean hath at any time entered into
my mouth.
9 But the voice answered me again from
heaven, What God hath cleansed, *that* call not
thou common.
10 And this was done three times: and all
were drawn up again into heaven.
11 And, behold, immediately there were
three men already come unto the house where I
was, sent from Cæs-a-re'a unto me.
12 And the spirit bade me go with them,
nothing doubting. Moreover these six brethren
accompanied me, and we entered into the
man's house:
13 And he shewed us how he had seen an
angel in his house, which stood and said unto
him, Send men to Jop'pa, and call for Si'mon,
whose surname is Pe'ter;
14 Who shall tell thee words, whereby thou
and all thy house shall be saved.
15 And as I began to speak, the Ho'ly Ghost
fell on them, as on us at the beginning.
16 Then remembered I the word of the Lord,
how that he said, John indeed baptized with
water; but ye shall be baptized with the Ho'ly
Ghost.
17 Forasmuch then as God gave them the
like gift as *he did* unto us, who believed on the
Lord Je'sus Christ; what was I, that I could
withstand God?
18 When they heard these things, they held
their peace, and glorified God, saying, Then
hath God also to the Gen'tiles granted repentance unto life.
19 ¶ Now they which were scattered abroad
upon the persecution that arose about Ste'phen
travelled as far as Phe-ni'ce, and Cy'prus, and
An'ti-och, preaching the word to none but unto
the Jews only.
20 And some of them were men of Cy'prus
and Cy-re'ne, which, when they were come to
An'ti-och, spake unto the Gre'cians, preaching
the Lord Je'sus.
21 And the hand of the Lord was with them:
and a great number believed, and turned unto
the Lord.
22 ¶ Then tidings of these things came unto
the ears of the church which was in Je-ru'sa-
lem: and they sent forth Bar'na-bas, that he
should go as far as An'ti-och.
23 Who, when he came, and had seen the
grace of God, was glad, and exhorted them all,
that with purpose of heart they would cleave
unto the Lord.
24 For he was a good man, and full of the
Ho'ly Ghost and of faith: and much people was
added unto the Lord.
25 Then departed Bar'na-bas to Tar'sus, for
to seek Saul:
26 And when he had found him, he brought
him unto An'ti-och. And it came to pass, that a
whole year they assembled themselves with the
church, and taught much people. And the disciples were called Chris'tians first in An'ti-och.
27 ¶ And in these days came prophets from
Je-ru'sa-lem unto An'ti-och.
28 And there stood up one of them named
Ag'a-bus, and signified by the spirit that there
should be great dearth throughout all the world:
which came to pass in the days of Clau'di-us
Cæ'sar.
29 Then the disciples, every man according
to his ability, determined to send relief unto the
brethren which dwelt in Ju-dæ'a:
30 Which also they did, and sent it to the elders by the hands of Bar'na-bas and Saul.

12 NOW about that time Her'od the king stretched forth *his* hands to vex certain of the church.

2 And he killed James the brother of John with the sword.

3 And because he saw it pleased the Jews, he proceeded further to take Pe'ter also. (Then were the days of unleavened bread.)

4 And when he had apprehended him, he put *him* in prison, and delivered *him* to four quaternions of soldiers to keep him; intending after Easter to bring him forth to the people.

5 Pe'ter therefore was kept in prison: but prayer was made without ceasing of the church unto God for him.

6 And when Her'od would have brought him forth, the same night Pe'ter was sleeping between two soldiers, bound with two chains: and the keepers before the door kept the prison.

7 And, behold, the angel of the Lord came upon *him,* and a light shined in the prison: and he smote Pe'ter on the side, and raised him up, saying, Arise up quickly. And his chains fell off from *his* hands.

8 And the angel said unto him, Gird thyself, and bind on thy sandals. And so he did. And he saith unto him, Cast thy garment about thee, and follow me.

9 And he went out, and followed him; and wist not that it was true which was done by the angel; but thought he saw a vision.

10 When they were past the first and the second ward, they came unto the iron gate that leadeth unto the city; which opened to them of his own accord: and they went out, and passed on through one street; and forthwith the angel departed from him.

11 And when Pe'ter was come to himself, he said, Now I know of a surety, that the Lord hath sent his angel, and hath delivered me out of the hand of Her'od, and *from* all the expectation of the people of the Jews.

12 And when he had considered *the thing,* he came to the house of Ma'ry the mother of John, whose surname was Mark; where many were gathered together praying.

13 And as Pe'ter knocked at the door of the gate, a damsel came to hearken, named Rho'da.

14 And when she knew Pe'ter's voice, she opened not the gate for gladness, but ran in, and told how Pe'ter stood before the gate.

15 And they said unto her, Thou art mad. But she constantly affirmed that it was even so. Then said they, It is his angel.

16 But Pe'ter continued knocking: and when they had opened *the door,* and saw him, they were astonished.

17 But he, beckoning unto them with the hand to hold their peace, declared unto them how the Lord had brought him out of the prison. And he said, Go shew these things unto James, and to the brethren. And he departed, and went into another place.

18 Now as soon as it was day, there was no small stir among the soldiers, what was become of Pe'ter.

19 And when Her'od had sought for him, and found him not, he examined the keepers, and commanded that *they* should be put to death. And he went down from Ju-dæ'a to Cæs-a-re'a, and *there* abode.

20 ¶ And Her'od was highly displeased with them of Tyre and Si'don: but they came with one accord to him, and, having made Blas'tus the king's chamberlain their friend, desired peace; because their country was nourished by the king's *country.*

21 And upon a set day Her'od, arrayed in royal apparel, sat upon his throne, and made an oration unto them.

22 And the people gave a shout, *saying, It is* the voice of a god, and not of a man.

23 And immediately the angel of the Lord smote him, because he gave not God the glory: and he was eaten of worms, and gave up the ghost.

24 ¶ But the word of God grew and multiplied.

25 And Bar'na-bas and Saul returned from Je-ru'sa-lem, when they had fulfilled *their* ministry, and took with them John, whose surname was Mark.

13 NOW there were in the church that was at An'ti-och certain prophets and teachers; as Bar'na-bas, and Sim'e-on that was called Ni'ger, and Lu'cius of Cy-re'ne, and Man'a-en, which had been brought up with Her'od the tetrarch, and Saul.

2 As they ministered to the Lord, and fasted, the Ho'ly Ghost said, Separate me Bar'na-bas and Saul for the work whereunto I have called them.

3 And when they had fasted and prayed, and laid *their* hands on them, they sent *them* away.

4 ¶ So they, being sent forth by the Ho'ly Ghost, departed unto Se-leu'ci-a; and from thence they sailed to Cy'prus.

5 And when they were at Sal'a-mis, they preached the word of God in the synagogues of the Jews: and they had also John to *their* minister.

6 And when they had gone through the isle unto Pa'phos, they found a certain sorcerer, a false prophet, a Jew, whose name *was* Bar-je'sus:

7 Which was with the deputy of the country, Ser'gi-us Pau'lus, a prudent man; who called for Bar'na-bas and Saul, and desired to hear the word of God.

8 But El'y-mas the sorcerer (for so is his name by interpretation) withstood them, seeking to turn away the deputy from the faith.

9 Then Saul, (who also *is called* Paul,) filled with the Ho'ly Ghost, set his eyes on him,

10 And said, O full of all subtilty and all mischief, *thou* child of the devil, *thou* enemy of all righteousness, wilt thou not cease to pervert the right ways of the Lord?

11 And now, behold, the hand of the Lord *is* upon thee, and thou shalt be blind, not seeing the sun for a season. And immediately there fell on him a mist and a darkness; and he went about seeking some to lead him by the hand.

12 Then the deputy, when he saw what was done, believed, being astonished at the doctrine of the Lord.

13 Now when Paul and his company loosed from Pa'phos, they came to Per'ga in Pam-phyl'i-a: and John departing from them returned to Je-ru'sa-lem.

14 ¶ But when they departed from Per'ga, they came to An'ti-och in Pi-sid'i-a, and went into the synagogue on the sabbath day, and sat down.

15 And after the reading of the law and the prophets the rulers of the synagogue sent unto them, saying, *Ye* men *and* brethren, if ye have any word of exhortation for the people, say on.

16 Then Paul stood up, and beckoning with *his* hand said, Men of Is'ra-el, ye that fear God, give audience.

17 The God of this people of Is'ra-el chose our fathers, and exalted the people when they

dwelt as strangers in the land of E'gypt, and with an high arm brought he them out of it.

18 And about the time of forty years suffered he their manners in the wilderness.

19 And when he had destroyed seven nations in the land of Cha'naan, he divided their land to them by lot.

20 And after that he gave *unto them* judges about the space of four hundred and fifty years, until Sam'u-el the prophet.

21 And afterward they desired a king: and God gave unto them Saul the son of Cis, a man of the tribe of Ben'ja-min, by the space of forty years.

22 And when he had removed him, he raised up unto them Da'vid to be their king; to whom also he gave testimony, and said, I have found Da'vid the *son* of Jes'se, a man after mine own heart, which shall fulfill all my will.

23 Of this man's seed hath God according to *his* promise raised unto Is'ra-el a Saviour, Je'sus:

24 When John had first preached before his coming the baptism of repentance to all the people of Is'ra-el.

25 And as John fulfilled his course, he said, Whom think ye that I am? I am not *he*. But, behold, there cometh one after me, whose shoes of *his* feet I am not worthy to loose.

26 Men *and* brethren, children of the stock of A'bra-ham, and whosoever among you feareth God, to you is the word of this salvation sent.

27 For they that dwell at Je-ru'sa-lem, and their rulers, because they knew him not, nor yet the voices of the prophets which are read every sabbath day, they have fulfilled *them* in condemning *him*.

28 And though they found no cause of death *in him*, yet desired they Pi'late that he should be slain.

29 And when they had fulfilled all that was written of him, they took *him* down from the tree, and laid *him* in a sepulchre.

30 But God raised him from the dead:

31 And he was seen many days of them which came up with him from Gal'i-lee to Je-ru'sa-lem, who are his witnesses unto the people.

32 And we declare unto you glad tidings, how that the promise which was made unto the fathers,

33 God hath fulfilled the same unto us their children, in that he hath raised up Je'sus again; as it is also written in the second psalm, Thou art my Son, this day have I begotten thee.

34 And as concerning that he raised him up from the dead, *now* no more to return to corruption, he said on this wise, I will give you the sure mercies of Da'vid.

35 Wherefore he saith also in another *psalm*, Thou shalt not suffer thine Holy One to see corruption.

36 For Da'vid, after he had served his own generation by the will of God, fell on sleep, and was laid unto his fathers, and saw corruption:

37 But he, whom God raised again, saw no corruption.

38 ¶ Be it known unto you therefore, men *and* brethren, that through this man is preached unto you the forgiveness of sins:

39 And by him all that believe are justified from all things, from which ye could not be justified by the law of Mo'ses.

40 Beware therefore, lest that come upon you, which is spoken of in the prophets;

41 Behold, ye despisers, and wonder, and perish: for I work a work in your days, a work which ye shall in no wise believe, though a man declare it unto you.

42 And when the Jews were gone out of the synagogue, the Gen'tiles besought that these words might be preached to them the next sabbath.

43 Now when the congregation was broken up, many of the Jews and religious proselytes followed Paul and Bar'na-bas: who, speaking to them, persuaded them to continue in the grace of God.

44 ¶ And the next sabbath day came almost the whole city together to hear the word of God.

45 But when the Jews saw the multitudes, they were filled with envy, and spake against those things which were spoken by Paul, contradicting and blaspheming.

46 Then Paul and Bar'na-bas waxed bold, and said, It was necessary that the word of God should first have been spoken to you: but seeing ye put it from you, and judge yourselves unworthy of everlasting life, lo, we turn to the Gen'tiles.

47 For so hath the Lord commanded us, *saying*, I have set thee to be a light of the Gen'tiles, that thou shouldest be for salvation unto the ends of the earth.

48 And when the Gen'tiles heard this, they were glad, and glorified the word of the Lord: and as many as were ordained to eternal life believed.

49 And the word of the Lord was published throughout all the region.

50 But the Jews stirred up the devout and honourable women, and the chief men of the city, and raised persecution against Paul and Bar'na-bas, and expelled them out of their coasts.

51 But they shook off the dust of their feet against them, and came unto I-co'ni-um.

52 And the disciples were filled with joy, and with the Ho'ly Ghost.

14

AND it came to pass in I-co'ni-um, that they went both together into the synagogue of the Jews, and so spake, that a great multitude both of the Jews and also of the Greeks believed.

2 But the unbelieving Jews stirred up the Gen'tiles, and made their minds evil affected against the brethren.

3 Long time therefore abode they speaking boldly in the Lord, which gave testimony unto the word of his grace, and granted signs and wonders to be done by their hands.

4 But the multitude of the city was divided: and part held with the Jews, and part with the apostles.

5 And when there was an assault made both of the Gen'tiles, and also of the Jews with their rulers, to use *them* despitefully, and to stone them,

6 They were ware of *it*, and fled unto Lys'tra and Der'be, cities of Lyc-a-o'ni-a, and unto the region that lieth round about:

7 And there they preached the gospel.

8 ¶ And there sat a certain man at Lys'tra, impotent in his feet, being a cripple from his mother's womb, who never had walked:

9 The same heard Paul speak: who stedfastly beholding him, and perceiving that he had faith to be healed,

10 Said with a loud voice, Stand upright on the feet. And he leaped and walked.

11 And when the people saw what Paul had done, they lifted up their voices, saying in the

speech of Lyc-a-o'ni-a, The gods are come down
to us in the likeness of men.
12 And they called Bar'na-bas, Ju'pi-ter; and
Paul, Mer-cu'ri-us, because he was the chief
speaker.
13 Then the priest of Ju'pi-ter, which was before their city, brought oxen and garlands unto
the gates, and would have done sacrifice with
the people.
14 *Which* when the apostles, Bar'na-bas and
Paul, heard *of*, they rent their clothes, and ran
in among the people, crying out,
15 And saying, Sirs, why do ye these things?
We also are men of like passions with you, and
preach unto you that ye should turn from these
vanities unto the living God, which made
heaven, and earth, and the sea, and all things
that are therein:
16 Who in times past suffered all nations to
walk in their own ways.
17 Nevertheless he left not himself without
witness, in that he did good, and gave us rain
from heaven, and fruitful seasons, filling our
hearts with food and gladness.
18 And with these sayings scarce restrained
they the people, that they had not done sacrifice
unto them.
19 ¶ And there came thither *certain* Jews
from An'ti-och and I-co'ni-um, who persuaded
the people, and, having stoned Paul, drew *him*
out of the city, supposing he had been dead.
20 Howbeit, as the disciples stood round
about him, he rose up, and came into the city:
and the next day he departed with Bar'na-bas to
Der'be.
21 And when they had preached the gospel
to that city, and had taught many, they returned
again to Lys'tra, and *to* I-co'ni-um, and An'ti-
och,
22 Confirming the souls of the disciples, *and*
exhorting them to continue in the faith, and
that we must through much tribulation enter
into the kingdom of God.
23 And when they had ordained them elders
in every church, and had prayed with fasting,
they commended them to the Lord, on whom
they believed.
24 And after they had passed throughout Pi-
sid'i-a, they came to Pam-phyl'i-a.
25 And when they had preached the word in
Per'ga, they went down into At'ta-li-a:
26 And thence sailed to An'ti-och, from
whence they had been recommended to the
grace of God for the work which they fulfilled.
27 And when they were come, and had gathered the church together, they rehearsed all
that God had done with them, and how he had
opened the door of faith unto the Gen'tiles.
28 And there they abode long time with the
disciples.

15 AND certain men which came down
from Ju-dæ'a taught the brethren, *and*
said, Except ye be circumcised after the manner of Mo'ses, ye cannot be saved.
2 When therefore Paul and Bar'na-bas had
no small dissension and disputation with them,
they determined that Paul and Bar'na-bas, and
certain other of them, should go up to Je-ru'sa-
lem unto the apostles and elders about this
question.
3 And being brought on their way by the
church, they passed through Phe-ni'ce and Sa-
ma'ri-a, declaring the conversion of the Gen'-
tiles: and they caused great joy unto all the
brethren.
4 And when they were come to Je-ru'sa-lem,
they were received of the church, and *of* the
apostles and elders, and they declared all things
that God had done with them.
5 But there rose up certain of the sect of the
Phar'i-sees which believed, saying, That it was
needful to circumcise them, and to command
them to keep the law of Mo'ses.
6 ¶ And the apostles and elders came together for to consider of this matter.
7 And when there had been much disputing,
Pe'ter rose up, and said unto them, Men *and*
brethren, ye know how that a good while ago
God made choice among us, that the Gen'tiles
by my mouth should hear the word of the gospel, and believe.
8 And God, which knoweth the hearts, bare
them witness, giving them the Ho'ly Ghost,
even as *he did* unto us;
9 And put no difference between us and
them, purifying their hearts by faith.
10 Now therefore why tempt ye God, to put a
yoke upon the neck of the disciples, which neither our fathers nor we were able to bear?
11 But we believe that through the grace of
the Lord Je'sus Christ we shall be saved, even
as they.
12 ¶ Then all the multitude kept silence, and
gave audience to Bar'na-bas and Paul, declaring
what miracles and wonders God had wrought
among the Gen'tiles by them.
13 ¶ And after they had held their peace,
James answered, saying, Men *and* brethren,
hearken unto me:
14 Sim'e-on hath declared how God at the
first did visit the Gen'tiles, to take out of them a
people for his name.
15 And to this agree the words of the prophets; as it is written,
16 After this I will return, and will build
again the tabernacle of Da'vid, which is fallen
down; and I will build again the ruins thereof,
and I will set it up:
17 That the residue of men might seek after
the Lord, and all the Gen'tiles, upon whom my
name is called, saith the Lord, who doeth all
these things.
18 Known unto God are all his works from
the beginning of the world.
19 Wherefore my sentence is, that we trouble not them, which from among the Gen'tiles
are turned to God:
20 But that we write unto them, that they abstain from pollutions of idols, and *from* fornication, and *from* things strangled, and *from*
blood.
21 For Mo'ses of old time hath in every city
them that preach him, being read in the synagogues every sabbath day.
22 Then pleased it the apostles and elders,
with the whole church, to send chosen men of
their own company to An'ti-och with Paul and
Bar'na-bas; *namely*, Ju'das surnamed Bar'sa-
bas, and Si'las, chief men among the brethren:
23 And they wrote *letters* by them after this
manner; The apostles and elders and brethren
send greeting unto the brethren which are of
the Gen'tiles in An'ti-och and Syr'i-a and Ci-li'-
cia:
24 Forasmuch as we have heard, that certain
which went out from us have troubled you with
words, subverting your souls, saying, *Ye must*
be circumcised, and keep the law: to whom we
gave no *such* commandment:
25 It seemed good unto us, being assembled
with one accord, to send chosen men unto you
with our beloved Bar'na-bas and Paul,

26 Men that have hazarded their lives for the name of our Lord Je'sus Christ.

27 We have sent therefore Ju'das and Si'las, who shall also tell *you* the same things by mouth.

28 For it seemed good to the Ho'ly Ghost, and to us, to lay upon you no greater burden than these necessary things;

29 That ye abstain from meats offered to idols, and from blood, and from things strangled, and from fornication: from which if ye keep yourselves, ye shall do well. Fare ye well.

30 So when they were dismissed, they came to An'ti-och: and when they had gathered the multitude together, they delivered the epistle:

31 *Which* when they had read, they rejoiced for the consolation.

32 And Ju'das and Si'las, being prophets also themselves, exhorted the brethren with many words, and confirmed *them*.

33 And after they had tarried *there* a space, they were let go in peace from the brethren unto the apostles.

34 Notwithstanding it pleased Si'las to abide there still.

35 Paul also and Bar'na-bas continued in An'ti-och, teaching and preaching the word of the Lord, with many others also.

36 ¶ And some days after Paul said unto Bar'na-bas, Let us go again and visit our brethren in every city where we have preached the word of the Lord, *and see* how they do.

37 And Bar'na-bas determined to take with them John, whose surname was Mark.

38 But Paul thought not good to take him with them, who departed from them from Pamphyl'i-a, and went not with them to the work.

39 And the contention was so sharp between them, that they departed asunder one from the other: and so Bar'na-bas took Mark, and sailed unto Cy'prus;

40 And Paul chose Si'las, and departed, being recommended by the brethren unto the grace of God.

41 And he went through Syr'i-a and Ci-li'cia, confirming the churches.

16 THEN came he to Der'be and Lys'tra: and, behold, a certain disciple was there, named Ti-mo'the-us, the son of a certain woman, which was a Jew'ess, and believed; but his father *was* a Greek:

2 Which was well reported of by the brethren that were at Lys'tra and I-co'ni-um.

3 Him would Paul have to go forth with him; and took and circumcised him because of the Jews which were in those quarters: for they knew all that his father was a Greek.

4 And as they went through the cities, they delivered them the decrees for to keep, that were ordained of the apostles and elders which were at Je-ru'sa-lem.

5 And so were the churches established in the faith, and increased in number daily.

6 Now when they had gone throughout Phryg'i-a and the region of Ga-la'tia, and were forbidden of the Ho'ly Ghost to preach the word in A'sia,

7 After they were come to Mys'ia, they assayed to go into Bi-thyn'i-a: but the Spirit suffered them not.

8 And they passing by Mys'ia came down to Tro'as.

9 And a vision appeared to Paul in the night; There stood a man of Mac-e-do'ni-a, and prayed him, saying, Come over into Mac-e-do'ni-a, and help us.

10 And after he had seen the vision, immediately we endeavoured to go into Mac-e-do'ni-a, assuredly gathering that the Lord had called us for to preach the gospel unto them.

11 Therefore loosing from Tro'as, we came with a straight course to Sam-o-thra'cia, and the next *day* to Ne-ap'o-lis;

12 And from thence to Phi-lip'pi, which is the chief city of that part of Mac-e-do'ni-a, *and* a colony: and we were in that city abiding certain days.

13 And on the sabbath we went out of the city by a river side, where prayer was wont to be made; and we sat down, and spake unto the women which resorted *thither*.

14 ¶ And a certain woman named Lyd'i-a, a seller of purple, of the city of Thy-a-ti'ra, which worshipped God, heard *us*: whose heart the Lord opened, that she attended unto the things which were spoken of Paul.

15 And when she was baptized, and her household, she besought *us*, saying, If ye have judged me to be faithful to the Lord, come into my house, and abide *there*. And she constrained us.

16 ¶ And it came to pass, as we went to prayer, a certain damsel possessed with a spirit of divination met us, which brought her masters much gain by soothsaying:

17 The same followed Paul and us, and cried, saying, These men are the servants of the most high God, which shew unto us the way of salvation.

18 And this did she many days. But Paul, being grieved, turned and said to the spirit, I command thee in the name of Je'sus Christ to come out of her. And he came out the same hour.

19 ¶ And when her masters saw that the hope of their gains was gone, they caught Paul and Si'las, and drew *them* into the marketplace unto the rulers,

20 And brought them to the magistrates, saying, These men, being Jews, do exceedingly trouble our city,

21 And teach customs, which are not lawful for us to receive, neither to observe, being Ro'mans.

22 And the multitude rose up together against them: and the magistrates rent off their clothes, and commanded to beat *them*.

23 And when they had laid many stripes upon them, they cast *them* into prison, charging the jailor to keep them safely:

24 Who, having received such a charge, thrust them into the inner prison, and made their feet fast in the stocks.

25 ¶ And at midnight Paul and Si'las prayed, and sang praises unto God: and the prisoners heard them.

26 And suddenly there was a great earthquake, so that the foundations of the prison were shaken: and immediately all the doors were opened, and every one's bands were loosed.

27 And the keeper of the prison awaking out of his sleep, and seeing the prison doors open, he drew out his sword, and would have killed himself, supposing that the prisoners had been fled.

28 But Paul cried with a loud voice, saying, Do thyself no harm: for we are all here.

29 Then he called for a light, and sprang in, and came trembling, and fell down before Paul and Si'las,

30 And brought them out, and said, Sirs, what must I do to be saved?

31 And they said, Believe on the Lord Je'sus Christ, and thou shalt be saved, and thy house.

32 And they spake unto him the word of the Lord, and to all that were in his house.

33 And he took them the same hour of the night, and washed *their* stripes; and was baptized, he and all his, straightway.

34 And when he had brought them into his house, he set meat before them, and rejoiced, believing in God with all his house.

35 And when it was day, the magistrates sent the serjeants, saying, Let those men go.

36 And the keeper of the prison told this saying to Paul, The magistrates have sent to let you go: now therefore depart, and go in peace.

37 But Paul said unto them, They have beaten us openly uncondemned, being Ro'mans, and have cast *us* into prison; and now do they thrust us out privily? nay verily; but let them come themselves and fetch us out.

38 And the serjeants told these words unto the magistrates: and they feared, when they heard that they were Ro'mans.

39 And they came and besought them, and brought *them* out, and desired *them* to depart out of the city.

40 And they went out of the prison, and entered into *the house of* Lyd'i-a: and when they had seen the brethren, they comforted them, and departed.

17 NOW when they had passed through Am-phip'o-lis and Ap-ol-lo'ni-a, they came to Thes-sa-lo-ni'ca, where was a synagogue of the Jews:

2 And Paul, as his manner was, went in unto them, and three sabbath days reasoned with them out of the scriptures,

3 Opening and alleging, that Christ must needs have suffered, and risen again from the dead; and that this Je'sus, whom I preach unto you, is Christ.

4 And some of them believed, and consorted with Paul and Si'las; and of the devout Greeks a great multitude, and of the chief women not a few.

5 ¶ But the Jews which believed not, moved with envy, took unto them certain lewd fellows of the baser sort, and gathered a company, and set all the city on an uproar, and assaulted the house of Ja'son, and sought to bring them out to the people.

6 And when they found them not, they drew Ja'son and certain brethren unto the rulers of the city, crying, These that have turned the world upside down are come hither also;

7 Whom Ja'son hath received: and these all do contrary to the decrees of Cæ'sar, saying that there is another king, *one* Je'sus.

8 And they troubled the people and the rulers of the city, when they heard these things.

9 And when they had taken security of Ja'son, and of the other, they let them go.

10 ¶ And the brethren immediately sent away Paul and Si'las by night unto Be-re'a: who coming *thither* went into the synagogue of the Jews.

11 These were more noble than those in Thes-sa-lo-ni'ca, in that they received the word with all readiness of mind, and searched the scriptures daily, whether those things were so.

12 Therefore many of them believed; also of honourable women which were Greeks, and of men, not a few.

13 But when the Jews of Thes-sa-lo-ni'ca had knowledge that the word of God was preached of Paul at Be-re'a, they came thither also, and stirred up the people.

14 And then immediately the brethren sent away Paul to go as it were to the sea: but Si'las and Ti-mo'the-us abode there still.

15 And they that conducted Paul brought him unto Ath'ens: and receiving a commandment unto Si'las and Ti-mo'the-us for to come to him with all speed, they departed.

16 ¶ Now while Paul waited for them at Ath'ens, his spirit was stirred in him, when he saw the city wholly given to idolatry.

17 Therefore disputed he in the synagogue with the Jews, and with the devout persons, and in the market daily with them that met with him.

18 Then certain philosophers of the Ep-i-cu-re'ans, and of the Sto'icks, encountered him. And some said, What will this babbler say? other some, He seemeth to be a setter forth of strange gods: because he preached unto them Je'sus, and the resurrection.

19 And they took him, and brought him unto Ar-e-op'a-gus, saying, May we know what this new doctrine, whereof thou speakest, *is?*

20 For thou bringest certain strange things to our ears: we would know therefore what these things mean.

21 (For all the Ath-e'ni-ans and strangers which were there spent their time in nothing else, but either to tell, or to hear some new thing.)

22 ¶ Then Paul stood in the midst of Mars' hill, and said, *Ye* men of Ath'ens, I perceive that in all things ye are too superstitious.

23 For as I passed by, and beheld your devotions, I found an altar with this inscription, TO THE UNKNOWN GOD. Whom therefore ye ignorantly worship, him declare I unto you.

24 God that made the world and all things therein, seeing that he is Lord of heaven and earth, dwelleth not in temples made with hands;

25 Neither is worshipped with men's hands, as though he needed any thing, seeing he giveth to all life and breath, and all things;

26 And hath made of one blood all nations of men for to dwell on all the face of the earth, and hath determined the times before appointed, and the bounds of their habitation;

27 That they should seek the Lord, if haply they might feel after him, and find him, though he be not far from every one of us:

28 For in him we live, and move, and have our being; as certain also of your own poets have said, For we are also his offspring.

29 Forasmuch then as we are the offspring of God, we ought not to think that the Godhead is like unto gold, or silver, or stone, graven by art and man's device.

30 And the times of this ignorance God winked at; but now commandeth all men every where to repent:

31 Because he hath appointed a day, in the which he will judge the world in righteousness by *that* man whom he hath ordained; *whereof* he hath given assurance unto all *men*, in that he hath raised him from the dead.

32 ¶ And when they heard of the resurrection of the dead, some mocked: and others said, We will hear thee again of this *matter*.

33 So Paul departed from among them.

34 Howbeit certain men clave unto him, and believed: among the which *was* Di-o-nys'ius the Ar-e-op'a-gite, and a woman named Dam'a-ris, and others with them.

18 AFTER these things Paul departed from
Ath'ens, and came to Cor'inth;
2 And found a certain Jew named A'qui-la,
born in Pon'tus, lately come from It'a-ly, with
his wife Pris-cil'la; (because that Clau'di-us had
commanded all Jews to depart from Rome:)
and came unto them.
3 And because he was of the same craft, he
abode with them, and wrought: for by their occupation they were tentmakers.
4 And he reasoned in the synagogue every
sabbath, and persuaded the Jews and the
Greeks.
5 And when Si'las and Ti-mo'the-us were
come from Mac-e-do'ni-a, Paul was pressed in
the spirit, and testified to the Jews *that* Je'sus
was Christ.
6 And when they opposed themselves, and
blasphemed, he shook *his* raiment, and said
unto them, Your blood *be* upon your own heads;
I *am* clean: from henceforth I will go unto the
Gen'tiles.
7 ¶ And he departed thence, and entered
into a certain *man's* house, named Jus'tus, *one*
that worshipped God, whose house joined hard
to the synagogue.
8 And Cris'pus, the chief ruler of the synagogue, believed on the Lord with all his house;
and many of the Co-rin'thi-ans hearing believed, and were baptized.
9 Then spake the Lord to Paul in the night by
a vision, Be not afraid, but speak, and hold not
thy peace:
10 For I am with thee, and no man shall set
on thee to hurt thee: for I have much people in
this city.
11 And he continued *there* a year and six
months, teaching the word of God among them.
12 ¶ And when Gal'li-o was the deputy of A-
cha'ia, the Jews made insurrection with one accord against Paul, and brought him to the judgment seat,
13 Saying, This *fellow* persuadeth men to
worship God contrary to the law.
14 And when Paul was now about to open *his*
mouth, Gal'li-o said unto the Jews, If it were a
matter of wrong or wicked lewdness, O *ye*
Jews, reason would that I should bear with you:
15 But if it be a question of words and
names, and *of* your law, look ye *to it;* for I will
be no judge of such *matters.*
16 And he drave them from the judgment
seat.
17 Then all the Greeks took Sos'the-nes, the
chief ruler of the synagogue, and beat *him* before the judgment seat. And Gal'li-o cared for
none of those things.
18 ¶ And Paul *after this* tarried *there* yet a
good while, and then took his leave of the
brethren, and sailed thence into Syr'i-a, and
with him Pris-cil'la and A'qui-la; having shorn
his head in Cen'-chre-a: for he had a vow.
19 And he came to Eph'e-sus, and left them
there: but he himself entered into the synagogue, and reasoned with the Jews.
20 When they desired *him* to tarry longer
time with them, he consented not;
21 But bade them farewell, saying, I must by
all means keep this feast that cometh in Je-ru'-
sa-lem: but I will return again unto you, if God
will. And he sailed from Eph'e-sus.
22 And when he had landed at Cæs-a-re'a,
and gone up, and saluted the church, he went
down to An'ti-och.
23 And after he had spent some time *there,*
he departed, and went over *all* the country of
Ga-la'tia and Phryg'i-a in order, strengthening
all the disciples.
24 ¶ And a certain Jew named A-pol'los,
born at Al-ex-an'dri-a, an eloquent man, *and*
mighty in the scriptures, came to Eph'e-sus.
25 This man was instructed in the way of the
Lord; and being fervent in the spirit, he spake
and taught diligently the things of the Lord,
knowing only the baptism of John.
26 And he began to speak boldly in the synagogue: whom when A'qui-la and Pris-cil'la had
heard, they took him unto *them,* and expounded
unto him the way of God more perfectly.
27 And when he was disposed to pass into A-
cha'ia, the brethren wrote, exhorting the disciples to receive him: who, when he was come,
helped them much which had believed through
grace:
28 For he mightily convinced the Jews, *and*
that publickly, shewing by the scriptures that
Je'sus was Christ.

19 AND it came to pass, that, while A-pol'-
los was at Cor'inth, Paul having passed
through the upper coasts came to Eph'e-sus:
and finding certain disciples,
2 He said unto them, Have ye received the
Ho'ly Ghost since ye believed? And they said
unto him, We have not so much as heard
whether there be any Ho'ly Ghost.
3 And he said unto them, Unto what then
were ye baptized? And they said, Unto John's
baptism.
4 Then said Paul, John verily baptized with
the baptism of repentance, saying unto the people, that they should believe on him which
should come after him, that is, on Christ Je'sus.
5 When they heard *this,* they were baptized
in the name of the Lord Je'sus.
6 And when Paul had laid *his* hands upon
them, the Ho'ly Ghost came on them; and they
spake with tongues, and prophesied.
7 And all the men were about twelve.
8 And he went into the synagogue, and spake
boldly for the space of three months, disputing
and persuading the things concerning the kingdom of God.
9 But when divers were hardened, and believed not, but spake evil of that way before the
multitude, he departed from them, and separated the disciples, disputing daily in the school
of one Ty-ran'nus.
10 And this continued by the space of two
years; so that all they which dwelt in A'sia
heard the word of the Lord Je'sus, both Jews
and Greeks.
11 And God wrought special miracles by the
hands of Paul:
12 So that from his body were brought unto
the sick handkerchiefs or aprons, and the diseases departed from them, and the evil spirits
went out of them.
13 ¶ Then certain of the vagabond Jews, ex-
orcists, took upon them to call over them which
had evil spirits the name of the Lord Je'sus, saying, We adjure you by Je'sus whom Paul
preacheth.
14 And there were seven sons of *one* Sce'va,
a Jew, *and* chief of the priests, which did so.
15 And the evil spirit answered and said, Je'-
sus I know, and Paul I know; but who are ye?
16 And the man in whom the evil spirit was
leaped on them, and overcame them, and prevailed against them, so that they fled out of that
house naked and wounded.
17 And this was known to all the Jews and
Greeks also dwelling at Eph'e-sus; and fear fell

on them all, and the name of the Lord Je'sus
was magnified.
18 And many that believed came, and confessed, and shewed their deeds.
19 Many of them also which used curious
arts brought their books together, and burned
them before all *men:* and they counted the price
of them, and found *it* fifty thousand *pieces* of
silver.
20 So mightily grew the word of God and
prevailed.
21 ¶ After these things were ended, Paul
purposed in the spirit, when he had passed
through Mac-e-do'ni-a and A-cha'ia, to go to Je-
ru'sa-lem, saying, After I have been there, I
must also see Rome.
22 So he sent into Mac-e-do'ni-a two of them
that ministered unto him, Ti-mo'the-us and E-
ras'tus; but he himself stayed in A'sia for a season.
23 And the same time there arose no small
stir about that way.
24 For a certain *man* named De-me'tri-us, a
silversmith, which made silver shrines for Di-
an'a, brought no small gain unto the craftsmen;
25 Whom he called together with the workmen of like occupation, and said, Sirs, ye know
that by this craft we have our wealth.
26 Moreover ye see and hear, that not alone
at Eph'e-sus, but almost throughout all A'sia,
this Paul hath persuaded and turned away
much people, saying that they be no gods,
which are made with hands:
27 So that not only this our craft is in danger
to be set at nought; but also that the temple of
the great goddess Di-an'a should be despised,
and her magnificence should be destroyed,
whom all A'sia and the world worshippeth.
28 And when they heard *these sayings,* they
were full of wrath, and cried out, saying, Great
is Di-an'a of the E-phe'sians.
29 And the whole city was filled with confusion: and having caught Ga'ius and Ar-is-tar'-
chus, men of Mac-e-do'ni-a, Paul's companions
in travel, they rushed with one accord into the
theatre.
30 And when Paul would have entered in
unto the people, the disciples suffered him not.
31 And certain of the chief of A'sia, which
were his friends, sent unto him, desiring *him*
that he would not adventure himself into the
theatre.
32 Some therefore cried one thing, and some
another: for the assembly was confused; and
the more part knew not wherefore they were
come together.
33 And they drew Al-ex-an'der out of the
multitude, the Jews putting him forward. And
Al-ex-an'der beckoned with the hand, and
would have made his defence unto the people.
34 But when they knew that he was a Jew, all
with one voice about the space of two hours
cried out, Great *is* Di-an'a of the E-phe'sians.
35 And when the townclerk had appeased
the people, he said, *Ye* men of Eph'e-sus, what
man is there that knoweth not how that the city
of the E-phe'sians is a worshipper of the great
goddess Di-an'a, and of the *image* which fell
down from Ju'pi-ter?
36 Seeing then that these things cannot be
spoken against, ye ought to be quiet, and to do
nothing rashly.
37 For ye have brought hither these men,
which are neither robbers of churches, nor yet
blasphemers of your goddess.
38 Wherefore if De-me'tri-us, and the craftsmen which are with him, have a matter against
any man, the law is open, and there are deputies: let them implead one another.
39 But if ye enquire any thing concerning
other matters, it shall be determined in a lawful
assembly.
40 For we are in danger to be called in question for this day's uproar, there being no cause
whereby we may give an account of this concourse.
41 And when he had thus spoken, he dismissed the assembly.

20 AND after the uproar was ceased, Paul
called unto *him* the disciples, and embraced *them,* and departed for to go into Mac-e-
do'ni-a.
2 And when he had gone over those parts,
and had given them much exhortation, he came
into Greece,
3 And *there* abode three months. And when
the Jews laid wait for him, as he was about to
sail into Syr'i-a, he purposed to return through
Mac-e-do'ni-a.
4 And there accompanied him into A'sia
Sop'a-ter of Be-re'a; and of the Thes-sa-lo'ni-
ans, Ar-is-tar'chus and Se-cun'dus; and Ga'ius
of Der'be, and Ti-mo'the-us; and of A'sia, Tych'-
i-cus and Troph'i-mus.
5 These going before tarried for us at Tro'as.
6 And we sailed away from Phi-lip'pi after
the days of unleavened bread, and came unto
them to Tro'as in five days; where we abode
seven days.
7 And upon the first *day* of the week, when
the disciples came together to break bread,
Paul preached unto them, ready to depart on
the morrow; and continued his speech until
midnight.
8 And there were many lights in the upper
chamber, where they were gathered together.
9 And there sat in a window a certain young
man named Eu'ty-chus, being fallen into a deep
sleep: and as Paul was long preaching, he sunk
down with sleep, and fell down from the third
loft, and was taken up dead.
10 And Paul went down, and fell on him, and
embracing *him* said, Trouble not yourselves; for
his life is in him.
11 When he therefore was come up again,
and had broken bread, and eaten, and talked a
long while, even till break of day, so he departed.
12 And they brought the young man alive,
and were not a little comforted.
13 ¶ And we went before to ship, and sailed
unto As'sos, there intending to take in Paul: for
so had he appointed, minding himself to go
afoot.
14 And when he met with us at As'sos, we
took him in, and came to Mit-y-le'ne.
15 And we sailed thence, and came the next
day over against Chi'os: and the next *day* we
arrived at Sa'mos, and tarried at Tro-gyl'li-um;
and the next *day* we came to Mi-le'tus.
16 For Paul had determined to sail by Eph'e-
sus, because he would not spend the time in A'-
sia: for he hasted, if it were possible for him, to
be at Je-ru'sa-lem the day of Pen'te-cost.
17 ¶ And from Mi-le'tus he sent to Eph'e-sus,
and called the elders of the church.
18 And when they were come to him, he said
unto them, Ye know, from the first day that I
came into A'sia, after what manner I have been
with you at all seasons,
19 Serving the Lord with all humility of
mind, and with many tears, and temptations,
which befell me by the lying in wait of the Jews:

20 *And* how I kept back nothing that was
profitable *unto you,* but have shewed you, and
have taught you publickly, and from house to
house,
21 Testifying both to the Jews, and also to
the Greeks, repentance toward God, and faith
toward our Lord Je'sus Christ.
22 And now, behold, I go bound in the spirit
unto Je-ru'sa-lem, not knowing the things that
shall befall me there:
23 Save that the Ho'ly Ghost witnesseth in
every city, saying that bonds and afflictions
abide me.
24 But none of these things move me, neither
count I my life dear unto myself, so that I might
finish my course with joy, and the ministry,
which I have received of the Lord Je'sus, to testify the gospel of the grace of God.
25 And now, behold, I know that ye all,
among whom I have gone preaching the kingdom of God, shall see my face no more.
26 Wherefore I take you to record this day,
that I *am* pure from the blood of all *men*.
27 For I have not shunned to declare unto
you all the counsel of God.
28 ¶ Take heed therefore unto yourselves,
and to all the flock, over the which the Ho'ly
Ghost hath made you overseers, to feed the
church of God, which he hath purchased with
his own blood.
29 For I know this, that after my departing
shall grievous wolves enter in among you, not
sparing the flock.
30 Also of your own selves shall men arise,
speaking perverse things, to draw away disciples after them.
31 Therefore watch, and remember, that by
the space of three years I ceased not to warn
every one night and day with tears.
32 And now, brethren, I commend you to
God, and to the word of his grace, which is able
to build you up, and to give you an inheritance
among all them which are sanctified.
33 I have coveted no man's silver, or gold, or
apparel.
34 Yea, ye yourselves know, that these hands
have ministered unto my necessities, and to
them that were with me.
35 I have shewed you all things, how that so
labouring ye ought to support the weak, and to
remember the words of the Lord Je'sus, how he
said, It is more blessed to give than to receive.
36 ¶ And when he had thus spoken, he
kneeled down, and prayed with them all.
37 And they all wept sore, and fell on Paul's
neck, and kissed him,
38 Sorrowing most of all for the words which
he spake, that they should see his face no more.
And they accompanied him unto the ship.

21 AND it came to pass, that after we were
gotten from them, and had launched, we
came with a straight course unto Co'os, and the
day following unto Rhodes, and from thence
unto Pat'a-ra:
2 And finding a ship sailing over unto Phe-
ni'cia, we went aboard, and set forth.
3 Now when we had discovered Cy'prus, we
left it on the left hand, and sailed into Syr'i-a,
and landed at Tyre: for there the ship was to
unlade her burden.
4 And finding disciples, we tarried there
seven days: who said to Paul through the Spirit,
that he should not go up to Je-ru'sa-lem.
5 And when we had accomplished those
days, we departed and went our way; and they
all brought us on our way, with wives and children, till *we were* out of the city: and we
kneeled down on the shore, and prayed.
6 And when we had taken our leave one of
another, we took ship; and they returned home
again.
7 And when we had finished *our* course from
Tyre, we came to Ptol-e-ma'is, and saluted the
brethren, and abode with them one day.
8 And the next *day* we that were of Paul's
company departed, and came unto Cæs-a-re'a:
and we entered into the house of Phil'ip the
evangelist, which was *one* of the seven; and
abode with him.
9 And the same man had four daughters, virgins, which did prophesy.
10 And as we tarried *there* many days, there
came down from Ju-dæ'a a certain prophet,
named Ag'a-bus.
11 And when he was come unto us, he took
Paul's girdle, and bound his own hands and
feet, and said, Thus saith the Ho'ly Ghost, So
shall the Jews at Je-ru'sa-lem bind the man that
owneth this girdle, and shall deliver *him* into
the hands of the Gen'tiles.
12 And when we heard these things, both we,
and they of that place, besought him not to go
up to Je-ru'sa-lem.
13 Then Paul answered, What mean ye to
weep and to break mine heart? for I am ready
not to be bound only, but also to die at Je-ru'sa-
lem for the name of the Lord Je'sus.
14 And when he would not be persuaded, we
ceased, saying, The will of the Lord be done.
15 And after those days we took up our carriages, and went up to Je-ru'sa-lem.
16 There went with us also *certain* of the disciples of Cæs-a-re-a, and brought with them
one Mna'son of Cy'prus, an old disciple, with
whom we should lodge.
17 And when we were come to Je-ru'sa-lem,
the brethren received us gladly.
18 And the *day* following Paul went in with
us unto James; and all the elders were present.
19 And when he had saluted them, he declared particularly what things God had
wrought among the Gen'tiles by his ministry.
20 And when they heard *it*, they glorified the
Lord, and said unto him, Thou seest, brother,
how many thousands of Jews there are which
believe; and they are all zealous of the law:
21 And they are informed of thee, that thou
teachest all the Jews which are among the
Gen'tiles to forsake Mo'ses, saying that they
ought not to circumcise *their* children, neither
to walk after the customs.
22 What is it therefore? the multitude must
needs come together: for they will hear that
thou art come.
23 Do therefore this that we say to thee: We
have four men which have a vow on them;
24 Them take, and purify thyself with them,
and be at charges with them, that they may
shave *their* heads: and all may know that those
things, whereof they were informed concerning
thee, are nothing; but *that* thou thyself also
walkest orderly, and keepest the law.
25 As touching the Gen'tiles which believe,
we have written *and* concluded that they observe no such thing, save only that they keep
themselves from *things* offered to idols, and
from blood, and from strangled, and from fornication.
26 Then Paul took the men, and the next day
purifying himself with them entered into the
temple, to signify the accomplishment of the
days of purification, until that an offering
should be offered for every one of them.

27 And when the seven days were almost ended, the Jews which were of A'sia, when they saw him in the temple, stirred up all the people, and laid hands on him,

28 Crying out, Men of Is'ra-el, help: This is the man, that teacheth all *men* every where against the people, and the law, and this place: and further brought Greeks also into the temple, and hath polluted this holy place.

29 (For they had seen before with him in the city Troph'i-mus an E-phe'sian, whom they supposed that Paul had brought into the temple.)

30 And all the city was moved, and the people ran together: and they took Paul, and drew him out of the temple: and forthwith the doors were shut.

31 And as they went about to kill him, tidings came unto the chief captain of the band, that all Je-ru'sa-lem was in an uproar.

32 Who immediately took soldiers and centurions, and ran down unto them: and when they saw the chief captain and the soldiers, they left beating of Paul.

33 Then the chief captain came near, and took him, and commanded *him* to be bound with two chains; and demanded who he was, and what he had done.

34 And some cried one thing, some another, among the multitude: and when he could not know the certainty for the tumult, he commanded him to be carried into the castle.

35 And when he came upon the stairs, so it was, that he was borne of the soldiers for the violence of the people.

36 For the multitude of the people followed after, crying, Away with him.

37 And as Paul was to be led into the castle, he said unto the chief captain, May I speak unto thee? Who said, Canst thou speak Greek?

38 Art not thou that E-gyp'tian, which before these days madest an uproar, and leddest out into the wilderness four thousand men that were murderers?

39 But Paul said, I am a man *which am* a Jew of Tar'sus, *a city* in Ci-li'cia, a citizen of no mean city: and, I beseech thee, suffer me to speak unto the people.

40 And when he had given him licence, Paul stood on the stairs, and beckoned with the hand unto the people. And when there was made a great silence, he spake unto *them* in the He'brew tongue, saying,

22 MEN, brethren, and fathers, hear ye my defence *which I make* now unto you.

2 (And when they heard that he spake in the He'brew tongue to them, they kept the more silence: and he saith,)

3 I am verily a man *which am* a Jew, born in Tar'sus, *a city* in Ci-li'cia, yet brought up in this city at the feet of Ga-ma'li-el, *and* taught according to the perfect manner of the law of the fathers, and was zealous toward God, as ye all are this day.

4 And I persecuted this way unto the death, binding and delivering into prisons both men and women.

5 As also the high priest doth bear me witness, and all the estate of the elders: from whom also I received letters unto the brethren, and went to Da-mas'cus, to bring them which were there bound unto Je-ru'sa-lem, for to be punished.

6 And it came to pass, that, as I made my journey, and was come nigh unto Da-mas'cus about noon, suddenly there shone from heaven a great light round about me.

7 And I fell unto the ground, and heard a voice saying unto me, Saul, Saul, why persecutest thou me?

8 And I answered, Who art thou, Lord? And he said unto me, I am Je'sus of Naz'a-reth, whom thou persecutest.

9 And they that were with me saw indeed the light, and were afraid; but they heard not the voice of him that spake to me.

10 And I said, What shall I do, Lord? And the Lord said unto me, Arise, and go into Da-mas'cus; and there it shall be told thee of all things which are appointed for thee to do.

11 And when I could not see for the glory of that light, being led by the hand of them that were with me, I came into Da-mas'cus.

12 And one An-a-ni'as, a devout man according to the law, having a good report of all the Jews which dwelt *there*,

13 Came unto me, and stood, and said unto me, Brother Saul, receive thy sight. And the same hour I looked up upon him.

14 And he said, The God of our fathers hath chosen thee, that thou shouldest know his will, and see that Just One, and shouldest hear the voice of his mouth.

15 For thou shalt be his witness unto all men of what thou hast seen and heard.

16 And now why tarriest thou? arise, and be baptized, and wash away thy sins, calling on the name of the Lord.

17 And it came to pass, that, when I was come again to Je-ru'sa-lem, even while I prayed in the temple, I was in a trance;

18 And saw him saying unto me, Make haste, and get thee quickly out of Je-ru'sa-lem: for they will not receive thy testimony concerning me.

19 And I said, Lord, they know that I imprisoned and beat in every synagogue them that believed on thee:

20 And when the blood of thy martyr Ste'phen was shed, I also was standing by, and consenting unto his death, and kept the raiment of them that slew him.

21 And he said unto me, Depart: for I will send thee far hence unto the Gen'tiles.

22 And they gave him audience unto this word, and *then* lifted up their voices, and said, Away with such a *fellow* from the earth: for it is not fit that he should live.

23 And as they cried out, and cast off *their* clothes, and threw dust into the air,

24 The chief captain commanded him to be brought into the castle, and bade that he should be examined by scourging; that he might know wherefore they cried so against him.

25 And as they bound him with thongs, Paul said unto the centurion that stood by, Is it lawful for you to scourge a man that is a Ro'man, and uncondemned?

26 When the centurion heard *that*, he went and told the chief captain, saying, Take heed what thou doest: for this man is a Ro'man.

27 Then the chief captain came, and said unto him, Tell me, art thou a Ro'man? He said, Yea.

28 And the chief captain answered, With a great sum obtained I this freedom. And Paul said, But I was *free* born.

29 Then straightway they departed from him which should have examined him: and the chief captain also was afraid, after he knew that he was a Ro'man, and because he had bound him.

30 On the morrow, because he would have known the certainty wherefore he was accused of the Jews, he loosed him from *his* bands, and

commanded the chief priests and all their council to appear, and brought Paul down, and set him before them.

23 AND Paul, earnestly beholding the council, said, Men *and* brethren, I have lived in all good conscience before God until this day.

2 And the high priest An-a-ni'as commanded them that stood by him to smite him on the mouth.

3 Then said Paul unto him, God shall smite thee, *thou* whited wall: for sittest thou to judge me after the law, and commandest me to be smitten contrary to the law?

4 And they that stood by said, Revilest thou God's high priest?

5 Then said Paul, I wist not, brethren, that he was the high priest: for it is written, Thou shalt not speak evil of the ruler of thy people.

6 But when Paul perceived that the one part were Sad'du-cees, and the other Phar'i-sees, he cried out in the council, Men *and* brethren, I am a Phar'i-see, the son of a Phar'i-see: of the hope and resurrection of the dead I am called in question.

7 And when he had so said, there arose a dissension between the Phar'i-sees and the Sad'du-cees: and the multitude was divided.

8 For the Sad'du-cees say that there is no resurrection, neither angel, nor spirit: but the Phar'i-sees confess both.

9 And there arose a great cry: and the scribes *that were* of the Phar'i-sees' part arose, and strove, saying, We find no evil in this man: but if a spirit or an angel hath spoken to him, let us not fight against God.

10 And when there arose a great dissension, the chief captain, fearing lest Paul should have been pulled in pieces of them, commanded the soldiers to go down, and to take him by force from among them, and to bring *him* into the castle.

11 And the night following the Lord stood by him, and said, Be of good cheer, Paul: for as thou hast testified of me in Je-ru'sa-lem, so must thou bear witness also at Rome.

12 And when it was day, certain of the Jews banded together, and bound themselves under a curse, saying that they would neither eat nor drink till they had killed Paul.

13 And they were more than forty which had made this conspiracy.

14 And they came to the chief priests and elders, and said, We have bound ourselves under a great curse, that we will eat nothing until we have slain Paul.

15 Now therefore ye with the council signify to the chief captain that he bring him down unto you to morrow, as though ye would enquire something more perfectly concerning him: and we, or ever he come near, are ready to kill him.

16 And when Paul's sister's son heard of their lying in wait, he went and entered into the castle, and told Paul.

17 Then Paul called one of the centurions unto *him*, and said, Bring this young man unto the chief captain: for he hath a certain thing to tell him.

18 So he took him, and brought *him* to the chief captain, and said, Paul the prisoner called me unto *him*, and prayed me to bring this young man unto thee, who hath something to say unto thee.

19 Then the chief captain took him by the hand, and went *with him* aside privately, and asked *him*, What is that thou hast to tell me?

20 And he said, The Jews have agreed to desire thee that thou wouldest bring down Paul to morrow into the council, as though they would enquire somewhat of him more perfectly.

21 But do not thou yield unto them: for there lie in wait for him of them more than forty men, which have bound themselves with an oath, that they will neither eat nor drink till they have killed him: and now are they ready, looking for a promise from thee.

22 So the chief captain *then* let the young man depart, and charged *him, See thou* tell no man that thou hast shewed these things to me.

23 And he called unto *him* two centurions, saying, Make ready two hundred soldiers to go to Cæs-a-re'a, and horsemen threescore and ten, and spearmen two hundred, at the third hour of the night;

24 And provide *them* beasts, that they may set Paul on, and bring *him* safe unto Fe'lix the governor.

25 And he wrote a letter after this manner:

26 Clau'di-us Lys'ias unto the most excellent governor Fe'lix *sendeth* greeting.

27 This man was taken of the Jews, and should have been killed of them: then came I with an army, and rescued him, having understood that he was a Ro'man.

28 And when I would have known the cause wherefore they accused him, I brought him forth into their council:

29 Whom I perceived to be accused of questions of their law, but to have nothing laid to his charge worthy of death or of bonds.

30 And when it was told me how that the Jews laid wait for the man, I sent straightway to thee, and gave commandment to his accusers also to say before thee what *they had* against him. Farewell.

31 Then the soldiers, as it was commanded them, took Paul, and brought *him* by night to An-tip'a-tris.

32 On the morrow they left the horsemen to go with him, and returned to the castle:

33 Who, when they came to Cæs-a-re'a, and delivered the epistle to the governor, presented Paul also before him.

34 And when the governor had read *the letter*, he asked of what province he was. And when he understood that *he was* of Ci-li'cia;

35 I will hear thee, said he, when thine accusers are also come. And he commanded him to be kept in Her'od's judgment hall.

24 AND after five days An-a-ni'as the high priest descended with the elders, and *with* a certain orator *named* Ter-tul'lus, who informed the governor against Paul.

2 And when he was called forth, Ter-tul'lus began to accuse *him*, saying, Seeing that by thee we enjoy great quietness, and that very worthy deeds are done unto this nation by thy providence,

3 We accept *it* always, and in all places, most noble Fe'lix, with all thankfulness.

4 Notwithstanding, that I be not further tedious unto thee, I pray thee that thou wouldest hear us of thy clemency a few words.

5 For we have found this man *a* pestilent *fellow*, and a mover of sedition among all the Jews throughout the world, and a ringleader of the sect of the Naz'a-renes:

6 Who also hath gone about to profane the temple: whom we took, and would have judged according to our law.

7 But the chief captain Lys'ias came *upon us*,

and with great violence took *him* away out of
our hands,
8 Commanding his accusers to come unto
thee: by examining of whom thyself mayest
take knowledge of all these things, whereof we
accuse him.
9 And the Jews also assented, saying that
these things were so.
10 Then Paul, after that the governor had
beckoned unto him to speak, answered, Forasmuch as I know that thou hast been of many
years a judge unto this nation, I do the more
cheerfully answer for myself:
11 Because that thou mayest understand,
that there are yet but twelve days since I went
up to Je-ru'sa-lem for to worship.
12 And they neither found me in the temple
disputing with any man, neither raising up the
people, neither in the synagogues, nor in the
city:
13 Neither can they prove the things whereof
they now accuse me.
14 But this I confess unto thee, that after the
way which they call heresy, so worship I the
God of my fathers, believing all things which
are written in the law and in the prophets:
15 And have hope toward God, which they
themselves also allow, that there shall be a resurrection of the dead, both of the just and unjust.
16 And herein do I exercise myself, to have
always a conscience void of offence toward
God, and *toward* men.
17 Now after many years I came to bring
alms to my nation, and offerings.
18 Whereupon certain Jews from A'sia found
me purified in the temple, neither with multitude, nor with tumult.
19 Who ought to have been here before thee,
and object, if they had ought against me.
20 Or else let these same *here* say, if they
have found any evil doing in me, while I stood
before the council,
21 Except it be for this one voice, that I cried
standing among them, Touching the resurrection of the dead I am called in question by you
this day.
22 And when Fe'lix heard these things, having more perfect knowledge of *that* way, he deferred them, and said, When Lys'ias the chief
captain shall come down, I will know the uttermost of your matter.
23 And he commanded a centurion to keep
Paul, and to let *him* have liberty, and that he
should forbid none of his acquaintance to minister or come unto him.
24 And after certain days, when Fe'lix came
with his wife Dru-sil'la, which was a Jew'ess, he
sent for Paul, and heard him concerning the
faith in Christ.
25 And as he reasoned of righteousness, temperance, and judgment to come, Fe'lix trembled, and answered, Go thy way for this time;
when I have a convenient season, I will call for
thee.
26 He hoped also that money should have
been given him of Paul, that he might loose
him: wherefore he sent for him the oftener, and
communed with him.
27 But after two years Por'ci-us Fes'tus came
into Fe'lix' room: and Fe'lix, willing to shew the
Jews a pleasure, left Paul bound.

25 NOW when Fes'tus was come into the
province, after three days he ascended
from Cæs-a-re'a to Je-ru'sa-lem.
2 Then the high priest and the chief of the
Jews informed him against Paul, and besought
him,
3 And desired favour against him, that he
would send for him to Je-ru'sa-lem, laying wait
in the way to kill him.
4 But Fes'tus answered, that Paul should be
kept at Cæs-a-re'a, and that he himself would
depart shortly *thither*.
5 Let them therefore, said he, which among
you are able, go down with *me*, and accuse this
man, if there be any wickedness in him.
6 And when he had tarried among them
more than ten days, he went down unto Cæs-a-
re'a; and the next day sitting on the judgment
seat commanded Paul to be brought.
7 And when he was come, the Jews which
came down from Je-ru'sa-lem stood round
about, and laid many and grievous complaints
against Paul, which they could not prove.
8 While he answered for himself, Neither
against the law of the Jews, neither against the
temple, nor yet against Caesar, have I offended
any thing at all.
9 But Fes'tus, willing to do the Jews a pleasure, answered Paul, and said, Wilt thou go up
to Je-ru'sa-lem, and there be judged of these
things before me?
10 Then said Paul, I stand at Cæ'sar's judgment seat, where I ought to be judged: to the
Jews have I done no wrong, as thou very well
knowest.
11 For if I be an offender, or have committed
any thing worthy of death, I refuse not to die:
but if there be none of these things whereof
these accuse me, no man may deliver me unto
them. I appeal unto Cæ'sar.
12 Then Fes'tus, when he had conferred with
the council, answered, Hast thou appealed unto
Cæ'sar? unto Cæ'sar shalt thou go.
13 And after certain days king A-grip'pa and
Ber-ni'ce came unto Cæs-a-re'a to salute Fes'-
tus.
14 And when they had been there many
days, Fes'tus declared Paul's cause unto the
king, saying, There is a certain man left in
bonds by Fe'lix:
15 About whom, when I was at Je-ru'sa-lem,
the chief priests and the elders of the Jews informed *me*, desiring *to have* judgment against
him.
16 To whom I answered, It is not the manner
of the Ro'mans to deliver any man to die, before
that he which is accused have the accusers face
to face, and have licence to answer for himself
concerning the crime laid against him.
17 Therefore, when they were come hither,
without any delay on the morrow I sat on the
judgment seat, and commanded the man to be
brought forth.
18 Against whom when the accusers stood
up, they brought none accusation of such things
as I supposed:
19 But had certain questions against him of
their own superstition, and of one Je'sus, which
was dead, whom Paul affirmed to be alive.
20 And because I doubted of such manner of
questions, I asked *him* whether he would go to
Je-ru'sa-lem, and there be judged of these matters.
21 But when Paul had appealed to be reserved unto the hearing of Au-gus'tus, I commanded him to be kept till I might send him to
Cæ'sar.
22 Then A-grip'pa said unto Fes'tus, I would
also hear the man myself. To morrow, said he,
thou shalt hear him.
23 And on the morrow, when A-grip'pa was

come, and Ber-ni′ce, with great pomp, and was
entered into the place of hearing, with the chief
captains, and principal men of the city, at Fes′-
tus′ commandment Paul was brought forth.
24 And Fes′tus said, King A-grip′pa, and all
men which are here present with us, ye see this
man, about whom all the multitude of the Jews
have dealt with me, both at Je-ru′sa-lem, and
also here, crying that he ought not to live any
longer.
25 But when I found that he had committed
nothing worthy of death, and that he himself
hath appealed to Au-gus′tus, I have determined
to send him.
26 Of whom I have no certain thing to write
unto my lord. Wherefore I have brought him
forth before you, and specially before thee, O
king A-grip′pa, that, after examination had, I
might have somewhat to write.
27 For it seemeth to me unreasonable to send
a prisoner, and not withal to signify the crimes
laid against him.

26 THEN A-grip′pa said unto Paul, Thou
art permitted to speak for thyself. Then
Paul stretched forth the hand, and answered for
himself:
2 I think myself happy, king A-grip′pa, because I shall answer for myself this day before
thee touching all the things whereof I am accused of the Jews:
3 Especially *because I know* thee to be expert in all customs and questions which are
among the Jews: wherefore I beseech thee to
hear me patiently.
4 My manner of life from my youth, which
was at the first among mine own nation at Je-
ru′sa-lem, know all the Jews;
5 Which knew me from the beginning, if they
would testify, that after the most straitest sect
of our religion I lived a Phar′i-see.
6 And now I stand and am judged for the
hope of the promise made of God unto our fathers:
7 Unto which *promise* our twelve tribes, instantly serving *God* day and night, hope to
come. For which hope's sake, king A-grip′pa, I
am accused of the Jews.
8 Why should it be thought a thing incredible
with you, that God should raise the dead?
9 I verily thought with myself, that I ought to
do many things contrary to the name of Je′sus
of Naz′a-reth.
10 Which thing I also did in Je-ru′sa-lem: and
many of the saints did I shut up in prison, having received authority from the chief priests;
and when they were put to death, I gave my
voice against *them*.
11 And I punished them oft in every synagogue, and compelled *them* to blaspheme; and
being exceedingly mad against them, I persecuted *them* even unto strange cities.
12 Whereupon as I went to Da-mas′cus with
authority and commission from the chief
priests,
13 At midday, O king, I saw in the way a
light from heaven, above the brightness of the
sun, shining round about me and them which
journeyed with me.
14 And when we were all fallen to the earth,
I heard a voice speaking unto me, and saying in
the He′brew tongue, Saul, Saul, why persecutest thou me? *it is* hard for thee to kick against
the pricks.
15 And I said, Who art thou, Lord? And he
said, I am Je′sus whom thou persecutest.
16 But rise, and stand upon thy feet: for I
have appeared unto thee for this purpose, to
make thee a minister and a witness both of
these things which thou hast seen, and of those
things in the which I will appear unto thee;
17 Delivering thee from the people, and *from*
the Gen′tiles, unto whom now I send thee,
18 To open their eyes, *and* to turn *them* from
darkness to light, and *from* the power of Sa′tan
unto God, that they may receive forgiveness of
sins, and inheritance among them which are
sanctified by faith that is in me.
19 Whereupon, O king A-grip′pa, I was not
disobedient unto the heavenly vision:
20 But shewed first unto them of Da-mas′-
cus, and at Je-ru′sa-lem, and throughout all the
coasts of Ju-dæ′a, and *then* to the Gen′tiles, that
they should repent and turn to God, and do
works meet for repentance.
21 For these causes the Jews caught me in
the temple, and went about to kill *me*.
22 Having therefore obtained help of God, I
continue unto this day, witnessing both to small
and great, saying none other things than those
which the prophets and Mo′ses did say should
come:
23 That Christ should suffer, *and* that he
should be the first that should rise from the
dead, and should shew light unto the people,
and to the Gen′tiles.
24 And as he thus spake for himself, Fes′tus
said with a loud voice, Paul thou art beside thyself; much learning doth make thee mad.
25 But he said, I am not mad, most noble
Fes′tus; but speak forth the words of truth and
soberness.
26 For the king knoweth of these things, before whom also I speak freely: for I am persuaded that none of these things are hidden
from him; for this thing was not done in a corner.
27 King A-grip′pa, believest thou the prophets? I know that thou believest.
28 Then A-grip′pa said unto Paul, Almost
thou persuadest me to be a Chris′tian.
29 And Paul said, I would to God, that not
only thou, but also all that hear me this day,
were both almost, and altogether such as I am,
except these bonds.
30 And when he had thus spoken, the king
rose up, and the governor, and Ber-ni′ce, and
they that sat with them:
31 And when they were gone aside, they
talked between themselves, saying, This man
doeth nothing worthy of death or of bonds.
32 Then said A-grip′pa unto Fes′tus, This
man might have been set at liberty, if he had
not appealed unto Cæ′sar.

27 AND when it was determined that we
should sail into It′a-ly, they delivered
Paul and certain other prisoners unto *one*
named Ju′lius, a centurion of Au-gus′tus' band.
2 And entering into a ship of Ad-ra-myt′ti-
um, we launched, meaning to sail by the coasts
of A′sia; *one* Ar-is-tar′chus, a Mac-e-do′ni-an of
Thes-sa-lo-ni′ca, being with us.
3 And the next *day* we touched at Si′don.
And Ju′lius courteously entreated Paul, and
gave *him* liberty to go unto his friends to refresh himself.
4 And when we had launched from thence,
we sailed under Cy′prus, because the winds
were contrary.
5 And when we had sailed over the sea of Ci-
li′cia and Pam-phyl′i-a, we came to My′ra, *a city*
of Ly′cia.
6 And there the centurion found a ship of Al-

ex-an'dri-a sailing into It'a-ly; and he put us therein.

7 And when we had sailed slowly many days, and scarce were come over against Cni'dus, the wind not suffering us, we sailed under Crete, over against Sal-mo'ne;

8 And, hardly passing it, came unto a place which is called The fair havens; nigh whereunto was the city *of* La-se'a.

9 Now when much time was spent, and when sailing was now dangerous, because the fast was now already past, Paul admonished *them,*

10 And said unto them, Sirs, I perceive that this voyage will be with hurt and much damage, not only of the lading and ship, but also of our lives.

11 Nevertheless the centurion believed the master and the owner of the ship, more than those things which were spoken by Paul.

12 And because the haven was not commodious to winter in, the more part advised to depart thence also, if by any means they might attain to Phe-ni'ce, *and there* to winter; *which is* an haven of Crete, and lieth toward the south west and north west.

13 And when the south wind blew softly, supposing that they had obtained *their* purpose, loosing *thence,* they sailed close by Crete.

14 But not long after there arose against it a tempestuous wind, called Eu-roc'ly-don.

15 And when the ship was caught, and could not bear up into the wind, we let *her* drive.

16 And running under a certain island which is called Clau'da, we had much work to come by the boat:

17 Which when they had taken up, they used helps, undergirding the ship; and, fearing lest they should fall into the quicksands, strake sail, and so were driven.

18 And we being exceedingly tossed with a tempest, the next *day* they lightened the ship;

19 And the third *day* we cast out with our own hands the tackling of the ship.

20 And when neither sun nor stars in many days appeared, and no small tempest lay on *us,* all hope that we should be saved was then taken away.

21 But after long abstinence Paul stood forth in the midst of them, and said, Sirs, ye should have hearkened unto me, and not have loosed from Crete, and to have gained this harm and loss.

22 And now I exhort you to be of good cheer: for there shall be no loss of *any man's* life among you, but of the ship.

23 For there stood by me this night the angel of God, whose I am, and whom I serve,

24 Saying, Fear not, Paul; thou must be brought before Cæsar: and, lo, God hath given thee all them that sail with thee.

25 Wherefore, sirs, be of good cheer: for I believe God, that it shall be even as it was told me.

26 Howbeit we must be cast upon a certain island.

27 But when the fourteenth night was come, as we were driven up and down in A'dri-a, about midnight the shipmen deemed that they drew near to some country;

28 And sounded, and found *it* twenty fathoms: and when they had gone a little further, they sounded again, and found *it* fifteen fathoms.

29 Then fearing lest we should have fallen upon rocks, they cast four anchors out of the stern, and wished for the day.

30 And as the shipmen were about to flee out of the ship, when they had let down the boat into the sea, under colour as though they would have cast anchors out of the foreship,

31 Paul said to the centurion and to the soldiers, Except these abide in the ship, ye cannot be saved.

32 Then the soldiers cut off the ropes of the boat, and let her fall off.

33 And while the day was coming on, Paul besought *them* all to take meat, saying, This day is the fourteenth day that ye have tarried and continued fasting, having taken nothing.

34 Wherefore I pray you to take *some* meat: for this is for your health: for there shall not an hair fall from the head of any of you.

35 And when he had thus spoken, he took bread, and gave thanks to God in presence of them all: and when he had broken *it,* he began to eat.

36 Then were they all of good cheer, and they also took *some* meat.

37 And we were in all in the ship two hundred threescore and sixteen souls.

38 And when they had eaten enough, they lightened the ship, and cast out the wheat into the sea.

39 And when it was day, they knew not the land: but they discovered a certain creek with a shore, into the which they were minded, if it were possible, to thrust in the ship.

40 And when they had taken up the anchors, they committed *themselves* unto the sea, and loosed the rudder bands, and hoised up the mainsail to the wind, and made toward shore.

41 And falling into a place where two seas met, they ran the ship aground; and the forepart stuck fast, and remained unmoveable, but the hinder part was broken with the violence of the waves.

42 And the soldiers' counsel was to kill the prisoners, lest any of them should swim out, and escape.

43 But the centurion, willing to save Paul, kept them from *their* purpose; and commanded that they which could swim should cast *themselves* first *into the sea,* and get to land:

44 And the rest, some on boards, and some on *broken pieces* of the ship. And so it came to pass, that they escaped all safe to land.

28 AND when they were escaped, then they knew that the island was called Mel'i-ta.

2 And the barbarous people shewed us no little kindness: for they kindled a fire, and received us every one, because of the present rain, and because of the cold.

3 And when Paul had gathered a bundle of sticks, and laid *them* on the fire, there came a viper out of the heat, and fastened on his hand.

4 And when the barbarians saw the *venomous* beast hang on his hand, they said among themselves, No doubt this man is a murderer, whom, though he hath escaped the sea, yet vengeance suffereth not to live.

5 And he shook off the beast into the fire, and felt no harm.

6 Howbeit they looked when he should have swollen, or fallen down dead suddenly: but after they had looked a great while, and saw no harm come to him, they changed their minds, and said that he was a god.

7 In the same quarters were possessions of the chief man of the island, whose name was Pub'li-us; who received us, and lodged us three days courteously.

8 And it came to pass, that the father of Pub'li-us lay sick of a fever and of a bloody flux: to

whom Paul entered in, and prayed, and laid his
hands on him, and healed him.
9 So when this was done, others also, which
had diseases in the island, came, and were
healed:
10 Who also honoured us with many hon-
ours; and when we departed, they laded *us* with
such things as were necessary.
11 And after three months we departed in a
ship of Al-ex-an'dri-a, which had wintered in
the isle, whose sign was Cas'tor and Pol'lux.
12 And landing at Syr'a-cuse, we tarried
there three days.
13 And from thence we fetched a compass,
and came to Rhe'gi-um: and after one day the
south wind blew, and we came the next day to
Pu-te'o-li:
14 Where we found brethren, and were desired to tarry with them seven days: and so we
went toward Rome.
15 And from thence, when the brethren
heard of us, they came to meet us as far as Ap'-
pi-i forum, and The three taverns: whom when
Paul saw, he thanked God, and took courage.
16 And when we came to Rome, the centurion delivered the prisoners to the captain of the
guard: but Paul was suffered to dwell by himself with a soldier that kept him.
17 And it came to pass, that after three days
Paul called the chief of the Jews together: and
when they were come together, he said unto
them, Men *and* brethren, though I have committed nothing against the people, or customs
of our fathers, yet was I delivered prisoner from
Je-ru'sa-lem into the hands of the Ro'mans.
18 Who, when they had examined me, would
have let *me* go, because there was no cause of
death in me.
19 But when the Jews spake against *it*, I constrained to appeal unto Cæ'sar; not that I had
ought to accuse my nation of.
20 For this cause therefore have I called for
you, to see *you*, and to speak with *you*: because
that for the hope of Is'ra-el I am bound with this
chain.
21 And they said unto him, We neither received letters out of Ju-dæ'a concerning thee,
neither any of the brethren that came shewed
or spake any harm of thee.
22 But we desire to hear of thee what thou
thinkest: for as concerning this sect, we know
that every where it is spoken against.
23 And when they had appointed him a day,
there came many to him into *his* lodging; to
whom he expounded and testified the kingdom
of God, persuading them concerning Je'sus,
both out of the law of Mo'ses, and *out of* the
prophets, from morning till evening.
24 And some believed the things which were
spoken, and some believed not.
25 And when they agreed not among themselves, they departed, after that Paul had spoken one word, Well spake the Ho'ly Ghost by E-
sa'ias the prophet unto our fathers,
26 Saying, Go unto this people, and say,
Hearing ye shall hear, and shall not understand;
and seeing ye shall see, and not perceive:
27 For the heart of this people is waxed
gross, and their ears are dull of hearing, and
their eyes have they closed; lest they should see
with *their* eyes, and hear with *their* ears, and
understand with *their* heart, and should be converted, and I should heal them.
28 Be it known therefore unto you, that the
salvation of God is sent unto the Gen'tiles, and
that they will hear it.
29 And when he had said these words, the
Jews departed, and had great reasoning among
themselves.
30 And Paul dwelt two whole years in his
own hired house, and received all that came in
unto him,
31 Preaching the kingdom of God, and teaching those things which concern the Lord Je'sus
Christ, with all confidence, no man forbidding
him.

THE LETTER OF PAUL TO THE

ROMANS

1 PAUL, a servant of Je'sus Christ, called *to*
be an apostle, separated unto the gospel of
God,
2 (Which he had promised afore by his
prophets in the holy scriptures,)
3 Concerning his Son Je'sus Christ our Lord,
which was made of the seed of Da'vid according to the flesh;
4 And declared *to be* the Son of God with
power, according to the spirit of holiness, by
the resurrection from the dead:
5 By whom we have received grace and
apostleship, for obedience to the faith among
all nations, for his name:
6 Among whom are ye also the called of Je'-
sus Christ:
7 To all that be in Rome, beloved of God,
called *to be* saints: Grace to you and peace from
God our Father, and the Lord Je'sus Christ.
8 First, I thank my God through Je'sus Christ
for you all, that your faith is spoken of throughout the whole world.
9 For God is my witness, whom I serve with
my spirit in the gospel of his Son, that without
ceasing I make mention of you always in my
prayers;
10 Making request, if by any means now at
length I might have a prosperous journey by the
will of God to come unto you.
11 For I long to see you, that I may impart
unto you some spiritual gift, to the end ye may
be established;
12 That is, that I may be comforted together
with you by the mutual faith both of you and
me.
13 Now I would not have you ignorant,
brethren, that oftentimes I purposed to come
unto you, (but was let hitherto,) that I might
have some fruit among you also, even as among
other Gen'tiles.
14 I am debtor both to the Greeks, and to the
Bar-ba'ri-ans; both to the wise, and to the unwise.
15 So, as much as in me is, I am ready to
preach the gospel to you that are at Rome also.
16 For I am not ashamed of the gospel of
Christ: for it is the power of God unto salvation
to every one that believeth; to the Jew first, and
also to the Greek.
17 For therein is the righteousness of God revealed from faith to faith: as it is written, The
just shall live by faith.
18 For the wrath of God is revealed from

heaven against all ungodliness and unrighteousness of men, who hold the truth in unrighteousness;

19 Because that which may be known of God is manifest in them; for God hath shewed *it* unto them.

20 For the invisible things of him from the creation of the world are clearly seen, being understood by the things that are made, *even* his eternal power and Godhead; so that they are without excuse:

21 Because that, when they knew God, they glorified *him* not as God, neither were thankful; but became vain in their imaginations, and their foolish heart was darkened.

22 Professing themselves to be wise, they became fools,

23 And changed the glory of the uncorruptible God into an image made like to corruptible man, and to birds, and fourfooted beasts, and creeping things.

24 Wherefore God also gave them up to uncleanness through the lusts of their own hearts, to dishonour their own bodies between themselves:

25 Who changed the truth of God into a lie, and worshipped and served the creature more than the Creator, who is blessed for ever. Amen.

26 For this cause God gave them up into vile affections: for even their women did change the natural use into that which is against nature:

27 And likewise also the men, leaving the natural use of the woman, burned in their lust one toward another; men with men working that which is unseemly, and receiving in themselves that recompence of their error which was meet.

28 And even as they did not like to retain God in *their* knowledge, God gave them over to a reprobate mind, to do those things which are not convenient;

29 Being filled with all unrighteousness, fornication, wickedness, covetousness, maliciousness; full of envy, murder, debate, deceit, malignity; whisperers,

30 Backbiters, haters of God, despiteful, proud, boasters, inventors of evil things, disobedient to parents,

31 Without understanding, covenantbreakers, without natural affection, implacable, unmerciful:

32 Who knowing the judgment of God, that they which commit such things are worthy of death, not only do the same, but have pleasure in them that do them.

2 THEREFORE thou art inexcusable, O man, whosoever thou art that judgest: for wherein thou judgest another, thou condemnest thyself; for thou that judgest doest the same things.

2 But we are sure that the judgment of God is according to truth against them which commit such things.

3 And thinkest thou this, O man, that judgest them which do such things, and doest the same, that thou shalt escape the judgment of God?

4 Or despisest thou the riches of his goodness and forbearance and longsuffering; not knowing that the goodness of God leadeth thee to repentance?

5 But after thy hardness and impenitent heart treasurest up unto thyself wrath against the day of wrath and revelation of the righteous judgment of God;

6 Who will render to every man according to his deeds:

7 To them who by patient continuance in well doing seek for glory and honour and immortality, eternal life:

8 But unto them that are contentious, and do not obey the truth, but obey unrighteousness, indignation and wrath,

9 Tribulation and anguish, upon every soul of man that doeth evil, of the Jew first, and also of the Gen'tile;

10 But glory, honour, and peace, to every man that worketh good, to the Jew first, and also to the Gentile:

11 For there is no respect of persons with God.

12 For as many as have sinned without law shall also perish without law: and as many as have sinned in the law shall be judged by the law;

13 (For not the hearers of the law *are* just before God, but the doers of the law shall be justified.

14 For when the Gen'tiles, which have not the law, do by nature the things contained in the law, these, having not the law, are a law unto themselves:

15 Which shew the work of the law written in their hearts, their conscience also bearing witness, and *their* thoughts the mean while accusing or else excusing one another;)

16 In the day when God shall judge the secrets of men by Je'sus Christ according to my gospel.

17 Behold, thou art called a Jew, and restest in the law, and makest thy boast of God,

18 And knowest *his* will, and approvest the things that are more excellent, being instructed out of the law;

19 And art confident that thou thyself art a guide of the blind, a light of them which are in darkness,

20 An instructor of the foolish, a teacher of babes, which hast the form of knowledge and of the truth in the law.

21 Thou therefore which teachest another, teachest thou not thyself? thou that preachest a man should not steal, dost thou steal?

22 Thou that sayest a man should not commit adultery, dost thou commit adultery? thou that abhorrest idols, dost thou commit sacrilege?

23 Thou that makest thy boast of the law, through breaking the law dishonourest thou God?

24 For the name of God is blasphemed among the Gen'tiles through you, as it is written.

25 For circumcision verily profiteth, if thou keep the law: but if thou be a breaker of the law, thy circumcision is made uncircumcision.

26 Therefore if the uncircumcision keep the righteousness of the law, shall not his uncircumcision be counted for circumcision?

27 And shall not uncircumcision which is by nature, if it fulfil the law, judge thee, who by the letter and circumcision dost transgress the law?

28 For he is not a Jew, which is one outwardly; neither *is that* circumcision, which is outward in the flesh:

29 But he *is* a Jew, which is one inwardly; and circumcision *is that* of the heart, in the spirit, *and* not in the letter; whose praise *is* not of men, but of God.

3 WHAT advantage then hath the Jew? or what profit *is there* of circumcision?

2 Much every way: chiefly, because that unto
them were committed the oracles of God.
3 For what if some did not believe? shall
their unbelief make the faith of God without effect?
4 God forbid: yea, let God be true, but every
man a liar; as it is written, That thou mightest
be justified in thy sayings, and mightest overcome when thou art judged.
5 But if our unrighteousness commend the
righteousness of God, what shall we say? *Is* God
unrighteous who taketh vengeance? (I speak as
a man)
6 God forbid: for then how shall God judge
the world?
7 For if the truth of God hath more abounded
through my lie unto his glory; why yet am I also
judged as a sinner?
8 And not *rather*, (as we be slanderously reported, and as some affirm that we say,) Let us
do evil, that good may come? whose damnation
is just.
9 What then? are we better *than they*? No, in
no wise: for we have before proved both Jews
and Gen'tiles, that they are all under sin;
10 As it is written, There is none righteous,
no, not one:
11 There is none that understandeth, there is
none that seeketh after God.
12 They are all gone out of the way, they are
together become unprofitable: there is none
that doeth good, no, not one.
13 Their throat *is* an open sepulchre; with
their tongues they have used deceit; the poison
of asps *is* under their lips:
14 Whose mouth *is* full of cursing and bitterness:
15 Their feet *are* swift to shed blood:
16 Destruction and misery *are* in their ways:
17 And the way of peace have they not
known:
18 There is no fear of God before their eyes.
19 Now we know that what things soever the
law saith, it saith to them who are under the
law: that every mouth may be stopped, and all
the world may become guilty before God.
20 Therefore by the deeds of the law there
shall no flesh be justified in his sight: for by the
law *is* the knowledge of sin.
21 But now the righteousness of God without
the law is manifested, being witnessed by the
law and the prophets;
22 Even the righteousness of God *which is* by
faith of Je'sus Christ unto all and upon all them
that believe: for there is no difference:
23 For all have sinned, and come short of the
glory of God;
24 Being justified freely by his grace through
the redemption that is in Christ Je'sus:
25 Whom God hath set forth *to be* a propitiation through faith in his blood, to declare his
righteousness for the remission of sins that are
past, through the forbearance of God;
26 To declare, *I say*, at this time his righteousness: that he might be just, and the justifier
of him which believeth in Je'sus.
27 Where *is* boasting then? It is excluded. By
what law? of works? Nay: but by the law of
faith.
28 Therefore we conclude that a man is justified by faith without the deeds of the law.
29 *Is he* the God of the Jews only? *is he* not
also of the Gen'tiles? Yes, of the Gen'tiles also:
30 Seeing *it is* one God, which shall justify
the circumcision by faith, and uncircumcision
through faith.
31 Do we then make void the law through
faith? God forbid: yea, we establish the law.

4 WHAT shall we say then that A'bra-ham
our father, as pertaining to the flesh, hath
found?
2 For if A'bra-ham were justified by works,
he hath *whereof* to glory; but not before God.
3 For what saith the scripture? A'bra-ham
believed God, and it was counted unto him for
righteousness.
4 Now to him that worketh is the reward not
reckoned of grace, but of debt.
5 But to him that worketh not, but believeth
on him that justifieth the ungodly, his faith is
counted for righteousness.
6 Even as Da'vid also describeth the blessedness of the man, unto whom God imputeth
righteousness without works,
7 *Saying*, Blessed *are* they whose iniquities
are forgiven, and whose sins are covered.
8 Blessed *is* the man to whom the Lord will
not impute sin.
9 *Cometh* this blessedness then upon the circumcision *only*, or upon the uncircumcision
also? for we say that faith was reckoned to A'-
bra-ham for righteousness.
10 How was it then reckoned? when he was
in circumcision, or in uncircumcision? Not in
circumcision, but in uncircumcision.
11 And he received the sign of circumcision,
a seal of the righteousness of faith which *he had*
yet being uncircumcised: that he might be the
father of all them that believe, though they be
not circumcised; that righteousness might be
imputed unto them also:
12 And the father of circumcision to them
who are not of the circumcision only, but who
also walk in the steps of that faith of our father
A'bra-ham, which *he had* being *yet* uncircumcised.
13 For the promise, that he should be the heir
of the world, *was* not to A'bra-ham, or to his
seed, through the law, but through the righteousness of faith.
14 For if they which are of the law *be* heirs,
faith is made void, and the promise of none effect:
15 Because the law worketh wrath: for
where no law is, *there is* no transgression.
16 Therefore *it is* of faith, that *it might be* by
grace; to the end the promise might be sure to
all the seed; not to that only which is of the law,
but to that also which is of the faith of A'bra-
ham; who is the father of us all,
17 (As it is written, I have made thee a father
of many nations,) before him whom he believed, *even* God, who quickeneth the dead, and
calleth those things which be not as though
they were.
18 Who against hope believed in hope, that
he might become the father of many nations,
according to that which was spoken, So shall
thy seed be.
19 And being not weak in faith, he considered not his own body now dead, when he was
about an hundred years old, neither yet the
deadness of Sa'-rah's womb:
20 He staggered not at the promise of God
through unbelief; but was strong in faith, giving
glory to God;
21 And being fully persuaded that, what he
had promised, he was able also to perform.
22 And therefore it was imputed to him for
righteousness.
23 Now it was not written for his sake alone,
that it was imputed to him;

24 But for us also, to whom it shall be imputed, if we believe on him that raised up Je'sus our Lord from the dead;

25 Who was delivered for our offences, and was raised again for our justification.

5 THEREFORE being justified by faith, we have peace with God through our Lord Je'sus Christ:

2 By whom also we have access by faith into this grace wherein we stand, and rejoice in hope of the glory of God.

3 And not only *so*, but we glory in tribulations also: knowing that tribulation worketh patience;

4 And patience, experience; and experience, hope:

5 And hope maketh not ashamed; because the love of God is shed abroad in our hearts by the Ho'ly Ghost which is given unto us.

6 For when we were yet without strength, in due time Christ died for the ungodly.

7 For scarcely for a righteous man will one die: yet peradventure for a good man some would even dare to die.

8 But God commendeth his love toward us, in that, while we were yet sinners, Christ died for us.

9 Much more then, being now justified by his blood, we shall be saved from wrath through him.

10 For if, when we were enemies, we were reconciled to God by the death of his Son, much more, being reconciled, we shall be saved by his life.

11 And not only *so*, but we also joy in God through our Lord Je'sus Christ, by whom we have now received the atonement.

12 Wherefore, as by one man sin entered into the world, and death by sin; and so death passed upon all men, for that all have sinned:

13 (For until the law sin was in the world: but sin is not imputed when there is no law.

14 Nevertheless death reigned from Ad'am to Mo'ses, even over them that had not sinned after the similitude of Ad'am's transgression, who is the figure of him that was to come.

15 But not as the offence, so also *is* the free gift. For if through the offence of one many be dead, much more the grace of God, and the gift by grace, *which is* by one man, Je'sus Christ, hath abounded unto many.

16 And not as *it was* by one that sinned, *so is* the gift: for the judgment *was* by one to condemnation, but the free gift *is* of many offences unto justification.

17 For if by one man's offence death reigned by one; much more they which receive abundance of grace and of the gift of righteousness shall reign in life by one, Je'sus Christ.)

18 Therefore as by the offence of one *judgment came* upon all men to condemnation; even so by the righteousness of one *the free gift came* upon all men unto justification of life.

19 For as by one man's disobedience many were made sinners, so by the obedience of one shall many be made righteous.

20 Moreover the law entered, that the offence might abound. But where sin abounded, grace did much more abound:

21 That as sin hath reigned unto death, even so might grace reign through righteousness unto eternal life by Je'sus Christ our Lord.

6 WHAT shall we say then? Shall we continue in sin, that grace may abound?

2 God forbid. How shall we, that are dead to sin, live any longer therein?

3 Know ye not, that so many of us as were baptized into Je'sus Christ were baptized into his death?

4 Therefore we are buried with him by baptism into death: that like as Christ was raised up from the dead by the glory of the Father, even so we also should walk in newness of life.

5 For if we have been planted together in the likeness of his death, we shall be also *in the likeness* of *his* resurrection:

6 Knowing this, that our old man is crucified with *him*, that the body of sin might be destroyed, that henceforth we should not serve sin.

7 For he that is dead is freed from sin.

8 Now if we be dead with Christ, we believe that we shall also live with him:

9 Knowing that Christ being raised from the dead dieth no more; death hath no more dominion over him.

10 For in that he died, he died unto sin once: but in that he liveth, he liveth unto God.

11 Likewise reckon ye also yourselves to be dead indeed unto sin, but alive unto God through Je'sus Christ our Lord.

12 Let not sin therefore reign in your mortal body, that ye should obey it in the lusts thereof.

13 Neither yield ye your members *as* instruments of unrighteousness unto sin: but yield yourselves unto God, as those that are alive from the dead, and your members *as* instruments of righteousness unto God.

14 For sin shall not have dominion over you: for ye are not under the law, but under grace.

15 What then? shall we sin, because we are not under the law, but under grace? God forbid.

16 Know ye not, that to whom ye yield yourselves servants to obey, his servants ye are to whom ye obey; whether of sin unto death, or of obedience unto righteousness?

17 But God be thanked, that ye were the servants of sin, but ye have obeyed from the heart that form of doctrine which was delivered you.

18 Being then made free from sin, ye became the servants of righteousness.

19 I speak after the manner of men because of the infirmity of your flesh: for as ye have yielded your members servants to uncleanness and to iniquity unto iniquity; even so now yield your members servants to righteousness unto holiness.

20 For when ye were the servants of sin, ye were free from righteousness.

21 What fruit had ye then in those things whereof ye are now ashamed? for the end of those things *is* death.

22 But now being made free from sin, and become servants to God, ye have your fruit unto holiness, and the end everlasting life.

23 For the wages of sin *is* death; but the gift of God *is* eternal life through Je'sus Christ our Lord.

7 KNOW ye not, brethren, (for I speak to them that know the law,) how that the law hath dominion over a man as long as he liveth?

2 For the woman which hath an husband is bound by the law to *her* husband so long as he liveth; but if the husband be dead, she is loosed from the law of *her* husband.

3 So then if, while *her* husband liveth, she be married to another man, she shall be called an adulteress: but if her husband be dead, she is free from that law; so that she is no adulteress, though she be married to another man.

4 Wherefore, my brethren, ye also are become dead to the law by the body of Christ; that
ye should be married to another, *even* to him
who is raised from the dead, that we should
bring forth fruit unto God.
5 For when we were in the flesh, the motions
of sins, which were by the law, did work in our
members to bring forth fruit unto death.
6 But now we are delivered from the law,
that being dead wherein we were held; that we
should serve in newness of spirit, and not *in* the
oldness of the letter.
7 What shall we say then? *Is* the law sin? God
forbid. Nay, I had not known sin, but by the
law: for I had not known lust, except the law
had said, Thou shalt not covet.
8 But sin, taking occasion by the comm-
mandment, wrought in me all manner of concupiscence. For without the law sin *was* dead.
9 For I was alive without the law once: but
when the commandment came, sin revived, and
I died.
10 And the commandment, which *was ordained* to life, I found *to be* unto death.
11 For sin, taking occasion by the commandment, deceived me, and by it slew *me*.
12 Wherefore the law *is* holy, and the commandment holy, and just, and good.
13 Was then that which is good made death
unto me? God forbid. But sin, that it might appear sin, working death in me by that which is
good; that sin by the commandment might become exceeding sinful.
14 For we know that the law is spiritual: but
I am carnal, sold under sin.
15 For that which I do I allow not: for what I
would, that do I not; but what I hate, that do I.
16 If then I do that which I would not, I consent unto the law that *it is* good.
17 Now then it is no more I that do it, but sin
that dwelleth in me.
18 For I know that in me (that is, in my
flesh,) dwelleth no good thing: for to will is present with me; but *how* to perform that which is
good I find not.
19 For the good that I would I do not: but the
evil which I would not, that I do.
20 Now if I do that I would not, it is no more
I that do it, but sin that dwelleth in me.
21 I find then a law, that, when I would do
good, evil is present with me.
22 For I delight in the law of God after the
inward man:
23 But I see another law in my members,
warring against the law of my mind, and bringing me into captivity to the law of sin which is
in my members.
24 O wretched man that I am! who shall deliver me from the body of this death?
25 I thank God through Je'sus Christ our
Lord. So then with the mind I myself serve the
law of God; but with the flesh the law of sin.

8 THERE *is* therefore now no condemnation
to them which are in Christ Je'sus, who
walk not after the flesh, but after the Spirit.
2 For the law of the Spirit of life in Christ
Je'sus hath made me free from the law of sin
and death.
3 For what the law could not do, in that it
was weak through the flesh, God sending his
own Son in the likeness of sinful flesh, and for
sin, condemned sin in the flesh:
4 That the righteousness of the law might be
fulfilled in us, who walk not after the flesh, but
after the Spirit.
5 For they that are after the flesh do mind the
things of the flesh; but they that are after the
Spirit the things of the Spirit.
6 For to be carnally minded *is* death; but to
be spiritually minded *is* life and peace.
7 Because the carnal mind *is* enmity against
God: for it is not subject to the law of God, neither indeed can be.
8 So then they that are in the flesh cannot
please God.
9 But ye are not in the flesh, but in the Spirit,
if so be that the Spirit of God dwell in you. Now
if any man have not the Spirit of Christ, he is
none of his.
10 And if Christ *be* in you, the body *is* dead
because of sin; but the Spirit *is* life because of
righteousness.
11 But if the Spirit of him that raised up Je'-
sus from the dead dwell in you, he that raised
up Christ from the dead shall also quicken your
mortal bodies by his Spirit that dwelleth in you.
12 Therefore, brethren, we are debtors, not
to the flesh, to live after the flesh.
13 For if ye live after the flesh, ye shall die:
but if ye through the Spirit do mortify the deeds
of the body, ye shall live.
14 For as many as are led by the Spirit of
God, they are the sons of God.
15 For ye have not received the spirit of
bondage again to fear; but ye have received the
Spirit of adoption, whereby we cry, Ab'ba, Father.
16 The Spirit itself beareth witness with our
spirit, that we are the children of God:
17 And if children, then heirs; heirs of God,
and joint-heirs with Christ; if so be that we suffer with *him*, that we may be also glorified together.
18 For I reckon that the sufferings of this
present time *are* not worthy *to be compared*
with the glory which shall be revealed in us.
19 For the earnest expectation of the creature waiteth for the manifestation of the sons of
God.
20 For the creature was made subject to vanity, not willingly, but by reason of him who hath
subjected *the same* in hope,
21 Because the creature itself also shall be
delivered from the bondage of corruption into
the glorious liberty of the children of God.
22 For we know that the whole creation
groaneth and travaileth in pain together until
now.
23 And not only *they*, but ourselves also,
which have the firstfruits of the Spirit, even we
ourselves groan within ourselves, waiting for
the adoption, *to wit*, the redemption of our
body.
24 For we are saved by hope: but hope that is
seen is not hope: for what a man seeth, why
doth he yet hope for?
25 But if we hope for that we see not, *then* do
we with patience wait for *it*.
26 Likewise the Spirit also helpeth our infirmities: for we know not what we should pray
for as we ought: but the Spirit itself maketh intercession for us with groanings which cannot
be uttered.
27 And he that searcheth the hearts knoweth
what *is* the mind of the Spirit, because he maketh intercession for the saints according to *the
will of* God.
28 And we know that all things work together for good to them that love God, to them
who are the called according to *his* purpose.
29 For whom he did foreknow, he also did
predestinate *to be* conformed to the image of

his Son, that he might be the firstborn among many brethren.

30 Moreover whom he did predestinate, them he also called: and whom he called, them he also justified: and whom he justified, them he also glorified.

31 What shall we then say to these things? If God *be* for us, who *can be* against us?

32 He that spared not his own Son, but delivered him up for us all, how shall he not with him also freely give us all things?

33 Who shall lay any thing to the charge of God's elect? *It is* God that justifieth.

34 Who *is* he that condemneth? *It is* Christ that died, yea rather, that is risen again, who is even at the right hand of God, who also maketh intercession for us.

35 Who shall separate us from the love of Christ? *shall* tribulation, or distress, or persecution, or famine, or nakedness, or peril, or sword?

36 As it is written, For thy sake we are killed all the day long; we are accounted as sheep for the slaughter.

37 Nay, in all these things we are more than conquerors through him that loved us.

38 For I am persuaded, that neither death, nor life, nor angels, nor principalities, nor powers, nor things present, nor things to come,

39 Nor height, nor depth, nor any other creature, shall be able to separate us from the love of God, which is in Christ Je'sus our Lord.

9 I SAY the truth in Christ, I lie not, my conscience also bearing me witness in the Ho'ly Ghost,

2 That I have great heaviness and continual sorrow in my heart.

3 For I could wish that myself were accursed from Christ for my brethren, my kinsmen according to the flesh:

4 Who are Is'ra-el-ites; to whom *pertaineth* the adoption, and the glory, and the covenants, and the giving of the law, and the service *of God,* and the promises;

5 Whose *are* the fathers, and of whom as concerning the flesh Christ *came,* who is over all, God blessed for ever. Amen.

6 Not as though the word of God hath taken none effect. For they *are* not all Is'ra-el, which are of Is'ra-el:

7 Neither, because they are the seed of A'bra-ham, *are they* all children: but, In I'saac shall thy seed be called.

8 That is, They which are the children of the flesh, these *are* not the children of God: but the children of the promise are counted for the seed.

9 For this *is* the word of promise, At this time will I come, and Sa'rah shall have a son.

10 And not only *this;* but when Re-bec'ca also had conceived by one, *even* by our father I'saac;

11 (For *the children* being not yet born, neither having done any good or evil, that the purpose of God according to election might stand, not of works, but of him that calleth;)

12 It was said unto her, The elder shall serve the younger.

13 As it is written, Ja'cob have I loved, but E'sau have I hated.

14 What shall we say then? *Is there* unrighteousness with God? God forbid.

15 For he saith to Mo'ses, I will have mercy on whom I will have mercy, and I will have compassion on whom I will have compassion.

16 So then *it is* not of him that willeth, nor of him that runneth, but of God that sheweth mercy.

17 For the scripture saith unto Pha'raoh, Even for this same purpose have I raised thee up, that I might shew my power in thee, and that my name might be declared throughout all the earth.

18 Therefore hath he mercy on whom he will *have mercy,* and whom he will he hardeneth.

19 Thou wilt say then unto me, Why doth he yet find fault? For who hath resisted his will?

20 Nay but, O man, who art thou that repliest against God? Shall the thing formed say to him that formed *it,* Why hast thou made me thus?

21 Hath not the potter power over the clay; of the same lump to make one vessel unto honour, and another unto dishonour?

22 *What* if God, willing to shew *his* wrath, and to make his power known, endured with much longsuffering the vessels of wrath fitted to destruction:

23 And that he might make known the riches of his glory on the vessels of mercy, which he had afore prepared unto glory,

24 Even us, whom he hath called, not of the Jews only, but also of the Gen'tiles?

25 As he saith also in O'see, I will call them my people, which were not my people; and her beloved, which was not beloved.

26 And it shall come to pass, *that* in the place where it was said unto them, Ye *are* not my people; there shall they be called the children of the living God.

27 E-sa'ias also crieth concerning Is'ra-el, Though the number of the children of Is'ra-el be as the sand of the sea, a remnant shall be saved:

28 For he will finish the work, and cut *it* short in righteousness: because a short work will the Lord make upon the earth.

29 And as E-sa'ias said before, Except the Lord of Sab'a-oth had left us a seed, we had been as Sod'om-a, and been made like unto Gomor'rha.

30 What shall we say then? That the Gen'tiles, which followed not after righteousness, have attained to righteousness, even the righteousness which is of faith.

31 But Is'ra-el, which followed after the law of righteousness, hath not attained to the law of righteousness.

32 Wherefore? Because *they sought it* not by faith, but as it were by the works of the law. For they stumbled at that stumblingstone;

33 As it is written, Behold, I lay in Si'on a stumblingstone and rock of offence: and whosoever believeth on him shall not be ashamed.

10 BRETHREN, my heart's desire and prayer to God for Is'ra-el is, that they might be saved.

2 For I bear them record that they have a zeal of God, but not according to knowledge.

3 For they being ignorant of God's righteousness, and going about to establish their own righteousness, have not submitted themselves unto the righteousness of God.

4 For Christ *is* the end of the law for righteousness to every one that believeth.

5 For Mo'ses describeth the righteousness which is of the law, That the man which doeth those things shall live by them.

6 But the righteousness which is of faith speaketh on this wise, Say not in thine heart, Who shall ascend into heaven? (that is, to bring Christ down *from above:*)

7 Or, Who shall descend into the deep? (that is, to bring up Christ again from the dead.)

8 But what saith it? The word is nigh thee, *even* in thy mouth, and in thy heart: that is, the word of faith, which we preach;

9 That if thou shalt confess with thy mouth the Lord Je'sus, and shalt believe in thine heart that God hath raised him from the dead, thou shalt be saved.

10 For with the heart man believeth unto righteousness; and with the mouth confession is made unto salvation.

11 For the scripture saith, Whosoever believeth on him shall not be ashamed.

12 For there is no difference between the Jew and the Greek: for the same Lord over all is rich unto all that call upon him.

13 For whosoever shall call upon the name of the Lord shall be saved.

14 How then shall they call on him in whom they have not believed? and how shall they believe in him of whom they have not heard? and how shall they hear without a preacher?

15 And how shall they preach, except they be sent? as it is written, How beautiful are the feet of them that preach the gospel of peace, and bring glad tidings of good things!

16 But they have not all obeyed the gospel. For E-sa'ias saith, Lord, who hath believed our report?

17 So then faith *cometh* by hearing, and hearing by the word of God.

18 But I say, Have they not heard? Yes verily, their sound went into all the earth, and their words unto the ends of the world.

19 But I say, Did not Is'ra-el know? First Mo'ses saith, I will provoke you to jealousy by *them that are* no people, *and* by a foolish nation I will anger you.

20 But E-sa'ias is very bold, and saith, I was found of them that sought me not; I was made manifest unto them that asked not after me.

21 But to Is'ra-el he saith, All day long I have stretched forth my hands unto a disobedient and gainsaying people.

11 I SAY then, Hath God cast away his people? God forbid. For I also am an Is'ra-el-ite, of the seed of A'bra-ham, *of* the tribe of Ben'ja-min.

2 God hath not cast away his people which he foreknew. Wot ye not what the scripture saith of E-li'as? how he maketh intercession to God against Is'ra-el, saying,

3 Lord, they have killed thy prophets, and digged down thine altars; and I am left alone, and they seek my life.

4 But what saith the answer of God unto him? I have reserved to myself seven thousand men, who have not bowed the knee to *the image of* Ba'al.

5 Even so then at this present time also there is a remnant according to the election of grace.

6 And if by grace, then *is it* no more of works: otherwise grace is no more grace. But if *it be* of works, then is it no more grace: otherwise work is no more work.

7 What then? Is'ra-el hath not obtained that which he seeketh for; but the election hath obtained it, and the rest were blinded

8 (According as it is written, God hath given them the spirit of slumber, eyes that they should not see, and ears that they should not hear;) unto this day.

9 And Da'vid saith, Let their table be made a snare, and a trap, and a stumblingblock, and a recompence unto them:

10 Let their eyes be darkened, that they may not see, and bow down their back alway.

11 I say then, Have they stumbled that they should fall? God forbid: but *rather* through their fall salvation *is come* unto the Gen'tiles, for to provoke them to jealousy.

12 Now if the fall of them *be* the riches of the world, and the diminishing of them the riches of the Gen'tiles; how much more their fulness?

13 For I speak to you Gen'tiles, inasmuch as I am the apostle of the Gen'tiles, I magnify mine office:

14 If by any means I may provoke to emulation *them which are* my flesh, and might save some of them.

15 For if the casting away of them *be* the reconciling of the world, what *shall* the receiving *of them be,* but life from the dead?

16 For if the firstfruit *be* holy, the lump *is* also *holy:* and if the root *be* holy, so *are* the branches.

17 And if some of the branches be broken off, and thou, being a wild olive tree, wert graffed in among them, and with them partakest of the root and fatness of the olive tree;

18 Boast not against the branches. But if thou boast, thou bearest not the root, but the root thee.

19 Thou wilt say then, The branches were broken off, that I might be graffed in.

20 Well; because of unbelief they were broken off, and thou standest by faith. Be not highminded, but fear:

21 For if God spared not the natural branches, *take heed* lest he also spare not thee.

22 Behold therefore the goodness and severity of God: on them which fell, severity; but toward thee, goodness, if thou continue in *his* goodness: otherwise thou also shalt be cut off.

23 And they also, if they abide not still in unbelief, shall be graffed in: for God is able to graff them in again.

24 For if thou wert cut out of the olive tree which is wild by nature, and wert graffed contrary to nature into a good olive tree: how much more shall these, which be the natural *branches,* be graffed into their own olive tree?

25 For I would not, brethren, that ye should be ignorant of this mystery, lest ye should be wise in your own conceits; that blindness in part is happened to Is'ra-el, until the fulness of the Gen'tiles be come in.

26 And so all Is'ra-el shall be saved: as it is written, There shall come out of Si'on the Deliverer, and shall turn away ungodliness from Ja'cob:

27 For this *is* my covenant unto them, when I shall take away their sins.

28 As concerning the gospel, *they are* enemies for your sakes: but as touching the election, *they are* beloved for the fathers' sakes.

29 For the gifts and calling of God *are* without repentance.

30 For as ye in times past have not believed God, yet have now obtained mercy through their unbelief:

31 Even so have these also now not believed, that through your mercy they also may obtain mercy.

32 For God hath concluded them all in unbelief, that he might have mercy upon all.

33 O the depth of the riches both of the wisdom and knowledge of God! how unsearchable *are* his judgments, and his ways past finding out!

34 For who hath known the mind of the Lord? or who hath been his counsellor?

35 Or who hath first given to him, and it shall be recompensed unto him again?

36 For of him, and through him, and to him, *are* all things: to whom *be* glory for ever. Amen.

12 I BESEECH you therefore, brethren, by the mercies of God, that ye present your bodies a living sacrifice, holy, acceptable unto God, *which is* your reasonable service.
2 And be not conformed to this world: but be ye transformed by the renewing of your mind, that ye may prove what *is* that good, and acceptable, and perfect, will of God.
3 For I say, through the grace given unto me, to every man that is among you, not to think *of himself* more highly than he ought to think; but to think soberly, according as God hath dealt to every man the measure of faith.
4 For as we have many members in one body, and all members have not the same office:
5 So we, *being* many, are one body in Christ, and every one members one of another.
6 Having then gifts differing according to the grace that is given to us, whether prophecy, *let us prophesy* according to the proportion of faith;
7 Or ministry, *let us wait* on *our* ministering: or he that teacheth, on teaching;
8 Or he that exhorteth, on exhortation: he that giveth, *let him do it* with simplicity; he that ruleth, with diligence; he that sheweth mercy, with cheerfulness.
9 *Let* love be without dissimulation. Abhor that which is evil; cleave to that which is good.
10 *Be* kindly affectioned one to another with brotherly love; in honour preferring one another;
11 Not slothful in business; fervent in spirit; serving the Lord;
12 Rejoicing in hope; patient in tribulation; continuing instant in prayer;
13 Distributing to the necessity of saints; given to hospitality.
14 Bless them which persecute you: bless, and curse not.
15 Rejoice with them that do rejoice, and weep with them that weep.
16 *Be* of the same mind one toward another. Mind not high things, but condescend to men of low estate. Be not wise in your own conceits.
17 Recompense to no man evil for evil. Provide things honest in the sight of all men.
18 If it be possible, as much as lieth in you, live peaceably with all men.
19 Dearly beloved, avenge not yourselves, but *rather* give place unto wrath: for it is written, Vengeance *is* mine; I will repay, saith the Lord.
20 Therefore if thine enemy hunger, feed him; if he thirst, give him drink: for in so doing thou shalt heap coals of fire on his head.
21 Be not overcome of evil, but overcome evil with good.

13 LET every soul be subject unto the higher powers. For there is no power but of God: the powers that be are ordained of God.
2 Whosoever therefore resisteth the power, resisteth the ordinance of God: and they that resist shall receive to themselves damnation.
3 For rulers are not a terror to good works, but to the evil. Wilt thou then not be afraid of the power? do that which is good, and thou shalt have praise of the same:
4 For he is the minister of God to thee for good. But if thou do that which is evil, be afraid; for he beareth not the sword in vain: for he is the minister of God, a revenger to *execute* wrath upon him that doeth evil.
5 Wherefore *ye* must needs be subject, not only for wrath, but also for conscience sake.
6 For for this cause pay ye tribute also: for they are God's ministers, attending continually upon this very thing.
7 Render therefore to all their dues: tribute to whom tribute *is due;* custom to whom custom; fear to whom fear; honour to whom honour.
8 Owe no man any thing, but to love one another: for he that loveth another hath fulfilled the law.
9 For this, Thou shalt not commit adultery, Thou shalt not kill, Thou shalt not steal, Thou shalt not bear false witness, Thou shalt not covet; and if *there be* any other commandment, it is briefly comprehended in this saying, namely, Thou shalt love thy neighbour as thyself.
10 Love worketh no ill to his neighbour: therefore love *is* the fulfilling of the law.
11 And that, knowing the time, that now *it is* high time to awake out of sleep: for now *is* our salvation nearer than when we believed.
12 The night is far spent, the day is at hand: let us therefore cast off the works of darkness, and let us put on the armour of light.
13 Let us walk honestly, as in the day; not in rioting and drunkenness, not in chambering and wantonness, not in strife and envying.
14 But put ye on the Lord Je'sus Christ, and make not provision for the flesh, to *fulfil* the lusts *thereof.*

14 HIM that is weak in the faith receive ye, *but* not to doubtful disputations.
2 For one believeth that he may eat all things: another, who is weak, eateth herbs.
3 Let not him that eateth despise him that eateth not; and let not him which eateth not judge him that eateth: for God hath received him.
4 Who art thou that judgest another man's servant? to his own master he standeth or falleth. Yea, he shall be holden up: for God is able to make him stand.
5 One man esteemeth one day above another: another esteemeth every day *alike.* Let every man be fully persuaded in his own mind.
6 He that regardeth the day, regardeth *it* unto the Lord; and he that regardeth not the day, to the Lord he doth not regard *it.* He that eateth, eateth to the Lord, for he giveth God thanks; and he that eateth not, to the Lord he eateth not, and giveth God thanks.
7 For none of us liveth to himself, and no man dieth to himself.
8 For whether we live, we live unto the Lord; and whether we die, we die unto the Lord: whether we live therefore, or die, we are the Lord's.
9 For to this end Christ both died, and rose, and revived, that he might be Lord both of the dead and living.
10 But why dost thou judge thy brother? or why dost thou set at nought thy brother? for we shall all stand before the judgment seat of Christ.
11 For it is written, *As* I live, saith the Lord, every knee shall bow to me, and every tongue shall confess to God.
12 So then every one of us shall give account of himself to God.
13 Let us not therefore judge one another any more: but judge this rather, that no man

put a stumblingblock or an occasion to fall in
his brother's way.
14 I know, and am persuaded by the Lord
Je'sus, that *there is* nothing unclean of itself:
but to him that esteemeth any thing to be unclean, to him *it is* unclean.
15 But if thy brother be grieved with *thy*
meat, now walkest thou not charitably. Destroy
not him with thy meat, for whom Christ died.
16 Let not then your good be evil spoken of:
17 For the kingdom of God is not meat and
drink; but righteousness, and peace, and joy in
the Ho'ly Ghost.
18 For he that in these things serveth Christ
is acceptable to God, and approved of men.
19 Let us therefore follow after the things
which make for peace, and things wherewith
one may edify another.
20 For meat destroy not the work of God. All
things indeed *are* pure; but *it is* evil for that
man who eateth with offence.
21 *It is* good neither to eat flesh, nor to drink
wine, nor *any thing* whereby thy brother stumbleth, or is offended, or is made weak.
22 Hast thou faith? have *it* to thyself before
God. Happy *is* he that condemneth not himself
in that thing which he alloweth.
23 And he that doubteth is damned if he eat,
because *he eateth* not of faith: for whatsoever *is*
not of faith is sin.

15 WE then that are strong ought to bear
the infirmities of the weak, and not to
please ourselves.
2 Let every one of us please *his* neighbour for
his good to edification.
3 For even Christ pleased not himself; but, as
it is written, The reproaches of them that reproached thee fell on me.
4 For whatsoever things were written aforetime were written for our learning, that we
through patience and comfort of the scriptures
might have hope.
5 Now the God of patience and consolation
grant you to be likeminded one toward another
according to Christ Je'sus:
6 That ye may with one mind *and* one mouth
glorify God, even the Father of our Lord Je'sus
Christ.
7 Wherefore receive ye one another, as
Christ also received us to the glory of God.
8 Now I say that Je'sus Christ was a minister
of the circumcision for the truth of God, to confirm the promises *made* unto the fathers:
9 And that the Gen'tiles might glorify God
for *his* mercy; as it is written, For this cause I
will confess to thee among the Gen'tiles, and
sing unto thy name.
10 And again he saith, Rejoice, ye Gen'tiles,
with his people.
11 And again, Praise the Lord, all ye Gen'-
tiles; and laud him, all ye people.
12 And again, E-sa'ias saith, There shall be a
root of Jes'se, and he that shall rise to reign
over the Gen'tiles; in him shall the Gen'tiles
trust.
13 Now the God of hope fill you with all joy
and peace in believing, that ye may abound in
hope, through the power of the Ho'ly Ghost.
14 And I myself also am persuaded of you,
my brethren, that ye also are full of goodness,
filled with all knowledge, able also to admonish
one another.
15 Nevertheless, brethren, I have written the
more boldly unto you in some sort, as putting
you in mind, because of the grace that is given
to me of God,
16 That I should be the minister of Je'sus
Christ to the Gen'tiles, ministering the gospel of
God, that the offering up of the Gen'tiles might
be acceptable, being sanctified by the Ho'ly
Ghost.
17 I have therefore whereof I may glory
through Je'sus Christ in those things which pertain to God.
18 For I will not dare to speak of any of those
things which Christ hath not wrought by me, to
make the Gen'tiles obedient, by word and deed,
19 Through mighty signs and wonders, by
the power of the Spirit of God; so that from Je-
ru'sa-lem, and round about unto Il-lyr'i-cum, I
have fully preached the gospel of Christ.
20 Yea, so have I strived to preach the gospel, not where Christ was named, lest I should
build upon another man's foundation:
21 But as it is written, To whom he was not
spoken of, they shall see: and they that have not
heard shall understand.
22 For which cause also I have been much
hindered from coming to you.
23 But now having no more place in these
parts, and having a great desire these many
years to come unto you;
24 Whensoever I take my journey into Spain,
I will come to you: for I trust to see you in my
journey, and to be brought on my way thitherward by you, if first I be somewhat filled with
your *company*.
25 But now I go unto Je-ru'sa-lem to minister
unto the saints.
26 For it hath pleased them of Mac-e-do'ni-a
and A-cha'ia to make a certain contribution for
the poor saints which are at Je-ru'sa-lem.
27 It hath pleased them verily; and their
debtors they are. For if the Gen'tiles have been
made partakers of their spiritual things, their
duty is also to minister unto them in carnal
things.
28 When therefore I have performed this,
and have sealed to them this fruit, I will come
by you into Spain.
29 And I am sure that, when I come unto
you, I shall come in the fulness of the blessing
of the gospel of Christ.
30 Now I beseech you, brethren, for the Lord
Je'sus Christ's sake, and for the love of the
Spirit, that ye strive together with me in *your*
prayers to God for me;
31 That I may be delivered from them that do
not believe in Ju-dæ'a; and that my service
which *I have* for Je-ru'sa-lem may be accepted
of the saints;
32 That I may come unto you with joy by the
will of God, and may with you be refreshed.
33 Now the God of peace *be* with you all.
Amen.

16 I COMMEND unto you Phe'be our sister, which is a servant of the church
which is at Cenchre-a:
2 That ye receive her in the Lord, as becometh saints, and that ye assist her in whatsoever
business she hath need of you: for she hath
been a succourer of many, and of myself also.
3 Greet Pris-cil'la and A'qui-la my helpers in
Christ Je'sus:
4 Who have for my life laid down their own
necks: unto whom not only I give thanks, but
also all the churches of the Gen'tiles.
5 Likewise *greet* the church that is in their
house. Salute my wellbeloved E-pæn'e-tus, who
is the firstfruits of A-cha'ia unto Christ.
6 Greet Ma'ry, who bestowed much labour
on us.

7 Salute An-dro-ni'cus and Ju'nia, my kinsmen, and my fellowprisoners, who are of note among the apostles, who also were in Christ before me.

8 Greet Am'pli-as my beloved in the Lord.

9 Salute Ur'bane, our helper in Christ, and Sta'chys my beloved.

10 Salute A-pelles approved in Christ. Salute them which are of Ar-is-to-bu'lus' *household*.

11 Salute He-ro'di-on my kinsman. Greet them that be of the *household* of Nar-cis'sus, which are in the Lord.

12 Salute Try-phe'na and Try-pho'sa, who labour in the Lord. Salute the beloved Per'sis, which laboured much in the Lord.

13 Salute Ru'fus chosen in the Lord, and his mother and mine.

14 Salute A-syn'cri-tus, Phle'gon, Her'mas, Pat'ro-bas, Her'mes, and the brethren which are with them.

15 Salute Phi-lolo'-gus, and Ju'lia, Ne're-us, and his sister, and O-lym'pas, and all the saints which are with them.

16 Salute one another with an holy kiss. The churches of Christ salute you.

17 Now I beseech you, brethren, mark them which cause divisions and offences contrary to the doctrine which ye have learned; and avoid them.

18 For they that are such serve not our Lord Je'sus Christ, but their own belly; and by good words and fair speeches deceive the hearts of the simple.

19 For your obedience is come abroad unto all *men*. I am glad therefore on your behalf: but yet I would have you wise unto that which is good, and simple concerning evil.

20 And the God of peace shall bruise Sa'tan under your feet shortly. The grace of our Lord Je'sus Christ *be* with you. Amen.

21 Ti-mo'the-us my workfellow, and Lu'cius, and Ja'son, and So-sip'a-ter, my kinsmen, salute you.

22 I Ter'tius, who wrote *this* epistle, salute you in the Lord.

23 Ga'ius mine host, and of the whole church, saluteth you. E-ras'tus the chamberlain of the city saluteth you, and Quar'tus a brother.

24 The grace of our Lord Je'sus Christ *be* with you all. Amen.

25 Now to him that is of power to stablish you according to my gospel, and the preaching of Je'sus Christ, according to the revelation of the mystery, which was kept secret since the world began,

26 But now is made manifest, and by the scriptures of the prophets, according to the commandment of the everlasting God, made known to all nations for the obedience of faith:

27 To God only wise, *be* glory through Je'sus Christ for ever. Amen.

Written to the Ro'mans from Co-rin'thus, *and sent* by Phe'be servant of the church at Cen'chre-a.

THE FIRST LETTER OF PAUL TO THE

CORINTHIANS

1 PAUL, called *to be* an apostle of Je'sus Christ through the will of God, and Sos'the-nes *our* brother,

2 Unto the church of God which is at Cor'inth, to them that are sanctified in Christ Je'sus, called *to be* saints, with all that in every place call upon the name of Je'sus Christ our Lord, both theirs and ours:

3 Grace *be* unto you, and peace, from God our Father, and *from* the Lord Je'sus Christ.

4 I thank my God always on your behalf, for the grace of God which is given you by Je'sus Christ;

5 That in every thing ye are enriched by him, in all utterance, and *in* all knowledge;

6 Even as the testimony of Christ was confirmed in you:

7 So that ye come behind in no gift; waiting for the coming of our Lord Je'sus Christ:

8 Who shall also confirm you unto the end, *that ye may be* blameless in the day of our Lord Je'sus Christ.

9 God *is* faithful, by whom ye were called unto the fellowship of his Son Je'sus Christ our Lord.

10 Now I beseech you, brethren, by the name of our Lord Je'sus Christ, that ye all speak the same thing, and *that* there be no divisions among you; but *that* ye be perfectly joined together in the same mind and in the same judgment.

11 For it hath been declared unto me of you, my brethren, by them *which are of the house* of Chlo'e, that there are contentions among you.

12 Now this I say, that every one of you saith, I am of Paul; and I of A-pol'los; and I of Ce'phas; and I of Christ.

13 Is Christ divided? was Paul crucified for you? or were ye baptized in the name of Paul?

14 I thank God that I baptized none of you, but Cris'pus and Ga'ius;

15 Lest any should say that I had baptized in mine own name.

16 And I baptized also the household of Steph'a-nas: besides, I know not whether I baptized any other.

17 For Christ sent me not to baptize, but to preach the gospel: not with wisdom of words, lest the cross of Christ should be made of none effect.

18 For the preaching of the cross is to them that perish foolishness; but unto us which are saved it is the power of God.

19 For it is written, I will destroy the wisdom of the wise, and will bring to nothing the understanding of the prudent.

20 Where *is* the wise? where *is* the scribe? where *is* the disputer of this world? hath not God made foolish the wisdom of this world?

21 For after that in the wisdom of God the world by wisdom knew not God, it pleased God by the foolishness of preaching to save them that believe.

22 For the Jews require a sign, and the Greeks seek after wisdom:

23 But we preach Christ crucified, unto the Jews a stumblingblock, and unto the Greeks foolishness;

24 But unto them which are called, both Jews and Greeks, Christ the power of God, and the wisdom of God.

25 Because the foolishness of God is wiser
than men; and the weakness of God is stronger
than men.
26 For ye see your calling, brethren, how that
not many wise men after the flesh, not many
mighty, not many noble, *are called:*
27 But God hath chosen the foolish things of
the world to confound the wise; and God hath
chosen the weak things of the world to confound the things which are mighty;
28 And base things of the world, and things
which are despised, hath God chosen, *yea,* and
things which are not, to bring to nought things
that are:
29 That no flesh should glory in his presence.
30 But of him are ye in Christ Je'sus, who of
God is made unto us wisdom, and righteousness, and sanctification, and redemption:
31 That, according as it is writen, He that
glorieth, let him glory in the Lord.

2 AND I, brethren, when I came to you,
came not with excellency of speech or of
wisdom, declaring unto you the testimony of
God.
2 For I determined not to know any thing
among you, save Je'sus Christ, and him crucified.
3 And I was with you in weakness, and in
fear, and in much trembling.
4 And my speech and my preaching *was* not
with enticing words of man's wisdom, but in
demonstration of the Spirit and of power:
5 That your faith should not stand in the wisdom of men, but in the power of God.
6 Howbeit we speak wisdom among them
that are perfect: yet not the wisdom of this
world, nor of the princes of this world, that
come to nought:
7 But we speak the wisdom of God in a mystery, *even* the hidden *wisdom,* which God ordained before the world unto our glory:
8 Which none of the princes of this world
knew: for had they known *it,* they would not
have crucified the Lord of glory.
9 But as it is written, Eye hath not seen, nor
ear heard, neither have entered into the heart of
man, the things which God hath prepared for
them that love him.
10 But God hath revealed *them* unto us by
his Spirit: for the Spirit searcheth all things,
yea, the deep things of God.
11 For what man knoweth the things of a
man, save the spirit of man which is in him?
even so the things of God knoweth no man, but
the Spirit of God.
12 Now we have received, not the spirit of
the world, but the spirit which is of God; that
we might know the things that are freely given
to us of God.
13 Which things also we speak, not in the
words which man's wisdom teacheth, but
which the Ho'ly Ghost teacheth; comparing
spiritual things with spiritual.
14 But the natural man receiveth not the
things of the Spirit of God: for they are foolishness unto him: neither can he know *them,* because they are spiritually discerned.
15 But he that is spiritual judgeth all things,
yet he himself is judged of no man.
16 For who hath known the mind of the
Lord, that he may instruct him? But we have
the mind of Christ.

3 AND I, brethren, could not speak unto you
as unto spiritual, but as unto carnal, *even*
as unto babes in Christ.
2 I have fed you with milk, and not with
meat: for hitherto ye were not able *to bear it,*
neither yet now are ye able.
3 For ye are yet carnal: for whereas *there is*
among you envying, and strife, and divisions,
are ye not carnal, and walk as men?
4 For while one saith, I am of Paul; and another, I *am* of A-pol'los; are ye not carnal?
5 Who then is Paul, and who *is* A-pol'los, but
ministers by whom ye believed, even as the
Lord gave to every man?
6 I have planted, A-pol'los watered; but God
gave the increase.
7 So then neither is he that planteth any
thing, neither he that watereth; but God that
giveth the increase.
8 Now he that planteth and he that watereth
are one: and every man shall receive his own
reward according to his own labour.
9 For we are labourers together with God: ye
are God's husbandry, *ye are* God's building.
10 According to the grace of God which is
given unto me, as a wise masterbuilder, I have
laid the foundation, and another buildeth
thereon. But let every man take heed how he
buildeth thereupon.
11 For other foundation can no man lay than
that is laid, which is Je'sus Christ.
12 Now if any man build upon this foundation gold, silver, precious stones, wood, hay,
stubble;
13 Every man's work shall be made manifest: for the day shall declare it, because it shall
be revealed by fire; and the fire shall try every
man's work of what sort it is.
14 If any man's work abide which he hath
built thereupon, he shall receive a reward.
15 If any man's work shall be burned, he
shall suffer loss: but he himself shall be saved;
yet so as by fire.
16 Know ye not that ye are the temple of
God, *that* the Spirit of God dwelleth in you?
17 If any man defile the temple of God, him
shall God destroy; for the temple of God is holy,
which *temple* ye are.
18 Let no man deceive himself. If any man
among you seemeth to be wise in this world, let
him become a fool, that he may be wise.
19 For the wisdom of this world is foolishness with God. For it is written, He taketh the
wise in their own craftiness.
20 And again, The Lord knoweth the
thoughts of the wise, that they are vain.
21 Therefore let no man glory in men. For all
things are yours;
22 Whether Paul or A-pol'los, or Ce'phas, or
the world, or life, or death, or things present, or
things to come; all are yours;
23 And ye are Christ's; and Christ *is* God's.

4 LET a man so account of us, as of the ministers of Christ, and stewards of the mysteries of God.
2 Moreover it is required in stewards, that a
man be found faithful.
3 But with me it is a very small thing that I
should be judged of you, or of man's judgment:
yea, I judge not mine own self.
4 For I know nothing by myself; yet am I not
hereby justified: but he that judgeth me is the
Lord.
5 Therefore judge nothing before the time,
until the Lord come, who both will bring to light
the hidden things of darkness, and will make
manifest the counsels of the hearts: and then
shall every man have praise of God.
6 And these things, brethren, I have in a fig-

ure transferred to myself and *to* A-pol'los for
your sakes; that ye might learn in us not to
think *of men* above that which is written, that
no one of you be puffed up for one against another.
7 For who maketh thee to differ *from another?* and what hast thou that thou didst not
receive? now if thou didst receive *it*, why dost
thou glory, as if thou hadst not received *it?*
8 Now ye are full, now ye are rich, ye have
reigned as kings without us: and I would to God
ye did reign, that we also might reign with you.
9 For I think that God hath set forth us the
apostles last, as it were appointed to death: for
we are made a spectacle unto the world, and to
angels, and to men.
10 We *are* fools for Christ's sake, but ye *are*
wise in Christ; we *are* weak, but ye *are* strong;
ye *are* honourable, but we *are* despised.
11 Even unto this present hour we both hunger, and thirst, and are naked, and are buffeted,
and have no certain dwellingplace;
12 And labour, working with our own hands:
being reviled, we bless; being persecuted, we
suffer it:
13 Being defamed, we intreat: we are made
as the filth of the world, *and are* the offscouring
of all things unto this day.
14 I write not these things to shame you, but
as my beloved sons I warn *you*.
15 For though ye have ten thousand instruc-
tors in Christ, yet *have ye* not many fathers: for
in Christ Je'sus I have begotten you through the
gospel.
16 Wherefore I beseech you, be ye followers
of me.
17 For this cause have I sent unto you Ti-
mo'the-us, who is my beloved son, and faithful
in the Lord, who shall bring you into remembrance of my ways which be in Christ, as I
teach every where in every church.
18 Now some are puffed up, as though I
would not come to you.
19 But I will come to you shortly, if the Lord
will, and will know, not the speech of them
which are puffed up, but the power.
20 For the kingdom of God *is* not in word,
but in power.
21 What will ye? shall I come unto you with a
rod, or in love, and *in* the spirit of meekness?

5 IT is reported commonly *that there is* fornication among you, and such fornication
as is not so much as named among the Gen'-
tiles, that one should have his father's wife.
2 And ye are puffed up, and have not rather
mourned, that he that hath done this deed
might be taken away from among you.
3 For I verily, as absent in body, but present
in spirit, have judged already, as though I were
present, *concerning* him that hath so done this
deed,
4 In the name of our Lord Je'sus Christ,
when ye are gathered together, and my spirit,
with the power of our Lord Je'sus Christ,
5 To deliver such an one unto Sa'tan for the
destruction of the flesh, that the spirit may be
saved in the day of the Lord Je'sus.
6 Your glorying *is* not good. Know ye not
that a little leaven leaveneth the whole lump?
7 Purge out therefore the old leaven, that ye
may be a new lump, as ye are unleavened. For
even Christ our passover is sacrificed for us:
8 Therefore let us keep the feast, not with old
leaven, neither with the leaven of malice and
wickedness; but with the unleavened *bread* of
sincerity and truth.
9 I wrote unto you in an epistle not to company with fornicators:
10 Yet not altogether with the fornicators of
this world, or with the covetous, or extortioners, or with idolaters; for then must ye needs go
out of the world.
11 But now I have written unto you not to
keep company, if any man that is called a
brother be a fornicator, or covetous, or an idolater, or a railer, or a drunkard, or an extortioner; with such an one no not to eat.
12 For what have I to do to judge them also
that are without? do not ye judge them that are
within?
13 But them that are without God judgeth.
Therefore put away from among yourselves
that wicked person.

6 DARE any of you, having a matter against
another, go to law before the unjust, and
not before the saints?
2 Do ye not know that the saints shall judge
the world? and if the world shall be judged by
you, are ye unworthy to judge the smallest matters?
3 Know ye not that we shall judge angels?
how much more things that pertain to this life?
4 If then ye have judgments of things pertaining to this life, set them to judge who are
least esteemed in the church.
5 I speak to your shame. Is it so, that there is
not a wise man among you? no, not one that
shall be able to judge between his brethren?
6 But brother goeth to law with brother, and
that before the unbelievers.
7 Now therefore there is utterly a fault
among you, because ye go to law one with another. Why do ye not rather take wrong? why
do ye not rather *suffer yourselves to* be defrauded?
8 Nay, ye do wrong, and defraud, and that
your brethren.
9 Know ye not that the unrighteous shall not
inherit the kingdom of God? Be not deceived:
neither fornicators, nor idolaters, nor adulterers, nor effeminate, nor abusers of themselves
with mankind,
10 Nor thieves, nor covetous, nor drunkards,
nor revilers, nor extortioners, shall inherit the
kingdom of God.
11 And such were some of you: but ye are
washed, but ye are sanctified, but ye are justified in the name of the Lord Je'sus, and by the
Spirit of our God.
12 All things are lawful unto me, but all
things are not expedient: all things are lawful
for me, but I will not be brought under the
power of any.
13 Meats for the belly, and the belly for
meats: but God shall destroy both it and them.
Now the body *is* not for fornication, but for the
Lord; and the Lord for the body.
14 And God hath both raised up the Lord,
and will also raise up us by his own power.
15 Know ye not that your bodies are the
members of Christ? shall I then take the members of Christ, and make *them* the members of
an harlot? God forbid.
16 What? know ye not that he which is
joined to an harlot is one body? for two, saith
he, shall be one flesh.
17 But he that is joined unto the Lord is one
spirit.
18 Flee fornication. Every sin that a man
doeth is without the body; but he that committeth fornication sinneth against his own body.
19 What? know ye not that your body is the

temple of the Ho'ly Ghost *which is* in you,
which ye have of God, and ye are not your own?
20 For ye are bought with a price: therefore
glorify God in your body, and in your spirit,
which are God's.

7 NOW concerning the things whereof ye
wrote unto me: *It is* good for a man not to
touch a woman.
2 Nevertheless, *to avoid* fornication, let every man have his own wife, and let every
woman have her own husband.
3 Let the husband render unto the wife due
benevolence: and likewise also the wife unto
the husband.
4 The wife hath not power of her own body,
but the husband: and likewise also the husband
hath not power of his own body, but the wife.
5 Defraud ye not one the other, except *it be*
with consent for a time, that ye may give yourselves to fasting and prayer; and come together
again, that Sa'tan tempt you not for your incon-
tinency.
6 But I speak this by permission, *and* not of
commandment.
7 For I would that all men were even as I
myself. But every man hath his proper gift of
God, one after this manner, and another after
that.
8 I say therefore to the unmarried and widows, It is good for them if they abide even as I.
9 But if they cannot contain, let them marry:
for it is better to marry than to burn.
10 And unto the married I command, *yet* not
I, but the Lord, Let not the wife depart from *her*
husband:
11 But and if she depart, let her remain unmarried, or be reconciled to *her* husband: and
let not the husband put away *his* wife.
12 But to the rest speak I, not the Lord: If any
brother hath a wife that believeth not, and she
be pleased to dwell with him, let him not put
her away.
13 And the woman which hath an husband
that believeth not, and if he be pleased to dwell
with her, let her not leave him.
14 For the unbelieving husband is sanctified
by the wife, and the unbelieving wife is sanctified by the husband: else were your children unclean; but now are they holy.
15 But if the unbelieving depart, let him depart. A brother or a sister is not under bondage
in such *cases:* but God hath called us to peace.
16 For what knowest thou, O wife, whether
thou shalt save *thy* husband? or how knowest
thou, O man, whether thou shalt save *thy* wife?
17 But as God hath distributed to every man,
as the Lord hath called every one, so let him
walk. And so ordain I in all churches.
18 Is any man called being circumcised? let
him not become uncircumcised. Is any called in
uncircumcision? let him not be circumcised.
19 Circumcision is nothing, and uncircumcision is nothing, but the keeping of the commandments of God.
20 Let every man abide in the same calling
wherein he was called.
21 Art thou called *being* a servant? care not
for it: but if thou mayest be made free, use *it*
rather.
22 For he that is called in the Lord, *being* a
servant, is the Lord's freeman: likewise also he
that is called, *being* free, is Christ's servant.
23 Ye are bought with a price; be not ye the
servants of men.
24 Brethren, let every man, wherein he is
called, therein abide with God.
25 Now concerning virgins I have no commandment of the Lord: yet I give my judgment,
as one that hath obtained mercy of the Lord to
be faithful.
26 I suppose therefore that this is good for
the present distress, *I say,* that *it is* good for a
man so to be.
27 Art thou bound unto a wife? seek not to
be loosed. Art thou loosed from a wife? seek not
a wife.
28 But and if thou marry, thou hast not
sinned; and if a virgin marry, she hath not
sinned. Nevertheless such shall have trouble in
the flesh: but I spare you.
29 But this I say, brethren, the time *is* short:
it remaineth, that both they that have wives be
as though they had none;
30 And they that weep, as though they wept
not; and they that rejoice, as though they rejoiced not; and they that buy, as though they
possessed not;
31 And they that use this world, as not abus-
ing *it:* for the fashion of this world passeth
away.
32 But I would have you without carefulness.
He that is unmarried careth for the things that
belong to the Lord, how he may please the
Lord:
33 But he that is married careth for the
things that are of the world, how he may please
his wife.
34 There is difference *also* between a wife
and a virgin. The unmarried woman careth for
the things of the Lord, that she may be holy
both in body and in spirit: but she that is married careth for the things of the world, how she
may please *her* husband.
35 And this I speak for your own profit; not
that I may cast a snare upon you, but for that
which is comely, and that ye may attend upon
the Lord without distraction.
36 But if any man think that he behaveth
himself uncomely toward his virgin, if she pass
the flower of *her* age, and need so require, let
him do what he will, he sinneth not: let them
marry.
37 Nevertheless he that standeth stedfast in
his heart, having no necessity, but hath power
over his own will, and hath so decreed in his
heart that he will keep his virgin, doeth well.
38 So then he that giveth *her* in marriage
doeth well; but he that giveth *her* not in marriage doeth better.
39 The wife is bound by the law as long as
her husband liveth; but if her husband be dead,
she is at liberty to be married to whom she will;
only in the Lord.
40 But she is happier if she so abide, after my
judgment: and I think also that I have the Spirit
of God.

8 NOW as touching things offered unto
idols, we know that we all have knowledge. Knowledge puffeth up, but charity edifieth.
2 And if any man think that he knoweth any
thing, he knoweth nothing yet as he ought to
know.
3 But if any man love God, the same is
known of him.
4 As concerning therefore the eating of those
things that are offered in sacrifice unto idols,
we know that an idol *is* nothing in the world,
and that *there is* none other God but one.
5 For though there be that are called gods,
whether in heaven or in earth, (as there be gods
many, and lords many,)

6 But to us *there is but* one God, the Father, of whom *are* all things, and we in him; and one Lord Je'sus Christ, by whom *are* all things, and we by him.

7 Howbeit *there is* not in every man that knowledge: for some with conscience of the idol unto this hour eat *it* as a thing offered unto an idol; and their conscience being weak is defiled.

8 But meat commmendeth us not to God: for neither, if we eat, are we the better; neither, if we eat not, are we the worse.

9 But take heed lest by any means this liberty of yours become a stumblingblock to them that are weak.

10 For if any man see thee which hast knowledge sit at meat in the idol's temple, shall not the conscience of him which is weak be emboldened to eat those things which are offered to idols;

11 And through thy knowledge shall the weak brother perish, for whom Christ died?

12 But when ye sin so against the brethren, and wound their weak conscience, ye sin against Christ.

13 Wherefore, if meat make my brother to offend, I will eat no flesh while the world standeth, lest I make my brother to offend.

9 AM I not an apostle? am I not free? have I not seen Je'sus Christ our Lord? are not ye my work in the Lord?

2 If I be not an apostle unto others, yet doubtless I am to you: for the seal of mine apostleship are ye in the Lord.

3 Mine answer to them that do examine me is this,

4 Have we not power to eat and to drink?

5 Have we not power to lead about a sister, a wife, as well as other apostles, and *as* the brethren of the Lord, and Ce'phas?

6 Or I only and Bar'na-bas, have not we power to forbear working?

7 Who goeth a warfare any time at his own charges? who planteth a vineyard, and eateth not of the fruit thereof? or who feedeth a flock, and eateth not of the milk of the flock?

8 Say I these things as a man? or saith not the law the same also?

9 For it is written in the law of Mo'ses, Thou shalt not muzzle the mouth of the ox that treadeth out the corn. Doth God take care for oxen?

10 Or saith he *it* altogether for our sakes? For our sakes, no doubt, *this* is written: that he that ploweth should plow in hope; and that he that thresheth in hope should be partaker of his hope.

11 If we have sown unto you spiritual things, *is it* a great thing if we shall reap your carnal things?

12 If others be partakers of *this* power over you, *are* not we rather? Nevertheless we have not used this power; but suffer all things, lest we should hinder the gospel of Christ.

13 Do ye not know that they which minister about holy things live *of the things* of the temple? and they which wait at the altar are partakers with the altar?

14 Even so hath the Lord ordained that they which preach the gospel should live of the gospel.

15 But I have used none of these things: neither have I written these things, that it should be so done unto me: for *it were* better for me to die, than that any man should make my glorying void.

16 For though I preach the gospel, I have nothing to glory of: for necessity is laid upon me; yea, woe is unto me, if I preach not the gospel!

17 For if I do this thing willingly, I have a reward: but if against my will, a dispensation *of the gospel* is committed unto me.

18 What is my reward then? *Verily* that, when I preach the gospel, I may make the gospel of Christ without charge, that I abuse not my power in the gospel.

19 For though I be free from all *men*, yet have I made myself servant unto all, that I might gain the more.

20 And unto the Jews I became as a Jew, that I might gain the Jews; to them that are under the law, as under the law, that I might gain them that are under the law;

21 To them that are without law, as without law, (being not without law to God, but under the law to Christ,) that I might gain them that are without law;

22 To the weak became I as weak, that I might gain the weak: I am made all things to all *men*, that I might by all means save some.

23 And this I do for the gospel's sake, that I might be partaker thereof with *you*.

24 Know ye not that they which run in a race run all, but one receiveth the prize? So run, that ye may obtain.

25 And every man that striveth for the mastery is temperate in all things. Now they *do it* to obtain a corruptible crown; but we an incorruptible.

26 I therefore so run, not as uncertainly; so fight I, not as one that beateth the air:

27 But I keep under my body, and bring *it* into subjection: lest that by any means, when I have preached to others, I myself should be a castaway.

10 MOREOVER, brethren, I would not that ye should be ignorant, how that all our fathers were under the cloud, and all passed through the sea;

2 And were all baptized unto Mo'ses in the cloud and in the sea;

3 And did all eat the same spiritual meat;

4 And did all drink the same spiritual drink: for they drank of that spiritual Rock that followed them: and that Rock was Christ.

5 But with many of them God was not well pleased: for they were overthrown in the wilderness.

6 Now these things were our examples, to the intent we should not lust after evil things, as they also lusted.

7 Neither be ye idolaters, as *were* some of them; as it is written, The people sat down to eat and drink, and rose up to play.

8 Neither let us commit fornication, as some of them committed, and fell in one day three and twenty thousand.

9 Neither let us tempt Christ, as some of them also tempted, and were destroyed of serpents.

10 Neither murmur ye, as some of them also murmured, and were destroyed of the destroyer.

11 Now all these things happened unto them for ensamples: and they are written for our admonition, upon whom the ends of the world are come.

12 Wherefore let him that thinketh he standeth take heed lest he fall.

13 There hath no temptation taken you but such as is common to man: but God *is* faithful, who will not suffer you to be tempted above

that ye are able; but will with the temptation
also make a way to escape, that ye may be able
to bear *it*.
14 Wherefore, my dearly beloved, flee from
idolatry.
15 I speak as to wise men; judge ye what I
say.
16 The cup of blessing which we bless, is it
not the communion of the blood of Christ? The
bread which we break, is it not the communion
of the body of Christ?
17 For we *being* many are one bread, *and*
one body: for we are all partakers of that one
bread.
18 Behold Is′ra-el after the flesh: are not they
which eat of the sacrifices partakers of the altar?
19 What say I then? that the idol is any thing,
or that which is offered in sacrifice to idols is
any thing?
20 But *I say*, that the things which the Gen′-
tiles sacrifice, they sacrifice to devils, and not to
God: and I would not that ye should have fellowship with devils.
21 Ye cannot drink the cup of the Lord, and
the cup of devils: ye cannot be partakers of the
Lord's table, and of the table of devils.
22 Do we provoke the Lord to jealousy? are
we stronger than he?
23 All things are lawful for me, but all things
are not expedient: all things are lawful for me,
but all things edify not.
24 Let no man seek his own, but every man
another's *wealth*.
25 Whatsoever is sold in the shambles, *that*
eat, asking no question for conscience sake:
26 For the earth *is* the Lord's, and the fulness
thereof.
27 If any of them that believe not bid you *to*
a feast, and ye be disposed to go; whatsoever is
set before you, eat, asking no question for conscience sake.
28 But if any man say unto you, This is offered in sacrifice unto idols, eat not for his sake
that shewed it, and for conscience sake: for the
earth *is* the Lord's, and the fulness thereof:
29 Conscience, I say, not thine own, but of
the other: for why is my liberty judged of another *man's* conscience?
30 For if I by grace be a partaker, why am I
evil spoken of for that for which I give thanks?
31 Whether therefore ye eat, or drink, or
whatsoever ye do, do all to the glory of God.
32 Give none offence, neither to the Jews,
nor to the Gen′tiles, nor to the church of God:
33 Even as I please all *men* in all *things*, not
seeking mine own profit, but the *profit* of many,
that they may be saved.

11 BE ye followers of me, even as I also *am*
of Christ.
2 Now I praise you, brethren, that ye remember me in all things, and keep the ordinances, as
I delivered *them* to you.
3 But I would have you know, that the head
of every man is Christ; and the head of the
woman *is* the man; and the head of Christ *is*
God.
4 Every man praying or prophesying, having
his head covered, dishonoureth his head.
5 But every woman that prayeth or prophesieth with *her* head uncovered dishonoureth her
head: for that is even all one as if she were
shaven.
6 For if the woman be not covered, let her
also be shorn: but if it be a shame for a woman
to be shorn or shaven, let her be covered.
7 For a man indeed ought not to cover *his*
head, forasmuch as he is the image and glory of
God: but the woman is the glory of the man.
8 For the man is not of the woman; but the
woman of the man.
9 Neither was the man created for the
woman; but the woman for the man.
10 For this cause ought the woman to have
power on *her* head because of the angels.
11 Nevertheless neither is the man without
the woman, neither the woman without the
man, in the Lord.
12 For as the woman *is* of the man, even so *is*
the man also by the woman; but all things of
God.
13 Judge in yourselves: is it comely that a
woman pray unto God uncovered?
14 Doth not even nature itself teach you,
that, if a man have long hair, it is a shame unto
him?
15 But if a woman have long hair, it is a glory
to her: for *her* hair is given her for a covering.
16 But if any man seem to be contentious, we
have no such custom, neither the churches of
God.
17 Now in this that I declare *unto you* I
praise *you* not, that ye come together not for
the better, but for the worse.
18 For first of all, when ye come together in
the church, I hear that there be divisions among
you; and I partly believe it.
19 For there must be also heresies among
you, that they which are approved may be
made manifest among you.
20 When ye come together therefore into one
place, *this* is not to eat the Lord's supper.
21 For in eating every one taketh before *oth-*
er his own supper: and one is hungry, and another is drunken.
22 What? have ye not houses to eat and to
drink in? or despise ye the church of God, and
shame them that have not? What shall I say to
you? shall I praise you in this? I praise *you* not.
23 For I have received of the Lord that which
also I delivered unto you, That the Lord Je′sus
the *same* night in which he was betrayed took
bread:
24 And when he had given thanks, he brake
it, and said, Take, eat: this is my body, which is
broken for you: this do in remembrance of me.
25 After the same manner also *he took* the
cup, when he had supped, saying, This cup is
the new testament in my blood: this do ye, as
oft as ye drink *it*, in remembrance of me.
26 For as often as ye eat this bread, and
drink this cup, ye do shew the Lord's death till
he come.
27 Wherefore whosoever shall eat this bread,
and drink *this* cup of the Lord, unworthily, shall
be guilty of the body and blood of the Lord.
28 But let a man examine himself, and so let
him eat of *that* bread, and drink of *that* cup.
29 For he that eateth and drinketh unworthily, eateth and drinketh damnation to himself,
not discerning the Lord's body.
30 For this cause many *are* weak and sickly
among you, and many sleep.
31 For if we would judge ourselves, we
should not be judged.
32 But when we are judged we are chastened
of the Lord, that we should not be condemned
with the world.
33 Wherefore, my brethren, when ye come
together to eat, tarry one for another.
34 And if any man hunger, let him eat at
home; that ye come not together unto condem-

nation. And the rest will I set in order when I
come.

12 NOW concerning spiritual *gifts*, brethren, I would not have you ignorant.
2 Ye know that ye were Gen'tiles, carried
away unto these dumb idols, even as ye were
led.
3 Wherefore I give you to understand, that
no man speaking by the Spirit of God calleth
Je'sus accursed: and *that* no man can say that
Je'sus is the Lord but by the Ho'ly Ghost.
4 Now there are diversities of gifts, but the
same Spirit.
5 And there are differences of administra-
tions, but the same Lord.
6 And there are diversities of operations, but
it is the same God which worketh all in all.
7 But the manifestation of the Spirit is given
to every man to profit withal.
8 For to one is given by the Spirit the word of
wisdom; to another the word of knowledge by
the same Spirit;
9 To another faith by the same Spirit; to another the gifts of healing by the same Spirit;
10 To another the working of miracles; to another prophecy; to another discerning of spirits;
to another *divers* kinds of tongues; to another
the interpretation of tongues:
11 But all these worketh that one and the
selfsame Spirit, dividing to every man severally
as he will.
12 For as the body is one, and hath many
members, and all the members of that one
body, being many, are one body: so also *is*
Christ.
13 For by one Spirit are we all baptized into
one body, whether *we be* Jews or Gen'tiles,
whether *we be* bond or free; and have been all
made to drink into one Spirit.
14 For the body is not one member, but
many.
15 If the foot shall say, Because I am not the
hand, I am not of the body; is it therefore not of
the body?
16 And if the ear shall say, Because I am not
the eye, I am not of the body; is it therefore not
of the body?
17 If the whole body *were* an eye, where
were the hearing? If the whole *were* hearing,
where *were* the smelling?
18 But now hath God set the members every
one of them in the body, as it hath pleased him.
19 And if they were all one member, where
were the body?
20 But now *are they* many members, yet but
one body.
21 And the eye cannot say unto the hand, I
have no need of thee: nor again the head to the
feet, I have no need of you.
22 Nay, much more those members of the
body, which seem to be more feeble, are necessary:
23 And those *members* of the body, which
we think to be less honourable, upon these we
bestow more abundant honour; and our uncomely *parts* have more abundant comeliness.
24 For our comely *parts* have no need: but
God hath tempered the body together, having
given more abundant honour to that *part* which
lacked:
25 That there should be no schism in the
body; but *that* the members should have the
same care one for another.
26 And whether one member suffer, all the
members suffer with it; or one member be honoured, all the members rejoice with it.
27 Now ye are the body of Christ, and members in particular.
28 And God hath set some in the church, first
apostles, secondarily prophets, thirdly teachers,
after that miracles, then gifts of healings, helps,
governments, diversities of tongues.
29 *Are* all apostles? *are* all prophets? *are* all
teachers? *are* all workers of miracles?
30 Have all the gifts of healing? do all speak
with tongues? do all interpret?
31 But covet earnestly the best gifts: and yet
shew I unto you a more excellent way.

13 THOUGH I speak with the tongues of
men and of angels, and have not charity,
I am become *as* sounding brass, or a tinkling
cymbal.
2 And though I have *the gift of* prophecy,
and understand all mysteries, and all knowledge; and though I have all faith, so that I could
remove mountains, and have not charity, I am
nothing.
3 And though I bestow all my goods to feed
the poor, and though I give my body to be
burned, and have not charity, it profiteth me
nothing.
4 Charity suffereth long, *and* is kind; charity
envieth not; charity vaunteth not itself, is not
puffed up,
5 Doth not behave itself unseemly, seeketh
not her own, is not easily provoked, thinketh no
evil;
6 Rejoiceth not in iniquity, but rejoiceth in
the truth;
7 Beareth all things, believeth all things, hop-
eth all things, endureth all things.
8 Charity never faileth: but whether *there be*
prophecies, they shall fail; whether *there be*
tongues, they shall cease; whether *there be*
knowledge, it shall vanish away.
9 For we know in part, and we prophesy in
part.
10 But when that which is perfect is come,
then that which is in part shall be done away.
11 When I was a child, I spake as a child, I
understood as a child, I thought as a child: but
when I became a man, I put away childish
things.
12 For now we see through a glass, darkly;
but then face to face: now I know in part; but
then shall I know even as also I am known.
13 And now abideth faith, hope, charity,
these three; but the greatest of these *is* charity.

14 FOLLOW after charity, and desire spiritual *gifts*, but rather that ye may prophesy.
2 For he that speaketh in an *unknown*
tongue speaketh not unto men, but unto God;
for no man understandeth *him;* howbeit in the
spirit he speaketh mysteries.
3 But he that prophesieth speaketh unto men
to edification, and exhortation, and comfort.
4 He that speaketh in an *unknown* tongue
edifieth himself; but he that prophesieth edifieth the church.
5 I would that ye all spake with tongues, but
rather that ye prophesied: for greater *is* he that
prophesieth than he that speaketh with
tongues, except he interpret, that the church
may receive edifying.
6 Now, brethren, if I come unto you speaking
with tongues, what shall I profit you, except I
shall speak to you either by revelation, or by
knowledge, or by prophesying, or by doctrine?
7 And even things without life giving sound,
whether pipe or harp, except they give a dis-

tinction in the sounds, how shall it be known
what is piped or harped?
8 For if the trumpet give an uncertain sound,
who shall prepare himself to the battle?
9 So likewise ye, except ye utter by the
tongue words easy to be understood, how shall
it be known what is spoken? for ye shall speak
into the air.
10 There are, it may be, so many kinds of
voices in the world, and none of them *is* without
signification.
11 Therefore if I know not the meaning of the
voice, I shall be unto him that speaketh a bar-
barian, and he that speaketh *shall be* a barbar-
ian unto me.
12 Even so ye, forasmuch as ye are zealous
of spiritual *gifts*, seek that ye may excel to the
edifying of the church.
13 Wherefore let him that speaketh in an *unknown* tongue pray that he may interpret.
14 For if I pray in an *unknown* tongue, my
spirit prayeth, but my understanding is unfruitful.
15 What is it then? I will pray with the spirit,
and I will pray with the understanding also: I
will sing with the spirit, and I will sing with the
understanding also.
16 Else when thou shalt bless with the spirit,
how shall he that occupieth the room of the unlearned say Amen at thy giving of thanks, seeing he understandeth not what thou sayest?
17 For thou verily givest thanks well, but the
other is not edified.
18 I thank my God, I speak with tongues
more than ye all:
19 Yet in the church I had rather speak five
words with my understanding, that *by my voice*
I might teach others also, than ten thousand
words in an *unknown* tongue.
20 Brethren, be not children in understanding: howbeit in malice be ye children, but in understanding be men.
21 In the law it is written, With *men of* other
tongues and other lips will I speak unto this
people; and yet for all that will they not hear
me, saith the Lord.
22 Wherefore tongues are for a sign, not to
them that believe, but to them that believe not:
but prophesying *serveth* not for them that believe not, but for them which believe.
23 If therefore the whole church be come together into one place, and all speak with
tongues, and there come in *those that are* unlearned, or unbelievers, will they not say that ye
are mad?
24 But if all prophesy, and there come in one
that believeth not, or *one* unlearned, he is convinced of all, he is judged of all:
25 And thus are the secrets of his heart made
manifest; and so falling down on *his* face he will
worship God, and report that God is in you of a
truth.
26 How is it then, brethren? when ye come
together, every one of you hath a psalm, hath a
doctrine, hath a tongue, hath a revelation, hath
an interpretation. Let all things be done unto
edifying.
27 If any man speak in an *unknown* tongue,
let it be by two, or at the most *by* three, and *that*
by course; and let one interpret.
28 But if there be no interpreter, let him keep
silence in the church; and let him speak to himself, and to God.
29 Let the prophets speak two or three, and
let the other judge.
30 If *any thing* be revealed to another that
sitteth by, let the first hold his peace.
31 For ye may all prophesy one by one, that
all may learn, and all may be comforted.
32 And the spirits of the prophets are subject
to the prophets.
33 For God is not *the author* of confusion,
but of peace, as in all churches of the saints.
34 Let your women keep silence in the
churches: for it is not permitted unto them to
speak; but *they are commanded* to be under
obedience, as also saith the law.
35 And if they will learn any thing, let them
ask their husbands at home: for it is a shame for
women to speak in the church.
36 What? came the word of God out from
you? or came it unto you only?
37 If any man think himself to be a prophet,
or spiritual, let him acknowledge that the things
that I write unto you are the commandments of
the Lord.
38 But if any man be ignorant, let him be ignorant.
39 Wherefore, brethren, covet to prophesy,
and forbid not to speak with tongues.
40 Let all things be done decently and in order.

15 MOREOVER, brethren, I declare unto
you the gospel which I preached unto
you, which also ye have received, and wherein
ye stand;
2 By which also ye are saved, if ye keep in
memory what I preached unto you, unless ye
have believed in vain.
3 For I delivered unto you first of all that
which I also received, how that Christ died for
our sins according to the scriptures;
4 And that he was buried, and that he rose
again the third day according to the scriptures:
5 And that he was seen of Ce'phas, then of
the twelve:
6 After that, he was seen of above five hundred brethren at once; of whom the greater part
remain unto this present, but some are fallen
asleep.
7 After that, he was seen of James; then of all
the apostles.
8 And last of all he was seen of me also, as of
one born out of due time.
9 For I am the least of the apostles, that am
not meet to be called an apostle, because I persecuted the church of God.
10 But by the grace of God I am what I am:
and his grace which *was bestowed* upon me
was not in vain; but I laboured more abundantly
than they all: yet not I, but the grace of God
which was with me.
11 Therefore whether *it were* I or they, so we
preach, and so ye believed.
12 Now if Christ be preached that he rose
from the dead, how say some among you that
there is no resurrection of the dead?
13 But if there be no resurrection of the dead,
then is Christ not risen:
14 And if Christ be not risen, then *is* our
preaching vain, and your faith *is* also vain.
15 Yea, and we are found false witnesses of
God; because we have testified of God that he
raised up Christ: whom he raised not up, if so
be that the dead rise not.
16 For if the dead rise not, then is not Christ
raised:
17 And if Christ be not raised, your faith *is*
vain; ye are yet in your sins.
18 Then they also which are fallen asleep in
Christ are perished.
19 If in this life only we have hope in Christ,
we are of all men most miserable.

20 But now is Christ risen from the dead, *and*
become the firstfruits of them that slept.
21 For since by man *came* death, by man
came also the resurrection of the dead.
22 For as in Ad'am all die, even so in Christ
shall all be made alive.
23 But every man in his own order: Christ
the firstfruits; afterward they that are Christ's
at his coming.
24 Then *cometh* the end, when he shall have
delivered up the kingdom to God, even the Father; when he shall have put down all rule and
all authority and power.
25 For he must reign, till he hath put all enemies under his feet.
26 The last enemy *that* shall be destroyed *is*
death.
27 For he hath put all things under his feet.
But when he saith all things are put under *him*,
it is manifest that he is excepted, which did put
all things under him.
28 And when all things shall be subdued unto
him, then shall the Son also himself be subject
unto him that put all things under him, that God
may be all in all.
29 Else what shall they do which are baptized for the dead, if the dead rise not at all?
why are they then baptized for the dead?
30 And why stand we in jeopardy every
hour?
31 I protest by your rejoicing which I have in
Christ Je'sus our Lord, I die daily.
32 If after the manner of men I have fought
with beasts at Eph'e-sus, what advantageth it
me, if the dead rise not? let us eat and drink; for
to morrow we die.
33 Be not deceived: evil communications
corrupt good manners.
34 Awake to righteousness, and sin not; for
some have not the knowledge of God: I speak
this to your shame.
35 But some *man* will say, How are the dead
raised up? and with what body do they come?
36 *Thou* fool, that which thou sowest is not
quickened, except it die:
37 And that which thou sowest, thou sowest
not that body that shall be, but bare grain, it
may chance of wheat, or of some other *grain:*
38 But God giveth it a body as it hath pleased
him, and to every seed his own body.
39 All flesh *is* not the same flesh: but *there is*
one *kind of* flesh of men, another flesh of
beasts, another of fishes, *and* another of birds.
40 *There are* also celestial bodies, and bodies
terrestrial: but the glory of the celestial *is* one,
and the *glory* of the terrestrial *is* another.
41 *There is* one glory of the sun, and another
glory of the moon, and another glory of the
stars: for *one* star differeth from *another* star in
glory.
42 So also *is* the resurrection of the dead. It
is sown in corruption: it is raised in incorruption:
43 It is sown in dishonour; it is raised in glory: it is sown in weakness; it is raised in power:
44 It is sown a natural body; it is raised a
spiritual body. There is a natural body, and
there is a spiritual body.
45 And so it is written, The first man Ad'am
was made a living soul; the last Ad'am *was*
made a quickening spirit.
46 Howbeit that *was* not first which is spiritual, but that which is natural; and afterward
that which is spiritual.
47 The first man *is* of the earth, earthy: the
second man *is* the Lord from heaven.
48 As *is* the earthy, such *are* they also that
are earthy: and as *is* the heavenly, such *are* they
also that are heavenly.
49 And as we have borne the image of the
earthy, we shall also bear the image of the
heavenly.
50 Now this I say, brethren, that flesh and
blood cannot inherit the kingdom of God; neither doth corruption inherit incorruption.
51 Behold, I shew you a mystery; We shall
not all sleep, but we shall all be changed,
52 In a moment, in the twinkling of an eye, at
the last trump: for the trumpet shall sound, and
the dead shall be raised incorruptible, and we
shall be changed.
53 For this corruptible must put on incorruption, and this mortal *must* put on immortality.
54 So when this corruptible shall have put on
incorruption, and this mortal shall have put on
immortality, then shall be brought to pass the
saying that is written, Death is swallowed up in
victory.
55 O death, where *is* thy sting? O grave,
where *is* thy victory?
56 The sting of death *is* sin; and the strength
of sin *is* the law.
57 But thanks *be* to God, which giveth us the
victory through our Lord Je'sus Christ.
58 Therefore, my beloved brethren, be ye
stedfast, unmoveable, always abounding in the
work of the Lord, forasmuch as ye know that
your labour is not in vain in the Lord.

16 NOW concerning the collection for the
saints, as I have given order to the
churches of Ga-la'tia, even so do ye.
2 Upon the first *day* of the week let every one
of you lay by him in store, as *God* hath prospered him, that there be no gatherings when I
come.
3 And when I come, whomsoever ye shall approve by *your* letters, them will I send to bring
your liberality unto Je-ru'sa-lem.
4 And if it be meet that I go also, they shall
go with me.
5 Now I will come unto you, when I shall
pass through Mac-e-do'ni-a: for I do pass
through Mac-e-do'ni-a.
6 And it may be that I will abide, yea, and
winter with you, that ye may bring me on my
journey whithersoever I go.
7 For I will not see you now by the way; but I
trust to tarry a while with you, if the Lord permit.
8 But I will tarry at Eph'e-sus until Pen'te-
cost.
9 For a great door and effectual is opened
unto me, and *there are* many adversaries.
10 Now if Ti-mo'the-us come, see that he
may be with you without fear: for he worketh
the work of the Lord, as I also *do*.
11 Let no man therefore despise him: but
conduct him forth in peace, that he may come
unto me: for I look for him with the brethren.
12 As touching *our* brother A-pol'los, I
greatly desired him to come unto you with the
brethren: but his will was not at all to come at
this time; but he will come when he shall have
convenient time.
13 Watch ye, stand fast in the faith, quit you
like men, be strong.
14 Let all your things be done with charity.
15 I beseech you, brethren, (ye know the
house of Steph'a-nas, that it is the firstfruits of
A-cha'ia, and *that* they have addicted themselves to the ministry of the saints,)

16 That ye submit yourselves unto such, and to every one that helpeth with *us*, and laboureth.

17 I am glad of the coming of Steph'a-nas and For-tu-na'tus and A-cha'i-cus: for that which was lacking on your part they have supplied.

18 For they have refreshed my spirit and yours: therefore acknowledge ye them that are such.

19 The churches of A'sia salute you. A'qui-la and Pris-cil'la salute you much in the Lord, with the church that is in their house.

20 All the brethren greet you. Greet ye one another with an holy kiss.

21 The salutation of *me* Paul with mine own hand.

22 If any man love not the Lord Je'sus Christ, let him be An-ath'e-ma Mar'an-a'tha.

23 The grace of our Lord Je'sus Christ *be* with you.

24 My love *be* with you all in Christ Je'sus. Amen.

The first *epistle* to the Co-rin'thi-ans was written from Phi-lip'pi by Steph'a-nas, and For-tu-na'tus, and A-cha'i-cus, and Ti-mo'the-us.

THE SECOND LETTER OF PAUL TO THE

CORINTHIANS

1 PAUL, an apostle of Je'sus Christ by the will of God, and Tim'o-thy *our* brother, unto the church of God which is at Cor'inth, with all the saints which are in all A-cha'ia:

2 Grace *be* to you and peace from God our Father, and *from* the Lord Je'sus Christ.

3 Blessed *be* God, even the Father of our Lord Je'sus Christ, the Father of mercies, and the God of all comfort;

4 Who comforteth us in all our tribulation, that we may be able to comfort them which are in any trouble, by the comfort wherewith we ourselves are comforted of God.

5 For as the sufferings of Christ abound in us, so our consolation also aboundeth by Christ.

6 And whether we be afflicted, *it is* for your consolation and salvation, which is effectual in the enduring of the same sufferings which we also suffer: or whether we be comforted, *it is* for your consolation and salvation.

7 And our hope of you *is* stedfast, knowing, that as ye are partakers of the sufferings, so *shall ye be* also of the consolation.

8 For we would not, brethren, have you ignorant of our trouble which came to us in A'sia, that we were pressed out of measure, above strength, insomuch that we despaired even of life:

9 But we had the sentence of death in ourselves, that we should not trust in ourselves, but in God which raiseth the dead:

10 Who delivered us from so great a death, and doth deliver: in whom we trust that he will yet deliver *us;*

11 Ye also helping together by prayer for us, that for the gift *bestowed* upon us by the means of many persons thanks may be given by many on our behalf.

12 For our rejoicing is this, the testimony of our conscience, that in simplicity and godly sincerity, not with fleshly wisdom, but by the grace of God, we have had our conversation in the world, and more abundantly to you-ward.

13 For we write none other things unto you, than what ye read or acknowledge; and I trust ye shall acknowledge even to the end;

14 As also ye have acknowledged us in part, that we are your rejoicing, even as ye also *are* ours in the day of the Lord Je'sus.

15 And in this confidence I was minded to come unto you before, that ye might have a second benefit;

16 And to pass by you into Mac-e-do'ni-a, and to come again out of Mac-e-do'ni-a unto you, and of you to be brought on my way toward Ju-dæ'a.

17 When I therefore was thus minded, did I use lightness? or the things that I purpose, do I purpose according to the flesh, that with me there should be yea yea, and nay nay?

18 But *as* God *is* true, our word toward you was not yea and nay.

19 For the Son of God, Je'sus Christ, who was preached among you by us, *even* by me and Sil-va'nus and Ti-mo'the-us, was not yea and nay, but in him was yea.

20 For all the promises of God in him *are* yea, and in him Amen, unto the glory of God by us.

21 Now he which stablisheth us with you in Christ, and hath anointed us, *is* God;

22 Who hath also sealed us, and given the earnest of the Spirit in our hearts.

23 Moreover I call God for a record upon my soul, that to spare you I came not as yet unto Cor'inth.

24 Not for that we have dominion over your faith, but are helpers of your joy: for by faith ye stand.

2 BUT I determined this with myself, that I would not come again to you in heaviness.

2 For if I make you sorry, who is he then that maketh me glad, but the same which is made sorry by me?

3 And I wrote this same unto you, lest, when I came, I should have sorrow from them of whom I ought to rejoice; having confidence in you all, that my joy is *the joy* of you all.

4 For out of much affliction and anguish of heart I wrote unto you with many tears; not that ye should be grieved, but that ye might know the love which I have more abundantly unto you.

5 But if any have caused grief, he hath not grieved me, but in part: that I may not overcharge you all.

6 Sufficient to such a man *is* this punishment, which *was inflicted* of many.

7 So that contrariwise ye *ought* rather to forgive *him*, and comfort *him*, lest perhaps such a one should be swallowed up with overmuch sorrow.

8 Wherefore I beseech you that ye would confirm *your* love toward him.

9 For to this end also did I write, that I might know the proof of you, whether ye be obedient in all things.

10 To whom ye forgive any thing, I *forgive* also: for if I forgave any thing, to whom I for-

gave *it*, for your sakes *forgave I it* in the person of Christ;

11 Lest Sa'tan should get an advantage of us: for we are not ignorant of his devices.

12 Furthermore, when I came to Tro'as to *preach* Christ's gospel, and a door was opened unto me of the Lord,

13 I had no rest in my spirit, because I found not Ti'tus my brother: but taking my leave of them, I went from thence into Mac-e-do'ni-a.

14 Now thanks *be* unto God, which always causeth us to triumph in Christ, and maketh manifest the savour of his knowledge by us in every place.

15 For we are unto God a sweet savour of Christ, in them that are saved, and in them that perish:

16 To the one *we are* the savour of death unto death; and to the other the savour of life unto life. And who *is* sufficient for these things?

17 For we are not as many, which corrupt the word of God: but as of sincerity, but as of God, in the sight of God speak we in Christ.

3 DO we begin again to commend ourselves? or need we, as some *others*, epistles of commendation to you, or *letters* of commendation from you?

2 Ye are our epistle written in our hearts, known and read of all men:

3 *Forasmuch as ye are* manifestly declared to be the epistle of Christ ministered by us, written not with ink, but with the Spirit of the living God; not in tables of stone, but in fleshy tables of the heart.

4 And such trust have we through Christ to Godward:

5 Not that we are sufficient of ourselves to think any thing as of ourselves; but our sufficiency *is* of God;

6 Who also hath made us able ministers of the new testament; not of the letter, but of the spirit: for the letter killeth, but the spirit giveth life.

7 But if the ministration of death, written *and* engraven in stones, was glorious, so that the children of Is'ra-el could not stedfastly behold the face of Mo'ses for the glory of his countenance; which *glory* was to be done away:

8 How shall not the ministration of the spirit be rather glorious?

9 For if the ministration of condemnation *be* glory, much more doth the ministration of righteousness exceed in glory.

10 For even that which was made glorious had no glory in this respect, by reason of the glory that excelleth.

11 For if that which is done away *was* glorious, much more that which remaineth *is* glorious.

12 Seeing then that we have such hope, we use great plainness of speech:

13 And not as Mo'ses, *which* put a veil over his face, that the children of Is'ra-el could not stedfastly look to the end of that which is abolished:

14 But their minds were blinded: for until this day remaineth the same veil untaken away in the reading of the old testament; which *veil* is done away in Christ.

15 But even unto this day, when Mo'ses is read, the veil is upon their heart.

16 Nevertheless when it shall turn to the Lord, the veil shall be taken away.

17 Now the Lord is that Spirit: and where the Spirit of the Lord *is*, there *is* liberty.

18 But we all, with open face beholding as in a glass the glory of the Lord, are changed into the same image from glory to glory, *even* as by the Spirit of the Lord.

4 THEREFORE seeing we have this ministry, as we have received mercy, we faint not;

2 But have renounced the hidden things of dishonesty, not walking in craftiness, nor handling the word of God deceitfully; but by manifestation of the truth commending ourselves to every man's conscience in the sight of God.

3 But if our gospel be hid, it is hid to them that are lost:

4 In whom the god of this world hath blinded the minds of them which believe not, lest the light of the glorious gospel of Christ, who is the image of God, should shine unto them.

5 For we preach not ourselves, but Christ Je'sus the Lord; and ourselves your servants for Je'sus' sake.

6 For God, who commanded the light to shine out of darkness, hath shined in our hearts, to *give* the light of the knowledge of the glory of God in the face of Je'sus Christ.

7 But we have this treasure in earthen vessels, that the excellency of the power may be of God, and not of us.

8 *We are* troubled on every side, yet not distressed; *we are* perplexed, but not in despair;

9 Persecuted, but not forsaken; cast down, but not destroyed;

10 Always bearing about in the body the dying of the Lord Je'sus, that the life also of Je'sus might be made manifest in our body.

11 For we which live are alway delivered unto death for Je'sus' sake, that the life also of Je'sus might be made manifest in our mortal flesh.

12 So then death worketh in us, but life in you.

13 We having the same spirit of faith, according as it is written, I believed, and therefore have I spoken; we also believe, and therefore speak;

14 Knowing that he which raised up the Lord Je'sus shall raise up us also by Je'sus, and shall present *us* with you.

15 For all things *are* for your sakes, that the abundant grace might through the thanksgiving of many redound to the glory of God.

16 For which cause we faint not; but though our outward man perish, yet the inward *man* is renewed day by day.

17 For our light affliction, which is but for a moment, worketh for us a far more exceeding *and* eternal weight of glory;

18 While we look not at the things which are seen, but at the things which are not seen: for the things which are seen *are* temporal; but the things which are not seen *are* eternal.

5 FOR we know that if our earthly house of *this* tabernacle were dissolved, we have a building of God, an house not made with hands, eternal in the heavens.

2 For in this we groan, earnestly desiring to be clothed upon with our house which is from heaven:

3 If so be that being clothed we shall not be found naked.

4 For we that are in *this* tabernacle do groan, being burdened: not for that we would be unclothed, but clothed upon, that mortality might be swallowed up of life.

5 Now he that hath wrought us for the self-

same thing *is* God, who also hath given unto us
the earnest of the Spirit.
6 Therefore *we are* always confident, knowing that, whilst we are at home in the body, we
are absent from the Lord:
7 (For we walk by faith, not by sight:)
8 We are confident, *I say*, and willing rather
to be absent from the body, and to be present
with the Lord.
9 Wherefore we labour, that, whether present or absent, we may be accepted of him.
10 For we must all appear before the judgment seat of Christ; that every one may receive
the things *done* in *his* body, according to that he
hath done, whether *it be* good or bad.
11 Knowing therefore the terror of the Lord,
we persuade men; but we are made manifest
unto God; and I trust also are made manifest in
your consciences.
12 For we commend not ourselves again
unto you, but give you occasion to glory on our
behalf, that ye may have somewhat to *cnswer*
them which glory in appearance, and not in
heart.
13 For whether we be beside ourselves, *it is*
to God: or whether we be sober, *it is* for your
cause.
14 For the love of Christ constraineth us; because we thus judge, that if one died for all,
then were all dead:
15 And *that* he died for all, that they which
live should not henceforth live unto themselves,
but unto him which died for them, and rose
again.
16 Wherefore henceforth know we no man
after the flesh: yea, though we have known
Christ after the flesh, yet now henceforth know
we *him* no more.
17 Therefore if any man *be* in Christ, *he is* a
new creature: old things are passed away; behold, all things are become new.
18 And all things *are* of God, who hath reconciled us to himself by Je'sus Christ, and hath
given to us the ministry of reconciliation;
19 To wit, that God was in Christ, reconciling
the world unto himself, not imputing their trespasses unto them; and hath committed unto us
the word of reconciliation.
20 Now then we are ambassadors for Christ,
as though God did beseech *you* by us: we pray
you in Christ's stead, be ye reconciled to God.
21 For he hath made him *to be* sin for us,
who knew no sin; that we might be made the
righteousness of God in him.

6 WE then, *as* workers together *with him*,
beseech *you* also that ye receive not the
grace of God in vain.
2 (For he saith, I have heard thee in a time
accepted, and in the day of salvation have I suc-
coured thee: behold, now *is* the accepted time;
behold, now *is* the day of salvation.)
3 Giving no offence in any thing, that the
ministry be not blamed:
4 But in all *things* approving ourselves as the
ministers of God, in much patience, in afflictions, in necessities, in distresses,
5 In stripes, in imprisonments, in tumults, in
labours, in watchings, in fastings;
6 By pureness, by knowledge, by longsuffering, by kindness, by the Ho'ly Ghost, by love
unfeigned,
7 By the word of truth, by the power of God,
by the armour of righteousness on the right
hand and on the left,
8 By honour and dishonour, by evil report
and good report: as deceivers, and *yet* true;
9 As unknown, and *yet* well known; as dying,
and, behold, we live; as chastened, and not
killed;
10 As sorrowful, yet alway rejoicing; as poor,
yet making many rich; as having nothing, and
yet possessing all things.
11 O *ye* Co-rin'thi-ans, our mouth is open
unto you, our heart is enlarged.
12 Ye are not straitened in us, but ye are
straitened in your own bowels.
13 Now for a recompence in the same, (I
speak as unto *my* children,) be ye also enlarged.
14 Be ye not unequally yoked together with
unbelievers: for what fellowship hath righteousness with unrighteousness? and what communion hath light with darkness?
15 And what concord hath Christ with Be'li-
al? or what part hath he that believeth with an
infidel?
16 And what agreement hath the temple of
God with idols? for ye are the temple of the living God; as God hath said, I will dwell in them,
and walk in *them;* and I will be their God, and
they shall be my people.
17 Wherefore come out from among them,
and be ye separate, saith the Lord, and touch
not the unclean *thing:* and I will receive you,
18 And will be a Father unto you, and ye
shall be my sons and daughters, saith the Lord
Almighty.

7 HAVING therefore these promises, dearly
beloved, let us cleanse ourselves from all
filthiness of the flesh and spirit, perfecting holiness in the fear of God.
2 Receive us; we have wronged no man, we
have corrupted no man, we have defrauded no
man.
3 I speak not *this* to condemn *you:* for I have
said before, that ye are in our hearts to die and
live with *you*.
4 Great *is* my boldness of speech toward you,
great *is* my glorying of you: I am filled with
comfort, I am exceeding joyful in all our tribulation.
5 For, when we were come into Mac-e-do'ni-
a, our flesh had no rest, but we were troubled
on every side; without *were* fightings, within
were fears.
6 Nevertheless God, that comforteth those
that are cast down, comforted us by the coming
of Ti'tus;
7 And not by his coming only, but by the
consolation wherewith he was comforted in
you, when he told us your earnest desire, your
mourning, your fervent mind toward me; so
that I rejoiced the more.
8 For though I made you sorry with a letter, I
do not repent, though I did repent: for I perceive that the same epistle hath made you
sorry, though *it were* but for a season.
9 Now I rejoice, not that ye were made sorry,
but that ye sorrowed to repentance: for ye were
made sorry after a godly manner, that ye might
receive damage by us in nothing.
10 For godly sorrow worketh repentance to
salvation not to be repented of: but the sorrow
of the world worketh death.
11 For behold this selfsame thing, that ye
sorrowed after a godly sort, what carefulness it
wrought in you, yea, *what* clearing of yourselves, yea, *what* indignation, yea, *what* fear,
yea, *what* vehement desire, yea, *what* zeal, yea,
what revenge! In all *things* ye have approved
yourselves to be clear in this matter.
12 Wherefore, though I wrote unto you, *I did*
it not for his cause that had done the wrong, nor

for his cause that suffered wrong, but that our care for you in the sight of God might appear unto you.

13 Therefore we were comforted in your comfort: yea, and exceedingly the more joyed we for the joy of Ti'tus, because his spirit was refreshed by you all.

14 For if I have boasted any thing to him of you, I am not ashamed; but as we spake all things to you in truth, even so our boasting, which *I made* before Ti'tus, is found a truth.

15 And his inward affection is more abundant toward you, whilst he remembereth the obedience of you all, how with fear and trembling ye received him.

16 I rejoice therefore that I have confidence in you in all *things*.

8 MOREOVER, brethren, we do you to wit of the grace of God bestowed on the churches of Mac-e-do'ni-a;

2 How that in a great trial of affliction the abundance of their joy and their deep poverty abounded unto the riches of their liberality.

3 For to *their* power, I bear record, yea, and beyond *their* power *they were* willing of themselves;

4 Praying us with much intreaty that we would receive the gift, and *take upon us* the fellowship of the ministering to the saints.

5 And *this they did,* not as we hoped, but first gave their own selves to the Lord, and unto us by the will of God.

6 Insomuch that we desired Ti'tus, that as he had begun, so he would also finish in you the same grace also.

7 Therefore, as ye abound in every *thing, in* faith, and utterance, and knowledge, and *in* all diligence, and *in* your love to us, *see* that ye abound in this grace also.

8 I speak not by commandment, but by occasion of the forwardness of others, and to prove the sincerity of your love.

9 For ye know the grace of our Lord Je'sus Christ, that, though he was rich, yet for your sakes he became poor, that ye through his poverty might be rich.

10 And herein I give *my* advice: for this is expedient for you, who have begun before, not only to do, but also to be forward a year ago.

11 Now therefore perform the doing *of it;* that as *there was* a readiness to will, so *there may be* a performance also out of that which ye have.

12 For if there be first a willing mind, *it is* accepted according to that a man hath, *and* not according to that he hath not.

13 For *I mean* not that other men be eased, and ye burdened:

14 But by an equality, *that* now at this time your abundance *may be a supply* for their want, that their abundance also may be *a supply* for your want: that there may be equality:

15 As it is written, He that *had gathered* much had nothing over; and he that *had gathered* little had no lack.

16 But thanks *be* to God, which put the same earnest care into the heart of Ti'tus for you.

17 For indeed he accepted the exhortation; but being more forward, of his own accord he went unto you.

18 And we have sent with him the brother, whose praise *is* in the gospel throughout all the churches;

19 And not *that* only, but who was also chosen of the churches to travel with us with this grace, which is administered by us to the glory of the same Lord, and *declaration of* your ready mind:

20 Avoiding this, that no man should blame us in this abundance which is administered by us:

21 Providing for honest things, not only in the sight of the Lord, but also in the sight of men.

22 And we have sent with them our brother, whom we have oftentimes proved diligent in many things, but now much more diligent, upon the great confidence which *I have* in you.

23 Whether *any do enquire* of Ti'tus, *he is* my partner and fellowhelper concerning you: or our brethren *be enquired of, they are* the messengers of the churches, *and* the glory of Christ.

24 Wherefore shew ye to them, and before the churches, the proof of your love, and of our boasting on your behalf.

9 FOR as touching the ministering to the saints, it is superfluous for me to write to you:

2 For I know the forwardness of your mind, for which I boast of you to them of Mac-e-do'ni-a, that A-cha'ia was ready a year ago; and your zeal hath provoked very many.

3 Yet have I sent the brethren, lest our boasting of you should be in vain in this behalf; that, as I said, ye may be ready:

4 Lest haply if they of Mac-e-do'ni-a come with me, and find you unprepared, we (that we say not, ye) should be ashamed in this same confident boasting.

5 Therefore I thought it necessary to exhort the brethren, that they would go before unto you, and make up beforehand your bounty, whereof ye had notice before, that the same might be ready, as *a matter of* bounty, and not as *of* covetousness.

6 But this *I say,* He which soweth sparingly shall reap also sparingly; and he which soweth bountifully shall reap also bountifully.

7 Every man according as he purposeth in his heart, *so let him give;* not grudgingly, or of necessity: for God loveth a cheerful giver.

8 And God *is* able to make all grace abound toward you; that ye, always having all sufficiency in all *things,* may abound to every good work:

9 (As it is written, He hath dispersed abroad; he hath given to the poor: his righteousness remaineth for ever.

10 Now he that ministereth seed to the sower both minister bread for *your* food, and multiply your seed sown, and increase the fruits of your righteousness;)

11 Being enriched in every thing to all bountifulness, which causeth through us thanksgiving to God.

12 For the administration of this service not only supplieth the want of the saints, but is abundant also by many thanksgivings unto God;

13 Whiles by the experiment of this ministration they glorify God for your professed subjection unto the gospel of Christ, and for *your* liberal distribution unto them, and unto all *men;*

14 And by their prayer for you, which long after you for the exceeding grace of God in you.

15 Thanks *be* unto God for his unspeakable gift.

10 NOW I Paul myself beseech you by the meekness and gentleness of Christ, who in presence *am* base among you, but being absent am bold toward you:

2 But I beseech *you,* that I may not be bold
when I am present with that confidence, wherewith I think to be bold against some, which
think of us as if we walked according to the
flesh.
3 For though we walk in the flesh, we do not
war after the flesh:
4 (For the weapons of our warfare *are* not
carnal, but mighty through God to the pulling
down of strong holds;)
5 Casting down imaginations, and every high
thing that exalteth itself against the knowledge
of God, and bringing into captivity every
thought to the obedience of Christ;
6 And having in a readiness to revenge all
disobedience, when your obedience is fulfilled.
7 Do ye look on things after the outward appearance? If any man trust to himself that he is
Christ's, let him of himself think this again,
that, as he *is* Christ's, even so *are* we Christ's.
8 For though I should boast somewhat more
of our authority, which the Lord hath given us
for edification, and not for your destruction, I
should not be ashamed:
9 That I may not seem as if I would terrify
you by letters.
10 For *his* letters, say they, *are* weighty and
powerful; but *his* bodily presence *is* weak, and
his speech contemptible.
11 Let such an one think this, that, such as
we are in word by letters when we are absent,
such *will we be* also in deed when we are present.
12 For we dare not make ourselves of the
number, or compare ourselves with some that
commend themselves; but they measuring
themselves by themselves, and comparing
themselves among themselves, are not wise.
13 But we will not boast of things without
our measure, but according to the measure of
the rule which God hath distributed to us, a
measure to reach even unto you.
14 For we stretch not ourselves beyond *our
measure,* as though we reached not unto you:
for we are come as far as to you also in *preaching* the gospel of Christ:
15 Not boasting of things without *our* measure, *that is,* of other men's labours; but having
hope, when your faith is increased, that we
shall be enlarged by you according to our rule
abundantly,
16 To preach the gospel in the *regions* beyond you, *and* not to boast in another man's
line of things made ready to our hand.
17 But he that glorieth, let him glory in the
Lord.
18 For not he that commendeth himself is
approved, but whom the Lord commendeth.

11 WOULD to God ye could bear with me a
little in *my* folly: and indeed bear with
me.
2 For I am jealous over you with godly jealousy: for I have espoused you to one husband,
that I may present *you as* a chaste virgin to
Christ.
3 But I fear, lest by any means, as the serpent
beguiled Eve through his subtilty, so your
minds should be corrupted from the simplicity
that is in Christ.
4 For if he that cometh preacheth another
Je'sus, whom we have not preached, or *if* ye
receive another spirit, which ye have not received, or another gospel, which ye have not
accepted, ye might well bear with *him.*
5 For I suppose I was not a whit behind the
very chiefest apostles.
6 But though *I be* rude in speech, yet not in
knowledge; but we have been throughly made
manifest among you in all things.
7 Have I committed an offence in abasing
myself that ye might be exalted, because I have
preached to you the gospel of God freely?
8 I robbed other churches, taking wages *of
them,* to do you service.
9 And when I was present with you, and
wanted, I was chargeable to no man: for that
which was lacking to me the brethren which
came from Mac-e-do'ni-a supplied: and in all
things I have kept myself from being burdensome unto you, and *so* will I keep *myself.*
10 As the truth of Christ is in me, no man
shall stop me of this boasting in the regions of
A-cha'ia.
11 Wherefore? because I love you not? God
knoweth.
12 But what I do, that I will do, that I may
cut off occasion from them which desire occasion; that wherein they glory, they may be
found even as we.
13 For such *are* false apostles, deceitful
workers, transforming themselves into the
apostles of Christ.
14 And no marvel; for Sa'tan himself is transformed into an angel of light.
15 Therefore *it is* no great thing if his ministers also be transformed as the ministers of
righteousness; whose end shall be according to
their works.
16 I say again, Let no man think me a fool; if
otherwise, yet as a fool receive me, that I may
boast myself a little.
17 That which I speak, I speak *it* not after the
Lord, but as it were foolishly, in this confidence
of boasting.
18 Seeing that many glory after the flesh, I
will glory also.
19 For ye suffer fools gladly, seeing ye *yourselves* are wise.
20 For ye suffer, if a man bring you into
bondage, if a man devour *you,* if a man take *of
you,* if a man exalt himself, if a man smite you
on the face.
21 I speak as concerning reproach, as though
we had been weak. Howbeit whereinsoever any
is bold, (I speak foolishly,) I am bold also.
22 Are they He'brews? so *am* I. Are they Is'-
ra-el-ites? so *am* I. Are they the seed of A'bra-
ham? so *am* I.
23 Are they ministers of Christ? (I speak as a
fool) I *am* more; in labours more abundant, in
stripes above measure, in prisons more frequent, in deaths oft.
24 Of the Jews five times received I forty
stripes save one.
25 Thrice was I beaten with rods, once was I
stoned, thrice I suffered shipwreck, a night and
a day I have been in the deep;
26 *In* journeyings often, *in* perils of waters,
in perils of robbers, *in* perils by *mine own* countrymen, *in* perils by the heathen, *in* perils in the
city, *in* perils in the wilderness, *in* perils in the
sea, *in* perils among false brethren;
27 In weariness and painfulness, in watchings often, in hunger and thirst, in fastings often, in cold and nakedness.
28 Beside those things that are without, that
which cometh upon me daily, the care of all the
churches.
29 Who is weak, and I am not weak? who is
offended, and I burn not?
30 If I must needs glory, I will glory of the
things which concern mine infirmities.
31 The God and Father of our Lord Je'sus

Christ, which is blessed for evermore, knoweth
that I lie not.
32 In Da-mas'cus the governor under Ar'e-
tas the king kept the city of the Dam'as-cenes
with a garrison, desirous to apprehend me:
33 And through a window in a basket was I
let down by the wall, and escaped his hands.

12 IT is not expedient for me doubtless to
glory. I will come to visions and revelations of the Lord.
2 I knew a man in Christ above fourteen
years ago, (whether in the body, I cannot tell; or
whether out of the body, I cannot tell: God
knoweth;) such an one caught up to the third
heaven.
3 And I knew such a man, (whether in the
body, or out of the body, I cannot tell: God
knoweth;)
4 How that he was caught up into paradise,
and heard unspeakable words, which it is not
lawful for a man to utter.
5 Of such an one will I glory: yet of myself I
will not glory, but in mine infirmities.
6 For though I would desire to glory, I shall
not be a fool; for I will say the truth: but *now* I
forbear, lest any man should think of me above
that which he seeth me *to be*, or *that* he heareth
of me.
7 And lest I should be exalted above measure
through the abundance of the revelations, there
was given to me a thorn in the flesh, the messenger of Sa'tan to buffet me, lest I should be
exalted above measure.
8 For this thing I besought the Lord thrice,
that it might depart from me.
9 And he said unto me, My grace is sufficient
for thee: for my strength is made perfect in
weakness. Most gladly therefore will I rather
glory in my infirmities, that the power of Christ
may rest upon me.
10 Therefore I take pleasure in infirmities, in
reproaches, in necessities, in persecutions, in
distresses for Christ's sake: for when I am
weak, then am I strong.
11 I am become a fool in glorying; ye have
compelled me: for I ought to have been commended of you: for in nothing am I behind the
very chiefest apostles, though I be nothing.
12 Truly the signs of an apostle were
wrought among you in all patience, in signs,
and wonders, and mighty deeds.
13 For what is it wherein ye were inferior to
other churches, except *it be* that I myself was
not burdensome to you? forgive me this wrong.
14 Behold, the third time I am ready to come
to you; and I will not be burdensome to you: for
I seek not yours, but you: for the children ought
not to lay up for the parents, but the parents for
the children.
15 And I will very gladly spend and be spent
for you; though the more abundantly I love you,
the less I be loved.
16 But be it so, I did not burden you: nevertheless, being crafty, I caught you with guile.
17 Did I make a gain of you by any of them
whom I sent unto you?
18 I desired Ti'tus, and with *him* I sent a
brother. Did Ti'tus make a gain of you? walked
we not in the same spirit? *walked we* not in the
same steps?
19 Again, think ye that we excuse ourselves
unto you? we speak before God in Christ: but
we do all things, dearly beloved, for your edifying.
20 For I fear, lest, when I come, I shall not
find you such as I would, and *that* I shall be
found unto you such as ye would not: lest *there*
be debates, envyings, wraths, strifes, backbit-
ings, whisperings, swellings, tumults:
21 *And* lest, when I come again, my God will
humble me among you, and *that* I shall bewail
many which have sinned already, and have not
repented of the uncleanness and fornication
and lasciviousness which they have committed.

13 THIS *is* the third *time* I am coming to
you. In the mouth of two or three witnesses shall every word be established.
2 I told you before, and foretell you, as if I
were present, the second time; and being absent
now I write to them which heretofore have
sinned, and to all other, that, if I come again, I
will not spare:
3 Since ye seek a proof of Christ speaking in
me, which to you-ward is not weak, but is
mighty in you.
4 For though he was crucified through weakness, yet he liveth by the power of God. For we
also are weak in him, but we shall live with him
by the power of God toward you.
5 Examine yourselves, whether ye be in the
faith; prove your own selves. Know ye not your
own selves, how that Je'sus Christ is in you, except ye be reprobates?
6 But I trust that ye shall know that we are
not reprobates.
7 Now I pray to God that ye do no evil; not
that we should appear approved, but that ye
should do that which is honest, though we be as
reprobates.
8 For we can do nothing against the truth,
but for the truth.
9 For we are glad, when we are weak, and ye
are strong: and this also we wish, *even* your
perfection.
10 Therefore I write these things being absent, lest being present I should use sharpness,
according to the power which the Lord hath
given me to edification, and not to destruction.
11 Finally, brethren, farewell. Be perfect, be
of good comfort, be of one mind, live in peace;
and the God of love and peace shall be with
you.
12 Greet one another with an holy kiss.
13 All the saints salute you.
14 The grace of the Lord Je'sus Christ, and
the love of God, and the communion of the Ho'-
ly Ghost, *be* with you all. Amen.

The second *epistle* to the Co-rin'thi-ans was written from Phi-lip'pi, *a city* of Mac-e-do'ni-a, by Ti'tus and Lu'cas.

THE LETTER OF PAUL TO THE

GALATIANS

1 PAUL, an apostle, (not of men, neither by man, but by Je'sus Christ, and God the Father, who raised him from the dead;)

2 And all the brethren which are with me, unto the churches of Ga-la'tia:

3 Grace *be* to you and peace from God the Father, and *from* our Lord Je'sus Christ,

4 Who gave himself for our sins, that he might deliver us from this present evil world, according to the will of God and our Father:

5 To whom *be* glory for ever and ever. Amen.

6 I marvel that ye are so soon removed from him that called you into the grace of Christ unto another gospel:

7 Which is not another; but there be some that trouble you, and would pervert the gospel of Christ.

8 But though we, or an angel from heaven, preach any other gospel unto you than that which we have preached unto you, let him be accursed.

9 As we said before, so say I now again, If any *man* preach any other gospel unto you than that ye have received, let him be accursed.

10 For do I now persuade men, or God? or do I seek to please men? for if I yet pleased men, I should not be the servant of Christ.

11 But I certify you, brethren, that the gospel which was preached of me is not after man.

12 For I neither received it of man, neither was I taught *it*, but by the revelation of Je'sus Christ.

13 For ye have heard of my conversation in time past in the Jews' religion, how that beyond measure I persecuted the church of God, and wasted it:

14 And profited in the Jews' religion above many my equals in mine own nation, being more exceedingly zealous of the traditions of my fathers.

15 But when it pleased God, who separated me from my mother's womb, and called *me* by his grace,

16 To reveal his Son in me, that I might preach him among the heathen; immediately I conferred not with flesh and blood:

17 Neither went I up to Je-ru'sa-lem to them which were apostles before me; but I went into A-ra'bi-a, and returned again unto Da-mas'cus.

18 Then after three years I went up to Je-ru'sa-lem to see Pe'ter, and abode with him fifteen days.

19 But other of the apostles saw I none, save James the Lord's brother.

20 Now the things which I write unto you, behold, before God, I lie not.

21 Afterwards I came into the regions of Syr'i-a and Ci-li'cia;

22 And was unknown by face unto the churches of Ju-dæ'a which were in Christ:

23 But they had heard only, That he which persecuted us in times past now preacheth the faith which once he destroyed.

24 And they glorified God in me.

2 THEN fourteen years after I went up again to Je-ru'sa-lem with Bar'na-bas, and took Ti'tus with *me* also.

2 And I went up by revelation, and communicated unto them that gospel which I preach among the Gen'tiles, but privately to them which were of reputation, lest by any means I should run, or had run, in vain.

3 But neither Ti'tus, who was with me, being a Greek, was compelled to be circumcised:

4 And that because of false brethren unawares brought in, who came in privily to spy out our liberty which we have in Christ Je'sus, that they might bring us into bondage:

5 To whom we gave place by subjection, no, not for an hour; that the truth of the gospel might continue with you.

6 But of these who seemed to be somewhat, (whatsoever they were, it maketh no matter to me: God accepteth no man's person:) for they who seemed *to be somewhat* in conference added nothing to me:

7 But contrariwise, when they saw that the gospel of the uncircumcision was committed unto me, as *the gospel* of the circumcision *was* unto Pe'ter;

8 (For he that wrought effectually in Pe'ter to the apostleship of the circumcision, the same was mighty in me toward the Gen'tiles:)

9 And when James, Ce'phas, and John, who seemed to be pillars, perceived the grace that was given unto me, they gave to me and Bar'na-bas the right hands of fellowship; that we *should go* unto the heathen, and they unto the circumcision.

10 Only *they would* that we should remember the poor; the same which I also was forward to do.

11 But when Pe'ter was come to An'ti-och, I withstood him to the face, because he was to be blamed.

12 For before that certain came from James, he did eat with the Gen'tiles: but when they were come, he withdrew and separated himself, fearing them which were of the circumcision.

13 And the other Jews dissembled likewise with him; insomuch that Bar'na-bas also was carried away with their dissimulation.

14 But when I saw that they walked not uprightly according to the truth of the gospel, I said unto Pe'ter before *them* all, If thou, being a Jew, livest after the manner of Gen'tiles, and not as do the Jews, why compellest thou the Gen'tiles to live as do the Jews?

15 We *who are* Jews by nature, and not sinners of the Gen'tiles,

16 Knowing that a man is not justified by the works of the law, but by the faith of Je'sus Christ, even we have believed in Je'sus Christ, that we might be justified by the faith of Christ, and not by the works of the law: for by the works of the law shall no flesh be justified.

17 But if, while we seek to be justified by Christ, we ourselves also are found sinners, *is* therefore Christ the minister of sin? God forbid.

18 For if I build again the things which I destroyed, I make myself a transgressor.

19 For I through the law am dead to the law, that I might live unto God.

20 I am crucified with Christ: nevertheless I live; yet not I, but Christ liveth in me: and the life which I now live in the flesh I live by the faith of the Son of God, who loved me, and gave himself for me.

21 I do not frustrate the grace of God: for if righteousness *come* by the law, then Christ is dead in vain.

3 O FOOLISH Ga-la'tians, who hath bewitched you, that ye should not obey the
truth, before whose eyes Je'sus Christ hath
been evidently set forth, crucified among you?
2 This only would I learn of you, Received ye
the Spirit by the works of the law, or by the
hearing of faith?
3 Are ye so foolish? having begun in the
Spirit, are ye now made perfect by the flesh?
4 Have ye suffered so many things in vain? if
it be yet in vain.
5 He therefore that ministereth to you the
Spirit, and worketh miracles among you, *doeth
he it* by the works of the law, or by the hearing
of faith?
6 Even as A'bra-ham believed God, and it
was accounted to him for righteousness.
7 Know ye therefore that they which are of
faith, the same are the children of A'bra-ham.
8 And the scripture, foreseeing that God
would justify the heathen through faith,
preached before the gospel unto A'bra-ham,
saying, In thee shall all nations be blessed.
9 So then they which be of faith are blessed
with faithful A'bra-ham.
10 For as many as are of the works of the law
are under the curse: for it is written, Cursed *is*
every one that continueth not in all things
which are written in the book of the law to do
them.
11 But that no man is justified by the law in
the sight of God, *it is* evident: for, The just shall
live by faith.
12 And the law is not of faith: but, The man
that doeth them shall live in them.
13 Christ hath redeemed us from the curse of
the law, being made a curse for us: for it is written, Cursed *is* every one that hangeth on a tree:
14 That the blessing of A'bra-ham might
come on the Gen'tiles through Je'sus Christ;
that we might receive the promise of the Spirit
through faith.
15 Brethren, I speak after the manner of
men; Though *it be* but a man's covenant, yet *if
it be* confirmed, no man disannulleth, or addeth
thereto.
16 Now to A'bra-ham and his seed were the
promises made. He saith not, And to seeds, as
of many; but as of one, And to thy seed, which
is Christ.
17 And this I say, *that* the covenant, that was
confirmed before of God in Christ, the law,
which was four hundred and thirty years after,
cannot disannul, that it should make the promise of none effect.
18 For if the inheritance *be* of the law, *it is* no
more of promise: but God gave *it* to A'bra-ham
by promise.
19 Wherefore then *serveth* the law? It was
added because of transgressions, till the seed
should come to whom the promise was made;
and it was ordained by angels in the hand of a
mediator.
20 Now a mediator is not *a mediator* of one,
but God is one.
21 *Is* the law then against the promises of
God? God forbid: for if there had been a law
given which could have given life, verily righteousness should have been by the law.
22 But the scripture hath concluded all under
sin, that the promise by faith of Je'sus Christ
might be given to them that believe.
23 But before faith came, we were kept under the law, shut up unto the faith which should
afterwards be revealed.
24 Wherefore the law was our schoolmaster
to bring us unto Christ, that we might be justified by faith.
25 But after that faith is come, we are no
longer under a schoolmaster.
26 For ye are all the children of God by faith
in Christ Je'sus.
27 For as many of you as have been baptized
into Christ have put on Christ.
28 There is neither Jew nor Greek, there is
neither bond nor free, there is neither male nor
female: for ye are all one in Christ Je'sus.
29 And if ye *be* Christ's, then are ye A'bra-
hams's seed, and heirs according to the promise.

4 NOW I say, *That* the heir, as long as he is a
child, differeth nothing from a servant,
though he be lord of all;
2 But is under tutors and governors until the
time appointed of the father.
3 Even so we, when we were children, were
in bondage under the elements of the world:
4 But when the fulness of the time was come,
God sent forth his Son, made of a woman, made
under the law,
5 To redeem them that were under the law,
that we might receive the adoption of sons.
6 And because ye are sons, God hath sent
forth the Spirit of his Son into your hearts, crying, Ab'ba, Father.
7 Wherefore thou art no more a servant, but
a son; and if a son, then an heir of God through
Christ.
8 Howbeit then, when ye knew not God, ye
did service unto them which by nature are no
gods.
9 But now, after that ye have known God, or
rather are known of God, how turn ye again to
the weak and beggarly elements, whereunto ye
desire again to be in bondage?
10 Ye observe days, and months, and times,
and years.
11 I am afraid of you, lest I have bestowed
upon you labour in vain.
12 Brethren, I beseech you, be as I *am;* for I
am as ye *are:* ye have not injured me at all.
13 Ye know how through infirmity of the
flesh I preached the gospel unto you at the first.
14 And my temptation which was in my flesh
ye despised not, nor rejected; but received me
as an angel of God, *even* as Christ Je'sus.
15 Where is then the blessedness ye spake
of? for I bear you record, that, if *it had been*
possible, ye would have plucked out your own
eyes, and have given them to me.
16 Am I therefore become your enemy, because I tell you the truth?
17 They zealously affect you, *but* not well;
yea, they would exclude you, that ye might affect them.
18 But *it is* good to be zealously affected always in *a* good *thing,* and not only when I am
present with you.
19 My little children, of whom I travail in
birth again until Christ be formed in you,
20 I desire to be present with you now, and
to change my voice; for I stand in doubt of you.
21 Tell me, ye that desire to be under the law,
do ye not hear the law?
22 For it is written, that A'bra-ham had two
sons, the one by a bondmaid, the other by a
freewoman.
23 But he *who was* of the bondwoman was
born after the flesh; but he of the freewoman
was by promise.
24 Which things are an allegory: for these
are the two covenants; the one from the mount

Si'nai, which gendereth to bondage, which is
A'gar.
25 For this A'gar is mount Si'nai in A-ra'bi-a,
and answereth to Je-ru'sa-lem which now is,
and is in bondage with her children.
26 But Je-ru'sa-lem which is above is free,
which is the mother of us all.
27 For it is written, Rejoice, *thou* barren that
bearest not; break forth and cry, thou that tra-
vailest not: for the desolate hath many more
children than she which hath an husband.
28 Now we, brethren, as I'saac was, are the
children of promise.
29 But as then he that was born after the
flesh persecuted him *that was born* after the
Spirit, even so *it is* now.
30 Nevertheless what saith the scripture?
Cast out the bondwoman and her son: for the
son of the bondwoman shall not be heir with
the son of the freewoman.
31 So then, brethren, we are not children of
the bondwoman, but of the free.

5 STAND fast therefore in the liberty wherewith Christ hath made us free, and be not
entangled again with the yoke of bondage.
2 Behold, I Paul say unto you, that if ye be
circumcised, Christ shall profit you nothing.
3 For I testify again to every man that is circumcised, that he is a debtor to do the whole
law.
4 Christ is become of no effect unto you,
whosoever of you are justified by the law; ye
are fallen from grace.
5 For we through the Spirit wait for the hope
of righteousness by faith.
6 For in Je'sus Christ neither circumcision
availeth any thing, nor uncircumcision; but
faith which worketh by love.
7 Ye did run well; who did hinder you that ye
should not obey the truth?
8 This persuasion *cometh* not of him that
calleth you.
9 A little leaven leaveneth the whole lump.
10 I have confidence in you through the Lord,
that ye will be none otherwise minded: but he
that troubleth you shall bear his judgment,
whosoever he be.
11 And I, brethren, if I yet preach circumcision, why do I yet suffer persecution? then is
the offence of the cross ceased.
12 I would they were even cut off which trouble you.
13 For, brethren, ye have been called unto
liberty; only *use* not liberty for an occasion to
the flesh, but by love serve one another.
14 For all the law is fulfilled in one word,
even in this; Thou shalt love thy neighbour as
thyself.
15 But if ye bite and devour one another,
take heed that ye be not consumed one of another.
16 *This* I say then, Walk in the Spirit, and ye
shall not fulfil the lust of the flesh.
17 For the flesh lusteth against the Spirit,
and the Spirit against the flesh: and these are
contrary the one to the other: so that ye cannot
do the things that ye would.
18 But if ye be led of the Spirit, ye are not
under the law.
19 Now the works of the flesh are manifest,
which are *these;* Adultery, fornication, uncleanness, lasciviousness,
20 Idolatry, witchcraft, hatred, variance,
emulations, wrath, strife, seditions, heresies,
21 Envyings, murders, drunkenness, revellings, and such like: of the which I tell you before, as I have also told *you* in time past, that
they which do such things shall not inherit the
kingdom of God.
22 But the fruit of the Spirit is love, joy,
peace, longsuffering, gentleness, goodness,
faith,
23 Meekness, temperance: against such
there is no law.
24 And they that are Christ's have crucified
the flesh with the affections and lusts.
25 If we live in the Spirit, let us also walk in
the Spirit.
26 Let us not be desirous of vain glory, provoking one another, envying one another.

6 BRETHREN, if a man be overtaken in a
fault, ye which are spiritual, restore such
an one in the spirit of meekness; considering
thyself, lest thou also be tempted.
2 Bear ye one another's burdens, and so fulfil
the law of Christ.
3 For if a man think himself to be something,
when he is nothing, he deceiveth himself.
4 But let every man prove his own work, and
then shall he have rejoicing in himself alone,
and not in another.
5 For every man shall bear his own burden.
6 Let him that is taught in the word communicate unto him that teacheth in all good things.
7 Be not deceived; God is not mocked: for
whatsoever a man soweth, that shall he also
reap.
8 For he that soweth to his flesh shall of the
flesh reap corruption; but he that soweth to the
Spirit shall of the Spirit reap life everlasting.
9 And let us not be weary in well doing: for
in due season we shall reap, if we faint not.
10 As we have therefore opportunity, let us
do good unto all *men,* especially unto them who
are of the household of faith.
11 Ye see how large a letter I have written
unto you with mine own hand.
12 As many as desire to make a fair shew in
the flesh, they constrain you to be circumcised;
only lest they should suffer persecution for the
cross of Christ.
13 For neither they themselves who are circumcised keep the law; but desire to have you
circumcised, that they may glory in your flesh.
14 But God forbid that I should glory, save in
the cross of our Lord Je'sus Christ, by whom
the world is crucified unto me, and I unto the
world.
15 For in Christ Je'sus neither circumcision
availeth any thing, nor uncircumcision, but a
new creature.
16 And as many as walk according to this
rule, peace *be* on them, and mercy, and upon
the Is'ra-el of God.
17 From henceforth let no man trouble me:
for I bear in my body the marks of the Lord
Je'sus.
18 Brethren, the grace of our Lord Je'sus
Christ *be* with your spirit. Amen.

Unto the Ga-la'tians written from Rome.

THE LETTER OF PAUL TO THE

EPHESIANS

1 PAUL, an apostle of Je'sus Christ by the
will of God, to the saints which are at Eph'-
e-sus, and to the faithful in Christ Je'sus:
2 Grace *be* to you, and peace, from God our
Father, and *from* the Lord Je'sus Christ.
3 Blessed *be* the God and Father of our Lord
Je'sus Christ, who hath blessed us with all spiritual blessings in heavenly *places* in Christ:
4 According as he hath chosen us in him before the foundation of the world, that we should
be holy and without blame before him in love:
5 Having predestinated us unto the adoption
of children by Je'sus Christ to himself, according to the good pleasure of his will,
6 To the praise of the glory of his grace,
wherein he hath made us accepted in the beloved.
7 In whom we have redemption through his
blood, the forgiveness of sins, according to the
riches of his grace;
8 Wherein he hath abounded toward us in all
wisdom and prudence;
9 Having made known unto us the mystery
of his will, according to his good pleasure which
he hath purposed in himself:
10 That in the dispensation of the fulness of
times he might gather together in one all things
in Christ, both which are in heaven, and which
are on earth; *even* in him:
11 In whom also we have obtained an inheritance, being predestinated according to the purpose of him who worketh all things after the
counsel of his own will:
12 That we should be to the praise of his glory, who first trusted in Christ.
13 In whom ye also *trusted,* after that ye
heard the word of truth, the gospel of your salvation: in whom also after that ye believed, ye
were sealed with that holy Spirit of promise,
14 Which is the earnest of our inheritance
until the redemption of the purchased possession, unto the praise of his glory.
15 Wherefore I also, after I heard of your
faith in the Lord Je'sus, and love unto all the
saints,
16 Cease not to give thanks for you, making
mention of you in my prayers;
17 That the God of our Lord Je'sus Christ,
the Father of glory, may give unto you the spirit
of wisdom and revelation in the knowledge of
him:
18 The eyes of your understanding being enlightened; that ye may know what is the hope of
his calling, and what the riches of the glory of
his inheritance in the saints,
19 And what *is* the exceeding greatness of
his power to us-ward who believe, according to
the working of his mighty power,
20 Which he wrought in Christ, when he
raised him from the dead, and set *him* at his
own right hand in the heavenly *places,*
21 Far above all principality, and power, and
might, and dominion, and every name that is
named, not only in this world, but also in that
which is to come:
22 And hath put all *things* under his feet, and
gave him *to be* the head over all *things* to the
church,
23 Which is his body, the fulness of him that
filleth all in all.

2 AND you *hath he quickened,* who were
dead in trespasses and sins;
2 Wherein in time past ye walked according
to the course of this world, according to the
prince of the power of the air, the spirit that
now worketh in the children of disobedience:
3 Among whom also we all had our conversation in times past in the lusts of our flesh, fulfilling the desires of the flesh and of the mind;
and were by nature the children of wrath, even
as others.
4 But God, who is rich in mercy, for his great
love wherewith he loved us,
5 Even when we were dead in sins, hath
quickened us together with Christ, (by grace ye
are saved;)
6 And hath raised *us* up together, and made
us sit together in heavenly *places* in Christ Je'-
sus:
7 That in the ages to come he might shew the
exceeding riches of his grace in *his* kindness
toward us through Christ Je'sus.
8 For by grace are ye saved through faith;
and that not of yourselves: *it is* the gift of God:
9 Not of works, lest any man should boast.
10 For we are his workmanship, created in
Christ Je'sus unto good works, which God hath
before ordained that we should walk in them.
11 Wherefore remember, that ye *being* in
time past Gen'tiles in the flesh, who are called
Uncircumcision by that which is called the Circumcision in the flesh made by hands;
12 That at that time ye were without Christ,
being aliens from the commonwealth of Is'ra-el,
and strangers from the covenants of promise,
having no hope, and without God in the world:
13 But now in Christ Je'sus ye who sometimes were far off are made nigh by the blood of
Christ.
14 For he is our peace, who hath made both
one, and hath broken down the middle wall of
partition *between us;*
15 Having abolished in his flesh the enmity,
even the law of commandments *contained* in
ordinances; for to make in himself of twain one
new man, *so* making peace;
16 And that he might reconcile both unto
God in one body by the cross, having slain the
enmity thereby:
17 And came and preached peace to you
which were afar off, and to them that were
nigh.
18 For through him we both have access by
one Spirit unto the Father.
19 Now therefore ye are no more strangers
and foreigners, but fellowcitizens with the
saints, and of the household of God;
20 And are built upon the foundation of the
apostles and prophets, Je'sus Christ himself
being the chief corner *stone;*
21 In whom all the building fitly framed together groweth unto an holy temple in the Lord:
22 In whom ye also are builded together for
an habitation of God through the Spirit.

3 FOR this cause I Paul, the prisoner of Je'-
sus Christ for you Gen'tiles,
2 If ye have heard of the dispensation of the
grace of God which is given me to you-ward:
3 How that by revelation he made known

unto me the mystery; (as I wrote afore in few
words,
4 Whereby, when ye read, ye may understand my knowledge in the mystery of Christ)
5 Which in other ages was not made known
unto the sons of men, as it is now revealed unto
his holy apostles and prophets by the Spirit;
6 That the Gen'tiles should be fellowheirs,
and of the same body, and partakers of his
promise in Christ by the gospel:
7 Whereof I was made a minister, according
to the gift of the grace of God given unto me by
the effectual working of his power.
8 Unto me, who am less than the least of all
saints, is this grace given, that I should preach
among the Gen'tiles the unsearchable riches of
Christ;
9 And to make all *men* see what *is* the fellowship of the mystery, which from the beginning
of the world hath been hid in God, who created
all things by Je'sus Christ:
10 To the intent that now unto the principalities and powers in heavenly *places* might be
known by the church the manifold wisdom of
God,
11 According to the eternal purpose which
he purposed in Christ Je'sus our Lord:
12 In whom we have boldness and access
with confidence by the faith of him.
13 Wherefore I desire that ye faint not at my
tribulations for you, which is your glory.
14 For this cause I bow my knees unto the
Father of our Lord Je'sus Christ,
15 Of whom the whole family in heaven and
earth is named,
16 That he would grant you, according to the
riches of his glory, to be strengthened with
might by his Spirit in the inner man;
17 That Christ may dwell in your hearts by
faith; that ye, being rooted and grounded in
love,
18 May be able to comprehend with all saints
what *is* the breadth, and length, and depth, and
height;
19 And to know the love of Christ, which
passeth knowledge, that ye might be filled with
all the fulness of God.
20 Now unto him that is able to do exceeding
abundantly above all that we ask or think, according to the power that worketh in us,
21 Unto him *be* glory in the church by Christ
Je'sus throughout all ages, world without end.
Amen.

4 I THEREFORE, the prisoner of the Lord,
beseech you that ye walk worthy of the vocation wherewith ye are called,
2 With all lowliness and meekness, with
longsuffering, forbearing one another in love;
3 Endeavouring to keep the unity of the
Spirit in the bond of peace.
4 *There is* one body, and one Spirit, even as
ye are called in one hope of your calling;
5 One Lord, one faith, one baptism,
6 One God and Father of all, who *is* above all,
and through all, and in you all.
7 But unto every one of us is given grace according to the measure of the gift of Christ.
8 Wherefore he saith, When he ascended up
on high, he led captivity captive, and gave gifts
unto men.
9 (Now that he ascended, what is it but that
he also descended first into the lower parts of
the earth?
10 He that descended is the same also that
ascended up far above all heavens, that he
might fill all things.)
11 And he gave some, apostles; and some,
prophets; and some, evangelists; and some, pastors and teachers;
12 For the perfecting of the saints, for the
work of the ministry, for the edifying of the
body of Christ:
13 Till we all come in the unity of the faith,
and of the knowledge of the Son of God, unto a
perfect man, unto the measure of the stature of
the fulness of Christ:
14 That we *henceforth* be no more children,
tossed to and fro, and carried about with every
wind of doctrine, by the sleight of men, *and*
cunning craftiness, whereby they lie in wait to
deceive;
15 But speaking the truth in love, may grow
up into him in all things, which is the head, *even*
Christ:
16 From whom the whole body fitly joined
together and compacted by that which every
joint supplieth, according to the effectual working in the measure of every part, maketh increase of the body unto the edifying of itself in
love.
17 This I say therefore, and testify in the
Lord, that ye henceforth walk not as other Gen'tiles walk, in the vanity of their mind,
18 Having the understanding darkened,
being alienated from the life of God through the
ignorance that is in them, because of the blindness of their heart:
19 Who being past feeling have given themselves over unto lasciviousness, to work all uncleanness with greediness.
20 But ye have not so learned Christ;
21 If so be that ye have heard him, and have
been taught by him, as the truth is in Je'sus:
22 That ye put off concerning the former
conversation the old man, which is corrupt according to the deceitful lusts;
23 And be renewed in the spirit of your mind;
24 And that ye put on the new man, which
after God is created in righteousness and true
holiness.
25 Wherefore putting away lying, speak every man truth with his neighbour: for we are
members one of another.
26 Be ye angry, and sin not: let not the sun go
down upon your wrath:
27 Neither give place to the devil.
28 Let him that stole steal no more: but
rather let him labour, working with *his* hands
the thing which is good, that he may have to
give to him that needeth.
29 Let no corrupt communication proceed
out of your mouth, but that which is good to the
use of edifying, that it may minister grace unto
the hearers.
30 And grieve not the holy Spirit of God,
whereby ye are sealed unto the day of redemption.
31 Let all bitterness, and wrath, and anger,
and clamour, and evil speaking, be put away
from you, with all malice:
32 And be ye kind one to another, tenderhearted, forgiving one another, even as God for
Christ's sake hath forgiven you.

5 BE ye therefore followers of God, as dear
children;
2 And walk in love, as Christ also hath loved
us, and hath given himself for us an offering
and a sacrifice to God for a sweetsmelling savour.
3 But fornication, and all uncleanness, or
covetousness, let it not be once named among
you, as becometh saints;

4 Neither filthiness, nor foolish talking, nor
jesting, which are not convenient: but rather
giving of thanks.
5 For this ye know, that no whoremonger,
nor unclean person, nor covetous man, who is
an idolater, hath any inheritance in the kingdom of Christ and of God.
6 Let no man deceive you with vain words:
for because of these things cometh the wrath of
God upon the children of disobedience.
7 Be not ye therefore partakers with them.
8 For ye were sometimes darkness, but now
are ye light in the Lord: walk as children of
light:
9 (For the fruit of the Spirit *is* in all goodness
and righteousness and truth;)
10 Proving what is acceptable unto the Lord.
11 And have no fellowship with the unfruitful works of darkness, but rather reprove *them*.
12 For it is a shame even to speak of those
things which are done of them in secret.
13 But all things that are reproved are made
manifest by the light: for whatsoever doth
make manifest is light.
14 Wherefore he saith, Awake thou that
sleepest, and arise from the dead, and Christ
shall give thee light.
15 See then that ye walk circumspectly, not
as fools, but as wise,
16 Redeeming the time, because the days are
evil.
17 Wherefore be ye not unwise, but understanding what the will of the Lord *is*.
18 And be not drunk with wine, wherein is
excess; but be filled with the Spirit;
19 Speaking to yourselves in psalms and
hymns and spiritual songs, singing and making
melody in your heart to the Lord;
20 Giving thanks always for all things unto
God and the Father in the name of our Lord
Je'sus Christ;
21 Submitting yourselves one to another in
the fear of God.
22 Wives, submit yourselves unto your own
husbands, as unto the Lord.
23 For the husband is the head of the wife,
even as Christ is the head of the church: and he
is the saviour of the body.
24 Therefore as the church is subject unto
Christ, so *let* the wives *be* to their own husbands in every thing.
25 Husbands, love your wives, even as Christ
also loved the church, and gave himself for it;
26 That he might sanctify and cleanse it with
the washing of water by the word,
27 That he might present it to himself a glorious church, not having spot, or wrinkle, or any
such thing; but that it should be holy and without blemish.
28 So ought men to love their wives as their
own bodies. He that loveth his wife loveth himself.
29 For no man ever yet hated his own flesh;
but nourisheth and cherisheth it, even as the
Lord the church:
30 For we are members of his body, of his
flesh, and of his bones.
31 For this cause shall a man leave his father
and mother, and shall be joined unto his wife,
and they two shall be one flesh.
32 This is a great mystery: but I speak concerning Christ and the church.
33 Nevertheless let every one of you in particular so love his wife even as himself; and the
wife *see* that she reverence *her* husband.

6 CHILDREN, obey your parents in the
Lord: for this is right.
2 Honour thy father and mother; which is the
first commandment with promise;
3 That it may be well with thee, and thou
mayest live long on the earth.
4 And, ye fathers, provoke not your children
to wrath: but bring them up in the nurture and
admonition of the Lord.
5 Servants, be obedient to them that are *your*
masters according to the flesh, with fear and
trembling, in singleness of your heart, as unto
Christ;
6 Not with eyeservice, as menpleasers; but
as the servants of Christ, doing the will of God
from the heart;
7 With good will doing service, as to the
Lord, and not to men:
8 Knowing that whatsoever good thing any
man doeth, the same shall he receive of the
Lord, whether *he be* bond or free.
9 And, ye masters, do the same things unto
them, forbearing threatening: knowing that
your Master also is in heaven; neither is there
respect of persons with him.
10 Finally, my brethren, be strong in the
Lord, and in the power of his might.
11 Put on the whole armour of God, that ye
may be able to stand against the wiles of the
devil.
12 For we wrestle not against flesh and
blood, but against principalities, against powers, against the rulers of the darkness of this
world, against spiritual wickedness in high
places.
13 Wherefore take unto you the whole armour of God, that ye may be able to withstand
in the evil day, and having done all, to stand.
14 Stand therefore, having your loins girt
about with truth, and having on the breastplate
of righteousness;
15 And your feet shod with the preparation
of the gospel of peace;
16 Above all, taking the shield of faith,
wherewith ye shall be able to quench all the fiery darts of the wicked.
17 And take the helmet of salvation, and the
sword of the Spirit, which is the word of God:
18 Praying always with all prayer and supplication in the Spirit, and watching thereunto
with all perseverance and supplication for all
saints;
19 And for me, that utterance may be given
unto me, that I may open my mouth boldly, to
make known the mystery of the gospel,
20 For which I am an ambassador in bonds:
that therein I may speak boldly, as I ought to
speak.
21 But that ye also may know my affairs, *and*
how I do, Tych'i-cus, a beloved brother and
faithful minister in the Lord, shall make known
to you all things:
22 Whom I have sent unto you for the same
purpose, that ye might know our affairs, and
that he might comfort your hearts.
23 Peace *be* to the brethren, and love with
faith, from God the Father and the Lord Je'sus
Christ.
24 Grace *be* with all them that love our Lord
Je'sus Christ in sincerity. Amen.

Written from Rome unto the E-phe'sians by Tych'i-cus.

THE LETTER OF PAUL TO THE

PHILIPPIANS

1 PAUL and Ti-mo'the-us, the servants of
Je'sus Christ, to all the saints in Christ Je'-
sus which are at Phi-lip'pi, with the bishops and
deacons:
2 Grace *be* unto you, and peace, from God
our Father, and *from* the Lord Je'sus Christ.
3 I thank my God upon every remembrance
of you,
4 Always in every prayer of mine for you all
making request with joy,
5 For your fellowship in the gospel from the
first day until now;
6 Being confident of this very thing, that he
which hath begun a good work in you will perform *it* until the day of Je'sus Christ:
7 Even as it is meet for me to think this of
you all, because I have you in my heart; inasmuch as both in my bonds, and in the defence
and confirmation of the gospel, ye all are partakers of my grace.
8 For God is my record, how greatly I long
after you all in the bowels of Je'sus Christ.
9 And this I pray, that your love may abound
yet more and more in knowledge and *in* all
judgment;
10 That ye may approve things that are excellent; that ye may be sincere and without offence till the day of Christ;
11 Being filled with the fruits of righteousness, which are by Je'sus Christ, unto the glory
and praise of God.
12 But I would ye should understand, brethren, that the things *which happened* unto me
have fallen out rather unto the furtherance of
the gospel;
13 So that my bonds in Christ are manifest in
all the palace, and in all other *places;*
14 And many of the brethren in the Lord,
waxing confident by my bonds, are much more
bold to speak the word without fear.
15 Some indeed preach Christ even of envy
and strife; and some also of good will:
16 The one preach Christ of contention, not
sincerely, supposing to add affliction to my
bonds:
17 But the other of love, knowing that I am
set for the defence of the gospel.
18 What then? notwithstanding, every way,
whether in pretence, or in truth, Christ is
preached; and I therein do rejoice, yea, and will
rejoice.
19 For I know that this shall turn to my salvation through your prayer, and the supply of
the Spirit of Je'sus Christ,
20 According to my earnest expectation and
my hope, that in nothing I shall be ashamed, but
that with all boldness, as always, *so* now also
Christ shall be magnified in my body, whether
it be by life, or by death.
21 For to me to live *is* Christ, and to die *is*
gain.
22 But if I live in the flesh, this *is* the fruit of
my labour: yet what I shall choose I wot not.
23 For I am in a strait betwixt two, having a
desire to depart, and to be with Christ; which is
far better:
24 Nevertheless to abide in the flesh *is* more
needful for you.
25 And having this confidence, I know that I
shall abide and continue with you all for your
furtherance and joy of faith;
26 That your rejoicing may be more abundant in Je'sus Christ for me by my coming to
you again.
27 Only let your conversation be as it becometh the gospel of Christ: that whether I come
and see you, or else be absent, I may hear of
your affairs, that ye stand fast in one spirit, with
one mind striving together for the faith of the
gospel;
28 And in nothing terrified by your adversaries: which is to them an evident token of perdition, but to you of salvation, and that of God.
29 For unto you it is given in the behalf of
Christ, not only to believe on him, but also to
suffer for his sake;
30 Having the same conflict which ye saw in
me, and now hear *to be* in me.

2 IF *there be* therefore any consolation in
Christ, if any comfort of love, if any fellowship of the Spirit, if any bowels and mercies,
2 Fulfil ye my joy, that ye be likeminded,
having the same love, *being* of one accord, of
one mind.
3 *Let* nothing *be done* through strife or vain-
glory; but in lowliness of mind let each esteem
other better than themselves.
4 Look not every man on his own things, but
every man also on the things of others.
5 Let this mind be in you, which was also in
Christ Je'sus:
6 Who, being in the form of God, thought it
not robbery to be equal with God:
7 But made himself of no reputation, and
took upon him the form of a servant, and was
made in the likeness of men:
8 And being found in fashion as a man, he
humbled himself, and became obedient unto
death, even the death of the cross.
9 Wherefore God also hath highly exalted
him, and given him a name which is above every name:
10 That at the name of Je'sus every knee
should bow, of *things* in heaven, and *things* in
earth, and *things* under the earth;
11 And *that* every tongue should confess
that Je'sus Christ *is* Lord, to the glory of God
the Father.
12 Wherefore, my beloved, as ye have always obeyed, not as in my presence only, but
now much more in my absence, work out your
own salvation with fear and trembling.
13 For it is God which worketh in you both to
will and to do of *his* good pleasure.
14 Do all things without murmurings and
disputings:
15 That ye may be blameless and harmless,
the sons of God, without rebuke, in the midst of
a crooked and perverse nation, among whom ye
shine as lights in the world;
16 Holding forth the word of life; that I may
rejoice in the day of Christ, that I have not run
in vain, neither laboured in vain.
17 Yea, and if I be offered upon the sacrifice
and service of your faith, I joy, and rejoice with
you all.
18 For the same cause also do ye joy, and
rejoice with me.
19 But I trust in the Lord Je'sus to send Ti-
mo'the-us shortly unto you, that I also may be
of good comfort, when I know your state.
20 For I have no man likeminded, who will
naturally care for your state.

21 For all seek their own, not the things which are Je'sus Christ's.

22 But ye know the proof of him, that, as a son with the father, he hath served with me in the gospel.

23 Him therefore I hope to send presently, so soon as I shall see how it will go with me.

24 But I trust in the Lord that I also myself shall come shortly.

25 Yet I supposed it necessary to send to you E-paph-ro-di'tus, my brother, and companion in labour, and fellowsoldier, but your messenger, and he that ministered to my wants.

26 For he longed after you all, and was full of heaviness, because that ye had heard that he had been sick.

27 For indeed he was sick nigh unto death: but God had mercy on him; and not on him only, but on me also, lest I should have sorrow upon sorrow.

28 I sent him therefore the more carefully, that, when ye see him again, ye may rejoice, and that I may be the less sorrowful.

29 Receive him therefore in the Lord with all gladness; and hold such in reputation:

30 Because for the work of Christ he was nigh unto death, not regarding his life, to supply your lack of service toward me.

3 FINALLY, my brethren, rejoice in the Lord. To write the same things to you, to me indeed *is* not grievous, but for you *it is* safe.

2 Beware of dogs, beware of evil workers, beware of the concision.

3 For we are the circumcision, which worship God in the spirit, and rejoice in Christ Je'sus, and have no confidence in the flesh.

4 Though I might also have confidence in the flesh. If any other man thinketh that he hath whereof he might trust in the flesh, I more:

5 Circumcised the eighth day, of the stock of Is'ra-el, *of* the tribe of Ben'ja-min, an He'brew of the He'brews; as touching the law, a Phar'i-see;

6 Concerning zeal, persecuting the church; touching the righteousness which is in the law, blameless.

7 But what things were gain to me, those I counted loss for Christ.

8 Yea doubtless, and I count all things *but* loss for the excellency of the knowledge of Christ Je'sus my Lord: for whom I have suffered the loss of all things, and do count them *but* dung, that I may win Christ.

9 And be found in him, not having mine own righteousness, which is of the law, but that which is through the faith of Christ, the righteousness which is of God by faith:

10 That I may know him, and the power of his resurrection, and the fellowship of his sufferings, being made conformable unto his death;

11 If by any means I might attain unto the resurrection of the dead.

12 Not as though I had already attained, either were already perfect: but I follow after, if that I may apprehend that for which also I am apprehended of Christ Je'sus.

13 Brethren, I count not myself to have apprehended: but *this* one thing *I do*, forgetting those things which are behind, and reaching forth unto those things which are before,

14 I press toward the mark for the prize of the high calling of God in Christ Je'sus.

15 Let us therefore, as many as be perfect, be thus minded: and if in any thing ye be otherwise minded, God shall reveal even this unto you.

16 Nevertheless, whereto we have already attained, let us walk by the same rule, let us mind the same thing.

17 Brethren, be followers together of me, and mark them which walk so as ye have us for an ensample.

18 (For many walk, of whom I have told you often, and now tell you even weeping, *that they are* the enemies of the cross of Christ:

19 Whose end *is* destruction, whose God *is their* belly, and *whose* glory *is* in their shame, who mind earthly things.)

20 For our conversation is in heaven; from whence also we look for the Saviour, the Lord Je'sus Christ:

21 Who shall change our vile body, that it may be fashioned like unto his glorious body, according to the working whereby he is able even to subdue all things unto himself.

4 THEREFORE, my brethren dearly beloved and longed for, my joy and crown, so stand fast in the Lord, *my* dearly beloved.

2 I beseech Eu-o'di-as, and beseech Syn'ty-che, that they be of the same mind in the Lord.

3 And I intreat thee also, true yokefellow, help those women which laboured with me in the gospel, with Clem'ent also, and *with* other my fellowlabourers, whose names *are* in the book of life.

4 Rejoice in the Lord alway: *and* again I say, Rejoice.

5 Let your moderation be known unto all men. The Lord *is* at hand.

6 Be careful for nothing; but in every thing by prayer and supplication with thanksgiving let your requests be made known unto God.

7 And the peace of God, which passeth all understanding, shall keep your hearts and minds through Christ Je'sus.

8 Finally, brethren, whatsoever things are true, whatsoever things *are* honest, whatsoever things *are* just, whatsoever things *are* pure, whatsoever things *are* lovely, whatsoever things *are* of good report; if *there be* any virtue, and if *there be* any praise, think on these things.

9 Those things, which ye have both learned, and received, and heard, and seen in me, do: and the God of peace shall be with you.

10 But I rejoiced in the Lord greatly, that now at the last your care of me hath flourished again; wherein ye were also careful, but ye lacked opportunity.

11 Not that I speak in respect of want: for I have learned, in whatsoever state I am, *therewith* to be content.

12 I know both how to be abased, and I know how to abound: every where and in all things I am instructed both to be full and to be hungry, both to abound and to suffer need.

13 I can do all things through Christ which strengtheneth me.

14 Notwithstanding ye have well done, that ye did communicate with my affliction.

15 Now ye Phi-lip'pi-ans know also, that in the beginning of the gospel, when I departed from Mac-e-do'ni-a, no church communicated with me as concerning giving and receiving, but ye only.

16 For even in Thes-sa-lo-ni'ca ye sent once and again unto my necessity.

17 Not because I desire a gift: but I desire fruit that may abound to your account.

18 But I have all, and abound: I am full, having received of E-paph-ro-di'tus the things

which were sent from you, an odour of a sweet
smell, a sacrifice acceptable, well pleasing to
God.
19 But my God shall supply all your need according to his riches in glory by Christ Je'sus.
20 Now unto God and our Father *be* glory for
ever and ever. Amen.
21 Salute every saint in Christ Je'sus. The
brethren which are with me greet you.
22 All the saints salute you, chiefly they that
are of Cæ'sar's household.
23 The grace of our Lord Je'sus Christ *be*
with you all. Amen.

It was written to the Phi-lip'pi-ans from Rome by E-
paph-ro-di'tus.

THE LETTER OF PAUL TO THE

COLOSSIANS

1 PAUL, an apostle of Je'sus Christ by the
will of God, and Ti-mo'the-us *our* brother,
2 To the saints and faithful brethren in Christ
which are at Co-los'se: Grace *be* unto you, and
peace, from God our Father and the Lord Je'sus
Christ.
3 We give thanks to God and the Father of
our Lord Je'sus Christ, praying always for you,
4 Since we heard of your faith in Christ Je'-
sus, and of the love *which ye have* to all the
saints,
5 For the hope which is laid up for you in
heaven, whereof ye heard before in the word of
the truth of the gospel;
6 Which is come unto you, as *it is* in all the
world; and bringeth forth fruit, as *it doth* also in
you, since the day ye heard *of it*, and knew the
grace of God in truth:
7 As ye also learned of Ep'a-phras our dear
fellowservant, who is for you a faithful minister
of Christ;
8 Who also declared unto us your love in the
Spirit.
9 For this cause we also, since the day we
heard *it*, do not cease to pray for you, and to
desire that ye might be filled with the knowledge of his will in all wisdom and spiritual understanding;
10 That ye might walk worthy of the Lord
unto all pleasing, being fruitful in every good
work, and increasing in the knowledge of God;
11 Strengthened with all might, according to
his glorious power, unto all patience and longsuffering with joyfulness;
12 Giving thanks unto the Father, which hath
made us meet to be partakers of the inheritance
of the saints in light:
13 Who hath delivered us from the power of
darkness, and hath translated *us* into the kingdom of his dear Son:
14 In whom we have redemption through his
blood, *even* the forgiveness of sins:
15 Who is the image of the invisible God, the
firstborn of every creature:
16 For by him were all things created, that
are in heaven, and that are in earth, visible and
invisible, whether *they be* thrones, or dominions, or principalities, or powers: all things
were created by him, and for him:
17 And he is before all things, and by him all
things consist.
18 And he is the head of the body, the
church: who is the beginning, the firstborn from
the dead; that in all *things* he might have the
preeminence.
19 For it pleased *the Father* that in him
should all fulness dwell;
20 And, having made peace through the
blood of his cross, by him to reconcile all things
unto himself; by him, *I say*, whether *they be*
things in earth, or things in heaven.
21 And you, that were sometime alienated
and enemies in *your* mind by wicked works, yet
now hath he reconciled
22 In the body of his flesh through death, to
present you holy and unblameable and unre-
proveable in his sight:
23 If ye continue in the faith grounded and
settled, and *be* not moved away from the hope
of the gospel, which ye have heard, *and* which
was preached to every creature which is under
heaven; whereof I Paul am made a minister;
24 Who now rejoice in my sufferings for you,
and fill up that which is behind of the afflictions
of Christ in my flesh for his body's sake, which
is the church:
25 Whereof I am made a minister, according
to the dispensation of God which is given to me
for you, to fulfil the word of God;
26 *Even* the mystery which hath been hid
from ages and from generations, but now is
made manifest to his saints:
27 To whom God would make known what *is*
the riches of the glory of this mystery among
the Gen'tiles; which is Christ in you, the hope of
glory:
28 Whom we preach, warning every man,
and teaching every man in all wisdom; that we
may present every man perfect in Christ Je'sus:
29 Whereunto I also labour, striving according to his working, which worketh in me mightily.

2 FOR I would that ye knew what great conflict I have for you, and *for* them at La-od-
i-ce'a, and *for* as many as have not seen my face
in the flesh;
2 That their hearts might be comforted,
being knit together in love, and unto all riches
of the full assurance of understanding, to the
acknowledgement of the mystery of God, and
of the Father, and of Christ;
3 In whom are hid all the treasures of wisdom and knowledge.
4 And this I say, lest any man should beguile
you with enticing words.
5 For though I be absent in the flesh, yet am I
with you in the spirit, joying and beholding
your order, and the stedfastness of your faith in
Christ.
6 As ye have therefore received Christ Je'sus
the Lord, *so* walk ye in him:
7 Rooted and built up in him, and stablished
in the faith, as ye have been taught, abounding
therein with thanksgiving.
8 Beware lest any man spoil you through philosophy and vain deceit, after the tradition of
men, after the rudiments of the world, and not
after Christ.

9 For in him dwelleth all the fulness of the Godhead bodily.
10 And ye are complete in him, which is the head of all principality and power:
11 In whom also ye are circumcised with the circumcison made without hands, in putting off the body of the sins of the flesh by the circumcision of Christ:
12 Buried with him in baptism, wherein also ye are risen with *him* through the faith of the operation of God, who hath raised him from the dead.
13 And you, being dead in your sins and the uncircumcision of your flesh, hath he quickened together with him, having forgiven you all trespasses;
14 Blotting out the handwriting of ordinances that was against us, which was contrary to us, and took it out of the way, nailing it to his cross;
15 *And* having spoiled principalities and powers, he made a shew of them openly, triumphing over them in it.
16 Let no man therefore judge you in meat, or in drink, or in respect of an holyday, or of the new moon, or of the sabbath *days*:
17 Which are a shadow of things to come; but the body *is* of Christ.
18 Let no man beguile you of your reward in a voluntary humility and worshipping of angels, intruding into those things which he hath not seen, vainly puffed up by his fleshly mind,
19 And not holding the Head, from which all the body by joints and bands having nourishment ministered, and knit together, increaseth with the increase of God.
20 Wherefore if ye be dead with Christ from the rudiments of the world, why, as though living in the world, are ye subject to ordinances,
21 (Touch not; taste not; handle not;
22 Which all are to perish with the using;) after the commandments and doctrines of men?
23 Which things have indeed a shew of wisdom in will worship, and humility, and neglecting of the body; not in any honour to the satisfying of the flesh.

3 IF ye then be risen with Christ, seek those things which are above, where Christ sitteth on the right hand of God.
2 Set your affection on things above, not on things on the earth.
3 For ye are dead, and your life is hid with Christ in God.
4 When Christ, *who is* our life, shall appear, then shall ye also appear with him in glory.
5 Mortify therefore your members which are upon the earth; fornication, uncleanness, inordinate affection, evil concupiscence, and covetousness, which is idolatry:
6 For which things' sake the wrath of God cometh on the children of disobedience:
7 In the which ye also walked some time, when ye lived in them.
8 But now ye also put off all these; anger, wrath, malice, blasphemy, filthy communication out of your mouth.
9 Lie not one to another, seeing that ye have put off the old man with his deeds;
10 And have put on the new *man*, which is renewed in knowledge after the image of him that created him:
11 Where there is neither Greek nor Jew, circumcision nor uncircumcision, Bar-ba'ri-an, Scyth'i-an, bond *nor* free: but Christ *is* all, and in all.
12 Put on therefore, as the elect of God, holy and beloved, bowels of mercies, kindness, humbleness of mind, meekness, longsuffering;
13 Forbearing one another, and forgiving one another, if any man have a quarrel against any: even as Christ forgave you, so also *do* ye.
14 And above all these things *put on* charity, which is the bond of perfectness.
15 And let the peace of God rule in your hearts, to the which also ye are called in one body; and be ye thankful.
16 Let the word of Christ dwell in you richly in all wisdom; teaching and admonishing one another in psalms and hymns and spiritual songs, singing with grace in your hearts to the Lord.
17 And whatsoever ye do in word or deed, *do* all in the name of the Lord Je'sus, giving thanks to God and the Father by him.
18 Wives, submit yourselves unto your own husbands, as it is fit in the Lord.
19 Husbands, love *your* wives, and be not bitter against them.
20 Children, obey *your* parents in all things: for this is well pleasing unto the Lord.
21 Fathers, provoke not your children *to anger*, lest they be discouraged.
22 Servants, obey in all things *your* masters according to the flesh; not with eyeservice, as menpleasers; but in singleness of heart, fearing God:
23 And whatsoever ye do, do *it* heartily, as to the Lord, and not unto men;
24 Knowing that of the Lord ye shall receive the reward of the inheritance: for ye serve the Lord Christ.
25 But he that doeth wrong shall receive for the wrong which he hath done: and there is no respect of persons.

4 MASTERS, give unto *your* servants that which is just and equal; knowing that ye also have a Master in heaven.
2 Continue in prayer, and watch in the same with thanksgiving;
3 Withal praying also for us, that God would open unto us a door of utterance, to speak the mystery of Christ, for which I am also in bonds:
4 That I may make it manifest, as I ought to speak.
5 Walk in wisdom toward them that are without, redeeming the time.
6 Let your speech *be* alway with grace, seasoned with salt, that ye may know how ye ought to answer every man.
7 All my state shall Tych'i-cus declare unto you, *who is* a beloved brother, and a faithful minister and fellowservant in the Lord:
8 Whom I have sent unto you for the same purpose, that he might know your estate, and comfort your hearts;
9 With O'nes'i-mus, a faithful and beloved brother, who is *one* of you. They shall make known unto you all things which *are done* here.
10 Ar-is-tar'chus my fellowprisoner saluteth you, and Mar'cus, sister's son to Bar'na-bas, (touching whom ye received commandments: if he come unto you, receive him;)
11 And Je'sus, which is called Jus'tus, who are of the circumcision. These only *are my* fellowworkers unto the kingdom of God, which have been a comfort unto me.
12 Ep'a-phras, who is *one* of you, a servant of Christ, saluteth you, always labouring fervently for you in prayers, that ye may stand perfect and complete in all the will of God.
13 For I bear him record, that he hath a great

zeal for you, and them *that are* in La-od-i-ce′a, and them in Hi-e-rap′o-lis.

14 Luke, the beloved physician, and De′mas, greet you.

15 Salute the brethren which are in La-od-i-ce′a, and Nym′phas, and the church which is in his house.

16 And when this epistle is read among you, cause that it be read also in the church of the La-od-i-ce′ans; and that ye likewise read the *epistle* from La-od-i-ce′a.

17 And say to Ar-chip′pus, Take heed to the ministry which thou hast received in the Lord, that thou fulfil it.

18 The salutation by the hand of me Paul. Remember my bonds. Grace *be* with you. Amen.

Written from Rome to the Co-los′si-ans by Tych′i-cus and O′nes′i-mus.

THE FIRST LETTER OF PAUL TO THE

THESSALONIANS

1 PAUL, and Sil-va′nus, and Ti-mo′the-us, unto the church of the Thes-sa-lo′ni-ans *which is* in God the Father and *in* the Lord Je′sus Christ: Grace *be* with you, and peace, from God our Father, and the Lord Je′sus Christ.

2 We give thanks to God always for you all, making mention of you in our prayers;

3 Remembering without ceasing your work of faith, and labour of love, and patience of hope in our Lord Je′sus Christ, in the sight of God and our Father;

4 Knowing, brethren beloved, your election of God.

5 For our gospel came not unto you in word only, but also in power, and in the Ho′ly Ghost, and in much assurance; as ye know what manner of men we were among you for your sake.

6 And ye became followers of us, and of the Lord, having received the word in much affliction, with joy of the Ho′ly Ghost:

7 So that ye were ensamples to all that believe in Mac-e-do′ni-a and A-cha′ia.

8 For from you sounded out the word of the Lord not only in Mac-e-do′ni-a and A-cha′ia, but also in every place your faith to God-ward is spread abroad; so that we need not to speak any thing.

9 For they themselves shew of us what manner of entering in we had unto you, and how ye turned to God from idols to serve the living and true God;

10 And to wait for his Son from heaven, whom he raised from the dead, *even* Je′sus, which delivered us from the wrath to come.

2 FOR yourselves, brethren, know our entrance in unto you, that it was not in vain:

2 But even after that we had suffered before, and were shamefully entreated, as ye know, at Phi-lip′pi, we were bold in our God to speak unto you the gospel of God with much contention.

3 For our exhortation *was* not of deceit, nor of uncleanness, nor in guile:

4 But as we were allowed of God to be put in trust with the gospel, even so we speak; not as pleasing men, but God, which trieth our hearts.

5 For neither at any time used we flattering words, as ye know, nor a cloke of covetousness; God *is* witness:

6 Nor of men sought we glory, neither of you, nor *yet* of others, when we might have been burdensome, as the apostles of Christ.

7 But we were gentle among you, even as a nurse cherisheth her children:

8 So being affectionately desirous of you, we were willing to have imparted unto you, not the gospel of God only, but also our own souls, because ye were dear unto us.

9 For ye remember, brethren, our labour and travail: for labouring night and day, because we would not be chargeable unto any of you, we preached unto you the gospel of God.

10 Ye *are* witnesses, and God *also*, how holily and justly and unblameably we behaved ourselves among you that believe:

11 As ye know how we exhorted and comforted and charged every one of you, as a father *doth* his children,

12 That ye would walk worthy of God, who hath called you unto his kingdom and glory.

13 For this cause also thank we God without ceasing, because, when ye received the word of God which ye heard of us, ye received *it* not *as* the word of men, but as it is in truth, the word of God, which effectually worketh also in you that believe.

14 For ye, brethren, became followers of the churches of God which in Ju-dæ′a are in Christ Je′sus: for ye also have suffered like things of your own countrymen, even as they *have* of the Jews:

15 Who both killed the Lord Je′sus, and their own prophets, and have persecuted us; and they please not God, and are contrary to all men:

16 Forbidding us to speak to the Gen′tiles that they might be saved, to fill up their sins alway: for the wrath is come upon them to the uttermost.

17 But we, brethren, being taken from you for a short time in presence, not in heart, endeavoured the more abundantly to see your face with great desire.

18 Wherefore we would have come unto you, even I Paul, once and again; but Sa′tan hindered us.

19 For what *is* our hope, or joy, or crown of rejoicing? *Are* not even ye in the presence of our Lord Je′sus Christ at his coming?

20 For ye are our glory and joy.

3 WHEREFORE when we could no longer forbear, we thought it good to be left at Ath′ens alone;

2 And sent Ti-mo′the-us, our brother, and minister of God, and our fellowlabourer in the gospel of Christ, to establish you, and to comfort you concerning your faith:

3 That no man should be moved by these afflictions: for yourselves know that we are appointed thereunto.

4 For verily, when we were with you, we told you before that we should suffer tribulation; even as it came to pass, and ye know.

5 For this cause, when I could no longer forbear, I sent to know your faith, lest by some

means the tempter have tempted you, and our
labour be in vain.
6 But now when Ti-mo'the-us came from you
unto us, and brought us good tidings of your
faith and charity, and that ye have good remembrance of us always, desiring greatly to see
us, as we also *to see* you:
7 Therefore, brethren, we were comforted
over you in all our affliction and distress by
your faith:
8 For now we live, if ye stand fast in the
Lord.
9 For what thanks can we render to God
again for you, for all the joy wherewith we joy
for your sakes before our God;
10 Night and day praying exceedingly that
we might see your face, and might perfect that
which is lacking in your faith?
11 Now God himself and our Father, and our
Lord Je'sus Christ, direct our way unto you.
12 And the Lord make you to increase and
abound in love one toward another, and toward
all *men*, even as we *do* toward you:
13 To the end he may stablish your hearts
unblameable in holiness before God, even our
Father, at the coming of our Lord Je'sus Christ
with all his saints.

4 FURTHERMORE then we beseech you,
brethren, and exhort *you* by the Lord Je'-
sus, that as ye have received of us how ye ought
to walk and to please God, so ye would abound
more and more.
2 For ye know what commandments we gave
you by the Lord Je'sus.
3 For this is the will of God, *even* your sanctification, that ye should abstain from fornication:
4 That every one of you should know how to
possess his vessel in sanctification and honour;
5 Not in the lust of concupiscence, even as
the Gen'tiles which know not God:
6 That no *man* go beyond and defraud his
brother in *any* matter: because that the Lord *is*
the avenger of all such, as we also have fore-
warned you and testified.
7 For God hath not called us unto uncleanness, but unto holiness.
8 He therefore that despiseth, despiseth not
man, but God, who hath also given unto us his
holy Spirit.
9 But as touching brotherly love ye need not
that I write unto you: for ye yourselves are
taught of God to love one another.
10 And indeed ye do it toward all the brethren which are in all Mac-e-do'ni-a: but we beseech you, brethren, that ye increase more and
more;
11 And that ye study to be quiet, and to do
your own business, and to work with your own
hands, as we commanded you;
12 That ye may walk honestly toward them
that are without, and *that* ye may have lack of
nothing.
13 But I would not have you to be ignorant,
brethren, concerning them which are asleep,
that ye sorrow not, even as others which have
no hope.
14 For if we believe that Je'sus died and rose
again, even so them also which sleep in Je'sus
will God bring with him.
15 For this we say unto you by the word of
the Lord, that we which are alive *and* remain
unto the coming of the Lord shall not prevent
them which are asleep.
16 For the Lord himself shall descend from
heaven with a shout, with the voice of the archangel, and with the trump of God: and the dead
in Christ shall rise first:
17 Then we which are alive *and* remain shall
be caught up together with them in the clouds,
to meet the Lord in the air: and so shall we ever
be with the Lord.
18 Wherefore comfort one another with
these words.

5 BUT of the times and the seasons, brethren, ye have no need that I write unto you.
2 For yourselves know perfectly that the day
of the Lord so cometh as a thief in the night.
3 For when they shall say, Peace and safety;
then sudden destruction cometh upon them, as
travail upon a woman with child; and they shall
not escape.
4 But ye, brethren, are not in darkness, that
that day should overtake you as a thief.
5 Ye are all the children of light, and the children of the day: we are not of the night, nor of
darkness.
6 Therefore let us not sleep, as *do* others; but
let us watch and be sober.
7 For they that sleep sleep in the night; and
they that be drunken are drunken in the night.
8 But let us, who are of the day, be sober,
putting on the breastplate of faith and love; and
for an helmet, the hope of salvation.
9 For God hath not appointed us to wrath,
but to obtain salvation by our Lord Je'sus
Christ,
10 Who died for us, that, whether we wake
or sleep, we should live together with him.
11 Wherefore comfort yourselves together,
and edify one another, even as also ye do.
12 And we beseech you, brethren, to know
them which labour among you, and are over
you in the Lord, and admonish you;
13 And to esteem them very highly in love
for their work's sake. *And* be at peace among
yourselves.
14 Now we exhort you, brethren, warn them
that are unruly, comfort the feebleminded, support the weak, be patient toward all *men*.
15 See that none render evil for evil unto any
man; but ever follow that which is good, both
among yourselves, and to all *men*.
16 Rejoice evermore.
17 Pray without ceasing.
18 In every thing give thanks: for this is the
will of God in Christ Je'sus concerning you.
19 Quench not the Spirit.
20 Despise not prophesyings.
21 Prove all things; hold fast that which is
good.
22 Abstain from all appearance of evil.
23 And the very God of peace sanctify you
wholly; and *I pray God* your whole spirit and
soul and body be preserved blameless unto the
coming of our Lord Je'sus Christ.
24 Faithful *is* he that calleth you, who also
will do *it*.
25 Brethren, pray for us.
26 Greet all the brethren with an holy kiss.
27 I charge you by the Lord that this epistle
be read unto all the holy brethren.
28 The grace of our Lord Je'sus Christ *be*
with you. Amen.

The first *epistle* unto the Thes-sa-lo'ni-ans was written from Ath'ens.

THE SECOND LETTER OF PAUL TO THE

THESSALONIANS

1 PAUL, and Sil-va'nus, and Ti-mo'the-us,
unto the church of the Thes-sa-lo'ni-ans in
God our Father and the Lord Je'sus Christ:
2 Grace unto you, and peace, from God our
Father and the Lord Je'sus Christ.
3 We are bound to thank God always for you,
brethren, as it is meet, because that your faith
groweth exceedingly, and the charity of every
one of you all toward each other aboundeth;
4 So that we ourselves glory in you in the
churches of God for your patience and faith in
all your persecutions and tribulations that ye
endure:
5 *Which is* a manifest token of the righteous
judgment of God, that ye may be counted worthy of the kingdom of God, for which ye also
suffer:
6 Seeing *it is* a righteous thing with God to
recompense tribulation to them that trouble
you;
7 And to you who are troubled rest with us,
when the Lord Je'sus shall be revealed from
heaven with his mighty angels,
8 In flaming fire taking vengeance on them
that know not God, and that obey not the gospel of our Lord Je'sus Christ:
9 Who shall be punished with everlasting destruction from the presence of the Lord, and
from the glory of his power;
10 When he shall come to be glorified in his
saints, and to be admired in all them that believe (because our testimony among you was
believed) in that day.
11 Wherefore also we pray always for you,
that our God would count you worthy of *this*
calling, and fulfil all the good pleasure of *his*
goodness, and the work of faith with power:
12 That the name of our Lord Je'sus Christ
may be glorified in you, and ye in him, according to the grace of our God and the Lord Je'sus
Christ.

2 NOW we beseech you, brethren, by the
coming of our Lord Je'sus Christ, and *by*
our gathering together unto him,
2 That ye be not soon shaken in mind, or be
troubled, neither by spirit, nor by word, nor by
letter as from us, as that the day of Christ is at
hand.
3 Let no man deceive you by any means: for
that day shall not come, except there come a
falling away first, and that man of sin be revealed, the son of perdition;
4 Who opposeth and exalteth himself above
all that is called God, or that is worshipped; so
that he as God sitteth in the temple of God,
shewing himself that he is God.
5 Remember ye not, that, when I was yet
with you, I told you these things?
6 And now ye know what withholdeth that
he might be revealed in his time.
7 For the mystery of iniquity doth already
work: only he who now letteth *will let,* until he
be taken out of the way.
8 And then shall that Wicked be revealed,
whom the Lord shall consume with the spirit of
his mouth, and shall destroy with the brightness of his coming:
9 *Even him,* whose coming is after the working of Sa'tan with all power and signs and lying
wonders,
10 And with all deceivableness of unrighteousness in them that perish; because they received not the love of the truth, that they might
be saved.
11 And for this cause God shall send them
strong delusion, that they should believe a lie:
12 That they all might be damned who believed not the truth, but had pleasure in unrighteousness.
13 But we are bound to give thanks alway to
God for you, brethren beloved of the Lord, because God hath from the beginning chosen you
to salvation through sanctification of the Spirit
and belief of the truth:
14 Whereunto he called you by our gospel, to
the obtaining of the glory of our Lord Je'sus
Christ.
15 Therefore, brethren, stand fast, and hold
the traditions which ye have been taught,
whether by word, or our epistle.
16 Now our Lord Je'sus Christ himself, and
God, even our Father, which hath loved us, and
hath given *us* everlasting consolation and good
hope through grace,
17 Comfort your hearts, and stablish you in
every good word and work.

3 FINALLY, brethren, pray for us, that the
word of the Lord may have *free* course,
and be glorified, even as *it is* with you:
2 And that we may be delivered from unreasonable and wicked men: for all *men* have not
faith.
3 But the Lord is faithful, who shall stablish
you, and keep *you* from evil.
4 And we have confidence in the Lord touching you, that ye both do and will do the things
which we command you.
5 And the Lord direct your hearts into the
love of God, and into the patient waiting for
Christ.
6 Now we command you, brethren, in the
name of our Lord Je'sus Christ, that ye withdraw yourselves from every brother that walketh disorderly, and not after the tradition which
he received of us.
7 For yourselves know how ye ought to follow us: for we behaved not ourselves disorderly
among you;
8 Neither did we eat any man's bread for
nought; but wrought with labour and travail
night and day, that we might not be chargeable
to any of you:
9 Not because we have not power, but to
make ourselves an ensample unto you to follow
us.
10 For even when we were with you, this we
commanded you, that if any would not work,
neither should he eat.
11 For we hear that there are some which
walk among you disorderly, working not at all,
but are busybodies.
12 Now them that are such we command and
exhort by our Lord Je'sus Christ, that with quietness they work, and eat their own bread.
13 But ye, brethren, be not weary in well
doing.
14 And if any man obey not our word by this
epistle, note that man, and have no company
with him, that he may be ashamed.
15 Yet count *him* not as an enemy, but admonish *him* as a brother.

16 Now the Lord of peace himself give you
peace always by all means. The Lord *be* with
you all.
17 The salutation of Paul with mine own
hand, which is the token in every epistle: so I
write.
18 The grace of our Lord Je'sus Christ *be*
with you all. Amen.

The second *epistle* to the Thes-sa-lo'ni-ans was written
from Ath'ens.

THE FIRST LETTER OF PAUL TO

TIMOTHY

1 PAUL, an apostle of Je'sus Christ by the
commandment of God our Saviour, and
Lord Je'sus Christ, *which is* our hope;
2 Unto Tim'o-thy, *my* own son in the faith:
Grace, mercy, *and* peace, from God our Father
and Je'sus Christ our Lord.
3 As I besought thee to abide still at Eph'e-
sus, when I went into Mac-e-do'ni-a, that thou
mightest charge some that they teach no other
doctrine,
4 Neither give heed to fables and endless genealogies, which minister questions, rather
than godly edifying which is in faith: *so do.*
5 Now the end of the commandment is charity out of a pure heart, and *of* a good conscience, and *of* faith unfeigned:
6 From which some having swerved have
turned aside unto vain jangling;
7 Desiring to be teachers of the law; understanding neither what they say, nor whereof
they affirm.
8 But we know that the law *is* good, if a man
use it lawfully;
9 Knowing this, that the law is not made for
a righteous man, but for the lawless and disobedient, for the ungodly and for sinners, for unholy and profane, for murderers of fathers and
murderers of mothers, for manslayers,
10 For whoremongers, for them that defile
themselves with mankind, for menstealers, for
liars, for perjured persons, and if there be any
other thing that is contrary to sound doctrine;
11 According to the glorious gospel of the
blessed God, which was committed to my trust.
12 And I thank Christ Je'sus our Lord, who
hath enabled me, for that he counted me faithful, putting me into the ministry;
13 Who was before a blasphemer, and a persecutor, and injurious: but I obtained mercy,
because I did *it* ignorantly in unbelief.
14 And the grace of our Lord was exceeding
abundant with faith and love which is in Christ
Je'sus.
15 This *is* a faithful saying, and worthy of all
acceptation, that Christ Je'sus came into the
world to save sinners; of whom I am chief.
16 Howbeit for this cause I obtained mercy,
that in me first Je'sus Christ might shew forth
all longsuffering, for a pattern to them which
should hereafter believe on him to life everlasting.
17 Now unto the King eternal, immortal, invisible, the only wise God, *be* honour and glory
for ever and ever. Amen.
18 This charge I commit unto thee, son Tim'-
o-thy, according to the prophecies which went
before on thee, that thou by them mightest war
a good warfare;
19 Holding faith, and a good conscience;
which some having put away concerning faith
have made shipwreck:
20 Of whom is Hy-me-næ'us and Al-ex-an'-
der; whom I have delivered unto Sa'tan, that
they may learn not to blaspheme.

2 I EXHORT therefore, that, first of all, supplications, prayers, intercessions, *and* giving of thanks, be made for all men;
2 For kings, and *for* all that are in authority;
that we may lead a quiet and peaceable life in
all godliness and honesty.
3 For this *is* good and acceptable in the sight
of God our Saviour;
4 Who will have all men to be saved, and to
come unto the knowledge of the truth.
5 For *there is* one God, and one mediator between God and men, the man Christ Je'sus;
6 Who gave himself a ransom for all, to be
testified in due time.
7 Whereunto I am ordained a preacher, and
an apostle, (I speak the truth in Christ, *and* lie
not;) a teacher of the Gen'tiles in faith and verity.
8 I will therefore that men pray every where,
lifting up holy hands, without wrath and doubting.
9 In like manner also, that women adorn
themselves in modest apparel, with shame-
facedness and sobriety; not with broided hair,
or gold, or pearls, or costly array;
10 But (which becometh women professing
godliness) with good works.
11 Let the woman learn in silence with all
subjection.
12 But I suffer not a woman to teach, nor to
usurp authority over the man, but to be in silence.
13 For Ad'am was first formed, then Eve.
14 And Ad'am was not deceived, but the
woman being deceived was in the transgression.
15 Notwithstanding she shall be saved in
childbearing, if they continue in faith and charity and holiness with sobriety.

3 THIS *is* a true saying, If a man desire the
office of a bishop, he desireth a good work.
2 A bishop then must be blameless, the husband of one wife, vigilant, sober, of good behaviour, given to hospitality, apt to teach;
3 Not given to wine, no striker, not greedy of
filthy lucre; but patient, not a brawler, not covetous;
4 One that ruleth well his own house, having
his children in subjection with all gravity;
5 (For if a man know not how to rule his own
house, how shall he take care of the church of
God?)
6 Not a novice, lest being lifted up with pride
he fall into the condemnation of the devil.
7 Moreover he must have a good report of
them which are without; lest he fall into reproach and the snare of the devil.
8 Likewise *must* the deacons *be* grave, not

doubletongued, not given to much wine, not greedy of filthy lucre;

9 Holding the mystery of the faith in a pure conscience.

10 And let these also first be proved; then let them use the office of a deacon, being *found* blameless.

11 Even so *must their* wives *be* grave, not slanderers, sober, faithful in all things.

12 Let the deacons be the husbands of one wife, ruling their children and their own houses well.

13 For they that have used the office of a deacon well purchase to themselves a good degree, and great boldness in the faith which is in Christ Je′sus.

14 These things write I unto thee, hoping to come unto thee shortly:

15 But if I tarry long, that thou mayest know how thou oughtest to behave thyself in the house of God, which is the church of the living God, the pillar and ground of the truth.

16 And without controversy great is the mystery of godliness: God was manifest in the flesh, justified in the Spirit, seen of angels, preached unto the Gen′tiles, believed on in the world, received up into glory.

4 NOW the Spirit speaketh expressly, that in the latter times some shall depart from the faith, giving heed to seducing spirits, and doctrines of devils;

2 Speaking lies in hypocrisy; having their conscience seared with a hot iron;

3 Forbidding to marry, *and commanding* to abstain from meats, which God hath created to be received with thanksgiving of them which believe and know the truth.

4 For every creature of God *is* good, and nothing to be refused, if it be received with thanksgiving:

5 For it is sanctified by the word of God and prayer.

6 If thou put the brethren in remembrance of these things, thou shalt be a good minister of Je′sus Christ, nourished up in the words of faith and of good doctrine, whereunto thou hast attained.

7 But refuse profane and old wives' fables, and exercise thyself *rather* unto godliness.

8 For bodily exercise profiteth little: but godliness is profitable unto all things, having promise of the life that now is, and of that which is to come.

9 This *is* a faithful saying and worthy of all acceptation.

10 For therefore we both labour and suffer reproach, because we trust in the living God, who is the Saviour of all men, specially of those that believe.

11 These things command and teach.

12 Let no man despise thy youth; but be thou an example of the believers, in word, in conversation, in charity, in spirit, in faith, in purity.

13 Till I come, give attendance to reading, to exhortation, to doctrine.

14 Neglect not the gift that is in thee, which was given thee by prophecy, with the laying on of the hands of the presbytery.

15 Meditate upon these things; give thyself wholly to them; that thy profiting may appear to all.

16 Take heed unto thyself, and unto the doctrine; continue in them: for in doing this thou shalt both save thyself, and them that hear thee.

5 REBUKE not an elder, but intreat *him* as a father; *and* the younger men as brethren;

2 The elder women as mothers; the younger as sisters, with all purity.

3 Honour widows that are widows indeed.

4 But if any widow have children or nephews, let them learn first to shew piety at home, and to requite their parents: for that is good and acceptable before God.

5 Now she that is a widow indeed, and desolate, trusteth in God, and continueth in supplications and prayers night and day.

6 But she that liveth in pleasure is dead while she liveth.

7 And these things give in charge, that they may be blameless.

8 But if any provide not for his own, and specially for those of his own house, he hath denied the faith, and is worse than an infidel.

9 Let not a widow be taken into the number under threescore years old, having been the wife of one man,

10 Well reported of for good works; if she have brought up children, if she have lodged strangers, if she have washed the saints' feet, if she have relieved the afflicted, if she have diligently followed every good work.

11 But the younger widows refuse: for when they have begun to wax wanton against Christ, they will marry;

12 Having damnation, because they have cast off their first faith.

13 And withal they learn *to be* idle, wandering about from house to house; and not only idle, but tattlers also and busybodies, speaking things which they ought not.

14 I will therefore that the younger women marry, bear children, guide the house, give none occasion to the adversary to speak reproachfully.

15 For some are already turned aside after Sa′tan.

16 If any man or woman that believeth have widows, let them relieve them, and let not the church be charged; that it may relieve them that are widows indeed.

17 Let the elders that rule well be counted worthy of double honour, especially they who labour in the word and doctrine.

18 For the scripture saith, Thou shalt not muzzle the ox that treadeth out the corn. And, The labourer *is* worthy of his reward.

19 Against an elder receive not an accusation, but before two or three witnesses.

20 Them that sin rebuke before all, that others also may fear.

21 I charge *thee* before God, and the Lord Je′sus Christ, and the elect angels, that thou observe these things without preferring one before another, doing nothing by partiality.

22 Lay hands suddenly on no man, neither be partaker of other men's sins: keep thyself pure.

23 Drink no longer water, but use a little wine for thy stomach's sake and thine often infirmities.

24 Some men's sins are open beforehand, going before to judgment; and some *men* they follow after.

25 Likewise also the good works *of some* are manifest beforehand; and they that are otherwise cannot be hid.

6 LET as many servants as are under the yoke count their own masters worthy of all honour, that the name of God and *his* doctrine be not blasphemed.

2 And they that have believing masters, let them not despise *them*, because they are brethren; but rather do *them* service, because they

are faithful and beloved, partakers of the benefit. These things teach and exhort.

3 If any man teach otherwise, and consent not to wholesome words, *even* the words of our Lord Je'sus Christ, and to the doctrine which is according to godliness;

4 He is proud, knowing nothing, but doting about questions and strifes of words, whereof cometh envy, strife, railings, evil surmisings,

5 Perverse disputings of men of corrupt minds, and destitute of the truth, supposing that gain is godliness: from such withdraw thyself.

6 But godliness with contentment is great gain.

7 For we brought nothing into *this* world, *and it is* certain we can carry nothing out.

8 And having food and raiment let us be therewith content.

9 But they that will be rich fall into temptation and a snare, and *into* many foolish and hurtful lusts, which drown men in destruction and perdition.

10 For the love of money is the root of all evil: which while some coveted after, they have erred from the faith, and pierced themselves through with many sorrows.

11 But thou, O man of God, flee these things; and follow after righteousness, godliness, faith, love, patience, meekness.

12 Fight the good fight of faith, lay hold on eternal life, whereunto thou art also called, and hast professed a good profession before many witnesses.

13 I give thee charge in the sight of God, who quickeneth all things, and *before* Christ Je'sus, who before Pon'ti-us Pi'late witnessed a good confession;

14 That thou keep *this* commandment without spot, unrebukeable, until the appearing of our Lord Je'sus Christ:

15 Which in his times he shall shew, *who is* the blessed and only Potentate, the King of kings, and Lord of lords;

16 Who only hath immortality, dwelling in the light which no man can approach unto; whom no man hath seen, nor can see: to whom *be* honour and power everlasting. Amen.

17 Charge them that are rich in this world, that they be not highminded, nor trust in uncertain riches, but in the living God, who giveth us richly all things to enjoy;

18 That they do good, that they be rich in good works, ready to distribute, willing to communicate;

19 Laying up in store for themselves a good foundation against the time to come, that they may lay hold on eternal life.

20 O Tim'o-thy, keep that which is committed to thy trust, avoiding profane *and* vain babblings, and oppositions of science falsely so called:

21 Which some professing have erred concerning the faith. Grace *be* with thee. Amen.

The first to Tim'o-thy was written from La-od-i-ce'a, which is the chiefest city of Phryg'i-a Pa-ca-ti-a'na.

THE SECOND LETTER OF PAUL TO

TIMOTHY

1 PAUL, an apostle of Je'sus Christ by the will of God, according to the promise of life which is in Christ Je'sus,

2 To Tim'o-thy, *my* dearly beloved son: Grace, mercy, *and* peace, from God the Father and Christ Je'sus our Lord.

3 I thank God, whom I serve from *my* forefathers with pure conscience, that without ceasing I have remembrance of thee in my prayers night and day;

4 Greatly desiring to see thee, being mindful of thy tears, that I may be filled with joy;

5 When I call to remembrance the unfeigned faith that is in thee, which dwelt first in thy grandmother Lo'is, and thy mother Eu'nice; and I am persuaded that in thee also.

6 Wherefore I put thee in remembrance that thou stir up the gift of God, which is in thee by the putting on of my hands.

7 For God hath not given us the spirit of fear; but of power, and of love, and of a sound mind.

8 Be not thou therefore ashamed of the testimony of our Lord, nor of me his prisoner: but be thou partaker of the afflictions of the gospel according to the power of God;

9 Who hath saved us, and called *us* with an holy calling, not according to our works, but according to his own purpose and grace, which was given us in Christ Je'sus before the world began,

10 But is now made manifest by the appearing of our Saviour Je'sus Christ, who hath abolished death, and hath brought life and immortality to light through the gospel:

11 Whereunto I am appointed a preacher, and an apostle, and a teacher of the Gen'tiles.

12 For the which cause I also suffer these things: nevertheless I am not ashamed: for I know whom I have believed, and am persuaded that he is able to keep that which I have committed unto him against that day.

13 Hold fast the form of sound words, which thou hast heard of me, in faith and love which is in Christ Je'sus.

14 That good thing which was committed unto thee keep by the Ho'ly Ghost which dwelleth in us.

15 This thou knowest, that all they which are in A'sia be turned away from me; of whom are Phy-gel'lus and Her-mog'e-nes.

16 The Lord give mercy unto the house of On-e-siph'o-rus; for he oft refreshed me, and was not ashamed of my chain:

17 But, when he was in Rome, he sought me out very diligently, and found *me*.

18 The Lord grant unto him that he may find mercy of the Lord in that day: and in how many things he ministered unto me at Eph'e-sus, thou knowest very well.

2 THOU therefore, my son, be strong in the grace that is in Christ Je'sus.

2 And the things that thou hast heard of me among many witnesses, the same commit thou to faithful men, who shall be able to teach others also.

3 Thou therefore endure hardness, as a good soldier of Je'sus Christ.

4 No man that warreth entangleth himself

with the affairs of *this* life; that he may please
him who hath chosen him to be a soldier.
5 And if a man also strive for masteries, *yet*
is he not crowned, except he strive lawfully.
6 The husbandman that laboureth must be
first partaker of the fruits.
7 Consider what I say; and the Lord give thee
understanding in all things.
8 Remember that Je'sus Christ of the seed of
Da'vid was raised from the dead according to
my gospel:
9 Wherein I suffer trouble, as an evil doer,
even unto bonds; but the word of God is not
bound.
10 Therefore I endure all things for the
elect's sakes, that they may also obtain the salvation which is in Christ Je'sus with eternal glory.
11 *It is* a faithful saying: For if we be dead
with *him,* we shall also live with *him:*
12 If we suffer, we shall also reign with *him:*
if we deny *him,* he also will deny us:
13 If we believe not, *yet* he abideth faithful:
he cannot deny himself.
14 Of these things put *them* in remembrance,
charging *them* before the Lord that they strive
not about words to no profit, *but* to the subverting of the hearers.
15 Study to shew thyself approved unto God,
a workman that needeth not to be ashamed,
rightly dividing the word of truth.
16 But shun profane *and* vain babblings: for
they will increase unto more ungodliness.
17 And their word will eat as doth a canker:
of whom is Hy-me-næ'us and Phi-le'tus;
18 Who concerning the truth have erred, saying that the resurrection is past already; and
overthrow the faith of some.
19 Nevertheless the foundation of God
standeth sure, having this seal, The Lord knoweth them that are his. And, Let every one that
nameth the name of Christ depart from iniquity.
20 But in a great house there are not only
vessels of gold and of silver, but also of wood
and of earth; and some to honour, and some to
dishonour.
21 If a man therefore purge himself from
these, he shall be a vessel unto honour, sanctified, and meet for the master's use, *and* prepared unto every good work.
22 Flee also youthful lusts: but follow righteousness, faith, charity, peace, with them that
call on the Lord out of a pure heart.
23 But foolish and unlearned questions
avoid, knowing that they do gender strifes.
24 And the servant of the Lord must not
strive; but be gentle unto all *men,* apt to teach,
patient,
25 In meekness instructing those that oppose
themselves; if God peradventure will give them
repentance to the acknowledging of the truth;
26 And *that* they may recover themselves
out of the snare of the devil, who are taken captive by him at his will.

3 THIS know also, that in the last days peril-
ous times shall come.
2 For men shall be lovers of their own selves,
covetous, boasters, proud, blasphemers, disobedient to parents, unthankful, unholy,
3 Without natural affection, trucebreakers,
false accusers, incontinent, fierce, despisers of
those that are good,
4 Traitors, heady, highminded, lovers of
pleasures more than lovers of God;
5 Having a form of godliness, but denying
the power thereof: from such turn away.
6 For of this sort are they which creep into
houses, and lead captive silly women laden
with sins, led away with divers lusts,
7 Ever learning, and never able to come to
the knowledge of the truth.
8 Now as Jan'nes and Jam'bres withstood
Mo'ses, so do these also resist the truth: men of
corrupt minds, reprobate concerning the faith.
9 But they shall proceed no further: for their
folly shall be manifest unto all *men,* as theirs
also was.
10 But thou hast fully known my doctrine,
manner of life, purpose, faith, longsuffering,
charity, patience,
11 Persecutions, afflictions, which came unto
me at An'ti-och, at I-co'ni-um, at Lys'tra; what
persecutions I endured: but out of *them* all the
Lord delivered me.
12 Yea, and all that will live godly in Christ
Je'sus shall suffer persecution.
13 But evil men and seducers shall wax
worse and worse, deceiving, and being deceived.
14 But continue thou in the things which
thou hast learned and hast been assured of,
knowing of whom thou hast learned *them;*
15 And that from a child thou hast known
the holy scriptures, which are able to make thee
wise unto salvation through faith which is in
Christ Je'sus.
16 All scripture *is* given by inspiration of
God, and *is* profitable for doctrine, for reproof,
for correction, for instruction in righteousness:
17 That the man of God may be perfect,
throughly furnished unto all good works.

4 I CHARGE *thee* therefore before God, and
the Lord Je'sus Christ, who shall judge the
quick and the dead at his appearing and his
kingdom;
2 Preach the word; be instant in season, out
of season; reprove, rebuke, exhort with all longsuffering and doctrine.
3 For the time will come when they will not
endure sound doctrine; but after their own lusts
shall they heap to themselves teachers, having
itching ears;
4 And they shall turn away *their* ears from
the truth, and shall be turned unto fables.
5 But watch thou in all things, endure afflictions, do the work of an evangelist, make full
proof of thy ministry.
6 For I am now ready to be offered, and the
time of my departure is at hand.
7 I have fought a good fight, I have finished
my course, I have kept the faith:
8 Henceforth there is laid up for me a crown
of righteousness, which the Lord, the righteous
judge, shall give me at that day: and not to me
only, but unto all them also that love his appearing.
9 Do thy diligence to come shortly unto me:
10 For De'mas hath forsaken me, having
loved this present world, and is departed unto
Thes-sa-lo-ni'ca; Cres'cens to Ga-la'tia, Ti'tus
unto Dal-ma'ti-a.
11 Only Luke is with me. Take Mark, and
bring him with thee: for he is profitable to me
for the ministry.
12 And Tych'i-cus have I sent to Eph'e-sus.
13 The cloke that I left at Tro'as with Car'-
pus, when thou comest, bring *with thee,* and the
books, *but* especially the parchments.

14 Al-ex-an'der the coppersmith did me much evil: the Lord reward him according to his works:

15 Of whom be thou ware also; for he hath greatly withstood our words.

16 At my first answer no man stood with me, but all *men* forsook me: *I pray God* that it may not be laid to their charge.

17 Notwithstanding the Lord stood with me, and strengthened me; that by me the preaching might be fully known, and *that* all the Gen'tiles might hear: and I was delivered out of the mouth of the lion.

18 And the Lord shall deliver me from every evil work, and will preserve *me* unto his heavenly kingdom: to whom *be* glory for ever and ever. Amen.

19 Salute Pris'ca and A'qui-la, and the household of On-e-siph'o-rus.

20 E-ras'tus abode at Cor'inth: but Troph'i-mus have I left at Mi-le'tum sick.

21 Do thy diligence to come before winter. Eu-bu'lus greeteth thee, and Pu'dens, and Li'-nus, and Clau'di-a, and all the brethren.

22 The Lord Je'sus Christ *be* with thy spirit. Grace *be* with you. Amen.

The second *epistle* unto Ti-mo'the-us, ordained the first bishop of the church of the E-phe'sians, was written from Rome, when Paul was brought before Ne'ro the second time.

THE LETTER OF PAUL TO

TITUS

1 PAUL, a servant of God, and an apostle of Je'sus Christ, according to the faith of God's elect, and the acknowledging of the truth which is after godliness;

2 In hope of eternal life, which God, that cannot lie, promised before the world began;

3 But hath in due times manifested his word through preaching, which is committed unto me according to the commandment of God our Saviour;

4 To Ti'tus, *mine* own son after the common faith: Grace, mercy, *and* peace, from God the Father and the Lord Je'sus Christ our Saviour.

5 For this cause left I thee in Crete, that thou shouldest set in order the things that are wanting, and ordain elders in every city, as I had appointed thee:

6 If any be blameless, the husband of one wife, having faithful children not accused of riot or unruly.

7 For a bishop must be blameless, as the steward of God; not selfwilled, not soon angry, not given to wine, no striker, not given to filthy lucre;

8 But a lover of hospitality, a lover of good men, sober, just, holy, temperate;

9 Holding fast the faithful word as he hath been taught, that he may be able by sound doctrine both to exhort and to convince the gainsayers.

10 For there are many unruly and vain talkers and deceivers, specially they of the circumcision:

11 Whose mouths must be stopped, who subvert whole houses, teaching things which they ought not, for filthy lucre's sake.

12 One of themselves, *even* a prophet of their own, said, The Cre'ti-ans *are* alway liars, evil beasts, slow bellies.

13 This witness is true. Wherefore rebuke them sharply, that they may be sound in the faith;

14 Not giving heed to Jew'ish fables, and commandments of men, that turn from the truth.

15 Unto the pure all things *are* pure: but unto them that are defiled and unbelieving *is* nothing pure; but even their mind and conscience is defiled.

16 They profess that they know God; but in works they deny *him*, being abominable, and disobedient, and unto every good work reprobate.

2 BUT speak thou the things which become sound doctrine:

2 That the aged men be sober, grave, temperate, sound in faith, in charity, in patience.

3 The aged women likewise, that *they be* in behaviour as becometh holiness, not false accusers, not given to much wine, teachers of good things;

4 That they may teach the young women to be sober, to love their husbands, to love their children,

5 *To be* discreet, chaste, keepers at home, good, obedient to their own husbands, that the word of God be not blasphemed.

6 Young men likewise exhort to be sober minded.

7 In all things shewing thyself a pattern of good works: in doctrine *shewing* uncorruptness, gravity, sincerity,

8 Sound speech, that cannot be condemned; that he that is of the contrary part may be ashamed, having no evil thing to say of you.

9 *Exhort* servants to be obedient unto their own masters, *and* to please *them* well in all things; not answering again;

10 Not purloining, but shewing all good fidelity; that they may adorn the doctrine of God our Saviour in all things.

11 For the grace of God that bringeth salvation hath appeared to all men,

12 Teaching us that, denying ungodliness and worldly lusts, we should live soberly, righteously, and godly, in this present world;

13 Looking for that blessed hope, and the glorious appearing of the great God and our Saviour Jesus Christ;

14 Who gave himself for us, that he might redeem us from all iniquity, and purify unto himself a peculiar people, zealous of good works.

15 These things speak, and exhort, and rebuke with all authority. Let no man despise thee.

3 PUT them in mind to be subject to principalities and powers, to obey magistrates, to be ready to every good work,

2 To speak evil of no man, to be no brawlers, *but* gentle, shewing all meekness unto all men.

3 For we ourselves also were sometimes foolish, disobedient, deceived, serving divers lusts and pleasures, living in malice and envy, hateful, *and* hating one another.

4 But after that the kindness and love of God our Saviour toward man appeared,

5 Not by works of righteousness which we have done, but according to his mercy he saved us, by the washing of regeneration, and renewing of the Ho'ly Ghost;

6 Which he shed on us abundantly through Je'sus Christ our Saviour;

7 That being justified by his grace, we should be made heirs according to the hope of eternal life.

8 *This is* a faithful saying, and these things I will that thou affirm constantly, that they which have believed in God might be careful to maintain good works. These things are good and profitable unto men.

9 But avoid foolish questions, and genealogies, and contentions, and strivings about the law; for they are unprofitable and vain.

10 A man that is an heretick after the first and second admonition reject;

11 Knowing that he that is such is subverted, and sinneth, being condemned of himself.

12 When I shall send Ar'te-mas unto thee, or Tych'i-cus, be diligent to come unto me to Ni-cop'o-lis: for I have determined there to winter.

13 Bring Ze'nas the lawyer and A-pol'los on their journey diligently, that nothing be wanting unto them.

14 And let ours also learn to maintain good works for necessary uses, that they be not unfruitful.

15 All that are with me salute thee. Greet them that love us in the faith. Grace *be* with you all. Amen.

It was written to Ti'tus, ordained the first bishop of the church of the Cre'ti-ans, from Ni-cop'o-lis of Mac-e-do'ni-a.

THE LETTER OF PAUL TO

PHILEMON

PAUL, a prisoner of Je'sus Christ, and Tim'o-thy *our* brother, unto Phi-le'mon our dearly beloved, and fellowlabourer,

2 And to *our* beloved Apph'i-a, and Ar-chip'-pus our fellowsoldier, and to the church in thy house:

3 Grace to you, and peace, from God our Father and the Lord Je'sus Christ.

4 I thank my God, making mention of thee always in my prayers,

5 Hearing of thy love and faith, which thou hast toward the Lord Je'sus, and toward all saints;

6 That the communication of thy faith may become effectual by the acknowledging of every good thing which is in you in Christ Je'sus.

7 For we have great joy and consolation in thy love, because the bowels of the saints are refreshed by thee, brother.

8 Wherefore, though I might be much bold in Christ to enjoin thee that which is convenient,

9 Yet for love's sake I rather beseech *thee*, being such an one as Paul the aged, and now also a prisoner of Je'sus Christ.

10 I beseech thee for my son O'nes'i-mus, whom I have begotten in my bonds:

11 Which in time past was to thee unprofitable, but now profitable to thee and to me:

12 Whom I have sent again: thou therefore receive him, that is, mine own bowels:

13 Whom I would have retained with me, that in thy stead he might have ministered unto me in the bonds of the gospel:

14 But without thy mind would I do nothing; that thy benefit should not be as it were of necessity, but willingly.

15 For perhaps he therefore departed for a season, that thou shouldest receive him for ever;

16 Not now as a servant, but above a servant, a brother beloved, specially to me, but how much more unto thee, both in the flesh, and in the Lord?

17 If thou count me therefore a partner, receive him as myself.

18 If he hath wronged thee, or oweth *thee* ought, put that on mine account;

19 I Paul have written *it* with mine own hand, I will repay *it*: albeit I do not say to thee how thou owest unto me even thine own self besides.

20 Yea, brother, let me have joy of thee in the Lord: refresh my bowels in the Lord.

21 Having confidence in thy obedience I wrote unto thee, knowing that thou wilt also do more than I say.

22 But withal prepare me also a lodging: for I trust that through your prayers I shall be given unto you.

23 There salute thee Ep'a-phras, my fellowprisoner in Christ Je'sus;

24 Mar'cus, Ar-is-tar'chus, De'mas, Lu'cas, my fellowlabourers.

25 The grace of our Lord Je'sus Christ *be* with your spirit. Amen.

Written from Rome to Phi-le'mon, by O'nes'i-mus, a servant.

THE LETTER TO THE

HEBREWS

1 GOD, who at sundry times and in divers manners spake in time past unto the fathers by the prophets,

2 Hath in these last days spoken unto us by *his* Son, whom he hath appointed heir of all things, by whom also he made the worlds;

3 Who being the brightness of *his* glory, and the express image of his person, and upholding all things by the word of his power, when he had by himself purged our sins, sat down on the right hand of the Majesty on high;

4 Being made so much better than the an-

gels, as he hath by inheritance obtained a more
excellent name than they.
5 For unto which of the angels said he at any
time, Thou art my son, this day have I begotten
thee? And again, I will be to him a Father, and
he shall be to me a Son?
6 And again, when he bringeth in the firstbe-
gotten into the world, he saith, And let all the
angels of God worship him.
7 And of the angels he saith, Who maketh his
angels spirits, and his ministers a flame of fire.
8 But unto the Son *he saith,* Thy throne, O
God, *is* for ever and ever: a sceptre of righteousness *is* the sceptre of thy kingdom.
9 Thou hast loved righteousness, and hated
iniquity; therefore God, *even* thy God, hath
anointed thee with the oil of gladness above thy
fellows.
10 And, Thou, Lord, in the beginning hast
laid the foundation of the earth; and the heavens are the works of thine hands:
11 They shall perish; but thou remainest; and
they all shall wax old as doth a garment;
12 And as a vesture shalt thou fold them up,
and they shall be changed: but thou art the
same, and thy years shall not fail.
13 But to which of the angels said he at any
time, Sit on my right hand, until I make thine
enemies thy footstool?
14 Are they not all ministering spirits, sent
forth to minister for them who shall be heirs of
salvation?

2 THEREFORE we ought to give the more
earnest heed to the things which we have
heard, lest at any time we should let *them* slip.
2 For if the word spoken by angels was stedfast, and every transgression and disobedience
received a just recompence of reward;
3 How shall we escape, if we neglect so great
salvation; which at the first began to be spoken
by the Lord, and was confirmed unto us by
them that heard *him;*
4 God also bearing *them* witness, both with
signs and wonders, and with divers miracles,
and gifts of the Ho'ly Ghost, according to his
own will?
5 For unto the angels hath he not put in subjection the world to come, whereof we speak.
6 But one in a certain place testified, saying,
What is man, that thou art mindful of him? or
the son of man, that thou visitest him?
7 Thou madest him a little lower than the angels; thou crownedst him with glory and honour, and didst set him over the works of thy
hands:
8 Thou hast put all things in subjection under
his feet. For in that he put all in subjection under him, he left nothing *that is* not put under
him. But now we see not yet all things put under him.
9 But we see Je'sus, who was made a little
lower than the angels for the suffering of death,
crowned with glory and honour; that he by the
grace of God should taste death for every man.
10 For it became him, for whom *are* all
things, and by whom *are* all things, in bringing
many sons unto glory, to make the captain of
their salvation perfect through sufferings.
11 For both he that sanctifieth and they who
are sanctified *are* all of one: for which cause he
is not ashamed to call them brethren,
12 Saying, I will declare thy name unto my
brethren, in the midst of the church will I sing
praise unto thee.
13 And again, I will put my trust in him. And
again, Behold I and the children which God
hath given me.
14 Forasmuch then as the children are partakers of flesh and blood, he also himself likewise took part of the same; that through death
he might destroy him that had the power of
death, that is, the devil;
15 And deliver them who through fear of
death were all their lifetime subject to bondage.
16 For verily he took not on *him the nature*
of angels; but he took on *him* the seed of A'bra-
ham.
17 Wherefore in all things it behoved him to
be made like unto *his* brethren, that he might be
a merciful and faithful high priest in things *per-*
taining to God, to make reconciliation for the
sins of the people.
18 For in that he himself hath suffered being
tempted, he is able to succour them that are
tempted.

3 WHEREFORE, holy brethren, partakers of
the heavenly calling, consider the Apostle
and High Priest of our profession, Christ Je'sus;
2 Who was faithful to him that appointed
him, as also Mo'ses *was faithful* in all his house.
3 For this *man* was counted worthy of more
glory than Mo'ses, inasmuch as he who hath
builded the house hath more honour than the
house.
4 For every house is builded by some *man;*
but he that built all things *is* God.
5 And Mo'ses verily *was* faithful in all his
house, as a servant, for a testimony of those
things which were to be spoken after;
6 But Christ as a son over his own house;
whose house are we, if we hold fast the confidence and the rejoicing of the hope firm unto
the end.
7 Wherefore (as the Ho'ly Ghost saith, To
day if ye will hear his voice,
8 Harden not your hearts, as in the provocation, in the day of temptation in the wilderness:
9 When your fathers tempted me, proved
me, and saw my works forty years.
10 Wherefore I was grieved with that generation, and said, They do alway err in *their*
heart; and they have not known my ways.
11 So I sware in my wrath, They shall not
enter into my rest.)
12 Take heed, brethren, lest there be in any
of you an evil heart of unbelief, in departing
from the living God.
13 But exhort one another daily, while it is
called To day; lest any of you be hardened
through the deceitfulness of sin.
14 For we are made partakers of Christ, if we
hold the beginning of our confidence stedfast
unto the end;
15 While it is said, To day if ye will hear his
voice, harden not your hearts, as in the provocation.
16 For some, when they had heard, did provoke: howbeit not all that came out of E'gypt by
Mo'ses.
17 But with whom was he grieved forty
years? *was it* not with them that had sinned,
whose carcases fell in the wilderness?
18 And to whom sware he that they should
not enter into his rest, but to them that believed
not?
19 So we see that they could not enter in because of unbelief.

4 LET us therefore fear, lest, a promise being
left *us* of entering into his rest, any of you
should seem to come short of it.

2 For unto us was the gospel preached, as well as unto them: but the word preached did not profit them, not being mixed with faith in them that heard *it*.

3 For we which have believed do enter into rest, as he said, As I have sworn in my wrath, if they shall enter into my rest: although the works were finished from the foundation of the world.

4 For he spake in a certain place of the seventh *day* on this wise, And God did rest the seventh day from all his works.

5 And in this *place* again, If they shall enter into my rest.

6 Seeing therefore it remaineth that some must enter therein, and they to whom it was first preached entered not in because of unbelief:

7 Again, he limiteth a certain day, saying in Da'vid, To day, after so long a time; as it is said, To day if ye will hear his voice, harden not your hearts.

8 For if Je'sus had given them rest, then would he not afterward have spoken of another day.

9 There remaineth therefore a rest to the people of God.

10 For he that is entered into his rest, he also hath ceased from his own works, as God *did* from his.

11 Let us labour therefore to enter into that rest, lest any man fall after the same example of unbelief.

12 For the word of God *is* quick, and powerful, and sharper than any twoedged sword, piercing even to the dividing asunder of soul and spirit, and of the joints and marrow, and *is* a discerner of the thoughts and intents of the heart.

13 Neither is there any creature that is not manifest in his sight: but all things *are* naked and opened unto the eyes of him with whom we have to do.

14 Seeing then that we have a great high priest, that is passed into the heavens, Je'sus the Son of God, let us hold fast *our* profession.

15 For we have not an high priest which cannot be touched with the feeling of our infirmities; but was in all points tempted like as *we are, yet* without sin.

16 Let us therefore come boldly unto the throne of grace, that we may obtain mercy, and find grace to help in time of need.

5 FOR every high priest taken from among men is ordained for men in things *pertaining* to God, that he may offer both gifts and sacrifices for sins:

2 Who can have compassion on the ignorant, and on them that are out of the way; for that he himself also is compassed with infirmity.

3 And by reason hereof he ought, as for the people, so also for himself, to offer for sins.

4 And no man taketh this honour unto himself, but he that is called of God, as *was* Aar'on.

5 So also Christ glorified not himself to be made an high priest; but he that said unto him, Thou art my Son, to day have I begotten thee.

6 As he saith also in another *place*, Thou *art* a priest for ever after the order of Mel-chis'e-dec.

7 Who in the days of his flesh, when he had offered up prayers and supplications with strong crying and tears unto him that was able to save him from death, and was heard in that he feared;

8 Though he were a Son, yet learned he obedience by the things which he suffered;

9 And being made perfect, he became the author of eternal salvation unto all them that obey him;

10 Called of God an high priest after the order of Mel-chis'e-dec.

11 Of whom we have many things to say, and hard to be uttered, seeing ye are dull of hearing.

12 For when for the time ye ought to be teachers, ye have need that one teach you again which *be* the first principles of the oracles of God; and are become such as have need of milk, and not of strong meat.

13 For every one that useth milk *is* unskilful in the word of righteousness: for he is a babe.

14 But strong meat belongeth to them that are of full age, *even* those who by reason of use have their senses exercised to discern both good and evil.

6 THEREFORE leaving the principles of the doctrine of Christ, let us go on unto perfection; not laying again the foundation of repentance from dead works, and of faith toward God,

2 Of the doctrine of baptisms, and of laying on of hands, and of resurrection of the dead, and of eternal judgment.

3 And this will we do, if God permit.

4 For *it is* impossible for those who were once enlightened, and have tasted of the heavenly gift, and were made partakers of the Ho'ly Ghost,

5 And have tasted the good word of God, and the powers of the world to come,

6 If they shall fall away, to renew them again unto repentance; seeing they crucify to themselves the Son of God afresh, and put *him* to an open shame.

7 For the earth which drinketh in the rain that cometh oft upon it, and bringeth forth herbs meet for them by whom it is dressed, receiveth blessing from God:

8 But that which beareth thorns and briers *is* rejected, and *is* nigh unto cursing; whose end *is* to be burned.

9 But, beloved, we are persuaded better things of you, and things that accompany salvation, though we thus speak.

10 For God *is* not unrighteous to forget your work and labour of love, which ye have shewed toward his name, in that ye have ministered to the saints, and do minister.

11 And we desire that every one of you do shew the same diligence to the full assurance of hope unto the end:

12 That ye be not slothful, but followers of them who through faith and patience inherit the promises.

13 For when God made promise to A'braham, because he could swear by no greater, he sware by himself,

14 Saying, Surely blessing I will bless thee, and multiplying I will multiply thee.

15 And so, after he had patiently endured, he obtained the promise.

16 For men verily swear by the greater: and an oath for confirmation *is* to them an end of all strife.

17 Wherein God, willing more abundantly to shew unto the heirs of promise the immutability of his counsel, confirmed *it* by an oath:

18 That by two immutable things, in which *it was* impossible for God to lie, we might have a strong consolation, who have fled for refuge to lay hold upon the hope set before us:

19 Which *hope* we have as an anchor of the soul, both sure and stedfast, and which entereth into that within the veil;

20 Whither the forerunner is for us entered, *even* Je'sus, made an high priest for ever after the order of Mel-chis'e-dec.

7 FOR this Mel-chis'e-dec, king of Sa'lem, priest of the most high God, who met A'bra-ham returning from the slaughter of the kings, and blessed him;

2 To whom also A'bra-ham gave a tenth part of all; first being by interpretation King of righteousness, and after that also King of Sa'lem, which is, King of peace;

3 Without father, without mother, without descent, having neither beginning of days, nor end of life; but made like unto the Son of God; abideth a priest continually.

4 Now consider how great this man *was,* unto whom even the patriarch A'bra-ham gave the tenth of the spoils.

5 And verily they that are of the sons of Le'vi, who receive the office of the priesthood, have a commandment to take tithes of the people according to the law, that is, of their brethren, though they come out of the loins of A'bra-ham:

6 But he whose descent is not counted from them received tithes of A'bra-ham, and blessed him that had the promises.

7 And without all contradiction the less is blessed of the better.

8 And here men that die receive tithes; but there he *receiveth them,* of whom it is witnessed that he liveth.

9 And as I may so say, Le'vi also, who receiveth tithes, payed tithes in A'bra-ham.

10 For he was yet in the loins of his father, when Mel-chis'e-dec met him.

11 If therefore perfection were by the Le-vit'i-cal priesthood, (for under it the people received the law,) what further need *was there* that another priest should rise after the order of Mel-chis'e-dec, and not be called after the order of Aar'on?

12 For the priesthood being changed, there is made of necessity a change also of the law.

13 For he of whom these things are spoken pertaineth to another tribe, of which no man gave attendance at the altar.

14 For *it is* evident that our Lord sprang out of Ju'da; of which tribe Mo'ses spake nothing concerning priesthood.

15 And it is yet far more evident: for that after the similitude of Mel-chis'e-dec there ariseth another priest,

16 Who is made, not after the law of a carnal commandment, but after the power of an endless life.

17 For he testifieth, Thou *art* a priest for ever after the order of Mel-chis'e-dec.

18 For there is verily a disannulling of the commandment going before for the weakness and unprofitableness thereof.

19 For the law made nothing perfect, but the bringing in of a better hope *did;* by the which we draw nigh unto God.

20 And inasmuch as not without an oath *he was made priest:*

21 (For those priests were made without an oath; but this with an oath by him that said unto him, The Lord sware and will not repent, Thou *art* a priest for ever after the order of Mel-chis'e-dec:)

22 By so much was Je'sus made a surety of a better testament.

23 And they truly were many priests, because they were not suffered to continue by reason of death:

24 But this *man,* because he continueth ever, hath an unchangeable priesthood.

25 Wherefore he is able also to save them to the uttermost that come unto God by him, seeing he ever liveth to make intercession for them.

26 For such an high priest became us, *who is* holy, harmless, undefiled, separate from sinners, and made higher than the heavens;

27 Who needeth not daily, as those high priests, to offer up sacrifice, first for his own sins, and then for the people's: for this he did once, when he offered up himself.

28 For the law maketh men high priests which have infirmity; but the word of the oath, which was since the law, *maketh* the Son, who is consecrated for evermore.

8 NOW of the things which we have spoken *this is* the sum: We have such an high priest, who is set on the right hand of the throne of the Majesty in the heavens;

2 A minister of the sanctuary, and of the true tabernacle, which the Lord pitched, and not man.

3 For every high priest is ordained to offer gifts and sacrifices: wherefore *it is* of necessity that this man have somewhat also to offer.

4 For if he were on earth, he should not be a priest, seeing that there are priests that offer gifts according to the law:

5 Who serve unto the example and shadow of heavenly things, as Mo'ses was admonished of God when he was about to make the tabernacle: for, See, saith he, *that* thou make all things according to the pattern shewed to thee in the mount.

6 But now hath he obtained a more excellent ministry, by how much also he is the mediator of a better covenant, which was established upon better promises.

7 For if that first *covenant* had been faultless, then should no place have been sought for the second.

8 For finding fault with them, he saith, Behold, the days come, saith the Lord, when I will make a new covenant with the house of Is'ra-el and with the house of Ju'dah:

9 Not according to the covenant that I made with their fathers in the day when I took them by the hand to lead them out of the land of E'gypt; because they continued not in my covenant, and I regarded them not, saith the Lord.

10 For this *is* the covenant that I will make with the house of Is'ra-el after those days, saith the Lord; I will put my laws into their mind, and write them in their hearts: and I will be to them a God, and they shall be to me a people:

11 And they shall not teach every man his neighbour, and every man his brother, saying, Know the Lord: for all shall know me, from the least to the greatest.

12 For I will be merciful to their unrighteousness, and their sins and their inquities will I remember no more.

13 In that he saith, A new *covenant,* he hath made the first old. Now that which decayeth and waxeth old *is* ready to vanish away.

9 THEN verily the first *covenant* had also ordinances of divine service, and a worldly sanctuary.

2 For there was a tabernacle made; the first,

wherein *was* the candlestick, and the table, and the shewbread; which is called the sanctuary.

3 And after the second veil, the tabernacle which is called the Holiest of all;

4 Which had the golden censer, and the ark of the covenant overlaid round about with gold, wherein *was* the golden pot that had manna, and Aar′on's rod that budded, and the tables of the covenant;

5 And over it the cherubims of glory shadowing the mercyseat; of which we cannot now speak particularly.

6 Now when these things were thus ordained, the priests went always into the first tabernacle, accomplishing the service *of God.*

7 But into the second *went* the high priest alone once every year, not without blood, which he offered for himself, and *for* the errors of the people:

8 The Ho′ly Ghost this signifying, that the way into the holiest of all was not yet made manifest, while as the first tabernacle was yet standing:

9 Which *was* a figure for the time then present, in which were offered both gifts, and sacrifices, that could not make him that did the service perfect, as pertaining to the conscience;

10 *Which stood* only in meats and drinks, and divers washings, and carnal ordinances, imposed *on them* until the time of reformation.

11 But Christ being come an high priest of good things to come, by a greater and more perfect tabernacle, not made with hands, that is to say, not of this building;

12 Neither by the blood of goats and calves, but by his own blood he entered in once into the holy place, having obtained eternal redemption *for us.*

13 For if the blood of bulls and of goats, and the ashes of an heifer sprinkling the unclean, sanctifieth to the purifying of the flesh:

14 How much more shall the blood of Christ, who through the eternal Spirit offered himself without spot to God, purge your conscience from dead works to serve the living God?

15 And for this cause he is the mediator of the new testament, that by means of death, for the redemption of the transgressions *that were* under the first testament, they which are called might receive the promise of eternal inheritance.

16 For where a testament *is,* there must also of necessity be the death of the testator.

17 For a testament *is* of force after men are dead: otherwise it is of no strength at all while the testator liveth.

18 Whereupon neither the first *testament* was dedicated without blood.

19 For when Mo′ses had spoken every precept to all the people according to the law, he took the blood of calves and of goats, with water, and scarlet wool, and hyssop, and sprinkled both the book, and all the people,

20 Saying, This *is* the blood of the testament which God hath enjoined unto you.

21 Moreover he sprinkled with blood both the tabernacle, and all the vessels of the ministry.

22 And almost all things are by the law purged with blood; and without shedding of blood is no remission.

23 *It was* therefore necessary that the patterns of things in the heavens should be purified with these; but the heavenly things themselves with better sacrifices than these.

24 For Christ is not entered into the holy places made with hands, *which are* the figures of the true; but into heaven itself, now to appear in the presence of God for us:

25 Nor yet that he should offer himself often, as the high priest entereth into the holy place every year with blood of others;

26 For then must he often have suffered since the foundation of the world: but now once in the end of the world hath he appeared to put away sin by the sacrifice of himself.

27 And as it is appointed unto men once to die, but after this the judgment:

28 So Christ was once offered to bear the sins of many; and unto them that look for him shall he appear the second time without sin unto salvation.

10 FOR the law having a shadow of good things to come, *and* not the very image of the things, can never with those sacrifices which they offered year by year continually make the comers thereunto perfect.

2 For then would they not have ceased to be offered? because that the worshippers once purged should have had no more conscience of sins.

3 But in those *sacrifices there is* a remembrance again *made* of sins every year.

4 For *it is* not possible that the blood of bulls and of goats should take away sins.

5 Wherefore when he cometh into the world, he saith, Sacrifice and offering thou wouldest not, but a body hast thou prepared me:

6 In burnt offerings and *sacrifices* for sin thou hast had no pleasure.

7 Then said I, Lo, I come (in the volume of the book it is written of me,) to do thy will, O God.

8 Above when he said, Sacrifice and offering and burnt offerings and *offering* for sin thou wouldest not, neither hadst pleasure *therein;* which are offered by the law;

9 Then said he, Lo, I come to do thy will, O God. He taketh away the first, that he may establish the second.

10 By the which will we are sanctified through the offering of the body of Je′sus Christ once *for all.*

11 And every priest standeth daily ministering and offering oftentimes the same sacrifices, which can never take away sins:

12 But this man, after he had offered one sacrifice for sins for ever, sat down on the right hand of God;

13 From henceforth expecting till his enemies be made his footstool.

14 For by one offering he hath perfected for ever them that are sanctified.

15 *Whereof* the Ho′ly Ghost also is a witness to us: for after that he had said before,

16 This *is* the covenant that I will make with them after those days, saith the Lord, I will put my laws into their hearts, and in their minds will I write them;

17 And their sins and iniquities will I remember no more.

18 Now where remission of these *is, there is* no more offering for sin.

19 Having therefore, brethren, boldness to enter into the holiest by the blood of Je′sus,

20 By a new and living way, which he hath consecrated for us, through the veil, that is to say, his flesh;

21 And *having* an high priest over the house of God;

22 Let us draw near with a true heart in full assurance of faith, having our hearts sprinkled

from an evil conscience, and our bodies washed
with pure water.
23 Let us hold fast the profession of *our* faith
without wavering; (for he *is* faithful that promised;)
24 And let us consider one another to provoke unto love and to good works:
25 Not forsaking the assembling of ourselves
together, as the manner of some *is;* but exhorting *one another:* and so much the more, as ye
see the day approaching.
26 For if we sin wilfully after that we have
received the knowledge of the truth, there remaineth no more sacrifice for sins,
27 But a certain fearful looking for of judgment and fiery indignation, which shall devour
the adversaries.
28 He that despised Mo'ses' law died without
mercy under two or three witnesses:
29 Of how much sorer punishment, suppose
ye, shall he be thought worthy, who hath trodden under foot the Son of God, and hath
counted the blood of the covenant, wherewith
he was sanctified, an unholy thing, and hath
done despite unto the Spirit of grace?
30 For we know him that hath said, Vengeance *belongeth* unto me, I will recompense,
saith the Lord. And again, The Lord shall judge
his people.
31 *It is* a fearful thing to fall into the hands of
the living God.
32 But call to remembrance the former days,
in which, after ye were illuminated, ye endured
a great fight of afflictions;
33 Partly, whilst ye were made a gazingstock
both by reproaches and afflictions; and partly,
whilst ye became companions of them that
were so used.
34 For ye had compassion of me in my
bonds, and took joyfully the spoiling of your
goods, knowing in yourselves that ye have in
heaven a better and an enduring substance.
35 Cast not away therefore your confidence,
which hath great recompence of reward.
36 For ye have need of patience, that, after
ye have done the will of God, ye might receive
the promise.
37 For yet a little while, and he that shall
come will come, and will not tarry.
38 Now the just shall live by faith: but if *any*
man draw back, my soul shall have no pleasure
in him.
39 But we are not of them who draw back
unto perdition; but of them that believe to the
saving of the soul.

11 NOW faith is the substance of things
hoped for, the evidence of things not
seen.
2 For by it the elders obtained a good report.
3 Through faith we understand that the
worlds were framed by the word of God, so that
things which are seen were not made of things
which do appear.
4 By faith A'bel offered unto God a more excellent sacrifice than Cain, by which he obtained witness that he was righteous, God testifying of his gifts: and by it he being dead yet
speaketh.
5 By faith E'noch was translated that he
should not see death; and was not found, because God had translated him: for before his
translation he had this testimony, that he
pleased God.
6 But without faith *it is* impossible to please
him: for he that cometh to God must believe
that he is, and *that* he is a rewarder of them
that diligently seek him.
7 By faith No'ah, being warned of God of
things not seen as yet, moved with fear, prepared an ark to the saving of his house; by the
which he condemned the world, and became
heir of the righteousness which is by faith.
8 By faith A'bra-ham, when he was called to
go out into a place which he should after receive for an inheritance, obeyed; and he went
out, not knowing whither he went.
9 By faith he sojourned in the land of promise, as *in* a strange country, dwelling in tabernacles with I'saac and Ja'cob, the heirs with him
of the same promise:
10 For he looked for a city which hath foundations, whose builder and maker *is* God.
11 Through faith also Sa'ra herself received
strength to conceive seed, and was delivered of
a child when she was past age, because she
judged him faithful who had promised.
12 Therefore sprang there even of one, and
him as good as dead, *so many* as the stars of the
sky in multitude, and as the sand which is by
the sea shore innumerable.
13 These all died in faith, not having received
the promises, but having seen them afar off,
and were persuaded of *them,* and embraced
them, and confessed that they were strangers
and pilgrims on the earth.
14 For they that say such things declare
plainly that they seek a country.
15 And truly, if they had been mindful of that
country from whence they came out, they
might have had opportunity to have returned.
16 But now they desire a better *country,* that
is, an heavenly: wherefore God is not ashamed
to be called their God: for he hath prepared for
them a city.
17 By faith A'bra-ham, when he was tried,
offered up I'saac: and he that had received the
promises offered up his only begotten *son,*
18 Of whom it was said, That in I'saac shall
thy seed be called:
19 Accounting that God *was* able to raise
him up, even from the dead; from whence also
he received him in a figure.
20 By faith I'saac blessed Ja'cob and E'sau
concerning things to come.
21 By faith Ja'cob, when he was a dying,
blessed both the sons of Jo'seph; and worshipped, *leaning* upon the top of his staff.
22 By faith Jo'seph, when he died, made
mention of the departing of the children of Is'-
ra-el; and gave commandment concerning his
bones.
23 By faith Mo'ses, when he was born, was
hid three months of his parents, because they
saw *he was* a proper child; and they were not
afraid of the king's commandment.
24 By faith Mo'ses, when he was come to
years, refused to be called the son of Pha'raoh's
daughter;
25 Choosing rather to suffer affliction with
the people of God, than to enjoy the pleasures
of sin for a season;
26 Esteeming the reproach of Christ greater
riches than the treasures in E'gypt: for he had
respect unto the recompence of the reward.
27 By faith he forsook E'gypt, not fearing the
wrath of the king: for he endured, as seeing him
who is invisible.
28 Through faith he kept the passover, and
the sprinkling of blood, lest he that destroyed
the firstborn should touch them.
29 By faith they passed through the Red sea

as by dry *land:* which the E-gyp'tians assaying to do were drowned.

30 By faith the walls of Jer'i-cho fell down, after they were compassed about seven days.

31 By faith the harlot Ra'hab perished not with them that believed not, when she had received the spies with peace.

32 And what shall I more say? for the time would fail me to tell of Ged'e-on, and *of* Ba'rak, and *of* Sam'son, and *of* Jeph'tha-e; *of* Da'vid also and Sam'u-el, and *of* the prophets:

33 Who through faith subdued kingdoms, wrought righteousness, obtained promises, stopped the mouths of lions,

34 Quenched the violence of fire, escaped the edge of the sword, out of weakness were made strong, waxed valiant in fight, turned to flight the armies of the aliens.

35 Women received their dead raised to life again: and others were tortured, not accepting deliverance; that they might obtain a better resurrection:

36 And others had trial of *cruel* mockings and scourgings, yea, moreover of bonds and imprisonment:

37 They were stoned, they were sawn asunder, were tempted, were slain with the sword: they wandered about in sheepskins and goatskins; being destitute, afflicted, tormented;

38 (Of whom the world was not worthy:) they wandered in deserts, and *in* mountains, and *in* dens and caves of the earth.

39 And these all, having obtained a good report through faith, received not the promise:

40 God having provided some better thing for us, that they without us should not be made perfect.

12 WHEREFORE seeing we also are compassed about with so great a cloud of witnesses, let us lay aside every weight, and the sin which doth so easily beset *us,* and let us run with patience the race that is set before us,

2 Looking unto Je'sus the author and finisher of *our* faith; who for the joy that was set before him endured the cross, despising the shame, and is set down at the right hand of the throne of God.

3 For consider him that endured such contradiction of sinners against himself, lest ye be wearied and faint in your minds.

4 Ye have not yet resisted unto blood, striving against sin.

5 And ye have forgotten the exhortation which speaketh unto you as unto children, My son, despise not thou the chastening of the Lord, nor faint when thou art rebuked of him:

6 For whom the Lord loveth he chasteneth, and scourgeth every son whom he receiveth.

7 If ye endure chastening, God dealeth with you as with sons; for what son is he whom the father chasteneth not?

8 But if ye be without chastisement, whereof all are partakers, then are ye bastards, and not sons.

9 Furthermore we have had fathers of our flesh which corrected *us,* and we gave *them* reverence: shall we not much rather be in subjection unto the Father of spirits, and live?

10 For they verily for a few days chastened *us* after their own pleasure; but he for *our* profit, that *we* might be partakers of his holiness.

11 Now no chastening for the present seemeth to be joyous, but grievous: nevertheless afterward it yieldeth the peaceable fruit of righteousness unto them which are exercised thereby.

12 Wherefore lift up the hands which hang down, and the feeble knees;

13 And make straight paths for your feet, lest that which is lame be turned out of the way; but let it rather be healed.

14 Follow peace with all *men,* and holiness, without which no man shall see the Lord:

15 Looking diligently lest any man fail of the grace of God; lest any root of bitterness springing up trouble *you,* and thereby many be defiled;

16 Lest there *be* any fornicator, or profane person, as E'sau, who for one morsel of meat sold his birthright.

17 For ye know how that afterward, when he would have inherited the blessing, he was rejected: for he found no place of repentance, though he sought it carefully with tears.

18 For ye are not come unto the mount that might be touched, and that burned with fire, nor unto blackness, and darkness, and tempest,

19 And the sound of a trumpet, and the voice of words; which *voice* they that heard intreated that the word should not be spoken to them any more:

20 (For they could not endure that which was commanded, And if so much as a beast touch the mountain, it shall be stoned, or thrust through with a dart:

21 And so terrible was the sight, *that* Mo'ses said, I exceedingly fear and quake:)

22 But ye are come unto mount Si'on, and unto the city of the living God, the heavenly Je-ru'sa-lem, and to an innumerable company of angels,

23 To the general assembly and church of the firstborn, which are written in heaven, and to God the Judge of all, and to the spirits of just men made perfect,

24 And to Je'sus the mediator of the new covenant, and to the blood of sprinkling, that speaketh better things than *that of* A'bel.

25 See that ye refuse not him that speaketh. For if they escaped not who refused him that spake on earth, much more *shall not* we *escape,* if we turn away from him that *speaketh* from heaven:

26 Whose voice then shook the earth: but now he hath promised, saying, Yet once more I shake not the earth only, but also heaven.

27 And this *word,* Yet once more, signifieth the removing of those things that are shaken, as of things that are made, that those things which cannot be shaken may remain.

28 Wherefore we receiving a kingdom which cannot be moved, let us have grace, whereby we may serve God acceptably with reverence and godly fear:

29 For our God *is* a consuming fire.

13 LET brotherly love continue.

2 Be not forgetful to entertain strangers: for thereby some have entertained angels unawares.

3 Remember them that are in bonds, as bound with them; *and* them which suffer adversity, as being yourselves also in the body.

4 Marriage *is* honourable in all, and the bed undefiled: but whoremongers and adulterers God will judge.

5 *Let your* conversation *be* without covetousness; *and be* content with such things as ye have: for he hath said, I will never leave thee, nor forsake thee.

6 So that we may boldly say, The Lord *is* my

helper, and I will not fear what man shall do
unto me.
7 Remember them which have the rule over
you, who have spoken unto you the word of
God: whose faith follow, considering the end of
their conversation.
8 Je'sus Christ the same yesterday, and to
day, and for ever.
9 Be not carried about with divers and
strange doctrines. For *it is* a good thing that the
heart be established with grace; not with meats,
which have not profited them that have been
occupied therein.
10 We have an altar, whereof they have no
right to eat which serve the tabernacle.
11 For the bodies of those beasts, whose
blood is brought into the sanctuary by the high
priest for sin, are burned without the camp.
12 Wherefore Je'sus also, that he might sanctify the people with his own blood, suffered
without the gate.
13 Let us go forth therefore unto him without
the camp, bearing his reproach.
14 For here have we no continuing city, but
we seek one to come.
15 By him therefore let us offer the sacrifice
of praise to God continually, that is, the fruit of
our lips giving thanks to his name.
16 But to do good and to communicate forget
not: for with such sacrifices God is well pleased.
17 Obey them that have the rule over you,
and submit yourselves: for they watch for your
souls, as they that must give account, that they
may do it with joy, and not with grief: for that *is*
unprofitable for you.
18 Pray for us: for we trust we have a good
conscience, in all things willing to live honestly.
19 But I beseech *you* the rather to do this,
that I may be restored to you the sooner.
20 Now the God of peace, that brought again
from the dead our Lord Je'sus, that great shepherd of the sheep, through the blood of the
everlasting covenant,
21 Make you perfect in every good work to
do his will, working in you that which is well-
pleasing in his sight, through Je'sus Christ; to
whom *be* glory for ever and ever. Amen.
22 And I beseech you, brethren, suffer the
word of exhortation: for I have written a letter
unto you in few words.
23 Know ye that *our* brother Tim'o-thy is set
at liberty; with whom, if he come shortly, I will
see you.
24 Salute all them that have the rule over
you, and all the saints. They of It'a-ly salute
you.
25 Grace *be* with you all. Amen.

Written to the He'brews from It'a-ly by Tim'o-thy.

THE LETTER OF

JAMES

1 JAMES, a servant of God and of the Lord
Je'sus Christ, to the twelve tribes which
are scattered abroad, greeting.
2 My brethren, count it all joy when ye fall
into divers temptations;
3 Knowing *this*, that the trying of your faith
worketh patience.
4 But let patience have *her* perfect work, that
ye may be perfect and entire, wanting nothing.
5 If any of you lack wisdom, let him ask of
God, that giveth to all *men* liberally, and up-
braideth not; and it shall be given him.
6 But let him ask in faith, nothing wavering.
For he that wavereth is like a wave of the sea
driven with the wind and tossed.
7 For let not that man think that he shall receive any thing of the Lord.
8 A double minded man *is* unstable in all his
ways.
9 Let the brother of low degree rejoice in that
he is exalted:
10 But the rich, in that he is made low: because as the flower of the grass he shall pass
away.
11 For the sun is no sooner risen with a burning heat, but it withereth the grass, and the
flower thereof falleth, and the grace of the fashion of it perisheth: so also shall the rich man
fade away in his ways.
12 Blessed *is* the man that endureth temptation: for when he is tried, he shall receive the
crown of life, which the Lord hath promised to
them that love him.
13 Let no man say when he is tempted, I am
tempted of God: for God cannot be tempted
with evil, neither tempteth he any man:
14 But every man is tempted, when he is
drawn away of his own lust, and enticed.
15 Then when lust hath conceived, it bringeth forth sin: and sin, when it is finished, bringeth forth death.
16 Do not err, my beloved brethren.
17 Every good gift and every perfect gift is
from above, and cometh down from the Father
of lights, with whom is no variableness, neither
shadow of turning.
18 Of his own will begat he us with the word
of truth, that we should be a kind of firstfruits
of his creatures.
19 Wherefore, my beloved brethren, let every man be swift to hear, slow to speak, slow to
wrath:
20 For the wrath of man worketh not the
righteousness of God.
21 Wherefore lay apart all filthiness and su-
perfluity of naughtiness, and receive with
meekness the engrafted word, which is able to
save your souls.
22 But be ye doers of the word, and not hearers only, deceiving your own selves.
23 For if any be a hearer of the word, and not
a doer, he is like unto a man beholding his natural face in a glass:
24 For he beholdeth himself, and goeth his
way, and straightway forgetteth what manner
of man he was.
25 But whoso looketh into the perfect law of
liberty, and continueth *therein*, he being not a
forgetful hearer, but a doer of the work, this
man shall be blessed in his deed.
26 If any man among you seem to be religious, and bridleth not his tongue, but deceiveth his own heart, this man's religion *is* vain.
27 Pure religion and undefiled before God
and the Father is this, To visit the fatherless and
widows in their affliction, *and* to keep himself
unspotted from the world.

2 MY brethren, have not the faith of our
Lord Je'sus Christ, *the Lord* of glory, with
respect of persons.
2 For if there come unto your assembly a
man with a gold ring, in goodly apparel, and
there come in also a poor man in vile raiment;
3 And ye have respect to him that weareth
the gay clothing, and say unto him, Sit thou
here in a good place; and say to the poor, Stand
thou there, or sit here under my footstool:
4 Are ye not then partial in yourselves, and
are become judges of evil thoughts?
5 Hearken, my beloved brethren, Hath not
God chosen the poor of this world rich in faith,
and heirs of the kingdom which he hath promised to them that love him?
6 But ye have despised the poor. Do not rich
men oppress you, and draw you before the
judgment seats?
7 Do not they blaspheme that worthy name
by the which ye are called?
8 If ye fulfil the royal law according to the
scripture, Thou shalt love thy neighbour as thyself, ye do well:
9 But if ye have respect to persons, ye commit sin, and are convinced of the law as transgressors.
10 For whosoever shall keep the whole law,
and yet offend in one *point,* he is guilty of all.
11 For he that said, Do not commit adultery,
said also, Do not kill. Now if thou commit no
adultery, yet if thou kill, thou art become a
transgressor of the law.
12 So speak ye, and so do, as they that shall
be judged by the law of liberty.
13 For he shall have judgment without mercy, that hath shewed no mercy; and mercy rejoiceth against judgment.
14 What *doth it* profit, my brethren, though a
man say he hath faith, and have not works? can
faith save him?
15 If a brother or sister be naked, and destitute of daily food,
16 And one of you say unto them, Depart in
peace, be *ye* warmed and filled; notwithstanding ye give them not those things which are
needful to the body; what *doth it* profit?
17 Even so faith, if it hath not works, is dead,
being alone.
18 Yea, a man may say, Thou hast faith, and
I have works: shew me thy faith without thy
works, and I will shew thee my faith by my
works.
19 Thou believest that there is one God; thou
doest well: the devils also believe, and tremble.
20 But wilt thou know, O vain man, that faith
without works is dead?
21 Was not A'bra-ham our father justified by
works, when he had offered I'saac his son upon
the altar?
22 Seest thou how faith wrought with his
works, and by works was faith made perfect?
23 And the scripture was fulfilled which
saith, A'bra-ham believed God, and it was imputed unto him for righteousness: and he was
called the Friend of God.
24 Ye see then how that by works a man is
justified, and not by faith only.
25 Likewise also was not Ra'hab the harlot
justified by works, when she had received the
messengers, and had sent *them* out another
way?
26 For as the body without the spirit is dead,
so faith without works is dead also.

3 MY brethren, be not many masters, knowing that we shall receive the greater condemnation.
2 For in many things we offend all. If any
man offend not in word, the same *is* a perfect
man, *and* able also to bridle the whole body.
3 Behold, we put bits in the horses' mouths,
that they may obey us; and we turn about their
whole body.
4 Behold also the ships, which though *they
be* so great, and *are* driven of fierce winds, yet
are they turned about with a very small helm,
whithersoever the governor listeth.
5 Even so the tongue is a little member, and
boasteth great things. Behold, how great a matter a little fire kindleth!
6 And the tongue *is* a fire, a world of iniquity:
so is the tongue among our members, that it
defileth the whole body, and setteth on fire the
course of nature; and it is set on fire of hell.
7 For every kind of beasts, and of birds, and
of serpents, and of things in the sea, is tamed,
and hath been tamed of mankind:
8 But the tongue can no man tame; *it is* an
unruly evil, full of deadly poison.
9 Therewith bless we God, even the Father;
and therewith curse we men, which are made
after the similitude of God.
10 Out of the same mouth proceedeth blessing and cursing. My brethren, these things
ought not so to be.
11 Doth a fountain send forth at the same
place sweet *water* and bitter?
12 Can the fig tree, my brethren, bear olive
berries? either a vine, figs? so *can* no fountain
both yield salt water and fresh.
13 Who *is* a wise man and endued with
knowledge among you? let him shew out of a
good conversation his works with meekness of
wisdom.
14 But if ye have bitter envying and strife in
your hearts, glory not, and lie not against the
truth.
15 This wisdom descendeth not from above,
but *is* earthly, sensual, devilish.
16 For where envying and strife *is,* there *is*
confusion and every evil work.
17 But the wisdom that is from above is first
pure, then peaceable, gentle, *and* easy to be intreated, full of mercy and good fruits, without
partiality, and without hypocrisy.
18 And the fruit of righteousness is sown in
peace of them that make peace.

4 FROM whence *come* wars and fightings
among you? *come they* not hence, *even* of
your lusts that war in your members?
2 Ye lust, and have not: ye kill, and desire to
have, and cannot obtain: ye fight and war, yet
ye have not, because ye ask not.
3 Ye ask, and receive not, because ye ask
amiss, that ye may consume *it* upon your lusts.
4 Ye adulterers and adulteresses, know ye
not that the friendship of the world is enmity
with God? whosoever therefore will be a friend
of the world is the enemy of God.
5 Do ye think that the scripture saith in vain,
The spirit that dwelleth in us lusteth to envy?
6 But he giveth more grace. Wherefore he
saith, God resisteth the proud, but giveth grace
unto the humble.
7 Submit yourselves therefore to God. Resist
the devil, and he will flee from you.
8 Draw nigh to God, and he will draw nigh to
you. Cleanse *your* hands, *ye* sinners; and purify
your hearts, *ye* double minded.

9 Be afflicted, and mourn, and weep: let your laughter be turned to mourning, and *your* joy to heaviness.

10 Humble yourselves in the sight of the Lord, and he shall lift you up.

11 Speak not evil one of another, brethren. He that speaketh evil of *his* brother, and judgeth his brother, speaketh evil of the law, and judgeth the law: but if thou judge the law, thou art not a doer of the law, but a judge.

12 There is one lawgiver, who is able to save and to destroy: who art thou that judgest another?

13 Go to now, ye that say, To day or to morrow we will go into such a city, and continue there a year, and buy and sell, and get gain:

14 Whereas ye know not what *shall be* on the morrow. For what *is* your life? It is even a vapour, that appeareth for a little time, and then vanisheth away.

15 For that ye *ought* to say, If the Lord will, we shall live, and do this, or that.

16 But now ye rejoice in your boastings: all such rejoicing is evil.

17 Therefore to him that knoweth to do good, and doeth *it* not, to him it is sin.

5 GO to now, *ye* rich men, weep and howl for your miseries that shall come upon *you.*

2 Your riches are corrupted, and your garments are motheaten.

3 Your gold and silver is cankered; and the rust of them shall be a witness against you, and shall eat your flesh as it were fire. Ye have heaped treasure together for the last days.

4 Behold, the hire of the labourers who have reaped down your fields, which is of you kept back by fraud, crieth: and the cries of them which have reaped are entered into the ears of the Lord of sab'a-oth.

5 Ye have lived in pleasure on the earth, and been wanton; ye have nourished your hearts, as in a day of slaughter.

6 Ye have condemned *and* killed the just; *and* he doth not resist you.

7 Be patient therefore, brethren, unto the coming of the Lord. Behold, the husbandman waiteth for the precious fruit of the earth, and hath long patience for it, until he receive the early and latter rain.

8 Be ye also patient; stablish your hearts: for the coming of the Lord draweth nigh.

9 Grudge not one against another, brethren, lest ye be condemned: behold, the judge standeth before the door.

10 Take, my brethren, the prophets, who have spoken in the name of the Lord, for an example of suffering affliction, and of patience.

11 Behold, we count them happy which endure. Ye have heard of the patience of Job, and have seen the end of the Lord; that the Lord is very pitiful, and of tender mercy.

12 But above all things, my brethren, swear not, neither by heaven, neither by the earth, neither by any other oath: but let your yea be yea; and *your* nay, nay; lest ye fall into condemnation.

13 Is any among you afflicted? let him pray. Is any merry? let him sing psalms.

14 Is any sick among you? let him call for the elders of the church; and let them pray over him, anointing him with oil in the name of the Lord:

15 And the prayer of faith shall save the sick, and the Lord shall raise him up; and if he have committed sins, they shall be forgiven him.

16 Confess *your* faults one to another, and pray one for another, that ye may be healed. The effectual fervent prayer of a righteous man availeth much.

17 E-li'as was a man subject to like passions as we are, and he prayed earnestly that it might not rain: and it rained not on the earth by the space of three years and six months.

18 And he prayed again, and the heaven gave rain, and the earth brought forth her fruit.

19 Brethren, if any of you do err from the truth, and one convert him;

20 Let him know, that he which converteth the sinner from the error of his way shall save a soul from death, and shall hide a multitude of sins.

THE FIRST LETTER OF

PETER

1 PE'TER, an apostle of Je'sus Christ, to the strangers scattered throughout Pon'tus, Ga-la'tia, Cap-pa-do'ci-a, A'sia, and Bi-thyn'i-a,

2 Elect according to the foreknowledge of God the Father, through sanctification of the Spirit, unto obedience and sprinkling of the blood of Je'sus Christ: Grace unto you, and peace, be multiplied.

3 Blessed *be* the God and Father of our Lord Je'sus Christ, which according to his abundant mercy hath begotten us again unto a lively hope by the resurrection of Je'sus Christ from the dead,

4 To an inheritance incorruptible, and undefiled, and that fadeth not away, reserved in heaven for you,

5 Who are kept by the power of God through faith unto salvation ready to be revealed in the last time.

6 Wherein ye greatly rejoice, though now for a season, if need be, ye are in heaviness through manifold temptations:

7 That the trial of your faith, being much more precious than of gold that perisheth, though it be tried with fire, might be found unto praise and honour and glory at the appearing of Je'sus Christ:

8 Whom having not seen, ye love; in whom, though now ye see *him* not, yet believing, ye rejoice with joy unspeakable and full of glory:

9 Receiving the end of your faith, *even* the salvation of *your* souls.

10 Of which salvation the prophets have enquired and searched diligently, who prophesied of the grace *that should come* unto you:

11 Searching what, or what manner of time the Spirit of Christ which was in them did signify, when it testified beforehand the sufferings of Christ, and the glory that should follow.

12 Unto whom it was revealed, that not unto themselves, but unto us they did minister the things, which are now reported unto you by them that have preached the gospel unto you with the Ho'ly Ghost sent down from heaven; which things the angels desire to look into.

13 Wherefore gird up the loins of your mind,

be sober, and hope to the end for the grace that is to be brought unto you at the revelation of Je'sus Christ;

14 As obedient children, not fashioning yourselves according to the former lusts in your ignorance:

15 But as he which hath called you is holy, so be ye holy in all manner of conversation;

16 Because it is written, Be ye holy; for I am holy.

17 And if ye call on the Father, who without respect of persons judgeth according to every man's work, pass the time of your sojourning *here* in fear:

18 Forasmuch as ye know that ye were not redeemed with corruptible things, *as* silver and gold, from your vain conversation *received* by tradition from your fathers;

19 But with the precious blood of Christ, as of a lamb without blemish and without spot:

20 Who verily was foreordained before the foundation of the world, but was manifest in these last times for you,

21 Who by him do believe in God, that raised him up from the dead, and gave him glory; that your faith and hope might be in God.

22 Seeing ye have purified your souls in obeying the truth through the Spirit unto unfeigned love of the brethren, *see that ye* love one another with a pure heart fervently:

23 Being born again, not of corruptible seed, but of incorruptible, by the word of God, which liveth and abideth for ever.

24 For all flesh *is* as grass, and all the glory of man as the flower of grass. The grass withereth, and the flower thereof falleth away:

25 But the word of the Lord endureth for ever. And this is the word which by the gospel is preached unto you.

2 WHEREFORE laying aside all malice, and all guile, and hypocrisies, and envies, and all evil speakings,

2 As newborn babes, desire the sincere milk of the word, that ye may grow thereby:

3 If so be ye have tasted that the Lord *is* gracious.

4 To whom coming, *as unto* a living stone, disallowed indeed of men, but chosen of God, *and* precious,

5 Ye also, as lively stones, are built up a spiritual house, an holy priesthood, to offer up spiritual sacrifices, acceptable to God by Je'sus Christ.

6 Wherefore also it is contained in the scripture, Behold, I lay in Si'on a chief corner stone, elect, precious: and he that believeth on him shall not be confounded.

7 Unto you therefore which believe *he is* precious: but unto them which be disobedient, the stone which the builders disallowed, the same is made the head of the corner,

8 And a stone of stumbling, and a rock of offence, *even to them* which stumble at the word, being disobedient: whereunto also they were appointed.

9 But ye *are* a chosen generation, a royal priesthood, an holy nation, a peculiar people; that ye should shew forth the praises of him who hath called you out of darkness into his marvellous light:

10 Which in time past *were* not a people, but *are* now the people of God: which had not obtained mercy, but now have obtained mercy.

11 Dearly beloved, I beseech *you* as strangers and pilgrims, abstain from fleshly lusts, which war against the soul;

12 Having your conversation honest among the Gen'tiles: that, whereas they speak against you as evildoers, they may by *your* good works, which they shall behold, glorify God in the day of visitation.

13 Submit yourselves to every ordinance of man for the Lord's sake: whether it be to the king, as supreme;

14 Or unto governors, as unto them that are sent by him for the punishment of evildoers, and for the praise of them that do well.

15 For so is the will of God, that with well doing ye may put to silence the ignorance of foolish men:

16 As free, and not using *your* liberty for a cloke of maliciousness, but as the servants of God.

17 Honour all *men*. Love the brotherhood. Fear God. Honour the king.

18 Servants, *be* subject to *your* masters with all fear; not only to the good and gentle, but also to the froward.

19 For this *is* thankworthy, if a man for conscience toward God endure grief, suffering wrongfully.

20 For what glory *is it*, if, when ye be buffeted for your faults, ye shall take it patiently? but if, when ye do well, and suffer *for it*, ye take it patiently, this *is* acceptable with God.

21 For even hereunto were ye called: because Christ also suffered for us, leaving us an example, that ye should follow his steps:

22 Who did no sin, neither was guile found in his mouth:

23 Who, when he was reviled, reviled not again; when he suffered, he threatened not; but committed *himself* to him that judgeth righteously:

24 Who his own self bare our sins in his own body on the tree, that we, being dead to sins, should live unto righteousness: by whose stripes ye were healed.

25 For ye were as sheep going astray; but are now returned unto the Shepherd and Bishop of your souls.

3 LIKEWISE ye wives, *be* in subjection to your own husbands; that, if any obey not the word, they also may without the word be won by the conversation of the wives;

2 While they behold your chaste conversation *coupled* with fear.

3 Whose adorning let it not be that outward *adorning* of plaiting the hair, and of wearing of gold, or of putting on of apparel;

4 But *let it be* the hidden man of the heart, in that which is not corruptible, *even the ornament* of a meek and quiet spirit, which is in the sight of God of great price.

5 For after this manner in the old time the holy women also, who trusted in God, adorned themselves, being in subjection unto their own husbands:

6 Even as Sa'ra obeyed A'bra-ham, calling him lord: whose daughters ye are, as long as ye do well, and are not afraid with any amazement.

7 Likewise, ye husbands, dwell with *them* according to knowledge, giving honour unto the wife, as unto the weaker vessel, and as being heirs together of the grace of life; that your prayers be not hindered.

8 Finally, *be ye* all of one mind, having compassion one of another, love as brethren, *be* pitiful, *be* courteous:

9 Not rendering evil for evil, or railing for railing: but contrariwise blessing; knowing that

ye are thereunto called, that ye should inherit a blessing.

10 For he that will love life, and see good days, let him refrain his tongue from evil, and his lips that they speak no guile:

11 Let him eschew evil, and do good; let him seek peace, and ensue it.

12 For the eyes of the Lord *are* over the righteous, and his ears *are open* unto their prayers: but the face of the Lord *is* against them that do evil.

13 And who *is* he that will harm you, if ye be followers of that which is good?

14 But and if ye suffer for righteousness' sake, happy *are ye:* and be not afraid of their terror, neither be troubled;

15 But sanctify the Lord God in your hearts: and *be* ready always to *give* an answer to every man that asketh you a reason of the hope that is in you with meekness and fear:

16 Having a good conscience; that, whereas they speak evil of you, as of evildoers, they may be ashamed that falsely accuse your good conversation in Christ.

17 For *it is* better, if the will of God be so, that ye suffer for well doing, than for evil doing.

18 For Christ also hath once suffered for sins, the just for the unjust, that he might bring us to God, being put to death in the flesh, but quickened by the Spirit:

19 By which also he went and preached unto the spirits in prison;

20 Which sometime were disobedient, when once the longsuffering of God waited in the days of No'ah, while the ark was a preparing, wherein few, that is, eight souls were saved by water.

21 The like figure whereunto *even* baptism doth also now save us (not the putting away of the filth of the flesh, but the answer of a good conscience toward God,) by the resurrection of Je'sus Christ:

22 Who is gone into heaven, and is on the right hand of God; angels and authorities and powers being made subject unto him.

4 FORASMUCH then as Christ hath suffered for us in the flesh, arm yourselves likewise with the same mind: for he that hath suffered in the flesh hath ceased from sin;

2 That he no longer should live the rest of *his* time in the flesh to the lusts of men, but to the will of God.

3 For the time past of *our* life may suffice us to have wrought the will of the Gen'tiles, when we walked in lasciviousness, lusts, excess of wine, revellings, banquetings, and abominable idolatries:

4 Wherein they think it strange that ye run not with *them* to the same excess of riot, speaking evil of *you:*

5 Who shall give account to him that is ready to judge the quick and the dead.

6 For for this cause was the gospel preached also to them that are dead, that they might be judged according to men in the flesh, but live according to God in the spirit.

7 But the end of all things is at hand: be ye therefore sober, and watch unto prayer.

8 And above all things have fervent charity among yourselves: for charity shall cover the multitude of sins.

9 Use hospitality one to another without grudging.

10 As every man hath received the gift, *even* *so* minister the same one to another, as good stewards of the manifold grace of God.

11 If any man speak, *let him speak* as the oracles of God; if any man minister, *let him do it* as of the ability which God giveth: that God in all things may be glorified through Je'sus Christ, to whom be praise and dominion for ever and ever. Amen.

12 Beloved, think it not strange concerning the fiery trial which is to try you, as though some strange thing happened unto you:

13 But rejoice, inasmuch as ye are partakers of Christ's sufferings; that, when his glory shall be revealed, ye may be glad also with exceeding joy.

14 If ye be reproached for the name of Christ, happy *are ye;* for the spirit of glory and of God resteth upon you: on their part he is evil spoken of, but on your part he is glorified.

15 But let none of you suffer as a murderer, or *as* a thief, or *as* an evildoer, or as a busybody in other men's matters.

16 Yet if *any man suffer* as a Chris'tian, let him not be ashamed; but let him glorify God on this behalf.

17 For the time *is come* that judgment must begin at the house of God: and if *it* first *begin* at us, what shall the end *be* of them that obey not the gospel of God?

18 And if the righteous scarcely be saved, where shall the ungodly and the sinner appear?

19 Wherefore let them that suffer according to the will of God commit the keeping of their souls *to him* in well doing, as unto a faithful Creator.

5 THE elders which are among you I exhort, who am also an elder, and a witness of the sufferings of Christ, and also a partaker of the glory that shall be revealed:

2 Feed the flock of God which is among you, taking the oversight *thereof,* not by constraint, but willingly; not for filthy lucre, but of a ready mind;

3 Neither as being lords over *God's* heritage, but being ensamples to the flock.

4 And when the chief Shepherd shall appear, ye shall receive a crown of glory that fadeth not away.

5 Likewise, ye younger, submit yourselves unto the elder. Yea, all *of you* be subject one to another, and be clothed with humility: for God resisteth the proud, and giveth grace to the humble.

6 Humble yourselves therefore under the mighty hand of God, that he may exalt you in due time:

7 Casting all your care upon him; for he careth for you.

8 Be sober, be vigilant; because your adversary the devil, as a roaring lion, walketh about, seeking whom he may devour:

9 Whom resist stedfast in the faith, knowing that the same afflictions are accomplished in your brethren that are in the world.

10 But the God of all grace, who hath called us unto his eternal glory by Christ Je'sus, after that ye have suffered a while, make you perfect, stablish, strengthen, settle *you.*

11 To him *be* glory and dominion for ever and ever. Amen.

12 By Sil-va'nus, a faithful brother unto you, as I suppose, I have written briefly, exhorting, and testifying that this is the true grace of God wherein ye stand.

13 The *church that is* at Bab'y-lon, elected together with *you,* saluteth you; and *so doth* Mar'cus my son.

14 Greet ye one another with a kiss of charity. Peace *be* with you all that are in Christ Je'sus. Amen.

THE SECOND LETTER OF

PETER

1 SI'MON Pe'ter, a servant and an apostle of Je'sus Christ, to them that have obtained like precious faith with us through the righteousness of God and our Saviour Je'sus Christ:

2 Grace and peace be multiplied unto you through the knowledge of God, and of Je'sus our Lord,

3 According as his divine power hath given unto us all things that *pertain* unto life and godliness, through the knowledge of him that hath called us to glory and virtue:

4 Whereby are given unto us exceeding great and precious promises: that by these ye might be partakers of the divine nature, having escaped the corruption that is in the world through lust.

5 And beside this, giving all diligence, add to your faith virtue; and to virtue knowledge;

6 And to knowledge temperance; and to temperance patience; and to patience godliness;

7 And to godliness brotherly kindness; and to brotherly kindness charity.

8 For if these things be in you, and abound, they make *you that ye shall* neither *be* barren nor unfruitful in the knowledge of our Lord Je'sus Christ.

9 But he that lacketh these things is blind, and cannot see afar off, and hath forgotten that he was purged from his old sins.

10 Wherefore the rather, brethren, give diligence to make your calling and election sure: for if ye do these things, ye shall never fall:

11 For so an entrance shall be ministered unto you abundantly into the everlasting kingdom of our Lord and Saviour Je'sus Christ.

12 Wherefore I will not be negligent to put you always in remembrance of these things, though ye know *them,* and be established in the present truth.

13 Yea, I think it meet, as long as I am in this tabernacle, to stir you up by putting *you* in remembrance;

14 Knowing that shortly I must put off *this* my tabernacle, even as our Lord Je'sus Christ hath shewed me.

15 Moreover I will endeavor that ye may be able after my decease to have these things always in remembrance.

16 For we have not followed cunningly devised fables, when we made known unto you the power and coming of our Lord Je'sus Christ, but were eyewitnesses of his majesty.

17 For he received from God the Father honour and glory, when there came such a voice to him from the excellent glory, This is my beloved Son, in whom I am well pleased.

18 And this voice which came from heaven we heard, when we were with him in the holy mount.

19 We have also a more sure word of prophecy; whereunto ye do well that ye take heed, as unto a light that shineth in a dark place, until the day dawn, and the day star arise in your hearts:

20 Knowing this first, that no prophecy of the scripture is of any private interpretation.

21 For the prophecy came not in old time by the will of man: but holy men of God spake *as they were* moved by the Ho'ly Ghost.

2 BUT there were false prophets also among the people, even as there shall be false teachers among you, who privily shall bring in damnable heresies, even denying the Lord that bought them, and bring upon themselves swift destruction.

2 And many shall follow their pernicious ways; by reason of whom the way of truth shall be evil spoken of.

3 And through covetousness shall they with feigned words make merchandise of you: whose judgment now of a long time lingereth not, and their damnation slumbereth not.

4 For if God spared not the angels that sinned, but cast *them* down to hell, and delivered *them* into chains of darkness, to be reserved unto judgment;

5 And spared not the old world, but saved No'ah the eighth *person,* a preacher of righteousness, bringing in the flood upon the world of the ungodly;

6 And turning the cities of Sod'om and Gomor'rha into ashes condemned *them* with an overthrow, making *them* an ensample unto those that after should live ungodly;

7 And delivered just Lot, vexed with the filthy conversation of the wicked:

8 (For that righteous man dwelling among them, in seeing and hearing, vexed *his* righteous soul from day to day with *their* unlawful deeds;)

9 The Lord knoweth how to deliver the godly out of temptations, and to reserve the unjust unto the day of judgment to be punished:

10 But chiefly them that walk after the flesh in the lust of uncleanness, and despise government. Presumptuous *are they,* selfwilled, they are not afraid to speak evil of dignities.

11 Whereas angels, which are greater in power and might, bring not railing accusation against them before the Lord.

12 But these, as natural brute beasts, made to be taken and destroyed, speak evil of the things that they understand not; and shall utterly perish in their own corruption;

13 And shall receive the reward of unrighteousness, *as* they that count it pleasure to riot in the day time. Spots *they are* and blemishes, sporting themselves with their own deceivings while they feast with you;

14 Having eyes full of adultery, and that cannot cease from sin; beguiling unstable souls: an heart they have exercised with covetous practices; cursed children:

15 Which have forsaken the right way, and are gone astray, following the way of Ba'laam *the son* of Bo'sor, who loved the wages of unrighteousness;

16 But was rebuked for his iniquity: the dumb ass speaking with man's voice forbad the madness of the prophet.

17 These are wells without water, clouds that

are carried with a tempest; to whom the mist of
darkness is reserved for ever.
18 For when they speak great swelling *words*
of vanity, they allure through the lusts of the
flesh, *through much* wantonness, those that
were clean escaped from them who live in error.
19 While they promise them liberty, they
themselves are the servants of corruption: for
of whom a man is overcome, of the same is he
brought in bondage.
20 For if after they have escaped the pollutions of the world through the knowledge of the
Lord and Saviour Je'sus Christ, they are again
entangled therein, and overcome, the latter end
is worse with them than the beginning.
21 For it had been better for them not to
have known the way of righteousness, than, after they have known *it*, to turn from the holy
commandment delivered unto them.
22 But it is happened unto them according to
the true proverb, The dog *is* turned to his own
vomit again; and the sow that was washed to
her wallowing in the mire.

3 THIS second epistle, beloved, I now write
unto you; in *both* which I stir up your pure
minds by way of remembrance:
2 That ye may be mindful of the words which
were spoken before by the holy prophets, and
of the commandment of us the apostles of the
Lord and Saviour:
3 Knowing this first, that there shall come in
the last days scoffers, walking after their own
lusts,
4 And saying, Where is the promise of his
coming? for since the fathers fell asleep, all
things continue as *they were* from the beginning
of the creation.
5 For this they willingly are ignorant of, that
by the word of God the heavens were of old,
and the earth standing out of the water and in
the water:
6 Whereby the world that then was, being
overflowed with water, perished:
7 But the heavens and the earth, which are
now, by the same word are kept in store, reserved unto fire against the day of judgment
and perdition of ungodly men.
8 But, beloved, be not ignorant of this one
thing, that one day *is* with the Lord as a thousand years, and a thousand years as one day.
9 The Lord is not slack concerning his promise, as some men count slackness; but is longsuffering to us-ward, not willing that any
should perish, but that all should come to repentance.
10 But the day of the Lord will come as a
thief in the night; in the which the heavens shall
pass away with a great noise, and the elements
shall melt with fervent heat, the earth also and
the works that are therein shall be burned up.
11 *Seeing* then *that* all these things shall be
dissolved, what manner *of persons* ought ye to
be in *all* holy conversation and godliness,
12 Looking for and hasting unto the coming
of the day of God, wherein the heavens being
on fire shall be dissolved, and the elements shall
melt with fervent heat?
13 Nevertheless we, according to his promise, look for new heavens and a new earth,
wherein dwelleth righteousness.
14 Wherefore, beloved, seeing that ye look
for such things, be diligent that ye may be
found of him in peace, without spot, and blameless.
15 And account *that* the longsuffering of our
Lord *is* salvation; even as our beloved brother
Paul also according to the wisdom given unto
him hath written unto you;
16 As also in all *his* epistles, speaking in
them of these things; in which are some things
hard to be understood, which they that are unlearned and unstable wrest, as *they do* also the
other scriptures, unto their own destruction.
17 Ye therefore, beloved, seeing ye know
these things before, beware lest ye also, being
led away with the error of the wicked, fall from
your own stedfastness.
18 But grow in grace, and *in* the knowledge
of our Lord and Saviour Je'sus Christ. To him
be glory both now and for ever. Amen.

THE FIRST LETTER OF

JOHN

1 THAT which was from the beginning,
which we have heard, which we have seen
with our eyes, which we have looked upon, and
our hands have handled, of the Word of life;
2 (For the life was manifested, and we have
seen *it*, and bear witness, and shew unto you
that eternal life, which was with the Father, and
was manifested unto us;)
3 That which we have seen and heard declare
we unto you, that ye also may have fellowship
with us: and truly our fellowship *is* with the Father, and with his Son Je'sus Christ.
4 And these things write we unto you, that
your joy may be full.
5 This then is the message which we have
heard of him, and declare unto you, that God is
light, and in him is no darkness at all.
6 If we say that we have fellowship with him,
and walk in darkness, we lie, and do not the
truth:
7 But if we walk in the light, as he is in the
light, we have fellowship one with another, and
the blood of Je'sus Christ his Son cleanseth us
from all sin.
8 If we say that we have no sin, we deceive
ourselves, and the truth is not in us.
9 If we confess our sins, he is faithful and
just to forgive us *our* sins, and to cleanse us
from all unrighteousness.
10 If we say that we have not sinned, we
make him a liar, and his word is not in us.

2 MY little children, these things write I unto
you, that ye sin not. And if any man sin, we
have an advocate with the Father, Je'sus Christ
the righteous:
2 And he is the propitiation for our sins: and
not for ours only, but also for *the sins of* the
whole world.
3 And hereby we do know that we know him,
if we keep his commandments.
4 He that saith, I know him, and keepeth not
his commandments, is a liar, and the truth is
not in him.

5 But whoso keepeth his word, in him verily is the love of God perfected: hereby know we that we are in him.

6 He that saith he abideth in him ought himself also so to walk, even as he walked.

7 Brethren, I write no new commandment unto you, but an old commandment which ye had from the beginning. The old commandment is the word which ye have heard from the beginning.

8 Again, a new commandment I write unto you, which thing is true in him and in you: because the darkness is past, and the true light now shineth.

9 He that saith he is in the light, and hateth his brother, is in darkness even until now.

10 He that loveth his brother abideth in the light, and there is none occasion of stumbling in him.

11 But he that hateth his brother is in darkness, and walketh in darkness, and knoweth not whither he goeth, because that darkness hath blinded his eyes.

12 I write unto you, little children, because your sins are forgiven you for his name's sake.

13 I write unto you, fathers, because ye have known him *that is* from the beginning. I write unto you, young men, because ye have overcome the wicked one. I write unto you, little children, because ye have known the Father.

14 I have written unto you, fathers, because ye have known him *that is* from the beginning. I have written unto you, young men, because ye are strong, and the word of God abideth in you, and ye have overcome the wicked one.

15 Love not the world, neither the things *that are* in the world. If any man love the world, the love of the Father is not in him.

16 For all that *is* in the world, the lust of the flesh, and the lust of the eyes, and the pride of life, is not of the Father, but is of the world.

17 And the world passeth away, and the lust thereof: but he that doeth the will of God abideth for ever.

18 Little children, it is the last time: and as ye have heard that antichrist shall come, even now are there many antichrists; whereby we know that it is the last time.

19 They went out from us, but they were not of us; for if they had been of us, they would *no doubt* have continued with us: but *they went out*, that they might be made manifest that they were not all of us.

20 But ye have an unction from the Holy One, and ye know all things.

21 I have not written unto you because ye know not the truth, but because ye know it, and that no lie is of the truth.

22 Who is a liar but he that denieth that Je'sus is the Christ? He is antichrist, that denieth the Father and the Son.

23 Whosoever denieth the Son, the same hath not the Father: [*but*] *he that acknowledgeth the Son hath the Father also*.

24 Let that therefore abide in you, which ye have heard from the beginning. If that which ye have heard from the beginning shall remain in you, ye also shall continue in the Son, and in the Father.

25 And this is the promise that he hath promised us, *even* eternal life.

26 These *things* have I written unto you concerning them that seduce you.

27 But the anointing which ye have received of him abideth in you, and ye need not that any man teach you: but as the same anointing teacheth you of all things, and is truth, and is no lie, and even as it hath taught you, ye shall abide in him.

28 And now, little children, abide in him; that, when he shall appear, we may have confidence, and not be ashamed before him at his coming.

29 If ye know that he is righteous, ye know that every one that doeth righteousness is born of him.

3 BEHOLD, what manner of love the Father hath bestowed upon us, that we should be called the sons of God: therefore the world knoweth us not, because it knew him not.

2 Beloved, now are we the sons of God, and it doth not yet appear what we shall be: but we know that, when he shall appear, we shall be like him; for we shall see him as he is.

3 And every man that hath this hope in him purifieth himself, even as he is pure.

4 Whosoever committeth sin transgresseth also the law: for sin is the transgression of the law.

5 And ye know that he was manifested to take away our sins; and in him is no sin.

6 Whosoever abideth in him sinneth not: whosoever sinneth hath not seen him, neither known him.

7 Little children, let no man deceive you: he that doeth righteousness is righteous, even as he is righteous.

8 He that committeth sin is of the devil; for the devil sinneth from the beginning. For this purpose the Son of God was manifested, that he might destroy the works of the devil.

9 Whosoever is born of God doth not commit sin; for his seed remaineth in him: and he cannot sin, because he is born of God.

10 In this the children of God are manifest, and the children of the devil: whosoever doeth not righteousness is not of God, neither he that loveth not his brother.

11 For this is the message that ye heard from the beginning, that we should love one another.

12 Not as Cain, *who* was of that wicked one, and slew his brother. And wherefore slew he him? Because his own works were evil, and his brother's righteous.

13 Marvel not, my brethren, if the world hate you.

14 We know that we have passed from death unto life, because we love the brethren. He that loveth not *his* brother abideth in death.

15 Whosoever hateth his brother is a murderer: and ye know that no murderer hath eternal life abiding in him.

16 Hereby perceive we the love *of God*, because he laid down his life for us: and we ought to lay down *our* lives for the brethren.

17 But whoso hath this world's good, and seeth his brother have need, and shutteth up his bowels *of compassion* from him, how dwelleth the love of God in him?

18 My little children, let us not love in word, neither in tongue; but in deed and in truth.

19 And hereby we know that we are of the truth, and shall assure our hearts before him.

20 For if our heart condemn us, God is greater than our heart, and knoweth all things.

21 Beloved, if our heart condemn us not, *then* have we confidence toward God.

22 And whatsoever we ask, we receive of him, because we keep his commandments, and do those things that are pleasing in his sight.

23 And this is his commandment, That we should believe on the name of his Son Je'sus

Christ, and love one another, as he gave us commandment.

24 And he that keepeth his commandments dwelleth in him, and he in him. And hereby we know that he abideth in us, by the Spirit which he hath given us.

4 BELOVED, believe not every spirit, but try the spirits whether they are of God: because many false prophets are gone out into the world.

2 Hereby know ye the Spirit of God: Every spirit that confesseth that Je'sus Christ is come in the flesh is of God:

3 And every spirit that confesseth not that Je'sus Christ is come in the flesh is not of God: and this is that *spirit* of antichrist, whereof ye have heard that it should come; and even now already is it in the world.

4 Ye are of God, little children, and have overcome them: because greater is he that is in you, than he that is in the world.

5 They are of the world: therefore speak they of the world, and the world heareth them.

6 We are of God: he that knoweth God heareth us; he that is not of God heareth not us. Hereby know we the spirit of truth, and the spirit of error.

7 Beloved, let us love one another: for love is of God; and every one that loveth is born of God, and knoweth God.

8 He that loveth not knoweth not God; for God is love.

9 In this was manifested the love of God toward us, because that God sent his only begotten Son into the world, that we might live through him.

10 Herein is love, not that we loved God, but that he loved us, and sent his Son *to be* the propitiation for our sins.

11 Beloved, if God so loved us, we ought also to love one another.

12 No man hath seen God at any time. If we love one another, God dwelleth in us, and his love is perfected in us.

13 Hereby know we that we dwell in him, and he in us, because he hath given us of his Spirit.

14 And we have seen and do testify that the Father sent the Son *to be* the Saviour of the world.

15 Whosoever shall confess that Je'sus is the Son of God, God dwelleth in him, and he in God.

16 And we have known and believed the love that God hath to us. God is love; and he that dwelleth in love dwelleth in God, and God in him.

17 Herein is our love made perfect, that we may have boldness in the day of judgment: because as he is, so are we in this world.

18 There is no fear in love; but perfect love casteth out fear: because fear hath torment. He that feareth is not made perfect in love.

19 We love him, because he first loved us.

20 If a man say, I love God, and hateth his brother, he is a liar: for he that loveth not his brother whom he hath seen, how can he love God whom he hath not seen?

21 And this commandment have we from him, That he who loveth God love his brother also.

5 WHOSOEVER believeth that Je'sus is the Christ is born of God: and every one that loveth him that begat loveth him also that is begotten of him.

2 By this we know that we love the children of God, when we love God, and keep his commandments.

3 For this is the love of God, that we keep his commandments: and his commandments are not grievous.

4 For whatsoever is born of God overcometh the world: and this is the victory that overcometh the world, *even* our faith.

5 Who is he that overcometh the world, but he that believeth that Je'sus is the Son of God?

6 This is he that came by water and blood, *even* Je'sus Christ; not by water only, but by water and blood. And it is the Spirit that beareth witness, because the Spirit is truth.

7 For there are three that bear record in heaven, the Father, the Word, and the Ho'ly Ghost: and these three are one.

8 And there are three that bear witness in earth, the spirit, and the water, and the blood: and these three agree in one.

9 If we receive the witness of men, the witness of God is greater: for this is the witness of God which he hath testified of his Son.

10 He that believeth on the Son of God hath the witness in himself: he that believeth not God hath made him a liar; because he believeth not the record that God gave of his Son.

11 And this is the record, that God hath given to us eternal life, and this life is in his Son.

12 He that hath the Son hath life; *and* he that hath not the Son of God hath not life.

13 These things have I written unto you that believe on the name of the Son of God; that ye may know that ye have eternal life, and that ye may believe on the name of the Son of God.

14 And this is the confidence that we have in him, that, if we ask any thing according to his will, he heareth us:

15 And if we know that he hear us, whatsoever we ask, we know that we have the petitions that we desired of him.

16 If any man see his brother sin a sin *which is* not unto death, he shall ask, and he shall give him life for them that sin not unto death. There is a sin unto death: I do not say that he shall pray for it.

17 All unrighteousness is sin: and there is a sin not unto death.

18 We know that whosoever is born of God sinneth not; but he that is begotten of God keepeth himself, and that wicked one toucheth him not.

19 *And* we know that we are of God, and the whole world lieth in wickedness.

20 And we know that the Son of God is come, and hath given us an understanding, that we may know him that is true, and we are in him that is true, *even* in his Son Je'sus Christ. This is the true God, and eternal life.

21 Little children, keep yourselves from idols. Amen.

THE SECOND LETTER OF

JOHN

THE elder unto the elect lady and her children, whom I love in the truth; and not I only, but also all they that have known the truth;

2 For the truth's sake, which dwelleth in us, and shall be with us for ever.

3 Grace be with you, mercy, *and* peace, from God the Father, and from the Lord Je'sus Christ, the Son of the Father, in truth and love.

4 I rejoiced greatly that I found of thy children walking in truth, as we have received a commandment from the Father.

5 And now I beseech thee, lady, not as though I wrote a new commandment unto thee, but that which we had from the beginning, that we love one another.

6 And this is love, that we walk after his commandments. This is the commandment, That, as ye have heard from the beginning, ye should walk in it.

7 For many deceivers are entered into the world, who confess not that Je'sus Christ is come in the flesh. This is a deceiver and an antichrist.

8 Look to yourselves, that we lose not those things which we have wrought, but that we receive a full reward.

9 Whosoever transgresseth, and abideth not in the doctrine of Christ, hath not God. He that abideth in the doctrine of Christ, he hath both the Father and the Son.

10 If there come any unto you, and bring not this doctrine, receive him not into *your* house, neither bid him God speed:

11 For he that biddeth him God speed is partaker of his evil deeds.

12 Having many things to write unto you, I would not *write* with paper and ink: but I trust to come unto you, and speak face to face, that our joy may be full.

13 The children of thy elect sister greet thee. Amen.

THE THIRD LETTER OF

JOHN

THE elder unto the wellbeloved Ga'ius, whom I love in the truth.

2 Beloved, I wish above all things that thou mayest prosper and be in health, even as thy soul prospereth.

3 For I rejoiced greatly, when the brethren came and testified of the truth that is in thee, even as thou walkest in the truth.

4 I have no greater joy than to hear that my children walk in truth.

5 Beloved, thou doest faithfully whatsoever thou doest to the brethren, and to strangers;

6 Which have borne witness of thy charity before the church: whom if thou bring forward on their journey after a godly sort, thou shalt do well:

7 Because that for his name's sake they went forth, taking nothing of the Gen'tiles.

8 We therefore ought to receive such, that we might be fellowhelpers to the truth.

9 I wrote unto the church: but Di-ot're-phes, who loveth to have the preeminence among them, receiveth us not.

10 Wherefore, if I come, I will remember his deeds which he doeth, prating against us with malicious words: and not content therewith, neither doth he himself receive the brethren, and forbiddeth them that would, and casteth *them* out of the church.

11 Beloved, follow not that which is evil, but that which is good. He that doeth good is of God: but he that doeth evil hath not seen God.

12 De-me'tri-us hath good report of all *men*, and of the truth itself: yea, and we *also* bear record; and ye know that our record is true.

13 I had many things to write, but I will not with ink and pen write unto thee:

14 But I trust I shall shortly see thee, and we shall speak face to face. Peace *be* to thee. *Our* friends salute thee. Greet the friends by name.

THE LETTER OF

JUDE

JUDE, the servant of Je'sus Christ, and brother of James, to them that are sanctified by God the Father, and preserved in Je'sus Christ, *and* called:

2 Mercy unto you, and peace, and love, be multiplied.

3 Beloved, when I gave all diligence to write unto you of the common salvation, it was needful for me to write unto you, and exhort *you* that ye should earnestly contend for the faith which was once delivered unto the saints.

4 For there are certain men crept in unawares, who were before of old ordained to this condemnation, ungodly men, turning the grace of our God into lasciviousness, and denying the only Lord God, and our Lord Je'sus Christ.

5 I will therefore put you in remembrance, though ye once knew this, how that the Lord, having saved the people out of the land of E'gypt, afterward destroyed them that believed not.

6 And the angels which kept not their first estate, but left their own habitation, he hath reserved in everlasting chains under darkness unto the judgment of the great day.

7 Even as Sod'om and Go-mor'rha, and the cities about them in like manner, giving themselves over to fornication, and going after

strange flesh, are set forth for an example, suffering the vengeance of eternal fire.

8 Likewise also these *filthy* dreamers defile the flesh, despise dominion, and speak evil of dignities.

9 Yet Mi'chael the archangel, when contending with the devil he disputed about the body of Mo'ses, durst not bring against him a railing accusation, but said, The Lord rebuke thee.

10 But these speak evil of those things which they know not: but what they know naturally, as brute beasts, in those things they corrupt themselves.

11 Woe unto them! for they have gone in the way of Cain, and ran greedily after the error of Ba'laam for reward, and perished in the gainsaying of Co're.

12 These are spots in your feasts of charity, when they feast with you, feeding themselves without fear: clouds *they are* without water, carried about of winds; trees whose fruit withereth, without fruit, twice dead, plucked up by the roots;

13 Raging waves of the sea, foaming out their own shame; wandering stars, to whom is reserved the blackness of darkness for ever.

14 And E'noch also, the seventh from Ad'am, prophesied of these, saying, Behold, the Lord cometh with ten thousands of his saints,

15 To execute judgment upon all, and to convince all that are ungodly among them of all their ungodly deeds which they have ungodly committed, and of all their hard *speeches* which ungodly sinners have spoken against him.

16 These are murmurers, complainers, walking after their own lusts; and their mouth speaketh great swelling *words*, having men's persons in admiration because of advantage.

17 But, beloved, remember ye the words which were spoken before of the apostles of our Lord Je'sus Christ;

18 How that they told you there should be mockers in the last time, who should walk after their own ungodly lusts.

19 These be they who separate themselves, sensual, having not the Spirit.

20 But ye, beloved, building up yourselves on your most holy faith, praying in the Ho'ly Ghost,

21 Keep yourselves in the love of God, looking for the mercy of our Lord Je'sus Christ unto eternal life.

22 And of some have compassion, making a difference:

23 And others save with fear, pulling *them* out of the fire; hating even the garment spotted by the flesh.

24 Now unto him that is able to keep you from falling, and to present *you* faultless before the presence of his glory with exceeding joy,

25 To the only wise God our Saviour, *be* glory and majesty, dominion and power, both now and ever. Amen.

THE

REVELATION TO JOHN

(The Apocalypse)

1 THE Revelation of Je'sus Christ, which God gave unto him, to shew unto his servants things which must shortly come to pass; and he sent and signified *it* by his angel unto his servant John:

2 Who bare record of the word of God, and of the testimony of Je'sus Christ, and of all things that he saw.

3 Blessed *is* he that readeth, and they that hear the words of this prophecy, and keep those things which are written therein for the time *is* at hand.

4 JOHN to the seven churches which are in A'sia: Grace *be* unto you, and peace, from him which is, and which was, and which is to come; and from the seven Spirits which are before his throne;

5 And from Je'sus Christ, *who is* the faithful witness, *and* the first begotten of the dead, and the prince of the kings of the earth. Unto him that loved us, and washed us from our sins in his own blood,

6 And hath made us kings and priests unto God and his Father; to him *be* glory and dominion for ever and ever. Amen.

7 Behold, he cometh with clouds; and every eye shall see him, and they *also* which pierced him: and all kindreds of the earth shall wail because of him. Even so, Amen.

8 I am Al'pha and O'me-ga, the beginning and the ending, saith the Lord, which is, and which was, and which is to come, the Almighty.

9 I John, who also am your brother, and companion in tribulation, and in the kingdom and patience of Je'sus Christ, was in the isle that is called Pat'mos, for the word of God, and for the testimony of Je'sus Christ.

10 I was in the Spirit on the Lord's day, and heard behind me a great voice, as of a trumpet,

11 Saying, I am Al'pha and O'me-ga, the first and the last: and, What thou seest, write in a book, and send *it* unto the seven churches which are in A'sia; unto Eph'e-sus, and unto Smyr'na, and unto Per'ga-mos, and unto Thy-a-ti'ra, and unto Sar'dis, and unto Phil-a-del'phi-a, and unto La-od-i-ce'a.

12 And I turned to see the voice that spake with me. And being turned, I saw seven golden candlesticks;

13 And in the midst of the seven candlesticks *one* like unto the Son of man, clothed with a garment down to the foot, and girt about the paps with a golden girdle.

14 His head and *his* hairs *were* white like wool, as white as snow; and his eyes *were* as a flame of fire;

15 And his feet like unto fine brass, as if they burned in a furnace; and his voice as the sound of many waters,

16 And he had in his right hand seven stars: and out of his mouth went a sharp twoedged sword: and his countenance *was* as the sun shineth in his strength.

17 And when I saw him, I fell at his feet as dead. And he laid his right hand upon me, saying unto me, Fear not; I am the first and the last:

18 *I am* he that liveth, and was dead; and, behold, I am alive for evermore, Amen; and have the keys of hell and of death.

19 Write the things which thou hast seen,

and the things which are, and the things which
shall be hereafter;
20 The mystery of the seven stars which thou
sawest in my right hand, and the seven golden
candlesticks. The seven stars are the angels of
the seven churches: and the seven candlesticks
which thou sawest are the seven churches.

2

UNTO the angel of the church of Eph'e-sus
write; These things saith he that holdeth
the seven stars in his right hand, who walketh
in the midst of the seven golden candlesticks;
2 I know thy works, and thy labour, and thy
patience, and how thou canst not bear them
which are evil: and thou hast tried them which
say they are apostles, and are not, and hast
found them liars:
3 And hast borne, and hast patience, and for
my name's sake hast laboured, and hast not
fainted.
4 Nevertheless I have *somewhat* against
thee, because thou hast left thy first love.
5 Remember therefore from whence thou art
fallen, and repent, and do the first works; or
else I will come unto thee quickly, and will remove thy candlestick out of his place, except
thou repent.
6 But this thou hast, that thou hatest the
deeds of the Nic-o-la'i-tanes, which I also hate.
7 He that hath an ear, let him hear what the
Spirit saith unto the churches; To him that overcometh will I give to eat of the tree of life,
which is in the midst of the paradise of God.
8 And unto the angel of the church in Smyr'-
na write; These things saith the first and the
last, which was dead, and is alive;
9 I know thy works, and tribulation, and poverty, (but thou art rich) and *I know* the blasphemy of them which say they are Jews, and
are not, but *are* the synagogue of Sa'tan.
10 Fear none of those things which thou
shalt suffer: behold, the devil shall cast *some* of
you into prison, that ye may be tried; and ye
shall have tribulation ten days: be thou faithful
unto death, and I will give thee a crown of life.
11 He that hath an ear, let him hear what the
Spirit saith unto the churches; He that overcometh shall not be hurt of the second death.
12 And to the angel of the church in Per'ga-
mos write; These things saith he which hath the
sharp sword with two edges;
13 I know thy works, and where thou dwellest, *even* where Sa'tan's seat *is*: and thou holdest fast my name, and hast not denied my faith,
even in those days wherein An'ti-pas *was* my
faithful martyr, who was slain among you,
where Sa'tan dwelleth.
14 But I have a few things against thee, because thou hast there them that hold the doctrine of Ba'laam, who taught Ba'lac to cast a
stumbling block before the children of Is'ra-el,
to eat things sacrificed unto idols, and to commit fornication.
15 So hast thou also them that hold the doctrine of the Nic-o-la'i-tanes, which thing I hate.
16 Repent; or else I will come unto thee
quickly, and will fight against them with the
sword of my mouth.
17 He that hath an ear, let him hear what the
Spirit saith unto the churches; To him that overcometh will I give to eat of the hidden manna,
and will give him a white stone, and in the stone
a new name written, which no man knoweth
saving he that receiveth *it*.
18 And unto the angel of the church in Thy-a-
ti'ra write; These things saith the Son of God,
who hath his eyes like unto a flame of fire, and
his feet *are* like fine brass;
19 I know thy works, and charity, and service, and faith, and thy patience, and thy works;
and the last *to be* more than the first.
20 Notwithstanding I have a few things
against thee, because thou sufferest that
woman Jez'e-bel, which calleth herself a prophetess, to teach and to seduce my servants to
commit fornication, and to eat things sacrificed
unto idols.
21 And I gave her space to repent of her fornication; and she repented not.
22 Behold, I will cast her into a bed, and
them that commit adultery with her into great
tribulation, except they repent of their deeds.
23 And I will kill her children with death; and
all the churches shall know that I am he which
searcheth the reins and hearts: and I will give
unto every one of you according to your works.
24 But unto you I say, and unto the rest in
Thy-a-ti'ra, as many as have not this doctrine,
and which have not known the depths of Sa'tan,
as they speak; I will put upon you none other
burden.
25 But that which ye have *already* hold fast
till I come.
26 And he that overcometh, and keepeth my
works unto the end, to him will I give power
over the nations:
27 And he shall rule them with a rod of iron;
as the vessels of a potter shall they be broken to
shivers: even as I received of my Father.
28 And I will give him the morning star.
29 He that hath an ear, let him hear what the
Spirit saith unto the churches.

3

AND unto the angel of the church in Sar'-
dis write; These things saith he that hath
the seven Spirits of God, and the seven stars; I
know thy works, that thou hast a name, that
thou livest, and art dead.
2 Be watchful, and strengthen the things
which remain, that are ready to die: for I have
not found thy works perfect before God.
3 Remember therefore how thou hast received and heard, and hold fast, and repent. If
therefore thou shalt not watch, I will come on
thee as a thief, and thou shalt not know what
hour I will come upon thee.
4 Thou hast a few names even in Sar'dis
which have not defiled their garments; and they
shall walk with me in white: for they are worthy.
5 He that overcometh, the same shall be
clothed in white raiment; and I will not blot out
his name out of the book of life, but I will confess his name before my Father, and before his
angels.
6 He that hath an ear, let him hear what the
Spirit saith unto the churches.
7 And to the angel of the church in Phil-a-del'-
phi-a write; These things saith he that is holy, he
that is true, he that hath the key of Da'vid, he
that openeth, and no man shutteth; and shutteth,
and no man openeth;
8 I know thy works: behold, I have set before
thee an open door, and no man can shut it: for
thou hast a little strength, and hast kept my
word, and hast not denied my name.
9 Behold, I will make them of the synagogue
of Sa'tan, which say they are Jews, and are not,
but do lie; behold, I will make them to come and
worship before thy feet, and to know that I
have loved thee.
10 Because thou hast kept the word of my
patience, I also will keep thee from the hour of

temptation, which shall come upon all the world, to try them that dwell upon the earth.

11 Behold, I come quickly: hold that fast which thou hast, that no man take thy crown.

12 Him that overcometh will I make a pillar in the temple of my God, and he shall go no more out: and I will write upon him the name of my God, and the name of the city of my God, *which is* new Je-ru'sa-lem, which cometh down out of heaven from my God: and *I will write upon him* my new name.

13 He that hath an ear, let him hear what the Spirit saith unto the churches.

14 And unto the angel of the church of the La-od-i-ce'ans write; These things saith the Amen, the faithful and true witness, the beginning of the creation of God;

15 I know thy works, that thou art neither cold nor hot: I would thou wert cold or hot.

16 So then because thou art lukewarm, and neither cold nor hot, I will spue thee out of my mouth.

17 Because thou sayest, I am rich, and increased with goods, and have need of nothing; and knowest not that thou art wretched, and miserable, and poor, and blind, and naked:

18 I counsel thee to buy of me gold tried in the fire, that thou mayest be rich; and white raiment, that thou mayest be clothed, and *that* the shame of thy nakedness do not appear; and anoint thine eyes with eyesalve, that thou mayest see.

19 As many as I love, I rebuke and chasten: be zealous therefore, and repent.

20 Behold, I stand at the door, and knock: if any man hear my voice, and open the door, I will come in to him, and will sup with him, and he with me.

21 To him that overcometh will I grant to sit with me in my throne, even as I also overcame, and am set down with my Father in his throne.

22 He that hath an ear, let him hear what the Spirit saith unto the churches.

4 AFTER this I looked, and, behold, a door *was* opened in heaven: and the first voice which I heard *was* as it were of a trumpet talking with me; which said, Come up hither, and I will shew thee things which must be hereafter.

2 And immediately I was in the spirit: and, behold, a throne was set in heaven, and *one* sat on the throne.

3 And he that sat was to look upon like a jasper and a sardine stone: and *there was* a rainbow round about the throne, in sight like unto an emerald.

4 And round about the throne *were* four and twenty seats: and upon the seats I saw four and twenty elders sitting, clothed in white raiment; and they had on their heads crowns of gold.

5 And out of the throne proceeded lightnings and thunderings and voices: and *there were* seven lamps of fire burning before the throne, which are the seven Spirits of God.

6 And before the throne *there was* a sea of glass like unto crystal: and in the midst of the throne, and round about the throne, *were* four beasts full of eyes before and behind.

7 And the first beast *was* like a lion, and the second beast like a calf, and the third beast had a face as a man, and the fourth beast *was* like a flying eagle.

8 And the four beasts had each of them six wings about *him;* and *they were* full of eyes within: and they rest not day and night, saying, Holy, holy, holy, Lord God Almighty, which was, and is, and is to come.

9 And when those beasts give glory and honour and thanks to him that sat on the throne, who liveth for ever and ever,

10 The four and twenty elders fall down before him that sat on the throne, and worship him that liveth for ever and ever, and cast their crowns before the throne, saying,

11 Thou art worthy, O Lord, to receive glory and honour and power: for thou hast created all things, and for thy pleasure they are and were created.

5 AND I saw in the right hand of him that sat on the throne a book written within and on the backside, sealed with seven seals.

2 And I saw a strong angel proclaiming with a loud voice, Who is worthy to open the book, and to loose the seals thereof?

3 And no man in heaven, nor in earth, neither under the earth, was able to open the book, neither to look thereon.

4 And I wept much, because no man was found worthy to open and to read the book, neither to look thereon.

5 And one of the elders saith unto me, Weep not: behold, the Lion of the tribe of Ju'da, the Root of Da'vid, hath prevailed to open the book, and to loose the seven seals thereof.

6 And I beheld, and, lo, in the midst of the throne, and of the four beasts, and in the midst of the elders, stood a Lamb as it had been slain, having seven horns and seven eyes, which are the seven Spirits of God sent forth into all the earth.

7 And he came and took the book out of the right hand of him that sat upon the throne.

8 And when he had taken the book, the four beasts and four *and* twenty elders fell down before the Lamb, having every one of them harps, and golden vials full of odours, which are the prayers of saints.

9 And they sung a new song, saying, Thou art worthy to take the book, and to open the seals thereof: for thou wast slain, and hast redeemed us to God by thy blood out of every kindred, and tongue, and people, and nation;

10 And hast made us unto our God kings and priests: and we shall reign on the earth.

11 And I beheld, and I heard the voice of many angels round about the throne and the beasts and the elders: and the number of them was ten thousand times ten thousand, and thousands of thousands;

12 Saying with a loud voice, Worthy is the Lamb that was slain to receive power, and riches, and wisdom, and strength, and honour, and glory, and blessing.

13 And every creature which is in heaven, and on the earth, and under the earth, and such as are in the sea, and all that are in them, heard I saying, Blessing, and honour, and glory, and power, *be* unto him that sitteth upon the throne, and unto the Lamb for ever and ever.

14 And the four beasts said, Amen. And the four *and* twenty elders fell down and worshipped him that liveth for ever and ever.

6 AND I saw when the Lamb opened one of the seals, and I heard, as it were the noise of thunder, one of the four beasts saying, Come and see.

2 And I saw, and behold a white horse: and he that sat on him had a bow; and a crown was given unto him: and he went forth conquering, and to conquer.

3 And when he had opened the second seal, I heard the second beast say, Come and see.

4 And there went out another horse *that was* red: and *power* was given to him that sat thereon to take peace from the earth, and that they should kill one another: and there was given unto him a great sword.

5 And when he had opened the third seal, I heard the third beast say, Come and see. And I beheld, and lo a black horse; and he that sat on him had a pair of balances in his hand.

6 And I heard a voice in the midst of the four beasts say, A measure of wheat for a penny, and three measures of barley for a penny; and *see* thou hurt not the oil and the wine.

7 And when he had opened the fourth seal, I heard the voice of the fourth beast say, Come and see.

8 And I looked, and behold a pale horse: and his name that sat on him was Death, and Hell followed with him. And power was given unto them over the fourth part of the earth, to kill with sword, and with hunger, and with death, and with the beasts of the earth.

9 And when he had opened the fifth seal, I saw under the altar the souls of them that were slain for the word of God, and for the testimony which they held:

10 And they cried with a loud voice, saying, How long, O Lord, holy and true, dost thou not judge and avenge our blood on them that dwell on the earth?

11 And white robes were given unto every one of them; and it was said unto them, that they should rest yet for a little season, until their fellowservants also and their brethren, that should be killed as they *were*, should be fulfilled.

12 And I beheld when he had opened the sixth seal, and, lo, there was a great earthquake; and the sun became black as sackcloth of hair, and the moon became as blood;

13 And the stars of heaven fell unto the earth, even as a fig tree casteth her untimely figs, when she is shaken of a mighty wind.

14 And the heaven departed as a scroll when it is rolled together; and every mountain and island were moved out of their places.

15 And the kings of the earth, and the great men, and the rich men, and the chief captains, and the mighty men, and every bondman, and every free man, hid themselves in the dens and in the rocks of the mountains;

16 And said to the mountains and rocks, Fall on us, and hide us from the face of him that sitteth on the throne, and from the wrath of the Lamb:

17 For the great day of his wrath is come; and who shall be able to stand?

7 AND after these things I saw four angels standing on the four corners of the earth, holding the four winds of the earth, that the wind should not blow on the earth, nor on the sea, nor on any tree.

2 And I saw another angel ascending from the east, having the seal of the living God: and he cried with a loud voice to the four angels, to whom it was given to hurt the earth and the sea,

3 Saying, Hurt not the earth, neither the sea, nor the trees, till we have sealed the servants of our God in their foreheads.

4 And I heard the number of them which were sealed: *and there were* sealed an hundred *and* forty *and* four thousand of all the tribes of the children of Is'ra-el.

5 Of the tribe of Ju'da *were* sealed twelve thousand. Of the tribe of Reu'ben *were* sealed twelve thousand. Of the tribe of Gad *were* sealed twelve thousand.

6 Of the tribe of A'ser *were* sealed twelve thousand. Of the tribe of Nep'tha-lim *were* sealed twelve thousand. Of the tribe of Ma-nas'-ses *were* sealed twelve thousand.

7 Of the tribe of Sim'e-on *were* sealed twelve thousand. Of the tribe of Le'vi *were* sealed twelve thousand. Of the tribe of Is'sa-char *were* sealed twelve thousand.

8 Of the tribe of Zab'u-lon *were* sealed twelve thousand. Of the tribe of Jo'seph *were* sealed twelve thousand. Of the tribe of Ben'ja-min *were* sealed twelve thousand.

9 After this I beheld, and, lo, a great multitude, which no man could number, of all nations, and kindreds, and people, and tongues, stood before the throne, and before the Lamb, clothed with white robes, and palms in their hands;

10 And cried with a loud voice, saying, Salvation to our God which sitteth upon the throne, and unto the Lamb.

11 And all the angels stood round about the throne, and *about* the elders and the four beasts, and fell before the throne on their faces, and worshipped God,

12 Saying, Amen: Blessing, and glory, and wisdom, and thanksgiving, and honour, and power, and might, *be* unto our God for ever and ever. Amen.

13 And one of the elders answered, saying unto me, What are these which are arrayed in white robes? and whence came they?

14 And I said unto him, Sir, thou knowest. And he said to me, These are they which came out of great tribulation, and have washed their robes, and made them white in the blood of the Lamb.

15 Therefore are they before the throne of God, and serve him day and night in his temple: and he that sitteth on the throne shall dwell among them.

16 They shall hunger no more, neither thirst any more; neither shall the sun light on them, nor any heat.

17 For the Lamb which is in the midst of the throne shall feed them, and shall lead them unto living fountains of waters: and God shall wipe away all tears from their eyes.

8 AND when he had opened the seventh seal, there was silence in heaven about the space of half an hour.

2 And I saw the seven angels which stood before God; and to them were given seven trumpets.

3 And another angel came and stood at the altar, having a golden censer; and there was given unto him much incense, that he should offer *it* with the prayers of all saints upon the golden altar which was before the throne.

4 And the smoke of the incense, *which came* with the prayers of the saints, ascended up before God out of the angel's hand.

5 And the angel took the censer, and filled it with fire of the altar, and cast *it* into the earth: and there were voices, and thunderings, and lightnings, and an earthquake.

6 And the seven angels which had the seven trumpets prepared themselves to sound.

7 The first angel sounded, and there followed hail and fire mingled with blood, and they were cast upon the earth: and the third part of trees was burnt up, and all green grass was burnt up.

8 And the second angel sounded, and as it were a great mountain burning with fire was

cast into the sea: and the third part of the sea
became blood;
9 And the third part of the creatures which
were in the sea, and had life, died; and the third
part of the ships were destroyed.
10 And the third angel sounded, and there
fell a great star from heaven, burning as it were
a lamp, and it fell upon the third part of the
rivers, and upon the fountains of waters;
11 And the name of the star is called Wormwood:
and the third part of the waters became
wormwood; and many men died of the waters,
because they were made bitter.
12 And the fourth angel sounded, and the
third part of the sun was smitten, and the third
part of the moon, and the third part of the stars;
so as the third part of them was darkened, and
the day shone not for a third part of it, and the
night likewise.
13 And I beheld, and heard an angel flying
through the midst of heaven, saying with a loud
voice, Woe, woe, woe, to the inhabiters of the
earth by reason of the other voices of the trumpet
of the three angels, which are yet to sound!

9 AND the fifth angel sounded, and I saw a
star fall from heaven unto the earth: and to
him was given the key of the bottomless pit.
2 And he opened the bottomless pit; and
there arose a smoke out of the pit, as the smoke
of a great furnace; and the sun and the air were
darkened by reason of the smoke of the pit.
3 And there came out of the smoke locusts
upon the earth: and unto them was given
power, as the scorpions of the earth have
power.
4 And it was commanded them that they
should not hurt the grass of the earth, neither
any green thing, neither any tree; but only those
men which have not the seal of God in their
foreheads.
5 And to them it was given that they should
not kill them, but that they should be tormented
five months: and their torment *was* as the torment
of a scorpion, when he striketh a man.
6 And in those days shall men seek death,
and shall not find it; and shall desire to die, and
death shall flee from them.
7 And the shapes of the locusts *were* like
unto horses prepared unto battle; and on their
heads *were* as it were crowns like gold, and
their faces *were* as the faces of men.
8 And they had hair as the hair of women,
and their teeth were as *the teeth* of lions.
9 And they had breastplates, as it were
breastplates of iron; and the sound of their
wings *was* as the sound of chariots of many
horses running to battle.
10 And they had tails like unto scorpions,
and there were stings in their tails: and their
power *was* to hurt men five months.
11 And they had a king over them, *which is*
the angel of the bottomless pit, whose name in
the He'brew tongue *is* A-bad'don, but in the
Greek tongue hath *his* name A-poll'yon.
12 One woe is past; *and*, behold, there come
two woes more hereafter.
13 And the sixth angel sounded, and I heard
a voice from the four horns of the golden altar
which is before God,
14 Saying to the sixth angel which had the
trumpet, Loose the four angels which are bound
in the great river Eu-phra'tes.
15 And the four angels were loosed, which
were prepared for an hour, and a day, and a
month, and a year, for to slay the third part of
men.
16 And the number of the army of the horsemen
were two hundred thousand thousand: and
I heard the number of them.
17 And thus I saw the horses in the vision,
and them that sat on them, having breastplates
of fire, and of jacinth, and brimstone: and the
heads of the horses *were* as the heads of lions;
and out of their mouths issued fire and smoke
and brimstone.
18 By these three was the third part of men
killed, by the fire, and by the smoke, and by the
brimstone, which issued out of their mouths.
19 For their power is in their mouth, and in
their tails: for their tails *were* like unto serpents,
and had heads, and with them they do hurt.
20 And the rest of the men which were not
killed by these plagues yet repented not of the
works of their hands, that they should not worship
devils, and idols of gold, and silver, and
brass, and stone, and of wood: which neither
can see, nor hear, nor walk:
21 Neither repented they of their murders,
nor of their sorceries, nor of their fornication,
nor of their thefts.

10 AND I saw another mighty angel come
down from heaven, clothed with a
cloud: and a rainbow *was* upon his head, and
his face *was* as it were the sun, and his feet as
pillars of fire:
2 And he had in his hand a little book open:
and he set his right foot upon the sea, and *his*
left *foot* on the earth,
3 And cried with a loud voice, as *when* a lion
roareth: and when he had cried, seven thunders
uttered their voices.
4 And when the seven thunders had uttered
their voices, I was about to write: and I heard a
voice from heaven saying unto me, Seal up
those things which the seven thunders uttered,
and write them not.
5 And the angel which I saw stand upon the
sea and upon the earth lifted up his hand to
heaven,
6 And sware by him that liveth for ever and
ever, who created heaven, and the things that
therein are, and the earth, and the things that
therein are, and the sea, and the things which
are therein, that there should be time no longer:
7 But in the days of the voice of the seventh
angel, when he shall begin to sound, the mystery
of God should be finished, as he hath declared
to his servants the prophets.
8 And the voice which I heard from heaven
spake unto me again, and said, Go *and* take the
little book which is open in the hand of the angel
which standeth upon the sea and upon the
earth.
9 And I went unto the angel, and said unto
him, Give me the little book. And he said unto
me, Take *it*, and eat it up; and it shall make thy
belly bitter, but it shall be in thy mouth sweet
as honey.
10 And I took the little book out of the angel's
hand, and ate it up; and it was in my
mouth sweet as honey: and as soon as I had
eaten it, my belly was bitter.
11 And he said unto me, Thou must prophesy
again before many peoples, and nations, and
tongues, and kings.

11 AND there was given me a reed like
unto a rod: and the angel stood, saying,
Rise, and measure the temple of God, and the
altar, and them that worship therein.
2 But the court which is without the temple
leave out, and measure it not; for it is given

unto the Gen'tiles: and the holy city shall they
tread under foot forty *and* two months.
3 And I will give *power* unto my two witnesses,
and they shall prophesy a thousand two
hundred *and* threescore days, clothed in sackcloth.
4 These are the two olive trees, and the two
candlesticks standing before the God of the
earth.
5 And if any man will hurt them, fire proceedeth
out of their mouth, and devoureth their
enemies: and if any man will hurt them, he
must in this manner be killed.
6 These have power to shut heaven, that it
rain not in the days of their prophecy: and have
power over waters to turn them to blood, and to
smite the earth with all plagues, as often as
they will.
7 And when they shall have finished their
testimony, the beast that ascendeth out of the
bottomless pit shall make war against them,
and shall overcome them, and kill them.
8 And their dead bodies *shall lie* in the street
of the great city, which spiritually is called
Sod'om and E'gypt, where also our Lord was
crucified.
9 And they of the people and kindreds and
tongues and nations shall see their dead bodies
three days and an half, and shall not suffer their
dead bodies to be put in graves.
10 And they that dwell upon the earth shall
rejoice over them, and make merry, and shall
send gifts one to another; because these two
prophets tormented them that dwelt on the
earth.
11 And after three days and an half the Spirit
of life from God entered into them, and they
stood upon their feet; and great fear fell upon
them which saw them.
12 And they heard a great voice from heaven
saying unto them, Come up hither. And they
ascended up to heaven in a cloud; and their enemies
beheld them.
13 And the same hour was there a great
earthquake, and the tenth part of the city fell,
and in the earthquake were slain of men seven
thousand: and the remnant were affrighted, and
gave glory to the God of heaven.
14 The second woe is past; *and*, behold, the
third woe cometh quickly.
15 And the seventh angel sounded; and there
were great voices in heaven, saying, The kingdoms
of this world are become *the kingdoms* of
our Lord, and of his Christ; and he shall reign
for ever and ever.
16 And the four and twenty elders, which sat
before God on their seats, fell upon their faces,
and worshipped God,
17 Saying, We give thee thanks, O Lord God
Almighty, which art, and wast, and art to come;
because thou hast taken to thee thy great
power, and hast reigned.
18 And the nations were angry, and thy
wrath is come, and the time of the dead, that
they should be judged, and that thou shouldest
give reward unto thy servants the prophets, and
to the saints, and them that fear thy name,
small and great; and shouldest destroy them
which destroy the earth.
19 And the temple of God was opened in
heaven, and there was seen in his temple the
ark of his testament; and there were lightnings,
and voices, and thunderings, and an earthquake,
and great hail.

12 AND there appeared a great wonder in
heaven; a woman clothed with the sun,
and the moon under her feet, and upon her head
a crown of twelve stars:
2 And she being with child cried, travailing
in birth, and pained to be delivered.
3 And there appeared another wonder in
heaven; and behold a great red dragon, having
seven heads and ten horns, and seven crowns
upon his heads.
4 And his tail drew the third part of the stars
of heaven, and did cast them to the earth: and
the dragon stood before the woman which was
ready to be delivered, for to devour her child as
soon as it was born.
5 And she brought forth a man child, who
was to rule all nations with a rod of iron: and
her child was caught up unto God, and *to* his
throne.
6 And the woman fled into the wilderness,
where she hath a place prepared of God, that
they should feed her there a thousand two hundred
and threescore days.
7 And there was war in heaven: Mi'chael and
his angels fought against the dragon; and the
dragon fought and his angels,
8 And prevailed not; neither was their place
found any more in heaven.
9 And the great dragon was cast out, that old
serpent, called the Dev'il, and Sa'tan, which
deceiveth the whole world: he was cast out into
the earth, and his angels were cast out with
him.
10 And I heard a loud voice saying in heaven,
Now is come salvation, and strength, and the
kingdom of our God, and the power of his
Christ: for the accuser of our brethren is cast
down, which accused them before our God day
and night.
11 And they overcame him by the blood of
the Lamb, and by the word of their testimony;
and they loved not their lives unto the death.
12 Therefore rejoice, *ye* heavens, and ye that
dwell in them. Woe to the inhabiters of the
earth and of the sea! for the devil is come down
unto you, having great wrath, because he knoweth
that he hath but a short time.
13 And when the dragon saw that he was
cast unto the earth, he persecuted the woman
which brought forth the man *child*.
14 And to the woman were given two wings
of a great eagle, that she might fly into the wilderness,
into her place, where she is nourished
for a time, and times, and half a time, from the
face of the serpent.
15 And the serpent cast out of his mouth water
as a flood after the woman, that he might
cause her to be carried away of the flood.
16 And the earth helped the woman, and the
earth opened her mouth, and swallowed up the
flood which the dragon cast out of his mouth.
17 And the dragon was wroth with the
woman, and went to make war with the remnant
of her seed, which keep the commandments
of God, and have the testimony of Je'sus
Christ.

13 AND I stood upon the sand of the sea,
and saw a beast rise up out of the sea,
having seven heads and ten horns, and upon his
horns ten crowns, and upon his heads the name
of blasphemy.
2 And the beast which I saw was like unto a
leopard, and his feet were as *the feet* of a bear,
and his mouth as the mouth of a lion: and the
dragon gave him his power, and his seat, and
great authority.
3 And I saw one of his heads as it were
wounded to death; and his deadly wound was

healed: and all the world wondered after the
beast.
4 And they worshipped the dragon which
gave power unto the beast: and they worshipped the beast, saying, Who *is* like unto the
beast? who is able to make war with him?
5 And there was given unto him a mouth
speaking great things and blasphemies; and
power was given unto him to continue forty
and two months.
6 And he opened his mouth in blasphemy
against God, to blaspheme his name, and his
tabernacle, and them that dwell in heaven.
7 And it was given unto him to make war
with the saints, and to overcome them: and
power was given him over all kindreds, and
tongues, and nations.
8 And all that dwell upon the earth shall worship him, whose names are not written in the
book of life of the Lamb slain from the foundation of the world.
9 If any man have an ear, let him hear.
10 He that leadeth into captivity shall go into
captivity: he that killeth with the sword must be
killed with the sword. Here is the patience and
the faith of the saints.
11 And I beheld another beast coming up out
of the earth; and he had two horns like a lamb,
and he spake as a dragon.
12 And he exerciseth all the power of the
first beast before him, and causeth the earth
and them which dwell therein to worship the
first beast, whose deadly wound was healed.
13 And he doeth great wonders, so that he
maketh fire come down from heaven on the
earth in the sight of men,
14 And deceiveth them that dwell on the
earth, by *the means of* those miracles which he
had power to do in the sight of the beast; saying
to them that dwell on the earth, that they
should make an image to the beast, which had
the wound by a sword, and did live.
15 And he had power to give life unto the
image of the beast, that the image of the beast
should both speak, and cause that as many as
would not worship the image of the beast
should be killed.
16 And he causeth all, both small and great,
rich and poor, free and bond, to receive a mark
in their right hand, or in their foreheads:
17 And that no man might buy or sell, save
he that had the mark, or the name of the beast,
or the number of his name.
18 Here is wisdom. Let him that hath understanding count the number of the beast: for it is
the number of a man; and his number *is* Six
hundred threescore *and* six.

14 AND I looked, and, lo, a Lamb stood on
the mount Si′on, and with him an hundred forty *and* four thousand, having his Father's name written in their foreheads.
2 And I heard a voice from heaven, as the
voice of many waters, and as the voice of a
great thunder: and I heard the voice of harpers
harping with their harps:
3 And they sung as it were a new song before
the throne, and before the four beasts, and the
elders: and no man could learn that song but
the hundred *and* forty *and* four thousand,
which were redeemed from the earth.
4 These are they which were not defiled with
women; for they are virgins. These are they
which follow the Lamb whithersoever he goeth.
These were redeemed from among men, *being*
the firstfruits unto God and to the Lamb.
5 And in their mouth was found no guile: for
they are without fault before the throne of God.
6 And I saw another angel fly in the midst of
heaven, having the everlasting gospel to preach
unto them that dwell on the earth, and to every
nation, and kindred, and tongue, and people,
7 Saying with a loud voice, Fear God, and
give glory to him; for the hour of his judgment
is come: and worship him that made heaven,
and earth, and the sea, and the fountains of waters.
8 And there followed another angel, saying,
Bab′y-lon is fallen, is fallen, that great city, because she made all nations drink of the wine of
the wrath of her fornication.
9 And the third angel followed them, saying
with a loud voice, If any man worship the beast
and his image, and receive *his* mark in his forehead, or in his hand,
10 The same shall drink of the wine of the
wrath of God, which is poured out without mixture into the cup of his indignation; and he shall
be tormented with fire and brimstone in the
presence of the holy angels, and in the presence
of the Lamb:
11 And the smoke of their torment ascendeth
up for ever and ever: and they have no rest day
nor night, who worship the beast and his image,
and whosoever receiveth the mark of his name.
12 Here is the patience of the saints: here *are*
they that keep the commandments of God, and
the faith of Je′sus.
13 And I heard the voice from heaven saying
unto me, Write, Blessed *are* the dead which die
in the Lord from henceforth: Yea, saith the
Spirit, that they may rest from their labours;
and their works do follow them.
14 And I looked, and behold a white cloud,
and upon the cloud *one* sat like unto the Son of
man, having on his head a golden crown, and in
his hand a sharp sickle.
15 And another angel came out of the temple, crying with a loud voice to him that sat on
the cloud, Thrust in thy sickle, and reap: for the
time is come for thee to reap; for the harvest of
the earth is ripe.
16 And he that sat on the cloud thrust in his
sickle on the earth; and the earth was reaped.
17 And another angel came out of the temple
which is in heaven, he also having a sharp
sickle.
18 And another angel came out from the altar, which had power over fire; and cried with a
loud cry to him that had the sharp sickle, saying, Thrust in thy sharp sickle, and gather the
clusters of the vine of the earth; for her grapes
are fully ripe.
19 And the angel thrust in his sickle into the
earth, and gathered the vine of the earth, and
cast *it* into the great winepress of the wrath of
God.
20 And the winepress was trodden without
the city, and blood came out of the winepress,
even unto the horse bridles, by the space of a
thousand *and* six hundred furlongs.

15 AND I saw another sign in heaven,
great and marvellous, seven angels having the seven last plagues; for in them is filled
up the wrath of God.
2 And I saw as it were a sea of glass mingled
with fire: and them that had gotten the victory
over the beast, and over his image, and over his
mark, *and* over the number of his name, stand
on the sea of glass, having the harps of God.
3 And they sing the song of Mo′ses the servant of God, and the song of the Lamb, saying,

Great and marvellous *are* thy works, Lord God
Almighty; just and true *are* thy ways, thou King
of saints.
4 Who shall not fear thee, O Lord, and glorify
thy name? for *thou* only *art* holy: for all nations
shall come and worship before thee; for thy
judgments are made manifest.
5 And after that I looked, and, behold, the
temple of the tabernacle of the testimony in
heaven was opened:
6 And the seven angels came out of the temple, having the seven plagues, clothed in pure
and white linen, and having their breasts girded
with golden girdles.
7 And one of the four beasts gave unto the
seven angels seven golden vials full of the
wrath of God, who liveth for ever and ever.
8 And the temple was filled with smoke from
the glory of God, and from his power; and no
man was able to enter into the temple, till the
seven plagues of the seven angels were fulfilled.

16 AND I heard a great voice out of the
temple saying to the seven angels, Go
your ways, and pour out the vials of the wrath
of God upon the earth.
2 And the first went, and poured out his vial
upon the earth; and there fell a noisome and
grievous sore upon the men which had the
mark of the beast, and *upon* them which worshipped his image.
3 And the second angel poured out his vial
upon the sea; and it became as the blood of a
dead *man:* and every living soul died in the sea.
4 And the third angel poured out his vial
upon the rivers and fountains of waters; and
they became blood.
5 And I heard the angel of the waters say,
Thou art righteous, O Lord, which art, and
wast, and shalt be, because thou hast judged
thus.
6 For they have shed the blood of saints and
prophets, and thou hast given them blood to
drink; for they are worthy.
7 And I heard another out of the altar say,
Even so, Lord God Almighty, true and righteous
are thy judgments.
8 And the fourth angel poured out his vial
upon the sun; and power was given unto him to
scorch men with fire.
9 And men were scorched with great heat,
and blasphemed the name of God, which hath
power over these plagues: and they repented
not to give him glory.
10 And the fifth angel poured out his vial
upon the seat of the beast; and his kingdom was
full of darkness; and they gnawed their tongues
for pain,
11 And blasphemed the God of heaven because of their pains and their sores, and repented not of their deeds.
12 And the sixth angel poured out his vial
upon the great river Eu-phra'tes; and the water
thereof was dried up, that the way of the kings
of the east might be prepared.
13 And I saw three unclean spirits like frogs
come out of the mouth of the dragon, and out of
the mouth of the beast, and out of the mouth of
the false prophet.
14 For they are the spirits of devils, working
miracles, *which* go forth unto the kings of the
earth and of the whole world, to gather them to
the battle of that great day of God Almighty.
15 Behold, I come as a thief. Blessed *is* he
that watcheth, and keepeth his garments, lest
he walk naked, and they see his shame.
16 And he gathered them together into a
place called in the He'brew tongue Ar-ma-ged'-
don.
17 And the seventh angel poured out his vial
into the air; and there came a great voice out of
the temple of heaven, from the throne, saying,
It is done.
18 And there were voices, and thunders, and
lightnings; and there was a great earthquake,
such as was not since men were upon the earth,
so mighty an earthquake, *and* so great.
19 And the great city was divided into three
parts, and the cities of the nations fell: and
great Bab'y-lon came in remembrance before
God, to give unto her the cup of the wine of the
fierceness of his wrath.
20 And every island fled away, and the
mountains were not found.
21 And there fell upon men a great hail out of
heaven, *every stone* about the weight of a talent: and men blasphemed God because of the
plague of the hail; for the plague thereof was
exceeding great.

17 AND there came one of the seven angels which had the seven vials, and
talked with me, saying unto me, Come hither; I
will shew unto thee the judgment of the great
whore that sitteth upon many waters:
2 With whom the kings of the earth have
committed fornication, and the inhabitants of
the earth have been made drunk with the wine
of her fornication.
3 So he carried me away in the spirit into the
wilderness: and I saw a woman sit upon a scarlet coloured beast, full of names of blasphemy,
having seven heads and ten horns.
4 And the woman was arrayed in purple and
scarlet colour, and decked with gold and precious stones and pearls, having a golden cup in
her hand full of abominations and filthiness of
her fornication:
5 And upon her forehead *was* a name written, MYSTERY, BAB'Y-LON THE GREAT,
THE MOTHER OF HARLOTS AND ABOMI-
NATIONS OF THE EARTH.
6 And I saw the woman drunken with the
blood of the saints, and with the blood of the
martyrs of Je'sus: and when I saw her, I wondered with great admiration.
7 And the angel said unto me, Wherefore
didst thou marvel? I will tell thee the mystery of
the woman, and of the beast that carrieth her,
which hath the seven heads and ten horns.
8 The beast that thou sawest was, and is not;
and shall ascend out of the bottomless pit, and
go into perdition: and they that dwell on the
earth shall wonder, whose names were not
written in the book of life from the foundation
of the world, when they behold the beast that
was, and is not, and yet is.
9 And here *is* the mind which hath wisdom.
The seven heads are seven mountains, on which
the woman sitteth.
10 And there are seven kings: five are fallen,
and one is, *and* the other is not yet come; and
when he cometh, he must continue a short
space.
11 And the beast that was, and is not, even
he is the eighth, and is of the seven, and goeth
into perdition.
12 And the ten horns which thou sawest are
ten kings, which have received no kingdom as
yet; but receive power as kings one hour with
the beast.
13 These have one mind, and shall give their
power and strength unto the beast.
14 These shall make war with the Lamb, and

the Lamb shall overcome them: for he is Lord of
lords, and King of kings: and they that are with
him *are* called, and chosen, and faithful.
15 And he saith unto me, The waters which
thou sawest, where the whore sitteth, are peoples, and multitudes, and nations, and tongues.
16 And the ten horns which thou sawest
upon the beast, these shall hate the whore, and
shall make her desolate and naked, and shall
eat her flesh, and burn her with fire.
17 For God hath put in their hearts to fulfil
his will, and to agree, and give their kingdom
unto the beast, until the words of God shall be
fulfilled.
18 And the woman which thou sawest is that
great city, which reigneth over the kings of the
earth.

18 AND after these things I saw another
angel come down from heaven, having
great power and the earth was lightened with
his glory.
2 And he cried mightily with a strong voice,
saying, Bab'y-lon the great is fallen, is fallen,
and is become the habitation of devils, and the
hold of every foul spirit, and a cage of every
unclean and hateful bird.
3 For all nations have drunk of the wine of
the wrath of her fornication, and the kings of
the earth have committed fornication with her,
and the merchants of the earth are waxed rich
through the abundance of her delicacies.
4 And I heard another voice from heaven,
saying, Come out of her, my people, that ye be
not partakers of her sins, and that ye receive
not of her plagues.
5 For her sins have reached unto heaven, and
God hath remembered her iniquities.
6 Reward her even as she rewarded you, and
double unto her double according to her works:
in the cup which she hath filled fill to her double.
7 How much she hath glorified herself, and
lived deliciously, so much torment and sorrow
give her: for she saith in her heart, I sit a queen,
and am no widow, and shall see no sorrow.
8 Therefore shall her plagues come in one
day, death, and mourning, and famine; and she
shall be utterly burned with fire: for strong *is*
the Lord God who judgeth her.
9 And the kings of the earth, who have committed fornication and lived deliciously with
her, shall bewail her, and lament for her, when
they shall see the smoke of her burning,
10 Standing afar off for the fear of her torment, saying, Alas, alas that great city Bab'y-
lon, that mighty city! for in one hour is thy judgment come.
11 And the merchants of the earth shall weep
and mourn over her; for no man buyeth their
merchandise any more:
12 The merchandise of gold, and silver, and
precious stones, and of pearls, and fine linen,
and purple, and silk, and scarlet, and all thyine
wood, and all manner vessels of ivory, and all
manner vessels of most precious wood, and of
brass, and iron, and marble,
13 And cinnamon, and odours, and ointments, and frankincense, and wine, and oil, and
fine flour, and wheat, and beasts, and sheep,
and horses, and chariots, and slaves, and souls
of men.
14 And the fruits that thy soul lusted after
are departed from thee, and all things which
were dainty and goodly are departed from thee,
and thou shalt find them no more at all.
15 The merchants of these things, which
were made rich by her, shall stand afar off for
the fear of her torment, weeping and wailing,
16 And saying, Alas, alas that great city, that
was clothed in fine linen, and purple, and scarlet, and decked with gold, and precious stones,
and pearls!
17 For in one hour so great riches is come to
nought. And every shipmaster, and all the company in ships, and sailors, and as many as trade
by sea, stood afar off,
18 And cried when they saw the smoke of
her burning, saying, What *city is* like unto this
great city!
19 And they cast dust on their heads, and
cried, weeping and wailing, saying, Alas, alas
that great city, wherein were made rich all that
had ships in the sea by reason of her costliness!
for in one hour is she made desolate.
20 Rejoice over her, *thou* heaven, and *ye* holy
apostles and prophets; for God hath avenged
you on her.
21 And a mighty angel took up a stone like a
great millstone, and cast *it* into the sea, saying,
Thus with violence shall that great city Bab'y-
lon be thrown down, and shall be found no
more at all.
22 And the voice of harpers, and musicians,
and of pipers, and trumpeters, shall be heard no
more at all in thee; and no craftsman, of whatsoever craft *he be*, shall be found any more in
thee; and the sound of a millstone shall be
heard no more at all in thee;
23 And the light of a candle shall shine no
more at all in thee; and the voice of the bridegroom and of the bride shall be heard no more
at all in thee: for thy merchants were the great
men of the earth; for by thy sorceries were all
nations deceived.
24 And in her was found the blood of prophets, and of saints, and of all that were slain
upon the earth.

19 AND after these things I heard a great
voice of much people in heaven, saying,
Al-le-lu'ia; Salvation, and glory, and honour,
and power, unto the Lord our God:
2 For true and righteous *are* his judgments:
for he hath judged the great whore, which did
corrupt the earth with her fornication, and hath
avenged the blood of his servants at her hand.
3 And again they said, Al-le-lu'ia. And her
smoke rose up for ever and ever.
4 And the four and twenty elders and the
four beasts fell down and worshipped God that
sat on the throne, saying, Amen; Al-le-lu'ia.
5 And a voice came out of the throne, saying,
Praise our God, all ye his servants, and ye that
fear him, both small and great.
6 And I heard as it were the voice of a great
multitude, and as the voice of many waters, and
as the voice of mighty thunderings, saying, Al-
le-luia: for the Lord God omnipotent reigneth.
7 Let us be glad and rejoice, and give honour
to him: for the marriage of the Lamb is come,
and his wife hath made herself ready.
8 And to her was granted that she should be
arrayed in fine linen, clean and white: for the
fine linen is the righteousness of saints.
9 And he saith unto me, Write, Blessed *are*
they which are called unto the marriage supper
of the Lamb. And he saith unto me, These are
the true sayings of God.
10 And I fell at his feet to worship him. And
he said unto me, See *thou do it* not: I am thy
fellowservant, and of thy brethren that have the
testimony of Je'sus: worship God: for the testimony of Je'sus is the spirit of prophecy.

11 And I saw heaven opened, and behold a white horse; and he that sat upon him *was* called Faithful and True, and in righteousness he doth judge and make war.

12 His eyes *were* as a flame of fire, and on his head *were* many crowns; and he had a name written, that no man knew, but he himself.

13 And he *was* clothed with a vesture dipped in blood: and his name is called The Word of God.

14 And the armies *which were* in heaven followed him upon white horses, clothed in fine linen, white and clean.

15 And out of his mouth goeth a sharp sword, that with it he should smite the nations: and he shall rule them with a rod of iron: and he treadeth the winepress of the fierceness and wrath of Almighty God.

16 And he hath on *his* vesture and on his thigh a name written, KING OF KINGS, AND LORD OF LORDS.

17 And I saw an angel standing in the sun; and he cried with a loud voice, saying to all the fowls that fly in the midst of heaven, Come and gather yourselves together unto the supper of the great God;

18 That ye may eat the flesh of kings, and the flesh of captains, and the flesh of mighty men, and the flesh of horses, and of them that sit on them, and the flesh of all *men, both* free and bond, both small and great.

19 And I saw the beast, and the kings of the earth, and their armies, gathered together to make war against him that sat on the horse, and against his army.

20 And the beast was taken, and with him the false prophet that wrought miracles before him with which he deceived them that had received the mark of the beast, and them that worshipped his image. These both were cast alive into a lake of fire burning with brimstone.

21 And the remnant were slain with the sword of him that sat upon the horse, which *sword* proceeded out of his mouth: and all the fowls were filled with their flesh.

20

AND I saw an angel come down from heaven, having the key of the bottomless pit and a great chain in his hand.

2 And he laid hold on the dragon, that old serpent, which is the Dev'il, and Sa'tan, and bound him a thousand years,

3 And cast him into the bottomless pit, and shut him up, and set a seal upon him, that he should deceive the nations no more, till the thousand years should be fulfilled: and after that he must be loosed a little season.

4 And I saw thrones, and they sat upon them, and judgment was given unto them: and *I saw* the souls of them that were beheaded for the witness of Je'sus, and for the word of God, and which had not worshipped the beast, neither his image, neither had received *his* mark upon their foreheads, or in their hands; and they lived and reigned with Christ a thousand years.

5 But the rest of the dead lived not again until the thousand years were finished. This *is* the first resurrection.

6 Blessed and holy *is* he that hath part in the first resurrection: on such the second death hath no power, but they shall be priests of God and of Christ, and shall reign with him a thousand years.

7 And when the thousand years are expired, Sa'tan shall be loosed out of his prison,

8 And shall go out to deceive the nations which are in the four quarters of the earth, Gog and Ma'gog, to gather them together to battle: the number of whom *is* as the sand of the sea.

9 And they went up on the breadth of the earth, and compassed the camp of the saints about, and the beloved city: and fire came down from God out of heaven and devoured them.

10 And the devil that deceived them was cast into the lake of fire and brimstone, where the beast and the false prophet *are,* and shall be tormented day and night for ever and ever.

11 And I saw a great white throne, and him that sat on it, from whose face the earth and the heaven fled away; and there was found no place for them.

12 And I saw the dead, small and great, stand before God; and the books were opened: and another book was opened, which is *the book* of life: and the dead were judged out of those things which were written in the books, according to their works.

13 And the sea gave up the dead which were in it; and death and hell delivered up the dead which were in them: and they were judged every man according to their works.

14 And death and hell were cast into the lake of fire. This is the second death.

15 And whosoever was not found written in the book of life was cast into the lake of fire.

21

AND I saw a new heaven and a new earth: for the first heaven and the first earth were passed away; and there was no more sea.

2 And I John saw the holy city, new Je-ru'salem, coming down from God out of heaven, prepared as a bride adorned for her husband.

3 And I heard a great voice out of heaven saying, Behold, the tabernacle of God *is* with men, and he will dwell with them, and they shall be his people, and God himself shall be with them, *and be* their God.

4 And God shall wipe away all tears from their eyes; and there shall be no more death, neither sorrow, nor crying, neither shall there be any more pain: for the former things are passed away.

5 And he that sat upon the throne said, Behold, I make all things new. And he said unto me, Write: for these words are true and faithful.

6 And he said unto me, It is done. I am Al'pha and O'me-ga, the beginning and the end. I will give unto him that is athirst of the fountain of the water of life freely.

7 He that overcometh shall inherit all things; and I will be his God, and he shall be my son.

8 But the fearful, and unbelieving, and the abominable, and murderers, and whoremongers, and sorcerers, and idolaters, and all liars, shall have their part in the lake which burneth with fire and brimstone: which is the second death.

9 And there came unto me one of the seven angels which had the seven vials full of the seven last plagues, and talked with me, saying, Come hither, I will shew thee the bride, the Lamb's wife.

10 And he carried me away in the spirit to a great and high mountain, and shewed me that great city, the holy Je-ru'sa-lem, descending out of heaven from God,

11 Having the glory of God: and her light *was* like unto a stone most precious, even like a jasper stone, clear as crystal;

12 And had a wall great and high, *and* had twelve gates, and at the gates twelve angels, and names written thereon, which are *the*

names of the twelve tribes of the children of
Is'ra-el:
13 On the east three gates; on the north three
gates; on the south three gates; and on the west
three gates.
14 And the wall of the city had twelve foundations, and in them the names of the twelve
apostles of the Lamb.
15 And he that talked with me had a golden
reed to measure the city, and the gates thereof,
and the wall thereof.
16 And the city lieth foursquare, and the
length is as large as the breadth: and he measured the city with the reed, twelve thousand
furlongs. The length and the breadth and the
height of it are equal.
17 And he measured the wall thereof, an
hundred *and* forty *and* four cubits, *according to*
the measure of a man, that is, of the angel.
18 And the building of the wall of it was *of*
jasper: and the city *was* pure gold, like unto
clear glass.
19 And the foundations of the wall of the city
were garnished with all manner of precious
stones. The first foundation *was* jasper; the second, sapphire; the third, a chalcedony; the
fourth, an emerald;
20 The fifth, sardonyx; the sixth, sardius; the
seventh, chrysolyte; the eighth, beryl; the ninth,
a topaz; the tenth, a chrysoprasus; the eleventh,
a jacinth; the twelfth, an amethyst.
21 And the twelve gates *were* twleve pearls;
every several gate was of one pearl: and the
street of the city *was* pure gold, as it were
transparent glass.
22 And I saw no temple therein: for the Lord
God Almighty and the Lamb are the temple of
it.
23 And the city had no need of the sun, neither of the moon, to shine in it: for the glory of
God did lighten it, and the Lamb *is* the light
thereof.
24 And the nations of them which are saved
shall walk in the light of it: and the kings of the
earth do bring their glory and honour into it.
25 And the gates of it shall not be shut at all
by day: for there shall be no night there.
26 And they shall bring the glory and honour
of the nations into it.
27 And there shall in no wise enter into it any
thing that defileth, neither *whatsoever* worketh
abomination, or *maketh* a lie: but they which
are written in the Lamb's book of life.

22 AND he shewed me a pure river of water of life, clear as crystal, proceeding
out of the throne of God and of the Lamb.
2 In the midst of the street of it, and on either
side of the river, *was there* the tree of life,
which bare twelve *manner of* fruits, *and*
yielded her fruit every month: and the leaves of
the tree *were* for the healing of the nations.
3 And there shall be no more curse: but the
throne of God and of the Lamb shall be in it;
and his servants shall serve him:
4 And they shall see his face; and his name
shall be in their foreheads.
5 And there shall be no night there; and they
need no candle, neither light of the sun; for the
Lord God giveth them light: and they shall reign
for ever and ever.
6 And he said unto me, These sayings *are*
faithful and true: and the Lord God of the holy
prophets sent his angel to shew unto his servants the things which must shortly be done.
7 Behold, I come quickly: blessed *is* he that
keepeth the sayings of the prophecy of this
book.
8 And I John saw these things, and heard
them. And when I had heard and seen, I fell
down to worship before the feet of the angel
which shewed me these things.
9 Then saith he unto me, See *thou do it* not:
for I am thy fellowservant, and of thy brethren
the prophets, and of them which keep the sayings of this book: worship God.
10 And he saith unto me, Seal not the sayings of the prophecy of this book: for the time is
at hand.
11 He that is unjust, let him be unjust still:
and he which is filthy, let him be filthy still: and
he that is righteous, let him be righteous still:
and he that is holy, let him be holy still.
12 And, behold, I come quickly; and my reward *is* with me, to give every man according
as his work shall be.
13 I am Al'pha and O'me-ga, the beginning
and the end, the first and the last.
14 Blessed *are* they that do his commandments, that they may have right to the tree of
life, and may enter in through the gates into the
city.
15 For without *are* dogs, and sorcerers, and
whoremongers, and murderers, and idolaters,
and whosoever loveth and maketh a lie.
16 I Je'sus have sent mine angel to testify
unto you these things in the churches. I am the
root and the offspring of Da'vid, *and* the bright
and morning star.
17 And the Spirit and the bride say, Come.
And let him that heareth say, Come. And let
him that is athirst come. And whosoever will,
let him take the water of life freely.
18 For I testify unto every man that heareth
the words of the prophecy of this book, If any
man shall add unto these things, God shall add
unto him the plagues that are written in this
book:
19 And if any man shall take away from the
words of the book of this prophecy, God shall
take away his part out of the book of life, and
out of the holy city, and *from* the things which
are written in this book.
20 He which testifieth these things saith,
Surely I come quickly. Amen. Even so, come,
Lord Je'sus.
21 The grace of our Lord Je'sus Christ *be*
with you all. Amen.

THE END OF THE NEW TESTAMENT.

HELPS TO BIBLE STUDY

A Short History of the Holy Bible

The Age of the Bible

The Holy Bible is not only the greatest and best of all books. Its history has been very difficult to trace, yet the same divine guidance that set its authors to work to write it has made Christians delve into the mists of the past to learn all about it. We find out more about it every day through the research of learned men, and things that are now hidden from us regarding it doubtless will be revealed in the course of time.

As to its authors and age, however, we know a very great deal. It was written by about forty different men and as it comes to us it took about sixteen hundred years to compose. We know pretty accurately that Moses began it about the year 1500 B. C. and that John, who wrote the last book, Revelation, finished it about the year 90 A. D., which estimate fills out the sixteen centuries.

The Bible gets its name from a Greek word which means "the little books." Gradually, in the course of many years, this word came to stand for something more than "little books," of which the Big Book was composed. It came to mean "the book," the "holy book," and finally it came to mean just what it means today—the Holy Book of Books.

This wonderful work is composed of two parts—the Old Testament and the New Testament. The Old Testament has in it thirty-nine books or parts. It contains God's account of the creation of the world, a history of the Jewish people and God's dealings with them, a number of books written by the great Jewish prophets in which are foretold the things that happen in the New Testament, as well as a number of beautiful books of purely a religious character, such as the Psalms.

The men who wrote the Old Testament left off work on it about four hundred years before Jesus Christ was born. The New Testament begins with the birth of Jesus and covers a period of about seventy-five years down to the time when the faith of Christianity was being extended by the men Jesus Himself chose to go out into the world and tell about it. The New Testament contains twenty-seven books, four of which are specially known as Gospels, because they tell particularly of the life of Jesus. The word "gospel" means "good tidings" or "good news," because of the tidings of salvation that it brings to those who read it.

Formation of the Bible and Languages

The student of the Bible must not think that the Book as he reads it is its original form. The men who wrote it did so with much labor, just as letters are now written, and on the things which were used by them just as we use paper. Not until the great art of printing was discovered was it possible to get a Bible such as we have. Instead readers of the Bible used many thousands of written pages, kept carefully bound together. Of these there were many copies, but not nearly enough to go around among those who wished to possess a copy.

The men who wrote the Bible used two or three different languages. In the Old Testament the older most were written in Hebrew, while portions were written in Aramaic, a language somewhat similar to Hebrew. The New Testament was written in a form of the Greek language. From these languages the Bible has been translated into almost every known tongue.

The growth of the Bible from two collections of smaller books into one grand whole was very slow, but God so directed the minds of men that they finally did the work and did it well. This was called forming the canon of Scripture. Canon is a word which means rod or rule. The term applied to the Bible means that it is the rule or form of God's word to mankind; in other words, the way God wants man to read what God has to say to him.

The canon of the Old Testament was formed first. This was done by the Jews themselves, probably about four hundred years before Christ's time. Their learned men gathered together all the nation's sacred writings and under divine guidance made one work of them. After Jesus died began the preparation of the New Testament by the men God directed to do the work. Then these were also gathered together and councils of religious and wise men discussed them. It took several hundred years to get them arranged in their present form.

Of course, there have been many different translations of the Bible. The first ones were made into Greek and Latin. From the best of these—one called the Septuagint, made at Alexandria, Egypt, about 270 B. C. to 150 B. C.—became an important source document.

The chapter and verse subdivisions of the Bible, the descriptive headings of chapters and the presence of italics, or sloping letters, in the text, did not exist in the original. The division into chapters, which was for greater ease of reading and quotation, was made in the thirteenth century by Cardinal Hugo or Archbishop Langton.

At a later period, probably 1551, one Robert Stephens made the division into verses. They are very imperfect and sometimes greatly obscure the meaning. The presence of italics is due to the fact that in many instances it was necessary to introduce words to make clear a meaning which could not be translated easily, or to supply dificiencies due to differences in language.

What the Books of the Bible Contain

The Holy Bible is divided into two great parts, called the Old Testament and the New Testament. Each is complete and distinct in itself as far as the subjects treated are concerned, but through both run God's revelation of Himself to man, His promise of salvation, His laws and wishes for man to follow.

The Books of the Old Testament

The thirty-nine books of the Old Testament are divided into four sub-divisions—the Pentateuch, the historical books, the poetical books and the prophetical books.

The Pentateuch contains the earliest Hebrew history and the Hebrew law as laid down by Moses. It consists of the five books of Genesis, Exodus, Leviticus, Numbers and Deuteronomy.

The historical books contain the further history of the Hebrews up to the time the writing of the Old Testament ceased. They consist of twelve books: Joshua, Judges, Ruth, 1 Samuel, 2 Samuel, 1 Kings, 2 Kings, 1 Chronicles, 2 Chronicles, Ezra, Nehemiah and Esther.

The poetical books contain such of the poetry and philosophy of the Hebrews as has been preserved. They consist of five books: Job, the Psalms, Proverbs, Ecclesiastes and the Song of Solomon, also known as the Canticles.

The prophetical books contain the warnings and utterance of the Hebrew prophets. There are seventeen of them—five major prophets and twelve minor prophets. The major ones are Isaiah, Jeremiah, Lamentations, Ezekiel and Daniel. The minor ones are Hosea, Joel, Amos, Obadiah, Jonah, Micah, Nahum, Habakkuk, Zephaniah, Haggai, Zechariah and Malachi.

The Pentateuch Books

GENESIS, as its name implies, tells of the beginning of things, how the world was made and man placed upon it, of the fall of man through sin in yielding to temptation, of God's original promise to man of salvation through righteousness. It also tells of the dispersion of man through the Flood and the beginning of the history of the Hebrews. Genesis contains fifty chapters and was written by Moses about 1500 B. C.

EXODUS gets its name from the fact that it tells of the departure or exodus of the Hebrews from Egypt. It also tells of the wanderings of the Hebrews in the wilderness and of the giving of the Law to the Israelites by God through Moses. It was written almost certainly by Moses about the year 1485 B. C. and contains forty chapters.

LEVITICUS is a continuation of the book of Exodus. It takes its name from the fact that it contains the ceremonial and religious law, the performance of which was entrusted to the tribe of the Levites. It contains twenty-seven chapters and was apparently written by Moses about the year 1470 B. C.

NUMBERS is so named because it specially tells of the census or numbering of the Hebrews. It also tells of the history of the Hebrews on their journeyings after leaving Egypt. It contains thirty-six chapters and apparently was written by Moses about 1460 B. C.

DEUTERONOMY, the last book of the Pentateuch, gets its name from the fact that it contains a second account of the giving of the Law. It exhorts to obedience. It contains also an account of the death of Moses, within sight of the Promised Land. The book contains thirty-four chapters and was written partially by Moses and partially by Joshua. The date of writing is about 1450 B. C.

The Historical Books

JOSHUA. This book begins the historical books. It tells of the entrance of the Israelites into the Promised Land and the conquest of it. It contains twenty-four chapters and was written partly by Joshua and partly by some unknown author, about 1410 B. C.

JUDGES is to the Old Testament what the Acts of the Apostles is to the New. It tells of the troubled times through which the Israelites passed after the death of Joshua and the raising up by God of leaders and reformers for the ruling and leading of the nation. It brings the student up to the time of Eli and probably was written largely by Samuel. It contains twenty-one chapters and covers a period of about three hundred years.

RUTH contains some history of great value regarding the early ancestry of Jesus, but is chiefly remarkable for the story of Naomi and of Ruth and Boaz. It contains only four chapters and its author and date are unknown.

SAMUEL. These two books take their name from the great prophet-judge. Both contain historical matter of great importance, including the careers of Eli and Samuel, the last of the Judges, and the first two kings of the Hebrews, Saul and David. Samuel wrote a part of the first book, while it is probable that Nathan and Jeremiah had a large share in the authorship of both of them. The first book contains thirty-one chapters and the second twenty-four.

KINGS. These two books continue the history of the Hebrews so far as the independent kingdom of Israel is concerned. The narrative runs from the death of David, through the greatness of the reign of Solomon and the wickedness of the kings that followed him, down to the destruction of Jerusalem and the first two Captivities. A period of about 425 years is covered. Both books may have been written by Jeremiah. The first contains twenty-two chapters and the second twenty-five.

CHRONICLES. These two books are really Hebrew national religious records. But they also contain a history of the kingdom of Judah and many important family records. The authors of the books, which contain twenty-nine and thirty-six chapters respectively, are believed to have been Ezra and Daniel.

EZRA takes up the history of the Jews, beginning with the return from the Captivity, and goes over a period of about eighty years, telling of the rebuilding of the Temple at Jerusalem and the religious reformation of the people. The author,

Ezra, was one of the greatest of the Jewish historians. The book contains ten chapters.

NEHEMIAH is a companion book to Ezra, continuing the history of the Jews after the Captivity. Its author, Nehemiah, was also a great Jewish historian. The book contains thirteen chapters.

ESTHER takes its name from its principal figure, the beautiful Hebrew queen of King Ahasuerus. It tells of her elevation to the throne and how she overthrew the conspiracy formed by Haman for the slaughter of the Jews. It contains ten chapters.

The Poetical Books

JOB. This is the first of the poetical books, and one of the most remarkable books of the whole Bible and has been the subject of much debate among Bible scholars. It is the story of Job, a patriarch, who was tested by God. It is full of great beauty and wisdom. In many ways it reminds the reader of Bunyan's "Pilgrim's Progress." Its authorship and date of writing are unknown. It contains forty-two chapters.

THE PSALMS form another of the Bible's wonderful Books. The book is really a manual for devotional reading, no matter what the condition of the reader's mind or what his needs. Every form of sorrow, joy, repentance, aspiration, prayer, or hope finds expression in one or another of the Psalms. Persons learned in Bible lore have divided the book into four parts, as follows: Davidic Psalms, or psalms attributed to David, 1 to 72 inclusive; Asaphic Psalms, or psalms attributed to Asaph, 73 to 89 inclusive; Psalms of the Captivity, or psalms written in prophecy of or during the Captivity, 90 to 106 inclusive; and Psalms of the Restoration, or psalms written in prophecy of or during the Restoration, 107 to 150 inclusive. All the psalms are poems. Their authorship doubtless includes many men, among them being Moses, David, Asaph, Ezra, Nehemiah and Jeremiah. The book contains one hundred and fifty chapters.

PROVERBS is a book of wisdom, a collection of wise sayings, attributed to Solomon, but probably only collected by him. It contains thirty-one chapters.

ECCLESIASTES is a companion book to Proverbs. Its title means "the preacher." Like Proverbs, it has been attributed to Solomon. It contains twelve chapters.

THE SONG OF SOLOMON is another of the Bible's remarkable poems. It has been regarded as telling in allegory of the love between Christ and His Church. It contains eight chapters and is doubtfully attributed to Solomon.

The Prophetical Books

ISAIAH. The first of the prophetical books of the Bible, which cover a period of four centuries. It takes its name from its author, the greatest of all the Hebrew prophets. This is the first book of the Old Testament in which there is a clear and undoubted reference to the coming of Jesus. In fact, the entire book is particularly rich in prophecy regarding the Lord Jesus Christ. Isaiah contains sixty-six chapters and was written about 700 B. C.

JEREMIAH gets its title from its supposed author, the prophet of that name. He takes the Hebrews to task for their worship of false gods and their sins, exhorts them to repentance and makes several prophecies regarding Jesus. The book contains fifty-two chapters.

LAMENTATIONS is also by Jeremiah. It is remarkable for its poetic beauty and arrangement. The theme is sorrow and lamentation for the sins of the Hebrews. It contains five chapters.

EZEKIEL gets its name from its author, Ezekiel, the Prophet of the Captivity. It is wonderfully rich in prophecy, foretelling the coming of Christ. It is to the Old Testament what Revelation is to the New. It contains forty-eight chapters.

DANIEL gets its name from its author, who was a man of princely rank. It is half history and half prophecy. In it is the story of Nebuchadnezzar. The book contains twelve chapters.

HOSEA is the first of the minor prophetical books. It is full of rebuke to the Jews for their wickednesses. The book contains fourteen chapters.

JOEL gets its name from its author, of whom little is known save that he lived about 830 B. C. He calls the people to repentance and foretells the coming of the Holy Spirit. The book contains three chapters.

AMOS follows much the same lines as Joel. The book contains nine chapters.

OBADIAH is the shortest of the prophetical books. It contains only one chapter.

JONAH tells the remarkable account of the prophet who tried to evade his mission, was swallowed by a huge fish, cast out and, finally, through fear of God, made to perform his duty. This is the first book of the Bible wherein is shown the thought of spreading the faith of God among other peoples than the Jews—in other words, the foreign missionary spirit. The book contains four chapters.

MICAH is remarkable for the fact that in it is foretold the birth of Jesus in Bethlehem. The book contains seven chapters.

NAHUM has much of the beautiful thought of Isaiah. Little is known of its author. The book contains three chapters.

HABAKKUK takes its name from its author, who is regarded as the prophet of faith. The Apostle Paul evidently was a deep student of this book, which contains three chapters, written in conversational form.

ZEPHANIAH was written by a prophet who was of royal blood. He particularly foretells the day of wrath and the reward of the good. The book contains three chapters.

HAGGAI takes its name from its author and contains two chapters.

ZECHARIAH contains many allusions to the coming of Jesus, even foretelling the entry into Jerusalem on an ass's colt, the betrayal and the sum of money Judas received for it. The book contains fourteen chapters.

MALACHI is the last book of the Old Testament and contains more prophesies regarding Christ. It contains four chapters.

The New Testament: Division into Four Parts

Like the Old Testament, the New Testament is divided into four parts—the historical books, which include the four Gospels and the Acts of the Apostles; the epistles of Paul; the general epistles; and Revelation, a prophetical book.

The historical books are the Gospels of Matthew, Mark, Luke, and John, and the Acts of the Apostles.

The epistles of Paul are Romans, 1 Corinthians, 2 Corinthians, Galatians, Ephesians, Philippians, Colossians, 1 Thessalonians, 2 Thessalonians, 1 Timothy, 2 Timothy, and Philemon.

The author of Hebrews is not known.

The general epistles are James, 1 Peter, 2 Peter, 1 John, 2 John, 3 John, and Jude.

The prophetical book is Revelation.

The Historical Books

The historical books of the New Testament differ from those of the Old Testament in that they tell of the life of Jesus and the spread of the faith He founded from the Jews, to whom He gave it first, to the other races of the earth, known as the Gentiles, by the men He commanded to do the work.

The first three of the four Gospels are called synoptical gospels, because they give a synopsis, or general view, of Christ's life. The fourth Gospel, that of John, is called the doctrinal Gospel, because it teaches specifically the doctrine of the divine nature of Christ as the Son of God. Four different points of view are expressed in the Gospels and to each of them interpreters of Scripture have assigned a symbol, based upon Ezekiel 1: 4–10. The Acts has often been called the Gospel of the Holy Spirit.

MATTHEW was the Gospel written for the Jews. It shows Jesus as the Messiah and King, in whom were fulfilled all the great Old Testament prophecies. Matthew, its author, was a Jew and a man of humble birth. It was written about A. D. 60. It has twenty-eight chapters.

MARK was the Gospel written for the Gentiles, especially the Romans. It sets forth character of Jesus as the Son of man. Mark, who wrote it, worked about the year A. D. 63, and probably obtained his facts from Peter. It contains sixteen chapters.

LUKE was the Gospel written for the Greeks. Its author was Luke, who seems to have been a physician of Gentile birth. He appears to have written under the guidance of Paul about the year A. D. 60. He especially sets forth the sacrificial character of Jesus as the Savior and Redeemer. This Gospel is peculiarly rich in matter not contained in the other Gospels. It contains twenty-four chapters and its symbol is an ox.

JOHN was the Gospel which may be said to have been directed to all mankind. John, its author, was the youngest of the apostles, and has been honored with the title of "the disciple whom Jesus loved." His Gospel is probably the greatest of all. It was written later than the others (probably about the year A. D. 85) and dwells upon Jesus as the Lord and Word made flesh. It contains twenty-one chapters.

THE ACTS OF THE APOSTLES takes its name from the fact that it is a history of the doings of the apostles for the first generation after the crucifixion of Jesus. It sets forth the coming of the Holy Spirit and the spread of the church under Peter and Paul. It was written by Luke. It contains twenty-eight chapters and was written about A. D. 63.

The Pauline Epistles

ROMANS. The epistles of Paul are very wonderful pieces of writing. As they are arranged in the Bible they begin with Romans. This was written to the Romans who were Christians and lays stress upon the "righteousness which is by faith." It exhorts its readers to lay aside racial differences and come together on a common basis as believers on Christ. It was written probably while Paul was at Corinth about the year A. D. 58, and contains sixteen chapters.

CORINTHIANS. These two books were written to the Christians at Corinth in Greece. In the latter Paul gives considerable autobiography. The first contains sixteen and the second thirteen chapters.

GALATIANS was written to the Christians of Galatia, in Asia Minor. Its chief theme is the freedom of the Gospel as opposed to the bondage of the law. It contains six chapters.

EPHESIANS takes its name from the fact that it was written to the people of Ephesus. In it Paul describes his ideal church and the work of each individual in it, with Jews and Gentiles as one body, with Christ as the common head. It contains six chapters and was written while Paul was in prison at Rome.

PHILIPPIANS was written to the church at Philippi. It gives thanks for the kindnesses bestowed upon the writer and offers good advice. It was written from prison in Rome and contains four chapters.

COLOSSIANS, written to the church at Colossi, dwells on the completeness of the church in Christ and gives warnings against heresies. It contains four chapters.

THESSALONIANS. These two books were probably the earliest of the Pauline epistles. They are full of the second coming of Christ and sound advice for their readers. They contain five and three chapters respectively.

TIMOTHY. These two books are letters written to Paul's helper and disciple, Timothy. Both are beautiful examples of pastoral wisdom. The last seems to have been written upon the eve of Paul's martyrdom, as is shown in the fourth chapter. They contain six and four chapters respectively.

TITUS is a letter in very much the same style as those to Timothy. It contains three chapters.

PHILEMON was written to a person of that name. It is remarkable because it shows the wonderfully sympathetic and just nature of Paul. It contains but one chapter.

HEBREWS is a doctrinal epistle, which particularly calls attention to the priesthood of Jesus Christ. It contains fourteen chapters.

The General Epistles

JAMES. This is the first of the general epistles and takes its name from its author. It is a great exhortation to patience and piety. It contains five chapters.

PETER. These two books take their name from that of their author. Their special themes are patience under persecution and holiness in living. They contain five and three chapters respectively.

JOHN. These three books are the work of that same "beloved disciple" who wrote the last Gospel. They are letters of a type highly spiritual. They contain five, one, and one chapters respectively.

JUDE takes its name from its author and is an admonition to all Christians to stand firm in the faith. It contains but one chapter.

The Prophetical Book

REVELATION is the title of the last book in the Bible. It was written by John, the author of the Gospel and Epistles that bear his name. It is the only truly prophetical book in the New Testament and is of very great beauty. It is full of a symbolism that is not always intelligible to its readers, which is strong proof of its prophetical character. Its theme is the end of all present mundane things and the coming of "the new heaven and the new earth." It contains twenty-two chapters.

CHART OF THE LIFE OF JESUS CHRIST

Ancestry	On one side God himself. On the other every phase of character, every human tendency represented in his genealogy.
Preparations for his coming	Universal peace. One empire. One language generally known. The Jews with the Scriptures in all lands. A general awakening.
Birth of Jesus about December, B.C. 5 Childhood and Youth	Home training. Bible study. Schooling. Different languages. Travel to Jerusalem. Great religious meetings. Village life. Work at a trade. Knowledge of his country's history and hopes. A perfect and beautiful character.
Preparations for his ministry	John the Baptist. Baptism. The Holy Spirit. The Voice from God. Temptation.
A.D. 27 Judea **First Year – Year of Beginnings**	**John's ministry of preparation began six months before Jesus began to preach, continued through the first year and three months into the second year.** First disciples. First miracle. First reform. First discourse. First tour. First Samaritan disciple. Healing of the nobleman's son.
A.D. 28 Galilee **Second Year – Year of Principles**	**Imprisonment of John the Baptist, March** The Pool of Bethesda. Organization. Choosing apostles. Sermon on the Mount. Miracles proving his authority and illustrating his work. Forgiveness of Sins. Seeking the lost. Life from the dead. The light of the world. Warnings and invitations. Parables. The year in which Jesus laid down and worked out many of the fundamental principles and truths of his kingdom.
A.D. 29 Galilee/Perea 2-3 months **Third Year – Year of Development**	**The Death of John the Baptist in March. Increasing opposition.** Feeding the five thousand. Miracles: The dropsical man, the ten lepers, blind Bartimeus. The transfiguration. At the feast of tabernacles. Discourses in the Temple. Healing of one born blind. The good shepherd. Parables: The great supper, the lost sheep, the lost coin, the prodigal son, the unjust steward, the rich man and Lazarus, the pounds.
A.D. 30 Perea **Last three months Jan. Feb. March**	Raising of Lazarus. Miracles. Parables. Instructions. Children. Zaccheus.
Saturday April 1–Saturday April 8 **Last Week**	Anointed at Bethany. Triumphal entry. Cleansing the Temple. Last great day of public teaching. Rest at Bethany. Passover/The Lord's Supper. The trial. The crucifixion. The burial. In the tomb.
Sunday April 9–Thursday May 18 **Resurrection Days**	Forty days. Eleven appearances, between April 9 and May 18, A.D. 30. The Ascension, Thursday, May 18 from Mount of Olives.
The Ever-Living Saviour	Return through the Holy Spirit. A Saviour in heaven. Ever abiding with his people. Coming again in his kingdom. A universal king, the world redeemed.

THE HARMONY OF THE LIFE OF CHRIST

BIRTH OF JOHN THE BAPTIST FORETOLD	St. Luke 1:5
BIRTH OF JESUS FORETOLD	St. Luke 1:26 St. Matthew 1:18
BIRTH AND NAMING OF JOHN	St. Luke 1:39
BIRTH OF JESUS	St. Luke 2:1 St. John 1:1–14
GENEALOGIES	St. Matthew 1:1 St. Luke 3:23
CIRCUMCISION AND NAMING OF JESUS	St. Luke 2:21
PRESENTATION OF JESUS IN THE TEMPLE	St. Luke 2:22
COMING OF THE WISE MEN	St. Matthew 2:1
FLIGHT TO–RETURN FROM EGYPT	St. Matthew 2:19
THE LAD JESUS IN THE TEMPLE	St. Luke 2:41
JOHN THE BAPTIST'S MINISTRY	St. Matthew 3:1 St. Mark 1:1 St. Luke 3:1 St. John 1:6, 15
THE BAPTISM OF JESUS	St. Matthew 3:13 St. Mark 1:9 St. Luke 3:21
THE TEMPTATION OF JESUS	St. Matthew 4:1 St. Mark 1:12 St. Luke 4:1
JESUS BEGINS HIS MINISTRY	St. Matthew 4:12 St. Mark 1:14 St. Luke 4:14
JOHN'S WITNESS OF JESUS	St. John 1:15
CALL OF FIRST DISCIPLES	St. John 1:35 St. Matthew 4:18 St. Mark 1:16 St. Luke 5:1
JESUS' SERMON ON THE MOUNT	St. Matthew 5, 6, 7 St. Luke 6:17
JESUS' FIRST MIRACLE	St. John 2:1
JESUS AT JERUSALEM	St. John 2:13
NICODEMUS VISITS JESUS	St. John 3:1
THE TWELVE	St. Matthew 10:2 St. Mark 3:13 St. Luke 6:13
THE TWELVE COMMISSIONED AND SENT FORTH	St. Matthew 10:1 St. Mark 3:13 St. Luke 9:1
THE TWELVE RETURN	St. Mark 6:30 St. Luke 9:10
JOHN THE BAPTIST'S DEATH	St. Matthew 14:1 St. Mark 6:14 St. Luke 9:7
PETER'S CONFESSION OF CHRIST	St. Matthew 16:13 St. Mark 8:27 St. Luke 9:18
JESUS FORETELLS HIS OWN DEATH	St. Matthew 16:21 St. Mark 8:31 St. Luke 9:22
THE TRANSFIGURATION (OF JESUS)	St. Matthew 17:1 St. Mark 9:2 St. Luke 9:28
THE SEVENTY SENT OUT: THEIR RETURN	St. Luke 10:1
THE RAISING OF LAZARUS	St. John 11:1
JESUS JOURNEYS TO JERUSALEM	St. Matthew 20:17 St. Mark 10:32 St. Luke 18:31
THE JEWS' COUNCIL PLOTS JESUS' DEATH	St. John 11:47 St. Matthew 26:3
JESUS' ARRIVAL AT BETHANY	St. John 12:1
JESUS ENTERS JERUSALEM	St. Matthew 21:1 St. Mark 11:1 St. Luke 19:29 St. John 12:12
JESUS CLEANSES THE TEMPLE	St. Matthew 21:12 St. Mark 11:15 St. Luke 19:45

Jesus Teaches in the Temple . . . . St. Matthew 21:23 St. Mark 11:27
St. Luke 20:1
Judas' Treacherous Plot . . . . St. Matthew 26:14 St. Mark 14:10
St. Luke 22:3
Preparation for the Passover . . . . St. Matthew 26:17 St. Mark 14:12
St. Luke 22:7
The Supper of the Last Evening . . . . St. Matthew 26:20 St. Mark 14:7
St. Luke 22:14
Jesus Washes His Disciples' Feet . . . . St. John 13:1
The Betrayer Revealed . . . . St. John 13:10
Jesus' Last Discourses to His Disciples . . . . St. John 13:31 St. John 17
Jesus Institutes "The Lord's
Supper" . . . . St. Matthew 26:26 St. Mark 22 St. Luke 22:19
Peter's Three Denials Foretold . . . . St. Matthew 26:34 St. Mark 14:30
St. Luke 22:34 St. John 13:38
Jesus' Agony in Gethsemane . . . . St. Matthew 26:36 St. Mark 14:32
St. Luke 22:39 St. John 18:1
The Betrayal and Arrest . . . . St. Matthew 26:47 St. Mark 14:43
St. Luke 22:47 St. John 18:2
Jesus Taken to Annas . . . . St. John 18:13
Before Caiaphas the High Priest . . . . St. Matthew 26:57 St. Mark 14:53
St. Luke 22:54 St. John 18:19
Peter's Three Denials . . . . St. Matthew 26:69 St. Mark 14:66
St. Luke 22:54 St. John 18:15
Jesus before the Council . . St. Matthew 27:1 St. Mark 15:1 St. Luke 22:66
Jesus before Pilate . . . . St. Matthew 27:2, 11 St. Mark 15:1
St. Luke 23:1 St. John 18:28
Pilate Declares Jesus Innocent . . . . St. Luke 23:4 St. John 19:4
Pilate Sends Jesus to Herod . . . . St. Luke 23:7
The Jews Reject Jesus . . . . St. Matthew 27:21, 25 St. Mark 15:6
St. Luke 23:18 St. John 18:40 St. John 19:15
Pilate Condemns Jesus to Death . . . . St. Matthew 27:26 St. Mark 15:15
St. Luke 23:24 St. John 19:16
Jesus Mocked by the
Soldiers . . . . St. Matthew 27:27 St. Mark 15:16 St. John 19:2
Jesus Led Away to be Crucified . . . . St. Matthew 27:31 St. Mark 15:20
St. Luke 23:33 St. John 19:18
The Crucifixion of Jesus . . . . St. Matthew 27:35 St. Mark 15:24
St. Luke 23:33 St. John 19:18
Jesus on the Cross . . . . St. Matthew 27:36 St. Mark 15:25
St. Luke 23:34 St. John 19:19
The Death of Jesus . . . . St. Matthew 27:50 St. Mark 15:37
St. Luke 23:46 St. John 19:30
The Centurion's
Witness . . . . St. Matthew 27:54 St. Mark 15:39 St. Luke 23:47
The Burial of Jesus . . . . St. Matthew 27:57 St. Mark 15:42
St. Luke 23:50 St. John 19:38

The Resurrection of Jesus . . . . St. Matthew 28:1 St. Mark 16:1
St. Luke 24:1 St. John 20:1

Appearances of Jesus After the Resurrection:

To Mary Magdalene . . . . St. Matthew 16:9 St. John 20:11
To the Women . . . . St. Matthew 28:1
To the Eleven . . . . St. Mark 16:14 St. John 20:19
To Two Going to Emmaus . . . . St. Mark 16:12 St. Luke 24:13
To the Eleven (a week later) . . . . St. John 20:26
To the Apostles in Galilee . . . . St. Mark 16:14 St. John 21:1
To Peter . . . . St. Luke 24:34 1 Corinthians 15:5
To Five Hundred Brethren in Galilee . . . . 1 Corinthians 15:6
To James . . . . 1 Corinthians 15:7
To Paul . . . . 1 Corinthians 15:8

Jesus' Commission to the Apostles . . . . St. Matthew 28:19 St. Mark 16:15
St. Luke 24:44
Jesus Talks with Peter . . . . St. John 21:15
The Ascension of Jesus . . . . St. Mark 16:9 St. Luke 24:50 Acts 1:4
The Descent of God the Holy Ghost . . . . Acts 2:1

THE MIRACLES OF OUR LORD

The First Miracle: Water Made Wine . . . . St. John 2:1
Many Healings . . . . St. Matthew 4:23 St. Matthew 8:16
St. Matthew 15:30 St. Mark 1:32
St. Luke 4:40 etc
A Leper . . . . St. Matthew 8:1–4 St. Mark 1:40 St. Luke 5:12
The Centurion's Servant . . . . St. Matthew 8:5 St. Luke 7:1
Peter's Wife's Mother . . . . St. Matthew 8:14 St. Mark 1:29 St. Luke 4:38
The Tempest Stilled . . . . . . St. Matthew 8:23 St. Mark 4:35 St. Luke 8:22
Two Demoniacs . . . . St. Matthew 8:28 St. Mark 5:1 St. Luke 8:26
A Palsied Man . . . . St. Matthew 9:1 St. Mark 2:1 St. Luke 5:18
The Twelve-Year Afflicted
Woman . . . . St. Matthew 9:20 St. Mark 5:25 St. Luke 8:43
Raising of Jairus' Daughter . St. Matthew 9:23 St. Mark 5:22 St. Luke 8:41
Two Blind Men . . . . St. Matthew 9:27
A Dumb Demoniac . . . . . St. Matthew 9:32 St. Matthew 12:22 St. Luke 14
A Man with a Withered
Hand . . . . St. Matthew 12:10 St. Mark 3:1 St. Luke 6:6
Five Thousand Fed . . . . St. Matthew 14:15 St. Mark 6:35
St. Luke 9:12 St. John 6:1
Jesus Walks on the Sea . . . St. Matthew 14:22 St. Mark 6:47 St. John 6:16
The Syrophenician's Daughter . . . . St. Matthew 15:21 St. Mark 7:24
Four Thousand Fed . . . . St. Matthew 15:32 St. Mark 8:1
The Epileptic Boy . . . . St. Matthew 17:14 St. Mark 9:14 St. Luke 9:37
Two Blind Men (Jericho) . . . . St. Matthew 20:30

A Man with an Unclean Spirit ....St. Mark 1:23 St. Luke 4:33
A Deaf Mute ....St. Mark 7:31
A Blind Man (Bethesda) ....St. Mark 8:22
Blind Bartimaeus ......St. Mark 10:46 St. Luke 18:35 St. Matthew 20:30
Draught of Fishes ....St. Luke 5:4
Raising of Widow's Son ....St. Luke 7:11
An Infirm Woman ....St. Luke 13:11
A Dropsical Man ....St. Luke 14:1
Ten Lepers ....St. Luke 17:11
Malchus' Ear Healed ....St. Luke 22:50
A Nobleman's Son ....St. John 4:46
A Cripple (Bethesda) ....St. John 5:1
A Man Born Blind ....St. John 9:1
Raising of Lazarus ....St. John 11:38
A Great Haul of Fishes ....St. John 21:1

THE PARABLES OF OUR LORD

The Builders ....St. Matthew 7:24–27 St. Luke 6:47–49
The Sower ....St. Matthew 13:3 St. Mark 4:1 St. Luke 8:4
The Wheat and the Tares ....St. Matthew 13:24–30
The Mustard Seed ......St. Matthew 13:31 St. Mark 4:30 St. Luke 13:18
The Leaven ....St. Matthew 13:33 St. Luke 13:20
The Hidden Treasure ....St. Matthew 13:44
The Pearl of Great Price ....St. Matthew 13:45
The Net ....St. Matthew 13:47
The Unmerciful Servant ....St. Matthew 18:23–35
The Laborers in the Vineyard ....St. Matthew 20:1–16
The Two Sons ....St. Matthew 21:28–32
The Wicked Husbandmen ....St. Matthew 21:33–46 St. Luke 20:9–18
The Marriage Feast ....St. Matthew 22:1–14
The Fig Tree ....St. Matthew 24:32
The Ten Virgins ....St. Matthew 25:1–13
The Talents ....St. Matthew 25:14–30
The Seed Growing Secretly ....St. Mark 4:26–29
The Good Samaritan ....St. Luke 10:25–37
The Rich Fool ....St. Luke 12:13–21
The Fruitless Fig Tree ....St. Luke 13:6–9
The Great Supper ....St. Luke 14:16–24
On Counting the Cost ....St. Luke 14:25–33
The Lost Sheep ....St. Luke 15:3–7
The Lost Coin ....St. Luke 15:8–10
The Lost Son ....St. Luke 15:11–32
The Dishonest Steward ....St. Luke 16:1–14
The Rich Man and Lazarus ....St. Luke 16:19–31
The Importunate Widow and Unjust Judge ....St. Luke 18:1–8
The Pharisee and Publican ....St. Luke 18:8–14
The Pounds ....St. Luke 19:11–27

THE APOSTLES AND THEIR HISTORY.

	Name.	Surname.	Parents.	Home.	Business.	Writings.	Work.	Death.
1	Simon.	Peter / Cephas = *Rock*.	Jonah.	*Early Life:* Bethsaida. *Later:* Capernaum.	Fisherman.	1 Peter. 2 Peter.	A missionary among the Jews, as far as Babylon, 1 Pet. 5:13. Probably = Rome.	*Trad.:* Crucified head downward, at Rome.
2	Andrew.		Jonah.	*Early Life:* Bethsaida. *Later:* Capernaum.	Fisherman.		*Tradition:* Preached in Scythia, Greece, and Asia Minor.	*Trad.:* Crucified on St. Andrew's cross (x).
3	James the greater or elder.	Boanerges, or *Sons of Thunder*.	Zebedee and Salome.	Bethsaida and afterward in Jerusalem.	Fisherman.		Preached in Jerusalem and Judea.	Beheaded by Herod, A.D. 41, at Jerusalem.
4	John, the beloved disciple.				Fisherman.	Gospel. 3 Epistles. Revelation.	Labored among the churches of Asia Minor, especially Ephesus.	Banished to Patmos, A.D. 95. Recalled. Died a natural death. *Trad.*
5	James the less or younger.		Alpheus or Cleophas and Mary.	Galilee.			Preached in Palestine and Egypt.	*Trad.:* Crucified in Egypt; or thrown from a pinnacle.
6	Jude.	Same as Thaddeus and Lebbeus.		Galilee.		Epistle.	Preached in Assyria and Persia. *Trad.*	Martyred in Persia. *Trad.*

THE APOSTLES AND THEIR HISTORY (*Continued*).

	NAME.	SURNAME.	PARENTS.	HOME.	BUSINESS.	WRITINGS.	WORK.	DEATH.
7	PHILIP.			Bethsaida.			Preached in Phrygia.	Died martyr at Hierapolis in Phrygia. *Trad.*
8	BARTHOLOMEW.	Nathaniel.		Cana of Galilee.				Flayed to death. *Trad.*
9	MATTHEW.	Levi.	Alpheus.	Capernaum.	Tax-collector.	Gospel.		*Trad.:* Died a martyr in Ethiopia.
10	THOMAS.	Didymus.		Galilee.			Claimed by the Syrian Christians as the founder of their church; perhaps also in Persia and India.	*Trad.:* Shot by arrows while at prayer.
11	SIMON.	The Cananæn, or *Zelotes.*		Galilee.				*Trad.:* Crucified.
12	JUDAS.	Iscariot.		Kerioth of Judea.			Betrayed the Lord Jesus.	Suicide.

REDI-REFERENCE

ANXIETY AND WORRY

Psalm 16:11; 37:1, 7; 43:5; Proverbs 16:7; Isaiah 41:10; Matthew 6:31-34; Philippians 4:6-9, 19; II Thessalonians 3:3; I Peter 5:7

ASSURANCE OF SALVATION

Matthew 24:35; John 5:24; 6:37; 10:27-30; 20:31; Romans 8:16, 31, 35-39; Hebrews 13:5; I John 5:11-13

BATTLE OF ARMAGEDDON

Revelation 14:14-20; 16:16

BEATITUDES

Matthew 5:3-12; Luke 20:23

BEREAVEMENT AND LOSS

Deuteronomy 31:8; Psalm 23; 27:10; 119:50

CHRISTIAN FELLOWSHIP

Psalm 122:1, 9; Matthew 18:20; John 13:34; Acts 2:42, 46; I Corinthians 1:9; Hebrews 10:24-25; I John 1:3, 7

CHRISTIAN'S ARMOR

Ephesians 6:11-18

COMFORT

Psalm 23; Lamentations 3:21-26; Matthew 5:4; 11:28-30; John 14:16-18; Romans 15:4; II Corinthians 1:3-5; II Thessalonians 2:16-17

CONFIDENCE

Psalm 27:3; Proverbs 3:26; 14:26; Isaiah 30:15; Galatians 6:9; Ephesians 3:11-12; Philippians 1:6; Hebrews 10:35; I Peter 2:9

CROWNS

I Corinthians 9:25; I Thessalonians 2:19-20; II Timothy 4:8; James 1:12; I Peter 5:2-4; Revelation 2:10

DANGER

Psalm 23:4; 32:7; 34:7, 17, 19; 91:1-2, 11; 121:1-8; Isaiah 43:2; Romans 14:8

DEATH

Psalm 23:4; 116:15; Romans 14:8; II Corinthians 5:1; Philippians 1:21; I Thessalonians 5:9-10; II Timothy 4:7-8; Hebrews 9:27; Revelation 21:4

DEITY OF CHRIST

Matthew 26:63-64; John 1:1-14, 18; 10:30; 14:9; 16:15; 17:10; 20:28; Romans 9:5; Colossians 1:15-19; 2:9; Titus 2:13; Hebrews 1:3, 8; I John 5:20

DIFFICULTIES

Romans 8:28; II Corinthians 4:17; Hebrews 5:8; 12:7, 11; Revelation 3:19

DISAPPOINTMENT

Psalm 43:5; 55:22; 126:6; John 14:27; II Corinthians 4:8-10

DISCOURAGEMENT

Joshua 1:9; Psalm 27:14; 43:5; John 14:1-3, 27; 16:33; 19:25-27; Colossians 1:5; Hebrews 4:16; I Peter 1:3-9; I John 5:14; Revelation 22:1-4

DIVORCE

Deuteronomy 24:1-4; Matthew 5:31-32; 19:3-12; Mark 10:2-12; Luke 16:18; I Corinthians 7:10-15

DOUBTFUL THINGS

Romans 14:1-23; I Corinthians 8:9, 13; Philippians 2:15; Colossians 3:2, 5-10, 17; I Thessalonians 5:22; Titus 2:12-14; James 4:4; I John 2:15-17

EXTERNAL PRESSURES

Joshua 1:9; Psalm 37:5; Romans 8:28; II Corinthians 12:9; I Peter 5:7; I John 5:4-5

FAITH

Romans 4:3; 10:17; Ephesians 2:8-9; Hebrews 11:1, 6; 12:2; James 1:3-6; I Peter 1:7

FEAR

Psalm 27:1; 56:11; 91:1-2; 121:1-8; Proverbs 3:25; 29:25; Isaiah 51:12; John 14:27; Romans 8:28-29, 31, 35-39; Philippians 4:19; II Timothy 1:7; I John 4:18; Jude 24-25

FORGIVENESS OF SIN

Psalm 32:5; 51; 103:3, 12; Proverbs 28:13; Isaiah 1:18; 55:7; James 5:15-16; I John 1:9

FORGIVING OTHERS

Proverbs 18:19; Matthew 5:44-47; 6:12, 14; 18:15-35; Mark 11:25-26; Luke 17:3-4; Ephesians 4:32; Colossians 3:13

FRIENDS AND FRIENDLINESS

Proverbs 18:24; John 13:35; 15:13-14; Galatians 6:1, 10

FRUIT OF THE SPIRIT

Galatians 5:22-23

GENEROSITY

I Chronicles 29:9; Psalm 37:21; Luke 6:38; Matthew 5:42; Proverbs 3:9-10; II Corinthians 9:6-7

GOD'S CARE

Psalm 31:19-20; 34:17-19; 91:1-2; Nahum 1:7; Ephesians 3:20; Philippians 4:19; I Peter 5:7; I John 4:16; Jude 24

GOLDEN RULE

Matthew 7:12; Luke 6:31

GREAT WHITE THRONE

Revelation 20:11-15

GROWING SPIRITUALLY

Ephesians 3:17-19; Colossians 1:9-11; 3:16; I Timothy 4:15; II Timothy 2:15; I Peter 2:2; II Peter 1:5-8; 3:18

GUIDANCE

Psalm 32:8; Isaiah 30:21; 58:11; Luke 1:79; John 16:13

GUILT

Psalm 32:1-2; Romans 8:1; II Corinthians 5:21; Ephesians 1:7; Colossians 2:9-17; Titus 3:5

HELL

Matthew 5:22; 13:42, 50; 18:8-9; 22:13; 25:41, 46; Mark 9:48; Jude 7

HELP AND CARE

II Chronicles 16:9; Psalm 34:7; 37:5, 24; 55:22; 91:4; Isaiah 50:9; 54:17; Hebrews 4:16; 13:5-6; I Peter 5:7

HOLY SPIRIT

Acts 5:3-4; I Corinthians 3:16; 6:19; 12:4-6; II Corinthians 13:14; I Peter 1:2

HONESTY

Romans 13:13; I Thessalonians 4:11-12; Hebrews 13:18; I Peter 2:11-12

HUMILITY

Proverbs 22:4; Micah 6:8; Acts 20:19; Romans 12:3; Philippians 2:3-4; I Peter 5:5-6

HUSBANDS

Genesis 18:19; Proverbs 23:13-14; I Corinthians 7:3; Ephesians 5:23-29; 6:4; I Peter 3:7

JESUS—
SAVIOUR OF THE WORLD

Matthew 1:21; Luke 19:10; John 3:16; 14:6; Acts 4:12; Romans 5:8; Ephesians 1:7; I John 5:12

JUDGMENT SEAT OF CHRIST

Matthew 6:2-4; 25:14-30; Luke 19:11-27; Romans 14:10-12; I Corinthians 3:9-15; II Corinthians 5:10; II Timothy 4:8

KINGDOM AGE

Isaiah 11:6-9; 14:7-8; 25:8-9; Revelation 20:1-6

LAKE OF FIRE

Revelation 20:14-15

LIBERTY

John 8:32, 36; Romans 6:6-7, 17-22; 7:6; 8:2; 14:1-23; I Corinthians 8:1-13; Galatians 2:21; 5:1, 13-14; Colossians 3:17; I Timothy 4:4

LIVING THE CHRISTIAN LIFE

Psalm 119:9-11; John 15:7; II Corinthians 5:17; Colossians 2:6; I Peter 2:2; I John 1:7

LONELINESS

Psalm 23; 27:10; 91:11; Isaiah 41:10; Matthew 28:20; Hebrews 13:5-6

LORD'S PRAYER

Matthew 6:9-15, Luke 11:1-13; I Corinthians 11:17-34

LORDSHIP

Luke 6:46; Romans 6:13-16; 10:9-10; 12:1-2; I Corinthians 6:19-20; Philippians 2:9-11

LOVE

John 3:16; 15:9-14; Romans 5:8; 8:35-39; I Corinthians 13; I John 3:1

MARK OF THE BEAST

Revelation 13

MARRIAGE SUPPER OF THE LAMB

Revelation 19:7-10

MAN'S NEED OF SALVATION

Isaiah 64:6; Romans 3:10, 23; 5:12; 6:23; Hebrews 9:27; I John 1:10

NATIONAL RESPONSIBILITIES

Psalm 33:12; Proverbs 14:34; 29:18; Romans 13:1-7; I Timothy 2:1-3; I Peter 2:13-17

NEW HEAVEN AND EARTH

Isaiah 65:17-25; Revelation 21-22

OBEDIENCE

I Samuel 15:22; Psalm 111:10; 119: 2; Ecclesiastes 12:13; Isaiah 1:19-20; Matthew 6:24; John 14:15, 21; Romans 6:16; II Corinthians 10:5; James 2:10; I John 3:22

OCCULT

Leviticus 20:27; Deuteronomy 18:9-12; I Samuel 28:7-12; II Kings 21:6; Isaiah 8:19; 19:3; 47:13-14; Acts 19:18-20; James 4:7

OCCUPATION

Genesis 2:15; Proverbs 14:23; Ecclesiastes 9:10; Romans 12:11-13; Ephesians 4:28; II Thessalonians 3:10-12

ONE HUNDRED & FORTY-FOUR THOUSAND

Revelation 7:4-8

OVERCOMING TEMPTATION

Isaiah 41:10; Matthew 26:41; I Corinthians 10:13; Philippians 1:6; II Thessalonians 3:3; James 4:7; I Peter 2:9

PARADISE AND HADES

Numbers 16:33; Luke 16:22-26; 23:43

PARENTS AND CHILDREN

Exodus 20:12; Psalm 148:12-13; Proverbs 1:8-9; 6:20-23; 23:22, 26; 28:7; Ephesians 6:1-4; Colossians 3:20-21; I Timothy 4:12; 5:4

PERSECUTION

Matthew 5:10-11; 10:22; Acts 5:41; 9:16; Romans 8:17; II Timothy 3:12; Hebrews 11:25; James 1:2-4; I Peter 2:20

PEACE

Isaiah 26:3-4; John 14:27; 16:33; Romans 5:1; Philippians 4:4-9; Colossians 3:15

PLAN OF SALVATION

Isaiah 55:7; John 1:12; 3:3; 5:24; Romans 10:9-10, 13; Ephesians 2:8-9; Titus 3:5-7; I John 5:11-13; Revelation 3:20

POWER OVER SATAN

James 4:7; I John 4:4

PRAISE AND GRATITUDE

Deuteronomy 8:10; I Samuel 12:24; II Chronicles 20; Psalm 34:1-4; 50:23; 51:15; 63:2-7; 100:4; 107:8; 139:14; 147:1; 150; Ephesians 5:18-20; Philippians 4:4-6; Colossians 3:15-17; I Thessalonians 5:18; Hebrews 13:15; I Peter 1:6-9

PRAYER

Psalm 10:17; 18:3; 86:5, 7; 145:18; Jeremiah 33:3; Joel 2:32; Matthew 7:7-8; 21:22; John 14:13-14; 15:7; Romans 10:9-13; Ephesians 6:18; Hebrews 4:14-16; James 5:16; I John 5:14-15

PROVISION

Psalm 23; 34:10; 37:3-4; 84:11; Isaiah 58:11; Matthew 6:33; II Corinthians 9:8; Ephesians 3:20; I Peter 1:3-5; II Peter 1:3-4

PURITY

Philippians 2:14-15; I Timothy 5:22; James 3:17; 4:8; I John 3:3

RAPTURE

I Corinthians 15:51-57; I Thessalonians 4:13-18

RETURN OF CHRIST

Luke 21:34-36; Acts 1:11; I Thessalonians 4:13-18; Titus 2:13; II Peter 3:8-14; I John 3:2-3

REWARDS

I Corinthians 3:11-15; Ephesians 5:27; 6:8; II Thessalonians 2:14; II Timothy 4:8; I John 3:1-2; Jude 24

SATAN

Isaiah 14:12-15; Ezekiel 28:12-19; James 4:7; II Peter 2:9; I John 4:4

SEAL JUDGMENTS

Revelation 6-7

SELF-IMAGE

I Samuel 16:7; Psalm 138:8; 139:14-16; Philippians 1:6; Hebrews 12:2

SELF-CONTROL

Proverbs 4:23-26; Romans 13:14; I Corinthians 9:25; 16:13; I Timothy 6:11-12; II Timothy 2:3-5

SEX AND MARRIAGE

Proverbs 5:18-19; Song of Solomon; I Corinthians 7; Ephesians 5:18-6:3; I Thessalonians 4:1-7; Hebrews 13:4; I Peter 3:1-9

SICKNESS

Psalm 41:3; 103:3; Matthew 4:23; John 11:4; James 5:13-15

SIN

Isaiah 53:5-6; 59:1-2; John 8:34; Romans 3:23; 6:23; Galatians 6:7-8

SIGNS OF THE TIMES

Physical Signs

Isaiah 35:1-2; Ezekiel 36:30; 38:14-16; 44:1-2; Daniel 11:40; 12:4; Matthew 24:7; 24:15; Luke 21:25-26; II Thessalonians 2:4; James 5:1-3; Revelation 11:1-2

Social Signs

Genesis 6:5; 13:13; 19:4-5; Deuteronomy 28:63-67; Ezekiel 34:11-13; 36:24; 38-39; Zechariah 12:2-3; Matthew 24:6, 9-10, 12, 37-39; Mark 7:21, 23; Luke 17:28-30; 21:24, 25, 29-33; 28:30; II Timothy 3:1-5; Revelation 9:13-21; 21:8; 22:15

Religious Signs

Daniel 8:23-25; 11:36-45; Joel 2:28-29; Matthew 24:5, 11, 13-14, 34; II Thessalonians 2:4-8; I Timothy 4:1; II Timothy 4:3-4; II Peter 2:1-2; 3:3-4; I John 5:19; Revelation 12:12; 13:1-18

SOCIAL RESPONSIBILITIES

Proverbs 19:17; Matthew 5:13-15; 10:42; Luke 3:10-11; Galatians 6:1-5; I John 3:17-18

SORROW

Job 5:17-18; Proverbs 10:22; Isaiah 53:4; Matthew 11:28-30; John 16:22; II Corinthians 1:3-5; 4:17-18; 6:10; I Thessalonians 4:13; I Peter 1:7; 4:12-13; Revelation 21:4

SPIRITUAL GIFTS

Romans 12:6-8; I Corinthians 12:14; Ephesians 4:11-12; I Peter 4:10

STRENGTH

Deuteronomy 33:25; Psalm 27:14; 28:7; Isaiah 40:29, 31; 41:10; II Corinthians 12:9; Philippians 4:13

STUDY

Psalm 19:7-11; 119:9, 11, 18; Acts 20:32; II Timothy 3:15-17; Hebrews 4:12; I Peter 2:2

SUFFERING

Romans 8:18; II Corinthians 1:5; Philippians 1:29; 3:10; II Timothy 2:12; I Peter 1:6-7; 2:19; 4:12-13, 16; 5:10

TEMPTATION

Psalm 94:17-18; Proverbs 28:13; Matthew 26:41; I Corinthians 10:12-13; Hebrews 2:18, 4:14-16; James 1:2-3, 12, 14; 4:7; I Peter 1:6; II Peter 2:9; I John 4:4; Jude 24

TEN COMMANDMENTS

Exodus 20

THOSE WHO HAVEN'T HEARD

John 6:45; 12:32; 16:8; Romans 1:19-20; 2:15, 18

TRIBULATION PERIOD

Daniel 9:24-27; Revelation 11:2-3; 13:5

TRUMPET JUDGMENTS

Revelation 8-9

TRUSTING

Psalm 5:11; 18:2; 37:5; Proverbs 3:5-6; Isaiah 12:2; 26:3

TWO WITNESSES

Revelation 11:3-12

UNPARDONABLE SIN

Matthew 12:22-32; Mark 3:22-30; Luke 11:14-23, 12:10; Hebrews 10:26; I John 5:16-17

VIAL JUDGMENTS

Revelation 16

VICTORY

II Chronicles 32:8; Romans 8:37; I Corinthians 15:57; II Corinthians 2:14; II Timothy 2:19; I John 5:4; Revelation 3:5; 21:7

WILL OF GOD

Psalm 37:4; 91:1-2; Proverbs 3:5-6; 4:26; Romans 14:5; Galatians 6:4; Ephesians 5:14-21; Philippians 2:12-13; I Thessalonians 4:3; I Peter 3:17

WITNESSING

Psalm 66:16; Proverbs 11:30; Matthew 5:16; Mark 5:19; Luke 24:48; Acts 1:8; Romans 1:16; II Corinthians 5:18-20; I Peter 3:15; 4:11

WIVES

Proverbs 11:6; 12:4; 14:1; 22:6, 15; 29:15; 31:10-31; I Timothy 3:11; Titus 2:3-5; I Peter 3:1-6

FAVORITE BIBLE STORIES

God's Work of Creation . . . . Genesis, Ch. 1
Adam and Eve . . . . Genesis, Ch. 2
Noah and the Ark . . . . Genesis, Ch. 6
God's Covenant with Noah . . . . Genesis, Ch. 9
Tower of Babel . . . . Genesis, Ch. 11
God's Call to Abram . . . . Genesis, Ch. 12
The Story of Lot . . . . Genesis, Ch. 19
Abraham and Isaac . . . . Genesis, Ch. 22
Isaac and Rebekah . . . . Genesis, Ch. 24
Jacob's Vision of a Ladder . . . . Genesis, Ch. 28
Jacob Wrestles with an Angel . . . . Genesis, Ch. 32
Joseph and His Brothers . . . . Genesis, Ch. 37
Joseph Interprets Pharaoh's Dream . . . . Genesis, Ch. 41
The Baby Moses . . . . Exodus, Ch. 2
The Burning Bush . . . . Exodus, Ch. 3
The First Passover . . . . Exodus, Ch. 12
The Crossing of the Red Sea . . . . Exodus, Ch. 14
The Quails and Manna . . . . Exodus, Ch. 16
The Ten Commandments . . . . Exodus, Ch. 20
The Battle of Jericho . . . . Joshua, Ch. 6
Joshua's Long Day . . . . Joshua, Ch. 10
The Sword of the Lord and Gideon . . . . Judges, Ch. 7
The Exploits of Samson . . . . Judges, Ch. 15
Samson and Delilah . . . . Judges, Ch. 16
Ruth and Naomi . . . . Ruth, Ch. 1
Ruth Gleans in the Field . . . . Ruth, Ch. 2
Samuel and Eli . . . . I Samuel, Ch. 3
David and Goliath . . . . I Samuel, Ch. 17
David and Jonathan . . . . I Samuel, Ch. 19
Saul Consults the Witch of Endor . . . . I Samuel, Ch. 28
David's Psalm of Thanksgiving . . . . II Samuel, Ch. 22
Solomon's Wisdom . . . . I Kings, Ch. 3
Solomon Builds the Temple . . . . I Kings, Ch. 6
The Queen of Sheba Visits Solomon . . . . I Kings, Ch. 10
Elijah and the Prophets of Baal . . . . I Kings, Ch. 18
Job's Prosperity Restored . . . . Job, Ch. 42
The Shepherd Psalm . . . . Psalm 23
Wisdom and Her Rewards . . . . Proverbs, Ch. 8
The Soft Answer . . . . Proverbs, Ch. 15
A Good Name is Better Than Riches . . . . Proverbs, Ch. 22
The Prince of Peace . . . . Isaiah, Ch. 9
Ezekiel's Vision of Cherubim and Wheels . . . . Ezekiel, Ch. 10
The Parable of the Dry Bones . . . . Ezekiel, Ch. 37

BIBLE DICTIONARY

AAR'ON (*mountaineer or enlightener*). Son of Amram and Jochebed, and elder brother of Moses and Miriam, Num. 26:59. Direct descendant of Levi by both parents. Called "the Levite," Ex. 4:14, when chosen as the "spokesman" of Moses. Married Elisheba, daughter of the prince of Judah, and had four sons, Nadab, Abihu, Eleazar, and Ithamar, Ex. 6:23. Eighty-three years old when introduced in the Bible. Mouthpiece and encourager of Moses before the Lord and the people of Israel, and in the Court of the Pharaoh, Ex. 4:30; 7:2. Miracle worker of the Exodus, Ex. 7:19. Helped Hur to stay the weary hands of Moses in the battle with Amalek, Ex. 17:9-12. In a weak moment yielded to idolatry among his people and incurred the wrath of Moses, Ex. 32. Consecrated to the priesthood by Moses, Ex. 29. Anointed and sanctified, with his sons, to minister in the priest's office, Ex. 40. Murmured against Moses at the instance of Miriam, but repented and joined Moses in prayer for Miriam's recovery, Num. 12. His authority in Israel vindicated by the miracle of the rod, Num. 17. Died on Mt. Hor, at age of one hundred and twenty-three years, and was succeeded in the priesthood by his son Eleazar, Num. 20:22-29. Office continued in his line till time of Eli. Restored to house of Eleazar by Solomon, 1 Kgs. 2:27.

A'BRA-HAM and **A'BRAM** (*father of a multitude*). Son of Terah, a dweller in Ur of the Chaldees, Gen. 11:25-31. Founder of the Jewish nation. Migrated from Chaldea to Haran. Moved thence to Canaan, to Egypt and back to Canaan, where he settled amid the oak-groves of Mamre. There confirmed in the thrice repeated promise that his seed should become a mighty nation, and his name changed from Abram to Abraham. Died, aged 175 years, and was buried in the tomb of Machpelah, Gen. 12.-26.

AD'AM (*red earth*). A city of Reuben, on Jordan, Josh. 3:16.

AD'AM (*red earth*). Used generically for man and woman, and translated *man* in Gen. 1:26, 27; 5:1; Job 20:29; 21:33; Ps. 68:18; 76:10.

AD'AM (*red earth*). The first man. Creative work of the sixth day. Placed in the "Garden of Eden." Tempted to eat of the forbidden fruit, fell under God's disfavor, and driven out of the Garden subject to the curse of sorrow and toil. Died at age of 930 years. Gen. 1:26, etc.; 2.-5.

A'MOS (*weighty*). One of the lesser prophets. Lived during reigns of Uzziah and Jeroboam II., Amos 1:1-7; 7:14-15. His book is 30th of O. T. It rebukes the sins of Israel and closes with God's promise. Book abounds in rural allusions.

AN'DREW (*manly*). An Apostle of Christ, John 1:35-40; Matt. 4:18. Brother of Simon Peter, native of Bethsaida, and fisherman. Original disciple of John the Baptist, Mark 13:3; John 4:6-13; 12:22.

AN'GEL (*messenger*). A messenger, 2 Sam. 2:5; Luke 7:24. In a spiritual sense, a messenger of God, Gen. 24:7; Heb. 1:14. Nature, Matt. 18:10. Number, 1 Kgs. 22:19; Matt. 26:53; Heb. 12:22. Strength, Ps. 103:20; Rev. 5:2. Activity, Isa. 6:2-6. Appearance, Matt. 28:2-4; Rev. 10:1, 2. Office, Isa. 6:1-3; Rev. 6:11; Matt. 13:49; 16:27; 24:31.

AN'TI-OCH (*after Antiochus*). (1) Capital of the Greek kings of Syria, on the Orontes. First Gentile church founded there, and disciples first called Christians there; Acts 11:19-21, 26. (2) A city of Pisidia, Acts 13:14. Starting point of the persecutions which followed Paul all through Asia Minor, Acts 14.

A-POL'LOS (*belonging to Apollo*). A learned Jew and Christian convert of Alexandria, who became a preacher and friend of Paul, Acts 18:24-28; 1 Cor. 3:6-9; Tit. 3:13.

ATH'ENS (*city of Athena, or Minerva*). Capital of Attica and chief seat of Grecian learning and civilization. Situate in S. E. part of the Grecian Peninsula, five miles from its seaport, the Piræus. Paul preached on its Areopagus or Mars' Hill, Acts 17:19-22, and founded a church there.

AU-GUS'TUS (*venerable*). Caius Julius Cæsar Octavianus, grand-nephew of, and heir to, Julius Cæsar. Made first emperor of Rome B.C. 27, with title of Augustus. During his reign Christ was born, Luke 2:1. Died A.D. 14, aged 76 years.

BAR'NA-BAS (*son of comfort*). Joseph or Joses, a convert of Cyprus, and companion of Paul, Acts 4:36; 9:27; 11:25, 26; 15:22-39.

BAR-THOL'O-MEW (*son of Tolmai*). One of the twelve apostles, Matt. 10:3; Mark 3:18; Luke 6:14; Acts 1:13; perhaps Nathanael in John 1:45.

BETH'-LE-HEM, BETH'LE-HEM (*house of bread*). (1) A town of Palestine, six miles S. of Jerusalem. First called Ephrath or Ephratah, Gen. 35: 16-19; 48:7. Called Bethlehem-judah after the conquest, Judg. 17:7. Home of Ruth, Ruth 1:19. Birthplace of David, 1 Sam. 17:12. Here Christ was born, Matt. 2:1, 2; Luke 2:15-18. (2) A town in Zebulun, Josh. 19:15.

CHRIST. The Anointed; the Messiah. A title of Jesus, the Saviour: at first with the article, "The Christ;" later, as part of a proper name, "Jesus Christ." [JESUS.]

COR'INTH (*ornament*). Anciently Ephyra; capital of Achaia. Destroyed by Rome, B.C. 146. Rebuilt by Julius Cæsar, B.C. 46, as a Roman colony. Paul founded a church there, Acts 18:1; 20: 2, 3.

DA-MAS'CUS. A city of Asia, 133 miles N. E. of Jerusalem, Gen. 14:15; 15:2. Adjacent region called "Syria of Damascus," 2 Sam. 8:5. Taken by David, 2 Sam. 8:6; and by Jeroboam, 2 Kgs. 14:28. Scene of Paul's conversion, Acts 9:1-27; 22:1-16.

DA'VID (*well-beloved*). Youngest son of Jesse, 1 Sam. 16:8-12, born at Bethlehem. Anointed king by Samuel, 1 Sam. 16:13. Re-anointed at Hebron, 2 Sam. 2:4. United his kingdom and raised it to great strength and splendor. Died at the age of 70, B.C. 1015, after a reign of seven and a half years over Judah and thirty-three years over the entire kingdom of Israel. History told in 1 Sam. 16. to 1 Kgs. 2.

DIS-CI'PLE (*learner*). Follower of Christ, Matt. 10:24; of John, Matt. 9:14. Applied specially to the twelve, Matt. 10:1; 11:1; 20:17.

E'GYPT (*Coptic land*). Northeastern country of Africa; the Hebrew "Mizraim," Gen. 10:6, and "Land of Ham," Ps. 105:23, 27. Bondage place of Israelites, Ex. 1.-14. Noted for Nile river, rich soil and gigantic ruins. Ancient religion monotheistic, with sun as central object; and attributes of nature in form of trinities. Vast temples and numerous priests. Kings called Pharaohs, who perpetuated their reins in obelisks, temples, sculptures, sphinxes, pyramids, etc. In intimate commerce with Hebrews, 1 Kgs. 3:1. Conquered Judea, 1 Kgs. 14:25, 26. Frequently mentioned in Scripture.

E-LI'JAH (*God is God*). (1) The prophet; Elias in N. T., Matt. 17:3. A Tishbite of Gilead; appears suddenly; is fed by ravens; restores the widow's son, 1 Kgs. 17:1-24; invokes fire on the prophets of Baal, 18:17-40; anoints Hazael, Jehu, and Elisha, 19.; denounces Ahab and Jezebel, 21:17-24; is translated in a chariot of fire, 2 Kgs. 2.; reappears on the mount of Transfiguration, Luke 9:28-35. (2) A son of Harim, Ez. 10:21.

EPH'E-SUS (*desirable*). Capital of Ionia, on the Ægean Sea. Noted for its commerce, learning, and architecture. Paul visited it, Acts 18:1-20, and founded a church there, to which he addressed one of his best epistles, Acts 19:1-10; 20:17-38.

E-PIS'TLE (*sending to*). In O. T. a letter, 2 Sam. 11:14; 2 Kgs. 5:5, 6; 2 Chr. 21:12; Ez. 4:6-11. In N. T., a formal tract containing Christian doctrine and salutary advice.

E-VAN'GEL-IST (*publisher of glad tidings*). One of the four writers of the gospels Matthew, Mark, Luke and John. A preacher of the gospel inferior in authority to the Apostles, Acts 8:14-19, and apparently to the prophets, Eph. 4:11, yet superior to the pastor and teacher, Acts 21:8; Eph. 4:11; 2 Tim.

4:5. A travelling and corresponding missionary, Acts 20:4, 5.

E-ZE'KI-EL (*strength of God*). One of the four greater prophets; carried captive to Babylon B.C. 598; entered the prophetic calling in fifth year of his captivity, Ezek. 1:1-3. Chapters 1.-24. of his book contain predictions before the fall of Jerusalem, and 25.-48. predictions after that event. The visions of the Temple, 40.-48. are a unique feature of the book.

EZ'RA (*help*). The famous scribe and priest, resident at Babylon, who returned to Jerusalem with his countrymen, B.C. 458, where he began instant reforms. He collected and revised the previous O. T. writings and largely settled the O. T. canon. His book, 15th of O. T., tells the story of the return and the establishment of a new order of things at Jerusalem and in Judea.

GA-LA'TIA (*land of the Galli, Gauls*). A central province of Asia Minor, and part of Paul's missionary field, Acts 16:6; 17:23; 2 Tim. 4:10.

GAL'I-LEE (*circle*). Originally the circuit containing the 20 towns given by Solomon to Hiram, Josh. 20:7; 1 Kgs. 9:11; 2 Kgs. 15:29. In time of Christ, one of the largest provinces of Palestine, in which he spent the greater part of his life and ministry. Luke 13:1; 23:6; John 1:43-47; Acts 1:11.

GETH-SEM'A-NE (*oil press*). Scene of Christ's agony and betrayal, at the foot of Olivet, near Jerusalem, Matt. 26:36-56; Mark 14:26-52; Luke 22:39-49; John 18:1-13.

GO-LI'ATH (*splendor*). The Philistine giant who defied the army of Israel, 1 Sam. 17:4-54. Another Goliath in 2 Sam. 21:19-22.

GREECE, GREEKS, GRE'CIANS. The well known country in S. E. of Europe, called also Hellas. Javan in O. T., Gen. 10:2-5; Isa. 46:19; Ezek. 27:13, 19; but direct in Dan. 8:21; 10:20; 11:2; Joel 3:6; Acts 20:2. Greek the original N. T. language.

HA-BAK'KUK (*embrace*). A minor prophet during reigns of Jehoiakim and Josiah. His book, thirteenth of the prophetic, denounces Chaldea, and concludes with a striking poem and prayer.

HAG'GA-I (*festive*). A minor prophet. His book, fifteenth of the prophetic, exhorts the Jews to crown the work of Zerubbabel.

HE'BREWS. "Abram the Hebrew," Gen. 14:13, that is, *eber,* the one who had "passed over" the Euphrates, westward. Hence, "seed" or descendants of Abraham. Among themselves, preferably, Israelites, from Gen. 32:28. Jews, *i.e.* Judahites, Judeans, after the captivity.

HER'OD (*heroic*). (1) Herod the Great, tetrarch of Judea, B.C. 41; King of Judea, B.C. 41-4; liberal, yet tyrannical and cruel. Issued murderous edict against children of Bethlehem, Matt. 2:16. (2) Herod Antipas, son of former; tetrarch of Galilee and Perea, B.C. 4-A.D. 39; murderer of John the Baptist, Matt. 14:1; Luke 3:19; 23:7-15; Acts 13:1. (3) Herod Philip, son of Herod the Great. Married Herodias, Matt. 14:3; Mark 6:17; Luke 3:19. Lived and died in private life. (4) Herod Philip II., son of Herod the Great, and tetrarch of Batanea, Ituraea, etc., B.C. 4-A.D. 34, Luke 3:1. (5) Herod Agrippa I., grandson of Herod the Great; tetrarch of Galilee; king of his grandfather's realm, A.D., 37-44, Acts 12:1-19. (6) Herod Agrippa II., son of former, and king of consolidated tetrarchies, A.D. 50-100, Acts 25:13-27; 26:1-28.

HIGH PRIEST. Chief priest, Aaron being the first. Originally a life office, limited to a line or family, Ex. 28:1; Lev. 21:10; Num. 3:32; 20:8; Deut. 10:6.

HO-SE'A (*help*). First of minor prophets. Prophetic career, B.C. 784-725, in Israel. Denounces the idolatries of Israel and Samaria. Style obscure.

I'SAAC (*laughter*). Son of Abraham, Gen. 17:17-22. Second of the patriarchs, and father of Jacob and Esau, Gen. 21.-35.

I-SA'IAH (*salvation of Jehovah*). Son of Amoz, Isa. 1:1, and first of greater prophets. His book, 23d of O. T., covers sixty years of prophecy, Isa. 1:1, at Jerusalem. It reproves the sins of the Jews and other nations, and foreshadows the coming of Christ. Called "prince of prophets." Poetically for Israel, Am. 7:9, 16.

IS'RA-EL (*who prevails with God*). Name given to Jacob, Gen. 32:28; 35:10; became national, Ex. 3:16; narrowed to northern kingdom after the revolt of the ten tribes from Judah, 1 Sam. 11:8; 2 Sam. 20:1; 1 Kgs. 12:16, with Shechem as capital, 1 Kgs. 12:25, and Tirzah as royal residence, 14:17; afterwards, capital at Samaria, 16:24. Kingdom lasted 254 years, with 19 kings, B.C. 975-721, when it fell a prey to the Assyrians. The returned of Israel blended with those of Judah.

JA'COB (*supplanter*). Son of Isaac and second born twin with Esau, Gen. 25:24-34. Bought Esau's birthright, fled to Padan-aram, married Rachel and Leah, wandered to Hebron, name changed to Israel, drifted to Egypt, where he died, aged 147 years, Gen. 25.-50.

JAMES (*Jacob*). (1) "The Greater" or "Elder," son of Zebedee and brother of John, Matt. 4:21, 22. A fisherman of Galilee, called to the Apostolate about A.D. 28, and styled Boanerges, Matt. 10:2, 3; Mark 3:14-18; Luke 6:12-16; Acts 1:13. Labored at Jerusalem. Beheaded by Herod, A.D. 44. (2) "The Less," another Apostle, son of Alphæus, Matt. 10:3; Mark 3:18; Luke 6:15. (3) Christ's brother, or more likely cousin, and identical with James the Less, Gal. 1:19. Compare Matt. 13:55; Mark 6:3; Acts 12:17. Resident at Jerusalem and author of The Epistle of James, written before A.D. 62 to the scattered Jews, urging good works as the groundwork and evidence of faith.

JE-HOSH'A-PHAT (*judged of God*). (1) Recorder under David and Solomon, 2 Sam. 8:16; 1 Kgs. 4:3. (2) A trumpeter, 1 Chr. 15:24. (3) Solomon's purveyor, 1 Kgs. 4:17. (4) Father of Jehu, 2 Kgs. 9:2-14. (5) Valley of Cedron, or else a visionary spot, Joel 3:2-12. (6) Son and successor of Asa on throne of Judah, B.C. 914-890. A God-fearing king, in close alliance with Israel, 1 Kgs. 15:24; 2 Kgs. 8:16; 2 Chr. 17.-21. 50.

JE-HO'VAH. "He that is." "I am," Ex. 3:14. The self-existent and eternal one. Hebrew word for God, generally rendered "Lord." Not pronounced; but Adonai, "Lord," or Elohim, "God," substituted, Ex. 6:3. [GOD.]

JER"E-MI'AH (*exalted*). (1) Second of greater prophets. His prophecies cover reins of Josiah, Jehoiakim, and Zedekiah, B.C. 628-586, and constitute the 24th O. T. book. Life one of vicissitude. Prophecies noted for boldness and beauty, and chiefly denunciative of Judah and her policy. Withdrew to Egypt, where he probably died. (2) Seven others in O. T., 2 Kgs. 23:31; 1 Chr. 12:4-13; 5:24; Neh. 10:2; 12:1, 12, 34; Jer. 35:3.

JE-RU'SA-LEM (*place of peace*). Capital of Hebrew monarchy and of kingdom of Judah, 24 miles west of Jordan and 37 east of the Mediterranean. "Salem," Ps. 76:2, and perhaps, Gen. 14:18. "Jebus," Judg. 19:10, 11. "Jebus-salem," Jerusalem, Josh. 10:1. "City of David," Zion, 1 Kgs. 8:1; 2 Kgs. 14:20. "City of Judah," 2 Chr. 25:28. "City of God," Ps. 46:4. "City of the great King," Ps. 48:2. "The holy city," Neh. 11:1. Captured and rebuilt by David, and made his capital, 2 Sam. 5:6-13; 1 Chr. 11:4-9. Destroyed by Nebuchadnezzar, B.C. 588. Rebuilt by returned captives. Captured by Alexander the Great, B.C. 332; by Antiochus, B.C. 203; by Rome, B.C. 63.

JE'SUS CHRIST. Jesus the Saviour; Christ, or Messiah, the anointed. Jesus the Christ. Name given to the long promised prophet and king, Matt. 11:3; Acts 19:4. Only begotten of God. Born of Mary at Bethlehem, B.C. 5; reared at Nazareth, baptized at age of 30, Luke 3:23. Ministerial career, extending over Galilee, Judea, and Perea, began A.D. 27 and ended with the crucifixion, April 7, A.D. 30. Matthew, Mark, and Luke record his Galilean ministry; John his Judean ministry. The four gospels embrace Christ's biography.

JOB (*persecuted*). (1) The pious and wealthy patriarch of Uz, whose poem constitutes the 18th O. T. book, and first of the poetical. It is a dramatic narrative of his life of vicissitude, the gist being, whether goodness can exist irrespective of reward. Poetry noted for its sublimity, pathos, and beauty. Authorship disputed. Oldest of sacred writings.

(2) Son of Issachar, Gen. 46:13. Jashub, 1 Chr. 7:1.

JO'EL (*Jehovah his God*). (1) Son of Pethuel and second of minor prophets. Probably of Judah and Contemporary with Uzziah, B.C. 810-758. His book, 29th of O. T., depicts calamities, rises into exhortation, and foreshadows the Messiah. (2) Son of Samuel, 1 Sam. 8:2. (3) Others in 1 Chr. 4:35; 5:4, 8, 12; 6:36; 7:3; 11:38; 15:7; 23:8; 27:20; 2 Chr. 29:12; Ez. 10:43; Neh. 11:9.

JOHN (*God's gift*). Johanan, contraction of Jehohanan. (1) Kinsman of the high priest, Acts 4:6. (2) Hebrew name of Mark, Acts 12:25; 13:5; 15:37. (3) John the Baptist, son of Zacharias. Birth foretold, Luke 1. Born about six months before Christ. Retired to wilderness. Emerged to preach and baptize. Baptized Jesus, Matt. 3. Imprisoned by Herod, Luke 3:1-22. Beheaded, Matt. 14:1-12. (4) John, Apostle and Evangelist; son of Zebedee, Matt. 4:21; a fisherman of Galilee, Luke 5:1-10; a favorite apostle, noted for zeal and firmness, John 13:23; 19:26; 20:2; 21:7. He remained at Jerusalem till about A.D. 65, when he went to Ephesus. Banished to Patmos, and released A.D. 96. His writings, doubtless done at Ephesus, are the fourth Gospel, giving Christ's ministry in Judea; his three epistles, and Revelation. (5) A frequent name among the Maccabees, 1 Macc.

JO'NAH (*dove*). Son of Amittai. Commissioned to denounce Nineveh. His book, 32d of O. T. and 5th of minor prophets, narrates his refusal, escape from drowning, final acceptance and successful ministry. Its lesson is God's providence over all nations.

JON'A-THAN (*God-given*). (1) A Levite, Judg. 17:7-13; 18. (2) Eldest son of Saul, and friend of David, 1 Sam. 13: 2, 3; 18:1-4; 19:1-7; 20. Fell in battle of Gilboa. David's lament, 2 Sam. 1:17-27. (3) Others in 2 Sam. 15:27, 36; 21:20, 21; 23:32; 1 Chr. 2:32, 33; 27:32; Ez. 8:6; 10:15; Neh. 12:11, 14, 35; Jer. 37:15, 20; 40:8.

JOR'DAN (*descender*). Chief river of Palestine, rising in the Anti-Libanus range, flowing southward, enlarging into Sea of Galilee, emptying into Dead Sea. A swift, narrow, yet fordable stream, with an entire course of about 200 miles, Gen. 13:10; Josh. 2:7; Judg. 3:28; 2 Sam. 10:17; Matt. 3:13.

JO'SEPH (*increase*). (1) Son of Jacob and Rachel, Gen. 37:3; sold into Egypt; promoted to high office by the Pharaoh; rescued his family from famine; settled them in Goshen; died at advanced age; bones carried back to Shechem, Gen. 37.-50. (2) An Isaacharite, Num. 13:7. (3) Two who returned, Ez. 10:42; Neh. 12:14. (4) Three of Christ's ancestors, Luke 3:24, 26, 30. (5) Husband of Mary, and a carpenter at Nazareth, Matt. 1:19; 13:55; Luke 3: 23; John 1:45. (6) Of Arimathea, a member of the Sanhedrim, who acknowledged Christ, Matt. 27:57-59; Mark 15:43; Luke 23:51. (7) The apostle Barsabas, substituted for Judas, Acts 1:23. (8) Frequent name in Apoc.

JU'DAH (*praise*). (1) Fourth son of Jacob, Gen. 29:35; 37:26-28; 43:3-10; 44:14-34. His tribe the largest, Num. 1:26, 27. Allotted the southern section of Canaan, Josh. 15:1-63. (2) Kingdom of, formed on disruption of Solomon's empire, out of Judah, Benjamin, Simeon, and part of Dan, with Jerusalem as capital, B.C. 975. Had 19 kings, and lasted for 389 years, till reduced by Nebuchadnezzar, B.C. 586. Outlived its rival, Israel, some 135 years. (3) City of Jerusalem, 2 Chr. 25:28. (4) A town in Naphtali, Josh. 19:34. (5) Persons in Ez. 3:9; 10:23; Neh. 11:9.

JU'DAS. Greek form of Judah. (1) Judah, Matt. 1:2, 3. (2) Iscariot, or of Kerioth. Betrayer of Christ, Matt. 10:4; Mark 3:19; Luke 6:16; John 6:71; 12: 6; 13:29. (3) Man of Damascus, Acts 9:11. (4) Barsabas, chief among the brethren, and prophet, Acts 15:22, 32. (5) A Galilean apostate, Acts 5:37. (6) Frequent name in Apoc.

JUDE, Jude 1:1. Judas, brother of James the Less, Luke 6:16; John 14:22; Acts 1:13; Matt. 13:55. Thaddæus, Lebbæus, Matt. 10:3; Mark 3:18. An Apostle and author of the epistle which bears his name, 26th N. T. book. Written about A.D. 65. Place not known.

JUDG'ES. Governors of Israel between Joshua and the kings. They were called to God, elective or usurpative. Qualification, martial or moral prowess.

Rule arbitrary. Fifteen are recorded. Period, B.C. 1400 - 1091, about 310 years. Book of Judges, 7th of O. T., probably compiled by Samuel. Its history is that of a tumultuous period, completing Joshua's conquests and leading to legitimate kingly rule.

LA'VER (*wash*). Brazen vessel holding water for priestly washings—hands, feet, and the sacrifices. Ex. 30:18-21; 38:8; 1 Kgs. 7:38-40; 2 Chr. 4:6.

LAW (*rule*). In Scripture, reference is nearly always to the Hebrew civil, moral, and ceremonial law, Matt. 5:17; John 1:17; Acts 25:8.

LEB'A-NON (*white*). Two mountain ranges running N. E., between which was Cœlo-Syria. The western is Libanus, or Lebanon proper. The eastern is Anti-Libanus, and skirted Palestine on the north, Deut. 1:7; Josh. 1:4. Many scripture allusions, Isa. 10:34; Jer. 22:23.

LE'VI (*joined*). (1) Third son of Jacob, Gen. 29:34; avenged Dinah's wrong, 34:25-31; cursed, 49:5-7; went to Egypt, Ex. 6:16; blessed, Ex. 32: 25-28. (2) Two of Christ's ancestors, Luke 3:24, 29. (3) Original name of Matthew, Mark 2:14; Luke 5:27, 29; compare Matt. 9:9.

LE'VITES. Descendants of Levi, Ex. 6:16-25; Lev. 25:32, etc.; Num. 35:2-8; Josh. 21:3. In above, the tribe is meant. But Levites came to mean the priestly branch, *i.e.,* descendants of Aaron, Josh. 3:3; 1 Kgs. 8:4; Ez. 2:70; John 1:19. Three Levitical lines, Kohathite, Gershonite, Merarite, Num. 3:17. Assigned 48 cities among the other tribes, Num. 35.

LORD (*loaf-guardian*). Jehovah, LORD, Gen. 15:4; Ps. 7., 100. Adonai, Lord, Christ, The Lord, Our Lord. Supreme ruler, and not the Saxon dignitary.

LORD'S SUP'PER. Substitute for the O. T. Paschal feast. Instituted by Christ the night before the crucifixion, as a reminder of his covenant with mankind, Matt. 26:19; Mark 14:16; Luke 22:13. "Breaking of bread," Acts 2:42; 20:7. "Communion," 1 Cor. 10:16. "Lord's Supper," only in 1 Cor. 11:20.

LUKE (*luminous*). Evangelist and physician, Col. 4:14; 2 Tim. 4:11. Author of third gospel and of Acts of the Apostles.

MAL'A-CHI (*God's messenger*). Last of minor prophets. Nothing known of nativity or lineage. Contemporary with Nehemiah, B.C. 445-433. His book foretells the coming of Christ and John the Baptist.

MARK (*polite, shining*). John Mark, Acts 12:12, 25; 15:37. John, Acts 13:5, 13. Mark, Acts 15:39. Convert of Peter, 1 Pet. 5:13. Companion of Paul, Col. 4:10. Author of second Gospel, which was probably written in Rome.

MA'RY (*rebellion*). Greek form of Miriam. (1) The bethrothed of Joseph and mother of Christ, Matt. 1:18-25; 12:46; Mark 6:3; Luke 8:19; John 2: 1-5; 19:26; Acts 1:14. (2) Wife of Cleophas, Matt. 27:56, 61; 28:1-9; Mark 16:1-8; Luke 24:1-10. (3) Mother of John Mark, Acts 12:12; Col. 4:10. (4) Sister of Martha and Lazarus, Luke 10: 41, 42; John 11, 12. (5) Mary Magdalene; *i.e.,* of Magdala, Matt. 28:1-10; Mark 16:1-10; Luke 24:10; John 20: 1-18. (6) A Roman convert, Rom. 16:6.

MAT'THEW (*gift of God*). Contraction of Mattathias. The Apostle and Evangelist. Levi in Luke, 5:27-29. Son of Alphæus, Mark 2:14. Tax-collector at Capernaum when called, Matt. 9:9. His gospel is first of N. T. Its original claimed to be the Hebrew, or Syro-Chaldaic, of Palestine. Time of writing placed at A.D. 60-66. Gist, to establish Jesus as O. T. Messiah.

MER'CY SEAT. Lid of the ark, Ex. 25:17-22; hence, covering, or atonement for sin, Heb. 9:5.

MI'CAH (*God-like*). (1) The erratic Ephraimite whose story is told in Judg. 17., 18. (2) Sixth of the minor prophets. Prophesied B.C. 750-698. He foretells the destruction of Samaria and Jerusalem, and prefigures the Messiah. (3) A Reubenite, 1 Chr. 5:5. (4) Grandson of Jonathan, 1 Chr. 8:34, 35. (5) A Levite, 1 Chr. 23:20. (6) Father of Abdon, 2 Chr. 24:20.

MIR'A-CLE (*wonderful*). In scripture, a supernatural event, Num. 22:28; 1 Kgs. 17:6; Matt. 9:18-33; 14:25.

MO'AB (*of his father*). Son of Lot by his daughter, and progenitor of the Moabites. The country lay east of the Dead Sea and south of the Arnon, Num.

21:13-15; 22.; Judg. 11:18. Though idolatrous, worshipping Chemosh, they were a strong, progressive people, holding Israel subject, Judg. 3:12-14; but finally subdued, 15-30; 2 Sam. 8:2; Isa. 15., 16.; Jer. 48.; Ruth 1., 2.

MO'SES (*drawn out*). The great leader and lawgiver of the Hebrews. Son of Amram, a Levite. Born in Egypt, about B.C. 1571. Adopted by Pharaoh's daughter, liberally educated, fled to Midian, Ex. 2. Called to lead the Exode, Ex. 3.-19. Promulgated the law, Ex. 20.-40.; Lev.; Num.; Deut. Died on Nebo, aged 120 years. Reputed author of Pentateuch and Job.

NA'HUM (*comforter*). Seventh of minor prophets. Probably an exile in Assyria. Approximate time of prophecy, B.C. 726-698. It relates to the fall of Nineveh. Noted for vigor and beauty.

NA'THAN (*given*). (1) Distinguished prophet, and royal adviser and biographer of David and Solomon, 2 Sam. 7:2-17; 12:1-22; 1 Kgs. 9:8-45; 1 Chr. 29:29; 2 Chr. 9:29. (2) A son of David, 1 Chr. 3:5; Luke 3:31. (3) Father of one of David's warriors, 2 Sam. 23:36. (4) A returned captive, Ez. 8:16.

NAZ'A-RETH (*separated*). A town of Galilee, now En-nazirah. Home of Jesus, Matt. 4:13; Mark 1:9; Luke 1:26; 4:16, 29; John 1:45, 46.

NE-HE-MI'AH (*consolidation*). (1) The Hebrew captive who returned, as leader of his people, to rebuild Jerusalem and administer its affairs. His book, 16th of O. T., B.C. 445-433, tells of his work. (2) Leader of returning captives, Ez. 2:2; Neh. 7:7. (3) An assistant wall-builder, Neh. 3:16.

NIC"O-DE'MUS (*people's victor*). The Pharisee ruler and timid convert who assisted at Christ's sepulture, John 3:1-10; 7:50; 19:39.

NILE (*dark blue*). The great river of Egypt, worshipped as a god, famous for its annual and fertilizing overflows and its many mouths. Name not mentioned in scripture, but alluded to as "the river," Gen. 41:1; Ex. 2:3; 7:21; "the river of Egypt," Gen. 15:18; "flood of Egypt," Am. 8:8; Sihor, "black," Josh. 13:3; Shihor, "dark blue," 1 Chr. 13:5; "Nachal of Egypt," "river of Cush," etc.

NIN'E-VEH (*dwelling of Ninus*). Capital of Assyria, on river Tigris. Founded by Asshur, Gen. 10:11. At height of its wealth and splendor during time of Jonah and Nahum, and burden of their prophecies. Taken by Medes about B.C. 750, and destroyed by combined Medes and Babylonians, B.C. 606, Jonah; Nah. 1.-3.; Zeph. 2:13. Among the ruins of Nineveh, which was supposed to embrace Nimrud and other suburbs, have been discovered many palaces and temples, and a richly sculptured obelisk whose references are to Syria and Israel.

NO'AH (*rest*). (1) Ninth in descent from Adam, Gen. 5:28-32. Chosen to build the ark, Gen. 6:8-22. Saved from the flood, with his three sons, Shem, Ham, and Japheth, Gen. 7., 8. Repeopled the earth, Gen. 9., 10. Died at age of 950 years. (2) A daughter of Zelophehad, Num. 26:33.

O"BA-DI'AH (*servant of God*). (1) A Judahite, 1 Chr. 3:21. (2) A chief of Issachar, 1 Chr. 7:3. (3) Son of Azel, 1 Chr. 8:38. (4) A Levite, 1 Chr. 9:16. (5) A Gadite, 1 Chr. 12:9. (6) A court officer under Ahab, 1 Kgs. 18:3-16. (7) A teacher of the law, 2 Chr. 17:7. (8) Others, in 1 Chr. 27:19; 2 Chr. 34:12; Ez. 8:9; Neh. 10:5; 12:25. (9) Fourth of minor prophets. Prophesied after capture of Jerusalem. His book, 31st of O. T., is a denunciation of Edom. Nothing known of his history.

PAL"ES-TI'NA, PAL'ES-TINE (*land of sojourners*). Philistia, land of the Philistines, Ps. 40:8; 83:7. Palestina, Ex. 15:14; Isa. 14:29, 31. Palestine, Joel 3:4. Canaan, Gen. 12:5; Ex. 15:15; Holy Land, Zech. 2:12. The indefinitely bounded region promised to Abraham, lying between the Mediterranean Sea and Jordan River and Dead Sea. It also embraced the Hebrew settlements beyond Jordan, Gen. 15:18; 17:8; Num. 24:2-12; Deut. 1:7.

PAR'A-BLE (*comparison*). Allegorical representation of something real in nature or human affairs, whence a moral is drawn. A favorite method of Oriental teaching, 2 Sam. 12:1-4; Isa. 5:1-7. Christ spoke over 30 parables, Matt. 13:3-8; 24-30, 31, 32, and elsewhere in Gospels.

PASS'O-VER (*passing over*). First of three great Jewish feasts, instituted in honor of the "passing over" of the Hebrew households by the destroying angel, Ex. 12., 13:3-10; 23:14-19; Lev. 23: 4-14. Called the "feast of unleavened bread." The Christian Passover is "The Lord's Supper," eucharist, Matt. 27:62; Luke 22:1-20; John 19:42.

PAUL (*small*). In Hebrew, Saul. Born at Tarsus in Cilicia, of Benjamite parents, about the beginning of 1st century; a Pharisee in faith; a tent-maker by trade, Phil. 3:5; Acts 18:3; 21:39; 23:6. Studied law with Gamaliel at Jerusalem; persecuted early Christians; converted near Damascus, Acts 5:34; 7:58; 9:1-22. Commissioned an apostle to the Gentiles, Acts 26:13-20. Carried the gospel to Asia Minor, Greece, and Rome. Author of fourteen epistles, amplifying the Christian faith. Supposably a martyr at Rome, A.D. 68.

PEN'TA-TEUCH (*five-fold book*). Greek name for the first five O. T. books, or books of Moses. Called Torah, "the law," by Hebrews.

PEN'TE-COST (*fiftieth day*). The Hebrew harvest-home festival, celebrated on fiftieth day from the Passover, or on the date of the giving of the law at Sinai, Ex. 23:16; 34:22; Lev. 23: 15-22; Num. 28. In the Christian Church, Pentecost is celebrated seven weeks after Easter, to commemorate the day in Acts 2:1-14.

PE'TER (*stone, rock*). Simon, or Simeon; son of Jonas, Matt. 16:17; Acts 15:14. A fisherman, resident at Capernaum, Matt. 8:14; called, Matt. 4:18-20; name changed to Peter, John 1:42. Founder of Christian Church among the Jews, Acts 2.; spokesman of the apostles, Acts 10.; author of two epistles; a probable martyr at Rome. His first epistle is dated from Babylon; his second is his valedictory. Both are advisory and exhortatory.

PHA'RAOH (*sun-king*). General name of Egyptian kings. Only a few are definitely named in the Bible. Different ones alluded to are, Gen. 12:15; 41.; Ex. 1:8; 5:1; 1 Chr. 4:18; 1 Kgs. 11: 18-22; 9:16; 2 Kgs. 18:21; Pharaoh-nechoh, 2 Kgs. 23:29; Pharaoh-hophra, Jer. 37:5-8.

PHIL'IP (*lover of horses*). (1) The apostle of Bethsaida, of whom little is known, Matt. 10:3; Mark 3:18; Luke 6:14; John 6:5-9; Acts 1:13. (2) The evangelist and deacon, resident at Cæsarea, and preacher throughout Samaria, Acts 6:5; 8:5-13; 21:8-10. (3) The tetrarch. [HEROD.] (4) Husband of Herodias, Matt. 14:3. [HEROD.] (5) Governor of Jerusalem under Antiochus, and regent of Syria, 2 Macc. 5:22. (6) Philip V., king of Macedonia, 1 Macc. 8:5. (7) King of Macedonia, B.C. 360-336, and father of Alexander the Great, 1 Macc. 1:1.

PHŒ-NI'CIA (*land of palm-trees*). Phenica in Acts 21:2. Phenice in Acts 11:19; 15:3. In O. T. referred to as Tyre and Sidon, or coasts of Tyre and Sidon. The small coast country north of Palestine, noted for its commercial enterprise, learning, and skill in arts. Included in the Land of Promise but never conquered, Josh. 13:4-6. David and Solomon employed its sailors and artisans, 2 Sam. 5:11; 1 Kgs. 5.

PI'LATE (*spear-armed*). Pontius Pilate in Matt. 27:2. Sixth Roman procurator of Judea, A.D. 26-36. Official residence at Cæsarea, with judicial visits to other places. Christ was brought before him at Jerusalem for judgment. He found no guilt, but lost his moral courage in the presence of the mob. Eventually banished to Gaul, Luke 23:1-7; John 18:27-40; 19.

PLAGUE (*blow*). Pestilential disease, Lev. 13:2-8; 26:25. Any calamitous visitation, Mark 5:29; Luke 7:21. The judgments of God on Egypt are called plagues. They were (1) Nile changed to blood, Ex. 7:14-25. (2) Visitation of frogs, Ex. 8:1-15. (3) Lice, Ex. 8:16-19. (4) Flies, Ex. 8:20-32. (5) Murrain, Ex. 9:1-7. (6) Boils, Ex. 9: 8-12. (7) Hail, Ex. 9:13-35. (8) Locusts, Ex. 10:1-20. (9) Darkness, Ex. 10:21-28. (10) Smiting of the firstborn, Ex. 12:29, 30.

PRIEST (*presbyter, elder*). Representative of man in things appertaining to God. Assistants of Moses as mediator,

Ex. 24:5. Function of priesthood conferred on Levites, Ex. 28. Priests divided into regular courses, 1 Chr. 24:1-19; 2 Chr. 23:8; Luke 1:5.

PROPH'ET (*speaking beforehand*). Who tells the future under God's inspiration. The prophetic order embraced political, as well as spiritual, advisers and warners. The books of seventeen—four greater and thirteen lesser prophets—are comprised in the O. T. Christ is the preeminent and eternal prophet, Luke 24:27, 44.

PSALMS (*play a stringed instrument*). In Hebrew, "Praises." The collection of one hundred and fifty lyrics which compose the nineteenth O. T. book. The liturgical hymnbook of the Hebrews, and accepted by early Christians. Authorship of seventy of them ascribed to David. The most perfect specimens of Hebrew poetry extant.

RED SEA. The arm of Gulf of Aden which separates Egypt from Arabia. "The sea," Ex. 14:2, 9, 16, 21, 28; 15:1-19; Josh. 24:6, 7. "Egyptian sea," Isa. 11:15. "Sea of *Suph*," *weedy* or *reedy sea,* translated "Red Sea," Ex. 10:19; 13:18; 15:4; 23:31; Num. 21:4. In N. T., the Greek "Erythrean," or Red Sea, Acts 7:36. At its head it separates into gulfs of Akaba and Suez, the latter of which the Israelites crossed.

REV"E-LA'TION (*veil drawn back*). (1) Scripturally, revealing truth through divine agency or by supernatural means, 2 Cor. 12:1-7. (2) Book of Revelation, or Apocalypse; last of N. T. books; written by the Apostle John, about A.D. 95-97, probably at Ephesus. It is a record of his inspired visions while a prisoner on the island of Patmos. Its aim is much disputed, but it is seemingly a prophetic panorama of church history to the end of time.

ROME, RO'MANS. First mentioned in Bible in 1 Macc. 1:10, when Rome was pushing her conquests in Palestine and Syria. The capital, Rome, is on the Tiber, about 15 miles from the sea. Founded B.C. 752. Governed by kings till B.C. 509; then by consuls till Augustus Cæsar became emperor, B.C. 30. At the Christian era Rome was virtual mistress of the civilized world. Empire declined rapidly after removal of capital to Constantinople by Constantine, A.D. 328. Gospel early introduced among Romans, but Christians persecuted till time of Constantine. Palestine was ruled from Rome by kings, procurators, governors, or proconsuls. Paul wrote his celebrated epistle to the Romans from Corinth, about A.D. 58, to show that Jew and Gentile were alike subject to sin and in equal need of justification and sanctification.

SAB'BATH (*rest*). Rest day, or seventh of the week, Gen. 2:2, 3. Became a Mosaic institution for rest and festal occasions, Ex. 16:23-30; 20:8-11; Lev. 19:3, 30; 23:3; 25:4-9; Deut. 5:12-15. Day for consulting prophets, 2 Kgs. 4:23. A day of teaching and joy, Neh. 8:1-12; Hos. 2:11. A whole week of time is implied in Matt. 28:1; Mark 16:1; Luke 24:1; John 20:1; Acts 20:7; 1 Cor. 16:2. Among Christians, the day after the Hebrew Sabbath, or seventh-day, gradually and till fully established, became the Sabbath, or first-day, in commemoration of the resurrection of Christ. Hence, "The Lord's Day," John 20:26; Acts 20:6-11; 1 Cor. 16:2; Rev. 1:10.

SAB'BATH DAY'S JOURNEY. Travel on the Sabbath was limited, Ex. 16:29. Custom seemed to sanction 2000 paces from the walls of a city as sufficient for all needs on the day of rest, Acts 1:12.

SAD'DU-CEES (*disciples of Zadok*). A Jewish sect, supposably Zadokites, 1 Kgs. 1:32-45, whose chief tenets were (1) rejection of the divinity of the Mosaic oral law and traditions; (2) rejection of the later O. T. books, but acceptance of the Mosaic teachings; (3) denial of angel and spiritual existence, and consequent immortality of the soul; (4) belief in the absolute moral freedom of man. Their hatred of Christianity was as bitter as that of the Pharisees, Matt. 3:7; Mark 12:18; Luke 20:27; Acts 4:1; 5:17; 23:6-10. Though composed of men of position, the sect was never very numerous nor influential, and it disappeared from history after the first century of the Christian era.

SALT SEA. The Dead Sea. "Sea of the plain," Deut. 4:49; 2 Kgs. 14:25.

"Salt sea," Deut. 3:17; Josh. 3:16; 12:3. "East sea," Ezek. 47:18; Joel 2:20; Zech. 14:8. "The sea," Ezek. 47:8. "Vale of Siddim," Gen. 14:3. "Sodomitish sea," 1 Esdr. 5:7. Title "Dead Sea" not found among Hebrew writers, but introduced by Greek authors. Situate 16 miles E. of Jerusalem; 46 miles long by 10 wide; 1300 feet below the level of the Mediterranean; waters intensely salt; receives waters of Jordan from the north; no outlet.

SA-MA'RI-A (*watch mountain*). (1) The kingdom of Samaria, synonymous with the kingdom of Israel, lay to the north of Judah. It varied in size at different times, but in general embraced the territory of the ten revolting tribes on either side of the Jordan, 1 Kgs. 13:32. Named from its capital, Samaria. In N. T. times, Samaria was one of the three subdivisions of Palestine, lying between Judea on the south and Galilee on the north. (2) Capital of the kingdom of Samaria or Israel, and located 30 miles north of Jerusalem. Founded by Omri, king of Israel, about B.C. 925, and called Samaria, after Shemer, from whom he bought the ground, 1 Kgs. 16:23, 24. It became a beautiful and strong city and remained the capital till Shalmaneser, the Assyrian, destroyed it and the empire, B.C. 721, 2 Kgs. 18:9-12. Herod rebuilt it and restored much of its ancient splendor, naming it Sebaste in honor of Augustus, who gave it to him. Philip preached the gospel there, Acts 8:5-9. It is now a modest village called Sebastiyeh, which perpetuates the name Sebaste, and is noted for its many ruins, chief of which is the famous colonnade, 3000 feet in length, 100 columns of which are still standing. Respecting the city the prophecy, Mic. 1:6, has been literally fulfilled.

SAM'SON (*sunlike*). Son of Manoah, of Dan, and judge of Israel for 20 years, Judg. 13:3-25. Noted for his great strength, marvellous exploits, and moral weakness. Contrary to the wishes of his parents, and to the law as laid down in Ex. 34:16, Deut. 7:3, he married a Philistine woman of Timnath, whom he deserted on account of her treachery, Judg. 14. Wishing to return to her, and finding her given to another, he wreaked his vengeance on the Philistines by burning their crops and slaughtering great numbers of them, Judg. 15:1-8. He was surrounded by 3000 of his enemies, while he dwelt on the rock Etam, and surrendered to them, but burst his bands, and routed them with great slaughter, Judg. 15:9-19. Again he was surrounded by enemies in Gaza, but escaped by carrying away the gates of the city. The secret of his strength was finally detected by Delilah, and he was imprisoned and made blind. He finally killed himself and numerous enemies by pulling down the pillars of the house in which they were feasting, Judg. 16.

SAM'U-EL (*God hath heard*). Son of Elkanah and Hannah, celebrated Hebrew prophet and last of the judges, 1 Sam. 1:19-28. Educated under Eli, 1 Sam. 3:4-14, and became his successor in the prophetic office. His sons proved so recreant that the people demanded a king, and Samuel anointed Saul, and resigned his authority to him, 1 Sam. 12. He also anointed David, Saul's successor, 1 Sam. 16:13. He died at Ramah, 1 Sam. 25:1. The two books which bear his name, the 9th and 10th of O. T., are called also First and Second Books of Kings. They were originally one book and contain the lives of Samuel, Saul, and David. The authorship is ascribed to a period subsequent to the secession of the ten tribes, and it is clearly an authorship different from Kings, for in Kings there are many references to the law, while in Samuel there are none. In Kings the Exile is alluded to; it is not so in Samuel. The plans of the two works vary; Samuel is biographical, Kings annalistic.

SAN'HE-DRIM, SAN'HE-DRIN (*seated together*). The supreme council of the Jewish nation, whose germ was in the seventy elders, Num. 11:16, 17, and further development in Jehoshaphat's tribunal, 2 Chr. 19:8-11. In full power after the captivity, and lasted till A.D. 425. The "great Sanhedrim" was composed of 71 priests, scribes, and elders, and presided over by the high priest. The "lesser Sanhedrims" were provincial courts in the towns, and composed of 23 members appointed by the "great Sanhedrim."The word usually appears as "council" in

N. T., Matt. 5:22; Mark 14:55; John 11:47; Acts 4:5-7. The members of the Sanhedrim embraced the three classes, priests, elders, and scribes. After the Roman conquest it had no control of the death power, but the confirmation and execution of capital sentences rested with the Roman procurator. Thus it was that while the Sanhedrim condemned Christ for blasphemy, he was not brought under the Roman judgment of death till accused by the Jews of treason, Matt. 26:65, 66; John 18:31; 19:12. The stoning of Stephen, Acts 7:57-59, was either due to mob excitement, or else illegal.

SA'RAH (*princess*). (1) Wife of Abraham and mother of Isaac, Gen. 11:29; 21:2, 3. Name changed from Sarai to Sarah, Gen. 17:15, 16. At Abraham's request she passed herself off as his sister during their sojourn in Egypt, Gen. 12:10-20, which angered the Pharaoh and led to their banishment. Relentless toward Hagar (whom she had given to Abraham as a concubine) when she bore Ishmael, and caused her to be banished to the desert, Gen. 16:5-16; deceitful when Isaac was promised, Gen. 18:15; cruel again toward Hagar on the occasion of Isaac's weaning, causing her to be banished finally from the household, Gen. 21:9-21. Commended for her faith, Heb. 11:11; and obedience, 1 Pet. 3:6. Died at age of 127 years and buried at Machpelah, Gen. 23. (2) Daughter of Asher, Num. 26:46.

SA'TAN (*adversary*). In O. T. a common noun, meaning enemy or adversary in general, 1 Sam. 29:4; 2 Sam. 19:22; except in Job 1:6, 12; 2:1; Zech. 3:1, where the word becomes a proper noun, and spiritual representative of evil. In N. T. sense, chief of the evil spirits; great adversary of man; the devil, Matt. 4:10; 25:41; Rev. 20, and elsewhere. Called also "the prince of this world;" "the wicked one;" "the tempter;" and in Rev. 12:9, the old serpent, the devil, and Satan.

SAUL (*wished*). (1) An early king of Edom, Gen. 36:37, 38. Shaul in 1 Chr. 1:48, 49. (2) A Benjamite, son of Kish, and first king of Israel. Anointed by Samuel; reigned B.C. 1095-1055; slain with his sons at Gilboa. His versatile career is described in 1 Sam. 9.-31. He stands in Bible history for the stature, strength, and ruggedness of character so essential to judges in times of danger or necessary reform, and for the bravery, generalship and self-confidence of one called on to institute a new empire. Of boundless ambition and erratic judgment, he usurped the priestly function, and drew the reproaches of the aged prophet Samuel, who had surrendered his line in anointing him. The announcement that royalty could not be perpetuated in his family drove him to inexcusable follies, yet with the courage of youth he fought his last despairing battle with the Philistines, and finished his course on his own sword. (3) Hebrew name of Paul, Acts 13:9.

SCRIBE (*writer*). The Hebrew scribe or writer appears to have been at first a court or military official, Ex. 5:6; Judg. 5:14; then secretary or recorder, for kings, priests, and prophets, 2 Sam. 8:17; 20:25; finally a secretary of state, doctor, or teacher, Ez. 7:6. Scribes became a class or guild, copyists and expounders of the law, and through their innovations fell under the same denunciations as priests and Pharisees, Matt. 23:1-33; Mark 7:5-13; Luke 5:30.

SERPENT (*creeper*). The Hebrew original embraces the entire serpent genus. Serpents numerous and venomous in Bible lands. The word appears in Scripture under various names; adder, supposably the cerastes, Gen. 49:17; asp, or cobra, Deut. 32:33; cockatrice, Jer. 8:17; viper, Job 20:16. Subtile, Gen. 3:1; wise, Matt. 10:16; poisonous, Prov. 23:32; sharp-tongued, Ps. 140:3; charmed, Ps. 58:5; emblem of wickedness, Matt. 23:33; cruelty, Pa. 58:4; treachery, Gen. 49:17; the devil, Rev. 12:9-15; fiery serpents sent as a punishment, Num. 21:6; sight of "brazen serpent," an antidote for poison of bite, Num. 21:8, 9; "fiery flying serpent," a probable allusion to dragon, Isa. 14:29.

SEV'EN. A favorite, and often symbolic, number among Hebrews, Gen. 2:2; 7:2; 41:2, 3. Used as a round number, 1 Sam. 2:5; Matt. 12:45. Type of abundance and completeness, Gen. 4:15, 24; Matt. 18:21, 22. These references, and other places, show a seventh day and seventh year sabbath and a seven times seventh year of Jubilee; also sacrificial animals limited to seven, and the golden candlesticks. Seven priests with seven trumpets surrounded Jericho for seven days, and seven times on the seventh day. In the Apocalypse we find seven churches, seven candlesticks, seven stars, seven seals, seven trumpets, seven vials, seven plagues, seven angels.

SHE'BA (*oath*). (1) Son of Bichri, a Benjamite, who revolted from David and was beheaded, 2 Sam. 20:1-22. (2) A Gadite chief, 1 Chr. 5:13. (3) A descendant of Ham, Gen. 10:7; 1 Chr. 1:9. (4) Son of Joktan, Gen. 10:28. (5) Son of Jokshan, Gen. 25:3; 1 Chr. 1:32. (6) The kingdom of Sheba, whose queen visited Solomon, 1 Kgs. 10:1-13; 2 Chr. 9:1-12. This country has been variously located in Africa, in Arabia, on the Persian Gulf, and in Arabia, on the Red Sea. The burden of authority identifies it with Yemen or Arabia Felix, on the Red Sea, and peopled by descendants of Sheba, son of Joktan. (7) A town in Simeon, Josh. 19:2. Probably the Shema of Josh. 15:26.

SHEEP. An important animal among Hebrews, and a main source of wealth. Shepherd's occupation highly respectable, Gen. 4:2; Ex. 3:1; 1 Sam. 16:11; Job 42:12, though odious to Egyptians. Used for sacrifices, Ex. 20:24; 29:38; Lev. 9:3; for food, 1 Sam. 25:18. Wool used for clothing, Lev. 13:47. Skins used for tabernacle coverings, Ex. 25:5. Paid as tribute, 2 Kgs. 3:4. Sheep and shepherd employed much figuratively, 2 Chr. 18:16; Ps. 119:176; Matt. 9:36; John 10:11; Heb. 13:20. The common sheep of Syria and Palestine was the broad-tailed variety.

SHEP'HERD (*herder of sheep*). A highly honorable occupation among pastoral Hebrews, engaged in by both sexes, Gen. 29:6; 30:29-35; Ex. 2:16-22. Often arduous and dangerous employment, Gen. 31:40; 1 Sam. 17:34. Equipment consisted of a sheepskin mantle, a scrip or wallet, a sling and crook. He led the flock to pasture in the morning, tended them by day and folded and watched them at night, Job 30:1; Luke 2:8; John 10:4. The office of sheep-master or chief shepherd was one of great trust as well as honor, 2 Kgs. 3:4; Heb. 13:20; 1 Pet. 5:4. It was the shepherd's duty to count the sheep daily and to tithe them, and he was held responsible for lost ones, Gen. 31:38, 39; Ex. 22:12, 13; Lev. 27:32; Jer. 33:13. Shepherd is used figuratively for Jehovah in Ps. 80:1; Jer. 31:10; for kings, Ezek. 34:10; in N. T. for Christ, John 10:11; Heb. 13:20; 1 Pet. 5:4. It is applied also to teachers in the synagogue and to those who preside over it. Hence pastor and minister of the gospel.

SI'LAS (*Silvanus, woody*). An eminent member of the early Christian church. Written Silvanus in Paul's epistles. Resided at Jerusalem as teacher, but accompanied Paul on his tours, and was his fellow-prisoner at Philippi. Said to have been bishop of Corinth, Acts 15:22, 32-34, 40; 17:14; 18:5; 2 Cor. 1:19; 1 Thess. 1:1.

SIM'E-ON (*who hears*). (1) Son of Jacob and Leah, Gen. 29:33. For the crime in Gen. 34:25-30 his father denounced him, Gen. 49:5-7. His tribe was small, Num. 1:22, 23; 26:14, and their inheritance a scattered portion of Canaan, Josh, 19:1-9. (2) Son of Judah in genealogy of Christ, Luke 3:30. (3) Simon Peter, Acts 15:14. (4) a venerable and pious Jew who blessed the child Jesus in the temple, Luke 2:25-35. (5) Simeon Niger, Acts 13:1. [NIGER.]

SI'MON (*Simeon*). (1) Several distinguished Jews bore this name during the Maccabean period. (2) A native of Samaria and famous sorcerer, who professed Christ for mercenary purposes, Acts 8:9-24. (3) Simon Peter, Matt. 4:18. [PETER.] (4) Simon the Canaanite, or Simon Zelotes, was a member of the party of the Zealots who advocated the Jewish ritual, and an apostle, Matt. 10:4. (5) Simon the brother of Jesus, Matt. 13:55; Mark 6:3. (6) Simon the Pharisee, in whose house a woman anointed the feet of Jesus, Luke 7:36-50. (7) Simon, the leper of Bethany, Matt. 26:6. (8) Simon of Cyrene, who was compelled to bear Christ's cross, Matt. 27:32; Mark 15:21; Luke 23:26. (9) The tanner of Joppa with whom Peter lodged, Acts 9:43. (10) Simon the father of Judas Iscariot, John 6:71; 13:2, 26.

SI'NAI (*bushy*). The peninsula of

Sinai lies between the two great arms of the Red Sea, Gulf of Akba on the east, and Gulf of Suez on the west. This region contains the mountain system of Horeb or Sinai, on one of whose mounts, or peaks, God appeared to Moses in the burning bush, Ex. 3:1-5, amid whose surrounding wilderness the wandering Israelites encamped, Ex. 19:1, 2, and from whose cloud-obscured heights the law was delivered to Moses, Ex. 19:3-25; 20.-40.; Lev. The numbering also took place there, Num. 1.-10.:1-12. The peninsula is a triangle whose base extends from the head of Suez to Akaba. This base is pierced by the plateau of Tih, the "desert of wandering," south of which are those tumultous mountain clusters above mentioned, central among which is Mount Sinai. The coast ranges along Akaba and Suez are systematic and elevated. The region was a dependency of Egypt from earliest times, but became subject to Rome.

SOL'O-MON (*peaceful*). Last of David's sons by Bathsheba. Named Jedidiah, "beloved of God," by Nathan, 1 Chr. 3:5; 2 Sam. 12:25. Placed in Nathan's care. Secured the throne according to David's pledge, 1 Kgs. 1:13-53, and much to the consternation of Adonijah, the legal successor. Reigned forty years, B.C. 1015-975. Confirmed his father's conquests, built the palace and temple, extended commerce, contracted favorable alliances, grew famous for wisdom, raised his kingdom to great wealth, splendor, and power, mingled justice with cruelty, endorsed true and false worship, encouraged literature, and wrote largely himself, fell a prey to the sensualities of his time and position, died leaving his kingdom under the eclipse of faction and on the edge of decay, 1 Kgs. 2.-11.; 2 Chr. 1.-9.

SPAIN. Anciently the whole peninsula of southwestern Europe, embracing Spain and Portugal; known to Greeks as Iberia and to Romans as Hispania. If identical with Tarshish, then known to Hebrews in Solomon's time; certainly to Phœnicians. Known to Paul, who contemplated a visit to it, Rom. 15:24-28. Christianity early introduced there.

SPIR'IT (*breath*). The breath, 2 Thess. 2:8. The vital principle, Eccl. 8:8. Elsewhere, the soul. [SOUL.] Holy Spirit, or Ghost, is the third person in the Trinity, 2 Cor. 13:14; Acts 15:28. Though Holy Spirit and Holy Ghost are synonymous in meaning, preference is given to the latter form in the Scriptures, Matt. 1:18; John 1:33; Acts 2:4; Rom. 5:5, and elsewhere, the former being used only four times.

STE'PHEN (*crown*). Chief of the first seven deacons, and first Christian martyr. A Greek convert of strong faith and great eloquence. Arrested and tried before the Sanhedrim, but stoned to death by an angry mob, before he had time to finish his defence. The date of his martyrdom is fixed at about A.D. 37. It was followed by the conversion of Saul, who was present at the stoning, and a bitter persecutor of early Christians at the time, Acts 6:5-15; 7., 8:1-3.

SYN'A-GOGUE (*led together*). The Jewish assembly for social and religious purposes seems to have had its origin during the captivity, or to have been an outgrowth of it, Ez. 8:15; Neh. 8:2; 9:1. The casual, or house, assemblages soon ran into regular congregations, with suitable buildings and stated meetings, at requisite points. These were the synagogues, often elaborate and costly, presided over by a chief, or rabbi, assisted by a council of elders, Mark 5:22, 35; Luke 4:20; John 16:2; Acts 18:8.

SYR'I-A. The Hebrew Aram. So indefinitely bounded at different times as to have been associated with Assyria (whence its name) and Babylon. More definitely the country to the north of Canaan, extending from the Tigris to the Mediterranean, and northward to the Taurus ranges. Damascus was the capital, and centre of wealth, learning, and power. Joshua subdued its petty kings, Josh. 11:2-18; David reduced it to submission, 2 Sam. 8., 10. During Solomon's reign it became independent, 1 Kgs. 11:23-25. The earliest recorded settlers in Syria were Hittites and other Hamitic races. The Shemitic element entered it from the southeast under Abraham and Chedorlaomer. After Syria became independent it was a persistent enemy of the Jews, 1 Kgs. 15:18-20; 20., 22.; 2 Kgs. 6:8-33; 7., 9:14, 15; 10:32, 33; 13:3, 14-25. The attempt of the Syrian king to ally Israel with him for the overthrow of Judah led Ahaz to call in the help of Assyria, and Syria was soon merged into the great Assyrian empire. It was conquered by Alexander the Great, B.C. 333, and finally fell to the lot of Seleucus Nicator, who made it the central province of his empire, with the capital at Antioch. The Syriac language was closely allied to the Hebrew.

TAB'ER-NA-CLE (*little shed or tent*). Tent of Jehovah, or movable sanctuary, which Moses was directed to erect in the wilderness, Ex. 25:8. Its plan, materials, and furnishings are described in Ex. 25:9-40; 26., 27. It could be readily taken down and set up and accompanied the Israelites during their wanderings, Ex. 40:38. During the conquest it was stationed at Gilgal, Josh. 4:19; 9:6; 10:15; and at Ebal, Josh. 8:30-35. After the conquest it was set up at Shiloh, Josh. 18:1, where it remained during the time of the Judges and where the ark was captured by the Philistines, 1 Sam. 4:17, 22. Sometime after the return of the ark it was taken to Jerusalem and placed in a new tabernacle, and finally in the temple, 2 Sam. 6:17; 1 Chr. 15:1, but the old structure was still venerated, as long as it remained at Shiloh. It was afterwards removed to Nob, 1 Sam. 21: 1-9, and in the reign of David to Gibeon, 1 Chr. 16:39; 21:29, where it was at the beginning of Solomon's reign. Some suppose that the tabernacle and its furniture were moved into Solomon's temple when it was completed.

TAL'ENT (*weight*). A Hebrew weight and denomination for money, equal to 3,000 shekels, or 93¾ pounds of silver, and varying in value from $1,550 to $2,000, Ex. 38:25; Matt. 18:24. The Attic, or Greek talent, was worth about $1,200; the Roman great talent, $500; the Roman small talent, $375.

TAR'SUS (*wing*). Chief city of Cilicia, Asia Minor, on river Cydnus, six miles from the Mediterranean. Birthplace of Paul and rival of Athens and Alexandria in literature and fine arts, Acts 9:11, 30; 11:25; 21:39; 22:3. At the mouth of the Cydnus were fine docks, and Tarsus had, at one time, considerable commercial importance. Some would identify it with Tarshish. It was founded by the Assyrian, Sardanapalus, and was captured by the Romans and made a free city. It is now represented by Tersons, a mean Turkish city with a fluctuating population.

TEM'PLE. (1) Solomon's temple erected at Jerusalem on Mount Moriah. David proposed to transform the tabernacle into a permanent temple at Jerusalem, and collected much material, but its construction was forbidden by the prophet Nathan, 1 Chr. 17.; 2 Sam. 7:7-29. Solomon completed the work after David's plans and with the assistance of Hiram, king of Tyre. He began to build in the fourth year of his reign, B.C. 1012, and finished and dedicated it B.C. 1005, 1 Chr. 21., 22., 28:11-19; 29:4-7; 1 Kgs. 6.-8.; 2 Chr. 3.-7. This costly and imposing structure, for the age, was pillaged several times during the Eastern invasions, and was finally destroyed during the last siege of Jerusalem by Nebuchadnezzar, B.C. 588. (2) The temple of Zerubbabel was begun in B.C. 534, by the returned captives under the lead of Zerubbabel and the patronage of King Cyrus of Persia. Owing to discords and direct opposition it was not completed till B.C. 515. It was much inferior to the first in cost and beauty, though one third larger in dimensions. It was partially destroyed by Antiochus Epiphanes, B.C. 163, and restored by Judas Maccabeus, Ez. 3.-6.; 2 Macc. 10:1-9. (3) Herod the Great removed the decayed temple of Zerubbabel and began the erection of a new one B.C. 17. This gorgeous and costly structure was not completed till the time of Herod Agrippa II., A.D. 64. It was of marble, after Græco-Roman designs, and was destroyed by the Romans under Titus, A.D. 70, thus verifying Mark 13:2.

THES"SA-LO-NI'CA. Ancient Thermæ, "hot springs;" now Salonika. Enlarged by Cassander and called Thessalonica after his wife, daughter of Alexander the Great. An important city of Macedonia, at the head of the Gulf of Thessalonica, or Thermæ. Paul visited it during his second tour and founded a strong church there, to whose members he wrote two epistles, Acts 17:1-9.

THOM'AS (*twin*). The cautious, susceptible, even doubtful, apostle, whose name, in Greek, was Didymus, "twin," Matt. 10:3; Mark 3:18; Luke 6:15; John 11:16; 14:5, 6; 20:24-29; Acts 1:13.

TIM'O-THY (*honoring God*). Son of Eunice, a Jewess, by a Gentile father. Born in Derbe or Lystra, Lycaonia, Acts 16:1; 2 Tim. 1:5. Converted by Paul and became a close friend and valuable assistant, Rom. 16:21; Heb. 13:23. Recipient of two of Paul's epistles, 15th and 16th N. T. books. The first was written to him while at Ephesus, probably from Macedonia, and about A.D. 65. The second seems to have been written from Rome some three years later. They are called pastoral epistles, because devoted to description of church work and earnest exhortation to faithfulness.

TITHE (*tenth*). One tenth of all produce of lands and herds was set apart, under the Levitical law, for the support of the Levites, and a tenth of their tenth went to the priests. There was tithe regulations among other nations, Gen. 14:20; 28:22; Lev. 27:30-33; Num. 18:21-32; Deut. 12:17, 18; 14:22-27. The Pharisees tithed their mint, anise, cummin, and rue, Matt. 23:23.

TI'TUS (*pleasant*). A distinguished Grecian who became a Christian convert and a companion of Paul in his trials and on his missionary tours, Tit. 1:4; Gal. 2:3-5; 2 Cor. 8:6, 16, 23. Entrusted with many important commissions, 2 Cor. 12:18; 2 Tim. 4:10; Tit. 1:5. Paul wrote an epistle to Titus, the 17th N. T. book, about A.D. 65, designed to instruct him in his ministerial duties in Crete, which were arduous, on account of the immorality of the people.

TONGUES. "And the whole earth was of one language, and of one speech," Gen. 11:1. Confusion of tongues and dispersion of peoples coincident, Gen. 11:7-9. "New tongues," Mark 16:17, is the first notice of a gift specially characteristic of the first outpouring of the Spirit. Ten days afterward the promise was fulfilled in the Pentecostal phenomenon, Acts 2:1-13.

TYRE (*rock*). The celebrated commercial city of Phœnicia on the Mediterranean coast. It fell to the lot of Asher, but was never conquered, Josh. 19:29. In intimate commercial relation with Hebrews, and King Hiram furnished and artificers and material for the temple and royal houses at Jerusalem, 2 Sam. 5:11; 1 Kgs. 5:1; 7:13; 9:11-14; 1 Chr. 14:1; 2 Chr. 2:2-18. The city was denounced by the prophets, Isa. 23:1-17; Jer. 27:3; Ezek. 26:3-21. It resisted the five-year siege of Shalmaneser and the thirteen-year siege of Nebuchadnezzar, but fell before that of Alexander. Referred to in N. T., Matt. 11:21, 22; 15:21; Mark 7:24. Paul visited it, Acts 21:3, 4.

UR (*light, region*). (1) Place where Abraham lived with his father Terah and his wife Sarah, before they started for the land of Canaan, Gen. 11:28, 31. Mentioned in Gen. 15:7, as of the Chaldees, and Acts 7:2, as in Mesopotamia. (2) Father of Eliphal, one of David's guard, 1 Chr. 11:35. Called Ahasbai in 2 Sam. 23:34.

ZAC-CHÆ'US (*just*). The rich chief among publicans, resident at Jericho, who climbed a tree to see Jesus pass, was invited down, became the host of Jesus, and was converted, Luke 19:1-10.

ZACH"A-RI'AS (*remembered by Jehovah*). Greek form of Zachariah. (1) The name is borne by many priests and laymen in the books of Esdras. (2) Father of John the Baptist and husband of Elizabeth. He was a priest of the course of Abia, or Abijah, 1 Chr. 24:10, and probably lived at Hebron, Luke 1:5-25, 57-80. (3) Son of Barachias, who was slain between the temple and the altar, Matt. 23:35; Luke 11:51.

ZEB'E-DEE (*God's portion*). A fisherman of Galilee, husband of Salome, and father of the apostles James the Great and John, Matt. 4:21; 27:56; Mark 1:19, 20; 15:40. His home is located at or near Bethsaida, and he appears to have been able to employ help in his occupation, Mark 1:20.

ZECH"A-RI'AH (*memory of God*). Son of Benechiah, Zech. 1:1; of Iddo, Ez. 5:1. Eleventh of the minor prophets and contemporary of Haggai, born in Babylon during the captivity, returned with Zerubbabel, Ez. 5:1; 6:14. The time of his prophecies is reckoned as between B.C. 520 and 518, during the period of building the second temple, whose completion was largely due to his energies as priest and prophet. His book, 38th of O. T., is divided into two parts. Chapters 1.-8. contain hopeful visions of the restored Hebrew state, exhortations to turn to Jehovah, warnings against God's enemies. Chapters 9.-14. are prophetic of the future fortunes of the theocracy, the conversion of Israel, the glorification of God's kingdom and of the coming of the Messiah. The style of the book is obscure. Many critics attribute the authorship of the second division of the book to Jeremiah. (2) A Reubenite chief, at time of the captivity by Tiglath-pileser, 1 Chr. 5:7. (3) A Korhite Levite, keeper of one of the doors of the tabernacle, 1 Chr. 9:21. (4) A son of Jehiel, 1 Chr. 9:37. (5) A Levite of the second order, one of the temple musicians, 1 Chr. 15:18, 20. (6) A priest who blew the trumpet before the ark on its return, 1 Chr. 15:24. (7) A Kohathite Levite, 1 Chr. 24:25. (8) A Merarite Levite, 1 Chr. 26:11. (9) A Manassite, 1 Chr. 27:21. (10) A prince of Judah in reign of Jehoshaphat, 2 Chr. 17:7. (11) Father of Jahaziel, 2 Chr. 20:14. (12) A son of Jehoshaphat, 2 Chr. 21:2. (13) Son of the high priest Jehoiada, in reign of Joash king of Judah, 2 Chr. 24:20, and probably same as the Zacharias of Matt. 23:35. (14) A prophet and royal counsellor in reign of Uzziah, 2 Chr. 16:5. (15) Father of Abijah, mother of King Hezekiah, 2 Chr. 29:1. (16) A member of the family of Asaph in time of Hezekiah, 2 Chr. 29:13. (17) A Kohathite Levite in the reign of Josiah, 2 Chr. 34:12. (18) One of the temple rulers in reign of Josiah, 2 Chr. 35:8. (19) Nine priests, Levites and returned captives in Ez. 8:3, 11, 16; 10:26; Neh. 8:4; 11:4, 5, 12; 12:16, 35, 41. (20) A witness for Isaiah, Isa. 8:2.

ZI'ON (*mount, sunny*). Zion or Sion in its literal and restricted sense was the celebrated mount in Jerusalem, the highest and southernmost or southwesternmost of the city. It was the original hill of the Jebusites, Josh. 15:63. After David became king, he captured it, "the stronghold of Zion," from the Jebusites, dwelt in the fort there, and greatly enlarged and strengthened its fortifications, calling it "the city of David," 2 Sam. 5:6-9; 1 Chr. 11:5-8. Despite David's prestige the name of Zion still clung to it, 1 Kgs. 8:1; 2 Kgs. 19:21, 31; 2 Chr. 5:2. The O. T. poets and prophets exalted the word Zion by frequent use and gave it a sacred turn, so that in time it came to type a sacred capital, Ps. 2:6; holy place, Ps. 137:2; 149:2; Isa, 30:19; God's chosen people, Ps. 51:18; 87:5; the Christian church, Heb. 12:22; the heavenly city, Rev. 14:1.

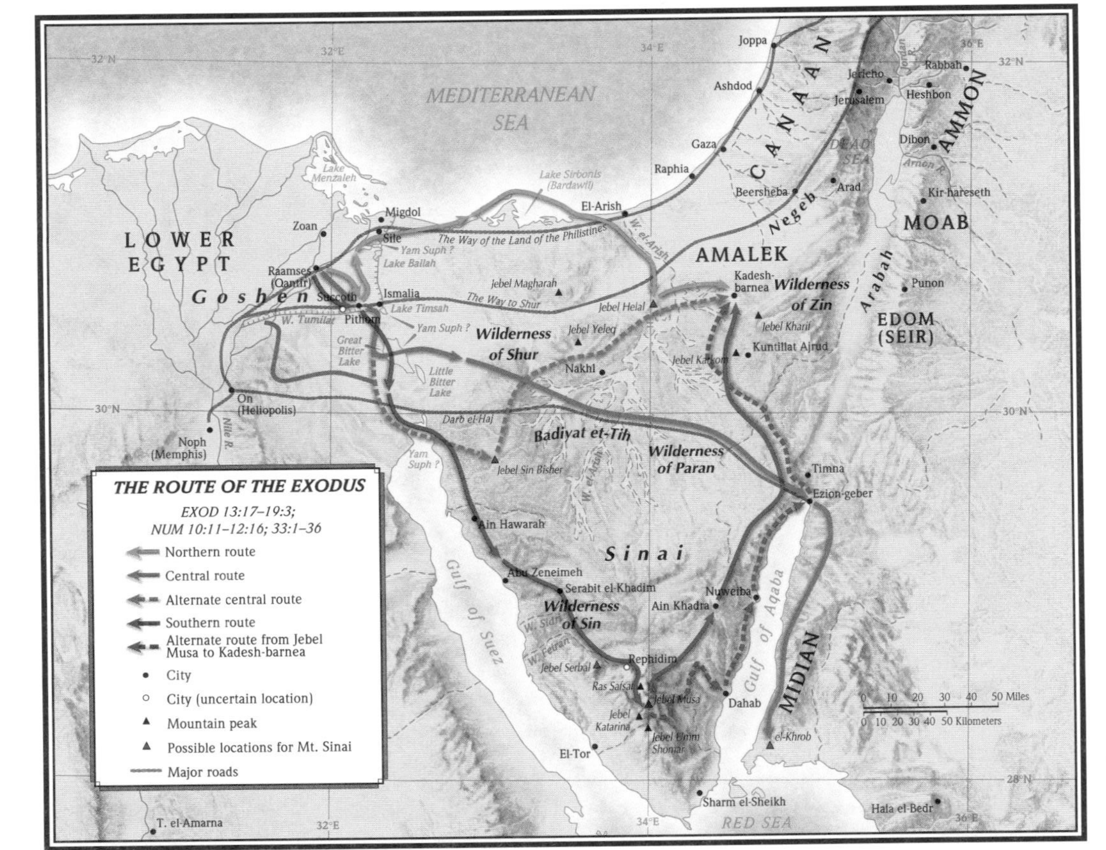
THE ROUTE OF THE EXODUS
EXOD 13:17–19:3;
NUM 10:11–12:16; 33:1–36
Northern route
Central route
Alternate central route
Southern route
Alternate route from Jebel Musa to Kadesh-barnea
City
City (uncertain location)
Mountain peak
Possible locations for Mt. Sinai
Major roads
MEDITERRANEAN SEA
LOWER EGYPT
Goshen
CANAAN
AMMON
MOAB
AMALEK
EDOM (SEIR)
MIDIAN
Sinai
Wilderness of Shur
Wilderness of Zin
Wilderness of Paran
Wilderness of Sin
Badiyat et-Tih
Negeb
Arabah
Gulf of Suez
Gulf of Aqaba
RED SEA
DEAD SEA
Lake Menzaleh
Lake Sirbonis (Bardawil)
Lake Ballah
Lake Timsah
Great Bitter Lake
Little Bitter Lake
Yam Suph ?
The Way of the Land of the Philistines
The Way to Shur
Darb el-Haj
W. Tumilat
W. el-Arish
W. Sidri
W. Feiran
Nile R.
Jordan R.
Arnon R.
Joppa
Ashdod
Gaza
Raphia
El-Arish
Migdol
Sile
Zoan
Raamses (Qantir)
Succoth
Pithom
Ismalia
On (Heliopolis)
Noph (Memphis)
T. el-Amarna
Jericho
Jerusalem
Rabbah
Heshbon
Dibon
Kir-hareseth
Arad
Beersheba
Punon
Kadesh-barnea
Kuntillat Ajrud
Nakhl
Timna
Ezion-geber
Ain Hawarah
Abu Zeneimeh
Serabit el-Khadim
Rephidim
Ain Khadra
Nuweiba
Dahab
El-Tor
Sharm el-Sheikh
Hala el-Bedr
Jebel Magharah
Jebel Helal
Jebel Yeleq
Jebel Kharif
Jebel Karkom
Jebel Sin Bisher
Jebel Serbal
Ras Safsaf
Jebel Musa
Jebel Katarina
Jebel Umm Shomar
el-Khrob
0 10 20 30 40 50 Miles
0 10 20 30 40 50 Kilometers
32°N
30°N
28°N
32°E
34°E
36°E

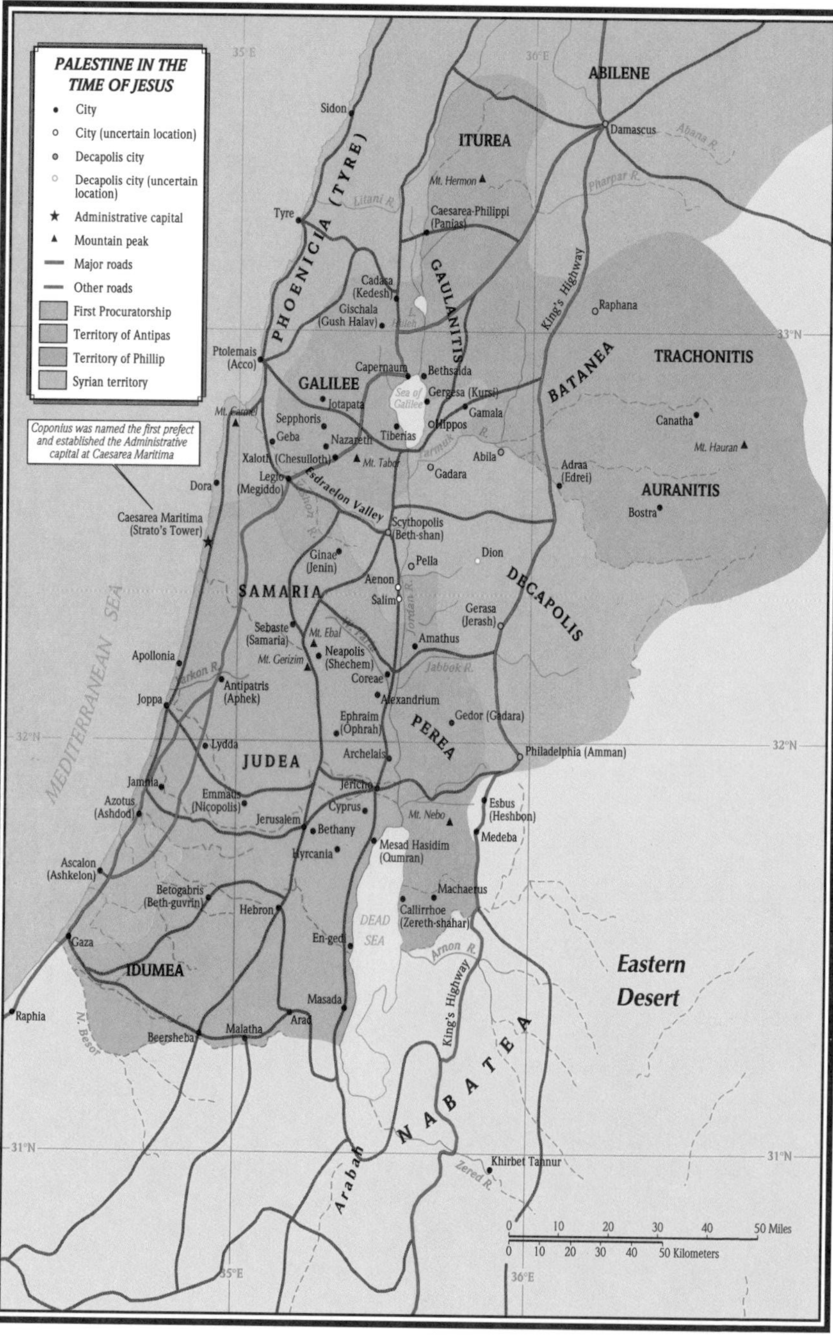

PALESTINE IN THE TIME OF JESUS
City
City (uncertain location)
Decapolis city
Decapolis city (uncertain location)
Administrative capital
Mountain peak
Major roads
Other roads
First Procuratorship
Territory of Antipas
Territory of Phillip
Syrian territory
Coponius was named the first prefect and established the Administrative capital at Caesarea Maritima
ABILENE
Damascus
Sidon
ITUREA
PHOENICIA (TYRE)
Mt. Hermon
Tyre
Caesarea-Philippi (Panias)
GAULANITIS
Cadasa (Kedesh)
Gischala (Gush Halav)
King's Highway
Raphana
Ptolemais (Acco)
GALILEE
Capernaum
Bethsaida
BATANEA
TRACHONITIS
Sea of Galilee
Gergesa (Kursi)
Jotapata
Gamala
Mt. Carmel
Sepphoris
Hippos
Canatha
Geba
Nazareth
Tiberias
Mt. Hauran
Xaloth (Chesulloth)
Mt. Tabor
Abila
Legio (Megiddo)
Gadara
Adraa (Edrei)
Dora
Esdraelon Valley
AURANITIS
Bostra
Caesarea Maritima (Strato's Tower)
Scythopolis (Beth-shan)
Ginae (Jenin)
Dion
Pella
DECAPOLIS
SAMARIA
Aenon
Salim
Jordan R.
Gerasa (Jerash)
Sebaste (Samaria)
Mt. Ebal
Amathus
MEDITERRANEAN SEA
Apollonia
Neapolis (Shechem)
Mt. Gerizim
Jabbok R.
Antipatris (Aphek)
Coreae
Joppa
Alexandrium
Ephraim (Ophrah)
Gedor (Gadara)
PEREA
32°N
Lydda
Philadelphia (Amman)
JUDEA
Archelais
Jamnia
Jericho
Emmaus (Nicopolis)
Esbus (Heshbon)
Azotus (Ashdod)
Cyprus
Jerusalem
Mt. Nebo
Bethany
Medeba
Mesad Hasidim (Qumran)
Hyrcania
Ascalon (Ashkelon)
Betogabris (Beth-guvrin)
Machaerus
Hebron
Callirrhoe (Zereth-shahar)
DEAD SEA
En-gedi
Gaza
Arnon R.
Eastern Desert
IDUMEA
Masada
Raphia
Arad
N. Besor
Beersheba
Malatha
NABATEA
Arabah
Khirbet Tannur
Zered R.
31°N
0 10 20 30 40 50 Miles
0 10 20 30 40 50 Kilometers
35°E
36°E

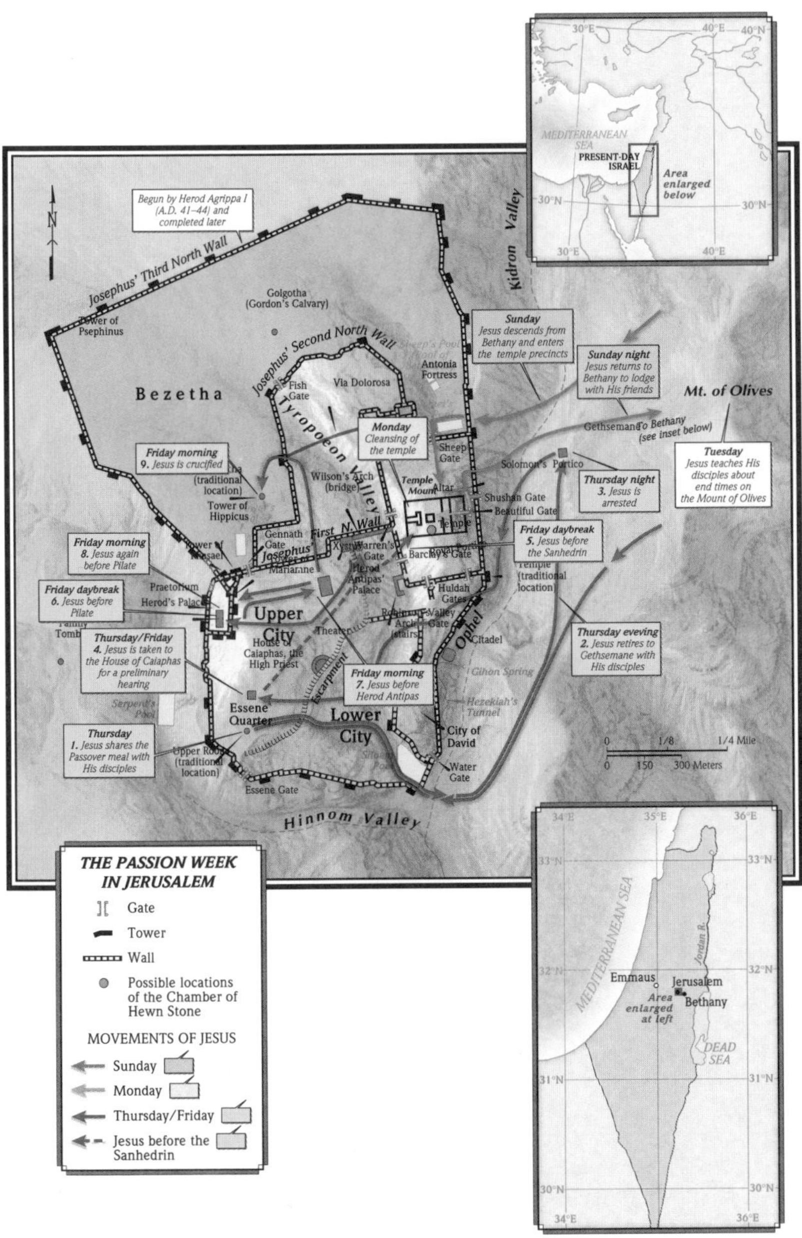
THE PASSION WEEK IN JERUSALEM
Gate
Tower
Wall
Possible locations of the Chamber of Hewn Stone
MOVEMENTS OF JESUS
Sunday
Monday
Thursday/Friday
Jesus before the Sanhedrin
Begun by Herod Agrippa I (A.D. 41–44) and completed later
Josephus' Third North Wall
Josephus' Second North Wall
Josephus' First N. Wall
Tower of Psephinus
Golgotha (Gordon's Calvary)
Bezetha
Fish Gate
Via Dolorosa
Antonia Fortress
Tyropoeon Valley
Kidron Valley
Mt. of Olives
Sunday
Jesus descends from Bethany and enters the temple precincts
Sunday night
Jesus returns to Bethany to lodge with His friends
Gethsemane
To Bethany (see inset below)
Monday
Cleansing of the temple
Sheep Gate
Solomon's Portico
Tuesday
Jesus teaches His disciples about end times on the Mount of Olives
Friday morning
9. Jesus is crucified
Wilson's Arch (bridge)
Temple Mount
Altar
Shushan Gate
Beautiful Gate
Temple
Thursday night
3. Jesus is arrested
Tower of Hippicus
Friday daybreak
5. Jesus before the Sanhedrin
Friday morning
8. Jesus again before Pilate
Gennath Gate
Xystus
Warren's Gate
Barclay's Gate
Royal Portico
Herod Antipas' Palace
Huldah Gates
Praetorium
Herod's Palace
Friday daybreak
6. Jesus before Pilate
Upper City
Theater
Valley Gate
Arch (stairs)
Ophel
Citadel
Thursday eveving
2. Jesus retires to Gethsemane with His disciples
Thursday/Friday
4. Jesus is taken to the House of Caiaphas for a preliminary hearing
House of Caiaphas, the High Priest
Escarpment
Gihon Spring
Friday morning
7. Jesus before Herod Antipas
Hezekiah's Tunnel
Essene Quarter
Lower City
City of David
Thursday
1. Jesus shares the Passover meal with His disciples
Upper Room (traditional location)
Water Gate
Essene Gate
Hinnom Valley
0
1/8
1/4 Mile
0
150
300 Meters
N
MEDITERRANEAN SEA
PRESENT-DAY ISRAEL
Area enlarged below
30°E
40°E
40°N
30°N
34°E
35°E
36°E
33°N
32°N
31°N
30°N
MEDITERRANEAN SEA
Jordan R.
Emmaus
Jerusalem
Bethany
Area enlarged at left
DEAD SEA

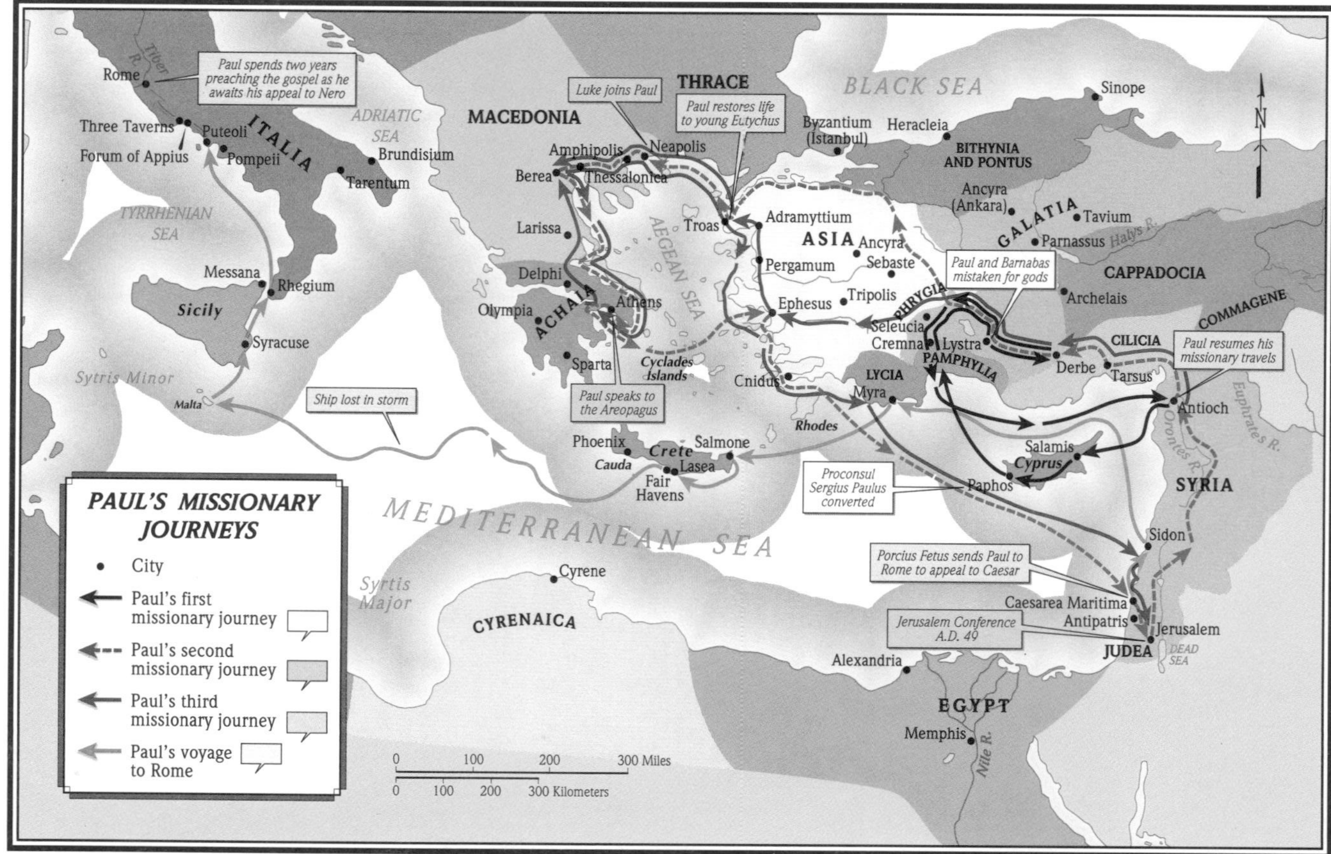

PAUL'S MISSIONARY JOURNEYS
City
Paul's first missionary journey
Paul's second missionary journey
Paul's third missionary journey
Paul's voyage to Rome
Paul spends two years preaching the gospel as he awaits his appeal to Nero
Luke joins Paul
Paul restores life to young Eutychus
Paul and Barnabas mistaken for gods
Paul resumes his missionary travels
Paul speaks to the Areopagus
Ship lost in storm
Proconsul Sergius Paulus converted
Porcius Fetus sends Paul to Rome to appeal to Caesar
Jerusalem Conference A.D. 49
Rome
Tiber R.
Three Taverns
Forum of Appius
Puteoli
Pompeii
ITALIA
ADRIATIC SEA
Brundisium
Tarentum
TYRRHENIAN SEA
Messana
Rhegium
Sicily
Syracuse
Sytris Minor
Malta
MACEDONIA
THRACE
Amphipolis
Neapolis
Berea
Thessalonica
Larissa
Delphi
Olympia
ACHAIA
Athens
Sparta
Cyclades Islands
AEGEAN SEA
Troas
Adramyttium
Pergamum
Ephesus
ASIA
Ancyra
Sebaste
Tripolis
Cnidus
Rhodes
Phoenix
Cauda
Crete
Salmone
Lasea
Fair Havens
BLACK SEA
Byzantium (Istanbul)
Heracleia
Sinope
BITHYNIA AND PONTUS
Ancyra (Ankara)
GALATIA
Tavium
Parnassus
Halys R.
CAPPADOCIA
Archelais
PHRYGIA
Seleucia
Cremna
Lystra
PAMPHYLIA
Derbe
CILICIA
Tarsus
COMMAGENE
LYCIA
Myra
Antioch
Orontes R.
Euphrates R.
Salamis
Cyprus
Paphos
SYRIA
Sidon
Caesarea Maritima
Antipatris
Jerusalem
JUDEA
DEAD SEA
MEDITERRANEAN SEA
Cyrene
Syrtis Major
CYRENAICA
Alexandria
EGYPT
Memphis
Nile R.
0 100 200 300 Miles
0 100 200 300 Kilometers
N